THE OFFICIAL®

1996 PRICE GUIDE TO

BASEBALL CARDS

BY

DR. JAMES BECKETT

FIFTEENTH EDITION

HOUSE OF COLLECTIBLES • NEW YORK

Important Notice: All of the information, including valuations, in this book has been compiled from the most reliable sources, and every effort has been made to eliminate errors and questionable data. Nevertheless, the possibility of error in a work of such scope always exists. The publisher will not be held responsible for losses which may occur in the purchase, sale or other transaction of items because of information contained herein. Readers who feel they have discovered errors are invited to write and inform us, so that they may be corrected in subsequent editions. Those seeking further information on the topics covered in this book are advised to refer to the complete line of *Official Price Guides* published by the House of Collectibles.

Published by:
House of Collectibles
201 East 50th Street
New York, New York 10022

Distributed by Ballantine Books, a division of Random House, Inc.,
New York, and simultaneously in Canada by
Random House of Canada Limited, Toronto.

Manufactured in the United States of America

ISSN: 0748-3317

ISBN: 0-876-37958-7

Fifteenth Edition: April 1995

10 9 8 7 6 5 4 3 2 1

Advertisers

About the Author

Jim Beckett, the leading authority on sport card values in the United States, maintains a wide range of activities in the world of sports. He possesses one of the finest collections of sports cards and autographs in the world, has made numerous appearances on radio and television, and has been frequently cited in many national publications. He was awarded the first "Special Achievement Award" for Contributions to the Hobby by the National Sports Collectors Convention in 1980, the "Jock-Jaspersen Award" for Hobby Dedication in 1983, and the "Buck Barker, Spirit of the Hobby" Award in 1991.

Dr. Beckett is the author of *The Sport Americana Baseball Card Price Guide, The Official Price Guide to Baseball Cards, The Sport Americana Price Guide to Baseball Collectibles, The Sport Americana Baseball Memorabilia and Autograph Price Guide, The Sport Americana Football Card Price Guide, The Official Price Guide to Football Cards, The Sport Americana Hockey Card Price Guide, The Official Price Guide to Hockey Cards, The Sport Americana Basketball Card Price Guide and Alphabetical Checklist, The Official Price Guide to Basketball Cards, and The Sport Americana Baseball Card Alphabetical Checklist.* In addition, he is the founder, publisher, and editor of *Beckett Baseball Card Monthly, Beckett Basketball Monthly, Beckett Football Card Monthly, Beckett Hockey Monthly, Beckett Focus on Future Stars, Beckett Racing Monthly, and Beckett Tribute* magazines.

Jim Beckett received his Ph.D. in Statistics from Southern Methodist University in 1975. Prior to starting Beckett Publications in 1984, Dr. Beckett served as an Associate Professor of Statistics at Bowling Green State University and as a vice president of a consulting firm in Dallas, Texas. He currently resides in Dallas with his wife, Patti, and their daughters, Christina, Rebecca, and Melissa.

How To Use This Book

Isn't it great? Every year this book gets bigger and bigger with all the new sets coming out. But even more exciting is that every year there are more collectors, more shows, more stores, and more interest in the cards we love so much. This edition has been enhanced and expanded from the previous edition. The cards you collect — who appears on them, what they look like, where they are from, and (most important to most of you) what their current values are — are enumerated within. Many of the features contained in the other *Beckett Price Guides* have been incorporated into this volume since condition grading, terminology, and many other aspects of collecting are common to the card hobby in general. We hope you find the book both interesting and useful in your collecting pursuits.

The *Beckett Guide* has been successful where other attempts have failed because it is complete, current, and valid. This Price Guide contains not just one, but three prices by condition for all the baseball cards listed. These account for most of the baseball cards in existence. The prices were added to the card lists just prior to printing and reflect not the author's opinions or desires but the going retail prices for each card, based on the marketplace (sports memorabilia conventions and shows, sports card shops, hobby papers, current mail-order catalogs, local club meetings, auction results, and other first-hand reportings of actually realized prices).

What is the best price guide available on the market today? Of course, card sellers prefer the price guide with the highest prices, while card buyers naturally prefer the one with the lowest prices. Accuracy, however, is the true test. Use the price guide trusted by more collectors and dealers than all the

Order with confidence...from Larry Fritsch Cards
America's 1st Full Time Dealer - Serving Collectors Since 1948

1995 BASEBALL SETS

Topps Complete Series #1 (396 Cards) **$39.95** Series #2 available soon. Write for details.

FLEER Complete Set (600 Cards) **$66.95** Insert (Chase) Cards singles available. Write for list.

DONRUSS Complete Set Series #1 (330 Cards) **$36.95** Series #2 available soon - Insert (Chase) card singles available now - Write for list.

SCORE Unopened Box Series #1 (432 Cards) **$37.95** Series #2 available soon - Write for details.

REPRINT SETS

WHO BUYS REPRINTS? THE TRUE COLLECTOR!

- 1890s Old Judge Type Set (80 cards) 34.95
- 1909 T204 Ramly (121 cads) 26.95
- 1909-11 T206 (523 cards) 59.95
- 1911 T205 (208 cards) 35.95
- 1922 E120 American Caramel (240) 29.95
- 1933 Goudey (240 cards) 44.95
- 1934 Goudey (96 cards) 29.95
- 1934-36 Diamond Stars (108 cards) 19.95
- 1938 Horrors of War (288 cards) 44.95
- 1939 Play Ball All 3 Series (161 cards) 26.95
- 1940 Play Ball (240 cards) 49.95
- 1941 Tip Top Bread (163) 24.95
- 1948 Bowman (48 cards) 7.95
- 1948 Bowman Basketball (72 cards) 24.95
- 1948 Bowman Football (108 cards) 24.95
- 1949 Bowman (240 cards) 37.95
- 1950 Bowman (252 cards) 44.95
- 1950 Bowman Football (144 cards) 34.95
- 1951 Bowman (324 cards) 49.95

We have many other reprints sets in stock, write for our latest catalog.

JUST A SAMPLE OF SETS AVAILABLE FROM OUR VAST INVENTORY!

(All sets are in EM to NrMT condition.) See shipping and insurance table. NOTE: All prices are subjects to change without notice.

BASEBALL SETS

- 1994 Topps Factory (792) $54.95
- 1994 Topps Traded (132) 19.95
- 1994 Fleer (720) 74.95
- 1994 Fleer Update (210) 21.95
- 1994 Bowman Box (288) 51.95
- 1994 Donruss #1 Box (468) 60.95
- 1994 Donruss #2 Box (468) 50.95
- 1994 Score #1 Box (504) 35.00
- 1994 Score #2 Box (504) 35.00
- 1993 Topps Factory (825) 43.95
- 1993 Topps Update (132) 14.95
- 1993 Fleer (720) 49.50
- 1993 Fleer Update (300) 21.00
- 1993 Donruss (792) 62.50
- 1993 Score (660) 57.50
- 1993 Upper Deck Fact. (840) 52.50
- 1992 Topps (792) 29.95
- 1992 Fleer (720) Factory 39.95
- 1992 Donruss (792) Factory 44.50
- 1992 Score (900) Factory 29.00
- 1992 Upper Deck Factory 47.50
- 1992 Topps Traded (132) 23.50
- 1992 Fleer Update (132) 180.00

BASEBALL SETS

- 1988 Topps (792) 27.95
- 1988 Fleer (660) Factory 38.50
- 1988 Score (660) Factory 23.50
- 1988 Donruss (660) Factory 25.00
- 1988 Topps Traded (132) 37.50
- 1988 Fleer Update (132) 15.95
- 1987 Topps (792) 34.95
- 1987 Fleer (660) Factory 99.50
- 1987 Donruss (660) Factory 75.00
- 1987 Topps Traded (132) 15.00
- 1987 Fleer Update (132) 14.95
- 1986 Topps (792) 50.00
- 1986 Topps Traded (132) 27.50
- 1986 Fleer (660) 127.50
- 1986 Fleer Update (132) 29.95
- 1986 Donruss (660) 200.00
- 1985 Topps (792) 110.00
- 1985 Topps Traded (132) 30.00
- 1985 Fleer (660) 190.00
- 1985 Fleer Update (132) 30.95
- 1985 Donruss (660) 235.00
- 1984 Topps (792) 80.00
- 1984 Topps Traded (132) 100.00

FREE!! 144 PAGE CATALOG FREE!!

The largest and best catalog in the hobby.

This 144 page issue is jam-packed with baseball, football, basketball, and hockey cards. Sets,singles, rookies, superstars, wax packs, reprints and much much more. If you need any card from 1880 - present - chances are good we have it. Our 60 page "One-Of-A-Kind" vintage card sale list (with grade & price) over 30,000 cards ready for shipment. New in this issue is our 20 page "3 Grade Special" where we list cards from 1954-1980. These cards are available in 3 different grades to help the collector looking to fill sets or just add to their collection. If the cards you're looking for aren't listed - use our "new concept" form, which makes over 8 million single cards available to you!! All this and more available in this catalog!

Send $2.00 or six 32¢ stamps to receive the next 3 issues free!!

- 1991 Topps (792) Factory 28.95
- 1991 Fleer (720) Factory 24.50
- 1991 Donruss (792) Factory 32.50
- 1991 Score (900) 30.00
- 1991 Upper Deck Factory 39.50
- 1991 Bowman (660) Factory 24.95
- 1991 Topps Traded (132) 14.50
- 1991 Fleer Update (132) 13.95
- 1990 Upper Deck Factory 45.75
- 1990 Bowman (528) Factory 22.95
- 1990 Donruss (715) Factory 25.50
- 1990 Topps (792) Factory 28.75
- 1990 Fleer (660) Factory 24.75
- 1990 Score Factory (714) 35.00
- 1990 Topps Traded (132) 11.75
- 1990 Fleer Update (132) 12.95
- 1989 Topps (792) Factory 24.50
- 1989 Fleer (660) 23.50
- 1989 Score (660) 21.50
- 1989 Donruss (660) Factory 28.50
- 1989 Bowman (484) Factory 21.95
- 1989 Topps Traded (132) 13.00
- 1989 Fleer Update (132) 13.95

- 1984 Fleer (660) 195.00
- 1984 Fleer Update (132) 995.00
- 1984 Donruss (660) 450.00
- 1983 Topps (792) 175.00
- 1983 Topps Traded (132) 125.00
- 1983 Fleer (660) 120.00
- 1983 Donruss (660) 150.00
- 1982 Topps Traded (132) 315.00
- 1982 Fleer (660) 95.00
- 1982 Donruss (660) 110.00
- 1981 Topps (726) 115.00
- 1981 Topps Traded (132) 50.00
- 1981 Fleer (660) 62.50
- 1981 Donruss (605) 65.00
- 1980 Topps (726) 300.00
- 1979 Topps (726) 225.00
- 1978 Topps (726) 325.00
- 1977 Topps (650) 425.00
- 1976 Topps (660) 450.00
- 1975 Topps (660) 825.00
- 1974 Topps (660) 650.00
- 1973 Topps (660) 1,125.00

FORGET THE NEW STUFF FOR FIVE MINUTES AND LET'S TALK CLASSICS!

UNTOUCHED 1975 Topps BASEBALL SETS

Brett Rookie, Yount Rookie, Carter Rookie, Rice Rookie and Many More!

YAH, WHO CAN AFFORD THAT??? YOU CAN!!! THAT'S WHO!!!

Larry Fritsch is the only person in the world with unopened cases of 1975s and we are cracking some open. Don't delay. The price will never be better on a virgin set of 1975 Topps direct from Topps. We grade these sets Excellent - mint to Near Mint as some printing and cutting flaws do exist.

COMPLETE SET (660 CARDS)

$749.95

plus $5.00 Shipping & Insurance

(As each set needs to be professionally hand collated just for you, when we receive your order, please allow 3-4 weeks for delivery.)

ALL AMERICAN GIRLS PROFESSIONAL BASEBALL LEAGUE CARD SET!!!

For the first time ever! A comprehensive set of the ALL AMERICAN GIRLS PROFESSIONAL BASEBALL LEAGUE. Larry Fritsch Cards has negotiated exclusive rights for this set. The set contains 230 cards of all the women who made this league a great success in the 1940's & 1950's. The fronts contain B&W photos with colored highlights, backs are two colored. Printed on high quality glossy stock. Available Now!!!

Special Introductory Prices
Complete Set (230) Cards

$19.95

NEGRO LEAGUE

Available now, a set of the great stars of the Negro Leagues. For the first time ever a set of cards on the Negro League using actual photographs. From 1898 until 1946, black men were banned from organized baseball. This set of 119 cards includes Satchell Paige, Josh Gibson, Cool Papa Bell, Buck Leonard. Also shown are many historic Negro uniforms.

- Complete Set of Negro League Cards (119 cards) $12.95
- 2 Complete Sets (238 cards) 22.50
- 5 Complete Sets (595 cards) 47.50

Add $5.00 shipping and insurance to all orders. Phone and Fax orders add an additional $5.00 for handling.

CHECK POLICY:

All personal checks will be held 15 working days for clearance. For fast service, please send postal money order. To receive Super Service it is necessary to send a POSTAL MONEY ORDER with your order. (All personal checks are held 15 days for clearance) Minimum charge order $20.00. WI residents add 5.5% sales tax

All prices subject to change. Call to verify prices.

WE ARE BUYING! (All cards and collectibles issued prior to 1969)
Before you sell... SEE US!! With over 46 years in card collecting (unchallenged by anyone), our reputation in beyond repute...We do Not make wild, unsubstantiated claims.. WE BUY CARDS AT A HIGHER PRICE THAN ANYONE. All purchases made are strictly confidential, we don't brag about our "Buys", we are private individuals. Try us. Our experience and knowledge...give us the edge...with a mailing list of over 110,000 active collectors, we have more exposure, we can pay higher prices...We will pay shipping (both ways if we do not buy your collection)...once card or 100,000...we treat each purchase alike. We also take items on consignment -call us for details.

(715) 344 - 8687

LARRY FRITSCH CARDS, INC.

735 Old Wausau Rd.,
P.O. Box 863 Dept. #526
Stevens Point, WI 54481

(715) 344 - 8687
FAX # (715) 344 - 1778

NEED SINGLE CARDS?

If you need single cards from 1880 to 1980, any sport, please write (send SASE) or call for a "NEW CONCEPT" form which makes over 8 million single cards available to you! Relive the history of sports with a single purchase. CALL OR WRITE TODAY.

others combined. Look for the *Beckett®* name. I won't put my name on anything I won't stake my reputation on. Not the lowest and not the highest — but the most accurate, with integrity.

To facilitate your use of this book, read the complete introductory section on the following pages before going to the pricing pages. Every collectible field has its own terminology; we've tried to capture most of these terms and definitions in our glossary. Please read carefully the section on grading and the condition of your cards, as you cannot determine which price column is appropriate for a given card without first knowing its condition.

Welcome to the world of baseball cards.

Advertising

Within this Price Guide you will find advertisements for sports memorabilia material, mail order, and retail sports collectibles establishments. All advertisements were accepted in good faith based on the reputation of the advertiser; however, neither the author, the publisher, the distributors, nor the other advertisers in this Price Guide accept any responsibility for any particular advertiser not complying with the terms of his or her ad.

Readers also should be aware that prices in advertisements are subject to change over the annual period before a new edition of this volume is issued each spring. When replying to an advertisement late in the baseball year, the reader should take this into account, and contact the dealer by phone or in writing for up-to-date price information. Should you come into contact with any of the advertisers in this guide as a result of their advertisement herein, please mention this source as your contact.

Prices in this Guide

Prices found in this guide reflect current retail rates just prior to the printing of this book. They do not reflect the FOR SALE prices of the author, the publisher, the distributors, the advertisers, or any card dealers associated with this guide. No one is obligated in any way to buy, sell or trade his or her cards based on these prices. The price listings were compiled by the author from actual buy/sell transactions at sports conventions, sports card shops, buy/sell advertisements in the hobby papers, for sale prices from dealer catalogs and price lists, and discussions with leading hobbyists in the U.S. and Canada. All prices are in U.S. dollars.

The Official Price Guide to Baseball Cards

1994 Baseball Cards Year In Review

by Tol Broome

Pop quiz question: What has seven card companies, 27 major sets and 115 different insert sets?

If you answered, "The 1994 baseball card hobby," you scored 100.

The year 1994 was the biggest ever for baseball cards in terms of the number of major sets and cards produced. Taken at face value, that simple fact wouldn't be newsworthy. At best, it would be old news. Practically everyone with more than a passing interest in our hobby knows the same thing could be said about each of the last 10 years.

Very few of us, though, had seen a year like 1993 when the baseball card boom officially hit the brakes and even had rolled back somewhat by the end of the year. Collecting was still fun, and business good for those who changed the way they catered to what was quickly becoming a buyer's market.

So entering 1994, everyone faced a more mature hobby. Manufacturers and dealers could no longer count on an ever-expanding field of customers. The scales had tipped from beginning hobbyists to more discriminating collectors with higher expectations and bigger budgets. Market saturation was out. Diversity, more product lines marked by reduced production, was in.

Competition may have demanded an increase in inserts and regular sets, but the true star of diversity was technology. Simply put, manufacturers could appeal to every taste imaginable because it was easier and cheaper to upgrade their sets. As a result, full-bleed photography, UV coating and gold foil became the rule rather than the exception.

Collectors were treated to the best-looking "basic" brands ever, and different tiers of premium sets came into sharper focus as manufacturers covered every niche of the marketplace. The demand for upscale design was no more evident than at the top end of the spectrum, where Leaf Limited and Bowman's Best joined Fleer Flair, Topps Finest and Upper Deck SP in the super-premium class.

Amid any upward rush, something has to give. During the frenzied days of the 1980s, it was bubble gum. In 1994, the under-a-dollar wax pack joined chewing gum as a novelty item. These days, it's more common for a collector to spend upwards of $50 on a box of cards than to plunk down pocket change for a wax pack.

Whether buying sets or packs, here's the expanded lineup of brands from major manufacturers hobbyists could choose from in 1994.

Basic Sets: Donruss, Fleer, Fleer Update, O-Pee-Chee, Pacific, Score, Topps, Topps Traded, Triple Play, Collector's Choice, Upper Deck Fun Pack.

Premium Sets: Bowman, Extra Bases, Leaf, Pinnacle, Select, Sportflics, Stadium Club, Studio, Ultra, Upper Deck.

Super-Premium Sets: Bowman's Best, Flair, Leaf Limited, Pacific Prisms, Finest, Upper Deck SP.

Judging by collector interest, the most popular 1994 sets were Bowman's Best, Donruss, Topps Finest, Leaf Limited, Pinnacle, Ultra and Upper Deck SP. But by no means did brand-new material dominate the marketplace. Vintage rebounded somewhat, and collectors stayed hot on the trail of 1992 Bowman, 1992 Fleer Update, 1993 Topps Finest and 1993 Upper Deck SP.

KIT YOUNG

"Serving Collectors Since 1976"

• Satisfaction Guaranteed •

INTRODUCTORY OFFER ½ PRICE SPECIAL

You can buy a Topps sample card from every year 1955-1991. This is a great chance to learn what cards looked like in the early years.

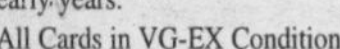

All Cards in VG-EX Condition

1 card from each year..........only $12.95
3 cards from each year.........only $37.95
6 cards from each year.........only $69.95

DO YOU RECEIVE THE HOBBY'S #1 CATALOGUE?

You should if you collect the following:

- 1950's-60's-70's Cards
- Rookie Cards
- Complete Sets
- Superstars
- Unopened Cases
- Investor Specials
- Football Cards
- Pre War Cards
- Card Lots
- Lesser Condition Cards
- Basketball Cards
- Rare & Unusual Items

To receive our catalogue (plus a new one every 30 days) send five (5) $.32 stamps.

We have just acquired the ultimate in sports memorabilia Gift Giving! An autographed baseball of a true living legend, the Yankee Clipper, Joltin' Joe.... Joe DiMaggio.

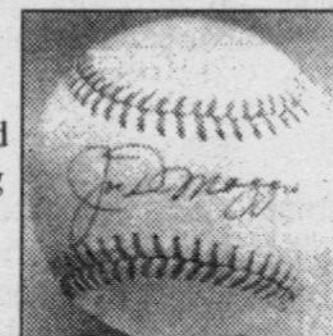

Each ball is accompanied with a special letter of authenticity issued by Scoreboard, Inc.

Special Sale Price $199.95.

TOPPS CARD LOTS

All cards VG-EX condition

	10 Diff.	25 Diff.	50 Diff.
1952	$65.00	$145.00	$275.00
1953	64.00	130.00	-
1954	58.00	129.00	-
1955	35.00	85.00	165.00
1956	40.00	95.00	175.00
1957	25.00	60.00	118.00
1958	20.00	45.00	86.00
1959	14.00	34.00	62.00
	50 Diff.	**100 Diff.**	**200 Diff.**
1960	$72.00	$135.00	$259.00
1961	67.00	135.00	259.00
1962	49.00	95.00	189.00
1963	42.00	83.00	-
1964	35.00	-	129.00
1965	31.00	59.00	116.00
1966	31.00	58.00	115.00
1967	31.00	58.00	115.00
1968	29.00	55.00	119.00
1969	29.00	55.00	105.00
1970	12.00	25.00	49.00
1971	14.00	27.00	54.00
1972	12.00	24.00	46.00
1973	11.00	21.00	-

BUYING CARDS

We have been buying cards through the mail (or at conventions) since 1976, and make hundreds of purchases each year. We will buy the following:

A) **Complete Collections** - including accumulations of all sizes
B) **Complete Sets** - from 1983 and older, including partial sets
C) **Star Cards** - Hall of Famers and Rookies, 1983 and older
D) **Older Cards** - All cards (Baseball & Football) before 1970, including Pre-War cards

If you have cards to sell, please call or write us. We will handle all transactions professionally and confidentially.

SPECIAL AUCTIONS

We offer special auctions of new and old cards, sets, lots & memorabilia several times a year. Many at bargain prices. Please send five (5) 32¢ stamps to receive our next three auctions.

Postage: Please include $3.25 per lot for introductory offer and lots under 200 cards. $4.25 per lot of 200 cards or more.

KIT YOUNG
DEPT. ZZ
11535 SORRENTO VALLEY ROAD, #403
SAN DIEGO, CA 92121

"SERVING COLLECTORS SINCE 1976"

Phone (619) 259-1300 Mon.-Fri. 8-6 PST
Fax (619) 259-1675 Sat. 8:30-5:30 PST

Less Is More

More major sets and inserts meant more choices for collectors and dealers. At the same time, more product lines didn't translate into a corresponding increase in the number of cards. Some manufacturers, for instance, trimmed the size of sets to offset the beefed up set lineup. Pinnacle weighed in at 80 cards lighter, from 620 in 1993 to 540 in 1994. Upper Deck went even further, dropping from 840 in 1993 to 550 cards.

"People really want to collect stars and rookies," explained Rich Bradley of Upper Deck. "Doing 800 cards, you are really digging down to unknown players to fill out the set. Most of our sets are smaller now because of that."

The year also saw the continued trend of another concession to the law (or perception) of supply and demand. As they had done in 1993, several companies announced production runs before releasing sets. Donruss announced the production of 17,500 cases, with 5,000 of which hobby-only. Leaf Limited delivered a grand total of 3,000 cases, and Pinnacle Brands capped its Select release at 4,950 cases of each series.

Pinnacle's Roy Whitehead said the company recognized a demand in the hobby for published limits at least on some of the card sets. "Limiting production has been a marketing decision, not a financial decision," said Whitehead. "In 1994 we were the only company that said we would print less. It guarantees scarcity and that demand will exceed supply."

Insertmania Continues

Insert cards continued to demand huge collector interest in 1994 as evidenced by the production of 115 different sets. Among those, the parallel set phenomenon came into its own. One company, Topps, kicked off the trend in 1992 with its Gold cards, juiced up versions of the regular cards inserted about one per box. In 1994, Pinnacle, Topps and Upper Deck spun off parallel inserts from a majority of their brands.

To stand out among the crowd, cardmakers added more of a "lottery" allure to their foil packs by inserting these scarce parallel inserts. Many complete set price tags quickly surpassed the $1,000 barrier and most of them remained above that heady mark throughout the year. Members of this four-digit club were Bowman's Best Refractors, Collector's Choice Gold Signature, Finest Refractors, Pinnacle Artist's Proofs, Pinnacle Museum Collection, Stadium Club First Day Issue and Upper Deck SP Holoview Red (actually a parallel version of an insert set).

The Pinnacle Artist's Proofs inserts towered over this exclusive parallel pack. Powered by Ken Griffey Jr., Frank Thomas and Cal Ripken Jr., the 540-card set hovered above the $4,000 level at the end of 1994.

The card designs for inserts ranged from the traditional to the innovative to the provocative. Donruss continued a 13-year old tradition with the production of a 30-card Diamond Kings set. Pinnacle used an innovative production technique called dufexing with its Museum Collection, one of the year's most attractive entries. Taking innovation a step further, Studio Editor's Choice ventured into the realm of multimedia with an "uncut film strip" look. Flair Hot Gloves, one of the few strong performers late in the year, built upon the cutting-edge die-cut design that started with 1993 Upper SP Platinum Power inserts.

Amid all the choices, collectors saw much less of one type of chase card: autographed inserts. As recently as 1992, insert cards were signed by 19 different superstars and hobby legends ranging from Cal Ripken to Ted Williams. In 1994 just Fleer and Upper Deck touted certified signatures.

Tim Salmon lent his hand to a 12-card insert set in the regular Fleer issue, and Darren Daulton and John Kruk signed cards for a 20-card Ultra Phillies Finest insert issue. In its Upper Deck set, the company included 3,000 cards featuring Griffey Jr. and Mickey Mantle. Each player signed 1,000 and both autographed another 1,000. A different insert carried the autograph of 1993 No. 1 draft pick Alex Rodriguez, who broke into the big leagues last season as Seattle's starting shortstop.

Ironically, autographed inserts have been all but chased from the market because they are too difficult to pull from packs.

"I don't think autographed cards sell one extra pack of cards of today's environment," explained Ted Taylor of Fleer. "They were the forerunner of insert cards. But they are so lean and so scarce that the odds of finding one have ultimately diminished their popularity."

One Strike and You're Out

No mention of the hobby in 1994 is complete without discussion of the Major League Baseball strike, which began Aug. 12 and caused a premature end to the season and a cancellation of the World Series for the first time since 1904. The hobby suffered because of the vacant ballparks, and two issues were postponed or canceled. Sportflics Rookie and Traded was revived as a retail-only product, and Series II from the Ted Williams Co. was dropped.

For the most part, card manufacturers were spared the full force of the strike. They had sold most of their 1994 product before play stopped, but dealers met mixed success moving their brand-new supplies without the help of a prime sales tool: television highlights.

"Where the strike had the most effect was with the casual collector," Upper Deck's Bradley said. "Those people will buy what is in the news. . . . Orel Hershiser testifying in court is just not good highlight material."

Still, there were exceptions to the softening market for recent releases. Tremendous pre-strike statistics sustained the popularity of many current superstars covering the spectrum from youth — Griffey, Thomas and Jeff Bagwell — to longtime favorites — Tony Gwynn, Greg Maddux, Don Mattingly, Kirby Puckett, Ripken and Matt Williams. George Brett and Nolan Ryan shared top billing among retired players possibly because they retired in 1993 and because the Hall of Fame certainly will open its doors to them in 1999.

Possibly because of the strike, vintage cards enjoyed a reversal of fortune after a bit of rough going just one year earlier. Dealers reported improved sales on material from the 1950s, '60s and early '70s, and attributed the upswing to frustrated collectors directing their attention away from players associated with the strike.

Changing of the Guard

Plenty of good highlight material captivated all hobbyists before the bats went silent. Whether the offensive explosion in '94 was the result of a juiced ball or expansion is subject to debate, the onslaught was dramatic. In terms of offense, the strike ended what might have been one of the most historically significant seasons in baseball history.

Thomas and Bagwell had legitimate chances at becoming the first Triple Crown winners since Carl Yastrzemski in 1967. The Big Hurt, however, would have faced a tough challenge from Griffey and Albert Belle in all three categories. And Bagwell was locked in a home run horse race with Williams and Bonds. He also was looking up at Gwynn in the batting race. Gwynn was batting .394 and was just three hits shy of the .400 mark when play stopped.

Thomas and Bagwell were named MVPs in the shortened season. Greg

Maddux won an unprecedented third straight NL Cy Young Award, and a revitalized David Cone won his first in the junior circuit. Rising stars such as Mike Piazza, Belle and Kenny Lofton also continued to shine in the hobby.

The strike also temporarily halted a couple of key statistical pursuits that could have a lasting impact on how collectors view some future Cooperstown residents. Thirty-eight year old Eddie Murray was well within striking distance of both 3,000 hits and 500 homers when play was stopped. And Dave Winfield's shot at 500 homers was put on hold 37 dingers shy. Gwynn, Wade Boggs, Paul Molitor and Puckett (all in search of 3,000 hits) and Jack Morris (a shot at 300 wins) also missed crucial playing time.

But the player with the most to lose was the incomparable Ripken, whose cards were some of the most popular in the entire hobby in '94. Baltimore's iron man was 122 games short of breaking Lou Gehrig's consecutive games streak of 2,130 at the time of the strike. With the off-season threat of the owners using replacement players to start the '95 campaign, Ripken faced the very real possibility of seeing his streak come to an end over baseball's worst labor dispute.

The Dodgers' Raul Mondesi upstaged all other rookies with scene-stealing play in all phases of the game. The rifle-armed right fielder batted .306 with 16 home runs, and he led the majors with 16 assists. He ran away with the NL Rookie of the Year Award, and his cards were the most sought after of all rookies. Other rookies who garnered considerable attention in the hobby included Carlos Delgado, Cliff Floyd, (AL ROY) Bob Hamelin, Jeffrey Hammonds, Ryan Klesko, Javier Lopez, Chan Ho Park, Manny Ramirez and Rondell White.

While many future superstars flashed signs of brilliance, one certified legend bowed out. The Cubs' Ryne Sandberg pre-empted the strike and shocked the baseball world by hanging up his spikes after playing just 34 games. Only one Sandberg highlight remains: his induction into the Hall of Fame as one of the game's greatest all-around second basemen.

What's in Store for 1995?

In 1995, our hobby will see the continuation of many trends distinguishing 1994. A protracted move toward premium sets is bringing about the virtual end to the foil pack for under $1. Only Score's basic packs could be purchased for less than a buck (99 cents) among the early releases. Even Topps has taken its basic set to the next level.

"This is probably the best Topps product ever," said Topps spokesman Marty Appel, as the '95 hobby season approached. "Every card has gold foil stamping and the photography is excellent. The look of the set is where our Stadium Club set was just a couple of years ago."

In 1995 and beyond, we will also see the card companies take more chances with their various product lines. Fleer offered a glimpse of this with its 1995 basic offering, which features an MTV look and six different card front designs.

Insertmania, too, will continue to evolve. Donruss planned to join the "limited production" insert set craze in '95 with a Printer's Proof set of its own, while Topps, Pinnacle, and Upper Deck planned various restrictions in production levels for some sets. Among the early releases, Collector's Choice SE came in one-fourth the size of 1994 Collector's Choice Series I.

Even with all the new trends evident in '94 and planned for '95, one thing is certain. The baseball card hobby is here to stay, and the major players have demonstrated that they have what it takes to react to the ever changing environment shaping our hobby.

Tol Broome is a freelance writer in Greensboro, N.C.

Introduction

Welcome to the exciting world of baseball card collecting, America's fastest-growing avocation. You have made a good choice in buying this book, since it will open up to you the entire panorama of this field in the simplest, most concise way. It is estimated that more than a third of a million different baseball cards have been issued during the past century. And the number of total cards put out by all manufacturers last year has been estimated at several billion, with an initial wholesale price of more than $1 billion. Sales of previously issued cards by dealers may account for a like or greater amount. With all that cardboard available in the marketplace, it should be no surprise that several million sports fans like you collect baseball cards today.

The growth of *Beckett Baseball Card Monthly* is another indication of this rising crescendo of popularity for baseball cards. Founded in 1984 by Dr. James Beckett, the author of this Price Guide, *Beckett Baseball Card Monthly* has grown to the pinnacle of the baseball card hobby with more than half a million readers anxiously awaiting each enjoyable issue.

So collecting baseball cards — while still pursued as a hobby with youthful exuberance by kids in the neighborhood — has also taken on the trappings of an industry, with thousands of full- and part-time card dealers, as well as vendors of supplies, clubs and conventions. In fact, each year since 1980 thousands of hobbyists have assembled for a National Sports Collectors Convention, at which hundreds of dealers have displayed their wares, seminars have been conducted, autographs penned by sports notables, and millions of cards changed hands. These colossal affairs have been staged in Los Angeles, Detroit, St. Louis, Chicago, New York, Anaheim, Arlington (Texas), San Francisco, Atlantic City, Atlanta and Houston. So baseball card collecting really is national in scope!

This increasing interest has been reflected in card values. As more collectors compete for available supplies, card prices (especially for premium-grade cards) rise. A national publication indicated a "very strong advance" in baseball card prices during the past decade. Which brings us back around again to the book you have in your hands. It is the best annual guide available to this exciting world of baseball cards. Read it and use it. May your enjoyment and your card collection increase in the coming months and years.

How to Collect

Each collection is personal and reflects the individuality of its owner. There are no set rules on how to collect cards. Since card collecting is a hobby or leisure pastime, what you collect, how much you collect, and how much time and money you spend collecting are entirely up to you. The funds you have available for collecting and your own personal taste should determine how you collect. Information and ideas presented here are intended to help you get the most enjoyment from this hobby.

It is impossible to collect every card ever produced. Therefore, beginners as well as intermediate and advanced collectors usually specialize in some way. One of the reasons this hobby is popular is that individual collectors can define and tailor their collecting methods to match their own tastes. To give you some ideas of the various approaches to collecting, we will list some of the more popular areas of specialization.

Many collectors select complete sets from particular years. For example, they may concentrate on assembling complete sets from all the years since their birth or since they became avid sports fans. They may try to collect a card for every player during that specified period of time.

Complete Baseball Card Sets

Regular Issues

1995 Topps	call for price
1994 Topps (792)	45.00
1993 Topps (825)	35.00
1992 Topps (792)	25.00
1991 Topps (792)	25.00
1990 Topps (792)	25.00
1990 thru 1994 All 5 sets for	145.00
1989 Topps (792)	25.00
1988 Topps (792)	25.00
1988 thru 1994 All 7 sets for	190.00
1987 Topps (792)	25.00
1986 Topps (792)	40.00
1986 thru 1995 All 9 sets for	250.00
1985 Topps (792)	85.00
1984 Topps (792)	70.00
1993 Topps Finest (199)	300.00
1994 Stadium Club Series 1 (270)	25.00
1993 Stadium Club Series 1 (300)	25.00
1992 Stadium Club Series 1 (300)	25.00
1992 Stadium Club Series 2 (300)	25.00
1992 Stadium Club Series 3 (300)	25.00
1992 Stadium Club Complete (900)	65.00
1993 Stadium Club Special All-Star (200)	30.00
1992 Stadium Club Skydome (200)	35.00
1991 Stadium Club Charter Member Set with Ryan Medallion (50)	50.00
1994 Bowman (682)	125.00
1993 Bowman (708)	120.00
1992 Bowman (705)	350.00
1991 Bowman (704)	20.00
1990 Bowman (528)	20.00
1989 Bowman (484)	20.00
1989 thru 1991 All 3 sets for	57.00
1995 Donruss	call for price
1994 Donruss (660)	60.00
1993 Donruss (792)	40.00
1992 Donruss (784)	25.00
1991 Donruss (784)	20.00
1990 Donruss (716)	15.00
1989 Donruss (660)	18.00
1988 Donruss (660)	22.00
1987 Donruss (660)	50.00
1987 thru 1994 All 8 sets for	225.00
1993 Leaf Series 2 (220)	25.00
1992 Leaf (528)	25.00
1993 Leaf Studio (220)	22.00
1995 Fleer (600)	50.00
1994 Fleer (720)	55.00
1993 Fleer (720)	44.00
1992 Fleer (720)	30.00
1991 Fleer (720)	15.00
1990 Fleer (660)	15.00
1989 Fleer (660)	23.00
1988 Fleer (660)	40.00
1987 Fleer (660)	85.00
1986 Fleer (660)	115.00
1993 Fleer Ultra Series 1 (300)	25.00
1992 Fleer Ultra Series 1 (300)	30.00
1992 Fleer Ultra Series 2 (300)	25.00
1991 Fleer Ultra (400)	28.00
1995 Score	call for price
1994 Score (660)	40.00
1993 Score (660)	45.00
1992 Score (900)	35.00
1991 Score (900)	25.00
1990 Score (704) Retail	20.00
1990 Score (714) Hobby	30.00
1989 Score (660)	20.00
1988 Score (660)	20.00
1994 Pinnacle Series 1 (270)	25.00
1994 Pinnacle Series 2 (270)	25.00
1993 Pinnacle Series 1 (310)	30.00
1992 Pinnacle Series 1 (310)	28.00
1992 Pinnacle Series 2 (310)	23.00
1995 Collectors Choice	call for price
1994 Collectors Choice (675) with 5 Gold Signature Cards	45.00
1994 Upper Deck (550)	55.00
1993 Upper Deck (840)	60.00
1992 Upper Deck (800)	40.00
1991 Upper Deck (800)	25.00
1990 Upper Deck (800)	30.00
1989 Upper Deck (800)	140.00
1993 Action Packed (84)	30.00
1992 Classic Minor League Update (50)	10.00
1991 Classic Draft Pick (50)	15.00
1990 Collect-A-Book (36)	10.00
1990 O-Pee-Chee (792)	30.00
1988 O-Pee-Chee (396)	16.00
1990 Sportflics (225)	40.00
1989 Sportflics (225)	35.00
1987 Sportflics (200)	30.00
1987 Sportflics Rookies (50)	15.00
1986 Sportflics Rookies (50)	20.00
1987 Sportflics Team Preview (26)	10.00

Traded or Update Issues

1994 Topps Traded (132)	35.00
1993 Topps Traded (132)	16.00
1992 Topps Traded (132)	25.00
1991 Topps Traded (132)	13.00
1990 Topps Traded (132)	9.00
1989 Topps Traded (132)	9.00
1988 Topps Traded (132)	25.00
1988 thru 1994 All 7 sets for	115.00
1987 Topps Traded (132)	11.00
1986 Topps Traded (132)	23.00
1985 Topps Traded (132)	30.00
'85-'94 All 10 sets for	175.00
1991 Donruss Rookies (56)	8.00
1990 Donruss Rookies (56)	9.00
1989 Donruss Rookies (56)	16.00
1988 Donruss Rookies (56)	24.00
1987 Donruss Rookies (56)	24.00
1994 Fleer Update (210)	29.00
1993 Fleer Final Edition (310)	18.00
1991 Fleer Update (132)	8.00
1990 Fleer Update (132)	10.00
1989 Fleer Update (132)	12.00
1988 Fleer Update (132)	18.00
1987 Fleer Update (132)	15.00
1986 Fleer Update (132)	30.00
1985 Fleer Update (132)	35.00
1991 Fleer Ultra Update (120)	65.00
1992 Score Traded (110)	35.00
1991 Score Traded (110)	8.00
1990 Score Traded (110)	14.00
1989 Score Traded (110)	14.00
1988 Score Traded (110)	65.00
1992 Pinnacle Rookies (30)	15.00
1992 Upper Deck High No. (100)	10.00
1991 Upper Deck High No. (100)	8.00
1991 Upper Deck Final Edition (100)	10.00
1990 Upper Deck High No. (100)	10.00
1989 Upper Deck High No. (100)	15.00

Specialty Sets

1993 Topps Black Gold (44)	16.00
1993 Topps Series 2 Gold (429)	65.00
1991 Topps '53 Archives (330)	85.00
1991 Topps '90 Major League Debut (171)	40.00
1990 Topps '89 Major League Debut (152)	17.00
1990 Topps Bigs (330)	30.00
1988 Topps Bigs (264)	30.00
1989 Topps Senior League (132)	9.00
1990 Topps Glossy All Stars (22)	6.00
1988 Topps Glossy All Stars (22)	6.00
1985 Topps Glossy All Stars (22)	6.00
1988 Topps Glossy Mail In All Stars (60)	10.00
1988 Topps United Kingdom (88)	7.00
1986 Topps Supers (60)	8.00
1985 Topps Home Run Kings (33)	12.00
1989 Donruss Traded (56)	8.00
1987 Donruss Highlights (56)	5.00
1987 Donruss Opening Day (272)	15.00
1987 Donruss All-Stars (64)	7.00
1986 Donruss All-Stars (64)	7.00
1989 Donruss All-Star Pop Ups (20)	6.00
1988 Donruss All-Star Pop Ups (20)	6.00
1986 Donruss All-Star Pop Ups (20)	6.00
1991 Donruss Large Diamond Kings (28)	12.00
1990 Donruss Large Diamond Kings (28)	12.00
1989 Donruss Large Diamond Kings (28)	12.00
1988 Donruss Large Diamond Kings (28)	12.00
1986 Donruss Large Diamond Kings (28)	12.00
1987 Fleer Minis (120)	10.00
1986 Fleer Minis (120)	12.00
1993 Fleer Excel Minor League (250)	55.00
1992 Pinnacle Team 2000 (80)	35.00
1989 Score Master (42)	12.00
1990 Score Young Superstars (84)	15.00
1989 Score Young Superstars (84)	20.00
1988 Score Young Superstars (80)	20.00
1992 Upper Deck Hologram (54)	30.00
1992 Upper Deck All-Star Fan Fest (54)	25.00
1992 Upper Deck Home Run Heroes (26)	30.00
1991 Upper Deck Silver Slugger (18)	30.00

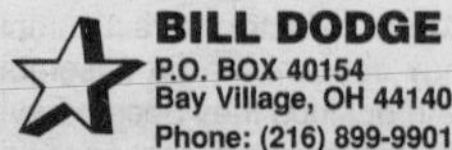

Seventeen years of quality mail order service

Many others wish to acquire only certain players. Usually such players are the superstars of the sport, but occasionally collectors will specialize in all the cards of players who attended a particular college or came from a certain town. Some collectors are only interested in the first cards or Rookie Cards of certain players. A handy guide for collectors interested in pursuing the hobby this way is the *Sport Americana Baseball Card Alphabetical Checklist No. 6.*

Another fun way to collect cards is by team. Most fans have a favorite team, and it is natural for that loyalty to be translated into a desire for cards of the players on that favorite team. For most of the recent years, team sets (all the cards from a given team for that year) are readily available at a reasonable price. *The Sport Americana Team Baseball Card Checklist* will open up this field to the collector.

Obtaining Cards

Several avenues are open to card collectors. Cards still can be purchased in the traditional way: by the pack at the local candy, grocery, drug or major discount stores.

But there are also thousands of card shops across the country that specialize in selling cards individually or by the pack, box, or set. Another alternative is the thousands of card shows held each month around the country, which feature anywhere from eight to 800 tables of sports cards and memorabilia for sale.

For many years, it has been possible to purchase complete sets of baseball cards through mail-order advertisers found in traditional sports media publications, such as *The Sporting News, Baseball Digest, Street & Smith yearbooks,* and others. These sets also are advertised in the card collecting periodicals. Many collectors will begin by subscribing to at least one of the hobby periodicals, all with good up-to-date information. In fact, subscription offers can be found in the advertising section of this book.

Most serious card collectors obtain old (and new) cards from one or more of several main sources:

- trading or buying from other collectors or dealers;
- responding to sale or auction ads in the hobby publications;
- buying at a local hobby store;
- attending sports collectibles shows or conventions.

We advise that you try all four methods since each has its own distinct advantages: (1) trading is a great way to make new friends; (2) hobby periodicals help you keep up with what's going on in the hobby (including when and where the conventions are happening); (3) stores provide the opportunity to enjoy personalized service and consider a great diversity of material in a relaxed sports-oriented atmosphere; and (4) shows allow you to choose from multiple dealers and thousands of cards under one roof in a competitive situation.

Preserving Your Cards

Cards are fragile. They must be handled properly in order to retain their value. Careless handling can easily result in creased or bent cards. It is, however, not recommended that tweezers or tongs be used to pick up your cards since such utensils might mar or indent card surfaces and thus reduce those cards' conditions and values.

In general, your cards should be handled directly as little as possible.

This is sometimes easier to say than to do.

Although there are still many who use custom boxes, storage trays, or even shoe boxes, plastic sheets are the preferred method of many collectors for storing cards.

A collection stored in plastic pages in a three-ring album allows you to view your collection at any time without the need to touch the card itself. Cards can also be kept in single holders (of various types and thickness) designed for the enjoyment of each card individually.

For a large collection, some collectors may use a combination of the above methods. When purchasing plastic sheets for your cards, be sure that you find the pocket size that fits the cards snugly. Don't put your 1951 Bowmans in a sheet designed to fit 1981 Topps.

Most hobby and collectibles shops and virtually all collectors' conventions will have these plastic pages available in quantity for the various sizes offered, or you can purchase them directly from the advertisers in this book.

Also, remember that pocket size isn't the only factor to consider when looking for plastic sheets. Other factors such as safety, economy, appearance, availability, or personal preference also may indicate which types of sheets a collector may want to buy.

Damp, sunny and/or hot conditions — no, this is not a weather forecast — are three elements to avoid in extremes if you are interested in preserving your collection.

- Too much (or too little) humidity can cause the gradual deterioration of a card;
- Direct, bright sun (or fluorescent light) over time will bleach out the color of a card;
- Extreme heat accelerates the decomposition of the card.

On the other hand, many cards have lasted more than 75 years without much scientific intervention. So be cautious, even if the above factors typically present a problem only when present in the extreme. It never hurts to be prudent.

Collecting vs. Investing

Collecting individual players and collecting complete sets are both popular vehicles for investment and speculation.

Most investors and speculators stock up on complete sets or on quantities of players they think have good investment potential.

There is obviously no guarantee in this book, or anywhere else for that matter, that cards will outperform the stock market or other investment alternatives in the future. After all, baseball cards do not pay quarterly dividends and cards cannot be sold at their "current values" as easily as stocks or bonds.

Nevertheless, investors have noticed a favorable long-term trend in the past performance of baseball and other sports collectibles, and certain cards and sets have outperformed just about any other investment in some years.

Many hobbyists maintain that the best investment is and always will be the building of a collection, which traditionally has held up better than outright speculation.

Some of the obvious questions are: Which cards? When to buy? When to sell? The best investment you can make is in your own education.

The more you know about your collection and the hobby, the more informed the decisions you will be able to make. We're not selling investment tips. We're selling information about the current value of baseball cards. It's up to you to use that information to your best advantage.

Terminology

Each hobby has its own language to describe its area of interest. The nomenclature traditionally used for trading cards is derived from the American Card Catalog, published in 1960 by Nostalgia Press. That catalog, written by Jefferson Burdick (who is called the "Father of Card Collecting" for his pioneering work), uses letter and number designations for each separate set of cards. The letter used in the ACC designation refers to the generic type of card. While both sport and non-sport issues are classified in the ACC, we shall confine ourselves to the sport issues. The following list defines the letters and their meanings as used by the American Card Catalog.

(none) or N - 19th Century U.S. Tobacco
B - Blankets
D - Bakery Inserts Including Bread
E - Early Candy and Gum
F - Food Inserts
H - Advertising
M - Periodicals
PC - Postcards
R - Candy and Gum since 1930

Following the letter prefix and an optional hyphen are one-, two-, or three-digit numbers,

R(-)999. These typically represent the company or entity issuing the cards. In several cases, the ACC number is extended by an additional hyphen and another one- or two-digit numerical suffix. For example, the 1957 Topps regular-series baseball card issue carries an ACC designation of R414-11. The "R" indicates a Candy or Gum card produced since 1930. The "414" is the ACC designation for Topps Chewing Gum baseball card issues, and the "11" is the ACC designation for the 1957 regular issue (Topps' eleventh baseball set). Like other traditional methods of identification, this system provides order to the process of cataloging cards; however, most serious collectors learn the ACC designation of the popular sets by repetition and familiarity, rather than by attempting to "figure out" what they might or should be. From 1948 forward, collectors and dealers commonly refer to all sets by their year, maker, type of issue, and any other distinguishing characteristic. For example, such a characteristic could be an unusual issue or one of several regular issues put out by a specific maker in a single year. Regional issues are usually referred to by year, maker, and sometimes by title or theme of the set.

Glossary/Legend

Our glossary defines terms used in the card collecting hobby and in this book. Many of these terms are also common to other types of sports memorabilia collecting. Some terms may have several meanings depending on use.

AA - Awesome Action
ACC - Acronym for American Card Catalog.
ALP - Alphabetical checklist.
ANN - Announcer.
AS - All-Star card. A card portraying an All-Star Player of the previous year that says "All-Star" on its face.
ASA - All-Star Advice
ATG - All-Time Great card.
ATL - All-Time Leaders card.
AW - Award Winner.
AU - With autograph.
BC - Bonus Card

BL - Blue letters.

BLANKET - A felt square (normally 5 to 6 inches) portraying a baseball player.

BOX - Card issued on a box or a card depicting a Boxer.

BRICK - A group of 50 or more cards having common characteristics that is intended to be bought, sold or traded as a unit.

CABINETS - Popular and highly valuable photographs on thick card stock produced in the 19th and early 20th century.

CC - Career Contributor.

CH - Community Heroes.

CHECKLIST - A list of the cards contained in a particular set. The list is always in numerical order if the cards are numbered. Some unnumbered sets are artificially numbered in alphabetical order, by team and alphabetically within the team, or by uniform number for convenience.

CL - Checklist card. A card that lists in order the cards and players in the set or series. Older checklist cards in Mint condition that have not been marked are very desirable and command premiums.

CO - Coach.

COIN - A small disc of metal or plastic portraying a player in its center.

COLLECTOR - A person who engages in the hobby of collecting cards primarily for his own enjoyment, with any profit motive being secondary.

COLLECTOR ISSUE - A set produced for the sake of the card itself with no product or service sponsor. It derives its name from the fact that most of these sets are produced for sale directly to the hobby market.

COM - Card issued by the Post Cereal Company through their mail-in offer.

COMBINATION CARD - A single card depicting two or more players (but not a team card).

COMM - Commissioner.

COMMON CARD - The typical card of any set; it has no premium value accruing from subject matter, numerical scarcity, popular demand, or anomaly.

CONVENTION - A gathering of dealers and collectors at a single location for the purpose of buying, selling, and trading sports memorabilia items. Conventions are open to the public and sometimes feature autograph guests, door prizes, contests, seminars, etc. They are frequently referred to simply as "shows."

CONVENTION ISSUE - A set produced in conjunction with a sports collectibles convention to commemorate or promote the show.

COOP - Cooperstown.

COR - Corrected card.

COUPON - See Tab.

CY - Cy Young Award.

DC - Draft Choice.

DD - Diamond Debut.

DEALER - A person who engages in buying, selling, and trading sports collectibles or supplies. A dealer may also be a collector, but as a dealer, his main goal is to earn a profit.

DIE-CUT - A card with part of its stock partially cut, allowing one or more parts to be folded or removed. After removal or appropriate folding, the remaining part of the card can frequently be made to stand up.

DISC - A circular-shaped card.

DISPLAY CARD - A sheet, usually containing three to nine cards, that is printed and used by the manufacturer to advertise and/or display the packages containing his products and cards. The backs of display cards are blank or contain advertisements.

DK - Diamond King.

DL - Division Leaders.

DP - Double Print (a card that was printed in double the quantity compared to the other cards in the same series) or a Draft Pick card.

DS - Diamond Skills.
DT - Dream Team.
EP - Elite Performer.
ERA - Earned Run Average.
ERR - Error card. A card with erroneous information, spelling, or depiction on either side of the card. Most errors are not corrected by the producing card company.
EXHIBIT - The generic name given to thick-stock, postcard-size cards with single color obverse pictures. The name is derived from the Exhibit Supply Co. of Chicago, the principal manufacturer of this type of card. These also are known as Arcade cards since they were found in many arcades.
FAN - Fantastic Finishers.
FDP - First or First Round Draft Pick.
FOIL - Foil embossed stamp on card.
FOLD - Foldout.
FRAN - The Franchise.
FS - Father/son card.
FULL SHEET - A complete sheet of cards that has not been cut up into individual cards by the manufacturer. Also called an uncut sheet.
FUN - Fun Cards.
GL - Green letters.
GS - Glow Stars.
HERO - Upper Deck Heros.
HES - Headline Stars.
HH - Hometown Heros.
HIGH NUMBER - The cards in the last series of numbers in a year in which such higher-numbered cards were printed or distributed in significantly lesser amounts than the lower-numbered cards. The high-number designation refers to a scarcity of the high-numbered cards. Not all years have high numbers in terms of this definition.
HL - Highlight card.
HOF - Hall of Fame, or a card that portrays a Hall of Famer (HOFer).
HOR - Horizontal pose on card as opposed to the standard vertical orientation found on most cards.
HS - Hot Shots.
I - Idols.
IA - In Action card.
IF - Infielder.
IN - Inside the Numbers.
INSERT - A card of a different type or any other sports collectible (typically a poster or sticker) contained and sold in the same package along with a card or cards of a major set. An insert card is either unnumbered or not numbered in the same sequence as the major set. Sometimes the inserts are randomly distributed and are not found in every pack.
ISSUE - Synonymous with set, but usually used in conjunction with a manufacturer, e.g., a Topps issue.
K - Strikeout.
KM - K-Man.
KP - Kid Picture.
KS - Kid Stars.
LAYERING - The separation or peeling of one or more layers of the card stock, usually at the corner of the card.
LEGITIMATE ISSUE - A set produced to promote or boost sales of a product or service, e.g., bubblegum, cereal, cigarettes, etc. Most collector issues are not legitimate issues in this sense.

LH - Little Hot Shots.

LHP - Lefthanded pitcher.

LID - A circular-shaped card (possibly with tab) that forms the top of the container for the product being promoted.

LL - League leaders or large letters on card.

MAJOR SET - A set produced by a national manufacturer of cards containing a large number of cards. Usually 100 or more different cards comprise a major set.

MB - Master Blaster.

MC - Members Choice.

MEM - Memorial card. For example, the 1990 Donruss and Topps Bart Giamatti cards.

MG - Manager.

MINI - A small card; for example, a 1975 Topps card of identical design but smaller dimensions than the regular Topps issue of 1975.

ML - Major League.

MVP - Most Valuable Player.

NAU - No autograph on card.

NH - No-Hitter.

NNOF - No Name on Front.

NOF - Name on Front.

NON-SPORT CARD - A card from a set whose major theme is a subject other than a sports subject. A card of a sports figure or event that is part of a non-sport set is still a non-sport card, e.g., while the "Look 'N' See" non-sport card set contains a card of Babe Ruth, a sports figure, that card is a non-sport card.

NOTCHING - The grooving of the card, usually caused by fingernails, rubber bands, or bumping card edges against other objects.

NT - Now and Then.

OBVERSE - The front, face, or pictured side of the card.

OF - Outfield or Outfielder.

OLY - Olympics Card.

ORG - Organist.

P - Pitcher or Pitching pose.

P1 - First Printing.

P2 - Second Printing.

P3 - Third Printing.

PANEL - An extended card that is composed of two or more individual cards. Often the panel forms the back part of the container for the product being promoted, e.g., a Hostess panel, a Bazooka panel, an Esskay Meat panel.

PCL - Pacific Coast League.

PLASTIC SHEET - A clear, plastic page that is punched for insertion into a binder (with standard three-ring spacing) containing pockets for displaying cards. Many different styles of sheets exist with pockets of varying sizes to hold the many differing card formats. Also called a display sheet or storage sheet.

PR - Printed name on back.

PREMIUM - A card, sometimes on photographic stock, that is purchased or obtained in conjunction with, or redemption for, another card or product. The premium is not packaged in the same unit as the primary item.

PRES - President.

PUZZLE CARD - A card whose back contains a part of a picture which, when joined correctly with other puzzle cards, forms the completed picture.

PUZZLE PIECE - A die-cut piece designed to interlock with similar pieces.

PV - ProVision.

PVC - Polyvinyl Chloride, a substance used to make many of the popular card display protective sheets. Non-PVC sheets are considered preferable for long-term storage of cards by many.

QS - Quick Start.

RARE - A card or series of cards of very limited availability. Unfortunately, "rare" is a subjective term frequently used indiscriminately to hype value. "Rare" cards are harder to obtain than "scarce" cards.

RB - Record Breaker.

REGIONAL - A card or set of cards issued and distributed only in a limited geographical area of the country.

REVERSE - The back or narrative side of the card.

RHP - Righthanded pitcher.

RIF - Rifleman.

ROY - Rookie of the Year.

RP - Relief pitcher.

RR - Rated Rookies (a subset featured in Donruss sets) or Rookie Rocker.

RRT - Rookie Rocket.

RS - Record Setter.

RT - Round Trippers.

SA - Super Action card.

SASE - Self-Addressed, Stamped Envelope.

SB - Stolen Bases.

SCARCE - A card or series of cards of limited availability. This subjective term is sometimes used indiscriminately to hype value. "Scarce" cards are not as difficult to obtain as "rare" cards.

SCR - Script name on back.

SD - San Diego Padres.

SEMI-HIGH - A card from the next to last series of a sequentially issued set. It has more value than an average card and generally less value than a high number. A card is not called a semi-high unless the next to last series in which it exists has an additional premium attached to it.

SERIES - The entire set of cards issued by a particular producer in a particular year; e.g., the 1971 Topps series. Also, within a particular set, series can refer to a group of (consecutively numbered) cards printed at the same time; e.g., the first series of the 1957 Topps issue (#'s1-88).

SET - One each of the entire run of cards of the same type produced by a particular manufacturer during a single year. In other words, if you have a complete set of 1976 Topps then you have every card from #1 up to and including #660, i.e., all of the different cards that were produced.

SF - Starflics.

SH - Shades (Score Pinnacle).

SI - Sidelines.

SKIP-NUMBERED - A set that has many unissued card numbers between the lowest number in the set and the highest number in the set; e.g., the 1948 Leaf baseball set contains 98 cards skip-numbered from #1 to #168. A major set in which a few numbers were not printed is not considered to be skip-numbered.

SLUG - Silver Slugger card (1991 Bowman).

SOT - Stars of Tomorrow.

SP - Single or Short Print (a card which was printed in lesser quantity compared to the other cards in the same series; see also DP and TP).

SPECIAL CARD - A card that portrays something other than a single player or team; for example, a card that portrays the previous year's statistical leaders or the results from the previous year's World Series.

SR - Star Rookies (Upper Deck).

SS - Shortstop.

ST - Stat Twins.

STA - Standouts.

STAMP - Adhesive-backed papers depicting a player. The stamp may be individual or in a sheet of many stamps. Moisture must be applied to the adhesive in order for the stamp to be attached to another surface.

STANDARD SIZE - Most modern sports cards measure 2-1/2 by 3-1/2 inches. Exceptions are noted in card descriptions throughout this book.

STAR CARD - A card that portrays a player of some repute, usually determined by his ability, however, sometimes referring to sheer popularity.

STICKER - A card with a removable layer that can be affixed to (stuck onto) another surface.

STOCK - The cardboard or paper on which the card is printed.

STRIP CARDS - A sheet or strip of cards, particularly popular in the 1920s and 1930s, with the individual cards usually separated by broken or dotted lines.

SUPERSTAR CARD - A card that portrays a superstar; e.g., a Hall of Famer or player with strong Hall of Fame potential.

SV - Super Veteran.

TAB - A card portion set off from the rest of the card, usually with perforations, that may be removed without damaging the central character or event depicted by the card.

TBC - Turn Back the Clock.

TC - Team Checklist.

TEAM CARD - A card that depicts an entire team.

TECH - The Technicians.

TEST SET - A set, usually containing a small number of cards, issued by a national card producer and distributed in a limited section or sections of the country. Presumably, the purpose of a test set is to test market appeal for a particular type of card.

TL - Team Leader.

TOP - Top Performers.

TP - Triple Print (a card that was printed in triple the quantity compared to the other cards in the same series).

TR - Trade reference on card.

TRIMMED - A card cut down from its original size. Trimmed cards are undesirable to most collectors.

UDCA - Upper Deck Classic Alumni.

UER - Uncorrected Error.

UMP - Umpire.

UP - Up Close and Personal.

USA - Team USA.

VAR - Variation card. One of two or more cards from the same series with the same number (or player with identical pose if the series is unnumbered) differing from one another by some aspect, the different feature stemming from the printing or stock of the card. This can be caused when the manufacturer of the cards notices an error in one or more of the cards, makes the changes, and then resumes the print run. In this case there will be two versions or variations of the same card. Sometimes one of the variations is relatively scarce.

VERT - Vertical pose on card.

WC - What's the Call?

WAS - Washington National League (1974 Topps).

WL - White letter on front.

WS - World Series card.
YL - Yellow letters on front
YT - Yellow team name on front.
* - to denote multi-sport sets.

Understanding Card Values

Determining Value

Why are some cards more valuable than others? Obviously, the economic laws of supply and demand are applicable to card collecting just as they are to any other field where a commodity is bought, sold or traded in a free, unregulated market.

Supply (the number of cards available on the market) is less than the total number of cards originally produced since attrition diminishes that original quantity. Each year a percentage of cards is typically thrown away, destroyed or otherwise lost to collectors. This percentage is much, much smaller today than it was in the past because more and more people have become increasingly aware of the value of their cards.

For those who collect only Mint condition cards, the supply of older cards can be quite small indeed. Until recently, collectors were not so conscious of the need to preserve the condition of their cards. For this reason, it is difficult to know exactly how many 1953 Topps are currently available, Mint or otherwise. It is generally accepted that there are fewer 1953 Topps available than 1963, 1973 or 1983 Topps cards. If demand were equal for each of these sets, the law of supply and demand would increase the price for the least available sets. Demand, however, is never equal for all sets, so price correlations can be complicated. The demand for a card is influenced by many factors. These include:

- the age of the card;
- the number of cards printed;
- the player(s) portrayed on the card;
- the attractiveness and popularity of the set;
- the physical condition of the card.

In general, (1) the older the card, (2) the fewer the number of the cards printed, (3) the more famous, popular and talented the player, (4) the more attractive and popular the set, and (5) the better the condition of the card, the higher the value of the card will be. There are exceptions to all but one of these factors: the condition of the card. Given two cards similar in all respects except condition, the one in the best condition will always be valued higher.

While those guidelines help to establish the value of a card, the countless exceptions and peculiarities make any simple, direct mathematical formula to determine card values impossible.

Regional Variation

Since the market varies from region to region, card prices of local players may be higher. This is known as a regional premium. How significant the premium is — and if there is any premium at all — depends on the local popularity of the team and the player.

The largest regional premiums usually do not apply to superstars, who often are so well-known nationwide that the prices of their key cards are too high for local dealers to realize a premium.

Lesser stars often command the strongest premiums. Their popularity is concentrated in their home region, creating local demand that greatly exceeds overall demand.

Regional premiums can apply to popular retired players and sometimes can be found in the areas where the players grew up or starred in college.

A regional discount is the converse of a regional premium. Regional discounts occur when a player has been so popular in his region for so long that local collectors and dealers have accumulated quantities of his key cards. The abundant supply may make the cards available in that area at the lowest prices anywhere.

Set Prices

A somewhat paradoxical situation exists in the price of a complete set vs. the combined cost of the individual cards in the set. In nearly every case, the sum of the prices for the individual cards is higher than the cost for the complete set. This is prevalent especially in the cards of the last few years. The reasons for this apparent anomaly stem from the habits of collectors and from the carrying costs to dealers. Today, each card in a set normally is produced in the same quantity as all other cards in its set.

Many collectors pick up only stars, superstars and particular teams. As a result, the dealer is left with a shortage of certain player cards and an abundance of others. He therefore incurs an expense in simply "carrying" these less desirable cards in stock. On the other hand, if he sells a complete set, he gets rid of large numbers of cards at one time. For this reason, he generally is willing to receive less money for a complete set. By doing this, he recovers all of his costs and also makes a profit.

The disparity between the price of the comlete set and the sum of the individual cards also has been influenced by the fact that some of the major manufacturers now are pre-collating card sets. Since "pulling" individual cards from the sets of all five manufacturers involves a specific type of labor (and cost), the singles or star card market is not affected significantly by pre-collation.

Set prices also do not include rare card varieties, unless specifically stated. Of course, the prices for sets do include one example of each type for the given set, but this is the least expensive variety.

Scarce Series

Scarce series occur because cards issued before 1974 were made available to the public each year in several series of finite numbers of cards, rather than all cards of the set being available for purchase at one time. At some point during the year, usually toward the end of the baseball season, interest in current year baseball cards waned. Consequently, the manufacturers produced smaller numbers of these later-series cards.

Nearly all nationwide issues from post-World War II manufacturers (1948 to 1973) exhibit these series variations. In the past, Topps, for example, may have issued series consisting of many different numbers of cards, including 55, 66, 80, 88 and others. Recently, Topps has settled on what is now its standard sheet size of 132 cards, six of which comprise its 792-card set.

While the number of cards within a given series is usually the same as the number of cards on one printed sheet, this is not always the case. For example, Bowman used 36 cards on its standard printed sheets, but in 1948 substituted 12 cards during later print runs of that year's baseball cards. Twelve of the cards from the initial sheet of 36 cards were removed and replaced by 12 different cards giving, in effect, a first series of 36 cards and a second series of 12 new cards. This replacement produced a scarcity of 24 cards — the 12 cards removed from the original sheet and the 12 new cards added to the sheet. A full sheet of 1948 Bowman cards (second printing) shows that card numbers 37 through 48 have replaced 12 of the cards on the first printing sheet.

The Topps Company also has created scarcities and/or excesses of certain cards in many of its sets. Topps, however, has most frequently gone the other direction by double printing some of the cards. Double printing causes an abundance of cards of the players who are on the same sheet more than one time. During the years from 1978 to 1981, Topps double printed 66 cards out of their large 726-card set. The Topps practice of double printing cards in earlier years is the most logical explanation for the known scarcities of particular cards in some of these Topps sets.

From 1988 through 1990, Donruss short printed and double printed certain cards in its major sets. Ostensibly this was because of its addition of bonus team MVP cards in its regular-issue wax packs.

We are always looking for information or photographs of printing sheets of cards for research. Each year, we try to update the hobby's knowledge of distribution anomalies. Please let us know at the address in this book if you have first-hand knowledge that would be helpful in this pursuit.

Grading Your Cards

Each hobby has its own grading terminology — stamps, coins, comic books, record collecting, etc. Collectors of sports cards are no exception. The one invariable criterion for determining the value of a card is its condition: The better the condition of the card, the more valuable it is. Condition grading, however, is subjective. Individual card dealers and collectors differ in the strictness of their grading, but the stated condition of a card should be determined without regard to whether it is being bought or sold.

No allowance is made for age. A 1952 card is judged by the same standards as a 1992 card. But there are specific sets and cards that are condition sensitive because of their border color, consistently poor centering, etc. Such cards and sets sometimes command premiums above the listed percentages in Mint condition.

Centering

Current centering terminology uses numbers representing the percentage of border on either side of the main design. Obviously, centering is diminished in importance for borderless cards such as Stadium Club.

Slightly Off-Center (60/40): A slightly off-center card is one that, upon close inspection, is found to have one border bigger than the opposite border. This degree once was offensive to only purists, but now some hobbyists try to avoid cards that are anything other than perfectly centered.

Off-Center (70/30): An off-center card has one border that is noticeably more than twice as wide as the opposite border.

Badly Off-Center (80/20 or worse): A badly off-center card has virtually no border on one side of the card.

Miscut: A miscut card actually shows part of the adjacent card in its larger border and consequently a corresponding amount of its card is cut off.

Corner Wear

Corner wear is the most scrutinized grading criteria in the hobby. These are the major categories of corner wear:

Corner with a slight touch of wear: The corner still is sharp, but there is a slight touch of wear showing. On a dark-bordered card, this shows as a dot of white.

Fuzzy corner: The corner still comes to a point, but the point has just begun to fray. A slightly "dinged" corner is considered the same as a fuzzy corner.

Slightly rounded corner: The fraying of the corner has increased to where there is only a hint of a point. Mild layering may be evident. A "dinged" corner is considered the same as a slightly rounded corner.

Rounded corner: The point is completely gone. Some layering is noticeable.

Badly rounded corner: The corner is completely round and rough. Severe layering is evident.

Creases

A third common defect is the crease. Thedegree of creasing in a card is difficult to show in a drawing or picture. On giving the specific condition of an expensive card for sale, the seller should note any creases additionally. Creases can be categorized as to severity according to the following scale:

Light Crease: A light crease is a crease that is barely noticeable upon close inspection. In fact, when cards are in plastic sheets or holders, a light crease may not be seen (until the card is taken out of the holder). A light crease on the front is much more serious than a light crease only on the card back.

Medium Crease: A medium crease is noticeable when held and studied at arm's length by the naked eye, but does not overly detract from the appearance of the card. It is an obvious crease, but not one that breaks the picture surface of the card.

Heavy Crease: A heavy crease is one that has torn or broken through the card's picture surface, e.g., puts a tear in the photo surface.

Alterations

Deceptive Trimming: This occurs when someone alters the card in order (1) to shave off edge wear, (2) to improve the sharpness of the corners, or (3) to improve centering — obviously their objective is to falsely increase the perceived value of the card to an unsuspecting buyer. The shrinkage usually is evident only if the trimmed card is compared to an adjacent full-sized card or if the trimmed card is itself measured.

Obvious Trimming: Obvious trimming is noticeable and unfortunate. It is usually performed by non-collectors who give no thought to the present or future value of their cards.

Deceptively Retouched Borders: This occurs when the borders (especially on those cards with dark borders) are touched up on the edges and corners with magic marker or crayons of appropriate color in order to make the card appear Mint.

Categorization of Defects

Miscellaneous Flaws

The following are common minor flaws that, depending on severity, lower a card's condition by one to four grades and often render it no better than Excellent-Mint: bubbles (lumps in surface), gum and wax stains, diamond cutting (slanted borders), notching, off-centered backs, paper wrinkles, scratched-off cartoons or puzzles on back, rubber band marks, scratches, surface impressions and warping.

The following are common serious flaws that, depending on severity, lower a card's condition at least four grades and often render it no better than Good: chemical or sun fading, erasure marks, mildew, miscutting (severe off-centering), holes, bleached or re-touched borders, tape marks, tears, trimming, water or coffee stains and writing.

Condition Guide

Grades

Mint (Mt) - A card with no flaws or wear. The card has four perfect corners, 60/40 or better centering from top to bottom and from left to right, original gloss, smooth edges and original color borders. A Mint card does not have print spots, color or focus imperfections.

Near Mint-Mint (NrMt-Mt) - A card with one minor flaw. Any one of the following would lower a Mint card to Near Mint-Mint: one corner with a slight touch of wear, barely noticeable print spots, color or focus imperfections. The card must have 60/40 or better centering in both directions, original gloss, smooth edges and original color borders.

Near Mint (NrMt) - A card with one minor flaw. Any one of the following would lower a Mint card to Near Mint: one fuzzy corner or two to four corners with slight touches of wear, 70/30 to 60/40 centering, slightly rough edges, minor print spots, color or focus imperfections. The card must have original gloss and original color borders.

Excellent-Mint (ExMt) - A card with two or three fuzzy, but not rounded, corners and centering no worse than 80/20. The card may have no more than two of the following: slightly rough edges, very slightly discolored borders, minor print spots, color or focus imperfections. The card must have original gloss.

Excellent (Ex) - A card with four fuzzy but definitely not rounded corners and centering no worse than 80/20. The card may have a small amount of original gloss lost, rough edges, slightly discolored borders and minor print spots, color or focus imperfections.

Very Good (Vg) - A card that has been handled but not abused: slightly rounded corners with slight layering, slight notching on edges, a significant amount of gloss lost from the surface but no scuffing and moderate discoloration of borders. The card may have a few light creases.

Good (G), Fair (F), Poor (P) - A well-worn, mishandled or abused card: badly rounded and layered corners, scuffing, most or all original gloss missing, seriously discolored borders, moderate or heavy creases, and one or more serious flaws. The grade of Good, Fair or Poor depends on the severity of wear and flaws. Good, Fair and Poor cards generally are used only as fillers.

The most widely used grades are defined above. Obviously, many cards will not perfectly fit one of the definitions.

Therefore, categories between the major grades known as in-between grades are used, such as Good to Very Good (G-Vg), Very Good to Excellent (VgEx), and Excellent-Mint to Near Mint (ExMt-NrMt). Such grades indicate a card with all qualities of the lower category but with at least a few qualities of the higher category.

The Officail Price Guide to Baseball Cards lists each card and set in three grades, with the middle grade valued at about 40-45% of the top grade, and the bottom grade valued at about 10-15% of the top grade.

The value of cards that fall between the listed columns can also be calculated using a percentage of the top grade. For example, a card that falls between the top and middle grades (Ex, ExMt or NrMt in most cases) will generally be valued at anywhere from 50% to 90% of the top grade.

Similarly, a card that falls between the middle and bottom grades (G-Vg, Vg or VgEx in most cases) will generally be valued at anywhere from 20% to 40% of the top grade.

There are also cases where cards are in better condition than the top grade or worse than the bottom grade. Cards that grade worse than the lowest grade are generally valued at 5-10% of the top grade.

Selling Your Cards

Just about every collector sells cards or will sell cards eventually. Someday you may be interested in selling your duplicates or maybe even your whole collection. You may sell to other collectors, friends or dealers. You may even sell cards you purchased from a certain dealer back to that same dealer. In any event, it helps to know some of the mechanics of the typical transaction between buyer and seller.

Dealers will buy cards in order to resell them to other collectors who are interested in the cards. Dealers will always pay a higher percentage for items that (in their opinion) can be resold quickly, and a much lower percentage for those items that are perceived as having low demand and hence are slow moving. In either case, dealers must buy at a price that allows for the expense of doing business and a margin for profit.

Many people think nothing of going into a department store and paying $15 for an item of clothing for which the store paid $5. But if you were selling your $15 card to a dealer and he offered you $5 for it, you might consider his mark-up unreasonable. To complete the analogy: Most department stores (and card dealers) that consistently pay $10 for $15 items eventually go out of business. An exception is when the dealer has lined up a willing buyer for the item(s) you are attempting to sell, or if the cards are so Hot that it's likely he'll likely have to hold the cards for just a short period of time.

In those cases, an offer of up to 75 percent of book value still will allow the dealer to make a reasonable profit considering the short time he will need to hold the merchandise. In general, however, most cards and collections will bring offers in the range of 25 to 50 percent of retail price. Also consider that most material from the last five to 10 years is plentiful. If that's what you're selling, don't be surprised if your best offer is well below that range.

History of Baseball Cards

Today's version of the baseball card, with its colorful and oft times high-tech fronts and backs, is a far cry from its earliest predecessors. The issue remains cloudy as to which was the very first baseball card ever produced, but the institution of baseball cards dates from the latter half of the 19th century, more than 100 years ago. Early issues, generally printed on heavy cardboard, were of poor quality, with photographs, drawings, and printing far short of today's standards.

Goodwin & Co., of New York, makers of Gypsy Queen, Old Judge, and other cigarette brands, is considered by many to be the first issuer of baseball and other sports cards. Its issues, predominantly sized 1-1/2 by 2-1/2 inches, generally consisted of photographs of baseball players, boxers, wrestlers, and other subjects mounted on stiff cardboard. More than 2,000 different photos of baseball players alone have been identified. These "Old Judges," a collective name commonly used for the Goodwin & Co. cards, were issued from 1886 to 1890 and are treasured parts of many collections today.

Among the other cigarette companies that issued baseball cards still attracting attention today are Allen & Ginter, D. Buchner & Co. (Gold Coin Chewing Tobacco), and P.H. Mayo & Brother. Cards from the first two companies bear colored line drawings, while the Mayos are sepia photographs on black cardboard. In addition to the small-size cards from this era, several tobacco companies issued cabinet-size baseball cards. These "cabinets" were considerably larger than the small cards, usually about 4-1/4 by 6-1/2 inches, and were printed on heavy stock. Goodwin & Co.'s Old Judge cabinets and the National Tobacco Works' "Newsboy" baseball photos are two that remain popular today.

By 1895, the American Tobacco Company began to dominate its competition. They discontinued baseball card inserts in their cigarette packages (actually slide boxes in those days). The lack of competition in the cigarette market had made these inserts unnecessary. This marked the end of the first era of baseball cards. At the dawn of the 20th century, few baseball cards were being issued. But once again, it was the cigarette companies — particularly, the American Tobacco Company — followed to a lesser extent by the candy and gum makers that revived the practice of including baseball cards with their products. The bulk of these cards, identified in the American Card Catalog (designated hereafter as ACC) as T or E cards for 20th century "Tobacco" or "Early Candy and Gum" issues, respectively, were released from 1909 to 1915.

This romantic and popular era of baseball card collecting produced many desirable items. The most outstanding is the fabled T-206 Honus Wagner card. Other perennial favorites among collectors are the T-206 Eddie Plank card, and the T-206 Magee error card. The former was once the second most valuable card and only recently relinquished that position to a more distinctive and aesthetically pleasing Napoleon Lajoie card from the 1933-34 Goudey Gum series. The latter misspells the player's name as "Magie," the most famous and most valuable blooper card.

The ingenuity and distinctiveness of this era has yet to be surpassed. Highlights include:

• the T-202 Hassan triple-folders, one of the best looking and the most distinctive cards ever issued;

• the durable T-201 Mecca double-folders, one of the first sets with players' records on the reverse;

• the T-3 Turkey Reds, the hobby's most popular cabinet card;

• the E-145 Cracker Jacks, the only major set containing Federal League player cards;

• the T-204 Ramlys, with their distinctive black-and-white oval photos and ornate gold borders.

These are but a few of the varieties issued during this period.

Increasing Popularity

While the American Tobacco Company dominated the field, several other tobacco companies, as well as clothing manufacturers, newspapers and periodicals, game makers, and companies whose identities remain anonymous, also issued cards during this period. In fact, the Collins-McCarthy Candy Company, makers of Zeenuts Pacific Coast League baseball cards, issued cards yearly from 1911 to 1938. Its record for continuous annual card production has been exceeded only by the Topps Chewing Gum Company. The era of the tobacco card issues closed with the onset of World War I, with the exception of the Red Man chewing tobacco sets produced from 1952 to 1955.

The next flurry of card issues broke out in the roaring and prosperous 1920s, the era of the E card. The caramel companies (National Caramel, American Caramel, York Caramel) were the leading distributors of these E cards. In addition, the strip card, a continous strip with several cards divided by dotted lines or other sectioning features, flourished during this time. While the E cards and the strip cards generally are considered less imaginative than the T cards or the recent candy and gum issues, they still are pursued by many advanced collectors.

Another significant event of the 1920s was the introduction of the arcade card. Taking its designation from its issuer, the Exhibit Supply Company of Chicago, it is usually known as the "Exhibit" card. Once a trademark of the penny arcades, amusement parks and county fairs across the country, Exhibit machines dispensed nearly postcard-size photos on thick stock for one penny.

These picture cards bore likenesses of a favorite cowboy, actor, actress or baseball player. Exhibit Supply and its associated companies produced baseball cards during a longer time span, although discontinuous, than any other manufacturer. Its first cards appeared in 1921, while its last issue was in 1966. In 1979, the Exhibit Supply Company was bought and somewhat revived by a collector/dealer who has since reprinted Exhibit photos of the past.

If the T card period, from 1909 to 1915, can be designated the "Golden Age" of baseball card collecting, then perhaps the "Silver Age" commenced with the introduction of the Big League Gum series of 239 cards in 1933 (a 240th card was added in 1934). These are the forerunners of today's baseball gum cards, and the Goudey Gum Company of Boston is responsible for their success. This era spanned the period from the Depression days of 1933 to America's formal involvement in World War II in 1941.

Goudey's attractive designs, with full-color line drawings on thick card stock, greatly influenced other cards being issued at that time. As a result, the most attractive and popular vintage cards in history were produced in this "Silver Age." The 1933 Goudey Big League Gum series also owes its popularity to the more than 40 Hall of Fame players in the set. These include four cards of Babe Ruth and two of Lou Gehrig. Goudey's reign continued in 1934, when it issued a 96-card set in color, together with the single remaining card from the 1933 series, #106, the Napoleon Lajoie card.

In addition to Goudey, several other bubblegum manufacturers issued baseball cards during this era. DeLong Gum Company issued an extremely attractive set in 1933. National Chicle Company's 192-card "Batter-Up" series of 1934-1936 became the largest die-cut set in card history. In addition, that company offered the popular "Diamond Stars" series during the same period. Other popular sets included the "Tattoo Orbit" set of 60 color cards issued in 1933 and Gum Products' 75-card "Double Play" set, featuring sepia depictions of two players per card.

In 1939, Gum Inc., which later became Bowman Gum, replaced Goudey Gum as the leading baseball card producer. In 1939 and the following year, it issued two important sets of black-and-white cards. In 1939, its "Play Ball America" set consisted of 162 cards. The larger, 240-card "Play Ball" set of 1940 still is considered by many to be the most attractive black-and-white cards ever produced. That firm introduced its only color set in 1941, consisting of 72 cards titled "Play Ball Sports Hall of Fame." Many of these were colored repeats of poses from the black-and-white 1940 series.

In addition to regular gum cards, many manufacturers distributed premium issues during the 1930s. These premiums were printed on paper or photographic stock, rather than card stock. They were much larger than the regular cards and were sold for a penny across the counter with gum (which was packaged separately from the premium). They often were redeemed at the store or through the mail in exchange for the wrappers of previously purchased gum cards, a la proof-of-purchase box-top premiums today. The gum premiums are scarcer than the card issues of the 1930s and in most cases no manufacturer's name is present.

World War II brought an end to this popular era of card collecting when paper and rubber shortages curtailed the production of bubblegum baseball cards. They were resurrected again in 1948 by the Bowman Gum Company (the direct descendant of Gum, Inc.). This marked the beginning of the modern era of card collecting.

In 1948, Bowman Gum issued a 48-card set in black and white consisting of one card and one slab of gum in every 1 cent pack. That same year, the Leaf Gum Company also issued a set of cards. Although rather poor in quality, these cards were issued in color. A squabble over the rights to use players' pictures developed between Bowman and Leaf. Eventually Leaf dropped out of the card market, but not before it had left a lasting heritage to the hobby by issuing some of the rarest cards now in existence. Leaf's baseball card series of 1948-49 contained 98 cards, skip numbered to #168 (not all numbers were printed). Of these 98 cards, 49 are relatively plentiful; the other 49, however, are rare and quite valuable.

Bowman continued its production of cards in 1949 with a color series of 240 cards. Because there are many scarce "high numbers," this series remains the most difficult Bowman regular issue to complete. Although the set was printed in color and commands great interest due to its scarcity, it is considered aesthetically inferior to the Goudey and National Chicle issues of the 1930s. In addition to the regular issue of 1949, Bowman also produced a set of 36 Pacific Coast League players. While this was not a regular issue, it still is prized by collectors. In fact, it has become the most valuable Bowman series.

In 1950 (representing Bowman's one-year monopoly of the baseball card market), the company began a string of top quality cards that continued until its demise in 1955. The 1950 series was itself something of an oddity because the low numbers, rather than the traditional high numbers, were the more difficult cards to obtain.

The year 1951 marked the beginning of the most competitive and perhaps the highest quality period of baseball card production. In that year, Topps Chewing Gum Company of Brooklyn entered the market. Topps' 1951 series consisted of two sets of 52 cards each, one set with red backs and the other with blue backs. In addition, Topps also issued 31 insert cards, three of which remain the rarest Topps cards ("Current All-Stars" Konstanty, Roberts and Stanky). The 1951 Topps cards were unattractive and paled in comparison to the 1951 Bowman issues. They were successful, however, and Topps has continued to produce cards ever since.

Intensified Competition

Topps issued a larger and more attractive card set in 1952. This larger size became standard for the next five years. (Bowman followed with larger-size baseball cards in 1953.) This 1952 Topps set has become, like the 1933 Goudey series and the T-206 white border series, the classic set of its era. The 407-card set is a collector's dream of scarcities, rarities, errors and variations. It also contains the first Topps issues of Mickey Mantle and Willie Mays.

As with Bowman and Leaf in the late 1940s, competition over player rights arose. Ensuing court battles occurred between Topps and Bowman. The market split due to stiff competition, and in January 1956, Topps bought out Bowman. (Topps, using the Bowman name, resurrected Bowman as a later label in 1989.) Topps remained essentially unchallenged as the primary producer of baseball cards through 1980. So, the story of major baseball card sets from 1956 through 1980 is by and large the story of Topps' issues. Notable exceptions include the small sets produced by Fleer Gum in 1959, 1960, 1961 and 1963, and the Kellogg's Cereal and Hostess Cakes baseball cards issued to promote their products.

A court decision in 1980 paved the way for two other large gum companies to enter (or reenter, in Fleer's case) the baseball card arena. Fleer, which had last made photo cards in 1963, and the Donruss Company (then a division of General Mills) secured rights to produce baseball cards of current players, thus breaking Topps' monopoly. Each company issued major card sets in 1981 with bubblegum products.

Then a higher court decision in that year overturned the lower court ruling against Topps. It appeared that Topps had regained its sole position as a producer of baseball cards. Undaunted by the revocation ruling, Fleer and Donruss continued to issue cards in 1982 but without bubblegum or any other edible product. Fleer issued its current player baseball cards with "team logo stickers," while Donruss issued its cards with a piece of a baseball jigsaw puzzle.

Since 1981, these three major baseball card producers all have thrived, sharing relatively equal recognition. Each has steadily increased its involvement in terms of numbers of issues per year. To the delight of collectors, their competition has generated novel, and in some cases exceptional, issues of current Major League Baseball players. Collectors also eagerly accepted the debut efforts of Score (1988) and Upper Deck (1989), the newest companies to enter the baseball card producing derby.

Upper Deck's successful entry into the market turned out to be very important. The company's card stock, photography, packaging and marketing gave baseball cards a new standard for quality, and began the "premium card" trend that continues today. The second premium baseball card set to be issued was the 1990 Leaf set, named for and issued by the parent company of Donruss. To gauge the significance of the premium card trend, one need only note that two of the most valuable post-1986 regular-issue cards are the 1989 Upper Deck Ken Griffey Jr. and 1990 Leaf Frank Thomas Rookie Cards.

Sharing the Pie

The impressive debut of Leaf in 1990 was followed by Studio, Ultra, and Stadium Club in 1991. Of those, Stadium Club made the biggest impact. In 1992, Bowman, and Pinnacle joined the premium fray. In 1992, Donruss and Fleer abandoned the traditional 50-cent pack market and instead produced premium sets comparable to (and presumably designed to compete against) Upper Deck's set. Those moves, combined with the almost instantaneous spread of premium cards to the other major team sports cards, serve as strong indicators that premium cards probably are here to stay. Bowman had been a lower-level product from 1989 to '91.

In 1993, Fleer, Topps and Upper Deck produced the first "superpremium" cards with Flair Finest SP. Judging by the success of both, the baseball card market is headed toward higher, not lower, price levels.

In 1994, the market swung even further toward high-end products with the introduction of Topps' Bowman's Best (a hybrid of prospect-oriented Bowman and the superpremium Finest) and Leaf Limited. Other 1994 debuts included Upper Deck's entry-level Collector's Choice, Fleer's oversized Extra Bases and Pinnacle's hobby-only Select.

Of course; the biggest news of 1994 was the strike that halted the season prematurely. While the baseball card hobby obviously suffered from the strike, there was no catastrophic market crash as some had feared. In fact, cards of standouts such as Ken Griffey Jr., Frank Thomas and Cal Ripken continued to sell well, and tough inserts such as Flair Hot Gloves and Upper Deck SP Holoview Die-Cuts experienced strong demand long after the strike.

Overall, inserts continued to dominate the hobby scene, although there were some market indications that collectors were tiring of the parallel chase cards first introduced by Topps in 1992.

All current major card producers have become increasingly aware of the organized collecting market. While the drugstores and grocery stores down the street remain major outlets for card sales, many issues now are distributed exclusively through hobby channels. Although no one can ever say what the future will bring, one only can surmise that the hobby market will play a significant role in future plans of all the major baseball card producers.

Additional Reading

With the increase in popularity of the hobby in recent years, there has been a corresponding increase in available literature. Below is a list of the books and periodicals that receive our highest recommendation and that we hope will further advance your knowledge and enjoyment of our great hobby.

Baseball Card Price Guide by Dr. James Beckett (Seventeenth Edition, $19.95, released 1995, published by Edgewater Book Company) — the most comprehensive Price Guide and checklist ever issued on baseball cards.

The Official Price Guide to Baseball Cards by Dr. James Beckett (Fifteenth Edition, $6.99, released 1995, published by The House of Collectibles) — an abridgment of *Baseball Card Price Guide* in a convenient and economical pocket-size format providing Dr. Beckett's pricing of the major baseball sets since 1948.

The Sport Americana Football Card Price Guide by Dr. James Beckett (Eleventh Edition, $16.95, released 1994, published by Edgewater Book Company) — the most comprehensive Price Guide and checklist ever issued on football cards. No serious football card hobbyist should be without it.

The Official Price Guide to Football Cards by Dr. James Beckett (Fourteenth Edition, $6.99, released 1994, published by The House of Collectibles) — an abridgment of *The Sport Americana Price Guide* listed above in a convenient and economical pocket-size format providing Dr. Beckett's pricing of the major football sets since 1948.

The Sport Americana Hockey Card Price Guide by Dr. James Beckett (Fourth Edition, $15.95, released 1994, published by Edgewater Book Company) — the most comprehensive Price Guide and checklist ever issued on hockey cards.

The Official Price Guide to Hockey Cards by Dr. James Beckett (Fourth Edition, $6.99, released 1994, published by The House of Collectibles) — an abridgment of *The Sport Americana Price Guide* listed above in a convenient and economical pocket-size format providing Dr. Beckett's pricing of the major hockey sets since 1951.

The Sport Americana Basketball Card Price Guide and Alphabetical Checklist by Dr. James Beckett (Fourth Edition, $15.95, released 1995, published by Edgewater Book Company) — the most comprehensive combination Price Guide and alphabetical checklist ever issued on basketball cards.

The Official Price Guide to Basketball Cards by Dr. James Beckett (Fourth Edition, $6.99, released 1994, published by The House of Collectibles) — an abridgment of *The Sport Americana Price Guide* listed above in a convenient and economical pocket-size format providing Dr. Beckett's pricing of the major basketball sets since 1948.

The Sport Americana Baseball Card Alphabetical Checklist by Dr. James Beckett (Sixth Edition, $15.95, released 1994, published by Edgewater Book Company) — an alphabetical listing, by the last name of the player portrayed on the card, of virtually all baseball cards (major league and minor league) produced through the 1992 major sets.

Beckett Baseball Card Monthly, published and edited by Dr. James Beckett — contains the most extensive and accepted monthly Price Guide, collectible glossy superstar covers, colorful feature articles, "Hot List" section, Convention Calendar, tips for beginners, "Readers Write" letters to and responses from the editor, autograph collecting tips and profiles of the sport's Hottest stars. Published every month, *BBCM* is the hobby's largest paid circulation periodical. *Beckett Football Card Monthly, Beckett Basketball Monthly, Beckett Hockey Monthly, Beckett Focus on Future Stars, Beckett Tribute* and *Beckett Racing Monthly* were built on the success of *BBCM*.

Acknowledgments

A great deal of diligence, hard work, and dedicated effort went into this year's volume. However, the high standards to which we hold ourselves could not have been met without the expert input and generous amount of time contributed by many people. Our sincere thanks are extended to each and every one of you.

Those who have worked closely with us on this and many other books have again proven themselves invaluable — Action Packed (Laurie Goldberg), Chris Benjamin, Levi Bleam, Peter Brennan, Ray Bright, Card Collectors Co., Cartophilium (Andrew Pywowarczuk), Classic (Mark Pokedoff), Barry Colla, Bill and Diane Dodge, David Festberg, Fleer (Jeff Massien and Ted Taylor), Steve Freedman, Gervise Ford, Larry and Jeff Fritsch, Tony Galovich, Georgia Music and Sports (Dick DeCourcey), Dick Gilkeson, Steve Gold (AU Sports), Bill Goodwin (St. Louis Baseball Cards), Mike and Howard Gordon, George Grauer, John Greenwald, Wayne Grove, Bill Haber, Bill Henderson, Jerry and Etta Hersh, Mike Hersh, Neil Hoppenworth, Jay and Mary Kasper, David Kohler (SportsCards Plus), Leaf (Vince Nauss and Traci Santiago), Paul Lewicki, Lew Lipset, Mike Livingston (University Trading Cards), Mark Macrae, Bill Madden, Michael McDonald (The Sports Page), Megacards (Dawn Ridgeway, Rick Starks), Mid-Atlantic Sports Cards (Bill Bossert), John Miller, Gary Mills, Brian Morris, Mike Mosier (Columbia City Collectibles Co.), B.A. Murry, Ralph Nozaki, Mike O'Brien, Oldies and Goodies (Nigel Spill), Pacific Trading Cards (Mike and Marty Cramer), Pinnacle (Roy Whitehead), Jack Pollard, Jeff Prillaman, Gavin Riley, Alan Rosen (Mr. Mint), Clifton Rouse, John Rumierz, San Diego Sport Collectibles (Bill Goepner and Nacho Arredondo), Kevin Savage (Sports Gallery), Gary Sawatski, Mike Schechter, Signature Rookies (Tim Johnson), Barry Sloate, John E. Spalding, Phil Spector (Scoreboard, Inc.), Sports Collectors Store, Frank Steele, Murvin Sterling, Lee Temanson, Topps (Marty Appel, Sy Berger, Bob Ibach), Treat (Harold Anderson), Ed Twombly (New England Bullpen), Upper Deck (Rich Bradley), Wayne Varner, Bill Vizas, Bill Wesslund (Portland Sports Card Co.), Ted Williams Card Company (Andy Abramson), Kit Young, Ted Zanidakis, and Bill Zimpleman. Finally we give a special acknowledgment to the late Dennis W. Eckes, "Mr. Sport Americana." The success of the Beckett Price Guides has always been the result of a team effort.

It is very difficult to be "accurate" — one can only do one's best. But this job is especially difficult since we're shooting at a moving target: Prices are fluctuating all the time. Having several full-time pricing experts has definitely proven to be better than just one, and I thank all of them for working together to provide you, our readers, with the most accurate prices possible.

Many people have provided price input, illustrative material, checklist verifications, errata, and/or background information. We should like to individually thank AbD Cards (Dale Wesolewski), Action Card Sales, Jerry Adamic, Johnny and Sandy Adams, Alex's MVP Cards & Comics, Doug Allen (Round Tripper Sportscards), Will Allison, Dennis Anderson, Ed Anderson, Shane Anderson, Bruce W. Andrews, Ellis Anmuth, Tom Antonowicz, Ric Apter, Jason Arasate, Clyde Archer, Matt Argento, Burl Armstrong, Neil Armstrong (World Series Cards), Todd Armstrong, B and J Sportscards, Dave Bailey, Shawn Bailey, Ball Four Cards (Frank and Steve Pemper), Frank and Vivian Barning, Bob Bartosz, Nathan Basford, Carl Berg, David Berman, Beulah Sports (Jeff Blatt), Brian Bigelow, George Birsic, B.J. Sportscollectables, David Boedicker (The Wild Pitch Inc.), Bob Boffa, Tim Bond (Tim's Cards & Comics), Brian W. Bottles, Bill Brandt, Jeff Breitenfield, John Brigandi, Chuck Brooks, Dan Bruner, Lesha Bundrick, Michael Bunker, John E. Burick, Ed Burkey Jr., Bubba Burnett, Virgil Burns,

California Card Co., Capital Cards, Danny Cariseo, Carl Carlson (C.T.S.), Jim Carr, Patrick Carroll, Carves Cards, Ira Cetron, Don Chaffee, Michael Chan, Sandy Chan, Ric Chandgie, Dwight Chapin, Ray Cherry, Bigg Wayne Christian, Dick Cianciotto, Derrick F. Clark, Bill Cochran, Don Coe, Tom Cohoon (Cardboard Dreams), Collection de Sport AZ (Ronald Villaneuve), Gary Collett, Andrew T. Collier, Charles A. Collins, Curt Cooter, Steven Cooter, Pedro Cortes, Rick Cosmen (RC Card Co.), Lou Costanzo (Champion Sports), Mike Coyne, Paul and Ryan Crabb, Kevin Crane, Taylor Crane, Chad Cripe, Brian Cunningham, Allen Custer, Donald L. Cutler, Eugene C. Dalager, Dave Dame, Brett Daniel, Tony Daniele III, Roy Datema, John Davidson, Travis Deaton, Dee's Baseball Cards (Dee Robinson), Tim DelVecchio, Steve Dempski, John Derossett, Mark Diamond, Gilberto Diaz Jr., Ken Dinerman (California Cruizers), Discount Dorothy, Walter J. Dodds Sr., Bill Dodson, Richard Dolloff (Dolloff Coin Center), Ron Dorsey, Double Play Baseball Cards, Richard Duglin (Baseball Cards-N-More), The Dugout, Kyle Dunbar, B.M. Dungan, Ken Edick (Home Plate of Utah), Randall Edwards, Rick Einhorn, Mark Ely, Todd Entenman, Doak Ewing, Bryan Failing, R.J. Faletti, John Fedak, Stephen A. Ferradino, Tom Ferrara, Louis Fineberg, Jay Finglass, L.V. Fischer, Fremont Fong, Perry Fong, Craig Frank, Mark Franke, Walter Franklin, Richard Galasso, Ray Garner, David Garza, David Gaumer, Georgetown Card Exchange, Richard Gibson Jr., Glenn A. Giesey, Dick Goddard, Dr. John R. Goldberg, Alvin Goldblum, Brian Goldner, Jeff Goldstein, Ron Gomez, Greg's Cards, Mike Grimm, Neil Gubitz (What-A-Card), Hall's Nostalgia, Hershell Hanks, Gregg Hara, Zac Hargis, Floyd Haynes (H and H Baseball Cards), Ben Heckert, Kevin Heimbigner, Dennis Heitland, Joel Hellman, Arthur W. Henkel, Hit and Run Cards (Jon, David, and Kirk Peterson), Gary Holcomb, Lyle Holcomb, Rich Hovorka, John Howard, Mark Hromalik, H.P. Hubert, Dennis Hughes, Harold Hull, Johnny Hustle Card Co., Tom Imboden, Chris Imbriaco, Vern Isenberg, Robert A. Ivanjack (Kit Young Cards), Dale Jackson, Hal Jarvis, Paul Jastrzembski, Jeff's Sports Cards, David Jenkins, Donn Jennings Cards, George Johnson, Robe Johnson, Stephen Jones, Steven L. Judd, Al Julian, Dave Jurgensmeier, John Just, Robert Just, Frank J. Katen, Jerry Katz (Bottom of the Ninth), Mark Kauffman, Allan Kaye, Rick Keplinger, Sam Kessler, Kevin's Kards, Larry B. Killian, Kingdom Collectibles, Inc., Philip C. Klutts, Steven Koenigsberg, Blake Krier, Neil Krohn, Scott Ku, Thomas Kunnecke, Gary Lambert, Matthew Lancaster (MC's Card and Hobby), Jason Lassic, Allan Latawiec, Gerald A. Lavelle, Dan Lavin, Richard S. Lawrence, William Lawrence, W.H. Lee, Morley Leeking, Ronald Lenhardt, Brian Lentz, Tom Leon, Leo's Sports Collectibles, Irv Lerner, Lisa Licitra, James Litopoulos, Larry Loeschen (A and J Sportscards), Allan Lowenberg, Kendall Loyd (Orlando Sportscards South), Robert Luce, David Macaray, Jim Macie, Joe Maddigan, David Madison, Rob Maerten, Pierre Marceau, Paul Marchant, Rich Markus, Bob Marquette, Brad L. Marten, Ronald L. Martin, Frank J. Masi, Bill Mastro, Duane Matthes, James S. Maxwell Jr., Dr. William McAvoy, Michael McCormick, Paul McCormick, McDag Productions Inc., Branson H. McKay, Tony McLaughlin, Mendal Mearkle, Ken Melanson, William Mendel, Eric Meredith, Blake Meyer (Lone Star Sportscards), Joe Michalowicz, Lee Milazzo, Jimmy Milburn, Cary S. Miller, David (Otis) Miller, Eldon Miller, George Miller, Wayne Miller, Dick Millerd, Mitchell's Baseball Cards, Perry Miyashita, Douglas Mo, William Munn, Mark Murphy, John Musacchio, National Sportscard Exchange, Bud Obermeyer, Francisco Ochoa, John O'Hara, Mike Orth, Ron Oser, Luther Owen, Earle Parrish, Clay Pasternack, Mickey Payne, Michael Perrotta, Doug and Zachary Perry, Tom Pfirrmann, Bob Pirro, George Pollitt, Don Prestia, Coy Priest, Bob Ragonese, Richard H. Ranck, Robert M. Ray, R.W. Ray, Phil Regli, Tom Reid, Glenn Renick, Rob Resnick, John Revell, Bill Rodman, Craig Roehrig, David H. Rogers, Michael H. Rosen, Martin Rotunno, Michael Runyan, Mark Rush, George Rusnak, Mark Russell, Terry Sack, Joe

Sak, Jennifer Salems, Barry Sanders, Everett Sands, Jon Sands, Dave Schau (Baseball Cards), Bruce M. Schwartz, Keith A. Schwartz, Charlie Seaver, Tom Shanyfelt, Steven C. Sharek, Art Smith, Ben Smith, Michael Smith, Jerry Sorice, Carl Specht, Sports Card Fan-Attic, The Sport Hobbyist, Dauer Stackpole, Norm Stapleton, Bill Steinberg, Bob Stern, Bill Stone, Tim Strandberg (East Texas Sports Cards), Edward Strauss, Strike Three, Richard Strobino, Superior Sport Card, Dr. Richard Swales, Paul Taglione, George Tahinos, Ian Taylor, Lyle Telfer, The Thirdhand Shoppe, Scott A. Thomas, Paul Thornton, Carl N. Thrower, Jim Thurtell, Bud Tompkins (Minnesota Connection), Philip J. Tremont, Ralph Triplette, Mike Trotta, Umpire's Choice Inc., Eric Unglaub, Nathan Voss, Steven Wagman, Jonathan Waldman, Terry Walker, T. Wall, Gary A. Walter, Mark Weber, Joe and John Weisenburger (The Wise Guys), Richard West, Mike Wheat, Richard Wiercinski, Don Williams (Robin's Nest of Dolls), Jeff Williams, Kent Williams, Craig Williamson, Opry Winston, Brandon Witz, John Wolf Jr., Jay Wolt (Cavalcade of Sports), Carl Womack, Pete Wooten, Peter Yee, Wes Young, Robert Zanze (Z-Cards and Sports), Dean Zindler, Tom Zmuda (Koinz & Kardz), and Tim Zwick.

Every year we make active solicitations for expert input. We are particularly appreciative of help (however extensive or cursory) provided for this volume. We receive many inquiries, comments and questions regarding material within this book. In fact, each and every one is read and digested. Time constraints, however, prevent us from personally replying. But keep sharing your knowledge. Your letters and input are part of the "big picture" of hobby information we can pass along to readers in our books and magazines. Even though we cannot respond to each letter, you are making significant contributions to the hobby through your interest and comments.

The effort to continually refine and improve this book also involves a growing number of people and types of expertise on our home team. Our company boasts a substantial Technical Services team, which strengthens our ability to provide comprehensive analysis of the marketplace. Technical Services capably handled numerous technical details and provided able assistance in the preparation of this edition.

Our baseball analysts played a major part in compiling this year's book, travelling thousands of miles during the past year to attend sports card shows and visit card shops around the United States and Canada. The Beckett baseball specialists are Theo Chen, Ben Ecklar, Mike Jaspersen, Eddie Kelly, Rich Klein, Tom Layberger, Grant Sandground and Dave Sliepka. Their detailed pricing analysis and careful proofreading were key contributions to the accuracy of this annual.

Theo Chen's coordination of pricing input as *Beckett Baseball Card Monthly* title analyst helped immeasurably, as did Tom Layberger's coordination of the pricing and description of sets listed in *BBCM.* As book title analyst, Rich Klein contributed his encyclopedic knowledge, which he combined with meticulous attention to detail during the proofing process.

The effort was directed by Technical Services manager Rich Olivieri. He was ably assisted by the rest of the Price Guide analysts: Pat Blandford, Dan Hitt, Allan Muir and Steve Smith. Also contributing to Technical Services functions were Jeff Allison, Jeany Finch, Tom Finch, Travis Raczynski, Gabriel Rangel, Brett Setter and Rob Springs.

The price gathering and analytical talents of this fine group of hobbyists have helped make our Beckett team stronger, while making this guide and its companion monthly Price Guide more widely recognized as the hobby's most reliable and relied upon sources of pricing information.

Granted, the production of any book is a total team effort. However, I owe special thanks to the members of our Book Team, who demonstrated extraordinary contributions to this massive undertaking. Managing editor Steve Wilson supervised a dedicated staff that continues to grow in expertise. He set up initial schedules and ensured that all deadlines were met, while looking for all the fine points to improve our process and presentation throughout the cycle.

Scott Layton, assistant manager of Special Projects, served as point man in the demanding area of new set entry and was a key person in the organization of both technological and people resources for the book. He was ably assisted by Beverly Mills and Maria Neubauer, who helped enter new sets (a record number this year), ensured the proper administration of our contributor Price Guide surveys and performed various other tasks. Also contributing to the Book Team effort was Teri McGahey.

Our computer experts, Rich Olivieri, Jordan Gallagher and the Information Services team, spent countless hours programming, testing and implementing new software to simplify the handling of thousands of prices that must be checked and updated for each edition of this book.

Airey Baringer made sure the production process ran smoothly, and Paul Kerutis coordinated the typesetting and was responsible for the card photos you see throughout the book. Matt Bowling contributed his design skills to enhance readability, and he pitched in along with Mary Gonzalez-Davis and Kaki Matheson during the arduous production cycle.

Carrie Ehrhardt spent tireless hours on the phone attending to the wishes of our dealer advertisers, and she was assisted by Loretta Gibbs. Once the ad specifications were delivered to our offices, John Marshall used his computer skills to turn raw copy into attractive display advertisements.

In the years since this guide debuted, Beckett Publications has grown beyond any rational expectation. A great many talented and hard working individuals have been instrumental in this growth and success. Our whole team is to be congratulated for what we together have accomplished. Our Beckett Publications team is led by Director of Finance Claire Backus, Vice Presidents Jeff Amano, Joe Galindo and Fred L. Reed III, and Senior Managers Beth Harwell, Mark Harwell, Pepper Hastings, Jay Johnson and Reed Poole. They are ably assisted by Dana Alecknavage, Theresa Anderson, Jeff Anthony, Chris Arends, Kelly Atkins, Kaye Ball, Marvin Bang, Barbara Barry, Nancy Bassi, James R. Beane, Therese Bellar, Christa Bencomo, Louise Bird, Cathryn Black, Amy Brougher, Bob Brown, Chris Calandro, Randy Calvert, Emily Camp, Mary Campana, Susan Catka, Jud Chappell, Albert Chavez, Evelyn Clark, Tommy Collins, Belinda Cross, Randy Cummings, Patrick Cunningham, Marlon DePaula, Marcelo Gomes DeSouza, Gail Docekal, Alejandro Egusquiza, Paulo Egusquiza, Eric Evans, Craig Ferris, Jorge Field, Sara Field, Jean Paul Figari, Kim Ford, Gayle Gasperin, Anita Gonzalez, Rosanna Gonzalez-Olaechea, Jeff Greer, Mary Gregory, Robert Gregory, Jenifer Grellhesl, Julie Grove, Patti Harris, Jenny Harwell, Joanna Hayden, Chris Hellem, Tracy Hinton, Tim Jaksa, Deliese Jaspersen, Julia Jernigan, Heidi Johnson, Wendy Kizer, Rudy Klancnik, Frances Knight, Jane Ann Layton, Sara Leeman, Benedito Leme, Lori Lindsey, Stanley Lira, Lisa Lujan, Sara Maneval, Louis Marroquin, Mike McAllister, Omar Mediano, Lisa Monaghan, Sherry Monday, Rob Moore, Mila Morante, Daniel Moscoso Jr., Mike Moss, Randy Mosty, Hugh Murphy, Shawn Murphy, Steve Naughton, Michael O'Hara, Lisa O'Neill, Stacy Olivieri, Mike Pagel, Wendy Pallugna, Laura Patterson, Mike Payne, Diego Picon, Tim Polzer, Fran Poole, Bob Richardson, Tina Riojas, Susan Sainz, Gary Santaniello, Janice Seydel, Elaine Simmons, Judi Smalling, Lynn Smith, Sheri Smith, Jeff Stanton, Laura Steele, Margaret Steele, Marcia Stoesz, Cindy Struble, Doree Tate, Peter Tepp, Jim Tereschuk, Jana Threatt, Larry Treachler, John Venable, Cindy Waisath, Patrick Wascovich, Carol Weaver and Mark Zeske. The whole Beckett Publications team has my thanks for jobs well done. Thank you, everyone.

I also thank my family, especially my wife, Patti, and our daughters, Christina, Rebecca, and Melissa, for putting up with me again.

1948 Bowman

The 48-card Bowman set of 1948 was the first major set of the post-war period. Each 2 1/16" by 2 1/2" card had a black and white photo of a current player, with his biographical information printed in black ink on a gray back. Due to the printing process and the 36-card sheet size upon which Bowman was then printing, the 12 cards marked with an SP in the checklist are scarcer numerically, as they were removed from the printing sheet in order to make room for the 12 high numbers (37-48). Many cards are found with over-printed, transposed, or blank backs. The set features the Rookie Cards of Hall of Famers Yogi Berra, Ralph Kiner, Stan Musial, Red Schoendienst, and Warren Spahn. Half of the cards in the set feature New York players (Yankees or Giants).

	NRMT	VG-E	GOOD
COMPLETE SET (48)	3600.00	1600.00	450.00
COMMON CARD (1-36)	20.00	9.00	2.50
COMMON CARD (37-48)	30.00	13.50	3.80

	NRMT	VG-E	GOOD
☐ 1 Bob Elliott	90.00	18.00	5.50
☐ 2 Ewell Blackwell	45.00	20.00	5.75
☐ 3 Ralph Kiner	140.00	65.00	17.50
☐ 4 Johnny Mize	100.00	45.00	12.50
☐ 5 Bob Feller	225.00	100.00	28.00
☐ 6 Yogi Berra	525.00	240.00	65.00
☐ 7 Pete Reiser SP	70.00	32.00	8.75
☐ 8 Phil Rizzuto SP	300.00	135.00	38.00
☐ 9 Walker Cooper	20.00	9.00	2.50
☐ 10 Buddy Rosar	20.00	9.00	2.50
☐ 11 Johnny Lindell	22.50	10.00	2.80
☐ 12 Johnny Sain	55.00	25.00	7.00
☐ 13 Willard Marshall SP	40.00	18.00	5.00
☐ 14 Allie Reynolds	50.00	23.00	6.25
☐ 15 Eddie Joost	20.00	9.00	2.50
☐ 16 Jack Lohrke SP	40.00	18.00	5.00
☐ 17 Enos Slaughter	100.00	45.00	12.50
☐ 18 Warren Spahn	300.00	135.00	38.00
☐ 19 Tommy Henrich	35.00	16.00	4.40
☐ 20 Buddy Kerr SP	40.00	18.00	5.00
☐ 21 Ferris Fain	25.00	11.50	3.10
☐ 22 Floyd Bevens SP	50.00	23.00	6.25
☐ 23 Larry Jansen	20.00	9.00	2.50
☐ 24 Dutch Leonard SP	40.00	18.00	5.00
☐ 25 Barney McCosky	20.00	9.00	2.50
☐ 26 Frank Shea SP	50.00	23.00	6.25
☐ 27 Sid Gordon	20.00	9.00	2.50
☐ 28 Emil Verban SP	40.00	18.00	5.00
☐ 29 Joe Page SP	55.00	25.00	7.00
☐ 30 Whitey Lockman SP	50.00	23.00	6.25
☐ 31 Bill McCahan	20.00	9.00	2.50
☐ 32 Bill Rigney	20.00	9.00	2.50
☐ 33 Bill Johnson	22.50	10.00	2.80
☐ 34 Sheldon Jones SP	40.00	18.00	5.00
☐ 35 Snuffy Stirnweiss	20.00	9.00	2.50
☐ 36 Stan Musial	800.00	350.00	100.00
☐ 37 Clint Hartung	30.00	13.50	3.80
☐ 38 Red Schoendienst	150.00	70.00	19.00
☐ 39 Augie Galan	30.00	13.50	3.80
☐ 40 Marty Marion	75.00	34.00	9.50
☐ 41 Rex Barney	35.00	16.00	4.40
☐ 42 Ray Poat	30.00	13.50	3.80
☐ 43 Bruce Edwards	30.00	13.50	3.80
☐ 44 Johnny Wyrostek	30.00	13.50	3.80
☐ 45 Hank Sauer	40.00	18.00	5.00
☐ 46 Herman Wehmeier	30.00	13.50	3.80
☐ 47 Bobby Thomson	80.00	36.00	10.00
☐ 48 Dave Koslo	55.00	13.50	3.80

1949 Bowman

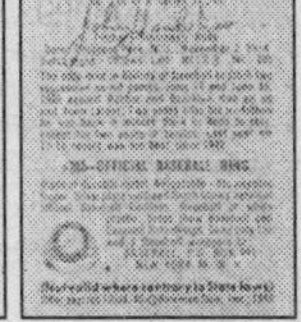

The cards in this 240-card set measure approximately 2 1/16" by 2 1/2". In 1949 Bowman took an intermediate step between black and white and full color with this set of tinted photos on colored backgrounds. Collectors should note the series price variations, which reflect some inconsistencies in the printing process. There are four major varieties in name printing, which are noted in the checklist below: NOF: name on front; NNOF: no name on front; PR: printed name on back; and SCR: script name on back. These variations resulted when Bowman used twelve of the lower numbers to fill out the last press sheet of 36 cards, adding to numbers 217-240. Cards 1-3 and 5-73 can be found with either gray or white backs. The set features the Rookie Cards of Hall of Famers Roy Campanella, Bob Lemon, Robin Roberts, Duke Snider, and Early Wynn as well as Rookie Cards of Richie Ashburn and Gil Hodges.

	NRMT	VG-E	GOOD
COMPLETE SET (240)	14000.	6300.	1800.
COMMON (1-3/5-36/73)	15.00	6.75	1.90
COMMON CARD (37-72)	15.00	6.75	1.90
COMMON CARD (4/74-108)	15.00	6.75	1.90
COMMON CARD (109-144)	15.00	6.75	1.90
COMMON CARD (145-180)	50.00	23.00	6.25
COMMON CARD (181-240)	50.00	23.00	6.25

	NRMT	VG-E	GOOD
☐ 1 Vern Bickford	80.00	16.00	4.80
☐ 2 Whitey Lockman	18.00	8.00	2.30
☐ 3 Bob Porterfield	18.00	8.00	2.30
☐ 4A Jerry Priddy NNOF	15.00	6.75	1.90

☐	4B	Jerry Priddy NOF	43.00	19.50	5.50
☐	5	Hank Sauer	15.00	6.75	1.90
☐	6	Phil Cavarretta	15.00	6.75	1.90
☐	7	Joe Dobson	15.00	6.75	1.90
☐	8	Murry Dickson	15.00	6.75	1.90
☐	9	Ferris Fain	18.00	8.00	2.30
☐	10	Ted Gray	15.00	6.75	1.90
☐	11	Lou Boudreau	60.00	27.00	7.50
☐	12	Cass Michaels	15.00	6.75	1.90
☐	13	Bob Chesnes	15.00	6.75	1.90
☐	14	Curt Simmons	35.00	16.00	4.40
☐	15	Ned Garver	15.00	6.75	1.90
☐	16	Al Kozar	15.00	6.75	1.90
☐	17	Earl Torgeson	15.00	6.75	1.90
☐	18	Bobby Thomson	35.00	16.00	4.40
☐	19	Bobby Brown	50.00	23.00	6.25
☐	20	Gene Hermanski	15.00	6.75	1.90
☐	21	Frank Baumholtz	18.00	8.00	2.30
☐	22	Peanuts Lowrey	15.00	6.75	1.90
☐	23	Bobby Doerr	65.00	29.00	8.25
☐	24	Stan Musial	500.00	230.00	65.00
☐	25	Carl Scheib	15.00	6.75	1.90
☐	26	George Kell	55.00	25.00	7.00
☐	27	Bob Feller	150.00	70.00	19.00
☐	28	Don Kolloway	15.00	6.75	1.90
☐	29	Ralph Kiner	100.00	45.00	12.50
☐	30	Andy Seminick	18.00	8.00	2.30
☐	31	Dick Kokos	15.00	6.75	1.90
☐	32	Eddie Yost	25.00	11.50	3.10
☐	33	Warren Spahn	160.00	70.00	20.00
☐	34	Dave Koslo	15.00	6.75	1.90
☐	35	Vic Raschi	55.00	25.00	7.00
☐	36	Pee Wee Reese	175.00	80.00	22.00
☐	37	Johnny Wyrostek	15.00	6.75	1.90
☐	38	Emil Verban	15.00	6.75	1.90
☐	39	Billy Goodman	15.00	6.75	1.90
☐	40	Red Munger	15.00	6.75	1.90
☐	41	Lou Brissie	15.00	6.75	1.90
☐	42	Hoot Evers	15.00	6.75	1.90
☐	43	Dale Mitchell	15.00	6.75	1.90
☐	44	Dave Philley	15.00	6.75	1.90
☐	45	Wally Westlake	15.00	6.75	1.90
☐	46	Robin Roberts	225.00	100.00	28.00
☐	47	Johnny Sain	35.00	16.00	4.40
☐	48	Willard Marshall	15.00	6.75	1.90
☐	49	Frank Shea	18.00	8.00	2.30
☐	50	Jackie Robinson	800.00	350.00	100.00
☐	51	Herman Wehmeier	15.00	6.75	1.90
☐	52	Johnny Schmitz	15.00	6.75	1.90
☐	53	Jack Kramer	15.00	6.75	1.90
☐	54	Marty Marion	30.00	13.50	3.80
☐	55	Eddie Joost	15.00	6.75	1.90
☐	56	Pat Mullin	15.00	6.75	1.90
☐	57	Gene Bearden	18.00	8.00	2.30
☐	58	Bob Elliott	18.00	8.00	2.30
☐	59	Jack Lohrke	15.00	6.75	1.90
☐	60	Yogi Berra	275.00	125.00	34.00
☐	61	Rex Barney	18.00	8.00	2.30
☐	62	Grady Hatton	15.00	6.75	1.90
☐	63	Andy Pafko	15.00	6.75	1.90
☐	64	Dom DiMaggio	35.00	16.00	4.40
☐	65	Enos Slaughter	75.00	34.00	9.50
☐	66	Elmer Valo	15.00	6.75	1.90
☐	67	Alvin Dark	35.00	16.00	4.40
☐	68	Sheldon Jones	15.00	6.75	1.90
☐	69	Tommy Henrich	35.00	16.00	4.40
☐	70	Carl Furillo	75.00	34.00	9.50
☐	71	Vern Stephens	15.00	6.75	1.90
☐	72	Tommy Holmes	18.00	8.00	2.30
☐	73	Billy Cox	30.00	13.50	3.80
☐	74	Tom McBride	15.00	6.75	1.90
☐	75	Eddie Mayo	15.00	6.75	1.90
☐	76	Bill Nicholson	15.00	6.75	1.90
☐	77	Ernie Bonham	15.00	6.75	1.90
☐	78A	Sam Zoldak NNOF	15.00	6.75	1.90
☐	78B	Sam Zoldak NOF	40.00	18.00	5.00
☐	79	Ron Northey	15.00	6.75	1.90
☐	80	Bill McCahan	15.00	6.75	1.90
☐	81	Virgil Stallcup	15.00	6.75	1.90
☐	82	Joe Page	15.00	6.75	1.90
☐	83A	Bob Scheffing NNOF	15.00	6.75	1.90
☐	83B	Bob Scheffing NOF	40.00	18.00	5.00
☐	84	Roy Campanella	700.00	325.00	90.00
☐	85A	Johnny Mize NNOF	90.00	40.00	11.50
☐	85B	Johnny Mize NOF	160.00	70.00	20.00
☐	86	Johnny Pesky	25.00	11.50	3.10
☐	87	Randy Gumpert	15.00	6.75	1.90
☐	88A	Bill Salkeld NNOF	15.00	6.75	1.90
☐	88B	Bill Salkeld NOF	40.00	18.00	5.00
☐	89	Mizell Platt	15.00	6.75	1.90
☐	90	Gil Coan	15.00	6.75	1.90
☐	91	Dick Wakefield	15.00	6.75	1.90
☐	92	Willie Jones	18.00	8.00	2.30
☐	93	Ed Stevens	15.00	6.75	1.90
☐	94	Mickey Vernon	35.00	16.00	4.40
☐	95	Howie Pollet	15.00	6.75	1.90
☐	96	Taft Wright	15.00	6.75	1.90
☐	97	Danny Litwhiler	15.00	6.75	1.90
☐	98A	Phil Rizzuto NNOF	150.00	70.00	19.00
☐	98B	Phil Rizzuto NOF	225.00	100.00	28.00
☐	99	Frank Gustine	15.00	6.75	1.90
☐	100	Gil Hodges	240.00	110.00	30.00
☐	101	Sid Gordon	15.00	6.75	1.90
☐	102	Stan Spence	15.00	6.75	1.90
☐	103	Joe Tipton	15.00	6.75	1.90
☐	104	Eddie Stanky	35.00	16.00	4.40
☐	105	Bill Kennedy	15.00	6.75	1.90
☐	106	Jake Early	15.00	6.75	1.90
☐	107	Eddie Lake	15.00	6.75	1.90
☐	108	Ken Heintzelman	15.00	6.75	1.90
☐	109A	Ed Fitzgerald SCR	15.00	6.75	1.90
☐	109B	Ed Fitzgerald PR	40.00	18.00	5.00
☐	110	Early Wynn	110.00	50.00	14.00
☐	111	Red Schoendienst	70.00	32.00	8.75
☐	112	Sam Chapman	15.00	6.75	1.90
☐	113	Ray LaManno	15.00	6.75	1.90
☐	114	Allie Reynolds	35.00	16.00	4.40
☐	115	Dutch Leonard	15.00	6.75	1.90
☐	116	Joe Hatton	15.00	6.75	1.90
☐	117	Walker Cooper	15.00	6.75	1.90
☐	118	Sam Mele	15.00	6.75	1.90
☐	119	Floyd Baker	15.00	6.75	1.90
☐	120	Cliff Fannin	15.00	6.75	1.90
☐	121	Mark Christman	15.00	6.75	1.90
☐	122	George Vico	15.00	6.75	1.90
☐	123	Johnny Blatnick	15.00	6.75	1.90
☐	124A	Danny Murtaugh SCR	24.00	11.00	3.00
☐	124B	Danny Murtaugh PR	45.00	20.00	5.75
☐	125	Ken Keltner	18.00	8.00	2.30
☐	126A	Al Brazle SCR	15.00	6.75	1.90
☐	126B	Al Brazle PR	40.00	18.00	5.00
☐	127A	Hank Majeski SCR	15.00	6.75	1.90
☐	127B	Hank Majeski PR	40.00	18.00	5.00
☐	128	Johnny VanderMeer	25.00	11.50	3.10
☐	129	Bill Johnson	18.00	8.00	2.30
☐	130	Harry Walker	15.00	6.75	1.90
☐	131	Paul Lehner	15.00	6.75	1.90
☐	132A	Al Evans SCR	15.00	6.75	1.90
☐	132B	Al Evans PR	40.00	18.00	5.00
☐	133	Aaron Robinson	15.00	6.75	1.90
☐	134	Hank Borowy	15.00	6.75	1.90
☐	135	Stan Rojek	15.00	6.75	1.90
☐	136	Hank Edwards	15.00	6.75	1.90
☐	137	Ted Wilks	15.00	6.75	1.90
☐	138	Buddy Rosar	15.00	6.75	1.90
☐	139	Hank Arft	15.00	6.75	1.90

	#	Player	NRMT	VG-E	GOOD
☐	140	Ray Scarborough	15.00	6.75	1.90
☐	141	Tony Lupien	15.00	6.75	1.90
☐	142	Eddie Waitkus	15.00	6.75	1.90
☐	143A	Bob Dillinger SCR	15.00	6.75	1.90
☐	143B	Bob Dillinger PR	40.00	18.00	5.00
☐	144	Mickey Haefner	15.00	6.75	1.90
☐	145	Sylvester Donnelly	50.00	23.00	6.25
☐	146	Mike McCormick	60.00	27.00	7.50
☐	147	Bert Singleton	50.00	23.00	6.25
☐	148	Bob Swift	50.00	23.00	6.25
☐	149	Roy Partee	50.00	23.00	6.25
☐	150	Allie Clark	50.00	23.00	6.25
☐	151	Mickey Harris	50.00	23.00	6.25
☐	152	Clarence Maddern	50.00	23.00	6.25
☐	153	Phil Masi	50.00	23.00	6.25
☐	154	Clint Hartung	60.00	27.00	7.50
☐	155	Mickey Guerra	50.00	23.00	6.25
☐	156	Al Zarilla	50.00	23.00	6.25
☐	157	Walt Masterson	50.00	23.00	6.25
☐	158	Harry Brecheen	50.00	23.00	6.25
☐	159	Glen Moulder	50.00	23.00	6.25
☐	160	Jim Blackburn	50.00	23.00	6.25
☐	161	Jocko Thompson	50.00	23.00	6.25
☐	162	Preacher Roe	125.00	57.50	15.50
☐	163	Clyde McCullough	50.00	23.00	6.25
☐	164	Vic Wertz	70.00	32.00	8.75
☐	165	Snuffy Stirnweiss	60.00	27.00	7.50
☐	166	Mike Tresh	50.00	23.00	6.25
☐	167	Babe Martin	50.00	23.00	6.25
☐	168	Doyle Lade	50.00	23.00	6.25
☐	169	Jeff Heath	50.00	23.00	6.25
☐	170	Bill Rigney	50.00	23.00	6.25
☐	171	Dick Fowler	50.00	23.00	6.25
☐	172	Eddie Pellagrini	50.00	23.00	6.25
☐	173	Eddie Stewart	50.00	23.00	6.25
☐	174	Terry Moore	100.00	45.00	12.50
☐	175	Luke Appling	125.00	57.50	15.50
☐	176	Ken Raffensberger	50.00	23.00	6.25
☐	177	Stan Lopata	60.00	27.00	7.50
☐	178	Tom Brown	60.00	27.00	7.50
☐	179	Hugh Casey	60.00	27.00	7.50
☐	180	Connie Berry	50.00	23.00	6.25
☐	181	Gus Niarhos	50.00	23.00	6.25
☐	182	Hal Peck	50.00	23.00	6.25
☐	183	Lou Stringer	50.00	23.00	6.25
☐	184	Bob Chipman	50.00	23.00	6.25
☐	185	Pete Reiser	100.00	45.00	12.50
☐	186	Buddy Kerr	50.00	23.00	6.25
☐	187	Phil Marchildon	50.00	23.00	6.25
☐	188	Karl Drews	50.00	23.00	6.25
☐	189	Earl Wooten	50.00	23.00	6.25
☐	190	Jim Hearn	50.00	23.00	6.25
☐	191	Joe Haynes	50.00	23.00	6.25
☐	192	Harry Gumbert	50.00	23.00	6.25
☐	193	Ken Trinkle	50.00	23.00	6.25
☐	194	Ralph Branca	100.00	45.00	12.50
☐	195	Eddie Bockman	50.00	23.00	6.25
☐	196	Fred Hutchinson	80.00	36.00	10.00
☐	197	Johnny Lindell	60.00	27.00	7.50
☐	198	Steve Gromek	50.00	23.00	6.25
☐	199	Tex Hughson	50.00	23.00	6.25
☐	200	Jess Dobernic	50.00	23.00	6.25
☐	201	Sibby Sisti	50.00	23.00	6.25
☐	202	Larry Jansen	50.00	23.00	6.25
☐	203	Barney McCosky	50.00	23.00	6.25
☐	204	Bob Savage	50.00	23.00	6.25
☐	205	Dick Sisler	60.00	27.00	7.50
☐	206	Bruce Edwards	50.00	23.00	6.25
☐	207	Johnny Hopp	50.00	23.00	6.25
☐	208	Dizzy Trout	50.00	23.00	6.25
☐	209	Charlie Keller	100.00	45.00	12.50
☐	210	Joe Gordon	100.00	45.00	12.50
☐	211	Boo Ferriss	50.00	23.00	6.25
☐	212	Ralph Hamner	50.00	23.00	6.25
☐	213	Red Barrett	50.00	23.00	6.25
☐	214	Richie Ashburn	500.00	230.00	65.00
☐	215	Kirby Higbe	50.00	23.00	6.25
☐	216	Schoolboy Rowe	60.00	27.00	7.50
☐	217	Marino Pieretti	50.00	23.00	6.25
☐	218	Dick Kryhoski	50.00	23.00	6.25
☐	219	Virgil Fire Trucks	60.00	27.00	7.50
☐	220	Johnny McCarthy	50.00	23.00	6.25
☐	221	Bob Muncrief	50.00	23.00	6.25
☐	222	Alex Kellner	50.00	23.00	6.25
☐	223	Bobby Hofman	50.00	23.00	6.25
☐	224	Satchel Paige	1000.00	450.00	125.00
☐	225	Jerry Coleman	90.00	40.00	11.50
☐	226	Duke Snider	1000.00	450.00	125.00
☐	227	Fritz Ostermueller	50.00	23.00	6.25
☐	228	Jackie Mayo	50.00	23.00	6.25
☐	229	Ed Lopat	125.00	57.50	15.50
☐	230	Augie Galan	50.00	23.00	6.25
☐	231	Earl Johnson	50.00	23.00	6.25
☐	232	George McQuinn	50.00	23.00	6.25
☐	233	Larry Doby	150.00	70.00	19.00
☐	234	Rip Sewell	50.00	23.00	6.25
☐	235	Jim Russell	50.00	23.00	6.25
☐	236	Fred Sanford	50.00	23.00	6.25
☐	237	Monte Kennedy	50.00	23.00	6.25
☐	238	Bob Lemon	240.00	110.00	30.00
☐	239	Frank McCormick	50.00	23.00	6.25
☐	240	Babe Young UER (Photo actually Bobby Young)	110.00	23.00	6.25

1950 Bowman

The cards in this 252-card set measure approximately 2 1/16" by 2 1/2". This set, marketed in 1950 by Bowman, represented a major improvement in terms of quality over their previous efforts. Each card was a beautifully colored line drawing developed from a simple photograph. The first 72 cards are the scarcest in the set, while the final 72 cards may be found with or without the copyright line. This was the only Bowman sports set to carry the famous "5-Star" logo. Key rookies in this set are Hank Bauer, Don Newcombe, and Al Rosen.

	NRMT	VG-E	GOOD
COMPLETE SET (252)	9000.00	4100.00	1150.00
COMMON CARD (1-36)	50.00	23.00	6.25
COMMON CARD (37-72)	50.00	23.00	6.25
COMMON CARD (73-108)	16.00	7.25	2.00
COMMON CARD (109-144)	16.00	7.25	2.00
COMMON CARD (145-180)	16.00	7.25	2.00
COMMON CARD (181-216)	16.00	7.25	2.00
COMMON CARD (217-252)	16.00	7.25	2.00

	#	Player			
☐	1	Mel Parnell	150.00	30.00	9.00
☐	2	Vern Stephens	55.00	25.00	7.00
☐	3	Dom DiMaggio	65.00	29.00	8.25
☐	4	Gus Zernial	60.00	27.00	7.50
☐	5	Bob Kuzava	50.00	23.00	6.25
☐	6	Bob Feller	180.00	80.00	23.00
☐	7	Jim Hegan	55.00	25.00	7.00
☐	8	George Kell	80.00	36.00	10.00
☐	9	Vic Wertz	55.00	25.00	7.00
☐	10	Tommy Henrich	65.00	29.00	8.25
☐	11	Phil Rizzuto	225.00	100.00	28.00
☐	12	Joe Page	50.00	23.00	6.25
☐	13	Ferris Fain	55.00	25.00	7.00
☐	14	Alex Kellner	50.00	23.00	6.25
☐	15	Al Kozar	50.00	23.00	6.25
☐	16	Roy Sievers	65.00	29.00	8.25
☐	17	Sid Hudson	50.00	23.00	6.25
☐	18	Eddie Robinson	50.00	23.00	6.25
☐	19	Warren Spahn	225.00	100.00	28.00
☐	20	Bob Elliott	55.00	25.00	7.00
☐	21	Pee Wee Reese	225.00	100.00	28.00
☐	22	Jackie Robinson	700.00	325.00	90.00
☐	23	Don Newcombe	150.00	70.00	19.00
☐	24	Johnny Schmitz	50.00	23.00	6.25
☐	25	Hank Sauer	50.00	23.00	6.25
☐	26	Grady Hatton	50.00	23.00	6.25
☐	27	Herman Wehmeier	50.00	23.00	6.25
☐	28	Bobby Thomson	65.00	29.00	8.25
☐	29	Eddie Stanky	55.00	25.00	7.00
☐	30	Eddie Waitkus	50.00	23.00	6.25
☐	31	Del Ennis	65.00	29.00	8.25
☐	32	Robin Roberts	150.00	70.00	19.00
☐	33	Ralph Kiner	100.00	45.00	12.50
☐	34	Murry Dickson	50.00	23.00	6.25
☐	35	Enos Slaughter	100.00	45.00	12.50
☐	36	Eddie Kazak	55.00	25.00	7.00
☐	37	Luke Appling	75.00	34.00	9.50
☐	38	Bill Wight	50.00	23.00	6.25
☐	39	Larry Doby	60.00	27.00	7.50
☐	40	Bob Lemon	75.00	34.00	9.50
☐	41	Hoot Evers	50.00	23.00	6.25
☐	42	Art Houtteman	50.00	23.00	6.25
☐	43	Bobby Doerr	75.00	34.00	9.50
☐	44	Joe Dobson	50.00	23.00	6.25
☐	45	Al Zarilla	50.00	23.00	6.25
☐	46	Yogi Berra	350.00	160.00	45.00
☐	47	Jerry Coleman	65.00	29.00	8.25
☐	48	Lou Brissie	50.00	23.00	6.25
☐	49	Elmer Valo	50.00	23.00	6.25
☐	50	Dick Kokos	50.00	23.00	6.25
☐	51	Ned Garver	50.00	23.00	6.25
☐	52	Sam Mele	50.00	23.00	6.25
☐	53	Clyde Vollmer	50.00	23.00	6.25
☐	54	Gil Coan	50.00	23.00	6.25
☐	55	Buddy Kerr	50.00	23.00	6.25
☐	56	Del Crandall	60.00	27.00	7.50
☐	57	Vern Bickford	50.00	23.00	6.25
☐	58	Carl Furillo	75.00	34.00	9.50
☐	59	Ralph Branca	65.00	29.00	8.25
☐	60	Andy Pafko	55.00	25.00	7.00
☐	61	Bob Rush	50.00	23.00	6.25
☐	62	Ted Kluszewski	100.00	45.00	12.50
☐	63	Ewell Blackwell	50.00	23.00	6.25
☐	64	Alvin Dark	65.00	29.00	8.25
☐	65	Dave Koslo	50.00	23.00	6.25
☐	66	Larry Jansen	55.00	25.00	7.00
☐	67	Willie Jones	50.00	23.00	6.25
☐	68	Curt Simmons	55.00	25.00	7.00
☐	69	Wally Westlake	50.00	23.00	6.25
☐	70	Bob Chesnes	50.00	23.00	6.25
☐	71	Red Schoendienst	75.00	34.00	9.50
☐	72	Howie Pollet	50.00	23.00	6.25
☐	73	Willard Marshall	16.00	7.25	2.00
☐	74	Johnny Antonelli	35.00	16.00	4.40
☐	75	Roy Campanella	275.00	125.00	34.00
☐	76	Rex Barney	20.00	9.00	2.50
☐	77	Duke Snider	275.00	125.00	34.00
☐	78	Mickey Owen	20.00	9.00	2.50
☐	79	Johnny VanderMeer	25.00	11.50	3.10
☐	80	Howard Fox	16.00	7.25	2.00
☐	81	Ron Northey	16.00	7.25	2.00
☐	82	Whitey Lockman	20.00	9.00	2.50
☐	83	Sheldon Jones	16.00	7.25	2.00
☐	84	Richie Ashburn	90.00	40.00	11.50
☐	85	Ken Heintzelman	16.00	7.25	2.00
☐	86	Stan Rojek	16.00	7.25	2.00
☐	87	Bill Werle	16.00	7.25	2.00
☐	88	Marty Marion	25.00	11.50	3.10
☐	89	Red Munger	16.00	7.25	2.00
☐	90	Harry Brecheen	20.00	9.00	2.50
☐	91	Cass Michaels	16.00	7.25	2.00
☐	92	Hank Majeski	16.00	7.25	2.00
☐	93	Gene Bearden	20.00	9.00	2.50
☐	94	Lou Boudreau	50.00	23.00	6.25
☐	95	Aaron Robinson	16.00	7.25	2.00
☐	96	Virgil Trucks	20.00	9.00	2.50
☐	97	Maurice McDermott	16.00	7.25	2.00
☐	98	Ted Williams	800.00	350.00	100.00
☐	99	Billy Goodman	20.00	9.00	2.50
☐	100	Vic Raschi	35.00	16.00	4.40
☐	101	Bobby Brown	35.00	16.00	4.40
☐	102	Billy Johnson	20.00	9.00	2.50
☐	103	Eddie Joost	16.00	7.25	2.00
☐	104	Sam Chapman	16.00	7.25	2.00
☐	105	Bob Dillinger	16.00	7.25	2.00
☐	106	Cliff Fannin	16.00	7.25	2.00
☐	107	Sam Dente	16.00	7.25	2.00
☐	108	Ray Scarborough	16.00	7.25	2.00
☐	109	Sid Gordon	16.00	7.25	2.00
☐	110	Tommy Holmes	20.00	9.00	2.50
☐	111	Walker Cooper	16.00	7.25	2.00
☐	112	Gil Hodges	100.00	45.00	12.50
☐	113	Gene Hermanski	16.00	7.25	2.00
☐	114	Wayne Terwilliger	16.00	7.25	2.00
☐	115	Roy Smalley	16.00	7.25	2.00
☐	116	Virgil Stallcup	16.00	7.25	2.00
☐	117	Bill Rigney	16.00	7.25	2.00
☐	118	Clint Hartung	16.00	7.25	2.00
☐	119	Dick Sisler	20.00	9.00	2.50
☐	120	John Thompson	16.00	7.25	2.00
☐	121	Andy Seminick	16.00	7.25	2.00
☐	122	Johnny Hopp	20.00	9.00	2.50
☐	123	Dino Restelli	16.00	7.25	2.00
☐	124	Clyde McCullough	16.00	7.25	2.00
☐	125	Del Rice	16.00	7.25	2.00
☐	126	Al Brazle	16.00	7.25	2.00
☐	127	Dave Philley	16.00	7.25	2.00
☐	128	Phil Masi	16.00	7.25	2.00
☐	129	Joe Gordon	16.00	7.25	2.00
☐	130	Dale Mitchell	20.00	9.00	2.50
☐	131	Steve Gromek	16.00	7.25	2.00
☐	132	Mickey Vernon	20.00	9.00	2.50
☐	133	Don Kolloway	16.00	7.25	2.00
☐	134	Paul Trout	16.00	7.25	2.00
☐	135	Pat Mullin	16.00	7.25	2.00
☐	136	Warren Rosar	16.00	7.25	2.00
☐	137	Johnny Pesky	20.00	9.00	2.50
☐	138	Allie Reynolds	35.00	16.00	4.40
☐	139	Johnny Mize	75.00	34.00	9.50
☐	140	Pete Suder	16.00	7.25	2.00
☐	141	Joe Coleman	16.00	7.25	2.00
☐	142	Sherm Lollar	25.00	11.50	3.10
☐	143	Eddie Stewart	16.00	7.25	2.00
☐	144	Al Evans	16.00	7.25	2.00
☐	145	Jack Graham	16.00	7.25	2.00
☐	146	Floyd Baker	16.00	7.25	2.00

☐ 147 Mike Garcia 32.00 14.50 4.00
☐ 148 Early Wynn 55.00 25.00 7.00
☐ 149 Bob Swift 16.00 7.25 2.00
☐ 150 George Vico 16.00 7.25 2.00
☐ 151 Fred Hutchinson 16.00 7.25 2.00
☐ 152 Ellis Kinder 16.00 7.25 2.00
☐ 153 Walt Masterson 16.00 7.25 2.00
☐ 154 Gus Niarhos 16.00 7.25 2.00
☐ 155 Frank Shea 20.00 9.00 2.50
☐ 156 Fred Sanford 20.00 9.00 2.50
☐ 157 Mike Guerra 16.00 7.25 2.00
☐ 158 Paul Lehner 16.00 7.25 2.00
☐ 159 Joe Tipton 16.00 7.25 2.00
☐ 160 Mickey Harris 16.00 7.25 2.00
☐ 161 Sherry Robertson 16.00 7.25 2.00
☐ 162 Eddie Yost 20.00 9.00 2.50
☐ 163 Earl Torgeson 16.00 7.25 2.00
☐ 164 Sibby Sisti 16.00 7.25 2.00
☐ 165 Bruce Edwards 16.00 7.25 2.00
☐ 166 Joe Hatton 16.00 7.25 2.00
☐ 167 Preacher Roe 35.00 16.00 4.40
☐ 168 Bob Scheffing 16.00 7.25 2.00
☐ 169 Hank Edwards 16.00 7.25 2.00
☐ 170 Dutch Leonard 16.00 7.25 2.00
☐ 171 Harry Gumbert 16.00 7.25 2.00
☐ 172 Peanuts Lowrey 16.00 7.25 2.00
☐ 173 Lloyd Merriman 16.00 7.25 2.00
☐ 174 Hank Thompson 25.00 11.50 3.10
☐ 175 Monte Kennedy 16.00 7.25 2.00
☐ 176 Sylvester Donnelly 16.00 7.25 2.00
☐ 177 Hank Borowy 16.00 7.25 2.00
☐ 178 Ed Fitzgerald 16.00 7.25 2.00
☐ 179 Chuck Diering 16.00 7.25 2.00
☐ 180 Harry Walker 16.00 7.25 2.00
☐ 181 Marino Pieretti 16.00 7.25 2.00
☐ 182 Sam Zoldak 16.00 7.25 2.00
☐ 183 Mickey Haefner 16.00 7.25 2.00
☐ 184 Randy Gumpert 16.00 7.25 2.00
☐ 185 Howie Judson 16.00 7.25 2.00
☐ 186 Ken Keltner 20.00 9.00 2.50
☐ 187 Lou Stringer 16.00 7.25 2.00
☐ 188 Earl Johnson 16.00 7.25 2.00
☐ 189 Owen Friend 16.00 7.25 2.00
☐ 190 Ken Wood 16.00 7.25 2.00
☐ 191 Dick Starr 16.00 7.25 2.00
☐ 192 Bob Chipman 16.00 7.25 2.00
☐ 193 Pete Reiser 25.00 11.50 3.10
☐ 194 Billy Cox 25.00 11.50 3.10
☐ 195 Phil Cavarretta 25.00 11.50 3.10
☐ 196 Doyle Lade 16.00 7.25 2.00
☐ 197 Johnny Wyrostek 16.00 7.25 2.00
☐ 198 Danny Litwhiler 16.00 7.25 2.00
☐ 199 Jack Kramer 16.00 7.25 2.00
☐ 200 Kirby Higbe 16.00 7.25 2.00
☐ 201 Pete Castiglione 16.00 7.25 2.00
☐ 202 Cliff Chambers 16.00 7.25 2.00
☐ 203 Danny Murtaugh 20.00 9.00 2.50
☐ 204 Granny Hamner 25.00 11.50 3.10
☐ 205 Mike Goliat 16.00 7.25 2.00
☐ 206 Stan Lopata 16.00 7.25 2.00
☐ 207 Max Lanier 16.00 7.25 2.00
☐ 208 Jim Hearn 16.00 7.25 2.00
☐ 209 Johnny Lindell 16.00 7.25 2.00
☐ 210 Ted Gray 16.00 7.25 2.00
☐ 211 Charlie Keller 20.00 9.00 2.50
☐ 212 Jerry Priddy 16.00 7.25 2.00
☐ 213 Carl Scheib 16.00 7.25 2.00
☐ 214 Dick Fowler 16.00 7.25 2.00
☐ 215 Ed Lopat 35.00 16.00 4.40
☐ 216 Bob Porterfield 20.00 9.00 2.50
☐ 217 Casey Stengel MG 110.00 50.00 14.00
☐ 218 Cliff Mapes 20.00 9.00 2.50
☐ 219 Hank Bauer 70.00 32.00 8.75
☐ 220 Leo Durocher MG 60.00 27.00 7.50
☐ 221 Don Mueller 32.00 14.50 4.00
☐ 222 Bobby Morgan 16.00 7.25 2.00
☐ 223 Jim Russell 16.00 7.25 2.00
☐ 224 Jack Banta 16.00 7.25 2.00
☐ 225 Eddie Sawyer MG 20.00 9.00 2.50
☐ 226 Jim Konstanty 40.00 18.00 5.00
☐ 227 Bob Miller 16.00 7.25 2.00
☐ 228 Bill Nicholson 20.00 9.00 2.50
☐ 229 Frank Frisch MG 45.00 20.00 5.75
☐ 230 Bill Serena 16.00 7.25 2.00
☐ 231 Preston Ward 16.00 7.25 2.00
☐ 232 Al Rosen 60.00 27.00 7.50
☐ 233 Allie Clark 16.00 7.25 2.00
☐ 234 Bobby Shantz 40.00 18.00 5.00
☐ 235 Harold Gilbert 16.00 7.25 2.00
☐ 236 Bob Cain 16.00 7.25 2.00
☐ 237 Bill Salkeld 16.00 7.25 2.00
☐ 238 Nippy Jones 16.00 7.25 2.00
☐ 239 Bill Howerton 16.00 7.25 2.00
☐ 240 Eddie Lake 16.00 7.25 2.00
☐ 241 Neil Berry 16.00 7.25 2.00
☐ 242 Dick Kryhoski 16.00 7.25 2.00
☐ 243 Johnny Groth 16.00 7.25 2.00
☐ 244 Dale Coogan 16.00 7.25 2.00
☐ 245 Al Papai 16.00 7.25 2.00
☐ 246 Walt Dropo 28.00 12.50 3.50
☐ 247 Irv Noren 25.00 11.50 3.10
☐ 248 Sam Jethroe 25.00 11.50 3.10
☐ 249 Snuffy Stirnweiss 20.00 9.00 2.50
☐ 250 Ray Coleman 16.00 7.25 2.00
☐ 251 John Moss 16.00 7.25 2.00
☐ 252 Billy DeMars 40.00 12.00 4.00

1951 Bowman

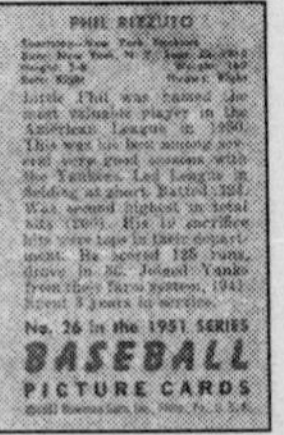

The cards in this 324-card set measure approximately 2 1/16" by 3 1/8". Many of the obverses of the cards appearing in the 1951 Bowman set are enlargements of those appearing in the previous year. The high number series (253-324) is highly valued and contains the true "Rookie" cards of Mickey Mantle and Willie Mays. Card number 195 depicts Paul Richards in caricature. George Kell's card (number 46) incorrectly lists him as being in the "1941" Bowman series. Player names are found printed in a panel on the front of the card. These cards were supposedly also sold in sheets in variety stores in the Philadelphia area.

	NRMT	VG-E	GOOD
COMPLETE SET (324)	17000.	7700.	2100.
COMMON CARD (1-36)	18.00	8.00	2.30
COMMON CARD (37-72)	15.00	6.75	1.90
COMMON CARD (73-108)	15.00	6.75	1.90
COMMON CARD (109-144)	15.00	6.75	1.90
COMMON CARD (145-180)	15.00	6.75	1.90
COMMON CARD (181-216)	15.00	6.75	1.90
COMMON CARD (217-252)	15.00	6.75	1.90
COMMON CARD (253-324)	40.00	18.00	5.00
☐ 1 Whitey Ford	750.00	150.00	45.00
☐ 2 Yogi Berra	350.00	160.00	45.00
☐ 3 Robin Roberts	80.00	36.00	10.00
☐ 4 Del Ennis	18.00	8.00	2.30
☐ 5 Dale Mitchell	20.00	9.00	2.50
☐ 6 Don Newcombe	40.00	18.00	5.00
☐ 7 Gil Hodges	90.00	40.00	11.50
☐ 8 Paul Lehner	18.00	8.00	2.30
☐ 9 Sam Chapman	18.00	8.00	2.30
☐ 10 Red Schoendienst	50.00	23.00	6.25
☐ 11 Red Munger	18.00	8.00	2.30
☐ 12 Hank Majeski	18.00	8.00	2.30
☐ 13 Eddie Stanky	18.00	8.00	2.30
☐ 14 Alvin Dark	30.00	13.50	3.80
☐ 15 Johnny Pesky	18.00	8.00	2.30
☐ 16 Maurice McDermott	18.00	8.00	2.30
☐ 17 Pete Castiglione	18.00	8.00	2.30
☐ 18 Gil Coan	18.00	8.00	2.30
☐ 19 Sid Gordon	18.00	8.00	2.30
☐ 20 Del Crandall UER (Misspelled Crandell on card)	20.00	9.00	2.50
☐ 21 Snuffy Stirnweiss	20.00	9.00	2.50
☐ 22 Hank Sauer	18.00	8.00	2.30
☐ 23 Hoot Evers	18.00	8.00	2.30
☐ 24 Ewell Blackwell	25.00	11.50	3.10
☐ 25 Vic Raschi	35.00	16.00	4.40
☐ 26 Phil Rizzuto	135.00	60.00	17.00
☐ 27 Jim Konstanty	18.00	8.00	2.30
☐ 28 Eddie Waitkus	18.00	8.00	2.30
☐ 29 Allie Clark	18.00	8.00	2.30
☐ 30 Bob Feller	120.00	55.00	15.00
☐ 31 Roy Campanella	225.00	100.00	28.00
☐ 32 Duke Snider	225.00	100.00	28.00
☐ 33 Bob Hooper	18.00	8.00	2.30
☐ 34 Marty Marion	25.00	11.50	3.10
☐ 35 Al Zarilla	18.00	8.00	2.30
☐ 36 Joe Dobson	18.00	8.00	2.30
☐ 37 Whitey Lockman	18.00	8.00	2.30
☐ 38 Al Evans	15.00	6.75	1.90
☐ 39 Ray Scarborough	15.00	6.75	1.90
☐ 40 Gus Bell	35.00	16.00	4.40
☐ 41 Eddie Yost	18.00	8.00	2.30
☐ 42 Vern Bickford	15.00	6.75	1.90
☐ 43 Billy DeMars	15.00	6.75	1.90
☐ 44 Roy Smalley	15.00	6.75	1.90
☐ 45 Art Houtteman	15.00	6.75	1.90
☐ 46 George Kell 1941 UER	55.00	25.00	7.00
☐ 47 Grady Hatton	15.00	6.75	1.90
☐ 48 Ken Raffensberger	15.00	6.75	1.90
☐ 49 Jerry Coleman	25.00	11.50	3.10
☐ 50 Johnny Mize	55.00	25.00	7.00
☐ 51 Andy Seminick	15.00	6.75	1.90
☐ 52 Dick Sisler	18.00	8.00	2.30
☐ 53 Bob Lemon	50.00	23.00	6.25
☐ 54 Ray Boone	35.00	16.00	4.40
☐ 55 Gene Hermanski	15.00	6.75	1.90
☐ 56 Ralph Branca	30.00	13.50	3.80
☐ 57 Alex Kellner	15.00	6.75	1.90
☐ 58 Enos Slaughter	55.00	25.00	7.00
☐ 59 Randy Gumpert	15.00	6.75	1.90
☐ 60 Chico Carrasquel	28.00	12.50	3.50
☐ 61 Jim Hearn	18.00	8.00	2.30
☐ 62 Lou Boudreau	50.00	23.00	6.25
☐ 63 Bob Dillinger	15.00	6.75	1.90
☐ 64 Bill Werle	15.00	6.75	1.90
☐ 65 Mickey Vernon	18.00	8.00	2.30
☐ 66 Bob Elliott	18.00	8.00	2.30
☐ 67 Roy Sievers	18.00	8.00	2.30
☐ 68 Dick Kokos	15.00	6.75	1.90
☐ 69 Johnny Schmitz	15.00	6.75	1.90
☐ 70 Ron Northey	15.00	6.75	1.90
☐ 71 Jerry Priddy	15.00	6.75	1.90
☐ 72 Lloyd Merriman	15.00	6.75	1.90
☐ 73 Tommy Byrne	15.00	6.75	1.90
☐ 74 Billy Johnson	18.00	8.00	2.30
☐ 75 Russ Meyer	15.00	6.75	1.90
☐ 76 Stan Lopata	15.00	6.75	1.90
☐ 77 Mike Goliat	15.00	6.75	1.90
☐ 78 Early Wynn	50.00	23.00	6.25
☐ 79 Jim Hegan	18.00	8.00	2.30
☐ 80 Pee Wee Reese	150.00	70.00	19.00
☐ 81 Carl Furillo	40.00	18.00	5.00
☐ 82 Joe Tipton	15.00	6.75	1.90
☐ 83 Carl Scheib	15.00	6.75	1.90
☐ 84 Barney McCosky	15.00	6.75	1.90
☐ 85 Eddie Kazak	15.00	6.75	1.90
☐ 86 Harry Brecheen	18.00	8.00	2.30
☐ 87 Floyd Baker	15.00	6.75	1.90
☐ 88 Eddie Robinson	15.00	6.75	1.90
☐ 89 Hank Thompson	18.00	8.00	2.30
☐ 90 Dave Koslo	18.00	8.00	2.30
☐ 91 Clyde Vollmer	15.00	6.75	1.90
☐ 92 Vern Stephens	18.00	8.00	2.30
☐ 93 Danny O'Connell	15.00	6.75	1.90
☐ 94 Clyde McCullough	15.00	6.75	1.90
☐ 95 Sherry Robertson	15.00	6.75	1.90
☐ 96 Sandy Consuegra	15.00	6.75	1.90
☐ 97 Bob Kuzava	15.00	6.75	1.90
☐ 98 Willard Marshall	15.00	6.75	1.90
☐ 99 Earl Torgeson	15.00	6.75	1.90
☐ 100 Sherm Lollar	18.00	8.00	2.30
☐ 101 Owen Friend	15.00	6.75	1.90
☐ 102 Dutch Leonard	15.00	6.75	1.90
☐ 103 Andy Pafko	18.00	8.00	2.30
☐ 104 Virgil Trucks	18.00	8.00	2.30
☐ 105 Don Kolloway	15.00	6.75	1.90
☐ 106 Pat Mullin	15.00	6.75	1.90
☐ 107 Johnny Wyrostek	15.00	6.75	1.90
☐ 108 Virgil Stallcup	15.00	6.75	1.90
☐ 109 Allie Reynolds	30.00	13.50	3.80
☐ 110 Bobby Brown	28.00	12.50	3.50
☐ 111 Curt Simmons	15.00	6.75	1.90
☐ 112 Willie Jones	15.00	6.75	1.90
☐ 113 Bill Nicholson	18.00	8.00	2.30
☐ 114 Sam Zoldak	15.00	6.75	1.90
☐ 115 Steve Gromek	15.00	6.75	1.90
☐ 116 Bruce Edwards	15.00	6.75	1.90
☐ 117 Eddie Miksis	15.00	6.75	1.90
☐ 118 Preacher Roe	30.00	13.50	3.80
☐ 119 Eddie Joost	15.00	6.75	1.90
☐ 120 Joe Coleman	15.00	6.75	1.90
☐ 121 Jerry Staley	15.00	6.75	1.90
☐ 122 Joe Garagiola	110.00	50.00	14.00
☐ 123 Howie Judson	15.00	6.75	1.90
☐ 124 Gus Niarhos	15.00	6.75	1.90
☐ 125 Bill Rigney	18.00	8.00	2.30
☐ 126 Bobby Thomson	30.00	13.50	3.80
☐ 127 Sal Maglie	50.00	23.00	6.25
☐ 128 Ellis Kinder	15.00	6.75	1.90
☐ 129 Matt Batts	15.00	6.75	1.90
☐ 130 Tom Saffell	15.00	6.75	1.90
☐ 131 Cliff Chambers	15.00	6.75	1.90
☐ 132 Cass Michaels	15.00	6.75	1.90
☐ 133 Sam Dente	15.00	6.75	1.90

☐ 134 Warren Spahn........ 110.00 50.00 14.00
☐ 135 Walker Cooper......... 15.00 6.75 1.90
☐ 136 Ray Coleman........... 15.00 6.75 1.90
☐ 137 Dick Starr................ 15.00 6.75 1.90
☐ 138 Phil Cavarretta......... 18.00 8.00 2.30
☐ 139 Doyle Lade.............. 15.00 6.75 1.90
☐ 140 Eddie Lake.............. 15.00 6.75 1.90
☐ 141 Fred Hutchinson...... 15.00 6.75 1.90
☐ 142 Aaron Robinson....... 15.00 6.75 1.90
☐ 143 Ted Kluszewski........ 40.00 18.00 5.00
☐ 144 Herman Wehmeier... 15.00 6.75 1.90
☐ 145 Fred Sanford........... 18.00 8.00 2.30
☐ 146 Johnny Hopp........... 18.00 8.00 2.30
☐ 147 Ken Heintzelman...... 15.00 6.75 1.90
☐ 148 Granny Hamner........ 15.00 6.75 1.90
☐ 149 Bubba Church.......... 15.00 6.75 1.90
☐ 150 Mike Garcia............. 18.00 8.00 2.30
☐ 151 Larry Doby.............. 32.00 14.50 4.00
☐ 152 Cal Abrams............. 15.00 6.75 1.90
☐ 153 Rex Barney.............. 18.00 8.00 2.30
☐ 154 Pete Suder.............. 15.00 6.75 1.90
☐ 155 Lou Brissie.............. 15.00 6.75 1.90
☐ 156 Del Rice.................. 15.00 6.75 1.90
☐ 157 Al Brazle................. 15.00 6.75 1.90
☐ 158 Chuck Diering.......... 15.00 6.75 1.90
☐ 159 Eddie Stewart.......... 15.00 6.75 1.90
☐ 160 Phil Masi................. 15.00 6.75 1.90
☐ 161 Wes Westrum.......... 15.00 6.75 1.90
☐ 162 Larry Jansen........... 18.00 8.00 2.30
☐ 163 Monte Kennedy........ 15.00 6.75 1.90
☐ 164 Bill Wight................ 15.00 6.75 1.90
☐ 165 Ted Williams.......... 750.00 350.00 95.00
☐ 166 Stan Rojek.............. 15.00 6.75 1.90
☐ 167 Murry Dickson......... 15.00 6.75 1.90
☐ 168 Sam Mele................ 15.00 6.75 1.90
☐ 169 Sid Hudson.............. 15.00 6.75 1.90
☐ 170 Sibby Sisti............... 15.00 6.75 1.90
☐ 171 Buddy Kerr.............. 15.00 6.75 1.90
☐ 172 Ned Garver.............. 15.00 6.75 1.90
☐ 173 Hank Arft................. 15.00 6.75 1.90
☐ 174 Mickey Owen........... 18.00 8.00 2.30
☐ 175 Wayne Terwilliger.... 15.00 6.75 1.90
☐ 176 Vic Wertz................ 18.00 8.00 2.30
☐ 177 Charlie Keller.......... 18.00 8.00 2.30
☐ 178 Ted Gray................. 15.00 6.75 1.90
☐ 179 Danny Litwhiler........ 15.00 6.75 1.90
☐ 180 Howie Fox............... 15.00 6.75 1.90
☐ 181 Casey Stengel MG.... 85.00 38.00 10.50
☐ 182 Tom Ferrick............. 15.00 6.75 1.90
☐ 183 Hank Bauer............. 30.00 13.50 3.80
☐ 184 Eddie Sawyer MG..... 18.00 8.00 2.30
☐ 185 Jimmy Bloodworth.. 15.00 6.75 1.90
☐ 186 Richie Ashburn........ 60.00 27.00 7.50
☐ 187 Al Rosen................. 24.00 11.00 3.00
☐ 188 Bobby Avila............. 15.00 6.75 1.90
☐ 189 Erv Palica................ 15.00 6.75 1.90
☐ 190 Joe Hatten............... 15.00 6.75 1.90
☐ 191 Billy Hitchcock......... 15.00 6.75 1.90
☐ 192 Hank Wyse............... 15.00 6.75 1.90
☐ 193 Ted Wilks................ 15.00 6.75 1.90
☐ 194 Peanuts Lowrey....... 15.00 6.75 1.90
☐ 195 Paul Richards MG... 18.00 8.00 2.30
(Caricature)
☐ 196 Billy Pierce.............. 30.00 13.50 3.80
☐ 197 Bob Cain................. 15.00 6.75 1.90
☐ 198 Monte Irvin........... 110.00 50.00 14.00
☐ 199 Sheldon Jones........ 15.00 6.75 1.90
☐ 200 Jack Kramer............ 15.00 6.75 1.90
☐ 201 Steve O'Neill MG...... 15.00 6.75 1.90
☐ 202 Mike Guerra............ 15.00 6.75 1.90
☐ 203 Vernon Law............. 30.00 13.50 3.80
☐ 204 Vic Lombardi........... 15.00 6.75 1.90
☐ 205 Mickey Grasso........ 15.00 6.75 1.90
☐ 206 Conrado Marrero..... 15.00 6.75 1.90
☐ 207 Billy Southworth MG 15.00 6.75 1.90
☐ 208 Blix Donnelly........... 15.00 6.75 1.90
☐ 209 Ken Wood............... 15.00 6.75 1.90
☐ 210 Les Moss................ 15.00 6.75 1.90
☐ 211 Hal Jeffcoat............. 15.00 6.75 1.90
☐ 212 Bob Rush................ 15.00 6.75 1.90
☐ 213 Neil Berry................ 15.00 6.75 1.90
☐ 214 Bob Swift................ 15.00 6.75 1.90
☐ 215 Ken Peterson.......... 15.00 6.75 1.90
☐ 216 Connie Ryan........... 15.00 6.75 1.90
☐ 217 Joe Page................. 15.00 6.75 1.90
☐ 218 Ed Lopat................. 30.00 13.50 3.80
☐ 219 Gene Woodling....... 40.00 18.00 5.00
☐ 220 Bob Miller............... 15.00 6.75 1.90
☐ 221 Dick Whitman.......... 15.00 6.75 1.90
☐ 222 Thurman Tucker...... 15.00 6.75 1.90
☐ 223 Johnny VanderMeer. 25.00 11.50 3.10
☐ 224 Billy Cox................. 15.00 6.75 1.90
☐ 225 Dan Bankhead......... 18.00 8.00 2.30
☐ 226 Jimmy Dykes MG..... 18.00 8.00 2.30
☐ 227 Bobby Schantz UER. 15.00 6.75 1.90
(Sic, Shantz)
☐ 228 Cloyd Boyer............ 18.00 8.00 2.30
☐ 229 Bill Howerton.......... 15.00 6.75 1.90
☐ 230 Max Lanier.............. 15.00 6.75 1.90
☐ 231 Luis Aloma.............. 15.00 6.75 1.90
☐ 232 Nelson Fox.......... 160.00 70.00 20.00
☐ 233 Leo Durocher MG.... 60.00 27.00 7.50
☐ 234 Clint Hartung........... 18.00 8.00 2.30
☐ 235 Jack Lohrke............ 15.00 6.75 1.90
☐ 236 Warren Rosar......... 15.00 6.75 1.90
☐ 237 Billy Goodman........ 18.00 8.00 2.30
☐ 238 Pete Reiser............. 18.00 8.00 2.30
☐ 239 Bill MacDonald........ 15.00 6.75 1.90
☐ 240 Joe Haynes............. 15.00 6.75 1.90
☐ 241 Irv Noren................. 18.00 8.00 2.30
☐ 242 Sam Jethroe........... 18.00 8.00 2.30
☐ 243 Johnny Antonelli...... 18.00 8.00 2.30
☐ 244 Cliff Fannin.............. 15.00 6.75 1.90
☐ 245 John Berardino........ 25.00 11.50 3.10
☐ 246 Bill Serena............... 15.00 6.75 1.90
☐ 247 Bob Ramazzotti........ 15.00 6.75 1.90
☐ 248 Johnny Klippstein.... 15.00 6.75 1.90
☐ 249 Johnny Groth........... 15.00 6.75 1.90
☐ 250 Hank Borowy........... 15.00 6.75 1.90
☐ 251 Willard Ramsdell...... 15.00 6.75 1.90
☐ 252 Dixie Howell............ 15.00 6.75 1.90
☐ 253 Mickey Mantle...... 8400.00 2900.00 850.00
☐ 254 Jackie Jensen........ 115.00 52.50 14.50
☐ 255 Milo Candini............ 40.00 18.00 5.00
☐ 256 Ken Sylvestri........... 40.00 18.00 5.00
☐ 257 Birdie Tebbetts........ 60.00 27.00 7.50
☐ 258 Luke Easter............ 60.00 27.00 7.50
☐ 259 Chuck Dressen MG.. 60.00 27.00 7.50
☐ 260 Carl Erskine.......... 115.00 52.50 14.50
☐ 261 Wally Moses........... 45.00 20.00 5.75
☐ 262 Gus Zernial............. 60.00 27.00 7.50
☐ 263 Howie Pollet............ 45.00 20.00 5.75
☐ 264 Don Richmond........ 40.00 18.00 5.00
☐ 265 Steve Bilko............. 45.00 20.00 5.75
☐ 266 Harry Dorish........... 40.00 18.00 5.00
☐ 267 Ken Holcombe......... 40.00 18.00 5.00
☐ 268 Don Mueller............ 50.00 23.00 6.25
☐ 269 Ray Noble............... 40.00 18.00 5.00
☐ 270 Willard Nixon.......... 40.00 18.00 5.00
☐ 271 Tommy Wright......... 40.00 18.00 5.00
☐ 272 Billy Meyer MG........ 40.00 18.00 5.00
☐ 273 Danny Murtaugh...... 45.00 20.00 5.75
☐ 274 George Metkovich.... 40.00 18.00 5.00
☐ 275 Bucky Harris MG..... 55.00 25.00 7.00
☐ 276 Frank Quinn............ 40.00 18.00 5.00
☐ 277 Roy Hartsfield......... 40.00 18.00 5.00

No.	Player	NRMT	VG-E	GOOD
☐ 278	Norman Roy	40.00	18.00	5.00
☐ 279	Jim Delsing	40.00	18.00	5.00
☐ 280	Frank Overmire	40.00	18.00	5.00
☐ 281	Al Widmar	40.00	18.00	5.00
☐ 282	Frank Frisch MG	75.00	34.00	9.50
☐ 283	Walt Dubiel	40.00	18.00	5.00
☐ 284	Gene Bearden	45.00	20.00	5.75
☐ 285	Johnny Lipon	40.00	18.00	5.00
☐ 286	Bob Usher	40.00	18.00	5.00
☐ 287	Jim Blackburn	40.00	18.00	5.00
☐ 288	Bobby Adams	40.00	18.00	5.00
☐ 289	Cliff Mapes	45.00	20.00	5.75
☐ 290	Bill Dickey CO	115.00	52.50	14.50
☐ 291	Tommy Henrich CO	60.00	27.00	7.50
☐ 292	Eddie Pellegrini	40.00	18.00	5.00
☐ 293	Ken Johnson	40.00	18.00	5.00
☐ 294	Jocko Thompson	40.00	18.00	5.00
☐ 295	Al Lopez MG	125.00	57.50	15.50
☐ 296	Bob Kennedy	45.00	20.00	5.75
☐ 297	Dave Philley	40.00	18.00	5.00
☐ 298	Joe Astroth	40.00	18.00	5.00
☐ 299	Clyde King	40.00	18.00	5.00
☐ 300	Hal Rice	40.00	18.00	5.00
☐ 301	Tommy Glaviano	40.00	18.00	5.00
☐ 302	Jim Busby	40.00	18.00	5.00
☐ 303	Marv Rotblatt	40.00	18.00	5.00
☐ 304	Al Gettell	40.00	18.00	5.00
☐ 305	Willie Mays	3800.00	1700.00	475.00
☐ 306	Jim Piersall	100.00	45.00	12.50
☐ 307	Walt Masterson	40.00	18.00	5.00
☐ 308	Ted Beard	40.00	18.00	5.00
☐ 309	Mel Queen	40.00	18.00	5.00
☐ 310	Erv Dusak	40.00	18.00	5.00
☐ 311	Mickey Harris	40.00	18.00	5.00
☐ 312	Gene Mauch	65.00	29.00	8.25
☐ 313	Ray Mueller	40.00	18.00	5.00
☐ 314	Johnny Sain	65.00	29.00	8.25
☐ 315	Zack Taylor MG	40.00	18.00	5.00
☐ 316	Duane Pillette	40.00	18.00	5.00
☐ 317	Smoky Burgess	85.00	38.00	10.50
☐ 318	Warren Hacker	40.00	18.00	5.00
☐ 319	Red Rolfe MG	55.00	25.00	7.00
☐ 320	Hal White	40.00	18.00	5.00
☐ 321	Earl Johnson	40.00	18.00	5.00
☐ 322	Luke Sewell MG	45.00	20.00	5.75
☐ 323	Joe Adcock	75.00	34.00	9.50
☐ 324	Johnny Pramesa	90.00	27.00	9.00

1952 Bowman

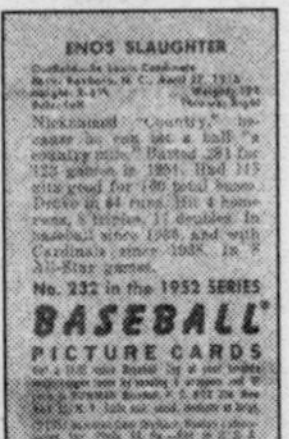

ENOS SLAUGHTER
No. 232 in the 1952 SERIES
BASEBALL
PICTURE CARDS

The cards in this 252-card set measure approximately 2 1/16" by 3 1/8". While the Bowman set of 1952 retained the card size introduced in 1951, it employed a modification of color tones from the two preceding years. The cards also appeared with a facsimile autograph on the front and, for the first time since 1949, premium advertising on the back. The 1952 set was apparently sold in sheets as well as in gum packs. Artwork for 15 cards that were never issued was discovered in the early 1980s. Notable Rookie Cards in this set are Lew Burdette, Gil McDougald, and Minnie Minoso.

	NRMT	VG-E	GOOD
COMPLETE SET (252)	7500.00	3400.00	950.00
COMMON CARD (1-36)	16.00	7.25	2.00
COMMON CARD (37-72)	16.00	7.25	2.00
COMMON CARD (73-108)	16.00	7.25	2.00
COMMON CARD (109-144)	16.00	7.25	2.00
COMMON CARD (145-180)	16.00	7.25	2.00
COMMON CARD (181-216)	16.00	7.25	2.00
COMMON CARD (217-252)	35.00	16.00	4.40

No.	Player	NRMT	VG-E	GOOD
☐ 1	Yogi Berra	425.00	130.00	42.50
☐ 2	Bobby Thomson	35.00	16.00	4.40
☐ 3	Fred Hutchinson	16.00	7.25	2.00
☐ 4	Robin Roberts	70.00	32.00	8.75
☐ 5	Minnie Minoso	110.00	50.00	14.00
☐ 6	Virgil Stallcup	16.00	7.25	2.00
☐ 7	Mike Garcia	20.00	9.00	2.50
☐ 8	Pee Wee Reese	120.00	55.00	15.00
☐ 9	Vern Stephens	20.00	9.00	2.50
☐ 10	Bob Hooper	16.00	7.25	2.00
☐ 11	Ralph Kiner	55.00	25.00	7.00
☐ 12	Max Surkont	16.00	7.25	2.00
☐ 13	Cliff Mapes	16.00	7.25	2.00
☐ 14	Cliff Chambers	16.00	7.25	2.00
☐ 15	Sam Mele	16.00	7.25	2.00
☐ 16	Turk Lown	16.00	7.25	2.00
☐ 17	Ed Lopat	35.00	16.00	4.40
☐ 18	Don Mueller	20.00	9.00	2.50
☐ 19	Bob Cain	16.00	7.25	2.00
☐ 20	Willie Jones	16.00	7.25	2.00
☐ 21	Nellie Fox	55.00	25.00	7.00
☐ 22	Willard Ramsdell	16.00	7.25	2.00
☐ 23	Bob Lemon	50.00	23.00	6.25
☐ 24	Carl Furillo	35.00	16.00	4.40
☐ 25	Mickey McDermott	16.00	7.25	2.00
☐ 26	Eddie Joost	16.00	7.25	2.00
☐ 27	Joe Garagiola	50.00	23.00	6.25
☐ 28	Roy Hartsfield	16.00	7.25	2.00
☐ 29	Ned Garver	16.00	7.25	2.00
☐ 30	Red Schoendienst	55.00	25.00	7.00
☐ 31	Eddie Yost	20.00	9.00	2.50
☐ 32	Eddie Miksis	16.00	7.25	2.00
☐ 33	Gil McDougald	70.00	32.00	8.75
☐ 34	Alvin Dark	16.00	7.25	2.00
☐ 35	Granny Hamner	16.00	7.25	2.00
☐ 36	Cass Michaels	16.00	7.25	2.00
☐ 37	Vic Raschi	25.00	11.50	3.10
☐ 38	Whitey Lockman	20.00	9.00	2.50
☐ 39	Vic Wertz	20.00	9.00	2.50
☐ 40	Bubba Church	16.00	7.25	2.00
☐ 41	Chico Carrasquel	20.00	9.00	2.50
☐ 42	Johnny Wyrostek	16.00	7.25	2.00
☐ 43	Bob Feller	110.00	50.00	14.00
☐ 44	Roy Campanella	225.00	100.00	28.00
☐ 45	Johnny Pesky	16.00	7.25	2.00
☐ 46	Carl Scheib	16.00	7.25	2.00
☐ 47	Pete Castiglione	16.00	7.25	2.00
☐ 48	Vern Bickford	16.00	7.25	2.00
☐ 49	Jim Hearn	16.00	7.25	2.00
☐ 50	Jerry Staley	16.00	7.25	2.00
☐ 51	Gil Coan	16.00	7.25	2.00

	No.	Player			
☐	52	Phil Rizzuto	120.00	55.00	15.00
☐	53	Richie Ashburn	60.00	27.00	7.50
☐	54	Billy Pierce	16.00	7.25	2.00
☐	55	Ken Raffensberger	16.00	7.25	2.00
☐	56	Clyde King	20.00	9.00	2.50
☐	57	Clyde Vollmer	16.00	7.25	2.00
☐	58	Hank Majeski	16.00	7.25	2.00
☐	59	Murry Dickson	16.00	7.25	2.00
☐	60	Sid Gordon	16.00	7.25	2.00
☐	61	Tommy Byrne	16.00	7.25	2.00
☐	62	Joe Presko	16.00	7.25	2.00
☐	63	Irv Noren	20.00	9.00	2.50
☐	64	Roy Smalley	16.00	7.25	2.00
☐	65	Hank Bauer	25.00	11.50	3.10
☐	66	Sal Maglie	20.00	9.00	2.50
☐	67	Johnny Groth	16.00	7.25	2.00
☐	68	Jim Busby	16.00	7.25	2.00
☐	69	Joe Adcock	16.00	7.25	2.00
☐	70	Carl Erskine	30.00	13.50	3.80
☐	71	Vernon Law	16.00	7.25	2.00
☐	72	Earl Torgeson	16.00	7.25	2.00
☐	73	Jerry Coleman	20.00	9.00	2.50
☐	74	Wes Westrum	18.00	8.00	2.30
☐	75	George Kell	40.00	18.00	5.00
☐	76	Del Ennis	16.00	7.25	2.00
☐	77	Eddie Robinson	16.00	7.25	2.00
☐	78	Lloyd Merriman	16.00	7.25	2.00
☐	79	Lou Brissie	16.00	7.25	2.00
☐	80	Gil Hodges	75.00	34.00	9.50
☐	81	Billy Goodman	18.00	8.00	2.30
☐	82	Gus Zernial	18.00	8.00	2.30
☐	83	Howie Pollet	16.00	7.25	2.00
☐	84	Sam Jethroe	18.00	8.00	2.30
☐	85	Marty Marion CO	20.00	9.00	2.50
☐	86	Cal Abrams	18.00	8.00	2.30
☐	87	Mickey Vernon	20.00	9.00	2.50
☐	88	Bruce Edwards	16.00	7.25	2.00
☐	89	Billy Hitchcock	16.00	7.25	2.00
☐	90	Larry Jansen	18.00	8.00	2.30
☐	91	Don Kolloway	16.00	7.25	2.00
☐	92	Eddie Waitkus	16.00	7.25	2.00
☐	93	Paul Richards MG	18.00	8.00	2.30
☐	94	Luke Sewell MG	18.00	8.00	2.30
☐	95	Luke Easter	18.00	8.00	2.30
☐	96	Ralph Branca	16.00	7.25	2.00
☐	97	Willard Marshall	16.00	7.25	2.00
☐	98	Jimmy Dykes MG	18.00	8.00	2.30
☐	99	Clyde McCullough	16.00	7.25	2.00
☐	100	Sibby Sisti	16.00	7.25	2.00
☐	101	Mickey Mantle	2400.00	1100.00	300.00
☐	102	Peanuts Lowrey	16.00	7.25	2.00
☐	103	Joe Haynes	16.00	7.25	2.00
☐	104	Hal Jeffcoat	16.00	7.25	2.00
☐	105	Bobby Brown	25.00	11.50	3.10
☐	106	Randy Gumpert	16.00	7.25	2.00
☐	107	Del Rice	16.00	7.25	2.00
☐	108	George Metkovich	18.00	8.00	2.30
☐	109	Tom Morgan	18.00	8.00	2.30
☐	110	Max Lanier	16.00	7.25	2.00
☐	111	Hoot Evers	16.00	7.25	2.00
☐	112	Smoky Burgess	20.00	9.00	2.50
☐	113	Al Zarilla	16.00	7.25	2.00
☐	114	Frank Hiller	16.00	7.25	2.00
☐	115	Larry Doby	25.00	11.50	3.10
☐	116	Duke Snider	180.00	80.00	23.00
☐	117	Bill Wight	16.00	7.25	2.00
☐	118	Ray Murray	16.00	7.25	2.00
☐	119	Bill Howerton	16.00	7.25	2.00
☐	120	Chet Nichols	16.00	7.25	2.00
☐	121	Al Corwin	16.00	7.25	2.00
☐	122	Billy Johnson	16.00	7.25	2.00
☐	123	Sid Hudson	16.00	7.25	2.00
☐	124	Birdie Tebbetts	18.00	8.00	2.30
☐	125	Howie Fox	16.00	7.25	2.00
☐	126	Phil Cavarretta	18.00	8.00	2.30
☐	127	Dick Sisler	16.00	7.25	2.00
☐	128	Don Newcombe	30.00	13.50	3.80
☐	129	Gus Niarhos	16.00	7.25	2.00
☐	130	Allie Clark	16.00	7.25	2.00
☐	131	Bob Swift	16.00	7.25	2.00
☐	132	Dave Cole	16.00	7.25	2.00
☐	133	Dick Kryhoski	16.00	7.25	2.00
☐	134	Al Brazle	16.00	7.25	2.00
☐	135	Mickey Harris	16.00	7.25	2.00
☐	136	Gene Hermanski	16.00	7.25	2.00
☐	137	Stan Rojek	16.00	7.25	2.00
☐	138	Ted Wilks	16.00	7.25	2.00
☐	139	Jerry Priddy	16.00	7.25	2.00
☐	140	Ray Scarborough	16.00	7.25	2.00
☐	141	Hank Edwards	16.00	7.25	2.00
☐	142	Early Wynn	50.00	23.00	6.25
☐	143	Sandy Consuegra	16.00	7.25	2.00
☐	144	Joe Hatton	16.00	7.25	2.00
☐	145	Johnny Mize	60.00	27.00	7.50
☐	146	Leo Durocher MG	50.00	23.00	6.25
☐	147	Marlin Stuart	16.00	7.25	2.00
☐	148	Ken Heintzelman	16.00	7.25	2.00
☐	149	Howie Judson	16.00	7.25	2.00
☐	150	Herman Wehmeier	16.00	7.25	2.00
☐	151	Al Rosen	25.00	11.50	3.10
☐	152	Billy Cox	16.00	7.25	2.00
☐	153	Fred Hatfield	16.00	7.25	2.00
☐	154	Ferris Fain	18.00	8.00	2.30
☐	155	Billy Meyer MG	16.00	7.25	2.00
☐	156	Warren Spahn	110.00	50.00	14.00
☐	157	Jim Delsing	16.00	7.25	2.00
☐	158	Bucky Harris MG	25.00	11.50	3.10
☐	159	Dutch Leonard	16.00	7.25	2.00
☐	160	Eddie Stanky	20.00	9.00	2.50
☐	161	Jackie Jensen	33.00	15.00	4.10
☐	162	Monte Irvin	50.00	23.00	6.25
☐	163	Johnny Lipon	16.00	7.25	2.00
☐	164	Connie Ryan	16.00	7.25	2.00
☐	165	Saul Rogovin	16.00	7.25	2.00
☐	166	Bobby Adams	16.00	7.25	2.00
☐	167	Bobby Avila	18.00	8.00	2.30
☐	168	Preacher Roe	20.00	9.00	2.50
☐	169	Walt Dropo	18.00	8.00	2.30
☐	170	Joe Astroth	16.00	7.25	2.00
☐	171	Mel Queen	16.00	7.25	2.00
☐	172	Ebba St.Claire	16.00	7.25	2.00
☐	173	Gene Bearden	16.00	7.25	2.00
☐	174	Mickey Grasso	16.00	7.25	2.00
☐	175	Randy Jackson	16.00	7.25	2.00
☐	176	Harry Brecheen	18.00	8.00	2.30
☐	177	Gene Woodling	18.00	8.00	2.30
☐	178	Dave Williams	20.00	9.00	2.50
☐	179	Pete Suder	16.00	7.25	2.00
☐	180	Ed Fitzgerald	16.00	7.25	2.00
☐	181	Joe Collins	20.00	9.00	2.50
☐	182	Dave Koslo	16.00	7.25	2.00
☐	183	Pat Mullin	16.00	7.25	2.00
☐	184	Curt Simmons	20.00	9.00	2.50
☐	185	Eddie Stewart	16.00	7.25	2.00
☐	186	Frank Smith	16.00	7.25	2.00
☐	187	Jim Hegan	18.00	8.00	2.30
☐	188	Charlie Dressen MG	20.00	9.00	2.50
☐	189	Jim Piersall	20.00	9.00	2.50
☐	190	Dick Fowler	16.00	7.25	2.00
☐	191	Bob Friend	25.00	11.50	3.10
☐	192	John Cusick	16.00	7.25	2.00
☐	193	Bobby Young	16.00	7.25	2.00
☐	194	Bob Porterfield	16.00	7.25	2.00
☐	195	Frank Baumholtz	16.00	7.25	2.00
☐	196	Stan Musial	525.00	240.00	65.00
☐	197	Charlie Silvera	16.00	7.25	2.00

	#	Player	NRMT	VG-E	GOOD
☐	198	Chuck Diering	16.00	7.25	2.00
☐	199	Ted Gray	16.00	7.25	2.00
☐	200	Ken Silvestri	16.00	7.25	2.00
☐	201	Ray Coleman	16.00	7.25	2.00
☐	202	Harry Perkowski	16.00	7.25	2.00
☐	203	Steve Gromek	16.00	7.25	2.00
☐	204	Andy Pafko	18.00	8.00	2.30
☐	205	Walt Masterson	16.00	7.25	2.00
☐	206	Elmer Valo	16.00	7.25	2.00
☐	207	George Strickland	16.00	7.25	2.00
☐	208	Walker Cooper	16.00	7.25	2.00
☐	209	Dick Littlefield	16.00	7.25	2.00
☐	210	Archie Wilson	16.00	7.25	2.00
☐	211	Paul Minner	16.00	7.25	2.00
☐	212	Solly Hemus	16.00	7.25	2.00
☐	213	Monte Kennedy	16.00	7.25	2.00
☐	214	Ray Boone	18.00	8.00	2.30
☐	215	Sheldon Jones	16.00	7.25	2.00
☐	216	Matt Batts	16.00	7.25	2.00
☐	217	Casey Stengel MG	140.00	65.00	17.50
☐	218	Willie Mays	1600.00	700.00	200.00
☐	219	Neil Berry	35.00	16.00	4.40
☐	220	Russ Meyer	35.00	16.00	4.40
☐	221	Lou Kretlow	35.00	16.00	4.40
☐	222	Dixie Howell	35.00	16.00	4.40
☐	223	Harry Simpson	35.00	16.00	4.40
☐	224	Johnny Schmitz	35.00	16.00	4.40
☐	225	Del Wilber	35.00	16.00	4.40
☐	226	Alex Kellner	35.00	16.00	4.40
☐	227	Clyde Sukeforth CO	35.00	16.00	4.40
☐	228	Bob Chipman	35.00	16.00	4.40
☐	229	Hank Arft	35.00	16.00	4.40
☐	230	Frank Shea	35.00	16.00	4.40
☐	231	Dee Fondy	35.00	16.00	4.40
☐	232	Enos Slaughter	80.00	36.00	10.00
☐	233	Bob Kuzava	35.00	16.00	4.40
☐	234	Fred Fitzsimmons CO	35.00	16.00	4.40
☐	235	Steve Souchock	35.00	16.00	4.40
☐	236	Tommy Brown	35.00	16.00	4.40
☐	237	Sherm Lollar	40.00	18.00	5.00
☐	238	Roy McMillan	35.00	16.00	4.40
☐	239	Dale Mitchell	40.00	18.00	5.00
☐	240	Billy Loes	38.00	17.00	4.70
☐	241	Mel Parnell	40.00	18.00	5.00
☐	242	Everett Kell	35.00	16.00	4.40
☐	243	Red Munger	35.00	16.00	4.40
☐	244	Lew Burdette	50.00	23.00	6.25
☐	245	George Schmees	35.00	16.00	4.40
☐	246	Jerry Snyder	35.00	16.00	4.40
☐	247	Johnny Pramesa	35.00	16.00	4.40
☐	248	Bill Werle	35.00	16.00	4.40
☐	249	Hank Thompson	40.00	18.00	5.00
☐	250	Ike Delock	35.00	16.00	4.40
☐	251	Jack Lohrke	35.00	16.00	4.40
☐	252	Frank Crosetti CO	110.00	28.00	8.75

1953 Bowman Color

The cards in this 160-card set measure approximately 2 1/2" by 3 3/4". The 1953 Bowman Color set, considered by many to be the best looking set of the modern era, contains Kodachrome photographs with no names or facsimile autographs on the face. Numbers 113 to 160 are somewhat more difficult to obtain, with numbers 113 to 128 being the most difficult. There are two cards of Al Corwin (126 and 149). There are no key Rookie Cards in this set.

	NRMT	VG-E	GOOD
COMPLETE SET (160)	11000.	5000.	1400.
COMMON CARD (1-96)	27.00	12.00	3.40
COMMON CARD (97-112)	30.00	13.50	3.80
COMMON CARD (113-128)	65.00	29.00	8.25
COMMON CARD (129-160)	60.00	27.00	7.50

	#	Player	NRMT	VG-E	GOOD
☐	1	Dave Williams	90.00	18.00	5.50
☐	2	Vic Wertz	30.00	13.50	3.80
☐	3	Sam Jethroe	30.00	13.50	3.80
☐	4	Art Houtteman	27.00	12.00	3.40
☐	5	Sid Gordon	27.00	12.00	3.40
☐	6	Joe Ginsberg	27.00	12.00	3.40
☐	7	Harry Chiti	27.00	12.00	3.40
☐	8	Al Rosen	50.00	23.00	6.25
☐	9	Phil Rizzuto	140.00	65.00	17.50
☐	10	Richie Ashburn	90.00	40.00	11.50
☐	11	Bobby Shantz	30.00	13.50	3.80
☐	12	Carl Erskine	40.00	18.00	5.00
☐	13	Gus Zernial	30.00	13.50	3.80
☐	14	Billy Loes	30.00	13.50	3.80
☐	15	Jim Busby	27.00	12.00	3.40
☐	16	Bob Friend	30.00	13.50	3.80
☐	17	Gerry Staley	27.00	12.00	3.40
☐	18	Nellie Fox	70.00	32.00	8.75
☐	19	Alvin Dark	30.00	13.50	3.80
☐	20	Don Lenhardt	27.00	12.00	3.40
☐	21	Joe Garagiola	60.00	27.00	7.50
☐	22	Bob Porterfield	27.00	12.00	3.40
☐	23	Herman Wehmeier	27.00	12.00	3.40
☐	24	Jackie Jensen	40.00	18.00	5.00
☐	25	Hoot Evers	27.00	12.00	3.40
☐	26	Roy McMillan	30.00	13.50	3.80
☐	27	Vic Raschi	40.00	18.00	5.00
☐	28	Smoky Burgess	30.00	13.50	3.80
☐	29	Bobby Avila	30.00	13.50	3.80
☐	30	Phil Cavarretta	30.00	13.50	3.80
☐	31	Jimmy Dykes MG	30.00	13.50	3.80
☐	32	Stan Musial	650.00	300.00	80.00
☐	33	Pee Wee Reese HOR	650.00	300.00	80.00
☐	34	Gil Coan	27.00	12.00	3.40
☐	35	Maurice McDermott	27.00	12.00	3.40
☐	36	Minnie Minoso	55.00	25.00	7.00
☐	37	Jim Wilson	27.00	12.00	3.40
☐	38	Harry Byrd	27.00	12.00	3.40
☐	39	Paul Richards MG	30.00	13.50	3.80
☐	40	Larry Doby	40.00	18.00	5.00
☐	41	Sammy White	27.00	12.00	3.40
☐	42	Tommy Brown	27.00	12.00	3.40
☐	43	Mike Garcia	30.00	13.50	3.80
☐	44	Berra/Bauer/Mantle	600.00	275.00	75.00
☐	45	Walt Dropo	30.00	13.50	3.80
☐	46	Roy Campanella	275.00	125.00	34.00
☐	47	Ned Garver	27.00	12.00	3.40
☐	48	Hank Sauer	30.00	13.50	3.80
☐	49	Eddie Stanky MG	30.00	13.50	3.80
☐	50	Lou Kretlow	27.00	12.00	3.40

☐ 51 Monte Irvin 65.00 29.00 8.25
☐ 52 Marty Marion MG....... 45.00 20.00 5.75
☐ 53 Del Rice 27.00 12.00 3.40
☐ 54 Chico Carrasquel........ 27.00 12.00 3.40
☐ 55 Leo Durocher MG 70.00 32.00 8.75
☐ 56 Bob Cain 27.00 12.00 3.40
☐ 57 Lou Boudreau MG...... 50.00 23.00 6.25
☐ 58 Willard Marshall......... 27.00 12.00 3.40
☐ 59 Mickey Mantle........ 2700.00 1200.00 350.00
☐ 60 Granny Hamner.......... 27.00 12.00 3.40
☐ 61 George Kell 60.00 27.00 7.50
☐ 62 Ted Kluszewski 60.00 27.00 7.50
☐ 63 Gil McDougald 60.00 27.00 7.50
☐ 64 Curt Simmons............ 30.00 13.50 3.80
☐ 65 Robin Roberts............ 75.00 34.00 9.50
☐ 66 Mel Parnell................. 30.00 13.50 3.80
☐ 67 Mel Clark.................... 27.00 12.00 3.40
☐ 68 Allie Reynolds 50.00 23.00 6.25
☐ 69 Charlie Grimm MG..... 30.00 13.50 3.80
☐ 70 Clint Courtney 27.00 12.00 3.40
☐ 71 Paul Minner 27.00 12.00 3.40
☐ 72 Ted Gray 27.00 12.00 3.40
☐ 73 Billy Pierce 27.00 12.00 3.40
☐ 74 Don Mueller 30.00 13.50 3.80
☐ 75 Saul Rogovin 27.00 12.00 3.40
☐ 76 Jim Hearn 27.00 12.00 3.40
☐ 77 Mickey Grasso 27.00 12.00 3.40
☐ 78 Carl Furillo 50.00 23.00 6.25
☐ 79 Ray Boone 30.00 13.50 3.80
☐ 80 Ralph Kiner................ 75.00 34.00 9.50
☐ 81 Enos Slaughter 70.00 32.00 8.75
☐ 82 Joe Astroth 27.00 12.00 3.40
☐ 83 Jack Daniels............... 30.00 13.50 3.80
☐ 84 Hank Bauer 40.00 18.00 5.00
☐ 85 Solly Hemus 27.00 12.00 3.40
☐ 86 Harry Simpson........... 27.00 12.00 3.40
☐ 87 Harry Perkowski 27.00 12.00 3.40
☐ 88 Joe Dobson................ 27.00 12.00 3.40
☐ 89 Sandy Consuegra....... 27.00 12.00 3.40
☐ 90 Joe Nuxhall 40.00 18.00 5.00
☐ 91 Steve Souchock 27.00 12.00 3.40
☐ 92 Gil Hodges 165.00 75.00 21.00
☐ 93 Phil Rizzuto and 275.00 125.00 34.00
Billy Martin
☐ 94 Bob Addis 27.00 12.00 3.40
☐ 95 Wally Moses CO......... 30.00 13.50 3.80
☐ 96 Sal Maglie 40.00 18.00 5.00
☐ 97 Eddie Mathews 250.00 115.00 31.00
☐ 98 Hector Rodriguez....... 30.00 13.50 3.80
☐ 99 Warren Spahn.......... 225.00 100.00 28.00
☐ 100 Bill Wight.................. 30.00 13.50 3.80
☐ 101 Red Schoendienst.... 75.00 34.00 9.50
☐ 102 Jim Hegan................ 35.00 16.00 4.40
☐ 103 Del Ennis.................. 35.00 16.00 4.40
☐ 104 Luke Easter 35.00 16.00 4.40
☐ 105 Eddie Joost.............. 30.00 13.50 3.80
☐ 106 Ken Raffensberger ... 30.00 13.50 3.80
☐ 107 Alex Kellner.............. 30.00 13.50 3.80
☐ 108 Bobby Adams 30.00 13.50 3.80
☐ 109 Ken Wood 30.00 13.50 3.80
☐ 110 Bob Rush.................. 30.00 13.50 3.80
☐ 111 Jim Dyck................... 30.00 13.50 3.80
☐ 112 Toby Atwell............... 30.00 13.50 3.80
☐ 113 Karl Drews 65.00 29.00 8.25
☐ 114 Bob Feller............... 275.00 125.00 34.00
☐ 115 Cloyd Boyer 65.00 29.00 8.25
☐ 116 Eddie Yost................ 70.00 32.00 8.75
☐ 117 Duke Snider 550.00 250.00 70.00
☐ 118 Billy Martin 250.00 115.00 31.00
☐ 119 Dale Mitchell 70.00 32.00 8.75
☐ 120 Marlin Stuart............ 65.00 29.00 8.25
☐ 121 Yogi Berra.............. 550.00 250.00 70.00
☐ 122 Bill Serena............... 65.00 29.00 8.25
☐ 123 Johnny Lipon........... 65.00 29.00 8.25
☐ 124 Charlie Dressen MG . 65.00 29.00 8.25
☐ 125 Fred Hatfield 65.00 29.00 8.25
☐ 126 Al Corwin 65.00 29.00 8.25
☐ 127 Dick Kryhoski........... 65.00 29.00 8.25
☐ 128 Whitey Lockman 65.00 29.00 8.25
☐ 129 Russ Meyer.............. 60.00 27.00 7.50
☐ 130 Cass Michaels.......... 60.00 27.00 7.50
☐ 131 Connie Ryan 60.00 27.00 7.50
☐ 132 Fred Hutchinson 65.00 29.00 8.25
☐ 133 Willie Jones 60.00 27.00 7.50
☐ 134 Johnny Pesky 65.00 29.00 8.25
☐ 135 Bobby Morgan 60.00 27.00 7.50
☐ 136 Jim Brideweser 60.00 27.00 7.50
☐ 137 Sam Dente 60.00 27.00 7.50
☐ 138 Bubba Church 60.00 27.00 7.50
☐ 139 Pete Runnels............ 65.00 29.00 8.25
☐ 140 Al Brazle................... 60.00 27.00 7.50
☐ 141 Frank Shea 60.00 27.00 7.50
☐ 142 Larry Miggins 60.00 27.00 7.50
☐ 143 Al Lopez MG 65.00 29.00 8.25
☐ 144 Warren Hacker......... 60.00 27.00 7.50
☐ 145 George Shuba.......... 65.00 29.00 8.25
☐ 146 Early Wynn 110.00 50.00 14.00
☐ 147 Clem Koshorek 60.00 27.00 7.50
☐ 148 Billy Goodman 65.00 29.00 8.25
☐ 149 Al Corwin 60.00 27.00 7.50
☐ 150 Carl Scheib 60.00 27.00 7.50
☐ 151 Joe Adcock 65.00 29.00 8.25
☐ 152 Clyde Vollmer 60.00 27.00 7.50
☐ 153 Whitey Ford 450.00 200.00 57.50
☐ 154 Turk Lown................ 60.00 27.00 7.50
☐ 155 Allie Clark................. 60.00 27.00 7.50
☐ 156 Max Surkont 60.00 27.00 7.50
☐ 157 Sherm Lollar............ 65.00 29.00 8.25
☐ 158 Howard Fox.............. 60.00 27.00 7.50
☐ 159 Mickey Vernon UER . 65.00 29.00 8.25
(Photo actually
Floyd Baker)
☐ 160 Cal Abrams 80.00 27.00 7.50

1953 Bowman B/W

The cards in this 64-card set measure approximately 2 1/2" by 3 3/4". Some collectors believe that the high cost of producing the 1953 color series forced Bowman to issue this set in black and white, since the two sets are identical in design except for the element of color. This set was also produced in fewer numbers than its color counterpart, and is popular among collectors for

the challenge involved in completing it. There are no key Rookie Cards in this set.

	NRMT	VG-E	GOOD
COMPLETE SET (64)	2400.00	1100.00	300.00
COMMON CARD (1-64)	32.00	14.50	4.00
☐ 1 Gus Bell	110.00	22.00	8.75
☐ 2 Willard Nixon	32.00	14.50	4.00
☐ 3 Bill Rigney....................	32.00	14.50	4.00
☐ 4 Pat Mullin	32.00	14.50	4.00
☐ 5 Dee Fondy.....................	32.00	14.50	4.00
☐ 6 Ray Murray	32.00	14.50	4.00
☐ 7 Andy Seminick.............	32.00	14.50	4.00
☐ 8 Pete Suder	32.00	14.50	4.00
☐ 9 Walt Masterson............	32.00	14.50	4.00
☐ 10 Dick Sisler..................	35.00	16.00	4.40
☐ 11 Dick Gernert................	32.00	14.50	4.00
☐ 12 Randy Jackson	32.00	14.50	4.00
☐ 13 Joe Tipton..................	32.00	14.50	4.00
☐ 14 Bill Nicholson.............	35.00	16.00	4.40
☐ 15 Johnny Mize	135.00	60.00	17.00
☐ 16 Stu Miller	40.00	18.00	5.00
☐ 17 Virgil Trucks	35.00	16.00	4.40
☐ 18 Billy Hoeft	32.00	14.50	4.00
☐ 19 Paul LaPalme.............	32.00	14.50	4.00
☐ 20 Eddie Robinson..........	32.00	14.50	4.00
☐ 21 Clarence Podbielan	32.00	14.50	4.00
☐ 22 Matt Batts	32.00	14.50	4.00
☐ 23 Wilmer Mizell..............	35.00	16.00	4.40
☐ 24 Del Wilber....................	32.00	14.50	4.00
☐ 25 Johnny Sain................	55.00	25.00	7.00
☐ 26 Preacher Roe	55.00	25.00	7.00
☐ 27 Bob Lemon	135.00	60.00	17.00
☐ 28 Hoyt Wilhelm	135.00	60.00	17.00
☐ 29 Sid Hudson..................	32.00	14.50	4.00
☐ 30 Walker Cooper	32.00	14.50	4.00
☐ 31 Gene Woodling	50.00	23.00	6.25
☐ 32 Rocky Bridges.............	32.00	14.50	4.00
☐ 33 Bob Kuzava..................	32.00	14.50	4.00
☐ 34 Ebba St.Claire	32.00	14.50	4.00
☐ 35 Johnny Wyrostek.......	32.00	14.50	4.00
☐ 36 Jim Piersall..................	50.00	23.00	6.25
☐ 37 Hal Jeffcoat.................	32.00	14.50	4.00
☐ 38 Dave Cole....................	32.00	14.50	4.00
☐ 39 Casey Stengel MG....	300.00	135.00	38.00
☐ 40 Larry Jansen	35.00	16.00	4.40
☐ 41 Bob Ramazzotti..........	32.00	14.50	4.00
☐ 42 Howie Judson	32.00	14.50	4.00
☐ 43 Hal Bevan.....................	32.00	14.50	4.00
☐ 44 Jim Delsing.................	32.00	14.50	4.00
☐ 45 Irv Noren.....................	35.00	16.00	4.40
☐ 46 Bucky Harris MG........	50.00	23.00	6.25
☐ 47 Jack Lohrke	32.00	14.50	4.00
☐ 48 Steve Ridzik................	32.00	14.50	4.00
☐ 49 Floyd Baker	32.00	14.50	4.00
☐ 50 Dutch Leonard	32.00	14.50	4.00
☐ 51 Lou Burdette	50.00	23.00	6.25
☐ 52 Ralph Branca	35.00	16.00	4.40
☐ 53 Morrie Martin.............	32.00	14.50	4.00
☐ 54 Bill Miller.....................	32.00	14.50	4.00
☐ 55 Don Johnson	32.00	14.50	4.00
☐ 56 Roy Smalley................	32.00	14.50	4.00
☐ 57 Andy Pafko	35.00	16.00	4.40
☐ 58 Jim Konstanty............	32.00	14.50	4.00
☐ 59 Duane Pillette.............	32.00	14.50	4.00
☐ 60 Billy Cox......................	40.00	18.00	5.00
☐ 61 Tom Gorman..............	32.00	14.50	4.00
☐ 62 Keith Thomas............	32.00	14.50	4.00
☐ 63 Steve Gromek	32.00	14.50	4.00
☐ 64 Andy Hansen.............	48.00	13.50	3.80

1954 Bowman

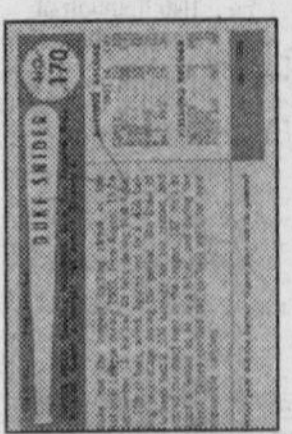

The cards in this 224-card set measure approximately 2 1/2" by 3 3/4". A contractual problem apparently resulted in the deletion of the number 66 Ted Williams card from this Bowman set, thereby creating a scarcity that is highly valued among collectors. The set price below does NOT include number 66 Williams but does include number 66 Jim Piersall, the apparent replacement for Williams in spite of the fact that Piersall was already number 210 to appear later in the set. Many errors in players' statistics exist (and some were corrected) while a few players' names were printed on the front, instead of appearing as a facsimile autograph. The notable Rookie Cards in this set are Harvey Kuenn and Don Larsen.

	NRMT	VG-E	GOOD
COMPLETE SET (224)	4000.00	1800.00	500.00
COMMON CARD (1-128)	10.00	4.50	1.25
COMMON CARD (129-224) ...	12.00	5.50	1.50
☐ 1 Phil Rizzuto................	150.00	45.00	15.00
☐ 2 Jackie Jensen	15.00	6.75	1.90
☐ 3 Marion Fricano.............	10.00	4.50	1.25
☐ 4 Bob Hooper..................	10.00	4.50	1.25
☐ 5 Billy Hunter	10.00	4.50	1.25
☐ 6 Nellie Fox	30.00	13.50	3.80
☐ 7 Walt Dropo	12.00	5.50	1.50
☐ 8 Jim Busby.....................	10.00	4.50	1.25
☐ 9 Dave Williams..............	10.00	4.50	1.25
☐ 10 Carl Erskine................	17.00	7.75	2.10
☐ 11 Sid Gordon	10.00	4.50	1.25
☐ 12 Roy McMillan..............	12.00	5.50	1.50
☐ 13 Paul Minner	10.00	4.50	1.25
☐ 14 Jerry Staley.................	10.00	4.50	1.25
☐ 15 Richie Ashburn	45.00	20.00	5.75
☐ 16 Jim Wilson..................	10.00	4.50	1.25
☐ 17 Tom Gorman..............	10.00	4.50	1.25
☐ 18 Hoot Evers..................	10.00	4.50	1.25
☐ 19 Bobby Shantz.............	10.00	4.50	1.25
☐ 20 Art Houtteman	10.00	4.50	1.25
☐ 21 Vic Wertz	12.00	5.50	1.50
☐ 22 Sam Mele....................	10.00	4.50	1.25
☐ 23 Harvey Kuenn	35.00	16.00	4.40
☐ 24 Bob Porterfield...........	10.00	4.50	1.25
☐ 25 Wes Westrum	12.00	5.50	1.50
☐ 26 Billy Cox.....................	10.00	4.50	1.25
☐ 27 Dick Cole.....................	10.00	4.50	1.25
☐ 28 Jim Greengrass..........	10.00	4.50	1.25
☐ 29 Johnny Klippstein	10.00	4.50	1.25
☐ 30 Del Rice	10.00	4.50	1:25

☐ 31	Smoky Burgess	12.00	5.50	1.50
☐ 32	Del Crandall	12.00	5.50	1.50
☐ 33A	Vic Raschi (No mention of trade on back)	20.00	9.00	2.50
☐ 33B	Vic Raschi (Traded to St.Louis)	35.00	16.00	4.40
☐ 34	Sammy White	10.00	4.50	1.25
☐ 35	Eddie Joost	10.00	4.50	1.25
☐ 36	George Strickland	10.00	4.50	1.25
☐ 37	Dick Kokos	10.00	4.50	1.25
☐ 38	Minnie Minoso	20.00	9.00	2.50
☐ 39	Ned Garver	10.00	4.50	1.25
☐ 40	Gil Coan	10.00	4.50	1.25
☐ 41	Alvin Dark	10.00	4.50	1.25
☐ 42	Billy Loes	12.00	5.50	1.50
☐ 43	Bob Friend	12.00	5.50	1.50
☐ 44	Harry Perkowski	10.00	4.50	1.25
☐ 45	Ralph Kiner	40.00	18.00	5.00
☐ 46	Rip Repulski	10.00	4.50	1.25
☐ 47	Granny Hamner	10.00	4.50	1.25
☐ 48	Jack Dittmer	10.00	4.50	1.25
☐ 49	Harry Byrd	10.00	4.50	1.25
☐ 50	George Kell	27.00	12.00	3.40
☐ 51	Alex Kellner	10.00	4.50	1.25
☐ 52	Joe Ginsberg	10.00	4.50	1.25
☐ 53	Don Lenhardt	10.00	4.50	1.25
☐ 54	Chico Carrasquel	10.00	4.50	1.25
☐ 55	Jim Delsing	10.00	4.50	1.25
☐ 56	Maurice McDermott	10.00	4.50	1.25
☐ 57	Hoyt Wilhelm	25.00	11.50	3.10
☐ 58	Pee Wee Reese	70.00	32.00	8.75
☐ 59	Bob Schultz	10.00	4.50	1.25
☐ 60	Fred Baczewski	10.00	4.50	1.25
☐ 61	Eddie Miksis	10.00	4.50	1.25
☐ 62	Enos Slaughter	40.00	18.00	5.00
☐ 63	Earl Torgeson	10.00	4.50	1.25
☐ 64	Eddie Mathews	50.00	23.00	6.25
☐ 65	Mickey Mantle	1100.00	500.00	140.00
☐ 66A	Ted Williams	4200.00	1250.00	425.00
☐ 66B	Jim Piersall	75.00	34.00	9.50
☐ 67	Carl Scheib	10.00	4.50	1.25
☐ 68	Bobby Avila	12.00	5.50	1.50
☐ 69	Clint Courtney	10.00	4.50	1.25
☐ 70	Willard Marshall	10.00	4.50	1.25
☐ 71	Ted Gray	10.00	4.50	1.25
☐ 72	Eddie Yost	12.00	5.50	1.50
☐ 73	Don Mueller	12.00	5.50	1.50
☐ 74	Jim Gilliam	27.00	12.00	3.40
☐ 75	Max Surkont	10.00	4.50	1.25
☐ 76	Joe Nuxhall	12.00	5.50	1.50
☐ 77	Bob Rush	10.00	4.50	1.25
☐ 78	Sal Yvars	10.00	4.50	1.25
☐ 79	Curt Simmons	12.00	5.50	1.50
☐ 80	Johnny Logan	10.00	4.50	1.25
☐ 81	Jerry Coleman	12.00	5.50	1.50
☐ 82	Billy Goodman	12.00	5.50	1.50
☐ 83	Ray Murray	10.00	4.50	1.25
☐ 84	Larry Doby	15.00	6.75	1.90
☐ 85	Jim Dyck	10.00	4.50	1.25
☐ 86	Harry Dorish	10.00	4.50	1.25
☐ 87	Don Lund	10.00	4.50	1.25
☐ 88	Tom Umphlett	10.00	4.50	1.25
☐ 89	Willie Mays	425.00	190.00	52.50
☐ 90	Roy Campanella	175.00	80.00	22.00
☐ 91	Cal Abrams	10.00	4.50	1.25
☐ 92	Ken Raffensberger	10.00	4.50	1.25
☐ 93	Bill Serena	10.00	4.50	1.25
☐ 94	Solly Hemus	10.00	4.50	1.25
☐ 95	Robin Roberts	45.00	20.00	5.75
☐ 96	Joe Adcock	12.00	5.50	1.50
☐ 97	Gil McDougald	20.00	9.00	2.50
☐ 98	Ellis Kinder	10.00	4.50	1.25
☐ 99	Pete Suder	10.00	4.50	1.25
☐ 100	Mike Garcia	12.00	5.50	1.50
☐ 101	Don Larsen	60.00	27.00	7.50
☐ 102	Billy Pierce	10.00	4.50	1.25
☐ 103	Steve Souchock	10.00	4.50	1.25
☐ 104	Frank Shea	10.00	4.50	1.25
☐ 105	Sal Maglie	15.00	6.75	1.90
☐ 106	Clem Labine	12.00	5.50	1.50
☐ 107	Paul LaPalme	10.00	4.50	1.25
☐ 108	Bobby Adams	10.00	4.50	1.25
☐ 109	Roy Smalley	10.00	4.50	1.25
☐ 110	Red Schoendienst	35.00	16.00	4.40
☐ 111	Murry Dickson	10.00	4.50	1.25
☐ 112	Andy Pafko	12.00	5.50	1.50
☐ 113	Allie Reynolds	18.00	8.00	2.30
☐ 114	Willard Nixon	10.00	4.50	1.25
☐ 115	Don Bollweg	10.00	4.50	1.25
☐ 116	Luke Easter	12.00	5.50	1.50
☐ 117	Dick Kryhoski	10.00	4.50	1.25
☐ 118	Bob Boyd	10.00	4.50	1.25
☐ 119	Fred Hatfield	10.00	4.50	1.25
☐ 120	Mel Hoderlein	10.00	4.50	1.25
☐ 121	Ray Katt	10.00	4.50	1.25
☐ 122	Carl Furillo	18.00	8.00	2.30
☐ 123	Toby Atwell	10.00	4.50	1.25
☐ 124	Gus Bell	12.00	5.50	1.50
☐ 125	Warren Hacker	10.00	4.50	1.25
☐ 126	Cliff Chambers	10.00	4.50	1.25
☐ 127	Del Ennis	12.00	5.50	1.50
☐ 128	Ebba St.Claire	10.00	4.50	1.25
☐ 129	Hank Bauer	20.00	9.00	2.50
☐ 130	Milt Bolling	12.00	5.50	1.50
☐ 131	Joe Astroth	12.00	5.50	1.50
☐ 132	Bob Feller	75.00	34.00	9.50
☐ 133	Duane Pillette	12.00	5.50	1.50
☐ 134	Luis Aloma	12.00	5.50	1.50
☐ 135	Johnny Pesky	12.00	5.50	1.50
☐ 136	Clyde Vollmer	12.00	5.50	1.50
☐ 137	Al Corwin	12.00	5.50	1.50
☐ 138	Gil Hodges	70.00	32.00	8.75
☐ 139	Preston Ward	12.00	5.50	1.50
☐ 140	Saul Rogovin	12.00	5.50	1.50
☐ 141	Joe Garagiola	40.00	18.00	5.00
☐ 142	Al Brazle	12.00	5.50	1.50
☐ 143	Willie Jones	12.00	5.50	1.50
☐ 144	Ernie Johnson	25.00	11.50	3.10
☐ 145	Billy Martin	55.00	25.00	7.00
☐ 146	Dick Gernert	12.00	5.50	1.50
☐ 147	Joe DeMaestri	12.00	5.50	1.50
☐ 148	Dale Mitchell	15.00	6.75	1.90
☐ 149	Bob Young	12.00	5.50	1.50
☐ 150	Cass Michaels	12.00	5.50	1.50
☐ 151	Pat Mullin	12.00	5.50	1.50
☐ 152	Mickey Vernon	15.00	6.75	1.90
☐ 153	Whitey Lockman	15.00	6.75	1.90
☐ 154	Don Newcombe	25.00	11.50	3.10
☐ 155	Frank Thomas	20.00	9.00	2.50
☐ 156	Rocky Bridges	12.00	5.50	1.50
☐ 157	Turk Lown	12.00	5.50	1.50
☐ 158	Stu Miller	15.00	6.75	1.90
☐ 159	Johnny Lindell	12.00	5.50	1.50
☐ 160	Danny O'Connell	12.00	5.50	1.50
☐ 161	Yogi Berra	175.00	80.00	22.00
☐ 162	Ted Lepcio	12.00	5.50	1.50
☐ 163A	Dave Philley (No mention of trade on back)	20.00	9.00	2.50
☐ 163B	Dave Philley (Traded to Cleveland)	36.00	16.00	4.50
☐ 164	Early Wynn	50.00	23.00	6.25
☐ 165	Johnny Groth	12.00	5.50	1.50
☐ 166	Sandy Consuegra	12.00	5.50	1.50

☐	167	Billy Hoeft	12.00	5.50	1.50
☐	168	Ed Fitzgerald	12.00	5.50	1.50
☐	169	Larry Jansen	15.00	6.75	1.90
☐	170	Duke Snider	165.00	75.00	21.00
☐	171	Carlos Bernier	12.00	5.50	1.50
☐	172	Andy Seminick	12.00	5.50	1.50
☐	173	Dee Fondy	12.00	5.50	1.50
☐	174	Pete Castiglione	12.00	5.50	1.50
☐	175	Mel Clark	12.00	5.50	1.50
☐	176	Vern Bickford	12.00	5.50	1.50
☐	177	Whitey Ford	90.00	40.00	11.50
☐	178	Del Wilber	12.00	5.50	1.50
☐	179	Morrie Martin	12.00	5.50	1.50
☐	180	Joe Tipton	12.00	5.50	1.50
☐	181	Les Moss	12.00	5.50	1.50
☐	182	Sherm Lollar	15.00	6.75	1.90
☐	183	Matt Batts	12.00	5.50	1.50
☐	184	Mickey Grasso	12.00	5.50	1.50
☐	185	Daryl Spencer	12.00	5.50	1.50
☐	186	Russ Meyer	12.00	5.50	1.50
☐	187	Vernon Law	15.00	6.75	1.90
☐	188	Frank Smith	12.00	5.50	1.50
☐	189	Randy Jackson	12.00	5.50	1.50
☐	190	Joe Presko	12.00	5.50	1.50
☐	191	Karl Drews	12.00	5.50	1.50
☐	192	Lou Burdette	20.00	9.00	2.50
☐	193	Eddie Robinson	12.00	5.50	1.50
☐	194	Sid Hudson	12.00	5.50	1.50
☐	195	Bob Cain	12.00	5.50	1.50
☐	196	Bob Lemon	38.00	17.00	4.70
☐	197	Lou Kretlow	12.00	5.50	1.50
☐	198	Virgil Trucks	15.00	6.75	1.90
☐	199	Steve Gromek	12.00	5.50	1.50
☐	200	Conrado Marrero	12.00	5.50	1.50
☐	201	Bobby Thomson	20.00	9.00	2.50
☐	202	George Shuba	15.00	6.75	1.90
☐	203	Vic Janowicz	20.00	9.00	2.50
☐	204	Jack Collum	12.00	5.50	1.50
☐	205	Hal Jeffcoat	12.00	5.50	1.50
☐	206	Steve Bilko	12.00	5.50	1.50
☐	207	Stan Lopata	12.00	5.50	1.50
☐	208	Johnny Antonelli	12.00	5.50	1.50
☐	209	Gene Woodling	12.00	5.50	1.50
☐	210	Jim Piersall	20.00	9.00	2.50
☐	211	Al Robertson	12.00	5.50	1.50
☐	212	Owen Friend	12.00	5.50	1.50
☐	213	Dick Littlefield	12.00	5.50	1.50
☐	214	Ferris Fain	15.00	6.75	1.90
☐	215	Johnny Bucha	12.00	5.50	1.50
☐	216	Jerry Snyder	12.00	5.50	1.50
☐	217	Hank Thompson	15.00	6.75	1.90
☐	218	Preacher Roe	20.00	9.00	2.50
☐	219	Hal Rice	12.00	5.50	1.50
☐	220	Hobie Landrith	12.00	5.50	1.50
☐	221	Frank Baumholtz	12.00	5.50	1.50
☐	222	Memo Luna	12.00	5.50	1.50
☐	223	Steve Ridzik	12.00	5.50	1.50
☐	224	Bill Bruton	30.00	5.50	1.50

1955 Bowman

The cards in this 320-card set measure approximately 2 1/2" by 3 3/4". The Bowman set of 1955 is known as the "TV set" because each player photograph is cleverly shown within a television set design. The set contains umpire cards, some transposed pictures (e.g., Johnsons and Bollings), an incorrect spelling for

Harvey Kuenn, and a traded line for Palica (all of which are noted in the checklist below). Some three-card advertising strips exist, the backs of these panels contain advertising for Bowman products. Advertising panels seen include Nellie Fox/Carl Furillo/Carl Erskine, Hank Aaron/Johnny Logan/Eddie Miksis, and a panel including Early Wynn and Pee Wee Reese. The notable Rookie Cards in this set are Elston Howard and Don Zimmer.

	NRMT	VG-E	GOOD
COMPLETE SET (320)	4800.00	2200.00	600.00
COMMON CARD (1-96)	8.00	3.60	1.00
COMMON CARD (97-224)	8.00	3.60	1.00
COMMON CARD (225-320)	16.00	7.25	2.00

☐	1	Hoyt Wilhelm	90.00	18.00	5.50
☐	2	Alvin Dark	12.00	5.50	1.50
☐	3	Joe Coleman	8.00	3.60	1.00
☐	4	Eddie Waitkus	8.00	3.60	1.00
☐	5	Jim Robertson	8.00	3.60	1.00
☐	6	Pete Suder	8.00	3.60	1.00
☐	7	Gene Baker	8.00	3.60	1.00
☐	8	Warren Hacker	8.00	3.60	1.00
☐	9	Gil McDougald	20.00	9.00	2.50
☐	10	Phil Rizzuto	70.00	32.00	8.75
☐	11	Bill Bruton	10.00	4.50	1.25
☐	12	Andy Pafko	10.00	4.50	1.25
☐	13	Clyde Vollmer	8.00	3.60	1.00
☐	14	Gus Keriazakos	8.00	3.60	1.00
☐	15	Frank Sullivan	8.00	3.60	1.00
☐	16	Jim Piersall	10.00	4.50	1.25
☐	17	Del Ennis	10.00	4.50	1.25
☐	18	Stan Lopata	8.00	3.60	1.00
☐	19	Bobby Avila	10.00	4.50	1.25
☐	20	Al Smith	10.00	4.50	1.25
☐	21	Don Hoak	8.00	3.60	1.00
☐	22	Roy Campanella	125.00	57.50	15.50
☐	23	Al Kaline	125.00	57.50	15.50
☐	24	Al Aber	8.00	3.60	1.00
☐	25	Minnie Minoso	20.00	9.00	2.50
☐	26	Virgil Trucks	10.00	4.50	1.25
☐	27	Preston Ward	8.00	3.60	1.00
☐	28	Dick Cole	8.00	3.60	1.00
☐	29	Red Schoendienst	25.00	11.50	3.10
☐	30	Bill Sarni	8.00	3.60	1.00
☐	31	Johnny Temple	13.00	5.75	1.65
☐	32	Wally Post	8.00	3.60	1.00
☐	33	Nellie Fox	22.00	10.00	2.80
☐	34	Clint Courtney	8.00	3.60	1.00
☐	35	Bill Tuttle	8.00	3.60	1.00
☐	36	Wayne Belardi	8.00	3.60	1.00
☐	37	Pee Wee Reese	65.00	29.00	8.25
☐	38	Early Wynn	27.00	12.00	3.40
☐	39	Bob Darnell	10.00	4.50	1.25
☐	40	Vic Wertz	10.00	4.50	1.25
☐	41	Mel Clark	8.00	3.60	1.00

☐ 42 Bob Greenwood 8.00 3.60 1.00
☐ 43 Bob Buhl 10.00 4.50 1.25
☐ 44 Danny O'Connell 8.00 3.60 1.00
☐ 45 Tom Umphlett 8.00 3.60 1.00
☐ 46 Mickey Vernon 10.00 4.50 1.25
☐ 47 Sammy White 8.00 3.60 1.00
☐ 48A Milt Bolling ERR 12.00 5.50 1.50
(Name on back is
Frank Bolling)
☐ 48B Milt Bolling COR 30.00 13.50 3.80
☐ 49 Jim Greengrass 8.00 3.60 1.00
☐ 50 Hobie Landrith 8.00 3.60 1.00
☐ 51 Elvin Tappe 8.00 3.60 1.00
☐ 52 Hal Rice 8.00 3.60 1.00
☐ 53 Alex Kellner 8.00 3.60 1.00
☐ 54 Don Bollweg 8.00 3.60 1.00
☐ 55 Cal Abrams 8.00 3.60 1.00
☐ 56 Billy Cox 10.00 4.50 1.25
☐ 57 Bob Friend 10.00 4.50 1.25
☐ 58 Frank Thomas 10.00 4.50 1.25
☐ 59 Whitey Ford 75.00 34.00 9.50
☐ 60 Enos Slaughter 32.00 14.50 4.00
☐ 61 Paul LaPalme 8.00 3.60 1.00
☐ 62 Royce Lint 8.00 3.60 1.00
☐ 63 Irv Noren 10.00 4.50 1.25
☐ 64 Curt Simmons 10.00 4.50 1.25
☐ 65 Don Zimmer 25.00 11.50 3.10
☐ 66 George Shuba 10.00 4.50 1.25
☐ 67 Don Larsen 20.00 9.00 2.50
☐ 68 Elston Howard 75.00 34.00 9.50
☐ 69 Billy Hunter 8.00 3.60 1.00
☐ 70 Lou Burdette 8.00 3.60 1.00
☐ 71 Dave Jolly 8.00 3.60 1.00
☐ 72 Chet Nichols 8.00 3.60 1.00
☐ 73 Eddie Yost 10.00 4.50 1.25
☐ 74 Jerry Snyder 8.00 3.60 1.00
☐ 75 Brooks Lawrence 8.00 3.60 1.00
☐ 76 Tom Poholsky 8.00 3.60 1.00
☐ 77 Jim McDonald 8.00 3.60 1.00
☐ 78 Gil Coan 8.00 3.60 1.00
☐ 79 Willie Miranda 8.00 3.60 1.00
☐ 80 Lou Limmer 8.00 3.60 1.00
☐ 81 Bobby Morgan 8.00 3.60 1.00
☐ 82 Lee Walls 8.00 3.60 1.00
☐ 83 Max Surkont 8.00 3.60 1.00
☐ 84 George Freese 8.00 3.60 1.00
☐ 85 Cass Michaels 8.00 3.60 1.00
☐ 86 Ted Gray 8.00 3.60 1.00
☐ 87 Randy Jackson 8.00 3.60 1.00
☐ 88 Steve Bilko 8.00 3.60 1.00
☐ 89 Lou Boudreau MG 25.00 11.50 3.10
☐ 90 Art Ditmar 8.00 3.60 1.00
☐ 91 Dick Marlowe 8.00 3.60 1.00
☐ 92 George Zuverink 8.00 3.60 1.00
☐ 93 Andy Seminick 8.00 3.60 1.00
☐ 94 Hank Thompson 10.00 4.50 1.25
☐ 95 Sal Maglie 12.00 5.50 1.50
☐ 96 Ray Narleski 8.00 3.60 1.00
☐ 97 Johnny Podres 20.00 9.00 2.50
☐ 98 Jim Gilliam 16.00 7.25 2.00
☐ 99 Jerry Coleman 10.00 4.50 1.25
☐ 100 Tom Morgan 8.00 3.60 1.00
☐ 101A Don Johnson ERR 12.00 5.50 1.50
(Photo actually
Ernie Johnson)
☐ 101B Don Johnson COR 30.00 13.50 3.80
☐ 102 Bobby Thomson 12.00 5.50 1.50
☐ 103 Eddie Mathews 38.00 17.00 4.70
☐ 104 Bob Porterfield 8.00 3.60 1.00
☐ 105 Johnny Schmitz 8.00 3.60 1.00
☐ 106 Del Rice 8.00 3.60 1.00
☐ 107 Solly Hemus 8.00 3.60 1.00
☐ 108 Lou Kretlow 8.00 3.60 1.00
☐ 109 Vern Stephens 10.00 4.50 1.25
☐ 110 Bob Miller 8.00 3.60 1.00
☐ 111 Steve Ridzik 8.00 3.60 1.00
☐ 112 Granny Hamner 8.00 3.60 1.00
☐ 113 Bob Hall 8.00 3.60 1.00
☐ 114 Vic Janowicz 10.00 4.50 1.25
☐ 115 Roger Bowman 8.00 3.60 1.00
☐ 116 Sandy Consuegra 8.00 3.60 1.00
☐ 117 Johnny Groth 8.00 3.60 1.00
☐ 118 Bobby Adams 8.00 3.60 1.00
☐ 119 Joe Astroth 8.00 3.60 1.00
☐ 120 Ed Burtschy 8.00 3.60 1.00
☐ 121 Rufus Crawford 8.00 3.60 1.00
☐ 122 Al Corwin 8.00 3.60 1.00
☐ 123 Marv Grissom 8.00 3.60 1.00
☐ 124 Johnny Antonelli 10.00 4.50 1.25
☐ 125 Paul Giel 10.00 4.50 1.25
☐ 126 Billy Goodman 10.00 4.50 1.25
☐ 127 Hank Majeski 8.00 3.60 1.00
☐ 128 Mike Garcia 10.00 4.50 1.25
☐ 129 Hal Naragon 8.00 3.60 1.00
☐ 130 Richie Ashburn 25.00 11.50 3.10
☐ 131 Willard Marshall 8.00 3.60 1.00
☐ 132A Harvey Kueen ERR 12.50 5.75 1.55
(Sic, Kuenn)
☐ 132B Harvey Kuenn COR 30.00 13.50 3.80
☐ 133 Charles King 8.00 3.60 1.00
☐ 134 Bob Feller 75.00 34.00 9.50
☐ 135 Lloyd Merriman 8.00 3.60 1.00
☐ 136 Rocky Bridges 8.00 3.60 1.00
☐ 137 Bob Talbot 8.00 3.60 1.00
☐ 138 Davey Williams 8.00 3.60 1.00
☐ 139 Shantz Brothers 8.00 3.60 1.00
(Wilmer and Bobby)
☐ 140 Bobby Shantz 10.00 4.50 1.25
☐ 141 Wes Westrum 10.00 4.50 1.25
☐ 142 Rudy Regalado 8.00 3.60 1.00
☐ 143 Don Newcombe 20.00 9.00 2.50
☐ 144 Art Houtteman 8.00 3.60 1.00
☐ 145 Bob Nieman 8.00 3.60 1.00
☐ 146 Don Liddle 8.00 3.60 1.00
☐ 147 Sam Mele 8.00 3.60 1.00
☐ 148 Bob Chakales 8.00 3.60 1.00
☐ 149 Cloyd Boyer 8.00 3.60 1.00
☐ 150 Billy Klaus 8.00 3.60 1.00
☐ 151 Jim Brideweser 8.00 3.60 1.00
☐ 152 Johnny Klippstein 8.00 3.60 1.00
☐ 153 Eddie Robinson 8.00 3.60 1.00
☐ 154 Frank Lary 13.00 5.75 1.65
☐ 155 Gerry Staley 8.00 3.60 1.00
☐ 156 Jim Hughes 10.00 4.50 1.25
☐ 157A Ernie Johnson ERR 12.00 5.50 1.50
(Photo actually
Don Johnson)
☐ 157B Ernie Johnson COR 30.00 13.50 3.80
☐ 158 Gil Hodges 40.00 18.00 5.00
☐ 159 Harry Byrd 8.00 3.60 1.00
☐ 160 Bill Skowron 25.00 11.50 3.10
☐ 161 Matt Batts 8.00 3.60 1.00
☐ 162 Charlie Maxwell 10.00 4.50 1.25
☐ 163 Sid Gordon 8.00 3.60 1.00
☐ 164 Toby Atwell 8.00 3.60 1.00
☐ 165 Maurice McDermott 8.00 3.60 1.00
☐ 166 Jim Busby 8.00 3.60 1.00
☐ 167 Bob Grim 15.00 6.75 1.90
☐ 168 Yogi Berra 100.00 45.00 12.50
☐ 169 Carl Furillo 20.00 9.00 2.50
☐ 170 Carl Erskine 20.00 9.00 2.50
☐ 171 Robin Roberts 27.00 12.00 3.40
☐ 172 Willie Jones 8.00 3.60 1.00
☐ 173 Chico Carrasquel 8.00 3.60 1.00
☐ 174 Sherm Lollar 10.00 4.50 1.25
☐ 175 Wilmer Shantz 8.00 3.60 1.00

☐ 176 Joe DeMaestri 8.00 3.60 1.00
☐ 177 Willard Nixon 8.00 3.60 1.00
☐ 178 Tom Brewer 8.00 3.60 1.00
☐ 179 Hank Aaron 240.00 110.00 30.00
☐ 180 Johnny Logan 10.00 4.50 1.25
☐ 181 Eddie Miksis 8.00 3.60 1.00
☐ 182 Bob Rush 8.00 3.60 1.00
☐ 183 Ray Katt 8.00 3.60 1.00
☐ 184 Willie Mays 240.00 110.00 30.00
☐ 185 Vic Raschi 8.00 3.60 1.00
☐ 186 Alex Grammas 8.00 3.60 1.00
☐ 187 Fred Hatfield 8.00 3.60 1.00
☐ 188 Ned Garver 8.00 3.60 1.00
☐ 189 Jack Collum 8.00 3.60 1.00
☐ 190 Fred Baczewski 8.00 3.60 1.00
☐ 191 Bob Lemon 25.00 11.50 3.10
☐ 192 George Strickland 8.00 3.60 1.00
☐ 193 Howie Judson 8.00 3.60 1.00
☐ 194 Joe Nuxhall 10.00 4.50 1.25
☐ 195A Erv Palica 10.00 4.50 1.25
(Without trade)
☐ 195B Erv Palica 30.00 13.50 3.80
(With trade)
☐ 196 Russ Meyer 10.00 4.50 1.25
☐ 197 Ralph Kiner 27.00 12.00 3.40
☐ 198 Dave Pope 8.00 3.60 1.00
☐ 199 Vernon Law 10.00 4.50 1.25
☐ 200 Dick Littlefield 8.00 3.60 1.00
☐ 201 Allie Reynolds 16.00 7.25 2.00
☐ 202 Mickey Mantle 650.00 300.00 80.00
☐ 203 Steve Gromek 8.00 3.60 1.00
☐ 204A Frank Bolling ERR .. 12.00 5.50 1.50
(Name on back is
Milt Bolling)
☐ 204B Frank Bolling COR . 30.00 13.50 3.80
☐ 205 Rip Repulski 8.00 3.60 1.00
☐ 206 Ralph Beard 8.00 3.60 1.00
☐ 207 Frank Shea 8.00 3.60 1.00
☐ 208 Ed Fitzgerald 8.00 3.60 1.00
☐ 209 Smoky Burgess 10.00 4.50 1.25
☐ 210 Earl Torgeson 8.00 3.60 1.00
☐ 211 Sonny Dixon 8.00 3.60 1.00
☐ 212 Jack Dittmer 8.00 3.60 1.00
☐ 213 George Kell 20.00 9.00 2.50
☐ 214 Billy Pierce 8.00 3.60 1.00
☐ 215 Bob Kuzava 8.00 3.60 1.00
☐ 216 Preacher Roe 12.00 5.50 1.50
☐ 217 Del Crandall 10.00 4.50 1.25
☐ 218 Joe Adcock 10.00 4.50 1.25
☐ 219 Whitey Lockman 10.00 4.50 1.25
☐ 220 Jim Hearn 8.00 3.60 1.00
☐ 221 Hector Brown 8.00 3.60 1.00
☐ 222 Russ Kemmerer 8.00 3.60 1.00
☐ 223 Hal Jeffcoat 8.00 3.60 1.00
☐ 224 Dee Fondy 8.00 3.60 1.00
☐ 225 Paul Richards MG 18.00 8.00 2.30
☐ 226 Bill McKinley UMP ... 25.00 11.50 3.10
☐ 227 Frank Baumholtz 16.00 7.25 2.00
☐ 228 John Phillips 16.00 7.25 2.00
☐ 229 Jim Brosnan 20.00 9.00 2.50
☐ 230 Al Brazle 16.00 7.25 2.00
☐ 231 Jim Konstanty 18.00 8.00 2.30
☐ 232 Birdie Tebbetts MG .. 18.00 8.00 2.30
☐ 233 Bill Serena 16.00 7.25 2.00
☐ 234 Dick Bartell CO 16.00 7.25 2.00
☐ 235 Joe Paparella UMP ... 25.00 11.50 3.10
☐ 236 Murry Dickson 16.00 7.25 2.00
☐ 237 Johnny Wyrostek 16.00 7.25 2.00
☐ 238 Eddie Stanky MG 16.00 7.25 2.00
☐ 239 Edwin Rommel UMP 25.00 11.50 3.10
☐ 240 Billy Loes 18.00 8.00 2.30
☐ 241 Johnny Pesky CO 16.00 7.25 2.00
☐ 242 Ernie Banks 300.00 135.00 38.00
☐ 243 Gus Bell 18.00 8.00 2.30
☐ 244 Duane Pillette 16.00 7.25 2.00
☐ 245 Bill Miller 16.00 7.25 2.00
☐ 246 Hank Bauer 35.00 16.00 4.40
☐ 247 Dutch Leonard CO ... 16.00 7.25 2.00
☐ 248 Harry Dorish 16.00 7.25 2.00
☐ 249 Billy Gardner 18.00 8.00 2.30
☐ 250 Larry Napp UMP 25.00 11.50 3.10
☐ 251 Stan Jok 16.00 7.25 2.00
☐ 252 Roy Smalley 16.00 7.25 2.00
☐ 253 Jim Wilson 16.00 7.25 2.00
☐ 254 Bennett Flowers 16.00 7.25 2.00
☐ 255 Pete Runnels 18.00 8.00 2.30
☐ 256 Owen Friend 16.00 7.25 2.00
☐ 257 Tom Alston 16.00 7.25 2.00
☐ 258 John Stevens UMP .. 25.00 11.50 3.10
☐ 259 Don Mossi 25.00 11.50 3.10
☐ 260 Edwin Hurley UMP ... 25.00 11.50 3.10
☐ 261 Walt Moryn 18.00 8.00 2.30
☐ 262 Jim Lemon 16.00 7.25 2.00
☐ 263 Eddie Joost 16.00 7.25 2.00
☐ 264 Bill Henry 16.00 7.25 2.00
☐ 265 Albert Barlick UMP ... 75.00 34.00 9.50
☐ 266 Mike Fornieles 16.00 7.25 2.00
☐ 267 Jim Honochick UMP 75.00 34.00 9.50
☐ 268 Roy Lee Hawes 16.00 7.25 2.00
☐ 269 Joe Amalfitano 20.00 9.00 2.50
☐ 270 Chico Fernandez 18.00 8.00 2.30
☐ 271 Bob Hooper 16.00 7.25 2.00
☐ 272 John Flaherty UMP .. 25.00 11.50 3.10
☐ 273 Bubba Church 16.00 7.25 2.00
☐ 274 Jim Delsing 16.00 7.25 2.00
☐ 275 William Grieve UMP. 25.00 11.50 3.10
☐ 276 Ike Delock 16.00 7.25 2.00
☐ 277 Ed Runge UMP 30.00 13.50 3.80
☐ 278 Charlie Neal 35.00 16.00 4.40
☐ 279 Hank Soar UMP 25.00 11.50 3.10
☐ 280 Clyde McCullough 16.00 7.25 2.00
☐ 281 Charles Berry UMP .. 25.00 11.50 3.10
☐ 282 Phil Cavarretta 16.00 7.25 2.00
☐ 283 Nestor Chylak UMP .. 25.00 11.50 3.10
☐ 284 Bill Jackowski UMP . 25.00 11.50 3.10
☐ 285 Walt Dropo 18.00 8.00 2.30
☐ 286 Frank Secory UMP ... 25.00 11.50 3.10
☐ 287 Ron Mrozinski 16.00 7.25 2.00
☐ 288 Dick Smith 16.00 7.25 2.00
☐ 289 Arthur Gore UMP 25.00 11.50 3.10
☐ 290 Hershell Freeman 16.00 7.25 2.00
☐ 291 Frank Dascoli UMP .. 25.00 11.50 3.10
☐ 292 Marv Blaylock 16.00 7.25 2.00
☐ 293 Thomas Gorman UMP 30.00 13.50 3.80
☐ 294 Wally Moses CO 18.00 8.00 2.30
☐ 295 Lee Ballanfant UMP . 25.00 11.50 3.10
☐ 296 Bill Virdon 35.00 16.00 4.40
☐ 297 Dusty Boggess UMP 25.00 11.50 3.10
☐ 298 Charlie Grimm MG ... 16.00 7.25 2.00
☐ 299 Lon Warneke UMP ... 30.00 13.50 3.80
☐ 300 Tommy Byrne 16.00 7.25 2.00
☐ 301 William Engeln UMP 25.00 11.50 3.10
☐ 302 Frank Malzone 30.00 13.50 3.80
☐ 303 Jocko Conlan UMP .. 75.00 34.00 9.50
☐ 304 Harry Chiti 16.00 7.25 2.00
☐ 305 Frank Umont UMP ... 25.00 11.50 3.10
☐ 306 Bob Cerv 25.00 11.50 3.10
☐ 307 Babe Pinelli UMP 30.00 13.50 3.80
☐ 308 Al Lopez MG 55.00 25.00 7.00
☐ 309 Hal Dixon UMP 25.00 11.50 3.10
☐ 310 Ken Lehman 18.00 8.00 2.30
☐ 311 Lawrence Goetz UMP 25.00 11.50 3.10
☐ 312 Bill Wight 16.00 7.25 2.00
☐ 313 Augie Donatelli UMP 40.00 18.00 5.00
☐ 314 Dale Mitchell 18.00 8.00 2.30
☐ 315 Cal Hubbard UMP 85.00 38.00 10.50

☐ 316	Marion Fricano	16.00	7.25	2.00
☐ 317	William Summers UMP	30.00	13.50	3.80
☐ 318	Sid Hudson	16.00	7.25	2.00
☐ 319	Al Schroll	16.00	7.25	2.00
☐ 320	George Susce Jr.	45.00	9.00	2.70

1989 Bowman

The 1989 Bowman set, which was actually produced by Topps, contains 484 cards measuring approximately 2 1/2" by 3 3/4". The fronts have white-bordered color photos with facsimile autographs and small Bowman logos. The backs are scarlet and feature charts detailing 1988 player performances vs. each team. The cards are checklisted below alphabetically according to teams in the AL and NL as follows: Baltimore Orioles (1-18), Boston Red Sox (19-36), California Angels (37-54), Chicago White Sox (55-72), Cleveland Indians (73-91), Detroit Tigers (92-109), Kansas City Royals (110-128), Milwaukee Brewers (129-146), Minnesota Twins (147-164), New York Yankees (165-183), Oakland Athletics (184-202), Seattle Mariners (203-220), Texas Rangers (221-238), Toronto Blue Jays (239-257), Atlanta Braves (262-279), Chicago Cubs (280-298), Cincinnati Reds (299-316), Houston Astros (317-334), Los Angeles Dodgers (335-352), Montreal Expos (353-370), New York Mets (371-389), Philadelphia Phillies (390-408), Pittsburgh Pirates (409-426), St. Louis Cardinals (427-444), San Diego Padres (445-462), and San Francisco Giants (463-480). Cards 258-261 form a father/son subset. The cards were released in midseason 1989 in wax, rack, and cello pack formats. Rookie Cards in this set include Jim Abbott, Steve Avery, Andy Benes, Rico Brogna, Royce Clayton, Ken Griffey Jr., Tino Martinez, Gary Sheffield, John Smoltz, Ed Sprague and Robin Ventura. Topps also produced a limited Bowman "Tiffany" set with reportedly only 6,000 sets being produced. This Tiffany version is valued approximately from five to eight times the values listed below.

	MINT	EXC	G-VG
COMPLETE SET (484)	15.00	6.75	1.90
COMPLETE FACT.SET (484)	15.00	6.75	1.90
COMMON CARD (1-484)	.05	.02	.01

☐ 1	Oswald Peraza	.05	.02	.01
☐ 2	Brian Holton	.05	.02	.01
☐ 3	Jose Bautista	.05	.02	.01
☐ 4	Pete Harnisch	.20	.09	.03
☐ 5	Dave Schmidt	.05	.02	.01
☐ 6	Gregg Olson	.25	.11	.03
☐ 7	Jeff Ballard	.05	.02	.01
☐ 8	Bob Melvin	.05	.02	.01
☐ 9	Cal Ripken	.50	.23	.06
☐ 10	Randy Milligan	.05	.02	.01
☐ 11	Juan Bell	.05	.02	.01
☐ 12	Billy Ripken	.05	.02	.01
☐ 13	Jim Traber	.05	.02	.01
☐ 14	Pete Stanicek	.05	.02	.01
☐ 15	Steve Finley	.25	.11	.03
☐ 16	Larry Sheets	.05	.02	.01
☐ 17	Phil Bradley	.05	.02	.01
☐ 18	Brady Anderson	.40	.18	.05
☐ 19	Lee Smith	.15	.07	.02
☐ 20	Tom Fischer	.05	.02	.01
☐ 21	Mike Boddicker	.05	.02	.01
☐ 22	Rob Murphy	.05	.02	.01
☐ 23	Wes Gardner	.05	.02	.01
☐ 24	John Dopson	.05	.02	.01
☐ 25	Bob Stanley	.05	.02	.01
☐ 26	Roger Clemens	.35	.16	.04
☐ 27	Rich Gedman	.05	.02	.01
☐ 28	Marty Barrett	.05	.02	.01
☐ 29	Luis Rivera	.05	.02	.01
☐ 30	Jody Reed	.05	.02	.01
☐ 31	Nick Esasky	.05	.02	.01
☐ 32	Wade Boggs	.20	.09	.03
☐ 33	Jim Rice	.15	.07	.02
☐ 34	Mike Greenwell	.10	.05	.01
☐ 35	Dwight Evans	.10	.05	.01
☐ 36	Ellis Burks	.10	.05	.01
☐ 37	Chuck Finley	.10	.05	.01
☐ 38	Kirk McCaskill	.05	.02	.01
☐ 39	Jim Abbott	.60	.25	.08
☐ 40	Bryan Harvey	.25	.11	.03
☐ 41	Bert Blyleven	.15	.07	.02
☐ 42	Mike Witt	.05	.02	.01
☐ 43	Bob McClure	.05	.02	.01
☐ 44	Bill Schroeder	.05	.02	.01
☐ 45	Lance Parrish	.10	.05	.01
☐ 46	Dick Schofield	.05	.02	.01
☐ 47	Wally Joyner	.10	.05	.01
☐ 48	Jack Howell	.05	.02	.01
☐ 49	Johnny Ray	.05	.02	.01
☐ 50	Chili Davis	.10	.05	.01
☐ 51	Tony Armas	.05	.02	.01
☐ 52	Claudell Washington	.05	.02	.01
☐ 53	Brian Downing	.05	.02	.01
☐ 54	Devon White	.10	.05	.01
☐ 55	Bobby Thigpen	.05	.02	.01
☐ 56	Bill Long	.05	.02	.01
☐ 57	Jerry Reuss	.05	.02	.01
☐ 58	Shawn Hillegas	.05	.02	.01
☐ 59	Melido Perez	.05	.02	.01
☐ 60	Jeff Bittiger	.05	.02	.01
☐ 61	Jack McDowell	.25	.11	.03
☐ 62	Carlton Fisk	.15	.07	.02
☐ 63	Steve Lyons	.05	.02	.01
☐ 64	Ozzie Guillen	.10	.05	.01
☐ 65	Robin Ventura	1.00	.45	.13
☐ 66	Fred Manrique	.05	.02	.01
☐ 67	Dan Pasqua	.05	.02	.01
☐ 68	Ivan Calderon	.05	.02	.01
☐ 69	Ron Kittle	.05	.02	.01
☐ 70	Daryl Boston	.05	.02	.01
☐ 71	Dave Gallagher	.05	.02	.01
☐ 72	Harold Baines	.10	.05	.01
☐ 73	Charles Nagy	.30	.14	.04

□ 74 John Farrell .05 .02 .01
□ 75 Kevin Wickander .05 .02 .01
□ 76 Greg Swindell .10 .05 .01
□ 77 Mike Walker .05 .02 .01
□ 78 Doug Jones .10 .05 .01
□ 79 Rich Yett .05 .02 .01
□ 80 Tom Candiotti .05 .02 .01
□ 81 Jesse Orosco .05 .02 .01
□ 82 Bud Black .05 .02 .01
□ 83 Andy Allanson .05 .02 .01
□ 84 Pete O'Brien .05 .02 .01
□ 85 Jerry Browne .05 .02 .01
□ 86 Brook Jacoby .05 .02 .01
□ 87 Mark Lewis .20 .09 .03
□ 88 Luis Aguayo .05 .02 .01
□ 89 Cory Snyder .05 .02 .01
□ 90 Oddibe McDowell .05 .02 .01
□ 91 Joe Carter .30 .14 .04
□ 92 Frank Tanana .05 .02 .01
□ 93 Jack Morris .15 .07 .02
□ 94 Doyle Alexander .05 .02 .01
□ 95 Steve Searcy .05 .02 .01
□ 96 Randy Bockus .05 .02 .01
□ 97 Jeff M. Robinson .05 .02 .01
□ 98 Mike Henneman .10 .05 .01
□ 99 Paul Gibson .05 .02 .01
□ 100 Frank Williams .05 .02 .01
□ 101 Matt Nokes .05 .02 .01
□ 102 Rico Brogna UER .50 .23 .06
(Misspelled Ricco on card back)
□ 103 Lou Whitaker .15 .07 .02
□ 104 Al Pedrique .05 .02 .01
□ 105 Alan Trammell .15 .07 .02
□ 106 Chris Brown .05 .02 .01
□ 107 Pat Sheridan .05 .02 .01
□ 108 Chet Lemon .05 .02 .01
□ 109 Keith Moreland .05 .02 .01
□ 110 Mel Stottlemyre Jr. .10 .05 .01
□ 111 Bret Saberhagen .10 .05 .01
□ 112 Floyd Bannister .05 .02 .01
□ 113 Jeff Montgomery .10 .05 .01
□ 114 Steve Farr .05 .02 .01
□ 115 Tom Gordon UER .20 .09 .03
(Front shows autograph of Don Gordon)
□ 116 Charlie Leibrandt .05 .02 .01
□ 117 Mark Gubicza .05 .02 .01
□ 118 Mike Macfarlane .10 .05 .01
□ 119 Bob Boone .10 .05 .01
□ 120 Kurt Stillwell .05 .02 .01
□ 121 George Brett .35 .16 .04
□ 122 Frank White .10 .05 .01
□ 123 Kevin Seitzer .05 .02 .01
□ 124 Willie Wilson .05 .02 .01
□ 125 Pat Tabler .05 .02 .01
□ 126 Bo Jackson .25 .11 .03
□ 127 Hugh Walker .05 .02 .01
□ 128 Danny Tartabull .10 .05 .01
□ 129 Teddy Higuera .05 .02 .01
□ 130 Don August .05 .02 .01
□ 131 Juan Nieves .05 .02 .01
□ 132 Mike Birkbeck .05 .02 .01
□ 133 Dan Plesac .05 .02 .01
□ 134 Chris Bosio .05 .02 .01
□ 135 Bill Wegman .05 .02 .01
□ 136 Chuck Crim .05 .02 .01
□ 137 B.J. Surhoff .05 .02 .01
□ 138 Joey Meyer .05 .02 .01
□ 139 Dale Sveum .05 .02 .01
□ 140 Paul Molitor .25 .11 .03
□ 141 Jim Gantner .05 .02 .01
□ 142 Gary Sheffield 1.00 .45 .13
□ 143 Greg Brock .05 .02 .01
□ 144 Robin Yount .25 .11 .03
□ 145 Glenn Braggs .05 .02 .01
□ 146 Rob Deer .05 .02 .01
□ 147 Fred Toliver .05 .02 .01
□ 148 Jeff Reardon .15 .07 .02
□ 149 Allan Anderson .05 .02 .01
□ 150 Frank Viola .10 .05 .01
□ 151 Shane Rawley .05 .02 .01
□ 152 Juan Berenguer .05 .02 .01
□ 153 Johnny Ard .05 .02 .01
□ 154 Tim Laudner .05 .02 .01
□ 155 Brian Harper .10 .05 .01
□ 156 Al Newman .05 .02 .01
□ 157 Kent Hrbek .10 .05 .01
□ 158 Gary Gaetti .05 .02 .01
□ 159 Wally Backman .05 .02 .01
□ 160 Gene Larkin .05 .02 .01
□ 161 Greg Gagne .05 .02 .01
□ 162 Kirby Puckett .50 .23 .06
□ 163 Dan Gladden .05 .02 .01
□ 164 Randy Bush .05 .02 .01
□ 165 Dave LaPoint .05 .02 .01
□ 166 Andy Hawkins .05 .02 .01
□ 167 Dave Righetti .05 .02 .01
□ 168 Lance McCullers .05 .02 .01
□ 169 Jimmy Jones .05 .02 .01
□ 170 Al Leiter .05 .02 .01
□ 171 John Candelaria .05 .02 .01
□ 172 Don Slaught .05 .02 .01
□ 173 Jamie Quirk .05 .02 .01
□ 174 Rafael Santana .05 .02 .01
□ 175 Mike Pagliarulo .05 .02 .01
□ 176 Don Mattingly .40 .18 .05
□ 177 Ken Phelps .05 .02 .01
□ 178 Steve Sax .05 .02 .01
□ 179 Dave Winfield .20 .09 .03
□ 180 Stan Jefferson .05 .02 .01
□ 181 Rickey Henderson .15 .07 .02
□ 182 Bob Brower .05 .02 .01
□ 183 Roberto Kelly .20 .09 .03
□ 184 Curt Young .05 .02 .01
□ 185 Gene Nelson .05 .02 .01
□ 186 Bob Welch .10 .05 .01
□ 187 Rick Honeycutt .05 .02 .01
□ 188 Dave Stewart .10 .05 .01
□ 189 Mike Moore .05 .02 .01
□ 190 Dennis Eckersley .15 .07 .02
□ 191 Eric Plunk .05 .02 .01
□ 192 Storm Davis .05 .02 .01
□ 193 Terry Steinbach .10 .05 .01
□ 194 Ron Hassey .05 .02 .01
□ 195 Stan Royer .05 .02 .01
□ 196 Walt Weiss .05 .02 .01
□ 197 Mark McGwire .15 .07 .02
□ 198 Carney Lansford .10 .05 .01
□ 199 Glenn Hubbard .05 .02 .01
□ 200 Dave Henderson .05 .02 .01
□ 201 Jose Canseco .30 .14 .04
□ 202 Dave Parker .15 .07 .02
□ 203 Scott Bankhead .05 .02 .01
□ 204 Tom Niedenfuer .05 .02 .01
□ 205 Mark Langston .15 .07 .02
□ 206 Erik Hanson .25 .11 .03
□ 207 Mike Jackson .05 .02 .01
□ 208 Dave Valle .05 .02 .01
□ 209 Scott Bradley .05 .02 .01
□ 210 Harold Reynolds .05 .02 .01
□ 211 Tino Martinez .25 .11 .03
□ 212 Rich Renteria .05 .02 .01
□ 213 Rey Quinones .05 .02 .01
□ 214 Jim Presley .05 .02 .01
□ 215 Alvin Davis .05 .02 .01

	No.	Player			
☐	216	Edgar Martinez	.10	.05	.01
☐	217	Darnell Coles	.05	.02	.01
☐	218	Jeffrey Leonard	.05	.02	.01
☐	219	Jay Buhner	.20	.09	.03
☐	220	Ken Griffey Jr.	6.00	2.70	.75
☐	221	Drew Hall	.05	.02	.01
☐	222	Bobby Witt	.10	.05	.01
☐	223	Jamie Moyer	.05	.02	.01
☐	224	Charlie Hough	.10	.05	.01
☐	225	Nolan Ryan	.75	.35	.09
☐	226	Jeff Russell	.05	.02	.01
☐	227	Jim Sundberg	.05	.02	.01
☐	228	Julio Franco	.10	.05	.01
☐	229	Buddy Bell	.10	.05	.01
☐	230	Scott Fletcher	.05	.02	.01
☐	231	Jeff Kunkel	.05	.02	.01
☐	232	Steve Buechele	.05	.02	.01
☐	233	Monty Fariss	.05	.02	.01
☐	234	Rick Leach	.05	.02	.01
☐	235	Ruben Sierra	.25	.11	.03
☐	236	Cecil Espy	.05	.02	.01
☐	237	Rafael Palmeiro	.25	.11	.03
☐	238	Pete Incaviglia	.10	.05	.01
☐	239	Dave Stieb	.10	.05	.01
☐	240	Jeff Musselman	.05	.02	.01
☐	241	Mike Flanagan	.05	.02	.01
☐	242	Todd Stottlemyre	.10	.05	.01
☐	243	Jimmy Key	.15	.07	.02
☐	244	Tony Castillo	.05	.02	.01
☐	245	Alex Sanchez	.05	.02	.01
☐	246	Tom Henke	.10	.05	.01
☐	247	John Cerutti	.05	.02	.01
☐	248	Ernie Whitt	.05	.02	.01
☐	249	Bob Brenly	.05	.02	.01
☐	250	Rance Mulliniks	.05	.02	.01
☐	251	Kelly Gruber	.05	.02	.01
☐	252	Ed Sprague	.25	.11	.03
☐	253	Fred McGriff	.25	.11	.03
☐	254	Tony Fernandez	.10	.05	.01
☐	255	Tom Lawless	.05	.02	.01
☐	256	George Bell	.10	.05	.01
☐	257	Jesse Barfield	.05	.02	.01
☐	258	Roberto Alomar w/Dad	.30	.14	.04
☐	259	Ken Griffey Jr./Sr.	1.25	.55	.16
☐	260	Cal Ripken Jr./Sr.	.25	.11	.03
☐	261	M.Stottlemyre Jr./Sr.	.05	.02	.01
☐	262	Zane Smith	.05	.02	.01
☐	263	Charlie Puleo	.05	.02	.01
☐	264	Derek Lilliquist	.05	.02	.01
☐	265	Paul Assenmacher	.05	.02	.01
☐	266	John Smoltz	.40	.18	.05
☐	267	Tom Glavine	.40	.18	.05
☐	268	Steve Avery	1.00	.45	.13
☐	269	Pete Smith	.05	.02	.01
☐	270	Jody Davis	.05	.02	.01
☐	271	Bruce Benedict	.05	.02	.01
☐	272	Andres Thomas	.05	.02	.01
☐	273	Gerald Perry	.05	.02	.01
☐	274	Ron Gant	.25	.11	.03
☐	275	Darrell Evans	.10	.05	.01
☐	276	Dale Murphy	.15	.07	.02
☐	277	Dion James	.05	.02	.01
☐	278	Lonnie Smith	.05	.02	.01
☐	279	Geronimo Berroa	.25	.11	.03
☐	280	Steve Wilson	.05	.02	.01
☐	281	Rick Sutcliffe	.10	.05	.01
☐	282	Kevin Coffman	.05	.02	.01
☐	283	Mitch Williams	.10	.05	.01
☐	284	Greg Maddux	.35	.16	.04
☐	285	Paul Kilgus	.05	.02	.01
☐	286	Mike Harkey	.05	.02	.01
☐	287	Lloyd McClendon	.05	.02	.01
☐	288	Damon Berryhill	.05	.02	.01
☐	289	Ty Griffin	.05	.02	.01
☐	290	Ryne Sandberg	.40	.18	.05
☐	291	Mark Grace	.25	.11	.03
☐	292	Curt Wilkerson	.05	.02	.01
☐	293	Vance Law	.05	.02	.01
☐	294	Shawon Dunston	.10	.05	.01
☐	295	Jerome Walton	.05	.02	.01
☐	296	Mitch Webster	.05	.02	.01
☐	297	Dwight Smith	.15	.07	.02
☐	298	Andre Dawson	.15	.07	.02
☐	299	Jeff Sellers	.05	.02	.01
☐	300	Jose Rijo	.15	.07	.02
☐	301	John Franco	.10	.05	.01
☐	302	Rick Mahler	.05	.02	.01
☐	303	Ron Robinson	.05	.02	.01
☐	304	Danny Jackson	.05	.02	.01
☐	305	Rob Dibble	.20	.09	.03
☐	306	Tom Browning	.05	.02	.01
☐	307	Bo Diaz	.05	.02	.01
☐	308	Manny Trillo	.05	.02	.01
☐	309	Chris Sabo	.25	.11	.03
☐	310	Ron Oester	.05	.02	.01
☐	311	Barry Larkin	.15	.07	.02
☐	312	Todd Benzinger	.05	.02	.01
☐	313	Paul O'Neill	.15	.07	.02
☐	314	Kal Daniels	.05	.02	.01
☐	315	Joel Youngblood	.05	.02	.01
☐	316	Eric Davis	.10	.05	.01
☐	317	Dave Smith	.05	.02	.01
☐	318	Mark Portugal	.10	.05	.01
☐	319	Brian Meyer	.05	.02	.01
☐	320	Jim Deshaies	.05	.02	.01
☐	321	Juan Agosto	.05	.02	.01
☐	322	Mike Scott	.05	.02	.01
☐	323	Rick Rhoden	.05	.02	.01
☐	324	Jim Clancy	.05	.02	.01
☐	325	Larry Andersen	.05	.02	.01
☐	326	Alex Trevino	.05	.02	.01
☐	327	Alan Ashby	.05	.02	.01
☐	328	Craig Reynolds	.05	.02	.01
☐	329	Bill Doran	.05	.02	.01
☐	330	Rafael Ramirez	.05	.02	.01
☐	331	Glenn Davis	.05	.02	.01
☐	332	Willie Ansley	.10	.05	.01
☐	333	Gerald Young	.05	.02	.01
☐	334	Cameron Drew	.05	.02	.01
☐	335	Jay Howell	.05	.02	.01
☐	336	Tim Belcher	.05	.02	.01
☐	337	Fernando Valenzuela	.05	.02	.01
☐	338	Ricky Horton	.05	.02	.01
☐	339	Tim Leary	.05	.02	.01
☐	340	Bill Bene	.05	.02	.01
☐	341	Orel Hershiser	.10	.05	.01
☐	342	Mike Scioscia	.05	.02	.01
☐	343	Rick Dempsey	.05	.02	.01
☐	344	Willie Randolph	.10	.05	.01
☐	345	Alfredo Griffin	.05	.02	.01
☐	346	Eddie Murray	.15	.07	.02
☐	347	Mickey Hatcher	.05	.02	.01
☐	348	Mike Sharperson	.05	.02	.01
☐	349	John Shelby	.05	.02	.01
☐	350	Mike Marshall	.05	.02	.01
☐	351	Kirk Gibson	.10	.05	.01
☐	352	Mike Davis	.05	.02	.01
☐	353	Bryn Smith	.05	.02	.01
☐	354	Pascual Perez	.05	.02	.01
☐	355	Kevin Gross	.05	.02	.01
☐	356	Andy McGaffigan	.05	.02	.01
☐	357	Brian Holman	.05	.02	.01
☐	358	Dave Wainhouse	.05	.02	.01
☐	359	Dennis Martinez	.10	.05	.01
☐	360	Tim Burke	.05	.02	.01
☐	361	Nelson Santovenia	.05	.02	.01

☐ 362 Tim Wallach .05 .02 .01
☐ 363 Spike Owen .05 .02 .01
☐ 364 Rex Hudler .05 .02 .01
☐ 365 Andres Galarraga .15 .07 .02
☐ 366 Otis Nixon .10 .05 .01
☐ 367 Hubie Brooks .05 .02 .01
☐ 368 Mike Aldrete .05 .02 .01
☐ 369 Tim Raines .15 .07 .02
☐ 370 Dave Martinez .05 .02 .01
☐ 371 Bob Ojeda .05 .02 .01
☐ 372 Ron Darling .10 .05 .01
☐ 373 Wally Whitehurst .05 .02 .01
☐ 374 Randy Myers .10 .05 .01
☐ 375 David Cone .20 .09 .03
☐ 376 Dwight Gooden .10 .05 .01
☐ 377 Sid Fernandez .10 .05 .01
☐ 378 Dave Proctor .05 .02 .01
☐ 379 Gary Carter .15 .07 .02
☐ 380 Keith Miller .05 .02 .01
☐ 381 Gregg Jefferies .35 .16 .04
☐ 382 Tim Teufel .05 .02 .01
☐ 383 Kevin Elster .05 .02 .01
☐ 384 Dave Magadan .05 .02 .01
☐ 385 Keith Hernandez .10 .05 .01
☐ 386 Mookie Wilson .10 .05 .01
☐ 387 Darryl Strawberry .15 .07 .02
☐ 388 Kevin McReynolds .10 .05 .01
☐ 389 Mark Carreon .05 .02 .01
☐ 390 Jeff Parrett .05 .02 .01
☐ 391 Mike Maddux .05 .02 .01
☐ 392 Don Carman .05 .02 .01
☐ 393 Bruce Ruffin .05 .02 .01
☐ 394 Ken Howell .05 .02 .01
☐ 395 Steve Bedrosian .05 .02 .01
☐ 396 Floyd Youmans .05 .02 .01
☐ 397 Larry McWilliams .05 .02 .01
☐ 398 Pat Combs .05 .02 .01
☐ 399 Steve Lake .05 .02 .01
☐ 400 Dickie Thon .05 .02 .01
☐ 401 Ricky Jordan .05 .02 .01
☐ 402 Mike Schmidt .25 .11 .03
☐ 403 Tom Herr .05 .02 .01
☐ 404 Chris James .05 .02 .01
☐ 405 Juan Samuel .05 .02 .01
☐ 406 Von Hayes .05 .02 .01
☐ 407 Ron Jones .05 .02 .01
☐ 408 Curt Ford .05 .02 .01
☐ 409 Bob Walk .05 .02 .01
☐ 410 Jeff D. Robinson .05 .02 .01
☐ 411 Jim Gott .05 .02 .01
☐ 412 Scott Medvin .05 .02 .01
☐ 413 John Smiley .05 .02 .01
☐ 414 Bob Kipper .05 .02 .01
☐ 415 Brian Fisher .05 .02 .01
☐ 416 Doug Drabek .15 .07 .02
☐ 417 Mike LaValliere .05 .02 .01
☐ 418 Ken Oberkfell .05 .02 .01
☐ 419 Sid Bream .05 .02 .01
☐ 420 Austin Manahan .05 .02 .01
☐ 421 Jose Lind .05 .02 .01
☐ 422 Bobby Bonilla .15 .07 .02
☐ 423 Glenn Wilson .05 .02 .01
☐ 424 Andy Van Slyke .15 .07 .02
☐ 425 Gary Redus .05 .02 .01
☐ 426 Barry Bonds .60 .25 .08
☐ 427 Don Heinkel .05 .02 .01
☐ 428 Ken Dayley .05 .02 .01
☐ 429 Todd Worrell .05 .02 .01
☐ 430 Brad DuVall .05 .02 .01
☐ 431 Jose DeLeon .05 .02 .01
☐ 432 Joe Magrane .05 .02 .01
☐ 433 John Ericks .05 .02 .01
☐ 434 Frank DiPino .05 .02 .01
☐ 435 Tony Pena .05 .02 .01
☐ 436 Ozzie Smith .30 .14 .04
☐ 437 Terry Pendleton .15 .07 .02
☐ 438 Jose Oquendo .05 .02 .01
☐ 439 Tim Jones .05 .02 .01
☐ 440 Pedro Guerrero .10 .05 .01
☐ 441 Milt Thompson .05 .02 .01
☐ 442 Willie McGee .10 .05 .01
☐ 443 Vince Coleman .10 .05 .01
☐ 444 Tom Brunansky .05 .02 .01
☐ 445 Walt Terrell .05 .02 .01
☐ 446 Eric Show .05 .02 .01
☐ 447 Mark Davis .05 .02 .01
☐ 448 Andy Benes .40 .18 .05
☐ 449 Ed Whitson .05 .02 .01
☐ 450 Dennis Rasmussen .05 .02 .01
☐ 451 Bruce Hurst .05 .02 .01
☐ 452 Pat Clements .05 .02 .01
☐ 453 Benito Santiago .10 .05 .01
☐ 454 Sandy Alomar Jr. .25 .11 .03
☐ 455 Garry Templeton .05 .02 .01
☐ 456 Jack Clark .10 .05 .01
☐ 457 Tim Flannery .05 .02 .01
☐ 458 Roberto Alomar .75 .35 .09
☐ 459 Carmelo Martinez .05 .02 .01
☐ 460 John Kruk .15 .07 .02
☐ 461 Tony Gwynn .30 .14 .04
☐ 462 Jerald Clark .05 .02 .01
☐ 463 Don Robinson .05 .02 .01
☐ 464 Craig Lefferts .05 .02 .01
☐ 465 Kelly Downs .05 .02 .01
☐ 466 Rick Reuschel .05 .02 .01
☐ 467 Scott Garrelts .05 .02 .01
☐ 468 Wil Tejada .05 .02 .01
☐ 469 Kirt Manwaring .05 .02 .01
☐ 470 Terry Kennedy .05 .02 .01
☐ 471 Jose Uribe .05 .02 .01
☐ 472 Royce Clayton .35 .16 .04
☐ 473 Robby Thompson .10 .05 .01
☐ 474 Kevin Mitchell .15 .07 .02
☐ 475 Ernest Riles .05 .02 .01
☐ 476 Will Clark .30 .14 .04
☐ 477 Donell Nixon .05 .02 .01
☐ 478 Candy Maldonado .05 .02 .01
☐ 479 Tracy Jones .05 .02 .01
☐ 480 Brett Butler .10 .05 .01
☐ 481 Checklist 1-121 .05 .02 .01
☐ 482 Checklist 122-242 .05 .02 .01
☐ 483 Checklist 243-363 .05 .02 .01
☐ 484 Checklist 364-484 .05 .02 .01

1990 Bowman

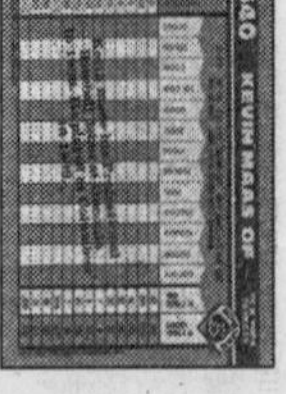

The 1990 Bowman set was issued in the standard card size of 2 1/2" by 3 1/2". This

was the second issue by Topps using the Bowman name. The set consists of 528 cards, increased from 1989's edition of 484 cards. The cards feature a white border with the player's photo inside and the Bowman logo on top. Again, the Bowman cards were issued with the backs featuring team by team statistics. The card numbering is in team order with the teams themselves being ordered alphabetically within each league. The set numbering is as follows: Atlanta Braves (1-20), Chicago Cubs (21-40), Cincinnati Reds (41-60), Houston Astros (61-81), Los Angeles Dodgers (82-101), Montreal Expos (102-121), New York Mets (122-142), Philadelphia Phillies (143-162), Pittsburgh Pirates (163-182), St. Louis Cardinals (183-202), San Diego Padres (203-222), San Francisco Giants (223-242), Baltimore Orioles (243-262), Boston Red Sox (263-282), California Angels (283-302), Chicago White Sox (303-322), Cleveland Indians (323-342), Detroit Tigers (343-362), Kansas City Royals (363-383), Milwaukee Brewers (384-404), Minnesota Twins (405-424), New York Yankees (425-444), Oakland A's (445-464), Seattle Mariners (465-484), Texas Rangers (485-503), and Toronto Blue Jays (504-524). Rookie Cards in this set include Moises Alou, Carlos Baerga, Scott Cooper, Delino DeShields, Cal Eldred, Travis Fryman, Leo Gomez, Juan Gonzalez, Tommy Greene, Marquis Grissom, Bob Hamelin, Chris Hoiles, Dave Hollins, Darryl Kile, Chuck Knoblauch, Ray Lankford, Kevin Maas, Ben McDonald, Jose Offerman, John Olerud, Sammy Sosa, Frank Thomas, Mo Vaughn, and Larry Walker. Topps also produced a Bowman Tiffany glossy set. Production of these Tiffany Bowmans was reported to be approximately 3,000 sets. These Tiffany versions are valued at approximately five to ten times the values listed below.

	MINT	EXC	G-VG
COMPLETE SET (528)	15.00	6.75	1.90
COMPLETE FACT.SET (528)	15.00	6.75	1.90
COMMON CARD (1-528)	.05	.02	.01
☐ 1 Tommy Greene	.15	.07	.02
☐ 2 Tom Glavine	.25	.11	.03
☐ 3 Andy Nezelek	.05	.02	.01
☐ 4 Mike Stanton	.05	.02	.01
☐ 5 Rick Luecken	.05	.02	.01
☐ 6 Kent Mercker	.25	.11	.03
☐ 7 Derek Lilliquist	.05	.02	.01
☐ 8 Charlie Leibrandt	.05	.02	.01
☐ 9 Steve Avery	.40	.18	.05
☐ 10 John Smoltz	.15	.07	.02
☐ 11 Mark Lemke	.10	.05	.01
☐ 12 Lonnie Smith	.05	.02	.01
☐ 13 Oddibe McDowell	.05	.02	.01
☐ 14 Tyler Houston	.05	.02	.01
☐ 15 Jeff Blauser	.10	.05	.01
☐ 16 Ernie Whitt	.05	.02	.01
☐ 17 Alexis Infante	.05	.02	.01
☐ 18 Jim Presley	.05	.02	.01
☐ 19 Dale Murphy	.15	.07	.02
☐ 20 Nick Esasky	.05	.02	.01
☐ 21 Rick Sutcliffe	.10	.05	.01
☐ 22 Mike Bielecki	.05	.02	.01
☐ 23 Steve Wilson	.05	.02	.01
☐ 24 Kevin Blankenship	.05	.02	.01
☐ 25 Mitch Williams	.10	.05	.01
☐ 26 Dean Wilkins	.05	.02	.01
☐ 27 Greg Maddux	.30	.14	.04
☐ 28 Mike Harkey	.05	.02	.01
☐ 29 Mark Grace	.20	.09	.03
☐ 30 Ryne Sandberg	.35	.16	.04
☐ 31 Greg Smith	.05	.02	.01
☐ 32 Dwight Smith	.05	.02	.01
☐ 33 Damon Berryhill	.05	.02	.01
☐ 34 Earl Cunningham UER (Errant * by the word "in")	.05	.02	.01
☐ 35 Jerome Walton	.05	.02	.01
☐ 36 Lloyd McClendon	.05	.02	.01
☐ 37 Ty Griffin	.05	.02	.01
☐ 38 Shawon Dunston	.05	.02	.01
☐ 39 Andre Dawson	.15	.07	.02
☐ 40 Luis Salazar	.05	.02	.01
☐ 41 Tim Layana	.05	.02	.01
☐ 42 Rob Dibble	.10	.05	.01
☐ 43 Tom Browning	.05	.02	.01
☐ 44 Danny Jackson	.05	.02	.01
☐ 45 Jose Rijo	.10	.05	.01
☐ 46 Scott Scudder	.05	.02	.01
☐ 47 Randy Myers UER (Career ERA .274, should be 2.74)	.10	.05	.01
☐ 48 Brian Lane	.05	.02	.01
☐ 49 Paul O'Neill	.10	.05	.01
☐ 50 Barry Larkin	.15	.07	.02
☐ 51 Reggie Jefferson	.05	.02	.01
☐ 52 Jeff Branson	.05	.02	.01
☐ 53 Chris Sabo	.10	.05	.01
☐ 54 Joe Oliver	.05	.02	.01
☐ 55 Todd Benzinger	.05	.02	.01
☐ 56 Rolando Roomes	.05	.02	.01
☐ 57 Hal Morris	.10	.05	.01
☐ 58 Eric Davis	.10	.05	.01
☐ 59 Scott Bryant	.05	.02	.01
☐ 60 Ken Griffey	.10	.05	.01
☐ 61 Darryl Kile	.20	.09	.03
☐ 62 Dave Smith	.05	.02	.01
☐ 63 Mark Portugal	.05	.02	.01
☐ 64 Jeff Juden	.15	.07	.02
☐ 65 Bill Gullickson	.05	.02	.01
☐ 66 Danny Darwin	.05	.02	.01
☐ 67 Larry Andersen	.05	.02	.01
☐ 68 Jose Cano	.05	.02	.01
☐ 69 Dan Schatzeder	.05	.02	.01
☐ 70 Jim Deshaies	.05	.02	.01
☐ 71 Mike Scott	.05	.02	.01
☐ 72 Gerald Young	.05	.02	.01
☐ 73 Ken Caminiti	.10	.05	.01
☐ 74 Ken Oberkfell	.05	.02	.01
☐ 75 Dave Rohde	.05	.02	.01
☐ 76 Bill Doran	.05	.02	.01
☐ 77 Andujar Cedeno	.15	.07	.02
☐ 78 Craig Biggio	.15	.07	.02
☐ 79 Karl Rhodes	.15	.07	.02
☐ 80 Glenn Davis	.05	.02	.01
☐ 81 Eric Anthony	.15	.07	.02
☐ 82 John Wetteland	.10	.05	.01
☐ 83 Jay Howell	.05	.02	.01
☐ 84 Orel Hershiser	.10	.05	.01
☐ 85 Tim Belcher	.05	.02	.01
☐ 86 Kiki Jones	.05	.02	.01
☐ 87 Mike Hartley	.05	.02	.01
☐ 88 Ramon Martinez	.10	.05	.01
☐ 89 Mike Scioscia	.05	.02	.01
☐ 90 Willie Randolph	.10	.05	.01
☐ 91 Juan Samuel	.05	.02	.01
☐ 92 Jose Offerman	.15	.07	.02

☐	93 Dave Hansen	.05	.02	.01
☐	94 Jeff Hamilton	.05	.02	.01
☐	95 Alfredo Griffin	.05	.02	.01
☐	96 Tom Goodwin	.05	.02	.01
☐	97 Kirk Gibson	.10	.05	.01
☐	98 Jose Vizcaino	.05	.02	.01
☐	99 Kal Daniels	.05	.02	.01
☐	100 Hubie Brooks	.05	.02	.01
☐	101 Eddie Murray	.15	.07	.02
☐	102 Dennis Boyd	.05	.02	.01
☐	103 Tim Burke	.05	.02	.01
☐	104 Bill Sampen	.05	.02	.01
☐	105 Brett Gideon	.05	.02	.01
☐	106 Mark Gardner	.05	.02	.01
☐	107 Howard Farmer	.05	.02	.01
☐	108 Mel Rojas	.10	.05	.01
☐	109 Kevin Gross	.05	.02	.01
☐	110 Dave Schmidt	.05	.02	.01
☐	111 Denny Martinez	.10	.05	.01
☐	112 Jerry Goff	.05	.02	.01
☐	113 Andres Galarraga	.15	.07	.02
☐	114 Tim Wallach	.05	.02	.01
☐	115 Marquis Grissom	.50	.23	.06
☐	116 Spike Owen	.05	.02	.01
☐	117 Larry Walker	.50	.23	.06
☐	118 Tim Raines	.15	.07	.02
☐	119 Delino DeShields	.25	.11	.03
☐	120 Tom Foley	.05	.02	.01
☐	121 Dave Martinez	.05	.02	.01
☐	122 Frank Viola UER (Career ERA .384, should be 3.84)	.10	.05	.01
☐	123 Julio Valera	.05	.02	.01
☐	124 Alejandro Pena	.05	.02	.01
☐	125 David Cone	.15	.07	.02
☐	126 Dwight Gooden	.10	.05	.01
☐	127 Kevin D. Brown	.05	.02	.01
☐	128 John Franco	.10	.05	.01
☐	129 Terry Bross	.05	.02	.01
☐	130 Blaine Beatty	.05	.02	.01
☐	131 Sid Fernandez	.10	.05	.01
☐	132 Mike Marshall	.05	.02	.01
☐	133 Howard Johnson	.10	.05	.01
☐	134 Jaime Roseboro	.10	.05	.01
☐	135 Alan Zinter	.05	.02	.01
☐	136 Keith Miller	.05	.02	.01
☐	137 Kevin Elster	.05	.02	.01
☐	138 Kevin McReynolds	.05	.02	.01
☐	139 Barry Lyons	.05	.02	.01
☐	140 Gregg Jefferies	.25	.11	.03
☐	141 Darryl Strawberry	.15	.07	.02
☐	142 Todd Hundley	.20	.09	.03
☐	143 Scott Service	.05	.02	.01
☐	144 Chuck Malone	.05	.02	.01
☐	145 Steve Ontiveros	.05	.02	.01
☐	146 Roger McDowell	.05	.02	.01
☐	147 Ken Howell	.05	.02	.01
☐	148 Pat Combs	.05	.02	.01
☐	149 Jeff Parrett	.05	.02	.01
☐	150 Chuck McElroy	.05	.02	.01
☐	151 Jason Grimsley	.05	.02	.01
☐	152 Len Dykstra	.15	.07	.02
☐	153 Mickey Morandini	.15	.07	.02
☐	154 John Kruk	.15	.07	.02
☐	155 Dickie Thon	.05	.02	.01
☐	156 Ricky Jordan	.05	.02	.01
☐	157 Jeff Jackson	.05	.02	.01
☐	158 Darren Daulton	.15	.07	.02
☐	159 Tom Herr	.05	.02	.01
☐	160 Von Hayes	.05	.02	.01
☐	161 Dave Hollins	.25	.11	.03
☐	162 Carmelo Martinez	.05	.02	.01
☐	163 Bob Walk	.05	.02	.01
☐	164 Doug Drabek	.15	.07	.02
☐	165 Walt Terrell	.05	.02	.01
☐	166 Bill Landrum	.05	.02	.01
☐	167 Scott Ruskin	.05	.02	.01
☐	168 Bob Patterson	.05	.02	.01
☐	169 Bobby Bonilla	.15	.07	.02
☐	170 Jose Lind	.05	.02	.01
☐	171 Andy Van Slyke	.15	.07	.02
☐	172 Mike LaValliere	.05	.02	.01
☐	173 Willie Greene	.25	.11	.03
☐	174 Jay Bell	.10	.05	.01
☐	175 Sid Bream	.05	.02	.01
☐	176 Tom Prince	.05	.02	.01
☐	177 Wally Backman	.05	.02	.01
☐	178 Moises Alou	.50	.23	.06
☐	179 Steve Carter	.05	.02	.01
☐	180 Gary Redus	.05	.02	.01
☐	181 Barry Bonds	.50	.23	.06
☐	182 Don Slaught UER (Card back shows headings for a pitcher)	.05	.02	.01
☐	183 Joe Magrane	.05	.02	.01
☐	184 Bryn Smith	.05	.02	.01
☐	185 Todd Worrell	.05	.02	.01
☐	186 Jose DeLeon	.05	.02	.01
☐	187 Frank DiPino	.05	.02	.01
☐	188 John Tudor	.05	.02	.01
☐	189 Howard Hilton	.05	.02	.01
☐	190 John Ericks	.05	.02	.01
☐	191 Ken Dayley	.05	.02	.01
☐	192 Ray Lankford	.40	.18	.05
☐	193 Todd Zeile	.15	.07	.02
☐	194 Willie McGee	.10	.05	.01
☐	195 Ozzie Smith	.25	.11	.03
☐	196 Milt Thompson	.05	.02	.01
☐	197 Terry Pendleton	.15	.07	.02
☐	198 Vince Coleman	.10	.05	.01
☐	199 Paul Coleman	.05	.02	.01
☐	200 Jose Oquendo	.05	.02	.01
☐	201 Pedro Guerrero	.10	.05	.01
☐	202 Tom Brunansky	.05	.02	.01
☐	203 Roger Smithberg	.05	.02	.01
☐	204 Eddie Whitson	.05	.02	.01
☐	205 Dennis Rasmussen	.05	.02	.01
☐	206 Craig Lefferts	.05	.02	.01
☐	207 Andy Benes	.15	.07	.02
☐	208 Bruce Hurst	.05	.02	.01
☐	209 Eric Show	.05	.02	.01
☐	210 Rafael Valdez	.05	.02	.01
☐	211 Joey Cora	.05	.02	.01
☐	212 Thomas Howard	.05	.02	.01
☐	213 Rob Nelson	.05	.02	.01
☐	214 Jack Clark	.10	.05	.01
☐	215 Garry Templeton	.05	.02	.01
☐	216 Fred Lynn	.10	.05	.01
☐	217 Tony Gwynn	.25	.11	.03
☐	218 Benito Santiago	.10	.05	.01
☐	219 Mike Pagliarulo	.05	.02	.01
☐	220 Joe Carter	.25	.11	.03
☐	221 Roberto Alomar	.40	.18	.05
☐	222 Bip Roberts	.10	.05	.01
☐	223 Rick Reuschel	.05	.02	.01
☐	224 Russ Swan	.05	.02	.01
☐	225 Eric Gunderson	.05	.02	.01
☐	226 Steve Bedrosian	.05	.02	.01
☐	227 Mike Remlinger	.05	.02	.01
☐	228 Scott Garrelts	.05	.02	.01
☐	229 Ernie Camacho	.05	.02	.01
☐	230 Andres Santana	.05	.02	.01
☐	231 Will Clark	.25	.11	.03
☐	232 Kevin Mitchell	.10	.05	.01
☐	233 Robby Thompson	.10	.05	.01
☐	234 Bill Bathe	.05	.02	.01

☐	235	Tony Perezchica	.05	.02	.01
☐	236	Gary Carter	.15	.07	.02
☐	237	Brett Butler	.10	.05	.01
☐	238	Matt Williams	.25	.11	.03
☐	239	Earnie Riles	.05	.02	.01
☐	240	Kevin Bass	.05	.02	.01
☐	241	Terry Kennedy	.05	.02	.01
☐	242	Steve Hosey	.15	.07	.02
☐	243	Ben McDonald	.40	.18	.05
☐	244	Jeff Ballard	.05	.02	.01
☐	245	Joe Price	.05	.02	.01
☐	246	Curt Schilling	.10	.05	.01
☐	247	Pete Harnisch	.10	.05	.01
☐	248	Mark Williamson	.05	.02	.01
☐	249	Gregg Olson	.10	.05	.01
☐	250	Chris Myers	.05	.02	.01
☐	251A	David Segui ERR (Missing vital stats at top of card back under name)	.30	.14	.04
☐	251B	David Segui COR	.15	.07	.02
☐	252	Joe Orsulak	.05	.02	.01
☐	253	Craig Worthington	.05	.02	.01
☐	254	Mickey Tettleton	.10	.05	.01
☐	255	Cal Ripken	.40	.18	.05
☐	256	Billy Ripken	.05	.02	.01
☐	257	Randy Milligan	.05	.02	.01
☐	258	Brady Anderson	.10	.05	.01
☐	259	Chris Hoiles	.25	.11	.03
☐	260	Mike Devereaux	.10	.05	.01
☐	261	Phil Bradley	.05	.02	.01
☐	262	Leo Gomez	.20	.09	.03
☐	263	Lee Smith	.15	.07	.02
☐	264	Mike Rochford	.05	.02	.01
☐	265	Jeff Reardon	.15	.07	.02
☐	266	Wes Gardner	.05	.02	.01
☐	267	Mike Boddicker	.05	.02	.01
☐	268	Roger Clemens	.30	.14	.04
☐	269	Rob Murphy	.05	.02	.01
☐	270	Mickey Pina	.10	.05	.01
☐	271	Tony Pena	.05	.02	.01
☐	272	Jody Reed	.05	.02	.01
☐	273	Kevin Romine	.05	.02	.01
☐	274	Mike Greenwell	.10	.05	.01
☐	275	Maurice Vaughn	.75	.35	.09
☐	276	Danny Heep	.05	.02	.01
☐	277	Scott Cooper	.25	.11	.03
☐	278	Greg Blosser	.15	.07	.02
☐	279	Dwight Evans UER (* by "1990 Team Breakdown")	.10	.05	.01
☐	280	Ellis Burks	.10	.05	.01
☐	281	Wade Boggs	.20	.09	.03
☐	282	Marty Barrett	.05	.02	.01
☐	283	Kirk McCaskill	.05	.02	.01
☐	284	Mark Langston	.15	.07	.02
☐	285	Bert Blyleven	.15	.07	.02
☐	286	Mike Fetters	.05	.02	.01
☐	287	Kyle Abbott	.05	.02	.01
☐	288	Jim Abbott	.15	.07	.02
☐	289	Chuck Finley	.10	.05	.01
☐	290	Gary DiSarcina	.05	.02	.01
☐	291	Dick Schofield	.05	.02	.01
☐	292	Devon White	.10	.05	.01
☐	293	Bobby Rose	.10	.05	.01
☐	294	Brian Downing	.05	.02	.01
☐	295	Lance Parrish	.10	.05	.01
☐	296	Jack Howell	.05	.02	.01
☐	297	Claudell Washington	.05	.02	.01
☐	298	John Orton	.05	.02	.01
☐	299	Wally Joyner	.10	.05	.01
☐	300	Lee Stevens	.05	.02	.01
☐	301	Chili Davis	.10	.05	.01
☐	302	Johnny Ray	.05	.02	.01
☐	303	Greg Hibbard	.05	.02	.01
☐	304	Eric King	.05	.02	.01
☐	305	Jack McDowell	.20	.09	.03
☐	306	Bobby Thigpen	.05	.02	.01
☐	307	Adam Peterson	.05	.02	.01
☐	308	Scott Radinsky	.05	.02	.01
☐	309	Wayne Edwards	.05	.02	.01
☐	310	Melido Perez	.05	.02	.01
☐	311	Robin Ventura	.50	.23	.06
☐	312	Sammy Sosa	.50	.23	.06
☐	313	Dan Pasqua	.05	.02	.01
☐	314	Carlton Fisk	.15	.07	.02
☐	315	Ozzie Guillen	.05	.02	.01
☐	316	Ivan Calderon	.05	.02	.01
☐	317	Daryl Boston	.05	.02	.01
☐	318	Craig Grebeck	.05	.02	.01
☐	319	Scott Fletcher	.05	.02	.01
☐	320	Frank Thomas	4.00	1.80	.50
☐	321	Steve Lyons	.05	.02	.01
☐	322	Carlos Martinez	.05	.02	.01
☐	323	Joe Skalski	.05	.02	.01
☐	324	Tom Candiotti	.05	.02	.01
☐	325	Greg Swindell	.10	.05	.01
☐	326	Steve Olin	.10	.05	.01
☐	327	Kevin Wickander	.05	.02	.01
☐	328	Doug Jones	.05	.02	.01
☐	329	Jeff Shaw	.05	.02	.01
☐	330	Kevin Bearse	.05	.02	.01
☐	331	Dion James	.05	.02	.01
☐	332	Jerry Browne	.05	.02	.01
☐	333	Joey Belle	1.50	.65	.19
☐	334	Felix Fermin	.05	.02	.01
☐	335	Candy Maldonado	.05	.02	.01
☐	336	Cory Snyder	.05	.02	.01
☐	337	Sandy Alomar Jr.	.10	.05	.01
☐	338	Mark Lewis	.05	.02	.01
☐	339	Carlos Baerga	1.00	.45	.13
☐	340	Chris James	.05	.02	.01
☐	341	Brook Jacoby	.05	.02	.01
☐	342	Keith Hernandez	.10	.05	.01
☐	343	Frank Tanana	.05	.02	.01
☐	344	Scott Aldred	.05	.02	.01
☐	345	Mike Henneman	.05	.02	.01
☐	346	Steve Wapnick	.05	.02	.01
☐	347	Greg Gohr	.05	.02	.01
☐	348	Eric Stone	.05	.02	.01
☐	349	Brian DuBois	.05	.02	.01
☐	350	Kevin Ritz	.05	.02	.01
☐	351	Rico Brogna	.15	.07	.02
☐	352	Mike Heath	.05	.02	.01
☐	353	Alan Trammell	.15	.07	.02
☐	354	Chet Lemon	.05	.02	.01
☐	355	Dave Bergman	.05	.02	.01
☐	356	Lou Whitaker	.15	.07	.02
☐	357	Cecil Fielder UER (* by "1990 Team Breakdown")	.15	.07	.02
☐	358	Milt Cuyler	.05	.02	.01
☐	359	Tony Phillips	.10	.05	.01
☐	360	Travis Fryman	1.00	.45	.13
☐	361	Ed Romero	.05	.02	.01
☐	362	Lloyd Moseby	.05	.02	.01
☐	363	Mark Gubicza	.05	.02	.01
☐	364	Bret Saberhagen	.10	.05	.01
☐	365	Tom Gordon	.10	.05	.01
☐	366	Steve Farr	.05	.02	.01
☐	367	Kevin Appier	.30	.14	.04
☐	368	Storm Davis	.05	.02	.01
☐	369	Mark Davis	.05	.02	.01
☐	370	Jeff Montgomery	.10	.05	.01
☐	371	Frank White	.10	.05	.01
☐	372	Brent Mayne	.05	.02	.01

☐	373 Bob Boone	.10	.05	.01
☐	374 Jim Eisenreich	.05	.02	.01
☐	375 Danny Tartabull	.10	.05	.01
☐	376 Kurt Stillwell	.05	.02	.01
☐	377 Bill Pecota	.05	.02	.01
☐	378 Bo Jackson	.15	.07	.02
☐	379 Bob Hamelin	.75	.35	.09
☐	380 Kevin Seitzer	.05	.02	.01
☐	381 Rey Palacios	.05	.02	.01
☐	382 George Brett	.30	.14	.04
☐	383 Gerald Perry	.05	.02	.01
☐	384 Teddy Higuera	.05	.02	.01
☐	385 Tom Filer	.05	.02	.01
☐	386 Dan Plesac	.05	.02	.01
☐	387 Cal Eldred	.25	.11	.03
☐	388 Jaime Navarro	.05	.02	.01
☐	389 Chris Bosio	.05	.02	.01
☐	390 Randy Veres	.05	.02	.01
☐	391 Gary Sheffield	.30	.14	.04
☐	392 George Canale	.05	.02	.01
☐	393 B.J. Surhoff	.05	.02	.01
☐	394 Tim McIntosh	.05	.02	.01
☐	395 Greg Brock	.05	.02	.01
☐	396 Greg Vaughn	.20	.09	.03
☐	397 Darryl Hamilton	.05	.02	.01
☐	398 Dave Parker	.15	.07	.02
☐	399 Paul Molitor	.20	.09	.03
☐	400 Jim Gantner	.05	.02	.01
☐	401 Rob Deer	.05	.02	.01
☐	402 Billy Spiers	.05	.02	.01
☐	403 Glenn Braggs	.05	.02	.01
☐	404 Robin Yount	.20	.09	.03
☐	405 Rick Aguilera	.10	.05	.01
☐	406 Johnny Ard	.10	.05	.01
☐	407 Kevin Tapani	.20	.09	.03
☐	408 Park Pittman	.05	.02	.01
☐	409 Allan Anderson	.05	.02	.01
☐	410 Juan Berenguer	.05	.02	.01
☐	411 Willie Banks	.15	.07	.02
☐	412 Rich Yett	.05	.02	.01
☐	413 Dave West	.05	.02	.01
☐	414 Greg Gagne	.05	.02	.01
☐	415 Chuck Knoblauch	.50	.23	.06
☐	416 Randy Bush	.05	.02	.01
☐	417 Gary Gaetti	.05	.02	.01
☐	418 Kent Hrbek	.10	.05	.01
☐	419 Al Newman	.05	.02	.01
☐	420 Danny Gladden	.05	.02	.01
☐	421 Paul Sorrento	.15	.07	.02
☐	422 Derek Parks	.05	.02	.01
☐	423 Scott Leius	.05	.02	.01
☐	424 Kirby Puckett	.35	.16	.04
☐	425 Willie Smith	.10	.05	.01
☐	426 Dave Righetti	.05	.02	.01
☐	427 Jeff D. Robinson	.05	.02	.01
☐	428 Alan Mills	.05	.02	.01
☐	429 Tim Leary	.05	.02	.01
☐	430 Pascual Perez	.05	.02	.01
☐	431 Alvaro Espinoza	.05	.02	.01
☐	432 Dave Winfield	.15	.07	.02
☐	433 Jesse Barfield	.05	.02	.01
☐	434 Randy Velarde	.05	.02	.01
☐	435 Rick Cerone	.05	.02	.01
☐	436 Steve Balboni	.05	.02	.01
☐	437 Mel Hall	.05	.02	.01
☐	438 Bob Geren	.05	.02	.01
☐	439 Bernie Williams	.25	.11	.03
☐	440 Kevin Maas	.05	.02	.01
☐	441 Mike Blowers	.05	.02	.01
☐	442 Steve Sax	.05	.02	.01
☐	443 Don Mattingly	.35	.16	.04
☐	444 Roberto Kelly	.10	.05	.01
☐	445 Mike Moore	.05	.02	.01
☐	446 Reggie Harris	.05	.02	.01
☐	447 Scott Sanderson	.05	.02	.01
☐	448 Dave Otto	.05	.02	.01
☐	449 Dave Stewart	.10	.05	.01
☐	450 Rick Honeycutt	.05	.02	.01
☐	451 Dennis Eckersley	.15	.07	.02
☐	452 Carney Lansford	.10	.05	.01
☐	453 Scott Hemond	.05	.02	.01
☐	454 Mark McGwire	.15	.07	.02
☐	455 Felix Jose	.10	.05	.01
☐	456 Terry Steinbach	.10	.05	.01
☐	457 Rickey Henderson	.15	.07	.02
☐	458 Dave Henderson	.05	.02	.01
☐	459 Mike Gallego	.05	.02	.01
☐	460 Jose Canseco	.30	.14	.04
☐	461 Walt Weiss	.05	.02	.01
☐	462 Ken Phelps	.05	.02	.01
☐	463 Darren Lewis	.25	.11	.03
☐	464 Ron Hassey	.05	.02	.01
☐	465 Roger Salkeld	.15	.07	.02
☐	466 Scott Bankhead	.05	.02	.01
☐	467 Keith Comstock	.05	.02	.01
☐	468 Randy Johnson	.30	.14	.04
☐	469 Erik Hanson	.10	.05	.01
☐	470 Mike Schooler	.05	.02	.01
☐	471 Gary Eave	.05	.02	.01
☐	472 Jeffrey Leonard	.05	.02	.01
☐	473 Dave Valle	.05	.02	.01
☐	474 Omar Vizquel	.05	.02	.01
☐	475 Pete O'Brien	.05	.02	.01
☐	476 Henry Cotto	.05	.02	.01
☐	477 Jay Buhner	.15	.07	.02
☐	478 Harold Reynolds	.05	.02	.01
☐	479 Alvin Davis	.05	.02	.01
☐	480 Darnell Coles	.05	.02	.01
☐	481 Ken Griffey Jr.	2.50	1.15	.30
☐	482 Greg Briley	.05	.02	.01
☐	483 Scott Bradley	.05	.02	.01
☐	484 Tino Martinez	.10	.05	.01
☐	485 Jeff Russell	.05	.02	.01
☐	486 Nolan Ryan	.75	.35	.09
☐	487 Robb Nen	.25	.11	.03
☐	488 Kevin Brown	.10	.05	.01
☐	489 Brian Bohanon	.05	.02	.01
☐	490 Ruben Sierra	.15	.07	.02
☐	491 Pete Incaviglia	.05	.02	.01
☐	492 Juan Gonzalez	2.00	.90	.25
☐	493 Steve Buechele	.05	.02	.01
☐	494 Scott Coolbaugh	.05	.02	.01
☐	495 Geno Petralli	.05	.02	.01
☐	496 Rafael Palmeiro	.15	.07	.02
☐	497 Julio Franco	.10	.05	.01
☐	498 Gary Pettis	.05	.02	.01
☐	499 Donald Harris	.05	.02	.01
☐	500 Monty Fariss	.10	.05	.01
☐	501 Harold Baines	.10	.05	.01
☐	502 Cecil Espy	.05	.02	.01
☐	503 Jack Daugherty	.05	.02	.01
☐	504 Willie Blair	.05	.02	.01
☐	505 Dave Stieb	.10	.05	.01
☐	506 Tom Henke	.10	.05	.01
☐	507 John Cerutti	.05	.02	.01
☐	508 Paul Kilgus	.05	.02	.01
☐	509 Jimmy Key	.10	.05	.01
☐	510 John Olerud	.60	.25	.08
☐	511 Ed Sprague	.10	.05	.01
☐	512 Manny Lee	.05	.02	.01
☐	513 Fred McGriff	.30	.14	.04
☐	514 Glenallen Hill	.05	.02	.01
☐	515 George Bell	.10	.05	.01
☐	516 Mookie Wilson	.05	.02	.01
☐	517 Luis Sojo	.05	.02	.01
☐	518 Nelson Liriano	.05	.02	.01

		MINT	EXC	G-VG
☐ 519	Kelly Gruber	.05	.02	.01
☐ 520	Greg Myers	.05	.02	.01
☐ 521	Pat Borders	.10	.05	.01
☐ 522	Junior Felix	.05	.02	.01
☐ 523	Eddie Zosky	.05	.02	.01
☐ 524	Tony Fernandez	.10	.05	.01
☐ 525	Checklist 1-132 UER (No copyright mark on the back)	.05	.02	.01
☐ 526	Checklist 133-264	.05	.02	.01
☐ 527	Checklist 265-396	.05	.02	.01
☐ 528	Checklist 397-528	.05	.02	.01

1991 Bowman

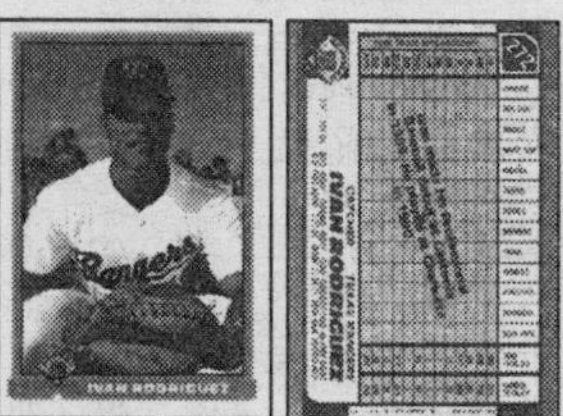

This 704-card standard size (2 1/2" by 3 1/2") set marked the third straight year that Topps issued a set using the Bowman name. The cards are arranged in team order by division as follows: AL East, AL West, NL East, and NL West. Some of the specials in the set include cards made for all the 1990 MVP's in each minor league, the leader sluggers by position (Silver Sluggers), and special cards commemorating long-time baseball figure Jimmie Reese, General Colin Powell, newly inducted Hall of Famer Rod Carew and Rickey Henderson's 938th Stolen Base. The cards themselves are designed just like the 1990 Bowman set while the backs again feature the innovative team by team breakdown of how the player did the previous year against a green background. The set numbering is as follows: Toronto Blue Jays (6-30), Milwaukee Brewers (31-56), Cleveland Indians (57-82), Baltimore Orioles (83-106), Boston Red Sox (107-130), Detroit Tigers (131-154), New York Yankees (155-179), California Angels (187-211), Oakland Athletics (212-238), Seattle Mariners (239-264), Texas Rangers (265-290), Kansas City Royals (291-316), Minnesota Twins (317-341), Chicago White Sox (342-366), St. Louis Cardinals (385-409), Chicago Cubs (411-433), Montreal Expos (434-459), New York Mets (460-484), Philadelphia Phillies (485-508), Pittsburgh Pirates (509-532), Houston Astros (539-565), Atlanta Braves (566-590), Los Angles Dodgers (591-615), San Fransico Giants (616-641), San Diego Padres (642-665), and Cincinnati Reds (666-691). Subsets include minor league MVP's (180-185/693-698), AL Silver Sluggers (367-375) and NL Silver Sluggers (376-384). There are two instances of misnumbering in the set; Ken Griffey (should be 255) and Ken Griffey Jr. are both numbered 246 and Donovan Osborne (should be 406) and Thomson/Branca share number 410. Rookie Cards in this set include Jeff Bagwell, Bret Boone, Jeromy Burnitz, Jeff Conine, Wil Cordero, Dave Fleming, Carlos Garcia, Pat Hentgen, Chipper Jones, Eric Karros, Steve Karsay, Ryan Klesko, Kenny Lofton, Javy Lopez, Sam Militello, Raul Mondesi, Mike Mussina, Marc Newfield, Donovan Osborne, Phil Plantier, Ivan Rodriguez, Tim Salmon, Reggie Sanders, Jim Thome, Todd Van Poppel, Rondell White, and Bob Wickman.

	MINT	EXC	G-VG
COMPLETE SET (704)	25.00	11.50	3.10
COMPLETE FACT.SET (704)	25.00	11.50	3.10
COMMON CARD (1-704)	.05	.02	.01

		MINT	EXC	G-VG
☐ 1	Rod Carew I	.10	.05	.01
☐ 2	Rod Carew II	.10	.05	.01
☐ 3	Rod Carew III	.10	.05	.01
☐ 4	Rod Carew IV	.10	.05	.01
☐ 5	Rod Carew V	.10	.05	.01
☐ 6	Willie Fraser	.05	.02	.01
☐ 7	John Olerud	.15	.07	.02
☐ 8	William Suero	.05	.02	.01
☐ 9	Roberto Alomar	.20	.09	.03
☐ 10	Todd Stottlemyre	.05	.02	.01
☐ 11	Joe Carter	.20	.09	.03
☐ 12	Steve Karsay	.40	.18	.05
☐ 13	Mark Whiten	.15	.07	.02
☐ 14	Pat Borders	.05	.02	.01
☐ 15	Mike Timlin	.05	.02	.01
☐ 16	Tom Henke	.10	.05	.01
☐ 17	Eddie Zosky	.05	.02	.01
☐ 18	Kelly Gruber	.05	.02	.01
☐ 19	Jimmy Key	.10	.05	.01
☐ 20	Jerry Schunk	.05	.02	.01
☐ 21	Manny Lee	.05	.02	.01
☐ 22	Dave Stieb	.10	.05	.01
☐ 23	Pat Hentgen	.40	.18	.05
☐ 24	Glenallen Hill	.05	.02	.01
☐ 25	Rene Gonzales	.05	.02	.01
☐ 26	Ed Sprague	.05	.02	.01
☐ 27	Ken Dayley	.05	.02	.01
☐ 28	Pat Tabler	.05	.02	.01
☐ 29	Denis Boucher	.05	.02	.01
☐ 30	Devon White	.10	.05	.01
☐ 31	Dante Bichette	.15	.07	.02
☐ 32	Paul Molitor	.15	.07	.02
☐ 33	Greg Vaughn	.10	.05	.01
☐ 34	Dan Plesac	.05	.02	.01
☐ 35	Chris George	.05	.02	.01
☐ 36	Tim McIntosh	.05	.02	.01
☐ 37	Franklin Stubbs	.05	.02	.01
☐ 38	Bo Dodson	.05	.02	.01
☐ 39	Ron Robinson	.05	.02	.01
☐ 40	Ed Nunez	.05	.02	.01
☐ 41	Greg Brock	.05	.02	.01
☐ 42	Jaime Navarro	.05	.02	.01
☐ 43	Chris Bosio	.05	.02	.01
☐ 44	B.J. Surhoff	.05	.02	.01
☐ 45	Chris Johnson	.05	.02	.01
☐ 46	Willie Randolph	.10	.05	.01
☐ 47	Narciso Elvira	.05	.02	.01
☐ 48	Jim Gantner	.05	.02	.01
☐ 49	Kevin Brown	.05	.02	.01

No.	Player			
☐ 50	Julio Machado	.05	.02	.01
☐ 51	Chuck Crim	.05	.02	.01
☐ 52	Gary Sheffield	.15	.07	.02
☐ 53	Angel Miranda	.05	.02	.01
☐ 54	Teddy Higuera	.05	.02	.01
☐ 55	Robin Yount	.15	.07	.02
☐ 56	Cal Eldred	.10	.05	.01
☐ 57	Sandy Alomar Jr.	.10	.05	.01
☐ 58	Greg Swindell	.05	.02	.01
☐ 59	Brook Jacoby	.05	.02	.01
☐ 60	Efrain Valdez	.05	.02	.01
☐ 61	Ever Magallanes	.05	.02	.01
☐ 62	Tom Candiotti	.05	.02	.01
☐ 63	Eric King	.05	.02	.01
☐ 64	Alex Cole	.05	.02	.01
☐ 65	Charles Nagy	.10	.05	.01
☐ 66	Mitch Webster	.05	.02	.01
☐ 67	Chris James	.05	.02	.01
☐ 68	Jim Thome	.60	.25	.08
☐ 69	Carlos Baerga	.30	.14	.04
☐ 70	Mark Lewis	.10	.05	.01
☐ 71	Jerry Browne	.05	.02	.01
☐ 72	Jesse Orosco	.05	.02	.01
☐ 73	Mike Huff	.05	.02	.01
☐ 74	Jose Escobar	.05	.02	.01
☐ 75	Jeff Manto	.05	.02	.01
☐ 76	Turner Ward	.15	.07	.02
☐ 77	Doug Jones	.05	.02	.01
☐ 78	Bruce Egloff	.05	.02	.01
☐ 79	Tim Costo	.05	.02	.01
☐ 80	Beau Allred	.05	.02	.01
☐ 81	Albert Belle	.40	.18	.05
☐ 82	John Farrell	.05	.02	.01
☐ 83	Glenn Davis	.05	.02	.01
☐ 84	Joe Orsulak	.05	.02	.01
☐ 85	Mark Williamson	.05	.02	.01
☐ 86	Ben McDonald	.15	.07	.02
☐ 87	Billy Ripken	.05	.02	.01
☐ 88	Leo Gomez	.10	.05	.01
☐ 89	Bob Melvin	.05	.02	.01
☐ 90	Jeff M. Robinson	.05	.02	.01
☐ 91	Jose Mesa	.05	.02	.01
☐ 92	Gregg Olson	.10	.05	.01
☐ 93	Mike Devereaux	.10	.05	.01
☐ 94	Luis Mercedes	.05	.02	.01
☐ 95	Arthur Rhodes	.15	.07	.02
☐ 96	Juan Bell	.05	.02	.01
☐ 97	Mike Mussina	1.50	.65	.19
☐ 98	Jeff Ballard	.05	.02	.01
☐ 99	Chris Hoiles	.15	.07	.02
☐ 100	Brady Anderson	.10	.05	.01
☐ 101	Bob Milacki	.05	.02	.01
☐ 102	David Segui	.05	.02	.01
☐ 103	Dwight Evans	.10	.05	.01
☐ 104	Cal Ripken	.35	.16	.04
☐ 105	Mike Linskey	.05	.02	.01
☐ 106	Jeff Tackett	.05	.02	.01
☐ 107	Jeff Reardon	.10	.05	.01
☐ 108	Dana Kiecker	.05	.02	.01
☐ 109	Ellis Burks	.10	.05	.01
☐ 110	Dave Owen	.05	.02	.01
☐ 111	Danny Darwin	.05	.02	.01
☐ 112	Mo Vaughn	.40	.18	.05
☐ 113	Jeff McNeely	.05	.02	.01
☐ 114	Tom Bolton	.05	.02	.01
☐ 115	Greg Blosser	.10	.05	.01
☐ 116	Mike Greenwell	.10	.05	.01
☐ 117	Phil Plantier	.30	.14	.04
☐ 118	Roger Clemens	.25	.11	.03
☐ 119	John Marzano	.05	.02	.01
☐ 120	Jody Reed	.05	.02	.01
☐ 121	Scott Taylor	.05	.02	.01
☐ 122	Jack Clark	.10	.05	.01
☐ 123	Derek Livernois	.05	.02	.01
☐ 124	Tony Pena	.05	.02	.01
☐ 125	Tom Brunansky	.05	.02	.01
☐ 126	Carlos Quintana	.05	.02	.01
☐ 127	Tim Naehring	.05	.02	.01
☐ 128	Matt Young	.05	.02	.01
☐ 129	Wade Boggs	.15	.07	.02
☐ 130	Kevin Morton	.05	.02	.01
☐ 131	Pete Incaviglia	.05	.02	.01
☐ 132	Rob Deer	.05	.02	.01
☐ 133	Bill Gullickson	.05	.02	.01
☐ 134	Rico Brogna	.15	.07	.02
☐ 135	Lloyd Moseby	.05	.02	.01
☐ 136	Cecil Fielder	.15	.07	.02
☐ 137	Tony Phillips	.05	.02	.01
☐ 138	Mark Leiter	.05	.02	.01
☐ 139	John Cerutti	.05	.02	.01
☐ 140	Mickey Tettleton	.10	.05	.01
☐ 141	Milt Cuyler	.10	.05	.01
☐ 142	Greg Gohr	.05	.02	.01
☐ 143	Tony Bernazard	.05	.02	.01
☐ 144	Dan Gakeler	.05	.02	.01
☐ 145	Travis Fryman	.40	.18	.05
☐ 146	Dan Petry	.05	.02	.01
☐ 147	Scott Aldred	.05	.02	.01
☐ 148	John DeSilva	.05	.02	.01
☐ 149	Rusty Meacham	.05	.02	.01
☐ 150	Lou Whitaker	.15	.07	.02
☐ 151	Dave Haas	.05	.02	.01
☐ 152	Luis de los Santos	.05	.02	.01
☐ 153	Ivan Cruz	.05	.02	.01
☐ 154	Alan Trammell	.15	.07	.02
☐ 155	Pat Kelly	.15	.07	.02
☐ 156	Carl Everett	.15	.07	.02
☐ 157	Greg Cadaret	.05	.02	.01
☐ 158	Kevin Maas	.05	.02	.01
☐ 159	Jeff Johnson	.05	.02	.01
☐ 160	Willie Smith	.05	.02	.01
☐ 161	Gerald Williams	.05	.02	.01
☐ 162	Mike Humphreys	.05	.02	.01
☐ 163	Alvaro Espinoza	.05	.02	.01
☐ 164	Matt Nokes	.05	.02	.01
☐ 165	Wade Taylor	.05	.02	.01
☐ 166	Roberto Kelly	.10	.05	.01
☐ 167	John Habyan	.05	.02	.01
☐ 168	Steve Farr	.05	.02	.01
☐ 169	Jesse Barfield	.05	.02	.01
☐ 170	Steve Sax	.05	.02	.01
☐ 171	Jim Leyritz	.05	.02	.01
☐ 172	Robert Eenhoorn	.05	.02	.01
☐ 173	Bernie Williams	.10	.05	.01
☐ 174	Scott Lusader	.05	.02	.01
☐ 175	Torey Lovullo	.05	.02	.01
☐ 176	Chuck Cary	.05	.02	.01
☐ 177	Scott Sanderson	.05	.02	.01
☐ 178	Don Mattingly	.30	.14	.04
☐ 179	Mel Hall	.05	.02	.01
☐ 180	Juan Gonzalez Minor League MVP	1.00	.45	.13
☐ 181	Hensley Meulens Minor League MVP	.05	.02	.01
☐ 182	Jose Offerman Minor League MVP	.10	.05	.01
☐ 183	Jeff Bagwell Minor League MVP	3.00	1.35	.40
☐ 184	Jeff Conine Minor League MVP	.50	.23	.06
☐ 185	Henry Rodriguez Minor League MVP	.20	.09	.03
☐ 186	Jimmie Reese CO	.15	.07	.02
☐ 187	Kyle Abbott	.05	.02	.01
☐ 188	Lance Parrish	.10	.05	.01
☐ 189	Rafael Montalvo	.05	.02	.01

	No.	Player			
☐	190	Floyd Bannister	.05	.02	.01
☐	191	Dick Schofield	.05	.02	.01
☐	192	Scott Lewis	.05	.02	.01
☐	193	Jeff D. Robinson	.05	.02	.01
☐	194	Kent Anderson	.05	.02	.01
☐	195	Wally Joyner	.10	.05	.01
☐	196	Chuck Finley	.10	.05	.01
☐	197	Luis Sojo	.05	.02	.01
☐	198	Jeff Richardson	.05	.02	.01
☐	199	Dave Parker	.15	.07	.02
☐	200	Jim Abbott	.15	.07	.02
☐	201	Junior Felix	.05	.02	.01
☐	202	Mark Langston	.15	.07	.02
☐	203	Tim Salmon	1.50	.65	.19
☐	204	Cliff Young	.05	.02	.01
☐	205	Scott Bailes	.05	.02	.01
☐	206	Bobby Rose	.05	.02	.01
☐	207	Gary Gaetti	.05	.02	.01
☐	208	Ruben Amaro	.05	.02	.01
☐	209	Luis Polonia	.05	.02	.01
☐	210	Dave Winfield	.15	.07	.02
☐	211	Bryan Harvey	.10	.05	.01
☐	212	Mike Moore	.05	.02	.01
☐	213	Rickey Henderson	.15	.07	.02
☐	214	Steve Chitren	.05	.02	.01
☐	215	Bob Welch	.05	.02	.01
☐	216	Terry Steinbach	.10	.05	.01
☐	217	Earnest Riles	.05	.02	.01
☐	218	Todd Van Poppel	.20	.09	.03
☐	219	Mike Gallego	.05	.02	.01
☐	220	Curt Young	.05	.02	.01
☐	221	Todd Burns	.05	.02	.01
☐	222	Vance Law	.05	.02	.01
☐	223	Eric Show	.05	.02	.01
☐	224	Don Peters	.05	.02	.01
☐	225	Dave Stewart	.10	.05	.01
☐	226	Dave Henderson	.05	.02	.01
☐	227	Jose Canseco	.20	.09	.03
☐	228	Walt Weiss	.05	.02	.01
☐	229	Dann Howitt	.05	.02	.01
☐	230	Willie Wilson	.05	.02	.01
☐	231	Harold Baines	.10	.05	.01
☐	232	Scott Hemond	.05	.02	.01
☐	233	Joe Slusarski	.05	.02	.01
☐	234	Mark McGwire	.15	.07	.02
☐	235	Kirk Dressendorfer	.05	.02	.01
☐	236	Craig Paquette	.05	.02	.01
☐	237	Dennis Eckersley	.15	.07	.02
☐	238	Dana Allison	.05	.02	.01
☐	239	Scott Bradley	.05	.02	.01
☐	240	Brian Holman	.05	.02	.01
☐	241	Mike Schooler	.05	.02	.01
☐	242	Rich DeLucia	.05	.02	.01
☐	243	Edgar Martinez	.10	.05	.01
☐	244	Henry Cotto	.05	.02	.01
☐	245	Omar Vizquel	.05	.02	.01
☐	246	Ken Griffey Jr. (See also 255)	1.50	.65	.19
☐	247	Jay Buhner	.10	.05	.01
☐	248	Bill Krueger	.05	.02	.01
☐	249	Dave Fleming	.15	.07	.02
☐	250	Patrick Lennon	.05	.02	.01
☐	251	Dave Valle	.05	.02	.01
☐	252	Harold Reynolds	.05	.02	.01
☐	253	Randy Johnson	.15	.07	.02
☐	254	Scott Bankhead	.05	.02	.01
☐	255	Ken Griffey UER (Card number is 246)	.10	.05	.01
☐	256	Greg Briley	.05	.02	.01
☐	257	Tino Martinez	.10	.05	.01
☐	258	Alvin Davis	.05	.02	.01
☐	259	Pete O'Brien	.05	.02	.01
☐	260	Erik Hanson	.05	.02	.01
☐	261	Bret Boone	.50	.23	.06
☐	262	Roger Salkeld	.10	.05	.01
☐	263	Dave Burba	.05	.02	.01
☐	264	Kerry Woodson	.05	.02	.01
☐	265	Julio Franco	.10	.05	.01
☐	266	Dan Peltier	.05	.02	.01
☐	267	Jeff Russell	.05	.02	.01
☐	268	Steve Buechele	.05	.02	.01
☐	269	Donald Harris	.05	.02	.01
☐	270	Robb Nen	.05	.02	.01
☐	271	Rich Gossage	.15	.07	.02
☐	272	Ivan Rodriguez	.50	.23	.06
☐	273	Jeff Huson	.05	.02	.01
☐	274	Kevin Brown	.10	.05	.01
☐	275	Dan Smith	.05	.02	.01
☐	276	Gary Pettis	.05	.02	.01
☐	277	Jack Daugherty	.05	.02	.01
☐	278	Mike Jeffcoat	.05	.02	.01
☐	279	Brad Arnsberg	.05	.02	.01
☐	280	Nolan Ryan	.60	.25	.08
☐	281	Eric McCray	.05	.02	.01
☐	282	Scott Chiamparino	.05	.02	.01
☐	283	Ruben Sierra	.15	.07	.02
☐	284	Geno Petralli	.05	.02	.01
☐	285	Monty Fariss	.10	.05	.01
☐	286	Rafael Palmeiro	.15	.07	.02
☐	287	Bobby Witt	.05	.02	.01
☐	288	Dean Palmer UER (Photo actually Dan Peltier)	.10	.05	.01
☐	289	Tony Scruggs	.05	.02	.01
☐	290	Kenny Rogers	.05	.02	.01
☐	291	Bret Saberhagen	.10	.05	.01
☐	292	Brian McRae	.30	.14	.04
☐	293	Storm Davis	.05	.02	.01
☐	294	Danny Tartabull	.10	.05	.01
☐	295	David Howard	.05	.02	.01
☐	296	Mike Boddicker	.05	.02	.01
☐	297	Joel Johnston	.05	.02	.01
☐	298	Tim Spehr	.05	.02	.01
☐	299	Hector Wagner	.05	.02	.01
☐	300	George Brett	.30	.14	.04
☐	301	Mike Macfarlane	.05	.02	.01
☐	302	Kirk Gibson	.10	.05	.01
☐	303	Harvey Pulliam	.05	.02	.01
☐	304	Jim Eisenreich	.05	.02	.01
☐	305	Kevin Seitzer	.05	.02	.01
☐	306	Mark Davis	.05	.02	.01
☐	307	Kurt Stillwell	.05	.02	.01
☐	308	Jeff Montgomery	.10	.05	.01
☐	309	Kevin Appier	.10	.05	.01
☐	310	Bob Hamelin	.40	.18	.05
☐	311	Tom Gordon	.10	.05	.01
☐	312	Kerwin Moore	.05	.02	.01
☐	313	Hugh Walker	.05	.02	.01
☐	314	Terry Shumpert	.05	.02	.01
☐	315	Warren Cromartie	.05	.02	.01
☐	316	Gary Thurman	.05	.02	.01
☐	317	Steve Bedrosian	.05	.02	.01
☐	318	Danny Gladden	.05	.02	.01
☐	319	Jack Morris	.15	.07	.02
☐	320	Kirby Puckett	.30	.14	.04
☐	321	Kent Hrbek	.10	.05	.01
☐	322	Kevin Tapani	.10	.05	.01
☐	323	Denny Neagle	.05	.02	.01
☐	324	Rich Garces	.05	.02	.01
☐	325	Larry Casian	.05	.02	.01
☐	326	Shane Mack	.10	.05	.01
☐	327	Allan Anderson	.05	.02	.01
☐	328	Junior Ortiz	.05	.02	.01
☐	329	Paul Abbott	.05	.02	.01
☐	330	Chuck Knoblauch	.25	.11	.03
☐	331	Chili Davis	.10	.05	.01

	No.	Player			
☐	332	Todd Ritchie	.15	.07	.02
☐	333	Brian Harper	.05	.02	.01
☐	334	Rick Aguilera	.10	.05	.01
☐	335	Scott Erickson	.05	.02	.01
☐	336	Pedro Munoz	.15	.07	.02
☐	337	Scott Leius	.05	.02	.01
☐	338	Greg Gagne	.05	.02	.01
☐	339	Mike Pagliarulo	.05	.02	.01
☐	340	Terry Leach	.05	.02	.01
☐	341	Willie Banks	.10	.05	.01
☐	342	Bobby Thigpen	.05	.02	.01
☐	343	Roberto Hernandez	.20	.09	.03
☐	344	Melido Perez	.05	.02	.01
☐	345	Carlton Fisk	.15	.07	.02
☐	346	Norberto Martin	.05	.02	.01
☐	347	Johnny Ruffin	.15	.07	.02
☐	348	Jeff Carter	.05	.02	.01
☐	349	Lance Johnson	.05	.02	.01
☐	350	Sammy Sosa	.15	.07	.02
☐	351	Alex Fernandez	.25	.11	.03
☐	352	Jack McDowell	.15	.07	.02
☐	353	Bob Wickman	.15	.07	.02
☐	354	Wilson Alvarez	.25	.11	.03
☐	355	Charlie Hough	.10	.05	.01
☐	356	Ozzie Guillen	.05	.02	.01
☐	357	Cory Snyder	.05	.02	.01
☐	358	Robin Ventura	.20	.09	.03
☐	359	Scott Fletcher	.05	.02	.01
☐	360	Cesar Bernhardt	.05	.02	.01
☐	361	Dan Pasqua	.05	.02	.01
☐	362	Tim Raines	.15	.07	.02
☐	363	Brian Drahman	.05	.02	.01
☐	364	Wayne Edwards	.05	.02	.01
☐	365	Scott Radinsky	.05	.02	.01
☐	366	Frank Thomas	2.00	.90	.25
☐	367	Cecil Fielder SLUG	.15	.07	.02
☐	368	Julio Franco SLUG	.05	.02	.01
☐	369	Kelly Gruber SLUG	.05	.02	.01
☐	370	Alan Trammell SLUG	.10	.05	.01
☐	371	Rickey Henderson SLUG	.10	.05	.01
☐	372	Jose Canseco SLUG	.20	.09	.03
☐	373	Ellis Burks SLUG	.05	.02	.01
☐	374	Lance Parrish SLUG	.05	.02	.01
☐	375	Dave Parker SLUG	.05	.02	.01
☐	376	Eddie Murray SLUG	.10	.05	.01
☐	377	Ryne Sandberg SLUG	.20	.09	.03
☐	378	Matt Williams SLUG	.15	.07	.02
☐	379	Barry Larkin SLUG	.10	.05	.01
☐	380	Barry Bonds SLUG	.20	.09	.03
☐	381	Bobby Bonilla SLUG	.10	.05	.01
☐	382	Darryl Strawberry SLUG	.10	.05	.01
☐	383	Benny Santiago SLUG	.05	.02	.01
☐	384	Don Robinson SLUG	.05	.02	.01
☐	385	Paul Coleman	.05	.02	.01
☐	386	Milt Thompson	.05	.02	.01
☐	387	Lee Smith	.15	.07	.02
☐	388	Ray Lankford	.15	.07	.02
☐	389	Tom Pagnozzi	.05	.02	.01
☐	390	Ken Hill	.15	.07	.02
☐	391	Jamie Moyer	.05	.02	.01
☐	392	Greg Carmona	.05	.02	.01
☐	393	John Ericks	.05	.02	.01
☐	394	Bob Tewksbury	.10	.05	.01
☐	395	Jose Oquendo	.05	.02	.01
☐	396	Rheal Cormier	.05	.02	.01
☐	397	Mike Milchin	.05	.02	.01
☐	398	Ozzie Smith	.20	.09	.03
☐	399	Aaron Holbert	.05	.02	.01
☐	400	Jose DeLeon	.05	.02	.01
☐	401	Felix Jose	.10	.05	.01
☐	402	Juan Agosto	.05	.02	.01
☐	403	Pedro Guerrero	.10	.05	.01
☐	404	Todd Zeile	.10	.05	.01
☐	405	Gerald Perry	.05	.02	.01
☐	406	Donovan Osborne UER (Card number is 410)	.15	.07	.02
☐	407	Bryn Smith	.05	.02	.01
☐	408	Bernard Gilkey	.10	.05	.01
☐	409	Rex Hudler	.05	.02	.01
☐	410	Thomson/Branca Shot. Bobby Thomson, Ralph Branca (See also 406)	.15	.07	.02
☐	411	Lance Dickson	.05	.02	.01
☐	412	Danny Jackson	.05	.02	.01
☐	413	Jerome Walton	.05	.02	.01
☐	414	Sean Cheetham	.05	.02	.01
☐	415	Joe Girardi	.05	.02	.01
☐	416	Ryne Sandberg	.25	.11	.03
☐	417	Mike Harkey	.05	.02	.01
☐	418	George Bell	.10	.05	.01
☐	419	Rick Wilkins	.15	.07	.02
☐	420	Earl Cunningham	.05	.02	.01
☐	421	Heathcliff Slocumb	.05	.02	.01
☐	422	Mike Bielecki	.05	.02	.01
☐	423	Jessie Hollins	.05	.02	.01
☐	424	Shawon Dunston	.05	.02	.01
☐	425	Dave Smith	.05	.02	.01
☐	426	Greg Maddux	.25	.11	.03
☐	427	Jose Vizcaino	.05	.02	.01
☐	428	Luis Salazar	.05	.02	.01
☐	429	Andre Dawson	.15	.07	.02
☐	430	Rick Sutcliffe	.10	.05	.01
☐	431	Paul Assenmacher	.05	.02	.01
☐	432	Erik Pappas	.05	.02	.01
☐	433	Mark Grace	.15	.07	.02
☐	434	Dennis Martinez	.10	.05	.01
☐	435	Marquis Grissom	.15	.07	.02
☐	436	Wil Cordero	.50	.23	.06
☐	437	Tim Wallach	.05	.02	.01
☐	438	Brian Barnes	.05	.02	.01
☐	439	Barry Jones	.05	.02	.01
☐	440	Ivan Calderon	.05	.02	.01
☐	441	Stan Spencer	.05	.02	.01
☐	442	Larry Walker	.15	.07	.02
☐	443	Chris Haney	.05	.02	.01
☐	444	Hector Rivera	.05	.02	.01
☐	445	Delino DeShields	.15	.07	.02
☐	446	Andres Galarraga	.15	.07	.02
☐	447	Gilberto Reyes	.05	.02	.01
☐	448	Willie Greene	.10	.05	.01
☐	449	Greg Colbrunn	.10	.05	.01
☐	450	Rondell White	1.00	.45	.13
☐	451	Steve Frey	.05	.02	.01
☐	452	Shane Andrews	.20	.09	.03
☐	453	Mike Fitzgerald	.05	.02	.01
☐	454	Spike Owen	.05	.02	.01
☐	455	Dave Martinez	.05	.02	.01
☐	456	Dennis Boyd	.05	.02	.01
☐	457	Eric Bullock	.05	.02	.01
☐	458	Reid Cornelius	.05	.02	.01
☐	459	Chris Nabholz	.05	.02	.01
☐	460	David Cone	.15	.07	.02
☐	461	Hubie Brooks	.05	.02	.01
☐	462	Sid Fernandez	.10	.05	.01
☐	463	Doug Simons	.05	.02	.01
☐	464	Howard Johnson	.10	.05	.01
☐	465	Chris Donnels	.05	.02	.01
☐	466	Anthony Young	.05	.02	.01
☐	467	Todd Hundley	.10	.05	.01
☐	468	Rick Cerone	.05	.02	.01
☐	469	Kevin Elster	.05	.02	.01
☐	470	Wally Whitehurst	.05	.02	.01
☐	471	Vince Coleman	.05	.02	.01
☐	472	Dwight Gooden	.10	.05	.01
☐	473	Charlie O'Brien	.05	.02	.01

	No.	Player			
☐	474	Jeromy Burnitz	.15	.07	.02
☐	475	John Franco	.10	.05	.01
☐	476	Daryl Boston	.05	.02	.01
☐	477	Frank Viola	.10	.05	.01
☐	478	D.J. Dozier	.05	.02	.01
☐	479	Kevin McReynolds	.05	.02	.01
☐	480	Tom Herr	.05	.02	.01
☐	481	Gregg Jefferies	.15	.07	.02
☐	482	Pete Schourek	.05	.02	.01
☐	483	Ron Darling	.05	.02	.01
☐	484	Dave Magadan	.05	.02	.01
☐	485	Andy Ashby	.05	.02	.01
☐	486	Dale Murphy	.15	.07	.02
☐	487	Von Hayes	.05	.02	.01
☐	488	Kim Batiste	.05	.02	.01
☐	489	Tony Longmire	.05	.02	.01
☐	490	Wally Backman	.05	.02	.01
☐	491	Jeff Jackson	.05	.02	.01
☐	492	Mickey Morandini	.05	.02	.01
☐	493	Darrel Akerfelds	.05	.02	.01
☐	494	Ricky Jordan	.05	.02	.01
☐	495	Randy Ready	.05	.02	.01
☐	496	Darrin Fletcher	.05	.02	.01
☐	497	Chuck Malone	.05	.02	.01
☐	498	Pat Combs	.05	.02	.01
☐	499	Dickie Thon	.05	.02	.01
☐	500	Roger McDowell	.05	.02	.01
☐	501	Len Dykstra	.15	.07	.02
☐	502	Joe Boever	.05	.02	.01
☐	503	John Kruk	.15	.07	.02
☐	504	Terry Mulholland	.05	.02	.01
☐	505	Wes Chamberlain	.05	.02	.01
☐	506	Mike Lieberthal	.10	.05	.01
☐	507	Darren Daulton	.15	.07	.02
☐	508	Charlie Hayes	.10	.05	.01
☐	509	John Smiley	.05	.02	.01
☐	510	Gary Varsho	.05	.02	.01
☐	511	Curt Wilkerson	.05	.02	.01
☐	512	Orlando Merced	.25	.11	.03
☐	513	Barry Bonds	.40	.18	.05
☐	514	Mike LaValliere	.05	.02	.01
☐	515	Doug Drabek	.15	.07	.02
☐	516	Gary Redus	.05	.02	.01
☐	517	William Pennyfeather	.05	.02	.01
☐	518	Randy Tomlin	.05	.02	.01
☐	519	Mike Zimmerman	.05	.02	.01
☐	520	Jeff King	.05	.02	.01
☐	521	Kurt Miller	.05	.02	.01
☐	522	Jay Bell	.10	.05	.01
☐	523	Bill Landrum	.05	.02	.01
☐	524	Zane Smith	.05	.02	.01
☐	525	Bobby Bonilla	.15	.07	.02
☐	526	Bob Walk	.05	.02	.01
☐	527	Austin Manahan	.05	.02	.01
☐	528	Joe Ausanio	.05	.02	.01
☐	529	Andy Van Slyke	.15	.07	.02
☐	530	Jose Lind	.05	.02	.01
☐	531	Carlos Garcia	.25	.11	.03
☐	532	Don Slaught	.05	.02	.01
☐	533	Gen.Colin Powell	.15	.07	.02
☐	534	Frank Bolick	.05	.02	.01
☐	535	Gary Scott	.05	.02	.01
☐	536	Nikco Riesgo	.05	.02	.01
☐	537	Reggie Sanders	.50	.23	.06
☐	538	Tim Howard	.05	.02	.01
☐	539	Ryan Bowen	.05	.02	.01
☐	540	Eric Anthony	.10	.05	.01
☐	541	Jim Deshaies	.05	.02	.01
☐	542	Tom Nevers	.05	.02	.01
☐	543	Ken Caminiti	.10	.05	.01
☐	544	Karl Rhodes	.05	.02	.01
☐	545	Xavier Hernandez	.05	.02	.01
☐	546	Mike Scott	.05	.02	.01
☐	547	Jeff Juden	.10	.05	.01
☐	548	Darryl Kile	.15	.07	.02
☐	549	Willie Ansley	.10	.05	.01
☐	550	Luis Gonzalez	.25	.11	.03
☐	551	Mike Simms	.05	.02	.01
☐	552	Mark Portugal	.05	.02	.01
☐	553	Jimmy Jones	.05	.02	.01
☐	554	Jim Clancy	.05	.02	.01
☐	555	Pete Harnisch	.10	.05	.01
☐	556	Craig Biggio	.15	.07	.02
☐	557	Eric Yelding	.05	.02	.01
☐	558	Dave Rohde	.05	.02	.01
☐	559	Casey Candaele	.05	.02	.01
☐	560	Curt Schilling	.10	.05	.01
☐	561	Steve Finley	.05	.02	.01
☐	562	Javier Ortiz	.05	.02	.01
☐	563	Andujar Cedeno	.10	.05	.01
☐	564	Rafael Ramirez	.05	.02	.01
☐	565	Kenny Lofton	2.00	.90	.25
☐	566	Steve Avery	.15	.07	.02
☐	567	Lonnie Smith	.05	.02	.01
☐	568	Kent Mercker	.10	.05	.01
☐	569	Chipper Jones	1.25	.55	.16
☐	570	Terry Pendleton	.15	.07	.02
☐	571	Otis Nixon	.10	.05	.01
☐	572	Juan Berenguer	.05	.02	.01
☐	573	Charlie Leibrandt	.05	.02	.01
☐	574	David Justice	.35	.16	.04
☐	575	Keith Mitchell	.15	.07	.02
☐	576	Tom Glavine	.20	.09	.03
☐	577	Greg Olson	.05	.02	.01
☐	578	Rafael Belliard	.05	.02	.01
☐	579	Ben Rivera	.05	.02	.01
☐	580	John Smoltz	.15	.07	.02
☐	581	Tyler Houston	.10	.05	.01
☐	582	Mark Wohlers	.15	.07	.02
☐	583	Ron Gant	.10	.05	.01
☐	584	Ramon Caraballo	.05	.02	.01
☐	585	Sid Bream	.05	.02	.01
☐	586	Jeff Treadway	.05	.02	.01
☐	587	Javy Lopez	1.00	.45	.13
☐	588	Deion Sanders	.30	.14	.04
☐	589	Mike Heath	.05	.02	.01
☐	590	Ryan Klesko	1.50	.65	.19
☐	591	Bob Ojeda	.05	.02	.01
☐	592	Alfredo Griffin	.05	.02	.01
☐	593	Raul Mondesi	3.00	1.35	.40
☐	594	Greg Smith	.05	.02	.01
☐	595	Orel Hershiser	.10	.05	.01
☐	596	Juan Samuel	.05	.02	.01
☐	597	Brett Butler	.10	.05	.01
☐	598	Gary Carter	.15	.07	.02
☐	599	Stan Javier	.05	.02	.01
☐	600	Kal Daniels	.05	.02	.01
☐	601	Jamie McAndrew	.05	.02	.01
☐	602	Mike Sharperson	.05	.02	.01
☐	603	Jay Howell	.05	.02	.01
☐	604	Eric Karros	.25	.11	.03
☐	605	Tim Belcher	.05	.02	.01
☐	606	Dan Opperman	.05	.02	.01
☐	607	Lenny Harris	.05	.02	.01
☐	608	Tom Goodwin	.10	.05	.01
☐	609	Darryl Strawberry	.15	.07	.02
☐	610	Ramon Martinez	.10	.05	.01
☐	611	Kevin Gross	.05	.02	.01
☐	612	Zakary Shinall	.05	.02	.01
☐	613	Mike Scioscia	.05	.02	.01
☐	614	Eddie Murray	.15	.07	.02
☐	615	Ronnie Walden	.05	.02	.01
☐	616	Will Clark	.20	.09	.03
☐	617	Adam Hyzdu	.05	.02	.01
☐	618	Matt Williams	.20	.09	.03
☐	619	Don Robinson	.05	.02	.01

	No.	Player			
☐	620	Jeff Brantley	.05	.02	.01
☐	621	Greg Litton	.05	.02	.01
☐	622	Steve Decker	.05	.02	.01
☐	623	Robby Thompson	.05	.02	.01
☐	624	Mark Leonard	.05	.02	.01
☐	625	Kevin Bass	.05	.02	.01
☐	626	Scott Garrelts	.05	.02	.01
☐	627	Jose Uribe	.05	.02	.01
☐	628	Eric Gunderson	.05	.02	.01
☐	629	Steve Hosey	.10	.05	.01
☐	630	Trevor Wilson	.05	.02	.01
☐	631	Terry Kennedy	.05	.02	.01
☐	632	Dave Righetti	.05	.02	.01
☐	633	Kelly Downs	.05	.02	.01
☐	634	Johnny Ard	.05	.02	.01
☐	635	Eric Christopherson	.05	.02	.01
☐	636	Kevin Mitchell	.10	.05	.01
☐	637	John Burkett	.10	.05	.01
☐	638	Kevin Rogers	.10	.05	.01
☐	639	Bud Black	.05	.02	.01
☐	640	Willie McGee	.10	.05	.01
☐	641	Royce Clayton	.15	.07	.02
☐	642	Tony Fernandez	.10	.05	.01
☐	643	Ricky Bones	.30	.14	.04
☐	644	Thomas Howard	.05	.02	.01
☐	645	Dave Staton	.05	.02	.01
☐	646	Jim Presley	.05	.02	.01
☐	647	Tony Gwynn	.25	.11	.03
☐	648	Marty Barrett	.05	.02	.01
☐	649	Scott Coolbaugh	.05	.02	.01
☐	650	Craig Lefferts	.05	.02	.01
☐	651	Eddie Whitson	.05	.02	.01
☐	652	Oscar Azocar	.05	.02	.01
☐	653	Wes Gardner	.05	.02	.01
☐	654	Bip Roberts	.05	.02	.01
☐	655	Robbie Beckett	.05	.02	.01
☐	656	Benito Santiago	.05	.02	.01
☐	657	Greg W.Harris	.05	.02	.01
☐	658	Jerald Clark	.05	.02	.01
☐	659	Fred McGriff	.20	.09	.03
☐	660	Larry Andersen	.05	.02	.01
☐	661	Bruce Hurst	.05	.02	.01
☐	662	Steve Martin	.05	.02	.01
☐	663	Rafael Valdez	.05	.02	.01
☐	664	Paul Faries	.05	.02	.01
☐	665	Andy Benes	.15	.07	.02
☐	666	Randy Myers	.10	.05	.01
☐	667	Rob Dibble	.05	.02	.01
☐	668	Glenn Sutko	.05	.02	.01
☐	669	Glenn Braggs	.05	.02	.01
☐	670	Billy Hatcher	.05	.02	.01
☐	671	Joe Oliver	.05	.02	.01
☐	672	Freddy Benavides	.05	.02	.01
☐	673	Barry Larkin	.15	.07	.02
☐	674	Chris Sabo	.10	.05	.01
☐	675	Mariano Duncan	.05	.02	.01
☐	676	Chris Jones	.05	.02	.01
☐	677	Gino Minutelli	.05	.02	.01
☐	678	Reggie Jefferson	.10	.05	.01
☐	679	Jack Armstrong	.05	.02	.01
☐	680	Chris Hammond	.10	.05	.01
☐	681	Jose Rijo	.10	.05	.01
☐	682	Bill Doran	.05	.02	.01
☐	683	Terry Lee	.05	.02	.01
☐	684	Tom Browning	.05	.02	.01
☐	685	Paul O'Neill	.10	.05	.01
☐	686	Eric Davis	.10	.05	.01
☐	687	Dan Wilson	.05	.02	.01
☐	688	Ted Power	.05	.02	.01
☐	689	Tim Layana	.05	.02	.01
☐	690	Norm Charlton	.05	.02	.01
☐	691	Hal Morris	.10	.05	.01
☐	692	Rickey Henderson	.15	.07	.02
☐	693	Sam Militello Minor League MVP	.05	.02	.01
☐	694	Matt Mieske Minor League MVP	.20	.09	.03
☐	695	Paul Russo Minor League MVP	.05	.02	.01
☐	696	Domingo Mota Minor League MVP	.05	.02	.01
☐	697	Todd Guggiana Minor League MVP	.05	.02	.01
☐	698	Marc Newfield Minor League MVP	.50	.23	.06
☐	699	Checklist 1-122	.05	.02	.01
☐	700	Checklist 123-244	.05	.02	.01
☐	701	Checklist 245-366	.05	.02	.01
☐	702	Checklist 367-471	.05	.02	.01
☐	703	Checklist 472-593	.05	.02	.01
☐	704	Checklist 594-704	.05	.02	.01

1992 Bowman

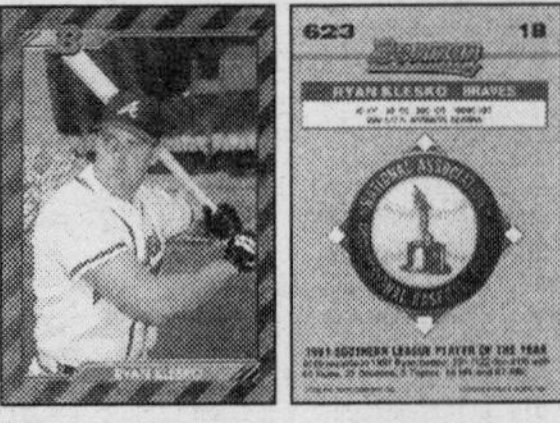

The cards in this 705-card set measure the standard size (2 1/2" by 3 1/2") and feature posed and action color player photos on a UV-coated white card face. A gradated orange bar accented with black diagonal stripes carries the player's name at the bottom right corner. The backs display close-up color photos and biography on a burlap-textured background. Below the photo, statistical information appears in a yellow-and-white grid with the player's name in a red bar at the top of the grid. Interspersed throughout the set are 45 special cards with an identical front design except for a textured gold-foil border. Each foil card has an extremely slight variation in that the photos are cropped differently. There is no additional value to either version. The foil cards were inserted one per wax pack and two per jumbo (23 regular cards) pack. These foil cards feature past and present Team USA players and minor league POY Award winners. Their backs have the same burlap background but display one of three emblems: 1) U.S. Baseball Federation; 2) Topps Team USA 1992; or 3) National Association of Professional Baseball Leagues. The player's name and biography are shown in a blue-and-white box above these emblems. Some of the regular and special cards picture players in civilian clothing who are still in the farm system. The cards are numbered on the back.

Rookie Cards in this set include Billy Ashley, Jason Bere, Carlos Delgado, Cliff Floyd, Alex Gonzalez, Bobby Jones, Pat Listach, David Nied, Melvin Nieves, Alex Ochoa, Jose Oliva, J.R. Phillips, Mike Piazza, Manny Ramirez, Scott Ruffcorn, Aaron Sele, Brien Taylor, Salomon Torres, Michael Tucker, Allen Watson, and Nigel Wilson.

	MINT	EXC	G-VG
COMPLETE SET (705)	350.00	160.00	45.00
COMMON CARD (1-705)	.15	.07	.02

		MINT	EXC	G-VG
☐ 1	Ivan Rodriguez	1.00	.25	.08
☐ 2	Kirk McCaskill	.15	.07	.02
☐ 3	Scott Livingstone	.15	.07	.02
☐ 4	Salomon Torres	1.00	.45	.13
☐ 5	Carlos Hernandez	.15	.07	.02
☐ 6	Dave Hollins	.60	.25	.08
☐ 7	Scott Fletcher	.15	.07	.02
☐ 8	Jorge Fabregas	.50	.23	.06
☐ 9	Andujar Cedeno	.20	.09	.03
☐ 10	Howard Johnson	.20	.09	.03
☐ 11	Trevor Hoffman	1.00	.45	.13
☐ 12	Roberto Kelly	.20	.09	.03
☐ 13	Gregg Jefferies	1.00	.45	.13
☐ 14	Marquis Grissom	1.00	.45	.13
☐ 15	Mike Ignasiak	.20	.09	.03
☐ 16	Jack Morris	.30	.14	.04
☐ 17	William Pennyfeather	.15	.07	.02
☐ 18	Todd Stottlemyre	.15	.07	.02
☐ 19	Chito Martinez	.15	.07	.02
☐ 20	Roberto Alomar	2.00	.90	.25
☐ 21	Sam Militello	.15	.07	.02
☐ 22	Hector Fajardo	.15	.07	.02
☐ 23	Paul Quantrill	.20	.09	.03
☐ 24	Chuck Knoblauch	1.00	.45	.13
☐ 25	Reggie Jefferson	.15	.07	.02
☐ 26	Jeremy McGarity	.15	.07	.02
☐ 27	Jerome Walton	.15	.07	.02
☐ 28	Chipper Jones	8.00	3.60	1.00
☐ 29	Brian Barber	.75	.35	.09
☐ 30	Ron Darling	.15	.07	.02
☐ 31	Roberto Petagine	1.25	.55	.16
☐ 32	Chuck Finley	.15	.07	.02
☐ 33	Edgar Martinez	.20	.09	.03
☐ 34	Napoleon Robinson	.20	.09	.03
☐ 35	Andy Van Slyke	.30	.14	.04
☐ 36	Bobby Thigpen	.15	.07	.02
☐ 37	Travis Fryman	2.00	.90	.25
☐ 38	Eric Christopherson	.15	.07	.02
☐ 39	Terry Mulholland	.15	.07	.02
☐ 40	Darryl Strawberry	.30	.14	.04
☐ 41	Manny Alexander	.30	.14	.04
☐ 42	Tracy Sanders	.30	.14	.04
☐ 43	Pete Incaviglia	.15	.07	.02
☐ 44	Kim Batiste	.15	.07	.02
☐ 45	Frankie Rodriguez	2.50	1.15	.30
☐ 46	Greg Swindell	.15	.07	.02
☐ 47	Delino DeShields	.30	.14	.04
☐ 48	John Ericks	.15	.07	.02
☐ 49	Franklin Stubbs	.15	.07	.02
☐ 50	Tony Gwynn	2.00	.90	.25
☐ 51	Clifton Garrett	.15	.07	.02
☐ 52	Mike Gardella	.20	.09	.03
☐ 53	Scott Erickson	.15	.07	.02
☐ 54	Gary Caraballo	.15	.07	.02
☐ 55	Jose Oliva	5.00	2.30	.60
☐ 56	Brook Fordyce	.15	.07	.02
☐ 57	Mark Whiten	.20	.09	.03
☐ 58	Joe Slusarski	.15	.07	.02
☐ 59	J.R. Phillips	4.00	1.80	.50
☐ 60	Barry Bonds	3.50	1.55	.45
☐ 61	Bob Milacki	.15	.07	.02
☐ 62	Keith Mitchell	.15	.07	.02
☐ 63	Angel Miranda	.15	.07	.02
☐ 64	Raul Mondesi	20.00	9.00	2.50
☐ 65	Brian Koelling	.15	.07	.02
☐ 66	Brian McRae	.50	.23	.06
☐ 67	John Patterson	.20	.09	.03
☐ 68	John Wetteland	.15	.07	.02
☐ 69	Wilson Alvarez	1.25	.55	.16
☐ 70	Wade Boggs	1.00	.45	.13
☐ 71	Darryl Ratliff	.15	.07	.02
☐ 72	Jeff Jackson	.15	.07	.02
☐ 73	Jeremy Hernandez	.20	.09	.03
☐ 74	Darryl Hamilton	.20	.09	.03
☐ 75	Rafael Belliard	.15	.07	.02
☐ 76	Rick Trlicek	.15	.07	.02
☐ 77	Felipe Crespo	.50	.23	.06
☐ 78	Carney Lansford	.20	.09	.03
☐ 79	Ryan Long	.40	.18	.05
☐ 80	Kirby Puckett	2.50	1.15	.30
☐ 81	Earl Cunningham	.15	.07	.02
☐ 82	Pedro Martinez	2.00	.90	.25
☐ 83	Scott Hatteberg	.30	.14	.04
☐ 84	Juan Gonzalez UER (65 doubles vs. Tigers)	5.00	2.30	.60
☐ 85	Robert Nutting	.15	.07	.02
☐ 86	Calvin Reese	1.25	.55	.16
☐ 87	Dave Silvestri	.20	.09	.03
☐ 88	Scott Ruffcorn	2.50	1.15	.30
☐ 89	Rick Aguilera	.20	.09	.03
☐ 90	Cecil Fielder	1.00	.45	.13
☐ 91	Kirk Dressendorfer	.15	.07	.02
☐ 92	Jerry DiPoto	.15	.07	.02
☐ 93	Mike Felder	.15	.07	.02
☐ 94	Craig Paquette	.20	.09	.03
☐ 95	Elvin Paulino	.20	.09	.03
☐ 96	Donovan Osborne	.15	.07	.02
☐ 97	Hubie Brooks	.15	.07	.02
☐ 98	Derek Lowe	.30	.14	.04
☐ 99	David Zancanaro	.20	.09	.03
☐ 100	Ken Griffey Jr.	15.00	6.75	1.90
☐ 101	Todd Hundley	.15	.07	.02
☐ 102	Mike Trombley	.30	.14	.04
☐ 103	Ricky Gutierrez	.30	.14	.04
☐ 104	Braulio Castillo	.15	.07	.02
☐ 105	Craig Lefferts	.15	.07	.02
☐ 106	Rick Sutcliffe	.20	.09	.03
☐ 107	Dean Palmer	.20	.09	.03
☐ 108	Henry Rodriguez	.60	.25	.08
☐ 109	Mark Clark	1.00	.45	.13
☐ 110	Kenny Lofton	9.00	4.00	1.15
☐ 111	Mark Carreon	.15	.07	.02
☐ 112	J.T. Bruett	.20	.09	.03
☐ 113	Gerald Williams	.20	.09	.03
☐ 114	Frank Thomas	15.00	6.75	1.90
☐ 115	Kevin Reimer	.15	.07	.02
☐ 116	Sammy Sosa	1.00	.45	.13
☐ 117	Mickey Tettleton	.20	.09	.03
☐ 118	Reggie Sanders	2.00	.90	.25
☐ 119	Trevor Wilson	.15	.07	.02
☐ 120	Cliff Brantley	.20	.09	.03
☐ 121	Spike Owen	.15	.07	.02
☐ 122	Jeff Montgomery	.20	.09	.03
☐ 123	Alex Sutherland	.15	.07	.02
☐ 124	Brien Taylor	1.50	.65	.19
☐ 125	Brian Williams	.40	.18	.05
☐ 126	Kevin Seitzer	.20	.09	.03
☐ 127	Carlos Delgado	12.00	5.50	1.50
☐ 128	Gary Scott	.15	.07	.02
☐ 129	Scott Cooper	.75	.35	.09
☐ 130	Domingo Jean	.40	.18	.05
☐ 131	Pat Mahomes	1.00	.45	.13

☐ 132 Mike Boddicker .15 .07 .02
☐ 133 Roberto Hernandez .20 .09 .03
☐ 134 Dave Valle .15 .07 .02
☐ 135 Kurt Stillwell .15 .07 .02
☐ 136 Brad Pennington .30 .14 .04
☐ 137 Jermaine Swinton .15 .07 .02
☐ 138 Ryan Hawblitzel .30 .14 .04
☐ 139 Tito Navarro .15 .07 .02
☐ 140 Sandy Alomar .20 .09 .03
☐ 141 Todd Benzinger .15 .07 .02
☐ 142 Danny Jackson .15 .07 .02
☐ 143 Melvin Nieves 3.00 1.35 .40
☐ 144 Jim Campanis .15 .07 .02
☐ 145 Luis Gonzalez .20 .09 .03
☐ 146 Dave Doorneweerd .30 .14 .04
☐ 147 Charlie Hayes .20 .09 .03
☐ 148 Greg Maddux 2.00 .90 .25
☐ 149 Brian Harper .15 .07 .02
☐ 150 Brent Miller .35 .16 .04
☐ 151 Shawn Estes .30 .14 .04
☐ 152 Mike Williams .30 .14 .04
☐ 153 Charlie Hough .20 .09 .03
☐ 154 Randy Myers .20 .09 .03
☐ 155 Kevin Young .30 .14 .04
☐ 156 Rick Wilkins .20 .09 .03
☐ 157 Terry Shumpert .15 .07 .02
☐ 158 Steve Karsay 2.50 1.15 .30
☐ 159 Gary DiSarcina .20 .09 .03
☐ 160 Deion Sanders 1.50 .65 .19
☐ 161 Tom Browning .15 .07 .02
☐ 162 Dickie Thon .15 .07 .02
☐ 163 Luis Mercedes .15 .07 .02
☐ 164 Riccardo Ingram .20 .09 .03
☐ 165 Tavo Alvarez .40 .18 .05
☐ 166 Rickey Henderson .75 .35 .09
☐ 167 Jaime Navarro .15 .07 .02
☐ 168 Billy Ashley 6.00 2.70 .75
☐ 169 Phil Dauphin .15 .07 .02
☐ 170 Ivan Cruz .15 .07 .02
☐ 171 Harold Baines .20 .09 .03
☐ 172 Bryan Harvey .20 .09 .03
☐ 173 Alex Cole .15 .07 .02
☐ 174 Curtis Shaw .15 .07 .02
☐ 175 Matt Williams 1.50 .65 .19
☐ 176 Felix Jose .20 .09 .03
☐ 177 Sam Horn .15 .07 .02
☐ 178 Randy Johnson .75 .35 .09
☐ 179 Ivan Calderon .15 .07 .02
☐ 180 Steve Avery 1.25 .55 .16
☐ 181 William Suero .15 .07 .02
☐ 182 Bill Swift .20 .09 .03
☐ 183 Howard Battle 1.00 .45 .13
☐ 184 Ruben Amaro .15 .07 .02
☐ 185 Jim Abbott .30 .14 .04
☐ 186 Mike Fitzgerald .15 .07 .02
☐ 187 Bruce Hurst .15 .07 .02
☐ 188 Jeff Juden .15 .07 .02
☐ 189 Jeromy Burnitz .75 .35 .09
☐ 190 Dave Burba .15 .07 .02
☐ 191 Kevin Brown .20 .09 .03
☐ 192 Patrick Lennon .15 .07 .02
☐ 193 Jeff McNeely .15 .07 .02
☐ 194 Wil Cordero 2.00 .90 .25
☐ 195 Chili Davis .20 .09 .03
☐ 196 Milt Cuyler .15 .07 .02
☐ 197 Von Hayes .15 .07 .02
☐ 198 Todd Revenig .15 .07 .02
☐ 199 Joel Johnston .15 .07 .02
☐ 200 Jeff Bagwell 8.00 3.60 1.00
☐ 201 Alex Fernandez 1.25 .55 .16
☐ 202 Todd Jones .30 .14 .04
☐ 203 Charles Nagy .20 .09 .03
☐ 204 Tim Raines .30 .14 .04
☐ 205 Kevin Maas .15 .07 .02
☐ 206 Julio Franco .20 .09 .03
☐ 207 Randy Velarde .15 .07 .02
☐ 208 Lance Johnson .15 .07 .02
☐ 209 Scott Leius .15 .07 .02
☐ 210 Derek Lee .20 .09 .03
☐ 211 Joe Sondrini .15 .07 .02
☐ 212 Royce Clayton .75 .35 .09
☐ 213 Chris George .15 .07 .02
☐ 214 Gary Sheffield .60 .25 .08
☐ 215 Mark Gubicza .15 .07 .02
☐ 216 Mike Moore .15 .07 .02
☐ 217 Rick Huisman .15 .07 .02
☐ 218 Jeff Russell .15 .07 .02
☐ 219 D.J. Dozier .20 .09 .03
☐ 220 Dave Martinez .15 .07 .02
☐ 221 Alan Newman .15 .07 .02
☐ 222 Nolan Ryan 8.00 3.60 1.00
☐ 223 Teddy Higuera .15 .07 .02
☐ 224 Damon Buford .30 .14 .04
☐ 225 Ruben Sierra .50 .23 .06
☐ 226 Tom Nevers .20 .09 .03
☐ 227 Tommy Greene .20 .09 .03
☐ 228 Nigel Wilson 1.50 .65 .19
☐ 229 John DeSilva .15 .07 .02
☐ 230 Bobby Witt .15 .07 .02
☐ 231 Greg Cadaret .15 .07 .02
☐ 232 John Vander Wal .20 .09 .03
☐ 233 Jack Clark .20 .09 .03
☐ 234 Bill Doran .15 .07 .02
☐ 235 Bobby Bonilla .30 .14 .04
☐ 236 Steve Olin .15 .07 .02
☐ 237 Derek Bell 1.00 .45 .13
☐ 238 David Cone .30 .14 .04
☐ 239 Victor Cole .20 .09 .03
☐ 240 Rod Bolton .30 .14 .04
☐ 241 Tom Pagnozzi .15 .07 .02
☐ 242 Rob Dibble .15 .07 .02
☐ 243 Michael Carter .15 .07 .02
☐ 244 Don Peters .15 .07 .02
☐ 245 Mike LaValliere .15 .07 .02
☐ 246 Joe Perona .15 .07 .02
☐ 247 Mitch Williams .20 .09 .03
☐ 248 Jay Buhner .20 .09 .03
☐ 249 Andy Benes .30 .14 .04
☐ 250 Alex Ochoa 3.00 1.35 .40
☐ 251 Greg Blosser .40 .18 .05
☐ 252 Jack Armstrong .15 .07 .02
☐ 253 Juan Samuel .15 .07 .02
☐ 254 Terry Pendleton .30 .14 .04
☐ 255 Ramon Martinez .20 .09 .03
☐ 256 Rico Brogna 1.00 .45 .13
☐ 257 John Smiley .15 .07 .02
☐ 258 Carl Everett 1.00 .45 .13
☐ 259 Tim Salmon 8.00 3.60 1.00
☐ 260 Will Clark 1.50 .65 .19
☐ 261 Ugueth Urbina 1.00 .45 .13
☐ 262 Jason Wood .30 .14 .04
☐ 263 Dave Magadan .15 .07 .02
☐ 264 Dante Bichette .50 .23 .06
☐ 265 Jose DeLeon .15 .07 .02
☐ 266 Mike Neill .30 .14 .04
☐ 267 Paul O'Neill .20 .09 .03
☐ 268 Anthony Young .15 .07 .02
☐ 269 Greg W. Harris .15 .07 .02
☐ 270 Todd Van Poppel .75 .35 .09
☐ 271 Pedro Castellano .30 .14 .04
☐ 272 Tony Phillips .15 .07 .02
☐ 273 Mike Gallego .15 .07 .02
☐ 274 Steve Cooke .75 .35 .09
☐ 275 Robin Ventura 1.00 .45 .13
☐ 276 Kevin Mitchell .20 .09 .03
☐ 277 Doug Linton .20 .09 .03

	No.	Player			
☐	278	Robert Eenhoorn	.15	.07	.02
☐	279	Gabe White	.75	.35	.09
☐	280	Dave Stewart	.20	.09	.03
☐	281	Mo Sanford	.15	.07	.02
☐	282	Greg Perschke	.20	.09	.03
☐	283	Kevin Flora	.15	.07	.02
☐	284	Jeff Williams	.15	.07	.02
☐	285	Keith Miller	.15	.07	.02
☐	286	Andy Ashby	.15	.07	.02
☐	287	Doug Dascenzo	.15	.07	.02
☐	288	Eric Karros	1.25	.55	.16
☐	289	Glenn Murray	1.25	.55	.16
☐	290	Troy Percival	.30	.14	.04
☐	291	Orlando Merced	.20	.09	.03
☐	292	Peter Hoy	.20	.09	.03
☐	293	Tony Fernandez	.20	.09	.03
☐	294	Juan Guzman	.40	.18	.05
☐	295	Jesse Barfield	.15	.07	.02
☐	296	Sid Fernandez	.20	.09	.03
☐	297	Scott Cepicky	.20	.09	.03
☐	298	Garret Anderson	2.00	.90	.25
☐	299	Cal Eldred	.75	.35	.09
☐	300	Ryne Sandberg	2.50	1.15	.30
☐	301	Jim Gantner	.15	.07	.02
☐	302	Mariano Rivera	.40	.18	.05
☐	303	Ron Lockett	.15	.07	.02
☐	304	Jose Offerman	.15	.07	.02
☐	305	Denny Martinez	.20	.09	.03
☐	306	Luis Ortiz	1.00	.45	.13
☐	307	David Howard	.15	.07	.02
☐	308	Russ Springer	.30	.14	.04
☐	309	Chris Howard	.20	.09	.03
☐	310	Kyle Abbott	.15	.07	.02
☐	311	Aaron Sele	6.00	2.70	.75
☐	312	David Justice	2.00	.90	.25
☐	313	Pete O'Brien	.15	.07	.02
☐	314	Greg Hansell	.75	.35	.09
☐	315	Dave Winfield	1.00	.45	.13
☐	316	Lance Dickson	.15	.07	.02
☐	317	Eric King	.15	.07	.02
☐	318	Vaughn Eshelman	.50	.23	.06
☐	319	Tim Belcher	.15	.07	.02
☐	320	Andres Galarraga	.75	.35	.09
☐	321	Scott Bullett	.15	.07	.02
☐	322	Doug Strange	.15	.07	.02
☐	323	Jerald Clark	.15	.07	.02
☐	324	Dave Righetti	.15	.07	.02
☐	325	Greg Hibbard	.15	.07	.02
☐	326	Eric Hillman	.15	.07	.02
☐	327	Shane Reynolds	1.50	.65	.19
☐	328	Chris Hammond	.15	.07	.02
☐	329	Albert Belle	4.00	1.80	.50
☐	330	Rich Becker	1.50	.65	.19
☐	331	Eddie Williams	.15	.07	.02
☐	332	Donald Harris	.15	.07	.02
☐	333	Dave Smith	.15	.07	.02
☐	334	Steve Fireovid	.15	.07	.02
☐	335	Steve Buechele	.15	.07	.02
☐	336	Mike Schooler	.15	.07	.02
☐	337	Kevin McReynolds	.15	.07	.02
☐	338	Hensley Meulens	.15	.07	.02
☐	339	Benji Gil	1.50	.65	.19
☐	340	Don Mattingly	2.50	1.15	.30
☐	341	Alvin Davis	.15	.07	.02
☐	342	Alan Mills	.15	.07	.02
☐	343	Kelly Downs	.15	.07	.02
☐	344	Leo Gomez	.15	.07	.02
☐	345	Tarrik Brock	.30	.14	.04
☐	346	Ryan Turner	.30	.14	.04
☐	347	John Smoltz	.30	.14	.04
☐	348	Bill Sampen	.15	.07	.02
☐	349	Paul Byrd	.40	.18	.05
☐	350	Mike Bordick	.15	.07	.02
☐	351	Jose Lind	.15	.07	.02
☐	352	David Wells	.15	.07	.02
☐	353	Barry Larkin	.30	.14	.04
☐	354	Bruce Ruffin	.15	.07	.02
☐	355	Luis Rivera	.15	.07	.02
☐	356	Sid Bream	.15	.07	.02
☐	357	Julian Vasquez	.15	.07	.02
☐	358	Jason Bere	10.00	4.50	1.25
☐	359	Ben McDonald	.60	.25	.08
☐	360	Scott Stahoviak	.60	.25	.08
☐	361	Kirt Manwaring	.15	.07	.02
☐	362	Jeff Johnson	.15	.07	.02
☐	363	Rob Deer	.15	.07	.02
☐	364	Tony Pena	.15	.07	.02
☐	365	Melido Perez	.15	.07	.02
☐	366	Clay Parker	.15	.07	.02
☐	367	Dale Sveum	.15	.07	.02
☐	368	Mike Scioscia	.15	.07	.02
☐	369	Roger Salkeld	.40	.18	.05
☐	370	Mike Stanley	.15	.07	.02
☐	371	Jack McDowell	.50	.23	.06
☐	372	Tim Wallach	.15	.07	.02
☐	373	Billy Ripken	.15	.07	.02
☐	374	Mike Christopher	.20	.09	.03
☐	375	Paul Molitor	1.00	.45	.13
☐	376	Dave Stieb	.20	.09	.03
☐	377	Pedro Guerrero	.20	.09	.03
☐	378	Russ Swan	.15	.07	.02
☐	379	Bob Ojeda	.15	.07	.02
☐	380	Donn Pall	.15	.07	.02
☐	381	Eddie Zosky	.15	.07	.02
☐	382	Darnell Coles	.15	.07	.02
☐	383	Tom Smith	.15	.07	.02
☐	384	Mark McGwire	.60	.25	.08
☐	385	Gary Carter	.30	.14	.04
☐	386	Rich Amaral	.15	.07	.02
☐	387	Alan Embree	.30	.14	.04
☐	388	Jonathan Hurst	.15	.07	.02
☐	389	Bobby Jones	5.00	2.30	.60
☐	390	Rico Rossy	.15	.07	.02
☐	391	Dan Smith	.15	.07	.02
☐	392	Terry Steinbach	.20	.09	.03
☐	393	Jon Farrell	.30	.14	.04
☐	394	Dave Anderson	.15	.07	.02
☐	395	Benny Santiago	.15	.07	.02
☐	396	Mark Wohlers	.20	.09	.03
☐	397	Mo Vaughn	2.00	.90	.25
☐	398	Randy Kramer	.15	.07	.02
☐	399	John Jaha	.75	.35	.09
☐	400	Cal Ripken	4.00	1.80	.50
☐	401	Ryan Bowen	.15	.07	.02
☐	402	Tim McIntosh	.15	.07	.02
☐	403	Bernard Gilkey	.20	.09	.03
☐	404	Junior Felix	.15	.07	.02
☐	405	Cris Colon	.15	.07	.02
☐	406	Marc Newfield	3.50	1.55	.45
☐	407	Bernie Williams	.20	.09	.03
☐	408	Jay Howell	.15	.07	.02
☐	409	Zane Smith	.15	.07	.02
☐	410	Jeff Shaw	.15	.07	.02
☐	411	Kerry Woodson	.15	.07	.02
☐	412	Wes Chamberlain	.15	.07	.02
☐	413	Dave Mlicki	.15	.07	.02
☐	414	Benny Distefano	.15	.07	.02
☐	415	Kevin Rogers	.20	.09	.03
☐	416	Tim Naehring	.15	.07	.02
☐	417	Clemente Nunez	.40	.18	.05
☐	418	Luis Sojo	.15	.07	.02
☐	419	Kevin Ritz	.15	.07	.02
☐	420	Omar Olivares	.15	.07	.02
☐	421	Manny Lee	.15	.07	.02
☐	422	Julio Valera	.15	.07	.02
☐	423	Omar Vizquel	.15	.07	.02

☐ 424 Darren Burton	.30	.14	.04
☐ 425 Mel Hall	.15	.07	.02
☐ 426 Dennis Powell	.15	.07	.02
☐ 427 Lee Stevens	.15	.07	.02
☐ 428 Glenn Davis	.15	.07	.02
☐ 429 Willie Greene	1.00	.45	.13
☐ 430 Kevin Wickander	.15	.07	.02
☐ 431 Dennis Eckersley	.30	.14	.04
☐ 432 Joe Orsulak	.15	.07	.02
☐ 433 Eddie Murray	.60	.25	.08
☐ 434 Matt Stairs	.15	.07	.02
☐ 435 Wally Joyner	.20	.09	.03
☐ 436 Rondell White	6.00	2.70	.75
☐ 437 Rob Maurer	.20	.09	.03
☐ 438 Joe Redfield	.15	.07	.02
☐ 439 Mark Lewis	.20	.09	.03
☐ 440 Darren Daulton	.50	.23	.06
☐ 441 Mike Henneman	.15	.07	.02
☐ 442 John Cangelosi	.15	.07	.02
☐ 443 Vince Moore	.60	.25	.08
☐ 444 John Wehner	.15	.07	.02
☐ 445 Kent Hrbek	.20	.09	.03
☐ 446 Mark McLemore	.15	.07	.02
☐ 447 Bill Wegman	.15	.07	.02
☐ 448 Robby Thompson	.15	.07	.02
☐ 449 Mark Anthony	.15	.07	.02
☐ 450 Archi Cianfrocco	.15	.07	.02
☐ 451 Johnny Ruffin	.15	.07	.02
☐ 452 Javy Lopez	6.00	2.70	.75
☐ 453 Greg Gohr	.15	.07	.02
☐ 454 Tim Scott	.20	.09	.03
☐ 455 Stan Belinda	.15	.07	.02
☐ 456 Darrin Jackson	.15	.07	.02
☐ 457 Chris Gardner	.15	.07	.02
☐ 458 Esteban Beltre	.20	.09	.03
☐ 459 Phil Plantier	.60	.25	.08
☐ 460 Jim Thome	4.00	1.80	.50
☐ 461 Mike Piazza	35.00	16.00	4.40
☐ 462 Matt Sinatro	.15	.07	.02
☐ 463 Scott Servais	.15	.07	.02
☐ 464 Brian Jordan	.75	.35	.09
☐ 465 Doug Drabek	.30	.14	.04
☐ 466 Carl Willis	.15	.07	.02
☐ 467 Bret Barberie	.15	.07	.02
☐ 468 Hal Morris	.20	.09	.03
☐ 469 Steve Sax	.15	.07	.02
☐ 470 Jerry Willard	.15	.07	.02
☐ 471 Dan Wilson	.15	.07	.02
☐ 472 Chris Hoiles	.30	.14	.04
☐ 473 Rheal Cormier	.15	.07	.02
☐ 474 John Morris	.15	.07	.02
☐ 475 Jeff Reardon	.20	.09	.03
☐ 476 Mark Leiter	.15	.07	.02
☐ 477 Tom Gordon	.20	.09	.03
☐ 478 Kent Bottenfield	.15	.07	.02
☐ 479 Gene Larkin	.15	.07	.02
☐ 480 Dwight Gooden	.20	.09	.03
☐ 481 B.J. Surhoff	.15	.07	.02
☐ 482 Andy Stankiewicz	.15	.07	.02
☐ 483 Tino Martinez	.20	.09	.03
☐ 484 Craig Biggio	.30	.14	.04
☐ 485 Denny Neagle	.15	.07	.02
☐ 486 Rusty Meacham	.15	.07	.02
☐ 487 Kal Daniels	.15	.07	.02
☐ 488 Dave Henderson	.15	.07	.02
☐ 489 Tim Costo	.15	.07	.02
☐ 490 Doug Davis	.15	.07	.02
☐ 491 Frank Viola	.20	.09	.03
☐ 492 Cory Snyder	.15	.07	.02
☐ 493 Chris Martin	.20	.09	.03
☐ 494 Dion James	.15	.07	.02
☐ 495 Randy Tomlin	.15	.07	.02
☐ 496 Greg Vaughn	.20	.09	.03
☐ 497 Dennis Cook	.15	.07	.02
☐ 498 Rosario Rodriguez	.15	.07	.02
☐ 499 Dave Staton	.15	.07	.02
☐ 500 George Brett	2.50	1.15	.30
☐ 501 Brian Barnes	.15	.07	.02
☐ 502 Butch Henry	.40	.18	.05
☐ 503 Harold Reynolds	.15	.07	.02
☐ 504 David Nied	3.00	1.35	.40
☐ 505 Lee Smith	.30	.14	.04
☐ 506 Steve Chitren	.15	.07	.02
☐ 507 Ken Hill	.30	.14	.04
☐ 508 Robbie Beckett	.15	.07	.02
☐ 509 Troy Afenir	.15	.07	.02
☐ 510 Kelly Gruber	.15	.07	.02
☐ 511 Bret Boone	2.50	1.15	.30
☐ 512 Jeff Branson	.15	.07	.02
☐ 513 Mike Jackson	.15	.07	.02
☐ 514 Pete Harnisch	.20	.09	.03
☐ 515 Chad Kreuter	.15	.07	.02
☐ 516 Joe Vitko	.30	.14	.04
☐ 517 Orel Hershiser	.20	.09	.03
☐ 518 John Doherty	.50	.23	.06
☐ 519 Jay Bell	.20	.09	.03
☐ 520 Mark Langston	.30	.14	.04
☐ 521 Dann Howitt	.15	.07	.02
☐ 522 Bobby Reed	.20	.09	.03
☐ 523 Roberto Munoz	.75	.35	.09
☐ 524 Todd Ritchie	.35	.16	.04
☐ 525 Bip Roberts	.15	.07	.02
☐ 526 Pat Listach	.50	.23	.06
☐ 527 Scott Brosius	.15	.07	.02
☐ 528 John Roper	2.00	.90	.25
☐ 529 Phil Hiatt	.50	.23	.06
☐ 530 Denny Walling	.15	.07	.02
☐ 531 Carlos Baerga	2.00	.90	.25
☐ 532 Manny Ramirez	15.00	6.75	1.90
☐ 533 Pat Clements UER	.15	.07	.02
(Mistakenly numbered 553)			
☐ 534 Ron Gant	.20	.09	.03
☐ 535 Pat Kelly	.20	.09	.03
☐ 536 Billy Spiers	.15	.07	.02
☐ 537 Darren Reed	.15	.07	.02
☐ 538 Ken Caminiti	.20	.09	.03
☐ 539 Butch Huskey	.75	.35	.09
☐ 540 Matt Nokes	.15	.07	.02
☐ 541 John Kruk	.40	.18	.05
☐ 542 John Jaha FOIL	.50	.23	.06
☐ 543 Justin Thompson	.50	.23	.06
☐ 544 Steve Hosey	.20	.09	.03
☐ 545 Joe Kmak	.20	.09	.03
☐ 546 John Franco	.20	.09	.03
☐ 547 Devon White	.20	.09	.03
☐ 548 Elston Hansen FOIL	.25	.11	.03
☐ 549 Ryan Klesko	10.00	4.50	1.25
☐ 550 Danny Tartabull	.20	.09	.03
☐ 551 Frank Thomas FOIL	25.00	11.50	3.10
☐ 552 Kevin Tapani	.20	.09	.03
☐ 553 Willie Banks	.15	.07	.02
(See also 533)			
☐ 554 B.J. Wallace FOIL	.75	.35	.09
☐ 555 Orlando Miller	2.00	.90	.25
☐ 556 Mark Smith	.75	.35	.09
☐ 557 Tim Wallach FOIL	.25	.11	.03
☐ 558 Bill Gullickson	.15	.07	.02
☐ 559 Derek Bell FOIL	.50	.23	.06
☐ 560 Joe Randa FOIL	.60	.25	.08
☐ 561 Frank Seminara	.15	.07	.02
☐ 562 Mark Gardner	.15	.07	.02
☐ 563 Rick Greene FOIL	.40	.18	.05
☐ 564 Gary Gaetti	.15	.07	.02
☐ 565 Ozzie Guillen	.15	.07	.02
☐ 566 Charles Nagy FOIL	.25	.11	.03
☐ 567 Mike Milchin	.15	.07	.02

☐ 568 Ben Shelton .15 .07 .02
☐ 569 Chris Roberts FOIL 2.00 .90 .25
☐ 570 Ellis Burks .20 .09 .03
☐ 571 Scott Scudder .15 .07 .02
☐ 572 Jim Abbott FOIL .40 .18 .05
☐ 573 Joe Carter 1.50 .65 .19
☐ 574 Steve Finley .15 .07 .02
☐ 575 Jim Olander FOIL .25 .11 .03
☐ 576 Carlos Garcia 1.25 .55 .16
☐ 577 Gregg Olson .15 .07 .02
☐ 578 Greg Swindell FOIL .25 .11 .03
☐ 579 Matt Williams FOIL 1.50 .65 .19
☐ 580 Mark Grace .30 .14 .04
☐ 581 Howard House FOIL .25 .11 .03
☐ 582 Luis Polonia .15 .07 .02
☐ 583 Erik Hanson .15 .07 .02
☐ 584 Salomon Torres FOIL .50 .23 .06
☐ 585 Carlton Fisk .50 .23 .06
☐ 586 Bret Saberhagen .20 .09 .03
☐ 587 Chad McConnell FOIL .60 .25 .08
☐ 588 Jimmy Key .20 .09 .03
☐ 589 Mike Macfarlane .15 .07 .02
☐ 590 Barry Bonds FOIL 3.00 1.35 .40
☐ 591 Jamie McAndrew .15 .07 .02
☐ 592 Shane Mack .20 .09 .03
☐ 593 Kerwin Moore .15 .07 .02
☐ 594 Joe Oliver .15 .07 .02
☐ 595 Chris Sabo UER .20 .09 .03
(715 Hits in '91; should be 175)
☐ 596 Alex Gonzalez 5.00 2.30 .60
☐ 597 Brett Butler .20 .09 .03
☐ 598 Mark Hutton .60 .25 .08
☐ 599 Andy Benes FOIL .40 .18 .05
☐ 600 Jose Canseco 1.50 .65 .19
☐ 601 Darryl Kile .30 .14 .04
☐ 602 Matt Stairs FOIL .25 .11 .03
☐ 603 Robert Butler FOIL .50 .23 .06
☐ 604 Willie McGee .20 .09 .03
☐ 605 Jack McDowell FOIL .50 .23 .06
☐ 606 Tom Candiotti .15 .07 .02
☐ 607 Ed Martel .15 .07 .02
☐ 608 Matt Mieske FOIL 1.00 .45 .13
☐ 609 Darrin Fletcher .15 .07 .02
☐ 610 Rafael Palmeiro 1.00 .45 .13
☐ 611 Bill Swift FOIL .30 .14 .04
☐ 612 Mike Mussina 3.00 1.35 .40
☐ 613 Vince Coleman .15 .07 .02
☐ 614 Scott Cepicky FOIL UER .25 .11 .03
(Bats: LEFLT)
☐ 615 Mike Greenwell .20 .09 .03
☐ 616 Kevin McGehee .30 .14 .04
☐ 617 Jeffrey Hammonds FOIL 6.00 2.70 .75
☐ 618 Scott Taylor .15 .07 .02
☐ 619 Dave Otto .15 .07 .02
☐ 620 Mark McGwire FOIL .60 .25 .08
☐ 621 Kevin Tatar .15 .07 .02
☐ 622 Steve Farr .15 .07 .02
☐ 623 Ryan Klesko FOIL 4.00 1.80 .50
☐ 624 Dave Fleming .20 .09 .03
☐ 625 Andre Dawson .50 .23 .06
☐ 626 Tino Martinez FOIL .30 .14 .04
☐ 627 Chad Curtis 1.25 .55 .16
☐ 628 Mickey Morandini .15 .07 .02
☐ 629 Gregg Olson FOIL .25 .11 .03
☐ 630 Lou Whitaker .30 .14 .04
☐ 631 Arthur Rhodes .20 .09 .03
☐ 632 Brandon Wilson .15 .07 .02
☐ 633 Lance Jennings .15 .07 .02
☐ 634 Allen Watson 1.25 .55 .16
☐ 635 Len Dykstra .50 .23 .06
☐ 636 Joe Girardi .15 .07 .02
☐ 637 Kiki Hernandez FOIL .25 .11 .03
☐ 638 Mike Hampton .40 .18 .05
☐ 639 Al Osuna .15 .07 .02
☐ 640 Kevin Appier .20 .09 .03
☐ 641 Rick Helling FOIL 1.25 .55 .16
☐ 642 Jody Reed .15 .07 .02
☐ 643 Ray Lankford 1.00 .45 .13
☐ 644 John Olerud 1.00 .45 .13
☐ 645 Paul Molitor FOIL 3.50 1.55 .45
☐ 646 Pat Borders .15 .07 .02
☐ 647 Mike Morgan .15 .07 .02
☐ 648 Larry Walker 1.00 .45 .13
☐ 649 Pedro Castellano FOIL .25 .11 .03
☐ 650 Fred McGriff 1.50 .65 .19
☐ 651 Walt Weiss .15 .07 .02
☐ 652 Calvin Murray FOIL .75 .35 .09
☐ 653 Dave Nilsson 1.50 .65 .19
☐ 654 Greg Pirkl 1.00 .45 .13
☐ 655 Robin Ventura FOIL 2.00 .90 .25
☐ 656 Mark Portugal .15 .07 .02
☐ 657 Roger McDowell .15 .07 .02
☐ 658 Rick Hirtensteiner .25 .11 .03
FOIL SP
☐ 659 Glenallen Hill .15 .07 .02
☐ 660 Greg Gagne .15 .07 .02
☐ 661 Charles Johnson FOIL 5.00 2.30 .60
☐ 662 Brian Hunter .15 .07 .02
☐ 663 Mark Lemke .15 .07 .02
☐ 664 Tim Belcher FOIL .25 .11 .03
☐ 665 Rich DeLucia .15 .07 .02
☐ 666 Bob Walk .15 .07 .02
☐ 667 Joe Carter FOIL 3.50 1.55 .45
☐ 668 Jose Guzman .15 .07 .02
☐ 669 Otis Nixon .15 .07 .02
☐ 670 Phil Nevin FOIL 2.50 1.15 .30
☐ 671 Eric Davis .20 .09 .03
☐ 672 Damion Easley .75 .35 .09
☐ 673 Will Clark FOIL 1.50 .65 .19
☐ 674 Mark Kiefer .20 .09 .03
☐ 675 Ozzie Smith 1.25 .55 .16
☐ 676 Manny Ramirez FOIL 6.00 2.70 .75
☐ 677 Gregg Olson .15 .07 .02
☐ 678 Cliff Floyd 12.00 5.50 1.50
☐ 679 Duane Singleton 1.00 .45 .13
☐ 680 Jose Rijo .20 .09 .03
☐ 681 Willie Randolph .20 .09 .03
☐ 682 Michael Tucker FOIL 5.00 2.30 .60
☐ 683 Darren Lewis .20 .09 .03
☐ 684 Dale Murphy .30 .14 .04
☐ 685 Mike Pagliarulo .15 .07 .02
☐ 686 Paul Miller .20 .09 .03
☐ 687 Mike Robertson .40 .18 .05
☐ 688 Mike Devereaux .20 .09 .03
☐ 689 Pedro Astacio 1.00 .45 .13
☐ 690 Alan Trammell .30 .14 .04
☐ 691 Roger Clemens 2.00 .90 .25
☐ 692 Bud Black .15 .07 .02
☐ 693 Turk Wendell .40 .18 .05
☐ 694 Barry Larkin FOIL 1.25 .55 .16
☐ 695 Todd Zeile .20 .09 .03
☐ 696 Pat Hentgen 2.00 .90 .25
☐ 697 Eddie Taubensee .15 .07 .02
☐ 698 Guillermo Velasquez .15 .07 .02
☐ 699 Tom Glavine .75 .35 .09
☐ 700 Robin Yount 1.00 .45 .13
☐ 701 Checklist 1-141 .15 .07 .02
☐ 702 Checklist 142-282 .15 .07 .02
☐ 703 Checklist 283-423 .15 .07 .02
☐ 704 Checklist 424-564 .15 .07 .02
☐ 705 Checklist 565-705 .15 .07 .02

1993 Bowman

This 708-card standard-size (2 1/2" by 3 1/2") set features white-bordered color action player photos on its fronts. The player's name appears in white lettering at the bottom right, with his last name printed on an ocher rectangle. The horizontal backs carry the player's name in green lettering above another color player photo on the left side, which displays his positon within a yellow circle at its lower right. His team name appears vertically in yellow lettering within a black rectangle near the left edge. The player's biography, career highlights, and stats appear on the right side. A simulated wooden strip across the top accents the back and carries the card's number. The 48 foil subset cards (339-374 and 693-704) feature sixteen 1992 MVPs of the Minor Leagues plus top prospects. One foil card was inserted into every 14-card pack. Rookie Cards in this set include Rene Arocha, James Baldwin, Trey Beamon, Marshall Boze, Roger Cedeno, Tim Clark, Danny Clyburn, Marty Cordova, Midre Cummings, Russ Davis, Kenny Felder, Jimmy Haynes, Lee Heath, Sterling Hitchcock, Brian L. Hunter, Derek Jeter, Jason Kendall, Mike Lansing, James Malave, Ray McDavid, Greg McMichael, Chad Mottola, James Mouton, Jose Pett, Kevin Roberson, J.T. Snow, Paul Spoljaric, Larry Sutton, Tony Tarasco, Steve Trachsel, Darrell Whitmore, and Preston Wilson.

	MINT	EXC	G-VG
COMPLETE SET (708)	75.00	34.00	9.50
COMMON CARD (1-708)	.10	.05	.01
COMMON FOIL (339-374)	.20	.09	.03
COMMON FOIL (693-704)	.20	.09	.03

	MINT	EXC	G-VG
☐ 1 Glenn Davis	.10	.05	.01
☐ 2 Hector Roa	.10	.05	.01
☐ 3 Ken Ryan	.30	.14	.04
☐ 4 Derek Wallace	.10	.05	.01
☐ 5 Jorge Fabregas	.10	.05	.01
☐ 6 Joe Oliver	.10	.05	.01
☐ 7 Brandon Wilson	.10	.05	.01
☐ 8 Mark Thompson	.25	.11	.03
☐ 9 Tracy Sanders	.10	.05	.01
☐ 10 Rich Renteria	.10	.05	.01
☐ 11 Lou Whitaker	.20	.09	.03
☐ 12 Brian Hunter	2.00	.90	.25
☐ 13 Joe Vitiello	1.00	.45	.13
☐ 14 Eric Karros	.15	.07	.02
☐ 15 Joe Kmak	.10	.05	.01
☐ 16 Tavo Alvarez	.10	.05	.01
☐ 17 Steve Dunn	.40	.18	.05
☐ 18 Tony Fernandez	.10	.05	.01
☐ 19 Melido Perez	.10	.05	.01
☐ 20 Mike Lieberthal	.10	.05	.01
☐ 21 Terry Steinbach	.15	.07	.02
☐ 22 Stan Belinda	.10	.05	.01
☐ 23 Jay Buhner	.15	.07	.02
☐ 24 Allen Watson	.10	.05	.01
☐ 25 Daryl Henderson	.15	.07	.02
☐ 26 Ray McDavid	.50	.23	.06
☐ 27 Shawn Green	1.50	.65	.19
☐ 28 Bud Black	.10	.05	.01
☐ 29 Sherman Obando	.20	.09	.03
☐ 30 Mike Hostetler	.15	.07	.02
☐ 31 Nate Minchey	.30	.14	.04
☐ 32 Randy Myers	.15	.07	.02
☐ 33 Brian Grebeck	.10	.05	.01
☐ 34 John Roper	.15	.07	.02
☐ 35 Larry Thomas	.15	.07	.02
☐ 36 Alex Cole	.10	.05	.01
☐ 37 Tom Kramer	.10	.05	.01
☐ 38 Matt Whisenant	.10	.05	.01
☐ 39 Chris Gomez	.60	.25	.08
☐ 40 Luis Gonzalez	.15	.07	.02
☐ 41 Kevin Appier	.15	.07	.02
☐ 42 Omar Daal	.10	.05	.01
☐ 43 Duane Singleton	.10	.05	.01
☐ 44 Bill Risley	.10	.05	.01
☐ 45 Pat Meares	.20	.09	.03
☐ 46 Butch Huskey	.10	.05	.01
☐ 47 Bobby Munoz	.10	.05	.01
☐ 48 Juan Bell	.10	.05	.01
☐ 49 Scott Lydy	.20	.09	.03
☐ 50 Dennis Moeller	.10	.05	.01
☐ 51 Marc Newfield	.40	.18	.05
☐ 52 Tripp Cromer	.10	.05	.01
☐ 53 Kurt Miller	.10	.05	.01
☐ 54 Jim Pena	.10	.05	.01
☐ 55 Juan Guzman	.15	.07	.02
☐ 56 Matt Williams	.60	.25	.08
☐ 57 Harold Reynolds	.10	.05	.01
☐ 58 Donnie Elliott	.10	.05	.01
☐ 59 Jon Shave	.10	.05	.01
☐ 60 Kevin Roberson	.10	.05	.01
☐ 61 Hilly Hathaway	.10	.05	.01
☐ 62 Jose Rijo	.15	.07	.02
☐ 63 Kerry Taylor	.25	.11	.03
☐ 64 Ryan Hawblitzel	.10	.05	.01
☐ 65 Glenallen Hill	.10	.05	.01
☐ 66 Ramon Martinez	.15	.07	.02
☐ 67 Travis Fryman	.30	.14	.04
☐ 68 Tom Nevers	.15	.07	.02
☐ 69 Phil Hiatt	.10	.05	.01
☐ 70 Tim Wallach	.10	.05	.01
☐ 71 B.J. Surhoff	.10	.05	.01
☐ 72 Rondell White	.60	.25	.08
☐ 73 Denny Hocking	.40	.18	.05
☐ 74 Mike Oquist	.10	.05	.01
☐ 75 Paul O'Neill	.15	.07	.02
☐ 76 Willie Banks	.10	.05	.01
☐ 77 Bob Welch	.10	.05	.01
☐ 78 Jose Sandoval	.10	.05	.01
☐ 79 Bill Haselman	.10	.05	.01
☐ 80 Rheal Cormier	.10	.05	.01
☐ 81 Dean Palmer	.15	.07	.02
☐ 82 Pat Gomez	.10	.05	.01
☐ 83 Steve Karsay	.25	.11	.03
☐ 84 Carl Hanselman	.10	.05	.01
☐ 85 T.R. Lewis	.20	.09	.03
☐ 86 Chipper Jones	.75	.35	.09

No.	Player			
87	Scott Hatteberg	.10	.05	.01
88	Greg Hibbard	.10	.05	.01
89	Lance Painter	.10	.05	.01
90	Chad Mottola	.30	.14	.04
91	Jason Bere	.75	.35	.09
92	Dante Bichette	.20	.09	.03
93	Sandy Alomar Jr.	.15	.07	.02
94	Carl Everett	.15	.07	.02
95	Danny Bautista	.30	.14	.04
96	Steve Finley	.10	.05	.01
97	David Cone	.20	.09	.03
98	Todd Hollandsworth	1.50	.65	.19
99	Matt Mieske	.15	.07	.02
100	Larry Walker	.20	.09	.03
101	Shane Mack	.15	.07	.02
102	Aaron Ledesma	.15	.07	.02
103	Andy Pettitte	.75	.35	.09
104	Kevin Stocker	.15	.07	.02
105	Mike Mohler	.10	.05	.01
106	Tony Menendez	.10	.05	.01
107	Derek Lowe	.10	.05	.01
108	Basil Shabazz	.10	.05	.01
109	Dan Smith	.10	.05	.01
110	Scott Sanders	.40	.18	.05
111	Todd Stottlemyre	.10	.05	.01
112	Benji Simonton	1.00	.45	.13
113	Rick Sutcliffe	.15	.07	.02
114	Lee Heath	.10	.05	.01
115	Jeff Russell	.10	.05	.01
116	Dave Stevens	.30	.14	.04
117	Mark Holzemer	.10	.05	.01
118	Tim Belcher	.10	.05	.01
119	Bobby Thigpen	.10	.05	.01
120	Roger Bailey	.20	.09	.03
121	Tony Mitchell	.40	.18	.05
122	Junior Felix	.10	.05	.01
123	Rich Robertson	.10	.05	.01
124	Andy Cook	.10	.05	.01
125	Brian Bevil	.25	.11	.03
126	Darryl Strawberry	.15	.07	.02
127	Cal Eldred	.15	.07	.02
128	Cliff Floyd	1.00	.45	.13
129	Alan Newman	.10	.05	.01
130	Howard Johnson	.10	.05	.01
131	Jim Abbott	.20	.09	.03
132	Chad McConnell	.10	.05	.01
133	Miguel Jimenez	.25	.11	.03
134	Brett Backlund	.10	.05	.01
135	John Cummings	.10	.05	.01
136	Brian Barber	.15	.07	.02
137	Rafael Palmeiro	.20	.09	.03
138	Tim Worrell	.10	.05	.01
139	Jose Pett	1.00	.45	.13
140	Barry Bonds	1.25	.55	.16
141	Damon Buford	.10	.05	.01
142	Jeff Blauser	.15	.07	.02
143	Frankie Rodriguez	.25	.11	.03
144	Mike Morgan	.10	.05	.01
145	Gary DiSarcina	.10	.05	.01
146	Calvin Reese	.15	.07	.02
147	Johnny Ruffin	.10	.05	.01
148	David Nied	.20	.09	.03
149	Charles Nagy	.10	.05	.01
150	Mike Myers	.10	.05	.01
151	Kenny Carlyle	.15	.07	.02
152	Eric Anthony	.10	.05	.01
153	Jose Lind	.10	.05	.01
154	Pedro Martinez	.20	.09	.03
155	Mark Kiefer	.10	.05	.01
156	Tim Laker	.10	.05	.01
157	Pat Mahomes	.10	.05	.01
158	Bobby Bonilla	.20	.09	.03
159	Domingo Jean	.10	.05	.01
160	Darren Daulton	.20	.09	.03
161	Mark McGwire	.20	.09	.03
162	Jason Kendall	1.00	.45	.13
163	Desi Relaford	.40	.18	.05
164	Ozzie Canseco	.10	.05	.01
165	Rick Helling	.15	.07	.02
166	Steve Pegues	.10	.05	.01
167	Paul Molitor	.40	.18	.05
168	Larry Carter	.15	.07	.02
169	Arthur Rhodes	.10	.05	.01
170	Damon Hollins	.60	.25	.08
171	Frank Viola	.15	.07	.02
172	Steve Trachsel	1.50	.65	.19
173	J.T. Snow	.20	.09	.03
174	Keith Gordon	.10	.05	.01
175	Carlton Fisk	.20	.09	.03
176	Jason Bates	.30	.14	.04
177	Mike Crosby	.10	.05	.01
178	Benny Santiago	.10	.05	.01
179	Mike Moore	.10	.05	.01
180	Jeff Juden	.10	.05	.01
181	Darren Burton	.10	.05	.01
182	Todd Williams	.20	.09	.03
183	John Jaha	.15	.07	.02
184	Mike Lansing	.30	.14	.04
185	Pedro Grifol	.10	.05	.01
186	Vince Coleman	.10	.05	.01
187	Pat Kelly	.10	.05	.01
188	Clemente Alvarez	.10	.05	.01
189	Ron Darling	.10	.05	.01
190	Orlando Merced	.15	.07	.02
191	Chris Bosio	.10	.05	.01
192	Steve Dixon	.10	.05	.01
193	Doug Dascenzo	.10	.05	.01
194	Ray Holbert	.25	.11	.03
195	Howard Battle	.20	.09	.03
196	Willie McGee	.15	.07	.02
197	John O'Donoghue	.10	.05	.01
198	Steve Avery	.20	.09	.03
199	Greg Blosser	.10	.05	.01
200	Ryne Sandberg	1.00	.45	.13
201	Joe Grahe	.10	.05	.01
202	Dan Wilson	.10	.05	.01
203	Domingo Martinez	.10	.05	.01
204	Andres Galarraga	.20	.09	.03
205	Jamie Taylor	.10	.05	.01
206	Darrell Whitmore	.20	.09	.03
207	Ben Blomdahl	.30	.14	.04
208	Doug Drabek	.20	.09	.03
209	Keith Miller	.10	.05	.01
210	Billy Ashley	.50	.23	.06
211	Mike Farrell	.10	.05	.01
212	John Wetteland	.10	.05	.01
213	Randy Tomlin	.10	.05	.01
214	Sid Fernandez	.10	.05	.01
215	Quilvio Veras	.50	.23	.06
216	Dave Hollins	.20	.09	.03
217	Mike Neill	.10	.05	.01
218	Andy Van Slyke	.20	.09	.03
219	Bret Boone	.20	.09	.03
220	Tom Pagnozzi	.10	.05	.01
221	Mike Welch	.20	.09	.03
222	Frank Seminara	.10	.05	.01
223	Ron Villone	.15	.07	.02
224	D.J. Thielen	.15	.07	.02
225	Cal Ripken	2.00	.90	.25
226	Pedro Borbon Jr.	.10	.05	.01
227	Carlos Quintana	.10	.05	.01
228	Tommy Shields	.15	.07	.02
229	Tim Salmon	.50	.23	.06
230	John Smiley	.10	.05	.01
231	Ellis Burks	.15	.07	.02
232	Pedro Castellano	.10	.05	.01

	No.	Player			
☐	233	Paul Byrd	.10	.05	.01
☐	234	Bryan Harvey	.15	.07	.02
☐	235	Scott Livingstone	.10	.05	.01
☐	236	James Mouton	.75	.35	.09
☐	237	Joe Randa	.15	.07	.02
☐	238	Pedro Astacio	.15	.07	.02
☐	239	Darryl Hamilton	.10	.05	.01
☐	240	Joey Eischen	.30	.14	.04
☐	241	Edgar Herrera	.25	.11	.03
☐	242	Dwight Gooden	.10	.05	.01
☐	243	Sam Militello	.10	.05	.01
☐	244	Ron Blazier	.30	.14	.04
☐	245	Ruben Sierra	.20	.09	.03
☐	246	Al Martin	.15	.07	.02
☐	247	Mike Felder	.10	.05	.01
☐	248	Bob Tewksbury	.10	.05	.01
☐	249	Craig Lefferts	.10	.05	.01
☐	250	Luis Lopez	.40	.18	.05
☐	251	Devon White	.15	.07	.02
☐	252	Will Clark	.40	.18	.05
☐	253	Mark Smith	.15	.07	.02
☐	254	Terry Pendleton	.20	.09	.03
☐	255	Aaron Sele	.50	.23	.06
☐	256	Jose Viera	.15	.07	.02
☐	257	Damion Easley	.15	.07	.02
☐	258	Rod Lofton	.10	.05	.01
☐	259	Chris Snopek	.50	.23	.06
☐	260	Quinton McCracken	.15	.07	.02
☐	261	Mike Matthews	.20	.09	.03
☐	262	Hector Carrasco	.30	.14	.04
☐	263	Rick Greene	.15	.07	.02
☐	264	Chris Holt	.50	.23	.06
☐	265	George Brett	1.25	.55	.16
☐	266	Rick Gorecki	.30	.14	.04
☐	267	Francisco Gamez	.10	.05	.01
☐	268	Marquis Grissom	.20	.09	.03
☐	269	Kevin Tapani UER (Misspelled Tapan on card front)	.10	.05	.01
☐	270	Ryan Thompson	.20	.09	.03
☐	271	Gerald Williams	.10	.05	.01
☐	272	Paul Fletcher	.10	.05	.01
☐	273	Lance Blankenship	.10	.05	.01
☐	274	Marty Neff	.10	.05	.01
☐	275	Shawn Estes	.10	.05	.01
☐	276	Rene Arocha	.20	.09	.03
☐	277	Scott Eyre	.25	.11	.03
☐	278	Phil Plantier	.20	.09	.03
☐	279	Paul Spoljaric	.30	.14	.04
☐	280	Chris Gambs	.10	.05	.01
☐	281	Harold Baines	.15	.07	.02
☐	282	Jose Oliva	.40	.18	.05
☐	283	Matt Whiteside	.10	.05	.01
☐	284	Brant Brown	.40	.18	.05
☐	285	Russ Springer	.10	.05	.01
☐	286	Chris Sabo	.15	.07	.02
☐	287	Ozzie Guillen	.10	.05	.01
☐	288	Marcus Moore	.25	.11	.03
☐	289	Chad Ogea	.30	.14	.04
☐	290	Walt Weiss	.10	.05	.01
☐	291	Brian Edmondson	.10	.05	.01
☐	292	Jimmy Gonzalez	.10	.05	.01
☐	293	Danny Miceli	.30	.14	.04
☐	294	Jose Offerman	.10	.05	.01
☐	295	Greg Vaughn	.15	.07	.02
☐	296	Frank Bolick	.10	.05	.01
☐	297	Mike Maksudian	.10	.05	.01
☐	298	John Franco	.10	.05	.01
☐	299	Danny Tartabull	.15	.07	.02
☐	300	Len Dykstra	.20	.09	.03
☐	301	Bobby Witt	.10	.05	.01
☐	302	Trey Beamon	1.50	.65	.19
☐	303	Tino Martinez	.15	.07	.02
☐	304	Aaron Holbert	.10	.05	.01
☐	305	Juan Gonzalez	1.00	.45	.13
☐	306	Billy Hall	.10	.05	.01
☐	307	Duane Ward	.15	.07	.02
☐	308	Rod Beck	.20	.09	.03
☐	309	Jose Mercedes	.10	.05	.01
☐	310	Otis Nixon	.10	.05	.01
☐	311	Gettys Glaze	.15	.07	.02
☐	312	Candy Maldonado	.10	.05	.01
☐	313	Chad Curtis	.15	.07	.02
☐	314	Tim Costo	.10	.05	.01
☐	315	Mike Robertson	.10	.05	.01
☐	316	Nigel Wilson	.20	.09	.03
☐	317	Greg McMichael	.20	.09	.03
☐	318	Scott Pose	.10	.05	.01
☐	319	Ivan Cruz	.10	.05	.01
☐	320	Greg Swindell	.10	.05	.01
☐	321	Kevin McReynolds	.10	.05	.01
☐	322	Tom Candiotti	.10	.05	.01
☐	323	Rob Wishnevski	.10	.05	.01
☐	324	Ken Hill	.15	.07	.02
☐	325	Kirby Puckett	1.25	.55	.16
☐	326	Tim Bogar	.10	.05	.01
☐	327	Mariano Rivera	.10	.05	.01
☐	328	Mitch Williams	.15	.07	.02
☐	329	Craig Paquette	.10	.05	.01
☐	330	Jay Bell	.15	.07	.02
☐	331	Jose Martinez	.25	.11	.03
☐	332	Rob Deer	.10	.05	.01
☐	333	Brook Fordyce	.10	.05	.01
☐	334	Matt Nokes	.10	.05	.01
☐	335	Derek Lee	.10	.05	.01
☐	336	Paul Ellis	.10	.05	.01
☐	337	Desi Wilson	.10	.05	.01
☐	338	Roberto Alomar	.75	.35	.09
☐	339	Jim Tatum FOIL	.20	.09	.03
☐	340	J.T. Snow FOIL	.20	.09	.03
☐	341	Tim Salmon FOIL	.50	.23	.06
☐	342	Russ Davis FOIL	.50	.23	.06
☐	343	Javy Lopez FOIL	.60	.25	.08
☐	344	Troy O'Leary FOIL	.20	.09	.03
☐	345	Marty Cordova FOIL	1.00	.45	.13
☐	346	Bubba Smith FOIL	.20	.09	.03
☐	347	Chipper Jones FOIL	.75	.35	.09
☐	348	Jessie Hollins FOIL	.20	.09	.03
☐	349	Willie Greene FOIL	.25	.11	.03
☐	350	Mark Thompson FOIL	.25	.11	.03
☐	351	Nigel Wilson FOIL	.30	.14	.04
☐	352	Todd Jones FOIL	.20	.09	.03
☐	353	Raul Mondesi FOIL	2.00	.90	.25
☐	354	Cliff Floyd FOIL	1.00	.45	.13
☐	355	Bobby Jones FOIL	.50	.23	.06
☐	356	Kevin Stocker FOIL	.25	.11	.03
☐	357	Midre Cummings FOIL	1.00	.45	.13
☐	358	Allen Watson FOIL	.20	.09	.03
☐	359	Ray McDavid FOIL	.50	.23	.06
☐	360	Steve Hosey FOIL	.20	.09	.03
☐	361	Brad Pennington FOIL	.20	.09	.03
☐	362	Frankie Rodriguez FOIL	.25	.11	.03
☐	363	Troy Percival FOIL	.20	.09	.03
☐	364	Jason Bere FOIL	.75	.35	.09
☐	365	Manny Ramirez FOIL	1.25	.55	.16
☐	366	Justin Thompson FOIL	.20	.09	.03
☐	367	Joe Vitiello FOIL	1.00	.45	.13
☐	368	Tyrone Hill FOIL	.25	.11	.03
☐	369	David McCarty FOIL	.25	.11	.03
☐	370	Brien Taylor FOIL	.30	.14	.04
☐	371	Todd Van Poppel FOIL	.25	.11	.03
☐	372	Marc Newfield FOIL	.40	.18	.05
☐	373	Terrell Lowery FOIL	.50	.23	.06
☐	374	Alex Gonzalez FOIL	.50	.23	.06
☐	375	Ken Griffey Jr.	3.00	1.35	.40
☐	376	Donovan Osborne	.10	.05	.01

	#	Player			
☐	377	Ritchie Moody	.10	.05	.01
☐	378	Shane Andrews	.25	.11	.03
☐	379	Carlos Delgado	1.00	.45	.13
☐	380	Bill Swift	.15	.07	.02
☐	381	Leo Gomez	.10	.05	.01
☐	382	Ron Gant	.15	.07	.02
☐	383	Scott Fletcher	.10	.05	.01
☐	384	Matt Walbeck	.10	.05	.01
☐	385	Chuck Finley	.10	.05	.01
☐	386	Kevin Mitchell	.15	.07	.02
☐	387	Wilson Alvarez UER (Misspelled Alverez on card front)	.20	.09	.03
☐	388	John Burke	.20	.09	.03
☐	389	Alan Embree	.10	.05	.01
☐	390	Trevor Hoffman	.10	.05	.01
☐	391	Alan Trammell	.20	.09	.03
☐	392	Todd Jones	.10	.05	.01
☐	393	Felix Jose	.10	.05	.01
☐	394	Orel Hershiser	.15	.07	.02
☐	395	Pat Listach	.15	.07	.02
☐	396	Gabe White	.15	.07	.02
☐	397	Dan Serafini	.40	.18	.05
☐	398	Todd Hundley	.10	.05	.01
☐	399	Wade Boggs	.20	.09	.03
☐	400	Tyler Green	.10	.05	.01
☐	401	Mike Bordick	.10	.05	.01
☐	402	Scott Bullett	.10	.05	.01
☐	403	LaGrande Russell	.10	.05	.01
☐	404	Ray Lankford	.20	.09	.03
☐	405	Nolan Ryan	3.00	1.35	.40
☐	406	Robbie Beckett	.10	.05	.01
☐	407	Brent Bowers	.25	.11	.03
☐	408	Adell Davenport	.10	.05	.01
☐	409	Brady Anderson	.15	.07	.02
☐	410	Tom Glavine	.20	.09	.03
☐	411	Doug Hecker	.25	.11	.03
☐	412	Jose Guzman	.10	.05	.01
☐	413	Luis Polonia	.10	.05	.01
☐	414	Brian Williams	.10	.05	.01
☐	415	Bo Jackson	.20	.09	.03
☐	416	Eric Young	.15	.07	.02
☐	417	Kenny Lofton	.75	.35	.09
☐	418	Orestes Destrade	.10	.05	.01
☐	419	Tony Phillips	.10	.05	.01
☐	420	Jeff Bagwell	1.50	.65	.19
☐	421	Mark Gardner	.10	.05	.01
☐	422	Brett Butler	.15	.07	.02
☐	423	Graeme Lloyd	.10	.05	.01
☐	424	Delino DeShields	.15	.07	.02
☐	425	Scott Erickson	.10	.05	.01
☐	426	Jeff Kent	.20	.09	.03
☐	427	Jimmy Key	.15	.07	.02
☐	428	Mickey Morandini	.10	.05	.01
☐	429	Marcos Armas	.10	.05	.01
☐	430	Don Slaught	.10	.05	.01
☐	431	Randy Johnson	.20	.09	.03
☐	432	Omar Olivares	.10	.05	.01
☐	433	Charlie Leibrandt	.10	.05	.01
☐	434	Kurt Stillwell	.10	.05	.01
☐	435	Scott Brow	.10	.05	.01
☐	436	Robby Thompson	.10	.05	.01
☐	437	Ben McDonald	.15	.07	.02
☐	438	Deion Sanders	.50	.23	.06
☐	439	Tony Pena	.10	.05	.01
☐	440	Mark Grace	.20	.09	.03
☐	441	Eduardo Perez	.20	.09	.03
☐	442	Tim Pugh	.10	.05	.01
☐	443	Scott Ruffcorn	.25	.11	.03
☐	444	Jay Gainer	.10	.05	.01
☐	445	Albert Belle	1.00	.45	.13
☐	446	Bret Barberie	.10	.05	.01
☐	447	Justin Mashore	.10	.05	.01
☐	448	Pete Harnisch	.10	.05	.01
☐	449	Greg Gagne	.10	.05	.01
☐	450	Eric Davis	.10	.05	.01
☐	451	Dave Mlicki	.10	.05	.01
☐	452	Moises Alou	.20	.09	.03
☐	453	Rick Aguilera	.15	.07	.02
☐	454	Eddie Murray	.20	.09	.03
☐	455	Bob Wickman	.10	.05	.01
☐	456	Wes Chamberlain	.10	.05	.01
☐	457	Brent Gates	.20	.09	.03
☐	458	Paul Wagner	.10	.05	.01
☐	459	Mike Hampton	.10	.05	.01
☐	460	Ozzie Smith	.50	.23	.06
☐	461	Tom Henke	.15	.07	.02
☐	462	Ricky Gutierrez	.10	.05	.01
☐	463	Jack Morris	.20	.09	.03
☐	464	Joel Chimelis	.15	.07	.02
☐	465	Gregg Olson	.10	.05	.01
☐	466	Javy Lopez	.60	.25	.08
☐	467	Scott Cooper	.15	.07	.02
☐	468	Willie Wilson	.10	.05	.01
☐	469	Mark Langston	.20	.09	.03
☐	470	Barry Larkin	.20	.09	.03
☐	471	Rod Bolton	.10	.05	.01
☐	472	Freddie Benavides	.10	.05	.01
☐	473	Ken Ramos	.10	.05	.01
☐	474	Chuck Carr	.10	.05	.01
☐	475	Cecil Fielder	.25	.11	.03
☐	476	Eddie Taubensee	.10	.05	.01
☐	477	Chris Eddy	.15	.07	.02
☐	478	Greg Hansell	.10	.05	.01
☐	479	Kevin Reimer	.10	.05	.01
☐	480	Denny Martinez	.15	.07	.02
☐	481	Chuck Knoblauch	.20	.09	.03
☐	482	Mike Draper	.10	.05	.01
☐	483	Spike Owen	.10	.05	.01
☐	484	Terry Mulholland	.10	.05	.01
☐	485	Dennis Eckersley	.20	.09	.03
☐	486	Blas Minor	.10	.05	.01
☐	487	Dave Fleming	.15	.07	.02
☐	488	Dan Cholowsky	.10	.05	.01
☐	489	Ivan Rodriguez	.20	.09	.03
☐	490	Gary Sheffield	.20	.09	.03
☐	491	Ed Sprague	.10	.05	.01
☐	492	Steve Hosey	.10	.05	.01
☐	493	Jimmy Haynes	1.00	.45	.13
☐	494	John Smoltz	.15	.07	.02
☐	495	Andre Dawson	.20	.09	.03
☐	496	Rey Sanchez	.10	.05	.01
☐	497	Ty Van Burkleo	.15	.07	.02
☐	498	Bobby Ayala	.35	.16	.04
☐	499	Tim Raines	.20	.09	.03
☐	500	Charlie Hayes	.15	.07	.02
☐	501	Paul Sorrento	.10	.05	.01
☐	502	Richie Lewis	.10	.05	.01
☐	503	Jason Pfaff	.10	.05	.01
☐	504	Ken Caminiti	.15	.07	.02
☐	505	Mike Macfarlane	.10	.05	.01
☐	506	Jody Reed	.10	.05	.01
☐	507	Bobby Hughes	.25	.11	.03
☐	508	Wil Cordero	.20	.09	.03
☐	509	George Tsamis	.10	.05	.01
☐	510	Bret Saberhagen	.15	.07	.02
☐	511	Derek Jeter	3.00	1.35	.40
☐	512	Gene Schall	.50	.23	.06
☐	513	Curtis Shaw	.10	.05	.01
☐	514	Steve Cooke	.10	.05	.01
☐	515	Edgar Martinez	.10	.05	.01
☐	516	Mike Milchin	.10	.05	.01
☐	517	Billy Ripken	.10	.05	.01
☐	518	Andy Benes	.15	.07	.02
☐	519	Juan de la Rosa	.10	.05	.01
☐	520	John Burkett	.15	.07	.02

☐ 521	Alex Ochoa	.30	.14	.04
☐ 522	Tony Tarasco	.40	.18	.05
☐ 523	Luis Ortiz	.15	.07	.02
☐ 524	Rick Wilkins	.10	.05	.01
☐ 525	Chris Turner	.10	.05	.01
☐ 526	Rob Dibble	.10	.05	.01
☐ 527	Jack McDowell	.20	.09	.03
☐ 528	Daryl Boston	.10	.05	.01
☐ 529	Bill Wertz	.10	.05	.01
☐ 530	Charlie Hough	.15	.07	.02
☐ 531	Sean Bergman	.10	.05	.01
☐ 532	Doug Jones	.10	.05	.01
☐ 533	Jeff Montgomery	.15	.07	.02
☐ 534	Roger Cedeno	1.50	.65	.19
☐ 535	Robin Yount	.40	.18	.05
☐ 536	Mo Vaughn	.20	.09	.03
☐ 537	Brian Harper	.10	.05	.01
☐ 538	Juan Castillo	.10	.05	.01
☐ 539	Steve Farr	.10	.05	.01
☐ 540	John Kruk	.20	.09	.03
☐ 541	Troy Neel	.15	.07	.02
☐ 542	Danny Clyburn	1.00	.45	.13
☐ 543	Jim Converse	.15	.07	.02
☐ 544	Gregg Jefferies	.20	.09	.03
☐ 545	Jose Canseco	.50	.23	.06
☐ 546	Julio Bruno	.25	.11	.03
☐ 547	Rob Butler	.15	.07	.02
☐ 548	Royce Clayton	.15	.07	.02
☐ 549	Chris Hoiles	.15	.07	.02
☐ 550	Greg Maddux	.75	.35	.09
☐ 551	Joe Ciccarella	.10	.05	.01
☐ 552	Ozzie Timmons	.30	.14	.04
☐ 553	Chili Davis	.15	.07	.02
☐ 554	Brian Koelling	.10	.05	.01
☐ 555	Frank Thomas	3.00	1.35	.40
☐ 556	Vinny Castilla	.10	.05	.01
☐ 557	Reggie Jefferson	.10	.05	.01
☐ 558	Rob Natal	.10	.05	.01
☐ 559	Mike Henneman	.10	.05	.01
☐ 560	Craig Biggio	.15	.07	.02
☐ 561	Billy Brewer	.15	.07	.02
☐ 562	Dan Melendez	.10	.05	.01
☐ 563	Kenny Felder	.35	.16	.04
☐ 564	Miguel Batista	.25	.11	.03
☐ 565	Dave Winfield	.20	.09	.03
☐ 566	Al Shirley	.10	.05	.01
☐ 567	Robert Eenhoorn	.10	.05	.01
☐ 568	Mike Williams	.10	.05	.01
☐ 569	Tanyon Sturtze	.30	.14	.04
☐ 570	Tim Wakefield	.10	.05	.01
☐ 571	Greg Pirkl	.10	.05	.01
☐ 572	Sean Lowe	.30	.14	.04
☐ 573	Terry Burrows	.10	.05	.01
☐ 574	Kevin Higgins	.15	.07	.02
☐ 575	Joe Carter	.40	.18	.05
☐ 576	Kevin Rogers	.10	.05	.01
☐ 577	Manny Alexander	.10	.05	.01
☐ 578	David Justice	.40	.18	.05
☐ 579	Brian Conroy	.10	.05	.01
☐ 580	Jessie Hollins	.10	.05	.01
☐ 581	Ron Watson	.10	.05	.01
☐ 582	Bip Roberts	.10	.05	.01
☐ 583	Tom Urbani	.10	.05	.01
☐ 584	Jason Hutchins	.10	.05	.01
☐ 585	Carlos Baerga	.40	.18	.05
☐ 586	Jeff Mutis	.10	.05	.01
☐ 587	Justin Thompson	.10	.05	.01
☐ 588	Orlando Miller	.20	.09	.03
☐ 589	Brian McRae	.20	.09	.03
☐ 590	Ramon Martinez	.15	.07	.02
☐ 591	Dave Nilsson	.15	.07	.02
☐ 592	Jose Vidro	.25	.11	.03
☐ 593	Rich Becker	.20	.09	.03
☐ 594	Preston Wilson	.40	.18	.05
☐ 595	Don Mattingly	1.25	.55	.16
☐ 596	Tony Longmire	.10	.05	.01
☐ 597	Kevin Seitzer	.10	.05	.01
☐ 598	Midre Cummings	1.00	.45	.13
☐ 599	Omar Vizquel	.10	.05	.01
☐ 600	Lee Smith	.20	.09	.03
☐ 601	David Hulse	.10	.05	.01
☐ 602	Darrell Sherman	.10	.05	.01
☐ 603	Alex Gonzalez	.50	.23	.06
☐ 604	Geronimo Pena	.10	.05	.01
☐ 605	Mike Devereaux	.15	.07	.02
☐ 606	Sterling Hitchcock	.20	.09	.03
☐ 607	Mike Greenwell	.15	.07	.02
☐ 608	Steve Buechele	.10	.05	.01
☐ 609	Troy Percival	.10	.05	.01
☐ 610	Roberto Kelly	.15	.07	.02
☐ 611	James Baldwin	2.00	.90	.25
☐ 612	Jerald Clark	.10	.05	.01
☐ 613	Albie Lopez	1.00	.45	.13
☐ 614	Dave Magadan	.10	.05	.01
☐ 615	Mickey Tettleton	.15	.07	.02
☐ 616	Sean Runyan	.15	.07	.02
☐ 617	Bob Hamelin	.40	.18	.05
☐ 618	Raul Mondesi	2.00	.90	.25
☐ 619	Tyrone Hill	.15	.07	.02
☐ 620	Darrin Fletcher	.10	.05	.01
☐ 621	Mike Trombley	.10	.05	.01
☐ 622	Jeromy Burnitz	.15	.07	.02
☐ 623	Bernie Williams	.15	.07	.02
☐ 624	Mike Farmer	.10	.05	.01
☐ 625	Rickey Henderson	.20	.09	.03
☐ 626	Carlos Garcia	.15	.07	.02
☐ 627	Jeff Darwin	.15	.07	.02
☐ 628	Todd Zeile	.15	.07	.02
☐ 629	Benji Gil	.15	.07	.02
☐ 630	Tony Gwynn	.75	.35	.09
☐ 631	Aaron Small	.25	.11	.03
☐ 632	Joe Rosselli	.40	.18	.05
☐ 633	Mike Mussina	.60	.25	.08
☐ 634	Ryan Klesko	1.00	.45	.13
☐ 635	Roger Clemens	.75	.35	.09
☐ 636	Sammy Sosa	.20	.09	.03
☐ 637	Orlando Palmeiro	.20	.09	.03
☐ 638	Willie Greene	.15	.07	.02
☐ 639	George Bell	.15	.07	.02
☐ 640	Garvin Alston	.15	.07	.02
☐ 641	Pete Janicki	.10	.05	.01
☐ 642	Chris Sheff	.15	.07	.02
☐ 643	Felipe Lira	.40	.18	.05
☐ 644	Roberto Petagine	.20	.09	.03
☐ 645	Wally Joyner	.15	.07	.02
☐ 646	Mike Piazza	3.00	1.35	.40
☐ 647	Jaime Navarro	.10	.05	.01
☐ 648	Jeff Hartsock	.15	.07	.02
☐ 649	David McCarty	.15	.07	.02
☐ 650	Bobby Jones	.50	.23	.06
☐ 651	Mark Hutton	.10	.05	.01
☐ 652	Kyle Abbott	.10	.05	.01
☐ 653	Steve Cox	.20	.09	.03
☐ 654	Jeff King	.10	.05	.01
☐ 655	Norm Charlton	.10	.05	.01
☐ 656	Mike Gulan	.15	.07	.02
☐ 657	Julio Franco	.15	.07	.02
☐ 658	Cameron Cairncross	.15	.07	.02
☐ 659	John Olerud	.20	.09	.03
☐ 660	Salomon Torres	.15	.07	.02
☐ 661	Brad Pennington	.10	.05	.01
☐ 662	Melvin Nieves	.20	.09	.03
☐ 663	Ivan Calderon	.10	.05	.01
☐ 664	Turk Wendell	.15	.07	.02
☐ 665	Chris Pritchett	.10	.05	.01
☐ 666	Reggie Sanders	.20	.09	.03

	No.	Player	MINT	EXC	G-VG
☐	667	Robin Ventura	.20	.09	.03
☐	668	Joe Girardi	.10	.05	.01
☐	669	Manny Ramirez	1.25	.55	.16
☐	670	Jeff Conine	.20	.09	.03
☐	671	Greg Gohr	.10	.05	.01
☐	672	Andujar Cedeno	.15	.07	.02
☐	673	Les Norman	.10	.05	.01
☐	674	Mike James	.10	.05	.01
☐	675	Marshall Boze	.30	.14	.04
☐	676	B.J. Wallace	.10	.05	.01
☐	677	Kent Hrbek	.15	.07	.02
☐	678	Jack Voigt	.15	.07	.02
☐	679	Brien Taylor	.20	.09	.03
☐	680	Curt Schilling	.15	.07	.02
☐	681	Todd Van Poppel	.15	.07	.02
☐	682	Kevin Young	.10	.05	.01
☐	683	Tommy Adams	.10	.05	.01
☐	684	Bernard Gilkey	.10	.05	.01
☐	685	Kevin Brown	.10	.05	.01
☐	686	Fred McGriff	.40	.18	.05
☐	687	Pat Borders	.10	.05	.01
☐	688	Kirt Manwaring	.10	.05	.01
☐	689	Sid Bream	.10	.05	.01
☐	690	John Valentin	.15	.07	.02
☐	691	Steve Olsen	.20	.09	.03
☐	692	Roberto Mejia	.20	.09	.03
☐	693	Carlos Delgado FOIL	1.00	.45	.13
☐	694	Steve Gibralter FOIL	.40	.18	.05
☐	695	Gary Mota FOIL	.25	.11	.03
☐	696	Jose Malave FOIL	1.25	.55	.16
☐	697	Larry Sutton FOIL	1.25	.55	.16
☐	698	Dan Frye FOIL	.30	.14	.04
☐	699	Tim Clark FOIL	.30	.14	.04
☐	700	Brian Rupp FOIL	.25	.11	.03
☐	701	Felipe Alou FOIL Moises Alou Father and Son	.20	.09	.03
☐	702	Barry Bonds FOIL Bobby Bonds Father and Son	.40	.18	.05
☐	703	Ken Griffey Sr. FOIL Ken Griffey Jr. Father and Son	1.00	.45	.13
☐	704	Brian McRae FOIL Hal McRae Father and Son	.30	.14	.04
☐	705	Checklist 1	.10	.05	.01
☐	706	Checklist 2	.10	.05	.01
☐	707	Checklist 3	.10	.05	.01
☐	708	Checklist 4	.10	.05	.01

1994 Bowman Previews

This 10-card set served as a preview to the 1994 Bowman set. The cards were randomly inserted in Stadium Club second series packs. Card fronts are similar to the full-bleed basic issue. The differences are a multi-colored foil stripe up the left-hand border with a red stripe at bottom. Red foil also surrounds the Bowman logo. In the upper right-hand corner is a blue foil Bowman Preview logo.The backs are identical to the basic issue with a horizontal layout containing a player photo, text and statistics.

	MINT	EXC	G-VG
COMPLETE SET (10)	50.00	23.00	6.25
COMMON CARD (1-10)	1.25	.55	.16

	No.	Player	MINT	EXC	G-VG
☐	1	Frank Thomas	20.00	9.00	2.50
☐	2	Mike Piazza	10.00	4.50	1.25
☐	3	Albert Belle	7.00	3.10	.85
☐	4	Javy Lopez	2.25	1.00	.30
☐	5	Cliff Floyd	3.00	1.35	.40
☐	6	Alex Gonzalez	1.25	.55	.16
☐	7	Ricky Bottalico	1.25	.55	.16
☐	8	Tony Clark	2.50	1.15	.30
☐	9	Mac Suzuki	2.50	1.15	.30
☐	10	James Mouton Foil	1.25	.55	.16

1994 Bowman

The 1994 Bowman set consists of 682 standard-size, full-bleed cards. In addition to a color photo on the front, there is a line of gold foil that runs up the far left side and across the bottom of the card. The player's name is also in gold foil at bottom and the Bowman logo at bottom left is enclosed in gold foil. Horizontal backs contain a player photo on the left and statistics and highlights on the right. There are 51 Foil cards (337-388) that include a number of top young stars and prospects. These foil cards were issued one per foil pack and two per jumbo. Rookie Cards include Brian Anderson, Alan Benes, John Hudek, Jason Jacome, Brooks Kieschnick, Chan Ho Park, Ruben Rivera and Will VanLandingham.

	MINT	EXC	G-VG
COMPLETE SET (682)	110.00	50.00	14.00
COMMON CARD (1-682)	.10	.05	.01

☐ 1 Joe Carter .40 .18 .05
☐ 2 Marcus Moore .10 .05 .01
☐ 3 Doug Creek .10 .05 .01
☐ 4 Pedro Martinez .20 .09 .03
☐ 5 Ken Griffey Jr. 3.00 1.35 .40
☐ 6 Greg Swindell .10 .05 .01
☐ 7 J.J. Johnson .10 .05 .01
☐ 8 Homer Bush .30 .14 .04
☐ 9 Arquimedez Pozo .75 .35 .09
☐ 10 Bryan Harvey .15 .07 .02
☐ 11 J.T. Snow .15 .07 .02
☐ 12 Alan Benes 1.00 .45 .13
☐ 13 Chad Kreuter .10 .05 .01
☐ 14 Eric Karros .15 .07 .02
☐ 15 Frank Thomas 3.00 1.35 .40
☐ 16 Bret Saberhagen .15 .07 .02
☐ 17 Terrell Lowery .20 .09 .03
☐ 18 Rod Bolton .10 .05 .01
☐ 19 Harold Baines .15 .07 .02
☐ 20 Matt Walbeck .10 .05 .01
☐ 21 Tom Glavine .20 .09 .03
☐ 22 Todd Jones .10 .05 .01
☐ 23 Alberto Castillo .10 .05 .01
☐ 24 Ruben Sierra .20 .09 .03
☐ 25 Don Mattingly 1.25 .55 .16
☐ 26 Mike Morgan .10 .05 .01
☐ 27 Jim Musselwhite .50 .23 .06
☐ 28 Matt Brunson .30 .14 .04
☐ 29 Adam Meinershagen .30 .14 .04
☐ 30 Joe Girardi .10 .05 .01
☐ 31 Shane Halter .10 .05 .01
☐ 32 Jose Paniagua .30 .14 .04
☐ 33 Paul Perkins .10 .05 .01
☐ 34 John Hudek .75 .35 .09
☐ 35 Frank Viola .10 .05 .01
☐ 36 David Lamb .25 .11 .03
☐ 37 Marshall Boze .10 .05 .01
☐ 38 Jorge Posada .10 .05 .01
☐ 39 Brian Anderson .75 .35 .09
☐ 40 Mark Whiten .15 .07 .02
☐ 41 Sean Bergman .10 .05 .01
☐ 42 Jose Parra .25 .11 .03
☐ 43 Mike Robertson .10 .05 .01
☐ 44 Pete Walker .10 .05 .01
☐ 45 Juan Gonzalez 1.00 .45 .13
☐ 46 Cleveland Ladell .20 .09 .03
☐ 47 Mark Smith .10 .05 .01
☐ 48 Kevin Jarvis .35 .16 .04
☐ 49 Amaury Telemaco .30 .14 .04
☐ 50 Andy Van Slyke .20 .09 .03
☐ 51 Rikkert Faneyte .10 .05 .01
☐ 52 Curtis Shaw .10 .05 .01
☐ 53 Matt Drews .50 .23 .06
☐ 54 Wilson Alvarez .20 .09 .03
☐ 55 Manny Ramirez .60 .25 .08
☐ 56 Bobby Munoz .10 .05 .01
☐ 57 Ed Sprague .10 .05 .01
☐ 58 Jamey Wright .40 .18 .05
☐ 59 Jeff Montgomery .15 .07 .02
☐ 60 Kirk Rueter .10 .05 .01
☐ 61 Edgar Martinez .10 .05 .01
☐ 62 Luis Gonzalez .10 .05 .01
☐ 63 Tim Vanegmond .10 .05 .01
☐ 64 Bip Roberts .10 .05 .01
☐ 65 John Jaha .10 .05 .01
☐ 66 Chuck Carr .10 .05 .01
☐ 67 Chuck Finley .10 .05 .01
☐ 68 Aaron Holbert .10 .05 .01
☐ 69 Cecil Fielder .20 .09 .03
☐ 70 Tom Engle .10 .05 .01
☐ 71 Ron Karkovice .10 .05 .01
☐ 72 Joe Orsulak .10 .05 .01
☐ 73 Duff Brumley .25 .11 .03
☐ 74 Craig Clayton .10 .05 .01
☐ 75 Cal Ripken 2.00 .90 .25
☐ 76 Brad Fulimer .25 .11 .03
☐ 77 Tony Tarasco .20 .09 .03
☐ 78 Terry Farrar .10 .05 .01
☐ 79 Matt Williams .50 .23 .06
☐ 80 Rickey Henderson .20 .09 .03
☐ 81 Terry Mulholland .10 .05 .01
☐ 82 Sammy Sosa .20 .09 .03
☐ 83 Paul Sorrento .10 .05 .01
☐ 84 Pete Incaviglia .10 .05 .01
☐ 85 Darren Hall .10 .05 .01
☐ 86 Scott Klingenbeck .10 .05 .01
☐ 87 Dario Perez .20 .09 .03
☐ 88 Ugueth Urbina .10 .05 .01
☐ 89 Dave Vanhof .20 .09 .03
☐ 90 Domingo Jean .10 .05 .01
☐ 91 Otis Nixon .10 .05 .01
☐ 92 Andres Berumen .10 .05 .01
☐ 93 Jose Valentin .10 .05 .01
☐ 94 Edgar Renteria .20 .09 .03
☐ 95 Chris Turner .10 .05 .01
☐ 96 Ray Lankford .20 .09 .03
☐ 97 Danny Bautista .15 .07 .02
☐ 98 Chan Ho Park 1.25 .55 .16
☐ 99 Glenn DiSarcina .15 .07 .02
☐ 100 Butch Huskey .10 .05 .01
☐ 101 Ivan Rodriguez .20 .09 .03
☐ 102 Johnny Ruffin .10 .05 .01
☐ 103 Alex Ochoa .20 .09 .03
☐ 104 Torii Hunter .30 .14 .04
☐ 105 Ryan Klesko .50 .23 .06
☐ 106 Jay Bell .15 .07 .02
☐ 107 Kurt Peltzer .10 .05 .01
☐ 108 Miguel Jimenez .15 .07 .02
☐ 109 Russ Davis .10 .05 .01
☐ 110 Derek Wallace .10 .05 .01
☐ 111 Keith Lockhart .10 .05 .01
☐ 112 Mike Lieberthal .10 .05 .01
☐ 113 Dave Stewart .15 .07 .02
☐ 114 Tom Schmidt .10 .05 .01
☐ 115 Brian McRae .15 .07 .02
☐ 116 Moises Alou .20 .09 .03
☐ 117 Dave Fleming .10 .05 .01
☐ 118 Jeff Bagwell 1.50 .65 .19
☐ 119 Luis Ortiz .10 .05 .01
☐ 120 Tony Gwynn .75 .35 .09
☐ 121 Jaime Navarro .10 .05 .01
☐ 122 Benny Santiago .10 .05 .01
☐ 123 Darrell Whitmore .15 .07 .02
☐ 124 John Mabry .40 .18 .05
☐ 125 Mickey Tettleton .15 .07 .02
☐ 126 Tom Candiotti .10 .05 .01
☐ 127 Tim Raines .20 .09 .03
☐ 128 Bobby Bonilla .20 .09 .03
☐ 129 John Dettmer .10 .05 .01
☐ 130 Hector Carrasco .10 .05 .01
☐ 131 Chris Hoiles .15 .07 .02
☐ 132 Rick Aguilera .15 .07 .02
☐ 133 David Justice .40 .18 .05
☐ 134 Esteban Loaiza .25 .11 .03
☐ 135 Barry Bonds 1.25 .55 .16
☐ 136 Bob Welch .10 .05 .01
☐ 137 Mike Stanley .10 .05 .01
☐ 138 Roberto Hernandez .10 .05 .01
☐ 139 Sandy Alomar .15 .07 .02
☐ 140 Darren Daulton .20 .09 .03
☐ 141 Angel Martinez .30 .14 .04
☐ 142 Howard Johnson .10 .05 .01
☐ 143 Bob Hamelin .20 .09 .03
☐ 144 J.J. Thobe .20 .09 .03
☐ 145 Roger Salkeld .10 .05 .01
☐ 146 Orlando Miller .15 .07 .02

□ 147 Dmitri Young .... .10 .05 .01
□ 148 Tim Hyers .... .20 .09 .03
□ 149 Mark Loretta .... .20 .09 .03
□ 150 Chris Hammond .... .10 .05 .01
□ 151 Joel Moore .... .25 .11 .03
□ 152 Todd Zeile .... .15 .07 .02
□ 153 Wil Cordero .... .20 .09 .03
□ 154 Chris Smith .... .10 .05 .01
□ 155 James Baldwin .... .50 .23 .06
□ 156 Edgardo Alfonzo .... .75 .35 .09
□ 157 Kym Ashworth .... .40 .18 .05
□ 158 Paul Bako .... .30 .14 .04
□ 159 Rick Krivda .... .30 .14 .04
□ 160 Pat Mahomes .... .10 .05 .01
□ 161 Damon Hollins .... .10 .05 .01
□ 162 Felix Martinez .... .25 .11 .03
□ 163 Jason Myers .... .50 .23 .06
□ 164 Izzy Molina .... .25 .11 .03
□ 165 Brien Taylor .... .20 .09 .03
□ 166 Kevin Orie .... .25 .11 .03
□ 167 Casey Whitten .... .30 .14 .04
□ 168 Tony Longmire .... .10 .05 .01
□ 169 John Olerud .... .20 .09 .03
□ 170 Mark Thompson .... .15 .07 .02
□ 171 Jorge Fabregas .... .10 .05 .01
□ 172 John Wetteland .... .10 .05 .01
□ 173 Dan Wilson .... .10 .05 .01
□ 174 Doug Drabek .... .20 .09 .03
□ 175 Jeffrey McNeely .... .10 .05 .01
□ 176 Melvin Nieves .... .20 .09 .03
□ 177 Doug Glanville .... .30 .14 .04
□ 178 Javier De La Hoya .... .15 .07 .02
□ 179 Chad Curtis .... .15 .07 .02
□ 180 Brian Barber .... .15 .07 .02
□ 181 Mike Henneman .... .10 .05 .01
□ 182 Jose Offerman .... .10 .05 .01
□ 183 Robert Ellis .... .20 .09 .03
□ 184 John Franco .... .10 .05 .01
□ 185 Benji Gil .... .15 .07 .02
□ 186 Hal Morris .... .15 .07 .02
□ 187 Chris Sabo .... .10 .05 .01
□ 188 Blaise Ilsley .... .10 .05 .01
□ 189 Steve Avery .... .20 .09 .03
□ 190 Rick White .... .10 .05 .01
□ 191 Rod Beck .... .15 .07 .02
□ 192 Mark McGwire UER .... .20 .09 .03
(No card number on back)
□ 193 Jim Abbott .... .20 .09 .03
□ 194 Randy Myers .... .10 .05 .01
□ 195 Kenny Lofton .... .75 .35 .09
□ 196 Mariano Duncan .... .10 .05 .01
□ 197 Lee Daniels .... .15 .07 .02
□ 198 Armando Reynoso .... .10 .05 .01
□ 199 Joe Randa .... .15 .07 .02
□ 200 Cliff Floyd .... .50 .23 .06
□ 201 Tim Harkrider .... .15 .07 .02
□ 202 Kevin Gallaher .... .10 .05 .01
□ 203 Scott Cooper .... .15 .07 .02
□ 204 Phil Stidham .... .10 .05 .01
□ 205 Jeff D'Amico .... .30 .14 .04
□ 206 Matt Whisenant .... .10 .05 .01
□ 207 De Shawn Warren .... .10 .05 .01
□ 208 Rene Arocha .... .15 .07 .02
□ 209 Tony Clark .... .75 .35 .09
□ 210 Jason Jacome .... 1.00 .45 .13
□ 211 Scott Christman .... .30 .14 .04
□ 212 Bill Pulsipher .... .60 .25 .08
□ 213 Dean Palmer .... .15 .07 .02
□ 214 Chad Mottola .... .15 .07 .02
□ 215 Manny Alexander .... .10 .05 .01
□ 216 Rich Becker .... .15 .07 .02
□ 217 Andre King .... .30 .14 .04
□ 218 Carlos Garcia .... .10 .05 .01
□ 219 Ron Pezzoni .... .10 .05 .01
□ 220 Steve Karsay .... .10 .05 .01
□ 221 Jose Musset .... .10 .05 .01
□ 222 Karl Rhodes .... .10 .05 .01
□ 223 Frank Cimorelli .... .10 .05 .01
□ 224 Kevin Jordan .... .40 .18 .05
□ 225 Duane Ward .... .10 .05 .01
□ 226 John Burke .... .15 .07 .02
□ 227 Mike Macfarlane .... .10 .05 .01
□ 228 Mike Lansing .... .15 .07 .02
□ 229 Chuck Knoblauch .... .20 .09 .03
□ 230 Ken Caminiti .... .15 .07 .02
□ 231 Gar Finnvold .... .10 .05 .01
□ 232 Derrek Lee .... .75 .35 .09
□ 233 Brady Anderson .... .15 .07 .02
□ 234 Vic Darensbourg .... .25 .11 .03
□ 235 Mark Langston .... .20 .09 .03
□ 236 T.J. Mathews .... .25 .11 .03
□ 237 Lou Whitaker .... .20 .09 .03
□ 238 Roger Cedeno .... .40 .18 .05
□ 239 Alex Fernandez .... .20 .09 .03
□ 240 Ryan Thompson .... .15 .07 .02
□ 241 Kerry Lacy .... .10 .05 .01
□ 242 Reggie Sanders .... .15 .07 .02
□ 243 Brad Pennington .... .10 .05 .01
□ 244 Bryan Eversgerd .... .10 .05 .01
□ 245 Greg Maddux .... .60 .25 .08
□ 246 Jason Kendall .... .20 .09 .03
□ 247 J.R. Phillips .... .20 .09 .03
□ 248 Bobby Witt .... .10 .05 .01
□ 249 Paul O'Neill .... .15 .07 .02
□ 250 Ryne Sandberg .... 1.00 .45 .13
□ 251 Charles Nagy .... .10 .05 .01
□ 252 Kevin Stocker .... .15 .07 .02
□ 253 Shawn Green .... .50 .23 .06
□ 254 Charlie Hayes .... .15 .07 .02
□ 255 Donnie Elliott .... .10 .05 .01
□ 256 Rob Fitzpatrick .... .10 .05 .01
□ 257 Tim Davis .... .10 .05 .01
□ 258 James Mouton .... .15 .07 .02
□ 259 Mike Greenwell .... .15 .07 .02
□ 260 Ray McDavid .... .10 .05 .01
□ 261 Mike Kelly .... .15 .07 .02
□ 262 Andy Larkin .... .75 .35 .09
□ 263 Marquis Riley UER .... .10 .05 .01
(No card number on back)
□ 264 Bob Tewksbury .... .10 .05 .01
□ 265 Brian Edmondson .... .10 .05 .01
□ 266 Eduardo Lantigua .... .20 .09 .03
□ 267 Brandon Wilson .... .10 .05 .01
□ 268 Mike Welch .... .10 .05 .01
□ 269 Tom Henke .... .10 .05 .01
□ 270 Calvin Reese .... .15 .07 .02
□ 271 Greg Zaun .... .20 .09 .03
□ 272 Todd Ritchie .... .10 .05 .01
□ 273 Javy Lopez .... .30 .14 .04
□ 274 Kevin Young .... .10 .05 .01
□ 275 Kirt Manwaring .... .10 .05 .01
□ 276 Bill Taylor .... .10 .05 .01
□ 277 Robert Eenhoorn .... .10 .05 .01
□ 278 Jessie Hollins .... .10 .05 .01
□ 279 Julian Tavarez .... .60 .25 .08
□ 280 Gene Schall .... .15 .07 .02
□ 281 Paul Molitor .... .40 .18 .05
□ 282 Neifi Perez .... .25 .11 .03
□ 283 Greg Gagne .... .10 .05 .01
□ 284 Marquis Grissom .... .20 .09 .03
□ 285 Randy Johnson .... .20 .09 .03
□ 286 Pete Harnisch .... .10 .05 .01
□ 287 Joel Bennett .... .30 .14 .04
□ 288 Derek Bell .... .15 .07 .02
□ 289 Darryl Hamilton .... .10 .05 .01
□ 290 Gary Sheffield .... .20 .09 .03

☐ 291 Eduardo Perez .15 .07 .02
☐ 292 Basil Shabazz .10 .05 .01
☐ 293 Eric Davis .10 .05 .01
☐ 294 Pedro Astacio .15 .07 .02
☐ 295 Robin Ventura .15 .07 .02
☐ 296 Jeff Kent .15 .07 .02
☐ 297 Rick Helling .10 .05 .01
☐ 298 Joe Oliver .10 .05 .01
☐ 299 Lee Smith .20 .09 .03
☐ 300 Dave Winfield .20 .09 .03
☐ 301 Deion Sanders .50 .23 .06
☐ 302 Ravelo Manzanillo .10 .05 .01
☐ 303 Mark Portugal .10 .05 .01
☐ 304 Brent Gates .20 .09 .03
☐ 305 Wade Boggs .20 .09 .03
☐ 306 Rick Wilkins .10 .05 .01
☐ 307 Carlos Baerga .40 .18 .05
☐ 308 Curt Schilling .10 .05 .01
☐ 309 Shannon Stewart .10 .05 .01
☐ 310 Darren Holmes .10 .05 .01
☐ 311 Robert Toth .25 .11 .03
☐ 312 Gabe White .10 .05 .01
☐ 313 Mac Suzuki .75 .35 .09
☐ 314 Alvin Morman .20 .09 .03
☐ 315 Mo Vaughn .20 .09 .03
☐ 316 Bryce Florie .10 .05 .01
☐ 317 Gabby Martinez .25 .11 .03
☐ 318 Carl Everett .15 .07 .02
☐ 319 Kerwin Moore .10 .05 .01
☐ 320 Tom Pagnozzi .10 .05 .01
☐ 321 Chris Gomez .20 .09 .03
☐ 322 Todd Williams .10 .05 .01
☐ 323 Pat Hentgen .15 .07 .02
☐ 324 Kirk Presley .75 .35 .09
☐ 325 Kevin Brown .10 .05 .01
☐ 326 Jason Isringhausen .60 .25 .08
☐ 327 Rick Forney .40 .18 .05
☐ 328 Carlos Pulido .15 .07 .02
☐ 329 Terrell Wade .75 .35 .09
☐ 330 Al Martin .10 .05 .01
☐ 331 Dan Carlson .25 .11 .03
☐ 332 Mark Acre .20 .09 .03
☐ 333 Sterling Hitchcock .15 .07 .02
☐ 334 Jon Ratliff .25 .11 .03
☐ 335 Alex Ramirez .50 .23 .06
☐ 336 Phil Geisler .30 .14 .04
☐ 337 Eddie Zambrano FOIL .10 .05 .01
☐ 338 Jim Thome FOIL .20 .09 .03
☐ 339 James Mouton FOIL .20 .09 .03
☐ 340 Cliff Floyd FOIL .50 .23 .06
☐ 341 Carlos Delgado FOIL .50 .23 .06
☐ 342 Roberto Petagine FOIL .15 .07 .02
☐ 343 Tim Clark FOIL .10 .05 .01
☐ 344 Bubba Smith FOIL .10 .05 .01
☐ 345 Randy Curtis FOIL .30 .14 .04
☐ 346 Joe Biasucci FOIL .20 .09 .03
☐ 347 D.J. Boston FOIL .20 .09 .03
☐ 348 Ruben Rivera FOIL 2.50 1.15 .30
☐ 349 Bryan Link FOIL .25 .11 .03
☐ 350 Mike Bell FOIL .40 .18 .05
☐ 351 Marty Watson FOIL .20 .09 .03
☐ 352 Jason Myers FOIL .50 .23 .06
☐ 353 Chipper Jones FOIL .40 .18 .05
☐ 354 Brooks Kieschnick FOIL 1.00 .45 .13
☐ 355 Calvin Reese FOIL .15 .07 .02
☐ 356 John Burke FOIL .15 .07 .02
☐ 357 Kurt Miller FOIL .10 .05 .01
☐ 358 Orlando Miller FOIL .15 .07 .02
☐ 359 Todd Hollandsworth FOIL .60 .25 .08
☐ 360 Rondell White FOIL .30 .14 .04
☐ 361 Bill Pulsipher FOIL .60 .25 .08
☐ 362 Tyler Green FOIL .10 .05 .01
☐ 363 Midre Cummings FOIL .25 .11 .03
☐ 364 Brian Barber FOIL .15 .07 .02
☐ 365 Melvin Nieves FOIL .20 .09 .03
☐ 366 Salomon Torres FOIL .15 .07 .02
☐ 367 Alex Ochoa FOIL .20 .09 .03
☐ 368 Frankie Rodriguez FOIL .20 .09 .03
☐ 369 Brian Anderson FOIL .75 .35 .09
☐ 370 James Baldwin FOIL .50 .23 .06
☐ 371 Manny Ramirez FOIL .60 .25 .08
☐ 372 Justin Thompson FOIL .10 .05 .01
☐ 373 Johnny Damon FOIL .40 .18 .05
☐ 374 Jeff D'Amico FOIL .30 .14 .04
☐ 375 Rich Becker FOIL .15 .07 .02
☐ 376 Derek Jeter FOIL .75 .35 .09
☐ 377 Steve Karsay FOIL .10 .05 .01
☐ 378 Mac Suzuki FOIL .75 .35 .09
☐ 379 Benji Gil FOIL .15 .07 .02
☐ 380 Alex Gonzalez FOIL .30 .14 .04
☐ 381 Jason Bere FOIL .40 .18 .05
☐ 382 Brett Butler FOIL .15 .07 .02
☐ 383 Jeff Conine FOIL .20 .09 .03
☐ 384 Darren Daulton FOIL .20 .09 .03
☐ 385 Jeff Kent FOIL .15 .07 .02
☐ 386 Don Mattingly FOIL 1.25 .55 .16
☐ 387 Mike Piazza FOIL 1.50 .65 .19
☐ 388 Ryne Sandberg FOIL 1.00 .45 .13
☐ 389 Rich Amaral .10 .05 .01
☐ 390 Craig Biggio .15 .07 .02
☐ 391 Jeff Suppan .60 .25 .08
☐ 392 Andy Benes .15 .07 .02
☐ 393 Cal Eldred .15 .07 .02
☐ 394 Jeff Conine .20 .09 .03
☐ 395 Tim Salmon .40 .18 .05
☐ 396 Ray Suplee .20 .09 .03
☐ 397 Tony Phillips .10 .05 .01
☐ 398 Ramon Martinez .15 .07 .02
☐ 399 Julio Franco .15 .07 .02
☐ 400 Dwight Gooden .10 .05 .01
☐ 401 Kevin Lomon .25 .11 .03
☐ 402 Jose Rijo .15 .07 .02
☐ 403 Mike Devereaux .15 .07 .02
☐ 404 Mike Zolecki .20 .09 .03
☐ 405 Fred McGriff .40 .18 .05
☐ 406 Danny Clyburn .30 .14 .04
☐ 407 Robby Thompson .10 .05 .01
☐ 408 Terry Steinbach .15 .07 .02
☐ 409 Luis Polonia .10 .05 .01
☐ 410 Mark Grace .20 .09 .03
☐ 411 Albert Belle .90 .40 .11
☐ 412 John Kruk .20 .09 .03
☐ 413 Scott Spiezio .40 .18 .05
☐ 414 Ellis Burks UER .15 .07 .02
(Name spelled Elkis on front)
☐ 415 Joe Vitiello .15 .07 .02
☐ 416 Tim Costo .10 .05 .01
☐ 417 Marc Newfield .20 .09 .03
☐ 418 Oscar Henriquez .30 .14 .04
☐ 419 Matt Perisho .25 .11 .03
☐ 420 Julio Bruno .10 .05 .01
☐ 421 Kenny Felder .20 .09 .03
☐ 422 Tyler Green .10 .05 .01
☐ 423 Jim Edmonds .10 .05 .01
☐ 424 Ozzie Smith .60 .25 .08
☐ 425 Rick Greene .15 .07 .02
☐ 426 Todd Hollandsworth .60 .25 .08
☐ 427 Eddie Pearson .50 .23 .06
☐ 428 Quilvio Veras .15 .07 .02
☐ 429 Kenny Rogers .10 .05 .01
☐ 430 Willie Greene .15 .07 .02
☐ 431 Vaughn Eshelman .10 .05 .01
☐ 432 Pat Meares .10 .05 .01
☐ 433 Jermaine Dye .75 .35 .09
☐ 434 Steve Cooke .10 .05 .01
☐ 435 Bill Swift .10 .05 .01

	No.	Player			
☐	436	Fausto Cruz	.25	.11	.03
☐	437	Mark Hutton	.10	.05	.01
☐	438	Brooks Kieschnick	1.00	.45	.13
☐	439	Yorkis Perez	.10	.05	.01
☐	440	Len Dykstra	.20	.09	.03
☐	441	Pat Borders	.10	.05	.01
☐	442	Doug Walls	.25	.11	.03
☐	443	Wally Joyner	.15	.07	.02
☐	444	Ken Hill	.15	.07	.02
☐	445	Eric Anthony	.10	.05	.01
☐	446	Mitch Williams	.10	.05	.01
☐	447	Cory Bailey	.20	.09	.03
☐	448	Dave Staton	.10	.05	.01
☐	449	Greg Vaughn	.15	.07	.02
☐	450	Dave Magadan	.10	.05	.01
☐	451	Chili Davis	.15	.07	.02
☐	452	Gerald Santos	.10	.05	.01
☐	453	Joe Perona	.10	.05	.01
☐	454	Delino DeShields	.15	.07	.02
☐	455	Jack McDowell	.20	.09	.03
☐	456	Todd Hundley	.10	.05	.01
☐	457	Ritchie Moody	.10	.05	.01
☐	458	Bret Boone	.20	.09	.03
☐	459	Ben McDonald	.15	.07	.02
☐	460	Kirby Puckett	1.25	.55	.16
☐	461	Gregg Olson	.10	.05	.01
☐	462	Rich Aude	.30	.14	.04
☐	463	John Burkett	.15	.07	.02
☐	464	Troy Neel	.15	.07	.02
☐	465	Jimmy Key	.15	.07	.02
☐	466	Ozzie Timmons	.15	.07	.02
☐	467	Eddie Murray	.20	.09	.03
☐	468	Mark Tranberg	.10	.05	.01
☐	469	Alex Gonzalez	.25	.11	.03
☐	470	David Nied	.20	.09	.03
☐	471	Barry Larkin	.20	.09	.03
☐	472	Brian Looney	.25	.11	.03
☐	473	Shawn Estes	.10	.05	.01
☐	474	A.J. Sager	.10	.05	.01
☐	475	Roger Clemens	.75	.35	.09
☐	476	Vince Moore	.10	.05	.01
☐	477	Scott Karl	.30	.14	.04
☐	478	Kurt Miller	.10	.05	.01
☐	479	Garret Anderson	.15	.07	.02
☐	480	Allen Watson	.10	.05	.01
☐	481	Jose Lima	.40	.18	.05
☐	482	Rick Gorecki	.10	.05	.01
☐	483	Jimmy Hurst	.75	.35	.09
☐	484	Preston Wilson	.10	.05	.01
☐	485	Will Clark	.40	.18	.05
☐	486	Mike Ferry	.20	.09	.03
☐	487	Curtis Goodwin	.30	.14	.04
☐	488	Mike Myers	.10	.05	.01
☐	489	Chipper Jones	.40	.18	.05
☐	490	Jeff King	.10	.05	.01
☐	491	Will VanLandingham	1.00	.45	.13
☐	492	Carlos Reyes	.10	.05	.01
☐	493	Andy Pettitte	.10	.05	.01
☐	494	Brant Brown	.10	.05	.01
☐	495	Daron Kirkreit	.10	.05	.01
☐	496	Ricky Bottalico	.30	.14	.04
☐	497	Devon White	.10	.05	.01
☐	498	Jason Johnson	.20	.09	.03
☐	499	Vince Coleman	.10	.05	.01
☐	500	Larry Walker	.20	.09	.03
☐	501	Bobby Ayala	.10	.05	.01
☐	502	Steve Finley	.10	.05	.01
☐	503	Scott Fletcher	.10	.05	.01
☐	504	Brad Ausmus	.10	.05	.01
☐	505	Scott Talanoa	.50	.23	.06
☐	506	Orestes Destrade	.10	.05	.01
☐	507	Gary DiSarcina	.10	.05	.01
☐	508	Willie Smith	.20	.09	.03

	No.	Player			
☐	509	Alan Trammell	.20	.09	.03
☐	510	Mike Piazza	1.50	.65	.19
☐	511	Ozzie Guillen	.10	.05	.01
☐	512	Jeromy Burnitz	.15	.07	.02
☐	513	Darren Oliver	.10	.05	.01
☐	514	Kevin Mitchell	.15	.07	.02
☐	515	Rafael Palmeiro	.20	.09	.03
☐	516	David McCarty	.15	.07	.02
☐	517	Jeff Blauser	.15	.07	.02
☐	518	Trey Beamon	.40	.18	.05
☐	519	Royce Clayton	.15	.07	.02
☐	520	Dennis Eckersley	.20	.09	.03
☐	521	Bernie Williams	.15	.07	.02
☐	522	Steve Buechele	.10	.05	.01
☐	523	Denny Martinez	.15	.07	.02
☐	524	Dave Hollins	.20	.09	.03
☐	525	Joey Hamilton	.75	.35	.09
☐	526	Andres Galarraga	.20	.09	.03
☐	527	Jeff Granger	.15	.07	.02
☐	528	Joey Eischen	.15	.07	.02
☐	529	Desi Relaford	.15	.07	.02
☐	530	Roberto Petagine	.15	.07	.02
☐	531	Andre Dawson	.20	.09	.03
☐	532	Ray Holbert	.10	.05	.01
☐	533	Duane Singleton	.10	.05	.01
☐	534	Kurt Abbott	.30	.14	.04
☐	535	Bo Jackson	.20	.09	.03
☐	536	Gregg Jefferies	.20	.09	.03
☐	537	David Mysel	.10	.05	.01
☐	538	Raul Mondesi	1.00	.45	.13
☐	539	Chris Snopek	.10	.05	.01
☐	540	Brook Fordyce	.10	.05	.01
☐	541	Ron Frazier	.15	.07	.02
☐	542	Brian Koelling	.10	.05	.01
☐	543	Jimmy Haynes	.10	.05	.01
☐	544	Marty Cordova	.15	.07	.02
☐	545	Jason Green	.25	.11	.03
☐	546	Orlando Merced	.15	.07	.02
☐	547	Lou Pote	.20	.09	.03
☐	548	Todd Van Poppel	.15	.07	.02
☐	549	Pat Kelly	.10	.05	.01
☐	550	Turk Wendell	.10	.05	.01
☐	551	Herb Perry	.25	.11	.03
☐	552	Ryan Karp	.25	.11	.03
☐	553	Juan Guzman	.15	.07	.02
☐	554	Bryan Rekar	.25	.11	.03
☐	555	Kevin Appier	.15	.07	.02
☐	556	Chris Schwab	.30	.14	.04
☐	557	Jay Buhner	.15	.07	.02
☐	558	Andujar Cedeno	.10	.05	.01
☐	559	Ryan McGuire	.50	.23	.06
☐	560	Ricky Gutierrez	.10	.05	.01
☐	561	Keith Kimsey	.30	.14	.04
☐	562	Tim Clark	.10	.05	.01
☐	563	Damion Easley	.10	.05	.01
☐	564	Clint Davis	.10	.05	.01
☐	565	Mike Moore	.10	.05	.01
☐	566	Orel Hershiser	.15	.07	.02
☐	567	Jason Bere	.40	.18	.05
☐	568	Kevin McReynolds	.10	.05	.01
☐	569	Leland Macon	.25	.11	.03
☐	570	John Courtright	.20	.09	.03
☐	571	Sid Fernandez	.10	.05	.01
☐	572	Chad Roper	.10	.05	.01
☐	573	Terry Pendleton	.10	.05	.01
☐	574	Danny Miceli	.10	.05	.01
☐	575	Joe Rosselli	.10	.05	.01
☐	576	Mike Bordick	.10	.05	.01
☐	577	Danny Tartabull	.15	.07	.02
☐	578	Jose Guzman	.10	.05	.01
☐	579	Omar Vizquel	.10	.05	.01
☐	580	Tommy Greene	.10	.05	.01
☐	581	Paul Spoljaric	.10	.05	.01

	No.	Player	MINT	EXC	G-VG
☐	582	Walt Weiss	.10	.05	.01
☐	583	Oscar Jimenez	.25	.11	.03
☐	584	Rod Henderson	.15	.07	.02
☐	585	Derek Lowe	.10	.05	.01
☐	586	Richard Hidalgo	.75	.35	.09
☐	587	Shayne Bennett	.10	.05	.01
☐	588	Tim Belk	.25	.11	.03
☐	589	Matt Mieske	.10	.05	.01
☐	590	Nigel Wilson	.15	.07	.02
☐	591	Jeff Knox	.25	.11	.03
☐	592	Bernard Gilkey	.10	.05	.01
☐	593	David Cone	.20	.09	.03
☐	594	Paul LoDuca	.30	.14	.04
☐	595	Scott Ruffcorn	.20	.09	.03
☐	596	Chris Roberts	.10	.05	.01
☐	597	Oscar Munoz	.10	.05	.01
☐	598	Scott Sullivan	.40	.18	.05
☐	599	Matt Jarvis	.25	.11	.03
☐	600	Jose Canseco	.40	.18	.05
☐	601	Tony Graffanino	.40	.18	.05
☐	602	Don Slaught	.10	.05	.01
☐	603	Brett King	.30	.14	.04
☐	604	Jose Herrera	.60	.25	.08
☐	605	Melido Perez	.10	.05	.01
☐	606	Mike Hubbard	.20	.09	.03
☐	607	Chad Ogea	.15	.07	.02
☐	608	Wayne Gomes	.25	.11	.03
☐	609	Roberto Alomar	.75	.35	.09
☐	610	Angel Echevarria	.20	.09	.03
☐	611	Jose Lind	.10	.05	.01
☐	612	Darrin Fletcher	.10	.05	.01
☐	613	Chris Bosio	.10	.05	.01
☐	614	Darryl Kile	.15	.07	.02
☐	615	Frankie Rodriguez	.20	.09	.03
☐	616	Phil Plantier	.15	.07	.02
☐	617	Pat Listach	.10	.05	.01
☐	618	Charlie Hough	.15	.07	.02
☐	619	Ryan Hancock	.30	.14	.04
☐	620	Darrel Deak	.30	.14	.04
☐	621	Travis Fryman	.20	.09	.03
☐	622	Brett Butler	.15	.07	.02
☐	623	Lance Johnson	.10	.05	.01
☐	624	Pete Smith	.10	.05	.01
☐	625	James Hurst	.10	.05	.01
☐	626	Roberto Kelly	.10	.05	.01
☐	627	Mike Mussina	.40	.18	.05
☐	628	Kevin Tapani	.10	.05	.01
☐	629	John Smoltz	.15	.07	.02
☐	630	Midre Cummings	.25	.11	.03
☐	631	Salomon Torres	.15	.07	.02
☐	632	Willie Adams	.10	.05	.01
☐	633	Derek Jeter	.75	.35	.09
☐	634	Steve Trachsel	.40	.18	.05
☐	635	Albie Lopez	.20	.09	.03
☐	636	Jason Moler	.10	.05	.01
☐	637	Carlos Delgado	.50	.23	.06
☐	638	Roberto Mejia	.15	.07	.02
☐	639	Darren Burton	.10	.05	.01
☐	640	B.J. Wallace	.10	.05	.01
☐	641	Brad Clontz	.60	.25	.08
☐	642	Billy Wagner	.60	.25	.08
☐	643	Aaron Sele	.35	.16	.04
☐	644	Cameron Cairncross	.10	.05	.01
☐	645	Brian Harper	.10	.05	.01
☐	646	Marc Valdes UER (No card number on back)	.30	.14	.04
☐	647	Mark Ratekin	.10	.05	.01
☐	648	Terry Bradshaw	.35	.16	.04
☐	649	Justin Thompson	.10	.05	.01
☐	650	Mike Busch	.25	.11	.03
☐	651	Joe Hall	.10	.05	.01
☐	652	Bobby Jones	.20	.09	.03
☐	653	Kelly Stinnett	.10	.05	.01
☐	654	Rod Steph	.25	.11	.03
☐	655	Jay Powell	.30	.14	.04
☐	656	Keith Garagozzo UER (No card number on back)	.20	.09	.03
☐	657	Todd Dunn	.10	.05	.01
☐	658	Charles Peterson	.40	.18	.05
☐	659	Darren Lewis	.10	.05	.01
☐	660	John Wasdin	.60	.25	.08
☐	661	Tate Seefried	.50	.23	.06
☐	662	Hector Trinidad	.30	.14	.04
☐	663	John Carter	.20	.09	.03
☐	664	Larry Mitchell	.10	.05	.01
☐	665	David Catlett	.30	.14	.04
☐	666	Dante Bichette	.20	.09	.03
☐	667	Felix Jose	.10	.05	.01
☐	668	Rondell White	.35	.16	.04
☐	669	Tino Martinez	.10	.05	.01
☐	670	Brian Hunter	.50	.23	.06
☐	671	Jose Malave	.30	.14	.04
☐	672	Archi Cianfrocco	.10	.05	.01
☐	673	Mike Matheny	.10	.05	.01
☐	674	Bret Barberie	.10	.05	.01
☐	675	Andrew Lorraine	.75	.35	.09
☐	676	Brian Jordan	.15	.07	.02
☐	677	Tim Belcher	.10	.05	.01
☐	678	Antonio Osuna	.25	.11	.03
☐	679	Checklist 1-184	.10	.05	.01
☐	680	Checklist 185-352	.10	.05	.01
☐	681	Checklist 353-498	.10	.05	.01
☐	682	Checklist 499-682	.10	.05	.01

1994 Bowman's Best

This 200-card standard-size set consists of 90 veteran stars, 90 rookies and prospects and 20 Mirror Image cards. The veteran cards have red backs and are designated 1R-90R. The rookies and prospects cards have blue backs and are designated 1B-90B. The Mirror Image cards feature a veteran star and a prospect matched by position. These cards are numbered 91-110. Subsets featured are Super Vet (1R-6R), Super Rookie (82R-90R), and Blue Chip (1B-11B). Rookie Cards include Brooks Kieschnick and Chan Ho Park.

	MINT	EXC	G-VG
COMPLETE SET (200)	110.00	50.00	14.00
COMMON BLUE CARD (1B-90B)	.50	.23	.06
COMMON RED CARD (1R-90R)	.50	.23	.06
COMMON MIR. IMG. (91-110)	1.00	.45	.13

	No.	Player	MINT	EXC	G-VG
☐	1B	Chipper Jones	1.25	.55	.16
☐	1R	Paul Molitor	1.50	.65	.19

☐	2B	Derek Jeter	2.50	1.15	.30
☐	2R	Eddie Murray	.75	.35	.09
☐	3B	Bill Pulsipher	2.00	.90	.25
☐	3R	Ozzie Smith	2.00	.90	.25
☐	4B	James Baldwin	2.00	.90	.25
☐	4R	Rickey Henderson	.75	.35	.09
☐	5B	Brooks Kieschnick	3.50	1.55	.45
☐	5R	Lee Smith	.75	.35	.09
☐	6B	Justin Thompson	.50	.23	.06
☐	6R	Dave Winfield	.75	.35	.09
☐	7B	Midre Cummings	1.00	.45	.13
☐	7R	Roberto Alomar	2.50	1.15	.30
☐	8B	Joey Hamilton	2.00	.90	.25
☐	8R	Matt Williams	2.00	.90	.25
☐	9B	Calvin Reese	.60	.25	.08
☐	9R	Mark Grace	.75	.35	.09
☐	10B	Brian Barber	.60	.25	.08
☐	10R	Lance Johnson	.50	.23	.06
☐	11B	John Burke	.60	.25	.08
☐	11R	Darren Daulton	.75	.35	.09
☐	12B	De Shawn Warren	.50	.23	.06
☐	12R	Tom Glavine	.75	.35	.09
☐	13B	Edgardo Alfonzo	2.50	1.15	.30
☐	13R	Gary Sheffield	.75	.35	.09
☐	14B	Eddie Pearson	1.75	.80	.22
☐	14R	Rod Beck	.60	.25	.08
☐	15B	Jimmy Haynes	.50	.23	.06
☐	15R	Fred McGriff	1.50	.65	.19
☐	16B	Danny Bautista	.60	.25	.08
☐	16R	Joe Carter	1.50	.65	.19
☐	17B	Roger Cedeno	1.25	.55	.16
☐	17R	Dante Bichette	.75	.35	.09
☐	18B	Jon Lieber	.75	.35	.09
☐	18R	Danny Tartabull	.60	.25	.08
☐	19B	Billy Wagner	2.00	.90	.25
☐	19R	Juan Gonzalez	3.50	1.55	.45
☐	20B	Tate Seefried	1.75	.80	.22
☐	20R	Steve Avery	.75	.35	.09
☐	21B	Chad Mottola	.50	.23	.06
☐	21R	John Wetteland	.50	.23	.06
☐	22B	Jose Malave	1.00	.45	.13
☐	22R	Ben McDonald	.60	.25	.08
☐	23B	Terrell Wade	2.50	1.15	.30
☐	23R	Jack McDowell	.75	.35	.09
☐	24B	Shane Andrews	.60	.25	.08
☐	24R	Jose Canseco	1.50	.65	.19
☐	25B	Chan Ho Park	4.00	1.80	.50
☐	25R	Tim Salmon	1.50	.65	.19
☐	26B	Kirk Presley	2.50	1.15	.30
☐	26R	Wilson Alvarez	.75	.35	.09
☐	27B	Robbie Beckett	.50	.23	.06
☐	27R	Gregg Jefferies	.75	.35	.09
☐	28B	Orlando Miller	.60	.25	.08
☐	28R	John Burkett	.60	.25	.08
☐	29B	Jorge Posada	.50	.23	.06
☐	29R	Greg Vaughn	.60	.25	.08
☐	30B	Frankie Rodriguez	.75	.35	.09
☐	30R	Robin Ventura	.60	.25	.08
☐	31B	Brian Hunter	1.75	.80	.22
☐	31R	Paul O'Neill	.60	.25	.08
☐	32B	Billy Ashley	1.25	.55	.16
☐	32R	Cecil Fielder	.75	.35	.09
☐	33B	Rondell White	1.00	.45	.13
☐	33R	Kevin Mitchell	.60	.25	.08
☐	34B	John Roper	.60	.25	.08
☐	34R	Jeff Conine	.75	.35	.09
☐	35B	Marc Valdes	.50	.23	.06
☐	35R	Carlos Baerga	1.50	.65	.19
☐	36B	Scott Ruffcorn	.75	.35	.09
☐	36R	Greg Maddux	2.50	1.15	.30
☐	37B	Rod Henderson	.50	.23	.06
☐	37R	Roger Clemens	2.50	1.15	.30
☐	38B	Curtis Goodwin	1.00	.45	.13
☐	38R	Deion Sanders	2.00	.90	.25
☐	39B	Russ Davis	1.25	.55	.16
☐	39R	Delino DeShields	.60	.25	.08
☐	40B	Rick Gorecki	.50	.23	.06
☐	40R	Ken Griffey Jr.	10.00	4.50	1.25
☐	41B	Johnny Damon	1.25	.55	.16
☐	41R	Albert Belle	3.50	1.55	.45
☐	42B	Roberto Petagine	.60	.25	.08
☐	42R	Wade Boggs	.75	.35	.09
☐	43B	Chris Snopek	.50	.23	.06
☐	43R	Andres Galarraga	.75	.35	.09
☐	44B	Mark Acre	.75	.35	.09
☐	44R	Aaron Sele	1.00	.45	.13
☐	45B	Todd Hollandsworth	2.00	.90	.25
☐	45R	Don Mattingly	4.00	1.80	.50
☐	46B	Shawn Green	2.00	.90	.25
☐	46R	David Cone	.75	.35	.09
☐	47B	John Carter	.75	.35	.09
☐	47R	Len Dykstra	.75	.35	.09
☐	48B	Jim Pittsley	1.00	.45	.13
☐	48R	Brett Butler	.60	.25	.08
☐	49B	John Wasdin	2.00	.90	.25
☐	49R	Bill Swift	.50	.23	.06
☐	50B	D.J. Boston	.75	.35	.09
☐	50R	Bobby Bonilla	.75	.35	.09
☐	51B	Tim Clark	.50	.23	.06
☐	51R	Rafael Palmeiro	.75	.35	.09
☐	52B	Alex Ochoa	.75	.35	.09
☐	52R	Moises Alou	.75	.35	.09
☐	53B	Chad Roper	.50	.23	.06
☐	53R	Jeff Bagwell	5.00	2.30	.60
☐	54B	Mike Kelly	.60	.25	.08
☐	54R	Mike Mussina	1.50	.65	.19
☐	55B	Brad Fullmer	.75	.35	.09
☐	55R	Frank Thomas	10.00	4.50	1.25
☐	56B	Carl Everett	.60	.25	.08
☐	56R	Jose Rijo	.60	.25	.08
☐	57B	Tim Belk	.75	.35	.09
☐	57R	Ruben Sierra	.75	.35	.09
☐	58B	Jimmy Hurst	2.50	1.15	.30
☐	58R	Randy Myers	.50	.23	.06
☐	59B	Mac Suzuki	2.50	1.15	.30
☐	59R	Barry Bonds	4.00	1.80	.50
☐	60B	Michael Moore	.50	.23	.06
☐	60R	Jimmy Key	.60	.25	.08
☐	61B	Alan Benes	3.50	1.55	.45
☐	61R	Travis Fryman	.75	.35	.09
☐	62B	Tony Clark	2.50	1.15	.30
☐	62R	John Olerud	.75	.35	.09
☐	63B	Edgar Renteria	.75	.35	.09
☐	63R	David Justice	1.50	.65	.19
☐	64B	Trey Beamon	1.25	.55	.16
☐	64R	Ray Lankford	.75	.35	.09
☐	65B	LaTroy Hawkins	2.50	1.15	.30
☐	65R	Bob Tewksbury	.50	.23	.06
☐	66B	Wayne Gomes	.75	.35	.09
☐	66R	Chuck Carr	.50	.23	.06
☐	67B	Ray McDavid	.50	.23	.06
☐	67R	Jay Buhner	.60	.25	.08
☐	68B	John Dettmer	.50	.23	.06
☐	68R	Kenny Lofton	3.00	1.35	.40
☐	69B	Willie Greene	.60	.25	.08
☐	69R	Marquis Grissom	.75	.35	.09
☐	70B	Dave Stevens	.50	.23	.06
☐	70R	Sammy Sosa	.75	.35	.09
☐	71B	Kevin Orie	.75	.35	.09
☐	71R	Cal Ripken	7.50	3.40	.95
☐	72B	Chad Ogea	.60	.25	.08
☐	72R	Ellis Burks	.60	.25	.08
☐	73B	Ben Van Ryn	.75	.35	.09
☐	73R	Jeff Montgomery	.60	.25	.08
☐	74B	Kym Ashworth	1.25	.55	.16
☐	74R	Julio Franco	.60	.25	.08

□ 75B Dmitri Young	.50	.23	.06
□ 75R Kirby Puckett	4.00	1.80	.50
□ 76B Herb Perry	.75	.35	.09
□ 76R Larry Walker	.75	.35	.09
□ 77B Joey Eischen	.60	.25	.08
□ 77R Andy Van Slyke	.75	.35	.09
□ 78B Arquimedez Pozo	2.50	1.15	.30
□ 78R Tony Gwynn	3.00	1.35	.40
□ 79B Ugueth Urbina	.50	.23	.06
□ 79R Will Clark	1.75	.80	.22
□ 80B Keith Williams	1.75	.80	.22
□ 80R Mo Vaughn	.75	.35	.09
□ 81B John Frascatore	.75	.35	.09
□ 81R Mike Piazza	5.00	2.30	.60
□ 82B Garey Ingram	.75	.35	.09
□ 82R James Mouton	.75	.35	.09
□ 83B Aaron Small	.50	.23	.06
□ 83R Carlos Delgado	2.00	.90	.25
□ 84B Olmedo Saenz	.75	.35	.09
□ 84R Ryan Klesko	1.50	.65	.19
□ 85B Jesus Tavarez	.75	.35	.09
□ 85R Javy Lopez	1.25	.55	.16
□ 86B Jose Silva	2.50	1.15	.30
□ 86R Raul Mondesi	3.50	1.55	.45
□ 87B Gerald Witasick Jr.	1.00	.45	.13
□ 87R Cliff Floyd	2.00	.90	.25
□ 88B Jay Maldonado	.75	.35	.09
□ 88R Manny Ramirez	2.50	1.15	.30
□ 89B Keith Heberling	1.25	.55	.16
□ 89R Hector Carrasco	.50	.23	.06
□ 90B Rusty Greer	2.00	.90	.25
□ 90R Jeff Granger	.60	.25	.08
□ 91 Frank Thomas Dmitri Young	5.00	2.30	.60
□ 92 Fred McGriff Brooks Kieschnick	1.75	.80	.22
□ 93 Matt Williams Shane Andrews	1.25	.55	.16
□ 94 Cal Ripken Kevin Orie	3.50	1.55	.45
□ 95 Barry Larkin Derek Jeter	1.25	.55	.16
□ 96 Ken Griffey Jr. Johnny Damon	7.00	3.10	.85
□ 97 Barry Bonds Rondell White	2.00	.90	.25
□ 98 Albert Belle Jimmy Hurst	1.50	.65	.19
□ 99 Raul Mondesi Ruben Rivera	6.00	2.70	.75
□ 100 Roger Clemens Scott Ruffcorn	1.50	.65	.19
□ 101 Greg Maddux John Wasdin	1.50	.65	.19
□ 102 Tim Salmon Chad Mottola	1.00	.45	.13
□ 103 Carlos Baerga Arquimedez Pozo	1.50	.65	.19
□ 104 Mike Piazza Bobby Hughes	2.50	1.15	.30
□ 105 Carlos Delgado Melvin Nieves	1.25	.55	.16
□ 106 Javy Lopez Jorge Posada	1.00	.45	.13
□ 107 Manny Ramirez Jose Malave	1.50	.65	.19
□ 108 Travis Fryman Chipper Jones	1.25	.55	.16
□ 109 Steve Avery Bill Pulsipher	1.25	.55	.16
□ 110 John Olerud Shawn Green	1.00	.45	.13

1994 Bowman's Best Refractors

This 200-card set is a parallel to the basic Bowman's Best issue. The cards were randomly inserted in packs at a rate of one in nine Bowman's Best packs. The only difference is the refractive finish that allows for a more glossy appearance. The cards are numbered with an "R" suffix.

	MINT	EXC	G-VG
COMPLETE SET (200)	1200.00	550.00	150.00
COMMON CARD	3.00	1.35	.40

*UNLISTED RED STARS: 8X to 15X VALUE
*MIRROR IMAGE STARS: 6X to 10X VALUE
*UNLISTED BLUE STARS: 4X to 8X VALUE

□ 40R Ken Griffey Jr.	125.00	57.50	15.50
□ 45R Don Mattingly	50.00	23.00	6.25
□ 53R Jeff Bagwell	60.00	27.00	7.50
□ 55R Frank Thomas	125.00	57.50	15.50
□ 59R Barry Bonds	50.00	23.00	6.25
□ 71R Cal Ripken	90.00	40.00	11.50
□ 75R Kirby Puckett	50.00	23.00	6.25
□ 81R Mike Piazza	60.00	27.00	7.50

1990 Classic Draft

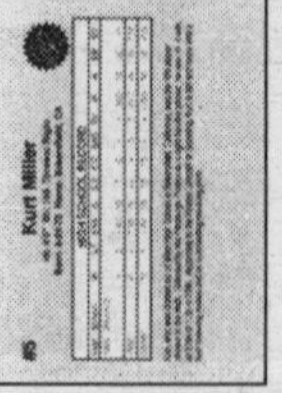

The 1990 Classic Draft Pick set is a standard-size (2 1/2" by 3 1/2"), 26-card set honoring the number one (first round) draft picks of 1990. According to the producer, the printing on this set was limited to 150,000 of each card. This was the first

Classic set that was not a game set or trivia set. Card numbers 2 and 22 were not issued.

	MINT	EXC	G-VG
COMPLETE SET (26)	12.00	5.50	1.50
COMMON CARD (1-26)	.10	.05	.01
□ 1 Chipper Jones	2.50	1.15	.30
□ 2 Not issued	.00	.00	.00
□ 3 Mike Lieberthal	.20	.09	.03
□ 4 Alex Fernandez	1.75	.80	.22
□ 5 Kurt Miller	.20	.09	.03
□ 6 Marc Newfield UER	1.75	.80	.22
□ 7 Dan Wilson	.20	.09	.03
□ 8 Tim Costo	.10	.05	.01
□ 9 Ron Walden	.10	.05	.01
□ 10 Carl Everett UER (Misspelled Evertt on card front)	.50	.23	.06
□ 11 Shane Andrews	.40	.18	.05
□ 12 Todd Ritchie	.20	.09	.03
□ 13 Donovan Osborne	.20	.09	.03
□ 14 Todd Van Poppel	.60	.25	.08
□ 15 Adam Hyzdu	.20	.09	.03
□ 16 Dan Smith	.10	.05	.01
□ 17 Jeromy Burnitz	.50	.23	.06
□ 18 Aaron Holbert	.20	.09	.03
□ 19 Eric Christopherson	.10	.05	.01
□ 20 Mike Mussina	3.00	1.35	.40
□ 21 Tom Nevers	.10	.05	.01
□ 22 Not issued	.00	.00	.00
□ 23 Lance Dickson	.10	.05	.01
□ 24 Rondell White	2.50	1.15	.30
□ 25 Robbie Beckett	.20	.09	.03
□ 26 Don Peters	.10	.05	.01
□ NNO Future Stars HOR Chipper Jones Rondell White (Checklist on back)	1.50	.65	.19

1991 Classic Draft

The premier edition of the 1991 Classic Draft Picks set contains 50 standard size (2 1/2" by 3 1/2") cards, plus a bonus card featuring Frankie Rodriguez. The production run was distributed between 330,000 hobby sets, 165,000 non-hobby sets, and 1,500 test sets. Each set includes a certificate of limited edition with a unique set number. The fronts display glossy color player photos, with maroon borders and a gray card face. The draft pick number, player's name, and position appear in the maroon border at the bottom of the picture. The horizontally oriented backs have biography and maroon border stripes intersecting at the upper corner. Also high school or college statistics and player profile are printed over a washed-out picture of a batter and catcher at home plate. The cards are numbered on the back. This set includes Brien Taylor, the first pick of the '91 draft. The Frankie Rodriguez bonus card was only included in hobby sets. Cards were checklisted by Classic based on draft order.

	MINT	EXC	G-VG
COMPLETE SET (50)	4.00	1.80	.50
COMMON CARD (1-50)	.05	.02	.01
□ 1 Brien Taylor	.25	.11	.03
□ 2 Mike Kelly	.50	.23	.06
□ 3 David McCarty	.25	.11	.03
□ 4 Dmitri Young	.30	.14	.04
□ 5 Joe Vitiello	.40	.18	.05
□ 6 Mark Smith	.10	.05	.01
□ 7 Tyler Green	.10	.05	.01
□ 8 Shawn Estes	.10	.05	.01
□ 9 Doug Glanville	.10	.05	.01
□ 10 Manny Ramirez	1.75	.80	.22
□ 11 Cliff Floyd	1.50	.65	.19
□ 12 Tyrone Hill	.10	.05	.01
□ 13 Eduardo Perez	.10	.05	.01
□ 14 Al Shirley	.10	.05	.01
□ 15 Benji Gil	.30	.14	.04
□ 16 Calvin Reese	.30	.14	.04
□ 17 Allen Watson	.10	.05	.01
□ 18 Brian Barber	.10	.05	.01
□ 19 Aaron Sele	.75	.35	.09
□ 20 Jon Farrell UER (Misspelled John)	.05	.02	.01
□ 21 Scott Ruffcorn	.50	.23	.06
□ 22 Brent Gates	.50	.23	.06
□ 23 Scott Stahoviak	.10	.05	.01
□ 24 Tom McKinnon	.05	.02	.01
□ 25 Shawn Livsey	.05	.02	.01
□ 26 Jason Pruitt	.05	.02	.01
□ 27 Greg Anthony	.05	.02	.01
□ 28 Justin Thompson	.10	.05	.01
□ 29 Steve Whitaker	.10	.05	.01
□ 30 Jorge Fabregas	.10	.05	.01
□ 31 Jeff Ware	.05	.02	.01
□ 32 Bobby Jones	.75	.35	.09
□ 33 J.J. Johnson	.10	.05	.01
□ 34 Mike Rossiter	.05	.02	.01
□ 35 Dan Cholowsky	.05	.02	.01
□ 36 Jimmy Gonzalez	.05	.02	.01
□ 37 Trever Miller UER (Misspelled Trevor)	.05	.02	.01
□ 38 Scott Hatteberg	.05	.02	.01
□ 39 Mike Groppuso	.05	.02	.01
□ 40 Ryan Long	.10	.05	.01
□ 41 Eddie Williams	.05	.02	.01
□ 42 Mike Durant	.05	.02	.01
□ 43 Buck McNabb	.05	.02	.01
□ 44 Jimmy Lewis	.05	.02	.01
□ 45 Eddie Ramos	.05	.02	.01
□ 46 Terry Horn	.05	.02	.01
□ 47 Jon Barnes	.05	.02	.01
□ 48 Shawn Curran	.05	.02	.01
□ 49 Tommy Adams	.05	.02	.01
□ 50 Trevor Mallory	.05	.02	.01
□ NNO Frankie Rodriguez Bonus card	.50	.23	.06

1992 Classic Draft Previews

These five baseball draft preview cards were inserted into Classic basketball draft pick foil packs and measure the standard size (2 1/2" by 3 1/2"). According to the backs, only 11,200 of each card were produced. The fronts display glossy color action player photos with white borders. The player's name appears in a teal stripe beneath the picture. This stripe intersects the Classic logo at the lower left corner, and the word "Preview" wraps around the top of the logo. The brightly colored backs display a drawing of a batter clad in a red-and-purple uniform with a stadium in the background. This picture is accented by two series of short purple diagonal stripes on the left and right. The picture is overprinted with silver foil lettering. The cards are numbered on the back.

	MINT	EXC	G-VG
COMPLETE SET (5)	32.00	14.50	4.00
COMMON CARD (BB1-BB5)	4.00	1.80	.50
☐ BB1 Phil Nevin	6.00	2.70	.75
☐ BB2 Paul Shuey	5.00	2.30	.60
☐ BB3 B.J. Wallace	4.00	1.80	.50
☐ BB4 Jeffrey Hammonds	18.00	8.00	2.30
☐ BB5 Chad Mottola	6.00	2.70	.75

1992 Classic Draft

The 1992 Classic Draft Picks set consists of 125 standard-size (2 1/2" by 3 1/2") cards. The set was sold in 16-card jumbo packs only to the hobby and periodical industries. The production run was reported to be 5,000 individually number cases, and no factory sets were produced. The fronts display color action player photos bordered in white. The player's name appears in a forest green stripe beneath the picture, and his position is printed in a small black bar. On a forest green background with white lettering, the backs present 1991 and 1992 college (and/or high school) statistics, player profile, and biography on the upper portion and a second color player photo on the lower portion. A ten-card flashback subset (cards 86-95) features Mike Mussina, Brien Taylor, and Mike Kelly. The cards are numbered on the back.

	MINT	EXC	G-VG
COMPLETE SET (125)	8.00	3.60	1.00
COMMON CARD (1-125)	.05	.02	.01
☐ 1 Phil Nevin	.30	.14	.04
☐ 2 Paul Shuey	.25	.11	.03
☐ 3 B.J. Wallace	.20	.09	.03
☐ 4 Jeffrey Hammonds	1.25	.55	.16
☐ 5 Chad Mottola	.30	.14	.04
☐ 6 Derek Jeter	1.25	.55	.16
☐ 7 Michael Tucker	.60	.25	.08
☐ 8 Derek Wallace	.05	.02	.01
☐ 9 Kenny Felder	.10	.05	.01
☐ 10 Chad McConnell	.10	.05	.01
☐ 11 Sean Lowe	.10	.05	.01
☐ 12 Ricky Greene	.05	.02	.01
☐ 13 Chris Roberts	.30	.14	.04
☐ 14 Shannon Stewart	.30	.14	.04
☐ 15 Benji Grigsby	.05	.02	.01
☐ 16 Jamie Arnold	.10	.05	.01
☐ 17 Rick Helling	.10	.05	.01
☐ 18 Jason Kendall	.50	.23	.06
☐ 19 Todd Steverson	.10	.05	.01
☐ 20 Dan Serafini	.10	.05	.01
☐ 21 Jeff Schmidt	.05	.02	.01
☐ 22 Sherard Clinkscales	.10	.05	.01
☐ 23 Ryan Luzinski	.05	.02	.01
☐ 24 Shon Walker	.10	.05	.01
☐ 25 Brandon Cromer	.10	.05	.01
☐ 26 Dave Landaker	.05	.02	.01
☐ 27 Michael Mathews	.10	.05	.01
☐ 28 Brian Sackinsky	.10	.05	.01
☐ 29 Jon Lieber	.50	.23	.06
☐ 30 Jim Rosenbohm	.05	.02	.01
☐ 31 DeShawn Warren	.10	.05	.01
☐ 32 Danny Clyburn	.50	.23	.06
☐ 33 Chris Smith	.10	.05	.01
☐ 34 Dwain Bostic	.05	.02	.01
☐ 35 Bobby Hughes	.10	.05	.01
☐ 36 Rick Magdellano	.10	.05	.01
☐ 37 Bob Wolcott	.10	.05	.01
☐ 38 Mike Gulan	.10	.05	.01
☐ 39 Yuri Sanchez	.05	.02	.01
☐ 40 Tony Sheffield	.10	.05	.01
☐ 41 Dan Melendez	.05	.02	.01
☐ 42 Jason Giambi	.10	.05	.01
☐ 43 Ritchie Moody	.05	.02	.01
☐ 44 Trey Beamon	.75	.35	.09
☐ 45 Tim Crabtree	.05	.02	.01
☐ 46 Chad Roper	.05	.02	.01
☐ 47 Mark Thompson	.10	.05	.01
☐ 48 Marquis Riley	.10	.05	.01
☐ 49 Tom Knauss	.05	.02	.01
☐ 50 Chris Holt	.10	.05	.01

☐ 51 Jonathan Nunnally	.10	.05	.01
☐ 52 Everett Stull	.10	.05	.01
☐ 53 Billy Owens	.25	.11	.03
☐ 54 Todd Etler	.10	.05	.01
☐ 55 Benji Simonton	.50	.23	.06
☐ 56 Dwight Maness	.05	.02	.01
☐ 57 Chris Eddy	.05	.02	.01
☐ 58 Brant Brown	.10	.05	.01
☐ 59 Trevor Humphry	.05	.02	.01
☐ 60 Chris Widger	.05	.02	.01
☐ 61 Steve Montgomery	.05	.02	.01
☐ 62 Chris Gomez	.50	.23	.06
☐ 63 Jared Baker	.05	.02	.01
☐ 64 Doug Hecker	.10	.05	.01
☐ 65 David Spykstra	.05	.02	.01
☐ 66 Scott Miller	.05	.02	.01
☐ 67 Carey Paige	.05	.02	.01
☐ 68 Dave Manning	.05	.02	.01
☐ 69 James Keith	.05	.02	.01
☐ 70 Levon Largusa	.05	.02	.01
☐ 71 Roger Bailey	.05	.02	.01
☐ 72 Rich Ireland	.05	.02	.01
☐ 73 Matt Williams	.05	.02	.01
☐ 74 Scott Gentile	.10	.05	.01
☐ 75 Hut Smith	.05	.02	.01
☐ 76 Rodney Henderson	.25	.11	.03
☐ 77 Mike Buddie	.05	.02	.01
☐ 78 Stephen Lyons	.05	.02	.01
☐ 79 John Burke	.05	.02	.01
☐ 80 Jim Pittsley	.30	.14	.04
☐ 81 Donnie Leshnock	.05	.02	.01
☐ 82 Cory Pearson	.05	.02	.01
☐ 83 Kurt Ehmann	.05	.02	.01
☐ 84 Bobby Bonds Jr.	.05	.02	.01
☐ 85 Steven Cox	.05	.02	.01
☐ 86 Brien Taylor FLB	.10	.05	.01
☐ 87 Mike Kelly FLB	.10	.05	.01
☐ 88 David McCarty FLB	.05	.02	.01
☐ 89 Dmitri Young FLB	.10	.05	.01
☐ 90 Joey Hamilton FLB	.10	.05	.01
☐ 91 Mark Smith FLB	.05	.02	.01
☐ 92 Doug Glanville FLB	.05	.02	.01
☐ 93 Mike Lieberthal FLB	.05	.02	.01
☐ 94 Joe Vitiello FLB	.10	.05	.01
☐ 95 Mike Mussina FLB	.40	.18	.05
☐ 96 Derek Hacopian	.05	.02	.01
☐ 97 Ted Corbin	.05	.02	.01
☐ 98 Carlton Fleming	.05	.02	.01
☐ 99 Aaron Rounsifer	.05	.02	.01
☐ 100 Chad Fox	.05	.02	.01
☐ 101 Chris Sheff	.05	.02	.01
☐ 102 Ben Jones	.05	.02	.01
☐ 103 David Post	.05	.02	.01
☐ 104 Jonnie Gendron	.05	.02	.01
☐ 105 Bob Juday	.05	.02	.01
☐ 106 David Becker	.05	.02	.01
☐ 107 Brandon Pico	.05	.02	.01
☐ 108 Tom Evans	.10	.05	.01
☐ 109 Jeff Faino	.05	.02	.01
☐ 110 Shawn Wills	.05	.02	.01
☐ 111 Derrick Cantrell	.05	.02	.01
☐ 112 Steve Rodriguez	.05	.02	.01
☐ 113 Ray Suplee	.05	.02	.01
☐ 114 Pat Leahy	.05	.02	.01
☐ 115 Matt Luke	.50	.23	.06
☐ 116 Jon McMullen	.05	.02	.01
☐ 117 Preston Wilson	.30	.14	.04
☐ 118 Gus Gandarillas	.05	.02	.01
☐ 119 Pete Janicki	.05	.02	.01
☐ 120 Byron Mathews	.05	.02	.01
☐ 121 Eric Owens	.05	.02	.01
☐ 122 John Lynch	.05	.02	.01
☐ 123 Mike Hickey	.05	.02	.01
☐ 124 Checklist 1	.05	.02	.01
☐ 125 Checklist 2	.05	.02	.01

1992 Classic Draft Foil Bonus

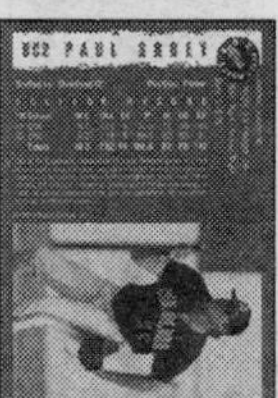

One of these twenty foil bonus cards was inserted in each 1992 Classic Draft Picks jumbo pack. The cards measure the standard size (2 1/2" by 3 1/2"). The photos and text of these bonus cards are identical to the regular issues, except that a silver foil coating has created a metallic sheen on the front, and the forest green backs have a faded look. A three-card flashback subset (cards BC18-BC20) features Brien Taylor, Mike Kelly, and Mike Mussina. The cards are numbered on the back.

	MINT	EXC	G-VG
COMPLETE SET (20)	8.00	3.60	1.00
COMMON CARD (BC1-BC20)	.20	.09	.03
☐ BC1 Phil Nevin	.50	.23	.06
☐ BC2 Paul Shuey	.40	.18	.05
☐ BC3 B.J. Wallace	.30	.14	.04
☐ BC4 Jeffrey Hammonds	2.00	.90	.25
☐ BC5 Chad Mottola	.50	.23	.06
☐ BC6 Derek Jeter	2.00	.90	.25
☐ BC7 Michael Tucker	.90	.40	.11
☐ BC8 Derek Wallace	.20	.09	.03
☐ BC9 Kenny Felder	.30	.14	.04
☐ BC10 Chad McConnell	.30	.14	.04
☐ BC11 Sean Lowe	.30	.14	.04
☐ BC12 Chris Roberts	.50	.23	.06
☐ BC13 Shannon Stewart	.50	.23	.06
☐ BC14 Benji Grisby	.20	.09	.03
☐ BC15 Jamie Arnold	.30	.14	.04
☐ BC16 Ryan Luzinski	.20	.09	.03
☐ BC17 Bobby Bonds Jr.	.20	.09	.03
☐ BC18 Brien Taylor (Flashback)	.30	.14	.04
☐ BC19 Mike Kelly (Flashback)	.30	.14	.04
☐ BC20 Mike Mussina (Flashback)	1.00	.45	.13

1994 Collector's Choice

Issued by Upper Deck, this 670 standard-size card set was issued in two series of

320 and 350. Factory sets contain five Gold Signature cards for a total of 675 cards. Card fronts feature color player action photos with white borders that are highlighted by vertical gray pinstripes. The player's name and team appear in white lettering at the bottom of the picture. The player's position appears within a black oval beneath an action player icon in a lower corner. The pinstripe border design reappears on the back, which carries another color player action photo in its upper portion. The player's name and position appear vertically within a team color-coded stripe along the photo's right side. A team logo appears at the lower left corner of the photo. Beneath the picture appear the player's biography and stats. Subsets include Rookie Class (1-20), First Draft Picks (21-30), Top Performers (306-315), Up Close (631-640) and Future Foundation (641-650). Rookie Cards include Brian Anderson, Michael Jordan, Brooks Kieschnick, Derrek Lee, Alex Rodriguez, Jose Silva and Terrell Wade.

	MINT	EXC	G-VG
COMPLETE SET (670)	30.00	13.50	3.80
COMPLETE FACT.SET (675)	35.00	16.00	4.40
COMPLETE SERIES 1 (320)	12.00	5.50	1.50
COMPLETE SERIES 2 (350)	18.00	8.00	2.30
COMMON CARD (1-320)	.05	.02	.01
COMMON CARD (321-670)	.05	.02	.01

Card	MINT	EXC	G-VG
☐ 1 Rich Becker	.15	.07	.02
☐ 2 Greg Blosser	.10	.05	.01
☐ 3 Midre Cummings	.20	.09	.03
☐ 4 Carlos Delgado	.35	.16	.04
☐ 5 Steve Dreyer	.15	.07	.02
☐ 6 Carl Everett	.15	.07	.02
☐ 7 Cliff Floyd	.35	.16	.04
☐ 8 Alex Gonzalez	.20	.09	.03
☐ 9 Shawn Green	.35	.16	.04
☐ 10 Butch Huskey	.10	.05	.01
☐ 11 Mark Hutton	.10	.05	.01
☐ 12 Miguel Jimenez	.15	.07	.02
☐ 13 Steve Karsay	.10	.05	.01
☐ 14 Marc Newfield	.15	.07	.02
☐ 15 Luis Ortiz	.10	.05	.01
☐ 16 Manny Ramirez	.40	.18	.05
☐ 17 Johnny Ruffin	.10	.05	.01
☐ 18 Scott Stahoviak	.10	.05	.01
☐ 19 Salomon Torres	.15	.07	.02
☐ 20 Gabe White	.10	.05	.01
☐ 21 Brian Anderson	.50	.23	.06
☐ 22 Wayne Gomes	.15	.07	.02
☐ 23 Jeff Granger	.13	.06	.02
☐ 24 Steve Soderstrom	.25	.11	.03
☐ 25 Trot Nixon	.50	.23	.06
☐ 26 Kirk Presley	.50	.23	.06
☐ 27 Matt Brunson	.20	.09	.03
☐ 28 Brooks Kieschnick	.60	.25	.08
☐ 29 Billy Wagner	.40	.18	.05
☐ 30 Matt Drews	.35	.16	.04
☐ 31 Kurt Abbott	.20	.09	.03
☐ 32 Luis Alicea	.05	.02	.01
☐ 33 Roberto Alomar	.50	.23	.06
☐ 34 Sandy Alomar Jr.	.08	.04	.01
☐ 35 Moises Alou	.10	.05	.01
☐ 36 Wilson Alvarez	.10	.05	.01
☐ 37 Rich Amaral	.05	.02	.01
☐ 38 Eric Anthony	.05	.02	.01
☐ 39 Luis Aquino	.05	.02	.01
☐ 40 Jack Armstrong	.05	.02	.01
☐ 41 Rene Arocha	.08	.04	.01
☐ 42 Rich Aude	.20	.09	.03
☐ 43 Brad Ausmus	.05	.02	.01
☐ 44 Steve Avery	.10	.05	.01
☐ 45 Bob Ayrault	.05	.02	.01
☐ 46 Willie Banks	.05	.02	.01
☐ 47 Bret Barberie	.05	.02	.01
☐ 48 Kim Batiste	.05	.02	.01
☐ 49 Rod Beck	.10	.05	.01
☐ 50 Jason Bere	.30	.14	.04
☐ 51 Sean Berry	.05	.02	.01
☐ 52 Dante Bichette	.10	.05	.01
☐ 53 Jeff Blauser	.08	.04	.01
☐ 54 Mike Blowers	.05	.02	.01
☐ 55 Tim Bogar	.05	.02	.01
☐ 56 Tom Bolton	.05	.02	.01
☐ 57 Ricky Bones	.05	.02	.01
☐ 58 Bobby Bonilla	.10	.05	.01
☐ 59 Bret Boone	.10	.05	.01
☐ 60 Pat Borders	.05	.02	.01
☐ 61 Mike Bordick	.05	.02	.01
☐ 62 Daryl Boston	.05	.02	.01
☐ 63 Ryan Bowen	.05	.02	.01
☐ 64 Jeff Branson	.05	.02	.01
☐ 65 George Brett	.75	.35	.09
☐ 66 Steve Buechele	.05	.02	.01
☐ 67 Dave Burba	.05	.02	.01
☐ 68 John Burkett	.08	.04	.01
☐ 69 Jeromy Burnitz	.08	.04	.01
☐ 70 Brett Butler	.05	.02	.01
☐ 71 Rob Butler	.05	.02	.01
☐ 72 Ken Caminiti	.08	.04	.01
☐ 73 Cris Carpenter	.05	.02	.01
☐ 74 Vinny Castilla	.05	.02	.01
☐ 75 Andujar Cedeno	.05	.02	.01
☐ 76 Wes Chamberlain	.05	.02	.01
☐ 77 Archi Cianfrocco	.05	.02	.01
☐ 78 Dave Clark	.05	.02	.01
☐ 79 Jerald Clark	.05	.02	.01
☐ 80 Royce Clayton	.08	.04	.01
☐ 81 David Cone	.10	.05	.01
☐ 82 Jeff Conine	.10	.05	.01
☐ 83 Steve Cooke	.05	.02	.01
☐ 84 Scott Cooper	.08	.04	.01
☐ 85 Joey Cora	.05	.02	.01
☐ 86 Tim Costo	.05	.02	.01
☐ 87 Chad Curtis	.08	.04	.01
☐ 88 Ron Darling	.05	.02	.01
☐ 89 Danny Darwin	.05	.02	.01
☐ 90 Rob Deer	.05	.02	.01
☐ 91 Jim Deshaies	.05	.02	.01
☐ 92 Delino DeShields	.08	.04	.01
☐ 93 Rob Dibble	.05	.02	.01
☐ 94 Gary DiSarcina	.05	.02	.01
☐ 95 Doug Drabek	.10	.05	.01
☐ 96 Scott Erickson	.05	.02	.01
☐ 97 Rikkert Faneyte	.05	.02	.01
☐ 98 Jeff Fassero	.05	.02	.01

☐ 99 Alex Fernandez	.10	.05	.01
☐ 100 Cecil Fielder	.10	.05	.01
☐ 101 Dave Fleming	.05	.02	.01
☐ 102 Darrin Fletcher	.05	.02	.01
☐ 103 Scott Fletcher	.05	.02	.01
☐ 104 Mike Gallego	.05	.02	.01
☐ 105 Carlos Garcia	.05	.02	.01
☐ 106 Jeff Gardner	.05	.02	.01
☐ 107 Brent Gates	.10	.05	.01
☐ 108 Benji Gil	.08	.04	.01
☐ 109 Bernard Gilkey	.05	.02	.01
☐ 110 Chris Gomez	.10	.05	.01
☐ 111 Luis Gonzalez	.05	.02	.01
☐ 112 Tom Gordon	.05	.02	.01
☐ 113 Jim Gott	.05	.02	.01
☐ 114 Mark Grace	.10	.05	.01
☐ 115 Tommy Greene	.05	.02	.01
☐ 116 Willie Greene	.08	.04	.01
☐ 117 Ken Griffey Jr.	2.00	.90	.25
☐ 118 Bill Gullickson	.05	.02	.01
☐ 119 Ricky Gutierrez	.05	.02	.01
☐ 120 Juan Guzman	.08	.04	.01
☐ 121 Chris Gwynn	.05	.02	.01
☐ 122 Tony Gwynn	.50	.23	.06
☐ 123 Jeffrey Hammonds	.25	.11	.03
☐ 124 Erik Hanson	.05	.02	.01
☐ 125 Gene Harris	.05	.02	.01
☐ 126 Greg W. Harris	.05	.02	.01
☐ 127 Bryan Harvey	.08	.04	.01
☐ 128 Billy Hatcher	.05	.02	.01
☐ 129 Hilly Hathaway	.05	.02	.01
☐ 130 Charlie Hayes	.08	.04	.01
☐ 131 Rickey Henderson	.10	.05	.01
☐ 132 Mike Henneman	.05	.02	.01
☐ 133 Pat Hentgen	.08	.04	.01
☐ 134 Roberto Hernandez	.05	.02	.01
☐ 135 Orel Hershiser	.08	.04	.01
☐ 136 Phil Hiatt	.10	.05	.01
☐ 137 Glenallen Hill	.05	.02	.01
☐ 138 Ken Hill	.08	.04	.01
☐ 139 Eric Hillman	.05	.02	.01
☐ 140 Chris Hoiles	.08	.04	.01
☐ 141 Dave Hollins	.10	.05	.01
☐ 142 David Hulse	.05	.02	.01
☐ 143 Todd Hundley	.05	.02	.01
☐ 144 Pete Incaviglia	.05	.02	.01
☐ 145 Danny Jackson	.05	.02	.01
☐ 146 John Jaha	.05	.02	.01
☐ 147 Domingo Jean	.05	.02	.01
☐ 148 Gregg Jefferies	.10	.05	.01
☐ 149 Reggie Jefferson	.05	.02	.01
☐ 150 Lance Johnson	.05	.02	.01
☐ 151 Bobby Jones	.15	.07	.02
☐ 152 Chipper Jones	.25	.11	.03
☐ 153 Todd Jones	.05	.02	.01
☐ 154 Brian Jordan	.08	.04	.01
☐ 155 Wally Joyner	.08	.04	.01
☐ 156 David Justice	.30	.14	.04
☐ 157 Ron Karkovice	.05	.02	.01
☐ 158 Eric Karros	.08	.04	.01
☐ 159 Jeff Kent	.08	.04	.01
☐ 160 Jimmy Key	.08	.04	.01
☐ 161 Mark Kiefer	.05	.02	.01
☐ 162 Darryl Kile	.08	.04	.01
☐ 163 Jeff King	.05	.02	.01
☐ 164 Wayne Kirby	.05	.02	.01
☐ 165 Ryan Klesko	.30	.14	.04
☐ 166 Chuck Knoblauch	.10	.05	.01
☐ 167 Chad Kreuter	.05	.02	.01
☐ 168 John Kruk	.10	.05	.01
☐ 169 Mark Langston	.10	.05	.01
☐ 170 Mike Lansing	.08	.04	.01
☐ 171 Barry Larkin	.10	.05	.01
☐ 172 Manny Lee	.05	.02	.01
☐ 173 Phil Leftwich	.05	.02	.01
☐ 174 Darren Lewis	.05	.02	.01
☐ 175 Derek Lilliquist	.05	.02	.01
☐ 176 Jose Lind	.05	.02	.01
☐ 177 Albie Lopez	.10	.05	.01
☐ 178 Javy Lopez	.20	.09	.03
☐ 179 Torey Lovullo	.05	.02	.01
☐ 180 Scott Lydy	.05	.02	.01
☐ 181 Mike Macfarlane	.05	.02	.01
☐ 182 Shane Mack	.08	.04	.01
☐ 183 Greg Maddux	.40	.18	.05
☐ 184 Dave Magadan	.05	.02	.01
☐ 185 Joe Magrane	.05	.02	.01
☐ 186 Kirk Manwaring	.05	.02	.01
☐ 187 Al Martin	.05	.02	.01
☐ 188 Pedro A. Martinez	.10	.05	.01
☐ 189 Pedro J. Martinez	.10	.05	.01
☐ 190 Ramon Martinez	.08	.04	.01
☐ 191 Tino Martinez	.05	.02	.01
☐ 192 Don Mattingly	.75	.35	.09
☐ 193 Derrick May	.05	.02	.01
☐ 194 David McCarty	.08	.04	.01
☐ 195 Ben McDonald	.08	.04	.01
☐ 196 Roger McDowell	.05	.02	.01
☐ 197 Fred McGriff UER (Stats on back have 73 stolen bases for 1989; should be 7)	.30	.14	.04
☐ 198 Mark McLemore	.05	.02	.01
☐ 199 Greg McMichael	.08	.04	.01
☐ 200 Jeff McNeely	.05	.02	.01
☐ 201 Brian McRae	.08	.04	.01
☐ 202 Pat Meares	.05	.02	.01
☐ 203 Roberto Mejia	.08	.04	.01
☐ 204 Orlando Merced	.08	.04	.01
☐ 205 Jose Mesa	.05	.02	.01
☐ 206 Blas Minor	.05	.02	.01
☐ 207 Angel Miranda	.05	.02	.01
☐ 208 Paul Molitor	.30	.14	.04
☐ 209 Raul Mondesi	.75	.35	.09
☐ 210 Jeff Montgomery	.08	.04	.01
☐ 211 Mickey Morandini	.05	.02	.01
☐ 212 Mike Morgan	.05	.02	.01
☐ 213 Jamie Moyer	.05	.02	.01
☐ 214 Bobby Munoz	.05	.02	.01
☐ 215 Troy Neel	.08	.04	.01
☐ 216 Dave Nilsson	.05	.02	.01
☐ 217 John O'Donoghue	.05	.02	.01
☐ 218 Paul O'Neill	.08	.04	.01
☐ 219 Jose Offerman	.05	.02	.01
☐ 220 Joe Oliver	.05	.02	.01
☐ 221 Greg Olson	.05	.02	.01
☐ 222 Donovan Osborne	.05	.02	.01
☐ 223 J. Owens	.05	.02	.01
☐ 224 Mike Pagliarulo	.05	.02	.01
☐ 225 Craig Paquette	.05	.02	.01
☐ 226 Roger Pavlik	.05	.02	.01
☐ 227 Brad Pennington	.05	.02	.01
☐ 228 Eduardo Perez	.08	.04	.01
☐ 229 Mike Perez	.05	.02	.01
☐ 230 Tony Phillips	.05	.02	.01
☐ 231 Hipolito Pichardo	.05	.02	.01
☐ 232 Phil Plantier	.08	.04	.01
☐ 233 Curtis Pride	.20	.09	.03
☐ 234 Tim Pugh	.05	.02	.01
☐ 235 Scott Radinsky	.05	.02	.01
☐ 236 Pat Rapp	.05	.02	.01
☐ 237 Kevin Reimer	.05	.02	.01
☐ 238 Armando Reynoso	.05	.02	.01
☐ 239 Jose Rijo	.08	.04	.01
☐ 240 Cal Ripken	1.25	.55	.16
☐ 241 Kevin Roberson	.05	.02	.01

☐ 242 Kenny Rogers .... .05 .02 .01
☐ 243 Kevin Rogers .... .05 .02 .01
☐ 244 Mel Rojas...................... .05 .02 .01
☐ 245 John Roper.................. .08 .04 .01
☐ 246 Kirk Rueter.................... .05 .02 .01
☐ 247 Scott Ruffcorn .... .10 .05 .01
☐ 248 Ken Ryan .... .05 .02 .01
☐ 249 Nolan Ryan .... 2.00 .90 .25
☐ 250 Bret Saberhagen .... .08 .04 .01
☐ 251 Tim Salmon .... .30 .14 .04
☐ 252 Reggie Sanders............ .08 .04 .01
☐ 253 Curt Schilling .... .05 .02 .01
☐ 254 David Segui.................. .05 .02 .01
☐ 255 Aaron Sele .... .20 .09 .03
☐ 256 Scott Servais................ .05 .02 .01
☐ 257 Gary Sheffield .... .10 .05 .01
☐ 258 Ruben Sierra................. .10 .05 .01
☐ 259 Don Slaught.................. .05 .02 .01
☐ 260 Lee Smith .... .10 .05 .01
☐ 261 Cory Snyder.................. .05 .02 .01
☐ 262 Paul Sorrento............... .05 .02 .01
☐ 263 Sammy Sosa................ .10 .05 .01
☐ 264 Bill Spiers .... .05 .02 .01
☐ 265 Mike Stanley .... .05 .02 .01
☐ 266 Dave Staton .... .05 .02 .01
☐ 267 Terry Steinbach............ .08 .04 .01
☐ 268 Kevin Stocker............... .08 .04 .01
☐ 269 Todd Stottlemyre .... .05 .02 .01
☐ 270 Doug Strange............... .05 .02 .01
☐ 271 Bill Swift .... .05 .02 .01
☐ 272 Kevin Tapani .... .05 .02 .01
☐ 273 Tony Tarasco .... .10 .05 .01
☐ 274 Julian Tavarez.............. .05 .02 .01
☐ 275 Mickey Tettleton .... .08 .04 .01
☐ 276 Ryan Thompson .... .08 .04 .01
☐ 277 Chris Turner.................. .05 .02 .01
☐ 278 John Valentin............... .08 .04 .01
☐ 279 Todd Van Poppel .... .08 .04 .01
☐ 280 Andy Van Slyke............ .10 .05 .01
☐ 281 Mo Vaughn................... .10 .05 .01
☐ 282 Robin Ventura.............. .08 .04 .01
☐ 283 Frank Viola.................... .05 .02 .01
☐ 284 Jose Vizcaino............... .05 .02 .01
☐ 285 Omar Vizquel .... .05 .02 .01
☐ 286 Larry Walker .... .10 .05 .01
☐ 287 Duane Ward................. .08 .04 .01
☐ 288 Allen Watson................ .05 .02 .01
☐ 289 Bill Wegman .... .05 .02 .01
☐ 290 Turk Wendell................ .05 .02 .01
☐ 291 Lou Whitaker .... .10 .05 .01
☐ 292 Devon White .... .08 .04 .01
☐ 293 Rondell White .... .20 .09 .03
☐ 294 Mark Whiten................. .08 .04 .01
☐ 295 Darrell Whitmore .... .08 .04 .01
☐ 296 Bob Wickman .... .05 .02 .01
☐ 297 Rick Wilkins.................. .05 .02 .01
☐ 298 Bernie Williams............ .08 .04 .01
☐ 299 Matt Williams............... .30 .14 .04
☐ 300 Woody Williams........... .05 .02 .01
☐ 301 Nigel Wilson .... .08 .04 .01
☐ 302 Dave Winfield............... .10 .05 .01
☐ 303 Anthony Young............ .05 .02 .01
☐ 304 Eric Young .... .08 .04 .01
☐ 305 Todd Zeile..................... .08 .04 .01
☐ 306 Jack McDowell TP .... .08 .04 .01
John Burkett
Tom Glavine
☐ 307 Randy Johnson TP....... .10 .05 .01
☐ 308 Randy Myers TP .... .05 .02 .01
☐ 309 Jack McDowell TP .... .08 .04 .01
☐ 310 Mike Piazza TP............. .50 .23 .06
☐ 311 Barry Bonds TP............ .40 .18 .05
☐ 312 Andres Galarraga TP.... .10 .05 .01
☐ 313 Juan Gonzalez TP......... .35 .16 .04
Barry Bonds
☐ 314 Albert Belle TP .... .30 .14 .04
☐ 315 Kenny Lofton TP .... .25 .11 .03
☐ 316 Barry Bonds.................. .20 .09 .03
Checklist 1-64
☐ 317 Ken Griffey Jr............... .50 .23 .06
Checklist 65-128
☐ 318 Mike Piazza .... .25 .11 .03
Checklist 129-192
☐ 319 Kirby Puckett .... .20 .09 .03
Checklist 193-256
☐ 320 Nolan Ryan .... .50 .23 .06
Checklist 257-320
☐ 321 Roberto Alomar .... .15 .07 .02
Checklist 321-370
☐ 322 Roger Clemens .... .15 .07 .02
Checklist 371-420
☐ 323 Juan Gonzalez.............. .20 .09 .03
Checklist 421-470
☐ 324 Ken Griffey Jr............... .50 .23 .06
Checklist 471-520
☐ 325 David Justice .... .15 .07 .02
Checklist 521-570
☐ 326 John Kruk .... .05 .02 .01
Checklist 571-620
☐ 327 Frank Thomas .... .50 .23 .06
Checklist 621-670
☐ 328 Tim Salmon .... .15 .07 .02
Angels TC
☐ 329 Jeff Bagwell .... .50 .23 .06
Astros TC
☐ 330 Mark McGwire .... .05 .02 .01
Athletics TC
☐ 331 Roberto Alomar .... .25 .11 .03
Blue Jays TC
☐ 332 David Justice .... .15 .07 .02
Braves TC
☐ 333 Pat Listach.................... .05 .02 .01
Brewers TC
☐ 334 Ozzie Smith.................. .20 .09 .03
Cardinals TC
☐ 335 Ryne Sandberg .... .35 .16 .04
Cubs TC
☐ 336 Mike Piazza.................. .50 .23 .06
Dodgers TC
☐ 337 Cliff Floyd..................... .15 .07 .02
Expos TC
☐ 338 Barry Bonds................. .40 .18 .05
Giants TC
☐ 339 Albert Belle .... .30 .14 .04
Indians TC
☐ 340 Ken Griffey Jr............ 1.00 .45 .13
Mariners TC
☐ 341 Gary Sheffield .... .05 .02 .01
Marlins TC
☐ 342 Dwight Gooden .... .05 .02 .01
Mets TC
☐ 343 Cal Ripken.................... .60 .25 .08
Orioles TC
☐ 344 Tony Gwynn................. .25 .11 .03
Padres TC
☐ 345 Lenny Dykstra.............. .05 .02 .01
Phillies TC
☐ 346 Andy Van Slyke............ .05 .02 .01
Pirates TC
☐ 347 Juan Gonzalez.............. .30 .14 .04
Rangers TC
☐ 348 Roger Clemens .... .25 .11 .03
Red Sox TC
☐ 349 Barry Larkin .... .05 .02 .01
Reds TC
☐ 350 Andres Galarraga .... .05 .02 .01

Rockies TC
☐ 351 Kevin Appier .05 .02 .01
Royals TC
☐ 352 Cecil Fielder .05 .02 .01
Tigers TC
☐ 353 Kirby Puckett .40 .18 .05
Twins TC
☐ 354 Frank Thomas 1.00 .45 .13
White Sox TC
☐ 355 Don Mattingly .40 .18 .05
Yankees TC
☐ 356 Bo Jackson .10 .05 .01
☐ 357 Randy Johnson .10 .05 .01
☐ 358 Darren Daulton .10 .05 .01
☐ 359 Charlie Hough .08 .04 .01
☐ 360 Andres Galarraga .10 .05 .01
☐ 361 Mike Felder .05 .02 .01
☐ 362 Chris Hammond .05 .02 .01
☐ 363 Shawon Dunston .05 .02 .01
☐ 364 Junior Felix .05 .02 .01
☐ 365 Ray Lankford .10 .05 .01
☐ 366 Darryl Strawberry .08 .04 .01
☐ 367 Dave Magadan .05 .02 .01
☐ 368 Gregg Olson .05 .02 .01
☐ 369 Lenny Dykstra .10 .05 .01
☐ 370 Darrin Jackson .05 .02 .01
☐ 371 Dave Stewart .08 .04 .01
☐ 372 Terry Pendleton .05 .02 .01
☐ 373 Arthur Rhodes .05 .02 .01
☐ 374 Benito Santiago .05 .02 .01
☐ 375 Travis Fryman .15 .07 .02
☐ 376 Scott Brosius .05 .02 .01
☐ 377 Stan Belinda .05 .02 .01
☐ 378 Derek Parks .05 .02 .01
☐ 379 Kevin Seitzer .05 .02 .01
☐ 380 Wade Boggs .10 .05 .01
☐ 381 Wally Whitehurst .05 .02 .01
☐ 382 Scott Leius .05 .02 .01
☐ 383 Danny Tartabull .08 .04 .01
☐ 384 Harold Reynolds .05 .02 .01
☐ 385 Tim Raines .10 .05 .01
☐ 386 Darryl Hamilton .05 .02 .01
☐ 387 Felix Fermin .05 .02 .01
☐ 388 Jim Eisenreich .05 .02 .01
☐ 389 Kurt Abbott .15 .07 .02
☐ 390 Kevin Appier .08 .04 .01
☐ 391 Chris Bosio .05 .02 .01
☐ 392 Randy Tomlin .05 .02 .01
☐ 393 Bob Hamelin .10 .05 .01
☐ 394 Kevin Gross .05 .02 .01
☐ 395 Wil Cordero .10 .05 .01
☐ 396 Joe Girardi .05 .02 .01
☐ 397 Orestes Destrade .05 .02 .01
☐ 398 Chris Haney .05 .02 .01
☐ 399 Xavier Hernandez .05 .02 .01
☐ 400 Mike Piazza 1.00 .45 .13
☐ 401 Alex Arias .05 .02 .01
☐ 402 Tom Candiotti .05 .02 .01
☐ 403 Kirk Gibson .08 .04 .01
☐ 404 Chuck Carr .05 .02 .01
☐ 405 Brady Anderson .08 .04 .01
☐ 406 Greg Gagne .05 .02 .01
☐ 407 Bruce Ruffin .05 .02 .01
☐ 408 Scott Hemond .05 .02 .01
☐ 409 Keith Miller .05 .02 .01
☐ 410 John Wetteland .05 .02 .01
☐ 411 Eric Anthony .05 .02 .01
☐ 412 Andre Dawson .10 .05 .01
☐ 413 Doug Henry .05 .02 .01
☐ 414 John Franco .05 .02 .01
☐ 415 Julio Franco .08 .04 .01
☐ 416 Dave Hansen .05 .02 .01
☐ 417 Mike Harkey .05 .02 .01
☐ 418 Jack Armstrong .05 .02 .01
☐ 419 Joe Orsulak .05 .02 .01
☐ 420 John Smoltz .08 .04 .01
☐ 421 Scott Livingstone .05 .02 .01
☐ 422 Darren Holmes .05 .02 .01
☐ 423 Ed Sprague .05 .02 .01
☐ 424 Jay Buhner .08 .04 .01
☐ 425 Kirby Puckett .75 .35 .09
☐ 426 Phil Clark .05 .02 .01
☐ 427 Anthony Young .05 .02 .01
☐ 428 Reggie Jefferson .05 .02 .01
☐ 429 Mariano Duncan .05 .02 .01
☐ 430 Tom Glavine .10 .05 .01
☐ 431 Dave Henderson .05 .02 .01
☐ 432 Melido Perez .05 .02 .01
☐ 433 Paul Wagner .05 .02 .01
☐ 434 Tim Worrell .05 .02 .01
☐ 435 Ozzie Guillen .05 .02 .01
☐ 436 Mike Butcher .05 .02 .01
☐ 437 Jim Deshaies .05 .02 .01
☐ 438 Kevin Young .05 .02 .01
☐ 439 Tom Browning .05 .02 .01
☐ 440 Mike Greenwell .08 .04 .01
☐ 441 Mike Stanton .05 .02 .01
☐ 442 John Doherty .05 .02 .01
☐ 443 John Dopson .05 .02 .01
☐ 444 Carlos Baerga .30 .14 .04
☐ 445 Jack McDowell .10 .05 .01
☐ 446 Kent Mercker .05 .02 .01
☐ 447 Ricky Jordan .05 .02 .01
☐ 448 Jerry Browne .05 .02 .01
☐ 449 Fernando Vina .05 .02 .01
☐ 450 Jim Abbott .10 .05 .01
☐ 451 Teddy Higuera .05 .02 .01
☐ 452 Tim Naehring .05 .02 .01
☐ 453 Jim Leyritz .05 .02 .01
☐ 454 Frank Castillo .05 .02 .01
☐ 455 Joe Carter .30 .14 .04
☐ 456 Craig Biggio .08 .04 .01
☐ 457 Geronimo Pena .05 .02 .01
☐ 458 Alejandro Pena .05 .02 .01
☐ 459 Mike Moore .05 .02 .01
☐ 460 Randy Myers .05 .02 .01
☐ 461 Greg Myers .05 .02 .01
☐ 462 Greg Hibbard .05 .02 .01
☐ 463 Jose Guzman .05 .02 .01
☐ 464 Tom Pagnozzi .05 .02 .01
☐ 465 Marquis Grissom .10 .05 .01
☐ 466 Tim Wallach .05 .02 .01
☐ 467 Joe Grahe .05 .02 .01
☐ 468 Bob Tewksbury .05 .02 .01
☐ 469 B.J. Surhoff .05 .02 .01
☐ 470 Kevin Mitchell .08 .04 .01
☐ 471 Bobby Witt .05 .02 .01
☐ 472 Milt Thompson .05 .02 .01
☐ 473 John Smiley .08 .04 .01
☐ 474 Jose Valentin .05 .02 .01
☐ 475 Harold Baines .35 .16 .04
☐ 476 Rick Aguilera .05 .02 .01
☐ 477 Edgar Martinez .05 .02 .01
☐ 478 Harold Baines .08 .04 .01
☐ 479 Bip Roberts .05 .02 .01
☐ 480 Edgar Martinez .05 .02 .01
☐ 481 Rheal Cormier .05 .02 .01
☐ 482 Hal Morris .08 .04 .01
☐ 483 Pat Kelly .05 .02 .01
☐ 484 Roberto Kelly .05 .02 .01
☐ 485 Chris Sabo .05 .02 .01
☐ 486 Kent Hrbek .08 .04 .01
☐ 487 Scott Kamieniecki .05 .02 .01
☐ 488 Walt Weiss .05 .02 .01
☐ 489 Karl Rhodes .05 .02 .01
☐ 490 Derek Bell .08 .04 .01

	No.	Player			
☐	491	Chili Davis	.08	.04	.01
☐	492	Brian Harper	.05	.02	.01
☐	493	Felix Jose	.05	.02	.01
☐	494	Trevor Hoffman	.05	.02	.01
☐	495	Dennis Eckersley	.10	.05	.01
☐	496	Pedro Astacio	.08	.04	.01
☐	497	Jay Bell	.08	.04	.01
☐	498	Randy Velarde	.05	.02	.01
☐	499	David Wells	.05	.02	.01
☐	500	Frank Thomas	2.00	.90	.25
☐	501	Mark Lemke	.05	.02	.01
☐	502	Mike Devereaux	.08	.04	.01
☐	503	Chuck McElroy	.05	.02	.01
☐	504	Luis Polonia	.05	.02	.01
☐	505	Damion Easley	.05	.02	.01
☐	506	Greg A. Harris	.05	.02	.01
☐	507	Chris James	.05	.02	.01
☐	508	Terry Mulholland	.05	.02	.01
☐	509	Pete Smith	.05	.02	.01
☐	510	Rickey Henderson	.10	.05	.01
☐	511	Sid Fernandez	.05	.02	.01
☐	512	Al Leiter	.05	.02	.01
☐	513	Doug Jones	.05	.02	.01
☐	514	Steve Farr	.05	.02	.01
☐	515	Chuck Finley	.05	.02	.01
☐	516	Bobby Thigpen	.05	.02	.01
☐	517	Jim Edmonds	.05	.02	.01
☐	518	Graeme Lloyd	.05	.02	.01
☐	519	Dwight Gooden	.05	.02	.01
☐	520	Pat Listach	.05	.02	.01
☐	521	Kevin Bass	.05	.02	.01
☐	522	Willie Banks	.05	.02	.01
☐	523	Steve Finley	.05	.02	.01
☐	524	Delino DeShields	.08	.04	.01
☐	525	Mark McGwire	.10	.05	.01
☐	526	Greg Swindell	.05	.02	.01
☐	527	Chris Nabholz	.05	.02	.01
☐	528	Scott Sanders	.05	.02	.01
☐	529	David Segui	.05	.02	.01
☐	530	Howard Johnson	.05	.02	.01
☐	531	Jaime Navarro	.05	.02	.01
☐	532	Jose Vizcaino	.05	.02	.01
☐	533	Mark Lewis	.05	.02	.01
☐	534	Pete Harnisch	.05	.02	.01
☐	535	Robby Thompson	.05	.02	.01
☐	536	Marcus Moore	.05	.02	.01
☐	537	Kevin Brown	.05	.02	.01
☐	538	Mark Clark	.05	.02	.01
☐	539	Sterling Hitchcock	.08	.04	.01
☐	540	Will Clark	.30	.14	.04
☐	541	Denis Boucher	.05	.02	.01
☐	542	Jack Morris	.10	.05	.01
☐	543	Pedro Munoz	.05	.02	.01
☐	544	Bret Boone	.10	.05	.01
☐	545	Ozzie Smith	.40	.18	.05
☐	546	Dennis Martinez	.08	.04	.01
☐	547	Dan Wilson	.05	.02	.01
☐	548	Rick Sutcliffe	.08	.04	.01
☐	549	Kevin McReynolds	.05	.02	.01
☐	550	Roger Clemens	.50	.23	.06
☐	551	Todd Benzinger	.05	.02	.01
☐	552	Bill Haselman	.05	.02	.01
☐	553	Bobby Munoz	.05	.02	.01
☐	554	Ellis Burks	.08	.04	.01
☐	555	Ryne Sandberg	.60	.25	.08
☐	556	Lee Smith	.10	.05	.01
☐	557	Danny Bautista	.08	.04	.01
☐	558	Rey Sanchez	.05	.02	.01
☐	559	Norm Charlton	.05	.02	.01
☐	560	Jose Canseco	.30	.14	.04
☐	561	Tim Belcher	.05	.02	.01
☐	562	Denny Neagle	.05	.02	.01
☐	563	Eric Davis	.05	.02	.01
☐	564	Jody Reed	.05	.02	.01
☐	565	Kenny Lofton	.50	.23	.06
☐	566	Gary Gaetti	.05	.02	.01
☐	567	Todd Worrell	.05	.02	.01
☐	568	Mark Portugal	.05	.02	.01
☐	569	Dick Schofield	.05	.02	.01
☐	570	Andy Benes	.08	.04	.01
☐	571	Zane Smith	.05	.02	.01
☐	572	Bobby Ayala	.05	.02	.01
☐	573	Chip Hale	.05	.02	.01
☐	574	Bob Welch	.05	.02	.01
☐	575	Deion Sanders	.40	.18	.05
☐	576	David Nied	.10	.05	.01
☐	577	Pat Mahomes	.05	.02	.01
☐	578	Charles Nagy	.05	.02	.01
☐	579	Otis Nixon	.05	.02	.01
☐	580	Dean Palmer	.08	.04	.01
☐	581	Roberto Petagine	.08	.04	.01
☐	582	Dwight Smith	.05	.02	.01
☐	583	Jeff Russell	.05	.02	.01
☐	584	Mark Dewey	.05	.02	.01
☐	585	Greg Vaughn	.08	.04	.01
☐	586	Brian Hunter	.05	.02	.01
☐	587	Willie McGee	.05	.02	.01
☐	588	Pedro J. Martinez	.10	.05	.01
☐	589	Roger Salkeld	.05	.02	.01
☐	590	Jeff Bagwell	1.00	.45	.13
☐	591	Spike Owen	.05	.02	.01
☐	592	Jeff Reardon	.08	.04	.01
☐	593	Erik Pappas	.05	.02	.01
☐	594	Brian Williams	.05	.02	.01
☐	595	Eddie Murray	.10	.05	.01
☐	596	Henry Rodriguez	.05	.02	.01
☐	597	Erik Hanson	.05	.02	.01
☐	598	Stan Javier	.05	.02	.01
☐	599	Mitch Williams	.05	.02	.01
☐	600	John Olerud	.10	.05	.01
☐	601	Vince Coleman	.05	.02	.01
☐	602	Damon Berryhill	.05	.02	.01
☐	603	Tom Brunansky	.05	.02	.01
☐	604	Robb Nen	.05	.02	.01
☐	605	Rafael Palmeiro	.10	.05	.01
☐	606	Cal Eldred	.08	.04	.01
☐	607	Jeff Brantley	.05	.02	.01
☐	608	Alan Mills	.05	.02	.01
☐	609	Jeff Nelson	.05	.02	.01
☐	610	Barry Bonds	.75	.35	.09
☐	611	Carlos Pulido	.15	.07	.02
☐	612	Tim Hyers	.15	.07	.02
☐	613	Steve Hosey	.05	.02	.01
☐	614	Brian Turang	.05	.02	.01
☐	615	Leo Gomez	.05	.02	.01
☐	616	Jesse Orosco	.05	.02	.01
☐	617	Dan Pasqua	.05	.02	.01
☐	618	Marvin Freeman	.05	.02	.01
☐	619	Tony Fernandez	.05	.02	.01
☐	620	Albert Belle	.60	.25	.08
☐	621	Eddie Taubensee	.05	.02	.01
☐	622	Mike Jackson	.05	.02	.01
☐	623	Jose Bautista	.05	.02	.01
☐	624	Jim Thome	.10	.05	.01
☐	625	Ivan Rodriguez	.10	.05	.01
☐	626	Ben Rivera	.05	.02	.01
☐	627	Dave Valle	.05	.02	.01
☐	628	Tom Henke	.05	.02	.01
☐	629	Omar Vizquel	.05	.02	.01
☐	630	Juan Gonzalez	.60	.25	.08
☐	631	Roberto Alomar UP	.25	.11	.03
☐	632	Barry Bonds UP	.40	.18	.05
☐	633	Juan Gonzalez UP	.35	.16	.04
☐	634	Ken Griffey Jr. UP	1.00	.45	.13
☐	635	Michael Jordan UP	4.00	1.80	.50
☐	636	David Justice UP	.15	.07	.02

☐ 637 Mike Piazza UP .... .50 .23 .06
☐ 638 Kirby Puckett UP .... .40 .18 .05
☐ 639 Tim Salmon UP .... .15 .07 .02
☐ 640 Frank Thomas UP ...... 1.00 .45 .13
☐ 641 Alan Benes FF .... .60 .25 .08
☐ 642 Johnny Damon FF .... .25 .11 .03
☐ 643 Brad Fullmer FF .... .15 .07 .02
☐ 644 Derek Jeter FF .... .50 .23 .06
☐ 645 Derrek Lee FF .... .50 .23 .06
☐ 646 Alex Ochoa FF .... .15 .07 .02
☐ 647 Alex Rodriguez FF ...... 3.00 1.35 .40
☐ 648 Jose Silva FF .... .50 .23 .06
☐ 649 Terrell Wade FF .... .50 .23 .06
☐ 650 Preston Wilson FF .... .10 .05 .01
☐ 651 Shane Andrews .... .08 .04 .01
☐ 652 James Baldwin .... .35 .16 .04
☐ 653 Ricky Bottalico .... .20 .09 .03
☐ 654 Tavo Alvarez .... .05 .02 .01
☐ 655 Donnie Elliott .... .05 .02 .01
☐ 656 Joey Eischen .... .08 .04 .01
☐ 657 Jason Giambi .... .05 .02 .01
☐ 658 Todd Hollandsworth .... .40 .18 .05
☐ 659 Brian L. Hunter .... .35 .16 .04
☐ 660 Charles Johnson .... .20 .09 .03
☐ 661 Michael Jordan 8.00 3.60 1.00
☐ 662 Jeff Juden .... .05 .02 .01
☐ 663 Mike Kelly .... .08 .04 .01
☐ 664 James Mouton .... .15 .07 .02
☐ 665 Ray Holbert .... .05 .02 .01
☐ 666 Pokey Reese .... .05 .02 .01
☐ 667 Ruben Santana .... .15 .07 .02
☐ 668 Paul Spoljaric .... .05 .02 .01
☐ 669 Luis Lopez .... .05 .02 .01
☐ 670 Matt Walbeck .... .05 .02 .01

1994 Collector's Choice Gold Signature

The 670-card Gold Foil Signature set is a parallel to the basic Collector's Choice issue. These cards were randomly inserted at a rate of one in 36 1994 Upper Deck Collector's Choice 12-card packs (11 regular issue cards plus the Gold Foil Signature insert). The other packs each contained one card from the more plentiful Silver Foil Signature set. Gold cards were also issued five per factory set. Gold Foil Signature cards share the same photo as the corresponding regular issue cards, but the borders on the basic player cards are enhanced with a layer of gold foil. Each card is stamped with a gold replica autograph. Some subset cards feature borderless designs (unlike the basic player cards), thus their corresponding borderless Gold Foil Signature cards differ only by the gold foil replica autograph. The Jeffrey Hammonds card has the signature of Orioles General Manager Roland Hemond.

	MINT	EXC	G-VG
COMPLETE SET (670)	4000.00	1800.00	500.00
COMPLETE SERIES 1 (320)	2000.00	900.00	250.00
COMPLETE SERIES 2 (350)	2000.00	900.00	250.00
COMMON CARD (1-320)	2.00	.90	.25
COMMON CARD (321-670)	2.00	.90	.25

*UNLISTED VETERAN STARS: 50X to 75X VALUE
*UNLISTED YOUNG STARS: 30X to 60X VALUE
*UNLISTED RCs: 20X to 40X VALUE

☐ 65 George Brett 100.00 45.00 12.50
☐ 117 Ken Griffey Jr. 150.00 70.00 19.00
☐ 192 Don Mattingly 60.00 27.00 7.50
☐ 240 Cal Ripken 100.00 45.00 12.50
☐ 249 Nolan Ryan 200.00 90.00 25.00
☐ 340 Ken Griffey Jr. TC..... 75.00 34.00 9.50
☐ 354 Frank Thomas TC..... 75.00 34.00 9.50
☐ 400 Mike Piazza 75.00 34.00 9.50
☐ 425 Kirby Puckett 60.00 27.00 7.50
☐ 500 Frank Thomas 150.00 70.00 19.00
☐ 555 Ryne Sandberg 50.00 23.00 6.25
☐ 590 Jeff Bagwell 75.00 34.00 9.50
☐ 610 Barry Bonds 50.00 23.00 6.25
☐ 634 Ken Griffey Jr. UP 75.00 34.00 9.50
☐ 635 Michael Jordan UP. 100.00 45.00 12.50
☐ 640 Frank Thomas UP 75.00 34.00 9.50
☐ 647 Alex Rodriguez....... 100.00 45.00 12.50
☐ 661 Michael Jordan 200.00 90.00 25.00

1994 Collector's Choice Silver Signature

This 670-card set is a parallel to the basic Collector's Choice set. One Silver Foil Signature card was inserted into every 12-card pack of 1994 Upper Deck Collector's Choice (11 regular issue cards plus one Signature card) unless there was a Gold Foil Signature card (which was randomly

inserted into one out of every 36 packs). Silver cards were also inserted at different rates in other pack forms. Each Silver Foil Signature card is identical in design to its corresponding regular issue card except for the silver replica autograph stamped into the UV coated card front. Regular issue cards have no replica autographs on them. As with the gold set, the Jeffrey Hammonds card has the signature of Orioles General Manager Roland Hemond.

	MINT	EXC	G-VG
COMPLETE SET (670)	200.00	90.00	25.00
COMPLETE SERIES 1 (320)	90.00	40.00	11.50
COMPLETE SERIES 2 (350)	110.00	50.00	14.00
COMMON CARD (1-320)	.10	.05	.01
COMMON CARD (321-670)	.10	.05	.01

*UNLISTED VETERAN STARS: 4X to 8X VALUE
*UNLISTED YOUNG STARS: 2.5X to 5X VALUE
*UNLISTED RCs: 1.5X to 3X VALUE

	MINT	EXC	G-VG
☐ 635 Michael Jordan UP	10.00	4.50	1.25
☐ 661 Michael Jordan	20.00	9.00	2.50

1994 Collector's Choice Home Run All-Stars

This 15-card set served as the eighth place prize in the Crash the Game contest, which was a promotion in both series of Collector's Choice. Horizontal fronts feature holographic images of the player that breaks through a brick wall. A small color photo of the player appears at left or right. The backs, outlined with bricks, features a small photo and text that appears over a stadium background. The cards are numbered with an "HA" prefix.

	MINT	EXC	G-VG
COMPLETE SET (8)	6.00	2.70	.75
COMMON CARD (HA1-HA8)	.25	.11	.03

	MINT	EXC	G-VG
☐ HA1 Juan Gonzalez	1.00	.45	.13
☐ HA2 Ken Griffey Jr.	3.00	1.35	.40
☐ HA3 Barry Bonds	1.25	.55	.16
☐ HA4 Bobby Bonilla	.25	.11	.03
☐ HA5 Cecil Fielder UER (Card number is HA4)	.45	.20	.06
☐ HA6 Albert Belle	1.00	.45	.13
☐ HA7 David Justice	.25	.11	.03
☐ HA8 Mike Piazza	1.50	.65	.19

1994 Collector's Choice Team vs. Team

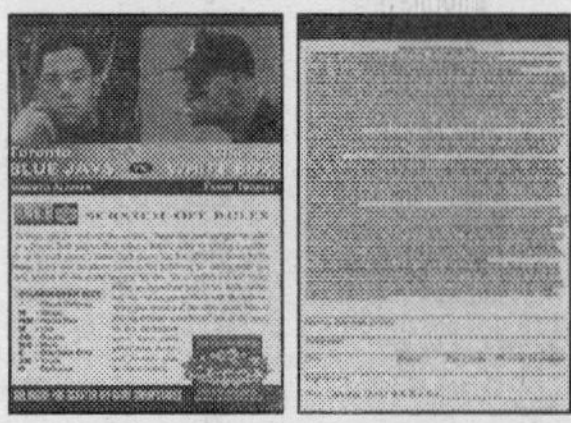

Issued one per second series pack, these 15 foldout, scratch-off game cards feature one team's lineup against the other. Various prizes were available through these game cards. The most plentiful, by far, was the eighth place Home Run All-Stars hologram set. Prizes were redeemable through October 31, 1994. Scratch-off rules and two small player photos are on the front with complete rules and provisions on the back. The cards fold out to expose the game portion. Cards that are scratched are half the values below.

	MINT	EXC	G-VG
COMPLETE SET (15)	5.00	2.30	.60
COMMON PAIR (1-15)	.25	.11	.03

*PRIZE BOX SCRATCHED: HALF VALUE

	MINT	EXC	G-VG
☐ 1 Roberto Alomar Toronto Blue Jays Frank Thomas Chicago White Sox	1.00	.45	.13
☐ 2 Barry Bonds Pittsburgh Pirates Ken Griffey	1.00	.45	.13
☐ 3 Roger Clemens Boston Red Sox Don Mattingly New York Yankees	.50	.23	.06
☐ 4 Lenny Dykstra Philadelphia Phillies David Justice Atlanta Braves	.25	.11	.03
☐ 5 Andres Galarraga Colorado Rockies Tony Gwynn San Diego Padres	.25	.11	.03
☐ 6 Dwight Goodens New York Mets Gary Sheffield Florida Marlins	.25	.11	.03

		MINT	EXC	G-VG
☐ 7	Ken Griffey Jr. Seattle Mariners Juan Gonzalez Texas Rangers	1.00	.45	.13
☐ 8	Barry Larkin Cincinnati Reds Jeff Bagwell Houston Astros	.50	.23	.06
☐ 9	Pat Listach Milwaukee Brewers Albert Belle Cleveland Indians	.25	.11	.03
☐ 10	Mark McGwire Oakland Athletics Tim Salmon California Angels	.25	.11	.03
☐ 11	Mike Piazza Los Angeles Dodgers Barry Bonds San Francisco Giants	.75	.35	.09
☐ 12	Kirby Puckett Minnesota Twins Brian McRae Kansas City Royals	.50	.23	.06
☐ 13	Cal Ripken Baltimore Orioles Cecil Fielder Detroit Tigers	.60	.25	.08
☐ 14	Ryne Sandberg Chicago Cubs Ozzie Smith St. Louis Cardinals	.50	.23	.06
☐ 15	Andy Van Slyke Pittsburgh Pirates Cliff Floyd Montreal Expos	.25	.11	.03

1995 Collector's Choice SE

The 1995 Collector's Choice SE set consists of 265 standard-size cards. One in every 216 packs was a Silver Super Pack, containing 12 silver signature cards. One in every 720 packs was a Gold Super Pack, containing 12 gold signature cards. The fronts feature color action player photos with blue borders. The player's name, position and the team name are printed on the bottom of the photo. The SE logo in blue-foil appears in a top corner. On a white background, the backs carry another color player photo with a short player biography, career stats and 1994 highlights. Subsets featured include Rookie Class (1-25), Record Pace (26-30), Stat Leaders (137-144), Fantasy Team (249-260).

	MINT	EXC	G-VG
COMPLETE SET (265)	25.00	11.50	3.10
COMMON CARD (1-265)	.10	.05	.01

		MINT	EXC	G-VG
☐ 1	Alex Rodriguez	1.25	.55	.16
☐ 2	Derek Jeter	.50	.23	.06
☐ 3	Dustin Hermanson	.10	.05	.01
☐ 4	Bill Pulsipher	.10	.05	.01
☐ 5	Terrell Wade	.10	.05	.01
☐ 6	Darren Dreifort	.10	.05	.01
☐ 7	LaTroy Hawkins	.10	.05	.01
☐ 8	Alex Ochoa	.20	.09	.03
☐ 9	Paul Wilson	.30	.14	.04
☐ 10	Rod Henderson	.10	.05	.01
☐ 11	Alan Benes	.25	.11	.03
☐ 12	Garret Anderson	.15	.07	.02
☐ 13	Armando Benitez	.10	.05	.01
☐ 14	Mark Thompson	.15	.07	.02
☐ 15	Andrew Lorraine	.10	.05	.01
☐ 16	Jose Silva	.10	.05	.01
☐ 17	Orlando Miller	.15	.07	.02
☐ 18	Russ Davis	.10	.05	.01
☐ 19	Jason Isringhausen	.10	.05	.01
☐ 20	Ray McDavid	.10	.05	.01
☐ 21	Tim VanEgmond	.10	.05	.01
☐ 22	Paul Shuey	.10	.05	.01
☐ 23	Steve Dunn	.15	.07	.02
☐ 24	Mike Lieberthal	.10	.05	.01
☐ 25	Chan Ho Park	.30	.14	.04
☐ 26	Ken Griffey Jr. RP	1.50	.65	.19
☐ 27	Tony Gwynn RP	.40	.18	.05
☐ 28	Chuck Knoblauch RP	.20	.09	.03
☐ 29	Frank Thomas RP	1.50	.65	.19
☐ 30	Matt Williams RP	.25	.11	.03
☐ 31	Chili Davis	.15	.07	.02
☐ 32	Chad Curtis	.15	.07	.02
☐ 33	Brian Anderson	.10	.05	.01
☐ 34	Chuck Finley	.10	.05	.01
☐ 35	Tim Salmon	.10	.05	.01
☐ 36	Bo Jackson	.20	.09	.03
☐ 37	Doug Drabek	.20	.09	.03
☐ 38	Craig Biggio	.15	.07	.02
☐ 39	Ken Caminiti	.15	.07	.02
☐ 40	Jeff Bagwell	1.50	.65	.19
☐ 41	Darryl Kile	.15	.07	.02
☐ 42	John Hudek	.10	.05	.01
☐ 43	Brian L. Hunter	.10	.05	.01
☐ 44	Dennis Eckersley	.20	.09	.03
☐ 45	Mark McGwire	.20	.09	.03
☐ 46	Brent Gates	.20	.09	.03
☐ 47	Steve Karsay	.10	.05	.01
☐ 48	Rickey Henderson	.20	.09	.03
☐ 49	Terry Steinbach	.15	.07	.02
☐ 50	Ruben Sierra	.20	.09	.03
☐ 51	Roberto Alomar	.60	.25	.08
☐ 52	Carlos Delgado	.35	.16	.04
☐ 53	Alex Gonzalez	.10	.05	.01
☐ 54	Joe Carter	.35	.16	.04
☐ 55	Paul Molitor	.40	.18	.05
☐ 56	Juan Guzman	.15	.07	.02
☐ 57	John Olerud	.20	.09	.03
☐ 58	Shawn Green	.20	.09	.03
☐ 59	Tom Glavine	.20	.09	.03
☐ 60	Greg Maddux	.60	.25	.08
☐ 61	Roberto Kelly	.10	.05	.01
☐ 62	Ryan Klesko	.35	.16	.04
☐ 63	Javy Lopez	.10	.05	.01
☐ 64	Jose Oliva	.20	.09	.03

No.	Player			
☐ 65	Fred McGriff	.35	.16	.04
☐ 66	Steve Avery	.20	.09	.03
☐ 67	David Justice	.35	.16	.04
☐ 68	Ricky Bones	.10	.05	.01
☐ 69	Cal Eldred	.15	.07	.02
☐ 70	Greg Vaughn	.15	.07	.02
☐ 71	Dave Nilsson	.10	.05	.01
☐ 72	Jose Valentin	.10	.05	.01
☐ 73	Matt Mieske	.10	.05	.01
☐ 74	Todd Zeile	.15	.07	.02
☐ 75	Ozzie Smith	.50	.23	.06
☐ 76	Bernard Gilkey	.10	.05	.01
☐ 77	Ray Lankford	.20	.09	.03
☐ 78	Bob Tewksbury	.10	.05	.01
☐ 79	Mark Whiten	.15	.07	.02
☐ 80	Gregg Jefferies	.20	.09	.03
☐ 81	Randy Myers	.10	.05	.01
☐ 82	Shawon Dunston	.10	.05	.01
☐ 83	Mark Grace	.20	.09	.03
☐ 84	Derrick May	.10	.05	.01
☐ 85	Sammy Sosa	.20	.09	.03
☐ 86	Steve Trachsel	.20	.09	.03
☐ 87	Brett Butler	.15	.07	.02
☐ 88	Delino DeShields	.15	.07	.02
☐ 89	Orel Hershiser	.15	.07	.02
☐ 90	Mike Piazza	1.25	.55	.16
☐ 91	Todd Hollandsworth	.10	.05	.01
☐ 92	Eric Karros	.15	.07	.02
☐ 93	Ramon Martinez	.15	.07	.02
☐ 94	Tim Wallach	.10	.05	.01
☐ 95	Raul Mondesi	.75	.35	.09
☐ 96	Larry Walker	.20	.09	.03
☐ 97	Wil Cordero	.15	.07	.02
☐ 98	Marquis Grissom	.20	.09	.03
☐ 99	Ken Hill	.15	.07	.02
☐ 100	Cliff Floyd	.35	.16	.04
☐ 101	Pedro J. Martinez	.20	.09	.03
☐ 102	John Wetteland	.10	.05	.01
☐ 103	Rondell White	.10	.05	.01
☐ 104	Moises Alou	.20	.09	.03
☐ 105	Barry Bonds	1.25	.55	.16
☐ 106	Darren Lewis	.10	.05	.01
☐ 107	Mark Portugal	.10	.05	.01
☐ 108	Matt Williams	.50	.23	.06
☐ 109	William VanLandingham	.10	.05	.01
☐ 110	Bill Swift	.10	.05	.01
☐ 111	Robby Thompson	.10	.05	.01
☐ 112	Rod Beck	.15	.07	.02
☐ 113	Darryl Strawberry	.15	.07	.02
☐ 114	Jim Thome	.20	.09	.03
☐ 115	Dave Winfield	.20	.09	.03
☐ 116	Eddie Murray	.20	.09	.03
☐ 117	Manny Ramirez	.40	.18	.05
☐ 118	Carlos Baerga	.40	.18	.05
☐ 119	Kenny Lofton	.75	.35	.09
☐ 120	Albert Belle	1.00	.45	.13
☐ 121	Mark Clark	.10	.05	.01
☐ 122	Dennis Martinez	.15	.07	.02
☐ 123	Randy Johnson	.20	.09	.03
☐ 124	Jay Buhner	.15	.07	.02
☐ 125	Ken Griffey Jr.	3.00	1.35	.40
☐ 126	Goose Gossage	.10	.05	.01
☐ 127	Tino Martinez	.10	.05	.01
☐ 128	Reggie Jefferson	.10	.05	.01
☐ 129	Edgar Martinez	.10	.05	.01
☐ 130	Gary Sheffield	.20	.09	.03
☐ 131	Pat Rapp	.10	.05	.01
☐ 132	Bret Barberie	.10	.05	.01
☐ 133	Chuck Carr	.10	.05	.01
☐ 134	Jeff Conine	.20	.09	.03
☐ 135	Charles Johnson	.10	.05	.01
☐ 136	Benito Santiago	.10	.05	.01
☐ 137	Matt Williams STL	.25	.11	.03
☐ 138	Jeff Bagwell STL	.60	.25	.08
☐ 139	Kenny Lofton STL	.40	.18	.05
☐ 140	Tony Gwynn STL	.35	.16	.04
☐ 141	Jimmy Key STL	.15	.07	.02
☐ 142	Greg Maddux STL	.30	.14	.04
☐ 143	Randy Johnson STL	.20	.09	.03
☐ 144	Lee Smith STL	.20	.09	.03
☐ 145	Bobby Bonilla	.20	.09	.03
☐ 146	Jason Jacome	.25	.11	.03
☐ 147	Jeff Kent	.15	.07	.02
☐ 148	Ryan Thompson	.15	.07	.02
☐ 149	Bobby Jones	.20	.09	.03
☐ 150	Bret Saberhagen	.15	.07	.02
☐ 151	John Franco	.10	.05	.01
☐ 152	Lee Smith	.20	.09	.03
☐ 153	Rafael Palmeiro	.20	.09	.03
☐ 154	Brady Anderson	.15	.07	.02
☐ 155	Cal Ripken	2.25	1.00	.30
☐ 156	Jeffrey Hammonds	.10	.05	.01
☐ 157	Mike Mussina	.40	.18	.05
☐ 158	Chris Hoiles	.15	.07	.02
☐ 159	Ben McDonald	.15	.07	.02
☐ 160	Tony Gwynn	.60	.25	.08
☐ 161	Joey Hamilton	.20	.09	.03
☐ 162	Andy Benes	.15	.07	.02
☐ 163	Trevor Hoffman	.10	.05	.01
☐ 164	Phil Plantier	.15	.07	.02
☐ 165	Derek Bell	.15	.07	.02
☐ 166	Bip Roberts	.10	.05	.01
☐ 167	Eddie Williams	.10	.05	.01
☐ 168	Fernando Valenzuela	.10	.05	.01
☐ 169	Mariano Duncan	.10	.05	.01
☐ 170	Lenny Dykstra	.20	.09	.03
☐ 171	Darren Daulton	.20	.09	.03
☐ 172	Danny Jackson	.10	.05	.01
☐ 173	Bobby Munoz	.10	.05	.01
☐ 174	Doug Jones	.10	.05	.01
☐ 175	Jay Bell	.15	.07	.02
☐ 176	Zane Smith	.10	.05	.01
☐ 177	Jon Lieber	.10	.05	.01
☐ 178	Carlos Garcia	.10	.05	.01
☐ 179	Orlando Merced	.10	.05	.01
☐ 180	Andy Van Slyke	.20	.09	.03
☐ 181	Rick Helling	.10	.05	.01
☐ 182	Rusty Greer	.15	.07	.02
☐ 183	Kenny Rogers	.10	.05	.01
☐ 184	Will Clark	.40	.18	.05
☐ 185	Jose Canseco	.40	.18	.05
☐ 186	Juan Gonzalez	1.00	.45	.13
☐ 187	Dean Palmer	.15	.07	.02
☐ 188	Ivan Rodriguez	.20	.09	.03
☐ 189	John Valentin	.15	.07	.02
☐ 190	Roger Clemens	.60	.25	.08
☐ 191	Aaron Sele	.20	.09	.03
☐ 192	Scott Cooper	.15	.07	.02
☐ 193	Mike Greenwell	.15	.07	.02
☐ 194	Mo Vaughn	.20	.09	.03
☐ 195	Andre Dawson	.20	.09	.03
☐ 196	Ron Gant	.15	.07	.02
☐ 197	Jose Rijo	.15	.07	.02
☐ 198	Bret Boone	.20	.09	.03
☐ 199	Deion Sanders	.50	.23	.06
☐ 200	Barry Larkin	.20	.09	.03
☐ 201	Hal Morris	.15	.07	.02
☐ 202	Reggie Sanders	.15	.07	.02
☐ 203	Kevin Mitchell	.15	.07	.02
☐ 204	Marvin Freeman	.10	.05	.01
☐ 205	Andres Galarraga	.20	.09	.03
☐ 206	Walt Weiss	.10	.05	.01
☐ 207	Charlie Hayes	.15	.07	.02
☐ 208	Dave Nied	.20	.09	.03
☐ 209	Dante Bichette	.20	.09	.03
☐ 210	David Cone	.20	.09	.03

☐ 211	Jeff Montgomery	.15	.07	.02
☐ 212	Felix Jose	.10	.05	.01
☐ 213	Mike Macfarlane	.10	.05	.01
☐ 214	Wally Joyner	.15	.07	.02
☐ 215	Bob Hamelin	.20	.09	.03
☐ 216	Brian McRae	.15	.07	.02
☐ 217	Kirk Gibson	.15	.07	.02
☐ 218	Lou Whitaker	.20	.09	.03
☐ 219	Chris Gomez	.15	.07	.02
☐ 220	Cecil Fielder	.20	.09	.03
☐ 221	Mickey Tettleton	.15	.07	.02
☐ 222	Travis Fryman	.25	.11	.03
☐ 223	Tony Phillips	.10	.05	.01
☐ 224	Rick Aguilera	.15	.07	.02
☐ 225	Scott Erickson	.10	.05	.01
☐ 226	Chuck Knoblauch	.20	.09	.03
☐ 227	Kent Hrbek	.15	.07	.02
☐ 228	Shane Mack	.15	.07	.02
☐ 229	Kevin Tapani	.10	.05	.01
☐ 230	Kirby Puckett	1.25	.55	.16
☐ 231	Julio Franco	.15	.07	.02
☐ 232	Jack McDowell	.20	.09	.03
☐ 233	Jason Bere	.30	.14	.04
☐ 234	Alex Fernandez	.20	.09	.03
☐ 235	Frank Thomas	3.00	1.35	.40
☐ 236	Ozzie Guillen	.10	.05	.01
☐ 237	Robin Ventura	.15	.07	.02
☐ 238	Michael Jordan	4.00	1.80	.50
☐ 239	Wilson Alvarez	.20	.09	.03
☐ 240	Don Mattingly	1.25	.55	.16
☐ 241	Jim Abbott	.20	.09	.03
☐ 242	Jim Leyritz	.10	.05	.01
☐ 243	Paul O'Neill	.15	.07	.02
☐ 244	Melido Perez	.10	.05	.01
☐ 245	Wade Boggs	.20	.09	.03
☐ 246	Mike Stanley	.10	.05	.01
☐ 247	Danny Tartabull	.10	.05	.01
☐ 248	Jimmy Key	.15	.07	.02
☐ 249	Greg Maddux FT	.30	.14	.04
☐ 250	Randy Johnson FT	.20	.09	.03
☐ 251	Bret Saberhagen FT	.15	.07	.02
☐ 252	John Wetteland FT	.10	.05	.01
☐ 253	Mike Piazza FT	.60	.25	.08
☐ 254	Jeff Bagwell FT	.60	.25	.08
☐ 255	Craig Biggio FT	.15	.07	.02
☐ 256	Matt Williams FT	.25	.11	.03
☐ 257	Wil Cordero FT	.10	.05	.01
☐ 258	Kenny Lofton FT	.40	.18	.05
☐ 259	Barry Bonds FT	.60	.25	.08
☐ 260	Dante Bichette FT	.20	.09	.03
☐ 261	Ken Griffey Jr. Checklist 1-53	.75	.35	.09
☐ 262	Goose Gossage Checklist 54-106	.10	.05	.01
☐ 263	Cal Ripken Checklist 107-159	.60	.25	.08
☐ 264	Kenny Rogers Checklist 160-212	.10	.05	.01
☐ 265	John Valentin Checklist 213-265	.10	.05	.01

1995 Collector's Choice SE Gold Signature

A parallel to the basic 265-card Collector's Choice set, each card features a gold-foil

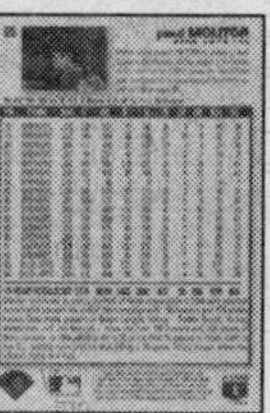

replica signature on it. Inserted one in 35 packs, the fronts feature color action player photos with blue borders. The player's name, position and the team name are printed on the bottom of the photo. The SE logo in blue-foil appears in a top corner. On a white background, the backs carry another color player photo with a short player biography, career stats and 1994 highlights. Following subsets are included in this set: Rookie Class (1-25), Record Pace (26-30), Stat Leaders (137-144), Fantasy Team (249-260), and Checklists (261-265).

	MINT	EXC	G-VG
COMPLETE SET (265)	900.00	400.00	115.00
COMMON CARD (1-265)	2.00	.90	.25

*UNLISTED VETERAN STARS: 18X to 30X VALUE
*UNLISTED YOUNG STARS: 15X to 25X VALUE

1995 Collector's Choice SE Silver Signature

A parallel to the basic 265-card Collector's Choice issue, each card has a silver-foil replica signature on the front. Inserted one in every pack, the fronts feature color action player photos with blue borders. The player's name, position and the team name are printed on the bottom of the photo. The SE logo in blue-foil appears in a top corner. On a white background, the backs carry another color player photo with a short player biography, career stats and 1994 highlights. Following subsets are included in this set:

Rookie Class (1-25), Record Pace (26-30), Stat Leaders (137-144), and Fantasy Team (249-260).

	MINT	EXC	G-VG
COMPLETE SET (265)	70.00	32.00	8.75
COMMON CARD (1-265)	.20	.09	.03

*UNLISTED VETERAN STARS: 1.5X to 3X VALUE
*UNLISTED YOUNG STARS: 1.25X to 2.5X VALUE

1981 Donruss

The cards in this 605-card set measure 2 1/2" by 3 1/2". In 1981 Donruss launched itself into the baseball card market with a set containing 600 numbered cards and five unnumbered checklists. Even though the five checklist cards are unnumbered, they are numbered below (601-605) for convenience in reference. The cards are printed on thin stock and more than one pose exists for several popular players. Numerous errors of the first print run were later corrected by the company. These are marked P1 and P2 in the checklist below. The key rookie cards in this set are Danny Ainge, Tim Raines, and Jeff Reardon.

	NRMT-MT	EXC	G-VG
COMPLETE SET (605)	45.00	20.00	5.75
COMMON CARD (1-605)	.10	.05	.01
☐ 1 Ozzie Smith	4.00	1.50	.45
☐ 2 Rollie Fingers	.50	.23	.06
☐ 3 Rick Wise	.10	.05	.01
☐ 4 Gene Richards	.10	.05	.01
☐ 5 Alan Trammell	1.75	.80	.22
☐ 6 Tom Brookens	.10	.05	.01
☐ 7A Duffy Dyer P1 (1980 batting average has decimal point)	.15	.07	.02
☐ 7B Duffy Dyer P2 (1980 batting average has no decimal point)	.10	.05	.01
☐ 8 Mark Fidrych	.15	.07	.02
☐ 9 Dave Rozema	.10	.05	.01
☐ 10 Ricky Peters	.10	.05	.01
☐ 11 Mike Schmidt	2.00	.90	.25
☐ 12 Willie Stargell	1.00	.45	.13
☐ 13 Tim Foli	.10	.05	.01
☐ 14 Manny Sanguillen	.15	.07	.02
☐ 15 Grant Jackson	.10	.05	.01
☐ 16 Eddie Solomon	.10	.05	.01
☐ 17 Omar Moreno	.10	.05	.01
☐ 18 Joe Morgan	1.00	.45	.13
☐ 19 Rafael Landestoy	.10	.05	.01
☐ 20 Bruce Bochy	.10	.05	.01
☐ 21 Joe Sambito	.10	.05	.01
☐ 22 Manny Trillo	.10	.05	.01
☐ 23A Dave Smith P1 (Line box around stats is not complete)	.15	.07	.02
☐ 23B Dave Smith P2 (Box totally encloses stats at top)	.15	.07	.02
☐ 24 Terry Puhl	.10	.05	.01
☐ 25 Bump Wills	.10	.05	.01
☐ 26A John Ellis P1 ERR (Photo on front shows Danny Walton)	.40	.18	.05
☐ 26B John Ellis P2 COR	.15	.07	.02
☐ 27 Jim Kern	.10	.05	.01
☐ 28 Richie Zisk	.10	.05	.01
☐ 29 John Mayberry	.10	.05	.01
☐ 30 Bob Davis	.10	.05	.01
☐ 31 Jackson Todd	.10	.05	.01
☐ 32 Alvis Woods	.10	.05	.01
☐ 33 Steve Carlton	2.00	.90	.25
☐ 34 Lee Mazzilli	.10	.05	.01
☐ 35 John Stearns	.10	.05	.01
☐ 36 Roy Lee Jackson	.10	.05	.01
☐ 37 Mike Scott	.10	.05	.01
☐ 38 Lamar Johnson	.10	.05	.01
☐ 39 Kevin Bell	.10	.05	.01
☐ 40 Ed Farmer	.10	.05	.01
☐ 41 Ross Baumgarten	.10	.05	.01
☐ 42 Leo Sutherland	.10	.05	.01
☐ 43 Dan Meyer	.10	.05	.01
☐ 44 Ron Reed	.10	.05	.01
☐ 45 Mario Mendoza	.10	.05	.01
☐ 46 Rick Honeycutt	.10	.05	.01
☐ 47 Glenn Abbott	.10	.05	.01
☐ 48 Leon Roberts	.10	.05	.01
☐ 49 Rod Carew	1.00	.45	.13
☐ 50 Bert Campaneris	.15	.07	.02
☐ 51A Tom Donahue P1 ERR. (Name on front misspelled Donahue)	.15	.07	.02
☐ 51B Tom Donohue P2 COR	.10	.05	.01
☐ 52 Dave Frost	.10	.05	.01
☐ 53 Ed Halicki	.10	.05	.01
☐ 54 Dan Ford	.10	.05	.01
☐ 55 Garry Maddox	.10	.05	.01
☐ 56A Steve Garvey P1 ("Surpassed 25 HR")	.75	.35	.09
☐ 56B Steve Garvey P2 ("Surpassed 21 HR")	.75	.35	.09
☐ 57 Bill Russell	.15	.07	.02
☐ 58 Don Sutton	.50	.23	.06
☐ 59 Reggie Smith	.15	.07	.02
☐ 60 Rick Monday	.15	.07	.02
☐ 61 Ray Knight	.15	.07	.02
☐ 62 Johnny Bench	1.50	.65	.19
☐ 63 Mario Soto	.10	.05	.01
☐ 64 Doug Bair	.10	.05	.01
☐ 65 George Foster	.15	.07	.02
☐ 66 Jeff Burroughs	.10	.05	.01
☐ 67 Keith Hernandez	.20	.09	.03
☐ 68 Tom Herr	.15	.07	.02
☐ 69 Bob Forsch	.10	.05	.01
☐ 70 John Fulgham	.10	.05	.01
☐ 71A Bobby Bonds P1 ERR.. (986 lifetime HR)	.20	.09	.03
☐ 71B Bobby Bonds P2 COR.. (326 lifetime HR)	.15	.07	.02

☐ 72A	Rennie Stennett P1 ("Breaking broke leg")	.15	.07	.02
☐ 72B	Rennie Stennett P2 (Word "broke" deleted)	.10	.05	.01
☐ 73	Joe Strain	.10	.05	.01
☐ 74	Ed Whitson	.10	.05	.01
☐ 75	Tom Griffin	.10	.05	.01
☐ 76	Billy North	.10	.05	.01
☐ 77	Gene Garber	.10	.05	.01
☐ 78	Mike Hargrove	.15	.07	.02
☐ 79	Dave Rosello	.10	.05	.01
☐ 80	Ron Hassey	.10	.05	.01
☐ 81	Sid Monge	.10	.05	.01
☐ 82A	Joe Charboneau P1 ('78 highlights, "For some reason")	.40	.18	.05
☐ 82B	Joe Charboneau P2 (Phrase "For some reason" deleted)	.40	.18	.05
☐ 83	Cecil Cooper	.15	.07	.02
☐ 84	Sal Bando	.15	.07	.02
☐ 85	Moose Haas	.10	.05	.01
☐ 86	Mike Caldwell	.10	.05	.01
☐ 87A	Larry Hisle P1 ('77 highlights, line ends with "28 RBI")	.15	.07	.02
☐ 87B	Larry Hisle P2 (Correct line "28 HR")	.10	.05	.01
☐ 88	Luis Gomez	.10	.05	.01
☐ 89	Larry Parrish	.10	.05	.01
☐ 90	Gary Carter	.75	.35	.09
☐ 91	Bill Gullickson	.30	.14	.04
☐ 92	Fred Norman	.10	.05	.01
☐ 93	Tommy Hutton	.10	.05	.01
☐ 94	Carl Yastrzemski	1.50	.65	.19
☐ 95	Glenn Hoffman	.10	.05	.01
☐ 96	Dennis Eckersley	1.00	.45	.13
☐ 97A	Tom Burgmeier P1 ERR (Throws: Right)	.15	.07	.02
☐ 97B	Tom Burgmeier P2 COR (Throws: Left)	.10	.05	.01
☐ 98	Win Remmerswaal	.10	.05	.01
☐ 99	Bob Horner	.15	.07	.02
☐ 100	George Brett	4.00	1.80	.50
☐ 101	Dave Chalk	.10	.05	.01
☐ 102	Dennis Leonard	.10	.05	.01
☐ 103	Renie Martin	.10	.05	.01
☐ 104	Amos Otis	.15	.07	.02
☐ 105	Graig Nettles	.15	.07	.02
☐ 106	Eric Soderholm	.10	.05	.01
☐ 107	Tommy John	.20	.09	.03
☐ 108	Tom Underwood	.10	.05	.01
☐ 109	Lou Piniella	.15	.07	.02
☐ 110	Mickey Klutts	.10	.05	.01
☐ 111	Bobby Murcer	.15	.07	.02
☐ 112	Eddie Murray	3.00	1.35	.40
☐ 113	Rick Dempsey	.15	.07	.02
☐ 114	Scott McGregor	.10	.05	.01
☐ 115	Ken Singleton	.15	.07	.02
☐ 116	Gary Roenicke	.10	.05	.01
☐ 117	Dave Revering	.10	.05	.01
☐ 118	Mike Norris	.10	.05	.01
☐ 119	Rickey Henderson	8.00	3.60	1.00
☐ 120	Mike Heath	.10	.05	.01
☐ 121	Dave Cash	.10	.05	.01
☐ 122	Randy Jones	.10	.05	.01
☐ 123	Eric Rasmussen	.10	.05	.01
☐ 124	Jerry Mumphrey	.10	.05	.01
☐ 125	Richie Hebner	.10	.05	.01
☐ 126	Mark Wagner	.10	.05	.01
☐ 127	Jack Morris	.50	.23	.06
☐ 128	Dan Petry	.15	.07	.02
☐ 129	Bruce Robbins	.10	.05	.01
☐ 130	Champ Summers	.10	.05	.01
☐ 131A	Pete Rose P1 (Last line ends with "see card 251")	2.00	.90	.25
☐ 131B	Pete Rose P2 (Last line corrected "see card 371")	2.00	.90	.25
☐ 132	Willie Stargell	1.00	.45	.13
☐ 133	Ed Ott	.10	.05	.01
☐ 134	Jim Bibby	.10	.05	.01
☐ 135	Bert Blyleven	.20	.09	.03
☐ 136	Dave Parker	.20	.09	.03
☐ 137	Bill Robinson	.15	.07	.02
☐ 138	Enos Cabell	.10	.05	.01
☐ 139	Dave Bergman	.10	.05	.01
☐ 140	J.R. Richard	.15	.07	.02
☐ 141	Ken Forsch	.10	.05	.01
☐ 142	Larry Bowa UER (Shortshop on front)	.15	.07	.02
☐ 143	Frank LaCorte UER (Photo actually Randy Niemann)	.10	.05	.01
☐ 144	Denny Walling	.10	.05	.01
☐ 145	Buddy Bell	.15	.07	.02
☐ 146	Ferguson Jenkins	.50	.23	.06
☐ 147	Dannny Darwin	.10	.05	.01
☐ 148	John Grubb	.10	.05	.01
☐ 149	Alfredo Griffin	.10	.05	.01
☐ 150	Jerry Garvin	.10	.05	.01
☐ 151	Paul Mirabella	.10	.05	.01
☐ 152	Rick Bosetti	.10	.05	.01
☐ 153	Dick Ruthven	.10	.05	.01
☐ 154	Frank Taveras	.10	.05	.01
☐ 155	Craig Swan	.10	.05	.01
☐ 156	Jeff Reardon	2.00	.90	.25
☐ 157	Steve Henderson	.10	.05	.01
☐ 158	Jim Morrison	.10	.05	.01
☐ 159	Glenn Borgmann	.10	.05	.01
☐ 160	LaMarr Hoyt	.15	.07	.02
☐ 161	Rich Wortham	.10	.05	.01
☐ 162	Thad Bosley	.10	.05	.01
☐ 163	Julio Cruz	.10	.05	.01
☐ 164A	Del Unser P1 (No "3B" heading)	.15	.07	.02
☐ 164B	Del Unser P2 (Batting record on back corrected ("3B")	.10	.05	.01
☐ 165	Jim Anderson	.10	.05	.01
☐ 166	Jim Beattie	.10	.05	.01
☐ 167	Shane Rawley	.10	.05	.01
☐ 168	Joe Simpson	.10	.05	.01
☐ 169	Rod Carew	1.00	.45	.13
☐ 170	Fred Patek	.10	.05	.01
☐ 171	Frank Tanana	.15	.07	.02
☐ 172	Alfredo Martinez	.10	.05	.01
☐ 173	Chris Knapp	.10	.05	.01
☐ 174	Joe Rudi	.15	.07	.02
☐ 175	Greg Luzinski	.15	.07	.02
☐ 176	Steve Garvey	.75	.35	.09
☐ 177	Joe Ferguson	.10	.05	.01
☐ 178	Bob Welch	.15	.07	.02
☐ 179	Dusty Baker	.20	.09	.03
☐ 180	Rudy Law	.10	.05	.01
☐ 181	Dave Concepcion	.15	.07	.02
☐ 182	Johnny Bench	1.50	.65	.19
☐ 183	Mike LaCoss	.10	.05	.01
☐ 184	Ken Griffey	.15	.07	.02
☐ 185	Dave Collins	.10	.05	.01
☐ 186	Brian Asselstine	.10	.05	.01
☐ 187	Garry Templeton	.15	.07	.02
☐ 188	Mike Phillips	.10	.05	.01
☐ 189	Pete Vuckovich	.15	.07	.02
☐ 190	John Urrea	.10	.05	.01

☐ 191	Tony Scott	.10	.05	.01
☐ 192	Darrell Evans	.15	.07	.02
☐ 193	Milt May	.10	.05	.01
☐ 194	Bob Knepper	.10	.05	.01
☐ 195	Randy Moffitt	.10	.05	.01
☐ 196	Larry Herndon	.10	.05	.01
☐ 197	Rick Camp	.10	.05	.01
☐ 198	Andre Thornton	.15	.07	.02
☐ 199	Tom Veryzer	.10	.05	.01
☐ 200	Gary Alexander	.10	.05	.01
☐ 201	Rick Waits	.10	.05	.01
☐ 202	Rick Manning	.10	.05	.01
☐ 203	Paul Molitor	3.00	1.35	.40
☐ 204	Jim Gantner	.15	.07	.02
☐ 205	Paul Mitchell	.10	.05	.01
☐ 206	Reggie Cleveland	.10	.05	.01
☐ 207	Sixto Lezcano	.10	.05	.01
☐ 208	Bruce Benedict	.10	.05	.01
☐ 209	Rodney Scott	.10	.05	.01
☐ 210	John Tamargo	.10	.05	.01
☐ 211	Bill Lee	.10	.05	.01
☐ 212	Andre Dawson UER (Middle name Fernando, should be Nolan)	1.50	.65	.19
☐ 213	Rowland Office	.10	.05	.01
☐ 214	Carl Yastrzemski	1.50	.65	.19
☐ 215	Jerry Remy	.10	.05	.01
☐ 216	Mike Torrez	.10	.05	.01
☐ 217	Skip Lockwood	.10	.05	.01
☐ 218	Fred Lynn	.15	.07	.02
☐ 219	Chris Chambliss	.15	.07	.02
☐ 220	Willie Aikens	.10	.05	.01
☐ 221	John Wathan	.10	.05	.01
☐ 222	Dan Quisenberry	.20	.09	.03
☐ 223	Willie Wilson	.10	.05	.01
☐ 224	Clint Hurdle	.10	.05	.01
☐ 225	Bob Watson	.15	.07	.02
☐ 226	Jim Spencer	.10	.05	.01
☐ 227	Ron Guidry	.15	.07	.02
☐ 228	Reggie Jackson	2.50	1.15	.30
☐ 229	Oscar Gamble	.10	.05	.01
☐ 230	Jeff Cox	.10	.05	.01
☐ 231	Luis Tiant	.15	.07	.02
☐ 232	Rich Dauer	.10	.05	.01
☐ 233	Dan Graham	.10	.05	.01
☐ 234	Mike Flanagan	.15	.07	.02
☐ 235	John Lowenstein	.10	.05	.01
☐ 236	Benny Ayala	.10	.05	.01
☐ 237	Wayne Gross	.10	.05	.01
☐ 238	Rick Langford	.10	.05	.01
☐ 239	Tony Armas	.15	.07	.02
☐ 240A	Bob Lacy P1 ERR (Name misspelled Bob "Lacy")	.20	.09	.03
☐ 240B	Bob Lacey P2 COR	.10	.05	.01
☐ 241	Gene Tenace	.10	.05	.01
☐ 242	Bob Shirley	.10	.05	.01
☐ 243	Gary Lucas	.10	.05	.01
☐ 244	Jerry Turner	.10	.05	.01
☐ 245	John Wockenfuss	.10	.05	.01
☐ 246	Stan Papi	.10	.05	.01
☐ 247	Milt Wilcox	.10	.05	.01
☐ 248	Dan Schatzeder	.10	.05	.01
☐ 249	Steve Kemp	.10	.05	.01
☐ 250	Jim Lentine	.10	.05	.01
☐ 251	Pete Rose	2.50	1.15	.30
☐ 252	Bill Madlock	.15	.07	.02
☐ 253	Dale Berra	.10	.05	.01
☐ 254	Kent Tekulve	.15	.07	.02
☐ 255	Enrique Romo	.10	.05	.01
☐ 256	Mike Easler	.10	.05	.01
☐ 257	Chuck Tanner MG	.10	.05	.01
☐ 258	Art Howe	.15	.07	.02
☐ 259	Alan Ashby	.10	.05	.01
☐ 260	Nolan Ryan	8.00	3.60	1.00
☐ 261A	Vern Ruhle P1 ERR (Photo on front actually Ken Forsch)	.40	.18	.05
☐ 261B	Vern Ruhle P2 COR	.15	.07	.02
☐ 262	Bob Boone	.15	.07	.02
☐ 263	Cesar Cedeno	.15	.07	.02
☐ 264	Jeff Leonard	.15	.07	.02
☐ 265	Pat Putnam	.10	.05	.01
☐ 266	Jon Matlack	.10	.05	.01
☐ 267	Dave Rajsich	.10	.05	.01
☐ 268	Billy Sample	.10	.05	.01
☐ 269	Damaso Garcia	.15	.07	.02
☐ 270	Tom Buskey	.10	.05	.01
☐ 271	Joey McLaughlin	.10	.05	.01
☐ 272	Barry Bonnell	.10	.05	.01
☐ 273	Tug McGraw	.15	.07	.02
☐ 274	Mike Jorgensen	.10	.05	.01
☐ 275	Pat Zachry	.10	.05	.01
☐ 276	Neil Allen	.10	.05	.01
☐ 277	Joel Youngblood	.10	.05	.01
☐ 278	Greg Pryor	.10	.05	.01
☐ 279	Britt Burns	.15	.07	.02
☐ 280	Rich Dotson	.15	.07	.02
☐ 281	Chet Lemon	.15	.07	.02
☐ 282	Rusty Kuntz	.10	.05	.01
☐ 283	Ted Cox	.10	.05	.01
☐ 284	Sparky Lyle	.15	.07	.02
☐ 285	Larry Cox	.10	.05	.01
☐ 286	Floyd Bannister	.10	.05	.01
☐ 287	Byron McLaughlin	.10	.05	.01
☐ 288	Rodney Craig	.10	.05	.01
☐ 289	Bobby Grich	.15	.07	.02
☐ 290	Dickie Thon	.15	.07	.02
☐ 291	Mark Clear	.10	.05	.01
☐ 292	Dave Lemanczyk	.10	.05	.01
☐ 293	Jason Thompson	.10	.05	.01
☐ 294	Rick Miller	.10	.05	.01
☐ 295	Lonnie Smith	.10	.05	.01
☐ 296	Ron Cey	.15	.07	.02
☐ 297	Steve Yeager	.10	.05	.01
☐ 298	Bobby Castillo	.10	.05	.01
☐ 299	Manny Mota	.15	.07	.02
☐ 300	Jay Johnstone	.15	.07	.02
☐ 301	Dan Driessen	.10	.05	.01
☐ 302	Joe Nolan	.10	.05	.01
☐ 303	Paul Householder	.10	.05	.01
☐ 304	Harry Spilman	.10	.05	.01
☐ 305	Cesar Geronimo	.10	.05	.01
☐ 306A	Gary Mathews P1 ERR (Name misspelled)	.20	.09	.03
☐ 306B	Gary Matthews P2 COR	.15	.07	.02
☐ 307	Ken Reitz	.10	.05	.01
☐ 308	Ted Simmons	.15	.07	.02
☐ 309	John Littlefield	.10	.05	.01
☐ 310	George Frazier	.10	.05	.01
☐ 311	Dane Iorg	.10	.05	.01
☐ 312	Mike Ivie	.10	.05	.01
☐ 313	Dennis Littlejohn	.10	.05	.01
☐ 314	Gary Lavelle	.10	.05	.01
☐ 315	Jack Clark	.15	.07	.02
☐ 316	Jim Wohlford	.10	.05	.01
☐ 317	Rick Matula	.10	.05	.01
☐ 318	Toby Harrah	.15	.07	.02
☐ 319A	Dwane Kuiper P1 ERR (Name misspelled)	.15	.07	.02
☐ 319B	Duane Kuiper P2 COR	.10	.05	.01
☐ 320	Len Barker	.10	.05	.01
☐ 321	Victor Cruz	.10	.05	.01
☐ 322	Dell Alston	.10	.05	.01
☐ 323	Robin Yount	3.00	1.35	.40

☐ 324 Charlie Moore .... .10 .05 .01
☐ 325 Lary Sorensen.............. .10 .05 .01
☐ 326A Gorman Thomas P1... .20 .09 .03
(2nd line on back:
"30 HR mark 4th")
☐ 326B Gorman Thomas P2... .15 .07 .02
("30 HR mark 3rd")
☐ 327 Bob Rodgers MG .... .10 .05 .01
☐ 328 Phil Niekro.................. .50 .23 .06
☐ 329 Chris Speier................ .10 .05 .01
☐ 330A Steve Rodgers P1...... .20 .09 .03
ERR (Name misspelled)
☐ 330B Steve Rogers P2 COR .10 .05 .01
☐ 331 Woodie Fryman............ .10 .05 .01
☐ 332 Warren Cromartie .... .10 .05 .01
☐ 333 Jerry White .... .10 .05 .01
☐ 334 Tony Perez................... .40 .18 .05
☐ 335 Carlton Fisk............... 1.50 .65 .19
☐ 336 Dick Drago.................... .10 .05 .01
☐ 337 Steve Renko................. .10 .05 .01
☐ 338 Jim Rice....................... .30 .14 .04
☐ 339 Jerry Royster .... .10 .05 .01
☐ 340 Frank White.................. .15 .07 .02
☐ 341 Jamie Quirk.................. .10 .05 .01
☐ 342A Paul Spittorff P1 ERR .15 .07 .02
(Name misspelled)
☐ 342B Paul Splittorff .... .10 .05 .01
P2 COR
☐ 343 Marty Pattin .... .10 .05 .01
☐ 344 Pete LaCock................. .10 .05 .01
☐ 345 Willie Randolph............ .15 .07 .02
☐ 346 Rick Cerone .... .10 .05 .01
☐ 347 Rich Gossage............... .20 .09 .03
☐ 348 Reggie Jackson.......... 2.00 .90 .25
☐ 349 Ruppert Jones .... .10 .05 .01
☐ 350 Dave McKay.................. .10 .05 .01
☐ 351 Yogi Berra CO .... .40 .18 .05
☐ 352 Doug DeCinces .... .15 .07 .02
☐ 353 Jim Palmer .... 1.00 .45 .13
☐ 354 Tippy Martinez .... .10 .05 .01
☐ 355 Al Bumbry..................... .15 .07 .02
☐ 356 Earl Weaver MG .... .15 .07 .02
☐ 357A Bob Picciolo P1 ERR . .15 .07 .02
(Name misspelled)
☐ 357B Rob Picciolo P2 COR. .10 .05 .01
☐ 358 Matt Keough .... .10 .05 .01
☐ 359 Dwayne Murphy............ .10 .05 .01
☐ 360 Brian Kingman .... .10 .05 .01
☐ 361 Bill Fahey .... .10 .05 .01
☐ 362 Steve Mura .... .10 .05 .01
☐ 363 Dennis Kinney.............. .10 .05 .01
☐ 364 Dave Winfield............ 2.50 1.15 .30
☐ 365 Lou Whitaker .... 1.00 .45 .13
☐ 366 Lance Parrish............... .20 .09 .03
☐ 367 Tim Corcoran................ .10 .05 .01
☐ 368 Pat Underwood............. .10 .05 .01
☐ 369 Al Cowens..................... .10 .05 .01
☐ 370 Sparky Anderson MG.... .15 .07 .02
☐ 371 Pete Rose .... 2.00 .90 .25
☐ 372 Phil Garner................... .15 .07 .02
☐ 373 Steve Nicosia............... .10 .05 .01
☐ 374 John Candelaria........... .15 .07 .02
☐ 375 Don Robinson............... .10 .05 .01
☐ 376 Lee Lacy .... .10 .05 .01
☐ 377 John Milner................... .10 .05 .01
☐ 378 Craig Reynolds .... .10 .05 .01
☐ 379A Luis Pujois P1 ERR.... .15 .07 .02
(Name misspelled)
☐ 379B Luis Pujols P2 COR ... .10 .05 .01
☐ 380 Joe Niekro.................... .15 .07 .02
☐ 381 Joaquin Andujar........... .15 .07 .02
☐ 382 Keith Moreland .... .15 .07 .02
☐ 383 Jose Cruz..................... .15 .07 .02
☐ 384 Bill Virdon MG .... .10 .05 .01
☐ 385 Jim Sundberg .... .15 .07 .02
☐ 386 Doc Medich................... .10 .05 .01
☐ 387 Al Oliver .... .15 .07 .02
☐ 388 Jim Norris...................... .10 .05 .01
☐ 389 Bob Bailor..................... .10 .05 .01
☐ 390 Ernie Whitt.................... .10 .05 .01
☐ 391 Otto Velez .... .10 .05 .01
☐ 392 Roy Howell .... .10 .05 .01
☐ 393 Bob Walk .... .35 .16 .04
☐ 394 Doug Flynn .... .10 .05 .01
☐ 395 Pete Falcone .... .10 .05 .01
☐ 396 Tom Hausman .... .10 .05 .01
☐ 397 Elliott Maddox............... .10 .05 .01
☐ 398 Mike Squires................. .10 .05 .01
☐ 399 Marvis Foley .... .10 .05 .01
☐ 400 Steve Trout .... .10 .05 .01
☐ 401 Wayne Nordhagen .... .10 .05 .01
☐ 402 Tony LaRussa MG .... .15 .07 .02
☐ 403 Bruce Bochte .... .10 .05 .01
☐ 404 Bake McBride................ .10 .05 .01
☐ 405 Jerry Narron .... .10 .05 .01
☐ 406 Rob Dressler................. .10 .05 .01
☐ 407 Dave Heaverlo.............. .10 .05 .01
☐ 408 Tom Paciorek................ .15 .07 .02
☐ 409 Carney Lansford .... .15 .07 .02
☐ 410 Brian Downing.............. .15 .07 .02
☐ 411 Don Aase .... .10 .05 .01
☐ 412 Jim Barr......................... .10 .05 .01
☐ 413 Don Baylor..................... .20 .09 .03
☐ 414 Jim Fregosi MG .... .10 .05 .01
☐ 415 Dallas Green MG.......... .10 .05 .01
☐ 416 Dave Lopes................... .15 .07 .02
☐ 417 Jerry Reuss.................. .15 .07 .02
☐ 418 Rick Sutcliffe................ .30 .14 .04
☐ 419 Derrel Thomas.............. .10 .05 .01
☐ 420 Tom Lasorda MG.......... .15 .07 .02
☐ 421 Charles Leibrandt......... .30 .14 .04
☐ 422 Tom Seaver............... 1.25 .55 .16
☐ 423 Ron Oester.................... .10 .05 .01
☐ 424 Junior Kennedy............ .10 .05 .01
☐ 425 Tom Seaver............... 1.50 .65 .19
☐ 426 Bobby Cox MG.............. .10 .05 .01
☐ 427 Leon Durham................ .15 .07 .02
☐ 428 Terry Kennedy.............. .10 .05 .01
☐ 429 Silvio Martinez............. .10 .05 .01
☐ 430 George Hendrick.......... .15 .07 .02
☐ 431 Red Schoendienst MG . .10 .05 .01
☐ 432 Johnnie LeMaster .... .10 .05 .01
☐ 433 Vida Blue...................... .15 .07 .02
☐ 434 John Montefusco.......... .10 .05 .01
☐ 435 Terry Whitfield.............. .10 .05 .01
☐ 436 Dave Bristol MG........... .10 .05 .01
☐ 437 Dale Murphy .... 1.00 .45 .13
☐ 438 Jerry Dybzinski .... .10 .05 .01
☐ 439 Jorge Orta..................... .10 .05 .01
☐ 440 Wayne Garland .... .10 .05 .01
☐ 441 Miguel Dilone................ .10 .05 .01
☐ 442 Dave Garcia MG .... .10 .05 .01
☐ 443 Don Money .... .10 .05 .01
☐ 444A Buck Martinez P1 ERR .15 .07 .02
(Reverse negative)
☐ 444B Buck Martinez............ .10 .05 .01
P2 COR
☐ 445 Jerry Augustine............ .10 .05 .01
☐ 446 Ben Oglivie................... .15 .07 .02
☐ 447 Jim Slaton..................... .10 .05 .01
☐ 448 Doyle Alexander........... .10 .05 .01
☐ 449 Tony Bernazard............ .10 .05 .01
☐ 450 Scott Sanderson .... .15 .07 .02
☐ 451 David Palmer .... .10 .05 .01
☐ 452 Stan Bahnsen............... .10 .05 .01
☐ 453 Dick Williams MG .... .10 .05 .01

☐	454 Rick Burleson	.10	.05	.01
☐	455 Gary Allenson	.10	.05	.01
☐	456 Bob Stanley	.10	.05	.01
☐	457A John Tudor P1 ERR	.35	.16	.04
	(Lifetime W-L "9.7")			
☐	457B John Tudor P2 COR	.35	.16	.04
	(Corrected "9-7")			
☐	458 Dwight Evans	.20	.09	.03
☐	459 Glenn Hubbard	.10	.05	.01
☐	460 U.L. Washington	.10	.05	.01
☐	461 Larry Gura	.10	.05	.01
☐	462 Rich Gale	.10	.05	.01
☐	463 Hal McRae	.20	.09	.03
☐	464 Jim Frey MG	.10	.05	.01
☐	465 Bucky Dent	.15	.07	.02
☐	466 Dennis Werth	.10	.05	.01
☐	467 Ron Davis	.10	.05	.01
☐	468 Reggie Jackson UER	2.00	.90	.25
	(32 HR in 1970, should be 23)			
☐	469 Bobby Brown	.10	.05	.01
☐	470 Mike Davis	.10	.05	.01
☐	471 Gaylord Perry	.50	.23	.06
☐	472 Mark Belanger	.15	.07	.02
☐	473 Jim Palmer	1.00	.45	.13
☐	474 Sammy Stewart	.10	.05	.01
☐	475 Tim Stoddard	.10	.05	.01
☐	476 Steve Stone	.15	.07	.02
☐	477 Jeff Newman	.10	.05	.01
☐	478 Steve McCatty	.10	.05	.01
☐	479 Billy Martin MG	.25	.11	.03
☐	480 Mitchell Page	.10	.05	.01
☐	481 Steve Carlton CY	1.00	.45	.13
☐	482 Bill Buckner	.15	.07	.02
☐	483A Ivan DeJesus P1 ERR	.15	.07	.02
	(Lifetime hits "702")			
☐	483B Ivan DeJesus P2 COR	.10	.05	.01
	(Lifetime hits "642")			
☐	484 Cliff Johnson	.10	.05	.01
☐	485 Lenny Randle	.10	.05	.01
☐	486 Larry Milbourne	.10	.05	.01
☐	487 Roy Smalley	.10	.05	.01
☐	488 John Castino	.10	.05	.01
☐	489 Ron Jackson	.10	.05	.01
☐	490A Dave Roberts P1	.15	.07	.02
	(Career Highlights: "Showed pop in")			
☐	490B Dave Roberts P2	.10	.05	.01
	("Declared himself")			
☐	491 George Brett MVP	2.50	1.15	.30
☐	492 Mike Cubbage	.10	.05	.01
☐	493 Rob Wilfong	.10	.05	.01
☐	494 Danny Goodwin	.10	.05	.01
☐	495 Jose Morales	.10	.05	.01
☐	496 Mickey Rivers	.15	.07	.02
☐	497 Mike Edwards	.10	.05	.01
☐	498 Mike Sadek	.10	.05	.01
☐	499 Lenn Sakata	.10	.05	.01
☐	500 Gene Michael MG	.10	.05	.01
☐	501 Dave Roberts	.10	.05	.01
☐	502 Steve Dillard	.10	.05	.01
☐	503 Jim Essian	.10	.05	.01
☐	504 Rance Mulliniks	.10	.05	.01
☐	505 Darrell Porter	.10	.05	.01
☐	506 Joe Torre MG	.15	.07	.02
☐	507 Terry Crowley	.10	.05	.01
☐	508 Bill Travers	.10	.05	.01
☐	509 Nelson Norman	.10	.05	.01
☐	510 Bob McClure	.10	.05	.01
☐	511 Steve Howe	.15	.07	.02
☐	512 Dave Rader	.10	.05	.01
☐	513 Mick Kelleher	.10	.05	.01
☐	514 Kiko Garcia	.10	.05	.01
☐	515 Larry Biittner	.10	.05	.01
☐	516A Willie Norwood P1	.15	.07	.02
	(Career Highlights "Spent most of")			
☐	516B Willie Norwood P2	.10	.05	.01
	("Traded to Seattle")			
☐	517 Bo Diaz	.10	.05	.01
☐	518 Juan Beniquez	.10	.05	.01
☐	519 Scot Thompson	.10	.05	.01
☐	520 Jim Tracy	.10	.05	.01
☐	521 Carlos Lezcano	.10	.05	.01
☐	522 Joe Amalfitano MG	.10	.05	.01
☐	523 Preston Hanna	.10	.05	.01
☐	524A Ray Burris P1	.15	.07	.02
	(Career Highlights: "Went on ...")			
☐	524B Ray Burris P2	.10	.05	.01
	("Drafted by ...")			
☐	525 Broderick Perkins	.10	.05	.01
☐	526 Mickey Hatcher	.10	.05	.01
☐	527 John Goryl MG	.10	.05	.01
☐	528 Dick Davis	.10	.05	.01
☐	529 Butch Wynegar	.10	.05	.01
☐	530 Sal Butera	.10	.05	.01
☐	531 Jerry Koosman	.15	.07	.02
☐	532A Geoff Zahn P1	.15	.07	.02
	(Career Highlights: "Was 2nd in")			
☐	532B Geoff Zahn P2	.10	.05	.01
	("Signed a 3 year")			
☐	533 Dennis Martinez	.15	.07	.02
☐	534 Gary Thomasson	.10	.05	.01
☐	535 Steve Macko	.10	.05	.01
☐	536 Jim Kaat	.15	.07	.02
☐	537 Best Hitters	2.50	1.15	.30
	George Brett			
	Rod Carew			
☐	538 Tim Raines	6.00	2.70	.75
☐	539 Keith Smith	.10	.05	.01
☐	540 Ken Macha	.10	.05	.01
☐	541 Burt Hooton	.10	.05	.01
☐	542 Butch Hobson	.15	.07	.02
☐	543 Bill Stein	.10	.05	.01
☐	544 Dave Stapleton	.10	.05	.01
☐	545 Bob Pate	.10	.05	.01
☐	546 Doug Corbett	.10	.05	.01
☐	547 Darrell Jackson	.10	.05	.01
☐	548 Pete Redfern	.10	.05	.01
☐	549 Roger Erickson	.10	.05	.01
☐	550 Al Hrabosky	.10	.05	.01
☐	551 Dick Tidrow	.10	.05	.01
☐	552 Dave Ford	.10	.05	.01
☐	553 Dave Kingman	.15	.07	.02
☐	554A Mike Vail P1	.15	.07	.02
	(Career Highlights: "After two ...")			
☐	554B Mike Vail P2	.10	.05	.01
	("Traded to ...")			
☐	555A Jerry Martin P1	.15	.07	.02
	(Career Highlights: "Overcame a ...")			
☐	555B Jerry Martin P2	.10	.05	.01
	("Traded to ...")			
☐	556A Jesus Figueroa P1	.15	.07	.02
	(Career Highlights: "Had an ...")			
☐	556B Jesus Figueroa P2	.10	.05	.01
	("Traded to ...")			
☐	557 Don Stanhouse	.10	.05	.01
☐	558 Barry Foote	.10	.05	.01
☐	559 Tim Blackwell	.10	.05	.01
☐	560 Bruce Sutter	.15	.07	.02
☐	561 Rick Reuschel	.15	.07	.02

☐ 562 Lynn McGlothen	.10	.05	.01
☐ 563A Bob Owchinko P1 (Career Highlights: "Traded to ...")	.10	.05	.01
☐ 563B Bob Owchinko P2 ("Involved in a ...")	.10	.05	.01
☐ 564 John Verhoeven	.10	.05	.01
☐ 565 Ken Landreaux	.10	.05	.01
☐ 566A Glen Adams P1 ERR (Name misspelled)	.15	.07	.02
☐ 566B Glenn Adams P2 COR	.10	.05	.01
☐ 567 Hosken Powell	.10	.05	.01
☐ 568 Dick Noles	.10	.05	.01
☐ 569 Danny Ainge	5.00	2.30	.60
☐ 570 Bobby Mattick MG	.10	.05	.01
☐ 571 Joe Lefebvre	.10	.05	.01
☐ 572 Bobby Clark	.10	.05	.01
☐ 573 Dennis Lamp	.10	.05	.01
☐ 574 Randy Lerch	.10	.05	.01
☐ 575 Mookie Wilson	.40	.18	.05
☐ 576 Ron LeFlore	.15	.07	.02
☐ 577 Jim Dwyer	.10	.05	.01
☐ 578 Bill Castro	.10	.05	.01
☐ 579 Greg Minton	.10	.05	.01
☐ 580 Mark Littell	.10	.05	.01
☐ 581 Andy Hassler	.10	.05	.01
☐ 582 Dave Stieb	.15	.07	.02
☐ 583 Ken Oberkfell	.10	.05	.01
☐ 584 Larry Bradford	.10	.05	.01
☐ 585 Fred Stanley	.10	.05	.01
☐ 586 Bill Caudill	.10	.05	.01
☐ 587 Doug Capilla	.10	.05	.01
☐ 588 George Riley	.10	.05	.01
☐ 589 Willie Hernandez	.15	.07	.02
☐ 590 Mike Schmidt MVP	1.50	.65	.19
☐ 591 Steve Stone CY	.10	.05	.01
☐ 592 Rick Sofield	.10	.05	.01
☐ 593 Bombo Rivera	.10	.05	.01
☐ 594 Gary Ward	.10	.05	.01
☐ 595A Dave Edwards P1 (Career Highlights: "Sidelined the")	.15	.07	.02
☐ 595B Dave Edwards P2 ("Traded to ...")	.10	.05	.01
☐ 596 Mike Proly	.10	.05	.01
☐ 597 Tommy Boggs	.10	.05	.01
☐ 598 Greg Gross	.10	.05	.01
☐ 599 Elias Sosa	.10	.05	.01
☐ 600 Pat Kelly	.10	.05	.01
☐ 601A Checklist 1-120 P1 ERR Unnumbered (51 Donahue)	.15	.05	.01
☐ 601B Checklist 1-120 P2 COR Unnumbered (51 Donohue)	.60	.05	.01
☐ 602 Checklist 121-240 Unnumbered	.15	.05	.01
☐ 603A Checklist 241-360 P1 ERR Unnumbered (306 Mathews)	.15	.05	.01
☐ 603B Checklist 241-360 P2 COR Unnumbered (306 Matthews)	.15	.05	.01
☐ 604A Checklist 361-480 P1 ERR Unnumbered (379 Pujois)	.15	.05	.01
☐ 604B Checklist 361-480 P2 COR Unnumbered (379 Pujols)	.15	.05	.01
☐ 605A Checklist 481-600 P1 ERR Unnumbered (566 Glen Adams)	.15	.05	.01
☐ 605B Checklist 481-600 P2 COR Unnumbered (566 Glenn Adams)	.15	.05	.01

1982 Donruss

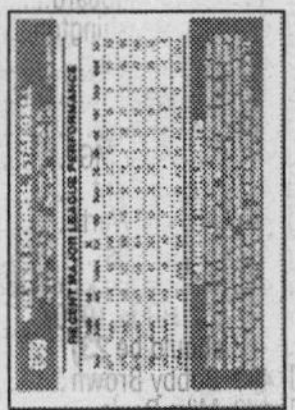

The 1982 Donruss set contains 653 numbered cards and the seven unnumbered checklists; each card measures 2 1/2" by 3 1/2". The first 26 cards of this set are entitled Donruss Diamond Kings (DK) and feature the artwork of Dick Perez of Perez-Steele Galleries. The set was marketed with puzzle pieces rather than with bubble gum. There are 63 pieces to the puzzle, which, when put together, make a collage of Babe Ruth entitled "Hall of Fame Diamond King." The card stock in this year's Donruss cards is considerably thicker than that of the 1981 cards. The seven unnumbered checklist cards are arbitrarily assigned numbers 654 through 660 and are listed at the end of the list below. Rookie Cards in this set include George Bell, Brett Butler, Kent Hrbek, Cal Ripken Jr., Steve Sax, Lee Smith, and Dave Stewart.

	NRMT-MT	EXC	G-VG
COMPLETE SET (660)	75.00	34.00	9.50
COMPLETE FACT.SET (660)	85.00	38.00	10.50
COMMON CARD (1-660)	.10	.05	.01
☐ 1 Pete Rose DK	2.00	.90	.25
☐ 2 Gary Carter DK	.40	.18	.05
☐ 3 Steve Garvey DK	.30	.14	.04
☐ 4 Vida Blue DK	.15	.07	.02
☐ 5A Alan Trammel DK ERR (Name misspelled)	1.00	.45	.13
☐ 5B Alan Trammell DK COR	.50	.23	.06
☐ 6 Len Barker DK	.15	.07	.02
☐ 7 Dwight Evans DK	.25	.11	.03
☐ 8 Rod Carew DK	.75	.35	.09
☐ 9 George Hendrick DK	.15	.07	.02
☐ 10 Phil Niekro DK	.25	.11	.03
☐ 11 Richie Zisk DK	.15	.07	.02
☐ 12 Dave Parker DK	.25	.11	.03
☐ 13 Nolan Ryan DK	5.00	2.30	.60
☐ 14 Ivan DeJesus DK	.15	.07	.02
☐ 15 George Brett DK	2.00	.90	.25
☐ 16 Tom Seaver DK	1.00	.45	.13
☐ 17 Dave Kingman DK	.15	.07	.02
☐ 18 Dave Winfield DK	1.50	.65	.19
☐ 19 Mike Norris DK	.15	.07	.02
☐ 20 Carlton Fisk DK	.75	.35	.09
☐ 21 Ozzie Smith DK	2.00	.90	.25

	#	Player			
☐	22	Roy Smalley DK	.15	.07	.02
☐	23	Buddy Bell DK	.15	.07	.02
☐	24	Ken Singleton DK	.15	.07	.02
☐	25	John Mayberry DK	.15	.07	.02
☐	26	Gorman Thomas DK	.15	.07	.02
☐	27	Earl Weaver MG	.15	.07	.02
☐	28	Rollie Fingers	.40	.18	.05
☐	29	Sparky Anderson MG	.15	.07	.02
☐	30	Dennis Eckersley	.75	.35	.09
☐	31	Dave Winfield	2.00	.90	.25
☐	32	Burt Hooton	.10	.05	.01
☐	33	Rick Waits	.10	.05	.01
☐	34	George Brett	3.50	1.55	.45
☐	35	Steve McCatty	.10	.05	.01
☐	36	Steve Rogers	.10	.05	.01
☐	37	Bill Stein	.10	.05	.01
☐	38	Steve Renko	.10	.05	.01
☐	39	Mike Squires	.10	.05	.01
☐	40	George Hendrick	.15	.07	.02
☐	41	Bob Knepper	.10	.05	.01
☐	42	Steve Carlton	1.00	.45	.13
☐	43	Larry Biittner	.10	.05	.01
☐	44	Chris Welsh	.10	.05	.01
☐	45	Steve Nicosia	.10	.05	.01
☐	46	Jack Clark	.15	.07	.02
☐	47	Chris Chambliss	.15	.07	.02
☐	48	Ivan DeJesus	.10	.05	.01
☐	49	Lee Mazzilli	.10	.05	.01
☐	50	Julio Cruz	.10	.05	.01
☐	51	Pete Redfern	.10	.05	.01
☐	52	Dave Stieb	.15	.07	.02
☐	53	Doug Corbett	.10	.05	.01
☐	54	George Bell	1.50	.65	.19
☐	55	Joe Simpson	.10	.05	.01
☐	56	Rusty Staub	.15	.07	.02
☐	57	Hector Cruz	.10	.05	.01
☐	58	Claudell Washington	.10	.05	.01
☐	59	Enrique Romo	.10	.05	.01
☐	60	Gary Lavelle	.10	.05	.01
☐	61	Tim Flannery	.10	.05	.01
☐	62	Joe Nolan	.10	.05	.01
☐	63	Larry Bowa	.15	.07	.02
☐	64	Sixto Lezcano	.10	.05	.01
☐	65	Joe Sambito	.10	.05	.01
☐	66	Bruce Kison	.10	.05	.01
☐	67	Wayne Nordhagen	.10	.05	.01
☐	68	Woodie Fryman	.10	.05	.01
☐	69	Billy Sample	.10	.05	.01
☐	70	Amos Otis	.15	.07	.02
☐	71	Matt Keough	.10	.05	.01
☐	72	Toby Harrah	.15	.07	.02
☐	73	Dave Righetti	.40	.18	.05
☐	74	Carl Yastrzemski	1.00	.45	.13
☐	75	Bob Welch	.15	.07	.02
☐	76A	Alan Trammel ERR (Name misspelled)	1.50	.65	.19
☐	76B	Alan Trammell COR	1.00	.45	.13
☐	77	Rick Dempsey	.15	.07	.02
☐	78	Paul Molitor	2.50	1.15	.30
☐	79	Dennis Martinez	.15	.07	.02
☐	80	Jim Slaton	.10	.05	.01
☐	81	Champ Summers	.10	.05	.01
☐	82	Carney Lansford	.15	.07	.02
☐	83	Barry Foote	.10	.05	.01
☐	84	Steve Garvey	.50	.23	.06
☐	85	Rick Manning	.10	.05	.01
☐	86	John Wathan	.10	.05	.01
☐	87	Brian Kingman	.10	.05	.01
☐	88	Andre Dawson UER (Middle name Fernando, should be Nolan)	1.25	.55	.16
☐	89	Jim Kern	.10	.05	.01
☐	90	Bobby Grich	.15	.07	.02
☐	91	Bob Forsch	.10	.05	.01
☐	92	Art Howe	.10	.05	.01
☐	93	Marty Bystrom	.10	.05	.01
☐	94	Ozzie Smith	3.00	1.35	.40
☐	95	Dave Parker	.20	.09	.03
☐	96	Doyle Alexander	.10	.05	.01
☐	97	Al Hrabosky	.10	.05	.01
☐	98	Frank Taveras	.10	.05	.01
☐	99	Tim Blackwell	.10	.05	.01
☐	100	Floyd Bannister	.10	.05	.01
☐	101	Alfredo Griffin	.10	.05	.01
☐	102	Dave Engle	.10	.05	.01
☐	103	Mario Soto	.10	.05	.01
☐	104	Ross Baumgarten	.10	.05	.01
☐	105	Ken Singleton	.15	.07	.02
☐	106	Ted Simmons	.15	.07	.02
☐	107	Jack Morris	.50	.23	.06
☐	108	Bob Watson	.15	.07	.02
☐	109	Dwight Evans	.20	.09	.03
☐	110	Tom Lasorda MG	.15	.07	.02
☐	111	Bert Blyleven	.20	.09	.03
☐	112	Dan Quisenberry	.15	.07	.02
☐	113	Rickey Henderson	3.50	1.55	.45
☐	114	Gary Carter	.60	.25	.08
☐	115	Brian Downing	.15	.07	.02
☐	116	Al Oliver	.15	.07	.02
☐	117	LaMarr Hoyt	.10	.05	.01
☐	118	Cesar Cedeno	.15	.07	.02
☐	119	Keith Moreland	.10	.05	.01
☐	120	Bob Shirley	.10	.05	.01
☐	121	Terry Kennedy	.10	.05	.01
☐	122	Frank Pastore	.10	.05	.01
☐	123	Gene Garber	.10	.05	.01
☐	124	Tony Pena	.15	.07	.02
☐	125	Allen Ripley	.10	.05	.01
☐	126	Randy Martz	.10	.05	.01
☐	127	Richie Zisk	.10	.05	.01
☐	128	Mike Scott	.15	.07	.02
☐	129	Lloyd Moseby	.10	.05	.01
☐	130	Rob Wilfong	.10	.05	.01
☐	131	Tim Stoddard	.10	.05	.01
☐	132	Gorman Thomas	.15	.07	.02
☐	133	Dan Petry	.10	.05	.01
☐	134	Bob Stanley	.10	.05	.01
☐	135	Lou Piniella	.15	.07	.02
☐	136	Pedro Guerrero	.15	.07	.02
☐	137	Len Barker	.10	.05	.01
☐	138	Rich Gale	.10	.05	.01
☐	139	Wayne Gross	.10	.05	.01
☐	140	Tim Wallach	1.25	.55	.16
☐	141	Gene Mauch MG	.10	.05	.01
☐	142	Doc Medich	.10	.05	.01
☐	143	Tony Bernazard	.10	.05	.01
☐	144	Bill Virdon MG	.10	.05	.01
☐	145	John Littlefield	.10	.05	.01
☐	146	Dave Bergman	.10	.05	.01
☐	147	Dick Davis	.10	.05	.01
☐	148	Tom Seaver	1.00	.45	.13
☐	149	Matt Sinatro	.10	.05	.01
☐	150	Chuck Tanner MG	.10	.05	.01
☐	151	Leon Durham	.10	.05	.01
☐	152	Gene Tenace	.10	.05	.01
☐	153	Al Bumbry	.15	.07	.02
☐	154	Mark Brouhard	.10	.05	.01
☐	155	Rick Peters	.10	.05	.01
☐	156	Jerry Remy	.10	.05	.01
☐	157	Rick Reuschel	.15	.07	.02
☐	158	Steve Howe	.10	.05	.01
☐	159	Alan Bannister	.10	.05	.01
☐	160	U.L. Washington	.10	.05	.01
☐	161	Rick Langford	.10	.05	.01
☐	162	Bill Gullickson	.15	.07	.02
☐	163	Mark Wagner	.10	.05	.01

☐ 164	Geoff Zahn	.10	.05	.01
☐ 165	Ron LeFlore	.15	.07	.02
☐ 166	Dane Iorg	.10	.05	.01
☐ 167	Joe Niekro	.15	.07	.02
☐ 168	Pete Rose	2.00	.90	.25
☐ 169	Dave Collins	.10	.05	.01
☐ 170	Rick Wise	.10	.05	.01
☐ 171	Jim Bibby	.10	.05	.01
☐ 172	Larry Herndon	.10	.05	.01
☐ 173	Bob Horner	.15	.07	.02
☐ 174	Steve Dillard	.10	.05	.01
☐ 175	Mookie Wilson	.15	.07	.02
☐ 176	Dan Meyer	.10	.05	.01
☐ 177	Fernando Arroyo	.10	.05	.01
☐ 178	Jackson Todd	.10	.05	.01
☐ 179	Darrell Jackson	.10	.05	.01
☐ 180	Alvis Woods	.10	.05	.01
☐ 181	Jim Anderson	.10	.05	.01
☐ 182	Dave Kingman	.15	.07	.02
☐ 183	Steve Henderson	.10	.05	.01
☐ 184	Brian Asselstine	.10	.05	.01
☐ 185	Rod Scurry	.10	.05	.01
☐ 186	Fred Breining	.10	.05	.01
☐ 187	Danny Boone	.10	.05	.01
☐ 188	Junior Kennedy	.10	.05	.01
☐ 189	Sparky Lyle	.15	.07	.02
☐ 190	Whitey Herzog MG	.15	.07	.02
☐ 191	Dave Smith	.10	.05	.01
☐ 192	Ed Ott	.10	.05	.01
☐ 193	Greg Luzinski	.15	.07	.02
☐ 194	Bill Lee	.10	.05	.01
☐ 195	Don Zimmer MG	.10	.05	.01
☐ 196	Hal McRae	.20	.09	.03
☐ 197	Mike Norris	.10	.05	.01
☐ 198	Duane Kuiper	.10	.05	.01
☐ 199	Rick Cerone	.10	.05	.01
☐ 200	Jim Rice	.20	.09	.03
☐ 201	Steve Yeager	.10	.05	.01
☐ 202	Tom Brookens	.10	.05	.01
☐ 203	Jose Morales	.10	.05	.01
☐ 204	Roy Howell	.10	.05	.01
☐ 205	Tippy Martinez	.10	.05	.01
☐ 206	Moose Haas	.10	.05	.01
☐ 207	Al Cowens	.10	.05	.01
☐ 208	Dave Stapleton	.10	.05	.01
☐ 209	Bucky Dent	.15	.07	.02
☐ 210	Ron Cey	.15	.07	.02
☐ 211	Jorge Orta	.10	.05	.01
☐ 212	Jamie Quirk	.10	.05	.01
☐ 213	Jeff Jones	.10	.05	.01
☐ 214	Tim Raines	2.50	1.15	.30
☐ 215	Jon Matlack	.10	.05	.01
☐ 216	Rod Carew	1.00	.45	.13
☐ 217	Jim Kaat	.15	.07	.02
☐ 218	Joe Pittman	.10	.05	.01
☐ 219	Larry Christenson	.10	.05	.01
☐ 220	Juan Bonilla	.10	.05	.01
☐ 221	Mike Easler	.10	.05	.01
☐ 222	Vida Blue	.15	.07	.02
☐ 223	Rick Camp	.10	.05	.01
☐ 224	Mike Jorgensen	.10	.05	.01
☐ 225	Jody Davis	.10	.05	.01
☐ 226	Mike Parrott	.10	.05	.01
☐ 227	Jim Clancy	.10	.05	.01
☐ 228	Hosken Powell	.10	.05	.01
☐ 229	Tom Hume	.10	.05	.01
☐ 230	Britt Burns	.10	.05	.01
☐ 231	Jim Palmer	1.00	.45	.13
☐ 232	Bob Rodgers MG	.10	.05	.01
☐ 233	Milt Wilcox	.10	.05	.01
☐ 234	Dave Revering	.10	.05	.01
☐ 235	Mike Torrez	.10	.05	.01
☐ 236	Robert Castillo	.10	.05	.01
☐ 237	Von Hayes	.15	.07	.02
☐ 238	Renie Martin	.10	.05	.01
☐ 239	Dwayne Murphy	.10	.05	.01
☐ 240	Rodney Scott	.10	.05	.01
☐ 241	Fred Patek	.10	.05	.01
☐ 242	Mickey Rivers	.10	.05	.01
☐ 243	Steve Trout	.10	.05	.01
☐ 244	Jose Cruz	.15	.07	.02
☐ 245	Manny Trillo	.10	.05	.01
☐ 246	Lary Sorensen	.10	.05	.01
☐ 247	Dave Edwards	.10	.05	.01
☐ 248	Dan Driessen	.10	.05	.01
☐ 249	Tommy Boggs	.10	.05	.01
☐ 250	Dale Berra	.10	.05	.01
☐ 251	Ed Whitson	.10	.05	.01
☐ 252	Lee Smith	8.00	3.60	1.00
☐ 253	Tom Paciorek	.15	.07	.02
☐ 254	Pat Zachry	.10	.05	.01
☐ 255	Luis Leal	.10	.05	.01
☐ 256	John Castino	.10	.05	.01
☐ 257	Rich Dauer	.10	.05	.01
☐ 258	Cecil Cooper	.15	.07	.02
☐ 259	Dave Rozema	.10	.05	.01
☐ 260	John Tudor	.15	.07	.02
☐ 261	Jerry Mumphrey	.10	.05	.01
☐ 262	Jay Johnstone	.15	.07	.02
☐ 263	Bo Diaz	.10	.05	.01
☐ 264	Dennis Leonard	.10	.05	.01
☐ 265	Jim Spencer	.10	.05	.01
☐ 266	John Milner	.10	.05	.01
☐ 267	Don Aase	.10	.05	.01
☐ 268	Jim Sundberg	.15	.07	.02
☐ 269	Lamar Johnson	.10	.05	.01
☐ 270	Frank LaCorte	.10	.05	.01
☐ 271	Barry Evans	.10	.05	.01
☐ 272	Enos Cabell	.10	.05	.01
☐ 273	Del Unser	.10	.05	.01
☐ 274	George Foster	.15	.07	.02
☐ 275	Brett Butler	3.00	1.35	.40
☐ 276	Lee Lacy	.10	.05	.01
☐ 277	Ken Reitz	.10	.05	.01
☐ 278	Keith Hernandez	.20	.09	.03
☐ 279	Doug DeCinces	.15	.07	.02
☐ 280	Charlie Moore	.10	.05	.01
☐ 281	Lance Parrish	.20	.09	.03
☐ 282	Ralph Houk MG	.10	.05	.01
☐ 283	Rich Gossage	.20	.09	.03
☐ 284	Jerry Reuss	.10	.05	.01
☐ 285	Mike Stanton	.10	.05	.01
☐ 286	Frank White	.15	.07	.02
☐ 287	Bob Owchinko	.10	.05	.01
☐ 288	Scott Sanderson	.15	.07	.02
☐ 289	Bump Wills	.10	.05	.01
☐ 290	Dave Frost	.10	.05	.01
☐ 291	Chet Lemon	.10	.05	.01
☐ 292	Tito Landrum	.10	.05	.01
☐ 293	Vern Ruhle	.10	.05	.01
☐ 294	Mike Schmidt	2.00	.90	.25
☐ 295	Sam Mejias	.10	.05	.01
☐ 296	Gary Lucas	.10	.05	.01
☐ 297	John Candelaria	.10	.05	.01
☐ 298	Jerry Martin	.10	.05	.01
☐ 299	Dale Murphy	.75	.35	.09
☐ 300	Mike Lum	.10	.05	.01
☐ 301	Tom Hausman	.10	.05	.01
☐ 302	Glenn Abbott	.10	.05	.01
☐ 303	Roger Erickson	.10	.05	.01
☐ 304	Otto Velez	.10	.05	.01
☐ 305	Danny Goodwin	.10	.05	.01
☐ 306	John Mayberry	.10	.05	.01
☐ 307	Lenny Randle	.10	.05	.01
☐ 308	Bob Bailor	.10	.05	.01
☐ 309	Jerry Morales	.10	.05	.01

☐ 310 Rufino Linares .10 .05 .01
☐ 311 Kent Tekulve .15 .07 .02
☐ 312 Joe Morgan .75 .35 .09
☐ 313 John Urrea .10 .05 .01
☐ 314 Paul Householder .10 .05 .01
☐ 315 Garry Maddox .10 .05 .01
☐ 316 Mike Ramsey .10 .05 .01
☐ 317 Alan Ashby .10 .05 .01
☐ 318 Bob Clark .10 .05 .01
☐ 319 Tony LaRussa MG .15 .07 .02
☐ 320 Charlie Lea .10 .05 .01
☐ 321 Danny Darwin .10 .05 .01
☐ 322 Cesar Geronimo .10 .05 .01
☐ 323 Tom Underwood .10 .05 .01
☐ 324 Andre Thornton .10 .05 .01
☐ 325 Rudy May .10 .05 .01
☐ 326 Frank Tanana .15 .07 .02
☐ 327 Dave Lopes .15 .07 .02
☐ 328 Richie Hebner .10 .05 .01
☐ 329 Mike Flanagan .15 .07 .02
☐ 330 Mike Caldwell .10 .05 .01
☐ 331 Scott McGregor .10 .05 .01
☐ 332 Jerry Augustine .10 .05 .01
☐ 333 Stan Papi .10 .05 .01
☐ 334 Rick Miller .10 .05 .01
☐ 335 Graig Nettles .15 .07 .02
☐ 336 Dusty Baker .20 .09 .03
☐ 337 Dave Garcia MG .10 .05 .01
☐ 338 Larry Gura .10 .05 .01
☐ 339 Cliff Johnson .10 .05 .01
☐ 340 Warren Cromartie .10 .05 .01
☐ 341 Steve Comer .10 .05 .01
☐ 342 Rick Burleson .10 .05 .01
☐ 343 John Martin .10 .05 .01
☐ 344 Craig Reynolds .10 .05 .01
☐ 345 Mike Proly .10 .05 .01
☐ 346 Ruppert Jones .10 .05 .01
☐ 347 Omar Moreno .10 .05 .01
☐ 348 Greg Minton .10 .05 .01
☐ 349 Rick Mahler .10 .05 .01
☐ 350 Alex Trevino .10 .05 .01
☐ 351 Mike Krukow .10 .05 .01
☐ 352A Shane Rawley ERR .75 .35 .09
(Photo of Jim Anderson)
☐ 352B Shane Rawley COR .10 .05 .01
☐ 353 Garth Iorg .10 .05 .01
☐ 354 Pete Mackanin .10 .05 .01
☐ 355 Paul Moskau .10 .05 .01
☐ 356 Richard Dotson .10 .05 .01
☐ 357 Steve Stone .15 .07 .02
☐ 358 Larry Hisle .10 .05 .01
☐ 359 Aurelio Lopez .10 .05 .01
☐ 360 Oscar Gamble .10 .05 .01
☐ 361 Tom Burgmeier .10 .05 .01
☐ 362 Terry Forster .10 .05 .01
☐ 363 Joe Charboneau .10 .05 .01
☐ 364 Ken Brett .10 .05 .01
☐ 365 Tony Armas .10 .05 .01
☐ 366 Chris Speier .10 .05 .01
☐ 367 Fred Lynn .15 .07 .02
☐ 368 Buddy Bell .15 .07 .02
☐ 369 Jim Essian .10 .05 .01
☐ 370 Terry Puhl .10 .05 .01
☐ 371 Greg Gross .10 .05 .01
☐ 372 Bruce Sutter .15 .07 .02
☐ 373 Joe Lefebvre .10 .05 .01
☐ 374 Ray Knight .15 .07 .02
☐ 375 Bruce Benedict .10 .05 .01
☐ 376 Tim Foli .10 .05 .01
☐ 377 Al Holland .10 .05 .01
☐ 378 Ken Kravec .10 .05 .01
☐ 379 Jeff Burroughs .10 .05 .01
☐ 380 Pete Falcone .10 .05 .01
☐ 381 Ernie Whitt .10 .05 .01
☐ 382 Brad Havens .10 .05 .01
☐ 383 Terry Crowley .10 .05 .01
☐ 384 Don Money .10 .05 .01
☐ 385 Dan Schatzeder .10 .05 .01
☐ 386 Gary Allenson .10 .05 .01
☐ 387 Yogi Berra CO .40 .18 .05
☐ 388 Ken Landreaux .10 .05 .01
☐ 389 Mike Hargrove .15 .07 .02
☐ 390 Darryl Motley .10 .05 .01
☐ 391 Dave McKay .10 .05 .01
☐ 392 Stan Bahnsen .10 .05 .01
☐ 393 Ken Forsch .10 .05 .01
☐ 394 Mario Mendoza .10 .05 .01
☐ 395 Jim Morrison .10 .05 .01
☐ 396 Mike Ivie .10 .05 .01
☐ 397 Broderick Perkins .10 .05 .01
☐ 398 Darrell Evans .15 .07 .02
☐ 399 Ron Reed .10 .05 .01
☐ 400 Johnny Bench 1.00 .45 .13
☐ 401 Steve Bedrosian .30 .14 .04
☐ 402 Bill Robinson .15 .07 .02
☐ 403 Bill Buckner .15 .07 .02
☐ 404 Ken Oberkfell .10 .05 .01
☐ 405 Cal Ripken 40.00 18.00 5.00
☐ 406 Jim Gantner .15 .07 .02
☐ 407 Kirk Gibson 1.25 .55 .16
☐ 408 Tony Perez .30 .14 .04
☐ 409 Tommy John UER .20 .09 .03
(Text says 52-56 as
Yankee, should be
52-26)
☐ 410 Dave Stewart 2.00 .90 .25
☐ 411 Dan Spillner .10 .05 .01
☐ 412 Willie Aikens .10 .05 .01
☐ 413 Mike Heath .10 .05 .01
☐ 414 Ray Burris .10 .05 .01
☐ 415 Leon Roberts .10 .05 .01
☐ 416 Mike Witt .15 .07 .02
☐ 417 Bob Molinaro .10 .05 .01
☐ 418 Steve Braun .10 .05 .01
☐ 419 Nolan Ryan UER 8.00 3.60 1.00
(Misnumbering of
Nolan's no-hitters
on card back)
☐ 420 Tug McGraw .15 .07 .02
☐ 421 Dave Concepcion .15 .07 .02
☐ 422A Juan Eichelberger .75 .35 .09
ERR (Photo of Gary Lucas)
☐ 422B Juan Eichelberger .10 .05 .01
COR
☐ 423 Rick Rhoden .10 .05 .01
☐ 424 Frank Robinson MG .30 .14 .04
☐ 425 Eddie Miller .10 .05 .01
☐ 426 Bill Caudill .10 .05 .01
☐ 427 Doug Flynn .10 .05 .01
☐ 428 Larry Andersen UER .10 .05 .01
(Misspelled Anderson
on card front)
☐ 429 Al Williams .10 .05 .01
☐ 430 Jerry Garvin .10 .05 .01
☐ 431 Glenn Adams .10 .05 .01
☐ 432 Barry Bonnell .10 .05 .01
☐ 433 Jerry Narron .10 .05 .01
☐ 434 John Stearns .10 .05 .01
☐ 435 Mike Tyson .10 .05 .01
☐ 436 Glenn Hubbard .10 .05 .01
☐ 437 Eddie Solomon .10 .05 .01
☐ 438 Jeff Leonard .10 .05 .01
☐ 439 Randy Bass .30 .14 .04
☐ 440 Mike LaCoss .10 .05 .01
☐ 441 Gary Matthews .15 .07 .02
☐ 442 Mark Littell .10 .05 .01

	#	Player			
☐	443	Don Sutton	.40	.18	.05
☐	444	John Harris	.10	.05	.01
☐	445	Vada Pinson CO	.15	.07	.02
☐	446	Elias Sosa	.10	.05	.01
☐	447	Charlie Hough	.15	.07	.02
☐	448	Willie Wilson	.15	.07	.02
☐	449	Fred Stanley	.10	.05	.01
☐	450	Tom Veryzer	.10	.05	.01
☐	451	Ron Davis	.10	.05	.01
☐	452	Mark Clear	.10	.05	.01
☐	453	Bill Russell	.15	.07	.02
☐	454	Lou Whitaker	.60	.25	.08
☐	455	Dan Graham	.10	.05	.01
☐	456	Reggie Cleveland	.10	.05	.01
☐	457	Sammy Stewart	.10	.05	.01
☐	458	Pete Vuckovich	.15	.07	.02
☐	459	John Wockenfuss	.10	.05	.01
☐	460	Glenn Hoffman	.10	.05	.01
☐	461	Willie Randolph	.15	.07	.02
☐	462	Fernando Valenzuela	.25	.11	.03
☐	463	Ron Hassey	.10	.05	.01
☐	464	Paul Splittorff	.10	.05	.01
☐	465	Rob Picciolo	.10	.05	.01
☐	466	Larry Parrish	.10	.05	.01
☐	467	Johnny Grubb	.10	.05	.01
☐	468	Dan Ford	.10	.05	.01
☐	469	Silvio Martinez	.10	.05	.01
☐	470	Kiko Garcia	.10	.05	.01
☐	471	Bob Boone	.15	.07	.02
☐	472	Luis Salazar	.10	.05	.01
☐	473	Randy Niemann	.10	.05	.01
☐	474	Tom Griffin	.10	.05	.01
☐	475	Phil Niekro	.40	.18	.05
☐	476	Hubie Brooks	.15	.07	.02
☐	477	Dick Tidrow	.10	.05	.01
☐	478	Jim Beattie	.10	.05	.01
☐	479	Damaso Garcia	.10	.05	.01
☐	480	Mickey Hatcher	.10	.05	.01
☐	481	Joe Price	.10	.05	.01
☐	482	Ed Farmer	.10	.05	.01
☐	483	Eddie Murray	2.00	.90	.25
☐	484	Ben Oglivie	.15	.07	.02
☐	485	Kevin Saucier	.10	.05	.01
☐	486	Bobby Murcer	.15	.07	.02
☐	487	Bill Campbell	.10	.05	.01
☐	488	Reggie Smith	.15	.07	.02
☐	489	Wayne Garland	.10	.05	.01
☐	490	Jim Wright	.10	.05	.01
☐	491	Billy Martin MG	.15	.07	.02
☐	492	Jim Fanning MG	.10	.05	.01
☐	493	Don Baylor	.20	.09	.03
☐	494	Rick Honeycutt	.10	.05	.01
☐	495	Carlton Fisk	1.25	.55	.16
☐	496	Denny Walling	.10	.05	.01
☐	497	Bake McBride	.10	.05	.01
☐	498	Darrell Porter	.10	.05	.01
☐	499	Gene Richards	.10	.05	.01
☐	500	Ron Oester	.10	.05	.01
☐	501	Ken Dayley	.10	.05	.01
☐	502	Jason Thompson	.10	.05	.01
☐	503	Milt May	.10	.05	.01
☐	504	Doug Bird	.10	.05	.01
☐	505	Bruce Bochte	.10	.05	.01
☐	506	Neil Allen	.10	.05	.01
☐	507	Joey McLaughlin	.10	.05	.01
☐	508	Butch Wynegar	.10	.05	.01
☐	509	Gary Roenicke	.10	.05	.01
☐	510	Robin Yount	2.00	.90	.25
☐	511	Dave Tobik	.10	.05	.01
☐	512	Rich Gedman	.10	.05	.01
☐	513	Gene Nelson	.10	.05	.01
☐	514	Rick Monday	.10	.05	.01
☐	515	Miguel Dilone	.10	.05	.01
☐	516	Clint Hurdle	.10	.05	.01
☐	517	Jeff Newman	.10	.05	.01
☐	518	Grant Jackson	.10	.05	.01
☐	519	Andy Hassler	.10	.05	.01
☐	520	Pat Putnam	.10	.05	.01
☐	521	Greg Pryor	.10	.05	.01
☐	522	Tony Scott	.10	.05	.01
☐	523	Steve Mura	.10	.05	.01
☐	524	Johnnie LeMaster	.10	.05	.01
☐	525	Dick Ruthven	.10	.05	.01
☐	526	John McNamara MG	.10	.05	.01
☐	527	Larry McWilliams	.10	.05	.01
☐	528	Johnny Ray	.10	.05	.01
☐	529	Pat Tabler	.15	.07	.02
☐	530	Tom Herr	.15	.07	.02
☐	531A	San Diego Chicken COR (With TM)	1.75	.80	.22
☐	531B	San Diego Chicken ERR (Without TM)	1.75	.80	.22
☐	532	Sal Butera	.10	.05	.01
☐	533	Mike Griffin	.10	.05	.01
☐	534	Kelvin Moore	.10	.05	.01
☐	535	Reggie Jackson	1.50	.65	.19
☐	536	Ed Romero	.10	.05	.01
☐	537	Derrel Thomas	.10	.05	.01
☐	538	Mike O'Berry	.10	.05	.01
☐	539	Jack O'Connor	.10	.05	.01
☐	540	Bob Ojeda	.35	.16	.04
☐	541	Roy Lee Jackson	.10	.05	.01
☐	542	Lynn Jones	.10	.05	.01
☐	543	Gaylord Perry	.40	.18	.05
☐	544A	Phil Garner ERR (Reverse negative)	.75	.35	.09
☐	544B	Phil Garner COR	.15	.07	.02
☐	545	Garry Templeton	.15	.07	.02
☐	546	Rafael Ramirez	.10	.05	.01
☐	547	Jeff Reardon	.50	.23	.06
☐	548	Ron Guidry	.15	.07	.02
☐	549	Tim Laudner	.10	.05	.01
☐	550	John Henry Johnson	.10	.05	.01
☐	551	Chris Bando	.10	.05	.01
☐	552	Bobby Brown	.10	.05	.01
☐	553	Larry Bradford	.10	.05	.01
☐	554	Scott Fletcher	.50	.23	.06
☐	555	Jerry Royster	.10	.05	.01
☐	556	Shooty Babitt UER (Spelled Babbitt on front)	.10	.05	.01
☐	557	Kent Hrbek	2.00	.90	.25
☐	558	Yankee Winners Ron Guidry Tommy John	.15	.07	.02
☐	559	Mark Bomback	.10	.05	.01
☐	560	Julio Valdez	.10	.05	.01
☐	561	Buck Martinez	.10	.05	.01
☐	562	Mike A. Marshall	.15	.07	.02
☐	563	Rennie Stennett	.10	.05	.01
☐	564	Steve Crawford	.10	.05	.01
☐	565	Bob Babcock	.10	.05	.01
☐	566	Johnny Podres CO	.15	.07	.02
☐	567	Paul Serna	.10	.05	.01
☐	568	Harold Baines	1.00	.45	.13
☐	569	Dave LaRoche	.10	.05	.01
☐	570	Lee May	.15	.07	.02
☐	571	Gary Ward	.10	.05	.01
☐	572	John Denny	.10	.05	.01
☐	573	Roy Smalley	.10	.05	.01
☐	574	Bob Brenly	.10	.05	.01
☐	575	Bronx Bombers Reggie Jackson Dave Winfield	2.25	1.00	.30
☐	576	Luis Pujols	.10	.05	.01
☐	577	Butch Hobson	.15	.07	.02

□ 578 Harvey Kuenn MG	.15	.07	.02
□ 579 Cal Ripken Sr. CO	.15	.07	.02
□ 580 Juan Berenguer	.10	.05	.01
□ 581 Benny Ayala	.10	.05	.01
□ 582 Vance Law	.10	.05	.01
□ 583 Rick Leach	.10	.05	.01
□ 584 George Frazier	.10	.05	.01
□ 585 Phillies Finest	1.50	.65	.19
Pete Rose			
Mike Schmidt			
□ 586 Joe Rudi	.10	.05	.01
□ 587 Juan Beniquez	.10	.05	.01
□ 588 Luis DeLeon	.10	.05	.01
□ 589 Craig Swan	.10	.05	.01
□ 590 Dave Chalk	.10	.05	.01
□ 591 Billy Gardner MG	.10	.05	.01
□ 592 Sal Bando	.15	.07	.02
□ 593 Bert Campaneris	.15	.07	.02
□ 594 Steve Kemp	.10	.05	.01
□ 595A Randy Lerch ERR	.75	.35	.09
(Braves)			
□ 595B Randy Lerch COR	.10	.05	.01
(Brewers)			
□ 596 Bryan Clark	.10	.05	.01
□ 597 Dave Ford	.10	.05	.01
□ 598 Mike Scioscia	.15	.07	.02
□ 599 John Lowenstein	.10	.05	.01
□ 600 Rene Lachemann MG	.10	.05	.01
□ 601 Mick Kelleher	.10	.05	.01
□ 602 Ron Jackson	.10	.05	.01
□ 603 Jerry Koosman	.15	.07	.02
□ 604 Dave Goltz	.10	.05	.01
□ 605 Ellis Valentine	.10	.05	.01
□ 606 Lonnie Smith	.15	.07	.02
□ 607 Joaquin Andujar	.15	.07	.02
□ 608 Garry Hancock	.10	.05	.01
□ 609 Jerry Turner	.10	.05	.01
□ 610 Bob Bonner	.10	.05	.01
□ 611 Jim Dwyer	.10	.05	.01
□ 612 Terry Bulling	.10	.05	.01
□ 613 Joel Youngblood	.10	.05	.01
□ 614 Larry Milbourne	.10	.05	.01
□ 615 Gene Roof UER	.10	.05	.01
(Name on front			
is Phil Roof)			
□ 616 Keith Drumwright	.10	.05	.01
□ 617 Dave Rosello	.10	.05	.01
□ 618 Rickey Keeton	.10	.05	.01
□ 619 Dennis Lamp	.10	.05	.01
□ 620 Sid Monge	.10	.05	.01
□ 621 Jerry White	.10	.05	.01
□ 622 Luis Aguayo	.10	.05	.01
□ 623 Jamie Easterly	.10	.05	.01
□ 624 Steve Sax	1.00	.45	.13
□ 625 Dave Roberts	.10	.05	.01
□ 626 Rick Bosetti	.10	.05	.01
□ 627 Terry Francona	.10	.05	.01
□ 628 Pride of Reds	1.25	.55	.16
Tom Seaver			
Johnny Bench			
□ 629 Paul Mirabella	.10	.05	.01
□ 630 Rance Mulliniks	.10	.05	.01
□ 631 Kevin Hickey	.10	.05	.01
□ 632 Reid Nichols	.10	.05	.01
□ 633 Dave Geisel	.10	.05	.01
□ 634 Ken Griffey	.10	.05	.01
□ 635 Bob Lemon MG	.15	.07	.02
□ 636 Orlando Sanchez	.10	.05	.01
□ 637 Bill Almon	.10	.05	.01
□ 638 Danny Ainge	2.00	.90	.25
□ 639 Willie Stargell	.75	.35	.09
□ 640 Bob Sykes	.10	.05	.01
□ 641 Ed Lynch	.10	.05	.01
□ 642 John Ellis	.10	.05	.01
□ 643 Ferguson Jenkins	.40	.18	.05
□ 644 Lenn Sakata	.10	.05	.01
□ 645 Julio Gonzalez	.10	.05	.01
□ 646 Jesse Orosco	.10	.05	.01
□ 647 Jerry Dybzinski	.10	.05	.01
□ 648 Tommy Davis CO	.15	.07	.02
□ 649 Ron Gardenhire	.10	.05	.01
□ 650 Felipe Alou CO	.15	.07	.02
□ 651 Harvey Haddix CO	.15	.07	.02
□ 652 Willie Upshaw	.10	.05	.01
□ 653 Bill Madlock	.15	.07	.02
□ 654A DK Checklist 1-26	.40	.05	.01
ERR (Unnumbered)			
(With Trammel)			
□ 654B DK Checklist 1-26	.15	.05	.01
COR (Unnumbered)			
(With Trammell)			
□ 655 Checklist 27-130	.15	.05	.01
(Unnumbered)			
□ 656 Checklist 131-234	.15	.05	.01
(Unnumbered)			
□ 657 Checklist 235-338	.15	.05	.01
(Unnumbered)			
□ 658 Checklist 339-442	.15	.05	.01
(Unnumbered)			
□ 659 Checklist 443-544	.15	.05	.01
(Unnumbered)			
□ 660 Checklist 545-653	.15	.05	.01
(Unnumbered)			

1983 Donruss

The cards in this 660-card set measure 2 1/2" by 3 1/2". The 1983 Donruss baseball set, issued with a 63-piece Diamond King puzzle, again leads off with a 26-card Diamond Kings (DK) series. Of the remaining 634 cards, two are combination cards, one portrays the San Diego Chicken, one shows the completed Ty Cobb puzzle, and seven are unnumbered checklist cards. The seven unnumbered checklist cards are arbitrarily assigned numbers 654 through 660 and are listed at the end of the list below. The Donruss logo and the year of issue are shown in the upper left corner of the obverse. The card backs have black print on yellow and white and are numbered on a small ball design. The complete set price below includes only the more common of each variation pair. The key Rookie Cards in this set are Wade Boggs, Julio Franco, Tony Gwynn, Howard Johnson, Willie McGee, Ryne Sandberg, and Frank Viola.

	NRMT-MT	EXC	G-VG
COMPLETE SET (660)	100.00	45.00	12.50
COMPLETE FACT.SET (660)	110.00	50.00	14.00
COMMON CARD (1-660)	.10	.05	.01
☐ 1 Fernando Valenzuela DK	.25	.11	.03
☐ 2 Rollie Fingers DK	.25	.11	.03
☐ 3 Reggie Jackson DK	.75	.35	.09
☐ 4 Jim Palmer DK	.50	.23	.06
☐ 5 Jack Morris DK	.20	.09	.03
☐ 6 George Foster DK	.15	.07	.02
☐ 7 Jim Sundberg DK	.15	.07	.02
☐ 8 Willie Stargell DK	.25	.11	.03
☐ 9 Dave Stieb DK	.15	.07	.02
☐ 10 Joe Niekro DK	.15	.07	.02
☐ 11 Rickey Henderson DK	1.50	.65	.19
☐ 12 Dale Murphy DK	.35	.16	.04
☐ 13 Toby Harrah DK	.15	.07	.02
☐ 14 Bill Buckner DK	.15	.07	.02
☐ 15 Willie Wilson DK	.15	.07	.02
☐ 16 Steve Carlton DK	.60	.25	.08
☐ 17 Ron Guidry DK	.20	.09	.03
☐ 18 Steve Rogers DK	.15	.07	.02
☐ 19 Kent Hrbek DK	.25	.11	.03
☐ 20 Keith Hernandez DK	.20	.09	.03
☐ 21 Floyd Bannister DK	.15	.07	.02
☐ 22 Johnny Bench DK	.50	.23	.06
☐ 23 Britt Burns DK	.15	.07	.02
☐ 24 Joe Morgan DK	.35	.16	.04
☐ 25 Carl Yastrzemski DK	.50	.23	.06
☐ 26 Terry Kennedy DK	.15	.07	.02
☐ 27 Gary Roenicke	.10	.05	.01
☐ 28 Dwight Bernard	.10	.05	.01
☐ 29 Pat Underwood	.10	.05	.01
☐ 30 Gary Allenson	.10	.05	.01
☐ 31 Ron Guidry	.15	.07	.02
☐ 32 Burt Hooton	.10	.05	.01
☐ 33 Chris Bando	.10	.05	.01
☐ 34 Vida Blue	.15	.07	.02
☐ 35 Rickey Henderson	2.50	1.15	.30
☐ 36 Ray Burris	.10	.05	.01
☐ 37 John Butcher	.10	.05	.01
☐ 38 Don Aase	.10	.05	.01
☐ 39 Jerry Koosman	.15	.07	.02
☐ 40 Bruce Sutter	.15	.07	.02
☐ 41 Jose Cruz	.15	.07	.02
☐ 42 Pete Rose	1.75	.80	.22
☐ 43 Cesar Cedeno	.15	.07	.02
☐ 44 Floyd Chiffer	.10	.05	.01
☐ 45 Larry McWilliams	.10	.05	.01
☐ 46 Alan Fowlkes	.10	.05	.01
☐ 47 Dale Murphy	.60	.25	.08
☐ 48 Doug Bird	.10	.05	.01
☐ 49 Hubie Brooks	.15	.07	.02
☐ 50 Floyd Bannister	.10	.05	.01
☐ 51 Jack O'Connor	.10	.05	.01
☐ 52 Steve Senteney	.10	.05	.01
☐ 53 Gary Gaetti	.60	.25	.08
☐ 54 Damaso Garcia	.10	.05	.01
☐ 55 Gene Nelson	.10	.05	.01
☐ 56 Mookie Wilson	.15	.07	.02
☐ 57 Allen Ripley	.10	.05	.01
☐ 58 Bob Horner	.15	.07	.02
☐ 59 Tony Pena	.15	.07	.02
☐ 60 Gary Lavelle	.10	.05	.01
☐ 61 Tim Lollar	.10	.05	.01
☐ 62 Frank Pastore	.10	.05	.01
☐ 63 Garry Maddox	.10	.05	.01
☐ 64 Bob Forsch	.10	.05	.01
☐ 65 Harry Spilman	.10	.05	.01
☐ 66 Geoff Zahn	.10	.05	.01
☐ 67 Salome Barojas	.10	.05	.01
☐ 68 David Palmer	.10	.05	.01
☐ 69 Charlie Hough	.15	.07	.02
☐ 70 Dan Quisenberry	.15	.07	.02
☐ 71 Tony Armas	.10	.05	.01
☐ 72 Rick Sutcliffe	.15	.07	.02
☐ 73 Steve Balboni	.10	.05	.01
☐ 74 Jerry Remy	.10	.05	.01
☐ 75 Mike Scioscia	.15	.07	.02
☐ 76 John Wockenfuss	.10	.05	.01
☐ 77 Jim Palmer	.75	.35	.09
☐ 78 Rollie Fingers	.35	.16	.04
☐ 79 Joe Nolan	.10	.05	.01
☐ 80 Pete Vuckovich	.10	.05	.01
☐ 81 Rick Leach	.10	.05	.01
☐ 82 Rick Miller	.10	.05	.01
☐ 83 Graig Nettles	.15	.07	.02
☐ 84 Ron Cey	.15	.07	.02
☐ 85 Miguel Dilone	.10	.05	.01
☐ 86 John Wathan	.10	.05	.01
☐ 87 Kelvin Moore	.10	.05	.01
☐ 88A Byrn Smith ERR (Sic, Bryn)	.15	.07	.02
☐ 88B Bryn Smith COR	.50	.23	.06
☐ 89 Dave Hostetler	.10	.05	.01
☐ 90 Rod Carew	.75	.35	.09
☐ 91 Lonnie Smith	.15	.07	.02
☐ 92 Bob Knepper	.10	.05	.01
☐ 93 Marty Bystrom	.10	.05	.01
☐ 94 Chris Welsh	.10	.05	.01
☐ 95 Jason Thompson	.10	.05	.01
☐ 96 Tom O'Malley	.10	.05	.01
☐ 97 Phil Niekro	.35	.16	.04
☐ 98 Neil Allen	.10	.05	.01
☐ 99 Bill Buckner	.15	.07	.02
☐ 100 Ed VandeBerg	.10	.05	.01
☐ 101 Jim Clancy	.10	.05	.01
☐ 102 Robert Castillo	.10	.05	.01
☐ 103 Bruce Berenyi	.10	.05	.01
☐ 104 Carlton Fisk	1.00	.45	.13
☐ 105 Mike Flanagan	.15	.07	.02
☐ 106 Cecil Cooper	.15	.07	.02
☐ 107 Jack Morris	.35	.16	.04
☐ 108 Mike Morgan	.10	.05	.01
☐ 109 Luis Aponte	.10	.05	.01
☐ 110 Pedro Guerrero	.15	.07	.02
☐ 111 Len Barker	.10	.05	.01
☐ 112 Willie Wilson	.15	.07	.02
☐ 113 Dave Beard	.10	.05	.01
☐ 114 Mike Gates	.10	.05	.01
☐ 115 Reggie Jackson	1.50	.65	.19
☐ 116 George Wright	.10	.05	.01
☐ 117 Vance Law	.10	.05	.01
☐ 118 Nolan Ryan	7.00	3.10	.85
☐ 119 Mike Krukow	.10	.05	.01
☐ 120 Ozzie Smith	2.00	.90	.25
☐ 121 Broderick Perkins	.10	.05	.01
☐ 122 Tom Seaver	1.00	.45	.13
☐ 123 Chris Chambliss	.15	.07	.02
☐ 124 Chuck Tanner MG	.10	.05	.01
☐ 125 Johnnie LeMaster	.10	.05	.01
☐ 126 Mel Hall	.50	.23	.06
☐ 127 Bruce Bochte	.10	.05	.01
☐ 128 Charlie Puleo	.10	.05	.01
☐ 129 Luis Leal	.10	.05	.01
☐ 130 John Pacella	.10	.05	.01
☐ 131 Glenn Gulliver	.10	.05	.01
☐ 132 Don Money	.10	.05	.01
☐ 133 Dave Rozema	.10	.05	.01
☐ 134 Bruce Hurst	.10	.05	.01
☐ 135 Rudy May	.10	.05	.01
☐ 136 Tom Lasorda MG	.15	.07	.02
☐ 137 Dan Spillner UER (Photo of Ed Whitson)	.10	.05	.01
☐ 138 Jerry Martin	.10	.05	.01

	#	Player			
☐	139	Mike Norris	.10	.05	.01
☐	140	Al Oliver	.15	.07	.02
☐	141	Daryl Sconiers	.10	.05	.01
☐	142	Lamar Johnson	.10	.05	.01
☐	143	Harold Baines	.50	.23	.06
☐	144	Alan Ashby	.10	.05	.01
☐	145	Garry Templeton	.10	.05	.01
☐	146	Al Holland	.10	.05	.01
☐	147	Bo Diaz	.10	.05	.01
☐	148	Dave Concepcion	.15	.07	.02
☐	149	Rick Camp	.10	.05	.01
☐	150	Jim Morrison	.10	.05	.01
☐	151	Randy Martz	.10	.05	.01
☐	152	Keith Hernandez	.20	.09	.03
☐	153	John Lowenstein	.10	.05	.01
☐	154	Mike Caldwell	.10	.05	.01
☐	155	Milt Wilcox	.10	.05	.01
☐	156	Rich Gedman	.10	.05	.01
☐	157	Rich Gossage	.20	.09	.03
☐	158	Jerry Reuss	.10	.05	.01
☐	159	Ron Hassey	.10	.05	.01
☐	160	Larry Gura	.10	.05	.01
☐	161	Dwayne Murphy	.10	.05	.01
☐	162	Woodie Fryman	.10	.05	.01
☐	163	Steve Comer	.10	.05	.01
☐	164	Ken Forsch	.10	.05	.01
☐	165	Dennis Lamp	.10	.05	.01
☐	166	David Green	.10	.05	.01
☐	167	Terry Puhl	.10	.05	.01
☐	168	Mike Schmidt (Wearing coach Hank King's uniform No. 37 instead of 20)	1.75	.80	.22
☐	169	Eddie Milner	.10	.05	.01
☐	170	John Curtis	.10	.05	.01
☐	171	Don Robinson	.10	.05	.01
☐	172	Rich Gale	.10	.05	.01
☐	173	Steve Bedrosian	.15	.07	.02
☐	174	Willie Hernandez	.15	.07	.02
☐	175	Ron Gardenhire	.10	.05	.01
☐	176	Jim Beattie	.10	.05	.01
☐	177	Tim Laudner	.10	.05	.01
☐	178	Buck Martinez	.10	.05	.01
☐	179	Kent Hrbek	.50	.23	.06
☐	180	Alfredo Griffin	.10	.05	.01
☐	181	Larry Andersen	.10	.05	.01
☐	182	Pete Falcone	.10	.05	.01
☐	183	Jody Davis	.10	.05	.01
☐	184	Glenn Hubbard	.10	.05	.01
☐	185	Dale Berra	.10	.05	.01
☐	186	Greg Minton	.10	.05	.01
☐	187	Gary Lucas	.10	.05	.01
☐	188	Dave Van Gorder	.10	.05	.01
☐	189	Bob Dernier	.10	.05	.01
☐	190	Willie McGee	1.50	.65	.19
☐	191	Dickie Thon	.10	.05	.01
☐	192	Bob Boone	.15	.07	.02
☐	193	Britt Burns	.10	.05	.01
☐	194	Jeff Reardon	.35	.16	.04
☐	195	Jon Matlack	.10	.05	.01
☐	196	Don Slaught	1.00	.45	.13
☐	197	Fred Stanley	.10	.05	.01
☐	198	Rick Manning	.10	.05	.01
☐	199	Dave Righetti	.15	.07	.02
☐	200	Dave Stapleton	.10	.05	.01
☐	201	Steve Yeager	.10	.05	.01
☐	202	Enos Cabell	.10	.05	.01
☐	203	Sammy Stewart	.10	.05	.01
☐	204	Moose Haas	.10	.05	.01
☐	205	Lenn Sakata	.10	.05	.01
☐	206	Charlie Moore	.10	.05	.01
☐	207	Alan Trammell	1.00	.45	.13
☐	208	Jim Rice	.20	.09	.03
☐	209	Roy Smalley	.10	.05	.01

	#	Player			
☐	210	Bill Russell	.15	.07	.02
☐	211	Andre Thornton	.10	.05	.01
☐	212	Willie Aikens	.10	.05	.01
☐	213	Dave McKay	.10	.05	.01
☐	214	Tim Blackwell	.10	.05	.01
☐	215	Buddy Bell	.15	.07	.02
☐	216	Doug DeCinces	.15	.07	.02
☐	217	Tom Herr	.15	.07	.02
☐	218	Frank LaCorte	.10	.05	.01
☐	219	Steve Carlton	1.00	.45	.13
☐	220	Terry Kennedy	.10	.05	.01
☐	221	Mike Easler	.10	.05	.01
☐	222	Jack Clark	.15	.07	.02
☐	223	Gene Garber	.10	.05	.01
☐	224	Scott Holman	.10	.05	.01
☐	225	Mike Proly	.10	.05	.01
☐	226	Terry Bulling	.10	.05	.01
☐	227	Jerry Garvin	.10	.05	.01
☐	228	Ron Davis	.10	.05	.01
☐	229	Tom Hume	.10	.05	.01
☐	230	Marc Hill	.10	.05	.01
☐	231	Dennis Martinez	.15	.07	.02
☐	232	Jim Gantner	.15	.07	.02
☐	233	Larry Pashnick	.10	.05	.01
☐	234	Dave Collins	.10	.05	.01
☐	235	Tom Burgmeier	.10	.05	.01
☐	236	Ken Landreaux	.10	.05	.01
☐	237	John Denny	.10	.05	.01
☐	238	Hal McRae	.20	.09	.03
☐	239	Matt Keough	.10	.05	.01
☐	240	Doug Flynn	.10	.05	.01
☐	241	Fred Lynn	.15	.07	.02
☐	242	Billy Sample	.10	.05	.01
☐	243	Tom Paciorek	.15	.07	.02
☐	244	Joe Sambito	.10	.05	.01
☐	245	Sid Monge	.10	.05	.01
☐	246	Ken Oberkfell	.10	.05	.01
☐	247	Joe Pittman UER (Photo of Juan Eichelberger)	.10	.05	.01
☐	248	Mario Soto	.10	.05	.01
☐	249	Claudell Washington	.10	.05	.01
☐	250	Rick Rhoden	.10	.05	.01
☐	251	Darrell Evans	.15	.07	.02
☐	252	Steve Henderson	.10	.05	.01
☐	253	Manny Castillo	.10	.05	.01
☐	254	Craig Swan	.10	.05	.01
☐	255	Joey McLaughlin	.10	.05	.01
☐	256	Pete Redfern	.10	.05	.01
☐	257	Ken Singleton	.15	.07	.02
☐	258	Robin Yount	2.00	.90	.25
☐	259	Elias Sosa	.10	.05	.01
☐	260	Bob Ojeda	.10	.05	.01
☐	261	Bobby Murcer	.15	.07	.02
☐	262	Candy Maldonado	.40	.18	.05
☐	263	Rick Waits	.10	.05	.01
☐	264	Greg Pryor	.10	.05	.01
☐	265	Bob Owchinko	.10	.05	.01
☐	266	Chris Speier	.10	.05	.01
☐	267	Bruce Kison	.10	.05	.01
☐	268	Mark Wagner	.10	.05	.01
☐	269	Steve Kemp	.10	.05	.01
☐	270	Phil Garner	.15	.07	.02
☐	271	Gene Richards	.10	.05	.01
☐	272	Renie Martin	.10	.05	.01
☐	273	Dave Roberts	.10	.05	.01
☐	274	Dan Driessen	.10	.05	.01
☐	275	Rufino Linares	.10	.05	.01
☐	276	Lee Lacy	.10	.05	.01
☐	277	Ryne Sandberg	25.00	11.50	3.10
☐	278	Darrell Porter	.10	.05	.01
☐	279	Cal Ripken	14.00	6.25	1.75
☐	280	Jamie Easterly	.10	.05	.01
☐	281	Bill Fahey	.10	.05	.01

☐ 282 Glenn Hoffman .10 .05 .01
☐ 283 Willie Randolph .15 .07 .02
☐ 284 Fernando Valenzuela .15 .07 .02
☐ 285 Alan Bannister .10 .05 .01
☐ 286 Paul Splittorff .10 .05 .01
☐ 287 Joe Rudi .10 .05 .01
☐ 288 Bill Gullickson .15 .07 .02
☐ 289 Danny Darwin .10 .05 .01
☐ 290 Andy Hassler .10 .05 .01
☐ 291 Ernesto Escarrega .10 .05 .01
☐ 292 Steve Mura .10 .05 .01
☐ 293 Tony Scott .10 .05 .01
☐ 294 Manny Trillo .10 .05 .01
☐ 295 Greg Harris .10 .05 .01
☐ 296 Luis DeLeon .10 .05 .01
☐ 297 Kent Tekulve .15 .07 .02
☐ 298 Atlee Hammaker .10 .05 .01
☐ 299 Bruce Benedict .10 .05 .01
☐ 300 Fergie Jenkins .35 .16 .04
☐ 301 Dave Kingman .15 .07 .02
☐ 302 Bill Caudill .10 .05 .01
☐ 303 John Castino .10 .05 .01
☐ 304 Ernie Whitt .10 .05 .01
☐ 305 Randy Johnson .10 .05 .01
☐ 306 Garth Iorg .10 .05 .01
☐ 307 Gaylord Perry .40 .18 .05
☐ 308 Ed Lynch .10 .05 .01
☐ 309 Keith Moreland .10 .05 .01
☐ 310 Rafael Ramirez .10 .05 .01
☐ 311 Bill Madlock .15 .07 .02
☐ 312 Milt May .10 .05 .01
☐ 313 John Montefusco .10 .05 .01
☐ 314 Wayne Krenchicki .10 .05 .01
☐ 315 George Vukovich .10 .05 .01
☐ 316 Joaquin Andujar .10 .05 .01
☐ 317 Craig Reynolds .10 .05 .01
☐ 318 Rick Burleson .10 .05 .01
☐ 319 Richard Dotson .10 .05 .01
☐ 320 Steve Rogers .10 .05 .01
☐ 321 Dave Schmidt .10 .05 .01
☐ 322 Bud Black .40 .18 .05
☐ 323 Jeff Burroughs .10 .05 .01
☐ 324 Von Hayes .15 .07 .02
☐ 325 Butch Wynegar .10 .05 .01
☐ 326 Carl Yastrzemski .75 .35 .09
☐ 327 Ron Roenicke .10 .05 .01
☐ 328 Howard Johnson 1.00 .45 .13
☐ 329 Rick Dempsey UER .15 .07 .02
(Posing as a left-handed batter)
☐ 330A Jim Slaton .10 .05 .01
(Bio printed black on white)
☐ 330B Jim Slaton .15 .07 .02
(Bio printed black on yellow)
☐ 331 Benny Ayala .10 .05 .01
☐ 332 Ted Simmons .15 .07 .02
☐ 333 Lou Whitaker .50 .23 .06
☐ 334 Chuck Rainey .10 .05 .01
☐ 335 Lou Piniella .15 .07 .02
☐ 336 Steve Sax .15 .07 .02
☐ 337 Toby Harrah .10 .05 .01
☐ 338 George Brett 3.00 1.35 .40
☐ 339 Dave Lopes .15 .07 .02
☐ 340 Gary Carter .40 .18 .05
☐ 341 John Grubb .10 .05 .01
☐ 342 Tim Foli .10 .05 .01
☐ 343 Jim Kaat .15 .07 .02
☐ 344 Mike LaCoss .10 .05 .01
☐ 345 Larry Christenson .10 .05 .01
☐ 346 Juan Bonilla .10 .05 .01
☐ 347 Omar Moreno .10 .05 .01
☐ 348 Chili Davis 1.25 .55 .16
☐ 349 Tommy Boggs .10 .05 .01
☐ 350 Rusty Staub .15 .07 .02
☐ 351 Bump Wills .10 .05 .01
☐ 352 Rick Sweet .10 .05 .01
☐ 353 Jim Gott .35 .16 .04
☐ 354 Terry Felton .10 .05 .01
☐ 355 Jim Kern .10 .05 .01
☐ 356 Bill Almon UER .10 .05 .01
(Expos/Mets in 1983, not Padres/Mets)
☐ 357 Tippy Martinez .10 .05 .01
☐ 358 Roy Howell .10 .05 .01
☐ 359 Dan Petry .10 .05 .01
☐ 360 Jerry Mumphrey .10 .05 .01
☐ 361 Mark Clear .10 .05 .01
☐ 362 Mike Marshall .10 .05 .01
☐ 363 Lary Sorensen .10 .05 .01
☐ 364 Amos Otis .15 .07 .02
☐ 365 Rick Langford .10 .05 .01
☐ 366 Brad Mills .10 .05 .01
☐ 367 Brian Downing .15 .07 .02
☐ 368 Mike Richardt .10 .05 .01
☐ 369 Aurelio Rodriguez .10 .05 .01
☐ 370 Dave Smith .10 .05 .01
☐ 371 Tug McGraw .15 .07 .02
☐ 372 Doug Bair .10 .05 .01
☐ 373 Ruppert Jones .10 .05 .01
☐ 374 Alex Trevino .10 .05 .01
☐ 375 Ken Dayley .10 .05 .01
☐ 376 Rod Scurry .10 .05 .01
☐ 377 Bob Brenly .10 .05 .01
☐ 378 Scot Thompson .10 .05 .01
☐ 379 Julio Cruz .10 .05 .01
☐ 380 John Stearns .10 .05 .01
☐ 381 Dale Murray .10 .05 .01
☐ 382 Frank Viola 1.50 .65 .19
☐ 383 Al Bumbry .15 .07 .02
☐ 384 Ben Oglivie .10 .05 .01
☐ 385 Dave Tobik .10 .05 .01
☐ 386 Bob Stanley .10 .05 .01
☐ 387 Andre Robertson .10 .05 .01
☐ 388 Jorge Orta .10 .05 .01
☐ 389 Ed Whitson .10 .05 .01
☐ 390 Don Hood .10 .05 .01
☐ 391 Tom Underwood .10 .05 .01
☐ 392 Tim Wallach .20 .09 .03
☐ 393 Steve Renko .10 .05 .01
☐ 394 Mickey Rivers .10 .05 .01
☐ 395 Greg Luzinski .15 .07 .02
☐ 396 Art Howe .10 .05 .01
☐ 397 Alan Wiggins .10 .05 .01
☐ 398 Jim Barr .10 .05 .01
☐ 399 Ivan DeJesus .10 .05 .01
☐ 400 Tom Lawless .10 .05 .01
☐ 401 Bob Walk .10 .05 .01
☐ 402 Jimmy Smith .10 .05 .01
☐ 403 Lee Smith 2.00 .90 .25
☐ 404 George Hendrick .15 .07 .02
☐ 405 Eddie Murray 1.50 .65 .19
☐ 406 Marshall Edwards .10 .05 .01
☐ 407 Lance Parrish .15 .07 .02
☐ 408 Carney Lansford .15 .07 .02
☐ 409 Dave Winfield 2.00 .90 .25
☐ 410 Bob Welch .15 .07 .02
☐ 411 Larry Milbourne .10 .05 .01
☐ 412 Dennis Leonard .10 .05 .01
☐ 413 Dan Meyer .10 .05 .01
☐ 414 Charlie Lea .10 .05 .01
☐ 415 Rick Honeycutt .10 .05 .01
☐ 416 Mike Witt .10 .05 .01
☐ 417 Steve Trout .10 .05 .01
☐ 418 Glenn Brummer .10 .05 .01

	No.	Player			
☐	419	Denny Walling	.10	.05	.01
☐	420	Gary Matthews	.15	.07	.02
☐	421	Charlie Leibrandt UER (Liebrandt on front of card)	.15	.07	.02
☐	422	Juan Eichelberger UER (Photo of Joe Pittman)	.10	.05	.01
☐	423	Cecilio Guante UER (Listed as Matt on card)	.15	.07	.02
☐	424	Bill Laskey	.10	.05	.01
☐	425	Jerry Royster	.10	.05	.01
☐	426	Dickie Noles	.10	.05	.01
☐	427	George Foster	.15	.07	.02
☐	428	Mike Moore	.60	.25	.08
☐	429	Gary Ward	.10	.05	.01
☐	430	Barry Bonnell	.10	.05	.01
☐	431	Ron Washington	.10	.05	.01
☐	432	Rance Mulliniks	.10	.05	.01
☐	433	Mike Stanton	.10	.05	.01
☐	434	Jesse Orosco	.10	.05	.01
☐	435	Larry Bowa	.15	.07	.02
☐	436	Biff Pocoroba	.10	.05	.01
☐	437	Johnny Ray	.10	.05	.01
☐	438	Joe Morgan	.60	.25	.08
☐	439	Eric Show	.15	.07	.02
☐	440	Larry Biittner	.10	.05	.01
☐	441	Greg Gross	.10	.05	.01
☐	442	Gene Tenace	.10	.05	.01
☐	443	Danny Heep	.10	.05	.01
☐	444	Bobby Clark	.10	.05	.01
☐	445	Kevin Hickey	.10	.05	.01
☐	446	Scott Sanderson	.10	.05	.01
☐	447	Frank Tanana	.15	.07	.02
☐	448	Cesar Geronimo	.10	.05	.01
☐	449	Jimmy Sexton	.10	.05	.01
☐	450	Mike Hargrove	.15	.07	.02
☐	451	Doyle Alexander	.10	.05	.01
☐	452	Dwight Evans	.15	.07	.02
☐	453	Terry Forster	.10	.05	.01
☐	454	Tom Brookens	.10	.05	.01
☐	455	Rich Dauer	.10	.05	.01
☐	456	Rob Picciolo	.10	.05	.01
☐	457	Terry Crowley	.10	.05	.01
☐	458	Ned Yost	.10	.05	.01
☐	459	Kirk Gibson	.75	.35	.09
☐	460	Reid Nichols	.10	.05	.01
☐	461	Oscar Gamble	.10	.05	.01
☐	462	Dusty Baker	.20	.09	.03
☐	463	Jack Perconte	.10	.05	.01
☐	464	Frank White	.15	.07	.02
☐	465	Mickey Klutts	.10	.05	.01
☐	466	Warren Cromartie	.10	.05	.01
☐	467	Larry Parrish	.10	.05	.01
☐	468	Bobby Grich	.15	.07	.02
☐	469	Dane Iorg	.10	.05	.01
☐	470	Joe Niekro	.15	.07	.02
☐	471	Ed Farmer	.10	.05	.01
☐	472	Tim Flannery	.10	.05	.01
☐	473	Dave Parker	.20	.09	.03
☐	474	Jeff Leonard	.10	.05	.01
☐	475	Al Hrabosky	.10	.05	.01
☐	476	Ron Hodges	.10	.05	.01
☐	477	Leon Durham	.10	.05	.01
☐	478	Jim Essian	.10	.05	.01
☐	479	Roy Lee Jackson	.10	.05	.01
☐	480	Brad Havens	.10	.05	.01
☐	481	Joe Price	.10	.05	.01
☐	482	Tony Bernazard	.10	.05	.01
☐	483	Scott McGregor	.10	.05	.01
☐	484	Paul Molitor	2.00	.90	.25
☐	485	Mike Ivie	.10	.05	.01
☐	486	Ken Griffey	.15	.07	.02
☐	487	Dennis Eckersley	.50	.23	.06
☐	488	Steve Garvey	.35	.16	.04
☐	489	Mike Fischlin	.10	.05	.01
☐	490	U.L. Washington	.10	.05	.01
☐	491	Steve McCatty	.10	.05	.01
☐	492	Roy Johnson	.10	.05	.01
☐	493	Don Baylor	.20	.09	.03
☐	494	Bobby Johnson	.10	.05	.01
☐	495	Mike Squires	.10	.05	.01
☐	496	Bert Roberge	.10	.05	.01
☐	497	Dick Ruthven	.10	.05	.01
☐	498	Tito Landrum	.10	.05	.01
☐	499	Sixto Lezcano	.10	.05	.01
☐	500	Johnny Bench	1.00	.45	.13
☐	501	Larry Whisenton	.10	.05	.01
☐	502	Manny Sarmiento	.10	.05	.01
☐	503	Fred Breining	.10	.05	.01
☐	504	Bill Campbell	.10	.05	.01
☐	505	Todd Cruz	.10	.05	.01
☐	506	Bob Bailor	.10	.05	.01
☐	507	Dave Stieb	.15	.07	.02
☐	508	Al Williams	.10	.05	.01
☐	509	Dan Ford	.10	.05	.01
☐	510	Gorman Thomas	.10	.05	.01
☐	511	Chet Lemon	.10	.05	.01
☐	512	Mike Torrez	.10	.05	.01
☐	513	Shane Rawley	.10	.05	.01
☐	514	Mark Belanger	.10	.05	.01
☐	515	Rodney Craig	.10	.05	.01
☐	516	Onix Concepcion	.10	.05	.01
☐	517	Mike Heath	.10	.05	.01
☐	518	Andre Dawson UER (Middle name Fernando, should be Nolan)	1.00	.45	.13
☐	519	Luis Sanchez	.10	.05	.01
☐	520	Terry Bogener	.10	.05	.01
☐	521	Rudy Law	.10	.05	.01
☐	522	Ray Knight	.15	.07	.02
☐	523	Joe Lefebvre	.10	.05	.01
☐	524	Jim Wohlford	.10	.05	.01
☐	525	Julio Franco	5.00	2.30	.60
☐	526	Ron Oester	.10	.05	.01
☐	527	Rick Mahler	.10	.05	.01
☐	528	Steve Nicosia	.10	.05	.01
☐	529	Junior Kennedy	.10	.05	.01
☐	530A	Whitey Herzog MG (Bio printed black on white)	.15	.07	.02
☐	530B	Whitey Herzog MG (Bio printed black on yellow)	.15	.07	.02
☐	531A	Don Sutton (Blue border on photo)	.35	.16	.04
☐	531B	Don Sutton (Green border on photo)	.35	.16	.04
☐	532	Mark Brouhard	.10	.05	.01
☐	533A	Sparky Anderson MG. (Bio printed black on white)	.15	.07	.02
☐	533B	Sparky Anderson MG. (Bio printed black on yellow)	.15	.07	.02
☐	534	Roger LaFrancois	.10	.05	.01
☐	535	George Frazier	.10	.05	.01
☐	536	Tom Niedenfuer	.10	.05	.01
☐	537	Ed Glynn	.10	.05	.01
☐	538	Lee May	.15	.07	.02
☐	539	Bob Kearney	.10	.05	.01
☐	540	Tim Raines	.75	.35	.09
☐	541	Paul Mirabella	.10	.05	.01
☐	542	Luis Tiant	.15	.07	.02

☐ 543 Ron LeFlore	.15	.07	.02
☐ 544 Dave LaPoint	.10	.05	.01
☐ 545 Randy Moffitt	.10	.05	.01
☐ 546 Luis Aguayo	.10	.05	.01
☐ 547 Brad Lesley	.10	.05	.01
☐ 548 Luis Salazar	.10	.05	.01
☐ 549 John Candelaria	.10	.05	.01
☐ 550 Dave Bergman	.10	.05	.01
☐ 551 Bob Watson	.15	.07	.02
☐ 552 Pat Tabler	.10	.05	.01
☐ 553 Brent Gaff	.10	.05	.01
☐ 554 Al Cowens	.10	.05	.01
☐ 555 Tom Brunansky	.15	.07	.02
☐ 556 Lloyd Moseby	.10	.05	.01
☐ 557A Pascual Perez ERR (Twins in glove)	2.00	.90	.25
☐ 557B Pascual Perez COR (Braves in glove)	.15	.07	.02
☐ 558 Willie Upshaw	.10	.05	.01
☐ 559 Richie Zisk	.10	.05	.01
☐ 560 Pat Zachry	.10	.05	.01
☐ 561 Jay Johnstone	.15	.07	.02
☐ 562 Carlos Diaz	.10	.05	.01
☐ 563 John Tudor	.15	.07	.02
☐ 564 Frank Robinson MG	.30	.14	.04
☐ 565 Dave Edwards	.10	.05	.01
☐ 566 Paul Householder	.10	.05	.01
☐ 567 Ron Reed	.10	.05	.01
☐ 568 Mike Ramsey	.10	.05	.01
☐ 569 Kiko Garcia	.10	.05	.01
☐ 570 Tommy John	.20	.09	.03
☐ 571 Tony LaRussa MG	.15	.07	.02
☐ 572 Joel Youngblood	.10	.05	.01
☐ 573 Wayne Tolleson	.10	.05	.01
☐ 574 Keith Creel	.10	.05	.01
☐ 575 Billy Martin MG	.15	.07	.02
☐ 576 Jerry Dybzinski	.10	.05	.01
☐ 577 Rick Cerone	.10	.05	.01
☐ 578 Tony Perez	.20	.09	.03
☐ 579 Greg Brock	.10	.05	.01
☐ 580 Glenn Wilson	.15	.07	.02
☐ 581 Tim Stoddard	.10	.05	.01
☐ 582 Bob McClure	.10	.05	.01
☐ 583 Jim Dwyer	.10	.05	.01
☐ 584 Ed Romero	.10	.05	.01
☐ 585 Larry Herndon	.10	.05	.01
☐ 586 Wade Boggs	18.00	8.00	2.30
☐ 587 Jay Howell	.15	.07	.02
☐ 588 Dave Stewart	.50	.23	.06
☐ 589 Bert Blyleven	.20	.09	.03
☐ 590 Dick Howser MG	.15	.07	.02
☐ 591 Wayne Gross	.10	.05	.01
☐ 592 Terry Francona	.10	.05	.01
☐ 593 Don Werner	.10	.05	.01
☐ 594 Bill Stein	.10	.05	.01
☐ 595 Jesse Barfield	.15	.07	.02
☐ 596 Bob Molinaro	.10	.05	.01
☐ 597 Mike Vail	.10	.05	.01
☐ 598 Tony Gwynn	25.00	11.50	3.10
☐ 599 Gary Rajsich	.10	.05	.01
☐ 600 Jerry Ujdur	.10	.05	.01
☐ 601 Cliff Johnson	.10	.05	.01
☐ 602 Jerry White	.10	.05	.01
☐ 603 Bryan Clark	.10	.05	.01
☐ 604 Joe Ferguson	.10	.05	.01
☐ 605 Guy Sularz	.10	.05	.01
☐ 606A Ozzie Virgil (Green border on photo)	.15	.07	.02
☐ 606B Ozzie Virgil (Orange border on photo)	.15	.07	.02
☐ 607 Terry Harper	.10	.05	.01
☐ 608 Harvey Kuenn MG	.15	.07	.02
☐ 609 Jim Sundberg	.15	.07	.02
☐ 610 Willie Stargell	.50	.23	.06
☐ 611 Reggie Smith	.15	.07	.02
☐ 612 Rob Wilfong	.10	.05	.01
☐ 613 The Niekro Brothers Joe Niekro Phil Niekro	.20	.09	.03
☐ 614 Lee Elia MG	.10	.05	.01
☐ 615 Mickey Hatcher	.10	.05	.01
☐ 616 Jerry Hairston	.10	.05	.01
☐ 617 John Martin	.10	.05	.01
☐ 618 Wally Backman	.10	.05	.01
☐ 619 Storm Davis	.10	.05	.01
☐ 620 Alan Knicely	.10	.05	.01
☐ 621 John Stuper	.10	.05	.01
☐ 622 Matt Sinatro	.10	.05	.01
☐ 623 Geno Petralli	.15	.07	.02
☐ 624 Duane Walker	.10	.05	.01
☐ 625 Dick Williams MG	.10	.05	.01
☐ 626 Pat Corrales MG	.10	.05	.01
☐ 627 Vern Ruhle	.10	.05	.01
☐ 628 Joe Torre MG	.15	.07	.02
☐ 629 Anthony Johnson	.10	.05	.01
☐ 630 Steve Howe	.10	.05	.01
☐ 631 Gary Woods	.10	.05	.01
☐ 632 LaMarr Hoyt	.10	.05	.01
☐ 633 Steve Swisher	.10	.05	.01
☐ 634 Terry Leach	.10	.05	.01
☐ 635 Jeff Newman	.10	.05	.01
☐ 636 Brett Butler	.75	.35	.09
☐ 637 Gary Gray	.10	.05	.01
☐ 638 Lee Mazzilli	.10	.05	.01
☐ 639A Ron Jackson ERR (A's in glove)	10.00	4.50	1.25
☐ 639B Ron Jackson COR (Angels in glove, red border on photo)	.10	.05	.01
☐ 639C Ron Jackson COR (Angels in glove, green border on photo)	.50	.23	.06
☐ 640 Juan Beniquez	.10	.05	.01
☐ 641 Dave Rucker	.10	.05	.01
☐ 642 Luis Pujols	.10	.05	.01
☐ 643 Rick Monday	.10	.05	.01
☐ 644 Hosken Powell	.10	.05	.01
☐ 645 The Chicken	.30	.14	.04
☐ 646 Dave Engle	.10	.05	.01
☐ 647 Dick Davis	.10	.05	.01
☐ 648 Frank Robinson Vida Blue Joe Morgan	.35	.16	.04
☐ 649 Al Chambers	.10	.05	.01
☐ 650 Jesus Vega	.10	.05	.01
☐ 651 Jeff Jones	.10	.05	.01
☐ 652 Marvis Foley	.10	.05	.01
☐ 653 Ty Cobb Puzzle Card	.25	.11	.03
☐ 654A Dick Perez/Diamond King Checklist 1-26 (Unnumbered) ERR (Word "checklist" omitted from back)	.25	.08	.01
☐ 654B Dick Perez/Diamond King Checklist 1-26 (Unnumbered) COR (Word "checklist" is on back)	.25	.08	.01
☐ 655 Checklist 27-130 (Unnumbered)	.15	.05	.01
☐ 656 Checklist 131-234 (Unnumbered)	.15	.05	.01

☐ 657 Checklist 235-338........ .15 .05 .01
(Unnumbered)
☐ 658 Checklist 339-442........ .15 .05 .01
(Unnumbered)
☐ 659 Checklist 443-544........ .15 .05 .01
(Unnumbered)
☐ 660 Checklist 545-653........ .15 .05 .01
(Unnumbered)

1984 Donruss

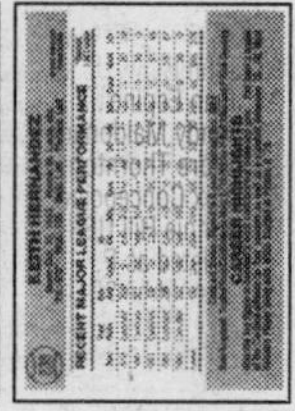

The 1984 Donruss set contains a total of 660 cards, each measuring 2 1/2" by 3 1/2"; however, only 658 are numbered. The first 26 cards in the set are again Diamond Kings (DK), although the drawings this year were styled differently and are easily differentiated from other DK issues. A new feature, Rated Rookies (RR), was introduced with this set with Bill Madden's 20 selections comprising numbers 27 through 46. Two "Living Legend" cards designated A (featuring Gaylord Perry and Rollie Fingers) and B (featuring Johnny Bench and Carl Yastrzemski) were issued as bonus cards in wax packs, but were not issued in the vending sets sold to hobby dealers. The seven unnumbered checklist cards are arbitrarily assigned numbers 652 through 658 and are listed at the end of the list below. The designs on the fronts of the Donruss cards changed considerably from the past two years. The backs contain statistics and are printed in green and black ink. The cards were distributed with a 63-piece puzzle of Duke Snider. There are no extra variation cards included in the complete set price below. The variation cards apparently resulted from a different printing for the factory sets as the Darling and Stenhouse no number variations as well as the Perez-Steel errors were corrected in the factory sets which were released later in the year. The key Rookie Cards in this set are Joe Carter, Ron Darling, Sid Fernandez, Tony Fernandez, Brian Harper, Tom Henke, Don Mattingly, Kevin McReynolds, Tony Phillips, Darryl Strawberry, and Andy Van Slyke.

	NRMT-MT	EXC	G-VG
COMPLETE SET (660)	250.00	115.00	31.00
COMPLETE FACT.SET (658)	300.00	135.00	38.00
COMMON CARD (1-658)	.30	.14	.04

☐ 1A Robin Yount DK ERR... 5.00 1.75 .50
(Perez Steel)
☐ 1B Robin Yount DK COR... 6.00 2.10 .60
☐ 2A Dave Concepcion DK...... .40 .18 .05
ERR (Perez Steel)
☐ 2B Dave Concepcion DK...... .50 .23 .06
COR
☐ 3A Dwayne Murphy DK....... .40 .18 .05
ERR (Perez Steel)
☐ 3B Dwayne Murphy DK....... .50 .23 .06
COR
☐ 4A John Castino DK ERR.... .40 .18 .05
(Perez Steel)
☐ 4B John Castino DK COR.... .50 .23 .06
☐ 5A Leon Durham DK ERR... .40 .18 .05
(Perez Steel)
☐ 5B Leon Durham DK COR.... .50 .23 .06
☐ 6A Rusty Staub DK ERR..... .40 .18 .05
(Perez Steel)
☐ 6B Rusty Staub DK COR..... .50 .23 .06
☐ 7A Jack Clark DK ERR .... .40 .18 .05
(Perez Steel)
☐ 7B Jack Clark DK COR .... .50 .23 .06
☐ 8A Dave Dravecky DK......... .40 .18 .05
ERR (Perez Steel)
☐ 8B Dave Dravecky DK......... .50 .23 .06
COR
☐ 9A Al Oliver DK ERR........... .40 .18 .05
(Perez Steel)
☐ 9B Al Oliver DK COR........... .50 .23 .06
☐ 10A Dave Righetti DK......... .40 .18 .05
ERR (Perez Steel)
☐ 10B Dave Righetti DK......... .50 .23 .06
COR
☐ 11A Hal McRae DK ERR...... .60 .25 .08
(Perez Steel)
☐ 11B Hal McRae DK COR..... .70 .30 .09
☐ 12A Ray Knight DK ERR..... .40 .18 .05
(Perez Steel)
☐ 12B Ray Knight DK COR..... .50 .23 .06
☐ 13A Bruce Sutter DK ERR... .40 .18 .05
(Perez Steel)
☐ 13B Bruce Sutter DK COR... .50 .23 .06
☐ 14A Bob Horner DK ERR.... .40 .18 .05
(Perez Steel)
☐ 14B Bob Horner DK COR.... .50 .23 .06
☐ 15A Lance Parrish DK......... .60 .25 .08
ERR (Perez Steel)
☐ 15B Lance Parrish DK......... .70 .30 .09
COR
☐ 16A Matt Young DK ERR.... .40 .18 .05
(Perez Steel)
☐ 16B Matt Young DK COR.... .50 .23 .06
☐ 17A Fred Lynn DK ERR....... .40 .18 .05
(Perez Steel)
(A's logo on back)
☐ 17B Fred Lynn DK COR....... .50 .23 .06
☐ 18A Ron Kittle DK ERR....... .40 .18 .05
(Perez Steel)
☐ 18B Ron Kittle DK COR....... .50 .23 .06
☐ 19A Jim Clancy DK ERR..... .40 .18 .05
(Perez Steel)
☐ 19B Jim Clancy DK COR..... .50 .23 .06
☐ 20A Bill Madlock DK ERR... .40 .18 .05
(Perez Steel)
☐ 20B Bill Madlock DK COR... .50 .23 .06
☐ 21A Larry Parrish DK.......... .40 .18 .05
ERR (Perez Steel)
☐ 21B Larry Parrish DK.......... .50 .23 .06
COR
☐ 22A Eddie Murray DK ERR 2.50 1.15 .30
(Perez Steel)
☐ 22B Eddie Murray DK COR 3.00 1.35 .40

	No.	Player			
☐	23A	Mike Schmidt DK ERR (Perez Steel)	4.00	1.80	.50
☐	23B	Mike Schmidt DK COR	4.50	2.00	.55
☐	24A	Pedro Guerrero DK ...... ERR (Perez Steel)	.40	.18	.05
☐	24B	Pedro Guerrero DK ...... COR	.50	.23	.06
☐	25A	Andre Thornton DK...... ERR (Perez Steel)	.40	.18	.05
☐	25B	Andre Thornton DK...... COR	.50	.23	.06
☐	26A	Wade Boggs DK ERR. (Perez Steel)	4.50	2.00	.55
☐	26B	Wade Boggs DK COR	5.00	2.30	.60
☐	27	Joel Skinner RR............	.30	.14	.04
☐	28	Tommy Dunbar RR........	.30	.14	.04
☐	29A	Mike Stenhouse RR..... ERR (No number on back)	.30	.14	.04
☐	29B	Mike Stenhouse RR... COR (Numbered on back)	2.00	.90	.25
☐	30A	Ron Darling RR ERR.. (No number on back)	1.50	.65	.19
☐	30B	Ron Darling RR COR . (Numbered on back)	4.00	1.80	.50
☐	31	Dion James RR.............	.50	.23	.06
☐	32	Tony Fernandez RR......	3.50	1.55	.45
☐	33	Angel Salazar RR	.30	.14	.04
☐	34	Kevin McReynolds RR .	1.25	.55	.16
☐	35	Dick Schofield RR..........	.50	.23	.06
☐	36	Brad Komminsk RR	.30	.14	.04
☐	37	Tim Teufel RR...............	.30	.14	.04
☐	38	Doug Frobel RR	.30	.14	.04
☐	39	Greg Gagne RR...........	1.50	.65	.19
☐	40	Mike Fuentes RR...........	.30	.14	.04
☐	41	Joe Carter RR	70.00	32.00	8.75
☐	42	Mike Brown RR............. (Angels OF)	.30	.14	.04
☐	43	Mike Jeffcoat RR	.30	.14	.04
☐	44	Sid Fernandez RR	2.50	1.15	.30
☐	45	Brian Dayett RR	.30	.14	.04
☐	46	Chris Smith RR..............	.30	.14	.04
☐	47	Eddie Murray	6.00	2.70	.75
☐	48	Robin Yount................	7.00	3.10	.85
☐	49	Lance Parrish................	.40	.18	.05
☐	50	Jim Rice.........................	.50	.23	.06
☐	51	Dave Winfield..............	7.00	3.10	.85
☐	52	Fernando Valenzuela......	.40	.18	.05
☐	53	George Brett	12.00	5.50	1.50
☐	54	Rickey Henderson........	8.00	3.60	1.00
☐	55	Gary Carter	1.50	.65	.19
☐	56	Buddy Bell......................	.40	.18	.05
☐	57	Reggie Jackson............	6.00	2.70	.75
☐	58	Harold Baines	1.00	.45	.13
☐	59	Ozzie Smith..................	7.00	3.10	.85
☐	60	Nolan Ryan UER .... (Text on back refers to 1972 as the year he struck out 383; the year was 1973)	30.00	13.50	3.80
☐	61	Pete Rose	5.00	2.30	.60
☐	62	Ron Oester......................	.30	.14	.04
☐	63	Steve Garvey................	1.00	.45	.13
☐	64	Jason Thompson	.30	.14	.04
☐	65	Jack Clark	.40	.18	.05
☐	66	Dale Murphy	1.75	.80	.22
☐	67	Leon Durham..................	.30	.14	.04
☐	68	Darryl Strawberry	12.00	5.50	1.50
☐	69	Richie Zisk.....................	.30	.14	.04
☐	70	Kent Hrbek......................	.75	.35	.09
☐	71	Dave Stieb......................	.40	.18	.05
☐	72	Ken Schrom....................	.30	.14	.04
☐	73	George Bell	.75	.35	.09

	No.	Player			
☐	74	John Moses....................	.30	.14	.04
☐	75	Ed Lynch........................	.30	.14	.04
☐	76	Chuck Rainey.................	.30	.14	.04
☐	77	Biff Pocoroba.................	.30	.14	.04
☐	78	Cecilio Guante................	.30	.14	.04
☐	79	Jim Barr.........................	.30	.14	.04
☐	80	Kurt Bevacqua................	.30	.14	.04
☐	81	Tom Foley......................	.30	.14	.04
☐	82	Joe Lefebvre	.30	.14	.04
☐	83	Andy Van Slyke	4.00	1.80	.50
☐	84	Bob Lillis MG	.30	.14	.04
☐	85	Ricky Adams..................	.30	.14	.04
☐	86	Jerry Hairston	.30	.14	.04
☐	87	Bob James.....................	.30	.14	.04
☐	88	Joe Altobelli MG............	.30	.14	.04
☐	89	Ed Romero......................	.30	.14	.04
☐	90	John Grubb....................	.30	.14	.04
☐	91	John Henry Johnson......	.30	.14	.04
☐	92	Juan Espino....................	.30	.14	.04
☐	93	Candy Maldonado..........	.30	.14	.04
☐	94	Andre Thornton..............	.30	.14	.04
☐	95	Onix Concepcion...........	.30	.14	.04
☐	96	Donnie Hill UER .... (Listed as P, should be 2B)	.40	.18	.05
☐	97	Andre Dawson UER ..... (Wrong middle name, should be Nolan)	5.00	2.30	.60
☐	98	Frank Tanana	.40	.18	.05
☐	99	Curt Wilkerson..............	.30	.14	.04
☐	100	Larry Gura......................	.30	.14	.04
☐	101	Dwayne Murphy...........	.30	.14	.04
☐	102	Tom Brennan	.30	.14	.04
☐	103	Dave Righetti	.40	.18	.05
☐	104	Steve Sax.....................	.40	.18	.05
☐	105	Dan Petry.....................	.40	.18	.05
☐	106	Cal Ripken................	32.00	14.50	4.00
☐	107	Paul Molitor UER .... ('83 stats should say .270 BA, 608 AB, and 164 hits)	8.00	3.60	1.00
☐	108	Fred Lynn.....................	.40	.18	.05
☐	109	Neil Allen......................	.30	.14	.04
☐	110	Joe Niekro.....................	.40	.18	.05
☐	111	Steve Carlton	4.50	2.00	.55
☐	112	Terry Kennedy.............	.30	.14	.04
☐	113	Bill Madlock................	.40	.18	.05
☐	114	Chili Davis...................	1.00	.45	.13
☐	115	Jim Gantner	.40	.18	.05
☐	116	Tom Seaver...............	6.00	2.70	.75
☐	117	Bill Buckner..................	.40	.18	.05
☐	118	Bill Caudill....................	.30	.14	.04
☐	119	Jim Clancy....................	.30	.14	.04
☐	120	John Castino.................	.30	.14	.04
☐	121	Dave Concepcion	.40	.18	.05
☐	122	Greg Luzinski...............	.40	.18	.05
☐	123	Mike Boddicker	.30	.14	.04
☐	124	Pete Ladd.....................	.30	.14	.04
☐	125	Juan Berenguer...........	.30	.14	.04
☐	126	John Montefusco	.30	.14	.04
☐	127	Ed Jurak........................	.30	.14	.04
☐	128	Tom Niedenfuer	.30	.14	.04
☐	129	Bert Blyleven...............	.50	.23	.06
☐	130	Bud Black.....................	.30	.14	.04
☐	131	Gorman Heimueller......	.30	.14	.04
☐	132	Dan Schatzeder...........	.30	.14	.04
☐	133	Ron Jackson	.30	.14	.04
☐	134	Tom Henke	1.75	.80	.22
☐	135	Kevin Hickey	.30	.14	.04
☐	136	Mike Scott.....................	.40	.18	.05
☐	137	Bo Diaz	.30	.14	.04
☐	138	Glenn Brummer	.30	.14	.04
☐	139	Sid Monge	.30	.14	.04

	No.	Player			
☐	140	Rich Gale	.30	.14	.04
☐	141	Brett Butler	1.00	.45	.13
☐	142	Brian Harper	1.50	.65	.19
☐	143	John Rabb	.30	.14	.04
☐	144	Gary Woods	.30	.14	.04
☐	145	Pat Putnam	.30	.14	.04
☐	146	Jim Acker	.30	.14	.04
☐	147	Mickey Hatcher	.30	.14	.04
☐	148	Todd Cruz	.30	.14	.04
☐	149	Tom Tellmann	.30	.14	.04
☐	150	John Wockenfuss	.30	.14	.04
☐	151	Wade Boggs	14.00	6.25	1.75
☐	152	Don Baylor	.50	.23	.06
☐	153	Bob Welch	.40	.18	.05
☐	154	Alan Bannister	.30	.14	.04
☐	155	Willie Aikens	.30	.14	.04
☐	156	Jeff Burroughs	.30	.14	.04
☐	157	Bryan Little	.30	.14	.04
☐	158	Bob Boone	.40	.18	.05
☐	159	Dave Hostetler	.30	.14	.04
☐	160	Jerry Dybzinski	.30	.14	.04
☐	161	Mike Madden	.30	.14	.04
☐	162	Luis DeLeon	.30	.14	.04
☐	163	Willie Hernandez	.40	.18	.05
☐	164	Frank Pastore	.30	.14	.04
☐	165	Rick Camp	.30	.14	.04
☐	166	Lee Mazzilli	.30	.14	.04
☐	167	Scot Thompson	.30	.14	.04
☐	168	Bob Forsch	.30	.14	.04
☐	169	Mike Flanagan	.30	.14	.04
☐	170	Rick Manning	.30	.14	.04
☐	171	Chet Lemon	.40	.18	.05
☐	172	Jerry Remy	.30	.14	.04
☐	173	Ron Guidry	.40	.18	.05
☐	174	Pedro Guerrero	.40	.18	.05
☐	175	Willie Wilson	.40	.18	.05
☐	176	Carney Lansford	.40	.18	.05
☐	177	Al Oliver	.40	.18	.05
☐	178	Jim Sundberg	.40	.18	.05
☐	179	Bobby Grich	.40	.18	.05
☐	180	Rich Dotson	.30	.14	.04
☐	181	Joaquin Andujar	.30	.14	.04
☐	182	Jose Cruz	.40	.18	.05
☐	183	Mike Schmidt	12.00	5.50	1.50
☐	184	Gary Redus	.50	.23	.06
☐	185	Garry Templeton	.30	.14	.04
☐	186	Tony Pena	.40	.18	.05
☐	187	Greg Minton	.30	.14	.04
☐	188	Phil Niekro	1.50	.65	.19
☐	189	Ferguson Jenkins	1.00	.45	.13
☐	190	Mookie Wilson	.40	.18	.05
☐	191	Jim Beattie	.30	.14	.04
☐	192	Gary Ward	.30	.14	.04
☐	193	Jesse Barfield	.40	.18	.05
☐	194	Pete Filson	.30	.14	.04
☐	195	Roy Lee Jackson	.30	.14	.04
☐	196	Rick Sweet	.30	.14	.04
☐	197	Jesse Orosco	.30	.14	.04
☐	198	Steve Lake	.30	.14	.04
☐	199	Ken Dayley	.30	.14	.04
☐	200	Manny Sarmiento	.30	.14	.04
☐	201	Mark Davis	.30	.14	.04
☐	202	Tim Flannery	.30	.14	.04
☐	203	Bill Scherrer	.30	.14	.04
☐	204	Al Holland	.30	.14	.04
☐	205	Dave Von Ohlen	.30	.14	.04
☐	206	Mike LaCoss	.30	.14	.04
☐	207	Juan Beniquez	.30	.14	.04
☐	208	Juan Agosto	.30	.14	.04
☐	209	Bobby Ramos	.30	.14	.04
☐	210	Al Bumbry	.40	.18	.05
☐	211	Mark Brouhard	.30	.14	.04
☐	212	Howard Bailey	.30	.14	.04
☐	213	Bruce Hurst	.40	.18	.05
☐	214	Bob Shirley	.30	.14	.04
☐	215	Pat Zachry	.30	.14	.04
☐	216	Julio Franco	2.50	1.15	.30
☐	217	Mike Armstrong	.30	.14	.04
☐	218	Dave Beard	.30	.14	.04
☐	219	Steve Rogers	.30	.14	.04
☐	220	John Butcher	.30	.14	.04
☐	221	Mike Smithson	.30	.14	.04
☐	222	Frank White	.40	.18	.05
☐	223	Mike Heath	.30	.14	.04
☐	224	Chris Bando	.30	.14	.04
☐	225	Roy Smalley	.30	.14	.04
☐	226	Dusty Baker	.50	.23	.06
☐	227	Lou Whitaker	2.50	1.15	.30
☐	228	John Lowenstein	.30	.14	.04
☐	229	Ben Oglivie	.30	.14	.04
☐	230	Doug DeCinces	.30	.14	.04
☐	231	Lonnie Smith	.40	.18	.05
☐	232	Ray Knight	.40	.18	.05
☐	233	Gary Matthews	.40	.18	.05
☐	234	Juan Bonilla	.30	.14	.04
☐	235	Rod Scurry	.30	.14	.04
☐	236	Atlee Hammaker	.30	.14	.04
☐	237	Mike Caldwell	.30	.14	.04
☐	238	Keith Hernandez	.50	.23	.06
☐	239	Larry Bowa	.40	.18	.05
☐	240	Tony Bernazard	.30	.14	.04
☐	241	Damaso Garcia	.30	.14	.04
☐	242	Tom Brunansky	.40	.18	.05
☐	243	Dan Driessen	.30	.14	.04
☐	244	Ron Kittle	.30	.14	.04
☐	245	Tim Stoddard	.30	.14	.04
☐	246	Bob L. Gibson (Brewers Pitcher)	.30	.14	.04
☐	247	Marty Castillo	.30	.14	.04
☐	248	Don Mattingly UER ("Traiing" on back)	55.00	25.00	7.00
☐	249	Jeff Newman	.30	.14	.04
☐	250	Alejandro Pena	.50	.23	.06
☐	251	Toby Harrah	.30	.14	.04
☐	252	Cesar Geronimo	.30	.14	.04
☐	253	Tom Underwood	.30	.14	.04
☐	254	Doug Flynn	.30	.14	.04
☐	255	Andy Hassler	.30	.14	.04
☐	256	Odell Jones	.30	.14	.04
☐	257	Rudy Law	.30	.14	.04
☐	258	Harry Spilman	.30	.14	.04
☐	259	Marty Bystrom	.30	.14	.04
☐	260	Dave Rucker	.30	.14	.04
☐	261	Ruppert Jones	.30	.14	.04
☐	262	Jeff R. Jones (Reds OF)	.30	.14	.04
☐	263	Gerald Perry	.40	.18	.05
☐	264	Gene Tenace	.30	.14	.04
☐	265	Brad Wellman	.30	.14	.04
☐	266	Dickie Noles	.30	.14	.04
☐	267	Jamie Allen	.30	.14	.04
☐	268	Jim Gott	.30	.14	.04
☐	269	Ron Davis	.30	.14	.04
☐	270	Benny Ayala	.30	.14	.04
☐	271	Ned Yost	.30	.14	.04
☐	272	Dave Rozema	.30	.14	.04
☐	273	Dave Stapleton	.30	.14	.04
☐	274	Lou Piniella	.40	.18	.05
☐	275	Jose Morales	.30	.14	.04
☐	276	Broderick Perkins	.30	.14	.04
☐	277	Butch Davis	.30	.14	.04
☐	278	Tony Phillips	4.00	1.80	.50
☐	279	Jeff Reardon	.50	.23	.06
☐	280	Ken Forsch	.30	.14	.04
☐	281	Pete O'Brien	.50	.23	.06
☐	282	Tom Paciorek	.40	.18	.05

	No.	Player	Mint	Ex	VG
☐	283	Frank LaCorte	.30	.14	.04
☐	284	Tim Lollar	.30	.14	.04
☐	285	Greg Gross	.30	.14	.04
☐	286	Alex Trevino	.30	.14	.04
☐	287	Gene Garber	.30	.14	.04
☐	288	Dave Parker	.50	.23	.06
☐	289	Lee Smith	3.00	1.35	.40
☐	290	Dave LaPoint	.30	.14	.04
☐	291	John Shelby	.30	.14	.04
☐	292	Charlie Moore	.30	.14	.04
☐	293	Alan Trammell	2.50	1.15	.30
☐	294	Tony Armas	.30	.14	.04
☐	295	Shane Rawley	.30	.14	.04
☐	296	Greg Brock	.30	.14	.04
☐	297	Hal McRae	.50	.23	.06
☐	298	Mike Davis	.30	.14	.04
☐	299	Tim Raines	2.00	.90	.25
☐	300	Bucky Dent	.40	.18	.05
☐	301	Tommy John	.50	.23	.06
☐	302	Carlton Fisk	4.00	1.80	.50
☐	303	Darrell Porter	.30	.14	.04
☐	304	Dickie Thon	.30	.14	.04
☐	305	Garry Maddox	.30	.14	.04
☐	306	Cesar Cedeno	.40	.18	.05
☐	307	Gary Lucas	.30	.14	.04
☐	308	Johnny Ray	.30	.14	.04
☐	309	Andy McGaffigan	.30	.14	.04
☐	310	Claudell Washington	.30	.14	.04
☐	311	Ryne Sandberg	20.00	9.00	2.50
☐	312	George Foster	.40	.18	.05
☐	313	Spike Owen	.50	.23	.06
☐	314	Gary Gaetti	.40	.18	.05
☐	315	Willie Upshaw	.30	.14	.04
☐	316	Al Williams	.30	.14	.04
☐	317	Jorge Orta	.30	.14	.04
☐	318	Orlando Mercado	.30	.14	.04
☐	319	Junior Ortiz	.30	.14	.04
☐	320	Mike Proly	.30	.14	.04
☐	321	Randy Johnson UER ('72-'82 stats are from Twins' Randy Johnson, '83 stats are from Braves' Randy Johnson)	.30	.14	.04
☐	322	Jim Morrison	.30	.14	.04
☐	323	Max Venable	.30	.14	.04
☐	324	Tony Gwynn	20.00	9.00	2.50
☐	325	Duane Walker	.30	.14	.04
☐	326	Ozzie Virgil	.30	.14	.04
☐	327	Jeff Lahti	.30	.14	.04
☐	328	Bill Dawley	.30	.14	.04
☐	329	Rob Wilfong	.30	.14	.04
☐	330	Marc Hill	.30	.14	.04
☐	331	Ray Burris	.30	.14	.04
☐	332	Allan Ramirez	.30	.14	.04
☐	333	Chuck Porter	.30	.14	.04
☐	334	Wayne Krenchicki	.30	.14	.04
☐	335	Gary Allenson	.30	.14	.04
☐	336	Bobby Meacham	.30	.14	.04
☐	337	Joe Beckwith	.30	.14	.04
☐	338	Rick Sutcliffe	.40	.18	.05
☐	339	Mark Huismann	.30	.14	.04
☐	340	Tim Conroy	.30	.14	.04
☐	341	Scott Sanderson	.30	.14	.04
☐	342	Larry Biittner	.30	.14	.04
☐	343	Dave Stewart	.50	.23	.06
☐	344	Darryl Motley	.30	.14	.04
☐	345	Chris Codiroli	.30	.14	.04
☐	346	Rich Behenna	.30	.14	.04
☐	347	Andre Robertson	.30	.14	.04
☐	348	Mike Marshall	.30	.14	.04
☐	349	Larry Herndon	.40	.18	.05
☐	350	Rich Dauer	.30	.14	.04
☐	351	Cecil Cooper	.40	.18	.05
☐	352	Rod Carew	2.50	1.15	.30
☐	353	Willie McGee	.60	.25	.08
☐	354	Phil Garner	.40	.18	.05
☐	355	Joe Morgan	1.50	.65	.19
☐	356	Luis Salazar	.30	.14	.04
☐	357	John Candelaria	.40	.18	.05
☐	358	Bill Laskey	.30	.14	.04
☐	359	Bob McClure	.30	.14	.04
☐	360	Dave Kingman	.40	.18	.05
☐	361	Ron Cey	.40	.18	.05
☐	362	Matt Young	.30	.14	.04
☐	363	Lloyd Moseby	.30	.14	.04
☐	364	Frank Viola	.75	.35	.09
☐	365	Eddie Milner	.30	.14	.04
☐	366	Floyd Bannister	.30	.14	.04
☐	367	Dan Ford	.30	.14	.04
☐	368	Moose Haas	.30	.14	.04
☐	369	Doug Bair	.30	.14	.04
☐	370	Ray Fontenot	.30	.14	.04
☐	371	Luis Aponte	.30	.14	.04
☐	372	Jack Fimple	.30	.14	.04
☐	373	Neal Heaton	.40	.18	.05
☐	374	Greg Pryor	.30	.14	.04
☐	375	Wayne Gross	.30	.14	.04
☐	376	Charlie Lea	.30	.14	.04
☐	377	Steve Lubratich	.30	.14	.04
☐	378	Jon Matlack	.30	.14	.04
☐	379	Julio Cruz	.30	.14	.04
☐	380	John Mizerock	.30	.14	.04
☐	381	Kevin Gross	.75	.35	.09
☐	382	Mike Ramsey	.30	.14	.04
☐	383	Doug Gwosdz	.30	.14	.04
☐	384	Kelly Paris	.30	.14	.04
☐	385	Pete Falcone	.30	.14	.04
☐	386	Milt May	.30	.14	.04
☐	387	Fred Breining	.30	.14	.04
☐	388	Craig Lefferts	.30	.14	.04
☐	389	Steve Henderson	.30	.14	.04
☐	390	Randy Moffitt	.30	.14	.04
☐	391	Ron Washington	.30	.14	.04
☐	392	Gary Roenicke	.30	.14	.04
☐	393	Tom Candiotti	1.50	.65	.19
☐	394	Larry Pashnick	.30	.14	.04
☐	395	Dwight Evans	.40	.18	.05
☐	396	Goose Gossage	.50	.23	.06
☐	397	Derrel Thomas	.30	.14	.04
☐	398	Juan Eichelberger	.30	.14	.04
☐	399	Leon Roberts	.30	.14	.04
☐	400	Dave Lopes	.40	.18	.05
☐	401	Bill Gullickson	.40	.18	.05
☐	402	Geoff Zahn	.30	.14	.04
☐	403	Billy Sample	.30	.14	.04
☐	404	Mike Squires	.30	.14	.04
☐	405	Craig Reynolds	.30	.14	.04
☐	406	Eric Show	.30	.14	.04
☐	407	John Denny	.30	.14	.04
☐	408	Dann Bilardello	.30	.14	.04
☐	409	Bruce Benedict	.30	.14	.04
☐	410	Kent Tekulve	.40	.18	.05
☐	411	Mel Hall	.40	.18	.05
☐	412	John Stuper	.30	.14	.04
☐	413	Rick Dempsey	.40	.18	.05
☐	414	Don Sutton	1.00	.45	.13
☐	415	Jack Morris	1.25	.55	.16
☐	416	John Tudor	.40	.18	.05
☐	417	Willie Randolph	.40	.18	.05
☐	418	Jerry Reuss	.30	.14	.04
☐	419	Don Slaught	.40	.18	.05
☐	420	Steve McCatty	.30	.14	.04
☐	421	Tim Wallach	.40	.18	.05
☐	422	Larry Parrish	.30	.14	.04
☐	423	Brian Downing	.40	.18	.05
☐	424	Britt Burns	.30	.14	.04

	#	Player			
☐	425	David Green	.30	.14	.04
☐	426	Jerry Mumphrey	.30	.14	.04
☐	427	Ivan DeJesus	.30	.14	.04
☐	428	Mario Soto	.30	.14	.04
☐	429	Gene Richards	.30	.14	.04
☐	430	Dale Berra	.30	.14	.04
☐	431	Darrell Evans	.40	.18	.05
☐	432	Glenn Hubbard	.30	.14	.04
☐	433	Jody Davis	.30	.14	.04
☐	434	Danny Heep	.30	.14	.04
☐	435	Ed Nunez	.30	.14	.04
☐	436	Bobby Castillo	.30	.14	.04
☐	437	Ernie Whitt	.30	.14	.04
☐	438	Scott Ullger	.30	.14	.04
☐	439	Doyle Alexander	.30	.14	.04
☐	440	Domingo Ramos	.30	.14	.04
☐	441	Craig Swan	.30	.14	.04
☐	442	Warren Brusstar	.30	.14	.04
☐	443	Len Barker	.30	.14	.04
☐	444	Mike Easler	.30	.14	.04
☐	445	Renie Martin	.30	.14	.04
☐	446	Dennis Rasmussen	.30	.14	.04
☐	447	Ted Power	.30	.14	.04
☐	448	Charles Hudson	.30	.14	.04
☐	449	Danny Cox	.60	.25	.08
☐	450	Kevin Bass	.30	.14	.04
☐	451	Daryl Sconiers	.30	.14	.04
☐	452	Scott Fletcher	.30	.14	.04
☐	453	Bryn Smith	.30	.14	.04
☐	454	Jim Dwyer	.30	.14	.04
☐	455	Rob Picciolo	.30	.14	.04
☐	456	Enos Cabell	.30	.14	.04
☐	457	Dennis Boyd	.40	.18	.05
☐	458	Butch Wynegar	.30	.14	.04
☐	459	Burt Hooton	.30	.14	.04
☐	460	Ron Hassey	.30	.14	.04
☐	461	Danny Jackson	1.50	.65	.19
☐	462	Bob Kearney	.30	.14	.04
☐	463	Terry Francona	.30	.14	.04
☐	464	Wayne Tolleson	.30	.14	.04
☐	465	Mickey Rivers	.30	.14	.04
☐	466	John Wathan	.30	.14	.04
☐	467	Bill Almon	.30	.14	.04
☐	468	George Vukovich	.30	.14	.04
☐	469	Steve Kemp	.30	.14	.04
☐	470	Ken Landreaux	.30	.14	.04
☐	471	Milt Wilcox	.30	.14	.04
☐	472	Tippy Martinez	.30	.14	.04
☐	473	Ted Simmons	.40	.18	.05
☐	474	Tim Foli	.30	.14	.04
☐	475	George Hendrick	.30	.14	.04
☐	476	Terry Puhl	.30	.14	.04
☐	477	Von Hayes	.30	.14	.04
☐	478	Bobby Brown	.30	.14	.04
☐	479	Lee Lacy	.30	.14	.04
☐	480	Joel Youngblood	.30	.14	.04
☐	481	Jim Slaton	.30	.14	.04
☐	482	Mike Fitzgerald	.30	.14	.04
☐	483	Keith Moreland	.30	.14	.04
☐	484	Ron Roenicke	.30	.14	.04
☐	485	Luis Leal	.30	.14	.04
☐	486	Bryan Oelkers	.30	.14	.04
☐	487	Bruce Berenyi	.30	.14	.04
☐	488	LaMarr Hoyt	.30	.14	.04
☐	489	Joe Nolan	.30	.14	.04
☐	490	Marshall Edwards	.30	.14	.04
☐	491	Mike Laga	.30	.14	.04
☐	492	Rick Cerone	.30	.14	.04
☐	493	Rick Miller UER (Listed as Mike on card front)	.30	.14	.04
☐	494	Rick Honeycutt	.30	.14	.04
☐	495	Mike Hargrove	.40	.18	.05

	#	Player			
☐	496	Joe Simpson	.30	.14	.04
☐	497	Keith Atherton	.30	.14	.04
☐	498	Chris Welsh	.30	.14	.04
☐	499	Bruce Kison	.30	.14	.04
☐	500	Bobby Johnson	.30	.14	.04
☐	501	Jerry Koosman	.40	.18	.05
☐	502	Frank DiPino	.30	.14	.04
☐	503	Tony Perez	1.00	.45	.13
☐	504	Ken Oberkfell	.30	.14	.04
☐	505	Mark Thurmond	.30	.14	.04
☐	506	Joe Price	.30	.14	.04
☐	507	Pascual Perez	.30	.14	.04
☐	508	Marvell Wynne	.30	.14	.04
☐	509	Mike Krukow	.30	.14	.04
☐	510	Dick Ruthven	.30	.14	.04
☐	511	Al Cowens	.30	.14	.04
☐	512	Cliff Johnson	.30	.14	.04
☐	513	Randy Bush	.30	.14	.04
☐	514	Sammy Stewart	.30	.14	.04
☐	515	Bill Schroeder	.30	.14	.04
☐	516	Aurelio Lopez	.40	.18	.05
☐	517	Mike G. Brown	.30	.14	.04
☐	518	Graig Nettles	.40	.18	.05
☐	519	Dave Sax	.30	.14	.04
☐	520	Jerry Willard	.30	.14	.04
☐	521	Paul Splittorff	.30	.14	.04
☐	522	Tom Burgmeier	.30	.14	.04
☐	523	Chris Speier	.30	.14	.04
☐	524	Bobby Clark	.30	.14	.04
☐	525	George Wright	.30	.14	.04
☐	526	Dennis Lamp	.30	.14	.04
☐	527	Tony Scott	.30	.14	.04
☐	528	Ed Whitson	.30	.14	.04
☐	529	Ron Reed	.30	.14	.04
☐	530	Charlie Puleo	.30	.14	.04
☐	531	Jerry Royster	.30	.14	.04
☐	532	Don Robinson	.30	.14	.04
☐	533	Steve Trout	.30	.14	.04
☐	534	Bruce Sutter	.40	.18	.05
☐	535	Bob Horner	.40	.18	.05
☐	536	Pat Tabler	.30	.14	.04
☐	537	Chris Chambliss	.40	.18	.05
☐	538	Bob Ojeda	.40	.18	.05
☐	539	Alan Ashby	.30	.14	.04
☐	540	Jay Johnstone	.40	.18	.05
☐	541	Bob Dernier	.30	.14	.04
☐	542	Brook Jacoby	.40	.18	.05
☐	543	U.L. Washington	.30	.14	.04
☐	544	Danny Darwin	.30	.14	.04
☐	545	Kiko Garcia	.30	.14	.04
☐	546	Vance Law UER (Listed as P on card front)	.30	.14	.04
☐	547	Tug McGraw	.40	.18	.05
☐	548	Dave Smith	.30	.14	.04
☐	549	Len Matuszek	.30	.14	.04
☐	550	Tom Hume	.30	.14	.04
☐	551	Dave Dravecky	.50	.23	.06
☐	552	Rick Rhoden	.30	.14	.04
☐	553	Duane Kuiper	.30	.14	.04
☐	554	Rusty Staub	.40	.18	.05
☐	555	Bill Campbell	.30	.14	.04
☐	556	Mike Torrez	.30	.14	.04
☐	557	Dave Henderson	.40	.18	.05
☐	558	Len Whitehouse	.30	.14	.04
☐	559	Barry Bonnell	.30	.14	.04
☐	560	Rick Lysander	.30	.14	.04
☐	561	Garth Iorg	.30	.14	.04
☐	562	Bryan Clark	.30	.14	.04
☐	563	Brian Giles	.30	.14	.04
☐	564	Vern Ruhle	.30	.14	.04
☐	565	Steve Bedrosian	.40	.18	.05
☐	566	Larry McWilliams	.30	.14	.04

☐ 567 Jeff Leonard UER .30 .14 .04
(Listed as P
on card front)
☐ 568 Alan Wiggins .30 .14 .04
☐ 569 Jeff Russell .75 .35 .09
☐ 570 Salome Barojas .30 .14 .04
☐ 571 Dane Iorg .30 .14 .04
☐ 572 Bob Knepper .30 .14 .04
☐ 573 Gary Lavelle .30 .14 .04
☐ 574 Gorman Thomas .30 .14 .04
☐ 575 Manny Trillo .30 .14 .04
☐ 576 Jim Palmer 3.00 1.35 .40
☐ 577 Dale Murray .30 .14 .04
☐ 578 Tom Brookens .40 .18 .05
☐ 579 Rich Gedman .30 .14 .04
☐ 580 Bill Doran .50 .23 .06
☐ 581 Steve Yeager .30 .14 .04
☐ 582 Dan Spillner .30 .14 .04
☐ 583 Dan Quisenberry .40 .18 .05
☐ 584 Rance Mulliniks .30 .14 .04
☐ 585 Storm Davis .40 .18 .05
☐ 586 Dave Schmidt .30 .14 .04
☐ 587 Bill Russell .30 .14 .04
☐ 588 Pat Sheridan .30 .14 .04
☐ 589 Rafael Ramirez .30 .14 .04
UER (A's on front)
☐ 590 Bud Anderson .30 .14 .04
☐ 591 George Frazier .30 .14 .04
☐ 592 Lee Tunnell .30 .14 .04
☐ 593 Kirk Gibson 1.50 .65 .19
☐ 594 Scott McGregor .30 .14 .04
☐ 595 Bob Bailor .30 .14 .04
☐ 596 Tommy Herr .40 .18 .05
☐ 597 Luis Sanchez .30 .14 .04
☐ 598 Dave Engle .30 .14 .04
☐ 599 Craig McMurtry .30 .14 .04
☐ 600 Carlos Diaz .30 .14 .04
☐ 601 Tom O'Malley .30 .14 .04
☐ 602 Nick Esasky .30 .14 .04
☐ 603 Ron Hodges .30 .14 .04
☐ 604 Ed VandeBerg .30 .14 .04
☐ 605 Alfredo Griffin .30 .14 .04
☐ 606 Glenn Hoffman .30 .14 .04
☐ 607 Hubie Brooks .40 .18 .05
☐ 608 Richard Barnes UER .30 .14 .04
(Photo of Neal Heaton)
☐ 609 Greg Walker .30 .14 .04
☐ 610 Ken Singleton .40 .18 .05
☐ 611 Mark Clear .30 .14 .04
☐ 612 Buck Martinez .30 .14 .04
☐ 613 Ken Griffey .40 .18 .05
☐ 614 Reid Nichols .30 .14 .04
☐ 615 Doug Sisk .30 .14 .04
☐ 616 Bob Brenly .30 .14 .04
☐ 617 Joey McLaughlin .30 .14 .04
☐ 618 Glenn Wilson .40 .18 .05
☐ 619 Bob Stoddard .30 .14 .04
☐ 620 Lenn Sakata UER .30 .14 .04
(Listed as Len
on card front)
☐ 621 Mike Young .30 .14 .04
☐ 622 John Stefero .30 .14 .04
☐ 623 Carmelo Martinez .30 .14 .04
☐ 624 Dave Bergman .30 .14 .04
☐ 625 Runnin' Reds UER 1.50 .65 .19
(Sic, Redbirds)
David Green
Willie McGee
Lonnie Smith
Ozzie Smith
☐ 626 Rudy May .30 .14 .04
☐ 627 Matt Keough .30 .14 .04
☐ 628 Jose DeLeon .40 .18 .05
☐ 629 Jim Essian .30 .14 .04
☐ 630 Darnell Coles .50 .23 .06
☐ 631 Mike Warren .30 .14 .04
☐ 632 Del Crandall MG .30 .14 .04
☐ 633 Dennis Martinez .40 .18 .05
☐ 634 Mike Moore .40 .18 .05
☐ 635 Lary Sorensen .30 .14 .04
☐ 636 Ricky Nelson .30 .14 .04
☐ 637 Omar Moreno .30 .14 .04
☐ 638 Charlie Hough .40 .18 .05
☐ 639 Dennis Eckersley 3.00 1.35 .40
☐ 640 Walt Terrell .30 .14 .04
☐ 641 Denny Walling .30 .14 .04
☐ 642 Dave Anderson .30 .14 .04
☐ 643 Jose Oquendo .50 .23 .06
☐ 644 Bob Stanley .30 .14 .04
☐ 645 Dave Geisel .30 .14 .04
☐ 646 Scott Garrelts .40 .18 .05
☐ 647 Gary Pettis .30 .14 .04
☐ 648 Duke Snider .50 .23 .06
Puzzle Card
☐ 649 Johnnie LeMaster .30 .14 .04
☐ 650 Dave Collins .30 .14 .04
☐ 651 The Chicken .50 .23 .06
☐ 652 DK Checklist 1-26 .35 .14 .04
(Unnumbered)
☐ 653 Checklist 27-130 .35 .14 .04
(Unnumbered)
☐ 654 Checklist 131-234 .35 .14 .04
(Unnumbered)
☐ 655 Checklist 235-338 .35 .14 .04
(Unnumbered)
☐ 656 Checklist 339-442 .35 .14 .04
(Unnumbered)
☐ 657 Checklist 443-546 .35 .14 .04
(Unnumbered)
☐ 658 Checklist 547-651 .35 .14 .04
(Unnumbered)
☐ A Living Legends A 5.00 2.30 .60
Gaylord Perry
Rollie Fingers
☐ B Living Legends B 9.00 4.00 1.15
Carl Yastrzemski
Johnny Bench

1985 Donruss

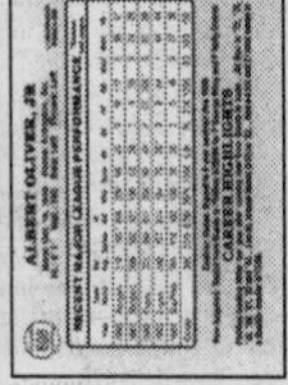

The cards in this 660-card set measure 2 1/2" by 3 1/2". The 1985 Donruss regular issue cards have fronts that feature jet black borders on which orange lines have been placed. The fronts contain the standard team logo, player's name, position, and Donruss logo. The cards were distributed with puzzle pieces from a Dick Perez

rendition of Lou Gehrig. The first 26 cards of the set feature Diamond Kings (DK), for the fourth year in a row; the artwork on the Diamond Kings was again produced by the Perez-Steele Galleries. Cards 27-46 feature Rated Rookies (RR). The unnumbered checklist cards are arbitrarily numbered below as numbers 654 through 660. Rookie Cards in this set include Roger Clemens, Alvin Davis, Eric Davis, Shawon Dunston, Dwight Gooden, Orel Hershiser, Jimmy Key, Mark Langston, Terry Pendleton, Kirby Puckett, Jose Rijo, Bret Saberhagen, and Danny Tartabull.

	NRMT-MT	EXC	G-VG
COMPLETE SET (660)	150.00	70.00	19.00
COMPLETE FACT.SET (660)	175.00	80.00	22.00
COMMON CARD (1-660)	.10	.05	.01
□ 1 Ryne Sandberg DK	3.50	1.55	.45
□ 2 Doug DeCinces DK	.15	.07	.02
□ 3 Richard Dotson DK	.15	.07	.02
□ 4 Bert Blyleven DK	.20	.09	.03
□ 5 Lou Whitaker DK	.35	.16	.04
□ 6 Dan Quisenberry DK	.15	.07	.02
□ 7 Don Mattingly DK	3.50	1.55	.45
□ 8 Carney Lansford DK	.15	.07	.02
□ 9 Frank Tanana DK	.15	.07	.02
□ 10 Willie Upshaw DK	.15	.07	.02
□ 11 Claudell Washington DK	.15	.07	.02
□ 12 Mike Marshall DK	.15	.07	.02
□ 13 Joaquin Andujar DK	.15	.07	.02
□ 14 Cal Ripken DK	4.00	1.80	.50
□ 15 Jim Rice DK	.20	.09	.03
□ 16 Don Sutton DK	.20	.09	.03
□ 17 Frank Viola DK	.20	.09	.03
□ 18 Alvin Davis DK	.15	.07	.02
□ 19 Mario Soto DK	.15	.07	.02
□ 20 Jose Cruz DK	.15	.07	.02
□ 21 Charlie Lea DK	.15	.07	.02
□ 22 Jesse Orosco DK	.15	.07	.02
□ 23 Juan Samuel DK	.15	.07	.02
□ 24 Tony Pena DK	.15	.07	.02
□ 25 Tony Gwynn DK	3.00	1.35	.40
□ 26 Bob Brenly DK	.15	.07	.02
□ 27 Danny Tartabull RR	4.00	1.80	.50
□ 28 Mike Bielecki RR	.10	.05	.01
□ 29 Steve Lyons RR	.10	.05	.01
□ 30 Jeff Reed RR	.10	.05	.01
□ 31 Tony Brewer RR	.10	.05	.01
□ 32 John Morris RR	.10	.05	.01
□ 33 Daryl Boston RR	.50	.23	.06
□ 34 Al Pulido RR	.10	.05	.01
□ 35 Steve Kiefer RR	.10	.05	.01
□ 36 Larry Sheets RR	.10	.05	.01
□ 37 Scott Bradley RR	.10	.05	.01
□ 38 Calvin Schiraldi RR	.10	.05	.01
□ 39 Shawon Dunston RR	1.00	.45	.13
□ 40 Charlie Mitchell RR	.10	.05	.01
□ 41 Billy Hatcher RR	.75	.35	.09
□ 42 Russ Stephans RR	.10	.05	.01
□ 43 Alejandro Sanchez RR	.10	.05	.01
□ 44 Steve Jeltz RR	.10	.05	.01
□ 45 Jim Traber RR	.10	.05	.01
□ 46 Doug Loman RR	.10	.05	.01
□ 47 Eddie Murray	2.00	.90	.25
□ 48 Robin Yount	2.50	1.15	.30
□ 49 Lance Parrish	.15	.07	.02
□ 50 Jim Rice	.20	.09	.03
□ 51 Dave Winfield	2.50	1.15	.30
□ 52 Fernando Valenzuela	.15	.07	.02
□ 53 George Brett	4.00	1.80	.50
□ 54 Dave Kingman	.15	.07	.02
□ 55 Gary Carter	.40	.18	.05
□ 56 Buddy Bell	.15	.07	.02
□ 57 Reggie Jackson	2.00	.90	.25
□ 58 Harold Baines	.20	.09	.03
□ 59 Ozzie Smith	2.50	1.15	.30
□ 60 Nolan Ryan UER (Set strikeout record in 1973, not 1972)	10.00	4.50	1.25
□ 61 Mike Schmidt	3.50	1.55	.45
□ 62 Dave Parker	.20	.09	.03
□ 63 Tony Gwynn	6.50	2.90	.80
□ 64 Tony Pena	.10	.05	.01
□ 65 Jack Clark	.15	.07	.02
□ 66 Dale Murphy	1.00	.45	.13
□ 67 Ryne Sandberg	7.00	3.10	.85
□ 68 Keith Hernandez	.20	.09	.03
□ 69 Alvin Davis	.25	.11	.03
□ 70 Kent Hrbek	.15	.07	.02
□ 71 Willie Upshaw	.10	.05	.01
□ 72 Dave Engle	.10	.05	.01
□ 73 Alfredo Griffin	.10	.05	.01
□ 74A Jack Perconte (Text on back four lines in length)	.10	.05	.01
□ 74B Jack Perconte (Text on back three lines in length)	.10	.05	.01
□ 75 Jesse Orosco	.10	.05	.01
□ 76 Jody Davis	.10	.05	.01
□ 77 Bob Horner	.10	.05	.01
□ 78 Larry McWilliams	.10	.05	.01
□ 79 Joel Youngblood	.10	.05	.01
□ 80 Alan Wiggins	.10	.05	.01
□ 81 Ron Oester	.10	.05	.01
□ 82 Ozzie Virgil	.10	.05	.01
□ 83 Ricky Horton	.10	.05	.01
□ 84 Bill Doran	.10	.05	.01
□ 85 Rod Carew	.75	.35	.09
□ 86 LaMarr Hoyt	.10	.05	.01
□ 87 Tim Wallach	.15	.07	.02
□ 88 Mike Flanagan	.10	.05	.01
□ 89 Jim Sundberg	.15	.07	.02
□ 90 Chet Lemon	.10	.05	.01
□ 91 Bob Stanley	.10	.05	.01
□ 92 Willie Randolph	.15	.07	.02
□ 93 Bill Russell	.15	.07	.02
□ 94 Julio Franco	.75	.35	.09
□ 95 Dan Quisenberry	.15	.07	.02
□ 96 Bill Caudill	.10	.05	.01
□ 97 Bill Gullickson	.15	.07	.02
□ 98 Danny Darwin	.10	.05	.01
□ 99 Curtis Wilkerson	.10	.05	.01
□ 100 Bud Black	.10	.05	.01
□ 101 Tony Phillips	.15	.07	.02
□ 102 Tony Bernazard	.10	.05	.01
□ 103 Jay Howell	.15	.07	.02
□ 104 Burt Hooton	.10	.05	.01
□ 105 Milt Wilcox	.10	.05	.01
□ 106 Rich Dauer	.10	.05	.01
□ 107 Don Sutton	.20	.09	.03
□ 108 Mike Witt	.10	.05	.01
□ 109 Bruce Sutter	.15	.07	.02
□ 110 Enos Cabell	.10	.05	.01
□ 111 John Denny	.10	.05	.01
□ 112 Dave Dravecky	.15	.07	.02
□ 113 Marvell Wynne	.10	.05	.01
□ 114 Johnnie LeMaster	.10	.05	.01
□ 115 Chuck Porter	.10	.05	.01
□ 116 John Gibbons	.10	.05	.01
□ 117 Keith Moreland	.10	.05	.01
□ 118 Darnell Coles	.10	.05	.01
□ 119 Dennis Lamp	.10	.05	.01

	No.	Player			
☐	120	Ron Davis	.10	.05	.01
☐	121	Nick Esasky	.10	.05	.01
☐	122	Vance Law	.10	.05	.01
☐	123	Gary Roenicke	.10	.05	.01
☐	124	Bill Schroeder	.10	.05	.01
☐	125	Dave Rozema	.10	.05	.01
☐	126	Bobby Meacham	.10	.05	.01
☐	127	Marty Barrett	.10	.05	.01
☐	128	R.J. Reynolds	.10	.05	.01
☐	129	Ernie Camacho UER (Photo of Rich Thompson)	.10	.05	.01
☐	130	Jorge Orta	.10	.05	.01
☐	131	Lary Sorensen	.10	.05	.01
☐	132	Terry Francona	.10	.05	.01
☐	133	Fred Lynn	.15	.07	.02
☐	134	Bob Jones	.10	.05	.01
☐	135	Jerry Hairston	.10	.05	.01
☐	136	Kevin Bass	.10	.05	.01
☐	137	Garry Maddox	.10	.05	.01
☐	138	Dave LaPoint	.10	.05	.01
☐	139	Kevin McReynolds	.15	.07	.02
☐	140	Wayne Krenchicki	.10	.05	.01
☐	141	Rafael Ramirez	.10	.05	.01
☐	142	Rod Scurry	.10	.05	.01
☐	143	Greg Minton	.10	.05	.01
☐	144	Tim Stoddard	.10	.05	.01
☐	145	Steve Henderson	.10	.05	.01
☐	146	George Bell	.20	.09	.03
☐	147	Dave Meier	.10	.05	.01
☐	148	Sammy Stewart	.10	.05	.01
☐	149	Mark Brouhard	.10	.05	.01
☐	150	Larry Herndon	.10	.05	.01
☐	151	Oil Can Boyd	.10	.05	.01
☐	152	Brian Dayett	.10	.05	.01
☐	153	Tom Niedenfuer	.10	.05	.01
☐	154	Brook Jacoby	.10	.05	.01
☐	155	Onix Concepcion	.10	.05	.01
☐	156	Tim Conroy	.10	.05	.01
☐	157	Joe Hesketh	.10	.05	.01
☐	158	Brian Downing	.15	.07	.02
☐	159	Tommy Dunbar	.10	.05	.01
☐	160	Marc Hill	.10	.05	.01
☐	161	Phil Garner	.15	.07	.02
☐	162	Jerry Davis	.10	.05	.01
☐	163	Bill Campbell	.10	.05	.01
☐	164	John Franco	1.50	.65	.19
☐	165	Len Barker	.10	.05	.01
☐	166	Benny Distefano	.10	.05	.01
☐	167	George Frazier	.10	.05	.01
☐	168	Tito Landrum	.10	.05	.01
☐	169	Cal Ripken	8.00	3.60	1.00
☐	170	Cecil Cooper	.15	.07	.02
☐	171	Alan Trammell	.75	.35	.09
☐	172	Wade Boggs	4.50	2.00	.55
☐	173	Don Baylor	.20	.09	.03
☐	174	Pedro Guerrero	.15	.07	.02
☐	175	Frank White	.15	.07	.02
☐	176	Rickey Henderson	2.50	1.15	.30
☐	177	Charlie Lea	.10	.05	.01
☐	178	Pete O'Brien	.15	.07	.02
☐	179	Doug DeCinces	.10	.05	.01
☐	180	Ron Kittle	.10	.05	.01
☐	181	George Hendrick	.10	.05	.01
☐	182	Joe Niekro	.15	.07	.02
☐	183	Juan Samuel	.10	.05	.01
☐	184	Mario Soto	.10	.05	.01
☐	185	Goose Gossage	.20	.09	.03
☐	186	Johnny Ray	.10	.05	.01
☐	187	Bob Brenly	.10	.05	.01
☐	188	Craig McMurtry	.10	.05	.01
☐	189	Leon Durham	.10	.05	.01
☐	190	Dwight Gooden	1.50	.65	.19
☐	191	Barry Bonnell	.10	.05	.01
☐	192	Tim Teufel	.10	.05	.01
☐	193	Dave Stieb	.15	.07	.02
☐	194	Mickey Hatcher	.10	.05	.01
☐	195	Jesse Barfield	.10	.05	.01
☐	196	Al Cowens	.10	.05	.01
☐	197	Hubie Brooks	.15	.07	.02
☐	198	Steve Trout	.10	.05	.01
☐	199	Glenn Hubbard	.10	.05	.01
☐	200	Bill Madlock	.15	.07	.02
☐	201	Jeff D. Robinson	.10	.05	.01
☐	202	Eric Show	.10	.05	.01
☐	203	Dave Concepcion	.15	.07	.02
☐	204	Ivan DeJesus	.10	.05	.01
☐	205	Neil Allen	.10	.05	.01
☐	206	Jerry Mumphrey	.10	.05	.01
☐	207	Mike C. Brown	.10	.05	.01
☐	208	Carlton Fisk	1.50	.65	.19
☐	209	Bryn Smith	.10	.05	.01
☐	210	Tippy Martinez	.10	.05	.01
☐	211	Dion James	.10	.05	.01
☐	212	Willie Hernandez	.10	.05	.01
☐	213	Mike Easler	.10	.05	.01
☐	214	Ron Guidry	.15	.07	.02
☐	215	Rick Honeycutt	.10	.05	.01
☐	216	Brett Butler	.20	.09	.03
☐	217	Larry Gura	.10	.05	.01
☐	218	Ray Burris	.10	.05	.01
☐	219	Steve Rogers	.10	.05	.01
☐	220	Frank Tanana UER (Bats Left listed twice on card back)	.15	.07	.02
☐	221	Ned Yost	.10	.05	.01
☐	222	Bret Saberhagen UER (18 career IP on back)	3.50	1.55	.45
☐	223	Mike Davis	.10	.05	.01
☐	224	Bert Blyleven	.20	.09	.03
☐	225	Steve Kemp	.10	.05	.01
☐	226	Jerry Reuss	.10	.05	.01
☐	227	Darrell Evans UER (80 homers in 1980)	.15	.07	.02
☐	228	Wayne Gross	.10	.05	.01
☐	229	Jim Gantner	.10	.05	.01
☐	230	Bob Boone	.15	.07	.02
☐	231	Lonnie Smith	.10	.05	.01
☐	232	Frank DiPino	.10	.05	.01
☐	233	Jerry Koosman	.15	.07	.02
☐	234	Graig Nettles	.15	.07	.02
☐	235	John Tudor	.15	.07	.02
☐	236	John Rabb	.10	.05	.01
☐	237	Rick Manning	.10	.05	.01
☐	238	Mike Fitzgerald	.10	.05	.01
☐	239	Gary Matthews	.10	.05	.01
☐	240	Jim Presley	.10	.05	.01
☐	241	Dave Collins	.10	.05	.01
☐	242	Gary Gaetti	.15	.07	.02
☐	243	Dann Bilardello	.10	.05	.01
☐	244	Rudy Law	.10	.05	.01
☐	245	John Lowenstein	.10	.05	.01
☐	246	Tom Tellmann	.10	.05	.01
☐	247	Howard Johnson	.35	.16	.04
☐	248	Ray Fontenot	.10	.05	.01
☐	249	Tony Armas	.10	.05	.01
☐	250	Candy Maldonado	.10	.05	.01
☐	251	Mike Jeffcoat	.10	.05	.01
☐	252	Dane Iorg	.10	.05	.01
☐	253	Bruce Bochte	.10	.05	.01
☐	254	Pete Rose	3.00	1.35	.40
☐	255	Don Aase	.10	.05	.01
☐	256	George Wright	.10	.05	.01
☐	257	Britt Burns	.10	.05	.01
☐	258	Mike Scott	.15	.07	.02
☐	259	Len Matuszek	.10	.05	.01
☐	260	Dave Rucker	.10	.05	.01

☐	261	Craig Lefferts	.15	.07	.02
☐	262	Jay Tibbs	.10	.05	.01
☐	263	Bruce Benedict	.10	.05	.01
☐	264	Don Robinson	.10	.05	.01
☐	265	Gary Lavelle	.10	.05	.01
☐	266	Scott Sanderson	.10	.05	.01
☐	267	Matt Young	.10	.05	.01
☐	268	Ernie Whitt	.10	.05	.01
☐	269	Houston Jimenez	.10	.05	.01
☐	270	Ken Dixon	.10	.05	.01
☐	271	Pete Ladd	.10	.05	.01
☐	272	Juan Berenguer	.10	.05	.01
☐	273	Roger Clemens	35.00	16.00	4.40
☐	274	Rick Cerone	.10	.05	.01
☐	275	Dave Anderson	.10	.05	.01
☐	276	George Vukovich	.10	.05	.01
☐	277	Greg Pryor	.10	.05	.01
☐	278	Mike Warren	.10	.05	.01
☐	279	Bob James	.10	.05	.01
☐	280	Bobby Grich	.15	.07	.02
☐	281	Mike Mason	.10	.05	.01
☐	282	Ron Reed	.10	.05	.01
☐	283	Alan Ashby	.10	.05	.01
☐	284	Mark Thurmond	.10	.05	.01
☐	285	Joe Lefebvre	.10	.05	.01
☐	286	Ted Power	.10	.05	.01
☐	287	Chris Chambliss	.15	.07	.02
☐	288	Lee Tunnell	.10	.05	.01
☐	289	Rich Bordi	.10	.05	.01
☐	290	Glenn Brummer	.10	.05	.01
☐	291	Mike Boddicker	.10	.05	.01
☐	292	Rollie Fingers	.20	.09	.03
☐	293	Lou Whitaker	.75	.35	.09
☐	294	Dwight Evans	.15	.07	.02
☐	295	Don Mattingly	8.00	3.60	1.00
☐	296	Mike Marshall	.10	.05	.01
☐	297	Willie Wilson	.15	.07	.02
☐	298	Mike Heath	.10	.05	.01
☐	299	Tim Raines	.60	.25	.08
☐	300	Larry Parrish	.10	.05	.01
☐	301	Geoff Zahn	.10	.05	.01
☐	302	Rich Dotson	.10	.05	.01
☐	303	David Green	.10	.05	.01
☐	304	Jose Cruz	.15	.07	.02
☐	305	Steve Carlton	1.25	.55	.16
☐	306	Gary Redus	.10	.05	.01
☐	307	Steve Garvey	.20	.09	.03
☐	308	Jose DeLeon	.10	.05	.01
☐	309	Randy Lerch	.10	.05	.01
☐	310	Claudell Washington	.10	.05	.01
☐	311	Lee Smith	1.00	.45	.13
☐	312	Darryl Strawberry	1.25	.55	.16
☐	313	Jim Beattie	.10	.05	.01
☐	314	John Butcher	.10	.05	.01
☐	315	Damaso Garcia	.10	.05	.01
☐	316	Mike Smithson	.10	.05	.01
☐	317	Luis Leal	.10	.05	.01
☐	318	Ken Phelps	.10	.05	.01
☐	319	Wally Backman	.10	.05	.01
☐	320	Ron Cey	.15	.07	.02
☐	321	Brad Komminsk	.10	.05	.01
☐	322	Jason Thompson	.10	.05	.01
☐	323	Frank Williams	.10	.05	.01
☐	324	Tim Lollar	.10	.05	.01
☐	325	Eric Davis	2.50	1.15	.30
☐	326	Von Hayes	.10	.05	.01
☐	327	Andy Van Slyke	1.00	.45	.13
☐	328	Craig Reynolds	.10	.05	.01
☐	329	Dick Schofield	.10	.05	.01
☐	330	Scott Fletcher	.10	.05	.01
☐	331	Jeff Reardon	.20	.09	.03
☐	332	Rick Dempsey	.10	.05	.01
☐	333	Ben Oglivie	.10	.05	.01
☐	334	Dan Petry	.10	.05	.01
☐	335	Jackie Gutierrez	.10	.05	.01
☐	336	Dave Righetti	.15	.07	.02
☐	337	Alejandro Pena	.10	.05	.01
☐	338	Mel Hall	.10	.05	.01
☐	339	Pat Sheridan	.10	.05	.01
☐	340	Keith Atherton	.10	.05	.01
☐	341	David Palmer	.10	.05	.01
☐	342	Gary Ward	.10	.05	.01
☐	343	Dave Stewart	.20	.09	.03
☐	344	Mark Gubicza	.50	.23	.06
☐	345	Carney Lansford	.15	.07	.02
☐	346	Jerry Willard	.10	.05	.01
☐	347	Ken Griffey	.15	.07	.02
☐	348	Franklin Stubbs	.10	.05	.01
☐	349	Aurelio Lopez	.10	.05	.01
☐	350	Al Bumbry	.15	.07	.02
☐	351	Charlie Moore	.10	.05	.01
☐	352	Luis Sanchez	.10	.05	.01
☐	353	Darrell Porter	.10	.05	.01
☐	354	Bill Dawley	.10	.05	.01
☐	355	Charles Hudson	.10	.05	.01
☐	356	Garry Templeton	.10	.05	.01
☐	357	Cecilio Guante	.10	.05	.01
☐	358	Jeff Leonard	.10	.05	.01
☐	359	Paul Molitor	3.00	1.35	.40
☐	360	Ron Gardenhire	.10	.05	.01
☐	361	Larry Bowa	.15	.07	.02
☐	362	Bob Kearney	.10	.05	.01
☐	363	Garth Iorg	.10	.05	.01
☐	364	Tom Brunansky	.15	.07	.02
☐	365	Brad Gulden	.10	.05	.01
☐	366	Greg Walker	.10	.05	.01
☐	367	Mike Young	.10	.05	.01
☐	368	Rick Waits	.10	.05	.01
☐	369	Doug Bair	.10	.05	.01
☐	370	Bob Shirley	.10	.05	.01
☐	371	Bob Ojeda	.15	.07	.02
☐	372	Bob Welch	.15	.07	.02
☐	373	Neal Heaton	.10	.05	.01
☐	374	Danny Jackson UER (Photo of Frank Wills)	.15	.07	.02
☐	375	Donnie Hill	.10	.05	.01
☐	376	Mike Stenhouse	.10	.05	.01
☐	377	Bruce Kison	.10	.05	.01
☐	378	Wayne Tolleson	.10	.05	.01
☐	379	Floyd Bannister	.10	.05	.01
☐	380	Vern Ruhle	.10	.05	.01
☐	381	Tim Corcoran	.10	.05	.01
☐	382	Kurt Kepshire	.10	.05	.01
☐	383	Bobby Brown	.10	.05	.01
☐	384	Dave Van Gorder	.10	.05	.01
☐	385	Rick Mahler	.10	.05	.01
☐	386	Lee Mazzilli	.10	.05	.01
☐	387	Bill Laskey	.10	.05	.01
☐	388	Thad Bosley	.10	.05	.01
☐	389	Al Chambers	.10	.05	.01
☐	390	Tony Fernandez	.50	.23	.06
☐	391	Ron Washington	.10	.05	.01
☐	392	Bill Swaggerty	.10	.05	.01
☐	393	Bob L. Gibson	.10	.05	.01
☐	394	Marty Castillo	.10	.05	.01
☐	395	Steve Crawford	.10	.05	.01
☐	396	Clay Christiansen	.10	.05	.01
☐	397	Bob Bailor	.10	.05	.01
☐	398	Mike Hargrove	.15	.07	.02
☐	399	Charlie Leibrandt	.10	.05	.01
☐	400	Tom Burgmeier	.10	.05	.01
☐	401	Razor Shines	.10	.05	.01
☐	402	Rob Wilfong	.10	.05	.01
☐	403	Tom Henke	.75	.35	.09
☐	404	Al Jones	.10	.05	.01
☐	405	Mike LaCoss	.10	.05	.01

	No.	Player			
☐	406	Luis DeLeon	.10	.05	.01
☐	407	Greg Gross	.10	.05	.01
☐	408	Tom Hume	.10	.05	.01
☐	409	Rick Camp	.10	.05	.01
☐	410	Milt May	.10	.05	.01
☐	411	Henry Cotto	.10	.05	.01
☐	412	David Von Ohlen	.10	.05	.01
☐	413	Scott McGregor	.10	.05	.01
☐	414	Ted Simmons	.15	.07	.02
☐	415	Jack Morris	.50	.23	.06
☐	416	Bill Buckner	.15	.07	.02
☐	417	Butch Wynegar	.10	.05	.01
☐	418	Steve Sax	.15	.07	.02
☐	419	Steve Balboni	.10	.05	.01
☐	420	Dwayne Murphy	.10	.05	.01
☐	421	Andre Dawson	1.50	.65	.19
☐	422	Charlie Hough	.15	.07	.02
☐	423	Tommy John	.20	.09	.03
☐	424A	Tom Seaver ERR (Photo of Floyd Bannister)	1.50	.65	.19
☐	424B	Tom Seaver COR	25.00	11.50	3.10
☐	425	Tommy Herr	.15	.07	.02
☐	426	Terry Puhl	.10	.05	.01
☐	427	Al Holland	.10	.05	.01
☐	428	Eddie Milner	.10	.05	.01
☐	429	Terry Kennedy	.10	.05	.01
☐	430	John Candelaria	.10	.05	.01
☐	431	Manny Trillo	.10	.05	.01
☐	432	Ken Oberkfell	.10	.05	.01
☐	433	Rick Sutcliffe	.15	.07	.02
☐	434	Ron Darling	.15	.07	.02
☐	435	Spike Owen	.10	.05	.01
☐	436	Frank Viola	.15	.07	.02
☐	437	Lloyd Moseby	.10	.05	.01
☐	438	Kirby Puckett	40.00	18.00	5.00
☐	439	Jim Clancy	.10	.05	.01
☐	440	Mike Moore	.15	.07	.02
☐	441	Doug Sisk	.10	.05	.01
☐	442	Dennis Eckersley	.50	.23	.06
☐	443	Gerald Perry	.10	.05	.01
☐	444	Dale Berra	.10	.05	.01
☐	445	Dusty Baker	.20	.09	.03
☐	446	Ed Whitson	.10	.05	.01
☐	447	Cesar Cedeno	.15	.07	.02
☐	448	Rick Schu	.10	.05	.01
☐	449	Joaquin Andujar	.10	.05	.01
☐	450	Mark Bailey	.10	.05	.01
☐	451	Ron Romanick	.10	.05	.01
☐	452	Julio Cruz	.10	.05	.01
☐	453	Miguel Dilone	.10	.05	.01
☐	454	Storm Davis	.10	.05	.01
☐	455	Jaime Cocanower	.10	.05	.01
☐	456	Barbaro Garbey	.10	.05	.01
☐	457	Rich Gedman	.10	.05	.01
☐	458	Phil Niekro	.20	.09	.03
☐	459	Mike Scioscia	.10	.05	.01
☐	460	Pat Tabler	.10	.05	.01
☐	461	Darryl Motley	.10	.05	.01
☐	462	Chris Codiroli	.10	.05	.01
☐	463	Doug Flynn	.10	.05	.01
☐	464	Billy Sample	.10	.05	.01
☐	465	Mickey Rivers	.10	.05	.01
☐	466	John Wathan	.10	.05	.01
☐	467	Bill Krueger	.10	.05	.01
☐	468	Andre Thornton	.10	.05	.01
☐	469	Rex Hudler	.10	.05	.01
☐	470	Sid Bream	.50	.23	.06
☐	471	Kirk Gibson	.20	.09	.03
☐	472	John Shelby	.10	.05	.01
☐	473	Moose Haas	.10	.05	.01
☐	474	Doug Corbett	.10	.05	.01
☐	475	Willie McGee	.15	.07	.02
☐	476	Bob Knepper	.10	.05	.01
☐	477	Kevin Gross	.10	.05	.01
☐	478	Carmelo Martinez	.10	.05	.01
☐	479	Kent Tekulve	.10	.05	.01
☐	480	Chili Davis	.15	.07	.02
☐	481	Bobby Clark	.10	.05	.01
☐	482	Mookie Wilson	.15	.07	.02
☐	483	Dave Owen	.10	.05	.01
☐	484	Ed Nunez	.10	.05	.01
☐	485	Rance Mulliniks	.10	.05	.01
☐	486	Ken Schrom	.10	.05	.01
☐	487	Jeff Russell	.15	.07	.02
☐	488	Tom Paciorek	.15	.07	.02
☐	489	Dan Ford	.10	.05	.01
☐	490	Mike Caldwell	.10	.05	.01
☐	491	Scottie Earl	.10	.05	.01
☐	492	Jose Rijo	3.00	1.35	.40
☐	493	Bruce Hurst	.15	.07	.02
☐	494	Ken Landreaux	.10	.05	.01
☐	495	Mike Fischlin	.10	.05	.01
☐	496	Don Slaught	.10	.05	.01
☐	497	Steve McCatty	.10	.05	.01
☐	498	Gary Lucas	.10	.05	.01
☐	499	Gary Pettis	.10	.05	.01
☐	500	Marvis Foley	.10	.05	.01
☐	501	Mike Squires	.10	.05	.01
☐	502	Jim Pankovits	.10	.05	.01
☐	503	Luis Aguayo	.10	.05	.01
☐	504	Ralph Citarella	.10	.05	.01
☐	505	Bruce Bochy	.10	.05	.01
☐	506	Bob Owchinko	.10	.05	.01
☐	507	Pascual Perez	.10	.05	.01
☐	508	Lee Lacy	.10	.05	.01
☐	509	Atlee Hammaker	.10	.05	.01
☐	510	Bob Dernier	.10	.05	.01
☐	511	Ed VandeBerg	.10	.05	.01
☐	512	Cliff Johnson	.10	.05	.01
☐	513	Len Whitehouse	.10	.05	.01
☐	514	Dennis Martinez	.15	.07	.02
☐	515	Ed Romero	.10	.05	.01
☐	516	Rusty Kuntz	.10	.05	.01
☐	517	Rick Miller	.10	.05	.01
☐	518	Dennis Rasmussen	.10	.05	.01
☐	519	Steve Yeager	.10	.05	.01
☐	520	Chris Bando	.10	.05	.01
☐	521	U.L. Washington	.10	.05	.01
☐	522	Curt Young	.10	.05	.01
☐	523	Angel Salazar	.10	.05	.01
☐	524	Curt Kaufman	.10	.05	.01
☐	525	Odell Jones	.10	.05	.01
☐	526	Juan Agosto	.10	.05	.01
☐	527	Denny Walling	.10	.05	.01
☐	528	Andy Hawkins	.10	.05	.01
☐	529	Sixto Lezcano	.10	.05	.01
☐	530	Skeeter Barnes	.10	.05	.01
☐	531	Randy Johnson	.10	.05	.01
☐	532	Jim Morrison	.10	.05	.01
☐	533	Warren Brusstar	.10	.05	.01
☐	534A	Jeff Pendleton ERR (Wrong first name)	3.00	1.35	.40
☐	534B	Terry Pendleton COR	15.00	6.75	1.90
☐	535	Vic Rodriguez	.10	.05	.01
☐	536	Bob McClure	.10	.05	.01
☐	537	Dave Bergman	.10	.05	.01
☐	538	Mark Clear	.10	.05	.01
☐	539	Mike Pagliarulo	.10	.05	.01
☐	540	Terry Whitfield	.10	.05	.01
☐	541	Joe Beckwith	.10	.05	.01
☐	542	Jeff Burroughs	.10	.05	.01
☐	543	Dan Schatzeder	.10	.05	.01
☐	544	Donnie Scott	.10	.05	.01
☐	545	Jim Slaton	.10	.05	.01
☐	546	Greg Luzinski	.15	.07	.02
☐	547	Mark Salas	.10	.05	.01

☐ 548 Dave Smith .10 .05 .01
☐ 549 John Wockenfuss .10 .05 .01
☐ 550 Frank Pastore .10 .05 .01
☐ 551 Tim Flannery .10 .05 .01
☐ 552 Rick Rhoden .10 .05 .01
☐ 553 Mark Davis .10 .05 .01
☐ 554 Jeff Dedmon .10 .05 .01
☐ 555 Gary Woods .10 .05 .01
☐ 556 Danny Heep .10 .05 .01
☐ 557 Mark Langston 2.25 1.00 .30
☐ 558 Darrell Brown .10 .05 .01
☐ 559 Jimmy Key 5.50 2.50 .70
☐ 560 Rick Lysander .10 .05 .01
☐ 561 Doyle Alexander .10 .05 .01
☐ 562 Mike Stanton .10 .05 .01
☐ 563 Sid Fernandez .50 .23 .06
☐ 564 Richie Hebner .10 .05 .01
☐ 565 Alex Trevino .10 .05 .01
☐ 566 Brian Harper .15 .07 .02
☐ 567 Dan Gladden .35 .16 .04
☐ 568 Luis Salazar .10 .05 .01
☐ 569 Tom Foley .10 .05 .01
☐ 570 Larry Andersen .10 .05 .01
☐ 571 Danny Cox .10 .05 .01
☐ 572 Joe Sambito .10 .05 .01
☐ 573 Juan Beniquez .10 .05 .01
☐ 574 Joel Skinner .10 .05 .01
☐ 575 Randy St.Claire .10 .05 .01
☐ 576 Floyd Rayford .10 .05 .01
☐ 577 Roy Howell .10 .05 .01
☐ 578 John Grubb .10 .05 .01
☐ 579 Ed Jurak .10 .05 .01
☐ 580 John Montefusco .10 .05 .01
☐ 581 Orel Hershiser 2.50 1.15 .30
☐ 582 Tom Waddell .10 .05 .01
☐ 583 Mark Huismann .10 .05 .01
☐ 584 Joe Morgan .50 .23 .06
☐ 585 Jim Wohlford .10 .05 .01
☐ 586 Dave Schmidt .10 .05 .01
☐ 587 Jeff Kunkel .10 .05 .01
☐ 588 Hal McRae .20 .09 .03
☐ 589 Bill Almon .10 .05 .01
☐ 590 Carmen Castillo .10 .05 .01
☐ 591 Omar Moreno .10 .05 .01
☐ 592 Ken Howell .10 .05 .01
☐ 593 Tom Brookens .10 .05 .01
☐ 594 Joe Nolan .10 .05 .01
☐ 595 Willie Lozado .10 .05 .01
☐ 596 Tom Nieto .10 .05 .01
☐ 597 Walt Terrell .10 .05 .01
☐ 598 Al Oliver .15 .07 .02
☐ 599 Shane Rawley .10 .05 .01
☐ 600 Denny Gonzalez .10 .05 .01
☐ 601 Mark Grant .10 .05 .01
☐ 602 Mike Armstrong .10 .05 .01
☐ 603 George Foster .15 .07 .02
☐ 604 Dave Lopes .15 .07 .02
☐ 605 Salome Barojas .10 .05 .01
☐ 606 Roy Lee Jackson .10 .05 .01
☐ 607 Pete Filson .10 .05 .01
☐ 608 Duane Walker .10 .05 .01
☐ 609 Glenn Wilson .10 .05 .01
☐ 610 Rafael Santana .10 .05 .01
☐ 611 Roy Smith .10 .05 .01
☐ 612 Ruppert Jones .10 .05 .01
☐ 613 Joe Cowley .10 .05 .01
☐ 614 Al Nipper UER .10 .05 .01
(Photo of Mike Brown)
☐ 615 Gene Nelson .10 .05 .01
☐ 616 Joe Carter 15.00 6.75 1.90
☐ 617 Ray Knight .15 .07 .02
☐ 618 Chuck Rainey .10 .05 .01
☐ 619 Dan Driessen .10 .05 .01
☐ 620 Daryl Sconiers .10 .05 .01
☐ 621 Bill Stein .10 .05 .01
☐ 622 Roy Smalley .10 .05 .01
☐ 623 Ed Lynch .10 .05 .01
☐ 624 Jeff Stone .10 .05 .01
☐ 625 Bruce Berenyi .10 .05 .01
☐ 626 Kelvin Chapman .10 .05 .01
☐ 627 Joe Price .10 .05 .01
☐ 628 Steve Bedrosian .10 .05 .01
☐ 629 Vic Mata .10 .05 .01
☐ 630 Mike Krukow .10 .05 .01
☐ 631 Phil Bradley .15 .07 .02
☐ 632 Jim Gott .10 .05 .01
☐ 633 Randy Bush .10 .05 .01
☐ 634 Tom Browning .75 .35 .09
☐ 635 Lou Gehrig .25 .11 .03
Puzzle Card
☐ 636 Reid Nichols .10 .05 .01
☐ 637 Dan Pasqua .30 .14 .04
☐ 638 German Rivera .10 .05 .01
☐ 639 Don Schulze .10 .05 .01
☐ 640A Mike Jones .10 .05 .01
(Text on back five lines in length)
☐ 640B Mike Jones .10 .05 .01
(Text on back four lines in length)
☐ 641 Pete Rose 3.00 1.35 .40
☐ 642 Wade Rowdon .10 .05 .01
☐ 643 Jerry Narron .10 .05 .01
☐ 644 Darrell Miller .10 .05 .01
☐ 645 Tim Hulett .20 .09 .03
☐ 646 Andy McGaffigan .10 .05 .01
☐ 647 Kurt Bevacqua .10 .05 .01
☐ 648 John Russell .10 .05 .01
☐ 649 Ron Robinson .10 .05 .01
☐ 650 Donnie Moore .10 .05 .01
☐ 651A Two for the Title 3.00 1.35 .40
Dave Winfield
Don Mattingly
(Yellow letters)
☐ 651B Two for the Title 8.00 3.60 1.00
Dave Winfield
Don Mattingly
(White letters)
☐ 652 Tim Laudner .10 .05 .01
☐ 653 Steve Farr .50 .23 .06
☐ 654 DK Checklist 1-26 .15 .05 .01
(Unnumbered)
☐ 655 Checklist 27-130 .15 .05 .01
(Unnumbered)
☐ 656 Checklist 131-234 .15 .05 .01
(Unnumbered)
☐ 657 Checklist 235-338 .15 .05 .01
(Unnumbered)
☐ 658 Checklist 339-442 .15 .05 .01
(Unnumbered)
☐ 659 Checklist 443-546 .15 .05 .01
(Unnumbered)
☐ 660 Checklist 547-653 .15 .05 .01
(Unnumbered)

1986 Donruss

The cards in this 660-card set measure 2 1/2" by 3 1/2". The 1986 Donruss regular issue cards have fronts that feature blue borders. The fronts contain the standard team logo, player's name, position, and

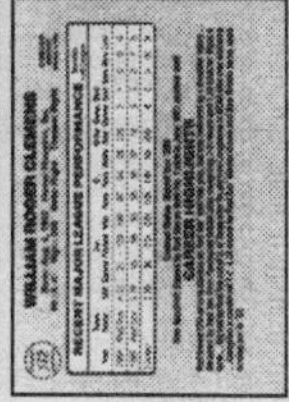

Donruss logo. The cards were distributed with puzzle pieces from a Dick Perez rendition of Hank Aaron. The first 26 cards of the set are Diamond Kings (DK), for the fifth year in a row; the artwork on the Diamond Kings was again produced by the Perez-Steele Galleries. Cards 27-46 again feature Rated Rookies (RR); Danny Tartabull is included in this subset for the second year in a row. The unnumbered checklist cards are arbitrarily numbered below as numbers 654 through 660. Rookie Cards in this set include Rick Aguilera, Jose Canseco, Vince Coleman, Kal Daniels, Darren Daulton, Len Dykstra, Cecil Fielder, Andres Galarraga, Fred McGriff, Paul O'Neill, and Mickey Tettleton.

	MINT	EXC	G-VG
COMPLETE SET (660)	110.00	50.00	14.00
COMPLETE FACT.SET (660)	120.00	55.00	15.00
COMMON CARD (1-660)	.10	.05	.01

		MINT	EXC	G-VG
☐ 1	Kirk Gibson DK	.15	.07	.02
☐ 2	Goose Gossage DK	.15	.07	.02
☐ 3	Willie McGee DK	.15	.07	.02
☐ 4	George Bell DK	.12	.05	.02
☐ 5	Tony Armas DK	.12	.05	.02
☐ 6	Chili Davis DK	.15	.07	.02
☐ 7	Cecil Cooper DK	.12	.05	.02
☐ 8	Mike Boddicker DK	.12	.05	.02
☐ 9	Dave Lopes DK	.12	.05	.02
☐ 10	Bill Doran DK	.12	.05	.02
☐ 11	Bret Saberhagen DK	.15	.07	.02
☐ 12	Brett Butler DK	.15	.07	.02
☐ 13	Harold Baines DK	.15	.07	.02
☐ 14	Mike Davis DK	.12	.05	.02
☐ 15	Tony Perez DK	.15	.07	.02
☐ 16	Willie Randolph DK	.12	.05	.02
☐ 17	Bob Boone DK	.12	.05	.02
☐ 18	Orel Hershiser DK	.15	.07	.02
☐ 19	Johnny Ray DK	.12	.05	.02
☐ 20	Gary Ward DK	.12	.05	.02
☐ 21	Rick Mahler DK	.12	.05	.02
☐ 22	Phil Bradley DK	.12	.05	.02
☐ 23	Jerry Koosman DK	.12	.05	.02
☐ 24	Tom Brunansky DK	.12	.05	.02
☐ 25	Andre Dawson DK	.35	.16	.04
☐ 26	Dwight Gooden DK	.12	.05	.02
☐ 27	Kal Daniels RR	.10	.05	.01
☐ 28	Fred McGriff RR	30.00	13.50	3.80
☐ 29	Cory Snyder RR	.10	.05	.01
☐ 30	Jose Guzman RR	.50	.23	.06
☐ 31	Ty Gainey RR	.10	.05	.01
☐ 32	Johnny Abrego RR	.10	.05	.01
☐ 33A	Andres Galarraga RR (No accent)	7.00	3.10	.85
☐ 33B	Andre's Galarraga RR (Accent over e)	7.00	3.10	.85
☐ 34	Dave Shipanoff RR	.10	.05	.01
☐ 35	Mark McLemore RR	.50	.23	.06
☐ 36	Marty Clary RR	.10	.05	.01
☐ 37	Paul O'Neill RR	4.00	1.80	.50
☐ 38	Danny Tartabull RR	.75	.35	.09
☐ 39	Jose Canseco RR	35.00	16.00	4.40
☐ 40	Juan Nieves RR	.10	.05	.01
☐ 41	Lance McCullers RR	.10	.05	.01
☐ 42	Rick Surhoff RR	.10	.05	.01
☐ 43	Todd Worrell RR	.30	.14	.04
☐ 44	Bob Kipper RR	.10	.05	.01
☐ 45	John Habyan RR	.10	.05	.01
☐ 46	Mike Woodard RR	.10	.05	.01
☐ 47	Mike Boddicker	.10	.05	.01
☐ 48	Robin Yount	1.25	.55	.16
☐ 49	Lou Whitaker	.20	.09	.03
☐ 50	Oil Can Boyd	.10	.05	.01
☐ 51	Rickey Henderson	1.50	.65	.19
☐ 52	Mike Marshall	.10	.05	.01
☐ 53	George Brett	2.50	1.15	.30
☐ 54	Dave Kingman	.15	.07	.02
☐ 55	Hubie Brooks	.10	.05	.01
☐ 56	Oddibe McDowell	.10	.05	.01
☐ 57	Doug DeCinces	.10	.05	.01
☐ 58	Britt Burns	.10	.05	.01
☐ 59	Ozzie Smith	1.25	.55	.16
☐ 60	Jose Cruz	.10	.05	.01
☐ 61	Mike Schmidt	1.25	.55	.16
☐ 62	Pete Rose	1.25	.55	.16
☐ 63	Steve Garvey	.20	.09	.03
☐ 64	Tony Pena	.10	.05	.01
☐ 65	Chili Davis	.15	.07	.02
☐ 66	Dale Murphy	.20	.09	.03
☐ 67	Ryne Sandberg	3.00	1.35	.40
☐ 68	Gary Carter	.20	.09	.03
☐ 69	Alvin Davis	.10	.05	.01
☐ 70	Kent Hrbek	.15	.07	.02
☐ 71	George Bell	.15	.07	.02
☐ 72	Kirby Puckett	9.00	4.00	1.15
☐ 73	Lloyd Moseby	.10	.05	.01
☐ 74	Bob Kearney	.10	.05	.01
☐ 75	Dwight Gooden	.40	.18	.05
☐ 76	Gary Matthews	.10	.05	.01
☐ 77	Rick Mahler	.10	.05	.01
☐ 78	Benny Distefano	.10	.05	.01
☐ 79	Jeff Leonard	.10	.05	.01
☐ 80	Kevin McReynolds	.15	.07	.02
☐ 81	Ron Oester	.10	.05	.01
☐ 82	John Russell	.10	.05	.01
☐ 83	Tommy Herr	.10	.05	.01
☐ 84	Jerry Mumphrey	.10	.05	.01
☐ 85	Ron Romanick	.10	.05	.01
☐ 86	Daryl Boston	.10	.05	.01
☐ 87	Andre Dawson	.75	.35	.09
☐ 88	Eddie Murray	1.00	.45	.13
☐ 89	Dion James	.10	.05	.01
☐ 90	Chet Lemon	.10	.05	.01
☐ 91	Bob Stanley	.10	.05	.01
☐ 92	Willie Randolph	.15	.07	.02
☐ 93	Mike Scioscia	.10	.05	.01
☐ 94	Tom Waddell	.10	.05	.01
☐ 95	Danny Jackson	.15	.07	.02
☐ 96	Mike Davis	.10	.05	.01
☐ 97	Mike Fitzgerald	.10	.05	.01
☐ 98	Gary Ward	.10	.05	.01
☐ 99	Pete O'Brien	.10	.05	.01
☐ 100	Bret Saberhagen	.50	.23	.06
☐ 101	Alfredo Griffin	.10	.05	.01
☐ 102	Brett Butler	.15	.07	.02
☐ 103	Ron Guidry	.15	.07	.02
☐ 104	Jerry Reuss	.10	.05	.01
☐ 105	Jack Morris	.15	.07	.02
☐ 106	Rick Dempsey	.10	.05	.01

☐ 107 Ray Burris	.10	.05	.01
☐ 108 Brian Downing	.15	.07	.02
☐ 109 Willie McGee	.15	.07	.02
☐ 110 Bill Doran	.10	.05	.01
☐ 111 Kent Tekulve	.10	.05	.01
☐ 112 Tony Gwynn	3.00	1.35	.40
☐ 113 Marvell Wynne	.10	.05	.01
☐ 114 David Green	.10	.05	.01
☐ 115 Jim Gantner	.10	.05	.01
☐ 116 George Foster	.15	.07	.02
☐ 117 Steve Trout	.10	.05	.01
☐ 118 Mark Langston	.50	.23	.06
☐ 119 Tony Fernandez	.15	.07	.02
☐ 120 John Butcher	.10	.05	.01
☐ 121 Ron Robinson	.10	.05	.01
☐ 122 Dan Spillner	.10	.05	.01
☐ 123 Mike Young	.10	.05	.01
☐ 124 Paul Molitor	1.50	.65	.19
☐ 125 Kirk Gibson	.20	.09	.03
☐ 126 Ken Griffey	.15	.07	.02
☐ 127 Tony Armas	.10	.05	.01
☐ 128 Mariano Duncan	.50	.23	.06
☐ 129 Pat Tabler	.10	.05	.01
☐ 130 Frank White	.15	.07	.02
☐ 131 Carney Lansford	.15	.07	.02
☐ 132 Vance Law	.10	.05	.01
☐ 133 Dick Schofield	.10	.05	.01
☐ 134 Wayne Tolleson	.10	.05	.01
☐ 135 Greg Walker	.10	.05	.01
☐ 136 Denny Walling	.10	.05	.01
☐ 137 Ozzie Virgil	.10	.05	.01
☐ 138 Ricky Horton	.10	.05	.01
☐ 139 LaMarr Hoyt	.10	.05	.01
☐ 140 Wayne Krenchicki	.10	.05	.01
☐ 141 Glenn Hubbard	.10	.05	.01
☐ 142 Cecilio Guante	.10	.05	.01
☐ 143 Mike Krukow	.10	.05	.01
☐ 144 Lee Smith	.50	.23	.06
☐ 145 Edwin Nunez	.10	.05	.01
☐ 146 Dave Stieb	.15	.07	.02
☐ 147 Mike Smithson	.10	.05	.01
☐ 148 Ken Dixon	.10	.05	.01
☐ 149 Danny Darwin	.10	.05	.01
☐ 150 Chris Pittaro	.10	.05	.01
☐ 151 Bill Buckner	.15	.07	.02
☐ 152 Mike Pagliarulo	.10	.05	.01
☐ 153 Bill Russell	.15	.07	.02
☐ 154 Brook Jacoby	.10	.05	.01
☐ 155 Pat Sheridan	.10	.05	.01
☐ 156 Mike Gallego	.20	.09	.03
☐ 157 Jim Wohlford	.10	.05	.01
☐ 158 Gary Pettis	.10	.05	.01
☐ 159 Toby Harrah	.10	.05	.01
☐ 160 Richard Dotson	.10	.05	.01
☐ 161 Bob Knepper	.10	.05	.01
☐ 162 Dave Dravecky	.15	.07	.02
☐ 163 Greg Gross	.10	.05	.01
☐ 164 Eric Davis	.35	.16	.04
☐ 165 Gerald Perry	.10	.05	.01
☐ 166 Rick Rhoden	.10	.05	.01
☐ 167 Keith Moreland	.10	.05	.01
☐ 168 Jack Clark	.15	.07	.02
☐ 169 Storm Davis	.10	.05	.01
☐ 170 Cecil Cooper	.15	.07	.02
☐ 171 Alan Trammell	.20	.09	.03
☐ 172 Roger Clemens	7.00	3.10	.85
☐ 173 Don Mattingly	3.00	1.35	.40
☐ 174 Pedro Guerrero	.15	.07	.02
☐ 175 Willie Wilson	.10	.05	.01
☐ 176 Dwayne Murphy	.10	.05	.01
☐ 177 Tim Raines	.30	.14	.04
☐ 178 Larry Parrish	.10	.05	.01
☐ 179 Mike Witt	.10	.05	.01
☐ 180 Harold Baines	.15	.07	.02
☐ 181 Vince Coleman UER (BA 2.67 on back)	.50	.23	.06
☐ 182 Jeff Heathcock	.10	.05	.01
☐ 183 Steve Carlton	.75	.35	.09
☐ 184 Mario Soto	.10	.05	.01
☐ 185 Goose Gossage	.15	.07	.02
☐ 186 Johnny Ray	.10	.05	.01
☐ 187 Dan Gladden	.10	.05	.01
☐ 188 Bob Horner	.10	.05	.01
☐ 189 Rick Sutcliffe	.15	.07	.02
☐ 190 Keith Hernandez	.15	.07	.02
☐ 191 Phil Bradley	.10	.05	.01
☐ 192 Tom Brunansky	.15	.07	.02
☐ 193 Jesse Barfield	.10	.05	.01
☐ 194 Frank Viola	.15	.07	.02
☐ 195 Willie Upshaw	.10	.05	.01
☐ 196 Jim Beattie	.10	.05	.01
☐ 197 Darryl Strawberry	.60	.25	.08
☐ 198 Ron Cey	.15	.07	.02
☐ 199 Steve Bedrosian	.10	.05	.01
☐ 200 Steve Kemp	.10	.05	.01
☐ 201 Manny Trillo	.10	.05	.01
☐ 202 Garry Templeton	.10	.05	.01
☐ 203 Dave Parker	.20	.09	.03
☐ 204 John Denny	.10	.05	.01
☐ 205 Terry Pendleton	.75	.35	.09
☐ 206 Terry Puhl	.10	.05	.01
☐ 207 Bobby Grich	.15	.07	.02
☐ 208 Ozzie Guillen	.75	.35	.09
☐ 209 Jeff Reardon	.20	.09	.03
☐ 210 Cal Ripken	5.00	2.30	.60
☐ 211 Bill Schroeder	.10	.05	.01
☐ 212 Dan Petry	.10	.05	.01
☐ 213 Jim Rice	.20	.09	.03
☐ 214 Dave Righetti	.15	.07	.02
☐ 215 Fernando Valenzuela	.15	.07	.02
☐ 216 Julio Franco	.35	.16	.04
☐ 217 Darryl Motley	.10	.05	.01
☐ 218 Dave Collins	.10	.05	.01
☐ 219 Tim Wallach	.15	.07	.02
☐ 220 George Wright	.10	.05	.01
☐ 221 Tommy Dunbar	.10	.05	.01
☐ 222 Steve Balboni	.10	.05	.01
☐ 223 Jay Howell	.10	.05	.01
☐ 224 Joe Carter	5.00	2.30	.60
☐ 225 Ed Whitson	.10	.05	.01
☐ 226 Orel Hershiser	.40	.18	.05
☐ 227 Willie Hernandez	.10	.05	.01
☐ 228 Lee Lacy	.10	.05	.01
☐ 229 Rollie Fingers	.20	.09	.03
☐ 230 Bob Boone	.15	.07	.02
☐ 231 Joaquin Andujar	.10	.05	.01
☐ 232 Craig Reynolds	.10	.05	.01
☐ 233 Shane Rawley	.10	.05	.01
☐ 234 Eric Show	.10	.05	.01
☐ 235 Jose DeLeon	.10	.05	.01
☐ 236 Jose Uribe	.10	.05	.01
☐ 237 Moose Haas	.10	.05	.01
☐ 238 Wally Backman	.10	.05	.01
☐ 239 Dennis Eckersley	.25	.11	.03
☐ 240 Mike Moore	.10	.05	.01
☐ 241 Damaso Garcia	.10	.05	.01
☐ 242 Tim Teufel	.10	.05	.01
☐ 243 Dave Concepcion	.15	.07	.02
☐ 244 Floyd Bannister	.10	.05	.01
☐ 245 Fred Lynn	.15	.07	.02
☐ 246 Charlie Moore	.10	.05	.01
☐ 247 Walt Terrell	.10	.05	.01
☐ 248 Dave Winfield	1.00	.45	.13
☐ 249 Dwight Evans	.15	.07	.02
☐ 250 Dennis Powell	.10	.05	.01
☐ 251 Andre Thornton	.10	.05	.01

☐	252 Onix Concepcion	.10	.05	.01
☐	253 Mike Heath	.10	.05	.01
☐	254A David Palmer ERR (Position 2B)	.10	.05	.01
☐	254B David Palmer COR (Position P)	.50	.23	.06
☐	255 Donnie Moore	.10	.05	.01
☐	256 Curtis Wilkerson	.10	.05	.01
☐	257 Julio Cruz	.10	.05	.01
☐	258 Nolan Ryan	6.00	2.70	.75
☐	259 Jeff Stone	.10	.05	.01
☐	260 John Tudor	.15	.07	.02
☐	261 Mark Thurmond	.10	.05	.01
☐	262 Jay Tibbs	.10	.05	.01
☐	263 Rafael Ramirez	.10	.05	.01
☐	264 Larry McWilliams	.10	.05	.01
☐	265 Mark Davis	.10	.05	.01
☐	266 Bob Dernier	.10	.05	.01
☐	267 Matt Young	.10	.05	.01
☐	268 Jim Clancy	.10	.05	.01
☐	269 Mickey Hatcher	.10	.05	.01
☐	270 Sammy Stewart	.10	.05	.01
☐	271 Bob L. Gibson	.10	.05	.01
☐	272 Nelson Simmons	.10	.05	.01
☐	273 Rich Gedman	.10	.05	.01
☐	274 Butch Wynegar	.10	.05	.01
☐	275 Ken Howell	.10	.05	.01
☐	276 Mel Hall	.10	.05	.01
☐	277 Jim Sundberg	.10	.05	.01
☐	278 Chris Codiroli	.10	.05	.01
☐	279 Herm Winningham	.10	.05	.01
☐	280 Rod Carew	.50	.23	.06
☐	281 Don Slaught	.10	.05	.01
☐	282 Scott Fletcher	.10	.05	.01
☐	283 Bill Dawley	.10	.05	.01
☐	284 Andy Hawkins	.10	.05	.01
☐	285 Glenn Wilson	.10	.05	.01
☐	286 Nick Esasky	.10	.05	.01
☐	287 Claudell Washington	.10	.05	.01
☐	288 Lee Mazzilli	.10	.05	.01
☐	289 Jody Davis	.10	.05	.01
☐	290 Darrell Porter	.10	.05	.01
☐	291 Scott McGregor	.10	.05	.01
☐	292 Ted Simmons	.15	.07	.02
☐	293 Aurelio Lopez	.10	.05	.01
☐	294 Marty Barrett	.10	.05	.01
☐	295 Dale Berra	.10	.05	.01
☐	296 Greg Brock	.10	.05	.01
☐	297 Charlie Leibrandt	.10	.05	.01
☐	298 Bill Krueger	.10	.05	.01
☐	299 Bryn Smith	.10	.05	.01
☐	300 Burt Hooton	.10	.05	.01
☐	301 Stu Cliburn	.10	.05	.01
☐	302 Luis Salazar	.10	.05	.01
☐	303 Ken Dayley	.10	.05	.01
☐	304 Frank DiPino	.10	.05	.01
☐	305 Von Hayes	.10	.05	.01
☐	306 Gary Redus	.10	.05	.01
☐	307 Craig Lefferts	.10	.05	.01
☐	308 Sammy Khalifa	.10	.05	.01
☐	309 Scott Garrelts	.10	.05	.01
☐	310 Rick Cerone	.10	.05	.01
☐	311 Shawon Dunston	.15	.07	.02
☐	312 Howard Johnson	.15	.07	.02
☐	313 Jim Presley	.10	.05	.01
☐	314 Gary Gaetti	.10	.05	.01
☐	315 Luis Leal	.10	.05	.01
☐	316 Mark Salas	.10	.05	.01
☐	317 Bill Caudill	.10	.05	.01
☐	318 Dave Henderson	.15	.07	.02
☐	319 Rafael Santana	.10	.05	.01
☐	320 Leon Durham	.10	.05	.01
☐	321 Bruce Sutter	.15	.07	.02
☐	322 Jason Thompson	.10	.05	.01
☐	323 Bob Brenly	.10	.05	.01
☐	324 Carmelo Martinez	.10	.05	.01
☐	325 Eddie Milner	.10	.05	.01
☐	326 Juan Samuel	.10	.05	.01
☐	327 Tom Nieto	.10	.05	.01
☐	328 Dave Smith	.10	.05	.01
☐	329 Urbano Lugo	.10	.05	.01
☐	330 Joel Skinner	.10	.05	.01
☐	331 Bill Gullickson	.15	.07	.02
☐	332 Floyd Rayford	.10	.05	.01
☐	333 Ben Oglivie	.10	.05	.01
☐	334 Lance Parrish	.15	.07	.02
☐	335 Jackie Gutierrez	.10	.05	.01
☐	336 Dennis Rasmussen	.10	.05	.01
☐	337 Terry Whitfield	.10	.05	.01
☐	338 Neal Heaton	.10	.05	.01
☐	339 Jorge Orta	.10	.05	.01
☐	340 Donnie Hill	.10	.05	.01
☐	341 Joe Hesketh	.10	.05	.01
☐	342 Charlie Hough	.10	.05	.01
☐	343 Dave Rozema	.10	.05	.01
☐	344 Greg Pryor	.10	.05	.01
☐	345 Mickey Tettleton	2.50	1.15	.30
☐	346 George Vukovich	.10	.05	.01
☐	347 Don Baylor	.20	.09	.03
☐	348 Carlos Diaz	.10	.05	.01
☐	349 Barbaro Garbey	.10	.05	.01
☐	350 Larry Sheets	.10	.05	.01
☐	351 Ted Higuera	.20	.09	.03
☐	352 Juan Beniquez	.10	.05	.01
☐	353 Bob Forsch	.10	.05	.01
☐	354 Mark Bailey	.10	.05	.01
☐	355 Larry Andersen	.10	.05	.01
☐	356 Terry Kennedy	.10	.05	.01
☐	357 Don Robinson	.10	.05	.01
☐	358 Jim Gott	.10	.05	.01
☐	359 Earnie Riles	.10	.05	.01
☐	360 John Christensen	.10	.05	.01
☐	361 Ray Fontenot	.10	.05	.01
☐	362 Spike Owen	.10	.05	.01
☐	363 Jim Acker	.10	.05	.01
☐	364 Ron Davis	.10	.05	.01
☐	365 Tom Hume	.10	.05	.01
☐	366 Carlton Fisk	.75	.35	.09
☐	367 Nate Snell	.10	.05	.01
☐	368 Rick Manning	.10	.05	.01
☐	369 Darrell Evans	.15	.07	.02
☐	370 Ron Hassey	.10	.05	.01
☐	371 Wade Boggs	2.50	1.15	.30
☐	372 Rick Honeycutt	.10	.05	.01
☐	373 Chris Bando	.10	.05	.01
☐	374 Bud Black	.10	.05	.01
☐	375 Steve Henderson	.10	.05	.01
☐	376 Charlie Lea	.10	.05	.01
☐	377 Reggie Jackson	1.25	.55	.16
☐	378 Dave Schmidt	.10	.05	.01
☐	379 Bob James	.10	.05	.01
☐	380 Glenn Davis	.10	.05	.01
☐	381 Tim Corcoran	.10	.05	.01
☐	382 Danny Cox	.10	.05	.01
☐	383 Tim Flannery	.10	.05	.01
☐	384 Tom Browning	.15	.07	.02
☐	385 Rick Camp	.10	.05	.01
☐	386 Jim Morrison	.10	.05	.01
☐	387 Dave LaPoint	.10	.05	.01
☐	388 Dave Lopes	.15	.07	.02
☐	389 Al Cowens	.10	.05	.01
☐	390 Doyle Alexander	.10	.05	.01
☐	391 Tim Laudner	.10	.05	.01
☐	392 Don Aase	.10	.05	.01
☐	393 Jaime Cocanower	.10	.05	.01
☐	394 Randy O'Neal	.10	.05	.01

☐	395	Mike Easler	.10	.05	.01
☐	396	Scott Bradley	.10	.05	.01
☐	397	Tom Niedenfuer	.10	.05	.01
☐	398	Jerry Willard	.10	.05	.01
☐	399	Lonnie Smith	.10	.05	.01
☐	400	Bruce Bochte	.10	.05	.01
☐	401	Terry Francona	.10	.05	.01
☐	402	Jim Slaton	.10	.05	.01
☐	403	Bill Stein	.10	.05	.01
☐	404	Tim Hulett	.10	.05	.01
☐	405	Alan Ashby	.10	.05	.01
☐	406	Tim Stoddard	.10	.05	.01
☐	407	Garry Maddox	.10	.05	.01
☐	408	Ted Power	.10	.05	.01
☐	409	Len Barker	.10	.05	.01
☐	410	Denny Gonzalez	.10	.05	.01
☐	411	George Frazier	.10	.05	.01
☐	412	Andy Van Slyke	.20	.09	.03
☐	413	Jim Dwyer	.10	.05	.01
☐	414	Paul Householder	.10	.05	.01
☐	415	Alejandro Sanchez	.10	.05	.01
☐	416	Steve Crawford	.10	.05	.01
☐	417	Dan Pasqua	.10	.05	.01
☐	418	Enos Cabell	.10	.05	.01
☐	419	Mike Jones	.10	.05	.01
☐	420	Steve Kiefer	.10	.05	.01
☐	421	Tim Burke	.10	.05	.01
☐	422	Mike Mason	.10	.05	.01
☐	423	Ruppert Jones	.10	.05	.01
☐	424	Jerry Hairston	.10	.05	.01
☐	425	Tito Landrum	.10	.05	.01
☐	426	Jeff Calhoun	.10	.05	.01
☐	427	Don Carman	.10	.05	.01
☐	428	Tony Perez	.20	.09	.03
☐	429	Jerry Davis	.10	.05	.01
☐	430	Bob Walk	.10	.05	.01
☐	431	Brad Wellman	.10	.05	.01
☐	432	Terry Forster	.10	.05	.01
☐	433	Billy Hatcher	.15	.07	.02
☐	434	Clint Hurdle	.10	.05	.01
☐	435	Ivan Calderon	.25	.11	.03
☐	436	Pete Filson	.10	.05	.01
☐	437	Tom Henke	.25	.11	.03
☐	438	Dave Engle	.10	.05	.01
☐	439	Tom Filer	.10	.05	.01
☐	440	Gorman Thomas	.10	.05	.01
☐	441	Rick Aguilera	1.50	.65	.19
☐	442	Scott Sanderson	.10	.05	.01
☐	443	Jeff Dedmon	.10	.05	.01
☐	444	Joe Orsulak	.25	.11	.03
☐	445	Atlee Hammaker	.10	.05	.01
☐	446	Jerry Royster	.10	.05	.01
☐	447	Buddy Bell	.15	.07	.02
☐	448	Dave Rucker	.10	.05	.01
☐	449	Ivan DeJesus	.10	.05	.01
☐	450	Jim Pankovits	.10	.05	.01
☐	451	Jerry Narron	.10	.05	.01
☐	452	Bryan Little	.10	.05	.01
☐	453	Gary Lucas	.10	.05	.01
☐	454	Dennis Martinez	.15	.07	.02
☐	455	Ed Romero	.10	.05	.01
☐	456	Bob Melvin	.10	.05	.01
☐	457	Glenn Hoffman	.10	.05	.01
☐	458	Bob Shirley	.10	.05	.01
☐	459	Bob Welch	.15	.07	.02
☐	460	Carmen Castillo	.10	.05	.01
☐	461	Dave Leeper OF	.10	.05	.01
☐	462	Tim Birtsas	.10	.05	.01
☐	463	Randy St.Claire	.10	.05	.01
☐	464	Chris Welsh	.10	.05	.01
☐	465	Greg Harris	.10	.05	.01
☐	466	Lynn Jones	.10	.05	.01
☐	467	Dusty Baker	.20	.09	.03
☐	468	Roy Smith	.10	.05	.01
☐	469	Andre Robertson	.10	.05	.01
☐	470	Ken Landreaux	.10	.05	.01
☐	471	Dave Bergman	.10	.05	.01
☐	472	Gary Roenicke	.10	.05	.01
☐	473	Pete Vuckovich	.10	.05	.01
☐	474	Kirk McCaskill	.25	.11	.03
☐	475	Jeff Lahti	.10	.05	.01
☐	476	Mike Scott	.10	.05	.01
☐	477	Darren Daulton	5.00	2.30	.60
☐	478	Graig Nettles	.15	.07	.02
☐	479	Bill Almon	.10	.05	.01
☐	480	Greg Minton	.10	.05	.01
☐	481	Randy Ready	.10	.05	.01
☐	482	Len Dykstra	5.00	2.30	.60
☐	483	Thad Bosley	.10	.05	.01
☐	484	Harold Reynolds	.50	.23	.06
☐	485	Al Oliver	.15	.07	.02
☐	486	Roy Smalley	.10	.05	.01
☐	487	John Franco	.15	.07	.02
☐	488	Juan Agosto	.10	.05	.01
☐	489	Al Pardo	.10	.05	.01
☐	490	Bill Wegman	.25	.11	.03
☐	491	Frank Tanana	.15	.07	.02
☐	492	Brian Fisher	.10	.05	.01
☐	493	Mark Clear	.10	.05	.01
☐	494	Len Matuszek	.10	.05	.01
☐	495	Ramon Romero	.10	.05	.01
☐	496	John Wathan	.10	.05	.01
☐	497	Rob Picciolo	.10	.05	.01
☐	498	U.L. Washington	.10	.05	.01
☐	499	John Candelaria	.10	.05	.01
☐	500	Duane Walker	.10	.05	.01
☐	501	Gene Nelson	.10	.05	.01
☐	502	John Mizerock	.10	.05	.01
☐	503	Luis Aguayo	.10	.05	.01
☐	504	Kurt Kepshire	.10	.05	.01
☐	505	Ed Wojna	.10	.05	.01
☐	506	Joe Price	.10	.05	.01
☐	507	Milt Thompson	.25	.11	.03
☐	508	Junior Ortiz	.10	.05	.01
☐	509	Vida Blue	.15	.07	.02
☐	510	Steve Engel	.10	.05	.01
☐	511	Karl Best	.10	.05	.01
☐	512	Cecil Fielder	15.00	6.75	1.90
☐	513	Frank Eufemia	.10	.05	.01
☐	514	Tippy Martinez	.10	.05	.01
☐	515	Billy Joe Robidoux	.10	.05	.01
☐	516	Bill Scherrer	.10	.05	.01
☐	517	Bruce Hurst	.15	.07	.02
☐	518	Rich Bordi	.10	.05	.01
☐	519	Steve Yeager	.10	.05	.01
☐	520	Tony Bernazard	.10	.05	.01
☐	521	Hal McRae	.20	.09	.03
☐	522	Jose Rijo	.50	.23	.06
☐	523	Mitch Webster	.10	.05	.01
☐	524	Jack Howell	.10	.05	.01
☐	525	Alan Bannister	.10	.05	.01
☐	526	Ron Kittle	.10	.05	.01
☐	527	Phil Garner	.15	.07	.02
☐	528	Kurt Bevacqua	.10	.05	.01
☐	529	Kevin Gross	.10	.05	.01
☐	530	Bo Diaz	.10	.05	.01
☐	531	Ken Oberkfell	.10	.05	.01
☐	532	Rick Reuschel	.10	.05	.01
☐	533	Ron Meridith	.10	.05	.01
☐	534	Steve Braun	.10	.05	.01
☐	535	Wayne Gross	.10	.05	.01
☐	536	Ray Searage	.10	.05	.01
☐	537	Tom Brookens	.10	.05	.01
☐	538	Al Nipper	.10	.05	.01
☐	539	Billy Sample	.10	.05	.01
☐	540	Steve Sax	.15	.07	.02

□ 541 Dan Quisenberry .... .15 .07 .02
□ 542 Tony Phillips .... .15 .07 .02
□ 543 Floyd Youmans .... .10 .05 .01
□ 544 Steve Buechele .... .50 .23 .06
□ 545 Craig Gerber .... .10 .05 .01
□ 546 Joe DeSa .... .10 .05 .01
□ 547 Brian Harper .... .15 .07 .02
□ 548 Kevin Bass .... .10 .05 .01
□ 549 Tom Foley .... .10 .05 .01
□ 550 Dave Van Gorder .... .10 .05 .01
□ 551 Bruce Bochy .... .10 .05 .01
□ 552 R.J. Reynolds .... .10 .05 .01
□ 553 Chris Brown .... .10 .05 .01
□ 554 Bruce Benedict .... .10 .05 .01
□ 555 Warren Brusstar .... .10 .05 .01
□ 556 Danny Heep .... .10 .05 .01
□ 557 Darnell Coles .... .10 .05 .01
□ 558 Greg Gagne .... .15 .07 .02
□ 559 Ernie Whitt .... .10 .05 .01
□ 560 Ron Washington .... .10 .05 .01
□ 561 Jimmy Key .... .75 .35 .09
□ 562 Billy Swift .... .60 .25 .08
□ 563 Ron Darling .... .15 .07 .02
□ 564 Dick Ruthven .... .10 .05 .01
□ 565 Zane Smith .... .10 .05 .01
□ 566 Sid Bream .... .15 .07 .02
□ 567A Joel Youngblood ERR .10 .05 .01
(Position P)
□ 567B Joel Youngblood COR .50 .23 .06
(Position IF)
□ 568 Mario Ramirez .... .10 .05 .01
□ 569 Tom Runnells .... .15 .07 .02
□ 570 Rick Schu .... .10 .05 .01
□ 571 Bill Campbell .... .10 .05 .01
□ 572 Dickie Thon .... .10 .05 .01
□ 573 Al Holland .... .10 .05 .01
□ 574 Reid Nichols .... .10 .05 .01
□ 575 Bert Roberge .... .10 .05 .01
□ 576 Mike Flanagan .... .10 .05 .01
□ 577 Tim Leary .... .10 .05 .01
□ 578 Mike Laga .... .10 .05 .01
□ 579 Steve Lyons .... .10 .05 .01
□ 580 Phil Niekro .... .20 .09 .03
□ 581 Gilberto Reyes .... .15 .07 .02
□ 582 Jamie Easterly .... .10 .05 .01
□ 583 Mark Gubicza .... .15 .07 .02
□ 584 Stan Javier .... .35 .16 .04
□ 585 Bill Laskey .... .10 .05 .01
□ 586 Jeff Russell .... .10 .05 .01
□ 587 Dickie Noles .... .10 .05 .01
□ 588 Steve Farr .... .15 .07 .02
□ 589 Steve Ontiveros .... .10 .05 .01
□ 590 Mike Hargrove .... .15 .07 .02
□ 591 Marty Bystrom .... .10 .05 .01
□ 592 Franklin Stubbs .... .10 .05 .01
□ 593 Larry Herndon .... .10 .05 .01
□ 594 Bill Swaggerty .... .10 .05 .01
□ 595 Carlos Ponce .... .10 .05 .01
□ 596 Pat Perry .... .10 .05 .01
□ 597 Ray Knight .... .15 .07 .02
□ 598 Steve Lombardozzi .... .10 .05 .01
□ 599 Brad Havens .... .10 .05 .01
□ 600 Pat Clements .... .10 .05 .01
□ 601 Joe Niekro .... .15 .07 .02
□ 602 Hank Aaron .... .15 .07 .02
Puzzle Card
□ 603 Dwayne Henry .... .10 .05 .01
□ 604 Mookie Wilson .... .15 .07 .02
□ 605 Buddy Biancalana .... .10 .05 .01
□ 606 Rance Mulliniks .... .10 .05 .01
□ 607 Alan Wiggins .... .10 .05 .01
□ 608 Joe Cowley .... .10 .05 .01
□ 609A Tom Seaver .... .75 .35 .09
(Green borders
on name)
□ 609B Tom Seaver .... 2.50 1.15 .30
(Yellow borders
on name)
□ 610 Neil Allen .... .10 .05 .01
□ 611 Don Sutton .... .20 .09 .03
□ 612 Fred Toliver .... .10 .05 .01
□ 613 Jay Baller .... .10 .05 .01
□ 614 Marc Sullivan .... .10 .05 .01
□ 615 John Grubb .... .10 .05 .01
□ 616 Bruce Kison .... .10 .05 .01
□ 617 Bill Madlock .... .15 .07 .02
□ 618 Chris Chambliss .... .15 .07 .02
□ 619 Dave Stewart .... .20 .09 .03
□ 620 Tim Lollar .... .10 .05 .01
□ 621 Gary Lavelle .... .10 .05 .01
□ 622 Charles Hudson .... .10 .05 .01
□ 623 Joel Davis .... .10 .05 .01
□ 624 Joe Johnson .... .10 .05 .01
□ 625 Sid Fernandez .... .15 .07 .02
□ 626 Dennis Lamp .... .10 .05 .01
□ 627 Terry Harper .... .10 .05 .01
□ 628 Jack Lazorko .... .10 .05 .01
□ 629 Roger McDowell .... .25 .11 .03
□ 630 Mark Funderburk .... .10 .05 .01
□ 631 Ed Lynch .... .10 .05 .01
□ 632 Rudy Law .... .10 .05 .01
□ 633 Roger Mason .... .10 .05 .01
□ 634 Mike Felder .... .15 .07 .02
□ 635 Ken Schrom .... .10 .05 .01
□ 636 Bob Ojeda .... .15 .07 .02
□ 637 Ed VandeBerg .... .10 .05 .01
□ 638 Bobby Meacham .... .10 .05 .01
□ 639 Cliff Johnson .... .10 .05 .01
□ 640 Garth Iorg .... .10 .05 .01
□ 641 Dan Driessen .... .10 .05 .01
□ 642 Mike Brown OF .... .10 .05 .01
□ 643 John Shelby .... .10 .05 .01
□ 644 Pete Rose .... .60 .25 .08
(Ty-Breaking)
□ 645 The Knuckle Brothers... .10 .05 .01
Phil Niekro
Joe Niekro
□ 646 Jesse Orosco .... .10 .05 .01
□ 647 Billy Beane .... .10 .05 .01
□ 648 Cesar Cedeno .... .15 .07 .02
□ 649 Bert Blyleven .... .20 .09 .03
□ 650 Max Venable .... .10 .05 .01
□ 651 Fleet Feet .... .10 .05 .01
Vince Coleman
Willie McGee
□ 652 Calvin Schiraldi .... .10 .05 .01
□ 653 King of Kings .... 1.00 .45 .13
(Pete Rose)
□ 654 Diamond Kings CL 1-26 .12 .05 .01
(Unnumbered)
□ 655A CL 1: 27-130 .... .12 .05 .01
(Unnumbered)
(45 Beane ERR)
□ 655B CL 1: 27-130 .... .50 .05 .01
(Unnumbered)
(45 Habyan COR)
□ 656 CL 2: 131-234 .... .12 .05 .01
(Unnumbered)
□ 657 CL 3: 235-338 .... .12 .05 .01
(Unnumbered)
□ 658 CL 4: 339-442 .... .12 .05 .01
(Unnumbered)
□ 659 CL 5: 443-546 .... .12 .05 .01
(Unnumbered)
□ 660 CL 6: 547-653 .... .12 .05 .01
(Unnumbered)

1986 Donruss Rookies

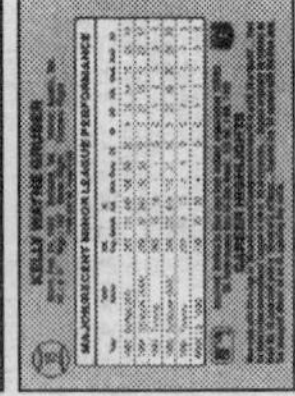

The 1986 Donruss "The Rookies" set features 56 cards plus a 15-piece puzzle of Hank Aaron. Cards are in full color and are standard size, 2 1/2" by 3 1/2". The set was distributed in a small green box with gold lettering. Although the set was wrapped in cellophane, the top card was number 1 Joyner, resulting in a percentage of the Joyner cards arriving in less than perfect condition. Donruss fixed the problem after it was called to their attention and even went so far as to include a customer service phone number in their second printing. Card fronts are similar in design to the 1986 Donruss regular issue except for the presence of "The Rookies" logo in the lower left corner and a bluish green border instead of a blue border. The key (extended) Rookie Cards in this set are Barry Bonds, Bobby Bonilla, Will Clark, Bo Jackson, Wally Joyner, John Kruk, Kevin Mitchell, and Ruben Sierra.

	MINT	EXC	G-VG
COMPLETE FACT.SET (56)	35.00	16.00	4.40
COMMON CARD (1-56)	.10	.05	.01
☐ 1 Wally Joyner	1.00	.45	.13
☐ 2 Tracy Jones	.10	.05	.01
☐ 3 Allan Anderson	.10	.05	.01
☐ 4 Ed Correa	.10	.05	.01
☐ 5 Reggie Williams	.10	.05	.01
☐ 6 Charlie Kerfeld	.10	.05	.01
☐ 7 Andres Galarraga	3.00	1.35	.40
☐ 8 Bob Tewksbury	.50	.23	.06
☐ 9 Al Newman	.10	.05	.01
☐ 10 Andres Thomas	.10	.05	.01
☐ 11 Barry Bonds	12.00	5.50	1.50
☐ 12 Juan Nieves	.10	.05	.01
☐ 13 Mark Eichhorn	.10	.05	.01
☐ 14 Dan Plesac	.10	.05	.01
☐ 15 Cory Snyder	.15	.07	.02
☐ 16 Kelly Gruber	.25	.11	.03
☐ 17 Kevin Mitchell	2.00	.90	.25
☐ 18 Steve Lombardozzi	.10	.05	.01
☐ 19 Mitch Williams	.40	.18	.05
☐ 20 John Cerutti	.10	.05	.01
☐ 21 Todd Worrell	.15	.07	.02
☐ 22 Jose Canseco	6.00	2.70	.75
☐ 23 Pete Incaviglia	.75	.35	.09
☐ 24 Jose Guzman	.25	.11	.03
☐ 25 Scott Bailes	.10	.05	.01
☐ 26 Greg Mathews	.10	.05	.01
☐ 27 Eric King	.10	.05	.01
☐ 28 Paul Assenmacher	.10	.05	.01
☐ 29 Jeff Sellers	.10	.05	.01
☐ 30 Bobby Bonilla	3.00	1.35	.40
☐ 31 Doug Drabek	1.50	.65	.19
☐ 32 Will Clark UER (Listed as throwing right, should be left)	8.00	3.60	1.00
☐ 33 Bip Roberts	.50	.23	.06
☐ 34 Jim Deshaies	.25	.11	.03
☐ 35 Mike LaValliere	.10	.05	.01
☐ 36 Scott Bankhead	.10	.05	.01
☐ 37 Dale Sveum	.10	.05	.01
☐ 38 Bo Jackson	4.00	1.80	.50
☐ 39 Robby Thompson	.60	.25	.08
☐ 40 Eric Plunk	.10	.05	.01
☐ 41 Bill Bathe	.10	.05	.01
☐ 42 John Kruk	1.50	.65	.19
☐ 43 Andy Allanson	.10	.05	.01
☐ 44 Mark Portugal	.75	.35	.09
☐ 45 Danny Tartabull	.75	.35	.09
☐ 46 Bob Kipper	.10	.05	.01
☐ 47 Gene Walter	.10	.05	.01
☐ 48 Rey Quinones UER (Misspelled Quinonez)	.10	.05	.01
☐ 49 Bobby Witt	.40	.18	.05
☐ 50 Bill Mooneyham	.10	.05	.01
☐ 51 John Cangelosi	.10	.05	.01
☐ 52 Ruben Sierra	5.00	2.30	.60
☐ 53 Rob Woodward	.10	.05	.01
☐ 54 Ed Hearn	.10	.05	.01
☐ 55 Joel McKeon	.10	.05	.01
☐ 56 Checklist 1-56	.10	.05	.01

1987 Donruss

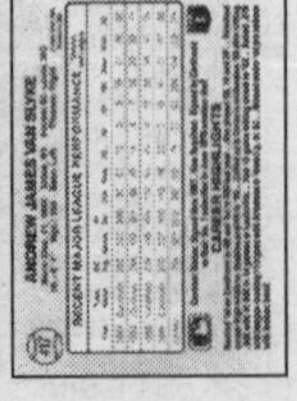

This 660-card set was distributed along with a puzzle of Roberto Clemente. The checklist cards are numbered throughout the set as multiples of 100. The wax pack boxes again contain four separate cards printed on the bottom of the box. Cards measure 2 1/2" by 3 1/2" and feature a black and gold border on the front; the backs are also done in black and gold on white card stock. The popular Diamond King subset returns for the sixth consecutive year. Some of the Diamond King (1-26) selections are repeats from prior years; Perez-Steele Galleries has indicated that a five-year rotation will be maintained in order to avoid depleting the pool of available worthy "kings" on some of the teams. Three of the Diamond Kings

have a variation (on the reverse) where the yellow strip behind the words "Donruss Diamond Kings" is not printed and, hence, the background is white. Rookie Cards in this set include Barry Bonds, Bobby Bonilla, Kevin Brown, Will Clark, David Cone, Chuck Finley, Mike Greenwell, Bo Jackson, Wally Joyner, Barry Larkin, Greg Maddux, Dave Magadan, Kevin Mitchell, Rafael Palmiero, Ruben Sierra, and Devon White. The backs of the cards in the factory sets are oriented differently than cards taken from wax packs, giving the appearance that one version or the other is upside down when sorting from the card backs.

	MINT	EXC	G-VG
COMPLETE SET (660)	40.00	18.00	5.00
COMPLETE FACT.SET (660)	40.00	18.00	5.00
COMMON CARD (1-660)	.06	.03	.01
☐ 1 Wally Joyner DK	.20	.09	.03
☐ 2 Roger Clemens DK	.50	.23	.06
☐ 3 Dale Murphy DK	.15	.07	.02
☐ 4 Darryl Strawberry DK	.15	.07	.02
☐ 5 Ozzie Smith DK	.30	.14	.04
☐ 6 Jose Canseco DK	.75	.35	.09
☐ 7 Charlie Hough DK	.10	.05	.01
☐ 8 Brook Jacoby DK	.10	.05	.01
☐ 9 Fred Lynn DK	.10	.05	.01
☐ 10 Rick Rhoden DK	.10	.05	.01
☐ 11 Chris Brown DK	.10	.05	.01
☐ 12 Von Hayes DK	.10	.05	.01
☐ 13 Jack Morris DK	.15	.07	.02
☐ 14A Kevin McReynolds DK ERR (Yellow strip missing on back)	.50	.23	.06
☐ 14B Kevin McReynolds DK COR	.15	.07	.02
☐ 15 George Brett DK	.40	.18	.05
☐ 16 Ted Higuera DK	.10	.05	.01
☐ 17 Hubie Brooks DK	.10	.05	.01
☐ 18 Mike Scott DK	.10	.05	.01
☐ 19 Kirby Puckett DK	.75	.35	.09
☐ 20 Dave Winfield DK	.35	.16	.04
☐ 21 Lloyd Moseby DK	.10	.05	.01
☐ 22A Eric Davis DK ERR (Yellow strip missing on back)	.60	.25	.08
☐ 22B Eric Davis DK COR	.15	.07	.02
☐ 23 Jim Presley DK	.10	.05	.01
☐ 24 Keith Moreland DK	.10	.05	.01
☐ 25A Greg Walker DK ERR (Yellow strip missing on back)	.50	.23	.06
☐ 25B Greg Walker DK COR	.10	.05	.01
☐ 26 Steve Sax DK	.10	.05	.01
☐ 27 DK Checklist 1-26	.10	.03	.01
☐ 28 B.J. Surhoff RR	.25	.11	.03
☐ 29 Randy Myers RR	1.00	.45	.13
☐ 30 Ken Gerhart RR	.06	.03	.01
☐ 31 Benito Santiago RR	.35	.16	.04
☐ 32 Greg Swindell RR	.75	.35	.09
☐ 33 Mike Birkbeck RR	.06	.03	.01
☐ 34 Terry Steinbach RR	.40	.18	.05
☐ 35 Bo Jackson RR	2.50	1.15	.30
☐ 36 Greg Maddux RR	8.00	3.60	1.00
☐ 37 Jim Lindeman RR	.06	.03	.01
☐ 38 Devon White RR	1.50	.65	.19
☐ 39 Eric Bell RR	.06	.03	.01
☐ 40 Willie Fraser RR	.06	.03	.01
☐ 41 Jerry Browne RR	.20	.09	.03
☐ 42 Chris James RR	.06	.03	.01
☐ 43 Rafael Palmeiro RR	4.00	1.80	.50
☐ 44 Pat Dodson RR	.06	.03	.01
☐ 45 Duane Ward RR	1.00	.45	.13
☐ 46 Mark McGwire RR	1.75	.80	.22
☐ 47 Bruce Fields RR UER (Photo actually Darnell Coles)	.06	.03	.01
☐ 48 Eddie Murray	.40	.18	.05
☐ 49 Ted Higuera	.06	.03	.01
☐ 50 Kirk Gibson	.10	.05	.01
☐ 51 Oil Can Boyd	.06	.03	.01
☐ 52 Don Mattingly	1.00	.45	.13
☐ 53 Pedro Guerrero	.10	.05	.01
☐ 54 George Brett	1.00	.45	.13
☐ 55 Jose Rijo	.15	.07	.02
☐ 56 Tim Raines	.15	.07	.02
☐ 57 Ed Correa	.06	.03	.01
☐ 58 Mike Witt	.06	.03	.01
☐ 59 Greg Walker	.06	.03	.01
☐ 60 Ozzie Smith	.60	.25	.08
☐ 61 Glenn Davis	.06	.03	.01
☐ 62 Glenn Wilson	.06	.03	.01
☐ 63 Tom Browning	.06	.03	.01
☐ 64 Tony Gwynn	1.00	.45	.13
☐ 65 R.J. Reynolds	.06	.03	.01
☐ 66 Will Clark	5.00	2.30	.60
☐ 67 Ozzie Virgil	.06	.03	.01
☐ 68 Rick Sutcliffe	.10	.05	.01
☐ 69 Gary Carter	.15	.07	.02
☐ 70 Mike Moore	.06	.03	.01
☐ 71 Bert Blyleven	.15	.07	.02
☐ 72 Tony Fernandez	.10	.05	.01
☐ 73 Kent Hrbek	.10	.05	.01
☐ 74 Lloyd Moseby	.06	.03	.01
☐ 75 Alvin Davis	.06	.03	.01
☐ 76 Keith Hernandez	.10	.05	.01
☐ 77 Ryne Sandberg	1.25	.55	.16
☐ 78 Dale Murphy	.15	.07	.02
☐ 79 Sid Bream	.06	.03	.01
☐ 80 Chris Brown	.06	.03	.01
☐ 81 Steve Garvey	.15	.07	.02
☐ 82 Mario Soto	.06	.03	.01
☐ 83 Shane Rawley	.06	.03	.01
☐ 84 Willie McGee	.10	.05	.01
☐ 85 Jose Cruz	.06	.03	.01
☐ 86 Brian Downing	.06	.03	.01
☐ 87 Ozzie Guillen	.10	.05	.01
☐ 88 Hubie Brooks	.06	.03	.01
☐ 89 Cal Ripken	1.50	.65	.19
☐ 90 Juan Nieves	.06	.03	.01
☐ 91 Lance Parrish	.10	.05	.01
☐ 92 Jim Rice	.15	.07	.02
☐ 93 Ron Guidry	.10	.05	.01
☐ 94 Fernando Valenzuela	.06	.03	.01
☐ 95 Andy Allanson	.06	.03	.01
☐ 96 Willie Wilson	.06	.03	.01
☐ 97 Jose Canseco	2.50	1.15	.30
☐ 98 Jeff Reardon	.15	.07	.02
☐ 99 Bobby Witt	.25	.11	.03
☐ 100 Checklist 28-133	.10	.03	.01
☐ 101 Jose Guzman	.10	.05	.01
☐ 102 Steve Balboni	.06	.03	.01
☐ 103 Tony Phillips	.10	.05	.01
☐ 104 Brook Jacoby	.06	.03	.01
☐ 105 Dave Winfield	.40	.18	.05
☐ 106 Orel Hershiser	.10	.05	.01
☐ 107 Lou Whitaker	.15	.07	.02
☐ 108 Fred Lynn	.10	.05	.01
☐ 109 Bill Wegman	.06	.03	.01
☐ 110 Donnie Moore	.06	.03	.01
☐ 111 Jack Clark	.10	.05	.01
☐ 112 Bob Knepper	.06	.03	.01
☐ 113 Von Hayes	.06	.03	.01

☐ 114	Bip Roberts	.30	.14	.04
☐ 115	Tony Pena	.06	.03	.01
☐ 116	Scott Garrelts	.06	.03	.01
☐ 117	Paul Molitor	.50	.23	.06
☐ 118	Darryl Strawberry	.25	.11	.03
☐ 119	Shawon Dunston	.10	.05	.01
☐ 120	Jim Presley	.06	.03	.01
☐ 121	Jesse Barfield	.06	.03	.01
☐ 122	Gary Gaetti	.06	.03	.01
☐ 123	Kurt Stillwell	.06	.03	.01
☐ 124	Joel Davis	.06	.03	.01
☐ 125	Mike Boddicker	.06	.03	.01
☐ 126	Robin Yount	.50	.23	.06
☐ 127	Alan Trammell	.15	.07	.02
☐ 128	Dave Righetti	.10	.05	.01
☐ 129	Dwight Evans	.10	.05	.01
☐ 130	Mike Scioscia	.06	.03	.01
☐ 131	Julio Franco	.20	.09	.03
☐ 132	Bret Saberhagen	.20	.09	.03
☐ 133	Mike Davis	.06	.03	.01
☐ 134	Joe Hesketh	.06	.03	.01
☐ 135	Wally Joyner	1.00	.45	.13
☐ 136	Don Slaught	.06	.03	.01
☐ 137	Daryl Boston	.06	.03	.01
☐ 138	Nolan Ryan	2.00	.90	.25
☐ 139	Mike Schmidt	.50	.23	.06
☐ 140	Tommy Herr	.06	.03	.01
☐ 141	Garry Templeton	.06	.03	.01
☐ 142	Kal Daniels	.06	.03	.01
☐ 143	Billy Sample	.06	.03	.01
☐ 144	Johnny Ray	.06	.03	.01
☐ 145	Rob Thompson	.40	.18	.05
☐ 146	Bob Dernier	.06	.03	.01
☐ 147	Danny Tartabull	.30	.14	.04
☐ 148	Ernie Whitt	.06	.03	.01
☐ 149	Kirby Puckett	2.00	.90	.25
☐ 150	Mike Young	.06	.03	.01
☐ 151	Ernest Riles	.06	.03	.01
☐ 152	Frank Tanana	.06	.03	.01
☐ 153	Rich Gedman	.06	.03	.01
☐ 154	Willie Randolph	.10	.05	.01
☐ 155	Bill Madlock	.10	.05	.01
☐ 156	Joe Carter	1.25	.55	.16
☐ 157	Danny Jackson	.10	.05	.01
☐ 158	Carney Lansford	.10	.05	.01
☐ 159	Bryn Smith	.06	.03	.01
☐ 160	Gary Pettis	.06	.03	.01
☐ 161	Oddibe McDowell	.06	.03	.01
☐ 162	John Cangelosi	.06	.03	.01
☐ 163	Mike Scott	.06	.03	.01
☐ 164	Eric Show	.06	.03	.01
☐ 165	Juan Samuel	.06	.03	.01
☐ 166	Nick Esasky	.06	.03	.01
☐ 167	Zane Smith	.06	.03	.01
☐ 168	Mike C. Brown OF	.06	.03	.01
☐ 169	Keith Moreland	.06	.03	.01
☐ 170	John Tudor	.06	.03	.01
☐ 171	Ken Dixon	.06	.03	.01
☐ 172	Jim Gantner	.06	.03	.01
☐ 173	Jack Morris	.15	.07	.02
☐ 174	Bruce Hurst	.06	.03	.01
☐ 175	Dennis Rasmussen	.06	.03	.01
☐ 176	Mike Marshall	.06	.03	.01
☐ 177	Dan Quisenberry	.10	.05	.01
☐ 178	Eric Plunk	.06	.03	.01
☐ 179	Tim Wallach	.10	.05	.01
☐ 180	Steve Buechele	.10	.05	.01
☐ 181	Don Sutton	.15	.07	.02
☐ 182	Dave Schmidt	.06	.03	.01
☐ 183	Terry Pendleton	.35	.16	.04
☐ 184	Jim Deshaies	.15	.07	.02
☐ 185	Steve Bedrosian	.06	.03	.01
☐ 186	Pete Rose	.50	.23	.06
☐ 187	Dave Dravecky	.10	.05	.01
☐ 188	Rick Reuschel	.06	.03	.01
☐ 189	Dan Gladden	.06	.03	.01
☐ 190	Rick Mahler	.06	.03	.01
☐ 191	Thad Bosley	.06	.03	.01
☐ 192	Ron Darling	.10	.05	.01
☐ 193	Matt Young	.06	.03	.01
☐ 194	Tom Brunansky	.06	.03	.01
☐ 195	Dave Stieb	.10	.05	.01
☐ 196	Frank Viola	.10	.05	.01
☐ 197	Tom Henke	.10	.05	.01
☐ 198	Karl Best	.06	.03	.01
☐ 199	Dwight Gooden	.10	.05	.01
☐ 200	Checklist 134-239	.10	.03	.01
☐ 201	Steve Trout	.06	.03	.01
☐ 202	Rafael Ramirez	.06	.03	.01
☐ 203	Bob Walk	.06	.03	.01
☐ 204	Roger Mason	.06	.03	.01
☐ 205	Terry Kennedy	.06	.03	.01
☐ 206	Ron Oester	.06	.03	.01
☐ 207	John Russell	.06	.03	.01
☐ 208	Greg Mathews	.06	.03	.01
☐ 209	Charlie Kerfeld	.06	.03	.01
☐ 210	Reggie Jackson	.50	.23	.06
☐ 211	Floyd Bannister	.06	.03	.01
☐ 212	Vance Law	.06	.03	.01
☐ 213	Rich Bordi	.06	.03	.01
☐ 214	Dan Plesac	.06	.03	.01
☐ 215	Dave Collins	.06	.03	.01
☐ 216	Bob Stanley	.06	.03	.01
☐ 217	Joe Niekro	.10	.05	.01
☐ 218	Tom Niedenfuer	.06	.03	.01
☐ 219	Brett Butler	.10	.05	.01
☐ 220	Charlie Leibrandt	.06	.03	.01
☐ 221	Steve Ontiveros	.06	.03	.01
☐ 222	Tim Burke	.06	.03	.01
☐ 223	Curtis Wilkerson	.06	.03	.01
☐ 224	Pete Incaviglia	.50	.23	.06
☐ 225	Lonnie Smith	.06	.03	.01
☐ 226	Chris Codiroli	.06	.03	.01
☐ 227	Scott Bailes	.06	.03	.01
☐ 228	Rickey Henderson	.50	.23	.06
☐ 229	Ken Howell	.06	.03	.01
☐ 230	Darnell Coles	.06	.03	.01
☐ 231	Don Aase	.06	.03	.01
☐ 232	Tim Leary	.06	.03	.01
☐ 233	Bob Boone	.10	.05	.01
☐ 234	Ricky Horton	.06	.03	.01
☐ 235	Mark Bailey	.06	.03	.01
☐ 236	Kevin Gross	.06	.03	.01
☐ 237	Lance McCullers	.06	.03	.01
☐ 238	Cecilio Guante	.06	.03	.01
☐ 239	Bob Melvin	.06	.03	.01
☐ 240	Billy Joe Robidoux	.06	.03	.01
☐ 241	Roger McDowell	.06	.03	.01
☐ 242	Leon Durham	.06	.03	.01
☐ 243	Ed Nunez	.06	.03	.01
☐ 244	Jimmy Key	.25	.11	.03
☐ 245	Mike Smithson	.06	.03	.01
☐ 246	Bo Diaz	.06	.03	.01
☐ 247	Carlton Fisk	.40	.18	.05
☐ 248	Larry Sheets	.06	.03	.01
☐ 249	Juan Castillo	.06	.03	.01
☐ 250	Eric King	.06	.03	.01
☐ 251	Doug Drabek	1.00	.45	.13
☐ 252	Wade Boggs	1.00	.45	.13
☐ 253	Mariano Duncan	.06	.03	.01
☐ 254	Pat Tabler	.06	.03	.01
☐ 255	Frank White	.10	.05	.01
☐ 256	Alfredo Griffin	.06	.03	.01
☐ 257	Floyd Youmans	.06	.03	.01
☐ 258	Rob Wilfong	.06	.03	.01
☐ 259	Pete O'Brien	.06	.03	.01

	No.	Player			
☐	260	Tim Hulett	.06	.03	.01
☐	261	Dickie Thon	.06	.03	.01
☐	262	Darren Daulton	.50	.23	.06
☐	263	Vince Coleman	.10	.05	.01
☐	264	Andy Hawkins	.06	.03	.01
☐	265	Eric Davis	.20	.09	.03
☐	266	Andres Thomas	.06	.03	.01
☐	267	Mike Diaz	.06	.03	.01
☐	268	Chili Davis	.10	.05	.01
☐	269	Jody Davis	.06	.03	.01
☐	270	Phil Bradley	.06	.03	.01
☐	271	George Bell	.10	.05	.01
☐	272	Keith Atherton	.06	.03	.01
☐	273	Storm Davis	.06	.03	.01
☐	274	Rob Deer	.06	.03	.01
☐	275	Walt Terrell	.06	.03	.01
☐	276	Roger Clemens	1.50	.65	.19
☐	277	Mike Easler	.06	.03	.01
☐	278	Steve Sax	.06	.03	.01
☐	279	Andre Thornton	.06	.03	.01
☐	280	Jim Sundberg	.06	.03	.01
☐	281	Bill Bathe	.06	.03	.01
☐	282	Jay Tibbs	.06	.03	.01
☐	283	Dick Schofield	.06	.03	.01
☐	284	Mike Mason	.06	.03	.01
☐	285	Jerry Hairston	.06	.03	.01
☐	286	Bill Doran	.06	.03	.01
☐	287	Tim Flannery	.06	.03	.01
☐	288	Gary Redus	.06	.03	.01
☐	289	John Franco	.10	.05	.01
☐	290	Paul Assenmacher	.06	.03	.01
☐	291	Joe Orsulak	.06	.03	.01
☐	292	Lee Smith	.20	.09	.03
☐	293	Mike Laga	.06	.03	.01
☐	294	Rick Dempsey	.06	.03	.01
☐	295	Mike Felder	.06	.03	.01
☐	296	Tom Brookens	.06	.03	.01
☐	297	Al Nipper	.06	.03	.01
☐	298	Mike Pagliarulo	.06	.03	.01
☐	299	Franklin Stubbs	.06	.03	.01
☐	300	Checklist 240-345	.10	.03	.01
☐	301	Steve Farr	.06	.03	.01
☐	302	Bill Mooneyham	.06	.03	.01
☐	303	Andres Galarraga	.60	.25	.08
☐	304	Scott Fletcher	.06	.03	.01
☐	305	Jack Howell	.06	.03	.01
☐	306	Russ Morman	.06	.03	.01
☐	307	Todd Worrell	.10	.05	.01
☐	308	Dave Smith	.06	.03	.01
☐	309	Jeff Stone	.06	.03	.01
☐	310	Ron Robinson	.06	.03	.01
☐	311	Bruce Bochy	.06	.03	.01
☐	312	Jim Winn	.06	.03	.01
☐	313	Mark Davis	.06	.03	.01
☐	314	Jeff Dedmon	.06	.03	.01
☐	315	Jamie Moyer	.20	.09	.03
☐	316	Wally Backman	.06	.03	.01
☐	317	Ken Phelps	.06	.03	.01
☐	318	Steve Lombardozzi	.06	.03	.01
☐	319	Rance Mulliniks	.06	.03	.01
☐	320	Tim Laudner	.06	.03	.01
☐	321	Mark Eichhorn	.06	.03	.01
☐	322	Lee Guetterman	.06	.03	.01
☐	323	Sid Fernandez	.10	.05	.01
☐	324	Jerry Mumphrey	.06	.03	.01
☐	325	David Palmer	.06	.03	.01
☐	326	Bill Almon	.06	.03	.01
☐	327	Candy Maldonado	.06	.03	.01
☐	328	John Kruk	1.50	.65	.19
☐	329	John Denny	.06	.03	.01
☐	330	Milt Thompson	.10	.05	.01
☐	331	Mike LaValliere	.06	.03	.01
☐	332	Alan Ashby	.06	.03	.01
☐	333	Doug Corbett	.06	.03	.01
☐	334	Ron Karkovice	.20	.09	.03
☐	335	Mitch Webster	.06	.03	.01
☐	336	Lee Lacy	.06	.03	.01
☐	337	Glenn Braggs	.06	.03	.01
☐	338	Dwight Lowry	.06	.03	.01
☐	339	Don Baylor	.15	.07	.02
☐	340	Brian Fisher	.06	.03	.01
☐	341	Reggie Williams	.06	.03	.01
☐	342	Tom Candiotti	.10	.05	.01
☐	343	Rudy Law	.06	.03	.01
☐	344	Curt Young	.06	.03	.01
☐	345	Mike Fitzgerald	.06	.03	.01
☐	346	Ruben Sierra	3.50	1.55	.45
☐	347	Mitch Williams	.30	.14	.04
☐	348	Jorge Orta	.06	.03	.01
☐	349	Mickey Tettleton	.10	.05	.01
☐	350	Ernie Camacho	.06	.03	.01
☐	351	Ron Kittle	.06	.03	.01
☐	352	Ken Landreaux	.06	.03	.01
☐	353	Chet Lemon	.06	.03	.01
☐	354	John Shelby	.06	.03	.01
☐	355	Mark Clear	.06	.03	.01
☐	356	Doug DeCinces	.06	.03	.01
☐	357	Ken Dayley	.06	.03	.01
☐	358	Phil Garner	.10	.05	.01
☐	359	Steve Jeltz	.06	.03	.01
☐	360	Ed Whitson	.06	.03	.01
☐	361	Barry Bonds	10.00	4.50	1.25
☐	362	Vida Blue	.10	.05	.01
☐	363	Cecil Cooper	.10	.05	.01
☐	364	Bob Ojeda	.06	.03	.01
☐	365	Dennis Eckersley	.15	.07	.02
☐	366	Mike Morgan	.06	.03	.01
☐	367	Willie Upshaw	.06	.03	.01
☐	368	Allan Anderson	.06	.03	.01
☐	369	Bill Gullickson	.06	.03	.01
☐	370	Bobby Thigpen	.20	.09	.03
☐	371	Juan Beniquez	.06	.03	.01
☐	372	Charlie Moore	.06	.03	.01
☐	373	Dan Petry	.06	.03	.01
☐	374	Rod Scurry	.06	.03	.01
☐	375	Tom Seaver	.40	.18	.05
☐	376	Ed VandeBerg	.06	.03	.01
☐	377	Tony Bernazard	.06	.03	.01
☐	378	Greg Pryor	.06	.03	.01
☐	379	Dwayne Murphy	.06	.03	.01
☐	380	Andy McGaffigan	.06	.03	.01
☐	381	Kirk McCaskill	.06	.03	.01
☐	382	Greg Harris	.06	.03	.01
☐	383	Rich Dotson	.06	.03	.01
☐	384	Craig Reynolds	.06	.03	.01
☐	385	Greg Gross	.06	.03	.01
☐	386	Tito Landrum	.06	.03	.01
☐	387	Craig Lefferts	.06	.03	.01
☐	388	Dave Parker	.15	.07	.02
☐	389	Bob Horner	.06	.03	.01
☐	390	Pat Clements	.06	.03	.01
☐	391	Jeff Leonard	.06	.03	.01
☐	392	Chris Speier	.06	.03	.01
☐	393	John Moses	.06	.03	.01
☐	394	Garth Iorg	.06	.03	.01
☐	395	Greg Gagne	.10	.05	.01
☐	396	Nate Snell	.06	.03	.01
☐	397	Bryan Clutterbuck	.06	.03	.01
☐	398	Darrell Evans	.10	.05	.01
☐	399	Steve Crawford	.06	.03	.01
☐	400	Checklist 346-451	.10	.03	.01
☐	401	Phil Lombardi	.06	.03	.01
☐	402	Rick Honeycutt	.06	.03	.01
☐	403	Ken Schrom	.06	.03	.01
☐	404	Bud Black	.06	.03	.01
☐	405	Donnie Hill	.06	.03	.01

	No.	Player			
☐	406	Wayne Krenchicki	.06	.03	.01
☐	407	Chuck Finley	.60	.25	.08
☐	408	Toby Harrah	.06	.03	.01
☐	409	Steve Lyons	.06	.03	.01
☐	410	Kevin Bass	.06	.03	.01
☐	411	Marvell Wynne	.06	.03	.01
☐	412	Ron Roenicke	.06	.03	.01
☐	413	Tracy Jones	.06	.03	.01
☐	414	Gene Garber	.06	.03	.01
☐	415	Mike Bielecki	.06	.03	.01
☐	416	Frank DiPino	.06	.03	.01
☐	417	Andy Van Slyke	.15	.07	.02
☐	418	Jim Dwyer	.06	.03	.01
☐	419	Ben Oglivie	.06	.03	.01
☐	420	Dave Bergman	.06	.03	.01
☐	421	Joe Sambito	.06	.03	.01
☐	422	Bob Tewksbury	.40	.18	.05
☐	423	Len Matuszek	.06	.03	.01
☐	424	Mike Kingery	.15	.07	.02
☐	425	Dave Kingman	.10	.05	.01
☐	426	Al Newman	.06	.03	.01
☐	427	Gary Ward	.06	.03	.01
☐	428	Ruppert Jones	.06	.03	.01
☐	429	Harold Baines	.10	.05	.01
☐	430	Pat Perry	.06	.03	.01
☐	431	Terry Puhl	.06	.03	.01
☐	432	Don Carman	.06	.03	.01
☐	433	Eddie Milner	.06	.03	.01
☐	434	LaMarr Hoyt	.06	.03	.01
☐	435	Rick Rhoden	.06	.03	.01
☐	436	Jose Uribe	.06	.03	.01
☐	437	Ken Oberkfell	.06	.03	.01
☐	438	Ron Davis	.06	.03	.01
☐	439	Jesse Orosco	.06	.03	.01
☐	440	Scott Bradley	.06	.03	.01
☐	441	Randy Bush	.06	.03	.01
☐	442	John Cerutti	.06	.03	.01
☐	443	Roy Smalley	.06	.03	.01
☐	444	Kelly Gruber	.10	.05	.01
☐	445	Bob Kearney	.06	.03	.01
☐	446	Ed Hearn	.06	.03	.01
☐	447	Scott Sanderson	.06	.03	.01
☐	448	Bruce Benedict	.06	.03	.01
☐	449	Junior Ortiz	.06	.03	.01
☐	450	Mike Aldrete	.06	.03	.01
☐	451	Kevin McReynolds	.10	.05	.01
☐	452	Rob Murphy	.06	.03	.01
☐	453	Kent Tekulve	.06	.03	.01
☐	454	Curt Ford	.06	.03	.01
☐	455	Dave Lopes	.10	.05	.01
☐	456	Bob Grich	.10	.05	.01
☐	457	Jose DeLeon	.06	.03	.01
☐	458	Andre Dawson	.35	.16	.04
☐	459	Mike Flanagan	.06	.03	.01
☐	460	Joey Meyer	.06	.03	.01
☐	461	Chuck Cary	.06	.03	.01
☐	462	Bill Buckner	.10	.05	.01
☐	463	Bob Shirley	.06	.03	.01
☐	464	Jeff Hamilton	.06	.03	.01
☐	465	Phil Niekro	.15	.07	.02
☐	466	Mark Gubicza	.06	.03	.01
☐	467	Jerry Willard	.06	.03	.01
☐	468	Bob Sebra	.06	.03	.01
☐	469	Larry Parrish	.06	.03	.01
☐	470	Charlie Hough	.10	.05	.01
☐	471	Hal McRae	.15	.07	.02
☐	472	Dave Leiper	.06	.03	.01
☐	473	Mel Hall	.06	.03	.01
☐	474	Dan Pasqua	.06	.03	.01
☐	475	Bob Welch	.10	.05	.01
☐	476	Johnny Grubb	.06	.03	.01
☐	477	Jim Traber	.06	.03	.01
☐	478	Chris Bosio	.25	.11	.03

	No.	Player			
☐	479	Mark McLemore	.06	.03	.01
☐	480	John Morris	.06	.03	.01
☐	481	Billy Hatcher	.10	.05	.01
☐	482	Dan Schatzeder	.06	.03	.01
☐	483	Rich Gossage	.15	.07	.02
☐	484	Jim Morrison	.06	.03	.01
☐	485	Bob Brenly	.06	.03	.01
☐	486	Bill Schroeder	.06	.03	.01
☐	487	Mookie Wilson	.10	.05	.01
☐	488	Dave Martinez	.20	.09	.03
☐	489	Harold Reynolds	.06	.03	.01
☐	490	Jeff Hearron	.06	.03	.01
☐	491	Mickey Hatcher	.06	.03	.01
☐	492	Barry Larkin	2.00	.90	.25
☐	493	Bob James	.06	.03	.01
☐	494	John Habyan	.06	.03	.01
☐	495	Jim Adduci	.06	.03	.01
☐	496	Mike Heath	.06	.03	.01
☐	497	Tim Stoddard	.06	.03	.01
☐	498	Tony Armas	.06	.03	.01
☐	499	Dennis Powell	.06	.03	.01
☐	500	Checklist 452-557	.10	.03	.01
☐	501	Chris Bando	.06	.03	.01
☐	502	David Cone	3.50	1.55	.45
☐	503	Jay Howell	.06	.03	.01
☐	504	Tom Foley	.06	.03	.01
☐	505	Ray Chadwick	.06	.03	.01
☐	506	Mike Loynd	.06	.03	.01
☐	507	Neil Allen	.06	.03	.01
☐	508	Danny Darwin	.06	.03	.01
☐	509	Rick Schu	.06	.03	.01
☐	510	Jose Oquendo	.06	.03	.01
☐	511	Gene Walter	.06	.03	.01
☐	512	Terry McGriff	.06	.03	.01
☐	513	Ken Griffey	.10	.05	.01
☐	514	Benny Distefano	.06	.03	.01
☐	515	Terry Mulholland	.60	.25	.08
☐	516	Ed Lynch	.06	.03	.01
☐	517	Bill Swift	.10	.05	.01
☐	518	Manny Lee	.06	.03	.01
☐	519	Andre David	.06	.03	.01
☐	520	Scott McGregor	.06	.03	.01
☐	521	Rick Manning	.06	.03	.01
☐	522	Willie Hernandez	.06	.03	.01
☐	523	Marty Barrett	.06	.03	.01
☐	524	Wayne Tolleson	.06	.03	.01
☐	525	Jose Gonzalez	.06	.03	.01
☐	526	Cory Snyder	.10	.05	.01
☐	527	Buddy Biancalana	.06	.03	.01
☐	528	Moose Haas	.06	.03	.01
☐	529	Wilfredo Tejada	.06	.03	.01
☐	530	Stu Cliburn	.06	.03	.01
☐	531	Dale Mohorcic	.06	.03	.01
☐	532	Ron Hassey	.06	.03	.01
☐	533	Ty Gainey	.06	.03	.01
☐	534	Jerry Royster	.06	.03	.01
☐	535	Mike Maddux	.06	.03	.01
☐	536	Ted Power	.06	.03	.01
☐	537	Ted Simmons	.10	.05	.01
☐	538	Rafael Belliard	.15	.07	.02
☐	539	Chico Walker	.06	.03	.01
☐	540	Bob Forsch	.06	.03	.01
☐	541	John Stefero	.06	.03	.01
☐	542	Dale Sveum	.06	.03	.01
☐	543	Mark Thurmond	.06	.03	.01
☐	544	Jeff Sellers	.06	.03	.01
☐	545	Joel Skinner	.06	.03	.01
☐	546	Alex Trevino	.06	.03	.01
☐	547	Randy Kutcher	.06	.03	.01
☐	548	Joaquin Andujar	.06	.03	.01
☐	549	Casey Candaele	.06	.03	.01
☐	550	Jeff Russell	.06	.03	.01
☐	551	John Candelaria	.06	.03	.01

☐ 552 Joe Cowley	.06	.03	.01
☐ 553 Danny Cox	.06	.03	.01
☐ 554 Denny Walling	.06	.03	.01
☐ 555 Bruce Ruffin	.15	.07	.02
☐ 556 Buddy Bell	.10	.05	.01
☐ 557 Jimmy Jones	.06	.03	.01
☐ 558 Bobby Bonilla	1.50	.65	.19
☐ 559 Jeff D. Robinson	.06	.03	.01
☐ 560 Ed Olwine	.06	.03	.01
☐ 561 Glenallen Hill	.35	.16	.04
☐ 562 Lee Mazzilli	.06	.03	.01
☐ 563 Mike G. Brown P	.06	.03	.01
☐ 564 George Frazier	.06	.03	.01
☐ 565 Mike Sharperson	.10	.05	.01
☐ 566 Mark Portugal	.50	.23	.06
☐ 567 Rick Leach	.06	.03	.01
☐ 568 Mark Langston	.15	.07	.02
☐ 569 Rafael Santana	.06	.03	.01
☐ 570 Manny Trillo	.06	.03	.01
☐ 571 Cliff Speck	.06	.03	.01
☐ 572 Bob Kipper	.06	.03	.01
☐ 573 Kelly Downs	.06	.03	.01
☐ 574 Randy Asadoor	.06	.03	.01
☐ 575 Dave Magadan	.25	.11	.03
☐ 576 Marvin Freeman	.20	.09	.03
☐ 577 Jeff Lahti	.06	.03	.01
☐ 578 Jeff Calhoun	.06	.03	.01
☐ 579 Gus Polidor	.06	.03	.01
☐ 580 Gene Nelson	.06	.03	.01
☐ 581 Tim Teufel	.06	.03	.01
☐ 582 Odell Jones	.06	.03	.01
☐ 583 Mark Ryal	.06	.03	.01
☐ 584 Randy O'Neal	.06	.03	.01
☐ 585 Mike Greenwell	1.00	.45	.13
☐ 586 Ray Knight	.10	.05	.01
☐ 587 Ralph Bryant	.10	.05	.01
☐ 588 Carmen Castillo	.06	.03	.01
☐ 589 Ed Wojna	.06	.03	.01
☐ 590 Stan Javier	.10	.05	.01
☐ 591 Jeff Musselman	.06	.03	.01
☐ 592 Mike Stanley	.75	.35	.09
☐ 593 Darrell Porter	.06	.03	.01
☐ 594 Drew Hall	.06	.03	.01
☐ 595 Rob Nelson	.06	.03	.01
☐ 596 Bryan Oelkers	.06	.03	.01
☐ 597 Scott Nielsen	.06	.03	.01
☐ 598 Brian Holton	.06	.03	.01
☐ 599 Kevin Mitchell	1.00	.45	.13
☐ 600 Checklist 558-660	.10	.03	.01
☐ 601 Jackie Gutierrez	.06	.03	.01
☐ 602 Barry Jones	.06	.03	.01
☐ 603 Jerry Narron	.06	.03	.01
☐ 604 Steve Lake	.06	.03	.01
☐ 605 Jim Pankovits	.06	.03	.01
☐ 606 Ed Romero	.06	.03	.01
☐ 607 Dave LaPoint	.06	.03	.01
☐ 608 Don Robinson	.06	.03	.01
☐ 609 Mike Krukow	.06	.03	.01
☐ 610 Dave Valle	.06	.03	.01
☐ 611 Len Dykstra	.60	.25	.08
☐ 612 Roberto Clemente PUZ	.35	.16	.04
☐ 613 Mike Trujillo	.06	.03	.01
☐ 614 Damaso Garcia	.06	.03	.01
☐ 615 Neal Heaton	.06	.03	.01
☐ 616 Juan Berenguer	.06	.03	.01
☐ 617 Steve Carlton	.35	.16	.04
☐ 618 Gary Lucas	.06	.03	.01
☐ 619 Geno Petralli	.06	.03	.01
☐ 620 Rick Aguilera	.25	.11	.03
☐ 621 Fred McGriff	3.00	1.35	.40
☐ 622 Dave Henderson	.10	.05	.01
☐ 623 Dave Clark	.15	.07	.02
☐ 624 Angel Salazar	.06	.03	.01
☐ 625 Randy Hunt	.06	.03	.01
☐ 626 John Gibbons	.06	.03	.01
☐ 627 Kevin Brown	1.00	.45	.13
☐ 628 Bill Dawley	.06	.03	.01
☐ 629 Aurelio Lopez	.06	.03	.01
☐ 630 Charles Hudson	.06	.03	.01
☐ 631 Ray Soff	.06	.03	.01
☐ 632 Ray Hayward	.06	.03	.01
☐ 633 Spike Owen	.06	.03	.01
☐ 634 Glenn Hubbard	.06	.03	.01
☐ 635 Kevin Elster	.06	.03	.01
☐ 636 Mike LaCoss	.06	.03	.01
☐ 637 Dwayne Henry	.06	.03	.01
☐ 638 Rey Quinones	.06	.03	.01
☐ 639 Jim Clancy	.06	.03	.01
☐ 640 Larry Andersen	.06	.03	.01
☐ 641 Calvin Schiraldi	.06	.03	.01
☐ 642 Stan Jefferson	.06	.03	.01
☐ 643 Marc Sullivan	.06	.03	.01
☐ 644 Mark Grant	.06	.03	.01
☐ 645 Cliff Johnson	.06	.03	.01
☐ 646 Howard Johnson	.10	.05	.01
☐ 647 Dave Sax	.06	.03	.01
☐ 648 Dave Stewart	.15	.07	.02
☐ 649 Danny Heep	.06	.03	.01
☐ 650 Joe Johnson	.06	.03	.01
☐ 651 Bob Brower	.06	.03	.01
☐ 652 Rob Woodward	.06	.03	.01
☐ 653 John Mizerock	.06	.03	.01
☐ 654 Tim Pyznarski	.06	.03	.01
☐ 655 Luis Aquino	.06	.03	.01
☐ 656 Mickey Brantley	.06	.03	.01
☐ 657 Doyle Alexander	.06	.03	.01
☐ 658 Sammy Stewart	.06	.03	.01
☐ 659 Jim Acker	.06	.03	.01
☐ 660 Pete Ladd	.10	.04	.01

1987 Donruss Rookies

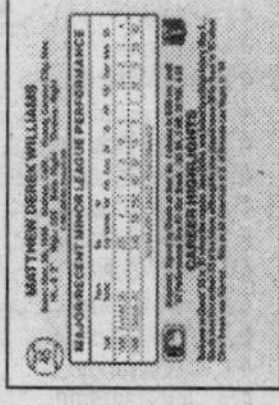

The 1987 Donruss "The Rookies" set features 56 cards plus a 15-piece puzzle of Roberto Clemente. Cards are in full color and are standard size, 2 1/2" by 3 1/2". The set was distributed in a small green and black box with gold lettering. Card fronts are similar in design to the 1987 Donruss regular issue except for the presence of "The Rookies" logo in the lower left corner and a green border instead of a black border. The key (extended) Rookie Cards in this set are Ellis Burks, Shane Mack, Luis Polonia, John Smiley, and Matt Williams.

	MINT	EXC	G-VG
COMPLETE FACT.SET (56)	18.00	8.00	2.30
COMMON CARD (1-56)	.07	.03	.01
☐ 1 Mark McGwire	1.50	.65	.19
☐ 2 Eric Bell	.07	.03	.01
☐ 3 Mark Williamson	.07	.03	.01
☐ 4 Mike Greenwell	.75	.35	.09
☐ 5 Ellis Burks	1.00	.45	.13
☐ 6 DeWayne Buice	.07	.03	.01
☐ 7 Mark McLemore	.07	.03	.01
☐ 8 Devon White	.75	.35	.09
☐ 9 Willie Fraser	.07	.03	.01
☐ 10 Les Lancaster	.07	.03	.01
☐ 11 Ken Williams	.07	.03	.01
☐ 12 Matt Nokes	.30	.14	.04
☐ 13 Jeff M. Robinson	.07	.03	.01
☐ 14 Bo Jackson	1.50	.65	.19
☐ 15 Kevin Seitzer	.25	.11	.03
☐ 16 Billy Ripken	.07	.03	.01
☐ 17 B.J. Surhoff	.10	.05	.01
☐ 18 Chuck Crim	.07	.03	.01
☐ 19 Mike Birkbeck	.07	.03	.01
☐ 20 Chris Bosio	.15	.07	.02
☐ 21 Les Straker	.07	.03	.01
☐ 22 Mark Davidson	.07	.03	.01
☐ 23 Gene Larkin	.07	.03	.01
☐ 24 Ken Gerhart	.07	.03	.01
☐ 25 Luis Polonia	.60	.25	.08
☐ 26 Terry Steinbach	.30	.14	.04
☐ 27 Mickey Brantley	.07	.03	.01
☐ 28 Mike Stanley	.50	.23	.06
☐ 29 Jerry Browne	.10	.05	.01
☐ 30 Todd Benzinger	.15	.07	.02
☐ 31 Fred McGriff	3.00	1.35	.40
☐ 32 Mike Henneman	.30	.14	.04
☐ 33 Casey Candaele	.07	.03	.01
☐ 34 Dave Magadan	.15	.07	.02
☐ 35 David Cone	2.50	1.15	.30
☐ 36 Mike Jackson	.20	.09	.03
☐ 37 John Mitchell	.07	.03	.01
☐ 38 Mike Dunne	.07	.03	.01
☐ 39 John Smiley	.35	.16	.04
☐ 40 Joe Magrane	.20	.09	.03
☐ 41 Jim Lindeman	.07	.03	.01
☐ 42 Shane Mack	.75	.35	.09
☐ 43 Stan Jefferson	.07	.03	.01
☐ 44 Benito Santiago	.25	.11	.03
☐ 45 Matt Williams	6.00	2.70	.75
☐ 46 Dave Meads	.07	.03	.01
☐ 47 Rafael Palmeiro	3.00	1.35	.40
☐ 48 Bill Long	.07	.03	.01
☐ 49 Bob Brower	.07	.03	.01
☐ 50 James Steels	.07	.03	.01
☐ 51 Paul Noce	.07	.03	.01
☐ 52 Greg Maddux	7.00	3.10	.85
☐ 53 Jeff Musselman	.07	.03	.01
☐ 54 Brian Holton	.07	.03	.01
☐ 55 Chuck Jackson	.07	.03	.01
☐ 56 Checklist 1-56	.07	.03	.01

1988 Donruss

This 660-card set was distributed along with a puzzle of Stan Musial. The six regular checklist cards are numbered throughout the set as multiples of 100. Cards measure 2 1/2" by 3 1/2" and feature a distinctive black and blue border on the front. The popular Diamond King subset returns for the seventh consecutive year. Rated Rookies are featured again as cards 28-47. Cards marked as SP (short printed) from 648-660 are more difficult to find than the other 13 SP's in the lower 600s. These 26 cards listed as SP were apparently pulled from the printing sheet to make room for the 26 Bonus MVP cards. Numbered with the prefix "BC" for bonus card, this 26-card set featuring the most valuable player from each of the 26 teams was randomly inserted in the wax and rack packs. The cards are distinguished by the MVP logo in the upper left corner of the obverse, and cards BC14-BC26 are considered to be more difficult to find than cards BC1-BC13. Six of the checklist cards were done two different ways to reflect the inclusion or exclusion of the Bonus MVP cards in the wax packs. In the checklist below, the A variations (for the checklist cards) are from the wax packs and the B variations are from the factory-collated sets. The key Rookie Cards in this set are Roberto Alomar, Jay Bell, Jeff Blauser, Jay Buhner, Ellis Burks, Mike Devereaux, Ron Gant, Tom Glavine, Mark Grace, Gregg Jefferies, Roberto Kelly, Jack McDowell, and Matt Williams. There was also a Kirby Puckett card issued as the package back of Donruss blister packs; it uses a different photo from both of Kirby's regular and Bonus MVP cards and is unnumbered on the back. The design pattern of the factory set card fronts is oriented differently from that of the regular wax pack cards.

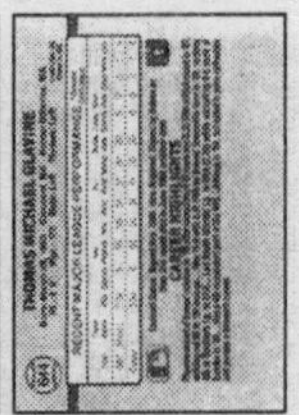

	MINT	EXC	G-VG
COMPLETE SET (660)	12.00	5.50	1.50
COMPLETE FACT.SET (660)	12.00	5.50	1.50
COMMON CARD (1-647)	.04	.02	.01
COMMON CARD SP (648-660)	.07	.03	.01
☐ 1 Mark McGwire DK	.25	.11	.03
☐ 2 Tim Raines DK	.10	.05	.01
☐ 3 Benito Santiago DK	.08	.04	.01
☐ 4 Alan Trammell DK	.10	.05	.01
☐ 5 Danny Tartabull DK	.10	.05	.01
☐ 6 Ron Darling DK	.08	.04	.01
☐ 7 Paul Molitor DK	.15	.07	.02
☐ 8 Devon White DK	.10	.05	.01
☐ 9 Andre Dawson DK	.10	.05	.01
☐ 10 Julio Franco DK	.10	.05	.01
☐ 11 Scott Fletcher DK	.08	.04	.01
☐ 12 Tony Fernandez DK	.08	.04	.01
☐ 13 Shane Rawley DK	.08	.04	.01
☐ 14 Kal Daniels DK	.08	.04	.01
☐ 15 Jack Clark DK	.08	.04	.01

☐ 16 Dwight Evans DK	.10	.05	.01
☐ 17 Tommy John DK	.10	.05	.01
☐ 18 Andy Van Slyke DK	.10	.05	.01
☐ 19 Gary Gaetti DK	.08	.04	.01
☐ 20 Mark Langston DK	.10	.05	.01
☐ 21 Will Clark DK	.25	.11	.03
☐ 22 Glenn Hubbard DK	.08	.04	.01
☐ 23 Billy Hatcher DK	.08	.04	.01
☐ 24 Bob Welch DK	.08	.04	.01
☐ 25 Ivan Calderon DK	.08	.04	.01
☐ 26 Cal Ripken DK	.35	.16	.04
☐ 27 DK Checklist 1-26	.06	.02	.01
☐ 28 Mackey Sasser RR	.04	.02	.01
☐ 29 Jeff Treadway RR	.04	.02	.01
☐ 30 Mike Campbell RR	.04	.02	.01
☐ 31 Lance Johnson RR	.40	.18	.05
☐ 32 Nelson Liriano RR	.04	.02	.01
☐ 33 Shawn Abner RR	.04	.02	.01
☐ 34 Roberto Alomar RR	3.00	1.35	.40
☐ 35 Shawn Hillegas RR	.04	.02	.01
☐ 36 Joey Meyer RR	.04	.02	.01
☐ 37 Kevin Elster RR	.04	.02	.01
☐ 38 Jose Lind RR	.15	.07	.02
☐ 39 Kirt Manwaring RR	.04	.02	.01
☐ 40 Mark Grace RR	1.25	.55	.16
☐ 41 Jody Reed RR	.20	.09	.03
☐ 42 John Farrell RR	.04	.02	.01
☐ 43 Al Leiter RR	.10	.05	.01
☐ 44 Gary Thurman RR	.04	.02	.01
☐ 45 Vicente Palacios RR	.04	.02	.01
☐ 46 Eddie Williams RR	.15	.07	.02
☐ 47 Jack McDowell RR	1.00	.45	.13
☐ 48 Ken Dixon	.04	.02	.01
☐ 49 Mike Birkbeck	.04	.02	.01
☐ 50 Eric King	.04	.02	.01
☐ 51 Roger Clemens	.40	.18	.05
☐ 52 Pat Clements	.04	.02	.01
☐ 53 Fernando Valenzuela	.04	.02	.01
☐ 54 Mark Gubicza	.04	.02	.01
☐ 55 Jay Howell	.04	.02	.01
☐ 56 Floyd Youmans	.04	.02	.01
☐ 57 Ed Correa	.04	.02	.01
☐ 58 DeWayne Buice	.04	.02	.01
☐ 59 Jose DeLeon	.04	.02	.01
☐ 60 Danny Cox	.04	.02	.01
☐ 61 Nolan Ryan	.75	.35	.09
☐ 62 Steve Bedrosian	.04	.02	.01
☐ 63 Tom Browning	.04	.02	.01
☐ 64 Mark Davis	.04	.02	.01
☐ 65 R.J. Reynolds	.04	.02	.01
☐ 66 Kevin Mitchell	.15	.07	.02
☐ 67 Ken Oberkfell	.04	.02	.01
☐ 68 Rick Sutcliffe	.10	.05	.01
☐ 69 Dwight Gooden	.10	.05	.01
☐ 70 Scott Bankhead	.04	.02	.01
☐ 71 Bert Blyleven	.15	.07	.02
☐ 72 Jimmy Key	.15	.07	.02
☐ 73 Les Straker	.04	.02	.01
☐ 74 Jim Clancy	.04	.02	.01
☐ 75 Mike Moore	.04	.02	.01
☐ 76 Ron Darling	.10	.05	.01
☐ 77 Ed Lynch	.04	.02	.01
☐ 78 Dale Murphy	.15	.07	.02
☐ 79 Doug Drabek	.15	.07	.02
☐ 80 Scott Garrelts	.04	.02	.01
☐ 81 Ed Whitson	.04	.02	.01
☐ 82 Rob Murphy	.04	.02	.01
☐ 83 Shane Rawley	.04	.02	.01
☐ 84 Greg Mathews	.04	.02	.01
☐ 85 Jim Deshaies	.04	.02	.01
☐ 86 Mike Witt	.04	.02	.01
☐ 87 Donnie Hill	.04	.02	.01
☐ 88 Jeff Reed	.04	.02	.01
☐ 89 Mike Boddicker	.04	.02	.01
☐ 90 Ted Higuera	.04	.02	.01
☐ 91 Walt Terrell	.04	.02	.01
☐ 92 Bob Stanley	.04	.02	.01
☐ 93 Dave Righetti	.04	.02	.01
☐ 94 Orel Hershiser	.10	.05	.01
☐ 95 Chris Bando	.04	.02	.01
☐ 96 Bret Saberhagen	.15	.07	.02
☐ 97 Curt Young	.04	.02	.01
☐ 98 Tim Burke	.04	.02	.01
☐ 99 Charlie Hough	.10	.05	.01
☐ 100A Checklist 28-137	.06	.02	.01
☐ 100B Checklist 28-133	.06	.02	.01
☐ 101 Bobby Witt	.10	.05	.01
☐ 102 George Brett	.40	.18	.05
☐ 103 Mickey Tettleton	.10	.05	.01
☐ 104 Scott Bailes	.04	.02	.01
☐ 105 Mike Pagliarulo	.04	.02	.01
☐ 106 Mike Scioscia	.04	.02	.01
☐ 107 Tom Brookens	.04	.02	.01
☐ 108 Ray Knight	.10	.05	.01
☐ 109 Dan Plesac	.04	.02	.01
☐ 110 Wally Joyner	.10	.05	.01
☐ 111 Bob Forsch	.04	.02	.01
☐ 112 Mike Scott	.04	.02	.01
☐ 113 Kevin Gross	.04	.02	.01
☐ 114 Benito Santiago	.10	.05	.01
☐ 115 Bob Kipper	.04	.02	.01
☐ 116 Mike Krukow	.04	.02	.01
☐ 117 Chris Bosio	.10	.05	.01
☐ 118 Sid Fernandez	.10	.05	.01
☐ 119 Jody Davis	.04	.02	.01
☐ 120 Mike Morgan	.04	.02	.01
☐ 121 Mark Eichhorn	.04	.02	.01
☐ 122 Jeff Reardon	.15	.07	.02
☐ 123 John Franco	.10	.05	.01
☐ 124 Richard Dotson	.04	.02	.01
☐ 125 Eric Bell	.04	.02	.01
☐ 126 Juan Nieves	.04	.02	.01
☐ 127 Jack Morris	.15	.07	.02
☐ 128 Rick Rhoden	.04	.02	.01
☐ 129 Rich Gedman	.04	.02	.01
☐ 130 Ken Howell	.04	.02	.01
☐ 131 Brook Jacoby	.04	.02	.01
☐ 132 Danny Jackson	.04	.02	.01
☐ 133 Gene Nelson	.04	.02	.01
☐ 134 Neal Heaton	.04	.02	.01
☐ 135 Willie Fraser	.04	.02	.01
☐ 136 Jose Guzman	.10	.05	.01
☐ 137 Ozzie Guillen	.10	.05	.01
☐ 138 Bob Knepper	.04	.02	.01
☐ 139 Mike Jackson	.10	.05	.01
☐ 140 Joe Magrane	.10	.05	.01
☐ 141 Jimmy Jones	.04	.02	.01
☐ 142 Ted Power	.04	.02	.01
☐ 143 Ozzie Virgil	.04	.02	.01
☐ 144 Felix Fermin	.04	.02	.01
☐ 145 Kelly Downs	.04	.02	.01
☐ 146 Shawon Dunston	.10	.05	.01
☐ 147 Scott Bradley	.04	.02	.01
☐ 148 Dave Stieb	.10	.05	.01
☐ 149 Frank Viola	.10	.05	.01
☐ 150 Terry Kennedy	.04	.02	.01
☐ 151 Bill Wegman	.04	.02	.01
☐ 152 Matt Nokes	.15	.07	.02
☐ 153 Wade Boggs	.25	.11	.03
☐ 154 Wayne Tolleson	.04	.02	.01
☐ 155 Mariano Duncan	.04	.02	.01
☐ 156 Julio Franco	.10	.05	.01
☐ 157 Charlie Leibrandt	.04	.02	.01
☐ 158 Terry Steinbach	.10	.05	.01
☐ 159 Mike Fitzgerald	.04	.02	.01
☐ 160 Jack Lazorko	.04	.02	.01

☐	161 Mitch Williams	.10	.05	.01
☐	162 Greg Walker	.04	.02	.01
☐	163 Alan Ashby	.04	.02	.01
☐	164 Tony Gwynn	.35	.16	.04
☐	165 Bruce Ruffin	.04	.02	.01
☐	166 Ron Robinson	.04	.02	.01
☐	167 Zane Smith	.04	.02	.01
☐	168 Junior Ortiz	.04	.02	.01
☐	169 Jamie Moyer	.04	.02	.01
☐	170 Tony Pena	.04	.02	.01
☐	171 Cal Ripken	.60	.25	.08
☐	172 B.J. Surhoff	.10	.05	.01
☐	173 Lou Whitaker	.15	.07	.02
☐	174 Ellis Burks	.40	.18	.05
☐	175 Ron Guidry	.10	.05	.01
☐	176 Steve Sax	.04	.02	.01
☐	177 Danny Tartabull	.10	.05	.01
☐	178 Carney Lansford	.10	.05	.01
☐	179 Casey Candaele	.04	.02	.01
☐	180 Scott Fletcher	.04	.02	.01
☐	181 Mark McLemore	.04	.02	.01
☐	182 Ivan Calderon	.10	.05	.01
☐	183 Jack Clark	.10	.05	.01
☐	184 Glenn Davis	.04	.02	.01
☐	185 Luis Aguayo	.04	.02	.01
☐	186 Bo Diaz	.04	.02	.01
☐	187 Stan Jefferson	.04	.02	.01
☐	188 Sid Bream	.04	.02	.01
☐	189 Bob Brenly	.04	.02	.01
☐	190 Dion James	.04	.02	.01
☐	191 Leon Durham	.04	.02	.01
☐	192 Jesse Orosco	.04	.02	.01
☐	193 Alvin Davis	.04	.02	.01
☐	194 Gary Gaetti	.04	.02	.01
☐	195 Fred McGriff	.40	.18	.05
☐	196 Steve Lombardozzi	.04	.02	.01
☐	197 Rance Mulliniks	.04	.02	.01
☐	198 Rey Quinones	.04	.02	.01
☐	199 Gary Carter	.15	.07	.02
☐	200A Checklist 138-247	.06	.02	.01
☐	200B Checklist 134-239	.06	.02	.01
☐	201 Keith Moreland	.04	.02	.01
☐	202 Ken Griffey	.10	.05	.01
☐	203 Tommy Gregg	.04	.02	.01
☐	204 Will Clark	.40	.18	.05
☐	205 John Kruk	.15	.07	.02
☐	206 Buddy Bell	.10	.05	.01
☐	207 Von Hayes	.04	.02	.01
☐	208 Tommy Herr	.04	.02	.01
☐	209 Craig Reynolds	.04	.02	.01
☐	210 Gary Pettis	.04	.02	.01
☐	211 Harold Baines	.10	.05	.01
☐	212 Vance Law	.04	.02	.01
☐	213 Ken Gerhart	.04	.02	.01
☐	214 Jim Gantner	.04	.02	.01
☐	215 Chet Lemon	.04	.02	.01
☐	216 Dwight Evans	.10	.05	.01
☐	217 Don Mattingly	.40	.18	.05
☐	218 Franklin Stubbs	.04	.02	.01
☐	219 Pat Tabler	.04	.02	.01
☐	220 Bo Jackson	.25	.11	.03
☐	221 Tony Phillips	.10	.05	.01
☐	222 Tim Wallach	.10	.05	.01
☐	223 Ruben Sierra	.25	.11	.03
☐	224 Steve Buechele	.04	.02	.01
☐	225 Frank White	.10	.05	.01
☐	226 Alfredo Griffin	.04	.02	.01
☐	227 Greg Swindell	.10	.05	.01
☐	228 Willie Randolph	.10	.05	.01
☐	229 Mike Marshall	.04	.02	.01
☐	230 Alan Trammell	.15	.07	.02
☐	231 Eddie Murray	.25	.11	.03
☐	232 Dale Sveum	.04	.02	.01
☐	233 Dick Schofield	.04	.02	.01
☐	234 Jose Oquendo	.04	.02	.01
☐	235 Bill Doran	.04	.02	.01
☐	236 Milt Thompson	.04	.02	.01
☐	237 Marvell Wynne	.04	.02	.01
☐	238 Bobby Bonilla	.20	.09	.03
☐	239 Chris Speier	.04	.02	.01
☐	240 Glenn Braggs	.04	.02	.01
☐	241 Wally Backman	.04	.02	.01
☐	242 Ryne Sandberg	.50	.23	.06
☐	243 Phil Bradley	.04	.02	.01
☐	244 Kelly Gruber	.04	.02	.01
☐	245 Tom Brunansky	.04	.02	.01
☐	246 Ron Oester	.04	.02	.01
☐	247 Bobby Thigpen	.04	.02	.01
☐	248 Fred Lynn	.10	.05	.01
☐	249 Paul Molitor	.25	.11	.03
☐	250 Darrell Evans	.10	.05	.01
☐	251 Gary Ward	.04	.02	.01
☐	252 Bruce Hurst	.04	.02	.01
☐	253 Bob Welch	.10	.05	.01
☐	254 Joe Carter	.30	.14	.04
☐	255 Willie Wilson	.04	.02	.01
☐	256 Mark McGwire	.35	.16	.04
☐	257 Mitch Webster	.04	.02	.01
☐	258 Brian Downing	.04	.02	.01
☐	259 Mike Stanley	.10	.05	.01
☐	260 Carlton Fisk	.15	.07	.02
☐	261 Billy Hatcher	.04	.02	.01
☐	262 Glenn Wilson	.04	.02	.01
☐	263 Ozzie Smith	.25	.11	.03
☐	264 Randy Ready	.04	.02	.01
☐	265 Kurt Stillwell	.04	.02	.01
☐	266 David Palmer	.04	.02	.01
☐	267 Mike Diaz	.04	.02	.01
☐	268 Robby Thompson	.10	.05	.01
☐	269 Andre Dawson	.15	.07	.02
☐	270 Lee Guetterman	.04	.02	.01
☐	271 Willie Upshaw	.04	.02	.01
☐	272 Randy Bush	.04	.02	.01
☐	273 Larry Sheets	.04	.02	.01
☐	274 Rob Deer	.04	.02	.01
☐	275 Kirk Gibson	.10	.05	.01
☐	276 Marty Barrett	.04	.02	.01
☐	277 Rickey Henderson	.20	.09	.03
☐	278 Pedro Guerrero	.10	.05	.01
☐	279 Brett Butler	.10	.05	.01
☐	280 Kevin Seitzer	.10	.05	.01
☐	281 Mike Davis	.04	.02	.01
☐	282 Andres Galarraga	.25	.11	.03
☐	283 Devon White	.15	.07	.02
☐	284 Pete O'Brien	.04	.02	.01
☐	285 Jerry Hairston	.04	.02	.01
☐	286 Kevin Bass	.04	.02	.01
☐	287 Carmelo Martinez	.04	.02	.01
☐	288 Juan Samuel	.04	.02	.01
☐	289 Kal Daniels	.04	.02	.01
☐	290 Albert Hall	.04	.02	.01
☐	291 Andy Van Slyke	.15	.07	.02
☐	292 Lee Smith	.15	.07	.02
☐	293 Vince Coleman	.10	.05	.01
☐	294 Tom Niedenfuer	.04	.02	.01
☐	295 Robin Yount	.20	.09	.03
☐	296 Jeff M. Robinson	.04	.02	.01
☐	297 Todd Benzinger	.10	.05	.01
☐	298 Dave Winfield	.20	.09	.03
☐	299 Mickey Hatcher	.04	.02	.01
☐	300A Checklist 248-357	.06	.02	.01
☐	300B Checklist 240-345	.06	.02	.01
☐	301 Bud Black	.04	.02	.01
☐	302 Jose Canseco	.40	.18	.05
☐	303 Tom Foley	.04	.02	.01
☐	304 Pete Incaviglia	.10	.05	.01

☐ 305 Bob Boone .10 .05 .01
☐ 306 Bill Long .04 .02 .01
☐ 307 Willie McGee .10 .05 .01
☐ 308 Ken Caminiti .50 .23 .06
☐ 309 Darren Daulton .15 .07 .02
☐ 310 Tracy Jones .04 .02 .01
☐ 311 Greg Booker .04 .02 .01
☐ 312 Mike LaValliere .04 .02 .01
☐ 313 Chili Davis .10 .05 .01
☐ 314 Glenn Hubbard .04 .02 .01
☐ 315 Paul Noce .04 .02 .01
☐ 316 Keith Hernandez .10 .05 .01
☐ 317 Mark Langston .15 .07 .02
☐ 318 Keith Atherton .04 .02 .01
☐ 319 Tony Fernandez .10 .05 .01
☐ 320 Kent Hrbek .10 .05 .01
☐ 321 John Cerutti .04 .02 .01
☐ 322 Mike Kingery .04 .02 .01
☐ 323 Dave Magadan .10 .05 .01
☐ 324 Rafael Palmeiro .50 .23 .06
☐ 325 Jeff Dedmon .04 .02 .01
☐ 326 Barry Bonds .60 .25 .08
☐ 327 Jeffrey Leonard .04 .02 .01
☐ 328 Tim Flannery .04 .02 .01
☐ 329 Dave Concepcion .10 .05 .01
☐ 330 Mike Schmidt .25 .11 .03
☐ 331 Bill Dawley .04 .02 .01
☐ 332 Larry Andersen .04 .02 .01
☐ 333 Jack Howell .04 .02 .01
☐ 334 Ken Williams .04 .02 .01
☐ 335 Bryn Smith .04 .02 .01
☐ 336 Billy Ripken .04 .02 .01
☐ 337 Greg Brock .04 .02 .01
☐ 338 Mike Heath .04 .02 .01
☐ 339 Mike Greenwell .15 .07 .02
☐ 340 Claudell Washington .04 .02 .01
☐ 341 Jose Gonzalez .04 .02 .01
☐ 342 Mel Hall .04 .02 .01
☐ 343 Jim Eisenreich .04 .02 .01
☐ 344 Tony Bernazard .04 .02 .01
☐ 345 Tim Raines .15 .07 .02
☐ 346 Bob Brower .04 .02 .01
☐ 347 Larry Parrish .04 .02 .01
☐ 348 Thad Bosley .04 .02 .01
☐ 349 Dennis Eckersley .15 .07 .02
☐ 350 Cory Snyder .04 .02 .01
☐ 351 Rick Cerone .04 .02 .01
☐ 352 John Shelby .04 .02 .01
☐ 353 Larry Herndon .04 .02 .01
☐ 354 John Habyan .04 .02 .01
☐ 355 Chuck Crim .04 .02 .01
☐ 356 Gus Polidor .04 .02 .01
☐ 357 Ken Dayley .04 .02 .01
☐ 358 Danny Darwin .04 .02 .01
☐ 359 Lance Parrish .10 .05 .01
☐ 360 James Steels .04 .02 .01
☐ 361 Al Pedrique .04 .02 .01
☐ 362 Mike Aldrete .04 .02 .01
☐ 363 Juan Castillo .04 .02 .01
☐ 364 Len Dykstra .20 .09 .03
☐ 365 Luis Quinones .04 .02 .01
☐ 366 Jim Presley .04 .02 .01
☐ 367 Lloyd Moseby .04 .02 .01
☐ 368 Kirby Puckett .50 .23 .06
☐ 369 Eric Davis .10 .05 .01
☐ 370 Gary Redus .04 .02 .01
☐ 371 Dave Schmidt .04 .02 .01
☐ 372 Mark Clear .04 .02 .01
☐ 373 Dave Bergman .04 .02 .01
☐ 374 Charles Hudson .04 .02 .01
☐ 375 Calvin Schiraldi .04 .02 .01
☐ 376 Alex Trevino .04 .02 .01
☐ 377 Tom Candiotti .04 .02 .01
☐ 378 Steve Farr .04 .02 .01
☐ 379 Mike Gallego .04 .02 .01
☐ 380 Andy McGaffigan .04 .02 .01
☐ 381 Kirk McCaskill .04 .02 .01
☐ 382 Oddibe McDowell .04 .02 .01
☐ 383 Floyd Bannister .04 .02 .01
☐ 384 Denny Walling .04 .02 .01
☐ 385 Don Carman .04 .02 .01
☐ 386 Todd Worrell .04 .02 .01
☐ 387 Eric Show .04 .02 .01
☐ 388 Dave Parker .15 .07 .02
☐ 389 Rick Mahler .04 .02 .01
☐ 390 Mike Dunne .04 .02 .01
☐ 391 Candy Maldonado .04 .02 .01
☐ 392 Bob Dernier .04 .02 .01
☐ 393 Dave Valle .04 .02 .01
☐ 394 Ernie Whitt .04 .02 .01
☐ 395 Juan Berenguer .04 .02 .01
☐ 396 Mike Young .04 .02 .01
☐ 397 Mike Felder .04 .02 .01
☐ 398 Willie Hernandez .04 .02 .01
☐ 399 Jim Rice .15 .07 .02
☐ 400A Checklist 358-467 .06 .02 .01
☐ 400B Checklist 346-451 .06 .02 .01
☐ 401 Tommy John .15 .07 .02
☐ 402 Brian Holton .04 .02 .01
☐ 403 Carmen Castillo .04 .02 .01
☐ 404 Jamie Quirk .04 .02 .01
☐ 405 Dwayne Murphy .04 .02 .01
☐ 406 Jeff Parrett .04 .02 .01
☐ 407 Don Sutton .15 .07 .02
☐ 408 Jerry Browne .04 .02 .01
☐ 409 Jim Winn .04 .02 .01
☐ 410 Dave Smith .04 .02 .01
☐ 411 Shane Mack .10 .05 .01
☐ 412 Greg Gross .04 .02 .01
☐ 413 Nick Esasky .04 .02 .01
☐ 414 Damaso Garcia .04 .02 .01
☐ 415 Brian Fisher .04 .02 .01
☐ 416 Brian Dayett .04 .02 .01
☐ 417 Curt Ford .04 .02 .01
☐ 418 Mark Williamson .04 .02 .01
☐ 419 Bill Schroeder .04 .02 .01
☐ 420 Mike Henneman .20 .09 .03
☐ 421 John Marzano .04 .02 .01
☐ 422 Ron Kittle .04 .02 .01
☐ 423 Matt Young .04 .02 .01
☐ 424 Steve Balboni .04 .02 .01
☐ 425 Luis Polonia .25 .11 .03
☐ 426 Randy St.Claire .04 .02 .01
☐ 427 Greg Harris .04 .02 .01
☐ 428 Johnny Ray .04 .02 .01
☐ 429 Ray Searage .04 .02 .01
☐ 430 Ricky Horton .04 .02 .01
☐ 431 Gerald Young .04 .02 .01
☐ 432 Rick Schu .04 .02 .01
☐ 433 Paul O'Neill .25 .11 .03
☐ 434 Rich Gossage .15 .07 .02
☐ 435 John Cangelosi .04 .02 .01
☐ 436 Mike LaCoss .04 .02 .01
☐ 437 Gerald Perry .04 .02 .01
☐ 438 Dave Martinez .04 .02 .01
☐ 439 Darryl Strawberry .15 .07 .02
☐ 440 John Moses .04 .02 .01
☐ 441 Greg Gagne .04 .02 .01
☐ 442 Jesse Barfield .04 .02 .01
☐ 443 George Frazier .04 .02 .01
☐ 444 Garth Iorg .04 .02 .01
☐ 445 Ed Nunez .04 .02 .01
☐ 446 Rick Aguilera .10 .05 .01
☐ 447 Jerry Mumphrey .04 .02 .01
☐ 448 Rafael Ramirez .04 .02 .01
☐ 449 John Smiley .20 .09 .03

☐	450 Atlee Hammaker	.04	.02	.01
☐	451 Lance McCullers	.04	.02	.01
☐	452 Guy Hoffman	.04	.02	.01
☐	453 Chris James	.04	.02	.01
☐	454 Terry Pendleton	.15	.07	.02
☐	455 Dave Meads	.04	.02	.01
☐	456 Bill Buckner	.10	.05	.01
☐	457 John Pawlowski	.04	.02	.01
☐	458 Bob Sebra	.04	.02	.01
☐	459 Jim Dwyer	.04	.02	.01
☐	460 Jay Aldrich	.04	.02	.01
☐	461 Frank Tanana	.04	.02	.01
☐	462 Oil Can Boyd	.04	.02	.01
☐	463 Dan Pasqua	.04	.02	.01
☐	464 Tim Crews	.10	.05	.01
☐	465 Andy Allanson	.04	.02	.01
☐	466 Bill Pecota	.04	.02	.01
☐	467 Steve Ontiveros	.04	.02	.01
☐	468 Hubie Brooks	.04	.02	.01
☐	469 Paul Kilgus	.04	.02	.01
☐	470 Dale Mohorcic	.04	.02	.01
☐	471 Dan Quisenberry	.10	.05	.01
☐	472 Dave Stewart	.10	.05	.01
☐	473 Dave Clark	.04	.02	.01
☐	474 Joel Skinner	.04	.02	.01
☐	475 Dave Anderson	.04	.02	.01
☐	476 Dan Petry	.04	.02	.01
☐	477 Carl Nichols	.04	.02	.01
☐	478 Ernest Riles	.04	.02	.01
☐	479 George Hendrick	.04	.02	.01
☐	480 John Morris	.04	.02	.01
☐	481 Manny Hernandez	.04	.02	.01
☐	482 Jeff Stone	.04	.02	.01
☐	483 Chris Brown	.04	.02	.01
☐	484 Mike Bielecki	.04	.02	.01
☐	485 Dave Dravecky	.10	.05	.01
☐	486 Rick Manning	.04	.02	.01
☐	487 Bill Almon	.04	.02	.01
☐	488 Jim Sundberg	.04	.02	.01
☐	489 Ken Phelps	.04	.02	.01
☐	490 Tom Henke	.10	.05	.01
☐	491 Dan Gladden	.04	.02	.01
☐	492 Barry Larkin	.20	.09	.03
☐	493 Fred Manrique	.04	.02	.01
☐	494 Mike Griffin	.04	.02	.01
☐	495 Mark Knudson	.04	.02	.01
☐	496 Bill Madlock	.10	.05	.01
☐	497 Tim Stoddard	.04	.02	.01
☐	498 Sam Horn	.04	.02	.01
☐	499 Tracy Woodson	.04	.02	.01
☐	500A Checklist 468-577	.06	.02	.01
☐	500B Checklist 452-557	.06	.02	.01
☐	501 Ken Schrom	.04	.02	.01
☐	502 Angel Salazar	.04	.02	.01
☐	503 Eric Plunk	.04	.02	.01
☐	504 Joe Hesketh	.04	.02	.01
☐	505 Greg Minton	.04	.02	.01
☐	506 Geno Petralli	.04	.02	.01
☐	507 Bob James	.04	.02	.01
☐	508 Robbie Wine	.04	.02	.01
☐	509 Jeff Calhoun	.04	.02	.01
☐	510 Steve Lake	.04	.02	.01
☐	511 Mark Grant	.04	.02	.01
☐	512 Frank Williams	.04	.02	.01
☐	513 Jeff Blauser	.50	.23	.06
☐	514 Bob Walk	.04	.02	.01
☐	515 Craig Lefferts	.04	.02	.01
☐	516 Manny Trillo	.04	.02	.01
☐	517 Jerry Reed	.04	.02	.01
☐	518 Rick Leach	.04	.02	.01
☐	519 Mark Davidson	.04	.02	.01
☐	520 Jeff Ballard	.04	.02	.01
☐	521 Dave Stapleton	.04	.02	.01
☐	522 Pat Sheridan	.04	.02	.01
☐	523 Al Nipper	.04	.02	.01
☐	524 Steve Trout	.04	.02	.01
☐	525 Jeff Hamilton	.04	.02	.01
☐	526 Tommy Hinzo	.04	.02	.01
☐	527 Lonnie Smith	.04	.02	.01
☐	528 Greg Cadaret	.04	.02	.01
☐	529 Bob McClure UER ("Rob" on front)	.04	.02	.01
☐	530 Chuck Finley	.10	.05	.01
☐	531 Jeff Russell	.04	.02	.01
☐	532 Steve Lyons	.04	.02	.01
☐	533 Terry Puhl	.04	.02	.01
☐	534 Eric Nolte	.04	.02	.01
☐	535 Kent Tekulve	.04	.02	.01
☐	536 Pat Pacillo	.04	.02	.01
☐	537 Charlie Puleo	.04	.02	.01
☐	538 Tom Prince	.04	.02	.01
☐	539 Greg Maddux	.75	.35	.09
☐	540 Jim Lindeman	.04	.02	.01
☐	541 Pete Stanicek	.04	.02	.01
☐	542 Steve Kiefer	.04	.02	.01
☐	543A Jim Morrison ERR (No decimal before lifetime average)	.30	.14	.04
☐	543B Jim Morrison COR	.04	.02	.01
☐	544 Spike Owen	.04	.02	.01
☐	545 Jay Buhner	.50	.23	.06
☐	546 Mike Devereaux	.40	.18	.05
☐	547 Jerry Don Gleaton	.04	.02	.01
☐	548 Jose Rijo	.15	.07	.02
☐	549 Dennis Martinez	.10	.05	.01
☐	550 Mike Loynd	.04	.02	.01
☐	551 Darrell Miller	.04	.02	.01
☐	552 Dave LaPoint	.04	.02	.01
☐	553 John Tudor	.04	.02	.01
☐	554 Rocky Childress	.04	.02	.01
☐	555 Wally Ritchie	.04	.02	.01
☐	556 Terry McGriff	.04	.02	.01
☐	557 Dave Leiper	.04	.02	.01
☐	558 Jeff D. Robinson	.04	.02	.01
☐	559 Jose Uribe	.04	.02	.01
☐	560 Ted Simmons	.10	.05	.01
☐	561 Les Lancaster	.04	.02	.01
☐	562 Keith A. Miller	.04	.02	.01
☐	563 Harold Reynolds	.04	.02	.01
☐	564 Gene Larkin	.04	.02	.01
☐	565 Cecil Fielder	.30	.14	.04
☐	566 Roy Smalley	.04	.02	.01
☐	567 Duane Ward	.10	.05	.01
☐	568 Bill Wilkinson	.04	.02	.01
☐	569 Howard Johnson	.10	.05	.01
☐	570 Frank DiPino	.04	.02	.01
☐	571 Pete Smith	.15	.07	.02
☐	572 Darnell Coles	.04	.02	.01
☐	573 Don Robinson	.04	.02	.01
☐	574 Rob Nelson UER (Career 0 RBI, but 1 RBI in '87)	.04	.02	.01
☐	575 Dennis Rasmussen	.04	.02	.01
☐	576 Steve Jeltz UER (Photo of Juan Samuel)	.04	.02	.01
☐	577 Tom Pagnozzi	.20	.09	.03
☐	578 Ty Gainey	.04	.02	.01
☐	579 Gary Lucas	.04	.02	.01
☐	580 Ron Hassey	.04	.02	.01
☐	581 Herm Winningham	.04	.02	.01
☐	582 Rene Gonzales	.04	.02	.01
☐	583 Brad Komminsk	.04	.02	.01
☐	584 Doyle Alexander	.04	.02	.01
☐	585 Jeff Sellers	.04	.02	.01
☐	586 Bill Gullickson	.04	.02	.01
☐	587 Tim Belcher	.10	.05	.01

☐ 588 Doug Jones .30 .14 .04
☐ 589 Melido Perez .20 .09 .03
☐ 590 Rick Honeycutt .04 .02 .01
☐ 591 Pascual Perez .04 .02 .01
☐ 592 Curt Wilkerson .04 .02 .01
☐ 593 Steve Howe .04 .02 .01
☐ 594 John Davis .04 .02 .01
☐ 595 Storm Davis .04 .02 .01
☐ 596 Sammy Stewart .04 .02 .01
☐ 597 Neil Allen .04 .02 .01
☐ 598 Alejandro Pena .04 .02 .01
☐ 599 Mark Thurmond .04 .02 .01
☐ 600A Checklist 578-660 .06 .02 .01
(BC1-BC26)
☐ 600B Checklist 558-660 .06 .02 .01
☐ 601 Jose Mesa .10 .05 .01
☐ 602 Don August .04 .02 .01
☐ 603 Terry Leach SP .07 .03 .01
☐ 604 Tom Newell .04 .02 .01
☐ 605 Randall Byers SP .07 .03 .01
☐ 606 Jim Gott .04 .02 .01
☐ 607 Harry Spilman .04 .02 .01
☐ 608 John Candelaria .04 .02 .01
☐ 609 Mike Brumley .04 .02 .01
☐ 610 Mickey Brantley .04 .02 .01
☐ 611 Jose Nunez SP .07 .03 .01
☐ 612 Tom Nieto .04 .02 .01
☐ 613 Rick Reuschel .04 .02 .01
☐ 614 Lee Mazzilli SP .07 .03 .01
☐ 615 Scott Lusader .04 .02 .01
☐ 616 Bobby Meacham .04 .02 .01
☐ 617 Kevin McReynolds SP .12 .05 .02
☐ 618 Gene Garber .04 .02 .01
☐ 619 Barry Lyons SP .07 .03 .01
☐ 620 Randy Myers .08 .04 .01
☐ 621 Donnie Moore .04 .02 .01
☐ 622 Domingo Ramos .04 .02 .01
☐ 623 Ed Romero .04 .02 .01
☐ 624 Greg Myers .04 .02 .01
☐ 625 Ripken Family .30 .14 .04
Cal Ripken Sr.
Cal Ripken Jr.
Billy Ripken
☐ 626 Pat Perry .04 .02 .01
☐ 627 Andres Thomas SP .07 .03 .01
☐ 628 Matt Williams SP 2.50 1.15 .30
☐ 629 Dave Hengel .04 .02 .01
☐ 630 Jeff Musselman SP .07 .03 .01
☐ 631 Tim Laudner .04 .02 .01
☐ 632 Bob Ojeda SP .07 .03 .01
☐ 633 Rafael Santana .04 .02 .01
☐ 634 Wes Gardner .04 .02 .01
☐ 635 Roberto Kelly SP 1.00 .45 .13
☐ 636 Mike Flanagan SP .07 .03 .01
☐ 637 Jay Bell .50 .23 .06
☐ 638 Bob Melvin .04 .02 .01
☐ 639 Damon Berryhill UER .15 .07 .02
(Bats: Swithch)
☐ 640 David Wells SP .25 .11 .03
☐ 641 Stan Musial PUZ .10 .05 .01
☐ 642 Doug Sisk .04 .02 .01
☐ 643 Keith Hughes .04 .02 .01
☐ 644 Tom Glavine 1.50 .65 .19
☐ 645 Al Newman .04 .02 .01
☐ 646 Scott Sanderson .04 .02 .01
☐ 647 Scott Terry .04 .02 .01
☐ 648 Tim Teufel SP .07 .03 .01
☐ 649 Garry Templeton SP .07 .03 .01
☐ 650 Manny Lee SP .07 .03 .01
☐ 651 Roger McDowell SP .07 .03 .01
☐ 652 Mookie Wilson SP .12 .05 .02
☐ 653 David Cone SP .50 .23 .06
☐ 654 Ron Gant SP 1.25 .55 .16
☐ 655 Joe Price SP .07 .03 .01
☐ 656 George Bell SP .12 .05 .02
☐ 657 Gregg Jefferies SP 2.50 1.15 .30
☐ 658 Todd Stottlemyre SP .30 .14 .04
☐ 659 Geronimo Berroa SP .60 .25 .08
☐ 660 Jerry Royster SP .07 .03 .01

1988 Donruss Rookies

The 1988 Donruss "The Rookies" set features 56 cards plus a 15-piece puzzle of Stan Musial. Cards are in full color and are standard size, 2 1/2" by 3 1/2". The set was distributed in a small green and black box with gold lettering. Card fronts are similar in design to the 1988 Donruss regular issue except for the presence of "The Rookies" logo in the lower right corner and a green and black border instead of a blue and black border on the fronts. Extended Rookie Cards in this set include Chris Sabo, Walt Weiss, Brady Anderson, Bryan Harvey, and Edgar Martinez.

	MINT	EXC	G-VG
COMPLETE FACT.SET (56)	16.00	7.25	2.00
COMMON CARD (1-56)	.07	.03	.01

☐ 1 Mark Grace 2.00 .90 .25
☐ 2 Mike Campbell .07 .03 .01
☐ 3 Todd Frohwirth .07 .03 .01
☐ 4 Dave Stapleton .07 .03 .01
☐ 5 Shawn Abner .07 .03 .01
☐ 6 Jose Cecena .07 .03 .01
☐ 7 Dave Gallagher .07 .03 .01
☐ 8 Mark Parent .07 .03 .01
☐ 9 Cecil Espy .07 .03 .01
☐ 10 Pete Smith .25 .11 .03
☐ 11 Jay Buhner 1.00 .45 .13
☐ 12 Pat Borders .50 .23 .06
☐ 13 Doug Jennings .07 .03 .01
☐ 14 Brady Anderson 1.00 .45 .13
☐ 15 Pete Stanicek .07 .03 .01
☐ 16 Roberto Kelly 1.00 .45 .13
☐ 17 Jeff Treadway .07 .03 .01
☐ 18 Walt Weiss .30 .14 .04
☐ 19 Paul Gibson .07 .03 .01
☐ 20 Tim Crews .10 .05 .01
☐ 21 Melido Perez .15 .07 .02
☐ 22 Steve Peters .07 .03 .01
☐ 23 Craig Worthington .07 .03 .01
☐ 24 John Trautwein .07 .03 .01

☐ 25 DeWayne Vaughn	.07	.03	.01
☐ 26 David Wells	.25	.11	.03
☐ 27 Al Leiter	.07	.03	.01
☐ 28 Tim Belcher	.07	.03	.01
☐ 29 Johnny Paredes	.07	.03	.01
☐ 30 Chris Sabo	.50	.23	.06
☐ 31 Damon Berryhill	.10	.05	.01
☐ 32 Randy Milligan	.25	.11	.03
☐ 33 Gary Thurman	.07	.03	.01
☐ 34 Kevin Elster	.07	.03	.01
☐ 35 Roberto Alomar	6.00	2.70	.75
☐ 36 Edgar Martinez UER (Photo of Edwin Nunez)	.75	.35	.09
☐ 37 Todd Stottlemyre	.25	.11	.03
☐ 38 Joey Meyer	.07	.03	.01
☐ 39 Carl Nichols	.07	.03	.01
☐ 40 Jack McDowell	1.00	.45	.13
☐ 41 Jose Bautista	.07	.03	.01
☐ 42 Sil Campusano	.07	.03	.01
☐ 43 John Dopson	.07	.03	.01
☐ 44 Jody Reed	.25	.11	.03
☐ 45 Darrin Jackson	.35	.16	.04
☐ 46 Mike Capel	.07	.03	.01
☐ 47 Ron Gant	1.00	.45	.13
☐ 48 John Davis	.07	.03	.01
☐ 49 Kevin Coffman	.07	.03	.01
☐ 50 Cris Carpenter	.07	.03	.01
☐ 51 Mackey Sasser	.07	.03	.01
☐ 52 Luis Alicea	.07	.03	.01
☐ 53 Bryan Harvey	1.00	.45	.13
☐ 54 Steve Ellsworth	.07	.03	.01
☐ 55 Mike Macfarlane	.50	.23	.06
☐ 56 Checklist 1-56	.07	.03	.01

1989 Donruss

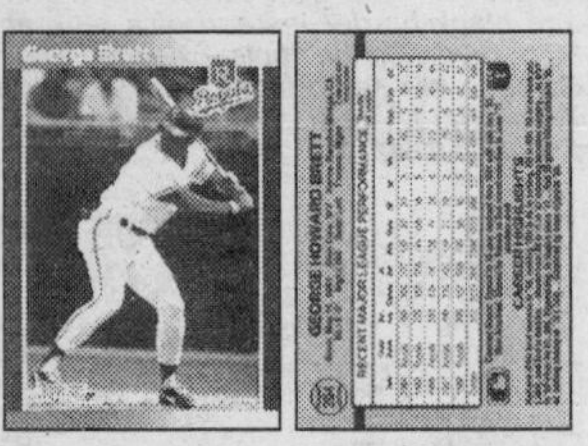

This 660-card set was distributed along with a puzzle of Warren Spahn. The six regular checklist cards are numbered throughout the set as multiples of 100. Cards measure 2 1/2" by 3 1/2" and feature a distinctive black side border with an alternating coating. The popular Diamond King subset returns for the eighth consecutive year. Rated Rookies are featured again as cards 28-47. The Donruss '89 logo appears in the lower left corner of every obverse. There are two variations that occur throughout most of the set. On the card backs "Denotes Led League" can be found with one asterisk to the left or with an asterisk on each side. On the card fronts the horizontal lines on the left and right borders can be glossy or non-glossy. Since both of these variation types are relatively minor and seem equally common, there is no premium value for either type. Rather than short-printing 26 cards in order to make room for printing the Bonus MVP's this year, Donruss apparently chose to double print 106 cards. These double prints are listed below by DP. Numbered with the prefix "BC" for bonus card, the 26-card set featuring the most valuable player from each of the 26 teams was randomly inserted in the wax and rack packs. These cards are distinguished by the bold MVP logo in the upper background of the obverse, and the four doubleprinted cards are denoted by "DP" in the checklist below. Rookie Cards in this set include Sandy Alomar Jr., Brady Anderson, Dante Bichette, Craig Biggio, Ken Griffey Jr., Randy Johnson, Felix Jose, Ramon Martinez, Hal Morris, Curt Schilling, Gary Sheffield, and John Smoltz.

	MINT	EXC	G-VG
COMPLETE SET (660)	12.00	5.50	1.50
COMPLETE FACT.SET (672)	15.00	6.75	1.90
COMMON CARD (1-660)	.05	.02	.01
COMMON CARD DP	.03	.01	.00

☐ 1 Mike Greenwell DK	.12	.05	.02
☐ 2 Bobby Bonilla DK DP	.12	.05	.02
☐ 3 Pete Incaviglia DK	.07	.03	.01
☐ 4 Chris Sabo DK DP	.07	.03	.01
☐ 5 Robin Yount DK	.10	.05	.01
☐ 6 Tony Gwynn DK DP	.10	.05	.01
☐ 7 Carlton Fisk DK UER (OF on back)	.12	.05	.02
☐ 8 Cory Snyder DK	.07	.03	.01
☐ 9 David Cone DK UER (Sic, "hurdlers")	.12	.05	.02
☐ 10 Kevin Seitzer DK	.07	.03	.01
☐ 11 Rick Reuschel DK	.07	.03	.01
☐ 12 Johnny Ray DK	.07	.03	.01
☐ 13 Dave Schmidt DK	.07	.03	.01
☐ 14 Andres Galarraga DK	.12	.05	.02
☐ 15 Kirk Gibson DK	.07	.03	.01
☐ 16 Fred McGriff DK	.15	.07	.02
☐ 17 Mark Grace DK	.12	.05	.02
☐ 18 Jeff M. Robinson DK	.07	.03	.01
☐ 19 Vince Coleman DK DP	.07	.03	.01
☐ 20 Dave Henderson DK	.07	.03	.01
☐ 21 Harold Reynolds DK	.07	.03	.01
☐ 22 Gerald Perry DK	.07	.03	.01
☐ 23 Frank Viola DK	.07	.03	.01
☐ 24 Steve Bedrosian DK	.07	.03	.01
☐ 25 Glenn Davis DK	.07	.03	.01
☐ 26 Don Mattingly DK UER (Doesn't mention Don's previous DK in 1985)	.25	.11	.03
☐ 27 DK Checklist 1-26 DP	.05	.02	.01
☐ 28 Sandy Alomar Jr. RR	.25	.11	.03
☐ 29 Steve Searcy RR	.05	.02	.01
☐ 30 Cameron Drew RR	.05	.02	.01
☐ 31 Gary Sheffield RR	1.00	.45	.13
☐ 32 Erik Hanson RR	.25	.11	.03
☐ 33 Ken Griffey Jr. RR	5.00	2.30	.60
☐ 34 Greg W. Harris RR	.05	.02	.01
☐ 35 Gregg Jefferies RR	.35	.16	.04
☐ 36 Luis Medina RR	.05	.02	.01
☐ 37 Carlos Quintana RR	.05	.02	.01
☐ 38 Felix Jose RR	.25	.11	.03
☐ 39 Cris Carpenter RR	.05	.02	.01
☐ 40 Ron Jones RR	.05	.02	.01
☐ 41 Dave West RR	.10	.05	.01

☐	42 Randy Johnson RR	.75	.35	.09
☐	43 Mike Harkey RR	.05	.02	.01
☐	44 Pete Harnisch RR DP	.15	.07	.02
☐	45 Tom Gordon RR DP	.15	.07	.02
☐	46 Gregg Olson RR DP	.25	.11	.03
☐	47 Alex Sanchez RR DP	.05	.02	.01
☐	48 Ruben Sierra	.25	.11	.03
☐	49 Rafael Palmeiro	.25	.11	.03
☐	50 Ron Gant	.25	.11	.03
☐	51 Cal Ripken	.50	.23	.06
☐	52 Wally Joyner	.10	.05	.01
☐	53 Gary Carter	.15	.07	.02
☐	54 Andy Van Slyke	.15	.07	.02
☐	55 Robin Yount	.25	.11	.03
☐	56 Pete Incaviglia	.10	.05	.01
☐	57 Greg Brock	.05	.02	.01
☐	58 Melido Perez	.05	.02	.01
☐	59 Craig Lefferts	.05	.02	.01
☐	60 Gary Pettis	.05	.02	.01
☐	61 Danny Tartabull	.10	.05	.01
☐	62 Guillermo Hernandez	.05	.02	.01
☐	63 Ozzie Smith	.30	.14	.04
☐	64 Gary Gaetti	.05	.02	.01
☐	65 Mark Davis	.05	.02	.01
☐	66 Lee Smith	.15	.07	.02
☐	67 Dennis Eckersley	.15	.07	.02
☐	68 Wade Boggs	.20	.09	.03
☐	69 Mike Scott	.05	.02	.01
☐	70 Fred McGriff	.25	.11	.03
☐	71 Tom Browning	.05	.02	.01
☐	72 Claudell Washington	.05	.02	.01
☐	73 Mel Hall	.05	.02	.01
☐	74 Don Mattingly	.40	.18	.05
☐	75 Steve Bedrosian	.05	.02	.01
☐	76 Juan Samuel	.05	.02	.01
☐	77 Mike Scioscia	.05	.02	.01
☐	78 Dave Righetti	.05	.02	.01
☐	79 Alfredo Griffin	.05	.02	.01
☐	80 Eric Davis UER (165 games in 1988, should be 135)	.10	.05	.01
☐	81 Juan Berenguer	.05	.02	.01
☐	82 Todd Worrell	.05	.02	.01
☐	83 Joe Carter	.25	.11	.03
☐	84 Steve Sax	.05	.02	.01
☐	85 Frank White	.10	.05	.01
☐	86 John Kruk	.15	.07	.02
☐	87 Rance Mulliniks	.05	.02	.01
☐	88 Alan Ashby	.05	.02	.01
☐	89 Charlie Leibrandt	.05	.02	.01
☐	90 Frank Tanana	.05	.02	.01
☐	91 Jose Canseco	.30	.14	.04
☐	92 Barry Bonds	.60	.25	.08
☐	93 Harold Reynolds	.05	.02	.01
☐	94 Mark McLemore	.05	.02	.01
☐	95 Mark McGwire	.15	.07	.02
☐	96 Eddie Murray	.15	.07	.02
☐	97 Tim Raines	.15	.07	.02
☐	98 Robby Thompson	.10	.05	.01
☐	99 Kevin McReynolds	.10	.05	.01
☐	100 Checklist 28-137	.05	.02	.01
☐	101 Carlton Fisk	.15	.07	.02
☐	102 Dave Martinez	.05	.02	.01
☐	103 Glenn Braggs	.05	.02	.01
☐	104 Dale Murphy	.15	.07	.02
☐	105 Ryne Sandberg	.40	.18	.05
☐	106 Dennis Martinez	.10	.05	.01
☐	107 Pete O'Brien	.05	.02	.01
☐	108 Dick Schofield	.05	.02	.01
☐	109 Henry Cotto	.05	.02	.01
☐	110 Mike Marshall	.05	.02	.01
☐	111 Keith Moreland	.05	.02	.01
☐	112 Tom Brunansky	.05	.02	.01
☐	113 Kelly Gruber UER (Wrong birthdate)	.05	.02	.01
☐	114 Brook Jacoby	.05	.02	.01
☐	115 Keith Brown	.05	.02	.01
☐	116 Matt Nokes	.05	.02	.01
☐	117 Keith Hernandez	.10	.05	.01
☐	118 Bob Forsch	.05	.02	.01
☐	119 Bert Blyleven UER (... 3000 strikeouts in 1987, should be 1986)	.15	.07	.02
☐	120 Willie Wilson	.05	.02	.01
☐	121 Tommy Gregg	.05	.02	.01
☐	122 Jim Rice	.15	.07	.02
☐	123 Bob Knepper	.05	.02	.01
☐	124 Danny Jackson	.05	.02	.01
☐	125 Eric Plunk	.05	.02	.01
☐	126 Brian Fisher	.05	.02	.01
☐	127 Mike Pagliarulo	.05	.02	.01
☐	128 Tony Gwynn	.30	.14	.04
☐	129 Lance McCullers	.05	.02	.01
☐	130 Andres Galarraga	.15	.07	.02
☐	131 Jose Uribe	.05	.02	.01
☐	132 Kirk Gibson UER (Wrong birthdate)	.10	.05	.01
☐	133 David Palmer	.05	.02	.01
☐	134 R.J. Reynolds	.05	.02	.01
☐	135 Greg Walker	.05	.02	.01
☐	136 Kirk McCaskill UER (Wrong birthdate)	.05	.02	.01
☐	137 Shawon Dunston	.10	.05	.01
☐	138 Andy Allanson	.05	.02	.01
☐	139 Rob Murphy	.05	.02	.01
☐	140 Mike Aldrete	.05	.02	.01
☐	141 Terry Kennedy	.05	.02	.01
☐	142 Scott Fletcher	.05	.02	.01
☐	143 Steve Balboni	.05	.02	.01
☐	144 Bret Saberhagen	.10	.05	.01
☐	145 Ozzie Virgil	.05	.02	.01
☐	146 Dale Sveum	.05	.02	.01
☐	147 Darryl Strawberry	.15	.07	.02
☐	148 Harold Baines	.10	.05	.01
☐	149 George Bell	.05	.02	.01
☐	150 Dave Parker	.15	.07	.02
☐	151 Bobby Bonilla	.15	.07	.02
☐	152 Mookie Wilson	.10	.05	.01
☐	153 Ted Power	.05	.02	.01
☐	154 Nolan Ryan	.75	.35	.09
☐	155 Jeff Reardon	.15	.07	.02
☐	156 Tim Wallach	.05	.02	.01
☐	157 Jamie Moyer	.05	.02	.01
☐	158 Rich Gossage	.15	.07	.02
☐	159 Dave Winfield	.20	.09	.03
☐	160 Von Hayes	.05	.02	.01
☐	161 Willie McGee	.10	.05	.01
☐	162 Rich Gedman	.05	.02	.01
☐	163 Tony Pena	.05	.02	.01
☐	164 Mike Morgan	.05	.02	.01
☐	165 Charlie Hough	.10	.05	.01
☐	166 Mike Stanley	.10	.05	.01
☐	167 Andre Dawson	.15	.07	.02
☐	168 Joe Boever	.05	.02	.01
☐	169 Pete Stanicek	.05	.02	.01
☐	170 Bob Boone	.10	.05	.01
☐	171 Ron Darling	.10	.05	.01
☐	172 Bob Walk	.05	.02	.01
☐	173 Rob Deer	.05	.02	.01
☐	174 Steve Buechele	.05	.02	.01
☐	175 Ted Higuera	.05	.02	.01
☐	176 Ozzie Guillen	.10	.05	.01
☐	177 Candy Maldonado	.05	.02	.01
☐	178 Doyle Alexander	.05	.02	.01
☐	179 Mark Gubicza	.05	.02	.01
☐	180 Alan Trammell	.15	.07	.02

	No.	Player			
☐	181	Vince Coleman	.10	.05	.01
☐	182	Kirby Puckett	.50	.23	.06
☐	183	Chris Brown	.05	.02	.01
☐	184	Marty Barrett	.05	.02	.01
☐	185	Stan Javier	.05	.02	.01
☐	186	Mike Greenwell	.10	.05	.01
☐	187	Billy Hatcher	.05	.02	.01
☐	188	Jimmy Key	.15	.07	.02
☐	189	Nick Esasky	.05	.02	.01
☐	190	Don Slaught	.05	.02	.01
☐	191	Cory Snyder	.05	.02	.01
☐	192	John Candelaria	.05	.02	.01
☐	193	Mike Schmidt	.25	.11	.03
☐	194	Kevin Gross	.05	.02	.01
☐	195	John Tudor	.05	.02	.01
☐	196	Neil Allen	.05	.02	.01
☐	197	Orel Hershiser	.10	.05	.01
☐	198	Kal Daniels	.05	.02	.01
☐	199	Kent Hrbek	.10	.05	.01
☐	200	Checklist 138-247	.05	.02	.01
☐	201	Joe Magrane	.05	.02	.01
☐	202	Scott Bailes	.05	.02	.01
☐	203	Tim Belcher	.05	.02	.01
☐	204	George Brett	.35	.16	.04
☐	205	Benito Santiago	.10	.05	.01
☐	206	Tony Fernandez	.10	.05	.01
☐	207	Gerald Young	.05	.02	.01
☐	208	Bo Jackson	.25	.11	.03
☐	209	Chet Lemon	.05	.02	.01
☐	210	Storm Davis	.05	.02	.01
☐	211	Doug Drabek	.15	.07	.02
☐	212	Mickey Brantley UER (Photo of Nelson Simmons)	.05	.02	.01
☐	213	Devon White	.10	.05	.01
☐	214	Dave Stewart	.10	.05	.01
☐	215	Dave Schmidt	.05	.02	.01
☐	216	Bryn Smith	.05	.02	.01
☐	217	Brett Butler	.10	.05	.01
☐	218	Bob Ojeda	.05	.02	.01
☐	219	Steve Rosenberg	.05	.02	.01
☐	220	Hubie Brooks	.05	.02	.01
☐	221	B.J. Surhoff	.05	.02	.01
☐	222	Rick Mahler	.05	.02	.01
☐	223	Rick Sutcliffe	.10	.05	.01
☐	224	Neal Heaton	.05	.02	.01
☐	225	Mitch Williams	.10	.05	.01
☐	226	Chuck Finley	.10	.05	.01
☐	227	Mark Langston	.15	.07	.02
☐	228	Jesse Orosco	.05	.02	.01
☐	229	Ed Whitson	.05	.02	.01
☐	230	Terry Pendleton	.15	.07	.02
☐	231	Lloyd Moseby	.05	.02	.01
☐	232	Greg Swindell	.10	.05	.01
☐	233	John Franco	.10	.05	.01
☐	234	Jack Morris	.15	.07	.02
☐	235	Howard Johnson	.10	.05	.01
☐	236	Glenn Davis	.05	.02	.01
☐	237	Frank Viola	.10	.05	.01
☐	238	Kevin Seitzer	.05	.02	.01
☐	239	Gerald Perry	.05	.02	.01
☐	240	Dwight Evans	.10	.05	.01
☐	241	Jim Deshaies	.05	.02	.01
☐	242	Bo Diaz	.05	.02	.01
☐	243	Carney Lansford	.10	.05	.01
☐	244	Mike LaValliere	.05	.02	.01
☐	245	Rickey Henderson	.15	.07	.02
☐	246	Roberto Alomar	.75	.35	.09
☐	247	Jimmy Jones	.05	.02	.01
☐	248	Pascual Perez	.05	.02	.01
☐	249	Will Clark	.30	.14	.04
☐	250	Fernando Valenzuela	.05	.02	.01
☐	251	Shane Rawley	.05	.02	.01
☐	252	Sid Bream	.05	.02	.01
☐	253	Steve Lyons	.05	.02	.01
☐	254	Brian Downing	.05	.02	.01
☐	255	Mark Grace	.25	.11	.03
☐	256	Tom Candiotti	.05	.02	.01
☐	257	Barry Larkin	.15	.07	.02
☐	258	Mike Krukow	.05	.02	.01
☐	259	Billy Ripken	.05	.02	.01
☐	260	Cecilio Guante	.05	.02	.01
☐	261	Scott Bradley	.05	.02	.01
☐	262	Floyd Bannister	.05	.02	.01
☐	263	Pete Smith	.05	.02	.01
☐	264	Jim Gantner UER (Wrong birthdate)	.05	.02	.01
☐	265	Roger McDowell	.05	.02	.01
☐	266	Bobby Thigpen	.05	.02	.01
☐	267	Jim Clancy	.05	.02	.01
☐	268	Terry Steinbach	.10	.05	.01
☐	269	Mike Dunne	.05	.02	.01
☐	270	Dwight Gooden	.10	.05	.01
☐	271	Mike Heath	.05	.02	.01
☐	272	Dave Smith	.05	.02	.01
☐	273	Keith Atherton	.05	.02	.01
☐	274	Tim Burke	.05	.02	.01
☐	275	Damon Berryhill	.05	.02	.01
☐	276	Vance Law	.05	.02	.01
☐	277	Rich Dotson	.05	.02	.01
☐	278	Lance Parrish	.10	.05	.01
☐	279	Denny Walling	.05	.02	.01
☐	280	Roger Clemens	.35	.16	.04
☐	281	Greg Mathews	.05	.02	.01
☐	282	Tom Niedenfuer	.05	.02	.01
☐	283	Paul Kilgus	.05	.02	.01
☐	284	Jose Guzman	.10	.05	.01
☐	285	Calvin Schiraldi	.05	.02	.01
☐	286	Charlie Puleo UER (Career ERA 4.24, should be 4.23)	.05	.02	.01
☐	287	Joe Orsulak	.05	.02	.01
☐	288	Jack Howell	.05	.02	.01
☐	289	Kevin Elster	.05	.02	.01
☐	290	Jose Lind	.05	.02	.01
☐	291	Paul Molitor	.25	.11	.03
☐	292	Cecil Espy	.05	.02	.01
☐	293	Bill Wegman	.05	.02	.01
☐	294	Dan Pasqua	.05	.02	.01
☐	295	Scott Garrelts UER (Wrong birthdate)	.05	.02	.01
☐	296	Walt Terrell	.05	.02	.01
☐	297	Ed Hearn	.05	.02	.01
☐	298	Lou Whitaker	.15	.07	.02
☐	299	Ken Dayley	.05	.02	.01
☐	300	Checklist 248-357	.05	.02	.01
☐	301	Tommy Herr	.05	.02	.01
☐	302	Mike Brumley	.05	.02	.01
☐	303	Ellis Burks	.10	.05	.01
☐	304	Curt Young UER (Wrong birthdate)	.05	.02	.01
☐	305	Jody Reed	.05	.02	.01
☐	306	Bill Doran	.05	.02	.01
☐	307	David Wells	.05	.02	.01
☐	308	Ron Robinson	.05	.02	.01
☐	309	Rafael Santana	.05	.02	.01
☐	310	Julio Franco	.10	.05	.01
☐	311	Jack Clark	.10	.05	.01
☐	312	Chris James	.05	.02	.01
☐	313	Milt Thompson	.05	.02	.01
☐	314	John Shelby	.05	.02	.01
☐	315	Al Leiter	.05	.02	.01
☐	316	Mike Davis	.05	.02	.01
☐	317	Chris Sabo	.25	.11	.03
☐	318	Greg Gagne	.05	.02	.01
☐	319	Jose Oquendo	.05	.02	.01
☐	320	John Farrell	.05	.02	.01

☐ 321 Franklin Stubbs .05 .02 .01
☐ 322 Kurt Stillwell .05 .02 .01
☐ 323 Shawn Abner .05 .02 .01
☐ 324 Mike Flanagan .05 .02 .01
☐ 325 Kevin Bass .05 .02 .01
☐ 326 Pat Tabler .05 .02 .01
☐ 327 Mike Henneman .10 .05 .01
☐ 328 Rick Honeycutt .05 .02 .01
☐ 329 John Smiley .05 .02 .01
☐ 330 Rey Quinones .05 .02 .01
☐ 331 Johnny Ray .05 .02 .01
☐ 332 Bob Welch .10 .05 .01
☐ 333 Larry Sheets .05 .02 .01
☐ 334 Jeff Parrett .05 .02 .01
☐ 335 Rick Reuschel UER .05 .02 .01
(For Don Robinson, should be Jeff)
☐ 336 Randy Myers .10 .05 .01
☐ 337 Ken Williams .05 .02 .01
☐ 338 Andy McGaffigan .05 .02 .01
☐ 339 Joey Meyer .05 .02 .01
☐ 340 Dion James .05 .02 .01
☐ 341 Les Lancaster .05 .02 .01
☐ 342 Tom Foley .05 .02 .01
☐ 343 Geno Petralli .05 .02 .01
☐ 344 Dan Petry .05 .02 .01
☐ 345 Alvin Davis .05 .02 .01
☐ 346 Mickey Hatcher .05 .02 .01
☐ 347 Marvell Wynne .05 .02 .01
☐ 348 Danny Cox .05 .02 .01
☐ 349 Dave Stieb .10 .05 .01
☐ 350 Jay Bell .15 .07 .02
☐ 351 Jeff Treadway .05 .02 .01
☐ 352 Luis Salazar .05 .02 .01
☐ 353 Len Dykstra .15 .07 .02
☐ 354 Juan Agosto .05 .02 .01
☐ 355 Gene Larkin .05 .02 .01
☐ 356 Steve Farr .05 .02 .01
☐ 357 Paul Assenmacher .05 .02 .01
☐ 358 Todd Benzinger .05 .02 .01
☐ 359 Larry Andersen .05 .02 .01
☐ 360 Paul O'Neill .15 .07 .02
☐ 361 Ron Hassey .05 .02 .01
☐ 362 Jim Gott .05 .02 .01
☐ 363 Ken Phelps .05 .02 .01
☐ 364 Tim Flannery .05 .02 .01
☐ 365 Randy Ready .05 .02 .01
☐ 366 Nelson Santovenia .05 .02 .01
☐ 367 Kelly Downs .05 .02 .01
☐ 368 Danny Heep .05 .02 .01
☐ 369 Phil Bradley .05 .02 .01
☐ 370 Jeff D. Robinson .05 .02 .01
☐ 371 Ivan Calderon .05 .02 .01
☐ 372 Mike Witt .05 .02 .01
☐ 373 Greg Maddux .35 .16 .04
☐ 374 Carmen Castillo .05 .02 .01
☐ 375 Jose Rijo .15 .07 .02
☐ 376 Joe Price .05 .02 .01
☐ 377 Rene Gonzales .05 .02 .01
☐ 378 Oddibe McDowell .05 .02 .01
☐ 379 Jim Presley .05 .02 .01
☐ 380 Brad Wellman .05 .02 .01
☐ 381 Tom Glavine .40 .18 .05
☐ 382 Dan Plesac .05 .02 .01
☐ 383 Wally Backman .05 .02 .01
☐ 384 Dave Gallagher .05 .02 .01
☐ 385 Tom Henke .10 .05 .01
☐ 386 Luis Polonia .10 .05 .01
☐ 387 Junior Ortiz .05 .02 .01
☐ 388 David Cone .20 .09 .03
☐ 389 Dave Bergman .05 .02 .01
☐ 390 Danny Darwin .05 .02 .01
☐ 391 Dan Gladden .05 .02 .01
☐ 392 John Dopson .05 .02 .01
☐ 393 Frank DiPino .05 .02 .01
☐ 394 Al Nipper .05 .02 .01
☐ 395 Willie Randolph .10 .05 .01
☐ 396 Don Carman .05 .02 .01
☐ 397 Scott Terry .05 .02 .01
☐ 398 Rick Cerone .05 .02 .01
☐ 399 Tom Pagnozzi .05 .02 .01
☐ 400 Checklist 358-467 .05 .02 .01
☐ 401 Mickey Tettleton .10 .05 .01
☐ 402 Curtis Wilkerson .05 .02 .01
☐ 403 Jeff Russell .05 .02 .01
☐ 404 Pat Perry .05 .02 .01
☐ 405 Jose Alvarez .05 .02 .01
☐ 406 Rick Schu .05 .02 .01
☐ 407 Sherman Corbett .05 .02 .01
☐ 408 Dave Magadan .05 .02 .01
☐ 409 Bob Kipper .05 .02 .01
☐ 410 Don August .05 .02 .01
☐ 411 Bob Brower .05 .02 .01
☐ 412 Chris Bosio .05 .02 .01
☐ 413 Jerry Reuss .05 .02 .01
☐ 414 Atlee Hammaker .05 .02 .01
☐ 415 Jim Walewander .05 .02 .01
☐ 416 Mike Macfarlane .10 .05 .01
☐ 417 Pat Sheridan .05 .02 .01
☐ 418 Pedro Guerrero .10 .05 .01
☐ 419 Allan Anderson .05 .02 .01
☐ 420 Mark Parent .05 .02 .01
☐ 421 Bob Stanley .05 .02 .01
☐ 422 Mike Gallego .05 .02 .01
☐ 423 Bruce Hurst .05 .02 .01
☐ 424 Dave Meads .05 .02 .01
☐ 425 Jesse Barfield .05 .02 .01
☐ 426 Rob Dibble .20 .09 .03
☐ 427 Joel Skinner .05 .02 .01
☐ 428 Ron Kittle .05 .02 .01
☐ 429 Rick Rhoden .05 .02 .01
☐ 430 Bob Dernier .05 .02 .01
☐ 431 Steve Jeltz .05 .02 .01
☐ 432 Rick Dempsey .05 .02 .01
☐ 433 Roberto Kelly .20 .09 .03
☐ 434 Dave Anderson .05 .02 .01
☐ 435 Herm Winningham .05 .02 .01
☐ 436 Al Newman .05 .02 .01
☐ 437 Jose DeLeon .05 .02 .01
☐ 438 Doug Jones .10 .05 .01
☐ 439 Brian Holton .05 .02 .01
☐ 440 Jeff Montgomery .10 .05 .01
☐ 441 Dickie Thon .05 .02 .01
☐ 442 Cecil Fielder .25 .11 .03
☐ 443 John Fishel .05 .02 .01
☐ 444 Jerry Don Gleaton .05 .02 .01
☐ 445 Paul Gibson .05 .02 .01
☐ 446 Walt Weiss .05 .02 .01
☐ 447 Glenn Wilson .05 .02 .01
☐ 448 Mike Moore .05 .02 .01
☐ 449 Chili Davis .10 .05 .01
☐ 450 Dave Henderson .05 .02 .01
☐ 451 Jose Bautista .05 .02 .01
☐ 452 Rex Hudler .05 .02 .01
☐ 453 Bob Brenly .05 .02 .01
☐ 454 Mackey Sasser .05 .02 .01
☐ 455 Daryl Boston .05 .02 .01
☐ 456 Mike R. Fitzgerald .05 .02 .01
☐ 457 Jeffrey Leonard .05 .02 .01
☐ 458 Bruce Sutter .10 .05 .01
☐ 459 Mitch Webster .05 .02 .01
☐ 460 Joe Hesketh .05 .02 .01
☐ 461 Bobby Witt .10 .05 .01
☐ 462 Stew Cliburn .05 .02 .01
☐ 463 Scott Bankhead .05 .02 .01
☐ 464 Ramon Martinez .50 .23 .06

	No.	Player			
☐	465	Dave Leiper	.05	.02	.01
☐	466	Luis Alicea	.05	.02	.01
☐	467	John Cerutti	.05	.02	.01
☐	468	Ron Washington	.05	.02	.01
☐	469	Jeff Reed	.05	.02	.01
☐	470	Jeff M. Robinson	.05	.02	.01
☐	471	Sid Fernandez	.10	.05	.01
☐	472	Terry Puhl	.05	.02	.01
☐	473	Charlie Lea	.05	.02	.01
☐	474	Israel Sanchez	.05	.02	.01
☐	475	Bruce Benedict	.05	.02	.01
☐	476	Oil Can Boyd	.05	.02	.01
☐	477	Craig Reynolds	.05	.02	.01
☐	478	Frank Williams	.05	.02	.01
☐	479	Greg Cadaret	.05	.02	.01
☐	480	Randy Kramer	.05	.02	.01
☐	481	Dave Eiland	.05	.02	.01
☐	482	Eric Show	.05	.02	.01
☐	483	Garry Templeton	.05	.02	.01
☐	484	Wallace Johnson	.05	.02	.01
☐	485	Kevin Mitchell	.15	.07	.02
☐	486	Tim Crews	.05	.02	.01
☐	487	Mike Maddux	.05	.02	.01
☐	488	Dave LaPoint	.05	.02	.01
☐	489	Fred Manrique	.05	.02	.01
☐	490	Greg Minton	.05	.02	.01
☐	491	Doug Dascenzo UER (Photo of Damon Berryhill)	.05	.02	.01
☐	492	Willie Upshaw	.05	.02	.01
☐	493	Jack Armstrong	.05	.02	.01
☐	494	Kirt Manwaring	.05	.02	.01
☐	495	Jeff Ballard	.05	.02	.01
☐	496	Jeff Kunkel	.05	.02	.01
☐	497	Mike Campbell	.05	.02	.01
☐	498	Gary Thurman	.05	.02	.01
☐	499	Zane Smith	.05	.02	.01
☐	500	Checklist 468-577 DP	.05	.02	.01
☐	501	Mike Birkbeck	.05	.02	.01
☐	502	Terry Leach	.05	.02	.01
☐	503	Shawn Hillegas	.05	.02	.01
☐	504	Manny Lee	.05	.02	.01
☐	505	Doug Jennings	.05	.02	.01
☐	506	Ken Oberkfell	.05	.02	.01
☐	507	Tim Teufel	.05	.02	.01
☐	508	Tom Brookens	.05	.02	.01
☐	509	Rafael Ramirez	.05	.02	.01
☐	510	Fred Toliver	.05	.02	.01
☐	511	Brian Holman	.05	.02	.01
☐	512	Mike Bielecki	.05	.02	.01
☐	513	Jeff Pico	.05	.02	.01
☐	514	Charles Hudson	.05	.02	.01
☐	515	Bruce Ruffin	.05	.02	.01
☐	516	Larry McWilliams UER. (New Richland, should be North Richland)	.05	.02	.01
☐	517	Jeff Sellers	.05	.02	.01
☐	518	John Costello	.05	.02	.01
☐	519	Brady Anderson	.40	.18	.05
☐	520	Craig McMurtry	.05	.02	.01
☐	521	Ray Hayward DP	.03	.01	.00
☐	522	Drew Hall DP	.03	.01	.00
☐	523	Mark Lemke DP	.10	.05	.01
☐	524	Oswald Peraza DP	.03	.01	.00
☐	525	Bryan Harvey DP	.25	.11	.03
☐	526	Rick Aguilera DP	.08	.04	.01
☐	527	Tom Prince DP	.03	.01	.00
☐	528	Mark Clear DP	.03	.01	.00
☐	529	Jerry Browne DP	.03	.01	.00
☐	530	Juan Castillo DP	.03	.01	.00
☐	531	Jack McDowell DP	.25	.11	.03
☐	532	Chris Speier DP	.03	.01	.00
☐	533	Darrell Evans DP	.08	.04	.01
☐	534	Luis Aquino DP	.03	.01	.00
☐	535	Eric King DP	.03	.01	.00
☐	536	Ken Hill DP	.60	.25	.08
☐	537	Randy Bush DP	.03	.01	.00
☐	538	Shane Mack DP	.08	.04	.01
☐	539	Tom Bolton DP	.03	.01	.00
☐	540	Gene Nelson DP	.03	.01	.00
☐	541	Wes Gardner DP	.03	.01	.00
☐	542	Ken Caminiti DP	.15	.07	.02
☐	543	Duane Ward DP	.10	.05	.01
☐	544	Norm Charlton DP	.15	.07	.02
☐	545	Hal Morris DP	.50	.23	.06
☐	546	Rich Yett DP	.03	.01	.00
☐	547	Hensley Meulens DP	.03	.01	.00
☐	548	Greg A. Harris DP	.03	.01	.00
☐	549	Darren Daulton DP	.13	.06	.02
☐	550	Jeff Hamilton DP	.03	.01	.00
☐	551	Luis Aguayo DP	.03	.01	.00
☐	552	Tim Leary DP	.03	.01	.00
☐	553	Ron Oester DP	.03	.01	.00
☐	554	Steve Lombardozzi DP	.03	.01	.00
☐	555	Tim Jones DP	.03	.01	.00
☐	556	Bud Black DP	.03	.01	.00
☐	557	Alejandro Pena DP	.03	.01	.00
☐	558	Jose DeJesus DP	.03	.01	.00
☐	559	Dennis Rasmussen DP	.03	.01	.00
☐	560	Pat Borders DP	.20	.09	.03
☐	561	Craig Biggio DP	.50	.23	.06
☐	562	Luis DeLosSantos DP	.03	.01	.00
☐	563	Fred Lynn DP	.08	.04	.01
☐	564	Todd Burns DP	.03	.01	.00
☐	565	Felix Fermin DP	.03	.01	.00
☐	566	Darnell Coles DP	.03	.01	.00
☐	567	Willie Fraser DP	.03	.01	.00
☐	568	Glenn Hubbard DP	.03	.01	.00
☐	569	Craig Worthington DP	.03	.01	.00
☐	570	Johnny Paredes DP	.03	.01	.00
☐	571	Don Robinson DP	.03	.01	.00
☐	572	Barry Lyons DP	.03	.01	.00
☐	573	Bill Long DP	.03	.01	.00
☐	574	Tracy Jones DP	.03	.01	.00
☐	575	Juan Nieves DP	.03	.01	.00
☐	576	Andres Thomas DP	.03	.01	.00
☐	577	Rolando Roomes DP	.03	.01	.00
☐	578	Luis Rivera UER DP (Wrong birthdate)	.03	.01	.00
☐	579	Chad Kreuter DP	.15	.07	.02
☐	580	Tony Armas DP	.03	.01	.00
☐	581	Jay Buhner	.20	.09	.03
☐	582	Ricky Horton DP	.03	.01	.00
☐	583	Andy Hawkins DP	.03	.01	.00
☐	584	Sil Campusano	.05	.02	.01
☐	585	Dave Clark	.05	.02	.01
☐	586	Van Snider DP	.03	.01	.00
☐	587	Todd Frohwirth DP	.03	.01	.00
☐	588	Warren Spahn DP PUZ	.10	.05	.01
☐	589	William Brennan	.05	.02	.01
☐	590	German Gonzalez	.05	.02	.01
☐	591	Ernie Whitt DP	.03	.01	.00
☐	592	Jeff Blauser	.15	.07	.02
☐	593	Spike Owen DP	.03	.01	.00
☐	594	Matt Williams	.40	.18	.05
☐	595	Lloyd McClendon DP	.03	.01	.00
☐	596	Steve Ontiveros	.05	.02	.01
☐	597	Scott Medvin	.05	.02	.01
☐	598	Hipolito Pena DP	.03	.01	.00
☐	599	Jerald Clark DP	.05	.02	.01
☐	600A	Checklist 578-660 DP (635 Kurt Schilling)	.25	.11	.03
☐	600B	Checklist 578-660 DP (635 Curt Schilling; MVP's not listed on checklist card)	.05	.02	.01
☐	600C	Checklist 578-660 DP	.05	.02	.01

	(635 Curt Schilling; MVP's listed following 660)			
☐	601 Carmelo Martinez DP	.03	.01	.00
☐	602 Mike LaCoss	.05	.02	.01
☐	603 Mike Devereaux	.10	.05	.01
☐	604 Alex Madrid DP	.03	.01	.00
☐	605 Gary Redus DP	.03	.01	.00
☐	606 Lance Johnson	.10	.05	.01
☐	607 Terry Clark DP	.03	.01	.00
☐	608 Manny Trillo DP	.03	.01	.00
☐	609 Scott Jordan	.10	.05	.01
☐	610 Jay Howell DP	.03	.01	.00
☐	611 Francisco Melendez	.05	.02	.01
☐	612 Mike Boddicker	.05	.02	.01
☐	613 Kevin Brown DP	.10	.05	.01
☐	614 Dave Valle	.05	.02	.01
☐	615 Tim Laudner DP	.03	.01	.00
☐	616 Andy Nezelek UER (Wrong birthdate)	.05	.02	.01
☐	617 Chuck Crim	.05	.02	.01
☐	618 Jack Savage DP	.03	.01	.00
☐	619 Adam Peterson	.05	.02	.01
☐	620 Todd Stottlemyre	.10	.05	.01
☐	621 Lance Blankenship	.05	.02	.01
☐	622 Miguel Garcia DP	.03	.01	.00
☐	623 Keith A. Miller DP	.03	.01	.00
☐	624 Ricky Jordan DP	.03	.01	.00
☐	625 Ernest Riles DP	.03	.01	.00
☐	626 John Moses DP	.03	.01	.00
☐	627 Nelson Liriano DP	.03	.01	.00
☐	628 Mike Smithson DP	.03	.01	.00
☐	629 Scott Sanderson	.05	.02	.01
☐	630 Dale Mohorcic	.05	.02	.01
☐	631 Marvin Freeman DP	.03	.01	.00
☐	632 Mike Young DP	.03	.01	.00
☐	633 Dennis Lamp	.05	.02	.01
☐	634 Dante Bichette DP	.75	.35	.09
☐	635 Curt Schilling DP	.40	.18	.05
☐	636 Scott May DP	.03	.01	.00
☐	637 Mike Schooler	.05	.02	.01
☐	638 Rick Leach	.05	.02	.01
☐	639 Tom Lampkin UER (Throws Left, should be Throws Right)	.05	.02	.01
☐	640 Brian Meyer	.05	.02	.01
☐	641 Brian Harper	.10	.05	.01
☐	642 John Smoltz	.40	.18	.05
☐	643 Jose Canseco (40/40 Club)	.20	.09	.03
☐	644 Bill Schroeder	.05	.02	.01
☐	645 Edgar Martinez	.10	.05	.01
☐	646 Dennis Cook	.05	.02	.01
☐	647 Barry Jones	.05	.02	.01
☐	648 Orel Hershiser (59 and Counting)	.10	.05	.01
☐	649 Rod Nichols	.05	.02	.01
☐	650 Jody Davis	.05	.02	.01
☐	651 Bob Milacki	.05	.02	.01
☐	652 Mike Jackson	.05	.02	.01
☐	653 Derek Lilliquist	.05	.02	.01
☐	654 Paul Mirabella	.05	.02	.01
☐	655 Mike Diaz	.05	.02	.01
☐	656 Jeff Musselman	.05	.02	.01
☐	657 Jerry Reed	.05	.02	.01
☐	658 Kevin Blankenship	.05	.02	.01
☐	659 Wayne Tolleson	.05	.02	.01
☐	660 Eric Hetzel	.05	.02	.01

1989 Donruss Rookies

The 1989 Donruss Rookies set contains 56 standard-size (2 1/2" by 3 1/2") cards. The fronts have green and black borders; the backs are green and feature career highlights. The cards were distributed as a boxed set through the Donruss Dealer Network. Rookie Cards in this set include Jim Abbott, Junior Felix, Steve Finley, Deion Sanders, and Jerome Walton.

		MINT	EXC	G-VG
	COMPLETE FACT.SET (56)	8.00	3.60	1.00
	COMMON CARD (1-56)	.05	.02	.01
☐	1 Gary Sheffield	1.50	.65	.19
☐	2 Gregg Jefferies	.40	.18	.05
☐	3 Ken Griffey Jr.	6.00	2.70	.75
☐	4 Tom Gordon	.20	.09	.03
☐	5 Billy Spiers	.05	.02	.01
☐	6 Deion Sanders	2.50	1.15	.30
☐	7 Donn Pall	.05	.02	.01
☐	8 Steve Carter	.05	.02	.01
☐	9 Francisco Oliveras	.05	.02	.01
☐	10 Steve Wilson	.05	.02	.01
☐	11 Bob Geren	.05	.02	.01
☐	12 Tony Castillo	.05	.02	.01
☐	13 Kenny Rogers	.35	.16	.04
☐	14 Carlos Martinez	.05	.02	.01
☐	15 Edgar Martinez	.10	.05	.01
☐	16 Jim Abbott	1.00	.45	.13
☐	17 Torey Lovullo	.05	.02	.01
☐	18 Mark Carreon	.05	.02	.01
☐	19 Geronimo Berroa	.30	.14	.04
☐	20 Luis Medina	.05	.02	.01
☐	21 Sandy Alomar Jr.	.25	.11	.03
☐	22 Bob Milacki	.05	.02	.01
☐	23 Joe Girardi	.15	.07	.02
☐	24 German Gonzalez	.05	.02	.01
☐	25 Craig Worthington	.05	.02	.01
☐	26 Jerome Walton	.05	.02	.01
☐	27 Gary Wayne	.05	.02	.01
☐	28 Tim Jones	.05	.02	.01
☐	29 Dante Bichette	.75	.35	.09
☐	30 Alexis Infante	.05	.02	.01
☐	31 Ken Hill	.75	.35	.09
☐	32 Dwight Smith	.15	.07	.02
☐	33 Luis de los Santos	.05	.02	.01
☐	34 Eric Yelding	.05	.02	.01
☐	35 Gregg Olson	.20	.09	.03
☐	36 Phil Stephenson	.05	.02	.01
☐	37 Ken Patterson	.05	.02	.01
☐	38 Rick Wrona	.05	.02	.01

☐ 39 Mike Brumley	.05	.02	.01
☐ 40 Cris Carpenter	.05	.02	.01
☐ 41 Jeff Brantley	.05	.02	.01
☐ 42 Ron Jones	.05	.02	.01
☐ 43 Randy Johnson	.75	.35	.09
☐ 44 Kevin Brown	.10	.05	.01
☐ 45 Ramon Martinez	.40	.18	.05
☐ 46 Greg W.Harris	.05	.02	.01
☐ 47 Steve Finley	.25	.11	.03
☐ 48 Randy Kramer	.05	.02	.01
☐ 49 Erik Hanson	.15	.07	.02
☐ 50 Matt Merullo	.05	.02	.01
☐ 51 Mike Devereaux	.10	.05	.01
☐ 52 Clay Parker	.05	.02	.01
☐ 53 Omar Vizquel	.20	.09	.03
☐ 54 Derek Lilliquist	.05	.02	.01
☐ 55 Junior Felix	.20	.09	.03
☐ 56 Checklist 1-56	.05	.02	.01

1990 Donruss

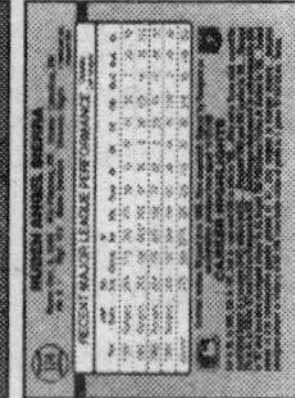

The 1990 Donruss set contains 716 standard-size (2 1/2" by 3 1/2") cards. The front borders are bright red. The horizontally oriented backs are amber. Cards numbered 1-26 are Diamond Kings; cards numbered 28-47 are Rated Rookies (RR). Numbered with the prefix "BC" for bonus card, a 26-card set featuring the most valuable player from each of the 26 teams was randomly inserted in all 1990 Donruss unopened pack formats. Card number 716 was added to the set shortly after the set's initial production, necessitating the checklist variation on card number 700. The set was the largest ever produced by Donruss, unfortunately it also had a large number of errors which were corrected after the cards were released. Every All-Star selection in the set has two versions, the statistical heading on the back is either "Recent Major League Performance" or "All-Star Game Performance." There are a number of cards that have been discovered to have minor printing flaws, which are insignificant variations, that collectors have found unworthy of price differentials. These very minor variations include numbers 1, 18, 154, 168, 206, 270, 321, 347, 405, 408, 425, 583, 585, 619, 637, 639, 699, 701, and 716. The factory sets were distributed without the Bonus Cards; thus there were again new checklist cards printed to reflect the exclusion of the Bonus Cards. These factory set checklist cards are the B variations below (except for 700C). Rookie Cards in this set include Delino DeShields, Juan Gonzalez, Tommy Greene, Marquis Grissom, Dave Justice, Ben McDonald, John Olerud, Dean Palmer, Sammy Sosa, and Larry Walker. The unusual number of cards in the set (716 plus 26 BC's, i.e., not divisible by 132) apparently led to 50 double-printed numbers, which are indicated in the checklists below (1990 Donruss and 1990 Donruss Bonus MVP's) by DP.

	MINT	EXC	G-VG
COMPLETE SET (716)	10.00	4.50	1.25
COMPLETE FACT.SET (728)	10.00	4.50	1.25
COMMON CARD (1-716)	.05	.02	.01
☐ 1 Bo Jackson DK	.20	.09	.03
☐ 2 Steve Sax DK	.08	.04	.01
☐ 3A Ruben Sierra DK ERR (No small line on top border on card back)	.30	.14	.04
☐ 3B Ruben Sierra DK COR	.25	.11	.03
☐ 4 Ken Griffey Jr. DK	.75	.35	.09
☐ 5 Mickey Tettleton DK	.08	.04	.01
☐ 6 Dave Stewart DK	.08	.04	.01
☐ 7 Jim Deshaies DK DP	.08	.04	.01
☐ 8 John Smoltz DK	.10	.05	.01
☐ 9 Mike Bielecki DK	.08	.04	.01
☐ 10A Brian Downing DK ERR (Reverse negative on card front)	.50	.23	.06
☐ 10B Brian Downing DK COR	.08	.04	.01
☐ 11 Kevin Mitchell DK	.10	.05	.01
☐ 12 Kelly Gruber DK	1.50	.65	.19
☐ 13 Joe Magrane DK	.08	.04	.01
☐ 14 John Franco DK	.08	.04	.01
☐ 15 Ozzie Guillen DK	.08	.04	.01
☐ 16 Lou Whitaker DK	.10	.05	.01
☐ 17 John Smiley DK	.08	.04	.01
☐ 18 Howard Johnson DK	.08	.04	.01
☐ 19 Willie Randolph DK	.08	.04	.01
☐ 20 Chris Bosio DK	.08	.04	.01
☐ 21 Tommy Herr DK DP	.08	.04	.01
☐ 22 Dan Gladden DK	.08	.04	.01
☐ 23 Ellis Burks DK	.10	.05	.01
☐ 24 Pete O'Brien DK	.08	.04	.01
☐ 25 Bryn Smith DK	.08	.04	.01
☐ 26 Ed Whitson DK DP	1.50	.65	.19
☐ 27 DK Checklist 1-27 DP (Comments on Perez-Steele on back)	.05	.02	.01
☐ 28 Robin Ventura RR	.50	.23	.06
☐ 29 Todd Zeile RR	.15	.07	.02
☐ 30 Sandy Alomar Jr. RR	.07	.03	.01
☐ 31 Kent Mercker RR	.25	.11	.03
☐ 32 Ben McDonald RR UER (Middle name Benard, not Benjamin)	.40	.18	.05
☐ 33A Juan Gonzalez RR ERR (Reverse negative)	5.00	2.30	.60
☐ 33B Juan Gonzalez RR COR	2.00	.90	.25
☐ 34 Eric Anthony RR	.15	.07	.02
☐ 35 Mike Fetters RR	.05	.02	.01
☐ 36 Marquis Grissom RR	.50	.23	.06
☐ 37 Greg Vaughn RR	.20	.09	.03
☐ 38 Brian DuBois RR	.05	.02	.01
☐ 39 Steve Avery RR UER (Born in MI, not NJ)	.40	.18	.05
☐ 40 Mark Gardner RR	.05	.02	.01
☐ 41 Andy Benes RR	.15	.07	.02

No.	Player			
☐ 42	Delino DeShields RR	.20	.09	.03
☐ 43	Scott Coolbaugh RR	.05	.02	.01
☐ 44	Pat Combs RR DP	.05	.02	.01
☐ 45	Alex Sanchez RR DP	.05	.02	.01
☐ 46	Kelly Mann RR DP	.05	.02	.01
☐ 47	Julio Machado RR DP	.05	.02	.01
☐ 48	Pete Incaviglia	.05	.02	.01
☐ 49	Shawon Dunston	.05	.02	.01
☐ 50	Jeff Treadway	.05	.02	.01
☐ 51	Jeff Ballard	.05	.02	.01
☐ 52	Claudell Washington	.05	.02	.01
☐ 53	Juan Samuel	.05	.02	.01
☐ 54	John Smiley	.05	.02	.01
☐ 55	Rob Deer	.05	.02	.01
☐ 56	Geno Petralli	.05	.02	.01
☐ 57	Chris Bosio	.05	.02	.01
☐ 58	Carlton Fisk	.15	.07	.02
☐ 59	Kirt Manwaring	.05	.02	.01
☐ 60	Chet Lemon	.05	.02	.01
☐ 61	Bo Jackson	.15	.07	.02
☐ 62	Doyle Alexander	.05	.02	.01
☐ 63	Pedro Guerrero	.07	.03	.01
☐ 64	Allan Anderson	.05	.02	.01
☐ 65	Greg W. Harris	.05	.02	.01
☐ 66	Mike Greenwell	.07	.03	.01
☐ 67	Walt Weiss	.05	.02	.01
☐ 68	Wade Boggs	.20	.09	.03
☐ 69	Jim Clancy	.05	.02	.01
☐ 70	Junior Felix	.05	.02	.01
☐ 71	Barry Larkin	.15	.07	.02
☐ 72	Dave LaPoint	.05	.02	.01
☐ 73	Joel Skinner	.05	.02	.01
☐ 74	Jesse Barfield	.05	.02	.01
☐ 75	Tommy Herr	.05	.02	.01
☐ 76	Ricky Jordan	.05	.02	.01
☐ 77	Eddie Murray	.15	.07	.02
☐ 78	Steve Sax	.05	.02	.01
☐ 79	Tim Belcher	.05	.02	.01
☐ 80	Danny Jackson	.05	.02	.01
☐ 81	Kent Hrbek	.07	.03	.01
☐ 82	Milt Thompson	.05	.02	.01
☐ 83	Brook Jacoby	.05	.02	.01
☐ 84	Mike Marshall	.05	.02	.01
☐ 85	Kevin Seitzer	.05	.02	.01
☐ 86	Tony Gwynn	.25	.11	.03
☐ 87	Dave Stieb	.07	.03	.01
☐ 88	Dave Smith	.05	.02	.01
☐ 89	Bret Saberhagen	.07	.03	.01
☐ 90	Alan Trammell	.15	.07	.02
☐ 91	Tony Phillips	.07	.03	.01
☐ 92	Doug Drabek	.15	.07	.02
☐ 93	Jeffrey Leonard	.05	.02	.01
☐ 94	Wally Joyner	.07	.03	.01
☐ 95	Carney Lansford	.07	.03	.01
☐ 96	Cal Ripken	.40	.18	.05
☐ 97	Andres Galarraga	.15	.07	.02
☐ 98	Kevin Mitchell	.07	.03	.01
☐ 99	Howard Johnson	.07	.03	.01
☐ 100A	Checklist 28-129	.05	.02	.01
☐ 100B	Checklist 28-125	.05	.02	.01
☐ 101	Melido Perez	.05	.02	.01
☐ 102	Spike Owen	.05	.02	.01
☐ 103	Paul Molitor	.20	.09	.03
☐ 104	Geronimo Berroa	.07	.03	.01
☐ 105	Ryne Sandberg	.35	.16	.04
☐ 106	Bryn Smith	.05	.02	.01
☐ 107	Steve Buechele	.05	.02	.01
☐ 108	Jim Abbott	.15	.07	.02
☐ 109	Alvin Davis	.05	.02	.01
☐ 110	Lee Smith	.15	.07	.02
☐ 111	Roberto Alomar	.40	.18	.05
☐ 112	Rick Reuschel	.05	.02	.01
☐ 113A	Kelly Gruber ERR (Born 2/22)	.05	.02	.01
☐ 113B	Kelly Gruber COR (Born 2/26; corrected in factory sets)	.05	.02	.01
☐ 114	Joe Carter	.25	.11	.03
☐ 115	Jose Rijo	.07	.03	.01
☐ 116	Greg Minton	.05	.02	.01
☐ 117	Bob Ojeda	.05	.02	.01
☐ 118	Glenn Davis	.05	.02	.01
☐ 119	Jeff Reardon	.15	.07	.02
☐ 120	Kurt Stillwell	.05	.02	.01
☐ 121	John Smoltz	.15	.07	.02
☐ 122	Dwight Evans	.07	.03	.01
☐ 123	Eric Yelding	.05	.02	.01
☐ 124	John Franco	.07	.03	.01
☐ 125	Jose Canseco	.30	.14	.04
☐ 126	Barry Bonds	.50	.23	.06
☐ 127	Lee Guetterman	.05	.02	.01
☐ 128	Jack Clark	.07	.03	.01
☐ 129	Dave Valle	.05	.02	.01
☐ 130	Hubie Brooks	.05	.02	.01
☐ 131	Ernest Riles	.05	.02	.01
☐ 132	Mike Morgan	.05	.02	.01
☐ 133	Steve Jeltz	.05	.02	.01
☐ 134	Jeff D. Robinson	.05	.02	.01
☐ 135	Ozzie Guillen	.05	.02	.01
☐ 136	Chili Davis	.07	.03	.01
☐ 137	Mitch Webster	.05	.02	.01
☐ 138	Jerry Browne	.05	.02	.01
☐ 139	Bo Diaz	.05	.02	.01
☐ 140	Robby Thompson	.07	.03	.01
☐ 141	Craig Worthington	.05	.02	.01
☐ 142	Julio Franco	.07	.03	.01
☐ 143	Brian Holman	.05	.02	.01
☐ 144	George Brett	.30	.14	.04
☐ 145	Tom Glavine	.25	.11	.03
☐ 146	Robin Yount	.20	.09	.03
☐ 147	Gary Carter	.15	.07	.02
☐ 148	Ron Kittle	.05	.02	.01
☐ 149	Tony Fernandez	.07	.03	.01
☐ 150	Dave Stewart	.07	.03	.01
☐ 151	Gary Gaetti	.05	.02	.01
☐ 152	Kevin Elster	.05	.02	.01
☐ 153	Gerald Perry	.05	.02	.01
☐ 154	Jesse Orosco	.05	.02	.01
☐ 155	Wally Backman	.05	.02	.01
☐ 156	Dennis Martinez	.07	.03	.01
☐ 157	Rick Sutcliffe	.07	.03	.01
☐ 158	Greg Maddux	.30	.14	.04
☐ 159	Andy Hawkins	.05	.02	.01
☐ 160	John Kruk	.15	.07	.02
☐ 161	Jose Oquendo	.05	.02	.01
☐ 162	John Dopson	.05	.02	.01
☐ 163	Joe Magrane	.05	.02	.01
☐ 164	Bill Ripken	.05	.02	.01
☐ 165	Fred Manrique	.05	.02	.01
☐ 166	Nolan Ryan UER (Did not lead NL in K's in '89 as he was in AL in '89)	.75	.35	.09
☐ 167	Damon Berryhill	.05	.02	.01
☐ 168	Dale Murphy	.15	.07	.02
☐ 169	Mickey Tettleton	.07	.03	.01
☐ 170A	Kirk McCaskill ERR (Born 4/19)	.05	.02	.01
☐ 170B	Kirk McCaskill COR (Born 4/9; corrected in factory sets)	.05	.02	.01
☐ 171	Dwight Gooden	.07	.03	.01
☐ 172	Jose Lind	.05	.02	.01
☐ 173	B.J. Surhoff	.05	.02	.01
☐ 174	Ruben Sierra	.15	.07	.02
☐ 175	Dan Plesac	.05	.02	.01

☐ 176 Dan Pasqua .05 .02 .01
☐ 177 Kelly Downs .05 .02 .01
☐ 178 Matt Nokes .05 .02 .01
☐ 179 Luis Aquino .05 .02 .01
☐ 180 Frank Tanana .05 .02 .01
☐ 181 Tony Pena .05 .02 .01
☐ 182 Dan Gladden .05 .02 .01
☐ 183 Bruce Hurst .05 .02 .01
☐ 184 Roger Clemens .30 .14 .04
☐ 185 Mark McGwire .15 .07 .02
☐ 186 Rob Murphy .05 .02 .01
☐ 187 Jim Deshaies .05 .02 .01
☐ 188 Fred McGriff .30 .14 .04
☐ 189 Rob Dibble .07 .03 .01
☐ 190 Don Mattingly .35 .16 .04
☐ 191 Felix Fermin .05 .02 .01
☐ 192 Roberto Kelly .07 .03 .01
☐ 193 Dennis Cook .05 .02 .01
☐ 194 Darren Daulton .15 .07 .02
☐ 195 Alfredo Griffin .05 .02 .01
☐ 196 Eric Plunk .05 .02 .01
☐ 197 Orel Hershiser .07 .03 .01
☐ 198 Paul O'Neill .07 .03 .01
☐ 199 Randy Bush .05 .02 .01
☐ 200A Checklist 130-231 .05 .02 .01
☐ 200B Checklist 126-223 .05 .02 .01
☐ 201 Ozzie Smith .25 .11 .03
☐ 202 Pete O'Brien .05 .02 .01
☐ 203 Jay Howell .05 .02 .01
☐ 204 Mark Gubicza .05 .02 .01
☐ 205 Ed Whitson .05 .02 .01
☐ 206 George Bell .07 .03 .01
☐ 207 Mike Scott .05 .02 .01
☐ 208 Charlie Leibrandt .05 .02 .01
☐ 209 Mike Heath .05 .02 .01
☐ 210 Dennis Eckersley .15 .07 .02
☐ 211 Mike LaValliere .05 .02 .01
☐ 212 Darnell Coles .05 .02 .01
☐ 213 Lance Parrish .07 .03 .01
☐ 214 Mike Moore .05 .02 .01
☐ 215 Steve Finley .07 .03 .01
☐ 216 Tim Raines .15 .07 .02
☐ 217A Scott Garrelts ERR .05 .02 .01
(Born 10/20)
☐ 217B Scott Garrelts COR .05 .02 .01
(Born 10/30; corrected in factory sets)
☐ 218 Kevin McReynolds .05 .02 .01
☐ 219 Dave Gallagher .05 .02 .01
☐ 220 Tim Wallach .05 .02 .01
☐ 221 Chuck Crim .05 .02 .01
☐ 222 Lonnie Smith .05 .02 .01
☐ 223 Andre Dawson .15 .07 .02
☐ 224 Nelson Santovenia .05 .02 .01
☐ 225 Rafael Palmeiro .15 .07 .02
☐ 226 Devon White .07 .03 .01
☐ 227 Harold Reynolds .05 .02 .01
☐ 228 Ellis Burks .07 .03 .01
☐ 229 Mark Parent .05 .02 .01
☐ 230 Will Clark .25 .11 .03
☐ 231 Jimmy Key .07 .03 .01
☐ 232 John Farrell .05 .02 .01
☐ 233 Eric Davis .07 .03 .01
☐ 234 Johnny Ray .05 .02 .01
☐ 235 Darryl Strawberry .15 .07 .02
☐ 236 Bill Doran .05 .02 .01
☐ 237 Greg Gagne .05 .02 .01
☐ 238 Jim Eisenreich .05 .02 .01
☐ 239 Tommy Gregg .05 .02 .01
☐ 240 Marty Barrett .05 .02 .01
☐ 241 Rafael Ramirez .05 .02 .01
☐ 242 Chris Sabo .07 .03 .01
☐ 243 Dave Henderson .05 .02 .01
☐ 244 Andy Van Slyke .15 .07 .02
☐ 245 Alvaro Espinoza .05 .02 .01
☐ 246 Garry Templeton .05 .02 .01
☐ 247 Gene Harris .05 .02 .01
☐ 248 Kevin Gross .05 .02 .01
☐ 249 Brett Butler .07 .03 .01
☐ 250 Willie Randolph .07 .03 .01
☐ 251 Roger McDowell .05 .02 .01
☐ 252 Rafael Belliard .05 .02 .01
☐ 253 Steve Rosenberg .05 .02 .01
☐ 254 Jack Howell .05 .02 .01
☐ 255 Marvell Wynne .05 .02 .01
☐ 256 Tom Candiotti .05 .02 .01
☐ 257 Todd Benzinger .05 .02 .01
☐ 258 Don Robinson .05 .02 .01
☐ 259 Phil Bradley .05 .02 .01
☐ 260 Cecil Espy .05 .02 .01
☐ 261 Scott Bankhead .05 .02 .01
☐ 262 Frank White .07 .03 .01
☐ 263 Andres Thomas .05 .02 .01
☐ 264 Glenn Braggs .05 .02 .01
☐ 265 David Cone .15 .07 .02
☐ 266 Bobby Thigpen .05 .02 .01
☐ 267 Nelson Liriano .05 .02 .01
☐ 268 Terry Steinbach .07 .03 .01
☐ 269 Kirby Puckett UER .35 .16 .04
(Back doesn't consider Joe Torre's .363 in '71)
☐ 270 Gregg Jefferies .25 .11 .03
☐ 271 Jeff Blauser .07 .03 .01
☐ 272 Cory Snyder .05 .02 .01
☐ 273 Roy Smith .05 .02 .01
☐ 274 Tom Foley .05 .02 .01
☐ 275 Mitch Williams .07 .03 .01
☐ 276 Paul Kilgus .05 .02 .01
☐ 277 Don Slaught .05 .02 .01
☐ 278 Von Hayes .05 .02 .01
☐ 279 Vince Coleman .07 .03 .01
☐ 280 Mike Boddicker .05 .02 .01
☐ 281 Ken Dayley .05 .02 .01
☐ 282 Mike Devereaux .07 .03 .01
☐ 283 Kenny Rogers .05 .02 .01
☐ 284 Jeff Russell .05 .02 .01
☐ 285 Jerome Walton .05 .02 .01
☐ 286 Derek Lilliquist .05 .02 .01
☐ 287 Joe Orsulak .05 .02 .01
☐ 288 Dick Schofield .05 .02 .01
☐ 289 Ron Darling .05 .02 .01
☐ 290 Bobby Bonilla .15 .07 .02
☐ 291 Jim Gantner .05 .02 .01
☐ 292 Bobby Witt .05 .02 .01
☐ 293 Greg Brock .05 .02 .01
☐ 294 Ivan Calderon .05 .02 .01
☐ 295 Steve Bedrosian .05 .02 .01
☐ 296 Mike Henneman .05 .02 .01
☐ 297 Tom Gordon .07 .03 .01
☐ 298 Lou Whitaker .15 .07 .02
☐ 299 Terry Pendleton .15 .07 .02
☐ 300A Checklist 232-333 .05 .02 .01
☐ 300B Checklist 224-321 .05 .02 .01
☐ 301 Juan Berenguer .05 .02 .01
☐ 302 Mark Davis .05 .02 .01
☐ 303 Nick Esasky .05 .02 .01
☐ 304 Rickey Henderson .15 .07 .02
☐ 305 Rick Cerone .05 .02 .01
☐ 306 Craig Biggio .15 .07 .02
☐ 307 Duane Ward .07 .03 .01
☐ 308 Tom Browning .05 .02 .01
☐ 309 Walt Terrell .05 .02 .01
☐ 310 Greg Swindell .07 .03 .01
☐ 311 Dave Righetti .05 .02 .01
☐ 312 Mike Maddux .05 .02 .01
☐ 313 Len Dykstra .15 .07 .02

☐ 314 Jose Gonzalez	.05	.02	.01
☐ 315 Steve Balboni	.05	.02	.01
☐ 316 Mike Scioscia	.05	.02	.01
☐ 317 Ron Oester	.05	.02	.01
☐ 318 Gary Wayne	.05	.02	.01
☐ 319 Todd Worrell	.05	.02	.01
☐ 320 Doug Jones	.05	.02	.01
☐ 321 Jeff Hamilton	.05	.02	.01
☐ 322 Danny Tartabull	.07	.03	.01
☐ 323 Chris James	.05	.02	.01
☐ 324 Mike Flanagan	.05	.02	.01
☐ 325 Gerald Young	.05	.02	.01
☐ 326 Bob Boone	.07	.03	.01
☐ 327 Frank Williams	.05	.02	.01
☐ 328 Dave Parker	.15	.07	.02
☐ 329 Sid Bream	.05	.02	.01
☐ 330 Mike Schooler	.05	.02	.01
☐ 331 Bert Blyleven	.15	.07	.02
☐ 332 Bob Welch	.05	.02	.01
☐ 333 Bob Milacki	.05	.02	.01
☐ 334 Tim Burke	.05	.02	.01
☐ 335 Jose Uribe	.05	.02	.01
☐ 336 Randy Myers	.07	.03	.01
☐ 337 Eric King	.05	.02	.01
☐ 338 Mark Langston	.15	.07	.02
☐ 339 Teddy Higuera	.05	.02	.01
☐ 340 Oddibe McDowell	.05	.02	.01
☐ 341 Lloyd McClendon	.05	.02	.01
☐ 342 Pascual Perez	.05	.02	.01
☐ 343 Kevin Brown UER (Signed is misspelled as signeed on back)	.07	.03	.01
☐ 344 Chuck Finley	.07	.03	.01
☐ 345 Erik Hanson	.07	.03	.01
☐ 346 Rich Gedman	.05	.02	.01
☐ 347 Bip Roberts	.07	.03	.01
☐ 348 Matt Williams	.25	.11	.03
☐ 349 Tom Henke	.07	.03	.01
☐ 350 Brad Komminsk	.05	.02	.01
☐ 351 Jeff Reed	.05	.02	.01
☐ 352 Brian Downing	.05	.02	.01
☐ 353 Frank Viola	.07	.03	.01
☐ 354 Terry Puhl	.05	.02	.01
☐ 355 Brian Harper	.07	.03	.01
☐ 356 Steve Farr	.05	.02	.01
☐ 357 Joe Boever	.05	.02	.01
☐ 358 Danny Heep	.05	.02	.01
☐ 359 Larry Andersen	.05	.02	.01
☐ 360 Rolando Roomes	.05	.02	.01
☐ 361 Mike Gallego	.05	.02	.01
☐ 362 Bob Kipper	.05	.02	.01
☐ 363 Clay Parker	.05	.02	.01
☐ 364 Mike Pagliarulo	.05	.02	.01
☐ 365 Ken Griffey Jr. UER (Signed through 1990, should be 1991)	2.50	1.15	.30
☐ 366 Rex Hudler	.05	.02	.01
☐ 367 Pat Sheridan	.05	.02	.01
☐ 368 Kirk Gibson	.07	.03	.01
☐ 369 Jeff Parrett	.05	.02	.01
☐ 370 Bob Walk	.05	.02	.01
☐ 371 Ken Patterson	.05	.02	.01
☐ 372 Bryan Harvey	.07	.03	.01
☐ 373 Mike Bielecki	.05	.02	.01
☐ 374 Tom Magrann	.05	.02	.01
☐ 375 Rick Mahler	.05	.02	.01
☐ 376 Craig Lefferts	.05	.02	.01
☐ 377 Gregg Olson	.07	.03	.01
☐ 378 Jamie Moyer	.05	.02	.01
☐ 379 Randy Johnson	.25	.11	.03
☐ 380 Jeff Montgomery	.07	.03	.01
☐ 381 Marty Clary	.05	.02	.01
☐ 382 Bill Spiers	.05	.02	.01
☐ 383 Dave Magadan	.05	.02	.01
☐ 384 Greg Hibbard	.05	.02	.01
☐ 385 Ernie Whitt	.05	.02	.01
☐ 386 Rick Honeycutt	.05	.02	.01
☐ 387 Dave West	.05	.02	.01
☐ 388 Keith Hernandez	.07	.03	.01
☐ 389 Jose Alvarez	.05	.02	.01
☐ 390 Joey Belle	1.50	.65	.19
☐ 391 Rick Aguilera	.07	.03	.01
☐ 392 Mike Fitzgerald	.05	.02	.01
☐ 393 Dwight Smith	.05	.02	.01
☐ 394 Steve Wilson	.05	.02	.01
☐ 395 Bob Geren	.05	.02	.01
☐ 396 Randy Ready	.05	.02	.01
☐ 397 Ken Hill	.15	.07	.02
☐ 398 Jody Reed	.05	.02	.01
☐ 399 Tom Brunansky	.05	.02	.01
☐ 400A Checklist 334-435	.05	.02	.01
☐ 400B Checklist 322-419	.05	.02	.01
☐ 401 Rene Gonzales	.05	.02	.01
☐ 402 Harold Baines	.07	.03	.01
☐ 403 Cecilio Guante	.05	.02	.01
☐ 404 Joe Girardi	.05	.02	.01
☐ 405A Sergio Valdez ERR (Card front shows black line crossing S in Sergio)	.15	.07	.02
☐ 405B Sergio Valdez COR	.05	.02	.01
☐ 406 Mark Williamson	.05	.02	.01
☐ 407 Glenn Hoffman	.05	.02	.01
☐ 408 Jeff Innis	.05	.02	.01
☐ 409 Randy Kramer	.05	.02	.01
☐ 410 Charlie O'Brien	.05	.02	.01
☐ 411 Charlie Hough	.05	.02	.01
☐ 412 Gus Polidor	.05	.02	.01
☐ 413 Ron Karkovice	.05	.02	.01
☐ 414 Trevor Wilson	.05	.02	.01
☐ 415 Kevin Ritz	.05	.02	.01
☐ 416 Gary Thurman	.05	.02	.01
☐ 417 Jeff M. Robinson	.05	.02	.01
☐ 418 Scott Terry	.05	.02	.01
☐ 419 Tim Laudner	.05	.02	.01
☐ 420 Dennis Rasmussen	.05	.02	.01
☐ 421 Luis Rivera	.05	.02	.01
☐ 422 Jim Corsi	.05	.02	.01
☐ 423 Dennis Lamp	.05	.02	.01
☐ 424 Ken Caminiti	.07	.03	.01
☐ 425 David Wells	.05	.02	.01
☐ 426 Norm Charlton	.07	.03	.01
☐ 427 Deion Sanders	.50	.23	.06
☐ 428 Dion James	.05	.02	.01
☐ 429 Chuck Cary	.05	.02	.01
☐ 430 Ken Howell	.05	.02	.01
☐ 431 Steve Lake	.05	.02	.01
☐ 432 Kal Daniels	.05	.02	.01
☐ 433 Lance McCullers	.05	.02	.01
☐ 434 Lenny Harris	.05	.02	.01
☐ 435 Scott Scudder	.05	.02	.01
☐ 436 Gene Larkin	.05	.02	.01
☐ 437 Dan Quisenberry	.07	.03	.01
☐ 438 Steve Olin	.07	.03	.01
☐ 439 Mickey Hatcher	.05	.02	.01
☐ 440 Willie Wilson	.05	.02	.01
☐ 441 Mark Grant	.05	.02	.01
☐ 442 Mookie Wilson	.05	.02	.01
☐ 443 Alex Trevino	.05	.02	.01
☐ 444 Pat Tabler	.05	.02	.01
☐ 445 Dave Bergman	.05	.02	.01
☐ 446 Todd Burns	.05	.02	.01
☐ 447 R.J. Reynolds	.05	.02	.01
☐ 448 Jay Buhner	.15	.07	.02
☐ 449 Lee Stevens	.05	.02	.01
☐ 450 Ron Hassey	.05	.02	.01

	No.	Player			
☐	451	Bob Melvin	.05	.02	.01
☐	452	Dave Martinez	.05	.02	.01
☐	453	Greg Litton	.05	.02	.01
☐	454	Mark Carreon	.05	.02	.01
☐	455	Scott Fletcher	.05	.02	.01
☐	456	Otis Nixon	.07	.03	.01
☐	457	Tony Fossas	.05	.02	.01
☐	458	John Russell	.05	.02	.01
☐	459	Paul Assenmacher	.05	.02	.01
☐	460	Zane Smith	.05	.02	.01
☐	461	Jack Daugherty	.05	.02	.01
☐	462	Rich Monteleone	.05	.02	.01
☐	463	Greg Briley	.05	.02	.01
☐	464	Mike Smithson	.05	.02	.01
☐	465	Benito Santiago	.07	.03	.01
☐	466	Jeff Brantley	.05	.02	.01
☐	467	Jose Nunez	.05	.02	.01
☐	468	Scott Bailes	.05	.02	.01
☐	469	Ken Griffey	.07	.03	.01
☐	470	Bob McClure	.05	.02	.01
☐	471	Mackey Sasser	.05	.02	.01
☐	472	Glenn Wilson	.05	.02	.01
☐	473	Kevin Tapani	.20	.09	.03
☐	474	Bill Buckner	.07	.03	.01
☐	475	Ron Gant	.20	.09	.03
☐	476	Kevin Romine	.05	.02	.01
☐	477	Juan Agosto	.05	.02	.01
☐	478	Herm Winningham	.05	.02	.01
☐	479	Storm Davis	.05	.02	.01
☐	480	Jeff King	.07	.03	.01
☐	481	Kevin Mmahat	.07	.03	.01
☐	482	Carmelo Martinez	.05	.02	.01
☐	483	Omar Vizquel	.05	.02	.01
☐	484	Jim Dwyer	.05	.02	.01
☐	485	Bob Knepper	.05	.02	.01
☐	486	Dave Anderson	.05	.02	.01
☐	487	Ron Jones	.05	.02	.01
☐	488	Jay Bell	.07	.03	.01
☐	489	Sammy Sosa	.50	.23	.06
☐	490	Kent Anderson	.05	.02	.01
☐	491	Domingo Ramos	.05	.02	.01
☐	492	Dave Clark	.05	.02	.01
☐	493	Tim Birtsas	.05	.02	.01
☐	494	Ken Oberkfell	.05	.02	.01
☐	495	Larry Sheets	.05	.02	.01
☐	496	Jeff Kunkel	.05	.02	.01
☐	497	Jim Presley	.05	.02	.01
☐	498	Mike Macfarlane	.05	.02	.01
☐	499	Pete Smith	.05	.02	.01
☐	500A	Checklist 436-537 DP	.05	.02	.01
☐	500B	Checklist 420-517	.05	.02	.01
☐	501	Gary Sheffield	.30	.14	.04
☐	502	Terry Bross	.05	.02	.01
☐	503	Jerry Kutzler	.05	.02	.01
☐	504	Lloyd Moseby	.05	.02	.01
☐	505	Curt Young	.05	.02	.01
☐	506	Al Newman	.05	.02	.01
☐	507	Keith Miller	.05	.02	.01
☐	508	Mike Stanton	.05	.02	.01
☐	509	Rich Yett	.05	.02	.01
☐	510	Tim Drummond	.05	.02	.01
☐	511	Joe Hesketh	.05	.02	.01
☐	512	Rick Wrona	.05	.02	.01
☐	513	Luis Salazar	.05	.02	.01
☐	514	Hal Morris	.07	.03	.01
☐	515	Terry Mulholland	.07	.03	.01
☐	516	John Morris	.05	.02	.01
☐	517	Carlos Quintana	.05	.02	.01
☐	518	Frank DiPino	.05	.02	.01
☐	519	Randy Milligan	.05	.02	.01
☐	520	Chad Kreuter	.05	.02	.01
☐	521	Mike Jeffcoat	.05	.02	.01
☐	522	Mike Harkey	.05	.02	.01
☐	523A	Andy Nezelek ERR (Born 10-24-85)	.05	.02	.01
☐	523B	Andy Nezelek COR (Corrected in factory sets: 10-25-65)	.15	.07	.02
☐	524	Dave Schmidt	.05	.02	.01
☐	525	Tony Armas	.05	.02	.01
☐	526	Barry Lyons	.05	.02	.01
☐	527	Rick Reed	.05	.02	.01
☐	528	Jerry Reuss	.05	.02	.01
☐	529	Dean Palmer	.25	.11	.03
☐	530	Jeff Peterek	.05	.02	.01
☐	531	Carlos Martinez	.05	.02	.01
☐	532	Atlee Hammaker	.05	.02	.01
☐	533	Mike Brumley	.05	.02	.01
☐	534	Terry Leach	.05	.02	.01
☐	535	Doug Strange	.05	.02	.01
☐	536	Jose DeLeon	.05	.02	.01
☐	537	Shane Rawley	.05	.02	.01
☐	538	Joey Cora	.05	.02	.01
☐	539	Eric Hetzel	.05	.02	.01
☐	540	Gene Nelson	.05	.02	.01
☐	541	Wes Gardner	.05	.02	.01
☐	542	Mark Portugal	.05	.02	.01
☐	543	Al Leiter	.05	.02	.01
☐	544	Jack Armstrong	.05	.02	.01
☐	545	Greg Cadaret	.05	.02	.01
☐	546	Rod Nichols	.05	.02	.01
☐	547	Luis Polonia	.07	.03	.01
☐	548	Charlie Hayes	.07	.03	.01
☐	549	Dickie Thon	.05	.02	.01
☐	550	Tim Crews	.05	.02	.01
☐	551	Dave Winfield	.15	.07	.02
☐	552	Mike Davis	.05	.02	.01
☐	553	Ron Robinson	.05	.02	.01
☐	554	Carmen Castillo	.05	.02	.01
☐	555	John Costello	.05	.02	.01
☐	556	Bud Black	.05	.02	.01
☐	557	Rick Dempsey	.05	.02	.01
☐	558	Jim Acker	.05	.02	.01
☐	559	Eric Show	.05	.02	.01
☐	560	Pat Borders	.07	.03	.01
☐	561	Danny Darwin	.05	.02	.01
☐	562	Rick Luecken	.05	.02	.01
☐	563	Edwin Nunez	.05	.02	.01
☐	564	Felix Jose	.07	.03	.01
☐	565	John Cangelosi	.05	.02	.01
☐	566	Bill Swift	.07	.03	.01
☐	567	Bill Schroeder	.05	.02	.01
☐	568	Stan Javier	.05	.02	.01
☐	569	Jim Traber	.05	.02	.01
☐	570	Wallace Johnson	.05	.02	.01
☐	571	Donell Nixon	.05	.02	.01
☐	572	Sid Fernandez	.07	.03	.01
☐	573	Lance Johnson	.07	.03	.01
☐	574	Andy McGaffigan	.05	.02	.01
☐	575	Mark Knudson	.05	.02	.01
☐	576	Tommy Greene	.15	.07	.02
☐	577	Mark Grace	.20	.09	.03
☐	578	Larry Walker	.50	.23	.06
☐	579	Mike Stanley	.05	.02	.01
☐	580	Mike Witt DP	.05	.02	.01
☐	581	Scott Bradley	.05	.02	.01
☐	582	Greg A. Harris	.05	.02	.01
☐	583A	Kevin Hickey ERR	.15	.07	.02
☐	583B	Kevin Hickey COR	.05	.02	.01
☐	584	Lee Mazzilli	.05	.02	.01
☐	585	Jeff Pico	.05	.02	.01
☐	586	Joe Oliver	.05	.02	.01
☐	587	Willie Fraser DP	.05	.02	.01
☐	588	Carl Yastrzemski Puzzle Card DP	.15	.07	.02
☐	589	Kevin Bass DP	.05	.02	.01

☐ 590 John Moses DP .05 .02 .01
☐ 591 Tom Pagnozzi DP .05 .02 .01
☐ 592 Tony Castillo DP .05 .02 .01
☐ 593 Jerald Clark DP .05 .02 .01
☐ 594 Dan Schatzeder .05 .02 .01
☐ 595 Luis Quinones DP .05 .02 .01
☐ 596 Pete Harnisch DP .07 .03 .01
☐ 597 Gary Redus .05 .02 .01
☐ 598 Mel Hall .05 .02 .01
☐ 599 Rick Schu .05 .02 .01
☐ 600A Checklist 538-639 .05 .02 .01
☐ 600B Checklist 518-617 .05 .02 .01
☐ 601 Mike Kingery DP .05 .02 .01
☐ 602 Terry Kennedy DP .05 .02 .01
☐ 603 Mike Sharperson DP .05 .02 .01
☐ 604 Don Carman DP .05 .02 .01
☐ 605 Jim Gott .05 .02 .01
☐ 606 Donn Pall DP .05 .02 .01
☐ 607 Rance Mulliniks .05 .02 .01
☐ 608 Curt Wilkerson DP .05 .02 .01
☐ 609 Mike Felder DP .05 .02 .01
☐ 610 Guillermo Hernandez DP .05 .02 .01
☐ 611 Candy Maldonado DP .05 .02 .01
☐ 612 Mark Thurmond DP .05 .02 .01
☐ 613 Rick Leach DP .05 .02 .01
☐ 614 Jerry Reed DP .05 .02 .01
☐ 615 Franklin Stubbs .05 .02 .01
☐ 616 Billy Hatcher DP .05 .02 .01
☐ 617 Don August DP .05 .02 .01
☐ 618 Tim Teufel .05 .02 .01
☐ 619 Shawn Hillegas DP .05 .02 .01
☐ 620 Manny Lee .05 .02 .01
☐ 621 Gary Ward DP .05 .02 .01
☐ 622 Mark Guthrie DP .05 .02 .01
☐ 623 Jeff Musselman DP .05 .02 .01
☐ 624 Mark Lemke DP .07 .03 .01
☐ 625 Fernando Valenzuela .05 .02 .01
☐ 626 Paul Sorrento DP .15 .07 .02
☐ 627 Glenallen Hill DP .05 .02 .01
☐ 628 Les Lancaster DP .05 .02 .01
☐ 629 Vance Law DP .05 .02 .01
☐ 630 Randy Velarde DP .05 .02 .01
☐ 631 Todd Frohwirth DP .05 .02 .01
☐ 632 Willie McGee .07 .03 .01
☐ 633 Dennis Boyd DP .05 .02 .01
☐ 634 Cris Carpenter DP .05 .02 .01
☐ 635 Brian Holton .05 .02 .01
☐ 636 Tracy Jones DP .05 .02 .01
☐ 637A Terry Steinbach AS .10 .05 .01
(Recent Major
League Performance)
☐ 637B Terry Steinbach AS .05 .02 .01
(All-Star Game
Performance)
☐ 638 Brady Anderson .07 .03 .01
☐ 639A Jack Morris ERR .15 .07 .02
(Card front shows
black line crossing
J in Jack)
☐ 639B Jack Morris COR .15 .07 .02
☐ 640 Jaime Navarro .05 .02 .01
☐ 641 Darrin Jackson .05 .02 .01
☐ 642 Mike Dyer .05 .02 .01
☐ 643 Mike Schmidt .25 .11 .03
☐ 644 Henry Cotto .05 .02 .01
☐ 645 John Cerutti .05 .02 .01
☐ 646 Francisco Cabrera .05 .02 .01
☐ 647 Scott Sanderson .05 .02 .01
☐ 648 Brian Meyer .05 .02 .01
☐ 649 Ray Searage .05 .02 .01
☐ 650A Bo Jackson AS .10 .05 .01
(Recent Major
League Performance)
☐ 650B Bo Jackson AS .07 .03 .01
(All-Star Game
Performance)
☐ 651 Steve Lyons .05 .02 .01
☐ 652 Mike LaCoss .05 .02 .01
☐ 653 Ted Power .05 .02 .01
☐ 654A Howard Johnson AS .10 .05 .01
(Recent Major
League Performance)
☐ 654B Howard Johnson AS .05 .02 .01
(All-Star Game
Performance)
☐ 655 Mauro Gozzo .05 .02 .01
☐ 656 Mike Blowers .05 .02 .01
☐ 657 Paul Gibson .05 .02 .01
☐ 658 Neal Heaton .05 .02 .01
☐ 659A Nolan Ryan 5000K 2.50 1.15 .30
(665 King of
Kings back) ERR
☐ 659B Nolan Ryan 5000K .50 .23 .06
COR (Still an error as
Ryan did not lead AL
in K's in '75)
☐ 660A Harold Baines AS 1.50 .65 .19
(Black line through
star on front;
Recent Major
League Performance)
☐ 660B Harold Baines AS 2.00 .90 .25
(Black line through
star on front;
All-Star Game
Performance)
☐ 660C Harold Baines AS .50 .23 .06
(Black line behind
star on front;
Recent Major
League Performance)
☐ 660D Harold Baines AS .05 .02 .01
(Black line behind
star on front;
All-Star Game
Performance)
☐ 661 Gary Pettis .05 .02 .01
☐ 662 Clint Zavaras .05 .02 .01
☐ 663A Rick Reuschel AS .10 .05 .01
(Recent Major
League Performance)
☐ 663B Rick Reuschel AS .05 .02 .01
(All-Star Game
Performance)
☐ 664 Alejandro Pena .05 .02 .01
☐ 665A Nolan Ryan KING 2.50 1.15 .30
(659 5000 K
back) ERR
☐ 665B Nolan Ryan KING COR .50 .23 .06
☐ 665C Nolan Ryan KING ERR .75 .35 .09
(No number on back;
in factory sets)
☐ 666 Ricky Horton .05 .02 .01
☐ 667 Curt Schilling .07 .03 .01
☐ 668 Bill Landrum .05 .02 .01
☐ 669 Todd Stottlemyre .07 .03 .01
☐ 670 Tim Leary .05 .02 .01
☐ 671 John Wetteland .07 .03 .01
☐ 672 Calvin Schiraldi .05 .02 .01
☐ 673A Ruben Sierra AS .25 .11 .03
(Recent Major
League Performance)
☐ 673B Ruben Sierra AS .10 .05 .01
(All-Star Game
Performance)
☐ 674A Pedro Guerrero AS .10 .05 .01

(Recent Major League Performance)
☐ 674B Pedro Guerrero AS .... .05 .02 .01
(All-Star Game Performance)
☐ 675 Ken Phelps .... .05 .02 .01
☐ 676A Cal Ripken AS .... .50 .23 .06
(Recent Major League Performance)
☐ 676B Cal Ripken AS .... .25 .11 .03
(All-Star Game Performance)
☐ 677 Denny Walling .... .05 .02 .01
☐ 678 Goose Gossage .... .15 .07 .02
☐ 679 Gary Mielke .... .05 .02 .01
☐ 680 Bill Bathe .... .05 .02 .01
☐ 681 Tom Lawless .... .05 .02 .01
☐ 682 Xavier Hernandez .... .05 .02 .01
☐ 683A Kirby Puckett AS .... .40 .18 .05
(Recent Major League Performance)
☐ 683B Kirby Puckett AS .... .20 .09 .03
(All-Star Game Performance)
☐ 684 Mariano Duncan .... .05 .02 .01
☐ 685 Ramon Martinez .... .07 .03 .01
☐ 686 Tim Jones .... .05 .02 .01
☐ 687 Tom Filer .... .05 .02 .01
☐ 688 Steve Lombardozzi .... .05 .02 .01
☐ 689 Bernie Williams .... .25 .11 .03
☐ 690 Chip Hale .... .05 .02 .01
☐ 691 Beau Allred .... .05 .02 .01
☐ 692A Ryne Sandberg AS .... .40 .18 .05
(Recent Major League Performance)
☐ 692B Ryne Sandberg AS .... .20 .09 .03
(All-Star Game Performance)
☐ 693 Jeff Huson .... .05 .02 .01
☐ 694 Curt Ford .... .05 .02 .01
☐ 695A Eric Davis AS .... .10 .05 .01
(Recent Major League Performance)
☐ 695B Eric Davis AS .... .05 .02 .01
(All-Star Game Performance)
☐ 696 Scott Lusader .... .05 .02 .01
☐ 697A Mark McGwire AS .... .10 .05 .01
(Recent Major League Performance)
☐ 697B Mark McGwire AS .... .07 .03 .01
(All-Star Game Performance)
☐ 698 Steve Cummings .... .05 .02 .01
☐ 699 George Canale .... .05 .02 .01
☐ 700A Checklist 640-715 .... .40 .05 .01
and BC1-BC26
☐ 700B Checklist 640-716 .... .10 .05 .01
and BC1-BC26
☐ 700C Checklist 618-716 .... .05 .02 .01
☐ 701A Julio Franco AS .... .10 .05 .01
(Recent Major League Performance)
☐ 701B Julio Franco AS .... .05 .02 .01
(All-Star Game Performance)
☐ 702 Dave Johnson (P) .... .05 .02 .01
☐ 703A Dave Stewart AS .... .10 .05 .01
(Recent Major League Performance)
☐ 703B Dave Stewart AS .... .05 .02 .01
(All-Star Game Performance)
☐ 704 David Justice .... 1.00 .45 .13
☐ 705A Tony Gwynn AS .... .25 .11 .03
(Recent Major League Performance)
☐ 705B Tony Gwynn AS .... .10 .05 .01
(All-Star Game Performance)
☐ 706 Greg Myers .... .05 .02 .01
☐ 707A Will Clark AS .... .25 .11 .03
(Recent Major League Performance)
☐ 707B Will Clark AS .... .15 .07 .02
(All-Star Game Performance)
☐ 708A Benito Santiago AS .... .10 .05 .01
(Recent Major League Performance)
☐ 708B Benito Santiago AS .... .05 .02 .01
(All-Star Game Performance)
☐ 709 Larry McWilliams .... .05 .02 .01
☐ 710A Ozzie Smith AS .... .10 .05 .01
(Recent Major League Performance)
☐ 710B Ozzie Smith AS .... .05 .02 .01
(All-Star Game Performance)
☐ 711 John Olerud .... .60 .25 .08
☐ 712A Wade Boggs AS .... .20 .09 .03
(Recent Major League Performance)
☐ 712B Wade Boggs AS .... .05 .02 .01
(All-Star Game Performance)
☐ 713 Gary Eave .... .05 .02 .01
☐ 714 Bob Tewksbury .... .07 .03 .01
☐ 715A Kevin Mitchell AS .... .10 .05 .01
(Recent Major League Performance)
☐ 715B Kevin Mitchell AS .... .05 .02 .01
(All-Star Game Performance)
☐ 716 Bart Giamatti COMM .... .20 .09 .03
(In Memoriam)

1990 Donruss Rookies

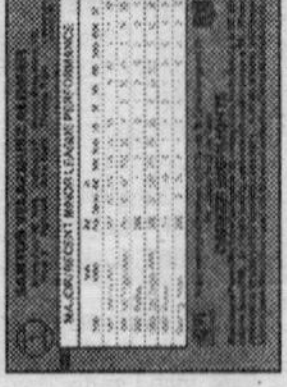

The 1990 Donruss Rookies set marked the fifth consecutive year that Donruss issued a boxed set honoring the best rookies of the season. This set, which used the 1990 Donruss design but featured a green bor-

der, was issued exclusively through the Donruss dealer network to hobby dealers. This 56-card, standard size, 2 1/2" by 3 1/2" set came in its own box and the words "The Rookies" are featured prominently on the front of the cards. The key Rookie Cards in this set are Carlos Baerga and Dave Hollins.

	MINT	EXC	G-VG
COMPLETE FACT.SET (56)	3.00	1.35	.40
COMMON CARD (1-56)	.05	.02	.01
☐ 1 Sandy Alomar Jr. UER (No stitches on baseball on Donruss logo on card front)	.08	.04	.01
☐ 2 John Olerud	.40	.18	.05
☐ 3 Pat Combs	.05	.02	.01
☐ 4 Brian DuBois	.05	.02	.01
☐ 5 Felix Jose	.08	.04	.01
☐ 6 Delino DeShields	.15	.07	.02
☐ 7 Mike Stanton	.08	.04	.01
☐ 8 Mike Munoz	.05	.02	.01
☐ 9 Craig Grebeck	.05	.02	.01
☐ 10 Joe Kraemer	.05	.02	.01
☐ 11 Jeff Huson	.05	.02	.01
☐ 12 Bill Sampen	.05	.02	.01
☐ 13 Brian Bohanon	.05	.02	.01
☐ 14 David Justice	.75	.35	.09
☐ 15 Robin Ventura	.50	.23	.06
☐ 16 Greg Vaughn	.25	.11	.03
☐ 17 Wayne Edwards	.05	.02	.01
☐ 18 Shawn Boskie	.05	.02	.01
☐ 19 Carlos Baerga	1.00	.45	.13
☐ 20 Mark Gardner	.05	.02	.01
☐ 21 Kevin Appier	.30	.14	.04
☐ 22 Mike Harkey	.05	.02	.01
☐ 23 Tim Layana	.05	.02	.01
☐ 24 Glenallen Hill	.05	.02	.01
☐ 25 Jerry Kutzler	.05	.02	.01
☐ 26 Mike Blowers	.05	.02	.01
☐ 27 Scott Ruskin	.05	.02	.01
☐ 28 Dana Kiecker	.05	.02	.01
☐ 29 Willie Blair	.05	.02	.01
☐ 30 Ben McDonald	.30	.14	.04
☐ 31 Todd Zeile	.10	.05	.01
☐ 32 Scott Coolbaugh	.05	.02	.01
☐ 33 Xavier Hernandez	.05	.02	.01
☐ 34 Mike Hartley	.05	.02	.01
☐ 35 Kevin Tapani	.15	.07	.02
☐ 36 Kevin Wickander	.05	.02	.01
☐ 37 Carlos Hernandez	.05	.02	.01
☐ 38 Brian Traxler	.05	.02	.01
☐ 39 Marty Brown	.05	.02	.01
☐ 40 Scott Radinsky	.05	.02	.01
☐ 41 Julio Machado	.05	.02	.01
☐ 42 Steve Avery	.40	.18	.05
☐ 43 Mark Lemke	.08	.04	.01
☐ 44 Alan Mills	.05	.02	.01
☐ 45 Marquis Grissom	.40	.18	.05
☐ 46 Greg Olson	.05	.02	.01
☐ 47 Dave Hollins	.25	.11	.03
☐ 48 Jerald Clark	.05	.02	.01
☐ 49 Eric Anthony	.08	.04	.01
☐ 50 Tim Drummond	.05	.02	.01
☐ 51 John Burkett	.25	.11	.03
☐ 52 Brent Knackert	.05	.02	.01
☐ 53 Jeff Shaw	.05	.02	.01
☐ 54 John Orton	.05	.02	.01
☐ 55 Terry Shumpert	.05	.02	.01
☐ 56 Checklist 1-56	.05	.02	.01

1991 Donruss

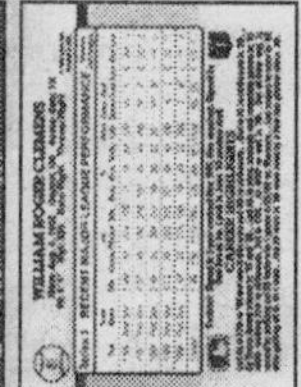

The 1991 Donruss set was issued in two series of 386 and 384 for of 770 cards. Twenty-two bonus cards, which can be considered part of the set, were randomly inserted in packs for a total of 792 cards. This set marked the first time Donruss issued cards in multiple series. First series cards feature a blue borders and second series green borders with some stripes and the players name in white against a red background. The cards measure the standard size of 2 1/2" by 3 1/2". The first 26 cards again feature the artwork of Dick Perez drawing each team's Diamond King. The first series also contains 20 Rated Rookie (RR) cards and nine All-Star cards (the AS cards are all American Leaguers in this first series). On cards 60, 70, 127, 182, 239, 294, 355, 368, and 377, the border stripes are red and yellow. As a separate promotion, wax packs were also given away with six and 12-packs of Coke and Diet Coke. Rookie Cards in the set include Wes Chamberlain, Jeff Conine, Luis Gonzalez, Brian McRae, Pedro Munoz, and Phil Plantier. The second series was issued approximately three months after the first series was issued. This series features the 26 MVP cards which Donruss had issued for the three previous years as their Bonus Cards, twenty more rated rookie cards and nine All-Star Cards (National Leaguers in this series). There were also special cards to honor the award winners and the heroes of the World Series.

	MINT	EXC	G-VG
COMPLETE SET (792)	10.00	4.50	1.25
COMPLETE W/4 LEAF PRVWS	12.00	5.50	1.50
COMPLETE W/4 STUDIO PRVWS	12.00	5.50	1.50
COMMON CARD (1-386)	.05	.02	.01
COMMON CARD (387-770)	.05	.02	.01
☐ 1 Dave Stieb DK	.05	.02	.01
☐ 2 Craig Biggio DK	.05	.02	.01
☐ 3 Cecil Fielder DK	.07	.03	.01
☐ 4 Barry Bonds DK	.25	.11	.03
☐ 5 Barry Larkin DK	.07	.03	.01
☐ 6 Dave Parker DK	.05	.02	.01
☐ 7 Len Dykstra DK	.07	.03	.01
☐ 8 Bobby Thigpen DK	.05	.02	.01
☐ 9 Roger Clemens DK	.15	.07	.02
☐ 10 Ron Gant DK UER (No trademark on team logo on back)	.05	.02	.01

☐ 11 Delino DeShields DK .... .07 .03 .01
☐ 12 Roberto Alomar DK UER .15 .07 .02
(No trademark on team logo on back)
☐ 13 Sandy Alomar Jr. DK ..... .05 .02 .01
☐ 14 Ryne Sandberg DK UER. .15 .07 .02
(Was DK in '85, not '83 as shown)
☐ 15 Ramon Martinez DK .... .05 .02 .01
☐ 16 Edgar Martinez DK .... .05 .02 .01
☐ 17 Dave Magadan DK .... .05 .02 .01
☐ 18 Matt Williams DK .... .07 .03 .01
☐ 19 Rafael Palmeiro DK .... .07 .03 .01
UER (No trademark on team logo on back)
☐ 20 Bob Welch DK .... .05 .02 .01
☐ 21 Dave Righetti DK .... .05 .02 .01
☐ 22 Brian Harper DK .... .05 .02 .01
☐ 23 Gregg Olson DK .... .05 .02 .01
☐ 24 Kurt Stillwell DK .... .05 .02 .01
☐ 25 Pedro Guerrero DK UER .05 .02 .01
(No trademark on team logo on back)
☐ 26 Chuck Finley DK UER ..... .05 .02 .01
(No trademark on team logo on back)
☐ 27 DK Checklist 1-27 .... .05 .02 .01
☐ 28 Tino Martinez RR .... .10 .05 .01
☐ 29 Mark Lewis RR .... .10 .05 .01
☐ 30 Bernard Gilkey RR .... .10 .05 .01
☐ 31 Hensley Meulens RR ...... .05 .02 .01
☐ 32 Derek Bell RR .... .10 .05 .01
☐ 33 Jose Offerman RR .... .10 .05 .01
☐ 34 Terry Bross RR .... .05 .02 .01
☐ 35 Leo Gomez RR .... .10 .05 .01
☐ 36 Derrick May RR .... .10 .05 .01
☐ 37 Kevin Morton RR .... .05 .02 .01
☐ 38 Moises Alou RR .... .25 .11 .03
☐ 39 Julio Valera RR .... .05 .02 .01
☐ 40 Milt Cuyler RR .... .05 .02 .01
☐ 41 Phil Plantier RR .... .30 .14 .04
☐ 42 Scott Chiamparino RR ... .05 .02 .01
☐ 43 Ray Lankford RR .... .20 .09 .03
☐ 44 Mickey Morandini RR .... .05 .02 .01
☐ 45 Dave Hansen RR .... .05 .02 .01
☐ 46 Kevin Belcher RR .... .05 .02 .01
☐ 47 Darrin Fletcher RR .... .05 .02 .01
☐ 48 Steve Sax AS .... .05 .02 .01
☐ 49 Ken Griffey Jr. AS .... .75 .35 .09
☐ 50A Jose Canseco AS ERR . .15 .07 .02
(Team in stat box should be AL, not A's)
☐ 50B Jose Canseco AS COR . .75 .35 .09
☐ 51 Sandy Alomar Jr. AS ...... .05 .02 .01
☐ 52 Cal Ripken AS .... .25 .11 .03
☐ 53 Rickey Henderson AS .... .10 .05 .01
☐ 54 Bob Welch AS .... .05 .02 .01
☐ 55 Wade Boggs AS .... .10 .05 .01
☐ 56 Mark McGwire AS .... .10 .05 .01
☐ 57A Jack McDowell ERR ..... .15 .07 .02
(Career stats do not include 1990)
☐ 57B Jack McDowell COR ..... .50 .23 .06
(Career include 1990)
☐ 58 Jose Lind .... .05 .02 .01
☐ 59 Alex Fernandez .... .25 .11 .03
☐ 60 Pat Combs .... .05 .02 .01
☐ 61 Mike Walker .... .05 .02 .01
☐ 62 Juan Samuel .... .05 .02 .01
☐ 63 Mike Blowers UER .... .05 .02 .01
(Last line has aseball, not baseball)
☐ 64 Mark Guthrie .... .05 .02 .01
☐ 65 Mark Salas .... .05 .02 .01
☐ 66 Tim Jones .... .05 .02 .01
☐ 67 Tim Leary .... .05 .02 .01
☐ 68 Andres Galarraga .... .15 .07 .02
☐ 69 Bob Milacki .... .05 .02 .01
☐ 70 Tim Belcher .... .05 .02 .01
☐ 71 Todd Zeile .... .10 .05 .01
☐ 72 Jerome Walton .... .05 .02 .01
☐ 73 Kevin Seitzer .... .05 .02 .01
☐ 74 Jerald Clark .... .05 .02 .01
☐ 75 John Smoltz UER .... .15 .07 .02
(Born in Detroit, not Warren)
☐ 76 Mike Henneman .... .05 .02 .01
☐ 77 Ken Griffey Jr. .... 1.50 .65 .19
☐ 78 Jim Abbott .... .15 .07 .02
☐ 79 Gregg Jefferies .... .15 .07 .02
☐ 80 Kevin Reimer .... .05 .02 .01
☐ 81 Roger Clemens .... .25 .11 .03
☐ 82 Mike Fitzgerald .... .05 .02 .01
☐ 83 Bruce Hurst UER .... .05 .02 .01
(Middle name is Lee, not Vee)
☐ 84 Eric Davis .... .10 .05 .01
☐ 85 Paul Molitor .... .15 .07 .02
☐ 86 Will Clark .... .20 .09 .03
☐ 87 Mike Bielecki .... .05 .02 .01
☐ 88 Bret Saberhagen .... .10 .05 .01
☐ 89 Nolan Ryan .... .60 .25 .08
☐ 90 Bobby Thigpen .... .05 .02 .01
☐ 91 Dickie Thon .... .05 .02 .01
☐ 92 Duane Ward .... .10 .05 .01
☐ 93 Luis Polonia .... .05 .02 .01
☐ 94 Terry Kennedy .... .05 .02 .01
☐ 95 Kent Hrbek .... .10 .05 .01
☐ 96 Danny Jackson .... .05 .02 .01
☐ 97 Sid Fernandez .... .10 .05 .01
☐ 98 Jimmy Key .... .10 .05 .01
☐ 99 Franklin Stubbs .... .05 .02 .01
☐ 100 Checklist 28-103 .... .05 .02 .01
☐ 101 R.J. Reynolds .... .05 .02 .01
☐ 102 Dave Stewart .... .10 .05 .01
☐ 103 Dan Pasqua .... .05 .02 .01
☐ 104 Dan Plesac .... .05 .02 .01
☐ 105 Mark McGwire .... .15 .07 .02
☐ 106 John Farrell .... .05 .02 .01
☐ 107 Don Mattingly .... .30 .14 .04
☐ 108 Carlton Fisk .... .15 .07 .02
☐ 109 Ken Oberkfell .... .05 .02 .01
☐ 110 Darrel Akerfelds .... .05 .02 .01
☐ 111 Gregg Olson .... .10 .05 .01
☐ 112 Mike Scioscia .... .05 .02 .01
☐ 113 Bryn Smith .... .05 .02 .01
☐ 114 Bob Geren .... .05 .02 .01
☐ 115 Tom Candiotti .... .05 .02 .01
☐ 116 Kevin Tapani .... .10 .05 .01
☐ 117 Jeff Treadway .... .05 .02 .01
☐ 118 Alan Trammell .... .15 .07 .02
☐ 119 Pete O'Brien .... .05 .02 .01
(Blue shading goes through stats)
☐ 120 Joel Skinner .... .05 .02 .01
☐ 121 Mike LaValliere .... .05 .02 .01
☐ 122 Dwight Evans .... .10 .05 .01
☐ 123 Jody Reed .... .05 .02 .01
☐ 124 Lee Guetterman .... .05 .02 .01
☐ 125 Tim Burke .... .05 .02 .01
☐ 126 Dave Johnson .... .05 .02 .01
☐ 127 Fernando Valenzuela .... .05 .02 .01
(Lower large stripe in yellow instead of blue) UER
☐ 128 Jose DeLeon .... .05 .02 .01

	No.	Player			
☐	129	Andre Dawson	.15	.07	.02
☐	130	Gerald Perry	.05	.02	.01
☐	131	Greg W. Harris	.05	.02	.01
☐	132	Tom Glavine	.20	.09	.03
☐	133	Lance McCullers	.05	.02	.01
☐	134	Randy Johnson	.15	.07	.02
☐	135	Lance Parrish UER (Born in McKeesport, not Clairton)	.10	.05	.01
☐	136	Mackey Sasser	.05	.02	.01
☐	137	Geno Petralli	.05	.02	.01
☐	138	Dennis Lamp	.05	.02	.01
☐	139	Dennis Martinez	.10	.05	.01
☐	140	Mike Pagliarulo	.05	.02	.01
☐	141	Hal Morris	.10	.05	.01
☐	142	Dave Parker	.15	.07	.02
☐	143	Brett Butler	.10	.05	.01
☐	144	Paul Assenmacher	.05	.02	.01
☐	145	Mark Gubicza	.05	.02	.01
☐	146	Charlie Hough	.10	.05	.01
☐	147	Sammy Sosa	.15	.07	.02
☐	148	Randy Ready	.05	.02	.01
☐	149	Kelly Gruber	.05	.02	.01
☐	150	Devon White	.10	.05	.01
☐	151	Gary Carter	.15	.07	.02
☐	152	Gene Larkin	.05	.02	.01
☐	153	Chris Sabo	.10	.05	.01
☐	154	David Cone	.15	.07	.02
☐	155	Todd Stottlemyre	.05	.02	.01
☐	156	Glenn Wilson	.05	.02	.01
☐	157	Bob Walk	.05	.02	.01
☐	158	Mike Gallego	.05	.02	.01
☐	159	Greg Hibbard	.05	.02	.01
☐	160	Chris Bosio	.05	.02	.01
☐	161	Mike Moore	.05	.02	.01
☐	162	Jerry Browne UER (Born Christiansted, should be St. Croix)	.05	.02	.01
☐	163	Steve Sax UER (No asterisk next to his 1989 At Bats)	.05	.02	.01
☐	164	Melido Perez	.05	.02	.01
☐	165	Danny Darwin	.05	.02	.01
☐	166	Roger McDowell	.05	.02	.01
☐	167	Bill Ripken	.05	.02	.01
☐	168	Mike Sharperson	.05	.02	.01
☐	169	Lee Smith	.15	.07	.02
☐	170	Matt Nokes	.05	.02	.01
☐	171	Jesse Orosco	.05	.02	.01
☐	172	Rick Aguilera	.10	.05	.01
☐	173	Jim Presley	.05	.02	.01
☐	174	Lou Whitaker	.15	.07	.02
☐	175	Harold Reynolds	.05	.02	.01
☐	176	Brook Jacoby	.05	.02	.01
☐	177	Wally Backman	.05	.02	.01
☐	178	Wade Boggs	.15	.07	.02
☐	179	Chuck Cary (Comma after DOB, not on other cards)	.05	.02	.01
☐	180	Tom Foley	.05	.02	.01
☐	181	Pete Harnisch	.10	.05	.01
☐	182	Mike Morgan	.05	.02	.01
☐	183	Bob Tewksbury	.10	.05	.01
☐	184	Joe Girardi	.05	.02	.01
☐	185	Storm Davis	.05	.02	.01
☐	186	Ed Whitson	.05	.02	.01
☐	187	Steve Avery UER (Born in New Jersey, should be Michigan)	.15	.07	.02
☐	188	Lloyd Moseby	.05	.02	.01
☐	189	Scott Bankhead	.05	.02	.01
☐	190	Mark Langston	.15	.07	.02
☐	191	Kevin McReynolds	.05	.02	.01
☐	192	Julio Franco	.10	.05	.01
☐	193	John Dopson	.05	.02	.01
☐	194	Dennis Boyd	.05	.02	.01
☐	195	Bip Roberts	.05	.02	.01
☐	196	Billy Hatcher	.05	.02	.01
☐	197	Edgar Diaz	.05	.02	.01
☐	198	Greg Litton	.05	.02	.01
☐	199	Mark Grace	.15	.07	.02
☐	200	Checklist 104-179	.05	.02	.01
☐	201	George Brett	.30	.14	.04
☐	202	Jeff Russell	.05	.02	.01
☐	203	Ivan Calderon	.05	.02	.01
☐	204	Ken Howell	.05	.02	.01
☐	205	Tom Henke	.10	.05	.01
☐	206	Bryan Harvey	.10	.05	.01
☐	207	Steve Bedrosian	.05	.02	.01
☐	208	Al Newman	.05	.02	.01
☐	209	Randy Myers	.10	.05	.01
☐	210	Daryl Boston	.05	.02	.01
☐	211	Manny Lee	.05	.02	.01
☐	212	Dave Smith	.05	.02	.01
☐	213	Don Slaught	.05	.02	.01
☐	214	Walt Weiss	.05	.02	.01
☐	215	Donn Pall	.05	.02	.01
☐	216	Jaime Navarro	.05	.02	.01
☐	217	Willie Randolph	.10	.05	.01
☐	218	Rudy Seanez	.05	.02	.01
☐	219	Jim Leyritz	.05	.02	.01
☐	220	Ron Karkovice	.05	.02	.01
☐	221	Ken Caminiti	.10	.05	.01
☐	222	Von Hayes	.05	.02	.01
☐	223	Cal Ripken	.35	.16	.04
☐	224	Lenny Harris	.05	.02	.01
☐	225	Milt Thompson	.05	.02	.01
☐	226	Alvaro Espinoza	.05	.02	.01
☐	227	Chris James	.05	.02	.01
☐	228	Dan Gladden	.05	.02	.01
☐	229	Jeff Blauser	.10	.05	.01
☐	230	Mike Heath	.05	.02	.01
☐	231	Omar Vizquel	.05	.02	.01
☐	232	Doug Jones	.05	.02	.01
☐	233	Jeff King	.05	.02	.01
☐	234	Luis Rivera	.05	.02	.01
☐	235	Ellis Burks	.10	.05	.01
☐	236	Greg Cadaret	.05	.02	.01
☐	237	Dave Martinez	.05	.02	.01
☐	238	Mark Williamson	.05	.02	.01
☐	239	Stan Javier	.05	.02	.01
☐	240	Ozzie Smith	.20	.09	.03
☐	241	Shawn Boskie	.05	.02	.01
☐	242	Tom Gordon	.10	.05	.01
☐	243	Tony Gwynn	.25	.11	.03
☐	244	Tommy Gregg	.05	.02	.01
☐	245	Jeff M. Robinson	.05	.02	.01
☐	246	Keith Comstock	.05	.02	.01
☐	247	Jack Howell	.05	.02	.01
☐	248	Keith Miller	.05	.02	.01
☐	249	Bobby Witt	.05	.02	.01
☐	250	Rob Murphy UER (Shown as on Reds in '89 in stats, should be Red Sox)	.05	.02	.01
☐	251	Spike Owen	.05	.02	.01
☐	252	Garry Templeton	.05	.02	.01
☐	253	Glenn Braggs	.05	.02	.01
☐	254	Ron Robinson	.05	.02	.01
☐	255	Kevin Mitchell	.10	.05	.01
☐	256	Les Lancaster	.05	.02	.01
☐	257	Mel Stottlemyre Jr.	.05	.02	.01
☐	258	Kenny Rogers UER (IP listed as 171, should be 172)	.05	.02	.01
☐	259	Lance Johnson	.05	.02	.01

☐ 260 John Kruk .15 .07 .02
☐ 261 Fred McGriff .20 .09 .03
☐ 262 Dick Schofield .05 .02 .01
☐ 263 Trevor Wilson .05 .02 .01
☐ 264 David West .05 .02 .01
☐ 265 Scott Scudder .05 .02 .01
☐ 266 Dwight Gooden .10 .05 .01
☐ 267 Willie Blair .05 .02 .01
☐ 268 Mark Portugal .05 .02 .01
☐ 269 Doug Drabek .15 .07 .02
☐ 270 Dennis Eckersley .15 .07 .02
☐ 271 Eric King .05 .02 .01
☐ 272 Robin Yount .15 .07 .02
☐ 273 Carney Lansford .10 .05 .01
☐ 274 Carlos Baerga .30 .14 .04
☐ 275 Dave Righetti .05 .02 .01
☐ 276 Scott Fletcher .05 .02 .01
☐ 277 Eric Yelding .05 .02 .01
☐ 278 Charlie Hayes .10 .05 .01
☐ 279 Jeff Ballard .05 .02 .01
☐ 280 Orel Hershiser .10 .05 .01
☐ 281 Jose Oquendo .05 .02 .01
☐ 282 Mike Witt .05 .02 .01
☐ 283 Mitch Webster .05 .02 .01
☐ 284 Greg Gagne .05 .02 .01
☐ 285 Greg Olson .05 .02 .01
☐ 286 Tony Phillips UER .05 .02 .01
(Born 4/15,
should be 4/25)
☐ 287 Scott Bradley .05 .02 .01
☐ 288 Cory Snyder UER .05 .02 .01
(In text, led is re-
peated and Inglewood is
misspelled as Englewood)
☐ 289 Jay Bell UER .10 .05 .01
(Born in Pensacola,
not Eglin AFB)
☐ 290 Kevin Romine .05 .02 .01
☐ 291 Jeff D. Robinson .05 .02 .01
☐ 292 Steve Frey UER .05 .02 .01
(Bats left,
should be right)
☐ 293 Craig Worthington .05 .02 .01
☐ 294 Tim Crews .05 .02 .01
☐ 295 Joe Magrane .05 .02 .01
☐ 296 Hector Villanueva .05 .02 .01
☐ 297 Terry Shumpert .05 .02 .01
☐ 298 Joe Carter .20 .09 .03
☐ 299 Kent Mercker UER .10 .05 .01
(IP listed as 53,
should be 52)
☐ 300 Checklist 180-255 .05 .02 .01
☐ 301 Chet Lemon .05 .02 .01
☐ 302 Mike Schooler .05 .02 .01
☐ 303 Dante Bichette .15 .07 .02
☐ 304 Kevin Elster .05 .02 .01
☐ 305 Jeff Huson .05 .02 .01
☐ 306 Greg A. Harris .05 .02 .01
☐ 307 Marquis Grissom UER .15 .07 .02
(Middle name Deon,
should be Dean)
☐ 308 Calvin Schiraldi .05 .02 .01
☐ 309 Mariano Duncan .05 .02 .01
☐ 310 Bill Spiers .05 .02 .01
☐ 311 Scott Garrelts .05 .02 .01
☐ 312 Mitch Williams .10 .05 .01
☐ 313 Mike Macfarlane .05 .02 .01
☐ 314 Kevin Brown .10 .05 .01
☐ 315 Robin Ventura .20 .09 .03
☐ 316 Darren Daulton .15 .07 .02
☐ 317 Pat Borders .05 .02 .01
☐ 318 Mark Eichhorn .05 .02 .01
☐ 319 Jeff Brantley .05 .02 .01
☐ 320 Shane Mack .10 .05 .01
☐ 321 Rob Dibble .05 .02 .01
☐ 322 John Franco .10 .05 .01
☐ 323 Junior Felix .05 .02 .01
☐ 324 Casey Candaele .05 .02 .01
☐ 325 Bobby Bonilla .15 .07 .02
☐ 326 Dave Henderson .05 .02 .01
☐ 327 Wayne Edwards .05 .02 .01
☐ 328 Mark Knudson .05 .02 .01
☐ 329 Terry Steinbach .10 .05 .01
☐ 330 Colby Ward UER .05 .02 .01
(No comma between
city and state)
☐ 331 Oscar Azocar .05 .02 .01
☐ 332 Scott Radinsky .05 .02 .01
☐ 333 Eric Anthony .10 .05 .01
☐ 334 Steve Lake .05 .02 .01
☐ 335 Bob Melvin .05 .02 .01
☐ 336 Kal Daniels .05 .02 .01
☐ 337 Tom Pagnozzi .05 .02 .01
☐ 338 Alan Mills .05 .02 .01
☐ 339 Steve Olin .05 .02 .01
☐ 340 Juan Berenguer .05 .02 .01
☐ 341 Francisco Cabrera .05 .02 .01
☐ 342 Dave Bergman .05 .02 .01
☐ 343 Henry Cotto .05 .02 .01
☐ 344 Sergio Valdez .05 .02 .01
☐ 345 Bob Patterson .05 .02 .01
☐ 346 John Marzano .05 .02 .01
☐ 347 Dana Kiecker .05 .02 .01
☐ 348 Dion James .05 .02 .01
☐ 349 Hubie Brooks .05 .02 .01
☐ 350 Bill Landrum .05 .02 .01
☐ 351 Bill Sampen .05 .02 .01
☐ 352 Greg Briley .05 .02 .01
☐ 353 Paul Gibson .05 .02 .01
☐ 354 Dave Eiland .05 .02 .01
☐ 355 Steve Finley .05 .02 .01
☐ 356 Bob Boone .10 .05 .01
☐ 357 Steve Buechele .05 .02 .01
☐ 358 Chris Hoiles .15 .07 .02
☐ 359 Larry Walker .15 .07 .02
☐ 360 Frank DiPino .05 .02 .01
☐ 361 Mark Grant .05 .02 .01
☐ 362 Dave Magadan .05 .02 .01
☐ 363 Robby Thompson .05 .02 .01
☐ 364 Lonnie Smith .05 .02 .01
☐ 365 Steve Farr .05 .02 .01
☐ 366 Dave Valle .05 .02 .01
☐ 367 Tim Naehring .05 .02 .01
☐ 368 Jim Acker .05 .02 .01
☐ 369 Jeff Reardon UER .10 .05 .01
(Born in Pittsfield,
not Dalton)
☐ 370 Tim Teufel .05 .02 .01
☐ 371 Juan Gonzalez 1.00 .45 .13
☐ 372 Luis Salazar .05 .02 .01
☐ 373 Rick Honeycutt .05 .02 .01
☐ 374 Greg Maddux .25 .11 .03
☐ 375 Jose Uribe UER .05 .02 .01
(Middle name Elta,
should be Alta)
☐ 376 Donnie Hill .05 .02 .01
☐ 377 Don Carman .05 .02 .01
☐ 378 Craig Grebeck .05 .02 .01
☐ 379 Willie Fraser .05 .02 .01
☐ 380 Glenallen Hill .05 .02 .01
☐ 381 Joe Oliver .05 .02 .01
☐ 382 Randy Bush .05 .02 .01
☐ 383 Alex Cole .05 .02 .01
☐ 384 Norm Charlton .05 .02 .01
☐ 385 Gene Nelson .05 .02 .01
☐ 386 Checklist 256-331 .05 .02 .01

	#	Player			
☐	387	Rickey Henderson MVP	.10	.05	.01
☐	388	Lance Parrish MVP	.05	.02	.01
☐	389	Fred McGriff MVP	.12	.05	.02
☐	390	Dave Parker MVP	.10	.05	.01
☐	391	Candy Maldonado MVP	.05	.02	.01
☐	392	Ken Griffey Jr. MVP	.75	.35	.09
☐	393	Gregg Olson MVP	.10	.05	.01
☐	394	Rafael Palmeiro MVP	.10	.05	.01
☐	395	Roger Clemens MVP	.15	.07	.02
☐	396	George Brett MVP	.15	.07	.02
☐	397	Cecil Fielder MVP	.10	.05	.01
☐	398	Brian Harper MVP UER (Major League Performance, should be Career)	.05	.02	.01
☐	399	Bobby Thigpen MVP	.05	.02	.01
☐	400	Roberto Kelly MVP UER (Second Base on front and OF on back)	.10	.05	.01
☐	401	Danny Darwin MVP	.05	.02	.01
☐	402	David Justice MVP	.15	.07	.02
☐	403	Lee Smith MVP	.10	.05	.01
☐	404	Ryne Sandberg MVP	.15	.07	.02
☐	405	Eddie Murray MVP	.10	.05	.01
☐	406	Tim Wallach MVP	.05	.02	.01
☐	407	Kevin Mitchell MVP	.10	.05	.01
☐	408	Darryl Strawberry MVP	.10	.05	.01
☐	409	Joe Carter MVP	.10	.05	.01
☐	410	Len Dykstra MVP	.10	.05	.01
☐	411	Doug Drabek MVP	.10	.05	.01
☐	412	Chris Sabo MVP	.05	.02	.01
☐	413	Paul Marak RR	.05	.02	.01
☐	414	Tim McIntosh RR	.05	.02	.01
☐	415	Brian Barnes RR	.05	.02	.01
☐	416	Eric Gunderson RR	.05	.02	.01
☐	417	Mike Gardiner RR	.05	.02	.01
☐	418	Steve Carter RR	.05	.02	.01
☐	419	Gerald Alexander RR	.05	.02	.01
☐	420	Rich Garces RR	.05	.02	.01
☐	421	Chuck Knoblauch RR	.25	.11	.03
☐	422	Scott Aldred RR	.05	.02	.01
☐	423	Wes Chamberlain RR	.05	.02	.01
☐	424	Lance Dickson RR	.05	.02	.01
☐	425	Greg Colbrunn RR	.10	.05	.01
☐	426	Rich DeLucia RR UER (Misspelled Delucia on card)	.05	.02	.01
☐	427	Jeff Conine RR	.50	.23	.06
☐	428	Steve Decker RR	.05	.02	.01
☐	429	Turner Ward RR	.15	.07	.02
☐	430	Mo Vaughn RR	.40	.18	.05
☐	431	Steve Chitren RR	.05	.02	.01
☐	432	Mike Benjamin RR	.05	.02	.01
☐	433	Ryne Sandberg AS	.15	.07	.02
☐	434	Len Dykstra AS	.10	.05	.01
☐	435	Andre Dawson AS	.10	.05	.01
☐	436A	Mike Scioscia AS (White star by name)	.05	.02	.01
☐	436B	Mike Scioscia AS (Yellow star by name)	.05	.02	.01
☐	437	Ozzie Smith AS	.10	.05	.01
☐	438	Kevin Mitchell AS	.05	.02	.01
☐	439	Jack Armstrong AS	.05	.02	.01
☐	440	Chris Sabo AS	.05	.02	.01
☐	441	Will Clark AS	.10	.05	.01
☐	442	Mel Hall	.05	.02	.01
☐	443	Mark Gardner	.05	.02	.01
☐	444	Mike Devereaux	.10	.05	.01
☐	445	Kirk Gibson	.10	.05	.01
☐	446	Terry Pendleton	.15	.07	.02
☐	447	Mike Harkey	.05	.02	.01
☐	448	Jim Eisenreich	.05	.02	.01
☐	449	Benito Santiago	.05	.02	.01
☐	450	Oddibe McDowell	.05	.02	.01
☐	451	Cecil Fielder	.15	.07	.02
☐	452	Ken Griffey	.10	.05	.01
☐	453	Bert Blyleven	.15	.07	.02
☐	454	Howard Johnson	.10	.05	.01
☐	455	Monty Fariss UER (Misspelled Farris on card)	.05	.02	.01
☐	456	Tony Pena	.05	.02	.01
☐	457	Tim Raines	.15	.07	.02
☐	458	Dennis Rasmussen	.05	.02	.01
☐	459	Luis Quinones	.05	.02	.01
☐	460	B.J. Surhoff	.05	.02	.01
☐	461	Ernest Riles	.05	.02	.01
☐	462	Rick Sutcliffe	.10	.05	.01
☐	463	Danny Tartabull	.10	.05	.01
☐	464	Pete Incaviglia	.05	.02	.01
☐	465	Carlos Martinez	.05	.02	.01
☐	466	Ricky Jordan	.05	.02	.01
☐	467	John Cerutti	.05	.02	.01
☐	468	Dave Winfield	.15	.07	.02
☐	469	Francisco Oliveras	.05	.02	.01
☐	470	Roy Smith	.05	.02	.01
☐	471	Barry Larkin	.15	.07	.02
☐	472	Ron Darling	.05	.02	.01
☐	473	David Wells	.05	.02	.01
☐	474	Glenn Davis	.05	.02	.01
☐	475	Neal Heaton	.05	.02	.01
☐	476	Ron Hassey	.05	.02	.01
☐	477	Frank Thomas	2.00	.90	.25
☐	478	Greg Vaughn	.10	.05	.01
☐	479	Todd Burns	.05	.02	.01
☐	480	Candy Maldonado	.05	.02	.01
☐	481	Dave LaPoint	.05	.02	.01
☐	482	Alvin Davis	.05	.02	.01
☐	483	Mike Scott	.05	.02	.01
☐	484	Dale Murphy	.15	.07	.02
☐	485	Ben McDonald	.15	.07	.02
☐	486	Jay Howell	.05	.02	.01
☐	487	Vince Coleman	.05	.02	.01
☐	488	Alfredo Griffin	.05	.02	.01
☐	489	Sandy Alomar Jr.	.10	.05	.01
☐	490	Kirby Puckett	.30	.14	.04
☐	491	Andres Thomas	.05	.02	.01
☐	492	Jack Morris	.15	.07	.02
☐	493	Matt Young	.05	.02	.01
☐	494	Greg Myers	.05	.02	.01
☐	495	Barry Bonds	.40	.18	.05
☐	496	Scott Cooper UER (No BA for 1990 and career)	.10	.05	.01
☐	497	Dan Schatzeder	.05	.02	.01
☐	498	Jesse Barfield	.05	.02	.01
☐	499	Jerry Goff	.05	.02	.01
☐	500	Checklist 332-408	.05	.02	.01
☐	501	Anthony Telford	.05	.02	.01
☐	502	Eddie Murray	.15	.07	.02
☐	503	Omar Olivares	.05	.02	.01
☐	504	Ryne Sandberg	.25	.11	.03
☐	505	Jeff Montgomery	.10	.05	.01
☐	506	Mark Parent	.05	.02	.01
☐	507	Ron Gant	.10	.05	.01
☐	508	Frank Tanana	.05	.02	.01
☐	509	Jay Buhner	.10	.05	.01
☐	510	Max Venable	.05	.02	.01
☐	511	Wally Whitehurst	.05	.02	.01
☐	512	Gary Pettis	.05	.02	.01
☐	513	Tom Brunansky	.05	.02	.01
☐	514	Tim Wallach	.05	.02	.01
☐	515	Craig Lefferts	.05	.02	.01
☐	516	Tim Layana	.05	.02	.01
☐	517	Darryl Hamilton	.10	.05	.01
☐	518	Rick Reuschel	.05	.02	.01

☐ 519	Steve Wilson	.05	.02	.01
☐ 520	Kurt Stillwell	.05	.02	.01
☐ 521	Rafael Palmeiro	.15	.07	.02
☐ 522	Ken Patterson	.05	.02	.01
☐ 523	Len Dykstra	.15	.07	.02
☐ 524	Tony Fernandez	.10	.05	.01
☐ 525	Kent Anderson	.05	.02	.01
☐ 526	Mark Leonard	.05	.02	.01
☐ 527	Allan Anderson	.05	.02	.01
☐ 528	Tom Browning	.05	.02	.01
☐ 529	Frank Viola	.10	.05	.01
☐ 530	John Olerud	.15	.07	.02
☐ 531	Juan Agosto	.05	.02	.01
☐ 532	Zane Smith	.05	.02	.01
☐ 533	Scott Sanderson	.05	.02	.01
☐ 534	Barry Jones	.05	.02	.01
☐ 535	Mike Felder	.05	.02	.01
☐ 536	Jose Canseco	.20	.09	.03
☐ 537	Felix Fermin	.05	.02	.01
☐ 538	Roberto Kelly	.10	.05	.01
☐ 539	Brian Holman	.05	.02	.01
☐ 540	Mark Davidson	.05	.02	.01
☐ 541	Terry Mulholland	.05	.02	.01
☐ 542	Randy Milligan	.05	.02	.01
☐ 543	Jose Gonzalez	.05	.02	.01
☐ 544	Craig Wilson	.05	.02	.01
☐ 545	Mike Hartley	.05	.02	.01
☐ 546	Greg Swindell	.05	.02	.01
☐ 547	Gary Gaetti	.05	.02	.01
☐ 548	David Justice	.35	.16	.04
☐ 549	Steve Searcy	.05	.02	.01
☐ 550	Erik Hanson	.05	.02	.01
☐ 551	Dave Stieb	.10	.05	.01
☐ 552	Andy Van Slyke	.15	.07	.02
☐ 553	Mike Greenwell	.10	.05	.01
☐ 554	Kevin Maas	.05	.02	.01
☐ 555	Delino DeShields	.15	.07	.02
☐ 556	Curt Schilling	.10	.05	.01
☐ 557	Ramon Martinez	.10	.05	.01
☐ 558	Pedro Guerrero	.10	.05	.01
☐ 559	Dwight Smith	.05	.02	.01
☐ 560	Mark Davis	.05	.02	.01
☐ 561	Shawn Abner	.05	.02	.01
☐ 562	Charlie Leibrandt	.05	.02	.01
☐ 563	John Shelby	.05	.02	.01
☐ 564	Bill Swift	.10	.05	.01
☐ 565	Mike Fetters	.05	.02	.01
☐ 566	Alejandro Pena	.05	.02	.01
☐ 567	Ruben Sierra	.15	.07	.02
☐ 568	Carlos Quintana	.05	.02	.01
☐ 569	Kevin Gross	.05	.02	.01
☐ 570	Derek Lilliquist	.05	.02	.01
☐ 571	Jack Armstrong	.05	.02	.01
☐ 572	Greg Brock	.05	.02	.01
☐ 573	Mike Kingery	.05	.02	.01
☐ 574	Greg Smith	.05	.02	.01
☐ 575	Brian McRae	.30	.14	.04
☐ 576	Jack Daugherty	.05	.02	.01
☐ 577	Ozzie Guillen	.05	.02	.01
☐ 578	Joe Boever	.05	.02	.01
☐ 579	Luis Sojo	.05	.02	.01
☐ 580	Chili Davis	.10	.05	.01
☐ 581	Don Robinson	.05	.02	.01
☐ 582	Brian Harper	.05	.02	.01
☐ 583	Paul O'Neill	.10	.05	.01
☐ 584	Bob Ojeda	.05	.02	.01
☐ 585	Mookie Wilson	.05	.02	.01
☐ 586	Rafael Ramirez	.05	.02	.01
☐ 587	Gary Redus	.05	.02	.01
☐ 588	Jamie Quirk	.05	.02	.01
☐ 589	Shawn Hillegas	.05	.02	.01
☐ 590	Tom Edens	.05	.02	.01
☐ 591	Joe Klink	.05	.02	.01
☐ 592	Charles Nagy	.10	.05	.01
☐ 593	Eric Plunk	.05	.02	.01
☐ 594	Tracy Jones	.05	.02	.01
☐ 595	Craig Biggio	.15	.07	.02
☐ 596	Jose DeJesus	.05	.02	.01
☐ 597	Mickey Tettleton	.10	.05	.01
☐ 598	Chris Gwynn	.05	.02	.01
☐ 599	Rex Hudler	.05	.02	.01
☐ 600	Checklist 409-506	.05	.02	.01
☐ 601	Jim Gott	.05	.02	.01
☐ 602	Jeff Manto	.05	.02	.01
☐ 603	Nelson Liriano	.05	.02	.01
☐ 604	Mark Lemke	.05	.02	.01
☐ 605	Clay Parker	.05	.02	.01
☐ 606	Edgar Martinez	.10	.05	.01
☐ 607	Mark Whiten	.15	.07	.02
☐ 608	Ted Power	.05	.02	.01
☐ 609	Tom Bolton	.05	.02	.01
☐ 610	Tom Herr	.05	.02	.01
☐ 611	Andy Hawkins UER (Pitched No-Hitter on 7/1, not 7/2)	.05	.02	.01
☐ 612	Scott Ruskin	.05	.02	.01
☐ 613	Ron Kittle	.05	.02	.01
☐ 614	John Wetteland	.10	.05	.01
☐ 615	Mike Perez	.05	.02	.01
☐ 616	Dave Clark	.05	.02	.01
☐ 617	Brent Mayne	.05	.02	.01
☐ 618	Jack Clark	.10	.05	.01
☐ 619	Marvin Freeman	.05	.02	.01
☐ 620	Edwin Nunez	.05	.02	.01
☐ 621	Russ Swan	.05	.02	.01
☐ 622	Johnny Ray	.05	.02	.01
☐ 623	Charlie O'Brien	.05	.02	.01
☐ 624	Joe Bitker	.05	.02	.01
☐ 625	Mike Marshall	.05	.02	.01
☐ 626	Otis Nixon	.10	.05	.01
☐ 627	Andy Benes	.15	.07	.02
☐ 628	Ron Oester	.05	.02	.01
☐ 629	Ted Higuera	.05	.02	.01
☐ 630	Kevin Bass	.05	.02	.01
☐ 631	Damon Berryhill	.05	.02	.01
☐ 632	Bo Jackson	.15	.07	.02
☐ 633	Brad Arnsberg	.05	.02	.01
☐ 634	Jerry Willard	.05	.02	.01
☐ 635	Tommy Greene	.10	.05	.01
☐ 636	Bob MacDonald	.05	.02	.01
☐ 637	Kirk McCaskill	.05	.02	.01
☐ 638	John Burkett	.10	.05	.01
☐ 639	Paul Abbott	.05	.02	.01
☐ 640	Todd Benzinger	.05	.02	.01
☐ 641	Todd Hundley	.10	.05	.01
☐ 642	George Bell	.10	.05	.01
☐ 643	Javier Ortiz	.05	.02	.01
☐ 644	Sid Bream	.05	.02	.01
☐ 645	Bob Welch	.05	.02	.01
☐ 646	Phil Bradley	.05	.02	.01
☐ 647	Bill Krueger	.05	.02	.01
☐ 648	Rickey Henderson	.15	.07	.02
☐ 649	Kevin Wickander	.05	.02	.01
☐ 650	Steve Balboni	.05	.02	.01
☐ 651	Gene Harris	.05	.02	.01
☐ 652	Jim Deshaies	.05	.02	.01
☐ 653	Jason Grimsley	.05	.02	.01
☐ 654	Joe Orsulak	.05	.02	.01
☐ 655	Jim Poole	.05	.02	.01
☐ 656	Felix Jose	.10	.05	.01
☐ 657	Denis Cook	.05	.02	.01
☐ 658	Tom Brookens	.05	.02	.01
☐ 659	Junior Ortiz	.05	.02	.01
☐ 660	Jeff Parrett	.05	.02	.01
☐ 661	Jerry Don Gleaton	.05	.02	.01
☐ 662	Brent Knackert	.05	.02	.01

☐ 663	Rance Mulliniks	.05	.02	.01
☐ 664	John Smiley	.05	.02	.01
☐ 665	Larry Andersen	.05	.02	.01
☐ 666	Willie McGee	.10	.05	.01
☐ 667	Chris Nabholz	.05	.02	.01
☐ 668	Brady Anderson	.10	.05	.01
☐ 669	Darren Holmes UER (19 CG's, should be 0)	.05	.02	.01
☐ 670	Ken Hill	.15	.07	.02
☐ 671	Gary Varsho	.05	.02	.01
☐ 672	Bill Pecota	.05	.02	.01
☐ 673	Fred Lynn	.10	.05	.01
☐ 674	Kevin D. Brown	.05	.02	.01
☐ 675	Dan Petry	.05	.02	.01
☐ 676	Mike Jackson	.05	.02	.01
☐ 677	Wally Joyner	.10	.05	.01
☐ 678	Danny Jackson	.05	.02	.01
☐ 679	Bill Haselman	.05	.02	.01
☐ 680	Mike Boddicker	.05	.02	.01
☐ 681	Mel Rojas	.05	.02	.01
☐ 682	Roberto Alomar	.25	.11	.03
☐ 683	David Justice ROY	.15	.07	.02
☐ 684	Chuck Crim	.05	.02	.01
☐ 685	Matt Williams	.20	.09	.03
☐ 686	Shawon Dunston	.05	.02	.01
☐ 687	Jeff Schulz	.05	.02	.01
☐ 688	John Barfield	.05	.02	.01
☐ 689	Gerald Young	.05	.02	.01
☐ 690	Luis Gonzalez	.25	.11	.03
☐ 691	Frank Wills	.05	.02	.01
☐ 692	Chuck Finley	.10	.05	.01
☐ 693	Sandy Alomar Jr. ROY	.05	.02	.01
☐ 694	Tim Drummond	.05	.02	.01
☐ 695	Herm Winningham	.05	.02	.01
☐ 696	Darryl Strawberry	.15	.07	.02
☐ 697	Al Leiter	.05	.02	.01
☐ 698	Karl Rhodes	.05	.02	.01
☐ 699	Stan Belinda	.05	.02	.01
☐ 700	Checklist 507-604	.05	.02	.01
☐ 701	Lance Blankenship	.05	.02	.01
☐ 702	Willie Stargell PUZ	.05	.02	.01
☐ 703	Jim Gantner	.05	.02	.01
☐ 704	Reggie Harris	.05	.02	.01
☐ 705	Rob Ducey	.05	.02	.01
☐ 706	Tim Hulett	.05	.02	.01
☐ 707	Atlee Hammaker	.05	.02	.01
☐ 708	Xavier Hernandez	.05	.02	.01
☐ 709	Chuck McElroy	.05	.02	.01
☐ 710	John Mitchell	.05	.02	.01
☐ 711	Carlos Hernandez	.05	.02	.01
☐ 712	Geronimo Pena	.05	.02	.01
☐ 713	Jim Neidlinger	.05	.02	.01
☐ 714	John Orton	.05	.02	.01
☐ 715	Terry Leach	.05	.02	.01
☐ 716	Mike Stanton	.05	.02	.01
☐ 717	Walt Terrell	.05	.02	.01
☐ 718	Luis Aquino	.05	.02	.01
☐ 719	Bud Black (Blue Jays uniform, but Giants logo)	.05	.02	.01
☐ 720	Bob Kipper	.05	.02	.01
☐ 721	Jeff Gray	.05	.02	.01
☐ 722	Jose Rijo	.10	.05	.01
☐ 723	Curt Young	.05	.02	.01
☐ 724	Jose Vizcaino	.05	.02	.01
☐ 725	Randy Tomlin	.05	.02	.01
☐ 726	Junior Noboa	.05	.02	.01
☐ 727	Bob Welch CY	.05	.02	.01
☐ 728	Gary Ward	.05	.02	.01
☐ 729	Rob Deer (Brewers uniform, but Tigers logo)	.05	.02	.01
☐ 730	David Segui	.05	.02	.01
☐ 731	Mark Carreon	.05	.02	.01
☐ 732	Vicente Palacios	.05	.02	.01
☐ 733	Sam Horn	.05	.02	.01
☐ 734	Howard Farmer	.05	.02	.01
☐ 735	Ken Dayley (Cardinals uniform, but Blue Jays logo)	.05	.02	.01
☐ 736	Kelly Mann	.05	.02	.01
☐ 737	Joe Grahe	.05	.02	.01
☐ 738	Kelly Downs	.05	.02	.01
☐ 739	Jimmy Kremers	.05	.02	.01
☐ 740	Kevin Appier	.10	.05	.01
☐ 741	Jeff Reed	.05	.02	.01
☐ 742	Jose Rijo WS	.10	.05	.01
☐ 743	Dave Rohde	.05	.02	.01
☐ 744	Dr.Dirt/Mr.Clean Len Dykstra Dale Murphy UER (No '91 Donruss logo on card front)	.10	.05	.01
☐ 745	Paul Sorrento	.10	.05	.01
☐ 746	Thomas Howard	.05	.02	.01
☐ 747	Matt Stark	.05	.02	.01
☐ 748	Harold Baines	.10	.05	.01
☐ 749	Doug Dascenzo	.05	.02	.01
☐ 750	Doug Drabek CY	.10	.05	.01
☐ 751	Gary Sheffield	.15	.07	.02
☐ 752	Terry Lee	.05	.02	.01
☐ 753	Jim Vatcher	.05	.02	.01
☐ 754	Lee Stevens	.05	.02	.01
☐ 755	Randy Veres	.05	.02	.01
☐ 756	Bill Doran	.05	.02	.01
☐ 757	Gary Wayne	.05	.02	.01
☐ 758	Pedro Munoz	.15	.07	.02
☐ 759	Chris Hammond	.10	.05	.01
☐ 760	Checklist 605-702	.05	.02	.01
☐ 761	Rickey Henderson MVP	.10	.05	.01
☐ 762	Barry Bonds MVP	.25	.11	.03
☐ 763	Billy Hatcher WS UER (Line 13, on should be one)	.05	.02	.01
☐ 764	Julio Machado	.05	.02	.01
☐ 765	Jose Mesa	.05	.02	.01
☐ 766	Willie Randolph WS	.05	.02	.01
☐ 767	Scott Erickson	.05	.02	.01
☐ 768	Travis Fryman	.50	.23	.06
☐ 769	Rich Rodriguez	.05	.02	.01
☐ 770	Checklist 703-770 and BC1-BC22	.05	.02	.01

1991 Donruss Elite

These special cards were inserted in the 1991 Donruss first and second series wax packs. Production was limited to a maxi-

mum of 10,000 cards for each card in the Elite series, and lesser production for the Sandberg Signature (5,000) and Ryan Legend (7,500) cards. The regular Elite cards are photos enclosed in a bronze marble borders which surround an evenly squared photo of the players. The Sandberg Signature card has a green marble border and is signed in a blue sharpie. The Nolan Ryan Legend card is a Dick Perez drawing with silver borders. The cards are all numbered on the back, 1 out of 10,000, etc. All of these special cards measure the standard, 2 1/2" by 3 1/2".

	MINT	EXC	G-VG
COMPLETE SET (10)	1200.00	550.00	150.00
COMMON CARD (1-8)	30.00	13.50	3.80
☐ 1 Barry Bonds	100.00	45.00	12.50
☐ 2 George Brett	120.00	55.00	15.00
☐ 3 Jose Canseco	70.00	32.00	8.75
☐ 4 Andre Dawson	50.00	23.00	6.25
☐ 5 Doug Drabek	30.00	13.50	3.80
☐ 6 Cecil Fielder	50.00	23.00	6.25
☐ 7 Rickey Henderson	50.00	23.00	6.25
☐ 8 Matt Williams	75.00	34.00	9.50
☐ L1 Nolan Ryan (Legend)	300.00	135.00	38.00
☐ S1 Ryne Sandberg (Signature Series)	450.00	200.00	57.50

1991 Donruss Rookies

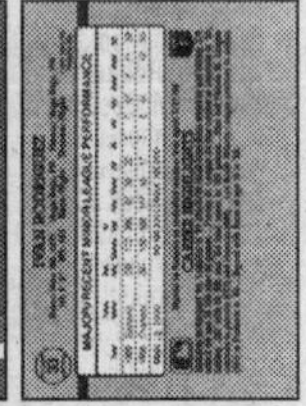

The 1991 Donruss Rookies set is a boxed set issued to honor the best rookies of the season. The cards measure the standard size (2 1/2" by 3 1/2"), and a mini puzzle featuring Hall of Famer Willie Stargell was included with the set. The fronts feature color action player photos, with white and red borders. Yellow and green stripes cut across the bottom of the card face, presenting the player's name and position. The words "The Rookies" and a baseball icon appear in the lower left corner of the picture. The horizontally oriented backs are printed in black on a green and white background, and present biography, statistics, and career highlights. The cards are numbered on the back. Rookie Cards showcased in this set include Jeff Bagwell, Chito Martinez, Orlando Merced, Dean Palmer, Ivan Rodriguez, Todd Van Poppel, and Rick Wilkins.

	MINT	EXC	G-VG
COMPLETE FACT.SET (56)	4.00	1.80	.50
COMMON CARD (1-56)	.05	.02	.01
☐ 1 Pat Kelly	.15	.07	.02
☐ 2 Rich DeLucia	.05	.02	.01
☐ 3 Wes Chamberlain	.05	.02	.01
☐ 4 Scott Leius	.05	.02	.01
☐ 5 Darryl Kile	.10	.05	.01
☐ 6 Milt Cuyler	.08	.04	.01
☐ 7 Todd Van Poppel	.20	.09	.03
☐ 8 Ray Lankford	.10	.05	.01
☐ 9 Brian R. Hunter	.15	.07	.02
☐ 10 Tony Perezchica	.05	.02	.01
☐ 11 Ced Landrum	.05	.02	.01
☐ 12 Dave Burba	.05	.02	.01
☐ 13 Ramon Garcia	.05	.02	.01
☐ 14 Ed Sprague	.05	.02	.01
☐ 15 Warren Newson	.05	.02	.01
☐ 16 Paul Faries	.05	.02	.01
☐ 17 Luis Gonzalez	.05	.02	.01
☐ 18 Charles Nagy	.08	.04	.01
☐ 19 Chris Hammond	.08	.04	.01
☐ 20 Frank Castillo	.05	.02	.01
☐ 21 Pedro Munoz	.05	.02	.01
☐ 22 Orlando Merced	.25	.11	.03
☐ 23 Jose Melendez	.05	.02	.01
☐ 24 Kirk Dressendorfer	.05	.02	.01
☐ 25 Heathcliff Slocumb	.05	.02	.01
☐ 26 Doug Simons	.05	.02	.01
☐ 27 Mike Timlin	.05	.02	.01
☐ 28 Jeff Fassero	.20	.09	.03
☐ 29 Mark Leiter	.05	.02	.01
☐ 30 Jeff Bagwell	3.00	1.35	.40
☐ 31 Brian McRae	.20	.09	.03
☐ 32 Mark Whiten	.05	.02	.01
☐ 33 Ivan Rodriguez	.50	.23	.06
☐ 34 Wade Taylor	.05	.02	.01
☐ 35 Darren Lewis	.08	.04	.01
☐ 36 Mo Vaughn	.40	.18	.05
☐ 37 Mike Remlinger	.05	.02	.01
☐ 38 Rick Wilkins	.15	.07	.02
☐ 39 Chuck Knoblauch	.25	.11	.03
☐ 40 Kevin Morton	.05	.02	.01
☐ 41 Carlos Rodriguez	.05	.02	.01
☐ 42 Mark Lewis	.08	.04	.01
☐ 43 Brent Mayne	.05	.02	.01
☐ 44 Chris Haney	.05	.02	.01
☐ 45 Denis Boucher	.05	.02	.01
☐ 46 Mike Gardiner	.05	.02	.01
☐ 47 Jeff Johnson	.05	.02	.01
☐ 48 Dean Palmer	.08	.04	.01
☐ 49 Chuck McElroy	.05	.02	.01
☐ 50 Chris Jones	.05	.02	.01
☐ 51 Scott Kamieniecki	.05	.02	.01
☐ 52 Al Osuna	.05	.02	.01
☐ 53 Rusty Meacham	.05	.02	.01
☐ 54 Chito Martinez	.05	.02	.01
☐ 55 Reggie Jefferson	.08	.04	.01
☐ 56 Checklist 1-56	.05	.02	.01

1992 Donruss

The 1992 Donruss set contains two series each featuring 396 cards, measuring the

standard size (2 1/2" by 3 1/2"). The front design features glossy color player photos with white borders. Two-toned blue stripes overlay the top and bottom of the picture, with the player's name printed in silver-and-black lettering above the bottom stripe. The horizontally oriented backs have a color headshot of the player (except on subset cards listed below), biography, career highlights, and recent Major League performance statistics (no earlier than 1987). The set includes Rated Rookies (1-20), AL All-Stars (21-30), Highlights (33, 94, 154, 215, 276), Rated Rookies (397-421), NL All-Stars (422-431), Highlights (434, 495, 555, 616, 677) and a puzzle of Hall of Famer Rod Carew. The cards are numbered on the back and checklisted below accordingly. Thirteen Diamond Kings cards featuring the artwork of Dick Perez were randomly inserted in first series foil packs and 13 more Diamond Kings were randomly inserted in second series foil packs. Inserted in both series foil and rack packs are 5,000 Cal Ripken Signature autographed cards, 7,500 Legend cards of Rickey Henderson, and 10,000 Elite cards each of Wade Boggs, Joe Carter, Will Clark, Dwight Gooden, Ken Griffey Jr., Tony Gwynn, Howard Johnson, Terry Pendleton, Kirby Puckett, and Frank Thomas. Rookie Cards in the set include Rod Beck, John Jaha, Pat Mahomes, Brian Williams, and Bob Zupcic.

	MINT	EXC	G-VG
COMPLETE SET (784)	15.00	6.75	1.90
COMPLETE HOBBY SET (788)	18.00	8.00	2.30
COMPLETE RETAIL SET (788)	18.00	8.00	2.30
COMPLETE SERIES 1 (396)	7.50	3.40	.95
COMPLETE SERIES 2 (388)	7.50	3.40	.95
COMMON CARD (1-396)	.05	.02	.01
COMMON CARD (397-784)	.05	.02	.01

	MINT	EXC	G-VG
☐ 1 Mark Wohlers RR	.10	.05	.01
☐ 2 Wil Cordero RR	.25	.11	.03
☐ 3 Kyle Abbott RR	.05	.02	.01
☐ 4 Dave Nilsson RR	.20	.09	.03
☐ 5 Kenny Lofton RR	1.25	.55	.16
☐ 6 Luis Mercedes RR	.10	.05	.01
☐ 7 Roger Salkeld RR	.10	.05	.01
☐ 8 Eddie Zosky RR	.10	.05	.01
☐ 9 Todd Van Poppel RR	.15	.07	.02
☐ 10 Frank Seminara RR	.05	.02	.01
☐ 11 Andy Ashby RR	.05	.02	.01
☐ 12 Reggie Jefferson RR	.05	.02	.01
☐ 13 Ryan Klesko RR	1.00	.45	.13
☐ 14 Carlos Garcia RR	.10	.05	.01
☐ 15 John Ramos RR	.05	.02	.01
☐ 16 Eric Karros RR	.15	.07	.02
☐ 17 Patrick Lennon RR	.05	.02	.01
☐ 18 Eddie Taubensee RR	.05	.02	.01
☐ 19 Roberto Hernandez RR	.10	.05	.01
☐ 20 D.J. Dozier RR	.10	.05	.01
☐ 21 Dave Henderson AS	.05	.02	.01
☐ 22 Cal Ripken AS	.25	.11	.03
☐ 23 Wade Boggs AS	.10	.05	.01
☐ 24 Ken Griffey Jr. AS	.75	.35	.09
☐ 25 Jack Morris AS	.10	.05	.01
☐ 26 Danny Tartabull AS	.10	.05	.01
☐ 27 Cecil Fielder AS	.10	.05	.01
☐ 28 Roberto Alomar AS	.15	.07	.02
☐ 29 Sandy Alomar Jr. AS	.05	.02	.01
☐ 30 Rickey Henderson AS	.10	.05	.01
☐ 31 Ken Hill	.10	.05	.01
☐ 32 John Habyan	.05	.02	.01
☐ 33 Otis Nixon HL	.05	.02	.01
☐ 34 Tim Wallach	.05	.02	.01
☐ 35 Cal Ripken	.40	.18	.05
☐ 36 Gary Carter	.15	.07	.02
☐ 37 Juan Agosto	.05	.02	.01
☐ 38 Doug Dascenzo	.05	.02	.01
☐ 39 Kirk Gibson	.10	.05	.01
☐ 40 Benito Santiago	.05	.02	.01
☐ 41 Otis Nixon	.05	.02	.01
☐ 42 Andy Allanson	.05	.02	.01
☐ 43 Brian Holman	.05	.02	.01
☐ 44 Dick Schofield	.05	.02	.01
☐ 45 Dave Magadan	.05	.02	.01
☐ 46 Rafael Palmeiro	.15	.07	.02
☐ 47 Jody Reed	.05	.02	.01
☐ 48 Ivan Calderon	.05	.02	.01
☐ 49 Greg W. Harris	.05	.02	.01
☐ 50 Chris Sabo	.10	.05	.01
☐ 51 Paul Molitor	.20	.09	.03
☐ 52 Robby Thompson	.05	.02	.01
☐ 53 Dave Smith	.05	.02	.01
☐ 54 Mark Davis	.05	.02	.01
☐ 55 Kevin Brown	.10	.05	.01
☐ 56 Donn Pall	.05	.02	.01
☐ 57 Len Dykstra	.15	.07	.02
☐ 58 Roberto Alomar	.25	.11	.03
☐ 59 Jeff D. Robinson	.05	.02	.01
☐ 60 Willie McGee	.10	.05	.01
☐ 61 Jay Buhner	.10	.05	.01
☐ 62 Mike Pagliarulo	.05	.02	.01
☐ 63 Paul O'Neill	.10	.05	.01
☐ 64 Hubie Brooks	.05	.02	.01
☐ 65 Kelly Gruber	.05	.02	.01
☐ 66 Ken Caminiti	.10	.05	.01
☐ 67 Gary Redus	.05	.02	.01
☐ 68 Harold Baines	.10	.05	.01
☐ 69 Charlie Hough	.10	.05	.01
☐ 70 B.J. Surhoff	.05	.02	.01
☐ 71 Walt Weiss	.05	.02	.01
☐ 72 Shawn Hillegas	.05	.02	.01
☐ 73 Roberto Kelly	.10	.05	.01
☐ 74 Jeff Ballard	.05	.02	.01
☐ 75 Craig Biggio	.10	.05	.01
☐ 76 Pat Combs	.05	.02	.01
☐ 77 Jeff M. Robinson	.05	.02	.01
☐ 78 Tim Belcher	.05	.02	.01
☐ 79 Cris Carpenter	.05	.02	.01
☐ 80 Checklist 1-79	.05	.02	.01
☐ 81 Steve Avery	.15	.07	.02
☐ 82 Chris James	.05	.02	.01
☐ 83 Brian Harper	.05	.02	.01
☐ 84 Charlie Leibrandt	.05	.02	.01
☐ 85 Mickey Tettleton	.10	.05	.01
☐ 86 Pete O'Brien	.05	.02	.01
☐ 87 Danny Darwin	.05	.02	.01
☐ 88 Bob Walk	.05	.02	.01
☐ 89 Jeff Reardon	.10	.05	.01

☐	90 Bobby Rose	.05	.02	.01
☐	91 Danny Jackson	.05	.02	.01
☐	92 John Morris	.05	.02	.01
☐	93 Bud Black	.05	.02	.01
☐	94 Tommy Greene HL	.05	.02	.01
☐	95 Rick Aguilera	.10	.05	.01
☐	96 Gary Gaetti	.05	.02	.01
☐	97 David Cone	.15	.07	.02
☐	98 John Olerud	.15	.07	.02
☐	99 Joel Skinner	.05	.02	.01
☐	100 Jay Bell	.10	.05	.01
☐	101 Bob Milacki	.05	.02	.01
☐	102 Norm Charlton	.05	.02	.01
☐	103 Chuck Crim	.05	.02	.01
☐	104 Terry Steinbach	.10	.05	.01
☐	105 Juan Samuel	.05	.02	.01
☐	106 Steve Howe	.05	.02	.01
☐	107 Rafael Belliard	.05	.02	.01
☐	108 Joey Cora	.05	.02	.01
☐	109 Tommy Greene	.10	.05	.01
☐	110 Gregg Olson	.05	.02	.01
☐	111 Frank Tanana	.05	.02	.01
☐	112 Lee Smith	.15	.07	.02
☐	113 Greg A. Harris	.05	.02	.01
☐	114 Dwayne Henry	.05	.02	.01
☐	115 Chili Davis	.10	.05	.01
☐	116 Kent Mercker	.05	.02	.01
☐	117 Brian Barnes	.05	.02	.01
☐	118 Rich DeLucia	.05	.02	.01
☐	119 Andre Dawson	.15	.07	.02
☐	120 Carlos Baerga	.20	.09	.03
☐	121 Mike LaValliere	.05	.02	.01
☐	122 Jeff Gray	.05	.02	.01
☐	123 Bruce Hurst	.05	.02	.01
☐	124 Alvin Davis	.05	.02	.01
☐	125 John Candelaria	.05	.02	.01
☐	126 Matt Nokes	.05	.02	.01
☐	127 George Bell	.10	.05	.01
☐	128 Bret Saberhagen	.10	.05	.01
☐	129 Jeff Russell	.05	.02	.01
☐	130 Jim Abbott	.15	.07	.02
☐	131 Bill Gullickson	.05	.02	.01
☐	132 Todd Zeile	.10	.05	.01
☐	133 Dave Winfield	.15	.07	.02
☐	134 Wally Whitehurst	.05	.02	.01
☐	135 Matt Williams	.20	.09	.03
☐	136 Tom Browning	.05	.02	.01
☐	137 Marquis Grissom	.15	.07	.02
☐	138 Erik Hanson	.05	.02	.01
☐	139 Rob Dibble	.05	.02	.01
☐	140 Don August	.05	.02	.01
☐	141 Tom Henke	.10	.05	.01
☐	142 Dan Pasqua	.05	.02	.01
☐	143 George Brett	.30	.14	.04
☐	144 Jerald Clark	.05	.02	.01
☐	145 Robin Ventura	.15	.07	.02
☐	146 Dale Murphy	.15	.07	.02
☐	147 Dennis Eckersley	.15	.07	.02
☐	148 Eric Yelding	.05	.02	.01
☐	149 Mario Diaz	.05	.02	.01
☐	150 Casey Candaele	.05	.02	.01
☐	151 Steve Olin	.05	.02	.01
☐	152 Luis Salazar	.05	.02	.01
☐	153 Kevin Maas	.05	.02	.01
☐	154 Nolan Ryan HL	.50	.23	.06
☐	155 Barry Jones	.05	.02	.01
☐	156 Chris Hoiles	.15	.07	.02
☐	157 Bobby Ojeda	.05	.02	.01
☐	158 Pedro Guerrero	.10	.05	.01
☐	159 Paul Assenmacher	.05	.02	.01
☐	160 Checklist 80-157	.05	.02	.01
☐	161 Mike Macfarlane	.05	.02	.01
☐	162 Craig Lefferts	.05	.02	.01
☐	163 Brian Hunter	.05	.02	.01
☐	164 Alan Trammell	.15	.07	.02
☐	165 Ken Griffey Jr.	1.50	.65	.19
☐	166 Lance Parrish	.10	.05	.01
☐	167 Brian Downing	.05	.02	.01
☐	168 John Barfield	.05	.02	.01
☐	169 Jack Clark	.10	.05	.01
☐	170 Chris Nabholz	.05	.02	.01
☐	171 Tim Teufel	.05	.02	.01
☐	172 Chris Hammond	.05	.02	.01
☐	173 Robin Yount	.20	.09	.03
☐	174 Dave Righetti	.05	.02	.01
☐	175 Joe Girardi	.05	.02	.01
☐	176 Mike Boddicker	.05	.02	.01
☐	177 Dean Palmer	.10	.05	.01
☐	178 Greg Hibbard	.05	.02	.01
☐	179 Randy Ready	.05	.02	.01
☐	180 Devon White	.10	.05	.01
☐	181 Mark Eichhorn	.05	.02	.01
☐	182 Mike Felder	.05	.02	.01
☐	183 Joe Klink	.05	.02	.01
☐	184 Steve Bedrosian	.05	.02	.01
☐	185 Barry Larkin	.15	.07	.02
☐	186 John Franco	.05	.02	.01
☐	187 Ed Sprague	.10	.05	.01
☐	188 Mark Portugal	.05	.02	.01
☐	189 Jose Lind	.05	.02	.01
☐	190 Bob Welch	.05	.02	.01
☐	191 Alex Fernandez	.15	.07	.02
☐	192 Gary Sheffield	.15	.07	.02
☐	193 Rickey Henderson	.15	.07	.02
☐	194 Rod Nichols	.05	.02	.01
☐	195 Scott Kamieniecki	.05	.02	.01
☐	196 Mike Flanagan	.05	.02	.01
☐	197 Steve Finley	.05	.02	.01
☐	198 Darren Daulton	.15	.07	.02
☐	199 Leo Gomez	.05	.02	.01
☐	200 Mike Morgan	.05	.02	.01
☐	201 Bob Tewksbury	.05	.02	.01
☐	202 Sid Bream	.05	.02	.01
☐	203 Sandy Alomar Jr.	.10	.05	.01
☐	204 Greg Gagne	.05	.02	.01
☐	205 Juan Berenguer	.05	.02	.01
☐	206 Cecil Fielder	.15	.07	.02
☐	207 Randy Johnson	.15	.07	.02
☐	208 Tony Pena	.05	.02	.01
☐	209 Doug Drabek	.15	.07	.02
☐	210 Wade Boggs	.15	.07	.02
☐	211 Bryan Harvey	.10	.05	.01
☐	212 Jose Vizcaino	.05	.02	.01
☐	213 Alonzo Powell	.05	.02	.01
☐	214 Will Clark	.20	.09	.03
☐	215 Rickey Henderson HL	.10	.05	.01
☐	216 Jack Morris	.15	.07	.02
☐	217 Junior Felix	.05	.02	.01
☐	218 Vince Coleman	.05	.02	.01
☐	219 Jimmy Key	.10	.05	.01
☐	220 Alex Cole	.05	.02	.01
☐	221 Bill Landrum	.05	.02	.01
☐	222 Randy Milligan	.05	.02	.01
☐	223 Jose Rijo	.10	.05	.01
☐	224 Greg Vaughn	.10	.05	.01
☐	225 Dave Stewart	.10	.05	.01
☐	226 Lenny Harris	.05	.02	.01
☐	227 Scott Sanderson	.05	.02	.01
☐	228 Jeff Blauser	.10	.05	.01
☐	229 Ozzie Guillen	.05	.02	.01
☐	230 John Kruk	.15	.07	.02
☐	231 Bob Melvin	.05	.02	.01
☐	232 Milt Cuyler	.05	.02	.01
☐	233 Felix Jose	.10	.05	.01
☐	234 Ellis Burks	.10	.05	.01
☐	235 Pete Harnisch	.10	.05	.01

	No.	Player			
□	236	Kevin Tapani	.05	.02	.01
□	237	Terry Pendleton	.15	.07	.02
□	238	Mark Gardner	.05	.02	.01
□	239	Harold Reynolds	.05	.02	.01
□	240	Checklist 158-237	.05	.02	.01
□	241	Mike Harkey	.05	.02	.01
□	242	Felix Fermin	.05	.02	.01
□	243	Barry Bonds	.40	.18	.05
□	244	Roger Clemens	.25	.11	.03
□	245	Dennis Rasmussen	.05	.02	.01
□	246	Jose DeLeon	.05	.02	.01
□	247	Orel Hershiser	.10	.05	.01
□	248	Mel Hall	.05	.02	.01
□	249	Rick Wilkins	.10	.05	.01
□	250	Tom Gordon	.05	.02	.01
□	251	Kevin Reimer	.05	.02	.01
□	252	Luis Polonia	.05	.02	.01
□	253	Mike Henneman	.05	.02	.01
□	254	Tom Pagnozzi	.05	.02	.01
□	255	Chuck Finley	.05	.02	.01
□	256	Mackey Sasser	.05	.02	.01
□	257	John Burkett	.10	.05	.01
□	258	Hal Morris	.05	.02	.01
□	259	Larry Walker	.15	.07	.02
□	260	Billy Swift	.10	.05	.01
□	261	Joe Oliver	.05	.02	.01
□	262	Julio Machado	.05	.02	.01
□	263	Todd Stottlemyre	.05	.02	.01
□	264	Matt Merullo	.05	.02	.01
□	265	Brent Mayne	.05	.02	.01
□	266	Thomas Howard	.05	.02	.01
□	267	Lance Johnson	.05	.02	.01
□	268	Terry Mulholland	.05	.02	.01
□	269	Rick Honeycutt	.05	.02	.01
□	270	Luis Gonzalez	.10	.05	.01
□	271	Jose Guzman	.05	.02	.01
□	272	Jimmy Jones	.05	.02	.01
□	273	Mark Lewis	.10	.05	.01
□	274	Rene Gonzales	.05	.02	.01
□	275	Jeff Johnson	.05	.02	.01
□	276	Dennis Martinez HL	.05	.02	.01
□	277	Delino DeShields	.15	.07	.02
□	278	Sam Horn	.05	.02	.01
□	279	Kevin Gross	.05	.02	.01
□	280	Jose Oquendo	.05	.02	.01
□	281	Mark Grace	.15	.07	.02
□	282	Mark Gubicza	.05	.02	.01
□	283	Fred McGriff	.20	.09	.03
□	284	Ron Gant	.10	.05	.01
□	285	Lou Whitaker	.15	.07	.02
□	286	Edgar Martinez	.10	.05	.01
□	287	Ron Tingley	.05	.02	.01
□	288	Kevin McReynolds	.05	.02	.01
□	289	Ivan Rodriguez	.15	.07	.02
□	290	Mike Gardiner	.05	.02	.01
□	291	Chris Haney	.05	.02	.01
□	292	Darrin Jackson	.05	.02	.01
□	293	Bill Doran	.05	.02	.01
□	294	Ted Higuera	.05	.02	.01
□	295	Jeff Brantley	.05	.02	.01
□	296	Les Lancaster	.05	.02	.01
□	297	Jim Eisenreich	.05	.02	.01
□	298	Ruben Sierra	.15	.07	.02
□	299	Scott Radinsky	.05	.02	.01
□	300	Jose DeJesus	.05	.02	.01
□	301	Mike Timlin	.05	.02	.01
□	302	Luis Sojo	.05	.02	.01
□	303	Kelly Downs	.05	.02	.01
□	304	Scott Bankhead	.05	.02	.01
□	305	Pedro Munoz	.10	.05	.01
□	306	Scott Scudder	.05	.02	.01
□	307	Kevin Elster	.05	.02	.01
□	308	Duane Ward	.10	.05	.01
□	309	Darryl Kile	.10	.05	.01
□	310	Orlando Merced	.10	.05	.01
□	311	Dave Henderson	.05	.02	.01
□	312	Tim Raines	.15	.07	.02
□	313	Mark Lee	.05	.02	.01
□	314	Mike Gallego	.05	.02	.01
□	315	Charles Nagy	.05	.02	.01
□	316	Jesse Barfield	.05	.02	.01
□	317	Todd Frohwirth	.05	.02	.01
□	318	Al Osuna	.05	.02	.01
□	319	Darrin Fletcher	.05	.02	.01
□	320	Checklist 238-316	.05	.02	.01
□	321	David Segui	.05	.02	.01
□	322	Stan Javier	.05	.02	.01
□	323	Bryn Smith	.05	.02	.01
□	324	Jeff Treadway	.05	.02	.01
□	325	Mark Whiten	.10	.05	.01
□	326	Kent Hrbek	.10	.05	.01
□	327	David Justice	.25	.11	.03
□	328	Tony Phillips	.05	.02	.01
□	329	Rob Murphy	.05	.02	.01
□	330	Kevin Morton	.05	.02	.01
□	331	John Smiley	.05	.02	.01
□	332	Luis Rivera	.05	.02	.01
□	333	Wally Joyner	.10	.05	.01
□	334	Heathcliff Slocumb	.05	.02	.01
□	335	Rick Cerone	.05	.02	.01
□	336	Mike Remlinger	.05	.02	.01
□	337	Mike Moore	.05	.02	.01
□	338	Lloyd McClendon	.05	.02	.01
□	339	Al Newman	.05	.02	.01
□	340	Kirk McCaskill	.05	.02	.01
□	341	Howard Johnson	.10	.05	.01
□	342	Greg Myers	.05	.02	.01
□	343	Kal Daniels	.05	.02	.01
□	344	Bernie Williams	.10	.05	.01
□	345	Shane Mack	.10	.05	.01
□	346	Gary Thurman	.05	.02	.01
□	347	Dante Bichette	.15	.07	.02
□	348	Mark McGwire	.15	.07	.02
□	349	Travis Fryman	.20	.09	.03
□	350	Ray Lankford	.15	.07	.02
□	351	Mike Jeffcoat	.05	.02	.01
□	352	Jack McDowell	.15	.07	.02
□	353	Mitch Williams	.10	.05	.01
□	354	Mike Devereaux	.10	.05	.01
□	355	Andres Galarraga	.15	.07	.02
□	356	Henry Cotto	.05	.02	.01
□	357	Scott Bailes	.05	.02	.01
□	358	Jeff Bagwell	.75	.35	.09
□	359	Scott Leius	.05	.02	.01
□	360	Zane Smith	.05	.02	.01
□	361	Bill Pecota	.05	.02	.01
□	362	Tony Fernandez	.10	.05	.01
□	363	Glenn Braggs	.05	.02	.01
□	364	Bill Spiers	.05	.02	.01
□	365	Vicente Palacios	.05	.02	.01
□	366	Tim Burke	.05	.02	.01
□	367	Randy Tomlin	.05	.02	.01
□	368	Kenny Rogers	.05	.02	.01
□	369	Brett Butler	.10	.05	.01
□	370	Pat Kelly	.10	.05	.01
□	371	Bip Roberts	.05	.02	.01
□	372	Gregg Jefferies	.15	.07	.02
□	373	Kevin Bass	.05	.02	.01
□	374	Ron Karkovice	.05	.02	.01
□	375	Paul Gibson	.05	.02	.01
□	376	Bernard Gilkey	.10	.05	.01
□	377	Dave Gallagher	.05	.02	.01
□	378	Bill Wegman	.05	.02	.01
□	379	Pat Borders	.05	.02	.01
□	380	Ed Whitson	.05	.02	.01
□	381	Gilberto Reyes	.05	.02	.01

☐	382	Russ Swan	.05	.02	.01
☐	383	Andy Van Slyke	.15	.07	.02
☐	384	Wes Chamberlain	.05	.02	.01
☐	385	Steve Chitren	.05	.02	.01
☐	386	Greg Olson	.05	.02	.01
☐	387	Brian McRae	.15	.07	.02
☐	388	Rich Rodriguez	.05	.02	.01
☐	389	Steve Decker	.05	.02	.01
☐	390	Chuck Knoblauch	.15	.07	.02
☐	391	Bobby Witt	.05	.02	.01
☐	392	Eddie Murray	.15	.07	.02
☐	393	Juan Gonzalez	.60	.25	.08
☐	394	Scott Ruskin	.05	.02	.01
☐	395	Jay Howell	.05	.02	.01
☐	396	Checklist 317-396	.05	.02	.01
☐	397	Royce Clayton RR	.15	.07	.02
☐	398	John Jaha RR	.15	.07	.02
☐	399	Dan Wilson RR	.05	.02	.01
☐	400	Archie Corbin RR	.10	.05	.01
☐	401	Barry Manuel RR	.10	.05	.01
☐	402	Kim Batiste RR	.05	.02	.01
☐	403	Pat Mahomes RR	.15	.07	.02
☐	404	Dave Fleming RR	.10	.05	.01
☐	405	Jeff Juden RR	.10	.05	.01
☐	406	Jim Thome RR	.40	.18	.05
☐	407	Sam Militello RR	.05	.02	.01
☐	408	Jeff Nelson RR	.10	.05	.01
☐	409	Anthony Young RR	.10	.05	.01
☐	410	Tino Martinez RR	.10	.05	.01
☐	411	Jeff Mutis RR	.10	.05	.01
☐	412	Rey Sanchez RR	.15	.07	.02
☐	413	Chris Gardner RR	.05	.02	.01
☐	414	John Vander Wal RR	.10	.05	.01
☐	415	Reggie Sanders RR	.25	.11	.03
☐	416	Brian Williams RR	.15	.07	.02
☐	417	Mo Sanford RR	.05	.02	.01
☐	418	David Weathers RR	.20	.09	.03
☐	419	Hector Fajardo RR	.05	.02	.01
☐	420	Steve Foster RR	.10	.05	.01
☐	421	Lance Dickson RR	.05	.02	.01
☐	422	Andre Dawson AS	.10	.05	.01
☐	423	Ozzie Smith AS	.10	.05	.01
☐	424	Chris Sabo AS	.05	.02	.01
☐	425	Tony Gwynn AS	.10	.05	.01
☐	426	Tom Glavine AS	.10	.05	.01
☐	427	Bobby Bonilla AS	.10	.05	.01
☐	428	Will Clark AS	.10	.05	.01
☐	429	Ryne Sandberg AS	.20	.09	.03
☐	430	Benito Santiago AS	.05	.02	.01
☐	431	Ivan Calderon AS	.05	.02	.01
☐	432	Ozzie Smith	.20	.09	.03
☐	433	Tim Leary	.05	.02	.01
☐	434	Bret Saberhagen HL	.05	.02	.01
☐	435	Mel Rojas	.05	.02	.01
☐	436	Ben McDonald	.10	.05	.01
☐	437	Tim Crews	.05	.02	.01
☐	438	Rex Hudler	.05	.02	.01
☐	439	Chico Walker	.05	.02	.01
☐	440	Kurt Stillwell	.05	.02	.01
☐	441	Tony Gwynn	.25	.11	.03
☐	442	John Smoltz	.10	.05	.01
☐	443	Lloyd Moseby	.05	.02	.01
☐	444	Mike Schooler	.05	.02	.01
☐	445	Joe Grahe	.05	.02	.01
☐	446	Dwight Gooden	.10	.05	.01
☐	447	Oil Can Boyd	.05	.02	.01
☐	448	John Marzano	.05	.02	.01
☐	449	Bret Barberie	.10	.05	.01
☐	450	Mike Maddux	.05	.02	.01
☐	451	Jeff Reed	.05	.02	.01
☐	452	Dale Sveum	.05	.02	.01
☐	453	Jose Uribe	.05	.02	.01
☐	454	Bob Scanlan	.05	.02	.01
☐	455	Kevin Appier	.10	.05	.01
☐	456	Jeff Huson	.05	.02	.01
☐	457	Ken Patterson	.05	.02	.01
☐	458	Ricky Jordan	.05	.02	.01
☐	459	Tom Candiotti	.05	.02	.01
☐	460	Lee Stevens	.05	.02	.01
☐	461	Rod Beck	.30	.14	.04
☐	462	Dave Valle	.05	.02	.01
☐	463	Scott Erickson	.05	.02	.01
☐	464	Chris Jones	.05	.02	.01
☐	465	Mark Carreon	.05	.02	.01
☐	466	Rob Ducey	.05	.02	.01
☐	467	Jim Corsi	.05	.02	.01
☐	468	Jeff King	.05	.02	.01
☐	469	Curt Young	.05	.02	.01
☐	470	Bo Jackson	.15	.07	.02
☐	471	Chris Bosio	.05	.02	.01
☐	472	Jamie Quirk	.05	.02	.01
☐	473	Jesse Orosco	.05	.02	.01
☐	474	Alvaro Espinoza	.05	.02	.01
☐	475	Joe Orsulak	.05	.02	.01
☐	476	Checklist 397-477	.05	.02	.01
☐	477	Gerald Young	.05	.02	.01
☐	478	Wally Backman	.05	.02	.01
☐	479	Juan Bell	.05	.02	.01
☐	480	Mike Scioscia	.05	.02	.01
☐	481	Omar Olivares	.05	.02	.01
☐	482	Francisco Cabrera	.05	.02	.01
☐	483	Greg Swindell UER (Shown on Indians, but listed on Reds)	.05	.02	.01
☐	484	Terry Leach	.05	.02	.01
☐	485	Tommy Gregg	.05	.02	.01
☐	486	Scott Aldred	.05	.02	.01
☐	487	Greg Briley	.05	.02	.01
☐	488	Phil Plantier	.15	.07	.02
☐	489	Curtis Wilkerson	.05	.02	.01
☐	490	Tom Brunansky	.05	.02	.01
☐	491	Mike Fetters	.05	.02	.01
☐	492	Frank Castillo	.05	.02	.01
☐	493	Joe Boever	.05	.02	.01
☐	494	Kirt Manwaring	.05	.02	.01
☐	495	Wilson Alvarez HL	.10	.05	.01
☐	496	Gene Larkin	.05	.02	.01
☐	497	Gary DiSarcina	.10	.05	.01
☐	498	Frank Viola	.10	.05	.01
☐	499	Manny Lee	.05	.02	.01
☐	500	Albert Belle	.40	.18	.05
☐	501	Stan Belinda	.05	.02	.01
☐	502	Dwight Evans	.10	.05	.01
☐	503	Eric Davis	.05	.02	.01
☐	504	Darren Holmes	.05	.02	.01
☐	505	Mike Bordick	.05	.02	.01
☐	506	Dave Hansen	.05	.02	.01
☐	507	Lee Guetterman	.05	.02	.01
☐	508	Keith Mitchell	.10	.05	.01
☐	509	Melido Perez	.05	.02	.01
☐	510	Dickie Thon	.05	.02	.01
☐	511	Mark Williamson	.05	.02	.01
☐	512	Mark Salas	.05	.02	.01
☐	513	Milt Thompson	.05	.02	.01
☐	514	Mo Vaughn	.20	.09	.03
☐	515	Jim Deshaies	.05	.02	.01
☐	516	Rich Garces	.05	.02	.01
☐	517	Lonnie Smith	.05	.02	.01
☐	518	Spike Owen	.05	.02	.01
☐	519	Tracy Jones	.05	.02	.01
☐	520	Greg Maddux	.20	.09	.03
☐	521	Carlos Martinez	.05	.02	.01
☐	522	Neal Heaton	.05	.02	.01
☐	523	Mike Greenwell	.10	.05	.01
☐	524	Andy Benes	.10	.05	.01
☐	525	Jeff Schaefer UER	.05	.02	.01

	(Photo of Tino Martinez)			
☐ 526	Mike Sharperson	.05	.02	.01
☐ 527	Wade Taylor	.05	.02	.01
☐ 528	Jerome Walton	.05	.02	.01
☐ 529	Storm Davis	.05	.02	.01
☐ 530	Jose Hernandez	.05	.02	.01
☐ 531	Mark Langston	.15	.07	.02
☐ 532	Rob Deer	.05	.02	.01
☐ 533	Geronimo Pena	.05	.02	.01
☐ 534	Juan Guzman	.10	.05	.01
☐ 535	Pete Schourek	.10	.05	.01
☐ 536	Todd Benzinger	.05	.02	.01
☐ 537	Billy Hatcher	.05	.02	.01
☐ 538	Tom Foley	.05	.02	.01
☐ 539	Dave Cochrane	.05	.02	.01
☐ 540	Mariano Duncan	.05	.02	.01
☐ 541	Edwin Nunez	.05	.02	.01
☐ 542	Rance Mulliniks	.05	.02	.01
☐ 543	Carlton Fisk	.15	.07	.02
☐ 544	Luis Aquino	.05	.02	.01
☐ 545	Ricky Bones	.10	.05	.01
☐ 546	Craig Grebeck	.05	.02	.01
☐ 547	Charlie Hayes	.10	.05	.01
☐ 548	Jose Canseco	.20	.09	.03
☐ 549	Andujar Cedeno	.10	.05	.01
☐ 550	Geno Petralli	.05	.02	.01
☐ 551	Javier Ortiz	.05	.02	.01
☐ 552	Rudy Seanez	.05	.02	.01
☐ 553	Rich Gedman	.05	.02	.01
☐ 554	Eric Plunk	.05	.02	.01
☐ 555	Nolan Ryan HL	.25	.11	.03
	(With Rich Gossage)			
☐ 556	Checklist 478-555	.05	.02	.01
☐ 557	Greg Colbrunn	.10	.05	.01
☐ 558	Chito Martinez	.05	.02	.01
☐ 559	Darryl Strawberry	.10	.05	.01
☐ 560	Luis Alicea	.05	.02	.01
☐ 561	Dwight Smith	.05	.02	.01
☐ 562	Terry Shumpert	.05	.02	.01
☐ 563	Jim Vatcher	.05	.02	.01
☐ 564	Deion Sanders	.25	.11	.03
☐ 565	Walt Terrell	.05	.02	.01
☐ 566	Dave Burba	.05	.02	.01
☐ 567	Dave Howard	.05	.02	.01
☐ 568	Todd Hundley	.05	.02	.01
☐ 569	Jack Daugherty	.05	.02	.01
☐ 570	Scott Cooper	.10	.05	.01
☐ 571	Bill Sampen	.05	.02	.01
☐ 572	Jose Melendez	.05	.02	.01
☐ 573	Freddie Benavides	.05	.02	.01
☐ 574	Jim Gantner	.05	.02	.01
☐ 575	Trevor Wilson	.05	.02	.01
☐ 576	Ryne Sandberg	.30	.14	.04
☐ 577	Kevin Seitzer	.05	.02	.01
☐ 578	Gerald Alexander	.05	.02	.01
☐ 579	Mike Huff	.05	.02	.01
☐ 580	Von Hayes	.05	.02	.01
☐ 581	Derek Bell	.10	.05	.01
☐ 582	Mike Stanley	.05	.02	.01
☐ 583	Kevin Mitchell	.10	.05	.01
☐ 584	Mike Jackson	.05	.02	.01
☐ 585	Dan Gladden	.05	.02	.01
☐ 586	Ted Power UER	.05	.02	.01
	(Wrong year given for signing with Reds)			
☐ 587	Jeff Innis	.05	.02	.01
☐ 588	Bob MacDonald	.05	.02	.01
☐ 589	Jose Tolentino	.05	.02	.01
☐ 590	Bob Patterson	.05	.02	.01
☐ 591	Scott Brosius	.05	.02	.01
☐ 592	Frank Thomas	1.50	.65	.19
☐ 593	Darryl Hamilton	.10	.05	.01
☐ 594	Kirk Dressendorfer	.05	.02	.01
☐ 595	Jeff Shaw	.05	.02	.01
☐ 596	Don Mattingly	.30	.14	.04
☐ 597	Glenn Davis	.05	.02	.01
☐ 598	Andy Mota	.05	.02	.01
☐ 599	Jason Grimsley	.05	.02	.01
☐ 600	Jimmy Poole	.05	.02	.01
☐ 601	Jim Gott	.05	.02	.01
☐ 602	Stan Royer	.05	.02	.01
☐ 603	Marvin Freeman	.05	.02	.01
☐ 604	Denis Boucher	.10	.05	.01
☐ 605	Denny Neagle	.10	.05	.01
☐ 606	Mark Lemke	.05	.02	.01
☐ 607	Jerry Don Gleaton	.05	.02	.01
☐ 608	Brent Knackert	.05	.02	.01
☐ 609	Carlos Quintana	.05	.02	.01
☐ 610	Bobby Bonilla	.15	.07	.02
☐ 611	Joe Hesketh	.05	.02	.01
☐ 612	Daryl Boston	.05	.02	.01
☐ 613	Shawon Dunston	.05	.02	.01
☐ 614	Danny Cox	.05	.02	.01
☐ 615	Darren Lewis	.10	.05	.01
☐ 616	Braves No-Hitter UER	.05	.02	.01
	Kent Mercker (Misspelled Merker on card front) Alejandro Pena Mark Wohlers			
☐ 617	Kirby Puckett	.30	.14	.04
☐ 618	Franklin Stubbs	.05	.02	.01
☐ 619	Chris Donnels	.05	.02	.01
☐ 620	David Wells UER	.05	.02	.01
	(Career Highlights in black not red)			
☐ 621	Mike Aldrete	.05	.02	.01
☐ 622	Bob Kipper	.05	.02	.01
☐ 623	Anthony Telford	.05	.02	.01
☐ 624	Randy Myers	.10	.05	.01
☐ 625	Willie Randolph	.10	.05	.01
☐ 626	Joe Slusarski	.05	.02	.01
☐ 627	John Wetteland	.05	.02	.01
☐ 628	Greg Cadaret	.05	.02	.01
☐ 629	Tom Glavine	.15	.07	.02
☐ 630	Wilson Alvarez	.15	.07	.02
☐ 631	Wally Ritchie	.05	.02	.01
☐ 632	Mike Mussina	.30	.14	.04
☐ 633	Mark Leiter	.05	.02	.01
☐ 634	Gerald Perry	.05	.02	.01
☐ 635	Matt Young	.05	.02	.01
☐ 636	Checklist 556-635	.05	.02	.01
☐ 637	Scott Hemond	.05	.02	.01
☐ 638	David West	.05	.02	.01
☐ 639	Jim Clancy	.05	.02	.01
☐ 640	Doug Piatt UER	.05	.02	.01
	(Not born in 1955 as on card; incorrect info on How Acquired)			
☐ 641	Omar Vizquel	.05	.02	.01
☐ 642	Rick Sutcliffe	.10	.05	.01
☐ 643	Glenallen Hill	.05	.02	.01
☐ 644	Gary Varsho	.05	.02	.01
☐ 645	Tony Fossas	.05	.02	.01
☐ 646	Jack Howell	.05	.02	.01
☐ 647	Jim Campanis	.05	.02	.01
☐ 648	Chris Gwynn	.05	.02	.01
☐ 649	Jim Leyritz	.05	.02	.01
☐ 650	Chuck McElroy	.05	.02	.01
☐ 651	Sean Berry	.10	.05	.01
☐ 652	Donald Harris	.05	.02	.01
☐ 653	Don Slaught	.05	.02	.01
☐ 654	Rusty Meacham	.05	.02	.01
☐ 655	Scott Terry	.05	.02	.01
☐ 656	Ramon Martinez	.10	.05	.01
☐ 657	Keith Miller	.05	.02	.01

☐ 658 Ramon Garcia .05 .02 .01
☐ 659 Milt Hill .10 .05 .01
☐ 660 Steve Frey .05 .02 .01
☐ 661 Bob McClure .05 .02 .01
☐ 662 Ced Landrum .05 .02 .01
☐ 663 Doug Henry .05 .02 .01
☐ 664 Candy Maldonado .05 .02 .01
☐ 665 Carl Willis .05 .02 .01
☐ 666 Jeff Montgomery .10 .05 .01
☐ 667 Craig Shipley .10 .05 .01
☐ 668 Warren Newson .05 .02 .01
☐ 669 Mickey Morandini .05 .02 .01
☐ 670 Brook Jacoby .05 .02 .01
☐ 671 Ryan Bowen .05 .02 .01
☐ 672 Bill Krueger .05 .02 .01
☐ 673 Rob Mallicoat .05 .02 .01
☐ 674 Doug Jones .05 .02 .01
☐ 675 Scott Livingstone .05 .02 .01
☐ 676 Danny Tartabull .10 .05 .01
☐ 677 Joe Carter HL .10 .05 .01
☐ 678 Cecil Espy .05 .02 .01
☐ 679 Randy Velarde .05 .02 .01
☐ 680 Bruce Ruffin .05 .02 .01
☐ 681 Ted Wood .05 .02 .01
☐ 682 Dan Plesac .05 .02 .01
☐ 683 Eric Bullock .05 .02 .01
☐ 684 Junior Ortiz .05 .02 .01
☐ 685 Dave Hollins .15 .07 .02
☐ 686 Dennis Martinez .10 .05 .01
☐ 687 Larry Andersen .05 .02 .01
☐ 688 Doug Simons .05 .02 .01
☐ 689 Tim Spehr .05 .02 .01
☐ 690 Calvin Jones .05 .02 .01
☐ 691 Mark Guthrie .05 .02 .01
☐ 692 Alfredo Griffin .05 .02 .01
☐ 693 Joe Carter .20 .09 .03
☐ 694 Terry Mathews .05 .02 .01
☐ 695 Pascual Perez .05 .02 .01
☐ 696 Gene Nelson .05 .02 .01
☐ 697 Gerald Williams .10 .05 .01
☐ 698 Chris Cron .05 .02 .01
☐ 699 Steve Buechele .05 .02 .01
☐ 700 Paul McClellan .05 .02 .01
☐ 701 Jim Lindeman .05 .02 .01
☐ 702 Francisco Oliveras .05 .02 .01
☐ 703 Rob Maurer .10 .05 .01
☐ 704 Pat Hentgen .20 .09 .03
☐ 705 Jaime Navarro .05 .02 .01
☐ 706 Mike Magnante .05 .02 .01
☐ 707 Nolan Ryan 1.00 .45 .13
☐ 708 Bobby Thigpen .05 .02 .01
☐ 709 John Cerutti .05 .02 .01
☐ 710 Steve Wilson .05 .02 .01
☐ 711 Hensley Meulens .05 .02 .01
☐ 712 Rheal Cormier .05 .02 .01
☐ 713 Scott Bradley .05 .02 .01
☐ 714 Mitch Webster .05 .02 .01
☐ 715 Roger Mason .05 .02 .01
☐ 716 Checklist 636-716 .05 .02 .01
☐ 717 Jeff Fassero .05 .02 .01
☐ 718 Cal Eldred .10 .05 .01
☐ 719 Sid Fernandez .10 .05 .01
☐ 720 Bob Zupcic .10 .05 .01
☐ 721 Jose Offerman .05 .02 .01
☐ 722 Cliff Brantley .10 .05 .01
☐ 723 Ron Darling .05 .02 .01
☐ 724 Dave Stieb .10 .05 .01
☐ 725 Hector Villanueva .05 .02 .01
☐ 726 Mike Hartley .05 .02 .01
☐ 727 Arthur Rhodes .10 .05 .01
☐ 728 Randy Bush .05 .02 .01
☐ 729 Steve Sax .05 .02 .01
☐ 730 Dave Otto .05 .02 .01
☐ 731 John Wehner .10 .05 .01
☐ 732 Dave Martinez .05 .02 .01
☐ 733 Ruben Amaro .05 .02 .01
☐ 734 Billy Ripken .05 .02 .01
☐ 735 Steve Farr .05 .02 .01
☐ 736 Shawn Abner .05 .02 .01
☐ 737 Gil Heredia .10 .05 .01
☐ 738 Ron Jones .05 .02 .01
☐ 739 Tony Castillo .05 .02 .01
☐ 740 Sammy Sosa .15 .07 .02
☐ 741 Julio Franco .10 .05 .01
☐ 742 Tim Naehring .05 .02 .01
☐ 743 Steve Wapnick .05 .02 .01
☐ 744 Craig Wilson .05 .02 .01
☐ 745 Darrin Chapin .10 .05 .01
☐ 746 Chris George .05 .02 .01
☐ 747 Mike Simms .05 .02 .01
☐ 748 Rosario Rodriguez .05 .02 .01
☐ 749 Skeeter Barnes .05 .02 .01
☐ 750 Roger McDowell .05 .02 .01
☐ 751 Dann Howitt .05 .02 .01
☐ 752 Paul Sorrento .05 .02 .01
☐ 753 Braulio Castillo .05 .02 .01
☐ 754 Yorkis Perez .05 .02 .01
☐ 755 Willie Fraser .05 .02 .01
☐ 756 Jeremy Hernandez .10 .05 .01
☐ 757 Curt Schilling .10 .05 .01
☐ 758 Steve Lyons .05 .02 .01
☐ 759 Dave Anderson .05 .02 .01
☐ 760 Willie Banks .05 .02 .01
☐ 761 Mark Leonard .05 .02 .01
☐ 762 Jack Armstrong .05 .02 .01
(Listed on Indians,
but shown on Reds)
☐ 763 Scott Servais .05 .02 .01
☐ 764 Ray Stephens .05 .02 .01
☐ 765 Junior Noboa .05 .02 .01
☐ 766 Jim Olander .05 .02 .01
☐ 767 Joe Magrane .05 .02 .01
☐ 768 Lance Blankenship .05 .02 .01
☐ 769 Mike Humphreys .10 .05 .01
☐ 770 Jarvis Brown .10 .05 .01
☐ 771 Damon Berryhill .05 .02 .01
☐ 772 Alejandro Pena .05 .02 .01
☐ 773 Jose Mesa .05 .02 .01
☐ 774 Gary Cooper .05 .02 .01
☐ 775 Carney Lansford .10 .05 .01
☐ 776 Mike Bielecki .05 .02 .01
(Shown on Cubs,
but listed on Braves)
☐ 777 Charlie O'Brien .05 .02 .01
☐ 778 Carlos Hernandez .05 .02 .01
☐ 779 Howard Farmer .05 .02 .01
☐ 780 Mike Stanton .05 .02 .01
☐ 781 Reggie Harris .05 .02 .01
☐ 782 Xavier Hernandez .05 .02 .01
☐ 783 Bryan Hickerson .05 .02 .01
☐ 784 Checklist 717-784 .05 .02 .01
and BC1-BC8

1992 Donruss Bonus Cards

The 1992 Donruss Bonus Cards set contains eight cards, measuring the standard size (2 1/2" by 3 1/2"). The cards are numbered on the back and checklisted below accordingly. The cards were randomly

inserted in foil packs of 1992 Donruss baseball cards.

	MINT	EXC	G-VG
COMPLETE SET (8)	1.50	.65	.19
COMMON CARD (BC1-BC8)	.12	.05	.02
☐ BC1 Cal Ripken MVP	.60	.25	.08
☐ BC2 Terry Pendleton MVP	.12	.05	.02
☐ BC3 Roger Clemens CY	.40	.18	.05
☐ BC4 Tom Glavine CY	.15	.07	.02
☐ BC5 Chuck Knoblauch ROY	.15	.07	.02
☐ BC6 Jeff Bagwell ROY	.75	.35	.09
☐ BC7 Colorado Rockies	.50	.23	.06
☐ BC8 Florida Marlins	.50	.23	.06

1992 Donruss Diamond Kings

These standard-size (2 1/2" by 3 1/2") cards were randomly inserted in 1992 Donruss I foil packs (cards 1-13 and the checklist only) and in 1992 Donruss II foil packs (cards 14-26). The fronts feature player portraits by noted sports artist Dick Perez. The words "Donruss Diamond Kings" are superimposed at the card top in a gold-trimmed blue and black banner, with the player's name in a similarly designed black stripe at the card bottom. On a white background with a dark blue border, the backs present career summary. The cards are numbered on the back with a DK prefix.

	MINT	EXC	G-VG
COMPLETE SET (27)	25.00	11.50	3.10
COMPLETE SERIES 1 (14)	17.00	7.75	2.10
COMPLETE SERIES 2 (13)	8.00	3.60	1.00
COMMON CARD (DK1-DK13)	.50	.23	.06
COMMON CARD (DK14-DK26)	.50	.23	.06
☐ DK1 Paul Molitor	2.00	.90	.25
☐ DK2 Will Clark	2.00	.90	.25
☐ DK3 Joe Carter	2.00	.90	.25
☐ DK4 Julio Franco	.75	.35	.09
☐ DK5 Cal Ripken	5.00	2.30	.60
☐ DK6 David Justice	2.00	.90	.25
☐ DK7 George Bell	.75	.35	.09
☐ DK8 Frank Thomas	10.00	4.50	1.25
☐ DK9 Wade Boggs	1.50	.65	.19
☐ DK10 Scott Sanderson	.50	.23	.06
☐ DK11 Jeff Bagwell	5.00	2.30	.60
☐ DK12 John Kruk	.75	.35	.09
☐ DK13 Felix Jose	.75	.35	.09
☐ DK14 Harold Baines	.75	.35	.09
☐ DK15 Dwight Gooden	.75	.35	.09
☐ DK16 Brian McRae	.75	.35	.09
☐ DK17 Jay Bell	.75	.35	.09
☐ DK18 Brett Butler	.75	.35	.09
☐ DK19 Hal Morris	.75	.35	.09
☐ DK20 Mark Langston	.75	.35	.09
☐ DK21 Scott Erickson	.50	.23	.06
☐ DK22 Randy Johnson	.75	.35	.09
☐ DK23 Greg Swindell	.50	.23	.06
☐ DK24 Dennis Martinez	.50	.23	.06
☐ DK25 Tony Phillips	.50	.23	.06
☐ DK26 Fred McGriff	2.00	.90	.25
☐ DK27 Checklist 1-26 DP (Dick Perez)	.30	.14	.04

1992 Donruss Elite

These cards were random inserts in 1992 Donruss foil packs. The numbering on the Elite cards is essentially a continuation of the series started the year before. The Signature Series Cal Ripken card was inserted in 1992 Donruss foil packs. Only 5,000 Ripken Signature Series cards were printed. The Rickey Henderson Legends Series card was inserted in 1992 Donruss foil packs; only 7,500 Henderson Legends cards were printed. All of these special limited cards are standard size, 2 1/2" by 3 1/2".

	MINT	EXC	G-VG
COMPLETE SET (12)	1000.00	450.00	125.00
COMMON CARD (9-18)	25.00	11.50	3.10
☐ 9 Wade Boggs	40.00	18.00	5.00
☐ 10 Joe Carter	60.00	27.00	7.50
☐ 11 Will Clark	60.00	27.00	7.50
☐ 12 Dwight Gooden	25.00	11.50	3.10
☐ 13 Ken Griffey Jr.	175.00	80.00	22.00
☐ 14 Tony Gwynn	60.00	27.00	7.50

☐	15 Howard Johnson	25.00	11.50	3.10
☐	16 Terry Pendleton	25.00	11.50	3.10
☐	17 Kirby Puckett	100.00	45.00	12.50
☐	18 Frank Thomas	175.00	80.00	22.00
☐	L2 Rickey Henderson (Legend Series)	100.00	45.00	12.50
☐	S2 Cal Ripken (Signature Series)	325.00	145.00	40.00

1992 Donruss Update

Four cards from this 22-card set were included in each retail factory set. Card numbers U1-U6 are Rated Rookie cards, while card numbers U7-U9 are Highlights cards. The cards measures the standard size (2 1/2" by 3 1/2") and features color action player photos with white borders. The photos are edged at the top and bottom by blue stripes of varying shades. The player's name overlaps the photo and the bottom border. The backs are horizontal with the Highlights, Rated Rookie, and regular cards presenting slightly different information. The Highlights cards describe a special career achievement and have a white blue-on-blue diagonal striped background. The Rated Rookie cards carry career highlights and recent statistics on a white and green-on-green diagonal striped background. The regular cards display a player close-up, statistics, career highlights, and biographical information. The cards are numbered on the back with a "U" prefix.

	MINT	EXC	G-VG
COMPLETE SET (22)	65.00	29.00	8.25
COMMON CARD (U1-U22)	1.00	.45	.13

☐	U1 Pat Listach RR	1.50	.65	.19
☐	U2 Andy Stankiewicz RR	1.00	.45	.13
☐	U3 Brian Jordan RR	2.50	1.15	.30
☐	U4 Dan Walters RR	1.00	.45	.13
☐	U5 Chad Curtis RR	4.00	1.80	.50
☐	U6 Kenny Lofton RR	40.00	18.00	5.00
☐	U7 Mark McGwire HL	3.00	1.35	.40
☐	U8 Eddie Murray HL	4.00	1.80	.50
☐	U9 Jeff Reardon HL	1.25	.55	.16
☐	U10 Frank Viola	1.25	.55	.16
☐	U11 Gary Sheffield	4.00	1.80	.50
☐	U12 George Bell	1.25	.55	.16
☐	U13 Rick Sutcliffe	1.00	.45	.13
☐	U14 Wally Joyner	1.00	.45	.13
☐	U15 Kevin Seitzer	1.00	.45	.13
☐	U16 Bill Krueger	1.00	.45	.13
☐	U17 Danny Tartabull	1.25	.55	.16
☐	U18 Dave Winfield	5.00	2.30	.60
☐	U19 Gary Carter	1.50	.65	.19
☐	U20 Bobby Bonilla	2.50	1.15	.30
☐	U21 Cory Snyder	1.00	.45	.13
☐	U22 Bill Swift	1.25	.55	.16

1992 Donruss Rookies

After six years of issuing "The Rookies" as a 56-card boxed set, Donruss expanded it to a 132-card set available only as a foil pack product. An additional 20 Phenom cards were randomly inserted in the packs (numbered 1-12 in 12-card foil packs and numbered 13-20 in 30-card jumbo packs). The cards measure the standard size (2 1/2" by 3 1/2"). The card design is the same as the 1992 Donruss regular issue except that the two-tone blue color bars have been replaced by green, as in the previous six Donruss Rookies sets. The cards are arranged in alphabetical order and numbered on the back. Rookie Cards in this set include Billy Ashley, Pedro Astacio, Chad Curtis, Brent Gates, Al Martin, David Nied, Manny Ramirez, and Tim Wakefield.

	MINT	EXC	G-VG
COMPLETE SET (132)	8.00	3.60	1.00
COMMON CARD (1-132)	.05	.02	.01

☐	1 Kyle Abbott	.05	.02	.01
☐	2 Troy Afenir	.05	.02	.01
☐	3 Rich Amaral	.05	.02	.01
☐	4 Ruben Amaro	.05	.02	.01
☐	5 Billy Ashley	.60	.25	.08
☐	6 Pedro Astacio	.15	.07	.02
☐	7 Jim Austin	.05	.02	.01
☐	8 Robert Ayrault	.08	.04	.01
☐	9 Kevin Baez	.08	.04	.01
☐	10 Esteban Beltre	.08	.04	.01
☐	11 Brian Bohanon	.05	.02	.01
☐	12 Kent Bottenfield	.05	.02	.01
☐	13 Jeff Branson	.05	.02	.01
☐	14 Brad Brink	.05	.02	.01
☐	15 John Briscoe	.05	.02	.01
☐	16 Doug Brocail	.05	.02	.01
☐	17 Rico Brogna	.05	.02	.01

	No.	Player			
☐	18	J.T. Bruett	.08	.04	.01
☐	19	Jacob Brumfield	.05	.02	.01
☐	20	Jim Bullinger	.05	.02	.01
☐	21	Kevin Campbell	.05	.02	.01
☐	22	Pedro Castellano	.15	.07	.02
☐	23	Mike Christopher	.05	.02	.01
☐	24	Archi Cianfrocco	.05	.02	.01
☐	25	Mark Clark	.20	.09	.03
☐	26	Craig Colbert	.05	.02	.01
☐	27	Victor Cole	.08	.04	.01
☐	28	Steve Cooke	.15	.07	.02
☐	29	Tim Costo	.05	.02	.01
☐	30	Chad Curtis	.15	.07	.02
☐	31	Doug Davis	.05	.02	.01
☐	32	Gary DiSarcina	.08	.04	.01
☐	33	John Doherty	.15	.07	.02
☐	34	Mike Draper	.05	.02	.01
☐	35	Monty Fariss	.05	.02	.01
☐	36	Bien Figueroa	.05	.02	.01
☐	37	John Flaherty	.08	.04	.01
☐	38	Tim Fortugno	.05	.02	.01
☐	39	Eric Fox	.08	.04	.01
☐	40	Jeff Frye	.08	.04	.01
☐	41	Ramon Garcia	.05	.02	.01
☐	42	Brent Gates	.25	.11	.03
☐	43	Tom Goodwin	.05	.02	.01
☐	44	Buddy Groom	.08	.04	.01
☐	45	Jeff Grotewold	.08	.04	.01
☐	46	Juan Guerrero	.08	.04	.01
☐	47	Johnny Guzman	.05	.02	.01
☐	48	Shawn Hare	.08	.04	.01
☐	49	Ryan Hawblitzel	.15	.07	.02
☐	50	Bert Hefferman	.05	.02	.01
☐	51	Butch Henry	.08	.04	.01
☐	52	Cesar Hernandez	.08	.04	.01
☐	53	Vince Horsman	.08	.04	.01
☐	54	Steve Hosey	.05	.02	.01
☐	55	Pat Howell	.08	.04	.01
☐	56	Peter Hoy	.08	.04	.01
☐	57	Jonathan Hurst	.05	.02	.01
☐	58	Mark Hutton	.15	.07	.02
☐	59	Shawn Jeter	.08	.04	.01
☐	60	Joel Johnston	.05	.02	.01
☐	61	Jeff Kent	.30	.14	.04
☐	62	Kurt Knudsen	.08	.04	.01
☐	63	Kevin Koslofski	.08	.04	.01
☐	64	Danny Leon	.08	.04	.01
☐	65	Jesse Levis	.08	.04	.01
☐	66	Tom Marsh	.08	.04	.01
☐	67	Ed Martel	.05	.02	.01
☐	68	Al Martin	.20	.09	.03
☐	69	Pedro Martinez	.25	.11	.03
☐	70	Derrick May	.08	.04	.01
☐	71	Matt Maysey	.08	.04	.01
☐	72	Russ McGinnis	.05	.02	.01
☐	73	Tim McIntosh	.05	.02	.01
☐	74	Jim McNamara	.08	.04	.01
☐	75	Jeff McNeely	.05	.02	.01
☐	76	Rusty Meacham	.05	.02	.01
☐	77	Tony Menendez	.05	.02	.01
☐	78	Henry Mercedes	.05	.02	.01
☐	79	Paul Miller	.08	.04	.01
☐	80	Joe Millette	.08	.04	.01
☐	81	Blas Minor	.08	.04	.01
☐	82	Dennis Moeller	.08	.04	.01
☐	83	Raul Mondesi	2.00	.90	.25
☐	84	Rob Natal	.08	.04	.01
☐	85	Troy Neel	.15	.07	.02
☐	86	David Nied	.30	.14	.04
☐	87	Jerry Nielson	.08	.04	.01
☐	88	Donovan Osborne	.05	.02	.01
☐	89	John Patterson	.08	.04	.01
☐	90	Roger Pavlik	.15	.07	.02
☐	91	Dan Peltier	.05	.02	.01
☐	92	Jim Pena	.05	.02	.01
☐	93	William Pennyfeather	.05	.02	.01
☐	94	Mike Perez	.05	.02	.01
☐	95	Hipolito Pichardo	.05	.02	.01
☐	96	Greg Pirkl	.15	.07	.02
☐	97	Harvey Pulliam	.05	.02	.01
☐	98	Manny Ramirez	1.50	.65	.19
☐	99	Pat Rapp	.15	.07	.02
☐	100	Jeff Reboulet	.05	.02	.01
☐	101	Darren Reed	.05	.02	.01
☐	102	Shane Reynolds	.20	.09	.03
☐	103	Bill Risley	.08	.04	.01
☐	104	Ben Rivera	.05	.02	.01
☐	105	Henry Rodriguez	.05	.02	.01
☐	106	Rico Rossy	.05	.02	.01
☐	107	Johnny Ruffin	.05	.02	.01
☐	108	Steve Scarsone	.08	.04	.01
☐	109	Tim Scott	.08	.04	.01
☐	110	Steve Shifflett	.08	.04	.01
☐	111	Dave Silvestri	.05	.02	.01
☐	112	Matt Stairs	.05	.02	.01
☐	113	William Suero	.05	.02	.01
☐	114	Jeff Tackett	.05	.02	.01
☐	115	Eddie Taubensee	.05	.02	.01
☐	116	Rick Trlicek	.05	.02	.01
☐	117	Scooter Tucker	.08	.04	.01
☐	118	Shane Turner	.08	.04	.01
☐	119	Julio Valera	.08	.04	.01
☐	120	Paul Wagner	.15	.07	.02
☐	121	Tim Wakefield	.05	.02	.01
☐	122	Mike Walker	.05	.02	.01
☐	123	Bruce Walton	.05	.02	.01
☐	124	Lenny Webster	.05	.02	.01
☐	125	Bob Wickman	.08	.04	.01
☐	126	Mike Williams	.15	.07	.02
☐	127	Kerry Woodson	.05	.02	.01
☐	128	Eric Young	.15	.07	.02
☐	129	Kevin Young	.15	.07	.02
☐	130	Pete Young	.05	.02	.01
☐	131	Checklist 1-66	.05	.02	.01
☐	132	Checklist 67-132	.05	.02	.01

1992 Donruss Rookies Phenoms

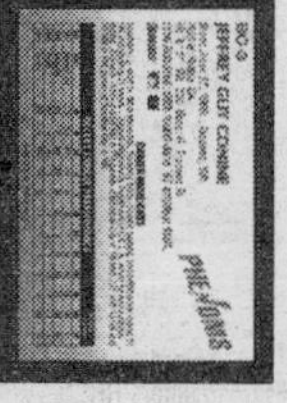

This 20-card set features baseball's most dynamic young prospects. The first 12 Phenom cards (1-12) were randomly inserted into 1992 Donruss The Rookies 12-card foil packs. The last eight Phenom cards (13-20) were randomly inserted in 30-card jumbo packs. The standard-size (2 1/2" by

3 1/2") cards display nonaction color photos that are accented by gold-foil border stripes on a predominantly black card face. The set title "Phenoms" appears in gold foil lettering above the picture, while the player's name is given in the bottom border. In a horizontal format, the backs present biography, career highlights, and recent career performance statistics in a white and gray box enclosed by black and gold borders. The cards are arranged alphabetically and numbered on the back with a "BC" prefix.

	MINT	EXC	G-VG
COMPLETE SET (20)	35.00	16.00	4.40
COMPLETE FOIL SET (12)	25.00	11.50	3.10
COMPLETE JUMBO SET (8)	10.00	4.50	1.25
COMMON CARD (BC1-BC12)	.50	.23	.06
COMMON CARD (BC13-BC20)	.50	.23	.06

	MINT	EXC	G-VG
☐ BC1 Moises Alou	2.00	.90	.25
☐ BC2 Bret Boone	2.00	.90	.25
☐ BC3 Jeff Conine	1.50	.65	.19
☐ BC4 Dave Fleming	.50	.23	.06
☐ BC5 Tyler Green	.50	.23	.06
☐ BC6 Eric Karros	1.00	.45	.13
☐ BC7 Pat Listach	.50	.23	.06
☐ BC8 Kenny Lofton	7.00	3.10	.85
☐ BC9 Mike Piazza	20.00	9.00	2.50
☐ BC10 Tim Salmon	5.00	2.30	.60
☐ BC11 Andy Stankiewicz	.50	.23	.06
☐ BC12 Dan Walters	.50	.23	.06
☐ BC13 Ramon Caraballo	.50	.23	.06
☐ BC14 Brian Jordan	.50	.23	.06
☐ BC15 Ryan Klesko	6.00	2.70	.75
☐ BC16 Sam Militello	.50	.23	.06
☐ BC17 Frank Seminara	.50	.23	.06
☐ BC18 Salomon Torres	1.00	.45	.13
☐ BC19 John Valentin	.50	.23	.06
☐ BC20 Wil Cordero	1.50	.65	.19

1993 Donruss

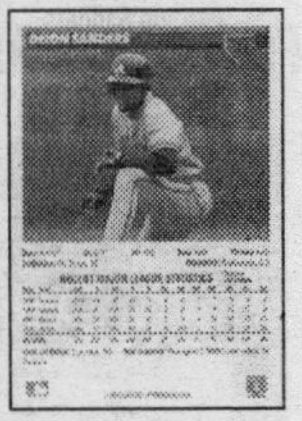

The 1993 Donruss set was issued in two series, each with 396 standard-size (2 1/2" by 3 1/2") cards. Several card subsets were randomly inserted in various Donruss products: Diamond Kings (featuring the artwork of Dick Perez and gold-foil stamping) in foil packs (1-15 in series I and 16-31 in series II); Elite series in all packs (18 in all, nine in each series); Spirit of the Game (reportedly packed approximately two per box) in regular foil and jumbo packs (20 in total with ten in each series); Long Ball Leaders in 26-card magazine distributor packs (1-9 in series I and 10-18 in series II); and MVP cards in 23-card jumbo packs (26 in total with 13 in each series). Will Clark Signature Series (2,500 in each series) and Robin Yount Legend Series (10,000) cards were randomly inserted throughout the packs. Finally a Rated Rookies subset spotlights 20 top prospects; these Rated Rookies are sprinkled thoughout the set and are designated by RR in the checklist below. The fronts feature glossy color action photos bordered in white. At the bottom of the picture, the team logo appears in a team color-coded diamond with the player's name in a color-coded bar extending to the right. The backs have a second color player photo with biography and recent major league statistics filling up the rest of the card. The cards are numbered in a team color-coded home plate icon at the upper right corner. Rookie Cards in this set include Rene Arocha and J.T. Snow.

	MINT	EXC	G-VG
COMPLETE SET (792)	30.00	13.50	3.80
COMPLETE SERIES 1 (396)	15.00	6.75	1.90
COMPLETE SERIES 2 (396)	15.00	6.75	1.90
COMMON CARD (1-396)	.05	.02	.01
COMMON CARD (397-792)	.05	.02	.01

	MINT	EXC	G-VG
☐ 1 Craig Lefferts	.05	.02	.01
☐ 2 Kent Mercker	.05	.02	.01
☐ 3 Phil Plantier	.10	.05	.01
☐ 4 Alex Arias	.05	.02	.01
☐ 5 Julio Valera	.05	.02	.01
☐ 6 Dan Wilson	.05	.02	.01
☐ 7 Frank Thomas	2.00	.90	.25
☐ 8 Eric Anthony	.05	.02	.01
☐ 9 Derek Lilliquist	.05	.02	.01
☐ 10 Rafael Bournigal	.08	.04	.01
☐ 11 Manny Alexander RR	.05	.02	.01
☐ 12 Bret Barberie	.05	.02	.01
☐ 13 Mickey Tettleton	.08	.04	.01
☐ 14 Anthony Young	.08	.04	.01
☐ 15 Tim Spehr	.05	.02	.01
☐ 16 Bob Ayrault	.05	.02	.01
☐ 17 Bill Wegman	.05	.02	.01
☐ 18 Jay Bell	.08	.04	.01
☐ 19 Rick Aguilera	.08	.04	.01
☐ 20 Todd Zeile	.08	.04	.01
☐ 21 Steve Farr	.05	.02	.01
☐ 22 Andy Benes	.08	.04	.01
☐ 23 Lance Blankenship	.05	.02	.01
☐ 24 Ted Wood	.05	.02	.01
☐ 25 Omar Vizquel	.05	.02	.01
☐ 26 Steve Avery	.10	.05	.01
☐ 27 Brian Bohanon	.05	.02	.01
☐ 28 Rick Wilkins	.05	.02	.01
☐ 29 Devon White	.08	.04	.01
☐ 30 Bobby Ayala	.20	.09	.03
☐ 31 Leo Gomez	.05	.02	.01
☐ 32 Mike Simms	.05	.02	.01
☐ 33 Ellis Burks	.08	.04	.01
☐ 34 Steve Wilson	.05	.02	.01
☐ 35 Jim Abbott	.10	.05	.01
☐ 36 Tim Wallach	.05	.02	.01
☐ 37 Wilson Alvarez	.10	.05	.01
☐ 38 Daryl Boston	.05	.02	.01
☐ 39 Sandy Alomar Jr.	.08	.04	.01
☐ 40 Mitch Williams	.08	.04	.01
☐ 41 Rico Brogna	.08	.04	.01

☐ 42 Gary Varsho .05 .02 .01
☐ 43 Kevin Appier .08 .04 .01
☐ 44 Eric Wedge RR .05 .02 .01
☐ 45 Dante Bichette .10 .05 .01
☐ 46 Jose Oquendo .05 .02 .01
☐ 47 Mike Trombley .05 .02 .01
☐ 48 Dan Walters .05 .02 .01
☐ 49 Gerald Williams .05 .02 .01
☐ 50 Bud Black .05 .02 .01
☐ 51 Bobby Witt .05 .02 .01
☐ 52 Mark Davis .05 .02 .01
☐ 53 Shawn Barton .08 .04 .01
☐ 54 Paul Assenmacher .05 .02 .01
☐ 55 Kevin Reimer .05 .02 .01
☐ 56 Billy Ashley RR .35 .16 .04
☐ 57 Eddie Zosky .05 .02 .01
☐ 58 Chris Sabo .08 .04 .01
☐ 59 Billy Ripken .05 .02 .01
☐ 60 Scooter Tucker .05 .02 .01
☐ 61 Tim Wakefield RR .05 .02 .01
☐ 62 Mitch Webster .05 .02 .01
☐ 63 Jack Clark .08 .04 .01
☐ 64 Mark Gardner .05 .02 .01
☐ 65 Lee Stevens .05 .02 .01
☐ 66 Todd Hundley .05 .02 .01
☐ 67 Bobby Thigpen .05 .02 .01
☐ 68 Dave Hollins .10 .05 .01
☐ 69 Jack Armstrong .05 .02 .01
☐ 70 Alex Cole .05 .02 .01
☐ 71 Mark Carreon .05 .02 .01
☐ 72 Todd Worrell .05 .02 .01
☐ 73 Steve Shifflett .05 .02 .01
☐ 74 Jerald Clark .05 .02 .01
☐ 75 Paul Molitor .30 .14 .04
☐ 76 Larry Carter .08 .04 .01
☐ 77 Rich Rowland RR .05 .02 .01
☐ 78 Damon Berryhill .05 .02 .01
☐ 79 Willie Banks .05 .02 .01
☐ 80 Hector Villanueva .05 .02 .01
☐ 81 Mike Gallego .05 .02 .01
☐ 82 Tim Belcher .05 .02 .01
☐ 83 Mike Bordick .05 .02 .01
☐ 84 Craig Biggio .08 .04 .01
☐ 85 Lance Parrish .08 .04 .01
☐ 86 Brett Butler .08 .04 .01
☐ 87 Mike Timlin .05 .02 .01
☐ 88 Brian Barnes .05 .02 .01
☐ 89 Brady Anderson .08 .04 .01
☐ 90 D.J. Dozier .08 .04 .01
☐ 91 Frank Viola .08 .04 .01
☐ 92 Darren Daulton .10 .05 .01
☐ 93 Chad Curtis .08 .04 .01
☐ 94 Zane Smith .05 .02 .01
☐ 95 George Bell .08 .04 .01
☐ 96 Rex Hudler .05 .02 .01
☐ 97 Mark Whiten .08 .04 .01
☐ 98 Tim Teufel .05 .02 .01
☐ 99 Kevin Ritz .05 .02 .01
☐ 100 Jeff Brantley .05 .02 .01
☐ 101 Jeff Conine .10 .05 .01
☐ 102 Vinny Castilla .05 .02 .01
☐ 103 Greg Vaughn .08 .04 .01
☐ 104 Steve Buechele .05 .02 .01
☐ 105 Darren Reed .05 .02 .01
☐ 106 Bip Roberts .05 .02 .01
☐ 107 John Habyan .05 .02 .01
☐ 108 Scott Servais .05 .02 .01
☐ 109 Walt Weiss .05 .02 .01
☐ 110 J.T. Snow RR .15 .07 .02
☐ 111 Jay Buhner .08 .04 .01
☐ 112 Darryl Strawberry .08 .04 .01
☐ 113 Roger Pavlik .08 .04 .01
☐ 114 Chris Nabholz .05 .02 .01
☐ 115 Pat Borders .05 .02 .01
☐ 116 Pat Howell .05 .02 .01
☐ 117 Gregg Olson .05 .02 .01
☐ 118 Curt Schilling .08 .04 .01
☐ 119 Roger Clemens .50 .23 .06
☐ 120 Victor Cole .05 .02 .01
☐ 121 Gary DiSarcina .05 .02 .01
☐ 122 Checklist 1-80 .05 .02 .01
(Gary Carter and
Kirt Manwaring
☐ 123 Steve Sax .05 .02 .01
☐ 124 Chuck Carr .05 .02 .01
☐ 125 Mark Lewis .05 .02 .01
☐ 126 Tony Gwynn .50 .23 .06
☐ 127 Travis Fryman .15 .07 .02
☐ 128 Dave Burba .05 .02 .01
☐ 129 Wally Joyner .08 .04 .01
☐ 130 John Smoltz .08 .04 .01
☐ 131 Cal Eldred .08 .04 .01
☐ 132 Checklist 81-159 .05 .02 .01
(Roberto Alomar and
Devon White)
☐ 133 Arthur Rhodes .05 .02 .01
☐ 134 Jeff Blauser .08 .04 .01
☐ 135 Scott Cooper .08 .04 .01
☐ 136 Doug Strange .05 .02 .01
☐ 137 Luis Sojo .05 .02 .01
☐ 138 Jeff Branson .05 .02 .01
☐ 139 Alex Fernandez .10 .05 .01
☐ 140 Ken Caminiti .08 .04 .01
☐ 141 Charles Nagy .05 .02 .01
☐ 142 Tom Candiotti .05 .02 .01
☐ 143 Willie Greene RR .08 .04 .01
☐ 144 John Vander Wal .05 .02 .01
☐ 145 Kurt Knudsen .05 .02 .01
☐ 146 John Franco .05 .02 .01
☐ 147 Eddie Pierce .05 .02 .01
☐ 148 Kim Batiste .05 .02 .01
☐ 149 Darren Holmes .05 .02 .01
☐ 150 Steve Cooke .05 .02 .01
☐ 151 Terry Jorgensen .05 .02 .01
☐ 152 Mark Clark .08 .04 .01
☐ 153 Randy Velarde .05 .02 .01
☐ 154 Greg W. Harris .05 .02 .01
☐ 155 Kevin Campbell .05 .02 .01
☐ 156 John Burkett .08 .04 .01
☐ 157 Kevin Mitchell .08 .04 .01
☐ 158 Deion Sanders .40 .18 .05
☐ 159 Jose Canseco .30 .14 .04
☐ 160 Jeff Hartsock .08 .04 .01
☐ 161 Tom Quinlan .05 .02 .01
☐ 162 Tim Pugh .05 .02 .01
☐ 163 Glenn Davis .05 .02 .01
☐ 164 Shane Reynolds .08 .04 .01
☐ 165 Jody Reed .05 .02 .01
☐ 166 Mike Sharperson .05 .02 .01
☐ 167 Scott Lewis .05 .02 .01
☐ 168 Dennis Martinez .08 .04 .01
☐ 169 Scott Radinsky .05 .02 .01
☐ 170 Dave Gallagher .05 .02 .01
☐ 171 Jim Thome .25 .11 .03
☐ 172 Terry Mulholland .05 .02 .01
☐ 173 Milt Cuyler .05 .02 .01
☐ 174 Bob Patterson .05 .02 .01
☐ 175 Jeff Montgomery .08 .04 .01
☐ 176 Tim Salmon RR .40 .18 .05
☐ 177 Franklin Stubbs .05 .02 .01
☐ 178 Donovan Osborne .05 .02 .01
☐ 179 Jeff Reboulet .05 .02 .01
☐ 180 Jeremy Hernandez .05 .02 .01
☐ 181 Charlie Hayes .08 .04 .01
☐ 182 Matt Williams .30 .14 .04
☐ 183 Mike Raczka .08 .04 .01

☐ 184	Francisco Cabrera	.05	.02	.01
☐ 185	Rich DeLucia	.05	.02	.01
☐ 186	Sammy Sosa	.10	.05	.01
☐ 187	Ivan Rodriguez	.10	.05	.01
☐ 188	Bret Boone RR	.10	.05	.01
☐ 189	Juan Guzman	.08	.04	.01
☐ 190	Tom Browning	.05	.02	.01
☐ 191	Randy Milligan	.05	.02	.01
☐ 192	Steve Finley	.05	.02	.01
☐ 193	John Patterson RR	.05	.02	.01
☐ 194	Kip Gross	.05	.02	.01
☐ 195	Tony Fossas	.05	.02	.01
☐ 196	Ivan Calderon	.05	.02	.01
☐ 197	Junior Felix	.05	.02	.01
☐ 198	Pate Schourek	.05	.02	.01
☐ 199	Craig Grebeck	.05	.02	.01
☐ 200	Juan Bell	.05	.02	.01
☐ 201	Glenallen Hill	.05	.02	.01
☐ 202	Danny Jackson	.05	.02	.01
☐ 203	John Kiely	.05	.02	.01
☐ 204	Bob Tewksbury	.05	.02	.01
☐ 205	Kevin Koslofski	.05	.02	.01
☐ 206	Craig Shipley	.05	.02	.01
☐ 207	John Jaha	.08	.04	.01
☐ 208	Royce Clayton	.08	.04	.01
☐ 209	Mike Piazza RR	2.00	.90	.25
☐ 210	Ron Gant	.08	.04	.01
☐ 211	Scott Erickson	.05	.02	.01
☐ 212	Doug Dascenzo	.05	.02	.01
☐ 213	Andy Stankiewicz	.05	.02	.01
☐ 214	Geronimo Berroa	.05	.02	.01
☐ 215	Dennis Eckersley	.10	.05	.01
☐ 216	Al Osuna	.05	.02	.01
☐ 217	Tino Martinez	.08	.04	.01
☐ 218	Henry Rodriguez	.05	.02	.01
☐ 219	Ed Sprague	.08	.04	.01
☐ 220	Ken Hill	.08	.04	.01
☐ 221	Chito Martinez	.05	.02	.01
☐ 222	Bret Saberhagen	.08	.04	.01
☐ 223	Mike Greenwell	.08	.04	.01
☐ 224	Mickey Morandini	.05	.02	.01
☐ 225	Chuck Finley	.05	.02	.01
☐ 226	Denny Neagle	.05	.02	.01
☐ 227	Kirk McCaskill	.05	.02	.01
☐ 228	Rheal Cormier	.05	.02	.01
☐ 229	Paul Sorrento	.05	.02	.01
☐ 230	Darrin Jackson	.05	.02	.01
☐ 231	Rob Deer	.05	.02	.01
☐ 232	Bill Swift	.08	.04	.01
☐ 233	Kevin McReynolds	.05	.02	.01
☐ 234	Terry Pendleton	.10	.05	.01
☐ 235	Dave Nilsson	.08	.04	.01
☐ 236	Chuck McElroy	.05	.02	.01
☐ 237	Derek Parks	.05	.02	.01
☐ 238	Norm Charlton	.05	.02	.01
☐ 239	Matt Nokes	.05	.02	.01
☐ 240	Juan Guerrero	.05	.02	.01
☐ 241	Jeff Parrett	.05	.02	.01
☐ 242	Ryan Thompson RR	.10	.05	.01
☐ 243	Dave Fleming	.08	.04	.01
☐ 244	Dave Hansen	.05	.02	.01
☐ 245	Monty Fariss	.05	.02	.01
☐ 246	Archi Cianfrocco	.05	.02	.01
☐ 247	Pat Hentgen	.08	.04	.01
☐ 248	Bill Pecota	.05	.02	.01
☐ 249	Ben McDonald	.08	.04	.01
☐ 250	Cliff Brantley	.05	.02	.01
☐ 251	John Valentin	.08	.04	.01
☐ 252	Jeff King	.05	.02	.01
☐ 253	Reggie Williams	.05	.02	.01
☐ 254	Checklist 160-238 (Damon Berryhill and Alex Arias)	.05	.02	.01
☐ 255	Ozzie Guillen	.05	.02	.01
☐ 256	Mike Perez	.05	.02	.01
☐ 257	Thomas Howard	.05	.02	.01
☐ 258	Kurt Stillwell	.05	.02	.01
☐ 259	Mike Henneman	.05	.02	.01
☐ 260	Steve Decker	.05	.02	.01
☐ 261	Brent Mayne	.05	.02	.01
☐ 262	Otis Nixon	.05	.02	.01
☐ 263	Mark Kiefer	.05	.02	.01
☐ 264	Checklist 239-317 (Don Mattingly and Mike Bordick)	.05	.02	.01
☐ 265	Richie Lewis	.05	.02	.01
☐ 266	Pat Gomez	.05	.02	.01
☐ 267	Scott Taylor	.05	.02	.01
☐ 268	Shawon Dunston	.05	.02	.01
☐ 269	Greg Myers	.05	.02	.01
☐ 270	Tim Costo	.05	.02	.01
☐ 271	Greg Hibbard	.05	.02	.01
☐ 272	Pete Harnisch	.05	.02	.01
☐ 273	Dave Mlicki	.05	.02	.01
☐ 274	Orel Hershiser	.08	.04	.01
☐ 275	Sean Berry RR	.05	.02	.01
☐ 276	Doug Simons	.05	.02	.01
☐ 277	John Doherty	.05	.02	.01
☐ 278	Eddie Murray	.10	.05	.01
☐ 279	Chris Haney	.05	.02	.01
☐ 280	Stan Javier	.05	.02	.01
☐ 281	Jaime Navarro	.05	.02	.01
☐ 282	Orlando Merced	.08	.04	.01
☐ 283	Kent Hrbek	.08	.04	.01
☐ 284	Bernard Gilkey	.05	.02	.01
☐ 285	Russ Springer	.05	.02	.01
☐ 286	Mike Maddux	.05	.02	.01
☐ 287	Eric Fox	.05	.02	.01
☐ 288	Mark Leonard	.05	.02	.01
☐ 289	Tim Leary	.05	.02	.01
☐ 290	Brian Hunter	.08	.04	.01
☐ 291	Donald Harris	.05	.02	.01
☐ 292	Bob Scanlan	.05	.02	.01
☐ 293	Turner Ward	.05	.02	.01
☐ 294	Hal Morris	.08	.04	.01
☐ 295	Jimmy Poole	.05	.02	.01
☐ 296	Doug Jones	.05	.02	.01
☐ 297	Tony Pena	.05	.02	.01
☐ 298	Ramon Martinez	.08	.04	.01
☐ 299	Tim Fortugno	.05	.02	.01
☐ 300	Marquis Grissom	.10	.05	.01
☐ 301	Lance Johnson	.05	.02	.01
☐ 302	Jeff Kent	.10	.05	.01
☐ 303	Reggie Jefferson	.05	.02	.01
☐ 304	Wes Chamberlain	.05	.02	.01
☐ 305	Shawn Hare	.05	.02	.01
☐ 306	Mike LaValliere	.05	.02	.01
☐ 307	Gregg Jefferies	.10	.05	.01
☐ 308	Troy Neel RR	.08	.04	.01
☐ 309	Pat Listach	.08	.04	.01
☐ 310	Geronimo Pena	.05	.02	.01
☐ 311	Pedro Munoz	.05	.02	.01
☐ 312	Guillermo Velasquez	.05	.02	.01
☐ 313	Roberto Kelly	.08	.04	.01
☐ 314	Mike Jackson	.05	.02	.01
☐ 315	Rickey Henderson	.10	.05	.01
☐ 316	Mark Lemke	.05	.02	.01
☐ 317	Erik Hanson	.05	.02	.01
☐ 318	Derrick May	.08	.04	.01
☐ 319	Geno Petralli	.05	.02	.01
☐ 320	Melvin Nieves RR	.10	.05	.01
☐ 321	Doug Linton	.05	.02	.01
☐ 322	Rob Dibble	.05	.02	.01
☐ 323	Chris Hoiles	.08	.04	.01
☐ 324	Jimmy Jones	.05	.02	.01
☐ 325	Dave Staton RR	.05	.02	.01

- ☐ 326 Pedro Martinez .10 .05 .01
- ☐ 327 Paul Quantrill .05 .02 .01
- ☐ 328 Greg Colbrunn .05 .02 .01
- ☐ 329 Hilly Hathaway .05 .02 .01
- ☐ 330 Jeff Innis .05 .02 .01
- ☐ 331 Ron Karkovice .05 .02 .01
- ☐ 332 Keith Shepherd .05 .02 .01
- ☐ 333 Alan Embree .05 .02 .01
- ☐ 334 Paul Wagner .05 .02 .01
- ☐ 335 Dave Haas .05 .02 .01
- ☐ 336 Ozzie Canseco .05 .02 .01
- ☐ 337 Bill Sampen .05 .02 .01
- ☐ 338 Rich Rodriguez .05 .02 .01
- ☐ 339 Dean Palmer .08 .04 .01
- ☐ 340 Greg Litton .05 .02 .01
- ☐ 341 Jim Tatum RR .05 .02 .01
- ☐ 342 Todd Haney .08 .04 .01
- ☐ 343 Larry Casian .05 .02 .01
- ☐ 344 Ryne Sandberg .60 .25 .08
- ☐ 345 Sterling Hitchcock .15 .07 .02
- ☐ 346 Chris Hammond .05 .02 .01
- ☐ 347 Vince Horsman .05 .02 .01
- ☐ 348 Butch Henry .05 .02 .01
- ☐ 349 Dann Howitt .05 .02 .01
- ☐ 350 Roger McDowell .05 .02 .01
- ☐ 351 Jack Morris .10 .05 .01
- ☐ 352 Bill Krueger .05 .02 .01
- ☐ 353 Cris Colon .05 .02 .01
- ☐ 354 Joe Vitko .05 .02 .01
- ☐ 355 Willie McGee .08 .04 .01
- ☐ 356 Jay Baller .05 .02 .01
- ☐ 357 Pat Mahomes .05 .02 .01
- ☐ 358 Roger Mason .05 .02 .01
- ☐ 359 Jerry Nielsen .05 .02 .01
- ☐ 360 Tom Pagnozzi .05 .02 .01
- ☐ 361 Kevin Baez .05 .02 .01
- ☐ 362 Tim Scott .05 .02 .01
- ☐ 363 Domingo Martinez .05 .02 .01
- ☐ 364 Kirt Manwaring .05 .02 .01
- ☐ 365 Rafael Palmeiro .10 .05 .01
- ☐ 366 Ray Lankford .10 .05 .01
- ☐ 367 Tim McIntosh .05 .02 .01
- ☐ 368 Jessie Hollins .08 .04 .01
- ☐ 369 Scott Leius .05 .02 .01
- ☐ 370 Bill Doran .05 .02 .01
- ☐ 371 Sam Militello .05 .02 .01
- ☐ 372 Ryan Bowen .05 .02 .01
- ☐ 373 Dave Henderson .05 .02 .01
- ☐ 374 Dan Smith RR .08 .04 .01
- ☐ 375 Steve Reed RR .08 .04 .01
- ☐ 376 Jose Offerman .05 .02 .01
- ☐ 377 Kevin Brown .05 .02 .01
- ☐ 378 Darrin Fletcher .05 .02 .01
- ☐ 379 Duane Ward .08 .04 .01
- ☐ 380 Wayne Kirby RR .05 .02 .01
- ☐ 381 Steve Scarsone .05 .02 .01
- ☐ 382 Mariano Duncan .05 .02 .01
- ☐ 383 Ken Ryan .20 .09 .03
- ☐ 384 Lloyd McClendon .05 .02 .01
- ☐ 385 Brian Holman .05 .02 .01
- ☐ 386 Braulio Castillo .05 .02 .01
- ☐ 387 Danny Leon .05 .02 .01
- ☐ 388 Omar Olivares .05 .02 .01
- ☐ 389 Kevin Wickander .05 .02 .01
- ☐ 390 Fred McGriff .30 .14 .04
- ☐ 391 Phil Clark .05 .02 .01
- ☐ 392 Darren Lewis .05 .02 .01
- ☐ 393 Phil Hiatt .05 .02 .01
- ☐ 394 Mike Morgan .05 .02 .01
- ☐ 395 Shane Mack .08 .04 .01
- ☐ 396 Checklist 318-396 .05 .02 .01 (Dennis Eckersley and Art Kusnyer CO)
- ☐ 397 David Segui .05 .02 .01
- ☐ 398 Rafael Belliard .05 .02 .01
- ☐ 399 Tim Naehring .05 .02 .01
- ☐ 400 Frank Castillo .05 .02 .01
- ☐ 401 Joe Grahe .05 .02 .01
- ☐ 402 Reggie Sanders .10 .05 .01
- ☐ 403 Roberto Hernandez .05 .02 .01
- ☐ 404 Luis Gonzalez .08 .04 .01
- ☐ 405 Carlos Baerga .30 .14 .04
- ☐ 406 Carlos Hernandez .05 .02 .01
- ☐ 407 Pedro Astacio RR .08 .04 .01
- ☐ 408 Mel Rojas .05 .02 .01
- ☐ 409 Scott Livingstone .05 .02 .01
- ☐ 410 Chico Walker .05 .02 .01
- ☐ 411 Brian McRae .10 .05 .01
- ☐ 412 Ben Rivera .05 .02 .01
- ☐ 413 Ricky Bones .05 .02 .01
- ☐ 414 Andy Van Slyke .10 .05 .01
- ☐ 415 Chuck Knoblauch .10 .05 .01
- ☐ 416 Luis Alicea .05 .02 .01
- ☐ 417 Bob Wickman .05 .02 .01
- ☐ 418 Doug Brocail .05 .02 .01
- ☐ 419 Scott Brosius .05 .02 .01
- ☐ 420 Rod Beck .10 .05 .01
- ☐ 421 Edgar Martinez .05 .02 .01
- ☐ 422 Ryan Klesko .60 .25 .08
- ☐ 423 Nolan Ryan 2.00 .90 .25
- ☐ 424 Rey Sanchez .05 .02 .01
- ☐ 425 Roberto Alomar .50 .23 .06
- ☐ 426 Barry Larkin .10 .05 .01
- ☐ 427 Mike Mussina .40 .18 .05
- ☐ 428 Jeff Bagwell 1.00 .45 .13
- ☐ 429 Mo Vaughn .10 .05 .01
- ☐ 430 Eric Karros .08 .04 .01
- ☐ 431 John Orton .05 .02 .01
- ☐ 432 Wil Cordero .10 .05 .01
- ☐ 433 Jack McDowell .10 .05 .01
- ☐ 434 Howard Johnson .05 .02 .01
- ☐ 435 Albert Belle .60 .25 .08
- ☐ 436 John Kruk .10 .05 .01
- ☐ 437 Skeeter Barnes .05 .02 .01
- ☐ 438 Don Slaught .05 .02 .01
- ☐ 439 Rusty Meacham .05 .02 .01
- ☐ 440 Tim Laker RR .05 .02 .01
- ☐ 441 Robin Yount .30 .14 .04
- ☐ 442 Brian Jordan .08 .04 .01
- ☐ 443 Kevin Tapani .05 .02 .01
- ☐ 444 Gary Sheffield .10 .05 .01
- ☐ 445 Rich Monteleone .05 .02 .01
- ☐ 446 Will Clark .30 .14 .04
- ☐ 447 Jerry Browne .05 .02 .01
- ☐ 448 Jeff Treadway .05 .02 .01
- ☐ 449 Mike Schooler .05 .02 .01
- ☐ 450 Mike Harkey .05 .02 .01
- ☐ 451 Julio Franco .08 .04 .01
- ☐ 452 Kevin Young RR .05 .02 .01
- ☐ 453 Kelly Gruber .05 .02 .01
- ☐ 454 Jose Rijo .08 .04 .01
- ☐ 455 Mike Devereaux .08 .04 .01
- ☐ 456 Andujar Cedeno .08 .04 .01
- ☐ 457 Damion Easley RR .08 .04 .01
- ☐ 458 Kevin Gross .05 .02 .01
- ☐ 459 Matt Young .05 .02 .01
- ☐ 460 Matt Stairs .05 .02 .01
- ☐ 461 Luis Polonia .05 .02 .01
- ☐ 462 Dwight Gooden .05 .02 .01
- ☐ 463 Warren Newson .05 .02 .01
- ☐ 464 Jose DeLeon .05 .02 .01
- ☐ 465 Jose Mesa .05 .02 .01
- ☐ 466 Danny Cox .05 .02 .01
- ☐ 467 Dan Gladden .05 .02 .01
- ☐ 468 Gerald Perry .05 .02 .01
- ☐ 469 Mike Boddicker .05 .02 .01

☐ 470 Jeff Gardner .05 .02 .01
☐ 471 Doug Henry .05 .02 .01
☐ 472 Mike Benjamin .05 .02 .01
☐ 473 Dan Peltier RR .05 .02 .01
☐ 474 Mike Stanton .05 .02 .01
☐ 475 John Smiley .05 .02 .01
☐ 476 Dwight Smith .05 .02 .01
☐ 477 Jim Leyritz .05 .02 .01
☐ 478 Dwayne Henry .05 .02 .01
☐ 479 Mark McGwire .10 .05 .01
☐ 480 Pete Incaviglia .05 .02 .01
☐ 481 Dave Cochrane .05 .02 .01
☐ 482 Eric Davis .05 .02 .01
☐ 483 John Olerud .10 .05 .01
☐ 484 Kent Bottenfield .05 .02 .01
☐ 485 Mark McLemore .05 .02 .01
☐ 486 Dave Magadan .05 .02 .01
☐ 487 John Marzano .05 .02 .01
☐ 488 Ruben Amaro .05 .02 .01
☐ 489 Rob Ducey .05 .02 .01
☐ 490 Stan Belinda .05 .02 .01
☐ 491 Dan Pasqua .05 .02 .01
☐ 492 Joe Magrane .05 .02 .01
☐ 493 Brook Jacoby .05 .02 .01
☐ 494 Gene Harris .05 .02 .01
☐ 495 Mark Leiter .05 .02 .01
☐ 496 Bryan Hickerson .05 .02 .01
☐ 497 Tom Gordon .05 .02 .01
☐ 498 Pete Smith .05 .02 .01
☐ 499 Chris Bosio .05 .02 .01
☐ 500 Shawn Boskie .05 .02 .01
☐ 501 Dave West .05 .02 .01
☐ 502 Milt Hill .05 .02 .01
☐ 503 Pat Kelly .05 .02 .01
☐ 504 Joe Boever .05 .02 .01
☐ 505 Terry Steinbach .08 .04 .01
☐ 506 Butch Huskey RR .05 .02 .01
☐ 507 David Valle .05 .02 .01
☐ 508 Mike Scioscia .05 .02 .01
☐ 509 Kenny Rogers .05 .02 .01
☐ 510 Moises Alou .10 .05 .01
☐ 511 David Wells .05 .02 .01
☐ 512 Mackey Sasser .05 .02 .01
☐ 513 Todd Frohwirth .05 .02 .01
☐ 514 Ricky Jordan .05 .02 .01
☐ 515 Mike Gardiner .05 .02 .01
☐ 516 Gary Redus .05 .02 .01
☐ 517 Gary Gaetti .05 .02 .01
☐ 518 Checklist .05 .02 .01
☐ 519 Carlton Fisk .10 .05 .01
☐ 520 Ozzie Smith .40 .18 .05
☐ 521 Rod Nichols .05 .02 .01
☐ 522 Benito Santiago .05 .02 .01
☐ 523 Bill Gullickson .05 .02 .01
☐ 524 Robby Thompson .05 .02 .01
☐ 525 Mike Macfarlane .05 .02 .01
☐ 526 Sid Bream .05 .02 .01
☐ 527 Darryl Hamilton .05 .02 .01
☐ 528 Checklist .05 .02 .01
☐ 529 Jeff Tackett .05 .02 .01
☐ 530 Greg Olson .05 .02 .01
☐ 531 Bob Zupcic .05 .02 .01
☐ 532 Mark Grace .10 .05 .01
☐ 533 Steve Frey .05 .02 .01
☐ 534 Dave Martinez .05 .02 .01
☐ 535 Robin Ventura .10 .05 .01
☐ 536 Casey Candaele .05 .02 .01
☐ 537 Kenny Lofton .50 .23 .06
☐ 538 Jay Howell .05 .02 .01
☐ 539 Fernando Ramsey RR .08 .04 .01
☐ 540 Larry Walker .10 .05 .01
☐ 541 Cecil Fielder .10 .05 .01
☐ 542 Lee Guetterman .05 .02 .01
☐ 543 Keith Miller .05 .02 .01
☐ 544 Len Dykstra .10 .05 .01
☐ 545 B.J. Surhoff .05 .02 .01
☐ 546 Bob Walk .05 .02 .01
☐ 547 Brian Harper .05 .02 .01
☐ 548 Lee Smith .10 .05 .01
☐ 549 Danny Tartabull .08 .04 .01
☐ 550 Frank Seminara .05 .02 .01
☐ 551 Henry Mercedes .05 .02 .01
☐ 552 Dave Righetti .05 .02 .01
☐ 553 Ken Griffey Jr. 2.00 .90 .25
☐ 554 Tom Glavine .10 .05 .01
☐ 555 Juan Gonzalez .60 .25 .08
☐ 556 Jim Bullinger .05 .02 .01
☐ 557 Derek Bell .08 .04 .01
☐ 558 Cesar Hernandez .05 .02 .01
☐ 559 Cal Ripken 1.50 .65 .19
☐ 560 Eddie Taubensee .05 .02 .01
☐ 561 John Flaherty .05 .02 .01
☐ 562 Todd Benzinger .05 .02 .01
☐ 563 Hubie Brooks .05 .02 .01
☐ 564 Delino DeShields .08 .04 .01
☐ 565 Tim Raines .10 .05 .01
☐ 566 Sid Fernandez .05 .02 .01
☐ 567 Steve Olin .05 .02 .01
☐ 568 Tommy Greene .08 .04 .01
☐ 569 Buddy Groom .05 .02 .01
☐ 570 Randy Tomlin .05 .02 .01
☐ 571 Hipolito Pichardo .05 .02 .01
☐ 572 Rene Arocha RR .15 .07 .02
☐ 573 Mike Fetters .05 .02 .01
☐ 574 Felix Jose .05 .02 .01
☐ 575 Gene Larkin .05 .02 .01
☐ 576 Bruce Hurst .05 .02 .01
☐ 577 Bernie Williams .08 .04 .01
☐ 578 Trevor Wilson .05 .02 .01
☐ 579 Bob Welch .05 .02 .01
☐ 580 David Justice .30 .14 .04
☐ 581 Randy Johnson .10 .05 .01
☐ 582 Jose Vizcaino .05 .02 .01
☐ 583 Jeff Huson .05 .02 .01
☐ 584 Rob Maurer RR .05 .02 .01
☐ 585 Todd Stottlemyre .05 .02 .01
☐ 586 Joe Oliver .05 .02 .01
☐ 587 Bob Milacki .05 .02 .01
☐ 588 Rob Murphy .05 .02 .01
☐ 589 Greg Pirkl RR .05 .02 .01
☐ 590 Lenny Harris .05 .02 .01
☐ 591 Luis Rivera .05 .02 .01
☐ 592 John Wetteland .05 .02 .01
☐ 593 Mark Langston .10 .05 .01
☐ 594 Bobby Bonilla .10 .05 .01
☐ 595 Esteban Beltre .05 .02 .01
☐ 596 Mike Hartley .05 .02 .01
☐ 597 Felix Fermin .05 .02 .01
☐ 598 Carlos Garcia .08 .04 .01
☐ 599 Frank Tanana .05 .02 .01
☐ 600 Pedro Guerrero .05 .02 .01
☐ 601 Terry Shumpert .05 .02 .01
☐ 602 Wally Whitehurst .05 .02 .01
☐ 603 Kevin Seitzer .05 .02 .01
☐ 604 Chris James .05 .02 .01
☐ 605 Greg Gohr RR .05 .02 .01
☐ 606 Mark Wohlers .05 .02 .01
☐ 607 Kirby Puckett .75 .35 .09
☐ 608 Greg Maddux .50 .23 .06
☐ 609 Don Mattingly .75 .35 .09
☐ 610 Greg Cadaret .05 .02 .01
☐ 611 Dave Stewart .08 .04 .01
☐ 612 Mark Portugal .05 .02 .01
☐ 613 Pete O'Brien .05 .02 .01
☐ 614 Bobby Ojeda .05 .02 .01
☐ 615 Joe Carter .30 .14 .04

☐ 616 Pete Young .05 .02 .01
☐ 617 Sam Horn .05 .02 .01
☐ 618 Vince Coleman .05 .02 .01
☐ 619 Wade Boggs .10 .05 .01
☐ 620 Todd Pratt .05 .02 .01
☐ 621 Ron Tingley .05 .02 .01
☐ 622 Doug Drabek .10 .05 .01
☐ 623 Scott Hemond .05 .02 .01
☐ 624 Tim Jones .05 .02 .01
☐ 625 Dennis Cook .05 .02 .01
☐ 626 Jose Melendez .05 .02 .01
☐ 627 Mike Munoz .05 .02 .01
☐ 628 Jim Pena .05 .02 .01
☐ 629 Gary Thurman .05 .02 .01
☐ 630 Charlie Leibrandt .05 .02 .01
☐ 631 Scott Fletcher .05 .02 .01
☐ 632 Andre Dawson .10 .05 .01
☐ 633 Greg Gagne .05 .02 .01
☐ 634 Greg Swindell .05 .02 .01
☐ 635 Kevin Maas .05 .02 .01
☐ 636 Xavier Hernandez .05 .02 .01
☐ 637 Ruben Sierra .10 .05 .01
☐ 638 Dmitri Young RR .08 .04 .01
☐ 639 Harold Reynolds .05 .02 .01
☐ 640 Tom Goodwin .05 .02 .01
☐ 641 Todd Burns .05 .02 .01
☐ 642 Jeff Fassero .05 .02 .01
☐ 643 Dave Winfield .10 .05 .01
☐ 644 Willie Randolph .08 .04 .01
☐ 645 Luis Mercedes .05 .02 .01
☐ 646 Dale Murphy .10 .05 .01
☐ 647 Danny Darwin .05 .02 .01
☐ 648 Dennis Moeller .05 .02 .01
☐ 649 Chuck Crim .05 .02 .01
☐ 650 Checklist .05 .02 .01
☐ 651 Shawn Abner .05 .02 .01
☐ 652 Tracy Woodson .05 .02 .01
☐ 653 Scott Scudder .05 .02 .01
☐ 654 Tom Lampkin .05 .02 .01
☐ 655 Alan Trammell .10 .05 .01
☐ 656 Cory Snyder .05 .02 .01
☐ 657 Chris Gwynn .05 .02 .01
☐ 658 Lonnie Smith .05 .02 .01
☐ 659 Jim Austin .05 .02 .01
☐ 660 Checklist .05 .02 .01
☐ 661 Tim Hulett .05 .02 .01
☐ 662 Marvin Freeman .05 .02 .01
☐ 663 Greg A. Harris .05 .02 .01
☐ 664 Heathcliff Slocumb .05 .02 .01
☐ 665 Mike Butcher .05 .02 .01
☐ 666 Steve Foster .05 .02 .01
☐ 667 Donn Pall .05 .02 .01
☐ 668 Darryl Kile .08 .04 .01
☐ 669 Jesse Levis .05 .02 .01
☐ 670 Jim Gott .05 .02 .01
☐ 671 Mark Hutton RR .05 .02 .01
☐ 672 Brian Drahman .05 .02 .01
☐ 673 Chad Kreuter .05 .02 .01
☐ 674 Tony Fernandez .05 .02 .01
☐ 675 Jose Lind .05 .02 .01
☐ 676 Kyle Abbott .05 .02 .01
☐ 677 Dan Plesac .05 .02 .01
☐ 678 Barry Bonds .75 .35 .09
☐ 679 Chili Davis .08 .04 .01
☐ 680 Stan Royer .05 .02 .01
☐ 681 Scott Kamieniecki .05 .02 .01
☐ 682 Carlos Martinez .05 .02 .01
☐ 683 Mike Moore .05 .02 .01
☐ 684 Candy Maldonado .05 .02 .01
☐ 685 Jeff Nelson .05 .02 .01
☐ 686 Lou Whitaker .10 .05 .01
☐ 687 Jose Guzman .05 .02 .01
☐ 688 Manny Lee .05 .02 .01
☐ 689 Bob MacDonald .05 .02 .01
☐ 690 Scott Bankhead .05 .02 .01
☐ 691 Alan Mills .05 .02 .01
☐ 692 Brian Williams .05 .02 .01
☐ 693 Tom Brunansky .05 .02 .01
☐ 694 Lenny Webster .05 .02 .01
☐ 695 Greg Briley .05 .02 .01
☐ 696 Paul O'Neill .08 .04 .01
☐ 697 Joey Cora .05 .02 .01
☐ 698 Charlie O'Brien .05 .02 .01
☐ 699 Junior Ortiz .05 .02 .01
☐ 700 Ron Darling .05 .02 .01
☐ 701 Tony Phillips .05 .02 .01
☐ 702 William Pennyfeather .05 .02 .01
☐ 703 Mark Gubicza .05 .02 .01
☐ 704 Steve Hosey RR .05 .02 .01
☐ 705 Henry Cotto .05 .02 .01
☐ 706 David Hulse .05 .02 .01
☐ 707 Mike Pagliarulo .05 .02 .01
☐ 708 Dave Stieb .05 .02 .01
☐ 709 Melido Perez .05 .02 .01
☐ 710 Jimmy Key .08 .04 .01
☐ 711 Jeff Russell .05 .02 .01
☐ 712 David Cone .10 .05 .01
☐ 713 Russ Swan .05 .02 .01
☐ 714 Mark Guthrie .05 .02 .01
☐ 715 Checklist .05 .02 .01
☐ 716 Al Martin RR .08 .04 .01
☐ 717 Randy Knorr .05 .02 .01
☐ 718 Mike Stanley .05 .02 .01
☐ 719 Rick Sutcliffe .08 .04 .01
☐ 720 Terry Leach .05 .02 .01
☐ 721 Chipper Jones RR .50 .23 .06
☐ 722 Jim Eisenreich .05 .02 .01
☐ 723 Tom Henke .08 .04 .01
☐ 724 Jeff Frye .05 .02 .01
☐ 725 Harold Baines .08 .04 .01
☐ 726 Scott Sanderson .05 .02 .01
☐ 727 Tom Foley .05 .02 .01
☐ 728 Bryan Harvey .08 .04 .01
☐ 729 Tom Edens .05 .02 .01
☐ 730 Eric Young .08 .04 .01
☐ 731 Dave Weathers .08 .04 .01
☐ 732 Spike Owen .05 .02 .01
☐ 733 Scott Aldred .05 .02 .01
☐ 734 Cris Carpenter .05 .02 .01
☐ 735 Dion James .05 .02 .01
☐ 736 Joe Girardi .05 .02 .01
☐ 737 Nigel Wilson RR .10 .05 .01
☐ 738 Scott Chiamparino .05 .02 .01
☐ 739 Jeff Reardon .08 .04 .01
☐ 740 Willie Blair .05 .02 .01
☐ 741 Jim Corsi .05 .02 .01
☐ 742 Ken Patterson .05 .02 .01
☐ 743 Andy Ashby .05 .02 .01
☐ 744 Rob Natal .05 .02 .01
☐ 745 Kevin Bass .05 .02 .01
☐ 746 Freddie Benavides .05 .02 .01
☐ 747 Chris Donnels .05 .02 .01
☐ 748 Kerry Woodson .05 .02 .01
☐ 749 Calvin Jones .05 .02 .01
☐ 750 Gary Scott .05 .02 .01
☐ 751 Joe Orsulak .05 .02 .01
☐ 752 Armando Reynoso .05 .02 .01
☐ 753 Monty Fariss .05 .02 .01
☐ 754 Billy Hatcher .05 .02 .01
☐ 755 Denis Boucher .05 .02 .01
☐ 756 Walt Weiss .05 .02 .01
☐ 757 Mike Fitzgerald .05 .02 .01
☐ 758 Rudy Seanez .05 .02 .01
☐ 759 Bret Barberie .05 .02 .01
☐ 760 Mo Sanford .05 .02 .01
☐ 761 Pedro Castellano .05 .02 .01

☐ 762	Chuck Carr	.05	.02	.01
☐ 763	Steve Howe	.05	.02	.01
☐ 764	Andres Galarraga	.10	.05	.01
☐ 765	Jeff Conine	.10	.05	.01
☐ 766	Ted Power	.05	.02	.01
☐ 767	Butch Henry	.05	.02	.01
☐ 768	Steve Decker	.05	.02	.01
☐ 769	Storm Davis	.05	.02	.01
☐ 770	Vinny Castilla	.05	.02	.01
☐ 771	Junior Felix	.05	.02	.01
☐ 772	Walt Terrell	.05	.02	.01
☐ 773	Brad Ausmus	.05	.02	.01
☐ 774	Jamie McAndrew	.05	.02	.01
☐ 775	Milt Thompson	.05	.02	.01
☐ 776	Charlie Hayes	.08	.04	.01
☐ 777	Jack Armstrong	.05	.02	.01
☐ 778	Dennis Rasmussen	.05	.02	.01
☐ 779	Darren Holmes	.05	.02	.01
☐ 780	Alex Arias	.05	.02	.01
☐ 781	Randy Bush	.05	.02	.01
☐ 782	Javy Lopez RR	.40	.18	.05
☐ 783	Dante Bichette	.10	.05	.01
☐ 784	John Johnstone	.05	.02	.01
☐ 785	Rene Gonzales	.05	.02	.01
☐ 786	Alex Cole	.05	.02	.01
☐ 787	Jeromy Burnitz RR	.08	.04	.01
☐ 788	Michael Huff	.05	.02	.01
☐ 789	Anthony Telford	.05	.02	.01
☐ 790	Jerald Clark	.05	.02	.01
☐ 791	Joel Johnston	.05	.02	.01
☐ 792	David Nied RR	.10	.05	.01

1993 Donruss Diamond Kings

These standard-size (2 1/2" by 3 1/2") cards were randomly inserted in 1993 Donruss packs. The cards are gold-foil stamped and feature on the fronts player portraits by noted sports artist Dick Perez. Inside green borders, the backs present career summaries. The first 15 cards were available in the first series of the 1993 Donruss and cards 16-31 were inserted with the second series. Diamond King numbers 27-28 honor the first draft picks of the new Florida Marlins and Colorado Rockies franchises. The cards are numbered on the back with a "DK" prefix. Collectors 16 years old and younger could enter Donruss' Diamond King contest by writing an essay of 75 words or less explaining who their favorite Diamond King player was and why. Winners were awarded one of 30 framed watercolors at the National Convention, held in Chicago, July 22-25, 1993.

	MINT	EXC	G-VG
COMPLETE SET (31)	30.00	13.50	3.80
COMPLETE SERIES 1 (15)	20.00	9.00	2.50
COMPLETE SERIES 2 (16)	10.00	4.50	1.25
COMMON CARD (DK1-DK15)	.50	.23	.06
COMMON CARD (DK16-DK31)	.50	.23	.06

☐ DK1	Ken Griffey Jr.	12.00	5.50	1.50
☐ DK2	Ryne Sandberg	4.00	1.80	.50
☐ DK3	Roger Clemens	3.00	1.35	.40
☐ DK4	Kirby Puckett	5.00	2.30	.60
☐ DK5	Bill Swift	.50	.23	.06
☐ DK6	Larry Walker	.75	.35	.09
☐ DK7	Juan Gonzalez	4.00	1.80	.50
☐ DK8	Wally Joyner	.50	.23	.06
☐ DK9	Andy Van Slyke	.50	.23	.06
☐ DK10	Robin Ventura	.75	.35	.09
☐ DK11	Bip Roberts	.50	.23	.06
☐ DK12	Roberto Kelly	.50	.23	.06
☐ DK13	Carlos Baerga	1.75	.80	.22
☐ DK14	Orel Hershiser	.50	.23	.06
☐ DK15	Cecil Fielder	1.25	.55	.16
☐ DK16	Robin Yount	1.75	.80	.22
☐ DK17	Darren Daulton	.50	.23	.06
☐ DK18	Mark McGwire	.75	.35	.09
☐ DK19	Tom Glavine	.75	.35	.09
☐ DK20	Roberto Alomar	3.00	1.35	.40
☐ DK21	Gary Sheffield	.75	.35	.09
☐ DK22	Bob Tewksbury	.50	.23	.06
☐ DK23	Brady Anderson	.50	.23	.06
☐ DK24	Craig Biggio	.75	.35	.09
☐ DK25	Eddie Murray	.75	.35	.09
☐ DK26	Luis Polonia	.50	.23	.06
☐ DK27	Nigel Wilson	.50	.23	.06
☐ DK28	David Nied	.50	.23	.06
☐ DK29	Pat Listach ROY	.50	.23	.06
☐ DK30	Eric Karros ROY	.50	.23	.06
☐ DK31	Checklist 1-31	.50	.23	.06

1993 Donruss Elite

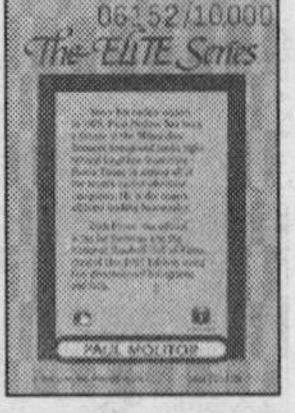

Cards 19-27 were random inserts in 1993 Donruss series I foil packs while cards 28-36 were inserted in series II packs. The numbering on the 1993 Elite cards follows consecutively after that of the 1992 Elite series cards, and each of the 10,000 Elite cards is serially numbered. The Signature Series Will Clark card was randomly inserted in 1993 Donruss foil packs; he personal-

ly autographed 5,000 cards. Featuring a Dick Perez portrait, the ten thousand Legends Series cards honor Robin Yount for his 3,000th hit achievement. All these special cards measure the standard size (2 1/2" by 3 1/2") and are numbered on the back. The front design of the Elite cards features a cutout color player photo superimposed on a neon-colored panel framed by a gray inner border and a variegated silver metallic outer border. The player's name appears in a neon-colored bar toward the bottom of the card. On a gray panel framed by a navy blue inner border and a two-toned blue outer border, the backs present player profile. The backs of the Elite cards also carry the serial number ("X of 10,000) as well as the card number.

	MINT	EXC	G-VG
COMPLETE SET (20)	800.00	350.00	100.00
COMMON CARD (19-27)	12.00	5.50	1.50
COMMON CARD (28-36)	12.00	5.50	1.50
☐ 19 Fred McGriff	30.00	13.50	3.80
☐ 20 Ryne Sandberg	75.00	34.00	9.50
☐ 21 Eddie Murray	12.00	5.50	1.50
☐ 22 Paul Molitor	30.00	13.50	3.80
☐ 23 Barry Larkin	12.00	5.50	1.50
☐ 24 Don Mattingly	75.00	34.00	9.50
☐ 25 Dennis Eckersley	12.00	5.50	1.50
☐ 26 Roberto Alomar	50.00	23.00	6.25
☐ 27 Edgar Martinez	12.00	5.50	1.50
☐ 28 Gary Sheffield	12.00	5.50	1.50
☐ 29 Darren Daulton	12.00	5.50	1.50
☐ 30 Larry Walker	12.00	5.50	1.50
☐ 31 Barry Bonds	75.00	34.00	9.50
☐ 32 Andy Van Slyke	12.00	5.50	1.50
☐ 33 Mark McGwire	12.00	5.50	1.50
☐ 34 Cecil Fielder	20.00	9.00	2.50
☐ 35 Dave Winfield	20.00	9.00	2.50
☐ 36 Juan Gonzalez	65.00	29.00	8.25
☐ L3 Robin Yount (Legend Series)	65.00	29.00	8.25
☐ S3 Will Clark AU (Signature Series)	200.00	90.00	25.00

1993 Donruss Long Ball Leaders

Randomly inserted in 26-card magazine distributor packs (1-9 in series I and 10-18 in series II), these standard-size (2 1/2" by 3 1/2") cards feature some of MLB's outstanding sluggers. The fronts feature full-bleed color action player photos with a red and bright yellow stripe design across the bottom that carries the player's name and team. The Donruss Long Ball Leaders icon rests on the stripe at the lower left. The player's longest home run is printed in gold foil at the upper left. The backs carry color photos of the ballpark in which the home run occurred and some facts about the player and his team. A red and yellow stripe, similar to the front, contains the words "1993 Edition." The cards are numbered on the back with an "LL" prefix.

	MINT	EXC	G-VG
COMPLETE SET (18)	80.00	36.00	10.00
COMPLETE SERIES 1 (9)	40.00	18.00	5.00
COMPLETE SERIES 2 (9)	40.00	18.00	5.00
COMMON CARD (LL1-LL9)	1.50	.65	.19
COMMON CARD (LL10-LL18)	1.50	.65	.19
☐ LL1 Rob Deer	1.50	.65	.19
☐ LL2 Fred McGriff	4.00	1.80	.50
☐ LL3 Albert Belle	8.00	3.60	1.00
☐ LL4 Mark McGwire	1.50	.65	.19
☐ LL5 David Justice	4.00	1.80	.50
☐ LL6 Jose Canseco	4.00	1.80	.50
☐ LL7 Kent Hrbek	1.50	.65	.19
☐ LL8 Roberto Alomar	6.00	2.70	.75
☐ LL9 Ken Griffey Jr.	25.00	11.50	3.10
☐ LL10 Frank Thomas	25.00	11.50	3.10
☐ LL11 Darryl Strawberry	1.50	.65	.19
☐ LL12 Felix Jose	1.50	.65	.19
☐ LL13 Cecil Fielder	2.50	1.15	.30
☐ LL14 Juan Gonzalez	8.00	3.60	1.00
☐ LL15 Ryne Sandberg	8.00	3.60	1.00
☐ LL16 Gary Sheffield	2.00	.90	.25
☐ LL17 Jeff Bagwell	12.00	5.50	1.50
☐ LL18 Larry Walker	2.00	.90	.25

1993 Donruss MVPs

Thirteen MVP cards were issued in each series, and they were randomly inserted in 23-card jumbo packs. The cards measure the standard size (2 1/2" by 3 1/2"). The fronts feature full-bleed color action player photos with a red, white, and blue ribbon design across the bottom that contains the player's name and team. The Donruss MVP icon is gold-foil stamped over the ribbon. The backs carry action player shots above *a ribbon design similar to the front, and below the ribbon a pink granite panel contains player information and 1992 Spotlight stats. The cards are numbered on the back with an "MVP" prefix.*

	MINT	EXC	G-VG
COMPLETE SET (26)	30.00	13.50	3.80
COMPLETE SERIES 1 (13)	10.00	4.50	1.25
COMPLETE SERIES 2 (13)	20.00	9.00	2.50
COMMON CARD (1-13)	.35	.16	.04
COMMON CARD (14-26)	.35	.16	.04

	MINT	EXC	G-VG
☐ 1 Luis Polonia	.35	.16	.04
☐ 2 Frank Thomas	8.00	3.60	1.00
☐ 3 George Brett	3.00	1.35	.40
☐ 4 Paul Molitor	1.25	.55	.16
☐ 5 Don Mattingly	3.00	1.35	.40
☐ 6 Roberto Alomar	2.00	.90	.25
☐ 7 Terry Pendleton	.35	.16	.04
☐ 8 Eric Karros	.35	.16	.04
☐ 9 Larry Walker	.55	.25	.07
☐ 10 Eddie Murray	.55	.25	.07
☐ 11 Darren Daulton	.55	.25	.07
☐ 12 Ray Lankford	.55	.25	.07
☐ 13 Will Clark	1.25	.55	.16
☐ 14 Cal Ripken	6.00	2.70	.75
☐ 15 Roger Clemens	2.00	.90	.25
☐ 16 Carlos Baerga	1.25	.55	.16
☐ 17 Cecil Fielder	.75	.35	.09
☐ 18 Kirby Puckett	3.00	1.35	.40
☐ 19 Mark McGwire	.35	.16	.04
☐ 20 Ken Griffey Jr.	8.00	3.60	1.00
☐ 21 Juan Gonzalez	2.50	1.15	.30
☐ 22 Ryne Sandberg	2.50	1.15	.30
☐ 23 Bip Roberts	.35	.16	.04
☐ 24 Jeff Bagwell	4.00	1.80	.50
☐ 25 Barry Bonds	3.00	1.35	.40
☐ 26 Gary Sheffield	.55	.25	.07

1993 Donruss Spirit of the Game

A new subset in 1993, these standard-size (2 1/2" by 3 1/2") cards were randomly inserted in 1993 Donruss packs and packed approximately two per box. Cards 1-10 were first-series inserts, and cards 11-20 were second-series inserts. The fronts feature borderless glossy color action player photos. The set title, "Spirit of the Game," is stamped in gold foil script across the top or bottom of the picture. The backs sport a second borderless color player photo; this photo concludes the action portrayed in the front photo. The caption to the second picture is printed in yellow block lettering. The cards are numbered on the back with an "SG" prefix.

	MINT	EXC	G-VG
COMPLETE SET (20)	20.00	9.00	2.50
COMPLETE SERIES 1 (10)	8.00	3.60	1.00
COMPLETE SERIES 2 (10)	12.00	5.50	1.50
COMMON CARD (SG1-SG10)	.60	.25	.08
COMMON CARD (SG11-SG20)	.60	.25	.08

	MINT	EXC	G-VG
☐ SG1 Mike Bordick Turning Two	.60	.25	.08
☐ SG2 David Justice Play at the Plate	1.50	.65	.19
☐ SG3 Roberto Alomar In There	2.50	1.15	.30
☐ SG4 Dennis Eckersley Pumped	.85	.40	.11
☐ SG5 Juan Gonzalez and Jose Canseco Dynamic Duo	3.00	1.35	.40
☐ SG6 George Bell and Frank Thomas ... Gone	2.50	1.15	.30
☐ SG7 Wade Boggs and Luis Polonia Safe or Out	.85	.40	.11
☐ SG8 Will Clark The Thrill	1.50	.65	.19
☐ SG9 Bip Roberts Safe at Home	.60	.25	.08
☐ SG10 Cecil Fielder Rob Deer Mickey Tettleton Thirty 3	.85	.40	.11
☐ SG11 Kenny Lofton Bag Bandit	2.50	1.15	.30
☐ SG12 Gary Sheffield Fred McGriff Back to Back	.60	.25	.08
☐ SG13 Greg Gagne Barry Larkin Range Rovers	.85	.40	.11
☐ SG14 Ryne Sandberg The Ball Stops Here	3.50	1.55	.45
☐ SG15 Carlos Baerga Gary Gaetti Over the Top	.60	.25	.08
☐ SG16 Danny Tartabull At the Wall	.60	.25	.08
☐ SG17 Brady Anderson Head First	.60	.25	.08
☐ SG18 Frank Thomas Big Hurt	10.00	4.50	1.25
☐ SG19 Kevin Gross No Hitter	.60	.25	.08
☐ SG20 Robin Yount 3,000 Hits	1.50	.65	.19

1994 Donruss

The 1994 Donruss set was issued in two separate series of 330 standard-size cards for a total of 660. The fronts feature borderless color player action photos on front. The player's name and position appear in gold

foil within a team color-coded stripe near the bottom. The team logo appears within a black rectangle framed by a team color near the bottom. The set name and year, stamped in gold foil, also appear in this rectangle. Most of the backs are horizontal, and feature another borderless color player action photo. A black rectangle framed by a team color appears on one side and carries the player's name, team, uniform number, and biography. The player's stats appear within ghosted stripes near the bottom. Rookie Cards include Curtis Pride and Julian Tavarez.

	MINT	EXC	G-VG
COMPLETE SET (660)	55.00	25.00	7.00
COMPLETE SERIES 1 (330)	30.00	13.50	3.80
COMPLETE SERIES 2 (330)	25.00	11.50	3.10
COMMON CARD (1-330)	.10	.05	.01
COMMON CARD (331-660)	.10	.05	.01

		MINT	EXC	G-VG
☐ 1	Nolan Ryan	3.00	1.35	.40
☐ 2	Mike Piazza	1.50	.65	.19
☐ 3	Moises Alou	.20	.09	.03
☐ 4	Ken Griffey Jr.	3.00	1.35	.40
☐ 5	Gary Sheffield	.20	.09	.03
☐ 6	Roberto Alomar	.75	.35	.09
☐ 7	John Kruk	.20	.09	.03
☐ 8	Gregg Olson	.10	.05	.01
☐ 9	Gregg Jefferies	.20	.09	.03
☐ 10	Tony Gwynn	.75	.35	.09
☐ 11	Chad Curtis	.15	.07	.02
☐ 12	Craig Biggio	.15	.07	.02
☐ 13	John Burkett	.15	.07	.02
☐ 14	Carlos Baerga	.40	.18	.05
☐ 15	Robin Yount	.40	.18	.05
☐ 16	Dennis Eckersley	.20	.09	.03
☐ 17	Dwight Gooden	.10	.05	.01
☐ 18	Ryne Sandberg	1.00	.45	.13
☐ 19	Rickey Henderson	.20	.09	.03
☐ 20	Jack McDowell	.20	.09	.03
☐ 21	Jay Bell	.15	.07	.02
☐ 22	Kevin Brown	.10	.05	.01
☐ 23	Robin Ventura	.15	.07	.02
☐ 24	Paul Molitor	.40	.18	.05
☐ 25	David Justice	.40	.18	.05
☐ 26	Rafael Palmeiro	.20	.09	.03
☐ 27	Cecil Fielder	.20	.09	.03
☐ 28	Chuck Knoblauch	.20	.09	.03
☐ 29	Dave Hollins	.20	.09	.03
☐ 30	Jimmy Key	.15	.07	.02
☐ 31	Mark Langston	.20	.09	.03
☐ 32	Darryl Kile	.15	.07	.02
☐ 33	Ruben Sierra	.20	.09	.03
☐ 34	Ron Gant	.15	.07	.02
☐ 35	Ozzie Smith	.60	.25	.08
☐ 36	Wade Boggs	.20	.09	.03
☐ 37	Marquis Grissom	.20	.09	.03
☐ 38	Will Clark	.40	.18	.05
☐ 39	Kenny Lofton	.75	.35	.09
☐ 40	Cal Ripken	2.25	1.00	.30
☐ 41	Steve Avery	.20	.09	.03
☐ 42	Mo Vaughn	.20	.09	.03
☐ 43	Brian McRae	.15	.07	.02
☐ 44	Mickey Tettleton	.15	.07	.02
☐ 45	Barry Larkin	.20	.09	.03
☐ 46	Charlie Hayes	.15	.07	.02
☐ 47	Kevin Appier	.15	.07	.02
☐ 48	Robby Thompson	.10	.05	.01
☐ 49	Juan Gonzalez	1.00	.45	.13
☐ 50	Paul O'Neill	.15	.07	.02
☐ 51	Marcos Armas	.10	.05	.01
☐ 52	Mike Butcher	.10	.05	.01
☐ 53	Ken Caminiti	.15	.07	.02
☐ 54	Pat Borders	.10	.05	.01
☐ 55	Pedro Munoz	.10	.05	.01
☐ 56	Tim Belcher	.10	.05	.01
☐ 57	Paul Assenmacher	.10	.05	.01
☐ 58	Damon Berryhill	.10	.05	.01
☐ 59	Ricky Bones	.10	.05	.01
☐ 60	Rene Arocha	.15	.07	.02
☐ 61	Shawn Boskie	.10	.05	.01
☐ 62	Pedro Astacio	.15	.07	.02
☐ 63	Frank Bolick	.10	.05	.01
☐ 64	Bud Black	.10	.05	.01
☐ 65	Sandy Alomar Jr.	.15	.07	.02
☐ 66	Rich Amaral	.10	.05	.01
☐ 67	Luis Aquino	.10	.05	.01
☐ 68	Kevin Baez	.10	.05	.01
☐ 69	Mike Devereaux	.15	.07	.02
☐ 70	Andy Ashby	.10	.05	.01
☐ 71	Larry Andersen	.10	.05	.01
☐ 72	Steve Cooke	.10	.05	.01
☐ 73	Mario Diaz	.10	.05	.01
☐ 74	Rob Deer	.10	.05	.01
☐ 75	Bobby Ayala	.10	.05	.01
☐ 76	Freddie Benavides	.10	.05	.01
☐ 77	Stan Belinda	.10	.05	.01
☐ 78	John Doherty	.10	.05	.01
☐ 79	Willie Banks	.10	.05	.01
☐ 80	Spike Owen	.10	.05	.01
☐ 81	Mike Bordick	.10	.05	.01
☐ 82	Chili Davis	.15	.07	.02
☐ 83	Luis Gonzalez	.10	.05	.01
☐ 84	Ed Sprague	.10	.05	.01
☐ 85	Jeff Reboulet	.10	.05	.01
☐ 86	Jason Bere	.40	.18	.05
☐ 87	Mark Hutton	.10	.05	.01
☐ 88	Jeff Blauser	.15	.07	.02
☐ 89	Cal Eldred	.15	.07	.02
☐ 90	Bernard Gilkey	.10	.05	.01
☐ 91	Frank Castillo	.10	.05	.01
☐ 92	Jim Gott	.10	.05	.01
☐ 93	Greg Colbrunn	.10	.05	.01
☐ 94	Jeff Brantley	.10	.05	.01
☐ 95	Jeremy Hernandez	.10	.05	.01
☐ 96	Norm Charlton	.10	.05	.01
☐ 97	Alex Arias	.10	.05	.01
☐ 98	John Franco	.10	.05	.01
☐ 99	Chris Hoiles	.15	.07	.02
☐ 100	Brad Ausmus	.10	.05	.01
☐ 101	Wes Chamberlain	.10	.05	.01
☐ 102	Mark Dewey	.10	.05	.01
☐ 103	Benji Gil	.15	.07	.02
☐ 104	John Dopson	.10	.05	.01
☐ 105	John Smiley	.10	.05	.01
☐ 106	David Nied	.20	.09	.03
☐ 107	George Brett	1.25	.55	.16
☐ 108	Kirk Gibson	.15	.07	.02
☐ 109	Larry Casian	.10	.05	.01
☐ 110	Checklist 1-82	.10	.05	.01

Ryne Sandberg

- ☐ 111 Brent Gates .20 .09 .03
- ☐ 112 Damion Easley .10 .05 .01
- ☐ 113 Pete Harnisch .10 .05 .01
- ☐ 114 Danny Cox .10 .05 .01
- ☐ 115 Kevin Tapani .10 .05 .01
- ☐ 116 Roberto Hernandez .10 .05 .01
- ☐ 117 Domingo Jean .10 .05 .01
- ☐ 118 Sid Bream .10 .05 .01
- ☐ 119 Doug Henry .10 .05 .01
- ☐ 120 Omar Olivares .10 .05 .01
- ☐ 121 Mike Harkey .10 .05 .01
- ☐ 122 Carlos Hernandez .10 .05 .01
- ☐ 123 Jeff Fassero .10 .05 .01
- ☐ 124 Dave Burba .10 .05 .01
- ☐ 125 Wayne Kirby .10 .05 .01
- ☐ 126 John Cummings .10 .05 .01
- ☐ 127 Bret Barberie .10 .05 .01
- ☐ 128 Todd Hundley .10 .05 .01
- ☐ 129 Tim Hulett .10 .05 .01
- ☐ 130 Phil Clark .10 .05 .01
- ☐ 131 Danny Jackson .10 .05 .01
- ☐ 132 Tom Foley .10 .05 .01
- ☐ 133 Donald Harris .10 .05 .01
- ☐ 134 Scott Fletcher .10 .05 .01
- ☐ 135 Johnny Ruffin .10 .05 .01
- ☐ 136 Jerald Clark .10 .05 .01
- ☐ 137 Billy Brewer .10 .05 .01
- ☐ 138 Dan Gladden .10 .05 .01
- ☐ 139 Eddie Guardado .10 .05 .01
- ☐ 140 Checklist 83-164 .10 .05 .01

Cal Ripken

- ☐ 141 Scott Hemond .10 .05 .01
- ☐ 142 Steve Frey .10 .05 .01
- ☐ 143 Xavier Hernandez .10 .05 .01
- ☐ 144 Mark Eichhorn .10 .05 .01
- ☐ 145 Ellis Burks .15 .07 .02
- ☐ 146 Jim Leyritz .10 .05 .01
- ☐ 147 Mark Lemke .10 .05 .01
- ☐ 148 Pat Listach .10 .05 .01
- ☐ 149 Donovan Osborne .10 .05 .01
- ☐ 150 Glenallen Hill .10 .05 .01
- ☐ 151 Orel Hershiser .15 .07 .02
- ☐ 152 Darrin Fletcher .10 .05 .01
- ☐ 153 Royce Clayton .15 .07 .02
- ☐ 154 Derek Lilliquist .10 .05 .01
- ☐ 155 Mike Felder .10 .05 .01
- ☐ 156 Jeff Conine .20 .09 .03
- ☐ 157 Ryan Thompson .15 .07 .02
- ☐ 158 Ben McDonald .15 .07 .02
- ☐ 159 Ricky Gutierrez .10 .05 .01
- ☐ 160 Terry Mulholland .10 .05 .01
- ☐ 161 Carlos Garcia .10 .05 .01
- ☐ 162 Tom Henke .10 .05 .01
- ☐ 163 Mike Greenwell .15 .07 .02
- ☐ 164 Thomas Howard .10 .05 .01
- ☐ 165 Joe Girardi .10 .05 .01
- ☐ 166 Hubie Brooks .10 .05 .01
- ☐ 167 Greg Gohr .10 .05 .01
- ☐ 168 Chip Hale .10 .05 .01
- ☐ 169 Rick Honeycutt .10 .05 .01
- ☐ 170 Hilly Hathaway .10 .05 .01
- ☐ 171 Todd Jones .10 .05 .01
- ☐ 172 Tony Fernandez .10 .05 .01
- ☐ 173 Bo Jackson .20 .09 .03
- ☐ 174 Bobby Munoz .10 .05 .01
- ☐ 175 Greg McMichael .15 .07 .02
- ☐ 176 Graeme Lloyd .10 .05 .01
- ☐ 177 Tom Pagnozzi .10 .05 .01
- ☐ 178 Derrick May .10 .05 .01
- ☐ 179 Pedro Martinez .20 .09 .03
- ☐ 180 Ken Hill .15 .07 .02
- ☐ 181 Bryan Hickerson .10 .05 .01
- ☐ 182 Jose Mesa .10 .05 .01
- ☐ 183 Dave Fleming .10 .05 .01
- ☐ 184 Henry Cotto .10 .05 .01
- ☐ 185 Jeff Kent .15 .07 .02
- ☐ 186 Mark McLemore .10 .05 .01
- ☐ 187 Trevor Hoffman .10 .05 .01
- ☐ 188 Todd Pratt .10 .05 .01
- ☐ 189 Blas Minor .10 .05 .01
- ☐ 190 Charlie Leibrandt .10 .05 .01
- ☐ 191 Tony Pena .10 .05 .01
- ☐ 192 Larry Luebbers .10 .05 .01
- ☐ 193 Greg W. Harris .10 .05 .01
- ☐ 194 David Cone .20 .09 .03
- ☐ 195 Bill Gullickson .10 .05 .01
- ☐ 196 Brian Harper .10 .05 .01
- ☐ 197 Steve Karsay .10 .05 .01
- ☐ 198 Greg Myers .10 .05 .01
- ☐ 199 Mark Portugal .10 .05 .01
- ☐ 200 Pat Hentgen .15 .07 .02
- ☐ 201 Mike LaValliere .10 .05 .01
- ☐ 202 Mike Stanley .10 .05 .01
- ☐ 203 Kent Mercker .10 .05 .01
- ☐ 204 Dave Nilsson .10 .05 .01
- ☐ 205 Erik Pappas .10 .05 .01
- ☐ 206 Mike Morgan .10 .05 .01
- ☐ 207 Roger McDowell .10 .05 .01
- ☐ 208 Mike Lansing .15 .07 .02
- ☐ 209 Kirt Manwaring .10 .05 .01
- ☐ 210 Randy Milligan .10 .05 .01
- ☐ 211 Erik Hanson .10 .05 .01
- ☐ 212 Orestes Destrade .10 .05 .01
- ☐ 213 Mike Maddux .10 .05 .01
- ☐ 214 Alan Mills .10 .05 .01
- ☐ 215 Tim Mauser .10 .05 .01
- ☐ 216 Ben Rivera .10 .05 .01
- ☐ 217 Don Slaught .10 .05 .01
- ☐ 218 Bob Patterson .10 .05 .01
- ☐ 219 Carlos Quintana .10 .05 .01
- ☐ 220 Checklist 165-247 .10 .05 .01

Tim Raines

- ☐ 221 Hal Morris .15 .07 .02
- ☐ 222 Darren Holmes .10 .05 .01
- ☐ 223 Chris Gwynn .10 .05 .01
- ☐ 224 Chad Kreuter .10 .05 .01
- ☐ 225 Mike Hartley .10 .05 .01
- ☐ 226 Scott Lydy .10 .05 .01
- ☐ 227 Eduardo Perez .15 .07 .02
- ☐ 228 Greg Swindell .10 .05 .01
- ☐ 229 Al Leiter .10 .05 .01
- ☐ 230 Scott Radinsky .10 .05 .01
- ☐ 231 Bob Wickman .10 .05 .01
- ☐ 232 Otis Nixon .10 .05 .01
- ☐ 233 Kevin Reimer .10 .05 .01
- ☐ 234 Geronimo Pena .10 .05 .01
- ☐ 235 Kevin Roberson .10 .05 .01
- ☐ 236 Jody Reed .10 .05 .01
- ☐ 237 Kirk Rueter .10 .05 .01
- ☐ 238 Willie McGee .10 .05 .01
- ☐ 239 Charles Nagy .10 .05 .01
- ☐ 240 Tim Leary .10 .05 .01
- ☐ 241 Carl Everett .15 .07 .02
- ☐ 242 Charlie O'Brien .10 .05 .01
- ☐ 243 Mike Pagliarulo .10 .05 .01
- ☐ 244 Kerry Taylor .10 .05 .01
- ☐ 245 Kevin Stocker .15 .07 .02
- ☐ 246 Joel Johnston .10 .05 .01
- ☐ 247 Geno Petralli .10 .05 .01
- ☐ 248 Jeff Russell .10 .05 .01
- ☐ 249 Joe Oliver .10 .05 .01
- ☐ 250 Roberto Mejia .15 .07 .02
- ☐ 251 Chris Haney .10 .05 .01
- ☐ 252 Bill Krueger .10 .05 .01
- ☐ 253 Shane Mack .15 .07 .02

☐ 254 Terry Steinbach .15 .07 .02
☐ 255 Luis Polonia .10 .05 .01
☐ 256 Eddie Taubensee .10 .05 .01
☐ 257 Dave Stewart .15 .07 .02
☐ 258 Tim Raines .20 .09 .03
☐ 259 Bernie Williams .15 .07 .02
☐ 260 John Smoltz .15 .07 .02
☐ 261 Kevin Seitzer .10 .05 .01
☐ 262 Bob Tewksbury .10 .05 .01
☐ 263 Bob Scanlan .10 .05 .01
☐ 264 Henry Rodriguez .10 .05 .01
☐ 265 Tim Scott .10 .05 .01
☐ 266 Scott Sanderson .10 .05 .01
☐ 267 Eric Plunk .10 .05 .01
☐ 268 Edgar Martinez .10 .05 .01
☐ 269 Charlie Hough .15 .07 .02
☐ 270 Joe Orsulak .10 .05 .01
☐ 271 Harold Reynolds .10 .05 .01
☐ 272 Tim Teufel .10 .05 .01
☐ 273 Bobby Thigpen .10 .05 .01
☐ 274 Randy Tomlin .10 .05 .01
☐ 275 Gary Redus .10 .05 .01
☐ 276 Ken Ryan .10 .05 .01
☐ 277 Tim Pugh .10 .05 .01
☐ 278 J. Owens .10 .05 .01
☐ 279 Phil Hiatt .20 .09 .03
☐ 280 Alan Trammell .20 .09 .03
☐ 281 Dave McCarty .15 .07 .02
☐ 282 Bob Welch .10 .05 .01
☐ 283 J.T. Snow .15 .07 .02
☐ 284 Brian Williams .10 .05 .01
☐ 285 Devon White .15 .07 .02
☐ 286 Steve Sax .10 .05 .01
☐ 287 Tony Tarasco .20 .09 .03
☐ 288 Bill Spiers .10 .05 .01
☐ 289 Allen Watson .10 .05 .01
☐ 290 Checklist 248-330 .10 .05 .01
Rickey Henderson
☐ 291 Jose Vizcaino .10 .05 .01
☐ 292 Darryl Strawberry .15 .07 .02
☐ 293 John Wetteland .10 .05 .01
☐ 294 Bill Swift .10 .05 .01
☐ 295 Jeff Treadway .10 .05 .01
☐ 296 Tino Martinez .10 .05 .01
☐ 297 Richie Lewis .10 .05 .01
☐ 298 Bret Saberhagen .15 .07 .02
☐ 299 Arthur Rhodes .10 .05 .01
☐ 300 Guillermo Velasquez .10 .05 .01
☐ 301 Milt Thompson .10 .05 .01
☐ 302 Doug Strange .10 .05 .01
☐ 303 Aaron Sele .30 .14 .04
☐ 304 Bip Roberts .10 .05 .01
☐ 305 Bruce Ruffin .10 .05 .01
☐ 306 Jose Lind .10 .05 .01
☐ 307 David Wells .10 .05 .01
☐ 308 Bobby Witt .10 .05 .01
☐ 309 Mark Wohlers .10 .05 .01
☐ 310 B.J. Surhoff .10 .05 .01
☐ 311 Mark Whiten .15 .07 .02
☐ 312 Turk Wendell .10 .05 .01
☐ 313 Raul Mondesi 1.00 .45 .13
☐ 314 Brian Turang .10 .05 .01
☐ 315 Chris Hammond .10 .05 .01
☐ 316 Tim Bogar .10 .05 .01
☐ 317 Brad Pennington .10 .05 .01
☐ 318 Tim Worrell .10 .05 .01
☐ 319 Mitch Williams .10 .05 .01
☐ 320 Rondell White .30 .14 .04
☐ 321 Frank Viola .10 .05 .01
☐ 322 Manny Ramirez .60 .25 .08
☐ 323 Gary Wayne .10 .05 .01
☐ 324 Mike Macfarlane .10 .05 .01
☐ 325 Russ Springer .10 .05 .01
☐ 326 Tim Wallach .10 .05 .01
☐ 327 Salomon Torres .15 .07 .02
☐ 328 Omar Vizquel .10 .05 .01
☐ 329 Andy Tomberlin .10 .05 .01
☐ 330 Chris Sabo .10 .05 .01
☐ 331 Mike Mussina .40 .18 .05
☐ 332 Andy Benes .15 .07 .02
☐ 333 Darren Daulton .20 .09 .03
☐ 334 Orlando Merced .15 .07 .02
☐ 335 Mark McGwire .20 .09 .03
☐ 336 Dave Winfield .20 .09 .03
☐ 337 Sammy Sosa .20 .09 .03
☐ 338 Eric Karros .15 .07 .02
☐ 339 Greg Vaughn .15 .07 .02
☐ 340 Don Mattingly 1.25 .55 .16
☐ 341 Frank Thomas 3.00 1.35 .40
☐ 342 Fred McGriff .40 .18 .05
☐ 343 Kirby Puckett 1.25 .55 .16
☐ 344 Roberto Kelly .15 .07 .02
☐ 345 Wally Joyner .15 .07 .02
☐ 346 Andres Galarraga .20 .09 .03
☐ 347 Bobby Bonilla .20 .09 .03
☐ 348 Benito Santiago .10 .05 .01
☐ 349 Barry Bonds 1.25 .55 .16
☐ 350 Delino DeShields .15 .07 .02
☐ 351 Albert Belle .90 .40 .11
☐ 352 Randy Johnson .20 .09 .03
☐ 353 Tim Salmon .40 .18 .05
☐ 354 John Olerud .20 .09 .03
☐ 355 Dean Palmer .15 .07 .02
☐ 356 Roger Clemens .75 .35 .09
☐ 357 Jim Abbott .20 .09 .03
☐ 358 Mark Grace .20 .09 .03
☐ 359 Ozzie Guillen .10 .05 .01
☐ 360 Lou Whitaker .20 .09 .03
☐ 361 Jose Rijo .15 .07 .02
☐ 362 Jeff Montgomery .15 .07 .02
☐ 363 Chuck Finley .10 .05 .01
☐ 364 Tom Glavine .20 .09 .03
☐ 365 Jeff Bagwell 1.50 .65 .19
☐ 366 Joe Carter .40 .18 .05
☐ 367 Ray Lankford .20 .09 .03
☐ 368 Ramon Martinez .15 .07 .02
☐ 369 Jay Buhner .15 .07 .02
☐ 370 Matt Williams .50 .23 .06
☐ 371 Larry Walker .20 .09 .03
☐ 372 Jose Canseco .40 .18 .05
☐ 373 Lenny Dykstra .20 .09 .03
☐ 374 Bryan Harvey .15 .07 .02
☐ 375 Andy Van Slyke .20 .09 .03
☐ 376 Ivan Rodriguez .20 .09 .03
☐ 377 Kevin Mitchell .15 .07 .02
☐ 378 Travis Fryman .25 .11 .03
☐ 379 Duane Ward .15 .07 .02
☐ 380 Greg Maddux .60 .25 .08
☐ 381 Scott Servais .10 .05 .01
☐ 382 Greg Olson .10 .05 .01
☐ 383 Rey Sanchez .10 .05 .01
☐ 384 Tom Kramer .10 .05 .01
☐ 385 David Valle .10 .05 .01
☐ 386 Eddie Murray .20 .09 .03
☐ 387 Kevin Higgins .10 .05 .01
☐ 388 Dan Wilson .10 .05 .01
☐ 389 Todd Frohwith .10 .05 .01
☐ 390 Gerald Williams .15 .07 .02
☐ 391 Hipolito Pichardo .10 .05 .01
☐ 392 Pat Meares .10 .05 .01
☐ 393 Luis Lopez .10 .05 .01
☐ 394 Ricky Jordan .10 .05 .01
☐ 395 Bob Walk .10 .05 .01
☐ 396 Sid Fernandez .10 .05 .01
☐ 397 Todd Worrell .10 .05 .01
☐ 398 Darryl Hamilton .10 .05 .01

	No.	Player			
☐	399	Randy Myers	.10	.05	.01
☐	400	Rod Brewer	.10	.05	.01
☐	401	Lance Blankenship	.10	.05	.01
☐	402	Steve Finley	.10	.05	.01
☐	403	Phil Leftwich	.10	.05	.01
☐	404	Juan Guzman	.15	.07	.02
☐	405	Anthony Young	.10	.05	.01
☐	406	Jeff Gardner	.10	.05	.01
☐	407	Ryan Bowen	.10	.05	.01
☐	408	Fernando Valenzuela	.10	.05	.01
☐	409	David West	.10	.05	.01
☐	410	Kenny Rogers	.10	.05	.01
☐	411	Bob Zupcic	.10	.05	.01
☐	412	Eric Young	.15	.07	.02
☐	413	Bret Boone	.20	.09	.03
☐	414	Danny Tartabull	.15	.07	.02
☐	415	Bob MacDonald	.10	.05	.01
☐	416	Ron Karkovice	.10	.05	.01
☐	417	Scott Cooper	.15	.07	.02
☐	418	Dante Bichette	.20	.09	.03
☐	419	Tripp Cromer	.15	.07	.02
☐	420	Billy Ashley	.20	.09	.03
☐	421	Roger Smithberg	.10	.05	.01
☐	422	Dennis Martinez	.15	.07	.02
☐	423	Mike Blowers	.10	.05	.01
☐	424	Darren Lewis	.10	.05	.01
☐	425	Junior Ortiz	.10	.05	.01
☐	426	Butch Huskey	.10	.05	.01
☐	427	Jimmy Poole	.10	.05	.01
☐	428	Walt Weiss	.10	.05	.01
☐	429	Scott Bankhead	.10	.05	.01
☐	430	Deion Sanders	.50	.23	.06
☐	431	Scott Bullett	.10	.05	.01
☐	432	Jeff Huson	.10	.05	.01
☐	433	Tyler Green	.10	.05	.01
☐	434	Billy Hatcher	.10	.05	.01
☐	435	Bob Hamelin	.20	.09	.03
☐	436	Reggie Sanders	.15	.07	.02
☐	437	Scott Erickson	.10	.05	.01
☐	438	Steve Reed	.10	.05	.01
☐	439	Randy Velarde	.10	.05	.01
☐	440	Checklist 331-412 (Tony Gwynn)	.10	.05	.01
☐	441	Terry Leach	.10	.05	.01
☐	442	Danny Bautista	.15	.07	.02
☐	443	Kent Hrbek	.15	.07	.02
☐	444	Rick Wilkins	.10	.05	.01
☐	445	Tony Phillips	.10	.05	.01
☐	446	Dion James	.10	.05	.01
☐	447	Joey Cora	.10	.05	.01
☐	448	Andre Dawson	.20	.09	.03
☐	449	Pedro Castellano	.10	.05	.01
☐	450	Tom Gordon	.10	.05	.01
☐	451	Rob Dibble	.10	.05	.01
☐	452	Ron Darling	.10	.05	.01
☐	453	Chipper Jones	.40	.18	.05
☐	454	Joe Grahe	.10	.05	.01
☐	455	Domingo Cedeno	.15	.07	.02
☐	456	Tom Edens	.10	.05	.01
☐	457	Mitch Webster	.10	.05	.01
☐	458	Jose Bautista	.10	.05	.01
☐	459	Troy O'Leary	.15	.07	.02
☐	460	Todd Zeile	.15	.07	.02
☐	461	Sean Berry	.10	.05	.01
☐	462	Brad Holman	.10	.05	.01
☐	463	Dave Martinez	.10	.05	.01
☐	464	Mark Lewis	.10	.05	.01
☐	465	Paul Carey	.10	.05	.01
☐	466	Jack Armstrong	.10	.05	.01
☐	467	David Telgheder	.10	.05	.01
☐	468	Gene Harris	.10	.05	.01
☐	469	Danny Darwin	.10	.05	.01
☐	470	Kim Batiste	.10	.05	.01
☐	471	Tim Wakefield	.10	.05	.01
☐	472	Craig Lefferts	.10	.05	.01
☐	473	Jacob Brumfield	.10	.05	.01
☐	474	Lance Painter	.15	.07	.02
☐	475	Milt Cuyler	.10	.05	.01
☐	476	Melido Perez	.10	.05	.01
☐	477	Derek Parks	.10	.05	.01
☐	478	Gary DiSarcina	.10	.05	.01
☐	479	Steve Bedrosian	.10	.05	.01
☐	480	Eric Anthony	.10	.05	.01
☐	481	Julio Franco	.15	.07	.02
☐	482	Tommy Greene	.10	.05	.01
☐	483	Pat Kelly	.10	.05	.01
☐	484	Nate Minchey	.15	.07	.02
☐	485	William Pennyfeather	.10	.05	.01
☐	486	Harold Baines	.15	.07	.02
☐	487	Howard Johnson	.10	.05	.01
☐	488	Angel Miranda	.10	.05	.01
☐	489	Scott Sanders	.15	.07	.02
☐	490	Shawon Dunston	.10	.05	.01
☐	491	Mel Rojas	.10	.05	.01
☐	492	Jeff Nelson	.10	.05	.01
☐	493	Archi Cianfrocco	.10	.05	.01
☐	494	Al Martin	.10	.05	.01
☐	495	Mike Gallego	.10	.05	.01
☐	496	Mike Henneman	.10	.05	.01
☐	497	Armando Reynoso	.10	.05	.01
☐	498	Mickey Morandini	.10	.05	.01
☐	499	Rick Renteria	.10	.05	.01
☐	500	Rick Sutcliffe	.15	.07	.02
☐	501	Bobby Jones	.25	.11	.03
☐	502	Gary Gaetti	.10	.05	.01
☐	503	Rick Aguilera	.15	.07	.02
☐	504	Todd Stottlemyre	.10	.05	.01
☐	505	Mike Mohler	.10	.05	.01
☐	506	Mike Stanton	.10	.05	.01
☐	507	Jose Guzman	.10	.05	.01
☐	508	Kevin Rogers	.10	.05	.01
☐	509	Chuck Carr	.10	.05	.01
☐	510	Chris Jones	.10	.05	.01
☐	511	Brent Mayne	.10	.05	.01
☐	512	Greg Harris	.10	.05	.01
☐	513	Dave Henderson	.10	.05	.01
☐	514	Eric Hillman	.15	.07	.02
☐	515	Dan Peltier	.10	.05	.01
☐	516	Craig Shipley	.10	.05	.01
☐	517	John Valentin	.15	.07	.02
☐	518	Wilson Alvarez	.20	.09	.03
☐	519	Andujar Cedeno	.10	.05	.01
☐	520	Troy Neel	.15	.07	.02
☐	521	Tom Candiotti	.10	.05	.01
☐	522	Matt Mieske	.10	.05	.01
☐	523	Jim Thome	.20	.09	.03
☐	524	Lou Frazier	.15	.07	.02
☐	525	Mike Jackson	.10	.05	.01
☐	526	Pedro Martinez	.20	.09	.03
☐	527	Roger Pavlik	.20	.09	.03
☐	528	Kent Bottenfield	.10	.05	.01
☐	529	Felix Jose	.10	.05	.01
☐	530	Mark Guthrie	.10	.05	.01
☐	531	Steve Farr	.10	.05	.01
☐	532	Craig Paquette	.10	.05	.01
☐	533	Doug Jones	.10	.05	.01
☐	534	Luis Alicea	.10	.05	.01
☐	535	Cory Snyder	.10	.05	.01
☐	536	Paul Sorrento	.10	.05	.01
☐	537	Nigel Wilson	.15	.07	.02
☐	538	Jeff King	.10	.05	.01
☐	539	Willie Greene	.15	.07	.02
☐	540	Kirk McCaskill	.10	.05	.01
☐	541	Al Osuna	.10	.05	.01
☐	542	Greg Hibbard	.10	.05	.01
☐	543	Brett Butler	.15	.07	.02

	No.	Player			
☐	544	Jose Valentin	.10	.05	.01
☐	545	Wil Cordero	.15	.07	.02
☐	546	Chris Bosio	.10	.05	.01
☐	547	Jamie Moyer	.10	.05	.01
☐	548	Jim Eisenreich	.10	.05	.01
☐	549	Vinny Castilla	.15	.07	.02
☐	550	Checklist 413-494 (Dave Winfield)	.10	.05	.01
☐	551	John Roper	.15	.07	.02
☐	552	Lance Johnson	.10	.05	.01
☐	553	Scott Kamieniecki	.10	.05	.01
☐	554	Mike Moore	.10	.05	.01
☐	555	Steve Buechele	.10	.05	.01
☐	556	Terry Pendleton	.20	.09	.03
☐	557	Todd Van Poppel	.15	.07	.02
☐	558	Rob Butler	.10	.05	.01
☐	559	Zane Smith	.10	.05	.01
☐	560	David Hulse	.15	.07	.02
☐	561	Tim Costo	.10	.05	.01
☐	562	John Habyan	.10	.05	.01
☐	563	Terry Jorgensen	.10	.05	.01
☐	564	Matt Nokes	.10	.05	.01
☐	565	Kevin McReynolds	.10	.05	.01
☐	566	Phil Plantier	.15	.07	.02
☐	567	Chris Turner	.10	.05	.01
☐	568	Carlos Delgado	.50	.23	.06
☐	569	John Jaha	.10	.05	.01
☐	570	Dwight Smith	.10	.05	.01
☐	571	John Vander Wal	.15	.07	.02
☐	572	Trevor Wilson	.10	.05	.01
☐	573	Felix Fermin	.10	.05	.01
☐	574	Marc Newfield	.20	.09	.03
☐	575	Jeromy Burnitz	.15	.07	.02
☐	576	Leo Gomez	.10	.05	.01
☐	577	Curt Schilling	.10	.05	.01
☐	578	Kevin Young	.10	.05	.01
☐	579	Jerry Spradlin	.10	.05	.01
☐	580	Curt Leskanic	.15	.07	.02
☐	581	Carl Willis	.10	.05	.01
☐	582	Alex Fernandez	.20	.09	.03
☐	583	Mark Holzemer	.15	.07	.02
☐	584	Domingo Martinez	.15	.07	.02
☐	585	Pete Smith	.10	.05	.01
☐	586	Brian Jordan	.15	.07	.02
☐	587	Kevin Gross	.10	.05	.01
☐	588	J.R. Phillips	.20	.09	.03
☐	589	Chris Nabholz	.10	.05	.01
☐	590	Bill Wertz	.15	.07	.02
☐	591	Derek Bell	.15	.07	.02
☐	592	Brady Anderson	.15	.07	.02
☐	593	Matt Turner	.10	.05	.01
☐	594	Pete Incaviglia	.10	.05	.01
☐	595	Greg Gagne	.10	.05	.01
☐	596	John Flaherty	.15	.07	.02
☐	597	Scott Livingstone	.10	.05	.01
☐	598	Rod Bolton	.10	.05	.01
☐	599	Mike Perez	.10	.05	.01
☐	600	Checklist 495-577 (Roger Clemens)	.10	.05	.01
☐	601	Tony Castillo	.10	.05	.01
☐	602	Henry Mercedes	.10	.05	.01
☐	603	Mike Fetters	.10	.05	.01
☐	604	Rod Beck	.15	.07	.02
☐	605	Damon Buford	.10	.05	.01
☐	606	Matt Whiteside	.15	.07	.02
☐	607	Shawn Green	.20	.09	.03
☐	608	Midre Cummings	.25	.11	.03
☐	609	Jeff McNeely	.10	.05	.01
☐	610	Danny Sheaffer	.15	.07	.02
☐	611	Paul Wagner	.10	.05	.01
☐	612	Torey Lovullo	.10	.05	.01
☐	613	Javy Lopez	.30	.14	.04
☐	614	Mariano Duncan	.10	.05	.01
☐	615	Doug Brocail	.10	.05	.01
☐	616	Dave Hansen	.10	.05	.01
☐	617	Ryan Klesko	.50	.23	.06
☐	618	Eric Davis	.10	.05	.01
☐	619	Scott Ruffcorn	.20	.09	.03
☐	620	Mike Trombley	.15	.07	.02
☐	621	Jaime Navarro	.10	.05	.01
☐	622	Rheal Cormier	.10	.05	.01
☐	623	Jose Offerman	.15	.07	.02
☐	624	David Segui	.10	.05	.01
☐	625	Robb Nen	.10	.05	.01
☐	626	Dave Gallagher	.10	.05	.01
☐	627	Julian Tavarez	.60	.25	.08
☐	628	Chris Gomez	.20	.09	.03
☐	629	Jeffrey Hammonds	.40	.18	.05
☐	630	Scott Brosius	.10	.05	.01
☐	631	Willie Blair	.10	.05	.01
☐	632	Doug Drabek	.20	.09	.03
☐	633	Bill Wegman	.10	.05	.01
☐	634	Jeff McKnight	.10	.05	.01
☐	635	Rich Rodriguez	.10	.05	.01
☐	636	Steve Trachsel	.40	.18	.05
☐	637	Buddy Groom	.15	.07	.02
☐	638	Sterling Hitchcock	.15	.07	.02
☐	639	Chuck McElroy	.10	.05	.01
☐	640	Rene Gonzales	.10	.05	.01
☐	641	Dan Plesac	.10	.05	.01
☐	642	Jeff Branson	.15	.07	.02
☐	643	Darrell Whitmore	.15	.07	.02
☐	644	Paul Quantrill	.10	.05	.01
☐	645	Rich Rowland	.10	.05	.01
☐	646	Curtis Pride	.30	.14	.04
☐	647	Erik Plantenberg	.10	.05	.01
☐	648	Albie Lopez	.20	.09	.03
☐	649	Rich Batchelor	.10	.05	.01
☐	650	Lee Smith	.20	.09	.03
☐	651	Cliff Floyd	.50	.23	.06
☐	652	Pete Schourek	.10	.05	.01
☐	653	Reggie Jefferson	.10	.05	.01
☐	654	Bill Haselman	.10	.05	.01
☐	655	Steve Hosey	.10	.05	.01
☐	656	Mark Clark	.10	.05	.01
☐	657	Mark Davis	.10	.05	.01
☐	658	Dave Magadan	.10	.05	.01
☐	659	Candy Maldonado	.10	.05	.01
☐	660	Checklist 578-660 (Mark Langston)	.10	.05	.01

1994 Donruss Special Edition

Issued in two series of 50 cards, this 100-card set of 1994 Donruss Special Edition

represents a Gold edition of the best players in the game. The first 50 cards correspond to cards 1-50 in the first series, while the second 50 cards correspond to cards 331-380 in the second series. The cards measure standard size. The full-bleed fronts display glossy color action photos accented by a holographic embossed foil stripe across the bottom containing the player's name and position. Intersecting the stripe is a similar foil box which carries the set name and player's team. The borderless backs have a second action player shot superimposed by a black panel containing the player's name, team, and biographical information. Statistics from 1993 and career averages are printed on ghosted stripes across the bottom. The backs are a mix of horizontal and vertical orientations. The card number appears in a holographic embossed foil box in the upper right corner.

	MINT	EXC	G-VG
COMPLETE SET (100)	30.00	13.50	3.80
COMPLETE SERIES 1 (50)	15.00	6.75	1.90
COMPLETE SERIES 2 (50)	15.00	6.75	1.90
COMMON CARD (1-50)	.25	.11	.03
COMMON CARD (51-100)	.25	.11	.03

*STARS: 1X to 2X BASIC CARDS

1994 Donruss Anniversary '84

Randomly inserted in hobby foil packs at a rate of one in 12, this ten-card standard-size set reproduces selected cards from the 1984 Donruss baseball set. The cards feature white bordered color player photos on their fronts. The player's name appears in yellow lettering within a colored stripe at the bottom. The player's gold-foil team name is shown within wavy gold-foil lines near the bottom of the photo. The horizontal and white-bordered back carries the player's name and biography within a green-colored stripe across the top. A white area below contains the player's stats and, within a green panel further below, his career highlights. The cards are numbered on the back at the bottom right as "X of 10," and also carry the numbers from the original 1984 set at the upper left.

	MINT	EXC	G-VG
COMPLETE SET (10)	60.00	27.00	7.50
COMMON CARD (1-10)	3.00	1.35	.40
☐ 1 Joe Carter	4.00	1.80	.50
☐ 2 Robin Yount	4.00	1.80	.50
☐ 3 George Brett	8.00	3.60	1.00
☐ 4 Rickey Henderson	3.00	1.35	.40
☐ 5 Nolan Ryan	20.00	9.00	2.50
☐ 6 Cal Ripken	15.00	6.75	1.90
☐ 7 Wade Boggs	3.00	1.35	.40
☐ 8 Don Mattingly	10.00	4.50	1.25
☐ 9 Ryne Sandberg	7.00	3.10	.85
☐ 10 Tony Gwynn	6.00	2.70	.75

1994 Donruss Award Winner Jumbos

This 10-card set was issued one per jumbo foil and Canadian foil boxes and spotlights players that won various awards in 1993. Cards 1-5 were included in first series boxes and 6-10 with the second series. The cards measure approximately 3 1/2" by 5". Ten-thousand of each card were produced. Card fronts are full-bleed with a color player photo and the Award Winner logo at the top. The backs are individually numbered out of 10,000.

	MINT	EXC	G-VG
COMPLETE SET (10)	130.00	57.50	16.50
COMPLETE SERIES 1 (5)	65.00	29.00	8.25
COMPLETE SERIES 2 (5)	65.00	29.00	8.25
COMMON CARD (1-5)	10.00	4.50	1.25
COMMON CARD (6-10)	4.00	1.80	.50

		MINT	EXC	G-VG
☐ 1	Barry Bonds MVP	15.00	6.75	1.90
☐ 2	Greg Maddux CY	10.00	4.50	1.25
☐ 3	Mike Piazza ROY	20.00	9.00	2.50
☐ 4	Barry Bonds Homerun King	15.00	6.75	1.90
☐ 5	Kirby Puckett AS MVP	15.00	6.75	1.90
☐ 6	Frank Thomas MVP	40.00	18.00	5.00
☐ 7	Jack McDowell CY	4.00	1.80	.50
☐ 8	Tim Salmon ROY	6.00	2.70	.75
☐ 9	Juan Gonzalez Homerun King	12.00	5.50	1.50
☐ 10	Paul Molitor WS MVP	6.00	2.70	.75

1994 Donruss Diamond Kings

This 30-card set was split in two series. Cards 1-14 and 29 were randomly inserted in first series packs, while cards 15-28 and 30 were inserted in second series packs. With each series, the insertion rate was one in nine. The cards measure the standard size. Jumbo versions of these cards were inserted one per retail box and command up to twice the values below. The fronts feature full-bleed player portraits by noted sports artist Dick Perez. Red and silver holographic foil lettering across the top provides the set title. The player's name is printed in gold script lettering across the bottom. On a yellow background the backs provide a career summary in red print with a narrow red border. The cards are numbered on the back with the prefix DK.

	MINT	EXC	G-VG
COMPLETE SET (30)	55.00	25.00	7.00
COMPLETE SERIES 1 (15)	25.00	11.50	3.10
COMPLETE SERIES 2 (15)	30.00	13.50	3.80
COMMON CARD (1-14/29)	.60	.25	.08
COMMON CARD (15-28/30)	.60	.25	.08

*JUMBO DK's: 1X to 2X VALUES BELOW

		MINT	EXC	G-VG
☐ 1	Barry Bonds	4.00	1.80	.50
☐ 2	Mo Vaughn	1.25	.55	.16
☐ 3	Steve Avery	1.25	.55	.16
☐ 4	Tim Salmon	2.00	.90	.25
☐ 5	Rick Wilkins	.60	.25	.08
☐ 6	Brian Harper	.60	.25	.08
☐ 7	Andres Galarraga	1.25	.55	.16
☐ 8	Albert Belle	3.00	1.35	.40
☐ 9	John Kruk	1.00	.45	.13
☐ 10	Ivan Rodriguez	1.25	.55	.16
☐ 11	Tony Gwynn	2.50	1.15	.30
☐ 12	Brian McRae	1.00	.45	.13
☐ 13	Bobby Bonilla	.60	.25	.08
☐ 14	Ken Griffey Jr.	10.00	4.50	1.25
☐ 15	Mike Piazza	5.00	2.30	.60
☐ 16	Don Mattingly	4.00	1.80	.50
☐ 17	Barry Larkin	1.25	.55	.16
☐ 18	Ruben Sierra	1.25	.55	.16
☐ 19	Orlando Merced	.60	.25	.08
☐ 20	Greg Vaughn	.60	.25	.08
☐ 21	Gregg Jefferies	1.25	.55	.16
☐ 22	Cecil Fielder	1.25	.55	.16
☐ 23	Moises Alou	1.00	.45	.13
☐ 24	John Olerud	1.25	.55	.16
☐ 25	Gary Sheffield	1.25	.55	.16
☐ 26	Mike Mussina	2.00	.90	.25
☐ 27	Jeff Bagwell	5.00	2.30	.60
☐ 28	Frank Thomas	10.00	4.50	1.25
☐ 29	Dave Winfield	1.25	.55	.16
☐ 30	Checklist	.60	.25	.08

1994 Donruss Dominators I

This ten-card, standard-size was randomly inserted in all packs at a rate of one in 12. The fronts displayed full-bleed color action shots with the set title printed along the bottom in gold and black lettering. The player's name appears within an oval gold bar. The horizontal backs carry a second player photo on approximately two-thirds of the card back. The remaining section contains statistics from the 1990s in a box with total number of homers printed prominently in white. The player's ranking in the 1990s is also listed. Jumbo Dominators (3 1/2" by 5") were issued one per hobby box and are valued up to twice the prices below.

	MINT	EXC	G-VG
COMPLETE SET (10)	25.00	11.50	3.10
COMMON CARD (1-10)	.60	.25	.08

*JUMBO DOMINATORS: 1X to 2X VALUES BELOW

		MINT	EXC	G-VG
☐ 1	Cecil Fielder	.60	.25	.08
☐ 2	Barry Bonds	4.00	1.80	.50
☐ 3	Fred McGriff	1.75	.80	.22
☐ 4	Matt Williams	2.00	.90	.25
☐ 5	Joe Carter	1.75	.80	.22
☐ 6	Juan Gonzalez	3.50	1.55	.45
☐ 7	Jose Canseco	1.75	.80	.22

	MINT	EXC	G-VG
☐ 8 Ron Gant	.60	.25	.08
☐ 9 Ken Griffey Jr.	10.00	4.50	1.25
☐ 10 Mark McGwire	.60	.25	.08

1994 Donruss Dominators II

Randomly inserted in all second series pack types, this 10-card standard-size set is arranged in descending order of batting average in the 1990s for these players. A total of 10,000 enlarged versions (3 1/2" by 5") of each card were printed, individually serially numbered and inserted in hobby foil pack boxes. The jumbo versions are valued up to twice the prices below. The fronts display full-bleed color action shots with the set title printed along the bottom in gold and black lettering. The player's name appears within an oval gold bar. The horizontal backs carry a second player photo on approximately two-thirds of the card back. The remaining section contains statistics from the 1990s in a box with batting average printed prominently in white. The player's ranking in the 1990s is also listed. The cards are numbered on the back.

	MINT	EXC	G-VG
COMPLETE SET (10)	30.00	13.50	3.80
COMMON CARD (1-10)	.60	.25	.08

*JUMBO DOMINATORS: 1X to 2X VALUES BELOW

	MINT	EXC	G-VG
☐ 1 Tony Gwynn	2.50	1.15	.30
☐ 2 Frank Thomas	10.00	4.50	1.25
☐ 3 Paul Molitor	1.25	.55	.16
☐ 4 Edgar Martinez	.60	.25	.08
☐ 5 Kirby Puckett	4.00	1.80	.50
☐ 6 Ken Griffey Jr.	10.00	4.50	1.25
☐ 7 Barry Bonds	4.00	1.80	.50
☐ 8 Willie McGee	.60	.25	.08
☐ 9 Lenny Dykstra	1.25	.55	.16
☐ 10 John Kruk	1.25	.55	.16

1994 Donruss Elite

This 12-card set was issued in two series of six. Using a continued numbering system

from previous years, cards 37-42 were randomly inserted in first series foil packs with cards 43-48 a second series offering. The cards measure the standard size. Only 10,000 of each card were produced. The color player photo inside a diamond design on the front rests on a marbleized panel framed by a red-and-white inner border and a silver foil outer border. Silver foil stripes radiate away from the edges of the picture. The player's name appears across the bottom of the front. The back design is similar, but with a color head shot in a small diamond and a player profile, both resting on a marbleized panel. The bottom carries the card number, the serial number, and the production run figure.

	MINT	EXC	G-VG
COMPLETE SET (12)	300.00	135.00	38.00
COMPLETE SERIES 1 (6)	150.00	70.00	19.00
COMPLETE SERIES 2 (6)	150.00	70.00	19.00
COMMON CARD (37-42)	10.00	4.50	1.25
COMMON CARD (43-48)	10.00	4.50	1.25

	MINT	EXC	G-VG
☐ 37 Frank Thomas	90.00	40.00	11.50
☐ 38 Tony Gwynn	20.00	9.00	2.50
☐ 39 Tim Salmon	15.00	6.75	1.90
☐ 40 Albert Belle	30.00	13.50	3.80
☐ 41 John Kruk	10.00	4.50	1.25
☐ 42 Juan Gonzalez	30.00	13.50	3.80
☐ 43 John Olerud	12.00	5.50	1.50
☐ 44 Barry Bonds	35.00	16.00	4.40
☐ 45 Ken Griffey Jr.	90.00	40.00	11.50
☐ 46 Mike Piazza	45.00	20.00	5.75
☐ 47 Jack McDowell	10.00	4.50	1.25
☐ 48 Andres Galarraga	12.00	5.50	1.50

1994 Donruss Long Ball Leaders

Inserted in second series hobby foil packs at a rate of one in 12, this 10-card set features some of top home run hitters and the distance of their longest home run of 1993. The card fronts have a color photo with a black right-hand border. Within the border is the Long Ball Leaders logo in silver foil. Also in silver foil at bottom, is the player's last name and the distance of the clout. Card backs contain a photo of the park with which the home run occurred as well as information such as the date, the pitcher and other particulars.

	MINT	EXC	G-VG
COMPLETE SET (10)	60.00	27.00	7.50
COMMON CARD (1-10)	1.50	.65	.19

	MINT	EXC	G-VG
☐ 1 Cecil Fielder	2.50	1.15	.30
☐ 2 Dean Palmer	1.50	.65	.19
☐ 3 Andres Galarraga	2.50	1.15	.30
☐ 4 Bo Jackson	2.50	1.15	.30
☐ 5 Ken Griffey Jr.	20.00	9.00	2.50
☐ 6 David Justice	3.00	1.35	.40
☐ 7 Mike Piazza	10.00	4.50	1.25
☐ 8 Frank Thomas	20.00	9.00	2.50
☐ 9 Barry Bonds	8.00	3.60	1.00
☐ 10 Juan Gonzalez	7.00	3.10	.85

1994 Donruss MVPs

Inserted at a rate of one per first and second series jumbo pack, this 28-card set was split into two series of 14; one player for each team. The first 14 are of National League players with the latter group being American Leaguers. Full-bleed card fronts feature an action photo of the player with "MVP" in large red (American League) or blue (National) letters at the bottom. The player's name and, for Amercian League player cards only, team name are beneath the "MVP". A number of white stars stretches up the left border. The backs, which are horizontal, contain a photo, 1993 statistics, a short write-up and white stars within blue foil along the left border.

	MINT	EXC	G-VG
COMPLETE SET (28)	50.00	23.00	6.25
COMPLETE SERIES 1 (14)	15.00	6.75	1.90
COMPLETE SERIES 2 (14)	35.00	16.00	4.40
COMMON CARD (1-14)	.50	.23	.06
COMMON CARD (15-28)	.60	.25	.08

	MINT	EXC	G-VG
☐ 1 David Justice	1.50	.65	.19
☐ 2 Mark Grace	.60	.25	.08
☐ 3 Jose Rijo	.50	.23	.06
☐ 4 Andres Galarraga	.75	.35	.09
☐ 5 Bryan Harvey	.50	.23	.06
☐ 6 Jeff Bagwell	5.00	2.30	.60
☐ 7 Mike Piazza	5.00	2.30	.60
☐ 8 Moises Alou	.60	.25	.08
☐ 9 Bobby Bonilla	.50	.23	.06
☐ 10 Len Dykstra	.75	.35	.09
☐ 11 Jeff King	.50	.23	.06
☐ 12 Gregg Jefferies	.75	.35	.09
☐ 13 Tony Gwynn	2.50	1.15	.30
☐ 14 Barry Bonds	4.00	1.80	.50
☐ 15 Cal Ripken	7.50	3.40	.95
☐ 16 Mo Vaughn	1.00	.45	.13
☐ 17 Tim Salmon	1.50	.65	.19
☐ 18 Frank Thomas	10.00	4.50	1.25
☐ 19 Albert Belle	3.50	1.55	.45
☐ 20 Cecil Fielder	1.00	.45	.13
☐ 21 Wally Joyner	.60	.25	.08
☐ 22 Greg Vaughn	.60	.25	.08
☐ 23 Kirby Puckett	4.00	1.80	.50
☐ 24 Don Mattingly	4.00	1.80	.50
☐ 25 Ruben Sierra	1.00	.45	.13
☐ 26 Ken Griffey Jr.	10.00	4.50	1.25
☐ 27 Juan Gonzalez	3.50	1.55	.45
☐ 28 John Olerud	1.00	.45	.13

1994 Donruss Spirit of the Game

Consisting of 10 cards, cards 1-5 were randomly inserted in first-series magazine jumbo packs and cards 6-10 in second series magazine jumbo packs. Measuring the standard-size, the set features horizontal designs on its borderless fronts that have color action player photos superposed upon triple exposure sepia-toned action shots. The set's title appears in dark brown cursive lettering within a prismatic-foil stripe across the bottom. The horizontal back carries a color player close-up that is superposed upon red, white, and blue bunting. An outstanding achievement by the player appears in gold lettering at the upper right, and a ghosted panel immediately below carries black-lettered text providing details. The cards are numbered on the back. Jumbo sized Spirit of the Game cards, individually numbered out of 10,000, were issued one per magazine jumbo box and carry no additional premium.

	MINT	EXC	G-VG
COMPLETE SET (10)	70.00	32.00	8.75
COMPLETE SERIES 1 (5)	40.00	18.00	5.00
COMPLETE SERIES 2 (5)	30.00	13.50	3.80
COMMON CARD (1-5)	1.50	.65	.19
COMMON CARD (6-10)	1.50	.65	.19
*JUMBO SOG: 1.5X VALUES BELOW			
☐ 1 John Olerud	1.50	.65	.19
☐ 2 Barry Bonds	8.00	3.60	1.00
☐ 3 Ken Griffey Jr.	20.00	9.00	2.50
☐ 4 Mike Piazza	10.00	4.50	1.25
☐ 5 Juan Gonzalez	7.00	3.10	.85
☐ 6 Frank Thomas	20.00	9.00	2.50
☐ 7 Tim Salmon	3.50	1.55	.45
☐ 8 David Justice	3.00	1.35	.40
☐ 9 Don Mattingly	8.00	3.60	1.00
☐ 10 Lenny Dykstra	1.50	.65	.19

1995 Donruss

The 1995 Donruss first series consists of 330 cards. The fronts feature borderless color action player photos. A second, smaller color player photo in a homeplate shape with team color-coded borders appears in the lower left corner. The player's position in silver-foil is above this smaller photo, while his name is printed in a silver-foil bar under the photo. The borderless backs carry a color action player cutout superimposed over the team logo, along with player biography and stats for the last five years. The cards are numbered on the back.

	MINT	EXC	G-VG
COMPLETE SERIES 1 (330)	20.00	9.00	2.50
COMMON CARD (1-330)	.10	.05	.01
☐ 1 David Justice	.40	.18	.05
☐ 2 Rene Arocha	.10	.05	.01
☐ 3 Sandy Alomar Jr.	.15	.07	.02
☐ 4 Luis Lopez	.10	.05	.01
☐ 5 Mike Piazza	1.25	.55	.16
☐ 6 Bobby Jones	.20	.09	.03
☐ 7 Damion Easley	.10	.05	.01
☐ 8 Barry Bonds	1.25	.55	.16
☐ 9 Mike Mussina	.40	.18	.05
☐ 10 Kevin Seitzer	.10	.05	.01
☐ 11 John Smiley	.10	.05	.01
☐ 12 Will VanLandingham	.10	.05	.01
☐ 13 Ron Darling	.10	.05	.01
☐ 14 Walt Weiss	.10	.05	.01
☐ 15 Mike Lansing	.10	.05	.01
☐ 16 Allen Watson	.10	.05	.01
☐ 17 Aaron Sele	.20	.09	.03
☐ 18 Randy Johnson	.20	.09	.03
☐ 19 Dean Palmer	.15	.07	.02
☐ 20 Jeff Bagwell	1.50	.65	.19
☐ 21 Curt Schilling	.10	.05	.01
☐ 22 Darrell Whitmore	.15	.07	.02
☐ 23 Steve Trachsel	.20	.09	.03
☐ 24 Dan Wilson	.10	.05	.01
☐ 25 Steve Finley	.10	.05	.01
☐ 26 Bret Boone	.20	.09	.03
☐ 27 Charles Johnson	.20	.09	.03
☐ 28 Mike Stanton	.10	.05	.01
☐ 29 Ismael Valdes	.10	.05	.01
☐ 30 Salomon Torres	.15	.07	.02
☐ 31 Eric Anthony	.10	.05	.01
☐ 32 Spike Owen	.10	.05	.01
☐ 33 Joey Cora	.10	.05	.01
☐ 34 Robert Eenhoorn	.10	.05	.01
☐ 35 Rick White	.10	.05	.01
☐ 36 Omar Vizquel	.10	.05	.01
☐ 37 Carlos Delgado	.35	.16	.04
☐ 38 Eddie Williams	.10	.05	.01
☐ 39 Shawon Dunston	.10	.05	.01
☐ 40 Darrin Fletcher	.10	.05	.01
☐ 41 Leo Gomez	.10	.05	.01
☐ 42 Juan Gonzalez	1.00	.45	.13
☐ 43 Luis Alicea	.10	.05	.01
☐ 44 Ken Ryan	.10	.05	.01
☐ 45 Lou Whitaker	.20	.09	.03
☐ 46 Mike Blowers	.10	.05	.01
☐ 47 Willie Blair	.10	.05	.01
☐ 48 Todd Van Poppel	.15	.07	.02
☐ 49 Roberto Alomar	.60	.25	.08
☐ 50 Ozzie Smith	.60	.25	.08
☐ 51 Sterling Hitchcock	.15	.07	.02
☐ 52 Mo Vaughn	.20	.09	.03
☐ 53 Rick Aguilera	.15	.07	.02
☐ 54 Kent Mercker	.10	.05	.01
☐ 55 Don Mattingly	1.25	.55	.16
☐ 56 Bob Scanlan	.10	.05	.01
☐ 57 Wilson Alvarez	.20	.09	.03
☐ 58 Jose Mesa	.10	.05	.01
☐ 59 Scott Kamieniecki	.10	.05	.01
☐ 60 Todd Jones	.10	.05	.01
☐ 61 John Kruk	.20	.09	.03
☐ 62 Mike Stanley	.10	.05	.01
☐ 63 Tino Martinez	.10	.05	.01
☐ 64 Eddie Zambrano	.10	.05	.01
☐ 65 Todd Hundley	.10	.05	.01
☐ 66 Jamie Moyer	.10	.05	.01
☐ 67 Rich Amaral	.10	.05	.01
☐ 68 Jose Valentin	.10	.05	.01
☐ 69 Alex Gonzalez	.10	.05	.01
☐ 70 Kurt Abbott	.10	.05	.01
☐ 71 Delino DeShields	.15	.07	.02
☐ 72 Brian Anderson	.20	.09	.03
☐ 73 John Vander Wal	.10	.05	.01
☐ 74 Turner Ward	.10	.05	.01
☐ 75 Tim Raines	.20	.09	.03
☐ 76 Mark Acre	.10	.05	.01
☐ 77 Jose Offerman	.10	.05	.01
☐ 78 Jimmy Key	.15	.07	.02
☐ 79 Mark Whiten	.15	.07	.02
☐ 80 Mark Gubicza	.10	.05	.01
☐ 81 Darren Hall	.10	.05	.01
☐ 82 Travis Fryman	.25	.11	.03
☐ 83 Cal Ripken	2.25	1.00	.30
☐ 84 Geronimo Berroa	.10	.05	.01
☐ 85 Bret Barberie	.10	.05	.01
☐ 86 Andy Ashby	.10	.05	.01
☐ 87 Steve Avery	.20	.09	.03
☐ 88 Rich Becker	.15	.07	.02

□ 89 John Valentin .15 .07 .02
□ 90 Glenallen Hill .10 .05 .01
□ 91 Carlos Garcia .10 .05 .01
□ 92 Dennis Martinez .15 .07 .02
□ 93 Pat Kelly .10 .05 .01
□ 94 Orlando Miller .15 .07 .02
□ 95 Felix Jose .10 .05 .01
□ 96 Mike Kingery .10 .05 .01
□ 97 Jeff Kent .15 .07 .02
□ 98 Pete Incaviglia .10 .05 .01
□ 99 Chad Curtis .15 .07 .02
□ 100 Thomas Howard .10 .05 .01
□ 101 Hector Carrasco .10 .05 .01
□ 102 Tom Pagnozzi .10 .05 .01
□ 103 Danny Tartabull .15 .07 .02
□ 104 Donnie Elliott .10 .05 .01
□ 105 Danny Jackson .10 .05 .01
□ 106 Steve Dunn .15 .07 .02
□ 107 Roger Salkeld .10 .05 .01
□ 108 Jeff King .10 .05 .01
□ 109 Cecil Fielder .20 .09 .03
□ 110 Checklist 1-82 .25 .11 .03
(Paul Molitor)
□ 111 Denny Neagle .10 .05 .01
□ 112 Troy Neel .15 .07 .02
□ 113 Rod Beck .15 .07 .02
□ 114 Alex Rodriguez 1.25 .55 .16
□ 115 Joey Eischen .10 .05 .01
□ 116 Tom Candiotti .10 .05 .01
□ 117 Ray McDavid .10 .05 .01
□ 118 Vince Coleman .10 .05 .01
□ 119 Pete Harnisch .10 .05 .01
□ 120 David Nied .20 .09 .03
□ 121 Pat Rapp .10 .05 .01
□ 122 Sammy Sosa .20 .09 .03
□ 123 Steve Reed .10 .05 .01
□ 124 Jose Oliva .20 .09 .03
□ 125 Ricky Bottalico .10 .05 .01
□ 126 Jose DeLeon .10 .05 .01
□ 127 Pat Hentgen .15 .07 .02
□ 128 Will Clark .40 .18 .05
□ 129 Mark Dewey .10 .05 .01
□ 130 Greg Vaughn .15 .07 .02
□ 131 Darren Dreifort .10 .05 .01
□ 132 Ed Sprague .10 .05 .01
□ 133 Lee Smith .20 .09 .03
□ 134 Charles Nagy .10 .05 .01
□ 135 Phil Plantier .15 .07 .02
□ 136 Jason Jacome .25 .11 .03
□ 137 Jose Lima .15 .07 .02
□ 138 J.R. Phillips .20 .09 .03
□ 139 J.T. Snow .10 .05 .01
□ 140 Michael Huff .10 .05 .01
□ 141 Billy Brewer .10 .05 .01
□ 142 Jeromy Burnitz .10 .05 .01
□ 143 Ricky Bones .10 .05 .01
□ 144 Carlos Rodriguez .10 .05 .01
□ 145 Luis Gonzalez .10 .05 .01
□ 146 Mark Lemke .10 .05 .01
□ 147 Al Martin .10 .05 .01
□ 148 Mike Bordick .10 .05 .01
□ 149 Robb Nen .10 .05 .01
□ 150 Wil Cordero .15 .07 .02
□ 151 Edgar Martinez .10 .05 .01
□ 152 Gerald Williams .10 .05 .01
□ 153 Esteban Beltre .10 .05 .01
□ 154 Mike Moore .10 .05 .01
□ 155 Mark Langston .20 .09 .03
□ 156 Mark Clark .10 .05 .01
□ 157 Bobby Ayala .10 .05 .01
□ 158 Rick Wilkins .10 .05 .01
□ 159 Bobby Munoz .10 .05 .01
□ 160 Checklist 83-164 .10 .05 .01
(Brett Butler)
□ 161 Scott Erickson .10 .05 .01
□ 162 Paul Molitor .40 .18 .05
□ 163 Jon Lieber .10 .05 .01
□ 164 Jason Grimsley .10 .05 .01
□ 165 Norberto Martin .10 .05 .01
□ 166 Javy Lopez .20 .09 .03
□ 167 Brian McRae .15 .07 .02
□ 168 Gary Sheffield .20 .09 .03
□ 169 Marcus Moore .10 .05 .01
□ 170 John Hudek .10 .05 .01
□ 171 Kelly Stinnett .10 .05 .01
□ 172 Chris Gomez .15 .07 .02
□ 173 Rey Sanchez .10 .05 .01
□ 174 Juan Guzman .15 .07 .02
□ 175 Chan Ho Park .30 .14 .04
□ 176 Terry Shumpert .10 .05 .01
□ 177 Steve Ontiveros .10 .05 .01
□ 178 Brad Ausmus .10 .05 .01
□ 179 Tim Davis .10 .05 .01
□ 180 Billy Ashley .20 .09 .03
□ 181 Vinny Castilla .10 .05 .01
□ 182 Bill Spiers .10 .05 .01
□ 183 Randy Knorr .10 .05 .01
□ 184 Brian Hunter .10 .05 .01
□ 185 Pat Meares .10 .05 .01
□ 186 Steve Buechele .10 .05 .01
□ 187 Kirt Manwaring .10 .05 .01
□ 188 Tim Naehring .10 .05 .01
□ 189 Matt Mieske .10 .05 .01
□ 190 Josias Manzanillo .10 .05 .01
□ 191 Greg McMichael .10 .05 .01
□ 192 Chuck Carr .10 .05 .01
□ 193 Midre Cummings .10 .05 .01
□ 194 Darryl Strawberry .15 .07 .02
□ 195 Greg Gagne .10 .05 .01
□ 196 Steve Cooke .10 .05 .01
□ 197 Woody Williams .10 .05 .01
□ 198 Ron Karkovice .10 .05 .01
□ 199 Phil Leftwich .10 .05 .01
□ 200 Jim Thome .20 .09 .03
□ 201 Brady Anderson .15 .07 .02
□ 202 Pedro Martinez .20 .09 .03
□ 203 Steve Karsay .10 .05 .01
□ 204 Reggie Sanders .15 .07 .02
□ 205 Bill Risley .10 .05 .01
□ 206 Jay Bell .15 .07 .02
□ 207 Kevin Brown .10 .05 .01
□ 208 Tim Scott .10 .05 .01
□ 209 Lenny Dykstra .20 .09 .03
□ 210 Willie Greene .15 .07 .02
□ 211 Jim Eisenreich .10 .05 .01
□ 212 Cliff Floyd .35 .16 .04
□ 213 Otis Nixon .10 .05 .01
□ 214 Eduardo Perez .15 .07 .02
□ 215 Manny Lee .10 .05 .01
□ 216 Armando Benitez .10 .05 .01
□ 217 Dave McCarty .15 .07 .02
□ 218 Scott Livingstone .10 .05 .01
□ 219 Chad Kreuter .10 .05 .01
□ 220 Checklist 165-246 .60 .25 .08
(Don Mattingly)
□ 221 Brian Jordan .15 .07 .02
□ 222 Matt Whiteside .10 .05 .01
□ 223 Jim Edmonds .10 .05 .01
□ 224 Tony Gwynn .60 .25 .08
□ 225 Jose Lind .10 .05 .01
□ 226 Marvin Freeman .10 .05 .01
□ 227 Ken Hill .15 .07 .02
□ 228 David Hulse .10 .05 .01
□ 229 Joe Hesketh .10 .05 .01
□ 230 Roberto Petagine .15 .07 .02
□ 231 Jeffrey Hammonds .10 .05 .01

	No.	Player	MINT	EXC	G-VG
☐	232	John Jaha	.10	.05	.01
☐	233	John Burkett	.15	.07	.02
☐	234	Hal Morris	.15	.07	.02
☐	235	Tony Castillo	.10	.05	.01
☐	236	Ryan Bowen	.10	.05	.01
☐	237	Wayne Kirby	.10	.05	.01
☐	238	Brent Mayne	.10	.05	.01
☐	239	Jim Bullinger	.10	.05	.01
☐	240	Mike Lieberthal	.10	.05	.01
☐	241	Barry Larkin	.20	.09	.03
☐	242	David Segui	.10	.05	.01
☐	243	Jose Bautista	.10	.05	.01
☐	244	Hector Fajardo	.10	.05	.01
☐	245	Orel Hershiser	.15	.07	.02
☐	246	James Mouton	.10	.05	.01
☐	247	Scott Leius	.10	.05	.01
☐	248	Tom Glavine	.20	.09	.03
☐	249	Danny Bautista	.10	.05	.01
☐	250	Jose Mercedes	.10	.05	.01
☐	251	Marquis Grissom	.20	.09	.03
☐	252	Charlie Hayes	.15	.07	.02
☐	253	Ryan Klesko	.35	.16	.04
☐	254	Vicente Palacios	.10	.05	.01
☐	255	Matias Carrillo	.10	.05	.01
☐	256	Gary DiSarcina	.10	.05	.01
☐	257	Kirk Gibson	.15	.07	.02
☐	258	Garey Ingram	.10	.05	.01
☐	259	Alex Fernandez	.20	.09	.03
☐	260	John Mabry	.10	.05	.01
☐	261	Chris Howard	.10	.05	.01
☐	262	Miguel Jimenez	.10	.05	.01
☐	263	Heath Slocumb	.10	.05	.01
☐	264	Albert Belle	1.00	.45	.13
☐	265	Dave Clark	.10	.05	.01
☐	266	Joe Orsulak	.10	.05	.01
☐	267	Joey Hamilton	.20	.09	.03
☐	268	Mark Portugal	.10	.05	.01
☐	269	Kevin Tapani	.10	.05	.01
☐	270	Sid Fernandez	.10	.05	.01
☐	271	Steve Dreyer	.10	.05	.01
☐	272	Denny Hocking	.10	.05	.01
☐	273	Troy O'Leary	.10	.05	.01
☐	274	Milt Cuyler	.10	.05	.01
☐	275	Frank Thomas	3.00	1.35	.40
☐	276	Jorge Fabregas	.10	.05	.01
☐	277	Mike Gallego	.10	.05	.01
☐	278	Mickey Morandini	.10	.05	.01
☐	279	Roberto Hernandez	.10	.05	.01
☐	280	Henry Rodriguez	.10	.05	.01
☐	281	Garret Anderson	.15	.07	.02
☐	282	Bob Wickman	.10	.05	.01
☐	283	Gar Finnvold	.10	.05	.01
☐	284	Paul O'Neill	.15	.07	.02
☐	285	Royce Clayton	.15	.07	.02
☐	286	Chuck Knoblauch	.20	.09	.03
☐	287	Johnny Ruffin	.10	.05	.01
☐	288	Dave Nilsson	.10	.05	.01
☐	289	David Cone	.20	.09	.03
☐	290	Chuck McElroy	.10	.05	.01
☐	291	Kevin Stocker	.15	.07	.02
☐	292	Jose Rijo	.15	.07	.02
☐	293	Sean Berry	.10	.05	.01
☐	294	Ozzie Guillen	.10	.05	.01
☐	295	Chris Hoiles	.15	.07	.02
☐	296	Kevin Foster	.10	.05	.01
☐	297	Jeff Frye	.10	.05	.01
☐	298	Lance Johnson	.10	.05	.01
☐	299	Mike Kelly	.15	.07	.02
☐	300	Ellis Burks	.15	.07	.02
☐	301	Roberto Kelly	.10	.05	.01
☐	302	Dante Bichette	.20	.09	.03
☐	303	Alvaro Espinoza	.10	.05	.01
☐	304	Alex Cole	.10	.05	.01
☐	305	Rickey Henderson	.20	.09	.03
☐	306	Dave Weathers	.10	.05	.01
☐	307	Shane Reynolds	.10	.05	.01
☐	308	Bobby Bonilla	.20	.09	.03
☐	309	Junior Felix	.10	.05	.01
☐	310	Jeff Fassero	.10	.05	.01
☐	311	Darren Lewis	.10	.05	.01
☐	312	John Doherty	.10	.05	.01
☐	313	Scott Servais	.10	.05	.01
☐	314	Rick Helling	.10	.05	.01
☐	315	Pedro Martinez	.20	.09	.03
☐	316	Wes Chamberlain	.10	.05	.01
☐	317	Bryan Eversgerd	.10	.05	.01
☐	318	Trevor Hoffman	.10	.05	.01
☐	319	John Patterson	.10	.05	.01
☐	320	Matt Walbeck	.10	.05	.01
☐	321	Jeff Montgomery	.15	.07	.02
☐	322	Mel Rojas	.10	.05	.01
☐	323	Eddie Taubensee	.10	.05	.01
☐	324	Ray Lankford	.20	.09	.03
☐	325	Jose Vizcaino	.10	.05	.01
☐	326	Carlos Baerga	.40	.18	.05
☐	327	Jack Voigt	.10	.05	.01
☐	328	Julio Franco	.15	.07	.02
☐	329	Brent Gates	.20	.09	.03
☐	330	Checklist 246-330 (Kirby Puckett)	.60	.25	.08

1995 Donruss Press Proofs

Parallel to the basic Donruss set, the Press Proofs are distinguished by the player's name, team name and Donruss logo being done in gold foil on front. The words "Press Proof are also in gold at the top. The first 20,000 cards of the production run were stamped as such and inserted at a rate of one in every 20 packs.

	MINT	EXC	G-VG
COMPLETE SERIES 1 (330)	1000.00	450.00	125.00
COMMON CARD (1-330)	2.00	.90	.25

*UNLISTED VETERAN STARS: 18X to 30X BASIC CARDS
*UNLISTED YOUNG STARS: 15X to 25X BASIC CARDS

1995 Donruss Bomb Squad

Randomly inserted one in every 24 retail packs and one in every 16 jumbo packs,

this set features the top six home run hitters in the National and American League. Each of the six cards shows a different slugger on the either side of the card. Both the fronts and backs are horizontal and feature the player photo with a bomber as background. There are foil bombs to the left indicating how many homers the player hit in 1994. A doggie tag indicates the player's position and rank among home run leaders in his league.

	MINT	EXC	G-VG
COMPLETE SET (6)	35.00	16.00	4.40
COMMON CARD (1-6)	2.00	.90	.25
☐ 1 Ken Griffey Jr. / Matt Williams	12.00	5.50	1.50
☐ 2 Frank Thomas / Jeff Bagwell	15.00	6.75	1.90
☐ 3 Albert Belle / Barry Bonds	7.00	3.10	.85
☐ 4 Jose Canseco / Fred McGriff	4.00	1.80	.50
☐ 5 Cecil Fielder / Andres Galarraga	2.00	.90	.25
☐ 6 Joe Carter / Kevin Mitchell	2.00	.90	.25

1995 Donruss Diamond Kings

The first series offering of the 1995 Donruss Diamond King set consists of 14 cards that were randomly inserted in first series packs. They measure the standard size. The fronts feature water color player portraits by noted sports artist Dick Perez. The player's name and "Diamond Kings" are in gold foil. The backs have a dark blue border with a player photo and text. The cards are numbered on back with a DK prefix.

	MINT	EXC	G-VG
COMPLETE SERIES 1 (14)	25.00	11.50	3.10
COMMON CARD (DK1-DK14)	1.00	.45	.13
☐ DK1 Frank Thomas	10.00	4.50	1.25
☐ DK2 Jeff Bagwell	5.00	2.30	.60
☐ DK3 Chili Davis	1.00	.45	.13
☐ DK4 Dante Bichette	1.50	.65	.19
☐ DK5 Ruben Sierra	1.50	.65	.19
☐ DK6 Jeff Conine	1.50	.65	.19
☐ DK7 Paul O'Neill	1.00	.45	.13
☐ DK8 Bobby Bonilla	1.00	.45	.13
☐ DK9 Joe Carter	2.00	.90	.25
☐ DK10 Moises Alou	1.50	.65	.19
☐ DK11 Kenny Lofton	3.00	1.35	.40
☐ DK12 Matt Williams	2.50	1.15	.30
☐ DK13 Kevin Seitzer	1.00	.45	.13
☐ DK14 Sammy Sosa	1.00	.45	.13

1995 Donruss Elite

Randomly inserted one in every 210 packs, the first series consists of six cards that are numbered (49-54) based on where the previous year's set left off. The fronts contain an action photo surrounded by a marble border. Silver holographic foil borders the card on all four sides. Limited to 10,000, the backs are individually numbered, contain a small photo and write-up.

	MINT	EXC	G-VG
COMPLETE SERIES 1 (6)	200.00	90.00	25.00
COMMON CARD (49-54)	10.00	4.50	1.25
☐ 49 Jeff Bagwell	50.00	23.00	6.25
☐ 50 Paul O'Neill	10.00	4.50	1.25
☐ 51 Greg Maddux	20.00	9.00	2.50
☐ 52 Mike Piazza	45.00	20.00	5.75
☐ 53 Matt Williams	18.00	8.00	2.30
☐ 54 Ken Griffey	90.00	40.00	11.50

1995 Donruss Long Ball Leaders

Inserted one in every 24 series one hobby packs, this set features eight top home run hitters. Metallic fronts have much ornamentation including a player photo, the length of

the player's home run, the stadium and the date. Horizontal backs have a player photo and photo of the stadium with which the home run occurred. The back also includes all the particulars concerning the home run.

	MINT	EXC	G-VG
COMPLETE SET (8)	30.00	13.50	3.80
COMMON CARD (1-8)	1.50	.65	.19
☐ 1 Frank Thomas	10.00	4.50	1.25
☐ 2 Fred McGriff	1.50	.65	.19
☐ 3 Ken Griffey Jr.	10.00	4.50	1.25
☐ 4 Matt Williams	2.00	.90	.25
☐ 5 Mike Piazza	4.00	1.80	.50
☐ 6 Jose Canseco	1.50	.65	.19
☐ 7 Barry Bonds	4.00	1.80	.50
☐ 8 Jeff Bagwell	5.00	2.30	.60

1994 Extra Bases

Measuring 2 1/2" by 4 3/4", this 400 card set was issued by Fleer. Full-bleed fronts contain a large color photo with the player's name and Extra Bases logo at the bottom. The backs are also full-bleed with a large player photo and statistics. The checklist was arranged alphabetically by team and league starting with the American League. Within each team, the player listings are alphabetical. The order is: Baltimore Orioles (1-14), Boston Red Sox (15-28), California Angels (29-39), Chicago White Sox (40-54), Cleveland Indians (55-70), Detroit Tigers (71-82), Kansas City Royals (83-97), Milwaukee Brewers (98-112), Minnesota Twins (113-126), New York Yankees (127-142), Oakland Athletics (143-157), Seattle Mariners (158-174), Texas Rangers (175-185), Toronto Blue Jays (186-198), Atlanta Braves (199-214), Chicago Cubs (215-226), Cincinnati Reds (227-241), Colorado Rockies (242-255), Florida Marlins (256-267), Houston Astros (268-282), Los Angeles Dodgers (283-298), Montreal Expos (299-314), New York Mets (315-328), Philadelphia Phillies (329-342), Pittsburgh Pirates (343-354), St. Louis Cardinals (355-366), San Diego Padres (367-380), and San Francisco Giants (381-395). Rookie Cards include Brian Anderson, Ray Durham, John Hudek, Brooks Kieschnick, Chan Ho Park and Mac Suzuki.

	MINT	EXC	G-VG
COMPLETE SET (400)	33.00	15.00	4.10
COMMON CARD (1-400)	.10	.05	.01
☐ 1 Brady Anderson	.15	.07	.02
☐ 2 Harold Baines	.15	.07	.02
☐ 3 Mike Devereaux	.15	.07	.02
☐ 4 Sid Fernandez	.10	.05	.01
☐ 5 Jeffrey Hammonds	.35	.16	.04
☐ 6 Chris Hoiles	.15	.07	.02
☐ 7 Ben McDonald	.15	.07	.02
☐ 8 Mark McLemore	.10	.05	.01
☐ 9 Mike Mussina	.40	.18	.05
☐ 10 Mike Oquist	.10	.05	.01
☐ 11 Rafael Palmeiro	.20	.09	.03
☐ 12 Cal Ripken	2.25	1.00	.30
☐ 13 Chris Sabo	.10	.05	.01
☐ 14 Lee Smith	.20	.09	.03
☐ 15 Wes Chamberlain	.10	.05	.01
☐ 16 Roger Clemens	.75	.35	.09
☐ 17 Scott Cooper	.15	.07	.02
☐ 18 Danny Darwin	.10	.05	.01
☐ 19 Andre Dawson	.20	.09	.03
☐ 20 Mike Greenwell	.15	.07	.02
☐ 21 Tim Naehring	.10	.05	.01
☐ 22 Otis Nixon	.10	.05	.01
☐ 23 Jeff Russell	.10	.05	.01
☐ 24 Ken Ryan	.10	.05	.01
☐ 25 Aaron Sele	.30	.14	.04
☐ 26 John Valentin	.15	.07	.02
☐ 27 Mo Vaughn	.20	.09	.03
☐ 28 Frank Viola	.10	.05	.01
☐ 29 Brian Anderson	.75	.35	.09
☐ 30 Chad Curtis	.15	.07	.02
☐ 31 Chili Davis	.15	.07	.02
☐ 32 Gary DiSarcina	.10	.05	.01
☐ 33 Damion Easley	.10	.05	.01
☐ 34 Jim Edmonds	.10	.05	.01
☐ 35 Chuck Finley	.10	.05	.01
☐ 36 Bo Jackson	.20	.09	.03
☐ 37 Mark Langston	.20	.09	.03
☐ 38 Harold Reynolds	.10	.05	.01
☐ 39 Tim Salmon	.40	.18	.05
☐ 40 Wilson Alvarez	.20	.09	.03
☐ 41 James Baldwin	.50	.23	.06
☐ 42 Jason Bere	.40	.18	.05
☐ 43 Joey Cora	.10	.05	.01
☐ 44 Ray Durham	1.25	.55	.16
☐ 45 Alex Fernandez	.20	.09	.03
☐ 46 Julio Franco	.15	.07	.02
☐ 47 Ozzie Guillen	.10	.05	.01
☐ 48 Darrin Jackson	.10	.05	.01
☐ 49 Lance Johnson	.10	.05	.01
☐ 50 Ron Karkovice	.10	.05	.01
☐ 51 Jack McDowell	.20	.09	.03

	No.	Player			
☐	52	Tim Raines	.20	.09	.03
☐	53	Frank Thomas	3.00	1.35	.40
☐	54	Robin Ventura	.15	.07	.02
☐	55	Sandy Alomar Jr.	.15	.07	.02
☐	56	Carlos Baerga	.40	.18	.05
☐	57	Albert Belle	1.00	.45	.13
☐	58	Mark Clark	.10	.05	.01
☐	59	Wayne Kirby	.10	.05	.01
☐	60	Kenny Lofton	.75	.35	.09
☐	61	Dennis Martinez	.15	.07	.02
☐	62	Jose Mesa	.10	.05	.01
☐	63	Jack Morris	.20	.09	.03
☐	64	Eddie Murray	.20	.09	.03
☐	65	Charles Nagy	.10	.05	.01
☐	66	Manny Ramirez	.60	.25	.08
☐	67	Paul Shuey	.10	.05	.01
☐	68	Paul Sorrento	.10	.05	.01
☐	69	Jim Thome	.20	.09	.03
☐	70	Omar Vizquel	.10	.05	.01
☐	71	Eric Davis	.10	.05	.01
☐	72	John Doherty	.10	.05	.01
☐	73	Cecil Fielder	.20	.09	.03
☐	74	Travis Fryman	.25	.11	.03
☐	75	Kirk Gibson	.15	.07	.02
☐	76	Gene Harris	.10	.05	.01
☐	77	Mike Henneman	.10	.05	.01
☐	78	Mike Moore	.10	.05	.01
☐	79	Tony Phillips	.10	.05	.01
☐	80	Mickey Tettleton	.15	.07	.02
☐	81	Alan Trammell	.20	.09	.03
☐	82	Lou Whitaker	.20	.09	.03
☐	83	Kevin Appier	.15	.07	.02
☐	84	Vince Coleman	.10	.05	.01
☐	85	David Cone	.20	.09	.03
☐	86	Gary Gaetti	.10	.05	.01
☐	87	Greg Gagne	.10	.05	.01
☐	88	Tom Gordon	.10	.05	.01
☐	89	Jeff Granger	.15	.07	.02
☐	90	Bob Hamelin	.20	.09	.03
☐	91	Dave Henderson	.10	.05	.01
☐	92	Felix Jose	.10	.05	.01
☐	93	Wally Joyner	.15	.07	.02
☐	94	Jose Lind	.10	.05	.01
☐	95	Mike Macfarlane	.10	.05	.01
☐	96	Brian McRae	.15	.07	.02
☐	97	Jeff Montgomery	.15	.07	.02
☐	98	Ricky Bones	.10	.05	.01
☐	99	Jeff Bronkey	.10	.05	.01
☐	100	Alex Diaz	.10	.05	.01
☐	101	Cal Eldred	.15	.07	.02
☐	102	Darryl Hamilton	.10	.05	.01
☐	103	Brian Harper	.10	.05	.01
☐	104	John Jaha	.10	.05	.01
☐	105	Pat Listach	.10	.05	.01
☐	106	Dave Nilsson	.10	.05	.01
☐	107	Jody Reed	.10	.05	.01
☐	108	Kevin Seitzer	.10	.05	.01
☐	109	Greg Vaughn	.15	.07	.02
☐	110	Turner Ward	.10	.05	.01
☐	111	Wes Weger	.10	.05	.01
☐	112	Bill Wegman	.10	.05	.01
☐	113	Rick Aguilera	.15	.07	.02
☐	114	Rich Becker	.15	.07	.02
☐	115	Alex Cole	.10	.05	.01
☐	116	Scott Erickson	.10	.05	.01
☐	117	Kent Hrbek	.15	.07	.02
☐	118	Chuck Knoblauch	.20	.09	.03
☐	119	Scott Leius	.10	.05	.01
☐	120	Shane Mack	.15	.07	.02
☐	121	Pat Mahomes	.10	.05	.01
☐	122	Pat Meares	.10	.05	.01
☐	123	Kirby Puckett	1.25	.55	.16
☐	124	Kevin Tapani	.10	.05	.01
☐	125	Matt Walbeck	.10	.05	.01
☐	126	Dave Winfield	.20	.09	.03
☐	127	Jim Abbott	.20	.09	.03
☐	128	Wade Boggs	.20	.09	.03
☐	129	Mike Gallego	.10	.05	.01
☐	130	Xavier Hernandez	.10	.05	.01
☐	131	Pat Kelly	.10	.05	.01
☐	132	Jimmy Key	.15	.07	.02
☐	133	Don Mattingly	1.25	.55	.16
☐	134	Terry Mulholland	.10	.05	.01
☐	135	Matt Nokes	.10	.05	.01
☐	136	Paul O'Neill	.15	.07	.02
☐	137	Melido Perez	.10	.05	.01
☐	138	Luis Polonia	.10	.05	.01
☐	139	Mike Stanley	.10	.05	.01
☐	140	Danny Tartabull	.15	.07	.02
☐	141	Randy Velarde	.10	.05	.01
☐	142	Bernie Williams	.15	.07	.02
☐	143	Mark Acre	.20	.09	.03
☐	144	Geronimo Berroa	.10	.05	.01
☐	145	Mike Bordick	.10	.05	.01
☐	146	Scott Brosius	.10	.05	.01
☐	147	Ron Darling	.10	.05	.01
☐	148	Dennis Eckersley	.20	.09	.03
☐	149	Brent Gates	.20	.09	.03
☐	150	Rickey Henderson	.20	.09	.03
☐	151	Stan Javier	.10	.05	.01
☐	152	Steve Karsay	.10	.05	.01
☐	153	Mark McGwire	.20	.09	.03
☐	154	Troy Neel	.15	.07	.02
☐	155	Ruben Sierra	.20	.09	.03
☐	156	Terry Steinbach	.15	.07	.02
☐	157	Bill Taylor	.10	.05	.01
☐	158	Rich Amaral	.10	.05	.01
☐	159	Eric Anthony	.10	.05	.01
☐	160	Bobby Ayala	.10	.05	.01
☐	161	Chris Bosio	.10	.05	.01
☐	162	Jay Buhner	.15	.07	.02
☐	163	Tim Davis	.10	.05	.01
☐	164	Felix Fermin	.10	.05	.01
☐	165	Dave Fleming	.10	.05	.01
☐	166	Ken Griffey Jr.	3.00	1.35	.40
☐	167	Reggie Jefferson	.10	.05	.01
☐	168	Randy Johnson	.20	.09	.03
☐	169	Edgar Martinez	.10	.05	.01
☐	170	Tino Martinez	.10	.05	.01
☐	171	Bill Risley	.10	.05	.01
☐	172	Roger Salkeld	.10	.05	.01
☐	173	Mac Suzuki	.75	.35	.09
☐	174	Dan Wilson	.10	.05	.01
☐	175	Kevin Brown	.10	.05	.01
☐	176	Jose Canseco	.40	.18	.05
☐	177	Will Clark	.40	.18	.05
☐	178	Juan Gonzalez	1.00	.45	.13
☐	179	Rick Helling	.10	.05	.01
☐	180	Tom Henke	.10	.05	.01
☐	181	Chris James	.10	.05	.01
☐	182	Manny Lee	.10	.05	.01
☐	183	Dean Palmer	.15	.07	.02
☐	184	Ivan Rodriguez	.20	.09	.03
☐	185	Kenny Rogers	.10	.05	.01
☐	186	Roberto Alomar	.75	.35	.09
☐	187	Pat Borders	.10	.05	.01
☐	188	Joe Carter	.40	.18	.05
☐	189	Carlos Delgado	.50	.23	.06
☐	190	Juan Guzman	.15	.07	.02
☐	191	Pat Hentgen	.15	.07	.02
☐	192	Paul Molitor	.40	.18	.05
☐	193	John Olerud	.20	.09	.03
☐	194	Ed Sprague	.10	.05	.01
☐	195	Dave Stewart	.15	.07	.02
☐	196	Todd Stottlemyre	.10	.05	.01
☐	197	Duane Ward	.10	.05	.01

☐ 198 Devon White .10 .05 .01
☐ 199 Steve Avery .20 .09 .03
☐ 200 Jeff Blauser .15 .07 .02
☐ 201 Tom Glavine .20 .09 .03
☐ 202 David Justice .40 .18 .05
☐ 203 Mike Kelly .15 .07 .02
☐ 204 Roberto Kelly .10 .05 .01
☐ 205 Ryan Klesko .50 .23 .06
☐ 206 Mark Lemke .10 .05 .01
☐ 207 Javy Lopez .30 .14 .04
☐ 208 Greg Maddux .60 .25 .08
☐ 209 Fred McGriff .40 .18 .05
☐ 210 Greg McMichael .15 .07 .02
☐ 211 Kent Mercker .10 .05 .01
☐ 212 Terry Pendleton .10 .05 .01
☐ 213 John Smoltz .15 .07 .02
☐ 214 Tony Tarasco .20 .09 .03
☐ 215 Willie Banks .10 .05 .01
☐ 216 Steve Buechele .10 .05 .01
☐ 217 Shawon Dunston .10 .05 .01
☐ 218 Mark Grace .20 .09 .03
☐ 219 Brooks Kieschnick 1.00 .45 .13
☐ 220 Derrick May .10 .05 .01
☐ 221 Randy Myers .10 .05 .01
☐ 222 Karl Rhodes .10 .05 .01
☐ 223 Rey Sanchez .10 .05 .01
☐ 224 Sammy Sosa .20 .09 .03
☐ 225 Steve Trachsel .40 .18 .05
☐ 226 Rick Wilkins .10 .05 .01
☐ 227 Bret Boone .20 .09 .03
☐ 228 Jeff Brantley .10 .05 .01
☐ 229 Tom Browning .10 .05 .01
☐ 230 Hector Carrasco .10 .05 .01
☐ 231 Rob Dibble .10 .05 .01
☐ 232 Erik Hanson .10 .05 .01
☐ 233 Barry Larkin .20 .09 .03
☐ 234 Kevin Mitchell .15 .07 .02
☐ 235 Hal Morris .15 .07 .02
☐ 236 Joe Oliver .10 .05 .01
☐ 237 Jose Rijo .15 .07 .02
☐ 238 Johnny Ruffin .10 .05 .01
☐ 239 Deion Sanders .50 .23 .06
☐ 240 Reggie Sanders .15 .07 .02
☐ 241 John Smiley .10 .05 .01
☐ 242 Dante Bichette .20 .09 .03
☐ 243 Ellis Burks .15 .07 .02
☐ 244 Andres Galarraga .20 .09 .03
☐ 245 Joe Girardi .10 .05 .01
☐ 246 Greg W. Harris .10 .05 .01
☐ 247 Charlie Hayes .15 .07 .02
☐ 248 Howard Johnson .10 .05 .01
☐ 249 Roberto Mejia .15 .07 .02
☐ 250 Marcus Moore .10 .05 .01
☐ 251 David Nied .20 .09 .03
☐ 252 Armando Reynoso .10 .05 .01
☐ 253 Bruce Ruffin .10 .05 .01
☐ 254 Mark Thompson .15 .07 .02
☐ 255 Walt Weiss .10 .05 .01
☐ 256 Kurt Abbott .30 .14 .04
☐ 257 Bret Barberie .10 .05 .01
☐ 258 Chuck Carr .10 .05 .01
☐ 259 Jeff Conine .20 .09 .03
☐ 260 Chris Hammond .10 .05 .01
☐ 261 Bryan Harvey .15 .07 .02
☐ 262 Jeremy Hernandez .10 .05 .01
☐ 263 Charlie Hough .15 .07 .02
☐ 264 Dave Magadan .10 .05 .01
☐ 265 Benito Santiago .10 .05 .01
☐ 266 Gary Sheffield .20 .09 .03
☐ 267 David Weathers .10 .05 .01
☐ 268 Jeff Bagwell 1.50 .65 .19
☐ 269 Craig Biggio .15 .07 .02
☐ 270 Ken Caminiti .15 .07 .02
☐ 271 Andujar Cedeno .10 .05 .01
☐ 272 Doug Drabek .20 .09 .03
☐ 273 Steve Finley .10 .05 .01
☐ 274 Luis Gonzalez .10 .05 .01
☐ 275 Pete Harnisch .10 .05 .01
☐ 276 John Hudek .75 .35 .09
☐ 277 Darryl Kile .15 .07 .02
☐ 278 Orlando Miller .15 .07 .02
☐ 279 James Mouton .20 .09 .03
☐ 280 Shane Reynolds .10 .05 .01
☐ 281 Scott Servais .10 .05 .01
☐ 282 Greg Swindell .10 .05 .01
☐ 283 Pedro Astacio .15 .07 .02
☐ 284 Brett Butler .15 .07 .02
☐ 285 Tom Candiotti .10 .05 .01
☐ 286 Delino DeShields .15 .07 .02
☐ 287 Kevin Gross .10 .05 .01
☐ 288 Orel Hershiser .15 .07 .02
☐ 289 Eric Karros .15 .07 .02
☐ 290 Ramon Martinez .15 .07 .02
☐ 291 Raul Mondesi 1.00 .45 .13
☐ 292 Jose Offerman .10 .05 .01
☐ 293 Chan Ho Park 1.25 .55 .16
☐ 294 Mike Piazza 1.50 .65 .19
☐ 295 Henry Rodriguez .10 .05 .01
☐ 296 Cory Snyder .10 .05 .01
☐ 297 Tim Wallach .10 .05 .01
☐ 298 Todd Worrell .10 .05 .01
☐ 299 Moises Alou .20 .09 .03
☐ 300 Sean Berry .10 .05 .01
☐ 301 Wil Cordero .20 .09 .03
☐ 302 Joey Eischen .15 .07 .02
☐ 303 Jeff Fassero .10 .05 .01
☐ 304 Darrin Fletcher .10 .05 .01
☐ 305 Cliff Floyd .50 .23 .06
☐ 306 Marquis Grissom .20 .09 .03
☐ 307 Ken Hill .15 .07 .02
☐ 308 Mike Lansing .15 .07 .02
☐ 309 Pedro Martinez .20 .09 .03
☐ 310 Mel Rojas .10 .05 .01
☐ 311 Kirk Rueter .10 .05 .01
☐ 312 Larry Walker .20 .09 .03
☐ 313 John Wetteland .10 .05 .01
☐ 314 Rondell White .30 .14 .04
☐ 315 Bobby Bonilla .20 .09 .03
☐ 316 John Franco .10 .05 .01
☐ 317 Dwight Gooden .10 .05 .01
☐ 318 Todd Hundley .10 .05 .01
☐ 319 Bobby Jones .25 .11 .03
☐ 320 Jeff Kent .15 .07 .02
☐ 321 Kevin McReynolds .10 .05 .01
☐ 322 Bill Pulsipher .60 .25 .08
☐ 323 Bret Saberhagen .15 .07 .02
☐ 324 David Segui .10 .05 .01
☐ 325 Pete Smith .10 .05 .01
☐ 326 Kelly Stinnett .10 .05 .01
☐ 327 Ryan Thompson .15 .07 .02
☐ 328 Jose Vizcaino .10 .05 .01
☐ 329 Ricky Bottalico .30 .14 .04
☐ 330 Darren Daulton .20 .09 .03
☐ 331 Mariano Duncan .10 .05 .01
☐ 332 Lenny Dykstra .20 .09 .03
☐ 333 Tommy Greene .10 .05 .01
☐ 334 Billy Hatcher .10 .05 .01
☐ 335 Dave Hollins .20 .09 .03
☐ 336 Pete Incaviglia .10 .05 .01
☐ 337 Danny Jackson .10 .05 .01
☐ 338 Doug Jones .10 .05 .01
☐ 339 Ricky Jordan .10 .05 .01
☐ 340 John Kruk .20 .09 .03
☐ 341 Curt Schilling .10 .05 .01
☐ 342 Kevin Stocker .15 .07 .02
☐ 343 Jay Bell .15 .07 .02

☐	344 Steve Cooke	.10	.05	.01
☐	345 Carlos Garcia	.10	.05	.01
☐	346 Brian Hunter	.10	.05	.01
☐	347 Jeff King	.10	.05	.01
☐	348 Al Martin	.10	.05	.01
☐	349 Orlando Merced	.15	.07	.02
☐	350 Denny Neagle	.10	.05	.01
☐	351 Don Slaught	.10	.05	.01
☐	352 Andy Van Slyke	.20	.09	.03
☐	353 Paul Wagner	.10	.05	.01
☐	354 Rick White	.10	.05	.01
☐	355 Luis Alicea	.10	.05	.01
☐	356 Rene Arocha	.15	.07	.02
☐	357 Rheal Cormier	.10	.05	.01
☐	358 Bernard Gilkey	.10	.05	.01
☐	359 Gregg Jefferies	.20	.09	.03
☐	360 Ray Lankford	.20	.09	.03
☐	361 Tom Pagnozzi	.10	.05	.01
☐	362 Mike Perez	.10	.05	.01
☐	363 Ozzie Smith	.60	.25	.08
☐	364 Bob Tewksbury	.10	.05	.01
☐	365 Mark Whiten	.15	.07	.02
☐	366 Todd Zeile	.15	.07	.02
☐	367 Andy Ashby	.10	.05	.01
☐	368 Brad Ausmus	.10	.05	.01
☐	369 Derek Bell	.15	.07	.02
☐	370 Andy Benes	.15	.07	.02
☐	371 Archi Cianfrocco	.10	.05	.01
☐	372 Tony Gwynn	.75	.35	.09
☐	373 Trevor Hoffman	.10	.05	.01
☐	374 Tim Hyers	.20	.09	.03
☐	375 Pedro Martinez	.20	.09	.03
☐	376 Phil Plantier	.15	.07	.02
☐	377 Bip Roberts	.10	.05	.01
☐	378 Scott Sanders	.10	.05	.01
☐	379 Dave Staton	.10	.05	.01
☐	380 Wally Whitehurst	.10	.05	.01
☐	381 Rod Beck	.15	.07	.02
☐	382 Todd Benzinger	.10	.05	.01
☐	383 Barry Bonds	1.25	.55	.16
☐	384 John Burkett	.15	.07	.02
☐	385 Royce Clayton	.15	.07	.02
☐	386 Bryan Hickerson	.10	.05	.01
☐	387 Mike Jackson	.10	.05	.01
☐	388 Darren Lewis	.10	.05	.01
☐	389 Kirt Manwaring	.10	.05	.01
☐	390 Willie McGee	.10	.05	.01
☐	391 Mark Portugal	.10	.05	.01
☐	392 Bill Swift	.10	.05	.01
☐	393 Robby Thompson	.10	.05	.01
☐	394 Salomon Torres	.15	.07	.02
☐	395 Matt Williams	.60	.25	.08
☐	396 Checklist 1-92	.10	.05	.01
☐	397 Checklist 93-189	.10	.05	.01
☐	398 Checklist 190-284	.10	.05	.01
☐	399 Checklist 285-380	.10	.05	.01
☐	400 Checklist 381-400/Inserts	.10	.05	.01

1994 Extra Bases Game Breakers

Consisting of 30 cards and randomly inserted in packs at a rate of three per eight, this set features top run producers from around the major leagues. The cards measure 2 1/2" by 4 11/16" and are horizontally designed. There are two photos on the front that bleed into one another. The back has a photo and career highlights.

		MINT	EXC	G-VG
	COMPLETE SET (30)	25.00	11.50	3.10
	COMMON CARD (1-30)	.25	.11	.03
☐	1 Jeff Bagwell	2.50	1.15	.30
☐	2 Rod Beck	.25	.11	.03
☐	3 Albert Belle	1.75	.80	.22
☐	4 Barry Bonds	2.00	.90	.25
☐	5 Jose Canseco	.75	.35	.09
☐	6 Joe Carter	.75	.35	.09
☐	7 Roger Clemens	1.25	.55	.16
☐	8 Darren Daulton	.45	.20	.06
☐	9 Lenny Dykstra	.45	.20	.06
☐	10 Cecil Fielder	.45	.20	.06
☐	11 Tom Glavine	.45	.20	.06
☐	12 Juan Gonzalez	1.75	.80	.22
☐	13 Mark Grace	.25	.11	.03
☐	14 Ken Griffey Jr.	5.00	2.30	.60
☐	15 David Justice	.75	.35	.09
☐	16 Greg Maddux	1.25	.55	.16
☐	17 Don Mattingly	2.00	.90	.25
☐	18 Ben McDonald	.25	.11	.03
☐	19 Fred McGriff	.75	.35	.09
☐	20 Paul Molitor	.75	.35	.09
☐	21 John Olerud	.45	.20	.06
☐	22 Mike Piazza	2.50	1.15	.30
☐	23 Kirby Puckett	2.00	.90	.25
☐	24 Cal Ripken	4.00	1.80	.50
☐	25 Tim Salmon	.75	.35	.09
☐	26 Gary Sheffield	.45	.20	.06
☐	27 Frank Thomas	5.00	2.30	.60
☐	28 Mo Vaughn	.45	.20	.06
☐	29 Matt Williams	1.00	.45	.13
☐	30 Dave Winfield	.45	.20	.06

1994 Extra Bases Major League Hopefuls

Randomly inserted in packs at a rate of one in eight, this 10-card set features top minor league performers. Cards measure 2 1/2" by 4 11/16". Computer generated fronts contain multiple player photos. The backs have a player photo and a write-up about the player's minor league exploits.

	MINT	EXC	G-VG
COMPLETE SET (10)	10.00	4.50	1.25
COMMON CARD (1-10)	.30	.14	.04
☐ 1 James Baldwin	1.00	.45	.13
☐ 2 Ricky Bottalico	.60	.25	.08
☐ 3 Ray Durham	2.50	1.15	.30
☐ 4 Joey Eischen	.30	.14	.04
☐ 5 Brooks Kieschnick	2.00	.90	.25
☐ 6 Orlando Miller	.75	.35	.09
☐ 7 Bill Pulsipher	2.00	.90	.25
☐ 8 Mac Suzuki	1.50	.65	.19
☐ 9 Mark Thompson	.30	.14	.04
☐ 10 Wes Weger	.30	.14	.04

1994 Extra Bases Rookie Standouts

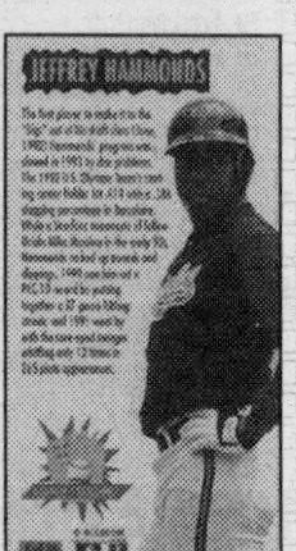

Randomly inserted in packs at a rate of one in four, this 20-card set features those that had potential for being top rookies in 1994. The cards measure 2 1/2" by 4 11/16". Card fronts have an action photo of the player. The background is somewhat blurred and a jagged outline appears around the player as if to allow him to stand out from the rest of the card. The backs have a player photo and text on a white background.

	MINT	EXC	G-VG
COMPLETE SET (20)	18.00	8.00	2.30
COMMON CARD (1-20)	.25	.11	.03
☐ 1 Kurt Abbott	.50	.23	.06
☐ 2 Brian Anderson	1.25	.55	.16
☐ 3 Hector Carrasco	.25	.11	.03
☐ 4 Tim Davis	.25	.11	.03
☐ 5 Carlos Delgado	1.50	.65	.19
☐ 6 Cliff Floyd	1.50	.65	.19
☐ 7 Bob Hamelin	1.00	.45	.13
☐ 8 Jeffrey Hammonds	1.00	.45	.13
☐ 9 Rick Helling	.25	.11	.03
☐ 10 Steve Karsay	.50	.23	.06
☐ 11 Ryan Klesko	1.75	.80	.22
☐ 12 Javy Lopez	1.00	.45	.13
☐ 13 Raul Mondesi	3.50	1.55	.45
☐ 14 James Mouton	.50	.23	.06
☐ 15 Chan Ho Park	2.00	.90	.25
☐ 16 Manny Ramirez	2.00	.90	.25
☐ 17 Tony Tarasco	.50	.23	.06
☐ 18 Steve Trachsel	.75	.35	.09
☐ 19 Rick White	.25	.11	.03
☐ 20 Rondell White	1.00	.45	.13

1994 Extra Bases Second Year Stars

Randomly inserted in packs at a rate of one in four, Second Year Stars takes a look at 20 top second year players and reflects on their rookie campaigns of 1993. The cards measure 2 1/2" by 4 11/16". Card fronts feature multiple photos including a large full bleed photo of the player and four smaller photos that give the appearance of being captured on film. These smaller photos run the length of the card and are on the left.

	MINT	EXC	G-VG
COMPLETE SET (20)	10.00	4.50	1.25
COMMON CARD (1-20)	.25	.11	.03
☐ 1 Bobby Ayala	.25	.11	.03
☐ 2 Jason Bere	1.00	.45	.13
☐ 3 Chuck Carr	.25	.11	.03
☐ 4 Jeff Conine	.40	.18	.05
☐ 5 Steve Cooke	.25	.11	.03

☐ 6	Wil Cordero	.40	.18	.05
☐ 7	Carlos Garcia	.25	.11	.03
☐ 8	Brent Gates	.40	.18	.05
☐ 9	Trevor Hoffman	.25	.11	.03
☐ 10	Wayne Kirby	.25	.11	.03
☐ 11	Al Martin	.25	.11	.03
☐ 12	Pedro Martinez	.40	.18	.05
☐ 13	Greg McMichael	.40	.18	.05
☐ 14	Troy Neel	.25	.11	.03
☐ 15	David Nied	.40	.18	.05
☐ 16	Mike Piazza	4.00	1.80	.50
☐ 17	Kirk Rueter	.40	.18	.05
☐ 18	Tim Salmon	1.25	.55	.16
☐ 19	Aaron Sele	.60	.25	.08
☐ 20	Kevin Stocker	.25	.11	.03

1993 Finest

These 199 standard-size (2 1/2" by 3 1/2") cards have metallic finishes on their fronts and feature color player action photos. The set's title appears at the top, and the player's name is shown at the bottom. The complete title of the set is Topps Baseball's Finest. The non-metallic, white-bordered horizontal back has a faded baseball action scene as a background and carries a color player action photo within a simulated metal frame on the left side. The player's name appears beneath the photo. The right side carries the set's title and the player's position, team, biography, and stats. The Mike Piazza card (199) was added to the set after the original 198 cards were released. The cards are numbered on the back. The key Rookie Card in this set is J.T. Snow.

	MINT	EXC	G-VG
COMPLETE SET (199)	250.00	115.00	31.00
COMMON CARD (1-199)	1.00	.45	.13

☐ 1	David Justice	4.50	2.00	.55
☐ 2	Lou Whitaker	2.00	.90	.25
☐ 3	Bryan Harvey	1.50	.65	.19
☐ 4	Carlos Garcia	1.50	.65	.19
☐ 5	Sid Fernandez	1.00	.45	.13
☐ 6	Brett Butler	1.50	.65	.19
☐ 7	Scott Cooper	1.50	.65	.19
☐ 8	B.J. Surhoff	1.00	.45	.13
☐ 9	Steve Finley	1.00	.45	.13
☐ 10	Curt Schilling	1.50	.65	.19
☐ 11	Jeff Bagwell	15.00	6.75	1.90
☐ 12	Alex Cole	1.00	.45	.13
☐ 13	John Olerud	2.00	.90	.25
☐ 14	John Smiley	1.00	.45	.13
☐ 15	Bip Roberts	1.00	.45	.13
☐ 16	Albert Belle	10.00	4.50	1.25
☐ 17	Duane Ward	1.50	.65	.19
☐ 18	Alan Trammell	2.00	.90	.25
☐ 19	Andy Benes	1.50	.65	.19
☐ 20	Reggie Sanders	1.50	.65	.19
☐ 21	Todd Zeile	1.50	.65	.19
☐ 22	Rick Aguilera	1.50	.65	.19
☐ 23	Dave Hollins	2.00	.90	.25
☐ 24	Jose Rijo	1.50	.65	.19
☐ 25	Matt Williams	6.00	2.70	.75
☐ 26	Sandy Alomar	1.50	.65	.19
☐ 27	Alex Fernandez	2.00	.90	.25
☐ 28	Ozzie Smith	6.00	2.70	.75
☐ 29	Ramon Martinez	1.50	.65	.19
☐ 30	Bernie Williams	1.50	.65	.19
☐ 31	Gary Sheffield	2.00	.90	.25
☐ 32	Eric Karros	1.50	.65	.19
☐ 33	Frank Viola	1.50	.65	.19
☐ 34	Kevin Young	1.00	.45	.13
☐ 35	Ken Hill	1.50	.65	.19
☐ 36	Tony Fernandez	1.00	.45	.13
☐ 37	Tim Wakefield	1.00	.45	.13
☐ 38	John Kruk	2.00	.90	.25
☐ 39	Chris Sabo	1.50	.65	.19
☐ 40	Marquis Grissom	2.00	.90	.25
☐ 41	Glenn Davis	1.00	.45	.13
☐ 42	Jeff Montgomery	1.50	.65	.19
☐ 43	Kenny Lofton	7.50	3.40	.95
☐ 44	John Burkett	1.50	.65	.19
☐ 45	Darryl Hamilton	1.00	.45	.13
☐ 46	Jim Abbott	2.00	.90	.25
☐ 47	Ivan Rodriguez	2.00	.90	.25
☐ 48	Eric Young	1.50	.65	.19
☐ 49	Mitch Williams	1.50	.65	.19
☐ 50	Harold Reynolds	1.00	.45	.13
☐ 51	Brian Harper	1.00	.45	.13
☐ 52	Rafael Palmeiro	2.00	.90	.25
☐ 53	Bret Saberhagen	1.50	.65	.19
☐ 54	Jeff Conine	2.00	.90	.25
☐ 55	Ivan Calderon	1.00	.45	.13
☐ 56	Juan Guzman	1.50	.65	.19
☐ 57	Carlos Baerga	4.50	2.00	.55
☐ 58	Charles Nagy	1.00	.45	.13
☐ 59	Wally Joyner	1.50	.65	.19
☐ 60	Charlie Hayes	1.50	.65	.19
☐ 61	Shane Mack	1.50	.65	.19
☐ 62	Pete Harnisch	1.00	.45	.13
☐ 63	George Brett	12.00	5.50	1.50
☐ 64	Lance Johnson	1.00	.45	.13
☐ 65	Ben McDonald	1.50	.65	.19
☐ 66	Bobby Bonilla	2.00	.90	.25
☐ 67	Terry Steinbach	1.50	.65	.19
☐ 68	Ron Gant	1.50	.65	.19
☐ 69	Doug Jones	1.00	.45	.13
☐ 70	Paul Molitor	4.50	2.00	.55
☐ 71	Brady Anderson	1.50	.65	.19
☐ 72	Chuck Finley	1.00	.45	.13
☐ 73	Mark Grace	2.00	.90	.25
☐ 74	Mike Devereaux	1.50	.65	.19
☐ 75	Tony Phillips	1.00	.45	.13
☐ 76	Chuck Knoblauch	2.00	.90	.25
☐ 77	Tony Gwynn	7.50	3.40	.95
☐ 78	Kevin Appier	1.50	.65	.19
☐ 79	Sammy Sosa	2.00	.90	.25
☐ 80	Mickey Tettleton	1.50	.65	.19
☐ 81	Felix Jose	1.00	.45	.13
☐ 82	Mark Langston	2.00	.90	.25
☐ 83	Gregg Jefferies	1.00	.45	.13
☐ 84	Andre Dawson AS	2.00	.90	.25
☐ 85	Greg Maddux AS	7.50	3.40	.95
☐ 86	Rickey Henderson AS	2.00	.90	.25

	No.	Player			
☐	87	Tom Glavine AS	2.00	.90	.25
☐	88	Roberto Alomar AS	7.50	3.40	.95
☐	89	Darryl Strawberry AS	1.50	.65	.19
☐	90	Wade Boggs AS	2.50	1.15	.30
☐	91	Bo Jackson AS	2.00	.90	.25
☐	92	Mark McGwire AS	2.00	.90	.25
☐	93	Robin Ventura AS	2.00	.90	.25
☐	94	Joe Carter AS	4.50	2.00	.55
☐	95	Lee Smith AS	2.00	.90	.25
☐	96	Cal Ripken AS	20.00	9.00	2.50
☐	97	Larry Walker AS	2.00	.90	.25
☐	98	Don Mattingly AS	12.00	5.50	1.50
☐	99	Jose Canseco AS	4.50	2.00	.55
☐	100	Dennis Eckersley AS	2.00	.90	.25
☐	101	Terry Pendleton AS	2.00	.90	.25
☐	102	Frank Thomas AS	30.00	13.50	3.80
☐	103	Barry Bonds AS	12.00	5.50	1.50
☐	104	Roger Clemens AS	7.50	3.40	.95
☐	105	Ryne Sandberg AS	10.00	4.50	1.25
☐	106	Fred McGriff AS	4.50	2.00	.55
☐	107	Nolan Ryan AS	35.00	16.00	4.40
☐	108	Will Clark AS	4.50	2.00	.55
☐	109	Pat Listach AS	1.50	.65	.19
☐	110	Ken Griffey Jr. AS	30.00	13.50	3.80
☐	111	Cecil Fielder AS	3.00	1.35	.40
☐	112	Kirby Puckett AS	12.00	5.50	1.50
☐	113	Dwight Gooden AS	1.00	.45	.13
☐	114	Barry Larkin AS	2.00	.90	.25
☐	115	David Cone AS	2.00	.90	.25
☐	116	Juan Gonzalez AS	10.00	4.50	1.25
☐	117	Kent Hrbek	1.50	.65	.19
☐	118	Tim Wallach	1.00	.45	.13
☐	119	Craig Biggio	1.50	.65	.19
☐	120	Roberto Kelly	1.50	.65	.19
☐	121	Gregg Olson	1.00	.45	.13
☐	122	Eddie Murray	2.00	.90	.25
☐	123	Wil Cordero	2.00	.90	.25
☐	124	Jay Buhner	1.50	.65	.19
☐	125	Carlton Fisk	2.00	.90	.25
☐	126	Eric Davis	1.00	.45	.13
☐	127	Doug Drabek	2.00	.90	.25
☐	128	Ozzie Guillen	1.00	.45	.13
☐	129	John Wetteland	1.00	.45	.13
☐	130	Andres Galarraga	2.00	.90	.25
☐	131	Ken Caminiti	1.50	.65	.19
☐	132	Tom Candiotti	1.00	.45	.13
☐	133	Pat Borders	1.00	.45	.13
☐	134	Kevin Brown	1.00	.45	.13
☐	135	Travis Fryman	3.00	1.35	.40
☐	136	Kevin Mitchell	1.50	.65	.19
☐	137	Greg Swindell	1.00	.45	.13
☐	138	Benito Santiago	1.00	.45	.13
☐	139	Reggie Jefferson	1.00	.45	.13
☐	140	Chris Bosio	1.00	.45	.13
☐	141	Deion Sanders	5.00	2.30	.60
☐	142	Scott Erickson	1.00	.45	.13
☐	143	Howard Johnson	1.00	.45	.13
☐	144	Orestes Destrade	1.50	.65	.19
☐	145	Jose Guzman	1.00	.45	.13
☐	146	Chad Curtis	1.50	.65	.19
☐	147	Cal Eldred	1.50	.65	.19
☐	148	Willie Greene	1.50	.65	.19
☐	149	Tommy Greene	1.50	.65	.19
☐	150	Erik Hanson	1.00	.45	.13
☐	151	Bob Welch	1.00	.45	.13
☐	152	John Jaha	1.50	.65	.19
☐	153	Harold Baines	1.50	.65	.19
☐	154	Randy Johnson	2.00	.90	.25
☐	155	Al Martin	1.50	.65	.19
☐	156	J.T. Snow	1.50	.65	.19
☐	157	Mike Mussina	6.00	2.70	.75
☐	158	Ruben Sierra	2.00	.90	.25
☐	159	Dean Palmer	1.50	.65	.19
☐	160	Steve Avery	2.00	.90	.25
☐	161	Julio Franco	1.50	.65	.19
☐	162	Dave Winfield	2.00	.90	.25
☐	163	Tim Salmon	4.50	2.00	.55
☐	164	Tom Henke	1.50	.65	.19
☐	165	Mo Vaughn	3.00	1.35	.40
☐	166	John Smoltz	1.50	.65	.19
☐	167	Danny Tartabull	1.50	.65	.19
☐	168	Delino DeShields	1.50	.65	.19
☐	169	Charlie Hough	1.50	.65	.19
☐	170	Paul O'Neill	1.50	.65	.19
☐	171	Darren Daulton	2.00	.90	.25
☐	172	Jack McDowell	2.00	.90	.25
☐	173	Junior Felix	1.00	.45	.13
☐	174	Jimmy Key	1.50	.65	.19
☐	175	George Bell	1.50	.65	.19
☐	176	Mike Stanton	1.00	.45	.13
☐	177	Len Dykstra	2.00	.90	.25
☐	178	Norm Charlton	1.00	.45	.13
☐	179	Eric Anthony	1.00	.45	.13
☐	180	Rob Dibble	1.00	.45	.13
☐	181	Otis Nixon	1.00	.45	.13
☐	182	Randy Myers	1.50	.65	.19
☐	183	Tim Raines	2.00	.90	.25
☐	184	Orel Hershiser	1.50	.65	.19
☐	185	Andy Van Slyke	2.00	.90	.25
☐	186	Mike Lansing	2.00	.90	.25
☐	187	Ray Lankford	2.00	.90	.25
☐	188	Mike Morgan	1.00	.45	.13
☐	189	Moises Alou	2.00	.90	.25
☐	190	Edgar Martinez	1.00	.45	.13
☐	191	John Franco	1.00	.45	.13
☐	192	Robin Yount	4.50	2.00	.55
☐	193	Bob Tewksbury	1.00	.45	.13
☐	194	Jay Bell	1.50	.65	.19
☐	195	Luis Gonzalez	1.50	.65	.19
☐	196	Dave Fleming	1.50	.65	.19
☐	197	Mike Greenwell	1.50	.65	.19
☐	198	David Nied	2.00	.90	.25
☐	199	Mike Piazza	30.00	13.50	3.80

1993 Finest Refractors

Randomly inserted in packs, these 199 standard-size (2 1/2" by 3 1/2") cards are identical to the regular-issue 1993 Topps Finest except that their fronts have been laminated with a plastic diffraction grating that gives the card a colorful 3-D appearance. The horizontal backs, however, are the same. A color player action photo appears on the left side within gold or silver

simulated picture frame. The player's name appears beneath. His position, team biography, and stats appear alongside on the right. All the back's design elements are superposed upon a ghosted and colorized baseball action photo. The cards are numbered on the back.

	MINT	EXC	G-VG
COMPLETE SET (199)	11000.	5000.	1400.
COMMON CARD (1-199)	20.00	9.00	2.50

*UNLISTED VETERAN STARS: 12X to 20X BASIC CARDS
*UNLISTED YOUNG STARS: 9X to 15X BASIC CARDS

	MINT	EXC	G-VG
☐ 1 David Justice	100.00	45.00	12.50
☐ 11 Jeff Bagwell	300.00	135.00	38.00
☐ 16 Albert Belle	200.00	90.00	25.00
☐ 25 Matt Williams	125.00	57.50	15.50
☐ 28 Ozzie Smith	125.00	57.50	15.50
☐ 43 Kenny Lofton	175.00	80.00	22.00
☐ 57 Carlos Baerga	100.00	45.00	12.50
☐ 63 George Brett	450.00	200.00	57.50
☐ 70 Paul Molitor	100.00	45.00	12.50
☐ 77 Tony Gwynn	175.00	80.00	22.00
☐ 85 Greg Maddux AS	175.00	80.00	22.00
☐ 88 Roberto Alomar AS	175.00	80.00	22.00
☐ 94 Joe Carter AS	100.00	45.00	12.50
☐ 96 Cal Ripken AS	900.00	400.00	115.00
☐ 98 Don Mattingly AS	250.00	115.00	31.00
☐ 99 Jose Canseco AS	100.00	45.00	12.50
☐ 102 Frank Thomas AS	700.00	325.00	90.00
☐ 103 Barry Bonds AS	250.00	115.00	31.00
☐ 104 Roger Clemens AS	175.00	80.00	22.00
☐ 105 Ryne Sandberg AS	225.00	100.00	28.00
☐ 106 Fred McGriff AS	100.00	45.00	12.50
☐ 107 Nolan Ryan AS	1000.00	450.00	125.00
☐ 108 Will Clark AS	100.00	45.00	12.50
☐ 110 Ken Griffey Jr. AS	700.00	325.00	90.00
☐ 112 Kirby Puckett AS	250.00	115.00	31.00
☐ 116 Juan Gonzalez AS	200.00	90.00	25.00
☐ 157 Mike Mussina	125.00	57.50	15.50
☐ 192 Robin Yount	100.00	45.00	12.50
☐ 199 Mike Piazza	250.00	115.00	31.00

1993 Finest All-Star Jumbos

These oversized (approximately 4" by 6") cards were inserted one card per sealed box of 1993 Topps Finest packs and feature reproductions of 33 players' cards from that set's All-Star subset. The cards are otherwise identical to that subset's cards. The fronts have a laminated metallic finish and feature color action player photo superposed on a diamond design. The horizontal back carries a color action player photo on the left side within a simulated metal picture frame. The player's name appears beneath. His position, team biography, and stats appear alongside on the right. All the back's design elements are superposed upon a ghosted and colorized baseball action photo. The cards are numbered on the back.

	MINT	EXC	G-VG
COMPLETE SET (33)	500.00	230.00	65.00
COMMON CARD (84-116)	4.00	1.80	.50

	MINT	EXC	G-VG
☐ 84 Andre Dawson AS	8.00	3.60	1.00
☐ 85 Greg Maddux AS	18.00	8.00	2.30
☐ 86 Rickey Henderson AS	8.00	3.60	1.00
☐ 87 Tom Glavine AS	8.00	3.60	1.00
☐ 88 Roberto Alomar AS	18.00	8.00	2.30
☐ 89 Darryl Strawberry AS	4.00	1.80	.50
☐ 90 Wade Boggs AS	8.00	3.60	1.00
☐ 91 Bo Jackson AS	8.00	3.60	1.00
☐ 92 Mark McGwire AS	4.00	1.80	.50
☐ 93 Robin Ventura AS	8.00	3.60	1.00
☐ 94 Joe Carter AS	12.00	5.50	1.50
☐ 95 Lee Smith AS	6.00	2.70	.75
☐ 96 Cal Ripken AS	55.00	25.00	7.00
☐ 97 Larry Walker AS	8.00	3.60	1.00
☐ 98 Don Mattingly AS	30.00	13.50	3.80
☐ 99 Jose Canseco AS	12.00	5.50	1.50
☐ 100 Dennis Eckersley AS	6.00	2.70	.75
☐ 101 Terry Pendleton AS	4.00	1.80	.50
☐ 102 Frank Thomas AS	75.00	34.00	9.50
☐ 103 Barry Bonds AS	30.00	13.50	3.80
☐ 104 Roger Clemens AS	18.00	8.00	2.30
☐ 105 Ryne Sandberg AS	25.00	11.50	3.10
☐ 106 Fred McGriff AS	12.00	5.50	1.50
☐ 107 Nolan Ryan AS	75.00	34.00	9.50
☐ 108 Will Clark AS	12.00	5.50	1.50
☐ 109 Pat Listach AS	4.00	1.80	.50
☐ 110 Ken Griffey Jr. AS	75.00	34.00	9.50
☐ 111 Cecil Fielder AS	8.00	3.60	1.00
☐ 112 Kirby Puckett AS	30.00	13.50	3.80
☐ 113 Dwight Gooden AS	4.00	1.80	.50
☐ 114 Barry Larkin AS	8.00	3.60	1.00
☐ 115 David Cone AS	6.00	2.70	.75
☐ 116 Juan Gonzalez AS	25.00	11.50	3.10

1994 Finest Pre-Production

This 40-card preview set is identical in design to the basic Finest set. Cards were randomly inserted at a rate of one in 36 in second series Topps packs and three cards were issued with each Topps factory set. The card numbers on back correspond to those of the regular issue. The only way to distinguish between the preview and basic cards is "Pre-Production" in small red letters on back.

	MINT	EXC	G-VG
COMPLETE SET (40)	200.00	90.00	25.00
COMMON CARD	3.00	1.35	.40

	MINT	EXC	G-VG
☐ 22P Deion Sanders	20.00	9.00	2.50
☐ 23P Jose Offerman	3.00	1.35	.40
☐ 26P Alex Fernandez	4.00	1.80	.50
☐ 31P Steve Finley	3.00	1.35	.40
☐ 35P Andres Galarraga	3.00	1.35	.40
☐ 43P Reggie Sanders	3.00	1.35	.40
☐ 47P Dave Hollins	4.00	1.80	.50
☐ 52P David Cone	6.00	2.70	.75
☐ 59P Dante Bichette	6.00	2.70	.75
☐ 61P Orlando Merced	3.00	1.35	.40
☐ 62P Brian McRae	6.00	2.70	.75
☐ 66P Mike Mussina	15.00	6.75	1.90
☐ 76P Mike Stanley	3.00	1.35	.40
☐ 78P Mark McGwire	6.00	2.70	.75
☐ 79P Pat Listach	3.00	1.35	.40
☐ 82P Dwight Gooden	3.00	1.35	.40
☐ 84P Phil Plantier	3.00	1.35	.40
☐ 90P Jeff Russell	3.00	1.35	.40
☐ 92P Gregg Jefferies	6.00	2.70	.75
☐ 93P Jose Guzman	3.00	1.35	.40
☐ 100P John Smoltz	6.00	2.70	.75
☐ 102P Jim Thome	3.00	1.35	.40
☐ 121P Moises Alou	3.00	1.35	.40
☐ 125P Devon White	4.00	1.80	.50
☐ 126P Ivan Rodriguez	6.00	2.70	.75
☐ 130P Dave Magadan	3.00	1.35	.40
☐ 136P Ozzie Smith	20.00	9.00	2.50
☐ 141P Chris Hoiles	3.00	1.35	.40
☐ 149P Jim Abbott	4.00	1.80	.50
☐ 151P Bill Swift	3.00	1.35	.40
☐ 154P Edgar Martinez	3.00	1.35	.40
☐ 157P J.T. Snow	3.00	1.35	.40
☐ 159P Alan Trammell	4.00	1.80	.50
☐ 163P Roberto Kelly	3.00	1.35	.40
☐ 166P Scott Erickson	3.00	1.35	.40
☐ 168P Scott Cooper	4.00	1.80	.50
☐ 169P Rod Beck	3.00	1.35	.40
☐ 177P Dean Palmer	3.00	1.35	.40
☐ 182P Todd Van Poppel	3.00	1.35	.40
☐ 185P Paul Sorrento	3.00	1.35	.40

1994 Finest

The 1994 Topps Finest baseball set consists of two series of 220 cards each, for a total of 440 cards. Each series includes 40 special design Finest cards: 20 top 1993 rookies (1-20), 20 top 1994 rookies (421-440) and 40 top veterans (201-240). These glossy and metallic cards have a color photo on front with green and gold borders. A color photo on back is accompanied by statistics and a "Finest Moment" note. Rookie Cards include Brian Anderson and Chan Ho Park.

	MINT	EXC	G-VG
COMPLETE SET (440)	200.00	90.00	25.00
COMPLETE SERIES 1 (220)	100.00	45.00	12.50
COMPLETE SERIES 2 (220)	100.00	45.00	12.50
COMMON CARD (1-220)	.50	.23	.06
COMMON CARD (221-440)	.50	.23	.06

	MINT	EXC	G-VG
☐ 1 Mike Piazza FIN	6.00	2.70	.75
☐ 2 Kevin Stocker FIN	.60	.25	.08
☐ 3 Greg McMichael FIN	.60	.25	.08
☐ 4 Jeff Conine FIN	.75	.35	.09
☐ 5 Rene Arocha FIN	.60	.25	.08
☐ 6 Aaron Sele FIN	1.25	.55	.16
☐ 7 Brent Gates FIN	.75	.35	.09
☐ 8 Chuck Carr FIN	.50	.23	.06
☐ 9 Kirk Rueter FIN	.50	.23	.06
☐ 10 Mike Lansing FIN	.60	.25	.08
☐ 11 Al Martin FIN	.50	.23	.06
☐ 12 Jason Bere FIN	1.50	.65	.19
☐ 13 Troy Neel FIN	.60	.25	.08
☐ 14 Armando Reynoso FIN	.50	.23	.06
☐ 15 Jeromy Burnitz FIN	.60	.25	.08
☐ 16 Rich Amaral FIN	.50	.23	.06
☐ 17 David McCarty FIN	.60	.25	.08
☐ 18 Tim Salmon FIN	1.75	.80	.22
☐ 19 Steve Cooke FIN	.50	.23	.06
☐ 20 Wil Cordero FIN	.75	.35	.09
☐ 21 Kevin Tapani	.50	.23	.06
☐ 22 Deion Sanders	2.00	.90	.25
☐ 23 Jose Offerman	.50	.23	.06
☐ 24 Mark Langston	.75	.35	.09
☐ 25 Ken Hill	.60	.25	.08
☐ 26 Alex Fernandez	.75	.35	.09
☐ 27 Jeff Blauser	.60	.25	.08
☐ 28 Royce Clayton	.60	.25	.08
☐ 29 Brad Ausmus	.50	.23	.06
☐ 30 Ryan Bowen	.50	.23	.06
☐ 31 Steve Finley	.50	.23	.06
☐ 32 Charlie Hayes	.60	.25	.08
☐ 33 Jeff Kent	.60	.25	.08
☐ 34 Mike Henneman	.50	.23	.06
☐ 35 Andres Galarraga	.75	.35	.09
☐ 36 Wayne Kirby	.50	.23	.06
☐ 37 Joe Oliver	.50	.23	.06
☐ 38 Terry Steinbach	.60	.25	.08
☐ 39 Ryan Thompson	.60	.25	.08
☐ 40 Luis Alicea	.50	.23	.06
☐ 41 Randy Velarde	.50	.23	.06
☐ 42 Bob Tewksbury	.50	.23	.06
☐ 43 Reggie Sanders	.60	.25	.08
☐ 44 Brian Williams	.50	.23	.06
☐ 45 Joe Orsulak	.50	.23	.06
☐ 46 Jose Lind	.50	.23	.06

	No.	Player			
☐	47	Dave Hollins	.75	.35	.09
☐	48	Graeme Lloyd	.50	.23	.06
☐	49	Jim Gott	.50	.23	.06
☐	50	Andre Dawson	.75	.35	.09
☐	51	Steve Buechele	.50	.23	.06
☐	52	David Cone	.75	.35	.09
☐	53	Ricky Gutierrez	.50	.23	.06
☐	54	Lance Johnson	.50	.23	.06
☐	55	Tino Martinez	.50	.23	.06
☐	56	Phil Hiatt	.50	.23	.06
☐	57	Carlos Garcia	.50	.23	.06
☐	58	Danny Darwin	.50	.23	.06
☐	59	Dante Bichette	.75	.35	.09
☐	60	Scott Kamieniecki	.50	.23	.06
☐	61	Orlando Merced	.60	.25	.08
☐	62	Brian McRae	.60	.25	.08
☐	63	Pat Kelly	.50	.23	.06
☐	64	Tom Henke	.50	.23	.06
☐	65	Jeff King	.50	.23	.06
☐	66	Mike Mussina	2.00	.90	.25
☐	67	Tim Pugh	.50	.23	.06
☐	68	Robby Thompson	.50	.23	.06
☐	69	Paul O'Neill	.60	.25	.08
☐	70	Hal Morris	.60	.25	.08
☐	71	Ron Karkovice	.50	.23	.06
☐	72	Joe Girardi	.50	.23	.06
☐	73	Eduardo Perez	.60	.25	.08
☐	74	Raul Mondesi	4.00	1.80	.50
☐	75	Mike Gallego	.50	.23	.06
☐	76	Mike Stanley	.50	.23	.06
☐	77	Kevin Roberson	.50	.23	.06
☐	78	Mark McGwire	.75	.35	.09
☐	79	Pat Listach	.50	.23	.06
☐	80	Eric Davis	.50	.23	.06
☐	81	Mike Bordick	.50	.23	.06
☐	82	Dwight Gooden	.50	.23	.06
☐	83	Mike Moore	.50	.23	.06
☐	84	Phil Plantier	.60	.25	.08
☐	85	Darren Lewis	.50	.23	.06
☐	86	Rick Wilkins	.50	.23	.06
☐	87	Darryl Strawberry	.60	.25	.08
☐	88	Rob Dibble	.50	.23	.06
☐	89	Greg Vaughn	.60	.25	.08
☐	90	Jeff Russell	.50	.23	.06
☐	91	Mark Lewis	.50	.23	.06
☐	92	Gregg Jefferies	.75	.35	.09
☐	93	Jose Guzman	.50	.23	.06
☐	94	Kenny Rogers	.50	.23	.06
☐	95	Mark Lemke	.50	.23	.06
☐	96	Mike Morgan	.50	.23	.06
☐	97	Andujar Cedeno	.50	.23	.06
☐	98	Orel Hershiser	.60	.25	.08
☐	99	Greg Swindell	.50	.23	.06
☐	100	John Smoltz	.60	.25	.08
☐	101	Pedro Martinez	.75	.35	.09
☐	102	Jim Thome	.75	.35	.09
☐	103	David Segui	.50	.23	.06
☐	104	Charles Nagy	.50	.23	.06
☐	105	Shane Mack	.60	.25	.08
☐	106	John Jaha	.50	.23	.06
☐	107	Tom Candiotti	.50	.23	.06
☐	108	David Wells	.50	.23	.06
☐	109	Bobby Jones	1.00	.45	.13
☐	110	Bob Hamelin	.75	.35	.09
☐	111	Bernard Gilkey	.50	.23	.06
☐	112	Chili Davis	.60	.25	.08
☐	113	Todd Stottlemyre	.50	.23	.06
☐	114	Derek Bell	.60	.25	.08
☐	115	Mark McLemore	.50	.23	.06
☐	116	Mark Whiten	.60	.25	.08
☐	117	Mike Devereaux	.60	.25	.08
☐	118	Terry Pendleton	.50	.23	.06
☐	119	Pat Meares	.50	.23	.06
☐	120	Pete Harnisch	.50	.23	.06
☐	121	Moises Alou	.75	.35	.09
☐	122	Jay Buhner	.60	.25	.08
☐	123	Wes Chamberlain	.50	.23	.06
☐	124	Mike Perez	.50	.23	.06
☐	125	Devon White	.50	.23	.06
☐	126	Ivan Rodriguez	.75	.35	.09
☐	127	Don Slaught	.50	.23	.06
☐	128	John Valentin	.60	.25	.08
☐	129	Jaime Navarro	.50	.23	.06
☐	130	Dave Magadan	.50	.23	.06
☐	131	Brady Anderson	.60	.25	.08
☐	132	Juan Guzman	.60	.25	.08
☐	133	John Wetteland	.50	.23	.06
☐	134	Dave Stewart	.60	.25	.08
☐	135	Scott Servais	.50	.23	.06
☐	136	Ozzie Smith	2.50	1.15	.30
☐	137	Darrin Fletcher	.50	.23	.06
☐	138	Jose Mesa	.50	.23	.06
☐	139	Wilson Alvarez	.75	.35	.09
☐	140	Pete Incaviglia	.50	.23	.06
☐	141	Chris Hoiles	.60	.25	.08
☐	142	Darryl Hamilton	.50	.23	.06
☐	143	Chuck Finley	.50	.23	.06
☐	144	Archi Cianfrocco	.50	.23	.06
☐	145	Bill Wegman	.50	.23	.06
☐	146	Joey Cora	.50	.23	.06
☐	147	Darrell Whitmore	.60	.25	.08
☐	148	David Hulse	.50	.23	.06
☐	149	Jim Abbott	.75	.35	.09
☐	150	Curt Schilling	.50	.23	.06
☐	151	Bill Swift	.50	.23	.06
☐	152	Tommy Greene	.50	.23	.06
☐	153	Roberto Mejia	.60	.25	.08
☐	154	Edgar Martinez	.50	.23	.06
☐	155	Roger Pavlik	.50	.23	.06
☐	156	Randy Tomlin	.50	.23	.06
☐	157	J.T. Snow	.60	.25	.08
☐	158	Bob Welch	.50	.23	.06
☐	159	Alan Trammell	.75	.35	.09
☐	160	Ed Sprague	.50	.23	.06
☐	161	Ben McDonald	.60	.25	.08
☐	162	Derrick May	.50	.23	.06
☐	163	Roberto Kelly	.50	.23	.06
☐	164	Bryan Harvey	.60	.25	.08
☐	165	Ron Gant	.60	.25	.08
☐	166	Scott Erickson	.50	.23	.06
☐	167	Anthony Young	.50	.23	.06
☐	168	Scott Cooper	.60	.25	.08
☐	169	Rod Beck	.60	.25	.08
☐	170	John Franco	.50	.23	.06
☐	171	Gary DiSarcina	.50	.23	.06
☐	172	Dave Fleming	.50	.23	.06
☐	173	Wade Boggs	1.25	.55	.16
☐	174	Kevin Appier	.60	.25	.08
☐	175	Jose Bautista	.50	.23	.06
☐	176	Wally Joyner	.60	.25	.08
☐	177	Dean Palmer	.60	.25	.08
☐	178	Tony Phillips	.50	.23	.06
☐	179	John Smiley	.50	.23	.06
☐	180	Charlie Hough	.60	.25	.08
☐	181	Scott Fletcher	.50	.23	.06
☐	182	Todd Van Poppel	.60	.25	.08
☐	183	Mike Blowers	.50	.23	.06
☐	184	Willie McGee	.50	.23	.06
☐	185	Paul Sorrento	.50	.23	.06
☐	186	Eric Young	.60	.25	.08
☐	187	Bret Barberie	.50	.23	.06
☐	188	Manny Lee	.50	.23	.06
☐	189	Jeff Branson	.50	.23	.06
☐	190	Jim Deshaies	.50	.23	.06
☐	191	Ken Caminiti	.60	.25	.08
☐	192	Tim Raines	.75	.35	.09

□ 193 Joe Grahe .50 .23 .06
□ 194 Hipolito Pichardo .50 .23 .06
□ 195 Denny Neagle .50 .23 .06
□ 196 Jeff Gardner .50 .23 .06
□ 197 Mike Benjamin .50 .23 .06
□ 198 Milt Thompson .50 .23 .06
□ 199 Bruce Ruffin .50 .23 .06
□ 200 Chris Hammond UER .50 .23 .06
(Back of card has Mariners; should be Marlins)
□ 201 Tony Gwynn FIN 3.00 1.35 .40
□ 202 Robin Ventura FIN .60 .25 .08
□ 203 Frank Thomas FIN 12.00 5.50 1.50
□ 204 Kirby Puckett FIN 5.00 2.30 .60
□ 205 Roberto Alomar FIN 3.00 1.35 .40
□ 206 Dennis Eckersley FIN .75 .35 .09
□ 207 Joe Carter FIN 1.75 .80 .22
□ 208 Albert Belle FIN 4.00 1.80 .50
□ 209 Greg Maddux FIN 3.00 1.35 .40
□ 210 Ryne Sandberg FIN 4.00 1.80 .50
□ 211 Juan Gonzalez FIN 4.00 1.80 .50
□ 212 Jeff Bagwell FIN 6.00 2.70 .75
□ 213 Randy Johnson FIN .75 .35 .09
□ 214 Matt Williams FIN 2.00 .90 .25
□ 215 Dave Winfield FIN .75 .35 .09
□ 216 Larry Walker FIN .75 .35 .09
□ 217 Roger Clemens FIN 3.00 1.35 .40
□ 218 Kenny Lofton FIN 3.00 1.35 .40
□ 219 Cecil Fielder FIN 1.25 .55 .16
□ 220 Darren Daulton FIN .75 .35 .09
□ 221 John Olerud FIN .75 .35 .09
□ 222 Jose Canseco FIN 1.75 .80 .22
□ 223 Rickey Henderson FIN .75 .35 .09
□ 224 Fred McGriff FIN 1.75 .80 .22
□ 225 Gary Sheffield FIN .75 .35 .09
□ 226 Jack McDowell FIN .75 .35 .09
□ 227 Rafael Palmeiro FIN .75 .35 .09
□ 228 Travis Fryman FIN 1.25 .55 .16
□ 229 Marquis Grissom FIN .75 .35 .09
□ 230 Barry Bonds FIN 4.00 1.80 .50
□ 231 Carlos Baerga FIN 1.75 .80 .22
□ 232 Ken Griffey Jr. FIN 12.00 5.50 1.50
□ 233 David Justice FIN 1.75 .80 .22
□ 234 Bobby Bonilla FIN .75 .35 .09
□ 235 Cal Ripken FIN 9.00 4.00 1.15
□ 236 Sammy Sosa FIN .75 .35 .09
□ 237 Len Dykstra FIN .75 .35 .09
□ 238 Will Clark FIN 1.75 .80 .22
□ 239 Paul Molitor FIN 1.75 .80 .22
□ 240 Barry Larkin FIN .75 .35 .09
□ 241 Bo Jackson .75 .35 .09
□ 242 Mitch Williams .50 .23 .06
□ 243 Ron Darling .50 .23 .06
□ 244 Darryl Kile .60 .25 .08
□ 245 Geronimo Berroa .50 .23 .06
□ 246 Gregg Olson .50 .23 .06
□ 247 Brian Harper .50 .23 .06
□ 248 Rheal Cormier .50 .23 .06
□ 249 Rey Sanchez .50 .23 .06
□ 250 Jeff Fassero .50 .23 .06
□ 251 Sandy Alomar .60 .25 .08
□ 252 Chris Bosio .50 .23 .06
□ 253 Andy Stankiewicz .50 .23 .06
□ 254 Harold Baines .60 .25 .08
□ 255 Andy Ashby .50 .23 .06
□ 256 Tyler Green .50 .23 .06
□ 257 Kevin Brown .50 .23 .06
□ 258 Mo Vaughn .75 .35 .09
□ 259 Mike Harkey .50 .23 .06
□ 260 Dave Henderson .50 .23 .06
□ 261 Kent Hrbek .60 .25 .08
□ 262 Darrin Jackson .50 .23 .06
□ 263 Bob Wickman .50 .23 .06
□ 264 Spike Owen .50 .23 .06
□ 265 Todd Jones .50 .23 .06
□ 266 Pat Borders .50 .23 .06
□ 267 Tom Glavine .75 .35 .09
□ 268 Dave Nilsson .50 .23 .06
□ 269 Rich Batchelor .50 .23 .06
□ 270 Delino DeShields .60 .25 .08
□ 271 Felix Fermin .50 .23 .06
□ 272 Orestes Destrade .50 .23 .06
□ 273 Mickey Morandini .50 .23 .06
□ 274 Otis Nixon .50 .23 .06
□ 275 Ellis Burks .60 .25 .08
□ 276 Greg Gagne .50 .23 .06
□ 277 John Doherty .50 .23 .06
□ 278 Julio Franco .60 .25 .08
□ 279 Bernie Williams .60 .25 .08
□ 280 Rick Aguilera .60 .25 .08
□ 281 Mickey Tettleton .60 .25 .08
□ 282 David Nied .75 .35 .09
□ 283 Johnny Ruffin .50 .23 .06
□ 284 Dan Wilson .50 .23 .06
□ 285 Omar Vizquel .50 .23 .06
□ 286 Willie Banks .50 .23 .06
□ 287 Erik Pappas .50 .23 .06
□ 288 Cal Eldred .60 .25 .08
□ 289 Bobby Witt .50 .23 .06
□ 290 Luis Gonzalez .50 .23 .06
□ 291 Greg Pirkl .50 .23 .06
□ 292 Alex Cole .50 .23 .06
□ 293 Ricky Bones .50 .23 .06
□ 294 Denis Boucher .50 .23 .06
□ 295 John Burkett .60 .25 .08
□ 296 Steve Trachsel 1.50 .65 .19
□ 297 Ricky Jordan .50 .23 .06
□ 298 Mark Dewey .50 .23 .06
□ 299 Jimmy Key .60 .25 .08
□ 300 Mike Macfarlane .50 .23 .06
□ 301 Tim Belcher .50 .23 .06
□ 302 Carlos Reyes .50 .23 .06
□ 303 Greg A. Harris .50 .23 .06
□ 304 Brian Anderson 3.00 1.35 .40
□ 305 Terry Mulholland .50 .23 .06
□ 306 Felix Jose .50 .23 .06
□ 307 Darren Holmes .50 .23 .06
□ 308 Jose Rijo .60 .25 .08
□ 309 Paul Wagner .50 .23 .06
□ 310 Bob Scanlan .50 .23 .06
□ 311 Mike Jackson .50 .23 .06
□ 312 Jose Vizcaino .50 .23 .06
□ 313 Rob Butler .50 .23 .06
□ 314 Kevin Seitzer .50 .23 .06
□ 315 Geronimo Pena .50 .23 .06
□ 316 Hector Carrasco .50 .23 .06
□ 317 Eddie Murray .75 .35 .09
□ 318 Roger Salkeld .50 .23 .06
□ 319 Todd Hundley .50 .23 .06
□ 320 Danny Jackson .50 .23 .06
□ 321 Kevin Young .50 .23 .06
□ 322 Mike Greenwell .60 .25 .08
□ 323 Kevin Mitchell .60 .25 .08
□ 324 Chuck Knoblauch .75 .35 .09
□ 325 Danny Tartabull .60 .25 .08
□ 326 Vince Coleman .50 .23 .06
□ 327 Marvin Freeman .50 .23 .06
□ 328 Andy Benes .60 .25 .08
□ 329 Mike Kelly .60 .25 .08
□ 330 Karl Rhodes .50 .23 .06
□ 331 Allen Watson .50 .23 .06
□ 332 Damion Easley .50 .23 .06
□ 333 Reggie Jefferson .50 .23 .06
□ 334 Kevin McReynolds .50 .23 .06
□ 335 Arthur Rhodes .50 .23 .06
□ 336 Brian Hunter .50 .23 .06

☐ 337 Tom Browning .50 .23 .06
☐ 338 Pedro Munoz .50 .23 .06
☐ 339 Billy Ripken .50 .23 .06
☐ 340 Gene Harris .50 .23 .06
☐ 341 Fernando Vina .50 .23 .06
☐ 342 Sean Berry .50 .23 .06
☐ 343 Pedro Astacio .60 .25 .08
☐ 344 B.J. Surhoff .50 .23 .06
☐ 345 Doug Drabek .75 .35 .09
☐ 346 Jody Reed .50 .23 .06
☐ 347 Ray Lankford .75 .35 .09
☐ 348 Steve Farr .50 .23 .06
☐ 349 Eric Anthony .50 .23 .06
☐ 350 Pete Smith .50 .23 .06
☐ 351 Lee Smith .75 .35 .09
☐ 352 Mariano Duncan .50 .23 .06
☐ 353 Doug Strange .50 .23 .06
☐ 354 Tim Bogar .50 .23 .06
☐ 355 Dave Weathers .50 .23 .06
☐ 356 Eric Karros .60 .25 .08
☐ 357 Randy Myers .50 .23 .06
☐ 358 Chad Curtis .60 .25 .08
☐ 359 Steve Avery .75 .35 .09
☐ 360 Brian Jordan .60 .25 .08
☐ 361 Tim Wallach .50 .23 .06
☐ 362 Pedro Martinez .75 .35 .09
☐ 363 Bip Roberts .50 .23 .06
☐ 364 Lou Whitaker .75 .35 .09
☐ 365 Luis Polonia .50 .23 .06
☐ 366 Benny Santiago .50 .23 .06
☐ 367 Brett Butler .60 .25 .08
☐ 368 Shawon Dunston .50 .23 .06
☐ 369 Kelly Stinnett .50 .23 .06
☐ 370 Chris Turner .50 .23 .06
☐ 371 Ruben Sierra .75 .35 .09
☐ 372 Greg A. Harris .50 .23 .06
☐ 373 Xavier Hernandez .50 .23 .06
☐ 374 Howard Johnson .50 .23 .06
☐ 375 Duane Ward .50 .23 .06
☐ 376 Roberto Hernandez .50 .23 .06
☐ 377 Scott Leius .50 .23 .06
☐ 378 Dave Valle .50 .23 .06
☐ 379 Sid Fernandez .50 .23 .06
☐ 380 Doug Jones .50 .23 .06
☐ 381 Zane Smith .50 .23 .06
☐ 382 Craig Biggio .60 .25 .08
☐ 383 Rick White .50 .23 .06
☐ 384 Tom Pagnozzi .50 .23 .06
☐ 385 Chris James .50 .23 .06
☐ 386 Bret Boone .75 .35 .09
☐ 387 Jeff Montgomery .60 .25 .08
☐ 388 Chad Kreuter .50 .23 .06
☐ 389 Greg Hibbard .50 .23 .06
☐ 390 Mark Grace .75 .35 .09
☐ 391 Phil Leftwich .50 .23 .06
☐ 392 Don Mattingly 5.00 2.30 .60
☐ 393 Ozzie Guillen .50 .23 .06
☐ 394 Gary Gaetti .50 .23 .06
☐ 395 Erik Hanson .50 .23 .06
☐ 396 Scott Brosius .50 .23 .06
☐ 397 Tom Gordon .50 .23 .06
☐ 398 Bill Gullickson .50 .23 .06
☐ 399 Matt Mieske .50 .23 .06
☐ 400 Pat Hentgen .60 .25 .08
☐ 401 Walt Weiss .50 .23 .06
☐ 402 Greg Blosser .50 .23 .06
☐ 403 Stan Javier .50 .23 .06
☐ 404 Doug Henry .50 .23 .06
☐ 405 Ramon Martinez .60 .25 .08
☐ 406 Frank Viola .50 .23 .06
☐ 407 Mike Hampton .50 .23 .06
☐ 408 Andy Van Slyke .75 .35 .09
☐ 409 Bobby Ayala .50 .23 .06
☐ 410 Todd Zeile .60 .25 .08
☐ 411 Jay Bell .60 .25 .08
☐ 412 Denny Martinez .60 .25 .08
☐ 413 Mark Portugal .50 .23 .06
☐ 414 Bobby Munoz .50 .23 .06
☐ 415 Kirt Manwaring .50 .23 .06
☐ 416 John Kruk .75 .35 .09
☐ 417 Trevor Hoffman .50 .23 .06
☐ 418 Chris Sabo .50 .23 .06
☐ 419 Bret Saberhagen .60 .25 .08
☐ 420 Chris Nabholz .50 .23 .06
☐ 421 James Mouton FIN 1.00 .45 .13
☐ 422 Tony Tarasco FIN .75 .35 .09
☐ 423 Carlos Delgado FIN 2.00 .90 .25
☐ 424 Rondell White FIN 1.25 .55 .16
☐ 425 Javy Lopez FIN 1.25 .55 .16
☐ 426 Chan Ho Park FIN 5.00 2.30 .60
☐ 427 Cliff Floyd FIN 2.00 .90 .25
☐ 428 Dave Staton FIN .50 .23 .06
☐ 429 J.R. Phillips FIN .75 .35 .09
☐ 430 Manny Ramirez FIN 2.50 1.15 .30
☐ 431 Kurt Abbott FIN 1.25 .55 .16
☐ 432 Melvin Nieves FIN .75 .35 .09
☐ 433 Alex Gonzalez FIN 1.00 .45 .13
☐ 434 Rick Helling FIN .50 .23 .06
☐ 435 Danny Bautista FIN .60 .25 .08
☐ 436 Matt Walbeck FIN .50 .23 .06
☐ 437 Ryan Klesko FIN 2.00 .90 .25
☐ 438 Steve Karsay FIN .50 .23 .06
☐ 439 Salomon Torres FIN .60 .25 .08
☐ 440 Scott Ruffcorn FIN .75 .35 .09

1994 Finest Refractors

The 1994 Topps Finest Refractors baseball set consists of two series of 220 cards each, for a total of 440 cards. These special cards were inserted at a rate of one in every nine packs. They are identical to the basic Finest card except for a more intense luster and 3-D appearance.

	MINT	EXC	G-VG
COMPLETE SET (440)	2500.00	1150.00	325.00
COMPLETE SERIES 1 (220)	1250.00	575.00	160.00
COMPLETE SERIES 2 (220)	1250.00	575.00	160.00
COMMON CARD (1-220)	3.00	1.35	.40
COMMON CARD (221-440)	3.00	1.35	.40

*UNLISTED VETERAN STARS: 5X to 10X BASIC CARDS
*UNLISTED YOUNG STARS: 3X to 6X BASIC CARDS
*UNLISTED RC's: 2X to 4X BASIC CARDS

☐ 1 Mike Piazza FIN	60.00	27.00	7.50
☐ 74 Raul Mondesi	40.00	18.00	5.00
☐ 203 Frank Thomas FIN	125.00	57.50	15.50
☐ 204 Kirby Puckett FIN	50.00	23.00	6.25
☐ 210 Ryne Sandberg FIN	40.00	18.00	5.00
☐ 212 Jeff Bagwell FIN	60.00	27.00	7.50
☐ 230 Barry Bonds FIN	50.00	23.00	6.25
☐ 232 Ken Griffey Jr. FIN	125.00	57.50	15.50
☐ 235 Cal Ripken FIN	90.00	40.00	11.50
☐ 392 Don Mattingly	50.00	23.00	6.25

1994 Finest Jumbos

Inserted one per Finest jumbo box, this 80-card set (3 1/2" by 5") was issued in two series of 40. Each of the 80 cards is identical in design to the special "Finest" cards from the basic Finest set. The "Finest" cards were designated to showcase top rookies, prospects and veterans. The card numbering is the same. Hence, the first series comprises of cards 1-20 and 201-220. The second series is cards 221-240 and 421-440.

	MINT	EXC	G-VG
COMPLETE SET (80)	450.00	200.00	57.50
COMPLETE SERIES 1 (40)	225.00	100.00	28.00
COMPLETE SERIES 2 (40)	225.00	100.00	28.00
COMMON CARD (1-20)	2.00	.90	.25
COMMON CARD (201-220)	2.00	.90	.25
COMMON CARD (221-240)	2.00	.90	.25
COMMON CARD (421-440)	2.00	.90	.25

*UNLISTED STARS: 3X BASIC CARDS

☐ 1 Mike Piazza	20.00	9.00	2.50
☐ 203 Frank Thomas	40.00	18.00	5.00
☐ 204 Kirby Puckett	15.00	6.75	1.90
☐ 210 Ryne Sandberg	12.00	5.50	1.50
☐ 212 Jeff Bagwell	20.00	9.00	2.50
☐ 230 Barry Bonds	15.00	6.75	1.90
☐ 232 Ken Griffey Jr.	40.00	18.00	5.00
☐ 235 Cal Ripken	30.00	13.50	3.80

1993 Flair

These 300 standard-size (2 1/2" by 3 1/2") cards are made from heavy 24 point board card stock, with an additional three points of high-gloss laminate on each side, and feature full-bleed color fronts that sport two photos of each player, one superposed upon the other. The Flair logo appears at the top and the player's name rests at the bottom, both stamped in gold foil. Another borderless color player action photo graces the back. Upon this slightly ghosted picture appear the player's stats and, with a gold foil start letter, career highlights. The player's team logo in the upper right rounds out the back. The cards are numbered in gold foil on the back, grouped alphabetically within teams, and checklisted below alphabetically according to teams for National League and American League as follows: Atlanta Braves (1-12), Chicago Cubs (13-23), Cincinnati Reds (24-34), Colorado Rockies (35-44), Florida Marlins (45-55), Houston Astros (56-67), Los Angeles Dodgers (68-77), Montreal Expos (78-88), New York Mets (89-96), Philadelphia Phillies (97-108), Pittsburgh Pirates (109-118), St. Louis Cardinals (119-130), San Diego Padres (131-136), San Francisco Giants (137-148), Baltimore Orioles (149-159), Boston Red Sox (160-169), California Angels (170-179), Chicago White Sox (180-190), Cleveland Indians (191-199), Detroit Tigers (200-211), Kansas City Royals (212-222), Milwaukee Brewers (223-232), Minnesota Twins (233-243), New York Yankees (244-255), Oakland Athletics (256-265), Seattle Mariners (266-276), Texas Rangers (277-286), and Toronto Blue Jays (287-297). The set closes with checklists (298-300). Rookie Cards in this set include Rene Arocha, David Hulse, Mike Lansing, and J.T. Snow.

	MINT	EXC	G-VG
COMPLETE SET (300)	90.00	40.00	11.50
COMMON CARD (1-300)	.20	.09	.03

☐ 1 Steve Avery	.40	.18	.05
☐ 2 Jeff Blauser	.30	.14	.04
☐ 3 Ron Gant	.30	.14	.04
☐ 4 Tom Glavine	.40	.18	.05
☐ 5 David Justice	1.25	.55	.16
☐ 6 Mark Lemke	.20	.09	.03
☐ 7 Greg Maddux	1.50	.65	.19
☐ 8 Fred McGriff	1.25	.55	.16
☐ 9 Terry Pendleton	.40	.18	.05
☐ 10 Deion Sanders	1.50	.65	.19
☐ 11 John Smoltz	.30	.14	.04
☐ 12 Mike Stanton	.20	.09	.03
☐ 13 Steve Buechele	.20	.09	.03
☐ 14 Mark Grace	.40	.18	.05
☐ 15 Greg Hibbard	.20	.09	.03
☐ 16 Derrick May	.30	.14	.04
☐ 17 Chuck McElroy	.20	.09	.03
☐ 18 Mike Morgan	.20	.09	.03
☐ 19 Randy Myers	.30	.14	.04

☐ 20 Ryne Sandberg .... 2.50 1.15 .30
☐ 21 Dwight Smith .... .20 .09 .03
☐ 22 Sammy Sosa .... .40 .18 .05
☐ 23 Jose Vizcaino .... .20 .09 .03
☐ 24 Tim Belcher .... .20 .09 .03
☐ 25 Rob Dibble .... .20 .09 .03
☐ 26 Roberto Kelly .... .30 .14 .04
☐ 27 Barry Larkin .... .40 .18 .05
☐ 28 Kevin Mitchell .... .30 .14 .04
☐ 29 Hal Morris .... .30 .14 .04
☐ 30 Joe Oliver .... .20 .09 .03
☐ 31 Jose Rijo .... .30 .14 .04
☐ 32 Bip Roberts .... .20 .09 .03
☐ 33 Chris Sabo .... .30 .14 .04
☐ 34 Reggie Sanders .... .40 .18 .05
☐ 35 Dante Bichette .... .40 .18 .05
☐ 36 Willie Blair .... .20 .09 .03
☐ 37 Jerald Clark .... .20 .09 .03
☐ 38 Alex Cole .... .20 .09 .03
☐ 39 Andres Galarraga .... .40 .18 .05
☐ 40 Joe Girardi .... .20 .09 .03
☐ 41 Charlie Hayes .... .30 .14 .04
☐ 42 Chris Jones .... .20 .09 .03
☐ 43 David Nied .... .40 .18 .05
☐ 44 Eric Young .... .30 .14 .04
☐ 45 Alex Arias .... .20 .09 .03
☐ 46 Jack Armstrong .... .20 .09 .03
☐ 47 Bret Barberie .... .20 .09 .03
☐ 48 Chuck Carr .... .20 .09 .03
☐ 49 Jeff Conine .... .40 .18 .05
☐ 50 Orestes Destrade .... .20 .09 .03
☐ 51 Chris Hammond .... .20 .09 .03
☐ 52 Bryan Harvey .... .30 .14 .04
☐ 53 Benito Santiago .... .20 .09 .03
☐ 54 Gary Sheffield .... .40 .18 .05
☐ 55 Walt Weiss .... .20 .09 .03
☐ 56 Eric Anthony .... .20 .09 .03
☐ 57 Jeff Bagwell .... 4.00 1.80 .50
☐ 58 Craig Biggio .... .30 .14 .04
☐ 59 Ken Caminiti .... .30 .14 .04
☐ 60 Andujar Cedeno .... .30 .14 .04
☐ 61 Doug Drabek .... .40 .18 .05
☐ 62 Steve Finley .... .20 .09 .03
☐ 63 Luis Gonzalez .... .30 .14 .04
☐ 64 Pete Harnisch .... .20 .09 .03
☐ 65 Doug Jones .... .20 .09 .03
☐ 66 Darryl Kile .... .30 .14 .04
☐ 67 Greg Swindell .... .20 .09 .03
☐ 68 Brett Butler .... .30 .14 .04
☐ 69 Jim Gott .... .20 .09 .03
☐ 70 Orel Hershiser .... .30 .14 .04
☐ 71 Eric Karros .... .30 .14 .04
☐ 72 Pedro Martinez .... .40 .18 .05
☐ 73 Ramon Martinez .... .30 .14 .04
☐ 74 Roger McDowell .... .20 .09 .03
☐ 75 Mike Piazza 8.00 3.60 1.00
☐ 76 Jody Reed .... .20 .09 .03
☐ 77 Tim Wallach .... .20 .09 .03
☐ 78 Moises Alou .... .40 .18 .05
☐ 79 Greg Colbrunn .... .20 .09 .03
☐ 80 Wil Cordero .... .40 .18 .05
☐ 81 Delino DeShields .... .30 .14 .04
☐ 82 Jeff Fassero .... .20 .09 .03
☐ 83 Marquis Grissom .... .40 .18 .05
☐ 84 Ken Hill .... .30 .14 .04
☐ 85 Mike Lansing .... .75 .35 .09
☐ 86 Dennis Martinez .... .30 .14 .04
☐ 87 Larry Walker .... .40 .18 .05
☐ 88 John Wetteland .... .20 .09 .03
☐ 89 Bobby Bonilla .... .40 .18 .05
☐ 90 Vince Coleman .... .20 .09 .03
☐ 91 Dwight Gooden .... .20 .09 .03
☐ 92 Todd Hundley .... .20 .09 .03

☐ 93 Howard Johnson .... .20 .09 .03
☐ 94 Eddie Murray .... .40 .18 .05
☐ 95 Joe Orsulak .... .20 .09 .03
☐ 96 Bret Saberhagen .... .30 .14 .04
☐ 97 Darren Daulton .... .40 .18 .05
☐ 98 Mariano Duncan .... .20 .09 .03
☐ 99 Len Dykstra .... .40 .18 .05
☐ 100 Jim Eisenreich .... .20 .09 .03
☐ 101 Tommy Greene .... .30 .14 .04
☐ 102 Dave Hollins .... .40 .18 .05
☐ 103 Pete Incaviglia .... .20 .09 .03
☐ 104 Danny Jackson .... .20 .09 .03
☐ 105 John Kruk .... .40 .18 .05
☐ 106 Terry Mulholland .... .20 .09 .03
☐ 107 Curt Schilling .... .30 .14 .04
☐ 108 Mitch Williams .... .30 .14 .04
☐ 109 Stan Belinda .... .20 .09 .03
☐ 110 Jay Bell .... .30 .14 .04
☐ 111 Steve Cooke .... .20 .09 .03
☐ 112 Carlos Garcia .... .30 .14 .04
☐ 113 Jeff King .... .20 .09 .03
☐ 114 Al Martin .... .30 .14 .04
☐ 115 Orlando Merced .... .30 .14 .04
☐ 116 Don Slaught .... .20 .09 .03
☐ 117 Andy Van Slyke .... .40 .18 .05
☐ 118 Tim Wakefield .... .20 .09 .03
☐ 119 Rene Arocha .... .50 .23 .06
☐ 120 Bernard Gilkey .... .20 .09 .03
☐ 121 Gregg Jefferies .... .40 .18 .05
☐ 122 Ray Lankford .... .40 .18 .05
☐ 123 Donovan Osborne .... .20 .09 .03
☐ 124 Tom Pagnozzi .... .20 .09 .03
☐ 125 Erik Pappas .... .20 .09 .03
☐ 126 Geronimo Pena .... .20 .09 .03
☐ 127 Lee Smith .... .40 .18 .05
☐ 128 Ozzie Smith .... 1.25 .55 .16
☐ 129 Bob Tewksbury .... .20 .09 .03
☐ 130 Mark Whiten .... .30 .14 .04
☐ 131 Derek Bell .... .30 .14 .04
☐ 132 Andy Benes .... .30 .14 .04
☐ 133 Tony Gwynn .... 2.00 .90 .25
☐ 134 Gene Harris .... .20 .09 .03
☐ 135 Trevor Hoffman .... .20 .09 .03
☐ 136 Phil Plantier .... .40 .18 .05
☐ 137 Rod Beck .... .40 .18 .05
☐ 138 Barry Bonds .... 3.00 1.35 .40
☐ 139 John Burkett .... .30 .14 .04
☐ 140 Will Clark .... 1.25 .55 .16
☐ 141 Royce Clayton .... .30 .14 .04
☐ 142 Mike Jackson .... .20 .09 .03
☐ 143 Darren Lewis .... .20 .09 .03
☐ 144 Kirt Manwaring .... .20 .09 .03
☐ 145 Willie McGee .... .20 .09 .03
☐ 146 Bill Swift .... .30 .14 .04
☐ 147 Robby Thompson .... .20 .09 .03
☐ 148 Matt Williams .... 1.25 .55 .16
☐ 149 Brady Anderson .... .30 .14 .04
☐ 150 Mike Devereaux .... .30 .14 .04
☐ 151 Chris Hoiles .... .30 .14 .04
☐ 152 Ben McDonald .... .30 .14 .04
☐ 153 Mark McLemore .... .20 .09 .03
☐ 154 Mike Mussina .... 1.50 .65 .19
☐ 155 Gregg Olson .... .20 .09 .03
☐ 156 Harold Reynolds .... .20 .09 .03
☐ 157 Cal Ripken UER .... 5.00 2.30 .60
(Back refers to his games streak going into 1992; should be 1993)
☐ 158 Rick Sutcliffe .... .30 .14 .04
☐ 159 Fernando Valenzuela .... .20 .09 .03
☐ 160 Roger Clemens .... 2.00 .90 .25
☐ 161 Scott Cooper .... .30 .14 .04
☐ 162 Andre Dawson .... .40 .18 .05
☐ 163 Scott Fletcher .... .20 .09 .03

☐ 164	Mike Greenwell	.30	.14	.04
☐ 165	Greg A. Harris	.20	.09	.03
☐ 166	Billy Hatcher	.20	.09	.03
☐ 167	Jeff Russell	.20	.09	.03
☐ 168	Mo Vaughn	.75	.35	.09
☐ 169	Frank Viola	.20	.09	.03
☐ 170	Chad Curtis	.30	.14	.04
☐ 171	Chili Davis	.30	.14	.04
☐ 172	Gary DiScarcina	.20	.09	.03
☐ 173	Damion Easley	.30	.14	.04
☐ 174	Chuck Finley	.20	.09	.03
☐ 175	Mark Langston	.40	.18	.05
☐ 176	Luis Polonia	.20	.09	.03
☐ 177	Tim Salmon	1.25	.55	.16
☐ 178	Scott Sanderson	.20	.09	.03
☐ 179	J.T.Snow	.40	.18	.05
☐ 180	Wilson Alvarez	.40	.18	.05
☐ 181	Ellis Burks	.30	.14	.04
☐ 182	Joey Cora	.20	.09	.03
☐ 183	Alex Fernandez	.40	.18	.05
☐ 184	Ozzie Guillen	.20	.09	.03
☐ 185	Roberto Hernandez	.20	.09	.03
☐ 186	Bo Jackson	.50	.23	.06
☐ 187	Lance Johnson	.20	.09	.03
☐ 188	Jack McDowell	.40	.18	.05
☐ 189	Frank Thomas	8.00	3.60	1.00
☐ 190	Robin Ventura	.40	.18	.05
☐ 191	Carlos Baerga	1.25	.55	.16
☐ 192	Albert Belle	2.50	1.15	.30
☐ 193	Wayne Kirby	.20	.09	.03
☐ 194	Derek Lilliquist	.20	.09	.03
☐ 195	Kenny Lofton	2.00	.90	.25
☐ 196	Carlos Martinez	.20	.09	.03
☐ 197	Jose Mesa	.20	.09	.03
☐ 198	Eric Plunk	.20	.09	.03
☐ 199	Paul Sorrento	.20	.09	.03
☐ 200	John Doherty	.20	.09	.03
☐ 201	Cecil Fielder	.60	.25	.08
☐ 202	Travis Fryman	.75	.35	.09
☐ 203	Kirk Gibson	.30	.14	.04
☐ 204	Mike Henneman	.20	.09	.03
☐ 205	Chad Kreuter	.20	.09	.03
☐ 206	Scott Livingstone	.20	.09	.03
☐ 207	Tony Phillips	.20	.09	.03
☐ 208	Mickey Tettleton	.30	.14	.04
☐ 209	Alan Trammell	.40	.18	.05
☐ 210	David Wells	.20	.09	.03
☐ 211	Lou Whitaker	.40	.18	.05
☐ 212	Kevin Appier	.30	.14	.04
☐ 213	George Brett	3.50	1.55	.45
☐ 214	David Cone	.40	.18	.05
☐ 215	Tom Gordon	.20	.09	.03
☐ 216	Phil Hiatt	.20	.09	.03
☐ 217	Felix Jose	.20	.09	.03
☐ 218	Wally Joyner	.30	.14	.04
☐ 219	Jose Lind	.20	.09	.03
☐ 220	Mike Macfarlane	.20	.09	.03
☐ 221	Brian McRae	.40	.18	.05
☐ 222	Jeff Montgomery	.30	.14	.04
☐ 223	Cal Eldred	.30	.14	.04
☐ 224	Darryl Hamilton	.20	.09	.03
☐ 225	John Jaha	.30	.14	.04
☐ 226	Pat Listach	.30	.14	.04
☐ 227	Graeme Lloyd	.20	.09	.03
☐ 228	Kevin Reimer	.20	.09	.03
☐ 229	Bill Spiers	.20	.09	.03
☐ 230	B.J.Surhoff	.20	.09	.03
☐ 231	Greg Vaughn	.30	.14	.04
☐ 232	Robin Yount	1.25	.55	.16
☐ 233	Rick Aguilera	.30	.14	.04
☐ 234	Jim Deshaies	.20	.09	.03
☐ 235	Brian Harper	.20	.09	.03
☐ 236	Kent Hrbek	.20	.09	.03
☐ 237	Chuck Knoblauch	.40	.18	.05
☐ 238	Shane Mack	.30	.14	.04
☐ 239	David McCarty	.30	.14	.04
☐ 240	Pedro Munoz	.20	.09	.03
☐ 241	Mike Pagliarulo	.20	.09	.03
☐ 242	Kirby Puckett	3.50	1.55	.45
☐ 243	Dave Winfield	.40	.18	.05
☐ 244	Jim Abbott	.40	.18	.05
☐ 245	Wade Boggs	.60	.25	.08
☐ 246	Pat Kelly	.20	.09	.03
☐ 247	Jimmy Key	.30	.14	.04
☐ 248	Jim Leyritz	.20	.09	.03
☐ 249	Don Mattingly	3.50	1.55	.45
☐ 250	Matt Nokes	.20	.09	.03
☐ 251	Paul O'Neill	.30	.14	.04
☐ 252	Mike Stanley	.20	.09	.03
☐ 253	Danny Tartabull	.30	.14	.04
☐ 254	Bob Wickman	.20	.09	.03
☐ 255	Bernie Williams	.30	.14	.04
☐ 256	Mike Bordick	.20	.09	.03
☐ 257	Dennis Eckersley	.40	.18	.05
☐ 258	Brent Gates	.40	.18	.05
☐ 259	Goose Gossage	.40	.18	.05
☐ 260	Rickey Henderson	.40	.18	.05
☐ 261	Mark McGwire	.40	.18	.05
☐ 262	Ruben Sierra	.40	.18	.05
☐ 263	Terry Steinbach	.30	.14	.04
☐ 264	Bob Welch	.20	.09	.03
☐ 265	Bobby Witt	.20	.09	.03
☐ 266	Rich Amaral	.20	.09	.03
☐ 267	Chris Bosio	.20	.09	.03
☐ 268	Jay Buhner	.30	.14	.04
☐ 269	Norm Charlton	.20	.09	.03
☐ 270	Ken Griffey Jr.	8.00	3.60	1.00
☐ 271	Erik Hanson	.20	.09	.03
☐ 272	Randy Johnson	.40	.18	.05
☐ 273	Edgar Martinez	.20	.09	.03
☐ 274	Tino Martinez	.30	.14	.04
☐ 275	Dave Valle	.20	.09	.03
☐ 276	Omar Vizquel	.20	.09	.03
☐ 277	Kevin Brown	.20	.09	.03
☐ 278	Jose Canseco	1.25	.55	.16
☐ 279	Julio Franco	.30	.14	.04
☐ 280	Juan Gonzalez	2.50	1.15	.30
☐ 281	Tom Henke	.30	.14	.04
☐ 282	David Hulse	.20	.09	.03
☐ 283	Rafael Palmeiro	.40	.18	.05
☐ 284	Dean Palmer	.30	.14	.04
☐ 285	Ivan Rodriguez	.40	.18	.05
☐ 286	Nolan Ryan	8.00	3.60	1.00
☐ 287	Roberto Alomar	1.50	.65	.19
☐ 288	Pat Borders	.20	.09	.03
☐ 289	Joe Carter	1.25	.55	.16
☐ 290	Juan Guzman	.30	.14	.04
☐ 291	Pat Hentgen	.30	.14	.04
☐ 292	Paul Molitor	1.25	.55	.16
☐ 293	John Olerud	.40	.18	.05
☐ 294	Ed Sprague	.20	.09	.03
☐ 295	Dave Stewart	.30	.14	.04
☐ 296	Duane Ward	.20	.09	.03
☐ 297	Devon White	.30	.14	.04
☐ 298	Checklist 1-100	.20	.09	.03
☐ 299	Checklist 101-200	.20	.09	.03
☐ 300	Checklist 201-300	.20	.09	.03

1993 Flair Wave of the Future

This 20-card standard-size (2 1/2" by 3 1/2") limited edition subset is made of the

same thick card stock as the regular-issue set and features full-bleed color player action photos on the fronts, with the Flair logo, player's name, and the "Wave of the Future" name and logo in gold foil, all superimposed upon an ocean breaker. The horizontal back carries the same wave photo, with a color player photo superposed on the right side. The Wave of the Future name and logo, along with the player's name and career hightlights, appear in gold foil on the left side. The cards are numbered on the back in gold foil with the numbering following alphabetical order of players' names.

	MINT	EXC	G-VG
COMPLETE SET (20)	70.00	32.00	8.75
COMMON CARD (1-20)	2.00	.90	.25
☐ 1 Jason Bere	6.00	2.70	.75
☐ 2 Jeromy Burnitz	2.00	.90	.25
☐ 3 Russ Davis	2.50	1.15	.30
☐ 4 Jim Edmonds	2.00	.90	.25
☐ 5 Cliff Floyd	6.00	2.70	.75
☐ 6 Jeffrey Hammonds	4.00	1.80	.50
☐ 7 Trevor Hoffman	2.00	.90	.25
☐ 8 Domingo Jean	2.00	.90	.25
☐ 9 David McCarty	2.50	1.15	.30
☐ 10 Bobby Munoz	2.50	1.15	.30
☐ 11 Brad Pennington	2.00	.90	.25
☐ 12 Mike Piazza	20.00	9.00	2.50
☐ 13 Manny Ramirez	8.00	3.60	1.00
☐ 14 John Roper	2.00	.90	.25
☐ 15 Tim Salmon	5.00	2.30	.60
☐ 16 Aaron Sele	4.00	1.80	.50
☐ 17 Allen Watson	2.50	1.15	.30
☐ 18 Rondell White	4.00	1.80	.50
☐ 19 Darrell Whitmore UER (Nigel Wilson back)	2.00	.90	.25
☐ 20 Nigel Wilson UER (Darrell Whitmore back)	2.50	1.15	.30

1994 Flair

For the second consecutive year Fleer issued a Flair brand. The set consists of 450 full bleed cards in two series of 250 and 200. The card stock is thicker than the traditional standard card. Card fronts feature two photos with the player's name and team name at the bottom in gold foil. The first letter of the player's last name appears within a gold shield to add style to this premium brand product. The backs are horizontal with a player photo and statistics. The team logo and player's name are done in gold foil. The cards are grouped alphabetically by team within each league as follows: Baltimore Orioles (1-9/251-258), Boston Red Sox (10-18/259-266), California Angels (19-27/267-274), Chicago White Sox (28-36/275-281), Cleveland Indians (37-45/282-290), Detroit Tigers (46-53/291-296), Kansas City Royals (54-62/297-302), Milwaukee Brewers (63-71/303-310), Minnesota Twins (72-79/311-317), New York Yankees (80-88/318-326), Oakland Athletics (89-97/327-334), Seattle Mariners (98-106/335-342), Texas Rangers (107-114/343-347), Toronto Blue Jays (115-123/348-351), Atlanta Braves (124-133/352-359), Chicago Cubs (134-142/360-364), Cincinnati Reds (143-150/365-371), Colorado Rockies (151-159/372-377), Florida Marlins (160-167/378-384), Houston Astros (168-176/385-392), Los Angeles Dodgers (177-185/393-399), Montreal Expos (186-194/400-406), New York Mets (195-203/407-410), Philadelphia Phillies (204-213/411-419), Pittsburgh Pirates (214-222/420-426), St. Louis Cardinals (223-230/427-432), San Diego Padres (231-237/433-441), and San Francisco Giants (238-247/442-448). Rookie Cards include Brian Anderson, John Hudek, Chan Ho Park, Alex Rodriguez and Will VanLandingham.

	MINT	EXC	G-VG
COMPLETE SET (450)	75.00	34.00	9.50
COMPLETE SERIES 1 (250)	40.00	18.00	5.00
COMPLETE SERIES 2 (200)	35.00	16.00	4.40
COMMON CARD (1-250)	.15	.07	.02
COMMON CARD (251-450)	.15	.07	.02
☐ 1 Harold Baines	.25	.11	.03
☐ 2 Jeffrey Hammonds	.50	.23	.06
☐ 3 Chris Hoiles	.25	.11	.03
☐ 4 Ben McDonald	.25	.11	.03
☐ 5 Mark McLemore	.15	.07	.02
☐ 6 Jamie Moyer	.15	.07	.02
☐ 7 Jim Poole	.15	.07	.02
☐ 8 Cal Ripken	4.00	1.80	.50
☐ 9 Chris Sabo	.15	.07	.02
☐ 10 Scott Bankhead	.15	.07	.02
☐ 11 Scott Cooper	.25	.11	.03
☐ 12 Danny Darwin	.15	.07	.02
☐ 13 Andre Dawson	.30	.14	.04
☐ 14 Billy Hatcher	.15	.07	.02
☐ 15 Aaron Sele	.50	.23	.06
☐ 16 John Valentin	.25	.11	.03
☐ 17 Dave Valle	.15	.07	.02
☐ 18 Mo Vaughn	.30	.14	.04
☐ 19 Brian Anderson	1.25	.55	.16

	#	Player			
☐	20	Gary DiSarcina	.15	.07	.02
☐	21	Jim Edmonds	.15	.07	.02
☐	22	Chuck Finley	.15	.07	.02
☐	23	Bo Jackson	.30	.14	.04
☐	24	Mark Leiter	.15	.07	.02
☐	25	Greg Myers	.15	.07	.02
☐	26	Eduardo Perez	.25	.11	.03
☐	27	Tim Salmon	.75	.35	.09
☐	28	Wilson Alvarez	.30	.14	.04
☐	29	Jason Bere	.60	.25	.08
☐	30	Alex Fernandez	.30	.14	.04
☐	31	Ozzie Guillen	.15	.07	.02
☐	32	Joe Hall	.15	.07	.02
☐	33	Darrin Jackson	.15	.07	.02
☐	34	Kirk McCaskill	.15	.07	.02
☐	35	Tim Raines	.30	.14	.04
☐	36	Frank Thomas	5.00	2.30	.60
☐	37	Carlos Baerga	.75	.35	.09
☐	38	Albert Belle	1.50	.65	.19
☐	39	Mark Clark	.15	.07	.02
☐	40	Wayne Kirby	.15	.07	.02
☐	41	Dennis Martinez	.25	.11	.03
☐	42	Charles Nagy	.15	.07	.02
☐	43	Manny Ramirez	1.00	.45	.13
☐	44	Paul Sorrento	.15	.07	.02
☐	45	Jim Thome	.30	.14	.04
☐	46	Eric Davis	.15	.07	.02
☐	47	John Doherty	.15	.07	.02
☐	48	Junior Felix	.15	.07	.02
☐	49	Cecil Fielder	.30	.14	.04
☐	50	Kirk Gibson	.25	.11	.03
☐	51	Mike Moore	.15	.07	.02
☐	52	Tony Phillips	.15	.07	.02
☐	53	Alan Trammell	.30	.14	.04
☐	54	Kevin Appier	.25	.11	.03
☐	55	Stan Belinda	.15	.07	.02
☐	56	Vince Coleman	.15	.07	.02
☐	57	Greg Gagne	.15	.07	.02
☐	58	Bob Hamelin	.30	.14	.04
☐	59	Dave Henderson	.15	.07	.02
☐	60	Wally Joyner	.25	.11	.03
☐	61	Mike Macfarlane	.15	.07	.02
☐	62	Jeff Montgomery	.25	.11	.03
☐	63	Ricky Bones	.15	.07	.02
☐	64	Jeff Bronkey	.15	.07	.02
☐	65	Alex Diaz	.15	.07	.02
☐	66	Cal Eldred	.25	.11	.03
☐	67	Darryl Hamilton	.15	.07	.02
☐	68	John Jaha	.15	.07	.02
☐	69	Mark Kiefer	.15	.07	.02
☐	70	Kevin Seitzer	.15	.07	.02
☐	71	Turner Ward	.15	.07	.02
☐	72	Rich Becker	.25	.11	.03
☐	73	Scott Erickson	.15	.07	.02
☐	74	Keith Garagozzo	.30	.14	.04
☐	75	Kent Hrbek	.25	.11	.03
☐	76	Scott Leius	.15	.07	.02
☐	77	Kirby Puckett	2.00	.90	.25
☐	78	Matt Walbeck	.15	.07	.02
☐	79	Dave Winfield	.30	.14	.04
☐	80	Mike Gallego	.15	.07	.02
☐	81	Xavier Hernandez	.15	.07	.02
☐	82	Jimmy Key	.25	.11	.03
☐	83	Jim Leyritz	.15	.07	.02
☐	84	Don Mattingly	2.00	.90	.25
☐	85	Matt Nokes	.15	.07	.02
☐	86	Paul O'Neill	.25	.11	.03
☐	87	Melido Perez	.15	.07	.02
☐	88	Danny Tartabull	.25	.11	.03
☐	89	Mike Bordick	.15	.07	.02
☐	90	Ron Darling	.15	.07	.02
☐	91	Dennis Eckersley	.30	.14	.04
☐	92	Stan Javier	.15	.07	.02

	#	Player			
☐	93	Steve Karsay	.15	.07	.02
☐	94	Mark McGwire	.30	.14	.04
☐	95	Troy Neel	.25	.11	.03
☐	96	Terry Steinbach	.25	.11	.03
☐	97	Bill Taylor	.15	.07	.02
☐	98	Eric Anthony	.15	.07	.02
☐	99	Chris Bosio	.15	.07	.02
☐	100	Tim Davis	.15	.07	.02
☐	101	Felix Fermin	.15	.07	.02
☐	102	Dave Fleming	.15	.07	.02
☐	103	Ken Griffey Jr.	5.00	2.30	.60
☐	104	Greg Hibbard	.15	.07	.02
☐	105	Reggie Jefferson	.15	.07	.02
☐	106	Tino Martinez	.15	.07	.02
☐	107	Jack Armstrong	.15	.07	.02
☐	108	Will Clark	.75	.35	.09
☐	109	Juan Gonzalez	1.75	.80	.22
☐	110	Rick Helling	.15	.07	.02
☐	111	Tom Henke	.15	.07	.02
☐	112	David Hulse	.15	.07	.02
☐	113	Manny Lee	.15	.07	.02
☐	114	Doug Strange	.15	.07	.02
☐	115	Roberto Alomar	1.25	.55	.16
☐	116	Joe Carter	.75	.35	.09
☐	117	Carlos Delgado	.75	.35	.09
☐	118	Pat Hentgen	.25	.11	.03
☐	119	Paul Molitor	.75	.35	.09
☐	120	John Olerud	.30	.14	.04
☐	121	Dave Stewart	.25	.11	.03
☐	122	Todd Stottlemyre	.15	.07	.02
☐	123	Mike Timlin	.15	.07	.02
☐	124	Jeff Blauser	.25	.11	.03
☐	125	Tom Glavine	.30	.14	.04
☐	126	David Justice	.75	.35	.09
☐	127	Mike Kelly	.25	.11	.03
☐	128	Ryan Klesko	.75	.35	.09
☐	129	Javy Lopez	.50	.23	.06
☐	130	Greg Maddux	1.00	.45	.13
☐	131	Fred McGriff	.75	.35	.09
☐	132	Kent Mercker	.15	.07	.02
☐	133	Mark Wohlers	.15	.07	.02
☐	134	Willie Banks	.15	.07	.02
☐	135	Steve Buechele	.15	.07	.02
☐	136	Shawon Dunston	.15	.07	.02
☐	137	Jose Guzman	.15	.07	.02
☐	138	Glenallen Hill	.15	.07	.02
☐	139	Randy Myers	.15	.07	.02
☐	140	Karl Rhodes	.15	.07	.02
☐	141	Ryne Sandberg	1.75	.80	.22
☐	142	Steve Trachsel	.60	.25	.08
☐	143	Bret Boone	.30	.14	.04
☐	144	Tom Browning	.15	.07	.02
☐	145	Hector Carrasco	.15	.07	.02
☐	146	Barry Larkin	.30	.14	.04
☐	147	Hal Morris	.25	.11	.03
☐	148	Jose Rijo	.25	.11	.03
☐	149	Reggie Sanders	.25	.11	.03
☐	150	John Smiley	.15	.07	.02
☐	151	Dante Bichette	.30	.14	.04
☐	152	Ellis Burks	.25	.11	.03
☐	153	Joe Girardi	.15	.07	.02
☐	154	Mike Harkey	.15	.07	.02
☐	155	Roberto Mejia	.25	.11	.03
☐	156	Marcus Moore	.15	.07	.02
☐	157	Armando Reynoso	.15	.07	.02
☐	158	Bruce Ruffin	.15	.07	.02
☐	159	Eric Young	.25	.11	.03
☐	160	Kurt Abbott	.50	.23	.06
☐	161	Jeff Conine	.30	.14	.04
☐	162	Orestes Destrade	.15	.07	.02
☐	163	Chris Hammond	.15	.07	.02
☐	164	Bryan Harvey	.25	.11	.03
☐	165	Dave Magadan	.15	.07	.02

☐ 166	Gary Sheffield	.30	.14	.04
☐ 167	David Weathers	.15	.07	.02
☐ 168	Andujar Cedeno	.15	.07	.02
☐ 169	Tom Edens	.15	.07	.02
☐ 170	Luis Gonzalez	.15	.07	.02
☐ 171	Pete Harnisch	.15	.07	.02
☐ 172	Todd Jones	.15	.07	.02
☐ 173	Darryl Kile	.25	.11	.03
☐ 174	James Mouton	.40	.18	.05
☐ 175	Scott Servais	.15	.07	.02
☐ 176	Mitch Williams	.15	.07	.02
☐ 177	Pedro Astacio	.25	.11	.03
☐ 178	Orel Hershiser	.25	.11	.03
☐ 179	Raul Mondesi	1.75	.80	.22
☐ 180	Jose Offerman	.15	.07	.02
☐ 181	Chan Ho Park	2.00	.90	.25
☐ 182	Mike Piazza	2.50	1.15	.30
☐ 183	Cory Snyder	.15	.07	.02
☐ 184	Tim Wallach	.15	.07	.02
☐ 185	Todd Worrell	.15	.07	.02
☐ 186	Sean Berry	.15	.07	.02
☐ 187	Wil Cordero	.30	.14	.04
☐ 188	Darrin Fletcher	.15	.07	.02
☐ 189	Cliff Floyd	.75	.35	.09
☐ 190	Marquis Grissom	.30	.14	.04
☐ 191	Rod Henderson	.40	.18	.05
☐ 192	Ken Hill	.25	.11	.03
☐ 193	Pedro Martinez	.30	.14	.04
☐ 194	Kirk Rueter	.15	.07	.02
☐ 195	Jeromy Burnitz	.25	.11	.03
☐ 196	John Franco	.15	.07	.02
☐ 197	Dwight Gooden	.15	.07	.02
☐ 198	Todd Hundley	.15	.07	.02
☐ 199	Bobby Jones	.40	.18	.05
☐ 200	Jeff Kent	.25	.11	.03
☐ 201	Mike Maddux	.15	.07	.02
☐ 202	Ryan Thompson	.25	.11	.03
☐ 203	Jose Vizcaino	.15	.07	.02
☐ 204	Darren Daulton	.30	.14	.04
☐ 205	Lenny Dykstra	.30	.14	.04
☐ 206	Jim Eisenreich	.15	.07	.02
☐ 207	Dave Hollins	.30	.14	.04
☐ 208	Danny Jackson	.15	.07	.02
☐ 209	Doug Jones	.15	.07	.02
☐ 210	Jeff Juden	.15	.07	.02
☐ 211	Ben Rivera	.15	.07	.02
☐ 212	Kevin Stocker	.25	.11	.03
☐ 213	Milt Thompson	.15	.07	.02
☐ 214	Jay Bell	.25	.11	.03
☐ 215	Steve Cooke	.15	.07	.02
☐ 216	Mark Dewey	.15	.07	.02
☐ 217	Al Martin	.15	.07	.02
☐ 218	Orlando Merced	.25	.11	.03
☐ 219	Don Slaught	.15	.07	.02
☐ 220	Zane Smith	.15	.07	.02
☐ 221	Rick White	.15	.07	.02
☐ 222	Kevin Young	.15	.07	.02
☐ 223	Rene Arocha	.25	.11	.03
☐ 224	Rheal Cormier	.15	.07	.02
☐ 225	Brian Jordan	.25	.11	.03
☐ 226	Ray Lankford	.30	.14	.04
☐ 227	Mike Perez	.15	.07	.02
☐ 228	Ozzie Smith	1.00	.45	.13
☐ 229	Mark Whiten	.25	.11	.03
☐ 230	Todd Zeile	.25	.11	.03
☐ 231	Derek Bell	.25	.11	.03
☐ 232	Archi Cianfrocco	.15	.07	.02
☐ 233	Ricky Gutierrez	.15	.07	.02
☐ 234	Trevor Hoffman	.15	.07	.02
☐ 235	Phil Plantier	.25	.11	.03
☐ 236	Dave Staton	.15	.07	.02
☐ 237	Wally Whitehurst	.15	.07	.02
☐ 238	Todd Benzinger	.15	.07	.02
☐ 239	Barry Bonds	2.00	.90	.25
☐ 240	John Burkett	.25	.11	.03
☐ 241	Royce Clayton	.25	.11	.03
☐ 242	Bryan Hickerson	.15	.07	.02
☐ 243	Mike Jackson	.15	.07	.02
☐ 244	Darren Lewis	.15	.07	.02
☐ 245	Kirt Manwaring	.15	.07	.02
☐ 246	Mark Portugal	.15	.07	.02
☐ 247	Salomon Torres	.25	.11	.03
☐ 248	Checklist 1-97	.15	.07	.02
☐ 249	Checklist 98-194	.15	.07	.02
☐ 250	Checklist 195-250/Inserts	.15	.07	.02
☐ 251	Brady Anderson	.25	.11	.03
☐ 252	Mike Devereaux	.25	.11	.03
☐ 253	Sid Fernandez	.15	.07	.02
☐ 254	Leo Gomez	.15	.07	.02
☐ 255	Mike Mussina	.75	.35	.09
☐ 256	Mike Oquist	.15	.07	.02
☐ 257	Rafael Palmeiro	.30	.14	.04
☐ 258	Lee Smith	.30	.14	.04
☐ 259	Damon Berryhill	.15	.07	.02
☐ 260	Wes Chamberlain	.15	.07	.02
☐ 261	Roger Clemens	1.25	.55	.16
☐ 262	Gar Finnvold	.15	.07	.02
☐ 263	Mike Greenwell	.25	.11	.03
☐ 264	Tim Naehring	.15	.07	.02
☐ 265	Otis Nixon	.15	.07	.02
☐ 266	Ken Ryan	.15	.07	.02
☐ 267	Chad Curtis	.25	.11	.03
☐ 268	Chili Davis	.25	.11	.03
☐ 269	Damion Easley	.15	.07	.02
☐ 270	Jorge Fabregas	.15	.07	.02
☐ 271	Mark Langston	.30	.14	.04
☐ 272	Phil Leftwich	.15	.07	.02
☐ 273	Harold Reynolds	.15	.07	.02
☐ 274	J.T. Snow	.25	.11	.03
☐ 275	Joey Cora	.15	.07	.02
☐ 276	Julio Franco	.25	.11	.03
☐ 277	Roberto Hernandez	.15	.07	.02
☐ 278	Lance Johnson	.15	.07	.02
☐ 279	Ron Karkovice	.15	.07	.02
☐ 280	Jack McDowell	.30	.14	.04
☐ 281	Robin Ventura	.25	.11	.03
☐ 282	Sandy Alomar Jr.	.25	.11	.03
☐ 283	Kenny Lofton	1.25	.55	.16
☐ 284	Jose Mesa	.15	.07	.02
☐ 285	Jack Morris	.30	.14	.04
☐ 286	Eddie Murray	.30	.14	.04
☐ 287	Chad Ogea	.25	.11	.03
☐ 288	Eric Plunk	.15	.07	.02
☐ 289	Paul Shuey	.25	.11	.03
☐ 290	Omar Vizquel	.15	.07	.02
☐ 291	Danny Bautista	.25	.11	.03
☐ 292	Travis Fryman	.30	.14	.04
☐ 293	Greg Gohr	.15	.07	.02
☐ 294	Chris Gomez	.35	.16	.04
☐ 295	Mickey Tettleton	.25	.11	.03
☐ 296	Lou Whitaker	.30	.14	.04
☐ 297	David Cone	.30	.14	.04
☐ 298	Gary Gaetti	.15	.07	.02
☐ 299	Tom Gordon	.15	.07	.02
☐ 300	Felix Jose	.15	.07	.02
☐ 301	Jose Lind	.15	.07	.02
☐ 302	Brian McRae	.25	.11	.03
☐ 303	Mike Fetters	.15	.07	.02
☐ 304	Brian Harper	.15	.07	.02
☐ 305	Pat Listach	.15	.07	.02
☐ 306	Matt Mieske	.15	.07	.02
☐ 307	Dave Nilsson	.15	.07	.02
☐ 308	Jody Reed	.15	.07	.02
☐ 309	Greg Vaughn	.25	.11	.03
☐ 310	Bill Wegman	.15	.07	.02
☐ 311	Rick Aguilera	.25	.11	.03

☐ 312 Alex Cole .15 .07 .02
☐ 313 Denny Hocking .15 .07 .02
☐ 314 Chuck Knoblauch .30 .14 .04
☐ 315 Shane Mack .25 .11 .03
☐ 316 Pat Meares .15 .07 .02
☐ 317 Kevin Tapani .15 .07 .02
☐ 318 Jim Abbott .30 .14 .04
☐ 319 Wade Boggs .30 .14 .04
☐ 320 Sterling Hitchcock .25 .11 .03
☐ 321 Pat Kelly .15 .07 .02
☐ 322 Terry Mulholland .15 .07 .02
☐ 323 Luis Polonia .15 .07 .02
☐ 324 Mike Stanley .15 .07 .02
☐ 325 Bob Wickman .15 .07 .02
☐ 326 Bernie Williams .25 .11 .03
☐ 327 Mark Acre .30 .14 .04
☐ 328 Geronimo Berroa .15 .07 .02
☐ 329 Scott Brosius .15 .07 .02
☐ 330 Brent Gates .30 .14 .04
☐ 331 Rickey Henderson .30 .14 .04
☐ 332 Carlos Reyes .15 .07 .02
☐ 333 Ruben Sierra .30 .14 .04
☐ 334 Bobby Witt .15 .07 .02
☐ 335 Bobby Ayala .15 .07 .02
☐ 336 Jay Buhner .25 .11 .03
☐ 337 Randy Johnson .30 .14 .04
☐ 338 Edgar Martinez .15 .07 .02
☐ 339 Bill Risley .15 .07 .02
☐ 340 Alex Rodriguez 8.00 3.60 1.00
☐ 341 Roger Salkeld .15 .07 .02
☐ 342 Dan Wilson .15 .07 .02
☐ 343 Kevin Brown .15 .07 .02
☐ 344 Jose Canseco .75 .35 .09
☐ 345 Dean Palmer .25 .11 .03
☐ 346 Ivan Rodriguez .30 .14 .04
☐ 347 Kenny Rogers .15 .07 .02
☐ 348 Pat Borders .15 .07 .02
☐ 349 Juan Guzman .25 .11 .03
☐ 350 Ed Sprague .15 .07 .02
☐ 351 Devon White .15 .07 .02
☐ 352 Steve Avery .30 .14 .04
☐ 353 Roberto Kelly .15 .07 .02
☐ 354 Mark Lemke .15 .07 .02
☐ 355 Greg McMichael .25 .11 .03
☐ 356 Terry Pendleton .15 .07 .02
☐ 357 John Smoltz .25 .11 .03
☐ 358 Mike Stanton .15 .07 .02
☐ 359 Tony Tarasco .30 .14 .04
☐ 360 Mark Grace .30 .14 .04
☐ 361 Derrick May .15 .07 .02
☐ 362 Rey Sanchez .15 .07 .02
☐ 363 Sammy Sosa .30 .14 .04
☐ 364 Rick Wilkins .15 .07 .02
☐ 365 Jeff Brantley .15 .07 .02
☐ 366 Tony Fernandez .15 .07 .02
☐ 367 Chuck McElroy .15 .07 .02
☐ 368 Kevin Mitchell .25 .11 .03
☐ 369 John Roper .25 .11 .03
☐ 370 Johnny Ruffin .15 .07 .02
☐ 371 Deion Sanders 1.00 .45 .13
☐ 372 Marvin Freeman .15 .07 .02
☐ 373 Andres Galarraga .30 .14 .04
☐ 374 Charlie Hayes .25 .11 .03
☐ 375 Nelson Liriano .15 .07 .02
☐ 376 David Nied .30 .14 .04
☐ 377 Walt Weiss .15 .07 .02
☐ 378 Bret Barberie .15 .07 .02
☐ 379 Jerry Browne .15 .07 .02
☐ 380 Chuck Carr .15 .07 .02
☐ 381 Greg Colbrunn .15 .07 .02
☐ 382 Charlie Hough .25 .11 .03
☐ 383 Kurt Miller .15 .07 .02
☐ 384 Benito Santiago .15 .07 .02
☐ 385 Jeff Bagwell 2.50 1.15 .30
☐ 386 Craig Biggio .25 .11 .03
☐ 387 Ken Caminiti .25 .11 .03
☐ 388 Doug Drabek .30 .14 .04
☐ 389 Steve Finley .15 .07 .02
☐ 390 John Hudek 1.25 .55 .16
☐ 391 Orlando Miller .25 .11 .03
☐ 392 Shane Reynolds .15 .07 .02
☐ 393 Brett Butler .25 .11 .03
☐ 394 Tom Candiotti .15 .07 .02
☐ 395 Delino DeShields .25 .11 .03
☐ 396 Kevin Gross .15 .07 .02
☐ 397 Eric Karros .25 .11 .03
☐ 398 Ramon Martinez .25 .11 .03
☐ 399 Henry Rodriguez .15 .07 .02
☐ 400 Moises Alou .30 .14 .04
☐ 401 Jeff Fassero .15 .07 .02
☐ 402 Mike Lansing .25 .11 .03
☐ 403 Mel Rojas .15 .07 .02
☐ 404 Larry Walker .30 .14 .04
☐ 405 John Wetteland .15 .07 .02
☐ 406 Gabe White .15 .07 .02
☐ 407 Bobby Bonilla .30 .14 .04
☐ 408 Josias Manzanillo .15 .07 .02
☐ 409 Bret Saberhagen .25 .11 .03
☐ 410 David Segui .15 .07 .02
☐ 411 Mariano Duncan .15 .07 .02
☐ 412 Tommy Greene .15 .07 .02
☐ 413 Billy Hatcher .15 .07 .02
☐ 414 Ricky Jordan .15 .07 .02
☐ 415 John Kruk .30 .14 .04
☐ 416 Bobby Munoz .15 .07 .02
☐ 417 Curt Schilling .15 .07 .02
☐ 418 Fernando Valenzuela .15 .07 .02
☐ 419 David West .15 .07 .02
☐ 420 Carlos Garcia .15 .07 .02
☐ 421 Brian Hunter .15 .07 .02
☐ 422 Jeff King .15 .07 .02
☐ 423 Jon Lieber .15 .07 .02
☐ 424 Ravelo Manzanillo .15 .07 .02
☐ 425 Denny Neagle .15 .07 .02
☐ 426 Andy Van Slyke .30 .14 .04
☐ 427 Bryan Eversgerd .15 .07 .02
☐ 428 Bernard Gilkey .15 .07 .02
☐ 429 Gregg Jefferies .30 .14 .04
☐ 430 Tom Pagnozzi .15 .07 .02
☐ 431 Bob Tewksbury .15 .07 .02
☐ 432 Allen Watson .15 .07 .02
☐ 433 Andy Ashby .15 .07 .02
☐ 434 Andy Benes .25 .11 .03
☐ 435 Donnie Elliott .15 .07 .02
☐ 436 Tony Gwynn 1.25 .55 .16
☐ 437 Joey Hamilton 1.00 .45 .13
☐ 438 Tim Hyers .35 .16 .04
☐ 439 Luis Lopez .15 .07 .02
☐ 440 Bip Roberts .15 .07 .02
☐ 441 Scott Sanders .15 .07 .02
☐ 442 Rod Beck .25 .11 .03
☐ 443 Dave Burba .15 .07 .02
☐ 444 Darryl Strawberry .25 .11 .03
☐ 445 Bill Swift .15 .07 .02
☐ 446 Robby Thompson .15 .07 .02
☐ 447 William VanLandingham 1.75 .80 .22
☐ 448 Matt Williams 1.00 .45 .13
☐ 449 Checklist 251-368 .15 .07 .02
☐ 450 Checklist 369-450/Inserts .15 .07 .02

1994 Flair Hot Glove

Randomly inserted in second series packs at a rate of one in 24, this set highlights 10

of the game's top players that also have outstanding defensive ability. The cards feature a special die-cut "glove" design with the player appearing within the glove. The back has a short write-up and a photo.

	MINT	EXC	G-VG
COMPLETE SET (10)	275.00	125.00	34.00
COMMON CARD (1-10)	12.00	5.50	1.50
☐ 1 Barry Bonds	30.00	13.50	3.80
☐ 2 Will Clark	12.00	5.50	1.50
☐ 3 Ken Griffey Jr.	85.00	38.00	10.50
☐ 4 Kenny Lofton	20.00	9.00	2.50
☐ 5 Greg Maddux	25.00	11.50	3.10
☐ 6 Don Mattingly	30.00	13.50	3.80
☐ 7 Kirby Puckett	30.00	13.50	3.80
☐ 8 Cal Ripken	65.00	29.00	8.25
☐ 9 Tim Salmon	12.00	5.50	1.50
☐ 10 Matt Williams	15.00	6.75	1.90

1994 Flair Hot Numbers

This 10-card set was randomly inserted in first series packs at a rate of one in 24. Metallic fronts feature a player photo with various numbers or statistics serving as background. The player's uniform number is part of the Hot Numbers logo at bottom left or right. The player's name is also at the bottom. The backs have a small photo centered in the middle surrounded by text highlighting achievements.

	MINT	EXC	G-VG
COMPLETE SET (10)	200.00	90.00	25.00
COMMON CARD (1-10)	8.00	3.60	1.00
☐ 1 Roberto Alomar	15.00	6.75	1.90
☐ 2 Carlos Baerga	10.00	4.50	1.25
☐ 3 Will Clark	10.00	4.50	1.25
☐ 4 Fred McGriff	10.00	4.50	1.25
☐ 5 Paul Molitor	10.00	4.50	1.25
☐ 6 John Olerud	8.00	3.60	1.00
☐ 7 Mike Piazza	30.00	13.50	3.80
☐ 8 Cal Ripken	40.00	18.00	5.00
☐ 9 Ryne Sandberg	20.00	9.00	2.50
☐ 10 Frank Thomas	60.00	27.00	7.50

1994 Flair Infield Power

Randomly inserted in second series packs at a rate of one in five, this 10-card standard-size set spotlights major league infielders who are power hitters. Card fronts feature a horizontal format with two photos of the player. The backs contain a short write-up with emphasis on power numbers. The back also has a small photo.

	MINT	EXC	G-VG
COMPLETE SET (10)	35.00	16.00	4.40
COMMON CARD (1-10)	1.00	.45	.13
☐ 1 Jeff Bagwell	8.00	3.60	1.00
☐ 2 Will Clark	2.25	1.00	.30
☐ 3 Darren Daulton	1.00	.45	.13
☐ 4 Don Mattingly	6.00	2.70	.75
☐ 5 Fred McGriff	2.25	1.00	.30
☐ 6 Rafael Palmeiro	1.00	.45	.13
☐ 7 Mike Piazza	8.00	3.60	1.00
☐ 8 Cal Ripken	12.00	5.50	1.50
☐ 9 Frank Thomas	15.00	6.75	1.90
☐ 10 Matt Williams	3.00	1.35	.40

1994 Flair Outfield Power

This 10-card set was randomly inserted in both first and second series packs at a rate of one in five. Two photos on the front feature the player fielding and hitting. The player's name and Outfield Power serve as a dividing point between the photos. The back contains a small photo and text.

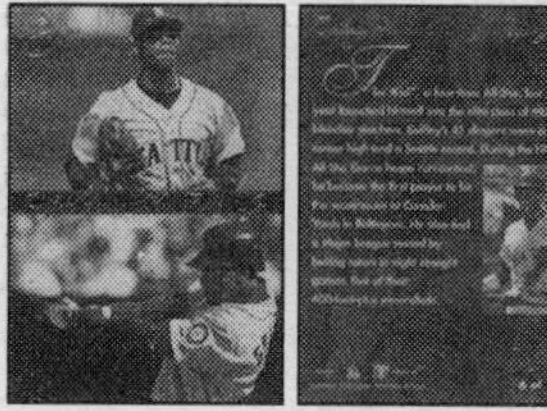

	MINT	EXC	G-VG
COMPLETE SET (10)	35.00	16.00	4.40
COMMON CARD (1-10)	1.00	.45	.13
☐ 1 Albert Belle	5.00	2.30	.60
☐ 2 Barry Bonds	6.00	2.70	.75
☐ 3 Joe Carter	2.25	1.00	.30
☐ 4 Lenny Dykstra	1.00	.45	.13
☐ 5 Juan Gonzalez	5.00	2.30	.60
☐ 6 Ken Griffey Jr.	15.00	6.75	1.90
☐ 7 David Justice	2.25	1.00	.30
☐ 8 Kirby Puckett	6.00	2.70	.75
☐ 9 Tim Salmon	2.25	1.00	.30
☐ 10 Dave Winfield	1.50	.65	.19

1994 Flair Wave of the Future I

This 10-card standard-size set takes a look at potential big league stars. Randomly inserted in first series packs at a rate of one in five, card fronts and backs have the player superimposed over a wavy colored background. The front has the Wave of the Future logo and a paragraph or two about the player along with a photo appears on the back.

	MINT	EXC	G-VG
COMPLETE SET (10)	35.00	16.00	4.40
COMMON CARD (1-10)	1.00	.45	.13
☐ 1 Kurt Abbott	1.00	.45	.13
☐ 2 Carlos Delgado	5.00	2.30	.60
☐ 3 Steve Karsay	1.00	.45	.13
☐ 4 Ryan Klesko	5.00	2.30	.60
☐ 5 Javy Lopez	3.00	1.35	.40
☐ 6 Raul Mondesi	10.00	4.50	1.25
☐ 7 James Mouton	1.00	.45	.13
☐ 8 Chan Ho Park	6.00	2.70	.75
☐ 9 Dave Staton	1.00	.45	.13
☐ 10 Rick White	1.00	.45	.13

1994 Flair Wave of the Future II

This 10-card standard-size set takes a look at potential big league stars. Randomly inserted in second series packs at a rate of one in five, card fronts and backs have the player superimposed over a wavy colored background. The front has the Wave of the Future logo and a paragraph about the player along with a photo on the back.

	MINT	EXC	G-VG
COMPLETE SET (10)	35.00	16.00	4.40
COMMON CARD (1-10)	1.00	.45	.13
☐ 1 Mark Acre	1.00	.45	.13
☐ 2 Chris Gomez	1.00	.45	.13
☐ 3 Joey Hamilton	5.00	2.30	.60
☐ 4 John Hudek	4.00	1.80	.50
☐ 5 Jon Lieber	1.00	.45	.13
☐ 6 Matt Mieske	1.00	.45	.13
☐ 7 Orlando Miller	2.00	.90	.25
☐ 8 Alex Rodriguez	20.00	9.00	2.50
☐ 9 Tony Tarasco	1.00	.45	.13
☐ 10 William VanLandingham	5.00	2.30	.60

1963 Fleer

The cards in this 66-card set measure 2 1/2" by 3 1/2". The Fleer set of current baseball players was marketed in 1963 in a gum card-style waxed wrapper package which contained a cherry cookie instead of gum. The cards were printed in sheets of 66 with the scarce card of Adcock apparently being replaced by the unnumbered checklist card for the final press run. The complete set price includes the checklist card. The catalog designation for this set is R418-4. The key Rookie Card in this set is Maury Wills. The set is basically arranged numerically in alphabetical order by teams which are also in alphabetical order.

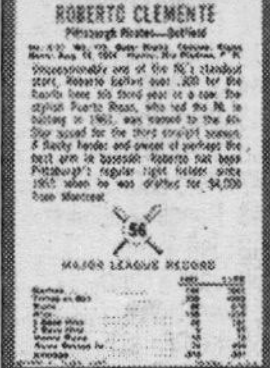

	NRMT	VG-E	GOOD
COMPLETE SET (67)	1800.00	800.00	230.00
COMMON CARD (1-66)	15.00	6.75	1.90
☐ 1 Steve Barber	25.00	7.50	2.50
☐ 2 Ron Hansen	15.00	6.75	1.90
☐ 3 Milt Pappas	20.00	9.00	2.50
☐ 4 Brooks Robinson	90.00	40.00	11.50
☐ 5 Willie Mays	200.00	90.00	25.00
☐ 6 Lou Clinton	15.00	6.75	1.90
☐ 7 Bill Monbouquette	15.00	6.75	1.90
☐ 8 Carl Yastrzemski	110.00	50.00	14.00
☐ 9 Ray Herbert	15.00	6.75	1.90
☐ 10 Jim Landis	15.00	6.75	1.90
☐ 11 Dick Donovan	15.00	6.75	1.90
☐ 12 Tito Francona	15.00	6.75	1.90
☐ 13 Jerry Kindall	15.00	6.75	1.90
☐ 14 Frank Lary	18.00	8.00	2.30
☐ 15 Dick Howser	18.00	8.00	2.30
☐ 16 Jerry Lumpe	15.00	6.75	1.90
☐ 17 Norm Siebern	15.00	6.75	1.90
☐ 18 Don Lee	15.00	6.75	1.90
☐ 19 Albie Pearson	18.00	8.00	2.30
☐ 20 Bob Rodgers	18.00	8.00	2.30
☐ 21 Leon Wagner	15.00	6.75	1.90
☐ 22 Jim Kaat	27.00	12.00	3.40
☐ 23 Vic Power	18.00	8.00	2.30
☐ 24 Rich Rollins	18.00	8.00	2.30
☐ 25 Bobby Richardson	30.00	13.50	3.80
☐ 26 Ralph Terry	18.00	8.00	2.30
☐ 27 Tom Cheney	15.00	6.75	1.90
☐ 28 Chuck Cottier	15.00	6.75	1.90
☐ 29 Jim Piersall	20.00	9.00	2.50
☐ 30 Dave Stenhouse	15.00	6.75	1.90
☐ 31 Glen Hobbie	15.00	6.75	1.90
☐ 32 Ron Santo	30.00	13.50	3.80
☐ 33 Gene Freese	15.00	6.75	1.90
☐ 34 Vada Pinson	20.00	9.00	2.50
☐ 35 Bob Purkey	15.00	6.75	1.90
☐ 36 Joe Amalfitano	15.00	6.75	1.90
☐ 37 Bob Aspromonte	15.00	6.75	1.90
☐ 38 Dick Farrell	15.00	6.75	1.90
☐ 39 Al Spangler	15.00	6.75	1.90
☐ 40 Tommy Davis	20.00	9.00	2.50
☐ 41 Don Drysdale	65.00	29.00	8.25
☐ 42 Sandy Koufax	200.00	90.00	25.00
☐ 43 Maury Wills	110.00	50.00	14.00
☐ 44 Frank Bolling	15.00	6.75	1.90
☐ 45 Warren Spahn	70.00	32.00	8.75
☐ 46 Joe Adcock SP	200.00	90.00	25.00
☐ 47 Roger Craig	18.00	8.00	2.30
☐ 48 Al Jackson	15.00	6.75	1.90
☐ 49 Rod Kanehl	15.00	6.75	1.90
☐ 50 Ruben Amaro	15.00	6.75	1.90
☐ 51 Johnny Callison	20.00	9.00	2.50
☐ 52 Clay Dalrymple	15.00	6.75	1.90
☐ 53 Don Demeter	15.00	6.75	1.90
☐ 54 Art Mahaffey	15.00	6.75	1.90
☐ 55 Smoky Burgess	20.00	9.00	2.50
☐ 56 Roberto Clemente	200.00	90.00	25.00
☐ 57 Roy Face	18.00	8.00	2.30
☐ 58 Vern Law	20.00	9.00	2.50
☐ 59 Bill Mazeroski	30.00	13.50	3.80
☐ 60 Ken Boyer	27.00	12.00	3.40
☐ 61 Bob Gibson	70.00	32.00	8.75
☐ 62 Gene Oliver	15.00	6.75	1.90
☐ 63 Bill White	25.00	11.50	3.10
☐ 64 Orlando Cepeda	35.00	16.00	4.40
☐ 65 Jim Davenport	15.00	6.75	1.90
☐ 66 Billy O'Dell	25.00	7.50	2.50
☐ NNO Checklist card	600.00	90.00	30.00

1981 Fleer

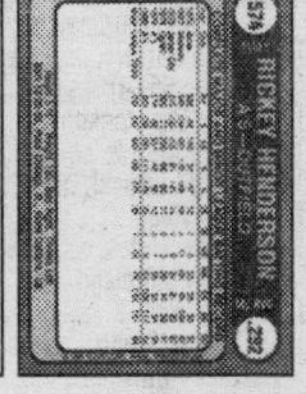

The cards in this 660-card set measure 2 1/2" by 3 1/2". This issue of cards marks Fleer's first entry into the current player baseball card market since 1963. Players from the same team are conveniently grouped together by number in the set. The teams are ordered (by 1980 standings) as follows: Philadelphia (1-27), Kansas City (28-50), Houston (51-78), New York Yankees (79-109), Los Angeles (110-141), Montreal (142-168), Baltimore (169-195), Cincinnati (196-220), Boston (221-241), Atlanta (242-267), California (268-290), Chicago Cubs (291-315), New York Mets (316-338), Chicago White Sox (339-350 and 352-359), Pittsburgh (360-386), Cleveland (387-408), Toronto (409-431), San Francisco (432-458), Detroit (459-483), San Diego (484-506), Milwaukee (507-527), St. Louis (528-550), Minnesota (551-571), Oakland (351 and 572-594), Seattle (595-616), and Texas (617-637). Cards 638-660 feature specials and checklists. The cards of pitchers in this set erroneously show a heading (on the card backs) of "Batting Record" over their career pitching statistics. There were three distinct printings: the two following the primary run were designed to correct numerous errors. The variations caused by these multiple printings are noted in the checklist below (P1, P2, or P3). The C. Nettles variation was corrected before the end of the first printing and thus is not included in the complete set consideration. The key Rookie Cards in this set are Danny Ainge, Harold Baines, Kirk Gibson, Jeff Reardon, and Fernando Valenzuela, whose first name was erroneously spelled Fernand on the card front.

	NRMT-MT	EXC	G-VG
COMPLETE SET (660)	45.00	20.00	5.75
COMMON CARD (1-660)	.10	.05	.01
☐ 1 Pete Rose UER (270 hits in '63, should be 170)	2.50	.80	.13
☐ 2 Larry Bowa	.15	.07	.02
☐ 3 Manny Trillo	.10	.05	.01
☐ 4 Bob Boone	.15	.07	.02
☐ 5 Mike Schmidt (See also 640A)	2.00	.90	.25
☐ 6A Steve Carlton P1 Pitcher of Year (See also 660A; Back "1066 Cardinals")	2.00	.90	.25
☐ 6B Steve Carlton P2 Pitcher of Year (Back "1066 Cardinals")	2.00	.90	.25
☐ 6C Steve Carlton P3 ("1966 Cardinals")	2.50	1.15	.30
☐ 7 Tug McGraw (See 657A)	.15	.07	.02
☐ 8 Larry Christenson	.10	.05	.01
☐ 9 Bake McBride	.10	.05	.01
☐ 10 Greg Luzinski	.15	.07	.02
☐ 11 Ron Reed	.10	.05	.01
☐ 12 Dickie Noles	.10	.05	.01
☐ 13 Keith Moreland	.15	.07	.02
☐ 14 Bob Walk	.30	.14	.04
☐ 15 Lonnie Smith	.10	.05	.01
☐ 16 Dick Ruthven	.10	.05	.01
☐ 17 Sparky Lyle	.15	.07	.02
☐ 18 Greg Gross	.10	.05	.01
☐ 19 Garry Maddox	.10	.05	.01
☐ 20 Nino Espinosa	.10	.05	.01
☐ 21 George Vukovich	.10	.05	.01
☐ 22 John Vukovich	.10	.05	.01
☐ 23 Ramon Aviles	.10	.05	.01
☐ 24A Ken Saucier P1 (Name on back "Ken")	.10	.05	.01
☐ 24B Ken Saucier P2 (Name on back "Ken")	.10	.05	.01
☐ 24C Kevin Saucier P3 (Name on back "Kevin")	.25	.11	.03
☐ 25 Randy Lerch	.10	.05	.01
☐ 26 Del Unser	.10	.05	.01
☐ 27 Tim McCarver	.20	.09	.03
☐ 28 George Brett (See also 655A)	4.00	1.80	.50
☐ 29 Willie Wilson (See also 653A)	.10	.05	.01
☐ 30 Paul Splittorff	.10	.05	.01
☐ 31 Dan Quisenberry	.20	.09	.03
☐ 32A Amos Otis P1 (Batting Pose; "Outfield"; 32 on back)	.15	.07	.02
☐ 32B Amos Otis P2 "Series Starter" (483 on back)	.15	.07	.02
☐ 33 Steve Busby	.10	.05	.01
☐ 34 U.L. Washington	.10	.05	.01
☐ 35 Dave Chalk	.10	.05	.01
☐ 36 Darrell Porter	.10	.05	.01
☐ 37 Marty Pattin	.10	.05	.01
☐ 38 Larry Gura	.10	.05	.01
☐ 39 Renie Martin	.10	.05	.01
☐ 40 Rich Gale	.10	.05	.01
☐ 41A Hal McRae P1 ("Royals" on front in black letters)	.50	.23	.06
☐ 41B Hal McRae P2 ("Royals" on front in blue letters)	.15	.07	.02
☐ 42 Dennis Leonard	.10	.05	.01
☐ 43 Willie Aikens	.10	.05	.01
☐ 44 Frank White	.15	.07	.02
☐ 45 Clint Hurdle	.10	.05	.01
☐ 46 John Wathan	.10	.05	.01
☐ 47 Pete LaCock	.10	.05	.01
☐ 48 Rance Mulliniks	.10	.05	.01
☐ 49 Jeff Twitty	.10	.05	.01
☐ 50 Jamie Quirk	.10	.05	.01
☐ 51 Art Howe	.15	.07	.02
☐ 52 Ken Forsch	.10	.05	.01
☐ 53 Vern Ruhle	.10	.05	.01
☐ 54 Joe Niekro	.15	.07	.02
☐ 55 Frank LaCorte	.10	.05	.01
☐ 56 J.R. Richard	.15	.07	.02
☐ 57 Nolan Ryan	8.00	3.60	1.00
☐ 58 Enos Cabell	.10	.05	.01
☐ 59 Cesar Cedeno	.15	.07	.02
☐ 60 Jose Cruz	.15	.07	.02
☐ 61 Bill Virdon MG	.10	.05	.01
☐ 62 Terry Puhl	.10	.05	.01
☐ 63 Joaquin Andujar	.15	.07	.02
☐ 64 Alan Ashby	.10	.05	.01
☐ 65 Joe Sambito	.10	.05	.01
☐ 66 Denny Walling	.10	.05	.01
☐ 67 Jeff Leonard	.15	.07	.02
☐ 68 Luis Pujols	.10	.05	.01
☐ 69 Bruce Bochy	.10	.05	.01
☐ 70 Rafael Landestoy	.10	.05	.01
☐ 71 Dave Smith	.10	.05	.01
☐ 72 Danny Heep	.10	.05	.01
☐ 73 Julio Gonzalez	.10	.05	.01
☐ 74 Craig Reynolds	.10	.05	.01
☐ 75 Gary Woods	.10	.05	.01
☐ 76 Dave Bergman	.10	.05	.01
☐ 77 Randy Niemann	.10	.05	.01
☐ 78 Joe Morgan	1.00	.45	.13
☐ 79 Reggie Jackson (See also 650A)	2.00	.90	.25
☐ 80 Bucky Dent	.15	.07	.02
☐ 81 Tommy John	.20	.09	.03
☐ 82 Luis Tiant	.15	.07	.02
☐ 83 Rick Cerone	.10	.05	.01
☐ 84 Dick Howser MG	.15	.07	.02
☐ 85 Lou Piniella	.15	.07	.02
☐ 86 Ron Davis	.10	.05	.01
☐ 87A Craig Nettles P1 ERR (Name on back misspelled "Craig")	10.00	4.50	1.25
☐ 87B Graig Nettles P2 COR ("Graig")	.25	.11	.03
☐ 88 Ron Guidry	.15	.07	.02
☐ 89 Rich Gossage	.20	.09	.03
☐ 90 Rudy May	.10	.05	.01
☐ 91 Gaylord Perry	.50	.23	.06
☐ 92 Eric Soderholm	.10	.05	.01
☐ 93 Bob Watson	.15	.07	.02
☐ 94 Bobby Murcer	.15	.07	.02
☐ 95 Bobby Brown	.10	.05	.01
☐ 96 Jim Spencer	.10	.05	.01
☐ 97 Tom Underwood	.10	.05	.01
☐ 98 Oscar Gamble	.10	.05	.01
☐ 99 Johnny Oates	.10	.05	.01
☐ 100 Fred Stanley	.10	.05	.01
☐ 101 Ruppert Jones	.10	.05	.01
☐ 102 Dennis Werth	.10	.05	.01
☐ 103 Joe Lefebvre	.10	.05	.01
☐ 104 Brian Doyle	.10	.05	.01
☐ 105 Aurelio Rodriguez	.10	.05	.01
☐ 106 Doug Bird	.10	.05	.01
☐ 107 Mike Griffin	.10	.05	.01
☐ 108 Tim Lollar	.10	.05	.01

☐ 109 Willie Randolph	.15	.07	.02
☐ 110 Steve Garvey	.75	.35	.09
☐ 111 Reggie Smith	.15	.07	.02
☐ 112 Don Sutton	.50	.23	.06
☐ 113 Burt Hooton	.10	.05	.01
☐ 114A Dave Lopes P1 (Small hand on back)	.50	.23	.06
☐ 114B Dave Lopes P2 (No hand)	.15	.07	.02
☐ 115 Dusty Baker	.20	.09	.03
☐ 116 Tom Lasorda MG	.15	.07	.02
☐ 117 Bill Russell	.15	.07	.02
☐ 118 Jerry Reuss UER ("Home:" omitted)	.15	.07	.02
☐ 119 Terry Forster	.10	.05	.01
☐ 120A Bob Welch P1 (Name on back is "Bob")	.25	.11	.03
☐ 120B Bob Welch P2 (Name on back is "Robert")	.40	.18	.05
☐ 121 Don Stanhouse	.10	.05	.01
☐ 122 Rick Monday	.15	.07	.02
☐ 123 Derrel Thomas	.10	.05	.01
☐ 124 Joe Ferguson	.10	.05	.01
☐ 125 Rick Sutcliffe	.30	.14	.04
☐ 126A Ron Cey P1 (Small hand on back)	.50	.23	.06
☐ 126B Ron Cey P2 (No hand)	.15	.07	.02
☐ 127 Dave Goltz	.10	.05	.01
☐ 128 Jay Johnstone	.15	.07	.02
☐ 129 Steve Yeager	.10	.05	.01
☐ 130 Gary Weiss	.10	.05	.01
☐ 131 Mike Scioscia	.50	.23	.06
☐ 132 Vic Davalillo	.10	.05	.01
☐ 133 Doug Rau	.10	.02	.00
☐ 134 Pepe Frias	.10	.05	.01
☐ 135 Mickey Hatcher	.10	.05	.01
☐ 136 Steve Howe	.15	.07	.02
☐ 137 Robert Castillo	.10	.05	.01
☐ 138 Gary Thomasson	.10	.05	.01
☐ 139 Rudy Law	.10	.05	.01
☐ 140 Fernando Valenzuela UER (Misspelled Fernand on card)	2.00	.90	.25
☐ 141 Manny Mota	.15	.07	.02
☐ 142 Gary Carter	.75	.35	.09
☐ 143 Steve Rogers	.10	.05	.01
☐ 144 Warren Cromartie	.10	.05	.01
☐ 145 Andre Dawson	1.50	.65	.19
☐ 146 Larry Parrish	.10	.05	.01
☐ 147 Rowland Office	.10	.05	.01
☐ 148 Ellis Valentine	.10	.05	.01
☐ 149 Dick Williams MG	.10	.05	.01
☐ 150 Bill Gullickson	.30	.14	.04
☐ 151 Elias Sosa	.10	.05	.01
☐ 152 John Tamargo	.10	.05	.01
☐ 153 Chris Speier	.10	.05	.01
☐ 154 Ron LeFlore	.15	.07	.02
☐ 155 Rodney Scott	.10	.05	.01
☐ 156 Stan Bahnsen	.10	.05	.01
☐ 157 Bill Lee	.10	.05	.01
☐ 158 Fred Norman	.10	.05	.01
☐ 159 Woodie Fryman	.10	.05	.01
☐ 160 David Palmer	.10	.05	.01
☐ 161 Jerry White	.10	.05	.01
☐ 162 Roberto Ramos	.10	.05	.01
☐ 163 John D'Acquisto	.10	.05	.01
☐ 164 Tommy Hutton	.10	.05	.01
☐ 165 Charlie Lea	.10	.05	.01
☐ 166 Scott Sanderson	.15	.07	.02
☐ 167 Ken Macha	.10	.05	.01
☐ 168 Tony Bernazard	.10	.05	.01
☐ 169 Jim Palmer	1.00	.45	.13
☐ 170 Steve Stone	.15	.07	.02
☐ 171 Mike Flanagan	.15	.07	.02
☐ 172 Al Bumbry	.15	.07	.02
☐ 173 Doug DeCinces	.15	.07	.02
☐ 174 Scott McGregor	.10	.05	.01
☐ 175 Mark Belanger	.15	.07	.02
☐ 176 Tim Stoddard	.10	.05	.01
☐ 177A Rick Dempsey P1 (Small hand on front)	.50	.23	.06
☐ 177B Rick Dempsey P2 (No hand)	.15	.07	.02
☐ 178 Earl Weaver MG	.15	.07	.02
☐ 179 Tippy Martinez	.15	.07	.02
☐ 180 Dennis Martinez	.15	.07	.02
☐ 181 Sammy Stewart	.10	.05	.01
☐ 182 Rich Dauer	.10	.05	.01
☐ 183 Lee May	.15	.07	.02
☐ 184 Eddie Murray	3.00	1.35	.40
☐ 185 Benny Ayala	.10	.05	.01
☐ 186 John Lowenstein	.10	.05	.01
☐ 187 Gary Roenicke	.10	.05	.01
☐ 188 Ken Singleton	.15	.07	.02
☐ 189 Dan Graham	.10	.05	.01
☐ 190 Terry Crowley	.10	.05	.01
☐ 191 Kiko Garcia	.10	.05	.01
☐ 192 Dave Ford	.10	.05	.01
☐ 193 Mark Corey	.10	.05	.01
☐ 194 Lenn Sakata	.10	.05	.01
☐ 195 Doug DeCinces	.15	.07	.02
☐ 196 Johnny Bench	1.50	.65	.19
☐ 197 Dave Concepcion	.15	.07	.02
☐ 198 Ray Knight	.15	.07	.02
☐ 199 Ken Griffey	.10	.05	.01
☐ 200 Tom Seaver	1.25	.55	.16
☐ 201 Dave Collins	.10	.05	.01
☐ 202A George Foster P1 Slugger (Number on back 216)	.15	.07	.02
☐ 202B George Foster P2 Slugger (Number on back 202)	.15	.07	.02
☐ 203 Junior Kennedy	.10	.05	.01
☐ 204 Frank Pastore	.10	.05	.01
☐ 205 Dan Driessen	.10	.05	.01
☐ 206 Hector Cruz	.10	.05	.01
☐ 207 Paul Moskau	.10	.05	.01
☐ 208 Charlie Leibrandt	.30	.14	.04
☐ 209 Harry Spilman	.10	.05	.01
☐ 210 Joe Price	.10	.05	.01
☐ 211 Tom Hume	.10	.05	.01
☐ 212 Joe Nolan	.10	.05	.01
☐ 213 Doug Bair	.10	.05	.01
☐ 214 Mario Soto	.10	.05	.01
☐ 215A Bill Bonham P1 (Small hand on back)	.50	.23	.06
☐ 215B Bill Bonham P2 (No hand)	.10	.05	.01
☐ 216 George Foster (See 202)	.15	.07	.02
☐ 217 Paul Householder	.10	.05	.01
☐ 218 Ron Oester	.10	.05	.01
☐ 219 Sam Mejias	.10	.05	.01
☐ 220 Sheldon Burnside	.10	.05	.01
☐ 221 Carl Yastrzemski	1.50	.65	.19
☐ 222 Jim Rice	.30	.14	.04
☐ 223 Fred Lynn	.15	.07	.02
☐ 224 Carlton Fisk	1.50	.65	.19
☐ 225 Rick Burleson	.10	.05	.01
☐ 226 Dennis Eckersley	1.00	.45	.13
☐ 227 Butch Hobson	.15	.07	.02
☐ 228 Tom Burgmeier	.10	.05	.01

	No.	Player			
☐	229	Garry Hancock	.10	.05	.01
☐	230	Don Zimmer MG	.10	.05	.01
☐	231	Steve Renko	.10	.05	.01
☐	232	Dwight Evans	.20	.09	.03
☐	233	Mike Torrez	.10	.05	.01
☐	234	Bob Stanley	.10	.05	.01
☐	235	Jim Dwyer	.10	.05	.01
☐	236	Dave Stapleton	.10	.05	.01
☐	237	Glenn Hoffman	.10	.05	.01
☐	238	Jerry Remy	.10	.05	.01
☐	239	Dick Drago	.10	.05	.01
☐	240	Bill Campbell	.10	.05	.01
☐	241	Tony Perez	.40	.18	.05
☐	242	Phil Niekro	.50	.23	.06
☐	243	Dale Murphy	1.00	.45	.13
☐	244	Bob Horner	.15	.07	.02
☐	245	Jeff Burroughs	.10	.05	.01
☐	246	Rick Camp	.10	.05	.01
☐	247	Bobby Cox MG	.10	.05	.01
☐	248	Bruce Benedict	.10	.05	.01
☐	249	Gene Garber	.10	.05	.01
☐	250	Jerry Royster	.10	.05	.01
☐	251A	Gary Matthews P1 (Small hand on back)	.50	.23	.06
☐	251B	Gary Matthews P2 (No hand)	.15	.07	.02
☐	252	Chris Chambliss	.15	.07	.02
☐	253	Luis Gomez	.10	.05	.01
☐	254	Bill Nahorodny	.10	.05	.01
☐	255	Doyle Alexander	.10	.05	.01
☐	256	Brian Asselstine	.10	.05	.01
☐	257	Biff Pocoroba	.10	.05	.01
☐	258	Mike Lum	.10	.05	.01
☐	259	Charlie Spikes	.10	.05	.01
☐	260	Glenn Hubbard	.10	.05	.01
☐	261	Tommy Boggs	.10	.05	.01
☐	262	Al Hrabosky	.10	.05	.01
☐	263	Rick Matula	.10	.05	.01
☐	264	Preston Hanna	.10	.05	.01
☐	265	Larry Bradford	.10	.05	.01
☐	266	Rafael Ramirez	.15	.07	.02
☐	267	Larry McWilliams	.10	.05	.01
☐	268	Rod Carew	1.00	.45	.13
☐	269	Bobby Grich	.15	.07	.02
☐	270	Carney Lansford	.15	.07	.02
☐	271	Don Baylor	.20	.09	.03
☐	272	Joe Rudi	.15	.07	.02
☐	273	Dan Ford	.10	.05	.01
☐	274	Jim Fregosi MG	.10	.05	.01
☐	275	Dave Frost	.10	.05	.01
☐	276	Frank Tanana	.15	.07	.02
☐	277	Dickie Thon	.15	.07	.02
☐	278	Jason Thompson	.10	.05	.01
☐	279	Rick Miller	.10	.05	.01
☐	280	Bert Campaneris	.15	.07	.02
☐	281	Tom Donohue	.10	.05	.01
☐	282	Brian Downing	.15	.07	.02
☐	283	Fred Patek	.10	.05	.01
☐	284	Bruce Kison	.10	.05	.01
☐	285	Dave LaRoche	.10	.05	.01
☐	286	Don Aase	.10	.05	.01
☐	287	Jim Barr	.10	.05	.01
☐	288	Alfredo Martinez	.10	.05	.01
☐	289	Larry Harlow	.10	.05	.01
☐	290	Andy Hassler	.10	.05	.01
☐	291	Dave Kingman	.15	.07	.02
☐	292	Bill Buckner	.15	.07	.02
☐	293	Rick Reuschel	.15	.07	.02
☐	294	Bruce Sutter	.15	.07	.02
☐	295	Jerry Martin	.10	.05	.01
☐	296	Scot Thompson	.10	.05	.01
☐	297	Ivan DeJesus	.10	.05	.01
☐	298	Steve Dillard	.10	.05	.01

	No.	Player			
☐	299	Dick Tidrow	.10	.05	.01
☐	300	Randy Martz	.10	.05	.01
☐	301	Lenny Randle	.10	.05	.01
☐	302	Lynn McGlothen	.10	.05	.01
☐	303	Cliff Johnson	.10	.05	.01
☐	304	Tim Blackwell	.10	.05	.01
☐	305	Dennis Lamp	.10	.05	.01
☐	306	Bill Caudill	.10	.05	.01
☐	307	Carlos Lezcano	.10	.05	.01
☐	308	Jim Tracy	.10	.05	.01
☐	309	Doug Capilla UER (Cubs on front but Braves on back)	.10	.05	.01
☐	310	Willie Hernandez	.15	.07	.02
☐	311	Mike Vail	.10	.05	.01
☐	312	Mike Krukow	.10	.05	.01
☐	313	Barry Foote	.10	.05	.01
☐	314	Larry Biittner	.10	.05	.01
☐	315	Mike Tyson	.10	.05	.01
☐	316	Lee Mazzilli	.10	.05	.01
☐	317	John Stearns	.10	.05	.01
☐	318	Alex Trevino	.10	.05	.01
☐	319	Craig Swan	.10	.05	.01
☐	320	Frank Taveras	.10	.05	.01
☐	321	Steve Henderson	.10	.05	.01
☐	322	Neil Allen	.10	.05	.01
☐	323	Mark Bomback	.10	.05	.01
☐	324	Mike Jorgensen	.10	.05	.01
☐	325	Joe Torre MG	.15	.07	.02
☐	326	Elliott Maddox	.10	.05	.01
☐	327	Pete Falcone	.10	.05	.01
☐	328	Ray Burris	.10	.05	.01
☐	329	Claudell Washington	.10	.05	.01
☐	330	Doug Flynn	.10	.05	.01
☐	331	Joel Youngblood	.10	.05	.01
☐	332	Bill Almon	.10	.05	.01
☐	333	Tom Hausman	.10	.05	.01
☐	334	Pat Zachry	.10	.05	.01
☐	335	Jeff Reardon	2.00	.90	.25
☐	336	Wally Backman	.15	.07	.02
☐	337	Dan Norman	.10	.05	.01
☐	338	Jerry Morales	.10	.05	.01
☐	339	Ed Farmer	.10	.05	.01
☐	340	Bob Molinaro	.10	.05	.01
☐	341	Todd Cruz	.10	.05	.01
☐	342A	Britt Burns P1 (Small hand on front)	.50	.23	.06
☐	342B	Britt Burns P2 (No hand)	.15	.07	.02
☐	343	Kevin Bell	.10	.05	.01
☐	344	Tony LaRussa MG	.15	.07	.02
☐	345	Steve Trout	.10	.05	.01
☐	346	Harold Baines	3.50	1.55	.45
☐	347	Richard Wortham	.10	.05	.01
☐	348	Wayne Nordhagen	.10	.05	.01
☐	349	Mike Squires	.10	.05	.01
☐	350	Lamar Johnson	.10	.05	.01
☐	351	Rickey Henderson (Most Stolen Bases AL)	5.00	2.30	.60
☐	352	Francisco Barrios	.10	.05	.01
☐	353	Thad Bosley	.10	.05	.01
☐	354	Chet Lemon	.10	.05	.01
☐	355	Bruce Kimm	.10	.05	.01
☐	356	Richard Dotson	.15	.07	.02
☐	357	Jim Morrison	.10	.05	.01
☐	358	Mike Proly	.10	.05	.01
☐	359	Greg Pryor	.10	.05	.01
☐	360	Dave Parker	.20	.09	.03
☐	361	Omar Moreno	.10	.05	.01
☐	362A	Kent Tekulve P1 (Back "1071 Waterbury" and "1078 Pirates")	.15	.07	.02
☐	362B	Kent Tekulve P2	.15	.07	.02

("1971 Waterbury" and "1978 Pirates")

☐ 363 Willie Stargell	1.00	.45	.13
☐ 364 Phil Garner	.15	.07	.02
☐ 365 Ed Ott	.10	.05	.01
☐ 366 Don Robinson	.10	.05	.01
☐ 367 Chuck Tanner MG	.10	.05	.01
☐ 368 Jim Rooker	.10	.05	.01
☐ 369 Dale Berra	.10	.05	.01
☐ 370 Jim Bibby	.10	.05	.01
☐ 371 Steve Nicosia	.10	.05	.01
☐ 372 Mike Easler	.10	.05	.01
☐ 373 Bill Robinson	.15	.07	.02
☐ 374 Lee Lacy	.10	.05	.01
☐ 375 John Candelaria	.15	.07	.02
☐ 376 Manny Sanguillen	.15	.07	.02
☐ 377 Rick Rhoden	.10	.05	.01
☐ 378 Grant Jackson	.10	.05	.01
☐ 379 Tim Foli	.10	.05	.01
☐ 380 Rod Scurry	.10	.05	.01
☐ 381 Bill Madlock	.15	.07	.02
☐ 382A Kurt Bevacqua P1 ERR (P on cap backwards)	.25	.11	.03
☐ 382B Kurt Bevacqua P2 COR	.10	.05	.01
☐ 383 Bert Blyleven	.20	.09	.03
☐ 384 Eddie Solomon	.10	.05	.01
☐ 385 Enrique Romo	.10	.05	.01
☐ 386 John Milner	.10	.05	.01
☐ 387 Mike Hargrove	.15	.07	.02
☐ 388 Jorge Orta	.10	.05	.01
☐ 389 Toby Harrah	.15	.07	.02
☐ 390 Tom Veryzer	.10	.05	.01
☐ 391 Miguel Dilone	.10	.05	.01
☐ 392 Dan Spillner	.10	.05	.01
☐ 393 Jack Brohamer	.10	.05	.01
☐ 394 Wayne Garland	.10	.05	.01
☐ 395 Sid Monge	.10	.05	.01
☐ 396 Rick Waits	.10	.05	.01
☐ 397 Joe Charboneau	.40	.18	.05
☐ 398 Gary Alexander	.10	.05	.01
☐ 399 Jerry Dybzinski	.10	.05	.01
☐ 400 Mike Stanton	.10	.05	.01
☐ 401 Mike Paxton	.10	.05	.01
☐ 402 Gary Gray	.10	.05	.01
☐ 403 Rick Manning	.10	.05	.01
☐ 404 Bo Diaz	.10	.05	.01
☐ 405 Ron Hassey	.10	.05	.01
☐ 406 Ross Grimsley	.10	.05	.01
☐ 407 Victor Cruz	.10	.05	.01
☐ 408 Len Barker	.10	.05	.01
☐ 409 Bob Bailor	.10	.05	.01
☐ 410 Otto Velez	.10	.05	.01
☐ 411 Ernie Whitt	.10	.05	.01
☐ 412 Jim Clancy	.10	.05	.01
☐ 413 Barry Bonnell	.10	.05	.01
☐ 414 Dave Stieb	.15	.07	.02
☐ 415 Damaso Garcia	.15	.07	.02
☐ 416 John Mayberry	.10	.05	.01
☐ 417 Roy Howell	.10	.05	.01
☐ 418 Danny Ainge	5.00	2.30	.60
☐ 419A Jesse Jefferson P1 (Back says Pirates)	.10	.05	.01
☐ 419B Jesse Jefferson P2 (Back says Pirates)	.10	.05	.01
☐ 419C Jesse Jefferson P3 (Back says Blue Jays)	.25	.11	.03
☐ 420 Joey McLaughlin	.10	.05	.01
☐ 421 Lloyd Moseby	.15	.07	.02
☐ 422 Alvis Woods	.10	.05	.01
☐ 423 Garth Iorg	.10	.05	.01
☐ 424 Doug Ault	.10	.05	.01
☐ 425 Ken Schrom	.10	.05	.01
☐ 426 Mike Willis	.10	.05	.01
☐ 427 Steve Braun	.10	.05	.01
☐ 428 Bob Davis	.10	.05	.01
☐ 429 Jerry Garvin	.10	.05	.01
☐ 430 Alfredo Griffin	.10	.05	.01
☐ 431 Bob Mattick MG	.10	.05	.01
☐ 432 Vida Blue	.15	.07	.02
☐ 433 Jack Clark	.15	.07	.02
☐ 434 Willie McCovey	1.00	.45	.13
☐ 435 Mike Ivie	.10	.05	.01
☐ 436A Darrel Evans P1 ERR (Name on front "Darrel")	.25	.11	.03
☐ 436B Darrell Evans P2 COR (Name on front "Darrell")	.15	.07	.02
☐ 437 Terry Whitfield	.10	.05	.01
☐ 438 Rennie Stennett	.10	.05	.01
☐ 439 John Montefusco	.10	.05	.01
☐ 440 Jim Wohlford	.10	.05	.01
☐ 441 Bill North	.10	.05	.01
☐ 442 Milt May	.10	.05	.01
☐ 443 Max Venable	.10	.05	.01
☐ 444 Ed Whitson	.10	.05	.01
☐ 445 Al Holland	.10	.05	.01
☐ 446 Randy Moffitt	.10	.05	.01
☐ 447 Bob Knepper	.10	.05	.01
☐ 448 Gary Lavelle	.10	.05	.01
☐ 449 Greg Minton	.10	.05	.01
☐ 450 Johnnie LeMaster	.10	.05	.01
☐ 451 Larry Herndon	.10	.05	.01
☐ 452 Rich Murray	.10	.05	.01
☐ 453 Joe Pettini	.10	.05	.01
☐ 454 Allen Ripley	.10	.05	.01
☐ 455 Dennis Littlejohn	.10	.05	.01
☐ 456 Tom Griffin	.10	.05	.01
☐ 457 Alan Hargesheimer	.10	.05	.01
☐ 458 Joe Strain	.10	.05	.01
☐ 459 Steve Kemp	.10	.05	.01
☐ 460 Sparky Anderson MG	.15	.07	.02
☐ 461 Alan Trammell	1.75	.80	.22
☐ 462 Mark Fidrych	.15	.07	.02
☐ 463 Lou Whitaker	1.00	.45	.13
☐ 464 Dave Rozema	.10	.05	.01
☐ 465 Milt Wilcox	.10	.05	.01
☐ 466 Champ Summers	.10	.05	.01
☐ 467 Lance Parrish	.20	.09	.03
☐ 468 Dan Petry	.15	.07	.02
☐ 469 Pat Underwood	.10	.05	.01
☐ 470 Rick Peters	.10	.05	.01
☐ 471 Al Cowens	.10	.05	.01
☐ 472 John Wockenfuss	.10	.05	.01
☐ 473 Tom Brookens	.10	.05	.01
☐ 474 Richie Hebner	.10	.05	.01
☐ 475 Jack Morris	.50	.23	.06
☐ 476 Jim Lentine	.10	.05	.01
☐ 477 Bruce Robbins	.10	.05	.01
☐ 478 Mark Wagner	.10	.05	.01
☐ 479 Tim Corcoran	.10	.05	.01
☐ 480A Stan Papi P1 (Front as Pitcher)	.15	.07	.02
☐ 480B Stan Papi P2 (Front as Shortstop)	.10	.05	.01
☐ 481 Kirk Gibson	3.50	1.55	.45
☐ 482 Dan Schatzeder	.10	.05	.01
☐ 483A Amos Otis P1 (See card 32)	.15	.07	.02
☐ 483B Amos Otis P2 (See card 32)	.15	.07	.02
☐ 484 Dave Winfield	2.50	1.15	.30
☐ 485 Rollie Fingers	.50	.23	.06
☐ 486 Gene Richards	.10	.05	.01

☐	487 Randy Jones	.10	.05	.01
☐	488 Ozzie Smith	3.50	1.55	.45
☐	489 Gene Tenace	.10	.05	.01
☐	490 Bill Fahey	.10	.05	.01
☐	491 John Curtis	.10	.05	.01
☐	492 Dave Cash	.10	.05	.01
☐	493A Tim Flannery P1 (Batting right)	.15	.07	.02
☐	493B Tim Flannery P2 (Batting left)	.10	.05	.01
☐	494 Jerry Mumphrey	.10	.05	.01
☐	495 Bob Shirley	.10	.05	.01
☐	496 Steve Mura	.10	.05	.01
☐	497 Eric Rasmussen	.10	.05	.01
☐	498 Broderick Perkins	.10	.05	.01
☐	499 Barry Evans	.10	.05	.01
☐	500 Chuck Baker	.10	.05	.01
☐	501 Luis Salazar	.10	.05	.01
☐	502 Gary Lucas	.10	.05	.01
☐	503 Mike Armstrong	.10	.05	.01
☐	504 Jerry Turner	.10	.05	.01
☐	505 Dennis Kinney	.10	.05	.01
☐	506 Willie Montanez UER (Misspelled Willy on card front)	.10	.05	.01
☐	507 Gorman Thomas	.15	.07	.02
☐	508 Ben Oglivie	.15	.07	.02
☐	509 Larry Hisle	.10	.05	.01
☐	510 Sal Bando	.15	.07	.02
☐	511 Robin Yount	3.00	1.35	.40
☐	512 Mike Caldwell	.10	.05	.01
☐	513 Sixto Lezcano	.10	.05	.01
☐	514A Bill Travers P1 ERR ("Jerry Augustine" with Augustine back)	.15	.07	.02
☐	514B Bill Travers P2 COR	.10	.05	.01
☐	515 Paul Molitor	3.00	1.35	.40
☐	516 Moose Haas	.10	.05	.01
☐	517 Bill Castro	.10	.05	.01
☐	518 Jim Slaton	.10	.05	.01
☐	519 Lary Sorensen	.10	.05	.01
☐	520 Bob McClure	.10	.05	.01
☐	521 Charlie Moore	.10	.05	.01
☐	522 Jim Gantner	.15	.07	.02
☐	523 Reggie Cleveland	.10	.05	.01
☐	524 Don Money	.10	.05	.01
☐	525 Bill Travers	.10	.05	.01
☐	526 Buck Martinez	.10	.05	.01
☐	527 Dick Davis	.10	.05	.01
☐	528 Ted Simmons	.15	.07	.02
☐	529 Garry Templeton	.15	.07	.02
☐	530 Ken Reitz	.10	.05	.01
☐	531 Tony Scott	.10	.05	.01
☐	532 Ken Oberkfell	.10	.05	.01
☐	533 Bob Sykes	.10	.05	.01
☐	534 Keith Smith	.10	.05	.01
☐	535 John Littlefield	.10	.05	.01
☐	536 Jim Kaat	.15	.07	.02
☐	537 Bob Forsch	.10	.05	.01
☐	538 Mike Phillips	.10	.05	.01
☐	539 Terry Landrum	.10	.05	.01
☐	540 Leon Durham	.15	.07	.02
☐	541 Terry Kennedy	.10	.05	.01
☐	542 George Hendrick	.15	.07	.02
☐	543 Dane Iorg	.10	.05	.01
☐	544 Mark Littell	.10	.05	.01
☐	545 Keith Hernandez	.20	.09	.03
☐	546 Silvio Martinez	.10	.05	.01
☐	547A Don Hood P1 ERR ("Pete Vuckovich" with Vuckovich back)	.15	.07	.02
☐	547B Don Hood P2 COR	.10	.05	.01
☐	548 Bobby Bonds	.15	.07	.02
☐	549 Mike Ramsey	.10	.05	.01
☐	550 Tom Herr	.15	.07	.02
☐	551 Roy Smalley	.10	.05	.01
☐	552 Jerry Koosman	.15	.07	.02
☐	553 Ken Landreaux	.10	.05	.01
☐	554 John Castino	.10	.05	.01
☐	555 Doug Corbett	.10	.05	.01
☐	556 Bombo Rivera	.10	.05	.01
☐	557 Ron Jackson	.10	.05	.01
☐	558 Butch Wynegar	.10	.05	.01
☐	559 Hosken Powell	.10	.05	.01
☐	560 Pete Redfern	.10	.05	.01
☐	561 Roger Erickson	.10	.05	.01
☐	562 Glenn Adams	.10	.05	.01
☐	563 Rick Sofield	.10	.05	.01
☐	564 Geoff Zahn	.10	.05	.01
☐	565 Pete Mackanin	.10	.05	.01
☐	566 Mike Cubbage	.10	.05	.01
☐	567 Darrell Jackson	.10	.05	.01
☐	568 Dave Edwards	.10	.05	.01
☐	569 Rob Wilfong	.10	.05	.01
☐	570 Sal Butera	.10	.05	.01
☐	571 Jose Morales	.10	.05	.01
☐	572 Rick Langford	.10	.05	.01
☐	573 Mike Norris	.10	.05	.01
☐	574 Rickey Henderson	8.00	3.60	1.00
☐	575 Tony Armas	.15	.07	.02
☐	576 Dave Revering	.10	.05	.01
☐	577 Jeff Newman	.10	.05	.01
☐	578 Bob Lacey	.10	.05	.01
☐	579 Brian Kingman	.10	.05	.01
☐	580 Mitchell Page	.10	.05	.01
☐	581 Billy Martin MG	.25	.11	.03
☐	582 Rob Picciolo	.10	.05	.01
☐	583 Mike Heath	.10	.05	.01
☐	584 Mickey Klutts	.10	.05	.01
☐	585 Orlando Gonzalez	.10	.05	.01
☐	586 Mike Davis	.10	.05	.01
☐	587 Wayne Gross	.10	.05	.01
☐	588 Matt Keough	.10	.05	.01
☐	589 Steve McCatty	.10	.05	.01
☐	590 Dwayne Murphy	.10	.05	.01
☐	591 Mario Guerrero	.10	.05	.01
☐	592 Dave McKay	.10	.05	.01
☐	593 Jim Essian	.10	.05	.01
☐	594 Dave Heaverlo	.10	.05	.01
☐	595 Maury Wills MG	.15	.07	.02
☐	596 Juan Beniquez	.10	.05	.01
☐	597 Rodney Craig	.10	.05	.01
☐	598 Jim Anderson	.10	.05	.01
☐	599 Floyd Bannister	.10	.05	.01
☐	600 Bruce Bochte	.10	.05	.01
☐	601 Julio Cruz	.10	.05	.01
☐	602 Ted Cox	.10	.05	.01
☐	603 Dan Meyer	.10	.05	.01
☐	604 Larry Cox	.10	.05	.01
☐	605 Bill Stein	.10	.05	.01
☐	606 Steve Garvey (Most Hits NL)	.50	.23	.06
☐	607 Dave Roberts	.10	.05	.01
☐	608 Leon Roberts	.10	.05	.01
☐	609 Reggie Walton	.10	.05	.01
☐	610 Dave Edler	.10	.05	.01
☐	611 Larry Milbourne	.10	.05	.01
☐	612 Kim Allen	.10	.05	.01
☐	613 Mario Mendoza	.10	.05	.01
☐	614 Tom Paciorek	.15	.07	.02
☐	615 Glenn Abbott	.10	.05	.01
☐	616 Joe Simpson	.10	.05	.01
☐	617 Mickey Rivers	.15	.07	.02
☐	618 Jim Kern	.10	.05	.01
☐	619 Jim Sundberg	.15	.07	.02
☐	620 Richie Zisk	.10	.05	.01

☐ 621 Jon Matlack .... .10 .05 .01
☐ 622 Ferguson Jenkins .... .50 .23 .06
☐ 623 Pat Corrales MG .... .10 .05 .01
☐ 624 Ed Figueroa .... .10 .05 .01
☐ 625 Buddy Bell .... .15 .07 .02
☐ 626 Al Oliver .... .15 .07 .02
☐ 627 Doc Medich .... .10 .05 .01
☐ 628 Bump Wills .... .10 .05 .01
☐ 629 Rusty Staub .... .15 .07 .02
☐ 630 Pat Putnam .... .10 .05 .01
☐ 631 John Grubb .... .10 .05 .01
☐ 632 Danny Darwin .... .15 .07 .02
☐ 633 Ken Clay .... .10 .05 .01
☐ 634 Jim Norris .... .10 .05 .01
☐ 635 John Butcher .... .10 .05 .01
☐ 636 Dave Roberts .... .10 .05 .01
☐ 637 Billy Sample .... .10 .05 .01
☐ 638 Carl Yastrzemski .... 1.50 .65 .19
☐ 639 Cecil Cooper .... .15 .07 .02
☐ 640A Mike Schmidt P1 ..... 2.00 .90 .25
(Portrait;
"Third Base";
number on back 5)
☐ 640B Mike Schmidt P2 ..... 2.00 .90 .25
("1980 Home Run King";
640 on back)
☐ 641A CL: Phils/Royals P1 ... .15 .05 .01
41 is Hal McRae
☐ 641B CL: Phils/Royals P2 ... .15 .05 .01
(41 is Hal McRae,
Double Threat)
☐ 642 CL: Astros/Yankees ...... .15 .05 .01
☐ 643 CL: Expos/Dodgers ...... .15 .05 .01
☐ 644A CL: Reds/Orioles P1 .. .15 .05 .01
(202 is George Foster;
Joe Nolan pitcher,
should be catcher)
☐ 644B CL: Reds/Orioles P2 .. .15 .05 .01
(202 is Foster Slugger;
Joe Nolan pitcher,
should be catcher)
☐ 645A Rose/Bowa/Schmidt 2.50 1.15 .30
Triple Threat P1
(No number on back)
☐ 645B Rose/Bowa/Schmidt 2.00 .90 .25
Triple Threat P2
(Back numbered 645)
☐ 646 CL: Braves/Red Sox ..... .15 .05 .01
☐ 647 CL: Cubs/Angels .... .15 .05 .01
☐ 648 CL: Mets/White Sox ..... .15 .05 .01
☐ 649 CL: Indians/Pirates .... .15 .05 .01
☐ 650A Reggie Jackson .... 2.00 .90 .25
Mr. Baseball P1
(Number on back 79)
☐ 650B Reggie Jackson .... 2.00 .90 .25
Mr. Baseball P2
(Number on back 650)
☐ 651 CL: Giants/Blue Jays .... .15 .05 .01
☐ 652A CL: Tigers/Padres P1 . .15 .05 .01
(483 is listed)
☐ 652B CL: Tigers/Padres P2 . .15 .05 .01
(483 is deleted)
☐ 653A Willie Wilson P1 .... .15 .07 .02
Most Hits Most Runs
(Number on back 29)
☐ 653B Willie Wilson P2 .... .15 .07 .02
Most Hits Most Runs
(Number on back 653)
☐ 654A CL:Brewers/Cards P1. .15 .05 .01
(514 Jerry Augustine;
547 Pete Vuckovich)
☐ 654B CL:Brewers/Cards P2. .15 .05 .01
(514 Billy Travers;
547 Don Hood)
☐ 655A George Brett P1 .... 4.00 1.80 .50
.390 Average
(Number on back 28)
☐ 655B George Brett P2 .... 4.00 1.80 .50
.390 Average
(Number on back 655)
☐ 656 CL: Twins/Oakland A's. .15 .05 .01
☐ 657A Tug McGraw P1 .... .15 .07 .02
Game Saver
(Number on back 7)
☐ 657B Tug McGraw P2 .... .15 .07 .02
Game Saver
(Number on back 657)
☐ 658 CL: Rangers/Mariners .. .15 .05 .01
☐ 659A Checklist P1 .... .15 .05 .01
of Special Cards
(Last lines on front,
Wilson Most Hits)
☐ 659B Checklist P2 .... .15 .05 .01
of Special Cards
(Last lines on front,
Otis Series Starter)
☐ 660A Steve Carlton P1 ...... 2.00 .90 .25
Golden Arm
(Back "1066 Cardinals";
Number on back 6)
☐ 660B Steve Carlton P2 ...... 2.00 .90 .25
Golden Arm
(Number on back 660;
Back "1066 Cardinals")
☐ 660C Steve Carlton P3 ...... 2.50 1.15 .30
Golden Arm
("1966 Cardinals")

1982 Fleer

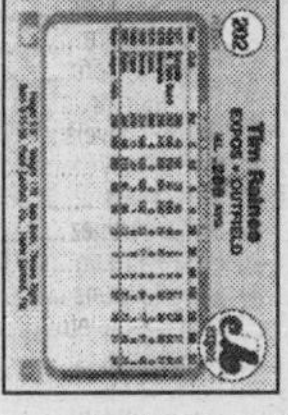

The cards in this 660-card set measure 2 1/2" by 3 1/2". The 1982 Fleer set is again ordered by teams; in fact, the players within each team are listed in alphabetical order. The teams are ordered (by 1981 standings) as follows: Los Angeles (1-29), New York Yankees (30-56), Cincinnati (57-84), Oakland (85-109), St. Louis (110-132), Milwaukee (133-156), Baltimore (157-182), Montreal (183-211), Houston (212-237), Philadelphia (238-262), Detroit (263-286), Boston (287-312), Texas (313-334), Chicago White Sox (335-358), Cleveland (359-382), San Francisco (383-403), Kansas City (404-427), Atlanta (428-449), California (450-474), Pittsburgh (475-501), Seattle (502-519), New York Mets (520-544), Minnesota (545-565), San Diego

(566-585), Chicago Cubs (586-607), and Toronto (608-627). Cards numbered 628 through 646 are special cards highlighting some of the stars and leaders of the 1981 season. The last 14 cards in the set (647-660) are checklist cards. The backs feature player statistics and a full-color team logo in the upper right-hand corner of each card. The complete set price below does not include any of the more valuable variation cards listed. Rookie Cards in this set include George Bell, Cal Ripken Jr., Steve Sax, Lee Smith, and Dave Stewart.

	NRMT-MT	EXC	G-VG
COMPLETE SET (660)	75.00	34.00	9.50
COMMON CARD (1-660)	.10	.05	.01
☐ 1 Dusty Baker	.20	.09	.03
☐ 2 Robert Castillo	.10	.05	.01
☐ 3 Ron Cey	.15	.07	.02
☐ 4 Terry Forster	.10	.05	.01
☐ 5 Steve Garvey	.50	.23	.06
☐ 6 Dave Goltz	.10	.05	.01
☐ 7 Pedro Guerrero	.15	.07	.02
☐ 8 Burt Hooton	.10	.05	.01
☐ 9 Steve Howe	.10	.05	.01
☐ 10 Jay Johnstone	.15	.07	.02
☐ 11 Ken Landreaux	.10	.05	.01
☐ 12 Dave Lopes	.15	.07	.02
☐ 13 Mike A. Marshall	.15	.07	.02
☐ 14 Bobby Mitchell	.10	.05	.01
☐ 15 Rick Monday	.10	.05	.01
☐ 16 Tom Niedenfuer	.10	.05	.01
☐ 17 Ted Power	.10	.05	.01
☐ 18 Jerry Reuss UER ("Home:" omitted)	.10	.05	.01
☐ 19 Ron Roenicke	.10	.05	.01
☐ 20 Bill Russell	.15	.07	.02
☐ 21 Steve Sax	1.00	.45	.13
☐ 22 Mike Scioscia	.15	.07	.02
☐ 23 Reggie Smith	.15	.07	.02
☐ 24 Dave Stewart	2.00	.90	.25
☐ 25 Rick Sutcliffe	.15	.07	.02
☐ 26 Derrel Thomas	.10	.05	.01
☐ 27 Fernando Valenzuela	.25	.11	.03
☐ 28 Bob Welch	.15	.07	.02
☐ 29 Steve Yeager	.10	.05	.01
☐ 30 Bobby Brown	.10	.05	.01
☐ 31 Rick Cerone	.10	.05	.01
☐ 32 Ron Davis	.10	.05	.01
☐ 33 Bucky Dent	.15	.07	.02
☐ 34 Barry Foote	.10	.05	.01
☐ 35 George Frazier	.10	.05	.01
☐ 36 Oscar Gamble	.10	.05	.01
☐ 37 Rich Gossage	.20	.09	.03
☐ 38 Ron Guidry	.15	.07	.02
☐ 39 Reggie Jackson	1.50	.65	.19
☐ 40 Tommy John	.20	.09	.03
☐ 41 Rudy May	.10	.05	.01
☐ 42 Larry Milbourne	.10	.05	.01
☐ 43 Jerry Mumphrey	.10	.05	.01
☐ 44 Bobby Murcer	.15	.07	.02
☐ 45 Gene Nelson	.10	.05	.01
☐ 46 Graig Nettles	.15	.07	.02
☐ 47 Johnny Oates	.10	.05	.01
☐ 48 Lou Piniella	.15	.07	.02
☐ 49 Willie Randolph	.15	.07	.02
☐ 50 Rick Reuschel	.15	.07	.02
☐ 51 Dave Revering	.10	.05	.01
☐ 52 Dave Righetti	.40	.18	.05
☐ 53 Aurelio Rodriguez	.10	.05	.01
☐ 54 Bob Watson	.15	.07	.02
☐ 55 Dennis Werth	.10	.05	.01
☐ 56 Dave Winfield	2.00	.90	.25
☐ 57 Johnny Bench	1.00	.45	.13
☐ 58 Bruce Berenyi	.10	.05	.01
☐ 59 Larry Biittner	.10	.05	.01
☐ 60 Scott Brown	.10	.05	.01
☐ 61 Dave Collins	.10	.05	.01
☐ 62 Geoff Combe	.10	.05	.01
☐ 63 Dave Concepcion	.15	.07	.02
☐ 64 Dan Driessen	.10	.05	.01
☐ 65 Joe Edelen	.10	.05	.01
☐ 66 George Foster	.15	.07	.02
☐ 67 Ken Griffey	.10	.05	.01
☐ 68 Paul Householder	.10	.05	.01
☐ 69 Tom Hume	.10	.05	.01
☐ 70 Junior Kennedy	.10	.05	.01
☐ 71 Ray Knight	.15	.07	.02
☐ 72 Mike LaCoss	.10	.05	.01
☐ 73 Rafael Landestoy	.10	.05	.01
☐ 74 Charlie Leibrandt	.10	.05	.01
☐ 75 Sam Mejias	.10	.05	.01
☐ 76 Paul Moskau	.10	.05	.01
☐ 77 Joe Nolan	.10	.05	.01
☐ 78 Mike O'Berry	.10	.05	.01
☐ 79 Ron Oester	.10	.05	.01
☐ 80 Frank Pastore	.10	.05	.01
☐ 81 Joe Price	.10	.05	.01
☐ 82 Tom Seaver	1.00	.45	.13
☐ 83 Mario Soto	.10	.05	.01
☐ 84 Mike Vail	.10	.05	.01
☐ 85 Tony Armas	.10	.05	.01
☐ 86 Shooty Babitt	.10	.05	.01
☐ 87 Dave Beard	.10	.05	.01
☐ 88 Rick Bosetti	.10	.05	.01
☐ 89 Keith Drumwright	.10	.05	.01
☐ 90 Wayne Gross	.10	.05	.01
☐ 91 Mike Heath	.10	.05	.01
☐ 92 Rickey Henderson	3.50	1.55	.45
☐ 93 Cliff Johnson	.10	.05	.01
☐ 94 Jeff Jones	.10	.05	.01
☐ 95 Matt Keough	.10	.05	.01
☐ 96 Brian Kingman	.10	.05	.01
☐ 97 Mickey Klutts	.10	.05	.01
☐ 98 Rick Langford	.10	.05	.01
☐ 99 Steve McCatty	.10	.05	.01
☐ 100 Dave McKay	.10	.05	.01
☐ 101 Dwayne Murphy	.10	.05	.01
☐ 102 Jeff Newman	.10	.05	.01
☐ 103 Mike Norris	.10	.05	.01
☐ 104 Bob Owchinko	.10	.05	.01
☐ 105 Mitchell Page	.10	.05	.01
☐ 106 Rob Picciolo	.10	.05	.01
☐ 107 Jim Spencer	.10	.05	.01
☐ 108 Fred Stanley	.10	.05	.01
☐ 109 Tom Underwood	.10	.05	.01
☐ 110 Joaquin Andujar	.15	.07	.02
☐ 111 Steve Braun	.10	.05	.01
☐ 112 Bob Forsch	.10	.05	.01
☐ 113 George Hendrick	.15	.07	.02
☐ 114 Keith Hernandez	.20	.09	.03
☐ 115 Tom Herr	.15	.07	.02
☐ 116 Dane Iorg	.10	.05	.01
☐ 117 Jim Kaat	.15	.07	.02
☐ 118 Tito Landrum	.10	.05	.01
☐ 119 Sixto Lezcano	.10	.05	.01
☐ 120 Mark Littell	.10	.05	.01
☐ 121 John Martin	.10	.05	.01
☐ 122 Silvio Martinez	.10	.05	.01
☐ 123 Ken Oberkfell	.10	.05	.01
☐ 124 Darrell Porter	.10	.05	.01
☐ 125 Mike Ramsey	.10	.05	.01
☐ 126 Orlando Sanchez	.10	.05	.01
☐ 127 Bob Shirley	.10	.05	.01

☐ 128 Lary Sorensen .10 .05 .01
☐ 129 Bruce Sutter .15 .07 .02
☐ 130 Bob Sykes .10 .05 .01
☐ 131 Garry Templeton .15 .07 .02
☐ 132 Gene Tenace .10 .05 .01
☐ 133 Jerry Augustine .10 .05 .01
☐ 134 Sal Bando .15 .07 .02
☐ 135 Mark Brouhard .10 .05 .01
☐ 136 Mike Caldwell .10 .05 .01
☐ 137 Reggie Cleveland .10 .05 .01
☐ 138 Cecil Cooper .15 .07 .02
☐ 139 Jamie Easterly .10 .05 .01
☐ 140 Marshall Edwards .10 .05 .01
☐ 141 Rollie Fingers .40 .18 .05
☐ 142 Jim Gantner .15 .07 .02
☐ 143 Moose Haas .10 .05 .01
☐ 144 Larry Hisle .10 .05 .01
☐ 145 Roy Howell .10 .05 .01
☐ 146 Rickey Keeton .10 .05 .01
☐ 147 Randy Lerch .10 .05 .01
☐ 148 Paul Molitor 2.50 1.15 .30
☐ 149 Don Money .10 .05 .01
☐ 150 Charlie Moore .10 .05 .01
☐ 151 Ben Oglivie .15 .07 .02
☐ 152 Ted Simmons .15 .07 .02
☐ 153 Jim Slaton .10 .05 .01
☐ 154 Gorman Thomas .15 .07 .02
☐ 155 Robin Yount 2.00 .90 .25
☐ 156 Pete Vuckovich .15 .07 .02
(Should precede Yount
in the team order)
☐ 157 Benny Ayala .10 .05 .01
☐ 158 Mark Belanger .15 .07 .02
☐ 159 Al Bumbry .15 .07 .02
☐ 160 Terry Crowley .10 .05 .01
☐ 161 Rich Dauer .10 .05 .01
☐ 162 Doug DeCinces .15 .07 .02
☐ 163 Rick Dempsey .15 .07 .02
☐ 164 Jim Dwyer .10 .05 .01
☐ 165 Mike Flanagan .15 .07 .02
☐ 166 Dave Ford .10 .05 .01
☐ 167 Dan Graham .10 .05 .01
☐ 168 Wayne Krenchicki .10 .05 .01
☐ 169 John Lowenstein .10 .05 .01
☐ 170 Dennis Martinez .15 .07 .02
☐ 171 Tippy Martinez .10 .05 .01
☐ 172 Scott McGregor .10 .05 .01
☐ 173 Jose Morales .10 .05 .01
☐ 174 Eddie Murray 2.00 .90 .25
☐ 175 Jim Palmer 1.00 .45 .13
☐ 176 Cal Ripken 40.00 18.00 5.00
(Fleer Ripken cards from 1982
through 1993 erroneously have 22
games played in 1981;not 23.)
☐ 177 Gary Roenicke .10 .05 .01
☐ 178 Lenn Sakata .10 .05 .01
☐ 179 Ken Singleton .15 .07 .02
☐ 180 Sammy Stewart .10 .05 .01
☐ 181 Tim Stoddard .10 .05 .01
☐ 182 Steve Stone .15 .07 .02
☐ 183 Stan Bahnsen .10 .05 .01
☐ 184 Ray Burris .10 .05 .01
☐ 185 Gary Carter .60 .25 .08
☐ 186 Warren Cromartie .10 .05 .01
☐ 187 Andre Dawson 1.25 .55 .16
☐ 188 Terry Francona .10 .05 .01
☐ 189 Woodie Fryman .10 .05 .01
☐ 190 Bill Gullickson .15 .07 .02
☐ 191 Grant Jackson .10 .05 .01
☐ 192 Wallace Johnson .10 .05 .01
☐ 193 Charlie Lea .10 .05 .01
☐ 194 Bill Lee .10 .05 .01
☐ 195 Jerry Manuel .10 .05 .01
☐ 196 Brad Mills .10 .05 .01
☐ 197 John Milner .10 .05 .01
☐ 198 Rowland Office .10 .05 .01
☐ 199 David Palmer .10 .05 .01
☐ 200 Larry Parrish .10 .05 .01
☐ 201 Mike Phillips .10 .05 .01
☐ 202 Tim Raines 2.50 1.15 .30
☐ 203 Bobby Ramos .10 .05 .01
☐ 204 Jeff Reardon .50 .23 .06
☐ 205 Steve Rogers .10 .05 .01
☐ 206 Scott Sanderson .15 .07 .02
☐ 207 Rodney Scott UER .25 .11 .03
(Photo actually
Tim Raines)
☐ 208 Elias Sosa .10 .05 .01
☐ 209 Chris Speier .10 .05 .01
☐ 210 Tim Wallach 1.25 .55 .16
☐ 211 Jerry White .10 .05 .01
☐ 212 Alan Ashby .10 .05 .01
☐ 213 Cesar Cedeno .15 .07 .02
☐ 214 Jose Cruz .15 .07 .02
☐ 215 Kiko Garcia .10 .05 .01
☐ 216 Phil Garner .15 .07 .02
☐ 217 Danny Heep .10 .05 .01
☐ 218 Art Howe .10 .05 .01
☐ 219 Bob Knepper .10 .05 .01
☐ 220 Frank LaCorte .10 .05 .01
☐ 221 Joe Niekro .15 .07 .02
☐ 222 Joe Pittman .10 .05 .01
☐ 223 Terry Puhl .10 .05 .01
☐ 224 Luis Pujols .10 .05 .01
☐ 225 Craig Reynolds .10 .05 .01
☐ 226 J.R. Richard .15 .07 .02
☐ 227 Dave Roberts .10 .05 .01
☐ 228 Vern Ruhle .10 .05 .01
☐ 229 Nolan Ryan 8.00 3.60 1.00
☐ 230 Joe Sambito .10 .05 .01
☐ 231 Tony Scott .10 .05 .01
☐ 232 Dave Smith .10 .05 .01
☐ 233 Harry Spilman .10 .05 .01
☐ 234 Don Sutton .40 .18 .05
☐ 235 Dickie Thon .10 .05 .01
☐ 236 Denny Walling .10 .05 .01
☐ 237 Gary Woods .10 .05 .01
☐ 238 Luis Aguayo .10 .05 .01
☐ 239 Ramon Aviles .10 .05 .01
☐ 240 Bob Boone .15 .07 .02
☐ 241 Larry Bowa .15 .07 .02
☐ 242 Warren Brusstar .10 .05 .01
☐ 243 Steve Carlton 1.00 .45 .13
☐ 244 Larry Christenson .10 .05 .01
☐ 245 Dick Davis .10 .05 .01
☐ 246 Greg Gross .10 .05 .01
☐ 247 Sparky Lyle .15 .07 .02
☐ 248 Garry Maddox .10 .05 .01
☐ 249 Gary Matthews .15 .07 .02
☐ 250 Bake McBride .10 .05 .01
☐ 251 Tug McGraw .15 .07 .02
☐ 252 Keith Moreland .10 .05 .01
☐ 253 Dickie Noles .10 .05 .01
☐ 254 Mike Proly .10 .05 .01
☐ 255 Ron Reed .10 .05 .01
☐ 256 Pete Rose 2.00 .90 .25
☐ 257 Dick Ruthven .10 .05 .01
☐ 258 Mike Schmidt 2.00 .90 .25
☐ 259 Lonnie Smith .15 .07 .02
☐ 260 Manny Trillo .10 .05 .01
☐ 261 Del Unser .10 .05 .01
☐ 262 George Vukovich .10 .05 .01
☐ 263 Tom Brookens .10 .05 .01
☐ 264 George Cappuzzello .10 .05 .01
☐ 265 Marty Castillo .10 .05 .01
☐ 266 Al Cowens .10 .05 .01

	No.	Player			
☐	267	Kirk Gibson	1.00	.45	.13
☐	268	Richie Hebner	.10	.05	.01
☐	269	Ron Jackson	.10	.05	.01
☐	270	Lynn Jones	.10	.05	.01
☐	271	Steve Kemp	.10	.05	.01
☐	272	Rick Leach	.10	.05	.01
☐	273	Aurelio Lopez	.10	.05	.01
☐	274	Jack Morris	.40	.18	.05
☐	275	Kevin Saucier	.10	.05	.01
☐	276	Lance Parrish	.20	.09	.03
☐	277	Rick Peters	.10	.05	.01
☐	278	Dan Petry	.10	.05	.01
☐	279	Dave Rozema	.10	.05	.01
☐	280	Stan Papi	.10	.05	.01
☐	281	Dan Schatzeder	.10	.05	.01
☐	282	Champ Summers	.10	.05	.01
☐	283	Alan Trammell	1.00	.45	.13
☐	284	Lou Whitaker	.60	.25	.08
☐	285	Milt Wilcox	.10	.05	.01
☐	286	John Wockenfuss	.10	.05	.01
☐	287	Gary Allenson	.10	.05	.01
☐	288	Tom Burgmeier	.10	.05	.01
☐	289	Bill Campbell	.10	.05	.01
☐	290	Mark Clear	.10	.05	.01
☐	291	Steve Crawford	.10	.05	.01
☐	292	Dennis Eckersley	.75	.35	.09
☐	293	Dwight Evans	.20	.09	.03
☐	294	Rich Gedman	.10	.05	.01
☐	295	Garry Hancock	.10	.05	.01
☐	296	Glenn Hoffman	.10	.05	.01
☐	297	Bruce Hurst	.10	.05	.01
☐	298	Carney Lansford	.15	.07	.02
☐	299	Rick Miller	.10	.05	.01
☐	300	Reid Nichols	.10	.05	.01
☐	301	Bob Ojeda	.35	.16	.04
☐	302	Tony Perez	.30	.14	.04
☐	303	Chuck Rainey	.10	.05	.01
☐	304	Jerry Remy	.10	.05	.01
☐	305	Jim Rice	.20	.09	.03
☐	306	Joe Rudi	.10	.05	.01
☐	307	Bob Stanley	.10	.05	.01
☐	308	Dave Stapleton	.10	.05	.01
☐	309	Frank Tanana	.15	.07	.02
☐	310	Mike Torrez	.10	.05	.01
☐	311	John Tudor	.15	.07	.02
☐	312	Carl Yastrzemski	1.00	.45	.13
☐	313	Buddy Bell	.15	.07	.02
☐	314	Steve Comer	.10	.05	.01
☐	315	Danny Darwin	.10	.05	.01
☐	316	John Ellis	.10	.05	.01
☐	317	John Grubb	.10	.05	.01
☐	318	Rick Honeycutt	.10	.05	.01
☐	319	Charlie Hough	.15	.07	.02
☐	320	Ferguson Jenkins	.40	.18	.05
☐	321	John Henry Johnson	.10	.05	.01
☐	322	Jim Kern	.10	.05	.01
☐	323	Jon Matlack	.10	.05	.01
☐	324	Doc Medich	.10	.05	.01
☐	325	Mario Mendoza	.10	.05	.01
☐	326	Al Oliver	.15	.07	.02
☐	327	Pat Putnam	.10	.05	.01
☐	328	Mickey Rivers	.10	.05	.01
☐	329	Leon Roberts	.10	.05	.01
☐	330	Billy Sample	.10	.05	.01
☐	331	Bill Stein	.10	.05	.01
☐	332	Jim Sundberg	.15	.07	.02
☐	333	Mark Wagner	.10	.05	.01
☐	334	Bump Wills	.10	.05	.01
☐	335	Bill Almon	.10	.05	.01
☐	336	Harold Baines	.75	.35	.09
☐	337	Ross Baumgarten	.10	.05	.01
☐	338	Tony Bernazard	.10	.05	.01
☐	339	Britt Burns	.10	.05	.01
☐	340	Richard Dotson	.10	.05	.01
☐	341	Jim Essian	.10	.05	.01
☐	342	Ed Farmer	.10	.05	.01
☐	343	Carlton Fisk	1.25	.55	.16
☐	344	Kevin Hickey	.10	.05	.01
☐	345	LaMarr Hoyt	.10	.05	.01
☐	346	Lamar Johnson	.10	.05	.01
☐	347	Jerry Koosman	.15	.07	.02
☐	348	Rusty Kuntz	.10	.05	.01
☐	349	Dennis Lamp	.10	.05	.01
☐	350	Ron LeFlore	.15	.07	.02
☐	351	Chet Lemon	.10	.05	.01
☐	352	Greg Luzinski	.15	.07	.02
☐	353	Bob Molinaro	.10	.05	.01
☐	354	Jim Morrison	.10	.05	.01
☐	355	Wayne Nordhagen	.10	.05	.01
☐	356	Greg Pryor	.10	.05	.01
☐	357	Mike Squires	.10	.05	.01
☐	358	Steve Trout	.10	.05	.01
☐	359	Alan Bannister	.10	.05	.01
☐	360	Len Barker	.10	.05	.01
☐	361	Bert Blyleven	.20	.09	.03
☐	362	Joe Charboneau	.10	.05	.01
☐	363	John Denny	.10	.05	.01
☐	364	Bo Diaz	.10	.05	.01
☐	365	Miguel Dilone	.10	.05	.01
☐	366	Jerry Dybzinski	.10	.05	.01
☐	367	Wayne Garland	.10	.05	.01
☐	368	Mike Hargrove	.15	.07	.02
☐	369	Toby Harrah	.15	.07	.02
☐	370	Ron Hassey	.10	.05	.01
☐	371	Von Hayes	.15	.07	.02
☐	372	Pat Kelly	.10	.05	.01
☐	373	Duane Kuiper	.10	.05	.01
☐	374	Rick Manning	.10	.05	.01
☐	375	Sid Monge	.10	.05	.01
☐	376	Jorge Orta	.10	.05	.01
☐	377	Dave Rosello	.10	.05	.01
☐	378	Dan Spillner	.10	.05	.01
☐	379	Mike Stanton	.10	.05	.01
☐	380	Andre Thornton	.15	.07	.02
☐	381	Tom Veryzer	.10	.05	.01
☐	382	Rick Waits	.10	.05	.01
☐	383	Doyle Alexander	.10	.05	.01
☐	384	Vida Blue	.15	.07	.02
☐	385	Fred Breining	.10	.05	.01
☐	386	Enos Cabell	.10	.05	.01
☐	387	Jack Clark	.15	.07	.02
☐	388	Darrell Evans	.15	.07	.02
☐	389	Tom Griffin	.10	.05	.01
☐	390	Larry Herndon	.10	.05	.01
☐	391	Al Holland	.10	.05	.01
☐	392	Gary Lavelle	.10	.05	.01
☐	393	Johnnie LeMaster	.10	.05	.01
☐	394	Jerry Martin	.10	.05	.01
☐	395	Milt May	.10	.05	.01
☐	396	Greg Minton	.10	.05	.01
☐	397	Joe Morgan	.75	.35	.09
☐	398	Joe Pettini	.10	.05	.01
☐	399	Allen Ripley	.10	.05	.01
☐	400	Billy Smith	.10	.05	.01
☐	401	Rennie Stennett	.10	.05	.01
☐	402	Ed Whitson	.10	.05	.01
☐	403	Jim Wohlford	.10	.05	.01
☐	404	Willie Aikens	.10	.05	.01
☐	405	George Brett	3.50	1.55	.45
☐	406	Ken Brett	.10	.05	.01
☐	407	Dave Chalk	.10	.05	.01
☐	408	Rich Gale	.10	.05	.01
☐	409	Cesar Geronimo	.10	.05	.01
☐	410	Larry Gura	.10	.05	.01
☐	411	Clint Hurdle	.10	.05	.01
☐	412	Mike Jones	.10	.05	.01

	No.	Player			
☐	413	Dennis Leonard	.10	.05	.01
☐	414	Renie Martin	.10	.05	.01
☐	415	Lee May	.15	.07	.02
☐	416	Hal McRae	.20	.09	.03
☐	417	Darryl Motley	.10	.05	.01
☐	418	Rance Mulliniks	.10	.05	.01
☐	419	Amos Otis	.15	.07	.02
☐	420	Ken Phelps	.10	.05	.01
☐	421	Jamie Quirk	.10	.05	.01
☐	422	Dan Quisenberry	.15	.07	.02
☐	423	Paul Splittorff	.10	.05	.01
☐	424	U.L. Washington	.10	.05	.01
☐	425	John Wathan	.10	.05	.01
☐	426	Frank White	.15	.07	.02
☐	427	Willie Wilson	.15	.07	.02
☐	428	Brian Asselstine	.10	.05	.01
☐	429	Bruce Benedict	.10	.05	.01
☐	430	Tommy Boggs	.10	.05	.01
☐	431	Larry Bradford	.10	.05	.01
☐	432	Rick Camp	.10	.05	.01
☐	433	Chris Chambliss	.15	.07	.02
☐	434	Gene Garber	.10	.05	.01
☐	435	Preston Hanna	.10	.05	.01
☐	436	Bob Horner	.15	.07	.02
☐	437	Glenn Hubbard	.10	.05	.01
☐	438A	All Hrabosky ERR (Height 5'1", All on reverse)	20.00	9.00	2.50
☐	438B	Al Hrabosky ERR (Height 5'1")	.60	.25	.08
☐	438C	Al Hrabosky (Height 5'10")	.15	.07	.02
☐	439	Rufino Linares	.10	.05	.01
☐	440	Rick Mahler	.10	.05	.01
☐	441	Ed Miller	.10	.05	.01
☐	442	John Montefusco	.10	.05	.01
☐	443	Dale Murphy	.75	.35	.09
☐	444	Phil Niekro	.40	.18	.05
☐	445	Gaylord Perry	.40	.18	.05
☐	446	Biff Pocoroba	.10	.05	.01
☐	447	Rafael Ramirez	.10	.05	.01
☐	448	Jerry Royster	.10	.05	.01
☐	449	Claudell Washington	.10	.05	.01
☐	450	Don Aase	.10	.05	.01
☐	451	Don Baylor	.20	.09	.03
☐	452	Juan Beniquez	.10	.05	.01
☐	453	Rick Burleson	.10	.05	.01
☐	454	Bert Campaneris	.15	.07	.02
☐	455	Rod Carew	1.00	.45	.13
☐	456	Bob Clark	.10	.05	.01
☐	457	Brian Downing	.15	.07	.02
☐	458	Dan Ford	.10	.05	.01
☐	459	Ken Forsch	.10	.05	.01
☐	460A	Dave Frost (5 mm space before ERA)	.10	.05	.01
☐	460B	Dave Frost (1 mm space)	.10	.05	.01
☐	461	Bobby Grich	.15	.07	.02
☐	462	Larry Harlow	.10	.05	.01
☐	463	John Harris	.10	.05	.01
☐	464	Andy Hassler	.10	.05	.01
☐	465	Butch Hobson	.15	.07	.02
☐	466	Jesse Jefferson	.10	.05	.01
☐	467	Bruce Kison	.10	.05	.01
☐	468	Fred Lynn	.15	.07	.02
☐	469	Angel Moreno	.10	.05	.01
☐	470	Ed Ott	.10	.05	.01
☐	471	Fred Patek	.10	.05	.01
☐	472	Steve Renko	.10	.05	.01
☐	473	Mike Witt	.10	.05	.01
☐	474	Geoff Zahn	.10	.05	.01
☐	475	Gary Alexander	.10	.05	.01
☐	476	Dale Berra	.10	.05	.01
☐	477	Kurt Bevacqua	.10	.05	.01
☐	478	Jim Bibby	.10	.05	.01
☐	479	John Candelaria	.10	.05	.01
☐	480	Victor Cruz	.10	.05	.01
☐	481	Mike Easler	.10	.05	.01
☐	482	Tim Foli	.10	.05	.01
☐	483	Lee Lacy	.10	.05	.01
☐	484	Vance Law	.10	.05	.01
☐	485	Bill Madlock	.15	.07	.02
☐	486	Willie Montanez	.10	.05	.01
☐	487	Omar Moreno	.10	.05	.01
☐	488	Steve Nicosia	.10	.05	.01
☐	489	Dave Parker	.20	.09	.03
☐	490	Tony Pena	.15	.07	.02
☐	491	Pascual Perez	.10	.05	.01
☐	492	Johnny Ray	.10	.05	.01
☐	493	Rick Rhoden	.10	.05	.01
☐	494	Bill Robinson	.15	.07	.02
☐	495	Don Robinson	.10	.05	.01
☐	496	Enrique Romo	.10	.05	.01
☐	497	Rod Scurry	.10	.05	.01
☐	498	Eddie Solomon	.10	.05	.01
☐	499	Willie Stargell	.75	.35	.09
☐	500	Kent Tekulve	.15	.07	.02
☐	501	Jason Thompson	.10	.05	.01
☐	502	Glenn Abbott	.10	.05	.01
☐	503	Jim Anderson	.10	.05	.01
☐	504	Floyd Bannister	.10	.05	.01
☐	505	Bruce Bochte	.10	.05	.01
☐	506	Jeff Burroughs	.10	.05	.01
☐	507	Bryan Clark	.10	.05	.01
☐	508	Ken Clay	.10	.05	.01
☐	509	Julio Cruz	.10	.05	.01
☐	510	Dick Drago	.10	.05	.01
☐	511	Gary Gray	.10	.05	.01
☐	512	Dan Meyer	.10	.05	.01
☐	513	Jerry Narron	.10	.05	.01
☐	514	Tom Paciorek	.15	.07	.02
☐	515	Casey Parsons	.10	.05	.01
☐	516	Lenny Randle	.10	.05	.01
☐	517	Shane Rawley	.10	.05	.01
☐	518	Joe Simpson	.10	.05	.01
☐	519	Richie Zisk	.10	.05	.01
☐	520	Neil Allen	.10	.05	.01
☐	521	Bob Bailor	.10	.05	.01
☐	522	Hubie Brooks	.15	.07	.02
☐	523	Mike Cubbage	.10	.05	.01
☐	524	Pete Falcone	.10	.05	.01
☐	525	Doug Flynn	.10	.05	.01
☐	526	Tom Hausman	.10	.05	.01
☐	527	Ron Hodges	.10	.05	.01
☐	528	Randy Jones	.10	.05	.01
☐	529	Mike Jorgensen	.10	.05	.01
☐	530	Dave Kingman	.15	.07	.02
☐	531	Ed Lynch	.10	.05	.01
☐	532	Mike G. Marshall	.10	.05	.01
☐	533	Lee Mazzilli	.10	.05	.01
☐	534	Dyar Miller	.10	.05	.01
☐	535	Mike Scott	.15	.07	.02
☐	536	Rusty Staub	.15	.07	.02
☐	537	John Stearns	.10	.05	.01
☐	538	Craig Swan	.10	.05	.01
☐	539	Frank Taveras	.10	.05	.01
☐	540	Alex Trevino	.10	.05	.01
☐	541	Ellis Valentine	.10	.05	.01
☐	542	Mookie Wilson	.15	.07	.02
☐	543	Joel Youngblood	.10	.05	.01
☐	544	Pat Zachry	.10	.05	.01
☐	545	Glenn Adams	.10	.05	.01
☐	546	Fernando Arroyo	.10	.05	.01
☐	547	John Verhoeven	.10	.05	.01
☐	548	Sal Butera	.10	.05	.01
☐	549	John Castino	.10	.05	.01

☐ 550	Don Cooper	.10	.05	.01
☐ 551	Doug Corbett	.10	.05	.01
☐ 552	Dave Engle	.10	.05	.01
☐ 553	Roger Erickson	.10	.05	.01
☐ 554	Danny Goodwin	.10	.05	.01
☐ 555A	Darrell Jackson (Black cap)	.60	.25	.08
☐ 555B	Darrell Jackson (Red cap with T)	.15	.07	.02
☐ 555C	Darrell Jackson (Red cap, no emblem)	3.00	1.35	.40
☐ 556	Pete Mackanin	.10	.05	.01
☐ 557	Jack O'Connor	.10	.05	.01
☐ 558	Hosken Powell	.10	.05	.01
☐ 559	Pete Redfern	.10	.05	.01
☐ 560	Roy Smalley	.10	.05	.01
☐ 561	Chuck Baker UER (Shortshop on front)	.10	.05	.01
☐ 562	Gary Ward	.10	.05	.01
☐ 563	Rob Wilfong	.10	.05	.01
☐ 564	Al Williams	.10	.05	.01
☐ 565	Butch Wynegar	.10	.05	.01
☐ 566	Randy Bass	.30	.14	.04
☐ 567	Juan Bonilla	.10	.05	.01
☐ 568	Danny Boone	.10	.05	.01
☐ 569	John Curtis	.10	.05	.01
☐ 570	Juan Eichelberger	.10	.05	.01
☐ 571	Barry Evans	.10	.05	.01
☐ 572	Tim Flannery	.10	.05	.01
☐ 573	Ruppert Jones	.10	.05	.01
☐ 574	Terry Kennedy	.10	.05	.01
☐ 575	Joe Lefebvre	.10	.05	.01
☐ 576A	John Littlefield ERR (Left handed; reverse negative)	200.00	90.00	25.00
☐ 576B	John Littlefield COR (Right handed)	.15	.07	.02
☐ 577	Gary Lucas	.10	.05	.01
☐ 578	Steve Mura	.10	.05	.01
☐ 579	Broderick Perkins	.10	.05	.01
☐ 580	Gene Richards	.10	.05	.01
☐ 581	Luis Salazar	.10	.05	.01
☐ 582	Ozzie Smith	3.00	1.35	.40
☐ 583	John Urrea	.10	.05	.01
☐ 584	Chris Welsh	.10	.05	.01
☐ 585	Rick Wise	.10	.05	.01
☐ 586	Doug Bird	.10	.05	.01
☐ 587	Tim Blackwell	.10	.05	.01
☐ 588	Bobby Bonds	.15	.07	.02
☐ 589	Bill Buckner	.15	.07	.02
☐ 590	Bill Caudill	.10	.05	.01
☐ 591	Hector Cruz	.10	.05	.01
☐ 592	Jody Davis	.10	.05	.01
☐ 593	Ivan DeJesus	.10	.05	.01
☐ 594	Steve Dillard	.10	.05	.01
☐ 595	Leon Durham	.10	.05	.01
☐ 596	Rawly Eastwick	.10	.05	.01
☐ 597	Steve Henderson	.10	.05	.01
☐ 598	Mike Krukow	.10	.05	.01
☐ 599	Mike Lum	.10	.05	.01
☐ 600	Randy Martz	.10	.05	.01
☐ 601	Jerry Morales	.10	.05	.01
☐ 602	Ken Reitz	.10	.05	.01
☐ 603A	Lee Smith ERR (Cubs logo reversed)	8.00	3.60	1.00
☐ 603B	Lee Smith COR	8.00	3.60	1.00
☐ 604	Dick Tidrow	.10	.05	.01
☐ 605	Jim Tracy	.10	.05	.01
☐ 606	Mike Tyson	.10	.05	.01
☐ 607	Ty Waller	.10	.05	.01
☐ 608	Danny Ainge	2.00	.90	.25
☐ 609	George Bell	1.50	.65	.19
☐ 610	Mark Bomback	.10	.05	.01
☐ 611	Barry Bonnell	.10	.05	.01
☐ 612	Jim Clancy	.10	.05	.01
☐ 613	Damaso Garcia	.10	.05	.01
☐ 614	Jerry Garvin	.10	.05	.01
☐ 615	Alfredo Griffin	.10	.05	.01
☐ 616	Garth Iorg	.10	.05	.01
☐ 617	Luis Leal	.10	.05	.01
☐ 618	Ken Macha	.10	.05	.01
☐ 619	John Mayberry	.10	.05	.01
☐ 620	Joey McLaughlin	.10	.05	.01
☐ 621	Lloyd Moseby	.10	.05	.01
☐ 622	Dave Stieb	.15	.07	.02
☐ 623	Jackson Todd	.10	.05	.01
☐ 624	Willie Upshaw	.10	.05	.01
☐ 625	Otto Velez	.10	.05	.01
☐ 626	Ernie Whitt	.10	.05	.01
☐ 627	Alvis Woods	.10	.05	.01
☐ 628	All Star Game Cleveland, Ohio	.15	.07	.02
☐ 629	All Star Infielders Frank White and Bucky Dent	.15	.07	.02
☐ 630	Big Red Machine Dan Driessen Dave Concepcion George Foster	.15	.07	.02
☐ 631	Bruce Sutter Top NL Relief Pitcher	.15	.07	.02
☐ 632	"Steve and Carlton" Steve Carlton and Carlton Fisk	1.00	.45	.13
☐ 633	Carl Yastrzemski 3000th Game	.60	.25	.08
☐ 634	Dynamic Duo Johnny Bench and Tom Seaver	1.00	.45	.13
☐ 635	West Meets East Fernando Valenzuela and Gary Carter	.15	.07	.02
☐ 636A	Fernando Valenzuela: NL SO King ("he" NL)	.20	.09	.03
☐ 636B	Fernando Valenzuela: NL SO King ("the" NL)	.15	.07	.02
☐ 637	Mike Schmidt Home Run King	1.00	.45	.13
☐ 638	NL All Stars Gary Carter and Dave Parker	.20	.09	.03
☐ 639	Perfect Game UER Len Barker and Bo Diaz (Catcher actually Ron Hassey)	.15	.07	.02
☐ 640	Pete and Re-Pete Pete Rose and Son	1.00	.45	.13
☐ 641	Phillies Finest Lonnie Smith Mike Schmidt Steve Carlton	.90	.40	.11
☐ 642	Red Sox Reunion Fred Lynn and Dwight Evans	.15	.07	.02
☐ 643	Rickey Henderson Most Hits and Runs	1.50	.65	.19
☐ 644	Rollie Fingers Most Saves AL	.40	.18	.05
☐ 645	Tom Seaver Most 1981 Wins	.75	.35	.09
☐ 646A	Yankee Powerhouse Reggie Jackson and Dave Winfield (Comma on back after outfielder)	2.25	1.00	.30

	No.	Card	NRMT-MT	EXC	G-VG
☐	646B	Yankee Powerhouse Reggie Jackson and Dave Winfield (No comma)	2.25	1.00	.30
☐	647	CL: Yankees/Dodgers	.15	.05	.01
☐	648	CL: A's/Reds	.15	.05	.01
☐	649	CL: Cards/Brewers	.15	.05	.01
☐	650	CL: Expos/Orioles	.15	.05	.01
☐	651	CL: Astros/Phillies	.15	.05	.01
☐	652	CL: Tigers/Red Sox	.15	.05	.01
☐	653	CL: Rangers/White Sox	.15	.05	.01
☐	654	CL: Giants/Indians	.15	.05	.01
☐	655	CL: Royals/Braves	.15	.05	.01
☐	656	CL: Angels/Pirates	.15	.05	.01
☐	657	CL: Mariners/Mets	.15	.05	.01
☐	658	CL: Padres/Twins	.15	.05	.01
☐	659	CL: Blue Jays/Cubs	.15	.05	.01
☐	660	Specials Checklist	.15	.05	.01

1983 Fleer

The cards in this 660-card set measure 2 1/2" by 3 1/2". In 1983, for the third straight year, Fleer has produced a baseball series numbering 660 cards. Of these, 1-628 are player cards, 629-646 are special cards, and 647-660 are checklist cards. The player cards are again ordered alphabetically within team. The team order relates back to each team's on-field performance during the previous year, i.e., World Champion Cardinals (1-25), AL Champion Brewers (26-51), Baltimore (52-75), California (76-103), Kansas City (104-128), Atlanta (129-152), Philadelphia (153-176), Boston (177-200), Los Angeles (201-227), Chicago White Sox (228-251), San Francisco (252-276), Montreal (277-301), Pittsburgh (302-326), Detroit (327-351), San Diego (352-375), New York Yankees (376-399), Cleveland (400-423), Toronto (424-444), Houston (445-469), Seattle (470-489), Chicago Cubs (490-512), Oakland (513-535), New York Mets (536-561), Texas (562-583), Cincinnati (584-606), and Minnesota (607-628). The front of each card has a colorful team logo at bottom left and the player's name and position at lower right. The reverses are done in shades of brown on white. The cards are numbered on the back next to a small black and white photo of the player. The key Rookie Cards in this set are Wade Boggs, Tony Gwynn, Howard Johnson, Willie McGee, Ryne Sandberg, and Frank Viola.

			NRMT-MT	EXC	G-VG
		COMPLETE SET (660)	100.00	45.00	12.50
		COMMON CARD (1-660)	.10	.05	.01
☐	1	Joaquin Andujar	.15	.07	.02
☐	2	Doug Bair	.10	.05	.01
☐	3	Steve Braun	.10	.05	.01
☐	4	Glenn Brummer	.10	.05	.01
☐	5	Bob Forsch	.10	.05	.01
☐	6	David Green	.10	.05	.01
☐	7	George Hendrick	.15	.07	.02
☐	8	Keith Hernandez	.20	.09	.03
☐	9	Tom Herr	.15	.07	.02
☐	10	Dane Iorg	.10	.05	.01
☐	11	Jim Kaat	.15	.07	.02
☐	12	Jeff Lahti	.10	.05	.01
☐	13	Tito Landrum	.10	.05	.01
☐	14	Dave LaPoint	.10	.05	.01
☐	15	Willie McGee	1.50	.65	.19
☐	16	Steve Mura	.10	.05	.01
☐	17	Ken Oberkfell	.10	.05	.01
☐	18	Darrell Porter	.10	.05	.01
☐	19	Mike Ramsey	.10	.05	.01
☐	20	Gene Roof	.10	.05	.01
☐	21	Lonnie Smith	.15	.07	.02
☐	22	Ozzie Smith	2.00	.90	.25
☐	23	John Stuper	.10	.05	.01
☐	24	Bruce Sutter	.15	.07	.02
☐	25	Gene Tenace	.10	.05	.01
☐	26	Jerry Augustine	.10	.05	.01
☐	27	Dwight Bernard	.10	.05	.01
☐	28	Mark Brouhard	.10	.05	.01
☐	29	Mike Caldwell	.10	.05	.01
☐	30	Cecil Cooper	.15	.07	.02
☐	31	Jamie Easterly	.10	.05	.01
☐	32	Marshall Edwards	.10	.05	.01
☐	33	Rollie Fingers	.35	.16	.04
☐	34	Jim Gantner	.15	.07	.02
☐	35	Moose Haas	.10	.05	.01
☐	36	Roy Howell	.10	.05	.01
☐	37	Pete Ladd	.10	.05	.01
☐	38	Bob McClure	.10	.05	.01
☐	39	Doc Medich	.10	.05	.01
☐	40	Paul Molitor	2.00	.90	.25
☐	41	Don Money	.10	.05	.01
☐	42	Charlie Moore	.10	.05	.01
☐	43	Ben Oglivie	.10	.05	.01
☐	44	Ed Romero	.10	.05	.01
☐	45	Ted Simmons	.15	.07	.02
☐	46	Jim Slaton	.10	.05	.01
☐	47	Don Sutton	.35	.16	.04
☐	48	Gorman Thomas	.10	.05	.01
☐	49	Pete Vuckovich	.10	.05	.01
☐	50	Ned Yost	.10	.05	.01
☐	51	Robin Yount	2.00	.90	.25
☐	52	Benny Ayala	.10	.05	.01
☐	53	Bob Bonner	.10	.05	.01
☐	54	Al Bumbry	.15	.07	.02
☐	55	Terry Crowley	.10	.05	.01
☐	56	Storm Davis	.10	.05	.01
☐	57	Rich Dauer	.10	.05	.01
☐	58	Rick Dempsey UER (Posing batting lefty)	.15	.07	.02
☐	59	Jim Dwyer	.10	.05	.01
☐	60	Mike Flanagan	.15	.07	.02
☐	61	Dan Ford	.10	.05	.01
☐	62	Glenn Gulliver	.10	.05	.01
☐	63	John Lowenstein	.10	.05	.01
☐	64	Dennis Martinez	.15	.07	.02
☐	65	Tippy Martinez	.10	.05	.01
☐	66	Scott McGregor	.10	.05	.01
☐	67	Eddie Murray	1.50	.65	.19
☐	68	Joe Nolan	.10	.05	.01

☐ 69 Jim Palmer	.75	.35	.09
☐ 70 Cal Ripken	14.00	6.25	1.75
☐ 71 Gary Roenicke	.10	.05	.01
☐ 72 Lenn Sakata	.10	.05	.01
☐ 73 Ken Singleton	.15	.07	.02
☐ 74 Sammy Stewart	.10	.05	.01
☐ 75 Tim Stoddard	.10	.05	.01
☐ 76 Don Aase	.10	.05	.01
☐ 77 Don Baylor	.20	.09	.03
☐ 78 Juan Beniquez	.10	.05	.01
☐ 79 Bob Boone	.15	.07	.02
☐ 80 Rick Burleson	.10	.05	.01
☐ 81 Rod Carew	.75	.35	.09
☐ 82 Bobby Clark	.10	.05	.01
☐ 83 Doug Corbett	.10	.05	.01
☐ 84 John Curtis	.10	.05	.01
☐ 85 Doug DeCinces	.15	.07	.02
☐ 86 Brian Downing	.15	.07	.02
☐ 87 Joe Ferguson	.10	.05	.01
☐ 88 Tim Foli	.10	.05	.01
☐ 89 Ken Forsch	.10	.05	.01
☐ 90 Dave Goltz	.10	.05	.01
☐ 91 Bobby Grich	.15	.07	.02
☐ 92 Andy Hassler	.10	.05	.01
☐ 93 Reggie Jackson	1.50	.65	.19
☐ 94 Ron Jackson	.10	.05	.01
☐ 95 Tommy John	.20	.09	.03
☐ 96 Bruce Kison	.10	.05	.01
☐ 97 Fred Lynn	.15	.07	.02
☐ 98 Ed Ott	.10	.05	.01
☐ 99 Steve Renko	.10	.05	.01
☐ 100 Luis Sanchez	.10	.05	.01
☐ 101 Rob Wilfong	.10	.05	.01
☐ 102 Mike Witt	.10	.05	.01
☐ 103 Geoff Zahn	.10	.05	.01
☐ 104 Willie Aikens	.10	.05	.01
☐ 105 Mike Armstrong	.10	.05	.01
☐ 106 Vida Blue	.15	.07	.02
☐ 107 Bud Black	.40	.18	.05
☐ 108 George Brett	3.00	1.35	.40
☐ 109 Bill Castro	.10	.05	.01
☐ 110 Onix Concepcion	.10	.05	.01
☐ 111 Dave Frost	.10	.05	.01
☐ 112 Cesar Geronimo	.10	.05	.01
☐ 113 Larry Gura	.10	.05	.01
☐ 114 Steve Hammond	.10	.05	.01
☐ 115 Don Hood	.10	.05	.01
☐ 116 Dennis Leonard	.10	.05	.01
☐ 117 Jerry Martin	.10	.05	.01
☐ 118 Lee May	.15	.07	.02
☐ 119 Hal McRae	.20	.09	.03
☐ 120 Amos Otis	.15	.07	.02
☐ 121 Greg Pryor	.10	.05	.01
☐ 122 Dan Quisenberry	.15	.07	.02
☐ 123 Don Slaught	1.00	.45	.13
☐ 124 Paul Splittorff	.10	.05	.01
☐ 125 U.L. Washington	.10	.05	.01
☐ 126 John Wathan	.10	.05	.01
☐ 127 Frank White	.15	.07	.02
☐ 128 Willie Wilson	.15	.07	.02
☐ 129 Steve Bedrosian UER (Height 6'33")	.15	.07	.02
☐ 130 Bruce Benedict	.10	.05	.01
☐ 131 Tommy Boggs	.10	.05	.01
☐ 132 Brett Butler	.75	.35	.09
☐ 133 Rick Camp	.10	.05	.01
☐ 134 Chris Chambliss	.15	.07	.02
☐ 135 Ken Dayley	.10	.05	.01
☐ 136 Gene Garber	.10	.05	.01
☐ 137 Terry Harper	.10	.05	.01
☐ 138 Bob Horner	.15	.07	.02
☐ 139 Glenn Hubbard	.10	.05	.01
☐ 140 Rufino Linares	.10	.05	.01
☐ 141 Rick Mahler	.10	.05	.01
☐ 142 Dale Murphy	.60	.25	.08
☐ 143 Phil Niekro	.35	.16	.04
☐ 144 Pascual Perez	.10	.05	.01
☐ 145 Biff Pocoroba	.10	.05	.01
☐ 146 Rafael Ramirez	.10	.05	.01
☐ 147 Jerry Royster	.10	.05	.01
☐ 148 Ken Smith	.10	.05	.01
☐ 149 Bob Walk	.10	.05	.01
☐ 150 Claudell Washington	.10	.05	.01
☐ 151 Bob Watson	.15	.07	.02
☐ 152 Larry Whisenton	.10	.05	.01
☐ 153 Porfirio Altamirano	.10	.05	.01
☐ 154 Marty Bystrom	.10	.05	.01
☐ 155 Steve Carlton	1.00	.45	.13
☐ 156 Larry Christenson	.10	.05	.01
☐ 157 Ivan DeJesus	.10	.05	.01
☐ 158 John Denny	.10	.05	.01
☐ 159 Bob Dernier	.10	.05	.01
☐ 160 Bo Diaz	.10	.05	.01
☐ 161 Ed Farmer	.10	.05	.01
☐ 162 Greg Gross	.10	.05	.01
☐ 163 Mike Krukow	.10	.05	.01
☐ 164 Garry Maddox	.10	.05	.01
☐ 165 Gary Matthews	.15	.07	.02
☐ 166 Tug McGraw	.15	.07	.02
☐ 167 Bob Molinaro	.10	.05	.01
☐ 168 Sid Monge	.10	.05	.01
☐ 169 Ron Reed	.10	.05	.01
☐ 170 Bill Robinson	.15	.07	.02
☐ 171 Pete Rose	1.75	.80	.22
☐ 172 Dick Ruthven	.10	.05	.01
☐ 173 Mike Schmidt	1.75	.80	.22
☐ 174 Manny Trillo	.10	.05	.01
☐ 175 Ozzie Virgil	.10	.05	.01
☐ 176 George Vukovich	.10	.05	.01
☐ 177 Gary Allenson	.10	.05	.01
☐ 178 Luis Aponte	.10	.05	.01
☐ 179 Wade Boggs	18.00	8.00	2.30
☐ 180 Tom Burgmeier	.10	.05	.01
☐ 181 Mark Clear	.10	.05	.01
☐ 182 Dennis Eckersley	.50	.23	.06
☐ 183 Dwight Evans	.15	.07	.02
☐ 184 Rich Gedman	.10	.05	.01
☐ 185 Glenn Hoffman	.10	.05	.01
☐ 186 Bruce Hurst	.15	.07	.02
☐ 187 Carney Lansford	.15	.07	.02
☐ 188 Rick Miller	.10	.05	.01
☐ 189 Reid Nichols	.10	.05	.01
☐ 190 Bob Ojeda	.15	.07	.02
☐ 191 Tony Perez	.20	.09	.03
☐ 192 Chuck Rainey	.10	.05	.01
☐ 193 Jerry Remy	.10	.05	.01
☐ 194 Jim Rice	.20	.09	.03
☐ 195 Bob Stanley	.10	.05	.01
☐ 196 Dave Stapleton	.10	.05	.01
☐ 197 Mike Torrez	.10	.05	.01
☐ 198 John Tudor	.15	.07	.02
☐ 199 Julio Valdez	.10	.05	.01
☐ 200 Carl Yastrzemski	.75	.35	.09
☐ 201 Dusty Baker	.20	.09	.03
☐ 202 Joe Beckwith	.10	.05	.01
☐ 203 Greg Brock	.10	.05	.01
☐ 204 Ron Cey	.15	.07	.02
☐ 205 Terry Forster	.10	.05	.01
☐ 206 Steve Garvey	.30	.14	.04
☐ 207 Pedro Guerrero	.15	.07	.02
☐ 208 Burt Hooton	.10	.05	.01
☐ 209 Steve Howe	.10	.05	.01
☐ 210 Ken Landreaux	.10	.05	.01
☐ 211 Mike Marshall	.10	.05	.01
☐ 212 Candy Maldonado	.40	.18	.05
☐ 213 Rick Monday	.10	.05	.01

- ☐ 214 Tom Niedenfuer .... .10 .05 .01
- ☐ 215 Jorge Orta .... .10 .05 .01
- ☐ 216 Jerry Reuss UER .... .10 .05 .01
  ("Home:" omitted)
- ☐ 217 Ron Roenicke .... .10 .05 .01
- ☐ 218 Vicente Romo .... .10 .05 .01
- ☐ 219 Bill Russell .... .15 .07 .02
- ☐ 220 Steve Sax .... .15 .07 .02
- ☐ 221 Mike Scioscia .... .15 .07 .02
- ☐ 222 Dave Stewart .... .50 .23 .06
- ☐ 223 Derrel Thomas .... .10 .05 .01
- ☐ 224 Fernando Valenzuela .... .15 .07 .02
- ☐ 225 Bob Welch .... .15 .07 .02
- ☐ 226 Ricky Wright .... .10 .05 .01
- ☐ 227 Steve Yeager .... .10 .05 .01
- ☐ 228 Bill Almon .... .10 .05 .01
- ☐ 229 Harold Baines .... .50 .23 .06
- ☐ 230 Salome Barojas .... .10 .05 .01
- ☐ 231 Tony Bernazard .... .10 .05 .01
- ☐ 232 Britt Burns .... .10 .05 .01
- ☐ 233 Richard Dotson .... .10 .05 .01
- ☐ 234 Ernesto Escarrega .... .10 .05 .01
- ☐ 235 Carlton Fisk .... 1.00 .45 .13
- ☐ 236 Jerry Hairston .... .10 .05 .01
- ☐ 237 Kevin Hickey .... .10 .05 .01
- ☐ 238 LaMarr Hoyt .... .10 .05 .01
- ☐ 239 Steve Kemp .... .10 .05 .01
- ☐ 240 Jim Kern .... .10 .05 .01
- ☐ 241 Ron Kittle .... .25 .11 .03
- ☐ 242 Jerry Koosman .... .15 .07 .02
- ☐ 243 Dennis Lamp .... .10 .05 .01
- ☐ 244 Rudy Law .... .10 .05 .01
- ☐ 245 Vance Law .... .10 .05 .01
- ☐ 246 Ron LeFlore .... .15 .07 .02
- ☐ 247 Greg Luzinski .... .15 .07 .02
- ☐ 248 Tom Paciorek .... .15 .07 .02
- ☐ 249 Aurelio Rodriguez .... .10 .05 .01
- ☐ 250 Mike Squires .... .10 .05 .01
- ☐ 251 Steve Trout .... .10 .05 .01
- ☐ 252 Jim Barr .... .10 .05 .01
- ☐ 253 Dave Bergman .... .10 .05 .01
- ☐ 254 Fred Breining .... .10 .05 .01
- ☐ 255 Bob Brenly .... .10 .05 .01
- ☐ 256 Jack Clark .... .15 .07 .02
- ☐ 257 Chili Davis .... 1.25 .55 .16
- ☐ 258 Darrell Evans .... .15 .07 .02
- ☐ 259 Alan Fowlkes .... .10 .05 .01
- ☐ 260 Rich Gale .... .10 .05 .01
- ☐ 261 Atlee Hammaker .... .10 .05 .01
- ☐ 262 Al Holland .... .10 .05 .01
- ☐ 263 Duane Kuiper .... .10 .05 .01
- ☐ 264 Bill Laskey .... .10 .05 .01
- ☐ 265 Gary Lavelle .... .10 .05 .01
- ☐ 266 Johnnie LeMaster .... .10 .05 .01
- ☐ 267 Renie Martin .... .10 .05 .01
- ☐ 268 Milt May .... .10 .05 .01
- ☐ 269 Greg Minton .... .10 .05 .01
- ☐ 270 Joe Morgan .... .60 .25 .08
- ☐ 271 Tom O'Malley .... .10 .05 .01
- ☐ 272 Reggie Smith .... .15 .07 .02
- ☐ 273 Guy Sularz .... .10 .05 .01
- ☐ 274 Champ Summers .... .10 .05 .01
- ☐ 275 Max Venable .... .10 .05 .01
- ☐ 276 Jim Wohlford .... .10 .05 .01
- ☐ 277 Ray Burris .... .10 .05 .01
- ☐ 278 Gary Carter .... .40 .18 .05
- ☐ 279 Warren Cromartie .... .10 .05 .01
- ☐ 280 Andre Dawson .... 1.00 .45 .13
- ☐ 281 Terry Francona .... .10 .05 .01
- ☐ 282 Doug Flynn .... .10 .05 .01
- ☐ 283 Woodie Fryman .... .10 .05 .01
- ☐ 284 Bill Gullickson .... .15 .07 .02
- ☐ 285 Wallace Johnson .... .10 .05 .01
- ☐ 286 Charlie Lea .... .10 .05 .01
- ☐ 287 Randy Lerch .... .10 .05 .01
- ☐ 288 Brad Mills .... .10 .05 .01
- ☐ 289 Dan Norman .... .10 .05 .01
- ☐ 290 Al Oliver .... .15 .07 .02
- ☐ 291 David Palmer .... .10 .05 .01
- ☐ 292 Tim Raines .... .75 .35 .09
- ☐ 293 Jeff Reardon .... .35 .16 .04
- ☐ 294 Steve Rogers .... .10 .05 .01
- ☐ 295 Scott Sanderson .... .10 .05 .01
- ☐ 296 Dan Schatzeder .... .10 .05 .01
- ☐ 297 Bryn Smith .... .10 .05 .01
- ☐ 298 Chris Speier .... .10 .05 .01
- ☐ 299 Tim Wallach .... .20 .09 .03
- ☐ 300 Jerry White .... .10 .05 .01
- ☐ 301 Joel Youngblood .... .10 .05 .01
- ☐ 302 Ross Baumgarten .... .10 .05 .01
- ☐ 303 Dale Berra .... .10 .05 .01
- ☐ 304 John Candelaria .... .10 .05 .01
- ☐ 305 Dick Davis .... .10 .05 .01
- ☐ 306 Mike Easler .... .10 .05 .01
- ☐ 307 Richie Hebner .... .10 .05 .01
- ☐ 308 Lee Lacy .... .10 .05 .01
- ☐ 309 Bill Madlock .... .15 .07 .02
- ☐ 310 Larry McWilliams .... .10 .05 .01
- ☐ 311 John Milner .... .10 .05 .01
- ☐ 312 Omar Moreno .... .10 .05 .01
- ☐ 313 Jim Morrison .... .10 .05 .01
- ☐ 314 Steve Nicosia .... .10 .05 .01
- ☐ 315 Dave Parker .... .20 .09 .03
- ☐ 316 Tony Pena .... .15 .07 .02
- ☐ 317 Johnny Ray .... .10 .05 .01
- ☐ 318 Rick Rhoden .... .10 .05 .01
- ☐ 319 Don Robinson .... .10 .05 .01
- ☐ 320 Enrique Romo .... .10 .05 .01
- ☐ 321 Manny Sarmiento .... .10 .05 .01
- ☐ 322 Rod Scurry .... .10 .05 .01
- ☐ 323 Jimmy Smith .... .10 .05 .01
- ☐ 324 Willie Stargell .... .50 .23 .06
- ☐ 325 Jason Thompson .... .10 .05 .01
- ☐ 326 Kent Tekulve .... .15 .07 .02
- ☐ 327A Tom Brookens .... .10 .05 .01
  (Short .375" brown box shaded in on card back)
- ☐ 327B Tom Brookens .... .10 .05 .01
  (Longer 1.25" brown box shaded in on card back)
- ☐ 328 Enos Cabell .... .10 .05 .01
- ☐ 329 Kirk Gibson .... .75 .35 .09
- ☐ 330 Larry Herndon .... .10 .05 .01
- ☐ 331 Mike Ivie .... .10 .05 .01
- ☐ 332 Howard Johnson .... 1.00 .45 .13
- ☐ 333 Lynn Jones .... .10 .05 .01
- ☐ 334 Rick Leach .... .10 .05 .01
- ☐ 335 Chet Lemon .... .10 .05 .01
- ☐ 336 Jack Morris .... .35 .16 .04
- ☐ 337 Lance Parrish .... .15 .07 .02
- ☐ 338 Larry Pashnick .... .10 .05 .01
- ☐ 339 Dan Petry .... .10 .05 .01
- ☐ 340 Dave Rozema .... .10 .05 .01
- ☐ 341 Dave Rucker .... .10 .05 .01
- ☐ 342 Elias Sosa .... .10 .05 .01
- ☐ 343 Dave Tobik .... .10 .05 .01
- ☐ 344 Alan Trammell .... 1.00 .45 .13
- ☐ 345 Jerry Turner .... .10 .05 .01
- ☐ 346 Jerry Ujdur .... .10 .05 .01
- ☐ 347 Pat Underwood .... .10 .05 .01
- ☐ 348 Lou Whitaker .... .50 .23 .06
- ☐ 349 Milt Wilcox .... .10 .05 .01
- ☐ 350 Glenn Wilson .... .15 .07 .02
- ☐ 351 John Wockenfuss .... .10 .05 .01
- ☐ 352 Kurt Bevacqua .... .10 .05 .01
- ☐ 353 Juan Bonilla .... .10 .05 .01

☐ 354 Floyd Chiffer .10 .05 .01
☐ 355 Luis DeLeon .10 .05 .01
☐ 356 Dave Dravecky .60 .25 .08
☐ 357 Dave Edwards .10 .05 .01
☐ 358 Juan Eichelberger .10 .05 .01
☐ 359 Tim Flannery .10 .05 .01
☐ 360 Tony Gwynn 25.00 11.50 3.10
☐ 361 Ruppert Jones .10 .05 .01
☐ 362 Terry Kennedy .10 .05 .01
☐ 363 Joe Lefebvre .10 .05 .01
☐ 364 Sixto Lezcano .10 .05 .01
☐ 365 Tim Lollar .10 .05 .01
☐ 366 Gary Lucas .10 .05 .01
☐ 367 John Montefusco .10 .05 .01
☐ 368 Broderick Perkins .10 .05 .01
☐ 369 Joe Pittman .10 .05 .01
☐ 370 Gene Richards .10 .05 .01
☐ 371 Luis Salazar .10 .05 .01
☐ 372 Eric Show .15 .07 .02
☐ 373 Garry Templeton .10 .05 .01
☐ 374 Chris Welsh .10 .05 .01
☐ 375 Alan Wiggins .10 .05 .01
☐ 376 Rick Cerone .10 .05 .01
☐ 377 Dave Collins .10 .05 .01
☐ 378 Roger Erickson .10 .05 .01
☐ 379 George Frazier .10 .05 .01
☐ 380 Oscar Gamble .10 .05 .01
☐ 381 Rich Gossage .20 .09 .03
☐ 382 Ken Griffey .15 .07 .02
☐ 383 Ron Guidry .15 .07 .02
☐ 384 Dave LaRoche .10 .05 .01
☐ 385 Rudy May .10 .05 .01
☐ 386 John Mayberry .10 .05 .01
☐ 387 Lee Mazzilli .10 .05 .01
☐ 388 Mike Morgan .10 .05 .01
☐ 389 Jerry Mumphrey .10 .05 .01
☐ 390 Bobby Murcer .15 .07 .02
☐ 391 Graig Nettles .15 .07 .02
☐ 392 Lou Piniella .15 .07 .02
☐ 393 Willie Randolph .15 .07 .02
☐ 394 Shane Rawley .10 .05 .01
☐ 395 Dave Righetti .15 .07 .02
☐ 396 Andre Robertson .10 .05 .01
☐ 397 Roy Smalley .10 .05 .01
☐ 398 Dave Winfield 2.00 .90 .25
☐ 399 Butch Wynegar .10 .05 .01
☐ 400 Chris Bando .10 .05 .01
☐ 401 Alan Bannister .10 .05 .01
☐ 402 Len Barker .10 .05 .01
☐ 403 Tom Brennan .10 .05 .01
☐ 404 Carmelo Castillo .10 .05 .01
☐ 405 Miguel Dilone .10 .05 .01
☐ 406 Jerry Dybzinski .10 .05 .01
☐ 407 Mike Fischlin .10 .05 .01
☐ 408 Ed Glynn UER .10 .05 .01
(Photo actually
Bud Anderson)
☐ 409 Mike Hargrove .15 .07 .02
☐ 410 Toby Harrah .10 .05 .01
☐ 411 Ron Hassey .10 .05 .01
☐ 412 Von Hayes .15 .07 .02
☐ 413 Rick Manning .10 .05 .01
☐ 414 Bake McBride .10 .05 .01
☐ 415 Larry Milbourne .10 .05 .01
☐ 416 Bill Nahorodny .10 .05 .01
☐ 417 Jack Perconte .10 .05 .01
☐ 418 Lary Sorensen .10 .05 .01
☐ 419 Dan Spillner .10 .05 .01
☐ 420 Rick Sutcliffe .15 .07 .02
☐ 421 Andre Thornton .10 .05 .01
☐ 422 Rick Waits .10 .05 .01
☐ 423 Eddie Whitson .10 .05 .01
☐ 424 Jesse Barfield .15 .07 .02
☐ 425 Barry Bonnell .10 .05 .01
☐ 426 Jim Clancy .10 .05 .01
☐ 427 Damaso Garcia .10 .05 .01
☐ 428 Jerry Garvin .10 .05 .01
☐ 429 Alfredo Griffin .10 .05 .01
☐ 430 Garth Iorg .10 .05 .01
☐ 431 Roy Lee Jackson .10 .05 .01
☐ 432 Luis Leal .10 .05 .01
☐ 433 Buck Martinez .10 .05 .01
☐ 434 Joey McLaughlin .10 .05 .01
☐ 435 Lloyd Moseby .10 .05 .01
☐ 436 Rance Mulliniks .10 .05 .01
☐ 437 Dale Murray .10 .05 .01
☐ 438 Wayne Nordhagen .10 .05 .01
☐ 439 Geno Petralli .15 .07 .02
☐ 440 Hosken Powell .10 .05 .01
☐ 441 Dave Stieb .15 .07 .02
☐ 442 Willie Upshaw .10 .05 .01
☐ 443 Ernie Whitt .10 .05 .01
☐ 444 Alvis Woods .10 .05 .01
☐ 445 Alan Ashby .10 .05 .01
☐ 446 Jose Cruz .15 .07 .02
☐ 447 Kiko Garcia .10 .05 .01
☐ 448 Phil Garner .15 .07 .02
☐ 449 Danny Heep .10 .05 .01
☐ 450 Art Howe .10 .05 .01
☐ 451 Bob Knepper .10 .05 .01
☐ 452 Alan Knicely .10 .05 .01
☐ 453 Ray Knight .15 .07 .02
☐ 454 Frank LaCorte .10 .05 .01
☐ 455 Mike LaCoss .10 .05 .01
☐ 456 Randy Moffitt .10 .05 .01
☐ 457 Joe Niekro .15 .07 .02
☐ 458 Terry Puhl .10 .05 .01
☐ 459 Luis Pujols .10 .05 .01
☐ 460 Craig Reynolds .10 .05 .01
☐ 461 Bert Roberge .10 .05 .01
☐ 462 Vern Ruhle .10 .05 .01
☐ 463 Nolan Ryan 7.00 3.10 .85
☐ 464 Joe Sambito .10 .05 .01
☐ 465 Tony Scott .10 .05 .01
☐ 466 Dave Smith .10 .05 .01
☐ 467 Harry Spilman .10 .05 .01
☐ 468 Dickie Thon .10 .05 .01
☐ 469 Denny Walling .10 .05 .01
☐ 470 Larry Andersen .10 .05 .01
☐ 471 Floyd Bannister .10 .05 .01
☐ 472 Jim Beattie .10 .05 .01
☐ 473 Bruce Bochte .10 .05 .01
☐ 474 Manny Castillo .10 .05 .01
☐ 475 Bill Caudill .10 .05 .01
☐ 476 Bryan Clark .10 .05 .01
☐ 477 Al Cowens .10 .05 .01
☐ 478 Julio Cruz .10 .05 .01
☐ 479 Todd Cruz .10 .05 .01
☐ 480 Gary Gray .10 .05 .01
☐ 481 Dave Henderson .15 .07 .02
☐ 482 Mike Moore .60 .25 .08
☐ 483 Gaylord Perry .40 .18 .05
☐ 484 Dave Revering .10 .05 .01
☐ 485 Joe Simpson .10 .05 .01
☐ 486 Mike Stanton .10 .05 .01
☐ 487 Rick Sweet .10 .05 .01
☐ 488 Ed VandeBerg .10 .05 .01
☐ 489 Richie Zisk .10 .05 .01
☐ 490 Doug Bird .10 .05 .01
☐ 491 Larry Bowa .15 .07 .02
☐ 492 Bill Buckner .15 .07 .02
☐ 493 Bill Campbell .10 .05 .01
☐ 494 Jody Davis .10 .05 .01
☐ 495 Leon Durham .10 .05 .01
☐ 496 Steve Henderson .10 .05 .01
☐ 497 Willie Hernandez .15 .07 .02

☐	498	Ferguson Jenkins	.35	.16	.04
☐	499	Jay Johnstone	.15	.07	.02
☐	500	Junior Kennedy	.10	.05	.01
☐	501	Randy Martz	.10	.05	.01
☐	502	Jerry Morales	.10	.05	.01
☐	503	Keith Moreland	.10	.05	.01
☐	504	Dickie Noles	.10	.05	.01
☐	505	Mike Proly	.10	.05	.01
☐	506	Allen Ripley	.10	.05	.01
☐	507	Ryne Sandberg UER (Should say High School in Spokane, Washington)	25.00	11.50	3.10
☐	508	Lee Smith	2.00	.90	.25
☐	509	Pat Tabler	.10	.05	.01
☐	510	Dick Tidrow	.10	.05	.01
☐	511	Bump Wills	.10	.05	.01
☐	512	Gary Woods	.10	.05	.01
☐	513	Tony Armas	.10	.05	.01
☐	514	Dave Beard	.10	.05	.01
☐	515	Jeff Burroughs	.10	.05	.01
☐	516	John D'Acquisto	.10	.05	.01
☐	517	Wayne Gross	.10	.05	.01
☐	518	Mike Heath	.10	.05	.01
☐	519	Rickey Henderson UER (Brock record listed as 120 steals)	3.00	1.35	.40
☐	520	Cliff Johnson	.10	.05	.01
☐	521	Matt Keough	.10	.05	.01
☐	522	Brian Kingman	.10	.05	.01
☐	523	Rick Langford	.10	.05	.01
☐	524	Dave Lopes	.15	.07	.02
☐	525	Steve McCatty	.10	.05	.01
☐	526	Dave McKay	.10	.05	.01
☐	527	Dan Meyer	.10	.05	.01
☐	528	Dwayne Murphy	.10	.05	.01
☐	529	Jeff Newman	.10	.05	.01
☐	530	Mike Norris	.10	.05	.01
☐	531	Bob Owchinko	.10	.05	.01
☐	532	Joe Rudi	.10	.05	.01
☐	533	Jimmy Sexton	.10	.05	.01
☐	534	Fred Stanley	.10	.05	.01
☐	535	Tom Underwood	.10	.05	.01
☐	536	Neil Allen	.10	.05	.01
☐	537	Wally Backman	.10	.05	.01
☐	538	Bob Bailor	.10	.05	.01
☐	539	Hubie Brooks	.15	.07	.02
☐	540	Carlos Diaz	.10	.05	.01
☐	541	Pete Falcone	.10	.05	.01
☐	542	George Foster	.15	.07	.02
☐	543	Ron Gardenhire	.10	.05	.01
☐	544	Brian Giles	.10	.05	.01
☐	545	Ron Hodges	.10	.05	.01
☐	546	Randy Jones	.10	.05	.01
☐	547	Mike Jorgensen	.10	.05	.01
☐	548	Dave Kingman	.15	.07	.02
☐	549	Ed Lynch	.10	.05	.01
☐	550	Jesse Orosco	.10	.05	.01
☐	551	Rick Ownbey	.10	.05	.01
☐	552	Charlie Puleo	.10	.05	.01
☐	553	Gary Rajsich	.10	.05	.01
☐	554	Mike Scott	.15	.07	.02
☐	555	Rusty Staub	.15	.07	.02
☐	556	John Stearns	.10	.05	.01
☐	557	Craig Swan	.10	.05	.01
☐	558	Ellis Valentine	.10	.05	.01
☐	559	Tom Veryzer	.10	.05	.01
☐	560	Mookie Wilson	.15	.07	.02
☐	561	Pat Zachry	.10	.05	.01
☐	562	Buddy Bell	.15	.07	.02
☐	563	John Butcher	.10	.05	.01
☐	564	Steve Comer	.10	.05	.01
☐	565	Danny Darwin	.10	.05	.01
☐	566	Bucky Dent	.15	.07	.02

☐	567	John Grubb	.10	.05	.01
☐	568	Rick Honeycutt	.10	.05	.01
☐	569	Dave Hostetler	.10	.05	.01
☐	570	Charlie Hough	.15	.07	.02
☐	571	Lamar Johnson	.10	.05	.01
☐	572	Jon Matlack	.10	.05	.01
☐	573	Paul Mirabella	.10	.05	.01
☐	574	Larry Parrish	.10	.05	.01
☐	575	Mike Richardt	.10	.05	.01
☐	576	Mickey Rivers	.10	.05	.01
☐	577	Billy Sample	.10	.05	.01
☐	578	Dave Schmidt	.10	.05	.01
☐	579	Bill Stein	.10	.05	.01
☐	580	Jim Sundberg	.15	.07	.02
☐	581	Frank Tanana	.15	.07	.02
☐	582	Mark Wagner	.10	.05	.01
☐	583	George Wright	.10	.05	.01
☐	584	Johnny Bench	1.00	.45	.13
☐	585	Bruce Berenyi	.10	.05	.01
☐	586	Larry Biittner	.10	.05	.01
☐	587	Cesar Cedeno	.15	.07	.02
☐	588	Dave Concepcion	.15	.07	.02
☐	589	Dan Driessen	.10	.05	.01
☐	590	Greg Harris	.10	.05	.01
☐	591	Ben Hayes	.10	.05	.01
☐	592	Paul Householder	.10	.05	.01
☐	593	Tom Hume	.10	.05	.01
☐	594	Wayne Krenchicki	.10	.05	.01
☐	595	Rafael Landestoy	.10	.05	.01
☐	596	Charlie Leibrandt	.15	.07	.02
☐	597	Eddie Milner	.10	.05	.01
☐	598	Ron Oester	.10	.05	.01
☐	599	Frank Pastore	.10	.05	.01
☐	600	Joe Price	.10	.05	.01
☐	601	Tom Seaver	1.00	.45	.13
☐	602	Bob Shirley	.10	.05	.01
☐	603	Mario Soto	.10	.05	.01
☐	604	Alex Trevino	.10	.05	.01
☐	605	Mike Vail	.10	.05	.01
☐	606	Duane Walker	.10	.05	.01
☐	607	Tom Brunansky	.15	.07	.02
☐	608	Bobby Castillo	.10	.05	.01
☐	609	John Castino	.10	.05	.01
☐	610	Ron Davis	.10	.05	.01
☐	611	Lenny Faedo	.10	.05	.01
☐	612	Terry Felton	.10	.05	.01
☐	613	Gary Gaetti	.60	.25	.08
☐	614	Mickey Hatcher	.10	.05	.01
☐	615	Brad Havens	.10	.05	.01
☐	616	Kent Hrbek	.60	.25	.08
☐	617	Randy Johnson	.10	.05	.01
☐	618	Tim Laudner	.10	.05	.01
☐	619	Jeff Little	.10	.05	.01
☐	620	Bobby Mitchell	.10	.05	.01
☐	621	Jack O'Connor	.10	.05	.01
☐	622	John Pacella	.10	.05	.01
☐	623	Pete Redfern	.10	.05	.01
☐	624	Jesus Vega	.10	.05	.01
☐	625	Frank Viola	1.50	.65	.19
☐	626	Ron Washington	.10	.05	.01
☐	627	Gary Ward	.10	.05	.01
☐	628	Al Williams	.10	.05	.01
☐	629	Red Sox All-Stars Carl Yastrzemski Dennis Eckersley Mark Clear	.75	.35	.09
☐	630	"300 Career Wins" Gaylord Perry and Terry Bulling 5/6/82	.25	.11	.03
☐	631	Pride of Venezuela Dave Concepcion and Manny Trillo	.15	.07	.02
☐	632	All-Star Infielders	.50	.23	.06

	Robin Yount and Buddy Bell			
☐ 633	Mr.Vet and Mr.Rookie..	.75	.35	.09
	Dave Winfield and Kent Hrbek			
☐ 634	Fountain of Youth	.60	.25	.08
	Willie Stargell and Pete Rose			
☐ 635	Big Chiefs	.15	.07	.02
	Toby Harrah and Andre Thornton			
☐ 636	Smith Brothers	.75	.35	.09
	Ozzie and Lonnie			
☐ 637	Base Stealers' Threat ...	.15	.07	.02
	Bo Diaz and Gary Carter			
☐ 638	All-Star Catchers..........	.40	.18	.05
	Carlton Fisk and Gary Carter			
☐ 639	The Silver Shoe..........	1.00	.45	.13
	Rickey Henderson			
☐ 640	Home Run Threats.......	.40	.18	.05
	Ben Oglivie and Reggie Jackson			
☐ 641	Two Teams Same Day .	.15	.07	.02
	Joel Youngblood August 4, 1982			
☐ 642	Last Perfect Game	.15	.07	.02
	Ron Hassey and Len Barker			
☐ 643	Black and Blue	.15	.07	.02
	Vida Blue			
☐ 644	Black and Blue	.15	.07	.02
	Bud Black			
☐ 645	Speed and Power.........	.60	.25	.08
	Reggie Jackson			
☐ 646	Speed and Power.......	1.00	.45	.13
	Rickey Henderson			
☐ 647	CL: Cards/Brewers.......	.15	.05	.01
☐ 648	CL: Orioles/Angels	.15	.05	.01
☐ 649	CL: Royals/Braves........	.15	.05	.01
☐ 650	CL: Phillies/Red Sox	.15	.05	.01
☐ 651	CL: Dodgers/White Sox	.15	.05	.01
☐ 652	CL: Giants/Expos	.15	.05	.01
☐ 653	CL: Pirates/Tigers	.15	.05	.01
☐ 654	CL: Padres/Yankees.....	.15	.05	.01
☐ 655	CL: Indians/Blue Jays ..	.15	.05	.01
☐ 656	CL: Astros/Mariners.....	.15	.05	.01
☐ 657	CL: Cubs/A's...............	.15	.05	.01
☐ 658	CL: Mets/Rangers	.15	.05	.01
☐ 659	CL: Reds/Twins............	.15	.05	.01
☐ 660	CL: Specials/Teams	.15	.05	.01

1984 Fleer

The cards in this 660-card set measure 2 1/2" by 3 1/2". The 1984 Fleer card set featured fronts with full-color team logos along with the player's name and position and the Fleer identification. The set features many imaginative photos, several multi-player cards, and many more action shots than the 1983 card set. The backs are quite similar to the 1983 backs except that blue rather than brown ink is used. The player cards are alphabetized within team and the teams are ordered by their 1983 season finish and won-lost record, e.g., Baltimore (1-23), Philadelphia (24-49), Chicago White Sox

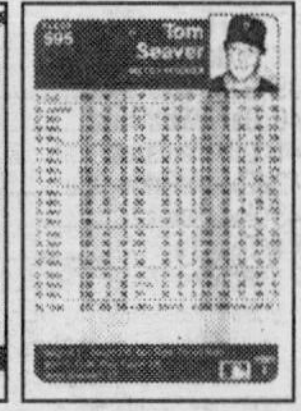

(50-73), Detroit (74-95), Los Angeles (96-118), New York Yankees (119-144), Toronto (145-169), Atlanta (170-193), Milwaukee (194-219), Houston (220-244), Pittsburgh (245-269), Montreal (270-293), San Diego (294-317), St. Louis (318-340), Kansas City (341-364), San Francisco (365-387), Boston (388-412), Texas (413-435), Oakland (436-461), Cincinnati (462-485), Chicago (486-507), California (508-532), Cleveland (533-555), Minnesota (556-579), New York Mets (580-603), and Seattle (604-625). Specials (626-646) and checklist cards (647-660) make up the end of the set. The key Rookie Cards in this set are Tony Fernandez, Don Mattingly, Kevin McReynolds, Juan Samuel, Darryl Strawberry, and Andy Van Slyke.

		NRMT-MT	EXC	G-VG
COMPLETE SET (660)		110.00	50.00	14.00
COMMON CARD (1-660)		.15	.07	.02
☐ 1	Mike Boddicker................	.20	.09	.03
☐ 2	Al Bumbry..........................	.20	.09	.03
☐ 3	Todd Cruz	.15	.07	.02
☐ 4	Rich Dauer........................	.15	.07	.02
☐ 5	Storm Davis......................	.15	.07	.02
☐ 6	Rick Dempsey...................	.15	.07	.02
☐ 7	Jim Dwyer..........................	.15	.07	.02
☐ 8	Mike Flanagan...................	.15	.07	.02
☐ 9	Dan Ford	.15	.07	.02
☐ 10	John Lowenstein............	.15	.07	.02
☐ 11	Dennis Martinez.............	.20	.09	.03
☐ 12	Tippy Martinez	.15	.07	.02
☐ 13	Scott McGregor	.15	.07	.02
☐ 14	Eddie Murray	4.00	1.80	.50
☐ 15	Joe Nolan.........................	.15	.07	.02
☐ 16	Jim Palmer	2.00	.90	.25
☐ 17	Cal Ripken..................	20.00	9.00	2.50
☐ 18	Gary Roenicke................	.15	.07	.02
☐ 19	Lenn Sakata	.15	.07	.02
☐ 20	John Shelby.....................	.15	.07	.02
☐ 21	Ken Singleton	.20	.09	.03
☐ 22	Sammy Stewart	.15	.07	.02
☐ 23	Tim Stoddard..................	.15	.07	.02
☐ 24	Marty Bystrom................	.15	.07	.02
☐ 25	Steve Carlton	3.00	1.35	.40
☐ 26	Ivan DeJesus	.15	.07	.02
☐ 27	John Denny......................	.15	.07	.02
☐ 28	Bob Dernier.....................	.15	.07	.02
☐ 29	Bo Diaz	.15	.07	.02
☐ 30	Kiko Garcia	.15	.07	.02
☐ 31	Greg Gross	.15	.07	.02
☐ 32	Kevin Gross	.40	.18	.05
☐ 33	Von Hayes.........................	.15	.07	.02
☐ 34	Willie Hernandez............	.20	.09	.03
☐ 35	Al Holland	.15	.07	.02
☐ 36	Charles Hudson	.15	.07	.02

☐ 37 Joe Lefebvre .15 .07 .02
☐ 38 Sixto Lezcano .15 .07 .02
☐ 39 Garry Maddox .15 .07 .02
☐ 40 Gary Matthews .20 .09 .03
☐ 41 Len Matuszek .15 .07 .02
☐ 42 Tug McGraw .20 .09 .03
☐ 43 Joe Morgan 1.00 .45 .13
☐ 44 Tony Perez .75 .35 .09
☐ 45 Ron Reed .15 .07 .02
☐ 46 Pete Rose 3.00 1.35 .40
☐ 47 Juan Samuel .75 .35 .09
☐ 48 Mike Schmidt 8.00 3.60 1.00
☐ 49 Ozzie Virgil .15 .07 .02
☐ 50 Juan Agosto .15 .07 .02
☐ 51 Harold Baines .50 .23 .06
☐ 52 Floyd Bannister .15 .07 .02
☐ 53 Salome Barojas .15 .07 .02
☐ 54 Britt Burns .15 .07 .02
☐ 55 Julio Cruz .15 .07 .02
☐ 56 Richard Dotson .15 .07 .02
☐ 57 Jerry Dybzinski .15 .07 .02
☐ 58 Carlton Fisk 2.50 1.15 .30
☐ 59 Scott Fletcher .15 .07 .02
☐ 60 Jerry Hairston .15 .07 .02
☐ 61 Kevin Hickey .15 .07 .02
☐ 62 Marc Hill .15 .07 .02
☐ 63 LaMarr Hoyt .15 .07 .02
☐ 64 Ron Kittle .15 .07 .02
☐ 65 Jerry Koosman .20 .09 .03
☐ 66 Dennis Lamp .15 .07 .02
☐ 67 Rudy Law .15 .07 .02
☐ 68 Vance Law .15 .07 .02
☐ 69 Greg Luzinski .20 .09 .03
☐ 70 Tom Paciorek .20 .09 .03
☐ 71 Mike Squires .15 .07 .02
☐ 72 Dick Tidrow .15 .07 .02
☐ 73 Greg Walker .15 .07 .02
☐ 74 Glenn Abbott .15 .07 .02
☐ 75 Howard Bailey .15 .07 .02
☐ 76 Doug Bair .15 .07 .02
☐ 77 Juan Berenguer .15 .07 .02
☐ 78 Tom Brookens .20 .09 .03
☐ 79 Enos Cabell .15 .07 .02
☐ 80 Kirk Gibson 1.00 .45 .13
☐ 81 John Grubb .15 .07 .02
☐ 82 Larry Herndon .20 .09 .03
☐ 83 Wayne Krenchicki .15 .07 .02
☐ 84 Rick Leach .15 .07 .02
☐ 85 Chet Lemon .20 .09 .03
☐ 86 Aurelio Lopez .20 .09 .03
☐ 87 Jack Morris .75 .35 .09
☐ 88 Lance Parrish .20 .09 .03
☐ 89 Dan Petry .20 .09 .03
☐ 90 Dave Rozema .15 .07 .02
☐ 91 Alan Trammell 1.75 .80 .22
☐ 92 Lou Whitaker 1.50 .65 .19
☐ 93 Milt Wilcox .15 .07 .02
☐ 94 Glenn Wilson .20 .09 .03
☐ 95 John Wockenfuss .15 .07 .02
☐ 96 Dusty Baker .30 .14 .04
☐ 97 Joe Beckwith .15 .07 .02
☐ 98 Greg Brock .15 .07 .02
☐ 99 Jack Fimple .15 .07 .02
☐ 100 Pedro Guerrero .20 .09 .03
☐ 101 Rick Honeycutt .15 .07 .02
☐ 102 Burt Hooton .15 .07 .02
☐ 103 Steve Howe .15 .07 .02
☐ 104 Ken Landreaux .15 .07 .02
☐ 105 Mike Marshall .15 .07 .02
☐ 106 Rick Monday .15 .07 .02
☐ 107 Jose Morales .15 .07 .02
☐ 108 Tom Niedenfuer .15 .07 .02
☐ 109 Alejandro Pena .35 .16 .04
☐ 110 Jerry Reuss UER .15 .07 .02
("Home:" omitted)
☐ 111 Bill Russell .20 .09 .03
☐ 112 Steve Sax .20 .09 .03
☐ 113 Mike Scioscia .15 .07 .02
☐ 114 Derrel Thomas .15 .07 .02
☐ 115 Fernando Valenzuela .20 .09 .03
☐ 116 Bob Welch .20 .09 .03
☐ 117 Steve Yeager .15 .07 .02
☐ 118 Pat Zachry .15 .07 .02
☐ 119 Don Baylor .30 .14 .04
☐ 120 Bert Campaneris .20 .09 .03
☐ 121 Rick Cerone .15 .07 .02
☐ 122 Ray Fontenot .15 .07 .02
☐ 123 George Frazier .15 .07 .02
☐ 124 Oscar Gamble .15 .07 .02
☐ 125 Rich Gossage .30 .14 .04
☐ 126 Ken Griffey .20 .09 .03
☐ 127 Ron Guidry .20 .09 .03
☐ 128 Jay Howell .20 .09 .03
☐ 129 Steve Kemp .15 .07 .02
☐ 130 Matt Keough .15 .07 .02
☐ 131 Don Mattingly 30.00 13.50 3.80
☐ 132 John Montefusco .15 .07 .02
☐ 133 Omar Moreno .15 .07 .02
☐ 134 Dale Murray .15 .07 .02
☐ 135 Graig Nettles .20 .09 .03
☐ 136 Lou Piniella .20 .09 .03
☐ 137 Willie Randolph .20 .09 .03
☐ 138 Shane Rawley .15 .07 .02
☐ 139 Dave Righetti .20 .09 .03
☐ 140 Andre Robertson .15 .07 .02
☐ 141 Bob Shirley .15 .07 .02
☐ 142 Roy Smalley .15 .07 .02
☐ 143 Dave Winfield 4.50 2.00 .55
☐ 144 Butch Wynegar .15 .07 .02
☐ 145 Jim Acker .15 .07 .02
☐ 146 Doyle Alexander .15 .07 .02
☐ 147 Jesse Barfield .20 .09 .03
☐ 148 George Bell .50 .23 .06
☐ 149 Barry Bonnell .15 .07 .02
☐ 150 Jim Clancy .15 .07 .02
☐ 151 Dave Collins .15 .07 .02
☐ 152 Tony Fernandez 2.50 1.15 .30
☐ 153 Damaso Garcia .15 .07 .02
☐ 154 Dave Geisel .15 .07 .02
☐ 155 Jim Gott .15 .07 .02
☐ 156 Alfredo Griffin .15 .07 .02
☐ 157 Garth Iorg .15 .07 .02
☐ 158 Roy Lee Jackson .15 .07 .02
☐ 159 Cliff Johnson .15 .07 .02
☐ 160 Luis Leal .15 .07 .02
☐ 161 Buck Martinez .15 .07 .02
☐ 162 Joey McLaughlin .15 .07 .02
☐ 163 Randy Moffitt .15 .07 .02
☐ 164 Lloyd Moseby .15 .07 .02
☐ 165 Rance Mulliniks .15 .07 .02
☐ 166 Jorge Orta .15 .07 .02
☐ 167 Dave Stieb .20 .09 .03
☐ 168 Willie Upshaw .15 .07 .02
☐ 169 Ernie Whitt .15 .07 .02
☐ 170 Len Barker .15 .07 .02
☐ 171 Steve Bedrosian .20 .09 .03
☐ 172 Bruce Benedict .15 .07 .02
☐ 173 Brett Butler .75 .35 .09
☐ 174 Rick Camp .15 .07 .02
☐ 175 Chris Chambliss .20 .09 .03
☐ 176 Ken Dayley .15 .07 .02
☐ 177 Pete Falcone .15 .07 .02
☐ 178 Terry Forster .15 .07 .02
☐ 179 Gene Garber .15 .07 .02
☐ 180 Terry Harper .15 .07 .02
☐ 181 Bob Horner .20 .09 .03

☐ 182	Glenn Hubbard	.15	.07	.02
☐ 183	Randy Johnson	.15	.07	.02
☐ 184	Craig McMurtry	.15	.07	.02
☐ 185	Donnie Moore	.15	.07	.02
☐ 186	Dale Murphy	1.25	.55	.16
☐ 187	Phil Niekro	.75	.35	.09
☐ 188	Pascual Perez	.15	.07	.02
☐ 189	Biff Pocoroba	.15	.07	.02
☐ 190	Rafael Ramirez	.15	.07	.02
☐ 191	Jerry Royster	.15	.07	.02
☐ 192	Claudell Washington	.15	.07	.02
☐ 193	Bob Watson	.20	.09	.03
☐ 194	Jerry Augustine	.15	.07	.02
☐ 195	Mark Brouhard	.15	.07	.02
☐ 196	Mike Caldwell	.15	.07	.02
☐ 197	Tom Candiotti	1.00	.45	.13
☐ 198	Cecil Cooper	.20	.09	.03
☐ 199	Rollie Fingers	.75	.35	.09
☐ 200	Jim Gantner	.20	.09	.03
☐ 201	Bob L. Gibson	.15	.07	.02
☐ 202	Moose Haas	.15	.07	.02
☐ 203	Roy Howell	.15	.07	.02
☐ 204	Pete Ladd	.15	.07	.02
☐ 205	Rick Manning	.15	.07	.02
☐ 206	Bob McClure	.15	.07	.02
☐ 207	Paul Molitor UER ('83 stats should say .270 BA and 608 AB)	5.00	2.30	.60
☐ 208	Don Money	.15	.07	.02
☐ 209	Charlie Moore	.15	.07	.02
☐ 210	Ben Oglivie	.15	.07	.02
☐ 211	Chuck Porter	.15	.07	.02
☐ 212	Ed Romero	.15	.07	.02
☐ 213	Ted Simmons	.20	.09	.03
☐ 214	Jim Slaton	.15	.07	.02
☐ 215	Don Sutton	.75	.35	.09
☐ 216	Tom Tellmann	.15	.07	.02
☐ 217	Pete Vuckovich	.15	.07	.02
☐ 218	Ned Yost	.15	.07	.02
☐ 219	Robin Yount	5.00	2.30	.60
☐ 220	Alan Ashby	.15	.07	.02
☐ 221	Kevin Bass	.15	.07	.02
☐ 222	Jose Cruz	.20	.09	.03
☐ 223	Bill Dawley	.15	.07	.02
☐ 224	Frank DiPino	.15	.07	.02
☐ 225	Bill Doran	.35	.16	.04
☐ 226	Phil Garner	.20	.09	.03
☐ 227	Art Howe	.15	.07	.02
☐ 228	Bob Knepper	.15	.07	.02
☐ 229	Ray Knight	.20	.09	.03
☐ 230	Frank LaCorte	.15	.07	.02
☐ 231	Mike LaCoss	.15	.07	.02
☐ 232	Mike Madden	.15	.07	.02
☐ 233	Jerry Mumphrey	.15	.07	.02
☐ 234	Joe Niekro	.20	.09	.03
☐ 235	Terry Puhl	.15	.07	.02
☐ 236	Luis Pujols	.15	.07	.02
☐ 237	Craig Reynolds	.15	.07	.02
☐ 238	Vern Ruhle	.15	.07	.02
☐ 239	Nolan Ryan	18.00	8.00	2.30
☐ 240	Mike Scott	.20	.09	.03
☐ 241	Tony Scott	.15	.07	.02
☐ 242	Dave Smith	.15	.07	.02
☐ 243	Dickie Thon	.15	.07	.02
☐ 244	Denny Walling	.15	.07	.02
☐ 245	Dale Berra	.15	.07	.02
☐ 246	Jim Bibby	.15	.07	.02
☐ 247	John Candelaria	.15	.07	.02
☐ 248	Jose DeLeon	.20	.09	.03
☐ 249	Mike Easler	.15	.07	.02
☐ 250	Cecilio Guante	.15	.07	.02
☐ 251	Richie Hebner	.15	.07	.02
☐ 252	Lee Lacy	.15	.07	.02
☐ 253	Bill Madlock	.20	.09	.03
☐ 254	Milt May	.15	.07	.02
☐ 255	Lee Mazzilli	.15	.07	.02
☐ 256	Larry McWilliams	.15	.07	.02
☐ 257	Jim Morrison	.15	.07	.02
☐ 258	Dave Parker	.30	.14	.04
☐ 259	Tony Pena	.20	.09	.03
☐ 260	Johnny Ray	.15	.07	.02
☐ 261	Rick Rhoden	.15	.07	.02
☐ 262	Don Robinson	.15	.07	.02
☐ 263	Manny Sarmiento	.15	.07	.02
☐ 264	Rod Scurry	.15	.07	.02
☐ 265	Kent Tekulve	.20	.09	.03
☐ 266	Gene Tenace	.15	.07	.02
☐ 267	Jason Thompson	.15	.07	.02
☐ 268	Lee Tunnell	.15	.07	.02
☐ 269	Marvell Wynne	.15	.07	.02
☐ 270	Ray Burris	.15	.07	.02
☐ 271	Gary Carter	.75	.35	.09
☐ 272	Warren Cromartie	.15	.07	.02
☐ 273	Andre Dawson	3.00	1.35	.40
☐ 274	Doug Flynn	.15	.07	.02
☐ 275	Terry Francona	.15	.07	.02
☐ 276	Bill Gullickson	.20	.09	.03
☐ 277	Bob James	.15	.07	.02
☐ 278	Charlie Lea	.15	.07	.02
☐ 279	Bryan Little	.15	.07	.02
☐ 280	Al Oliver	.20	.09	.03
☐ 281	Tim Raines	1.25	.55	.16
☐ 282	Bobby Ramos	.15	.07	.02
☐ 283	Jeff Reardon	.35	.16	.04
☐ 284	Steve Rogers	.15	.07	.02
☐ 285	Scott Sanderson	.15	.07	.02
☐ 286	Dan Schatzeder	.15	.07	.02
☐ 287	Bryn Smith	.15	.07	.02
☐ 288	Chris Speier	.15	.07	.02
☐ 289	Manny Trillo	.15	.07	.02
☐ 290	Mike Vail	.15	.07	.02
☐ 291	Tim Wallach	.20	.09	.03
☐ 292	Chris Welsh	.15	.07	.02
☐ 293	Jim Wohlford	.15	.07	.02
☐ 294	Kurt Bevacqua	.15	.07	.02
☐ 295	Juan Bonilla	.15	.07	.02
☐ 296	Bobby Brown	.15	.07	.02
☐ 297	Luis DeLeon	.15	.07	.02
☐ 298	Dave Dravecky	.20	.09	.03
☐ 299	Tim Flannery	.15	.07	.02
☐ 300	Steve Garvey	.75	.35	.09
☐ 301	Tony Gwynn	12.00	5.50	1.50
☐ 302	Andy Hawkins	.15	.07	.02
☐ 303	Ruppert Jones	.15	.07	.02
☐ 304	Terry Kennedy	.15	.07	.02
☐ 305	Tim Lollar	.15	.07	.02
☐ 306	Gary Lucas	.15	.07	.02
☐ 307	Kevin McReynolds	1.00	.45	.13
☐ 308	Sid Monge	.15	.07	.02
☐ 309	Mario Ramirez	.15	.07	.02
☐ 310	Gene Richards	.15	.07	.02
☐ 311	Luis Salazar	.15	.07	.02
☐ 312	Eric Show	.15	.07	.02
☐ 313	Elias Sosa	.15	.07	.02
☐ 314	Garry Templeton	.15	.07	.02
☐ 315	Mark Thurmond	.15	.07	.02
☐ 316	Ed Whitson	.15	.07	.02
☐ 317	Alan Wiggins	.15	.07	.02
☐ 318	Neil Allen	.15	.07	.02
☐ 319	Joaquin Andujar	.15	.07	.02
☐ 320	Steve Braun	.15	.07	.02
☐ 321	Glenn Brummer	.15	.07	.02
☐ 322	Bob Forsch	.15	.07	.02
☐ 323	David Green	.15	.07	.02
☐ 324	George Hendrick	.15	.07	.02
☐ 325	Tom Herr	.20	.09	.03

☐ 326 Dane Iorg .15 .07 .02
☐ 327 Jeff Lahti .15 .07 .02
☐ 328 Dave LaPoint .15 .07 .02
☐ 329 Willie McGee .40 .18 .05
☐ 330 Ken Oberkfell .15 .07 .02
☐ 331 Darrell Porter .15 .07 .02
☐ 332 Jamie Quirk .15 .07 .02
☐ 333 Mike Ramsey .15 .07 .02
☐ 334 Floyd Rayford .15 .07 .02
☐ 335 Lonnie Smith .20 .09 .03
☐ 336 Ozzie Smith 4.00 1.80 .50
☐ 337 John Stuper .15 .07 .02
☐ 338 Bruce Sutter .20 .09 .03
☐ 339 Andy Van Slyke UER 3.00 1.35 .40
(Batting and throwing both wrong on card back)
☐ 340 Dave Von Ohlen .15 .07 .02
☐ 341 Willie Aikens .15 .07 .02
☐ 342 Mike Armstrong .15 .07 .02
☐ 343 Bud Black .15 .07 .02
☐ 344 George Brett 8.00 3.60 1.00
☐ 345 Onix Concepcion .15 .07 .02
☐ 346 Keith Creel .15 .07 .02
☐ 347 Larry Gura .15 .07 .02
☐ 348 Don Hood .15 .07 .02
☐ 349 Dennis Leonard .15 .07 .02
☐ 350 Hal McRae .30 .14 .04
☐ 351 Amos Otis .20 .09 .03
☐ 352 Gaylord Perry .35 .16 .04
☐ 353 Greg Pryor .15 .07 .02
☐ 354 Dan Quisenberry .20 .09 .03
☐ 355 Steve Renko .15 .07 .02
☐ 356 Leon Roberts .15 .07 .02
☐ 357 Pat Sheridan .15 .07 .02
☐ 358 Joe Simpson .15 .07 .02
☐ 359 Don Slaught .20 .09 .03
☐ 360 Paul Splittorff .15 .07 .02
☐ 361 U.L. Washington .15 .07 .02
☐ 362 John Wathan .15 .07 .02
☐ 363 Frank White .20 .09 .03
☐ 364 Willie Wilson .20 .09 .03
☐ 365 Jim Barr .15 .07 .02
☐ 366 Dave Bergman .15 .07 .02
☐ 367 Fred Breining .15 .07 .02
☐ 368 Bob Brenly .15 .07 .02
☐ 369 Jack Clark .20 .09 .03
☐ 370 Chili Davis .50 .23 .06
☐ 371 Mark Davis .15 .07 .02
☐ 372 Darrell Evans .20 .09 .03
☐ 373 Atlee Hammaker .15 .07 .02
☐ 374 Mike Krukow .15 .07 .02
☐ 375 Duane Kuiper .15 .07 .02
☐ 376 Bill Laskey .15 .07 .02
☐ 377 Gary Lavelle .15 .07 .02
☐ 378 Johnnie LeMaster .15 .07 .02
☐ 379 Jeff Leonard .15 .07 .02
☐ 380 Randy Lerch .15 .07 .02
☐ 381 Renie Martin .15 .07 .02
☐ 382 Andy McGaffigan .15 .07 .02
☐ 383 Greg Minton .15 .07 .02
☐ 384 Tom O'Malley .15 .07 .02
☐ 385 Max Venable .15 .07 .02
☐ 386 Brad Wellman .15 .07 .02
☐ 387 Joel Youngblood .15 .07 .02
☐ 388 Gary Allenson .15 .07 .02
☐ 389 Luis Aponte .15 .07 .02
☐ 390 Tony Armas .15 .07 .02
☐ 391 Doug Bird .15 .07 .02
☐ 392 Wade Boggs 8.00 3.60 1.00
☐ 393 Dennis Boyd .20 .09 .03
☐ 394 Mike Brown UER P .15 .07 .02
(shown with record of 31-104)
☐ 395 Mark Clear .15 .07 .02
☐ 396 Dennis Eckersley 1.50 .65 .19
☐ 397 Dwight Evans .20 .09 .03
☐ 398 Rich Gedman .15 .07 .02
☐ 399 Glenn Hoffman .15 .07 .02
☐ 400 Bruce Hurst .20 .09 .03
☐ 401 John Henry Johnson .15 .07 .02
☐ 402 Ed Jurak .15 .07 .02
☐ 403 Rick Miller .15 .07 .02
☐ 404 Jeff Newman .15 .07 .02
☐ 405 Reid Nichols .15 .07 .02
☐ 406 Bob Ojeda .20 .09 .03
☐ 407 Jerry Remy .15 .07 .02
☐ 408 Jim Rice .30 .14 .04
☐ 409 Bob Stanley .15 .07 .02
☐ 410 Dave Stapleton .15 .07 .02
☐ 411 John Tudor .20 .09 .03
☐ 412 Carl Yastrzemski 2.00 .90 .25
☐ 413 Buddy Bell .20 .09 .03
☐ 414 Larry Biittner .15 .07 .02
☐ 415 John Butcher .15 .07 .02
☐ 416 Danny Darwin .15 .07 .02
☐ 417 Bucky Dent .20 .09 .03
☐ 418 Dave Hostetler .15 .07 .02
☐ 419 Charlie Hough .20 .09 .03
☐ 420 Bobby Johnson .15 .07 .02
☐ 421 Odell Jones .15 .07 .02
☐ 422 Jon Matlack .15 .07 .02
☐ 423 Pete O'Brien .35 .16 .04
☐ 424 Larry Parrish .15 .07 .02
☐ 425 Mickey Rivers .15 .07 .02
☐ 426 Billy Sample .15 .07 .02
☐ 427 Dave Schmidt .15 .07 .02
☐ 428 Mike Smithson .15 .07 .02
☐ 429 Bill Stein .15 .07 .02
☐ 430 Dave Stewart .30 .14 .04
☐ 431 Jim Sundberg .20 .09 .03
☐ 432 Frank Tanana .20 .09 .03
☐ 433 Dave Tobik .15 .07 .02
☐ 434 Wayne Tolleson .15 .07 .02
☐ 435 George Wright .15 .07 .02
☐ 436 Bill Almon .15 .07 .02
☐ 437 Keith Atherton .15 .07 .02
☐ 438 Dave Beard .15 .07 .02
☐ 439 Tom Burgmeier .15 .07 .02
☐ 440 Jeff Burroughs .15 .07 .02
☐ 441 Chris Codiroli .15 .07 .02
☐ 442 Tim Conroy .15 .07 .02
☐ 443 Mike Davis .15 .07 .02
☐ 444 Wayne Gross .15 .07 .02
☐ 445 Garry Hancock .15 .07 .02
☐ 446 Mike Heath .15 .07 .02
☐ 447 Rickey Henderson 4.50 2.00 .55
☐ 448 Donnie Hill .15 .07 .02
☐ 449 Bob Kearney .15 .07 .02
☐ 450 Bill Krueger .15 .07 .02
☐ 451 Rick Langford .15 .07 .02
☐ 452 Carney Lansford .20 .09 .03
☐ 453 Dave Lopes .20 .09 .03
☐ 454 Steve McCatty .15 .07 .02
☐ 455 Dan Meyer .15 .07 .02
☐ 456 Dwayne Murphy .15 .07 .02
☐ 457 Mike Norris .15 .07 .02
☐ 458 Ricky Peters .15 .07 .02
☐ 459 Tony Phillips 3.00 1.35 .40
☐ 460 Tom Underwood .15 .07 .02
☐ 461 Mike Warren .15 .07 .02
☐ 462 Johnny Bench 2.00 .90 .25
☐ 463 Bruce Berenyi .15 .07 .02
☐ 464 Dann Bilardello .15 .07 .02
☐ 465 Cesar Cedeno .20 .09 .03
☐ 466 Dave Concepcion .20 .09 .03
☐ 467 Dan Driessen .15 .07 .02

☐ 468 Nick Esasky .15 .07 .02
☐ 469 Rich Gale .15 .07 .02
☐ 470 Ben Hayes .15 .07 .02
☐ 471 Paul Householder .15 .07 .02
☐ 472 Tom Hume .15 .07 .02
☐ 473 Alan Knicely .15 .07 .02
☐ 474 Eddie Milner .15 .07 .02
☐ 475 Ron Oester .15 .07 .02
☐ 476 Kelly Paris .15 .07 .02
☐ 477 Frank Pastore .15 .07 .02
☐ 478 Ted Power .15 .07 .02
☐ 479 Joe Price .15 .07 .02
☐ 480 Charlie Puleo .15 .07 .02
☐ 481 Gary Redus .30 .14 .04
☐ 482 Bill Scherrer .15 .07 .02
☐ 483 Mario Soto .15 .07 .02
☐ 484 Alex Trevino .15 .07 .02
☐ 485 Duane Walker .15 .07 .02
☐ 486 Larry Bowa .20 .09 .03
☐ 487 Warren Brusstar .15 .07 .02
☐ 488 Bill Buckner .20 .09 .03
☐ 489 Bill Campbell .15 .07 .02
☐ 490 Ron Cey .20 .09 .03
☐ 491 Jody Davis .15 .07 .02
☐ 492 Leon Durham .15 .07 .02
☐ 493 Mel Hall .20 .09 .03
☐ 494 Ferguson Jenkins .50 .23 .06
☐ 495 Jay Johnstone .20 .09 .03
☐ 496 Craig Lefferts .15 .07 .02
☐ 497 Carmelo Martinez .15 .07 .02
☐ 498 Jerry Morales .15 .07 .02
☐ 499 Keith Moreland .15 .07 .02
☐ 500 Dickie Noles .15 .07 .02
☐ 501 Mike Proly .15 .07 .02
☐ 502 Chuck Rainey .15 .07 .02
☐ 503 Dick Ruthven .15 .07 .02
☐ 504 Ryne Sandberg 12.00 5.50 1.50
☐ 505 Lee Smith 1.50 .65 .19
☐ 506 Steve Trout .15 .07 .02
☐ 507 Gary Woods .15 .07 .02
☐ 508 Juan Beniquez .15 .07 .02
☐ 509 Bob Boone .20 .09 .03
☐ 510 Rick Burleson .15 .07 .02
☐ 511 Rod Carew 1.50 .65 .19
☐ 512 Bobby Clark .15 .07 .02
☐ 513 John Curtis .15 .07 .02
☐ 514 Doug DeCinces .15 .07 .02
☐ 515 Brian Downing .20 .09 .03
☐ 516 Tim Foli .15 .07 .02
☐ 517 Ken Forsch .15 .07 .02
☐ 518 Bobby Grich .20 .09 .03
☐ 519 Andy Hassler .15 .07 .02
☐ 520 Reggie Jackson 3.50 1.55 .45
☐ 521 Ron Jackson .15 .07 .02
☐ 522 Tommy John .30 .14 .04
☐ 523 Bruce Kison .15 .07 .02
☐ 524 Steve Lubratich .15 .07 .02
☐ 525 Fred Lynn .20 .09 .03
☐ 526 Gary Pettis .15 .07 .02
☐ 527 Luis Sanchez .15 .07 .02
☐ 528 Daryl Sconiers .15 .07 .02
☐ 529 Ellis Valentine .15 .07 .02
☐ 530 Rob Wilfong .15 .07 .02
☐ 531 Mike Witt .15 .07 .02
☐ 532 Geoff Zahn .15 .07 .02
☐ 533 Bud Anderson .15 .07 .02
☐ 534 Chris Bando .15 .07 .02
☐ 535 Alan Bannister .15 .07 .02
☐ 536 Bert Blyleven .30 .14 .04
☐ 537 Tom Brennan .15 .07 .02
☐ 538 Jamie Easterly .15 .07 .02
☐ 539 Juan Eichelberger .15 .07 .02
☐ 540 Jim Essian .15 .07 .02
☐ 541 Mike Fischlin .15 .07 .02
☐ 542 Julio Franco 2.00 .90 .25
☐ 543 Mike Hargrove .20 .09 .03
☐ 544 Toby Harrah .15 .07 .02
☐ 545 Ron Hassey .15 .07 .02
☐ 546 Neal Heaton .20 .09 .03
☐ 547 Bake McBride .15 .07 .02
☐ 548 Broderick Perkins .15 .07 .02
☐ 549 Lary Sorensen .15 .07 .02
☐ 550 Dan Spillner .15 .07 .02
☐ 551 Rick Sutcliffe .20 .09 .03
☐ 552 Pat Tabler .15 .07 .02
☐ 553 Gorman Thomas .15 .07 .02
☐ 554 Andre Thornton .15 .07 .02
☐ 555 George Vukovich .15 .07 .02
☐ 556 Darrell Brown .15 .07 .02
☐ 557 Tom Brunansky .20 .09 .03
☐ 558 Randy Bush .15 .07 .02
☐ 559 Bobby Castillo .15 .07 .02
☐ 560 John Castino .15 .07 .02
☐ 561 Ron Davis .15 .07 .02
☐ 562 Dave Engle .15 .07 .02
☐ 563 Lenny Faedo .15 .07 .02
☐ 564 Pete Filson .15 .07 .02
☐ 565 Gary Gaetti .20 .09 .03
☐ 566 Mickey Hatcher .15 .07 .02
☐ 567 Kent Hrbek .50 .23 .06
☐ 568 Rusty Kuntz .15 .07 .02
☐ 569 Tim Laudner .15 .07 .02
☐ 570 Rick Lysander .15 .07 .02
☐ 571 Bobby Mitchell .15 .07 .02
☐ 572 Ken Schrom .15 .07 .02
☐ 573 Ray Smith .15 .07 .02
☐ 574 Tim Teufel .15 .07 .02
☐ 575 Frank Viola .60 .25 .08
☐ 576 Gary Ward .15 .07 .02
☐ 577 Ron Washington .15 .07 .02
☐ 578 Len Whitehouse .15 .07 .02
☐ 579 Al Williams .15 .07 .02
☐ 580 Bob Bailor .15 .07 .02
☐ 581 Mark Bradley .15 .07 .02
☐ 582 Hubie Brooks .20 .09 .03
☐ 583 Carlos Diaz .15 .07 .02
☐ 584 George Foster .20 .09 .03
☐ 585 Brian Giles .15 .07 .02
☐ 586 Danny Heep .15 .07 .02
☐ 587 Keith Hernandez .30 .14 .04
☐ 588 Ron Hodges .15 .07 .02
☐ 589 Scott Holman .15 .07 .02
☐ 590 Dave Kingman .20 .09 .03
☐ 591 Ed Lynch .15 .07 .02
☐ 592 Jose Oquendo .25 .11 .03
☐ 593 Jesse Orosco .15 .07 .02
☐ 594 Junior Ortiz .15 .07 .02
☐ 595 Tom Seaver 3.50 1.55 .45
☐ 596 Doug Sisk .15 .07 .02
☐ 597 Rusty Staub .20 .09 .03
☐ 598 John Stearns .15 .07 .02
☐ 599 Darryl Strawberry 7.00 3.10 .85
☐ 600 Craig Swan .15 .07 .02
☐ 601 Walt Terrell .15 .07 .02
☐ 602 Mike Torrez .15 .07 .02
☐ 603 Mookie Wilson .20 .09 .03
☐ 604 Jamie Allen .15 .07 .02
☐ 605 Jim Beattie .15 .07 .02
☐ 606 Tony Bernazard .15 .07 .02
☐ 607 Manny Castillo .15 .07 .02
☐ 608 Bill Caudill .15 .07 .02
☐ 609 Bryan Clark .15 .07 .02
☐ 610 Al Cowens .15 .07 .02
☐ 611 Dave Henderson .20 .09 .03
☐ 612 Steve Henderson .15 .07 .02
☐ 613 Orlando Mercado .15 .07 .02

□ 614 Mike Moore .... .20 .09 .03
□ 615 Ricky Nelson UER .... .15 .07 .02
(Jamie Nelson's
stats on back)
□ 616 Spike Owen .... .30 .14 .04
□ 617 Pat Putnam .... .15 .07 .02
□ 618 Ron Roenicke .... .15 .07 .02
□ 619 Mike Stanton .... .15 .07 .02
□ 620 Bob Stoddard .... .15 .07 .02
□ 621 Rick Sweet .... .15 .07 .02
□ 622 Roy Thomas .... .15 .07 .02
□ 623 Ed VandeBerg .... .15 .07 .02
□ 624 Matt Young .... .15 .07 .02
□ 625 Richie Zisk .... .15 .07 .02
□ 626 Fred Lynn .... .20 .09 .03
1982 AS Game RB
□ 627 Manny Trillo .... .20 .09 .03
1983 AS Game RB
□ 628 Steve Garvey .... .35 .16 .04
NL Iron Man
□ 629 Rod Carew .... .50 .23 .06
AL Batting Runner-Up
□ 630 Wade Boggs .... 2.50 1.15 .30
AL Batting Champion
□ 631 Tim Raines: Letting .... .60 .25 .08
Go of the Raines
□ 632 Al Oliver .... .20 .09 .03
Double Trouble
□ 633 Steve Sax .... .20 .09 .03
AS Second Base
□ 634 Dickie Thon .... .20 .09 .03
AS Shortstop
□ 635 Ace Firemen .... .20 .09 .03
Dan Quisenberry
and Tippy Martinez
□ 636 Reds Reunited .... 1.00 .45 .13
Joe Morgan
Pete Rose
Tony Perez
□ 637 Backstop Stars .... .25 .11 .03
Lance Parrish
Bob Boone
□ 638 George Brett and .... 2.00 .90 .25
Gaylord Perry
Pine Tar 7/24/83
□ 639 1983 No Hitters .... .20 .09 .03
Dave Righetti
Mike Warren
Bob Forsch
□ 640 Johnny Bench and .... 2.00 .90 .25
Carl Yastrzemski
Retiring Superstars
□ 641 Gaylord Perry .... .35 .16 .04
Going Out In Style
□ 642 Steve Carlton .... 1.00 .45 .13
300 Club and
Strikeout Record
□ 643 Joe Altobelli and .... .20 .09 .03
Paul Owens
World Series Managers
□ 644 Rick Dempsey .... .20 .09 .03
World Series MVP
□ 645 Mike Boddicker .... .20 .09 .03
WS Rookie Winner
□ 646 Scott McGregor .... .20 .09 .03
WS Clincher
□ 647 CL: Orioles/Royals .... .20 .07 .02
Joe Altobelli MG
□ 648 CL: Phillies/Giants .... .20 .07 .02
Paul Owens MG
□ 649 CL: White Sox/Red Sox .20 .07 .02
Tony LaRussa MG
□ 650 CL: Tigers/Rangers .... .20 .07 .02
Sparky Anderson MG
□ 651 CL: Dodgers/A's .... .20 .07 .02
Tommy Lasorda MG
□ 652 CL: Yankees/Reds .... .20 .07 .02
Billy Martin MG
□ 653 CL: Blue Jays/Cubs .... .20 .07 .02
Bobby Cox MG
□ 654 CL: Braves/Angels .... .20 .07 .02
Joe Torre MG
□ 655 CL: Brewers/Indians .... .20 .07 .02
Rene Lachemann MG
□ 656 CL: Astros/Twins .... .20 .07 .02
Bob Lillis MG
□ 657 CL: Pirates/Mets .... .20 .07 .02
Chuck Tanner MG
□ 658 CL: Expos/Mariners .... .20 .07 .02
Bill Virdon MG
□ 659 CL: Padres/Specials .... .20 .07 .02
Dick Williams MG
□ 660 CL: Cardinals/Teams .... .20 .07 .02
Whitey Herzog MG

1984 Fleer Update

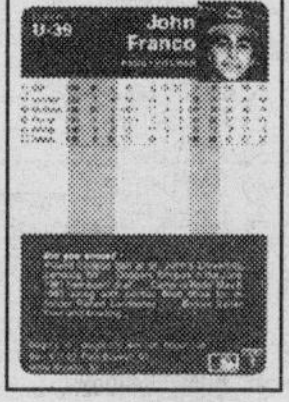

The cards in this 132-card set measure 2 1/2" by 3 1/2". For the first time, the Fleer Gum Company issued a traded, extended, or update set. The purpose of the set was the same as the traded sets issued by Topps over the past four years, i.e., to portray players with their proper team for the current year and to portray rookies who were not in their regular issue. Like the Topps Traded sets of the past four years, the Fleer Update sets were distributed through hobby dealers only. The set was quite popular with collectors, and, apparently, the print run was relatively short, as the set was quickly in short supply and exhibited a rapid and dramatic price increase. The cards are numbered on the back with a U prefix; the order corresponds to the alphabetical order of the subjects' names. The (extended) Rookie Cards in this set are Roger Clemens, Ron Darling, Alvin Davis, John Franco, Dwight Gooden, Jimmy Key, Mark Langston, Kirby Puckett, Jose Rijo, and Bret Saberhagen. Collectors are urged to be careful if purchasing single cards of Clemens, Darling, Gooden, Puckett, Rose, or Saberhagen as these specific cards have been illegally reprinted. These fakes are blurry when compared to the real cards.

	NRMT-MT	EXC	G-VG
COMPLETE FACT.SET (132)	700.00	325.00	90.00
COMMON CARD (1-132)	.60	.25	.08

	NRMT-MT	EXC	G-VG
☐ 1 Willie Aikens	.60	.25	.08
☐ 2 Luis Aponte	.60	.25	.08
☐ 3 Mark Bailey	.60	.25	.08
☐ 4 Bob Bailor	.60	.25	.08
☐ 5 Dusty Baker	1.00	.45	.13
☐ 6 Steve Balboni	.60	.25	.08
☐ 7 Alan Bannister	.60	.25	.08
☐ 8 Marty Barrett	.75	.35	.09
☐ 9 Dave Beard	.60	.25	.08
☐ 10 Joe Beckwith	.60	.25	.08
☐ 11 Dave Bergman	.60	.25	.08
☐ 12 Tony Bernazard	.60	.25	.08
☐ 13 Bruce Bochte	.60	.25	.08
☐ 14 Barry Bonnell	.60	.25	.08
☐ 15 Phil Bradley	.75	.35	.09
☐ 16 Fred Breining	.60	.25	.08
☐ 17 Mike C. Brown	.60	.25	.08
☐ 18 Bill Buckner	.75	.35	.09
☐ 19 Ray Burris	.60	.25	.08
☐ 20 John Butcher	.60	.25	.08
☐ 21 Brett Butler	2.50	1.15	.30
☐ 22 Enos Cabell	.60	.25	.08
☐ 23 Bill Campbell	.60	.25	.08
☐ 24 Bill Caudill	.60	.25	.08
☐ 25 Bobby Clark	.60	.25	.08
☐ 26 Bryan Clark	.60	.25	.08
☐ 27 Roger Clemens	300.00	135.00	38.00
☐ 28 Jaime Cocanower	.60	.25	.08
☐ 29 Ron Darling	2.50	1.15	.30
☐ 30 Alvin Davis	1.25	.55	.16
☐ 31 Bob Dernier	.60	.25	.08
☐ 32 Carlos Diaz	.60	.25	.08
☐ 33 Mike Easler	.60	.25	.08
☐ 34 Dennis Eckersley	15.00	6.75	1.90
☐ 35 Jim Essian	.60	.25	.08
☐ 36 Darrell Evans	.75	.35	.09
☐ 37 Mike Fitzgerald	.60	.25	.08
☐ 38 Tim Foli	.60	.25	.08
☐ 39 John Franco	8.00	3.60	1.00
☐ 40 George Frazier	.60	.25	.08
☐ 41 Rich Gale	.60	.25	.08
☐ 42 Barbaro Garbey	.60	.25	.08
☐ 43 Dwight Gooden	16.00	7.25	2.00
☐ 44 Rich Gossage	1.00	.45	.13
☐ 45 Wayne Gross	.60	.25	.08
☐ 46 Mark Gubicza	2.00	.90	.25
☐ 47 Jackie Gutierrez	.60	.25	.08
☐ 48 Toby Harrah	.60	.25	.08
☐ 49 Ron Hassey	.60	.25	.08
☐ 50 Richie Hebner	.60	.25	.08
☐ 51 Willie Hernandez	.75	.35	.09
☐ 52 Ed Hodge	.60	.25	.08
☐ 53 Ricky Horton	.60	.25	.08
☐ 54 Art Howe	.60	.25	.08
☐ 55 Dane Iorg	.60	.25	.08
☐ 56 Brook Jacoby	.75	.35	.09
☐ 57 Dion James	.75	.35	.09
☐ 58 Mike Jeffcoat	.60	.25	.08
☐ 59 Ruppert Jones	.60	.25	.08
☐ 60 Bob Kearney	.60	.25	.08
☐ 61 Jimmy Key	38.00	17.00	4.70
☐ 62 Dave Kingman	.75	.35	.09
☐ 63 Brad Komminsk	.60	.25	.08
☐ 64 Jerry Koosman	.75	.35	.09
☐ 65 Wayne Krenchicki	.60	.25	.08
☐ 66 Rusty Kuntz	.60	.25	.08
☐ 67 Frank LaCorte	.60	.25	.08
☐ 68 Dennis Lamp	.60	.25	.08
☐ 69 Tito Landrum	.60	.25	.08
☐ 70 Mark Langston	18.00	8.00	2.30
☐ 71 Rick Leach	.60	.25	.08
☐ 72 Craig Lefferts	.75	.35	.09
☐ 73 Gary Lucas	.60	.25	.08
☐ 74 Jerry Martin	.60	.25	.08
☐ 75 Carmelo Martinez	.60	.25	.08
☐ 76 Mike Mason	.60	.25	.08
☐ 77 Gary Matthews	.75	.35	.09
☐ 78 Andy McGaffigan	.60	.25	.08
☐ 79 Joey McLaughlin	.60	.25	.08
☐ 80 Joe Morgan	6.00	2.70	.75
☐ 81 Darryl Motley	.60	.25	.08
☐ 82 Graig Nettles	.75	.35	.09
☐ 83 Phil Niekro	3.00	1.35	.40
☐ 84 Ken Oberkfell	.60	.25	.08
☐ 85 Al Oliver	.75	.35	.09
☐ 86 Jorge Orta	.60	.25	.08
☐ 87 Amos Otis	.75	.35	.09
☐ 88 Bob Owchinko	.60	.25	.08
☐ 89 Dave Parker	1.00	.45	.13
☐ 90 Jack Perconte	.60	.25	.08
☐ 91 Tony Perez	3.00	1.35	.40
☐ 92 Gerald Perry	.60	.25	.08
☐ 93 Kirby Puckett	325.00	145.00	40.00
☐ 94 Shane Rawley	.60	.25	.08
☐ 95 Floyd Rayford	.60	.25	.08
☐ 96 Ron Reed	.60	.25	.08
☐ 97 R.J. Reynolds	.60	.25	.08
☐ 98 Gene Richards	.60	.25	.08
☐ 99 Jose Rijo	30.00	13.50	3.80
☐ 100 Jeff D. Robinson	.60	.25	.08
☐ 101 Ron Romanick	.60	.25	.08
☐ 102 Pete Rose	30.00	13.50	3.80
☐ 103 Bret Saberhagen	30.00	13.50	3.80
☐ 104 Scott Sanderson	.60	.25	.08
☐ 105 Dick Schofield	1.00	.45	.13
☐ 106 Tom Seaver	20.00	9.00	2.50
☐ 107 Jim Slaton	.60	.25	.08
☐ 108 Mike Smithson	.60	.25	.08
☐ 109 Lary Sorensen	.60	.25	.08
☐ 110 Tim Stoddard	.60	.25	.08
☐ 111 Jeff Stone	.60	.25	.08
☐ 112 Champ Summers	.60	.25	.08
☐ 113 Jim Sundberg	.75	.35	.09
☐ 114 Rick Sutcliffe	.75	.35	.09
☐ 115 Craig Swan	.60	.25	.08
☐ 116 Derrel Thomas	.60	.25	.08
☐ 117 Gorman Thomas	.60	.25	.08
☐ 118 Alex Trevino	.60	.25	.08
☐ 119 Manny Trillo	.60	.25	.08
☐ 120 John Tudor	.75	.35	.09
☐ 121 Tom Underwood	.60	.25	.08
☐ 122 Mike Vail	.60	.25	.08
☐ 123 Tom Waddell	.60	.25	.08
☐ 124 Gary Ward	.60	.25	.08
☐ 125 Terry Whitfield	.60	.25	.08
☐ 126 Curtis Wilkerson	.60	.25	.08
☐ 127 Frank Williams	.60	.25	.08
☐ 128 Glenn Wilson	.60	.25	.08
☐ 129 John Wockenfuss	.60	.25	.08
☐ 130 Ned Yost	.60	.25	.08
☐ 131 Mike Young	.60	.25	.08
☐ 132 Checklist 1-132	.60	.25	.08

1985 Fleer

The cards in this 660-card set measure 2 1/2" by 3 1/2". The 1985 Fleer set features fronts that contain the team logo along with

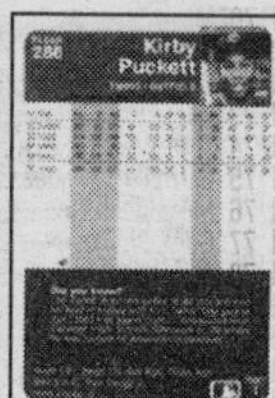

the player's name and position. The borders enclosing the photo are color-coded to correspond to the player's team. In each case, the color is one of the standard colors of that team, e.g., orange for Baltimore, red for St. Louis, etc. The backs feature the same name, number, and statistics format that Fleer has been using over the past few years. The cards are ordered alphabetically within team. The teams are ordered based on their respective performance during the prior year, e.g., World Champion Detroit Tigers (1-25), NL Champion San Diego (26-48), Chicago Cubs (49-71), New York Mets (72-95), Toronto (96-119), New York Yankees (120-147), Boston (148-169), Baltimore (170-195), Kansas City (196-218), St. Louis (219-243), Philadelphia (244-269), Minnesota (270-292), California (293-317), Atlanta (318-342), Houston (343-365), Los Angeles (366-391), Montreal (392-413), Oakland (414-436), Cleveland (437-460), Pittsburgh (461-481), Seattle (482-505), Chicago White Sox (506-530), Cincinnati (531-554), Texas (555-575), Milwaukee (576-601), and San Francisco (602-625). Subsets include Specials (626-643) and Major League Prospects (644-653). The black and white photo on the reverse is included for the third straight year. This set is noted for containing the Rookie Cards of Roger Clemens, Eric Davis, Shawon Dunston, Dwight Gooden, Orel Hershiser, Jimmy Key, Mark Langston, Terry Pendleton, Kirby Puckett, Jose Rijo, Bret Saberhagen, and Danny Tartabull.

	NRMT-MT	EXC	G-VG
COMPLETE SET (660)	140.00	65.00	17.50
COMMON CARD (1-660)	.10	.05	.01
☐ 1 Doug Bair	.10	.05	.01
☐ 2 Juan Berenguer	.10	.05	.01
☐ 3 Dave Bergman	.10	.05	.01
☐ 4 Tom Brookens	.10	.05	.01
☐ 5 Marty Castillo	.10	.05	.01
☐ 6 Darrell Evans	.15	.07	.02
☐ 7 Barbaro Garbey	.10	.05	.01
☐ 8 Kirk Gibson	.20	.09	.03
☐ 9 John Grubb	.10	.05	.01
☐ 10 Willie Hernandez	.10	.05	.01
☐ 11 Larry Herndon	.10	.05	.01
☐ 12 Howard Johnson	.35	.16	.04
☐ 13 Ruppert Jones	.10	.05	.01
☐ 14 Rusty Kuntz	.10	.05	.01
☐ 15 Chet Lemon	.10	.05	.01
☐ 16 Aurelio Lopez	.10	.05	.01
☐ 17 Sid Monge	.10	.05	.01
☐ 18 Jack Morris	.50	.23	.06
☐ 19 Lance Parrish	.15	.07	.02
☐ 20 Dan Petry	.10	.05	.01
☐ 21 Dave Rozema	.10	.05	.01
☐ 22 Bill Scherrer	.10	.05	.01
☐ 23 Alan Trammell	.75	.35	.09
☐ 24 Lou Whitaker	.75	.35	.09
☐ 25 Milt Wilcox	.10	.05	.01
☐ 26 Kurt Bevacqua	.10	.05	.01
☐ 27 Greg Booker	.10	.05	.01
☐ 28 Bobby Brown	.10	.05	.01
☐ 29 Luis DeLeon	.10	.05	.01
☐ 30 Dave Dravecky	.15	.07	.02
☐ 31 Tim Flannery	.10	.05	.01
☐ 32 Steve Garvey	.20	.09	.03
☐ 33 Rich Gossage	.20	.09	.03
☐ 34 Tony Gwynn	6.50	2.90	.80
☐ 35 Greg Harris	.10	.05	.01
☐ 36 Andy Hawkins	.10	.05	.01
☐ 37 Terry Kennedy	.10	.05	.01
☐ 38 Craig Lefferts	.15	.07	.02
☐ 39 Tim Lollar	.10	.05	.01
☐ 40 Carmelo Martinez	.10	.05	.01
☐ 41 Kevin McReynolds	.15	.07	.02
☐ 42 Graig Nettles	.15	.07	.02
☐ 43 Luis Salazar	.10	.05	.01
☐ 44 Eric Show	.10	.05	.01
☐ 45 Garry Templeton	.10	.05	.01
☐ 46 Mark Thurmond	.10	.05	.01
☐ 47 Ed Whitson	.10	.05	.01
☐ 48 Alan Wiggins	.10	.05	.01
☐ 49 Rich Bordi	.10	.05	.01
☐ 50 Larry Bowa	.15	.07	.02
☐ 51 Warren Brusstar	.10	.05	.01
☐ 52 Ron Cey	.15	.07	.02
☐ 53 Henry Cotto	.10	.05	.01
☐ 54 Jody Davis	.10	.05	.01
☐ 55 Bob Dernier	.10	.05	.01
☐ 56 Leon Durham	.10	.05	.01
☐ 57 Dennis Eckersley	.50	.23	.06
☐ 58 George Frazier	.10	.05	.01
☐ 59 Richie Hebner	.10	.05	.01
☐ 60 Dave Lopes	.15	.07	.02
☐ 61 Gary Matthews	.10	.05	.01
☐ 62 Keith Moreland	.10	.05	.01
☐ 63 Rick Reuschel	.15	.07	.02
☐ 64 Dick Ruthven	.10	.05	.01
☐ 65 Ryne Sandberg	7.00	3.10	.85
☐ 66 Scott Sanderson	.10	.05	.01
☐ 67 Lee Smith	1.00	.45	.13
☐ 68 Tim Stoddard	.10	.05	.01
☐ 69 Rick Sutcliffe	.15	.07	.02
☐ 70 Steve Trout	.10	.05	.01
☐ 71 Gary Woods	.10	.05	.01
☐ 72 Wally Backman	.10	.05	.01
☐ 73 Bruce Berenyi	.10	.05	.01
☐ 74 Hubie Brooks UER (Kelvin Chapman's stats on card back)	.15	.07	.02
☐ 75 Kelvin Chapman	.10	.05	.01
☐ 76 Ron Darling	.15	.07	.02
☐ 77 Sid Fernandez	.50	.23	.06
☐ 78 Mike Fitzgerald	.10	.05	.01
☐ 79 George Foster	.15	.07	.02
☐ 80 Brent Gaff	.10	.05	.01
☐ 81 Ron Gardenhire	.10	.05	.01
☐ 82 Dwight Gooden	1.50	.65	.19
☐ 83 Tom Gorman	.10	.05	.01
☐ 84 Danny Heep	.10	.05	.01
☐ 85 Keith Hernandez	.20	.09	.03
☐ 86 Ray Knight	.15	.07	.02
☐ 87 Ed Lynch	.10	.05	.01
☐ 88 Jose Oquendo	.10	.05	.01
☐ 89 Jesse Orosco	.10	.05	.01

□ 90 Rafael Santana .10 .05 .01
□ 91 Doug Sisk .10 .05 .01
□ 92 Rusty Staub .15 .07 .02
□ 93 Darryl Strawberry 1.25 .55 .16
□ 94 Walt Terrell .10 .05 .01
□ 95 Mookie Wilson .15 .07 .02
□ 96 Jim Acker .10 .05 .01
□ 97 Willie Aikens .10 .05 .01
□ 98 Doyle Alexander .10 .05 .01
□ 99 Jesse Barfield .10 .05 .01
□ 100 George Bell .20 .09 .03
□ 101 Jim Clancy .10 .05 .01
□ 102 Dave Collins .10 .05 .01
□ 103 Tony Fernandez .50 .23 .06
□ 104 Damaso Garcia .10 .05 .01
□ 105 Jim Gott .10 .05 .01
□ 106 Alfredo Griffin .10 .05 .01
□ 107 Garth Iorg .10 .05 .01
□ 108 Roy Lee Jackson .10 .05 .01
□ 109 Cliff Johnson .10 .05 .01
□ 110 Jimmy Key 5.50 2.50 .70
□ 111 Dennis Lamp .10 .05 .01
□ 112 Rick Leach .10 .05 .01
□ 113 Luis Leal .10 .05 .01
□ 114 Buck Martinez .10 .05 .01
□ 115 Lloyd Moseby .10 .05 .01
□ 116 Rance Mulliniks .10 .05 .01
□ 117 Dave Stieb .15 .07 .02
□ 118 Willie Upshaw .10 .05 .01
□ 119 Ernie Whitt .10 .05 .01
□ 120 Mike Armstrong .10 .05 .01
□ 121 Don Baylor .20 .09 .03
□ 122 Marty Bystrom .10 .05 .01
□ 123 Rick Cerone .10 .05 .01
□ 124 Joe Cowley .10 .05 .01
□ 125 Brian Dayett .10 .05 .01
□ 126 Tim Foli .10 .05 .01
□ 127 Ray Fontenot .10 .05 .01
□ 128 Ken Griffey .15 .07 .02
□ 129 Ron Guidry .15 .07 .02
□ 130 Toby Harrah .10 .05 .01
□ 131 Jay Howell .15 .07 .02
□ 132 Steve Kemp .10 .05 .01
□ 133 Don Mattingly 8.00 3.60 1.00
□ 134 Bobby Meacham .10 .05 .01
□ 135 John Montefusco .10 .05 .01
□ 136 Omar Moreno .10 .05 .01
□ 137 Dale Murray .10 .05 .01
□ 138 Phil Niekro .20 .09 .03
□ 139 Mike Pagliarulo .10 .05 .01
□ 140 Willie Randolph .15 .07 .02
□ 141 Dennis Rasmussen .10 .05 .01
□ 142 Dave Righetti .15 .07 .02
□ 143 Jose Rijo 3.00 1.35 .40
□ 144 Andre Robertson .10 .05 .01
□ 145 Bob Shirley .10 .05 .01
□ 146 Dave Winfield 2.50 1.15 .30
□ 147 Butch Wynegar .10 .05 .01
□ 148 Gary Allenson .10 .05 .01
□ 149 Tony Armas .10 .05 .01
□ 150 Marty Barrett .10 .05 .01
□ 151 Wade Boggs 4.50 2.00 .55
□ 152 Dennis Boyd .10 .05 .01
□ 153 Bill Buckner .15 .07 .02
□ 154 Mark Clear .10 .05 .01
□ 155 Roger Clemens 35.00 16.00 4.40
□ 156 Steve Crawford .10 .05 .01
□ 157 Mike Easler .10 .05 .01
□ 158 Dwight Evans .15 .07 .02
□ 159 Rich Gedman .10 .05 .01
□ 160 Jackie Gutierrez .15 .07 .02
(Wade Boggs
shown on deck)
□ 161 Bruce Hurst .15 .07 .02
□ 162 John Henry Johnson .10 .05 .01
□ 163 Rick Miller .10 .05 .01
□ 164 Reid Nichols .10 .05 .01
□ 165 Al Nipper .10 .05 .01
□ 166 Bob Ojeda .15 .07 .02
□ 167 Jerry Remy .10 .05 .01
□ 168 Jim Rice .20 .09 .03
□ 169 Bob Stanley .10 .05 .01
□ 170 Mike Boddicker .10 .05 .01
□ 171 Al Bumbry .15 .07 .02
□ 172 Todd Cruz .10 .05 .01
□ 173 Rich Dauer .10 .05 .01
□ 174 Storm Davis .10 .05 .01
□ 175 Rick Dempsey .10 .05 .01
□ 176 Jim Dwyer .10 .05 .01
□ 177 Mike Flanagan .10 .05 .01
□ 178 Dan Ford .10 .05 .01
□ 179 Wayne Gross .10 .05 .01
□ 180 John Lowenstein .10 .05 .01
□ 181 Dennis Martinez .15 .07 .02
□ 182 Tippy Martinez .10 .05 .01
□ 183 Scott McGregor .10 .05 .01
□ 184 Eddie Murray 2.00 .90 .25
□ 185 Joe Nolan .10 .05 .01
□ 186 Floyd Rayford .10 .05 .01
□ 187 Cal Ripken 8.00 3.60 1.00
□ 188 Gary Roenicke .10 .05 .01
□ 189 Lenn Sakata .10 .05 .01
□ 190 John Shelby .10 .05 .01
□ 191 Ken Singleton .15 .07 .02
□ 192 Sammy Stewart .10 .05 .01
□ 193 Bill Swaggerty .10 .05 .01
□ 194 Tom Underwood .10 .05 .01
□ 195 Mike Young .10 .05 .01
□ 196 Steve Balboni .10 .05 .01
□ 197 Joe Beckwith .10 .05 .01
□ 198 Bud Black .10 .05 .01
□ 199 George Brett 4.00 1.80 .50
□ 200 Onix Concepcion .10 .05 .01
□ 201 Mark Gubicza .50 .23 .06
□ 202 Larry Gura .10 .05 .01
□ 203 Mark Huismann .10 .05 .01
□ 204 Dane Iorg .10 .05 .01
□ 205 Danny Jackson .15 .07 .02
□ 206 Charlie Leibrandt .10 .05 .01
□ 207 Hal McRae .20 .09 .03
□ 208 Darryl Motley .10 .05 .01
□ 209 Jorge Orta .10 .05 .01
□ 210 Greg Pryor .10 .05 .01
□ 211 Dan Quisenberry .15 .07 .02
□ 212 Bret Saberhagen 3.50 1.55 .45
□ 213 Pat Sheridan .10 .05 .01
□ 214 Don Slaught .15 .07 .02
□ 215 U.L. Washington .10 .05 .01
□ 216 John Wathan .10 .05 .01
□ 217 Frank White .15 .07 .02
□ 218 Willie Wilson .15 .07 .02
□ 219 Neil Allen .10 .05 .01
□ 220 Joaquin Andujar .10 .05 .01
□ 221 Steve Braun .10 .05 .01
□ 222 Danny Cox .10 .05 .01
□ 223 Bob Forsch .10 .05 .01
□ 224 David Green .10 .05 .01
□ 225 George Hendrick .10 .05 .01
□ 226 Tom Herr .15 .07 .02
□ 227 Ricky Horton .10 .05 .01
□ 228 Art Howe .10 .05 .01
□ 229 Mike Jorgensen .10 .05 .01
□ 230 Kurt Kepshire .10 .05 .01
□ 231 Jeff Lahti .10 .05 .01
□ 232 Tito Landrum .10 .05 .01
□ 233 Dave LaPoint .10 .05 .01

	No.	Player			
☐	234	Willie McGee	.15	.07	.02
☐	235	Tom Nieto	.10	.05	.01
☐	236	Terry Pendleton	3.00	1.35	.40
☐	237	Darrell Porter	.10	.05	.01
☐	238	Dave Rucker	.10	.05	.01
☐	239	Lonnie Smith	.10	.05	.01
☐	240	Ozzie Smith	2.50	1.15	.30
☐	241	Bruce Sutter	.15	.07	.02
☐	242	Andy Van Slyke UER (Bats Right, Throws Left)	1.00	.45	.13
☐	243	Dave Von Ohlen	.10	.05	.01
☐	244	Larry Andersen	.10	.05	.01
☐	245	Bill Campbell	.10	.05	.01
☐	246	Steve Carlton	1.25	.55	.16
☐	247	Tim Corcoran	.10	.05	.01
☐	248	Ivan DeJesus	.10	.05	.01
☐	249	John Denny	.10	.05	.01
☐	250	Bo Diaz	.10	.05	.01
☐	251	Greg Gross	.10	.05	.01
☐	252	Kevin Gross	.10	.05	.01
☐	253	Von Hayes	.10	.05	.01
☐	254	Al Holland	.10	.05	.01
☐	255	Charles Hudson	.10	.05	.01
☐	256	Jerry Koosman	.15	.07	.02
☐	257	Joe Lefebvre	.10	.05	.01
☐	258	Sixto Lezcano	.10	.05	.01
☐	259	Garry Maddox	.10	.05	.01
☐	260	Len Matuszek	.10	.05	.01
☐	261	Tug McGraw	.15	.07	.02
☐	262	Al Oliver	.15	.07	.02
☐	263	Shane Rawley	.10	.05	.01
☐	264	Juan Samuel	.10	.05	.01
☐	265	Mike Schmidt	3.50	1.55	.45
☐	266	Jeff Stone	.10	.05	.01
☐	267	Ozzie Virgil	.10	.05	.01
☐	268	Glenn Wilson	.10	.05	.01
☐	269	John Wockenfuss	.10	.05	.01
☐	270	Darrell Brown	.10	.05	.01
☐	271	Tom Brunansky	.15	.07	.02
☐	272	Randy Bush	.10	.05	.01
☐	273	John Butcher	.10	.05	.01
☐	274	Bobby Castillo	.10	.05	.01
☐	275	Ron Davis	.10	.05	.01
☐	276	Dave Engle	.10	.05	.01
☐	277	Pete Filson	.10	.05	.01
☐	278	Gary Gaetti	.15	.07	.02
☐	279	Mickey Hatcher	.10	.05	.01
☐	280	Ed Hodge	.10	.05	.01
☐	281	Kent Hrbek	.15	.07	.02
☐	282	Houston Jimenez	.10	.05	.01
☐	283	Tim Laudner	.10	.05	.01
☐	284	Rick Lysander	.10	.05	.01
☐	285	Dave Meier	.10	.05	.01
☐	286	Kirby Puckett	40.00	18.00	5.00
☐	287	Pat Putnam	.10	.05	.01
☐	288	Ken Schrom	.10	.05	.01
☐	289	Mike Smithson	.10	.05	.01
☐	290	Tim Teufel	.10	.05	.01
☐	291	Frank Viola	.15	.07	.02
☐	292	Ron Washington	.10	.05	.01
☐	293	Don Aase	.10	.05	.01
☐	294	Juan Beniquez	.10	.05	.01
☐	295	Bob Boone	.15	.07	.02
☐	296	Mike C. Brown	.10	.05	.01
☐	297	Rod Carew	.75	.35	.09
☐	298	Doug Corbett	.10	.05	.01
☐	299	Doug DeCinces	.10	.05	.01
☐	300	Brian Downing	.15	.07	.02
☐	301	Ken Forsch	.10	.05	.01
☐	302	Bobby Grich	.15	.07	.02
☐	303	Reggie Jackson	2.00	.90	.25
☐	304	Tommy John	.20	.09	.03

	No.	Player			
☐	305	Curt Kaufman	.10	.05	.01
☐	306	Bruce Kison	.10	.05	.01
☐	307	Fred Lynn	.15	.07	.02
☐	308	Gary Pettis	.10	.05	.01
☐	309	Ron Romanick	.10	.05	.01
☐	310	Luis Sanchez	.10	.05	.01
☐	311	Dick Schofield	.10	.05	.01
☐	312	Daryl Sconiers	.10	.05	.01
☐	313	Jim Slaton	.10	.05	.01
☐	314	Derrel Thomas	.10	.05	.01
☐	315	Rob Wilfong	.10	.05	.01
☐	316	Mike Witt	.10	.05	.01
☐	317	Geoff Zahn	.10	.05	.01
☐	318	Len Barker	.10	.05	.01
☐	319	Steve Bedrosian	.10	.05	.01
☐	320	Bruce Benedict	.10	.05	.01
☐	321	Rick Camp	.10	.05	.01
☐	322	Chris Chambliss	.15	.07	.02
☐	323	Jeff Dedmon	.10	.05	.01
☐	324	Terry Forster	.10	.05	.01
☐	325	Gene Garber	.10	.05	.01
☐	326	Albert Hall	.10	.05	.01
☐	327	Terry Harper	.10	.05	.01
☐	328	Bob Horner	.10	.05	.01
☐	329	Glenn Hubbard	.10	.05	.01
☐	330	Randy Johnson	.10	.05	.01
☐	331	Brad Komminsk	.10	.05	.01
☐	332	Rick Mahler	.10	.05	.01
☐	333	Craig McMurtry	.10	.05	.01
☐	334	Donnie Moore	.10	.05	.01
☐	335	Dale Murphy	1.00	.45	.13
☐	336	Ken Oberkfell	.10	.05	.01
☐	337	Pascual Perez	.10	.05	.01
☐	338	Gerald Perry	.10	.05	.01
☐	339	Rafael Ramirez	.10	.05	.01
☐	340	Jerry Royster	.10	.05	.01
☐	341	Alex Trevino	.10	.05	.01
☐	342	Claudell Washington	.10	.05	.01
☐	343	Alan Ashby	.10	.05	.01
☐	344	Mark Bailey	.10	.05	.01
☐	345	Kevin Bass	.10	.05	.01
☐	346	Enos Cabell	.10	.05	.01
☐	347	Jose Cruz	.15	.07	.02
☐	348	Bill Dawley	.10	.05	.01
☐	349	Frank DiPino	.10	.05	.01
☐	350	Bill Doran	.10	.05	.01
☐	351	Phil Garner	.15	.07	.02
☐	352	Bob Knepper	.10	.05	.01
☐	353	Mike LaCoss	.10	.05	.01
☐	354	Jerry Mumphrey	.10	.05	.01
☐	355	Joe Niekro	.15	.07	.02
☐	356	Terry Puhl	.10	.05	.01
☐	357	Craig Reynolds	.10	.05	.01
☐	358	Vern Ruhle	.10	.05	.01
☐	359	Nolan Ryan	10.00	4.50	1.25
☐	360	Joe Sambito	.10	.05	.01
☐	361	Mike Scott	.15	.07	.02
☐	362	Dave Smith	.10	.05	.01
☐	363	Julio Solano	.10	.05	.01
☐	364	Dickie Thon	.10	.05	.01
☐	365	Denny Walling	.10	.05	.01
☐	366	Dave Anderson	.10	.05	.01
☐	367	Bob Bailor	.10	.05	.01
☐	368	Greg Brock	.10	.05	.01
☐	369	Carlos Diaz	.10	.05	.01
☐	370	Pedro Guerrero	.15	.07	.02
☐	371	Orel Hershiser	2.50	1.15	.30
☐	372	Rick Honeycutt	.10	.05	.01
☐	373	Burt Hooton	.10	.05	.01
☐	374	Ken Howell	.10	.05	.01
☐	375	Ken Landreaux	.10	.05	.01
☐	376	Candy Maldonado	.10	.05	.01
☐	377	Mike Marshall	.10	.05	.01

☐ 378 Tom Niedenfuer	.10	.05	.01
☐ 379 Alejandro Pena	.10	.05	.01
☐ 380 Jerry Reuss UER ("Home:" omitted)	.10	.05	.01
☐ 381 R.J. Reynolds	.10	.05	.01
☐ 382 German Rivera	.10	.05	.01
☐ 383 Bill Russell	.15	.07	.02
☐ 384 Steve Sax	.15	.07	.02
☐ 385 Mike Scioscia	.10	.05	.01
☐ 386 Franklin Stubbs	.10	.05	.01
☐ 387 Fernando Valenzuela	.15	.07	.02
☐ 388 Bob Welch	.15	.07	.02
☐ 389 Terry Whitfield	.10	.05	.01
☐ 390 Steve Yeager	.10	.05	.01
☐ 391 Pat Zachry	.10	.05	.01
☐ 392 Fred Breining	.10	.05	.01
☐ 393 Gary Carter	.40	.18	.05
☐ 394 Andre Dawson	1.50	.65	.19
☐ 395 Miguel Dilone	.10	.05	.01
☐ 396 Dan Driessen	.10	.05	.01
☐ 397 Doug Flynn	.10	.05	.01
☐ 398 Terry Francona	.10	.05	.01
☐ 399 Bill Gullickson	.15	.07	.02
☐ 400 Bob James	.10	.05	.01
☐ 401 Charlie Lea	.10	.05	.01
☐ 402 Bryan Little	.10	.05	.01
☐ 403 Gary Lucas	.10	.05	.01
☐ 404 David Palmer	.10	.05	.01
☐ 405 Tim Raines	.60	.25	.08
☐ 406 Mike Ramsey	.10	.05	.01
☐ 407 Jeff Reardon	.20	.09	.03
☐ 408 Steve Rogers	.10	.05	.01
☐ 409 Dan Schatzeder	.10	.05	.01
☐ 410 Bryn Smith	.10	.05	.01
☐ 411 Mike Stenhouse	.10	.05	.01
☐ 412 Tim Wallach	.15	.07	.02
☐ 413 Jim Wohlford	.10	.05	.01
☐ 414 Bill Almon	.10	.05	.01
☐ 415 Keith Atherton	.10	.05	.01
☐ 416 Bruce Bochte	.10	.05	.01
☐ 417 Tom Burgmeier	.10	.05	.01
☐ 418 Ray Burris	.10	.05	.01
☐ 419 Bill Caudill	.10	.05	.01
☐ 420 Chris Codiroli	.10	.05	.01
☐ 421 Tim Conroy	.10	.05	.01
☐ 422 Mike Davis	.10	.05	.01
☐ 423 Jim Essian	.10	.05	.01
☐ 424 Mike Heath	.10	.05	.01
☐ 425 Rickey Henderson	2.50	1.15	.30
☐ 426 Donnie Hill	.10	.05	.01
☐ 427 Dave Kingman	.15	.07	.02
☐ 428 Bill Krueger	.10	.05	.01
☐ 429 Carney Lansford	.15	.07	.02
☐ 430 Steve McCatty	.10	.05	.01
☐ 431 Joe Morgan	.50	.23	.06
☐ 432 Dwayne Murphy	.10	.05	.01
☐ 433 Tony Phillips	.15	.07	.02
☐ 434 Lary Sorensen	.10	.05	.01
☐ 435 Mike Warren	.10	.05	.01
☐ 436 Curt Young	.10	.05	.01
☐ 437 Luis Aponte	.10	.05	.01
☐ 438 Chris Bando	.10	.05	.01
☐ 439 Tony Bernazard	.10	.05	.01
☐ 440 Bert Blyleven	.20	.09	.03
☐ 441 Brett Butler	.20	.09	.03
☐ 442 Ernie Camacho	.10	.05	.01
☐ 443 Joe Carter	15.00	6.75	1.90
☐ 444 Carmelo Castillo	.10	.05	.01
☐ 445 Jamie Easterly	.10	.05	.01
☐ 446 Steve Farr	.50	.23	.06
☐ 447 Mike Fischlin	.10	.05	.01
☐ 448 Julio Franco	.75	.35	.09
☐ 449 Mel Hall	.10	.05	.01
☐ 450 Mike Hargrove	.15	.07	.02
☐ 451 Neal Heaton	.10	.05	.01
☐ 452 Brook Jacoby	.10	.05	.01
☐ 453 Mike Jeffcoat	.10	.05	.01
☐ 454 Don Schulze	.10	.05	.01
☐ 455 Roy Smith	.10	.05	.01
☐ 456 Pat Tabler	.10	.05	.01
☐ 457 Andre Thornton	.10	.05	.01
☐ 458 George Vukovich	.10	.05	.01
☐ 459 Tom Waddell	.10	.05	.01
☐ 460 Jerry Willard	.10	.05	.01
☐ 461 Dale Berra	.10	.05	.01
☐ 462 John Candelaria	.10	.05	.01
☐ 463 Jose DeLeon	.10	.05	.01
☐ 464 Doug Frobel	.10	.05	.01
☐ 465 Cecilio Guante	.10	.05	.01
☐ 466 Brian Harper	.15	.07	.02
☐ 467 Lee Lacy	.10	.05	.01
☐ 468 Bill Madlock	.15	.07	.02
☐ 469 Lee Mazzilli	.10	.05	.01
☐ 470 Larry McWilliams	.10	.05	.01
☐ 471 Jim Morrison	.10	.05	.01
☐ 472 Tony Pena	.10	.05	.01
☐ 473 Johnny Ray	.10	.05	.01
☐ 474 Rick Rhoden	.10	.05	.01
☐ 475 Don Robinson	.10	.05	.01
☐ 476 Rod Scurry	.10	.05	.01
☐ 477 Kent Tekulve	.10	.05	.01
☐ 478 Jason Thompson	.10	.05	.01
☐ 479 John Tudor	.15	.07	.02
☐ 480 Lee Tunnell	.10	.05	.01
☐ 481 Marvell Wynne	.10	.05	.01
☐ 482 Salome Barojas	.10	.05	.01
☐ 483 Dave Beard	.10	.05	.01
☐ 484 Jim Beattie	.10	.05	.01
☐ 485 Barry Bonnell	.10	.05	.01
☐ 486 Phil Bradley	.15	.07	.02
☐ 487 Al Cowens	.10	.05	.01
☐ 488 Alvin Davis	.25	.11	.03
☐ 489 Dave Henderson	.15	.07	.02
☐ 490 Steve Henderson	.10	.05	.01
☐ 491 Bob Kearney	.10	.05	.01
☐ 492 Mark Langston	2.25	1.00	.30
☐ 493 Larry Milbourne	.10	.05	.01
☐ 494 Paul Mirabella	.10	.05	.01
☐ 495 Mike Moore	.15	.07	.02
☐ 496 Edwin Nunez	.10	.05	.01
☐ 497 Spike Owen	.10	.05	.01
☐ 498 Jack Perconte	.10	.05	.01
☐ 499 Ken Phelps	.10	.05	.01
☐ 500 Jim Presley	.10	.05	.01
☐ 501 Mike Stanton	.10	.05	.01
☐ 502 Bob Stoddard	.10	.05	.01
☐ 503 Gorman Thomas	.10	.05	.01
☐ 504 Ed VandeBerg	.10	.05	.01
☐ 505 Matt Young	.10	.05	.01
☐ 506 Juan Agosto	.10	.05	.01
☐ 507 Harold Baines	.20	.09	.03
☐ 508 Floyd Bannister	.10	.05	.01
☐ 509 Britt Burns	.10	.05	.01
☐ 510 Julio Cruz	.10	.05	.01
☐ 511 Richard Dotson	.10	.05	.01
☐ 512 Jerry Dybzinski	.10	.05	.01
☐ 513 Carlton Fisk	1.50	.65	.19
☐ 514 Scott Fletcher	.10	.05	.01
☐ 515 Jerry Hairston	.10	.05	.01
☐ 516 Marc Hill	.10	.05	.01
☐ 517 LaMarr Hoyt	.10	.05	.01
☐ 518 Ron Kittle	.10	.05	.01
☐ 519 Rudy Law	.10	.05	.01
☐ 520 Vance Law	.10	.05	.01
☐ 521 Greg Luzinski	.15	.07	.02
☐ 522 Gene Nelson	.10	.05	.01

☐ 523 Tom Paciorek .15 .07 .02
☐ 524 Ron Reed .10 .05 .01
☐ 525 Bert Roberge .10 .05 .01
☐ 526 Tom Seaver 1.50 .65 .19
☐ 527 Roy Smalley .10 .05 .01
☐ 528 Dan Spillner .10 .05 .01
☐ 529 Mike Squires .10 .05 .01
☐ 530 Greg Walker .10 .05 .01
☐ 531 Cesar Cedeno .15 .07 .02
☐ 532 Dave Concepcion .15 .07 .02
☐ 533 Eric Davis 2.50 1.15 .30
☐ 534 Nick Esasky .10 .05 .01
☐ 535 Tom Foley .10 .05 .01
☐ 536 John Franco UER 1.50 .65 .19
(Koufax misspelled
as Kofax on back)
☐ 537 Brad Gulden .10 .05 .01
☐ 538 Tom Hume .10 .05 .01
☐ 539 Wayne Krenchicki .10 .05 .01
☐ 540 Andy McGaffigan .10 .05 .01
☐ 541 Eddie Milner .10 .05 .01
☐ 542 Ron Oester .10 .05 .01
☐ 543 Bob Owchinko .10 .05 .01
☐ 544 Dave Parker .20 .09 .03
☐ 545 Frank Pastore .10 .05 .01
☐ 546 Tony Perez .20 .09 .03
☐ 547 Ted Power .10 .05 .01
☐ 548 Joe Price .10 .05 .01
☐ 549 Gary Redus .10 .05 .01
☐ 550 Pete Rose 2.50 1.15 .30
☐ 551 Jeff Russell .15 .07 .02
☐ 552 Mario Soto .10 .05 .01
☐ 553 Jay Tibbs .10 .05 .01
☐ 554 Duane Walker .10 .05 .01
☐ 555 Alan Bannister .10 .05 .01
☐ 556 Buddy Bell .15 .07 .02
☐ 557 Danny Darwin .10 .05 .01
☐ 558 Charlie Hough .15 .07 .02
☐ 559 Bobby Jones .10 .05 .01
☐ 560 Odell Jones .10 .05 .01
☐ 561 Jeff Kunkel .10 .05 .01
☐ 562 Mike Mason .10 .05 .01
☐ 563 Pete O'Brien .15 .07 .02
☐ 564 Larry Parrish .10 .05 .01
☐ 565 Mickey Rivers .10 .05 .01
☐ 566 Billy Sample .10 .05 .01
☐ 567 Dave Schmidt .10 .05 .01
☐ 568 Donnie Scott .10 .05 .01
☐ 569 Dave Stewart .20 .09 .03
☐ 570 Frank Tanana .15 .07 .02
☐ 571 Wayne Tolleson .10 .05 .01
☐ 572 Gary Ward .10 .05 .01
☐ 573 Curtis Wilkerson .10 .05 .01
☐ 574 George Wright .10 .05 .01
☐ 575 Ned Yost .10 .05 .01
☐ 576 Mark Brouhard .10 .05 .01
☐ 577 Mike Caldwell .10 .05 .01
☐ 578 Bobby Clark .10 .05 .01
☐ 579 Jaime Cocanower .10 .05 .01
☐ 580 Cecil Cooper .15 .07 .02
☐ 581 Rollie Fingers .20 .09 .03
☐ 582 Jim Gantner .10 .05 .01
☐ 583 Moose Haas .10 .05 .01
☐ 584 Dion James .10 .05 .01
☐ 585 Pete Ladd .10 .05 .01
☐ 586 Rick Manning .10 .05 .01
☐ 587 Bob McClure .10 .05 .01
☐ 588 Paul Molitor 3.00 1.35 .40
☐ 589 Charlie Moore .10 .05 .01
☐ 590 Ben Oglivie .10 .05 .01
☐ 591 Chuck Porter .10 .05 .01
☐ 592 Randy Ready .10 .05 .01
☐ 593 Ed Romero .10 .05 .01
☐ 594 Bill Schroeder .10 .05 .01
☐ 595 Ray Searage .10 .05 .01
☐ 596 Ted Simmons .15 .07 .02
☐ 597 Jim Sundberg .15 .07 .02
☐ 598 Don Sutton .20 .09 .03
☐ 599 Tom Tellmann .10 .05 .01
☐ 600 Rick Waits .10 .05 .01
☐ 601 Robin Yount 2.50 1.15 .30
☐ 602 Dusty Baker .20 .09 .03
☐ 603 Bob Brenly .10 .05 .01
☐ 604 Jack Clark .15 .07 .02
☐ 605 Chili Davis .15 .07 .02
☐ 606 Mark Davis .10 .05 .01
☐ 607 Dan Gladden .35 .16 .04
☐ 608 Atlee Hammaker .10 .05 .01
☐ 609 Mike Krukow .10 .05 .01
☐ 610 Duane Kuiper .10 .05 .01
☐ 611 Bob Lacey .10 .05 .01
☐ 612 Bill Laskey .10 .05 .01
☐ 613 Gary Lavelle .10 .05 .01
☐ 614 Johnnie LeMaster .10 .05 .01
☐ 615 Jeff Leonard .10 .05 .01
☐ 616 Randy Lerch .10 .05 .01
☐ 617 Greg Minton .10 .05 .01
☐ 618 Steve Nicosia .10 .05 .01
☐ 619 Gene Richards .10 .05 .01
☐ 620 Jeff D. Robinson .10 .05 .01
☐ 621 Scot Thompson .10 .05 .01
☐ 622 Manny Trillo .10 .05 .01
☐ 623 Brad Wellman .10 .05 .01
☐ 624 Frank Williams .10 .05 .01
☐ 625 Joel Youngblood .10 .05 .01
☐ 626 Cal Ripken IA 4.00 1.80 .50
☐ 627 Mike Schmidt IA 1.50 .65 .19
☐ 628 Giving The Signs .15 .07 .02
Sparky Anderson
☐ 629 AL Pitcher's Nightmare 1.50 .65 .19
Dave Winfield
Rickey Henderson
☐ 630 NL Pitcher's Nightmare 1.50 .65 .19
Mike Schmidt
Ryne Sandberg
☐ 631 NL All-Stars 1.00 .45 .13
Darryl Strawberry
Gary Carter
Steve Garvey
Ozzie Smith
☐ 632 A-S Winning Battery .25 .11 .03
Gary Carter
Charlie Lea
☐ 633 NL Pennant Clinchers .25 .11 .03
Steve Garvey
Rich Gossage
☐ 634 NL Rookie Phenoms .15 .07 .02
Dwight Gooden
Juan Samuel
☐ 635 Toronto's Big Guns .15 .07 .02
Willie Upshaw
☐ 636 Toronto's Big Guns .15 .07 .02
Lloyd Moseby
☐ 637 HOLLAND: Al Holland .15 .07 .02
☐ 638 TUNNELL: Lee Tunnell .15 .07 .02
☐ 639 500th Homer 1.00 .45 .13
Reggie Jackson
☐ 640 4000th Hit 1.25 .55 .16
Pete Rose
☐ 641 Father and Son 5.00 2.30 .60
Cal Ripken Jr. and Sr.
☐ 642 Cubs: Division Champs .15 .07 .02
☐ 643 Two Perfect Games .15 .07 .02
and One No-Hitter:
Mike Witt
David Palmer

Jack Morris			
☐ 644 Willie Lozado and Vic Mata	.10	.05	.01
☐ 645 Kelly Gruber and Randy O'Neal	.50	.23	.06
☐ 646 Jose Roman and Joel Skinner	.10	.05	.01
☐ 647 Steve Kiefer and Danny Tartabull	4.00	1.80	.50
☐ 648 Rob Deer and Alejandro Sanchez	.50	.23	.06
☐ 649 Billy Hatcher and Shawon Dunston	1.00	.45	.13
☐ 650 Ron Robinson and Mike Bielecki	.10	.05	.01
☐ 651 Zane Smith and Paul Zuvella	.35	.16	.04
☐ 652 Joe Hesketh and Glenn Davis	.50	.23	.06
☐ 653 John Russell and Steve Jeltz	.10	.05	.01
☐ 654 CL: Tigers/Padres and Cubs/Mets	.15	.05	.01
☐ 655 CL: Blue Jays/Yankees and Red Sox/Orioles	.15	.05	.01
☐ 656 CL: Royals/Cardinals and Phillies/Twins	.15	.05	.01
☐ 657 CL: Angels/Braves and Astros/Dodgers	.15	.05	.01
☐ 658 CL: Expos/A's and Indians/Pirates	.15	.05	.01
☐ 659 CL: Mariners/White Sox and Reds/Rangers	.15	.05	.01
☐ 660 CL: Brewers/Giants and Special Cards	.15	.05	.01

1985 Fleer Update

This 132-card set was issued late in the collecting year and features new players and players on new teams compared to the 1985 Fleer regular issue cards. Cards measure 2 1/2" by 3 1/2" and were distributed together as a complete set in a special box. The cards are numbered with a U prefix and are ordered alphabetically by the player's name. This set features the Extended Rookie Cards of Tom Browning, Ivan Calderon, Vince Coleman, Darren Daulton, Mariano Duncan, Ozzie Guillen, Teddy Higuera, and Mickey Tettleton.

	NRMT-MT	EXC	G-VG
COMPLETE FACT.SET (132)	30.00	13.50	3.80
COMMON CARD (1-132)	.15	.07	.02

☐ 1 Don Aase	.15	.07	.02
☐ 2 Bill Almon	.15	.07	.02
☐ 3 Dusty Baker	.30	.14	.04
☐ 4 Dale Berra	.15	.07	.02
☐ 5 Karl Best	.15	.07	.02
☐ 6 Tim Birtsas	.15	.07	.02
☐ 7 Vida Blue	.20	.09	.03
☐ 8 Rich Bordi	.15	.07	.02
☐ 9 Daryl Boston	.35	.16	.04
☐ 10 Hubie Brooks	.20	.09	.03
☐ 11 Chris Brown	.15	.07	.02
☐ 12 Tom Browning	.75	.35	.09
☐ 13 Al Bumbry	.15	.07	.02
☐ 14 Tim Burke	.15	.07	.02
☐ 15 Ray Burris	.15	.07	.02
☐ 16 Jeff Burroughs	.15	.07	.02
☐ 17 Ivan Calderon	.40	.18	.05
☐ 18 Jeff Calhoun	.15	.07	.02
☐ 19 Bill Campbell	.15	.07	.02
☐ 20 Don Carman	.15	.07	.02
☐ 21 Gary Carter	.40	.18	.05
☐ 22 Bobby Castillo	.15	.07	.02
☐ 23 Bill Caudill	.15	.07	.02
☐ 24 Rick Cerone	.15	.07	.02
☐ 25 Jack Clark	.20	.09	.03
☐ 26 Pat Clements	.15	.07	.02
☐ 27 Stewart Cliburn	.15	.07	.02
☐ 28 Vince Coleman	1.00	.45	.13
☐ 29 Dave Collins	.15	.07	.02
☐ 30 Fritz Connally	.15	.07	.02
☐ 31 Henry Cotto	.15	.07	.02
☐ 32 Danny Darwin	.15	.07	.02
☐ 33 Darren Daulton	15.00	6.75	1.90
☐ 34 Jerry Davis	.15	.07	.02
☐ 35 Brian Dayett	.15	.07	.02
☐ 36 Ken Dixon	.15	.07	.02
☐ 37 Tommy Dunbar	.15	.07	.02
☐ 38 Mariano Duncan	1.00	.45	.13
☐ 39 Bob Fallon	.15	.07	.02
☐ 40 Brian Fisher	.15	.07	.02
☐ 41 Mike Fitzgerald	.15	.07	.02
☐ 42 Ray Fontenot	.15	.07	.02
☐ 43 Greg Gagne	.40	.18	.05
☐ 44 Oscar Gamble	.15	.07	.02
☐ 45 Jim Gott	.15	.07	.02
☐ 46 David Green	.15	.07	.02
☐ 47 Alfredo Griffin	.15	.07	.02
☐ 48 Ozzie Guillen	2.00	.90	.25
☐ 49 Toby Harrah	.15	.07	.02
☐ 50 Ron Hassey	.15	.07	.02
☐ 51 Rickey Henderson	3.00	1.35	.40
☐ 52 Steve Henderson	.15	.07	.02
☐ 53 George Hendrick	.15	.07	.02
☐ 54 Teddy Higuera	.25	.11	.03
☐ 55 Al Holland	.15	.07	.02
☐ 56 Burt Hooton	.15	.07	.02
☐ 57 Jay Howell	.15	.07	.02
☐ 58 LaMarr Hoyt	.15	.07	.02
☐ 59 Tim Hulett	.25	.11	.03
☐ 60 Bob James	.15	.07	.02
☐ 61 Cliff Johnson	.15	.07	.02
☐ 62 Howard Johnson	.40	.18	.05
☐ 63 Ruppert Jones	.15	.07	.02
☐ 64 Steve Kemp	.15	.07	.02
☐ 65 Bruce Kison	.15	.07	.02
☐ 66 Mike LaCoss	.15	.07	.02
☐ 67 Lee Lacy	.15	.07	.02
☐ 68 Dave LaPoint	.15	.07	.02
☐ 69 Gary Lavelle	.15	.07	.02
☐ 70 Vance Law	.15	.07	.02
☐ 71 Manny Lee	.15	.07	.02
☐ 72 Sixto Lezcano	.15	.07	.02
☐ 73 Tim Lollar	.15	.07	.02

☐ 74 Urbano Lugo	.15	.07	.02
☐ 75 Fred Lynn	.20	.09	.03
☐ 76 Steve Lyons	.15	.07	.02
☐ 77 Mickey Mahler	.15	.07	.02
☐ 78 Ron Mathis	.15	.07	.02
☐ 79 Len Matuszek	.15	.07	.02
☐ 80 Oddibe McDowell UER (Part of bio actually Roger's)	.40	.18	.05
☐ 81 Roger McDowell UER (Part of bio actually Oddibe's)	.40	.18	.05
☐ 82 Donnie Moore	.15	.07	.02
☐ 83 Ron Musselman	.15	.07	.02
☐ 84 Al Oliver	.20	.09	.03
☐ 85 Joe Orsulak	.60	.25	.08
☐ 86 Dan Pasqua	.25	.11	.03
☐ 87 Chris Pittaro	.15	.07	.02
☐ 88 Rick Reuschel	.20	.09	.03
☐ 89 Earnie Riles	.15	.07	.02
☐ 90 Jerry Royster	.15	.07	.02
☐ 91 Dave Rozema	.15	.07	.02
☐ 92 Dave Rucker	.15	.07	.02
☐ 93 Vern Ruhle	.15	.07	.02
☐ 94 Mark Salas	.15	.07	.02
☐ 95 Luis Salazar	.15	.07	.02
☐ 96 Joe Sambito	.15	.07	.02
☐ 97 Billy Sample	.15	.07	.02
☐ 98 Alejandro Sanchez	.15	.07	.02
☐ 99 Calvin Schiraldi	.15	.07	.02
☐ 100 Rick Schu	.15	.07	.02
☐ 101 Larry Sheets	.15	.07	.02
☐ 102 Ron Shephard	.15	.07	.02
☐ 103 Nelson Simmons	.15	.07	.02
☐ 104 Don Slaught	.15	.07	.02
☐ 105 Roy Smalley	.15	.07	.02
☐ 106 Lonnie Smith	.15	.07	.02
☐ 107 Nate Snell	.15	.07	.02
☐ 108 Lary Sorensen	.15	.07	.02
☐ 109 Chris Speier	.15	.07	.02
☐ 110 Mike Stenhouse	.15	.07	.02
☐ 111 Tim Stoddard	.15	.07	.02
☐ 112 John Stuper	.15	.07	.02
☐ 113 Jim Sundberg	.20	.09	.03
☐ 114 Bruce Sutter	.20	.09	.03
☐ 115 Don Sutton	.30	.14	.04
☐ 116 Bruce Tanner	.15	.07	.02
☐ 117 Kent Tekulve	.15	.07	.02
☐ 118 Walt Terrell	.15	.07	.02
☐ 119 Mickey Tettleton	5.00	2.30	.60
☐ 120 Rich Thompson	.15	.07	.02
☐ 121 Louis Thornton	.15	.07	.02
☐ 122 Alex Trevino	.15	.07	.02
☐ 123 John Tudor	.15	.07	.02
☐ 124 Jose Uribe	.15	.07	.02
☐ 125 Dave Valle	.25	.11	.03
☐ 126 Dave Von Ohlen	.15	.07	.02
☐ 127 Curt Wardle	.15	.07	.02
☐ 128 U.L. Washington	.15	.07	.02
☐ 129 Ed Whitson	.15	.07	.02
☐ 130 Herm Winningham	.15	.07	.02
☐ 131 Rich Yett	.15	.07	.02
☐ 132 Checklist U1-U132	.15	.07	.02

1986 Fleer

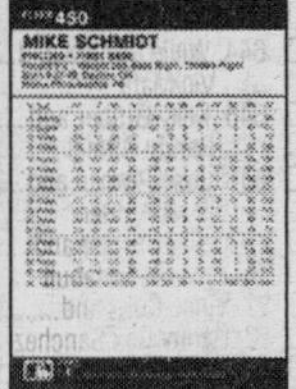

The cards in this 660-card set measure 2 1/2" by 3 1/2". The 1986 Fleer set features fronts that contain the team logo along with the player's name and position. The player cards are alphabetized within team and the teams are ordered by their 1985 season finish and won-lost record, e.g., Kansas City (1-25), St. Louis (26-49), Toronto (50-73), New York Mets (74-97), New York Yankees (98-122), Los Angeles (123-147), California (148-171), Cincinnati (172-196), Chicago White Sox (197-220), Detroit (221-243), Montreal (244-267), Baltimore (268-291), Houston (292-314), San Diego (315-338), Boston (339-360), Chicago Cubs (361-385), Minnesota (386-409), Oakland (410-432), Philadelphia (433-457), Seattle (458-481), Milwaukee (482-506), Atlanta (507-532), San Francisco (533-555), Texas (556-578), Cleveland (579-601), and Pittsburgh (602-625). Subsets include Specials (626-643) and Major League Prospects (644-653). The border enclosing the photo is dark blue. The backs feature the same name, number, and statistics format that Fleer has been using over the past few years. The Dennis and Tippy Martinez cards were apparently switched in the set numbering, as their adjacent numbers (279 and 280) were reversed on the Orioles checklist card. The set includes the Rookie Cards of Rick Aguilera, Jose Canseco, Vince Coleman, Darren Daulton, Len Dykstra, Cecil Fielder, Paul O'Neill, Benito Santiago, and Mickey Tettleton.

	MINT	EXC	G-VG
COMPLETE SET (660)	100.00	45.00	12.50
COMPLETE FACT.SET (660)	110.00	50.00	14.00
COMMON CARD (1-660)	.10	.05	.01
☐ 1 Steve Balboni	.15	.07	.02
☐ 2 Joe Beckwith	.10	.05	.01
☐ 3 Buddy Biancalana	.10	.05	.01
☐ 4 Bud Black	.10	.05	.01
☐ 5 George Brett	2.50	1.15	.30
☐ 6 Onix Concepcion	.10	.05	.01
☐ 7 Steve Farr	.15	.07	.02
☐ 8 Mark Gubicza	.15	.07	.02
☐ 9 Dane Iorg	.10	.05	.01
☐ 10 Danny Jackson	.15	.07	.02
☐ 11 Lynn Jones	.10	.05	.01
☐ 12 Mike Jones	.10	.05	.01
☐ 13 Charlie Leibrandt	.10	.05	.01
☐ 14 Hal McRae	.20	.09	.03
☐ 15 Omar Moreno	.10	.05	.01
☐ 16 Darryl Motley	.10	.05	.01
☐ 17 Jorge Orta	.10	.05	.01
☐ 18 Dan Quisenberry	.15	.07	.02
☐ 19 Bret Saberhagen	.50	.23	.06
☐ 20 Pat Sheridan	.10	.05	.01
☐ 21 Lonnie Smith	.10	.05	.01

	Player			
☐	22 Jim Sundberg	.10	.05	.01
☐	23 John Wathan	.10	.05	.01
☐	24 Frank White	.15	.07	.02
☐	25 Willie Wilson	.10	.05	.01
☐	26 Joaquin Andujar	.10	.05	.01
☐	27 Steve Braun	.10	.05	.01
☐	28 Bill Campbell	.10	.05	.01
☐	29 Cesar Cedeno	.15	.07	.02
☐	30 Jack Clark	.15	.07	.02
☐	31 Vince Coleman	.50	.23	.06
☐	32 Danny Cox	.10	.05	.01
☐	33 Ken Dayley	.10	.05	.01
☐	34 Ivan DeJesus	.10	.05	.01
☐	35 Bob Forsch	.10	.05	.01
☐	36 Brian Harper	.15	.07	.02
☐	37 Tom Herr	.10	.05	.01
☐	38 Ricky Horton	.10	.05	.01
☐	39 Kurt Kepshire	.10	.05	.01
☐	40 Jeff Lahti	.10	.05	.01
☐	41 Tito Landrum	.10	.05	.01
☐	42 Willie McGee	.15	.07	.02
☐	43 Tom Nieto	.10	.05	.01
☐	44 Terry Pendleton	.75	.35	.09
☐	45 Darrell Porter	.10	.05	.01
☐	46 Ozzie Smith	1.25	.55	.16
☐	47 John Tudor	.15	.07	.02
☐	48 Andy Van Slyke	.20	.09	.03
☐	49 Todd Worrell	.30	.14	.04
☐	50 Jim Acker	.10	.05	.01
☐	51 Doyle Alexander	.10	.05	.01
☐	52 Jesse Barfield	.10	.05	.01
☐	53 George Bell	.15	.07	.02
☐	54 Jeff Burroughs	.10	.05	.01
☐	55 Bill Caudill	.10	.05	.01
☐	56 Jim Clancy	.10	.05	.01
☐	57 Tony Fernandez	.15	.07	.02
☐	58 Tom Filer	.10	.05	.01
☐	59 Damaso Garcia	.10	.05	.01
☐	60 Tom Henke	.25	.11	.03
☐	61 Garth Iorg	.10	.05	.01
☐	62 Cliff Johnson	.10	.05	.01
☐	63 Jimmy Key	.75	.35	.09
☐	64 Dennis Lamp	.10	.05	.01
☐	65 Gary Lavelle	.10	.05	.01
☐	66 Buck Martinez	.10	.05	.01
☐	67 Lloyd Moseby	.10	.05	.01
☐	68 Rance Mulliniks	.10	.05	.01
☐	69 Al Oliver	.15	.07	.02
☐	70 Dave Stieb	.15	.07	.02
☐	71 Louis Thornton	.10	.05	.01
☐	72 Willie Upshaw	.10	.05	.01
☐	73 Ernie Whitt	.10	.05	.01
☐	74 Rick Aguilera	1.25	.55	.16
☐	75 Wally Backman	.10	.05	.01
☐	76 Gary Carter	.20	.09	.03
☐	77 Ron Darling	.15	.07	.02
☐	78 Len Dykstra	5.00	2.30	.60
☐	79 Sid Fernandez	.15	.07	.02
☐	80 George Foster	.15	.07	.02
☐	81 Dwight Gooden	.40	.18	.05
☐	82 Tom Gorman	.10	.05	.01
☐	83 Danny Heep	.10	.05	.01
☐	84 Keith Hernandez	.20	.09	.03
☐	85 Howard Johnson	.15	.07	.02
☐	86 Ray Knight	.15	.07	.02
☐	87 Terry Leach	.10	.05	.01
☐	88 Ed Lynch	.10	.05	.01
☐	89 Roger McDowell	.25	.11	.03
☐	90 Jesse Orosco	.10	.05	.01
☐	91 Tom Paciorek	.15	.07	.02
☐	92 Ronn Reynolds	.10	.05	.01
☐	93 Rafael Santana	.10	.05	.01
☐	94 Doug Sisk	.10	.05	.01
☐	95 Rusty Staub	.15	.07	.02
☐	96 Darryl Strawberry	.60	.25	.08
☐	97 Mookie Wilson	.15	.07	.02
☐	98 Neil Allen	.10	.05	.01
☐	99 Don Baylor	.20	.09	.03
☐	100 Dale Berra	.10	.05	.01
☐	101 Rich Bordi	.10	.05	.01
☐	102 Marty Bystrom	.10	.05	.01
☐	103 Joe Cowley	.10	.05	.01
☐	104 Brian Fisher	.10	.05	.01
☐	105 Ken Griffey	.15	.07	.02
☐	106 Ron Guidry	.15	.07	.02
☐	107 Ron Hassey	.10	.05	.01
☐	108 Rickey Henderson UER (SB Record of 120, sic)	1.50	.65	.19
☐	109 Don Mattingly	3.00	1.35	.40
☐	110 Bobby Meacham	.10	.05	.01
☐	111 John Montefusco	.10	.05	.01
☐	112 Phil Niekro	.20	.09	.03
☐	113 Mike Pagliarulo	.10	.05	.01
☐	114 Dan Pasqua	.10	.05	.01
☐	115 Willie Randolph	.15	.07	.02
☐	116 Dave Righetti	.15	.07	.02
☐	117 Andre Robertson	.10	.05	.01
☐	118 Billy Sample	.10	.05	.01
☐	119 Bob Shirley	.10	.05	.01
☐	120 Ed Whitson	.10	.05	.01
☐	121 Dave Winfield	1.00	.45	.13
☐	122 Butch Wynegar	.10	.05	.01
☐	123 Dave Anderson	.10	.05	.01
☐	124 Bob Bailor	.10	.05	.01
☐	125 Greg Brock	.10	.05	.01
☐	126 Enos Cabell	.10	.05	.01
☐	127 Bobby Castillo	.10	.05	.01
☐	128 Carlos Diaz	.10	.05	.01
☐	129 Mariano Duncan	.50	.23	.06
☐	130 Pedro Guerrero	.15	.07	.02
☐	131 Orel Hershiser	.40	.18	.05
☐	132 Rick Honeycutt	.10	.05	.01
☐	133 Ken Howell	.10	.05	.01
☐	134 Ken Landreaux	.10	.05	.01
☐	135 Bill Madlock	.15	.07	.02
☐	136 Candy Maldonado	.10	.05	.01
☐	137 Mike Marshall	.10	.05	.01
☐	138 Len Matuszek	.10	.05	.01
☐	139 Tom Niedenfuer	.10	.05	.01
☐	140 Alejandro Pena	.10	.05	.01
☐	141 Jerry Reuss	.10	.05	.01
☐	142 Bill Russell	.15	.07	.02
☐	143 Steve Sax	.15	.07	.02
☐	144 Mike Scioscia	.10	.05	.01
☐	145 Fernando Valenzuela	.15	.07	.02
☐	146 Bob Welch	.15	.07	.02
☐	147 Terry Whitfield	.10	.05	.01
☐	148 Juan Beniquez	.10	.05	.01
☐	149 Bob Boone	.15	.07	.02
☐	150 John Candelaria	.10	.05	.01
☐	151 Rod Carew	.50	.23	.06
☐	152 Stewart Cliburn	.10	.05	.01
☐	153 Doug DeCinces	.10	.05	.01
☐	154 Brian Downing	.15	.07	.02
☐	155 Ken Forsch	.10	.05	.01
☐	156 Craig Gerber	.10	.05	.01
☐	157 Bobby Grich	.15	.07	.02
☐	158 George Hendrick	.10	.05	.01
☐	159 Al Holland	.10	.05	.01
☐	160 Reggie Jackson	1.25	.55	.16
☐	161 Ruppert Jones	.10	.05	.01
☐	162 Urbano Lugo	.10	.05	.01
☐	163 Kirk McCaskill	.25	.11	.03
☐	164 Donnie Moore	.10	.05	.01
☐	165 Gary Pettis	.10	.05	.01
☐	166 Ron Romanick	.10	.05	.01

	#	Player			
☐	167	Dick Schofield	.10	.05	.01
☐	168	Daryl Sconiers	.10	.05	.01
☐	169	Jim Slaton	.10	.05	.01
☐	170	Don Sutton	.20	.09	.03
☐	171	Mike Witt	.10	.05	.01
☐	172	Buddy Bell	.15	.07	.02
☐	173	Tom Browning	.15	.07	.02
☐	174	Dave Concepcion	.15	.07	.02
☐	175	Eric Davis	.35	.16	.04
☐	176	Bo Diaz	.10	.05	.01
☐	177	Nick Esasky	.10	.05	.01
☐	178	John Franco	.15	.07	.02
☐	179	Tom Hume	.10	.05	.01
☐	180	Wayne Krenchicki	.10	.05	.01
☐	181	Andy McGaffigan	.10	.05	.01
☐	182	Eddie Milner	.10	.05	.01
☐	183	Ron Oester	.10	.05	.01
☐	184	Dave Parker	.20	.09	.03
☐	185	Frank Pastore	.10	.05	.01
☐	186	Tony Perez	.20	.09	.03
☐	187	Ted Power	.10	.05	.01
☐	188	Joe Price	.10	.05	.01
☐	189	Gary Redus	.10	.05	.01
☐	190	Ron Robinson	.10	.05	.01
☐	191	Pete Rose	1.25	.55	.16
☐	192	Mario Soto	.10	.05	.01
☐	193	John Stuper	.10	.05	.01
☐	194	Jay Tibbs	.10	.05	.01
☐	195	Dave Van Gorder	.10	.05	.01
☐	196	Max Venable	.10	.05	.01
☐	197	Juan Agosto	.10	.05	.01
☐	198	Harold Baines	.15	.07	.02
☐	199	Floyd Bannister	.10	.05	.01
☐	200	Britt Burns	.10	.05	.01
☐	201	Julio Cruz	.10	.05	.01
☐	202	Joel Davis	.10	.05	.01
☐	203	Richard Dotson	.10	.05	.01
☐	204	Carlton Fisk	.75	.35	.09
☐	205	Scott Fletcher	.10	.05	.01
☐	206	Ozzie Guillen	.75	.35	.09
☐	207	Jerry Hairston	.10	.05	.01
☐	208	Tim Hulett	.10	.05	.01
☐	209	Bob James	.10	.05	.01
☐	210	Ron Kittle	.10	.05	.01
☐	211	Rudy Law	.10	.05	.01
☐	212	Bryan Little	.10	.05	.01
☐	213	Gene Nelson	.10	.05	.01
☐	214	Reid Nichols	.10	.05	.01
☐	215	Luis Salazar	.10	.05	.01
☐	216	Tom Seaver	.75	.35	.09
☐	217	Dan Spillner	.10	.05	.01
☐	218	Bruce Tanner	.10	.05	.01
☐	219	Greg Walker	.10	.05	.01
☐	220	Dave Wehrmeister	.10	.05	.01
☐	221	Juan Berenguer	.10	.05	.01
☐	222	Dave Bergman	.10	.05	.01
☐	223	Tom Brookens	.10	.05	.01
☐	224	Darrell Evans	.15	.07	.02
☐	225	Barbaro Garbey	.10	.05	.01
☐	226	Kirk Gibson	.20	.09	.03
☐	227	John Grubb	.10	.05	.01
☐	228	Willie Hernandez	.10	.05	.01
☐	229	Larry Herndon	.10	.05	.01
☐	230	Chet Lemon	.10	.05	.01
☐	231	Aurelio Lopez	.10	.05	.01
☐	232	Jack Morris	.20	.09	.03
☐	233	Randy O'Neal	.10	.05	.01
☐	234	Lance Parrish	.15	.07	.02
☐	235	Dan Petry	.10	.05	.01
☐	236	Alejandro Sanchez	.10	.05	.01
☐	237	Bill Scherrer	.10	.05	.01
☐	238	Nelson Simmons	.10	.05	.01
☐	239	Frank Tanana	.15	.07	.02
☐	240	Walt Terrell	.10	.05	.01
☐	241	Alan Trammell	.20	.09	.03
☐	242	Lou Whitaker	.20	.09	.03
☐	243	Milt Wilcox	.10	.05	.01
☐	244	Hubie Brooks	.10	.05	.01
☐	245	Tim Burke	.10	.05	.01
☐	246	Andre Dawson	.60	.25	.08
☐	247	Mike Fitzgerald	.10	.05	.01
☐	248	Terry Francona	.10	.05	.01
☐	249	Bill Gullickson	.15	.07	.02
☐	250	Joe Hesketh	.10	.05	.01
☐	251	Bill Laskey	.10	.05	.01
☐	252	Vance Law	.10	.05	.01
☐	253	Charlie Lea	.10	.05	.01
☐	254	Gary Lucas	.10	.05	.01
☐	255	David Palmer	.10	.05	.01
☐	256	Tim Raines	.30	.14	.04
☐	257	Jeff Reardon	.20	.09	.03
☐	258	Bert Roberge	.10	.05	.01
☐	259	Dan Schatzeder	.10	.05	.01
☐	260	Bryn Smith	.10	.05	.01
☐	261	Randy St.Claire	.10	.05	.01
☐	262	Scot Thompson	.10	.05	.01
☐	263	Tim Wallach	.15	.07	.02
☐	264	U.L. Washington	.10	.05	.01
☐	265	Mitch Webster	.10	.05	.01
☐	266	Herm Winningham	.10	.05	.01
☐	267	Floyd Youmans	.10	.05	.01
☐	268	Don Aase	.10	.05	.01
☐	269	Mike Boddicker	.10	.05	.01
☐	270	Rich Dauer	.10	.05	.01
☐	271	Storm Davis	.10	.05	.01
☐	272	Rick Dempsey	.10	.05	.01
☐	273	Ken Dixon	.10	.05	.01
☐	274	Jim Dwyer	.10	.05	.01
☐	275	Mike Flanagan	.10	.05	.01
☐	276	Wayne Gross	.10	.05	.01
☐	277	Lee Lacy	.10	.05	.01
☐	278	Fred Lynn	.15	.07	.02
☐	279	Tippy Martinez	.10	.05	.01
☐	280	Dennis Martinez	.15	.07	.02
☐	281	Scott McGregor	.10	.05	.01
☐	282	Eddie Murray	1.00	.45	.13
☐	283	Floyd Rayford	.10	.05	.01
☐	284	Cal Ripken	5.00	2.30	.60
☐	285	Gary Roenicke	.10	.05	.01
☐	286	Larry Sheets	.10	.05	.01
☐	287	John Shelby	.10	.05	.01
☐	288	Nate Snell	.10	.05	.01
☐	289	Sammy Stewart	.10	.05	.01
☐	290	Alan Wiggins	.10	.05	.01
☐	291	Mike Young	.10	.05	.01
☐	292	Alan Ashby	.10	.05	.01
☐	293	Mark Bailey	.10	.05	.01
☐	294	Kevin Bass	.10	.05	.01
☐	295	Jeff Calhoun	.10	.05	.01
☐	296	Jose Cruz	.10	.05	.01
☐	297	Glenn Davis	.10	.05	.01
☐	298	Bill Dawley	.10	.05	.01
☐	299	Frank DiPino	.10	.05	.01
☐	300	Bill Doran	.10	.05	.01
☐	301	Phil Garner	.15	.07	.02
☐	302	Jeff Heathcock	.10	.05	.01
☐	303	Charlie Kerfeld	.10	.05	.01
☐	304	Bob Knepper	.10	.05	.01
☐	305	Ron Mathis	.10	.05	.01
☐	306	Jerry Mumphrey	.10	.05	.01
☐	307	Jim Pankovits	.10	.05	.01
☐	308	Terry Puhl	.10	.05	.01
☐	309	Craig Reynolds	.10	.05	.01
☐	310	Nolan Ryan	6.00	2.70	.75
☐	311	Mike Scott	.10	.05	.01
☐	312	Dave Smith	.10	.05	.01

☐ 313 Dickie Thon .10 .05 .01
☐ 314 Denny Walling .10 .05 .01
☐ 315 Kurt Bevacqua .10 .05 .01
☐ 316 Al Bumbry .10 .05 .01
☐ 317 Jerry Davis .10 .05 .01
☐ 318 Luis DeLeon .10 .05 .01
☐ 319 Dave Dravecky .15 .07 .02
☐ 320 Tim Flannery .10 .05 .01
☐ 321 Steve Garvey .20 .09 .03
☐ 322 Rich Gossage .20 .09 .03
☐ 323 Tony Gwynn 3.00 1.35 .40
☐ 324 Andy Hawkins .10 .05 .01
☐ 325 LaMarr Hoyt .10 .05 .01
☐ 326 Roy Lee Jackson .10 .05 .01
☐ 327 Terry Kennedy .10 .05 .01
☐ 328 Craig Lefferts .10 .05 .01
☐ 329 Carmelo Martinez .10 .05 .01
☐ 330 Lance McCullers .10 .05 .01
☐ 331 Kevin McReynolds .15 .07 .02
☐ 332 Graig Nettles .15 .07 .02
☐ 333 Jerry Royster .10 .05 .01
☐ 334 Eric Show .10 .05 .01
☐ 335 Tim Stoddard .10 .05 .01
☐ 336 Garry Templeton .10 .05 .01
☐ 337 Mark Thurmond .10 .05 .01
☐ 338 Ed Wojna .10 .05 .01
☐ 339 Tony Armas .10 .05 .01
☐ 340 Marty Barrett .10 .05 .01
☐ 341 Wade Boggs 2.50 1.15 .30
☐ 342 Dennis Boyd .10 .05 .01
☐ 343 Bill Buckner .15 .07 .02
☐ 344 Mark Clear .10 .05 .01
☐ 345 Roger Clemens 7.00 3.10 .85
☐ 346 Steve Crawford .10 .05 .01
☐ 347 Mike Easler .10 .05 .01
☐ 348 Dwight Evans .15 .07 .02
☐ 349 Rich Gedman .10 .05 .01
☐ 350 Jackie Gutierrez .10 .05 .01
☐ 351 Glenn Hoffman .10 .05 .01
☐ 352 Bruce Hurst .15 .07 .02
☐ 353 Bruce Kison .10 .05 .01
☐ 354 Tim Lollar .10 .05 .01
☐ 355 Steve Lyons .10 .05 .01
☐ 356 Al Nipper .10 .05 .01
☐ 357 Bob Ojeda .15 .07 .02
☐ 358 Jim Rice .20 .09 .03
☐ 359 Bob Stanley .10 .05 .01
☐ 360 Mike Trujillo .10 .05 .01
☐ 361 Thad Bosley .10 .05 .01
☐ 362 Warren Brusstar .10 .05 .01
☐ 363 Ron Cey .15 .07 .02
☐ 364 Jody Davis .10 .05 .01
☐ 365 Bob Dernier .10 .05 .01
☐ 366 Shawon Dunston .15 .07 .02
☐ 367 Leon Durham .10 .05 .01
☐ 368 Dennis Eckersley .25 .11 .03
☐ 369 Ray Fontenot .10 .05 .01
☐ 370 George Frazier .10 .05 .01
☐ 371 Billy Hatcher .15 .07 .02
☐ 372 Dave Lopes .15 .07 .02
☐ 373 Gary Matthews .10 .05 .01
☐ 374 Ron Meridith .10 .05 .01
☐ 375 Keith Moreland .10 .05 .01
☐ 376 Reggie Patterson .10 .05 .01
☐ 377 Dick Ruthven .10 .05 .01
☐ 378 Ryne Sandberg 3.00 1.35 .40
☐ 379 Scott Sanderson .10 .05 .01
☐ 380 Lee Smith .50 .23 .06
☐ 381 Lary Sorensen .10 .05 .01
☐ 382 Chris Speier .10 .05 .01
☐ 383 Rick Sutcliffe .15 .07 .02
☐ 384 Steve Trout .10 .05 .01
☐ 385 Gary Woods .10 .05 .01
☐ 386 Bert Blyleven .20 .09 .03
☐ 387 Tom Brunansky .15 .07 .02
☐ 388 Randy Bush .10 .05 .01
☐ 389 John Butcher .10 .05 .01
☐ 390 Ron Davis .10 .05 .01
☐ 391 Dave Engle .10 .05 .01
☐ 392 Frank Eufemia .10 .05 .01
☐ 393 Pete Filson .10 .05 .01
☐ 394 Gary Gaetti .10 .05 .01
☐ 395 Greg Gagne .15 .07 .02
☐ 396 Mickey Hatcher .10 .05 .01
☐ 397 Kent Hrbek .15 .07 .02
☐ 398 Tim Laudner .10 .05 .01
☐ 399 Rick Lysander .10 .05 .01
☐ 400 Dave Meier .10 .05 .01
☐ 401 Kirby Puckett UER 9.00 4.00 1.15
(Card has him in NL, should be AL)
☐ 402 Mark Salas .10 .05 .01
☐ 403 Ken Schrom .10 .05 .01
☐ 404 Roy Smalley .10 .05 .01
☐ 405 Mike Smithson .10 .05 .01
☐ 406 Mike Stenhouse .10 .05 .01
☐ 407 Tim Teufel .10 .05 .01
☐ 408 Frank Viola .15 .07 .02
☐ 409 Ron Washington .10 .05 .01
☐ 410 Keith Atherton .10 .05 .01
☐ 411 Dusty Baker .20 .09 .03
☐ 412 Tim Birtsas .10 .05 .01
☐ 413 Bruce Bochte .10 .05 .01
☐ 414 Chris Codiroli .10 .05 .01
☐ 415 Dave Collins .10 .05 .01
☐ 416 Mike Davis .10 .05 .01
☐ 417 Alfredo Griffin .10 .05 .01
☐ 418 Mike Heath .10 .05 .01
☐ 419 Steve Henderson .10 .05 .01
☐ 420 Donnie Hill .10 .05 .01
☐ 421 Jay Howell .10 .05 .01
☐ 422 Tommy John .20 .09 .03
☐ 423 Dave Kingman .15 .07 .02
☐ 424 Bill Krueger .10 .05 .01
☐ 425 Rick Langford .10 .05 .01
☐ 426 Carney Lansford .15 .07 .02
☐ 427 Steve McCatty .10 .05 .01
☐ 428 Dwayne Murphy .10 .05 .01
☐ 429 Steve Ontiveros .10 .05 .01
☐ 430 Tony Phillips .15 .07 .02
☐ 431 Jose Rijo .50 .23 .06
☐ 432 Mickey Tettleton 2.50 1.15 .30
☐ 433 Luis Aguayo .10 .05 .01
☐ 434 Larry Andersen .10 .05 .01
☐ 435 Steve Carlton .75 .35 .09
☐ 436 Don Carman .10 .05 .01
☐ 437 Tim Corcoran .10 .05 .01
☐ 438 Darren Daulton 5.00 2.30 .60
☐ 439 John Denny .10 .05 .01
☐ 440 Tom Foley .10 .05 .01
☐ 441 Greg Gross .10 .05 .01
☐ 442 Kevin Gross .10 .05 .01
☐ 443 Von Hayes .10 .05 .01
☐ 444 Charles Hudson .10 .05 .01
☐ 445 Garry Maddox .10 .05 .01
☐ 446 Shane Rawley .10 .05 .01
☐ 447 Dave Rucker .10 .05 .01
☐ 448 John Russell .10 .05 .01
☐ 449 Juan Samuel .10 .05 .01
☐ 450 Mike Schmidt 1.25 .55 .16
☐ 451 Rick Schu .10 .05 .01
☐ 452 Dave Shipanoff .10 .05 .01
☐ 453 Dave Stewart .20 .09 .03
☐ 454 Jeff Stone .10 .05 .01
☐ 455 Kent Tekulve .10 .05 .01
☐ 456 Ozzie Virgil .10 .05 .01

☐ 457	Glenn Wilson	.10	.05	.01
☐ 458	Jim Beattie	.10	.05	.01
☐ 459	Karl Best	.10	.05	.01
☐ 460	Barry Bonnell	.10	.05	.01
☐ 461	Phil Bradley	.10	.05	.01
☐ 462	Ivan Calderon	.25	.11	.03
☐ 463	Al Cowens	.10	.05	.01
☐ 464	Alvin Davis	.10	.05	.01
☐ 465	Dave Henderson	.15	.07	.02
☐ 466	Bob Kearney	.10	.05	.01
☐ 467	Mark Langston	.50	.23	.06
☐ 468	Bob Long	.10	.05	.01
☐ 469	Mike Moore	.10	.05	.01
☐ 470	Edwin Nunez	.10	.05	.01
☐ 471	Spike Owen	.10	.05	.01
☐ 472	Jack Perconte	.10	.05	.01
☐ 473	Jim Presley	.10	.05	.01
☐ 474	Donnie Scott	.10	.05	.01
☐ 475	Bill Swift	.60	.25	.08
☐ 476	Danny Tartabull	.75	.35	.09
☐ 477	Gorman Thomas	.10	.05	.01
☐ 478	Roy Thomas	.10	.05	.01
☐ 479	Ed VandeBerg	.10	.05	.01
☐ 480	Frank Wills	.10	.05	.01
☐ 481	Matt Young	.10	.05	.01
☐ 482	Ray Burris	.10	.05	.01
☐ 483	Jaime Cocanower	.10	.05	.01
☐ 484	Cecil Cooper	.15	.07	.02
☐ 485	Danny Darwin	.10	.05	.01
☐ 486	Rollie Fingers	.20	.09	.03
☐ 487	Jim Gantner	.10	.05	.01
☐ 488	Bob L. Gibson	.10	.05	.01
☐ 489	Moose Haas	.10	.05	.01
☐ 490	Teddy Higuera	.20	.09	.03
☐ 491	Paul Householder	.10	.05	.01
☐ 492	Pete Ladd	.10	.05	.01
☐ 493	Rick Manning	.10	.05	.01
☐ 494	Bob McClure	.10	.05	.01
☐ 495	Paul Molitor	1.50	.65	.19
☐ 496	Charlie Moore	.10	.05	.01
☐ 497	Ben Oglivie	.10	.05	.01
☐ 498	Randy Ready	.10	.05	.01
☐ 499	Earnie Riles	.10	.05	.01
☐ 500	Ed Romero	.10	.05	.01
☐ 501	Bill Schroeder	.10	.05	.01
☐ 502	Ray Searage	.10	.05	.01
☐ 503	Ted Simmons	.15	.07	.02
☐ 504	Pete Vuckovich	.10	.05	.01
☐ 505	Rick Waits	.10	.05	.01
☐ 506	Robin Yount	1.25	.55	.16
☐ 507	Len Barker	.10	.05	.01
☐ 508	Steve Bedrosian	.10	.05	.01
☐ 509	Bruce Benedict	.10	.05	.01
☐ 510	Rick Camp	.10	.05	.01
☐ 511	Rick Cerone	.10	.05	.01
☐ 512	Chris Chambliss	.15	.07	.02
☐ 513	Jeff Dedmon	.10	.05	.01
☐ 514	Terry Forster	.10	.05	.01
☐ 515	Gene Garber	.10	.05	.01
☐ 516	Terry Harper	.10	.05	.01
☐ 517	Bob Horner	.10	.05	.01
☐ 518	Glenn Hubbard	.10	.05	.01
☐ 519	Joe Johnson	.10	.05	.01
☐ 520	Brad Komminsk	.10	.05	.01
☐ 521	Rick Mahler	.10	.05	.01
☐ 522	Dale Murphy	.20	.09	.03
☐ 523	Ken Oberkfell	.10	.05	.01
☐ 524	Pascual Perez	.10	.05	.01
☐ 525	Gerald Perry	.10	.05	.01
☐ 526	Rafael Ramirez	.10	.05	.01
☐ 527	Steve Shields	.10	.05	.01
☐ 528	Zane Smith	.10	.05	.01
☐ 529	Bruce Sutter	.15	.07	.02
☐ 530	Milt Thompson	.25	.11	.03
☐ 531	Claudell Washington	.10	.05	.01
☐ 532	Paul Zuvella	.10	.05	.01
☐ 533	Vida Blue	.15	.07	.02
☐ 534	Bob Brenly	.10	.05	.01
☐ 535	Chris Brown	.10	.05	.01
☐ 536	Chili Davis	.15	.07	.02
☐ 537	Mark Davis	.10	.05	.01
☐ 538	Rob Deer	.25	.11	.03
☐ 539	Dan Driessen	.10	.05	.01
☐ 540	Scott Garrelts	.10	.05	.01
☐ 541	Dan Gladden	.10	.05	.01
☐ 542	Jim Gott	.10	.05	.01
☐ 543	David Green	.10	.05	.01
☐ 544	Atlee Hammaker	.10	.05	.01
☐ 545	Mike Jeffcoat	.10	.05	.01
☐ 546	Mike Krukow	.10	.05	.01
☐ 547	Dave LaPoint	.10	.05	.01
☐ 548	Jeff Leonard	.10	.05	.01
☐ 549	Greg Minton	.10	.05	.01
☐ 550	Alex Trevino	.10	.05	.01
☐ 551	Manny Trillo	.10	.05	.01
☐ 552	Jose Uribe	.10	.05	.01
☐ 553	Brad Wellman	.10	.05	.01
☐ 554	Frank Williams	.10	.05	.01
☐ 555	Joel Youngblood	.10	.05	.01
☐ 556	Alan Bannister	.10	.05	.01
☐ 557	Glenn Brummer	.10	.05	.01
☐ 558	Steve Buechele	.50	.23	.06
☐ 559	Jose Guzman	.50	.23	.06
☐ 560	Toby Harrah	.10	.05	.01
☐ 561	Greg Harris	.10	.05	.01
☐ 562	Dwayne Henry	.10	.05	.01
☐ 563	Burt Hooton	.10	.05	.01
☐ 564	Charlie Hough	.15	.07	.02
☐ 565	Mike Mason	.10	.05	.01
☐ 566	Oddibe McDowell	.10	.05	.01
☐ 567	Dickie Noles	.10	.05	.01
☐ 568	Pete O'Brien	.10	.05	.01
☐ 569	Larry Parrish	.10	.05	.01
☐ 570	Dave Rozema	.10	.05	.01
☐ 571	Dave Schmidt	.10	.05	.01
☐ 572	Don Slaught	.10	.05	.01
☐ 573	Wayne Tolleson	.10	.05	.01
☐ 574	Duane Walker	.10	.05	.01
☐ 575	Gary Ward	.10	.05	.01
☐ 576	Chris Welsh	.10	.05	.01
☐ 577	Curtis Wilkerson	.10	.05	.01
☐ 578	George Wright	.10	.05	.01
☐ 579	Chris Bando	.10	.05	.01
☐ 580	Tony Bernazard	.10	.05	.01
☐ 581	Brett Butler	.15	.07	.02
☐ 582	Ernie Camacho	.10	.05	.01
☐ 583	Joe Carter	5.00	2.30	.60
☐ 584	Carmen Castillo	.10	.05	.01
☐ 585	Jamie Easterly	.10	.05	.01
☐ 586	Julio Franco	.35	.16	.04
☐ 587	Mel Hall	.10	.05	.01
☐ 588	Mike Hargrove	.15	.07	.02
☐ 589	Neal Heaton	.10	.05	.01
☐ 590	Brook Jacoby	.10	.05	.01
☐ 591	Otis Nixon	1.00	.45	.13
☐ 592	Jerry Reed	.10	.05	.01
☐ 593	Vern Ruhle	.10	.05	.01
☐ 594	Pat Tabler	.10	.05	.01
☐ 595	Rich Thompson	.10	.05	.01
☐ 596	Andre Thornton	.10	.05	.01
☐ 597	Dave Von Ohlen	.10	.05	.01
☐ 598	George Vukovich	.10	.05	.01
☐ 599	Tom Waddell	.10	.05	.01
☐ 600	Curt Wardle	.10	.05	.01
☐ 601	Jerry Willard	.10	.05	.01
☐ 602	Bill Almon	.10	.05	.01

☐ 603 Mike Bielecki .... .10 .05 .01
☐ 604 Sid Bream .... .15 .07 .02
☐ 605 Mike C. Brown .... .10 .05 .01
☐ 606 Pat Clements .... .10 .05 .01
☐ 607 Jose DeLeon .... .10 .05 .01
☐ 608 Denny Gonzalez .... .10 .05 .01
☐ 609 Cecilio Guante .... .10 .05 .01
☐ 610 Steve Kemp .... .10 .05 .01
☐ 611 Sammy Khalifa .... .10 .05 .01
☐ 612 Lee Mazzilli .... .10 .05 .01
☐ 613 Larry McWilliams .... .10 .05 .01
☐ 614 Jim Morrison .... .10 .05 .01
☐ 615 Joe Orsulak .... .25 .11 .03
☐ 616 Tony Pena .... .10 .05 .01
☐ 617 Johnny Ray .... .10 .05 .01
☐ 618 Rick Reuschel .... .10 .05 .01
☐ 619 R.J. Reynolds .... .10 .05 .01
☐ 620 Rick Rhoden .... .10 .05 .01
☐ 621 Don Robinson .... .10 .05 .01
☐ 622 Jason Thompson .... .10 .05 .01
☐ 623 Lee Tunnell .... .10 .05 .01
☐ 624 Jim Winn .... .10 .05 .01
☐ 625 Marvell Wynne .... .10 .05 .01
☐ 626 Dwight Gooden IA .... .15 .07 .02
☐ 627 Don Mattingly IA .... 1.25 .55 .16
☐ 628 4192 (Pete Rose) .... .60 .25 .08
☐ 629 3000 Career Hits .... .35 .16 .04
Rod Carew
☐ 630 300 Career Wins .... .40 .18 .05
Tom Seaver
Phil Niekro
☐ 631 Ouch (Don Baylor) .... .15 .07 .02
☐ 632 Instant Offense .... .40 .18 .05
Darryl Strawberry
Tim Raines
☐ 633 Shortstops Supreme .. 1.50 .65 .19
Cal Ripken
Alan Trammell
☐ 634 Boggs and "Hero" .... 1.50 .65 .19
Wade Boggs
George Brett
☐ 635 Braves Dynamic Duo ... .15 .07 .02
Bob Horner
Dale Murphy
☐ 636 Cardinal Ignitors .... .15 .07 .02
Willie McGee
Vince Coleman
☐ 637 Terror on Basepaths .... .15 .07 .02
Vince Coleman
☐ 638 Charlie Hustle / Dr.K .... .60 .25 .08
Pete Rose
Dwight Gooden
☐ 639 1984 and 1985 AL ..... 1.25 .55 .16
Batting Champs
Wade Boggs
Don Mattingly
☐ 640 NL West Sluggers .... .25 .11 .03
Dale Murphy
Steve Garvey
Dave Parker
☐ 641 Staff Aces .... .15 .07 .02
Fernando Valenzuela
Dwight Gooden
☐ 642 Blue Jay Stoppers .... .30 .14 .04
Jimmy Key
Dave Stieb
☐ 643 AL All-Star Backstops .. .20 .09 .03
Carlton Fisk
Rich Gedman
☐ 644 Gene Walter and .... 2.00 .90 .25
Benito Santiago
☐ 645 Mike Woodard and .... .10 .05 .01
Colin Ward
☐ 646 Kal Daniels and .... 3.50 1.55 .45
Paul O'Neill
☐ 647 Andres Galarraga and 6.00 2.70 .75
Fred Toliver
☐ 648 Bob Kipper and .... .10 .05 .01
Curt Ford
☐ 649 Jose Canseco and 22.00 10.00 2.80
Eric Plunk
☐ 650 Mark McLemore and .... .40 .18 .05
Gus Polidor
☐ 651 Rob Woodward and ..... .10 .05 .01
Mickey Brantley
☐ 652 Billy Joe Robidoux and .10 .05 .01
Mark Funderburk
☐ 653 Cecil Fielder and 12.00 5.50 1.50
Cory Snyder
☐ 654 CL: Royals/Cardinals .... .15 .05 .01
Blue Jays/Mets
☐ 655 CL: Yankees/Dodgers ... .15 .05 .01
Angels/Reds UER
(168 Darly Sconiers)
☐ 656 CL: White Sox/Tigers ... .15 .05 .01
Expos/Orioles
(279 Dennis,
280 Tippy)
☐ 657 CL: Astros/Padres .... .15 .05 .01
Red Sox/Cubs
☐ 658 CL: Twins/A's .... .15 .05 .01
Phillies/Mariners
☐ 659 CL: Brewers/Braves ..... .15 .05 .01
Giants/Rangers
☐ 660 CL: Indians/Pirates .... .15 .05 .01
Special Cards

1986 Fleer All-Stars

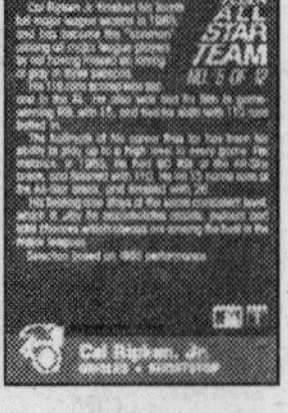

Randomly inserted in wax and cello packs, this 12-card set features top stars. Cards measure 2 1/2" by 3 1/2" and feature attractive red backgrounds (American Leaguers) and blue backgrounds (National Leaguers). The 12 selections cover each position, left and right-handed starting pitchers, a reliever, and a designated hitter.

	MINT	EXC	G-VG
COMPLETE SET (12)	30.00	13.50	3.80
COMMON CARD (1-12)	.25	.11	.03

☐ 1 Don Mattingly .... 7.50 3.40 .95
☐ 2 Tom Herr .... .25 .11 .03
☐ 3 George Brett .... 7.50 3.40 .95
☐ 4 Gary Carter .... .50 .23 .06
☐ 5 Cal Ripken 12.00 5.50 1.50

	MINT	EXC	G-VG
☐ 6 Dave Parker	.35	.16	.04
☐ 7 Rickey Henderson UER (Misspelled Ricky on card back)	4.00	1.80	.50
☐ 8 Pedro Guerrero	.35	.16	.04
☐ 9 Dan Quisenberry	.25	.11	.03
☐ 10 Dwight Gooden	.75	.35	.09
☐ 11 Gorman Thomas	.25	.11	.03
☐ 12 John Tudor	.25	.11	.03

1986 Fleer Future Hall of Famers

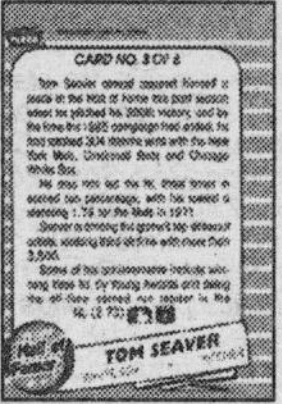

These attractive cards were issued as inserts with the Fleer three-packs. They are the same size as the regular issue (2 1/2" by 3 1/2") and feature players that Fleer predicts will be "Future Hall of Famers." The card backs describe career highlights, records, and honors won by the player. The cards are numbered on the back; Pete Rose is given the honor of being card number 1.

	MINT	EXC	G-VG
COMPLETE SET (6)	20.00	9.00	2.50
COMMON CARD (1-6)	2.00	.90	.25
☐ 1 Pete Rose	3.50	1.55	.45
☐ 2 Steve Carlton	2.50	1.15	.30
☐ 3 Tom Seaver	2.50	1.15	.30
☐ 4 Rod Carew	2.00	.90	.25
☐ 5 Nolan Ryan	12.00	5.50	1.50
☐ 6 Reggie Jackson	3.00	1.35	.40

1986 Fleer Update

This 132-card set was distributed by Fleer to dealers as a complete set in a custom box. In addition to the complete set of 132 cards, the box also contains 25 Team Logo Stickers. The card fronts look very similar to the 1986 Fleer regular issue. The cards are numbered (with a U prefix) alphabetically according to player's last name. Cards measure the standard size, 2 1/2" by 3 1/2". The (extended) Rookie Cards in this set include Barry Bonds, Bobby Bonilla, Will Clark, Doug Drabek, Wally Joyner, John Kruk, Kevin Mitchell, and Ruben Sierra.

	MINT	EXC	G-VG
COMPLETE FACT.SET (132)	24.00	11.00	3.00
COMMON CARD (1-132)	.07	.03	.01
☐ 1 Mike Aldrete	.07	.03	.01
☐ 2 Andy Allanson	.07	.03	.01
☐ 3 Neil Allen	.07	.03	.01
☐ 4 Joaquin Andujar	.07	.03	.01
☐ 5 Paul Assenmacher	.07	.03	.01
☐ 6 Scott Bailes	.07	.03	.01
☐ 7 Jay Baller	.07	.03	.01
☐ 8 Scott Bankhead	.07	.03	.01
☐ 9 Bill Bathe	.07	.03	.01
☐ 10 Don Baylor	.15	.07	.02
☐ 11 Billy Beane	.07	.03	.01
☐ 12 Steve Bedrosian	.07	.03	.01
☐ 13 Juan Beniquez	.07	.03	.01
☐ 14 Barry Bonds	9.00	4.00	1.15
☐ 15 Bobby Bonilla UER (Wrong birthday)	2.50	1.15	.30
☐ 16 Rich Bordi	.07	.03	.01
☐ 17 Bill Campbell	.07	.03	.01
☐ 18 Tom Candiotti	.10	.05	.01
☐ 19 John Cangelosi	.07	.03	.01
☐ 20 Jose Canseco UER (Headings on back for a pitcher)	6.00	2.70	.75
☐ 21 Chuck Cary	.07	.03	.01
☐ 22 Juan Castillo	.07	.03	.01
☐ 23 Rick Cerone	.07	.03	.01
☐ 24 John Cerutti	.07	.03	.01
☐ 25 Will Clark	7.00	3.10	.85
☐ 26 Mark Clear	.07	.03	.01
☐ 27 Darnell Coles	.07	.03	.01
☐ 28 Dave Collins	.07	.03	.01
☐ 29 Tim Conroy	.07	.03	.01
☐ 30 Ed Correa	.07	.03	.01
☐ 31 Joe Cowley	.07	.03	.01
☐ 32 Bill Dawley	.07	.03	.01
☐ 33 Rob Deer	.20	.09	.03
☐ 34 John Denny	.07	.03	.01
☐ 35 Jim Deshaies	.20	.09	.03
☐ 36 Doug Drabek	1.50	.65	.19
☐ 37 Mike Easler	.07	.03	.01
☐ 38 Mark Eichhorn	.07	.03	.01
☐ 39 Dave Engle	.07	.03	.01
☐ 40 Mike Fischlin	.07	.03	.01
☐ 41 Scott Fletcher	.07	.03	.01
☐ 42 Terry Forster	.07	.03	.01
☐ 43 Terry Francona	.07	.03	.01
☐ 44 Andres Galarraga	2.50	1.15	.30
☐ 45 Lee Guetterman	.07	.03	.01
☐ 46 Bill Gullickson	.10	.05	.01
☐ 47 Jackie Gutierrez	.07	.03	.01
☐ 48 Moose Haas	.07	.03	.01
☐ 49 Billy Hatcher	.10	.05	.01
☐ 50 Mike Heath	.07	.03	.01
☐ 51 Guy Hoffman	.07	.03	.01
☐ 52 Tom Hume	.07	.03	.01
☐ 53 Pete Incaviglia	.75	.35	.09
☐ 54 Dane Iorg	.07	.03	.01
☐ 55 Chris James	.07	.03	.01
☐ 56 Stan Javier	.25	.11	.03
☐ 57 Tommy John	.15	.07	.02
☐ 58 Tracy Jones	.07	.03	.01
☐ 59 Wally Joyner	1.00	.45	.13
☐ 60 Wayne Krenchicki	.07	.03	.01
☐ 61 John Kruk	1.50	.65	.19
☐ 62 Mike LaCoss	.07	.03	.01
☐ 63 Pete Ladd	.07	.03	.01
☐ 64 Dave LaPoint	.07	.03	.01
☐ 65 Mike LaValliere	.07	.03	.01
☐ 66 Rudy Law	.07	.03	.01

☐ 67	Dennis Leonard	.07	.03	.01
☐ 68	Steve Lombardozzi	.07	.03	.01
☐ 69	Aurelio Lopez	.07	.03	.01
☐ 70	Mickey Mahler	.07	.03	.01
☐ 71	Candy Maldonado	.07	.03	.01
☐ 72	Roger Mason	.07	.03	.01
☐ 73	Greg Mathews	.07	.03	.01
☐ 74	Andy McGaffigan	.07	.03	.01
☐ 75	Joel McKeon	.07	.03	.01
☐ 76	Kevin Mitchell	1.50	.65	.19
☐ 77	Bill Mooneyham	.07	.03	.01
☐ 78	Omar Moreno	.07	.03	.01
☐ 79	Jerry Mumphrey	.07	.03	.01
☐ 80	Al Newman	.07	.03	.01
☐ 81	Phil Niekro	.15	.07	.02
☐ 82	Randy Niemann	.07	.03	.01
☐ 83	Juan Nieves	.07	.03	.01
☐ 84	Bob Ojeda	.10	.05	.01
☐ 85	Rick Ownbey	.07	.03	.01
☐ 86	Tom Paciorek	.10	.05	.01
☐ 87	David Palmer	.07	.03	.01
☐ 88	Jeff Parrett	.07	.03	.01
☐ 89	Pat Perry	.07	.03	.01
☐ 90	Dan Plesac	.07	.03	.01
☐ 91	Darrell Porter	.07	.03	.01
☐ 92	Luis Quinones	.07	.03	.01
☐ 93	Rey Quinones UER (Misspelled Quinonez)	.07	.03	.01
☐ 94	Gary Redus	.07	.03	.01
☐ 95	Jeff Reed	.07	.03	.01
☐ 96	Bip Roberts	.50	.23	.06
☐ 97	Billy Joe Robidoux	.07	.03	.01
☐ 98	Gary Roenicke	.07	.03	.01
☐ 99	Ron Roenicke	.07	.03	.01
☐ 100	Angel Salazar	.07	.03	.01
☐ 101	Joe Sambito	.07	.03	.01
☐ 102	Billy Sample	.07	.03	.01
☐ 103	Dave Schmidt	.07	.03	.01
☐ 104	Ken Schrom	.07	.03	.01
☐ 105	Ruben Sierra	5.00	2.30	.60
☐ 106	Ted Simmons	.10	.05	.01
☐ 107	Sammy Stewart	.07	.03	.01
☐ 108	Kurt Stillwell	.07	.03	.01
☐ 109	Dale Sveum	.07	.03	.01
☐ 110	Tim Teufel	.07	.03	.01
☐ 111	Bob Tewksbury	.40	.18	.05
☐ 112	Andres Thomas	.07	.03	.01
☐ 113	Jason Thompson	.07	.03	.01
☐ 114	Milt Thompson	.10	.05	.01
☐ 115	Robby Thompson	.50	.23	.06
☐ 116	Jay Tibbs	.07	.03	.01
☐ 117	Fred Toliver	.07	.03	.01
☐ 118	Wayne Tolleson	.07	.03	.01
☐ 119	Alex Trevino	.07	.03	.01
☐ 120	Manny Trillo	.07	.03	.01
☐ 121	Ed VandeBerg	.07	.03	.01
☐ 122	Ozzie Virgil	.07	.03	.01
☐ 123	Tony Walker	.07	.03	.01
☐ 124	Gene Walter	.07	.03	.01
☐ 125	Duane Ward	.75	.35	.09
☐ 126	Jerry Willard	.07	.03	.01
☐ 127	Mitch Williams	.35	.16	.04
☐ 128	Reggie Williams	.07	.03	.01
☐ 129	Bobby Witt	.35	.16	.04
☐ 130	Marvell Wynne	.07	.03	.01
☐ 131	Steve Yeager	.07	.03	.01
☐ 132	Checklist 1-132	.07	.03	.01

1987 Fleer

This 660-card set features a distinctive blue border, which fades to white on the card

fronts. The backs are printed in blue, red, and pink on white card stock. The bottom of the card back shows an innovative graph of the player's ability, e.g., "He's got the stuff" for pitchers and "How he's hitting 'em," for hitters. Cards are numbered on the back and are again the standard 2 1/2" by 3 1/2". Cards are again organized numerically by teams, i.e., World Champion Mets (1-25), Boston Red Sox (26-48), Houston Astros (49-72), California Angels (73-95), New York Yankees (96-120), Texas Rangers (121-143), Detroit Tigers (144-168), Philadelphia Phillies (169-192), Cincinnati Reds (193-218), Toronto Blue Jays (219-240), Cleveland Indians (241-263), San Francisco Giants (264-288), St. Louis Cardinals (289-312), Montreal Expos (313-337), Milwaukee Brewers (338-361), Kansas City Royals (362-384), Oakland A's (385-410), San Diego Padres (411-435), Los Angeles Dodgers (436-460), Baltimore Orioles (461-483), Chicago White Sox (484-508), Atlanta Braves (509-532), Minnesota Twins (533-554), Chicago Cubs (555-578), Seattle Mariners (579-600), and Pittsburgh Pirates (601-624). The last 36 cards in the set consist of Specials (625-643), Rookie Pairs (644-653), and checklists (654-660). The key Rookie Cards in this set are Barry Bonds, Bobby Bonilla, Will Clark, Doug Drabek, Chuck Finley, Bo Jackson, Wally Joyner, John Kruk, Barry Larkin, Dave Magadan, Kevin Mitchell, Kevin Seitzer, Ruben Sierra, Greg Swindell, and Devon White. Fleer also produced a "limited" edition version of this set with glossy coating and packaged in a "tin." However, this glossy tin set was apparently not limited enough (estimated between 75,000 and 100,000 1987 tin sets produced by Fleer), since the values of the "tin" glossy cards are now the same as the values of the regular set cards.

		MINT	EXC	G-VG
	COMPLETE SET (660)	80.00	36.00	10.00
	COMPLETE FACT.SET (672)	80.00	36.00	10.00
	COMMON CARD (1-660)	.08	.04	.01
☐ 1	Rick Aguilera	.40	.18	.05
☐ 2	Richard Anderson	.08	.04	.01
☐ 3	Wally Backman	.08	.04	.01
☐ 4	Gary Carter	.15	.07	.02
☐ 5	Ron Darling	.12	.05	.02
☐ 6	Len Dykstra	1.00	.45	.13
☐ 7	Kevin Elster	.08	.04	.01
☐ 8	Sid Fernandez	.12	.05	.02
☐ 9	Dwight Gooden	.25	.11	.03

	No.	Player			
☐	10	Ed Hearn	.08	.04	.01
☐	11	Danny Heep	.08	.04	.01
☐	12	Keith Hernandez	.12	.05	.02
☐	13	Howard Johnson	.12	.05	.02
☐	14	Ray Knight	.12	.05	.02
☐	15	Lee Mazzilli	.08	.04	.01
☐	16	Roger McDowell	.08	.04	.01
☐	17	Kevin Mitchell	2.00	.90	.25
☐	18	Randy Niemann	.08	.04	.01
☐	19	Bob Ojeda	.08	.04	.01
☐	20	Jesse Orosco	.08	.04	.01
☐	21	Rafael Santana	.08	.04	.01
☐	22	Doug Sisk	.08	.04	.01
☐	23	Darryl Strawberry	.30	.14	.04
☐	24	Tim Teufel	.08	.04	.01
☐	25	Mookie Wilson	.12	.05	.02
☐	26	Tony Armas	.08	.04	.01
☐	27	Marty Barrett	.08	.04	.01
☐	28	Don Baylor	.15	.07	.02
☐	29	Wade Boggs	1.50	.65	.19
☐	30	Oil Can Boyd	.08	.04	.01
☐	31	Bill Buckner	.12	.05	.02
☐	32	Roger Clemens	3.00	1.35	.40
☐	33	Steve Crawford	.08	.04	.01
☐	34	Dwight Evans	.12	.05	.02
☐	35	Rich Gedman	.08	.04	.01
☐	36	Dave Henderson	.12	.05	.02
☐	37	Bruce Hurst	.08	.04	.01
☐	38	Tim Lollar	.08	.04	.01
☐	39	Al Nipper	.08	.04	.01
☐	40	Spike Owen	.08	.04	.01
☐	41	Jim Rice	.15	.07	.02
☐	42	Ed Romero	.08	.04	.01
☐	43	Joe Sambito	.08	.04	.01
☐	44	Calvin Schiraldi	.08	.04	.01
☐	45	Tom Seaver	.50	.23	.06
☐	46	Jeff Sellers	.08	.04	.01
☐	47	Bob Stanley	.08	.04	.01
☐	48	Sammy Stewart	.08	.04	.01
☐	49	Larry Andersen	.08	.04	.01
☐	50	Alan Ashby	.08	.04	.01
☐	51	Kevin Bass	.08	.04	.01
☐	52	Jeff Calhoun	.08	.04	.01
☐	53	Jose Cruz	.08	.04	.01
☐	54	Danny Darwin	.08	.04	.01
☐	55	Glenn Davis	.08	.04	.01
☐	56	Jim Deshaies	.30	.14	.04
☐	57	Bill Doran	.08	.04	.01
☐	58	Phil Garner	.12	.05	.02
☐	59	Billy Hatcher	.12	.05	.02
☐	60	Charlie Kerfeld	.08	.04	.01
☐	61	Bob Knepper	.08	.04	.01
☐	62	Dave Lopes	.12	.05	.02
☐	63	Aurelio Lopez	.08	.04	.01
☐	64	Jim Pankovits	.08	.04	.01
☐	65	Terry Puhl	.08	.04	.01
☐	66	Craig Reynolds	.08	.04	.01
☐	67	Nolan Ryan	3.50	1.55	.45
☐	68	Mike Scott	.08	.04	.01
☐	69	Dave Smith	.08	.04	.01
☐	70	Dickie Thon	.08	.04	.01
☐	71	Tony Walker	.08	.04	.01
☐	72	Denny Walling	.08	.04	.01
☐	73	Bob Boone	.12	.05	.02
☐	74	Rick Burleson	.08	.04	.01
☐	75	John Candelaria	.08	.04	.01
☐	76	Doug Corbett	.08	.04	.01
☐	77	Doug DeCinces	.08	.04	.01
☐	78	Brian Downing	.08	.04	.01
☐	79	Chuck Finley	1.00	.45	.13
☐	80	Terry Forster	.08	.04	.01
☐	81	Bob Grich	.12	.05	.02
☐	82	George Hendrick	.08	.04	.01
☐	83	Jack Howell	.08	.04	.01
☐	84	Reggie Jackson	.75	.35	.09
☐	85	Ruppert Jones	.08	.04	.01
☐	86	Wally Joyner	1.50	.65	.19
☐	87	Gary Lucas	.08	.04	.01
☐	88	Kirk McCaskill	.08	.04	.01
☐	89	Donnie Moore	.08	.04	.01
☐	90	Gary Pettis	.08	.04	.01
☐	91	Vern Ruhle	.08	.04	.01
☐	92	Dick Schofield	.08	.04	.01
☐	93	Don Sutton	.15	.07	.02
☐	94	Rob Wilfong	.08	.04	.01
☐	95	Mike Witt	.08	.04	.01
☐	96	Doug Drabek	1.50	.65	.19
☐	97	Mike Easler	.08	.04	.01
☐	98	Mike Fischlin	.08	.04	.01
☐	99	Brian Fisher	.08	.04	.01
☐	100	Ron Guidry	.12	.05	.02
☐	101	Rickey Henderson	1.00	.45	.13
☐	102	Tommy John	.15	.07	.02
☐	103	Ron Kittle	.08	.04	.01
☐	104	Don Mattingly	1.50	.65	.19
☐	105	Bobby Meacham	.08	.04	.01
☐	106	Joe Niekro	.12	.05	.02
☐	107	Mike Pagliarulo	.08	.04	.01
☐	108	Dan Pasqua	.08	.04	.01
☐	109	Willie Randolph	.12	.05	.02
☐	110	Dennis Rasmussen	.08	.04	.01
☐	111	Dave Righetti	.12	.05	.02
☐	112	Gary Roenicke	.08	.04	.01
☐	113	Rod Scurry	.08	.04	.01
☐	114	Bob Shirley	.08	.04	.01
☐	115	Joel Skinner	.08	.04	.01
☐	116	Tim Stoddard	.08	.04	.01
☐	117	Bob Tewksbury	.75	.35	.09
☐	118	Wayne Tolleson	.08	.04	.01
☐	119	Claudell Washington	.08	.04	.01
☐	120	Dave Winfield	.60	.25	.08
☐	121	Steve Buechele	.12	.05	.02
☐	122	Ed Correa	.08	.04	.01
☐	123	Scott Fletcher	.08	.04	.01
☐	124	Jose Guzman	.12	.05	.02
☐	125	Toby Harrah	.08	.04	.01
☐	126	Greg Harris	.08	.04	.01
☐	127	Charlie Hough	.12	.05	.02
☐	128	Pete Incaviglia	.75	.35	.09
☐	129	Mike Mason	.08	.04	.01
☐	130	Oddibe McDowell	.08	.04	.01
☐	131	Dale Mohorcic	.08	.04	.01
☐	132	Pete O'Brien	.08	.04	.01
☐	133	Tom Paciorek	.12	.05	.02
☐	134	Larry Parrish	.08	.04	.01
☐	135	Geno Petralli	.08	.04	.01
☐	136	Darrell Porter	.08	.04	.01
☐	137	Jeff Russell	.08	.04	.01
☐	138	Ruben Sierra	7.00	3.10	.85
☐	139	Don Slaught	.08	.04	.01
☐	140	Gary Ward	.08	.04	.01
☐	141	Curtis Wilkerson	.08	.04	.01
☐	142	Mitch Williams	.40	.18	.05
☐	143	Bobby Witt UER (Tulsa misspelled as Tusla; ERA should be 6.43, not .643)	.50	.23	.06
☐	144	Dave Bergman	.08	.04	.01
☐	145	Tom Brookens	.08	.04	.01
☐	146	Bill Campbell	.08	.04	.01
☐	147	Chuck Cary	.08	.04	.01
☐	148	Darnell Coles	.08	.04	.01
☐	149	Dave Collins	.08	.04	.01
☐	150	Darrell Evans	.12	.05	.02
☐	151	Kirk Gibson	.12	.05	.02
☐	152	John Grubb	.08	.04	.01

☐ 153	Willie Hernandez	.08	.04	.01
☐ 154	Larry Herndon	.08	.04	.01
☐ 155	Eric King	.08	.04	.01
☐ 156	Chet Lemon	.08	.04	.01
☐ 157	Dwight Lowry	.08	.04	.01
☐ 158	Jack Morris	.15	.07	.02
☐ 159	Randy O'Neal	.08	.04	.01
☐ 160	Lance Parrish	.12	.05	.02
☐ 161	Dan Petry	.08	.04	.01
☐ 162	Pat Sheridan	.08	.04	.01
☐ 163	Jim Slaton	.08	.04	.01
☐ 164	Frank Tanana	.08	.04	.01
☐ 165	Walt Terrell	.08	.04	.01
☐ 166	Mark Thurmond	.08	.04	.01
☐ 167	Alan Trammell	.15	.07	.02
☐ 168	Lou Whitaker	.15	.07	.02
☐ 169	Luis Aguayo	.08	.04	.01
☐ 170	Steve Bedrosian	.08	.04	.01
☐ 171	Don Carman	.08	.04	.01
☐ 172	Darren Daulton	1.00	.45	.13
☐ 173	Greg Gross	.08	.04	.01
☐ 174	Kevin Gross	.08	.04	.01
☐ 175	Von Hayes	.08	.04	.01
☐ 176	Charles Hudson	.08	.04	.01
☐ 177	Tom Hume	.08	.04	.01
☐ 178	Steve Jeltz	.08	.04	.01
☐ 179	Mike Maddux	.08	.04	.01
☐ 180	Shane Rawley	.08	.04	.01
☐ 181	Gary Redus	.08	.04	.01
☐ 182	Ron Roenicke	.08	.04	.01
☐ 183	Bruce Ruffin	.25	.11	.03
☐ 184	John Russell	.08	.04	.01
☐ 185	Juan Samuel	.08	.04	.01
☐ 186	Dan Schatzeder	.08	.04	.01
☐ 187	Mike Schmidt	.75	.35	.09
☐ 188	Rick Schu	.08	.04	.01
☐ 189	Jeff Stone	.08	.04	.01
☐ 190	Kent Tekulve	.08	.04	.01
☐ 191	Milt Thompson	.12	.05	.02
☐ 192	Glenn Wilson	.08	.04	.01
☐ 193	Buddy Bell	.12	.05	.02
☐ 194	Tom Browning	.08	.04	.01
☐ 195	Sal Butera	.08	.04	.01
☐ 196	Dave Concepcion	.12	.05	.02
☐ 197	Kal Daniels	.08	.04	.01
☐ 198	Eric Davis	.20	.09	.03
☐ 199	John Denny	.08	.04	.01
☐ 200	Bo Diaz	.08	.04	.01
☐ 201	Nick Esasky	.08	.04	.01
☐ 202	John Franco	.12	.05	.02
☐ 203	Bill Gullickson	.08	.04	.01
☐ 204	Barry Larkin	4.00	1.80	.50
☐ 205	Eddie Milner	.08	.04	.01
☐ 206	Rob Murphy	.08	.04	.01
☐ 207	Ron Oester	.08	.04	.01
☐ 208	Dave Parker	.15	.07	.02
☐ 209	Tony Perez	.15	.07	.02
☐ 210	Ted Power	.08	.04	.01
☐ 211	Joe Price	.08	.04	.01
☐ 212	Ron Robinson	.08	.04	.01
☐ 213	Pete Rose	.75	.35	.09
☐ 214	Mario Soto	.08	.04	.01
☐ 215	Kurt Stillwell	.08	.04	.01
☐ 216	Max Venable	.08	.04	.01
☐ 217	Chris Welsh	.08	.04	.01
☐ 218	Carl Willis	.08	.04	.01
☐ 219	Jesse Barfield	.08	.04	.01
☐ 220	George Bell	.12	.05	.02
☐ 221	Bill Caudill	.08	.04	.01
☐ 222	John Cerutti	.08	.04	.01
☐ 223	Jim Clancy	.08	.04	.01
☐ 224	Mark Eichhorn	.08	.04	.01
☐ 225	Tony Fernandez	.12	.05	.02
☐ 226	Damaso Garcia	.08	.04	.01
☐ 227	Kelly Gruber ERR (Wrong birth year)	.12	.05	.02
☐ 228	Tom Henke	.12	.05	.02
☐ 229	Garth Iorg	.08	.04	.01
☐ 230	Joe Johnson	.08	.04	.01
☐ 231	Cliff Johnson	.08	.04	.01
☐ 232	Jimmy Key	.40	.18	.05
☐ 233	Dennis Lamp	.08	.04	.01
☐ 234	Rick Leach	.08	.04	.01
☐ 235	Buck Martinez	.08	.04	.01
☐ 236	Lloyd Moseby	.08	.04	.01
☐ 237	Rance Mulliniks	.08	.04	.01
☐ 238	Dave Stieb	.12	.05	.02
☐ 239	Willie Upshaw	.08	.04	.01
☐ 240	Ernie Whitt	.08	.04	.01
☐ 241	Andy Allanson	.08	.04	.01
☐ 242	Scott Bailes	.08	.04	.01
☐ 243	Chris Bando	.08	.04	.01
☐ 244	Tony Bernazard	.08	.04	.01
☐ 245	John Butcher	.08	.04	.01
☐ 246	Brett Butler	.12	.05	.02
☐ 247	Ernie Camacho	.08	.04	.01
☐ 248	Tom Candiotti	.12	.05	.02
☐ 249	Joe Carter	1.50	.65	.19
☐ 250	Carmen Castillo	.08	.04	.01
☐ 251	Julio Franco	.25	.11	.03
☐ 252	Mel Hall	.08	.04	.01
☐ 253	Brook Jacoby	.08	.04	.01
☐ 254	Phil Niekro	.15	.07	.02
☐ 255	Otis Nixon	.08	.04	.01
☐ 256	Dickie Noles	.08	.04	.01
☐ 257	Bryan Oelkers	.08	.04	.01
☐ 258	Ken Schrom	.08	.04	.01
☐ 259	Don Schulze	.08	.04	.01
☐ 260	Cory Snyder	.12	.05	.02
☐ 261	Pat Tabler	.08	.04	.01
☐ 262	Andre Thornton	.08	.04	.01
☐ 263	Rich Yett	.08	.04	.01
☐ 264	Mike Aldrete	.08	.04	.01
☐ 265	Juan Berenguer	.08	.04	.01
☐ 266	Vida Blue	.12	.05	.02
☐ 267	Bob Brenly	.08	.04	.01
☐ 268	Chris Brown	.08	.04	.01
☐ 269	Will Clark	16.00	7.25	2.00
☐ 270	Chili Davis	.12	.05	.02
☐ 271	Mark Davis	.08	.04	.01
☐ 272	Kelly Downs	.08	.04	.01
☐ 273	Scott Garrelts	.08	.04	.01
☐ 274	Dan Gladden	.08	.04	.01
☐ 275	Mike Krukow	.08	.04	.01
☐ 276	Randy Kutcher	.08	.04	.01
☐ 277	Mike LaCoss	.08	.04	.01
☐ 278	Jeff Leonard	.08	.04	.01
☐ 279	Candy Maldonado	.08	.04	.01
☐ 280	Roger Mason	.08	.04	.01
☐ 281	Bob Melvin	.08	.04	.01
☐ 282	Greg Minton	.08	.04	.01
☐ 283	Jeff D. Robinson	.08	.04	.01
☐ 284	Harry Spilman	.08	.04	.01
☐ 285	Robby Thompson	.75	.35	.09
☐ 286	Jose Uribe	.08	.04	.01
☐ 287	Frank Williams	.08	.04	.01
☐ 288	Joel Youngblood	.08	.04	.01
☐ 289	Jack Clark	.12	.05	.02
☐ 290	Vince Coleman	.12	.05	.02
☐ 291	Tim Conroy	.08	.04	.01
☐ 292	Danny Cox	.08	.04	.01
☐ 293	Ken Dayley	.08	.04	.01
☐ 294	Curt Ford	.08	.04	.01
☐ 295	Bob Forsch	.08	.04	.01
☐ 296	Tom Herr	.08	.04	.01
☐ 297	Ricky Horton	.08	.04	.01

	No.	Player			
☐	298	Clint Hurdle	.08	.04	.01
☐	299	Jeff Lahti	.08	.04	.01
☐	300	Steve Lake	.08	.04	.01
☐	301	Tito Landrum	.08	.04	.01
☐	302	Mike LaValliere	.08	.04	.01
☐	303	Greg Mathews	.08	.04	.01
☐	304	Willie McGee	.12	.05	.02
☐	305	Jose Oquendo	.08	.04	.01
☐	306	Terry Pendleton	.50	.23	.06
☐	307	Pat Perry	.08	.04	.01
☐	308	Ozzie Smith	1.00	.45	.13
☐	309	Ray Soff	.08	.04	.01
☐	310	John Tudor	.08	.04	.01
☐	311	Andy Van Slyke UER (Bats R, Throws L)	.15	.07	.02
☐	312	Todd Worrell	.12	.05	.02
☐	313	Dann Bilardello	.08	.04	.01
☐	314	Hubie Brooks	.08	.04	.01
☐	315	Tim Burke	.08	.04	.01
☐	316	Andre Dawson	.50	.23	.06
☐	317	Mike Fitzgerald	.08	.04	.01
☐	318	Tom Foley	.08	.04	.01
☐	319	Andres Galarraga	1.00	.45	.13
☐	320	Joe Hesketh	.08	.04	.01
☐	321	Wallace Johnson	.08	.04	.01
☐	322	Wayne Krenchicki	.08	.04	.01
☐	323	Vance Law	.08	.04	.01
☐	324	Dennis Martinez	.12	.05	.02
☐	325	Bob McClure	.08	.04	.01
☐	326	Andy McGaffigan	.08	.04	.01
☐	327	Al Newman	.08	.04	.01
☐	328	Tim Raines	.15	.07	.02
☐	329	Jeff Reardon	.15	.07	.02
☐	330	Luis Rivera	.08	.04	.01
☐	331	Bob Sebra	.08	.04	.01
☐	332	Bryn Smith	.08	.04	.01
☐	333	Jay Tibbs	.08	.04	.01
☐	334	Tim Wallach	.12	.05	.02
☐	335	Mitch Webster	.08	.04	.01
☐	336	Jim Wohlford	.08	.04	.01
☐	337	Floyd Youmans	.08	.04	.01
☐	338	Chris Bosio	.40	.18	.05
☐	339	Glenn Braggs	.08	.04	.01
☐	340	Rick Cerone	.08	.04	.01
☐	341	Mark Clear	.08	.04	.01
☐	342	Bryan Clutterbuck	.08	.04	.01
☐	343	Cecil Cooper	.12	.05	.02
☐	344	Rob Deer	.08	.04	.01
☐	345	Jim Gantner	.08	.04	.01
☐	346	Ted Higuera	.08	.04	.01
☐	347	John Henry Johnson	.08	.04	.01
☐	348	Tim Leary	.08	.04	.01
☐	349	Rick Manning	.08	.04	.01
☐	350	Paul Molitor	.75	.35	.09
☐	351	Charlie Moore	.08	.04	.01
☐	352	Juan Nieves	.08	.04	.01
☐	353	Ben Oglivie	.08	.04	.01
☐	354	Dan Plesac	.08	.04	.01
☐	355	Ernest Riles	.08	.04	.01
☐	356	Billy Joe Robidoux	.08	.04	.01
☐	357	Bill Schroeder	.08	.04	.01
☐	358	Dale Sveum	.08	.04	.01
☐	359	Gorman Thomas	.08	.04	.01
☐	360	Bill Wegman	.08	.04	.01
☐	361	Robin Yount	.75	.35	.09
☐	362	Steve Balboni	.08	.04	.01
☐	363	Scott Bankhead	.08	.04	.01
☐	364	Buddy Biancalana	.08	.04	.01
☐	365	Bud Black	.08	.04	.01
☐	366	George Brett	2.00	.90	.25
☐	367	Steve Farr	.08	.04	.01
☐	368	Mark Gubicza	.08	.04	.01
☐	369	Bo Jackson	5.00	2.30	.60
☐	370	Danny Jackson	.12	.05	.02
☐	371	Mike Kingery	.20	.09	.03
☐	372	Rudy Law	.08	.04	.01
☐	373	Charlie Leibrandt	.08	.04	.01
☐	374	Dennis Leonard	.08	.04	.01
☐	375	Hal McRae	.15	.07	.02
☐	376	Jorge Orta	.08	.04	.01
☐	377	Jamie Quirk	.08	.04	.01
☐	378	Dan Quisenberry	.12	.05	.02
☐	379	Bret Saberhagen	.35	.16	.04
☐	380	Angel Salazar	.08	.04	.01
☐	381	Lonnie Smith	.08	.04	.01
☐	382	Jim Sundberg	.08	.04	.01
☐	383	Frank White	.12	.05	.02
☐	384	Willie Wilson	.08	.04	.01
☐	385	Joaquin Andujar	.08	.04	.01
☐	386	Doug Bair	.08	.04	.01
☐	387	Dusty Baker	.15	.07	.02
☐	388	Bruce Bochte	.08	.04	.01
☐	389	Jose Canseco	5.00	2.30	.60
☐	390	Chris Codiroli	.08	.04	.01
☐	391	Mike Davis	.08	.04	.01
☐	392	Alfredo Griffin	.08	.04	.01
☐	393	Moose Haas	.08	.04	.01
☐	394	Donnie Hill	.08	.04	.01
☐	395	Jay Howell	.08	.04	.01
☐	396	Dave Kingman	.12	.05	.02
☐	397	Carney Lansford	.12	.05	.02
☐	398	Dave Leiper	.08	.04	.01
☐	399	Bill Mooneyham	.08	.04	.01
☐	400	Dwayne Murphy	.08	.04	.01
☐	401	Steve Ontiveros	.08	.04	.01
☐	402	Tony Phillips	.12	.05	.02
☐	403	Eric Plunk	.08	.04	.01
☐	404	Jose Rijo	.15	.07	.02
☐	405	Terry Steinbach	.75	.35	.09
☐	406	Dave Stewart	.15	.07	.02
☐	407	Mickey Tettleton	.12	.05	.02
☐	408	Dave Von Ohlen	.08	.04	.01
☐	409	Jerry Willard	.08	.04	.01
☐	410	Curt Young	.08	.04	.01
☐	411	Bruce Bochy	.08	.04	.01
☐	412	Dave Dravecky	.12	.05	.02
☐	413	Tim Flannery	.08	.04	.01
☐	414	Steve Garvey	.15	.07	.02
☐	415	Rich Gossage	.15	.07	.02
☐	416	Tony Gwynn	2.00	.90	.25
☐	417	Andy Hawkins	.08	.04	.01
☐	418	LaMarr Hoyt	.08	.04	.01
☐	419	Terry Kennedy	.08	.04	.01
☐	420	John Kruk	2.00	.90	.25
☐	421	Dave LaPoint	.08	.04	.01
☐	422	Craig Lefferts	.08	.04	.01
☐	423	Carmelo Martinez	.08	.04	.01
☐	424	Lance McCullers	.08	.04	.01
☐	425	Kevin McReynolds	.12	.05	.02
☐	426	Graig Nettles	.12	.05	.02
☐	427	Bip Roberts	.50	.23	.06
☐	428	Jerry Royster	.08	.04	.01
☐	429	Benito Santiago	.30	.14	.04
☐	430	Eric Show	.08	.04	.01
☐	431	Bob Stoddard	.08	.04	.01
☐	432	Garry Templeton	.08	.04	.01
☐	433	Gene Walter	.08	.04	.01
☐	434	Ed Whitson	.08	.04	.01
☐	435	Marvell Wynne	.08	.04	.01
☐	436	Dave Anderson	.08	.04	.01
☐	437	Greg Brock	.08	.04	.01
☐	438	Enos Cabell	.08	.04	.01
☐	439	Mariano Duncan	.08	.04	.01
☐	440	Pedro Guerrero	.12	.05	.02
☐	441	Orel Hershiser	.12	.05	.02
☐	442	Rick Honeycutt	.08	.04	.01

	No.	Player			
☐	443	Ken Howell	.08	.04	.01
☐	444	Ken Landreaux	.08	.04	.01
☐	445	Bill Madlock	.12	.05	.02
☐	446	Mike Marshall	.08	.04	.01
☐	447	Len Matuszek	.08	.04	.01
☐	448	Tom Niedenfuer	.08	.04	.01
☐	449	Alejandro Pena	.08	.04	.01
☐	450	Dennis Powell	.08	.04	.01
☐	451	Jerry Reuss	.08	.04	.01
☐	452	Bill Russell	.12	.05	.02
☐	453	Steve Sax	.08	.04	.01
☐	454	Mike Scioscia	.08	.04	.01
☐	455	Franklin Stubbs	.08	.04	.01
☐	456	Alex Trevino	.08	.04	.01
☐	457	Fernando Valenzuela	.08	.04	.01
☐	458	Ed VandeBerg	.08	.04	.01
☐	459	Bob Welch	.12	.05	.02
☐	460	Reggie Williams	.08	.04	.01
☐	461	Don Aase	.08	.04	.01
☐	462	Juan Beniquez	.08	.04	.01
☐	463	Mike Boddicker	.08	.04	.01
☐	464	Juan Bonilla	.08	.04	.01
☐	465	Rich Bordi	.08	.04	.01
☐	466	Storm Davis	.08	.04	.01
☐	467	Rick Dempsey	.08	.04	.01
☐	468	Ken Dixon	.08	.04	.01
☐	469	Jim Dwyer	.08	.04	.01
☐	470	Mike Flanagan	.08	.04	.01
☐	471	Jackie Gutierrez	.08	.04	.01
☐	472	Brad Havens	.08	.04	.01
☐	473	Lee Lacy	.08	.04	.01
☐	474	Fred Lynn	.12	.05	.02
☐	475	Scott McGregor	.08	.04	.01
☐	476	Eddie Murray	.75	.35	.09
☐	477	Tom O'Malley	.08	.04	.01
☐	478	Cal Ripken	3.00	1.35	.40
☐	479	Larry Sheets	.08	.04	.01
☐	480	John Shelby	.08	.04	.01
☐	481	Nate Snell	.08	.04	.01
☐	482	Jim Traber	.08	.04	.01
☐	483	Mike Young	.08	.04	.01
☐	484	Neil Allen	.08	.04	.01
☐	485	Harold Baines	.12	.05	.02
☐	486	Floyd Bannister	.08	.04	.01
☐	487	Daryl Boston	.08	.04	.01
☐	488	Ivan Calderon	.08	.04	.01
☐	489	John Cangelosi	.08	.04	.01
☐	490	Steve Carlton	.50	.23	.06
☐	491	Joe Cowley	.08	.04	.01
☐	492	Julio Cruz	.08	.04	.01
☐	493	Bill Dawley	.08	.04	.01
☐	494	Jose DeLeon	.08	.04	.01
☐	495	Richard Dotson	.08	.04	.01
☐	496	Carlton Fisk	.50	.23	.06
☐	497	Ozzie Guillen	.12	.05	.02
☐	498	Jerry Hairston	.08	.04	.01
☐	499	Ron Hassey	.08	.04	.01
☐	500	Tim Hulett	.08	.04	.01
☐	501	Bob James	.08	.04	.01
☐	502	Steve Lyons	.08	.04	.01
☐	503	Joel McKeon	.08	.04	.01
☐	504	Gene Nelson	.08	.04	.01
☐	505	Dave Schmidt	.08	.04	.01
☐	506	Ray Searage	.08	.04	.01
☐	507	Bobby Thigpen	.30	.14	.04
☐	508	Greg Walker	.08	.04	.01
☐	509	Jim Acker	.08	.04	.01
☐	510	Doyle Alexander	.08	.04	.01
☐	511	Paul Assenmacher	.08	.04	.01
☐	512	Bruce Benedict	.08	.04	.01
☐	513	Chris Chambliss	.12	.05	.02
☐	514	Jeff Dedmon	.08	.04	.01
☐	515	Gene Garber	.08	.04	.01

	No.	Player			
☐	516	Ken Griffey	.12	.05	.02
☐	517	Terry Harper	.08	.04	.01
☐	518	Bob Horner	.08	.04	.01
☐	519	Glenn Hubbard	.08	.04	.01
☐	520	Rick Mahler	.08	.04	.01
☐	521	Omar Moreno	.08	.04	.01
☐	522	Dale Murphy	.15	.07	.02
☐	523	Ken Oberkfell	.08	.04	.01
☐	524	Ed Olwine	.08	.04	.01
☐	525	David Palmer	.08	.04	.01
☐	526	Rafael Ramirez	.08	.04	.01
☐	527	Billy Sample	.08	.04	.01
☐	528	Ted Simmons	.12	.05	.02
☐	529	Zane Smith	.08	.04	.01
☐	530	Bruce Sutter	.12	.05	.02
☐	531	Andres Thomas	.08	.04	.01
☐	532	Ozzie Virgil	.08	.04	.01
☐	533	Allan Anderson	.08	.04	.01
☐	534	Keith Atherton	.08	.04	.01
☐	535	Billy Beane	.08	.04	.01
☐	536	Bert Blyleven	.15	.07	.02
☐	537	Tom Brunansky	.08	.04	.01
☐	538	Randy Bush	.08	.04	.01
☐	539	George Frazier	.08	.04	.01
☐	540	Gary Gaetti	.08	.04	.01
☐	541	Greg Gagne	.12	.05	.02
☐	542	Mickey Hatcher	.08	.04	.01
☐	543	Neal Heaton	.08	.04	.01
☐	544	Kent Hrbek	.12	.05	.02
☐	545	Roy Lee Jackson	.08	.04	.01
☐	546	Tim Laudner	.08	.04	.01
☐	547	Steve Lombardozzi	.08	.04	.01
☐	548	Mark Portugal	.75	.35	.09
☐	549	Kirby Puckett	4.00	1.80	.50
☐	550	Jeff Reed	.08	.04	.01
☐	551	Mark Salas	.08	.04	.01
☐	552	Roy Smalley	.08	.04	.01
☐	553	Mike Smithson	.08	.04	.01
☐	554	Frank Viola	.12	.05	.02
☐	555	Thad Bosley	.08	.04	.01
☐	556	Ron Cey	.12	.05	.02
☐	557	Jody Davis	.08	.04	.01
☐	558	Ron Davis	.08	.04	.01
☐	559	Bob Dernier	.08	.04	.01
☐	560	Frank DiPino	.08	.04	.01
☐	561	Shawon Dunston UER (Wrong birth year listed on card back)	.12	.05	.02
☐	562	Leon Durham	.08	.04	.01
☐	563	Dennis Eckersley	.25	.11	.03
☐	564	Terry Francona	.08	.04	.01
☐	565	Dave Gumpert	.08	.04	.01
☐	566	Guy Hoffman	.08	.04	.01
☐	567	Ed Lynch	.08	.04	.01
☐	568	Gary Matthews	.08	.04	.01
☐	569	Keith Moreland	.08	.04	.01
☐	570	Jamie Moyer	.30	.14	.04
☐	571	Jerry Mumphrey	.08	.04	.01
☐	572	Ryne Sandberg	2.00	.90	.25
☐	573	Scott Sanderson	.08	.04	.01
☐	574	Lee Smith	.25	.11	.03
☐	575	Chris Speier	.08	.04	.01
☐	576	Rick Sutcliffe	.12	.05	.02
☐	577	Manny Trillo	.08	.04	.01
☐	578	Steve Trout	.08	.04	.01
☐	579	Karl Best	.08	.04	.01
☐	580	Scott Bradley	.08	.04	.01
☐	581	Phil Bradley	.08	.04	.01
☐	582	Mickey Brantley	.08	.04	.01
☐	583	Mike G. Brown P	.08	.04	.01
☐	584	Alvin Davis	.08	.04	.01
☐	585	Lee Guetterman	.08	.04	.01
☐	586	Mark Huismann	.08	.04	.01

☐ 587 Bob Kearney	.08	.04	.01
☐ 588 Pete Ladd	.08	.04	.01
☐ 589 Mark Langston	.15	.07	.02
☐ 590 Mike Moore	.08	.04	.01
☐ 591 Mike Morgan	.08	.04	.01
☐ 592 John Moses	.08	.04	.01
☐ 593 Ken Phelps	.08	.04	.01
☐ 594 Jim Presley	.08	.04	.01
☐ 595 Rey Quinones UER (Quinonez on front)	.08	.04	.01
☐ 596 Harold Reynolds	.08	.04	.01
☐ 597 Billy Swift	.12	.05	.02
☐ 598 Danny Tartabull	.50	.23	.06
☐ 599 Steve Yeager	.08	.04	.01
☐ 600 Matt Young	.08	.04	.01
☐ 601 Bill Almon	.08	.04	.01
☐ 602 Rafael Belliard	.20	.09	.03
☐ 603 Mike Bielecki	.08	.04	.01
☐ 604 Barry Bonds	35.00	16.00	4.40
☐ 605 Bobby Bonilla	3.50	1.55	.45
☐ 606 Sid Bream	.08	.04	.01
☐ 607 Mike C. Brown	.08	.04	.01
☐ 608 Pat Clements	.08	.04	.01
☐ 609 Mike Diaz	.08	.04	.01
☐ 610 Cecilio Guante	.08	.04	.01
☐ 611 Barry Jones	.08	.04	.01
☐ 612 Bob Kipper	.08	.04	.01
☐ 613 Larry McWilliams	.08	.04	.01
☐ 614 Jim Morrison	.08	.04	.01
☐ 615 Joe Orsulak	.08	.04	.01
☐ 616 Junior Ortiz	.08	.04	.01
☐ 617 Tony Pena	.08	.04	.01
☐ 618 Johnny Ray	.08	.04	.01
☐ 619 Rick Reuschel	.08	.04	.01
☐ 620 R.J. Reynolds	.08	.04	.01
☐ 621 Rick Rhoden	.08	.04	.01
☐ 622 Don Robinson	.08	.04	.01
☐ 623 Bob Walk	.08	.04	.01
☐ 624 Jim Winn	.08	.04	.01
☐ 625 Youthful Power Pete Incaviglia Jose Canseco	.60	.25	.08
☐ 626 300 Game Winners Don Sutton Phil Niekro	.15	.07	.02
☐ 627 AL Firemen Dave Righetti Don Aase	.10	.05	.01
☐ 628 Rookie All-Stars Wally Joyner Jose Canseco	.60	.25	.08
☐ 629 Magic Mets Gary Carter Sid Fernandez Dwight Gooden Keith Hernandez Darryl Strawberry	.25	.11	.03
☐ 630 NL Best Righties Mike Scott Mike Krukow	.10	.05	.01
☐ 631 Sensational Southpaws Fernando Valenzuela John Franco	.10	.05	.01
☐ 632 Count'Em Bob Horner	.10	.05	.01
☐ 633 AL Pitcher's Nightmare Jose Canseco Jim Rice Kirby Puckett	1.00	.45	.13
☐ 634 All-Star Battery Gary Carter Roger Clemens	.35	.16	.04
☐ 635 4000 Strikeouts Steve Carlton	.20	.09	.03
☐ 636 Big Bats at First Glenn Davis Eddie Murray	.15	.07	.02
☐ 637 On Base Wade Boggs Keith Hernandez	.20	.09	.03
☐ 638 Sluggers Left Side Don Mattingly Darryl Strawberry	.50	.23	.06
☐ 639 Former MVP's Dave Parker Ryne Sandberg	.25	.11	.03
☐ 640 Dr. K and Super K Dwight Gooden Roger Clemens	.40	.18	.05
☐ 641 AL West Stoppers Mike Witt Charlie Hough	.10	.05	.01
☐ 642 Doubles and Triples Juan Samuel Tim Raines	.15	.07	.02
☐ 643 Outfielders with Punch Harold Baines Jesse Barfield	.10	.05	.01
☐ 644 Dave Clark and Greg Swindell	1.00	.45	.13
☐ 645 Ron Karkovice and Russ Morman	.40	.18	.05
☐ 646 Devon White and Willie Fraser	2.50	1.15	.30
☐ 647 Mike Stanley and Jerry Browne	1.00	.45	.13
☐ 648 Dave Magadan and Phil Lombardi	.40	.18	.05
☐ 649 Jose Gonzalez and Ralph Bryant	.08	.04	.01
☐ 650 Jimmy Jones and Randy Asadoor	.08	.04	.01
☐ 651 Tracy Jones and Marvin Freeman	.30	.14	.04
☐ 652 John Stefero and Kevin Seitzer	.40	.18	.05
☐ 653 Rob Nelson and Steve Fireovid	.08	.04	.01
☐ 654 CL: Mets/Red Sox Astros/Angels	.10	.04	.01
☐ 655 CL: Yankees/Rangers Tigers/Phillies	.10	.04	.01
☐ 656 CL: Reds/Blue Jays Indians/Giants ERR (230/231 wrong)	.10	.04	.01
☐ 657 CL: Cardinals/Expos Brewers/Royals	.10	.04	.01
☐ 658 CL: A's/Padres Dodgers/Orioles	.10	.04	.01
☐ 659 CL: White Sox/Braves Twins/Cubs	.10	.04	.01
☐ 660 CL: Mariners/Pirates Special Cards ER (580/581 wrong)	.10	.04	.01

1987 Fleer All-Stars

This 12-card set was distributed as an insert in packs of the Fleer regular issue. The cards measure 2 1/2" by 3 1/2" and are designed with a color player photo superimposed on a gray or black background with

yellow stars. The player's name, team, and position are printed in orange on black or gray at the bottom of the obverse. The card backs are done predominantly in gray, red, and black. Cards are numbered on the back in the upper right hand corner.

	MINT	EXC	G-VG
COMPLETE SET (12)	22.00	10.00	2.80
COMMON CARD (1-12)	.30	.14	.04

	MINT	EXC	G-VG
☐ 1 Don Mattingly	5.50	2.50	.70
☐ 2 Gary Carter	.50	.23	.06
☐ 3 Tony Fernandez	.30	.14	.04
☐ 4 Steve Sax	.30	.14	.04
☐ 5 Kirby Puckett	8.00	3.60	1.00
☐ 6 Mike Schmidt	3.50	1.55	.45
☐ 7 Mike Easler	.30	.14	.04
☐ 8 Todd Worrell	.30	.14	.04
☐ 9 George Bell	.30	.14	.04
☐ 10 Fernando Valenzuela	.30	.14	.04
☐ 11 Roger Clemens	6.00	2.70	.75
☐ 12 Tim Raines	.75	.35	.09

1987 Fleer Headliners

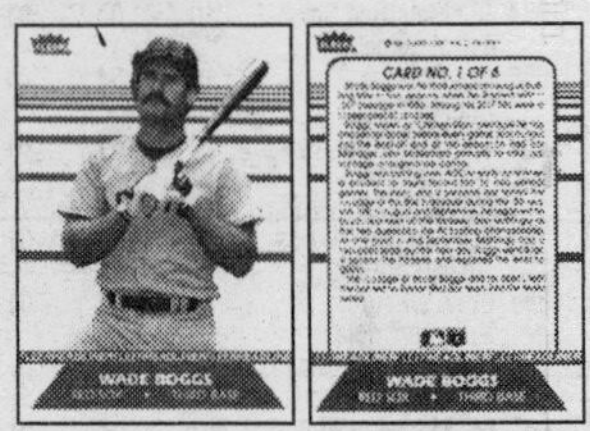

This six-card set was distributed as a special insert in rack packs as well as with three-pack wax pack rack packs. The obverse features the player photo against a beige background with irregular red stripes. The cards measure 2 1/2" by 3 1/2". The cards are numbered on the back. The checklist below also lists each player's team affiliation.

	MINT	EXC	G-VG
COMPLETE SET (6)	7.00	3.10	.85
COMMON CARD (1-6)	.60	.25	.08

	MINT	EXC	G-VG
☐ 1 Wade Boggs	2.00	.90	.25
☐ 2 Jose Canseco	3.00	1.35	.40
☐ 3 Dwight Gooden	.60	.25	.08
☐ 4 Rickey Henderson	2.00	.90	.25
☐ 5 Keith Hernandez	.60	.25	.08
☐ 6 Jim Rice	.60	.25	.08

1987 Fleer Update

This 132-card set was distributed by Fleer to dealers as a complete set in a custom box. In addition to the complete set of 132 cards, the box also contains 25 Team Logo stickers. The card fronts look very similar to the 1987 Fleer regular issue. The cards are numbered (with a U prefix) alphabetically according to player's last name. Cards measure the standard size, 2 1/2" by 3 1/2". Fleer misalphabetized Jim Winn in their set numbering by putting him ahead of the next four players listed. The key (extended) Rookie Cards in this set are Ellis Burks, Mike Greenwell, Greg Maddux, Fred McGriff, Mark McGwire and Matt Williams. Fleer also produced a "limited" edition version of this set with glossy coating and packaged in a "tin." However, this glossy tin set was apparently not limited enough (estimated between 75,000 and 100,000 1987 Update tin sets produced by Fleer), since the values of the "tin" glossy cards are now the same as the values of the cards in the regular set.

	MINT	EXC	G-VG
COMPLETE FACT.SET (132)	12.00	5.50	1.50
COMMON CARD (1-132)	.05	.02	.01

	MINT	EXC	G-VG
☐ 1 Scott Bankhead	.05	.02	.01
☐ 2 Eric Bell	.05	.02	.01
☐ 3 Juan Beniquez	.05	.02	.01
☐ 4 Juan Berenguer	.05	.02	.01
☐ 5 Mike Birkbeck	.05	.02	.01
☐ 6 Randy Bockus	.05	.02	.01
☐ 7 Rod Booker	.05	.02	.01
☐ 8 Thad Bosley	.05	.02	.01
☐ 9 Greg Brock	.05	.02	.01
☐ 10 Bob Brower	.05	.02	.01
☐ 11 Chris Brown	.05	.02	.01
☐ 12 Jerry Browne	.10	.05	.01
☐ 13 Ralph Bryant	.05	.02	.01
☐ 14 DeWayne Buice	.05	.02	.01
☐ 15 Ellis Burks	1.00	.45	.13
☐ 16 Casey Candaele	.05	.02	.01

☐ 17 Steve Carlton .35 .16 .04
☐ 18 Juan Castillo .05 .02 .01
☐ 19 Chuck Crim .05 .02 .01
☐ 20 Mark Davidson .05 .02 .01
☐ 21 Mark Davis .05 .02 .01
☐ 22 Storm Davis .05 .02 .01
☐ 23 Bill Dawley .05 .02 .01
☐ 24 Andre Dawson .40 .18 .05
☐ 25 Brian Dayett .05 .02 .01
☐ 26 Rick Dempsey .05 .02 .01
☐ 27 Ken Dowell .05 .02 .01
☐ 28 Dave Dravecky .10 .05 .01
☐ 29 Mike Dunne .05 .02 .01
☐ 30 Dennis Eckersley .20 .09 .03
☐ 31 Cecil Fielder 1.50 .65 .19
☐ 32 Brian Fisher .05 .02 .01
☐ 33 Willie Fraser .05 .02 .01
☐ 34 Ken Gerhart .05 .02 .01
☐ 35 Jim Gott .05 .02 .01
☐ 36 Dan Gladden .05 .02 .01
☐ 37 Mike Greenwell .75 .35 .09
☐ 38 Cecilio Guante .05 .02 .01
☐ 39 Albert Hall .05 .02 .01
☐ 40 Atlee Hammaker .05 .02 .01
☐ 41 Mickey Hatcher .05 .02 .01
☐ 42 Mike Heath .05 .02 .01
☐ 43 Neal Heaton .05 .02 .01
☐ 44 Mike Henneman .30 .14 .04
☐ 45 Guy Hoffman .05 .02 .01
☐ 46 Charles Hudson .05 .02 .01
☐ 47 Chuck Jackson .05 .02 .01
☐ 48 Mike Jackson .20 .09 .03
☐ 49 Reggie Jackson .50 .23 .06
☐ 50 Chris James .05 .02 .01
☐ 51 Dion James .05 .02 .01
☐ 52 Stan Javier .10 .05 .01
☐ 53 Stan Jefferson .05 .02 .01
☐ 54 Jimmy Jones .05 .02 .01
☐ 55 Tracy Jones .05 .02 .01
☐ 56 Terry Kennedy .05 .02 .01
☐ 57 Mike Kingery .10 .05 .01
☐ 58 Ray Knight .10 .05 .01
☐ 59 Gene Larkin .05 .02 .01
☐ 60 Mike LaValliere .05 .02 .01
☐ 61 Jack Lazorko .05 .02 .01
☐ 62 Terry Leach .05 .02 .01
☐ 63 Rick Leach .05 .02 .01
☐ 64 Craig Lefferts .05 .02 .01
☐ 65 Jim Lindeman .05 .02 .01
☐ 66 Bill Long .05 .02 .01
☐ 67 Mike Loynd .05 .02 .01
☐ 68 Greg Maddux 6.00 2.70 .75
☐ 69 Bill Madlock .10 .05 .01
☐ 70 Dave Magadan .15 .07 .02
☐ 71 Joe Magrane .15 .07 .02
☐ 72 Fred Manrique .05 .02 .01
☐ 73 Mike Mason .05 .02 .01
☐ 74 Lloyd McClendon .05 .02 .01
☐ 75 Fred McGriff 3.00 1.35 .40
☐ 76 Mark McGwire 1.50 .65 .19
☐ 77 Mark McLemore .05 .02 .01
☐ 78 Kevin McReynolds .10 .05 .01
☐ 79 Dave Meads .05 .02 .01
☐ 80 Greg Minton .05 .02 .01
☐ 81 John Mitchell .05 .02 .01
☐ 82 Kevin Mitchell .50 .23 .06
☐ 83 John Morris .05 .02 .01
☐ 84 Jeff Musselman .05 .02 .01
☐ 85 Randy Myers .75 .35 .09
☐ 86 Gene Nelson .05 .02 .01
☐ 87 Joe Niekro .10 .05 .01
☐ 88 Tom Nieto .05 .02 .01
☐ 89 Reid Nichols .05 .02 .01
☐ 90 Matt Nokes .30 .14 .04
☐ 91 Dickie Noles .05 .02 .01
☐ 92 Edwin Nunez .05 .02 .01
☐ 93 Jose Nunez .05 .02 .01
☐ 94 Paul O'Neill 1.25 .55 .16
☐ 95 Jim Paciorek .05 .02 .01
☐ 96 Lance Parrish .10 .05 .01
☐ 97 Bill Pecota .05 .02 .01
☐ 98 Tony Pena .05 .02 .01
☐ 99 Luis Polonia .50 .23 .06
☐ 100 Randy Ready .05 .02 .01
☐ 101 Jeff Reardon .15 .07 .02
☐ 102 Gary Redus .05 .02 .01
☐ 103 Rick Rhoden .05 .02 .01
☐ 104 Wally Ritchie .05 .02 .01
☐ 105 Jeff M. Robinson UER .05 .02 .01
(Wrong Jeff's stats on back)
☐ 106 Mark Salas .05 .02 .01
☐ 107 Dave Schmidt .05 .02 .01
☐ 108 Kevin Seitzer UER .15 .07 .02
(Wrong birth year)
☐ 109 John Shelby .05 .02 .01
☐ 110 John Smiley .40 .18 .05
☐ 111 Lary Sorensen .05 .02 .01
☐ 112 Chris Speier .05 .02 .01
☐ 113 Randy St.Claire .05 .02 .01
☐ 114 Jim Sundberg .05 .02 .01
☐ 115 B.J. Surhoff .25 .11 .03
☐ 116 Greg Swindell .35 .16 .04
☐ 117 Danny Tartabull .35 .16 .04
☐ 118 Dorn Taylor .05 .02 .01
☐ 119 Lee Tunnell .05 .02 .01
☐ 120 Ed VandeBerg .05 .02 .01
☐ 121 Andy Van Slyke .15 .07 .02
☐ 122 Gary Ward .05 .02 .01
☐ 123 Devon White .75 .35 .09
☐ 124 Alan Wiggins .05 .02 .01
☐ 125 Bill Wilkinson .05 .02 .01
☐ 126 Jim Winn .05 .02 .01
☐ 127 Frank Williams .05 .02 .01
☐ 128 Ken Williams .05 .02 .01
☐ 129 Matt Williams 5.00 2.30 .60
☐ 130 Herm Willingham .05 .02 .01
☐ 131 Matt Young .05 .02 .01
☐ 132 Checklist 1-132 .05 .02 .01

1988 Fleer

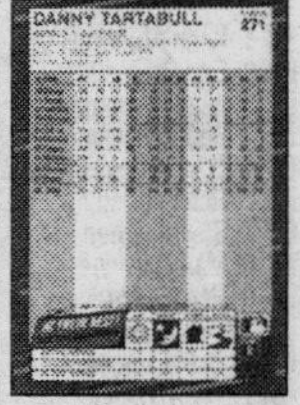

This 660-card set features a distinctive white background with red and blue diagonal stripes across the card. The backs are printed in gray and red on white card stock. The bottom of the card back shows an inno-

vative breakdown of the player's demonstrated ability with respect to day, night, home, and road games. Cards are numbered on the back and are again the standard 2 1/2" by 3 1/2". Cards are again organized numerically by teams, i.e., World Champion Twins (1-25), St. Louis Cardinals (26-50), Detroit Tigers (51-75), San Francisco Giants (76-101), Toronto Blue Jays (102-126), New York Mets (127-154), Milwaukee Brewers (155-178), Montreal Expos (179-201), New York Yankees (202-226), Cincinnati Reds (227-250), Kansas City Royals (251-274), Oakland A's (275-296), Philadelphia Phillies (297-320), Pittsburgh Pirates (321-342), Boston Red Sox (343-367), Seattle Mariners (368-390), Chicago White Sox (391-413), Chicago Cubs (414-436), Houston Astros (437-460), Texas Rangers (461-483), California Angels (484-507), Los Angeles Dodgers (508-530), Atlanta Braves (531-552), Baltimore Orioles (553-575), San Diego Padres (576-599), and Cleveland Indians (600-621). The last 39 cards in the set consist of Specials (622-640), Rookie Pairs (641-653), and checklists (654-660). Cards 90 and 91 are incorrectly numbered on the checklist card number 654. Rookie Cards in this set include Jay Bell, Jeff Blauser, John Burkett, Ellis Burks, Ken Caminiti, Mike Devereaux, Ron Gant, Tom Glavine, Mark Grace, Gregg Jefferies, Roberto Kelly, Edgar Martinez, Jack McDowell, Jeff Montgomery, and Matt Williams. A subset of "Stadium Cards" was randomly inserted throughout the packs. These cards pictured all 26 stadiums used by Major League Baseball and presented facts about these ballparks. Fleer also produced a "limited" edition version of this set with glossy coating and packaged in a "tin." However, this tin set was apparently not limited enough (estimated between 40,000 and 60,000 1988 tin sets produced by Fleer), since the values of the "tin" glossy cards are now only double the values of the respective cards in the regular set.

	MINT	EXC	G-VG
COMPLETE SET (660)	25.00	11.50	3.10
COMPLETE RETAIL SET (660)	28.00	12.50	3.50
COMPLETE HOBBY SET (672)	30.00	13.50	3.80
COMMON CARD (1-660)	.06	.03	.01

		MINT	EXC	G-VG
☐ 1	Keith Atherton	.06	.03	.01
☐ 2	Don Baylor	.15	.07	.02
☐ 3	Juan Berenguer	.06	.03	.01
☐ 4	Bert Blyleven	.15	.07	.02
☐ 5	Tom Brunansky	.06	.03	.01
☐ 6	Randy Bush	.06	.03	.01
☐ 7	Steve Carlton	.30	.14	.04
☐ 8	Mark Davidson	.06	.03	.01
☐ 9	George Frazier	.06	.03	.01
☐ 10	Gary Gaetti	.06	.03	.01
☐ 11	Greg Gagne	.06	.03	.01
☐ 12	Dan Gladden	.06	.03	.01
☐ 13	Kent Hrbek	.10	.05	.01
☐ 14	Gene Larkin	.06	.03	.01
☐ 15	Tim Laudner	.06	.03	.01
☐ 16	Steve Lombardozzi	.06	.03	.01
☐ 17	Al Newman	.06	.03	.01
☐ 18	Joe Niekro	.10	.05	.01
☐ 19	Kirby Puckett	1.00	.45	.13
☐ 20	Jeff Reardon	.15	.07	.02
☐ 21A	Dan Schatzeder ERR (Misspelled Schatzader on card front)	.10	.05	.01
☐ 21B	Dan Schatzeder COR	.06	.03	.01
☐ 22	Roy Smalley	.06	.03	.01
☐ 23	Mike Smithson	.06	.03	.01
☐ 24	Les Straker	.06	.03	.01
☐ 25	Frank Viola	.10	.05	.01
☐ 26	Jack Clark	.10	.05	.01
☐ 27	Vince Coleman	.10	.05	.01
☐ 28	Danny Cox	.06	.03	.01
☐ 29	Bill Dawley	.06	.03	.01
☐ 30	Ken Dayley	.06	.03	.01
☐ 31	Doug DeCinces	.06	.03	.01
☐ 32	Curt Ford	.06	.03	.01
☐ 33	Bob Forsch	.06	.03	.01
☐ 34	David Green	.06	.03	.01
☐ 35	Tom Herr	.06	.03	.01
☐ 36	Ricky Horton	.06	.03	.01
☐ 37	Lance Johnson	.75	.35	.09
☐ 38	Steve Lake	.06	.03	.01
☐ 39	Jim Lindeman	.06	.03	.01
☐ 40	Joe Magrane	.15	.07	.02
☐ 41	Greg Mathews	.06	.03	.01
☐ 42	Willie McGee	.10	.05	.01
☐ 43	John Morris	.06	.03	.01
☐ 44	Jose Oquendo	.06	.03	.01
☐ 45	Tony Pena	.06	.03	.01
☐ 46	Terry Pendleton	.15	.07	.02
☐ 47	Ozzie Smith	.40	.18	.05
☐ 48	John Tudor	.06	.03	.01
☐ 49	Lee Tunnell	.06	.03	.01
☐ 50	Todd Worrell	.06	.03	.01
☐ 51	Doyle Alexander	.06	.03	.01
☐ 52	Dave Bergman	.06	.03	.01
☐ 53	Tom Brookens	.06	.03	.01
☐ 54	Darrell Evans	.10	.05	.01
☐ 55	Kirk Gibson	.10	.05	.01
☐ 56	Mike Heath	.06	.03	.01
☐ 57	Mike Henneman	.30	.14	.04
☐ 58	Willie Hernandez	.06	.03	.01
☐ 59	Larry Herndon	.06	.03	.01
☐ 60	Eric King	.06	.03	.01
☐ 61	Chet Lemon	.06	.03	.01
☐ 62	Scott Lusader	.06	.03	.01
☐ 63	Bill Madlock	.10	.05	.01
☐ 64	Jack Morris	.15	.07	.02
☐ 65	Jim Morrison	.06	.03	.01
☐ 66	Matt Nokes	.25	.11	.03
☐ 67	Dan Petry	.06	.03	.01
☐ 68A	Jeff M. Robinson ERR (Stats for Jeff D. Robinson on card back, Born 12-13-60)	.25	.11	.03
☐ 68B	Jeff M. Robinson COR (Born 12-14-61)	.06	.03	.01
☐ 69	Pat Sheridan	.06	.03	.01
☐ 70	Nate Snell	.06	.03	.01
☐ 71	Frank Tanana	.06	.03	.01
☐ 72	Walt Terrell	.06	.03	.01
☐ 73	Mark Thurmond	.06	.03	.01
☐ 74	Alan Trammell	.15	.07	.02
☐ 75	Lou Whitaker	.15	.07	.02
☐ 76	Mike Aldrete	.06	.03	.01
☐ 77	Bob Brenly	.06	.03	.01
☐ 78	Will Clark	1.25	.55	.16
☐ 79	Chili Davis	.10	.05	.01
☐ 80	Kelly Downs	.06	.03	.01
☐ 81	Dave Dravecky	.10	.05	.01
☐ 82	Scott Garrelts	.06	.03	.01
☐ 83	Atlee Hammaker	.06	.03	.01
☐ 84	Dave Henderson	.10	.05	.01

☐ 85 Mike Krukow .06 .03 .01
☐ 86 Mike LaCoss .06 .03 .01
☐ 87 Craig Lefferts .06 .03 .01
☐ 88 Jeff Leonard .06 .03 .01
☐ 89 Candy Maldonado .06 .03 .01
☐ 90 Eddie Milner .06 .03 .01
☐ 91 Bob Melvin .06 .03 .01
☐ 92 Kevin Mitchell .15 .07 .02
☐ 93 Jon Perlman .06 .03 .01
☐ 94 Rick Reuschel .06 .03 .01
☐ 95 Don Robinson .06 .03 .01
☐ 96 Chris Speier .06 .03 .01
☐ 97 Harry Spilman .06 .03 .01
☐ 98 Robby Thompson .10 .05 .01
☐ 99 Jose Uribe .06 .03 .01
☐ 100 Mark Wasinger .06 .03 .01
☐ 101 Matt Williams 5.00 2.30 .60
☐ 102 Jesse Barfield .06 .03 .01
☐ 103 George Bell .10 .05 .01
☐ 104 Juan Beniquez .06 .03 .01
☐ 105 John Cerutti .06 .03 .01
☐ 106 Jim Clancy .06 .03 .01
☐ 107 Rob Ducey .06 .03 .01
☐ 108 Mark Eichhorn .06 .03 .01
☐ 109 Tony Fernandez .10 .05 .01
☐ 110 Cecil Fielder .60 .25 .08
☐ 111 Kelly Gruber .06 .03 .01
☐ 112 Tom Henke .10 .05 .01
☐ 113A Garth Iorg ERR .25 .11 .03
(Misspelled lorq
on card front)
☐ 113B Garth Iorg COR .06 .03 .01
☐ 114 Jimmy Key .15 .07 .02
☐ 115 Rick Leach .06 .03 .01
☐ 116 Manny Lee .06 .03 .01
☐ 117 Nelson Liriano .06 .03 .01
☐ 118 Fred McGriff 2.00 .90 .25
☐ 119 Lloyd Moseby .06 .03 .01
☐ 120 Rance Mulliniks .06 .03 .01
☐ 121 Jeff Musselman .06 .03 .01
☐ 122 Jose Nunez .06 .03 .01
☐ 123 Dave Stieb .10 .05 .01
☐ 124 Willie Upshaw .06 .03 .01
☐ 125 Duane Ward .35 .16 .04
☐ 126 Ernie Whitt .06 .03 .01
☐ 127 Rick Aguilera .10 .05 .01
☐ 128 Wally Backman .06 .03 .01
☐ 129 Mark Carreon .20 .09 .03
☐ 130 Gary Carter .15 .07 .02
☐ 131 David Cone 1.00 .45 .13
☐ 132 Ron Darling .10 .05 .01
☐ 133 Len Dykstra .40 .18 .05
☐ 134 Sid Fernandez .10 .05 .01
☐ 135 Dwight Gooden .10 .05 .01
☐ 136 Keith Hernandez .10 .05 .01
☐ 137 Gregg Jefferies 4.00 1.80 .50
☐ 138 Howard Johnson .10 .05 .01
☐ 139 Terry Leach .06 .03 .01
☐ 140 Barry Lyons .06 .03 .01
☐ 141 Dave Magadan .10 .05 .01
☐ 142 Roger McDowell .06 .03 .01
☐ 143 Kevin McReynolds .10 .05 .01
☐ 144 Keith A. Miller .06 .03 .01
☐ 145 John Mitchell .06 .03 .01
☐ 146 Randy Myers .35 .16 .04
☐ 147 Bob Ojeda .06 .03 .01
☐ 148 Jesse Orosco .06 .03 .01
☐ 149 Rafael Santana .06 .03 .01
☐ 150 Doug Sisk .06 .03 .01
☐ 151 Darryl Strawberry .15 .07 .02
☐ 152 Tim Teufel .06 .03 .01
☐ 153 Gene Walter .06 .03 .01
☐ 154 Mookie Wilson .10 .05 .01
☐ 155 Jay Aldrich .06 .03 .01
☐ 156 Chris Bosio .10 .05 .01
☐ 157 Glenn Braggs .06 .03 .01
☐ 158 Greg Brock .06 .03 .01
☐ 159 Juan Castillo .06 .03 .01
☐ 160 Mark Clear .06 .03 .01
☐ 161 Cecil Cooper .10 .05 .01
☐ 162 Chuck Crim .06 .03 .01
☐ 163 Rob Deer .06 .03 .01
☐ 164 Mike Felder .06 .03 .01
☐ 165 Jim Gantner .06 .03 .01
☐ 166 Ted Higuera .06 .03 .01
☐ 167 Steve Kiefer .06 .03 .01
☐ 168 Rick Manning .06 .03 .01
☐ 169 Paul Molitor .40 .18 .05
☐ 170 Juan Nieves .06 .03 .01
☐ 171 Dan Plesac .06 .03 .01
☐ 172 Earnest Riles .06 .03 .01
☐ 173 Bill Schroeder .06 .03 .01
☐ 174 Steve Stanicek .06 .03 .01
☐ 175 B.J. Surhoff .10 .05 .01
☐ 176 Dale Sveum .06 .03 .01
☐ 177 Bill Wegman .06 .03 .01
☐ 178 Robin Yount .40 .18 .05
☐ 179 Hubie Brooks .06 .03 .01
☐ 180 Tim Burke .06 .03 .01
☐ 181 Casey Candaele .06 .03 .01
☐ 182 Mike Fitzgerald .06 .03 .01
☐ 183 Tom Foley .06 .03 .01
☐ 184 Andres Galarraga .50 .23 .06
☐ 185 Neal Heaton .06 .03 .01
☐ 186 Wallace Johnson .06 .03 .01
☐ 187 Vance Law .06 .03 .01
☐ 188 Dennis Martinez .10 .05 .01
☐ 189 Bob McClure .06 .03 .01
☐ 190 Andy McGaffigan .06 .03 .01
☐ 191 Reid Nichols .06 .03 .01
☐ 192 Pascual Perez .06 .03 .01
☐ 193 Tim Raines .15 .07 .02
☐ 194 Jeff Reed .06 .03 .01
☐ 195 Bob Sebra .06 .03 .01
☐ 196 Bryn Smith .06 .03 .01
☐ 197 Randy St.Claire .06 .03 .01
☐ 198 Tim Wallach .10 .05 .01
☐ 199 Mitch Webster .06 .03 .01
☐ 200 Herm Winningham .06 .03 .01
☐ 201 Floyd Youmans .06 .03 .01
☐ 202 Brad Arnsberg .06 .03 .01
☐ 203 Rick Cerone .06 .03 .01
☐ 204 Pat Clements .06 .03 .01
☐ 205 Henry Cotto .06 .03 .01
☐ 206 Mike Easler .06 .03 .01
☐ 207 Ron Guidry .10 .05 .01
☐ 208 Bill Gullickson .06 .03 .01
☐ 209 Rickey Henderson .40 .18 .05
☐ 210 Charles Hudson .06 .03 .01
☐ 211 Tommy John .15 .07 .02
☐ 212 Roberto Kelly 1.50 .65 .19
☐ 213 Ron Kittle .06 .03 .01
☐ 214 Don Mattingly .60 .25 .08
☐ 215 Bobby Meacham .06 .03 .01
☐ 216 Mike Pagliarulo .06 .03 .01
☐ 217 Dan Pasqua .06 .03 .01
☐ 218 Willie Randolph .10 .05 .01
☐ 219 Rick Rhoden .06 .03 .01
☐ 220 Dave Righetti .06 .03 .01
☐ 221 Jerry Royster .06 .03 .01
☐ 222 Tim Stoddard .06 .03 .01
☐ 223 Wayne Tolleson .06 .03 .01
☐ 224 Gary Ward .06 .03 .01
☐ 225 Claudell Washington .06 .03 .01
☐ 226 Dave Winfield .35 .16 .04
☐ 227 Buddy Bell .10 .05 .01

☐ 228 Tom Browning .06 .03 .01
☐ 229 Dave Concepcion .10 .05 .01
☐ 230 Kal Daniels .06 .03 .01
☐ 231 Eric Davis .10 .05 .01
☐ 232 Bo Diaz .06 .03 .01
☐ 233 Nick Esasky .06 .03 .01
(Has a dollar sign
before '87 SB totals)
☐ 234 John Franco .10 .05 .01
☐ 235 Guy Hoffman .06 .03 .01
☐ 236 Tom Hume .06 .03 .01
☐ 237 Tracy Jones .06 .03 .01
☐ 238 Bill Landrum .06 .03 .01
☐ 239 Barry Larkin .30 .14 .04
☐ 240 Terry McGriff .06 .03 .01
☐ 241 Rob Murphy .06 .03 .01
☐ 242 Ron Oester .06 .03 .01
☐ 243 Dave Parker .15 .07 .02
☐ 244 Pat Perry .06 .03 .01
☐ 245 Ted Power .06 .03 .01
☐ 246 Dennis Rasmussen .06 .03 .01
☐ 247 Ron Robinson .06 .03 .01
☐ 248 Kurt Stillwell .06 .03 .01
☐ 249 Jeff Treadway .06 .03 .01
☐ 250 Frank Williams .06 .03 .01
☐ 251 Steve Balboni .06 .03 .01
☐ 252 Bud Black .06 .03 .01
☐ 253 Thad Bosley .06 .03 .01
☐ 254 George Brett .75 .35 .09
☐ 255 John Davis .06 .03 .01
☐ 256 Steve Farr .06 .03 .01
☐ 257 Gene Garber .06 .03 .01
☐ 258 Jerry Don Gleaton .06 .03 .01
☐ 259 Mark Gubicza .06 .03 .01
☐ 260 Bo Jackson .75 .35 .09
☐ 261 Danny Jackson .06 .03 .01
☐ 262 Ross Jones .06 .03 .01
☐ 263 Charlie Leibrandt .06 .03 .01
☐ 264 Bill Pecota .06 .03 .01
☐ 265 Melido Perez .35 .16 .04
☐ 266 Jamie Quirk .06 .03 .01
☐ 267 Dan Quisenberry .10 .05 .01
☐ 268 Bret Saberhagen .15 .07 .02
☐ 269 Angel Salazar .06 .03 .01
☐ 270 Kevin Seitzer UER .10 .05 .01
(Wrong birth year)
☐ 271 Danny Tartabull .10 .05 .01
☐ 272 Gary Thurman .06 .03 .01
☐ 273 Frank White .10 .05 .01
☐ 274 Willie Wilson .06 .03 .01
☐ 275 Tony Bernazard .06 .03 .01
☐ 276 Jose Canseco 1.00 .45 .13
☐ 277 Mike Davis .06 .03 .01
☐ 278 Storm Davis .06 .03 .01
☐ 279 Dennis Eckersley .15 .07 .02
☐ 280 Alfredo Griffin .06 .03 .01
☐ 281 Rick Honeycutt .06 .03 .01
☐ 282 Jay Howell .06 .03 .01
☐ 283 Reggie Jackson .50 .23 .06
☐ 284 Dennis Lamp .06 .03 .01
☐ 285 Carney Lansford .10 .05 .01
☐ 286 Mark McGwire 1.00 .45 .13
☐ 287 Dwayne Murphy .06 .03 .01
☐ 288 Gene Nelson .06 .03 .01
☐ 289 Steve Ontiveros .06 .03 .01
☐ 290 Tony Phillips .10 .05 .01
☐ 291 Eric Plunk .06 .03 .01
☐ 292 Luis Polonia .60 .25 .08
☐ 293 Rick Rodriguez .06 .03 .01
☐ 294 Terry Steinbach .10 .05 .01
☐ 295 Dave Stewart .10 .05 .01
☐ 296 Curt Young .06 .03 .01
☐ 297 Luis Aguayo .06 .03 .01
☐ 298 Steve Bedrosian .06 .03 .01
☐ 299 Jeff Calhoun .06 .03 .01
☐ 300 Don Carman .06 .03 .01
☐ 301 Todd Frohwirth .06 .03 .01
☐ 302 Greg Gross .06 .03 .01
☐ 303 Kevin Gross .06 .03 .01
☐ 304 Von Hayes .06 .03 .01
☐ 305 Keith Hughes .06 .03 .01
☐ 306 Mike Jackson .15 .07 .02
☐ 307 Chris James .06 .03 .01
☐ 308 Steve Jeltz .06 .03 .01
☐ 309 Mike Maddux .06 .03 .01
☐ 310 Lance Parrish .10 .05 .01
☐ 311 Shane Rawley .06 .03 .01
☐ 312 Wally Ritchie .06 .03 .01
☐ 313 Bruce Ruffin .06 .03 .01
☐ 314 Juan Samuel .06 .03 .01
☐ 315 Mike Schmidt .40 .18 .05
☐ 316 Rick Schu .06 .03 .01
☐ 317 Jeff Stone .06 .03 .01
☐ 318 Kent Tekulve .06 .03 .01
☐ 319 Milt Thompson .06 .03 .01
☐ 320 Glenn Wilson .06 .03 .01
☐ 321 Rafael Belliard .06 .03 .01
☐ 322 Barry Bonds 2.00 .90 .25
☐ 323 Bobby Bonilla UER .40 .18 .05
(Wrong birth year)
☐ 324 Sid Bream .06 .03 .01
☐ 325 John Cangelosi .06 .03 .01
☐ 326 Mike Diaz .06 .03 .01
☐ 327 Doug Drabek .15 .07 .02
☐ 328 Mike Dunne .06 .03 .01
☐ 329 Brian Fisher .06 .03 .01
☐ 330 Brett Gideon .06 .03 .01
☐ 331 Terry Harper .06 .03 .01
☐ 332 Bob Kipper .06 .03 .01
☐ 333 Mike LaValliere .06 .03 .01
☐ 334 Jose Lind .25 .11 .03
☐ 335 Junior Ortiz .06 .03 .01
☐ 336 Vicente Palacios .06 .03 .01
☐ 337 Bob Patterson .06 .03 .01
☐ 338 Al Pedrique .06 .03 .01
☐ 339 R.J. Reynolds .06 .03 .01
☐ 340 John Smiley .35 .16 .04
☐ 341 Andy Van Slyke UER .15 .07 .02
(Wrong batting and
throwing listed)
☐ 342 Bob Walk .06 .03 .01
☐ 343 Marty Barrett .06 .03 .01
☐ 344 Todd Benzinger .15 .07 .02
☐ 345 Wade Boggs .50 .23 .06
☐ 346 Tom Bolton .06 .03 .01
☐ 347 Oil-Can Boyd .06 .03 .01
☐ 348 Ellis Burks 1.00 .45 .13
☐ 349 Roger Clemens .75 .35 .09
☐ 350 Steve Crawford .06 .03 .01
☐ 351 Dwight Evans .10 .05 .01
☐ 352 Wes Gardner .06 .03 .01
☐ 353 Rich Gedman .06 .03 .01
☐ 354 Mike Greenwell .40 .18 .05
☐ 355 Sam Horn .06 .03 .01
☐ 356 Bruce Hurst .06 .03 .01
☐ 357 John Marzano .06 .03 .01
☐ 358 Al Nipper .06 .03 .01
☐ 359 Spike Owen .06 .03 .01
☐ 360 Jody Reed .30 .14 .04
☐ 361 Jim Rice .15 .07 .02
☐ 362 Ed Romero .06 .03 .01
☐ 363 Kevin Romine .06 .03 .01
☐ 364 Joe Sambito .06 .03 .01
☐ 365 Calvin Schiraldi .06 .03 .01
☐ 366 Jeff Sellers .06 .03 .01
☐ 367 Bob Stanley .06 .03 .01

	No.	Player			
☐	368	Scott Bankhead	.06	.03	.01
☐	369	Phil Bradley	.06	.03	.01
☐	370	Scott Bradley	.06	.03	.01
☐	371	Mickey Brantley	.06	.03	.01
☐	372	Mike Campbell	.06	.03	.01
☐	373	Alvin Davis	.06	.03	.01
☐	374	Lee Guetterman	.06	.03	.01
☐	375	Dave Hengel	.06	.03	.01
☐	376	Mike Kingery	.06	.03	.01
☐	377	Mark Langston	.15	.07	.02
☐	378	Edgar Martinez	1.00	.45	.13
☐	379	Mike Moore	.06	.03	.01
☐	380	Mike Morgan	.06	.03	.01
☐	381	John Moses	.06	.03	.01
☐	382	Donell Nixon	.06	.03	.01
☐	383	Edwin Nunez	.06	.03	.01
☐	384	Ken Phelps	.06	.03	.01
☐	385	Jim Presley	.06	.03	.01
☐	386	Rey Quinones	.06	.03	.01
☐	387	Jerry Reed	.06	.03	.01
☐	388	Harold Reynolds	.06	.03	.01
☐	389	Dave Valle	.06	.03	.01
☐	390	Bill Wilkinson	.06	.03	.01
☐	391	Harold Baines	.10	.05	.01
☐	392	Floyd Bannister	.06	.03	.01
☐	393	Daryl Boston	.06	.03	.01
☐	394	Ivan Calderon	.10	.05	.01
☐	395	Jose DeLeon	.06	.03	.01
☐	396	Richard Dotson	.06	.03	.01
☐	397	Carlton Fisk	.15	.07	.02
☐	398	Ozzie Guillen	.10	.05	.01
☐	399	Ron Hassey	.06	.03	.01
☐	400	Donnie Hill	.06	.03	.01
☐	401	Bob James	.06	.03	.01
☐	402	Dave LaPoint	.06	.03	.01
☐	403	Bill Lindsey	.06	.03	.01
☐	404	Bill Long	.06	.03	.01
☐	405	Steve Lyons	.06	.03	.01
☐	406	Fred Manrique	.06	.03	.01
☐	407	Jack McDowell	2.00	.90	.25
☐	408	Gary Redus	.06	.03	.01
☐	409	Ray Searage	.06	.03	.01
☐	410	Bobby Thigpen	.06	.03	.01
☐	411	Greg Walker	.06	.03	.01
☐	412	Ken Williams	.06	.03	.01
☐	413	Jim Winn	.06	.03	.01
☐	414	Jody Davis	.06	.03	.01
☐	415	Andre Dawson	.40	.18	.05
☐	416	Brian Dayett	.06	.03	.01
☐	417	Bob Dernier	.06	.03	.01
☐	418	Frank DiPino	.06	.03	.01
☐	419	Shawon Dunston	.10	.05	.01
☐	420	Leon Durham	.06	.03	.01
☐	421	Les Lancaster	.06	.03	.01
☐	422	Ed Lynch	.06	.03	.01
☐	423	Greg Maddux	2.50	1.15	.30
☐	424	Dave Martinez	.06	.03	.01
☐	425A	Keith Moreland ERR (Photo actually Jody Davis)	1.50	.65	.19
☐	425B	Keith Moreland COR (Bat on shoulder)	.10	.05	.01
☐	426	Jamie Moyer	.06	.03	.01
☐	427	Jerry Mumphrey	.06	.03	.01
☐	428	Paul Noce	.06	.03	.01
☐	429	Rafael Palmeiro	1.50	.65	.19
☐	430	Wade Rowdon	.06	.03	.01
☐	431	Ryne Sandberg	1.00	.45	.13
☐	432	Scott Sanderson	.06	.03	.01
☐	433	Lee Smith	.15	.07	.02
☐	434	Jim Sundberg	.06	.03	.01
☐	435	Rick Sutcliffe	.10	.05	.01
☐	436	Manny Trillo	.06	.03	.01
☐	437	Juan Agosto	.06	.03	.01
☐	438	Larry Andersen	.06	.03	.01
☐	439	Alan Ashby	.06	.03	.01
☐	440	Kevin Bass	.06	.03	.01
☐	441	Ken Caminiti	1.25	.55	.16
☐	442	Rocky Childress	.06	.03	.01
☐	443	Jose Cruz	.06	.03	.01
☐	444	Danny Darwin	.06	.03	.01
☐	445	Glenn Davis	.06	.03	.01
☐	446	Jim Deshaies	.06	.03	.01
☐	447	Bill Doran	.06	.03	.01
☐	448	Ty Gainey	.06	.03	.01
☐	449	Billy Hatcher	.06	.03	.01
☐	450	Jeff Heathcock	.06	.03	.01
☐	451	Bob Knepper	.06	.03	.01
☐	452	Rob Mallicoat	.06	.03	.01
☐	453	Dave Meads	.06	.03	.01
☐	454	Craig Reynolds	.06	.03	.01
☐	455	Nolan Ryan	1.50	.65	.19
☐	456	Mike Scott	.06	.03	.01
☐	457	Dave Smith	.06	.03	.01
☐	458	Denny Walling	.06	.03	.01
☐	459	Robbie Wine	.06	.03	.01
☐	460	Gerald Young	.06	.03	.01
☐	461	Bob Brower	.06	.03	.01
☐	462A	Jerry Browne ERR (Photo actually Bob Brower, white player)	1.50	.65	.19
☐	462B	Jerry Browne COR (Black player)	.10	.05	.01
☐	463	Steve Buechele	.06	.03	.01
☐	464	Edwin Correa	.06	.03	.01
☐	465	Cecil Espy	.06	.03	.01
☐	466	Scott Fletcher	.06	.03	.01
☐	467	Jose Guzman	.10	.05	.01
☐	468	Greg Harris	.06	.03	.01
☐	469	Charlie Hough	.10	.05	.01
☐	470	Pete Incaviglia	.10	.05	.01
☐	471	Paul Kilgus	.06	.03	.01
☐	472	Mike Loynd	.06	.03	.01
☐	473	Oddibe McDowell	.06	.03	.01
☐	474	Dale Mohorcic	.06	.03	.01
☐	475	Pete O'Brien	.06	.03	.01
☐	476	Larry Parrish	.06	.03	.01
☐	477	Geno Petralli	.06	.03	.01
☐	478	Jeff Russell	.06	.03	.01
☐	479	Ruben Sierra	.75	.35	.09
☐	480	Mike Stanley	.10	.05	.01
☐	481	Curtis Wilkerson	.06	.03	.01
☐	482	Mitch Williams	.10	.05	.01
☐	483	Bobby Witt	.10	.05	.01
☐	484	Tony Armas	.06	.03	.01
☐	485	Bob Boone	.10	.05	.01
☐	486	Bill Buckner	.10	.05	.01
☐	487	DeWayne Buice	.06	.03	.01
☐	488	Brian Downing	.06	.03	.01
☐	489	Chuck Finley	.10	.05	.01
☐	490	Willie Fraser UER (Wrong bio stats, for George Hendrick)	.06	.03	.01
☐	491	Jack Howell	.06	.03	.01
☐	492	Ruppert Jones	.06	.03	.01
☐	493	Wally Joyner	.10	.05	.01
☐	494	Jack Lazorko	.06	.03	.01
☐	495	Gary Lucas	.06	.03	.01
☐	496	Kirk McCaskill	.06	.03	.01
☐	497	Mark McLemore	.06	.03	.01
☐	498	Darrell Miller	.06	.03	.01
☐	499	Greg Minton	.06	.03	.01
☐	500	Donnie Moore	.06	.03	.01
☐	501	Gus Polidor	.06	.03	.01
☐	502	Johnny Ray	.06	.03	.01

☐ 503 Mark Ryal .06 .03 .01
☐ 504 Dick Schofield .06 .03 .01
☐ 505 Don Sutton .15 .07 .02
☐ 506 Devon White .20 .09 .03
☐ 507 Mike Witt .06 .03 .01
☐ 508 Dave Anderson .06 .03 .01
☐ 509 Tim Belcher .10 .05 .01
☐ 510 Ralph Bryant .06 .03 .01
☐ 511 Tim Crews .10 .05 .01
☐ 512 Mike Devereaux .75 .35 .09
☐ 513 Mariano Duncan .06 .03 .01
☐ 514 Pedro Guerrero .10 .05 .01
☐ 515 Jeff Hamilton .06 .03 .01
☐ 516 Mickey Hatcher .06 .03 .01
☐ 517 Brad Havens .06 .03 .01
☐ 518 Orel Hershiser .10 .05 .01
☐ 519 Shawn Hillegas .06 .03 .01
☐ 520 Ken Howell .06 .03 .01
☐ 521 Tim Leary .06 .03 .01
☐ 522 Mike Marshall .06 .03 .01
☐ 523 Steve Sax .06 .03 .01
☐ 524 Mike Scioscia .06 .03 .01
☐ 525 Mike Sharperson .06 .03 .01
☐ 526 John Shelby .06 .03 .01
☐ 527 Franklin Stubbs .06 .03 .01
☐ 528 Fernando Valenzuela .06 .03 .01
☐ 529 Bob Welch .10 .05 .01
☐ 530 Matt Young .06 .03 .01
☐ 531 Jim Acker .06 .03 .01
☐ 532 Paul Assenmacher .06 .03 .01
☐ 533 Jeff Blauser 1.00 .45 .13
☐ 534 Joe Boever .06 .03 .01
☐ 535 Martin Clary .06 .03 .01
☐ 536 Kevin Coffman .06 .03 .01
☐ 537 Jeff Dedmon .06 .03 .01
☐ 538 Ron Gant 2.00 .90 .25
☐ 539 Tom Glavine 3.50 1.55 .45
☐ 540 Ken Griffey .10 .05 .01
☐ 541 Albert Hall .06 .03 .01
☐ 542 Glenn Hubbard .06 .03 .01
☐ 543 Dion James .06 .03 .01
☐ 544 Dale Murphy .15 .07 .02
☐ 545 Ken Oberkfell .06 .03 .01
☐ 546 David Palmer .06 .03 .01
☐ 547 Gerald Perry .06 .03 .01
☐ 548 Charlie Puleo .06 .03 .01
☐ 549 Ted Simmons .10 .05 .01
☐ 550 Zane Smith .06 .03 .01
☐ 551 Andres Thomas .06 .03 .01
☐ 552 Ozzie Virgil .06 .03 .01
☐ 553 Don Aase .06 .03 .01
☐ 554 Jeff Ballard .06 .03 .01
☐ 555 Eric Bell .06 .03 .01
☐ 556 Mike Boddicker .06 .03 .01
☐ 557 Ken Dixon .06 .03 .01
☐ 558 Jim Dwyer .06 .03 .01
☐ 559 Ken Gerhart .06 .03 .01
☐ 560 Rene Gonzales .06 .03 .01
☐ 561 Mike Griffin .06 .03 .01
☐ 562 John Habyan UER .06 .03 .01
(Misspelled Hayban on both sides of card)
☐ 563 Terry Kennedy .06 .03 .01
☐ 564 Ray Knight .10 .05 .01
☐ 565 Lee Lacy .06 .03 .01
☐ 566 Fred Lynn .10 .05 .01
☐ 567 Eddie Murray .35 .16 .04
☐ 568 Tom Niedenfuer .06 .03 .01
☐ 569 Bill Ripken .06 .03 .01
☐ 570 Cal Ripken 1.25 .55 .16
☐ 571 Dave Schmidt .06 .03 .01
☐ 572 Larry Sheets .06 .03 .01
☐ 573 Pete Stanicek .06 .03 .01
☐ 574 Mark Williamson .06 .03 .01
☐ 575 Mike Young .06 .03 .01
☐ 576 Shawn Abner .06 .03 .01
☐ 577 Greg Booker .06 .03 .01
☐ 578 Chris Brown .06 .03 .01
☐ 579 Keith Comstock .06 .03 .01
☐ 580 Joey Cora .20 .09 .03
☐ 581 Mark Davis .06 .03 .01
☐ 582 Tim Flannery .10 .05 .01
(With surfboard)
☐ 583 Goose Gossage .15 .07 .02
☐ 584 Mark Grant .06 .03 .01
☐ 585 Tony Gwynn .60 .25 .08
☐ 586 Andy Hawkins .06 .03 .01
☐ 587 Stan Jefferson .06 .03 .01
☐ 588 Jimmy Jones .06 .03 .01
☐ 589 John Kruk .35 .16 .04
☐ 590 Shane Mack .10 .05 .01
☐ 591 Carmelo Martinez .06 .03 .01
☐ 592 Lance McCullers UER .06 .03 .01
(6'11" tall)
☐ 593 Eric Nolte .06 .03 .01
☐ 594 Randy Ready .06 .03 .01
☐ 595 Luis Salazar .06 .03 .01
☐ 596 Benito Santiago .10 .05 .01
☐ 597 Eric Show .06 .03 .01
☐ 598 Garry Templeton .06 .03 .01
☐ 599 Ed Whitson .06 .03 .01
☐ 600 Scott Bailes .06 .03 .01
☐ 601 Chris Bando .06 .03 .01
☐ 602 Jay Bell 1.00 .45 .13
☐ 603 Brett Butler .10 .05 .01
☐ 604 Tom Candiotti .06 .03 .01
☐ 605 Joe Carter .75 .35 .09
☐ 606 Carmen Castillo .06 .03 .01
☐ 607 Brian Dorsett .06 .03 .01
☐ 608 John Farrell .06 .03 .01
☐ 609 Julio Franco .10 .05 .01
☐ 610 Mel Hall .06 .03 .01
☐ 611 Tommy Hinzo .06 .03 .01
☐ 612 Brook Jacoby .06 .03 .01
☐ 613 Doug Jones .50 .23 .06
☐ 614 Ken Schrom .06 .03 .01
☐ 615 Cory Snyder .06 .03 .01
☐ 616 Sammy Stewart .06 .03 .01
☐ 617 Greg Swindell .10 .05 .01
☐ 618 Pat Tabler .06 .03 .01
☐ 619 Ed VandeBerg .06 .03 .01
☐ 620 Eddie Williams .30 .14 .04
☐ 621 Rich Yett .06 .03 .01
☐ 622 Slugging Sophomores .10 .05 .01
Wally Joyner
Cory Snyder
☐ 623 Dominican Dynamite .06 .03 .01
George Bell
Pedro Guerrero
☐ 624 Oakland's Power Team .60 .25 .08
Mark McGwire
Jose Canseco
☐ 625 Classic Relief .06 .03 .01
Dave Righetti
Dan Plesac
☐ 626 All Star Righties .10 .05 .01
Bret Saberhagen
Mike Witt
Jack Morris
☐ 627 Game Closers .06 .03 .01
John Franco
Steve Bedrosian
☐ 628 Masters/Double Play .40 .18 .05
Ozzie Smith
Ryne Sandberg
☐ 629 Rookie Record Setter .35 .16 .04

Mark McGwire			
☐ 630 Changing the Guard	.25	.11	.03
Mike Greenwell			
Ellis Burks			
Todd Benzinger			
☐ 631 NL Batting Champs	.25	.11	.03
Tony Gwynn			
Tim Raines			
☐ 632 Pitching Magic	.06	.03	.01
Mike Scott			
Orel Hershiser			
☐ 633 Big Bats at First	.20	.09	.03
Pat Tabler			
Mark McGwire			
☐ 634 Hitting King/Thief	.20	.09	.03
Tony Gwynn			
Vince Coleman			
☐ 635 Slugging Shortstops	.30	.14	.04
Tony Fernandez			
Cal Ripken			
Alan Trammell			
☐ 636 Tried/True Sluggers	.25	.11	.03
Mike Schmidt			
Gary Carter			
☐ 637 Crunch Time	.06	.03	.01
Darryl Strawberry			
Eric Davis			
☐ 638 AL All-Stars	.25	.11	.03
Matt Nokes			
Kirby Puckett			
☐ 639 NL All-Stars	.10	.05	.01
Keith Hernandez			
Dale Murphy			
☐ 640 The O's Brothers	.50	.23	.06
Billy Ripken			
Cal Ripken			
☐ 641 Mark Grace and	2.50	1.15	.30
Darrin Jackson			
☐ 642 Damon Berryhill and ..	1.00	.45	.13
Jeff Montgomery			
☐ 643 Felix Fermin and	.08	.04	.01
Jesse Reid			
☐ 644 Greg Myers and	.08	.04	.01
Greg Tabor			
☐ 645 Joey Meyer and	.08	.04	.01
Jim Eppard			
☐ 646 Adam Peterson and	.08	.04	.01
Randy Velarde			
☐ 647 Pete Smith and	.35	.16	.04
Chris Gwynn			
☐ 648 Tom Newell and	.08	.04	.01
Greg Jelks			
☐ 649 Mario Diaz and	.08	.04	.01
Clay Parker			
☐ 650 Jack Savage and	.08	.04	.01
Todd Simmons			
☐ 651 John Burkett and	1.50	.65	.19
Kirt Manwaring			
☐ 652 Dave Otto and	.40	.18	.05
Walt Weiss			
☐ 653 Jeff King and	.60	.25	.08
Randell Byers			
☐ 654 CL: Twins/Cards	.06	.03	.01
Tigers/Giants UER			
(90 Bob Melvin,			
91 Eddie Milner)			
☐ 655 CL: Blue Jays/Mets	.06	.03	.01
Brewers/Expos UER			
(Mets listed before			
Blue Jays on card)			
☐ 656 CL: Yankees/Reds	.06	.03	.01
Royals/A's			
☐ 657 CL: Phillies/Pirates	.06	.03	.01
Red Sox/Mariners			
☐ 658 CL: White Sox/Cubs	.06	.03	.01
Astros/Rangers			
☐ 659 CL: Angels/Dodgers	.06	.03	.01
Braves/Orioles			
☐ 660 CL: Padres/Indians	.06	.03	.01
Rookies/Specials			

1988 Fleer All-Stars

The cards in this 12-card set measure the standard, 2 1/2" by 3 1/2". These cards were inserted (randomly) in wax and cello packs of the 1988 Fleer regular issue set. The cards show the player silhouetted against a light green background with dark green stripes. The player's name, team, and position are printed in yellow at the bottom of the obverse. The card backs are done predominantly in green, white, and black. Cards are numbered on the back. These 12 cards are considered a separate set in their own right and are not typically included in a complete set of the regular issue 1988 Fleer cards. The players are the "best" at each position, three pitchers, eight position players, and a designated hitter.

	MINT	EXC	G-VG
COMPLETE SET (12)	8.00	3.60	1.00
COMMON CARD (1-12)	.25	.11	.03
☐ 1 Matt Nokes	.25	.11	.03
☐ 2 Tom Henke	.25	.11	.03
☐ 3 Ted Higuera	.25	.11	.03
☐ 4 Roger Clemens	4.00	1.80	.50
☐ 5 George Bell	.40	.18	.05
☐ 6 Andre Dawson	1.00	.45	.13
☐ 7 Eric Davis	.40	.18	.05
☐ 8 Wade Boggs	1.50	.65	.19
☐ 9 Alan Trammell	.40	.18	.05
☐ 10 Juan Samuel	.25	.11	.03
☐ 11 Jack Clark	.25	.11	.03
☐ 12 Paul Molitor	1.50	.65	.19

1988 Fleer Headliners

This six-card set was distributed as a special insert in rack packs. The obverse features the player photo superimposed on a

gray newsprint background. The cards measure 2 1/2" by 3 1/2". The cards are printed in red, black, and white on the back describing why that particular player made headlines the previous season. The cards are numbered on the back.

	MINT	EXC	G-VG
COMPLETE SET (6)	5.00	2.30	.60
COMMON CARD (1-6)	.60	.25	.08

	MINT	EXC	G-VG
☐ 1 Don Mattingly	2.50	1.15	.30
☐ 2 Mark McGwire	1.00	.45	.13
☐ 3 Jack Morris	.60	.25	.08
☐ 4 Darryl Strawberry	.60	.25	.08
☐ 5 Dwight Gooden	.60	.25	.08
☐ 6 Tim Raines	.60	.25	.08

1988 Fleer Update

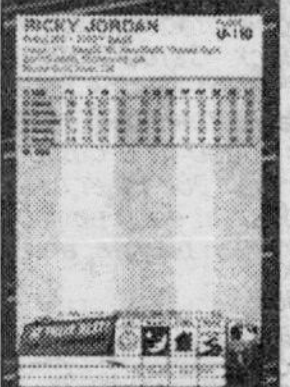

This 132-card set was distributed by Fleer to dealers as a complete set in a custom box. In addition to the complete set of 132 cards, the box also contains 25 Team Logo stickers.The card fronts look very similar to the 1988 Fleer regular issue. The cards are numbered (with a U prefix) alphabetically according to player's last name. Cards measure the standard size, 2 1/2" by 3 1/2". This was the first Fleer Update set to adopt the Fleer "alphabetical within team" numbering system. The key (extended) Rookie Cards in this set are Roberto Alomar, Craig Biggio, Bryan Harvey, Chris Sabo, and John Smoltz. Fleer also produced a "limited" edition version of this set with glossy coating and packaged in a "tin." However, this tin set was apparently not limited enough (estimated between 40,000 and 60,000 1988 Update tin sets produced by Fleer), since the values of the "tin" glossy cards are now only double the values of the respective cards in the regular set.

	MINT	EXC	G-VG
COMPLETE FACT.SET (132)	15.00	6.75	1.90
COMMON CARD (1-132)	.05	.02	.01

	MINT	EXC	G-VG
☐ 1 Jose Bautista	.05	.02	.01
☐ 2 Joe Orsulak	.05	.02	.01
☐ 3 Doug Sisk	.05	.02	.01
☐ 4 Craig Worthington	.05	.02	.01
☐ 5 Mike Boddicker	.05	.02	.01
☐ 6 Rick Cerone	.05	.02	.01
☐ 7 Larry Parrish	.05	.02	.01
☐ 8 Lee Smith	.15	.07	.02
☐ 9 Mike Smithson	.05	.02	.01
☐ 10 John Trautwein	.05	.02	.01
☐ 11 Sherman Corbett	.05	.02	.01
☐ 12 Chili Davis	.08	.04	.01
☐ 13 Jim Eppard	.05	.02	.01
☐ 14 Bryan Harvey	1.00	.45	.13
☐ 15 John Davis	.05	.02	.01
☐ 16 Dave Gallagher	.05	.02	.01
☐ 17 Ricky Horton	.05	.02	.01
☐ 18 Dan Pasqua	.05	.02	.01
☐ 19 Melido Perez	.25	.11	.03
☐ 20 Jose Segura	.05	.02	.01
☐ 21 Andy Allanson	.05	.02	.01
☐ 22 Jon Perlman	.05	.02	.01
☐ 23 Domingo Ramos	.05	.02	.01
☐ 24 Rick Rodriguez	.05	.02	.01
☐ 25 Willie Upshaw	.05	.02	.01
☐ 26 Paul Gibson	.05	.02	.01
☐ 27 Don Heinkel	.05	.02	.01
☐ 28 Ray Knight	.08	.04	.01
☐ 29 Gary Pettis	.05	.02	.01
☐ 30 Luis Salazar	.05	.02	.01
☐ 31 Mike Macfarlane	.50	.23	.06
☐ 32 Jeff Montgomery	.50	.23	.06
☐ 33 Ted Power	.05	.02	.01
☐ 34 Israel Sanchez	.05	.02	.01
☐ 35 Kurt Stillwell	.05	.02	.01
☐ 36 Pat Tabler	.05	.02	.01
☐ 37 Don August	.05	.02	.01
☐ 38 Darryl Hamilton	.50	.23	.06
☐ 39 Jeff Leonard	.05	.02	.01
☐ 40 Joey Meyer	.05	.02	.01
☐ 41 Allan Anderson	.05	.02	.01
☐ 42 Brian Harper	.08	.04	.01
☐ 43 Tom Herr	.05	.02	.01
☐ 44 Charlie Lea	.05	.02	.01
☐ 45 John Moses (Listed as Hohn on checklist card)	.05	.02	.01
☐ 46 John Candelaria	.05	.02	.01
☐ 47 Jack Clark	.08	.04	.01
☐ 48 Richard Dotson	.05	.02	.01
☐ 49 Al Leiter	.10	.05	.01
☐ 50 Rafael Santana	.05	.02	.01
☐ 51 Don Slaught	.05	.02	.01
☐ 52 Todd Burns	.05	.02	.01
☐ 53 Dave Henderson	.08	.04	.01
☐ 54 Doug Jennings	.05	.02	.01
☐ 55 Dave Parker	.10	.05	.01
☐ 56 Walt Weiss	.30	.14	.04
☐ 57 Bob Welch	.08	.04	.01
☐ 58 Henry Cotto	.05	.02	.01
☐ 59 Mario Diaz UER (Listed as Marion on card front)	.05	.02	.01
☐ 60 Mike Jackson	.05	.02	.01
☐ 61 Bill Swift	.08	.04	.01
☐ 62 Jose Cecena	.05	.02	.01
☐ 63 Ray Hayward	.05	.02	.01
☐ 64 Jim Steels UER (Listed as Jim Steele on card back)	.05	.02	.01

☐ 65 Pat Borders	.50	.23	.06
☐ 66 Sil Campusano	.05	.02	.01
☐ 67 Mike Flanagan	.05	.02	.01
☐ 68 Todd Stottlemyre	.30	.14	.04
☐ 69 David Wells	.25	.11	.03
☐ 70 Jose Alvarez	.05	.02	.01
☐ 71 Paul Runge	.05	.02	.01
☐ 72 Cesar Jimenez (Card was intended for German Jiminez, it's his photo)	.05	.02	.01
☐ 73 Pete Smith	.25	.11	.03
☐ 74 John Smoltz	2.00	.90	.25
☐ 75 Damon Berryhill	.15	.07	.02
☐ 76 Goose Gossage	.10	.05	.01
☐ 77 Mark Grace	2.00	.90	.25
☐ 78 Darrin Jackson	.20	.09	.03
☐ 79 Vance Law	.05	.02	.01
☐ 80 Jeff Pico	.05	.02	.01
☐ 81 Gary Varsho	.05	.02	.01
☐ 82 Tim Birtsas	.05	.02	.01
☐ 83 Rob Dibble	.40	.18	.05
☐ 84 Danny Jackson	.05	.02	.01
☐ 85 Paul O'Neill	.50	.23	.06
☐ 86 Jose Rijo	.10	.05	.01
☐ 87 Chris Sabo	.50	.23	.06
☐ 88 John Fishel	.05	.02	.01
☐ 89 Craig Biggio	2.00	.90	.25
☐ 90 Terry Puhl	.05	.02	.01
☐ 91 Rafael Ramirez	.05	.02	.01
☐ 92 Louie Meadows	.05	.02	.01
☐ 93 Kirk Gibson	.10	.05	.01
☐ 94 Alfredo Griffin	.05	.02	.01
☐ 95 Jay Howell	.05	.02	.01
☐ 96 Jesse Orosco	.05	.02	.01
☐ 97 Alejandro Pena	.05	.02	.01
☐ 98 Tracy Woodson	.05	.02	.01
☐ 99 John Dopson	.05	.02	.01
☐ 100 Brian Holman	.05	.02	.01
☐ 101 Rex Hudler	.05	.02	.01
☐ 102 Jeff Parrett	.05	.02	.01
☐ 103 Nelson Santovenia	.05	.02	.01
☐ 104 Kevin Elster	.05	.02	.01
☐ 105 Jeff Innis	.05	.02	.01
☐ 106 Mackey Sasser	.05	.02	.01
☐ 107 Phil Bradley	.05	.02	.01
☐ 108 Danny Clay	.05	.02	.01
☐ 109 Greg Harris	.05	.02	.01
☐ 110 Ricky Jordan	.25	.11	.03
☐ 111 David Palmer	.05	.02	.01
☐ 112 Jim Gott	.05	.02	.01
☐ 113 Tommy Gregg UER (Photo of Randy Milligan)	.05	.02	.01
☐ 114 Barry Jones	.05	.02	.01
☐ 115 Randy Milligan	.25	.11	.03
☐ 116 Luis Alicea	.05	.02	.01
☐ 117 Tom Brunansky	.05	.02	.01
☐ 118 John Costello	.05	.02	.01
☐ 119 Jose DeLeon	.05	.02	.01
☐ 120 Bob Horner	.05	.02	.01
☐ 121 Scott Terry	.05	.02	.01
☐ 122 Roberto Alomar	5.00	2.30	.60
☐ 123 Dave Leiper	.05	.02	.01
☐ 124 Keith Moreland	.05	.02	.01
☐ 125 Mark Parent	.05	.02	.01
☐ 126 Dennis Rasmussen	.05	.02	.01
☐ 127 Randy Bockus	.05	.02	.01
☐ 128 Brett Butler	.08	.04	.01
☐ 129 Donell Nixon	.05	.02	.01
☐ 130 Earnest Riles	.05	.02	.01
☐ 131 Roger Samuels	.05	.02	.01
☐ 132 Checklist U1-U132	.05	.02	.01

1989 Fleer

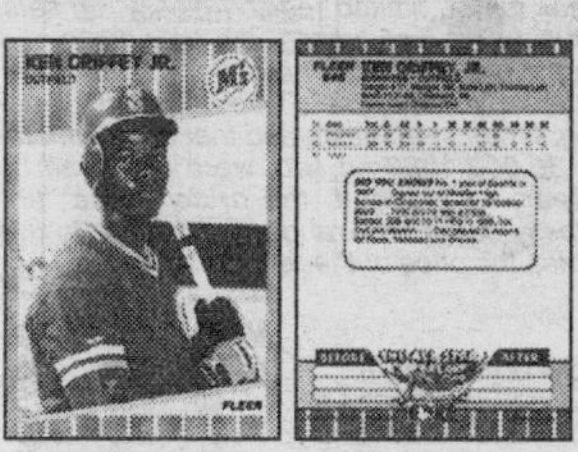

This 660-card set features a distinctive gray border background with white and yellow trim. The backs are printed in gray, black, and yellow on white card stock. The bottom of the card back shows an innovative breakdown of the player's demonstrated ability with respect to his performance before and after the All-Star break. Cards are numbered on the back and are again the standard 2 1/2" by 3 1/2". Cards are again organized numerically by teams and alphabetically within teams: Oakland A's (1-26), New York Mets (27-52), Los Angeles Dodgers (53-77), Boston Red Sox (78-101), Minnesota Twins (102-127), Detroit Tigers (128-151), Cincinnati Reds (152-175), Milwaukee Brewers (176-200), Pittsburgh Pirates (201-224), Toronto Blue Jays (225-248), New York Yankees (249-274), Kansas City Royals (275-298), San Diego Padres (299-322), San Francisco Giants (323-347), Houston Astros (348-370), Montreal Expos (371-395), Cleveland Indians (396-417), Chicago Cubs (418-442), St. Louis Cardinals (443-466), California Angels (467-490), Chicago White Sox (491-513), Texas Rangers (514-537), Seattle Mariners (538-561), Philadelphia Phillies (562-584), Atlanta Braves (585-605), and Baltimore Orioles (606-627). However, pairs 148/149, 153/154, 272/273, 283/284, and 367/368 were apparently mis-alphabetized by Fleer. The last 33 cards in the set consist of Specials (628-639), Rookie Pairs (640-653), and checklists (654-660). Due to the early beginning of production of this set, it seemed Fleer "presumed" that the A's would win the World Series, since they are listed as the first team in the numerical order; in fact, Fleer had the Mets over the underdog (but eventual World Champion) Dodgers as well. Fleer later reported that they merely arranged the teams according to team record due to the early printing date. Approximately half of the California Angels players have white rather than yellow halos. Certain Oakland A's player cards have red instead of green lines for front photo borders. Checklist cards are available either with or without positions listed for each player. Rookie Cards in this set include Sandy Alomar Jr., Brady Anderson, Dante Bichette, Craig Biggio, Ken Griffey Jr., Charlie Hayes, Ken Hill, Randy Johnson, Felix Jose, Ramon Martinez, Hal

Morris, Gary Sheffield, and John Smoltz. Fleer also produced the last of their three-year run of "limited" edition glossy, tin sets. This tin set was limited, but only compared to the previous year, as collector and dealer interest in the tin sets was apparently waning. It has been estimated that approximately 30,000 1989 tin sets were produced by Fleer; as a result, the price of the "tin" glossy cards now ranges from three to five times the price of the regular set cards.

	MINT	EXC	G-VG
COMPLETE SET (660)	14.00	6.25	1.75
COMPLETE RETAIL SET (660)	14.00	6.25	1.75
COMPLETE HOBBY SET (672)	16.00	7.25	2.00
COMMON CARD (1-660)	.05	.02	.01

	MINT	EXC	G-VG
☐ 1 Don Baylor	.15	.07	.02
☐ 2 Lance Blankenship	.05	.02	.01
☐ 3 Todd Burns UER (Wrong birthdate; before/after All-Star stats missing)	.05	.02	.01
☐ 4 Greg Cadaret UER (All-Star Break stats show 3 losses, should be 2)	.05	.02	.01
☐ 5 Jose Canseco	.30	.14	.04
☐ 6 Storm Davis	.05	.02	.01
☐ 7 Dennis Eckersley	.15	.07	.02
☐ 8 Mike Gallego	.05	.02	.01
☐ 9 Ron Hassey	.05	.02	.01
☐ 10 Dave Henderson	.05	.02	.01
☐ 11 Rick Honeycutt	.05	.02	.01
☐ 12 Glenn Hubbard	.05	.02	.01
☐ 13 Stan Javier	.05	.02	.01
☐ 14 Doug Jennings	.05	.02	.01
☐ 15 Felix Jose	.25	.11	.03
☐ 16 Carney Lansford	.10	.05	.01
☐ 17 Mark McGwire	.15	.07	.02
☐ 18 Gene Nelson	.05	.02	.01
☐ 19 Dave Parker	.15	.07	.02
☐ 20 Eric Plunk	.05	.02	.01
☐ 21 Luis Polonia	.10	.05	.01
☐ 22 Terry Steinbach	.10	.05	.01
☐ 23 Dave Stewart	.10	.05	.01
☐ 24 Walt Weiss	.05	.02	.01
☐ 25 Bob Welch	.10	.05	.01
☐ 26 Curt Young	.05	.02	.01
☐ 27 Rick Aguilera	.10	.05	.01
☐ 28 Wally Backman	.05	.02	.01
☐ 29 Mark Carreon UER (After All-Star Break batting 7.14)	.05	.02	.01
☐ 30 Gary Carter	.15	.07	.02
☐ 31 David Cone	.20	.09	.03
☐ 32 Ron Darling	.10	.05	.01
☐ 33 Len Dykstra	.15	.07	.02
☐ 34 Kevin Elster	.05	.02	.01
☐ 35 Sid Fernandez	.10	.05	.01
☐ 36 Dwight Gooden	.10	.05	.01
☐ 37 Keith Hernandez	.10	.05	.01
☐ 38 Gregg Jefferies	.35	.16	.04
☐ 39 Howard Johnson	.10	.05	.01
☐ 40 Terry Leach	.05	.02	.01
☐ 41 Dave Magadan UER (Bio says 15 doubles, should be 13)	.05	.02	.01
☐ 42 Bob McClure	.05	.02	.01
☐ 43 Roger McDowell UER (Led Mets with 58, should be 62)	.05	.02	.01
☐ 44 Kevin McReynolds	.10	.05	.01
☐ 45 Keith A. Miller	.05	.02	.01
☐ 46 Randy Myers	.10	.05	.01
☐ 47 Bob Ojeda	.05	.02	.01
☐ 48 Mackey Sasser	.05	.02	.01
☐ 49 Darryl Strawberry	.15	.07	.02
☐ 50 Tim Teufel	.05	.02	.01
☐ 51 Dave West	.10	.05	.01
☐ 52 Mookie Wilson	.10	.05	.01
☐ 53 Dave Anderson	.05	.02	.01
☐ 54 Tim Belcher	.05	.02	.01
☐ 55 Mike Davis	.05	.02	.01
☐ 56 Mike Devereaux	.10	.05	.01
☐ 57 Kirk Gibson	.10	.05	.01
☐ 58 Alfredo Griffin	.05	.02	.01
☐ 59 Chris Gwynn	.05	.02	.01
☐ 60 Jeff Hamilton	.05	.02	.01
☐ 61A Danny Heep (Home: Lake Hills)	.40	.18	.05
☐ 61B Danny Heep (Home: San Antonio)	.10	.05	.01
☐ 62 Orel Hershiser	.10	.05	.01
☐ 63 Brian Holton	.05	.02	.01
☐ 64 Jay Howell	.05	.02	.01
☐ 65 Tim Leary	.05	.02	.01
☐ 66 Mike Marshall	.05	.02	.01
☐ 67 Ramon Martinez	.50	.23	.06
☐ 68 Jesse Orosco	.05	.02	.01
☐ 69 Alejandro Pena	.05	.02	.01
☐ 70 Steve Sax	.05	.02	.01
☐ 71 Mike Scioscia	.05	.02	.01
☐ 72 Mike Sharperson	.05	.02	.01
☐ 73 John Shelby	.05	.02	.01
☐ 74 Franklin Stubbs	.05	.02	.01
☐ 75 John Tudor	.05	.02	.01
☐ 76 Fernando Valenzuela	.05	.02	.01
☐ 77 Tracy Woodson	.05	.02	.01
☐ 78 Marty Barrett	.05	.02	.01
☐ 79 Todd Benzinger	.05	.02	.01
☐ 80 Mike Boddicker UER (Rochester in '76, should be '78)	.05	.02	.01
☐ 81 Wade Boggs	.20	.09	.03
☐ 82 Oil Can Boyd	.05	.02	.01
☐ 83 Ellis Burks	.10	.05	.01
☐ 84 Rick Cerone	.05	.02	.01
☐ 85 Roger Clemens	.35	.16	.04
☐ 86 Steve Curry	.05	.02	.01
☐ 87 Dwight Evans	.10	.05	.01
☐ 88 Wes Gardner	.05	.02	.01
☐ 89 Rich Gedman	.05	.02	.01
☐ 90 Mike Greenwell	.10	.05	.01
☐ 91 Bruce Hurst	.05	.02	.01
☐ 92 Dennis Lamp	.05	.02	.01
☐ 93 Spike Owen	.05	.02	.01
☐ 94 Larry Parrish UER (Before All-Star Break batting 1.90)	.05	.02	.01
☐ 95 Carlos Quintana	.05	.02	.01
☐ 96 Jody Reed	.05	.02	.01
☐ 97 Jim Rice	.15	.07	.02
☐ 98A Kevin Romine ERR (Photo actually Randy Kutcher batting)	.40	.18	.05
☐ 98B Kevin Romine COR (Arms folded)	.10	.05	.01
☐ 99 Lee Smith	.15	.07	.02
☐ 100 Mike Smithson	.05	.02	.01
☐ 101 Bob Stanley	.05	.02	.01
☐ 102 Allan Anderson	.05	.02	.01
☐ 103 Keith Atherton	.05	.02	.01
☐ 104 Juan Berenguer	.05	.02	.01
☐ 105 Bert Blyleven	.15	.07	.02

☐ 106 Eric Bullock UER .... .05 .02 .01
(Bats/Throws Right, should be Left)
☐ 107 Randy Bush .... .05 .02 .01
☐ 108 John Christensen .... .05 .02 .01
☐ 109 Mark Davidson .... .05 .02 .01
☐ 110 Gary Gaetti .... .05 .02 .01
☐ 111 Greg Gagne .... .05 .02 .01
☐ 112 Dan Gladden .... .05 .02 .01
☐ 113 German Gonzalez .... .05 .02 .01
☐ 114 Brian Harper .... .10 .05 .01
☐ 115 Tom Herr .... .05 .02 .01
☐ 116 Kent Hrbek .... .10 .05 .01
☐ 117 Gene Larkin .... .05 .02 .01
☐ 118 Tim Laudner .... .05 .02 .01
☐ 119 Charlie Lea .... .05 .02 .01
☐ 120 Steve Lombardozzi .... .05 .02 .01
☐ 121A John Moses .... .40 .18 .05
(Home: Tempe)
☐ 121B John Moses .... .10 .05 .01
(Home: Phoenix)
☐ 122 Al Newman .... .05 .02 .01
☐ 123 Mark Portugal .... .10 .05 .01
☐ 124 Kirby Puckett .... .50 .23 .06
☐ 125 Jeff Reardon .... .15 .07 .02
☐ 126 Fred Toliver .... .05 .02 .01
☐ 127 Frank Viola .... .10 .05 .01
☐ 128 Doyle Alexander .... .05 .02 .01
☐ 129 Dave Bergman .... .05 .02 .01
☐ 130A Tom Brookens ERR .... .75 .35 .09
(Mike Heath back)
☐ 130B Tom Brookens COR .... .10 .05 .01
☐ 131 Paul Gibson .... .05 .02 .01
☐ 132A Mike Heath ERR .... .75 .35 .09
(Tom Brookens back)
☐ 132B Mike Heath COR .... .10 .05 .01
☐ 133 Don Heinkel .... .05 .02 .01
☐ 134 Mike Henneman .... .10 .05 .01
☐ 135 Guillermo Hernandez .... .05 .02 .01
☐ 136 Eric King .... .05 .02 .01
☐ 137 Chet Lemon .... .05 .02 .01
☐ 138 Fred Lynn UER .... .10 .05 .01
('74, '75 stats missing)
☐ 139 Jack Morris .... .15 .07 .02
☐ 140 Matt Nokes .... .05 .02 .01
☐ 141 Gary Pettis .... .05 .02 .01
☐ 142 Ted Power .... .05 .02 .01
☐ 143 Jeff M. Robinson .... .05 .02 .01
☐ 144 Luis Salazar .... .05 .02 .01
☐ 145 Steve Searcy .... .05 .02 .01
☐ 146 Pat Sheridan .... .05 .02 .01
☐ 147 Frank Tanana .... .05 .02 .01
☐ 148 Alan Trammell .... .15 .07 .02
☐ 149 Walt Terrell .... .05 .02 .01
☐ 150 Jim Walewander .... .05 .02 .01
☐ 151 Lou Whitaker .... .15 .07 .02
☐ 152 Tim Birtsas .... .05 .02 .01
☐ 153 Tom Browning .... .05 .02 .01
☐ 154 Keith Brown .... .05 .02 .01
☐ 155 Norm Charlton .... .15 .07 .02
☐ 156 Dave Concepcion .... .10 .05 .01
☐ 157 Kal Daniels .... .05 .02 .01
☐ 158 Eric Davis .... .10 .05 .01
☐ 159 Bo Diaz .... .05 .02 .01
☐ 160 Rob Dibble .... .20 .09 .03
☐ 161 Nick Esasky .... .05 .02 .01
☐ 162 John Franco .... .10 .05 .01
☐ 163 Danny Jackson .... .05 .02 .01
☐ 164 Barry Larkin .... .15 .07 .02
☐ 165 Rob Murphy .... .05 .02 .01
☐ 166 Paul O'Neill .... .15 .07 .02
☐ 167 Jeff Reed .... .05 .02 .01
☐ 168 Jose Rijo .... .15 .07 .02
☐ 169 Ron Robinson .... .05 .02 .01
☐ 170 Chris Sabo .... .25 .11 .03
☐ 171 Candy Sierra .... .05 .02 .01
☐ 172 Van Snider .... .05 .02 .01
☐ 173A Jeff Treadway 9.00 4.00 1.15
(Target registration mark above head on front in light blue)
☐ 173B Jeff Treadway .... .05 .02 .01
(No target on front)
☐ 174 Frank Williams .... .05 .02 .01
(After All-Star Break stats are jumbled)
☐ 175 Herm Winningham .... .05 .02 .01
☐ 176 Jim Adduci .... .05 .02 .01
☐ 177 Don August .... .05 .02 .01
☐ 178 Mike Birkbeck .... .05 .02 .01
☐ 179 Chris Bosio .... .05 .02 .01
☐ 180 Glenn Braggs .... .05 .02 .01
☐ 181 Greg Brock .... .05 .02 .01
☐ 182 Mark Clear .... .05 .02 .01
☐ 183 Chuck Crim .... .05 .02 .01
☐ 184 Rob Deer .... .05 .02 .01
☐ 185 Tom Filer .... .05 .02 .01
☐ 186 Jim Gantner .... .05 .02 .01
☐ 187 Darryl Hamilton .... .25 .11 .03
☐ 188 Ted Higuera .... .05 .02 .01
☐ 189 Odell Jones .... .05 .02 .01
☐ 190 Jeffrey Leonard .... .05 .02 .01
☐ 191 Joey Meyer .... .05 .02 .01
☐ 192 Paul Mirabella .... .05 .02 .01
☐ 193 Paul Molitor .... .25 .11 .03
☐ 194 Charlie O'Brien .... .05 .02 .01
☐ 195 Dan Plesac .... .05 .02 .01
☐ 196 Gary Sheffield .... 1.25 .55 .16
☐ 197 B.J. Surhoff .... .05 .02 .01
☐ 198 Dale Sveum .... .05 .02 .01
☐ 199 Bill Wegman .... .05 .02 .01
☐ 200 Robin Yount .... .25 .11 .03
☐ 201 Rafael Belliard .... .05 .02 .01
☐ 202 Barry Bonds .... .60 .25 .08
☐ 203 Bobby Bonilla .... .15 .07 .02
☐ 204 Sid Bream .... .05 .02 .01
☐ 205 Benny Distefano .... .05 .02 .01
☐ 206 Doug Drabek .... .15 .07 .02
☐ 207 Mike Dunne .... .05 .02 .01
☐ 208 Felix Fermin .... .05 .02 .01
☐ 209 Brian Fisher .... .05 .02 .01
☐ 210 Jim Gott .... .05 .02 .01
☐ 211 Bob Kipper .... .05 .02 .01
☐ 212 Dave LaPoint .... .05 .02 .01
☐ 213 Mike LaValliere .... .05 .02 .01
☐ 214 Jose Lind .... .05 .02 .01
☐ 215 Junior Ortiz .... .05 .02 .01
☐ 216 Vicente Palacios .... .05 .02 .01
☐ 217 Tom Prince .... .05 .02 .01
☐ 218 Gary Redus .... .05 .02 .01
☐ 219 R.J. Reynolds .... .05 .02 .01
☐ 220 Jeff D. Robinson .... .05 .02 .01
☐ 221 John Smiley .... .05 .02 .01
☐ 222 Andy Van Slyke .... .15 .07 .02
☐ 223 Bob Walk .... .05 .02 .01
☐ 224 Glenn Wilson .... .05 .02 .01
☐ 225 Jesse Barfield .... .05 .02 .01
☐ 226 George Bell .... .10 .05 .01
☐ 227 Pat Borders .... .25 .11 .03
☐ 228 John Cerutti .... .05 .02 .01
☐ 229 Jim Clancy .... .05 .02 .01
☐ 230 Mark Eichhorn .... .05 .02 .01
☐ 231 Tony Fernandez .... .10 .05 .01
☐ 232 Cecil Fielder .... .25 .11 .03

	Player			
☐ 233	Mike Flanagan	.05	.02	.01
☐ 234	Kelly Gruber	.05	.02	.01
☐ 235	Tom Henke	.10	.05	.01
☐ 236	Jimmy Key	.15	.07	.02
☐ 237	Rick Leach	.05	.02	.01
☐ 238	Manny Lee UER (Bio says regular shortstop, sic, Tony Fernandez)	.05	.02	.01
☐ 239	Nelson Liriano	.05	.02	.01
☐ 240	Fred McGriff	.25	.11	.03
☐ 241	Lloyd Moseby	.05	.02	.01
☐ 242	Rance Mulliniks	.05	.02	.01
☐ 243	Jeff Musselman	.05	.02	.01
☐ 244	Dave Stieb	.10	.05	.01
☐ 245	Todd Stottlemyre	.10	.05	.01
☐ 246	Duane Ward	.10	.05	.01
☐ 247	David Wells	.15	.07	.02
☐ 248	Ernie Whitt UER (HR total 21, should be 121)	.05	.02	.01
☐ 249	Luis Aguayo	.05	.02	.01
☐ 250A	Neil Allen (Home: Sarasota, FL)	.75	.35	.09
☐ 250B	Neil Allen (Home: Syosset, NY)	.10	.05	.01
☐ 251	John Candelaria	.05	.02	.01
☐ 252	Jack Clark	.10	.05	.01
☐ 253	Richard Dotson	.05	.02	.01
☐ 254	Rickey Henderson	.15	.07	.02
☐ 255	Tommy John	.15	.07	.02
☐ 256	Roberto Kelly	.20	.09	.03
☐ 257	Al Leiter	.05	.02	.01
☐ 258	Don Mattingly	.40	.18	.05
☐ 259	Dale Mohorcic	.05	.02	.01
☐ 260	Hal Morris	.50	.23	.06
☐ 261	Scott Nielsen	.05	.02	.01
☐ 262	Mike Pagliarulo UER (Wrong birthdate)	.05	.02	.01
☐ 263	Hipolito Pena	.05	.02	.01
☐ 264	Ken Phelps	.05	.02	.01
☐ 265	Willie Randolph	.10	.05	.01
☐ 266	Rick Rhoden	.05	.02	.01
☐ 267	Dave Righetti	.05	.02	.01
☐ 268	Rafael Santana	.05	.02	.01
☐ 269	Steve Shields	.05	.02	.01
☐ 270	Joel Skinner	.05	.02	.01
☐ 271	Don Slaught	.05	.02	.01
☐ 272	Claudell Washington	.05	.02	.01
☐ 273	Gary Ward	.05	.02	.01
☐ 274	Dave Winfield	.20	.09	.03
☐ 275	Luis Aquino	.05	.02	.01
☐ 276	Floyd Bannister	.05	.02	.01
☐ 277	George Brett	.35	.16	.04
☐ 278	Bill Buckner	.10	.05	.01
☐ 279	Nick Capra	.05	.02	.01
☐ 280	Jose DeJesus	.05	.02	.01
☐ 281	Steve Farr	.05	.02	.01
☐ 282	Jerry Don Gleaton	.05	.02	.01
☐ 283	Mark Gubicza	.05	.02	.01
☐ 284	Tom Gordon UER (16.2 innings in '88, should be 15.2)	.20	.09	.03
☐ 285	Bo Jackson	.25	.11	.03
☐ 286	Charlie Leibrandt	.05	.02	.01
☐ 287	Mike Macfarlane	.10	.05	.01
☐ 288	Jeff Montgomery	.10	.05	.01
☐ 289	Bill Pecota UER (Photo actually Brad Wellman)	.05	.02	.01
☐ 290	Jamie Quirk	.05	.02	.01
☐ 291	Bret Saberhagen	.10	.05	.01
☐ 292	Kevin Seitzer	.05	.02	.01
☐ 293	Kurt Stillwell	.05	.02	.01
☐ 294	Pat Tabler	.05	.02	.01
☐ 295	Danny Tartabull	.10	.05	.01
☐ 296	Gary Thurman	.05	.02	.01
☐ 297	Frank White	.10	.05	.01
☐ 298	Willie Wilson	.05	.02	.01
☐ 299	Roberto Alomar	.75	.35	.09
☐ 300	Sandy Alomar Jr. UER (Wrong birthdate, says 6/16/66, should say 6/18/66)	.30	.14	.04
☐ 301	Chris Brown	.05	.02	.01
☐ 302	Mike Brumley UER (133 hits in '88, should be 134)	.05	.02	.01
☐ 303	Mark Davis	.05	.02	.01
☐ 304	Mark Grant	.05	.02	.01
☐ 305	Tony Gwynn	.30	.14	.04
☐ 306	Greg W. Harris	.05	.02	.01
☐ 307	Andy Hawkins	.05	.02	.01
☐ 308	Jimmy Jones	.05	.02	.01
☐ 309	John Kruk	.15	.07	.02
☐ 310	Dave Leiper	.05	.02	.01
☐ 311	Carmelo Martinez	.05	.02	.01
☐ 312	Lance McCullers	.05	.02	.01
☐ 313	Keith Moreland	.05	.02	.01
☐ 314	Dennis Rasmussen	.05	.02	.01
☐ 315	Randy Ready UER (1214 games in '88, should be 114)	.05	.02	.01
☐ 316	Benito Santiago	.10	.05	.01
☐ 317	Eric Show	.05	.02	.01
☐ 318	Todd Simmons	.05	.02	.01
☐ 319	Garry Templeton	.05	.02	.01
☐ 320	Dickie Thon	.05	.02	.01
☐ 321	Ed Whitson	.05	.02	.01
☐ 322	Marvell Wynne	.05	.02	.01
☐ 323	Mike Aldrete	.05	.02	.01
☐ 324	Brett Butler	.10	.05	.01
☐ 325	Will Clark UER (Three consecutive 100 RBI seasons)	.30	.14	.04
☐ 326	Kelly Downs UER ('88 stats missing)	.05	.02	.01
☐ 327	Dave Dravecky	.10	.05	.01
☐ 328	Scott Garrelts	.05	.02	.01
☐ 329	Atlee Hammaker	.05	.02	.01
☐ 330	Charlie Hayes	.50	.23	.06
☐ 331	Mike Krukow	.05	.02	.01
☐ 332	Craig Lefferts	.05	.02	.01
☐ 333	Candy Maldonado	.05	.02	.01
☐ 334	Kirt Manwaring UER (Bats Rights)	.05	.02	.01
☐ 335	Bob Melvin	.05	.02	.01
☐ 336	Kevin Mitchell	.15	.07	.02
☐ 337	Donell Nixon	.05	.02	.01
☐ 338	Tony Perezchica	.05	.02	.01
☐ 339	Joe Price	.05	.02	.01
☐ 340	Rick Reuschel	.05	.02	.01
☐ 341	Earnest Riles	.05	.02	.01
☐ 342	Don Robinson	.05	.02	.01
☐ 343	Chris Speier	.05	.02	.01
☐ 344	Robby Thompson UER (West Plam Beach)	.10	.05	.01
☐ 345	Jose Uribe	.05	.02	.01
☐ 346	Matt Williams	.40	.18	.05
☐ 347	Trevor Wilson	.05	.02	.01
☐ 348	Juan Agosto	.05	.02	.01
☐ 349	Larry Andersen	.05	.02	.01
☐ 350A	Alan Ashby ERR (Throws Rig)	3.00	1.35	.40
☐ 350B	Alan Ashby COR	.05	.02	.01
☐ 351	Kevin Bass	.05	.02	.01

☐ 352 Buddy Bell .10 .05 .01
☐ 353 Craig Biggio .60 .25 .08
☐ 354 Danny Darwin .05 .02 .01
☐ 355 Glenn Davis .05 .02 .01
☐ 356 Jim Deshaies .05 .02 .01
☐ 357 Bill Doran .05 .02 .01
☐ 358 John Fishel .05 .02 .01
☐ 359 Billy Hatcher .05 .02 .01
☐ 360 Bob Knepper .05 .02 .01
☐ 361 Louie Meadows UER .05 .02 .01
(Bio says 10 EBH's and 6 SB's in '88, should be 3 and 4)
☐ 362 Dave Meads .05 .02 .01
☐ 363 Jim Pankovits .05 .02 .01
☐ 364 Terry Puhl .05 .02 .01
☐ 365 Rafael Ramirez .05 .02 .01
☐ 366 Craig Reynolds .05 .02 .01
☐ 367 Mike Scott .05 .02 .01
(Card number listed as 368 on Astros CL)
☐ 368 Nolan Ryan .75 .35 .09
(Card number listed as 367 on Astros CL)
☐ 369 Dave Smith .05 .02 .01
☐ 370 Gerald Young .05 .02 .01
☐ 371 Hubie Brooks .05 .02 .01
☐ 372 Tim Burke .05 .02 .01
☐ 373 John Dopson .05 .02 .01
☐ 374 Mike R. Fitzgerald .05 .02 .01
Montreal Expos
☐ 375 Tom Foley .05 .02 .01
☐ 376 Andres Galarraga UER .15 .07 .02
(Home: Caracus)
☐ 377 Neal Heaton .05 .02 .01
☐ 378 Joe Hesketh .05 .02 .01
☐ 379 Brian Holman .05 .02 .01
☐ 380 Rex Hudler .05 .02 .01
☐ 381 Randy Johnson UER .75 .35 .09
(Innings for '85 and '86 shown as 27 and 120, should be 27.1 and 119.2)
☐ 382 Wallace Johnson .05 .02 .01
☐ 383 Tracy Jones .05 .02 .01
☐ 384 Dave Martinez .05 .02 .01
☐ 385 Dennis Martinez .10 .05 .01
☐ 386 Andy McGaffigan .05 .02 .01
☐ 387 Otis Nixon .10 .05 .01
☐ 388 Johnny Paredes .05 .02 .01
☐ 389 Jeff Parrett .05 .02 .01
☐ 390 Pascual Perez .05 .02 .01
☐ 391 Tim Raines .15 .07 .02
☐ 392 Luis Rivera .05 .02 .01
☐ 393 Nelson Santovenia .05 .02 .01
☐ 394 Bryn Smith .05 .02 .01
☐ 395 Tim Wallach .05 .02 .01
☐ 396 Andy Allanson UER .05 .02 .01
(1214 hits in '88, should be 114)
☐ 397 Rod Allen .05 .02 .01
☐ 398 Scott Bailes .05 .02 .01
☐ 399 Tom Candiotti .05 .02 .01
☐ 400 Joe Carter .25 .11 .03
☐ 401 Carmen Castillo UER .05 .02 .01
(After All-Star Break batting 2.50)
☐ 402 Dave Clark UER .05 .02 .01
(Card front shows position as Rookie; after All-Star Break batting 3.14)
☐ 403 John Farrell UER .05 .02 .01
(Typo in runs allowed in '88)
☐ 404 Julio Franco .10 .05 .01
☐ 405 Don Gordon .05 .02 .01
☐ 406 Mel Hall .05 .02 .01
☐ 407 Brad Havens .05 .02 .01
☐ 408 Brook Jacoby .05 .02 .01
☐ 409 Doug Jones .10 .05 .01
☐ 410 Jeff Kaiser .05 .02 .01
☐ 411 Luis Medina .05 .02 .01
☐ 412 Cory Snyder .05 .02 .01
☐ 413 Greg Swindell .10 .05 .01
☐ 414 Ron Tingley UER .05 .02 .01
(Hit HR in first ML at-bat, should be first AL at-bat)
☐ 415 Willie Upshaw .05 .02 .01
☐ 416 Ron Washington .05 .02 .01
☐ 417 Rich Yett .05 .02 .01
☐ 418 Damon Berryhill .05 .02 .01
☐ 419 Mike Bielecki .05 .02 .01
☐ 420 Doug Dascenzo .05 .02 .01
☐ 421 Jody Davis UER .05 .02 .01
(Braves stats for '88 missing)
☐ 422 Andre Dawson .15 .07 .02
☐ 423 Frank DiPino .05 .02 .01
☐ 424 Shawon Dunston .10 .05 .01
☐ 425 Rich Gossage .15 .07 .02
☐ 426 Mark Grace UER .35 .16 .04
(Minor League stats for '88 missing)
☐ 427 Mike Harkey .05 .02 .01
☐ 428 Darrin Jackson .10 .05 .01
☐ 429 Les Lancaster .05 .02 .01
☐ 430 Vance Law .05 .02 .01
☐ 431 Greg Maddux .40 .18 .05
☐ 432 Jamie Moyer .05 .02 .01
☐ 433 Al Nipper .05 .02 .01
☐ 434 Rafael Palmeiro UER .25 .11 .03
(170 hits in '88, should be 178)
☐ 435 Pat Perry .05 .02 .01
☐ 436 Jeff Pico .05 .02 .01
☐ 437 Ryne Sandberg .40 .18 .05
☐ 438 Calvin Schiraldi .05 .02 .01
☐ 439 Rick Sutcliffe .10 .05 .01
☐ 440A Manny Trillo ERR 3.00 1.35 .40
(Throws Rig)
☐ 440B Manny Trillo COR .05 .02 .01
☐ 441 Gary Varsho UER .05 .02 .01
(Wrong birthdate; .303 should be .302; 11/28 should be 9/19)
☐ 442 Mitch Webster .05 .02 .01
☐ 443 Luis Alicea .05 .02 .01
☐ 444 Tom Brunansky .05 .02 .01
☐ 445 Vince Coleman UER .10 .05 .01
(Third straight with 83, should be fourth straight with 81)
☐ 446 John Costello UER .05 .02 .01
(Home California, should be New York)
☐ 447 Danny Cox .05 .02 .01
☐ 448 Ken Dayley .05 .02 .01
☐ 449 Jose DeLeon .05 .02 .01
☐ 450 Curt Ford .05 .02 .01
☐ 451 Pedro Guerrero .10 .05 .01
☐ 452 Bob Horner .05 .02 .01
☐ 453 Tim Jones .05 .02 .01
☐ 454 Steve Lake .05 .02 .01
☐ 455 Joe Magrane UER .05 .02 .01
(Des Moines, IO)

	No.	Player			
☐	456	Greg Mathews	.05	.02	.01
☐	457	Willie McGee	.10	.05	.01
☐	458	Larry McWilliams	.05	.02	.01
☐	459	Jose Oquendo	.05	.02	.01
☐	460	Tony Pena	.05	.02	.01
☐	461	Terry Pendleton	.15	.07	.02
☐	462	Steve Peters UER (Lives in Harrah, not Harah)	.05	.02	.01
☐	463	Ozzie Smith	.30	.14	.04
☐	464	Scott Terry	.05	.02	.01
☐	465	Denny Walling	.05	.02	.01
☐	466	Todd Worrell	.05	.02	.01
☐	467	Tony Armas UER (Before All-Star Break batting 2.39)	.05	.02	.01
☐	468	Dante Bichette	.75	.35	.09
☐	469	Bob Boone	.10	.05	.01
☐	470	Terry Clark	.05	.02	.01
☐	471	Stew Cliburn	.05	.02	.01
☐	472	Mike Cook UER (TM near Angels logo missing from front)	.05	.02	.01
☐	473	Sherman Corbett	.05	.02	.01
☐	474	Chili Davis	.10	.05	.01
☐	475	Brian Downing	.05	.02	.01
☐	476	Jim Eppard	.05	.02	.01
☐	477	Chuck Finley	.10	.05	.01
☐	478	Willie Fraser	.05	.02	.01
☐	479	Bryan Harvey UER (ML record shows 0-0, should be 7-5)	.25	.11	.03
☐	480	Jack Howell	.05	.02	.01
☐	481	Wally Joyner UER (Yorba Linda, GA)	.10	.05	.01
☐	482	Jack Lazorko	.05	.02	.01
☐	483	Kirk McCaskill	.05	.02	.01
☐	484	Mark McLemore	.05	.02	.01
☐	485	Greg Minton	.05	.02	.01
☐	486	Dan Petry	.05	.02	.01
☐	487	Johnny Ray	.05	.02	.01
☐	488	Dick Schofield	.05	.02	.01
☐	489	Devon White	.10	.05	.01
☐	490	Mike Witt	.05	.02	.01
☐	491	Harold Baines	.10	.05	.01
☐	492	Daryl Boston	.05	.02	.01
☐	493	Ivan Calderon UER ('80 stats shifted)	.05	.02	.01
☐	494	Mike Diaz	.05	.02	.01
☐	495	Carlton Fisk	.15	.07	.02
☐	496	Dave Gallagher	.05	.02	.01
☐	497	Ozzie Guillen	.10	.05	.01
☐	498	Shawn Hillegas	.05	.02	.01
☐	499	Lance Johnson	.10	.05	.01
☐	500	Barry Jones	.05	.02	.01
☐	501	Bill Long	.05	.02	.01
☐	502	Steve Lyons	.05	.02	.01
☐	503	Fred Manrique	.05	.02	.01
☐	504	Jack McDowell	.30	.14	.04
☐	505	Donn Pall	.05	.02	.01
☐	506	Kelly Paris	.05	.02	.01
☐	507	Dan Pasqua	.05	.02	.01
☐	508	Ken Patterson	.05	.02	.01
☐	509	Melido Perez	.05	.02	.01
☐	510	Jerry Reuss	.05	.02	.01
☐	511	Mark Salas	.05	.02	.01
☐	512	Bobby Thigpen UER ('86 ERA 4.69, should be 4.68)	.05	.02	.01
☐	513	Mike Woodard	.05	.02	.01
☐	514	Bob Brower	.05	.02	.01
☐	515	Steve Buechele	.05	.02	.01
☐	516	Jose Cecena	.05	.02	.01
☐	517	Cecil Espy	.05	.02	.01
☐	518	Scott Fletcher	.05	.02	.01
☐	519	Cecilio Guante ('87 Yankee stats are off-centered)	.05	.02	.01
☐	520	Jose Guzman	.10	.05	.01
☐	521	Ray Hayward	.05	.02	.01
☐	522	Charlie Hough	.10	.05	.01
☐	523	Pete Incaviglia	.10	.05	.01
☐	524	Mike Jeffcoat	.05	.02	.01
☐	525	Paul Kilgus	.05	.02	.01
☐	526	Chad Kreuter	.15	.07	.02
☐	527	Jeff Kunkel	.05	.02	.01
☐	528	Oddibe McDowell	.05	.02	.01
☐	529	Pete O'Brien	.05	.02	.01
☐	530	Geno Petralli	.05	.02	.01
☐	531	Jeff Russell	.05	.02	.01
☐	532	Ruben Sierra	.25	.11	.03
☐	533	Mike Stanley	.10	.05	.01
☐	534A	Ed VandeBerg ERR (Throws Lef)	3.00	1.35	.40
☐	534B	Ed VandeBerg COR	.05	.02	.01
☐	535	Curtis Wilkerson ERR (Pitcher headings at bottom)	.05	.02	.01
☐	536	Mitch Williams	.10	.05	.01
☐	537	Bobby Witt UER ('85 ERA .643, should be 6.43)	.10	.05	.01
☐	538	Steve Balboni	.05	.02	.01
☐	539	Scott Bankhead	.05	.02	.01
☐	540	Scott Bradley	.05	.02	.01
☐	541	Mickey Brantley	.05	.02	.01
☐	542	Jay Buhner	.20	.09	.03
☐	543	Mike Campbell	.05	.02	.01
☐	544	Darnell Coles	.05	.02	.01
☐	545	Henry Cotto	.05	.02	.01
☐	546	Alvin Davis	.05	.02	.01
☐	547	Mario Diaz	.05	.02	.01
☐	548	Ken Griffey Jr.	6.00	2.70	.75
☐	549	Erik Hanson	.25	.11	.03
☐	550	Mike Jackson UER (Lifetime ERA 3.345, should be 3.45)	.05	.02	.01
☐	551	Mark Langston	.15	.07	.02
☐	552	Edgar Martinez	.10	.05	.01
☐	553	Bill McGuire	.05	.02	.01
☐	554	Mike Moore	.05	.02	.01
☐	555	Jim Presley	.05	.02	.01
☐	556	Rey Quinones	.05	.02	.01
☐	557	Jerry Reed	.05	.02	.01
☐	558	Harold Reynolds	.05	.02	.01
☐	559	Mike Schooler	.05	.02	.01
☐	560	Bill Swift	.10	.05	.01
☐	561	Dave Valle	.05	.02	.01
☐	562	Steve Bedrosian	.05	.02	.01
☐	563	Phil Bradley	.05	.02	.01
☐	564	Don Carman	.05	.02	.01
☐	565	Bob Dernier	.05	.02	.01
☐	566	Marvin Freeman	.05	.02	.01
☐	567	Todd Frohwirth	.05	.02	.01
☐	568	Greg Gross	.05	.02	.01
☐	569	Kevin Gross	.05	.02	.01
☐	570	Greg A. Harris	.05	.02	.01
☐	571	Von Hayes	.05	.02	.01
☐	572	Chris James	.05	.02	.01
☐	573	Steve Jeltz	.05	.02	.01
☐	574	Ron Jones UER (Led IL in '88 with 85, should be 75)	.05	.02	.01
☐	575	Ricky Jordan	.05	.02	.01
☐	576	Mike Maddux	.05	.02	.01
☐	577	David Palmer	.05	.02	.01

☐ 578 Lance Parrish	.10	.05	.01
☐ 579 Shane Rawley	.05	.02	.01
☐ 580 Bruce Ruffin	.05	.02	.01
☐ 581 Juan Samuel	.05	.02	.01
☐ 582 Mike Schmidt	.25	.11	.03
☐ 583 Kent Tekulve	.05	.02	.01
☐ 584 Milt Thompson UER (19 hits in '88, should be 109)	.05	.02	.01
☐ 585 Jose Alvarez	.05	.02	.01
☐ 586 Paul Assenmacher	.05	.02	.01
☐ 587 Bruce Benedict	.05	.02	.01
☐ 588 Jeff Blauser	.15	.07	.02
☐ 589 Terry Blocker	.05	.02	.01
☐ 590 Ron Gant	.25	.11	.03
☐ 591 Tom Glavine	.40	.18	.05
☐ 592 Tommy Gregg	.05	.02	.01
☐ 593 Albert Hall	.05	.02	.01
☐ 594 Dion James	.05	.02	.01
☐ 595 Rick Mahler	.05	.02	.01
☐ 596 Dale Murphy	.15	.07	.02
☐ 597 Gerald Perry	.05	.02	.01
☐ 598 Charlie Puleo	.05	.02	.01
☐ 599 Ted Simmons	.10	.05	.01
☐ 600 Pete Smith	.05	.02	.01
☐ 601 Zane Smith	.05	.02	.01
☐ 602 John Smoltz	.40	.18	.05
☐ 603 Bruce Sutter	.10	.05	.01
☐ 604 Andres Thomas	.05	.02	.01
☐ 605 Ozzie Virgil	.05	.02	.01
☐ 606 Brady Anderson	.40	.18	.05
☐ 607 Jeff Ballard	.05	.02	.01
☐ 608 Jose Bautista	.05	.02	.01
☐ 609 Ken Gerhart	.05	.02	.01
☐ 610 Terry Kennedy	.05	.02	.01
☐ 611 Eddie Murray	.15	.07	.02
☐ 612 Carl Nichols UER (Before All-Star Break batting 1.88)	.05	.02	.01
☐ 613 Tom Niedenfuer	.05	.02	.01
☐ 614 Joe Orsulak	.05	.02	.01
☐ 615 Oswald Peraza UER (Shown as Oswaldo)	.05	.02	.01
☐ 616A Bill Ripken ERR (Rick Face written on knob of bat)	10.00	4.50	1.25
☐ 616B Bill Ripken (Bat knob whited out)	45.00	20.00	5.75
☐ 616C Bill Ripken (Words on bat knob scribbled out)	10.00	4.50	1.25
☐ 616D Bill Ripken DP (Black box covering bat knob)	.10	.05	.01
☐ 617 Cal Ripken	.50	.23	.06
☐ 618 Dave Schmidt	.05	.02	.01
☐ 619 Rick Schu	.05	.02	.01
☐ 620 Larry Sheets	.05	.02	.01
☐ 621 Doug Sisk	.05	.02	.01
☐ 622 Pete Stanicek	.05	.02	.01
☐ 623 Mickey Tettleton	.10	.05	.01
☐ 624 Jay Tibbs	.05	.02	.01
☐ 625 Jim Traber	.05	.02	.01
☐ 626 Mark Williamson	.05	.02	.01
☐ 627 Craig Worthington	.05	.02	.01
☐ 628 Speed/Power Jose Canseco	.20	.09	.03
☐ 629 Pitcher Perfect Tom Browning	.05	.02	.01
☐ 630 Like Father/Like Sons Roberto Alomar Sandy Alomar Jr. (Names on card listed in wrong order) UER	.40	.18	.05
☐ 631 NL All Stars UER Will Clark Rafael Palmeiro (Gallaraga, sic; Clark 3 consecutive 100 RBI seasons; third with 102 RBI's)	.30	.14	.04
☐ 632 Homeruns - Coast to Coast UER Darryl Strawberry Will Clark (Homeruns should be two words)	.25	.11	.03
☐ 633 Hot Corners - Hot Hitters UER Wade Boggs Carney Lansford (Boggs hit .366 in '86, should be '88)	.10	.05	.01
☐ 634 Triple A's Jose Canseco Terry Steinbach Mark McGwire	.25	.11	.03
☐ 635 Dual Heat Mark Davis Dwight Gooden	.05	.02	.01
☐ 636 NL Pitching Power UER Danny Jackson David Cone (Hersheiser, sic)	.10	.05	.01
☐ 637 Cannon Arms UER Chris Sabo Bobby Bonilla (Bobby Bonds, sic)	.10	.05	.01
☐ 638 Double Trouble UER Andres Galarraga (Misspelled Gallaraga on card back) Gerald Perry	.10	.05	.01
☐ 639 Power Center Kirby Puckett Eric Davis	.15	.07	.02
☐ 640 Steve Wilson and Cameron Drew	.05	.02	.01
☐ 641 Kevin Brown and Kevin Reimer	.40	.18	.05
☐ 642 Brad Pounders and Jerald Clark	.05	.02	.01
☐ 643 Mike Capel and Drew Hall	.05	.02	.01
☐ 644 Joe Girardi and Rolando Roomes	.15	.07	.02
☐ 645 Lenny Harris and Marty Brown	.05	.02	.01
☐ 646 Luis DeLosSantos and Jim Campbell	.05	.02	.01
☐ 647 Randy Kramer and Miguel Garcia	.05	.02	.01
☐ 648 Torey Lovullo and Robert Palacios	.05	.02	.01
☐ 649 Jim Corsi and Bob Milacki	.05	.02	.01
☐ 650 Grady Hall and Mike Rochford	.05	.02	.01
☐ 651 Terry Taylor and Vance Lovelace	.05	.02	.01
☐ 652 Ken Hill and Dennis Cook	.75	.35	.09
☐ 653 Scott Service and Shane Turner	.05	.02	.01
☐ 654 CL: Oakland/Mets Dodgers/Red Sox (10 Hendersor;	.05	.02	.01

68 Jess Orosco)

		MINT	EXC	G-VG
☐ 655A	CL: Twins/Tigers ERR Reds/Brewers (179 Boslo and Twins/Tigers positions listed)	.10	.02	.01
☐ 655B	CL: Twins/Tigers COR Reds/Brewers (179 Boslo but Twins/Tigers positions not listed)	.10	.02	.01
☐ 656	CL: Pirates/Blue Jays Yankees/Royals (225 Jess Barfield)	.05	.02	.01
☐ 657	CL: Padres/Giants Astros/Expos (367/368 wrong)	.05	.02	.01
☐ 658	CL: Indians/Cubs Cardinals/Angels (449 Deleon)	.05	.02	.01
☐ 659	CL: White Sox/Rangers Mariners/Phillies	.05	.02	.01
☐ 660	CL: Braves/Orioles Specials/Checklists (632 hyphenated differently and 650 Hali; 595 Rich Mahler; 619 Rich Schu)	.05	.02	.01

1989 Fleer All-Stars

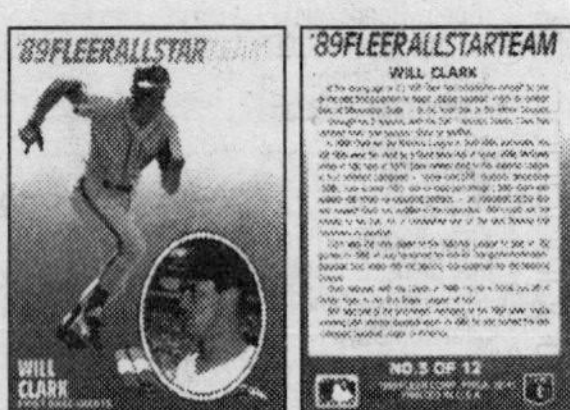

This twelve-card subset was randomly inserted in Fleer wax packs (15 regular cards) and Fleer value packs (36 regular cards). The players selected are the 1989 Fleer Major League All-Star team. One player has been selected for each position along with a DH and three pitchers. The cards are attractively designed and are standard size, 2 1/2" by 3 1/2". The cards are numbered on the backs and feature a distinctive green background on the card fronts.

	MINT	EXC	G-VG
COMPLETE SET (12)	5.00	2.30	.60
COMMON CARD (1-12)	.20	.09	.03
☐ 1 Bobby Bonilla	.40	.18	.05
☐ 2 Jose Canseco	1.50	.65	.19
☐ 3 Will Clark	1.50	.65	.19
☐ 4 Dennis Eckersley	.30	.14	.04
☐ 5 Julio Franco	.30	.14	.04
☐ 6 Mike Greenwell	.30	.14	.04
☐ 7 Orel Hershiser	.30	.14	.04
☐ 8 Paul Molitor	1.00	.45	.13
☐ 9 Mike Scioscia	.20	.09	.03
☐ 10 Darryl Strawberry	.30	.14	.04
☐ 11 Alan Trammell	.40	.18	.05
☐ 12 Frank Viola	.30	.14	.04

1989 Fleer For The Record

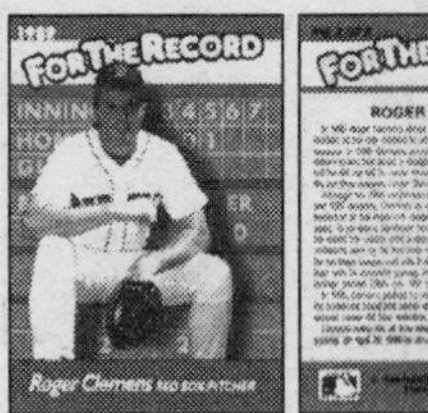

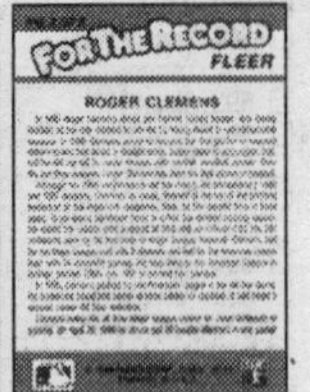

This six-card subset was distributed randomly (as an insert) in Fleer rack packs. These cards are standard size, 2 1/2" by 3 1/2" and are quite attractive. The set is subtitled "For The Record" and commemorates record-breaking events for those players from the previous season. The cards are numbered on the backs. The card backs are printed in red, black, and gray on white card stock.

	MINT	EXC	G-VG
COMPLETE SET (6)	6.00	2.70	.75
COMMON CARD (1-6)	.25	.11	.03
☐ 1 Wade Boggs	1.00	.45	.13
☐ 2 Roger Clemens	1.50	.65	.19
☐ 3 Andres Galarraga	1.00	.45	.13
☐ 4 Kirk Gibson	.25	.11	.03
☐ 5 Greg Maddux	2.50	1.15	.30
☐ 6 Don Mattingly UER (Won batting title '83, should say '84)	2.00	.90	.25

1989 Fleer Update

The 1989 Fleer Update set contains 132 standard-size (2 1/2" by 3 1/2") cards. The fronts are gray with white pinstripes. The vertically oriented backs show lifetime stats and performance "Before and After the All-Star Break". The set numbering is in team order with players within teams ordered alphabetically. The set does includes special cards for Nolan Ryan's 5,000th strikeout and Mike Schmidt's retirement. Rookie Cards include Kevin Appier, Joey (Albert) Belle, Deion Sanders, Greg Vaughn Robin Ventura and Todd Zeile. Fleer did NOT produce a limited (tin) edition version of this set

with glossy coating. The card numbering is in alphabetical order within teams with the teams themselves alphabetized within league. Cards are numbered with a U prefix.

	MINT	EXC	G-VG
COMPLETE FACT.SET (132)	7.00	3.10	.85
COMMON CARD (1-132)	.05	.02	.01

	MINT	EXC	G-VG
☐ 1 Phil Bradley	.05	.02	.01
☐ 2 Mike Devereaux	.08	.04	.01
☐ 3 Steve Finley	.25	.11	.03
☐ 4 Kevin Hickey	.05	.02	.01
☐ 5 Brian Holton	.05	.02	.01
☐ 6 Bob Milacki	.05	.02	.01
☐ 7 Randy Milligan	.05	.02	.01
☐ 8 John Dopson	.05	.02	.01
☐ 9 Nick Esasky	.05	.02	.01
☐ 10 Rob Murphy	.05	.02	.01
☐ 11 Jim Abbott	1.00	.45	.13
☐ 12 Bert Blyleven	.10	.05	.01
☐ 13 Jeff Manto	.05	.02	.01
☐ 14 Bob McClure	.05	.02	.01
☐ 15 Lance Parrish	.08	.04	.01
☐ 16 Lee Stevens	.05	.02	.01
☐ 17 Claudell Washington	.05	.02	.01
☐ 18 Mark Davis	.05	.02	.01
☐ 19 Eric King	.05	.02	.01
☐ 20 Ron Kittle	.05	.02	.01
☐ 21 Matt Merullo	.05	.02	.01
☐ 22 Steve Rosenberg	.05	.02	.01
☐ 23 Robin Ventura	1.00	.45	.13
☐ 24 Keith Atherton	.05	.02	.01
☐ 25 Joey Belle	3.00	1.35	.40
☐ 26 Jerry Browne	.05	.02	.01
☐ 27 Felix Fermin	.05	.02	.01
☐ 28 Brad Komminsk	.05	.02	.01
☐ 29 Pete O'Brien	.05	.02	.01
☐ 30 Mike Brumley	.05	.02	.01
☐ 31 Tracy Jones	.05	.02	.01
☐ 32 Mike Schwabe	.05	.02	.01
☐ 33 Gary Ward	.05	.02	.01
☐ 34 Frank Williams	.05	.02	.01
☐ 35 Kevin Appier	1.00	.45	.13
☐ 36 Bob Boone	.08	.04	.01
☐ 37 Luis DeLosSantos	.05	.02	.01
☐ 38 Jim Eisenreich	.05	.02	.01
☐ 39 Jaime Navarro	.25	.11	.03
☐ 40 Bill Spiers	.05	.02	.01
☐ 41 Greg Vaughn	.75	.35	.09
☐ 42 Randy Veres	.05	.02	.01
☐ 43 Wally Backman	.05	.02	.01
☐ 44 Shane Rawley	.05	.02	.01
☐ 45 Steve Balboni	.05	.02	.01
☐ 46 Jesse Barfield	.05	.02	.01
☐ 47 Alvaro Espinoza	.05	.02	.01
☐ 48 Bob Geren	.05	.02	.01
☐ 49 Mel Hall	.05	.02	.01
☐ 50 Andy Hawkins	.05	.02	.01
☐ 51 Hensley Meulens	.05	.02	.01
☐ 52 Steve Sax	.05	.02	.01
☐ 53 Deion Sanders	1.75	.80	.22
☐ 54 Rickey Henderson	.25	.11	.03
☐ 55 Mike Moore	.05	.02	.01
☐ 56 Tony Phillips	.08	.04	.01
☐ 57 Greg Briley	.05	.02	.01
☐ 58 Gene Harris	.10	.05	.01
☐ 59 Randy Johnson	.75	.35	.09
☐ 60 Jeffrey Leonard	.05	.02	.01
☐ 61 Dennis Powell	.05	.02	.01
☐ 62 Omar Vizquel	.20	.09	.03
☐ 63 Kevin Brown	.08	.04	.01
☐ 64 Julio Franco	.08	.04	.01
☐ 65 Jamie Moyer	.05	.02	.01
☐ 66 Rafael Palmeiro	.25	.11	.03
☐ 67 Nolan Ryan	1.50	.65	.19
☐ 68 Francisco Cabrera	.15	.07	.02
☐ 69 Junior Felix	.20	.09	.03
☐ 70 Al Leiter	.05	.02	.01
☐ 71 Alex Sanchez	.05	.02	.01
☐ 72 Geronimo Berroa	.35	.16	.04
☐ 73 Derek Lilliquist	.05	.02	.01
☐ 74 Lonnie Smith	.05	.02	.01
☐ 75 Jeff Treadway	.05	.02	.01
☐ 76 Paul Kilgus	.05	.02	.01
☐ 77 Lloyd McClendon	.05	.02	.01
☐ 78 Scott Sanderson	.05	.02	.01
☐ 79 Dwight Smith	.15	.07	.02
☐ 80 Jerome Walton	.05	.02	.01
☐ 81 Mitch Williams	.08	.04	.01
☐ 82 Steve Wilson	.05	.02	.01
☐ 83 Todd Benzinger	.05	.02	.01
☐ 84 Ken Griffey	.08	.04	.01
☐ 85 Rick Mahler	.05	.02	.01
☐ 86 Rolando Roomes	.05	.02	.01
☐ 87 Scott Scudder	.05	.02	.01
☐ 88 Jim Clancy	.05	.02	.01
☐ 89 Rick Rhoden	.05	.02	.01
☐ 90 Dan Schatzeder	.05	.02	.01
☐ 91 Mike Morgan	.05	.02	.01
☐ 92 Eddie Murray	.25	.11	.03
☐ 93 Willie Randolph	.08	.04	.01
☐ 94 Ray Searage	.05	.02	.01
☐ 95 Mike Aldrete	.05	.02	.01
☐ 96 Kevin Gross	.05	.02	.01
☐ 97 Mark Langston	.10	.05	.01
☐ 98 Spike Owen	.05	.02	.01
☐ 99 Zane Smith	.05	.02	.01
☐ 100 Don Aase	.05	.02	.01
☐ 101 Barry Lyons	.05	.02	.01
☐ 102 Juan Samuel	.05	.02	.01
☐ 103 Wally Whitehurst	.05	.02	.01
☐ 104 Dennis Cook	.05	.02	.01
☐ 105 Len Dykstra	.10	.05	.01
☐ 106 Charlie Hayes	.40	.18	.05
☐ 107 Tommy Herr	.05	.02	.01
☐ 108 Ken Howell	.05	.02	.01
☐ 109 John Kruk	.10	.05	.01
☐ 110 Roger McDowell	.05	.02	.01
☐ 111 Terry Mulholland	.08	.04	.01
☐ 112 Jeff Parrett	.05	.02	.01
☐ 113 Neal Heaton	.05	.02	.01
☐ 114 Jeff King	.08	.04	.01
☐ 115 Randy Kramer	.05	.02	.01
☐ 116 Bill Landrum	.05	.02	.01
☐ 117 Cris Carpenter	.05	.02	.01
☐ 118 Frank DiPino	.05	.02	.01
☐ 119 Ken Hill	.60	.25	.08
☐ 120 Dan Quisenberry	.08	.04	.01
☐ 121 Milt Thompson	.05	.02	.01
☐ 122 Todd Zeile	.60	.25	.08

☐ 123	Jack Clark	.08	.04	.01
☐ 124	Bruce Hurst	.05	.02	.01
☐ 125	Mark Parent	.05	.02	.01
☐ 126	Bip Roberts	.08	.04	.01
☐ 127	Jeff Brantley UER (Photo actually Joe Kmak)	.05	.02	.01
☐ 128	Terry Kennedy	.05	.02	.01
☐ 129	Mike LaCoss	.05	.02	.01
☐ 130	Greg Litton	.05	.02	.01
☐ 131	Mike Schmidt	.50	.23	.06
☐ 132	Checklist 1-132	.05	.02	.01

1990 Fleer

The 1990 Fleer set contains 660 standard-size (2 1/2" by 3 1/2") cards. The outer front borders are white; the inner, ribbon-like borders are different depending on the team. The vertically oriented backs are white, red, pink, and navy. The set is again ordered numerically by teams, followed by combination cards, rookie prospect pairs, and checklists. Just as with the 1989 set, Fleer incorrectly anticipated the outcome of the 1989 Playoffs according to the team ordering. The A's, listed first, did win the World Series, but their opponents were the Giants, not the Cubs. Fleer later reported that they merely arranged the teams according to regular season team record due to the early printing date. The complete team ordering is as follows: Oakland A's (1-24), Chicago Cubs (25-49), San Francisco Giants (50-75), Toronto Blue Jays (76-99), Kansas City Royals (100-124), California Angels (125-148), San Diego Padres (149-171), Baltimore Orioles (172-195), New York Mets (196-219), Houston Astros (220-241), St. Louis Cardinals (242-265), Boston Red Sox (266-289), Texas Rangers (290-315), Milwaukee Brewers (316-340), Montreal Expos (341-364), Minnesota Twins (365-388), Los Angeles Dodgers (389-411), Cincinnati Reds (412-435), New York Yankees (436-458), Pittsburgh Pirates (459-482), Cleveland Indians (483-504), Seattle Mariners (505-528), Chicago White Sox (529-551), Philadelphia Phillies (552-573), Atlanta Braves (574-598), and Detroit Tigers (599-620). Rookie Cards in this set include Moises Alou, Eric Anthony, Alex Cole, Delino DeShields, Juan Gonzalez, Tommy Greene, Marquis Grissom, Dave Justice, Derrick May, Ben McDonald, Sammy Sosa, and Larry Walker. The following five cards have minor printing differences, 6, 162, 260, 469, and 550; these differences are so minor that collectors have deemed them not significant enough to effect a price differential. Fleer also produced a separate set for Canada. The Canadian set only differs from the regular set in that it shows copyright "FLEER LTD./LTEE PTD. IN CANADA" on the card backs. Although these Canadian cards were undoubtedly produced in much lesser quantities compared to the U.S. issue, the fact that the versions are so similar has kept the demand (and the price differential) for the Canadian cards down.

	MINT	EXC	G-VG
COMPLETE SET (660)	10.00	4.50	1.25
COMPLETE RETAIL SET (660)	10.00	4.50	1.25
COMPLETE HOBBY SET (672)	10.00	4.50	1.25
COMMON CARD (1-660)	.05	.02	.01

☐ 1	Lance Blankenship	.05	.02	.01
☐ 2	Todd Burns	.05	.02	.01
☐ 3	Jose Canseco	.30	.14	.04
☐ 4	Jim Corsi	.05	.02	.01
☐ 5	Storm Davis	.05	.02	.01
☐ 6	Dennis Eckersley	.15	.07	.02
☐ 7	Mike Gallego	.05	.02	.01
☐ 8	Ron Hassey	.05	.02	.01
☐ 9	Dave Henderson	.05	.02	.01
☐ 10	Rickey Henderson	.15	.07	.02
☐ 11	Rick Honeycutt	.05	.02	.01
☐ 12	Stan Javier	.05	.02	.01
☐ 13	Felix Jose	.10	.05	.01
☐ 14	Carney Lansford	.10	.05	.01
☐ 15	Mark McGwire UER (1989 runs listed as 4, should be 74)	.15	.07	.02
☐ 16	Mike Moore	.05	.02	.01
☐ 17	Gene Nelson	.05	.02	.01
☐ 18	Dave Parker	.15	.07	.02
☐ 19	Tony Phillips	.10	.05	.01
☐ 20	Terry Steinbach	.10	.05	.01
☐ 21	Dave Stewart	.10	.05	.01
☐ 22	Walt Weiss	.05	.02	.01
☐ 23	Bob Welch	.05	.02	.01
☐ 24	Curt Young	.05	.02	.01
☐ 25	Paul Assenmacher	.05	.02	.01
☐ 26	Damon Berryhill	.05	.02	.01
☐ 27	Mike Bielecki	.05	.02	.01
☐ 28	Kevin Blankenship	.05	.02	.01
☐ 29	Andre Dawson	.15	.07	.02
☐ 30	Shawon Dunston	.05	.02	.01
☐ 31	Joe Girardi	.05	.02	.01
☐ 32	Mark Grace	.20	.09	.03
☐ 33	Mike Harkey	.05	.02	.01
☐ 34	Paul Kilgus	.05	.02	.01
☐ 35	Les Lancaster	.05	.02	.01
☐ 36	Vance Law	.05	.02	.01
☐ 37	Greg Maddux	.30	.14	.04
☐ 38	Lloyd McClendon	.05	.02	.01
☐ 39	Jeff Pico	.05	.02	.01
☐ 40	Ryne Sandberg	.35	.16	.04
☐ 41	Scott Sanderson	.05	.02	.01
☐ 42	Dwight Smith	.05	.02	.01
☐ 43	Rick Sutcliffe	.10	.05	.01
☐ 44	Jerome Walton	.05	.02	.01
☐ 45	Mitch Webster	.05	.02	.01
☐ 46	Curt Wilkerson	.05	.02	.01
☐ 47	Dean Wilkins	.05	.02	.01

	No.	Player			
☐	48	Mitch Williams	.10	.05	.01
☐	49	Steve Wilson	.05	.02	.01
☐	50	Steve Bedrosian	.05	.02	.01
☐	51	Mike Benjamin	.05	.02	.01
☐	52	Jeff Brantley	.05	.02	.01
☐	53	Brett Butler	.10	.05	.01
☐	54	Will Clark UER ("Did You Know" says first in runs, should say tied for first)	.25	.11	.03
☐	55	Kelly Downs	.05	.02	.01
☐	56	Scott Garrelts	.05	.02	.01
☐	57	Atlee Hammaker	.05	.02	.01
☐	58	Terry Kennedy	.05	.02	.01
☐	59	Mike LaCoss	.05	.02	.01
☐	60	Craig Lefferts	.05	.02	.01
☐	61	Greg Litton	.05	.02	.01
☐	62	Candy Maldonado	.05	.02	.01
☐	63	Kirt Manwaring UER (No '88 Phoenix stats as noted in box)	.05	.02	.01
☐	64	Randy McCament	.05	.02	.01
☐	65	Kevin Mitchell	.10	.05	.01
☐	66	Donell Nixon	.05	.02	.01
☐	67	Ken Oberkfell	.05	.02	.01
☐	68	Rick Reuschel	.05	.02	.01
☐	69	Ernest Riles	.05	.02	.01
☐	70	Don Robinson	.05	.02	.01
☐	71	Pat Sheridan	.05	.02	.01
☐	72	Chris Speier	.05	.02	.01
☐	73	Robby Thompson	.10	.05	.01
☐	74	Jose Uribe	.05	.02	.01
☐	75	Matt Williams	.25	.11	.03
☐	76	George Bell	.10	.05	.01
☐	77	Pat Borders	.10	.05	.01
☐	78	John Cerutti	.05	.02	.01
☐	79	Junior Felix	.05	.02	.01
☐	80	Tony Fernandez	.10	.05	.01
☐	81	Mike Flanagan	.05	.02	.01
☐	82	Mauro Gozzo	.05	.02	.01
☐	83	Kelly Gruber	.05	.02	.01
☐	84	Tom Henke	.10	.05	.01
☐	85	Jimmy Key	.10	.05	.01
☐	86	Manny Lee	.05	.02	.01
☐	87	Nelson Liriano UER (Should say "led the IL" instead of "led the TL")	.05	.02	.01
☐	88	Lee Mazzilli	.05	.02	.01
☐	89	Fred McGriff	.30	.14	.04
☐	90	Lloyd Moseby	.05	.02	.01
☐	91	Rance Mulliniks	.05	.02	.01
☐	92	Alex Sanchez	.05	.02	.01
☐	93	Dave Stieb	.10	.05	.01
☐	94	Todd Stottlemyre	.10	.05	.01
☐	95	Duane Ward UER (Double line of '87 Syracuse stats)	.10	.05	.01
☐	96	David Wells	.05	.02	.01
☐	97	Ernie Whitt	.05	.02	.01
☐	98	Frank Wills	.05	.02	.01
☐	99	Mookie Wilson	.05	.02	.01
☐	100	Kevin Appier	.30	.14	.04
☐	101	Luis Aquino	.05	.02	.01
☐	102	Bob Boone	.10	.05	.01
☐	103	George Brett	.30	.14	.04
☐	104	Jose DeJesus	.05	.02	.01
☐	105	Luis De Los Santos	.05	.02	.01
☐	106	Jim Eisenreich	.05	.02	.01
☐	107	Steve Farr	.05	.02	.01
☐	108	Tom Gordon	.10	.05	.01
☐	109	Mark Gubicza	.05	.02	.01
☐	110	Bo Jackson	.15	.07	.02
☐	111	Terry Leach	.05	.02	.01
☐	112	Charlie Leibrandt	.05	.02	.01
☐	113	Rick Luecken	.05	.02	.01
☐	114	Mike Macfarlane	.05	.02	.01
☐	115	Jeff Montgomery	.10	.05	.01
☐	116	Bret Saberhagen	.10	.05	.01
☐	117	Kevin Seitzer	.05	.02	.01
☐	118	Kurt Stillwell	.05	.02	.01
☐	119	Pat Tabler	.05	.02	.01
☐	120	Danny Tartabull	.10	.05	.01
☐	121	Gary Thurman	.05	.02	.01
☐	122	Frank White	.10	.05	.01
☐	123	Willie Wilson	.05	.02	.01
☐	124	Matt Winters	.05	.02	.01
☐	125	Jim Abbott	.15	.07	.02
☐	126	Tony Armas	.05	.02	.01
☐	127	Dante Bichette	.20	.09	.03
☐	128	Bert Blyleven	.15	.07	.02
☐	129	Chili Davis	.10	.05	.01
☐	130	Brian Downing	.05	.02	.01
☐	131	Mike Fetters	.05	.02	.01
☐	132	Chuck Finley	.10	.05	.01
☐	133	Willie Fraser	.05	.02	.01
☐	134	Bryan Harvey	.10	.05	.01
☐	135	Jack Howell	.05	.02	.01
☐	136	Wally Joyner	.10	.05	.01
☐	137	Jeff Manto	.05	.02	.01
☐	138	Kirk McCaskill	.05	.02	.01
☐	139	Bob McClure	.05	.02	.01
☐	140	Greg Minton	.05	.02	.01
☐	141	Lance Parrish	.10	.05	.01
☐	142	Dan Petry	.05	.02	.01
☐	143	Johnny Ray	.05	.02	.01
☐	144	Dick Schofield	.05	.02	.01
☐	145	Lee Stevens	.05	.02	.01
☐	146	Claudell Washington	.05	.02	.01
☐	147	Devon White	.10	.05	.01
☐	148	Mike Witt	.05	.02	.01
☐	149	Roberto Alomar	.40	.18	.05
☐	150	Sandy Alomar Jr.	.10	.05	.01
☐	151	Andy Benes	.15	.07	.02
☐	152	Jack Clark	.10	.05	.01
☐	153	Pat Clements	.05	.02	.01
☐	154	Joey Cora	.05	.02	.01
☐	155	Mark Davis	.05	.02	.01
☐	156	Mark Grant	.05	.02	.01
☐	157	Tony Gwynn	.25	.11	.03
☐	158	Greg W. Harris	.05	.02	.01
☐	159	Bruce Hurst	.05	.02	.01
☐	160	Darrin Jackson	.05	.02	.01
☐	161	Chris James	.05	.02	.01
☐	162	Carmelo Martinez	.05	.02	.01
☐	163	Mike Pagliarulo	.05	.02	.01
☐	164	Mark Parent	.05	.02	.01
☐	165	Dennis Rasmussen	.05	.02	.01
☐	166	Bip Roberts	.10	.05	.01
☐	167	Benito Santiago	.10	.05	.01
☐	168	Calvin Schiraldi	.05	.02	.01
☐	169	Eric Show	.05	.02	.01
☐	170	Garry Templeton	.05	.02	.01
☐	171	Ed Whitson	.05	.02	.01
☐	172	Brady Anderson	.10	.05	.01
☐	173	Jeff Ballard	.05	.02	.01
☐	174	Phil Bradley	.05	.02	.01
☐	175	Mike Devereaux	.10	.05	.01
☐	176	Steve Finley	.10	.05	.01
☐	177	Pete Harnisch	.10	.05	.01
☐	178	Kevin Hickey	.05	.02	.01
☐	179	Brian Holton	.05	.02	.01
☐	180	Ben McDonald	.40	.18	.05
☐	181	Bob Melvin	.05	.02	.01
☐	182	Bob Milacki	.05	.02	.01
☐	183	Randy Milligan UER	.05	.02	.01

(Double line of '87 stats)
- ☐ 184 Gregg Olson .10 .05 .01
- ☐ 185 Joe Orsulak .05 .02 .01
- ☐ 186 Bill Ripken .05 .02 .01
- ☐ 187 Cal Ripken .40 .18 .05
- ☐ 188 Dave Schmidt .05 .02 .01
- ☐ 189 Larry Sheets .05 .02 .01
- ☐ 190 Mickey Tettleton .10 .05 .01
- ☐ 191 Mark Thurmond .05 .02 .01
- ☐ 192 Jay Tibbs .05 .02 .01
- ☐ 193 Jim Traber .05 .02 .01
- ☐ 194 Mark Williamson .05 .02 .01
- ☐ 195 Craig Worthington .05 .02 .01
- ☐ 196 Don Aase .05 .02 .01
- ☐ 197 Blaine Beatty .05 .02 .01
- ☐ 198 Mark Carreon .05 .02 .01
- ☐ 199 Gary Carter .15 .07 .02
- ☐ 200 David Cone .15 .07 .02
- ☐ 201 Ron Darling .05 .02 .01
- ☐ 202 Kevin Elster .05 .02 .01
- ☐ 203 Sid Fernandez .10 .05 .01
- ☐ 204 Dwight Gooden .10 .05 .01
- ☐ 205 Keith Hernandez .10 .05 .01
- ☐ 206 Jeff Innis .05 .02 .01
- ☐ 207 Gregg Jefferies .25 .11 .03
- ☐ 208 Howard Johnson .10 .05 .01
- ☐ 209 Barry Lyons UER .05 .02 .01 (Double line of '87 stats)
- ☐ 210 Dave Magadan .05 .02 .01
- ☐ 211 Kevin McReynolds .05 .02 .01
- ☐ 212 Jeff Musselman .05 .02 .01
- ☐ 213 Randy Myers .10 .05 .01
- ☐ 214 Bob Ojeda .05 .02 .01
- ☐ 215 Juan Samuel .05 .02 .01
- ☐ 216 Mackey Sasser .05 .02 .01
- ☐ 217 Darryl Strawberry .15 .07 .02
- ☐ 218 Tim Teufel .05 .02 .01
- ☐ 219 Frank Viola .10 .05 .01
- ☐ 220 Juan Agosto .05 .02 .01
- ☐ 221 Larry Andersen .05 .02 .01
- ☐ 222 Eric Anthony .15 .07 .02
- ☐ 223 Kevin Bass .05 .02 .01
- ☐ 224 Craig Biggio .15 .07 .02
- ☐ 225 Ken Caminiti .10 .05 .01
- ☐ 226 Jim Clancy .05 .02 .01
- ☐ 227 Danny Darwin .05 .02 .01
- ☐ 228 Glenn Davis .05 .02 .01
- ☐ 229 Jim Deshaies .05 .02 .01
- ☐ 230 Bill Doran .05 .02 .01
- ☐ 231 Bob Forsch .05 .02 .01
- ☐ 232 Brian Meyer .05 .02 .01
- ☐ 233 Terry Puhl .05 .02 .01
- ☐ 234 Rafael Ramirez .05 .02 .01
- ☐ 235 Rick Rhoden .05 .02 .01
- ☐ 236 Dan Schatzeder .05 .02 .01
- ☐ 237 Mike Scott .05 .02 .01
- ☐ 238 Dave Smith .05 .02 .01
- ☐ 239 Alex Trevino .05 .02 .01
- ☐ 240 Glenn Wilson .05 .02 .01
- ☐ 241 Gerald Young .05 .02 .01
- ☐ 242 Tom Brunansky .05 .02 .01
- ☐ 243 Cris Carpenter .05 .02 .01
- ☐ 244 Alex Cole .10 .05 .01
- ☐ 245 Vince Coleman .10 .05 .01
- ☐ 246 John Costello .05 .02 .01
- ☐ 247 Ken Dayley .05 .02 .01
- ☐ 248 Jose DeLeon .05 .02 .01
- ☐ 249 Frank DiPino .05 .02 .01
- ☐ 250 Pedro Guerrero .10 .05 .01
- ☐ 251 Ken Hill .15 .07 .02
- ☐ 252 Joe Magrane .05 .02 .01
- ☐ 253 Willie McGee UER .10 .05 .01 (No decimal point before 353)
- ☐ 254 John Morris .05 .02 .01
- ☐ 255 Jose Oquendo .05 .02 .01
- ☐ 256 Tony Pena .05 .02 .01
- ☐ 257 Terry Pendleton .15 .07 .02
- ☐ 258 Ted Power .05 .02 .01
- ☐ 259 Dan Quisenberry .10 .05 .01
- ☐ 260 Ozzie Smith .25 .11 .03
- ☐ 261 Scott Terry .05 .02 .01
- ☐ 262 Milt Thompson .05 .02 .01
- ☐ 263 Denny Walling .05 .02 .01
- ☐ 264 Todd Worrell .05 .02 .01
- ☐ 265 Todd Zeile .15 .07 .02
- ☐ 266 Marty Barrett .05 .02 .01
- ☐ 267 Mike Boddicker .05 .02 .01
- ☐ 268 Wade Boggs .20 .09 .03
- ☐ 269 Ellis Burks .10 .05 .01
- ☐ 270 Rick Cerone .05 .02 .01
- ☐ 271 Roger Clemens .30 .14 .04
- ☐ 272 John Dopson .05 .02 .01
- ☐ 273 Nick Esasky .05 .02 .01
- ☐ 274 Dwight Evans .10 .05 .01
- ☐ 275 Wes Gardner .05 .02 .01
- ☐ 276 Rich Gedman .05 .02 .01
- ☐ 277 Mike Greenwell .10 .05 .01
- ☐ 278 Danny Heep .05 .02 .01
- ☐ 279 Eric Hetzel .05 .02 .01
- ☐ 280 Dennis Lamp .05 .02 .01
- ☐ 281 Rob Murphy UER .05 .02 .01 ('89 stats say Reds, should say Red Sox)
- ☐ 282 Joe Price .05 .02 .01
- ☐ 283 Carlos Quintana .05 .02 .01
- ☐ 284 Jody Reed .05 .02 .01
- ☐ 285 Luis Rivera .05 .02 .01
- ☐ 286 Kevin Romine .05 .02 .01
- ☐ 287 Lee Smith .15 .07 .02
- ☐ 288 Mike Smithson .05 .02 .01
- ☐ 289 Bob Stanley .05 .02 .01
- ☐ 290 Harold Baines .10 .05 .01
- ☐ 291 Kevin Brown .10 .05 .01
- ☐ 292 Steve Buechele .05 .02 .01
- ☐ 293 Scott Coolbaugh .05 .02 .01
- ☐ 294 Jack Daugherty .05 .02 .01
- ☐ 295 Cecil Espy .05 .02 .01
- ☐ 296 Julio Franco .10 .05 .01
- ☐ 297 Juan Gonzalez 2.00 .90 .25
- ☐ 298 Cecilio Guante .05 .02 .01
- ☐ 299 Drew Hall .05 .02 .01
- ☐ 300 Charlie Hough .10 .05 .01
- ☐ 301 Pete Incaviglia .05 .02 .01
- ☐ 302 Mike Jeffcoat .05 .02 .01
- ☐ 303 Chad Kreuter .05 .02 .01
- ☐ 304 Jeff Kunkel .05 .02 .01
- ☐ 305 Rick Leach .05 .02 .01
- ☐ 306 Fred Manrique .05 .02 .01
- ☐ 307 Jamie Moyer .05 .02 .01
- ☐ 308 Rafael Palmeiro .15 .07 .02
- ☐ 309 Geno Petralli .05 .02 .01
- ☐ 310 Kevin Reimer .05 .02 .01
- ☐ 311 Kenny Rogers .05 .02 .01
- ☐ 312 Jeff Russell .05 .02 .01
- ☐ 313 Nolan Ryan .75 .35 .09
- ☐ 314 Ruben Sierra .15 .07 .02
- ☐ 315 Bobby Witt .05 .02 .01
- ☐ 316 Chris Bosio .05 .02 .01
- ☐ 317 Glenn Braggs UER .05 .02 .01 (Stats say 111 K's, but bio says 117 K's)
- ☐ 318 Greg Brock .05 .02 .01
- ☐ 319 Chuck Crim .05 .02 .01

☐ 320 Rob Deer .05 .02 .01
☐ 321 Mike Felder .05 .02 .01
☐ 322 Tom Filer .05 .02 .01
☐ 323 Tony Fossas .05 .02 .01
☐ 324 Jim Gantner .05 .02 .01
☐ 325 Darryl Hamilton .10 .05 .01
☐ 326 Teddy Higuera .05 .02 .01
☐ 327 Mark Knudson .05 .02 .01
☐ 328 Bill Krueger UER .05 .02 .01
('86 stats missing)
☐ 329 Tim McIntosh .05 .02 .01
☐ 330 Paul Molitor .20 .09 .03
☐ 331 Jaime Navarro .05 .02 .01
☐ 332 Charlie O'Brien .05 .02 .01
☐ 333 Jeff Peterek .05 .02 .01
☐ 334 Dan Plesac .05 .02 .01
☐ 335 Jerry Reuss .05 .02 .01
☐ 336 Gary Sheffield UER .30 .14 .04
(Bio says played for 3 teams in '87, but stats say in '88)
☐ 337 Bill Spiers .05 .02 .01
☐ 338 B.J. Surhoff .05 .02 .01
☐ 339 Greg Vaughn .15 .07 .02
☐ 340 Robin Yount .20 .09 .03
☐ 341 Hubie Brooks .05 .02 .01
☐ 342 Tim Burke .05 .02 .01
☐ 343 Mike Fitzgerald .05 .02 .01
☐ 344 Tom Foley .05 .02 .01
☐ 345 Andres Galarraga .15 .07 .02
☐ 346 Damaso Garcia .05 .02 .01
☐ 347 Marquis Grissom .50 .23 .06
☐ 348 Kevin Gross .05 .02 .01
☐ 349 Joe Hesketh .05 .02 .01
☐ 350 Jeff Huson .05 .02 .01
☐ 351 Wallace Johnson .05 .02 .01
☐ 352 Mark Langston .15 .07 .02
☐ 353A Dave Martinez 3.00 1.35 .40
(Yellow on front)
☐ 353B Dave Martinez .05 .02 .01
(Red on front)
☐ 354 Dennis Martinez UER .10 .05 .01
('87 ERA is 616, should be 6.16)
☐ 355 Andy McGaffigan .05 .02 .01
☐ 356 Otis Nixon .10 .05 .01
☐ 357 Spike Owen .05 .02 .01
☐ 358 Pascual Perez .05 .02 .01
☐ 359 Tim Raines .15 .07 .02
☐ 360 Nelson Santovenia .05 .02 .01
☐ 361 Bryn Smith .05 .02 .01
☐ 362 Zane Smith .05 .02 .01
☐ 363 Larry Walker .50 .23 .06
☐ 364 Tim Wallach .05 .02 .01
☐ 365 Rick Aguilera .10 .05 .01
☐ 366 Allan Anderson .05 .02 .01
☐ 367 Wally Backman .05 .02 .01
☐ 368 Doug Baker .05 .02 .01
☐ 369 Juan Berenguer .05 .02 .01
☐ 370 Randy Bush .05 .02 .01
☐ 371 Carmen Castillo .05 .02 .01
☐ 372 Mike Dyer .05 .02 .01
☐ 373 Gary Gaetti .05 .02 .01
☐ 374 Greg Gagne .05 .02 .01
☐ 375 Dan Gladden .05 .02 .01
☐ 376 German Gonzalez UER .05 .02 .01
(Bio says 31 saves in '88, but stats say 30)
☐ 377 Brian Harper .10 .05 .01
☐ 378 Kent Hrbek .10 .05 .01
☐ 379 Gene Larkin .05 .02 .01
☐ 380 Tim Laudner UER .05 .02 .01
(No decimal point before '85 BA of 238)
☐ 381 John Moses .05 .02 .01
☐ 382 Al Newman .05 .02 .01
☐ 383 Kirby Puckett .35 .16 .04
☐ 384 Shane Rawley .05 .02 .01
☐ 385 Jeff Reardon .15 .07 .02
☐ 386 Roy Smith .05 .02 .01
☐ 387 Gary Wayne .05 .02 .01
☐ 388 Dave West .05 .02 .01
☐ 389 Tim Belcher .05 .02 .01
☐ 390 Tim Crews UER .05 .02 .01
(Stats say 163 IP for '83, but bio says 136)
☐ 391 Mike Davis .05 .02 .01
☐ 392 Rick Dempsey .05 .02 .01
☐ 393 Kirk Gibson .10 .05 .01
☐ 394 Jose Gonzalez .05 .02 .01
☐ 395 Alfredo Griffin .05 .02 .01
☐ 396 Jeff Hamilton .05 .02 .01
☐ 397 Lenny Harris .05 .02 .01
☐ 398 Mickey Hatcher .05 .02 .01
☐ 399 Orel Hershiser .10 .05 .01
☐ 400 Jay Howell .05 .02 .01
☐ 401 Mike Marshall .05 .02 .01
☐ 402 Ramon Martinez .10 .05 .01
☐ 403 Mike Morgan .05 .02 .01
☐ 404 Eddie Murray .15 .07 .02
☐ 405 Alejandro Pena .05 .02 .01
☐ 406 Willie Randolph .10 .05 .01
☐ 407 Mike Scioscia .05 .02 .01
☐ 408 Ray Searage .05 .02 .01
☐ 409 Fernando Valenzuela .05 .02 .01
☐ 410 Jose Vizcaino .05 .02 .01
☐ 411 John Wetteland .10 .05 .01
☐ 412 Jack Armstrong .05 .02 .01
☐ 413 Todd Benzinger UER .05 .02 .01
(Bio says .323 at Pawtucket, but stats say .321)
☐ 414 Tim Birtsas .05 .02 .01
☐ 415 Tom Browning .05 .02 .01
☐ 416 Norm Charlton .10 .05 .01
☐ 417 Eric Davis .10 .05 .01
☐ 418 Rob Dibble .10 .05 .01
☐ 419 John Franco .10 .05 .01
☐ 420 Ken Griffey .10 .05 .01
☐ 421 Chris Hammond .15 .07 .02
(No 1989 used for "Did Not Play" stat, actually did play for Nashville in 1989)
☐ 422 Danny Jackson .05 .02 .01
☐ 423 Barry Larkin .15 .07 .02
☐ 424 Tim Leary .05 .02 .01
☐ 425 Rick Mahler .05 .02 .01
☐ 426 Joe Oliver .05 .02 .01
☐ 427 Paul O'Neill .10 .05 .01
☐ 428 Luis Quinones UER .05 .02 .01
('86-'88 stats are omitted from card but included in totals)
☐ 429 Jeff Reed .05 .02 .01
☐ 430 Jose Rijo .10 .05 .01
☐ 431 Ron Robinson .05 .02 .01
☐ 432 Rolando Roomes .05 .02 .01
☐ 433 Chris Sabo .10 .05 .01
☐ 434 Scott Scudder .05 .02 .01
☐ 435 Herm Winningham .05 .02 .01
☐ 436 Steve Balboni .05 .02 .01
☐ 437 Jesse Barfield .05 .02 .01
☐ 438 Mike Blowers .05 .02 .01
☐ 439 Tom Brookens .05 .02 .01
☐ 440 Greg Cadaret .05 .02 .01

	No.	Player			
☐	441	Alvaro Espinoza UER (Career games say 218, should be 219)	.05	.02	.01
☐	442	Bob Geren	.05	.02	.01
☐	443	Lee Guetterman	.05	.02	.01
☐	444	Mel Hall	.05	.02	.01
☐	445	Andy Hawkins	.05	.02	.01
☐	446	Roberto Kelly	.10	.05	.01
☐	447	Don Mattingly	.35	.16	.04
☐	448	Lance McCullers	.05	.02	.01
☐	449	Hensley Meulens	.05	.02	.01
☐	450	Dale Mohorcic	.05	.02	.01
☐	451	Clay Parker	.05	.02	.01
☐	452	Eric Plunk	.05	.02	.01
☐	453	Dave Righetti	.05	.02	.01
☐	454	Deion Sanders	.50	.23	.06
☐	455	Steve Sax	.05	.02	.01
☐	456	Don Slaught	.05	.02	.01
☐	457	Walt Terrell	.05	.02	.01
☐	458	Dave Winfield	.15	.07	.02
☐	459	Jay Bell	.10	.05	.01
☐	460	Rafael Belliard	.05	.02	.01
☐	461	Barry Bonds	.50	.23	.06
☐	462	Bobby Bonilla	.15	.07	.02
☐	463	Sid Bream	.05	.02	.01
☐	464	Benny Distefano	.05	.02	.01
☐	465	Doug Drabek	.15	.07	.02
☐	466	Jim Gott	.05	.02	.01
☐	467	Billy Hatcher UER (.1 hits for Cubs in 1984)	.05	.02	.01
☐	468	Neal Heaton	.05	.02	.01
☐	469	Jeff King	.10	.05	.01
☐	470	Bob Kipper	.05	.02	.01
☐	471	Randy Kramer	.05	.02	.01
☐	472	Bill Landrum	.05	.02	.01
☐	473	Mike LaValliere	.05	.02	.01
☐	474	Jose Lind	.05	.02	.01
☐	475	Junior Ortiz	.05	.02	.01
☐	476	Gary Redus	.05	.02	.01
☐	477	Rick Reed	.05	.02	.01
☐	478	R.J. Reynolds	.05	.02	.01
☐	479	Jeff D. Robinson	.05	.02	.01
☐	480	John Smiley	.05	.02	.01
☐	481	Andy Van Slyke	.15	.07	.02
☐	482	Bob Walk	.05	.02	.01
☐	483	Andy Allanson	.05	.02	.01
☐	484	Scott Bailes	.05	.02	.01
☐	485	Joey Belle UER (Has Jay Bell "Did You Know")	1.25	.55	.16
☐	486	Bud Black	.05	.02	.01
☐	487	Jerry Browne	.05	.02	.01
☐	488	Tom Candiotti	.05	.02	.01
☐	489	Joe Carter	.25	.11	.03
☐	490	Dave Clark (No '84 stats)	.05	.02	.01
☐	491	John Farrell	.05	.02	.01
☐	492	Felix Fermin	.05	.02	.01
☐	493	Brook Jacoby	.05	.02	.01
☐	494	Dion James	.05	.02	.01
☐	495	Doug Jones	.05	.02	.01
☐	496	Brad Komminsk	.05	.02	.01
☐	497	Rod Nichols	.05	.02	.01
☐	498	Pete O'Brien	.05	.02	.01
☐	499	Steve Olin	.10	.05	.01
☐	500	Jesse Orosco	.05	.02	.01
☐	501	Joel Skinner	.05	.02	.01
☐	502	Cory Snyder	.05	.02	.01
☐	503	Greg Swindell	.10	.05	.01
☐	504	Rich Yett	.05	.02	.01
☐	505	Scott Bankhead	.05	.02	.01
☐	506	Scott Bradley	.05	.02	.01
☐	507	Greg Briley UER (28 SB's in bio, but 27 in stats)	.05	.02	.01
☐	508	Jay Buhner	.15	.07	.02
☐	509	Darnell Coles	.05	.02	.01
☐	510	Keith Comstock	.05	.02	.01
☐	511	Henry Cotto	.05	.02	.01
☐	512	Alvin Davis	.05	.02	.01
☐	513	Ken Griffey Jr.	2.50	1.15	.30
☐	514	Erik Hanson	.10	.05	.01
☐	515	Gene Harris	.05	.02	.01
☐	516	Brian Holman	.05	.02	.01
☐	517	Mike Jackson	.05	.02	.01
☐	518	Randy Johnson	.20	.09	.03
☐	519	Jeffrey Leonard	.05	.02	.01
☐	520	Edgar Martinez	.10	.05	.01
☐	521	Dennis Powell	.05	.02	.01
☐	522	Jim Presley	.05	.02	.01
☐	523	Jerry Reed	.05	.02	.01
☐	524	Harold Reynolds	.05	.02	.01
☐	525	Mike Schooler	.05	.02	.01
☐	526	Bill Swift	.10	.05	.01
☐	527	Dave Valle	.05	.02	.01
☐	528	Omar Vizquel	.05	.02	.01
☐	529	Ivan Calderon	.05	.02	.01
☐	530	Carlton Fisk UER (Bellow Falls, should be Bellows Falls)	.15	.07	.02
☐	531	Scott Fletcher	.05	.02	.01
☐	532	Dave Gallagher	.05	.02	.01
☐	533	Ozzie Guillen	.05	.02	.01
☐	534	Greg Hibbard	.05	.02	.01
☐	535	Shawn Hillegas	.05	.02	.01
☐	536	Lance Johnson	.10	.05	.01
☐	537	Eric King	.05	.02	.01
☐	538	Ron Kittle	.05	.02	.01
☐	539	Steve Lyons	.05	.02	.01
☐	540	Carlos Martinez	.05	.02	.01
☐	541	Tom McCarthy	.05	.02	.01
☐	542	Matt Merullo (Had 5 ML runs scored entering '90, not 6)	.05	.02	.01
☐	543	Donn Pall UER (Stats say pro career began in '85, bio says '88)	.05	.02	.01
☐	544	Dan Pasqua	.05	.02	.01
☐	545	Ken Patterson	.05	.02	.01
☐	546	Melido Perez	.05	.02	.01
☐	547	Steve Rosenberg	.05	.02	.01
☐	548	Sammy Sosa	.50	.23	.06
☐	549	Bobby Thigpen	.05	.02	.01
☐	550	Robin Ventura	.50	.23	.06
☐	551	Greg Walker	.05	.02	.01
☐	552	Don Carman	.05	.02	.01
☐	553	Pat Combs (6 walks for Phillies in '89 in stats, brief bio says 4)	.05	.02	.01
☐	554	Dennis Cook	.05	.02	.01
☐	555	Darren Daulton	.15	.07	.02
☐	556	Len Dykstra	.15	.07	.02
☐	557	Curt Ford	.05	.02	.01
☐	558	Charlie Hayes	.10	.05	.01
☐	559	Von Hayes	.05	.02	.01
☐	560	Tommy Herr	.05	.02	.01
☐	561	Ken Howell	.05	.02	.01
☐	562	Steve Jeltz	.05	.02	.01
☐	563	Ron Jones	.05	.02	.01
☐	564	Ricky Jordan UER (Duplicate line of statistics on back)	.05	.02	.01
☐	565	John Kruk	.15	.07	.02

- ☐ 566 Steve Lake .... .05 .02 .01
- ☐ 567 Roger McDowell .... .05 .02 .01
- ☐ 568 Terry Mulholland UER.. .10 .05 .01
  ("Did You Know" refers to Dave Magadan)
- ☐ 569 Dwayne Murphy.......... .05 .02 .01
- ☐ 570 Jeff Parrett.......... .05 .02 .01
- ☐ 571 Randy Ready.......... .05 .02 .01
- ☐ 572 Bruce Ruffin.......... .05 .02 .01
- ☐ 573 Dickie Thon.......... .05 .02 .01
- ☐ 574 Jose Alvarez UER.......... .05 .02 .01
  ('78 and '79 stats are reversed)
- ☐ 575 Geronimo Berroa .... .10 .05 .01
- ☐ 576 Jeff Blauser.......... .10 .05 .01
- ☐ 577 Joe Boever.......... .05 .02 .01
- ☐ 578 Marty Clary UER .... .05 .02 .01
  (No comma between city and state)
- ☐ 579 Jody Davis .... .05 .02 .01
- ☐ 580 Mark Eichhorn .... .05 .02 .01
- ☐ 581 Darrell Evans.......... .10 .05 .01
- ☐ 582 Ron Gant.......... .20 .09 .03
- ☐ 583 Tom Glavine.......... .25 .11 .03
- ☐ 584 Tommy Greene .... .15 .07 .02
- ☐ 585 Tommy Gregg.......... .05 .02 .01
- ☐ 586 David Justice UER ..... 1.00 .45 .13
  (Actually had 16 2B in Sumter in '86)
- ☐ 587 Mark Lemke.......... .10 .05 .01
- ☐ 588 Derek Lilliquist.......... .05 .02 .01
- ☐ 589 Oddibe McDowell.......... .05 .02 .01
- ☐ 590 Kent Mercker ERA.......... .25 .11 .03
  (Bio says 2.75 ERA, stats say 2.68 ERA)
- ☐ 591 Dale Murphy .... .15 .07 .02
- ☐ 592 Gerald Perry.......... .05 .02 .01
- ☐ 593 Lonnie Smith .... .05 .02 .01
- ☐ 594 Pete Smith .... .05 .02 .01
- ☐ 595 John Smoltz.......... .15 .07 .02
- ☐ 596 Mike Stanton UER.......... .05 .02 .01
  (No comma between city and state)
- ☐ 597 Andres Thomas.......... .05 .02 .01
- ☐ 598 Jeff Treadway .... .05 .02 .01
- ☐ 599 Doyle Alexander.......... .05 .02 .01
- ☐ 600 Dave Bergman .... .05 .02 .01
- ☐ 601 Brian DuBois.......... .05 .02 .01
- ☐ 602 Paul Gibson .... .05 .02 .01
- ☐ 603 Mike Heath.......... .05 .02 .01
- ☐ 604 Mike Henneman.......... .05 .02 .01
- ☐ 605 Guillermo Hernandez ... .05 .02 .01
- ☐ 606 Shawn Holman .... .05 .02 .01
- ☐ 607 Tracy Jones .... .05 .02 .01
- ☐ 608 Chet Lemon .... .05 .02 .01
- ☐ 609 Fred Lynn.......... .10 .05 .01
- ☐ 610 Jack Morris.......... .15 .07 .02
- ☐ 611 Matt Nokes .... .05 .02 .01
- ☐ 612 Gary Pettis .... .05 .02 .01
- ☐ 613 Kevin Ritz.......... .05 .02 .01
- ☐ 614 Jeff M. Robinson .... .05 .02 .01
  ('88 stats are not in line)
- ☐ 615 Steve Searcy.......... .05 .02 .01
- ☐ 616 Frank Tanana .... .05 .02 .01
- ☐ 617 Alan Trammell.......... .15 .07 .02
- ☐ 618 Gary Ward.......... .05 .02 .01
- ☐ 619 Lou Whitaker .... .15 .07 .02
- ☐ 620 Frank Williams .... .05 .02 .01
- ☐ 621A George Brett '80 ...... 1.50 .65 .19
  ERR (Had 10 .390 hitting seasons)
- ☐ 621B George Brett '80 .... .25 .11 .03
  COR
- ☐ 622 Fern.Valenzuela '81 .... .05 .02 .01
- ☐ 623 Dale Murphy '82 .... .05 .02 .01
- ☐ 624A Cal Ripken '83 ERR . 5.00 2.30 .60
  (Misspelled Ripkin on card back)
- ☐ 624B Cal Ripken '83 COR ... .25 .11 .03
- ☐ 625 Ryne Sandberg '84 ...... .25 .11 .03
- ☐ 626 Don Mattingly '85 .... .15 .07 .02
- ☐ 627 Roger Clemens '86 ...... .15 .07 .02
- ☐ 628 George Bell '87 .... .05 .02 .01
- ☐ 629 Jose Canseco '88 UER. .15 .07 .02
  (Reggie won MVP in '83, should say '73)
- ☐ 630A Will Clark '89 ERR ... 1.00 .45 .13
  (32 total bases on card back)
- ☐ 630B Will Clark '89 COR..... .15 .07 .02
  (321 total bases; technically still an error, listing only 24 runs)
- ☐ 631 Game Savers.......... .05 .02 .01
  Mark Davis
  Mitch Williams
- ☐ 632 Boston Igniters .... .10 .05 .01
  Wade Boggs
  Mike Greenwell
- ☐ 633 Starter and Stopper ..... .05 .02 .01
  Mark Gubicza
  Jeff Russell
- ☐ 634 League's Best .... .15 .07 .02
  Shortstops
  Tony Fernandez
  Cal Ripken
- ☐ 635 Human Dynamos.......... .15 .07 .02
  Kirby Puckett
  Bo Jackson
- ☐ 636 300 Strikeout Club.......... .25 .11 .03
  Nolan Ryan
  Mike Scott
- ☐ 637 The Dynamic Duo .... .10 .05 .01
  Will Clark
  Kevin Mitchell
- ☐ 638 AL All-Stars.......... .20 .09 .03
  Don Mattingly
  Mark McGwire
- ☐ 639 NL East Rivals.......... .15 .07 .02
  Howard Johnson
  Ryne Sandberg
- ☐ 640 Rudy Seanez.......... .05 .02 .01
  Colin Charland
- ☐ 641 George Canale.......... .05 .02 .01
  Kevin Maas UER
  (Canale listed as INF on front, 1B on back)
- ☐ 642 Kelly Mann.......... .05 .02 .01
  and Dave Hansen
- ☐ 643 Greg Smith .... .05 .02 .01
  and Stu Tate
- ☐ 644 Tom Drees.......... .05 .02 .01
  and Dann Howitt
- ☐ 645 Mike Roesler.......... .20 .09 .03
  and Derrick May
- ☐ 646 Scott Hemond.......... .05 .02 .01
  and Mark Gardner
- ☐ 647 John Orton.......... .05 .02 .01
  and Scott Leius
- ☐ 648 Rich Monteleone.......... .05 .02 .01
  and Dana Williams
- ☐ 649 Mike Huff.......... .05 .02 .01
  and Steve Frey
- ☐ 650 Chuck McElroy.......... .50 .23 .06
  and Moises Alou

		MINT	EXC	G-VG
☐ 651	Bobby Rose and Mike Hartley	.05	.02	.01
☐ 652	Matt Kinzer and Wayne Edwards	.05	.02	.01
☐ 653	Delino DeShields and Jason Grimsley	.20	.09	.03
☐ 654	CL: A's/Cubs Giants/Blue Jays	.05	.02	.01
☐ 655	CL: Royals/Angels Padres/Orioles	.05	.02	.01
☐ 656	CL: Mets/Astros Cards/Red Sox	.05	.02	.01
☐ 657	CL: Rangers/Brewers Expos/Twins	.05	.02	.01
☐ 658	CL: Dodgers/Reds Yankees/Pirates	.05	.02	.01
☐ 659	CL: Indians/Mariners White Sox/Phillies	.05	.02	.01
☐ 660A	CL: Braves/Tigers Specials/Checklists (Checklist-660 in smaller print on card front)	.10	.02	.01
☐ 660B	CL: Braves/Tigers Specials/Checklists (Checklist-660 in normal print on card front)	.10	.02	.01

1990 Fleer All-Stars

The 1990 Fleer All-Star insert set includes 12 standard-size (2 1/2" by 3 1/2") cards. The fronts are white with a light gray screen and bright red stripes. The vertically oriented backs are red, pink and white. The player selection for the set is Fleer's opinion of the best Major League at each position. Cards were individually distributed as an insert in 33-card cellos and random wax packs.

	MINT	EXC	G-VG
COMPLETE SET (12)	5.00	2.30	.60
COMMON CARD (1-12)	.15	.07	.02

		MINT	EXC	G-VG
☐ 1	Harold Baines	.30	.14	.04
☐ 2	Will Clark	1.00	.45	.13
☐ 3	Mark Davis	.15	.07	.02
☐ 4	Howard Johnson UER (In middle of 5th line, the is misspelled th)	.15	.07	.02
☐ 5	Joe Magrane	.15	.07	.02
☐ 6	Kevin Mitchell	.30	.14	.04
☐ 7	Kirby Puckett	1.50	.65	.19
☐ 8	Cal Ripken	2.00	.90	.25
☐ 9	Ryne Sandberg	1.50	.65	.19
☐ 10	Mike Scott	.15	.07	.02
☐ 11	Ruben Sierra	.50	.23	.06
☐ 12	Mickey Tettleton	.30	.14	.04

1990 Fleer League Standouts

This six-card subset was distributed one per 45-card rack packs. These cards are standard size, 2 1/2" by 3 1/2" and are quite attractive. The set is subtitled "Standouts" and commemorates outstanding events for those players from the previous season. The cards are numbered on the backs. The card backs are printed on white card stock.

	MINT	EXC	G-VG
COMPLETE SET (6)	5.00	2.30	.60
COMMON CARD (1-6)	.60	.25	.08

		MINT	EXC	G-VG
☐ 1	Barry Larkin	.60	.25	.08
☐ 2	Don Mattingly	2.00	.90	.25
☐ 3	Darryl Strawberry	.60	.25	.08
☐ 4	Jose Canseco	1.25	.55	.16
☐ 5	Wade Boggs	1.00	.45	.13
☐ 6	Mark Grace UER (Chris Sabo misspelled as Cris)	.75	.35	.09

1990 Fleer Soaring Stars

The 1990 Fleer Soaring Stars set was issued by Fleer in their jumbo cello packs. This 12-card, standard-size (2 1/2" by 3 1/2") set featured 12 of the most popular young players entering the 1990 season. The set gives the visual impression of rockets exploding in the air to honor these young players.

	MINT	EXC	G-VG
COMPLETE SET (12)	22.00	10.00	2.80
COMMON CARD (1-12)	.40	.18	.05

☐ 1 Todd Zeile	.75	.35	.09
☐ 2 Mike Stanton	.40	.18	.05
☐ 3 Larry Walker	3.00	1.35	.40
☐ 4 Robin Ventura	3.00	1.35	.40
☐ 5 Scott Coolbaugh	.40	.18	.05
☐ 6 Ken Griffey Jr.	15.00	6.75	1.90
☐ 7 Tom Gordon	.50	.23	.06
☐ 8 Jerome Walton	.40	.18	.05
☐ 9 Junior Felix	.40	.18	.05
☐ 10 Jim Abbott	1.25	.55	.16
☐ 11 Ricky Jordan	.40	.18	.05
☐ 12 Dwight Smith	.40	.18	.05

1990 Fleer Update

The 1990 Fleer Update set contains 132 standard-size (2 1/2" by 3 1/2") cards. This set marked the seventh consecutive year Fleer issued an end of season Update set. The set was issued exclusively as a boxed set through hobby dealers. The set is checklisted alphabetically by team for each league and then alphabetically within each team. The fronts are styled the same as the 1990 Fleer regular issue set. The backs are numbered with the prefix "U" for Update. Rookie Cards in this set include Carlos Baerga, Chuck Carr, Alex Fernandez, Travis Fryman, Chris Hoiles, Dave Hollins, Jose Offerman, John Olerud, Frank Thomas, and Mark Whiten.

	MINT	EXC	G-VG
COMPLETE FACT.SET (132)	6.00	2.70	.75
COMMON CARD (1-132)	.05	.02	.01
☐ 1 Steve Avery	.40	.18	.05
☐ 2 Francisco Cabrera	.05	.02	.01
☐ 3 Nick Esasky	.05	.02	.01
☐ 4 Jim Kremers	.05	.02	.01
☐ 5 Greg Olson	.05	.02	.01
☐ 6 Jim Presley	.05	.02	.01
☐ 7 Shawn Boskie	.05	.02	.01
☐ 8 Joe Kraemer	.05	.02	.01
☐ 9 Luis Salazar	.05	.02	.01
☐ 10 Hector Villanueva	.05	.02	.01
☐ 11 Glenn Braggs	.05	.02	.01
☐ 12 Mariano Duncan	.05	.02	.01
☐ 13 Billy Hatcher	.05	.02	.01
☐ 14 Tim Layana	.05	.02	.01
☐ 15 Hal Morris	.08	.04	.01
☐ 16 Javier Ortiz	.05	.02	.01
☐ 17 Dave Rohde	.05	.02	.01
☐ 18 Eric Yelding	.05	.02	.01
☐ 19 Hubie Brooks	.05	.02	.01
☐ 20 Kal Daniels	.05	.02	.01
☐ 21 Dave Hansen	.05	.02	.01
☐ 22 Mike Hartley	.05	.02	.01
☐ 23 Stan Javier	.05	.02	.01
☐ 24 Jose Offerman	.15	.07	.02
☐ 25 Juan Samuel	.05	.02	.01
☐ 26 Dennis Boyd	.05	.02	.01
☐ 27 Delino DeShields	.15	.07	.02
☐ 28 Steve Frey	.05	.02	.01
☐ 29 Mark Gardner	.05	.02	.01
☐ 30 Chris Nabholz	.05	.02	.01
☐ 31 Bill Sampen	.05	.02	.01
☐ 32 Dave Schmidt	.05	.02	.01
☐ 33 Daryl Boston	.05	.02	.01
☐ 34 Chuck Carr	.25	.11	.03
☐ 35 John Franco	.08	.04	.01
☐ 36 Todd Hundley	.20	.09	.03
☐ 37 Julio Machado	.05	.02	.01
☐ 38 Alejandro Pena	.05	.02	.01
☐ 39 Darren Reed	.05	.02	.01
☐ 40 Kelvin Torve	.05	.02	.01
☐ 41 Darrel Akerfelds	.05	.02	.01
☐ 42 Jose DeJesus	.05	.02	.01
☐ 43 Dave Hollins UER (Misspelled Dane on card back)	.25	.11	.03
☐ 44 Carmelo Martinez	.05	.02	.01
☐ 45 Brad Moore	.05	.02	.01
☐ 46 Dale Murphy	.10	.05	.01
☐ 47 Wally Backman	.05	.02	.01
☐ 48 Stan Belinda	.05	.02	.01
☐ 49 Bob Patterson	.05	.02	.01
☐ 50 Ted Power	.05	.02	.01
☐ 51 Don Slaught	.05	.02	.01
☐ 52 Geronimo Pena	.05	.02	.01
☐ 53 Lee Smith	.10	.05	.01
☐ 54 John Tudor	.05	.02	.01
☐ 55 Joe Carter	.25	.11	.03
☐ 56 Thomas Howard	.05	.02	.01
☐ 57 Craig Lefferts	.05	.02	.01
☐ 58 Rafael Valdez	.05	.02	.01
☐ 59 Dave Anderson	.05	.02	.01
☐ 60 Kevin Bass	.05	.02	.01
☐ 61 John Burkett	.25	.11	.03
☐ 62 Gary Carter	.10	.05	.01
☐ 63 Rick Parker	.05	.02	.01
☐ 64 Trevor Wilson	.05	.02	.01
☐ 65 Chris Hoiles	.25	.11	.03
☐ 66 Tim Hulett	.05	.02	.01
☐ 67 Dave Johnson	.05	.02	.01
☐ 68 Curt Schilling	.08	.04	.01
☐ 69 David Segui	.15	.07	.02
☐ 70 Tom Brunansky	.05	.02	.01
☐ 71 Greg A. Harris	.05	.02	.01
☐ 72 Dana Kiecker	.05	.02	.01
☐ 73 Tim Naehring	.20	.09	.03
☐ 74 Tony Pena	.05	.02	.01

☐ 75 Jeff Reardon	.10	.05	.01
☐ 76 Jerry Reed	.05	.02	.01
☐ 77 Mark Eichhorn	.05	.02	.01
☐ 78 Mark Langston	.10	.05	.01
☐ 79 John Orton	.05	.02	.01
☐ 80 Luis Polonia	.08	.04	.01
☐ 81 Dave Winfield	.10	.05	.01
☐ 82 Cliff Young	.05	.02	.01
☐ 83 Wayne Edwards	.05	.02	.01
☐ 84 Alex Fernandez	.50	.23	.06
☐ 85 Craig Grebeck	.05	.02	.01
☐ 86 Scott Radinsky	.05	.02	.01
☐ 87 Frank Thomas	4.00	1.80	.50
☐ 88 Beau Allred	.05	.02	.01
☐ 89 Sandy Alomar Jr.	.08	.04	.01
☐ 90 Carlos Baerga	1.00	.45	.13
☐ 91 Kevin Bearse	.05	.02	.01
☐ 92 Chris James	.05	.02	.01
☐ 93 Candy Maldonado	.05	.02	.01
☐ 94 Jeff Manto	.05	.02	.01
☐ 95 Cecil Fielder	.20	.09	.03
☐ 96 Travis Fryman	1.00	.45	.13
☐ 97 Lloyd Moseby	.05	.02	.01
☐ 98 Edwin Nunez	.05	.02	.01
☐ 99 Tony Phillips	.08	.04	.01
☐ 100 Larry Sheets	.05	.02	.01
☐ 101 Mark Davis	.05	.02	.01
☐ 102 Storm Davis	.05	.02	.01
☐ 103 Gerald Perry	.05	.02	.01
☐ 104 Terry Shumpert	.05	.02	.01
☐ 105 Edgar Diaz	.05	.02	.01
☐ 106 Dave Parker	.10	.05	.01
☐ 107 Tim Drummond	.05	.02	.01
☐ 108 Junior Ortiz	.05	.02	.01
☐ 109 Park Pittman	.05	.02	.01
☐ 110 Kevin Tapani	.20	.09	.03
☐ 111 Oscar Azocar	.05	.02	.01
☐ 112 Jim Leyritz	.15	.07	.02
☐ 113 Kevin Maas	.05	.02	.01
☐ 114 Alan Mills	.05	.02	.01
☐ 115 Matt Nokes	.05	.02	.01
☐ 116 Pascual Perez	.05	.02	.01
☐ 117 Ozzie Canseco	.05	.02	.01
☐ 118 Scott Sanderson	.05	.02	.01
☐ 119 Tino Martinez	.08	.04	.01
☐ 120 Jeff Schaefer	.05	.02	.01
☐ 121 Matt Young	.05	.02	.01
☐ 122 Brian Bohanon	.05	.02	.01
☐ 123 Jeff Huson	.05	.02	.01
☐ 124 Ramon Manon	.05	.02	.01
☐ 125 Gary Mielke UER (Shown as Blue Jay on front)	.05	.02	.01
☐ 126 Willie Blair	.05	.02	.01
☐ 127 Glenallen Hill	.05	.02	.01
☐ 128 John Olerud UER (Listed as throwing right, should be left)	.60	.25	.08
☐ 129 Luis Sojo	.05	.02	.01
☐ 130 Mark Whiten	.25	.11	.03
☐ 131 Nolan Ryan	.75	.35	.09
☐ 132 Checklist U1-U132	.05	.02	.01

1991 Fleer

The 1991 Fleer set consists of 720 cards which measure the now standard size of 2 1/2" by 3 1/2". This set marks Fleer's eleventh consecutive year of issuing sets of

current players. This set does not have what has been a Fleer tradition in recent years, the two-player rookie cards and there are less two-player special cards than in prior years. Apparently this was an attempt by Fleer to increase the number of single player cards in the set. The design features solid yellow borders with the information in black indicating name, position, and team. The backs feature beautiful full-color photos along with the career statistics and a biography for those players where there is room. The set is again ordered numerically by teams, followed by combination cards, rookie prospect pairs, and checklists. Again Fleer incorrectly anticipated the outcome of the 1990 Playoffs according to the team ordering. The A's, listed first, did not win the World Series and their opponents (and Series winners) were the Reds, not the Pirates. Fleer later reported that they merely arranged the teams according to regular season team record due to the early printing date. The complete team ordering is as follows: Oakland A's (1-28), Pittsburgh Pirates (29-54), Cincinnati Reds (55-82), Boston Red Sox (83-113), Chicago White Sox (114-139), New York Mets (140-166), Toronto Blue Jays (167-192), Los Angeles Dodgers (193-223), Montreal Expos (224-251), San Francisco Giants (252-277), Texas Rangers (278-304), California Angels (305-330), Detroit Tigers (331-357), Cleveland Indians (358-385), Philadelphia Phillies (386-412), Chicago Cubs (413-441), Seattle Mariners (442-465), Baltimore Orioles (466-496), Houston Astros (497-522) San Diego Padres (523-548), Kansas City Royals (549-575), Milwaukee Brewers (576-601), Minnesota Twins (602-627), St. Louis Cardinals (628-654), New York Yankees (655-680), and Atlanta Braves (681-708). A number of the cards in the set can be found with photos cropped (very slightly) differently as Fleer used two separate printers in their attempt to maximize production. Rookie Cards in this set include Wes Chamberlain, Jeff Conine, Carlos Garcia, Luis Gonzalez, Brian McRae, Pedro Munoz, Phil Plantier, and Randy Tomlin.

	MINT	EXC	G-VG
COMPLETE SET (720)	10.00	4.50	1.25
COMPLETE RETAIL SET (732)	12.00	5.50	1.50
COMPLETE HOBBY SET (732)	12.00	5.50	1.50
COMMON CARD (1-720)	.05	.02	.01
☐ 1 Troy Afenir	.05	.02	.01
☐ 2 Harold Baines	.10	.05	.01

- ☐ 3 Lance Blankenship .... .05 .02 .01
- ☐ 4 Todd Burns .... .05 .02 .01
- ☐ 5 Jose Canseco .... .20 .09 .03
- ☐ 6 Dennis Eckersley .... .15 .07 .02
- ☐ 7 Mike Gallego .... .05 .02 .01
- ☐ 8 Ron Hassey .... .05 .02 .01
- ☐ 9 Dave Henderson .... .05 .02 .01
- ☐ 10 Rickey Henderson .... .15 .07 .02
- ☐ 11 Rick Honeycutt .... .05 .02 .01
- ☐ 12 Doug Jennings .... .05 .02 .01
- ☐ 13 Joe Klink .... .05 .02 .01
- ☐ 14 Carney Lansford .... .10 .05 .01
- ☐ 15 Darren Lewis .... .10 .05 .01
- ☐ 16 Willie McGee UER .... .10 .05 .01
  (Height 6'11")
- ☐ 17 Mark McGwire UER .... .15 .07 .02
  (183 extra base hits in 1987)
- ☐ 18 Mike Moore .... .05 .02 .01
- ☐ 19 Gene Nelson .... .05 .02 .01
- ☐ 20 Dave Otto .... .05 .02 .01
- ☐ 21 Jamie Quirk .... .05 .02 .01
- ☐ 22 Willie Randolph .... .10 .05 .01
- ☐ 23 Scott Sanderson .... .05 .02 .01
- ☐ 24 Terry Steinbach .... .10 .05 .01
- ☐ 25 Dave Stewart .... .10 .05 .01
- ☐ 26 Walt Weiss .... .05 .02 .01
- ☐ 27 Bob Welch .... .05 .02 .01
- ☐ 28 Curt Young .... .05 .02 .01
- ☐ 29 Wally Backman .... .05 .02 .01
- ☐ 30 Stan Belinda UER .... .05 .02 .01
  (Born in Huntington, should be State College)
- ☐ 31 Jay Bell .... .10 .05 .01
- ☐ 32 Rafael Belliard .... .05 .02 .01
- ☐ 33 Barry Bonds .... .40 .18 .05
- ☐ 34 Bobby Bonilla .... .15 .07 .02
- ☐ 35 Sid Bream .... .05 .02 .01
- ☐ 36 Doug Drabek .... .15 .07 .02
- ☐ 37 Carlos Garcia .... .25 .11 .03
- ☐ 38 Neal Heaton .... .05 .02 .01
- ☐ 39 Jeff King .... .05 .02 .01
- ☐ 40 Bob Kipper .... .05 .02 .01
- ☐ 41 Bill Landrum .... .05 .02 .01
- ☐ 42 Mike LaValliere .... .05 .02 .01
- ☐ 43 Jose Lind .... .05 .02 .01
- ☐ 44 Carmelo Martinez .... .05 .02 .01
- ☐ 45 Bob Patterson .... .05 .02 .01
- ☐ 46 Ted Power .... .05 .02 .01
- ☐ 47 Gary Redus .... .05 .02 .01
- ☐ 48 R.J. Reynolds .... .05 .02 .01
- ☐ 49 Don Slaught .... .05 .02 .01
- ☐ 50 John Smiley .... .05 .02 .01
- ☐ 51 Zane Smith .... .05 .02 .01
- ☐ 52 Randy Tomlin .... .05 .02 .01
- ☐ 53 Andy Van Slyke .... .15 .07 .02
- ☐ 54 Bob Walk .... .05 .02 .01
- ☐ 55 Jack Armstrong .... .05 .02 .01
- ☐ 56 Todd Benzinger .... .05 .02 .01
- ☐ 57 Glenn Braggs .... .05 .02 .01
- ☐ 58 Keith Brown .... .05 .02 .01
- ☐ 59 Tom Browning .... .05 .02 .01
- ☐ 60 Norm Charlton .... .05 .02 .01
- ☐ 61 Eric Davis .... .10 .05 .01
- ☐ 62 Rob Dibble .... .05 .02 .01
- ☐ 63 Bill Doran .... .05 .02 .01
- ☐ 64 Mariano Duncan .... .05 .02 .01
- ☐ 65 Chris Hammond .... .10 .05 .01
- ☐ 66 Billy Hatcher .... .05 .02 .01
- ☐ 67 Danny Jackson .... .05 .02 .01
- ☐ 68 Barry Larkin .... .15 .07 .02
- ☐ 69 Tim Layana .... .05 .02 .01
  (Black line over made in first text line)
- ☐ 70 Terry Lee .... .05 .02 .01
- ☐ 71 Rick Mahler .... .05 .02 .01
- ☐ 72 Hal Morris .... .10 .05 .01
- ☐ 73 Randy Myers .... .10 .05 .01
- ☐ 74 Ron Oester .... .05 .02 .01
- ☐ 75 Joe Oliver .... .05 .02 .01
- ☐ 76 Paul O'Neill .... .10 .05 .01
- ☐ 77 Luis Quinones .... .05 .02 .01
- ☐ 78 Jeff Reed .... .05 .02 .01
- ☐ 79 Jose Rijo .... .10 .05 .01
- ☐ 80 Chris Sabo .... .10 .05 .01
- ☐ 81 Scott Scudder .... .05 .02 .01
- ☐ 82 Herm Winningham .... .05 .02 .01
- ☐ 83 Larry Andersen .... .05 .02 .01
- ☐ 84 Marty Barrett .... .05 .02 .01
- ☐ 85 Mike Boddicker .... .05 .02 .01
- ☐ 86 Wade Boggs .... .15 .07 .02
- ☐ 87 Tom Bolton .... .05 .02 .01
- ☐ 88 Tom Brunansky .... .05 .02 .01
- ☐ 89 Ellis Burks .... .10 .05 .01
- ☐ 90 Roger Clemens .... .25 .11 .03
- ☐ 91 Scott Cooper .... .10 .05 .01
- ☐ 92 John Dopson .... .05 .02 .01
- ☐ 93 Dwight Evans .... .10 .05 .01
- ☐ 94 Wes Gardner .... .05 .02 .01
- ☐ 95 Jeff Gray .... .05 .02 .01
- ☐ 96 Mike Greenwell .... .10 .05 .01
- ☐ 97 Greg A. Harris .... .05 .02 .01
- ☐ 98 Daryl Irvine .... .05 .02 .01
- ☐ 99 Dana Kiecker .... .05 .02 .01
- ☐ 100 Randy Kutcher .... .05 .02 .01
- ☐ 101 Dennis Lamp .... .05 .02 .01
- ☐ 102 Mike Marshall .... .05 .02 .01
- ☐ 103 John Marzano .... .05 .02 .01
- ☐ 104 Rob Murphy .... .05 .02 .01
- ☐ 105 Tim Naehring .... .05 .02 .01
- ☐ 106 Tony Pena .... .05 .02 .01
- ☐ 107 Phil Plantier .... .30 .14 .04
- ☐ 108 Carlos Quintana .... .05 .02 .01
- ☐ 109 Jeff Reardon .... .10 .05 .01
- ☐ 110 Jerry Reed .... .05 .02 .01
- ☐ 111 Jody Reed .... .05 .02 .01
- ☐ 112 Luis Rivera UER .... .05 .02 .01
  (Born 1/3/84)
- ☐ 113 Kevin Romine .... .05 .02 .01
- ☐ 114 Phil Bradley .... .05 .02 .01
- ☐ 115 Ivan Calderon .... .05 .02 .01
- ☐ 116 Wayne Edwards .... .05 .02 .01
- ☐ 117 Alex Fernandez .... .25 .11 .03
- ☐ 118 Carlton Fisk .... .15 .07 .02
- ☐ 119 Scott Fletcher .... .05 .02 .01
- ☐ 120 Craig Grebeck .... .05 .02 .01
- ☐ 121 Ozzie Guillen .... .05 .02 .01
- ☐ 122 Greg Hibbard .... .05 .02 .01
- ☐ 123 Lance Johnson UER .... .05 .02 .01
  (Born Cincinnati, should be Lincoln Heights)
- ☐ 124 Barry Jones .... .05 .02 .01
- ☐ 125 Ron Karkovice .... .05 .02 .01
- ☐ 126 Eric King .... .05 .02 .01
- ☐ 127 Steve Lyons .... .05 .02 .01
- ☐ 128 Carlos Martinez .... .05 .02 .01
- ☐ 129 Jack McDowell UER .... .15 .07 .02
  (Stanford misspelled as Standford on back)
- ☐ 130 Donn Pall .... .05 .02 .01
  (No dots over any i's in text)
- ☐ 131 Dan Pasqua .... .05 .02 .01
- ☐ 132 Ken Patterson .... .05 .02 .01
- ☐ 133 Melido Perez .... .05 .02 .01
- ☐ 134 Adam Peterson .... .05 .02 .01

☐ 135 Scott Radinsky .05 .02 .01
☐ 136 Sammy Sosa .15 .07 .02
☐ 137 Bobby Thigpen .05 .02 .01
☐ 138 Frank Thomas 2.00 .90 .25
☐ 139 Robin Ventura .20 .09 .03
☐ 140 Daryl Boston .05 .02 .01
☐ 141 Chuck Carr .10 .05 .01
☐ 142 Mark Carreon .05 .02 .01
☐ 143 David Cone .15 .07 .02
☐ 144 Ron Darling .05 .02 .01
☐ 145 Kevin Elster .05 .02 .01
☐ 146 Sid Fernandez .10 .05 .01
☐ 147 John Franco .10 .05 .01
☐ 148 Dwight Gooden .10 .05 .01
☐ 149 Tom Herr .05 .02 .01
☐ 150 Todd Hundley .10 .05 .01
☐ 151 Gregg Jefferies .15 .07 .02
☐ 152 Howard Johnson .10 .05 .01
☐ 153 Dave Magadan .05 .02 .01
☐ 154 Kevin McReynolds .05 .02 .01
☐ 155 Keith Miller UER .05 .02 .01
(Text says Rochester in '87, stats say Tidewater, mixed up with other Keith Miller)
☐ 156 Bob Ojeda .05 .02 .01
☐ 157 Tom O'Malley .05 .02 .01
☐ 158 Alejandro Pena .05 .02 .01
☐ 159 Darren Reed .05 .02 .01
☐ 160 Mackey Sasser .05 .02 .01
☐ 161 Darryl Strawberry .15 .07 .02
☐ 162 Tim Teufel .05 .02 .01
☐ 163 Kelvin Torve .05 .02 .01
☐ 164 Julio Valera .05 .02 .01
☐ 165 Frank Viola .10 .05 .01
☐ 166 Wally Whitehurst .05 .02 .01
☐ 167 Jim Acker .05 .02 .01
☐ 168 Derek Bell .10 .05 .01
☐ 169 George Bell .10 .05 .01
☐ 170 Willie Blair .05 .02 .01
☐ 171 Pat Borders .05 .02 .01
☐ 172 John Cerutti .05 .02 .01
☐ 173 Junior Felix .05 .02 .01
☐ 174 Tony Fernandez .10 .05 .01
☐ 175 Kelly Gruber UER .05 .02 .01
(Born in Houston, should be Bellaire)
☐ 176 Tom Henke .10 .05 .01
☐ 177 Glenallen Hill .05 .02 .01
☐ 178 Jimmy Key .10 .05 .01
☐ 179 Manny Lee .05 .02 .01
☐ 180 Fred McGriff .20 .09 .03
☐ 181 Rance Mulliniks .05 .02 .01
☐ 182 Greg Myers .05 .02 .01
☐ 183 John Olerud UER .15 .07 .02
(Listed as throwing right, should be left)
☐ 184 Luis Sojo .05 .02 .01
☐ 185 Dave Stieb .10 .05 .01
☐ 186 Todd Stottlemyre .05 .02 .01
☐ 187 Duane Ward .10 .05 .01
☐ 188 David Wells .05 .02 .01
☐ 189 Mark Whiten .15 .07 .02
☐ 190 Ken Williams .05 .02 .01
☐ 191 Frank Wills .05 .02 .01
☐ 192 Mookie Wilson .05 .02 .01
☐ 193 Don Aase .05 .02 .01
☐ 194 Tim Belcher UER .05 .02 .01
(Born Sparta, Ohio, should say Mt. Gilead)
☐ 195 Hubie Brooks .05 .02 .01
☐ 196 Dennis Cook .05 .02 .01
☐ 197 Tim Crews .05 .02 .01
☐ 198 Kal Daniels .05 .02 .01
☐ 199 Kirk Gibson .10 .05 .01
☐ 200 Jim Gott .05 .02 .01
☐ 201 Alfredo Griffin .05 .02 .01
☐ 202 Chris Gwynn .05 .02 .01
☐ 203 Dave Hansen .05 .02 .01
☐ 204 Lenny Harris .05 .02 .01
☐ 205 Mike Hartley .05 .02 .01
☐ 206 Mickey Hatcher .05 .02 .01
☐ 207 Carlos Hernandez .05 .02 .01
☐ 208 Orel Hershiser .10 .05 .01
☐ 209 Jay Howell UER .05 .02 .01
(No 1982 Yankee stats)
☐ 210 Mike Huff .05 .02 .01
☐ 211 Stan Javier .05 .02 .01
☐ 212 Ramon Martinez .10 .05 .01
☐ 213 Mike Morgan .05 .02 .01
☐ 214 Eddie Murray .15 .07 .02
☐ 215 Jim Neidlinger .05 .02 .01
☐ 216 Jose Offerman .10 .05 .01
☐ 217 Jim Poole .05 .02 .01
☐ 218 Juan Samuel .05 .02 .01
☐ 219 Mike Scioscia .05 .02 .01
☐ 220 Ray Searage .05 .02 .01
☐ 221 Mike Sharperson .05 .02 .01
☐ 222 Fernando Valenzuela .05 .02 .01
☐ 223 Jose Vizcaino .05 .02 .01
☐ 224 Mike Aldrete .05 .02 .01
☐ 225 Scott Anderson .05 .02 .01
☐ 226 Dennis Boyd .05 .02 .01
☐ 227 Tim Burke .05 .02 .01
☐ 228 Delino DeShields .15 .07 .02
☐ 229 Mike Fitzgerald .05 .02 .01
☐ 230 Tom Foley .05 .02 .01
☐ 231 Steve Frey .05 .02 .01
☐ 232 Andres Galarraga .15 .07 .02
☐ 233 Mark Gardner .05 .02 .01
☐ 234 Marquis Grissom .15 .07 .02
☐ 235 Kevin Gross .05 .02 .01
(No date given for first Expos win)
☐ 236 Drew Hall .05 .02 .01
☐ 237 Dave Martinez .05 .02 .01
☐ 238 Dennis Martinez .10 .05 .01
☐ 239 Dale Mohorcic .05 .02 .01
☐ 240 Chris Nabholz .05 .02 .01
☐ 241 Otis Nixon .10 .05 .01
☐ 242 Junior Noboa .05 .02 .01
☐ 243 Spike Owen .05 .02 .01
☐ 244 Tim Raines .15 .07 .02
☐ 245 Mel Rojas UER .05 .02 .01
(Stats show 3.60 ERA, bio says 3.19 ERA)
☐ 246 Scott Ruskin .05 .02 .01
☐ 247 Bill Sampen .05 .02 .01
☐ 248 Nelson Santovenia .05 .02 .01
☐ 249 Dave Schmidt .05 .02 .01
☐ 250 Larry Walker .15 .07 .02
☐ 251 Tim Wallach .05 .02 .01
☐ 252 Dave Anderson .05 .02 .01
☐ 253 Kevin Bass .05 .02 .01
☐ 254 Steve Bedrosian .05 .02 .01
☐ 255 Jeff Brantley .05 .02 .01
☐ 256 John Burkett .10 .05 .01
☐ 257 Brett Butler .10 .05 .01
☐ 258 Gary Carter .15 .07 .02
☐ 259 Will Clark .20 .09 .03
☐ 260 Steve Decker .05 .02 .01
☐ 261 Kelly Downs .05 .02 .01
☐ 262 Scott Garrelts .05 .02 .01
☐ 263 Terry Kennedy .05 .02 .01
☐ 264 Mike LaCoss .05 .02 .01
☐ 265 Mark Leonard .05 .02 .01

	No.	Player			
☐	266	Greg Litton	.05	.02	.01
☐	267	Kevin Mitchell	.10	.05	.01
☐	268	Randy O'Neal	.05	.02	.01
☐	269	Rick Parker	.05	.02	.01
☐	270	Rick Reuschel	.05	.02	.01
☐	271	Ernest Riles	.05	.02	.01
☐	272	Don Robinson	.05	.02	.01
☐	273	Robby Thompson	.05	.02	.01
☐	274	Mark Thurmond	.05	.02	.01
☐	275	Jose Uribe	.05	.02	.01
☐	276	Matt Williams	.20	.09	.03
☐	277	Trevor Wilson	.05	.02	.01
☐	278	Gerald Alexander	.05	.02	.01
☐	279	Brad Arnsberg	.05	.02	.01
☐	280	Kevin Belcher	.05	.02	.01
☐	281	Joe Bitker	.05	.02	.01
☐	282	Kevin Brown	.10	.05	.01
☐	283	Steve Buechele	.05	.02	.01
☐	284	Jack Daugherty	.05	.02	.01
☐	285	Julio Franco	.10	.05	.01
☐	286	Juan Gonzalez	1.00	.45	.13
☐	287	Bill Haselman	.05	.02	.01
☐	288	Charlie Hough	.10	.05	.01
☐	289	Jeff Huson	.05	.02	.01
☐	290	Pete Incaviglia	.05	.02	.01
☐	291	Mike Jeffcoat	.05	.02	.01
☐	292	Jeff Kunkel	.05	.02	.01
☐	293	Gary Mielke	.05	.02	.01
☐	294	Jamie Moyer	.05	.02	.01
☐	295	Rafael Palmeiro	.15	.07	.02
☐	296	Geno Petralli	.05	.02	.01
☐	297	Gary Pettis	.05	.02	.01
☐	298	Kevin Reimer	.05	.02	.01
☐	299	Kenny Rogers	.05	.02	.01
☐	300	Jeff Russell	.05	.02	.01
☐	301	John Russell	.05	.02	.01
☐	302	Nolan Ryan	.60	.25	.08
☐	303	Ruben Sierra	.15	.07	.02
☐	304	Bobby Witt	.05	.02	.01
☐	305	Jim Abbott UER (Text on back states he won Sullivan Award (outstanding amateur athlete) in 1989;should be '88)	.15	.07	.02
☐	306	Kent Anderson	.05	.02	.01
☐	307	Dante Bichette	.15	.07	.02
☐	308	Bert Blyleven	.15	.07	.02
☐	309	Chili Davis	.10	.05	.01
☐	310	Brian Downing	.05	.02	.01
☐	311	Mark Eichhorn	.05	.02	.01
☐	312	Mike Fetters	.05	.02	.01
☐	313	Chuck Finley	.10	.05	.01
☐	314	Willie Fraser	.05	.02	.01
☐	315	Bryan Harvey	.10	.05	.01
☐	316	Donnie Hill	.05	.02	.01
☐	317	Wally Joyner	.10	.05	.01
☐	318	Mark Langston	.15	.07	.02
☐	319	Kirk McCaskill	.05	.02	.01
☐	320	John Orton	.05	.02	.01
☐	321	Lance Parrish	.10	.05	.01
☐	322	Luis Polonia UER (1984 Madfison, should be Madison)	.05	.02	.01
☐	323	Johnny Ray	.05	.02	.01
☐	324	Bobby Rose	.05	.02	.01
☐	325	Dick Schofield	.05	.02	.01
☐	326	Rick Schu	.05	.02	.01
☐	327	Lee Stevens	.05	.02	.01
☐	328	Devon White	.10	.05	.01
☐	329	Dave Winfield	.15	.07	.02
☐	330	Cliff Young	.05	.02	.01
☐	331	Dave Bergman	.05	.02	.01
☐	332	Phil Clark	.05	.02	.01
☐	333	Darnell Coles	.05	.02	.01
☐	334	Milt Cuyler	.05	.02	.01
☐	335	Cecil Fielder	.15	.07	.02
☐	336	Travis Fryman	.40	.18	.05
☐	337	Paul Gibson	.05	.02	.01
☐	338	Jerry Don Gleaton	.05	.02	.01
☐	339	Mike Heath	.05	.02	.01
☐	340	Mike Henneman	.05	.02	.01
☐	341	Chet Lemon	.05	.02	.01
☐	342	Lance McCullers	.05	.02	.01
☐	343	Jack Morris	.15	.07	.02
☐	344	Lloyd Moseby	.05	.02	.01
☐	345	Edwin Nunez	.05	.02	.01
☐	346	Clay Parker	.05	.02	.01
☐	347	Dan Petry	.05	.02	.01
☐	348	Tony Phillips	.05	.02	.01
☐	349	Jeff M. Robinson	.05	.02	.01
☐	350	Mark Salas	.05	.02	.01
☐	351	Mike Schwabe	.05	.02	.01
☐	352	Larry Sheets	.05	.02	.01
☐	353	John Shelby	.05	.02	.01
☐	354	Frank Tanana	.05	.02	.01
☐	355	Alan Trammell	.15	.07	.02
☐	356	Gary Ward	.05	.02	.01
☐	357	Lou Whitaker	.15	.07	.02
☐	358	Beau Allred	.05	.02	.01
☐	359	Sandy Alomar Jr.	.10	.05	.01
☐	360	Carlos Baerga	.30	.14	.04
☐	361	Kevin Bearse	.05	.02	.01
☐	362	Tom Brookens	.05	.02	.01
☐	363	Jerry Browne UER (No dot over i in first text line)	.05	.02	.01
☐	364	Tom Candiotti	.05	.02	.01
☐	365	Alex Cole	.05	.02	.01
☐	366	John Farrell UER (Born in Neptune, should be Monmouth)	.05	.02	.01
☐	367	Felix Fermin	.05	.02	.01
☐	368	Keith Hernandez	.10	.05	.01
☐	369	Brook Jacoby	.05	.02	.01
☐	370	Chris James	.05	.02	.01
☐	371	Dion James	.05	.02	.01
☐	372	Doug Jones	.05	.02	.01
☐	373	Candy Maldonado	.05	.02	.01
☐	374	Steve Olin	.05	.02	.01
☐	375	Jesse Orosco	.05	.02	.01
☐	376	Rudy Seanez	.10	.05	.01
☐	377	Joel Skinner	.05	.02	.01
☐	378	Cory Snyder	.05	.02	.01
☐	379	Greg Swindell	.05	.02	.01
☐	380	Sergio Valdez	.05	.02	.01
☐	381	Mike Walker	.05	.02	.01
☐	382	Colby Ward	.05	.02	.01
☐	383	Turner Ward	.15	.07	.02
☐	384	Mitch Webster	.05	.02	.01
☐	385	Kevin Wickander	.05	.02	.01
☐	386	Darrel Akerfelds	.05	.02	.01
☐	387	Joe Boever	.05	.02	.01
☐	388	Rod Booker	.05	.02	.01
☐	389	Sil Campusano	.05	.02	.01
☐	390	Don Carman	.05	.02	.01
☐	391	Wes Chamberlain	.05	.02	.01
☐	392	Pat Combs	.05	.02	.01
☐	393	Darren Daulton	.15	.07	.02
☐	394	Jose DeJesus	.05	.02	.01
☐	395	Len Dykstra	.15	.07	.02
☐	396	Jason Grimsley	.05	.02	.01
☐	397	Charlie Hayes	.10	.05	.01
☐	398	Von Hayes	.05	.02	.01
☐	399	David Hollins UER (Atl-bats, should say at-bats)	.05	.02	.01
☐	400	Ken Howell	.05	.02	.01

□ 401 Ricky Jordan .05 .02 .01
□ 402 John Kruk .15 .07 .02
□ 403 Steve Lake .05 .02 .01
□ 404 Chuck Malone .05 .02 .01
□ 405 Roger McDowell UER .05 .02 .01
(Says Phillies is saves, should say in)
□ 406 Chuck McElroy .05 .02 .01
□ 407 Mickey Morandini .05 .02 .01
□ 408 Terry Mulholland .05 .02 .01
□ 409 Dale Murphy .15 .07 .02
□ 410A Randy Ready ERR .05 .02 .01
(No Brewers stats listed for 1983)
□ 410B Randy Ready COR .05 .02 .01
□ 411 Bruce Ruffin .05 .02 .01
□ 412 Dickie Thon .05 .02 .01
□ 413 Paul Assenmacher .05 .02 .01
□ 414 Damon Berryhill .05 .02 .01
□ 415 Mike Bielecki .05 .02 .01
□ 416 Shawn Boskie .05 .02 .01
□ 417 Dave Clark .05 .02 .01
□ 418 Doug Dascenzo .05 .02 .01
□ 419A Andre Dawson ERR .15 .07 .02
(No stats for 1976)
□ 419B Andre Dawson COR .15 .07 .02
□ 420 Shawon Dunston .05 .02 .01
□ 421 Joe Girardi .05 .02 .01
□ 422 Mark Grace .15 .07 .02
□ 423 Mike Harkey .05 .02 .01
□ 424 Les Lancaster .05 .02 .01
□ 425 Bill Long .05 .02 .01
□ 426 Greg Maddux .25 .11 .03
□ 427 Derrick May .10 .05 .01
□ 428 Jeff Pico .05 .02 .01
□ 429 Domingo Ramos .05 .02 .01
□ 430 Luis Salazar .05 .02 .01
□ 431 Ryne Sandberg .25 .11 .03
□ 432 Dwight Smith .05 .02 .01
□ 433 Greg Smith .05 .02 .01
□ 434 Rick Sutcliffe .10 .05 .01
□ 435 Gary Varsho .05 .02 .01
□ 436 Hector Villanueva .05 .02 .01
□ 437 Jerome Walton .05 .02 .01
□ 438 Curtis Wilkerson .05 .02 .01
□ 439 Mitch Williams .10 .05 .01
□ 440 Steve Wilson .05 .02 .01
□ 441 Marvell Wynne .05 .02 .01
□ 442 Scott Bankhead .05 .02 .01
□ 443 Scott Bradley .05 .02 .01
□ 444 Greg Briley .05 .02 .01
□ 445 Mike Brumley UER .05 .02 .01
(Text 40 SB's in 1988, stats say 41)
□ 446 Jay Buhner .10 .05 .01
□ 447 Dave Burba .05 .02 .01
□ 448 Henry Cotto .05 .02 .01
□ 449 Alvin Davis .05 .02 .01
□ 450A Ken Griffey Jr. 1.50 .65 .19
(Bat .300)
□ 450B Ken Griffey Jr. 1.50 .65 .19
(Bat around .300)
□ 451 Erik Hanson .05 .02 .01
□ 452 Gene Harris UER .05 .02 .01
(63 career runs, should be 73)
□ 453 Brian Holman .05 .02 .01
□ 454 Mike Jackson .05 .02 .01
□ 455 Randy Johnson .15 .07 .02
□ 456 Jeffrey Leonard .05 .02 .01
□ 457 Edgar Martinez .10 .05 .01
□ 458 Tino Martinez .10 .05 .01
□ 459 Pete O'Brien UER .05 .02 .01
(1987 BA .266, should be .286)
□ 460 Harold Reynolds .05 .02 .01
□ 461 Mike Schooler .05 .02 .01
□ 462 Bill Swift .10 .05 .01
□ 463 David Valle .05 .02 .01
□ 464 Omar Vizquel .05 .02 .01
□ 465 Matt Young .05 .02 .01
□ 466 Brady Anderson .10 .05 .01
□ 467 Jeff Ballard UER .05 .02 .01
(Missing top of right parenthesis after Saberhagen in last text line)
□ 468 Juan Bell .05 .02 .01
□ 469A Mike Devereaux .10 .05 .01
(First line of text ends with six)
□ 469B Mike Devereaux .10 .05 .01
(First line of text ends with runs)
□ 470 Steve Finley .05 .02 .01
□ 471 Dave Gallagher .05 .02 .01
□ 472 Leo Gomez .10 .05 .01
□ 473 Rene Gonzales .05 .02 .01
□ 474 Pete Harnisch .10 .05 .01
□ 475 Kevin Hickey .05 .02 .01
□ 476 Chris Hoiles .15 .07 .02
□ 477 Sam Horn .05 .02 .01
□ 478 Tim Hulett .05 .02 .01
(Photo shows National Leaguer sliding into second base)
□ 479 Dave Johnson .05 .02 .01
□ 480 Ron Kittle UER .05 .02 .01
(Edmonton misspelled as Edmundton)
□ 481 Ben McDonald .15 .07 .02
□ 482 Bob Melvin .05 .02 .01
□ 483 Bob Milacki .05 .02 .01
□ 484 Randy Milligan .05 .02 .01
□ 485 John Mitchell .05 .02 .01
□ 486 Gregg Olson .10 .05 .01
□ 487 Joe Orsulak .05 .02 .01
□ 488 Joe Price .05 .02 .01
□ 489 Bill Ripken .05 .02 .01
□ 490 Cal Ripken .35 .16 .04
□ 491 Curt Schilling .10 .05 .01
□ 492 David Segui .05 .02 .01
□ 493 Anthony Telford .05 .02 .01
□ 494 Mickey Tettleton .10 .05 .01
□ 495 Mark Williamson .05 .02 .01
□ 496 Craig Worthington .05 .02 .01
□ 497 Juan Agosto .05 .02 .01
□ 498 Eric Anthony .10 .05 .01
□ 499 Craig Biggio .15 .07 .02
□ 500 Ken Caminiti UER .10 .05 .01
(Born 4/4, should be 4/21)
□ 501 Casey Candaele .05 .02 .01
□ 502 Andujar Cedeno .10 .05 .01
□ 503 Danny Darwin .05 .02 .01
□ 504 Mark Davidson .05 .02 .01
□ 505 Glenn Davis .05 .02 .01
□ 506 Jim Deshaies .05 .02 .01
□ 507 Luis Gonzalez .25 .11 .03
□ 508 Bill Gullickson .05 .02 .01
□ 509 Xavier Hernandez .05 .02 .01
□ 510 Brian Meyer .05 .02 .01
□ 511 Ken Oberkfell .05 .02 .01
□ 512 Mark Portugal .05 .02 .01
□ 513 Rafael Ramirez .05 .02 .01
□ 514 Karl Rhodes .05 .02 .01

	No.	Player			
☐	515	Mike Scott	.05	.02	.01
☐	516	Mike Simms	.05	.02	.01
☐	517	Dave Smith	.05	.02	.01
☐	518	Franklin Stubbs	.05	.02	.01
☐	519	Glenn Wilson	.05	.02	.01
☐	520	Eric Yelding UER (Text has 63 steals, stats have 64, which is correct)	.05	.02	.01
☐	521	Gerald Young	.05	.02	.01
☐	522	Shawn Abner	.05	.02	.01
☐	523	Roberto Alomar	.25	.11	.03
☐	524	Andy Benes	.15	.07	.02
☐	525	Joe Carter	.20	.09	.03
☐	526	Jack Clark	.10	.05	.01
☐	527	Joey Cora	.05	.02	.01
☐	528	Paul Faries	.05	.02	.01
☐	529	Tony Gwynn	.25	.11	.03
☐	530	Atlee Hammaker	.05	.02	.01
☐	531	Greg W. Harris	.05	.02	.01
☐	532	Thomas Howard	.05	.02	.01
☐	533	Bruce Hurst	.05	.02	.01
☐	534	Craig Lefferts	.05	.02	.01
☐	535	Derek Lilliquist	.05	.02	.01
☐	536	Fred Lynn	.10	.05	.01
☐	537	Mike Pagliarulo	.05	.02	.01
☐	538	Mark Parent	.05	.02	.01
☐	539	Dennis Rasmussen	.05	.02	.01
☐	540	Bip Roberts	.05	.02	.01
☐	541	Richard Rodriguez	.05	.02	.01
☐	542	Benito Santiago	.05	.02	.01
☐	543	Calvin Schiraldi	.05	.02	.01
☐	544	Eric Show	.05	.02	.01
☐	545	Phil Stephenson	.05	.02	.01
☐	546	Garry Templeton UER (Born 3/24/57, should be 3/24/56)	.05	.02	.01
☐	547	Ed Whitson	.05	.02	.01
☐	548	Eddie Williams	.05	.02	.01
☐	549	Kevin Appier	.10	.05	.01
☐	550	Luis Aquino	.05	.02	.01
☐	551	Bob Boone	.10	.05	.01
☐	552	George Brett	.30	.14	.04
☐	553	Jeff Conine	.50	.23	.06
☐	554	Steve Crawford	.05	.02	.01
☐	555	Mark Davis	.05	.02	.01
☐	556	Storm Davis	.05	.02	.01
☐	557	Jim Eisenreich	.05	.02	.01
☐	558	Steve Farr	.05	.02	.01
☐	559	Tom Gordon	.10	.05	.01
☐	560	Mark Gubicza	.05	.02	.01
☐	561	Bo Jackson	.15	.07	.02
☐	562	Mike Macfarlane	.05	.02	.01
☐	563	Brian McRae	.30	.14	.04
☐	564	Jeff Montgomery	.10	.05	.01
☐	565	Bill Pecota	.05	.02	.01
☐	566	Gerald Perry	.05	.02	.01
☐	567	Bret Saberhagen	.10	.05	.01
☐	568	Jeff Schulz	.05	.02	.01
☐	569	Kevin Seitzer	.05	.02	.01
☐	570	Terry Shumpert	.05	.02	.01
☐	571	Kurt Stillwell	.05	.02	.01
☐	572	Danny Tartabull	.10	.05	.01
☐	573	Gary Thurman	.05	.02	.01
☐	574	Frank White	.10	.05	.01
☐	575	Willie Wilson	.05	.02	.01
☐	576	Chris Bosio	.05	.02	.01
☐	577	Greg Brock	.05	.02	.01
☐	578	George Canale	.05	.02	.01
☐	579	Chuck Crim	.05	.02	.01
☐	580	Rob Deer	.05	.02	.01
☐	581	Edgar Diaz	.05	.02	.01
☐	582	Tom Edens	.05	.02	.01
☐	583	Mike Felder	.05	.02	.01
☐	584	Jim Gantner	.05	.02	.01
☐	585	Darryl Hamilton	.10	.05	.01
☐	586	Ted Higuera	.05	.02	.01
☐	587	Mark Knudson	.05	.02	.01
☐	588	Bill Krueger	.05	.02	.01
☐	589	Tim McIntosh	.05	.02	.01
☐	590	Paul Mirabella	.05	.02	.01
☐	591	Paul Molitor	.15	.07	.02
☐	592	Jaime Navarro	.05	.02	.01
☐	593	Dave Parker	.15	.07	.02
☐	594	Dan Plesac	.05	.02	.01
☐	595	Ron Robinson	.05	.02	.01
☐	596	Gary Sheffield	.15	.07	.02
☐	597	Bill Spiers	.05	.02	.01
☐	598	B.J. Surhoff	.05	.02	.01
☐	599	Greg Vaughn	.10	.05	.01
☐	600	Randy Veres	.05	.02	.01
☐	601	Robin Yount	.15	.07	.02
☐	602	Rick Aguilera	.10	.05	.01
☐	603	Allan Anderson	.05	.02	.01
☐	604	Juan Berenguer	.05	.02	.01
☐	605	Randy Bush	.05	.02	.01
☐	606	Carmen Castillo	.05	.02	.01
☐	607	Tim Drummond	.05	.02	.01
☐	608	Scott Erickson	.05	.02	.01
☐	609	Gary Gaetti	.05	.02	.01
☐	610	Greg Gagne	.05	.02	.01
☐	611	Dan Gladden	.05	.02	.01
☐	612	Mark Guthrie	.05	.02	.01
☐	613	Brian Harper	.05	.02	.01
☐	614	Kent Hrbek	.10	.05	.01
☐	615	Gene Larkin	.05	.02	.01
☐	616	Terry Leach	.05	.02	.01
☐	617	Nelson Liriano	.05	.02	.01
☐	618	Shane Mack	.10	.05	.01
☐	619	John Moses	.05	.02	.01
☐	620	Pedro Munoz	.15	.07	.02
☐	621	Al Newman	.05	.02	.01
☐	622	Junior Ortiz	.05	.02	.01
☐	623	Kirby Puckett	.30	.14	.04
☐	624	Roy Smith	.05	.02	.01
☐	625	Kevin Tapani	.10	.05	.01
☐	626	Gary Wayne	.05	.02	.01
☐	627	David West	.05	.02	.01
☐	628	Cris Carpenter	.05	.02	.01
☐	629	Vince Coleman	.05	.02	.01
☐	630	Ken Dayley	.05	.02	.01
☐	631	Jose DeLeon	.05	.02	.01
☐	632	Frank DiPino	.05	.02	.01
☐	633	Bernard Gilkey	.10	.05	.01
☐	634	Pedro Guerrero	.10	.05	.01
☐	635	Ken Hill	.15	.07	.02
☐	636	Felix Jose	.10	.05	.01
☐	637	Ray Lankford	.15	.07	.02
☐	638	Joe Magrane	.05	.02	.01
☐	639	Tom Niedenfuer	.05	.02	.01
☐	640	Jose Oquendo	.05	.02	.01
☐	641	Tom Pagnozzi	.05	.02	.01
☐	642	Terry Pendleton	.15	.07	.02
☐	643	Mike Perez	.05	.02	.01
☐	644	Bryn Smith	.05	.02	.01
☐	645	Lee Smith	.15	.07	.02
☐	646	Ozzie Smith	.20	.09	.03
☐	647	Scott Terry	.05	.02	.01
☐	648	Bob Tewksbury	.10	.05	.01
☐	649	Milt Thompson	.05	.02	.01
☐	650	John Tudor	.05	.02	.01
☐	651	Denny Walling	.05	.02	.01
☐	652	Craig Wilson	.05	.02	.01
☐	653	Todd Worrell	.05	.02	.01
☐	654	Todd Zeile	.10	.05	.01
☐	655	Oscar Azocar	.05	.02	.01

☐ 656 Steve Balboni UER (Born 1/5/57, should be 1/16)	.05	.02	.01
☐ 657 Jesse Barfield	.05	.02	.01
☐ 658 Greg Cadaret	.05	.02	.01
☐ 659 Chuck Cary	.05	.02	.01
☐ 660 Rick Cerone	.05	.02	.01
☐ 661 Dave Eiland	.05	.02	.01
☐ 662 Alvaro Espinoza	.05	.02	.01
☐ 663 Bob Geren	.05	.02	.01
☐ 664 Lee Guetterman	.05	.02	.01
☐ 665 Mel Hall	.05	.02	.01
☐ 666 Andy Hawkins	.05	.02	.01
☐ 667 Jimmy Jones	.05	.02	.01
☐ 668 Roberto Kelly	.10	.05	.01
☐ 669 Dave LaPoint UER (No '81 Brewers stats, totals also are wrong)	.05	.02	.01
☐ 670 Tim Leary	.05	.02	.01
☐ 671 Jim Leyritz	.05	.02	.01
☐ 672 Kevin Maas	.05	.02	.01
☐ 673 Don Mattingly	.30	.14	.04
☐ 674 Matt Nokes	.05	.02	.01
☐ 675 Pascual Perez	.05	.02	.01
☐ 676 Eric Plunk	.05	.02	.01
☐ 677 Dave Righetti	.05	.02	.01
☐ 678 Jeff D. Robinson	.05	.02	.01
☐ 679 Steve Sax	.05	.02	.01
☐ 680 Mike Witt	.05	.02	.01
☐ 681 Steve Avery UER (Born in New Jersey, should say Michigan)	.15	.07	.02
☐ 682 Mike Bell	.05	.02	.01
☐ 683 Jeff Blauser	.10	.05	.01
☐ 684 Francisco Cabrera UER (Born 10/16, should say 10/10)	.05	.02	.01
☐ 685 Tony Castillo	.05	.02	.01
☐ 686 Marty Clary UER (Shown pitching righty, but bio has left)	.05	.02	.01
☐ 687 Nick Esasky	.05	.02	.01
☐ 688 Ron Gant	.10	.05	.01
☐ 689 Tom Glavine	.20	.09	.03
☐ 690 Mark Grant	.05	.02	.01
☐ 691 Tommy Gregg	.05	.02	.01
☐ 692 Dwayne Henry	.05	.02	.01
☐ 693 David Justice	.35	.16	.04
☐ 694 Jimmy Kremers	.05	.02	.01
☐ 695 Charlie Leibrandt	.05	.02	.01
☐ 696 Mark Lemke	.05	.02	.01
☐ 697 Oddibe McDowell	.05	.02	.01
☐ 698 Greg Olson	.05	.02	.01
☐ 699 Jeff Parrett	.05	.02	.01
☐ 700 Jim Presley	.05	.02	.01
☐ 701 Victor Rosario	.05	.02	.01
☐ 702 Lonnie Smith	.05	.02	.01
☐ 703 Pete Smith	.05	.02	.01
☐ 704 John Smoltz	.15	.07	.02
☐ 705 Mike Stanton	.10	.05	.01
☐ 706 Andres Thomas	.05	.02	.01
☐ 707 Jeff Treadway	.05	.02	.01
☐ 708 Jim Vatcher	.05	.02	.01
☐ 709 Home Run Kings Ryne Sandberg Cecil Fielder	.12	.05	.02
☐ 710 2nd Generation Stars Barry Bonds Ken Griffey Jr.	.60	.25	.08
☐ 711 NLCS Team Leaders Bobby Bonilla Barry Larkin	.10	.05	.01
☐ 712 Top Game Savers Bobby Thigpen John Franco	.05	.02	.01
☐ 713 Chicago's 100 Club Andre Dawson Ryne Sandberg UER (Ryno misspelled Rhino)	.10	.05	.01
☐ 714 CL:A's/Pirates Reds/Red Sox	.05	.02	.01
☐ 715 CL:White Sox/Mets Blue Jays/Dodgers	.05	.02	.01
☐ 716 CL:Expos/Giants Rangers/Angels	.05	.02	.01
☐ 717 CL:Tigers/Indians Phillies/Cubs	.05	.02	.01
☐ 718 CL:Mariners/Orioles Astros/Padres	.05	.02	.01
☐ 719 CL:Royals/Brewers Twins/Cardinals	.05	.02	.01
☐ 720 CL:Yankees/Braves Superstars/Specials	.05	.02	.01

1991 Fleer All-Stars

For the sixth consecutive year Fleer issued an All-Star insert set. This year the cards were only available in Fleer cello packs. This ten-card set measures the standard size of 2 1/2" by 3 1/2" and is reminiscent of the 1971 Topps Greatest Moments set with two pictures on the (black-bordered) front as well as a photo on the back.

	MINT	EXC	G-VG
COMPLETE SET (10)	18.00	8.00	2.30
COMMON CARD (1-10)	.50	.23	.06
☐ 1 Ryne Sandberg	3.00	1.35	.40
☐ 2 Barry Larkin	.50	.23	.06
☐ 3 Matt Williams	1.75	.80	.22
☐ 4 Cecil Fielder	1.00	.45	.13
☐ 5 Barry Bonds	3.50	1.55	.45
☐ 6 Rickey Henderson	1.00	.45	.13
☐ 7 Ken Griffey Jr.	10.00	4.50	1.25
☐ 8 Jose Canseco	1.75	.80	.22
☐ 9 Benito Santiago	.50	.23	.06
☐ 10 Roger Clemens	2.00	.90	.25

1991 Fleer Pro-Visions

This 12-card subset is in the standard size of 2 1/2" by 3 1/2" and features drawings by

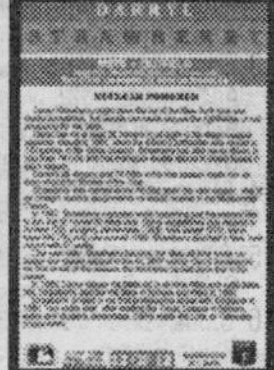

talented artist Terry Smith on the front of the card with a description on the back explaining why the card is painted in that way. These cards were only available in Fleer wax and Rak packs. The formal description of this set is the 1991 Fleer Pro-Visions TM Sports Art Cards. The cards have distinctive black borders.

	MINT	EXC	G-VG
COMPLETE SET (12)	4.00	1.80	.50
COMMON CARD (1-12)	.20	.09	.03
☐ 1 Kirby Puckett UER (.326 average, should be .328)	1.00	.45	.13
☐ 2 Will Clark UER (On tenth line, pennant misspelled pennent)	.50	.23	.06
☐ 3 Ruben Sierra UER (No apostrophe in hasn't)	.30	.14	.04
☐ 4 Mark McGwire UER (Fisk won ROY in '72, not '82)	.20	.09	.03
☐ 5 Bo Jackson (Bio says 6', others have him at 6'1")	.30	.14	.04
☐ 6 Jose Canseco UER (Bio 6'3", 230, text has 6'4", 240)	.50	.23	.06
☐ 7 Dwight Gooden UER (2.80 ERA in Lynchburg, should be 2.50)	.20	.09	.03
☐ 8 Mike Greenwell UER (.328 BA and 87 RBI, should be .325 and 95)	.20	.09	.03
☐ 9 Roger Clemens	.60	.25	.08
☐ 10 Eric Davis	.20	.09	.03
☐ 11 Don Mattingly	1.00	.45	.13
☐ 12 Darryl Strawberry	.20	.09	.03

1991 Fleer Pro-Visions Factory

This four-card set was inserted only into factory sets. The standard-size (2 1/2" by 3 1/2") cards feature on the fronts colorful player portraits by artist Terry Smith. The pictures are bordered in white, with the player's name immediately below in red lettering. The backs of each card have different colors as well as biography and career highlights. The cards are numbered on the back.

	MINT	EXC	G-VG
COMPLETE SET (4)	2.50	1.15	.30
COMMON CARD (1-4)	.25	.11	.03
☐ 1 Barry Bonds, Pittsburgh Pirates	1.25	.55	.16
☐ 2 Rickey Henderson, Oakland Athletics	.60	.25	.08
☐ 3 Ryne Sandberg, Chicago Cubs	1.25	.55	.16
☐ 4 Dave Stewart, Oakland Athletics	.25	.11	.03

1991 Fleer Update

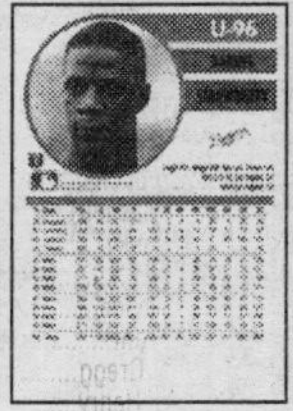

The 1991 Fleer Update set contains 132 cards measuring the standard size (2 1/2" by 3 1/2"). The glossy color action photos on the fronts are placed on a yellow card face and accentuated by black lines above and below. The backs have a head shot (circular format), biography, and complete Major League statistics. The cards are checklisted below alphabetically within and according to teams for each league as follows: Baltimore Orioles (1-3), Boston Red Sox (4-7), California Angels (8-10), Chicago White Sox (11-15), Cleveland Indians (16-21), Detroit Tigers (22-24), Kansas City Royals (25-28), Milwaukee Brewers (29-35), Minnesota Twins (36-41), New York Yankees (42-49), Oakland Athletics (50-51), Seattle Mariners (52-57), Texas Rangers (58-62), Toronto Blue Jays (63-69), Atlanta Braves (70-76), Chicago Cubs (77-83), Cincinnati Reds (84-86), Houston Astros (87-90), Los Angeles Dodgers (91-96), Montreal Expos (97-99), New York Mets (100-104), Philadelphia Phillies (105-110),

Pittsburgh Pirates (111-115), St. Louis Cardinals (116-119), San Diego Padres (120-127), and San Francisco Giants (128-131). The key Rookie Cards in this set are Jeff Bagwell and Ivan Rodriguez. Cards are numbered with a "U" prefix.

	MINT	EXC	G-VG
COMPLETE FACT.SET (132)	4.00	1.80	.50
COMMON CARD (1-132)	.05	.02	.01

	MINT	EXC	G-VG
☐ 1 Glenn Davis	.05	.02	.01
☐ 2 Dwight Evans	.08	.04	.01
☐ 3 Jose Mesa	.05	.02	.01
☐ 4 Jack Clark	.08	.04	.01
☐ 5 Danny Darwin	.05	.02	.01
☐ 6 Steve Lyons	.05	.02	.01
☐ 7 Mo Vaughn	.40	.18	.05
☐ 8 Floyd Bannister	.05	.02	.01
☐ 9 Gary Gaetti	.05	.02	.01
☐ 10 Dave Parker	.10	.05	.01
☐ 11 Joey Cora	.05	.02	.01
☐ 12 Charlie Hough	.08	.04	.01
☐ 13 Matt Merullo	.05	.02	.01
☐ 14 Warren Newson	.05	.02	.01
☐ 15 Tim Raines	.10	.05	.01
☐ 16 Albert Belle	.50	.23	.06
☐ 17 Glenallen Hill	.05	.02	.01
☐ 18 Shawn Hillegas	.05	.02	.01
☐ 19 Mark Lewis	.08	.04	.01
☐ 20 Charles Nagy	.08	.04	.01
☐ 21 Mark Whiten	.10	.05	.01
☐ 22 John Cerutti	.05	.02	.01
☐ 23 Rob Deer	.05	.02	.01
☐ 24 Mickey Tettleton	.08	.04	.01
☐ 25 Warren Cromartie	.05	.02	.01
☐ 26 Kirk Gibson	.08	.04	.01
☐ 27 David Howard	.05	.02	.01
☐ 28 Brent Mayne	.05	.02	.01
☐ 29 Dante Bichette	.10	.05	.01
☐ 30 Mark Lee	.05	.02	.01
☐ 31 Julio Machado	.05	.02	.01
☐ 32 Edwin Nunez	.05	.02	.01
☐ 33 Willie Randolph	.08	.04	.01
☐ 34 Franklin Stubbs	.05	.02	.01
☐ 35 Bill Wegman	.05	.02	.01
☐ 36 Chili Davis	.08	.04	.01
☐ 37 Chuck Knoblauch	.25	.11	.03
☐ 38 Scott Leius	.05	.02	.01
☐ 39 Jack Morris	.10	.05	.01
☐ 40 Mike Pagliarulo	.05	.02	.01
☐ 41 Lenny Webster	.05	.02	.01
☐ 42 John Habyan	.05	.02	.01
☐ 43 Steve Howe	.05	.02	.01
☐ 44 Jeff Johnson	.05	.02	.01
☐ 45 Scott Kamieniecki	.05	.02	.01
☐ 46 Pat Kelly	.15	.07	.02
☐ 47 Hensley Meulens	.05	.02	.01
☐ 48 Wade Taylor	.05	.02	.01
☐ 49 Bernie Williams	.08	.04	.01
☐ 50 Kirk Dressendorfer	.05	.02	.01
☐ 51 Ernest Riles	.05	.02	.01
☐ 52 Rich DeLucia	.05	.02	.01
☐ 53 Tracy Jones	.05	.02	.01
☐ 54 Bill Krueger	.05	.02	.01
☐ 55 Alonzo Powell	.05	.02	.01
☐ 56 Jeff Schaefer	.05	.02	.01
☐ 57 Russ Swan	.05	.02	.01
☐ 58 John Barfield	.05	.02	.01
☐ 59 Rich Gossage	.10	.05	.01
☐ 60 Jose Guzman	.05	.02	.01
☐ 61 Dean Palmer	.08	.04	.01
☐ 62 Ivan Rodriguez	.50	.23	.06
☐ 63 Roberto Alomar	.25	.11	.03
☐ 64 Tom Candiotti	.05	.02	.01
☐ 65 Joe Carter	.20	.09	.03
☐ 66 Ed Sprague	.05	.02	.01
☐ 67 Pat Tabler	.05	.02	.01
☐ 68 Mike Timlin	.05	.02	.01
☐ 69 Devon White	.08	.04	.01
☐ 70 Rafael Belliard	.05	.02	.01
☐ 71 Juan Berenguer	.05	.02	.01
☐ 72 Sid Bream	.05	.02	.01
☐ 73 Marvin Freeman	.05	.02	.01
☐ 74 Kent Mercker	.08	.04	.01
☐ 75 Otis Nixon	.08	.04	.01
☐ 76 Terry Pendleton	.10	.05	.01
☐ 77 George Bell	.08	.04	.01
☐ 78 Danny Jackson	.05	.02	.01
☐ 79 Chuck McElroy	.05	.02	.01
☐ 80 Gary Scott	.05	.02	.01
☐ 81 Heathcliff Slocumb	.05	.02	.01
☐ 82 Dave Smith	.05	.02	.01
☐ 83 Rick Wilkins	.15	.07	.02
☐ 84 Freddie Benavides	.05	.02	.01
☐ 85 Ted Power	.05	.02	.01
☐ 86 Mo Sanford	.05	.02	.01
☐ 87 Jeff Bagwell	3.00	1.35	.40
☐ 88 Steve Finley	.05	.02	.01
☐ 89 Pete Harnisch	.08	.04	.01
☐ 90 Darryl Kile	.10	.05	.01
☐ 91 Brett Butler	.08	.04	.01
☐ 92 John Candelaria	.05	.02	.01
☐ 93 Gary Carter	.10	.05	.01
☐ 94 Kevin Gross	.05	.02	.01
☐ 95 Bob Ojeda	.05	.02	.01
☐ 96 Darryl Strawberry	.05	.02	.01
☐ 97 Ivan Calderon	.05	.02	.01
☐ 98 Ron Hassey	.05	.02	.01
☐ 99 Gilberto Reyes	.05	.02	.01
☐ 100 Hubie Brooks	.05	.02	.01
☐ 101 Rick Cerone	.05	.02	.01
☐ 102 Vince Coleman	.05	.02	.01
☐ 103 Jeff Innis	.05	.02	.01
☐ 104 Pete Schourek	.05	.02	.01
☐ 105 Andy Ashby	.05	.02	.01
☐ 106 Wally Backman	.05	.02	.01
☐ 107 Darrin Fletcher	.05	.02	.01
☐ 108 Tommy Greene	.08	.04	.01
☐ 109 John Morris	.05	.02	.01
☐ 110 Mitch Williams	.08	.04	.01
☐ 111 Lloyd McClendon	.05	.02	.01
☐ 112 Orlando Merced	.25	.11	.03
☐ 113 Vicente Palacios	.05	.02	.01
☐ 114 Gary Varsho	.05	.02	.01
☐ 115 John Wehner	.05	.02	.01
☐ 116 Rex Hudler	.05	.02	.01
☐ 117 Tim Jones	.05	.02	.01
☐ 118 Geronimo Pena	.05	.02	.01
☐ 119 Gerald Perry	.05	.02	.01
☐ 120 Larry Andersen	.05	.02	.01
☐ 121 Jerald Clark	.05	.02	.01
☐ 122 Scott Coolbaugh	.05	.02	.01
☐ 123 Tony Fernandez	.08	.04	.01
☐ 124 Darrin Jackson	.05	.02	.01
☐ 125 Fred McGriff	.20	.09	.03
☐ 126 Jose Mota	.05	.02	.01
☐ 127 Tim Teufel	.05	.02	.01
☐ 128 Bud Black	.05	.02	.01
☐ 129 Mike Felder	.05	.02	.01
☐ 130 Willie McGee	.08	.04	.01
☐ 131 Dave Righetti	.05	.02	.01
☐ 132 Checklist U1-U132	.05	.02	.01

1992 Fleer

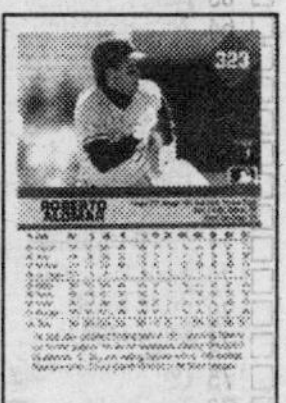

The 1992 Fleer set contains 720 cards measuring the standard size (2 1/2" by 3 1/2"). The card fronts shade from metallic pale green to white as one moves down the face. The team logo and player's name appear to the right of the picture, running the length of the card. The top portion of the backs has a different color player photo and biography, while the bottom portion includes statistics and player profile. The cards are checklisted below alphabetically within and according to teams for each league as follows: Baltimore Orioles (1-31), Boston Red Sox (32-49), California Angels (50-73), Chicago White Sox (74-101), Cleveland Indians (102-126), Detroit Tigers (127-149), Kansas City Royals (150-172), Milwaukee Brewers (173-194), Minnesota Twins (195-220), New York Yankees (221-247), Oakland Athletics (248-272), Seattle Mariners (273-296), Texas Rangers (297-321), Toronto Blue Jays (322-348), Atlanta Braves (349-374), Chicago Cubs (375-397), Cincinnati Reds (398-423), Houston Astros (424-446), Los Angeles Dodgers (447-471), Montreal Expos (472-494), New York Mets (495-520), Philadelphia Phillies (521-547), Pittsburgh Pirates (548-573), St. Louis Cardinals (574-596), San Diego Padres (597-624), and San Francisco Giants (625-651). Topical subsets feature Major League Prospects (652-680), Record Setters (681-687), League Leaders (688-697), Super Star Specials (698-707) and Pro Visions (708-713). Rookie Cards in the set include Rod Beck.

	MINT	EXC	G-VG
COMPLETE SET (720)	15.00	6.75	1.90
COMPLETE HOBBY SET (732)	25.00	11.50	3.10
COMPLETE RETAIL SET (732)	25.00	11.50	3.10
COMMON CARD (1-720)	.05	.02	.01

	MINT	EXC	G-VG
☐ 1 Brady Anderson	.10	.05	.01
☐ 2 Jose Bautista	.05	.02	.01
☐ 3 Juan Bell	.05	.02	.01
☐ 4 Glenn Davis	.05	.02	.01
☐ 5 Mike Devereaux	.10	.05	.01
☐ 6 Dwight Evans	.10	.05	.01
☐ 7 Mike Flanagan	.05	.02	.01
☐ 8 Leo Gomez	.05	.02	.01
☐ 9 Chris Hoiles	.15	.07	.02
☐ 10 Sam Horn	.05	.02	.01
☐ 11 Tim Hulett	.05	.02	.01
☐ 12 Dave Johnson	.05	.02	.01
☐ 13 Chito Martinez	.05	.02	.01
☐ 14 Ben McDonald	.10	.05	.01
☐ 15 Bob Melvin	.05	.02	.01
☐ 16 Luis Mercedes	.05	.02	.01
☐ 17 Jose Mesa	.05	.02	.01
☐ 18 Bob Milacki	.05	.02	.01
☐ 19 Randy Milligan	.05	.02	.01
☐ 20 Mike Mussina UER (Card back refers to him as Jeff)	.30	.14	.04
☐ 21 Gregg Olson	.05	.02	.01
☐ 22 Joe Orsulak	.05	.02	.01
☐ 23 Jim Poole	.05	.02	.01
☐ 24 Arthur Rhodes	.10	.05	.01
☐ 25 Billy Ripken	.05	.02	.01
☐ 26 Cal Ripken	.40	.18	.05
☐ 27 David Segui	.05	.02	.01
☐ 28 Roy Smith	.05	.02	.01
☐ 29 Anthony Telford	.05	.02	.01
☐ 30 Mark Williamson	.05	.02	.01
☐ 31 Craig Worthington	.05	.02	.01
☐ 32 Wade Boggs	.15	.07	.02
☐ 33 Tom Bolton	.05	.02	.01
☐ 34 Tom Brunansky	.05	.02	.01
☐ 35 Ellis Burks	.10	.05	.01
☐ 36 Jack Clark	.10	.05	.01
☐ 37 Roger Clemens	.25	.11	.03
☐ 38 Danny Darwin	.05	.02	.01
☐ 39 Mike Greenwell	.10	.05	.01
☐ 40 Joe Hesketh	.05	.02	.01
☐ 41 Daryl Irvine	.05	.02	.01
☐ 42 Dennis Lamp	.05	.02	.01
☐ 43 Tony Pena	.05	.02	.01
☐ 44 Phil Plantier	.15	.07	.02
☐ 45 Carlos Quintana	.05	.02	.01
☐ 46 Jeff Reardon	.10	.05	.01
☐ 47 Jody Reed	.05	.02	.01
☐ 48 Luis Rivera	.05	.02	.01
☐ 49 Mo Vaughn	.20	.09	.03
☐ 50 Jim Abbott	.15	.07	.02
☐ 51 Kyle Abbott	.05	.02	.01
☐ 52 Ruben Amaro Jr.	.05	.02	.01
☐ 53 Scott Bailes	.05	.02	.01
☐ 54 Chris Beasley	.05	.02	.01
☐ 55 Mark Eichhorn	.05	.02	.01
☐ 56 Mike Fetters	.05	.02	.01
☐ 57 Chuck Finley	.05	.02	.01
☐ 58 Gary Gaetti	.05	.02	.01
☐ 59 Dave Gallagher	.05	.02	.01
☐ 60 Donnie Hill	.05	.02	.01
☐ 61 Bryan Harvey UER (Lee Smith led the Majors with 47 saves)	.10	.05	.01
☐ 62 Wally Joyner	.10	.05	.01
☐ 63 Mark Langston	.15	.07	.02
☐ 64 Kirk McCaskill	.05	.02	.01
☐ 65 John Orton	.05	.02	.01
☐ 66 Lance Parrish	.10	.05	.01
☐ 67 Luis Polonia	.05	.02	.01
☐ 68 Bobby Rose	.05	.02	.01
☐ 69 Dick Schofield	.05	.02	.01
☐ 70 Luis Sojo	.05	.02	.01
☐ 71 Lee Stevens	.05	.02	.01
☐ 72 Dave Winfield	.15	.07	.02
☐ 73 Cliff Young	.05	.02	.01
☐ 74 Wilson Alvarez	.15	.07	.02
☐ 75 Esteban Beltre	.10	.05	.01
☐ 76 Joey Cora	.05	.02	.01
☐ 77 Brian Drahman	.05	.02	.01
☐ 78 Alex Fernandez	.15	.07	.02
☐ 79 Carlton Fisk	.15	.07	.02
☐ 80 Scott Fletcher	.05	.02	.01

☐ 81 Craig Grebeck	.05	.02	.01
☐ 82 Ozzie Guillen	.05	.02	.01
☐ 83 Greg Hibbard	.05	.02	.01
☐ 84 Charlie Hough	.10	.05	.01
☐ 85 Mike Huff	.05	.02	.01
☐ 86 Bo Jackson	.15	.07	.02
☐ 87 Lance Johnson	.05	.02	.01
☐ 88 Ron Karkovice	.05	.02	.01
☐ 89 Jack McDowell	.15	.07	.02
☐ 90 Matt Merullo	.05	.02	.01
☐ 91 Warren Newson	.05	.02	.01
☐ 92 Donn Pall UER (Called Dunn on card back)	.05	.02	.01
☐ 93 Dan Pasqua	.05	.02	.01
☐ 94 Ken Patterson	.05	.02	.01
☐ 95 Melido Perez	.05	.02	.01
☐ 96 Scott Radinsky	.05	.02	.01
☐ 97 Tim Raines	.15	.07	.02
☐ 98 Sammy Sosa	.15	.07	.02
☐ 99 Bobby Thigpen	.05	.02	.01
☐ 100 Frank Thomas	1.50	.65	.19
☐ 101 Robin Ventura	.15	.07	.02
☐ 102 Mike Aldrete	.05	.02	.01
☐ 103 Sandy Alomar Jr.	.10	.05	.01
☐ 104 Carlos Baerga	.20	.09	.03
☐ 105 Albert Belle	.40	.18	.05
☐ 106 Willie Blair	.05	.02	.01
☐ 107 Jerry Browne	.05	.02	.01
☐ 108 Alex Cole	.05	.02	.01
☐ 109 Felix Fermin	.05	.02	.01
☐ 110 Glenallen Hill	.05	.02	.01
☐ 111 Shawn Hillegas	.05	.02	.01
☐ 112 Chris James	.05	.02	.01
☐ 113 Reggie Jefferson	.05	.02	.01
☐ 114 Doug Jones	.05	.02	.01
☐ 115 Eric King	.05	.02	.01
☐ 116 Mark Lewis	.10	.05	.01
☐ 117 Carlos Martinez	.05	.02	.01
☐ 118 Charles Nagy UER (Throws right, but card says left)	.05	.02	.01
☐ 119 Rod Nichols	.05	.02	.01
☐ 120 Steve Olin	.05	.02	.01
☐ 121 Jesse Orosco	.05	.02	.01
☐ 122 Rudy Seanez	.05	.02	.01
☐ 123 Joel Skinner	.05	.02	.01
☐ 124 Greg Swindell	.05	.02	.01
☐ 125 Jim Thome	.40	.18	.05
☐ 126 Mark Whiten	.10	.05	.01
☐ 127 Scott Aldred	.05	.02	.01
☐ 128 Andy Allanson	.05	.02	.01
☐ 129 John Cerutti	.05	.02	.01
☐ 130 Milt Cuyler	.05	.02	.01
☐ 131 Mike Dalton	.05	.02	.01
☐ 132 Rob Deer	.05	.02	.01
☐ 133 Cecil Fielder	.15	.07	.02
☐ 134 Travis Fryman	.20	.09	.03
☐ 135 Dan Gakeler	.05	.02	.01
☐ 136 Paul Gibson	.05	.02	.01
☐ 137 Bill Gullickson	.05	.02	.01
☐ 138 Mike Henneman	.05	.02	.01
☐ 139 Pete Incaviglia	.05	.02	.01
☐ 140 Mark Leiter	.05	.02	.01
☐ 141 Scott Livingstone	.05	.02	.01
☐ 142 Lloyd Moseby	.05	.02	.01
☐ 143 Tony Phillips	.05	.02	.01
☐ 144 Mark Salas	.05	.02	.01
☐ 145 Frank Tanana	.05	.02	.01
☐ 146 Walt Terrell	.05	.02	.01
☐ 147 Mickey Tettleton	.10	.05	.01
☐ 148 Alan Trammell	.15	.07	.02
☐ 149 Lou Whitaker	.15	.07	.02
☐ 150 Kevin Appier	.10	.05	.01
☐ 151 Luis Aquino	.05	.02	.01
☐ 152 Todd Benzinger	.05	.02	.01
☐ 153 Mike Boddicker	.05	.02	.01
☐ 154 George Brett	.30	.14	.04
☐ 155 Storm Davis	.05	.02	.01
☐ 156 Jim Eisenreich	.05	.02	.01
☐ 157 Kirk Gibson	.10	.05	.01
☐ 158 Tom Gordon	.05	.02	.01
☐ 159 Mark Gubicza	.05	.02	.01
☐ 160 David Howard	.05	.02	.01
☐ 161 Mike Macfarlane	.05	.02	.01
☐ 162 Brent Mayne	.05	.02	.01
☐ 163 Brian McRae	.15	.07	.02
☐ 164 Jeff Montgomery	.10	.05	.01
☐ 165 Bill Pecota	.05	.02	.01
☐ 166 Harvey Pulliam	.05	.02	.01
☐ 167 Bret Saberhagen	.10	.05	.01
☐ 168 Kevin Seitzer	.05	.02	.01
☐ 169 Terry Shumpert	.05	.02	.01
☐ 170 Kurt Stillwell	.05	.02	.01
☐ 171 Danny Tartabull	.10	.05	.01
☐ 172 Gary Thurman	.05	.02	.01
☐ 173 Dante Bichette	.15	.07	.02
☐ 174 Kevin D. Brown	.05	.02	.01
☐ 175 Chuck Crim	.05	.02	.01
☐ 176 Jim Gantner	.05	.02	.01
☐ 177 Darryl Hamilton	.10	.05	.01
☐ 178 Ted Higuera	.05	.02	.01
☐ 179 Darren Holmes	.05	.02	.01
☐ 180 Mark Lee	.05	.02	.01
☐ 181 Julio Machado	.05	.02	.01
☐ 182 Paul Molitor	.20	.09	.03
☐ 183 Jaime Navarro	.05	.02	.01
☐ 184 Edwin Nunez	.05	.02	.01
☐ 185 Dan Plesac	.05	.02	.01
☐ 186 Willie Randolph	.10	.05	.01
☐ 187 Ron Robinson	.05	.02	.01
☐ 188 Gary Sheffield	.15	.07	.02
☐ 189 Bill Spiers	.05	.02	.01
☐ 190 B.J. Surhoff	.05	.02	.01
☐ 191 Dale Sveum	.05	.02	.01
☐ 192 Greg Vaughn	.10	.05	.01
☐ 193 Bill Wegman	.05	.02	.01
☐ 194 Robin Yount	.20	.09	.03
☐ 195 Rick Aguilera	.10	.05	.01
☐ 196 Allan Anderson	.05	.02	.01
☐ 197 Steve Bedrosian	.05	.02	.01
☐ 198 Randy Bush	.05	.02	.01
☐ 199 Larry Casian	.05	.02	.01
☐ 200 Chili Davis	.10	.05	.01
☐ 201 Scott Erickson	.05	.02	.01
☐ 202 Greg Gagne	.05	.02	.01
☐ 203 Dan Gladden	.05	.02	.01
☐ 204 Brian Harper	.05	.02	.01
☐ 205 Kent Hrbek	.10	.05	.01
☐ 206 Chuck Knoblauch UER (Career hit total of 59 is wrong)	.15	.07	.02
☐ 207 Gene Larkin	.05	.02	.01
☐ 208 Terry Leach	.05	.02	.01
☐ 209 Scott Leius	.05	.02	.01
☐ 210 Shane Mack	.10	.05	.01
☐ 211 Jack Morris	.15	.07	.02
☐ 212 Pedro Munoz	.10	.05	.01
☐ 213 Denny Neagle	.10	.05	.01
☐ 214 Al Newman	.05	.02	.01
☐ 215 Junior Ortiz	.05	.02	.01
☐ 216 Mike Pagliarulo	.05	.02	.01
☐ 217 Kirby Puckett	.30	.14	.04
☐ 218 Paul Sorrento	.05	.02	.01
☐ 219 Kevin Tapani	.05	.02	.01
☐ 220 Lenny Webster	.05	.02	.01

	#	Player			
☐	221	Jesse Barfield	.05	.02	.01
☐	222	Greg Cadaret	.05	.02	.01
☐	223	Dave Eiland	.05	.02	.01
☐	224	Alvaro Espinoza	.05	.02	.01
☐	225	Steve Farr	.05	.02	.01
☐	226	Bob Geren	.05	.02	.01
☐	227	Lee Guetterman	.05	.02	.01
☐	228	John Habyan	.05	.02	.01
☐	229	Mel Hall	.05	.02	.01
☐	230	Steve Howe	.05	.02	.01
☐	231	Mike Humphreys	.10	.05	.01
☐	232	Scott Kamieniecki	.05	.02	.01
☐	233	Pat Kelly	.10	.05	.01
☐	234	Roberto Kelly	.10	.05	.01
☐	235	Tim Leary	.05	.02	.01
☐	236	Kevin Maas	.05	.02	.01
☐	237	Don Mattingly	.30	.14	.04
☐	238	Hensley Meulens	.05	.02	.01
☐	239	Matt Nokes	.05	.02	.01
☐	240	Pascual Perez	.05	.02	.01
☐	241	Eric Plunk	.05	.02	.01
☐	242	John Ramos	.05	.02	.01
☐	243	Scott Sanderson	.05	.02	.01
☐	244	Steve Sax	.05	.02	.01
☐	245	Wade Taylor	.05	.02	.01
☐	246	Randy Velarde	.05	.02	.01
☐	247	Bernie Williams	.10	.05	.01
☐	248	Troy Afenir	.05	.02	.01
☐	249	Harold Baines	.10	.05	.01
☐	250	Lance Blankenship	.05	.02	.01
☐	251	Mike Bordick	.05	.02	.01
☐	252	Jose Canseco	.20	.09	.03
☐	253	Steve Chitren	.05	.02	.01
☐	254	Ron Darling	.05	.02	.01
☐	255	Dennis Eckersley	.15	.07	.02
☐	256	Mike Gallego	.05	.02	.01
☐	257	Dave Henderson	.05	.02	.01
☐	258	Rickey Henderson UER (Wearing 24 on front and 22 on back)	.15	.07	.02
☐	259	Rick Honeycutt	.05	.02	.01
☐	260	Brook Jacoby	.05	.02	.01
☐	261	Carney Lansford	.10	.05	.01
☐	262	Mark McGwire	.15	.07	.02
☐	263	Mike Moore	.05	.02	.01
☐	264	Gene Nelson	.05	.02	.01
☐	265	Jamie Quirk	.05	.02	.01
☐	266	Joe Slusarski	.05	.02	.01
☐	267	Terry Steinbach	.10	.05	.01
☐	268	Dave Stewart	.10	.05	.01
☐	269	Todd Van Poppel	.15	.07	.02
☐	270	Walt Weiss	.05	.02	.01
☐	271	Bob Welch	.05	.02	.01
☐	272	Curt Young	.05	.02	.01
☐	273	Scott Bradley	.05	.02	.01
☐	274	Greg Briley	.05	.02	.01
☐	275	Jay Buhner	.10	.05	.01
☐	276	Henry Cotto	.05	.02	.01
☐	277	Alvin Davis	.05	.02	.01
☐	278	Rich DeLucia	.05	.02	.01
☐	279	Ken Griffey Jr.	1.50	.65	.19
☐	280	Erik Hanson	.05	.02	.01
☐	281	Brian Holman	.05	.02	.01
☐	282	Mike Jackson	.05	.02	.01
☐	283	Randy Johnson	.15	.07	.02
☐	284	Tracy Jones	.05	.02	.01
☐	285	Bill Krueger	.05	.02	.01
☐	286	Edgar Martinez	.10	.05	.01
☐	287	Tino Martinez	.10	.05	.01
☐	288	Rob Murphy	.05	.02	.01
☐	289	Pete O'Brien	.05	.02	.01
☐	290	Alonzo Powell	.05	.02	.01
☐	291	Harold Reynolds	.05	.02	.01
☐	292	Mike Schooler	.05	.02	.01
☐	293	Russ Swan	.05	.02	.01
☐	294	Bill Swift	.10	.05	.01
☐	295	Dave Valle	.05	.02	.01
☐	296	Omar Vizquel	.05	.02	.01
☐	297	Gerald Alexander	.05	.02	.01
☐	298	Brad Arnsberg	.05	.02	.01
☐	299	Kevin Brown	.10	.05	.01
☐	300	Jack Daugherty	.05	.02	.01
☐	301	Mario Diaz	.05	.02	.01
☐	302	Brian Downing	.05	.02	.01
☐	303	Julio Franco	.10	.05	.01
☐	304	Juan Gonzalez	.60	.25	.08
☐	305	Rich Gossage	.15	.07	.02
☐	306	Jose Guzman	.05	.02	.01
☐	307	Jose Hernandez	.05	.02	.01
☐	308	Jeff Huson	.05	.02	.01
☐	309	Mike Jeffcoat	.05	.02	.01
☐	310	Terry Mathews	.05	.02	.01
☐	311	Rafael Palmeiro	.15	.07	.02
☐	312	Dean Palmer	.10	.05	.01
☐	313	Geno Petralli	.05	.02	.01
☐	314	Gary Pettis	.05	.02	.01
☐	315	Kevin Reimer	.05	.02	.01
☐	316	Ivan Rodriguez	.15	.07	.02
☐	317	Kenny Rogers	.05	.02	.01
☐	318	Wayne Rosenthal	.05	.02	.01
☐	319	Jeff Russell	.05	.02	.01
☐	320	Nolan Ryan	1.00	.45	.13
☐	321	Ruben Sierra	.15	.07	.02
☐	322	Jim Acker	.05	.02	.01
☐	323	Roberto Alomar	.25	.11	.03
☐	324	Derek Bell	.10	.05	.01
☐	325	Pat Borders	.05	.02	.01
☐	326	Tom Candiotti	.05	.02	.01
☐	327	Joe Carter	.20	.09	.03
☐	328	Rob Ducey	.05	.02	.01
☐	329	Kelly Gruber	.05	.02	.01
☐	330	Juan Guzman	.10	.05	.01
☐	331	Tom Henke	.10	.05	.01
☐	332	Jimmy Key	.10	.05	.01
☐	333	Manny Lee	.05	.02	.01
☐	334	Al Leiter	.05	.02	.01
☐	335	Bob MacDonald	.05	.02	.01
☐	336	Candy Maldonado	.05	.02	.01
☐	337	Rance Mulliniks	.05	.02	.01
☐	338	Greg Myers	.05	.02	.01
☐	339	John Olerud UER (1991 BA has .256, but text says .258)	.15	.07	.02
☐	340	Ed Sprague	.10	.05	.01
☐	341	Dave Stieb	.10	.05	.01
☐	342	Todd Stottlemyre	.05	.02	.01
☐	343	Mike Timlin	.05	.02	.01
☐	344	Duane Ward	.10	.05	.01
☐	345	David Wells	.05	.02	.01
☐	346	Devon White	.10	.05	.01
☐	347	Mookie Wilson	.05	.02	.01
☐	348	Eddie Zosky	.10	.05	.01
☐	349	Steve Avery	.15	.07	.02
☐	350	Mike Bell	.05	.02	.01
☐	351	Rafael Belliard	.05	.02	.01
☐	352	Juan Berenguer	.05	.02	.01
☐	353	Jeff Blauser	.10	.05	.01
☐	354	Sid Bream	.05	.02	.01
☐	355	Francisco Cabrera	.05	.02	.01
☐	356	Marvin Freeman	.05	.02	.01
☐	357	Ron Gant	.10	.05	.01
☐	358	Tom Glavine	.15	.07	.02
☐	359	Brian Hunter	.05	.02	.01
☐	360	David Justice	.20	.09	.03
☐	361	Charlie Leibrandt	.05	.02	.01
☐	362	Mark Lemke	.05	.02	.01

☐ 363	Kent Mercker	.05	.02	.01
☐ 364	Keith Mitchell	.10	.05	.01
☐ 365	Greg Olson	.05	.02	.01
☐ 366	Terry Pendleton	.15	.07	.02
☐ 367	Armando Reynoso	.05	.02	.01
☐ 368	Deion Sanders	.25	.11	.03
☐ 369	Lonnie Smith	.05	.02	.01
☐ 370	Pete Smith	.05	.02	.01
☐ 371	John Smoltz	.10	.05	.01
☐ 372	Mike Stanton	.10	.05	.01
☐ 373	Jeff Treadway	.05	.02	.01
☐ 374	Mark Wohlers	.10	.05	.01
☐ 375	Paul Assenmacher	.05	.02	.01
☐ 376	George Bell	.10	.05	.01
☐ 377	Shawn Boskie	.05	.02	.01
☐ 378	Frank Castillo	.05	.02	.01
☐ 379	Andre Dawson	.15	.07	.02
☐ 380	Shawon Dunston	.05	.02	.01
☐ 381	Mark Grace	.15	.07	.02
☐ 382	Mike Harkey	.05	.02	.01
☐ 383	Danny Jackson	.05	.02	.01
☐ 384	Les Lancaster	.05	.02	.01
☐ 385	Ced Landrum	.05	.02	.01
☐ 386	Greg Maddux	.20	.09	.03
☐ 387	Derrick May	.10	.05	.01
☐ 388	Chuck McElroy	.05	.02	.01
☐ 389	Ryne Sandberg	.30	.14	.04
☐ 390	Heathcliff Slocumb	.05	.02	.01
☐ 391	Dave Smith	.05	.02	.01
☐ 392	Dwight Smith	.05	.02	.01
☐ 393	Rick Sutcliffe	.10	.05	.01
☐ 394	Hector Villanueva	.05	.02	.01
☐ 395	Chico Walker	.05	.02	.01
☐ 396	Jerome Walton	.05	.02	.01
☐ 397	Rick Wilkins	.10	.05	.01
☐ 398	Jack Armstrong	.05	.02	.01
☐ 399	Freddie Benavides	.05	.02	.01
☐ 400	Glenn Braggs	.05	.02	.01
☐ 401	Tom Browning	.05	.02	.01
☐ 402	Norm Charlton	.05	.02	.01
☐ 403	Eric Davis	.05	.02	.01
☐ 404	Rob Dibble	.05	.02	.01
☐ 405	Bill Doran	.05	.02	.01
☐ 406	Mariano Duncan	.05	.02	.01
☐ 407	Kip Gross	.05	.02	.01
☐ 408	Chris Hammond	.05	.02	.01
☐ 409	Billy Hatcher	.05	.02	.01
☐ 410	Chris Jones	.05	.02	.01
☐ 411	Barry Larkin	.15	.07	.02
☐ 412	Hal Morris	.10	.05	.01
☐ 413	Randy Myers	.10	.05	.01
☐ 414	Joe Oliver	.05	.02	.01
☐ 415	Paul O'Neill	.10	.05	.01
☐ 416	Ted Power	.05	.02	.01
☐ 417	Luis Quinones	.05	.02	.01
☐ 418	Jeff Reed	.05	.02	.01
☐ 419	Jose Rijo	.10	.05	.01
☐ 420	Chris Sabo	.10	.05	.01
☐ 421	Reggie Sanders	.20	.09	.03
☐ 422	Scott Scudder	.05	.02	.01
☐ 423	Glenn Sutko	.05	.02	.01
☐ 424	Eric Anthony	.05	.02	.01
☐ 425	Jeff Bagwell	.75	.35	.09
☐ 426	Craig Biggio	.10	.05	.01
☐ 427	Ken Caminiti	.10	.05	.01
☐ 428	Casey Candaele	.05	.02	.01
☐ 429	Mike Capel	.05	.02	.01
☐ 430	Andujar Cedeno	.10	.05	.01
☐ 431	Jim Corsi	.05	.02	.01
☐ 432	Mark Davidson	.05	.02	.01
☐ 433	Steve Finley	.05	.02	.01
☐ 434	Luis Gonzalez	.10	.05	.01
☐ 435	Pete Harnisch	.10	.05	.01
☐ 436	Dwayne Henry	.05	.02	.01
☐ 437	Xavier Hernandez	.05	.02	.01
☐ 438	Jimmy Jones	.05	.02	.01
☐ 439	Darryl Kile	.10	.05	.01
☐ 440	Rob Mallicoat	.05	.02	.01
☐ 441	Andy Mota	.05	.02	.01
☐ 442	Al Osuna	.05	.02	.01
☐ 443	Mark Portugal	.05	.02	.01
☐ 444	Scott Servais	.05	.02	.01
☐ 445	Mike Simms	.05	.02	.01
☐ 446	Gerald Young	.05	.02	.01
☐ 447	Tim Belcher	.05	.02	.01
☐ 448	Brett Butler	.10	.05	.01
☐ 449	John Candelaria	.05	.02	.01
☐ 450	Gary Carter	.15	.07	.02
☐ 451	Dennis Cook	.05	.02	.01
☐ 452	Tim Crews	.05	.02	.01
☐ 453	Kal Daniels	.05	.02	.01
☐ 454	Jim Gott	.05	.02	.01
☐ 455	Alfredo Griffin	.05	.02	.01
☐ 456	Kevin Gross	.05	.02	.01
☐ 457	Chris Gwynn	.05	.02	.01
☐ 458	Lenny Harris	.05	.02	.01
☐ 459	Orel Hershiser	.10	.05	.01
☐ 460	Jay Howell	.05	.02	.01
☐ 461	Stan Javier	.05	.02	.01
☐ 462	Eric Karros	.15	.07	.02
☐ 463	Ramon Martinez UER (Card says bats right, should be left)	.10	.05	.01
☐ 464	Roger McDowell UER (Wins add up to 54, totals have 51)	.05	.02	.01
☐ 465	Mike Morgan	.05	.02	.01
☐ 466	Eddie Murray	.15	.07	.02
☐ 467	Jose Offerman	.05	.02	.01
☐ 468	Bob Ojeda	.05	.02	.01
☐ 469	Juan Samuel	.05	.02	.01
☐ 470	Mike Scioscia	.05	.02	.01
☐ 471	Darryl Strawberry	.10	.05	.01
☐ 472	Bret Barberie	.05	.02	.01
☐ 473	Brian Barnes	.05	.02	.01
☐ 474	Eric Bullock	.05	.02	.01
☐ 475	Ivan Calderon	.05	.02	.01
☐ 476	Delino DeShields	.15	.07	.02
☐ 477	Jeff Fassero	.05	.02	.01
☐ 478	Mike Fitzgerald	.05	.02	.01
☐ 479	Steve Frey	.05	.02	.01
☐ 480	Andres Galarraga	.15	.07	.02
☐ 481	Mark Gardner	.05	.02	.01
☐ 482	Marquis Grissom	.15	.07	.02
☐ 483	Chris Haney	.05	.02	.01
☐ 484	Barry Jones	.05	.02	.01
☐ 485	Dave Martinez	.05	.02	.01
☐ 486	Dennis Martinez	.10	.05	.01
☐ 487	Chris Nabholz	.05	.02	.01
☐ 488	Spike Owen	.05	.02	.01
☐ 489	Gilberto Reyes	.05	.02	.01
☐ 490	Mel Rojas	.05	.02	.01
☐ 491	Scott Ruskin	.05	.02	.01
☐ 492	Bill Sampen	.05	.02	.01
☐ 493	Larry Walker	.15	.07	.02
☐ 494	Tim Wallach	.05	.02	.01
☐ 495	Daryl Boston	.05	.02	.01
☐ 496	Hubie Brooks	.05	.02	.01
☐ 497	Tim Burke	.05	.02	.01
☐ 498	Mark Carreon	.05	.02	.01
☐ 499	Tony Castillo	.05	.02	.01
☐ 500	Vince Coleman	.05	.02	.01
☐ 501	David Cone	.15	.07	.02
☐ 502	Kevin Elster	.05	.02	.01
☐ 503	Sid Fernandez	.10	.05	.01
☐ 504	John Franco	.05	.02	.01

☐ 505 Dwight Gooden	.10	.05	.01
☐ 506 Todd Hundley	.05	.02	.01
☐ 507 Jeff Innis	.05	.02	.01
☐ 508 Gregg Jefferies	.15	.07	.02
☐ 509 Howard Johnson	.10	.05	.01
☐ 510 Dave Magadan	.05	.02	.01
☐ 511 Terry McDaniel	.10	.05	.01
☐ 512 Kevin McReynolds	.05	.02	.01
☐ 513 Keith Miller	.05	.02	.01
☐ 514 Charlie O'Brien	.05	.02	.01
☐ 515 Mackey Sasser	.05	.02	.01
☐ 516 Pete Schourek	.10	.05	.01
☐ 517 Julio Valera	.05	.02	.01
☐ 518 Frank Viola	.10	.05	.01
☐ 519 Wally Whitehurst	.05	.02	.01
☐ 520 Anthony Young	.10	.05	.01
☐ 521 Andy Ashby	.05	.02	.01
☐ 522 Kim Batiste	.05	.02	.01
☐ 523 Joe Boever	.05	.02	.01
☐ 524 Wes Chamberlain	.05	.02	.01
☐ 525 Pat Combs	.05	.02	.01
☐ 526 Danny Cox	.05	.02	.01
☐ 527 Darren Daulton	.15	.07	.02
☐ 528 Jose DeJesus	.05	.02	.01
☐ 529 Len Dykstra	.15	.07	.02
☐ 530 Darrin Fletcher	.05	.02	.01
☐ 531 Tommy Greene	.10	.05	.01
☐ 532 Jason Grimsley	.05	.02	.01
☐ 533 Charlie Hayes	.10	.05	.01
☐ 534 Von Hayes	.05	.02	.01
☐ 535 Dave Hollins	.15	.07	.02
☐ 536 Ricky Jordan	.05	.02	.01
☐ 537 John Kruk	.15	.07	.02
☐ 538 Jim Lindeman	.05	.02	.01
☐ 539 Mickey Morandini	.05	.02	.01
☐ 540 Terry Mulholland	.05	.02	.01
☐ 541 Dale Murphy	.15	.07	.02
☐ 542 Randy Ready	.05	.02	.01
☐ 543 Wally Ritchie UER (Letters in data are cut off on card)	.05	.02	.01
☐ 544 Bruce Ruffin	.05	.02	.01
☐ 545 Steve Searcy	.05	.02	.01
☐ 546 Dickie Thon	.05	.02	.01
☐ 547 Mitch Williams	.10	.05	.01
☐ 548 Stan Belinda	.05	.02	.01
☐ 549 Jay Bell	.10	.05	.01
☐ 550 Barry Bonds	.40	.18	.05
☐ 551 Bobby Bonilla	.15	.07	.02
☐ 552 Steve Buechele	.05	.02	.01
☐ 553 Doug Drabek	.15	.07	.02
☐ 554 Neal Heaton	.05	.02	.01
☐ 555 Jeff King	.05	.02	.01
☐ 556 Bob Kipper	.05	.02	.01
☐ 557 Bill Landrum	.05	.02	.01
☐ 558 Mike LaValliere	.05	.02	.01
☐ 559 Jose Lind	.05	.02	.01
☐ 560 Lloyd McClendon	.05	.02	.01
☐ 561 Orlando Merced	.10	.05	.01
☐ 562 Bob Patterson	.05	.02	.01
☐ 563 Joe Redfield	.05	.02	.01
☐ 564 Gary Redus	.05	.02	.01
☐ 565 Rosario Rodriguez	.05	.02	.01
☐ 566 Don Slaught	.05	.02	.01
☐ 567 John Smiley	.05	.02	.01
☐ 568 Zane Smith	.05	.02	.01
☐ 569 Randy Tomlin	.05	.02	.01
☐ 570 Andy Van Slyke	.15	.07	.02
☐ 571 Gary Varsho	.05	.02	.01
☐ 572 Bob Walk	.05	.02	.01
☐ 573 John Wehner UER (Actually played for Carolina in 1991, not Cards)	.10	.05	.01

☐ 574 Juan Agosto	.05	.02	.01
☐ 575 Cris Carpenter	.05	.02	.01
☐ 576 Jose DeLeon	.05	.02	.01
☐ 577 Rich Gedman	.05	.02	.01
☐ 578 Bernard Gilkey	.10	.05	.01
☐ 579 Pedro Guerrero	.10	.05	.01
☐ 580 Ken Hill	.10	.05	.01
☐ 581 Rex Hudler	.05	.02	.01
☐ 582 Felix Jose	.10	.05	.01
☐ 583 Ray Lankford	.15	.07	.02
☐ 584 Omar Olivares	.05	.02	.01
☐ 585 Jose Oquendo	.05	.02	.01
☐ 586 Tom Pagnozzi	.05	.02	.01
☐ 587 Geronimo Pena	.05	.02	.01
☐ 588 Mike Perez	.05	.02	.01
☐ 589 Gerald Perry	.05	.02	.01
☐ 590 Bryn Smith	.05	.02	.01
☐ 591 Lee Smith	.15	.07	.02
☐ 592 Ozzie Smith	.20	.09	.03
☐ 593 Scott Terry	.05	.02	.01
☐ 594 Bob Tewksbury	.05	.02	.01
☐ 595 Milt Thompson	.05	.02	.01
☐ 596 Todd Zeile	.10	.05	.01
☐ 597 Larry Andersen	.05	.02	.01
☐ 598 Oscar Azocar	.05	.02	.01
☐ 599 Andy Benes	.10	.05	.01
☐ 600 Ricky Bones	.10	.05	.01
☐ 601 Jerald Clark	.05	.02	.01
☐ 602 Pat Clements	.05	.02	.01
☐ 603 Paul Faries	.05	.02	.01
☐ 604 Tony Fernandez	.10	.05	.01
☐ 605 Tony Gwynn	.25	.11	.03
☐ 606 Greg W. Harris	.05	.02	.01
☐ 607 Thomas Howard	.05	.02	.01
☐ 608 Bruce Hurst	.05	.02	.01
☐ 609 Darrin Jackson	.05	.02	.01
☐ 610 Tom Lampkin	.05	.02	.01
☐ 611 Craig Lefferts	.05	.02	.01
☐ 612 Jim Lewis	.05	.02	.01
☐ 613 Mike Maddux	.05	.02	.01
☐ 614 Fred McGriff	.20	.09	.03
☐ 615 Jose Melendez	.05	.02	.01
☐ 616 Jose Mota	.05	.02	.01
☐ 617 Dennis Rasmussen	.05	.02	.01
☐ 618 Bip Roberts	.05	.02	.01
☐ 619 Rich Rodriguez	.05	.02	.01
☐ 620 Benito Santiago	.05	.02	.01
☐ 621 Craig Shipley	.10	.05	.01
☐ 622 Tim Teufel	.05	.02	.01
☐ 623 Kevin Ward	.05	.02	.01
☐ 624 Ed Whitson	.05	.02	.01
☐ 625 Dave Anderson	.05	.02	.01
☐ 626 Kevin Bass	.05	.02	.01
☐ 627 Rod Beck	.30	.14	.04
☐ 628 Bud Black	.05	.02	.01
☐ 629 Jeff Brantley	.05	.02	.01
☐ 630 John Burkett	.10	.05	.01
☐ 631 Will Clark	.20	.09	.03
☐ 632 Royce Clayton	.15	.07	.02
☐ 633 Steve Decker	.05	.02	.01
☐ 634 Kelly Downs	.05	.02	.01
☐ 635 Mike Felder	.05	.02	.01
☐ 636 Scott Garrelts	.05	.02	.01
☐ 637 Eric Gunderson	.05	.02	.01
☐ 638 Bryan Hickerson	.05	.02	.01
☐ 639 Darren Lewis	.10	.05	.01
☐ 640 Greg Litton	.05	.02	.01
☐ 641 Kirt Manwaring	.05	.02	.01
☐ 642 Paul McClellan	.05	.02	.01
☐ 643 Willie McGee	.10	.05	.01
☐ 644 Kevin Mitchell	.10	.05	.01
☐ 645 Francisco Oliveras	.05	.02	.01

☐ 646 Mike Remlinger............ .05 .02 .01
☐ 647 Dave Righetti............... .05 .02 .01
☐ 648 Robby Thompson........ .05 .02 .01
☐ 649 Jose Uribe.................... .05 .02 .01
☐ 650 Matt Williams.............. .20 .09 .03
☐ 651 Trevor Wilson.............. .05 .02 .01
☐ 652 Tom Goodwin MLP UER .05 .02 .01
(Timed in 3.5,
should be be timed)
☐ 653 Terry Bross MLP.......... .05 .02 .01
☐ 654 Mike Christopher MLP. .05 .02 .01
☐ 655 Kenny Lofton MLP..... 1.25 .55 .16
☐ 656 Chris Cron MLP........... .05 .02 .01
☐ 657 Willie Banks MLP......... .05 .02 .01
☐ 658 Pat Rice MLP............... .05 .02 .01
☐ 659A Rob Maurer MLP ERR 1.00 .45 .13
(Name misspelled as
Mauer on card front)
☐ 659B Rob Maurer MLP COR .10 .05 .01
☐ 660 Don Harris MLP........... .05 .02 .01
☐ 661 Henry Rodriguez MLP.. .05 .02 .01
☐ 662 Cliff Brantley MLP........ .10 .05 .01
☐ 663 Mike Linskey MLP UER .05 .02 .01
(220 pounds in data,
200 in text)
☐ 664 Gary DiSarcina MLP..... .10 .05 .01
☐ 665 Gil Heredia MLP........... .10 .05 .01
☐ 666 Vinny Castilla MLP....... .05 .02 .01
☐ 667 Paul Abbott MLP.......... .05 .02 .01
☐ 668 Monty Fariss MLP UER .05 .02 .01
(Called Paul on back)
☐ 669 Jarvis Brown MLP........ .10 .05 .01
☐ 670 Wayne Kirby MLP......... .15 .07 .02
☐ 671 Scott Brosius MLP....... .05 .02 .01
☐ 672 Bob Hamelin MLP........ .25 .11 .03
☐ 673 Joel Johnston MLP...... .05 .02 .01
☐ 674 Tim Spehr MLP............ .05 .02 .01
☐ 675A Jeff Gardner MLP ERR .10 .05 .01
(P on front,
should be SS)
☐ 675B Jeff Gardner MLP COR 1.00 .45 .13
☐ 676 Rico Rossy MLP.......... .05 .02 .01
☐ 677 Roberto Hernandez MLP .10 .05 .01
☐ 678 Ted Wood MLP............ .05 .02 .01
☐ 679 Cal Eldred MLP............ .10 .05 .01
☐ 680 Sean Berry MLP........... .10 .05 .01
☐ 681 Rickey Henderson RS.. .10 .05 .01
☐ 682 Nolan Ryan RS............. .50 .23 .06
☐ 683 Dennis Martinez RS..... .05 .02 .01
☐ 684 Wilson Alvarez RS....... .10 .05 .01
☐ 685 Joe Carter RS............... .10 .05 .01
☐ 686 Dave Winfield RS......... .10 .05 .01
☐ 687 David Cone RS............. .10 .05 .01
☐ 688 Jose Canseco LL UER.. .10 .05 .01
(Text on back has 42 stolen
bases in '88; should be 40)
☐ 689 Howard Johnson LL..... .05 .02 .01
☐ 690 Julio Franco LL............ .05 .02 .01
☐ 691 Terry Pendleton LL...... .10 .05 .01
☐ 692 Cecil Fielder LL............ .10 .05 .01
☐ 693 Scott Erickson LL......... .05 .02 .01
☐ 694 Tom Glavine LL............ .10 .05 .01
☐ 695 Dennis Martinez LL...... .05 .02 .01
☐ 696 Bryan Harvey LL.......... .05 .02 .01
☐ 697 Lee Smith LL................ .10 .05 .01
☐ 698 Super Siblings............. .10 .05 .01
Roberto Alomar
Sandy Alomar Jr.
☐ 699 The Indispensables...... .10 .05 .01
Bobby Bonilla
Will Clark
☐ 700 Teamwork..................... .05 .02 .01
Mark Wohlers
Kent Mercker
Alejandro Pena
☐ 701 Tiger Tandems............. .40 .18 .05
Stacy Jones
Bo Jackson
Gregg Olson
Frank Thomas
☐ 702 The Ignitors................. .10 .05 .01
Paul Molitor
Brett Butler
☐ 703 Indispensables II.......... .25 .11 .03
Cal Ripken
Joe Carter
☐ 704 Power Packs................ .15 .07 .02
Barry Larkin
Kirby Puckett
☐ 705 Today and Tomorrow... .15 .07 .02
Mo Vaughn
Cecil Fielder
☐ 706 Teenage Sensations..... .05 .02 .01
Ramon Martinez
Ozzie Guillen
☐ 707 Designated Hitters....... .05 .02 .01
Harold Baines
Wade Boggs
☐ 708 Robin Yount PV........... .10 .05 .01
☐ 709 Ken Griffey Jr. PV UER .75 .35 .09
(Missing quotations on
back; BA has .322, but
was actually .327)
☐ 710 Nolan Ryan PV............ .50 .23 .06
☐ 711 Cal Ripken PV.............. .25 .11 .03
☐ 712 Frank Thomas PV......... .75 .35 .09
☐ 713 David Justice PV.......... .15 .07 .02
☐ 714 Checklist 1-101............ .05 .02 .01
☐ 715 Checklist 102-194........ .05 .02 .01
☐ 716 Checklist 195-296........ .05 .02 .01
☐ 717 Checklist 297-397........ .05 .02 .01
☐ 718 Checklist 398-494........ .05 .02 .01
☐ 719 Checklist 495-596........ .05 .02 .01
☐ 720A Checklist 597-720 ERR .05 .02 .01
(659 Rob Mauer)
☐ 720B Checklist 597-720 COR .05 .02 .01
(659 Rob Maurer)

1992 Fleer All-Stars

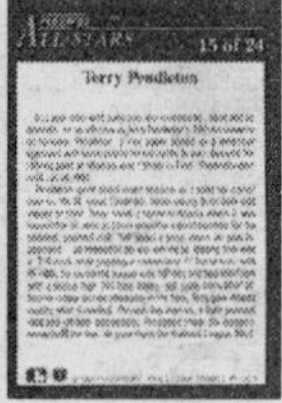

The 24-card All-Stars series was randomly inserted in 1992 Fleer wax packs (fin-sealed single packs). The cards measure the standard size (2 1/2" by 3 1/2"). The glossy color photos on the fronts are bordered in black and accented above and below with gold stripes and lettering. A diamond with a color head shot of the player is

superimposed at the lower right corner of the picture. The player's name and the words "Fleer '92 All-Stars" appear above and below the picture respectively in gold foil lettering. On a white background with black borders, the back has career highlights with the words "Fleer '92 All-Stars" appearing at the top in yellow lettering. The cards are numbered on the back.

	MINT	EXC	G-VG
COMPLETE SET (24)	40.00	18.00	5.00
COMMON CARD (1-24)	.75	.35	.09
☐ 1 Felix Jose	1.00	.45	.13
☐ 2 Tony Gwynn	2.00	.90	.25
☐ 3 Barry Bonds	3.50	1.55	.45
☐ 4 Bobby Bonilla	1.00	.45	.13
☐ 5 Mike LaValliere	.75	.35	.09
☐ 6 Tom Glavine	1.00	.45	.13
☐ 7 Ramon Martinez	1.00	.45	.13
☐ 8 Lee Smith	1.00	.45	.13
☐ 9 Mickey Tettleton	.75	.35	.09
☐ 10 Scott Erickson	.75	.35	.09
☐ 11 Frank Thomas	10.00	4.50	1.25
☐ 12 Danny Tartabull	1.00	.45	.13
☐ 13 Will Clark	2.00	.90	.25
☐ 14 Ryne Sandberg	3.00	1.35	.40
☐ 15 Terry Pendleton	1.00	.45	.13
☐ 16 Barry Larkin	1.00	.45	.13
☐ 17 Rafael Palmeiro	1.50	.65	.19
☐ 18 Julio Franco	1.00	.45	.13
☐ 19 Robin Ventura	1.00	.45	.13
☐ 20 Cal Ripken UER (Candidte; total bases misspelled as based)	5.00	2.30	.60
☐ 21 Joe Carter	2.00	.90	.25
☐ 22 Kirby Puckett	3.50	1.55	.45
☐ 23 Ken Griffey Jr.	10.00	4.50	1.25
☐ 24 Jose Canseco	2.00	.90	.25

1992 Fleer Roger Clemens

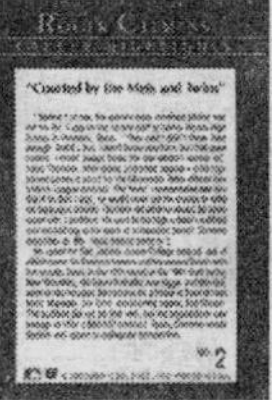

Roger Clemens served as a spokesperson for Fleer during 1992 and was the exclusive subject of this 15-card set. The first 12-card Roger Clemens "Career Highlights" subseries was randomly inserted in 1992 Fleer packs. Two-thousand signed cards were randomly inserted in wax packs and could also be won by entering a drawing. However, these cards are uncertifiable as they do not have any distinguishable marks. Moreover, a three-card Clemens subset (13-15) was available through a special mail-in offer. The cards measure the standard size (2 1/2" by 3 1/2"). The glossy color photos on the fronts are bordered in black and accented with gold stripes and lettering on the top of the card. On a pale yellow background with black borders, the back has player profile and career highlights. The cards are numbered on the back.

	MINT	EXC	G-VG
COMPLETE SET (12)	10.00	4.50	1.25
COMMON CLEMENS (1-12)	1.00	.45	.13
COMMON SEND-OFF (13-15)	1.00	.45	.13
☐ 1 Quiet Storm	1.00	.45	.13
☐ 2 Courted By Mets and Twins	1.00	.45	.13
☐ 3 The Show	1.00	.45	.13
☐ 4 Rocket Launched	1.00	.45	.13
☐ 5 Time Of Trial	1.00	.45	.13
☐ 6 Break Through	1.00	.45	.13
☐ 7 Play It Again Roger	1.00	.45	.13
☐ 8 Business As Usual	1.00	.45	.13
☐ 9 Heeee's Back	1.00	.45	.13
☐ 10 Blood, Sweat, and Tears	1.00	.45	.13
☐ 11 Prime Of Life	1.00	.45	.13
☐ 12 Man For Every Season	1.00	.45	.13
☐ 13 Cooperstown Bound	1.00	.45	.13
☐ 14 The Heat of the Moment	1.00	.45	.13
☐ 15 Final Words Q and A with "The Rocket"	1.00	.45	.13

1992 Fleer Lumber Company

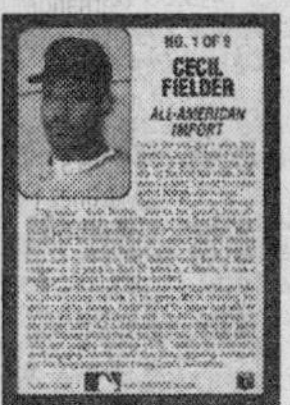

The 1992 Fleer Lumber Company set features nine outstanding hitters in Major League Baseball. The cards measure the standard size (2 1/2" by 3 1/2"). Inside a black glossy frame, the fronts display color action player photos, with the player's name printed in black in a gold foil bar beneath the picture. The wider right border contains the catch phrase "The Lumber Co." in the shape of a baseball bat, complete with woodgrain streaks. The backs carry a color head shot and, on a tan panel, a summary of the player's hitting performance and records. The cards are numbered on the back with an "L" prefix.

	MINT	EXC	G-VG
COMPLETE SET (9)	10.00	4.50	1.25
COMMON CARD (L1-L9)	.75	.35	.09
☐ L1 Cecil Fielder	1.50	.65	.19
☐ L2 Mickey Tettleton	.75	.35	.09
☐ L3 Darryl Strawberry	.75	.35	.09
☐ L4 Ryne Sandberg	3.50	1.55	.45
☐ L5 Jose Canseco	2.00	.90	.25
☐ L6 Matt Williams	2.00	.90	.25
☐ L7 Cal Ripken	5.00	2.30	.60
☐ L8 Barry Bonds	3.50	1.55	.45
☐ L9 Ron Gant	.75	.35	.09

1992 Fleer Rookie Sensations

The 20-card Fleer Rookie Sensations series was randomly inserted in 1992 Fleer 35-card cello packs. The cards measure the standard size (2 1/2" by 3 1/2"). The glossy color photos on the fronts have a white border on a royal blue card face. The words "Rookie Sensations" appear above the picture in gold foil lettering, while the player's name appears on a gold foil plaque beneath the picture. On a light blue background with royal blue borders, the backs have career summary. The cards are numbered on the back. Through a mail-in offer for ten Fleer baseball card wrappers and 1.00 for postage and handling, Fleer offered an uncut 8 1/2" by 11" numbered promo sheet picturing ten of the 20-card set on each side in a reduced-size front-only format. The offer indicated an expiration date of July 31, 1992, or whenever the production quantity of 250,000 sheets was exhausted.

	MINT	EXC	G-VG
COMPLETE SET (20)	70.00	32.00	8.75
COMMON CARD (1-20)	1.00	.45	.13
☐ 1 Frank Thomas	35.00	16.00	4.40
☐ 2 Todd Van Poppel	1.50	.65	.19
☐ 3 Orlando Merced	1.50	.65	.19
☐ 4 Jeff Bagwell	18.00	8.00	2.30
☐ 5 Jeff Fassero	1.00	.45	.13
☐ 6 Darren Lewis	1.50	.65	.19
☐ 7 Milt Cuyler	1.00	.45	.13
☐ 8 Mike Timlin	1.00	.45	.13
☐ 9 Brian McRae	2.00	.90	.25
☐ 10 Chuck Knoblauch	3.00	1.35	.40
☐ 11 Rich DeLucia	1.00	.45	.13
☐ 12 Ivan Rodriguez	3.00	1.35	.40
☐ 13 Juan Guzman	2.00	.90	.25
☐ 14 Steve Chitren	1.00	.45	.13
☐ 15 Mark Wohlers	1.00	.45	.13
☐ 16 Wes Chamberlain	1.00	.45	.13
☐ 17 Ray Lankford	2.50	1.15	.30
☐ 18 Chito Martinez	1.00	.45	.13
☐ 19 Phil Plantier	2.00	.90	.25
☐ 20 Scott Leius UER (Misspelled Lieus on card front)	1.00	.45	.13

1992 Fleer Smoke 'n Heat

This 12-card set features outstanding major league pitchers, especially the premier fastball pitchers in both leagues. The cards were randomly inserted in Fleer's 1992 Christmas baseball set. The cards measure the standard size (2 1/2" by 3 1/2"). The front design features color action player photos bordered in black. The player's name appears in a gold foil bar beneath the picture, and the words "Smoke 'n Heat" are printed vertically in the wider right border. Within black borders and on a background of yellow shading to orange, the backs carry a color head shot and player profile. The cards are numbered on the back with an "S" prefix.

	MINT	EXC	G-VG
COMPLETE SET (12)	10.00	4.50	1.25
COMMON CARD (S1-S12)	.50	.23	.06
☐ S1 Lee Smith	.75	.35	.09
☐ S2 Jack McDowell	.50	.23	.06
☐ S3 David Cone	.75	.35	.09
☐ S4 Roger Clemens	2.50	1.15	.30
☐ S5 Nolan Ryan	8.00	3.60	1.00
☐ S6 Scott Erickson	.50	.23	.06
☐ S7 Tom Glavine	1.25	.55	.16
☐ S8 Dwight Gooden	.50	.23	.06
☐ S9 Andy Benes	.75	.35	.09
☐ S10 Steve Avery	1.50	.65	.19
☐ S11 Randy Johnson	1.00	.45	.13
☐ S12 Jim Abbott	.50	.23	.06

1992 Fleer Team Leaders

The 20-card Fleer Team Leaders series was randomly inserted in 1992 Fleer 42-card rack packs. The cards measure the standard size (2 1/2" by 3 1/2"). The glossy color photos on the fronts are bordered in white and green. Two gold foil stripes below the picture intersect a diamond-shaped "Team Leaders" emblem. On a pale green background with green borders, the backs have career summary. The cards are numbered on the back.

	MINT	EXC	G-VG
COMPLETE SET (20)	75.00	34.00	9.50
COMMON CARD (1-20)	1.50	.65	.19
☐ 1 Don Mattingly	10.00	4.50	1.25
☐ 2 Howard Johnson	1.50	.65	.19
☐ 3 Chris Sabo UER (Where he it, should be Where he hit)	1.50	.65	.19
☐ 4 Carlton Fisk	2.00	.90	.25
☐ 5 Kirby Puckett	10.00	4.50	1.25
☐ 6 Cecil Fielder	3.50	1.55	.45
☐ 7 Tony Gwynn	5.00	2.30	.60
☐ 8 Will Clark	5.00	2.30	.60
☐ 9 Bobby Bonilla	2.00	.90	.25
☐ 10 Len Dykstra	2.00	.90	.25
☐ 11 Tom Glavine	2.00	.90	.25
☐ 12 Rafael Palmeiro	4.00	1.80	.50
☐ 13 Wade Boggs	4.00	1.80	.50
☐ 14 Joe Carter	5.00	2.30	.60
☐ 15 Ken Griffey Jr.	35.00	16.00	4.40
☐ 16 Darryl Strawberry	2.00	.90	.25
☐ 17 Cal Ripken	16.00	7.25	2.00
☐ 18 Danny Tartabull	2.00	.90	.25
☐ 19 Jose Canseco	5.00	2.30	.60
☐ 20 Andre Dawson	2.00	.90	.25

1992 Fleer Update

The 1992 Fleer Update set contains 132 cards measuring the standard size (2 1/2" by 3 1/2"). Factory sets included a four-card, black-bordered "92 Headliners" insert set for a total of 136 cards. The basic card fronts have color action player photos with a metallic blue-green border that fades to white as one moves down the card face. The team logo, player's name, and his position appear in the wider right border. The top half of the backs has a close-up photo, while the bottom half carry biography and complete career statistics. The cards are checklisted below alphabetically within and according to teams for each league as follows: Baltimore Orioles (1-3), Boston Red Sox (4-6), California Angels (7-11), Chicago White Sox (12-14), Cleveland Indians (15-18), Detroit Tigers (19-25), Kansas City Royals (26-32), Milwaukee Brewers (33-38), Minnesota Twins (39-41), New York Yankees (42-46), Oakland Athletics (47-53), Seattle Mariners (54-58), Texas Rangers (59-62), Toronto Blue Jays (63-67), Atlanta Braves (68-71), Chicago Cubs (72-77), Cincinnati Reds (78-84), Houston Astros (85-88), Los Angeles Dodgers (89-94), Montreal Expos (95-100), New York Mets (101-107), Philadelphia Phillies (108-112), Pittsburgh Pirates (113-117), St. Louis Cardinals (118-121), San Diego Padres (122-126), and San Francisco Giants (127-132). The cards are numbered on the back with a "U" prefix. Rookie Cards in this set include Chad Curtis, Damion Easley, John Jaha, Jeff Kent, Pat Listach, Pat Mahomes, Al Martin, Troy Neel, David Nied, Mike Piazza, Tim Wakefield, and Eric Young.

	MINT	EXC	G-VG
COMPLETE FACT.SET (136)	150.00	70.00	19.00
COMPLETE SET (132)	120.00	55.00	15.00
COMMON CARD (1-132)	.25	.11	.03
☐ 1 Todd Frohwirth	.25	.11	.03
☐ 2 Alan Mills	.25	.11	.03
☐ 3 Rick Sutcliffe	.35	.16	.04
☐ 4 John Valentin	1.50	.65	.19
☐ 5 Frank Viola	.35	.16	.04
☐ 6 Bob Zupcic	.25	.11	.03
☐ 7 Mike Butcher	.25	.11	.03
☐ 8 Chad Curtis	2.50	1.15	.30
☐ 9 Damion Easley	1.50	.65	.19
☐ 10 Tim Salmon	15.00	6.75	1.90
☐ 11 Julio Valera	.25	.11	.03
☐ 12 George Bell	.35	.16	.04
☐ 13 Roberto Hernandez	.35	.16	.04
☐ 14 Shawn Jeter	.25	.11	.03
☐ 15 Thomas Howard	.25	.11	.03
☐ 16 Jesse Levis	.25	.11	.03
☐ 17 Kenny Lofton	25.00	11.50	3.10
☐ 18 Paul Sorrento	.25	.11	.03
☐ 19 Rico Brogna	.35	.16	.04
☐ 20 John Doherty	1.00	.45	.13
☐ 21 Dan Gladden	.25	.11	.03
☐ 22 Buddy Groom	.25	.11	.03

☐ 23 Shawn Hare .25 .11 .03
☐ 24 John Kiely .25 .11 .03
☐ 25 Kurt Knudsen .35 .16 .04
☐ 26 Gregg Jefferies 1.50 .65 .19
☐ 27 Wally Joyner .35 .16 .04
☐ 28 Kevin Koslofski .25 .11 .03
☐ 29 Kevin McReynolds .25 .11 .03
☐ 30 Rusty Meacham .25 .11 .03
☐ 31 Keith Miller .25 .11 .03
☐ 32 Hipolito Pichardo .25 .11 .03
☐ 33 James Austin .25 .11 .03
☐ 34 Scott Fletcher .25 .11 .03
☐ 35 John Jaha 1.50 .65 .19
☐ 36 Pat Listach 1.00 .45 .13
☐ 37 Dave Nilsson 3.00 1.35 .40
☐ 38 Kevin Seitzer .25 .11 .03
☐ 39 Tom Edens .25 .11 .03
☐ 40 Pat Mahomes 2.00 .90 .25
☐ 41 John Smiley .25 .11 .03
☐ 42 Charlie Hayes .35 .16 .04
☐ 43 Sam Militello .25 .11 .03
☐ 44 Andy Stankiewicz .25 .11 .03
☐ 45 Danny Tartabull .35 .16 .04
☐ 46 Bob Wickman .35 .16 .04
☐ 47 Jerry Browne .25 .11 .03
☐ 48 Kevin Campbell .25 .11 .03
☐ 49 Vince Horsman .25 .11 .03
☐ 50 Troy Neel 2.00 .90 .25
☐ 51 Ruben Sierra .75 .35 .09
☐ 52 Bruce Walton .25 .11 .03
☐ 53 Willie Wilson .25 .11 .03
☐ 54 Bret Boone 4.00 1.80 .50
☐ 55 Dave Fleming .35 .16 .04
☐ 56 Kevin Mitchell .50 .23 .06
☐ 57 Jeff Nelson .25 .11 .03
☐ 58 Shane Turner .25 .11 .03
☐ 59 Jose Canseco 4.00 1.80 .50
☐ 60 Jeff Frye .25 .11 .03
☐ 61 Danny Leon .25 .11 .03
☐ 62 Roger Pavlik .60 .25 .08
☐ 63 David Cone .50 .23 .06
☐ 64 Pat Hentgen 4.00 1.80 .50
☐ 65 Randy Knorr .25 .11 .03
☐ 66 Jack Morris .50 .23 .06
☐ 67 Dave Winfield 2.50 1.15 .30
☐ 68 David Nied 6.00 2.70 .75
☐ 69 Otis Nixon .25 .11 .03
☐ 70 Alejandro Pena .25 .11 .03
☐ 71 Jeff Reardon .35 .16 .04
☐ 72 Alex Arias .35 .16 .04
☐ 73 Jim Bullinger .25 .11 .03
☐ 74 Mike Morgan .25 .11 .03
☐ 75 Rey Sanchez .75 .35 .09
☐ 76 Bob Scanlan .25 .11 .03
☐ 77 Sammy Sosa 2.00 .90 .25
☐ 78 Scott Bankhead .25 .11 .03
☐ 79 Tim Belcher .25 .11 .03
☐ 80 Steve Foster .25 .11 .03
☐ 81 Willie Greene 2.00 .90 .25
☐ 82 Bip Roberts .35 .16 .04
☐ 83 Scott Ruskin .25 .11 .03
☐ 84 Greg Swindell .25 .11 .03
☐ 85 Juan Guerrero .25 .11 .03
☐ 86 Butch Henry .25 .11 .03
☐ 87 Doug Jones .25 .11 .03
☐ 88 Brian Williams .75 .35 .09
☐ 89 Tom Candiotti .25 .11 .03
☐ 90 Eric Davis .35 .16 .04
☐ 91 Carlos Hernandez .25 .11 .03
☐ 92 Mike Piazza 70.00 32.00 8.75
☐ 93 Mike Sharperson .25 .11 .03
☐ 94 Eric Young .75 .35 .09
☐ 95 Moises Alou 5.00 2.30 .60
☐ 96 Greg Colbrunn .35 .16 .04
☐ 97 Wil Cordero 4.00 1.80 .50
☐ 98 Ken Hill 2.00 .90 .25
☐ 99 John Vander Wal .25 .11 .03
☐ 100 John Wetteland .25 .11 .03
☐ 101 Bobby Bonilla .50 .23 .06
☐ 102 Eric Hillman .25 .11 .03
☐ 103 Pat Howell .25 .11 .03
☐ 104 Jeff Kent 5.00 2.30 .60
☐ 105 Dick Schofield .25 .11 .03
☐ 106 Ryan Thompson 4.00 1.80 .50
☐ 107 Chico Walker .25 .11 .03
☐ 108 Juan Bell .25 .11 .03
☐ 109 Mariano Duncan .25 .11 .03
☐ 110 Jeff Grotewold .25 .11 .03
☐ 111 Ben Rivera .25 .11 .03
☐ 112 Curt Schilling .35 .16 .04
☐ 113 Victor Cole .25 .11 .03
☐ 114 Albert Martin 3.00 1.35 .40
☐ 115 Roger Mason .25 .11 .03
☐ 116 Blas Minor .25 .11 .03
☐ 117 Tim Wakefield .25 .11 .03
☐ 118 Mark Clark 2.00 .90 .25
☐ 119 Rheal Cormier .25 .11 .03
☐ 120 Donovan Osborne .25 .11 .03
☐ 121 Todd Worrell .25 .11 .03
☐ 122 Jeremy Hernandez .25 .11 .03
☐ 123 Randy Myers .35 .16 .04
☐ 124 Frank Seminara .25 .11 .03
☐ 125 Gary Sheffield 1.50 .65 .19
☐ 126 Dan Walters .25 .11 .03
☐ 127 Steve Hosey .35 .16 .04
☐ 128 Mike Jackson .25 .11 .03
☐ 129 Jim Pena .25 .11 .03
☐ 130 Cory Snyder .25 .11 .03
☐ 131 Bill Swift .35 .16 .04
☐ 132 Checklist U1-U132 .25 .11 .03

1992 Fleer Update Headliners

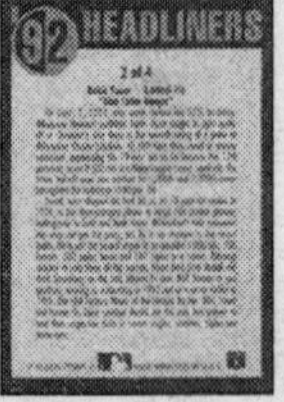

This four card set featuring top 1992 achievements was included with the 1992 Fleer Update factory set. The cards are black bordered with a color photo and gold foil on front. The backs have detailed information concerning the record or performance.

	MINT	EXC	G-VG
COMPLETE SET (4)	30.00	13.50	3.80
COMMON CARD (H1-H4)	1.00	.45	.13

		MINT	EXC	G-VG
☐ H1	Ken Griffey Jr.	25.00	11.50	3.10
☐ H2	Robin Yount	3.00	1.35	.40
☐ H3	Jeff Reardon	1.00	.45	.13
☐ H4	Cecil Fielder	2.50	1.15	.30

1993 Fleer

The 1993 Fleer baseball set contains two series of 360 cards each measuring the standard size (2 1/2" by 3 1/2"). Randomly inserted in the first series wax packs were a three-card Golden Moments subset, a 12-card NL All-Stars subset, an 18-card Major League Prospects subset, and three Pro-Visions cards. The fronts show glossy color action player photos bordered in silver. A team color-coded stripe edges the left side of the picture and carries the player's name and team name. On a background that shades from white to silver, the horizontally oriented backs have the player's last name in team-color coded block lettering, a cut out color player photo, and a box displaying biographical and statistical information. The cards are checklisted below alphabetically within and according to teams for each league as follows: Atlanta Braves (1-16), Chicago Cubs (17-28), Cincinnati Reds (29-44), Houston Astros (45-56), Los Angeles Dodgers (57-69), Montreal Expos (70-83), New York Mets (84-96), Philadelphia Phillies (97-109), Pittsburgh Pirates (110-123), St. Louis Cardinals (124-136), San Diego Padres (137-149), San Francisco Giants (150-162), Baltimore Orioles (163-175), Boston Red Sox (176-186), California Angels (187-198), Chicago White Sox (199-211), Cleveland Indians (212-223), Detroit Tigers (224-234), Kansas City Royals (235-246), Milwaukee Brewers (247-260), Minnesota Twins (261-275), New York Yankees (276-289), Oakland Athletics (290-303), Seattle Mariners (304-316), Texas Rangers (317-329), and Toronto Blue Jays (330-343). Topical subsets featured include League Leaders (344-348), NL Round Trippers (349-353), and Super Star Specials (354-357). The set concludes with checklists (358-360). The second series consists of 360 cards and includes cards of players from the expansion teams, the Florida Marlins and the Colorado Rockies. Three Golden Moments cards, three Pro-Vision cards, 18 Major League Prospects cards, and 12 American League All-Stars cards were inserted in series II wax packs. The rack packs included ten Team Leader cards while the jumbo packs offered ten Rookie Sensations. The 12-card Tom Glavine "Career Highlights" set continued to be randomly inserted in all series II cards; though some cards were autographed, series I wax variations were not repeated in series II. The cards are numbered on the back, grouped alphabetically within teams, and checklisted below alphabetically according to teams for each league as follows: Atlanta Braves (361-372), Chicago Cubs (373-385), Cincinnati Reds (386-400), Colorado Rockies (401-416), Florida Marlins (417-431), Houston Astros (432-442), Los Angeles Dodgers (443-456), Montreal Expos (457-465), New York Mets (466-482), Philadelphia Phillies (483-498), Pittsburgh Pirates (499-506), St. Louis Cardinals (507-517), San Diego Padres (518-525), San Francisco Giants (526-540), Baltimore Orioles (541-553), Boston Red Sox (554-567), California Angels (568-578), Chicago White Sox (579-589), Cleveland Indians (590-602), Detroit Tigers (603-614), Kansas City Royals (615-627), Milwaukee Brewers (628-636), Minnesota Twins (637-646), New York Yankees (647-658), Oakland Athletics (659-669), Seattle Mariners (670-681), Texas Rangers (682-690), and Toronto Blue Jays (691-703). The set closes with the following topical subsets: League Leaders (704-708), AL Round Trippers (709-713), Super Star Specials (714-717), and checklists (718-720).

	MINT	EXC	G-VG
COMPLETE SET (720)	45.00	20.00	5.75
COMPLETE SERIES 1 (360)	22.50	10.00	2.80
COMPLETE SERIES 2 (360)	22.50	10.00	2.80
COMMON CARD (1-360)	.05	.02	.01
COMMON CARD (361-720)	.05	.02	.01

		MINT	EXC	G-VG
☐ 1	Steve Avery	.10	.05	.01
☐ 2	Sid Bream	.05	.02	.01
☐ 3	Ron Gant	.08	.04	.01
☐ 4	Tom Glavine	.10	.05	.01
☐ 5	Brian Hunter	.08	.04	.01
☐ 6	Ryan Klesko	.60	.25	.08
☐ 7	Charlie Leibrandt	.05	.02	.01
☐ 8	Kent Mercker	.05	.02	.01
☐ 9	David Nied	.10	.05	.01
☐ 10	Otis Nixon	.05	.02	.01
☐ 11	Greg Olson	.05	.02	.01
☐ 12	Terry Pendleton	.10	.05	.01
☐ 13	Deion Sanders	.40	.18	.05
☐ 14	John Smoltz	.08	.04	.01
☐ 15	Mike Stanton	.05	.02	.01
☐ 16	Mark Wohlers	.05	.02	.01
☐ 17	Paul Assenmacher	.05	.02	.01
☐ 18	Steve Buechele	.05	.02	.01
☐ 19	Shawon Dunston	.05	.02	.01
☐ 20	Mark Grace	.10	.05	.01
☐ 21	Derrick May	.08	.04	.01
☐ 22	Chuck McElroy	.05	.02	.01
☐ 23	Mike Morgan	.05	.02	.01
☐ 24	Rey Sanchez	.05	.02	.01
☐ 25	Ryne Sandberg	.60	.25	.08
☐ 26	Bob Scanlan	.05	.02	.01
☐ 27	Sammy Sosa	.10	.05	.01
☐ 28	Rick Wilkins	.05	.02	.01

☐ 29 Bobby Ayala .20 .09 .03
☐ 30 Tim Belcher .05 .02 .01
☐ 31 Jeff Branson .05 .02 .01
☐ 32 Norm Charlton .05 .02 .01
☐ 33 Steve Foster .05 .02 .01
☐ 34 Willie Greene .08 .04 .01
☐ 35 Chris Hammond .05 .02 .01
☐ 36 Milt Hill .05 .02 .01
☐ 37 Hal Morris .08 .04 .01
☐ 38 Joe Oliver .05 .02 .01
☐ 39 Paul O'Neill .08 .04 .01
☐ 40 Tim Pugh .05 .02 .01
☐ 41 Jose Rijo .08 .04 .01
☐ 42 Bip Roberts .05 .02 .01
☐ 43 Chris Sabo .08 .04 .01
☐ 44 Reggie Sanders .10 .05 .01
☐ 45 Eric Anthony .05 .02 .01
☐ 46 Jeff Bagwell 1.00 .45 .13
☐ 47 Craig Biggio .08 .04 .01
☐ 48 Joe Boever .05 .02 .01
☐ 49 Casey Candaele .05 .02 .01
☐ 50 Steve Finley .05 .02 .01
☐ 51 Luis Gonzalez .08 .04 .01
☐ 52 Pete Harnisch .05 .02 .01
☐ 53 Xavier Hernandez .05 .02 .01
☐ 54 Doug Jones .05 .02 .01
☐ 55 Eddie Taubensee .08 .04 .01
☐ 56 Brian Williams .05 .02 .01
☐ 57 Pedro Astacio .08 .04 .01
☐ 58 Todd Benzinger .05 .02 .01
☐ 59 Brett Butler .08 .04 .01
☐ 60 Tom Candiotti .05 .02 .01
☐ 61 Lenny Harris .05 .02 .01
☐ 62 Carlos Hernandez .08 .04 .01
☐ 63 Orel Hershiser .08 .04 .01
☐ 64 Eric Karros .08 .04 .01
☐ 65 Ramon Martinez .08 .04 .01
☐ 66 Jose Offerman .05 .02 .01
☐ 67 Mike Scioscia .05 .02 .01
☐ 68 Mike Sharperson .05 .02 .01
☐ 69 Eric Young .08 .04 .01
☐ 70 Moises Alou .10 .05 .01
☐ 71 Ivan Calderon .05 .02 .01
☐ 72 Archi Cianfrocco .08 .04 .01
☐ 73 Wil Cordero .10 .05 .01
☐ 74 Delino DeShields .08 .04 .01
☐ 75 Mark Gardner .05 .02 .01
☐ 76 Ken Hill .08 .04 .01
☐ 77 Tim Laker .05 .02 .01
☐ 78 Chris Nabholz .05 .02 .01
☐ 79 Mel Rojas .05 .02 .01
☐ 80 John Vander Wal UER .05 .02 .01
(Misspelled Vander Wall in letters on back)
☐ 81 Larry Walker .10 .05 .01
☐ 82 Tim Wallach .05 .02 .01
☐ 83 John Wetteland .05 .02 .01
☐ 84 Bobby Bonilla .10 .05 .01
☐ 85 Daryl Boston .05 .02 .01
☐ 86 Sid Fernandez .05 .02 .01
☐ 87 Eric Hillman .05 .02 .01
☐ 88 Todd Hundley .05 .02 .01
☐ 89 Howard Johnson .05 .02 .01
☐ 90 Jeff Kent .10 .05 .01
☐ 91 Eddie Murray .10 .05 .01
☐ 92 Bill Pecota .05 .02 .01
☐ 93 Bret Saberhagen .08 .04 .01
☐ 94 Dick Schofield .05 .02 .01
☐ 95 Pete Schourek .08 .04 .01
☐ 96 Anthony Young .08 .04 .01
☐ 97 Ruben Amaro Jr. .05 .02 .01
☐ 98 Juan Bell .05 .02 .01
☐ 99 Wes Chamberlain .05 .02 .01
☐ 100 Darren Daulton .10 .05 .01
☐ 101 Mariano Duncan .05 .02 .01
☐ 102 Mike Hartley .05 .02 .01
☐ 103 Ricky Jordan .05 .02 .01
☐ 104 John Kruk .10 .05 .01
☐ 105 Mickey Morandini .05 .02 .01
☐ 106 Terry Mulholland .05 .02 .01
☐ 107 Ben Rivera .05 .02 .01
☐ 108 Curt Schilling .08 .04 .01
☐ 109 Keith Shepherd .05 .02 .01
☐ 110 Stan Belinda .05 .02 .01
☐ 111 Jay Bell .08 .04 .01
☐ 112 Barry Bonds .75 .35 .09
☐ 113 Jeff King .05 .02 .01
☐ 114 Mike LaValliere .05 .02 .01
☐ 115 Jose Lind .05 .02 .01
☐ 116 Roger Mason .05 .02 .01
☐ 117 Orlando Merced .08 .04 .01
☐ 118 Bob Patterson .05 .02 .01
☐ 119 Don Slaught .05 .02 .01
☐ 120 Zane Smith .05 .02 .01
☐ 121 Randy Tomlin .05 .02 .01
☐ 122 Andy Van Slyke .10 .05 .01
☐ 123 Tim Wakefield .05 .02 .01
☐ 124 Rheal Cormier .05 .02 .01
☐ 125 Bernard Gilkey .05 .02 .01
☐ 126 Felix Jose .05 .02 .01
☐ 127 Ray Lankford .10 .05 .01
☐ 128 Bob McClure .05 .02 .01
☐ 129 Donovan Osborne .05 .02 .01
☐ 130 Tom Pagnozzi .05 .02 .01
☐ 131 Geronimo Pena .05 .02 .01
☐ 132 Mike Perez .05 .02 .01
☐ 133 Lee Smith .10 .05 .01
☐ 134 Bob Tewksbury .05 .02 .01
☐ 135 Todd Worrell .05 .02 .01
☐ 136 Todd Zeile .08 .04 .01
☐ 137 Jerald Clark .05 .02 .01
☐ 138 Tony Gwynn .50 .23 .06
☐ 139 Greg W. Harris .05 .02 .01
☐ 140 Jeremy Hernandez .05 .02 .01
☐ 141 Darrin Jackson .05 .02 .01
☐ 142 Mike Maddux .05 .02 .01
☐ 143 Fred McGriff .30 .14 .04
☐ 144 Jose Melendez .05 .02 .01
☐ 145 Rich Rodriguez .05 .02 .01
☐ 146 Frank Seminara .05 .02 .01
☐ 147 Gary Sheffield .10 .05 .01
☐ 148 Kurt Stillwell .05 .02 .01
☐ 149 Dan Walters .05 .02 .01
☐ 150 Rod Beck .10 .05 .01
☐ 151 Bud Black .05 .02 .01
☐ 152 Jeff Brantley .05 .02 .01
☐ 153 John Burkett .08 .04 .01
☐ 154 Will Clark .30 .14 .04
☐ 155 Royce Clayton .08 .04 .01
☐ 156 Mike Jackson .05 .02 .01
☐ 157 Darren Lewis .05 .02 .01
☐ 158 Kirt Manwaring .05 .02 .01
☐ 159 Willie McGee .08 .04 .01
☐ 160 Cory Snyder .05 .02 .01
☐ 161 Bill Swift .08 .04 .01
☐ 162 Trevor Wilson .05 .02 .01
☐ 163 Brady Anderson .08 .04 .01
☐ 164 Glenn Davis .05 .02 .01
☐ 165 Mike Devereaux .08 .04 .01
☐ 166 Todd Frohwirth .05 .02 .01
☐ 167 Leo Gomez .05 .02 .01
☐ 168 Chris Hoiles .08 .04 .01
☐ 169 Ben McDonald .08 .04 .01
☐ 170 Randy Milligan .05 .02 .01
☐ 171 Alan Mills .05 .02 .01
☐ 172 Mike Mussina .40 .18 .05

☐ 173 Gregg Olson .05 .02 .01
☐ 174 Arthur Rhodes .05 .02 .01
☐ 175 David Segui .05 .02 .01
☐ 176 Ellis Burks .08 .04 .01
☐ 177 Roger Clemens .50 .23 .06
☐ 178 Scott Cooper .08 .04 .01
☐ 179 Danny Darwin .05 .02 .01
☐ 180 Tony Fossas .05 .02 .01
☐ 181 Paul Quantrill .05 .02 .01
☐ 182 Jody Reed .05 .02 .01
☐ 183 John Valentin .08 .04 .01
☐ 184 Mo Vaughn .10 .05 .01
☐ 185 Frank Viola .08 .04 .01
☐ 186 Bob Zupcic .05 .02 .01
☐ 187 Jim Abbott .10 .05 .01
☐ 188 Gary DiSarcina .08 .04 .01
☐ 189 Damion Easley .08 .04 .01
☐ 190 Junior Felix .05 .02 .01
☐ 191 Chuck Finley .05 .02 .01
☐ 192 Joe Grahe .05 .02 .01
☐ 193 Bryan Harvey .08 .04 .01
☐ 194 Mark Langston .10 .05 .01
☐ 195 John Orton .05 .02 .01
☐ 196 Luis Polonia .05 .02 .01
☐ 197 Tim Salmon .40 .18 .05
☐ 198 Luis Sojo .05 .02 .01
☐ 199 Wilson Alvarez .10 .05 .01
☐ 200 George Bell .08 .04 .01
☐ 201 Alex Fernandez .10 .05 .01
☐ 202 Craig Grebeck .05 .02 .01
☐ 203 Ozzie Guillen .05 .02 .01
☐ 204 Lance Johnson .05 .02 .01
☐ 205 Ron Karkovice .05 .02 .01
☐ 206 Kirk McCaskill .05 .02 .01
☐ 207 Jack McDowell .10 .05 .01
☐ 208 Scott Radinsky .05 .02 .01
☐ 209 Tim Raines .10 .05 .01
☐ 210 Frank Thomas 2.00 .90 .25
☐ 211 Robin Ventura .10 .05 .01
☐ 212 Sandy Alomar Jr. .08 .04 .01
☐ 213 Carlos Baerga .30 .14 .04
☐ 214 Dennis Cook .05 .02 .01
☐ 215 Thomas Howard .05 .02 .01
☐ 216 Mark Lewis .08 .04 .01
☐ 217 Derek Lilliquist .05 .02 .01
☐ 218 Kenny Lofton .50 .23 .06
☐ 219 Charles Nagy .05 .02 .01
☐ 220 Steve Olin .05 .02 .01
☐ 221 Paul Sorrento .05 .02 .01
☐ 222 Jim Thome .25 .11 .03
☐ 223 Mark Whiten .08 .04 .01
☐ 224 Milt Cuyler .05 .02 .01
☐ 225 Rob Deer .05 .02 .01
☐ 226 John Doherty .05 .02 .01
☐ 227 Cecil Fielder .10 .05 .01
☐ 228 Travis Fryman .15 .07 .02
☐ 229 Mike Henneman .05 .02 .01
☐ 230 John Kiely UER .05 .02 .01
(Card has batting stats of Pat Kelly)
☐ 231 Kurt Knudsen .05 .02 .01
☐ 232 Scott Livingstone .08 .04 .01
☐ 233 Tony Phillips .05 .02 .01
☐ 234 Mickey Tettleton .08 .04 .01
☐ 235 Kevin Appier .08 .04 .01
☐ 236 George Brett .75 .35 .09
☐ 237 Tom Gordon .05 .02 .01
☐ 238 Gregg Jefferies .10 .05 .01
☐ 239 Wally Joyner .08 .04 .01
☐ 240 Kevin Koslofski .05 .02 .01
☐ 241 Mike Macfarlane .05 .02 .01
☐ 242 Brian McRae .10 .05 .01
☐ 243 Rusty Meacham .05 .02 .01
☐ 244 Keith Miller .05 .02 .01
☐ 245 Jeff Montgomery .08 .04 .01
☐ 246 Hipolito Pichardo .05 .02 .01
☐ 247 Ricky Bones .05 .02 .01
☐ 248 Cal Eldred .08 .04 .01
☐ 249 Mike Fetters .05 .02 .01
☐ 250 Darryl Hamilton .05 .02 .01
☐ 251 Doug Henry .05 .02 .01
☐ 252 John Jaha .08 .04 .01
☐ 253 Pat Listach .08 .04 .01
☐ 254 Paul Molitor .30 .14 .04
☐ 255 Jaime Navarro .05 .02 .01
☐ 256 Kevin Seitzer .05 .02 .01
☐ 257 B.J. Surhoff .05 .02 .01
☐ 258 Greg Vaughn .08 .04 .01
☐ 259 Bill Wegman .05 .02 .01
☐ 260 Robin Yount .30 .14 .04
☐ 261 Rick Aguilera .08 .04 .01
☐ 262 Chili Davis .08 .04 .01
☐ 263 Scott Erickson .05 .02 .01
☐ 264 Greg Gagne .05 .02 .01
☐ 265 Mark Guthrie .05 .02 .01
☐ 266 Brian Harper .05 .02 .01
☐ 267 Kent Hrbek .08 .04 .01
☐ 268 Terry Jorgensen .05 .02 .01
☐ 269 Gene Larkin .05 .02 .01
☐ 270 Scott Leius .05 .02 .01
☐ 271 Pat Mahomes .05 .02 .01
☐ 272 Pedro Munoz .05 .02 .01
☐ 273 Kirby Puckett .75 .35 .09
☐ 274 Kevin Tapani .05 .02 .01
☐ 275 Carl Willis .05 .02 .01
☐ 276 Steve Farr .05 .02 .01
☐ 277 John Habyan .05 .02 .01
☐ 278 Mel Hall .05 .02 .01
☐ 279 Charlie Hayes .08 .04 .01
☐ 280 Pat Kelly .05 .02 .01
☐ 281 Don Mattingly .75 .35 .09
☐ 282 Sam Militello .05 .02 .01
☐ 283 Matt Nokes .05 .02 .01
☐ 284 Melido Perez .05 .02 .01
☐ 285 Andy Stankiewicz .05 .02 .01
☐ 286 Danny Tartabull .08 .04 .01
☐ 287 Randy Velarde .05 .02 .01
☐ 288 Bob Wickman .05 .02 .01
☐ 289 Bernie Williams .08 .04 .01
☐ 290 Lance Blankenship .05 .02 .01
☐ 291 Mike Bordick .08 .04 .01
☐ 292 Jerry Browne .05 .02 .01
☐ 293 Dennis Eckersley .10 .05 .01
☐ 294 Rickey Henderson .10 .05 .01
☐ 295 Vince Horsman .05 .02 .01
☐ 296 Mark McGwire .10 .05 .01
☐ 297 Jeff Parrett .05 .02 .01
☐ 298 Ruben Sierra .10 .05 .01
☐ 299 Terry Steinbach .08 .04 .01
☐ 300 Walt Weiss .05 .02 .01
☐ 301 Bob Welch .05 .02 .01
☐ 302 Willie Wilson .05 .02 .01
☐ 303 Bobby Witt .05 .02 .01
☐ 304 Bret Boone .10 .05 .01
☐ 305 Jay Buhner .08 .04 .01
☐ 306 Dave Fleming .08 .04 .01
☐ 307 Ken Griffey Jr. 2.00 .90 .25
☐ 308 Erik Hanson .05 .02 .01
☐ 309 Edgar Martinez .05 .02 .01
☐ 310 Tino Martinez .08 .04 .01
☐ 311 Jeff Nelson .05 .02 .01
☐ 312 Dennis Powell .05 .02 .01
☐ 313 Mike Schooler .05 .02 .01
☐ 314 Russ Swan .05 .02 .01
☐ 315 Dave Valle .05 .02 .01
☐ 316 Omar Vizquel .05 .02 .01

☐ 317 Kevin Brown .05 .02 .01
☐ 318 Todd Burns .05 .02 .01
☐ 319 Jose Canseco .30 .14 .04
☐ 320 Julio Franco .08 .04 .01
☐ 321 Jeff Frye .05 .02 .01
☐ 322 Juan Gonzalez .60 .25 .08
☐ 323 Jose Guzman .05 .02 .01
☐ 324 Jeff Huson .05 .02 .01
☐ 325 Dean Palmer .08 .04 .01
☐ 326 Kevin Reimer .05 .02 .01
☐ 327 Ivan Rodriguez .10 .05 .01
☐ 328 Kenny Rogers .05 .02 .01
☐ 329 Dan Smith .05 .02 .01
☐ 330 Roberto Alomar .40 .18 .05
☐ 331 Derek Bell .08 .04 .01
☐ 332 Pat Borders .05 .02 .01
☐ 333 Joe Carter .30 .14 .04
☐ 334 Kelly Gruber .05 .02 .01
☐ 335 Tom Henke .08 .04 .01
☐ 336 Jimmy Key .08 .04 .01
☐ 337 Manny Lee .05 .02 .01
☐ 338 Candy Maldonado .05 .02 .01
☐ 339 John Olerud .10 .05 .01
☐ 340 Todd Stottlemyre .05 .02 .01
☐ 341 Duane Ward .08 .04 .01
☐ 342 Devon White .08 .04 .01
☐ 343 Dave Winfield .10 .05 .01
☐ 344 Edgar Martinez LL .05 .02 .01
☐ 345 Cecil Fielder LL .08 .04 .01
☐ 346 Kenny Lofton LL .25 .11 .03
☐ 347 Jack Morris LL .08 .04 .01
☐ 348 Roger Clemens LL .25 .11 .03
☐ 349 Fred McGriff RT .15 .07 .02
☐ 350 Barry Bonds RT .40 .18 .05
☐ 351 Gary Sheffield RT .08 .04 .01
☐ 352 Darren Daulton RT .08 .04 .01
☐ 353 Dave Hollins RT .08 .04 .01
☐ 354 Brothers in Blue .05 .02 .01
Pedro Martinez
Ramon Martinez
☐ 355 Power Packs .15 .07 .02
Ivan Rodriguez
Kirby Puckett
☐ 356 Triple Threats .15 .07 .02
Ryne Sandberg
Gary Sheffield
☐ 357 Infield Trifecta .15 .07 .02
Roberto Alomar
Chuck Knoblauch
Carlos Baerga
☐ 358 Checklist 1-120 .05 .02 .01
☐ 359 Checklist 121-240 .05 .02 .01
☐ 360 Checklist 241-360 .05 .02 .01
☐ 361 Rafael Belliard .05 .02 .01
☐ 362 Damon Berryhill .05 .02 .01
☐ 363 Mike Bielecki .05 .02 .01
☐ 364 Jeff Blauser .08 .04 .01
☐ 365 Francisco Cabrera .05 .02 .01
☐ 366 Marvin Freeman .05 .02 .01
☐ 367 David Justice .30 .14 .04
☐ 368 Mark Lemke .05 .02 .01
☐ 369 Alejandro Pena .05 .02 .01
☐ 370 Jeff Reardon .08 .04 .01
☐ 371 Lonnie Smith .05 .02 .01
☐ 372 Pete Smith .05 .02 .01
☐ 373 Shawn Boskie .05 .02 .01
☐ 374 Jim Bullinger .05 .02 .01
☐ 375 Frank Castillo .05 .02 .01
☐ 376 Doug Dascenzo .05 .02 .01
☐ 377 Andre Dawson .10 .05 .01
☐ 378 Mike Harkey .05 .02 .01
☐ 379 Greg Hibbard .05 .02 .01
☐ 380 Greg Maddux .40 .18 .05
☐ 381 Ken Patterson .05 .02 .01
☐ 382 Jeff D. Robinson .05 .02 .01
☐ 383 Luis Salazar .05 .02 .01
☐ 384 Dwight Smith .05 .02 .01
☐ 385 Jose Vizcaino .05 .02 .01
☐ 386 Scott Bankhead .05 .02 .01
☐ 387 Tom Browning .05 .02 .01
☐ 388 Darnell Coles .05 .02 .01
☐ 389 Rob Dibble .05 .02 .01
☐ 390 Bill Doran .05 .02 .01
☐ 391 Dwayne Henry .05 .02 .01
☐ 392 Cesar Hernandez .05 .02 .01
☐ 393 Roberto Kelly .08 .04 .01
☐ 394 Barry Larkin .10 .05 .01
☐ 395 Dave Martinez .05 .02 .01
☐ 396 Kevin Mitchell .08 .04 .01
☐ 397 Jeff Reed .05 .02 .01
☐ 398 Scott Ruskin .05 .02 .01
☐ 399 Greg Swindell .05 .02 .01
☐ 400 Dan Wilson .05 .02 .01
☐ 401 Andy Ashby .05 .02 .01
☐ 402 Freddie Benavides .05 .02 .01
☐ 403 Dante Bichette .10 .05 .01
☐ 404 Willie Blair .05 .02 .01
☐ 405 Denis Boucher .05 .02 .01
☐ 406 Vinny Castilla .05 .02 .01
☐ 407 Braulio Castillo .05 .02 .01
☐ 408 Alex Cole .05 .02 .01
☐ 409 Andres Galarraga .10 .05 .01
☐ 410 Joe Girardi .05 .02 .01
☐ 411 Butch Henry .05 .02 .01
☐ 412 Darren Holmes .05 .02 .01
☐ 413 Calvin Jones .05 .02 .01
☐ 414 Steve Reed .08 .04 .01
☐ 415 Kevin Ritz .05 .02 .01
☐ 416 Jim Tatum .05 .02 .01
☐ 417 Jack Armstrong .05 .02 .01
☐ 418 Bret Barberie .05 .02 .01
☐ 419 Ryan Bowen .05 .02 .01
☐ 420 Cris Carpenter .05 .02 .01
☐ 421 Chuck Carr .05 .02 .01
☐ 422 Scott Chiamparino .05 .02 .01
☐ 423 Jeff Conine .10 .05 .01
☐ 424 Jim Corsi .05 .02 .01
☐ 425 Steve Decker .05 .02 .01
☐ 426 Chris Donnels .05 .02 .01
☐ 427 Monty Fariss .05 .02 .01
☐ 428 Bob Natal .05 .02 .01
☐ 429 Pat Rapp .08 .04 .01
☐ 430 Dave Weathers .08 .04 .01
☐ 431 Nigel Wilson .10 .05 .01
☐ 432 Ken Caminiti .08 .04 .01
☐ 433 Andujar Cedeno .08 .04 .01
☐ 434 Tom Edens .05 .02 .01
☐ 435 Juan Guerrero .05 .02 .01
☐ 436 Pete Incaviglia .05 .02 .01
☐ 437 Jimmy Jones .05 .02 .01
☐ 438 Darryl Kile .08 .04 .01
☐ 439 Rob Murphy .05 .02 .01
☐ 440 Al Osuna .05 .02 .01
☐ 441 Mark Portugal .05 .02 .01
☐ 442 Scott Servais .05 .02 .01
☐ 443 John Candelaria .05 .02 .01
☐ 444 Tim Crews .05 .02 .01
☐ 445 Eric Davis .05 .02 .01
☐ 446 Tom Goodwin .05 .02 .01
☐ 447 Jim Gott .05 .02 .01
☐ 448 Kevin Gross .05 .02 .01
☐ 449 Dave Hansen .05 .02 .01
☐ 450 Jay Howell .05 .02 .01
☐ 451 Roger McDowell .05 .02 .01
☐ 452 Bob Ojeda .05 .02 .01
☐ 453 Henry Rodriguez .05 .02 .01

	No.	Player			
☐	454	Darryl Strawberry	.08	.04	.01
☐	455	Mitch Webster	.05	.02	.01
☐	456	Steve Wilson	.05	.02	.01
☐	457	Brian Barnes	.05	.02	.01
☐	458	Sean Berry	.05	.02	.01
☐	459	Jeff Fassero	.05	.02	.01
☐	460	Darrin Fletcher	.05	.02	.01
☐	461	Marquis Grissom	.10	.05	.01
☐	462	Dennis Martinez	.08	.04	.01
☐	463	Spike Owen	.05	.02	.01
☐	464	Matt Stairs	.05	.02	.01
☐	465	Sergio Valdez	.05	.02	.01
☐	466	Kevin Bass	.05	.02	.01
☐	467	Vince Coleman	.05	.02	.01
☐	468	Mark Dewey	.05	.02	.01
☐	469	Kevin Elster	.05	.02	.01
☐	470	Tony Fernandez	.05	.02	.01
☐	471	John Franco	.05	.02	.01
☐	472	Dave Gallagher	.05	.02	.01
☐	473	Paul Gibson	.05	.02	.01
☐	474	Dwight Gooden	.05	.02	.01
☐	475	Lee Guetterman	.05	.02	.01
☐	476	Jeff Innis	.05	.02	.01
☐	477	Dave Magadan	.05	.02	.01
☐	478	Charlie O'Brien	.05	.02	.01
☐	479	Willie Randolph	.08	.04	.01
☐	480	Mackey Sasser	.05	.02	.01
☐	481	Ryan Thompson	.10	.05	.01
☐	482	Chico Walker	.05	.02	.01
☐	483	Kyle Abbott	.05	.02	.01
☐	484	Bob Ayrault	.05	.02	.01
☐	485	Kim Batiste	.05	.02	.01
☐	486	Cliff Brantley	.05	.02	.01
☐	487	Jose DeLeon	.05	.02	.01
☐	488	Len Dykstra	.10	.05	.01
☐	489	Tommy Greene	.08	.04	.01
☐	490	Jeff Grotewold	.05	.02	.01
☐	491	Dave Hollins	.10	.05	.01
☐	492	Danny Jackson	.05	.02	.01
☐	493	Stan Javier	.05	.02	.01
☐	494	Tom Marsh	.05	.02	.01
☐	495	Greg Mathews	.05	.02	.01
☐	496	Dale Murphy	.10	.05	.01
☐	497	Todd Pratt	.05	.02	.01
☐	498	Mitch Williams	.08	.04	.01
☐	499	Danny Cox	.05	.02	.01
☐	500	Doug Drabek	.10	.05	.01
☐	501	Carlos Garcia	.08	.04	.01
☐	502	Lloyd McClendon	.05	.02	.01
☐	503	Denny Neagle	.05	.02	.01
☐	504	Gary Redus	.05	.02	.01
☐	505	Bob Walk	.05	.02	.01
☐	506	John Wehner	.05	.02	.01
☐	507	Luis Alicea	.05	.02	.01
☐	508	Mark Clark	.08	.04	.01
☐	509	Pedro Guerrero	.05	.02	.01
☐	510	Rex Hudler	.05	.02	.01
☐	511	Brian Jordan	.08	.04	.01
☐	512	Omar Olivares	.05	.02	.01
☐	513	Jose Oquendo	.05	.02	.01
☐	514	Gerald Perry	.05	.02	.01
☐	515	Bryn Smith	.05	.02	.01
☐	516	Craig Wilson	.05	.02	.01
☐	517	Tracy Woodson	.05	.02	.01
☐	518	Larry Andersen	.05	.02	.01
☐	519	Andy Benes	.08	.04	.01
☐	520	Jim Deshaies	.05	.02	.01
☐	521	Bruce Hurst	.05	.02	.01
☐	522	Randy Myers	.08	.04	.01
☐	523	Benito Santiago	.05	.02	.01
☐	524	Tim Scott	.05	.02	.01
☐	525	Tim Teufel	.05	.02	.01
☐	526	Mike Benjamin	.05	.02	.01
☐	527	Dave Burba	.05	.02	.01
☐	528	Craig Colbert	.05	.02	.01
☐	529	Mike Felder	.05	.02	.01
☐	530	Bryan Hickerson	.05	.02	.01
☐	531	Chris James	.05	.02	.01
☐	532	Mark Leonard	.05	.02	.01
☐	533	Greg Litton	.05	.02	.01
☐	534	Francisco Oliveras	.05	.02	.01
☐	535	John Patterson	.05	.02	.01
☐	536	Jim Pena	.05	.02	.01
☐	537	Dave Righetti	.05	.02	.01
☐	538	Robby Thompson	.05	.02	.01
☐	539	Jose Uribe	.05	.02	.01
☐	540	Matt Williams	.40	.18	.05
☐	541	Storm Davis	.05	.02	.01
☐	542	Sam Horn	.05	.02	.01
☐	543	Tim Hulett	.05	.02	.01
☐	544	Craig Lefferts	.05	.02	.01
☐	545	Chito Martinez	.05	.02	.01
☐	546	Mark McLemore	.05	.02	.01
☐	547	Luis Mercedes	.05	.02	.01
☐	548	Bob Milacki	.05	.02	.01
☐	549	Joe Orsulak	.05	.02	.01
☐	550	Billy Ripken	.05	.02	.01
☐	551	Cal Ripken	1.25	.55	.16
☐	552	Rick Sutcliffe	.08	.04	.01
☐	553	Jeff Tackett	.05	.02	.01
☐	554	Wade Boggs	.10	.05	.01
☐	555	Tom Brunansky	.05	.02	.01
☐	556	Jack Clark	.05	.02	.01
☐	557	John Dopson	.05	.02	.01
☐	558	Mike Gardiner	.05	.02	.01
☐	559	Mike Greenwell	.08	.04	.01
☐	560	Greg A. Harris	.05	.02	.01
☐	561	Billy Hatcher	.05	.02	.01
☐	562	Joe Hesketh	.05	.02	.01
☐	563	Tony Pena	.05	.02	.01
☐	564	Phil Plantier	.10	.05	.01
☐	565	Luis Rivera	.05	.02	.01
☐	566	Herm Winningham	.05	.02	.01
☐	567	Matt Young	.05	.02	.01
☐	568	Bert Blyleven	.10	.05	.01
☐	569	Mike Butcher	.05	.02	.01
☐	570	Chuck Crim	.05	.02	.01
☐	571	Chad Curtis	.08	.04	.01
☐	572	Tim Fortugno	.05	.02	.01
☐	573	Steve Frey	.05	.02	.01
☐	574	Gary Gaetti	.05	.02	.01
☐	575	Scott Lewis	.05	.02	.01
☐	576	Lee Stevens	.05	.02	.01
☐	577	Ron Tingley	.05	.02	.01
☐	578	Julio Valera	.05	.02	.01
☐	579	Shawn Abner	.05	.02	.01
☐	580	Joey Cora	.05	.02	.01
☐	581	Chris Cron	.05	.02	.01
☐	582	Carlton Fisk	.10	.05	.01
☐	583	Roberto Hernandez	.05	.02	.01
☐	584	Charlie Hough	.08	.04	.01
☐	585	Terry Leach	.05	.02	.01
☐	586	Donn Pall	.05	.02	.01
☐	587	Dan Pasqua	.05	.02	.01
☐	588	Steve Sax	.05	.02	.01
☐	589	Bobby Thigpen	.05	.02	.01
☐	590	Albert Belle	.60	.25	.08
☐	591	Felix Fermin	.05	.02	.01
☐	592	Glenallen Hill	.05	.02	.01
☐	593	Brook Jacoby	.05	.02	.01
☐	594	Reggie Jefferson	.05	.02	.01
☐	595	Carlos Martinez	.05	.02	.01
☐	596	Jose Mesa	.05	.02	.01
☐	597	Rod Nichols	.05	.02	.01
☐	598	Junior Ortiz	.05	.02	.01
☐	599	Eric Plunk	.05	.02	.01

☐ 600 Ted Power .05 .02 .01
☐ 601 Scott Scudder .05 .02 .01
☐ 602 Kevin Wickander .05 .02 .01
☐ 603 Skeeter Barnes .05 .02 .01
☐ 604 Mark Carreon .05 .02 .01
☐ 605 Dan Gladden .05 .02 .01
☐ 606 Bill Gullickson .05 .02 .01
☐ 607 Chad Kreuter .05 .02 .01
☐ 608 Mark Leiter .05 .02 .01
☐ 609 Mike Munoz .05 .02 .01
☐ 610 Rich Rowland .05 .02 .01
☐ 611 Frank Tanana .05 .02 .01
☐ 612 Walt Terrell .05 .02 .01
☐ 613 Alan Trammell .10 .05 .01
☐ 614 Lou Whitaker .10 .05 .01
☐ 615 Luis Aquino .05 .02 .01
☐ 616 Mike Boddicker .05 .02 .01
☐ 617 Jim Eisenreich .05 .02 .01
☐ 618 Mark Gubicza .05 .02 .01
☐ 619 David Howard .05 .02 .01
☐ 620 Mike Magnante .05 .02 .01
☐ 621 Brent Mayne .05 .02 .01
☐ 622 Kevin McReynolds .05 .02 .01
☐ 623 Ed Pierce .05 .02 .01
☐ 624 Bill Sampen .05 .02 .01
☐ 625 Steve Shifflett .05 .02 .01
☐ 626 Gary Thurman .05 .02 .01
☐ 627 Curtis Wilkerson .05 .02 .01
☐ 628 Chris Bosio .05 .02 .01
☐ 629 Scott Fletcher .05 .02 .01
☐ 630 Jim Gantner .05 .02 .01
☐ 631 Dave Nilsson .08 .04 .01
☐ 632 Jesse Orosco .05 .02 .01
☐ 633 Dan Plesac .05 .02 .01
☐ 634 Ron Robinson .05 .02 .01
☐ 635 Bill Spiers .05 .02 .01
☐ 636 Franklin Stubbs .05 .02 .01
☐ 637 Willie Banks .05 .02 .01
☐ 638 Randy Bush .05 .02 .01
☐ 639 Chuck Knoblauch .10 .05 .01
☐ 640 Shane Mack .08 .04 .01
☐ 641 Mike Pagliarulo .05 .02 .01
☐ 642 Jeff Reboulet .05 .02 .01
☐ 643 John Smiley .05 .02 .01
☐ 644 Mike Trombley .05 .02 .01
☐ 645 Gary Wayne .05 .02 .01
☐ 646 Lenny Webster .05 .02 .01
☐ 647 Tim Burke .05 .02 .01
☐ 648 Mike Gallego .05 .02 .01
☐ 649 Dion James .05 .02 .01
☐ 650 Jeff Johnson .05 .02 .01
☐ 651 Scott Kamieniecki .05 .02 .01
☐ 652 Kevin Maas .05 .02 .01
☐ 653 Rich Monteleone .05 .02 .01
☐ 654 Jerry Nielsen .05 .02 .01
☐ 655 Scott Sanderson .05 .02 .01
☐ 656 Mike Stanley .05 .02 .01
☐ 657 Gerald Williams .05 .02 .01
☐ 658 Curt Young .05 .02 .01
☐ 659 Harold Baines .08 .04 .01
☐ 660 Kevin Campbell .05 .02 .01
☐ 661 Ron Darling .05 .02 .01
☐ 662 Kelly Downs .05 .02 .01
☐ 663 Eric Fox .05 .02 .01
☐ 664 Dave Henderson .05 .02 .01
☐ 665 Rick Honeycutt .05 .02 .01
☐ 666 Mike Moore .05 .02 .01
☐ 667 Jamie Quirk .05 .02 .01
☐ 668 Jeff Russell .05 .02 .01
☐ 669 Dave Stewart .08 .04 .01
☐ 670 Greg Briley .05 .02 .01
☐ 671 Dave Cochrane .05 .02 .01
☐ 672 Henry Cotto .05 .02 .01
☐ 673 Rich DeLucia .05 .02 .01
☐ 674 Brian Fisher .05 .02 .01
☐ 675 Mark Grant .05 .02 .01
☐ 676 Randy Johnson .10 .05 .01
☐ 677 Tim Leary .05 .02 .01
☐ 678 Pete O'Brien .05 .02 .01
☐ 679 Lance Parrish .08 .04 .01
☐ 680 Harold Reynolds .05 .02 .01
☐ 681 Shane Turner .05 .02 .01
☐ 682 Jack Daugherty .05 .02 .01
☐ 683 David Hulse .05 .02 .01
☐ 684 Terry Mathews .05 .02 .01
☐ 685 Al Newman .05 .02 .01
☐ 686 Edwin Nunez .05 .02 .01
☐ 687 Rafael Palmeiro .10 .05 .01
☐ 688 Roger Pavlik .08 .04 .01
☐ 689 Geno Petralli .05 .02 .01
☐ 690 Nolan Ryan 2.00 .90 .25
☐ 691 David Cone .10 .05 .01
☐ 692 Alfredo Griffin .05 .02 .01
☐ 693 Juan Guzman .08 .04 .01
☐ 694 Pat Hentgen .08 .04 .01
☐ 695 Randy Knorr .05 .02 .01
☐ 696 Bob MacDonald .05 .02 .01
☐ 697 Jack Morris .10 .05 .01
☐ 698 Ed Sprague .05 .02 .01
☐ 699 Dave Stieb .05 .02 .01
☐ 700 Pat Tabler .05 .02 .01
☐ 701 Mike Timlin .05 .02 .01
☐ 702 David Wells .05 .02 .01
☐ 703 Eddie Zosky .05 .02 .01
☐ 704 Gary Sheffield LL .08 .04 .01
☐ 705 Darren Daulton LL .08 .04 .01
☐ 706 Marquis Grissom LL .08 .04 .01
☐ 707 Greg Maddux LL .20 .09 .03
☐ 708 Bill Swift LL .05 .02 .01
☐ 709 Juan Gonzalez RT .35 .16 .04
☐ 710 Mark McGwire RT .08 .04 .01
☐ 711 Cecil Fielder RT .08 .04 .01
☐ 712 Albert Belle RT .30 .14 .04
☐ 713 Joe Carter RT .15 .07 .02
☐ 714 Cecil Fielder SS .50 .23 .06
Frank Thomas
Power Brokers
☐ 715 Larry Walker SS .08 .04 .01
Darren Daulton
Unsung Heroes
☐ 716 Edgar Martinez SS .05 .02 .01
Robin Ventura
Hot Corner Hammers
☐ 717 Roger Clemens SS .15 .07 .02
Dennis Eckersley
Start to Finish
☐ 718 Checklist 361-480 .05 .02 .01
☐ 719 Checklist 481-600 .05 .02 .01
☐ 720 Checklist 601-720 .05 .02 .01

1993 Fleer All-Stars AL

This 12-card standard-size (2 1/2" by 3 1/2") set was randomly inserted in series II wax packs. The horizontal fronts feature a color close-up photo cut out and superposed upon a black-and-white action scene framed by white borders. The player's name and the word "All-Stars" are printed in gold foil lettering across the bottom of the pic-

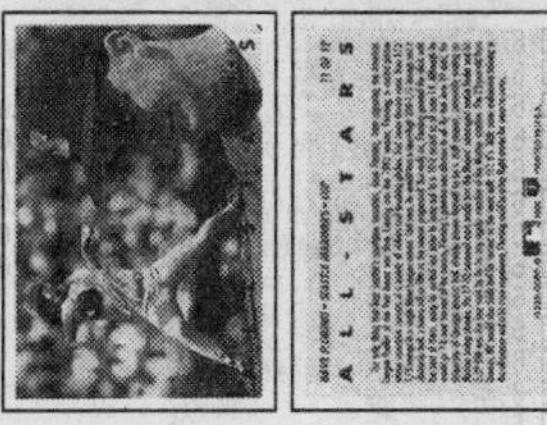

ture. On a pastel yellow panel, each horizontal back carries a career summary. The cards are numbered on the back "No. X of 12."

	MINT	EXC	G-VG
COMPLETE SET (12)	35.00	16.00	4.40
COMMON CARD (1-12)	.60	.25	.08
☐ 1 Frank Thomas	12.00	5.50	1.50
☐ 2 Roberto Alomar	3.00	1.35	.40
☐ 3 Edgar Martinez	.60	.25	.08
☐ 4 Pat Listach	.60	.25	.08
☐ 5 Cecil Fielder	.60	.25	.08
☐ 6 Juan Gonzalez	4.00	1.80	.50
☐ 7 Ken Griffey Jr.	12.00	5.50	1.50
☐ 8 Joe Carter	1.75	.80	.22
☐ 9 Kirby Puckett	5.00	2.30	.60
☐ 10 Brian Harper	.60	.25	.08
☐ 11 Dave Fleming	.60	.25	.08
☐ 12 Jack McDowell	.85	.40	.11

1993 Fleer All-Stars NL

This 12-card standard-size (2 1/2" by 3 1/2") set was randomly inserted in 1993 Fleer series I wax packs. Cards 1-12 feature National League All-Stars. The horizontal fronts feature a color close-up photo cut out and superimposed on a black-and-white action scene framed by white borders. The player's name and the word "All-Stars" are printed in gold foil lettering across the bottom of the picture. On a pastel yellow panel, the horizontal backs carry career summary. The cards are numbered on the back "No. X of 12."

	MINT	EXC	G-VG
COMPLETE SET (12)	12.00	5.50	1.50
COMMON CARD (1-12)	.60	.25	.08
☐ 1 Fred McGriff	1.75	.80	.22
☐ 2 Delino DeShields	.60	.25	.08
☐ 3 Gary Sheffield	.85	.40	.11
☐ 4 Barry Larkin	.85	.40	.11
☐ 5 Felix Jose	.60	.25	.08
☐ 6 Larry Walker	.85	.40	.11
☐ 7 Barry Bonds	5.00	2.30	.60
☐ 8 Andy Van Slyke	.60	.25	.08
☐ 9 Darren Daulton	.60	.25	.08
☐ 10 Greg Maddux	3.00	1.35	.40
☐ 11 Tom Glavine	.60	.25	.08
☐ 12 Lee Smith	.60	.25	.08

1993 Fleer Tom Glavine

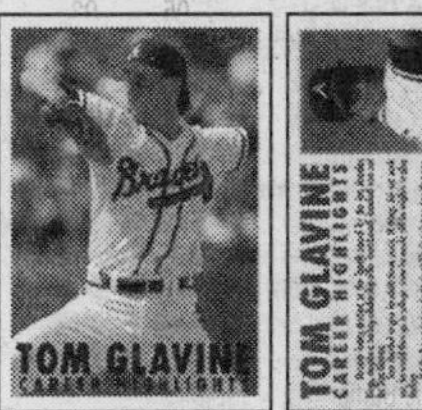

As part of the Signature Series, this 12-card set spotlights Tom Glavine. An additional three cards (13-15) were available via a mail-in offer and are generally considered to be a sepearate set. The cards measure the standard size (2 1/2" by 3 1/2"). The fronts feature glossy color action photos with white borders. The player's name and the words "Career Highlights" appear in gold foil block lettering across the bottom of the picture. The horizontal backs carry a small close-up color photo and summarize chapters of Glavine's career. The cards are numbered on the back at the lower left corner. Reportedly, a filmmaking problem during production resulted in eight variations in this 12-card insert set. Different backs appear on eight of the 12 cards. Cards 1-4 and 7-10 in wax packs feature card-back text variations from those included in the rack and jumbo magazine packs. The text differences occur in the first few words of text on the card back. No corrections were made in Series I. The correct Glavine cards appeared in Series II wax, rack, and jumbo magazine packs.

	MINT	EXC	G-VG
COMPLETE SET (12)	4.00	1.80	.50
COMMON GLAVINE (1-12)	.50	.23	.06
COMMON SEND-OFF (13-15)	2.00	.90	.25

☐ 1A Tom Glavine .... .50 .23 .06
The Glavine family ...
(Throwing to first)
☐ 1B Tom Glavine .... .50 .23 .06
Tom Glavine's dream ...
(Throwing to first)
☐ 2A Tom Glavine .... .50 .23 .06
High School baseball ...
(Pitching, with arm behind head, shot from left side)
☐ 2B Tom Glavine .... .50 .23 .06
After Winning ...
(Pitching, with arm behind head, shot from left side)
☐ 3A Tom Glavine .... .50 .23 .06
Despite being drafted ...
(Pitching, close-up shot from left side)
☐ 3B Tom Glavine .... .50 .23 .06
Little Leaguers ...
(Pitching, close-up shot from left side)
☐ 4A Tom Glavine .... .50 .23 .06
Unflappable is ...
(Pitching, shot from almost directly in front)
☐ 4B Tom Glavine .... .50 .23 .06
Will success spoil ...
(Pitching, shot from almost directly in front)
☐ 5 Tom Glavine .... .50 .23 .06
In 1989 Tom ...
(Pitching, shot from right angle)
☐ 6 Tom Glavine .... .50 .23 .06
Tom Glavine had ...
(Pitching, with ball below waist)
☐ 7A Tom Glavine .... .50 .23 .06
Tom Glavine's dream ...
(Pitching, close-up shot with ball behind head)
☐ 7B Tom Glavine .... .50 .23 .06
The Glavine family ...
(Pitching, close-up shot with ball behind head)
☐ 8A Tom Glavine .... .50 .23 .06
After Winning ...
(Pitching, shot from directly in front)
☐ 8B Tom Glavine .... .50 .23 .06
High School baseball ...
(Pitching, shot from directly in front)
☐ 9A Tom Glavine .... .50 .23 .06
Little Leaguers ...
(Pitching, just after release with left leg in air)
☐ 9B Tom Glavine .... .50 .23 .06
Despite being drafted ...
(Pitching, just after release with left leg in air)
☐ 10A Tom Glavine .... .50 .23 .06
Will success spoil ...
(Pitching, ball below waist and right leg slightly raised)
☐ 10B Tom Glavine .... .50 .23 .06
Unflappable is ...
(Pitching, ball below waist and right leg slightly raised)
☐ 11 Tom Glavine .... .50 .23 .06
What makes Tom ...
(Batting)
☐ 12 Tom Glavine .... .50 .23 .06
It was a day ...
(Pitching, close-up shot wearing dark blue top)
☐ 13 Tom Glavine .... 2.00 .90 .25
(Pitching; follow through)
☐ 14 Tom Glavine .... 2.00 .90 .25
(Pitching; first base dugout view)
☐ 15 Tom Glavine .... 2.00 .90 .25
(Pitching; batter's point of view)
☐ AU Tom Glavine AU 75.00 34.00 9.50
(Certified signature)

1993 Fleer Golden Moments I

This three-card standard-size (2 1/2" by 3 1/2") set was randomly inserted in 1993 Fleer series I wax packs. The fronts feature glossy color action photos framed by thin aqua and white lines and a black outer border. A gold foil baseball icon appears at each corner of the picture, and the player's name and the set title "Golden Moments" appears in a gold foil bar toward the bottom of the picture. The black-bordered backs have a similar design to that on the fronts, only with a small color head shot and a summary of the player's outstanding achievement on a white panel. The cards are unnumbered and checklisted below in alphabetical order.

	MINT	EXC	G-VG
COMPLETE SET (3)	6.00	2.70	.75
COMMON CARD (1-3)	.50	.23	.06

☐ 1 George Brett .... 5.00 2.30 .60
3,000 Hits
☐ 2 Mickey Morandini .... .50 .23 .06
Unassisted Triple Play
☐ 3 Dave Winfield.................. 1.00 .45 .13
Oldest Player with 100 RBI Season

1993 Fleer Golden Moments II

Randomly inserted in series II wax packs, these three standard-size (2 1/2" by 3 1/2")

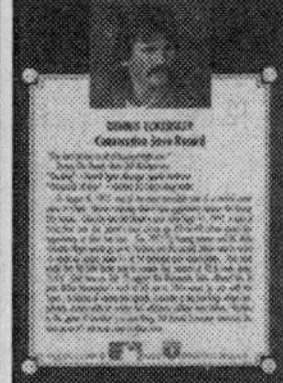

cards feature on their fronts black-bordered color player action shots trimmed with white and blue lines. The player's name and the set's title appear at the bottom within a gold-foil banner, and gold-foil baseball icons appear in each corner. The black-bordered backs display a color player head shot at their tops. A description of the Golden Moment feat performed by the player follows below within a white panel trimmed with white and blue lines and set off by white baseball icons in each corner. The cards are unnumbered and checklisted below in alphabetical order.

	MINT	EXC	G-VG
COMPLETE SET (3)	12.00	5.50	1.50
COMMON CARD (1-3)	1.00	.45	.13
☐ 1 Dennis Eckersley Consecutive Saves Record	1.50	.65	.19
☐ 2 Bip Roberts Ties NL Consecutive Hits Record	1.00	.45	.13
☐ 3 Frank Thomas and Juan Gonzalez 100 Plus RBI Seasons, First Two Years	10.00	4.50	1.25

1993 Fleer Major League Prospects I

Randomly inserted in series I wax packs, these 18 standard-size (2 1/2" by 3 1/2") cards feature black-bordered color player action photos on their fronts. The player's name appears in gold foil at the top, and the set's name and logo appear in gold foil and black at the bottom. The black-bordered horizontal back carries a color player head shot in the upper left. The player's name, biography, and career highlights are displayed on a white background alongside and below. The cards are numbered on the back. The key card in this set is Mike Piazza.

	MINT	EXC	G-VG
COMPLETE SET (18)	30.00	13.50	3.80
COMMON CARD (1-18)	.60	.25	.08
☐ 1 Melvin Nieves	1.50	.65	.19
☐ 2 Sterling Hitchcock	.85	.40	.11
☐ 3 Tim Costo	.60	.25	.08
☐ 4 Manny Alexander	.85	.40	.11
☐ 5 Alan Embree	.85	.40	.11
☐ 6 Kevin Young	.85	.40	.11
☐ 7 J.T. Snow	.85	.40	.11
☐ 8 Russ Springer	.60	.25	.08
☐ 9 Billy Ashley	4.00	1.80	.50
☐ 10 Kevin Rogers	.60	.25	.08
☐ 11 Steve Hosey	.60	.25	.08
☐ 12 Eric Wedge	.60	.25	.08
☐ 13 Mike Piazza	20.00	9.00	2.50
☐ 14 Jesse Levis	.60	.25	.08
☐ 15 Rico Brogna	.85	.40	.11
☐ 16 Alex Arias	.60	.25	.08
☐ 17 Rod Brewer	.60	.25	.08
☐ 18 Troy Neel	.85	.40	.11

1993 Fleer Major League Prospects II

Randomly inserted in series II wax packs, these 18 standard-size (2 1/2" by 3 1/2") cards feature black-bordered color player action photos on their fronts. The player's name appears in gold foil at the top, and the set's name and logo appear in gold foil and black at the bottom. The black-bordered horizontal back carries a color player head shot in the upper left. The player's name, biography, and career highlights are displayed on the white background alongside and below. The cards are numbered on the back.

	MINT	EXC	G-VG
COMPLETE SET (18)	15.00	6.75	1.90
COMMON CARD (1-18)	.60	.25	.08

☐ 1 Scooter Tucker	.60	.25	.08
☐ 2 Kerry Woodson	.60	.25	.08
☐ 3 Greg Colbrunn	.85	.40	.11
☐ 4 Pedro Martinez	1.50	.65	.19
☐ 5 Dave Silvestri	.60	.25	.08
☐ 6 Kent Bottenfield	.60	.25	.08
☐ 7 Rafael Bournigal	.60	.25	.08
☐ 8 J.T. Bruett	.60	.25	.08
☐ 9 Dave Mlicki	.85	.40	.11
☐ 10 Paul Wagner	.60	.25	.08
☐ 11 Mike Williams	.60	.25	.08
☐ 12 Henry Mercedes	.60	.25	.08
☐ 13 Scott Taylor	.60	.25	.08
☐ 14 Dennis Moeller	.60	.25	.08
☐ 15 Javy Lopez	4.00	1.80	.50
☐ 16 Steve Cooke	.85	.40	.11
☐ 17 Pete Young	.60	.25	.08
☐ 18 Ken Ryan	.85	.40	.11

1993 Fleer Pro-Visions I

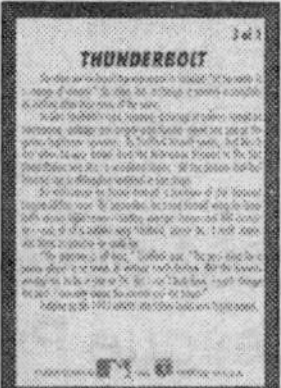

Randomly inserted in series I wax packs, these three standard-size (2 1/2" by 3 1/2") cards feature black-bordered fanciful color artwork of the players in action. The player's name appears in gold foil within the bottom black margin of each. The back carries player career highlights within a black-bordered white panel. The cards are numbered on the back.

	MINT	EXC	G-VG
COMPLETE SET (3)	4.00	1.80	.50
COMMON CARD (1-3)	1.00	.45	.13
☐ 1 Roberto Alomar	3.00	1.35	.40
☐ 2 Dennis Eckersley	1.00	.45	.13
☐ 3 Gary Sheffield	1.00	.45	.13

1993 Fleer Pro-Visions II

Randomly inserted in series II wax packs, these three standard-size (2 1/2" by 3 1/2") cards feature black-bordered fanciful color artwork of the players in action. The player's

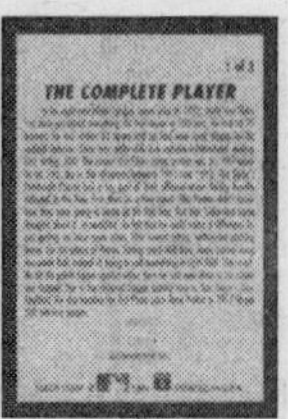

name appears in gold foil within the bottom black margin of each. The back carries player career highlights within a black-bordered white panel. The cards are numbered on the back.

	MINT	EXC	G-VG
COMPLETE SET (3)	3.00	1.35	.40
COMMON CARD (1-3)	.60	.25	.08
☐ 1 Andy Van Slyke	.60	.25	.08
☐ 2 Tom Glavine	1.25	.55	.16
☐ 3 Cecil Fielder	1.25	.55	.16

1993 Fleer Rookie Sensations I

Randomly inserted in series I cello packs, these ten standard-size (2 1/2" by 3 1/2") cards feature on their blue-bordered fronts cutout color player photos, each superposed upon a silver-colored background. The set's title and the player's name appear in gold foil in an upper corner. The back has the same blue-bordered and silver-colored background design. A color player head shot appears in the upper left and the player's career highlights follow alongside and below. The cards are numbered on the back "X of 10."

	MINT	EXC	G-VG
COMPLETE SET (10)	20.00	9.00	2.50
COMMON CARD (1-10)	1.00	.45	.13
☐ 1 Kenny Lofton	12.00	5.50	1.50
☐ 2 Cal Eldred	1.50	.65	.19
☐ 3 Pat Listach	1.00	.45	.13
☐ 4 Roberto Hernandez	1.50	.65	.19

☐ 5 Dave Fleming	1.00	.45	.13
☐ 6 Eric Karros	1.00	.45	.13
☐ 7 Reggie Sanders	2.50	1.15	.30
☐ 8 Derrick May	1.00	.45	.13
☐ 9 Mike Perez	1.00	.45	.13
☐ 10 Donovan Osborne	1.00	.45	.13

1993 Fleer Rookie Sensations II

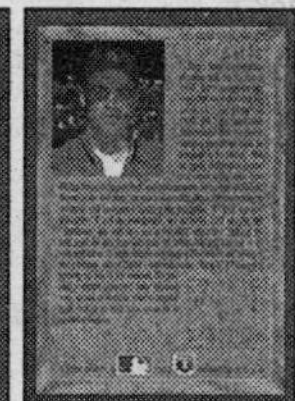

Randomly inserted in series II cello packs, these ten standard-size (2 1/2" by 3 1/2") cards feature on their blue-bordered fronts cutout color player photos, each superposed upon a silver-colored background. The set's title and the player's name appear in gold foil in an upper corner. The backs have the same blue-bordered and silver-colored background design. A color player head shot appears in the upper left and the player's career highlights follow alongside and below. The cards are numbered on the back.

	MINT	EXC	G-VG
COMPLETE SET (10)	10.00	4.50	1.25
COMMON CARD (1-10)	1.00	.45	.13
☐ 1 Moises Alou	4.00	1.80	.50
☐ 2 Pedro Astacio	1.50	.65	.19
☐ 3 Jim Austin	1.00	.45	.13
☐ 4 Chad Curtis	2.00	.90	.25
☐ 5 Gary DiSarcina	1.00	.45	.13
☐ 6 Scott Livingstone	1.00	.45	.13
☐ 7 Sam Militello	1.00	.45	.13
☐ 8 Arthur Rhodes	1.50	.65	.19
☐ 9 Tim Wakefield	1.00	.45	.13
☐ 10 Bob Zupcic	1.00	.45	.13

1993 Fleer Team Leaders AL

One Fleer Team Leader AL or Fleer Tom Glavine was inserted into each series I rack pack. Each of the ten tan-bordered standard-size (2 1/2" by 3 1/2") cards comprising this set feature a posed color player

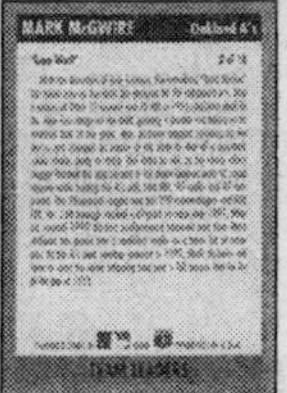

photo on its front with a smaller cutout color action photo superposed in a lower corner. The player's name and the set's title appear vertically in gold foil along the left side within team color-coded bars. The tan-bordered backs carry the player's name and team at the top within a team color-coded bar, and the set's title at the bottom within another team color-coded bar. Between these, the player's career highlights appear on a white background. The cards are numbered on the back.

	MINT	EXC	G-VG
COMPLETE SET (10)	75.00	34.00	9.50
COMMON CARD (1-10)	1.50	.65	.19
☐ 1 Kirby Puckett	12.00	5.50	1.50
☐ 2 Mark McGwire	1.50	.65	.19
☐ 3 Pat Listach	1.50	.65	.19
☐ 4 Roger Clemens	8.00	3.60	1.00
☐ 5 Frank Thomas	30.00	13.50	3.80
☐ 6 Carlos Baerga	4.50	2.00	.55
☐ 7 Brady Anderson	1.50	.65	.19
☐ 8 Juan Gonzalez	10.00	4.50	1.25
☐ 9 Roberto Alomar	8.00	3.60	1.00
☐ 10 Ken Griffey Jr.	30.00	13.50	3.80

1993 Fleer Team Leaders NL

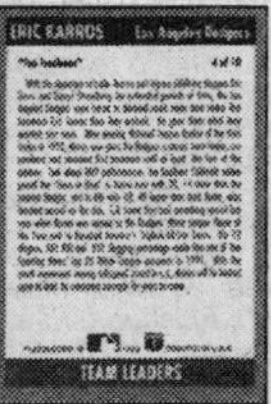

One Fleer Team Leader NL or Fleer Tom Glavine was inserted into each series II rack pack. Each of the ten tan-bordered standard-size (2 1/2" by 3 1/2") cards feature a posed color player photo on its front with a smaller cutout color action photo superposed in a lower corner. The player's name and the set's title appear vertically in

gold foil along the left side within team-colored bars. The tan-bordered backs carry the player's name and team at the top within a team color-coded bar, and the set's title at the bottom within another team color-coded bar. Between these, the player's career highlights appear on a white background. The cards are numbered on the back.

	MINT	EXC	G-VG
COMPLETE SET (10)	35.00	16.00	4.40
COMMON CARD (1-10)	1.50	.65	.19

	MINT	EXC	G-VG
☐ 1 Will Clark	4.50	2.00	.55
☐ 2 Terry Pendleton	1.50	.65	.19
☐ 3 Ray Lankford	2.50	1.15	.30
☐ 4 Eric Karros	1.50	.65	.19
☐ 5 Gary Sheffield	2.50	1.15	.30
☐ 6 Ryne Sandberg	10.00	4.50	1.25
☐ 7 Marquis Grissom	1.50	.65	.19
☐ 8 John Kruk	2.50	1.15	.30
☐ 9 Jeff Bagwell	15.00	6.75	1.90
☐ 10 Andy Van Slyke	1.50	.65	.19

1993 Fleer Final Edition

The cards are numbered on the back (with an "F" prefix), grouped alphabetically within teams, and checklisted below alphabetically according to teams for the National League and American League as follows: Atlanta Braves (1-5), Chicago Cubs (6-13), Cincinnati Reds (14-20), Colorado Rockies (21-47), Florida Marlins (48-75), Houston Astros (76-80), Los Angeles Dodgers (81-87), Montreal Expos (88- 97), New York Mets (98-107), Philadelphia Phillies (108-112), Pittsburgh Pirates (113-122), St. Louis Cardinals (123-133), San Diego Padres (134-148), San Francisco Giants (149-155), Baltimore Orioles (156-168), Boston Red Sox (169- 178), California Angels (179-191), Chicago White Sox (192- 198), Cleveland Indians (199-208), Detroit Tigers (209-214), Kansas City Royals (215-221), Milwaukee Brewers (222-232), Minnesota Twins (233-241), New York Yankees (242-252), Oakland Athletics (253-262), Seattle Mariners (263-276), Texas Rangers (277-285), and Toronto Blue Jays (286-297). The set closes with checklist cards (298-300). Rookie Cards in this set include Rene Arocha, Russ Davis, Scott Lydy, J.T. Snow, Tony Tarasco, and Darrell Whitmore.

	MINT	EXC	G-VG
COMPLETE FACT.SET (310)	15.00	6.75	1.90
COMPLETE SET (300)	10.00	4.50	1.25
COMMON CARD (1-300)	.05	.02	.01

	MINT	EXC	G-VG
☐ 1 Steve Bedrosian	.05	.02	.01
☐ 2 Jay Howell	.05	.02	.01
☐ 3 Greg Maddux	.40	.18	.05
☐ 4 Greg McMichael	.15	.07	.02
☐ 5 Tony Tarasco	.25	.11	.03
☐ 6 Jose Bautista	.05	.02	.01
☐ 7 Jose Guzman	.05	.02	.01
☐ 8 Greg Hibbard	.05	.02	.01
☐ 9 Candy Maldonado	.05	.02	.01
☐ 10 Randy Myers	.08	.04	.01
☐ 11 Matt Walbeck	.05	.02	.01
☐ 12 Turk Wendell	.08	.04	.01
☐ 13 Willie Wilson	.05	.02	.01
☐ 14 Greg Cadaret	.05	.02	.01
☐ 15 Roberto Kelly	.08	.04	.01
☐ 16 Randy Milligan	.05	.02	.01
☐ 17 Kevin Mitchell	.08	.04	.01
☐ 18 Jeff Reardon	.08	.04	.01
☐ 19 John Roper	.08	.04	.01
☐ 20 John Smiley	.05	.02	.01
☐ 21 Andy Ashby	.05	.02	.01
☐ 22 Dante Bichette	.10	.05	.01
☐ 23 Willie Blair	.05	.02	.01
☐ 24 Pedro Castellano	.05	.02	.01
☐ 25 Vinny Castilla	.05	.02	.01
☐ 26 Jerald Clark	.05	.02	.01
☐ 27 Alex Cole	.05	.02	.01
☐ 28 Scott Fredrickson	.08	.04	.01
☐ 29 Jay Gainer	.05	.02	.01
☐ 30 Andres Galarraga	.10	.05	.01
☐ 31 Joe Girardi	.05	.02	.01
☐ 32 Ryan Hawblitzel	.05	.02	.01
☐ 33 Charlie Hayes	.08	.04	.01
☐ 34 Darren Holmes	.05	.02	.01
☐ 35 Chris Jones	.05	.02	.01
☐ 36 David Nied	.10	.05	.01
☐ 37 J.Owens	.05	.02	.01
☐ 38 Lance Painter	.05	.02	.01
☐ 39 Jeff Parrett	.05	.02	.01
☐ 40 Steve Reed	.05	.02	.01
☐ 41 Armando Reynoso	.05	.02	.01
☐ 42 Bruce Ruffin	.05	.02	.01
☐ 43 Danny Sheaffer	.08	.04	.01
☐ 44 Keith Shepherd	.05	.02	.01
☐ 45 Jim Tatum	.05	.02	.01
☐ 46 Gary Wayne	.05	.02	.01
☐ 47 Eric Young	.08	.04	.01
☐ 48 Luis Aquino	.05	.02	.01
☐ 49 Alex Arias	.05	.02	.01
☐ 50 Jack Armstrong	.05	.02	.01
☐ 51 Bret Barberie	.05	.02	.01
☐ 52 Geronimo Berroa	.05	.02	.01
☐ 53 Ryan Bowen	.05	.02	.01
☐ 54 Greg Briley	.05	.02	.01
☐ 55 Cris Carpenter	.05	.02	.01
☐ 56 Chuck Carr	.05	.02	.01
☐ 57 Jeff Conine	.10	.05	.01
☐ 58 Jim Corsi	.05	.02	.01
☐ 59 Orestes Destrade	.05	.02	.01
☐ 60 Junior Felix	.05	.02	.01
☐ 61 Chris Hammond	.05	.02	.01
☐ 62 Bryan Harvey	.08	.04	.01
☐ 63 Charlie Hough	.08	.04	.01
☐ 64 Joe Klink	.05	.02	.01

	#	Player			
☐	65	Richie Lewis UER (Refers to place of birth and residence as Illinois instead of Indiana)	.05	.02	.01
☐	66	Mitch Lyden	.08	.04	.01
☐	67	Bob Natal	.05	.02	.01
☐	68	Scott Pose	.05	.02	.01
☐	69	Rich Renteria	.05	.02	.01
☐	70	Benito Santiago	.05	.02	.01
☐	71	Gary Sheffield	.10	.05	.01
☐	72	Matt Turner	.08	.04	.01
☐	73	Walt Weiss	.05	.02	.01
☐	74	Darrell Whitmore	.15	.07	.02
☐	75	Nigel Wilson	.10	.05	.01
☐	76	Kevin Bass	.05	.02	.01
☐	77	Doug Drabek	.10	.05	.01
☐	78	Tom Edens	.05	.02	.01
☐	79	Chris James	.05	.02	.01
☐	80	Greg Swindell	.05	.02	.01
☐	81	Omar Daal	.05	.02	.01
☐	82	Raul Mondesi	1.50	.65	.19
☐	83	Jody Reed	.05	.02	.01
☐	84	Cory Snyder	.05	.02	.01
☐	85	Rick Trlicek	.05	.02	.01
☐	86	Tim Wallach	.05	.02	.01
☐	87	Todd Worrell	.05	.02	.01
☐	88	Tavo Alvarez	.05	.02	.01
☐	89	Frank Bolick	.05	.02	.01
☐	90	Kent Bottenfield	.05	.02	.01
☐	91	Greg Colbrunn	.05	.02	.01
☐	92	Cliff Floyd	.60	.25	.08
☐	93	Lou Frazier	.08	.04	.01
☐	94	Mike Gardiner	.05	.02	.01
☐	95	Mike Lansing	.20	.09	.03
☐	96	Bill Risley	.05	.02	.01
☐	97	Jeff Shaw	.05	.02	.01
☐	98	Kevin Baez	.05	.02	.01
☐	99	Tim Bogar	.05	.02	.01
☐	100	Jeromy Burnitz	.05	.02	.01
☐	101	Mike Draper	.08	.04	.01
☐	102	Darrin Jackson	.05	.02	.01
☐	103	Mike Maddux	.05	.02	.01
☐	104	Joe Orsulak	.05	.02	.01
☐	105	Doug Saunders	.05	.02	.01
☐	106	Frank Tanana	.05	.02	.01
☐	107	Dave Telgheder	.05	.02	.01
☐	108	Larry Andersen	.05	.02	.01
☐	109	Jim Eisenreich	.05	.02	.01
☐	110	Pete Incaviglia	.05	.02	.01
☐	111	Danny Jackson	.05	.02	.01
☐	112	David West	.05	.02	.01
☐	113	Al Martin	.08	.04	.01
☐	114	Blas Minor	.05	.02	.01
☐	115	Dennis Moeller	.05	.02	.01
☐	116	William Pennyfeather	.05	.02	.01
☐	117	Rich Robertson	.05	.02	.01
☐	118	Ben Shelton	.05	.02	.01
☐	119	Lonnie Smith	.05	.02	.01
☐	120	Freddie Toliver	.05	.02	.01
☐	121	Paul Wagner	.05	.02	.01
☐	122	Kevin Young	.05	.02	.01
☐	123	Rene Arocha	.15	.07	.02
☐	124	Gregg Jefferies	.10	.05	.01
☐	125	Paul Kilgus	.05	.02	.01
☐	126	Les Lancaster	.05	.02	.01
☐	127	Joe Magrane	.05	.02	.01
☐	128	Rob Murphy	.05	.02	.01
☐	129	Erik Pappas	.05	.02	.01
☐	130	Stan Royer	.05	.02	.01
☐	131	Ozzie Smith	.40	.18	.05
☐	132	Tom Urbani	.05	.02	.01
☐	133	Mark Whiten	.08	.04	.01
☐	134	Derek Bell	.08	.04	.01
☐	135	Doug Brocail	.05	.02	.01
☐	136	Phil Clark	.05	.02	.01
☐	137	Mark Ettles	.05	.02	.01
☐	138	Jeff Gardner	.05	.02	.01
☐	139	Pat Gomez	.05	.02	.01
☐	140	Ricky Gutierrez	.05	.02	.01
☐	141	Gene Harris	.05	.02	.01
☐	142	Kevin Higgins	.08	.04	.01
☐	143	Trevor Hoffman	.05	.02	.01
☐	144	Phil Plantier	.10	.05	.01
☐	145	Kerry Taylor	.15	.07	.02
☐	146	Guillermo Velasquez	.05	.02	.01
☐	147	Wally Whitehurst	.05	.02	.01
☐	148	Tim Worrell	.05	.02	.01
☐	149	Todd Benzinger	.05	.02	.01
☐	150	Barry Bonds	.75	.35	.09
☐	151	Greg Brummett	.05	.02	.01
☐	152	Mark Carreon	.05	.02	.01
☐	153	Dave Martinez	.05	.02	.01
☐	154	Jeff Reed	.05	.02	.01
☐	155	Kevin Rogers	.05	.02	.01
☐	156	Harold Baines	.08	.04	.01
☐	157	Damon Buford	.05	.02	.01
☐	158	Paul Carey	.05	.02	.01
☐	159	Jeffrey Hammonds	.40	.18	.05
☐	160	Jamie Moyer	.05	.02	.01
☐	161	Sherman Obando	.15	.07	.02
☐	162	John O'Donoghue	.05	.02	.01
☐	163	Brad Pennington	.05	.02	.01
☐	164	Jim Poole	.05	.02	.01
☐	165	Harold Reynolds	.05	.02	.01
☐	166	Fernando Valenzuela	.05	.02	.01
☐	167	Jack Voigt	.08	.04	.01
☐	168	Mark Williamson	.05	.02	.01
☐	169	Scott Bankhead	.05	.02	.01
☐	170	Greg Blosser	.05	.02	.01
☐	171	Jim Byrd	.05	.02	.01
☐	172	Ivan Calderson	.05	.02	.01
☐	173	Andre Dawson	.10	.05	.01
☐	174	Scott Fletcher	.05	.02	.01
☐	175	Jose Melendez	.05	.02	.01
☐	176	Carlos Quintana	.05	.02	.01
☐	177	Jeff Russell	.05	.02	.01
☐	178	Aaron Sele	.40	.18	.05
☐	179	Rod Correia	.08	.04	.01
☐	180	Chili Davis	.08	.04	.01
☐	181	Jim Edmonds	.30	.14	.04
☐	182	Rene Gonzales	.05	.02	.01
☐	183	Hilly Hathaway	.05	.02	.01
☐	184	Torey Lovullo	.05	.02	.01
☐	185	Greg Myers	.05	.02	.01
☐	186	Gene Nelson	.05	.02	.01
☐	187	Troy Percival	.05	.02	.01
☐	188	Scott Sanderson	.05	.02	.01
☐	189	Darryl Scott	.05	.02	.01
☐	190	J.T. Snow	.15	.07	.02
☐	191	Russ Springer	.05	.02	.01
☐	192	Jason Bere	.50	.23	.06
☐	193	Rodney Bolton	.05	.02	.01
☐	194	Ellis Burks	.08	.04	.01
☐	195	Bo Jackson	.10	.05	.01
☐	196	Mike LaValliere	.05	.02	.01
☐	197	Scott Ruffcorn	.20	.09	.03
☐	198	Jeff Schwartz	.05	.02	.01
☐	199	Jerry DiPoto	.08	.04	.01
☐	200	Alvaro Espinoza	.05	.02	.01
☐	201	Wayne Kirby	.05	.02	.01
☐	202	Tom Kramer	.05	.02	.01
☐	203	Jesse Levis	.05	.02	.01
☐	204	Manny Ramirez	.75	.35	.09
☐	205	Jeff Treadway	.05	.02	.01
☐	206	Bill Wertz	.05	.02	.01
☐	207	Cliff Young	.05	.02	.01
☐	208	Matt Young	.05	.02	.01

☐ 209 Kirk Gibson	.08	.04	.01
☐ 210 Greg Gohr	.05	.02	.01
☐ 211 Bill Krueger	.05	.02	.01
☐ 212 Bob MacDonald	.05	.02	.01
☐ 213 Mike Moore	.05	.02	.01
☐ 214 David Wells	.05	.02	.01
☐ 215 Billy Brewer	.08	.04	.01
☐ 216 David Cone	.10	.05	.01
☐ 217 Greg Gagne	.05	.02	.01
☐ 218 Mark Gardner	.05	.02	.01
☐ 219 Chris Haney	.05	.02	.01
☐ 220 Phil Hiatt	.05	.02	.01
☐ 221 Jose Lind	.05	.02	.01
☐ 222 Juan Bell	.05	.02	.01
☐ 223 Tom Brunansky	.05	.02	.01
☐ 224 Mike Ignasiak	.05	.02	.01
☐ 225 Joe Kmak	.05	.02	.01
☐ 226 Tom Lampkin	.05	.02	.01
☐ 227 Graeme Lloyd	.05	.02	.01
☐ 228 Carlos Maldonado	.05	.02	.01
☐ 229 Matt Mieske	.08	.04	.01
☐ 230 Angel Miranda	.05	.02	.01
☐ 231 Troy O'Leary	.05	.02	.01
☐ 232 Kevin Reimer	.05	.02	.01
☐ 233 Larry Casian	.05	.02	.01
☐ 234 Jim Deshaies	.05	.02	.01
☐ 235 Eddie Guardado	.05	.02	.01
☐ 236 Chip Hale	.05	.02	.01
☐ 237 Mike Maksudian	.05	.02	.01
☐ 238 David McCarty	.08	.04	.01
☐ 239 Pat Meares	.15	.07	.02
☐ 240 George Tsamis	.05	.02	.01
☐ 241 Dave Winfield	.10	.05	.01
☐ 242 Jim Abbott	.10	.05	.01
☐ 243 Wade Boggs	.10	.05	.01
☐ 244 Andy Cook	.05	.02	.01
☐ 245 Russ Davis	.30	.14	.04
☐ 246 Mike Humphreys	.05	.02	.01
☐ 247 Jimmy Key	.08	.04	.01
☐ 248 Jim Leyritz	.05	.02	.01
☐ 249 Bobby Munoz	.05	.02	.01
☐ 250 Paul O'Neill	.08	.04	.01
☐ 251 Spike Owen	.05	.02	.01
☐ 252 Dave Silvestri	.05	.02	.01
☐ 253 Marcos Armas	.05	.02	.01
☐ 254 Brent Gates	.10	.05	.01
☐ 255 Goose Gossage	.10	.05	.01
☐ 256 Scott Lydy	.15	.07	.02
☐ 257 Henry Mercedes	.05	.02	.01
☐ 258 Mike Mohler	.05	.02	.01
☐ 259 Troy Neel	.08	.04	.01
☐ 260 Edwin Nunez	.05	.02	.01
☐ 261 Craig Paquette	.05	.02	.01
☐ 262 Kevin Seitzer	.05	.02	.01
☐ 263 Rich Amaral	.05	.02	.01
☐ 264 Mike Blowers	.05	.02	.01
☐ 265 Chris Bosio	.05	.02	.01
☐ 266 Norm Charlton	.05	.02	.01
☐ 267 Jim Converse	.15	.07	.02
☐ 268 John Cummings	.05	.02	.01
☐ 269 Mike Felder	.05	.02	.01
☐ 270 Mike Hampton	.05	.02	.01
☐ 271 Bill Haselman	.05	.02	.01
☐ 272 Dwayne Henry	.05	.02	.01
☐ 273 Greg Litton	.05	.02	.01
☐ 274 Mackey Sasser	.05	.02	.01
☐ 275 Lee Tinsley	.05	.02	.01
☐ 276 David Wainhouse	.05	.02	.01
☐ 277 Jeff Bronkey	.08	.04	.01
☐ 278 Benji Gil	.08	.04	.01
☐ 279 Tom Henke	.08	.04	.01
☐ 280 Charlie Leibrandt	.05	.02	.01
☐ 281 Robb Nen	.05	.02	.01
☐ 282 Bill Ripken	.05	.02	.01
☐ 283 Jon Shave	.05	.02	.01
☐ 284 Doug Strange	.05	.02	.01
☐ 285 Matt Whiteside	.05	.02	.01
☐ 286 Scott Brow	.05	.02	.01
☐ 287 Willie Canate	.05	.02	.01
☐ 288 Tony Castillo	.05	.02	.01
☐ 289 Domingo Cedeno	.05	.02	.01
☐ 290 Darnell Coles	.05	.02	.01
☐ 291 Danny Cox	.05	.02	.01
☐ 292 Mark Eichhorn	.05	.02	.01
☐ 293 Tony Fernandez	.05	.02	.01
☐ 294 Al Leiter	.05	.02	.01
☐ 295 Paul Molitor	.30	.14	.04
☐ 296 Dave Stewart	.08	.04	.01
☐ 297 Woody Williams	.05	.02	.01
☐ 298 Checklist F1-F100	.05	.02	.01
☐ 299 Checklist F101-F200	.05	.02	.01
☐ 300 Checklist F201-F300	.05	.02	.01

1994 Fleer

The 1994 Fleer baseball set consists of 720 standard-size cards. The white-bordered fronts feature color player action photos. In one corner, the player's name and position appear in a gold foil lettered arc; his team logo appears within. The backs are also white-bordered and feature a color player photo, some action, others posed. One side of the picture is ghosted and color-screened, and carries the player's name, biography, and career highlights. The bottom of the photo is also color-screened and ghosted, and carries the player's statistics. The cards are numbered on the back, grouped alphabetically within teams, and checklisted below alphabetically according to teams for each league as follows: Baltimore Orioles (1-24), Boston Red Sox (25-47), California Angels (48-72), Chicago White Sox (73-97), Cleveland Indians (98-123), Detroit Tigers (124-146), Kansas City Royals (147-172), Milwaukee Brewers (173-197), Minnesota Twins (198-223), New York Yankees (224-251), Oakland Athletics (252-277), Seattle Mariners (278-301), Texas Rangers (302-323), Toronto Blue Jays (324-349), Atlanta Braves (350-378), Chicago Cubs (379-403), Cincinnati Reds (404-431), Colorado Rockies (432-457), Florida Marlins (458-481), Houston Astros (482-503), Los Angeles Dodgers (504-530), Montreal Expos (531-556), New York Mets

(557-580), Philadelphia Phillies (581-604), Pittsburgh Pirates (605-626), St. Louis Cardinals (627-651), San Diego Padres (652-679), and San Francisco Giants (680-705). The set closes with a Superstar Specials (706-713) subset.

	MINT	EXC	G-VG
COMPLETE SET (720)	50.00	23.00	6.25
COMMON CARD (1-720)	.10	.05	.01

	No.	Player	MINT	EXC	G-VG
☐	1	Brady Anderson	.15	.07	.02
☐	2	Harold Baines	.15	.07	.02
☐	3	Mike Devereaux	.15	.07	.02
☐	4	Todd Frohwirth	.10	.05	.01
☐	5	Jeffrey Hammonds	.30	.14	.04
☐	6	Chris Hoiles	.15	.07	.02
☐	7	Tim Hulett	.10	.05	.01
☐	8	Ben McDonald	.15	.07	.02
☐	9	Mark McLemore	.10	.05	.01
☐	10	Alan Mills	.10	.05	.01
☐	11	Jamie Moyer	.10	.05	.01
☐	12	Mike Mussina	.40	.18	.05
☐	13	Gregg Olson	.10	.05	.01
☐	14	Mike Pagliarulo	.10	.05	.01
☐	15	Brad Pennington	.10	.05	.01
☐	16	Jim Poole	.10	.05	.01
☐	17	Harold Reynolds	.10	.05	.01
☐	18	Arthur Rhodes	.10	.05	.01
☐	19	Cal Ripken	2.25	1.00	.30
☐	20	David Segui	.10	.05	.01
☐	21	Rick Sutcliffe	.15	.07	.02
☐	22	Fernando Valenzuela	.10	.05	.01
☐	23	Jack Voigt	.10	.05	.01
☐	24	Mark Williamson	.10	.05	.01
☐	25	Scott Bankhead	.10	.05	.01
☐	26	Roger Clemens	.60	.25	.08
☐	27	Scott Cooper	.15	.07	.02
☐	28	Danny Darwin	.10	.05	.01
☐	29	Andre Dawson	.20	.09	.03
☐	30	Rob Deer	.10	.05	.01
☐	31	John Dopson	.10	.05	.01
☐	32	Scott Fletcher	.10	.05	.01
☐	33	Mike Greenwell	.15	.07	.02
☐	34	Greg A. Harris	.10	.05	.01
☐	35	Billy Hatcher	.10	.05	.01
☐	36	Bob Melvin	.10	.05	.01
☐	37	Tony Pena	.10	.05	.01
☐	38	Paul Quantrill	.10	.05	.01
☐	39	Carlos Quintana	.10	.05	.01
☐	40	Ernest Riles	.10	.05	.01
☐	41	Jeff Russell	.10	.05	.01
☐	42	Ken Ryan	.10	.05	.01
☐	43	Aaron Sele	.30	.14	.04
☐	44	John Valentin	.15	.07	.02
☐	45	Mo Vaughn	.20	.09	.03
☐	46	Frank Viola	.10	.05	.01
☐	47	Bob Zupcic	.10	.05	.01
☐	48	Mike Butcher	.10	.05	.01
☐	49	Rod Correia	.10	.05	.01
☐	50	Chad Curtis	.15	.07	.02
☐	51	Chili Davis	.15	.07	.02
☐	52	Gary DiSarcina	.10	.05	.01
☐	53	Damion Easley	.10	.05	.01
☐	54	Jim Edmonds	.10	.05	.01
☐	55	Chuck Finley	.10	.05	.01
☐	56	Steve Frey	.10	.05	.01
☐	57	Rene Gonzales	.10	.05	.01
☐	58	Joe Grahe	.10	.05	.01
☐	59	Hilly Hathaway	.10	.05	.01
☐	60	Stan Javier	.10	.05	.01
☐	61	Mark Langston	.20	.09	.03
☐	62	Phil Leftwich	.10	.05	.01
☐	63	Torey Lovullo	.10	.05	.01
☐	64	Joe Magrane	.10	.05	.01
☐	65	Greg Myers	.10	.05	.01
☐	66	Ken Patterson	.10	.05	.01
☐	67	Eduardo Perez	.15	.07	.02
☐	68	Luis Polonia	.10	.05	.01
☐	69	Tim Salmon	.40	.18	.05
☐	70	J.T. Snow	.15	.07	.02
☐	71	Ron Tingley	.10	.05	.01
☐	72	Julio Valera	.10	.05	.01
☐	73	Wilson Alvarez	.20	.09	.03
☐	74	Tim Belcher	.10	.05	.01
☐	75	George Bell	.15	.07	.02
☐	76	Jason Bere	.40	.18	.05
☐	77	Rod Bolton	.10	.05	.01
☐	78	Ellis Burks	.15	.07	.02
☐	79	Joey Cora	.10	.05	.01
☐	80	Alex Fernandez	.20	.09	.03
☐	81	Craig Grebeck	.10	.05	.01
☐	82	Ozzie Guillen	.10	.05	.01
☐	83	Roberto Hernandez	.10	.05	.01
☐	84	Bo Jackson	.20	.09	.03
☐	85	Lance Johnson	.10	.05	.01
☐	86	Ron Karkovice	.10	.05	.01
☐	87	Mike LaValliere	.10	.05	.01
☐	88	Kirk McCaskill	.10	.05	.01
☐	89	Jack McDowell	.20	.09	.03
☐	90	Warren Newson	.10	.05	.01
☐	91	Dan Pasqua	.10	.05	.01
☐	92	Scott Radinsky	.10	.05	.01
☐	93	Tim Raines	.20	.09	.03
☐	94	Steve Sax	.10	.05	.01
☐	95	Jeff Schwarz	.15	.07	.02
☐	96	Frank Thomas	3.00	1.35	.40
☐	97	Robin Ventura	.15	.07	.02
☐	98	Sandy Alomar Jr.	.15	.07	.02
☐	99	Carlos Baerga	.40	.18	.05
☐	100	Albert Belle	.90	.40	.11
☐	101	Mark Clark	.10	.05	.01
☐	102	Jerry DiPoto	.15	.07	.02
☐	103	Alvaro Espinoza	.10	.05	.01
☐	104	Felix Fermin	.10	.05	.01
☐	105	Jeremy Hernandez	.10	.05	.01
☐	106	Reggie Jefferson	.10	.05	.01
☐	107	Wayne Kirby	.10	.05	.01
☐	108	Tom Kramer	.10	.05	.01
☐	109	Mark Lewis	.10	.05	.01
☐	110	Derek Lilliquist	.10	.05	.01
☐	111	Kenny Lofton	.75	.35	.09
☐	112	Candy Maldonado	.10	.05	.01
☐	113	Jose Mesa	.10	.05	.01
☐	114	Jeff Mutis	.10	.05	.01
☐	115	Charles Nagy	.10	.05	.01
☐	116	Bob Ojeda	.10	.05	.01
☐	117	Junior Ortiz	.10	.05	.01
☐	118	Eric Plunk	.10	.05	.01
☐	119	Manny Ramirez	.60	.25	.08
☐	120	Paul Sorrento	.10	.05	.01
☐	121	Jim Thome	.20	.09	.03
☐	122	Jeff Treadway	.10	.05	.01
☐	123	Bill Wertz	.10	.05	.01
☐	124	Skeeter Barnes	.10	.05	.01
☐	125	Milt Cuyler	.10	.05	.01
☐	126	Eric Davis	.10	.05	.01
☐	127	John Doherty	.10	.05	.01
☐	128	Cecil Fielder	.20	.09	.03
☐	129	Travis Fryman	.25	.11	.03
☐	130	Kirk Gibson	.15	.07	.02
☐	131	Dan Gladden	.10	.05	.01
☐	132	Greg Gohr	.10	.05	.01
☐	133	Chris Gomez	.20	.09	.03
☐	134	Bill Gullickson	.10	.05	.01
☐	135	Mike Henneman	.10	.05	.01

	No.	Player			
☐	136	Kurt Knudsen	.10	.05	.01
☐	137	Chad Kreuter	.10	.05	.01
☐	138	Bill Krueger	.10	.05	.01
☐	139	Scott Livingstone	.10	.05	.01
☐	140	Bob MacDonald	.10	.05	.01
☐	141	Mike Moore	.10	.05	.01
☐	142	Tony Phillips	.10	.05	.01
☐	143	Mickey Tettleton	.15	.07	.02
☐	144	Alan Trammell	.20	.09	.03
☐	145	David Wells	.10	.05	.01
☐	146	Lou Whitaker	.20	.09	.03
☐	147	Kevin Appier	.15	.07	.02
☐	148	Stan Belinda	.10	.05	.01
☐	149	George Brett	1.25	.55	.16
☐	150	Billy Brewer	.10	.05	.01
☐	151	Hubie Brooks	.10	.05	.01
☐	152	David Cone	.20	.09	.03
☐	153	Gary Gaetti	.10	.05	.01
☐	154	Greg Gagne	.10	.05	.01
☐	155	Tom Gordon	.10	.05	.01
☐	156	Mark Gubicza	.10	.05	.01
☐	157	Chris Gwynn	.10	.05	.01
☐	158	John Habyan	.10	.05	.01
☐	159	Chris Haney	.10	.05	.01
☐	160	Phil Hiatt	.20	.09	.03
☐	161	Felix Jose	.10	.05	.01
☐	162	Wally Joyner	.15	.07	.02
☐	163	Jose Lind	.10	.05	.01
☐	164	Mike Macfarlane	.10	.05	.01
☐	165	Mike Magnante	.10	.05	.01
☐	166	Brent Mayne	.10	.05	.01
☐	167	Brian McRae	.15	.07	.02
☐	168	Kevin McReynolds	.10	.05	.01
☐	169	Keith Miller	.10	.05	.01
☐	170	Jeff Montgomery	.15	.07	.02
☐	171	Hipolito Pichardo	.10	.05	.01
☐	172	Rico Rossy	.10	.05	.01
☐	173	Juan Bell	.10	.05	.01
☐	174	Ricky Bones	.10	.05	.01
☐	175	Cal Eldred	.15	.07	.02
☐	176	Mike Fetters	.10	.05	.01
☐	177	Darryl Hamilton	.10	.05	.01
☐	178	Doug Henry	.10	.05	.01
☐	179	Mike Ignasiak	.10	.05	.01
☐	180	John Jaha	.10	.05	.01
☐	181	Pat Listach	.10	.05	.01
☐	182	Graeme Lloyd	.10	.05	.01
☐	183	Matt Mieske	.10	.05	.01
☐	184	Angel Miranda	.10	.05	.01
☐	185	Jaime Navarro	.10	.05	.01
☐	186	Dave Nilsson	.10	.05	.01
☐	187	Troy O'Leary	.10	.05	.01
☐	188	Jesse Orosco	.10	.05	.01
☐	189	Kevin Reimer	.10	.05	.01
☐	190	Kevin Seitzer	.10	.05	.01
☐	191	Bill Spiers	.10	.05	.01
☐	192	B.J. Surhoff	.10	.05	.01
☐	193	Dickie Thon	.10	.05	.01
☐	194	Jose Valentin	.10	.05	.01
☐	195	Greg Vaughn	.15	.07	.02
☐	196	Bill Wegman	.10	.05	.01
☐	197	Robin Yount	.40	.18	.05
☐	198	Rick Aguilera	.15	.07	.02
☐	199	Willie Banks	.10	.05	.01
☐	200	Bernardo Brito	.10	.05	.01
☐	201	Larry Casian	.10	.05	.01
☐	202	Scott Erickson	.10	.05	.01
☐	203	Eddie Guardado	.10	.05	.01
☐	204	Mark Guthrie	.10	.05	.01
☐	205	Chip Hale	.10	.05	.01
☐	206	Brian Harper	.10	.05	.01
☐	207	Mike Hartley	.10	.05	.01
☐	208	Kent Hrbek	.15	.07	.02
☐	209	Terry Jorgensen	.10	.05	.01
☐	210	Chuck Knoblauch	.20	.09	.03
☐	211	Gene Larkin	.10	.05	.01
☐	212	Shane Mack	.15	.07	.02
☐	213	David McCarty	.15	.07	.02
☐	214	Pat Meares	.10	.05	.01
☐	215	Pedro Munoz	.10	.05	.01
☐	216	Derek Parks	.10	.05	.01
☐	217	Kirby Puckett	1.25	.55	.16
☐	218	Jeff Reboulet	.10	.05	.01
☐	219	Kevin Tapani	.10	.05	.01
☐	220	Mike Trombley	.10	.05	.01
☐	221	George Tsamis	.10	.05	.01
☐	222	Carl Willis	.10	.05	.01
☐	223	Dave Winfield	.20	.09	.03
☐	224	Jim Abbott	.20	.09	.03
☐	225	Paul Assenmacher	.10	.05	.01
☐	226	Wade Boggs	.20	.09	.03
☐	227	Russ Davis	.10	.05	.01
☐	228	Steve Farr	.10	.05	.01
☐	229	Mike Gallego	.10	.05	.01
☐	230	Paul Gibson	.10	.05	.01
☐	231	Steve Howe	.10	.05	.01
☐	232	Dion James	.10	.05	.01
☐	233	Domingo Jean	.10	.05	.01
☐	234	Scott Kamieniecki	.10	.05	.01
☐	235	Pat Kelly	.10	.05	.01
☐	236	Jimmy Key	.15	.07	.02
☐	237	Jim Leyritz	.10	.05	.01
☐	238	Kevin Maas	.10	.05	.01
☐	239	Don Mattingly	1.25	.55	.16
☐	240	Rich Monteleone	.10	.05	.01
☐	241	Bobby Munoz	.10	.05	.01
☐	242	Matt Nokes	.10	.05	.01
☐	243	Paul O'Neill	.15	.07	.02
☐	244	Spike Owen	.10	.05	.01
☐	245	Melido Perez	.10	.05	.01
☐	246	Lee Smith	.20	.09	.03
☐	247	Mike Stanley	.10	.05	.01
☐	248	Danny Tartabull	.15	.07	.02
☐	249	Randy Velarde	.10	.05	.01
☐	250	Bob Wickman	.10	.05	.01
☐	251	Bernie Williams	.15	.07	.02
☐	252	Mike Aldrete	.10	.05	.01
☐	253	Marcos Armas	.10	.05	.01
☐	254	Lance Blankenship	.10	.05	.01
☐	255	Mike Bordick	.10	.05	.01
☐	256	Scott Brosius	.10	.05	.01
☐	257	Jerry Browne	.10	.05	.01
☐	258	Ron Darling	.10	.05	.01
☐	259	Kelly Downs	.10	.05	.01
☐	260	Dennis Eckersley	.20	.09	.03
☐	261	Brent Gates	.20	.09	.03
☐	262	Goose Gossage	.20	.09	.03
☐	263	Scott Hemond	.10	.05	.01
☐	264	Dave Henderson	.10	.05	.01
☐	265	Rick Honeycutt	.10	.05	.01
☐	266	Vince Horsman	.10	.05	.01
☐	267	Scott Lydy	.10	.05	.01
☐	268	Mark McGwire	.20	.09	.03
☐	269	Mike Mohler	.10	.05	.01
☐	270	Troy Neel	.15	.07	.02
☐	271	Edwin Nunez	.10	.05	.01
☐	272	Craig Paquette	.10	.05	.01
☐	273	Ruben Sierra	.20	.09	.03
☐	274	Terry Steinbach	.15	.07	.02
☐	275	Todd Van Poppel	.15	.07	.02
☐	276	Bob Welch	.10	.05	.01
☐	277	Bobby Witt	.10	.05	.01
☐	278	Rich Amaral	.10	.05	.01
☐	279	Mike Blowers	.10	.05	.01
☐	280	Bret Boone UER (Name spelled Brett on front)	.20	.09	.03

- ☐ 281 Chris Bosio .10 .05 .01
- ☐ 282 Jay Buhner .15 .07 .02
- ☐ 283 Norm Charlton .10 .05 .01
- ☐ 284 Mike Felder .10 .05 .01
- ☐ 285 Dave Fleming .10 .05 .01
- ☐ 286 Ken Griffey Jr. 3.00 1.35 .40
- ☐ 287 Erik Hanson .10 .05 .01
- ☐ 288 Bill Haselman .10 .05 .01
- ☐ 289 Brad Holman .10 .05 .01
- ☐ 290 Randy Johnson .20 .09 .03
- ☐ 291 Tim Leary .10 .05 .01
- ☐ 292 Greg Litton .10 .05 .01
- ☐ 293 Dave Magadan .10 .05 .01
- ☐ 294 Edgar Martinez .10 .05 .01
- ☐ 295 Tino Martinez .10 .05 .01
- ☐ 296 Jeff Nelson .10 .05 .01
- ☐ 297 Erik Plantenberg .10 .05 .01
- ☐ 298 Mackey Sasser .10 .05 .01
- ☐ 299 Brian Turang .10 .05 .01
- ☐ 300 Dave Valle .10 .05 .01
- ☐ 301 Omar Vizquel .10 .05 .01
- ☐ 302 Brian Bohanon .10 .05 .01
- ☐ 303 Kevin Brown .10 .05 .01
- ☐ 304 Jose Canseco UER .40 .18 .05
  (Back mentions 1991 as his 40/40 MVP season; should be '88)
- ☐ 305 Mario Diaz .10 .05 .01
- ☐ 306 Julio Franco .15 .07 .02
- ☐ 307 Juan Gonzalez 1.00 .45 .13
- ☐ 308 Tom Henke .10 .05 .01
- ☐ 309 David Hulse .10 .05 .01
- ☐ 310 Manny Lee .10 .05 .01
- ☐ 311 Craig Lefferts .10 .05 .01
- ☐ 312 Charlie Leibrandt .10 .05 .01
- ☐ 313 Rafael Palmeiro .20 .09 .03
- ☐ 314 Dean Palmer .15 .07 .02
- ☐ 315 Roger Pavlik .10 .05 .01
- ☐ 316 Dan Peltier .10 .05 .01
- ☐ 317 Gene Petralli .10 .05 .01
- ☐ 318 Gary Redus .10 .05 .01
- ☐ 319 Ivan Rodriguez .20 .09 .03
- ☐ 320 Kenny Rogers .10 .05 .01
- ☐ 321 Nolan Ryan 3.00 1.35 .40
- ☐ 322 Doug Strange .10 .05 .01
- ☐ 323 Matt Whiteside .10 .05 .01
- ☐ 324 Roberto Alomar .60 .25 .08
- ☐ 325 Pat Borders .10 .05 .01
- ☐ 326 Joe Carter .40 .18 .05
- ☐ 327 Tony Castillo .10 .05 .01
- ☐ 328 Darnell Coles .10 .05 .01
- ☐ 329 Danny Cox .10 .05 .01
- ☐ 330 Mark Eichhorn .10 .05 .01
- ☐ 331 Tony Fernandez .10 .05 .01
- ☐ 332 Alfredo Griffin .10 .05 .01
- ☐ 333 Juan Guzman .15 .07 .02
- ☐ 334 Rickey Henderson .20 .09 .03
- ☐ 335 Pat Hentgen .15 .07 .02
- ☐ 336 Randy Knorr .10 .05 .01
- ☐ 337 Al Leiter .10 .05 .01
- ☐ 338 Paul Molitor .40 .18 .05
- ☐ 339 Jack Morris .20 .09 .03
- ☐ 340 John Olerud .20 .09 .03
- ☐ 341 Dick Schofield .10 .05 .01
- ☐ 342 Ed Sprague .10 .05 .01
- ☐ 343 Dave Stewart .15 .07 .02
- ☐ 344 Todd Stottlemyre .10 .05 .01
- ☐ 345 Mike Timlin .10 .05 .01
- ☐ 346 Duane Ward .15 .07 .02
- ☐ 347 Turner Ward .10 .05 .01
- ☐ 348 Devon White .15 .07 .02
- ☐ 349 Woody Williams .10 .05 .01
- ☐ 350 Steve Avery .20 .09 .03
- ☐ 351 Steve Bedrosian .10 .05 .01
- ☐ 352 Rafael Belliard .10 .05 .01
- ☐ 353 Damon Berryhill .10 .05 .01
- ☐ 354 Jeff Blauser .15 .07 .02
- ☐ 355 Sid Bream .10 .05 .01
- ☐ 356 Francisco Cabrera .10 .05 .01
- ☐ 357 Marvin Freeman .10 .05 .01
- ☐ 358 Ron Gant .15 .07 .02
- ☐ 359 Tom Glavine .20 .09 .03
- ☐ 360 Jay Howell .10 .05 .01
- ☐ 361 David Justice .40 .18 .05
- ☐ 362 Ryan Klesko .50 .23 .06
- ☐ 363 Mark Lemke .10 .05 .01
- ☐ 364 Javy Lopez .30 .14 .04
- ☐ 365 Greg Maddux .60 .25 .08
- ☐ 366 Fred McGriff .40 .18 .05
- ☐ 367 Greg McMichael .15 .07 .02
- ☐ 368 Kent Mercker .10 .05 .01
- ☐ 369 Otis Nixon .10 .05 .01
- ☐ 370 Greg Olson .10 .05 .01
- ☐ 371 Bill Pecota .10 .05 .01
- ☐ 372 Terry Pendleton .20 .09 .03
- ☐ 373 Deion Sanders .50 .23 .06
- ☐ 374 Pete Smith .10 .05 .01
- ☐ 375 John Smoltz .15 .07 .02
- ☐ 376 Mike Stanton .10 .05 .01
- ☐ 377 Tony Tarasco .20 .09 .03
- ☐ 378 Mark Wohlers .10 .05 .01
- ☐ 379 Jose Bautista .10 .05 .01
- ☐ 380 Shawn Boskie .10 .05 .01
- ☐ 381 Steve Buechele .10 .05 .01
- ☐ 382 Frank Castillo .10 .05 .01
- ☐ 383 Mark Grace .20 .09 .03
- ☐ 384 Jose Guzman .10 .05 .01
- ☐ 385 Mike Harkey .10 .05 .01
- ☐ 386 Greg Hibbard .10 .05 .01
- ☐ 387 Glenallen Hill .10 .05 .01
- ☐ 388 Steve Lake .10 .05 .01
- ☐ 389 Derrick May .10 .05 .01
- ☐ 390 Chuck McElroy .10 .05 .01
- ☐ 391 Mike Morgan .10 .05 .01
- ☐ 392 Randy Myers .10 .05 .01
- ☐ 393 Dan Plesac .10 .05 .01
- ☐ 394 Kevin Roberson .10 .05 .01
- ☐ 395 Rey Sanchez .10 .05 .01
- ☐ 396 Ryne Sandberg 1.00 .45 .13
- ☐ 397 Bob Scanlan .10 .05 .01
- ☐ 398 Dwight Smith .10 .05 .01
- ☐ 399 Sammy Sosa .20 .09 .03
- ☐ 400 Jose Vizcaino .10 .05 .01
- ☐ 401 Rick Wilkins .10 .05 .01
- ☐ 402 Willie Wilson .10 .05 .01
- ☐ 403 Eric Yelding .10 .05 .01
- ☐ 404 Bobby Ayala .10 .05 .01
- ☐ 405 Jeff Branson .10 .05 .01
- ☐ 406 Tom Browning .10 .05 .01
- ☐ 407 Jacob Brumfield .10 .05 .01
- ☐ 408 Tim Costo .10 .05 .01
- ☐ 409 Rob Dibble .10 .05 .01
- ☐ 410 Willie Greene .15 .07 .02
- ☐ 411 Thomas Howard .10 .05 .01
- ☐ 412 Roberto Kelly .15 .07 .02
- ☐ 413 Bill Landrum .10 .05 .01
- ☐ 414 Barry Larkin .20 .09 .03
- ☐ 415 Larry Luebbers .10 .05 .01
- ☐ 416 Kevin Mitchell .15 .07 .02
- ☐ 417 Hal Morris .15 .07 .02
- ☐ 418 Joe Oliver .10 .05 .01
- ☐ 419 Tim Pugh .10 .05 .01
- ☐ 420 Jeff Reardon .15 .07 .02
- ☐ 421 Jose Rijo .15 .07 .02
- ☐ 422 Bip Roberts .10 .05 .01
- ☐ 423 John Roper .15 .07 .02
- ☐ 424 Johnny Ruffin .10 .05 .01

☐ 425 Chris Sabo .10 .05 .01
☐ 426 Juan Samuel .10 .05 .01
☐ 427 Reggie Sanders .15 .07 .02
☐ 428 Scott Service .10 .05 .01
☐ 429 John Smiley .10 .05 .01
☐ 430 Jerry Spradlin .10 .05 .01
☐ 431 Kevin Wickander .10 .05 .01
☐ 432 Freddie Benavides .10 .05 .01
☐ 433 Dante Bichette .20 .09 .03
☐ 434 Willie Blair .10 .05 .01
☐ 435 Daryl Boston .10 .05 .01
☐ 436 Kent Bottenfield .10 .05 .01
☐ 437 Vinny Castilla .10 .05 .01
☐ 438 Jerald Clark .10 .05 .01
☐ 439 Alex Cole .10 .05 .01
☐ 440 Andres Galarraga .20 .09 .03
☐ 441 Joe Girardi .10 .05 .01
☐ 442 Greg W. Harris .10 .05 .01
☐ 443 Charlie Hayes .15 .07 .02
☐ 444 Darren Holmes .10 .05 .01
☐ 445 Chris Jones .10 .05 .01
☐ 446 Roberto Mejia .15 .07 .02
☐ 447 David Nied .20 .09 .03
☐ 448 J. Owens .10 .05 .01
☐ 449 Jeff Parrett .10 .05 .01
☐ 450 Steve Reed .10 .05 .01
☐ 451 Armando Reynoso .10 .05 .01
☐ 452 Bruce Ruffin .10 .05 .01
☐ 453 Mo Sanford .10 .05 .01
☐ 454 Danny Sheaffer .10 .05 .01
☐ 455 Jim Tatum .10 .05 .01
☐ 456 Gary Wayne .10 .05 .01
☐ 457 Eric Young .15 .07 .02
☐ 458 Luis Aquino .10 .05 .01
☐ 459 Alex Arias .10 .05 .01
☐ 460 Jack Armstrong .10 .05 .01
☐ 461 Bret Barberie .10 .05 .01
☐ 462 Ryan Bowen .10 .05 .01
☐ 463 Chuck Carr .10 .05 .01
☐ 464 Jeff Conine .20 .09 .03
☐ 465 Henry Cotto .10 .05 .01
☐ 466 Orestes Destrade .10 .05 .01
☐ 467 Chris Hammond .10 .05 .01
☐ 468 Bryan Harvey .15 .07 .02
☐ 469 Charlie Hough .15 .07 .02
☐ 470 Joe Klink .10 .05 .01
☐ 471 Richie Lewis .10 .05 .01
☐ 472 Bob Natal .10 .05 .01
☐ 473 Pat Rapp .10 .05 .01
☐ 474 Rich Renteria .10 .05 .01
☐ 475 Rich Rodriguez .10 .05 .01
☐ 476 Benito Santiago .10 .05 .01
☐ 477 Gary Sheffield .20 .09 .03
☐ 478 Matt Turner .10 .05 .01
☐ 479 David Weathers .10 .05 .01
☐ 480 Walt Weiss .10 .05 .01
☐ 481 Darrell Whitmore .15 .07 .02
☐ 482 Eric Anthony .10 .05 .01
☐ 483 Jeff Bagwell 1.50 .65 .19
☐ 484 Kevin Bass .10 .05 .01
☐ 485 Craig Biggio .15 .07 .02
☐ 486 Ken Caminiti .15 .07 .02
☐ 487 Andujar Cedeno .10 .05 .01
☐ 488 Chris Donnels .10 .05 .01
☐ 489 Doug Drabek .20 .09 .03
☐ 490 Steve Finley .10 .05 .01
☐ 491 Luis Gonzalez .10 .05 .01
☐ 492 Pete Harnisch .10 .05 .01
☐ 493 Xavier Hernandez .10 .05 .01
☐ 494 Doug Jones .10 .05 .01
☐ 495 Todd Jones .10 .05 .01
☐ 496 Darryl Kile .15 .07 .02
☐ 497 Al Osuna .10 .05 .01
☐ 498 Mark Portugal .10 .05 .01
☐ 499 Scott Servais .10 .05 .01
☐ 500 Greg Swindell .10 .05 .01
☐ 501 Eddie Taubensee .10 .05 .01
☐ 502 Jose Uribe .10 .05 .01
☐ 503 Brian Williams .10 .05 .01
☐ 504 Billy Ashley .20 .09 .03
☐ 505 Pedro Astacio .15 .07 .02
☐ 506 Brett Butler .15 .07 .02
☐ 507 Tom Candiotti .10 .05 .01
☐ 508 Omar Daal .10 .05 .01
☐ 509 Jim Gott .10 .05 .01
☐ 510 Kevin Gross .10 .05 .01
☐ 511 Dave Hansen .10 .05 .01
☐ 512 Carlos Hernandez .10 .05 .01
☐ 513 Orel Hershiser .10 .05 .01
☐ 514 Eric Karros .15 .07 .02
☐ 515 Pedro Martinez .20 .09 .03
☐ 516 Ramon Martinez .15 .07 .02
☐ 517 Roger McDowell .10 .05 .01
☐ 518 Raul Mondesi 1.00 .45 .13
☐ 519 Jose Offerman .10 .05 .01
☐ 520 Mike Piazza 1.50 .65 .19
☐ 521 Jody Reed .10 .05 .01
☐ 522 Henry Rodriguez .10 .05 .01
☐ 523 Mike Sharperson .10 .05 .01
☐ 524 Cory Snyder .10 .05 .01
☐ 525 Darryl Strawberry .15 .07 .02
☐ 526 Rick Trlicek .10 .05 .01
☐ 527 Tim Wallach .10 .05 .01
☐ 528 Mitch Webster .10 .05 .01
☐ 529 Steve Wilson .10 .05 .01
☐ 530 Todd Worrell .10 .05 .01
☐ 531 Moises Alou .20 .09 .03
☐ 532 Brian Barnes .10 .05 .01
☐ 533 Sean Berry .10 .05 .01
☐ 534 Greg Colbrunn .10 .05 .01
☐ 535 Delino DeShields .15 .07 .02
☐ 536 Jeff Fassero .10 .05 .01
☐ 537 Darrin Fletcher .10 .05 .01
☐ 538 Cliff Floyd .50 .23 .06
☐ 539 Lou Frazier .10 .05 .01
☐ 540 Marquis Grissom .20 .09 .03
☐ 541 Butch Henry .10 .05 .01
☐ 542 Ken Hill .15 .07 .02
☐ 543 Mike Lansing .15 .07 .02
☐ 544 Brian Looney .25 .11 .03
☐ 545 Dennis Martinez .15 .07 .02
☐ 546 Chris Nabholz .10 .05 .01
☐ 547 Randy Ready .10 .05 .01
☐ 548 Mel Rojas .10 .05 .01
☐ 549 Kirk Rueter .10 .05 .01
☐ 550 Tim Scott .10 .05 .01
☐ 551 Jeff Shaw .10 .05 .01
☐ 552 Tim Spehr .10 .05 .01
☐ 553 John VanderWal .10 .05 .01
☐ 554 Larry Walker .20 .09 .03
☐ 555 John Wetteland .10 .05 .01
☐ 556 Rondell White .30 .14 .04
☐ 557 Tim Bogar .10 .05 .01
☐ 558 Bobby Bonilla .20 .09 .03
☐ 559 Jeromy Burnitz .15 .07 .02
☐ 560 Sid Fernandez .10 .05 .01
☐ 561 John Franco .10 .05 .01
☐ 562 Dave Gallagher .10 .05 .01
☐ 563 Dwight Gooden .10 .05 .01
☐ 564 Eric Hillman .10 .05 .01
☐ 565 Todd Hundley .10 .05 .01
☐ 566 Jeff Innis .10 .05 .01
☐ 567 Darrin Jackson .10 .05 .01
☐ 568 Howard Johnson .10 .05 .01
☐ 569 Bobby Jones .20 .09 .03
☐ 570 Jeff Kent .15 .07 .02

☐ 571 Mike Maddux .10 .05 .01
☐ 572 Jeff McKnight .10 .05 .01
☐ 573 Eddie Murray .20 .09 .03
☐ 574 Charlie O'Brien .10 .05 .01
☐ 575 Joe Orsulak .10 .05 .01
☐ 576 Bret Saberhagen .15 .07 .02
☐ 577 Pete Schourek .10 .05 .01
☐ 578 Dave Telgheder .10 .05 .01
☐ 579 Ryan Thompson .15 .07 .02
☐ 580 Anthony Young .10 .05 .01
☐ 581 Ruben Amaro .10 .05 .01
☐ 582 Larry Andersen .10 .05 .01
☐ 583 Kim Batiste .10 .05 .01
☐ 584 Wes Chamberlain .10 .05 .01
☐ 585 Darren Daulton .20 .09 .03
☐ 586 Mariano Duncan .10 .05 .01
☐ 587 Lenny Dykstra .20 .09 .03
☐ 588 Jim Eisenreich .10 .05 .01
☐ 589 Tommy Greene .10 .05 .01
☐ 590 Dave Hollins .20 .09 .03
☐ 591 Pete Incaviglia .10 .05 .01
☐ 592 Danny Jackson .10 .05 .01
☐ 593 Ricky Jordan .10 .05 .01
☐ 594 John Kruk .20 .09 .03
☐ 595 Roger Mason .10 .05 .01
☐ 596 Mickey Morandini .10 .05 .01
☐ 597 Terry Mulholland .10 .05 .01
☐ 598 Todd Pratt .10 .05 .01
☐ 599 Ben Rivera .10 .05 .01
☐ 600 Curt Schilling .10 .05 .01
☐ 601 Kevin Stocker .15 .07 .02
☐ 602 Milt Thompson .10 .05 .01
☐ 603 David West .10 .05 .01
☐ 604 Mitch Williams .10 .05 .01
☐ 605 Jay Bell .15 .07 .02
☐ 606 Dave Clark .10 .05 .01
☐ 607 Steve Cooke .10 .05 .01
☐ 608 Tom Foley .10 .05 .01
☐ 609 Carlos Garcia .10 .05 .01
☐ 610 Joel Johnston .10 .05 .01
☐ 611 Jeff King .10 .05 .01
☐ 612 Al Martin .10 .05 .01
☐ 613 Lloyd McClendon .10 .05 .01
☐ 614 Orlando Merced .15 .07 .02
☐ 615 Blas Minor .10 .05 .01
☐ 616 Denny Neagle .10 .05 .01
☐ 617 Mark Petkovsek .15 .07 .02
☐ 618 Tom Prince .10 .05 .01
☐ 619 Don Slaught .10 .05 .01
☐ 620 Zane Smith .10 .05 .01
☐ 621 Randy Tomlin .10 .05 .01
☐ 622 Andy Van Slyke .20 .09 .03
☐ 623 Paul Wagner .10 .05 .01
☐ 624 Tim Wakefield .10 .05 .01
☐ 625 Bob Walk .10 .05 .01
☐ 626 Kevin Young .10 .05 .01
☐ 627 Luis Alicea .10 .05 .01
☐ 628 Rene Arocha .15 .07 .02
☐ 629 Rod Brewer .10 .05 .01
☐ 630 Rheal Cormier .10 .05 .01
☐ 631 Bernard Gilkey .10 .05 .01
☐ 632 Lee Guetterman .10 .05 .01
☐ 633 Gregg Jefferies .20 .09 .03
☐ 634 Brian Jordan .15 .07 .02
☐ 635 Les Lancaster .10 .05 .01
☐ 636 Ray Lankford .20 .09 .03
☐ 637 Rob Murphy .10 .05 .01
☐ 638 Omar Olivares .10 .05 .01
☐ 639 Jose Oquendo .10 .05 .01
☐ 640 Donovan Osborne .10 .05 .01
☐ 641 Tom Pagnozzi .10 .05 .01
☐ 642 Erik Pappas .10 .05 .01
☐ 643 Geronimo Pena .10 .05 .01
☐ 644 Mike Perez .10 .05 .01
☐ 645 Gerald Perry .10 .05 .01
☐ 646 Ozzie Smith .60 .25 .08
☐ 647 Bob Tewksbury .10 .05 .01
☐ 648 Allen Watson .10 .05 .01
☐ 649 Mark Whiten .15 .07 .02
☐ 650 Tracy Woodson .10 .05 .01
☐ 651 Todd Zeile .15 .07 .02
☐ 652 Andy Ashby .10 .05 .01
☐ 653 Brad Ausmus .10 .05 .01
☐ 654 Billy Bean .10 .05 .01
☐ 655 Derek Bell .15 .07 .02
☐ 656 Andy Benes .15 .07 .02
☐ 657 Doug Brocail .10 .05 .01
☐ 658 Jarvis Brown .10 .05 .01
☐ 659 Archi Cianfrocco .10 .05 .01
☐ 660 Phil Clark .10 .05 .01
☐ 661 Mark Davis .10 .05 .01
☐ 662 Jeff Gardner .10 .05 .01
☐ 663 Pat Gomez .10 .05 .01
☐ 664 Ricky Gutierrez .10 .05 .01
☐ 665 Tony Gwynn .75 .35 .09
☐ 666 Gene Harris .10 .05 .01
☐ 667 Kevin Higgins .10 .05 .01
☐ 668 Trevor Hoffman .10 .05 .01
☐ 669 Pedro Martinez .20 .09 .03
☐ 670 Tim Mauser .10 .05 .01
☐ 671 Melvin Nieves .20 .09 .03
☐ 672 Phil Plantier .15 .07 .02
☐ 673 Frank Seminara .10 .05 .01
☐ 674 Craig Shipley .10 .05 .01
☐ 675 Kerry Taylor .10 .05 .01
☐ 676 Tim Teufel .10 .05 .01
☐ 677 Guillermo Velasquez .10 .05 .01
☐ 678 Wally Whitehurst .10 .05 .01
☐ 679 Tim Worrell .10 .05 .01
☐ 680 Rod Beck .15 .07 .02
☐ 681 Mike Benjamin .10 .05 .01
☐ 682 Todd Benzinger .10 .05 .01
☐ 683 Bud Black .10 .05 .01
☐ 684 Barry Bonds 1.25 .55 .16
☐ 685 Jeff Brantley .10 .05 .01
☐ 686 Dave Burba .10 .05 .01
☐ 687 John Burkett .15 .07 .02
☐ 688 Mark Carreon .10 .05 .01
☐ 689 Will Clark .40 .18 .05
☐ 690 Royce Clayton .15 .07 .02
☐ 691 Bryan Hickerson .10 .05 .01
☐ 692 Mike Jackson .10 .05 .01
☐ 693 Darren Lewis .10 .05 .01
☐ 694 Kirt Manwaring .10 .05 .01
☐ 695 Dave Martinez .10 .05 .01
☐ 696 Willie McGee .10 .05 .01
☐ 697 John Patterson .10 .05 .01
☐ 698 Jeff Reed .10 .05 .01
☐ 699 Kevin Rogers .10 .05 .01
☐ 700 Scott Sanderson .10 .05 .01
☐ 701 Steve Scarsone .10 .05 .01
☐ 702 Billy Swift .10 .05 .01
☐ 703 Robby Thompson .10 .05 .01
☐ 704 Matt Williams .50 .23 .06
☐ 705 Trevor Wilson .10 .05 .01
☐ 706 Brave New World .10 .05 .01
Fred McGriff
Ron Gant
David Justice
☐ 707 1-2 Punch .10 .05 .01
John Olerud
Paul Molitor
☐ 708 American Heat .10 .05 .01
Mike Mussina
Jack McDowell
☐ 709 Together Again .10 .05 .01

		MINT	EXC	G-VG
	Lou Whitaker Alan Trammell			
☐ 710	Lone Star Lumber	.30	.14	.04
	Rafael Palmeiro Juan Gonzalez			
☐ 711	Batmen	.10	.05	.01
	Brett Butler Tony Gwyn			
☐ 712	Twin Peaks	.40	.18	.05
	Kirby Puckett Chuck Knoblauch			
☐ 713	Back to Back	.50	.23	.06
	Mike Piazza Eric Karros			
☐ 714	Checklist 1-130	.10	.05	.01
☐ 715	Checklist 131-261	.10	.05	.01
☐ 716	Checklist 262-392	.10	.05	.01
☐ 717	Checklist 393-522	.10	.05	.01
☐ 718	Checklist 523-652	.10	.05	.01
☐ 719	Checklist 653-720/Inserts	.10	.05	.01
☐ 720	Insert Checklist	.10	.05	.01

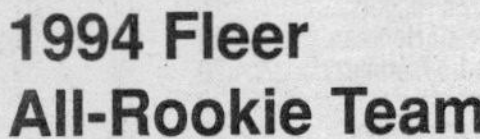

1994 Fleer All-Rookie Team

Collectors could redeem an All-Rookie Team Exchange card by mail for this nine-card set of top 1994 rookies at each position as chosen by Fleer. None of these players were in the basic 1994 Fleer set. The exchange card was randomly inserted into all pack types.

	MINT	EXC	G-VG
COMPLETE SET (9)	15.00	6.75	1.90
COMMON CARD (M1-M9)	1.00	.45	.13
☐ M1 Kurt Abbott	1.50	.65	.19
☐ M2 Rich Becker	1.00	.45	.13
☐ M3 Carlos Delgado	5.00	2.30	.60
☐ M4 Jorge Fabregas	1.00	.45	.13
☐ M5 Bob Hamelin	3.00	1.35	.40
☐ M6 John Hudek	3.00	1.35	.40
☐ M7 Tim Hyers	1.00	.45	.13
☐ M8 Luis S.Lopez	1.00	.45	.13
☐ M9 James Mouton	1.00	.45	.13
☐ NNO Exp. All-Rookie Exch.	3.00	1.35	.40

1994 Fleer All-Stars

Fleer issued this 50-card set in 1994, to commemorate the All-Stars of the 1993 season. The cards were exclusively avail able in the Fleer wax packs at a rate of one in two. The set features 25 American League (1-25) and 25 National League (26-50) All-Stars. The cards measure standard size. The full-bleed fronts feature color action player cut-out photos with an American flag background. The player's name is stamped in gold foil along the bottom edge adjacent to a 1993 All-Stars Game logo. The borderless backs carry a

similar flag background with a player head shot near the bottom. The player's name and career highlights round out the back.

	MINT	EXC	G-VG
COMPLETE SET (50)	25.00	11.50	3.10
COMMON CARD (1-50)	.25	.11	.03
☐ 1 Roberto Alomar	1.00	.45	.13
☐ 2 Carlos Baerga	.60	.25	.08
☐ 3 Albert Belle	1.25	.55	.16
☐ 4 Wade Boggs	.50	.23	.06
☐ 5 Joe Carter	.60	.25	.08
☐ 6 Scott Cooper	.25	.11	.03
☐ 7 Cecil Fielder	.50	.23	.06
☐ 8 Travis Fryman	.50	.23	.06
☐ 9 Juan Gonzalez	1.25	.55	.16
☐ 10 Ken Griffey Jr.	4.00	1.80	.50
☐ 11 Pat Hentgen	.35	.16	.04
☐ 12 Randy Johnson	.50	.23	.06
☐ 13 Jimmy Key	.35	.16	.04
☐ 14 Mark Langston	.25	.11	.03
☐ 15 Jack McDowell	.50	.23	.06
☐ 16 Paul Molitor	.60	.25	.08
☐ 17 Jeff Montgomery	.25	.11	.03
☐ 18 Mike Mussina	.75	.35	.09
☐ 19 John Olerud	.50	.23	.06
☐ 20 Kirby Puckett	1.50	.65	.19
☐ 21 Cal Ripken	3.00	1.35	.40
☐ 22 Ivan Rodriguez	.50	.23	.06
☐ 23 Frank Thomas	4.00	1.80	.50
☐ 24 Greg Vaughn	.25	.11	.03
☐ 25 Duane Ward	.25	.11	.03
☐ 26 Steve Avery	.50	.23	.06
☐ 27 Rod Beck	.35	.16	.04
☐ 28 Jay Bell	.25	.11	.03
☐ 29 Andy Benes	.35	.16	.04
☐ 30 Jeff Blauser	.25	.11	.03
☐ 31 Barry Bonds	1.50	.65	.19
☐ 32 Bobby Bonilla	.35	.16	.04
☐ 33 John Burkett	.35	.16	.04
☐ 34 Darren Daulton	.50	.23	.06
☐ 35 Andres Galarraga	.50	.23	.06
☐ 36 Tom Glavine	.50	.23	.06
☐ 37 Mark Grace	.35	.16	.04
☐ 38 Marquis Grissom	.50	.23	.06
☐ 39 Tony Gwynn	1.00	.45	.13
☐ 40 Bryan Harvey	.25	.11	.03
☐ 41 Dave Hollins	.35	.16	.04
☐ 42 David Justice	.60	.25	.08
☐ 43 Darryl Kile	.25	.11	.03
☐ 44 John Kruk	.35	.16	.04
☐ 45 Barry Larkin	.50	.23	.06
☐ 46 Terry Mulholland	.25	.11	.03
☐ 47 Mike Piazza	2.00	.90	.25
☐ 48 Ryne Sandberg	1.25	.55	.16
☐ 49 Gary Sheffield	.50	.23	.06
☐ 50 John Smoltz	.35	.16	.04

1994 Fleer Award Winners

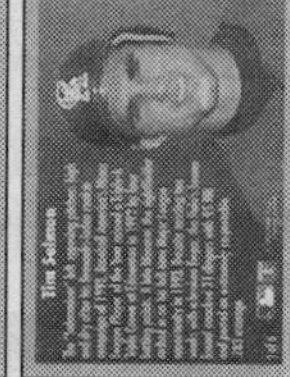

Randomly inserted in foil packs at a rate of one in 37, this six-card standard-size set spotlights six outstanding players who received awards. Inside beige borders, the horizontal fronts feature three views of the same color player photo. The words "Fleer Award Winners" and the player's name are printed in gold foil toward the bottom. The backs have a similar design to the fronts, only with one color player cutout and a season summary.

	MINT	EXC	G-VG
COMPLETE SET (6)	12.00	5.50	1.50
COMMON CARD (1-6)	.50	.23	.06
☐ 1 Frank Thomas AL Most Valuable Player	6.00	2.70	.75
☐ 2 Barry Bonds NL Most Valuable Player	2.50	1.15	.30
☐ 3 Jack McDowell AL Pitcher of the Year	.50	.23	.06
☐ 4 Greg Maddux NL Pitcher of the Year	1.50	.65	.19
☐ 5 Tim Salmon AL Rookie of the Year	.90	.40	.11
☐ 6 Mike Piazza NL Rookie of the Year	3.00	1.35	.40

1994 Fleer Golden Moments

Standard-size and jumbo-size (3 1/2" by 5") Golden Moments were distributed in various forms. The standard-size cards were issued one per blue retail jumbo pack. A shrink-wrapped package containing a jumbo set was issued one per Fleer hobby case. Jumbos were later issued for retail purposes. The front feature borderless color player action photos. The player's name, along with his golden moment accomplishment, appear in gold foil at the bottom. The set's title appears in gold foil at the top. The back carries another borderless color player photo, which fades on one side into a color background for the white-lettered narrative

of the player's golden moment. The production number out of a total of 10,000 appears near the bottom of the jumbos. The standard-size cards are not individually numbered.

	MINT	EXC	G-VG
COMPLETE SET (10)	40.00	18.00	5.00
COMMON CARD (1-10)	.60	.25	.08
*JUMBO GM's: SAME VALUES AS BELOW			
☐ 1 Mark Whiten	.60	.25	.08
☐ 2 Carlos Baerga	2.00	.90	.25
☐ 3 Dave Winfield	.60	.25	.08
☐ 4 Ken Griffey Jr.	12.00	5.50	1.50
☐ 5 Bo Jackson	.60	.25	.08
☐ 6 George Brett	5.00	2.30	.60
☐ 7 Nolan Ryan	12.00	5.50	1.50
☐ 8 Fred McGriff	2.00	.90	.25
☐ 9 Frank Thomas	12.00	5.50	1.50
☐ 10 Chris Bosio Jim Abbott Darryl Kile	.60	.25	.08

1994 Fleer League Leaders

Randomly inserted in all pack types at arate of one in 17, this 28-card standard-size set features six statistical leaders each for the American (1-6) and the National (7-12) Leagues. Inside a beige border, the fronts feature a color action player cutout superimposed on a black-and-white player photo. The player's name and the set title are gold foil stamped in the bottom border, while the player's achievement is printed vertically along the right edge of the picture. The horizontal backs have a color close-up shot on the left portion and a player summary on the right.

	MINT	EXC	G-VG
COMPLETE SET (12)	10.00	4.50	1.25
COMMON CARD (1-12)	.25	.11	.03
☐ 1 John Olerud AL Batting Crown	.45	.20	.06
☐ 2 Albert Belle AL RBI Leader	1.75	.80	.22
☐ 3 Rafael Palmeiro AL Runs Scored Leader	.45	.20	.06
☐ 4 Kenny Lofton AL Stolen Base Leader	1.50	.65	.19
☐ 5 Jack McDowell AL Winningest Pitcher	.45	.20	.06
☐ 6 Kevin Appier AL ERA Leader	.25	.11	.03
☐ 7 Andres Galarraga NL Batting Crown	.45	.20	.06
☐ 8 Barry Bonds NL RBI Leader	2.50	1.15	.30
☐ 9 Lenny Dykstra NL Runs Scored Leader	.45	.20	.06
☐ 10 Chuck Carr NL Stolen Base Leader	.25	.11	.03
☐ 11 Tom Glavine NL Winningest Pitcher	.45	.20	.06
☐ 12 Greg Maddux NL ERA Leader	1.50	.65	.19

1994 Fleer Lumber Company

Randomly inserted in jumbo packs at a rate of one in five, this ten-card standard-size set features the best hitters in the game. The full-bleed fronts have a color action player cutout on a wood background. The player's name, team name, and the set title "Lumber Company" appear in an oval-shaped seal burned in the wood, just as one would find on a bat. On a background consisting of wooden bats laying on infield sand, the backs present a color headshot and a player profile on a ghosted panel. The cards are numbered alphabetically.

	MINT	EXC	G-VG
COMPLETE SET (10)	15.00	6.75	1.90
COMMON CARD (1-10)	.50	.23	.06
☐ 1 Albert Belle	1.75	.80	.22
☐ 2 Barry Bonds	2.50	1.15	.30
☐ 3 Ron Gant	.50	.23	.06
☐ 4 Juan Gonzalez	2.00	.90	.25
☐ 5 Ken Griffey Jr.	6.00	2.70	.75
☐ 6 David Justice	.90	.40	.11
☐ 7 Fred McGriff	.90	.40	.11
☐ 8 Rafael Palmeiro	.50	.23	.06
☐ 9 Frank Thomas	6.00	2.70	.75
☐ 10 Matt Williams	1.25	.55	.16

1994 Fleer Major League Prospects

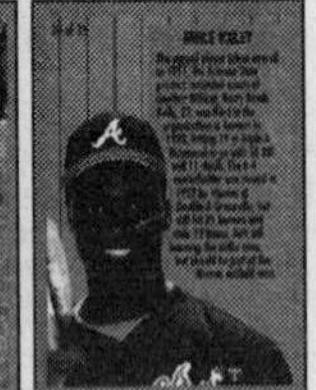

Randomly inserted in all pack types at a rate of one in six, this 35-card standard-size set showcases some of the outstanding young players in Major League Baseball. Inside beige borders, the fronts display color action photos superimposed over ghosted versions of the team logos. The set title and the player's name are gold foil stamped across the bottom of the card. On a beige background with thin blue pin-stripes, the backs show a color player cutout and, on a powder blue panel, a player profile. The cards are numbered on the back "X of 35."

	MINT	EXC	G-VG
COMPLETE SET (35)	20.00	9.00	2.50
COMMON CARD (1-35)	.25	.11	.03
☐ 1 Kurt Abbott	1.00	.45	.13
☐ 2 Brian Anderson	2.50	1.15	.30
☐ 3 Rich Aude	.75	.35	.09
☐ 4 Cory Bailey	.50	.23	.06
☐ 5 Danny Bautista	.50	.23	.06
☐ 6 Marty Cordova	.75	.35	.09
☐ 7 Tripp Cromer	.25	.11	.03
☐ 8 Midre Cummings	1.00	.45	.13
☐ 9 Carlos Delgado	3.00	1.35	.40
☐ 10 Steve Dreyer	.25	.11	.03
☐ 11 Steve Dunn	.50	.23	.06
☐ 12 Jeff Granger	1.25	.55	.16
☐ 13 Tyrone Hill	.50	.23	.06
☐ 14 Denny Hocking	.75	.35	.09
☐ 15 John Hope	.50	.23	.06
☐ 16 Butch Huskey	.50	.23	.06
☐ 17 Miguel Jimenez	.50	.23	.06
☐ 18 Chipper Jones	2.50	1.15	.30
☐ 19 Steve Karsay	.75	.35	.09
☐ 20 Mike Kelly	1.25	.55	.16
☐ 21 Mike Lieberthal	.50	.23	.06
☐ 22 Albie Lopez	.75	.35	.09
☐ 23 Jeff McNeely	.50	.23	.06

		MINT	EXC	G-VG
☐ 24	Dan Miceli	.50	.23	.06
☐ 25	Nate Minchey	.50	.23	.06
☐ 26	Marc Newfield	1.00	.45	.13
☐ 27	Darren Oliver	.50	.23	.06
☐ 28	Luis Ortiz	.25	.11	.03
☐ 29	Curtis Pride	1.00	.45	.13
☐ 30	Roger Salkeld	.50	.23	.06
☐ 31	Scott Sanders	.25	.11	.03
☐ 32	Dave Staton	.50	.23	.06
☐ 33	Salomon Torres	.50	.23	.06
☐ 34	Steve Trachsel	1.00	.45	.13
☐ 35	Chris Turner	.25	.11	.03

1994 Fleer Pro-Visions

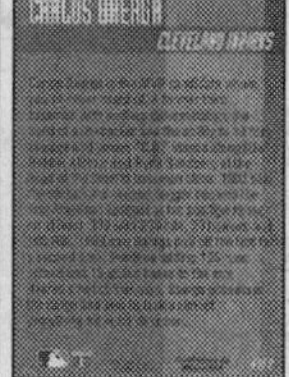

Randomly inserted in all pack types at a rate of one in 12, this nine-card standard-size set features on its fronts colorful artistic player caricatures with surrealistic backgrounds drawn by illustrator Wayne Still. The player's name is gold foil stamped at the lower right corner. When all nine cards are placed in order in a collector sheet, the backgrounds fit together to form a composite. The backs shade from one bright color to another and present career summaries.

		MINT	EXC	G-VG
COMPLETE SET (9)		5.00	2.30	.60
COMMON CARD (1-9)		.25	.11	.03
☐ 1	Darren Daulton	.25	.11	.03
☐ 2	John Olerud	.25	.11	.03
☐ 3	Matt Williams	.75	.35	.09
☐ 4	Carlos Baerga	.60	.25	.08
☐ 5	Ozzie Smith	.75	.35	.09
☐ 6	Juan Gonzalez	1.25	.55	.16
☐ 7	Jack McDowell	.25	.11	.03
☐ 8	Mike Piazza	2.00	.90	.25
☐ 9	Tony Gwynn	1.00	.45	.13

1994 Fleer Rookie Sensations

Randomly inserted in jumbo packs at a rate of one in four, this 20-card standard-size set features outstanding rookies. The fronts are "double exposed," with a player action cutout superimposed over a second photo. The team logo also appears in the team

color-coded background. The set title is gold foil stamped toward the top, and the player's name is gold foil stamped on a team color-coded ribbon toward the bottom. On a white background featuring a ghosted version of the team logo, the backs have a player cutout photo and a season summary.

		MINT	EXC	G-VG
COMPLETE SET (20)		20.00	9.00	2.50
COMMON CARD (1-20)		.50	.23	.06
☐ 1	Rene Arocha	.50	.23	.06
☐ 2	Jason Bere	2.00	.90	.25
☐ 3	Jeromy Burnitz	.50	.23	.06
☐ 4	Chuck Carr	.50	.23	.06
☐ 5	Jeff Conine	.50	.23	.06
☐ 6	Steve Cooke	.50	.23	.06
☐ 7	Cliff Floyd	2.50	1.15	.30
☐ 8	Jeffrey Hammonds	2.00	.90	.25
☐ 9	Wayne Kirby	.50	.23	.06
☐ 10	Mike Lansing	.50	.23	.06
☐ 11	Al Martin	.50	.23	.06
☐ 12	Greg McMichael	.50	.23	.06
☐ 13	Troy Neel	.50	.23	.06
☐ 14	Mike Piazza	8.00	3.60	1.00
☐ 15	Armando Reynoso	.50	.23	.06
☐ 16	Kirk Rueter	.50	.23	.06
☐ 17	Tim Salmon	2.25	1.00	.30
☐ 18	Aaron Sele	1.25	.55	.16
☐ 19	J.T. Snow	.50	.23	.06
☐ 20	Kevin Stocker	.50	.23	.06

1994 Fleer Tim Salmon

Spotlighting American League Rookie of the Year Tim Salmon, this 15-card standard size set was issued in two forms. Cards 1-12 were randomly inserted in packs (one in eight) and 13-15 were available through a

mail-in offer. Ten wrappers and 1.50 were necessary to acquire the mail-ins. Salmon autographed more than 2,000 of his cards. The cards feature a borderless all-foil, spectra-etched design and UV coating on both sides. The fronts feature cutout color action shots of Salmon that are superposed upon the silvery foil-and-etched design. His name appears in gold lettering near the bottom, along with the words "A.L. Rookie of the Year" in silver lettering within a gold bar. The back carries a color photo of Salmon on the right side. His name appears in ocher lettering in the upper left, followed below by career highlights in black lettering. The cards are numbered on the back.

	MINT	EXC	G-VG
COMPLETE SET (12)	40.00	18.00	5.00
COMMON SALMON (1-12)	4.00	1.80	.50
COMMON MAIL-IN (13-15)	5.00	2.30	.60

	MINT	EXC	G-VG
☐ 1 Tim Salmon (Watching flight of ball after hit)	4.00	1.80	.50
☐ 2 Tim Salmon (Trotting in to catch ball)	4.00	1.80	.50
☐ 3 Tim Salmon (Follow through, weight on front leg)	4.00	1.80	.50
☐ 4 Tim Salmon (Middle of swing, horizontal pose)	4.00	1.80	.50
☐ 5 Tim Salmon (Sliding into base)	4.00	1.80	.50
☐ 6 Tim Salmon (Pose swing, end of bat in camera angle)	4.00	1.80	.50
☐ 7 Tim Salmon (Running with shades on)	4.00	1.80	.50
☐ 8 Tim Salmon (Bat cocked, awaiting pitch)	4.00	1.80	.50
☐ 9 Tim Salmon (Adjusting batting gloves, bat under arm)	4.00	1.80	.50
☐ 10 Tim Salmon (Running to base)	4.00	1.80	.50
☐ 11 Tim Salmon (Awaiting pitch, shot from left side with catcher in view)	4.00	1.80	.50
☐ 12 Tim Salmon (Ready to play)	4.00	1.80	.50
☐ 13 Tim Salmon (Awaiting a pitch)	5.00	2.30	.60
☐ 14 Tim Salmon (Fielding)	5.00	2.30	.60
☐ 15 Tim Salmon (Running the bases)	5.00	2.30	.60
☐ AU Tim Salmon AU (Certified autograph)	70.00	32.00	8.75

1994 Fleer Smoke 'n Heat

Randomly inserted in wax packs at a rate of one in 36, this 12-card standard-size set

showcases the best pitchers in the game. On the fronts, color action player cutouts are superimposed on a red-and-gold fiery background that has a metallic sheen to it. The set title "Smoke 'n Heat" is printed in large block lettering. On a reddish marbleized background, the backs have another player cutout and season summary.

	MINT	EXC	G-VG
COMPLETE SET (12)	80.00	36.00	10.00
COMMON CARD (1-12)	2.00	.90	.25

	MINT	EXC	G-VG
☐ 1 Roger Clemens	10.00	4.50	1.25
☐ 2 David Cone	3.00	1.35	.40
☐ 3 Juan Guzman	2.00	.90	.25
☐ 4 Pete Harnisch	2.00	.90	.25
☐ 5 Randy Johnson	3.00	1.35	.40
☐ 6 Mark Langston	2.00	.90	.25
☐ 7 Greg Maddux	10.00	4.50	1.25
☐ 8 Mike Mussina	6.00	2.70	.75
☐ 9 Jose Rijo	2.00	.90	.25
☐ 10 Nolan Ryan	40.00	18.00	5.00
☐ 11 Curt Schilling	2.00	.90	.25
☐ 12 John Smoltz	3.00	1.35	.40

1994 Fleer Team Leaders

Randomly inserted in all pack types, this 28-card standard-size set features Fleer's selected top player from each of the 28 major league teams. The fronts feature a action player cutout superposed on a larger close-up photo with a team color-coded background, all inside beige borders. The set title, player's name, team name, and position are printed in gold foil across the bottom. On a white background with a

ghosted version of the team logo, the horizontal backs carry a second color player cutout and a summary of the player's performance. The card numbering is arranged alphabetically by city according to the American (1-14) and the National (15-28) Leagues.

	MINT	EXC	G-VG
COMPLETE SET (28)	25.00	11.50	3.10
COMMON CARD (1-28)	.50	.23	.06

	MINT	EXC	G-VG
☐ 1 Cal Ripken	4.50	2.00	.55
☐ 2 Mo Vaughn	.75	.35	.09
☐ 3 Tim Salmon	.90	.40	.11
☐ 4 Frank Thomas	6.00	2.70	.75
☐ 5 Carlos Baerga	.90	.40	.11
☐ 6 Cecil Fielder	.75	.35	.09
☐ 7 Brian McRae	.75	.35	.09
☐ 8 Greg Vaughn	.50	.23	.06
☐ 9 Kirby Puckett	2.50	1.15	.30
☐ 10 Don Mattingly	2.50	1.15	.30
☐ 11 Mark McGwire	.50	.23	.06
☐ 12 Ken Griffey Jr.	6.00	2.70	.75
☐ 13 Juan Gonzalez	2.00	.90	.25
☐ 14 Paul Molitor	.90	.40	.11
☐ 15 David Justice	.90	.40	.11
☐ 16 Ryne Sandberg	2.00	.90	.25
☐ 17 Barry Larkin	.75	.35	.09
☐ 18 Andres Galarraga	.75	.35	.09
☐ 19 Gary Sheffield	.75	.35	.09
☐ 20 Jeff Bagwell	3.00	1.35	.40
☐ 21 Mike Piazza	3.00	1.35	.40
☐ 22 Marquis Grissom	.75	.35	.09
☐ 23 Bobby Bonilla	.50	.23	.06
☐ 24 Lenny Dykstra	.75	.35	.09
☐ 25 Jay Bell	.50	.23	.06
☐ 26 Gregg Jefferies	.75	.35	.09
☐ 27 Tony Gwynn	1.50	.65	.19
☐ 28 Will Clark	.90	.40	.11

1994 Fleer Update

This 200-card standard-size set highlights traded players in their new uniforms and promising young rookies. A ten card Diamond Tribute set was included in each factory set for a total of 210 cards. The cards are numbered on the back, grouped alphabetically by team by league as follows: Baltimore Orioles (1-8), Boston Red Sox (9-14), California Angels (15-22), Chicago White Sox (23-30), Cleveland Indians (31-38), Detroit Tigers (39-46), Kansas City Royals (47-51), Milwaukee Brewers (52-58), Minnesota Twins (59-66), New York Yankees (67-71), Oakland Athletics (72-78), Seattle Mariners (79-88), Texas Rangers (89-95), Toronto Blue Jays (96-100), Atlanta Braves (101-105), Chicago Cubs (106-113), Cincinnati Reds (114-121), Colorado Rockies (122-131), Florida Marlins (132-139), Houston Astros (140-147), Los Angeles Dodgers (148-151), Montreal Expos (152-155), New York Mets (156-163), Philadelphia Phillies (164-171), Pittsburgh Pirates (172-177), St. Louis Cardinals (178-183), San Diego Padres (184-191), and San Francisco Giants (192-198). Rookie Cards include Brian Anderson, John Hudek, Chan Ho Park, Alex Rodriguez and Will VanLandingham.

	MINT	EXC	G-VG
COMPLETE FACT.SET (210)	25.00	11.50	3.10
COMPLETE SET (200)	18.00	8.00	2.30
COMMON CARD (U1-U200)	.15	.07	.02

	MINT	EXC	G-VG
☐ U1 Mark Eichhorn	.15	.07	.02
☐ U2 Sid Fernandez	.15	.07	.02
☐ U3 Leo Gomez	.15	.07	.02
☐ U4 Mike Oquist	.15	.07	.02
☐ U5 Rafael Palmeiro	.30	.14	.04
☐ U6 Chris Sabo	.15	.07	.02
☐ U7 Dwight Smith	.15	.07	.02
☐ U8 Lee Smith	.30	.14	.04
☐ U9 Damon Berryhill	.15	.07	.02
☐ U10 Wes Chamberlain	.15	.07	.02
☐ U11 Gar Finnvold	.15	.07	.02
☐ U12 Chris Howard	.15	.07	.02
☐ U13 Tim Naehring	.15	.07	.02
☐ U14 Otis Nixon	.15	.07	.02
☐ U15 Brian Anderson	2.00	.90	.25
☐ U16 Jorge Fabregas	.15	.07	.02
☐ U17 Rex Hudler	.15	.07	.02
☐ U18 Bo Jackson	.30	.14	.04
☐ U19 Mark Leiter	.15	.07	.02
☐ U20 Spike Owen	.15	.07	.02
☐ U21 Harold Reynolds	.15	.07	.02
☐ U22 Chris Turner	.15	.07	.02
☐ U23 Dennis Cook	.15	.07	.02
☐ U24 Jose DeLeon	.15	.07	.02
☐ U25 Julio Franco	.20	.09	.03
☐ U26 Joe Hall	.15	.07	.02
☐ U27 Darrin Jackson	.15	.07	.02
☐ U28 Dane Johnson	.15	.07	.02
☐ U29 Norberto Martin	.15	.07	.02
☐ U30 Scott Sanderson	.15	.07	.02
☐ U31 Jason Grimsley	.15	.07	.02
☐ U32 Dennis Martinez	.20	.09	.03
☐ U33 Jack Morris	.30	.14	.04
☐ U34 Eddie Murray	.30	.14	.04
☐ U35 Chad Ogea	.20	.09	.03
☐ U36 Tony Pena	.15	.07	.02
☐ U37 Paul Shuey	.20	.09	.03
☐ U38 Omar Vizquel	.15	.07	.02
☐ U39 Danny Bautista	.20	.09	.03
☐ U40 Tim Belcher	.15	.07	.02
☐ U41 Joe Boever	.15	.07	.02
☐ U42 Storm Davis	.15	.07	.02
☐ U43 Junior Felix	.15	.07	.02
☐ U44 Mike Gardiner	.15	.07	.02
☐ U45 Buddy Groom	.15	.07	.02
☐ U46 Juan Samuel	.15	.07	.02
☐ U47 Vince Coleman	.15	.07	.02
☐ U48 Bob Hamelin	.30	.14	.04
☐ U49 Dave Henderson	.15	.07	.02

□	U50	Rusty Meacham	.15	.07	.02
□	U51	Terry Shumpert	.15	.07	.02
□	U52	Jeff Bronkey	.15	.07	.02
□	U53	Alex Diaz	.15	.07	.02
□	U54	Brian Harper	.15	.07	.02
□	U55	Jose Mercedes	.15	.07	.02
□	U56	Jody Reed	.15	.07	.02
□	U57	Bob Scanlan	.15	.07	.02
□	U58	Turner Ward	.15	.07	.02
□	U59	Rich Becker	.20	.09	.03
□	U60	Alex Cole	.15	.07	.02
□	U61	Denny Hocking	.15	.07	.02
□	U62	Scott Leius	.15	.07	.02
□	U63	Pat Mahomes	.15	.07	.02
□	U64	Carlos Pulido	.40	.18	.05
□	U65	Dave Stevens	.15	.07	.02
□	U66	Matt Walbeck	.15	.07	.02
□	U67	Xavier Hernandez	.15	.07	.02
□	U68	Sterling Hitchcock	.20	.09	.03
□	U69	Terry Mulholland	.15	.07	.02
□	U70	Luis Polonia	.15	.07	.02
□	U71	Gerald Williams	.15	.07	.02
□	U72	Mark Acre	.40	.18	.05
□	U73	Geronimo Berroa	.15	.07	.02
□	U74	Rickey Henderson	.30	.14	.04
□	U75	Stan Javier	.15	.07	.02
□	U76	Steve Karsay	.15	.07	.02
□	U77	Carlos Reyes	.15	.07	.02
□	U78	Bill Taylor	.15	.07	.02
□	U79	Eric Anthony	.15	.07	.02
□	U80	Bobby Ayala	.15	.07	.02
□	U81	Tim Davis	.15	.07	.02
□	U82	Felix Fermin	.15	.07	.02
□	U83	Reggie Jefferson	.15	.07	.02
□	U84	Keith Mitchell	.15	.07	.02
□	U85	Bill Risley	.15	.07	.02
□	U86	Alex Rodriguez	10.00	4.50	1.25
□	U87	Roger Salkeld	.15	.07	.02
□	U88	Dan Wilson	.15	.07	.02
□	U89	Cris Carpenter	.15	.07	.02
□	U90	Will Clark	1.00	.45	.13
□	U91	Jeff Frye	.15	.07	.02
□	U92	Rick Helling	.15	.07	.02
□	U93	Chris James	.15	.07	.02
□	U94	Oddibe McDowell	.15	.07	.02
□	U95	Billy Ripken	.15	.07	.02
□	U96	Carlos Delgado	1.25	.55	.16
□	U97	Alex Gonzalez	.60	.25	.08
□	U98	Shawn Green	1.25	.55	.16
□	U99	Darren Hall	.15	.07	.02
□	U100	Mike Huff	.15	.07	.02
□	U101	Mike Kelly	.20	.09	.03
□	U102	Roberto Kelly	.15	.07	.02
□	U103	Charlie O'Brien	.15	.07	.02
□	U104	Jose Oliva	.50	.23	.06
□	U105	Gregg Olson	.15	.07	.02
□	U106	Willie Banks	.15	.07	.02
□	U107	Jim Bullinger	.15	.07	.02
□	U108	Chuck Crim	.15	.07	.02
□	U109	Shawon Dunston	.15	.07	.02
□	U110	Karl Rhodes	.15	.07	.02
□	U111	Steve Trachsel	1.00	.45	.13
□	U112	Anthony Young	.15	.07	.02
□	U113	Eddie Zambrano	.15	.07	.02
□	U114	Bret Boone	.30	.14	.04
□	U115	Jeff Brantley	.15	.07	.02
□	U116	Hector Carrasco	.15	.07	.02
□	U117	Tony Fernandez	.15	.07	.02
□	U118	Tim Fortugno	.15	.07	.02
□	U119	Erik Hanson	.15	.07	.02
□	U120	Chuck McElroy	.15	.07	.02
□	U121	Deion Sanders	1.25	.55	.16
□	U122	Ellis Burks	.20	.09	.03
□	U123	Marvin Freeman	.15	.07	.02
□	U124	Mike Harkey	.15	.07	.02
□	U125	Howard Johnson	.15	.07	.02
□	U126	Mike Kingery	.15	.07	.02
□	U127	Nelson Liriano	.15	.07	.02
□	U128	Marcus Moore	.15	.07	.02
□	U129	Mike Munoz	.15	.07	.02
□	U130	Kevin Ritz	.15	.07	.02
□	U131	Walt Weiss	.15	.07	.02
□	U132	Kurt Abbott	.75	.35	.09
□	U133	Jerry Browne	.15	.07	.02
□	U134	Greg Colbrunn	.15	.07	.02
□	U135	Jeremy Hernandez	.15	.07	.02
□	U136	Dave Magadan	.15	.07	.02
□	U137	Kurt Miller	.15	.07	.02
□	U138	Robb Nen	.15	.07	.02
□	U139	Jesus Tavarez	.40	.18	.05
□	U140	Sid Bream	.15	.07	.02
□	U141	Tom Edens	.15	.07	.02
□	U142	Tony Eusebio	.15	.07	.02
□	U143	John Hudek	2.00	.90	.25
□	U144	Brian Hunter	1.25	.55	.16
□	U145	Orlando Miller	.20	.09	.03
□	U146	James Mouton	.40	.18	.05
□	U147	Shane Reynolds	.15	.07	.02
□	U148	Rafael Bournigal	.15	.07	.02
□	U149	Delino DeShields	.20	.09	.03
□	U150	Garey Ingram	.40	.18	.05
□	U151	Chan Ho Park	3.00	1.35	.40
□	U152	Wil Cordero	.30	.14	.04
□	U153	Pedro Martinez	.30	.14	.04
□	U154	Randy Milligan	.15	.07	.02
□	U155	Lenny Webster	.15	.07	.02
□	U156	Rico Brogna	.15	.07	.02
□	U157	Josias Manzanillo	.15	.07	.02
□	U158	Kevin McReynolds	.15	.07	.02
□	U159	Mike Remlinger	.15	.07	.02
□	U160	David Segui	.15	.07	.02
□	U161	Pete Smith	.15	.07	.02
□	U162	Kelly Stinnett	.15	.07	.02
□	U163	Jose Vizcaino	.15	.07	.02
□	U164	Billy Hatcher	.15	.07	.02
□	U165	Doug Jones	.15	.07	.02
□	U166	Mike Lieberthal	.15	.07	.02
□	U167	Tony Longmire	.15	.07	.02
□	U168	Bobby Munoz	.15	.07	.02
□	U169	Paul Quantrill	.15	.07	.02
□	U170	Heathcliff Slocumb	.15	.07	.02
□	U171	Fernando Valenzuela	.15	.07	.02
□	U172	Mark Dewey	.15	.07	.02
□	U173	Brian R. Hunter	.15	.07	.02
□	U174	Jon Lieber	.50	.23	.06
□	U175	Ravelo Manzanillo	.15	.07	.02
□	U176	Dan Miceli	.15	.07	.02
□	U177	Rick White	.15	.07	.02
□	U178	Bryan Eversgerd	.15	.07	.02
□	U179	John Habyan	.15	.07	.02
□	U180	Terry McGriff	.15	.07	.02
□	U181	Vicente Palacios	.15	.07	.02
□	U182	Rich Rodriguez	.15	.07	.02
□	U183	Rick Sutcliffe	.20	.09	.03
□	U184	Donnie Elliott	.15	.07	.02
□	U185	Joey Hamilton	2.00	.90	.25
□	U186	Tim Hyers	.50	.23	.06
□	U187	Luis Lopez	.15	.07	.02
□	U188	Ray McDavid	.15	.07	.02
□	U189	Bip Roberts	.15	.07	.02
□	U190	Scott Sanders	.15	.07	.02
□	U191	Eddie Williams	.15	.07	.02
□	U192	Steve Frey	.15	.07	.02
□	U193	Pat Gomez	.15	.07	.02
□	U194	Rich Monteleone	.15	.07	.02
□	U195	Mark Portugal	.15	.07	.02

		MINT	EXC	G-VG
☐ U196	Darryl Strawberry	.20	.09	.03
☐ U197	Salomon Torres	.20	.09	.03
☐ U198	Will VanLandingham	2.50	1.15	.30
☐ U199	Checklist 1-102	.15	.07	.02
☐ U200	Checklist 103-200/Ins.	.15	.07	.02

1994 Fleer Update Diamond Tribute

This 10-card standard-size set was included one per 1994 Fleer Update factory set. The set consists of some of baseball's elite performers. Card fronts feature the player superimposed over a background of a sky and images of baseballs. The backs are similar with the exception of a small write-up containing career highlights.

	MINT	EXC	G-VG
COMPLETE SET (10)	7.00	3.10	.85
COMMON CARD (1-10)	.25	.11	.03
☐ 1 Barry Bonds	1.50	.65	.19
☐ 2 Joe Carter	.60	.25	.08
☐ 3 Will Clark	.60	.25	.08
☐ 4 Roger Clemens	.90	.40	.11
☐ 5 Tony Gwynn	.90	.40	.11
☐ 6 Don Mattingly	1.50	.65	.19
☐ 7 Fred McGriff	.60	.25	.08
☐ 8 Eddie Murray	.25	.11	.03
☐ 9 Kirby Puckett	1.50	.65	.19
☐ 10 Cal Ripken	2.00	.90	.25

1995 Fleer

The 1995 Fleer set consists of 600 standard-size cards issued as one series. Full-bleed fronts have two player photos and, atypical of baseball cards fronts, biographical information such as height, weight, etc. The backgrounds are multi-colored. The backs are horizontal and contain year-by-year statistics along with a photo. The checklist is arranged alphabetically by teams within each league as follows: Baltimore Orioles (1-22), Boston Red Sox (23-43), Detroit Tigers (44-64), New York Yankees (65-86), Toronto Blue Jays (87-108), Chicago White Sox (109-129), Cleveland Indians (130-151), Kansas City Royals (152-173), Milwaukee Brewers (174-195), Minnesota Twins (196-217), California Angels (218-237), Oakland Athletics (238-257), Seattle Mariners (258-279), Texas Rangers (280-298), Atlanta Braves (299-322), Florida Marlins (323-343), Montreal Expos (344-364), New York Mets (365-385), Philadelphia Phillies (386-407), Chicago Cubs (408-428), Cincinnati Reds (429-450), Houston Astros (451-471), Pittsburgh Pirates (472-492), St. Louis Cardinals (493-513), Colorado Rockies (514-531), Los Angeles Dodgers (532-552), San Diego Padres (553-566), and San Francisco Giants (572-593).

	MINT	EXC	G-VG
COMPLETE SET (600)	40.00	18.00	5.00
COMMON CARD (1-600)	.10	.05	.01
☐ 1 Brady Anderson	.10	.05	.01
☐ 2 Harold Baines	.15	.07	.02
☐ 3 Damon Buford	.10	.05	.01
☐ 4 Mike Devereaux	.15	.07	.02
☐ 5 Mark Eichhorn	.10	.05	.01
☐ 6 Sid Fernandez	.10	.05	.01
☐ 7 Leo Gomez	.10	.05	.01
☐ 8 Jeffrey Hammonds	.20	.09	.03
☐ 9 Chris Hoiles	.15	.07	.02
☐ 10 Rick Krivda	.10	.05	.01
☐ 11 Ben McDonald	.15	.07	.02
☐ 12 Mark McLemore	.10	.05	.01
☐ 13 Alan Mills	.10	.05	.01
☐ 14 Jamie Moyer	.10	.05	.01
☐ 15 Mike Mussina	.40	.18	.05
☐ 16 Mike Oquist	.10	.05	.01
☐ 17 Rafael Palmeiro	.20	.09	.03
☐ 18 Arthur Rhodes	.10	.05	.01
☐ 19 Cal Ripken	2.25	1.00	.30
☐ 20 Chris Sabo	.10	.05	.01
☐ 21 Lee Smith	.20	.09	.03
☐ 22 Jack Voigt	.10	.05	.01
☐ 23 Damon Berryhill	.10	.05	.01
☐ 24 Tom Brunansky	.10	.05	.01
☐ 25 Wes Chamberlain	.10	.05	.01
☐ 26 Roger Clemens	.60	.25	.08
☐ 27 Scott Cooper	.15	.07	.02
☐ 28 Andre Dawson	.20	.09	.03
☐ 29 Gar Finnvold	.10	.05	.01
☐ 30 Tony Fossas	.10	.05	.01
☐ 31 Mike Greenwell	.10	.05	.01
☐ 32 Joe Hesketh	.10	.05	.01
☐ 33 Chris Howard	.10	.05	.01
☐ 34 Chris Nabholz	.10	.05	.01
☐ 35 Tim Naehring	.10	.05	.01
☐ 36 Otis Nixon	.10	.05	.01
☐ 37 Carlos Rodriguez	.10	.05	.01
☐ 38 Rich Rowland	.10	.05	.01
☐ 39 Ken Ryan	.10	.05	.01
☐ 40 Aaron Sele	.20	.09	.03
☐ 41 John Valentin	.10	.05	.01
☐ 42 Mo Vaughn	.20	.09	.03
☐ 43 Frank Viola	.10	.05	.01
☐ 44 Danny Bautista	.10	.05	.01

☐ 45 Joe Boever	.10	.05	.01
☐ 46 Milt Cuyler	.10	.05	.01
☐ 47 Storm Davis	.10	.05	.01
☐ 48 John Doherty	.10	.05	.01
☐ 49 Junior Felix	.10	.05	.01
☐ 50 Cecil Fielder	.20	.09	.03
☐ 51 Travis Fryman	.25	.11	.03
☐ 52 Mike Gardiner	.10	.05	.01
☐ 53 Kirk Gibson	.10	.05	.01
☐ 54 Chris Gomez	.15	.07	.02
☐ 55 Buddy Groom	.10	.05	.01
☐ 56 Mike Henneman	.10	.05	.01
☐ 57 Chad Kreuter	.10	.05	.01
☐ 58 Mike Moore	.10	.05	.01
☐ 59 Tony Phillips	.15	.07	.02
☐ 60 Juan Samuel	.10	.05	.01
☐ 61 Mickey Tettleton	.10	.05	.01
☐ 62 Alan Trammell	.15	.07	.02
☐ 63 David Wells	.10	.05	.01
☐ 64 Lou Whitaker	.15	.07	.02
☐ 65 Jim Abbott	.15	.07	.02
☐ 66 Joe Ausanio	.10	.05	.01
☐ 67 Wade Boggs	.20	.09	.03
☐ 68 Mike Gallego	.10	.05	.01
☐ 69 Xavier Hernandez	.10	.05	.01
☐ 70 Sterling Hitchcock	.10	.05	.01
☐ 71 Steve Howe	.10	.05	.01
☐ 72 Scott Kamieniecki	.10	.05	.01
☐ 73 Pat Kelly	.10	.05	.01
☐ 74 Jimmy Key	.20	.09	.03
☐ 75 Jim Leyritz	.10	.05	.01
☐ 76 Don Mattingly	1.25	.55	.16
☐ 77 Terry Mulholland	.10	.05	.01
☐ 78 Paul O'Neill	.20	.09	.03
☐ 79 Melido Perez	.10	.05	.01
☐ 80 Luis Polonia	.10	.05	.01
☐ 81 Mike Stanley	.10	.05	.01
☐ 82 Danny Tartabull	.15	.07	.02
☐ 83 Randy Velarde	.10	.05	.01
☐ 84 Bob Wickman	.10	.05	.01
☐ 85 Bernie Williams	.10	.05	.01
☐ 86 Gerald Williams	.10	.05	.01
☐ 87 Roberto Alomar	.60	.25	.08
☐ 88 Pat Borders	.10	.05	.01
☐ 89 Joe Carter	.40	.18	.05
☐ 90 Tony Castillo	.10	.05	.01
☐ 91 Brad Cornett	.15	.07	.02
☐ 92 Carlos Delgado	.35	.16	.04
☐ 93 Alex Gonzalez	.15	.07	.02
☐ 94 Shawn Green	.10	.05	.01
☐ 95 Juan Guzman	.15	.07	.02
☐ 96 Darren Hall	.10	.05	.01
☐ 97 Pat Hentgen	.15	.07	.02
☐ 98 Mike Huff	.10	.05	.01
☐ 99 Randy Knorr	.10	.05	.01
☐ 100 Al Leiter	.10	.05	.01
☐ 101 Paul Molitor	.40	.18	.05
☐ 102 John Olerud	.20	.09	.03
☐ 103 Dick Schofield	.10	.05	.01
☐ 104 Ed Sprague	.10	.05	.01
☐ 105 Dave Stewart	.15	.07	.02
☐ 106 Todd Stottlemyre	.10	.05	.01
☐ 107 Devon White	.15	.07	.02
☐ 108 Woody Williams	.10	.05	.01
☐ 109 Wilson Alvarez	.20	.09	.03
☐ 110 Paul Assenmacher	.10	.05	.01
☐ 111 Jason Bere	.35	.16	.04
☐ 112 Dennis Cook	.10	.05	.01
☐ 113 Joey Cora	.10	.05	.01
☐ 114 Jose DeLeon	.10	.05	.01
☐ 115 Alex Fernandez	.20	.09	.03
☐ 116 Julio Franco	.15	.07	.02
☐ 117 Craig Grebeck	.10	.05	.01
☐ 118 Ozzie Guillen	.10	.05	.01
☐ 119 Roberto Hernandez	.10	.05	.01
☐ 120 Darrin Jackson	.10	.05	.01
☐ 121 Lance Johnson	.10	.05	.01
☐ 122 Ron Karkovice	.10	.05	.01
☐ 123 Mike LaValliere	.10	.05	.01
☐ 124 Norberto Martin	.10	.05	.01
☐ 125 Kirk McCaskill	.10	.05	.01
☐ 126 Jack McDowell	.20	.09	.03
☐ 127 Tim Raines	.15	.07	.02
☐ 128 Frank Thomas	3.00	1.35	.40
☐ 129 Robin Ventura	.20	.09	.03
☐ 130 Sandy Alomar Jr.	.15	.07	.02
☐ 131 Carlos Baerga	.40	.18	.05
☐ 132 Albert Belle	1.00	.45	.13
☐ 133 Mark Clark	.10	.05	.01
☐ 134 Alvaro Espinoza	.10	.05	.01
☐ 135 Jason Grimsley	.10	.05	.01
☐ 136 Wayne Kirby	.10	.05	.01
☐ 137 Kenny Lofton	.75	.35	.09
☐ 138 Albie Lopez	.10	.05	.01
☐ 139 Dennis Martinez	.10	.05	.01
☐ 140 Jose Mesa	.10	.05	.01
☐ 141 Eddie Murray	.20	.09	.03
☐ 142 Charles Nagy	.10	.05	.01
☐ 143 Tony Pena	.10	.05	.01
☐ 144 Eric Plunk	.10	.05	.01
☐ 145 Manny Ramirez	.40	.18	.05
☐ 146 Jeff Russell	.10	.05	.01
☐ 147 Paul Shuey	.15	.07	.02
☐ 148 Paul Sorrento	.10	.05	.01
☐ 149 Jim Thome	.20	.09	.03
☐ 150 Omar Vizquel	.10	.05	.01
☐ 151 Dave Winfield	.20	.09	.03
☐ 152 Kevin Appier	.10	.05	.01
☐ 153 Billy Brewer	.10	.05	.01
☐ 154 Vince Coleman	.10	.05	.01
☐ 155 David Cone	.20	.09	.03
☐ 156 Gary Gaetti	.10	.05	.01
☐ 157 Greg Gagne	.10	.05	.01
☐ 158 Tom Gordon	.10	.05	.01
☐ 159 Mark Gubicza	.10	.05	.01
☐ 160 Bob Hamelin	.20	.09	.03
☐ 161 Dave Henderson	.10	.05	.01
☐ 162 Felix Jose	.10	.05	.01
☐ 163 Wally Joyner	.15	.07	.02
☐ 164 Jose Lind	.10	.05	.01
☐ 165 Mike Macfarlane	.10	.05	.01
☐ 166 Mike Magnante	.10	.05	.01
☐ 167 Brent Mayne	.10	.05	.01
☐ 168 Brian McRae	.20	.09	.03
☐ 169 Rusty Meacham	.10	.05	.01
☐ 170 Jeff Montgomery	.10	.05	.01
☐ 171 Hipolito Pichardo	.10	.05	.01
☐ 172 Terry Shumpert	.10	.05	.01
☐ 173 Michael Tucker	.15	.07	.02
☐ 174 Ricky Bones	.10	.05	.01
☐ 175 Jeff Cirillo	.10	.05	.01
☐ 176 Alex Diaz	.10	.05	.01
☐ 177 Cal Eldred	.10	.05	.01
☐ 178 Mike Fetters	.10	.05	.01
☐ 179 Darryl Hamilton	.10	.05	.01
☐ 180 Brian Harper	.10	.05	.01
☐ 181 John Jaha	.10	.05	.01
☐ 182 Pat Listach	.10	.05	.01
☐ 183 Graeme Lloyd	.10	.05	.01
☐ 184 Jose Mercedes	.10	.05	.01
☐ 185 Matt Mieske	.15	.07	.02
☐ 186 Dave Nilsson	.10	.05	.01
☐ 187 Jody Reed	.10	.05	.01
☐ 188 Bob Scanlan	.10	.05	.01
☐ 189 Kevin Seitzer	.10	.05	.01
☐ 190 Bill Spiers	.10	.05	.01

	#	Player			
☐	191	B.J. Surhoff	.10	.05	.01
☐	192	Jose Valentin	.10	.05	.01
☐	193	Greg Vaughn	.15	.07	.02
☐	194	Turner Ward	.10	.05	.01
☐	195	Bill Wegman	.10	.05	.01
☐	196	Rick Aguilera	.10	.05	.01
☐	197	Rich Becker	.10	.05	.01
☐	198	Alex Cole	.10	.05	.01
☐	199	Marty Cordova	.10	.05	.01
☐	200	Steve Dunn	.10	.05	.01
☐	201	Scott Erickson	.10	.05	.01
☐	202	Mark Guthrie	.10	.05	.01
☐	203	Chip Hale	.10	.05	.01
☐	204	LaTroy Hawkins	.10	.05	.01
☐	205	Denny Hocking	.10	.05	.01
☐	206	Chuck Knoblauch	.15	.07	.02
☐	207	Scott Leius	.10	.05	.01
☐	208	Shane Mack	.10	.05	.01
☐	209	Pat Mahomes	.10	.05	.01
☐	210	Pat Meares	.10	.05	.01
☐	211	Pedro Munoz	.10	.05	.01
☐	212	Kirby Puckett	1.25	.55	.16
☐	213	Jeff Reboulet	.10	.05	.01
☐	214	Dave Stevens	.10	.05	.01
☐	215	Kevin Tapani	.10	.05	.01
☐	216	Matt Walbeck	.10	.05	.01
☐	217	Carl Willis	.10	.05	.01
☐	218	Brian Anderson	.20	.09	.03
☐	219	Chad Curtis	.10	.05	.01
☐	220	Chili Davis	.15	.07	.02
☐	221	Gary DiSarcina	.10	.05	.01
☐	222	Damion Easley	.10	.05	.01
☐	223	Jim Edmonds	.10	.05	.01
☐	224	Chuck Finley	.10	.05	.01
☐	225	Joe Grahe	.10	.05	.01
☐	226	Rex Hudler	.10	.05	.01
☐	227	Bo Jackson	.20	.09	.03
☐	228	Mark Langston	.15	.07	.02
☐	229	Phil Leftwich	.10	.05	.01
☐	230	Mark Leiter	.10	.05	.01
☐	231	Spike Owen	.10	.05	.01
☐	232	Bob Patterson	.10	.05	.01
☐	233	Troy Percival	.10	.05	.01
☐	234	Eduardo Perez	.10	.05	.01
☐	235	Tim Salmon	.20	.09	.03
☐	236	J.T. Snow	.10	.05	.01
☐	237	Chris Turner	.10	.05	.01
☐	238	Mark Acre	.10	.05	.01
☐	239	Geronimo Berroa	.10	.05	.01
☐	240	Mike Bordick	.10	.05	.01
☐	241	John Briscoe	.10	.05	.01
☐	242	Scott Brosius	.10	.05	.01
☐	243	Ron Darling	.10	.05	.01
☐	244	Dennis Eckersley	.15	.07	.02
☐	245	Brent Gates	.10	.05	.01
☐	246	Rickey Henderson	.20	.09	.03
☐	247	Stan Javier	.10	.05	.01
☐	248	Steve Karsay	.10	.05	.01
☐	249	Mark McGwire	.20	.09	.03
☐	250	Troy Neel	.10	.05	.01
☐	251	Steve Ontiveros	.10	.05	.01
☐	252	Carlos Reyes	.10	.05	.01
☐	253	Ruben Sierra	.20	.09	.03
☐	254	Terry Steinbach	.15	.07	.02
☐	255	Bill Taylor	.10	.05	.01
☐	256	Todd Van Poppel	.15	.07	.02
☐	257	Bobby Witt	.10	.05	.01
☐	258	Rich Amaral	.10	.05	.01
☐	259	Eric Anthony	.10	.05	.01
☐	260	Bobby Ayala	.10	.05	.01
☐	261	Mike Blowers	.10	.05	.01
☐	262	Chris Bosio	.10	.05	.01
☐	263	Jay Buhner	.15	.07	.02
☐	264	John Cummings	.10	.05	.01
☐	265	Tim Davis	.10	.05	.01
☐	266	Felix Fermin	.10	.05	.01
☐	267	Dave Fleming	.10	.05	.01
☐	268	Goose Gossage	.15	.07	.02
☐	269	Ken Griffey Jr.	3.00	1.35	.40
☐	270	Reggie Jefferson	.10	.05	.01
☐	271	Randy Johnson	.20	.09	.03
☐	272	Edgar Martinez	.10	.05	.01
☐	273	Tino Martinez	.10	.05	.01
☐	274	Greg Pirkl	.10	.05	.01
☐	275	Bill Risley	.10	.05	.01
☐	276	Roger Salkeld	.10	.05	.01
☐	277	Luis Sojo	.10	.05	.01
☐	278	Mac Suzuki	.15	.07	.02
☐	279	Dan Wilson	.10	.05	.01
☐	280	Kevin Brown	.10	.05	.01
☐	281	Jose Canseco	.40	.18	.05
☐	282	Cris Carpenter	.10	.05	.01
☐	283	Will Clark	.40	.18	.05
☐	284	Jeff Frye	.10	.05	.01
☐	285	Juan Gonzalez	1.00	.45	.13
☐	286	Rick Helling	.10	.05	.01
☐	287	Tom Henke	.10	.05	.01
☐	288	David Hulse	.10	.05	.01
☐	289	Chris James	.10	.05	.01
☐	290	Manny Lee	.10	.05	.01
☐	291	Oddibe McDowell	.10	.05	.01
☐	292	Dean Palmer	.10	.05	.01
☐	293	Roger Pavlik	.10	.05	.01
☐	294	Bill Ripken	.10	.05	.01
☐	295	Ivan Rodriguez	.20	.09	.03
☐	296	Kenny Rogers	.10	.05	.01
☐	297	Doug Strange	.10	.05	.01
☐	298	Matt Whiteside	.10	.05	.01
☐	299	Steve Avery	.20	.09	.03
☐	300	Steve Bedrosian	.10	.05	.01
☐	301	Rafael Belliard	.10	.05	.01
☐	302	Jeff Blauser	.15	.07	.02
☐	303	Dave Gallagher	.10	.05	.01
☐	304	Tom Glavine	.20	.09	.03
☐	305	David Justice	.40	.18	.05
☐	306	Mike Kelly	.10	.05	.01
☐	307	Roberto Kelly	.10	.05	.01
☐	308	Ryan Klesko	.35	.16	.04
☐	309	Mark Lemke	.10	.05	.01
☐	310	Javy Lopez	.15	.07	.02
☐	311	Greg Maddux	.60	.25	.08
☐	312	Fred McGriff	.40	.18	.05
☐	313	Greg McMichael	.10	.05	.01
☐	314	Kent Mercker	.10	.05	.01
☐	315	Charlie O'Brien	.10	.05	.01
☐	316	Jose Oliva	.15	.07	.02
☐	317	Terry Pendleton	.10	.05	.01
☐	318	John Smoltz	.20	.09	.03
☐	319	Mike Stanton	.10	.05	.01
☐	320	Tony Tarasco	.15	.07	.02
☐	321	Terrell Wade	.10	.05	.01
☐	322	Mark Wohlers	.10	.05	.01
☐	323	Kurt Abbott	.10	.05	.01
☐	324	Luis Aquino	.10	.05	.01
☐	325	Bret Barberie	.10	.05	.01
☐	326	Ryan Bowen	.10	.05	.01
☐	327	Jerry Browne	.10	.05	.01
☐	328	Chuck Carr	.10	.05	.01
☐	329	Matias Carrillo	.10	.05	.01
☐	330	Greg Colbrunn	.10	.05	.01
☐	331	Jeff Conine	.20	.09	.03
☐	332	Mark Gardner	.10	.05	.01
☐	333	Chris Hammond	.10	.05	.01
☐	334	Bryan Harvey	.10	.05	.01
☐	335	Richie Lewis	.10	.05	.01
☐	336	Dave Magadan	.10	.05	.01

	#	Player			
☐	337	Terry Mathews	.10	.05	.01
☐	338	Robb Nen	.10	.05	.01
☐	339	Yorkis Perez	.10	.05	.01
☐	340	Pat Rapp	.10	.05	.01
☐	341	Benito Santiago	.10	.05	.01
☐	342	Gary Sheffield	.20	.09	.03
☐	343	Dave Weathers	.10	.05	.01
☐	344	Moises Alou	.20	.09	.03
☐	345	Sean Berry	.10	.05	.01
☐	346	Wil Cordero	.15	.07	.02
☐	347	Joey Eischen	.10	.05	.01
☐	348	Jeff Fassero	.10	.05	.01
☐	349	Darrin Fletcher	.10	.05	.01
☐	350	Cliff Floyd	.35	.16	.04
☐	351	Marquis Grissom	.20	.09	.03
☐	352	Butch Henry	.10	.05	.01
☐	353	Gil Heredia	.10	.05	.01
☐	354	Ken Hill	.20	.09	.03
☐	355	Mike Lansing	.10	.05	.01
☐	356	Pedro Martinez	.15	.07	.02
☐	357	Mel Rojas	.10	.05	.01
☐	358	Kirk Rueter	.10	.05	.01
☐	359	Tim Scott	.10	.05	.01
☐	360	Jeff Shaw	.10	.05	.01
☐	361	Larry Walker	.20	.09	.03
☐	362	Lenny Webster	.10	.05	.01
☐	363	John Wetteland	.10	.05	.01
☐	364	Rondell White	.20	.09	.03
☐	365	Bobby Bonilla	.15	.07	.02
☐	366	Rico Brogna	.10	.05	.01
☐	367	Jeromy Burnitz	.10	.05	.01
☐	368	John Franco	.10	.05	.01
☐	369	Dwight Gooden	.10	.05	.01
☐	370	Todd Hundley	.10	.05	.01
☐	371	Jason Jacome	.25	.11	.03
☐	372	Bobby Jones	.15	.07	.02
☐	373	Jeff Kent	.10	.05	.01
☐	374	Jim Lindeman	.10	.05	.01
☐	375	Josias Manzanillo	.10	.05	.01
☐	376	Roger Mason	.10	.05	.01
☐	377	Kevin McReynolds	.10	.05	.01
☐	378	Joe Orsulak	.10	.05	.01
☐	379	Bill Pulsipher	.20	.09	.03
☐	380	Bret Saberhagen	.15	.07	.02
☐	381	David Segui	.10	.05	.01
☐	382	Pete Smith	.10	.05	.01
☐	383	Kelly Stinnett	.10	.05	.01
☐	384	Ryan Thompson	.10	.05	.01
☐	385	Jose Vizcaino	.10	.05	.01
☐	386	Toby Borland	.10	.05	.01
☐	387	Ricky Bottalico	.10	.05	.01
☐	388	Darren Daulton	.20	.09	.03
☐	389	Mariano Duncan	.10	.05	.01
☐	390	Lenny Dykstra	.20	.09	.03
☐	391	Jim Eisenreich	.10	.05	.01
☐	392	Tommy Greene	.10	.05	.01
☐	393	Dave Hollins	.15	.07	.02
☐	394	Pete Incaviglia	.10	.05	.01
☐	395	Danny Jackson	.10	.05	.01
☐	396	Doug Jones	.10	.05	.01
☐	397	Ricky Jordan	.10	.05	.01
☐	398	John Kruk	.15	.07	.02
☐	399	Mike Lieberthal	.15	.07	.02
☐	400	Tony Longmire	.10	.05	.01
☐	401	Mickey Morandini	.10	.05	.01
☐	402	Bobby Munoz	.15	.07	.02
☐	403	Curt Schilling	.10	.05	.01
☐	404	Heathcliff Slocumb	.10	.05	.01
☐	405	Kevin Stocker	.15	.07	.02
☐	406	Fernando Valenzuela	.10	.05	.01
☐	407	David West	.10	.05	.01
☐	408	Willie Banks	.10	.05	.01
☐	409	Jose Bautista	.10	.05	.01
☐	410	Steve Buechele	.10	.05	.01
☐	411	Jim Bullinger	.10	.05	.01
☐	412	Chuck Crim	.10	.05	.01
☐	413	Shawon Dunston	.10	.05	.01
☐	414	Kevin Foster	.10	.05	.01
☐	415	Mark Grace	.15	.07	.02
☐	416	Jose Hernandez	.10	.05	.01
☐	417	Glenallen Hill	.10	.05	.01
☐	418	Brooks Kieschnick	.25	.11	.03
☐	419	Derrick May	.15	.07	.02
☐	420	Randy Myers	.10	.05	.01
☐	421	Dan Plesac	.10	.05	.01
☐	422	Karl Rhodes	.10	.05	.01
☐	423	Rey Sanchez	.10	.05	.01
☐	424	Sammy Sosa	.20	.09	.03
☐	425	Steve Trachsel	.15	.07	.02
☐	426	Rick Wilkins	.10	.05	.01
☐	427	Anthony Young	.10	.05	.01
☐	428	Eddie Zambrano	.10	.05	.01
☐	429	Bret Boone	.20	.09	.03
☐	430	Jeff Branson	.10	.05	.01
☐	431	Jeff Brantley	.10	.05	.01
☐	432	Hector Carrasco	.10	.05	.01
☐	433	Brian Dorsett	.10	.05	.01
☐	434	Tony Fernandez	.10	.05	.01
☐	435	Tim Fortugno	.10	.05	.01
☐	436	Erik Hanson	.10	.05	.01
☐	437	Thomas Howard	.10	.05	.01
☐	438	Kevin Jarvis	.10	.05	.01
☐	439	Barry Larkin	.20	.09	.03
☐	440	Chuck McElroy	.10	.05	.01
☐	441	Kevin Mitchell	.15	.07	.02
☐	442	Hal Morris	.15	.07	.02
☐	443	Jose Rijo	.15	.07	.02
☐	444	John Roper	.10	.05	.01
☐	445	Johnny Ruffin	.10	.05	.01
☐	446	Deion Sanders	.60	.25	.08
☐	447	Reggie Sanders	.10	.05	.01
☐	448	Pete Schourek	.10	.05	.01
☐	449	John Smiley	.10	.05	.01
☐	450	Eddie Taubensee	.10	.05	.01
☐	451	Jeff Bagwell	1.50	.65	.19
☐	452	Kevin Bass	.10	.05	.01
☐	453	Craig Biggio	.15	.07	.02
☐	454	Ken Caminiti	.15	.07	.02
☐	455	Andujar Cedeno	.10	.05	.01
☐	456	Doug Drabek	.15	.07	.02
☐	457	Tony Eusebio	.10	.05	.01
☐	458	Mike Felder	.10	.05	.01
☐	459	Steve Finley	.10	.05	.01
☐	460	Luis Gonzalez	.10	.05	.01
☐	461	Mike Hampton	.10	.05	.01
☐	462	Pete Harnisch	.10	.05	.01
☐	463	John Hudek	.10	.05	.01
☐	464	Todd Jones	.10	.05	.01
☐	465	Darryl Kile	.10	.05	.01
☐	466	James Mouton	.10	.05	.01
☐	467	Shane Reynolds	.10	.05	.01
☐	468	Scott Servais	.10	.05	.01
☐	469	Greg Swindell	.10	.05	.01
☐	470	Dave Veres	.15	.07	.02
☐	471	Brian Williams	.10	.05	.01
☐	472	Jay Bell	.15	.07	.02
☐	473	Jacob Brumfield	.10	.05	.01
☐	474	Dave Clark	.10	.05	.01
☐	475	Steve Cooke	.10	.05	.01
☐	476	Midre Cummings	.10	.05	.01
☐	477	Mark Dewey	.10	.05	.01
☐	478	Tom Foley	.10	.05	.01
☐	479	Carlos Garcia	.10	.05	.01
☐	480	Jeff King	.10	.05	.01
☐	481	Jon Lieber	.10	.05	.01
☐	482	Ravelo Manzanillo	.10	.05	.01

☐ 483 Al Martin .10 .05 .01
☐ 484 Orlando Merced .10 .05 .01
☐ 485 Danny Miceli .10 .05 .01
☐ 486 Denny Neagle .10 .05 .01
☐ 487 Lance Parrish .10 .05 .01
☐ 488 Don Slaught .10 .05 .01
☐ 489 Zane Smith .10 .05 .01
☐ 490 Andy Van Slyke .10 .05 .01
☐ 491 Paul Wagner .10 .05 .01
☐ 492 Rick White .10 .05 .01
☐ 493 Luis Alicea .10 .05 .01
☐ 494 Rene Arocha .10 .05 .01
☐ 495 Rheal Cormier .10 .05 .01
☐ 496 Bryan Eversgerd .10 .05 .01
☐ 497 Bernard Gilkey .10 .05 .01
☐ 498 John Habyan .10 .05 .01
☐ 499 Gregg Jefferies .20 .09 .03
☐ 500 Brian Jordan .10 .05 .01
☐ 501 Ray Lankford .15 .07 .02
☐ 502 John Mabry .10 .05 .01
☐ 503 Terry McGriff .10 .05 .01
☐ 504 Tom Pagnozzi .10 .05 .01
☐ 505 Vicente Palacios .10 .05 .01
☐ 506 Geronimo Pena .10 .05 .01
☐ 507 Gerald Perry .10 .05 .01
☐ 508 Rich Rodriguez .10 .05 .01
☐ 509 Ozzie Smith .60 .25 .08
☐ 510 Bob Tewksbury .10 .05 .01
☐ 511 Allen Watson .10 .05 .01
☐ 512 Mark Whiten .15 .07 .02
☐ 513 Todd Zeile .10 .05 .01
☐ 514 Dante Bichette .20 .09 .03
☐ 515 Willie Blair .10 .05 .01
☐ 516 Ellis Burks .15 .07 .02
☐ 517 Marvin Freeman .10 .05 .01
☐ 518 Andres Galarraga .20 .09 .03
☐ 519 Joe Girardi .10 .05 .01
☐ 520 Greg W. Harris .10 .05 .01
☐ 521 Charlie Hayes .15 .07 .02
☐ 522 Mike Kingery .10 .05 .01
☐ 523 Nelson Liriano .10 .05 .01
☐ 524 Mike Munoz .10 .05 .01
☐ 525 David Nied .20 .09 .03
☐ 526 Steve Reed .10 .05 .01
☐ 527 Kevin Ritz .10 .05 .01
☐ 528 Bruce Ruffin .10 .05 .01
☐ 529 John Vander Wal .10 .05 .01
☐ 530 Walt Weiss .10 .05 .01
☐ 531 Eric Young .10 .05 .01
☐ 532 Billy Ashley .20 .09 .03
☐ 533 Pedro Astacio .10 .05 .01
☐ 534 Rafael Bournigal .10 .05 .01
☐ 535 Brett Butler .10 .05 .01
☐ 536 Tom Candiotti .10 .05 .01
☐ 537 Omar Daal .10 .05 .01
☐ 538 Delino DeShields .15 .07 .02
☐ 539 Darren Dreifort .10 .05 .01
☐ 540 Kevin Gross .10 .05 .01
☐ 541 Orel Hershiser .15 .07 .02
☐ 542 Garey Ingram .10 .05 .01
☐ 543 Eric Karros .10 .05 .01
☐ 544 Ramon Martinez .15 .07 .02
☐ 545 Raul Mondesi .75 .35 .09
☐ 546 Chan Ho Park .30 .14 .04
☐ 547 Mike Piazza 1.25 .55 .16
☐ 548 Henry Rodriguez .10 .05 .01
☐ 549 Rudy Seanez .10 .05 .01
☐ 550 Ismael Valdes .10 .05 .01
☐ 551 Tim Wallach .10 .05 .01
☐ 552 Todd Worrell .10 .05 .01
☐ 553 Andy Ashby .10 .05 .01
☐ 554 Brad Ausmus .10 .05 .01
☐ 555 Derek Bell .15 .07 .02
☐ 556 Andy Benes .15 .07 .02
☐ 557 Phil Clark .10 .05 .01
☐ 558 Donnie Elliott .10 .05 .01
☐ 559 Ricky Gutierrez .10 .05 .01
☐ 560 Tony Gwynn .60 .25 .08
☐ 561 Joey Hamilton .20 .09 .03
☐ 562 Trevor Hoffman .10 .05 .01
☐ 563 Luis Lopez .10 .05 .01
☐ 564 Pedro A. Martinez .20 .09 .03
☐ 565 Tim Mauser .10 .05 .01
☐ 566 Phil Plantier .15 .07 .02
☐ 567 Bip Roberts .10 .05 .01
☐ 568 Scott Sanders .10 .05 .01
☐ 569 Craig Shipley .10 .05 .01
☐ 570 Jeff Tabaka .10 .05 .01
☐ 571 Eddie Williams .10 .05 .01
☐ 572 Rod Beck .20 .09 .03
☐ 573 Mike Benjamin .10 .05 .01
☐ 574 Barry Bonds 1.25 .55 .16
☐ 575 Dave Burba .10 .05 .01
☐ 576 John Burkett .15 .07 .02
☐ 577 Mark Carreon .10 .05 .01
☐ 578 Royce Clayton .15 .07 .02
☐ 579 Steve Frey .10 .05 .01
☐ 580 Bryan Hickerson .10 .05 .01
☐ 581 Mike Jackson .10 .05 .01
☐ 582 Darren Lewis .10 .05 .01
☐ 583 Kirt Manwaring .10 .05 .01
☐ 584 Rich Monteleone .10 .05 .01
☐ 585 John Patterson .10 .05 .01
☐ 586 J.R. Phillips .15 .07 .02
☐ 587 Mark Portugal .10 .05 .01
☐ 588 Joe Rosselli .10 .05 .01
☐ 589 Darryl Strawberry .15 .07 .02
☐ 590 Bill Swift .15 .07 .02
☐ 591 Robby Thompson .10 .05 .01
☐ 592 Will VanLandingham .10 .05 .01
☐ 593 Matt Williams .50 .23 .06
☐ 594 Checklist 1-121 .10 .05 .01
☐ 595 Checklist 122-245 .10 .05 .01
☐ 596 Checklist 246-369 .10 .05 .01
☐ 597 Checklist 370-492 .10 .05 .01
☐ 598 Checklist 493-600 .10 .05 .01
☐ 599 Inserts Checklist .10 .05 .01
☐ 600 Inserts Checklist .10 .05 .01
☐ NNO All-Rookie Exchange 15.00 6.75 1.90

1995 Fleer All-Stars

Randomly inserted in all pack types at a rate of one in three, this 25-card set showcases those that participated in the 1994 mid-season classic held in Pittsburgh. Horizontally designed, the fronts contain

photos of American League stars with the back protraying the National League player from the same position. On each side, the 1994 All-Star Game logo appears in gold foil as does either the A.L. or N.L. logo in silver foil.

	MINT	EXC	G-VG
COMPLETE SET (25)	15.00	6.75	1.90
COMMON CARD (1-25)	.25	.11	.03
☐ 1 Ivan Rodriguez Mike Piazza	1.00	.45	.13
☐ 2 Frank Thomas Gregg Jefferies	3.00	1.35	.40
☐ 3 Robert Alomar Mariano Duncan	.50	.23	.06
☐ 4 Wade Boggs Matt Williams	.60	.25	.08
☐ 5 Cal Ripken Jr. Ozzie Smith	2.50	1.15	.30
☐ 6 Joe Carter Barry Bonds	1.00	.45	.13
☐ 7 Ken Griffey Jr. Tony Gwynn	4.00	1.80	.50
☐ 8 Kirby Puckett David Justice	1.25	.55	.16
☐ 9 Jimmy Key Greg Maddux	.50	.23	.06
☐ 10 Chuck Knoblauch Wil Cordero	.25	.11	.03
☐ 11 Scott Cooper Ken Caminiti	.25	.11	.03
☐ 12 Will Clark Carlos Garcia	.50	.23	.06
☐ 13 Paul Molitor Jeff Bagwell	1.75	.80	.22
☐ 14 Travis Fryman Craig Biggio	.25	.11	.03
☐ 15 Mickey Tettleton Fred McGriff	.50	.23	.06
☐ 16 Kenny Lofton Moises Alou	.60	.25	.08
☐ 17 Albert Belle Marquis Grissom	.75	.35	.09
☐ 18 Paul O'Neill Dante Bichette	.25	.11	.03
☐ 19 David Cone Ken Hill	.25	.11	.03
☐ 20 Mike Mussina Doug Drabek	.50	.23	.06
☐ 21 Randy Johnson John Hudek	.25	.11	.03
☐ 22 Pat Hentgen Danny Jackson	.25	.11	.03
☐ 23 Wilson Alvarez Rod Beck	.25	.11	.03
☐ 24 Lee Smith Randy Myers	.25	.11	.03
☐ 25 Jason Bere Doug Jones	.25	.11	.03

1995 Fleer Award Winners

Randomly inserted in all pack types at a rate of one in 24, this six card set highlights the major award winners of 1994. Card

fronts feature action photos that are full-bleed on the right border and have gold border on the left. Within the gold border are the player's name and Fleer Award Winner. The backs contain a photo with text that references 1994 accomplishments.

	MINT	EXC	G-VG
COMPLETE SET (6)	15.00	6.75	1.90
COMMON CARD (1-6)	1.00	.45	.13
☐ 1 Frank Thomas AL MVP	8.00	3.60	1.00
☐ 2 Jeff Bagwell NL MVP	4.00	1.80	.50
☐ 3 David Cone AL Pitcher of the Year	1.00	.45	.13
☐ 4 Greg Maddux NL Pitcher of the Year	2.50	1.15	.30
☐ 5 Bob Hamelin AL ROY	1.00	.45	.13
☐ 6 Raul Mondesi NL ROY	2.50	1.15	.30

1995 Fleer League Leaders

Randomly inserted in all pack types at a rate of one in 12, this 10-card set features 1994 American and National League leaders in various categories. The horizontal cards have player photos on front and back. The back also has a brief write-up concerning the accomplishment.

	MINT	EXC	G-VG
COMPLETE SET (10)	15.00	6.75	1.90
COMMON CARD (1-10)	.75	.35	.09

☐ 1 Paul O'Neill AL Batting Leader	.75	.35	.09
☐ 2 Ken Griffey Jr. AL Home Run Leader	6.00	2.70	.75
☐ 3 Kirby Puckett AL RBI Leader	2.50	1.15	.30
☐ 4 Jimmy Key AL Winningest Pitcher	.75	.35	.09
☐ 5 Randy Johnson AL Strikeout Leader	.75	.35	.09
☐ 6 Tony Gwynn NL Batting Leader	2.00	.90	.25
☐ 7 Matt Williams NL Home Run Leader	1.75	.80	.22
☐ 8 Jeff Bagwell NL RBI Leader	3.00	1.35	.40
☐ 9 Greg Maddux Ken Hill NL Winningest Pitchers	2.00	.90	.25
☐ 10 Andy Benes NL Strikeout Leader	.75	.35	.09

1995 Fleer Lumber Company

Randomly inserted in retail packs at a rate of one in 24, this set highlights 10 of the game's top sluggers. Full-bleed card fronts feature an action photo with the Lumber Company logo, which includes the player's name, toward the bottom of the photo. Card backs have a player photo and woodgrain background with a write-up that highlights individual achievements.

	MINT	EXC	G-VG
COMPLETE SET (10)	40.00	18.00	5.00
COMMON CARD (1-10)	1.00	.45	.13
☐ 1 Jeff Bagwell	6.00	2.70	.75
☐ 2 Albert Belle	3.00	1.35	.40
☐ 3 Barry Bonds	4.00	1.80	.50
☐ 4 Jose Canseco	2.00	.90	.25
☐ 5 Joe Carter	2.00	.90	.25
☐ 6 Ken Griffey Jr.	12.00	5.50	1.50
☐ 7 Fred McGriff	2.00	.90	.25
☐ 8 Kevin Mitchell	1.00	.45	.13
☐ 9 Frank Thomas	12.00	5.50	1.50
☐ 10 Matt Williams	2.50	1.15	.30

1995 Fleer Major League Prospects

Randomly inserted in all pack types at a rate of one in six, this 10-card set spotlights major league hopefuls. Card fronts feature a player photo with the words "Major League Prospects" serving as part of the background. The player's name and team appear in silver foil at the bottom. The backs have a photo and a write-up on his minor league career.

	MINT	EXC	G-VG
COMPLETE SET (10)	15.00	6.75	1.90
COMMON CARD (1-10)	.50	.23	.06
☐ 1 Garret Anderson	.50	.23	.06
☐ 2 James Baldwin	1.25	.55	.16
☐ 3 Alan Benes	1.25	.55	.16
☐ 4 Armando Benitez	.50	.23	.06
☐ 5 Ray Durham	1.50	.65	.19
☐ 6 Brian L. Hunter	1.50	.65	.19
☐ 7 Derek Jeter	2.00	.90	.25
☐ 8 Charles Johnson	1.50	.65	.19
☐ 9 Orlando Miller	.50	.23	.06
☐ 10 Alex Rodriguez	5.00	2.30	.60

1995 Fleer Pro-Visions

Randomly inserted in all pack types at a rate of one in nine, this six card set features top players illustrated by Wayne Anthony

Still. The colorful artwork on front features the player in a surrealistic setting. The backs offer write-up on the player's previous season.

	MINT	EXC	G-VG
COMPLETE SET (6)	4.00	1.80	.50
COMMON CARD (1-6)	.50	.23	.06
☐ 1 Mike Mussina	.75	.35	.09
☐ 2 Raul Mondesi	1.00	.45	.13
☐ 3 Jeff Bagwell	2.00	.90	.25
☐ 4 Greg Maddux	1.00	.45	.13
☐ 5 Tim Salmon	.50	.23	.06
☐ 6 Manny Ramirez	.75	.35	.09

1995 Fleer Rookie Sensations

Randomly inserted in 18-card packs, this 20-card set features top rookies from the 1994 season. The fronts have full-bleed color photos with the team and player's name in gold foil along the right edge. The backs also have full-bleed color photos along with player information.

	MINT	EXC	G-VG
COMPLETE SET (20)	50.00	23.00	6.25
COMMON CARD (1-20)	1.25	.55	.16
☐ 1 Kurt Abbott	1.25	.55	.16
☐ 2 Rico Brogna	1.25	.55	.16
☐ 3 Hector Carrasco	1.25	.55	.16
☐ 4 Kevin Foster	1.25	.55	.16
☐ 5 Chris Gomez	1.25	.55	.16
☐ 6 Darren Hall	1.25	.55	.16
☐ 7 Bob Hamelin	3.00	1.35	.40
☐ 8 Joey Hamilton	3.50	1.55	.45
☐ 9 John Hudek	3.00	1.35	.40
☐ 10 Ryan Klesko	5.00	2.30	.60
☐ 11 Javy Lopez	4.00	1.80	.50
☐ 12 Matt Mieske	1.25	.55	.16
☐ 13 Raul Mondesi	8.00	3.60	1.00
☐ 14 Manny Ramirez	6.00	2.70	.75
☐ 15 Shane Reynolds	1.25	.55	.16
☐ 16 Bill Risley	1.25	.55	.16
☐ 17 Johnny Ruffin	1.25	.55	.16
☐ 18 Steve Trachsel	3.00	1.35	.40
☐ 19 Will VanLandingham	3.50	1.55	.45
☐ 20 Rondell White	4.00	1.80	.50

1995 Fleer Team Leaders

Randomly inserted in 12-card hobby packs at a rate of one in 24, this 28-card set features top players from each team. Each team is represented with card the has the team's leading hitter on one side with the leading pitcher on the other side. The team logo, "Team Leaders" and the player's name are gold foil stamped on front and back.

	MINT	EXC	G-VG
COMPLETE SET (28)	100.00	45.00	12.50
COMMON PAIR (1-28)	1.50	.65	.19
☐ 1 Cal Ripken Jr. / Mike Mussina	15.00	6.75	1.90
☐ 2 Mo Vaughn / Roger Clemens	6.00	2.70	.75
☐ 3 Tim Salmon / Chuck Finley	1.50	.65	.19
☐ 4 Frank Thomas / Jack McDowell	20.00	9.00	2.50
☐ 5 Albert Belle / Dennis Martinez	5.00	2.30	.60
☐ 6 Cecil Fielder / Mike Moore	1.50	.65	.19
☐ 7 Bob Hamelin / David Cone	1.50	.65	.19
☐ 8 Greg Vaughn / Ricky Bones	1.50	.65	.19
☐ 9 Kirby Puckett / Rick Aguilera	7.00	3.10	.85
☐ 10 Don Mattingly / Jimmy Key	7.00	3.10	.85
☐ 11 Ruben Sierra / Dennis Eckersley	1.50	.65	.19
☐ 12 Ken Griffey Jr. / Randy Johnson	20.00	9.00	2.50
☐ 13 Jose Canseco / Kenny Rogers	3.50	1.55	.45
☐ 14 Joe Carter / Pat Hentgen	3.50	1.55	.45
☐ 15 David Justice / Greg Maddux	6.00	2.70	.75
☐ 16 Sammy Sosa / Steve Trachsel	1.50	.65	.19
☐ 17 Kevin Mitchell / Jose Rijo	1.50	.65	.19
☐ 18 Dante Bichette / Bruce Ruffin	1.50	.65	.19
☐ 19 Jeff Conine / Robb Nen	1.50	.65	.19
☐ 20 Jeff Bagwell / Doug Drabek	10.00	4.50	1.25

Card	MINT	EXC	G-VG
☐ 21 Mike Piazza Ramon Martinez	8.00	3.60	1.00
☐ 22 Moises Alou Ken Hill	1.50	.65	.19
☐ 23 Bobby Bonilla Bret Saberhagen	1.50	.65	.19
☐ 24 Darren Daulton Danny Jackson	1.50	.65	.19
☐ 25 Jay Bell Zane Smith	1.50	.65	.19
☐ 26 Gregg Jefferies Bob Tewksbury	1.50	.65	.19
☐ 27 Tony Gwynn Andy Benes	5.00	2.30	.60
☐ 28 Matt Williams Rod Beck	3.50	1.55	.45

1991 Front Row Draft

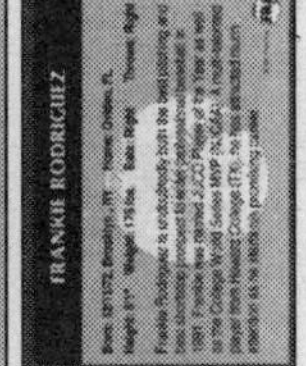

This 50-card premier edition set includes 27 of the top 40 eligible players from the 1991 Baseball Draft. The cards measure the standard size (2 1/2" by 3 1/2"), and only 240,000 sets were produced. Each set contains a numbered card registering the set and one card from a limited Draft Pick subset as a bonus card. In exchange for returning the bonus card, the collector received card number 50 (Benji Gil), a mini-update set (51-54; sent to the first 120,000 respondents), and one card from a five-card Frankie Rodriguez bonus set. The photos on both sides of the card are highlighted with an ultra violet finish. The obverse has glossy color player photos bordered in gray, with the player's name in black lettering below the picture. The words "Front Row" appear in a baseball in the upper right corner, while the words "'91 Draft Pick" appear in a diamond in the lower left corner. The reverse has a color photo of the player in little league, biography, statistics, and career achievements. The cards are numbered on the back.

	MINT	EXC	G-VG
COMPLETE SET (50)	4.00	1.80	.50
COMMON CARD (1-49)	.05	.02	.01
*GOLD: 4X VALUES BELOW			
*SILVER: 2X VALUES BELOW			

Card	MINT	EXC	G-VG
☐ 1 Frankie Rodriguez	.50	.23	.06
☐ 2 Aaron Sele	.75	.35	.09
☐ 3 Chad Schoenvogel	.05	.02	.01
☐ 4 Scott Ruffcorn	.50	.23	.06
☐ 5 Dan Cholowski UER (Name should be spelled Cholowsky)	.15	.07	.02
☐ 6 Gene Schall	.25	.11	.03
☐ 7 Trever Miller	.05	.02	.01
☐ 8 Chris Durkin	.05	.02	.01
☐ 9 Mike Neill	.05	.02	.01
☐ 10 Kevin Stocker	.10	.05	.01
☐ 11 Bobby Jones	.75	.35	.09
☐ 12 Jon Farrell	.05	.02	.01
☐ 13 Ronnie Allen	.05	.02	.01
☐ 14 Mike Rossiter	.05	.02	.01
☐ 15 Scott Hatteberg	.05	.02	.01
☐ 16 Rodney Pedraza	.15	.07	.02
☐ 17 Mike Durant	.05	.02	.01
☐ 18 Ryan Long	.15	.07	.02
☐ 19 Greg Anthony	.05	.02	.01
☐ 20 Jon Barnes	.05	.02	.01
☐ 21 Brian Barber	.10	.05	.01
☐ 22 Brent Gates	.50	.23	.06
☐ 23 Calvin Reese	.30	.14	.04
☐ 24 Terry Horn	.05	.02	.01
☐ 25 Scott Stahoviak	.10	.05	.01
☐ 26 Jason Pruitt	.05	.02	.01
☐ 27 Shawn Curran	.05	.02	.01
☐ 28 Jimmy Lewis	.05	.02	.01
☐ 29 Alex Ochoa	.30	.14	.04
☐ 30 Joe DeBerry	.05	.02	.01
☐ 31 Justin Thompson	.10	.05	.01
☐ 32 Jimmy Gonzalez	.05	.02	.01
☐ 33 Eddie Ramos	.05	.02	.01
☐ 34 Tyler Green	.10	.05	.01
☐ 35 Toby Rumfield	.10	.05	.01
☐ 36 Dave Doornenweerd	.05	.02	.01
☐ 37 Jeff Hostetler	.05	.02	.01
☐ 38 Shawn Livsey	.05	.02	.01
☐ 39 Mike Groppuso	.05	.02	.01
☐ 40 Steve Whitaker	.10	.05	.01
☐ 41 Tom McKinnon	.05	.02	.01
☐ 42 Buck McNabb	.05	.02	.01
☐ 43 Al Shirley	.10	.05	.01
☐ 44 Allen Watson UER (Misspelled Allan)	.10	.05	.01
☐ 45 Bill Bliss	.05	.02	.01
☐ 46 Todd Hollandsworth	.40	.18	.05
☐ 47 Manny Ramirez	1.75	.80	.22
☐ 48 J.J. Johnson	.10	.05	.01
☐ 49 Cliff Floyd	1.50	.65	.19
☐ 50A Bonus Card	1.75	.80	.22
☐ 50B Benji Gil	.40	.18	.05
☐ 51B Herb Perry	.20	.09	.03
☐ 52B Tarrik Brock	.15	.07	.02
☐ 53B Trevor Mallory	.15	.07	.02
☐ 54B Chris Pritchett	.20	.09	.03
☐ FR1 Frankie Rodriguez Pitching (Just after release, forward knee bent)	.50	.23	.06
☐ FR2 Frankie Rodriguez Pitching (Ball in hand behind body, in wind up)	.50	.23	.06
☐ FR3 Frankie Rodriguez Batting stance (Almost at middle of swing)	.50	.23	.06
☐ FR4 Frankie Rodriguez Pitching (Just after release, forward leg straight)	.50	.23	.06
☐ FR5 Frankie Rodriguez Batting stance (Bat cocked above shoulder, waiting for pitch)	.50	.23	.06

1992 Front Row Draft

This 100-card set measures the standard size (2 1/2" by 3 1/2") and features color action player photos. According to Front Row, the production run was 10,000 wax cases and 2,500 30-set factory cases (both were individually numbered). Gold and silver foil stamped cards were randomly inserted into wax packs. Also randomly inserted were pure gold cards of Ken Griffey Jr. and Frank Thomas and HOFer signature cards of Brooks Robinson, Yogi Berra, Whitey Ford and others. The fronts feature color action player photos with blue borders that fade as one moves down the card face. The words "Draft Pick '92" appear in a yellow stripe that cuts across the card top, intersecting the Front Row logo at the upper right corner. The player's name in a yellow bar toward the bottom complete the front. On a tan panel featuring the Front Row logo, the horizontally oriented backs carry a color photo of the player in little league, biography, complete amateur statistics, and career achievements. The cards are numbered on the back.

	MINT	EXC	G-VG
COMPLETE SET (100)	8.00	3.60	1.00
COMMON CARD (1-100)	.05	.02	.01
*GOLD: 4X VALUES BELOW			
*SILVER: 2X VALUES BELOW			

		MINT	EXC	G-VG
☐ 1	Dan Melendez	.12	.05	.02
☐ 2	Billy Owens	.25	.11	.03
☐ 3	Sherard Clinkscales	.10	.05	.01
☐ 4	Tim Moore	.05	.02	.01
☐ 5	Michael Hickey	.05	.02	.01
☐ 6	Kenny Carlyle	.05	.02	.01
☐ 7	Todd Steverson	.25	.11	.03
☐ 8	Ted Corbin	.05	.02	.01
☐ 9	Tim Crabtree	.05	.02	.01
☐ 10	Jason Angel	.05	.02	.01
☐ 11	Mike Gulan	.15	.07	.02
☐ 12	Jared Baker	.05	.02	.01
☐ 13	Mike Buddie	.05	.02	.01
☐ 14	Brandon Pico	.05	.02	.01
☐ 15	Jonathan Nunnally	.15	.07	.02
☐ 16	Scott Patton	.05	.02	.01
☐ 17	Tony Sheffield	.05	.02	.01
☐ 18	Danny Clyburn	.50	.23	.06
☐ 19	Tom Knauss	.05	.02	.01
☐ 20	Carey Paige	.12	.05	.02
☐ 21	Keith Johnson	.05	.02	.01
☐ 22	Larry Mitchell	.05	.02	.01
☐ 23	Tim Leger	.05	.02	.01
☐ 24	Doug Hecker	.20	.09	.03
☐ 25	Aaron Thatcher	.05	.02	.01
☐ 26	Marquis Riley	.12	.05	.02
☐ 27	Jamie Taylor	.05	.02	.01
☐ 28	Don Wengert	.05	.02	.01
☐ 29	Jason Moler	.35	.16	.04
☐ 30	Kevin Kloek	.20	.09	.03
☐ 31	Kevin Pearson	.05	.02	.01
☐ 32	David Mysel	.05	.02	.01
☐ 33	Chris Holt	.15	.07	.02
☐ 34	Chris Gomez	.50	.23	.06
☐ 35	Joe Hamilton	.05	.02	.01
☐ 36	Brandon Cromer	.05	.02	.01
☐ 37	Lloyd Peever	.12	.05	.02
☐ 38	Gordon Sanchez	.05	.02	.01
☐ 39	Michael Tucker Bonus Card	1.50	.65	.19
☐ 40	Jason Giambi	.35	.16	.04
☐ 41	Sean Runyan	.05	.02	.01
☐ 42	Jamie Keefe	.15	.07	.02
☐ 43	Scott Gentile	.10	.05	.01
☐ 44	Michael Tucker	.60	.25	.08
☐ 45	Scott Klingenbeck	.20	.09	.03
☐ 46	Ed Christian	.05	.02	.01
☐ 47	Scott Miller	.05	.02	.01
☐ 48	Rick Navarro	.05	.02	.01
☐ 49	Bill Selby	.05	.02	.01
☐ 50	Chris Roberts	.30	.14	.04
☐ 51	John Dillinger	.05	.02	.01
☐ 52	Keith Johns	.05	.02	.01
☐ 53	Matt Williams	.05	.02	.01
☐ 54	Garvin Alston	.05	.02	.01
☐ 55	Derek Jeter	1.25	.55	.16
☐ 56	Chris Eddy	.05	.02	.01
☐ 57	Jeff Schmidt	.05	.02	.01
☐ 58	Chris Petersen	.05	.02	.01
☐ 59	Chris Sheff	.05	.02	.01
☐ 60	Chad Roper	.15	.07	.02
☐ 61	Rich Ireland	.12	.05	.02
☐ 62	Tibor Brown	.05	.02	.01
☐ 63	Todd Etler	.12	.05	.02
☐ 64	John Turlais	.05	.02	.01
☐ 65	Shawn Holcomb	.05	.02	.01
☐ 66	Ben Jones	.05	.02	.01
☐ 67	Marcel Galligani	.05	.02	.01
☐ 68	Troy Penix	.20	.09	.03
☐ 69	Matt Luke	.50	.23	.06
☐ 70	David Post	.05	.02	.01
☐ 71	Michael Warner	.05	.02	.01
☐ 72	Alexis Aranzamendi	.05	.02	.01
☐ 73	Larry Hingle	.05	.02	.01
☐ 74	Shon Walker	.25	.11	.03
☐ 75	Mark Thompson	.20	.09	.03
☐ 76	John Lieber	.50	.23	.06
☐ 77	Wes Weger	.30	.14	.04
☐ 78	Mike Smith	.10	.05	.01
☐ 79	Ritchie Moody	.12	.05	.02
☐ 80	B.J. Wallace	.20	.09	.03
☐ 81	Rick Helling	.40	.18	.05
☐ 82	Chad Mottola	.30	.14	.04
☐ 83	Brant Brown	.20	.09	.03
☐ 84	Steve Rodriguez	.05	.02	.01
☐ 85	John Vanhof	.05	.02	.01
☐ 86	Brian Wolf	.05	.02	.01
☐ 87	Steve Montgomery	.05	.02	.01
☐ 88	Eric Owens	.15	.07	.02
☐ 89	Jason Kendall	.50	.23	.06
☐ 90	Bob Bennett	.05	.02	.01
☐ 91	Joe Petcka	.15	.07	.02
☐ 92	Jim Rosenbohm	.05	.02	.01
☐ 93	David Manning	.05	.02	.01
☐ 94	Davie Landaker	.20	.09	.03
☐ 95	Dan Kyslinger	.05	.02	.01
☐ 96	Roger Bailey	.12	.05	.02

☐ 97 Jon Zuber	.20	.09	.03
☐ 98 Steve Cox	.05	.02	.01
☐ 99 Chris Widger	.05	.02	.01
☐ 100 Checklist 1-100	.05	.02	.01

1993 Fun Pack

This 225-card set measures the standard-size (2 1/2" by 3 1/2") and has fronts that display action player photos on a bright multicolored background. The team name is printed in yellow at the top right and the player's name appears below the photo within the irregular green border. The pink- and yellow-bordered back carries a cartoon with a trivia question above. The answer appears in fine print along the right side. The player's biography, statistics, and career highlights are shown beneath the cartoon, and his name, team, and position are displayed in the upper right. The bottom white margin carrying the Upper Deck and MLBPA logos rounds out the back. Topical subsets featured are Stars of Tomorrow (1-9), Hot Shots (10-21), Kid Stars (22-27), Upper Deck Heroes (28-36), All-Star Advice (210-215), All-Star Fold Outs (216-220), and Checklists (221-225) and randomly numbered Glow Stars. The Hot Shots were available by mail and in retail packs. The cards are numbered on the back. Card numbers 37-209 are arranged alphabetically according to team names, with each team subset beginning with a Glow Star card as follows: California Angels (37-41), Houston Astros (42-47), Oakland Athletics (48-53), Toronto Blue Jays (54-60), Atlanta Braves (61-68), Milwaukee Brewers (69-73), St. Louis Cardinals (74-79), Chicago Cubs (80-85), Los Angeles Dodgers (86-92), Montreal Expos (93-98), San Francisco Giants (99-104), Cleveland Indians (105-110), Seattle Mariners (111-116), Florida Marlins (117-122), New York Mets (123-129), Baltimore Orioles (130-135), San Diego Padres (136-141), Philadelphia Phillies (142-147), Pittsburgh Pirates (148-152), Texas Rangers (153-160), Boston Red Sox (161-166), Cincinnati Reds (167-172), Colorado Rockies (173-178), Kansas City Royals (179-184), Detroit Tigers (185-190), Minnesota Twins (191-196), Chicago White Sox (197-203), and New York Yankees (204-209). The only noteworthy Rookie Card in this set is J.T. Snow.

	MINT	EXC	G-VG
COMPLETE SET (225)	30.00	13.50	3.80
COMMON CARD (1-225)	.05	.02	.01

☐ 1 Wil Cordero SOT	.10	.05	.01
☐ 2 Brent Gates SOT	.10	.05	.01
☐ 3 Benji Gil SOT	.08	.04	.01
☐ 4 Phil Hiatt SOT	.05	.02	.01
☐ 5 David McCarty SOT	.08	.04	.01
☐ 6 Mike Piazza SOT	2.00	.90	.25
☐ 7 Tim Salmon SOT	.40	.18	.05
☐ 8 J.T. Snow SOT	.15	.07	.02
☐ 9 Kevin Young SOT	.05	.02	.01
☐ 10 Roberto Alomar HS	1.00	.45	.13
☐ 11 Barry Bonds HS	1.50	.65	.19
☐ 12 Jose Canseco HS	.60	.25	.08
☐ 13 Will Clark HS	.60	.25	.08
☐ 14 Roger Clemens HS	1.00	.45	.13
☐ 15 Juan Gonzalez HS	1.25	.55	.16
☐ 16 Ken Griffey Jr. HS	4.00	1.80	.50
☐ 17 Mark McGwire HS	.25	.11	.03
☐ 18 Nolan Ryan HS	4.00	1.80	.50
☐ 19 Ryne Sandberg HS	1.25	.55	.16
☐ 20 Gary Sheffield HS	.25	.11	.03
☐ 21 Frank Thomas HS	4.00	1.80	.50
☐ 22 Roberto Alomar KS	.25	.11	.03
☐ 23 Roger Clemens KS	.25	.11	.03
☐ 24 Ken Griffey Jr. KS	1.00	.45	.13
☐ 25 Gary Sheffield KS	.08	.04	.01
☐ 26 Nolan Ryan KS	1.00	.45	.13
☐ 27 Frank Thomas KS	1.00	.45	.13
☐ 28 Reggie Jackson HERO	.15	.07	.02
☐ 29 Roger Clemens HERO	.25	.11	.03
☐ 30 Ken Griffey Jr. HERO	1.00	.45	.13
☐ 31 Bo Jackson HERO	.08	.04	.01
☐ 32 Cal Ripken HERO	.75	.35	.09
☐ 33 Nolan Ryan HERO	1.00	.45	.13
☐ 34 Deion Sanders HERO	.10	.05	.01
☐ 35 Ozzie Smith HERO	.20	.09	.03
☐ 36 Frank Thomas HERO	1.00	.45	.13
☐ 37 Tim Salmon GS	.20	.09	.03
☐ 38 Chili Davis	.08	.04	.01
☐ 39 Chuck Finley	.05	.02	.01
☐ 40 Mark Langston	.10	.05	.01
☐ 41 Luis Polonia	.05	.02	.01
☐ 42 Jeff Bagwell GS	.50	.23	.06
☐ 43 Jeff Bagwell	1.00	.45	.13
☐ 44 Craig Biggio	.08	.04	.01
☐ 45 Ken Caminiti	.08	.04	.01
☐ 46 Doug Drabek	.10	.05	.01
☐ 47 Steve Finley	.05	.02	.01
☐ 48 Mark McGwire GS	.08	.04	.01
☐ 49 Dennis Eckersley	.10	.05	.01
☐ 50 Rickey Henderson	.10	.05	.01
☐ 51 Mark McGwire	.10	.05	.01
☐ 52 Ruben Sierra	.10	.05	.01
☐ 53 Terry Steinbach	.08	.04	.01
☐ 54 Roberto Alomar GS	.25	.11	.03
☐ 55 Roberto Alomar	.50	.23	.06
☐ 56 Joe Carter	.30	.14	.04
☐ 57 Juan Guzman	.08	.04	.01
☐ 58 Paul Molitor	.30	.14	.04
☐ 59 Jack Morris	.10	.05	.01
☐ 60 John Olerud	.10	.05	.01
☐ 61 Tom Glavine GS	.08	.04	.01
☐ 62 Steve Avery	.10	.05	.01
☐ 63 Tom Glavine	.10	.05	.01
☐ 64 David Justice	.30	.14	.04
☐ 65 Greg Maddux	.40	.18	.05
☐ 66 Terry Pendleton	.10	.05	.01
☐ 67 Deion Sanders	.40	.18	.05
☐ 68 John Smoltz	.08	.04	.01
☐ 69 Robin Yount GS	.15	.07	.02
☐ 70 Cal Eldred	.08	.04	.01
☐ 71 Pat Listach	.08	.04	.01
☐ 72 Greg Vaughn	.08	.04	.01
☐ 73 Robin Yount	.30	.14	.04

☐ 74	Ozzie Smith GS	.20	.09	.03
☐ 75	Gregg Jefferies	.10	.05	.01
☐ 76	Ray Lankford	.10	.05	.01
☐ 77	Lee Smith	.10	.05	.01
☐ 78	Ozzie Smith	.40	.18	.05
☐ 79	Bob Tewksbury	.05	.02	.01
☐ 80	Ryne Sandberg GS	.40	.18	.05
☐ 81	Mark Grace	.10	.05	.01
☐ 82	Mike Morgan	.05	.02	.01
☐ 83	Randy Myers	.08	.04	.01
☐ 84	Ryne Sandberg	.75	.35	.09
☐ 85	Sammy Sosa	.10	.05	.01
☐ 86	Eric Karros GS	.08	.04	.01
☐ 87	Brett Butler	.08	.04	.01
☐ 88	Orel Hershiser	.08	.04	.01
☐ 89	Eric Karros	.08	.04	.01
☐ 90	Ramon Martinez	.08	.04	.01
☐ 91	Jose Offerman	.05	.02	.01
☐ 92	Darryl Strawberry	.08	.04	.01
☐ 93	Marquis Grissom GS	.08	.04	.01
☐ 94	Delino DeShields	.08	.04	.01
☐ 95	Marquis Grissom	.10	.05	.01
☐ 96	Ken Hill	.08	.04	.01
☐ 97	Dennis Martinez	.08	.04	.01
☐ 98	Larry Walker	.10	.05	.01
☐ 99	Barry Bonds GS	.40	.18	.05
☐ 100	Barry Bonds	.75	.35	.09
☐ 101	Will Clark	.30	.14	.04
☐ 102	Bill Swift	.08	.04	.01
☐ 103	Robby Thompson	.05	.02	.01
☐ 104	Matt Williams	.30	.14	.04
☐ 105	Carlos Baerga GS	.15	.07	.02
☐ 106	Sandy Alomar Jr.	.08	.04	.01
☐ 107	Carlos Baerga	.30	.14	.04
☐ 108	Albert Belle	.60	.25	.08
☐ 109	Kenny Lofton	.50	.23	.06
☐ 110	Charles Nagy	.05	.02	.01
☐ 111	Ken Griffey Jr. GS	1.00	.45	.13
☐ 112	Jay Buhner	.08	.04	.01
☐ 113	Dave Fleming	.08	.04	.01
☐ 114	Ken Griffey Jr.	2.00	.90	.25
☐ 115	Randy Johnson	.10	.05	.01
☐ 116	Edgar Martinez	.05	.02	.01
☐ 117	Benito Santiago GS	.05	.02	.01
☐ 118	Bret Barberie	.05	.02	.01
☐ 119	Jeff Conine	.10	.05	.01
☐ 120	Brian Harvey	.05	.02	.01
☐ 121	Benito Santiago	.05	.02	.01
☐ 122	Walt Weiss	.05	.02	.01
☐ 123	Dwight Gooden GS	.05	.02	.01
☐ 124	Bobby Bonilla	.10	.05	.01
☐ 125	Tony Fernandez	.05	.02	.01
☐ 126	Dwight Gooden	.05	.02	.01
☐ 127	Howard Johnson	.05	.02	.01
☐ 128	Eddie Murray	.10	.05	.01
☐ 129	Bret Saberhagen	.08	.04	.01
☐ 130	Cal Ripken GS	.75	.35	.09
☐ 131	Brady Anderson	.08	.04	.01
☐ 132	Mike Devereaux	.08	.04	.01
☐ 133	Ben McDonald	.08	.04	.01
☐ 134	Mike Mussina	.40	.18	.05
☐ 135	Cal Ripken	1.50	.65	.19
☐ 136	Fred McGriff GS	.15	.07	.02
☐ 137	Andy Benes	.08	.04	.01
☐ 138	Tony Gwynn	.50	.23	.06
☐ 139	Fred McGriff	.30	.14	.04
☐ 140	Phil Plantier	.10	.05	.01
☐ 141	Gary Sheffield	.10	.05	.01
☐ 142	Darren Daulton GS	.08	.04	.01
☐ 143	Darren Daulton	.10	.05	.01
☐ 144	Len Dykstra	.10	.05	.01
☐ 145	Dave Hollins	.10	.05	.01
☐ 146	John Kruk	.10	.05	.01
☐ 147	Mitch Williams	.08	.04	.01
☐ 148	Andy Van Slyke GS	.08	.04	.01
☐ 149	Jay Bell	.08	.04	.01
☐ 150	Zane Smith	.05	.02	.01
☐ 151	Andy Van Slyke	.10	.05	.01
☐ 152	Tim Wakefield	.05	.02	.01
☐ 153	Juan Gonzalez GS	.30	.14	.04
☐ 154	Kevin Brown	.05	.02	.01
☐ 155	Jose Canseco	.30	.14	.04
☐ 156	Juan Gonzalez	.60	.25	.08
☐ 157	Rafael Palmeiro	.10	.05	.01
☐ 158	Dean Palmer	.08	.04	.01
☐ 159	Ivan Rodriguez	.10	.05	.01
☐ 160	Nolan Ryan	2.00	.90	.25
☐ 161	Roger Clemens GS	.25	.11	.03
☐ 162	Roger Clemens	.50	.23	.06
☐ 163	Andre Dawson	.10	.05	.01
☐ 164	Mike Greenwell	.08	.04	.01
☐ 165	Tony Pena	.05	.02	.01
☐ 166	Frank Viola	.08	.04	.01
☐ 167	Barry Larkin GS	.08	.04	.01
☐ 168	Rob Dibble	.05	.02	.01
☐ 169	Roberto Kelly	.08	.04	.01
☐ 170	Barry Larkin	.10	.05	.01
☐ 171	Kevin Mitchell	.08	.04	.01
☐ 172	Bip Roberts	.05	.02	.01
☐ 173	Andres Galarraga GS	.08	.04	.01
☐ 174	Dante Bichette	.10	.05	.01
☐ 175	Jerald Clark	.05	.02	.01
☐ 176	Andres Galarraga	.10	.05	.01
☐ 177	Charlie Hayes	.08	.04	.01
☐ 178	David Nied	.10	.05	.01
☐ 179	David Cone GS	.05	.02	.01
☐ 180	Kevin Appier	.08	.04	.01
☐ 181	George Brett	.75	.35	.09
☐ 182	David Cone	.10	.05	.01
☐ 183	Felix Jose	.05	.02	.01
☐ 184	Wally Joyner	.08	.04	.01
☐ 185	Cecil Fielder GS	.08	.04	.01
☐ 186	Cecil Fielder	.10	.05	.01
☐ 187	Travis Fryman	.15	.07	.02
☐ 188	Tony Phillips	.05	.02	.01
☐ 189	Mickey Tettleton	.08	.04	.01
☐ 190	Lou Whitaker	.10	.05	.01
☐ 191	Kirby Puckett GS	.40	.18	.05
☐ 192	Scott Erickson	.05	.02	.01
☐ 193	Chuck Knoblauch	.10	.05	.01
☐ 194	Shane Mack	.08	.04	.01
☐ 195	Kirby Puckett	.75	.35	.09
☐ 196	Dave Winfield	.10	.05	.01
☐ 197	Frank Thomas GS	1.00	.45	.13
☐ 198	George Bell	.08	.04	.01
☐ 199	Bo Jackson	.10	.05	.01
☐ 200	Jack McDowell	.10	.05	.01
☐ 201	Tim Raines	.10	.05	.01
☐ 202	Frank Thomas	2.00	.90	.25
☐ 203	Robin Ventura	.10	.05	.01
☐ 204	Jim Abbott GS	.10	.05	.01
☐ 205	Jim Abbott	.10	.05	.01
☐ 206	Wade Boggs	.10	.05	.01
☐ 207	Jimmy Key	.08	.04	.01
☐ 208	Don Mattingly	.75	.35	.09
☐ 209	Danny Tartabull	.08	.04	.01
☐ 210	Brett Butler ASA	.05	.02	.01
☐ 211	Tony Gwynn ASA	.10	.05	.01
☐ 212	Rickey Henderson ASA	.08	.04	.01
☐ 213	Ramon Martinez ASA	.05	.02	.01
☐ 214	Nolan Ryan ASA	1.00	.45	.13
☐ 215	Ozzie Smith ASA	.10	.05	.01
☐ 216	Marquis Grissom FOLD	.10	.05	.01
☐ 217	Dean Palmer FOLD	.08	.04	.01
☐ 218	Cal Ripken FOLD	.75	.35	.09
☐ 219	Delon Sanders FOLD	.10	.05	.01

		MINT	EXC	G-VG
☐ 220	Darryl Strawberry FOLD	.05	.02	.01
☐ 221	David McCarty CL	.08	.04	.01
☐ 222	Barry Bonds CL	.40	.18	.05
☐ 223	Juan Gonzalez CL	.35	.16	.04
☐ 224	Ken Griffey Jr. CL	1.00	.45	.13
☐ 225	Frank Thomas CL	1.00	.45	.13
☐ NNO	Hot Shots Card Punched	.15	.07	.02
☐ NNO	Hot Shots Card Expired	.30	.14	.04

1993 Fun Pack All-Stars

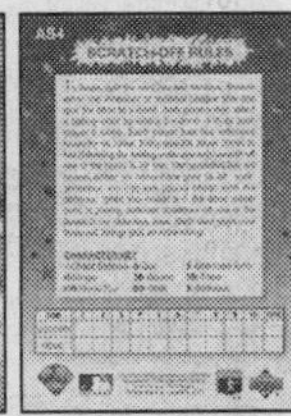

Randomly inserted in 1993 Upper Deck Fun Packs, these nine foldouts measure the standard size (2 1/2" by 3 1/2") when closed and 2 1/2" by 7" when opened. The front of each features side-by-side color action photos of an American League and a National League player. The set's title appears above the photos within a blue stripe. The players' names appear within an irregular white stripe near the bottom. The blue-and-white back carries the rules for playing the scratch-off game and a section to keep score. The actual scratch-off line-ups appear when the card is opened. The American League players and their scratch-off circles are displayed within the reddish left side of the foldout, and their National League counterparts appear within the bluish right side. The scratch-offs are numbered on the back with an "AS" prefix.

	MINT	EXC	G-VG
COMPLETE SET (9)	20.00	9.00	2.50
COMMON PAIR (AS1-AS9)	.75	.35	.09

		MINT	EXC	G-VG
☐ AS1	Frank Thomas Fred McGriff	5.00	2.30	.60
☐ AS2	Ivan Rodriguez Darren Daulton	.75	.35	.09
☐ AS3	Mark McGwire Will Clark	1.25	.55	.16
☐ AS4	Roberto Alomar Ryne Sandberg	2.50	1.15	.30
☐ AS5	Robin Ventura Terry Pendleton	.75	.35	.09
☐ AS6	Cal Ripken Ozzie Smith	3.50	1.55	.45
☐ AS7	Juan Gonzalez Barry Bonds	3.50	1.55	.45
☐ AS8	Ken Griffey Jr. Marquis Grissom	5.00	2.30	.60
☐ AS9	Kirby Puckett Tony Gwynn	2.50	1.15	.30

1994 Fun Pack

Issued by Upper Deck for the second straight year, the Fun Pack set consists of 240 cards. Bright yellow and green borders surround a color player photo on the front. The backs, with much the same color scheme, are horizontal and contain a cartoon relating to the player and statistics. The following subsets are included in this set: Stars of Tomorrow (1-9), Standouts (175-192), Pro-Files (193-198), Headline Stars (199-207), What's the Call (208-216), Foldouts (217-225) and Fun Cards (226-234). Michael Jordan's Rookie Card is in this set.

	MINT	EXC	G-VG
COMPLETE SET (240)	50.00	23.00	6.25
COMMON CARD (1-240)	.10	.05	.01

		MINT	EXC	G-VG
☐ 1	Manny Ramirez	.60	.25	.08
☐ 2	Cliff Floyd	.50	.23	.06
☐ 3	Rondell White	.30	.14	.04
☐ 4	Carlos Delgado	.50	.23	.06
☐ 5	Chipper Jones	.40	.18	.05
☐ 6	Javy Lopez	.30	.14	.04
☐ 7	Ryan Klesko	.50	.23	.06
☐ 8	Steve Karsay	.10	.05	.01
☐ 9	Rich Becker	.15	.07	.02
☐ 10	Gary Sheffield	.20	.09	.03
☐ 11	Jeffrey Hammonds	.30	.14	.04
☐ 12	Roberto Alomar	.75	.35	.09
☐ 13	Brent Gates	.20	.09	.03
☐ 14	Andres Galarraga	.20	.09	.03
☐ 15	Tim Salmon	.40	.18	.05
☐ 16	Dwight Gooden	.10	.05	.01
☐ 17	Mark Grace	.20	.09	.03
☐ 18	Andy Van Slyke	.20	.09	.03
☐ 19	Juan Gonzalez	1.00	.45	.13
☐ 20	Mickey Tettleton	.15	.07	.02
☐ 21	Roger Clemens	.75	.35	.09
☐ 22	Will Clark	.40	.18	.05
☐ 23	David Justice	.40	.18	.05
☐ 24	Ken Griffey Jr.	3.00	1.35	.40
☐ 25	Barry Bonds	1.25	.55	.16
☐ 26	Bill Swift	.10	.05	.01
☐ 27	Fred McGriff	.40	.18	.05
☐ 28	Randy Myers	.10	.05	.01
☐ 29	Joe Carter	.40	.18	.05
☐ 30	Nigel Wilson	.15	.07	.02
☐ 31	Mike Piazza	1.50	.65	.19
☐ 32	Dave Winfield	.20	.09	.03
☐ 33	Steve Avery	.20	.09	.03
☐ 34	Kirby Puckett	1.25	.55	.16
☐ 35	Frank Thomas	3.00	1.35	.40
☐ 36	Aaron Sele	.30	.14	.04
☐ 37	Ricky Gutierrez	.10	.05	.01
☐ 38	Curt Schilling	.10	.05	.01
☐ 39	Mike Greenwell	.15	.07	.02

☐	40 Andy Benes	.15	.07	.02
☐	41 Kevin Brown	.10	.05	.01
☐	42 Mo Vaughn	.20	.09	.03
☐	43 Dennis Eckersley	.20	.09	.03
☐	44 Ken Hill	.15	.07	.02
☐	45 Cecil Fielder	.20	.09	.03
☐	46 Bobby Jones	.25	.11	.03
☐	47 Tom Glavine	.20	.09	.03
☐	48 Wally Joyner	.15	.07	.02
☐	49 Ellis Burks	.15	.07	.02
☐	50 Jason Bere	.40	.18	.05
☐	51 Randy Johnson	.20	.09	.03
☐	52 Darryl Kile	.15	.07	.02
☐	53 Jeff Montgomery	.15	.07	.02
☐	54 Alex Fernandez	.20	.09	.03
☐	55 Kevin Appier	.15	.07	.02
☐	56 Brian McRae	.15	.07	.02
☐	57 John Wetteland	.10	.05	.01
☐	58 Bob Tewksbury	.10	.05	.01
☐	59 Todd Van Poppel	.15	.07	.02
☐	60 Ryne Sandberg	1.00	.45	.13
☐	61 Bret Barberie	.10	.05	.01
☐	62 Phil Plantier	.15	.07	.02
☐	63 Chris Hoiles	.15	.07	.02
☐	64 Tony Phillips	.10	.05	.01
☐	65 Salomon Torres	.15	.07	.02
☐	66 Juan Guzman	.15	.07	.02
☐	67 Paul O'Neill	.15	.07	.02
☐	68 Dante Bichette	.20	.09	.03
☐	69 Lenny Dykstra	.20	.09	.03
☐	70 Ivan Rodriguez	.20	.09	.03
☐	71 Dean Palmer	.15	.07	.02
☐	72 Brett Butler	.15	.07	.02
☐	73 Rick Aguilera	.15	.07	.02
☐	74 Robby Thompson	.10	.05	.01
☐	75 Jim Abbott	.20	.09	.03
☐	76 Al Martin	.10	.05	.01
☐	77 Roberto Hernandez	.10	.05	.01
☐	78 Jay Buhner	.15	.07	.02
☐	79 Devon White	.10	.05	.01
☐	80 Travis Fryman	.25	.11	.03
☐	81 Jeromy Burnitz	.15	.07	.02
☐	82 John Burkett	.15	.07	.02
☐	83 Orlando Merced	.15	.07	.02
☐	84 Jose Rijo	.15	.07	.02
☐	85 Eddie Murray	.20	.09	.03
☐	86 Howard Johnson	.10	.05	.01
☐	87 Chuck Carr	.10	.05	.01
☐	88 Pedro J. Martinez	.20	.09	.03
☐	89 Charlie Hayes	.15	.07	.02
☐	90 Matt Williams	.50	.23	.06
☐	91 Steve Finley	.10	.05	.01
☐	92 Pat Listach	.10	.05	.01
☐	93 Sandy Alomar Jr.	.15	.07	.02
☐	94 Delino DeShields	.15	.07	.02
☐	95 Rod Beck	.15	.07	.02
☐	96 Todd Zeile UER (Card misnumbered 97)	.15	.07	.02
☐	97 Duane Ward UER (Card misnumbered 98)	.10	.05	.01
☐	98 Darryl Hamilton	.10	.05	.01
☐	99 John Olerud	.20	.09	.03
☐	100 Andre Dawson	.20	.09	.03
☐	101 Ozzie Smith	.60	.25	.08
☐	102 Rick Wilkins	.10	.05	.01
☐	103 Alan Trammell	.20	.09	.03
☐	104 Jeff Blauser	.15	.07	.02
☐	105 Bret Boone	.20	.09	.03
☐	106 J.T. Snow	.15	.07	.02
☐	107 Kenny Lofton	.75	.35	.09
☐	108 Cal Ripken	2.25	1.00	.30
☐	109 Carlos Baerga	.40	.18	.05
☐	110 Bip Roberts	.10	.05	.01
☐	111 Barry Larkin	.20	.09	.03
☐	112 Mark Langston	.20	.09	.03
☐	113 Ozzie Guillen	.10	.05	.01
☐	114 Chad Curtis	.15	.07	.02
☐	115 Dave Hollins	.20	.09	.03
☐	116 Reggie Sanders	.15	.07	.02
☐	117 Jeff Conine	.20	.09	.03
☐	118 Mark Whiten	.15	.07	.02
☐	119 Tony Gwynn	.75	.35	.09
☐	120 John Kruk	.20	.09	.03
☐	121 Eduardo Perez	.15	.07	.02
☐	122 Walt Weiss	.10	.05	.01
☐	123 Don Mattingly	1.25	.55	.16
☐	124 Rickey Henderson	.20	.09	.03
☐	125 Mark McGwire	.20	.09	.03
☐	126 Wade Boggs	.20	.09	.03
☐	127 Bobby Bonilla	.20	.09	.03
☐	128 Jeff King	.10	.05	.01
☐	129 Jack McDowell	.20	.09	.03
☐	130 Albert Belle	1.00	.45	.13
☐	131 Greg Maddux	.60	.25	.08
☐	132 Dennis Martinez	.15	.07	.02
☐	133 Jose Canseco	.40	.18	.05
☐	134 Bryan Harvey	.15	.07	.02
☐	135 Dave Fleming	.10	.05	.01
☐	136 Larry Walker	.20	.09	.03
☐	137 Ken Caminiti	.15	.07	.02
☐	138 Doug Drabek	.20	.09	.03
☐	139 Alex Gonzalez	.20	.09	.03
☐	140 Darren Daulton	.20	.09	.03
☐	141 Ruben Sierra	.20	.09	.03
☐	142 Kirk Rueter	.10	.05	.01
☐	143 Raul Mondesi	1.00	.45	.13
☐	144 Greg Vaughn	.15	.07	.02
☐	145 Danny Tartabull	.15	.07	.02
☐	146 Eric Karros	.15	.07	.02
☐	147 Chuck Knoblauch	.20	.09	.03
☐	148 Mike Mussina	.40	.18	.05
☐	149 Brady Anderson	.15	.07	.02
☐	150 Paul Molitor	.40	.18	.05
☐	151 Bo Jackson	.20	.09	.03
☐	152 Jeff Bagwell	1.50	.65	.19
☐	153 Gregg Jefferies	.20	.09	.03
☐	154 Rafael Palmeiro	.20	.09	.03
☐	155 Orel Hershiser	.15	.07	.02
☐	156 Derek Bell	.15	.07	.02
☐	157 Jeff Kent	.15	.07	.02
☐	158 Craig Biggio	.15	.07	.02
☐	159 Marquis Grissom	.20	.09	.03
☐	160 Matt Mieske	.10	.05	.01
☐	161 Jay Bell	.15	.07	.02
☐	162 Sammy Sosa	.20	.09	.03
☐	163 Robin Ventura	.15	.07	.02
☐	164 Deion Sanders	.50	.23	.06
☐	165 Jimmy Key	.15	.07	.02
☐	166 Cal Eldred	.15	.07	.02
☐	167 David McCarty	.15	.07	.02
☐	168 Carlos Garcia	.10	.05	.01
☐	169 Willie Greene	.15	.07	.02
☐	170 Michael Jordan	12.00	5.50	1.50
☐	171 Roberto Mejia	.15	.07	.02
☐	172 Phil Hiatt UER (Card misnumbered 72)	.10	.05	.01
☐	173 Marc Newfield	.20	.09	.03
☐	174 Kevin Stocker	.15	.07	.02
☐	175 Randy Johnson STA	.15	.07	.02
☐	176 Ivan Rodriguez STA	.15	.07	.02
☐	177 Frank Thomas STA	1.50	.65	.19
☐	178 Roberto Alomar STA	.40	.18	.05
☐	179 Travis Fryman STA	.15	.07	.02
☐	180 Cal Ripken STA	1.00	.45	.13
☐	181 Juan Gonzalez STA	.50	.23	.06
☐	182 Ken Griffey Jr. STA	1.50	.65	.19

☐ 183 Albert Belle STA	.50	.23	.06
☐ 184 Greg Maddux STA	.30	.14	.04
☐ 185 Mike Piazza STA	.75	.35	.09
☐ 186 Fred McGriff STA	.20	.09	.03
☐ 187 Robby Thompson STA.	.10	.05	.01
☐ 188 Matt Williams STA	.15	.07	.02
☐ 189 Jeff Blauser STA	.15	.07	.02
☐ 190 Barry Bonds STA	.60	.25	.08
☐ 191 Lenny Dykstra STA	.15	.07	.02
☐ 192 David Justice STA	.20	.09	.03
☐ 193 Ken Griffey Jr. PF	1.50	.65	.19
☐ 194 Barry Bonds PF	.60	.25	.08
☐ 195 Frank Thomas PF	1.50	.65	.19
☐ 196 Juan Gonzalez PF	.50	.23	.06
☐ 197 Randy Johnson PF	.15	.07	.02
☐ 198 Chuck Carr PF	.10	.05	.01
☐ 199 Barry Bonds HES Juan Gonzalez	1.00	.45	.13
☐ 200 Ken Griffey Jr. HES Don Mattingly	2.00	.90	.25
☐ 201 Roberto Alomar HES Carlos Baerga	.50	.23	.06
☐ 202 Dave Winfield HES Robin Yount	.30	.14	.04
☐ 203 Mike Piazza HES Tim Salmon	1.00	.45	.13
☐ 204 Albert Belle HES Frank Thomas	2.00	.90	.25
☐ 205 Cliff Floyd HES Rondell White	.50	.23	.06
☐ 206 Kirby Puckett HES Tony Gwynn	.75	.35	.09
☐ 207 Roger Clemens HES Greg Maddux	.50	.23	.06
☐ 208 Mike Piazza WC	.75	.35	.09
☐ 209 Jose Canseco WC	.40	.18	.05
☐ 210 Frank Thomas WC	1.50	.65	.19
☐ 211 Roberto Alomar WC	.40	.18	.05
☐ 212 Barry Bonds WC	.60	.25	.08
☐ 213 Rickey Henderson WC.	.15	.07	.02
☐ 214 John Kruk WC	.15	.07	.02
☐ 215 Juan Gonzalez WC	.50	.23	.06
☐ 216 Ken Griffey Jr. WC	1.50	.65	.19
☐ 217 Roberto Alomar FOLD	.40	.18	.05
☐ 218 Craig Biggio FOLD	.10	.05	.01
☐ 219 Cal Ripken FOLD	1.00	.45	.13
☐ 220 Mike Piazza FOLD	.75	.35	.09
☐ 221 Brent Gates FOLD	.20	.09	.03
☐ 222 Walt Weiss FOLD	.10	.05	.01
☐ 223 Bobby Bonilla FOLD	.10	.05	.01
☐ 224 Ken Griffey Jr. FOLD	1.50	.65	.19
☐ 225 Barry Bonds FOLD	.60	.25	.08
☐ 226 Barry Bonds FUN	.60	.25	.08
☐ 227 Joe Carter FUN	.20	.09	.03
☐ 228 Mike Greenwell FUN	.10	.05	.01
☐ 229 Ken Griffey Jr. FUN	1.50	.65	.19
☐ 230 John Kruk FUN	.15	.07	.02
☐ 231 Mike Piazza FUN	.75	.35	.09
☐ 232 Kirby Puckett FUN	.60	.25	.08
☐ 233 John Smoltz FUN	.15	.07	.02
☐ 234 Rick Wilkins FUN	.10	.05	.01
☐ 235 Checklist 1-40 (Ken Griffey Jr.)	1.50	.65	.19
☐ 236 Checklist 41-80 (Frank Thomas)	1.50	.65	.19
☐ 237 Checklist 81-120 (Barry Bonds)	.60	.25	.08
☐ 238 Checklist 121-160 (Mike Piazza)	.75	.35	.09
☐ 239 Checklist 161-200 (Tim Salmon)	.30	.14	.04
☐ 240 Checklist 201-240 (Juan Gonzalez)	.50	.23	.06

1948-49 Leaf

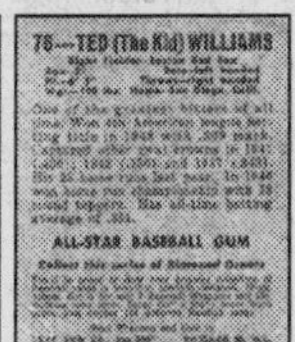

The cards in this 98-card set measure 2 3/8" by 2 7/8". The 1948-49 Leaf set was the first post-war baseball series issued in color. In hobby circles, it has been speculated that the set was issued in the spring of 1949. This effort was not entirely successful due to a lack of refinement which resulted in many color variations and cards out of register. In addition, the set was skip numbered from 1-168, with 49 of the 98 cards printed in limited quantities (marked with SP in the checklist). Cards 102 and 136 have variations, and cards are sometimes found with overprinted or incorrect backs. The notable rookie cards in this set include Stan Musial, Satchel Paige, and Jackie Robinson.

	NRMT	VG-E	GOOD
COMPLETE SET (98)	25000.	11300.	3100.
COMMON CARD (1-168)	25.00	11.50	3.10
☐ 1 Joe DiMaggio	2150.00	800.00	160.00
☐ 3 Babe Ruth	2500.00	1150.00	325.00
☐ 4 Stan Musial	850.00	375.00	105.00
☐ 5 Virgil Trucks SP	350.00	160.00	45.00
☐ 8 Satchel Paige SP	2100.00	950.00	275.00
☐ 10 Dizzy Trout	28.00	12.50	3.50
☐ 11 Phil Rizzuto	250.00	115.00	31.00
☐ 13 Cass Michaels SP	250.00	115.00	31.00
☐ 14 Billy Johnson	28.00	12.50	3.50
☐ 17 Frank Overmire	25.00	11.50	3.10
☐ 19 Johnny Wyrostek SP	250.00	115.00	31.00
☐ 20 Hank Sauer SP	350.00	160.00	45.00
☐ 22 Al Evans	25.00	11.50	3.10
☐ 26 Sam Chapman	25.00	11.50	3.10
☐ 27 Mickey Harris	25.00	11.50	3.10
☐ 28 Jim Hegan	25.00	11.50	3.10
☐ 29 Elmer Valo	25.00	11.50	3.10
☐ 30 Billy Goodman SP	300.00	135.00	38.00
☐ 31 Lou Brissie	25.00	11.50	3.10
☐ 32 Warren Spahn	275.00	125.00	34.00
☐ 33 Peanuts Lowrey SP	250.00	115.00	31.00
☐ 36 Al Zarilla SP	250.00	115.00	31.00
☐ 38 Ted Kluszewski	125.00	57.50	15.50
☐ 39 Ewell Blackwell	55.00	25.00	7.00
☐ 42 Kent Peterson	25.00	11.50	3.10
☐ 43 Ed Stevens SP	250.00	115.00	31.00
☐ 45 Ken Keltner SP	250.00	115.00	31.00
☐ 46 Johnny Mize	110.00	50.00	14.00
☐ 47 George Vico	25.00	11.50	3.10
☐ 48 Johnny Schmitz SP	250.00	115.00	31.00
☐ 49 Del Ennis	40.00	18.00	5.00
☐ 50 Dick Wakefield	25.00	11.50	3.10
☐ 51 Al Dark SP	400.00	180.00	50.00
☐ 53 Johnny VanderMeer	50.00	23.00	6.25

☐ 54 Bobby Adams SP	250.00	115.00	31.00
☐ 55 Tommy Henrich SP	400.00	180.00	50.00
☐ 56 Larry Jansen UER (Misspelled Jensen)	25.00	11.50	3.10
☐ 57 Bob McCall	25.00	11.50	3.10
☐ 59 Luke Appling	85.00	38.00	10.50
☐ 61 Jake Early	25.00	11.50	3.10
☐ 62 Eddie Joost SP	250.00	115.00	31.00
☐ 63 Barney McCosky SP	250.00	115.00	31.00
☐ 65 Robert Elliott UER (Misspelled Elliot on card front)	40.00	18.00	5.00
☐ 66 Orval Grove SP	250.00	115.00	31.00
☐ 68 Eddie Miller SP	250.00	115.00	31.00
☐ 70 Honus Wagner	275.00	125.00	34.00
☐ 72 Hank Edwards	25.00	11.50	3.10
☐ 73 Pat Seerey	25.00	11.50	3.10
☐ 75 Dom DiMaggio SP	500.00	230.00	65.00
☐ 76 Ted Williams	850.00	375.00	105.00
☐ 77 Roy Smalley	25.00	11.50	3.10
☐ 78 Hoot Evers SP	250.00	115.00	31.00
☐ 79 Jackie Robinson	850.00	375.00	105.00
☐ 81 Whitey Kurowski SP	250.00	115.00	31.00
☐ 82 Johnny Lindell	28.00	12.50	3.50
☐ 83 Bobby Doerr	110.00	50.00	14.00
☐ 84 Sid Hudson	25.00	11.50	3.10
☐ 85 Dave Philley SP	300.00	135.00	38.00
☐ 86 Ralph Weigel	25.00	11.50	3.10
☐ 88 Frank Gustine SP	250.00	115.00	31.00
☐ 91 Ralph Kiner	175.00	80.00	22.00
☐ 93 Bob Feller SP	1250.00	575.00	160.00
☐ 95 George Stirnweiss	25.00	11.50	3.10
☐ 97 Marty Marion	55.00	25.00	7.00
☐ 98 Hal Newhouser SP	600.00	275.00	75.00
☐ 102A Gene Hermansk ERR	250.00	115.00	31.00
☐ 102B Gene Hermansk COR	28.00	12.50	3.50
☐ 104 Eddie Stewart SP	250.00	115.00	31.00
☐ 106 Lou Boudreau	100.00	45.00	12.50
☐ 108 Matt Batts SP	250.00	115.00	31.00
☐ 111 Jerry Priddy	25.00	11.50	3.10
☐ 113 Dutch Leonard SP	250.00	115.00	31.00
☐ 117 Joe Gordon	35.00	16.00	4.40
☐ 120 George Kell SP	550.00	250.00	70.00
☐ 121 Johnny Pesky SP	350.00	160.00	45.00
☐ 123 Cliff Fannin SP	250.00	115.00	31.00
☐ 125 Andy Pafko	25.00	11.50	3.10
☐ 127 Enos Slaughter SP	650.00	300.00	80.00
☐ 128 Buddy Rosar	25.00	11.50	3.10
☐ 129 Kirby Higbe SP	250.00	115.00	31.00
☐ 131 Sid Gordon SP	250.00	115.00	31.00
☐ 133 Tommy Holmes SP	400.00	180.00	50.00
☐ 136A Cliff Aberson (Full sleeve)	25.00	11.50	3.10
☐ 136B Cliff Aberson (Short sleeve)	250.00	115.00	31.00
☐ 137 Harry Walker SP	250.00	115.00	31.00
☐ 138 Larry Doby SP	500.00	230.00	65.00
☐ 139 Johnny Hopp	25.00	11.50	3.10
☐ 142 Danny Murtaugh SP	350.00	160.00	45.00
☐ 143 Dick Sisler SP	250.00	115.00	31.00
☐ 144 Bob Dillinger SP	250.00	115.00	31.00
☐ 146 Pete Reiser SP	400.00	180.00	50.00
☐ 149 Hank Majeski SP	250.00	115.00	31.00
☐ 153 Floyd Baker SP	250.00	115.00	31.00
☐ 158 Harry Brecheen SP	350.00	160.00	45.00
☐ 159 Mizell Platt	25.00	11.50	3.10
☐ 160 Bob Scheffing SP	250.00	115.00	31.00
☐ 161 Vern Stephens SP	350.00	160.00	45.00
☐ 163 Fred Hutchinson SP	350.00	160.00	45.00
☐ 165 Dale Mitchell SP	350.00	160.00	45.00
☐ 168 Phil Cavarretta SP	400.00	160.00	45.00

1960 Leaf

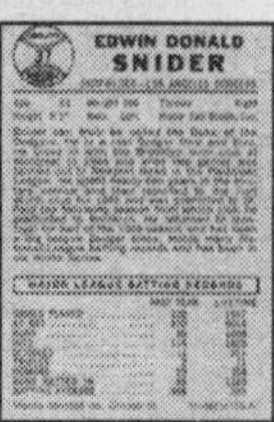

The cards in this 144-card set measure 2 1/2" by 3 1/2". The 1960 Leaf set was issued in a regular gum package style but with a marble instead of gum. The series was a joint production by Sports Novelties, Inc., and Leaf, two Chicago-based companies. Cards 73-144 are more difficult to find than the lower numbers. Photo variations exist (probably proof cards) for the seven cards listed with an asterisk and there is a well-known error card, number 25 showing Brooks Lawrence (in a Reds uniform) with Jim Grant's name on front, and Grant's biography and record on back. The corrected version with Grant's photo is the more difficult variety. The only notable Rookie Card in this set is Dallas Green. The complete set price below includes both versions of Jim Grant.

	NRMT	VG-E	GOOD
COMPLETE SET (145)	1250.00	575.00	160.00
COMMON CARD (1-72)	3.00	1.35	.40
COMMON CARD (73-144)	20.00	9.00	2.50
☐ 1 Luis Aparicio *	24.00	6.00	1.90
☐ 2 Woody Held	3.00	1.35	.40
☐ 3 Frank Lary	4.00	1.80	.50
☐ 4 Camilo Pascual	4.00	1.80	.50
☐ 5 Pancho Herrera	3.00	1.35	.40
☐ 6 Felipe Alou	8.00	3.60	1.00
☐ 7 Benjamin Daniels	3.00	1.35	.40
☐ 8 Roger Craig	4.00	1.80	.50
☐ 9 Eddie Kasko	3.00	1.35	.40
☐ 10 Bob Grim	4.00	1.80	.50
☐ 11 Jim Busby	3.00	1.35	.40
☐ 12 Ken Boyer	8.00	3.60	1.00
☐ 13 Bob Boyd	3.00	1.35	.40
☐ 14 Sam Jones	4.00	1.80	.50
☐ 15 Larry Jackson	4.00	1.80	.50
☐ 16 Elroy Face	3.00	1.35	.40
☐ 17 Walt Moryn *	3.00	1.35	.40
☐ 18 Jim Gilliam	4.00	1.80	.50
☐ 19 Don Newcombe	4.00	1.80	.50
☐ 20 Glen Hobbie	3.00	1.35	.40
☐ 21 Pedro Ramos	3.00	1.35	.40
☐ 22 Ryne Duren	3.00	1.35	.40
☐ 23 Joey Jay *	4.00	1.80	.50
☐ 24 Lou Berberet	3.00	1.35	.40
☐ 25A Jim Grant ERR (Photo actually Brooks Lawrence)	14.00	6.25	1.75
☐ 25B Jim Grant COR	24.00	11.00	3.00
☐ 26 Tom Borland	3.00	1.35	.40

☐ 27 Brooks Robinson 40.00 18.00 5.00
☐ 28 Jerry Adair .... 3.00 1.35 .40
☐ 29 Ron Jackson .... 3.00 1.35 .40
☐ 30 George Strickland .... 3.00 1.35 .40
☐ 31 Rocky Bridges .... 3.00 1.35 .40
☐ 32 Bill Tuttle .... 3.00 1.35 .40
☐ 33 Ken Hunt .... 3.00 1.35 .40
☐ 34 Hal Griggs .... 3.00 1.35 .40
☐ 35 Jim Coates * .... 3.00 1.35 .40
☐ 36 Brooks Lawrence .... 3.00 1.35 .40
☐ 37 Duke Snider 45.00 20.00 5.75
☐ 38 Al Spangler .... 3.00 1.35 .40
☐ 39 Jim Owens .... 3.00 1.35 .40
☐ 40 Bill Virdon .... 3.00 1.35 .40
☐ 41 Ernie Broglio .... 4.00 1.80 .50
☐ 42 Andre Rodgers .... 3.00 1.35 .40
☐ 43 Julio Becquer .... 3.00 1.35 .40
☐ 44 Tony Taylor .... 4.00 1.80 .50
☐ 45 Jerry Lynch .... 4.00 1.80 .50
☐ 46 Cletis Boyer .... 3.00 1.35 .40
☐ 47 Jerry Lumpe .... 3.00 1.35 .40
☐ 48 Charlie Maxwell .... 4.00 1.80 .50
☐ 49 Jim Perry .... 3.00 1.35 .40
☐ 50 Danny McDevitt .... 3.00 1.35 .40
☐ 51 Juan Pizarro .... 3.00 1.35 .40
☐ 52 Dallas Green 12.00 5.50 1.50
☐ 53 Bob Friend .... 4.00 1.80 .50
☐ 54 Jack Sanford .... 4.00 1.80 .50
☐ 55 Jim Rivera .... 3.00 1.35 .40
☐ 56 Ted Wills .... 3.00 1.35 .40
☐ 57 Milt Pappas .... 4.00 1.80 .50
☐ 58 Hal Smith * .... 3.00 1.35 .40
☐ 59 Bobby Avila .... 3.00 1.35 .40
☐ 60 Clem Labine .... 4.00 1.80 .50
☐ 61 Norman Rehm * .... 3.00 1.35 .40
☐ 62 John Gabler .... 3.00 1.35 .40
☐ 63 John Tsitouris .... 3.00 1.35 .40
☐ 64 Dave Sisler .... 3.00 1.35 .40
☐ 65 Vic Power .... 4.00 1.80 .50
☐ 66 Earl Battey .... 3.00 1.35 .40
☐ 67 Bob Purkey .... 3.00 1.35 .40
☐ 68 Moe Drabowsky .... 4.00 1.80 .50
☐ 69 Hoyt Wilhelm 14.00 6.25 1.75
☐ 70 Humberto Robinson .... 3.00 1.35 .40
☐ 71 Whitey Herzog 8.00 3.60 1.00
☐ 72 Dick Donovan * .... 3.00 1.35 .40
☐ 73 Gordon Jones 22.00 10.00 2.80
☐ 74 Joe Hicks 20.00 9.00 2.50
☐ 75 Ray Culp 25.00 11.50 3.10
☐ 76 Dick Drott 20.00 9.00 2.50
☐ 77 Bob Duliba 20.00 9.00 2.50
☐ 78 Art Ditmar 20.00 9.00 2.50
☐ 79 Steve Korcheck 20.00 9.00 2.50
☐ 80 Henry Mason 20.00 9.00 2.50
☐ 81 Harry Simpson 20.00 9.00 2.50
☐ 82 Gene Green 20.00 9.00 2.50
☐ 83 Bob Shaw 20.00 9.00 2.50
☐ 84 Howard Reed 20.00 9.00 2.50
☐ 85 Dick Stigman 20.00 9.00 2.50
☐ 86 Rip Repulski 20.00 9.00 2.50
☐ 87 Seth Morehead 20.00 9.00 2.50
☐ 88 Camilo Carreon 20.00 9.00 2.50
☐ 89 John Blanchard 20.00 9.00 2.50
☐ 90 Billy Hoeft 20.00 9.00 2.50
☐ 91 Fred Hopke 20.00 9.00 2.50
☐ 92 Joe Martin 20.00 9.00 2.50
☐ 93 Wally Shannon 20.00 9.00 2.50
☐ 94 Two Hal Smith's 30.00 13.50 3.80
Hal R. Smith
Hal W. Smith
☐ 95 Al Schroll 20.00 9.00 2.50
☐ 96 John Kucks 20.00 9.00 2.50
☐ 97 Tom Morgan 20.00 9.00 2.50
☐ 98 Willie Jones 20.00 9.00 2.50
☐ 99 Marshall Renfroe 20.00 9.00 2.50
☐ 100 Willie Tasby 20.00 9.00 2.50
☐ 101 Irv Noren 20.00 9.00 2.50
☐ 102 Russ Snyder 20.00 9.00 2.50
☐ 103 Bob Turley 20.00 9.00 2.50
☐ 104 Jim Woods 20.00 9.00 2.50
☐ 105 Ronnie Kline 20.00 9.00 2.50
☐ 106 Steve Bilko 20.00 9.00 2.50
☐ 107 Elmer Valo 20.00 9.00 2.50
☐ 108 Tom McAvoy 20.00 9.00 2.50
☐ 109 Stan Williams 22.00 10.00 2.80
☐ 110 Earl Averill Jr. 20.00 9.00 2.50
☐ 111 Lee Walls 20.00 9.00 2.50
☐ 112 Paul Richards MG 22.00 10.00 2.80
☐ 113 Ed Sadowski 20.00 9.00 2.50
☐ 114 Stover McIlwain 20.00 9.00 2.50
☐ 115 Chuck Tanner UER 25.00 11.50 3.10
(Photo actually
Ken Kuhn)
☐ 116 Lou Klimchock 20.00 9.00 2.50
☐ 117 Neil Chrisley 20.00 9.00 2.50
☐ 118 John Callison 25.00 11.50 3.10
☐ 119 Hal Smith 20.00 9.00 2.50
☐ 120 Carl Sawatski 20.00 9.00 2.50
☐ 121 Frank Leja 20.00 9.00 2.50
☐ 122 Earl Torgeson 20.00 9.00 2.50
☐ 123 Art Schult 20.00 9.00 2.50
☐ 124 Jim Brosnan 22.00 10.00 2.80
☐ 125 Sparky Anderson 75.00 34.00 9.50
☐ 126 Joe Pignatano 20.00 9.00 2.50
☐ 127 Rocky Nelson 20.00 9.00 2.50
☐ 128 Orlando Cepeda 65.00 29.00 8.25
☐ 129 Daryl Spencer 20.00 9.00 2.50
☐ 130 Ralph Lumenti 20.00 9.00 2.50
☐ 131 Sam Taylor 20.00 9.00 2.50
☐ 132 Harry Brecheen CO 22.00 10.00 2.80
☐ 133 Johnny Groth 20.00 9.00 2.50
☐ 134 Wayne Terwilliger 20.00 9.00 2.50
☐ 135 Kent Hadley 20.00 9.00 2.50
☐ 136 Faye Throneberry 20.00 9.00 2.50
☐ 137 Jack Meyer 20.00 9.00 2.50
☐ 138 Chuck Cottier 20.00 9.00 2.50
☐ 139 Joe DeMaestri 20.00 9.00 2.50
☐ 140 Gene Freese 20.00 9.00 2.50
☐ 141 Curt Flood 30.00 13.50 3.80
☐ 142 Gino Cimoli 20.00 9.00 2.50
☐ 143 Clay Dalrymple 20.00 9.00 2.50
☐ 144 Jim Bunning 60.00 18.00 4.80

1990 Leaf

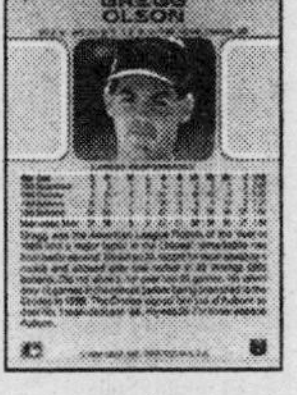

The 1990 Leaf set was another major, premium set introduced by Donruss in 1990.

This set, which was produced on high quality paper stock, was issued in two separate series of 264 cards each. The second series was issued approximately six weeks after the release of the first series. The cards are in the standard size of 2 1/2" by 3 1/2" and have full-color photos on both the front and the back of the cards. The first card of the set includes a brief history of the Leaf company and the checklists feature player photos in a style very reminiscent to the Topps checklists of the late 1960s. The card style is very similar to Upper Deck, but the Leaf sets were only distributed through hobby channels and were not available in factory sets. Rookie Cards in the set include Eric Anthony, Carlos Baerga, Delino DeShields, Bernard Gilkey, Marquis Grissom, Chris Hoiles, David Justice, Kevin Maas, Ben McDonald, Jose Offerman, John Olerud, Sammy Sosa, Kevin Tapani, Frank Thomas, Larry Walker, and Mark Whiten. Each pack contained 15 cards and one three-piece puzzle card of a 63-piece Yogi Berra "Donruss Hall of Fame Diamond King" puzzle.

	MINT	EXC	G-VG
COMPLETE SET (528)	250.00	115.00	31.00
COMPLETE SERIES 1 (264)	120.00	55.00	15.00
COMPLETE SERIES 2 (264)	130.00	57.50	16.50
COMMON CARD (1-264)	.20	.09	.03
COMMON CARD (265-528)	.20	.09	.03

☐ 1	Introductory Card	.20	.09	.03
☐ 2	Mike Henneman	.20	.09	.03
☐ 3	Steve Bedrosian	.20	.09	.03
☐ 4	Mike Scott	.20	.09	.03
☐ 5	Allan Anderson	.20	.09	.03
☐ 6	Rick Sutcliffe	.30	.14	.04
☐ 7	Gregg Olson	.20	.09	.03
☐ 8	Kevin Elster	.20	.09	.03
☐ 9	Pete O'Brien	.20	.09	.03
☐ 10	Carlton Fisk	.50	.23	.06
☐ 11	Joe Magrane	.20	.09	.03
☐ 12	Roger Clemens	3.00	1.35	.40
☐ 13	Tom Glavine	3.00	1.35	.40
☐ 14	Tom Gordon	.30	.14	.04
☐ 15	Todd Benzinger	.20	.09	.03
☐ 16	Hubie Brooks	.20	.09	.03
☐ 17	Roberto Kelly	.75	.35	.09
☐ 18	Barry Larkin	.75	.35	.09
☐ 19	Mike Boddicker	.20	.09	.03
☐ 20	Roger McDowell	.20	.09	.03
☐ 21	Nolan Ryan	8.00	3.60	1.00
☐ 22	John Farrell	.20	.09	.03
☐ 23	Bruce Hurst	.20	.09	.03
☐ 24	Wally Joyner	.30	.14	.04
☐ 25	Greg Maddux	8.00	3.60	1.00
☐ 26	Chris Bosio	.20	.09	.03
☐ 27	John Cerutti	.20	.09	.03
☐ 28	Tim Burke	.20	.09	.03
☐ 29	Dennis Eckersley	.50	.23	.06
☐ 30	Glenn Davis	.20	.09	.03
☐ 31	Jim Abbott	1.50	.65	.19
☐ 32	Mike LaValliere	.20	.09	.03
☐ 33	Andres Thomas	.20	.09	.03
☐ 34	Lou Whitaker	.40	.18	.05
☐ 35	Alvin Davis	.20	.09	.03
☐ 36	Melido Perez	.20	.09	.03
☐ 37	Craig Biggio	1.25	.55	.16
☐ 38	Rick Aguilera	.30	.14	.04
☐ 39	Pete Harnisch	.50	.23	.06
☐ 40	David Cone	1.50	.65	.19
☐ 41	Scott Garrelts	.20	.09	.03
☐ 42	Jay Howell	.20	.09	.03
☐ 43	Eric King	.20	.09	.03
☐ 44	Pedro Guerrero	.30	.14	.04
☐ 45	Mike Bielecki	.20	.09	.03
☐ 46	Bob Boone	.30	.14	.04
☐ 47	Kevin Brown	.30	.14	.04
☐ 48	Jerry Browne	.20	.09	.03
☐ 49	Mike Scioscia	.20	.09	.03
☐ 50	Chuck Cary	.20	.09	.03
☐ 51	Wade Boggs	2.00	.90	.25
☐ 52	Von Hayes	.20	.09	.03
☐ 53	Tony Fernandez	.30	.14	.04
☐ 54	Dennis Martinez	.30	.14	.04
☐ 55	Tom Candiotti	.20	.09	.03
☐ 56	Andy Benes	1.25	.55	.16
☐ 57	Rob Dibble	.20	.09	.03
☐ 58	Chuck Crim	.20	.09	.03
☐ 59	John Smoltz	1.00	.45	.13
☐ 60	Mike Heath	.20	.09	.03
☐ 61	Kevin Gross	.20	.09	.03
☐ 62	Mark McGwire	1.50	.65	.19
☐ 63	Bert Blyleven	.40	.18	.05
☐ 64	Bob Walk	.20	.09	.03
☐ 65	Mickey Tettleton	.30	.14	.04
☐ 66	Sid Fernandez	.30	.14	.04
☐ 67	Terry Kennedy	.20	.09	.03
☐ 68	Fernando Valenzuela	.20	.09	.03
☐ 69	Don Mattingly	4.00	1.80	.50
☐ 70	Paul O'Neill	.50	.23	.06
☐ 71	Robin Yount	2.00	.90	.25
☐ 72	Bret Saberhagen	.40	.18	.05
☐ 73	Geno Petralli	.20	.09	.03
☐ 74	Brook Jacoby	.20	.09	.03
☐ 75	Roberto Alomar	4.00	1.80	.50
☐ 76	Devon White	.60	.25	.08
☐ 77	Jose Lind	.20	.09	.03
☐ 78	Pat Combs	.20	.09	.03
☐ 79	Dave Stieb	.30	.14	.04
☐ 80	Tim Wallach	.20	.09	.03
☐ 81	Dave Stewart	.30	.14	.04
☐ 82	Eric Anthony	.50	.23	.06
☐ 83	Randy Bush	.20	.09	.03
☐ 84	Checklist 1-88 (Rickey Henderson)	.30	.14	.04
☐ 85	Jaime Navarro	.20	.09	.03
☐ 86	Tommy Gregg	.20	.09	.03
☐ 87	Frank Tanana	.20	.09	.03
☐ 88	Omar Vizquel	.50	.23	.06
☐ 89	Ivan Calderon	.20	.09	.03
☐ 90	Vince Coleman	.30	.14	.04
☐ 91	Barry Bonds	5.00	2.30	.60
☐ 92	Randy Milligan	.20	.09	.03
☐ 93	Frank Viola	.30	.14	.04
☐ 94	Matt Williams	6.00	2.70	.75
☐ 95	Alfredo Griffin	.20	.09	.03
☐ 96	Steve Sax	.20	.09	.03
☐ 97	Gary Gaetti	.20	.09	.03
☐ 98	Ryne Sandberg	3.50	1.55	.45
☐ 99	Danny Tartabull	.20	.09	.03
☐ 100	Rafael Palmeiro	2.00	.90	.25
☐ 101	Jesse Orosco	.20	.09	.03
☐ 102	Garry Templeton	.20	.09	.03
☐ 103	Frank DiPino	.20	.09	.03
☐ 104	Tony Pena	.20	.09	.03
☐ 105	Dickie Thon	.20	.09	.03
☐ 106	Kelly Gruber	.20	.09	.03
☐ 107	Marquis Grissom	5.00	2.30	.60
☐ 108	Jose Canseco	3.00	1.35	.40
☐ 109	Mike Blowers	.20	.09	.03
☐ 110	Tom Browning	.20	.09	.03
☐ 111	Greg Vaughn	2.00	.90	.25

□ 112 Oddibe McDowell .20 .09 .03
□ 113 Gary Ward .20 .09 .03
□ 114 Jay Buhner .75 .35 .09
□ 115 Eric Show .20 .09 .03
□ 116 Bryan Harvey .50 .23 .06
□ 117 Andy Van Slyke .40 .18 .05
□ 118 Jeff Ballard .20 .09 .03
□ 119 Barry Lyons .20 .09 .03
□ 120 Kevin Mitchell .40 .18 .05
□ 121 Mike Gallego .20 .09 .03
□ 122 Dave Smith .20 .09 .03
□ 123 Kirby Puckett 4.00 1.80 .50
□ 124 Jerome Walton .20 .09 .03
□ 125 Bo Jackson 2.00 .90 .25
□ 126 Harold Baines .30 .14 .04
□ 127 Scott Bankhead .20 .09 .03
□ 128 Ozzie Guillen .30 .14 .04
□ 129 Jose Oquendo UER .20 .09 .03
(League misspelled as Legue)
□ 130 John Dopson .20 .09 .03
□ 131 Charlie Hayes 1.00 .45 .13
□ 132 Fred McGriff 3.00 1.35 .40
□ 133 Chet Lemon .20 .09 .03
□ 134 Gary Carter .40 .18 .05
□ 135 Rafael Ramirez .20 .09 .03
□ 136 Shane Mack .30 .14 .04
□ 137 Mark Grace UER 1.00 .45 .13
(Card back has OB:L, should be B:L)
□ 138 Phil Bradley .20 .09 .03
□ 139 Dwight Gooden .30 .14 .04
□ 140 Harold Reynolds .20 .09 .03
□ 141 Scott Fletcher .20 .09 .03
□ 142 Ozzie Smith 1.50 .65 .19
□ 143 Mike Greenwell .30 .14 .04
□ 144 Pete Smith .20 .09 .03
□ 145 Mark Gubicza .20 .09 .03
□ 146 Chris Sabo .20 .09 .03
□ 147 Ramon Martinez 1.00 .45 .13
□ 148 Tim Leary .20 .09 .03
□ 149 Randy Myers .30 .14 .04
□ 150 Jody Reed .20 .09 .03
□ 151 Bruce Ruffin .20 .09 .03
□ 152 Jeff Russell .20 .09 .03
□ 153 Doug Jones .20 .09 .03
□ 154 Tony Gwynn 3.00 1.35 .40
□ 155 Mark Langston .40 .18 .05
□ 156 Mitch Williams .30 .14 .04
□ 157 Gary Sheffield 5.00 2.30 .60
□ 158 Tom Henke .30 .14 .04
□ 159 Oil Can Boyd .20 .09 .03
□ 160 Rickey Henderson 1.25 .55 .16
□ 161 Bill Doran .20 .09 .03
□ 162 Chuck Finley .30 .14 .04
□ 163 Jeff King .30 .14 .04
□ 164 Nick Esasky .20 .09 .03
□ 165 Cecil Fielder 1.50 .65 .19
□ 166 Dave Valle .20 .09 .03
□ 167 Robin Ventura 4.00 1.80 .50
□ 168 Jim Deshaies .20 .09 .03
□ 169 Juan Berenguer .20 .09 .03
□ 170 Craig Worthington .20 .09 .03
□ 171 Gregg Jeffries 3.50 1.55 .45
□ 172 Will Clark 3.00 1.35 .40
□ 173 Kirk Gibson .30 .14 .04
□ 174 Checklist 89-176 .30 .14 .04
(Carlton Fisk)
□ 175 Bobby Thigpen .20 .09 .03
□ 176 John Tudor .20 .09 .03
□ 177 Andre Dawson .60 .25 .08
□ 178 George Brett 4.00 1.80 .50
□ 179 Steve Buechele .20 .09 .03
□ 180 Joey Belle 18.00 8.00 2.30
□ 181 Eddie Murray .75 .35 .09
□ 182 Bob Geren .20 .09 .03
□ 183 Rob Murphy .20 .09 .03
□ 184 Tom Herr .20 .09 .03
□ 185 George Bell .30 .14 .04
□ 186 Spike Owen .20 .09 .03
□ 187 Cory Snyder .20 .09 .03
□ 188 Fred Lynn .30 .14 .04
□ 189 Eric Davis .30 .14 .04
□ 190 Dave Parker .40 .18 .05
□ 191 Jeff Blauser .40 .18 .05
□ 192 Matt Nokes .20 .09 .03
□ 193 Delino DeShields 2.50 1.15 .30
□ 194 Scott Sanderson .20 .09 .03
□ 195 Lance Parrish .30 .14 .04
□ 196 Bobby Bonilla .75 .35 .09
□ 197 Cal Ripken UER 6.00 2.70 .75
(Reistertown, should be Reisterstown)
□ 198 Kevin McReynolds .20 .09 .03
□ 199 Robby Thompson .30 .14 .04
□ 200 Tim Belcher .20 .09 .03
□ 201 Jesse Barfield .20 .09 .03
□ 202 Mariano Duncan .20 .09 .03
□ 203 Bill Spiers .20 .09 .03
□ 204 Frank White .30 .14 .04
□ 205 Julio Franco .30 .14 .04
□ 206 Greg Swindell .30 .14 .04
□ 207 Benito Santiago .30 .14 .04
□ 208 Johnny Ray .20 .09 .03
□ 209 Gary Redus .20 .09 .03
□ 210 Jeff Parrett .20 .09 .03
□ 211 Jimmy Key .75 .35 .09
□ 212 Tim Raines .40 .18 .05
□ 213 Carney Lansford .30 .14 .04
□ 214 Gerald Young .20 .09 .03
□ 215 Gene Larkin .20 .09 .03
□ 216 Dan Plesac .20 .09 .03
□ 217 Lonnie Smith .20 .09 .03
□ 218 Alan Trammell .40 .18 .05
□ 219 Jeffrey Leonard .20 .09 .03
□ 220 Sammy Sosa 5.00 2.30 .60
□ 221 Todd Zeile 1.00 .45 .13
□ 222 Bill Landrum .20 .09 .03
□ 223 Mike Devereaux .30 .14 .04
□ 224 Mike Marshall .20 .09 .03
□ 225 Jose Uribe .20 .09 .03
□ 226 Juan Samuel .20 .09 .03
□ 227 Mel Hall .20 .09 .03
□ 228 Kent Hrbek .30 .14 .04
□ 229 Shawon Dunston .20 .09 .03
□ 230 Kevin Seitzer .20 .09 .03
□ 231 Pete Incaviglia .20 .09 .03
□ 232 Sandy Alomar Jr. .30 .14 .04
□ 233 Bip Roberts .30 .14 .04
□ 234 Scott Terry .20 .09 .03
□ 235 Dwight Evans .30 .14 .04
□ 236 Ricky Jordan .30 .14 .04
□ 237 John Olerud 6.00 2.70 .75
□ 238 Zane Smith .20 .09 .03
□ 239 Walt Weiss .20 .09 .03
□ 240 Alvaro Espinoza .20 .09 .03
□ 241 Billy Hatcher .20 .09 .03
□ 242 Paul Molitor 2.00 .90 .25
□ 243 Dale Murphy .40 .18 .05
□ 244 Dave Bergman .20 .09 .03
□ 245 Ken Griffey Jr. 35.00 16.00 4.40
□ 246 Ed Whitson .20 .09 .03
□ 247 Kirk McCaskill .20 .09 .03
□ 248 Jay Bell .30 .14 .04
□ 249 Ben McDonald 4.00 1.80 .50
□ 250 Darryl Strawberry .40 .18 .05

☐ 251 Brett Butler .30 .14 .04
☐ 252 Terry Steinbach .30 .14 .04
☐ 253 Ken Caminiti .30 .14 .04
☐ 254 Dan Gladden .20 .09 .03
☐ 255 Dwight Smith .20 .09 .03
☐ 256 Kurt Stillwell .20 .09 .03
☐ 257 Ruben Sierra 1.50 .65 .19
☐ 258 Mike Schooler .20 .09 .03
☐ 259 Lance Johnson .50 .23 .06
☐ 260 Terry Pendleton .20 .09 .03
☐ 261 Ellis Burks .30 .14 .04
☐ 262 Len Dykstra 1.00 .45 .13
☐ 263 Mookie Wilson .20 .09 .03
☐ 264 Checklist 177-264 .50 .23 .06
(Nolan Ryan) UER
(No TM after Ranger
logo)
☐ 265 No Hit King 5.00 2.30 .60
(Nolan Ryan)
☐ 266 Brian DuBois .20 .09 .03
☐ 267 Don Robinson .20 .09 .03
☐ 268 Glenn Wilson .20 .09 .03
☐ 269 Kevin Tapani 1.25 .55 .16
☐ 270 Marvell Wynne .20 .09 .03
☐ 271 Billy Ripken .20 .09 .03
☐ 272 Howard Johnson .30 .14 .04
☐ 273 Brian Holman .20 .09 .03
☐ 274 Dan Pasqua .20 .09 .03
☐ 275 Ken Dayley .20 .09 .03
☐ 276 Jeff Reardon .40 .18 .05
☐ 277 Jim Presley .20 .09 .03
☐ 278 Jim Eisenreich .20 .09 .03
☐ 279 Danny Jackson .20 .09 .03
☐ 280 Orel Hershiser .30 .14 .04
☐ 281 Andy Hawkins .20 .09 .03
☐ 282 Jose Rijo .40 .18 .05
☐ 283 Luis Rivera .20 .09 .03
☐ 284 John Kruk .50 .23 .06
☐ 285 Jeff Huson .20 .09 .03
☐ 286 Joel Skinner .20 .09 .03
☐ 287 Jack Clark .30 .14 .04
☐ 288 Chili Davis .30 .14 .04
☐ 289 Joe Girardi .20 .09 .03
☐ 290 B.J. Surhoff .20 .09 .03
☐ 291 Luis Sojo .20 .09 .03
☐ 292 Tom Foley .20 .09 .03
☐ 293 Mike Moore .20 .09 .03
☐ 294 Ken Oberkfell .20 .09 .03
☐ 295 Luis Polonia .30 .14 .04
☐ 296 Doug Drabek .30 .14 .04
☐ 297 David Justice 10.00 4.50 1.25
☐ 298 Paul Gibson .20 .09 .03
☐ 299 Edgar Martinez .50 .23 .06
☐ 300 Frank Thomas UER 85.00 38.00 10.50
(No B in front
of birthdate)
☐ 301 Eric Yelding .20 .09 .03
☐ 302 Greg Gagne .20 .09 .03
☐ 303 Brad Komminsk .20 .09 .03
☐ 304 Ron Darling .20 .09 .03
☐ 305 Kevin Bass .20 .09 .03
☐ 306 Jeff Hamilton .20 .09 .03
☐ 307 Ron Karkovice .20 .09 .03
☐ 308 Milt Thompson UER .50 .23 .06
(Ray Lankford pictured
on card back)
☐ 309 Mike Harkey .20 .09 .03
☐ 310 Mel Stottlemyre Jr. .20 .09 .03
☐ 311 Kenny Rogers .75 .35 .09
☐ 312 Mitch Webster .20 .09 .03
☐ 313 Kal Daniels .20 .09 .03
☐ 314 Matt Nokes .20 .09 .03
☐ 315 Dennis Lamp .20 .09 .03
☐ 316 Ken Howell .20 .09 .03
☐ 317 Glenallen Hill .20 .09 .03
☐ 318 Dave Martinez .20 .09 .03
☐ 319 Chris James .20 .09 .03
☐ 320 Mike Pagliarulo .20 .09 .03
☐ 321 Hal Morris 1.00 .45 .13
☐ 322 Rob Deer .20 .09 .03
☐ 323 Greg Olson .20 .09 .03
☐ 324 Tony Phillips .40 .18 .05
☐ 325 Larry Walker 6.00 2.70 .75
☐ 326 Ron Hassey .20 .09 .03
☐ 327 Jack Howell .20 .09 .03
☐ 328 John Smiley .20 .09 .03
☐ 329 Steve Finley .30 .14 .04
☐ 330 Dave Magadan .20 .09 .03
☐ 331 Greg Litton .20 .09 .03
☐ 332 Mickey Hatcher .20 .09 .03
☐ 333 Lee Guetterman .20 .09 .03
☐ 334 Norm Charlton .20 .09 .03
☐ 335 Edgar Diaz .20 .09 .03
☐ 336 Willie Wilson .20 .09 .03
☐ 337 Bobby Witt .30 .14 .04
☐ 338 Candy Maldonado .20 .09 .03
☐ 339 Craig Lefferts .20 .09 .03
☐ 340 Dante Bichette 3.00 1.35 .40
☐ 341 Wally Backman .20 .09 .03
☐ 342 Dennis Cook .20 .09 .03
☐ 343 Pat Borders .20 .09 .03
☐ 344 Wallace Johnson .20 .09 .03
☐ 345 Willie Randolph .30 .14 .04
☐ 346 Danny Darwin .20 .09 .03
☐ 347 Al Newman .20 .09 .03
☐ 348 Mark Knudson .20 .09 .03
☐ 349 Joe Boever .20 .09 .03
☐ 350 Larry Sheets .20 .09 .03
☐ 351 Mike Jackson .20 .09 .03
☐ 352 Wayne Edwards .20 .09 .03
☐ 353 Bernard Gilkey 1.50 .65 .19
☐ 354 Don Slaught .20 .09 .03
☐ 355 Joe Orsulak .20 .09 .03
☐ 356 John Franco .30 .14 .04
☐ 357 Jeff Brantley .20 .09 .03
☐ 358 Mike Morgan .20 .09 .03
☐ 359 Deion Sanders 7.00 3.10 .85
☐ 360 Terry Leach .20 .09 .03
☐ 361 Les Lancaster .20 .09 .03
☐ 362 Storm Davis .20 .09 .03
☐ 363 Scott Coolbaugh .20 .09 .03
☐ 364 Checklist 265-352 .30 .14 .04
(Ozzie Smith)
☐ 365 Cecilio Guante .20 .09 .03
☐ 366 Joey Cora .20 .09 .03
☐ 367 Willie McGee .30 .14 .04
☐ 368 Jerry Reed .20 .09 .03
☐ 369 Darren Daulton .75 .35 .09
☐ 370 Manny Lee .20 .09 .03
☐ 371 Mark Gardner .20 .09 .03
☐ 372 Rick Honeycutt .20 .09 .03
☐ 373 Steve Balboni .20 .09 .03
☐ 374 Jack Armstrong .20 .09 .03
☐ 375 Charlie O'Brien .20 .09 .03
☐ 376 Ron Gant 1.50 .65 .19
☐ 377 Lloyd Moseby .20 .09 .03
☐ 378 Gene Harris .20 .09 .03
☐ 379 Joe Carter 2.50 1.15 .30
☐ 380 Scott Bailes .20 .09 .03
☐ 381 R.J. Reynolds .20 .09 .03
☐ 382 Bob Melvin .20 .09 .03
☐ 383 Tim Teufel .20 .09 .03
☐ 384 John Burkett 1.00 .45 .13
☐ 385 Felix Jose .50 .23 .06
☐ 386 Larry Andersen .20 .09 .03
☐ 387 David West .20 .09 .03

☐ 388 Luis Salazar .20 .09 .03
☐ 389 Mike Macfarlane .50 .23 .06
☐ 390 Charlie Hough .30 .14 .04
☐ 391 Greg Briley .20 .09 .03
☐ 392 Donn Pall .20 .09 .03
☐ 393 Bryn Smith .20 .09 .03
☐ 394 Carlos Quintana .20 .09 .03
☐ 395 Steve Lake .20 .09 .03
☐ 396 Mark Whiten 1.50 .65 .19
☐ 397 Edwin Nunez .20 .09 .03
☐ 398 Rick Parker .20 .09 .03
☐ 399 Mark Portugal .20 .09 .03
☐ 400 Roy Smith .20 .09 .03
☐ 401 Hector Villanueva .20 .09 .03
☐ 402 Bob Milacki .20 .09 .03
☐ 403 Alejandro Pena .20 .09 .03
☐ 404 Scott Bradley .20 .09 .03
☐ 405 Ron Kittle .20 .09 .03
☐ 406 Bob Tewksbury .30 .14 .04
☐ 407 Wes Gardner .20 .09 .03
☐ 408 Ernie Whitt .20 .09 .03
☐ 409 Terry Shumpert .20 .09 .03
☐ 410 Tim Layana .20 .09 .03
☐ 411 Chris Gwynn .20 .09 .03
☐ 412 Jeff D. Robinson .20 .09 .03
☐ 413 Scott Scudder .20 .09 .03
☐ 414 Kevin Romine .20 .09 .03
☐ 415 Jose DeJesus .20 .09 .03
☐ 416 Mike Jeffcoat .20 .09 .03
☐ 417 Rudy Seanez .20 .09 .03
☐ 418 Mike Dunne .20 .09 .03
☐ 419 Dick Schofield .20 .09 .03
☐ 420 Steve Wilson .20 .09 .03
☐ 421 Bill Krueger .20 .09 .03
☐ 422 Junior Felix .20 .09 .03
☐ 423 Drew Hall .20 .09 .03
☐ 424 Curt Young .20 .09 .03
☐ 425 Franklin Stubbs .20 .09 .03
☐ 426 Dave Winfield 1.50 .65 .19
☐ 427 Rick Reed .20 .09 .03
☐ 428 Charlie Leibrandt .20 .09 .03
☐ 429 Jeff M. Robinson .20 .09 .03
☐ 430 Erik Hanson .30 .14 .04
☐ 431 Barry Jones .20 .09 .03
☐ 432 Alex Trevino .20 .09 .03
☐ 433 John Moses .20 .09 .03
☐ 434 Dave Johnson .20 .09 .03
☐ 435 Mackey Sasser .20 .09 .03
☐ 436 Rick Leach .20 .09 .03
☐ 437 Lenny Harris .20 .09 .03
☐ 438 Carlos Martinez .20 .09 .03
☐ 439 Rex Hudler .20 .09 .03
☐ 440 Domingo Ramos .20 .09 .03
☐ 441 Gerald Perry .20 .09 .03
☐ 442 Jeff Russell .20 .09 .03
☐ 443 Carlos Baerga 10.00 4.50 1.25
☐ 444 Checklist 353-440 .35 .16 .04
(Will Clark)
☐ 445 Stan Javier .20 .09 .03
☐ 446 Kevin Maas .20 .09 .03
☐ 447 Tom Brunansky .20 .09 .03
☐ 448 Carmelo Martinez .20 .09 .03
☐ 449 Willie Blair .20 .09 .03
☐ 450 Andres Galarraga 1.50 .65 .19
☐ 451 Bud Black .20 .09 .03
☐ 452 Greg W. Harris .20 .09 .03
☐ 453 Joe Oliver .20 .09 .03
☐ 454 Greg Brock .20 .09 .03
☐ 455 Jeff Treadway .20 .09 .03
☐ 456 Lance McCullers .20 .09 .03
☐ 457 Dave Schmidt .20 .09 .03
☐ 458 Todd Burns .20 .09 .03
☐ 459 Max Venable .20 .09 .03
☐ 460 Neal Heaton .20 .09 .03
☐ 461 Mark Williamson .20 .09 .03
☐ 462 Keith Miller .20 .09 .03
☐ 463 Mike LaCoss .20 .09 .03
☐ 464 Jose Offerman .40 .18 .05
☐ 465 Jim Leyritz .60 .25 .08
☐ 466 Glenn Braggs .20 .09 .03
☐ 467 Ron Robinson .20 .09 .03
☐ 468 Mark Davis .20 .09 .03
☐ 469 Gary Pettis .20 .09 .03
☐ 470 Keith Hernandez .30 .14 .04
☐ 471 Dennis Rasmussen .20 .09 .03
☐ 472 Mark Eichhorn .20 .09 .03
☐ 473 Ted Power .20 .09 .03
☐ 474 Terry Mulholland .30 .14 .04
☐ 475 Todd Stottlemyre .30 .14 .04
☐ 476 Jerry Goff .20 .09 .03
☐ 477 Gene Nelson .20 .09 .03
☐ 478 Rich Gedman .20 .09 .03
☐ 479 Brian Harper .30 .14 .04
☐ 480 Mike Felder .20 .09 .03
☐ 481 Steve Avery 5.00 2.30 .60
☐ 482 Jack Morris .30 .14 .04
☐ 483 Randy Johnson 2.50 1.15 .30
☐ 484 Scott Radinsky .20 .09 .03
☐ 485 Jose DeLeon .20 .09 .03
☐ 486 Stan Belinda .20 .09 .03
☐ 487 Brian Holton .20 .09 .03
☐ 488 Mark Carreon .20 .09 .03
☐ 489 Trevor Wilson .20 .09 .03
☐ 490 Mike Sharperson .20 .09 .03
☐ 491 Alan Mills .20 .09 .03
☐ 492 John Candelaria .20 .09 .03
☐ 493 Paul Assenmacher .20 .09 .03
☐ 494 Steve Crawford .20 .09 .03
☐ 495 Brad Arnsberg .20 .09 .03
☐ 496 Sergio Valdez .20 .09 .03
☐ 497 Mark Parent .20 .09 .03
☐ 498 Tom Pagnozzi .30 .14 .04
☐ 499 Greg A. Harris .20 .09 .03
☐ 500 Randy Ready .20 .09 .03
☐ 501 Duane Ward .30 .14 .04
☐ 502 Nelson Santovenia .20 .09 .03
☐ 503 Joe Klink .20 .09 .03
☐ 504 Eric Plunk .20 .09 .03
☐ 505 Jeff Reed .20 .09 .03
☐ 506 Ted Higuera .20 .09 .03
☐ 507 Joe Hesketh .20 .09 .03
☐ 508 Dan Petry .20 .09 .03
☐ 509 Matt Young .20 .09 .03
☐ 510 Jerald Clark .20 .09 .03
☐ 511 John Orton .20 .09 .03
☐ 512 Scott Ruskin .20 .09 .03
☐ 513 Chris Hoiles 2.50 1.15 .30
☐ 514 Daryl Boston .20 .09 .03
☐ 515 Francisco Oliveras .20 .09 .03
☐ 516 Ozzie Canseco .20 .09 .03
☐ 517 Xavier Hernandez .20 .09 .03
☐ 518 Fred Manrique .20 .09 .03
☐ 519 Shawn Boskie .20 .09 .03
☐ 520 Jeff Montgomery .30 .14 .04
☐ 521 Jack Daugherty .20 .09 .03
☐ 522 Keith Comstock .20 .09 .03
☐ 523 Greg Hibbard .20 .09 .03
☐ 524 Lee Smith .50 .23 .06
☐ 525 Dana Kiecker .20 .09 .03
☐ 526 Darrel Akerfelds .20 .09 .03
☐ 527 Greg Myers .20 .09 .03
☐ 528 Checklist 441-528 .35 .16 .04
(Ryne Sandberg)

1991 Leaf Previews

The 1991 Leaf Previews set consists of 26 cards measuring the standard size (2 1/2" by 3 1/2"). The front design has color action player photos, with white and silver borders. Black photo mounts are drawn in at the corners of the pictures, just as one would find in an old-fashioned photo album. The back has a color head shot and biography in the top portion on a black background. A red stripe cuts across the card, and career statistics are given below it on a silver background. The words "1991 Preview Card" appear in white block lettering beneath the statistics. The cards are numbered on the back. Cards from this set were issued as inserts (four at a time) inside specially marked 1991 Donruss hobby factory sets.

	MINT	EXC	G-VG
COMPLETE SET (26)	60.00	27.00	7.50
COMMON CARD (1-26)	1.25	.55	.16
☐ 1 David Justice	7.00	3.10	.85
☐ 2 Ryne Sandberg	7.00	3.10	.85
☐ 3 Barry Larkin	2.00	.90	.25
☐ 4 Craig Biggio	2.00	.90	.25
☐ 5 Ramon Martinez	2.00	.90	.25
☐ 6 Tim Wallach	1.25	.55	.16
☐ 7 Dwight Gooden	1.25	.55	.16
☐ 8 Len Dykstra	2.00	.90	.25
☐ 9 Barry Bonds	8.00	3.60	1.00
☐ 10 Ray Lankford	4.00	1.80	.50
☐ 11 Tony Gwynn	6.00	2.70	.75
☐ 12 Will Clark	6.00	2.70	.75
☐ 13 Leo Gomez	2.00	.90	.25
☐ 14 Wade Boggs	4.00	1.80	.50
☐ 15 Chuck Finley UER (Position on card back is First Base)	1.25	.55	.16
☐ 16 Carlton Fisk	3.00	1.35	.40
☐ 17 Sandy Alomar Jr.	1.25	.55	.16
☐ 18 Cecil Fielder	4.00	1.80	.50
☐ 19 Bo Jackson	3.00	1.35	.40
☐ 20 Paul Molitor	4.00	1.80	.50
☐ 21 Kirby Puckett	7.00	3.10	.85
☐ 22 Don Mattingly	7.00	3.10	.85
☐ 23 Rickey Henderson	4.00	1.80	.50
☐ 24 Tino Martinez	1.25	.55	.16
☐ 25 Nolan Ryan	15.00	6.75	1.90
☐ 26 Dave Stieb	1.25	.55	.16

1991 Leaf

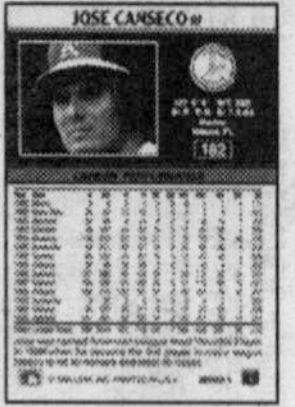

This 528-card standard size 2 1/2" by 3 1/2" set marks the second year Donruss has produced a two-series premium set using the Leaf name. This set features a photo of the player which is surrounded by black and white borders. The whole card is framed in gray borders. The Leaf logo is in the upper right corner of the card. The back of the card features a gray, red and black back with white lettering on the black background and black lettering on the gray and red backgrounds. The backs of the cards also features biographical and statistical information along with a write-up when room is provided. The set was issued using the Donruss dealer distribution network with very little Leaf product being released in other fashions. The cards are numbered on the back. Rookie Cards in the set include Wes Chamberlain, Brian McRae, Orlando Merced, Denny Neagle, and Randy Tomlin.

	MINT	EXC	G-VG
COMPLETE SET (528)	20.00	9.00	2.50
COMPLETE SERIES 1 (264)	10.00	4.50	1.25
COMPLETE SERIES 2 (264)	10.00	4.50	1.25
COMMON CARD (1-264)	.05	.02	.01
COMMON CARD (265-528)	.05	.02	.01
☐ 1 The Leaf Card	.05	.02	.01
☐ 2 Kurt Stillwell	.05	.02	.01
☐ 3 Bobby Witt	.05	.02	.01
☐ 4 Tony Phillips	.05	.02	.01
☐ 5 Scott Garrelts	.05	.02	.01
☐ 6 Greg Swindell	.05	.02	.01
☐ 7 Billy Ripken	.05	.02	.01
☐ 8 Dave Martinez	.05	.02	.01
☐ 9 Kelly Gruber	.05	.02	.01
☐ 10 Juan Samuel	.05	.02	.01
☐ 11 Brian Holman	.05	.02	.01
☐ 12 Craig Biggio	.20	.09	.03
☐ 13 Lonnie Smith	.05	.02	.01
☐ 14 Ron Robinson	.05	.02	.01
☐ 15 Mike LaValliere	.05	.02	.01
☐ 16 Mark Davis	.05	.02	.01
☐ 17 Jack Daugherty	.05	.02	.01
☐ 18 Mike Henneman	.05	.02	.01
☐ 19 Mike Greenwell	.10	.05	.01
☐ 20 Dave Magadan	.05	.02	.01
☐ 21 Mark Williamson	.05	.02	.01
☐ 22 Marquis Grissom	.30	.14	.04
☐ 23 Pat Borders	.05	.02	.01
☐ 24 Mike Scioscia	.05	.02	.01
☐ 25 Shawon Dunston	.05	.02	.01

☐	26 Randy Bush	.05	.02	.01
☐	27 John Smoltz	.20	.09	.03
☐	28 Chuck Crim	.05	.02	.01
☐	29 Don Slaught	.05	.02	.01
☐	30 Mike Macfarlane	.05	.02	.01
☐	31 Wally Joyner	.10	.05	.01
☐	32 Pat Combs	.05	.02	.01
☐	33 Tony Pena	.05	.02	.01
☐	34 Howard Johnson	.10	.05	.01
☐	35 Leo Gomez	.10	.05	.01
☐	36 Spike Owen	.05	.02	.01
☐	37 Eric Davis	.10	.05	.01
☐	38 Roberto Kelly	.10	.05	.01
☐	39 Jerome Walton	.05	.02	.01
☐	40 Shane Mack	.10	.05	.01
☐	41 Kent Mercker	.10	.05	.01
☐	42 B.J. Surhoff	.05	.02	.01
☐	43 Jerry Browne	.05	.02	.01
☐	44 Lee Smith	.20	.09	.03
☐	45 Chuck Finley	.10	.05	.01
☐	46 Terry Mulholland	.05	.02	.01
☐	47 Tom Bolton	.05	.02	.01
☐	48 Tom Herr	.05	.02	.01
☐	49 Jim Deshaies	.05	.02	.01
☐	50 Walt Weiss	.05	.02	.01
☐	51 Hal Morris	.10	.05	.01
☐	52 Lee Guetterman	.05	.02	.01
☐	53 Paul Assenmacher	.05	.02	.01
☐	54 Brian Harper	.05	.02	.01
☐	55 Paul Gibson	.05	.02	.01
☐	56 John Burkett	.10	.05	.01
☐	57 Doug Jones	.05	.02	.01
☐	58 Jose Oquendo	.05	.02	.01
☐	59 Dick Schofield	.05	.02	.01
☐	60 Dickie Thon	.05	.02	.01
☐	61 Ramon Martinez	.10	.05	.01
☐	62 Jay Buhner	.10	.05	.01
☐	63 Mark Portugal	.05	.02	.01
☐	64 Bob Welch	.05	.02	.01
☐	65 Chris Sabo	.10	.05	.01
☐	66 Chuck Cary	.05	.02	.01
☐	67 Mark Langston	.20	.09	.03
☐	68 Joe Boever	.05	.02	.01
☐	69 Jody Reed	.05	.02	.01
☐	70 Alejandro Pena	.05	.02	.01
☐	71 Jeff King	.05	.02	.01
☐	72 Tom Pagnozzi	.05	.02	.01
☐	73 Joe Oliver	.05	.02	.01
☐	74 Mike Witt	.05	.02	.01
☐	75 Hector Villanueva	.05	.02	.01
☐	76 Dan Gladden	.05	.02	.01
☐	77 David Justice	.60	.25	.08
☐	78 Mike Gallego	.05	.02	.01
☐	79 Tom Candiotti	.05	.02	.01
☐	80 Ozzie Smith	.25	.11	.03
☐	81 Luis Polonia	.05	.02	.01
☐	82 Randy Ready	.05	.02	.01
☐	83 Greg A. Harris	.05	.02	.01
☐	84 Checklist 1-92 Dave Justice	.05	.02	.01
☐	85 Kevin Mitchell	.10	.05	.01
☐	86 Mark McLemore	.05	.02	.01
☐	87 Terry Steinbach	.10	.05	.01
☐	88 Tom Browning	.05	.02	.01
☐	89 Matt Nokes	.05	.02	.01
☐	90 Mike Harkey	.05	.02	.01
☐	91 Omar Vizquel	.05	.02	.01
☐	92 Dave Bergman	.05	.02	.01
☐	93 Matt Williams	.35	.16	.04
☐	94 Steve Olin	.05	.02	.01
☐	95 Craig Wilson	.05	.02	.01
☐	96 Dave Stieb	.10	.05	.01
☐	97 Ruben Sierra	.20	.09	.03

☐	98 Jay Howell	.05	.02	.01
☐	99 Scott Bradley	.05	.02	.01
☐	100 Eric Yelding	.05	.02	.01
☐	101 Rickey Henderson	.35	.16	.04
☐	102 Jeff Reed	.05	.02	.01
☐	103 Jimmy Key	.10	.05	.01
☐	104 Terry Shumpert	.05	.02	.01
☐	105 Kenny Rogers	.05	.02	.01
☐	106 Cecil Fielder	.35	.16	.04
☐	107 Robby Thompson	.05	.02	.01
☐	108 Alex Cole	.05	.02	.01
☐	109 Randy Milligan	.05	.02	.01
☐	110 Andres Galarraga	.20	.09	.03
☐	111 Bill Spiers	.05	.02	.01
☐	112 Kal Daniels	.05	.02	.01
☐	113 Henry Cotto	.05	.02	.01
☐	114 Casey Candaele	.05	.02	.01
☐	115 Jeff Blauser	.10	.05	.01
☐	116 Robin Yount	.30	.14	.04
☐	117 Ben McDonald	.20	.09	.03
☐	118 Bret Saberhagen	.10	.05	.01
☐	119 Juan Gonzalez	2.00	.90	.25
☐	120 Lou Whitaker	.20	.09	.03
☐	121 Ellis Burks	.10	.05	.01
☐	122 Charlie O'Brien	.05	.02	.01
☐	123 John Smiley	.05	.02	.01
☐	124 Tim Burke	.05	.02	.01
☐	125 John Olerud	.40	.18	.05
☐	126 Eddie Murray	.20	.09	.03
☐	127 Greg Maddux	.40	.18	.05
☐	128 Kevin Tapani	.10	.05	.01
☐	129 Ron Gant	.10	.05	.01
☐	130 Jay Bell	.10	.05	.01
☐	131 Chris Hoiles	.20	.09	.03
☐	132 Tom Gordon	.10	.05	.01
☐	133 Kevin Seitzer	.05	.02	.01
☐	134 Jeff Huson	.05	.02	.01
☐	135 Jerry Don Gleaton	.05	.02	.01
☐	136 Jeff Brantley UER (Photo actually Rick Leach on back)	.05	.02	.01
☐	137 Felix Fermin	.05	.02	.01
☐	138 Mike Devereaux	.10	.05	.01
☐	139 Delino DeShields	.20	.09	.03
☐	140 David Wells	.05	.02	.01
☐	141 Tim Crews	.05	.02	.01
☐	142 Erik Hanson	.05	.02	.01
☐	143 Mark Davidson	.05	.02	.01
☐	144 Tommy Gregg	.05	.02	.01
☐	145 Jim Gantner	.05	.02	.01
☐	146 Jose Lind	.05	.02	.01
☐	147 Danny Tartabull	.10	.05	.01
☐	148 Geno Petralli	.05	.02	.01
☐	149 Travis Fryman	1.00	.45	.13
☐	150 Tim Naehring	.10	.05	.01
☐	151 Kevin McReynolds	.05	.02	.01
☐	152 Joe Orsulak	.05	.02	.01
☐	153 Steve Frey	.05	.02	.01
☐	154 Duane Ward	.10	.05	.01
☐	155 Stan Javier	.05	.02	.01
☐	156 Damon Berryhill	.05	.02	.01
☐	157 Gene Larkin	.05	.02	.01
☐	158 Greg Olson	.05	.02	.01
☐	159 Mark Knudson	.05	.02	.01
☐	160 Carmelo Martinez	.05	.02	.01
☐	161 Storm Davis	.05	.02	.01
☐	162 Jim Abbott	.20	.09	.03
☐	163 Len Dykstra	.20	.09	.03
☐	164 Tom Brunansky	.05	.02	.01
☐	165 Dwight Gooden	.10	.05	.01
☐	166 Jose Mesa	.05	.02	.01
☐	167 Oil Can Boyd	.05	.02	.01
☐	168 Barry Larkin	.20	.09	.03

	#	Player			
☐	169	Scott Sanderson	.05	.02	.01
☐	170	Mark Grace	.20	.09	.03
☐	171	Mark Guthrie	.05	.02	.01
☐	172	Tom Glavine	.60	.25	.08
☐	173	Gary Sheffield	.35	.16	.04
☐	174	Checklist 93-184 Roger Clemens	.15	.07	.02
☐	175	Chris James	.05	.02	.01
☐	176	Milt Thompson	.05	.02	.01
☐	177	Donnie Hill	.05	.02	.01
☐	178	Wes Chamberlain	.05	.02	.01
☐	179	John Marzano	.05	.02	.01
☐	180	Frank Viola	.10	.05	.01
☐	181	Eric Anthony	.10	.05	.01
☐	182	Jose Canseco	.50	.23	.06
☐	183	Scott Scudder	.05	.02	.01
☐	184	Dave Eiland	.05	.02	.01
☐	185	Luis Salazar	.05	.02	.01
☐	186	Pedro Munoz	.20	.09	.03
☐	187	Steve Searcy	.05	.02	.01
☐	188	Don Robinson	.05	.02	.01
☐	189	Sandy Alomar Jr.	.10	.05	.01
☐	190	Jose DeLeon	.05	.02	.01
☐	191	John Orton	.05	.02	.01
☐	192	Darren Daulton	.20	.09	.03
☐	193	Mike Morgan	.05	.02	.01
☐	194	Greg Briley	.05	.02	.01
☐	195	Karl Rhodes	.05	.02	.01
☐	196	Harold Baines	.10	.05	.01
☐	197	Bill Doran	.05	.02	.01
☐	198	Alvaro Espinoza	.05	.02	.01
☐	199	Kirk McCaskill	.05	.02	.01
☐	200	Jose DeJesus	.05	.02	.01
☐	201	Jack Clark	.10	.05	.01
☐	202	Daryl Boston	.05	.02	.01
☐	203	Randy Tomlin	.05	.02	.01
☐	204	Pedro Guerrero	.10	.05	.01
☐	205	Billy Hatcher	.05	.02	.01
☐	206	Tim Leary	.05	.02	.01
☐	207	Ryne Sandberg	.75	.35	.09
☐	208	Kirby Puckett	.75	.35	.09
☐	209	Charlie Leibrandt	.05	.02	.01
☐	210	Rick Honeycutt	.05	.02	.01
☐	211	Joel Skinner	.05	.02	.01
☐	212	Rex Hudler	.05	.02	.01
☐	213	Bryan Harvey	.10	.05	.01
☐	214	Charlie Hayes	.10	.05	.01
☐	215	Matt Young	.05	.02	.01
☐	216	Terry Kennedy	.05	.02	.01
☐	217	Carl Nichols	.05	.02	.01
☐	218	Mike Moore	.05	.02	.01
☐	219	Paul O'Neill	.10	.05	.01
☐	220	Steve Sax	.05	.02	.01
☐	221	Shawn Boskie	.05	.02	.01
☐	222	Rich DeLucia	.05	.02	.01
☐	223	Lloyd Moseby	.05	.02	.01
☐	224	Mike Kingery	.05	.02	.01
☐	225	Carlos Baerga	.60	.25	.08
☐	226	Bryn Smith	.05	.02	.01
☐	227	Todd Stottlemyre	.05	.02	.01
☐	228	Julio Franco	.10	.05	.01
☐	229	Jim Gott	.05	.02	.01
☐	230	Mike Schooler	.05	.02	.01
☐	231	Steve Finley	.05	.02	.01
☐	232	Dave Henderson	.05	.02	.01
☐	233	Luis Quinones	.05	.02	.01
☐	234	Mark Whiten	.20	.09	.03
☐	235	Brian McRae	.50	.23	.06
☐	236	Rich Gossage	.20	.09	.03
☐	237	Rob Deer	.05	.02	.01
☐	238	Will Clark	.60	.25	.08
☐	239	Albert Belle	1.25	.55	.16
☐	240	Bob Melvin	.05	.02	.01
☐	241	Larry Walker	.30	.14	.04
☐	242	Dante Bichette	.25	.11	.03
☐	243	Orel Hershiser	.10	.05	.01
☐	244	Pete O'Brien	.05	.02	.01
☐	245	Pete Harnisch	.10	.05	.01
☐	246	Jeff Treadway	.05	.02	.01
☐	247	Julio Machado	.05	.02	.01
☐	248	Dave Johnson	.05	.02	.01
☐	249	Kirk Gibson	.10	.05	.01
☐	250	Kevin Brown	.10	.05	.01
☐	251	Milt Cuyler	.05	.02	.01
☐	252	Jeff Reardon	.10	.05	.01
☐	253	David Cone	.20	.09	.03
☐	254	Gary Redus	.05	.02	.01
☐	255	Junior Noboa	.05	.02	.01
☐	256	Greg Myers	.05	.02	.01
☐	257	Dennis Cook	.05	.02	.01
☐	258	Joe Girardi	.05	.02	.01
☐	259	Allan Anderson	.05	.02	.01
☐	260	Paul Marak	.05	.02	.01
☐	261	Barry Bonds	1.00	.45	.13
☐	262	Juan Bell	.05	.02	.01
☐	263	Russ Morman	.05	.02	.01
☐	264	Checklist 185-264 and BC1-BC12 George Brett	.20	.09	.03
☐	265	Jerald Clark	.05	.02	.01
☐	266	Dwight Evans	.10	.05	.01
☐	267	Roberto Alomar	1.00	.45	.13
☐	268	Danny Jackson	.05	.02	.01
☐	269	Brian Downing	.05	.02	.01
☐	270	John Cerutti	.05	.02	.01
☐	271	Robin Ventura	.75	.35	.09
☐	272	Gerald Perry	.05	.02	.01
☐	273	Wade Boggs	.20	.09	.03
☐	274	Dennis Martinez	.10	.05	.01
☐	275	Andy Benes	.20	.09	.03
☐	276	Tony Fossas	.05	.02	.01
☐	277	Franklin Stubbs	.05	.02	.01
☐	278	John Kruk	.20	.09	.03
☐	279	Kevin Gross	.05	.02	.01
☐	280	Von Hayes	.05	.02	.01
☐	281	Frank Thomas	4.00	1.80	.50
☐	282	Rob Dibble	.05	.02	.01
☐	283	Mel Hall	.05	.02	.01
☐	284	Rick Mahler	.05	.02	.01
☐	285	Dennis Eckersley	.20	.09	.03
☐	286	Bernard Gilkey	.10	.05	.01
☐	287	Dan Plesac	.05	.02	.01
☐	288	Jason Grimsley	.05	.02	.01
☐	289	Mark Lewis	.10	.05	.01
☐	290	Tony Gwynn	.40	.18	.05
☐	291	Jeff Russell	.05	.02	.01
☐	292	Curt Schilling	.10	.05	.01
☐	293	Pascual Perez	.05	.02	.01
☐	294	Jack Morris	.20	.09	.03
☐	295	Hubie Brooks	.05	.02	.01
☐	296	Alex Fernandez	.50	.23	.06
☐	297	Harold Reynolds	.05	.02	.01
☐	298	Craig Worthington	.05	.02	.01
☐	299	Willie Wilson	.05	.02	.01
☐	300	Mike Maddux	.05	.02	.01
☐	301	Dave Righetti	.05	.02	.01
☐	302	Paul Molitor	.35	.16	.04
☐	303	Gary Gaetti	.05	.02	.01
☐	304	Terry Pendleton	.20	.09	.03
☐	305	Kevin Elster	.05	.02	.01
☐	306	Scott Fletcher	.05	.02	.01
☐	307	Jeff Robinson	.05	.02	.01
☐	308	Jesse Barfield	.05	.02	.01
☐	309	Mike LaCoss	.05	.02	.01
☐	310	Andy Van Slyke	.20	.09	.03
☐	311	Glenallen Hill	.05	.02	.01

	No.	Player			
☐	312	Bud Black	.05	.02	.01
☐	313	Kent Hrbek	.10	.05	.01
☐	314	Tim Teufel	.05	.02	.01
☐	315	Tony Fernandez	.10	.05	.01
☐	316	Beau Allred	.05	.02	.01
☐	317	Curtis Wilkerson	.05	.02	.01
☐	318	Bill Sampen	.05	.02	.01
☐	319	Randy Johnson	.25	.11	.03
☐	320	Mike Heath	.05	.02	.01
☐	321	Sammy Sosa	.30	.14	.04
☐	322	Mickey Tettleton	.10	.05	.01
☐	323	Jose Vizcaino	.05	.02	.01
☐	324	John Candelaria	.05	.02	.01
☐	325	Dave Howard	.05	.02	.01
☐	326	Jose Rijo	.10	.05	.01
☐	327	Todd Zeile	.10	.05	.01
☐	328	Gene Nelson	.05	.02	.01
☐	329	Dwayne Henry	.05	.02	.01
☐	330	Mike Boddicker	.05	.02	.01
☐	331	Ozzie Guillen	.05	.02	.01
☐	332	Sam Horn	.05	.02	.01
☐	333	Wally Whitehurst	.05	.02	.01
☐	334	Dave Parker	.20	.09	.03
☐	335	George Brett	.60	.25	.08
☐	336	Bobby Thigpen	.05	.02	.01
☐	337	Ed Whitson	.05	.02	.01
☐	338	Ivan Calderon	.05	.02	.01
☐	339	Mike Pagliarulo	.05	.02	.01
☐	340	Jack McDowell	.20	.09	.03
☐	341	Dana Kiecker	.05	.02	.01
☐	342	Fred McGriff	.50	.23	.06
☐	343	Mark Lee	.05	.02	.01
☐	344	Alfredo Griffin	.05	.02	.01
☐	345	Scott Bankhead	.05	.02	.01
☐	346	Darrin Jackson	.05	.02	.01
☐	347	Rafael Palmeiro	.35	.16	.04
☐	348	Steve Farr	.05	.02	.01
☐	349	Hensley Meulens	.05	.02	.01
☐	350	Danny Cox	.05	.02	.01
☐	351	Alan Trammell	.20	.09	.03
☐	352	Edwin Nunez	.05	.02	.01
☐	353	Joe Carter	.40	.18	.05
☐	354	Eric Show	.05	.02	.01
☐	355	Vance Law	.05	.02	.01
☐	356	Jeff Gray	.05	.02	.01
☐	357	Bobby Bonilla	.20	.09	.03
☐	358	Ernest Riles	.05	.02	.01
☐	359	Ron Hassey	.05	.02	.01
☐	360	Willie McGee	.10	.05	.01
☐	361	Mackey Sasser	.05	.02	.01
☐	362	Glenn Braggs	.05	.02	.01
☐	363	Mario Diaz	.05	.02	.01
☐	364	Checklist 265-356 Barry Bonds	.20	.09	.03
☐	365	Kevin Bass	.05	.02	.01
☐	366	Pete Incaviglia	.05	.02	.01
☐	367	Luis Sojo UER (1989 stats interspersed with 1990's)	.05	.02	.01
☐	368	Lance Parrish	.10	.05	.01
☐	369	Mark Leonard	.05	.02	.01
☐	370	Heathcliff Slocumb	.05	.02	.01
☐	371	Jimmy Jones	.05	.02	.01
☐	372	Ken Griffey Jr.	3.50	1.55	.45
☐	373	Chris Hammond	.10	.05	.01
☐	374	Chili Davis	.10	.05	.01
☐	375	Joey Cora	.05	.02	.01
☐	376	Ken Hill	.20	.09	.03
☐	377	Darryl Strawberry	.20	.09	.03
☐	378	Ron Darling	.05	.02	.01
☐	379	Sid Bream	.05	.02	.01
☐	380	Bill Swift	.10	.05	.01
☐	381	Shawn Abner	.05	.02	.01
☐	382	Eric King	.05	.02	.01
☐	383	Mickey Morandini	.05	.02	.01
☐	384	Carlton Fisk	.20	.09	.03
☐	385	Steve Lake	.05	.02	.01
☐	386	Mike Jeffcoat	.05	.02	.01
☐	387	Darren Holmes	.05	.02	.01
☐	388	Tim Wallach	.05	.02	.01
☐	389	George Bell	.10	.05	.01
☐	390	Craig Lefferts	.05	.02	.01
☐	391	Ernie Whitt	.05	.02	.01
☐	392	Felix Jose	.10	.05	.01
☐	393	Kevin Maas	.05	.02	.01
☐	394	Devon White	.10	.05	.01
☐	395	Otis Nixon	.10	.05	.01
☐	396	Chuck Knoblauch	.60	.25	.08
☐	397	Scott Coolbaugh	.05	.02	.01
☐	398	Glenn Davis	.05	.02	.01
☐	399	Manny Lee	.05	.02	.01
☐	400	Andre Dawson	.20	.09	.03
☐	401	Scott Chiamparino	.05	.02	.01
☐	402	Bill Gullickson	.05	.02	.01
☐	403	Lance Johnson	.05	.02	.01
☐	404	Juan Agosto	.05	.02	.01
☐	405	Danny Darwin	.05	.02	.01
☐	406	Barry Jones	.05	.02	.01
☐	407	Larry Andersen	.05	.02	.01
☐	408	Luis Rivera	.05	.02	.01
☐	409	Jaime Navarro	.05	.02	.01
☐	410	Roger McDowell	.05	.02	.01
☐	411	Brett Butler	.10	.05	.01
☐	412	Dale Murphy	.20	.09	.03
☐	413	Tim Raines UER (Listed as hitting .500 in 1980, should be .050)	.20	.09	.03
☐	414	Norm Charlton	.05	.02	.01
☐	415	Greg Cadaret	.05	.02	.01
☐	416	Chris Nabholz	.05	.02	.01
☐	417	Dave Stewart	.10	.05	.01
☐	418	Rich Gedman	.05	.02	.01
☐	419	Willie Randolph	.10	.05	.01
☐	420	Mitch Williams	.10	.05	.01
☐	421	Brook Jacoby	.05	.02	.01
☐	422	Greg W. Harris	.05	.02	.01
☐	423	Nolan Ryan	1.50	.65	.19
☐	424	Dave Rohde	.05	.02	.01
☐	425	Don Mattingly	.75	.35	.09
☐	426	Greg Gagne	.05	.02	.01
☐	427	Vince Coleman	.05	.02	.01
☐	428	Dan Pasqua	.05	.02	.01
☐	429	Alvin Davis	.05	.02	.01
☐	430	Cal Ripken	.75	.35	.09
☐	431	Jamie Quirk	.05	.02	.01
☐	432	Benito Santiago	.05	.02	.01
☐	433	Jose Uribe	.05	.02	.01
☐	434	Candy Maldonado	.05	.02	.01
☐	435	Junior Felix	.05	.02	.01
☐	436	Deion Sanders	.50	.23	.06
☐	437	John Franco	.10	.05	.01
☐	438	Greg Hibbard	.05	.02	.01
☐	439	Floyd Bannister	.05	.02	.01
☐	440	Steve Howe	.05	.02	.01
☐	441	Steve Decker	.05	.02	.01
☐	442	Vicente Palacios	.05	.02	.01
☐	443	Pat Tabler	.05	.02	.01
☐	444	Checklist 357-448 Darryl Strawberry	.05	.02	.01
☐	445	Mike Felder	.05	.02	.01
☐	446	Al Newman	.05	.02	.01
☐	447	Chris Donnels	.05	.02	.01
☐	448	Rich Rodriguez	.05	.02	.01
☐	449	Turner Ward	.20	.09	.03
☐	450	Bob Walk	.05	.02	.01
☐	451	Gilberto Reyes	.05	.02	.01

	#	Player	MINT	EXC	G-VG
☐	452	Mike Jackson	.05	.02	.01
☐	453	Rafael Belliard	.05	.02	.01
☐	454	Wayne Edwards	.05	.02	.01
☐	455	Andy Allanson	.05	.02	.01
☐	456	Dave Smith	.05	.02	.01
☐	457	Gary Carter	.20	.09	.03
☐	458	Warren Cromartie	.05	.02	.01
☐	459	Jack Armstrong	.05	.02	.01
☐	460	Bob Tewksbury	.10	.05	.01
☐	461	Joe Klink	.05	.02	.01
☐	462	Xavier Hernandez	.05	.02	.01
☐	463	Scott Radinsky	.05	.02	.01
☐	464	Jeff Robinson	.05	.02	.01
☐	465	Gregg Jefferies	.35	.16	.04
☐	466	Denny Neagle	.05	.02	.01
☐	467	Carmelo Martinez	.05	.02	.01
☐	468	Donn Pall	.05	.02	.01
☐	469	Bruce Hurst	.05	.02	.01
☐	470	Eric Bullock	.05	.02	.01
☐	471	Rick Aguilera	.10	.05	.01
☐	472	Charlie Hough	.10	.05	.01
☐	473	Carlos Quintana	.05	.02	.01
☐	474	Marty Barrett	.05	.02	.01
☐	475	Kevin D. Brown	.05	.02	.01
☐	476	Bobby Ojeda	.05	.02	.01
☐	477	Edgar Martinez	.10	.05	.01
☐	478	Bip Roberts	.05	.02	.01
☐	479	Mike Flanagan	.05	.02	.01
☐	480	John Habyan	.05	.02	.01
☐	481	Larry Casian	.05	.02	.01
☐	482	Wally Backman	.05	.02	.01
☐	483	Doug Dascenzo	.05	.02	.01
☐	484	Rick Dempsey	.05	.02	.01
☐	485	Ed Sprague	.05	.02	.01
☐	486	Steve Chitren	.05	.02	.01
☐	487	Mark McGwire	.20	.09	.03
☐	488	Roger Clemens	.50	.23	.06
☐	489	Orlando Merced	.40	.18	.05
☐	490	Rene Gonzales	.05	.02	.01
☐	491	Mike Stanton	.05	.02	.01
☐	492	Al Osuna	.05	.02	.01
☐	493	Rick Cerone	.05	.02	.01
☐	494	Mariano Duncan	.05	.02	.01
☐	495	Zane Smith	.05	.02	.01
☐	496	John Morris	.05	.02	.01
☐	497	Frank Tanana	.05	.02	.01
☐	498	Junior Ortiz	.05	.02	.01
☐	499	Dave Winfield	.25	.11	.03
☐	500	Gary Varsho	.05	.02	.01
☐	501	Chico Walker	.05	.02	.01
☐	502	Ken Caminiti	.10	.05	.01
☐	503	Ken Griffey	.10	.05	.01
☐	504	Randy Myers	.10	.05	.01
☐	505	Steve Bedrosian	.05	.02	.01
☐	506	Cory Snyder	.05	.02	.01
☐	507	Cris Carpenter	.05	.02	.01
☐	508	Tim Belcher	.05	.02	.01
☐	509	Jeff Hamilton	.05	.02	.01
☐	510	Steve Avery	.60	.25	.08
☐	511	Dave Valle	.05	.02	.01
☐	512	Tom Lampkin	.05	.02	.01
☐	513	Shawn Hillegas	.05	.02	.01
☐	514	Reggie Jefferson	.10	.05	.01
☐	515	Ron Karkovice	.05	.02	.01
☐	516	Doug Drabek	.20	.09	.03
☐	517	Tom Henke	.10	.05	.01
☐	518	Chris Bosio	.05	.02	.01
☐	519	Gregg Olson	.10	.05	.01
☐	520	Bob Scanlan	.05	.02	.01
☐	521	Alonzo Powell	.05	.02	.01
☐	522	Jeff Ballard	.05	.02	.01
☐	523	Ray Lankford	.40	.18	.05
☐	524	Tommy Greene	.10	.05	.01
☐	525	Mike Timlin	.05	.02	.01
☐	526	Juan Berenguer	.05	.02	.01
☐	527	Scott Erickson	.05	.02	.01
☐	528	Checklist 449-528 and BC13-BC26 Sandy Alomar Jr.	.05	.02	.01

1991 Leaf Gold Rookies

This 26-card standard size (2 1/2" by 3 1/2") set was issued by Leaf as an adjunct (inserted in packs) to their 1991 Leaf regular issue. The set features some of the most popular prospects active in baseball. This set marks the first time Leaf Inc. and/or Donruss had produced a card utilizing any of the first 24 young players. The first twelve cards were issued as random inserts in with the first series of 1991 Leaf foil packs. The rest were issued as random inserts in with the second series. The card numbers have a BC prefix. The earliest Leaf Gold Rookie cards issued with the first series can sometimes be found with erroneous regular numbered backs 265 through 276 instead of the correct BC1 through BC12. These numbered variations are very tough to find and are valued at ten times the values listed below.

	MINT	EXC	G-VG
COMPLETE SET (26)	40.00	18.00	5.00
COMMON CARD (BC1-BC12)	1.00	.45	.13
COMMON CARD (BC13-BC26)	1.00	.45	.13

	#	Player	MINT	EXC	G-VG
☐	BC1	Scott Leius	1.00	.45	.13
☐	BC2	Luis Gonzalez	1.50	.65	.19
☐	BC3	Wil Cordero	4.00	1.80	.50
☐	BC4	Gary Scott	1.00	.45	.13
☐	BC5	Willie Banks	1.00	.45	.13
☐	BC6	Arthur Rhodes	1.50	.65	.19
☐	BC7	Mo Vaughn	5.00	2.30	.60
☐	BC8	Henry Rodriguez	1.00	.45	.13
☐	BC9	Todd Van Poppel	2.00	.90	.25
☐	BC10	Reggie Sanders	4.00	1.80	.50
☐	BC11	Rico Brogna	2.50	1.15	.30
☐	BC12	Mike Mussina	8.00	3.60	1.00
☐	BC13	Kirk Dressendorfer	1.00	.45	.13
☐	BC14	Jeff Bagwell	15.00	6.75	1.90
☐	BC15	Pete Schourek	1.50	.65	.19
☐	BC16	Wade Taylor	1.00	.45	.13
☐	BC17	Pat Kelly	1.50	.65	.19

		MINT	EXC	G-VG
☐ BC18	Tim Costo	1.00	.45	.13
☐ BC19	Roger Salkeld	1.00	.45	.13
☐ BC20	Andujar Cedeno	1.50	.65	.19
☐ BC21	Ryan Klesko UER (1990 Sumter BA .289; should be .368)	9.00	4.00	1.15
☐ BC22	Mike Huff	1.00	.45	.13
☐ BC23	Anthony Young	1.50	.65	.19
☐ BC24	Eddie Zosky	1.00	.45	.13
☐ BC25	Nolan Ryan UER No Hitter 7 (Word other repeated in 7th line)	3.00	1.35	.40
☐ BC26	Rickey Henderson Record Steal	1.00	.45	.13

1992 Leaf Previews

Four Leaf Preview cards were included in each 1992 Donruss hobby factory set. The cards are standard size, 2 1/2" by 3 1/2". The cards were intended to show collectors and dealers the style of the 1992 Leaf set. The fronts carry glossy color player photos framed by silver borders. The player's name, position, and the team logo appear in a black stripe beneath the picture. The horizontal backs have a second color photo, with biography, statistics (on a white panel), and player profile filling out the rest of the card. The cards are numbered on the back.

	MINT	EXC	G-VG
COMPLETE SET (26)	60.00	27.00	7.50
COMMON CARD (1-26)	1.00	.45	.13

		MINT	EXC	G-VG
☐ 1	Steve Avery	2.50	1.15	.30
☐ 2	Ryne Sandberg	6.00	2.70	.75
☐ 3	Chris Sabo	1.00	.45	.13
☐ 4	Jeff Bagwell	8.00	3.60	1.00
☐ 5	Darryl Strawberry	1.50	.65	.19
☐ 6	Bret Barberie	1.00	.45	.13
☐ 7	Howard Johnson	1.00	.45	.13
☐ 8	John Kruk	1.50	.65	.19
☐ 9	Andy Van Slyke	1.50	.65	.19
☐ 10	Felix Jose	1.50	.65	.19
☐ 11	Fred McGriff	3.00	1.35	.40
☐ 12	Will Clark	3.00	1.35	.40
☐ 13	Cal Ripken	9.00	4.00	1.15
☐ 14	Phil Plantier	2.00	.90	.25
☐ 15	Lee Stevens	1.00	.45	.13
☐ 16	Frank Thomas	18.00	8.00	2.30
☐ 17	Mark Whiten	1.50	.65	.19
☐ 18	Cecil Fielder	2.00	.90	.25
☐ 19	George Brett	6.00	2.70	.75
☐ 20	Robin Yount	2.50	1.15	.30
☐ 21	Scott Erickson	1.00	.45	.13
☐ 22	Don Mattingly	6.00	2.70	.75
☐ 23	Jose Canseco	3.00	1.35	.40
☐ 24	Ken Griffey Jr.	18.00	8.00	2.30
☐ 25	Nolan Ryan	15.00	6.75	1.90
☐ 26	Joe Carter	3.00	1.35	.40

1992 Leaf

The 1992 Leaf set consists of 528 cards, issued in two series each with 264 cards measuring the standard size (2 1/2" by 3 1/2"). The fronts feature color action player photos on a silver card face. The player's name appears in a black bar edged at the bottom by a thin red stripe. The team logo overlaps the bar at the right corner. The horizontally oriented backs have color action player photos on left portion of the card. The right portion carries the player's name and team logo in a black bar as well as career statistics and career highlights in a white box. The card backs have a silver background. The cards are numbered on the back. Leaf also produced a Gold Foil Version of the complete set (series I and II), featuring gold metallic ink and gold foil highlights instead of the traditional silver. One of these "black gold inserts" was included in each 15-card foil pack. Twelve "Gold Leaf Rookie" bonus cards, numbered BC1-BC12, were randomly inserted in first series foil packs and twelve, numbered BC13-24, were randomly inserted in second series foil packs. Rookie Cards in the set include Archi Cianfrocco, Chris Gardner, Brian Jordan, Jeff Kent, and Pat Listach.

	MINT	EXC	G-VG
COMPLETE SET (528)	18.00	8.00	2.30
COMPLETE SERIES 1 (264)	9.00	4.00	1.15
COMPLETE SERIES 2 (264)	9.00	4.00	1.15
COMMON CARD (1-264)	.05	.02	.01
COMMON CARD (265-528)	.05	.02	.01

		MINT	EXC	G-VG
☐ 1	Jim Abbott	.05	.02	.01
☐ 2	Cal Eldred	.10	.05	.01
☐ 3	Bud Black	.05	.02	.01
☐ 4	Dave Howard	.05	.02	.01
☐ 5	Luis Sojo	.05	.02	.01
☐ 6	Gary Scott	.05	.02	.01
☐ 7	Joe Oliver	.05	.02	.01

☐ 8 Chris Gardner	.05	.02	.01
☐ 9 Sandy Alomar Jr.	.10	.05	.01
☐ 10 Greg W. Harris	.05	.02	.01
☐ 11 Doug Drabek	.20	.09	.03
☐ 12 Darryl Hamilton	.10	.05	.01
☐ 13 Mike Mussina	.50	.23	.06
☐ 14 Kevin Tapani	.05	.02	.01
☐ 15 Ron Gant	.10	.05	.01
☐ 16 Mark McGwire	.20	.09	.03
☐ 17 Robin Ventura	.20	.09	.03
☐ 18 Pedro Guerrero	.10	.05	.01
☐ 19 Roger Clemens	.35	.16	.04
☐ 20 Steve Farr	.05	.02	.01
☐ 21 Frank Tanana	.05	.02	.01
☐ 22 Joe Hesketh	.05	.02	.01
☐ 23 Erik Hanson	.05	.02	.01
☐ 24 Greg Cadaret	.05	.02	.01
☐ 25 Rex Hudler	.05	.02	.01
☐ 26 Mark Grace	.20	.09	.03
☐ 27 Kelly Gruber	.05	.02	.01
☐ 28 Jeff Bagwell	1.25	.55	.16
☐ 29 Darryl Strawberry	.10	.05	.01
☐ 30 Dave Smith	.05	.02	.01
☐ 31 Kevin Appier	.10	.05	.01
☐ 32 Steve Chitren	.05	.02	.01
☐ 33 Kevin Gross	.05	.02	.01
☐ 34 Rick Aguilera	.10	.05	.01
☐ 35 Juan Guzman	.10	.05	.01
☐ 36 Joe Orsulak	.05	.02	.01
☐ 37 Tim Raines	.20	.09	.03
☐ 38 Harold Reynolds	.05	.02	.01
☐ 39 Charlie Hough	.10	.05	.01
☐ 40 Tony Phillips	.05	.02	.01
☐ 41 Nolan Ryan	1.50	.65	.19
☐ 42 Vince Coleman	.05	.02	.01
☐ 43 Andy Van Slyke	.20	.09	.03
☐ 44 Tim Burke	.05	.02	.01
☐ 45 Luis Polonia	.05	.02	.01
☐ 46 Tom Browning	.05	.02	.01
☐ 47 Willie McGee	.10	.05	.01
☐ 48 Gary DiSarcina	.10	.05	.01
☐ 49 Mark Lewis	.10	.05	.01
☐ 50 Phil Plantier	.20	.09	.03
☐ 51 Doug Dascenzo	.05	.02	.01
☐ 52 Cal Ripken	.60	.25	.08
☐ 53 Pedro Munoz	.10	.05	.01
☐ 54 Carlos Hernandez	.05	.02	.01
☐ 55 Jerald Clark	.05	.02	.01
☐ 56 Jeff Brantley	.05	.02	.01
☐ 57 Don Mattingly	.50	.23	.06
☐ 58 Roger McDowell	.05	.02	.01
☐ 59 Steve Avery	.20	.09	.03
☐ 60 John Olerud	.20	.09	.03
☐ 61 Bill Gullickson	.05	.02	.01
☐ 62 Juan Gonzalez	.90	.40	.11
☐ 63 Felix Jose	.10	.05	.01
☐ 64 Robin Yount	.20	.09	.03
☐ 65 Greg Briley	.05	.02	.01
☐ 66 Steve Finley	.05	.02	.01
☐ 67 Checklist 1-88 Frank Thomas	.05	.02	.01
☐ 68 Tom Gordon	.05	.02	.01
☐ 69 Rob Dibble	.05	.02	.01
☐ 70 Glenallen Hill	.05	.02	.01
☐ 71 Calvin Jones	.05	.02	.01
☐ 72 Joe Girardi	.05	.02	.01
☐ 73 Barry Larkin	.20	.09	.03
☐ 74 Andy Benes	.10	.05	.01
☐ 75 Milt Cuyler	.05	.02	.01
☐ 76 Kevin Bass	.05	.02	.01
☐ 77 Pete Harnisch	.10	.05	.01
☐ 78 Wilson Alvarez	.20	.09	.03
☐ 79 Mike Devereaux	.10	.05	.01
☐ 80 Doug Henry	.05	.02	.01
☐ 81 Orel Hershiser	.10	.05	.01
☐ 82 Shane Mack	.10	.05	.01
☐ 83 Mike Macfarlane	.05	.02	.01
☐ 84 Thomas Howard	.05	.02	.01
☐ 85 Alex Fernandez	.20	.09	.03
☐ 86 Reggie Jefferson	.05	.02	.01
☐ 87 Leo Gomez	.05	.02	.01
☐ 88 Mel Hall	.05	.02	.01
☐ 89 Mike Greenwell	.10	.05	.01
☐ 90 Jeff Russell	.05	.02	.01
☐ 91 Steve Buechele	.05	.02	.01
☐ 92 David Cone	.20	.09	.03
☐ 93 Kevin Reimer	.05	.02	.01
☐ 94 Mark Lemke	.05	.02	.01
☐ 95 Bob Tewksbury	.05	.02	.01
☐ 96 Zane Smith	.05	.02	.01
☐ 97 Mark Eichhorn	.05	.02	.01
☐ 98 Kirby Puckett	.50	.23	.06
☐ 99 Paul O'Neill	.10	.05	.01
☐ 100 Dennis Eckersley	.20	.09	.03
☐ 101 Duane Ward	.10	.05	.01
☐ 102 Matt Nokes	.05	.02	.01
☐ 103 Mo Vaughn	.30	.14	.04
☐ 104 Pat Kelly	.10	.05	.01
☐ 105 Ron Karkovice	.05	.02	.01
☐ 106 Bill Spiers	.05	.02	.01
☐ 107 Gary Gaetti	.05	.02	.01
☐ 108 Mackey Sasser	.05	.02	.01
☐ 109 Robby Thompson	.05	.02	.01
☐ 110 Marvin Freeman	.05	.02	.01
☐ 111 Jimmy Key	.10	.05	.01
☐ 112 Dwight Gooden	.10	.05	.01
☐ 113 Charlie Leibrandt	.05	.02	.01
☐ 114 Devon White	.10	.05	.01
☐ 115 Charles Nagy	.05	.02	.01
☐ 116 Rickey Henderson	.20	.09	.03
☐ 117 Paul Assenmacher	.05	.02	.01
☐ 118 Junior Felix	.05	.02	.01
☐ 119 Julio Franco	.10	.05	.01
☐ 120 Norm Charlton	.05	.02	.01
☐ 121 Scott Servais	.05	.02	.01
☐ 122 Gerald Perry	.05	.02	.01
☐ 123 Brian McRae	.20	.09	.03
☐ 124 Don Slaught	.05	.02	.01
☐ 125 Juan Samuel	.05	.02	.01
☐ 126 Harold Baines	.10	.05	.01
☐ 127 Scott Livingstone	.05	.02	.01
☐ 128 Jay Buhner	.10	.05	.01
☐ 129 Darrin Jackson	.05	.02	.01
☐ 130 Luis Mercedes	.05	.02	.01
☐ 131 Brian Harper	.05	.02	.01
☐ 132 Howard Johnson	.10	.05	.01
☐ 133 Checklist 89-176 Nolan Ryan	.05	.02	.01
☐ 134 Dante Bichette	.20	.09	.03
☐ 135 Dave Righetti	.05	.02	.01
☐ 136 Jeff Montgomery	.10	.05	.01
☐ 137 Joe Grahe	.05	.02	.01
☐ 138 Delino DeShields	.20	.09	.03
☐ 139 Jose Rijo	.10	.05	.01
☐ 140 Ken Caminiti	.10	.05	.01
☐ 141 Steve Olin	.05	.02	.01
☐ 142 Kurt Stillwell	.05	.02	.01
☐ 143 Jay Bell	.10	.05	.01
☐ 144 Jaime Navarro	.05	.02	.01
☐ 145 Ben McDonald	.10	.05	.01
☐ 146 Greg Gagne	.05	.02	.01
☐ 147 Jeff Blauser	.10	.05	.01
☐ 148 Carney Lansford	.10	.05	.01
☐ 149 Ozzie Guillen	.05	.02	.01
☐ 150 Milt Thompson	.05	.02	.01
☐ 151 Jeff Reardon	.10	.05	.01

☐ 152 Scott Sanderson .05 .02 .01
☐ 153 Cecil Fielder .20 .09 .03
☐ 154 Greg A. Harris .05 .02 .01
☐ 155 Rich DeLucia .05 .02 .01
☐ 156 Roberto Kelly .10 .05 .01
☐ 157 Bryn Smith .05 .02 .01
☐ 158 Chuck McElroy .05 .02 .01
☐ 159 Tom Henke .10 .05 .01
☐ 160 Luis Gonzalez .10 .05 .01
☐ 161 Steve Wilson .05 .02 .01
☐ 162 Shawn Boskie .05 .02 .01
☐ 163 Mark Davis .05 .02 .01
☐ 164 Mike Moore .05 .02 .01
☐ 165 Mike Scioscia .05 .02 .01
☐ 166 Scott Erickson .05 .02 .01
☐ 167 Todd Stottlemyre .05 .02 .01
☐ 168 Alvin Davis .05 .02 .01
☐ 169 Greg Hibbard .05 .02 .01
☐ 170 David Valle .05 .02 .01
☐ 171 Dave Winfield .20 .09 .03
☐ 172 Alan Trammell .20 .09 .03
☐ 173 Kenny Rogers .05 .02 .01
☐ 174 John Franco .05 .02 .01
☐ 175 Jose Lind .05 .02 .01
☐ 176 Pete Schourek .10 .05 .01
☐ 177 Von Hayes .05 .02 .01
☐ 178 Chris Hammond .05 .02 .01
☐ 179 John Burkett .10 .05 .01
☐ 180 Dickie Thon .05 .02 .01
☐ 181 Joel Skinner .05 .02 .01
☐ 182 Scott Cooper .10 .05 .01
☐ 183 Andre Dawson .20 .09 .03
☐ 184 Billy Ripken .05 .02 .01
☐ 185 Kevin Mitchell .10 .05 .01
☐ 186 Brett Butler .10 .05 .01
☐ 187 Tony Fernandez .10 .05 .01
☐ 188 Cory Snyder .05 .02 .01
☐ 189 John Habyan .05 .02 .01
☐ 190 Dennis Martinez .10 .05 .01
☐ 191 John Smoltz .10 .05 .01
☐ 192 Greg Myers .05 .02 .01
☐ 193 Rob Deer .05 .02 .01
☐ 194 Ivan Rodriguez .20 .09 .03
☐ 195 Ray Lankford .20 .09 .03
☐ 196 Bill Wegman .05 .02 .01
☐ 197 Edgar Martinez .10 .05 .01
☐ 198 Darryl Kile .10 .05 .01
☐ 199 Checklist 177-264 .05 .02 .01
Cal Ripken
☐ 200 Brent Mayne .05 .02 .01
☐ 201 Larry Walker .20 .09 .03
☐ 202 Carlos Baerga .30 .14 .04
☐ 203 Russ Swan .05 .02 .01
☐ 204 Mike Morgan .05 .02 .01
☐ 205 Hal Morris .10 .05 .01
☐ 206 Tony Gwynn .35 .16 .04
☐ 207 Mark Leiter .05 .02 .01
☐ 208 Kirt Manwaring .05 .02 .01
☐ 209 Al Osuna .05 .02 .01
☐ 210 Bobby Thigpen .05 .02 .01
☐ 211 Chris Hoiles .20 .09 .03
☐ 212 B.J. Surhoff .05 .02 .01
☐ 213 Lenny Harris .05 .02 .01
☐ 214 Scott Leius .05 .02 .01
☐ 215 Gregg Jefferies .20 .09 .03
☐ 216 Bruce Hurst .05 .02 .01
☐ 217 Steve Sax .05 .02 .01
☐ 218 Dave Otto .05 .02 .01
☐ 219 Sam Horn .05 .02 .01
☐ 220 Charlie Hayes .10 .05 .01
☐ 221 Frank Viola .10 .05 .01
☐ 222 Jose Guzman .05 .02 .01
☐ 223 Gary Redus .05 .02 .01
☐ 224 Dave Gallagher .05 .02 .01
☐ 225 Dean Palmer .10 .05 .01
☐ 226 Greg Olson .05 .02 .01
☐ 227 Jose DeLeon .05 .02 .01
☐ 228 Mike LaValliere .05 .02 .01
☐ 229 Mark Langston .20 .09 .03
☐ 230 Chuck Knoblauch .20 .09 .03
☐ 231 Bill Doran .05 .02 .01
☐ 232 Dave Henderson .05 .02 .01
☐ 233 Roberto Alomar .35 .16 .04
☐ 234 Scott Fletcher .05 .02 .01
☐ 235 Tim Naehring .05 .02 .01
☐ 236 Mike Gallego .05 .02 .01
☐ 237 Lance Johnson .05 .02 .01
☐ 238 Paul Molitor .25 .11 .03
☐ 239 Dan Gladden .05 .02 .01
☐ 240 Willie Randolph .10 .05 .01
☐ 241 Will Clark .30 .14 .04
☐ 242 Sid Bream .05 .02 .01
☐ 243 Derek Bell .10 .05 .01
☐ 244 Bill Pecota .05 .02 .01
☐ 245 Terry Pendleton .20 .09 .03
☐ 246 Randy Ready .05 .02 .01
☐ 247 Jack Armstrong .05 .02 .01
☐ 248 Todd Van Poppel .20 .09 .03
☐ 249 Shawon Dunston .05 .02 .01
☐ 250 Bobby Rose .05 .02 .01
☐ 251 Jeff Huson .05 .02 .01
☐ 252 Bip Roberts .05 .02 .01
☐ 253 Doug Jones .05 .02 .01
☐ 254 Lee Smith .20 .09 .03
☐ 255 George Brett .50 .23 .06
☐ 256 Randy Tomlin .05 .02 .01
☐ 257 Todd Benzinger .05 .02 .01
☐ 258 Dave Stewart .10 .05 .01
☐ 259 Mark Carreon .05 .02 .01
☐ 260 Pete O'Brien .05 .02 .01
☐ 261 Tim Teufel .05 .02 .01
☐ 262 Bob Milacki .05 .02 .01
☐ 263 Mark Guthrie .05 .02 .01
☐ 264 Darrin Fletcher .05 .02 .01
☐ 265 Omar Vizquel .05 .02 .01
☐ 266 Chris Bosio .05 .02 .01
☐ 267 Jose Canseco .30 .14 .04
☐ 268 Mike Boddicker .05 .02 .01
☐ 269 Lance Parrish .10 .05 .01
☐ 270 Jose Vizcaino .05 .02 .01
☐ 271 Chris Sabo .10 .05 .01
☐ 272 Royce Clayton .20 .09 .03
☐ 273 Marquis Grissom .20 .09 .03
☐ 274 Fred McGriff .30 .14 .04
☐ 275 Barry Bonds .60 .25 .08
☐ 276 Greg Vaughn .10 .05 .01
☐ 277 Gregg Olson .05 .02 .01
☐ 278 Dave Hollins .20 .09 .03
☐ 279 Tom Glavine .20 .09 .03
☐ 280 Bryan Hickerson .05 .02 .01
☐ 281 Scott Radinsky .05 .02 .01
☐ 282 Omar Olivares .05 .02 .01
☐ 283 Ivan Calderon .05 .02 .01
☐ 284 Kevin Maas .05 .02 .01
☐ 285 Mickey Tettleton .10 .05 .01
☐ 286 Wade Boggs .20 .09 .03
☐ 287 Stan Belinda .05 .02 .01
☐ 288 Bret Barberie .05 .02 .01
☐ 289 Jose Oquendo .05 .02 .01
☐ 290 Frank Castillo .05 .02 .01
☐ 291 Dave Stieb .10 .05 .01
☐ 292 Tommy Greene .10 .05 .01
☐ 293 Eric Karros .20 .09 .03
☐ 294 Greg Maddux .30 .14 .04
☐ 295 Jim Eisenreich .05 .02 .01
☐ 296 Rafael Palmeiro .20 .09 .03

297	Ramon Martinez	.10	.05	.01
298	Tim Wallach	.05	.02	.01
299	Jim Thome	.60	.25	.08
300	Chito Martinez	.05	.02	.01
301	Mitch Williams	.10	.05	.01
302	Randy Johnson	.20	.09	.03
303	Carlton Fisk	.20	.09	.03
304	Travis Fryman	.30	.14	.04
305	Bobby Witt	.05	.02	.01
306	Dave Magadan	.05	.02	.01
307	Alex Cole	.05	.02	.01
308	Bobby Bonilla	.20	.09	.03
309	Bryan Harvey	.10	.05	.01
310	Rafael Belliard	.05	.02	.01
311	Mariano Duncan	.05	.02	.01
312	Chuck Crim	.05	.02	.01
313	John Kruk	.20	.09	.03
314	Ellis Burks	.10	.05	.01
315	Craig Biggio	.10	.05	.01
316	Glenn Davis	.05	.02	.01
317	Ryne Sandberg	.50	.23	.06
318	Mike Sharperson	.05	.02	.01
319	Rich Rodriguez	.05	.02	.01
320	Lee Guetterman	.05	.02	.01
321	Benito Santiago	.05	.02	.01
322	Jose Offerman	.05	.02	.01
323	Tony Pena	.05	.02	.01
324	Pat Borders	.05	.02	.01
325	Mike Henneman	.05	.02	.01
326	Kevin Brown	.10	.05	.01
327	Chris Nabholz	.05	.02	.01
328	Franklin Stubbs	.05	.02	.01
329	Tino Martinez	.10	.05	.01
330	Mickey Morandini	.05	.02	.01
331	Checklist 265-352 Ryne Sandberg	.05	.02	.01
332	Mark Gubicza	.05	.02	.01
333	Bill Landrum	.05	.02	.01
334	Mark Whiten	.10	.05	.01
335	Darren Daulton	.20	.09	.03
336	Rick Wilkins	.10	.05	.01
337	Brian Jordan	.20	.09	.03
338	Kevin Ward	.05	.02	.01
339	Ruben Amaro	.05	.02	.01
340	Trevor Wilson	.05	.02	.01
341	Andujar Cedeno	.10	.05	.01
342	Michael Huff	.05	.02	.01
343	Brady Anderson	.10	.05	.01
344	Craig Grebeck	.05	.02	.01
345	Bobby Ojeda	.05	.02	.01
346	Mike Pagliarulo	.05	.02	.01
347	Terry Shumpert	.05	.02	.01
348	Dann Bilardello	.05	.02	.01
349	Frank Thomas	2.50	1.15	.30
350	Albert Belle	.60	.25	.08
351	Jose Mesa	.05	.02	.01
352	Rich Monteleone	.05	.02	.01
353	Bob Walk	.05	.02	.01
354	Monty Fariss	.05	.02	.01
355	Luis Rivera	.05	.02	.01
356	Anthony Young	.05	.02	.01
357	Geno Petralli	.05	.02	.01
358	Otis Nixon	.05	.02	.01
359	Tom Pagnozzi	.05	.02	.01
360	Reggie Sanders	.30	.14	.04
361	Lee Stevens	.05	.02	.01
362	Kent Hrbek	.10	.05	.01
363	Orlando Merced	.10	.05	.01
364	Mike Bordick	.05	.02	.01
365	Dion James UER (Blue Jays logo on card back)	.05	.02	.01
366	Jack Clark	.10	.05	.01
367	Mike Stanley	.05	.02	.01
368	Randy Velarde	.05	.02	.01
369	Dan Pasqua	.05	.02	.01
370	Pat Listach	.15	.07	.02
371	Mike Fitzgerald	.05	.02	.01
372	Tom Foley	.05	.02	.01
373	Matt Williams	.30	.14	.04
374	Brian Hunter	.05	.02	.01
375	Joe Carter	.30	.14	.04
376	Bret Saberhagen	.10	.05	.01
377	Mike Stanton	.05	.02	.01
378	Hubie Brooks	.05	.02	.01
379	Eric Bell	.05	.02	.01
380	Walt Weiss	.05	.02	.01
381	Danny Jackson	.05	.02	.01
382	Manny Lee	.05	.02	.01
383	Ruben Sierra	.20	.09	.03
384	Greg Swindell	.05	.02	.01
385	Ryan Bowen	.05	.02	.01
386	Kevin Ritz	.05	.02	.01
387	Curtis Wilkerson	.05	.02	.01
388	Gary Varsho	.05	.02	.01
389	Dave Hansen	.05	.02	.01
390	Bob Welch	.05	.02	.01
391	Lou Whitaker	.20	.09	.03
392	Ken Griffey Jr.	2.50	1.15	.30
393	Mike Maddux	.05	.02	.01
394	Arthur Rhodes	.10	.05	.01
395	Chili Davis	.10	.05	.01
396	Eddie Murray	.20	.09	.03
397	Checklist 353-440 Robin Yount	.05	.02	.01
398	Dave Cochrane	.05	.02	.01
399	Kevin Seitzer	.05	.02	.01
400	Ozzie Smith	.25	.11	.03
401	Paul Sorrento	.05	.02	.01
402	Les Lancaster	.05	.02	.01
403	Junior Noboa	.05	.02	.01
404	David Justice	.35	.16	.04
405	Andy Ashby	.05	.02	.01
406	Danny Tartabull	.10	.05	.01
407	Bill Swift	.10	.05	.01
408	Craig Lefferts	.05	.02	.01
409	Tom Candiotti	.05	.02	.01
410	Lance Blankenship	.05	.02	.01
411	Jeff Tackett	.05	.02	.01
412	Sammy Sosa	.20	.09	.03
413	Jody Reed	.05	.02	.01
414	Bruce Ruffin	.05	.02	.01
415	Gene Larkin	.05	.02	.01
416	John Vander Wal	.10	.05	.01
417	Tim Belcher	.05	.02	.01
418	Steve Frey	.05	.02	.01
419	Dick Schofield	.05	.02	.01
420	Jeff King	.05	.02	.01
421	Kim Batiste	.05	.02	.01
422	Jack McDowell	.20	.09	.03
423	Damon Berryhill	.05	.02	.01
424	Gary Wayne	.05	.02	.01
425	Jack Morris	.20	.09	.03
426	Moises Alou	.20	.09	.03
427	Mark McLemore	.05	.02	.01
428	Juan Guerrero	.10	.05	.01
429	Scott Scudder	.05	.02	.01
430	Eric Davis	.05	.02	.01
431	Joe Slusarski	.05	.02	.01
432	Todd Zeile	.10	.05	.01
433	Dwayne Henry	.05	.02	.01
434	Cliff Brantley	.10	.05	.01
435	Butch Henry	.15	.07	.02
436	Todd Worrell	.05	.02	.01
437	Bob Scanlan	.05	.02	.01
438	Wally Joyner	.10	.05	.01

☐	439 John Flaherty	.10	.05	.01
☐	440 Brian Downing	.05	.02	.01
☐	441 Darren Lewis	.10	.05	.01
☐	442 Gary Carter	.20	.09	.03
☐	443 Wally Ritchie	.05	.02	.01
☐	444 Chris Jones	.05	.02	.01
☐	445 Jeff Kent	.50	.23	.06
☐	446 Gary Sheffield	.20	.09	.03
☐	447 Ron Darling	.05	.02	.01
☐	448 Deion Sanders	.30	.14	.04
☐	449 Andres Galarraga	.20	.09	.03
☐	450 Chuck Finley	.05	.02	.01
☐	451 Derek Lilliquist	.05	.02	.01
☐	452 Carl Willis	.05	.02	.01
☐	453 Wes Chamberlain	.05	.02	.01
☐	454 Roger Mason	.05	.02	.01
☐	455 Spike Owen	.05	.02	.01
☐	456 Thomas Howard	.05	.02	.01
☐	457 Dave Martinez	.05	.02	.01
☐	458 Pete Incaviglia	.05	.02	.01
☐	459 Keith A. Miller	.05	.02	.01
☐	460 Mike Fetters	.05	.02	.01
☐	461 Paul Gibson	.05	.02	.01
☐	462 George Bell	.10	.05	.01
☐	463 Checklist 441-528 Bobby Bonilla	.05	.02	.01
☐	464 Terry Mulholland	.05	.02	.01
☐	465 Storm Davis	.05	.02	.01
☐	466 Gary Pettis	.05	.02	.01
☐	467 Randy Bush	.05	.02	.01
☐	468 Ken Hill	.10	.05	.01
☐	469 Rheal Cormier	.05	.02	.01
☐	470 Andy Stankiewicz	.05	.02	.01
☐	471 Dave Burba	.05	.02	.01
☐	472 Henry Cotto	.05	.02	.01
☐	473 Dale Sveum	.05	.02	.01
☐	474 Rich Gossage	.20	.09	.03
☐	475 William Suero	.05	.02	.01
☐	476 Doug Strange	.05	.02	.01
☐	477 Bill Krueger	.05	.02	.01
☐	478 John Wetteland	.05	.02	.01
☐	479 Melido Perez	.05	.02	.01
☐	480 Lonnie Smith	.05	.02	.01
☐	481 Mike Jackson	.05	.02	.01
☐	482 Mike Gardiner	.05	.02	.01
☐	483 David Wells	.05	.02	.01
☐	484 Barry Jones	.05	.02	.01
☐	485 Scott Bankhead	.05	.02	.01
☐	486 Terry Leach	.05	.02	.01
☐	487 Vince Horsman	.10	.05	.01
☐	488 Dave Eiland	.05	.02	.01
☐	489 Alejandro Pena	.05	.02	.01
☐	490 Julio Valera	.05	.02	.01
☐	491 Joe Boever	.05	.02	.01
☐	492 Paul Miller	.10	.05	.01
☐	493 Archi Cianfrocco	.05	.02	.01
☐	494 Dave Fleming	.10	.05	.01
☐	495 Kyle Abbott	.05	.02	.01
☐	496 Chad Kreuter	.05	.02	.01
☐	497 Chris James	.05	.02	.01
☐	498 Donnie Hill	.05	.02	.01
☐	499 Jacob Brumfield	.10	.05	.01
☐	500 Ricky Bones	.10	.05	.01
☐	501 Terry Steinbach	.10	.05	.01
☐	502 Bernard Gilkey	.10	.05	.01
☐	503 Dennis Cook	.05	.02	.01
☐	504 Len Dykstra	.20	.09	.03
☐	505 Mike Bielecki	.05	.02	.01
☐	506 Bob Kipper	.05	.02	.01
☐	507 Jose Melendez	.05	.02	.01
☐	508 Rick Sutcliffe	.10	.05	.01
☐	509 Ken Patterson	.05	.02	.01
☐	510 Andy Allanson	.05	.02	.01
☐	511 Al Newman	.05	.02	.01
☐	512 Mark Gardner	.05	.02	.01
☐	513 Jeff Schaefer	.05	.02	.01
☐	514 Jim McNamara	.10	.05	.01
☐	515 Peter Hoy	.10	.05	.01
☐	516 Curt Schilling	.10	.05	.01
☐	517 Kirk McCaskill	.05	.02	.01
☐	518 Chris Gwynn	.05	.02	.01
☐	519 Sid Fernandez	.10	.05	.01
☐	520 Jeff Parrett	.05	.02	.01
☐	521 Scott Ruskin	.05	.02	.01
☐	522 Kevin McReynolds	.05	.02	.01
☐	523 Rick Cerone	.05	.02	.01
☐	524 Jesse Orosco	.05	.02	.01
☐	525 Troy Afenir	.05	.02	.01
☐	526 John Smiley	.05	.02	.01
☐	527 Dale Murphy	.20	.09	.03
☐	528 Leaf Set Card	.05	.02	.01

1992 Leaf Black Gold

This 528-card standard-size (2 1/2" by 3 1/2") set was issued in two 264-card series. These Black Gold cards were inserted one per foil pack. The cards are similar to the regular issue Leaf cards, except that the card face is black rather than silver and accented by a gold foil inner border. Likewise, the horizontal backs have a gold rather than a silver background. The cards are numbered on the back.

	MINT	EXC	G-VG
COMPLETE SET (528)	140.00	65.00	17.50
COMPLETE SERIES 1 (264)	70.00	32.00	8.75
COMPLETE SERIES 2 (264)	70.00	32.00	8.75
COMMON CARD (1-264)	.15	.07	.02
COMMON CARD (265-528)	.15	.07	.02

*VETERAN STARS: 5X to 10X BASIC CARDS
*YOUNG STARS: 3X to 6X BASIC CARDS

1992 Leaf Gold Rookies

This 24-card standard-size (2 1/2" by 3 1/2") set honors 1992's most promising

newcomers. The first 12 cards were randomly inserted in Leaf series I foil packs, while the second 12 cards were featured only in series II packs. The card numbers show a BC prefix. The fronts display full-bleed color action photos highlighted by gold foil border stripes. A gold foil diamond appears at the corners of the picture frame, and the player's name appears in a black bar that extends between the bottom two diamonds. On a gold background, the horizontally oriented backs feature a second color player photo, biography, and, on a white panel, career statistics and career summary. The cards are numbered on the back.

	MINT	EXC	G-VG
COMPLETE SET (24)	20.00	9.00	2.50
COMPLETE SERIES 1 (12)	8.00	3.60	1.00
COMPLETE SERIES 2 (12)	12.00	5.50	1.50
COMMON CARD (BC1-BC12)	.30	.14	.04
COMMON CARD (BC13-BC24)	.30	.14	.04

	MINT	EXC	G-VG
☐ BC1 Chad Curtis	1.00	.45	.13
☐ BC2 Brent Gates	1.25	.55	.16
☐ BC3 Pedro Martinez	1.25	.55	.16
☐ BC4 Kenny Lofton	6.00	2.70	.75
☐ BC5 Turk Wendell	.30	.14	.04
☐ BC6 Mark Hutton	.30	.14	.04
☐ BC7 Todd Hundley	.30	.14	.04
☐ BC8 Matt Stairs	.30	.14	.04
☐ BC9 Eddie Taubensee	.30	.14	.04
☐ BC10 David Nied	1.50	.65	.19
☐ BC11 Salomon Torres	1.00	.45	.13
☐ BC12 Bret Boone	1.50	.65	.19
☐ BC13 Johnny Ruffin	.30	.14	.04
☐ BC14 Ed Martel	.30	.14	.04
☐ BC15 Rick Trlicek	.30	.14	.04
☐ BC16 Raul Mondesi	10.00	4.50	1.25
☐ BC17 Pat Mahomes	1.00	.45	.13
☐ BC18 Dan Wilson	.30	.14	.04
☐ BC19 Donovan Osborne	.30	.14	.04
☐ BC20 Dave Silvestri	.30	.14	.04
☐ BC21 Gary DiSarcina	.30	.14	.04
☐ BC22 Denny Neagle	.30	.14	.04
☐ BC23 Steve Hosey	.30	.14	.04
☐ BC24 John Doherty	.30	.14	.04

1993 Leaf

The 1993 Leaf baseball set consists of three series of 220, 220, and 110 cards, respectively. Three insert subsets, Gold Leaf Rookies, Heading for the Hall, and Frank Thomas, were randomly packed in the 14-card foil packs. Two other insert sets, Gold Leaf All Stars and Fasttrack, were randomly packed only in jumbo and magazine distributor packs respectively. Players from five MLB teams were found only in second series packs to show them in their new uniforms (Colorado Rockies, Florida Marlins, Cincinnati Reds, California Angels, and Seattle Mariners). All the cards measure the standard size (2 1/2" by 3 1/2"). The fronts feature color action photos that are full-bleed except at the bottom where a diagonal black stripe (gold-foil stamped with the player's name) separates the picture from a team color-coded slate triangle. The Leaf seal embossed with gold foil is superimposed at the lower right corner. The backs have the same design as the fronts, only the player action shot is cutout and superimposed on a cityscape background. A holographic team logo appears in the upper left corner, while biography and statistics are printed diagonally across the bottom of the photo. The cards are numbered on the back. Rookie Cards in this set include Marcos Armas, Greg McMichael, J. Owens, Kevin Roberson, J.T. Snow, and Tony Tarasco.

	MINT	EXC	G-VG
COMPLETE SET (550)	50.00	23.00	6.25
COMPLETE SERIES 1 (220)	20.00	9.00	2.50
COMPLETE SERIES 2 (220)	20.00	9.00	2.50
COMPLETE UPDATE (110)	10.00	4.50	1.25
COMMON CARD (1-220)	.10	.05	.01
COMMON CARD (221-440)	.10	.05	.01
COMMON CARD (441-550)	.10	.05	.01

	MINT	EXC	G-VG
☐ 1 Ben McDonald	.15	.07	.02
☐ 2 Sid Fernandez	.10	.05	.01
☐ 3 Juan Guzman	.15	.07	.02
☐ 4 Curt Schilling	.15	.07	.02
☐ 5 Ivan Rodriguez	.20	.09	.03
☐ 6 Don Slaught	.10	.05	.01
☐ 7 Terry Steinbach	.15	.07	.02
☐ 8 Todd Zeile	.15	.07	.02
☐ 9 Andy Stankiewicz	.10	.05	.01
☐ 10 Tim Teufel	.10	.05	.01
☐ 11 Marvin Freeman	.10	.05	.01
☐ 12 Jim Austin	.10	.05	.01
☐ 13 Bob Scanlan	.10	.05	.01
☐ 14 Rusty Meacham	.10	.05	.01
☐ 15 Casey Candaele	.10	.05	.01
☐ 16 Travis Fryman	.25	.11	.03
☐ 17 Jose Offerman	.10	.05	.01
☐ 18 Albert Belle	1.00	.45	.13
☐ 19 John Vander Wal	.10	.05	.01
☐ 20 Dan Pasqua	.10	.05	.01

	#	Player			
☐	21	Frank Viola	.15	.07	.02
☐	22	Terry Mulholland	.10	.05	.01
☐	23	Gregg Olson	.10	.05	.01
☐	24	Randy Tomlin	.10	.05	.01
☐	25	Todd Stottlemyre	.10	.05	.01
☐	26	Jose Oquendo	.10	.05	.01
☐	27	Julio Franco	.15	.07	.02
☐	28	Tony Gwynn	.75	.35	.09
☐	29	Ruben Sierra	.20	.09	.03
☐	30	Robby Thompson	.10	.05	.01
☐	31	Jim Bullinger	.10	.05	.01
☐	32	Rick Aguilera	.15	.07	.02
☐	33	Scott Servais	.10	.05	.01
☐	34	Cal Eldred	.15	.07	.02
☐	35	Mike Piazza	3.00	1.35	.40
☐	36	Brent Mayne	.10	.05	.01
☐	37	Wil Cordero	.20	.09	.03
☐	38	Milt Cuyler	.10	.05	.01
☐	39	Howard Johnson	.10	.05	.01
☐	40	Kenny Lofton	.75	.35	.09
☐	41	Alex Fernandez	.20	.09	.03
☐	42	Denny Neagle	.10	.05	.01
☐	43	Tony Pena	.10	.05	.01
☐	44	Bob Tewksbury	.10	.05	.01
☐	45	Glenn Davis	.10	.05	.01
☐	46	Fred McGriff	.40	.18	.05
☐	47	John Olerud	.20	.09	.03
☐	48	Steve Hosey	.10	.05	.01
☐	49	Rafael Palmeiro	.20	.09	.03
☐	50	David Justice	.40	.18	.05
☐	51	Pete Harnisch	.10	.05	.01
☐	52	Sam Militello	.10	.05	.01
☐	53	Orel Hershiser	.15	.07	.02
☐	54	Pat Mahomes	.10	.05	.01
☐	55	Greg Colbrunn	.10	.05	.01
☐	56	Greg Vaughn	.15	.07	.02
☐	57	Vince Coleman	.10	.05	.01
☐	58	Brian McRae	.20	.09	.03
☐	59	Len Dykstra	.20	.09	.03
☐	60	Dan Gladden	.10	.05	.01
☐	61	Ted Power	.10	.05	.01
☐	62	Donovan Osborne	.10	.05	.01
☐	63	Ron Karkovice	.10	.05	.01
☐	64	Frank Seminara	.10	.05	.01
☐	65	Bob Zupcic	.10	.05	.01
☐	66	Kirt Manwaring	.10	.05	.01
☐	67	Mike Devereaux	.15	.07	.02
☐	68	Mark Lemke	.10	.05	.01
☐	69	Devon White	.15	.07	.02
☐	70	Sammy Sosa	.20	.09	.03
☐	71	Pedro Astacio	.15	.07	.02
☐	72	Dennis Eckersley	.20	.09	.03
☐	73	Chris Nabholz	.10	.05	.01
☐	74	Melido Perez	.10	.05	.01
☐	75	Todd Hundley	.10	.05	.01
☐	76	Kent Hrbek	.15	.07	.02
☐	77	Mickey Morandini	.10	.05	.01
☐	78	Tim McIntosh	.10	.05	.01
☐	79	Andy Van Slyke	.20	.09	.03
☐	80	Kevin McReynolds	.10	.05	.01
☐	81	Mike Henneman	.10	.05	.01
☐	82	Greg W. Harris	.10	.05	.01
☐	83	Sandy Alomar Jr.	.15	.07	.02
☐	84	Mike Jackson	.10	.05	.01
☐	85	Ozzie Guillen	.10	.05	.01
☐	86	Jeff Blauser	.15	.07	.02
☐	87	John Valentin	.15	.07	.02
☐	88	Rey Sanchez	.10	.05	.01
☐	89	Rick Sutcliffe	.15	.07	.02
☐	90	Luis Gonzalez	.15	.07	.02
☐	91	Jeff Fassero	.10	.05	.01
☐	92	Kenny Rogers	.10	.05	.01
☐	93	Bret Saberhagen	.15	.07	.02
☐	94	Bob Welch	.10	.05	.01
☐	95	Darren Daulton	.20	.09	.03
☐	96	Mike Gallego	.10	.05	.01
☐	97	Orlando Merced	.15	.07	.02
☐	98	Chuck Knoblauch	.20	.09	.03
☐	99	Bernard Gilkey	.10	.05	.01
☐	100	Billy Ashley	.50	.23	.06
☐	101	Kevin Appier	.15	.07	.02
☐	102	Jeff Brantley	.10	.05	.01
☐	103	Bill Gullickson	.10	.05	.01
☐	104	John Smoltz	.15	.07	.02
☐	105	Paul Sorrento	.10	.05	.01
☐	106	Steve Buechele	.10	.05	.01
☐	107	Steve Sax	.10	.05	.01
☐	108	Andujar Cedeno	.15	.07	.02
☐	109	Billy Hatcher	.10	.05	.01
☐	110	Checklist	.10	.05	.01
☐	111	Alan Mills	.10	.05	.01
☐	112	John Franco	.10	.05	.01
☐	113	Jack Morris	.20	.09	.03
☐	114	Mitch Williams	.15	.07	.02
☐	115	Nolan Ryan	3.00	1.35	.40
☐	116	Jay Bell	.15	.07	.02
☐	117	Mike Bordick	.10	.05	.01
☐	118	Geronimo Pena	.10	.05	.01
☐	119	Danny Tartabull	.15	.07	.02
☐	120	Checklist	.10	.05	.01
☐	121	Steve Avery	.20	.09	.03
☐	122	Ricky Bones	.10	.05	.01
☐	123	Mike Morgan	.10	.05	.01
☐	124	Jeff Montgomery	.15	.07	.02
☐	125	Jeff Bagwell	1.50	.65	.19
☐	126	Tony Phillips	.10	.05	.01
☐	127	Lenny Harris	.10	.05	.01
☐	128	Glenallen Hill	.10	.05	.01
☐	129	Marquis Grissom	.20	.09	.03
☐	130	Gerald Williams UER (Bernie Williams picture and stats)	.10	.05	.01
☐	131	Greg A. Harris	.10	.05	.01
☐	132	Tommy Greene	.15	.07	.02
☐	133	Chris Hoiles	.15	.07	.02
☐	134	Bob Walk	.10	.05	.01
☐	135	Duane Ward	.15	.07	.02
☐	136	Tom Pagnozzi	.10	.05	.01
☐	137	Jeff Huson	.10	.05	.01
☐	138	Kurt Stillwell	.10	.05	.01
☐	139	Dave Henderson	.10	.05	.01
☐	140	Darrin Jackson	.10	.05	.01
☐	141	Frank Castillo	.10	.05	.01
☐	142	Scott Erickson	.10	.05	.01
☐	143	Darryl Kile	.15	.07	.02
☐	144	Bill Wegman	.10	.05	.01
☐	145	Steve Wilson	.10	.05	.01
☐	146	George Brett	1.25	.55	.16
☐	147	Moises Alou	.20	.09	.03
☐	148	Lou Whitaker	.20	.09	.03
☐	149	Chico Walker	.10	.05	.01
☐	150	Jerry Browne	.10	.05	.01
☐	151	Kirk McCaskill	.10	.05	.01
☐	152	Zane Smith	.10	.05	.01
☐	153	Matt Young	.10	.05	.01
☐	154	Lee Smith	.20	.09	.03
☐	155	Leo Gomez	.10	.05	.01
☐	156	Dan Walters	.10	.05	.01
☐	157	Pat Borders	.10	.05	.01
☐	158	Matt Williams	.60	.25	.08
☐	159	Dean Palmer	.15	.07	.02
☐	160	John Patterson	.10	.05	.01
☐	161	Doug Jones	.10	.05	.01
☐	162	John Habyan	.10	.05	.01
☐	163	Pedro Martinez	.20	.09	.03
☐	164	Carl Willis	.10	.05	.01

☐ 165 Darrin Fletcher .10 .05 .01
☐ 166 B.J. Surhoff .10 .05 .01
☐ 167 Eddie Murray .20 .09 .03
☐ 168 Keith Miller .10 .05 .01
☐ 169 Ricky Jordan .10 .05 .01
☐ 170 Juan Gonzalez 1.00 .45 .13
☐ 171 Charles Nagy .10 .05 .01
☐ 172 Mark Clark .15 .07 .02
☐ 173 Bobby Thigpen .10 .05 .01
☐ 174 Tim Scott .10 .05 .01
☐ 175 Scott Cooper .15 .07 .02
☐ 176 Royce Clayton .15 .07 .02
☐ 177 Brady Anderson .15 .07 .02
☐ 178 Sid Bream .10 .05 .01
☐ 179 Derek Bell .15 .07 .02
☐ 180 Otis Nixon .10 .05 .01
☐ 181 Kevin Gross .10 .05 .01
☐ 182 Ron Darling .10 .05 .01
☐ 183 John Wetteland .10 .05 .01
☐ 184 Mike Stanley .10 .05 .01
☐ 185 Jeff Kent .20 .09 .03
☐ 186 Brian Harper .10 .05 .01
☐ 187 Mariano Duncan .10 .05 .01
☐ 188 Robin Yount .40 .18 .05
☐ 189 Al Martin .15 .07 .02
☐ 190 Eddie Zosky .10 .05 .01
☐ 191 Mike Munoz .10 .05 .01
☐ 192 Andy Benes .15 .07 .02
☐ 193 Dennis Cook .10 .05 .01
☐ 194 Bill Swift .15 .07 .02
☐ 195 Frank Thomas 3.00 1.35 .40
☐ 196 Damon Berryhill .10 .05 .01
☐ 197 Mike Greenwell .15 .07 .02
☐ 198 Mark Grace .20 .09 .03
☐ 199 Darryl Hamilton .10 .05 .01
☐ 200 Derrick May .15 .07 .02
☐ 201 Ken Hill .15 .07 .02
☐ 202 Kevin Brown .10 .05 .01
☐ 203 Dwight Gooden .10 .05 .01
☐ 204 Bobby Witt .10 .05 .01
☐ 205 Juan Bell .10 .05 .01
☐ 206 Kevin Maas .10 .05 .01
☐ 207 Jeff King .10 .05 .01
☐ 208 Scott Leius .10 .05 .01
☐ 209 Rheal Cormier .10 .05 .01
☐ 210 Darryl Strawberry .15 .07 .02
☐ 211 Tom Gordon .10 .05 .01
☐ 212 Bud Black .10 .05 .01
☐ 213 Mickey Tettleton .15 .07 .02
☐ 214 Pete Smith .10 .05 .01
☐ 215 Felix Fermin .10 .05 .01
☐ 216 Rick Wilkins .10 .05 .01
☐ 217 George Bell .15 .07 .02
☐ 218 Eric Anthony .10 .05 .01
☐ 219 Pedro Munoz .10 .05 .01
☐ 220 Checklist .10 .05 .01
☐ 221 Lance Blankenship .10 .05 .01
☐ 222 Deion Sanders .60 .25 .08
☐ 223 Craig Biggio .15 .07 .02
☐ 224 Ryne Sandberg 1.00 .45 .13
☐ 225 Ron Gant .15 .07 .02
☐ 226 Tom Brunansky .10 .05 .01
☐ 227 Chad Curtis .15 .07 .02
☐ 228 Joe Carter .40 .18 .05
☐ 229 Brian Jordan .15 .07 .02
☐ 230 Brett Butler .15 .07 .02
☐ 231 Frank Bolick .10 .05 .01
☐ 232 Rod Beck .20 .09 .03
☐ 233 Carlos Baerga .40 .18 .05
☐ 234 Eric Karros .15 .07 .02
☐ 235 Jack Armstrong .10 .05 .01
☐ 236 Bobby Bonilla .20 .09 .03
☐ 237 Don Mattingly 1.25 .55 .16
☐ 238 Jeff Gardner .10 .05 .01
☐ 239 Dave Hollins .20 .09 .03
☐ 240 Steve Cooke .10 .05 .01
☐ 241 Jose Canseco .40 .18 .05
☐ 242 Ivan Calderon .10 .05 .01
☐ 243 Tim Belcher .10 .05 .01
☐ 244 Freddie Benavides .10 .05 .01
☐ 245 Roberto Alomar .75 .35 .09
☐ 246 Rob Deer .10 .05 .01
☐ 247 Will Clark .40 .18 .05
☐ 248 Mike Felder .10 .05 .01
☐ 249 Harold Baines .15 .07 .02
☐ 250 David Cone .20 .09 .03
☐ 251 Mark Guthrie .10 .05 .01
☐ 252 Ellis Burks .15 .07 .02
☐ 253 Jim Abbott .20 .09 .03
☐ 254 Chili Davis .15 .07 .02
☐ 255 Chris Bosio .10 .05 .01
☐ 256 Bret Barberie .10 .05 .01
☐ 257 Hal Morris .15 .07 .02
☐ 258 Dante Bichette .20 .09 .03
☐ 259 Storm Davis .10 .05 .01
☐ 260 Gary DiSarcina .10 .05 .01
☐ 261 Ken Caminiti .15 .07 .02
☐ 262 Paul Molitor .40 .18 .05
☐ 263 Joe Oliver .10 .05 .01
☐ 264 Pat Listach .15 .07 .02
☐ 265 Gregg Jefferies .20 .09 .03
☐ 266 Jose Guzman .10 .05 .01
☐ 267 Eric Davis .10 .05 .01
☐ 268 Delino DeShields .15 .07 .02
☐ 269 Barry Bonds 1.25 .55 .16
☐ 270 Mike Bielecki .10 .05 .01
☐ 271 Jay Buhner .15 .07 .02
☐ 272 Scott Pose .10 .05 .01
☐ 273 Tony Fernandez .10 .05 .01
☐ 274 Chito Martinez .10 .05 .01
☐ 275 Phil Plantier .20 .09 .03
☐ 276 Pete Incaviglia .10 .05 .01
☐ 277 Carlos Garcia .15 .07 .02
☐ 278 Tom Henke .15 .07 .02
☐ 279 Roger Clemens .75 .35 .09
☐ 280 Rob Dibble .10 .05 .01
☐ 281 Daryl Boston .10 .05 .01
☐ 282 Greg Gagne .10 .05 .01
☐ 283 Cecil Fielder .20 .09 .03
☐ 284 Carlton Fisk .20 .09 .03
☐ 285 Wade Boggs .20 .09 .03
☐ 286 Damion Easley .15 .07 .02
☐ 287 Norm Charlton .10 .05 .01
☐ 288 Jeff Conine .20 .09 .03
☐ 289 Roberto Kelly .15 .07 .02
☐ 290 Jerald Clark .10 .05 .01
☐ 291 Rickey Henderson .20 .09 .03
☐ 292 Chuck Finley .10 .05 .01
☐ 293 Doug Drabek .20 .09 .03
☐ 294 Dave Stewart .15 .07 .02
☐ 295 Tom Glavine .20 .09 .03
☐ 296 Jaime Navarro .10 .05 .01
☐ 297 Ray Lankford .20 .09 .03
☐ 298 Greg Hibbard .10 .05 .01
☐ 299 Jody Reed .10 .05 .01
☐ 300 Dennis Martinez .15 .07 .02
☐ 301 Dave Martinez .10 .05 .01
☐ 302 Reggie Jefferson .10 .05 .01
☐ 303 John Cummings .10 .05 .01
☐ 304 Orestes Destrade .10 .05 .01
☐ 305 Mike Maddux .10 .05 .01
☐ 306 David Segui .10 .05 .01
☐ 307 Gary Sheffield .20 .09 .03
☐ 308 Danny Jackson .10 .05 .01
☐ 309 Craig Lefferts .10 .05 .01
☐ 310 Andre Dawson .20 .09 .03

☐ 311 Barry Larkin .20 .09 .03
☐ 312 Alex Cole .10 .05 .01
☐ 313 Mark Gardner .10 .05 .01
☐ 314 Kirk Gibson .15 .07 .02
☐ 315 Shane Mack .15 .07 .02
☐ 316 Bo Jackson .20 .09 .03
☐ 317 Jimmy Key .15 .07 .02
☐ 318 Greg Myers .10 .05 .01
☐ 319 Ken Griffey Jr. 3.00 1.35 .40
☐ 320 Monty Fariss .10 .05 .01
☐ 321 Kevin Mitchell .15 .07 .02
☐ 322 Andres Galarraga .20 .09 .03
☐ 323 Mark McGwire .20 .09 .03
☐ 324 Mark Langston .20 .09 .03
☐ 325 Steve Finley .10 .05 .01
☐ 326 Greg Maddux .75 .35 .09
☐ 327 Dave Nilsson .15 .07 .02
☐ 328 Ozzie Smith .60 .25 .08
☐ 329 Candy Maldonado .10 .05 .01
☐ 330 Checklist .10 .05 .01
☐ 331 Tim Pugh .10 .05 .01
☐ 332 Joe Girardi .10 .05 .01
☐ 333 Junior Felix .10 .05 .01
☐ 334 Greg Swindell .10 .05 .01
☐ 335 Ramon Martinez .15 .07 .02
☐ 336 Sean Berry .10 .05 .01
☐ 337 Joe Orsulak .10 .05 .01
☐ 338 Wes Chamberlain .10 .05 .01
☐ 339 Stan Belinda .10 .05 .01
☐ 340 Checklist UER .10 .05 .01
(306 Luis Mercedes)
☐ 341 Bruce Hurst .10 .05 .01
☐ 342 John Burkett .15 .07 .02
☐ 343 Mike Mussina .60 .25 .08
☐ 344 Scott Fletcher .10 .05 .01
☐ 345 Rene Gonzales .10 .05 .01
☐ 346 Roberto Hernandez .10 .05 .01
☐ 347 Carlos Martinez .10 .05 .01
☐ 348 Bill Krueger .10 .05 .01
☐ 349 Felix Jose .10 .05 .01
☐ 350 John Jaha .15 .07 .02
☐ 351 Willie Banks .10 .05 .01
☐ 352 Matt Nokes .10 .05 .01
☐ 353 Kevin Seitzer .10 .05 .01
☐ 354 Erik Hanson .10 .05 .01
☐ 355 David Hulse .10 .05 .01
☐ 356 Domingo Martinez .10 .05 .01
☐ 357 Greg Olson .10 .05 .01
☐ 358 Randy Myers .15 .07 .02
☐ 359 Tom Browning .10 .05 .01
☐ 360 Charlie Hayes .15 .07 .02
☐ 361 Bryan Harvey .15 .07 .02
☐ 362 Eddie Taubensee .10 .05 .01
☐ 363 Tim Wallach .10 .05 .01
☐ 364 Mel Rojas .10 .05 .01
☐ 365 Frank Tanana .10 .05 .01
☐ 366 John Kruk .20 .09 .03
☐ 367 Tim Laker .10 .05 .01
☐ 368 Rich Rodriguez .10 .05 .01
☐ 369 Darren Lewis .10 .05 .01
☐ 370 Harold Reynolds .10 .05 .01
☐ 371 Jose Melendez .10 .05 .01
☐ 372 Joe Grahe .10 .05 .01
☐ 373 Lance Johnson .10 .05 .01
☐ 374 Jose Mesa .10 .05 .01
☐ 375 Scott Livingstone .10 .05 .01
☐ 376 Wally Joyner .15 .07 .02
☐ 377 Kevin Reimer .10 .05 .01
☐ 378 Kirby Puckett 1.25 .55 .16
☐ 379 Paul O'Neill .15 .07 .02
☐ 380 Randy Johnson .20 .09 .03
☐ 381 Manny Lee .10 .05 .01
☐ 382 Dick Schofield .10 .05 .01
☐ 383 Darren Holmes .10 .05 .01
☐ 384 Charlie Hough .15 .07 .02
☐ 385 John Orton .10 .05 .01
☐ 386 Edgar Martinez .10 .05 .01
☐ 387 Terry Pendleton .20 .09 .03
☐ 388 Dan Plesac .10 .05 .01
☐ 389 Jeff Reardon .15 .07 .02
☐ 390 David Nied .20 .09 .03
☐ 391 Dave Magadan .10 .05 .01
☐ 392 Larry Walker .20 .09 .03
☐ 393 Ben Rivera .10 .05 .01
☐ 394 Lonnie Smith .10 .05 .01
☐ 395 Craig Shipley .10 .05 .01
☐ 396 Willie McGee .15 .07 .02
☐ 397 Arthur Rhodes .10 .05 .01
☐ 398 Mike Stanton .10 .05 .01
☐ 399 Luis Polonia .10 .05 .01
☐ 400 Jack McDowell .20 .09 .03
☐ 401 Mike Moore .10 .05 .01
☐ 402 Jose Lind .10 .05 .01
☐ 403 Bill Spiers .10 .05 .01
☐ 404 Kevin Tapani .10 .05 .01
☐ 405 Spike Owen .10 .05 .01
☐ 406 Tino Martinez .15 .07 .02
☐ 407 Charlie Leibrandt .10 .05 .01
☐ 408 Ed Sprague .10 .05 .01
☐ 409 Bryn Smith .10 .05 .01
☐ 410 Benito Santiago .10 .05 .01
☐ 411 Jose Rijo .15 .07 .02
☐ 412 Pete O'Brien .10 .05 .01
☐ 413 Willie Wilson .10 .05 .01
☐ 414 Bip Roberts .10 .05 .01
☐ 415 Eric Young .15 .07 .02
☐ 416 Walt Weiss .10 .05 .01
☐ 417 Milt Thompson .10 .05 .01
☐ 418 Chris Sabo .15 .07 .02
☐ 419 Scott Sanderson .10 .05 .01
☐ 420 Tim Raines .20 .09 .03
☐ 421 Alan Trammell .20 .09 .03
☐ 422 Mike Macfarlane .10 .05 .01
☐ 423 Dave Winfield .20 .09 .03
☐ 424 Bob Wickman .10 .05 .01
☐ 425 David Valle .10 .05 .01
☐ 426 Gary Redus .10 .05 .01
☐ 427 Turner Ward .10 .05 .01
☐ 428 Reggie Sanders .20 .09 .03
☐ 429 Todd Worrell .10 .05 .01
☐ 430 Julio Valera .10 .05 .01
☐ 431 Cal Ripken 2.00 .90 .25
☐ 432 Mo Vaughn .20 .09 .03
☐ 433 John Smiley .10 .05 .01
☐ 434 Omar Vizquel .10 .05 .01
☐ 435 Billy Ripken .10 .05 .01
☐ 436 Cory Snyder .10 .05 .01
☐ 437 Carlos Quintana .10 .05 .01
☐ 438 Omar Olivares .10 .05 .01
☐ 439 Robin Ventura .20 .09 .03
☐ 440 Checklist .10 .05 .01
☐ 441 Kevin Higgins .15 .07 .02
☐ 442 Carlos Hernandez .10 .05 .01
☐ 443 Dan Peltier .10 .05 .01
☐ 444 Derek Lilliquist .10 .05 .01
☐ 445 Tim Salmon .50 .23 .06
☐ 446 Sherman Obando .20 .09 .03
☐ 447 Pat Kelly .10 .05 .01
☐ 448 Todd Van Poppel .15 .07 .02
☐ 449 Mark Whiten .15 .07 .02
☐ 450 Checklist .10 .05 .01
☐ 451 Pat Meares .20 .09 .03
☐ 452 Tony Tarasco .40 .18 .05
☐ 453 Chris Gwynn .10 .05 .01
☐ 454 Armando Reynoso .10 .05 .01
☐ 455 Danny Darwin .10 .05 .01

☐ 456	Willie Greene	.15	.07	.02
☐ 457	Mike Blowers	.10	.05	.01
☐ 458	Kevin Roberson	.10	.05	.01
☐ 459	Graeme Lloyd	.10	.05	.01
☐ 460	David West	.10	.05	.01
☐ 461	Joey Cora	.10	.05	.01
☐ 462	Alex Arias	.10	.05	.01
☐ 463	Chad Kreuter	.10	.05	.01
☐ 464	Mike Lansing	.30	.14	.04
☐ 465	Mike Timlin	.10	.05	.01
☐ 466	Paul Wagner	.10	.05	.01
☐ 467	Mark Portugal	.10	.05	.01
☐ 468	Jim Leyritz	.10	.05	.01
☐ 469	Ryan Klesko	1.00	.45	.13
☐ 470	Mario Diaz	.10	.05	.01
☐ 471	Guillermo Velasquez	.10	.05	.01
☐ 472	Fernando Valenzuela	.10	.05	.01
☐ 473	Raul Mondesi	2.00	.90	.25
☐ 474	Mike Pagliarulo	.10	.05	.01
☐ 475	Chris Hammond	.10	.05	.01
☐ 476	Torey Lovullo	.10	.05	.01
☐ 477	Trevor Wilson	.10	.05	.01
☐ 478	Marcos Armas	.10	.05	.01
☐ 479	Dave Gallagher	.10	.05	.01
☐ 480	Jeff Treadway	.10	.05	.01
☐ 481	Jeff Branson	.10	.05	.01
☐ 482	Dickie Thon	.10	.05	.01
☐ 483	Eduardo Perez	.15	.07	.02
☐ 484	David Wells	.10	.05	.01
☐ 485	Brian Williams	.10	.05	.01
☐ 486	Domingo Cedeno	.10	.05	.01
☐ 487	Tom Candiotti	.10	.05	.01
☐ 488	Steve Frey	.10	.05	.01
☐ 489	Greg McMichael	.20	.09	.03
☐ 490	Marc Newfield	.30	.14	.04
☐ 491	Larry Andersen	.10	.05	.01
☐ 492	Damon Buford	.10	.05	.01
☐ 493	Ricky Gutierrez	.10	.05	.01
☐ 494	Jeff Russell	.10	.05	.01
☐ 495	Vinny Castilla	.10	.05	.01
☐ 496	Wilson Alvarez	.20	.09	.03
☐ 497	Scott Bullett	.10	.05	.01
☐ 498	Larry Casian	.10	.05	.01
☐ 499	Jose Vizcaino	.10	.05	.01
☐ 500	J.T. Snow	.15	.07	.02
☐ 501	Bryan Hickerson	.10	.05	.01
☐ 502	Jeremy Hernandez	.10	.05	.01
☐ 503	Jeromy Burnitz	.15	.07	.02
☐ 504	Steve Farr	.10	.05	.01
☐ 505	J. Owens	.10	.05	.01
☐ 506	Craig Paquette	.10	.05	.01
☐ 507	Jim Eisenreich	.10	.05	.01
☐ 508	Matt Whiteside	.10	.05	.01
☐ 509	Luis Aquino	.10	.05	.01
☐ 510	Mike LaValliere	.10	.05	.01
☐ 511	Jim Gott	.10	.05	.01
☐ 512	Mark McLemore	.10	.05	.01
☐ 513	Randy Milligan	.10	.05	.01
☐ 514	Gary Gaetti	.10	.05	.01
☐ 515	Lou Frazier	.15	.07	.02
☐ 516	Rich Amaral	.10	.05	.01
☐ 517	Gene Harris	.10	.05	.01
☐ 518	Aaron Sele	.50	.23	.06
☐ 519	Mark Wohlers	.10	.05	.01
☐ 520	Scott Kamieniecki	.10	.05	.01
☐ 521	Kent Mercker	.10	.05	.01
☐ 522	Jim Deshaies	.10	.05	.01
☐ 523	Kevin Stocker	.15	.07	.02
☐ 524	Jason Bere	.75	.35	.09
☐ 525	Tim Bogar	.10	.05	.01
☐ 526	Brad Pennington	.10	.05	.01
☐ 527	Curt Leskanic	.10	.05	.01
☐ 528	Wayne Kirby	.10	.05	.01
☐ 529	Tim Costo	.10	.05	.01
☐ 530	Doug Henry	.10	.05	.01
☐ 531	Trevor Hoffman	.10	.05	.01
☐ 532	Kelly Gruber	.10	.05	.01
☐ 533	Mike Harkey	.10	.05	.01
☐ 534	John Doherty	.10	.05	.01
☐ 535	Erik Pappas	.10	.05	.01
☐ 536	Brent Gates	.20	.09	.03
☐ 537	Roger McDowell	.10	.05	.01
☐ 538	Chris Haney	.10	.05	.01
☐ 539	Blas Minor	.10	.05	.01
☐ 540	Pat Hentgen	.15	.07	.02
☐ 541	Chuck Carr	.10	.05	.01
☐ 542	Doug Strange	.10	.05	.01
☐ 543	Xavier Hernandez	.10	.05	.01
☐ 544	Paul Quantrill	.10	.05	.01
☐ 545	Anthony Young	.10	.05	.01
☐ 546	Bret Boone	.20	.09	.03
☐ 547	Dwight Smith	.10	.05	.01
☐ 548	Bobby Munoz	.10	.05	.01
☐ 549	Russ Springer	.10	.05	.01
☐ 550	Roger Pavlik	.15	.07	.02
☐ DW	Dave Winfield 3000 Hits	2.50	1.15	.30
☐ FT	Frank Thomas AU/3500 (Certified autograph)	300.00	135.00	38.00

1993 Leaf Fasttrack

These 20 standard-size (2 1/2" by 3 1/2") cards were randomly inserted into 1993 Leaf retail packs; the first ten were series I inserts, the second ten were series II inserts. The fronts feature color player action photos that are borderless, except in the lower right corner, where an oblique white stripe carries the motion-streaked set title. Beneath this is a black stripe that contains the player's name and team name and, further below, a black marbleized design. The gold-foil-embossed Leaf seal appears in an upper corner. The similarly designed backs carry a second color player action photo. The player's name, position, biography, and career highlights appear above and parallel to the oblique corner design. The player's prismatic-foil-embossed team name appears in an upper corner. The cards are numbered on the back.

	MINT	EXC	G-VG
COMPLETE SET (20)	100.00	45.00	12.50
COMPLETE SERIES 1 (10)	60.00	27.00	7.50

COMPLETE SERIES 2 (10)	40.00	18.00	5.00
COMMON CARD (1-10)	2.00	.90	.25
COMMON CARD (11-20)	2.00	.90	.25
☐ 1 Frank Thomas	35.00	16.00	4.40
☐ 2 Tim Wakefield	2.00	.90	.25
☐ 3 Kenny Lofton	9.00	4.00	1.15
☐ 4 Mike Mussina	7.00	3.10	.85
☐ 5 Juan Gonzalez	12.00	5.50	1.50
☐ 6 Chuck Knoblauch	3.00	1.35	.40
☐ 7 Eric Karros	2.00	.90	.25
☐ 8 Ray Lankford	3.00	1.35	.40
☐ 9 Juan Guzman	2.00	.90	.25
☐ 10 Pat Listach	2.00	.90	.25
☐ 11 Carlos Baerga	5.00	2.30	.60
☐ 12 Felix Jose	2.00	.90	.25
☐ 13 Steve Avery	3.00	1.35	.40
☐ 14 Robin Ventura	3.00	1.35	.40
☐ 15 Ivan Rodriguez	3.00	1.35	.40
☐ 16 Cal Eldred	2.00	.90	.25
☐ 17 Jeff Bagwell	18.00	8.00	2.30
☐ 18 David Justice	5.00	2.30	.60
☐ 19 Travis Fryman	4.00	1.80	.50
☐ 20 Marquis Grissom	3.00	1.35	.40

1993 Leaf Gold All-Stars

These 20 standard-size (2 1/2" by 3 1/2") cards were randomly inserted into 1993 Leaf jumbo packs; the first ten were series I inserts, the second ten were series II inserts. One side of each card features a color player action photo of a National League All-Star that is borderless, except in the lower right corner, where oblique red, white, and blue stripes carry the set's title, with the word "Stars" printed in gold foil. Beneath this is a black marbleized design that contains the player's name in white lettering, and his position, which is printed in gold foil. The gold-foil-embossed Leaf seal appears in an upper corner. The design of the other side is almost identical and carries a color player action photo of an American League All-Star. The AL side carries the year and copyright symbol, and the Major League Baseball and MLBPA logos. The NL side carries the card's number.

	MINT	EXC	G-VG
COMPLETE SET (20)	40.00	18.00	5.00
COMPLETE SERIES 1 (10)	18.00	8.00	2.30
COMPLETE SERIES 2 (10)	22.00	10.00	2.80
COMMON PAIR (1-10)	.75	.35	.09
COMMON PAIR (11-20)	.75	.35	.09
☐ 1 Ivan Rodriguez Darren Daulton	1.00	.45	.13
☐ 2 Don Mattingly Fred McGriff	3.00	1.35	.40
☐ 3 Cecil Fielder Jeff Bagwell	3.50	1.55	.45
☐ 4 Carlos Baerga Ryne Sandberg	3.00	1.35	.40
☐ 5 Chuck Knoblauch Delino DeShields	.75	.35	.09
☐ 6 Robin Ventura Terry Pendleton	1.00	.45	.13
☐ 7 Ken Griffey Jr. Andy Van Slyke	6.00	2.70	.75
☐ 8 Joe Carter Dave Justice	1.75	.80	.22
☐ 9 Jose Canseco Tony Gwynn	2.50	1.15	.30
☐ 10 Dennis Eckersley Rob Dibble	.75	.35	.09
☐ 11 Mark McGwire Will Clark	1.25	.55	.16
☐ 12 Frank Thomas Mark Grace	6.00	2.70	.75
☐ 13 Roberto Alomar Craig Biggio	1.75	.80	.22
☐ 14 Cal Ripken Barry Larkin	4.00	1.80	.50
☐ 15 Edgar Martinez Gary Sheffield	.75	.35	.09
☐ 16 Rickey Henderson Barry Bonds	4.00	1.80	.50
☐ 17 Kirby Puckett Reggie Sanders	3.00	1.35	.40
☐ 18 Jim Abbott Tom Glavine	1.00	.45	.13
☐ 19 Nolan Ryan Greg Maddux	8.00	3.60	1.00
☐ 20 Roger Clemens Doug Drabek	1.75	.80	.22

1993 Leaf Gold Rookies

These 20 cards of promising newcomers were randomly inserted into 1993 Leaf foil packs; the first ten in series I packs, the last ten in series II packs. The front of each standard-size (2 1/2" by 3 1/2") card fea-

tures a borderless color player action shot. The player's name appears in white cursive lettering within a wide gray lithic stripe near the bottom, which is set off by gold-foil lines and carries the set's title in simulated bas-relief. The gold foil-embossed Leaf seal appears in an upper corner. The back carries another borderless color player action photo, which is cut out and projected upon a picture of the player's ballpark. His prismatic foil-embossed team logo appears in an upper corner. His name and biography, along with his 1992 minor league stats within a gray lithic stripe, appear near the bottom. The cards are numbered on the back.

	MINT	EXC	G-VG
COMPLETE SET (20)	50.00	23.00	6.25
COMPLETE SERIES 1 (10)	25.00	11.50	3.10
COMPLETE SERIES 2 (10)	25.00	11.50	3.10
COMMON CARD (1-10)	1.00	.45	.13
COMMON CARD (11-20)	1.00	.45	.13
☐ 1 Kevin Young	1.00	.45	.13
☐ 2 Wil Cordero	4.00	1.80	.50
☐ 3 Mark Kiefer	1.00	.45	.13
☐ 4 Gerald Williams	1.00	.45	.13
☐ 5 Brandon Wilson	1.00	.45	.13
☐ 6 Greg Gohr	1.00	.45	.13
☐ 7 Ryan Thompson	2.50	1.15	.30
☐ 8 Tim Wakefield	1.00	.45	.13
☐ 9 Troy Neel	1.50	.65	.19
☐ 10 Tim Salmon	12.00	5.50	1.50
☐ 11 Kevin Rogers	1.00	.45	.13
☐ 12 Rod Bolton	1.00	.45	.13
☐ 13 Ken Ryan	1.50	.65	.19
☐ 14 Phil Hiatt	1.00	.45	.13
☐ 15 Rene Arocha	1.50	.65	.19
☐ 16 Nigel Wilson	2.00	.90	.25
☐ 17 J.T. Snow	2.00	.90	.25
☐ 18 Benji Gil	2.50	1.15	.30
☐ 19 Chipper Jones	12.00	5.50	1.50
☐ 20 Darrell Sherman	1.00	.45	.13

1993 Leaf Heading for the Hall

Randomly inserted into all 1993 Leaf packs, this ten-card standard-size (2 1/2" by 3 1/2") set features potential Hall of Famers. Cards 1-5 were series I inserts and cards 6-10 were series II inserts. The fronts feature borderless color player action shots, with the player's name appearing within a lithic banner near the bottom, below the set's logo. The gold foil-embossed Leaf seal appears in an upper corner. The horizontal backs carry a cutout color player action photo superposed upon an exterior view of the Hall of Fame building and a blowup of a road map of the Cooperstown area. A Hall of Fame-style plaque appears on the right, which bears the player's name, likeness, and achievements that merit his induction into the Hall. The cards are numbered on the back.

	MINT	EXC	G-VG
COMPLETE SET (10)	40.00	18.00	5.00
COMPLETE SERIES 1 (5)	20.00	9.00	2.50
COMPLETE SERIES 2 (5)	20.00	9.00	2.50
COMMON CARD (1-5)	1.50	.65	.19
COMMON CARD (6-10)	3.50	1.55	.45
☐ 1 Nolan Ryan	12.00	5.50	1.50
☐ 2 Tony Gwynn	4.00	1.80	.50
☐ 3 Robin Yount	2.50	1.15	.30
☐ 4 Eddie Murray	1.50	.65	.19
☐ 5 Cal Ripken	9.00	4.00	1.15
☐ 6 Roger Clemens	4.00	1.80	.50
☐ 7 George Brett	6.00	2.70	.75
☐ 8 Ryne Sandberg	5.00	2.30	.60
☐ 9 Kirby Puckett	6.00	2.70	.75
☐ 10 Ozzie Smith	3.50	1.55	.45

1993 Leaf Frank Thomas

This ten-card set spotlights Chicago White Sox slugger Frank Thomas. The standard-size (2 1/2" by 3 1/2") cards were randomly inserted into all forms of Leaf packs. The full-bleed fronts carry color action shots with "Frank" stamped in large prismatic foil letters across the bottom of the picture. A black oval containing a one-word description of Thomas' baseball-playing style overlays on the name. The borderless backs contain a color portrait bordered on the top half by the Chicago skyline. Below the portrait is a gray-bordered career highlight. The White Sox logo is stamped in prismatic foil in the upper left. The cards are numbered on the back. Five cards were inserted in each of the two series.

	MINT	EXC	G-VG
COMPLETE SET (10)	40.00	18.00	5.00
COMPLETE SERIES 1 (5)	20.00	9.00	2.50
COMPLETE SERIES 2 (5)	20.00	9.00	2.50
COMMON THOMAS (1-10)	5.00	2.30	.60
□ 1 Frank Thomas Aggressive	5.00	2.30	.60
□ 2 Frank Thomas Serious	5.00	2.30	.60
□ 3 Frank Thomas Intense	5.00	2.30	.60
□ 4 Frank Thomas Confident	5.00	2.30	.60
□ 5 Frank Thomas Assertive	5.00	2.30	.60
□ 6 Frank Thomas Power	5.00	2.30	.60
□ 7 Frank Thomas Control	5.00	2.30	.60
□ 8 Frank Thomas Strength	5.00	2.30	.60
□ 9 Frank Thomas Concentration	5.00	2.30	.60
□ 10 Frank Thomas Preparation	5.00	2.30	.60

1993 Leaf Update Gold All-Stars

Randomly inserted in Update packs, this ten-card standard-size (2 1/2" by 3 1/2") set has the same card design as the 1993 Leaf Gold All-Stars set, featuring color player action shots on both sides: American League All-Stars on one side, and their National League All-Star counterparts on the other. The photos are borderless, except at the bottom, where a diagonal red, white, and blue stripe carries the set's title; with the words "All-Stars" printed in gold foil within the white portion. The player's name appears in white lettering, along with his position printed in gold-foil, within the dark marbleized triangle section beneath the stripe. The gold-foil Leaf logo appears in an upper corner on both sides. The cards are numbered on the NL All-Star side. Leaf Update was an exclusive hobby only product and thus had far lower production figures than the first two series of Leaf product printed earlier this year. A total of 6,250 Leaf Update cases were produced.

	MINT	EXC	G-VG
COMPLETE SET (10)	20.00	9.00	2.50
COMMON PAIR (1-10)	.75	.35	.09
□ 1 Mark Langston Terry Mulholland	.75	.35	.09
□ 2 Ivan Rodriguez Darren Daulton	1.00	.45	.13
□ 3 John Olerud John Kruk	1.00	.45	.13
□ 4 Roberto Alomar Ryne Sandberg	3.50	1.55	.45
□ 5 Wade Boggs Gary Sheffield	1.00	.45	.13
□ 6 Cal Ripken Barry Larkin	5.00	2.30	.60
□ 7 Kirby Puckett Bobby Bonds	5.00	2.30	.60
□ 8 Ken Griffey Jr. Marquis Grissom	7.00	3.10	.85
□ 9 Joe Carter David Justice	2.00	.90	.25
□ 10 Paul Molitor Mark Grace	1.25	.55	.16

1993 Leaf Update Gold Rookies

Randomly inserted in Update packs, this five-card standard-size (2 1/2" by 3 1/2") set has the same card design as the 1993 Leaf Gold Rookies set, featuring borderless color player action shots on its fronts. The player's name appears near the bottom in cursive white lettering within a broad gray lithic stripe set of by gold-foil lines. The set's title appears within the stripe in simulated bas-relief. The gold-foil leaf logo resides in an upper corner. The back carries a color action player shot that has been superposed upon a borderless photo of the player's home ballpark. The player's prismatic-foil team logo appears in an upper corner. The player's 1992 premajor league stats are displayed within a gray lithic stripe near the bottom. His name and biography appear in black lettering above. The cards are numbered on the back.

	MINT	EXC	G-VG
COMPLETE SET (5)	25.00	11.50	3.10
COMMON CARD (1-5)	1.50	.65	.19

		MINT	EXC	G-VG
☐ 1	Allen Watson	1.50	.65	.19
☐ 2	Jeffrey Hammonds	4.00	1.80	.50
☐ 3	Dave McCarty	1.50	.65	.19
☐ 4	Mike Piazza	20.00	9.00	2.50
☐ 5	Roberto Mejia	1.50	.65	.19

1993 Leaf Update Frank Thomas Jumbos

One of these oversized cards was inserted on top of the packs in each sealed Update box. Since 6,250 cases were produced, and each case contained 12 boxes, then 7,500 of each card were produced. The cards measure approximately 4 7/8" by 6 3/4", but otherwise are identical to the regular 1993 Leaf Frank Thomas cards. The fronts feature color action shots of Thomas that are borderless, except at the bottom, where a broad dark margin carries the name "Frank" in bold and large silver-foil lettering. Each card's subtitle appears within an elongated black capsule that is superposed upon the silver-foil letters. The back carries a closeup of Thomas that appears within a rectangle framed by a gray line. This rectangle is superposed upon a background view of the Chicago skyline, which fades to gray toward the bottom. Thomas' name and career highlights appear below the photo, and his team's logo appears in prismatic foil at the upper left. The cards are numbered on the back and also carry the production number out of a total of 7,500.

	MINT	EXC	G-VG
COMPLETE SET (10)	90.00	40.00	11.50
COMMON THOMAS (1-10)	10.00	4.50	1.25
☐ 1 Frank Thomas Aggressive	10.00	4.50	1.25
☐ 2 Frank Thomas Serious	10.00	4.50	1.25
☐ 3 Frank Thomas Intense	10.00	4.50	1.25
☐ 4 Frank Thomas Confident	10.00	4.50	1.25
☐ 5 Frank Thomas Assertive	10.00	4.50	1.25
☐ 6 Frank Thomas Power	10.00	4.50	1.25
☐ 7 Frank Thomas Control	10.00	4.50	1.25
☐ 8 Frank Thomas Strength	10.00	4.50	1.25
☐ 9 Frank Thomas Concentration	10.00	4.50	1.25
☐ 10 Frank Thomas Preparation	10.00	4.50	1.25

1994 Leaf

The 1994 Leaf baseball set consists of two series of 220 cards for a total of 440. All the cards measure the standard size. The fronts feature color action player photos, with team color-coded designs on the bottom. The player's name and the Leaf logo are foil stamped, the team name appears under the player's name. The backs carry a photo of the player's home stadium in the background with a silhouetted photo of the player in the foreground. Additionally, a headshot appears in a ticket stub-like design with biographical information, while player statistics appear on the bottom. Cards featuring players from the Texas Rangers, Cleveland Indians, Milwaukee Brewers and Houston Astros were held out of the first series in order to have up-to-date photography in each team's new uniforms. A limited number of players from the San Francisco Giants are featured in the first series because of minor modifications to the team's uniforms. Randomly inserted in hobby packs at a rate of one in 36 was a stamped version of Frank Thomas' 1990 Leaf rookie card.

	MINT	EXC	G-VG
COMPLETE SET (440)	30.00	13.50	3.80
COMPLETE SERIES 1 (220)	14.00	6.25	1.75
COMPLETE SERIES 2 (220)	16.00	7.25	2.00
COMMON CARD (1-220)	.10	.05	.01
COMMON CARD (221-440)	.10	.05	.01
☐ 1 Cal Ripken	2.25	1.00	.30
☐ 2 Tony Tarasco	.20	.09	.03
☐ 3 Joe Girardi	.10	.05	.01
☐ 4 Bernie Williams	.15	.07	.02
☐ 5 Chad Kreuter	.10	.05	.01
☐ 6 Troy Neel	.15	.07	.02
☐ 7 Tom Pagnozzi	.10	.05	.01
☐ 8 Kirk Rueter	.10	.05	.01
☐ 9 Chris Bosio	.10	.05	.01
☐ 10 Dwight Gooden	.10	.05	.01

☐ 11 Mariano Duncan .... .10 .05 .01
☐ 12 Jay Bell .... .15 .07 .02
☐ 13 Lance Johnson .... .10 .05 .01
☐ 14 Richie Lewis .... .10 .05 .01
☐ 15 Dave Martinez .... .10 .05 .01
☐ 16 Orel Hershiser .... .15 .07 .02
☐ 17 Rob Butler .... .10 .05 .01
☐ 18 Glenallen Hill .... .10 .05 .01
☐ 19 Chad Curtis .... .15 .07 .02
☐ 20 Mike Stanton .... .10 .05 .01
☐ 21 Tim Wallach .... .10 .05 .01
☐ 22 Milt Thompson .... .10 .05 .01
☐ 23 Kevin Young .... .10 .05 .01
☐ 24 John Smiley .... .10 .05 .01
☐ 25 Jeff Montgomery .... .15 .07 .02
☐ 26 Robin Ventura .... .15 .07 .02
☐ 27 Scott Lydy .... .10 .05 .01
☐ 28 Todd Stottlemyre .... .10 .05 .01
☐ 29 Mark Whiten .... .15 .07 .02
☐ 30 Robby Thompson .... .10 .05 .01
☐ 31 Bobby Bonilla .... .20 .09 .03
☐ 32 Andy Ashby .... .10 .05 .01
☐ 33 Greg Myers .... .10 .05 .01
☐ 34 Billy Hatcher .... .10 .05 .01
☐ 35 Brad Holman .... .10 .05 .01
☐ 36 Mark McLemore .... .10 .05 .01
☐ 37 Scott Sanders .... .10 .05 .01
☐ 38 Jim Abbott .... .20 .09 .03
☐ 39 David Wells .... .10 .05 .01
☐ 40 Roberto Kelly .... .10 .05 .01
☐ 41 Jeff Conine .... .20 .09 .03
☐ 42 Sean Berry .... .10 .05 .01
☐ 43 Mark Grace .... .20 .09 .03
☐ 44 Eric Young .... .15 .07 .02
☐ 45 Rick Aguilera .... .15 .07 .02
☐ 46 Chipper Jones .... .40 .18 .05
☐ 47 Mel Rojas .... .10 .05 .01
☐ 48 Ryan Thompson .... .15 .07 .02
☐ 49 Al Martin .... .10 .05 .01
☐ 50 Cecil Fielder .... .20 .09 .03
☐ 51 Pat Kelly .... .10 .05 .01
☐ 52 Kevin Tapani .... .10 .05 .01
☐ 53 Tim Costo .... .10 .05 .01
☐ 54 Dave Hollins .... .20 .09 .03
☐ 55 Kirt Manwaring .... .10 .05 .01
☐ 56 Gregg Jefferies .... .20 .09 .03
☐ 57 Ron Darling .... .10 .05 .01
☐ 58 Bill Haselman .... .10 .05 .01
☐ 59 Phil Plantier .... .15 .07 .02
☐ 60 Frank Viola .... .10 .05 .01
☐ 61 Todd Zeile .... .15 .07 .02
☐ 62 Bret Barberie .... .10 .05 .01
☐ 63 Roberto Mejia .... .15 .07 .02
☐ 64 Chuck Knoblauch .... .20 .09 .03
☐ 65 Jose Lind .... .10 .05 .01
☐ 66 Brady Anderson .... .15 .07 .02
☐ 67 Ruben Sierra .... .20 .09 .03
☐ 68 Jose Vizcaino .... .10 .05 .01
☐ 69 Joe Grahe .... .10 .05 .01
☐ 70 Kevin Appier .... .15 .07 .02
☐ 71 Wilson Alvarez .... .20 .09 .03
☐ 72 Tom Candiotti .... .10 .05 .01
☐ 73 John Burkett .... .15 .07 .02
☐ 74 Anthony Young .... .10 .05 .01
☐ 75 Scott Cooper .... .15 .07 .02
☐ 76 Nigel Wilson .... .15 .07 .02
☐ 77 John Valentin .... .15 .07 .02
☐ 78 Dave McCarty .... .15 .07 .02
☐ 79 Archi Cianfrocco .... .10 .05 .01
☐ 80 Lou Whitaker .... .20 .09 .03
☐ 81 Dante Bichette .... .20 .09 .03
☐ 82 Mark Dewey .... .10 .05 .01
☐ 83 Danny Jackson .... .10 .05 .01
☐ 84 Harold Baines .... .15 .07 .02
☐ 85 Todd Benzinger .... .10 .05 .01
☐ 86 Damion Easley .... .10 .05 .01
☐ 87 Danny Cox .... .10 .05 .01
☐ 88 Jose Bautista .... .10 .05 .01
☐ 89 Mike Lansing .... .15 .07 .02
☐ 90 Phil Hiatt .... .10 .05 .01
☐ 91 Tim Pugh .... .10 .05 .01
☐ 92 Tino Martinez .... .10 .05 .01
☐ 93 Raul Mondesi .... 1.00 .45 .13
☐ 94 Greg Maddux .... .60 .25 .08
☐ 95 Al Leiter .... .10 .05 .01
☐ 96 Benito Santiago .... .10 .05 .01
☐ 97 Lenny Dykstra .... .20 .09 .03
☐ 98 Sammy Sosa .... .20 .09 .03
☐ 99 Tim Bogar .... .10 .05 .01
☐ 100 Checklist 1-73 .... .10 .05 .01
A.L. East Logos
☐ 101 Deion Sanders .... .50 .23 .06
☐ 102 Bobby Witt .... .10 .05 .01
☐ 103 Wil Cordero .... .20 .09 .03
☐ 104 Rich Amaral .... .10 .05 .01
☐ 105 Mike Mussina .... .50 .23 .06
☐ 106 Reggie Sanders .... .15 .07 .02
☐ 107 Ozzie Guillen .... .10 .05 .01
☐ 108 Paul O'Neill .... .15 .07 .02
☐ 109 Tim Salmon .... .40 .18 .05
☐ 110 Rheal Cormier .... .10 .05 .01
☐ 111 Billy Ashley .... .20 .09 .03
☐ 112 Jeff Kent .... .15 .07 .02
☐ 113 Derek Bell .... .15 .07 .02
☐ 114 Danny Darwin .... .10 .05 .01
☐ 115 Chip Hale .... .10 .05 .01
☐ 116 Tim Raines .... .20 .09 .03
☐ 117 Ed Sprague .... .10 .05 .01
☐ 118 Darrin Fletcher .... .10 .05 .01
☐ 119 Darren Holmes .... .10 .05 .01
☐ 120 Alan Trammell .... .20 .09 .03
☐ 121 Don Mattingly .... 1.25 .55 .16
☐ 122 Greg Gagne .... .10 .05 .01
☐ 123 Jose Offerman .... .10 .05 .01
☐ 124 Joe Orsulak .... .10 .05 .01
☐ 125 Jack McDowell .... .20 .09 .03
☐ 126 Barry Larkin .... .20 .09 .03
☐ 127 Ben McDonald .... .15 .07 .02
☐ 128 Mike Bordick .... .10 .05 .01
☐ 129 Devon White .... .10 .05 .01
☐ 130 Mike Perez .... .10 .05 .01
☐ 131 Jay Buhner .... .15 .07 .02
☐ 132 Phil Leftwich .... .10 .05 .01
☐ 133 Tommy Greene .... .10 .05 .01
☐ 134 Charlie Hayes .... .15 .07 .02
☐ 135 Don Slaught .... .10 .05 .01
☐ 136 Mike Gallego .... .10 .05 .01
☐ 137 Dave Winfield .... .20 .09 .03
☐ 138 Steve Avery .... .20 .09 .03
☐ 139 Derrick May .... .10 .05 .01
☐ 140 Bryan Harvey .... .15 .07 .02
☐ 141 Wally Joyner .... .15 .07 .02
☐ 142 Andre Dawson .... .20 .09 .03
☐ 143 Andy Benes .... .15 .07 .02
☐ 144 John Franco .... .10 .05 .01
☐ 145 Jeff King .... .10 .05 .01
☐ 146 Joe Oliver .... .10 .05 .01
☐ 147 Bill Gullikson .... .10 .05 .01
☐ 148 Armando Reynoso .... .10 .05 .01
☐ 149 Dave Fleming .... .10 .05 .01
☐ 150 Checklist 74-166 .... .10 .05 .01
A.L. Central Logos
☐ 151 Todd Van Poppel .... .15 .07 .02
☐ 152 Bernard Gilkey .... .10 .05 .01
☐ 153 Kevin Gross .... .10 .05 .01
☐ 154 Mike Devereaux .... .15 .07 .02

	No.	Player			
☐	155	Tim Wakefield	.10	.05	.01
☐	156	Andres Galarraga	.20	.09	.03
☐	157	Pat Meares	.10	.05	.01
☐	158	Jim Leyritz	.10	.05	.01
☐	159	Mike Macfarlane	.10	.05	.01
☐	160	Tony Phillips	.10	.05	.01
☐	161	Brent Gates	.20	.09	.03
☐	162	Mark Langston	.20	.09	.03
☐	163	Allen Watson	.10	.05	.01
☐	164	Randy Johnson	.20	.09	.03
☐	165	Doug Brocail	.10	.05	.01
☐	166	Rob Dibble	.10	.05	.01
☐	167	Roberto Hernandez	.10	.05	.01
☐	168	Felix Jose	.10	.05	.01
☐	169	Steve Cooke	.10	.05	.01
☐	170	Darren Daulton	.20	.09	.03
☐	171	Eric Karros	.15	.07	.02
☐	172	Geronimo Pena	.10	.05	.01
☐	173	Gary DiSarcina	.10	.05	.01
☐	174	Marquis Grissom	.20	.09	.03
☐	175	Joey Cora	.10	.05	.01
☐	176	Jim Eisenreich	.10	.05	.01
☐	177	Brad Pennington	.10	.05	.01
☐	178	Terry Steinbach	.15	.07	.02
☐	179	Pat Borders	.10	.05	.01
☐	180	Steve Buechele	.10	.05	.01
☐	181	Jeff Fassero	.10	.05	.01
☐	182	Mike Greenwell	.15	.07	.02
☐	183	Mike Henneman	.10	.05	.01
☐	184	Ron Karkovice	.10	.05	.01
☐	185	Pat Hentgen	.15	.07	.02
☐	186	Jose Guzman	.10	.05	.01
☐	187	Brett Butler	.15	.07	.02
☐	188	Charlie Hough	.15	.07	.02
☐	189	Terry Pendleton	.10	.05	.01
☐	190	Melido Perez	.10	.05	.01
☐	191	Orestes Destrade	.10	.05	.01
☐	192	Mike Morgan	.10	.05	.01
☐	193	Joe Carter	.40	.18	.05
☐	194	Jeff Blauser	.15	.07	.02
☐	195	Chris Hoiles	.15	.07	.02
☐	196	Ricky Gutierrez	.10	.05	.01
☐	197	Mike Moore	.10	.05	.01
☐	198	Carl Willis	.10	.05	.01
☐	199	Aaron Sele	.25	.11	.03
☐	200	Checklist 147-220 A.L. West Logos	.10	.05	.01
☐	201	Tim Naehring	.10	.05	.01
☐	202	Scott Livingstone	.10	.05	.01
☐	203	Luis Alicea	.10	.05	.01
☐	204	Torey Lovullo	.10	.05	.01
☐	205	Jim Gott	.10	.05	.01
☐	206	Bob Wickman	.10	.05	.01
☐	207	Greg McMichael	.15	.07	.02
☐	208	Scott Brosius	.10	.05	.01
☐	209	Chris Gwynn	.10	.05	.01
☐	210	Steve Sax	.10	.05	.01
☐	211	Dick Schofield	.10	.05	.01
☐	212	Robb Nen	.10	.05	.01
☐	213	Ben Rivera	.10	.05	.01
☐	214	Vinny Castilla	.10	.05	.01
☐	215	Jamie Moyer	.10	.05	.01
☐	216	Wally Whitehurst	.10	.05	.01
☐	217	Frank Castillo	.10	.05	.01
☐	218	Mike Blowers	.10	.05	.01
☐	219	Tim Scott	.10	.05	.01
☐	220	Paul Wagner	.10	.05	.01
☐	221	Jeff Bagwell	1.50	.65	.19
☐	222	Ricky Bones	.10	.05	.01
☐	223	Sandy Alomar Jr.	.15	.07	.02
☐	224	Rod Beck	.15	.07	.02
☐	225	Roberto Alomar	.75	.35	.09
☐	226	Jack Armstrong	.10	.05	.01
☐	227	Scott Erickson	.10	.05	.01
☐	228	Rene Arocha	.15	.07	.02
☐	229	Eric Anthony	.10	.05	.01
☐	230	Jeromy Burnitz	.15	.07	.02
☐	231	Kevin Brown	.10	.05	.01
☐	232	Tim Belcher	.10	.05	.01
☐	233	Bret Boone	.20	.09	.03
☐	234	Dennis Eckersley	.20	.09	.03
☐	235	Tom Glavine	.20	.09	.03
☐	236	Craig Biggio	.15	.07	.02
☐	237	Pedro Astacio	.15	.07	.02
☐	238	Ryan Bowen	.10	.05	.01
☐	239	Brad Ausmus	.10	.05	.01
☐	240	Vince Coleman	.10	.05	.01
☐	241	Jason Bere	.40	.18	.05
☐	242	Ellis Burks	.15	.07	.02
☐	243	Wes Chamberlain	.10	.05	.01
☐	244	Ken Caminiti	.15	.07	.02
☐	245	Willie Banks	.10	.05	.01
☐	246	Sid Fernandez	.10	.05	.01
☐	247	Carlos Baerga	.40	.18	.05
☐	248	Carlos Garcia	.10	.05	.01
☐	249	Jose Canseco	.40	.18	.05
☐	250	Alex Diaz	.10	.05	.01
☐	251	Albert Belle	1.00	.45	.13
☐	252	Moises Alou	.20	.09	.03
☐	253	Bobby Ayala	.10	.05	.01
☐	254	Tony Gwynn	.75	.35	.09
☐	255	Roger Clemens	.75	.35	.09
☐	256	Eric Davis	.10	.05	.01
☐	257	Wade Boggs	.20	.09	.03
☐	258	Chili Davis	.15	.07	.02
☐	259	Rickey Henderson	.20	.09	.03
☐	260	Andujar Cedeno	.10	.05	.01
☐	261	Cris Carpenter	.10	.05	.01
☐	262	Juan Guzman	.15	.07	.02
☐	263	David Justice	.40	.18	.05
☐	264	Barry Bonds	1.25	.55	.16
☐	265	Pete Incaviglia	.10	.05	.01
☐	266	Tony Fernandez	.10	.05	.01
☐	267	Cal Eldred	.15	.07	.02
☐	268	Alex Fernandez	.20	.09	.03
☐	269	Kent Hrbek	.15	.07	.02
☐	270	Steve Farr	.10	.05	.01
☐	271	Doug Drabek	.20	.09	.03
☐	272	Brian Jordan	.15	.07	.02
☐	273	Xavier Hernandez	.10	.05	.01
☐	274	David Cone	.20	.09	.03
☐	275	Brian Hunter	.10	.05	.01
☐	276	Mike Harkey	.10	.05	.01
☐	277	Delino DeShields	.15	.07	.02
☐	278	David Hulse	.10	.05	.01
☐	279	Mickey Tettleton	.15	.07	.02
☐	280	Kevin McReynolds	.10	.05	.01
☐	281	Darryl Hamilton	.10	.05	.01
☐	282	Ken Hill	.10	.05	.01
☐	283	Wayne Kirby	.10	.05	.01
☐	284	Chris Hammond	.10	.05	.01
☐	285	Mo Vaughn	.20	.09	.03
☐	286	Ryan Klesko	.50	.23	.06
☐	287	Rick Wilkins	.10	.05	.01
☐	288	Bill Swift	.10	.05	.01
☐	289	Rafael Palmeiro	.20	.09	.03
☐	290	Brian Harper	.10	.05	.01
☐	291	Chris Turner	.10	.05	.01
☐	292	Luis Gonzalez	.10	.05	.01
☐	293	Kenny Rogers	.10	.05	.01
☐	294	Kirby Puckett	1.25	.55	.16
☐	295	Mike Stanley	.10	.05	.01
☐	296	Carlos Reyes	.10	.05	.01
☐	297	Charles Nagy	.10	.05	.01
☐	298	Reggie Jefferson	.10	.05	.01
☐	299	Bip Roberts	.10	.05	.01

☐	300 Darrin Jackson	.10	.05	.01
☐	301 Mike Jackson	.10	.05	.01
☐	302 Dave Nilsson	.10	.05	.01
☐	303 Ramon Martinez	.15	.07	.02
☐	304 Bobby Jones	.25	.11	.03
☐	305 Johnny Ruffin	.10	.05	.01
☐	306 Brian McRae	.15	.07	.02
☐	307 Bo Jackson	.20	.09	.03
☐	308 Dave Stewart	.15	.07	.02
☐	309 John Smoltz	.15	.07	.02
☐	310 Dennis Martinez	.15	.07	.02
☐	311 Dean Palmer	.15	.07	.02
☐	312 David Nied	.20	.09	.03
☐	313 Eddie Murray	.20	.09	.03
☐	314 Darryl Kile	.15	.07	.02
☐	315 Rick Sutcliffe	.15	.07	.02
☐	316 Shawon Dunston	.10	.05	.01
☐	317 John Jaha	.10	.05	.01
☐	318 Salomon Torres	.15	.07	.02
☐	319 Gary Sheffield	.20	.09	.03
☐	320 Curt Schilling	.10	.05	.01
☐	321 Greg Vaughn	.15	.07	.02
☐	322 Jay Howell	.10	.05	.01
☐	323 Todd Hundley	.10	.05	.01
☐	324 Chris Sabo	.10	.05	.01
☐	325 Stan Javier	.10	.05	.01
☐	326 Willie Greene	.15	.07	.02
☐	327 Hipolito Pichardo	.10	.05	.01
☐	328 Doug Strange	.10	.05	.01
☐	329 Dan Wilson	.10	.05	.01
☐	330 Checklist 221-293 N.L. East Logos	.10	.05	.01
☐	331 Omar Vizquel	.10	.05	.01
☐	332 Scott Servais	.10	.05	.01
☐	333 Bob Tewksbury	.10	.05	.01
☐	334 Matt Williams	.50	.23	.06
☐	335 Tom Foley	.10	.05	.01
☐	336 Jeff Russell	.10	.05	.01
☐	337 Scott Leius	.10	.05	.01
☐	338 Ivan Rodriguez	.20	.09	.03
☐	339 Kevin Seitzer	.10	.05	.01
☐	340 Jose Rijo	.15	.07	.02
☐	341 Eduardo Perez	.15	.07	.02
☐	342 Kirk Gibson	.15	.07	.02
☐	343 Randy Milligan	.10	.05	.01
☐	344 Edgar Martinez	.10	.05	.01
☐	345 Fred McGriff	.40	.18	.05
☐	346 Kurt Abbott	.30	.14	.04
☐	347 John Kruk	.20	.09	.03
☐	348 Mike Felder	.10	.05	.01
☐	349 Dave Staton	.10	.05	.01
☐	350 Kenny Lofton	.75	.35	.09
☐	351 Graeme Lloyd	.10	.05	.01
☐	352 David Segui	.10	.05	.01
☐	353 Danny Tartabull	.15	.07	.02
☐	354 Bob Welch	.10	.05	.01
☐	355 Duane Ward	.10	.05	.01
☐	356 Karl Rhodes	.10	.05	.01
☐	357 Lee Smith	.20	.09	.03
☐	358 Chris James	.10	.05	.01
☐	359 Walt Weiss	.10	.05	.01
☐	360 Pedro Munoz	.10	.05	.01
☐	361 Paul Sorrento	.10	.05	.01
☐	362 Todd Worrell	.10	.05	.01
☐	363 Bob Hamelin	.20	.09	.03
☐	364 Julio Franco	.15	.07	.02
☐	365 Roberto Petagine	.15	.07	.02
☐	366 Willie McGee	.10	.05	.01
☐	367 Pedro Martinez	.20	.09	.03
☐	368 Ken Griffey Jr.	3.00	1.35	.40
☐	369 B.J. Surhoff	.10	.05	.01
☐	370 Kevin Mitchell	.15	.07	.02
☐	371 John Doherty	.10	.05	.01
☐	372 Manny Lee	.10	.05	.01
☐	373 Terry Mulholland	.10	.05	.01
☐	374 Zane Smith	.10	.05	.01
☐	375 Otis Nixon	.10	.05	.01
☐	376 Jody Reed	.10	.05	.01
☐	377 Doug Jones	.10	.05	.01
☐	378 John Olerud	.20	.09	.03
☐	379 Greg Swindell	.10	.05	.01
☐	380 Checklist 294-366 N.L. Central Logos	.10	.05	.01
☐	381 Royce Clayton	.15	.07	.02
☐	382 Jim Thome	.20	.09	.03
☐	383 Steve Finley	.10	.05	.01
☐	384 Ray Lankford	.20	.09	.03
☐	385 Henry Rodriguez	.10	.05	.01
☐	386 Dave Magadan	.10	.05	.01
☐	387 Gary Redus	.10	.05	.01
☐	388 Orlando Merced	.15	.07	.02
☐	389 Tom Gordon	.10	.05	.01
☐	390 Luis Polonia	.10	.05	.01
☐	391 Mark McGwire	.20	.09	.03
☐	392 Mark Lemke	.10	.05	.01
☐	393 Doug Henry	.10	.05	.01
☐	394 Chuck Finley	.10	.05	.01
☐	395 Paul Molitor	.40	.18	.05
☐	396 Randy Myers	.10	.05	.01
☐	397 Larry Walker	.20	.09	.03
☐	398 Pete Harnisch	.10	.05	.01
☐	399 Darren Lewis	.10	.05	.01
☐	400 Frank Thomas	3.00	1.35	.40
☐	401 Jack Morris	.20	.09	.03
☐	402 Greg Hibbard	.10	.05	.01
☐	403 Jeffrey Hammonds	.40	.18	.05
☐	404 Will Clark	.40	.18	.05
☐	405 Travis Fryman	.25	.11	.03
☐	406 Scott Sanderson	.10	.05	.01
☐	407 Gene Harris	.10	.05	.01
☐	408 Chuck Carr	.10	.05	.01
☐	409 Ozzie Smith	.60	.25	.08
☐	410 Kent Mercker	.10	.05	.01
☐	411 Andy Van Slyke	.20	.09	.03
☐	412 Jimmy Key	.15	.07	.02
☐	413 Pat Mahomes	.10	.05	.01
☐	414 John Wetteland	.10	.05	.01
☐	415 Todd Jones	.10	.05	.01
☐	416 Greg Harris	.10	.05	.01
☐	417 Kevin Stocker	.15	.07	.02
☐	418 Juan Gonzalez	1.00	.45	.13
☐	419 Pete Smith	.10	.05	.01
☐	420 Pat Listach	.10	.05	.01
☐	421 Trevor Hoffman	.10	.05	.01
☐	422 Scott Fletcher	.10	.05	.01
☐	423 Mark Lewis	.10	.05	.01
☐	424 Mickey Morandini	.10	.05	.01
☐	425 Ryne Sandberg	1.00	.45	.13
☐	426 Erik Hanson	.10	.05	.01
☐	427 Gary Gaetti	.10	.05	.01
☐	428 Harold Reynolds	.10	.05	.01
☐	429 Mark Portugal	.10	.05	.01
☐	430 David Valle	.10	.05	.01
☐	431 Mitch Williams	.10	.05	.01
☐	432 Howard Johnson	.10	.05	.01
☐	433 Hal Morris	.15	.07	.02
☐	434 Tom Henke	.10	.05	.01
☐	435 Shane Mack	.15	.07	.02
☐	436 Mike Piazza	1.50	.65	.19
☐	437 Bret Saberhagen	.15	.07	.02
☐	438 Jose Mesa	.10	.05	.01
☐	439 Jaime Navarro	.10	.05	.01
☐	440 Checklist 367-440 N.L. West Logos	.10	.05	.01
☐	A300 Frank Thomas Leaf 5th Anniversary	5.00	2.30	.60

1994 Leaf Clean-Up Crew

Inserted in magazine jumbo packs at a rate of one in 12, this 12-card set was issued in two series of six. Full-bleed fronts contain an action photo with the Clean-Up Crew logo at bottom right and the player's name in a colored band toward bottom left. The backs contain a photo and 1993 statistics when batting fourth. The home plate area serves as background.

	MINT	EXC	G-VG
COMPLETE SET (12)	50.00	23.00	6.25
COMPLETE SERIES 1 (6)	10.00	4.50	1.25
COMPLETE SERIES 2 (6)	40.00	18.00	5.00
COMMON CARD (1-6)	2.00	.90	.25
COMMON CARD (7-12)	2.00	.90	.25

	MINT	EXC	G-VG
☐ 1 Larry Walker	4.00	1.80	.50
☐ 2 Andres Galarraga	4.00	1.80	.50
☐ 3 Dave Hollins	2.00	.90	.25
☐ 4 Bobby Bonilla	2.00	.90	.25
☐ 5 Cecil Fielder	4.00	1.80	.50
☐ 6 Danny Tartabull	2.00	.90	.25
☐ 7 Juan Gonzalez	12.00	5.50	1.50
☐ 8 Joe Carter	5.00	2.30	.60
☐ 9 Fred McGriff	5.00	2.30	.60
☐ 10 Matt Williams	7.00	3.10	.85
☐ 11 Albert Belle	12.00	5.50	1.50
☐ 12 Harold Baines	2.00	.90	.25

1994 Leaf Gamers

A close-up photo of the player highlights this 12-card set that was issued in two series of six. They were randomly inserted in jumbo packs at a rate of one in eight. The player's name appears at the top of the photo with the Leaf Gamers hologram logo at the bottom. The backs feature a variety of color photos including a frame by frame series resembling a film strip. There is also a small write-up.

	MINT	EXC	G-VG
COMPLETE SET (12)	150.00	70.00	19.00
COMPLETE SERIES 1 (6)	65.00	29.00	8.25
COMPLETE SERIES 2 (6)	85.00	38.00	10.50
COMMON CARD (1-6)	3.00	1.35	.40
COMMON CARD (7-12)	3.00	1.35	.40

	MINT	EXC	G-VG
☐ 1 Ken Griffey Jr.	40.00	18.00	5.00
☐ 2 Lenny Dykstra	3.00	1.35	.40
☐ 3 Juan Gonzalez	12.00	5.50	1.50
☐ 4 Don Mattingly	15.00	6.75	1.90
☐ 5 David Justice	6.00	2.70	.75
☐ 6 Mark Grace	3.00	1.35	.40
☐ 7 Frank Thomas	40.00	18.00	5.00
☐ 8 Barry Bonds	15.00	6.75	1.90
☐ 9 Kirby Puckett	15.00	6.75	1.90
☐ 10 Will Clark	7.00	3.10	.85
☐ 11 John Kruk	3.00	1.35	.40
☐ 12 Mike Piazza	20.00	9.00	2.50

1994 Leaf Gold Rookies

This set, which was randomly inserted in all packs at a rate of one in 18, features ten of the hottest young stars in the majors. A color player cutout is layed over a dark brownish background that contains "94 Gold Leaf Rookie". The player's name and team appear at the bottom in silver. Horizontal backs include career highlights and two photos.

	MINT	EXC	G-VG
COMPLETE SET (20)	35.00	16.00	4.40
COMPLETE SERIES 1 (10)	20.00	9.00	2.50
COMPLETE SERIES 2 (10)	15.00	6.75	1.90
COMMON CARD (1-10)	.60	.25	.08
COMMON CARD (11-20)	.60	.25	.08

	MINT	EXC	G-VG
☐ 1 Javy Lopez	2.50	1.15	.30
☐ 2 Rondell White	2.50	1.15	.30
☐ 3 Butch Huskey	.60	.25	.08
☐ 4 Midre Cummings	1.50	.65	.19
☐ 5 Scott Ruffcorn	1.25	.55	.16

☐ 6 Manny Ramirez	5.00	2.30	.60
☐ 7 Danny Bautista	.60	.25	.08
☐ 8 Russ Davis	.60	.25	.08
☐ 9 Steve Karsay	1.00	.45	.13
☐ 10 Carlos Delgado	4.00	1.80	.50
☐ 11 Bob Hamelin	2.50	1.15	.30
☐ 12 Marcus Moore	.60	.25	.08
☐ 13 Miguel Jimenez	.60	.25	.08
☐ 14 Matt Walbeck	.60	.25	.08
☐ 15 James Mouton	1.00	.45	.13
☐ 16 Rich Becker	1.00	.45	.13
☐ 17 Brian Anderson	3.00	1.35	.40
☐ 18 Cliff Floyd	4.00	1.80	.50
☐ 19 Steve Trachsel	1.50	.65	.19
☐ 20 Hector Carrasco	.60	.25	.08

1994 Leaf Gold Stars

Randomly inserted in all packs at a rate of one in 90, the 15 cards in this set are individually numbered and limited to 10,000 per player. The cards were issued in two series with eight cards in series one and seven in series two. The fronts are bordered by gold and have a green marble appearance with the player appearing within a diamond (outlined in gold) in the card's upper half. The player's name, gold facsimile autograph and team name appear below the photo. The backs are similar to the fronts except for 1993 highlights and the individual numbering. They are numbered "X/10,000".

	MINT	EXC	G-VG
COMPLETE SET (15)	375.00	170.00	47.50
COMPLETE SERIES 1 (8)	200.00	90.00	25.00
COMPLETE SERIES 2 (7)	175.00	80.00	22.00
COMMON CARD (1-8)	10.00	4.50	1.25
COMMON CARD (9-15)	10.00	4.50	1.25

☐ 1 Roberto Alomar	20.00	9.00	2.50
☐ 2 Barry Bonds	35.00	16.00	4.40
☐ 3 David Justice	15.00	6.75	1.90
☐ 4 Ken Griffey Jr.	90.00	40.00	11.50
☐ 5 Lenny Dykstra	10.00	4.50	1.25
☐ 6 Don Mattingly	35.00	16.00	4.40
☐ 7 Andres Galarraga	10.00	4.50	1.25
☐ 8 Greg Maddux	20.00	9.00	2.50
☐ 9 Carlos Baerga	15.00	6.75	1.90
☐ 10 Paul Molitor	15.00	6.75	1.90
☐ 11 Frank Thomas	90.00	40.00	11.50
☐ 12 John Olerud	10.00	4.50	1.25
☐ 13 Juan Gonzalez	30.00	13.50	3.80
☐ 14 Fred McGriff	15.00	6.75	1.90
☐ 15 Jack McDowell	10.00	4.50	1.25

1994 Leaf MVP Contenders

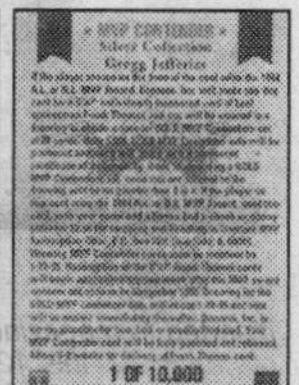

This 30-card set contains 15 players from each league who were projected to be 1994 MVP hopefuls. These unnumbered cards were randomly inserted in all second series packs at a rate of one in 36. If the player appearing on the card was named his league's MVP (Frank Thomas American League and Jeff Bagwell National League), the card could be redeemed for a 5" x 7" Frank Thomas card individually numbered out of 20,000. Also, the collector was entered in a drawing for a special Gold MVP Contenders set. The fronts contain a color player photo with a black and white National or American League logo serving as a background. The backs contain all the rules and read "1 of 10,000". The expiration for redeeming Thomas and Bagwell cards was early February 1995.

	MINT	EXC	G-VG
COMPLETE SET (30)	200.00	90.00	25.00
COMMON AL PLAYER (A1-A15)	2.00	.90	.25
COMMON NL PLAYER (N1-N15)	2.00	.90	.25

☐ A1 Carlos Baerga	4.50	2.00	.55
☐ A2 Albert Belle	10.00	4.50	1.25
☐ A3 Jose Canseco	4.50	2.00	.55
☐ A4 Joe Carter	4.50	2.00	.55
☐ A5 Will Clark	4.50	2.00	.55
☐ A6 Cecil Fielder	2.00	.90	.25
☐ A7 Juan Gonzalez	10.00	4.50	1.25
☐ A8 Ken Griffey Jr.	30.00	13.50	3.80
☐ A9 Paul Molitor	4.50	2.00	.55
☐ A10 Rafael Palmeiro	2.00	.90	.25
☐ A11 Kirby Puckett	12.00	5.50	1.50
☐ A12 Cal Ripken	20.00	9.00	2.50
☐ A13 Frank Thomas	30.00	13.50	3.80
☐ A14 Mo Vaughn	2.00	.90	.25
☐ A15 AL Bonus Card	2.00	.90	.25
☐ N1 Jeff Bagwell	18.00	8.00	2.30
☐ N2 Dante Bichette	2.00	.90	.25
☐ N3 Barry Bonds	12.00	5.50	1.50
☐ N4 Darren Daulton	2.00	.90	.25
☐ N5 Andres Galarraga	2.00	.90	.25
☐ N6 Gregg Jefferies	2.00	.90	.25

☐ N7 Dave Justice	4.50	2.00	.55
☐ N8 Ray Lankford	2.00	.90	.25
☐ N9 Barry Larkin	2.00	.90	.25
☐ N10 Fred McGriff	4.50	2.00	.55
☐ N11 Mike Piazza	15.00	6.75	1.90
☐ N12 Deion Sanders	6.00	2.70	.75
☐ N13 Gary Sheffield	2.00	.90	.25
☐ N14 Matt Williams	6.00	2.70	.75
☐ N15 NL Bonus Card	2.00	.90	.25

1994 Leaf Power Brokers

Inserted in second series retail and hobby foil packs at a rate of one in 12, this 10-card set spotlights top sluggers. Both fronts and backs are horizontal. The fronts have a small player cutout with a black background and "Power Brokers" dominating the card. Fireworks appear within "Power". The backs contain various pie charts that document the player's home run tendencies as far as home vs. away etc. There is also a small photo.

	MINT	EXC	G-VG
COMPLETE SET (10)	25.00	11.50	3.10
COMMON CARD (1-10)	1.00	.45	.13
☐ 1 Frank Thomas	8.00	3.60	1.00
☐ 2 David Justice	1.25	.55	.16
☐ 3 Barry Bonds	3.00	1.35	.40
☐ 4 Juan Gonzalez	2.50	1.15	.30
☐ 5 Ken Griffey Jr.	8.00	3.60	1.00
☐ 6 Mike Piazza	4.00	1.80	.50
☐ 7 Cecil Fielder	1.00	.45	.13
☐ 8 Fred McGriff	1.25	.55	.16
☐ 9 Joe Carter	1.25	.55	.16
☐ 10 Albert Belle	2.50	1.15	.30

1994 Leaf Slideshow

Randomly inserted in first and second series packs at a rate of one in 54, these ten standard-size cards simulate mounted photographic slides, but the images of the players are actually printed on acetate. The color transparencies can be seen best when they are held up to the light. The front of each transparency is framed by a simulated white slide holder, which at its bottom bears the player's name and the game from which the photo was shot. The insert sets's title is shown in blue and merges with the blue-edged bottom. The remaining edges are black. The back, in addition to the appearance of the slide's reverse image, carries comments about the player from Frank Thomas.

	MINT	EXC	G-VG
COMPLETE SET (10)	70.00	32.00	8.75
COMPLETE SERIES 1 (5)	35.00	16.00	4.40
COMPLETE SERIES 2 (5)	35.00	16.00	4.40
COMMON CARD (1-5)	2.00	.90	.25
COMMON CARD (6-10)	2.00	.90	.25
☐ 1 Frank Thomas	20.00	9.00	2.50
☐ 2 Mike Piazza	10.00	4.50	1.25
☐ 3 Darren Daulton	2.00	.90	.25
☐ 4 Ryne Sandberg	7.00	3.10	.85
☐ 5 Roberto Alomar	5.00	2.30	.60
☐ 6 Barry Bonds	8.00	3.60	1.00
☐ 7 Juan Gonzalez	7.00	3.10	.85
☐ 8 Tim Salmon	3.50	1.55	.45
☐ 9 Ken Griffey Jr.	20.00	9.00	2.50
☐ 10 David Justice	3.50	1.55	.45

1994 Leaf Statistical Standouts

Inserted in retail and hobby foil packs at a rate of one in 12, this 10-card set features players that had significant statistical achievements in 1993. For example: Cal Ripken's home run record for a shortstop.

Card fronts contain a player photo that stands out from a background that is the colors of that player's team. The back contains a photo and statistical information.

	MINT	EXC	G-VG
COMPLETE SET (10)	25.00	11.50	3.10
COMMON CARD (1-10)	1.00	.45	.13
☐ 1 Frank Thomas	8.00	3.60	1.00
☐ 2 Barry Bonds	3.00	1.35	.40
☐ 3 Juan Gonzalez	2.50	1.15	.30
☐ 4 Mike Piazza	4.00	1.80	.50
☐ 5 Greg Maddux	2.00	.90	.25
☐ 6 Ken Griffey Jr.	8.00	3.60	1.00
☐ 7 Joe Carter	1.25	.55	.16
☐ 8 Dave Winfield	1.00	.45	.13
☐ 9 Tony Gwynn	2.00	.90	.25
☐ 10 Cal Ripken	6.00	2.70	.75

1994 Leaf Limited

This 160-card standard-size set was issued exclusively to hobby dealers. The fronts display silver holographic Spectra Tech foiling and a silhouetted player action photo over full silver foil. The backs contain silver holographic Spectra Tech foil, two photos, and a quote about the player by well-known baseball personalities. The cards are numbered on the back, grouped alphabetically within teams, and checklisted below alphabetically according to teams for each league as follows: Baltimore Orioles (1-6), Boston Red Sox (7-12), California Angels (13-18), Chicago White Sox (19-25), Cleveland Indians (26-30), Detroit Tigers (31-35), Kansas City Royals (36-41), Milwaukee Brewers (42-47), Minnesota Twins (48-52), New York Yankees (53-58), Oakland Athletics (59-63), Seattle Mariners (64-69), Texas Rangers (70-74), Toronto Blue Jays (75-80), Atlanta Braves (81-88), Chicago Cubs (89-93), Cincinnati Reds (94-99), Colorado Rockies (100-104), Florida Marlins (105-109), Houston Astros (110-115), Los Angeles Dodgers (116-122), Montreal Expos (123-128), New York Mets (129-133), Philadelphia Phillies (134-138), Pittsburgh Pirates (139-143), St. Louis Cardinals (144-149), San Diego Padres (150-154), and San Francisco Giants (155-160). The only Rookie Card is Brian Anderson.

	MINT	EXC	G-VG
COMPLETE SET (160)	175.00	80.00	22.00
COMMON CARD (1-160)	1.00	.45	.13
☐ 1 Jeffrey Hammonds	2.00	.90	.25
☐ 2 Ben McDonald	1.50	.65	.19
☐ 3 Mike Mussina	3.00	1.35	.40
☐ 4 Rafael Palmeiro	2.00	.90	.25
☐ 5 Cal Ripken	15.00	6.75	1.90
☐ 6 Lee Smith	2.00	.90	.25
☐ 7 Roger Clemens	5.00	2.30	.60
☐ 8 Scott Cooper	1.50	.65	.19
☐ 9 Andre Dawson	2.00	.90	.25
☐ 10 Mike Greenwell	1.50	.65	.19
☐ 11 Aaron Sele	2.50	1.15	.30
☐ 12 Mo Vaughn	2.00	.90	.25
☐ 13 Brian Anderson	5.00	2.30	.60
☐ 14 Chad Curtis	1.50	.65	.19
☐ 15 Chili Davis	1.50	.65	.19
☐ 16 Gary DiSarcina	1.00	.45	.13
☐ 17 Mark Langston	2.00	.90	.25
☐ 18 Tim Salmon	3.00	1.35	.40
☐ 19 Wilson Alvarez	2.00	.90	.25
☐ 20 Jason Bere	3.00	1.35	.40
☐ 21 Julio Franco	1.50	.65	.19
☐ 22 Jack McDowell	2.00	.90	.25
☐ 23 Tim Raines	2.00	.90	.25
☐ 24 Frank Thomas	20.00	9.00	2.50
☐ 25 Robin Ventura	1.50	.65	.19
☐ 26 Carlos Baerga	3.00	1.35	.40
☐ 27 Albert Belle	7.00	3.10	.85
☐ 28 Kenny Lofton	5.00	2.30	.60
☐ 29 Eddie Murray	2.00	.90	.25
☐ 30 Manny Ramirez	4.00	1.80	.50
☐ 31 Cecil Fielder	2.00	.90	.25
☐ 32 Travis Fryman	2.00	.90	.25
☐ 33 Mickey Tettleton	1.50	.65	.19
☐ 34 Alan Trammell	2.00	.90	.25
☐ 35 Lou Whitaker	2.00	.90	.25
☐ 36 David Cone	2.00	.90	.25
☐ 37 Gary Gaetti	1.00	.45	.13
☐ 38 Greg Gagne	1.00	.45	.13
☐ 39 Bob Hamelin	2.50	1.15	.30
☐ 40 Wally Joyner	1.50	.65	.19
☐ 41 Brian McRae	1.50	.65	.19
☐ 42 Ricky Bones	1.00	.45	.13
☐ 43 Brian Harper	1.00	.45	.13
☐ 44 John Jaha	1.00	.45	.13
☐ 45 Pat Listach	1.00	.45	.13
☐ 46 Dave Nilsson	1.00	.45	.13
☐ 47 Greg Vaughn	1.50	.65	.19
☐ 48 Kent Hrbek	1.50	.65	.19
☐ 49 Chuck Knoblauch	2.00	.90	.25
☐ 50 Shane Mack	1.50	.65	.19
☐ 51 Kirby Puckett	8.00	3.60	1.00
☐ 52 Dave Winfield	2.00	.90	.25
☐ 53 Jim Abbott	2.00	.90	.25
☐ 54 Wade Boggs	2.00	.90	.25
☐ 55 Jimmy Key	1.50	.65	.19
☐ 56 Don Mattingly	8.00	3.60	1.00
☐ 57 Paul O'Neill	1.50	.65	.19
☐ 58 Danny Tartabull	1.50	.65	.19
☐ 59 Dennis Eckersley	2.00	.90	.25
☐ 60 Rickey Henderson	2.00	.90	.25
☐ 61 Mark McGwire	2.00	.90	.25
☐ 62 Troy Neel	1.50	.65	.19
☐ 63 Ruben Sierra	2.00	.90	.25
☐ 64 Eric Anthony	1.00	.45	.13
☐ 65 Jay Buhner	1.50	.65	.19
☐ 66 Ken Griffey Jr.	20.00	9.00	2.50
☐ 67 Randy Johnson	2.00	.90	.25
☐ 68 Edgar Martinez	1.00	.45	.13
☐ 69 Tino Martinez	1.00	.45	.13

☐	70 Jose Canseco	3.00	1.35	.40
☐	71 Will Clark	3.00	1.35	.40
☐	72 Juan Gonzalez	7.00	3.10	.85
☐	73 Dean Palmer	1.50	.65	.19
☐	74 Ivan Rodriguez	2.00	.90	.25
☐	75 Roberto Alomar	5.00	2.30	.60
☐	76 Joe Carter	3.00	1.35	.40
☐	77 Carlos Delgado	3.00	1.35	.40
☐	78 Paul Molitor	3.00	1.35	.40
☐	79 John Olerud	2.00	.90	.25
☐	80 Devon White	1.00	.45	.13
☐	81 Steve Avery	2.00	.90	.25
☐	82 Tom Glavine	2.00	.90	.25
☐	83 David Justice	3.00	1.35	.40
☐	84 Roberto Kelly	1.00	.45	.13
☐	85 Ryan Klesko	3.50	1.55	.45
☐	86 Javy Lopez	2.50	1.15	.30
☐	87 Greg Maddux	5.00	2.30	.60
☐	88 Fred McGriff	3.00	1.35	.40
☐	89 Shawon Dunston	1.00	.45	.13
☐	90 Mark Grace	2.00	.90	.25
☐	91 Derrick May	1.00	.45	.13
☐	92 Sammy Sosa	2.00	.90	.25
☐	93 Rick Wilkins	1.00	.45	.13
☐	94 Bret Boone	2.00	.90	.25
☐	95 Barry Larkin	2.00	.90	.25
☐	96 Kevin Mitchell	1.50	.65	.19
☐	97 Hal Morris	1.50	.65	.19
☐	98 Deion Sanders	3.50	1.55	.45
☐	99 Reggie Sanders	1.50	.65	.19
☐	100 Dante Bichette	2.00	.90	.25
☐	101 Ellis Burks	1.50	.65	.19
☐	102 Andres Galarraga	2.00	.90	.25
☐	103 Joe Girardi	1.00	.45	.13
☐	104 Charlie Hayes	1.50	.65	.19
☐	105 Chuck Carr	1.00	.45	.13
☐	106 Jeff Conine	2.00	.90	.25
☐	107 Bryan Harvey	1.50	.65	.19
☐	108 Benito Santiago	1.00	.45	.13
☐	109 Gary Sheffield	2.00	.90	.25
☐	110 Jeff Bagwell	10.00	4.50	1.25
☐	111 Craig Biggio	1.50	.65	.19
☐	112 Ken Caminiti	1.50	.65	.19
☐	113 Andujar Cedeno	1.00	.45	.13
☐	114 Doug Drabek	2.00	.90	.25
☐	115 Luis Gonzalez	1.00	.45	.13
☐	116 Brett Butler	1.50	.65	.19
☐	117 Delino DeShields	1.50	.65	.19
☐	118 Eric Karros	1.50	.65	.19
☐	119 Raul Mondesi	7.00	3.10	.85
☐	120 Mike Piazza	10.00	4.50	1.25
☐	121 Henry Rodriguez	1.00	.45	.13
☐	122 Tim Wallach	1.00	.45	.13
☐	123 Moises Alou	2.00	.90	.25
☐	124 Cliff Floyd	3.00	1.35	.40
☐	125 Marquis Grissom	2.00	.90	.25
☐	126 Ken Hill	1.50	.65	.19
☐	127 Larry Walker	2.00	.90	.25
☐	128 John Wetteland	1.00	.45	.13
☐	129 Bobby Bonilla	2.00	.90	.25
☐	130 John Franco	1.00	.45	.13
☐	131 Jeff Kent	1.50	.65	.19
☐	132 Bret Saberhagen	1.50	.65	.19
☐	133 Ryan Thompson	1.50	.65	.19
☐	134 Darren Daulton	2.00	.90	.25
☐	135 Mariano Duncan	1.00	.45	.13
☐	136 Lenny Dykstra	2.00	.90	.25
☐	137 Danny Jackson	1.00	.45	.13
☐	138 John Kruk	1.50	.65	.19
☐	139 Jay Bell	1.50	.65	.19
☐	140 Jeff King	1.00	.45	.13
☐	141 Al Martin	1.00	.45	.13
☐	142 Orlando Merced	1.50	.65	.19
☐	143 Andy Van Slyke	2.00	.90	.25
☐	144 Bernard Gilkey	1.00	.45	.13
☐	145 Gregg Jefferies	2.00	.90	.25
☐	146 Ray Lankford	2.00	.90	.25
☐	147 Ozzie Smith	4.00	1.80	.50
☐	148 Mark Whiten	1.50	.65	.19
☐	149 Todd Zeile	1.50	.65	.19
☐	150 Derek Bell	1.50	.65	.19
☐	151 Andy Benes	1.50	.65	.19
☐	152 Tony Gwynn	5.00	2.30	.60
☐	153 Phil Plantier	1.50	.65	.19
☐	154 Bip Roberts	1.00	.45	.13
☐	155 Rod Beck	1.50	.65	.19
☐	156 Barry Bonds	8.00	3.60	1.00
☐	157 John Burkett	1.50	.65	.19
☐	158 Royce Clayton	1.50	.65	.19
☐	159 Bill Swift	1.00	.45	.13
☐	160 Matt Williams	4.00	1.80	.50

1994 Leaf Limited Gold All-Stars

Randomly inserted in packs at a rate of one in eight, this 18-card standard-size set features the starting players at each position in both the National and American leagues for the 1994 All-Star Game. They are identical in design to the basic Limited product except for being gold and individually numbered out of 10,000.

	MINT	EXC	G-VG
COMPLETE SET (18)	450.00	200.00	57.50
COMMON CARD (1-18)	8.00	3.60	1.00

☐	1 Frank Thomas	90.00	40.00	11.50
☐	2 Gregg Jefferies	12.00	5.50	1.50
☐	3 Roberto Alomar	20.00	9.00	2.50
☐	4 Mariano Duncan	8.00	3.60	1.00
☐	5 Wade Boggs	12.00	5.50	1.50
☐	6 Matt Williams	18.00	8.00	2.30
☐	7 Cal Ripken	65.00	29.00	8.25
☐	8 Ozzie Smith	18.00	8.00	2.30
☐	9 Kirby Puckett	35.00	16.00	4.40
☐	10 Barry Bonds	35.00	16.00	4.40
☐	11 Ken Griffey Jr.	90.00	40.00	11.50
☐	12 Tony Gwynn	20.00	9.00	2.50
☐	13 Joe Carter	14.00	6.25	1.75
☐	14 David Justice	14.00	6.25	1.75
☐	15 Ivan Rodriguez	12.00	5.50	1.50
☐	16 Mike Piazza	45.00	20.00	5.75
☐	17 Jimmy Key	8.00	3.60	1.00
☐	18 Greg Maddux	20.00	9.00	2.50

1994 Leaf Limited Rookies

This 80-card standard-size set was issued exclusively to hobby dealers. The set showcases top rookies and prospects of 1994. The fronts display silver holographic Spectra Tech foiling and a silhouetted player action photo over full silver foil. The word "Rookies" appears in black letters above the Leaf Limited logo at top. The backs contain silver holographic Spectra Tech foil, two photos, and a quote about the player by well-known baseball personalities.

	MINT	EXC	G-VG
COMPLETE SET (80)	75.00	34.00	9.50
COMMON CARD (1-80)	.60	.25	.08

	MINT	EXC	G-VG
☐ 1 Charles Johnson	2.00	.90	.25
☐ 2 Rico Brogna	.60	.25	.08
☐ 3 Melvin Nieves	1.00	.45	.13
☐ 4 Rich Becker	1.00	.45	.13
☐ 5 Russ Davis	1.50	.65	.19
☐ 6 Matt Mieske	.60	.25	.08
☐ 7 Paul Shuey	.60	.25	.08
☐ 8 Hector Carrasco	.60	.25	.08
☐ 9 J.R. Phillips	1.00	.45	.13
☐ 10 Scott Ruffcorn	1.00	.45	.13
☐ 11 Kurt Abbott	1.50	.65	.19
☐ 12 Danny Bautista	.60	.25	.08
☐ 13 Rick White	.60	.25	.08
☐ 14 Steve Dunn	.60	.25	.08
☐ 15 Joe Ausanio	.60	.25	.08
☐ 16 Salomon Torres	.60	.25	.08
☐ 17 Ricky Bottalico	1.25	.55	.16
☐ 18 Johnny Ruffin	.60	.25	.08
☐ 19 Kevin Foster	1.25	.55	.16
☐ 20 William VanLandingham	4.00	1.80	.50
☐ 21 Troy O'Leary	.60	.25	.08
☐ 22 Mark Acre	1.00	.45	.13
☐ 23 Norberto Martin	.60	.25	.08
☐ 24 Jason Jacome	4.00	1.80	.50
☐ 25 Steve Trachsel	2.00	.90	.25
☐ 26 Denny Hocking	.60	.25	.08
☐ 27 Mike Lieberthal	.60	.25	.08
☐ 28 Gerald Williams	.60	.25	.08
☐ 29 John Mabry	2.00	.90	.25
☐ 30 Greg Blosser	.60	.25	.08
☐ 31 Carl Everett	.60	.25	.08
☐ 32 Steve Karsay	1.00	.45	.13
☐ 33 Jose Valentin	.60	.25	.08
☐ 34 Jon Lieber	1.25	.55	.16
☐ 35 Chris Gomez	1.00	.45	.13
☐ 36 Jesus Tavarez	1.00	.45	.13
☐ 37 Tony Longmire	.60	.25	.08
☐ 38 Luis Lopez	.60	.25	.08
☐ 39 Matt Walbeck	.60	.25	.08
☐ 40 Rikkert Faneyte	.60	.25	.08
☐ 41 Shane Reynolds	.60	.25	.08
☐ 42 Joey Hamilton	1.75	.80	.22
☐ 43 Ismael Valdes	1.00	.45	.13
☐ 44 Danny Miceli	.60	.25	.08
☐ 45 Darren Bragg	1.50	.65	.19
☐ 46 Alex Gonzalez	1.50	.65	.19
☐ 47 Rick Helling	.60	.25	.08
☐ 48 Jose Oliva	1.00	.45	.13
☐ 49 Jim Edmonds	.60	.25	.08
☐ 50 Miguel Jimenez	.60	.25	.08
☐ 51 Tony Eusebio	.60	.25	.08
☐ 52 Shawn Green	2.00	.90	.25
☐ 53 Billy Ashley	1.50	.65	.19
☐ 54 Rondell White	1.50	.65	.19
☐ 55 Cory Bailey	1.00	.45	.13
☐ 56 Tim Davis	.60	.25	.08
☐ 57 John Hudek	3.00	1.35	.40
☐ 58 Darren Hall	.60	.25	.08
☐ 59 Darren Dreifort	.60	.25	.08
☐ 60 Mike Kelly	.60	.25	.08
☐ 61 Marcus Moore	.60	.25	.08
☐ 62 Garret Anderson	.60	.25	.08
☐ 63 Brian Hunter	2.00	.90	.25
☐ 64 Mark Smith	.60	.25	.08
☐ 65 Garey Ingram	1.00	.45	.13
☐ 66 Rusty Greer	2.50	1.15	.30
☐ 67 Marc Newfield	1.00	.45	.13
☐ 68 Gar Finnvold	.60	.25	.08
☐ 69 Paul Spoljaric	.60	.25	.08
☐ 70 Ray McDavid	.60	.25	.08
☐ 71 Orlando Miller	.60	.25	.08
☐ 72 Jorge Fabregas	.60	.25	.08
☐ 73 Ray Holbert	.60	.25	.08
☐ 74 Armando Benitez	2.00	.90	.25
☐ 75 Ernie Young	2.00	.90	.25
☐ 76 James Mouton	1.00	.45	.13
☐ 77 Robert Perez	1.25	.55	.16
☐ 78 Chan Ho Park	5.00	2.30	.60
☐ 79 Roger Salkeld	.60	.25	.08
☐ 80 Tony Tarasco	1.00	.45	.13

1994 Leaf Limited Rookies Phenoms

This 10-card set was randomly inserted in Leaf Limited Rookies packs at a rate of approximately of one in eight. Limited to 5,000, the set showcases top 1994 rookies. The fronts are designed much like the

Limited Rookies except the card is comprised of gold foil instead of silver. Gold backs are also virtually identical to the Limited Rookies in terms of content and layout. The cards are individually numbered on back out of 5,000.

	MINT	EXC	G-VG
COMPLETE SET (10)	250.00	115.00	31.00
COMMON CARD (1-10)	12.00	5.50	1.50
☐ 1 Raul Mondesi	50.00	23.00	6.25
☐ 2 Bob Hamelin	15.00	6.75	1.90
☐ 3 Midre Cummings	12.00	5.50	1.50
☐ 4 Carlos Delgado	25.00	11.50	3.10
☐ 5 Cliff Floyd	25.00	11.50	3.10
☐ 6 Jeffrey Hammonds	15.00	6.75	1.90
☐ 7 Ryan Klesko	25.00	11.50	3.10
☐ 8 Javy Lopez	15.00	6.75	1.90
☐ 9 Manny Ramirez	30.00	13.50	3.80
☐ 10 Alex Rodriguez	75.00	34.00	9.50

1991 OPC Premier

The 1991 O-Pee-Chee Premier set contains 132 standard-size (2 1/2" by 3 1/2") cards. The fronts feature color action player photos on a white card face. All the pictures are bordered in gold above, while the color of the border stripes on the other three sides varies from card to card. The player's name, team name, and position (the last item in English and French) appear below the picture. In a horizontal format, the backs have a color head shot and the team logo in a circular format. Biography and statistics (1990 and career) are presented on an orange and yellow striped background. The cards are arranged in alphabetical order and numbered on the back. Small packs of these cards were given out at the Fan Fest to commemorate the 1991 All-Star Game in Canada. Rookie Cards in this set include Jeff Conine.

	MINT	EXC	G-VG
COMPLETE SET (132)	10.00	4.50	1.25
COMPLETE FACT.SET (132)	15.00	6.75	1.90
COMMON CARD (1-132)	.05	.02	.01
☐ 1 Roberto Alomar	.35	.16	.04
☐ 2 Sandy Alomar Jr.	.10	.05	.01
☐ 3 Moises Alou	.25	.11	.03
☐ 4 Brian Barnes	.05	.02	.01
☐ 5 Steve Bedrosian	.05	.02	.01
☐ 6 George Bell	.10	.05	.01
☐ 7 Juan Bell	.05	.02	.01
☐ 8 Albert Belle	.50	.23	.06
☐ 9 Bud Black	.05	.02	.01
☐ 10 Mike Boddicker	.05	.02	.01
☐ 11 Wade Boggs	.15	.07	.02
☐ 12 Barry Bonds	.50	.23	.06
☐ 13 Denis Boucher	.05	.02	.01
☐ 14 George Brett	.30	.14	.04
☐ 15 Hubie Brooks	.05	.02	.01
☐ 16 Brett Butler	.10	.05	.01
☐ 17 Ivan Calderon	.05	.02	.01
☐ 18 Jose Canseco	.25	.11	.03
☐ 19 Gary Carter	.15	.07	.02
☐ 20 Joe Carter	.20	.09	.03
☐ 21 Jack Clark	.10	.05	.01
☐ 22 Will Clark	.25	.11	.03
☐ 23 Roger Clemens	.30	.14	.04
☐ 24 Alex Cole	.05	.02	.01
☐ 25 Vince Coleman	.05	.02	.01
☐ 26 Jeff Conine	.50	.23	.06
☐ 27 Milt Cuyler	.05	.02	.01
☐ 28 Danny Darwin	.05	.02	.01
☐ 29 Eric Davis	.10	.05	.01
☐ 30 Glenn Davis	.05	.02	.01
☐ 31 Andre Dawson	.15	.07	.02
☐ 32 Ken Dayley	.05	.02	.01
☐ 33 Steve Decker	.05	.02	.01
☐ 34 Delino DeShields	.15	.07	.02
☐ 35 Lance Dickson	.05	.02	.01
☐ 36 Kirk Dressendorfer	.05	.02	.01
☐ 37 Shawon Dunston	.05	.02	.01
☐ 38 Dennis Eckersley	.15	.07	.02
☐ 39 Dwight Evans	.10	.05	.01
☐ 40 Howard Farmer	.05	.02	.01
☐ 41 Junior Felix	.05	.02	.01
☐ 42 Alex Fernandez	.25	.11	.03
☐ 43 Tony Fernandez	.10	.05	.01
☐ 44 Cecil Fielder	.15	.07	.02
☐ 45 Carlton Fisk	.15	.07	.02
☐ 46 Willie Fraser	.05	.02	.01
☐ 47 Gary Gaetti	.05	.02	.01
☐ 48 Andres Galarraga	.15	.07	.02
☐ 49 Ron Gant	.10	.05	.01
☐ 50 Kirk Gibson	.10	.05	.01
☐ 51 Bernard Gilkey	.10	.05	.01
☐ 52 Leo Gomez	.10	.05	.01
☐ 53 Rene Gonzales	.05	.02	.01
☐ 54 Juan Gonzalez	1.00	.45	.13
☐ 55 Dwight Gooden	.10	.05	.01
☐ 56 Ken Griffey Jr.	1.50	.65	.19
☐ 57 Kelly Gruber	.05	.02	.01
☐ 58 Pedro Guerrero	.05	.02	.01
☐ 59 Tony Gwynn	.25	.11	.03
☐ 60 Chris Hammond	.05	.02	.01
☐ 61 Ron Hassey	.05	.02	.01
☐ 62 Rickey Henderson 939 Stolen Bases	.15	.07	.02
☐ 63 Tom Henke	.10	.05	.01
☐ 64 Orel Hershiser	.10	.05	.01
☐ 65 Chris Hoiles	.15	.07	.02
☐ 66 Todd Hundley	.10	.05	.01
☐ 67 Pete Incaviglia	.05	.02	.01
☐ 68 Danny Jackson	.05	.02	.01
☐ 69 Barry Jones	.05	.02	.01
☐ 70 David Justice	.35	.16	.04
☐ 71 Jimmy Key	.10	.05	.01
☐ 72 Ray Lankford	.15	.07	.02
☐ 73 Darren Lewis	.10	.05	.01
☐ 74 Kevin Maas	.05	.02	.01
☐ 75 Denny Martinez	.10	.05	.01
☐ 76 Tino Martinez	.10	.05	.01

#	Player	MINT	EXC	G-VG
77	Don Mattingly	.30	.14	.04
78	Willie McGee	.10	.05	.01
79	Fred McGriff	.20	.09	.03
80	Hensley Meulens	.05	.02	.01
81	Kevin Mitchell	.10	.05	.01
82	Paul Molitor	.20	.09	.03
83	Mickey Morandini	.05	.02	.01
84	Jack Morris	.15	.07	.02
85	Dale Murphy	.15	.07	.02
86	Eddie Murray	.15	.07	.02
87	Chris Nabholz	.05	.02	.01
88	Tim Naehring	.05	.02	.01
89	Otis Nixon	.10	.05	.01
90	Jose Offerman	.10	.05	.01
91	Bob Ojeda	.05	.02	.01
92	John Olerud	.20	.09	.03
93	Gregg Olson	.10	.05	.01
94	Dave Parker	.15	.07	.02
95	Terry Pendleton	.15	.07	.02
96	Kirby Puckett	.30	.14	.04
97	Tim Raines	.15	.07	.02
98	Jeff Reardon	.10	.05	.01
99	Dave Righetti	.05	.02	.01
100	Cal Ripken	.50	.23	.06
101	Mel Rojas	.05	.02	.01
102	Nolan Ryan 7th No-Hitter	1.00	.45	.13
103	Ryne Sandberg	.25	.11	.03
104	Scott Sanderson	.05	.02	.01
105	Benny Santiago	.05	.02	.01
106	Pete Schourek	.05	.02	.01
107	Gary Scott	.05	.02	.01
108	Terry Shumpert	.05	.02	.01
109	Ruben Sierra	.15	.07	.02
110	Doug Simons	.05	.02	.01
111	Dave Smith	.05	.02	.01
112	Ozzie Smith	.20	.09	.03
113	Cory Snyder	.05	.02	.01
114	Luis Sojo	.05	.02	.01
115	Dave Stewart	.10	.05	.01
116	Dave Stieb	.15	.07	.02
117	Darryl Strawberry	.15	.07	.02
118	Pat Tabler	.05	.02	.01
119	Wade Taylor	.05	.02	.01
120	Bobby Thigpen	.05	.02	.01
121	Frank Thomas	2.00	.90	.25
122	Mike Timlin	.05	.02	.01
123	Alan Trammell	.15	.07	.02
124	Mo Vaughn	.40	.18	.05
125	Tim Wallach	.10	.05	.01
126	Devon White	.15	.07	.02
127	Mark Whiten	.15	.07	.02
128	Bernie Williams	.10	.05	.01
129	Willie Wilson	.05	.02	.01
130	Dave Winfield	.15	.07	.02
131	Robin Yount	.20	.09	.03
132	Checklist 1-132	.05	.02	.01

1992 OPC Premier

The 1992 O-Pee-Chee Premier baseball set consists of 198 cards, each measuring the standard-size (2 1/2" by 3 1/2"). The fronts feature a mix of color action and posed player photos bordered in white. Gold stripes edge the picture on top and below, while colored stripes edge the pictures on the left and right sides. The player's name, position, and team appear in the

bottom white border. In addition to a color head shot, the backs carry biography and the team logo on a panel that shades from green to blue as well as statistics on a black panel. The cards are numbered on the back. The most notable Rookie Card in the set is Rod Beck.

	MINT	EXC	G-VG
COMPLETE SET (198)	10.00	4.50	1.25
COMPLETE FACT.SET (198)	15.00	6.75	1.90
COMMON CARD (1-198)	.05	.02	.01

#	Player	MINT	EXC	G-VG
1	Wade Boggs	.15	.07	.02
2	John Smiley	.05	.02	.01
3	Checklist 1-99	.05	.02	.01
4	Ron Gant	.10	.05	.01
5	Mike Bordick	.05	.02	.01
6	Charlie Hayes	.10	.05	.01
7	Kevin Morton	.05	.02	.01
8	Checklist 100-198	.05	.02	.01
9	Chris Gwynn	.05	.02	.01
10	Melido Perez	.05	.02	.01
11	Dan Gladden	.05	.02	.01
12	Brian McRae	.15	.07	.02
13	Dennis Martinez	.10	.05	.01
14	Bob Scanlan	.05	.02	.01
15	Julio Franco	.10	.05	.01
16	Ruben Amaro	.05	.02	.01
17	Mo Sanford	.05	.02	.01
18	Scott Bankhead	.05	.02	.01
19	Dickie Thon	.05	.02	.01
20	Chris James	.05	.02	.01
21	Mike Huff	.05	.02	.01
22	Orlando Merced	.10	.05	.01
23	Chris Sabo	.05	.02	.01
24	Jose Canseco	.20	.09	.03
25	Reggie Sanders	.20	.09	.03
26	Chris Nabholz	.05	.02	.01
27	Kevin Seitzer	.05	.02	.01
28	Ryan Bowen	.05	.02	.01
29	Gary Carter	.15	.07	.02
30	Wayne Rosenthal	.05	.02	.01
31	Alan Trammell	.15	.07	.02
32	Doug Drabek	.15	.07	.02
33	Craig Shipley	.05	.02	.01
34	Ryne Sandberg	.30	.14	.04
35	Chuck Knoblauch	.15	.07	.02
36	Bret Barberie	.10	.05	.01
37	Tim Naehring	.05	.02	.01
38	Omar Olivares	.05	.02	.01
39	Royce Clayton	.15	.07	.02
40	Brent Mayne	.05	.02	.01
41	Darrin Fletcher	.10	.05	.01
42	Howard Johnson	.10	.05	.01
43	Steve Sax	.05	.02	.01
44	Greg Swindell	.05	.02	.01
45	Andre Dawson	.15	.07	.02
46	Kent Hrbek	.10	.05	.01

☐ 47	Dwight Gooden	.10	.05	.01
☐ 48	Mark Leiter	.05	.02	.01
☐ 49	Tom Glavine	.15	.07	.02
☐ 50	Mo Vaughn	.20	.09	.03
☐ 51	Doug Jones	.05	.02	.01
☐ 52	Brian Barnes	.05	.02	.01
☐ 53	Rob Dibble	.05	.02	.01
☐ 54	Kevin McReynolds	.05	.02	.01
☐ 55	Ivan Rodriguez	.15	.07	.02
☐ 56	Scott Livingstone UER (Photo actually Travis Fryman)	.05	.02	.01
☐ 57	Mike Magnante	.05	.02	.01
☐ 58	Pete Schourek	.05	.02	.01
☐ 59	Frank Thomas	1.50	.65	.19
☐ 60	Kirk McCaskill	.05	.02	.01
☐ 61	Wally Joyner	.10	.05	.01
☐ 62	Rick Aguilera	.10	.05	.01
☐ 63	Eric Karros	.15	.07	.02
☐ 64	Tino Martinez	.05	.02	.01
☐ 65	Bryan Hickerson	.05	.02	.01
☐ 66	Ruben Sierra	.15	.07	.02
☐ 67	Willie Randolph	.10	.05	.01
☐ 68	Bill Landrum	.05	.02	.01
☐ 69	Bip Roberts	.05	.02	.01
☐ 70	Cecil Fielder	.15	.07	.02
☐ 71	Pat Kelly	.10	.05	.01
☐ 72	Kenny Lofton	1.25	.55	.16
☐ 73	John Franco	.05	.02	.01
☐ 74	Phil Plantier	.15	.07	.02
☐ 75	Dave Martinez	.05	.02	.01
☐ 76	Warren Newson	.05	.02	.01
☐ 77	Chito Martinez	.05	.02	.01
☐ 78	Brian Hunter	.05	.02	.01
☐ 79	Jack Morris	.15	.07	.02
☐ 80	Eric King	.05	.02	.01
☐ 81	Nolan Ryan	1.00	.45	.13
☐ 82	Bret Saberhagen	.10	.05	.01
☐ 83	Roberto Kelly	.10	.05	.01
☐ 84	Ozzie Smith	.20	.09	.03
☐ 85	Chuck McElroy	.05	.02	.01
☐ 86	Carlton Fisk	.15	.07	.02
☐ 87	Mike Mussina	.30	.14	.04
☐ 88	Mark Carreon	.05	.02	.01
☐ 89	Ken Hill	.10	.05	.01
☐ 90	Rick Cerone	.05	.02	.01
☐ 91	Deion Sanders	.25	.11	.03
☐ 92	Don Mattingly	.35	.16	.04
☐ 93	Danny Tartabull	.10	.05	.01
☐ 94	Keith Miller	.05	.02	.01
☐ 95	Gregg Jefferies	.15	.07	.02
☐ 96	Barry Larkin	.15	.07	.02
☐ 97	Kevin Mitchell	.10	.05	.01
☐ 98	Rick Sutcliffe	.10	.05	.01
☐ 99	Mark McGwire	.15	.07	.02
☐ 100	Albert Belle	.40	.18	.05
☐ 101	Gregg Olson	.05	.02	.01
☐ 102	Kirby Puckett	.35	.16	.04
☐ 103	Luis Gonzalez	.10	.05	.01
☐ 104	Randy Myers	.10	.05	.01
☐ 105	Roger Clemens	.25	.11	.03
☐ 106	Tony Gwynn	.25	.11	.03
☐ 107	Jeff Bagwell	.75	.35	.09
☐ 108	John Wetteland	.05	.02	.01
☐ 109	Bernie Williams	.10	.05	.01
☐ 110	Scott Kamieniecki	.05	.02	.01
☐ 111	Robin Yount	.20	.09	.03
☐ 112	Dean Palmer	.10	.05	.01
☐ 113	Tim Belcher	.05	.02	.01
☐ 114	George Brett	.30	.14	.04
☐ 115	Frank Viola	.10	.05	.01
☐ 116	Kelly Gruber	.05	.02	.01
☐ 117	David Justice	.25	.11	.03
☐ 118	Scott Leius	.05	.02	.01
☐ 119	Jeff Fassero	.05	.02	.01
☐ 120	Sammy Sosa	.15	.07	.02
☐ 121	Al Osuna	.05	.02	.01
☐ 122	Wilson Alvarez	.05	.02	.01
☐ 123	Jose Offerman	.10	.05	.01
☐ 124	Mel Rojas	.05	.02	.01
☐ 125	Shawon Dunston	.05	.02	.01
☐ 126	Pete Incaviglia	.05	.02	.01
☐ 127	Von Hayes	.05	.02	.01
☐ 128	Dave Gallagher	.05	.02	.01
☐ 129	Eric Davis	.05	.02	.01
☐ 130	Roberto Alomar	.25	.11	.03
☐ 131	Mike Gallego	.05	.02	.01
☐ 132	Robin Ventura	.15	.07	.02
☐ 133	Bill Swift	.10	.05	.01
☐ 134	John Kruk	.15	.07	.02
☐ 135	Craig Biggio	.10	.05	.01
☐ 136	Eddie Taubensee	.05	.02	.01
☐ 137	Cal Ripken	.40	.18	.05
☐ 138	Charles Nagy	.05	.02	.01
☐ 139	Jose Melendez	.05	.02	.01
☐ 140	Jim Abbott	.15	.07	.02
☐ 141	Paul Molitor	.20	.09	.03
☐ 142	Tom Candiotti	.05	.02	.01
☐ 143	Bobby Bonilla	.15	.07	.02
☐ 144	Matt Williams	.20	.09	.03
☐ 145	Brett Butler	.10	.05	.01
☐ 146	Will Clark	.20	.09	.03
☐ 147	Rickey Henderson	.15	.07	.02
☐ 148	Ray Lankford	.15	.07	.02
☐ 149	Bill Pecota	.05	.02	.01
☐ 150	Dave Winfield	.15	.07	.02
☐ 151	Darren Lewis	.10	.05	.01
☐ 152	Bob MacDonald	.05	.02	.01
☐ 153	David Segui	.05	.02	.01
☐ 154	Benny Santiago	.05	.02	.01
☐ 155	Chuck Finley	.05	.02	.01
☐ 156	Andujar Cedeno	.10	.05	.01
☐ 157	Barry Bonds	.40	.18	.05
☐ 158	Joe Grahe	.05	.02	.01
☐ 159	Frank Castillo	.05	.02	.01
☐ 160	Dave Burba	.05	.02	.01
☐ 161	Leo Gomez	.05	.02	.01
☐ 162	Orel Hershiser	.10	.05	.01
☐ 163	Delino DeShields	.15	.07	.02
☐ 164	Sandy Alomar Jr.	.10	.05	.01
☐ 165	Denny Neagle	.05	.02	.01
☐ 166	Fred McGriff	.20	.09	.03
☐ 167	Ken Griffey Jr.	1.50	.65	.19
☐ 168	Juan Guzman	.10	.05	.01
☐ 169	Bobby Rose	.05	.02	.01
☐ 170	Steve Avery	.15	.07	.02
☐ 171	Rich DeLucia	.05	.02	.01
☐ 172	Mike Timlin	.05	.02	.01
☐ 173	Randy Johnson	.15	.07	.02
☐ 174	Paul Gibson	.05	.02	.01
☐ 175	David Cone	.15	.07	.02
☐ 176	Marquis Grissom	.15	.07	.02
☐ 177	Kurt Stillwell	.05	.02	.01
☐ 178	Mark Whiten	.10	.05	.01
☐ 179	Darryl Strawberry	.10	.05	.01
☐ 180	Mike Morgan	.05	.02	.01
☐ 181	Scott Scudder	.05	.02	.01
☐ 182	George Bell	.15	.07	.02
☐ 183	Alvin Davis	.05	.02	.01
☐ 184	Len Dykstra	.15	.07	.02
☐ 185	Kyle Abbott	.05	.02	.01
☐ 186	Chris Haney	.05	.02	.01
☐ 187	Junior Noboa	.05	.02	.01
☐ 188	Dennis Eckersley	.15	.07	.02
☐ 189	Derek Bell	.10	.05	.01
☐ 190	Lee Smith	.15	.07	.02

		MINT	EXC	G-VG
☐ 191	Andres Galarraga	.15	.07	.02
☐ 192	Jack Armstrong	.05	.02	.01
☐ 193	Eddie Murray	.15	.07	.02
☐ 194	Joe Carter	.20	.09	.03
☐ 195	Terry Pendleton	.15	.07	.02
☐ 196	Darryl Kile	.10	.05	.01
☐ 197	Rod Beck	.30	.14	.04
☐ 198	Hubie Brooks	.05	.02	.01

1993 O-Pee-Chee

The 1993 O-Pee-Chee baseball set consists of 396 cards measuring the standard size (2 1/2" by 3 1/2"). This is the first year that the regular series differs from the series that Topps issued. The set was sold in wax packs with eight cards plus a random insert card from either a four-card World Series Heroes subset or an 18-card World Series Champions subset. The fronts features color action player photos with white borders. The player's name appears in a silver stripe across the bottom that overlaps the O-Pee-Chee logo. The backs display color close-ups next to a panel containing biographical data. The panel and a stripe at the bottom reflect the team colors. A white box in the center of the card contains statistics and bilingual (English and French) career highlights. The cards are numbered on the back. The only noteworthy Rookie Card in this set is David Hulse.

		MINT	EXC	G-VG
	COMPLETE SET (396)	50.00	23.00	6.25
	COMMON CARD (1-396)	.10	.05	.01
☐ 1	Jim Abbott Now with Yankees, 12/6/92	.30	.14	.04
☐ 2	Eric Anthony	.10	.05	.01
☐ 3	Harold Baines	.20	.09	.03
☐ 4	Roberto Alomar	1.00	.45	.13
☐ 5	Steve Avery	.30	.14	.04
☐ 6	James Austin	.10	.05	.01
☐ 7	Mark Wohlers	.10	.05	.01
☐ 8	Steve Buechele	.10	.05	.01
☐ 9	Pedro Astacio	.20	.09	.03
☐ 10	Moises Alou	.20	.09	.03
☐ 11	Rod Beck	.30	.14	.04
☐ 12	Sandy Alomar	.20	.09	.03
☐ 13	Bret Boone	.30	.14	.04
☐ 14	Bryan Harvey	.20	.09	.03
☐ 15	Bobby Bonilla	.30	.14	.04
☐ 16	Brady Anderson	.20	.09	.03
☐ 17	Andy Benes	.20	.09	.03
☐ 18	Ruben Amaro	.10	.05	.01
☐ 19	Jay Bell	.20	.09	.03
☐ 20	Kevin Brown	.10	.05	.01
☐ 21	Scott Bankhead Now with Red Sox, 12/8/92	.10	.05	.01
☐ 22	Denis Boucher	.10	.05	.01
☐ 23	Kevin Appier	.20	.09	.03
☐ 24	Pat Kelly	.10	.05	.01
☐ 25	Rick Aguilera	.20	.09	.03
☐ 26	George Bell	.20	.09	.03
☐ 27	Steve Farr	.10	.05	.01
☐ 28	Chad Curtis	.30	.14	.04
☐ 29	Jeff Bagwell	2.00	.90	.25
☐ 30	Lance Blankenship	.10	.05	.01
☐ 31	Derek Bell	.20	.09	.03
☐ 32	Damon Berryhill	.10	.05	.01
☐ 33	Ricky Bones	.10	.05	.01
☐ 34	Rheal Cormier	.10	.05	.01
☐ 35	Andre Dawson Now with Red Sox, 12/2/92	.30	.14	.04
☐ 36	Brett Butler	.10	.05	.01
☐ 37	Sean Berry	.10	.05	.01
☐ 38	Bud Black	.10	.05	.01
☐ 39	Carlos Baerga	.60	.25	.08
☐ 40	Jay Buhner	.20	.09	.03
☐ 41	Charlie Hough	.20	.09	.03
☐ 42	Sid Fernandez	.10	.05	.01
☐ 43	Luis Mercedes	.10	.05	.01
☐ 44	Jerald Clark Now with Rockies, 11/17/92	.10	.05	.01
☐ 45	Wes Chamberlain	.10	.05	.01
☐ 46	Barry Bonds Now with Giants, 12/8/92	1.50	.65	.19
☐ 47	Jose Canseco	.60	.25	.08
☐ 48	Tim Belcher	.10	.05	.01
☐ 49	David Nied	.30	.14	.04
☐ 50	George Brett	1.50	.65	.19
☐ 51	Cecil Fielder	.30	.14	.04
☐ 52	Chili Davis Now with Angels, 12/11/92	.20	.09	.03
☐ 53	Alex Fernandez	.30	.14	.04
☐ 54	Charlie Hayes Now with Rockies, 11/17/92	.20	.09	.03
☐ 55	Rob Ducey	.10	.05	.01
☐ 56	Craig Biggio	.20	.09	.03
☐ 57	Mike Bordick	.10	.05	.01
☐ 58	Pat Borders	.10	.05	.01
☐ 59	Jeff Blauser	.20	.09	.03
☐ 60	Chris Bosio Now with Mariners, 12/3/92	.10	.05	.01
☐ 61	Bernard Gilkey	.20	.09	.03
☐ 62	Shawon Dunston	.10	.05	.01
☐ 63	Tom Candiotti	.10	.05	.01
☐ 64	Darrin Fletcher	.10	.05	.01
☐ 65	Jeff Brantley	.10	.05	.01
☐ 66	Albert Belle	1.25	.55	.16
☐ 67	Dave Fleming	.10	.05	.01
☐ 68	John Franco	.10	.05	.01
☐ 69	Glenn Davis	.10	.05	.01
☐ 70	Tony Fernandez Now with Mets, 10/26/92	.10	.05	.01
☐ 71	Darren Daulton	.30	.14	.04
☐ 72	Doug Drabek	.30	.14	.04

Now with Astros,
12/1/92
☐ 73 Julio Franco .20 .09 .03
☐ 74 Tom Browning .10 .05 .01
☐ 75 Tom Gordon .10 .05 .01
☐ 76 Travis Fryman .30 .14 .04
☐ 77 Scott Erickson .10 .05 .01
☐ 78 Carlton Fisk .30 .14 .04
☐ 79 Roberto Kelly .20 .09 .03
Now with Reds,
11/3/92
☐ 80 Gary DiSarcina .10 .05 .01
☐ 81 Ken Caminiti .10 .05 .01
☐ 82 Ron Darling .10 .05 .01
☐ 83 Joe Carter .60 .25 .08
☐ 84 Sid Bream .10 .05 .01
☐ 85 Cal Eldred .20 .09 .03
☐ 86 Mark Grace .30 .14 .04
☐ 87 Eric Davis .10 .05 .01
☐ 88 Ivan Calderon .10 .05 .01
Now with Red Sox,
12/8/92
☐ 89 John Burkett .20 .09 .03
☐ 90 Felix Fermin .10 .05 .01
☐ 91 Ken Griffey Jr. 4.00 1.80 .50
☐ 92 Dwight Gooden .10 .05 .01
☐ 93 Mike Devereaux .20 .09 .03
☐ 94 Tony Gwynn .75 .35 .09
☐ 95 Mariano Duncan .10 .05 .01
☐ 96 Jeff King .10 .05 .01
☐ 97 Juan Gonzalez 1.25 .55 .16
☐ 98 Norm Charlton .10 .05 .01
Now with Mariners,
11/17/92
☐ 99 Mark Gubicza .10 .05 .01
☐ 100 Danny Gladden .10 .05 .01
☐ 101 Greg Gagne .10 .05 .01
Now with Royals,
12/8/92
☐ 102 Ozzie Guillen .10 .05 .01
☐ 103 Don Mattingly 1.50 .65 .19
☐ 104 Damion Easley .20 .09 .03
☐ 105 Casey Candaele .10 .05 .01
☐ 106 Dennis Eckersley .30 .14 .04
☐ 107 David Cone .30 .14 .04
Now with Royals,
12/8/92
☐ 108 Ron Gant .20 .09 .03
☐ 109 Mike Fetters .10 .05 .01
☐ 110 Mike Harkey .10 .05 .01
☐ 111 Kevin Gross .10 .05 .01
☐ 112 Archi Cianfrocco .10 .05 .01
☐ 113 Will Clark .60 .25 .08
☐ 114 Glenallen Hill .10 .05 .01
☐ 115 Erik Hanson .10 .05 .01
☐ 116 Todd Hundley .10 .05 .01
☐ 117 Leo Gomez .10 .05 .01
☐ 118 Bruce Hurst .10 .05 .01
☐ 119 Len Dykstra .30 .14 .04
☐ 120 Jose Lind .10 .05 .01
Now with Royals,
11/19/92
☐ 121 Jose Guzman .10 .05 .01
Now with Cubs,
12/1/92
☐ 122 Rob Dibble .10 .05 .01
☐ 123 Gregg Jefferies .30 .14 .04
☐ 124 Bill Gullickson .10 .05 .01
☐ 125 Brian Harper .10 .05 .01
☐ 126 Roberto Hernandez .10 .05 .01
☐ 127 Sam Militello .10 .05 .01
☐ 128 Junior Felix .10 .05 .01
Now with Marlins,
11/17/92
☐ 129 Andujar Cedeno .20 .09 .03
☐ 130 Rickey Henderson .30 .14 .04
☐ 131 Bob MacDonald .10 .05 .01
☐ 132 Tom Glavine .30 .14 .04
☐ 133 Scott Fletcher .10 .05 .01
Now with Red Sox,
11/30/92
☐ 134 Brian Jordan .20 .09 .03
☐ 135 Greg Maddux .75 .35 .09
Now with Braves,
12/9/92
☐ 136 Orel Hershiser .20 .09 .03
☐ 137 Greg Colbrunn .10 .05 .01
☐ 138 Royce Clayton .20 .09 .03
☐ 139 Thomas Howard .10 .05 .01
☐ 140 Randy Johnson .30 .14 .04
☐ 141 Jeff Innis .10 .05 .01
☐ 142 Chris Hoiles .20 .09 .03
☐ 143 Darrin Jackson .10 .05 .01
☐ 144 Tommy Greene .10 .05 .01
☐ 145 Mike LaValliere .10 .05 .01
☐ 146 David Hulse .10 .05 .01
☐ 147 Barry Larkin .30 .14 .04
☐ 148 Wally Joyner .20 .09 .03
☐ 149 Mike Henneman .10 .05 .01
☐ 150 Kent Hrbek .20 .09 .03
☐ 151 Bo Jackson .30 .14 .04
☐ 152 Rich Monteleone .10 .05 .01
☐ 153 Chuck Finley .10 .05 .01
☐ 154 Steve Finley .10 .05 .01
☐ 155 Dave Henderson .10 .05 .01
☐ 156 Kelly Gruber .10 .05 .01
Now with Angels,
12/8/92
☐ 157 Brian Hunter .10 .05 .01
☐ 158 Darryl Hamilton .10 .05 .01
☐ 159 Derrick May .20 .09 .03
☐ 160 Jay Howell .10 .05 .01
☐ 161 Wil Cordero .30 .14 .04
☐ 162 Bryan Hickerson .10 .05 .01
☐ 163 Reggie Jefferson .10 .05 .01
☐ 164 Edgar Martinez .10 .05 .01
☐ 165 Nigel Wilson .30 .14 .04
☐ 166 Howard Johnson .10 .05 .01
☐ 167 Tim Hulett .10 .05 .01
☐ 168 Mike Maddux .10 .05 .01
Now with Mets,
12/17/92
☐ 169 Dave Hollins .30 .14 .04
☐ 170 Zane Smith .10 .05 .01
☐ 171 Rafael Palmeiro .30 .14 .04
☐ 172 Dave Martinez .10 .05 .01
Now with Giants,
12/9/92
☐ 173 Rusty Meacham .10 .05 .01
☐ 174 Mark Leiter .10 .05 .01
☐ 175 Chuck Knoblauch .30 .14 .04
☐ 176 Lance Johnson .10 .05 .01
☐ 177 Matt Nokes .10 .05 .01
☐ 178 Luis Gonzalez .20 .09 .03
☐ 179 Jack Morris .20 .09 .03
☐ 180 David Justice .60 .25 .08
☐ 181 Doug Henry .10 .05 .01
☐ 182 Felix Jose .10 .05 .01
☐ 183 Delino DeShields .20 .09 .03
☐ 184 Rene Gonzales .10 .05 .01
☐ 185 Pete Harnisch .10 .05 .01
☐ 186 Mike Moore .10 .05 .01
Now with Tigers,
12/9/92
☐ 187 Juan Guzman .10 .05 .01
☐ 188 John Olerud .30 .14 .04
☐ 189 Ryan Klesko 1.25 .55 .16

☐ 190 John Jaha	.10	.05	.01
☐ 191 Ray Lankford	.30	.14	.04
☐ 192 Jeff Fassero	.10	.05	.01
☐ 193 Darren Lewis	.20	.09	.03
☐ 194 Mark Lewis	.10	.05	.01
☐ 195 Alan Mills	.10	.05	.01
☐ 196 Wade Boggs Now with Yankees, 12/15/92	.30	.14	.04
☐ 197 Hal Morris	.20	.09	.03
☐ 198 Ron Karkovice	.10	.05	.01
☐ 199 Joe Grahe	.10	.05	.01
☐ 200 Butch Henry Now with Rockies, 11/17/92	.10	.05	.01
☐ 201 Mark McGwire	.30	.14	.04
☐ 202 Tom Henke Now with Rangers, 12/15/92	.20	.09	.03
☐ 203 Ed Sprague	.10	.05	.01
☐ 204 Charlie Leibrandt Now with Rangers, 12/9/92	.10	.05	.01
☐ 205 Pat Listach	.20	.09	.03
☐ 206 Omar Olivares	.10	.05	.01
☐ 207 Mike Morgan	.10	.05	.01
☐ 208 Eric Karros	.20	.09	.03
☐ 209 Marquis Grissom	.30	.14	.04
☐ 210 Willie McGee	.10	.05	.01
☐ 211 Derek Lilliquist	.10	.05	.01
☐ 212 Tino Martinez	.10	.05	.01
☐ 213 Jeff Kent	.30	.14	.04
☐ 214 Mike Mussina	.75	.35	.09
☐ 215 Randy Myers Now with Cubs, 12/9/92	.10	.05	.01
☐ 216 John Kruk	.30	.14	.04
☐ 217 Tom Brunansky	.10	.05	.01
☐ 218 Paul O'Neill Now with Yankees, 11/3/92	.20	.09	.03
☐ 219 Scott Livingstone	.10	.05	.01
☐ 220 John Valentin	.20	.09	.03
☐ 221 Eddie Zosky	.10	.05	.01
☐ 222 Pete Smith	.10	.05	.01
☐ 223 Bill Wegman	.10	.05	.01
☐ 224 Todd Zeile	.20	.09	.03
☐ 225 Tim Wallach Now with Dodgers, 12/24/92	.10	.05	.01
☐ 226 Mitch Williams	.20	.09	.03
☐ 227 Tim Wakefield	.10	.05	.01
☐ 228 Frank Viola	.20	.09	.03
☐ 229 Nolan Ryan	4.00	1.80	.50
☐ 230 Kirk McCaskill	.10	.05	.01
☐ 231 Melido Perez	.10	.05	.01
☐ 232 Mark Langston	.30	.14	.04
☐ 233 Xavier Hernandez	.10	.05	.01
☐ 234 Jerry Browne	.10	.05	.01
☐ 235 Dave Stieb Now with White Sox, 12/8/92	.10	.05	.01
☐ 236 Mark Lemke	.10	.05	.01
☐ 237 Paul Molitor Now with Blue Jays, 12/7/92	.60	.25	.08
☐ 238 Geronimo Pena	.10	.05	.01
☐ 239 Ken Hill	.20	.09	.03
☐ 240 Jack Clark	.20	.09	.03
☐ 241 Greg Myers	.10	.05	.01
☐ 242 Pete Incaviglia Now with Phillies, 12/8/92	.10	.05	.01
☐ 243 Ruben Sierra	.30	.14	.04
☐ 244 Todd Stottlemyre	.10	.05	.01
☐ 245 Pat Hentgen	.20	.09	.03
☐ 246 Melvin Nieves	.30	.14	.04
☐ 247 Jaime Navarro	.10	.05	.01
☐ 248 Donovan Osborne	.10	.05	.01
☐ 249 Brian Barnes	.10	.05	.01
☐ 250 Cory Snyder Now with Dodgers, 12/5/92	.10	.05	.01
☐ 251 Kenny Lofton	1.00	.45	.13
☐ 252 Kevin Mitchell Now with Reds, 11/17/92	.20	.09	.03
☐ 253 Dave Magadan Now with Marlins, 12/8/92	.10	.05	.01
☐ 254 Ben McDonald	.20	.09	.03
☐ 255 Fred McGriff	.50	.23	.06
☐ 256 Mickey Morandini	.10	.05	.01
☐ 257 Randy Tomlin	.10	.05	.01
☐ 258 Dean Palmer	.20	.09	.03
☐ 259 Roger Clemens	.75	.35	.09
☐ 260 Joe Oliver	.10	.05	.01
☐ 261 Jeff Montgomery	.20	.09	.03
☐ 262 Tony Phillips	.10	.05	.01
☐ 263 Shane Mack	.20	.09	.03
☐ 264 Jack McDowell	.30	.14	.04
☐ 265 Mike Macfarlane	.10	.05	.01
☐ 266 Luis Polonia	.10	.05	.01
☐ 267 Doug Jones	.10	.05	.01
☐ 268 Terry Steinbach	.20	.09	.03
☐ 269 Jimmy Key Now with Yankees, 12/10/92	.20	.09	.03
☐ 270 Pat Tabler	.10	.05	.01
☐ 271 Otis Nixon	.10	.05	.01
☐ 272 Dave Nilsson	.20	.09	.03
☐ 273 Tom Pagnozzi	.10	.05	.01
☐ 274 Ryne Sandberg	1.25	.55	.16
☐ 275 Ramon Martinez	.20	.09	.03
☐ 276 Tim Laker	.10	.05	.01
☐ 277 Bill Swift	.10	.05	.01
☐ 278 Charles Nagy	.10	.05	.01
☐ 279 Harold Reynolds Now with Orioles, 12/11/92	.10	.05	.01
☐ 280 Eddie Murray	.30	.14	.04
☐ 281 Gregg Olson	.10	.05	.01
☐ 282 Frank Seminara	.10	.05	.01
☐ 283 Terry Mulholland	.10	.05	.01
☐ 284 Kevin Reimer Now with Brewers, 11/17/92	.10	.05	.01
☐ 285 Mike Greenwell	.20	.09	.03
☐ 286 Jose Rijo	.20	.09	.03
☐ 287 Brian McRae	.30	.14	.04
☐ 288 Frank Tanana Now with Mets, 12/10/92	.10	.05	.01
☐ 289 Pedro Munoz	.10	.05	.01
☐ 290 Tim Raines	.30	.14	.04
☐ 291 Andy Stankiewicz	.10	.05	.01
☐ 292 Tim Salmon	.75	.35	.09
☐ 293 Jimmy Jones	.10	.05	.01
☐ 294 Dave Stewart Now with Blue Jays, 12/8/92	.20	.09	.03
☐ 295 Mike Timlin	.10	.05	.01
☐ 296 Greg Olson	.10	.05	.01
☐ 297 Dan Plesac Now with Cubs, 21/8/92	.10	.05	.01

□ 298 Mike Perez .10 .05 .01
□ 299 Jose Offerman .10 .05 .01
□ 300 Denny Martinez .20 .09 .03
□ 301 Robby Thompson .10 .05 .01
□ 302 Bret Saberhagen .20 .09 .03
□ 303 Joe Orsulak .10 .05 .01
Now with Mets,
12/18/92
□ 304 Tim Naehring .10 .05 .01
□ 305 Bip Roberts .10 .05 .01
□ 306 Kirby Puckett 1.50 .65 .19
□ 307 Steve Sax .10 .05 .01
□ 308 Danny Tartabull .20 .09 .03
□ 309 Jeff Juden .10 .05 .01
□ 310 Duane Ward .20 .09 .03
□ 311 Alejandro Pena .10 .05 .01
Now with Pirates,
12/10/92
□ 312 Kevin Seitzer .10 .05 .01
□ 313 Ozzie Smith .75 .35 .09
□ 314 Mike Piazza 4.00 1.80 .50
□ 315 Chris Nabholz .10 .05 .01
□ 316 Tony Pena .10 .05 .01
□ 317 Gary Sheffield .30 .14 .04
□ 318 Mark Portugal .10 .05 .01
□ 319 Walt Weiss .10 .05 .01
Now with Marlins,
11/17/92
□ 320 Manny Lee .10 .05 .01
Now with Rangers,
12/19/92
□ 321 David Wells .10 .05 .01
□ 322 Terry Pendleton .30 .14 .04
□ 323 Billy Spiers .10 .05 .01
□ 324 Lee Smith .30 .14 .04
□ 325 Bob Scanlan .10 .05 .01
□ 326 Mike Scioscia .10 .05 .01
□ 327 Spike Owen .10 .05 .01
Now with Yankees,
12/4/92
□ 328 Mackey Sasser .10 .05 .01
Now with Mariners,
12/23/92
□ 329 Arthur Rhodes .10 .05 .01
□ 330 Ben Rivera .10 .05 .01
□ 331 Ivan Rodriguez .10 .05 .01
□ 332 Phil Plantier .20 .09 .03
Now with Padres,
12/10/92
□ 333 Chris Sabo .10 .05 .01
□ 334 Mickey Tettleton .20 .09 .03
□ 335 John Smiley .10 .05 .01
Now with Reds,
11/30/92
□ 336 Bobby Thigpen .10 .05 .01
□ 337 Randy Velarde .10 .05 .01
□ 338 Luis Sojo .10 .05 .01
Now with Blue Jays,
12/8/92
□ 339 Scott Servais .10 .05 .01
□ 340 Bob Welch .10 .05 .01
□ 341 Devon White .30 .14 .04
□ 342 Jeff Reardon .20 .09 .03
□ 343 B.J. Surhoff .10 .05 .01
□ 344 Bob Tewksbury .10 .05 .01
□ 345 Jose Vizcaino .10 .05 .01
□ 346 Mike Sharperson .10 .05 .01
□ 347 Mel Rojas .10 .05 .01
□ 348 Matt Williams .60 .25 .08
□ 349 Steve Olin .10 .05 .01
□ 350 Mike Schooler .10 .05 .01
□ 351 Ryan Thompson .30 .14 .04
□ 352 Cal Ripken 3.00 1.35 .40
□ 353 Benito Santiago .20 .09 .03
Now with Marlins,
12/16/92
□ 354 Curt Schilling .20 .09 .03
□ 355 Andy Van Slyke .20 .09 .03
□ 356 Kenny Rogers .10 .05 .01
□ 357 Jody Reed .10 .05 .01
Now with Dodgers,
11/17/92
□ 358 Reggie Sanders .30 .14 .04
□ 359 Kevin McReynolds .10 .05 .01
□ 360 Alan Trammell .30 .14 .04
□ 361 Kevin Tapani .20 .09 .03
□ 362 Frank Thomas 4.00 1.80 .50
□ 363 Bernie Williams .20 .09 .03
□ 364 John Smoltz .10 .05 .01
□ 365 Robin Yount .60 .25 .08
□ 366 John Wetteland .10 .05 .01
□ 367 Bob Zupcic .10 .05 .01
□ 368 Julio Valera .10 .05 .01
□ 369 Brian Williams .10 .05 .01
□ 370 Willie Wilson .10 .05 .01
Now with Cubs,
12/18/92
□ 371 Dave Winfield .30 .14 .04
Now with Twins,
12/17/92
□ 372 Deion Sanders .75 .35 .09
□ 373 Greg Vaughn .20 .09 .03
□ 374 Todd Worrell .10 .05 .01
Now with Dodgers,
12/9/92
□ 375 Darryl Strawberry .20 .09 .03
□ 376 John Vander Wal .10 .05 .01
□ 377 Mike Benjamin .10 .05 .01
□ 378 Mark Whiten .20 .09 .03
□ 379 Omar Vizquel .10 .05 .01
□ 380 Anthony Young .10 .05 .01
□ 381 Rick Sutcliffe .20 .09 .03
□ 382 Candy Maldonado .10 .05 .01
Now with Cubs,
12/11/92
□ 383 Francisco Cabrera .10 .05 .01
□ 384 Larry Walker .30 .14 .04
□ 385 Scott Cooper .20 .09 .03
□ 386 Gerald Williams .10 .05 .01
□ 387 Robin Ventura .10 .05 .01
□ 388 Carl Willis .10 .05 .01
□ 389 Lou Whitaker .30 .14 .04
□ 390 Hipolito Pichardo .10 .05 .01
□ 391 Rudy Seanez .10 .05 .01
□ 392 Greg Swindell .10 .05 .01
Now with Astros,
12/4/92
□ 393 Mo Vaughn .30 .14 .04
□ 394 Checklist 1-132 .10 .05 .01
□ 395 Checklist 133-264 .10 .05 .01
□ 396 Checklist 265-396 .10 .05 .01

1993 O-Pee-Chee World Champions

This 18-card subset was randomly inserted in 1993 O-Pee-Chee wax packs and features the Toronto Blue Jays, the 1992 World Series Champions. The standard-size (2 1/2" by 3 1/2") cards are similar to the regular issue, with glossy color action

player photos with white borders on the fronts. They differ in having a gold (rather than silver) stripe across the bottom, which intersects a 1992 World Champions logo. The backs carry statistics on a burnt orange box against a light blue panel with bilingual (English and French) career highlights. The cards are numbered on the back.

	MINT	EXC	G-VG
COMPLETE SET (18)	3.50	1.55	.45
COMMON CARD (1-18)	.20	.09	.03
☐ 1 Roberto Alomar	.75	.35	.09
☐ 2 Pat Borders	.20	.09	.03
☐ 3 Joe Carter	.50	.23	.06
☐ 4 David Cone	.35	.16	.04
☐ 5 Kelly Gruber	.20	.09	.03
☐ 6 Juan Guzman	.20	.09	.03
☐ 7 Tom Henke	.20	.09	.03
☐ 8 Jimmy Key	.35	.16	.04
☐ 9 Manny Lee	.20	.09	.03
☐ 10 Candy Maldonado	.20	.09	.03
☐ 11 Jack Morris	.35	.16	.04
☐ 12 John Olerud	.35	.16	.04
☐ 13 Ed Sprague	.20	.09	.03
☐ 14 Todd Stottlemyre	.20	.09	.03
☐ 15 Duane Ward	.20	.09	.03
☐ 16 Devon White	.35	.16	.04
☐ 17 Dave Winfield	.35	.16	.04
☐ 18 Cito Gaston MG	.20	.09	.03

1993 O-Pee-Chee World Series Heroes

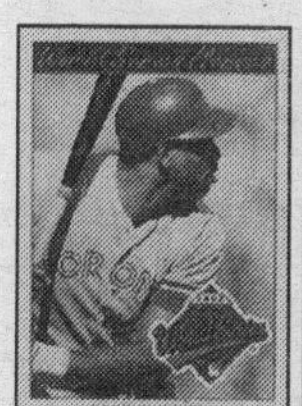

This four-card subset was randomly inserted in 1993 O-Pee-Chee wax packs. These cards were more difficult to find than the 18-card World Series Champions insert set. The cards measure the standard size (2 1/2" by 3 1/2"). The fronts feature color action player photos with white borders. The words "World Series Heroes" appear in a dark blue stripe above the picture, while the player's name is printed in the bottom white border. A 1992 World Series logo overlays the picture at the lower right corner. Over a ghosted version of the 1992 World Series logo, the backs summarize, in English and French, the player's outstanding performance in the 1992 World Series. The cards are numbered on the back in alphabetical order by player's name.

	MINT	EXC	G-VG
COMPLETE SET (4)	.75	.35	.09
COMMON CARD (1-4)	.25	.11	.03
☐ 1 Pat Borders	.25	.11	.03
☐ 2 Jimmy Key	.35	.16	.04
☐ 3 Ed Sprague	.25	.11	.03
☐ 4 Dave Winfield	.35	.16	.04

1993 OPC Premier

The 1993 O-Pee-Chee Premier set consists of 132 cards measuring the standard size (2 1/2" by 3 1/2"). The foil packs contain eight regular cards and one Star Performer insert card. The white-bordered fronts feature a mix of color action and posed player photos. The player's name and position are printed in the lower left border. The backs carry a color head shot, biography, 1992 statistics, and the team logo. The cards are numbered on the back. According to O-Pee-Chee, only 4,000 cases were produced. Randomly inserted throughout the foil packs were a 22-card Foil Star Performer subset and a four-card Top Draft Picks subset. Rookie Cards in this set include Rene Arocha and J.T. Snow.

	MINT	EXC	G-VG
COMPLETE SET (132)	6.00	2.70	.75
COMMON CARD (1-132)	.05	.02	.01
☐ 1 Barry Bonds	.75	.35	.09
☐ 2 Chad Curtis	.08	.04	.01
☐ 3 Chris Bosio	.05	.02	.01
☐ 4 Cal Eldred	.08	.04	.01
☐ 5 Dan Walters	.05	.02	.01
☐ 6 Rene Arocha	.15	.07	.02

☐ 7 Delino DeShields	.08	.04	.01
☐ 8 Spike Owen	.05	.02	.01
☐ 9 Jeff Russell	.05	.02	.01
☐ 10 Phil Plantier	.10	.05	.01
☐ 11 Mike Christopher	.05	.02	.01
☐ 12 Darren Daulton	.10	.05	.01
☐ 13 Scott Cooper	.08	.04	.01
☐ 14 Paul O'Neill	.08	.04	.01
☐ 15 Jimmy Key	.08	.04	.01
☐ 16 Dickie Thon	.05	.02	.01
☐ 17 Greg Gohr	.05	.02	.01
☐ 18 Andre Dawson	.10	.05	.01
☐ 19 Steve Cooke	.05	.02	.01
☐ 20 Tony Fernandez	.05	.02	.01
☐ 21 Mark Gardner	.05	.02	.01
☐ 22 Dave Martinez	.05	.02	.01
☐ 23 Jose Guzman	.05	.02	.01
☐ 24 Chili Davis	.08	.04	.01
☐ 25 Randy Knorr	.05	.02	.01
☐ 26 Mike Piazza	2.00	.90	.25
☐ 27 Benji Gil	.08	.04	.01
☐ 28 Dave Winfield	.10	.05	.01
☐ 29 Wil Cordero	.10	.05	.01
☐ 30 Butch Henry	.05	.02	.01
☐ 31 Eric Young	.08	.04	.01
☐ 32 Orestes Destrade	.08	.04	.01
☐ 33 Randy Myers	.08	.04	.01
☐ 34 Tom Brunansky	.05	.02	.01
☐ 35 Dan Wilson	.05	.02	.01
☐ 36 Juan Guzman	.08	.04	.01
☐ 37 Tim Salmon	.35	.16	.04
☐ 38 Bill Krueger	.05	.02	.01
☐ 39 Larry Walker	.10	.05	.01
☐ 40 David Hulse	.05	.02	.01
☐ 41 Ken Ryan	.20	.09	.03
☐ 42 Jose Lind	.05	.02	.01
☐ 43 Benny Santiago	.05	.02	.01
☐ 44 Ray Lankford	.10	.05	.01
☐ 45 Dave Stewart	.08	.04	.01
☐ 46 Don Mattingly	.75	.35	.09
☐ 47 Fernando Valenzuela	.05	.02	.01
☐ 48 Scott Fletcher	.05	.02	.01
☐ 49 Wade Boggs	.10	.05	.01
☐ 50 Norm Charlton	.05	.02	.01
☐ 51 Carlos Baerga	.30	.14	.04
☐ 52 John Olerud	.10	.05	.01
☐ 53 Willie Wilson	.05	.02	.01
☐ 54 Dennis Moeller	.05	.02	.01
☐ 55 Joe Orsulak	.05	.02	.01
☐ 56 John Smiley	.05	.02	.01
☐ 57 Al Martin	.08	.04	.01
☐ 58 Andres Galarraga	.10	.05	.01
☐ 59 Billy Ripken	.05	.02	.01
☐ 60 Dave Stieb	.08	.04	.01
☐ 61 Dave Magadan	.05	.02	.01
☐ 62 Todd Worrell	.05	.02	.01
☐ 63 Sherman Obando	.15	.07	.02
☐ 64 Kent Bottenfield	.05	.02	.01
☐ 65 Vinny Castilla	.05	.02	.01
☐ 66 Charlie Hayes	.08	.04	.01
☐ 67 Mike Hartley	.05	.02	.01
☐ 68 Harold Baines	.08	.04	.01
☐ 69 John Cummings	.05	.02	.01
☐ 70 J.T. Snow	.15	.07	.02
☐ 71 Graeme Lloyd	.05	.02	.01
☐ 72 Frank Bolick	.05	.02	.01
☐ 73 Doug Drabek	.10	.05	.01
☐ 74 Milt Thompson	.05	.02	.01
☐ 75 Tim Pugh	.05	.02	.01
☐ 76 John Kruk	.10	.05	.01
☐ 77 Tom Henke	.08	.04	.01
☐ 78 Kevin Young	.05	.02	.01
☐ 79 Ryan Thompson	.10	.05	.01
☐ 80 Mike Hampton	.05	.02	.01
☐ 81 Jose Canseco	.30	.14	.04
☐ 82 Mike Lansing	.20	.09	.03
☐ 83 Candy Maldonado	.05	.02	.01
☐ 84 Alex Arias	.05	.02	.01
☐ 85 Troy Neel	.08	.04	.01
☐ 86 Greg Swindell	.05	.02	.01
☐ 87 Tim Wallach	.05	.02	.01
☐ 88 Andy Van Slyke	.10	.05	.01
☐ 89 Harold Reynolds	.05	.02	.01
☐ 90 Bryan Harvey	.08	.04	.01
☐ 91 Jerald Clark	.05	.02	.01
☐ 92 David Cone	.10	.05	.01
☐ 93 Ellis Burks	.08	.04	.01
☐ 94 Scott Bankhead	.05	.02	.01
☐ 95 Pete Incaviglia	.05	.02	.01
☐ 96 Cecil Fielder	.10	.05	.01
☐ 97 Sean Berry	.05	.02	.01
☐ 98 Gregg Jefferies	.10	.05	.01
☐ 99 Billy Brewer	.05	.02	.01
☐ 100 Scott Sanderson	.05	.02	.01
☐ 101 Walt Weiss	.05	.02	.01
☐ 102 Travis Fryman	.15	.07	.02
☐ 103 Barry Larkin	.10	.05	.01
☐ 104 Darren Holmes	.05	.02	.01
☐ 105 Ivan Calderon	.05	.02	.01
☐ 106 Terry Jorgensen	.05	.02	.01
☐ 107 David Nied	.10	.05	.01
☐ 108 Tim Bogar	.05	.02	.01
☐ 109 Roberto Kelly	.05	.02	.01
☐ 110 Mike Moore	.05	.02	.01
☐ 111 Carlos Garcia	.08	.04	.01
☐ 112 Mike Bielecki	.05	.02	.01
☐ 113 Trevor Hoffman	.05	.02	.01
☐ 114 Rich Amaral	.05	.02	.01
☐ 115 Jody Reed	.05	.02	.01
☐ 116 Charlie Liebrandt	.05	.02	.01
☐ 117 Greg Gagne	.05	.02	.01
☐ 118 Darrell Sherman	.05	.02	.01
☐ 119 Jeff Conine	.10	.05	.01
☐ 120 Tim Laker	.05	.02	.01
☐ 121 Kevin Seitzer	.05	.02	.01
☐ 122 Jeff Mutis	.05	.02	.01
☐ 123 Rico Rossy	.05	.02	.01
☐ 124 Paul Molitor	.10	.05	.01
☐ 125 Cal Ripken	1.50	.65	.19
☐ 126 Greg Maddux	.50	.23	.06
☐ 127 Greg McMichael	.15	.07	.02
☐ 128 Felix Jose	.05	.02	.01
☐ 129 Dick Schofield	.05	.02	.01
☐ 130 Jim Abbott	.10	.05	.01
☐ 131 Kevin Reimer	.05	.02	.01
☐ 132 Checklist 1-132	.05	.02	.01

1993 OPC Premier Star Performers

The 1993 O-Pee-Chee Premier Star Performers set was inserted one card per 1993 O-Pee-Chee Premier foil packs. The 22-card set measures the standard size (2 1/2" by 3 1/2"). The fronts display a gold outer border with a narrow white inner border that frames a color action player photo. The subset title is printed on a green stripe across the top of the photo and the player's name and position are printed below the photo on the lower border. The backs con-

tain a kelly-green border surrounding a white box that carries a player head shot, biography and career summary in both French and English. A ghosted team logo appears beneath the career summary. The cards are numbered on the back. A 22-card standard-size (2 1/2" by 3 1/2") set of Foil Star Performers was randomly inserted in foil packs. The gold foil-stamped set logo rests in a lower corner. The Foil Star Performers are valued at a multiple of the regular Star Performers cards.

	MINT	EXC	G-VG
COMPLETE SET (22)	10.00	4.50	1.25
COMMON CARD (1-22)	.10	.05	.01

*FOIL STARS: 12.5X TO 25X VALUES BELOW

	MINT	EXC	G-VG
☐ 1 Frank Thomas	2.00	.90	.25
☐ 2 Fred McGriff	.30	.14	.04
☐ 3 Roberto Alomar	.50	.23	.06
☐ 4 Ryne Sandberg	.60	.25	.08
☐ 5 Edgar Martinez	.10	.05	.01
☐ 6 Gary Sheffield	.15	.07	.02
☐ 7 Juan Gonzalez	.60	.25	.08
☐ 8 Eric Karros	.10	.05	.01
☐ 9 Ken Griffey Jr.	2.00	.90	.25
☐ 10 Deion Sanders	.40	.18	.05
☐ 11 Kirby Puckett	.75	.35	.09
☐ 12 Will Clark	.30	.14	.04
☐ 13 Joe Carter	.30	.14	.04
☐ 14 Barry Bonds	.75	.35	.09
☐ 15 Pat Listach	.10	.05	.01
☐ 16 Mark McGwire	.10	.05	.01
☐ 17 Kenny Lofton	.50	.23	.06
☐ 18 Roger Clemens	.50	.23	.06
☐ 19 Greg Maddux	.50	.23	.06
☐ 20 Nolan Ryan	2.00	.90	.25
☐ 21 Tom Glavine	.15	.07	.02
☐ 22 Dennis Eckersley	.10	.05	.01

1993 OPC Premier Top Draft Picks

Randomly inserted in foil packs, this four-card standard-size (2 1/2" by 3 1/2") set features the top two draft picks of the Toronto Blue Jays and Montreal Expos. Each borderless front carries a posed color player photo, with the player's name and team appearing vertically in gold foil within a team color-coded stripe. The set's gold foil-highlighted logo rests in a lower corner. The back carries a posed player color headshot in the upper left of a mottled, light blue panel. The player's team's logo appears alongside, and his career highlights follow below. The cards are numbered on the back.

	MINT	EXC	G-VG
COMPLETE SET (4)	10.00	4.50	1.25
COMMON CARD (1-4)	1.50	.65	.19

	MINT	EXC	G-VG
☐ 1 B.J. Wallace	1.50	.65	.19
☐ 2 Shannon Stewart	4.00	1.80	.50
☐ 3 Rod Henderson	2.50	1.15	.30
☐ 4 Todd Steverson	3.00	1.35	.40

1994 O-Pee-Chee

The 1994 O-Pee-Chee baseball set consists of 270 standard-size cards. Card fronts feature color player photos with a black border up the left side. Within the border is the team name. The player's name and position (bilingual) are in colored bar at the bottom. The back has a large color photo that is ghosted by a statistical box at the bottom.

	MINT	EXC	G-VG
COMPLETE SET (270)	18.00	8.00	2.30
COMMON CARD (1-270)	.05	.02	.01

	MINT	EXC	G-VG
☐ 1 Paul Molitor	.30	.14	.04
☐ 2 Kirt Manwaring	.05	.02	.01
☐ 3 Brady Anderson	.08	.04	.01
☐ 4 Scott Cooper	.08	.04	.01
☐ 5 Kevin Stocker	.08	.04	.01
☐ 6 Alex Fernandez	.10	.05	.01
☐ 7 Jeff Montgomery	.08	.04	.01
☐ 8 Danny Tartabull	.08	.04	.01
☐ 9 Damion Easley	.05	.02	.01
☐ 10 Andujar Cedeno	.05	.02	.01

☐ 11 Steve Karsay .05 .02 .01
☐ 12 Dave Stewart .08 .04 .01
☐ 13 Fred McGriff .30 .14 .04
☐ 14 Jaime Navarro .05 .02 .01
☐ 15 Allen Watson .05 .02 .01
☐ 16 Ryne Sandberg .60 .25 .08
☐ 17 Arthur Rhodes .05 .02 .01
☐ 18 Marquis Grissom .10 .05 .01
☐ 19 John Burkett .08 .04 .01
☐ 20 Robby Thompson .05 .02 .01
☐ 21 Denny Martinez .08 .04 .01
☐ 22 Ken Griffey Jr. 2.00 .90 .25
☐ 23 Orestes Destrade .05 .02 .01
☐ 24 Dwight Gooden .05 .02 .01
☐ 25 Rafael Palmeiro .10 .05 .01
☐ 26 Pedro Martinez .10 .05 .01
☐ 27 Wes Chamberlain .05 .02 .01
☐ 28 Juan Gonzalez .60 .25 .08
☐ 29 Kevin Mitchell .08 .04 .01
☐ 30 Dante Bichette .10 .05 .01
☐ 31 Howard Johnson .05 .02 .01
☐ 32 Mickey Tettleton .08 .04 .01
☐ 33 Robin Ventura .08 .04 .01
☐ 34 Terry Mulholland .05 .02 .01
☐ 35 Bernie Williams .08 .04 .01
☐ 36 Eduardo Perez .08 .04 .01
☐ 37 Rickey Henderson .10 .05 .01
☐ 38 Terry Pendleton .05 .02 .01
☐ 39 John Smoltz .08 .04 .01
☐ 40 Derrick May .05 .02 .01
☐ 41 Pedro Martinez .10 .05 .01
☐ 42 Mark Portugal .05 .02 .01
☐ 43 Albert Belle .60 .25 .08
☐ 44 Edgar Martinez .05 .02 .01
☐ 45 Gary Sheffield .10 .05 .01
☐ 46 Bret Saberhagen .08 .04 .01
☐ 47 Ricky Gutierrez .05 .02 .01
☐ 48 Orlando Merced .08 .04 .01
☐ 49 Mike Greenwell .08 .04 .01
☐ 50 Jose Rijo .08 .04 .01
☐ 51 Jeff Granger .08 .04 .01
☐ 52 Mike Henneman .05 .02 .01
☐ 53 Dave Winfield .10 .05 .01
☐ 54 Don Mattingly .75 .35 .09
☐ 55 J.T. Snow .08 .04 .01
☐ 56 Todd Van Poppel .08 .04 .01
☐ 57 Chipper Jones .25 .11 .03
☐ 58 Darryl Hamilton .05 .02 .01
☐ 59 Delino DeShields .05 .02 .01
☐ 60 Rondell White .20 .09 .03
☐ 61 Eric Anthony .05 .02 .01
☐ 62 Charlie Hough .08 .04 .01
☐ 63 Sid Fernandez .05 .02 .01
☐ 64 Derek Bell .08 .04 .01
☐ 65 Phil Plantier .08 .04 .01
☐ 66 Curt Schilling .05 .02 .01
☐ 67 Roger Clemens .40 .18 .05
☐ 68 Jose Lind .05 .02 .01
☐ 69 Andres Galarraga .10 .05 .01
☐ 70 Tim Belcher .05 .02 .01
☐ 71 Ron Karkovice .05 .02 .01
☐ 72 Alan Trammell .10 .05 .01
☐ 73 Pete Harnisch .05 .02 .01
☐ 74 Mark McGwire .10 .05 .01
☐ 75 Ryan Klesko .30 .14 .04
☐ 76 Ramon Martinez .08 .04 .01
☐ 77 Gregg Jefferies .10 .05 .01
☐ 78 Steve Buechele .05 .02 .01
☐ 79 Bill Swift .05 .02 .01
☐ 80 Matt Williams .40 .18 .05
☐ 81 Randy Johnson .10 .05 .01
☐ 82 Mike Mussina .30 .14 .04
☐ 83 Andy Benes .08 .04 .01
☐ 84 Dave Staton .05 .02 .01
☐ 85 Steve Cooke .05 .02 .01
☐ 86 Andy Van Slyke .10 .05 .01
☐ 87 Ivan Rodriguez .10 .05 .01
☐ 88 Frank Viola .05 .02 .01
☐ 89 Aaron Sele .20 .09 .03
☐ 90 Ellis Burks .08 .04 .01
☐ 91 Wally Joyner .08 .04 .01
☐ 92 Rick Aguilera .08 .04 .01
☐ 93 Kirby Puckett .75 .35 .09
☐ 94 Roberto Hernandez .05 .02 .01
☐ 95 Mike Stanley .05 .02 .01
☐ 96 Roberto Alomar .40 .18 .05
☐ 97 James Mouton .15 .07 .02
☐ 98 Chad Curtis .08 .04 .01
☐ 99 Mitch Williams .05 .02 .01
☐ 100 Carlos Delgado .30 .14 .04
☐ 101 Greg Maddux .40 .18 .05
☐ 102 Brian Harper .05 .02 .01
☐ 103 Tom Pagnozzi .05 .02 .01
☐ 104 Jose Offerman .05 .02 .01
☐ 105 John Wetteland .05 .02 .01
☐ 106 Carlos Baerga .30 .14 .04
☐ 107 Dave Magadan .05 .02 .01
☐ 108 Bobby Jones .15 .07 .02
☐ 109 Tony Gwynn .50 .23 .06
☐ 110 Jeromy Burnitz .08 .04 .01
☐ 111 Bip Roberts .05 .02 .01
☐ 112 Carlos Garcia .05 .02 .01
☐ 113 Jeff Russell .05 .02 .01
☐ 114 Armando Reynoso .05 .02 .01
☐ 115 Ozzie Guillen .05 .02 .01
☐ 116 Bo Jackson .10 .05 .01
☐ 117 Terry Steinbach .08 .04 .01
☐ 118 Deion Sanders .35 .16 .04
☐ 119 Randy Myers .05 .02 .01
☐ 120 Mark Whiten .08 .04 .01
☐ 121 Manny Ramirez .40 .18 .05
☐ 122 Ben McDonald .08 .04 .01
☐ 123 Darren Daulton .10 .05 .01
☐ 124 Kevin Young .05 .02 .01
☐ 125 Barry Larkin .10 .05 .01
☐ 126 Cecil Fielder .10 .05 .01
☐ 127 Frank Thomas 2.00 .90 .25
☐ 128 Luis Polonia .05 .02 .01
☐ 129 Steve Finley .05 .02 .01
☐ 130 John Olerud .10 .05 .01
☐ 131 John Jaha .05 .02 .01
☐ 132 Darren Lewis .05 .02 .01
☐ 133 Orel Hershiser .08 .04 .01
☐ 134 Chris Bosio .05 .02 .01
☐ 135 Ryan Thompson .08 .04 .01
☐ 136 Chris Sabo .05 .02 .01
☐ 137 Tommy Greene .05 .02 .01
☐ 138 Andre Dawson .10 .05 .01
☐ 139 Roberto Kelly .05 .02 .01
☐ 140 Ken Hill .08 .04 .01
☐ 141 Greg Gagne .05 .02 .01
☐ 142 Julio Franco .08 .04 .01
☐ 143 Chili Davis .08 .04 .01
☐ 144 Dennis Eckersley .10 .05 .01
☐ 145 Joe Carter .30 .14 .04
☐ 146 Mark Grace .10 .05 .01
☐ 147 Mike Piazza 1.00 .45 .13
☐ 148 J.R. Phillips .10 .05 .01
☐ 149 Rich Amaral .05 .02 .01
☐ 150 Benny Santiago .05 .02 .01
☐ 151 Jeff King .05 .02 .01
☐ 152 Dean Palmer .08 .04 .01
☐ 153 Hal Morris .08 .04 .01
☐ 154 Mike Macfarlane .05 .02 .01
☐ 155 Chuck Knoblauch .10 .05 .01
☐ 156 Pat Kelly .05 .02 .01

	No.	Player			
☐	157	Greg Swindell	.05	.02	.01
☐	158	Chuck Finley	.05	.02	.01
☐	159	Devon White	.05	.02	.01
☐	160	Duane Ward	.05	.02	.01
☐	161	Sammy Sosa	.10	.05	.01
☐	162	Javy Lopez	.20	.09	.03
☐	163	Eric Karros	.08	.04	.01
☐	164	Royce Clayton	.08	.04	.01
☐	165	Salomon Torres	.08	.04	.01
☐	166	Jeff Kent	.08	.04	.01
☐	167	Chris Hoiles	.08	.04	.01
☐	168	Len Dykstra	.10	.05	.01
☐	169	Jose Canseco	.30	.14	.04
☐	170	Bret Boone	.10	.05	.01
☐	171	Charlie Hayes	.08	.04	.01
☐	172	Lou Whitaker	.10	.05	.01
☐	173	Jack McDowell	.10	.05	.01
☐	174	Jimmy Key	.08	.04	.01
☐	175	Mark Langston	.10	.05	.01
☐	176	Darryl Kile	.08	.04	.01
☐	177	Juan Guzman	.08	.04	.01
☐	178	Pat Borders	.05	.02	.01
☐	179	Cal Eldred	.08	.04	.01
☐	180	Jose Guzman	.05	.02	.01
☐	181	Ozzie Smith	.40	.18	.05
☐	182	Rod Beck	.08	.04	.01
☐	183	Dave Fleming	.05	.02	.01
☐	184	Eddie Murray	.10	.05	.01
☐	185	Cal Ripken	1.50	.65	.19
☐	186	Dave Hollins	.10	.05	.01
☐	187	Will Clark	.30	.14	.04
☐	188	Otis Nixon	.05	.02	.01
☐	189	Joe Oliver	.05	.02	.01
☐	190	Roberto Mejia	.08	.04	.01
☐	191	Felix Jose	.05	.02	.01
☐	192	Tony Phillips	.05	.02	.01
☐	193	Wade Boggs	.10	.05	.01
☐	194	Tim Salmon	.30	.14	.04
☐	195	Ruben Sierra	.10	.05	.01
☐	196	Steve Avery	.10	.05	.01
☐	197	B.J. Surhoff	.05	.02	.01
☐	198	Todd Zeile	.08	.04	.01
☐	199	Raul Mondesi UER (No card number on back)	.75	.35	.09
☐	200	Barry Bonds	.75	.35	.09
☐	201	Sandy Alomar	.08	.04	.01
☐	202	Bobby Bonilla	.10	.05	.01
☐	203	Mike Devereaux	.08	.04	.01
☐	204	Rickey Bottalico	.20	.09	.03
☐	205	Kevin Brown	.05	.02	.01
☐	206	Jason Bere	.25	.11	.03
☐	207	Reggie Sanders	.08	.04	.01
☐	208	David Nied	.10	.05	.01
☐	209	Travis Fryman	.15	.07	.02
☐	210	James Baldwin	.35	.16	.04
☐	211	Jim Abbott	.10	.05	.01
☐	212	Jeff Bagwell	1.00	.45	.13
☐	213	Bob Welch	.05	.02	.01
☐	214	Jeff Blauser	.08	.04	.01
☐	215	Brett Butler	.08	.04	.01
☐	216	Pat Listach	.05	.02	.01
☐	217	Bob Tewksbury	.05	.02	.01
☐	218	Mike Lansing	.08	.04	.01
☐	219	Wayne Kirby	.05	.02	.01
☐	220	Chuck Carr	.05	.02	.01
☐	221	Harold Baines	.08	.04	.01
☐	222	Jay Bell	.08	.04	.01
☐	223	Ciff Floyd	.30	.14	.04
☐	224	Rob Dibble	.05	.02	.01
☐	225	Kevin Appier	.08	.04	.01
☐	226	Eric Davis	.05	.02	.01
☐	227	Matt Walbeck	.05	.02	.01
☐	228	Tim Raines	.10	.05	.01
☐	229	Paul O'Neill	.08	.04	.01
☐	230	Craig Biggio	.05	.02	.01
☐	231	Brent Gates	.10	.05	.01
☐	232	Rob Butler	.05	.02	.01
☐	233	David Justice	.30	.14	.04
☐	234	Rene Arocha	.05	.02	.01
☐	235	Mike Morgan	.05	.02	.01
☐	236	Denis Boucher	.05	.02	.01
☐	237	Kenny Lofton	.50	.23	.06
☐	238	Jeff Conine	.10	.05	.01
☐	239	Bryan Harvey	.08	.04	.01
☐	240	Danny Jackson	.05	.02	.01
☐	241	Al Martin	.05	.02	.01
☐	242	Tom Henke	.05	.02	.01
☐	243	Erik Hanson	.05	.02	.01
☐	244	Walt Weiss	.05	.02	.01
☐	245	Brian McRae	.08	.04	.01
☐	246	Kevin Tapani	.05	.02	.01
☐	247	David McCarty	.08	.04	.01
☐	248	Doug Drabek	.10	.05	.01
☐	249	Troy Neel	.08	.04	.01
☐	250	Tom Glavine	.10	.05	.01
☐	251	Ray Lankford	.10	.05	.01
☐	252	Wil Cordero	.10	.05	.01
☐	253	Larry Walker	.10	.05	.01
☐	254	Charles Nagy	.05	.02	.01
☐	255	Kirk Rueter	.05	.02	.01
☐	256	John Franco	.05	.02	.01
☐	257	John Kruk	.10	.05	.01
☐	258	Alex Gonzalez	.20	.09	.03
☐	259	Mo Vaughn	.10	.05	.01
☐	260	David Cone	.10	.05	.01
☐	261	Kent Hrbek	.08	.04	.01
☐	262	Lance Johnson	.05	.02	.01
☐	263	Luis Gonzalez	.05	.02	.01
☐	264	Mike Bordick	.05	.02	.01
☐	265	Ed Sprague	.05	.02	.01
☐	266	Moises Alou	.10	.05	.01
☐	267	Omar Vizquel	.05	.02	.01
☐	268	Jay Buhner	.08	.04	.01
☐	269	Checklist	.05	.02	.01
☐	270	Checklist	.05	.02	.01

1994 O-Pee-Chee All-Star Redemptions

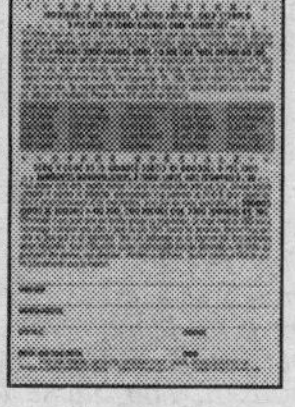

Inserted one per pack, this standard-size, 25-card redemption set features some of the game's top stars. White borders surround a color player photo on front. The backs contain redemption information. Any

five cards from this set and $20 CDN could be redeemed for a foil version of the jumbo set that was issued one per wax box. The redemption deadline was September 30, 1994.

	MINT	EXC	G-VG
COMPLETE SET (25)	12.00	5.50	1.50
COMMON CARD (1-25)	.20	.09	.03

*FOIL JUMBOS: 3X TO 6X VALUES BELOW
*REGULAR JUMBOS: 3X TO 6X VALUES BELOW

	MINT	EXC	G-VG
☐ 1 Frank Thomas	3.00	1.35	.40
☐ 2 Paul Molitor	.40	.18	.05
☐ 3 Barry Bonds	1.25	.55	.16
☐ 4 Juan Gonzalez	1.00	.45	.13
☐ 5 Jeff Bagwell	1.50	.65	.19
☐ 6 Carlos Baerga	.40	.18	.05
☐ 7 Ryne Sandberg	1.00	.45	.13
☐ 8 Ken Griffey Jr.	3.00	1.35	.40
☐ 9 Mike Piazza	1.50	.65	.19
☐ 10 Tim Salmon	.40	.18	.05
☐ 11 Marquis Grissom	.30	.14	.04
☐ 12 Albert Belle	1.00	.45	.13
☐ 13 Fred McGriff	.40	.18	.05
☐ 14 Jack McDowell	.20	.09	.03
☐ 15 Cal Ripken	2.25	1.00	.30
☐ 16 John Olerud	.30	.14	.04
☐ 17 Kirby Puckett	1.25	.55	.16
☐ 18 Roger Clemens	.75	.35	.09
☐ 19 Larry Walker	.30	.14	.04
☐ 20 Cecil Fielder	.30	.14	.04
☐ 21 Roberto Alomar	.75	.35	.09
☐ 22 Greg Maddux	.75	.35	.09
☐ 23 Joe Carter	.40	.18	.05
☐ 24 David Justice	.40	.18	.05
☐ 25 Kenny Lofton	.75	.35	.09

1994 O-Pee-Chee Diamond Dynamos

This 18-card set was randomly inserted in packs at a rate of one in 18. Card fronts have full-bleed color photos with the player's name and set name in red foil at the bottom. The backs have a small player photo and text over a white background.

	MINT	EXC	G-VG
COMPLETE SET (18)	40.00	18.00	5.00
COMMON CARD (1-18)	1.50	.65	.19

	MINT	EXC	G-VG
☐ 1 Mike Piazza	20.00	9.00	2.50
☐ 2 Robert Mejia	2.00	.90	.25
☐ 3 Wayne Kirby	1.50	.65	.19
☐ 4 Kevin Stocker	1.50	.65	.19
☐ 5 Chris Gomez	2.00	.90	.25
☐ 6 Bobby Jones	1.50	.65	.19
☐ 7 David McCarty	1.50	.65	.19
☐ 8 Kirk Rueter	2.00	.90	.25
☐ 9 J.T. Snow	1.50	.65	.19
☐ 10 Wil Cordero	2.00	.90	.25
☐ 11 Tim Salmon	6.00	2.70	.75
☐ 12 Jeff Conine	2.00	.90	.25
☐ 13 Jason Bere	5.00	2.30	.60
☐ 14 Greg McMichael	1.50	.65	.19
☐ 15 Brent Gates	2.00	.90	.25
☐ 16 Allen Watson	2.00	.90	.25
☐ 17 Aaron Sele	1.50	.65	.19
☐ 18 Carlos Garcia	1.50	.65	.19

1994 O-Pee-Chee Hot Prospects

Randomly inserted in packs at a rate of one in 36, this set consist of nine top prospects. The card fronts feature a full-bleed color photo with a solid color background. The player's name is in gold foil at the bottom and the Hot Prospects logo is at top right. An orange back contains a player photo and statistics.

	MINT	EXC	G-VG
COMPLETE SET (9)	40.00	18.00	5.00
COMMON CARD (1-9)	1.50	.65	.19

	MINT	EXC	G-VG
☐ 1 Cliff Floyd	6.00	2.70	.75
☐ 2 James Mouton	1.50	.65	.19
☐ 3 Salomon Torres	1.50	.65	.19
☐ 4 Raul Mondesi	14.00	6.25	1.75
☐ 5 Carlos Delgado	6.00	2.70	.75
☐ 6 Manny Ramirez	8.00	3.60	1.00
☐ 7 Javy Lopez	4.00	1.80	.50
☐ 8 Alex Gonzalez	3.00	1.35	.40
☐ 9 Ryan Klesko	7.00	3.10	.85

1994 O-Pee-Chee World Champions

This nine card set features members of the 1993 World Series champion Toronto Blue

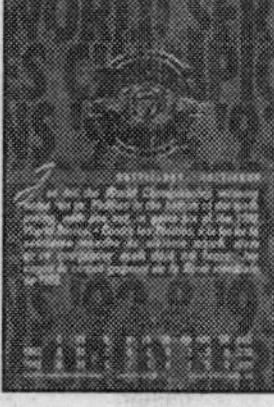

Jays. Randomly inserted in packs at a rate of one 36, the player is superimposed over a background containing the phrase, "1993 World Series Champions". The backs contain World Series statistics from 1992 and 1993 and highlights.

	MINT	EXC	G-VG
COMPLETE SET (9)	20.00	9.00	2.50
COMMON CARD (1-9)	1.25	.55	.16
☐ 1 Rickey Henderson	2.50	1.15	.30
☐ 2 Devon White	1.75	.80	.22
☐ 3 Paul Molitor	4.00	1.80	.50
☐ 4 Joe Carter	4.00	1.80	.50
☐ 5 John Olerud	1.75	.80	.22
☐ 6 Roberto Alomar	6.00	2.70	.75
☐ 7 Ed Sprague	1.25	.55	.16
☐ 8 Pat Borders	1.25	.55	.16
☐ 9 Tony Fernandez	1.25	.55	.16

1994 Pacific

The 660 cards comprising this set measure the standard size and feature color player action shots on their fronts that are borderless, except at the bottom, where a team color-coded marbleized border set off by a gold-foil line carries the team color-coded player's name. The set's gold-foil-stamped crown logo rests at the lower left. The back carries another color player action photo that is bordered only at the bottom, where the photo appears "torn away," revealing the gray marbleized area that carries the player's name, biography in both English and Spanish, statistics, and a ghosted team logo. The cards are numbered on the back, grouped alphabetically within teams, and checklisted below alphabetically according to teams as follows: Atlanta Braves (1-23), Baltimore Orioles (24-47), Boston Red Sox (48-70), California Angels (71-93), Chicago Cubs (94-117), Chicago White Sox (118-140), Cincinnati Reds (141-163), Cleveland Indians (164-186), Colorado Rockies (187-209), Detroit Tigers (210-232), Florida Marlins (233-255), Houston Astros (256-278), Kansas City Royals (279-301), Los Angeles Dodgers (302-324), Milwaukee Brewers (325-348), Minnesota Twins (349-371), Montreal Expos (372-394), New York Mets (395-419), New York Yankees (420-443), Oakland Athletics (444-466), Philadelphia Phillies (467-490), Pittsburgh Pirates (491-514), San Diego Padres (515-537), San Francisco Giants (538-560), Seattle Mariners (561-584), St. Louis Cardinals (585-608), Texas Rangers (609-631), and Toronto Blue Jays (632-654). The set closes with an Award Winners subset (655-660).

	MINT	EXC	G-VG
COMPLETE SET (660)	40.00	18.00	5.00
COMMON CARD (1-660)	.05	.02	.01
☐ 1 Steve Avery	.15	.07	.02
☐ 2 Steve Bedrosian	.05	.02	.01
☐ 3 Damon Berryhill	.05	.02	.01
☐ 4 Jeff Blauser	.10	.05	.01
☐ 5 Sid Bream	.05	.02	.01
☐ 6 Francisco Cabrera	.05	.02	.01
☐ 7 Ramon Caraballo	.05	.02	.01
☐ 8 Ron Gant	.10	.05	.01
☐ 9 Tom Glavine	.15	.07	.02
☐ 10 Chipper Jones	.25	.11	.03
☐ 11 David Justice	.30	.14	.04
☐ 12 Ryan Klesko	.30	.14	.04
☐ 13 Mark Lemke	.05	.02	.01
☐ 14 Javy Lopez	.20	.09	.03
☐ 15 Greg Maddux	.40	.18	.05
☐ 16 Fred McGriff	.30	.14	.04
☐ 17 Greg McMichael	.10	.05	.01
☐ 18 Kent Mercker	.05	.02	.01
☐ 19 Otis Nixon	.05	.02	.01
☐ 20 Terry Pendleton	.05	.02	.01
☐ 21 Deion Sanders	.35	.16	.04
☐ 22 John Smoltz	.10	.05	.01
☐ 23 Tony Tarasco	.15	.07	.02
☐ 24 Manny Alexander	.05	.02	.01
☐ 25 Brady Anderson	.10	.05	.01
☐ 26 Harold Baines	.10	.05	.01
☐ 27 Damon Buford	.05	.02	.01
☐ 28 Paul Carey	.05	.02	.01
☐ 29 Mike Devereaux	.10	.05	.01
☐ 30 Todd Frohwirth	.05	.02	.01
☐ 31 Leo Gomez	.05	.02	.01
☐ 32 Jeffrey Hammonds	.25	.11	.03
☐ 33 Chris Hoiles	.10	.05	.01
☐ 34 Tim Hulett	.05	.02	.01
☐ 35 Ben McDonald	.10	.05	.01
☐ 36 Mark McLemore	.05	.02	.01
☐ 37 Alan Mills	.05	.02	.01
☐ 38 Mike Mussina	.35	.16	.04
☐ 39 Sherman Obando	.05	.02	.01
☐ 40 Gregg Olson	.05	.02	.01
☐ 41 Mike Pagliarulo	.05	.02	.01
☐ 42 Jim Poole	.05	.02	.01
☐ 43 Harold Reynolds	.05	.02	.01
☐ 44 Cal Ripken	1.50	.65	.19
☐ 45 David Segui	.05	.02	.01
☐ 46 Fernando Valenzuela	.05	.02	.01
☐ 47 Jack Voigt	.05	.02	.01

☐	48 Scott Bankhead	.05	.02	.01
☐	49 Roger Clemens	.40	.18	.05
☐	50 Scott Cooper	.10	.05	.01
☐	51 Danny Darwin	.05	.02	.01
☐	52 Andre Dawson	.15	.07	.02
☐	53 John Dopson	.05	.02	.01
☐	54 Scott Fletcher	.05	.02	.01
☐	55 Tony Fossas	.05	.02	.01
☐	56 Mike Greenwell	.10	.05	.01
☐	57 Billy Hatcher	.05	.02	.01
☐	58 Jeff McNeely	.05	.02	.01
☐	59 Jose Melendez	.05	.02	.01
☐	60 Tim Naehring	.05	.02	.01
☐	61 Tony Pena	.05	.02	.01
☐	62 Carlos Quintana	.05	.02	.01
☐	63 Paul Quantrill	.05	.02	.01
☐	64 Luis Rivera	.05	.02	.01
☐	65 Jeff Russell	.05	.02	.01
☐	66 Aaron Sele	.20	.09	.03
☐	67 John Valentin	.10	.05	.01
☐	68 Mo Vaughn	.15	.07	.02
☐	69 Frank Viola	.05	.02	.01
☐	70 Bob Zupcic	.05	.02	.01
☐	71 Mike Butcher	.05	.02	.01
☐	72 Rod Correia	.05	.02	.01
☐	73 Chad Curtis	.10	.05	.01
☐	74 Chili Davis	.10	.05	.01
☐	75 Gary DiSarcina	.05	.02	.01
☐	76 Damion Easley	.05	.02	.01
☐	77 John Farrell	.05	.02	.01
☐	78 Chuck Finley	.05	.02	.01
☐	79 Joe Grahe	.05	.02	.01
☐	80 Stan Javier	.05	.02	.01
☐	81 Mark Langston	.15	.07	.02
☐	82 Phil Leftwich	.05	.02	.01
☐	83 Torey Lovullo	.05	.02	.01
☐	84 Joe Magrane	.05	.02	.01
☐	85 Greg Myers	.05	.02	.01
☐	86 Eduardo Perez	.10	.05	.01
☐	87 Luis Polonia	.05	.02	.01
☐	88 Tim Salmon	.30	.14	.04
☐	89 J.T. Snow	.10	.05	.01
☐	90 Kurt Stillwell	.05	.02	.01
☐	91 Ron Tingley	.05	.02	.01
☐	92 Chris Turner	.05	.02	.01
☐	93 Julio Valera	.05	.02	.01
☐	94 Jose Bautista	.05	.02	.01
☐	95 Shawn Boskie	.05	.02	.01
☐	96 Steve Buechele	.05	.02	.01
☐	97 Frank Castillo	.05	.02	.01
☐	98 Mark Grace UER (stats have 98 home runs in 1993; should be 14)	.15	.07	.02
☐	99 Jose Guzman	.05	.02	.01
☐	100 Mike Harkey	.05	.02	.01
☐	101 Greg Hibbard	.05	.02	.01
☐	102 Doug Jennings	.05	.02	.01
☐	103 Derrick May	.05	.02	.01
☐	104 Mike Morgan	.05	.02	.01
☐	105 Randy Myers	.05	.02	.01
☐	106 Karl Rhodes	.05	.02	.01
☐	107 Kevin Roberson	.05	.02	.01
☐	108 Rey Sanchez	.05	.02	.01
☐	109 Ryne Sandberg	.60	.25	.08
☐	110 Tommy Shields	.05	.02	.01
☐	111 Dwight Smith	.05	.02	.01
☐	112 Sammy Sosa	.15	.07	.02
☐	113 Jose Vizcaino	.05	.02	.01
☐	114 Turk Wendell	.05	.02	.01
☐	115 Rick Wilkins	.05	.02	.01
☐	116 Willie Wilson	.05	.02	.01
☐	117 Eduardo Zambrano	.05	.02	.01
☐	118 Wilson Alvarez	.15	.07	.02
☐	119 Tim Belcher	.05	.02	.01
☐	120 Jason Bere	.25	.11	.03
☐	121 Rodney Bolton	.05	.02	.01
☐	122 Ellis Burks	.10	.05	.01
☐	123 Joey Cora	.05	.02	.01
☐	124 Alex Fernandez	.15	.07	.02
☐	125 Ozzie Guillen	.05	.02	.01
☐	126 Craig Grebeck	.05	.02	.01
☐	127 Roberto Hernandez	.05	.02	.01
☐	128 Bo Jackson	.15	.07	.02
☐	129 Lance Johnson	.05	.02	.01
☐	130 Ron Karkovice	.05	.02	.01
☐	131 Mike LaValliere	.05	.02	.01
☐	132 Norberto Martin	.05	.02	.01
☐	133 Kirk McCaskill	.05	.02	.01
☐	134 Jack McDowell	.15	.07	.02
☐	135 Scott Radinsky	.05	.02	.01
☐	136 Tim Raines	.15	.07	.02
☐	137 Steve Sax	.05	.02	.01
☐	138 Frank Thomas	2.00	.90	.25
☐	139 Dan Pasqua	.05	.02	.01
☐	140 Robin Ventura	.10	.05	.01
☐	141 Jeff Branson	.05	.02	.01
☐	142 Tom Browning	.05	.02	.01
☐	143 Jacob Brumfield	.05	.02	.01
☐	144 Tim Costo	.05	.02	.01
☐	145 Rob Dibble	.05	.02	.01
☐	146 Brian Dorsett	.05	.02	.01
☐	147 Steve Foster	.05	.02	.01
☐	148 Cesar Hernandez	.05	.02	.01
☐	149 Roberto Kelly	.05	.02	.01
☐	150 Barry Larkin	.15	.07	.02
☐	151 Larry Luebbers	.05	.02	.01
☐	152 Kevin Mitchell	.10	.05	.01
☐	153 Joe Oliver	.05	.02	.01
☐	154 Tim Pugh	.05	.02	.01
☐	155 Jeff Reardon	.10	.05	.01
☐	156 Jose Rijo	.10	.05	.01
☐	157 Bip Roberts	.05	.02	.01
☐	158 Chris Sabo	.05	.02	.01
☐	159 Juan Samuel	.05	.02	.01
☐	160 Reggie Sanders	.10	.05	.01
☐	161 John Smiley	.05	.02	.01
☐	162 Jerry Spradlin	.05	.02	.01
☐	163 Gary Varsho	.05	.02	.01
☐	164 Sandy Alomar Jr.	.10	.05	.01
☐	165 Albert Belle	.60	.25	.08
☐	166 Carlos Baerga	.30	.14	.04
☐	167 Mark Clark	.05	.02	.01
☐	168 Alvaro Espinoza	.05	.02	.01
☐	169 Felix Fermin	.05	.02	.01
☐	170 Reggie Jefferson	.05	.02	.01
☐	171 Wayne Kirby	.05	.02	.01
☐	172 Tom Kramer	.05	.02	.01
☐	173 Kenny Lofton	.50	.23	.06
☐	174 Jesse Levis	.05	.02	.01
☐	175 Candy Maldonado	.05	.02	.01
☐	176 Carlos Martinez	.05	.02	.01
☐	177 Jose Mesa	.05	.02	.01
☐	178 Jeff Mutis	.05	.02	.01
☐	179 Charles Nagy	.05	.02	.01
☐	180 Bob Ojeda	.05	.02	.01
☐	181 Junior Ortiz	.05	.02	.01
☐	182 Eric Plunk	.05	.02	.01
☐	183 Manny Ramirez	.40	.18	.05
☐	184 Jeff Treadway	.05	.02	.01
☐	185 Bill Wertz	.05	.02	.01
☐	186 Paul Sorrento	.05	.02	.01
☐	187 Freddie Benavides	.05	.02	.01
☐	188 Dante Bichette	.15	.07	.02
☐	189 Willie Blair	.05	.02	.01
☐	190 Daryl Boston	.05	.02	.01
☐	191 Pedro Castellano	.05	.02	.01

☐ 192 Vinny Castilla .05 .02 .01
☐ 193 Jerald Clark .05 .02 .01
☐ 194 Alex Cole .05 .02 .01
☐ 195 Andres Galarraga .15 .07 .02
☐ 196 Joe Girardi .05 .02 .01
☐ 197 Charlie Hayes .10 .05 .01
☐ 198 Darren Holmes .05 .02 .01
☐ 199 Chris Jones .05 .02 .01
☐ 200 Curt Leskanic .05 .02 .01
☐ 201 Roberto Mejia .10 .05 .01
☐ 202 David Nied .15 .07 .02
☐ 203 J. Owens .05 .02 .01
☐ 204 Steve Reed .05 .02 .01
☐ 205 Armando Reynoso .05 .02 .01
☐ 206 Bruce Ruffin .05 .02 .01
☐ 207 Keith Shepherd .05 .02 .01
☐ 208 Jim Tatum .05 .02 .01
☐ 209 Eric Young .10 .05 .01
☐ 210 Skeeter Barnes .05 .02 .01
☐ 211 Danny Bautista .10 .05 .01
☐ 212 Tom Bolton .05 .02 .01
☐ 213 Eric Davis .05 .02 .01
☐ 214 Storm Davis .05 .02 .01
☐ 215 Cecil Fielder .15 .07 .02
☐ 216 Travis Fryman .20 .09 .03
☐ 217 Kirk Gibson .10 .05 .01
☐ 218 Dan Gladden .05 .02 .01
☐ 219 John Doherty .05 .02 .01
☐ 220 Chris Gomez .15 .07 .02
☐ 221 David Haas .05 .02 .01
☐ 222 Bill Krueger .05 .02 .01
☐ 223 Chad Kreuter .05 .02 .01
☐ 224 Mark Leiter .05 .02 .01
☐ 225 Bob MacDonald .05 .02 .01
☐ 226 Mike Moore .05 .02 .01
☐ 227 Tony Phillips .05 .02 .01
☐ 228 Rich Rowland .05 .02 .01
☐ 229 Mickey Tettleton .10 .05 .01
☐ 230 Alan Trammell .15 .07 .02
☐ 231 Lou Whitaker .15 .07 .02
☐ 232 David Wells .05 .02 .01
☐ 233 Luis Aquino .05 .02 .01
☐ 234 Alex Arias .05 .02 .01
☐ 235 Jack Armstrong .05 .02 .01
☐ 236 Ryan Bowen .05 .02 .01
☐ 237 Chuck Carr .05 .02 .01
☐ 238 Matias Carrillo .05 .02 .01
☐ 239 Jeff Conine .15 .07 .02
☐ 240 Henry Cotto .05 .02 .01
☐ 241 Orestes Destrade .05 .02 .01
☐ 242 Chris Hammond .05 .02 .01
☐ 243 Bryan Harvey .10 .05 .01
☐ 244 Charlie Hough .10 .05 .01
☐ 245 Richie Lewis .05 .02 .01
☐ 246 Mitch Lyden .05 .02 .01
☐ 247 Dave Magadan .05 .02 .01
☐ 248 Bob Natal .05 .02 .01
☐ 249 Benito Santiago .05 .02 .01
☐ 250 Gary Sheffield .15 .07 .02
☐ 251 Matt Turner .05 .02 .01
☐ 252 David Weathers .05 .02 .01
☐ 253 Walt Weiss .05 .02 .01
☐ 254 Darrell Whitmore .10 .05 .01
☐ 255 Nigel Wilson .10 .05 .01
☐ 256 Eric Anthony .05 .02 .01
☐ 257 Jeff Bagwell 1.00 .45 .13
☐ 258 Kevin Bass .05 .02 .01
☐ 259 Craig Biggio .10 .05 .01
☐ 260 Ken Caminiti .10 .05 .01
☐ 261 Andujar Cedeno .05 .02 .01
☐ 262 Chris Donnels .05 .02 .01
☐ 263 Doug Drabek .15 .07 .02
☐ 264 Tom Edens .05 .02 .01
☐ 265 Steve Finley .05 .02 .01
☐ 266 Luis Gonzalez .05 .02 .01
☐ 267 Pete Harnisch .05 .02 .01
☐ 268 Xavier Hernandez .05 .02 .01
☐ 269 Todd Jones .05 .02 .01
☐ 270 Darryl Kile .10 .05 .01
☐ 271 Al Osuna .05 .02 .01
☐ 272 Rick Parker .05 .02 .01
☐ 273 Mark Portugal .05 .02 .01
☐ 274 Scott Servais .05 .02 .01
☐ 275 Greg Swindell .05 .02 .01
☐ 276 Eddie Taubensee .05 .02 .01
☐ 277 Jose Uribe .05 .02 .01
☐ 278 Brian Williams .05 .02 .01
☐ 279 Kevin Appier .10 .05 .01
☐ 280 Billy Brewer .05 .02 .01
☐ 281 David Cone .15 .07 .02
☐ 282 Greg Gagne .05 .02 .01
☐ 283 Tom Gordon .05 .02 .01
☐ 284 Chris Gwynn .05 .02 .01
☐ 285 John Habyan .05 .02 .01
☐ 286 Chris Haney .05 .02 .01
☐ 287 Phil Hiatt .05 .02 .01
☐ 288 David Howard .05 .02 .01
☐ 289 Felix Jose .05 .02 .01
☐ 290 Wally Joyner .10 .05 .01
☐ 291 Kevin Koslofski .05 .02 .01
☐ 292 Jose Lind .05 .02 .01
☐ 293 Brent Mayne .05 .02 .01
☐ 294 Mike Macfarlane .05 .02 .01
☐ 295 Brian McRae .10 .05 .01
☐ 296 Kevin McReynolds .05 .02 .01
☐ 297 Keith Miller .05 .02 .01
☐ 298 Jeff Montgomery .10 .05 .01
☐ 299 Hipolito Pichardo .05 .02 .01
☐ 300 Rico Rossy .05 .02 .01
☐ 301 Curtis Wilkerson .05 .02 .01
☐ 302 Pedro Astacio .10 .05 .01
☐ 303 Rafael Bournigal .05 .02 .01
☐ 304 Brett Butler .10 .05 .01
☐ 305 Tom Candiotti .05 .02 .01
☐ 306 Omar Daal .05 .02 .01
☐ 307 Jim Gott .05 .02 .01
☐ 308 Kevin Gross .05 .02 .01
☐ 309 Dave Hansen .05 .02 .01
☐ 310 Carlos Hernandez .05 .02 .01
☐ 311 Orel Hershiser .10 .05 .01
☐ 312 Eric Karros .10 .05 .01
☐ 313 Pedro Martinez .15 .07 .02
☐ 314 Ramon Martinez .10 .05 .01
☐ 315 Roger McDowell .05 .02 .01
☐ 316 Raul Mondesi .75 .35 .09
☐ 317 Jose Offerman .05 .02 .01
☐ 318 Mike Piazza 1.00 .45 .13
☐ 319 Jody Reed .05 .02 .01
☐ 320 Henry Rodriguez .05 .02 .01
☐ 321 Cory Snyder .05 .02 .01
☐ 322 Darryl Strawberry .10 .05 .01
☐ 323 Tim Wallach .05 .02 .01
☐ 324 Steve Wilson .05 .02 .01
☐ 325 Juan Bell .05 .02 .01
☐ 326 Ricky Bones .05 .02 .01
☐ 327 Alex Diaz .05 .02 .01
☐ 328 Cal Eldred .10 .05 .01
☐ 329 Darryl Hamilton .05 .02 .01
☐ 330 Doug Henry .05 .02 .01
☐ 331 John Jaha .05 .02 .01
☐ 332 Pat Listach .05 .02 .01
☐ 333 Graeme Lloyd .05 .02 .01
☐ 334 Carlos Maldonado .05 .02 .01
☐ 335 Angel Miranda .05 .02 .01
☐ 336 Jaime Navarro .05 .02 .01
☐ 337 Dave Nilsson .05 .02 .01

☐ 338 Rafael Novoa	.05	.02	.01
☐ 339 Troy O'Leary	.05	.02	.01
☐ 340 Jesse Orosco	.05	.02	.01
☐ 341 Kevin Seitzer	.05	.02	.01
☐ 342 Bill Spiers	.05	.02	.01
☐ 343 William Suero	.05	.02	.01
☐ 344 B.J. Surhoff	.05	.02	.01
☐ 345 Dickie Thon	.05	.02	.01
☐ 346 Jose Valentin	.05	.02	.01
☐ 347 Greg Vaughn	.10	.05	.01
☐ 348 Robin Yount	.30	.14	.04
☐ 349 Willie Banks	.05	.02	.01
☐ 350 Bernardo Brito	.05	.02	.01
☐ 351 Scott Erickson	.05	.02	.01
☐ 352 Mark Guthrie	.05	.02	.01
☐ 353 Chip Hale	.05	.02	.01
☐ 354 Brian Harper	.05	.02	.01
☐ 355 Kent Hrbek	.10	.05	.01
☐ 356 Terry Jorgensen	.05	.02	.01
☐ 357 Chuck Knoblauch	.15	.07	.02
☐ 358 Gene Larkin	.05	.02	.01
☐ 359 Scott Leius	.05	.02	.01
☐ 360 Shane Mack	.10	.05	.01
☐ 361 David McCarty	.10	.05	.01
☐ 362 Pat Meares	.05	.02	.01
☐ 363 Pedro Munoz	.05	.02	.01
☐ 364 Derek Parks	.05	.02	.01
☐ 365 Kirby Puckett	.75	.35	.09
☐ 366 Jeff Reboulet	.05	.02	.01
☐ 367 Kevin Tapani	.05	.02	.01
☐ 368 Mike Trombley	.05	.02	.01
☐ 369 George Tsamis	.05	.02	.01
☐ 370 Carl Willis	.05	.02	.01
☐ 371 Dave Winfield	.15	.07	.02
☐ 372 Moises Alou	.15	.07	.02
☐ 373 Brian Barnes	.05	.02	.01
☐ 374 Sean Berry	.05	.02	.01
☐ 375 Frank Bolick	.05	.02	.01
☐ 376 Wil Cordero	.15	.07	.02
☐ 377 Delino DeShields	.10	.05	.01
☐ 378 Jeff Fassero	.05	.02	.01
☐ 379 Darrin Fletcher	.05	.02	.01
☐ 380 Cliff Floyd	.30	.14	.04
☐ 381 Lou Frazier	.05	.02	.01
☐ 382 Marquis Grissom	.15	.07	.02
☐ 383 Gil Heredia	.05	.02	.01
☐ 384 Mike Lansing	.10	.05	.01
☐ 385 Oreste Marrero	.15	.07	.02
☐ 386 Dennis Martinez	.10	.05	.01
☐ 387 Curtis Pride	.20	.09	.03
☐ 388 Mel Rojas	.05	.02	.01
☐ 389 Kirk Rueter	.05	.02	.01
☐ 390 Joe Siddall	.05	.02	.01
☐ 391 John Vander Wal	.05	.02	.01
☐ 392 Larry Walker	.15	.07	.02
☐ 393 John Wetteland	.05	.02	.01
☐ 394 Rondell White	.20	.09	.03
☐ 395 Tim Bogar	.05	.02	.01
☐ 396 Bobby Bonilla	.15	.07	.02
☐ 397 Jeromy Burnitz	.10	.05	.01
☐ 398 Mike Draper	.05	.02	.01
☐ 399 Sid Fernandez	.05	.02	.01
☐ 400 John Franco	.05	.02	.01
☐ 401 Dave Gallagher	.05	.02	.01
☐ 402 Dwight Gooden	.05	.02	.01
☐ 403 Eric Hillman	.05	.02	.01
☐ 404 Todd Hundley	.05	.02	.01
☐ 405 Butch Huskey	.05	.02	.01
☐ 406 Jeff Innis	.05	.02	.01
☐ 407 Howard Johnson	.05	.02	.01
☐ 408 Jeff Kent	.10	.05	.01
☐ 409 Ced Landrum	.05	.02	.01
☐ 410 Mike Maddux	.05	.02	.01
☐ 411 Josias Manzanillo	.05	.02	.01
☐ 412 Jeff McKnight	.05	.02	.01
☐ 413 Eddie Murray	.15	.07	.02
☐ 414 Tito Navarro	.05	.02	.01
☐ 415 Joe Orsulak	.05	.02	.01
☐ 416 Bret Saberhagen	.10	.05	.01
☐ 417 Dave Telgheder	.05	.02	.01
☐ 418 Ryan Thompson	.10	.05	.01
☐ 419 Chico Walker	.05	.02	.01
☐ 420 Jim Abbott	.15	.07	.02
☐ 421 Wade Boggs	.15	.07	.02
☐ 422 Mike Gallego	.05	.02	.01
☐ 423 Mark Hutton	.05	.02	.01
☐ 424 Dion James	.05	.02	.01
☐ 425 Domingo Jean	.05	.02	.01
☐ 426 Pat Kelly	.05	.02	.01
☐ 427 Jimmy Key	.10	.05	.01
☐ 428 Jim Leyritz	.05	.02	.01
☐ 429 Kevin Maas	.05	.02	.01
☐ 430 Don Mattingly	.75	.35	.09
☐ 431 Bobby Munoz	.05	.02	.01
☐ 432 Matt Nokes	.05	.02	.01
☐ 433 Paul O'Neill	.10	.05	.01
☐ 434 Spike Owen	.05	.02	.01
☐ 435 Melido Perez	.05	.02	.01
☐ 436 Lee Smith	.15	.07	.02
☐ 437 Andy Stankiewicz	.05	.02	.01
☐ 438 Mike Stanley	.05	.02	.01
☐ 439 Danny Tartabull	.10	.05	.01
☐ 440 Randy Velarde	.05	.02	.01
☐ 441 Bernie Williams	.10	.05	.01
☐ 442 Gerald Williams	.05	.02	.01
☐ 443 Mike Witt	.05	.02	.01
☐ 444 Marcos Armas	.05	.02	.01
☐ 445 Lance Blankenship	.05	.02	.01
☐ 446 Mike Bordick	.05	.02	.01
☐ 447 Ron Darling	.05	.02	.01
☐ 448 Dennis Eckersley	.15	.07	.02
☐ 449 Brent Gates	.15	.07	.02
☐ 450 Goose Gossage	.15	.07	.02
☐ 451 Scott Hemond	.05	.02	.01
☐ 452 Dave Henderson	.05	.02	.01
☐ 453 Shawn Hillegas	.05	.02	.01
☐ 454 Rick Honeycutt	.05	.02	.01
☐ 455 Scott Lydy	.05	.02	.01
☐ 456 Mark McGwire	.15	.07	.02
☐ 457 Henry Mercedes	.05	.02	.01
☐ 458 Mike Mohler	.05	.02	.01
☐ 459 Troy Neel	.10	.05	.01
☐ 460 Edwin Nunez	.05	.02	.01
☐ 461 Craig Paquette	.05	.02	.01
☐ 462 Ruben Sierra	.15	.07	.02
☐ 463 Terry Steinbach	.10	.05	.01
☐ 464 Todd Van Poppel	.10	.05	.01
☐ 465 Bob Welch	.05	.02	.01
☐ 466 Bobby Witt	.05	.02	.01
☐ 467 Ruben Amaro	.05	.02	.01
☐ 468 Larry Andersen	.05	.02	.01
☐ 469 Kim Batiste	.05	.02	.01
☐ 470 Wes Chamberlain	.05	.02	.01
☐ 471 Darren Daulton	.15	.07	.02
☐ 472 Mariano Duncan	.05	.02	.01
☐ 473 Len Dykstra	.15	.07	.02
☐ 474 Jim Eisenreich	.05	.02	.01
☐ 475 Tommy Greene	.05	.02	.01
☐ 476 Dave Hollins	.15	.07	.02
☐ 477 Pete Incaviglia	.05	.02	.01
☐ 478 Danny Jackson	.05	.02	.01
☐ 479 John Kruk	.15	.07	.02
☐ 480 Tony Longmire	.05	.02	.01
☐ 481 Jeff Manto	.05	.02	.01
☐ 482 Mickey Morandini	.05	.02	.01
☐ 483 Terry Mulholland	.05	.02	.01

	#	Player			
☐	484	Todd Pratt	.05	.02	.01
☐	485	Ben Rivera	.05	.02	.01
☐	486	Curt Schilling	.05	.02	.01
☐	487	Kevin Stocker	.10	.05	.01
☐	488	Milt Thompson	.05	.02	.01
☐	489	David West	.05	.02	.01
☐	490	Mitch Williams	.05	.02	.01
☐	491	Jeff Ballard	.05	.02	.01
☐	492	Jay Bell	.10	.05	.01
☐	493	Scott Bullett	.05	.02	.01
☐	494	Dave Clark	.05	.02	.01
☐	495	Steve Cooke	.05	.02	.01
☐	496	Midre Cummings	.25	.11	.03
☐	497	Mark Dewey	.05	.02	.01
☐	498	Carlos Garcia	.05	.02	.01
☐	499	Jeff King	.05	.02	.01
☐	500	Al Martin	.05	.02	.01
☐	501	Lloyd McClendon	.05	.02	.01
☐	502	Orlando Merced	.10	.05	.01
☐	503	Blas Minor	.05	.02	.01
☐	504	Denny Neagle	.05	.02	.01
☐	505	Tom Prince	.05	.02	.01
☐	506	Don Slaught	.05	.02	.01
☐	507	Zane Smith	.05	.02	.01
☐	508	Randy Tomlin	.05	.02	.01
☐	509	Andy Van Slyke	.15	.07	.02
☐	510	Paul Wagner	.05	.02	.01
☐	511	Tim Wakefield	.05	.02	.01
☐	512	Bob Walk	.05	.02	.01
☐	513	John Wehner	.05	.02	.01
☐	514	Kevin Young	.05	.02	.01
☐	515	Billy Bean	.05	.02	.01
☐	516	Andy Benes	.10	.05	.01
☐	517	Derek Bell	.10	.05	.01
☐	518	Doug Brocail	.05	.02	.01
☐	519	Jarvis Brown	.05	.02	.01
☐	520	Phil Clark	.05	.02	.01
☐	521	Mark Davis	.05	.02	.01
☐	522	Jeff Gardner	.05	.02	.01
☐	523	Pat Gomez	.05	.02	.01
☐	524	Ricky Gutierrez	.05	.02	.01
☐	525	Tony Gwynn	.50	.23	.06
☐	526	Gene Harris	.05	.02	.01
☐	527	Kevin Higgins	.05	.02	.01
☐	528	Trevor Hoffman	.05	.02	.01
☐	529	Luis Lopez	.05	.02	.01
☐	530	Pedro Martinez	.15	.07	.02
☐	531	Melvin Nieves	.15	.07	.02
☐	532	Phil Plantier	.10	.05	.01
☐	533	Frank Seminara	.05	.02	.01
☐	534	Craig Shipley	.05	.02	.01
☐	535	Tim Teufel	.05	.02	.01
☐	536	Guillermo Velasquez	.05	.02	.01
☐	537	Wally Whittehurst	.05	.02	.01
☐	538	Rod Beck	.10	.05	.01
☐	539	Todd Benzinger	.05	.02	.01
☐	540	Barry Bonds	.75	.35	.09
☐	541	Jeff Brantley	.05	.02	.01
☐	542	Dave Burba	.05	.02	.01
☐	543	John Burkett	.10	.05	.01
☐	544	Will Clark	.30	.14	.04
☐	545	Royce Clayton	.10	.05	.01
☐	546	Bryan Hickerson	.05	.02	.01
☐	547	Mike Jackson	.05	.02	.01
☐	548	Darren Lewis	.05	.02	.01
☐	549	Kirt Manwaring	.05	.02	.01
☐	550	Dave Martinez	.05	.02	.01
☐	551	Willie McGee	.05	.02	.01
☐	552	Jeff Reed	.05	.02	.01
☐	553	Dave Righetti	.05	.02	.01
☐	554	Kevin Rogers	.05	.02	.01
☐	555	Steve Scarsone	.05	.02	.01
☐	556	Bill Swift	.05	.02	.01
☐	557	Robby Thompson	.05	.02	.01
☐	558	Salomon Torres	.10	.05	.01
☐	559	Matt Williams	.35	.16	.04
☐	560	Trevor Wilson	.05	.02	.01
☐	561	Rich Amaral	.05	.02	.01
☐	562	Mike Blowers	.05	.02	.01
☐	563	Chris Bosio	.05	.02	.01
☐	564	Jay Buhner	.10	.05	.01
☐	565	Norm Charlton	.05	.02	.01
☐	566	Jim Converse	.05	.02	.01
☐	567	Rich DeLucia	.05	.02	.01
☐	568	Mike Felder	.05	.02	.01
☐	569	Dave Fleming	.05	.02	.01
☐	570	Ken Griffey Jr.	2.00	.90	.25
☐	571	Bill Haselman	.05	.02	.01
☐	572	Dwayne Henry	.05	.02	.01
☐	573	Brad Holman	.05	.02	.01
☐	574	Randy Johnson	.15	.07	.02
☐	575	Greg Litton	.05	.02	.01
☐	576	Edgar Martinez	.05	.02	.01
☐	577	Tino Martinez	.05	.02	.01
☐	578	Jeff Nelson	.05	.02	.01
☐	579	Marc Newfield	.15	.07	.02
☐	580	Roger Salkeld	.05	.02	.01
☐	581	Mackey Sasser	.05	.02	.01
☐	582	Brian Turang	.05	.02	.01
☐	583	Omar Vizquel	.05	.02	.01
☐	584	Dave Valle	.05	.02	.01
☐	585	Luis Alicea	.05	.02	.01
☐	586	Rene Arocha	.10	.05	.01
☐	587	Rheal Cormier	.05	.02	.01
☐	588	Tripp Cromer	.05	.02	.01
☐	589	Bernard Gilkey	.05	.02	.01
☐	590	Lee Guetterman	.05	.02	.01
☐	591	Gregg Jefferies	.15	.07	.02
☐	592	Tim Jones	.05	.02	.01
☐	593	Paul Kilgus	.05	.02	.01
☐	594	Les Lancaster	.05	.02	.01
☐	595	Omar Olivares	.05	.02	.01
☐	596	Jose Oquendo	.05	.02	.01
☐	597	Donovan Osborne	.05	.02	.01
☐	598	Tom Pagnozzi	.05	.02	.01
☐	599	Erik Pappas	.05	.02	.01
☐	600	Geronimo Pena	.05	.02	.01
☐	601	Mike Perez	.05	.02	.01
☐	602	Gerald Perry	.05	.02	.01
☐	603	Stan Royer	.05	.02	.01
☐	604	Ozzie Smith	.40	.18	.05
☐	605	Bob Tewksbury	.05	.02	.01
☐	606	Allen Watson	.05	.02	.01
☐	607	Mark Whiten	.10	.05	.01
☐	608	Todd Zeile	.10	.05	.01
☐	609	Jeff Bronkey	.05	.02	.01
☐	610	Kevin Brown	.05	.02	.01
☐	611	Jose Canseco	.30	.14	.04
☐	612	Doug Dascenzo	.05	.02	.01
☐	613	Butch Davis	.05	.02	.01
☐	614	Mario Diaz	.05	.02	.01
☐	615	Julio Franco	.10	.05	.01
☐	616	Benji Gil	.10	.05	.01
☐	617	Juan Gonzalez	.60	.25	.08
☐	618	Tom Henke	.05	.02	.01
☐	619	Jeff Huson	.05	.02	.01
☐	620	David Hulse	.05	.02	.01
☐	621	Craig Lefferts	.05	.02	.01
☐	622	Rafael Palmeiro	.15	.07	.02
☐	623	Dean Palmer	.10	.05	.01
☐	624	Bob Patterson	.05	.02	.01
☐	625	Roger Pavlik	.05	.02	.01
☐	626	Gary Redus	.05	.02	.01
☐	627	Ivan Rodriguez	.15	.07	.02
☐	628	Kenny Rogers	.05	.02	.01
☐	629	Jon Shave	.05	.02	.01

☐ 630	Doug Strange	.05	.02	.01
☐ 631	Matt Whiteside	.05	.02	.01
☐ 632	Roberto Alomar	.40	.18	.05
☐ 633	Pat Borders	.05	.02	.01
☐ 634	Scott Brow	.05	.02	.01
☐ 635	Rob Butler	.05	.02	.01
☐ 636	Joe Carter	.30	.14	.04
☐ 637	Tony Castillo	.05	.02	.01
☐ 638	Mark Eichhorn	.05	.02	.01
☐ 639	Tony Fernandez	.05	.02	.01
☐ 640	Huck Flener	.05	.02	.01
☐ 641	Alfredo Griffin	.05	.02	.01
☐ 642	Juan Guzman	.10	.05	.01
☐ 643	Rickey Henderson	.15	.07	.02
☐ 644	Pat Hentgen	.10	.05	.01
☐ 645	Randy Knorr	.05	.02	.01
☐ 646	Al Leiter	.05	.02	.01
☐ 647	Domingo Martinez	.05	.02	.01
☐ 648	Paul Molitor	.30	.14	.04
☐ 649	Jack Morris	.15	.07	.02
☐ 650	John Olerud	.15	.07	.02
☐ 651	Ed Sprague	.05	.02	.01
☐ 652	Dave Stewart	.10	.05	.01
☐ 653	Devon White	.05	.02	.01
☐ 654	Woody Williams	.05	.02	.01
☐ 655	Barry Bonds MVP	.40	.18	.05
☐ 656	Greg Maddux CY	.20	.09	.03
☐ 657	Jack McDowell CY	.10	.05	.01
☐ 658	Mike Piazza ROY	.50	.23	.06
☐ 659	Tim Salmon ROY	.15	.07	.02
☐ 660	Frank Thomas MVP	1.00	.45	.13

1994 Pacific All-Latino

Randomly inserted in Pacific purple foil packs at a rate of one in 25, this 20-card set spotlights the greatest Latin players chosen by the Pacific staff. Print run was limited to 8,000 sets. The cards measure the standard size. The fronts feature a full-bleed color player photo with gold foil stamping. The player's name in gold foil appears on the bottom of the photo. Superimposed on the player's native country's flag, the horizontal backs show a close-up color player photo on the left, while 1993 highlights, printed in English and Spanish, appear on the right. The set subdivides into American League (1-10) and National League (11-20) players.

		MINT	EXC	G-VG
COMPLETE SET (20)		30.00	13.50	3.80
COMMON CARD (1-20)		1.00	.45	.13
☐ 1	Benito Santiago	1.00	.45	.13
☐ 2	Dave Magadan	1.00	.45	.13
☐ 3	Andres Galarraga	1.50	.65	.19
☐ 4	Luis Gonzalez	1.00	.45	.13
☐ 5	Jose Offerman	1.00	.45	.13
☐ 6	Bobby Bonilla	1.00	.45	.13
☐ 7	Dennis Martinez	1.00	.45	.13
☐ 8	Mariano Duncan	1.00	.45	.13
☐ 9	Orlando Merced	1.00	.45	.13
☐ 10	Jose Rijo	1.50	.65	.19
☐ 11	Danny Tartabull	1.00	.45	.13
☐ 12	Ruben Sierra	1.50	.65	.19
☐ 13	Ivan Rodriguez	1.50	.65	.19
☐ 14	Juan Gonzalez	8.00	3.60	1.00
☐ 15	Jose Canseco	4.00	1.80	.50
☐ 16	Rafael Palmeiro	1.50	.65	.19
☐ 17	Roberto Alomar	6.00	2.70	.75
☐ 18	Eduardo Perez	1.00	.45	.13
☐ 19	Alex Fernandez	1.50	.65	.19
☐ 20	Omar Vizquel	1.00	.45	.13

1994 Pacific Gold Prisms

Randomly inserted in Pacific purple foil packs at a rate of one in 25, this 20-card prism "Home Run Leaders" set honors the top 1993 home run leaders. Print run was reportedly limited to 8,000 sets. The cards measure standard size. The fronts feature a cut-out color player photo against a gold prism background. The player's name appears at the bottom, highlighted in team colors. Superimposed on a baseball field, the horizontal backs show a close-up color player photo on the left, while the number of home runs the player hit in 1993 is highlighted on a large baseball icon on the right. The set subdivides into American League (1-10) and National League (11-20) players. The cards are numbered on the back.

		MINT	EXC	G-VG
COMPLETE SET (20)		100.00	45.00	12.50
COMMON CARD (1-20)		1.50	.65	.19
☐ 1	Juan Gonzalez	8.00	3.60	1.00
☐ 2	Ken Griffey Jr.	25.00	11.50	3.10
☐ 3	Frank Thomas	25.00	11.50	3.10
☐ 4	Albert Belle	8.00	3.60	1.00
☐ 5	Rafael Palmeiro	2.50	1.15	.30

☐ 6	Joe Carter	4.00	1.80	.50
☐ 7	Dean Palmer	1.50	.65	.19
☐ 8	Mickey Tettleton	1.50	.65	.19
☐ 9	Tim Salmon	4.00	1.80	.50
☐ 10	Danny Tartabull	1.50	.65	.19
☐ 11	Barry Bonds	10.00	4.50	1.25
☐ 12	David Justice	4.00	1.80	.50
☐ 13	Matt Williams	5.00	2.30	.60
☐ 14	Fred McGriff	4.00	1.80	.50
☐ 15	Ron Gant	1.50	.65	.19
☐ 16	Mike Piazza	12.00	5.50	1.50
☐ 17	Bobby Bonilla	1.50	.65	.19
☐ 18	Phil Plantier	1.50	.65	.19
☐ 19	Sammy Sosa	2.50	1.15	.30
☐ 20	Rick Wilkins	1.50	.65	.19

1994 Pacific Silver Prisms

Randomly inserted in Pacific foil packs, this 36-card set is also known as "Jewels of the Crown". The print run was reportedly limited to 8,000 sets. The cards measure the standard size. The fronts feature a cut-out color player photo against a prism background that is either circular or triangular. The triangular versions were randomly inserted in purple packs and the circular one per black retail pack. The circular versions are valued between 25 to 50 percent of the triangular. The player's name appears at the bottom, highlighted in team colors. On a red velvet background, the horizontal backs show a close-up color player photo on the left, while highlights of the 1993 season in English and Spanish are printed over a unique jewel design on the right. The set divides into American League (1-18) and National League (19-36) players.

	MINT	EXC	G-VG
COMPLETE SET (36)	140.00	65.00	17.50
COMMON CARD (1-36)	1.50	.65	.19
*CIRCULAR: .25X TO .50X VALUES BELOW			

☐ 1	Robin Yount	4.00	1.80	.50
☐ 2	Juan Gonzalez	8.00	3.60	1.00
☐ 3	Rafael Palmeiro	2.50	1.15	.30
☐ 4	Paul Molitor	4.00	1.80	.50
☐ 5	Roberto Alomar	6.00	2.70	.75
☐ 6	John Olerud	2.50	1.15	.30
☐ 7	Randy Johnson	2.50	1.15	.30
☐ 8	Ken Griffey Jr.	25.00	11.50	3.10
☐ 9	Wade Boggs	2.50	1.15	.30
☐ 10	Don Mattingly	10.00	4.50	1.25
☐ 11	Kirby Puckett	10.00	4.50	1.25
☐ 12	Tim Salmon	4.00	1.80	.50
☐ 13	Frank Thomas	25.00	11.50	3.10
☐ 14	Fernando Valenzuela	1.50	.65	.19
☐ 15	Cal Ripken	18.00	8.00	2.30
☐ 16	Carlos Baerga	4.00	1.80	.50
☐ 17	Kenny Lofton	6.00	2.70	.75
☐ 18	Cecil Fielder	2.50	1.15	.30
☐ 19	John Burkett	1.50	.65	.19
☐ 20	Andres Galarraga	2.50	1.15	.30
☐ 21	Charlie Hayes	1.50	.65	.19
☐ 22	Orestes Destrade	1.50	.65	.19
☐ 23	Jeff Conine	2.50	1.15	.30
☐ 24	Jeff Bagwell	12.00	5.50	1.50
☐ 25	Mark Grace	1.50	.65	.19
☐ 26	Ryne Sandberg	8.00	3.60	1.00
☐ 27	Gregg Jefferies	2.50	1.15	.30
☐ 28	Barry Bonds	10.00	4.50	1.25
☐ 29	Mike Piazza	12.00	5.50	1.50
☐ 30	Greg Maddux	6.00	2.70	.75
☐ 31	Darren Daulton	2.50	1.15	.30
☐ 32	John Kruk	2.50	1.15	.30
☐ 33	Lenny Dykstra	2.50	1.15	.30
☐ 34	Orlando Merced	1.50	.65	.19
☐ 35	Tony Gwynn	6.00	2.70	.75
☐ 36	Robby Thompson	1.50	.65	.19

1992 Pinnacle

The 1992 Score Pinnacle baseball set consists of two series each with 310 cards measuring the standard size (2 1/2" by 3 1/2"). Series I count goods pack had 16 cards per pack, while the cello pack featured 27 cards. Two 12-card bonus subsets, displaying the artwork of Chris Greco, were randomly inserted in series I and II count good packs. The fronts feature glossy color player photos, on a black background accented by thin white borders. On a black background, the horizontally oriented backs carry a close-up portrait, statistics (1991 and career), and an in-depth player profile. An anti-counterfeit device appears in the bottom border of each card back. Special subsets featured include '92 Rookie Prospects (52, 55, 168, 247-261, 263-280), Idols (281-286), Sidelines (287-294), Draft Picks (295-304), Shades (305-310), Idols (584-591), Sidelines (592-596), Shades (601-605), Grips (606-612), and Technicians (614-620). The cards are num-

bered on the back. Rookie Cards in the set include Chad Curtis, Cliff Floyd, Benji Gil, Tyler Green, Bobby Jones, Pat Listach, Manny Ramirez, Scott Ruffcorn, Al Shirley, Allen Watson, and Bob Zupcic.

	MINT	EXC	G-VG
COMPLETE SET (620)	40.00	18.00	5.00
COMPLETE SERIES 1 (310)	25.00	11.50	3.10
COMPLETE SERIES 2 (310)	15.00	6.75	1.90
COMMON CARD (1-310)	.10	.05	.01
COMMON CARD (311-620)	.10	.05	.01

	No.	Player	MINT	EXC	G-VG
☐	1	Frank Thomas	4.00	1.80	.50
☐	2	Benito Santiago	.10	.05	.01
☐	3	Carlos Baerga	.50	.23	.06
☐	4	Cecil Fielder	.30	.14	.04
☐	5	Barry Larkin	.25	.11	.03
☐	6	Ozzie Smith	.40	.18	.05
☐	7	Willie McGee	.15	.07	.02
☐	8	Paul Molitor	.30	.14	.04
☐	9	Andy Van Slyke	.25	.11	.03
☐	10	Ryne Sandberg	.75	.35	.09
☐	11	Kevin Seitzer	.10	.05	.01
☐	12	Len Dykstra	.25	.11	.03
☐	13	Edgar Martinez	.15	.07	.02
☐	14	Ruben Sierra	.25	.11	.03
☐	15	Howard Johnson	.15	.07	.02
☐	16	Dave Henderson	.10	.05	.01
☐	17	Devon White	.15	.07	.02
☐	18	Terry Pendleton	.25	.11	.03
☐	19	Steve Finley	.10	.05	.01
☐	20	Kirby Puckett	1.00	.45	.13
☐	21	Orel Hershiser	.15	.07	.02
☐	22	Hal Morris	.15	.07	.02
☐	23	Don Mattingly	1.00	.45	.13
☐	24	Delino DeShields	.25	.11	.03
☐	25	Dennis Eckersley	.25	.11	.03
☐	26	Ellis Burks	.15	.07	.02
☐	27	Jay Buhner	.15	.07	.02
☐	28	Matt Williams	.50	.23	.06
☐	29	Lou Whitaker	.25	.11	.03
☐	30	Alex Fernandez	.30	.14	.04
☐	31	Albert Belle	1.00	.45	.13
☐	32	Todd Zeile	.15	.07	.02
☐	33	Tony Pena	.10	.05	.01
☐	34	Jay Bell	.15	.07	.02
☐	35	Rafael Palmeiro	.30	.14	.04
☐	36	Wes Chamberlain	.10	.05	.01
☐	37	George Bell	.15	.07	.02
☐	38	Robin Yount	.30	.14	.04
☐	39	Vince Coleman	.10	.05	.01
☐	40	Bruce Hurst	.10	.05	.01
☐	41	Harold Baines	.15	.07	.02
☐	42	Chuck Finley	.10	.05	.01
☐	43	Ken Caminiti	.15	.07	.02
☐	44	Ben McDonald	.15	.07	.02
☐	45	Roberto Alomar	.50	.23	.06
☐	46	Chili Davis	.15	.07	.02
☐	47	Bill Doran	.10	.05	.01
☐	48	Jerald Clark	.10	.05	.01
☐	49	Jose Lind	.10	.05	.01
☐	50	Nolan Ryan	3.00	1.35	.40
☐	51	Phil Plantier	.25	.11	.03
☐	52	Gary DiSarcina	.15	.07	.02
☐	53	Kevin Bass	.10	.05	.01
☐	54	Pat Kelly	.15	.07	.02
☐	55	Mark Wohlers	.15	.07	.02
☐	56	Walt Weiss	.10	.05	.01
☐	57	Lenny Harris	.10	.05	.01
☐	58	Ivan Calderon	.10	.05	.01
☐	59	Harold Reynolds	.10	.05	.01
☐	60	George Brett	1.00	.45	.13
☐	61	Gregg Olson	.10	.05	.01
☐	62	Orlando Merced	.15	.07	.02
☐	63	Steve Decker	.10	.05	.01
☐	64	John Franco	.10	.05	.01
☐	65	Greg Maddux	.50	.23	.06
☐	66	Alex Cole	.10	.05	.01
☐	67	Dave Hollins	.25	.11	.03
☐	68	Kent Hrbek	.15	.07	.02
☐	69	Tom Pagnozzi	.10	.05	.01
☐	70	Jeff Bagwell	2.00	.90	.25
☐	71	Jim Gantner	.10	.05	.01
☐	72	Matt Nokes	.10	.05	.01
☐	73	Brian Harper	.10	.05	.01
☐	74	Andy Benes	.15	.07	.02
☐	75	Tom Glavine	.25	.11	.03
☐	76	Terry Steinbach	.15	.07	.02
☐	77	Dennis Martinez	.15	.07	.02
☐	78	John Olerud	.25	.11	.03
☐	79	Ozzie Guillen	.10	.05	.01
☐	80	Darryl Strawberry	.15	.07	.02
☐	81	Gary Gaetti	.10	.05	.01
☐	82	Dave Righetti	.10	.05	.01
☐	83	Chris Hoiles	.25	.11	.03
☐	84	Andujar Cedeno	.15	.07	.02
☐	85	Jack Clark	.15	.07	.02
☐	86	David Howard	.10	.05	.01
☐	87	Bill Gullickson	.10	.05	.01
☐	88	Bernard Gilkey	.15	.07	.02
☐	89	Kevin Elster	.10	.05	.01
☐	90	Kevin Maas	.10	.05	.01
☐	91	Mark Lewis	.10	.05	.01
☐	92	Greg Vaughn	.15	.07	.02
☐	93	Bret Barberie	.10	.05	.01
☐	94	Dave Smith	.10	.05	.01
☐	95	Roger Clemens	.60	.25	.08
☐	96	Doug Drabek	.25	.11	.03
☐	97	Omar Vizquel	.10	.05	.01
☐	98	Jose Guzman	.10	.05	.01
☐	99	Juan Samuel	.10	.05	.01
☐	100	David Justice	.50	.23	.06
☐	101	Tom Browning	.10	.05	.01
☐	102	Mark Gubicza	.10	.05	.01
☐	103	Mickey Morandini	.10	.05	.01
☐	104	Ed Whitson	.10	.05	.01
☐	105	Lance Parrish	.15	.07	.02
☐	106	Scott Erickson	.10	.05	.01
☐	107	Jack McDowell	.25	.11	.03
☐	108	Dave Stieb	.15	.07	.02
☐	109	Mike Moore	.10	.05	.01
☐	110	Travis Fryman	.50	.23	.06
☐	111	Dwight Gooden	.15	.07	.02
☐	112	Fred McGriff	.50	.23	.06
☐	113	Alan Trammell	.25	.11	.03
☐	114	Roberto Kelly	.15	.07	.02
☐	115	Andre Dawson	.25	.11	.03
☐	116	Bill Landrum	.10	.05	.01
☐	117	Brian McRae	.25	.11	.03
☐	118	B.J. Surhoff	.10	.05	.01
☐	119	Chuck Knoblauch	.35	.16	.04
☐	120	Steve Olin	.15	.07	.02
☐	121	Robin Ventura	.25	.11	.03
☐	122	Will Clark	.50	.23	.06
☐	123	Tino Martinez	.15	.07	.02
☐	124	Dale Murphy	.25	.11	.03
☐	125	Pete O'Brien	.10	.05	.01
☐	126	Ray Lankford	.25	.11	.03
☐	127	Juan Gonzalez	1.50	.65	.19
☐	128	Ron Gant	.15	.07	.02
☐	129	Marquis Grissom	.25	.11	.03
☐	130	Jose Canseco	.60	.25	.08
☐	131	Mike Greenwell	.15	.07	.02
☐	132	Mark Langston	.25	.11	.03
☐	133	Brett Butler	.15	.07	.02

☐ 134	Kelly Gruber	.10	.05	.01
☐ 135	Chris Sabo	.15	.07	.02
☐ 136	Mark Grace	.25	.11	.03
☐ 137	Tony Fernandez	.15	.07	.02
☐ 138	Glenn Davis	.10	.05	.01
☐ 139	Pedro Munoz	.15	.07	.02
☐ 140	Craig Biggio	.15	.07	.02
☐ 141	Pete Schourek	.15	.07	.02
☐ 142	Mike Boddicker	.10	.05	.01
☐ 143	Robby Thompson	.10	.05	.01
☐ 144	Mel Hall	.10	.05	.01
☐ 145	Bryan Harvey	.15	.07	.02
☐ 146	Mike LaValliere	.10	.05	.01
☐ 147	John Kruk	.25	.11	.03
☐ 148	Joe Carter	.50	.23	.06
☐ 149	Greg Olson	.10	.05	.01
☐ 150	Julio Franco	.15	.07	.02
☐ 151	Darryl Hamilton	.15	.07	.02
☐ 152	Felix Fermin	.10	.05	.01
☐ 153	Jose Offerman	.10	.05	.01
☐ 154	Paul O'Neill	.15	.07	.02
☐ 155	Tommy Greene	.15	.07	.02
☐ 156	Ivan Rodriguez	.30	.14	.04
☐ 157	Dave Stewart	.15	.07	.02
☐ 158	Jeff Reardon	.15	.07	.02
☐ 159	Felix Jose	.15	.07	.02
☐ 160	Doug Dascenzo	.10	.05	.01
☐ 161	Tim Wallach	.10	.05	.01
☐ 162	Dan Plesac	.10	.05	.01
☐ 163	Luis Gonzalez	.15	.07	.02
☐ 164	Mike Henneman	.10	.05	.01
☐ 165	Mike Devereaux	.15	.07	.02
☐ 166	Luis Polonia	.10	.05	.01
☐ 167	Mike Sharperson	.10	.05	.01
☐ 168	Chris Donnels	.10	.05	.01
☐ 169	Greg W. Harris	.10	.05	.01
☐ 170	Deion Sanders	.50	.23	.06
☐ 171	Mike Schooler	.10	.05	.01
☐ 172	Jose DeJesus	.10	.05	.01
☐ 173	Jeff Montgomery	.15	.07	.02
☐ 174	Milt Cuyler	.10	.05	.01
☐ 175	Wade Boggs	.25	.11	.03
☐ 176	Kevin Tapani	.10	.05	.01
☐ 177	Bill Spiers	.10	.05	.01
☐ 178	Tim Raines	.25	.11	.03
☐ 179	Randy Milligan	.10	.05	.01
☐ 180	Rob Dibble	.10	.05	.01
☐ 181	Kirt Manwaring	.10	.05	.01
☐ 182	Pascual Perez	.10	.05	.01
☐ 183	Juan Guzman	.15	.07	.02
☐ 184	John Smiley	.10	.05	.01
☐ 185	David Segui	.10	.05	.01
☐ 186	Omar Olivares	.10	.05	.01
☐ 187	Joe Slusarski	.10	.05	.01
☐ 188	Erik Hanson	.10	.05	.01
☐ 189	Mark Portugal	.10	.05	.01
☐ 190	Walt Terrell	.10	.05	.01
☐ 191	John Smoltz	.15	.07	.02
☐ 192	Wilson Alvarez	.30	.14	.04
☐ 193	Jimmy Key	.15	.07	.02
☐ 194	Larry Walker	.25	.11	.03
☐ 195	Lee Smith	.25	.11	.03
☐ 196	Pete Harnisch	.15	.07	.02
☐ 197	Mike Harkey	.10	.05	.01
☐ 198	Frank Tanana	.10	.05	.01
☐ 199	Terry Mulholland	.10	.05	.01
☐ 200	Cal Ripken	1.00	.45	.13
☐ 201	Dave Magadan	.10	.05	.01
☐ 202	Bud Black	.10	.05	.01
☐ 203	Terry Shumpert	.10	.05	.01
☐ 204	Mike Mussina	.75	.35	.09
☐ 205	Mo Vaughn	.50	.23	.06
☐ 206	Steve Farr	.10	.05	.01
☐ 207	Darrin Jackson	.10	.05	.01
☐ 208	Jerry Browne	.10	.05	.01
☐ 209	Jeff Russell	.10	.05	.01
☐ 210	Mike Scioscia	.10	.05	.01
☐ 211	Rick Aguilera	.15	.07	.02
☐ 212	Jaime Navarro	.10	.05	.01
☐ 213	Randy Tomlin	.10	.05	.01
☐ 214	Bobby Thigpen	.10	.05	.01
☐ 215	Mark Gardner	.10	.05	.01
☐ 216	Norm Charlton	.10	.05	.01
☐ 217	Mark McGwire	.25	.11	.03
☐ 218	Skeeter Barnes	.10	.05	.01
☐ 219	Bob Tewksbury	.10	.05	.01
☐ 220	Junior Felix	.10	.05	.01
☐ 221	Sam Horn	.10	.05	.01
☐ 222	Jody Reed	.10	.05	.01
☐ 223	Luis Sojo	.10	.05	.01
☐ 224	Jerome Walton	.10	.05	.01
☐ 225	Darryl Kile	.15	.07	.02
☐ 226	Mickey Tettleton	.15	.07	.02
☐ 227	Dan Pasqua	.10	.05	.01
☐ 228	Jim Gott	.10	.05	.01
☐ 229	Bernie Williams	.15	.07	.02
☐ 230	Shane Mack	.15	.07	.02
☐ 231	Steve Avery	.30	.14	.04
☐ 232	Dave Valle	.10	.05	.01
☐ 233	Mark Leonard	.10	.05	.01
☐ 234	Spike Owen	.10	.05	.01
☐ 235	Gary Sheffield	.25	.11	.03
☐ 236	Steve Chitren	.10	.05	.01
☐ 237	Zane Smith	.10	.05	.01
☐ 238	Tom Gordon	.10	.05	.01
☐ 239	Jose Oquendo	.10	.05	.01
☐ 240	Todd Stottlemyre	.10	.05	.01
☐ 241	Darren Daulton	.25	.11	.03
☐ 242	Tim Naehring	.10	.05	.01
☐ 243	Tony Phillips	.10	.05	.01
☐ 244	Shawon Dunston	.10	.05	.01
☐ 245	Manny Lee	.10	.05	.01
☐ 246	Mike Pagliarulo	.10	.05	.01
☐ 247	Jim Thome	1.00	.45	.13
☐ 248	Luis Mercedes	.10	.05	.01
☐ 249	Cal Eldred	.15	.07	.02
☐ 250	Derek Bell	.15	.07	.02
☐ 251	Arthur Rhodes	.15	.07	.02
☐ 252	Scott Cooper	.15	.07	.02
☐ 253	Roberto Hernandez	.15	.07	.02
☐ 254	Mo Sanford	.10	.05	.01
☐ 255	Scott Servais	.10	.05	.01
☐ 256	Eric Karros	.25	.11	.03
☐ 257	Andy Mota	.10	.05	.01
☐ 258	Keith Mitchell	.10	.05	.01
☐ 259	Joel Johnston	.10	.05	.01
☐ 260	John Wehner	.10	.05	.01
☐ 261	Gino Minutelli	.10	.05	.01
☐ 262	Greg Gagne	.10	.05	.01
☐ 263	Stan Royer	.10	.05	.01
☐ 264	Carlos Garcia	.15	.07	.02
☐ 265	Andy Ashby	.10	.05	.01
☐ 266	Kim Batiste	.10	.05	.01
☐ 267	Julio Valera	.10	.05	.01
☐ 268	Royce Clayton	.25	.11	.03
☐ 269	Gary Scott	.10	.05	.01
☐ 270	Kirk Dressendorfer	.10	.05	.01
☐ 271	Sean Berry	.15	.07	.02
☐ 272	Lance Dickson	.10	.05	.01
☐ 273	Rob Maurer	.15	.07	.02
☐ 274	Scott Brosius	.10	.05	.01
☐ 275	Dave Fleming	.15	.07	.02
☐ 276	Lenny Webster	.10	.05	.01
☐ 277	Mike Humphreys	.15	.07	.02
☐ 278	Freddie Benavides	.10	.05	.01
☐ 279	Harvey Pulliam	.10	.05	.01

☐	280 Jeff Carter	.10	.05	.01
☐	281 Jim Abbott I Nolan Ryan	.60	.25	.08
☐	282 Wade Boggs I George Brett	.30	.14	.04
☐	283 Ken Griffey Jr. I Rickey Henderson	.75	.35	.09
☐	284 Wally Joyner I Dale Murphy	.15	.07	.02
☐	285 Chuck Knoblauch I Ozzie Smith	.25	.11	.03
☐	286 Robin Ventura I Lou Gehrig	.25	.11	.03
☐	287 Robin Yount SIDE	.15	.07	.02
☐	288 Bob Tewksbury SIDE	.10	.05	.01
☐	289 Kirby Puckett SIDE	.40	.18	.05
☐	290 Kenny Lofton SIDE	1.00	.45	.13
☐	291 Jack McDowell SIDE	.15	.07	.02
☐	292 John Burkett SIDE	.15	.07	.02
☐	293 Dwight Smith SIDE	.10	.05	.01
☐	294 Nolan Ryan SIDE	1.25	.55	.16
☐	295 Manny Ramirez DP	4.00	1.80	.50
☐	296 Cliff Floyd DP UER (Throws right, not left as indicated on back)	3.00	1.35	.40
☐	297 Al Shirley DP	.20	.09	.03
☐	298 Brian Barber DP	.20	.09	.03
☐	299 Jon Farrell DP	.15	.07	.02
☐	300 Scott Ruffcorn DP	.60	.25	.08
☐	301 Tyrone Hill DP	.20	.09	.03
☐	302 Benji Gil DP	.50	.23	.06
☐	303 Tyler Green DP	.20	.09	.03
☐	304 Allen Watson DP	.30	.14	.04
☐	305 Jay Buhner SH	.15	.07	.02
☐	306 Roberto Alomar SH	.25	.11	.03
☐	307 Chuck Knoblauch SH	.15	.07	.02
☐	308 Darryl Strawberry SH	.10	.05	.01
☐	309 Danny Tartabull SH	.10	.05	.01
☐	310 Bobby Bonilla SH	.15	.07	.02
☐	311 Mike Felder	.10	.05	.01
☐	312 Storm Davis	.10	.05	.01
☐	313 Tim Teufel	.10	.05	.01
☐	314 Tom Brunansky	.10	.05	.01
☐	315 Rex Hudler	.10	.05	.01
☐	316 Dave Otto	.10	.05	.01
☐	317 Jeff King	.10	.05	.01
☐	318 Dan Gladden	.10	.05	.01
☐	319 Bill Pecota	.10	.05	.01
☐	320 Franklin Stubbs	.10	.05	.01
☐	321 Gary Carter	.25	.11	.03
☐	322 Melido Perez	.10	.05	.01
☐	323 Eric Davis	.10	.05	.01
☐	324 Greg Myers	.10	.05	.01
☐	325 Pete Incaviglia	.10	.05	.01
☐	326 Von Hayes	.10	.05	.01
☐	327 Greg Swindell	.10	.05	.01
☐	328 Steve Sax	.10	.05	.01
☐	329 Chuck McElroy	.10	.05	.01
☐	330 Gregg Jefferies	.30	.14	.04
☐	331 Joe Oliver	.10	.05	.01
☐	332 Paul Faries	.10	.05	.01
☐	333 David West	.10	.05	.01
☐	334 Craig Grebeck	.10	.05	.01
☐	335 Chris Hammond	.10	.05	.01
☐	336 Billy Ripken	.10	.05	.01
☐	337 Scott Sanderson	.10	.05	.01
☐	338 Dick Schofield	.10	.05	.01
☐	339 Bob Milacki	.10	.05	.01
☐	340 Kevin Reimer	.10	.05	.01
☐	341 Jose DeLeon	.10	.05	.01
☐	342 Henry Cotto	.10	.05	.01
☐	343 Daryl Boston	.10	.05	.01
☐	344 Kevin Gross	.10	.05	.01
☐	345 Milt Thompson	.10	.05	.01
☐	346 Luis Rivera	.10	.05	.01
☐	347 Al Osuna	.10	.05	.01
☐	348 Rob Deer	.10	.05	.01
☐	349 Tim Leary	.10	.05	.01
☐	350 Mike Stanton	.10	.05	.01
☐	351 Dean Palmer	.15	.07	.02
☐	352 Trevor Wilson	.10	.05	.01
☐	353 Mark Eichhorn	.10	.05	.01
☐	354 Scott Aldred	.10	.05	.01
☐	355 Mark Whiten	.15	.07	.02
☐	356 Leo Gomez	.10	.05	.01
☐	357 Rafael Belliard	.10	.05	.01
☐	358 Carlos Quintana	.10	.05	.01
☐	359 Mark Davis	.10	.05	.01
☐	360 Chris Nabholz	.10	.05	.01
☐	361 Carlton Fisk	.25	.11	.03
☐	362 Joe Orsulak	.10	.05	.01
☐	363 Eric Anthony	.10	.05	.01
☐	364 Greg Hibbard	.10	.05	.01
☐	365 Scott Leius	.10	.05	.01
☐	366 Hensley Meulens	.10	.05	.01
☐	367 Chris Bosio	.10	.05	.01
☐	368 Brian Downing	.10	.05	.01
☐	369 Sammy Sosa	.25	.11	.03
☐	370 Stan Belinda	.10	.05	.01
☐	371 Joe Grahe	.10	.05	.01
☐	372 Luis Salazar	.10	.05	.01
☐	373 Lance Johnson	.10	.05	.01
☐	374 Kal Daniels	.10	.05	.01
☐	375 Dave Winfield	.30	.14	.04
☐	376 Brook Jacoby	.10	.05	.01
☐	377 Mariano Duncan	.10	.05	.01
☐	378 Ron Darling	.10	.05	.01
☐	379 Randy Johnson	.25	.11	.03
☐	380 Chito Martinez	.10	.05	.01
☐	381 Andres Galarraga	.25	.11	.03
☐	382 Willie Randolph	.15	.07	.02
☐	383 Charles Nagy	.10	.05	.01
☐	384 Tim Belcher	.10	.05	.01
☐	385 Duane Ward	.15	.07	.02
☐	386 Vicente Palacios	.10	.05	.01
☐	387 Mike Gallego	.10	.05	.01
☐	388 Rich DeLucia	.10	.05	.01
☐	389 Scott Radinsky	.10	.05	.01
☐	390 Damon Berryhill	.10	.05	.01
☐	391 Kirk McCaskill	.10	.05	.01
☐	392 Pedro Guerrero	.15	.07	.02
☐	393 Kevin Mitchell	.15	.07	.02
☐	394 Dickie Thon	.10	.05	.01
☐	395 Bobby Bonilla	.25	.11	.03
☐	396 Bill Wegman	.10	.05	.01
☐	397 Dave Martinez	.10	.05	.01
☐	398 Rick Sutcliffe	.15	.07	.02
☐	399 Larry Andersen	.10	.05	.01
☐	400 Tony Gwynn	.60	.25	.08
☐	401 Rickey Henderson	.25	.11	.03
☐	402 Greg Cadaret	.10	.05	.01
☐	403 Keith Miller	.10	.05	.01
☐	404 Bip Roberts	.15	.07	.02
☐	405 Kevin Brown	.15	.07	.02
☐	406 Mitch Williams	.15	.07	.02
☐	407 Frank Viola	.15	.07	.02
☐	408 Darren Lewis	.15	.07	.02
☐	409 Bob Welch	.10	.05	.01
☐	410 Bob Walk	.10	.05	.01
☐	411 Todd Frohwirth	.10	.05	.01
☐	412 Brian Hunter	.10	.05	.01
☐	413 Ron Karkovice	.10	.05	.01
☐	414 Mike Morgan	.10	.05	.01
☐	415 Joe Hesketh	.10	.05	.01
☐	416 Don Slaught	.10	.05	.01
☐	417 Tom Henke	.15	.07	.02

☐ 418	Kurt Stillwell	.10	.05	.01
☐ 419	Hector Villaneuva	.10	.05	.01
☐ 420	Glenallen Hill	.10	.05	.01
☐ 421	Pat Borders	.10	.05	.01
☐ 422	Charlie Hough	.15	.07	.02
☐ 423	Charlie Leibrandt	.10	.05	.01
☐ 424	Eddie Murray	.25	.11	.03
☐ 425	Jesse Barfield	.10	.05	.01
☐ 426	Mark Lemke	.10	.05	.01
☐ 427	Kevin McReynolds	.10	.05	.01
☐ 428	Gilberto Reyes	.10	.05	.01
☐ 429	Ramon Martinez	.15	.07	.02
☐ 430	Steve Buechele	.10	.05	.01
☐ 431	David Wells	.10	.05	.01
☐ 432	Kyle Abbott	.10	.05	.01
☐ 433	John Habyan	.10	.05	.01
☐ 434	Kevin Appier	.15	.07	.02
☐ 435	Gene Larkin	.10	.05	.01
☐ 436	Sandy Alomar Jr.	.15	.07	.02
☐ 437	Mike Jackson	.10	.05	.01
☐ 438	Todd Benzinger	.10	.05	.01
☐ 439	Teddy Higuera	.10	.05	.01
☐ 440	Reggie Sanders	.50	.23	.06
☐ 441	Mark Carreon	.10	.05	.01
☐ 442	Bret Saberhagen	.15	.07	.02
☐ 443	Gene Nelson	.10	.05	.01
☐ 444	Jay Howell	.10	.05	.01
☐ 445	Roger McDowell	.10	.05	.01
☐ 446	Sid Bream	.10	.05	.01
☐ 447	Mackey Sasser	.10	.05	.01
☐ 448	Bill Swift	.15	.07	.02
☐ 449	Hubie Brooks	.10	.05	.01
☐ 450	David Cone	.25	.11	.03
☐ 451	Bobby Witt	.10	.05	.01
☐ 452	Brady Anderson	.15	.07	.02
☐ 453	Lee Stevens	.10	.05	.01
☐ 454	Luis Aquino	.10	.05	.01
☐ 455	Carney Lansford	.15	.07	.02
☐ 456	Carlos Hernandez	.10	.05	.01
☐ 457	Danny Jackson	.10	.05	.01
☐ 458	Gerald Young	.10	.05	.01
☐ 459	Tom Candiotti	.10	.05	.01
☐ 460	Billy Hatcher	.10	.05	.01
☐ 461	John Wetteland	.10	.05	.01
☐ 462	Mike Bordick	.10	.05	.01
☐ 463	Don Robinson	.10	.05	.01
☐ 464	Jeff Johnson	.10	.05	.01
☐ 465	Lonnie Smith	.10	.05	.01
☐ 466	Paul Assenmacher	.10	.05	.01
☐ 467	Alvin Davis	.10	.05	.01
☐ 468	Jim Eisenreich	.10	.05	.01
☐ 469	Brent Mayne	.10	.05	.01
☐ 470	Jeff Brantley	.10	.05	.01
☐ 471	Tim Burke	.10	.05	.01
☐ 472	Pat Mahomes	.25	.11	.03
☐ 473	Ryan Bowen	.10	.05	.01
☐ 474	Bryn Smith	.10	.05	.01
☐ 475	Mike Flanagan	.10	.05	.01
☐ 476	Reggie Jefferson	.10	.05	.01
☐ 477	Jeff Blauser	.15	.07	.02
☐ 478	Craig Lefferts	.10	.05	.01
☐ 479	Todd Worrell	.10	.05	.01
☐ 480	Scott Scudder	.10	.05	.01
☐ 481	Kirk Gibson	.15	.07	.02
☐ 482	Kenny Rogers	.10	.05	.01
☐ 483	Jack Morris	.25	.11	.03
☐ 484	Russ Swan	.10	.05	.01
☐ 485	Mike Huff	.10	.05	.01
☐ 486	Ken Hill	.15	.07	.02
☐ 487	Geronimo Pena	.10	.05	.01
☐ 488	Charlie O'Brien	.10	.05	.01
☐ 489	Mike Maddux	.10	.05	.01
☐ 490	Scott Livingstone	.10	.05	.01
☐ 491	Carl Willis	.10	.05	.01
☐ 492	Kelly Downs	.10	.05	.01
☐ 493	Dennis Cook	.10	.05	.01
☐ 494	Joe Magrane	.10	.05	.01
☐ 495	Bob Kipper	.10	.05	.01
☐ 496	Jose Mesa	.10	.05	.01
☐ 497	Charlie Hayes	.15	.07	.02
☐ 498	Joe Girardi	.10	.05	.01
☐ 499	Doug Jones	.10	.05	.01
☐ 500	Barry Bonds	1.00	.45	.13
☐ 501	Bill Krueger	.10	.05	.01
☐ 502	Glenn Braggs	.10	.05	.01
☐ 503	Eric King	.10	.05	.01
☐ 504	Frank Castillo	.10	.05	.01
☐ 505	Mike Gardiner	.10	.05	.01
☐ 506	Cory Snyder	.10	.05	.01
☐ 507	Steve Howe	.10	.05	.01
☐ 508	Jose Rijo	.15	.07	.02
☐ 509	Sid Fernandez	.15	.07	.02
☐ 510	Archi Cianfrocco	.10	.05	.01
☐ 511	Mark Guthrie	.10	.05	.01
☐ 512	Bob Ojeda	.10	.05	.01
☐ 513	John Doherty	.20	.09	.03
☐ 514	Dante Bichette	.25	.11	.03
☐ 515	Juan Berenguer	.10	.05	.01
☐ 516	Jeff M. Robinson	.10	.05	.01
☐ 517	Mike Macfarlane	.10	.05	.01
☐ 518	Matt Young	.10	.05	.01
☐ 519	Otis Nixon	.10	.05	.01
☐ 520	Brian Holman	.10	.05	.01
☐ 521	Chris Haney	.10	.05	.01
☐ 522	Jeff Kent	.75	.35	.09
☐ 523	Chad Curtis	.35	.16	.04
☐ 524	Vince Horsman	.15	.07	.02
☐ 525	Rod Nichols	.10	.05	.01
☐ 526	Peter Hoy	.15	.07	.02
☐ 527	Shawn Boskie	.10	.05	.01
☐ 528	Alejandro Pena	.10	.05	.01
☐ 529	Dave Burba	.10	.05	.01
☐ 530	Ricky Jordan	.10	.05	.01
☐ 531	Dave Silvestri	.10	.05	.01
☐ 532	John Patterson UER (Listed as being born in 1960; should be 1967)	.15	.07	.02
☐ 533	Jeff Branson	.10	.05	.01
☐ 534	Derrick May	.15	.07	.02
☐ 535	Esteban Beltre	.15	.07	.02
☐ 536	Jose Melendez	.10	.05	.01
☐ 537	Wally Joyner	.15	.07	.02
☐ 538	Eddie Taubensee	.10	.05	.01
☐ 539	Jim Abbott	.25	.11	.03
☐ 540	Brian Williams	.15	.07	.02
☐ 541	Donovan Osborne	.10	.05	.01
☐ 542	Patrick Lennon	.10	.05	.01
☐ 543	Mike Groppuso	.10	.05	.01
☐ 544	Jarvis Brown	.15	.07	.02
☐ 545	Shawn Livsey	.10	.05	.01
☐ 546	Jeff Ware	.10	.05	.01
☐ 547	Danny Tartabull	.15	.07	.02
☐ 548	Bobby Jones	1.00	.45	.13
☐ 549	Ken Griffey Jr.	4.00	1.80	.50
☐ 550	Rey Sanchez	.15	.07	.02
☐ 551	Pedro Astacio	.25	.11	.03
☐ 552	Juan Guerrero	.15	.07	.02
☐ 553	Jacob Brumfield	.15	.07	.02
☐ 554	Ben Rivera	.10	.05	.01
☐ 555	Brian Jordan	.20	.09	.03
☐ 556	Denny Neagle	.10	.05	.01
☐ 557	Cliff Brantley	.15	.07	.02
☐ 558	Anthony Young	.10	.05	.01
☐ 559	John Vander Wal	.15	.07	.02
☐ 560	Monty Fariss	.10	.05	.01
☐ 561	Russ Springer	.15	.07	.02

☐ 562 Pat Listach	.20	.09	.03
☐ 563 Pat Hentgen	.60	.25	.08
☐ 564 Andy Stankiewicz	.10	.05	.01
☐ 565 Mike Perez	.10	.05	.01
☐ 566 Mike Bielecki	.10	.05	.01
☐ 567 Butch Henry	.15	.07	.02
☐ 568 Dave Nilsson	.40	.18	.05
☐ 569 Scott Hatteberg	.15	.07	.02
☐ 570 Ruben Amaro Jr.	.10	.05	.01
☐ 571 Todd Hundley	.10	.05	.01
☐ 572 Moises Alou	.30	.14	.04
☐ 573 Hector Fajardo	.10	.05	.01
☐ 574 Todd Van Poppel	.25	.11	.03
☐ 575 Willie Banks	.10	.05	.01
☐ 576 Bob Zupcic	.15	.07	.02
☐ 577 J.J. Johnson	.20	.09	.03
☐ 578 John Burkett	.15	.07	.02
☐ 579 Trever Miller	.10	.05	.01
☐ 580 Scott Bankhead	.10	.05	.01
☐ 581 Rich Amaral	.10	.05	.01
☐ 582 Kenny Lofton	3.00	1.35	.40
☐ 583 Matt Stairs	.10	.05	.01
☐ 584 Don Mattingly Rod Carew IDOLS	.30	.14	.04
☐ 585 Steve Avery Jack Morris IDOLS	.15	.07	.02
☐ 586 Roberto Alomar Sandy Alomar SR. IDOLS	.20	.09	.03
☐ 587 Scott Sanderson Scott Sanderson IDOLS	.10	.05	.01
☐ 588 David Justice Willie Stargell IDOLS	.20	.09	.03
☐ 589 Rex Hudler Roger Staubach IDOLS	.25	.11	.03
☐ 590 David Cone Jackie Gleason IDOLS	.15	.07	.02
☐ 591 Tony Gwynn Willie Davis IDOLS	.20	.09	.03
☐ 592 Orel Hershiser SIDE	.15	.07	.02
☐ 593 John Wetteland SIDE	.10	.05	.01
☐ 594 Tom Glavine SIDE	.15	.07	.02
☐ 595 Randy Johnson SIDE	.15	.07	.02
☐ 596 Jim Gott SIDE	.10	.05	.01
☐ 597 Donald Harris	.10	.05	.01
☐ 598 Shawn Hare	.15	.07	.02
☐ 599 Chris Gardner	.10	.05	.01
☐ 600 Rusty Meacham	.10	.05	.01
☐ 601 Benito Santiago	.10	.05	.01
☐ 602 Eric Davis SHADE	.10	.05	.01
☐ 603 Jose Lind SHADE	.10	.05	.01
☐ 604 David Justice SHADE	.25	.11	.03
☐ 605 Tim Raines SHADE	.15	.07	.02
☐ 606 Randy Tomlin GRIP	.10	.05	.01
☐ 607 Jack McDowell GRIP	.15	.07	.02
☐ 608 Greg Maddux GRIP	.20	.09	.03
☐ 609 Charles Nagy GRIP	.10	.05	.01
☐ 610 Tom Candiotti GRIP	.10	.05	.01
☐ 611 David Cone GRIP	.15	.07	.02
☐ 612 Steve Avery GRIP	.15	.07	.02
☐ 613 Rod Beck GRIP	.75	.35	.09
☐ 614 Rickey Henderson TECH	.15	.07	.02
☐ 615 Benito Santiago TECH	.10	.05	.01
☐ 616 Ruben Sierra TECH	.15	.07	.02
☐ 617 Ryne Sandberg TECH	.40	.18	.05
☐ 618 Nolan Ryan TECH	1.25	.55	.16
☐ 619 Brett Butler TECH	.10	.05	.01
☐ 620 David Justice TECH	.25	.11	.03

1992 Pinnacle Rookie Idols

This 18-card insert set is a spin-off on the Idols subset featured in the regular series. The set features full-bleed color photos of 18 rookies along with their pick of sports figures or other individuals who had the greatest impact on their careers. The standard-size (2 1/2" by 3 1/2") cards were randomly inserted in Series II wax packs. Both sides of the cards are horizontally oriented. The fronts carry a close-up photo of the rookie superimposed on an action game shot of his idol. On a background that shades from white to light blue, the backs feature text comparing the two players flanked by a color photo of each player. The cards are numbered on the back.

	MINT	EXC	G-VG
COMPLETE SET (18)	140.00	65.00	17.50
COMMON PAIR (1-18)	3.00	1.35	.40
☐ 1 Reggie Sanders and Eric Davis	8.00	3.60	1.00
☐ 2 Hector Fajardo and Jim Abbott	3.00	1.35	.40
☐ 3 Gary Cooper and George Brett	16.00	7.25	2.00
☐ 4 Mark Wohlers and Roger Clemens	12.00	5.50	1.50
☐ 5 Luis Mercedes and Julio Franco	3.00	1.35	.40
☐ 6 Willie Banks and Doc Gooden	3.00	1.35	.40
☐ 7 Kenny Lofton and Rickey Henderson	30.00	13.50	3.80
☐ 8 Keith Mitchell and Dave Henderson	3.00	1.35	.40
☐ 9 Kim Batiste and Barry Larkin	3.00	1.35	.40
☐ 10 Todd Hundley and Thurman Munson	4.00	1.80	.50
☐ 11 Eddie Zosky and Cal Ripken	20.00	9.00	2.50
☐ 12 Todd Van Poppel and Nolan Ryan	40.00	18.00	5.00
☐ 13 Jim Thome and Ryne Sandberg	25.00	11.50	3.10
☐ 14 Dave Fleming and Bobby Murcer	3.00	1.35	.40
☐ 15 Royce Clayton and Ozzie Smith	12.00	5.50	1.50
☐ 16 Donald Harris	3.00	1.35	.40

and Darryl Strawberry			
☐ 17 Chad Curtis	5.00	2.30	.60
and Alan Trammell			
☐ 18 Derek Bell	8.00	3.60	1.00
and Dave Winfield			

1992 Pinnacle Slugfest

This 15-card set measures the standard size (2 1/2" by 3 1/2"). The horizontally oriented fronts feature glossy photos of players at bat. The player's name is printed in gold and the word "Slugfest" is printed in red in a black border across the bottom of the picture. The back design includes a color action player photo on the right half of the card, and statistics and a career summary on the left. The cards are numbered on the back. The cards were issued as an insert with specially marked cello packs.

	MINT	EXC	G-VG
COMPLETE SET (15)	45.00	20.00	5.75
COMMON CARD (1-15)	1.00	.45	.13
☐ 1 Cecil Fielder	1.50	.65	.19
☐ 2 Mark McGwire	1.00	.45	.13
☐ 3 Jose Canseco	2.50	1.15	.30
☐ 4 Barry Bonds	4.00	1.80	.50
☐ 5 David Justice	2.00	.90	.25
☐ 6 Bobby Bonilla	1.00	.45	.13
☐ 7 Ken Griffey Jr.	12.00	5.50	1.50
☐ 8 Ron Gant	1.00	.45	.13
☐ 9 Ryne Sandberg	4.00	1.80	.50
☐ 10 Ruben Sierra	1.00	.45	.13
☐ 11 Frank Thomas	12.00	5.50	1.50
☐ 12 Will Clark	2.50	1.15	.30
☐ 13 Kirby Puckett	4.00	1.80	.50
☐ 14 Cal Ripken	6.00	2.70	.75
☐ 15 Jeff Bagwell	6.00	2.70	.75

1992 Pinnacle Team Pinnacle

This 12-card, double-sided subset features the National League and American League All-Star team as selected by Pinnacle. The

standard-size (2 1/2" by 3 1/2") were randomly inserted in Series I wax packs. There is one card per position, including two cards for pitchers and two cards for relief pitchers for a total set of twelve. The cards feature illustrations by sports artist Chris Greco of the National League All-Star on one side and the American League All-Star on the other. The words "Team Pinnacle" are printed vertically down the left side of the card in red for American League on one side and blue for National League on the other. The player's name appears in a gold stripe at the bottom. There is no text. The cards are numbered in the black bottom stripe on the side featuring the National League All-Star.

	MINT	EXC	G-VG
COMPLETE SET (12)	140.00	65.00	17.50
COMMON PAIR (1-12)	5.00	2.30	.60
☐ 1 Roger Clemens	12.00	5.50	1.50
and Ramon Martinez			
☐ 2 Jim Abbott	12.00	5.50	1.50
and Steve Avery			
☐ 3 Ivan Rodriguez	8.00	3.60	1.00
and Benito Santiago			
☐ 4 Frank Thomas	50.00	23.00	6.25
and Will Clark			
☐ 5 Roberto Alomar	30.00	13.50	3.80
and Ryne Sandberg			
☐ 6 Robin Ventura	15.00	6.75	1.90
and Matt Williams			
☐ 7 Cal Ripken	30.00	13.50	3.80
and Barry Larkin			
☐ 8 Danny Tartabull	20.00	9.00	2.50
and Barry Bonds			
☐ 9 Ken Griffey Jr.	40.00	18.00	5.00
and Brett Butler			
☐ 10 Ruben Sierra	15.00	6.75	1.90
and Dave Justice			
☐ 11 Dennis Eckersley	6.00	2.70	.75
and Rob Dibble			
☐ 12 Scott Radinsky	5.00	2.30	.60
and John Franco			

1992 Pinnacle Team 2000

This 80-card standard-size (2 1/2" by 3 1/2") set focuses on young players who will be still be stars in the year 2000. Cards 1-40 were inserted in Series 1 jumbo packs

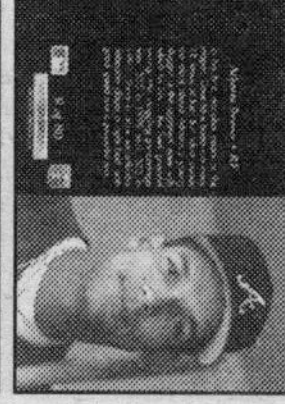

while cards 41-80 were featured in Series 2 jumbo packs. The fronts features action color player photos. The cards are bordered by a 1/2" black stripe that runs along the left edge and bottom forming a right angle. The two ends of the black stripe are sloped. The words "Team 2000" and the player's name appear in gold foil in the stripe. The team logo is displayed in the lower left corner. The horizontally oriented backs show a close-up color player photo and a career summary on a black background. The cards are numbered on the back.

	MINT	EXC	G-VG
COMPLETE SET (80)	30.00	13.50	3.80
COMPLETE SERIES 1 (40)	20.00	9.00	2.50
COMPLETE SERIES 2 (40)	10.00	4.50	1.25
COMMON CARD (1-40)	.15	.07	.02
COMMON CARD (41-80)	.15	.07	.02

		MINT	EXC	G-VG
☐ 1	Mike Mussina	1.00	.45	.13
☐ 2	Phil Plantier	.15	.07	.02
☐ 3	Frank Thomas	5.00	2.30	.60
☐ 4	Travis Fryman	.60	.25	.08
☐ 5	Kevin Appier	.15	.07	.02
☐ 6	Chuck Knoblauch	.40	.18	.05
☐ 7	Pat Kelly	.15	.07	.02
☐ 8	Ivan Rodriguez	.40	.18	.05
☐ 9	David Justice	.60	.25	.08
☐ 10	Jeff Bagwell	2.50	1.15	.30
☐ 11	Marquis Grissom	.25	.11	.03
☐ 12	Andy Benes	.15	.07	.02
☐ 13	Gregg Olson	.15	.07	.02
☐ 14	Kevin Morton	.15	.07	.02
☐ 15	Tim Naehring	.15	.07	.02
☐ 16	Dave Hollins	.25	.11	.03
☐ 17	Sandy Alomar Jr.	.15	.07	.02
☐ 18	Albert Belle	1.25	.55	.16
☐ 19	Charles Nagy	.15	.07	.02
☐ 20	Brian McRae	.25	.11	.03
☐ 21	Larry Walker	.25	.11	.03
☐ 22	Delino DeShields	.25	.11	.03
☐ 23	Jeff Johnson	.15	.07	.02
☐ 24	Bernie Williams	.15	.07	.02
☐ 25	Jose Offerman	.15	.07	.02
☐ 26	Juan Gonzalez	2.00	.90	.25
☐ 27A	Juan Guzman (Pinnacle logo at top)	.25	.11	.03
☐ 27B	Juan Guzman (Pinnacle logo at bottom)	.25	.11	.03
☐ 28	Eric Anthony	.15	.07	.02
☐ 29	Brian Hunter	.15	.07	.02
☐ 30	John Smoltz	.25	.11	.03
☐ 31	Deion Sanders	.50	.23	.06
☐ 32	Greg Maddux	.60	.25	.08
☐ 33	Andujar Cedeno	.15	.07	.02
☐ 34	Royce Clayton	.15	.07	.02
☐ 35	Kenny Lofton	3.00	1.35	.40
☐ 36	Cal Eldred	.15	.07	.02
☐ 37	Jim Thome	1.25	.55	.16
☐ 38	Gary DiSarcina	.15	.07	.02
☐ 39	Brian Jordan	.30	.14	.04
☐ 40	Chad Curtis	.40	.18	.05
☐ 41	Ben McDonald	.25	.11	.03
☐ 42	Jim Abbott	.15	.07	.02
☐ 43	Robin Ventura	.30	.14	.04
☐ 44	Milt Cuyler	.15	.07	.02
☐ 45	Gregg Jefferies	.30	.14	.04
☐ 46	Scott Radinsky	.15	.07	.02
☐ 47	Ken Griffey Jr.	5.00	2.30	.60
☐ 48	Roberto Alomar	.75	.35	.09
☐ 49	Ramon Martinez	.25	.11	.03
☐ 50	Bret Barberie	.15	.07	.02
☐ 51	Ray Lankford	.15	.07	.02
☐ 52	Leo Gomez	.15	.07	.02
☐ 53	Tommy Greene	.15	.07	.02
☐ 54	Mo Vaughn	.60	.25	.08
☐ 55	Sammy Sosa	.25	.11	.03
☐ 56	Carlos Baerga	.60	.25	.08
☐ 57	Mark Lewis	.15	.07	.02
☐ 58	Tom Gordon	.15	.07	.02
☐ 59	Gary Sheffield	.25	.11	.03
☐ 60	Scott Erickson	.15	.07	.02
☐ 61	Pedro Munoz	.15	.07	.02
☐ 62	Tino Martinez	.15	.07	.02
☐ 63	Darren Lewis	.15	.07	.02
☐ 64	Dean Palmer	.15	.07	.02
☐ 65	John Olerud	.15	.07	.02
☐ 66	Steve Avery	.40	.18	.05
☐ 67	Pete Harnisch	.15	.07	.02
☐ 68	Luis Gonzalez	.15	.07	.02
☐ 69	Kim Batiste	.15	.07	.02
☐ 70	Reggie Sanders	.60	.25	.08
☐ 71	Luis Mercedes	.15	.07	.02
☐ 72	Todd Van Poppel	.15	.07	.02
☐ 73	Gary Scott	.15	.07	.02
☐ 74	Monty Fariss	.15	.07	.02
☐ 75	Kyle Abbott	.15	.07	.02
☐ 76	Eric Karros	.50	.23	.06
☐ 77	Mo Sanford	.15	.07	.02
☐ 78	Todd Hundley	.15	.07	.02
☐ 79	Reggie Jefferson	.15	.07	.02
☐ 80	Pat Mahomes	.35	.16	.04

1992 Pinnacle Rookies

This 30-card boxed set features top rookies of the 1992 season, with at least one player from each team. A total of 180,000 sets were produced. The fronts feature full-bleed

color action player photos except at the bottom where a team-color coded bar carries the player's name (in gold foil lettering) and a black bar has the words "1992 Rookie." The team logo appears in a gold foil circle at the lower right corner. The horizontally oriented backs carry a second large color player photo, again edged at the bottom by a team-color coded bar with the player's name and a black bar carrying a player profile. The cards are numbered on the back.

	MINT	EXC	G-VG
COMPLETE FACT.SET (30)	7.50	3.40	.95
COMMON CARD (1-30)	.10	.05	.01
☐ 1 Luis Mercedes	.10	.05	.01
☐ 2 Scott Cooper	.10	.05	.01
☐ 3 Kenny Lofton	4.00	1.80	.50
☐ 4 John Doherty	.20	.09	.03
☐ 5 Pat Listach	.20	.09	.03
☐ 6 Andy Stankiewicz	.10	.05	.01
☐ 7 Derek Bell	.30	.14	.04
☐ 8 Gary DiSarcina	.10	.05	.01
☐ 9 Roberto Hernandez	.10	.05	.01
☐ 10 Joel Johnston	.10	.05	.01
☐ 11 Pat Mahomes	.40	.18	.05
☐ 12 Todd Van Poppel	.25	.11	.03
☐ 13 Dave Fleming	.15	.07	.02
☐ 14 Monty Fariss	.10	.05	.01
☐ 15 Gary Scott	.10	.05	.01
☐ 16 Moises Alou	.50	.23	.06
☐ 17 Todd Hundley	.10	.05	.01
☐ 18 Kim Batiste	.10	.05	.01
☐ 19 Denny Neagle	.10	.05	.01
☐ 20 Donovan Osborne	.10	.05	.01
☐ 21 Mark Wohlers	.10	.05	.01
☐ 22 Reggie Sanders	.75	.35	.09
☐ 23 Brian Williams	.10	.05	.01
☐ 24 Eric Karros	.50	.23	.06
☐ 25 Frank Seminara	.10	.05	.01
☐ 26 Royce Clayton	.15	.07	.02
☐ 27 Dave Nilsson	.60	.25	.08
☐ 28 Matt Stairs	.10	.05	.01
☐ 29 Chad Curtis	.50	.23	.06
☐ 30 Carlos Hernandez	.10	.05	.01

1993 Pinnacle

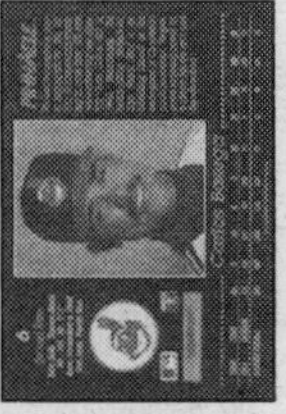

The 1993 Score Pinnacle baseball set contains 620 standard-size (2 1/2" by 3 1/2") cards issued in two series. A ten-card Team Pinnacle subset was randomly inserted in Series I packs, and a ten-card Rookie Team Pinnacle subset was randomly inserted in Series II, as was the ten-card Tribute subset. The fronts feature color action player photos bordered in white and set on a black card face. The player's name appears below the photo, the player's team is above. The horizontal backs are black and carry a color close-up in the center and reversed out text including biographical information, career highlights, and statistics. The set includes the following topical subsets: Rookies (238-288, 575-620), Now and Then (289-296, 470-476), Idols (297-303, 477-483), Hometown Heroes (304-310, 484-490), and Draft Picks (455-469). The cards are numbered on the back. Rookie Cards in this set include Rene Arocha, Derek Jeter, Jason Kendall, J.T. Snow, and Todd Steverson.

	MINT	EXC	G-VG
COMPLETE SET (620)	50.00	23.00	6.25
COMPLETE SERIES 1 (310)	25.00	11.50	3.10
COMPLETE SERIES 2 (310)	25.00	11.50	3.10
COMMON CARD (1-310)	.10	.05	.01
COMMON CARD (311-620)	.10	.05	.01
☐ 1 Gary Sheffield	.20	.09	.03
☐ 2 Cal Eldred	.15	.07	.02
☐ 3 Larry Walker	.20	.09	.03
☐ 4 Deion Sanders	.50	.23	.06
☐ 5 Dave Fleming	.15	.07	.02
☐ 6 Carlos Baerga	.40	.18	.05
☐ 7 Bernie Williams	.15	.07	.02
☐ 8 John Kruk	.20	.09	.03
☐ 9 Jimmy Key	.15	.07	.02
☐ 10 Jeff Bagwell	1.50	.65	.19
☐ 11 Jim Abbott	.20	.09	.03
☐ 12 Terry Steinbach	.15	.07	.02
☐ 13 Bob Tewksbury	.10	.05	.01
☐ 14 Eric Karros	.15	.07	.02
☐ 15 Ryne Sandberg	1.00	.45	.13
☐ 16 Will Clark	.40	.18	.05
☐ 17 Edgar Martinez	.10	.05	.01
☐ 18 Eddie Murray	.20	.09	.03
☐ 19 Andy Van Slyke	.20	.09	.03
☐ 20 Cal Ripken	2.00	.90	.25
☐ 21 Ivan Rodriguez	.20	.09	.03
☐ 22 Barry Larkin	.20	.09	.03
☐ 23 Don Mattingly	1.25	.55	.16
☐ 24 Gregg Jefferies	.20	.09	.03
☐ 25 Roger Clemens	.75	.35	.09
☐ 26 Cecil Fielder	.25	.11	.03
☐ 27 Kent Hrbek	.15	.07	.02
☐ 28 Robin Ventura	.20	.09	.03
☐ 29 Rickey Henderson	.20	.09	.03
☐ 30 Roberto Alomar	.75	.35	.09
☐ 31 Luis Polonia	.10	.05	.01
☐ 32 Andujar Cedeno	.15	.07	.02
☐ 33 Pat Listach	.15	.07	.02
☐ 34 Mark Grace	.20	.09	.03
☐ 35 Otis Nixon	.10	.05	.01
☐ 36 Felix Jose	.10	.05	.01
☐ 37 Mike Sharperson	.10	.05	.01
☐ 38 Dennis Martinez	.15	.07	.02
☐ 39 Willie McGee	.15	.07	.02
☐ 40 Kenny Lofton	.75	.35	.09
☐ 41 Randy Johnson	.20	.09	.03
☐ 42 Andy Benes	.15	.07	.02
☐ 43 Bobby Bonilla	.20	.09	.03
☐ 44 Mike Mussina	.60	.25	.08
☐ 45 Len Dykstra	.20	.09	.03
☐ 46 Ellis Burks	.15	.07	.02

☐ 47 Chris Sabo .15 .07 .02
☐ 48 Jay Bell .15 .07 .02
☐ 49 Jose Canseco .40 .18 .05
☐ 50 Craig Biggio .15 .07 .02
☐ 51 Wally Joyner .15 .07 .02
☐ 52 Mickey Tettleton .15 .07 .02
☐ 53 Tim Raines .20 .09 .03
☐ 54 Brian Harper .10 .05 .01
☐ 55 Rene Gonzales .10 .05 .01
☐ 56 Mark Langston .20 .09 .03
☐ 57 Jack Morris .20 .09 .03
☐ 58 Mark McGwire .20 .09 .03
☐ 59 Ken Caminiti .15 .07 .02
☐ 60 Terry Pendleton .20 .09 .03
☐ 61 Dave Nilsson .15 .07 .02
☐ 62 Tom Pagnozzi .10 .05 .01
☐ 63 Mike Morgan .10 .05 .01
☐ 64 Darryl Strawberry .15 .07 .02
☐ 65 Charles Nagy .10 .05 .01
☐ 66 Ken Hill .15 .07 .02
☐ 67 Matt Williams .50 .23 .06
☐ 68 Jay Buhner .15 .07 .02
☐ 69 Vince Coleman .10 .05 .01
☐ 70 Brady Anderson .15 .07 .02
☐ 71 Fred McGriff .40 .18 .05
☐ 72 Ben McDonald .15 .07 .02
☐ 73 Terry Mulholland .10 .05 .01
☐ 74 Randy Tomlin .10 .05 .01
☐ 75 Nolan Ryan 3.00 1.35 .40
☐ 76 Frank Viola UER .15 .07 .02
(Card incorrectly states he has a surgically repaired elbow)
☐ 77 Jose Rijo .15 .07 .02
☐ 78 Shane Mack .15 .07 .02
☐ 79 Travis Fryman .25 .11 .03
☐ 80 Jack McDowell .20 .09 .03
☐ 81 Mark Gubicza .10 .05 .01
☐ 82 Matt Nokes .10 .05 .01
☐ 83 Bert Blyleven .20 .09 .03
☐ 84 Eric Anthony .10 .05 .01
☐ 85 Mike Bordick .10 .05 .01
☐ 86 John Olerud .20 .09 .03
☐ 87 B.J.Surhoff .10 .05 .01
☐ 88 Bernard Gilkey .10 .05 .01
☐ 89 Shawon Dunston .10 .05 .01
☐ 90 Tom Glavine .20 .09 .03
☐ 91 Brett Butler .15 .07 .02
☐ 92 Moises Alou .20 .09 .03
☐ 93 Albert Belle 1.00 .45 .13
☐ 94 Darren Lewis .10 .05 .01
☐ 95 Omar Vizquel .10 .05 .01
☐ 96 Dwight Gooden .10 .05 .01
☐ 97 Gregg Olson .10 .05 .01
☐ 98 Tony Gwynn .75 .35 .09
☐ 99 Darren Daulton .20 .09 .03
☐ 100 Dennis Eckersley .20 .09 .03
☐ 101 Rob Dibble .10 .05 .01
☐ 102 Mike Greenwell .15 .07 .02
☐ 103 Jose Lind .10 .05 .01
☐ 104 Julio Franco .15 .07 .02
☐ 105 Tom Gordon .10 .05 .01
☐ 106 Scott Livingstone .10 .05 .01
☐ 107 Chuck Knoblauch .20 .09 .03
☐ 108 Frank Thomas 3.00 1.35 .40
☐ 109 Melido Perez .10 .05 .01
☐ 110 Ken Griffey Jr. 3.00 1.35 .40
☐ 111 Harold Baines .15 .07 .02
☐ 112 Gary Gaetti .10 .05 .01
☐ 113 Pete Harnisch .10 .05 .01
☐ 114 David Wells .10 .05 .01
☐ 115 Charlie Leibrandt .10 .05 .01
☐ 116 Ray Lankford .20 .09 .03
☐ 117 Kevin Seitzer .10 .05 .01
☐ 118 Robin Yount .40 .18 .05
☐ 119 Lenny Harris .10 .05 .01
☐ 120 Chris James .10 .05 .01
☐ 121 Delino DeShields .15 .07 .02
☐ 122 Kirt Manwaring .10 .05 .01
☐ 123 Glenallen Hill .10 .05 .01
☐ 124 Hensley Meulens .10 .05 .01
☐ 125 Darrin Jackson .10 .05 .01
☐ 126 Todd Hundley .10 .05 .01
☐ 127 Dave Hollins .20 .09 .03
☐ 128 Sam Horn .10 .05 .01
☐ 129 Roberto Hernandez .10 .05 .01
☐ 130 Vicente Palacios .10 .05 .01
☐ 131 George Brett 1.25 .55 .16
☐ 132 Dave Martinez .10 .05 .01
☐ 133 Kevin Appier .15 .07 .02
☐ 134 Pat Kelly .10 .05 .01
☐ 135 Pedro Munoz .10 .05 .01
☐ 136 Mark Carreon .10 .05 .01
☐ 137 Lance Johnson .10 .05 .01
☐ 138 Devon White .15 .07 .02
☐ 139 Julio Valera .10 .05 .01
☐ 140 Eddie Taubensee .10 .05 .01
☐ 141 Willie Wilson .10 .05 .01
☐ 142 Stan Belinda .10 .05 .01
☐ 143 John Smoltz .15 .07 .02
☐ 144 Darryl Hamilton .10 .05 .01
☐ 145 Sammy Sosa .20 .09 .03
☐ 146 Carlos Hernandez .10 .05 .01
☐ 147 Tom Candiotti .10 .05 .01
☐ 148 Mike Felder .10 .05 .01
☐ 149 Rusty Meacham .10 .05 .01
☐ 150 Ivan Calderon .10 .05 .01
☐ 151 Pete O'Brien .10 .05 .01
☐ 152 Erik Hanson .10 .05 .01
☐ 153 Billy Ripken .10 .05 .01
☐ 154 Kurt Stillwell .10 .05 .01
☐ 155 Jeff Kent .20 .09 .03
☐ 156 Mickey Morandini .10 .05 .01
☐ 157 Randy Milligan .10 .05 .01
☐ 158 Reggie Sanders .20 .09 .03
☐ 159 Luis Rivera .10 .05 .01
☐ 160 Orlando Merced .15 .07 .02
☐ 161 Dean Palmer .15 .07 .02
☐ 162 Mike Perez .10 .05 .01
☐ 163 Scott Erickson .10 .05 .01
☐ 164 Kevin McReynolds .10 .05 .01
☐ 165 Kevin Maas .10 .05 .01
☐ 166 Ozzie Guillen .10 .05 .01
☐ 167 Rob Deer .10 .05 .01
☐ 168 Danny Tartabull .15 .07 .02
☐ 169 Lee Stevens .10 .05 .01
☐ 170 Dave Henderson .10 .05 .01
☐ 171 Derek Bell .15 .07 .02
☐ 172 Steve Finley .10 .05 .01
☐ 173 Greg Olson .10 .05 .01
☐ 174 Geronimo Pena .10 .05 .01
☐ 175 Paul Quantrill .10 .05 .01
☐ 176 Steve Buechele .10 .05 .01
☐ 177 Kevin Gross .10 .05 .01
☐ 178 Tim Wallach .10 .05 .01
☐ 179 Dave Valle .10 .05 .01
☐ 180 Dave Silvestri .10 .05 .01
☐ 181 Bud Black .10 .05 .01
☐ 182 Henry Rodriguez .10 .05 .01
☐ 183 Tim Teufel .10 .05 .01
☐ 184 Mark McLemore .10 .05 .01
☐ 185 Bret Saberhagen .15 .07 .02
☐ 186 Chris Hoiles .15 .07 .02
☐ 187 Ricky Jordan .10 .05 .01
☐ 188 Don Slaught .10 .05 .01
☐ 189 Mo Vaughn .20 .09 .03

	No.	Player			
☐	190	Joe Oliver	.10	.05	.01
☐	191	Juan Gonzalez	1.00	.45	.13
☐	192	Scott Leius	.10	.05	.01
☐	193	Milt Cuyler	.10	.05	.01
☐	194	Chris Haney	.10	.05	.01
☐	195	Ron Karkovice	.10	.05	.01
☐	196	Steve Farr	.10	.05	.01
☐	197	John Orton	.10	.05	.01
☐	198	Kelly Gruber	.10	.05	.01
☐	199	Ron Darling	.10	.05	.01
☐	200	Ruben Sierra	.20	.09	.03
☐	201	Chuck Finley	.10	.05	.01
☐	202	Mike Moore	.10	.05	.01
☐	203	Pat Borders	.10	.05	.01
☐	204	Sid Bream	.10	.05	.01
☐	205	Todd Zeile	.15	.07	.02
☐	206	Rick Wilkins	.10	.05	.01
☐	207	Jim Gantner	.10	.05	.01
☐	208	Frank Castillo	.10	.05	.01
☐	209	Dave Hansen	.10	.05	.01
☐	210	Trevor Wilson	.10	.05	.01
☐	211	Sandy Alomar Jr.	.15	.07	.02
☐	212	Sean Berry	.10	.05	.01
☐	213	Tino Martinez	.15	.07	.02
☐	214	Chito Martinez	.10	.05	.01
☐	215	Dan Walters	.10	.05	.01
☐	216	John Franco	.10	.05	.01
☐	217	Glenn Davis	.10	.05	.01
☐	218	Mariano Duncan	.10	.05	.01
☐	219	Mike LaValliere	.10	.05	.01
☐	220	Rafael Palmeiro	.20	.09	.03
☐	221	Jack Clark	.10	.05	.01
☐	222	Hal Morris	.15	.07	.02
☐	223	Ed Sprague	.10	.05	.01
☐	224	John Valentin	.15	.07	.02
☐	225	Sam Militello	.10	.05	.01
☐	226	Bob Wickman	.10	.05	.01
☐	227	Damion Easley	.15	.07	.02
☐	228	John Jaha	.15	.07	.02
☐	229	Bob Ayrault	.10	.05	.01
☐	230	Mo Sanford	.10	.05	.01
☐	231	Walt Weiss	.10	.05	.01
☐	232	Dante Bichette	.20	.09	.03
☐	233	Steve Decker	.10	.05	.01
☐	234	Jerald Clark	.10	.05	.01
☐	235	Bryan Harvey	.15	.07	.02
☐	236	Joe Girardi	.10	.05	.01
☐	237	Dave Magadan	.10	.05	.01
☐	238	David Nied	.20	.09	.03
☐	239	Eric Wedge	.10	.05	.01
☐	240	Rico Brogna	.10	.05	.01
☐	241	J.T.Bruett	.10	.05	.01
☐	242	Jonathan Hurst	.10	.05	.01
☐	243	Bret Boone	.20	.09	.03
☐	244	Manny Alexander	.10	.05	.01
☐	245	Scooter Tucker	.10	.05	.01
☐	246	Troy Neel	.15	.07	.02
☐	247	Eddie Zosky	.10	.05	.01
☐	248	Melvin Nieves	.20	.09	.03
☐	249	Ryan Thompson	.20	.09	.03
☐	250	Shawn Barton	.15	.07	.02
☐	251	Ryan Klesko	1.00	.45	.13
☐	252	Mike Piazza	3.00	1.35	.40
☐	253	Steve Hosey	.10	.05	.01
☐	254	Shane Reynolds	.15	.07	.02
☐	255	Dan Wilson	.10	.05	.01
☐	256	Tom Marsh	.10	.05	.01
☐	257	Barry Manuel	.10	.05	.01
☐	258	Paul Miller	.10	.05	.01
☐	259	Pedro Martinez	.20	.09	.03
☐	260	Steve Cooke	.10	.05	.01
☐	261	Johnny Guzman	.10	.05	.01
☐	262	Mike Butcher	.10	.05	.01
☐	263	Bien Figueroa	.10	.05	.01
☐	264	Rich Rowland	.10	.05	.01
☐	265	Shawn Jeter	.10	.05	.01
☐	266	Gerald Williams	.10	.05	.01
☐	267	Derek Parks	.10	.05	.01
☐	268	Henry Mercedes	.10	.05	.01
☐	269	David Hulse	.10	.05	.01
☐	270	Tim Pugh	.10	.05	.01
☐	271	William Suero	.10	.05	.01
☐	272	Ozzie Canseco	.10	.05	.01
☐	273	Fernando Ramsey	.15	.07	.02
☐	274	Bernardo Brito	.10	.05	.01
☐	275	Dave Mlicki	.10	.05	.01
☐	276	Tim Salmon	.50	.23	.06
☐	277	Mike Raczka	.15	.07	.02
☐	278	Ken Ryan	.30	.14	.04
☐	279	Rafael Bournigal	.15	.07	.02
☐	280	Wil Cordero	.20	.09	.03
☐	281	Billy Ashley	.50	.23	.06
☐	282	Paul Wagner	.10	.05	.01
☐	283	Blas Minor	.10	.05	.01
☐	284	Rick Trlicek	.10	.05	.01
☐	285	Willie Greene	.15	.07	.02
☐	286	Ted Wood	.10	.05	.01
☐	287	Phil Clark	.10	.05	.01
☐	288	Jesse Levis	.10	.05	.01
☐	289	Tony Gwynn NT	.40	.18	.05
☐	290	Nolan Ryan NT	1.50	.65	.19
☐	291	Dennis Martinez NT	.10	.05	.01
☐	292	Eddie Murray NT	.15	.07	.02
☐	293	Robin Yount NT	.15	.07	.02
☐	294	George Brett NT	.60	.25	.08
☐	295	Dave Winfield NT	.15	.07	.02
☐	296	Bert Blyleven NT	.10	.05	.01
☐	297	Jeff Bagwell I	.60	.25	.08
☐	298	John Smoltz I	.15	.07	.02
☐	299	Larry Walker I	.15	.07	.02
☐	300	Gary Sheffield I	.15	.07	.02
☐	301	Ivan Rodriguez I	.15	.07	.02
☐	302	Delino DeShields I	.15	.07	.02
☐	303	Tim Salmon I	.20	.09	.03
☐	304	Bernard Gilkey HH	.10	.05	.01
☐	305	Cal Ripken HH	1.00	.45	.13
☐	306	Barry Larkin HH	.15	.07	.02
☐	307	Kent Hrbek HH	.10	.05	.01
☐	308	Rickey Henderson HH	.15	.07	.02
☐	309	Darryl Strawberry HH	.15	.07	.02
☐	310	John Franco HH	.10	.05	.01
☐	311	Todd Stottlemyre	.10	.05	.01
☐	312	Luis Gonzalez	.15	.07	.02
☐	313	Tommy Greene	.15	.07	.02
☐	314	Randy Velarde	.10	.05	.01
☐	315	Steve Avery	.20	.09	.03
☐	316	Jose Oquendo	.10	.05	.01
☐	317	Rey Sanchez	.10	.05	.01
☐	318	Greg Vaughn	.15	.07	.02
☐	319	Orel Hershiser	.15	.07	.02
☐	320	Paul Sorrento	.10	.05	.01
☐	321	Royce Clayton	.15	.07	.02
☐	322	John Vander Wal	.10	.05	.01
☐	323	Henry Cotto	.10	.05	.01
☐	324	Pete Schourek	.10	.05	.01
☐	325	David Segui	.10	.05	.01
☐	326	Arthur Rhodes	.10	.05	.01
☐	327	Bruce Hurst	.10	.05	.01
☐	328	Wes Chamberlain	.10	.05	.01
☐	329	Ozzie Smith	.60	.25	.08
☐	330	Scott Cooper	.15	.07	.02
☐	331	Felix Fermin	.10	.05	.01
☐	332	Mike Macfarlane	.10	.05	.01
☐	333	Dan Gladden	.10	.05	.01
☐	334	Kevin Tapani	.10	.05	.01
☐	335	Steve Sax	.10	.05	.01

☐ 336 Jeff Montgomery .15 .07 .02
☐ 337 Gary DiSarcina .10 .05 .01
☐ 338 Lance Blankenship .10 .05 .01
☐ 339 Brian Williams .10 .05 .01
☐ 340 Duane Ward .15 .07 .02
☐ 341 Chuck McElroy .10 .05 .01
☐ 342 Joe Magrane .10 .05 .01
☐ 343 Jaime Navarro .10 .05 .01
☐ 344 David Justice .40 .18 .05
☐ 345 Jose Offerman .10 .05 .01
☐ 346 Marquis Grissom .20 .09 .03
☐ 347 Bill Swift .15 .07 .02
☐ 348 Jim Thome .40 .18 .05
☐ 349 Archi Cianfrocco .10 .05 .01
☐ 350 Anthony Young .10 .05 .01
☐ 351 Leo Gomez .10 .05 .01
☐ 352 Bill Gullickson .10 .05 .01
☐ 353 Alan Trammell .20 .09 .03
☐ 354 Dan Pasqua .10 .05 .01
☐ 355 Jeff King .10 .05 .01
☐ 356 Kevin Brown .10 .05 .01
☐ 357 Tim Belcher .10 .05 .01
☐ 358 Bip Roberts .10 .05 .01
☐ 359 Brent Mayne .10 .05 .01
☐ 360 Rheal Cormier .10 .05 .01
☐ 361 Mark Guthrie .10 .05 .01
☐ 362 Craig Grebeck .10 .05 .01
☐ 363 Andy Stankiewicz .10 .05 .01
☐ 364 Juan Guzman .15 .07 .02
☐ 365 Bobby Witt .10 .05 .01
☐ 366 Mark Portugal .10 .05 .01
☐ 367 Brian McRae .20 .09 .03
☐ 368 Mark Lemke .10 .05 .01
☐ 369 Bill Wegman .10 .05 .01
☐ 370 Donovan Osborne .10 .05 .01
☐ 371 Derrick May .15 .07 .02
☐ 372 Carl Willis .10 .05 .01
☐ 373 Chris Nabholz .10 .05 .01
☐ 374 Mark Lewis .10 .05 .01
☐ 375 John Burkett .15 .07 .02
☐ 376 Luis Mercedes .10 .05 .01
☐ 377 Ramon Martinez .15 .07 .02
☐ 378 Kyle Abbott .10 .05 .01
☐ 379 Mark Wohlers .10 .05 .01
☐ 380 Bob Walk .10 .05 .01
☐ 381 Kenny Rogers .10 .05 .01
☐ 382 Tim Naehring .10 .05 .01
☐ 383 Alex Fernandez .20 .09 .03
☐ 384 Keith Miller .10 .05 .01
☐ 385 Mike Henneman .10 .05 .01
☐ 386 Rick Aguilera .15 .07 .02
☐ 387 George Bell .15 .07 .02
☐ 388 Mike Gallego .10 .05 .01
☐ 389 Howard Johnson .10 .05 .01
☐ 390 Kim Batiste .10 .05 .01
☐ 391 Jerry Browne .10 .05 .01
☐ 392 Damon Berryhill .10 .05 .01
☐ 393 Ricky Bones .10 .05 .01
☐ 394 Omar Olivares .10 .05 .01
☐ 395 Mike Harkey .10 .05 .01
☐ 396 Pedro Astacio .15 .07 .02
☐ 397 John Wetteland .10 .05 .01
☐ 398 Rod Beck .20 .09 .03
☐ 399 Thomas Howard .10 .05 .01
☐ 400 Mike Devereaux .15 .07 .02
☐ 401 Tim Wakefield .10 .05 .01
☐ 402 Curt Schilling .15 .07 .02
☐ 403 Zane Smith .10 .05 .01
☐ 404 Bob Zupcic .10 .05 .01
☐ 405 Tom Browning .10 .05 .01
☐ 406 Tony Phillips .10 .05 .01
☐ 407 John Doherty .10 .05 .01
☐ 408 Pat Mahomes .10 .05 .01
☐ 409 John Habyan .10 .05 .01
☐ 410 Steve Olin .10 .05 .01
☐ 411 Chad Curtis .15 .07 .02
☐ 412 Joe Grahe .10 .05 .01
☐ 413 John Patterson .10 .05 .01
☐ 414 Brian Hunter .10 .05 .01
☐ 415 Doug Henry .10 .05 .01
☐ 416 Lee Smith .20 .09 .03
☐ 417 Bob Scanlan .10 .05 .01
☐ 418 Kent Mercker .10 .05 .01
☐ 419 Mel Rojas .10 .05 .01
☐ 420 Mark Whiten .15 .07 .02
☐ 421 Carlton Fisk .20 .09 .03
☐ 422 Candy Maldonado .10 .05 .01
☐ 423 Doug Drabek .20 .09 .03
☐ 424 Wade Boggs .20 .09 .03
☐ 425 Mark Davis .10 .05 .01
☐ 426 Kirby Puckett 1.25 .55 .16
☐ 427 Joe Carter .40 .18 .05
☐ 428 Paul Molitor .40 .18 .05
☐ 429 Eric Davis .10 .05 .01
☐ 430 Darryl Kile .15 .07 .02
☐ 431 Jeff Parrett .10 .05 .01
☐ 432 Jeff Blauser .15 .07 .02
☐ 433 Dan Plesac .10 .05 .01
☐ 434 Andres Galarraga .20 .09 .03
☐ 435 Jim Gott .10 .05 .01
☐ 436 Jose Mesa .10 .05 .01
☐ 437 Ben Rivera .10 .05 .01
☐ 438 Dave Winfield .20 .09 .03
☐ 439 Norm Charlton .10 .05 .01
☐ 440 Chris Bosio .10 .05 .01
☐ 441 Wilson Alvarez .20 .09 .03
☐ 442 Dave Stewart .15 .07 .02
☐ 443 Doug Jones .10 .05 .01
☐ 444 Jeff Russell .10 .05 .01
☐ 445 Ron Gant .15 .07 .02
☐ 446 Paul O'Neill .15 .07 .02
☐ 447 Charlie Hayes .15 .07 .02
☐ 448 Joe Hesketh .10 .05 .01
☐ 449 Chris Hammond .10 .05 .01
☐ 450 Hipolito Pichardo .10 .05 .01
☐ 451 Scott Radinsky .10 .05 .01
☐ 452 Bobby Thigpen .10 .05 .01
☐ 453 Xavier Hernandez .10 .05 .01
☐ 454 Lonnie Smith .10 .05 .01
☐ 455 Jamie Arnold DP .25 .11 .03
☐ 456 B.J. Wallace DP .10 .05 .01
☐ 457 Derek Jeter DP 3.00 1.35 .40
☐ 458 Jason Kendall DP 1.00 .45 .13
☐ 459 Rick Helling DP .15 .07 .02
☐ 460 Derek Wallace DP .10 .05 .01
☐ 461 Sean Lowe DP .30 .14 .04
☐ 462 Shannon Stewart DP .40 .18 .05
☐ 463 Benji Grigsby DP .20 .09 .03
☐ 464 Todd Steverson DP .30 .14 .04
☐ 465 Dan Serafini DP .40 .18 .05
☐ 466 Michael Tucker DP .40 .18 .05
☐ 467 Chris Roberts DP .20 .09 .03
☐ 468 Pete Janicki DP .10 .05 .01
☐ 469 Jeff Schmidt DP .10 .05 .01
☐ 470 Don Mattingly NT .60 .25 .08
☐ 471 Cal Ripken NT 1.00 .45 .13
☐ 472 Jack Morris NT .15 .07 .02
☐ 473 Terry Pendleton NT .10 .05 .01
☐ 474 Dennis Eckersley NT .15 .07 .02
☐ 475 Carlton Fisk NT .15 .07 .02
☐ 476 Wade Boggs NT .15 .07 .02
☐ 477 Len Dykstra I .15 .07 .02
☐ 478 Danny Tartabull I .15 .07 .02
☐ 479 Jeff Conine I .15 .07 .02
☐ 480 Gregg Jefferies I .15 .07 .02
☐ 481 Paul Molitor I .20 .09 .03

	#	Player			
☐	482	John Valentin I	.10	.05	.01
☐	483	Alex Arias I	.10	.05	.01
☐	484	Barry Bonds HH	.60	.25	.08
☐	485	Doug Drabek HH	.10	.05	.01
☐	486	Dave Winfield HH	.15	.07	.02
☐	487	Brett Butler HH	.10	.05	.01
☐	488	Harold Baines HH	.10	.05	.01
☐	489	David Cone HH	.10	.05	.01
☐	490	Willie McGee HH	.10	.05	.01
☐	491	Robby Thompson	.10	.05	.01
☐	492	Pete Incaviglia	.10	.05	.01
☐	493	Manny Lee	.10	.05	.01
☐	494	Rafael Belliard	.10	.05	.01
☐	495	Scott Fletcher	.10	.05	.01
☐	496	Jeff Frye	.10	.05	.01
☐	497	Andre Dawson	.20	.09	.03
☐	498	Mike Scioscia	.10	.05	.01
☐	499	Spike Owen	.10	.05	.01
☐	500	Sid Fernandez	.10	.05	.01
☐	501	Joe Orsulak	.10	.05	.01
☐	502	Benito Santiago	.10	.05	.01
☐	503	Dale Murphy	.20	.09	.03
☐	504	Barry Bonds	1.25	.55	.16
☐	505	Jose Guzman	.10	.05	.01
☐	506	Tony Pena	.10	.05	.01
☐	507	Greg Swindell	.10	.05	.01
☐	508	Mike Pagliarulo	.10	.05	.01
☐	509	Lou Whitaker	.20	.09	.03
☐	510	Greg Gagne	.10	.05	.01
☐	511	Butch Henry	.10	.05	.01
☐	512	Jeff Brantley	.10	.05	.01
☐	513	Jack Armstrong	.10	.05	.01
☐	514	Danny Jackson	.10	.05	.01
☐	515	Junior Felix	.10	.05	.01
☐	516	Milt Thompson	.10	.05	.01
☐	517	Greg Maddux	.75	.35	.09
☐	518	Eric Young	.15	.07	.02
☐	519	Jody Reed	.10	.05	.01
☐	520	Roberto Kelly	.15	.07	.02
☐	521	Darren Holmes	.10	.05	.01
☐	522	Craig Lefferts	.10	.05	.01
☐	523	Charlie Hough	.15	.07	.02
☐	524	Bo Jackson	.20	.09	.03
☐	525	Bill Spiers	.10	.05	.01
☐	526	Orestes Destrade	.10	.05	.01
☐	527	Greg Hibbard	.10	.05	.01
☐	528	Roger McDowell	.10	.05	.01
☐	529	Cory Snyder	.10	.05	.01
☐	530	Harold Reynolds	.10	.05	.01
☐	531	Kevin Reimer	.10	.05	.01
☐	532	Rick Sutcliffe	.15	.07	.02
☐	533	Tony Fernandez	.10	.05	.01
☐	534	Tom Brunansky	.10	.05	.01
☐	535	Jeff Reardon	.15	.07	.02
☐	536	Chili Davis	.15	.07	.02
☐	537	Bob Ojeda	.10	.05	.01
☐	538	Greg Colbrunn	.10	.05	.01
☐	539	Phil Plantier	.20	.09	.03
☐	540	Brian Jordan	.15	.07	.02
☐	541	Pete Smith	.10	.05	.01
☐	542	Frank Tanana	.10	.05	.01
☐	543	John Smiley	.10	.05	.01
☐	544	David Cone	.20	.09	.03
☐	545	Daryl Boston	.10	.05	.01
☐	546	Tom Henke	.15	.07	.02
☐	547	Bill Krueger	.10	.05	.01
☐	548	Freddie Benavides	.10	.05	.01
☐	549	Randy Myers	.15	.07	.02
☐	550	Reggie Jefferson	.10	.05	.01
☐	551	Kevin Mitchell	.15	.07	.02
☐	552	Dave Stieb	.10	.05	.01
☐	553	Bret Barberie	.10	.05	.01
☐	554	Tim Crews	.10	.05	.01
☐	555	Doug Dascenzo	.10	.05	.01
☐	556	Alex Cole	.10	.05	.01
☐	557	Jeff Innis	.10	.05	.01
☐	558	Carlos Garcia	.15	.07	.02
☐	559	Steve Howe	.10	.05	.01
☐	560	Kirk McCaskill	.10	.05	.01
☐	561	Frank Seminara	.10	.05	.01
☐	562	Cris Carpenter	.10	.05	.01
☐	563	Mike Stanley	.10	.05	.01
☐	564	Carlos Quintana	.10	.05	.01
☐	565	Mitch Williams	.15	.07	.02
☐	566	Juan Bell	.10	.05	.01
☐	567	Eric Fox	.10	.05	.01
☐	568	Al Leiter	.10	.05	.01
☐	569	Mike Stanton	.10	.05	.01
☐	570	Scott Kamieniecki	.10	.05	.01
☐	571	Ryan Bowen	.10	.05	.01
☐	572	Andy Ashby	.10	.05	.01
☐	573	Bob Welch	.10	.05	.01
☐	574	Scott Sanderson	.10	.05	.01
☐	575	Joe Kmak	.10	.05	.01
☐	576	Scott Pose	.10	.05	.01
☐	577	Ricky Gutierrez	.10	.05	.01
☐	578	Mike Trombley	.10	.05	.01
☐	579	Sterling Hitchcock	.20	.09	.03
☐	580	Rodney Bolton	.10	.05	.01
☐	581	Tyler Green	.10	.05	.01
☐	582	Tim Costo	.10	.05	.01
☐	583	Tim Laker	.10	.05	.01
☐	584	Steve Reed	.15	.07	.02
☐	585	Tom Kramer	.10	.05	.01
☐	586	Robb Nen	.10	.05	.01
☐	587	Jim Tatum	.10	.05	.01
☐	588	Frank Bolick	.10	.05	.01
☐	589	Kevin Young	.10	.05	.01
☐	590	Matt Whiteside	.10	.05	.01
☐	591	Cesar Hernandez	.10	.05	.01
☐	592	Mike Mohler	.10	.05	.01
☐	593	Alan Embree	.10	.05	.01
☐	594	Terry Jorgensen	.10	.05	.01
☐	595	John Cummings	.10	.05	.01
☐	596	Domingo Martinez	.10	.05	.01
☐	597	Benji Gil	.15	.07	.02
☐	598	Todd Pratt	.10	.05	.01
☐	599	Rene Arocha	.20	.09	.03
☐	600	Dennis Moeller	.10	.05	.01
☐	601	Jeff Conine	.20	.09	.03
☐	602	Trevor Hoffman	.10	.05	.01
☐	603	Daniel Smith	.10	.05	.01
☐	604	Lee Tinsley	.10	.05	.01
☐	605	Dan Peltier	.10	.05	.01
☐	606	Billy Brewer	.15	.07	.02
☐	607	Matt Walbeck	.10	.05	.01
☐	608	Richie Lewis	.10	.05	.01
☐	609	J.T. Snow	.15	.07	.02
☐	610	Pat Gomez	.10	.05	.01
☐	611	Phil Hiatt	.10	.05	.01
☐	612	Alex Arias	.10	.05	.01
☐	613	Kevin Rogers	.10	.05	.01
☐	614	Al Martin	.15	.07	.02
☐	615	Greg Gohr	.10	.05	.01
☐	616	Graeme Lloyd	.10	.05	.01
☐	617	Kent Bottenfield	.10	.05	.01
☐	618	Chuck Carr	.10	.05	.01
☐	619	Darrell Sherman	.10	.05	.01
☐	620	Mike Lansing	.30	.14	.04

1993 Pinnacle Expansion Opening Day

This nine-card set of 1993 Pinnacle Expansion Opening Day was issued to commemorate openning day for the two 1993 expansion teams, the Colorado Rockies and the Florida Marlins. The cards measure standard size (2 1/2" by 3 1/2"). The full-bleed fronts feature glossy color action player photos. Across the bottom is a team color-coded bar containing the player's name, position, and opening day date. A logo for the Expansion Draft is printed in the lower right corner. An anti-counterfeit device is printed in the bottom black border. The backs carry the same design as the fronts with a player from the Rockies appearing on one side and a Marlin's player on the flip side. The cards are numbered on both sides.

	MINT	EXC	G-VG
COMPLETE SET (9)	20.00	9.00	2.50
COMMON PAIR (1-9)	1.00	.45	.13
☐ 1 Charlie Hough David Nied	4.00	1.80	.50
☐ 2 Benito Santiago Joe Girardi	1.00	.45	.13
☐ 3 Orestes Destrade Andres Galarraga	6.00	2.70	.75
☐ 4 Bret Barberie Eric Young	1.50	.65	.19
☐ 5 Dave Magadan Charlie Hayes	1.50	.65	.19
☐ 6 Walt Weiss Freddie Benavides	1.00	.45	.13
☐ 7 Jeff Conine Jerald Clark	5.00	2.30	.60
☐ 8 Scott Pose Alex Cole	1.00	.45	.13
☐ 9 Junior Felix Dante Bichette	4.00	1.80	.50

1993 Pinnacle Rookie Team Pinnacle

These ten standard-size (2 1/2" by 3 1/2") cards were randomly inserted in Series II foil packs and each features an American League rookie on one side and a National League rookie on the other. Both sides feature black-bordered color player paintings that resemble grainy photographs and are trimmed by a thin white line. Each double-sided card displays paintings by artist Christopher Greco. The player's name, position, and league appear in white lettering within a colored stripe beneath the picture, blue for the American League, red for the National League. The set's title appears in gold foil above each painting. The cards are numbered on the front and back. According to Score, the chances of finding a Rookie Team Pinnacle card are not less than one in 90 packs.

	MINT	EXC	G-VG
COMPLETE SET (10)	150.00	70.00	19.00
COMMON PAIR (1-10)	5.00	2.30	.60
☐ 1 Pedro Martinez Mike Trombley	5.00	2.30	.60
☐ 2 Kevin Rogers Sterling Hitchcock	5.00	2.30	.60
☐ 3 Mike Piazza Jesse Levis	70.00	32.00	8.75
☐ 4 Ryan Klesko J.T. Snow	30.00	13.50	3.80
☐ 5 John Patterson Bret Boone	5.00	2.30	.60
☐ 6 Kevin Young Domingo Martinez	5.00	2.30	.60
☐ 7 Wil Cordero Manny Alexander	5.00	2.30	.60
☐ 8 Steve Hosey Tim Salmon	20.00	9.00	2.50
☐ 9 Ryan Thompson Gerald Williams	5.00	2.30	.60
☐ 10 Melvin Nieves David Hulse	5.00	2.30	.60

1993 Pinnacle Slugfest

These 30 standard-size (2 1/2" by 3 1/2") cards salute baseball's top hitters and were randomly inserted in series II 27-card superpacks. The fronts feature color player action shots that are borderless, except at the bottom, where a black stripe carries the player's name in white lettering. The set's title appears below in black lettering within a gold foil stripe. The horizontal back carries a posed color player photo on its right side. On the left side appears the player's name, the set's title, and the player's career highlights and team logo. The cards are numbered on the back.

	MINT	EXC	G-VG
COMPLETE SET (30)	50.00	23.00	6.25
COMMON CARD (1-30)	.75	.35	.09
☐ 1 Juan Gonzalez	5.00	2.30	.60
☐ 2 Mark McGwire	.75	.35	.09
☐ 3 Cecil Fielder	1.50	.65	.19
☐ 4 Joe Carter	2.25	1.00	.30
☐ 5 Fred McGriff	2.25	1.00	.30
☐ 6 Barry Bonds	6.00	2.70	.75
☐ 7 Gary Sheffield	1.00	.45	.13
☐ 8 Dave Hollins	.75	.35	.09
☐ 9 Frank Thomas	15.00	6.75	1.90
☐ 10 Danny Tartabull	.75	.35	.09
☐ 11 Albert Belle	5.00	2.30	.60
☐ 12 Ruben Sierra	1.00	.45	.13
☐ 13 Larry Walker	1.00	.45	.13
☐ 14 Jeff Bagwell	7.50	3.40	.95
☐ 15 David Justice	2.25	1.00	.30
☐ 16 Kirby Puckett	6.00	2,70	.75
☐ 17 John Kruk	1.00	.45	.13
☐ 18 Howard Johnson	.75	.35	.09
☐ 19 Darryl Strawberry	.75	.35	.09
☐ 20 Will Clark	2.25	1.00	.30
☐ 21 Kevin Mitchell	.75	.35	.09
☐ 22 Mickey Tettleton	.75	.35	.09
☐ 23 Don Mattingly	6.00	2.70	.75
☐ 24 Jose Canseco	2.50	1.15	.30
☐ 25 George Bell	.75	.35	.09
☐ 26 Andre Dawson	1.00	.45	.13
☐ 27 Ryne Sandberg	5.00	2.30	.60
☐ 28 Ken Griffey Jr.	15.00	6.75	1.90
☐ 29 Carlos Baerga	2.25	1.00	.30
☐ 30 Travis Fryman	1.50	.65	.19

1993 Pinnacle Team Pinnacle

This ten-card Team Pinnacle subset was randomly inserted in first series foil packs. According to Score, the chances of finding one are not less than one in 24 packs. Each double-sided card displays paintings by artist Christopher Greco. One side features the best player at his position in the American League, while the opposite has his National League counterpart. A special bonus Team Pinnacle card (11) was available to collectors only through a mail-in offer for ten 1993 Pinnacle baseball wrappers plus 1.50 for shipping and handling. Moreover, hobby dealers who ordered Pinnacle received two bonus cards and an advertisement display promoting the offer.

	MINT	EXC	G-VG
COMPLETE SET (10)	125.00	57.50	15.50
COMMON PAIR (1-10/B11)	5.00	2.30	.60
☐ 1 Greg Maddux Mike Mussina	12.00	5.50	1.50
☐ 2 Tom Glavine John Smiley	5.00	2.30	.60
☐ 3 Darren Daulton Ivan Rodriguez	5.00	2.30	.60
☐ 4 Fred McGriff Frank Thomas	40.00	18.00	5.00
☐ 5 Delino DeShields Carlos Baerga	10.00	4.50	1.25
☐ 6 Gary Sheffield Edgar Martinez	5.00	2.30	.60
☐ 7 Ozzie Smith Pat Listach	10.00	4.50	1.25
☐ 8 Barry Bonds Juan Gonzalez	25.00	11.50	3.10
☐ 9 Andy Van Slyke Kirby Puckett	12.00	5.50	1.50
☐ 10 Larry Walker Joe Carter	5.00	2.30	.60
☐ B11 Rob Dibble Rick Aguilera	5.00	2.30	.60

1993 Pinnacle Team 2001

This 30-card standard-size (2 1/2" by 3 1/2") set salutes players expected to be stars in the year 2001. The cards were inserted one per pack in first series 27-card superpacks and feature color player action shots on their fronts. These photos are borderless at the top and right, and black-bordered on the bottom and left. The player's name appears in gold-foil in the bottom margin, and his gold-foil-encircled team logo rests in the bottom left. The set's title appears vertically in gold foil in the left margin. The horizontal back carries a posed color player photo in its right half, and on the left, the player's name in gold foil, followed by his team name, position, and career highlights. The set's vertical title reappears in gold foil near the left edge. The cards are numbered on the back.

	MINT	EXC	G-VG
COMPLETE SET (30)	40.00	18.00	5.00
COMMON CARD (1-30)	.75	.35	.09
☐ 1 Wil Cordero	.75	.35	.09
☐ 2 Cal Eldred	.75	.35	.09
☐ 3 Mike Mussina	3.00	1.35	.40
☐ 4 Chuck Knoblauch	.75	.35	.09
☐ 5 Melvin Nieves	.75	.35	.09
☐ 6 Tim Wakefield	.75	.35	.09
☐ 7 Carlos Baerga	2.25	1.00	.30
☐ 8 Bret Boone	.75	.35	.09
☐ 9 Jeff Bagwell	7.50	3.40	.95
☐ 10 Travis Fryman	1.50	.65	.19
☐ 11 Royce Clayton	1.00	.45	.13
☐ 12 Delino DeShields	.75	.35	.09
☐ 13 Juan Gonzalez	5.00	2.30	.60
☐ 14 Pedro Martinez	.75	.35	.09
☐ 15 Bernie Williams	.75	.35	.09
☐ 16 Billy Ashley	2.00	.90	.25
☐ 17 Marquis Grissom	1.00	.45	.13
☐ 18 Kenny Lofton	4.00	1.80	.50
☐ 19 Ray Lankford	1.00	.45	.13
☐ 20 Tim Salmon	3.00	1.35	.40
☐ 21 Steve Hosey	.75	.35	.09
☐ 22 Charles Nagy	.75	.35	.09
☐ 23 Dave Fleming	.75	.35	.09
☐ 24 Reggie Sanders	.75	.35	.09
☐ 25 Sam Militello	.75	.35	.09
☐ 26 Eric Karros	.75	.35	.09
☐ 27 Ryan Klesko	3.50	1.55	.45
☐ 28 Dean Palmer	.75	.35	.09
☐ 29 Ivan Rodriguez	.75	.35	.09
☐ 30 Sterling Hitchcock	.75	.35	.09

1993 Pinnacle Tribute

Randomly inserted in second-series packs, these ten standard-size (2 1/2" by 3 1/2") cards pay tribute to two recent retirees from baseball: George Brett (1-5), and Nolan Ryan (6-10). Score estimates that the chances of finding a tribute chase card are not less than one in 24 count good packs. The fronts feature black-bordered color player action shots that are framed by a thin white line. The player's name appears in white lettering within the black bottom margin. Printed vertically, "Tribute" appears in gold foil along the right edge. The black back carries a color player photo toward the upper left. The player's name and the card's title appear below in gold-colored lettering. Career highlights follow in white. The set's title reappears vertically in gold-colored lettering. The cards are numbered on the back.

	MINT	EXC	G-VG
COMPLETE SET (10)	70.00	32.00	8.75
COMMON BRETT (1-5)	6.00	2.70	.75
COMMON RYAN (6-10)	10.00	4.50	1.25
☐ 1 George Brett Kansas City Royalty	6.00	2.70	.75
☐ 2 George Brett The Chase for .400	6.00	2.70	.75
☐ 3 George Brett Pine Tar Pandemonium	6.00	2.70	.75
☐ 4 George Brett MVP and a World Series, Too	6.00	2.70	.75
☐ 5 George Brett 3,000 or Bust	6.00	2.70	.75
☐ 6 Nolan Ryan The Rookie	10.00	4.50	1.25
☐ 7 Nolan Ryan Angel of No Mercy	10.00	4.50	1.25
☐ 8 Nolan Ryan Astronomical Success	10.00	4.50	1.25
☐ 9 Nolan Ryan 5,000 Ks	10.00	4.50	1.25
☐ 10 Nolan Ryan No-Hitter No. 7	10.00	4.50	1.25

1994 Pinnacle

The 540-card 1994 Pinnacle set was issued in two series of 270. The fronts feature full-bleed color action player photos. In one of the upper corners, the new Pinnacle logo appears with the brand name immediately below in small white lettering. Toward the bottom, the player's last name in gold foil on a black bar overlays a two-color emblem carrying his first name and his team name. On most of the backs, a ghosted version of the front picture forms the background for a player cutout, biography, and statistics. The series closes with a Rookie Prospects subset (224-261) and a Draft Picks subset (262-270). The cards are numbered on the back. Rookie Cards include Brian Anderson, Brooks Kieschnick, Derrek Lee, Trot Nixon and Kirk Presley.

	MINT	EXC	G-VG
COMPLETE SET (540)	30.00	13.50	3.80
COMPLETE SERIES 1 (270)	15.00	6.75	1.90
COMPLETE SERIES 2 (270)	15.00	6.75	1.90
COMMON CARD (1-270)	.10	.05	.01
COMMON CARD (271-540)	.10	.05	.01

	MINT	EXC	G-VG
☐ 1 Frank Thomas	3.00	1.35	.40
☐ 2 Carlos Baerga	.40	.18	.05
☐ 3 Sammy Sosa	.20	.09	.03
☐ 4 Tony Gwynn	.75	.35	.09
☐ 5 John Olerud	.20	.09	.03
☐ 6 Ryne Sandberg	1.00	.45	.13
☐ 7 Moises Alou	.20	.09	.03
☐ 8 Steve Avery	.20	.09	.03
☐ 9 Tim Salmon	.40	.18	.05
☐ 10 Cecil Fielder	.20	.09	.03
☐ 11 Greg Maddux	.60	.25	.08
☐ 12 Barry Larkin	.20	.09	.03
☐ 13 Mike Devereaux	.15	.07	.02
☐ 14 Charlie Hayes	.15	.07	.02
☐ 15 Albert Belle	1.00	.45	.13
☐ 16 Andy Van Slyke	.20	.09	.03
☐ 17 Mo Vaughn	.20	.09	.03
☐ 18 Brian McRae	.15	.07	.02
☐ 19 Cal Eldred	.15	.07	.02
☐ 20 Craig Biggio	.15	.07	.02
☐ 21 Kirby Puckett	1.25	.55	.16
☐ 22 Derek Bell	.15	.07	.02
☐ 23 Don Mattingly	1.25	.55	.16
☐ 24 John Burkett	.15	.07	.02
☐ 25 Roger Clemens	.75	.35	.09
☐ 26 Barry Bonds	1.25	.55	.16
☐ 27 Paul Molitor	.40	.18	.05
☐ 28 Mike Piazza	1.50	.65	.19
☐ 29 Robin Ventura	.15	.07	.02
☐ 30 Jeff Conine	.20	.09	.03
☐ 31 Wade Boggs	.20	.09	.03
☐ 32 Dennis Eckersley	.20	.09	.03
☐ 33 Bobby Bonilla	.20	.09	.03
☐ 34 Lenny Dykstra	.20	.09	.03
☐ 35 Manny Alexander	.10	.05	.01
☐ 36 Ray Lankford	.20	.09	.03
☐ 37 Greg Vaughn	.15	.07	.02
☐ 38 Chuck Finley	.10	.05	.01
☐ 39 Todd Benzinger	.10	.05	.01
☐ 40 David Justice	.40	.18	.05
☐ 41 Rob Dibble	.10	.05	.01
☐ 42 Tom Henke	.10	.05	.01
☐ 43 David Nied	.20	.09	.03
☐ 44 Sandy Alomar Jr.	.15	.07	.02
☐ 45 Pete Harnisch	.10	.05	.01
☐ 46 Jeff Russell	.10	.05	.01
☐ 47 Terry Mulholland	.15	.07	.02
☐ 48 Kevin Appier	.15	.07	.02
☐ 49 Randy Tomlin	.10	.05	.01
☐ 50 Cal Ripken	2.25	1.00	.30
☐ 51 Andy Benes	.15	.07	.02
☐ 52 Jimmy Key	.15	.07	.02
☐ 53 Kirt Manwaring	.10	.05	.01
☐ 54 Kevin Tapani	.10	.05	.01
☐ 55 Jose Guzman	.10	.05	.01
☐ 56 Todd Stottlemyre	.10	.05	.01
☐ 57 Jack McDowell	.20	.09	.03
☐ 58 Orel Hershiser	.15	.07	.02
☐ 59 Chris Hammond	.10	.05	.01
☐ 60 Chris Nabholz	.10	.05	.01
☐ 61 Ruben Sierra	.20	.09	.03
☐ 62 Dwight Gooden	.10	.05	.01
☐ 63 John Kruk	.20	.09	.03
☐ 64 Omar Vizquel	.10	.05	.01
☐ 65 Tim Naehring	.10	.05	.01
☐ 66 Dwight Smith	.10	.05	.01
☐ 67 Mickey Tettleton	.15	.07	.02
☐ 68 J.T. Snow	.15	.07	.02
☐ 69 Greg McMichael	.15	.07	.02
☐ 70 Kevin Mitchell	.15	.07	.02
☐ 71 Kevin Brown	.10	.05	.01
☐ 72 Scott Cooper	.15	.07	.02
☐ 73 Jim Thome	.20	.09	.03
☐ 74 Joe Girardi	.10	.05	.01
☐ 75 Eric Anthony	.10	.05	.01
☐ 76 Orlando Merced	.15	.07	.02
☐ 77 Felix Jose	.10	.05	.01
☐ 78 Tommy Greene	.10	.05	.01
☐ 79 Bernard Gilkey	.10	.05	.01
☐ 80 Phil Plantier	.15	.07	.02
☐ 81 Danny Tartabull	.15	.07	.02
☐ 82 Trevor Wilson	.10	.05	.01
☐ 83 Chuck Knoblauch	.20	.09	.03
☐ 84 Rick Wilkins	.10	.05	.01
☐ 85 Devon White	.15	.07	.02
☐ 86 Lance Johnson	.10	.05	.01
☐ 87 Eric Karros	.15	.07	.02
☐ 88 Gary Sheffield	.20	.09	.03
☐ 89 Wil Cordero	.20	.09	.03
☐ 90 Ron Darling	.10	.05	.01
☐ 91 Darren Daulton	.20	.09	.03
☐ 92 Joe Orsulak	.10	.05	.01
☐ 93 Steve Cooke	.10	.05	.01
☐ 94 Darryl Hamilton	.10	.05	.01
☐ 95 Aaron Sele	.25	.11	.03
☐ 96 John Doherty	.10	.05	.01
☐ 97 Gary DiSarcina	.10	.05	.01
☐ 98 Jeff Blauser	.15	.07	.02
☐ 99 John Smiley	.10	.05	.01
☐ 100 Ken Griffey Jr.	3.00	1.35	.40
☐ 101 Dean Palmer	.15	.07	.02

	#	Player			
☐	102	Felix Fermin	.10	.05	.01
☐	103	Jerald Clark	.10	.05	.01
☐	104	Doug Drabek	.20	.09	.03
☐	105	Curt Schilling	.10	.05	.01
☐	106	Jeff Montgomery	.15	.07	.02
☐	107	Rene Arocha	.15	.07	.02
☐	108	Carlos Garcia	.10	.05	.01
☐	109	Wally Whitehurst	.10	.05	.01
☐	110	Jim Abbott	.20	.09	.03
☐	111	Royce Clayton	.15	.07	.02
☐	112	Chris Hoiles	.15	.07	.02
☐	113	Mike Morgan	.10	.05	.01
☐	114	Joe Magrane	.10	.05	.01
☐	115	Tom Candiotti	.10	.05	.01
☐	116	Ron Karkovice	.10	.05	.01
☐	117	Ryan Bowen	.10	.05	.01
☐	118	Rod Beck	.15	.07	.02
☐	119	John Wetteland	.10	.05	.01
☐	120	Terry Steinbach	.15	.07	.02
☐	121	Dave Hollins	.20	.09	.03
☐	122	Jeff Kent	.15	.07	.02
☐	123	Ricky Bones	.10	.05	.01
☐	124	Brian Jordan	.15	.07	.02
☐	125	Chad Kreuter	.10	.05	.01
☐	126	John Valentin	.15	.07	.02
☐	127	Hilly Hathaway	.10	.05	.01
☐	128	Wilson Alvarez	.20	.09	.03
☐	129	Tino Martinez	.10	.05	.01
☐	130	Rodney Bolton	.10	.05	.01
☐	131	David Segui	.10	.05	.01
☐	132	Wayne Kirby	.15	.07	.02
☐	133	Eric Young	.15	.07	.02
☐	134	Scott Servais	.10	.05	.01
☐	135	Scott Radinsky	.10	.05	.01
☐	136	Bret Barberie	.10	.05	.01
☐	137	John Roper	.15	.07	.02
☐	138	Ricky Gutierrez	.10	.05	.01
☐	139	Bernie Williams	.15	.07	.02
☐	140	Bud Black	.10	.05	.01
☐	141	Jose Vizcaino	.10	.05	.01
☐	142	Gerald Williams	.15	.07	.02
☐	143	Duane Ward	.15	.07	.02
☐	144	Danny Jackson	.10	.05	.01
☐	145	Allen Watson	.10	.05	.01
☐	146	Scott Fletcher	.10	.05	.01
☐	147	Delino DeShields	.15	.07	.02
☐	148	Shane Mack	.15	.07	.02
☐	149	Jim Eisenreich	.10	.05	.01
☐	150	Troy Neel	.15	.07	.02
☐	151	Jay Bell	.15	.07	.02
☐	152	B.J. Surhoff	.10	.05	.01
☐	153	Mark Whiten	.15	.07	.02
☐	154	Mike Henneman	.10	.05	.01
☐	155	Todd Hundley	.10	.05	.01
☐	156	Greg Myers	.10	.05	.01
☐	157	Ryan Klesko	.50	.23	.06
☐	158	Dave Fleming	.10	.05	.01
☐	159	Mickey Morandini	.10	.05	.01
☐	160	Blas Minor	.10	.05	.01
☐	161	Reggie Jefferson	.10	.05	.01
☐	162	David Hulse	.15	.07	.02
☐	163	Greg Swindell	.10	.05	.01
☐	164	Roberto Hernandez	.10	.05	.01
☐	165	Brady Anderson	.15	.07	.02
☐	166	Jack Armstrong	.10	.05	.01
☐	167	Phil Clark	.10	.05	.01
☐	168	Melido Perez	.10	.05	.01
☐	169	Darren Lewis	.10	.05	.01
☐	170	Sam Horn	.10	.05	.01
☐	171	Mike Harkey	.10	.05	.01
☐	172	Juan Guzman	.15	.07	.02
☐	173	Bob Natal	.15	.07	.02
☐	174	Deion Sanders	.50	.23	.06
☐	175	Carlos Quintana	.10	.05	.01
☐	176	Mel Rojas	.10	.05	.01
☐	177	Willie Banks	.10	.05	.01
☐	178	Ben Rivera	.10	.05	.01
☐	179	Kenny Lofton	.75	.35	.09
☐	180	Leo Gomez	.10	.05	.01
☐	181	Roberto Mejia	.15	.07	.02
☐	182	Mike Perez	.10	.05	.01
☐	183	Travis Fryman	.25	.11	.03
☐	184	Ben McDonald	.15	.07	.02
☐	185	Steve Frey	.10	.05	.01
☐	186	Kevin Young	.10	.05	.01
☐	187	Dave Magadan	.10	.05	.01
☐	188	Bobby Munoz	.15	.07	.02
☐	189	Pat Rapp	.10	.05	.01
☐	190	Jose Offerman	.15	.07	.02
☐	191	Vinny Castilla	.10	.05	.01
☐	192	Ivan Calderon	.10	.05	.01
☐	193	Ken Caminiti	.15	.07	.02
☐	194	Benji Gil	.15	.07	.02
☐	195	Chuck Carr	.10	.05	.01
☐	196	Derrick May	.10	.05	.01
☐	197	Pat Kelly	.10	.05	.01
☐	198	Jeff Brantley	.10	.05	.01
☐	199	Jose Lind	.10	.05	.01
☐	200	Steve Buechele	.10	.05	.01
☐	201	Wes Chamberlain	.10	.05	.01
☐	202	Eduardo Perez	.15	.07	.02
☐	203	Bret Saberhagen	.15	.07	.02
☐	204	Gregg Jefferies	.20	.09	.03
☐	205	Darrin Fletcher	.10	.05	.01
☐	206	Kent Hrbek	.15	.07	.02
☐	207	Kim Batiste	.10	.05	.01
☐	208	Jeff King	.10	.05	.01
☐	209	Donovan Osborne	.10	.05	.01
☐	210	Dave Nilsson	.10	.05	.01
☐	211	Al Martin	.10	.05	.01
☐	212	Mike Moore	.10	.05	.01
☐	213	Sterling Hitchcock	.15	.07	.02
☐	214	Geronimo Pena	.10	.05	.01
☐	215	Kevin Higgins	.15	.07	.02
☐	216	Norm Charlton	.10	.05	.01
☐	217	Don Slaught	.10	.05	.01
☐	218	Mitch Williams	.10	.05	.01
☐	219	Derek Lilliquist	.10	.05	.01
☐	220	Armando Reynoso	.10	.05	.01
☐	221	Kenny Rogers	.10	.05	.01
☐	222	Doug Jones	.10	.05	.01
☐	223	Luis Aquino	.10	.05	.01
☐	224	Mike Oquist	.15	.07	.02
☐	225	Darryl Scott	.10	.05	.01
☐	226	Kurt Abbott	.30	.14	.04
☐	227	Andy Tomberlin	.10	.05	.01
☐	228	Norberto Martin	.15	.07	.02
☐	229	Pedro Castellano	.10	.05	.01
☐	230	Curtis Pride	.30	.14	.04
☐	231	Jeff McNeely	.10	.05	.01
☐	232	Scott Lydy	.10	.05	.01
☐	233	Darren Oliver	.10	.05	.01
☐	234	Danny Bautista	.15	.07	.02
☐	235	Butch Huskey	.10	.05	.01
☐	236	Chipper Jones	.40	.18	.05
☐	237	Eddie Zambrano	.10	.05	.01
☐	238	Domingo Jean	.10	.05	.01
☐	239	Javy Lopez	.30	.14	.04
☐	240	Nigel Wilson	.15	.07	.02
☐	241	Drew Denson	.10	.05	.01
☐	242	Raul Mondesi	1.00	.45	.13
☐	243	Luis Ortiz	.10	.05	.01
☐	244	Manny Ramirez	.60	.25	.08
☐	245	Greg Blosser	.10	.05	.01
☐	246	Rondell White	.30	.14	.04
☐	247	Steve Karsay	.10	.05	.01

	Player			
☐ 248	Scott Stahoviak	.10	.05	.01
☐ 249	Jose Valentin	.15	.07	.02
☐ 250	Marc Newfield	.20	.09	.03
☐ 251	Keith Kessinger	.10	.05	.01
☐ 252	Carl Everett	.15	.07	.02
☐ 253	John O'Donoghue	.10	.05	.01
☐ 254	Turk Wendell	.10	.05	.01
☐ 255	Scott Ruffcorn	.20	.09	.03
☐ 256	Tony Tarasco	.20	.09	.03
☐ 257	Andy Cook	.15	.07	.02
☐ 258	Matt Mieske	.10	.05	.01
☐ 259	Luis Lopez	.10	.05	.01
☐ 260	Ramon Caraballo	.15	.07	.02
☐ 261	Salomon Torres	.15	.07	.02
☐ 262	Brooks Kieschnick	1.00	.45	.13
☐ 263	Daron Kirkreit	.15	.07	.02
☐ 264	Bill Wagner	.60	.25	.08
☐ 265	Matt Drews	.50	.23	.06
☐ 266	Scott Christman	.30	.14	.04
☐ 267	Torii Hunter	.30	.14	.04
☐ 268	Jamey Wright	.40	.18	.05
☐ 269	Jeff Granger	.20	.09	.03
☐ 270	Trot Nixon	.75	.35	.09
☐ 271	Randy Myers	.10	.05	.01
☐ 272	Trevor Hoffman	.10	.05	.01
☐ 273	Bob Wickman	.10	.05	.01
☐ 274	Willie McGee	.10	.05	.01
☐ 275	Hipolito Pichardo	.10	.05	.01
☐ 276	Bobby Witt	.10	.05	.01
☐ 277	Gregg Olson	.10	.05	.01
☐ 278	Randy Johnson	.20	.09	.03
☐ 279	Robb Nen	.10	.05	.01
☐ 280	Paul O'Neill	.15	.07	.02
☐ 281	Lou Whitaker	.20	.09	.03
☐ 282	Chad Curtis	.15	.07	.02
☐ 283	Doug Henry	.10	.05	.01
☐ 284	Tom Glavine	.20	.09	.03
☐ 285	Mike Greenwell	.15	.07	.02
☐ 286	Roberto Kelly	.10	.05	.01
☐ 287	Roberto Alomar	.75	.35	.09
☐ 288	Charlie Hough	.15	.07	.02
☐ 289	Alex Fernandez	.20	.09	.03
☐ 290	Jeff Bagwell	1.50	.65	.19
☐ 291	Wally Joyner	.15	.07	.02
☐ 292	Andujar Cedeno	.10	.05	.01
☐ 293	Rick Aguilera	.15	.07	.02
☐ 294	Darryl Strawberry	.15	.07	.02
☐ 295	Mike Mussina	.40	.18	.05
☐ 296	Jeff Gardner	.10	.05	.01
☐ 297	Chris Gwynn	.10	.05	.01
☐ 298	Matt Williams	.60	.25	.08
☐ 299	Brent Gates	.20	.09	.03
☐ 300	Mark McGwire	.20	.09	.03
☐ 301	Jim Deshaies	.10	.05	.01
☐ 302	Edgar Martinez	.10	.05	.01
☐ 303	Danny Darwin	.10	.05	.01
☐ 304	Pat Meares	.10	.05	.01
☐ 305	Benito Santiago	.10	.05	.01
☐ 306	Jose Canseco	.40	.18	.05
☐ 307	Jim Gott	.10	.05	.01
☐ 308	Paul Sorrento	.10	.05	.01
☐ 309	Scott Kamieniecki	.10	.05	.01
☐ 310	Larry Walker	.20	.09	.03
☐ 311	Mark Langston	.20	.09	.03
☐ 312	John Jaha	.10	.05	.01
☐ 313	Stan Javier	.10	.05	.01
☐ 314	Hal Morris	.15	.07	.02
☐ 315	Robby Thompson	.10	.05	.01
☐ 316	Pat Hentgen	.15	.07	.02
☐ 317	Tom Gordon	.10	.05	.01
☐ 318	Joey Cora	.10	.05	.01
☐ 319	Luis Alicea	.10	.05	.01
☐ 320	Andre Dawson	.20	.09	.03
☐ 321	Darryl Kile	.15	.07	.02
☐ 322	Jose Rijo	.15	.07	.02
☐ 323	Luis Gonzalez	.10	.05	.01
☐ 324	Billy Ashley	.20	.09	.03
☐ 325	David Cone	.20	.09	.03
☐ 326	Bill Swift	.10	.05	.01
☐ 327	Phil Hiatt	.10	.05	.01
☐ 328	Craig Paquette	.10	.05	.01
☐ 329	Bob Welch	.10	.05	.01
☐ 330	Tony Phillips	.10	.05	.01
☐ 331	Archi Cianfrocco	.10	.05	.01
☐ 332	Dave Winfield	.20	.09	.03
☐ 333	David McCarty	.15	.07	.02
☐ 334	Al Leiter	.10	.05	.01
☐ 335	Tom Browning	.10	.05	.01
☐ 336	Mark Grace	.20	.09	.03
☐ 337	Jose Mesa	.10	.05	.01
☐ 338	Mike Stanley	.10	.05	.01
☐ 339	Roger McDowell	.10	.05	.01
☐ 340	Damion Easley	.10	.05	.01
☐ 341	Angel Miranda	.10	.05	.01
☐ 342	John Smoltz	.15	.07	.02
☐ 343	Jay Buhner	.15	.07	.02
☐ 344	Bryan Harvey	.15	.07	.02
☐ 345	Joe Carter	.40	.18	.05
☐ 346	Dante Bichette	.20	.09	.03
☐ 347	Jason Bere	.40	.18	.05
☐ 348	Frank Viola	.10	.05	.01
☐ 349	Ivan Rodriguez	.20	.09	.03
☐ 350	Juan Gonzalez	1.00	.45	.13
☐ 351	Steve Finley	.10	.05	.01
☐ 352	Mike Felder	.10	.05	.01
☐ 353	Ramon Martinez	.15	.07	.02
☐ 354	Greg Gagne	.10	.05	.01
☐ 355	Ken Hill	.15	.07	.02
☐ 356	Pedro Munoz	.10	.05	.01
☐ 357	Todd Van Poppel	.15	.07	.02
☐ 358	Marquis Grissom	.20	.09	.03
☐ 359	Milt Cuyler	.10	.05	.01
☐ 360	Reggie Sanders	.15	.07	.02
☐ 361	Scott Erickson	.10	.05	.01
☐ 362	Billy Hatcher	.10	.05	.01
☐ 363	Gene Harris	.10	.05	.01
☐ 364	Rene Gonzales	.10	.05	.01
☐ 365	Kevin Rogers	.10	.05	.01
☐ 366	Eric Plunk	.10	.05	.01
☐ 367	Todd Zeile	.10	.05	.01
☐ 368	John Franco	.10	.05	.01
☐ 369	Brett Butler	.15	.07	.02
☐ 370	Bill Spiers	.10	.05	.01
☐ 371	Terry Pendleton	.10	.05	.01
☐ 372	Chris Bosio	.10	.05	.01
☐ 373	Orestes Destrade	.10	.05	.01
☐ 374	Dave Stewart	.15	.07	.02
☐ 375	Darren Holmes	.10	.05	.01
☐ 376	Doug Strange	.10	.05	.01
☐ 377	Brian Turang	.10	.05	.01
☐ 378	Carl Willis	.10	.05	.01
☐ 379	Mark McLemore	.10	.05	.01
☐ 380	Bobby Jones	.25	.11	.03
☐ 381	Scott Sanders	.10	.05	.01
☐ 382	Kirk Rueter	.10	.05	.01
☐ 383	Randy Velarde	.10	.05	.01
☐ 384	Fred McGriff	.40	.18	.05
☐ 385	Charles Nagy	.10	.05	.01
☐ 386	Rich Amaral	.10	.05	.01
☐ 387	Geronimo Berroa	.10	.05	.01
☐ 388	Eric Davis	.10	.05	.01
☐ 389	Ozzie Smith	.60	.25	.08
☐ 390	Alex Arias	.10	.05	.01
☐ 391	Brad Ausmus	.10	.05	.01
☐ 392	Cliff Floyd	.50	.23	.06
☐ 393	Roger Salkeld	.10	.05	.01

☐	394 Jim Edmonds	.10	.05	.01
☐	395 Jeromy Burnitz	.15	.07	.02
☐	396 Dave Staton	.10	.05	.01
☐	397 Rob Butler	.10	.05	.01
☐	398 Marcos Armas	.10	.05	.01
☐	399 Darrell Whitmore	.15	.07	.02
☐	400 Ryan Thompson	.15	.07	.02
☐	401 Ross Powell	.10	.05	.01
☐	402 Joe Oliver	.10	.05	.01
☐	403 Paul Carey	.10	.05	.01
☐	404 Bob Hamelin	.20	.09	.03
☐	405 Chris Turner	.10	.05	.01
☐	406 Nate Minchey	.15	.07	.02
☐	407 Lonnie Maclin	.20	.09	.03
☐	408 Harold Baines	.15	.07	.02
☐	409 Brian Williams	.10	.05	.01
☐	410 Johnny Ruffin	.10	.05	.01
☐	411 Julian Tavarez	.60	.25	.08
☐	412 Mark Hutton	.10	.05	.01
☐	413 Carlos Delgado	.50	.23	.06
☐	414 Chris Gomez	.20	.09	.03
☐	415 Mike Hampton	.10	.05	.01
☐	416 Alex Diaz	.10	.05	.01
☐	417 Jeffrey Hammonds	.35	.16	.04
☐	418 Jayhawk Owens	.10	.05	.01
☐	419 J.R. Phillips	.20	.09	.03
☐	420 Cory Bailey	.20	.09	.03
☐	421 Denny Hocking	.10	.05	.01
☐	422 Jon Shave	.10	.05	.01
☐	423 Damon Buford	.10	.05	.01
☐	424 Troy O'Leary	.10	.05	.01
☐	425 Tripp Cromer	.10	.05	.01
☐	426 Albie Lopez	.20	.09	.03
☐	427 Tony Fernandez	.10	.05	.01
☐	428 Ozzie Guillen	.10	.05	.01
☐	429 Alan Trammell	.25	.11	.03
☐	430 John Wasdin	.60	.25	.08
☐	431 Marc Valdes	.25	.11	.03
☐	432 Brian Anderson	.75	.35	.09
☐	433 Matt Brunson	.30	.14	.04
☐	434 Wayne Gomes	.25	.11	.03
☐	435 Jay Powell	.30	.14	.04
☐	436 Kirk Presley	.75	.35	.09
☐	437 Jon Ratliff	.25	.11	.03
☐	438 Derrek Lee	.75	.35	.09
☐	439 Tom Pagnozzi	.10	.05	.01
☐	440 Kent Mercker	.10	.05	.01
☐	441 Phil Leftwich	.10	.05	.01
☐	442 Jamie Moyer	.10	.05	.01
☐	443 John Flaherty	.10	.05	.01
☐	444 Mark Wohlers	.10	.05	.01
☐	445 Jose Bautista	.10	.05	.01
☐	446 Andres Galarraga	.20	.09	.03
☐	447 Mark Lemke	.10	.05	.01
☐	448 Tim Wakefield	.10	.05	.01
☐	449 Pat Listach	.10	.05	.01
☐	450 Rickey Henderson	.20	.09	.03
☐	451 Mike Gallego	.10	.05	.01
☐	452 Bob Tewksbury	.10	.05	.01
☐	453 Kirk Gibson	.15	.07	.02
☐	454 Pedro Astacio	.15	.07	.02
☐	455 Mike Lansing	.15	.07	.02
☐	456 Sean Berry	.10	.05	.01
☐	457 Bob Walk	.10	.05	.01
☐	458 Chili Davis	.15	.07	.02
☐	459 Ed Sprague	.10	.05	.01
☐	460 Kevin Stocker	.15	.07	.02
☐	461 Mike Stanton	.10	.05	.01
☐	462 Tim Raines	.20	.09	.03
☐	463 Mike Bordick	.10	.05	.01
☐	464 David Wells	.10	.05	.01
☐	465 Tim Laker	.10	.05	.01
☐	466 Cory Snyder	.10	.05	.01
☐	467 Alex Cole	.10	.05	.01
☐	468 Pete Incaviglia	.10	.05	.01
☐	469 Roger Pavlik	.10	.05	.01
☐	470 Greg W. Harris	.10	.05	.01
☐	471 Xavier Hernandez	.10	.05	.01
☐	472 Erik Hanson	.10	.05	.01
☐	473 Jesse Orosco	.10	.05	.01
☐	474 Greg Colbrunn	.10	.05	.01
☐	475 Harold Reynolds	.10	.05	.01
☐	476 Greg A. Harris	.10	.05	.01
☐	477 Pat Borders	.10	.05	.01
☐	478 Melvin Nieves	.20	.09	.03
☐	479 Mariano Duncan	.10	.05	.01
☐	480 Greg Hibbard	.10	.05	.01
☐	481 Tim Pugh	.10	.05	.01
☐	482 Bobby Ayala	.10	.05	.01
☐	483 Sid Fernandez	.10	.05	.01
☐	484 Tim Wallach	.10	.05	.01
☐	485 Randy Milligan	.10	.05	.01
☐	486 Walt Weiss	.10	.05	.01
☐	487 Matt Walbeck	.10	.05	.01
☐	488 Mike Macfarlane	.10	.05	.01
☐	489 Jerry Browne	.10	.05	.01
☐	490 Chris Sabo	.10	.05	.01
☐	491 Tim Belcher	.10	.05	.01
☐	492 Spike Owen	.10	.05	.01
☐	493 Rafael Palmeiro	.20	.09	.03
☐	494 Brian Harper	.10	.05	.01
☐	495 Eddie Murray	.20	.09	.03
☐	496 Ellis Burks	.15	.07	.02
☐	497 Karl Rhodes	.10	.05	.01
☐	498 Otis Nixon	.10	.05	.01
☐	499 Lee Smith	.20	.09	.03
☐	500 Bip Roberts	.10	.05	.01
☐	501 Pedro Martinez	.20	.09	.03
☐	502 Brian Hunter	.10	.05	.01
☐	503 Tyler Green	.10	.05	.01
☐	504 Bruce Hurst	.10	.05	.01
☐	505 Alex Gonzalez	.30	.14	.04
☐	506 Mark Portugal	.10	.05	.01
☐	507 Bob Ojeda	.10	.05	.01
☐	508 Dave Henderson	.10	.05	.01
☐	509 Bo Jackson	.20	.09	.03
☐	510 Bret Boone	.20	.09	.03
☐	511 Mark Eichhorn	.10	.05	.01
☐	512 Luis Polonia	.10	.05	.01
☐	513 Will Clark	.40	.18	.05
☐	514 Dave Valle	.10	.05	.01
☐	515 Dan Wilson	.10	.05	.01
☐	516 Dennis Martinez	.15	.07	.02
☐	517 Jim Leyritz	.10	.05	.01
☐	518 Howard Johnson	.10	.05	.01
☐	519 Jody Reed	.10	.05	.01
☐	520 Julio Franco	.15	.07	.02
☐	521 Jeff Reardon	.15	.07	.02
☐	522 Willie Greene	.15	.07	.02
☐	523 Shawon Dunston	.10	.05	.01
☐	524 Keith Mitchell	.10	.05	.01
☐	525 Rick Helling	.10	.05	.01
☐	526 Mark Kiefer	.10	.05	.01
☐	527 Chan Ho Park	1.25	.55	.16
☐	528 Tony Longmire	.10	.05	.01
☐	529 Rich Becker	.15	.07	.02
☐	530 Tim Hyers	.10	.05	.01
☐	531 Darrin Jackson	.10	.05	.01
☐	532 Jack Morris	.20	.09	.03
☐	533 Rick White	.10	.05	.01
☐	534 Mike Kelly	.15	.07	.02
☐	535 James Mouton	.20	.09	.03
☐	536 Steve Trachsel	.40	.18	.05
☐	537 Tony Eusebio	.10	.05	.01
☐	538 Kelly Stinnett	.10	.05	.01
☐	539 Paul Spoljaric	.10	.05	.01

☐ 540 Darren Dreifort	.10	.05	.01
☐ SR1 Carlos Delgado Super Rookie	25.00	11.50	3.10

1994 Pinnacle Artist's Proofs

Randomly inserted at a rate of one in 26 hobby and retail packs, this 540-card set parallels that of the basic Pinnacle issue. Each card is embossed with a gold-foil-stamped "Artist's Proof" logo just above the player name. The Pinnacle logo is also done in gold foil. Just 1,000 of each card were printed.

	MINT	EXC	G-VG
COMPLETE SET (540)	4000.00	1800.00	500.00
COMPLETE SERIES 1 (270)	2500.00	1150.00	325.00
COMPLETE SERIES 2 (270)	1500.00	700.00	190.00
COMMON CARD (1-270)	3.00	1.35	.40
COMMON CARD (271-540)	3.00	1.35	.40

*UNLISTED VETERAN STARS: 30X to 60X BASIC CARDS
*UNLISTED YOUNG STARS: 25X to 50X BASIC CARDS
*UNLISTED RCs: 20X to 40X BASIC CARDS

☐ 1 Frank Thomas	150.00	70.00	19.00
☐ 6 Ryne Sandberg	50.00	23.00	6.25
☐ 21 Kirby Puckett	60.00	27.00	7.50
☐ 23 Don Mattingly	60.00	27.00	7.50
☐ 26 Barry Bonds	60.00	27.00	7.50
☐ 28 Mike Piazza	75.00	34.00	9.50
☐ 50 Cal Ripken	110.00	50.00	14.00
☐ 100 Ken Griffey Jr.	150.00	70.00	19.00
☐ 242 Raul Mondesi	50.00	23.00	6.25
☐ 290 Jeff Bagwell	75.00	34.00	9.50

1994 Pinnacle Museum Collection

This 540-card set is a parallel dufex to that of the basic Pinnacle issue. They were randomly inserted at a rate of one in four hobby and retail packs. A Museum Collection logo replaces the anti-counterfeit device. Only 6,500 of each card were printed.

	MINT	EXC	G-VG
COMPLETE SET (540)	1500.00	700.00	190.00
COMPLETE SERIES 1 (270)	900.00	400.00	115.00
COMPLETE SERIES 2 (270)	600.00	275.00	75.00
COMMON CARD (1-270)	1.50	.65	.19
COMMON CARD (271-540)	1.50	.65	.19

*UNLISTED VETERAN STARS: 10X to 20X BASIC CARDS
*UNLISTED YOUNG STARS: 7.5X to 15X BASIC CARDS
*UNLISTED RCs: 6X to 12X BASIC CARDS

☐ 1 Frank Thomas	60.00	27.00	7.50
☐ 6 Ryne Sandberg	20.00	9.00	2.50
☐ 21 Kirby Puckett	25.00	11.50	3.10
☐ 23 Don Mattingly	25.00	11.50	3.10
☐ 26 Barry Bonds	25.00	11.50	3.10
☐ 28 Mike Piazza	30.00	13.50	3.80
☐ 50 Cal Ripken	40.00	18.00	5.00
☐ 100 Ken Griffey Jr.	60.00	27.00	7.50
☐ 242 Raul Mondesi	20.00	9.00	2.50
☐ 290 Jeff Bagwell	30.00	13.50	3.80

1994 Pinnacle Rookie Team Pinnacle

These nine double-front cards of the "Rookie Team Pinnacle" set feature a top AL and a top NL rookie prospect by position. The insertion rate for these is one per 48 packs. These special portrait cards were painted by artists Christopher Greco and Ron DeFelice. The front features the National League player and card number. Both sides contain a gold Rookie Team Pinnacle logo.

	MINT	EXC	G-VG
COMPLETE SET (9)	125.00	57.50	15.50
COMMON PAIR (1-9)	5.00	2.30	.60

		MINT	EXC	G-VG
☐ 1	Carlos Delgado / Javier Lopez	25.00	11.50	3.10
☐ 2	Bob Hamelin / J.R. Phillips	15.00	6.75	1.90
☐ 3	Jon Shave / Keith Kessinger	5.00	2.30	.60
☐ 4	Luis Ortiz / Butch Huskey	7.00	3.10	.85
☐ 5	Kurt Abbott / Chipper Jones	15.00	6.75	1.90
☐ 6	Manny Ramirez / Rondell White	30.00	13.50	3.80
☐ 7	Jeffrey Hammonds / Cliff Floyd	25.00	11.50	3.10
☐ 8	Marc Newfield / Nigel Wilson	5.00	2.30	.60
☐ 9	Mark Hutton / Salomon Torres	7.00	3.10	.85

1994 Pinnacle Run Creators

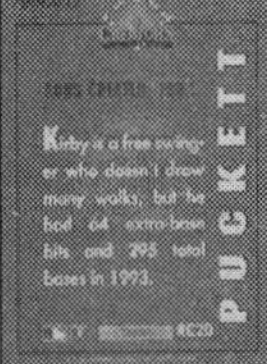

Randomly inserted at an approximate rate of one in four jumbo packs, this 22-card standard-size set spotlights top run producers. The player stands out from a solid background on front. His last name and the Pinnacle logo run up the right border in gold foil. The Run Creators logo is at bottom center. A solid colored back contains the team logo as background to statistical highlights including runs created.

	MINT	EXC	G-VG
COMPLETE SET (44)	175.00	80.00	22.00
COMPLETE SERIES 1 (22)	100.00	45.00	12.50
COMPLETE SERIES 2 (22)	75.00	34.00	9.50
COMMON CARD (RC1-RC22)	1.25	.55	.16
COMMON CARD (RC23-RC44)	1.25	.55	.16

		MINT	EXC	G-VG
☐ RC1	John Olerud	2.00	.90	.25
☐ RC2	Frank Thomas	20.00	9.00	2.50
☐ RC3	Ken Griffey Jr.	20.00	9.00	2.50
☐ RC4	Paul Molitor	3.00	1.35	.40
☐ RC5	Rafael Palmeiro	2.00	.90	.25
☐ RC6	Roberto Alomar	5.00	2.30	.60
☐ RC7	Juan Gonzalez	7.00	3.10	.85
☐ RC8	Albert Belle	7.00	3.10	.85
☐ RC9	Travis Fryman	2.50	1.15	.30
☐ RC10	Rickey Henderson	2.00	.90	.25
☐ RC11	Tony Phillips	1.25	.55	.16
☐ RC12	Mo Vaughn	2.00	.90	.25
☐ RC13	Tim Salmon	3.00	1.35	.40
☐ RC14	Kenny Lofton	5.00	2.30	.60
☐ RC15	Carlos Baerga	3.00	1.35	.40
☐ RC16	Greg Vaughn	1.25	.55	.16
☐ RC17	Jay Buhner	1.50	.65	.19
☐ RC18	Chris Hoiles	1.25	.55	.16
☐ RC19	Mickey Tettleton	1.25	.55	.16
☐ RC20	Kirby Puckett	8.00	3.60	1.00
☐ RC21	Danny Tartabull	1.50	.65	.19
☐ RC22	Devon White	1.50	.65	.19
☐ RC23	Barry Bonds	8.00	3.60	1.00
☐ RC24	Lenny Dykstra	2.00	.90	.25
☐ RC25	John Kruk	1.50	.65	.19
☐ RC26	Fred McGriff	3.00	1.35	.40
☐ RC27	Gregg Jefferies	2.00	.90	.25
☐ RC28	Mike Piazza	10.00	4.50	1.25
☐ RC29	Jeff Blauser	1.25	.55	.16
☐ RC30	Andres Galarraga	2.00	.90	.25
☐ RC31	Darren Daulton	2.00	.90	.25
☐ RC32	David Justice	3.00	1.35	.40
☐ RC33	Craig Biggio	1.50	.65	.19
☐ RC34	Mark Grace	1.50	.65	.19
☐ RC35	Tony Gwynn	5.00	2.30	.60
☐ RC36	Jeff Bagwell	10.00	4.50	1.25
☐ RC37	Jay Bell	1.25	.55	.16
☐ RC38	Marquis Grissom	2.00	.90	.25
☐ RC39	Matt Williams	4.00	1.80	.50
☐ RC40	Charlie Hayes	1.25	.55	.16
☐ RC41	Dante Bichette	2.00	.90	.25
☐ RC42	Bernard Gilkey	1.25	.55	.16
☐ RC43	Brett Butler	1.25	.55	.16
☐ RC44	Rick Wilkins	1.25	.55	.16

1994 Pinnacle Team Pinnacle

Identical in design to the Rookie Team Pinnacle set, these double-front cards feature top players from each of the nine positions. Randomly inserted in second series hobby and retail packs at a rate of one in 48, these special portrait cards were painted by artists Christopher Greco and Ron DeFelice. The front features the National League player and card number. Both sides contain a gold Team Pinnacle logo.

	MINT	EXC	G-VG
COMPLETE SET (9)	200.00	90.00	25.00
COMMON PAIR (1-9)	12.00	5.50	1.50

		MINT	EXC	G-VG
☐ 1	Jeff Bagwell / Frank Thomas	75.00	34.00	9.50
☐ 2	Carlos Baerga / Robby Thompson	12.00	5.50	1.50
☐ 3	Matt Williams	12.00	5.50	1.50

Dean Palmer
- ☐ 4 Cal Ripken.................... 40.00 18.00 5.00
  Jay Bell
- ☐ 5 Ivan Rodriguez............ 25.00 11.50 3.10
  Mike Piazza
- ☐ 6 Lenny Dykstra............. 50.00 23.00 6.25
  Ken Griffey Jr.
- ☐ 7 Juan Gonzalez............. 30.00 13.50 3.80
  Barry Bonds
- ☐ 8 Tim Salmon 15.00 6.75 1.90
  Dave Justice
- ☐ 9 Greg Maddux............... 15.00 6.75 1.90
  Jack McDowell

1994 Pinnacle Tribute

Randomly inserted in hobby packs at a rate of one in 18, this 18-card set was issued in two series of nine. Showcasing some of the top superstar veterans, the fronts have a color player photo with "Tribute" up the left border in a black stripe. The player's name appears at the bottom with a notation given to describe the player. The backs are primarily black with a close-up photo of the player. The cards are numbered with a TR prefix.

	MINT	EXC	G-VG
COMPLETE SET (18)	100.00	45.00	12.50
COMPLETE SERIES 1 (9)	40.00	18.00	5.00
COMPLETE SERIES 2 (9)	60.00	27.00	7.50
COMMON CARD (TR1-TR9)	1.25	.55	.16
COMMON CARD (TR10-TR18)	1.25	.55	.16

☐ TR1 Paul Molitor	3.00	1.35	.40
☐ TR2 Jim Abbott	1.25	.55	.16
☐ TR3 Dave Winfield	1.75	.80	.22
☐ TR4 Bo Jackson	1.75	.80	.22
☐ TR5 David Justice	3.00	1.35	.40
☐ TR6 Len Dykstra	1.75	.80	.22
☐ TR7 Mike Piazza	10.00	4.50	1.25
☐ TR8 Barry Bonds	8.00	3.60	1.00
☐ TR9 Randy Johnson	1.75	.80	.22
☐ TR10 Ozzie Smith	4.00	1.80	.50
☐ TR11 Mark Whiten	1.25	.55	.16
☐ TR12 Greg Maddux	5.00	2.30	.60
☐ TR13 Cal Ripken	15.00	6.75	1.90
☐ TR14 Frank Thomas	20.00	9.00	2.50
☐ TR15 Juan Gonzalez	7.00	3.10	.85
☐ TR16 Roberto Alomar	5.00	2.30	.60
☐ TR17 Ken Griffey Jr.	20.00	9.00	2.50
☐ TR18 Lee Smith	1.75	.80	.22

1988 Score

This 660-card set was distributed by Major League Marketing. Cards measure 2 1/2" by 3 1/2" and feature six distinctive border colors on the front. Highlights (652-660) and Rookie Prospects (623-647) are included in the set. Reggie Jackson's career is honored with a five-card subset on cards 500-504. Card number 501, showing Reggie as a member of the Baltimore Orioles, is one of the few opportunities collectors have to visually remember (on a regular card) Reggie's one-year stay with the Orioles. The set is distinguished by the fact that each card back shows a full-color picture of the player. Rookie Cards in this set include Jeff Blauser, Ellis Burks, Mike Devereaux, Ron Gant, Tom Glavine, Gregg Jefferies, Roberto Kelly, Jeff Montgomery, and Matt Williams. The company also produced a very limited "glossy" set, that is valued at ten times the value of the regular (non-glossy) set. Although exact production quantities of this glossy set are not known, it has been speculated, but not confirmed, that 5,000 glossy sets were produced. It is generally accepted that the number of Score glossy sets produced in 1988 was much smaller (estimated only 10 percent to 15 percent as many) than the number of Topps Tiffany or Fleer Tin sets. These Score glossy cards, when bought or sold individually, are valued approximately five to ten times the values listed below.

	MINT	EXC	G-VG
COMPLETE SET (660)	15.00	6.75	1.90
COMPLETE FACT.SET (660)	18.00	8.00	2.30
COMMON CARD (1-660)	.05	.02	.01

☐ 1 Don Mattingly	.40	.18	.05
☐ 2 Wade Boggs	.25	.11	.03
☐ 3 Tim Raines	.15	.07	.02
☐ 4 Andre Dawson	.15	.07	.02
☐ 5 Mark McGwire	.35	.16	.04
☐ 6 Kevin Seitzer	.10	.05	.01
☐ 7 Wally Joyner	.10	.05	.01
☐ 8 Jesse Barfield	.05	.02	.01
☐ 9 Pedro Guerrero	.10	.05	.01
☐ 10 Eric Davis	.10	.05	.01
☐ 11 George Brett	.40	.18	.05
☐ 12 Ozzie Smith	.30	.14	.04
☐ 13 Rickey Henderson	.25	.11	.03
☐ 14 Jim Rice	.15	.07	.02
☐ 15 Matt Nokes	.15	.07	.02

☐ 16 Mike Schmidt .25 .11 .03
☐ 17 Dave Parker .15 .07 .02
☐ 18 Eddie Murray .20 .09 .03
☐ 19 Andres Galarraga .25 .11 .03
☐ 20 Tony Fernandez .10 .05 .01
☐ 21 Kevin McReynolds .10 .05 .01
☐ 22 B.J. Surhoff .10 .05 .01
☐ 23 Pat Tabler .05 .02 .01
☐ 24 Kirby Puckett .50 .23 .06
☐ 25 Benny Santiago .10 .05 .01
☐ 26 Ryne Sandberg .50 .23 .06
☐ 27 Kelly Downs .10 .05 .01
(Will Clark in background, out of focus)
☐ 28 Jose Cruz .05 .02 .01
☐ 29 Pete O'Brien .05 .02 .01
☐ 30 Mark Langston .15 .07 .02
☐ 31 Lee Smith .15 .07 .02
☐ 32 Juan Samuel .05 .02 .01
☐ 33 Kevin Bass .05 .02 .01
☐ 34 R.J. Reynolds .05 .02 .01
☐ 35 Steve Sax .05 .02 .01
☐ 36 John Kruk .15 .07 .02
☐ 37 Alan Trammell .15 .07 .02
☐ 38 Chris Bosio .10 .05 .01
☐ 39 Brook Jacoby .05 .02 .01
☐ 40 Willie McGee UER .10 .05 .01
(Excited misspelled as excitd)
☐ 41 Dave Magadan .10 .05 .01
☐ 42 Fred Lynn .10 .05 .01
☐ 43 Kent Hrbek .10 .05 .01
☐ 44 Brian Downing .05 .02 .01
☐ 45 Jose Canseco .40 .18 .05
☐ 46 Jim Presley .05 .02 .01
☐ 47 Mike Stanley .10 .05 .01
☐ 48 Tony Pena .05 .02 .01
☐ 49 David Cone .35 .16 .04
☐ 50 Rick Sutcliffe .10 .05 .01
☐ 51 Doug Drabek .15 .07 .02
☐ 52 Bill Doran .05 .02 .01
☐ 53 Mike Scioscia .05 .02 .01
☐ 54 Candy Maldonado .05 .02 .01
☐ 55 Dave Winfield .20 .09 .03
☐ 56 Lou Whitaker .15 .07 .02
☐ 57 Tom Henke .10 .05 .01
☐ 58 Ken Gerhart .05 .02 .01
☐ 59 Glenn Braggs .05 .02 .01
☐ 60 Julio Franco .10 .05 .01
☐ 61 Charlie Leibrandt .05 .02 .01
☐ 62 Gary Gaetti .05 .02 .01
☐ 63 Bob Boone .10 .05 .01
☐ 64 Luis Polonia .25 .11 .03
☐ 65 Dwight Evans .10 .05 .01
☐ 66 Phil Bradley .05 .02 .01
☐ 67 Mike Boddicker .05 .02 .01
☐ 68 Vince Coleman .10 .05 .01
☐ 69 Howard Johnson .10 .05 .01
☐ 70 Tim Wallach .10 .05 .01
☐ 71 Keith Moreland .05 .02 .01
☐ 72 Barry Larkin .20 .09 .03
☐ 73 Alan Ashby .05 .02 .01
☐ 74 Rick Rhoden .05 .02 .01
☐ 75 Darrell Evans .10 .05 .01
☐ 76 Dave Stieb .10 .05 .01
☐ 77 Dan Plesac .05 .02 .01
☐ 78 Will Clark UER .40 .18 .05
(Born 3/17/64, should be 3/13/64)
☐ 79 Frank White .10 .05 .01
☐ 80 Joe Carter .30 .14 .04
☐ 81 Mike Witt .05 .02 .01
☐ 82 Terry Steinbach .10 .05 .01
☐ 83 Alvin Davis .05 .02 .01
☐ 84 Tommy Herr .10 .05 .01
(Will Clark shown sliding into second)
☐ 85 Vance Law .05 .02 .01
☐ 86 Kal Daniels .05 .02 .01
☐ 87 Rick Honeycutt UER .05 .02 .01
(Wrong years for stats on back)
☐ 88 Alfredo Griffin .05 .02 .01
☐ 89 Bret Saberhagen .15 .07 .02
☐ 90 Bert Blyleven .15 .07 .02
☐ 91 Jeff Reardon .15 .07 .02
☐ 92 Cory Snyder .05 .02 .01
☐ 93A Greg Walker ERR 3.00 1.35 .40
(93 of 66)
☐ 93B Greg Walker COR .05 .02 .01
(93 of 660)
☐ 94 Joe Magrane .10 .05 .01
☐ 95 Rob Deer .05 .02 .01
☐ 96 Ray Knight .10 .05 .01
☐ 97 Casey Candaele .05 .02 .01
☐ 98 John Cerutti .05 .02 .01
☐ 99 Buddy Bell .10 .05 .01
☐ 100 Jack Clark .10 .05 .01
☐ 101 Eric Bell .05 .02 .01
☐ 102 Willie Wilson .05 .02 .01
☐ 103 Dave Schmidt .05 .02 .01
☐ 104 Dennis Eckersley UER .15 .07 .02
(Complete games stats are wrong)
☐ 105 Don Sutton .15 .07 .02
☐ 106 Danny Tartabull .10 .05 .01
☐ 107 Fred McGriff .40 .18 .05
☐ 108 Les Straker .05 .02 .01
☐ 109 Lloyd Moseby .05 .02 .01
☐ 110 Roger Clemens .40 .18 .05
☐ 111 Glenn Hubbard .05 .02 .01
☐ 112 Ken Williams .05 .02 .01
☐ 113 Ruben Sierra .25 .11 .03
☐ 114 Stan Jefferson .05 .02 .01
☐ 115 Milt Thompson .05 .02 .01
☐ 116 Bobby Bonilla .20 .09 .03
☐ 117 Wayne Tolleson .05 .02 .01
☐ 118 Matt Williams 2.00 .90 .25
☐ 119 Chet Lemon .05 .02 .01
☐ 120 Dale Sveum .05 .02 .01
☐ 121 Dennis Boyd .05 .02 .01
☐ 122 Brett Butler .10 .05 .01
☐ 123 Terry Kennedy .05 .02 .01
☐ 124 Jack Howell .05 .02 .01
☐ 125 Curt Young .05 .02 .01
☐ 126A Dave Valle ERR .10 .05 .01
(Misspelled Dale on card front)
☐ 126B Dave Valle COR .05 .02 .01
☐ 127 Curt Wilkerson .05 .02 .01
☐ 128 Tim Teufel .05 .02 .01
☐ 129 Ozzie Virgil .05 .02 .01
☐ 130 Brian Fisher .05 .02 .01
☐ 131 Lance Parrish .10 .05 .01
☐ 132 Tom Browning .05 .02 .01
☐ 133A Larry Andersen ERR .10 .05 .01
(Misspelled Anderson on card front)
☐ 133B Larry Andersen COR .05 .02 .01
☐ 134A Bob Brenly ERR .10 .05 .01
(Misspelled Brenley on card front)
☐ 134B Bob Brenly COR .05 .02 .01
☐ 135 Mike Marshall .05 .02 .01
☐ 136 Gerald Perry .05 .02 .01
☐ 137 Bobby Meacham .05 .02 .01

☐ 138 Larry Herndon .05 .02 .01
☐ 139 Fred Manrique .05 .02 .01
☐ 140 Charlie Hough .10 .05 .01
☐ 141 Ron Darling .10 .05 .01
☐ 142 Herm Winningham .05 .02 .01
☐ 143 Mike Diaz .05 .02 .01
☐ 144 Mike Jackson .10 .05 .01
☐ 145 Denny Walling .05 .02 .01
☐ 146 Robby Thompson .10 .05 .01
☐ 147 Franklin Stubbs .05 .02 .01
☐ 148 Albert Hall .05 .02 .01
☐ 149 Bobby Witt .10 .05 .01
☐ 150 Lance McCullers .05 .02 .01
☐ 151 Scott Bradley .05 .02 .01
☐ 152 Mark McLemore .05 .02 .01
☐ 153 Tim Laudner .05 .02 .01
☐ 154 Greg Swindell .10 .05 .01
☐ 155 Marty Barrett .05 .02 .01
☐ 156 Mike Heath .05 .02 .01
☐ 157 Gary Ward .05 .02 .01
☐ 158A Lee Mazzilli ERR .10 .05 .01
(Misspelled Mazilli
on card front)
☐ 158B Lee Mazzilli COR .05 .02 .01
☐ 159 Tom Foley .05 .02 .01
☐ 160 Robin Yount .20 .09 .03
☐ 161 Steve Bedrosian .05 .02 .01
☐ 162 Bob Walk .05 .02 .01
☐ 163 Nick Esasky .05 .02 .01
☐ 164 Ken Caminiti .50 .23 .06
☐ 165 Jose Uribe .05 .02 .01
☐ 166 Dave Anderson .05 .02 .01
☐ 167 Ed Whitson .05 .02 .01
☐ 168 Ernie Whitt .05 .02 .01
☐ 169 Cecil Cooper .10 .05 .01
☐ 170 Mike Pagliarulo .05 .02 .01
☐ 171 Pat Sheridan .05 .02 .01
☐ 172 Chris Bando .05 .02 .01
☐ 173 Lee Lacy .05 .02 .01
☐ 174 Steve Lombardozzi .05 .02 .01
☐ 175 Mike Greenwell .15 .07 .02
☐ 176 Greg Minton .05 .02 .01
☐ 177 Moose Haas .05 .02 .01
☐ 178 Mike Kingery .05 .02 .01
☐ 179 Greg A. Harris .05 .02 .01
☐ 180 Bo Jackson .25 .11 .03
☐ 181 Carmelo Martinez .05 .02 .01
☐ 182 Alex Trevino .05 .02 .01
☐ 183 Ron Oester .05 .02 .01
☐ 184 Danny Darwin .05 .02 .01
☐ 185 Mike Krukow .05 .02 .01
☐ 186 Rafael Palmeiro .50 .23 .06
☐ 187 Tim Burke .05 .02 .01
☐ 188 Roger McDowell .05 .02 .01
☐ 189 Garry Templeton .05 .02 .01
☐ 190 Terry Pendleton .15 .07 .02
☐ 191 Larry Parrish .05 .02 .01
☐ 192 Rey Quinones .05 .02 .01
☐ 193 Joaquin Andujar .05 .02 .01
☐ 194 Tom Brunansky .05 .02 .01
☐ 195 Donnie Moore .05 .02 .01
☐ 196 Dan Pasqua .05 .02 .01
☐ 197 Jim Gantner .05 .02 .01
☐ 198 Mark Eichhorn .05 .02 .01
☐ 199 John Grubb .05 .02 .01
☐ 200 Bill Ripken .05 .02 .01
☐ 201 Sam Horn .05 .02 .01
☐ 202 Todd Worrell .05 .02 .01
☐ 203 Terry Leach .05 .02 .01
☐ 204 Garth Iorg .05 .02 .01
☐ 205 Brian Dayett .05 .02 .01
☐ 206 Bo Diaz .05 .02 .01
☐ 207 Craig Reynolds .05 .02 .01
☐ 208 Brian Holton .05 .02 .01
☐ 209 Marvell Wynne UER .05 .02 .01
(Misspelled Marvelle
on card front)
☐ 210 Dave Concepcion .10 .05 .01
☐ 211 Mike Davis .05 .02 .01
☐ 212 Devon White .15 .07 .02
☐ 213 Mickey Brantley .05 .02 .01
☐ 214 Greg Gagne .05 .02 .01
☐ 215 Oddibe McDowell .05 .02 .01
☐ 216 Jimmy Key .15 .07 .02
☐ 217 Dave Bergman .05 .02 .01
☐ 218 Calvin Schiraldi .05 .02 .01
☐ 219 Larry Sheets .05 .02 .01
☐ 220 Mike Easler .05 .02 .01
☐ 221 Kurt Stillwell .05 .02 .01
☐ 222 Chuck Jackson .05 .02 .01
☐ 223 Dave Martinez .05 .02 .01
☐ 224 Tim Leary .05 .02 .01
☐ 225 Steve Garvey .15 .07 .02
☐ 226 Greg Mathews .05 .02 .01
☐ 227 Doug Sisk .05 .02 .01
☐ 228 Dave Henderson .10 .05 .01
(Wearing Red Sox uniform;
Red Sox logo on back)
☐ 229 Jimmy Dwyer .05 .02 .01
☐ 230 Larry Owen .05 .02 .01
☐ 231 Andre Thornton .05 .02 .01
☐ 232 Mark Salas .05 .02 .01
☐ 233 Tom Brookens .05 .02 .01
☐ 234 Greg Brock .05 .02 .01
☐ 235 Rance Mulliniks .05 .02 .01
☐ 236 Bob Brower .05 .02 .01
☐ 237 Joe Niekro .10 .05 .01
☐ 238 Scott Bankhead .05 .02 .01
☐ 239 Doug DeCinces .05 .02 .01
☐ 240 Tommy John .15 .07 .02
☐ 241 Rich Gedman .05 .02 .01
☐ 242 Ted Power .05 .02 .01
☐ 243 Dave Meads .05 .02 .01
☐ 244 Jim Sundberg .05 .02 .01
☐ 245 Ken Oberkfell .05 .02 .01
☐ 246 Jimmy Jones .05 .02 .01
☐ 247 Ken Landreaux .05 .02 .01
☐ 248 Jose Oquendo .05 .02 .01
☐ 249 John Mitchell .05 .02 .01
☐ 250 Don Baylor .15 .07 .02
☐ 251 Scott Fletcher .05 .02 .01
☐ 252 Al Newman .05 .02 .01
☐ 253 Carney Lansford .10 .05 .01
☐ 254 Johnny Ray .05 .02 .01
☐ 255 Gary Pettis .05 .02 .01
☐ 256 Ken Phelps .05 .02 .01
☐ 257 Rick Leach .05 .02 .01
☐ 258 Tim Stoddard .05 .02 .01
☐ 259 Ed Romero .05 .02 .01
☐ 260 Sid Bream .05 .02 .01
☐ 261A Tom Niedenfuer ERR .10 .05 .01
(Misspelled Neidenfuer
on card front)
☐ 261B Tom Niedenfuer COR .05 .02 .01
☐ 262 Rick Dempsey .05 .02 .01
☐ 263 Lonnie Smith .05 .02 .01
☐ 264 Bob Forsch .05 .02 .01
☐ 265 Barry Bonds .75 .35 .09
☐ 266 Willie Randolph .10 .05 .01
☐ 267 Mike Ramsey .05 .02 .01
☐ 268 Don Slaught .05 .02 .01
☐ 269 Mickey Tettleton .10 .05 .01
☐ 270 Jerry Reuss .05 .02 .01
☐ 271 Marc Sullivan .05 .02 .01
☐ 272 Jim Morrison .05 .02 .01
☐ 273 Steve Balboni .05 .02 .01

No.	Player			
☐ 274	Dick Schofield	.05	.02	.01
☐ 275	John Tudor	.05	.02	.01
☐ 276	Gene Larkin	.05	.02	.01
☐ 277	Harold Reynolds	.05	.02	.01
☐ 278	Jerry Browne	.05	.02	.01
☐ 279	Willie Upshaw	.05	.02	.01
☐ 280	Ted Higuera	.05	.02	.01
☐ 281	Terry McGriff	.05	.02	.01
☐ 282	Terry Puhl	.05	.02	.01
☐ 283	Mark Wasinger	.05	.02	.01
☐ 284	Luis Salazar	.05	.02	.01
☐ 285	Ted Simmons	.10	.05	.01
☐ 286	John Shelby	.05	.02	.01
☐ 287	John Smiley	.25	.11	.03
☐ 288	Curt Ford	.05	.02	.01
☐ 289	Steve Crawford	.05	.02	.01
☐ 290	Dan Quisenberry	.10	.05	.01
☐ 291	Alan Wiggins	.05	.02	.01
☐ 292	Randy Bush	.05	.02	.01
☐ 293	John Candelaria	.05	.02	.01
☐ 294	Tony Phillips	.10	.05	.01
☐ 295	Mike Morgan	.05	.02	.01
☐ 296	Bill Wegman	.05	.02	.01
☐ 297A	Terry Francona ERR (Misspelled Franconia on card front)	.10	.05	.01
☐ 297B	Terry Francona COR	.05	.02	.01
☐ 298	Mickey Hatcher	.05	.02	.01
☐ 299	Andres Thomas	.05	.02	.01
☐ 300	Bob Stanley	.05	.02	.01
☐ 301	Al Pedrique	.05	.02	.01
☐ 302	Jim Lindeman	.05	.02	.01
☐ 303	Wally Backman	.05	.02	.01
☐ 304	Paul O'Neill	.25	.11	.03
☐ 305	Hubie Brooks	.05	.02	.01
☐ 306	Steve Buechele	.05	.02	.01
☐ 307	Bobby Thigpen	.05	.02	.01
☐ 308	George Hendrick	.05	.02	.01
☐ 309	John Moses	.05	.02	.01
☐ 310	Ron Guidry	.10	.05	.01
☐ 311	Bill Schroeder	.05	.02	.01
☐ 312	Jose Nunez	.05	.02	.01
☐ 313	Bud Black	.05	.02	.01
☐ 314	Joe Sambito	.05	.02	.01
☐ 315	Scott McGregor	.05	.02	.01
☐ 316	Rafael Santana	.05	.02	.01
☐ 317	Frank Williams	.05	.02	.01
☐ 318	Mike Fitzgerald	.05	.02	.01
☐ 319	Rick Mahler	.05	.02	.01
☐ 320	Jim Gott	.05	.02	.01
☐ 321	Mariano Duncan	.05	.02	.01
☐ 322	Jose Guzman	.10	.05	.01
☐ 323	Lee Guetterman	.05	.02	.01
☐ 324	Dan Gladden	.05	.02	.01
☐ 325	Gary Carter	.15	.07	.02
☐ 326	Tracy Jones	.05	.02	.01
☐ 327	Floyd Youmans	.05	.02	.01
☐ 328	Bill Dawley	.05	.02	.01
☐ 329	Paul Noce	.05	.02	.01
☐ 330	Angel Salazar	.05	.02	.01
☐ 331	Goose Gossage	.15	.07	.02
☐ 332	George Frazier	.05	.02	.01
☐ 333	Ruppert Jones	.05	.02	.01
☐ 334	Billy Joe Robidoux	.05	.02	.01
☐ 335	Mike Scott	.05	.02	.01
☐ 336	Randy Myers	.10	.05	.01
☐ 337	Bob Sebra	.05	.02	.01
☐ 338	Eric Show	.05	.02	.01
☐ 339	Mitch Williams	.10	.05	.01
☐ 340	Paul Molitor	.25	.11	.03
☐ 341	Gus Polidor	.05	.02	.01
☐ 342	Steve Trout	.05	.02	.01
☐ 343	Jerry Don Gleaton	.05	.02	.01
☐ 344	Bob Knepper	.05	.02	.01
☐ 345	Mitch Webster	.05	.02	.01
☐ 346	John Morris	.05	.02	.01
☐ 347	Andy Hawkins	.05	.02	.01
☐ 348	Dave Leiper	.05	.02	.01
☐ 349	Ernest Riles	.05	.02	.01
☐ 350	Dwight Gooden	.10	.05	.01
☐ 351	Dave Righetti	.05	.02	.01
☐ 352	Pat Dodson	.05	.02	.01
☐ 353	John Habyan	.05	.02	.01
☐ 354	Jim Deshaies	.05	.02	.01
☐ 355	Butch Wynegar	.05	.02	.01
☐ 356	Bryn Smith	.05	.02	.01
☐ 357	Matt Young	.05	.02	.01
☐ 358	Tom Pagnozzi	.20	.09	.03
☐ 359	Floyd Rayford	.05	.02	.01
☐ 360	Darryl Strawberry	.15	.07	.02
☐ 361	Sal Butera	.05	.02	.01
☐ 362	Domingo Ramos	.05	.02	.01
☐ 363	Chris Brown	.05	.02	.01
☐ 364	Jose Gonzalez	.05	.02	.01
☐ 365	Dave Smith	.05	.02	.01
☐ 366	Andy McGaffigan	.05	.02	.01
☐ 367	Stan Javier	.05	.02	.01
☐ 368	Henry Cotto	.05	.02	.01
☐ 369	Mike Birkbeck	.05	.02	.01
☐ 370	Len Dykstra	.25	.11	.03
☐ 371	Dave Collins	.05	.02	.01
☐ 372	Spike Owen	.05	.02	.01
☐ 373	Geno Petralli	.05	.02	.01
☐ 374	Ron Karkovice	.05	.02	.01
☐ 375	Shane Rawley	.05	.02	.01
☐ 376	DeWayne Buice	.05	.02	.01
☐ 377	Bill Pecota	.05	.02	.01
☐ 378	Leon Durham	.05	.02	.01
☐ 379	Ed Olwine	.05	.02	.01
☐ 380	Bruce Hurst	.05	.02	.01
☐ 381	Bob McClure	.05	.02	.01
☐ 382	Mark Thurmond	.05	.02	.01
☐ 383	Buddy Biancalana	.05	.02	.01
☐ 384	Tim Conroy	.05	.02	.01
☐ 385	Tony Gwynn	.35	.16	.04
☐ 386	Greg Gross	.05	.02	.01
☐ 387	Barry Lyons	.05	.02	.01
☐ 388	Mike Felder	.05	.02	.01
☐ 389	Pat Clements	.05	.02	.01
☐ 390	Ken Griffey	.10	.05	.01
☐ 391	Mark Davis	.05	.02	.01
☐ 392	Jose Rijo	.15	.07	.02
☐ 393	Mike Young	.05	.02	.01
☐ 394	Willie Fraser	.05	.02	.01
☐ 395	Dion James	.05	.02	.01
☐ 396	Steve Shields	.05	.02	.01
☐ 397	Randy St.Claire	.05	.02	.01
☐ 398	Danny Jackson	.05	.02	.01
☐ 399	Cecil Fielder	.30	.14	.04
☐ 400	Keith Hernandez	.10	.05	.01
☐ 401	Don Carman	.05	.02	.01
☐ 402	Chuck Crim	.05	.02	.01
☐ 403	Rob Woodward	.05	.02	.01
☐ 404	Junior Ortiz	.05	.02	.01
☐ 405	Glenn Wilson	.05	.02	.01
☐ 406	Ken Howell	.05	.02	.01
☐ 407	Jeff Kunkel	.05	.02	.01
☐ 408	Jeff Reed	.05	.02	.01
☐ 409	Chris James	.05	.02	.01
☐ 410	Zane Smith	.05	.02	.01
☐ 411	Ken Dixon	.05	.02	.01
☐ 412	Ricky Horton	.05	.02	.01
☐ 413	Frank DiPino	.05	.02	.01
☐ 414	Shane Mack	.10	.05	.01
☐ 415	Danny Cox	.05	.02	.01
☐ 416	Andy Van Slyke	.15	.07	.02

	Card			
☐	417 Danny Heep	.05	.02	.01
☐	418 John Cangelosi	.05	.02	.01
☐	419A John Christensen ERR (Christiansen on card front)	.10	.05	.01
☐	419B John Christensen COR	.05	.02	.01
☐	420 Joey Cora	.15	.07	.02
☐	421 Mike LaValliere	.05	.02	.01
☐	422 Kelly Gruber	.05	.02	.01
☐	423 Bruce Benedict	.05	.02	.01
☐	424 Len Matuszek	.05	.02	.01
☐	425 Kent Tekulve	.05	.02	.01
☐	426 Rafael Ramirez	.05	.02	.01
☐	427 Mike Flanagan	.05	.02	.01
☐	428 Mike Gallego	.05	.02	.01
☐	429 Juan Castillo	.05	.02	.01
☐	430 Neal Heaton	.05	.02	.01
☐	431 Phil Garner	.10	.05	.01
☐	432 Mike Dunne	.05	.02	.01
☐	433 Wallace Johnson	.05	.02	.01
☐	434 Jack O'Connor	.05	.02	.01
☐	435 Steve Jeltz	.05	.02	.01
☐	436 Donell Nixon	.05	.02	.01
☐	437 Jack Lazorko	.05	.02	.01
☐	438 Keith Comstock	.05	.02	.01
☐	439 Jeff D. Robinson	.05	.02	.01
☐	440 Graig Nettles	.10	.05	.01
☐	441 Mel Hall	.05	.02	.01
☐	442 Gerald Young	.05	.02	.01
☐	443 Gary Redus	.05	.02	.01
☐	444 Charlie Moore	.05	.02	.01
☐	445 Bill Madlock	.10	.05	.01
☐	446 Mark Clear	.05	.02	.01
☐	447 Greg Booker	.05	.02	.01
☐	448 Rick Schu	.05	.02	.01
☐	449 Ron Kittle	.05	.02	.01
☐	450 Dale Murphy	.15	.07	.02
☐	451 Bob Dernier	.05	.02	.01
☐	452 Dale Mohorcic	.05	.02	.01
☐	453 Rafael Belliard	.05	.02	.01
☐	454 Charlie Puleo	.05	.02	.01
☐	455 Dwayne Murphy	.05	.02	.01
☐	456 Jim Eisenreich	.10	.05	.01
☐	457 David Palmer	.05	.02	.01
☐	458 Dave Stewart	.10	.05	.01
☐	459 Pascual Perez	.05	.02	.01
☐	460 Glenn Davis	.05	.02	.01
☐	461 Dan Petry	.05	.02	.01
☐	462 Jim Winn	.05	.02	.01
☐	463 Darrell Miller	.05	.02	.01
☐	464 Mike Moore	.05	.02	.01
☐	465 Mike LaCoss	.05	.02	.01
☐	466 Steve Farr	.05	.02	.01
☐	467 Jerry Mumphrey	.05	.02	.01
☐	468 Kevin Gross	.05	.02	.01
☐	469 Bruce Bochy	.05	.02	.01
☐	470 Orel Hershiser	.10	.05	.01
☐	471 Eric King	.05	.02	.01
☐	472 Ellis Burks	.40	.18	.05
☐	473 Darren Daulton	.15	.07	.02
☐	474 Mookie Wilson	.10	.05	.01
☐	475 Frank Viola	.10	.05	.01
☐	476 Ron Robinson	.05	.02	.01
☐	477 Bob Melvin	.05	.02	.01
☐	478 Jeff Musselman	.05	.02	.01
☐	479 Charlie Kerfeld	.05	.02	.01
☐	480 Richard Dotson	.05	.02	.01
☐	481 Kevin Mitchell	.15	.07	.02
☐	482 Gary Roenicke	.05	.02	.01
☐	483 Tim Flannery	.05	.02	.01
☐	484 Rich Yett	.05	.02	.01
☐	485 Pete Incaviglia	.10	.05	.01
☐	486 Rick Cerone	.05	.02	.01
☐	487 Tony Armas	.05	.02	.01
☐	488 Jerry Reed	.05	.02	.01
☐	489 Dave Lopes	.10	.05	.01
☐	490 Frank Tanana	.05	.02	.01
☐	491 Mike Loynd	.05	.02	.01
☐	492 Bruce Ruffin	.05	.02	.01
☐	493 Chris Speier	.05	.02	.01
☐	494 Tom Hume	.05	.02	.01
☐	495 Jesse Orosco	.05	.02	.01
☐	496 Robbie Wine UER (Misspelled Robby on card front)	.05	.02	.01
☐	497 Jeff Montgomery	.50	.23	.06
☐	498 Jeff Dedmon	.05	.02	.01
☐	499 Luis Aguayo	.05	.02	.01
☐	500 Reggie Jackson (Oakland A's)	.30	.14	.04
☐	501 Reggie Jackson (Baltimore Orioles)	.30	.14	.04
☐	502 Reggie Jackson (New York Yankees)	.30	.14	.04
☐	503 Reggie Jackson (California Angels)	.30	.14	.04
☐	504 Reggie Jackson (Oakland A's)	.30	.14	.04
☐	505 Billy Hatcher	.05	.02	.01
☐	506 Ed Lynch	.05	.02	.01
☐	507 Willie Hernandez	.05	.02	.01
☐	508 Jose DeLeon	.05	.02	.01
☐	509 Joel Youngblood	.05	.02	.01
☐	510 Bob Welch	.10	.05	.01
☐	511 Steve Ontiveros	.05	.02	.01
☐	512 Randy Ready	.05	.02	.01
☐	513 Juan Nieves	.05	.02	.01
☐	514 Jeff Russell	.05	.02	.01
☐	515 Von Hayes	.05	.02	.01
☐	516 Mark Gubicza	.05	.02	.01
☐	517 Ken Dayley	.05	.02	.01
☐	518 Don Aase	.05	.02	.01
☐	519 Rick Reuschel	.05	.02	.01
☐	520 Mike Henneman	.20	.09	.03
☐	521 Rick Aguilera	.10	.05	.01
☐	522 Jay Howell	.05	.02	.01
☐	523 Ed Correa	.05	.02	.01
☐	524 Manny Trillo	.05	.02	.01
☐	525 Kirk Gibson	.10	.05	.01
☐	526 Wally Ritchie	.05	.02	.01
☐	527 Al Nipper	.05	.02	.01
☐	528 Atlee Hammaker	.05	.02	.01
☐	529 Shawon Dunston	.10	.05	.01
☐	530 Jim Clancy	.05	.02	.01
☐	531 Tom Paciorek	.10	.05	.01
☐	532 Joel Skinner	.05	.02	.01
☐	533 Scott Garrelts	.05	.02	.01
☐	534 Tom O'Malley	.05	.02	.01
☐	535 John Franco	.10	.05	.01
☐	536 Paul Kilgus	.05	.02	.01
☐	537 Darrell Porter	.05	.02	.01
☐	538 Walt Terrell	.05	.02	.01
☐	539 Bill Long	.05	.02	.01
☐	540 George Bell	.10	.05	.01
☐	541 Jeff Sellers	.05	.02	.01
☐	542 Joe Boever	.05	.02	.01
☐	543 Steve Howe	.05	.02	.01
☐	544 Scott Sanderson	.05	.02	.01
☐	545 Jack Morris	.15	.07	.02
☐	546 Todd Benzinger	.10	.05	.01
☐	547 Steve Henderson	.05	.02	.01
☐	548 Eddie Milner	.05	.02	.01
☐	549 Jeff M. Robinson	.05	.02	.01
☐	550 Cal Ripken	.60	.25	.08
☐	551 Jody Davis	.05	.02	.01
☐	552 Kirk McCaskill	.05	.02	.01

☐ 553	Craig Lefferts	.05	.02	.01
☐ 554	Darnell Coles	.05	.02	.01
☐ 555	Phil Niekro	.15	.07	.02
☐ 556	Mike Aldrete	.05	.02	.01
☐ 557	Pat Perry	.05	.02	.01
☐ 558	Juan Agosto	.05	.02	.01
☐ 559	Rob Murphy	.05	.02	.01
☐ 560	Dennis Rasmussen	.05	.02	.01
☐ 561	Manny Lee	.05	.02	.01
☐ 562	Jeff Blauser	.50	.23	.06
☐ 563	Bob Ojeda	.05	.02	.01
☐ 564	Dave Dravecky	.10	.05	.01
☐ 565	Gene Garber	.05	.02	.01
☐ 566	Ron Roenicke	.05	.02	.01
☐ 567	Tommy Hinzo	.05	.02	.01
☐ 568	Eric Nolte	.05	.02	.01
☐ 569	Ed Hearn	.05	.02	.01
☐ 570	Mark Davidson	.05	.02	.01
☐ 571	Jim Walewander	.05	.02	.01
☐ 572	Donnie Hill UER (84 Stolen Base total listed as 7)	.05	.02	.01
☐ 573	Jamie Moyer	.05	.02	.01
☐ 574	Ken Schrom	.05	.02	.01
☐ 575	Nolan Ryan	.75	.35	.09
☐ 576	Jim Acker	.05	.02	.01
☐ 577	Jamie Quirk	.05	.02	.01
☐ 578	Jay Aldrich	.05	.02	.01
☐ 579	Claudell Washington	.05	.02	.01
☐ 580	Jeff Leonard	.05	.02	.01
☐ 581	Carmen Castillo	.05	.02	.01
☐ 582	Daryl Boston	.05	.02	.01
☐ 583	Jeff DeWillis	.05	.02	.01
☐ 584	John Marzano	.05	.02	.01
☐ 585	Bill Gullickson	.05	.02	.01
☐ 586	Andy Allanson	.05	.02	.01
☐ 587	Lee Tunnell UER (1987 stat line reads .4.84 ERA)	.05	.02	.01
☐ 588	Gene Nelson	.05	.02	.01
☐ 589	Dave LaPoint	.05	.02	.01
☐ 590	Harold Baines	.10	.05	.01
☐ 591	Bill Buckner	.10	.05	.01
☐ 592	Carlton Fisk	.15	.07	.02
☐ 593	Rick Manning	.05	.02	.01
☐ 594	Doug Jones	.30	.14	.04
☐ 595	Tom Candiotti	.05	.02	.01
☐ 596	Steve Lake	.05	.02	.01
☐ 597	Jose Lind	.15	.07	.02
☐ 598	Ross Jones	.05	.02	.01
☐ 599	Gary Matthews	.05	.02	.01
☐ 600	Fernando Valenzuela	.05	.02	.01
☐ 601	Dennis Martinez	.10	.05	.01
☐ 602	Les Lancaster	.05	.02	.01
☐ 603	Ozzie Guillen	.10	.05	.01
☐ 604	Tony Bernazard	.05	.02	.01
☐ 605	Chili Davis	.10	.05	.01
☐ 606	Roy Smalley	.05	.02	.01
☐ 607	Ivan Calderon	.10	.05	.01
☐ 608	Jay Tibbs	.05	.02	.01
☐ 609	Guy Hoffman	.05	.02	.01
☐ 610	Doyle Alexander	.05	.02	.01
☐ 611	Mike Bielecki	.05	.02	.01
☐ 612	Shawn Hillegas	.05	.02	.01
☐ 613	Keith Atherton	.05	.02	.01
☐ 614	Eric Plunk	.05	.02	.01
☐ 615	Sid Fernandez	.10	.05	.01
☐ 616	Dennis Lamp	.05	.02	.01
☐ 617	Dave Engle	.05	.02	.01
☐ 618	Harry Spilman	.05	.02	.01
☐ 619	Don Robinson	.05	.02	.01
☐ 620	John Farrell	.05	.02	.01
☐ 621	Nelson Liriano	.05	.02	.01
☐ 622	Floyd Bannister	.05	.02	.01
☐ 623	Randy Milligan	.25	.11	.03
☐ 624	Kevin Elster	.05	.02	.01
☐ 625	Jody Reed	.20	.09	.03
☐ 626	Shawn Abner	.05	.02	.01
☐ 627	Kirt Manwaring	.05	.02	.01
☐ 628	Pete Stanicek	.05	.02	.01
☐ 629	Rob Ducey	.05	.02	.01
☐ 630	Steve Kiefer	.05	.02	.01
☐ 631	Gary Thurman	.05	.02	.01
☐ 632	Darrel Akerfelds	.05	.02	.01
☐ 633	Dave Clark	.05	.02	.01
☐ 634	Roberto Kelly	.50	.23	.06
☐ 635	Keith Hughes	.05	.02	.01
☐ 636	John Davis	.05	.02	.01
☐ 637	Mike Devereaux	.40	.18	.05
☐ 638	Tom Glavine	1.50	.65	.19
☐ 639	Keith A. Miller	.05	.02	.01
☐ 640	Chris Gwynn UER (Wrong batting and throwing on back)	.15	.07	.02
☐ 641	Tim Crews	.10	.05	.01
☐ 642	Mackey Sasser	.05	.02	.01
☐ 643	Vicente Palacios	.05	.02	.01
☐ 644	Kevin Romine	.05	.02	.01
☐ 645	Gregg Jefferies	1.50	.65	.19
☐ 646	Jeff Treadway	.05	.02	.01
☐ 647	Ron Gant	1.00	.45	.13
☐ 648	Mark McGwire and Matt Nokes (Rookie Sluggers)	.20	.09	.03
☐ 649	Eric Davis and Tim Raines (Speed and Power)	.10	.05	.01
☐ 650	Don Mattingly and Jack Clark	.20	.09	.03
☐ 651	Tony Fernandez, Alan Trammell, and Cal Ripken	.25	.11	.03
☐ 652	Vince Coleman HL 100 Stolen Bases	.05	.02	.01
☐ 653	Kirby Puckett HL 10 Hits in a Row	.25	.11	.03
☐ 654	Benito Santiago HL Hitting Streak	.05	.02	.01
☐ 655	Juan Nieves HL No Hitter	.05	.02	.01
☐ 656	Steve Bedrosian HL Saves Record	.05	.02	.01
☐ 657	Mike Schmidt HL 500 Homers	.15	.07	.02
☐ 658	Don Mattingly HL Home Run Streak	.25	.11	.03
☐ 659	Mark McGwire HL Rookie HR Record	.15	.07	.02
☐ 660	Paul Molitor HL Hitting Streak	.15	.07	.02

1988 Score Rookie/Traded

This 110-card set featured traded players (1-65) and rookies (66-110) for the 1988 season. The cards are distinguishable from the regular Score set by the orange borders and by the fact that the numbering on the back has a T suffix. The cards are standard size, 2 1/2" by 3 1/2", and were distributed

by Score as a collated set in a special collector box along with some trivia cards. Score also produced a limited "glossy" Rookie and Traded set, that is valued at three times the value of the regular (non-glossy) set. It should be noted that the set itself (non-glossy) is now considered somewhat scarce. Apparently Score's first attempt at a Rookie/Traded set was produced very conservatively, resulting in a set which is now recognized as being much tougher to find than the other Rookie/Traded sets from the other major companies of that year. The key (extended) Rookie Cards in this set are Roberto Alomar, Brady Anderson, Craig Biggio, Pat Borders, Jay Buhner, Orestes Destrade, Rob Dibble, Mark Grace, Darryl Hamilton, Bryan Harvey, Mike Macfarlane, Jack McDowell, Melido Perez, Chris Sabo, Todd Stottlemyre, and Walt Weiss.

	MINT	EXC	G-VG
COMPLETE FACT.SET (110)	60.00	27.00	7.50
COMMON CARD (1T-110T)	.20	.09	.03
☐ 1T Jack Clark	.25	.11	.03
☐ 2T Danny Jackson	.20	.09	.03
☐ 3T Brett Butler	.25	.11	.03
☐ 4T Kurt Stillwell	.20	.09	.03
☐ 5T Tom Brunansky	.20	.09	.03
☐ 6T Dennis Lamp	.20	.09	.03
☐ 7T Jose DeLeon	.20	.09	.03
☐ 8T Tom Herr	.20	.09	.03
☐ 9T Keith Moreland	.20	.09	.03
☐ 10T Kirk Gibson	.25	.11	.03
☐ 11T Bud Black	.20	.09	.03
☐ 12T Rafael Ramirez	.20	.09	.03
☐ 13T Luis Salazar	.20	.09	.03
☐ 14T Goose Gossage	.35	.16	.04
☐ 15T Bob Welch	.25	.11	.03
☐ 16T Vance Law	.20	.09	.03
☐ 17T Ray Knight	.25	.11	.03
☐ 18T Dan Quisenberry	.25	.11	.03
☐ 19T Don Slaught	.20	.09	.03
☐ 20T Lee Smith	.35	.16	.04
☐ 21T Rick Cerone	.20	.09	.03
☐ 22T Pat Tabler	.20	.09	.03
☐ 23T Larry McWilliams	.20	.09	.03
☐ 24T Ricky Horton	.20	.09	.03
☐ 25T Graig Nettles	.25	.11	.03
☐ 26T Dan Petry	.20	.09	.03
☐ 27T Jose Rijo	.75	.35	.09
☐ 28T Chili Davis	.25	.11	.03
☐ 29T Dickie Thon	.20	.09	.03
☐ 30T Mackey Sasser	.20	.09	.03
☐ 31T Mickey Tettleton	.40	.18	.05
☐ 32T Rick Dempsey	.20	.09	.03
☐ 33T Ron Hassey	.20	.09	.03
☐ 34T Phil Bradley	.20	.09	.03
☐ 35T Jay Howell	.20	.09	.03
☐ 36T Bill Buckner	.25	.11	.03
☐ 37T Alfredo Griffin	.20	.09	.03
☐ 38T Gary Pettis	.20	.09	.03
☐ 39T Calvin Schiraldi	.20	.09	.03
☐ 40T John Candelaria	.20	.09	.03
☐ 41T Joe Orsulak	.20	.09	.03
☐ 42T Willie Upshaw	.20	.09	.03
☐ 43T Herm Winningham	.20	.09	.03
☐ 44T Ron Kittle	.20	.09	.03
☐ 45T Bob Dernier	.20	.09	.03
☐ 46T Steve Balboni	.20	.09	.03
☐ 47T Steve Shields	.20	.09	.03
☐ 48T Henry Cotto	.20	.09	.03
☐ 49T Dave Henderson	.25	.11	.03
☐ 50T Dave Parker	.35	.16	.04
☐ 51T Mike Young	.20	.09	.03
☐ 52T Mark Salas	.20	.09	.03
☐ 53T Mike Davis	.20	.09	.03
☐ 54T Rafael Santana	.20	.09	.03
☐ 55T Don Baylor	.35	.16	.04
☐ 56T Dan Pasqua	.20	.09	.03
☐ 57T Ernest Riles	.20	.09	.03
☐ 58T Glenn Hubbard	.20	.09	.03
☐ 59T Mike Smithson	.20	.09	.03
☐ 60T Richard Dotson	.20	.09	.03
☐ 61T Jerry Reuss	.20	.09	.03
☐ 62T Mike Jackson	.20	.09	.03
☐ 63T Floyd Bannister	.20	.09	.03
☐ 64T Jesse Orosco	.20	.09	.03
☐ 65T Larry Parrish	.20	.09	.03
☐ 66T Jeff Bittiger	.20	.09	.03
☐ 67T Ray Hayward	.20	.09	.03
☐ 68T Ricky Jordan	.50	.23	.06
☐ 69T Tommy Gregg	.20	.09	.03
☐ 70T Brady Anderson	2.00	.90	.25
☐ 71T Jeff Montgomery	2.00	.90	.25
☐ 72T Darryl Hamilton	1.50	.65	.19
☐ 73T Cecil Espy	.20	.09	.03
☐ 74T Greg Briley	.20	.09	.03
☐ 75T Joey Meyer	.20	.09	.03
☐ 76T Mike Macfarlane	1.50	.65	.19
☐ 77T Oswald Peraza	.20	.09	.03
☐ 78T Jack Armstrong	.20	.09	.03
☐ 79T Don Heinkel	.20	.09	.03
☐ 80T Mark Grace	10.00	4.50	1.25
☐ 81T Steve Curry	.20	.09	.03
☐ 82T Damon Berryhill	.40	.18	.05
☐ 83T Steve Ellsworth	.20	.09	.03
☐ 84T Pete Smith	.40	.18	.05
☐ 85T Jack McDowell	10.00	4.50	1.25
☐ 86T Rob Dibble	.75	.35	.09
☐ 87T Bryan Harvey UER (Games Pitched 47, Innings 5)	2.00	.90	.25
☐ 88T John Dopson	.20	.09	.03
☐ 89T Dave Gallagher	.20	.09	.03
☐ 90T Todd Stottlemyre	1.00	.45	.13
☐ 91T Mike Schooler	.20	.09	.03
☐ 92T Don Gordon	.20	.09	.03
☐ 93T Sil Campusano	.20	.09	.03
☐ 94T Jeff Pico	.20	.09	.03
☐ 95T Jay Buhner	6.00	2.70	.75
☐ 96T Nelson Santovenia	.20	.09	.03
☐ 97T Al Leiter	.30	.14	.04
☐ 98T Luis Alicea	.20	.09	.03
☐ 99T Pat Borders	1.50	.65	.19
☐ 100T Chris Sabo	2.00	.90	.25
☐ 101T Tim Belcher	.20	.09	.03
☐ 102T Walt Weiss	.75	.35	.09
☐ 103T Craig Biggio	7.00	3.10	.85

☐ 104T	Don August	.20	.09	.03
☐ 105T	Roberto Alomar	35.00	16.00	4.40
☐ 106T	Todd Burns	.20	.09	.03
☐ 107T	John Costello	.20	.09	.03
☐ 108T	Melido Perez	.75	.35	.09
☐ 109T	Darrin Jackson	1.00	.45	.13
☐ 110T	Orestes Destrade	.20	.09	.03

1989 Score

This 660-card set was distributed by Major League Marketing. Cards measure 2 1/2" by 3 1/2" and feature six distinctive inner border (inside a white outer border) colors on the front. Highlights (652-660) and Rookie Prospects (621-651) are included in the set. The set is distinguished by the fact that each card back shows a full-color picture (portrait) of the player. Score "missed" many of the mid-season and later trades; there are numerous examples of inconsistency with regard to the treatment of these players. Study as examples of this inconsistency of handling of late trades, cards numbered 49, 71, 77, 83, 106, 126, 139, 145, 173, 177, 242, 348, 384, 420, 439, 488, 494, and 525. Rookie Cards in this set include Sandy Alomar Jr., Brady Anderson, Craig Biggio, Charlie Hayes, Randy Johnson, Felix Jose, Ramon Martinez, Gary Sheffield, and John Smoltz.

	MINT	EXC	G-VG
COMPLETE SET (660)	15.00	6.75	1.90
COMPLETE FACT.SET (660)	15.00	6.75	1.90
COMMON CARD (1-660)	.05	.02	.01

☐ 1	Jose Canseco	.30	.14	.04
☐ 2	Andre Dawson	.15	.07	.02
☐ 3	Mark McGwire	.15	.07	.02
☐ 4	Benito Santiago	.10	.05	.01
☐ 5	Rick Reuschel	.05	.02	.01
☐ 6	Fred McGriff	.25	.11	.03
☐ 7	Kal Daniels	.05	.02	.01
☐ 8	Gary Gaetti	.05	.02	.01
☐ 9	Ellis Burks	.10	.05	.01
☐ 10	Darryl Strawberry	.15	.07	.02
☐ 11	Julio Franco	.10	.05	.01
☐ 12	Lloyd Moseby	.05	.02	.01
☐ 13	Jeff Pico	.05	.02	.01
☐ 14	Johnny Ray	.05	.02	.01
☐ 15	Cal Ripken	.50	.23	.06
☐ 16	Dick Schofield	.05	.02	.01
☐ 17	Mel Hall	.05	.02	.01
☐ 18	Bill Ripken	.05	.02	.01
☐ 19	Brook Jacoby	.05	.02	.01
☐ 20	Kirby Puckett	.50	.23	.06
☐ 21	Bill Doran	.05	.02	.01
☐ 22	Pete O'Brien	.05	.02	.01
☐ 23	Matt Nokes	.05	.02	.01
☐ 24	Brian Fisher	.05	.02	.01
☐ 25	Jack Clark	.10	.05	.01
☐ 26	Gary Pettis	.05	.02	.01
☐ 27	Dave Valle	.05	.02	.01
☐ 28	Willie Wilson	.05	.02	.01
☐ 29	Curt Young	.05	.02	.01
☐ 30	Dale Murphy	.15	.07	.02
☐ 31	Barry Larkin	.15	.07	.02
☐ 32	Dave Stewart	.10	.05	.01
☐ 33	Mike LaValliere	.05	.02	.01
☐ 34	Glenn Hubbard	.05	.02	.01
☐ 35	Ryne Sandberg	.40	.18	.05
☐ 36	Tony Pena	.05	.02	.01
☐ 37	Greg Walker	.05	.02	.01
☐ 38	Von Hayes	.05	.02	.01
☐ 39	Kevin Mitchell	.15	.07	.02
☐ 40	Tim Raines	.15	.07	.02
☐ 41	Keith Hernandez	.10	.05	.01
☐ 42	Keith Moreland	.05	.02	.01
☐ 43	Ruben Sierra	.25	.11	.03
☐ 44	Chet Lemon	.05	.02	.01
☐ 45	Willie Randolph	.10	.05	.01
☐ 46	Andy Allanson	.05	.02	.01
☐ 47	Candy Maldonado	.05	.02	.01
☐ 48	Sid Bream	.05	.02	.01
☐ 49	Denny Walling	.05	.02	.01
☐ 50	Dave Winfield	.20	.09	.03
☐ 51	Alvin Davis	.05	.02	.01
☐ 52	Cory Snyder	.05	.02	.01
☐ 53	Hubie Brooks	.05	.02	.01
☐ 54	Chili Davis	.10	.05	.01
☐ 55	Kevin Seitzer	.05	.02	.01
☐ 56	Jose Uribe	.05	.02	.01
☐ 57	Tony Fernandez	.10	.05	.01
☐ 58	Tim Teufel	.05	.02	.01
☐ 59	Oddibe McDowell	.05	.02	.01
☐ 60	Les Lancaster	.05	.02	.01
☐ 61	Billy Hatcher	.05	.02	.01
☐ 62	Dan Gladden	.05	.02	.01
☐ 63	Marty Barrett	.05	.02	.01
☐ 64	Nick Esasky	.05	.02	.01
☐ 65	Wally Joyner	.10	.05	.01
☐ 66	Mike Greenwell	.10	.05	.01
☐ 67	Ken Williams	.05	.02	.01
☐ 68	Bob Horner	.05	.02	.01
☐ 69	Steve Sax	.05	.02	.01
☐ 70	Rickey Henderson	.15	.07	.02
☐ 71	Mitch Webster	.05	.02	.01
☐ 72	Rob Deer	.05	.02	.01
☐ 73	Jim Presley	.05	.02	.01
☐ 74	Albert Hall	.05	.02	.01
☐ 75A	George Brett ERR (At age 33)	.75	.35	.09
☐ 75B	George Brett COR (At age 35)	.35	.16	.04
☐ 76	Brian Downing	.05	.02	.01
☐ 77	Dave Martinez	.05	.02	.01
☐ 78	Scott Fletcher	.05	.02	.01
☐ 79	Phil Bradley	.05	.02	.01
☐ 80	Ozzie Smith	.30	.14	.04
☐ 81	Larry Sheets	.05	.02	.01
☐ 82	Mike Aldrete	.05	.02	.01
☐ 83	Darnell Coles	.05	.02	.01
☐ 84	Len Dykstra	.15	.07	.02
☐ 85	Jim Rice	.15	.07	.02
☐ 86	Jeff Treadway	.05	.02	.01
☐ 87	Jose Lind	.05	.02	.01

☐ 88 Willie McGee .10 .05 .01
☐ 89 Mickey Brantley .05 .02 .01
☐ 90 Tony Gwynn .30 .14 .04
☐ 91 R.J. Reynolds .05 .02 .01
☐ 92 Milt Thompson .05 .02 .01
☐ 93 Kevin McReynolds .10 .05 .01
☐ 94 Eddie Murray UER .20 .09 .03
('86 batting .205, should be .305)
☐ 95 Lance Parrish .10 .05 .01
☐ 96 Ron Kittle .05 .02 .01
☐ 97 Gerald Young .05 .02 .01
☐ 98 Ernie Whitt .05 .02 .01
☐ 99 Jeff Reed .05 .02 .01
☐ 100 Don Mattingly .40 .18 .05
☐ 101 Gerald Perry .05 .02 .01
☐ 102 Vance Law .05 .02 .01
☐ 103 John Shelby .05 .02 .01
☐ 104 Chris Sabo .25 .11 .03
☐ 105 Danny Tartabull .10 .05 .01
☐ 106 Glenn Wilson .05 .02 .01
☐ 107 Mark Davidson .05 .02 .01
☐ 108 Dave Parker .15 .07 .02
☐ 109 Eric Davis .10 .05 .01
☐ 110 Alan Trammell .15 .07 .02
☐ 111 Ozzie Virgil .05 .02 .01
☐ 112 Frank Tanana .05 .02 .01
☐ 113 Rafael Ramirez .05 .02 .01
☐ 114 Dennis Martinez .10 .05 .01
☐ 115 Jose DeLeon .05 .02 .01
☐ 116 Bob Ojeda .05 .02 .01
☐ 117 Doug Drabek .15 .07 .02
☐ 118 Andy Hawkins .05 .02 .01
☐ 119 Greg Maddux .35 .16 .04
☐ 120 Cecil Fielder UER .25 .11 .03
(Photo on back reversed)
☐ 121 Mike Scioscia .05 .02 .01
☐ 122 Dan Petry .05 .02 .01
☐ 123 Terry Kennedy .05 .02 .01
☐ 124 Kelly Downs .05 .02 .01
☐ 125 Greg Gross UER .05 .02 .01
(Gregg on back)
☐ 126 Fred Lynn .10 .05 .01
☐ 127 Barry Bonds .60 .25 .08
☐ 128 Harold Baines .10 .05 .01
☐ 129 Doyle Alexander .05 .02 .01
☐ 130 Kevin Elster .05 .02 .01
☐ 131 Mike Heath .05 .02 .01
☐ 132 Teddy Higuera .05 .02 .01
☐ 133 Charlie Leibrandt .05 .02 .01
☐ 134 Tim Laudner .05 .02 .01
☐ 135A Ray Knight ERR .50 .23 .06
(Reverse negative)
☐ 135B Ray Knight COR .15 .07 .02
☐ 136 Howard Johnson .10 .05 .01
☐ 137 Terry Pendleton .15 .07 .02
☐ 138 Andy McGaffigan .05 .02 .01
☐ 139 Ken Oberkfell .05 .02 .01
☐ 140 Butch Wynegar .05 .02 .01
☐ 141 Rob Murphy .05 .02 .01
☐ 142 Rich Renteria .05 .02 .01
☐ 143 Jose Guzman .10 .05 .01
☐ 144 Andres Galarraga .15 .07 .02
☐ 145 Ricky Horton .05 .02 .01
☐ 146 Frank DiPino .05 .02 .01
☐ 147 Glenn Braggs .05 .02 .01
☐ 148 John Kruk .15 .07 .02
☐ 149 Mike Schmidt .25 .11 .03
☐ 150 Lee Smith .15 .07 .02
☐ 151 Robin Yount .20 .09 .03
☐ 152 Mark Eichhorn .05 .02 .01
☐ 153 DeWayne Buice .05 .02 .01
☐ 154 B.J. Surhoff .05 .02 .01
☐ 155 Vince Coleman .10 .05 .01
☐ 156 Tony Phillips .10 .05 .01
☐ 157 Willie Fraser .05 .02 .01
☐ 158 Lance McCullers .05 .02 .01
☐ 159 Greg Gagne .05 .02 .01
☐ 160 Jesse Barfield .05 .02 .01
☐ 161 Mark Langston .15 .07 .02
☐ 162 Kurt Stillwell .05 .02 .01
☐ 163 Dion James .05 .02 .01
☐ 164 Glenn Davis .05 .02 .01
☐ 165 Walt Weiss .05 .02 .01
☐ 166 Dave Concepcion .10 .05 .01
☐ 167 Alfredo Griffin .05 .02 .01
☐ 168 Don Heinkel .05 .02 .01
☐ 169 Luis Rivera .05 .02 .01
☐ 170 Shane Rawley .05 .02 .01
☐ 171 Darrell Evans .10 .05 .01
☐ 172 Robby Thompson .10 .05 .01
☐ 173 Jody Davis .05 .02 .01
☐ 174 Andy Van Slyke .15 .07 .02
☐ 175 Wade Boggs UER .20 .09 .03
(Bio says .364, should be .356)
☐ 176 Garry Templeton .05 .02 .01
('85 stats off-centered)
☐ 177 Gary Redus .05 .02 .01
☐ 178 Craig Lefferts .05 .02 .01
☐ 179 Carney Lansford .10 .05 .01
☐ 180 Ron Darling .10 .05 .01
☐ 181 Kirk McCaskill .05 .02 .01
☐ 182 Tony Armas .05 .02 .01
☐ 183 Steve Farr .05 .02 .01
☐ 184 Tom Brunansky .05 .02 .01
☐ 185 Bryan Harvey UER .25 .11 .03
('87 games 47, should be 3)
☐ 186 Mike Marshall .05 .02 .01
☐ 187 Bo Diaz .05 .02 .01
☐ 188 Willie Upshaw .05 .02 .01
☐ 189 Mike Pagliarulo .05 .02 .01
☐ 190 Mike Krukow .05 .02 .01
☐ 191 Tommy Herr .05 .02 .01
☐ 192 Jim Pankovits .05 .02 .01
☐ 193 Dwight Evans .10 .05 .01
☐ 194 Kelly Gruber .05 .02 .01
☐ 195 Bobby Bonilla .15 .07 .02
☐ 196 Wallace Johnson .05 .02 .01
☐ 197 Dave Stieb .10 .05 .01
☐ 198 Pat Borders .25 .11 .03
☐ 199 Rafael Palmeiro .25 .11 .03
☐ 200 Dwight Gooden .10 .05 .01
☐ 201 Pete Incaviglia .10 .05 .01
☐ 202 Chris James .05 .02 .01
☐ 203 Marvell Wynne .05 .02 .01
☐ 204 Pat Sheridan .05 .02 .01
☐ 205 Don Baylor .15 .07 .02
☐ 206 Paul O'Neill .15 .07 .02
☐ 207 Pete Smith .05 .02 .01
☐ 208 Mark McLemore .05 .02 .01
☐ 209 Henry Cotto .05 .02 .01
☐ 210 Kirk Gibson .10 .05 .01
☐ 211 Claudell Washington .05 .02 .01
☐ 212 Randy Bush .05 .02 .01
☐ 213 Joe Carter .25 .11 .03
☐ 214 Bill Buckner .10 .05 .01
☐ 215 Bert Blyleven UER .15 .07 .02
(Wrong birth year)
☐ 216 Brett Butler .10 .05 .01
☐ 217 Lee Mazzilli .05 .02 .01
☐ 218 Spike Owen .05 .02 .01
☐ 219 Bill Swift .10 .05 .01

☐ 220 Tim Wallach .05 .02 .01
☐ 221 David Cone .20 .09 .03
☐ 222 Don Carman .05 .02 .01
☐ 223 Rich Gossage .15 .07 .02
☐ 224 Bob Walk .05 .02 .01
☐ 225 Dave Righetti .05 .02 .01
☐ 226 Kevin Bass .05 .02 .01
☐ 227 Kevin Gross .05 .02 .01
☐ 228 Tim Burke .05 .02 .01
☐ 229 Rick Mahler .05 .02 .01
☐ 230 Lou Whitaker UER .15 .07 .02
(252 games in '85, should be 152)
☐ 231 Luis Alicea .05 .02 .01
☐ 232 Roberto Alomar .75 .35 .09
☐ 233 Bob Boone .10 .05 .01
☐ 234 Dickie Thon .05 .02 .01
☐ 235 Shawon Dunston .10 .05 .01
☐ 236 Pete Stanicek .05 .02 .01
☐ 237 Craig Biggio .60 .25 .08
(Inconsistent design, portrait on front)
☐ 238 Dennis Boyd .05 .02 .01
☐ 239 Tom Candiotti .05 .02 .01
☐ 240 Gary Carter .15 .07 .02
☐ 241 Mike Stanley .10 .05 .01
☐ 242 Ken Phelps .05 .02 .01
☐ 243 Chris Bosio .05 .02 .01
☐ 244 Les Straker .05 .02 .01
☐ 245 Dave Smith .05 .02 .01
☐ 246 John Candelaria .05 .02 .01
☐ 247 Joe Orsulak .05 .02 .01
☐ 248 Storm Davis .05 .02 .01
☐ 249 Floyd Bannister UER .05 .02 .01
(ML Batting Record)
☐ 250 Jack Morris .15 .07 .02
☐ 251 Bret Saberhagen .10 .05 .01
☐ 252 Tom Niedenfuer .05 .02 .01
☐ 253 Neal Heaton .05 .02 .01
☐ 254 Eric Show .05 .02 .01
☐ 255 Juan Samuel .05 .02 .01
☐ 256 Dale Sveum .05 .02 .01
☐ 257 Jim Gott .05 .02 .01
☐ 258 Scott Garrelts .05 .02 .01
☐ 259 Larry McWilliams .05 .02 .01
☐ 260 Steve Bedrosian .05 .02 .01
☐ 261 Jack Howell .05 .02 .01
☐ 262 Jay Tibbs .05 .02 .01
☐ 263 Jamie Moyer .05 .02 .01
☐ 264 Doug Sisk .05 .02 .01
☐ 265 Todd Worrell .05 .02 .01
☐ 266 John Farrell .05 .02 .01
☐ 267 Dave Collins .05 .02 .01
☐ 268 Sid Fernandez .10 .05 .01
☐ 269 Tom Brookens .05 .02 .01
☐ 270 Shane Mack .10 .05 .01
☐ 271 Paul Kilgus .05 .02 .01
☐ 272 Chuck Crim .05 .02 .01
☐ 273 Bob Knepper .05 .02 .01
☐ 274 Mike Moore .05 .02 .01
☐ 275 Guillermo Hernandez .05 .02 .01
☐ 276 Dennis Eckersley .15 .07 .02
☐ 277 Graig Nettles .10 .05 .01
☐ 278 Rich Dotson .05 .02 .01
☐ 279 Larry Herndon .05 .02 .01
☐ 280 Gene Larkin .05 .02 .01
☐ 281 Roger McDowell .05 .02 .01
☐ 282 Greg Swindell .10 .05 .01
☐ 283 Juan Agosto .05 .02 .01
☐ 284 Jeff M. Robinson .05 .02 .01
☐ 285 Mike Dunne .05 .02 .01
☐ 286 Greg Mathews .05 .02 .01
☐ 287 Kent Tekulve .05 .02 .01
☐ 288 Jerry Mumphrey .05 .02 .01
☐ 289 Jack McDowell .30 .14 .04
☐ 290 Frank Viola .10 .05 .01
☐ 291 Mark Gubicza .05 .02 .01
☐ 292 Dave Schmidt .05 .02 .01
☐ 293 Mike Henneman .10 .05 .01
☐ 294 Jimmy Jones .05 .02 .01
☐ 295 Charlie Hough .10 .05 .01
☐ 296 Rafael Santana .05 .02 .01
☐ 297 Chris Speier .05 .02 .01
☐ 298 Mike Witt .05 .02 .01
☐ 299 Pascual Perez .05 .02 .01
☐ 300 Nolan Ryan .75 .35 .09
☐ 301 Mitch Williams .10 .05 .01
☐ 302 Mookie Wilson .10 .05 .01
☐ 303 Mackey Sasser .05 .02 .01
☐ 304 John Cerutti .05 .02 .01
☐ 305 Jeff Reardon .15 .07 .02
☐ 306 Randy Myers UER .10 .05 .01
(6 hits in '87, should be 61)
☐ 307 Greg Brock .05 .02 .01
☐ 308 Bob Welch .10 .05 .01
☐ 309 Jeff D. Robinson .05 .02 .01
☐ 310 Harold Reynolds .05 .02 .01
☐ 311 Jim Walewander .05 .02 .01
☐ 312 Dave Magadan .05 .02 .01
☐ 313 Jim Gantner .05 .02 .01
☐ 314 Walt Terrell .05 .02 .01
☐ 315 Wally Backman .05 .02 .01
☐ 316 Luis Salazar .05 .02 .01
☐ 317 Rick Rhoden .05 .02 .01
☐ 318 Tom Henke .10 .05 .01
☐ 319 Mike Macfarlane .10 .05 .01
☐ 320 Dan Plesac .05 .02 .01
☐ 321 Calvin Schiraldi .05 .02 .01
☐ 322 Stan Javier .05 .02 .01
☐ 323 Devon White .10 .05 .01
☐ 324 Scott Bradley .05 .02 .01
☐ 325 Bruce Hurst .05 .02 .01
☐ 326 Manny Lee .05 .02 .01
☐ 327 Rick Aguilera .10 .05 .01
☐ 328 Bruce Ruffin .05 .02 .01
☐ 329 Ed Whitson .05 .02 .01
☐ 330 Bo Jackson .25 .11 .03
☐ 331 Ivan Calderon .05 .02 .01
☐ 332 Mickey Hatcher .05 .02 .01
☐ 333 Barry Jones .05 .02 .01
☐ 334 Ron Hassey .05 .02 .01
☐ 335 Bill Wegman .05 .02 .01
☐ 336 Damon Berryhill .05 .02 .01
☐ 337 Steve Ontiveros .05 .02 .01
☐ 338 Dan Pasqua .05 .02 .01
☐ 339 Bill Pecota .05 .02 .01
☐ 340 Greg Cadaret .05 .02 .01
☐ 341 Scott Bankhead .05 .02 .01
☐ 342 Ron Guidry .10 .05 .01
☐ 343 Danny Heep .05 .02 .01
☐ 344 Bob Brower .05 .02 .01
☐ 345 Rich Gedman .05 .02 .01
☐ 346 Nelson Santovenia .05 .02 .01
☐ 347 George Bell .10 .05 .01
☐ 348 Ted Power .05 .02 .01
☐ 349 Mark Grant .05 .02 .01
☐ 350A Roger Clemens ERR 3.00 1.35 .40
(778 career wins)
☐ 350B Roger Clemens COR .35 .16 .04
(78 career wins)
☐ 351 Bill Long .05 .02 .01
☐ 352 Jay Bell .15 .07 .02
☐ 353 Steve Balboni .05 .02 .01
☐ 354 Bob Kipper .05 .02 .01
☐ 355 Steve Jeltz .05 .02 .01

	No.	Player			
☐	356	Jesse Orosco	.05	.02	.01
☐	357	Bob Dernier	.05	.02	.01
☐	358	Mickey Tettleton	.10	.05	.01
☐	359	Duane Ward	.10	.05	.01
☐	360	Darrin Jackson	.10	.05	.01
☐	361	Rey Quinones	.05	.02	.01
☐	362	Mark Grace	.50	.23	.06
☐	363	Steve Lake	.05	.02	.01
☐	364	Pat Perry	.05	.02	.01
☐	365	Terry Steinbach	.10	.05	.01
☐	366	Alan Ashby	.05	.02	.01
☐	367	Jeff Montgomery	.10	.05	.01
☐	368	Steve Buechele	.05	.02	.01
☐	369	Chris Brown	.05	.02	.01
☐	370	Orel Hershiser	.10	.05	.01
☐	371	Todd Benzinger	.05	.02	.01
☐	372	Ron Gant	.25	.11	.03
☐	373	Paul Assenmacher	.05	.02	.01
☐	374	Joey Meyer	.05	.02	.01
☐	375	Neil Allen	.05	.02	.01
☐	376	Mike Davis	.05	.02	.01
☐	377	Jeff Parrett	.05	.02	.01
☐	378	Jay Howell	.05	.02	.01
☐	379	Rafael Belliard	.05	.02	.01
☐	380	Luis Polonia UER (2 triples in '87, should be 10)	.10	.05	.01
☐	381	Keith Atherton	.05	.02	.01
☐	382	Kent Hrbek	.10	.05	.01
☐	383	Bob Stanley	.05	.02	.01
☐	384	Dave LaPoint	.05	.02	.01
☐	385	Rance Mulliniks	.05	.02	.01
☐	386	Melido Perez	.05	.02	.01
☐	387	Doug Jones	.10	.05	.01
☐	388	Steve Lyons	.05	.02	.01
☐	389	Alejandro Pena	.05	.02	.01
☐	390	Frank White	.10	.05	.01
☐	391	Pat Tabler	.05	.02	.01
☐	392	Eric Plunk	.05	.02	.01
☐	393	Mike Maddux	.05	.02	.01
☐	394	Allan Anderson	.05	.02	.01
☐	395	Bob Brenly	.05	.02	.01
☐	396	Rick Cerone	.05	.02	.01
☐	397	Scott Terry	.05	.02	.01
☐	398	Mike Jackson	.05	.02	.01
☐	399	Bobby Thigpen UER (Bio says 37 saves in '88, should be 34)	.05	.02	.01
☐	400	Don Sutton	.15	.07	.02
☐	401	Cecil Espy	.05	.02	.01
☐	402	Junior Ortiz	.05	.02	.01
☐	403	Mike Smithson	.05	.02	.01
☐	404	Bud Black	.05	.02	.01
☐	405	Tom Foley	.05	.02	.01
☐	406	Andres Thomas	.05	.02	.01
☐	407	Rick Sutcliffe	.10	.05	.01
☐	408	Brian Harper	.10	.05	.01
☐	409	John Smiley	.05	.02	.01
☐	410	Juan Nieves	.05	.02	.01
☐	411	Shawn Abner	.05	.02	.01
☐	412	Wes Gardner	.05	.02	.01
☐	413	Darren Daulton	.15	.07	.02
☐	414	Juan Berenguer	.05	.02	.01
☐	415	Charles Hudson	.05	.02	.01
☐	416	Rick Honeycutt	.05	.02	.01
☐	417	Greg Booker	.05	.02	.01
☐	418	Tim Belcher	.05	.02	.01
☐	419	Don August	.05	.02	.01
☐	420	Dale Mohorcic	.05	.02	.01
☐	421	Steve Lombardozzi	.05	.02	.01
☐	422	Atlee Hammaker	.05	.02	.01
☐	423	Jerry Don Gleaton	.05	.02	.01
☐	424	Scott Bailes	.05	.02	.01
☐	425	Bruce Sutter	.10	.05	.01
☐	426	Randy Ready	.05	.02	.01
☐	427	Jerry Reed	.05	.02	.01
☐	428	Bryn Smith	.05	.02	.01
☐	429	Tim Leary	.05	.02	.01
☐	430	Mark Clear	.05	.02	.01
☐	431	Terry Leach	.05	.02	.01
☐	432	John Moses	.05	.02	.01
☐	433	Ozzie Guillen	.10	.05	.01
☐	434	Gene Nelson	.05	.02	.01
☐	435	Gary Ward	.05	.02	.01
☐	436	Luis Aguayo	.05	.02	.01
☐	437	Fernando Valenzuela	.05	.02	.01
☐	438	Jeff Russell UER (Saves total does not add up correctly)	.05	.02	.01
☐	439	Cecilio Guante	.05	.02	.01
☐	440	Don Robinson	.05	.02	.01
☐	441	Rick Anderson	.05	.02	.01
☐	442	Tom Glavine	.40	.18	.05
☐	443	Daryl Boston	.05	.02	.01
☐	444	Joe Price	.05	.02	.01
☐	445	Stewart Cliburn	.05	.02	.01
☐	446	Manny Trillo	.05	.02	.01
☐	447	Joel Skinner	.05	.02	.01
☐	448	Charlie Puleo	.05	.02	.01
☐	449	Carlton Fisk	.15	.07	.02
☐	450	Will Clark	.30	.14	.04
☐	451	Otis Nixon	.10	.05	.01
☐	452	Rick Schu	.05	.02	.01
☐	453	Todd Stottlemyre UER (ML Batting Record)	.10	.05	.01
☐	454	Tim Birtsas	.05	.02	.01
☐	455	Dave Gallagher	.05	.02	.01
☐	456	Barry Lyons	.05	.02	.01
☐	457	Fred Manrique	.05	.02	.01
☐	458	Ernest Riles	.05	.02	.01
☐	459	Doug Jennings	.05	.02	.01
☐	460	Joe Magrane	.05	.02	.01
☐	461	Jamie Quirk	.05	.02	.01
☐	462	Jack Armstrong	.05	.02	.01
☐	463	Bobby Witt	.10	.05	.01
☐	464	Keith A. Miller	.05	.02	.01
☐	465	Todd Burns	.05	.02	.01
☐	466	John Dopson	.05	.02	.01
☐	467	Rich Yett	.05	.02	.01
☐	468	Craig Reynolds	.05	.02	.01
☐	469	Dave Bergman	.05	.02	.01
☐	470	Rex Hudler	.05	.02	.01
☐	471	Eric King	.05	.02	.01
☐	472	Joaquin Andujar	.05	.02	.01
☐	473	Sil Campusano	.05	.02	.01
☐	474	Terry Mulholland	.10	.05	.01
☐	475	Mike Flanagan	.05	.02	.01
☐	476	Greg A. Harris	.05	.02	.01
☐	477	Tommy John	.15	.07	.02
☐	478	Dave Anderson	.05	.02	.01
☐	479	Fred Toliver	.05	.02	.01
☐	480	Jimmy Key	.15	.07	.02
☐	481	Donell Nixon	.05	.02	.01
☐	482	Mark Portugal	.10	.05	.01
☐	483	Tom Pagnozzi	.05	.02	.01
☐	484	Jeff Kunkel	.05	.02	.01
☐	485	Frank Williams	.05	.02	.01
☐	486	Jody Reed	.05	.02	.01
☐	487	Roberto Kelly	.20	.09	.03
☐	488	Shawn Hillegas UER (165 innings in '87, should be 165.2)	.05	.02	.01
☐	489	Jerry Reuss	.05	.02	.01
☐	490	Mark Davis	.05	.02	.01
☐	491	Jeff Sellers	.05	.02	.01
☐	492	Zane Smith	.05	.02	.01

☐ 493 Al Newman .... .05 .02 .01
☐ 494 Mike Young .... .05 .02 .01
☐ 495 Larry Parrish .... .05 .02 .01
☐ 496 Herm Winningham .... .05 .02 .01
☐ 497 Carmen Castillo .... .05 .02 .01
☐ 498 Joe Hesketh .... .05 .02 .01
☐ 499 Darrell Miller .... .05 .02 .01
☐ 500 Mike LaCoss .... .05 .02 .01
☐ 501 Charlie Lea .... .05 .02 .01
☐ 502 Bruce Benedict .... .05 .02 .01
☐ 503 Chuck Finley .... .10 .05 .01
☐ 504 Brad Wellman .... .05 .02 .01
☐ 505 Tim Crews .... .05 .02 .01
☐ 506 Ken Gerhart .... .05 .02 .01
☐ 507A Brian Holton ERR .... .05 .02 .01
(Born 1/25/65 Denver, should be 11/29/59 in McKeesport)
☐ 507B Brian Holton COR .... 3.00 1.35 .40
☐ 508 Dennis Lamp .... .05 .02 .01
☐ 509 Bobby Meacham UER .... .05 .02 .01
('84 games 099)
☐ 510 Tracy Jones .... .05 .02 .01
☐ 511 Mike R. Fitzgerald .... .05 .02 .01
☐ 512 Jeff Bittiger .... .05 .02 .01
☐ 513 Tim Flannery .... .05 .02 .01
☐ 514 Ray Hayward .... .05 .02 .01
☐ 515 Dave Leiper .... .05 .02 .01
☐ 516 Rod Scurry .... .05 .02 .01
☐ 517 Carmelo Martinez .... .05 .02 .01
☐ 518 Curtis Wilkerson .... .05 .02 .01
☐ 519 Stan Jefferson .... .05 .02 .01
☐ 520 Dan Quisenberry .... .10 .05 .01
☐ 521 Lloyd McClendon .... .05 .02 .01
☐ 522 Steve Trout .... .05 .02 .01
☐ 523 Larry Andersen .... .05 .02 .01
☐ 524 Don Aase .... .05 .02 .01
☐ 525 Bob Forsch .... .05 .02 .01
☐ 526 Geno Petralli .... .05 .02 .01
☐ 527 Angel Salazar .... .05 .02 .01
☐ 528 Mike Schooler .... .05 .02 .01
☐ 529 Jose Oquendo .... .05 .02 .01
☐ 530 Jay Buhner UER .... .20 .09 .03
(Wearing 43 on front, listed as 34 on back)
☐ 531 Tom Bolton .... .05 .02 .01
☐ 532 Al Nipper .... .05 .02 .01
☐ 533 Dave Henderson .... .05 .02 .01
☐ 534 John Costello .... .05 .02 .01
☐ 535 Donnie Moore .... .05 .02 .01
☐ 536 Mike Laga .... .05 .02 .01
☐ 537 Mike Gallego .... .05 .02 .01
☐ 538 Jim Clancy .... .05 .02 .01
☐ 539 Joel Youngblood .... .05 .02 .01
☐ 540 Rick Leach .... .05 .02 .01
☐ 541 Kevin Romine .... .05 .02 .01
☐ 542 Mark Salas .... .05 .02 .01
☐ 543 Greg Minton .... .05 .02 .01
☐ 544 Dave Palmer .... .05 .02 .01
☐ 545 Dwayne Murphy UER .... .05 .02 .01
(Game-sinning)
☐ 546 Jim Deshaies .... .05 .02 .01
☐ 547 Don Gordon .... .05 .02 .01
☐ 548 Ricky Jordan .... .05 .02 .01
☐ 549 Mike Boddicker .... .05 .02 .01
☐ 550 Mike Scott .... .05 .02 .01
☐ 551 Jeff Ballard .... .05 .02 .01
☐ 552A Jose Rijo ERR .... .50 .23 .06
(Uniform listed as 27 on back)
☐ 552B Jose Rijo COR .... .15 .07 .02
(Uniform listed as 24 on back)
☐ 553 Danny Darwin .... .05 .02 .01
☐ 554 Tom Browning .... .05 .02 .01
☐ 555 Danny Jackson .... .05 .02 .01
☐ 556 Rick Dempsey .... .05 .02 .01
☐ 557 Jeffrey Leonard .... .05 .02 .01
☐ 558 Jeff Musselman .... .05 .02 .01
☐ 559 Ron Robinson .... .05 .02 .01
☐ 560 John Tudor .... .05 .02 .01
☐ 561 Don Slaught UER .... .05 .02 .01
(237 games in 1987)
☐ 562 Dennis Rasmussen .... .05 .02 .01
☐ 563 Brady Anderson .... .40 .18 .05
☐ 564 Pedro Guerrero .... .10 .05 .01
☐ 565 Paul Molitor .... .25 .11 .03
☐ 566 Terry Clark .... .05 .02 .01
☐ 567 Terry Puhl .... .05 .02 .01
☐ 568 Mike Campbell .... .05 .02 .01
☐ 569 Paul Mirabella .... .05 .02 .01
☐ 570 Jeff Hamilton .... .05 .02 .01
☐ 571 Oswald Peraza .... .05 .02 .01
☐ 572 Bob McClure .... .05 .02 .01
☐ 573 Jose Bautista .... .05 .02 .01
☐ 574 Alex Trevino .... .05 .02 .01
☐ 575 John Franco .... .10 .05 .01
☐ 576 Mark Parent .... .05 .02 .01
☐ 577 Nelson Liriano .... .05 .02 .01
☐ 578 Steve Shields .... .05 .02 .01
☐ 579 Odell Jones .... .05 .02 .01
☐ 580 Al Leiter .... .05 .02 .01
☐ 581 Dave Stapleton .... .05 .02 .01
☐ 582 World Series '88 .... .10 .05 .01
Orel Hershiser
Jose Canseco
Kirk Gibson
Dave Stewart
☐ 583 Donnie Hill .... .05 .02 .01
☐ 584 Chuck Jackson .... .05 .02 .01
☐ 585 Rene Gonzales .... .05 .02 .01
☐ 586 Tracy Woodson .... .05 .02 .01
☐ 587 Jim Adduci .... .05 .02 .01
☐ 588 Mario Soto .... .05 .02 .01
☐ 589 Jeff Blauser .... .15 .07 .02
☐ 590 Jim Traber .... .05 .02 .01
☐ 591 Jon Perlman .... .05 .02 .01
☐ 592 Mark Williamson .... .05 .02 .01
☐ 593 Dave Meads .... .05 .02 .01
☐ 594 Jim Eisenreich .... .05 .02 .01
☐ 595A Paul Gibson P1 .... 1.00 .45 .13
☐ 595B Paul Gibson P2 .... .05 .02 .01
(Airbrushed leg on player in background)
☐ 596 Mike Birkbeck .... .05 .02 .01
☐ 597 Terry Francona .... .05 .02 .01
☐ 598 Paul Zuvella .... .05 .02 .01
☐ 599 Franklin Stubbs .... .05 .02 .01
☐ 600 Gregg Jefferies .... .35 .16 .04
☐ 601 John Cangelosi .... .05 .02 .01
☐ 602 Mike Sharperson .... .05 .02 .01
☐ 603 Mike Diaz .... .05 .02 .01
☐ 604 Gary Varsho .... .05 .02 .01
☐ 605 Terry Blocker .... .05 .02 .01
☐ 606 Charlie O'Brien .... .05 .02 .01
☐ 607 Jim Eppard .... .05 .02 .01
☐ 608 John Davis .... .05 .02 .01
☐ 609 Ken Griffey .... .10 .05 .01
☐ 610 Buddy Bell .... .10 .05 .01
☐ 611 Ted Simmons UER .... .10 .05 .01
('78 stats Cardinal)
☐ 612 Matt Williams .... .40 .18 .05
☐ 613 Danny Cox .... .05 .02 .01
☐ 614 Al Pedrique .... .05 .02 .01
☐ 615 Ron Oester .... .05 .02 .01
☐ 616 John Smoltz .... .40 .18 .05

☐ 617 Bob Melvin	.05	.02	.01
☐ 618 Rob Dibble	.20	.09	.03
☐ 619 Kirt Manwaring	.05	.02	.01
☐ 620 Felix Fermin	.05	.02	.01
☐ 621 Doug Dascenzo	.05	.02	.01
☐ 622 Bill Brennan	.05	.02	.01
☐ 623 Carlos Quintana	.05	.02	.01
☐ 624 Mike Harkey UER (13 and 31 walks in '88, should be 35 and 33)	.05	.02	.01
☐ 625 Gary Sheffield	1.00	.45	.13
☐ 626 Tom Prince	.05	.02	.01
☐ 627 Steve Searcy	.05	.02	.01
☐ 628 Charlie Hayes (Listed as outfielder)	.40	.18	.05
☐ 629 Felix Jose UER (Modesto misspelled as Modesta)	.30	.14	.04
☐ 630 Sandy Alomar Jr. (Inconsistent design, portrait on front)	.25	.11	.03
☐ 631 Derek Lilliquist	.05	.02	.01
☐ 632 Geronimo Berroa	.30	.14	.04
☐ 633 Luis Medina	.05	.02	.01
☐ 634 Tom Gordon UER (Height 6'0")	.20	.09	.03
☐ 635 Ramon Martinez	.50	.23	.06
☐ 636 Craig Worthington	.05	.02	.01
☐ 637 Edgar Martinez	.10	.05	.01
☐ 638 Chad Kreuter	.15	.07	.02
☐ 639 Ron Jones	.05	.02	.01
☐ 640 Van Snider	.05	.02	.01
☐ 641 Lance Blankenship	.05	.02	.01
☐ 642 Dwight Smith UER (10 HR's in '87, should be 18)	.15	.07	.02
☐ 643 Cameron Drew	.05	.02	.01
☐ 644 Jerald Clark	.05	.02	.01
☐ 645 Randy Johnson	.75	.35	.09
☐ 646 Norm Charlton	.15	.07	.02
☐ 647 Todd Frohwirth UER (Southpaw on back)	.05	.02	.01
☐ 648 Luis De Los Santos	.05	.02	.01
☐ 649 Tim Jones	.05	.02	.01
☐ 650 Dave West UER (ML hits 3, should be 6)	.10	.05	.01
☐ 651 Bob Milacki	.05	.02	.01
☐ 652 Wrigley Field HL (Let There Be Lights)	.05	.02	.01
☐ 653 Orel Hershiser HL (The Streak)	.10	.05	.01
☐ 654A Wade Boggs HL ERR (Wade Whacks 'Em) ("seaason" on back)	3.00	1.35	.40
☐ 654B Wade Boggs HL COR. (Wade Whacks 'Em)	.05	.02	.01
☐ 655 Jose Canseco HL (One of a Kind)	.20	.09	.03
☐ 656 Doug Jones HL (Doug Sets Saves)	.05	.02	.01
☐ 657 Rickey Henderson HL (Rickey Rocks 'Em)	.10	.05	.01
☐ 658 Tom Browning HL (Tom Perfect Pitches)	.05	.02	.01
☐ 659 Mike Greenwell HL (Greenwell Gamers)	.05	.02	.01
☐ 660 Boston Red Sox HL (Joe Morgan MG, Sox Sock 'Em)	.05	.02	.01

1989 Score Rookie/Traded

The 1989 Score Rookie and Traded set contains 110 standard-size (2 1/2" by 3 1/2") cards. The fronts have coral green borders with pink diamonds at the bottom. The vertically oriented backs have color facial shots, career stats, and biographical information. Cards 1-80 feature traded players; cards 81-110 feature 1989 rookies. The set was distributed in a blue box with 10 Magic Motion trivia cards. Rookie Cards in this set include Jim Abbott, Joey (Albert) Belle, Junior Felix, Ken Griffey Jr., Ken Hill, Gregg Olson, Jerome Walton, and John Wetteland.

	MINT	EXC	G-VG
COMPLETE FACT.SET (110)	10.00	4.50	1.25
COMMON CARD (1T-110T)	.05	.02	.01
☐ 1T Rafael Palmeiro	.30	.14	.04
☐ 2T Nolan Ryan	1.50	.65	.19
☐ 3T Jack Clark	.08	.04	.01
☐ 4T Dave LaPoint	.05	.02	.01
☐ 5T Mike Moore	.05	.02	.01
☐ 6T Pete O'Brien	.05	.02	.01
☐ 7T Jeffrey Leonard	.05	.02	.01
☐ 8T Rob Murphy	.05	.02	.01
☐ 9T Tom Herr	.05	.02	.01
☐ 10T Claudell Washington	.05	.02	.01
☐ 11T Mike Pagliarulo	.05	.02	.01
☐ 12T Steve Lake	.05	.02	.01
☐ 13T Spike Owen	.05	.02	.01
☐ 14T Andy Hawkins	.05	.02	.01
☐ 15T Todd Benzinger	.05	.02	.01
☐ 16T Mookie Wilson	.08	.04	.01
☐ 17T Bert Blyleven	.10	.05	.01
☐ 18T Jeff Treadway	.05	.02	.01
☐ 19T Bruce Hurst	.05	.02	.01
☐ 20T Steve Sax	.05	.02	.01
☐ 21T Juan Samuel	.05	.02	.01
☐ 22T Jesse Barfield	.05	.02	.01
☐ 23T Carmen Castillo	.05	.02	.01
☐ 24T Terry Leach	.05	.02	.01
☐ 25T Mark Langston	.10	.05	.01
☐ 26T Eric King	.05	.02	.01
☐ 27T Steve Balboni	.05	.02	.01
☐ 28T Len Dykstra	.10	.05	.01
☐ 29T Keith Moreland	.05	.02	.01
☐ 30T Terry Kennedy	.05	.02	.01
☐ 31T Eddie Murray	.25	.11	.03
☐ 32T Mitch Williams	.08	.04	.01
☐ 33T Jeff Parrett	.05	.02	.01

☐	34T Wally Backman	.05	.02	.01
☐	35T Julio Franco	.08	.04	.01
☐	36T Lance Parrish	.08	.04	.01
☐	37T Nick Esasky	.05	.02	.01
☐	38T Luis Polonia	.08	.04	.01
☐	39T Kevin Gross	.05	.02	.01
☐	40T John Dopson	.05	.02	.01
☐	41T Willie Randolph	.08	.04	.01
☐	42T Jim Clancy	.05	.02	.01
☐	43T Tracy Jones	.05	.02	.01
☐	44T Phil Bradley	.05	.02	.01
☐	45T Milt Thompson	.05	.02	.01
☐	46T Chris James	.05	.02	.01
☐	47T Scott Fletcher	.05	.02	.01
☐	48T Kal Daniels	.05	.02	.01
☐	49T Steve Bedrosian	.05	.02	.01
☐	50T Rickey Henderson	.25	.11	.03
☐	51T Dion James	.05	.02	.01
☐	52T Tim Leary	.05	.02	.01
☐	53T Roger McDowell	.05	.02	.01
☐	54T Mel Hall	.05	.02	.01
☐	55T Dickie Thon	.05	.02	.01
☐	56T Zane Smith	.05	.02	.01
☐	57T Danny Heep	.05	.02	.01
☐	58T Bob McClure	.05	.02	.01
☐	59T Brian Holton	.05	.02	.01
☐	60T Randy Ready	.05	.02	.01
☐	61T Bob Melvin	.05	.02	.01
☐	62T Harold Baines	.08	.04	.01
☐	63T Lance McCullers	.05	.02	.01
☐	64T Jody Davis	.05	.02	.01
☐	65T Darrell Evans	.08	.04	.01
☐	66T Joel Youngblood	.05	.02	.01
☐	67T Frank Viola	.08	.04	.01
☐	68T Mike Aldrete	.05	.02	.01
☐	69T Greg Cadaret	.05	.02	.01
☐	70T John Kruk	.10	.05	.01
☐	71T Pat Sheridan	.05	.02	.01
☐	72T Oddibe McDowell	.05	.02	.01
☐	73T Tom Brookens	.05	.02	.01
☐	74T Bob Boone	.08	.04	.01
☐	75T Walt Terrell	.05	.02	.01
☐	76T Joel Skinner	.05	.02	.01
☐	77T Randy Johnson	.75	.35	.09
☐	78T Felix Fermin	.05	.02	.01
☐	79T Rick Mahler	.05	.02	.01
☐	80T Richard Dotson	.05	.02	.01
☐	81T Cris Carpenter	.05	.02	.01
☐	82T Bill Spiers	.05	.02	.01
☐	83T Junior Felix	.20	.09	.03
☐	84T Joe Girardi	.15	.07	.02
☐	85T Jerome Walton	.05	.02	.01
☐	86T Greg Litton	.05	.02	.01
☐	87T Greg W.Harris	.05	.02	.01
☐	88T Jim Abbott	1.00	.45	.13
☐	89T Kevin Brown	.08	.04	.01
☐	90T John Wetteland	.50	.23	.06
☐	91T Gary Wayne	.05	.02	.01
☐	92T Rich Monteleone	.05	.02	.01
☐	93T Bob Geren	.05	.02	.01
☐	94T Clay Parker	.05	.02	.01
☐	95T Steve Finley	.25	.11	.03
☐	96T Gregg Olson	.25	.11	.03
☐	97T Ken Patterson	.05	.02	.01
☐	98T Ken Hill	.60	.25	.08
☐	99T Scott Scudder	.05	.02	.01
☐	100T Ken Griffey Jr.	6.00	2.70	.75
☐	101T Jeff Brantley	.05	.02	.01
☐	102T Donn Pall	.05	.02	.01
☐	103T Carlos Martinez	.05	.02	.01
☐	104T Joe Oliver	.25	.11	.03
☐	105T Omar Vizquel	.20	.09	.03
☐	106T Joey Belle	3.00	1.35	.40
☐	107T Kenny Rogers	.35	.16	.04
☐	108T Mark Carreon	.05	.02	.01
☐	109T Rolando Roomes	.05	.02	.01
☐	110T Pete Harnisch	.25	.11	.03

1990 Score

The 1990 Score set contains 704 standard-size (2 1/2" by 3 1/2") cards. The front borders are red, blue, green or white. The vertically oriented backs are white with borders that match the fronts, and feature color mugshots. Cards numbered 661-682 contain the first round draft picks subset noted as DC for "draft choice" in the checklist below. Cards numbered 683-695 contain the "Dream Team" subset noted by DT in the checklist below. Rookie Cards in this set include Scott Cooper, Delino DeShields, Cal Eldred, Juan Gonzalez, Tommy Greene, Marquis Grissom, Dave Justice, Chuck Knoblauch, Kevin Maas, Ben McDonald, John Olerud, Dean Palmer, Sammy Sosa, Frank Thomas, Mo Vaughn, and Larry Walker. A ten-card set of Dream Team Rookies was inserted into each hobby factory set, but was not included in retail factory sets. These cards carry a B prefix on the card number and include a player at each position plus a commemorative card honoring the late Baseball Commissioner A. Bartlett Giamatti.

	MINT	EXC	G-VG
COMPLETE SET (704)	15.00	6.75	1.90
COMPLETE RETAIL SET (704)	15.00	6.75	1.90
COMPLETE HOBBY SET (714)	20.00	9.00	2.50
COMMON CARD (1-704)	.05	.02	.01

☐	1 Don Mattingly	.35	.16	.04
☐	2 Cal Ripken	.40	.18	.05
☐	3 Dwight Evans	.10	.05	.01
☐	4 Barry Bonds	.50	.23	.06
☐	5 Kevin McReynolds	.05	.02	.01
☐	6 Ozzie Guillen	.05	.02	.01
☐	7 Terry Kennedy	.05	.02	.01
☐	8 Bryan Harvey	.10	.05	.01
☐	9 Alan Trammell	.15	.07	.02
☐	10 Cory Snyder	.05	.02	.01
☐	11 Jody Reed	.05	.02	.01
☐	12 Roberto Alomar	.40	.18	.05
☐	13 Pedro Guerrero	.10	.05	.01
☐	14 Gary Redus	.05	.02	.01
☐	15 Marty Barrett	.05	.02	.01

☐ 16 Ricky Jordan	.05	.02	.01
☐ 17 Joe Magrane	.05	.02	.01
☐ 18 Sid Fernandez	.10	.05	.01
☐ 19 Richard Dotson	.05	.02	.01
☐ 20 Jack Clark	.10	.05	.01
☐ 21 Bob Walk	.05	.02	.01
☐ 22 Ron Karkovice	.05	.02	.01
☐ 23 Lenny Harris	.05	.02	.01
☐ 24 Phil Bradley	.05	.02	.01
☐ 25 Andres Galarraga	.15	.07	.02
☐ 26 Brian Downing	.05	.02	.01
☐ 27 Dave Martinez	.05	.02	.01
☐ 28 Eric King	.05	.02	.01
☐ 29 Barry Lyons	.05	.02	.01
☐ 30 Dave Schmidt	.05	.02	.01
☐ 31 Mike Boddicker	.05	.02	.01
☐ 32 Tom Foley	.05	.02	.01
☐ 33 Brady Anderson	.10	.05	.01
☐ 34 Jim Presley	.05	.02	.01
☐ 35 Lance Parrish	.10	.05	.01
☐ 36 Von Hayes	.05	.02	.01
☐ 37 Lee Smith	.15	.07	.02
☐ 38 Herm Winningham	.05	.02	.01
☐ 39 Alejandro Pena	.05	.02	.01
☐ 40 Mike Scott	.05	.02	.01
☐ 41 Joe Orsulak	.05	.02	.01
☐ 42 Rafael Ramirez	.05	.02	.01
☐ 43 Gerald Young	.05	.02	.01
☐ 44 Dick Schofield	.05	.02	.01
☐ 45 Dave Smith	.05	.02	.01
☐ 46 Dave Magadan	.05	.02	.01
☐ 47 Dennis Martinez	.10	.05	.01
☐ 48 Greg Minton	.05	.02	.01
☐ 49 Milt Thompson	.05	.02	.01
☐ 50 Orel Hershiser	.10	.05	.01
☐ 51 Bip Roberts	.10	.05	.01
☐ 52 Jerry Browne	.05	.02	.01
☐ 53 Bob Ojeda	.05	.02	.01
☐ 54 Fernando Valenzuela	.05	.02	.01
☐ 55 Matt Nokes	.05	.02	.01
☐ 56 Brook Jacoby	.05	.02	.01
☐ 57 Frank Tanana	.05	.02	.01
☐ 58 Scott Fletcher	.05	.02	.01
☐ 59 Ron Oester	.05	.02	.01
☐ 60 Bob Boone	.10	.05	.01
☐ 61 Dan Gladden	.05	.02	.01
☐ 62 Darnell Coles	.05	.02	.01
☐ 63 Gregg Olson	.10	.05	.01
☐ 64 Todd Burns	.05	.02	.01
☐ 65 Todd Benzinger	.05	.02	.01
☐ 66 Dale Murphy	.15	.07	.02
☐ 67 Mike Flanagan	.05	.02	.01
☐ 68 Jose Oquendo	.05	.02	.01
☐ 69 Cecil Espy	.05	.02	.01
☐ 70 Chris Sabo	.10	.05	.01
☐ 71 Shane Rawley	.05	.02	.01
☐ 72 Tom Brunansky	.05	.02	.01
☐ 73 Vance Law	.05	.02	.01
☐ 74 B.J. Surhoff	.05	.02	.01
☐ 75 Lou Whitaker	.15	.07	.02
☐ 76 Ken Caminiti UER (Euclid, Ohio should be Hanford, California)	.10	.05	.01
☐ 77 Nelson Liriano	.05	.02	.01
☐ 78 Tommy Gregg	.05	.02	.01
☐ 79 Don Slaught	.05	.02	.01
☐ 80 Eddie Murray	.15	.07	.02
☐ 81 Joe Boever	.05	.02	.01
☐ 82 Charlie Leibrandt	.05	.02	.01
☐ 83 Jose Lind	.05	.02	.01
☐ 84 Tony Phillips	.05	.02	.01
☐ 85 Mitch Webster	.05	.02	.01
☐ 86 Dan Plesac	.05	.02	.01
☐ 87 Rick Mahler	.05	.02	.01
☐ 88 Steve Lyons	.05	.02	.01
☐ 89 Tony Fernandez	.10	.05	.01
☐ 90 Ryne Sandberg	.35	.16	.04
☐ 91 Nick Esasky	.05	.02	.01
☐ 92 Luis Salazar	.05	.02	.01
☐ 93 Pete Incaviglia	.05	.02	.01
☐ 94 Ivan Calderon	.05	.02	.01
☐ 95 Jeff Treadway	.05	.02	.01
☐ 96 Kurt Stillwell	.05	.02	.01
☐ 97 Gary Sheffield	.30	.14	.04
☐ 98 Jeffrey Leonard	.05	.02	.01
☐ 99 Andres Thomas	.05	.02	.01
☐ 100 Roberto Kelly	.10	.05	.01
☐ 101 Alvaro Espinoza	.05	.02	.01
☐ 102 Greg Gagne	.05	.02	.01
☐ 103 John Farrell	.05	.02	.01
☐ 104 Willie Wilson	.05	.02	.01
☐ 105 Glenn Braggs	.05	.02	.01
☐ 106 Chet Lemon	.05	.02	.01
☐ 107A Jamie Moyer ERR (Scintilating)	.05	.02	.01
☐ 107B Jamie Moyer COR (Scintillating)	.10	.05	.01
☐ 108 Chuck Crim	.05	.02	.01
☐ 109 Dave Valle	.05	.02	.01
☐ 110 Walt Weiss	.05	.02	.01
☐ 111 Larry Sheets	.05	.02	.01
☐ 112 Don Robinson	.05	.02	.01
☐ 113 Danny Heep	.05	.02	.01
☐ 114 Carmelo Martinez	.05	.02	.01
☐ 115 Dave Gallagher	.05	.02	.01
☐ 116 Mike LaValliere	.05	.02	.01
☐ 117 Bob McClure	.05	.02	.01
☐ 118 Rene Gonzales	.05	.02	.01
☐ 119 Mark Parent	.05	.02	.01
☐ 120 Wally Joyner	.10	.05	.01
☐ 121 Mark Gubicza	.05	.02	.01
☐ 122 Tony Pena	.05	.02	.01
☐ 123 Carmen Castillo	.05	.02	.01
☐ 124 Howard Johnson	.10	.05	.01
☐ 125 Steve Sax	.05	.02	.01
☐ 126 Tim Belcher	.05	.02	.01
☐ 127 Tim Burke	.05	.02	.01
☐ 128 Al Newman	.05	.02	.01
☐ 129 Dennis Rasmussen	.05	.02	.01
☐ 130 Doug Jones	.05	.02	.01
☐ 131 Fred Lynn	.10	.05	.01
☐ 132 Jeff Hamilton	.05	.02	.01
☐ 133 German Gonzalez	.05	.02	.01
☐ 134 John Morris	.05	.02	.01
☐ 135 Dave Parker	.15	.07	.02
☐ 136 Gary Pettis	.05	.02	.01
☐ 137 Dennis Boyd	.05	.02	.01
☐ 138 Candy Maldonado	.05	.02	.01
☐ 139 Rick Cerone	.05	.02	.01
☐ 140 George Brett	.30	.14	.04
☐ 141 Dave Clark	.05	.02	.01
☐ 142 Dickie Thon	.05	.02	.01
☐ 143 Junior Ortiz	.05	.02	.01
☐ 144 Don August	.05	.02	.01
☐ 145 Gary Gaetti	.05	.02	.01
☐ 146 Kirt Manwaring	.05	.02	.01
☐ 147 Jeff Reed	.05	.02	.01
☐ 148 Jose Alvarez	.05	.02	.01
☐ 149 Mike Schooler	.05	.02	.01
☐ 150 Mark Grace	.20	.09	.03
☐ 151 Geronimo Berroa	.10	.05	.01
☐ 152 Barry Jones	.05	.02	.01
☐ 153 Geno Petralli	.05	.02	.01
☐ 154 Jim Deshaies	.05	.02	.01
☐ 155 Barry Larkin	.15	.07	.02
☐ 156 Alfredo Griffin	.05	.02	.01

☐ 157 Tom Henke .10 .05 .01
☐ 158 Mike Jeffcoat .05 .02 .01
☐ 159 Bob Welch .05 .02 .01
☐ 160 Julio Franco .10 .05 .01
☐ 161 Henry Cotto .05 .02 .01
☐ 162 Terry Steinbach .10 .05 .01
☐ 163 Damon Berryhill .05 .02 .01
☐ 164 Tim Crews .05 .02 .01
☐ 165 Tom Browning .05 .02 .01
☐ 166 Fred Manrique .05 .02 .01
☐ 167 Harold Reynolds .05 .02 .01
☐ 168A Ron Hassey ERR .05 .02 .01
(27 on back)
☐ 168B Ron Hassey COR 1.00 .45 .13
(24 on back)
☐ 169 Shawon Dunston .05 .02 .01
☐ 170 Bobby Bonilla .15 .07 .02
☐ 171 Tommy Herr .05 .02 .01
☐ 172 Mike Heath .05 .02 .01
☐ 173 Rich Gedman .05 .02 .01
☐ 174 Bill Ripken .05 .02 .01
☐ 175 Pete O'Brien .05 .02 .01
☐ 176A Lloyd McClendon ERR .75 .35 .09
(Uniform number on back listed as 1)
☐ 176B Lloyd McClendon COR .05 .02 .01
(Uniform number on back listed as 10)
☐ 177 Brian Holton .05 .02 .01
☐ 178 Jeff Blauser .10 .05 .01
☐ 179 Jim Eisenreich .05 .02 .01
☐ 180 Bert Blyleven .15 .07 .02
☐ 181 Rob Murphy .05 .02 .01
☐ 182 Bill Doran .05 .02 .01
☐ 183 Curt Ford .05 .02 .01
☐ 184 Mike Henneman .05 .02 .01
☐ 185 Eric Davis .10 .05 .01
☐ 186 Lance McCullers .05 .02 .01
☐ 187 Steve Davis .05 .02 .01
☐ 188 Bill Wegman .05 .02 .01
☐ 189 Brian Harper .10 .05 .01
☐ 190 Mike Moore .05 .02 .01
☐ 191 Dale Mohorcic .05 .02 .01
☐ 192 Tim Wallach .05 .02 .01
☐ 193 Keith Hernandez .10 .05 .01
☐ 194 Dave Righetti .05 .02 .01
☐ 195A Bret Saberhagen ERR .10 .05 .01
(Joke)
☐ 195B Bret Saberhagen COR .10 .05 .01
(Joker)
☐ 196 Paul Kilgus .05 .02 .01
☐ 197 Bud Black .05 .02 .01
☐ 198 Juan Samuel .05 .02 .01
☐ 199 Kevin Seitzer .05 .02 .01
☐ 200 Darryl Strawberry .15 .07 .02
☐ 201 Dave Stieb .10 .05 .01
☐ 202 Charlie Hough .10 .05 .01
☐ 203 Jack Morris .15 .07 .02
☐ 204 Rance Mulliniks .05 .02 .01
☐ 205 Alvin Davis .05 .02 .01
☐ 206 Jack Howell .05 .02 .01
☐ 207 Ken Patterson .05 .02 .01
☐ 208 Terry Pendleton .15 .07 .02
☐ 209 Craig Lefferts .05 .02 .01
☐ 210 Kevin Brown UER .10 .05 .01
(First mention of '89 Rangers should be '88)
☐ 211 Dan Petry .05 .02 .01
☐ 212 Dave Leiper .05 .02 .01
☐ 213 Daryl Boston .05 .02 .01
☐ 214 Kevin Hickey .05 .02 .01
☐ 215 Mike Krukow .05 .02 .01
☐ 216 Terry Francona .05 .02 .01
☐ 217 Kirk McCaskill .05 .02 .01
☐ 218 Scott Bailes .05 .02 .01
☐ 219 Bob Forsch .05 .02 .01
☐ 220A Mike Aldrete ERR .05 .02 .01
(25 on back)
☐ 220B Mike Aldrete COR .10 .05 .01
(24 on back)
☐ 221 Steve Buechele .05 .02 .01
☐ 222 Jesse Barfield .05 .02 .01
☐ 223 Juan Berenguer .05 .02 .01
☐ 224 Andy McGaffigan .05 .02 .01
☐ 225 Pete Smith .05 .02 .01
☐ 226 Mike Witt .05 .02 .01
☐ 227 Jay Howell .05 .02 .01
☐ 228 Scott Bradley .05 .02 .01
☐ 229 Jerome Walton .05 .02 .01
☐ 230 Greg Swindell .10 .05 .01
☐ 231 Atlee Hammaker .05 .02 .01
☐ 232A Mike Devereaux ERR .10 .05 .01
(RF on front)
☐ 232B Mike Devereaux COR 1.00 .45 .13
(CF on front)
☐ 233 Ken Hill .15 .07 .02
☐ 234 Craig Worthington .05 .02 .01
☐ 235 Scott Terry .05 .02 .01
☐ 236 Brett Butler .10 .05 .01
☐ 237 Doyle Alexander .05 .02 .01
☐ 238 Dave Anderson .05 .02 .01
☐ 239 Bob Milacki .05 .02 .01
☐ 240 Dwight Smith .05 .02 .01
☐ 241 Otis Nixon .10 .05 .01
☐ 242 Pat Tabler .05 .02 .01
☐ 243 Derek Lilliquist .05 .02 .01
☐ 244 Danny Tartabull .10 .05 .01
☐ 245 Wade Boggs .20 .09 .03
☐ 246 Scott Garrelts .05 .02 .01
(Should say Relief Pitcher on front)
☐ 247 Spike Owen .05 .02 .01
☐ 248 Norm Charlton .10 .05 .01
☐ 249 Gerald Perry .05 .02 .01
☐ 250 Nolan Ryan .75 .35 .09
☐ 251 Kevin Gross .05 .02 .01
☐ 252 Randy Milligan .05 .02 .01
☐ 253 Mike LaCoss .05 .02 .01
☐ 254 Dave Bergman .05 .02 .01
☐ 255 Tony Gwynn .25 .11 .03
☐ 256 Felix Fermin .05 .02 .01
☐ 257 Greg W. Harris .05 .02 .01
☐ 258 Junior Felix .05 .02 .01
☐ 259 Mark Davis .05 .02 .01
☐ 260 Vince Coleman .10 .05 .01
☐ 261 Paul Gibson .05 .02 .01
☐ 262 Mitch Williams .10 .05 .01
☐ 263 Jeff Russell .05 .02 .01
☐ 264 Omar Vizquel .05 .02 .01
☐ 265 Andre Dawson .15 .07 .02
☐ 266 Storm Davis .05 .02 .01
☐ 267 Guillermo Hernandez .05 .02 .01
☐ 268 Mike Felder .05 .02 .01
☐ 269 Tom Candiotti .05 .02 .01
☐ 270 Bruce Hurst .05 .02 .01
☐ 271 Fred McGriff .30 .14 .04
☐ 272 Glenn Davis .05 .02 .01
☐ 273 John Franco .10 .05 .01
☐ 274 Rich Yett .05 .02 .01
☐ 275 Craig Biggio .15 .07 .02
☐ 276 Gene Larkin .05 .02 .01
☐ 277 Rob Dibble .10 .05 .01
☐ 278 Randy Bush .05 .02 .01
☐ 279 Kevin Bass .05 .02 .01
☐ 280A Bo Jackson ERR .20 .09 .03
(Watham)

	#	Player			
☐	280B	Bo Jackson COR (Wathan)	.50	.23	.06
☐	281	Wally Backman	.05	.02	.01
☐	282	Larry Andersen	.05	.02	.01
☐	283	Chris Bosio	.05	.02	.01
☐	284	Juan Agosto	.05	.02	.01
☐	285	Ozzie Smith	.25	.11	.03
☐	286	George Bell	.10	.05	.01
☐	287	Rex Hudler	.05	.02	.01
☐	288	Pat Borders	.10	.05	.01
☐	289	Danny Jackson	.05	.02	.01
☐	290	Carlton Fisk	.15	.07	.02
☐	291	Tracy Jones	.05	.02	.01
☐	292	Allan Anderson	.05	.02	.01
☐	293	Johnny Ray	.05	.02	.01
☐	294	Lee Guetterman	.05	.02	.01
☐	295	Paul O'Neill	.10	.05	.01
☐	296	Carney Lansford	.10	.05	.01
☐	297	Tom Brookens	.05	.02	.01
☐	298	Claudell Washington	.05	.02	.01
☐	299	Hubie Brooks	.05	.02	.01
☐	300	Will Clark	.25	.11	.03
☐	301	Kenny Rogers	.05	.02	.01
☐	302	Darrell Evans	.10	.05	.01
☐	303	Greg Briley	.05	.02	.01
☐	304	Donn Pall	.05	.02	.01
☐	305	Teddy Higuera	.05	.02	.01
☐	306	Dan Pasqua	.05	.02	.01
☐	307	Dave Winfield	.15	.07	.02
☐	308	Dennis Powell	.05	.02	.01
☐	309	Jose DeLeon	.05	.02	.01
☐	310	Roger Clemens UER (Dominate, should say dominant)	.30	.14	.04
☐	311	Melido Perez	.05	.02	.01
☐	312	Devon White	.10	.05	.01
☐	313	Dwight Gooden	.10	.05	.01
☐	314	Carlos Martinez	.05	.02	.01
☐	315	Dennis Eckersley	.15	.07	.02
☐	316	Clay Parker UER (Height 6'11")	.05	.02	.01
☐	317	Rick Honeycutt	.05	.02	.01
☐	318	Tim Laudner	.05	.02	.01
☐	319	Joe Carter	.25	.11	.03
☐	320	Robin Yount	.20	.09	.03
☐	321	Felix Jose	.10	.05	.01
☐	322	Mickey Tettleton	.10	.05	.01
☐	323	Mike Gallego	.05	.02	.01
☐	324	Edgar Martinez	.10	.05	.01
☐	325	Dave Henderson	.05	.02	.01
☐	326	Chili Davis	.10	.05	.01
☐	327	Steve Balboni	.05	.02	.01
☐	328	Jody Davis	.05	.02	.01
☐	329	Shawn Hillegas	.05	.02	.01
☐	330	Jim Abbott	.15	.07	.02
☐	331	John Dopson	.05	.02	.01
☐	332	Mark Williamson	.05	.02	.01
☐	333	Jeff D. Robinson	.05	.02	.01
☐	334	John Smiley	.05	.02	.01
☐	335	Bobby Thigpen	.05	.02	.01
☐	336	Garry Templeton	.05	.02	.01
☐	337	Marvell Wynne	.05	.02	.01
☐	338A	Ken Griffey ERR (Uniform number on back listed as 25)	.10	.05	.01
☐	338B	Ken Griffey COR (Uniform number on back listed as 30)	1.50	.65	.19
☐	339	Steve Finley	.10	.05	.01
☐	340	Ellis Burks	.10	.05	.01
☐	341	Frank Williams	.05	.02	.01
☐	342	Mike Morgan	.05	.02	.01
☐	343	Kevin Mitchell	.10	.05	.01
☐	344	Joel Youngblood	.05	.02	.01
☐	345	Mike Greenwell	.10	.05	.01
☐	346	Glenn Wilson	.05	.02	.01
☐	347	John Costello	.05	.02	.01
☐	348	Wes Gardner	.05	.02	.01
☐	349	Jeff Ballard	.05	.02	.01
☐	350	Mark Thurmond UER (ERA is 192, should be 1.92)	.05	.02	.01
☐	351	Randy Myers	.10	.05	.01
☐	352	Shawn Abner	.05	.02	.01
☐	353	Jesse Orosco	.05	.02	.01
☐	354	Greg Walker	.05	.02	.01
☐	355	Pete Harnisch	.10	.05	.01
☐	356	Steve Farr	.05	.02	.01
☐	357	Dave LaPoint	.05	.02	.01
☐	358	Willie Fraser	.05	.02	.01
☐	359	Mickey Hatcher	.05	.02	.01
☐	360	Rickey Henderson	.15	.07	.02
☐	361	Mike Fitzgerald	.05	.02	.01
☐	362	Bill Schroeder	.05	.02	.01
☐	363	Mark Carreon	.05	.02	.01
☐	364	Ron Jones	.05	.02	.01
☐	365	Jeff Montgomery	.10	.05	.01
☐	366	Bill Krueger	.05	.02	.01
☐	367	John Cangelosi	.05	.02	.01
☐	368	Jose Gonzalez	.05	.02	.01
☐	369	Greg Hibbard	.05	.02	.01
☐	370	John Smoltz	.15	.07	.02
☐	371	Jeff Brantley	.05	.02	.01
☐	372	Frank White	.10	.05	.01
☐	373	Ed Whitson	.05	.02	.01
☐	374	Willie McGee	.10	.05	.01
☐	375	Jose Canseco	.30	.14	.04
☐	376	Randy Ready	.05	.02	.01
☐	377	Don Aase	.05	.02	.01
☐	378	Tony Armas	.05	.02	.01
☐	379	Steve Bedrosian	.05	.02	.01
☐	380	Chuck Finley	.10	.05	.01
☐	381	Kent Hrbek	.10	.05	.01
☐	382	Jim Gantner	.05	.02	.01
☐	383	Mel Hall	.05	.02	.01
☐	384	Mike Marshall	.05	.02	.01
☐	385	Mark McGwire	.15	.07	.02
☐	386	Wayne Tolleson	.05	.02	.01
☐	387	Brian Holman	.05	.02	.01
☐	388	John Wetteland	.10	.05	.01
☐	389	Darren Daulton	.15	.07	.02
☐	390	Rob Deer	.05	.02	.01
☐	391	John Moses	.05	.02	.01
☐	392	Todd Worrell	.05	.02	.01
☐	393	Chuck Cary	.05	.02	.01
☐	394	Stan Javier	.05	.02	.01
☐	395	Willie Randolph	.10	.05	.01
☐	396	Bill Buckner	.10	.05	.01
☐	397	Robby Thompson	.10	.05	.01
☐	398	Mike Scioscia	.05	.02	.01
☐	399	Lonnie Smith	.05	.02	.01
☐	400	Kirby Puckett	.35	.16	.04
☐	401	Mark Langston	.15	.07	.02
☐	402	Danny Darwin	.05	.02	.01
☐	403	Greg Maddux	.30	.14	.04
☐	404	Lloyd Moseby	.05	.02	.01
☐	405	Rafael Palmeiro	.15	.07	.02
☐	406	Chad Kreuter	.05	.02	.01
☐	407	Jimmy Key	.10	.05	.01
☐	408	Tim Birtsas	.05	.02	.01
☐	409	Tim Raines	.15	.07	.02
☐	410	Dave Stewart	.10	.05	.01
☐	411	Eric Yelding	.05	.02	.01
☐	412	Kent Anderson	.05	.02	.01
☐	413	Les Lancaster	.05	.02	.01
☐	414	Rick Dempsey	.05	.02	.01

	No.	Player			
☐	415	Randy Johnson	.20	.09	.03
☐	416	Gary Carter	.15	.07	.02
☐	417	Rolando Roomes	.05	.02	.01
☐	418	Dan Schatzeder	.05	.02	.01
☐	419	Bryn Smith	.05	.02	.01
☐	420	Ruben Sierra	.15	.07	.02
☐	421	Steve Jeltz	.05	.02	.01
☐	422	Ken Oberkfell	.05	.02	.01
☐	423	Sid Bream	.05	.02	.01
☐	424	Jim Clancy	.05	.02	.01
☐	425	Kelly Gruber	.05	.02	.01
☐	426	Rick Leach	.05	.02	.01
☐	427	Len Dykstra	.15	.07	.02
☐	428	Jeff Pico	.05	.02	.01
☐	429	John Cerutti	.05	.02	.01
☐	430	David Cone	.15	.07	.02
☐	431	Jeff Kunkel	.05	.02	.01
☐	432	Luis Aquino	.05	.02	.01
☐	433	Ernie Whitt	.05	.02	.01
☐	434	Bo Diaz	.05	.02	.01
☐	435	Steve Lake	.05	.02	.01
☐	436	Pat Perry	.05	.02	.01
☐	437	Mike Davis	.05	.02	.01
☐	438	Cecilio Guante	.05	.02	.01
☐	439	Duane Ward	.10	.05	.01
☐	440	Andy Van Slyke	.15	.07	.02
☐	441	Gene Nelson	.05	.02	.01
☐	442	Luis Polonia	.10	.05	.01
☐	443	Kevin Elster	.05	.02	.01
☐	444	Keith Moreland	.05	.02	.01
☐	445	Roger McDowell	.05	.02	.01
☐	446	Ron Darling	.05	.02	.01
☐	447	Ernest Riles	.05	.02	.01
☐	448	Mookie Wilson	.05	.02	.01
☐	449A	Billy Spiers ERR (No birth year)	.75	.35	.09
☐	449B	Billy Spiers COR (Born in 1966)	.05	.02	.01
☐	450	Rick Sutcliffe	.10	.05	.01
☐	451	Nelson Santovenia	.05	.02	.01
☐	452	Andy Allanson	.05	.02	.01
☐	453	Bob Melvin	.05	.02	.01
☐	454	Benito Santiago	.10	.05	.01
☐	455	Jose Uribe	.05	.02	.01
☐	456	Bill Landrum	.05	.02	.01
☐	457	Bobby Witt	.05	.02	.01
☐	458	Kevin Romine	.05	.02	.01
☐	459	Lee Mazzilli	.05	.02	.01
☐	460	Paul Molitor	.20	.09	.03
☐	461	Ramon Martinez	.10	.05	.01
☐	462	Frank DiPino	.05	.02	.01
☐	463	Walt Terrell	.05	.02	.01
☐	464	Bob Geren	.05	.02	.01
☐	465	Rick Reuschel	.05	.02	.01
☐	466	Mark Grant	.05	.02	.01
☐	467	John Kruk	.15	.07	.02
☐	468	Gregg Jefferies	.25	.11	.03
☐	469	R.J. Reynolds	.05	.02	.01
☐	470	Harold Baines	.10	.05	.01
☐	471	Dennis Lamp	.05	.02	.01
☐	472	Tom Gordon	.10	.05	.01
☐	473	Terry Puhl	.05	.02	.01
☐	474	Curt Wilkerson	.05	.02	.01
☐	475	Dan Quisenberry	.10	.05	.01
☐	476	Oddibe McDowell	.05	.02	.01
☐	477	Zane Smith UER (Career ERA .393)	.05	.02	.01
☐	478	Franklin Stubbs	.05	.02	.01
☐	479	Wallace Johnson	.05	.02	.01
☐	480	Jay Tibbs	.05	.02	.01
☐	481	Tom Glavine	.25	.11	.03
☐	482	Manny Lee	.05	.02	.01
☐	483	Joe Hesketh UER (Says Rookiess on back, should say Rookies)	.05	.02	.01
☐	484	Mike Bielecki	.05	.02	.01
☐	485	Greg Brock	.05	.02	.01
☐	486	Pascual Perez	.05	.02	.01
☐	487	Kirk Gibson	.10	.05	.01
☐	488	Scott Sanderson	.05	.02	.01
☐	489	Domingo Ramos	.05	.02	.01
☐	490	Kal Daniels	.05	.02	.01
☐	491A	David Wells ERR (Reverse negative photo on card back)	1.50	.65	.19
☐	491B	David Wells COR	.05	.02	.01
☐	492	Jerry Reed	.05	.02	.01
☐	493	Eric Show	.05	.02	.01
☐	494	Mike Pagliarulo	.05	.02	.01
☐	495	Ron Robinson	.05	.02	.01
☐	496	Brad Komminsk	.05	.02	.01
☐	497	Greg Litton	.05	.02	.01
☐	498	Chris James	.05	.02	.01
☐	499	Luis Quinones	.05	.02	.01
☐	500	Frank Viola	.10	.05	.01
☐	501	Tim Teufel UER (Twins '85, the s is lower case, should be upper case)	.05	.02	.01
☐	502	Terry Leach	.05	.02	.01
☐	503	Matt Williams UER (Wearing 10 on front, listed as 9 on back)	.25	.11	.03
☐	504	Tim Leary	.05	.02	.01
☐	505	Doug Drabek	.15	.07	.02
☐	506	Mariano Duncan	.05	.02	.01
☐	507	Charlie Hayes	.10	.05	.01
☐	508	Joey Belle	1.00	.45	.13
☐	509	Pat Sheridan	.05	.02	.01
☐	510	Mackey Sasser	.05	.02	.01
☐	511	Jose Rijo	.10	.05	.01
☐	512	Mike Smithson	.05	.02	.01
☐	513	Gary Ward	.05	.02	.01
☐	514	Dion James	.05	.02	.01
☐	515	Jim Gott	.05	.02	.01
☐	516	Drew Hall	.05	.02	.01
☐	517	Doug Bair	.05	.02	.01
☐	518	Scott Scudder	.05	.02	.01
☐	519	Rick Aguilera	.10	.05	.01
☐	520	Rafael Belliard	.05	.02	.01
☐	521	Jay Buhner	.15	.07	.02
☐	522	Jeff Reardon	.15	.07	.02
☐	523	Steve Rosenberg	.05	.02	.01
☐	524	Randy Velarde	.05	.02	.01
☐	525	Jeff Musselman	.05	.02	.01
☐	526	Bill Long	.05	.02	.01
☐	527	Gary Wayne	.05	.02	.01
☐	528	Dave Johnson (P)	.05	.02	.01
☐	529	Ron Kittle	.05	.02	.01
☐	530	Erik Hanson UER (5th line on back says seson, should say season)	.10	.05	.01
☐	531	Steve Wilson	.05	.02	.01
☐	532	Joey Meyer	.05	.02	.01
☐	533	Curt Young	.05	.02	.01
☐	534	Kelly Downs	.05	.02	.01
☐	535	Joe Girardi	.05	.02	.01
☐	536	Lance Blankenship	.05	.02	.01
☐	537	Greg Mathews	.05	.02	.01
☐	538	Donell Nixon	.05	.02	.01
☐	539	Mark Knudson	.05	.02	.01
☐	540	Jeff Wetherby	.05	.02	.01
☐	541	Darrin Jackson	.05	.02	.01
☐	542	Terry Mulholland	.10	.05	.01
☐	543	Eric Hetzel	.05	.02	.01

☐ 544 Rick Reed .... .05 .02 .01
☐ 545 Dennis Cook .... .05 .02 .01
☐ 546 Mike Jackson.............. .05 .02 .01
☐ 547 Brian Fisher................. .05 .02 .01
☐ 548 Gene Harris.................. .10 .05 .01
☐ 549 Jeff King .... .10 .05 .01
☐ 550 Dave Dravecky .... .10 .05 .01
☐ 551 Randy Kutcher.............. .05 .02 .01
☐ 552 Mark Portugal............... .05 .02 .01
☐ 553 Jim Corsi .... .05 .02 .01
☐ 554 Todd Stottlemyre.......... .10 .05 .01
☐ 555 Scott Bankhead............ .05 .02 .01
☐ 556 Ken Dayley................... .05 .02 .01
☐ 557 Rick Wrona .... .05 .02 .01
☐ 558 Sammy Sosa................ .50 .23 .06
☐ 559 Keith Miller .... .05 .02 .01
☐ 560 Ken Griffey Jr............. 2.50 1.15 .30
☐ 561A Ryne Sandberg HL · 10.00 4.50 1.25
ERR (Position on front listed as 3B)
☐ 561B Ryne Sandberg HL COR .20 .09 .03
☐ 562 Billy Hatcher .... .05 .02 .01
☐ 563 Jay Bell .... .10 .05 .01
☐ 564 Jack Daugherty............ .05 .02 .01
☐ 565 Rich Monteleone.......... .05 .02 .01
☐ 566 Bo Jackson AS-MVP.... .05 .02 .01
☐ 567 Tony Fossas................ .05 .02 .01
☐ 568 Roy Smith..................... .05 .02 .01
☐ 569 Jaime Navarro.............. .05 .02 .01
☐ 570 Lance Johnson .... .10 .05 .01
☐ 571 Mike Dyer .... .05 .02 .01
☐ 572 Kevin Ritz..................... .05 .02 .01
☐ 573 Dave West..................... .05 .02 .01
☐ 574 Gary Mielke.................. .05 .02 .01
☐ 575 Scott Lusader .... .05 .02 .01
☐ 576 Joe Oliver..................... .05 .02 .01
☐ 577 Sandy Alomar Jr. .... .10 .05 .01
☐ 578 Andy Benes UER.......... .15 .07 .02
(Extra comma between day and year)
☐ 579 Tim Jones..................... .05 .02 .01
☐ 580 Randy McCament .... .05 .02 .01
☐ 581 Curt Schilling .... .10 .05 .01
☐ 582 John Orton.................... .05 .02 .01
☐ 583A Milt Cuyler ERR .... .75 .35 .09
(998 games)
☐ 583B Milt Cuyler COR......... .05 .02 .01
(98 games; the extra 9 was ghosted out and may still be visible)
☐ 584 Eric Anthony .... .15 .07 .02
☐ 585 Greg Vaughn................ .20 .09 .03
☐ 586 Deion Sanders .... .50 .23 .06
☐ 587 Jose DeJesus.............. .05 .02 .01
☐ 588 Chip Hale .... .05 .02 .01
☐ 589 John Olerud .... .60 .25 .08
☐ 590 Steve Olin .... .10 .05 .01
☐ 591 Marquis Grissom .... .50 .23 .06
☐ 592 Moises Alou................. .50 .23 .06
☐ 593 Mark Lemke.................. .10 .05 .01
☐ 594 Dean Palmer .... .25 .11 .03
☐ 595 Robin Ventura.............. .50 .23 .06
☐ 596 Tino Martinez .... .10 .05 .01
☐ 597 Mike Huff....................... .05 .02 .01
☐ 598 Scott Hemond.............. .05 .02 .01
☐ 599 Wally Whitehurst .... .05 .02 .01
☐ 600 Todd Zeile.................... .15 .07 .02
☐ 601 Glenallen Hill................ .05 .02 .01
☐ 602 Hal Morris..................... .10 .05 .01
☐ 603 Juan Bell...................... .05 .02 .01
☐ 604 Bobby Rose .... .10 .05 .01
☐ 605 Matt Merullo .... .05 .02 .01
☐ 606 Kevin Maas .... .05 .02 .01
☐ 607 Randy Nosek................ .05 .02 .01
☐ 608A Billy Bates................. .10 .05 .01
(Text mentions 12 triples in tenth line)
☐ 608B Billy Bates.................. .10 .05 .01
(Text has no mention of triples)
☐ 609 Mike Stanton................ .05 .02 .01
☐ 610 Mauro Gozzo................ .05 .02 .01
☐ 611 Charles Nagy............... .25 .11 .03
☐ 612 Scott Coolbaugh .... .05 .02 .01
☐ 613 Jose Vizcaino.............. .05 .02 .01
☐ 614 Greg Smith .... .05 .02 .01
☐ 615 Jeff Huson .... .05 .02 .01
☐ 616 Mickey Weston .... .05 .02 .01
☐ 617 John Pawlowski........... .05 .02 .01
☐ 618A Joe Skalski ERR......... .05 .02 .01
(27 on back)
☐ 618B Joe Skalski COR ...... 1.00 .45 .13
(67 on back)
☐ 619 Bernie Williams........... .25 .11 .03
☐ 620 Shawn Holman .... .05 .02 .01
☐ 621 Gary Eave..................... .05 .02 .01
☐ 622 Darrin Fletcher UER ..... .10 .05 .01
(Elmherst, should be Elmhurst)
☐ 623 Pat Combs................... .05 .02 .01
☐ 624 Mike Blowers............... .05 .02 .01
☐ 625 Kevin Appier .... .30 .14 .04
☐ 626 Pat Austin..................... .05 .02 .01
☐ 627 Kelly Mann.................... .05 .02 .01
☐ 628 Matt Kinzer .... .10 .05 .01
☐ 629 Chris Hammond........... .15 .07 .02
☐ 630 Dean Wilkins................ .05 .02 .01
☐ 631 Larry Walker UER .... .50 .23 .06
(Uniform number 55 on front and 33 on back; Home is Maple Ridge, not Maple River)
☐ 632 Blaine Beatty............... .05 .02 .01
☐ 633A Tommy Barrett ERR... .05 .02 .01
(29 on back)
☐ 633B Tommy Barrett COR 2.00 .90 .25
(14 on back)
☐ 634 Stan Belinda................ .05 .02 .01
☐ 635 Mike (Tex) Smith .... .05 .02 .01
☐ 636 Hensley Meulens......... .05 .02 .01
☐ 637 Juan Gonzalez UER.... 2.00 .90 .25
(Sarasots on back, should be Sarasota)
☐ 638 Lenny Webster............. .05 .02 .01
☐ 639 Mark Gardner............... .05 .02 .01
☐ 640 Tommy Greene .... .15 .07 .02
☐ 641 Mike Hartley................. .05 .02 .01
☐ 642 Phil Stephenson........... .05 .02 .01
☐ 643 Kevin Mmahat.............. .05 .02 .01
☐ 644 Ed Whited .... .05 .02 .01
☐ 645 Delino DeShields......... .20 .09 .03
☐ 646 Kevin Blankenship........ .05 .02 .01
☐ 647 Paul Sorrento............... .15 .07 .02
☐ 648 Mike Roesler................ .05 .02 .01
☐ 649 Jason Grimsley .... .05 .02 .01
☐ 650 David Justice .... 1.00 .45 .13
☐ 651 Scott Cooper................ .25 .11 .03
☐ 652 Dave Eiland.................. .05 .02 .01
☐ 653 Mike Munoz.................. .05 .02 .01
☐ 654 Jeff Fischer .... .05 .02 .01
☐ 655 Terry Jorgensen........... .05 .02 .01
☐ 656 George Canale............. .05 .02 .01
☐ 657 Brian DuBois UER......... .05 .02 .01
(Misspelled Dubois on card)
☐ 658 Carlos Quintana .... .05 .02 .01

☐ 659 Luis de los Santos	.05	.02	.01
☐ 660 Jerald Clark	.05	.02	.01
☐ 661 Donald Harris DC	.05	.02	.01
☐ 662 Paul Coleman DC	.05	.02	.01
☐ 663 Frank Thomas DC	4.00	1.80	.50
☐ 664 Brent Mayne DC	.05	.02	.01
☐ 665 Eddie Zosky DC	.05	.02	.01
☐ 666 Steve Hosey DC	.15	.07	.02
☐ 667 Scott Bryant DC	.05	.02	.01
☐ 668 Tom Goodwin DC	.05	.02	.01
☐ 669 Cal Eldred DC	.25	.11	.03
☐ 670 Earl Cunningham DC	.05	.02	.01
☐ 671 Alan Zinter DC	.05	.02	.01
☐ 672 Chuck Knoblauch DC	.50	.23	.06
☐ 673 Kyle Abbott DC	.05	.02	.01
☐ 674 Roger Salkeld DC	.15	.07	.02
☐ 675 Maurice Vaughn DC	.75	.35	.09
☐ 676 Keith(Kiki) Jones DC	.05	.02	.01
☐ 677 Tyler Houston DC	.05	.02	.01
☐ 678 Jeff Jackson DC	.05	.02	.01
☐ 679 Greg Gohr DC	.05	.02	.01
☐ 680 Ben McDonald DC	.40	.18	.05
☐ 681 Greg Blosser DC	.15	.07	.02
☐ 682 Willie Green DC UER (Name misspelled on card, should be Greene)	.25	.11	.03
☐ 683 Wade Boggs DT UER (Text says 215 hits in '89, should be 205)	.20	.09	.03
☐ 684 Will Clark DT	.20	.09	.03
☐ 685 Tony Gwynn DT UER (Text reads battling instead of batting)	.15	.07	.02
☐ 686 Rickey Henderson DT	.15	.07	.02
☐ 687 Bo Jackson DT	.20	.09	.03
☐ 688 Mark Langston DT	.15	.07	.02
☐ 689 Barry Larkin DT	.15	.07	.02
☐ 690 Kirby Puckett DT	.25	.11	.03
☐ 691 Ryne Sandberg DT	.25	.11	.03
☐ 692 Mike Scott DT	.10	.05	.01
☐ 693A Terry Steinbach DT ERR (cathers)	.10	.05	.01
☐ 693B Terry Steinbach DT COR (catchers)	.10	.05	.01
☐ 694 Bobby Thigpen DT	.10	.05	.01
☐ 695 Mitch Williams DT	.10	.05	.01
☐ 696 Nolan Ryan HL	.35	.16	.04
☐ 697 Bo Jackson FB/BB	1.50	.65	.19
☐ 698 Rickey Henderson ALCS-MVP	.10	.05	.01
☐ 699 Will Clark NLCS-MVP	.15	.07	.02
☐ 700 WS Games 1/2 (Dave Stewart and Mike Moore)	.05	.02	.01
☐ 701 Lights Out: Candlestick 5:04pm (10/17/89)	.10	.05	.01
☐ 702 WS Game 3 Bashers Blast Giants (Carney Lansford, Ricky Henderson, Jose Canseco, Dave Henderson)	.05	.02	.01
☐ 703 WS Game 4/Wrap-up A's Sweep Battle of of the Bay (A's Celebrate)	.05	.02	.01
☐ 704 Wade Boggs HL Wade Raps 200	.15	.07	.02

1990 Score Rookie Dream Team

A ten-card set of Dream Team Rookies was inserted into each hobby factory set, but was not included in retail factory sets. These standard size (2 1/2" by 3 1/2") cards carry a B prefix on the card number and include a player at each position plus a commemorative card honoring the late Baseball Commissioner A. Bartlett Giamatti.

	MINT	EXC	G-VG
COMPLETE SET (10)	6.00	2.70	.75
COMMON CARD (B1-B10)	.20	.09	.03
☐ B1 A.Bartlett Giamatti COMM MEM	.50	.23	.06
☐ B2 Pat Combs	.20	.09	.03
☐ B3 Todd Zeile	.50	.23	.06
☐ B4 Luis de los Santos	.20	.09	.03
☐ B5 Mark Lemke	.35	.16	.04
☐ B6 Robin Ventura	2.00	.90	.25
☐ B7 Jeff Huson	.20	.09	.03
☐ B8 Greg Vaughn	1.00	.45	.13
☐ B9 Marquis Grissom	2.00	.90	.25
☐ B10 Eric Anthony	.35	.16	.04

1990 Score Rookie/Traded

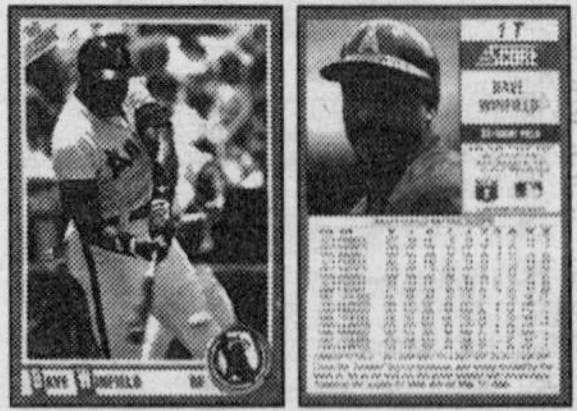

The 1990 Score Rookie and Traded set marks the third consecutive year Score has issued an end of the year set to mark trades and give rookies early cards. The set con-

sists of 110 cards each measuring the standard size of 2 1/2" by 3 1/2". The first 66 cards are traded players while the last 44 cards are rookie cards. Included in the set are multi-sport athletes Eric Lindros (hockey) and D.J. Dozier (football). Rookie Cards in the set include Carlos Baerga, Derek Bell, Dave Hollins, and Ray Lankford.

	MINT	EXC	G-VG
COMPLETE FACT.SET (110)	10.00	4.50	1.25
COMMON CARD (1T-110T)	.05	.02	.01

	MINT	EXC	G-VG
☐ 1T Dave Winfield	.10	.05	.01
☐ 2T Kevin Bass	.05	.02	.01
☐ 3T Nick Esasky	.05	.02	.01
☐ 4T Mitch Webster	.05	.02	.01
☐ 5T Pascual Perez	.05	.02	.01
☐ 6T Gary Pettis	.05	.02	.01
☐ 7T Tony Pena	.05	.02	.01
☐ 8T Candy Maldonado	.05	.02	.01
☐ 9T Cecil Fielder	.20	.09	.03
☐ 10T Carmelo Martinez	.05	.02	.01
☐ 11T Mark Langston	.10	.05	.01
☐ 12T Dave Parker	.10	.05	.01
☐ 13T Don Slaught	.05	.02	.01
☐ 14T Tony Phillips	.08	.04	.01
☐ 15T John Franco	.08	.04	.01
☐ 16T Randy Myers	.08	.04	.01
☐ 17T Jeff Reardon	.10	.05	.01
☐ 18T Sandy Alomar Jr.	.08	.04	.01
☐ 19T Joe Carter	.40	.18	.05
☐ 20T Fred Lynn	.08	.04	.01
☐ 21T Storm Davis	.05	.02	.01
☐ 22T Craig Lefferts	.05	.02	.01
☐ 23T Pete O'Brien	.05	.02	.01
☐ 24T Dennis Boyd	.05	.02	.01
☐ 25T Lloyd Moseby	.05	.02	.01
☐ 26T Mark Davis	.05	.02	.01
☐ 27T Tim Leary	.05	.02	.01
☐ 28T Gerald Perry	.05	.02	.01
☐ 29T Don Aase	.05	.02	.01
☐ 30T Ernie Whitt	.05	.02	.01
☐ 31T Dale Murphy	.10	.05	.01
☐ 32T Alejandro Pena	.05	.02	.01
☐ 33T Juan Samuel	.05	.02	.01
☐ 34T Hubie Brooks	.05	.02	.01
☐ 35T Gary Carter	.10	.05	.01
☐ 36T Jim Presley	.05	.02	.01
☐ 37T Wally Backman	.05	.02	.01
☐ 38T Matt Nokes	.05	.02	.01
☐ 39T Dan Petry	.05	.02	.01
☐ 40T Franklin Stubbs	.05	.02	.01
☐ 41T Jeff Huson	.05	.02	.01
☐ 42T Billy Hatcher	.05	.02	.01
☐ 43T Terry Leach	.05	.02	.01
☐ 44T Phil Bradley	.05	.02	.01
☐ 45T Claudell Washington	.05	.02	.01
☐ 46T Luis Polonia	.08	.04	.01
☐ 47T Daryl Boston	.05	.02	.01
☐ 48T Lee Smith	.10	.05	.01
☐ 49T Tom Brunansky	.05	.02	.01
☐ 50T Mike Witt	.05	.02	.01
☐ 51T Willie Randolph	.08	.04	.01
☐ 52T Stan Javier	.05	.02	.01
☐ 53T Brad Komminsk	.05	.02	.01
☐ 54T John Candelaria	.05	.02	.01
☐ 55T Bryn Smith	.05	.02	.01
☐ 56T Glenn Braggs	.05	.02	.01
☐ 57T Keith Hernandez	.08	.04	.01
☐ 58T Ken Oberkfell	.05	.02	.01
☐ 59T Steve Jeltz	.05	.02	.01
☐ 60T Chris James	.05	.02	.01
☐ 61T Scott Sanderson	.05	.02	.01
☐ 62T Bill Long	.05	.02	.01
☐ 63T Rick Cerone	.05	.02	.01
☐ 64T Scott Bailes	.05	.02	.01
☐ 65T Larry Sheets	.05	.02	.01
☐ 66T Junior Ortiz	.05	.02	.01
☐ 67T Francisco Cabrera	.05	.02	.01
☐ 68T Gary DiSarcina	.05	.02	.01
☐ 69T Greg Olson	.05	.02	.01
☐ 70T Beau Allred	.05	.02	.01
☐ 71T Oscar Azocar	.05	.02	.01
☐ 72T Kent Mercker	.25	.11	.03
☐ 73T John Burkett	.25	.11	.03
☐ 74T Carlos Baerga	1.00	.45	.13
☐ 75T Dave Hollins	.25	.11	.03
☐ 76T Todd Hundley	.20	.09	.03
☐ 77T Rick Parker	.05	.02	.01
☐ 78T Steve Cummings	.05	.02	.01
☐ 79T Bill Sampen	.05	.02	.01
☐ 80T Jerry Kutzler	.05	.02	.01
☐ 81T Derek Bell	.25	.11	.03
☐ 82T Kevin Tapani	.20	.09	.03
☐ 83T Jim Leyritz	.15	.07	.02
☐ 84T Ray Lankford	.40	.18	.05
☐ 85T Wayne Edwards	.05	.02	.01
☐ 86T Frank Thomas	4.00	1.80	.50
☐ 87T Tim Naehring	.20	.09	.03
☐ 88T Willie Blair	.05	.02	.01
☐ 89T Alan Mills	.05	.02	.01
☐ 90T Scott Radinsky	.05	.02	.01
☐ 91T Howard Farmer	.05	.02	.01
☐ 92T Julio Machado	.05	.02	.01
☐ 93T Rafael Valdez	.05	.02	.01
☐ 94T Shawn Boskie	.05	.02	.01
☐ 95T David Segui	.15	.07	.02
☐ 96T Chris Hoiles	.25	.11	.03
☐ 97T D.J. Dozier	.05	.02	.01
☐ 98T Hector Villanueva	.05	.02	.01
☐ 99T Eric Gunderson	.05	.02	.01
☐ 100T Eric Lindros	4.00	1.80	.50
☐ 101T Dave Otto	.05	.02	.01
☐ 102T Dana Kiecker	.05	.02	.01
☐ 103T Tim Drummond	.05	.02	.01
☐ 104T Mickey Pina	.05	.02	.01
☐ 105T Craig Grebeck	.05	.02	.01
☐ 106T Bernard Gilkey	.25	.11	.03
☐ 107T Tim Layana	.05	.02	.01
☐ 108T Scott Chiamparino	.05	.02	.01
☐ 109T Steve Avery	.50	.23	.06
☐ 110T Terry Shumpert	.05	.02	.01

1991 Score

The 1991 Score set contains 893 cards. The cards feature a solid color border fram-

ing the full-color photo of the cards. The cards measure the standard card size of 2 1/2" by 3 1/2" and also feature Score trademark full-color photos on the back. The backs also include a brief biography on each player. This set marks the fourth consecutive year that Score has issued a major set but the first time Score issued the set in two series. Score also reused their successful Dream Team concept by using non-baseball photos of Today's stars. Series one contains 441 cards and ends with the Annie Leibowitz photo of Jose Canseco used in American Express ads. This first series also includes 49 Rookie Prospects (331-379), 12 First Round Draft Picks (380-393), and five each of the Master Blaster (402-406), K-Man (407-411), and Rifleman (412-416) subsets. The All-Star sets in the first series are all American Leaguers (which are all caricatures). Rookie Cards in the set include Jeromy Burnitz, Wes Chamberlain, Chipper Jones, Steve Karsay, Brian McRae, Mike Mussina, Marc Newfield, Phil Plantier, Todd Van Poppel, and Rondell White. There are a number of pitchers whose card backs show Innings Pitched totals which do not equal the added year-by-year total; the following card numbers were affected, 4, 24, 29, 30, 51, 81, 109, 111, 118, 141, 150, 156, 177, 204, 218, 232, 235, 255, 287, 289, 311, and 328. The second series was issued approximately three months after the release of series one and included many of the special cards Score is noted for, e.g., the continuation of the Dream Team set begun in Series One, All-Star Cartoons featuring National Leaguers, a continuation of the 1990 first round draft picks, and 61 rookie prospects. An American Flag card (737) was issued to honor the American soldiers involved in Desert Storm.

	MINT	EXC	G-VG
COMPLETE SET (893)	15.00	6.75	1.90
COMPLETE FACT.SET (900)	20.00	9.00	2.50
COMMON CARD (1-441)	.05	.02	.01
COMMON CARD (442-893)	.05	.02	.01

	MINT	EXC	G-VG
☐ 1 Jose Canseco	.20	.09	.03
☐ 2 Ken Griffey Jr.	1.50	.65	.19
☐ 3 Ryne Sandberg	.25	.11	.03
☐ 4 Nolan Ryan	.60	.25	.08
☐ 5 Bo Jackson	.15	.07	.02
☐ 6 Bret Saberhagen UER (In bio, missed misspelled as mised)	.10	.05	.01
☐ 7 Will Clark	.20	.09	.03
☐ 8 Ellis Burks	.10	.05	.01
☐ 9 Joe Carter	.20	.09	.03
☐ 10 Rickey Henderson	.15	.07	.02
☐ 11 Ozzie Guillen	.05	.02	.01
☐ 12 Wade Boggs	.15	.07	.02
☐ 13 Jerome Walton	.05	.02	.01
☐ 14 John Franco	.10	.05	.01
☐ 15 Ricky Jordan UER (League misspelled as legue)	.05	.02	.01
☐ 16 Wally Backman	.05	.02	.01
☐ 17 Rob Dibble	.05	.02	.01
☐ 18 Glenn Braggs	.05	.02	.01
☐ 19 Cory Snyder	.05	.02	.01
☐ 20 Kal Daniels	.05	.02	.01
☐ 21 Mark Langston	.15	.07	.02
☐ 22 Kevin Gross	.05	.02	.01
☐ 23 Don Mattingly UER (First line, ' is missing from Yankee)	.30	.14	.04
☐ 24 Dave Righetti	.05	.02	.01
☐ 25 Roberto Alomar	.25	.11	.03
☐ 26 Robby Thompson	.05	.02	.01
☐ 27 Jack McDowell	.15	.07	.02
☐ 28 Bip Roberts UER (Bio reads playd)	.05	.02	.01
☐ 29 Jay Howell	.05	.02	.01
☐ 30 Dave Stieb UER (17 wins in bio, 18 in stats)	.10	.05	.01
☐ 31 Johnny Ray	.05	.02	.01
☐ 32 Steve Sax	.05	.02	.01
☐ 33 Terry Mulholland	.05	.02	.01
☐ 34 Lee Guetterman	.05	.02	.01
☐ 35 Tim Raines	.15	.07	.02
☐ 36 Scott Fletcher	.05	.02	.01
☐ 37 Lance Parrish	.10	.05	.01
☐ 38 Tony Phillips UER (Born 4/15, should be 4/25)	.05	.02	.01
☐ 39 Todd Stottlemyre	.05	.02	.01
☐ 40 Alan Trammell	.15	.07	.02
☐ 41 Todd Burns	.05	.02	.01
☐ 42 Mookie Wilson	.05	.02	.01
☐ 43 Chris Bosio	.05	.02	.01
☐ 44 Jeffrey Leonard	.05	.02	.01
☐ 45 Doug Jones	.05	.02	.01
☐ 46 Mike Scott UER (In first line, dominate should read dominating)	.05	.02	.01
☐ 47 Andy Hawkins	.05	.02	.01
☐ 48 Harold Reynolds	.05	.02	.01
☐ 49 Paul Molitor	.15	.07	.02
☐ 50 John Farrell	.05	.02	.01
☐ 51 Danny Darwin	.05	.02	.01
☐ 52 Jeff Blauser	.10	.05	.01
☐ 53 John Tudor UER (41 wins in '81)	.05	.02	.01
☐ 54 Milt Thompson	.05	.02	.01
☐ 55 David Justice	.35	.16	.04
☐ 56 Greg Olson	.05	.02	.01
☐ 57 Willie Blair	.05	.02	.01
☐ 58 Rick Parker	.05	.02	.01
☐ 59 Shawn Boskie	.05	.02	.01
☐ 60 Kevin Tapani	.05	.02	.01
☐ 61 Dave Hollins	.15	.07	.02
☐ 62 Scott Radinsky	.05	.02	.01
☐ 63 Francisco Cabrera	.05	.02	.01
☐ 64 Tim Layana	.05	.02	.01
☐ 65 Jim Leyritz	.05	.02	.01
☐ 66 Wayne Edwards	.05	.02	.01
☐ 67 Lee Stevens	.05	.02	.01
☐ 68 Bill Sampen UER (Fourth line, long is spelled along)	.05	.02	.01
☐ 69 Craig Grebeck UER (Born in Cerritos, not Johnstown)	.05	.02	.01
☐ 70 John Burkett	.10	.05	.01
☐ 71 Hector Villanueva	.05	.02	.01
☐ 72 Oscar Azocar	.05	.02	.01
☐ 73 Alan Mills	.05	.02	.01
☐ 74 Carlos Baerga	.30	.14	.04
☐ 75 Charles Nagy	.10	.05	.01
☐ 76 Tim Drummond	.05	.02	.01
☐ 77 Dana Kiecker	.05	.02	.01

#	Player			
☐ 78	Tom Edens	.05	.02	.01
☐ 79	Kent Mercker	.10	.05	.01
☐ 80	Steve Avery	.15	.07	.02
☐ 81	Lee Smith	.15	.07	.02
☐ 82	Dave Martinez	.05	.02	.01
☐ 83	Dave Winfield	.15	.07	.02
☐ 84	Bill Spiers	.05	.02	.01
☐ 85	Dan Pasqua	.05	.02	.01
☐ 86	Randy Milligan	.05	.02	.01
☐ 87	Tracy Jones	.05	.02	.01
☐ 88	Greg Myers	.05	.02	.01
☐ 89	Keith Hernandez	.10	.05	.01
☐ 90	Todd Benzinger	.05	.02	.01
☐ 91	Mike Jackson	.05	.02	.01
☐ 92	Mike Stanley	.05	.02	.01
☐ 93	Candy Maldonado	.05	.02	.01
☐ 94	John Kruk UER (No decimal point before 1990 BA)	.15	.07	.02
☐ 95	Cal Ripken UER (Genius spelled genuis)	.35	.16	.04
☐ 96	Willie Fraser	.05	.02	.01
☐ 97	Mike Felder	.05	.02	.01
☐ 98	Bill Landrum	.05	.02	.01
☐ 99	Chuck Crim	.05	.02	.01
☐ 100	Chuck Finley	.10	.05	.01
☐ 101	Kirt Manwaring	.05	.02	.01
☐ 102	Jaime Navarro	.05	.02	.01
☐ 103	Dickie Thon	.05	.02	.01
☐ 104	Brian Downing	.05	.02	.01
☐ 105	Jim Abbott	.15	.07	.02
☐ 106	Tom Brookens	.05	.02	.01
☐ 107	Darryl Hamilton UER (Bio info is for Jeff Hamilton)	.10	.05	.01
☐ 108	Bryan Harvey	.10	.05	.01
☐ 109	Greg A. Harris UER (Shown pitching lefty, bio says righty)	.05	.02	.01
☐ 110	Greg Swindell	.05	.02	.01
☐ 111	Juan Berenguer	.05	.02	.01
☐ 112	Mike Heath	.05	.02	.01
☐ 113	Scott Bradley	.05	.02	.01
☐ 114	Jack Morris	.15	.07	.02
☐ 115	Barry Jones	.05	.02	.01
☐ 116	Kevin Romine	.05	.02	.01
☐ 117	Garry Templeton	.05	.02	.01
☐ 118	Scott Sanderson	.05	.02	.01
☐ 119	Roberto Kelly	.10	.05	.01
☐ 120	George Brett	.30	.14	.04
☐ 121	Oddibe McDowell	.05	.02	.01
☐ 122	Jim Acker	.05	.02	.01
☐ 123	Bill Swift UER (Born 12/27/61, should be 10/27)	.10	.05	.01
☐ 124	Eric King	.05	.02	.01
☐ 125	Jay Buhner	.10	.05	.01
☐ 126	Matt Young	.05	.02	.01
☐ 127	Alvaro Espinoza	.05	.02	.01
☐ 128	Greg Hibbard	.05	.02	.01
☐ 129	Jeff M. Robinson	.05	.02	.01
☐ 130	Mike Greenwell	.10	.05	.01
☐ 131	Dion James	.05	.02	.01
☐ 132	Donn Pall UER (1988 ERA in stats 0.00)	.05	.02	.01
☐ 133	Lloyd Moseby	.05	.02	.01
☐ 134	Randy Velarde	.05	.02	.01
☐ 135	Allan Anderson	.05	.02	.01
☐ 136	Mark Davis	.05	.02	.01
☐ 137	Eric Davis	.10	.05	.01
☐ 138	Phil Stephenson	.05	.02	.01
☐ 139	Felix Fermin	.05	.02	.01
☐ 140	Pedro Guerrero	.10	.05	.01
☐ 141	Charlie Hough	.10	.05	.01
☐ 142	Mike Henneman	.05	.02	.01
☐ 143	Jeff Montgomery	.10	.05	.01
☐ 144	Lenny Harris	.05	.02	.01
☐ 145	Bruce Hurst	.05	.02	.01
☐ 146	Eric Anthony	.10	.05	.01
☐ 147	Paul Assenmacher	.05	.02	.01
☐ 148	Jesse Barfield	.05	.02	.01
☐ 149	Carlos Quintana	.05	.02	.01
☐ 150	Dave Stewart	.10	.05	.01
☐ 151	Roy Smith	.05	.02	.01
☐ 152	Paul Gibson	.05	.02	.01
☐ 153	Mickey Hatcher	.05	.02	.01
☐ 154	Jim Eisenreich	.05	.02	.01
☐ 155	Kenny Rogers	.05	.02	.01
☐ 156	Dave Schmidt	.05	.02	.01
☐ 157	Lance Johnson	.05	.02	.01
☐ 158	Dave West	.05	.02	.01
☐ 159	Steve Balboni	.05	.02	.01
☐ 160	Jeff Brantley	.05	.02	.01
☐ 161	Craig Biggio	.15	.07	.02
☐ 162	Brook Jacoby	.05	.02	.01
☐ 163	Dan Gladden	.05	.02	.01
☐ 164	Jeff Reardon UER (Total IP shown as 943.2, should be 943.1)	.10	.05	.01
☐ 165	Mark Carreon	.05	.02	.01
☐ 166	Mel Hall	.05	.02	.01
☐ 167	Gary Mielke	.05	.02	.01
☐ 168	Cecil Fielder	.15	.07	.02
☐ 169	Darrin Jackson	.05	.02	.01
☐ 170	Rick Aguilera	.10	.05	.01
☐ 171	Walt Weiss	.05	.02	.01
☐ 172	Steve Farr	.05	.02	.01
☐ 173	Jody Reed	.05	.02	.01
☐ 174	Mike Jeffcoat	.05	.02	.01
☐ 175	Mark Grace	.15	.07	.02
☐ 176	Larry Sheets	.05	.02	.01
☐ 177	Bill Gullickson	.05	.02	.01
☐ 178	Chris Gwynn	.05	.02	.01
☐ 179	Melido Perez	.05	.02	.01
☐ 180	Sid Fernandez UER (779 runs in 1990)	.10	.05	.01
☐ 181	Tim Burke	.05	.02	.01
☐ 182	Gary Pettis	.05	.02	.01
☐ 183	Rob Murphy	.05	.02	.01
☐ 184	Craig Lefferts	.05	.02	.01
☐ 185	Howard Johnson	.10	.05	.01
☐ 186	Ken Caminiti	.10	.05	.01
☐ 187	Tim Belcher	.05	.02	.01
☐ 188	Greg Cadaret	.05	.02	.01
☐ 189	Matt Williams	.20	.09	.03
☐ 190	Dave Magadan	.05	.02	.01
☐ 191	Geno Petralli	.05	.02	.01
☐ 192	Jeff D. Robinson	.05	.02	.01
☐ 193	Jim Deshaies	.05	.02	.01
☐ 194	Willie Randolph	.10	.05	.01
☐ 195	George Bell	.10	.05	.01
☐ 196	Hubie Brooks	.05	.02	.01
☐ 197	Tom Gordon	.10	.05	.01
☐ 198	Mike Fitzgerald	.05	.02	.01
☐ 199	Mike Pagliarulo	.05	.02	.01
☐ 200	Kirby Puckett	.30	.14	.04
☐ 201	Shawon Dunston	.05	.02	.01
☐ 202	Dennis Boyd	.05	.02	.01
☐ 203	Junior Felix UER (Text has him in NL)	.05	.02	.01
☐ 204	Alejandro Pena	.05	.02	.01
☐ 205	Pete Smith	.05	.02	.01
☐ 206	Tom Glavine UER (Lefty spelled leftie)	.20	.09	.03
☐ 207	Luis Salazar	.05	.02	.01
☐ 208	John Smoltz	.15	.07	.02

☐ 209 Doug Dascenzo .05 .02 .01
☐ 210 Tim Wallach .05 .02 .01
☐ 211 Greg Gagne .05 .02 .01
☐ 212 Mark Gubicza .05 .02 .01
☐ 213 Mark Parent .05 .02 .01
☐ 214 Ken Oberkfell .05 .02 .01
☐ 215 Gary Carter .15 .07 .02
☐ 216 Rafael Palmeiro .15 .07 .02
☐ 217 Tom Niedenfuer .05 .02 .01
☐ 218 Dave LaPoint .05 .02 .01
☐ 219 Jeff Treadway .05 .02 .01
☐ 220 Mitch Williams UER .10 .05 .01
('89 ERA shown as 2.76, should be 2.64)
☐ 221 Jose DeLeon .05 .02 .01
☐ 222 Mike LaValliere .05 .02 .01
☐ 223 Darrel Akerfelds .05 .02 .01
☐ 224A Kent Anderson ERR .10 .05 .01
(First line, flachy should read flashy)
☐ 224B Kent Anderson COR .10 .05 .01
(Corrected in factory sets)
☐ 225 Dwight Evans .10 .05 .01
☐ 226 Gary Redus .05 .02 .01
☐ 227 Paul O'Neill .10 .05 .01
☐ 228 Marty Barrett .05 .02 .01
☐ 229 Tom Browning .05 .02 .01
☐ 230 Terry Pendleton .15 .07 .02
☐ 231 Jack Armstrong .05 .02 .01
☐ 232 Mike Boddicker .05 .02 .01
☐ 233 Neal Heaton .05 .02 .01
☐ 234 Marquis Grissom .15 .07 .02
☐ 235 Bert Blyleven .15 .07 .02
☐ 236 Curt Young .05 .02 .01
☐ 237 Don Carman .05 .02 .01
☐ 238 Charlie Hayes .10 .05 .01
☐ 239 Mark Knudson .05 .02 .01
☐ 240 Todd Zeile .10 .05 .01
☐ 241 Larry Walker UER .15 .07 .02
(Maple River, should be Maple Ridge)
☐ 242 Jerald Clark .05 .02 .01
☐ 243 Jeff Ballard .05 .02 .01
☐ 244 Jeff King .05 .02 .01
☐ 245 Tom Brunansky .05 .02 .01
☐ 246 Darren Daulton .15 .07 .02
☐ 247 Scott Terry .05 .02 .01
☐ 248 Rob Deer .05 .02 .01
☐ 249 Brady Anderson UER .10 .05 .01
(1990 Hagerstown 1 hit, should say 13 hits)
☐ 250 Len Dykstra .15 .07 .02
☐ 251 Greg W. Harris .05 .02 .01
☐ 252 Mike Hartley .05 .02 .01
☐ 253 Joey Cora .05 .02 .01
☐ 254 Ivan Calderon .05 .02 .01
☐ 255 Ted Power .05 .02 .01
☐ 256 Sammy Sosa .15 .07 .02
☐ 257 Steve Buechele .05 .02 .01
☐ 258 Mike Devereaux UER .10 .05 .01
(No comma between city and state)
☐ 259 Brad Komminsk UER .05 .02 .01
(Last text line, Ba should be BA)
☐ 260 Teddy Higuera .05 .02 .01
☐ 261 Shawn Abner .05 .02 .01
☐ 262 Dave Valle .05 .02 .01
☐ 263 Jeff Huson .05 .02 .01
☐ 264 Edgar Martinez .10 .05 .01
☐ 265 Carlton Fisk .15 .07 .02
☐ 266 Steve Finley .05 .02 .01
☐ 267 John Wetteland .10 .05 .01
☐ 268 Kevin Appier .10 .05 .01
☐ 269 Steve Lyons .05 .02 .01
☐ 270 Mickey Tettleton .10 .05 .01
☐ 271 Luis Rivera .05 .02 .01
☐ 272 Steve Jeltz .05 .02 .01
☐ 273 R.J. Reynolds .05 .02 .01
☐ 274 Carlos Martinez .05 .02 .01
☐ 275 Dan Plesac .05 .02 .01
☐ 276 Mike Morgan UER .05 .02 .01
(Total IP shown as 1149.1, should be 1149)
☐ 277 Jeff Russell .05 .02 .01
☐ 278 Pete Incaviglia .05 .02 .01
☐ 279 Kevin Seitzer UER .05 .02 .01
(Bio has 200 hits twice and .300 four times, should be once and three times)
☐ 280 Bobby Thigpen .05 .02 .01
☐ 281 Stan Javier UER .05 .02 .01
(Born 1/9, should say 9/1)
☐ 282 Henry Cotto .05 .02 .01
☐ 283 Gary Wayne .05 .02 .01
☐ 284 Shane Mack .10 .05 .01
☐ 285 Brian Holman .05 .02 .01
☐ 286 Gerald Perry .05 .02 .01
☐ 287 Steve Crawford .05 .02 .01
☐ 288 Nelson Liriano .05 .02 .01
☐ 289 Don Aase .05 .02 .01
☐ 290 Randy Johnson .15 .07 .02
☐ 291 Harold Baines .10 .05 .01
☐ 292 Kent Hrbek .10 .05 .01
☐ 293A Les Lancaster ERR .05 .02 .01
(No comma between Dallas and Texas)
☐ 293B Les Lancaster COR .05 .02 .01
(Corrected in factory sets)
☐ 294 Jeff Musselman .05 .02 .01
☐ 295 Kurt Stillwell .05 .02 .01
☐ 296 Stan Belinda .05 .02 .01
☐ 297 Lou Whitaker .15 .07 .02
☐ 298 Glenn Wilson .05 .02 .01
☐ 299 Omar Vizquel UER .05 .02 .01
(Born 5/15, should be 4/24, there is a decimal before GP total for '90)
☐ 300 Ramon Martinez .10 .05 .01
☐ 301 Dwight Smith .05 .02 .01
☐ 302 Tim Crews .05 .02 .01
☐ 303 Lance Blankenship .05 .02 .01
☐ 304 Sid Bream .05 .02 .01
☐ 305 Rafael Ramirez .05 .02 .01
☐ 306 Steve Wilson .05 .02 .01
☐ 307 Mackey Sasser .05 .02 .01
☐ 308 Franklin Stubbs .05 .02 .01
☐ 309 Jack Daugherty UER .05 .02 .01
(Born 6/3/60, should say July)
☐ 310 Eddie Murray .15 .07 .02
☐ 311 Bob Welch .05 .02 .01
☐ 312 Brian Harper .05 .02 .01
☐ 313 Lance McCullers .05 .02 .01
☐ 314 Dave Smith .05 .02 .01
☐ 315 Bobby Bonilla .15 .07 .02
☐ 316 Jerry Don Gleaton .05 .02 .01
☐ 317 Greg Maddux .25 .11 .03
☐ 318 Keith Miller .05 .02 .01
☐ 319 Mark Portugal .05 .02 .01
☐ 320 Robin Ventura .20 .09 .03
☐ 321 Bob Ojeda .05 .02 .01

	No.	Player			
☐	322	Mike Harkey	.05	.02	.01
☐	323	Jay Bell	.10	.05	.01
☐	324	Mark McGwire	.15	.07	.02
☐	325	Gary Gaetti	.05	.02	.01
☐	326	Jeff Pico	.05	.02	.01
☐	327	Kevin McReynolds	.05	.02	.01
☐	328	Frank Tanana	.05	.02	.01
☐	329	Eric Yelding UER (Listed as 6'3", should be 5'11")	.05	.02	.01
☐	330	Barry Bonds	.40	.18	.05
☐	331	Brian McRae UER (No comma between city and state)	.30	.14	.04
☐	332	Pedro Munoz	.15	.07	.02
☐	333	Daryl Irvine	.05	.02	.01
☐	334	Chris Hoiles	.15	.07	.02
☐	335	Thomas Howard	.05	.02	.01
☐	336	Jeff Schulz	.05	.02	.01
☐	337	Jeff Manto	.05	.02	.01
☐	338	Beau Allred	.05	.02	.01
☐	339	Mike Bordick	.15	.07	.02
☐	340	Todd Hundley	.10	.05	.01
☐	341	Jim Vatcher UER (Height 6'9", should be 5'9")	.05	.02	.01
☐	342	Luis Sojo	.05	.02	.01
☐	343	Jose Offerman UER (Born 1969, should say 1968)	.10	.05	.01
☐	344	Pete Coachman	.05	.02	.01
☐	345	Mike Benjamin	.05	.02	.01
☐	346	Ozzie Canseco	.05	.02	.01
☐	347	Tim McIntosh	.05	.02	.01
☐	348	Phil Plantier	.30	.14	.04
☐	349	Terry Shumpert	.05	.02	.01
☐	350	Darren Lewis	.10	.05	.01
☐	351	David Walsh	.05	.02	.01
☐	352A	Scott Chiamparino ERR (Bats left, should be right)	.10	.05	.01
☐	352B	Scott Chiamparino COR (corrected in factory sets)	.10	.05	.01
☐	353	Julio Valera UER (Progressed misspelled as progessed)	.05	.02	.01
☐	354	Anthony Telford	.05	.02	.01
☐	355	Kevin Wickander	.05	.02	.01
☐	356	Tim Naehring	.05	.02	.01
☐	357	Jim Poole	.05	.02	.01
☐	358	Mark Whiten UER (Shown hitting lefty, bio says righty)	.15	.07	.02
☐	359	Terry Wells	.05	.02	.01
☐	360	Rafael Valdez	.05	.02	.01
☐	361	Mel Stottlemyre Jr.	.05	.02	.01
☐	362	David Segui	.05	.02	.01
☐	363	Paul Abbott	.05	.02	.01
☐	364	Steve Howard	.05	.02	.01
☐	365	Karl Rhodes	.05	.02	.01
☐	366	Rafael Novoa	.05	.02	.01
☐	367	Joe Grahe	.05	.02	.01
☐	368	Darren Reed	.05	.02	.01
☐	369	Jeff McKnight	.05	.02	.01
☐	370	Scott Leius	.05	.02	.01
☐	371	Mark Dewey	.05	.02	.01
☐	372	Mark Lee UER (Shown hitting lefty, bio says righty, born in Dakota, should say North Dakota)	.05	.02	.01
☐	373	Rosario Rodriguez (Shown hitting lefty, bio says righty) UER	.05	.02	.01
☐	374	Chuck McElroy	.05	.02	.01
☐	375	Mike Bell	.05	.02	.01
☐	376	Mickey Morandini	.05	.02	.01
☐	377	Bill Haselman	.05	.02	.01
☐	378	Dave Pavlas	.05	.02	.01
☐	379	Derrick May	.10	.05	.01
☐	380	Jeromy Burnitz FDP	.15	.07	.02
☐	381	Donald Peters FDP	.05	.02	.01
☐	382	Alex Fernandez FDP	.25	.11	.03
☐	383	Mike Mussina FDP	1.50	.65	.19
☐	384	Dan Smith FDP	.05	.02	.01
☐	385	Lance Dickson FDP	.05	.02	.01
☐	386	Carl Everett FDP	.15	.07	.02
☐	387	Thomas Nevers FDP	.05	.02	.01
☐	388	Adam Hyzdu FDP	.05	.02	.01
☐	389	Todd Van Poppel FDP	.20	.09	.03
☐	390	Rondell White FDP	1.00	.45	.13
☐	391	Marc Newfield FDP	.50	.23	.06
☐	392	Julio Franco AS	.05	.02	.01
☐	393	Wade Boggs AS	.10	.05	.01
☐	394	Ozzie Guillen AS	.05	.02	.01
☐	395	Cecil Fielder AS	.10	.05	.01
☐	396	Ken Griffey Jr. AS	.75	.35	.09
☐	397	Rickey Henderson AS	.10	.05	.01
☐	398	Jose Canseco AS	.15	.07	.02
☐	399	Roger Clemens AS	.15	.07	.02
☐	400	Sandy Alomar Jr. AS	.05	.02	.01
☐	401	Bobby Thigpen AS	.05	.02	.01
☐	402	Bobby Bonilla MB	.10	.05	.01
☐	403	Eric Davis MB	.05	.02	.01
☐	404	Fred McGriff MB	.15	.07	.02
☐	405	Glenn Davis MB	.05	.02	.01
☐	406	Kevin Mitchell MB	.05	.02	.01
☐	407	Rob Dibble KM	.05	.02	.01
☐	408	Ramon Martinez KM	.05	.02	.01
☐	409	David Cone KM	.10	.05	.01
☐	410	Bobby Witt KM	.05	.02	.01
☐	411	Mark Langston KM	.10	.05	.01
☐	412	Bo Jackson RIF	.10	.05	.01
☐	413	Shawon Dunston RIF UER (In the baseball, should say in baseball)	.05	.02	.01
☐	414	Jesse Barfield RIF	.05	.02	.01
☐	415	Ken Caminiti RIF	.05	.02	.01
☐	416	Benito Santiago RIF	.05	.02	.01
☐	417	Nolan Ryan HL	.35	.16	.04
☐	418	Bobby Thigpen HL UER (Back refers to Hal McRae Jr., should say Brian McRae)	.05	.02	.01
☐	419	Ramon Martinez HL	.05	.02	.01
☐	420	Bo Jackson HL	.10	.05	.01
☐	421	Carlton Fisk HL	.10	.05	.01
☐	422	Jimmy Key	.10	.05	.01
☐	423	Junior Noboa	.05	.02	.01
☐	424	Al Newman	.05	.02	.01
☐	425	Pat Borders	.05	.02	.01
☐	426	Von Hayes	.05	.02	.01
☐	427	Tim Teufel	.05	.02	.01
☐	428	Eric Plunk UER (Text says Eric's had, no apostrophe needed)	.05	.02	.01
☐	429	John Moses	.05	.02	.01
☐	430	Mike Witt	.05	.02	.01
☐	431	Otis Nixon	.10	.05	.01
☐	432	Tony Fernandez	.10	.05	.01
☐	433	Rance Mulliniks	.05	.02	.01
☐	434	Dan Petry	.05	.02	.01
☐	435	Bob Geren	.05	.02	.01
☐	436	Steve Frey	.05	.02	.01
☐	437	Jamie Moyer	.05	.02	.01

No.	Player			
☐ 438	Junior Ortiz	.05	.02	.01
☐ 439	Tom O'Malley	.05	.02	.01
☐ 440	Pat Combs	.05	.02	.01
☐ 441	Jose Canseco DT	.75	.35	.09
☐ 442	Alfredo Griffin	.05	.02	.01
☐ 443	Andres Galarraga	.15	.07	.02
☐ 444	Bryn Smith	.05	.02	.01
☐ 445	Andre Dawson	.15	.07	.02
☐ 446	Juan Samuel	.05	.02	.01
☐ 447	Mike Aldrete	.05	.02	.01
☐ 448	Ron Gant	.10	.05	.01
☐ 449	Fernando Valenzuela	.05	.02	.01
☐ 450	Vince Coleman UER (Should say topped majors in steals four times, not three times)	.05	.02	.01
☐ 451	Kevin Mitchell	.10	.05	.01
☐ 452	Spike Owen	.05	.02	.01
☐ 453	Mike Bielecki	.05	.02	.01
☐ 454	Dennis Martinez	.10	.05	.01
☐ 455	Brett Butler	.10	.05	.01
☐ 456	Ron Darling	.05	.02	.01
☐ 457	Dennis Rasmussen	.05	.02	.01
☐ 458	Ken Howell	.05	.02	.01
☐ 459	Steve Bedrosian	.05	.02	.01
☐ 460	Frank Viola	.10	.05	.01
☐ 461	Jose Lind	.05	.02	.01
☐ 462	Chris Sabo	.10	.05	.01
☐ 463	Dante Bichette	.15	.07	.02
☐ 464	Rick Mahler	.05	.02	.01
☐ 465	John Smiley	.05	.02	.01
☐ 466	Devon White	.10	.05	.01
☐ 467	John Orton	.05	.02	.01
☐ 468	Mike Stanton	.05	.02	.01
☐ 469	Billy Hatcher	.05	.02	.01
☐ 470	Wally Joyner	.10	.05	.01
☐ 471	Gene Larkin	.05	.02	.01
☐ 472	Doug Drabek	.15	.07	.02
☐ 473	Gary Sheffield	.15	.07	.02
☐ 474	David Wells	.05	.02	.01
☐ 475	Andy Van Slyke	.15	.07	.02
☐ 476	Mike Gallego	.05	.02	.01
☐ 477	B.J. Surhoff	.05	.02	.01
☐ 478	Gene Nelson	.05	.02	.01
☐ 479	Mariano Duncan	.05	.02	.01
☐ 480	Fred McGriff	.20	.09	.03
☐ 481	Jerry Browne	.05	.02	.01
☐ 482	Alvin Davis	.05	.02	.01
☐ 483	Bill Wegman	.05	.02	.01
☐ 484	Dave Parker	.15	.07	.02
☐ 485	Dennis Eckersley	.15	.07	.02
☐ 486	Erik Hanson UER (Basketball misspelled as baseketball)	.05	.02	.01
☐ 487	Bill Ripken	.05	.02	.01
☐ 488	Tom Candiotti	.05	.02	.01
☐ 489	Mike Schooler	.05	.02	.01
☐ 490	Gregg Olson	.10	.05	.01
☐ 491	Chris James	.05	.02	.01
☐ 492	Pete Harnisch	.10	.05	.01
☐ 493	Julio Franco	.10	.05	.01
☐ 494	Greg Briley	.05	.02	.01
☐ 495	Ruben Sierra	.15	.07	.02
☐ 496	Steve Olin	.05	.02	.01
☐ 497	Mike Fetters	.05	.02	.01
☐ 498	Mark Williamson	.05	.02	.01
☐ 499	Bob Tewksbury	.10	.05	.01
☐ 500	Tony Gwynn	.25	.11	.03
☐ 501	Randy Myers	.10	.05	.01
☐ 502	Keith Comstock	.05	.02	.01
☐ 503	Craig Worthington UER (DeCinces misspelled DiCinces on back)	.05	.02	.01
☐ 504	Mark Eichhorn UER (Stats incomplete, doesn't have '89 Braves stint)	.05	.02	.01
☐ 505	Barry Larkin	.15	.07	.02
☐ 506	Dave Johnson	.05	.02	.01
☐ 507	Bobby Witt	.05	.02	.01
☐ 508	Joe Orsulak	.05	.02	.01
☐ 509	Pete O'Brien	.05	.02	.01
☐ 510	Brad Arnsberg	.05	.02	.01
☐ 511	Storm Davis	.05	.02	.01
☐ 512	Bob Milacki	.05	.02	.01
☐ 513	Bill Pecota	.05	.02	.01
☐ 514	Glenallen Hill	.05	.02	.01
☐ 515	Danny Tartabull	.10	.05	.01
☐ 516	Mike Moore	.05	.02	.01
☐ 517	Ron Robinson UER (577 K's in 1990)	.05	.02	.01
☐ 518	Mark Gardner	.05	.02	.01
☐ 519	Rick Wrona	.05	.02	.01
☐ 520	Mike Scioscia	.05	.02	.01
☐ 521	Frank Wills	.05	.02	.01
☐ 522	Greg Brock	.05	.02	.01
☐ 523	Jack Clark	.10	.05	.01
☐ 524	Bruce Ruffin	.05	.02	.01
☐ 525	Robin Yount	.15	.07	.02
☐ 526	Tom Foley	.05	.02	.01
☐ 527	Pat Perry	.05	.02	.01
☐ 528	Greg Vaughn	.10	.05	.01
☐ 529	Wally Whitehurst	.05	.02	.01
☐ 530	Norm Charlton	.05	.02	.01
☐ 531	Marvell Wynne	.05	.02	.01
☐ 532	Jim Gantner	.05	.02	.01
☐ 533	Greg Litton	.05	.02	.01
☐ 534	Manny Lee	.05	.02	.01
☐ 535	Scott Bailes	.05	.02	.01
☐ 536	Charlie Leibrandt	.05	.02	.01
☐ 537	Roger McDowell	.05	.02	.01
☐ 538	Andy Benes	.15	.07	.02
☐ 539	Rick Honeycutt	.05	.02	.01
☐ 540	Dwight Gooden	.10	.05	.01
☐ 541	Scott Garrelts	.05	.02	.01
☐ 542	Dave Clark	.05	.02	.01
☐ 543	Lonnie Smith	.05	.02	.01
☐ 544	Rick Reuschel	.05	.02	.01
☐ 545	Delino DeShields UER (Rockford misspelled as Rock Ford in '88)	.15	.07	.02
☐ 546	Mike Sharperson	.05	.02	.01
☐ 547	Mike Kingery	.05	.02	.01
☐ 548	Terry Kennedy	.05	.02	.01
☐ 549	David Cone	.15	.07	.02
☐ 550	Orel Hershiser	.10	.05	.01
☐ 551	Matt Nokes	.05	.02	.01
☐ 552	Eddie Williams	.05	.02	.01
☐ 553	Frank DiPino	.05	.02	.01
☐ 554	Fred Lynn	.10	.05	.01
☐ 555	Alex Cole	.05	.02	.01
☐ 556	Terry Leach	.05	.02	.01
☐ 557	Chet Lemon	.05	.02	.01
☐ 558	Paul Mirabella	.05	.02	.01
☐ 559	Bill Long	.05	.02	.01
☐ 560	Phil Bradley	.05	.02	.01
☐ 561	Duane Ward	.10	.05	.01
☐ 562	Dave Bergman	.05	.02	.01
☐ 563	Eric Show	.05	.02	.01
☐ 564	Xavier Hernandez	.05	.02	.01
☐ 565	Jeff Parrett	.05	.02	.01
☐ 566	Chuck Cary	.05	.02	.01
☐ 567	Ken Hill	.15	.07	.02
☐ 568	Bob Welch Hand (Complement should be compliment) UER	.05	.02	.01

☐	569 John Mitchell	.05	.02	.01
☐	570 Travis Fryman	.50	.23	.06
☐	571 Derek Lilliquist	.05	.02	.01
☐	572 Steve Lake	.05	.02	.01
☐	573 John Barfield	.05	.02	.01
☐	574 Randy Bush	.05	.02	.01
☐	575 Joe Magrane	.05	.02	.01
☐	576 Eddie Diaz	.05	.02	.01
☐	577 Casey Candaele	.05	.02	.01
☐	578 Jesse Orosco	.05	.02	.01
☐	579 Tom Henke	.10	.05	.01
☐	580 Rick Cerone UER (Actually his third go-round with Yankees)	.05	.02	.01
☐	581 Drew Hall	.05	.02	.01
☐	582 Tony Castillo	.05	.02	.01
☐	583 Jimmy Jones	.05	.02	.01
☐	584 Rick Reed	.05	.02	.01
☐	585 Joe Girardi	.05	.02	.01
☐	586 Jeff Gray	.05	.02	.01
☐	587 Luis Polonia	.05	.02	.01
☐	588 Joe Klink	.05	.02	.01
☐	589 Rex Hudler	.05	.02	.01
☐	590 Kirk McCaskill	.05	.02	.01
☐	591 Juan Agosto	.05	.02	.01
☐	592 Wes Gardner	.05	.02	.01
☐	593 Rich Rodriguez	.05	.02	.01
☐	594 Mitch Webster	.05	.02	.01
☐	595 Kelly Gruber	.05	.02	.01
☐	596 Dale Mohorcic	.05	.02	.01
☐	597 Willie McGee	.10	.05	.01
☐	598 Bill Krueger	.05	.02	.01
☐	599 Bob Walk UER (Cards says he's 33, but actually he's 34)	.05	.02	.01
☐	600 Kevin Maas	.05	.02	.01
☐	601 Danny Jackson	.05	.02	.01
☐	602 Craig McMurtry UER (Anonymously misspelled anonimously)	.05	.02	.01
☐	603 Curtis Wilkerson	.05	.02	.01
☐	604 Adam Peterson	.05	.02	.01
☐	605 Sam Horn	.05	.02	.01
☐	606 Tommy Gregg	.05	.02	.01
☐	607 Ken Dayley	.05	.02	.01
☐	608 Carmelo Castillo	.05	.02	.01
☐	609 John Shelby	.05	.02	.01
☐	610 Don Slaught	.05	.02	.01
☐	611 Calvin Schiraldi	.05	.02	.01
☐	612 Dennis Lamp	.05	.02	.01
☐	613 Andres Thomas	.05	.02	.01
☐	614 Jose Gonzalez	.05	.02	.01
☐	615 Randy Ready	.05	.02	.01
☐	616 Kevin Bass	.05	.02	.01
☐	617 Mike Marshall	.05	.02	.01
☐	618 Daryl Boston	.05	.02	.01
☐	619 Andy McGaffigan	.05	.02	.01
☐	620 Joe Oliver	.05	.02	.01
☐	621 Jim Gott	.05	.02	.01
☐	622 Jose Oquendo	.05	.02	.01
☐	623 Jose DeJesus	.05	.02	.01
☐	624 Mike Brumley	.05	.02	.01
☐	625 John Olerud	.15	.07	.02
☐	626 Ernest Riles	.05	.02	.01
☐	627 Gene Harris	.05	.02	.01
☐	628 Jose Uribe	.05	.02	.01
☐	629 Darnell Coles	.05	.02	.01
☐	630 Carney Lansford	.10	.05	.01
☐	631 Tim Leary	.05	.02	.01
☐	632 Tim Hulett	.05	.02	.01
☐	633 Kevin Elster	.05	.02	.01
☐	634 Tony Fossas	.05	.02	.01
☐	635 Francisco Oliveras	.05	.02	.01
☐	636 Bob Patterson	.05	.02	.01
☐	637 Gary Ward	.05	.02	.01
☐	638 Rene Gonzales	.05	.02	.01
☐	639 Don Robinson	.05	.02	.01
☐	640 Darryl Strawberry	.15	.07	.02
☐	641 Dave Anderson	.05	.02	.01
☐	642 Scott Scudder	.05	.02	.01
☐	643 Reggie Harris UER (Hepatitis misspelled as hepititis)	.05	.02	.01
☐	644 Dave Henderson	.05	.02	.01
☐	645 Ben McDonald	.15	.07	.02
☐	646 Bob Kipper	.05	.02	.01
☐	647 Hal Morris UER (It's should be its)	.10	.05	.01
☐	648 Tim Birtsas	.05	.02	.01
☐	649 Steve Searcy	.05	.02	.01
☐	650 Dale Murphy	.15	.07	.02
☐	651 Ron Oester	.05	.02	.01
☐	652 Mike LaCoss	.05	.02	.01
☐	653 Ron Jones	.05	.02	.01
☐	654 Kelly Downs	.05	.02	.01
☐	655 Roger Clemens	.25	.11	.03
☐	656 Herm Winningham	.05	.02	.01
☐	657 Trevor Wilson	.05	.02	.01
☐	658 Jose Rijo	.10	.05	.01
☐	659 Dann Bilardello UER (Bio has 13 games, 1 hit, and 32 AB, stats show 19, 2, and 37)	.05	.02	.01
☐	660 Gregg Jefferies	.15	.07	.02
☐	661 Doug Drabek AS UER (Through is misspelled though)	.07	.03	.01
☐	662 Randy Myers AS	.05	.02	.01
☐	663 Benny Santiago AS	.05	.02	.01
☐	664 Will Clark AS	.15	.07	.02
☐	665 Ryne Sandberg AS	.20	.09	.03
☐	666 Barry Larkin AS UER (Line 13, coolly misspelled cooly)	.07	.03	.01
☐	667 Matt Williams AS	.07	.03	.01
☐	668 Barry Bonds AS	.25	.11	.03
☐	669 Eric Davis AS	.05	.02	.01
☐	670 Bobby Bonilla AS	.07	.03	.01
☐	671 Chipper Jones FDP	1.25	.55	.16
☐	672 Eric Christopherson FDP	.05	.02	.01
☐	673 Robbie Beckett FDP	.05	.02	.01
☐	674 Shane Andrews FDP	.20	.09	.03
☐	675 Steve Karsay FDP	.40	.18	.05
☐	676 Aaron Holbert FDP	.05	.02	.01
☐	677 Donovan Osborne FDP	.15	.07	.02
☐	678 Todd Ritchie FDP	.15	.07	.02
☐	679 Ron Walden FDP	.05	.02	.01
☐	680 Tim Costo FDP	.05	.02	.01
☐	681 Dan Wilson FDP	.05	.02	.01
☐	682 Kurt Miller FDP	.05	.02	.01
☐	683 Mike Lieberthal FDP	.10	.05	.01
☐	684 Roger Clemens KM	.15	.07	.02
☐	685 Dwight Gooden KM	.10	.05	.01
☐	686 Nolan Ryan KM	.35	.16	.04
☐	687 Frank Viola KM	.05	.02	.01
☐	688 Erik Hanson KM	.05	.02	.01
☐	689 Matt Williams MB	.10	.05	.01
☐	690 Jose Canseco MB UER (Mammoth misspelled as monmouth)	.15	.07	.02
☐	691 Darryl Strawberry MB	.10	.05	.01
☐	692 Bo Jackson MB	.10	.05	.01
☐	693 Cecil Fielder MB	.10	.05	.01
☐	694 Sandy Alomar Jr. RF	.05	.02	.01
☐	695 Cory Snyder RF	.05	.02	.01

☐ 696 Eric Davis RF	.05	.02	.01
☐ 697 Ken Griffey Jr. RF	1.00	.45	.13
☐ 698 Andy Van Slyke RF UER (Line 2, outfielders does not need)	.10	.05	.01
☐ 699 Langston/Witt NH Mark Langston Mike Witt	.05	.02	.01
☐ 700 Randy Johnson NH	.10	.05	.01
☐ 701 Nolan Ryan NH	.30	.14	.04
☐ 702 Dave Stewart NH	.05	.02	.01
☐ 703 Fernando Valenzuela NH	.05	.02	.01
☐ 704 Andy Hawkins NH	.05	.02	.01
☐ 705 Melido Perez NH	.05	.02	.01
☐ 706 Terry Mulholland NH	.05	.02	.01
☐ 707 Dave Stieb NH	.05	.02	.01
☐ 708 Brian Barnes	.05	.02	.01
☐ 709 Bernard Gilkey	.10	.05	.01
☐ 710 Steve Decker	.05	.02	.01
☐ 711 Paul Faries	.05	.02	.01
☐ 712 Paul Marak	.05	.02	.01
☐ 713 Wes Chamberlain	.05	.02	.01
☐ 714 Kevin Belcher	.05	.02	.01
☐ 715 Dan Boone UER (IP adds up to 101, but card has 101.2)	.05	.02	.01
☐ 716 Steve Adkins	.05	.02	.01
☐ 717 Geronimo Pena	.05	.02	.01
☐ 718 Howard Farmer	.05	.02	.01
☐ 719 Mark Leonard	.05	.02	.01
☐ 720 Tom Lampkin	.05	.02	.01
☐ 721 Mike Gardiner	.05	.02	.01
☐ 722 Jeff Conine	.50	.23	.06
☐ 723 Efrain Valdez	.05	.02	.01
☐ 724 Chuck Malone	.05	.02	.01
☐ 725 Leo Gomez	.10	.05	.01
☐ 726 Paul McClellan	.05	.02	.01
☐ 727 Mark Leiter	.05	.02	.01
☐ 728 Rich DeLucia UER (Line 2, all told is written alltold)	.05	.02	.01
☐ 729 Mel Rojas	.05	.02	.01
☐ 730 Hector Wagner	.05	.02	.01
☐ 731 Ray Lankford	.15	.07	.02
☐ 732 Turner Ward	.15	.07	.02
☐ 733 Gerald Alexander	.05	.02	.01
☐ 734 Scott Anderson	.05	.02	.01
☐ 735 Tony Perezchica	.05	.02	.01
☐ 736 Jimmy Kremers	.05	.02	.01
☐ 737 American Flag (Pray for Peace)	.25	.11	.03
☐ 738 Mike York	.05	.02	.01
☐ 739 Mike Rochford	.05	.02	.01
☐ 740 Scott Aldred	.05	.02	.01
☐ 741 Rico Brogna	.15	.07	.02
☐ 742 Dave Burba	.05	.02	.01
☐ 743 Ray Stephens	.05	.02	.01
☐ 744 Eric Gunderson	.05	.02	.01
☐ 745 Troy Afenir	.05	.02	.01
☐ 746 Jeff Shaw	.05	.02	.01
☐ 747 Orlando Merced	.25	.11	.03
☐ 748 Omar Olivares UER (Line 9, league is misspelled legaue)	.05	.02	.01
☐ 749 Jerry Kutzler	.05	.02	.01
☐ 750 Mo Vaughn UER (44 SB's in 1990)	.40	.18	.05
☐ 751 Matt Stark	.05	.02	.01
☐ 752 Randy Hennis	.05	.02	.01
☐ 753 Andujar Cedeno	.10	.05	.01
☐ 754 Kelvin Torve	.05	.02	.01
☐ 755 Joe Kraemer	.05	.02	.01
☐ 756 Phil Clark	.05	.02	.01
☐ 757 Ed Vosberg	.05	.02	.01
☐ 758 Mike Perez	.05	.02	.01
☐ 759 Scott Lewis	.05	.02	.01
☐ 760 Steve Chitren	.05	.02	.01
☐ 761 Ray Young	.05	.02	.01
☐ 762 Andres Santana	.05	.02	.01
☐ 763 Rodney McCray	.05	.02	.01
☐ 764 Sean Berry UER (Name misspelled Barry on card front)	.15	.07	.02
☐ 765 Brent Mayne	.05	.02	.01
☐ 766 Mike Simms	.05	.02	.01
☐ 767 Glenn Sutko	.05	.02	.01
☐ 768 Gary DiSarcina	.10	.05	.01
☐ 769 George Brett HL	.20	.09	.03
☐ 770 Cecil Fielder HL	.10	.05	.01
☐ 771 Jim Presley	.05	.02	.01
☐ 772 John Dopson	.05	.02	.01
☐ 773 Bo Jackson Breaker	.10	.05	.01
☐ 774 Brent Knackert UER (Born in 1954, shown throwing righty, but bio says lefty)	.05	.02	.01
☐ 775 Bill Doran UER (Reds in NL East)	.05	.02	.01
☐ 776 Dick Schofield	.05	.02	.01
☐ 777 Nelson Santovenia	.05	.02	.01
☐ 778 Mark Guthrie	.05	.02	.01
☐ 779 Mark Lemke	.05	.02	.01
☐ 780 Terry Steinbach	.10	.05	.01
☐ 781 Tom Bolton	.05	.02	.01
☐ 782 Randy Tomlin	.05	.02	.01
☐ 783 Jeff Kunkel	.05	.02	.01
☐ 784 Felix Jose	.10	.05	.01
☐ 785 Rick Sutcliffe	.10	.05	.01
☐ 786 John Cerutti	.05	.02	.01
☐ 787 Jose Vizcaino UER (Offerman, not Opperman)	.05	.02	.01
☐ 788 Curt Schilling	.10	.05	.01
☐ 789 Ed Whitson	.05	.02	.01
☐ 790 Tony Pena	.05	.02	.01
☐ 791 John Candelaria	.05	.02	.01
☐ 792 Carmelo Martinez	.05	.02	.01
☐ 793 Sandy Alomar Jr. UER (Indian's should say Indians')	.10	.05	.01
☐ 794 Jim Neidlinger	.05	.02	.01
☐ 795 Barry Larkin WS and Chris Sabo	.10	.05	.01
☐ 796 Paul Sorrento	.10	.05	.01
☐ 797 Tom Pagnozzi	.05	.02	.01
☐ 798 Tino Martinez	.10	.05	.01
☐ 799 Scott Ruskin UER (Text says first three seasons but lists averages for four)	.05	.02	.01
☐ 800 Kirk Gibson	.10	.05	.01
☐ 801 Walt Terrell	.05	.02	.01
☐ 802 John Russell	.05	.02	.01
☐ 803 Chili Davis	.10	.05	.01
☐ 804 Chris Nabholz	.05	.02	.01
☐ 805 Juan Gonzalez	1.00	.45	.13
☐ 806 Ron Hassey	.05	.02	.01
☐ 807 Todd Worrell	.05	.02	.01
☐ 808 Tommy Greene	.10	.05	.01
☐ 809 Joel Skinner UER (Joel, not Bob, was drafted in 1979)	.05	.02	.01
☐ 810 Benito Santiago	.05	.02	.01
☐ 811 Pat Tabler UER (Line 3, always misspelled alway)	.05	.02	.01
☐ 812 Scott Erickson UER	.05	.02	.01

(Record spelled rcord)
☐ 813 Moises Alou .25 .11 .03
☐ 814 Dale Sveum .05 .02 .01
☐ 815 Ryne Sandberg MANYR .25 .11 .03
☐ 816 Rick Dempsey .05 .02 .01
☐ 817 Scott Bankhead .05 .02 .01
☐ 818 Jason Grimsley .05 .02 .01
☐ 819 Doug Jennings .05 .02 .01
☐ 820 Tom Herr .05 .02 .01
☐ 821 Rob Ducey .05 .02 .01
☐ 822 Luis Quinones .05 .02 .01
☐ 823 Greg Minton .05 .02 .01
☐ 824 Mark Grant .05 .02 .01
☐ 825 Ozzie Smith UER .15 .07 .02
(Shortstop misspelled shortsop)
☐ 826 Dave Eiland .05 .02 .01
☐ 827 Danny Heep .05 .02 .01
☐ 828 Hensley Meulens .05 .02 .01
☐ 829 Charlie O'Brien .05 .02 .01
☐ 830 Glenn Davis .05 .02 .01
☐ 831 John Marzano UER .05 .02 .01
(International misspelled Internaional)
☐ 832 Steve Ontiveros .05 .02 .01
☐ 833 Ron Karkovice .05 .02 .01
☐ 834 Jerry Goff .05 .02 .01
☐ 835 Ken Griffey .10 .05 .01
☐ 836 Kevin Reimer .05 .02 .01
☐ 837 Randy Kutcher UER .05 .02 .01
(Infectious misspelled infectous)
☐ 838 Mike Blowers .05 .02 .01
☐ 839 Mike Macfarlane .05 .02 .01
☐ 840 Frank Thomas UER 2.00 .90 .25
(1989 Sarasota stats, 15 games but 188 AB)
☐ 841 The Griffeys 1.00 .45 .13
Ken Griffey Jr.
Ken Griffey Sr.
☐ 842 Jack Howell .05 .02 .01
☐ 843 Goose Gozzo .05 .02 .01
☐ 844 Gerald Young .05 .02 .01
☐ 845 Zane Smith .05 .02 .01
☐ 846 Kevin Brown .10 .05 .01
☐ 847 Sil Campusano .05 .02 .01
☐ 848 Larry Andersen .05 .02 .01
☐ 849 Cal Ripken FRAN .30 .14 .04
☐ 850 Roger Clemens FRAN .15 .07 .02
☐ 851 Sandy Alomar Jr. FRAN .05 .02 .01
☐ 852 Alan Trammell FRAN .10 .05 .01
☐ 853 George Brett FRAN .25 .11 .03
☐ 854 Robin Yount FRAN .10 .05 .01
☐ 855 Kirby Puckett FRAN .25 .11 .03
☐ 856 Don Mattingly FRAN .25 .11 .03
☐ 857 Rickey Henderson FRAN .10 .05 .01
☐ 858 Ken Griffey Jr. FRAN .75 .35 .09
☐ 859 Ruben Sierra FRAN .10 .05 .01
☐ 860 John Olerud FRAN .10 .05 .01
☐ 861 David Justice FRAN .15 .07 .02
☐ 862 Ryne Sandberg FRAN .25 .11 .03
☐ 863 Eric Davis FRAN .05 .02 .01
☐ 864 Darryl Strawberry FRAN .10 .05 .01
☐ 865 Tim Wallach FRAN .05 .02 .01
☐ 866 Dwight Gooden FRAN .10 .05 .01
☐ 867 Len Dykstra FRAN .10 .05 .01
☐ 868 Barry Bonds FRAN .25 .11 .03
☐ 869 Todd Zeile FRAN UER .05 .02 .01
(Powerful misspelled as poweful)
☐ 870 Benito Santiago FRAN .05 .02 .01
☐ 871 Will Clark FRAN .15 .07 .02
☐ 872 Craig Biggio FRAN .10 .05 .01
☐ 873 Wally Joyner FRAN .05 .02 .01
☐ 874 Frank Thomas FRAN 1.00 .45 .13
☐ 875 Rickey Henderson MVP .10 .05 .01
☐ 876 Barry Bonds MVP .25 .11 .03
☐ 877 Bob Welch CY .05 .02 .01
☐ 878 Doug Drabek CY .10 .05 .01
☐ 879 Sandy Alomar Jr ROY .05 .02 .01
☐ 880 David Justice ROY .15 .07 .02
☐ 881 Damon Berryhill .05 .02 .01
☐ 882 Frank Viola DT .10 .05 .01
☐ 883 Dave Stewart DT .10 .05 .01
☐ 884 Doug Jones DT .10 .05 .01
☐ 885 Randy Myers DT .10 .05 .01
☐ 886 Will Clark DT .30 .14 .04
☐ 887 Roberto Alomar DT .40 .18 .05
☐ 888 Barry Larkin DT .12 .05 .02
☐ 889 Wade Boggs DT .20 .09 .03
☐ 890 Rickey Henderson DT .15 .07 .02
☐ 891 Kirby Puckett DT .40 .18 .05
☐ 892 Ken Griffey Jr DT 1.50 .65 .19
☐ 893 Benny Santiago DT .10 .05 .01

1991 Score Cooperstown

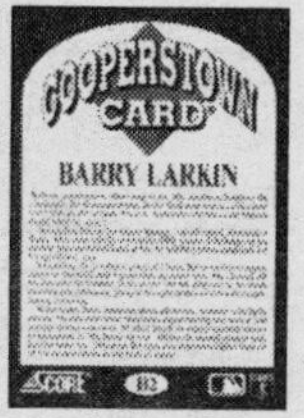

This seven-card set measures the standard 2 1/2" by 3 1/2" and was available only as an insert with 1991 Score factory sets. The card design is not like the regular 1991 Score cards. The card front features a portrait of the player in an oval on a white background. The words "Cooperstown Card" are prominently displayed on the card front. The cards are numbered on the back with a B prefix.

	MINT	EXC	G-VG
COMPLETE SET (7)	8.00	3.60	1.00
COMMON CARD (B1-B7)	.50	.23	.06
☐ B1 Wade Boggs	.75	.35	.09
☐ B2 Barry Larkin	.50	.23	.06
☐ B3 Ken Griffey Jr.	5.00	2.30	.60
☐ B4 Rickey Henderson	.75	.35	.09
☐ B5 George Brett	1.75	.80	.22
☐ B6 Will Clark	1.00	.45	.13
☐ B7 Nolan Ryan	3.50	1.55	.45

1991 Score Hot Rookies

This ten-card set measures the standard size (2 1/2" by 3 1/2"), and one of these cards was inserted in the 1991 Score blister (100-card) packs. The front features a color action player photo, with white borders and the words "Hot Rookie" in yellow above the picture. The card background shades from orange to yellow to orange as one moves down the card face. In a horizontal format, the left half of the back has a color head shot, while the right half has career summary. The cards are numbered on the back.

	MINT	EXC	G-VG
COMPLETE SET (10)	20.00	9.00	2.50
COMMON CARD (1-10)	.50	.23	.06
☐ 1 David Justice	2.50	1.15	.30
☐ 2 Kevin Maas	.50	.23	.06
☐ 3 Hal Morris	.75	.35	.09
☐ 4 Frank Thomas	12.00	5.50	1.50
☐ 5 Jeff Conine	2.00	.90	.25
☐ 6 Sandy Alomar Jr.	.50	.23	.06
☐ 7 Ray Lankford	1.50	.65	.19
☐ 8 Steve Decker	.50	.23	.06
☐ 9 Juan Gonzalez	6.00	2.70	.75
☐ 10 Jose Offerman	.50	.23	.06

1991 Score Mickey Mantle

This seven-card set measures the standard 2 1/2" by 3 1/2" and features Mickey Mantle at various points in his career. This set was released to dealers and media members on Score's mailing list and was individually numbered on the back. This numbered dealer/media set was limited to 5,000 sets produced. The cards were sent in seven-card packs in the Yankees colors. The fronts are full-color glossy shots of Mantle while the backs are in a horizontal format with a full-color photo and some narrative information. The pictures have red and white borders, with the caption appearing in a blue stripe below the photo. The card number and the set serial number appear on the back. These were essentially the same cards Score used in their second series promotion.

	MINT	EXC	G-VG
COMPLETE SET (7)	250.00	115.00	31.00
COMMON MANTLE (1-7)	40.00	18.00	5.00
*PROMO CARDS: 1.25X VALUES BELOW			
☐ 1 The Rookie (With Billy Martin)	40.00	18.00	5.00
☐ 2 Triple Crown	40.00	18.00	5.00
☐ 3 World Series	40.00	18.00	5.00
☐ 4 Going, Going, Gone	40.00	18.00	5.00
☐ 5 Speed and Grace	40.00	18.00	5.00
☐ 6 A True Yankee	40.00	18.00	5.00
☐ 7 Twilight	40.00	18.00	5.00
☐ AU Mickey Mantle AU (Autographed with certified signature)	500.00	230.00	65.00

1991 Score Rookie/Traded

The 1991 Score Rookie and Traded set contains 110 standard-size (2 1/2" by 3 1/2") player cards and 10 "World Series II" magic motion trivia cards. The front design features glossy color action photos, with white and purple borders on a mauve card face. The player's name, team, and position are given above the pictures. In a horizontal format, the left portion of the back has a color head shot and biography, while the right portion has statistics and player profile on a pale yellow background. The cards are numbered on the back. Cards 1T-80T feature traded players, while cards 81T-110T focus on rookies. The only noteworthy

Rookie Cards in the set are Jeff Bagwell, Luis Gonzalez, Ivan Rodriguez, and Rick Wilkins.

	MINT	EXC	G-VG
COMPLETE FACT.SET (110)	4.00	1.80	.50
COMMON CARD (1T-110T)	.05	.02	.01
☐ 1T Bo Jackson	.20	.09	.03
☐ 2T Mike Flanagan	.05	.02	.01
☐ 3T Pete Incaviglia	.05	.02	.01
☐ 4T Jack Clark	.08	.04	.01
☐ 5T Hubie Brooks	.05	.02	.01
☐ 6T Ivan Calderon	.05	.02	.01
☐ 7T Glenn Davis	.05	.02	.01
☐ 8T Wally Backman	.05	.02	.01
☐ 9T Dave Smith	.05	.02	.01
☐ 10T Tim Raines	.10	.05	.01
☐ 11T Joe Carter	.20	.09	.03
☐ 12T Sid Bream	.05	.02	.01
☐ 13T George Bell	.08	.04	.01
☐ 14T Steve Bedrosian	.05	.02	.01
☐ 15T Willie Wilson	.05	.02	.01
☐ 16T Darryl Strawberry	.05	.02	.01
☐ 17T Danny Jackson	.05	.02	.01
☐ 18T Kirk Gibson	.08	.04	.01
☐ 19T Willie McGee	.08	.04	.01
☐ 20T Junior Felix	.05	.02	.01
☐ 21T Steve Farr	.05	.02	.01
☐ 22T Pat Tabler	.05	.02	.01
☐ 23T Brett Butler	.08	.04	.01
☐ 24T Danny Darwin	.05	.02	.01
☐ 25T Mickey Tettleton	.08	.04	.01
☐ 26T Gary Carter	.10	.05	.01
☐ 27T Mitch Williams	.08	.04	.01
☐ 28T Candy Maldonado	.05	.02	.01
☐ 29T Otis Nixon	.08	.04	.01
☐ 30T Brian Downing	.05	.02	.01
☐ 31T Tom Candiotti	.05	.02	.01
☐ 32T John Candelaria	.05	.02	.01
☐ 33T Rob Murphy	.05	.02	.01
☐ 34T Deion Sanders	.30	.14	.04
☐ 35T Willie Randolph	.08	.04	.01
☐ 36T Pete Harnisch	.08	.04	.01
☐ 37T Dante Bichette	.10	.05	.01
☐ 38T Garry Templeton	.05	.02	.01
☐ 39T Gary Gaetti	.05	.02	.01
☐ 40T John Cerutti	.05	.02	.01
☐ 41T Rick Cerone	.05	.02	.01
☐ 42T Mike Pagliarulo	.05	.02	.01
☐ 43T Ron Hassey	.05	.02	.01
☐ 44T Roberto Alomar	.20	.09	.03
☐ 45T Mike Boddicker	.05	.02	.01
☐ 46T Bud Black	.05	.02	.01
☐ 47T Rob Deer	.05	.02	.01
☐ 48T Devon White	.08	.04	.01
☐ 49T Luis Sojo	.05	.02	.01
☐ 50T Terry Pendleton	.10	.05	.01
☐ 51T Kevin Gross	.05	.02	.01
☐ 52T Mike Huff	.05	.02	.01
☐ 53T Dave Righetti	.05	.02	.01
☐ 54T Matt Young	.05	.02	.01
☐ 55T Earnest Riles	.05	.02	.01
☐ 56T Bill Gullickson	.05	.02	.01
☐ 57T Vince Coleman	.05	.02	.01
☐ 58T Fred McGriff	.20	.09	.03
☐ 59T Franklin Stubbs	.05	.02	.01
☐ 60T Eric King	.05	.02	.01
☐ 61T Cory Snyder	.05	.02	.01
☐ 62T Dwight Evans	.08	.04	.01
☐ 63T Gerald Perry	.05	.02	.01
☐ 64T Eric Show	.05	.02	.01
☐ 65T Shawn Hillegas	.05	.02	.01
☐ 66T Tony Fernandez	.08	.04	.01
☐ 67T Tim Teufel	.05	.02	.01
☐ 68T Mitch Webster	.05	.02	.01
☐ 69T Mike Heath	.05	.02	.01
☐ 70T Chili Davis	.08	.04	.01
☐ 71T Larry Andersen	.05	.02	.01
☐ 72T Gary Varsho	.05	.02	.01
☐ 73T Juan Berenguer	.05	.02	.01
☐ 74T Jack Morris	.10	.05	.01
☐ 75T Barry Jones	.05	.02	.01
☐ 76T Rafael Belliard	.05	.02	.01
☐ 77T Steve Buechele	.05	.02	.01
☐ 78T Scott Sanderson	.05	.02	.01
☐ 79T Bob Ojeda	.05	.02	.01
☐ 80T Curt Schilling	.08	.04	.01
☐ 81T Brian Drahman	.05	.02	.01
☐ 82T Ivan Rodriguez	.50	.23	.06
☐ 83T David Howard	.05	.02	.01
☐ 84T Heathcliff Slocumb	.05	.02	.01
☐ 85T Mike Timlin	.05	.02	.01
☐ 86T Darryl Kile	.10	.05	.01
☐ 87T Pete Schourek	.05	.02	.01
☐ 88T Bruce Walton	.05	.02	.01
☐ 89T Al Osuna	.05	.02	.01
☐ 90T Gary Scott	.05	.02	.01
☐ 91T Doug Simons	.05	.02	.01
☐ 92T Chris Jones	.05	.02	.01
☐ 93T Chuck Knoblauch	.25	.11	.03
☐ 94T Dana Allison	.05	.02	.01
☐ 95T Erik Pappas	.05	.02	.01
☐ 96T Jeff Bagwell	3.00	1.35	.40
☐ 97T Kirk Dressendorfer	.05	.02	.01
☐ 98T Freddie Benavides	.05	.02	.01
☐ 99T Luis Gonzalez	.25	.11	.03
☐ 100T Wade Taylor	.05	.02	.01
☐ 101T Ed Sprague	.05	.02	.01
☐ 102T Bob Scanlan	.05	.02	.01
☐ 103T Rick Wilkins	.15	.07	.02
☐ 104T Chris Donnels	.05	.02	.01
☐ 105T Joe Slusarski	.05	.02	.01
☐ 106T Mark Lewis	.08	.04	.01
☐ 107T Pat Kelly	.15	.07	.02
☐ 108T John Briscoe	.05	.02	.01
☐ 109T Luis Lopez	.05	.02	.01
☐ 110T Jeff Johnson	.05	.02	.01

1992 Score

The 1992 Score set marked the second year that Score released their set in two different series. The first series contains 442 cards measuring the standard size (2 1/2" by 3 1/2"). The second series contains 451 more cards sequentially numbered. The

glossy color action photos on the fronts are bordered above and below by stripes of the same color, and a thicker, different color stripe runs the length of the card to one side of the picture. The backs have a color close-up shot in the upper right corner, with biography, complete career statistics, and player profile printed on a yellow background. Hall of Famer Joe DiMaggio is remembered in a five-card subset. He autographed 2,500 cards; 2,495 of these were randomly inserted in Series I packs, while the other five were given away through a mail-in sweepstakes. Another 150,000 unsigned DiMaggio cards were inserted in Series I Count Goods packs only. Score later extended its DiMaggio promotion to Series I blister packs; one hundred signed and twelve thousand unsigned cards were randomly inserted in these packs. Also a special "World Series II" trivia card was inserted into each pack. These cards highlight crucial games and heroes from past Octobers. Topical subsets included in the set focus on Rookie Prospects (395-424), No-Hit Club (425-428), Highlights (429-430), AL All-Stars (431-440; with color montages displaying Chris Greco's player caricatures), Dream Team (441-442), Rookie Prospects (736-772, 814-877), NL All-Stars (773-782), Highlights (783, 795-797), No-Hit Club (784-787), Draft Picks (799-810), Memorabilia (878-882), and Dream Team (883-893). All of the Rookie Prospects (736-772) can be found with or without the Rookie Prospect stripe. The cards are numbered on the back. Rookie Cards in the set include Cliff Floyd, Brent Gates, Benji Gil, Tyler Green, Manny Ramirez, Scott Ruffcorn, Aaron Sele, Allen Watson, and Bob Zupcic. Chuck Knoblauch, 1991 American League Rookie of the Year, autographed 3,000 of his own 1990 Score Draft Pick cards (card number 672) in gold ink, 2,989 were randomly inserted in Series 2 poly packs, while the other 11 were given away in a sweepstakes. The backs of these Knoblauch autograph cards have special holograms to differentiate them.

	MINT	EXC	G-VG
COMPLETE SET (893)	18.00	8.00	2.30
COMPLETE FACT.SET (910)	25.00	11.50	3.10
COMPLETE SERIES 1 (442)	9.00	4.00	1.15
COMPLETE SERIES 2 (451)	9.00	4.00	1.15
COMMON CARD (1-442)	.05	.02	.01
COMMON CARD (443-893)	.05	.02	.01

	MINT	EXC	G-VG
□ 1 Ken Griffey Jr.	1.50	.65	.19
□ 2 Nolan Ryan	1.00	.45	.13
□ 3 Will Clark	.20	.09	.03
□ 4 David Justice	.20	.09	.03
□ 5 Dave Henderson	.05	.02	.01
□ 6 Bret Saberhagen	.10	.05	.01
□ 7 Fred McGriff	.20	.09	.03
□ 8 Erik Hanson	.05	.02	.01
□ 9 Darryl Strawberry	.10	.05	.01
□ 10 Dwight Gooden	.10	.05	.01
□ 11 Juan Gonzalez	.60	.25	.08
□ 12 Mark Langston	.15	.07	.02
□ 13 Lonnie Smith	.05	.02	.01
□ 14 Jeff Montgomery	.10	.05	.01
□ 15 Roberto Alomar	.25	.11	.03
□ 16 Delino DeShields	.15	.07	.02
□ 17 Steve Bedrosian	.05	.02	.01
□ 18 Terry Pendleton	.15	.07	.02
□ 19 Mark Carreon	.05	.02	.01
□ 20 Mark McGwire	.15	.07	.02
□ 21 Roger Clemens	.25	.11	.03
□ 22 Chuck Crim	.05	.02	.01
□ 23 Don Mattingly	.30	.14	.04
□ 24 Dickie Thon	.05	.02	.01
□ 25 Ron Gant	.10	.05	.01
□ 26 Milt Cuyler	.05	.02	.01
□ 27 Mike Macfarlane	.05	.02	.01
□ 28 Dan Gladden	.05	.02	.01
□ 29 Melido Perez	.05	.02	.01
□ 30 Willie Randolph	.10	.05	.01
□ 31 Albert Belle	.40	.18	.05
□ 32 Dave Winfield	.15	.07	.02
□ 33 Jimmy Jones	.05	.02	.01
□ 34 Kevin Gross	.05	.02	.01
□ 35 Andres Galarraga	.15	.07	.02
□ 36 Mike Devereaux	.10	.05	.01
□ 37 Chris Bosio	.05	.02	.01
□ 38 Mike LaValliere	.05	.02	.01
□ 39 Gary Gaetti	.05	.02	.01
□ 40 Felix Jose	.10	.05	.01
□ 41 Alvaro Espinoza	.05	.02	.01
□ 42 Rick Aguilera	.10	.05	.01
□ 43 Mike Gallego	.05	.02	.01
□ 44 Eric Davis	.05	.02	.01
□ 45 George Bell	.10	.05	.01
□ 46 Tom Brunansky	.05	.02	.01
□ 47 Steve Farr	.05	.02	.01
□ 48 Duane Ward	.10	.05	.01
□ 49 David Wells	.05	.02	.01
□ 50 Cecil Fielder	.15	.07	.02
□ 51 Walt Weiss	.05	.02	.01
□ 52 Todd Zeile	.10	.05	.01
□ 53 Doug Jones	.05	.02	.01
□ 54 Bob Walk	.05	.02	.01
□ 55 Rafael Palmeiro	.15	.07	.02
□ 56 Rob Deer	.05	.02	.01
□ 57 Paul O'Neill	.10	.05	.01
□ 58 Jeff Reardon	.10	.05	.01
□ 59 Randy Ready	.05	.02	.01
□ 60 Scott Erickson	.05	.02	.01
□ 61 Paul Molitor	.20	.09	.03
□ 62 Jack McDowell	.15	.07	.02
□ 63 Jim Acker	.05	.02	.01
□ 64 Jay Buhner	.10	.05	.01
□ 65 Travis Fryman	.20	.09	.03
□ 66 Marquis Grissom	.15	.07	.02
□ 67 Mike Harkey	.05	.02	.01
□ 68 Luis Polonia	.05	.02	.01
□ 69 Ken Caminiti	.10	.05	.01
□ 70 Chris Sabo	.10	.05	.01
□ 71 Gregg Olson	.05	.02	.01
□ 72 Carlton Fisk	.15	.07	.02
□ 73 Juan Samuel	.05	.02	.01
□ 74 Todd Stottlemyre	.05	.02	.01
□ 75 Andre Dawson	.15	.07	.02
□ 76 Alvin Davis	.05	.02	.01
□ 77 Bill Doran	.05	.02	.01
□ 78 B.J. Surhoff	.05	.02	.01
□ 79 Kirk McCaskill	.05	.02	.01
□ 80 Dale Murphy	.15	.07	.02
□ 81 Jose DeLeon	.05	.02	.01
□ 82 Alex Fernandez	.15	.07	.02
□ 83 Ivan Calderon	.05	.02	.01
□ 84 Brent Mayne	.05	.02	.01
□ 85 Jody Reed	.05	.02	.01
□ 86 Randy Tomlin	.05	.02	.01
□ 87 Randy Milligan	.05	.02	.01
□ 88 Pascual Perez	.05	.02	.01

□ 89 Hensley Meulens	.05	.02	.01
□ 90 Joe Carter	.20	.09	.03
□ 91 Mike Moore	.05	.02	.01
□ 92 Ozzie Guillen	.05	.02	.01
□ 93 Shawn Hillegas	.05	.02	.01
□ 94 Chili Davis	.10	.05	.01
□ 95 Vince Coleman	.05	.02	.01
□ 96 Jimmy Key	.10	.05	.01
□ 97 Billy Ripken	.05	.02	.01
□ 98 Dave Smith	.05	.02	.01
□ 99 Tom Bolton	.05	.02	.01
□ 100 Barry Larkin	.15	.07	.02
□ 101 Kenny Rogers	.05	.02	.01
□ 102 Mike Boddicker	.05	.02	.01
□ 103 Kevin Elster	.05	.02	.01
□ 104 Ken Hill	.10	.05	.01
□ 105 Charlie Leibrandt	.05	.02	.01
□ 106 Pat Combs	.05	.02	.01
□ 107 Hubie Brooks	.05	.02	.01
□ 108 Julio Franco	.10	.05	.01
□ 109 Vicente Palacios	.05	.02	.01
□ 110 Kal Daniels	.05	.02	.01
□ 111 Bruce Hurst	.05	.02	.01
□ 112 Willie McGee	.10	.05	.01
□ 113 Ted Power	.05	.02	.01
□ 114 Milt Thompson	.05	.02	.01
□ 115 Doug Drabek	.15	.07	.02
□ 116 Rafael Belliard	.05	.02	.01
□ 117 Scott Garrelts	.05	.02	.01
□ 118 Terry Mulholland	.05	.02	.01
□ 119 Jay Howell	.05	.02	.01
□ 120 Danny Jackson	.05	.02	.01
□ 121 Scott Ruskin	.05	.02	.01
□ 122 Robin Ventura	.15	.07	.02
□ 123 Bip Roberts	.05	.02	.01
□ 124 Jeff Russell	.05	.02	.01
□ 125 Hal Morris	.10	.05	.01
□ 126 Teddy Higuera	.05	.02	.01
□ 127 Luis Sojo	.05	.02	.01
□ 128 Carlos Baerga	.20	.09	.03
□ 129 Jeff Ballard	.05	.02	.01
□ 130 Tom Gordon	.05	.02	.01
□ 131 Sid Bream	.05	.02	.01
□ 132 Rance Mulliniks	.05	.02	.01
□ 133 Andy Benes	.10	.05	.01
□ 134 Mickey Tettleton	.10	.05	.01
□ 135 Rich DeLucia	.05	.02	.01
□ 136 Tom Pagnozzi	.05	.02	.01
□ 137 Harold Baines	.10	.05	.01
□ 138 Danny Darwin	.05	.02	.01
□ 139 Kevin Bass	.05	.02	.01
□ 140 Chris Nabholz	.05	.02	.01
□ 141 Pete O'Brien	.05	.02	.01
□ 142 Jeff Treadway	.05	.02	.01
□ 143 Mickey Morandini	.05	.02	.01
□ 144 Eric King	.05	.02	.01
□ 145 Danny Tartabull	.10	.05	.01
□ 146 Lance Johnson	.05	.02	.01
□ 147 Casey Candaele	.05	.02	.01
□ 148 Felix Fermin	.05	.02	.01
□ 149 Rich Rodriguez	.05	.02	.01
□ 150 Dwight Evans	.10	.05	.01
□ 151 Joe Klink	.05	.02	.01
□ 152 Kevin Reimer	.05	.02	.01
□ 153 Orlando Merced	.10	.05	.01
□ 154 Mel Hall	.05	.02	.01
□ 155 Randy Myers	.10	.05	.01
□ 156 Greg A. Harris	.05	.02	.01
□ 157 Jeff Brantley	.05	.02	.01
□ 158 Jim Eisenreich	.05	.02	.01
□ 159 Luis Rivera	.05	.02	.01
□ 160 Cris Carpenter	.05	.02	.01
□ 161 Bruce Ruffin	.05	.02	.01

□ 162 Omar Vizquel	.05	.02	.01
□ 163 Gerald Alexander	.05	.02	.01
□ 164 Mark Guthrie	.05	.02	.01
□ 165 Scott Lewis	.05	.02	.01
□ 166 Bill Sampen	.05	.02	.01
□ 167 Dave Anderson	.05	.02	.01
□ 168 Kevin McReynolds	.05	.02	.01
□ 169 Jose Vizcaino	.05	.02	.01
□ 170 Bob Geren	.05	.02	.01
□ 171 Mike Morgan	.05	.02	.01
□ 172 Jim Gott	.05	.02	.01
□ 173 Mike Pagliarulo	.05	.02	.01
□ 174 Mike Jeffcoat	.05	.02	.01
□ 175 Craig Lefferts	.05	.02	.01
□ 176 Steve Finley	.05	.02	.01
□ 177 Wally Backman	.05	.02	.01
□ 178 Kent Mercker	.05	.02	.01
□ 179 John Cerutti	.05	.02	.01
□ 180 Jay Bell	.10	.05	.01
□ 181 Dale Sveum	.05	.02	.01
□ 182 Greg Gagne	.05	.02	.01
□ 183 Donnie Hill	.05	.02	.01
□ 184 Rex Hudler	.05	.02	.01
□ 185 Pat Kelly	.10	.05	.01
□ 186 Jeff D. Robinson	.05	.02	.01
□ 187 Jeff Gray	.05	.02	.01
□ 188 Jerry Willard	.05	.02	.01
□ 189 Carlos Quintana	.05	.02	.01
□ 190 Dennis Eckersley	.15	.07	.02
□ 191 Kelly Downs	.05	.02	.01
□ 192 Gregg Jefferies	.15	.07	.02
□ 193 Darrin Fletcher	.05	.02	.01
□ 194 Mike Jackson	.05	.02	.01
□ 195 Eddie Murray	.15	.07	.02
□ 196 Bill Landrum	.05	.02	.01
□ 197 Eric Yelding	.05	.02	.01
□ 198 Devon White	.10	.05	.01
□ 199 Larry Walker	.15	.07	.02
□ 200 Ryne Sandberg	.30	.14	.04
□ 201 Dave Magadan	.05	.02	.01
□ 202 Steve Chitren	.05	.02	.01
□ 203 Scott Fletcher	.05	.02	.01
□ 204 Dwayne Henry	.05	.02	.01
□ 205 Scott Coolbaugh	.05	.02	.01
□ 206 Tracy Jones	.05	.02	.01
□ 207 Von Hayes	.05	.02	.01
□ 208 Bob Melvin	.05	.02	.01
□ 209 Scott Scudder	.05	.02	.01
□ 210 Luis Gonzalez	.10	.05	.01
□ 211 Scott Sanderson	.05	.02	.01
□ 212 Chris Donnels	.05	.02	.01
□ 213 Heathcliff Slocumb	.05	.02	.01
□ 214 Mike Timlin	.05	.02	.01
□ 215 Brian Harper	.05	.02	.01
□ 216 Juan Berenguer UER (Decimal point missing in IP total)	.05	.02	.01
□ 217 Mike Henneman	.05	.02	.01
□ 218 Bill Spiers	.05	.02	.01
□ 219 Scott Terry	.05	.02	.01
□ 220 Frank Viola	.10	.05	.01
□ 221 Mark Eichhorn	.05	.02	.01
□ 222 Ernest Riles	.05	.02	.01
□ 223 Ray Lankford	.15	.07	.02
□ 224 Pete Harnisch	.10	.05	.01
□ 225 Bobby Bonilla	.15	.07	.02
□ 226 Mike Scioscia	.05	.02	.01
□ 227 Joel Skinner	.05	.02	.01
□ 228 Brian Holman	.05	.02	.01
□ 229 Gilberto Reyes	.05	.02	.01
□ 230 Matt Williams	.20	.09	.03
□ 231 Jaime Navarro	.05	.02	.01
□ 232 Jose Rijo	.10	.05	.01

☐	233 Atlee Hammaker	.05	.02	.01
☐	234 Tim Teufel	.05	.02	.01
☐	235 John Kruk	.15	.07	.02
☐	236 Kurt Stillwell	.05	.02	.01
☐	237 Dan Pasqua	.05	.02	.01
☐	238 Tim Crews	.05	.02	.01
☐	239 Dave Gallagher	.05	.02	.01
☐	240 Leo Gomez	.05	.02	.01
☐	241 Steve Avery	.15	.07	.02
☐	242 Bill Gullickson	.05	.02	.01
☐	243 Mark Portugal	.05	.02	.01
☐	244 Lee Guetterman	.05	.02	.01
☐	245 Benito Santiago	.05	.02	.01
☐	246 Jim Gantner	.05	.02	.01
☐	247 Robby Thompson	.05	.02	.01
☐	248 Terry Shumpert	.05	.02	.01
☐	249 Mike Bell	.05	.02	.01
☐	250 Harold Reynolds	.05	.02	.01
☐	251 Mike Felder	.05	.02	.01
☐	252 Bill Pecota	.05	.02	.01
☐	253 Bill Krueger	.05	.02	.01
☐	254 Alfredo Griffin	.05	.02	.01
☐	255 Lou Whitaker	.15	.07	.02
☐	256 Roy Smith	.05	.02	.01
☐	257 Jerald Clark	.05	.02	.01
☐	258 Sammy Sosa	.15	.07	.02
☐	259 Tim Naehring	.05	.02	.01
☐	260 Dave Righetti	.05	.02	.01
☐	261 Paul Gibson	.05	.02	.01
☐	262 Chris James	.05	.02	.01
☐	263 Larry Andersen	.05	.02	.01
☐	264 Storm Davis	.05	.02	.01
☐	265 Jose Lind	.05	.02	.01
☐	266 Greg Hibbard	.05	.02	.01
☐	267 Norm Charlton	.05	.02	.01
☐	268 Paul Kilgus	.05	.02	.01
☐	269 Greg Maddux	.20	.09	.03
☐	270 Ellis Burks	.10	.05	.01
☐	271 Frank Tanana	.05	.02	.01
☐	272 Gene Larkin	.05	.02	.01
☐	273 Ron Hassey	.05	.02	.01
☐	274 Jeff M. Robinson	.05	.02	.01
☐	275 Steve Howe	.05	.02	.01
☐	276 Daryl Boston	.05	.02	.01
☐	277 Mark Lee	.05	.02	.01
☐	278 Jose Segura	.05	.02	.01
☐	279 Lance Blankenship	.05	.02	.01
☐	280 Don Slaught	.05	.02	.01
☐	281 Russ Swan	.05	.02	.01
☐	282 Bob Tewksbury	.05	.02	.01
☐	283 Geno Petralli	.05	.02	.01
☐	284 Shane Mack	.10	.05	.01
☐	285 Bob Scanlan	.05	.02	.01
☐	286 Tim Leary	.05	.02	.01
☐	287 John Smoltz	.10	.05	.01
☐	288 Pat Borders	.05	.02	.01
☐	289 Mark Davidson	.05	.02	.01
☐	290 Sam Horn	.05	.02	.01
☐	291 Lenny Harris	.05	.02	.01
☐	292 Franklin Stubbs	.05	.02	.01
☐	293 Thomas Howard	.05	.02	.01
☐	294 Steve Lyons	.05	.02	.01
☐	295 Francisco Oliveras	.05	.02	.01
☐	296 Terry Leach	.05	.02	.01
☐	297 Barry Jones	.05	.02	.01
☐	298 Lance Parrish	.10	.05	.01
☐	299 Wally Whitehurst	.05	.02	.01
☐	300 Bob Welch	.05	.02	.01
☐	301 Charlie Hayes	.10	.05	.01
☐	302 Charlie Hough	.10	.05	.01
☐	303 Gary Redus	.05	.02	.01
☐	304 Scott Bradley	.05	.02	.01
☐	305 Jose Oquendo	.05	.02	.01

☐	306 Pete Incaviglia	.05	.02	.01
☐	307 Marvin Freeman	.05	.02	.01
☐	308 Gary Pettis	.05	.02	.01
☐	309 Joe Slusarski	.05	.02	.01
☐	310 Kevin Seitzer	.05	.02	.01
☐	311 Jeff Reed	.05	.02	.01
☐	312 Pat Tabler	.05	.02	.01
☐	313 Mike Maddux	.05	.02	.01
☐	314 Bob Milacki	.05	.02	.01
☐	315 Eric Anthony	.05	.02	.01
☐	316 Dante Bichette	.15	.07	.02
☐	317 Steve Decker	.10	.05	.01
☐	318 Jack Clark	.10	.05	.01
☐	319 Doug Dascenzo	.05	.02	.01
☐	320 Scott Leius	.05	.02	.01
☐	321 Jim Lindeman	.05	.02	.01
☐	322 Bryan Harvey	.10	.05	.01
☐	323 Spike Owen	.05	.02	.01
☐	324 Roberto Kelly	.10	.05	.01
☐	325 Stan Belinda	.05	.02	.01
☐	326 Joey Cora	.05	.02	.01
☐	327 Jeff Innis	.05	.02	.01
☐	328 Willie Wilson	.05	.02	.01
☐	329 Juan Agosto	.05	.02	.01
☐	330 Charles Nagy	.05	.02	.01
☐	331 Scott Bailes	.05	.02	.01
☐	332 Pete Schourek	.10	.05	.01
☐	333 Mike Flanagan	.05	.02	.01
☐	334 Omar Olivares	.05	.02	.01
☐	335 Dennis Lamp	.05	.02	.01
☐	336 Tommy Greene	.10	.05	.01
☐	337 Randy Velarde	.05	.02	.01
☐	338 Tom Lampkin	.05	.02	.01
☐	339 John Russell	.05	.02	.01
☐	340 Bob Kipper	.05	.02	.01
☐	341 Todd Burns	.05	.02	.01
☐	342 Ron Jones	.05	.02	.01
☐	343 Dave Valle	.05	.02	.01
☐	344 Mike Heath	.05	.02	.01
☐	345 John Olerud	.15	.07	.02
☐	346 Gerald Young	.05	.02	.01
☐	347 Ken Patterson	.05	.02	.01
☐	348 Les Lancaster	.05	.02	.01
☐	349 Steve Crawford	.05	.02	.01
☐	350 John Candelaria	.05	.02	.01
☐	351 Mike Aldrete	.05	.02	.01
☐	352 Mariano Duncan	.05	.02	.01
☐	353 Julio Machado	.05	.02	.01
☐	354 Ken Williams	.05	.02	.01
☐	355 Walt Terrell	.05	.02	.01
☐	356 Mitch Williams	.10	.05	.01
☐	357 Al Newman	.05	.02	.01
☐	358 Bud Black	.05	.02	.01
☐	359 Joe Hesketh	.05	.02	.01
☐	360 Paul Assenmacher	.05	.02	.01
☐	361 Bo Jackson	.15	.07	.02
☐	362 Jeff Blauser	.10	.05	.01
☐	363 Mike Brumley	.05	.02	.01
☐	364 Jim Deshaies	.05	.02	.01
☐	365 Brady Anderson	.10	.05	.01
☐	366 Chuck McElroy	.05	.02	.01
☐	367 Matt Merullo	.05	.02	.01
☐	368 Tim Belcher	.05	.02	.01
☐	369 Luis Aquino	.05	.02	.01
☐	370 Joe Oliver	.05	.02	.01
☐	371 Greg Swindell	.05	.02	.01
☐	372 Lee Stevens	.05	.02	.01
☐	373 Mark Knudson	.05	.02	.01
☐	374 Bill Wegman	.05	.02	.01
☐	375 Jerry Don Gleaton	.05	.02	.01
☐	376 Pedro Guerrero	.10	.05	.01
☐	377 Randy Bush	.05	.02	.01
☐	378 Greg W. Harris	.05	.02	.01

☐ 379	Eric Plunk	.05	.02	.01
☐ 380	Jose DeJesus	.05	.02	.01
☐ 381	Bobby Witt	.05	.02	.01
☐ 382	Curtis Wilkerson	.05	.02	.01
☐ 383	Gene Nelson	.05	.02	.01
☐ 384	Wes Chamberlain	.10	.05	.01
☐ 385	Tom Henke	.10	.05	.01
☐ 386	Mark Lemke	.05	.02	.01
☐ 387	Greg Briley	.05	.02	.01
☐ 388	Rafael Ramirez	.05	.02	.01
☐ 389	Tony Fossas	.05	.02	.01
☐ 390	Henry Cotto	.05	.02	.01
☐ 391	Tim Hulett	.05	.02	.01
☐ 392	Dean Palmer	.10	.05	.01
☐ 393	Glenn Braggs	.05	.02	.01
☐ 394	Mark Salas	.05	.02	.01
☐ 395	Rusty Meacham	.05	.02	.01
☐ 396	Andy Ashby	.05	.02	.01
☐ 397	Jose Melendez	.05	.02	.01
☐ 398	Warren Newson	.05	.02	.01
☐ 399	Frank Castillo	.05	.02	.01
☐ 400	Chito Martinez	.05	.02	.01
☐ 401	Bernie Williams	.10	.05	.01
☐ 402	Derek Bell	.10	.05	.01
☐ 403	Javier Ortiz	.05	.02	.01
☐ 404	Tim Sherrill	.05	.02	.01
☐ 405	Rob MacDonald	.05	.02	.01
☐ 406	Phil Plantier	.15	.07	.02
☐ 407	Troy Afenir	.05	.02	.01
☐ 408	Gino Minutelli	.05	.02	.01
☐ 409	Reggie Jefferson	.05	.02	.01
☐ 410	Mike Remlinger	.05	.02	.01
☐ 411	Carlos Rodriguez	.05	.02	.01
☐ 412	Joe Redfield	.05	.02	.01
☐ 413	Alonzo Powell	.05	.02	.01
☐ 414	Scott Livingstone UER (Travis Fryman, not Woody, should be referenced on back)	.05	.02	.01
☐ 415	Scott Kamieniecki	.05	.02	.01
☐ 416	Tim Spehr	.05	.02	.01
☐ 417	Brian Hunter	.05	.02	.01
☐ 418	Ced Landrum	.05	.02	.01
☐ 419	Bret Barberie	.05	.02	.01
☐ 420	Kevin Morton	.05	.02	.01
☐ 421	Doug Henry	.05	.02	.01
☐ 422	Doug Piatt	.05	.02	.01
☐ 423	Pat Rice	.05	.02	.01
☐ 424	Juan Guzman	.10	.05	.01
☐ 425	Nolan Ryan NH	.50	.23	.06
☐ 426	Tommy Greene NH	.05	.02	.01
☐ 427	Bob Milacki and Mike Flanagan NH (Mark Williamson and Gregg Olson)	.05	.02	.01
☐ 428	Wilson Alvarez NH	.10	.05	.01
☐ 429	Otis Nixon HL	.05	.02	.01
☐ 430	Rickey Henderson HL	.10	.05	.01
☐ 431	Cecil Fielder AS	.10	.05	.01
☐ 432	Julio Franco AS	.05	.02	.01
☐ 433	Cal Ripken AS	.20	.09	.03
☐ 434	Wade Boggs AS	.10	.05	.01
☐ 435	Joe Carter AS	.10	.05	.01
☐ 436	Ken Griffey Jr. AS	.75	.35	.09
☐ 437	Ruben Sierra AS	.10	.05	.01
☐ 438	Scott Erickson AS	.05	.02	.01
☐ 439	Tom Henke AS	.05	.02	.01
☐ 440	Terry Steinbach AS	.05	.02	.01
☐ 441	Rickey Henderson DT	.10	.05	.01
☐ 442	Ryne Sandberg DT	.30	.14	.04
☐ 443	Otis Nixon	.05	.02	.01
☐ 444	Scott Radinsky	.05	.02	.01
☐ 445	Mark Grace	.15	.07	.02
☐ 446	Tony Pena	.05	.02	.01
☐ 447	Billy Hatcher	.05	.02	.01
☐ 448	Glenallen Hill	.05	.02	.01
☐ 449	Chris Gwynn	.05	.02	.01
☐ 450	Tom Glavine	.15	.07	.02
☐ 451	John Habyan	.05	.02	.01
☐ 452	Al Osuna	.05	.02	.01
☐ 453	Tony Phillips	.05	.02	.01
☐ 454	Greg Cadaret	.05	.02	.01
☐ 455	Rob Dibble	.05	.02	.01
☐ 456	Rick Honeycutt	.05	.02	.01
☐ 457	Jerome Walton	.05	.02	.01
☐ 458	Mookie Wilson	.05	.02	.01
☐ 459	Mark Gubicza	.05	.02	.01
☐ 460	Craig Biggio	.10	.05	.01
☐ 461	Dave Cochrane	.05	.02	.01
☐ 462	Keith Miller	.05	.02	.01
☐ 463	Alex Cole	.05	.02	.01
☐ 464	Pete Smith	.05	.02	.01
☐ 465	Brett Butler	.10	.05	.01
☐ 466	Jeff Huson	.05	.02	.01
☐ 467	Steve Lake	.05	.02	.01
☐ 468	Lloyd Moseby	.05	.02	.01
☐ 469	Tim McIntosh	.05	.02	.01
☐ 470	Dennis Martinez	.10	.05	.01
☐ 471	Greg Myers	.05	.02	.01
☐ 472	Mackey Sasser	.05	.02	.01
☐ 473	Junior Ortiz	.05	.02	.01
☐ 474	Greg Olson	.05	.02	.01
☐ 475	Steve Sax	.05	.02	.01
☐ 476	Ricky Jordan	.05	.02	.01
☐ 477	Max Venable	.05	.02	.01
☐ 478	Brian McRae	.15	.07	.02
☐ 479	Doug Simons	.05	.02	.01
☐ 480	Rickey Henderson	.15	.07	.02
☐ 481	Gary Varsho	.05	.02	.01
☐ 482	Carl Willis	.05	.02	.01
☐ 483	Rick Wilkins	.10	.05	.01
☐ 484	Donn Pall	.05	.02	.01
☐ 485	Edgar Martinez	.10	.05	.01
☐ 486	Tom Foley	.05	.02	.01
☐ 487	Mark Williamson	.05	.02	.01
☐ 488	Jack Armstrong	.05	.02	.01
☐ 489	Gary Carter	.15	.07	.02
☐ 490	Ruben Sierra	.15	.07	.02
☐ 491	Gerald Perry	.05	.02	.01
☐ 492	Rob Murphy	.05	.02	.01
☐ 493	Zane Smith	.05	.02	.01
☐ 494	Darryl Kile	.10	.05	.01
☐ 495	Kelly Gruber	.05	.02	.01
☐ 496	Jerry Browne	.05	.02	.01
☐ 497	Darryl Hamilton	.10	.05	.01
☐ 498	Mike Stanton	.05	.02	.01
☐ 499	Mark Leonard	.05	.02	.01
☐ 500	Jose Canseco	.20	.09	.03
☐ 501	Dave Martinez	.05	.02	.01
☐ 502	Jose Guzman	.05	.02	.01
☐ 503	Terry Kennedy	.05	.02	.01
☐ 504	Ed Sprague	.10	.05	.01
☐ 505	Frank Thomas UER (His Gulf Coast League stats are wrong)	1.50	.65	.19
☐ 506	Darren Daulton	.15	.07	.02
☐ 507	Kevin Tapani	.05	.02	.01
☐ 508	Luis Salazar	.05	.02	.01
☐ 509	Paul Faries	.05	.02	.01
☐ 510	Sandy Alomar Jr.	.10	.05	.01
☐ 511	Jeff King	.05	.02	.01
☐ 512	Gary Thurman	.05	.02	.01
☐ 513	Chris Hammond	.05	.02	.01
☐ 514	Pedro Munoz	.10	.05	.01
☐ 515	Alan Trammell	.15	.07	.02
☐ 516	Geronimo Pena	.05	.02	.01

	#	Player			
☐	517	Rodney McCray UER (Stole 6 bases in 1990, not 5; career totals are correct at 7)	.05	.02	.01
☐	518	Manny Lee	.05	.02	.01
☐	519	Junior Felix	.05	.02	.01
☐	520	Kirk Gibson	.10	.05	.01
☐	521	Darrin Jackson	.05	.02	.01
☐	522	John Burkett	.10	.05	.01
☐	523	Jeff Johnson	.05	.02	.01
☐	524	Jim Corsi	.05	.02	.01
☐	525	Robin Yount	.20	.09	.03
☐	526	Jamie Quirk	.05	.02	.01
☐	527	Bob Ojeda	.05	.02	.01
☐	528	Mark Lewis	.05	.02	.01
☐	529	Bryn Smith	.05	.02	.01
☐	530	Kent Hrbek	.10	.05	.01
☐	531	Dennis Boyd	.05	.02	.01
☐	532	Ron Karkovice	.05	.02	.01
☐	533	Don August	.05	.02	.01
☐	534	Todd Frohwirth	.05	.02	.01
☐	535	Wally Joyner	.10	.05	.01
☐	536	Dennis Rasmussen	.05	.02	.01
☐	537	Andy Allanson	.05	.02	.01
☐	538	Goose Gossage	.15	.07	.02
☐	539	John Marzano	.05	.02	.01
☐	540	Cal Ripken	.40	.18	.05
☐	541	Bill Swift UER (Brewers logo on front)	.10	.05	.01
☐	542	Kevin Appier	.10	.05	.01
☐	543	Dave Bergman	.05	.02	.01
☐	544	Bernard Gilkey	.10	.05	.01
☐	545	Mike Greenwell	.10	.05	.01
☐	546	Jose Uribe	.05	.02	.01
☐	547	Jesse Orosco	.05	.02	.01
☐	548	Bob Patterson	.05	.02	.01
☐	549	Mike Stanley	.05	.02	.01
☐	550	Howard Johnson	.10	.05	.01
☐	551	Joe Orsulak	.05	.02	.01
☐	552	Dick Schofield	.05	.02	.01
☐	553	Dave Hollins	.15	.07	.02
☐	554	David Segui	.05	.02	.01
☐	555	Barry Bonds	.40	.18	.05
☐	556	Mo Vaughn	.20	.09	.03
☐	557	Craig Wilson	.05	.02	.01
☐	558	Bobby Rose	.05	.02	.01
☐	559	Rod Nichols	.05	.02	.01
☐	560	Len Dykstra	.15	.07	.02
☐	561	Craig Grebeck	.05	.02	.01
☐	562	Darren Lewis	.10	.05	.01
☐	563	Todd Benzinger	.05	.02	.01
☐	564	Ed Whitson	.05	.02	.01
☐	565	Jesse Barfield	.05	.02	.01
☐	566	Lloyd McClendon	.05	.02	.01
☐	567	Dan Plesac	.05	.02	.01
☐	568	Danny Cox	.05	.02	.01
☐	569	Skeeter Barnes	.05	.02	.01
☐	570	Bobby Thigpen	.05	.02	.01
☐	571	Deion Sanders	.25	.11	.03
☐	572	Chuck Knoblauch	.15	.07	.02
☐	573	Matt Nokes	.05	.02	.01
☐	574	Herm Winningham	.05	.02	.01
☐	575	Tom Candiotti	.05	.02	.01
☐	576	Jeff Bagwell	.75	.35	.09
☐	577	Brook Jacoby	.05	.02	.01
☐	578	Chico Walker	.05	.02	.01
☐	579	Brian Downing	.05	.02	.01
☐	580	Dave Stewart	.10	.05	.01
☐	581	Francisco Cabrera	.05	.02	.01
☐	582	Rene Gonzales	.05	.02	.01
☐	583	Stan Javier	.05	.02	.01
☐	584	Randy Johnson	.15	.07	.02
☐	585	Chuck Finley	.05	.02	.01
☐	586	Mark Gardner	.05	.02	.01
☐	587	Mark Whiten	.10	.05	.01
☐	588	Garry Templeton	.05	.02	.01
☐	589	Gary Sheffield	.15	.07	.02
☐	590	Ozzie Smith	.20	.09	.03
☐	591	Candy Maldonado	.05	.02	.01
☐	592	Mike Sharperson	.05	.02	.01
☐	593	Carlos Martinez	.05	.02	.01
☐	594	Scott Bankhead	.05	.02	.01
☐	595	Tim Wallach	.05	.02	.01
☐	596	Tino Martinez	.10	.05	.01
☐	597	Roger McDowell	.05	.02	.01
☐	598	Cory Snyder	.05	.02	.01
☐	599	Andujar Cedeno	.10	.05	.01
☐	600	Kirby Puckett	.30	.14	.04
☐	601	Rick Parker	.05	.02	.01
☐	602	Todd Hundley	.05	.02	.01
☐	603	Greg Litton	.05	.02	.01
☐	604	Dave Johnson	.05	.02	.01
☐	605	John Franco	.05	.02	.01
☐	606	Mike Fetters	.05	.02	.01
☐	607	Luis Alicea	.05	.02	.01
☐	608	Trevor Wilson	.05	.02	.01
☐	609	Rob Ducey	.05	.02	.01
☐	610	Ramon Martinez	.10	.05	.01
☐	611	Dave Burba	.05	.02	.01
☐	612	Dwight Smith	.05	.02	.01
☐	613	Kevin Maas	.05	.02	.01
☐	614	John Costello	.05	.02	.01
☐	615	Glenn Davis	.05	.02	.01
☐	616	Shawn Abner	.05	.02	.01
☐	617	Scott Hemond	.05	.02	.01
☐	618	Tom Prince	.05	.02	.01
☐	619	Wally Ritchie	.05	.02	.01
☐	620	Jim Abbott	.15	.07	.02
☐	621	Charlie O'Brien	.05	.02	.01
☐	622	Jack Daugherty	.05	.02	.01
☐	623	Tommy Gregg	.05	.02	.01
☐	624	Jeff Shaw	.05	.02	.01
☐	625	Tony Gwynn	.25	.11	.03
☐	626	Mark Leiter	.05	.02	.01
☐	627	Jim Clancy	.05	.02	.01
☐	628	Tim Layana	.05	.02	.01
☐	629	Jeff Schaefer	.05	.02	.01
☐	630	Lee Smith	.15	.07	.02
☐	631	Wade Taylor	.05	.02	.01
☐	632	Mike Simms	.05	.02	.01
☐	633	Terry Steinbach	.10	.05	.01
☐	634	Shawon Dunston	.05	.02	.01
☐	635	Tim Raines	.15	.07	.02
☐	636	Kirt Manwaring	.05	.02	.01
☐	637	Warren Cromartie	.05	.02	.01
☐	638	Luis Quinones	.05	.02	.01
☐	639	Greg Vaughn	.10	.05	.01
☐	640	Kevin Mitchell	.10	.05	.01
☐	641	Chris Hoiles	.15	.07	.02
☐	642	Tom Browning	.05	.02	.01
☐	643	Mitch Webster	.05	.02	.01
☐	644	Steve Olin	.05	.02	.01
☐	645	Tony Fernandez	.10	.05	.01
☐	646	Juan Bell	.05	.02	.01
☐	647	Joe Boever	.05	.02	.01
☐	648	Carney Lansford	.10	.05	.01
☐	649	Mike Benjamin	.05	.02	.01
☐	650	George Brett	.30	.14	.04
☐	651	Tim Burke	.05	.02	.01
☐	652	Jack Morris	.15	.07	.02
☐	653	Orel Hershiser	.10	.05	.01
☐	654	Mike Schooler	.05	.02	.01
☐	655	Andy Van Slyke	.15	.07	.02
☐	656	Dave Stieb	.10	.05	.01
☐	657	Dave Clark	.05	.02	.01
☐	658	Ben McDonald	.10	.05	.01

- ☐ 659 John Smiley .05 .02 .01
- ☐ 660 Wade Boggs .15 .07 .02
- ☐ 661 Eric Bullock .05 .02 .01
- ☐ 662 Eric Show .05 .02 .01
- ☐ 663 Lenny Webster .05 .02 .01
- ☐ 664 Mike Huff .05 .02 .01
- ☐ 665 Rick Sutcliffe .10 .05 .01
- ☐ 666 Jeff Manto .05 .02 .01
- ☐ 667 Mike Fitzgerald .05 .02 .01
- ☐ 668 Matt Young .05 .02 .01
- ☐ 669 Dave West .05 .02 .01
- ☐ 670 Mike Hartley .05 .02 .01
- ☐ 671 Curt Schilling .10 .05 .01
- ☐ 672 Brian Bohanon .05 .02 .01
- ☐ 673 Cecil Espy .05 .02 .01
- ☐ 674 Joe Grahe .05 .02 .01
- ☐ 675 Sid Fernandez .10 .05 .01
- ☐ 676 Edwin Nunez .05 .02 .01
- ☐ 677 Hector Villanueva .05 .02 .01
- ☐ 678 Sean Berry .10 .05 .01
- ☐ 679 Dave Eiland .05 .02 .01
- ☐ 680 Dave Cone .15 .07 .02
- ☐ 681 Mike Bordick .05 .02 .01
- ☐ 682 Tony Castillo .05 .02 .01
- ☐ 683 John Barfield .05 .02 .01
- ☐ 684 Jeff Hamilton .05 .02 .01
- ☐ 685 Ken Dayley .05 .02 .01
- ☐ 686 Carmelo Martinez .05 .02 .01
- ☐ 687 Mike Capel .05 .02 .01
- ☐ 688 Scott Chiamparino .05 .02 .01
- ☐ 689 Rich Gedman .05 .02 .01
- ☐ 690 Rich Monteleone .05 .02 .01
- ☐ 691 Alejandro Pena .05 .02 .01
- ☐ 692 Oscar Azocar .05 .02 .01
- ☐ 693 Jim Poole .05 .02 .01
- ☐ 694 Mike Gardiner .05 .02 .01
- ☐ 695 Steve Buechele .05 .02 .01
- ☐ 696 Rudy Seanez .05 .02 .01
- ☐ 697 Paul Abbott .05 .02 .01
- ☐ 698 Steve Searcy .05 .02 .01
- ☐ 699 Jose Offerman .05 .02 .01
- ☐ 700 Ivan Rodriguez .15 .07 .02
- ☐ 701 Joe Girardi .05 .02 .01
- ☐ 702 Tony Perezchica .05 .02 .01
- ☐ 703 Paul McClellan .05 .02 .01
- ☐ 704 David Howard .05 .02 .01
- ☐ 705 Dan Petry .05 .02 .01
- ☐ 706 Jack Howell .05 .02 .01
- ☐ 707 Jose Mesa .05 .02 .01
- ☐ 708 Randy St. Claire .05 .02 .01
- ☐ 709 Kevin Brown .10 .05 .01
- ☐ 710 Ron Darling .05 .02 .01
- ☐ 711 Jason Grimsley .05 .02 .01
- ☐ 712 John Orton .05 .02 .01
- ☐ 713 Shawn Boskie .05 .02 .01
- ☐ 714 Pat Clements .05 .02 .01
- ☐ 715 Brian Barnes .05 .02 .01
- ☐ 716 Luis Lopez .05 .02 .01
- ☐ 717 Bob McClure .05 .02 .01
- ☐ 718 Mark Davis .05 .02 .01
- ☐ 719 Dann Bilardello .05 .02 .01
- ☐ 720 Tom Edens .05 .02 .01
- ☐ 721 Willie Fraser .05 .02 .01
- ☐ 722 Curt Young .05 .02 .01
- ☐ 723 Neal Heaton .05 .02 .01
- ☐ 724 Craig Worthington .05 .02 .01
- ☐ 725 Mel Rojas .05 .02 .01
- ☐ 726 Daryl Irvine .05 .02 .01
- ☐ 727 Roger Mason .05 .02 .01
- ☐ 728 Kirk Dressendorfer .05 .02 .01
- ☐ 729 Scott Aldred .05 .02 .01
- ☐ 730 Willie Blair .05 .02 .01
- ☐ 731 Allan Anderson .05 .02 .01
- ☐ 732 Dana Kiecker .05 .02 .01
- ☐ 733 Jose Gonzalez .05 .02 .01
- ☐ 734 Brian Drahman .05 .02 .01
- ☐ 735 Brad Komminsk .05 .02 .01
- ☐ 736 Arthur Rhodes .10 .05 .01
- ☐ 737 Terry Mathews .05 .02 .01
- ☐ 738 Jeff Fassero .05 .02 .01
- ☐ 739 Mike Magnante .05 .02 .01
- ☐ 740 Kip Gross .05 .02 .01
- ☐ 741 Jim Hunter .05 .02 .01
- ☐ 742 Jose Mota .05 .02 .01
- ☐ 743 Joe Bitker .05 .02 .01
- ☐ 744 Tim Mauser .05 .02 .01
- ☐ 745 Ramon Garcia .05 .02 .01
- ☐ 746 Rod Beck .30 .14 .04
- ☐ 747 Jim Austin .05 .02 .01
- ☐ 748 Keith Mitchell .05 .02 .01
- ☐ 749 Wayne Rosenthal .05 .02 .01
- ☐ 750 Bryan Hickerson .05 .02 .01
- ☐ 751 Bruce Egloff .05 .02 .01
- ☐ 752 John Wehner .05 .02 .01
- ☐ 753 Darren Holmes .05 .02 .01
- ☐ 754 Dave Hansen .05 .02 .01
- ☐ 755 Mike Mussina .30 .14 .04
- ☐ 756 Anthony Young .10 .05 .01
- ☐ 757 Ron Tingley .05 .02 .01
- ☐ 758 Ricky Bones .10 .05 .01
- ☐ 759 Mark Wohlers .10 .05 .01
- ☐ 760 Wilson Alvarez .15 .07 .02
- ☐ 761 Harvey Pulliam .05 .02 .01
- ☐ 762 Ryan Bowen .05 .02 .01
- ☐ 763 Terry Bross .05 .02 .01
- ☐ 764 Joel Johnston .05 .02 .01
- ☐ 765 Terry McDaniel .05 .02 .01
- ☐ 766 Esteban Beltre .05 .02 .01
- ☐ 767 Rob Maurer .05 .02 .01
- ☐ 768 Ted Wood .05 .02 .01
- ☐ 769 Mo Sanford .05 .02 .01
- ☐ 770 Jeff Carter .05 .02 .01
- ☐ 771 Gil Heredia .05 .02 .01
- ☐ 772 Monty Fariss .05 .02 .01
- ☐ 773 Will Clark AS .10 .05 .01
- ☐ 774 Ryne Sandberg AS .20 .09 .03
- ☐ 775 Barry Larkin AS .10 .05 .01
- ☐ 776 Howard Johnson AS .05 .02 .01
- ☐ 777 Barry Bonds AS .25 .11 .03
- ☐ 778 Brett Butler AS .05 .02 .01
- ☐ 779 Tony Gwynn AS .20 .09 .03
- ☐ 780 Ramon Martinez AS .05 .02 .01
- ☐ 781 Lee Smith AS .10 .05 .01
- ☐ 782 Mike Scioscia AS .05 .02 .01
- ☐ 783 Dennis Martinez HL UER .05 .02 .01
  (Card has both 13th
  and 15th perfect game
  in Major League history)
- ☐ 784 Dennis Martinez NH .05 .02 .01
- ☐ 785 Mark Gardner NH .05 .02 .01
- ☐ 786 Bret Saberhagen NH .05 .02 .01
- ☐ 787 Kent Mercker NH .05 .02 .01
  Mark Wohlers
  Alejandro Pena
- ☐ 788 Cal Ripken MVP .30 .14 .04
- ☐ 789 Terry Pendleton MVP .10 .05 .01
- ☐ 790 Roger Clemens CY .15 .07 .02
- ☐ 791 Tom Glavine CY .10 .05 .01
- ☐ 792 Chuck Knoblauch ROY .10 .05 .01
- ☐ 793 Jeff Bagwell ROY .40 .18 .05
- ☐ 794 Cal Ripken MANYR .30 .14 .04
- ☐ 795 David Cone HL .10 .05 .01
- ☐ 796 Kirby Puckett HL .20 .09 .03
- ☐ 797 Steve Avery HL .10 .05 .01
- ☐ 798 Jack Morris HL .10 .05 .01
- ☐ 799 Allen Watson DC .15 .07 .02

☐ 800	Manny Ramirez DC	1.50	.65	.19
☐ 801	Cliff Floyd DC	1.25	.55	.16
☐ 802	Al Shirley DC	.15	.07	.02
☐ 803	Brian Barber DC	.15	.07	.02
☐ 804	Jon Farrell DC	.15	.07	.02
☐ 805	Brent Gates DC	.25	.11	.03
☐ 806	Scott Ruffcorn DC	.25	.11	.03
☐ 807	Tyrone Hill DC	.15	.07	.02
☐ 808	Benji Gil DC	.20	.09	.03
☐ 809	Aaron Sele DC	.60	.25	.08
☐ 810	Tyler Green DC	.15	.07	.02
☐ 811	Chris Jones	.05	.02	.01
☐ 812	Steve Wilson	.05	.02	.01
☐ 813	Freddie Benavides	.05	.02	.01
☐ 814	Don Wakamatsu	.05	.02	.01
☐ 815	Mike Humphreys	.10	.05	.01
☐ 816	Scott Servais	.05	.02	.01
☐ 817	Rico Rossy	.05	.02	.01
☐ 818	John Ramos	.05	.02	.01
☐ 819	Rob Mallicoat	.05	.02	.01
☐ 820	Milt Hill	.05	.02	.01
☐ 821	Carlos Garcia	.10	.05	.01
☐ 822	Stan Royer	.05	.02	.01
☐ 823	Jeff Plympton	.05	.02	.01
☐ 824	Braulio Castillo	.05	.02	.01
☐ 825	David Haas	.05	.02	.01
☐ 826	Luis Mercedes	.10	.05	.01
☐ 827	Eric Karros	.15	.07	.02
☐ 828	Shawn Hare	.10	.05	.01
☐ 829	Reggie Sanders	.20	.09	.03
☐ 830	Tom Goodwin	.05	.02	.01
☐ 831	Dan Gakeler	.05	.02	.01
☐ 832	Stacy Jones	.10	.05	.01
☐ 833	Kim Batiste	.05	.02	.01
☐ 834	Cal Eldred	.10	.05	.01
☐ 835	Chris George	.05	.02	.01
☐ 836	Wayne Housie	.05	.02	.01
☐ 837	Mike Ignasiak	.05	.02	.01
☐ 838	Josias Manzanillo	.10	.05	.01
☐ 839	Jim Olander	.05	.02	.01
☐ 840	Gary Cooper	.05	.02	.01
☐ 841	Royce Clayton	.15	.07	.02
☐ 842	Hector Fajardo	.05	.02	.01
☐ 843	Blaine Beatty	.05	.02	.01
☐ 844	Jorge Pedre	.05	.02	.01
☐ 845	Kenny Lofton	1.00	.45	.13
☐ 846	Scott Brosius	.05	.02	.01
☐ 847	Chris Cron	.05	.02	.01
☐ 848	Denis Boucher	.05	.02	.01
☐ 849	Kyle Abbott	.05	.02	.01
☐ 850	Bob Zupcic	.05	.02	.01
☐ 851	Rheal Cormier	.05	.02	.01
☐ 852	Jim Lewis	.05	.02	.01
☐ 853	Anthony Telford	.05	.02	.01
☐ 854	Cliff Brantley	.10	.05	.01
☐ 855	Kevin Campbell	.05	.02	.01
☐ 856	Craig Shipley	.10	.05	.01
☐ 857	Chuck Carr	.10	.05	.01
☐ 858	Tony Eusebio	.05	.02	.01
☐ 859	Jim Thome	.40	.18	.05
☐ 860	Vinny Castilla	.05	.02	.01
☐ 861	Dann Howitt	.05	.02	.01
☐ 862	Kevin Ward	.05	.02	.01
☐ 863	Steve Wapnick	.05	.02	.01
☐ 864	Rod Brewer	.05	.02	.01
☐ 865	Todd Van Poppel	.15	.07	.02
☐ 866	Jose Hernandez	.05	.02	.01
☐ 867	Amalio Carreno	.10	.05	.01
☐ 868	Calvin Jones	.05	.02	.01
☐ 869	Jeff Gardner	.05	.02	.01
☐ 870	Jarvis Brown	.05	.02	.01
☐ 871	Eddie Taubensee	.05	.02	.01
☐ 872	Andy Mota	.05	.02	.01
☐ 873	Chris Haney	.05	.02	.01
☐ 874	Roberto Hernandez	.10	.05	.01
☐ 875	Laddie Renfroe	.05	.02	.01
☐ 876	Scott Cooper	.10	.05	.01
☐ 877	Armando Reynoso	.05	.02	.01
☐ 878	Ty Cobb MEMO	.25	.11	.03
☐ 879	Babe Ruth MEMO	.30	.14	.04
☐ 880	Honus Wagner MEMO	.15	.07	.02
☐ 881	Lou Gehrig MEMO	.25	.11	.03
☐ 882	Satchel Paige MEMO	.15	.07	.02
☐ 883	Will Clark DT	.20	.09	.03
☐ 884	Cal Ripken DT	.40	.18	.05
☐ 885	Wade Boggs DT	.10	.05	.01
☐ 886	Kirby Puckett DT	.35	.16	.04
☐ 887	Tony Gwynn DT	.20	.09	.03
☐ 888	Craig Biggio DT	.05	.02	.01
☐ 889	Scott Erickson DT	.05	.02	.01
☐ 890	Tom Glavine DT	.10	.05	.01
☐ 891	Rob Dibble DT	.05	.02	.01
☐ 892	Mitch Williams DT	.05	.02	.01
☐ 893	Frank Thomas DT	1.50	.65	.19
☐ X672	Chuck Knoblauch AU (1990 Score card, autographed with special hologram on back)	60.00	27.00	7.50

1992 Score Joe DiMaggio

This five-card standard-size (2 1/2" by 3 1/2") set was issued in honor of one of baseball's all-time greats, Joe DiMaggio. Supposedly 30,000 of each card were produced. On a white card face, the fronts have vintage photos that have been colorized and accented by red, white, and blue border stripes. The player's name appears in an orange bar and the card title in a white banner beneath the picture. The backs feature a different colorized player photo and career highlights (on gray), framed between a red top stripe and a navy blue bottom stripe. The cards are numbered on the back.

	MINT	EXC	G-VG
COMPLETE SET (5)	200.00	90.00	25.00
COMMON DIMAGGIO (1-5)	40.00	18.00	5.00
☐ 1 Joe DiMaggio The Minors	40.00	18.00	5.00
☐ 2 Joe DiMaggio The Rookie	40.00	18.00	5.00

☐ 3 Joe DiMaggio............... 40.00 18.00 5.00
The MVP
☐ 4 Joe DiMaggio............... 40.00 18.00 5.00
The Streak
☐ 5 Joe DiMaggio............... 40.00 18.00 5.00
The Legend
☐ AU Joe DiMaggio AU 600.00 275.00 75.00
(Autographed with
certified signature)

1992 Score Factory Inserts

This 17-card insert set was included in 1992 Score factory sets and consists of four topical subsets. Cards B1-B7 capture a moment from each game of the 1991 World Series. Cards B8-B11 are Cooperstown cards, honoring future Hall of Famers. Cards B12-B14 form a "Joe D" subset paying tribute to Joe DiMaggio. Cards B15-B17, subtitled "Yaz", conclude the set by commemorating Carl Yastrzemski's heroic feats twenty-five years ago in winning the Triple Crown and lifting the Red Sox to their first American League pennant in 21 years. The cards measure the standard size (2 1/2" by 3 1/2"), and each subset displays a different front design. The World Series cards carry full-bleed color action photos except for a blue stripe at the bottom, while the Cooperstown cards have a color portrait on a white card face. Both the DiMaggio and Yastrzemski subsets have action photos with silver borders; they differ in that the DiMaggio photos are black and white, the Yastrzemski photos color. The DiMaggio and Yastrzemski subsets are numbered on the back within each subset (e.g., "1 of 3") and as a part of the 17-card insert set (e.g., "B1"). In the DiMaggio and Yastrzemski subsets, Score varied the insert set slightly in retail versus hobby factory sets. In the hobby set, the DiMaggio cards display different black-and-white photos that are bordered beneath by a dark blue stripe (the stripe is green in the retail factory insert). On the backs, these hobby inserts have a red stripe at the bottom; the same stripe is dark blue on the retail inserts. The Yastrzemski cards in the hobby set have different color photos on their fronts than the retail inserts.

	MINT	EXC	G-VG
COMPLETE SET (17)	10.00	4.50	1.25
COMMON WS (B1-B7)...............	.30	.14	.04
COMMON COOP. (B8-B11)......	1.00	.45	.13
COMMON DIMAGGIO (B12-B14)	2.00	.90	.25
COMMON YAZ (B15-B17)..........	.50	.23	.06

☐ B1 1991 WS Game 1 .... .30 .14 .04
(Greg) Gagne powers
Twins to win
☐ B2 1991 WS Game 2 .... .30 .14 .04
(Scott) Leius lifts
Twins to 2-0 lead
☐ B3 1991 WS Game 3 .... .30 .14 .04
(Mark) Lemke leaves
Twins limp
(David Justice)
☐ B4 1991 WS Game 4 .... .30 .14 .04
Braves gain series tie
(Lonnie Smith and
Brian Harper)
☐ B5 1991 WS Game 5 .... 1.75 .80 .22
Braves bomb Twins
(David Justice)
☐ B6 1991 WS Game 6 .... 3.00 1.35 .40
Kirby (Puckett) keeps
the Twins alive
☐ B7 1991 WS Game 7 .... .30 .14 .04
A Classic win for the
Twins (Gene Larkin)
☐ B8 Carlton Fisk.................. 1.00 .45 .13
Cooperstown Card
☐ B9 Ozzie Smith.................. 2.50 1.15 .30
Cooperstown Card
☐ B10 Dave Winfield .... 1.75 .80 .22
Cooperstown Card
☐ B11 Robin Yount .... 2.00 .90 .25
Cooperstown Card
☐ B12 Joe DiMaggio .... 2.00 .90 .25
The Hard Hitter
☐ B13 Joe DiMaggio .... 2.00 .90 .25
The Stylish Fielder
☐ B14 Joe DiMaggio .... 2.00 .90 .25
The Championship Player
☐ B15 Carl Yastrzemski.......... .50 .23 .06
The Impossible Dream
☐ B16 Carl Yastrzemski.......... .50 .23 .06
The Triple Crown
☐ B17 Carl Yastrzemski.......... .50 .23 .06
The World Series

1992 Score Franchise

This four-card set features three all-time greats, Stan Musial, Mickey Mantle, and Carl Yastrzemski, and measures the standard size (2 1/2" by 3 1/2"). Each former player autographed 2,000 of his 1992 Score cards, and 500 of the combo cards were signed by all three. In addition to these signed cards, Score produced 600,000 unsigned cards (150,000 of each Franchise card), and both signed and unsigned cards were randomly inserted in 1992 Score Series II poly packs, blister packs, and cello packs. The first three cards feature color

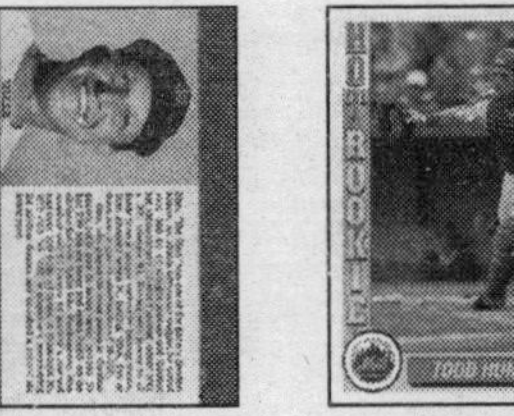

action photos of each player. The fourth is horizontally oriented and pictures each player in a batting stance. A forest green stripe borders the top and bottom. The words "The Franchise" and the Score logo appear at the top, and the player's name is printed on the green stripe at the bottom. The backs of the first three cards have a close-up photo and a career summary. The fourth card is a combo card, summarizing the career of all three players. The cards are numbered on the back.

	MINT	EXC	G-VG
COMPLETE SET (4)	32.00	14.50	4.00
COMMON CARD (1-4)	8.00	3.60	1.00
☐ 1 Stan Musial	8.00	3.60	1.00
☐ 2 Mickey Mantle	14.00	6.25	1.75
☐ 3 Carl Yastrzemski	8.00	3.60	1.00
☐ 4 The Franchise Players Stan Musial Mickey Mantle Carl Yastrzemski	10.00	4.50	1.25
☐ AU1 Stan Musial (Autographed with certified signature)	250.00	115.00	31.00
☐ AU2 Mickey Mantle (Autographed with certified signature)	500.00	230.00	65.00
☐ AU3 Carl Yastrzemski (Autographed with certified signature)	175.00	80.00	22.00
☐ AU4 Franchise Players Stan Musial Mickey Mantle Carl Yastrzemski (Autographed with certified signatures of all three)	1500.00	700.00	190.00

1992 Score Hot Rookies

This ten-card set measures the standard size (2 1/2" by 3 1/2"). The front design features color action player photos on a white face. The words "Hot Rookie" appear in orange and yellow vertically along the left edge of the photo, and the team logo is in the lower left corner. The player's name is printed in yellow on a red box accented with a shadow detail. The Score brand mark is superimposed on the lower right corner of the picture. The horizontally oriented backs display color close-up photos. As on the fronts, the words "Hot Rookie" appear along the left photo edge. The player's name is also printed on the back as it is on the front. A career summary is shown in a graded orange background. The cards are numbered on the back.

	MINT	EXC	G-VG
COMPLETE SET (10)	12.00	5.50	1.50
COMMON CARD (1-10)	.50	.23	.06
☐ 1 Cal Eldred	1.00	.45	.13
☐ 2 Royce Clayton	.75	.35	.09
☐ 3 Kenny Lofton	8.00	3.60	1.00
☐ 4 Todd Van Poppel	1.00	.45	.13
☐ 5 Scott Cooper	1.00	.45	.13
☐ 6 Todd Hundley	.50	.23	.06
☐ 7 Tino Martinez	.50	.23	.06
☐ 8 Anthony Telford	.50	.23	.06
☐ 9 Derek Bell	1.00	.45	.13
☐ 10 Reggie Jefferson	.50	.23	.06

1992 Score Impact Players

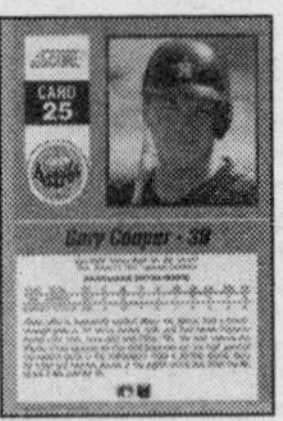

The 1992 Score Impact Players insert set was issued in two series each with 45 cards with the respective series of the 1992 regular issue Score cards. Five cards from the 45-card first (second) series were randomly inserted in each 1992 Score I (II) jumbo pack. The cards measure the standard size (2 1/2" by 3 1/2") and the fronts feature full-bleed color action player photos. The pic-

tures are enhanced by a wide vertical stripe running near the left edge containing the words "90's Impact Player" and a narrower stripe at the bottom printed with the player's name. The stripes are team color-coded and intersect at the team logo in the lower left corner. The backs display close-up color player photos. The picture borders and background colors reflect the team's colors. A white box below the photo contains biographical and statistical information as well as a career summary. The cards are numbered on the back.

	MINT	EXC	G-VG
COMPLETE SET (90)	20.00	9.00	2.50
COMPLETE SERIES 1 (45)	14.00	6.25	1.75
COMPLETE SERIES 2 (45)	6.00	2.70	.75
COMMON CARD (1-45)	.10	.05	.01
COMMON CARD (46-90)	.10	.05	.01

	MINT	EXC	G-VG
☐ 1 Chuck Knoblauch	.35	.16	.04
☐ 2 Jeff Bagwell	2.00	.90	.25
☐ 3 Juan Guzman	.10	.05	.01
☐ 4 Milt Cuyler	.10	.05	.01
☐ 5 Ivan Rodriguez	.15	.07	.02
☐ 6 Rich DeLucia	.10	.05	.01
☐ 7 Orlando Merced	.10	.05	.01
☐ 8 Ray Lankford	.10	.05	.01
☐ 9 Brian Hunter	.10	.05	.01
☐ 10 Roberto Alomar	.50	.23	.06
☐ 11 Wes Chamberlain	.10	.05	.01
☐ 12 Steve Avery	.30	.14	.04
☐ 13 Scott Erickson	.10	.05	.01
☐ 14 Jim Abbott	.15	.07	.02
☐ 15 Mark Whiten	.10	.05	.01
☐ 16 Leo Gomez	.10	.05	.01
☐ 17 Doug Henry	.10	.05	.01
☐ 18 Brent Mayne	.10	.05	.01
☐ 19 Charles Nagy	.10	.05	.01
☐ 20 Phil Plantier	.10	.05	.01
☐ 21 Mo Vaughn	.50	.23	.06
☐ 22 Craig Biggio	.15	.07	.02
☐ 23 Derek Bell	.10	.05	.01
☐ 24 Royce Clayton	.10	.05	.01
☐ 25 Gary Cooper	.10	.05	.01
☐ 26 Scott Cooper	.10	.05	.01
☐ 27 Juan Gonzalez	1.50	.65	.19
☐ 28 Ken Griffey Jr.	3.50	1.55	.45
☐ 29 Larry Walker	.15	.07	.02
☐ 30 John Smoltz	.15	.07	.02
☐ 31 Todd Hundley	.10	.05	.01
☐ 32 Kenny Lofton	2.50	1.15	.30
☐ 33 Andy Mota	.10	.05	.01
☐ 34 Todd Zeile	.15	.07	.02
☐ 35 Arthur Rhodes	.10	.05	.01
☐ 36 Jim Thome	1.00	.45	.13
☐ 37 Todd Van Poppel	.10	.05	.01
☐ 38 Mark Wohlers	.10	.05	.01
☐ 39 Anthony Young	.10	.05	.01
☐ 40 Sandy Alomar Jr.	.10	.05	.01
☐ 41 John Olerud	.10	.05	.01
☐ 42 Robin Ventura	.25	.11	.03
☐ 43 Frank Thomas	4.00	1.80	.50
☐ 44 David Justice	.50	.23	.06
☐ 45 Hal Morris	.10	.05	.01
☐ 46 Ruben Sierra	.15	.07	.02
☐ 47 Travis Fryman	.50	.23	.06
☐ 48 Mike Mussina	.75	.35	.09
☐ 49 Tom Glavine	.25	.11	.03
☐ 50 Barry Larkin	.15	.07	.02
☐ 51 Will Clark	.40	.18	.05
☐ 52 Jose Canseco	.40	.18	.05
☐ 53 Bo Jackson	.25	.11	.03
☐ 54 Dwight Gooden	.10	.05	.01
☐ 55 Barry Bonds	1.00	.45	.13
☐ 56 Fred McGriff	.40	.18	.05
☐ 57 Roger Clemens	.50	.23	.06
☐ 58 Benito Santiago	.10	.05	.01
☐ 59 Darryl Strawberry	.15	.07	.02
☐ 60 Cecil Fielder	.25	.11	.03
☐ 61 John Franco	.10	.05	.01
☐ 62 Matt Williams	.40	.18	.05
☐ 63 Marquis Grissom	.15	.07	.02
☐ 64 Danny Tartabull	.15	.07	.02
☐ 65 Ron Gant	.10	.05	.01
☐ 66 Paul O'Neill	.15	.07	.02
☐ 67 Devon White	.15	.07	.02
☐ 68 Rafael Palmeiro	.25	.11	.03
☐ 69 Tom Gordon	.10	.05	.01
☐ 70 Shawon Dunston	.10	.05	.01
☐ 71 Rob Dibble	.10	.05	.01
☐ 72 Eddie Zosky	.10	.05	.01
☐ 73 Jack McDowell	.15	.07	.02
☐ 74 Len Dykstra	.15	.07	.02
☐ 75 Ramon Martinez	.15	.07	.02
☐ 76 Reggie Sanders	.50	.23	.06
☐ 77 Greg Maddux	.40	.18	.05
☐ 78 Ellis Burks	.15	.07	.02
☐ 79 John Smiley	.10	.05	.01
☐ 80 Roberto Kelly	.10	.05	.01
☐ 81 Ben McDonald	.10	.05	.01
☐ 82 Mark Lewis	.10	.05	.01
☐ 83 Jose Rijo	.15	.07	.02
☐ 84 Ozzie Guillen	.10	.05	.01
☐ 85 Lance Dickson	.10	.05	.01
☐ 86 Kim Batiste	.10	.05	.01
☐ 87 Gregg Olson	.10	.05	.01
☐ 88 Andy Benes	.10	.05	.01
☐ 89 Cal Eldred	.10	.05	.01
☐ 90 David Cone	.15	.07	.02

1992 Score Rookie/Traded

The 1992 Score Rookie and Traded set contains 110 standard-size (2 1/2" by 3 1/2") cards featuring traded veterans and rookies. The fronts display color action player photos edged on one side by an orange stripe that fades to white as one moves down the card face. The player's name appears in a purple bar above the picture, while his position is printed in a purple bar below the picture. The backs carry a color close-up photo, biography, and on a yellow panel, batting or pitching statistics and

career summary. The cards are numbered on the back with the "T" suffix. The set is arranged numerically such that cards 1T-79T are traded players and cards 80T-110T feature rookies. Rookie Cards in this set include Chad Curtis, Brian Jordan, and Jeff Kent.

	MINT	EXC	G-VG
COMPLETE FACT.SET (110)	30.00	13.50	3.80
COMMON CARD (1T-110T)	.10	.05	.01
☐ 1T Gary Sheffield	.50	.23	.06
☐ 2T Kevin Seitzer	.10	.05	.01
☐ 3T Danny Tartabull	.15	.07	.02
☐ 4T Steve Sax	.10	.05	.01
☐ 5T Bobby Bonilla	.20	.09	.03
☐ 6T Frank Viola	.15	.07	.02
☐ 7T Dave Winfield	1.00	.45	.13
☐ 8T Rick Sutcliffe	.15	.07	.02
☐ 9T Jose Canseco	1.50	.65	.19
☐ 10T Greg Swindell	.10	.05	.01
☐ 11T Eddie Murray	.50	.23	.06
☐ 12T Randy Myers	.15	.07	.02
☐ 13T Wally Joyner	.15	.07	.02
☐ 14T Kenny Lofton	8.00	3.60	1.00
☐ 15T Jack Morris	.20	.09	.03
☐ 16T Charlie Hayes	.15	.07	.02
☐ 17T Pete Incaviglia	.10	.05	.01
☐ 18T Kevin Mitchell	.15	.07	.02
☐ 19T Kurt Stillwell	.10	.05	.01
☐ 20T Bret Saberhagen	.15	.07	.02
☐ 21T Steve Buechele	.10	.05	.01
☐ 22T John Smiley	.10	.05	.01
☐ 23T Sammy Sosa	.60	.25	.08
☐ 24T George Bell	.15	.07	.02
☐ 25T Curt Schilling	.15	.07	.02
☐ 26T Dick Schofield	.10	.05	.01
☐ 27T David Cone	.20	.09	.03
☐ 28T Dan Gladden	.10	.05	.01
☐ 29T Kirk McCaskill	.10	.05	.01
☐ 30T Mike Gallego	.10	.05	.01
☐ 31T Kevin McReynolds	.10	.05	.01
☐ 32T Bill Swift	.15	.07	.02
☐ 33T Dave Martinez	.10	.05	.01
☐ 34T Storm Davis	.10	.05	.01
☐ 35T Willie Randolph	.15	.07	.02
☐ 36T Melido Perez	.10	.05	.01
☐ 37T Mark Carreon	.10	.05	.01
☐ 38T Doug Jones	.10	.05	.01
☐ 39T Gregg Jefferies	.75	.35	.09
☐ 40T Mike Jackson	.10	.05	.01
☐ 41T Dickie Thon	.10	.05	.01
☐ 42T Eric King	.10	.05	.01
☐ 43T Herm Winningham	.10	.05	.01
☐ 44T Derek Lilliquist	.10	.05	.01
☐ 45T Dave Anderson	.10	.05	.01
☐ 46T Jeff Reardon	.15	.07	.02
☐ 47T Scott Bankhead	.10	.05	.01
☐ 48T Cory Snyder	.10	.05	.01
☐ 49T Al Newman	.10	.05	.01
☐ 50T Keith Miller	.10	.05	.01
☐ 51T Dave Burba	.10	.05	.01
☐ 52T Bill Pecota	.10	.05	.01
☐ 53T Chuck Crim	.10	.05	.01
☐ 54T Mariano Duncan	.10	.05	.01
☐ 55T Dave Gallagher	.10	.05	.01
☐ 56T Chris Gwynn	.10	.05	.01
☐ 57T Scott Ruskin	.10	.05	.01
☐ 58T Jack Armstrong	.10	.05	.01
☐ 59T Gary Carter	.20	.09	.03
☐ 60T Andres Galarraga	.75	.35	.09
☐ 61T Ken Hill	.15	.07	.02
☐ 62T Eric Davis	.10	.05	.01
☐ 63T Ruben Sierra	.40	.18	.05
☐ 64T Darrin Fletcher	.10	.05	.01
☐ 65T Tim Belcher	.10	.05	.01
☐ 66T Mike Morgan	.10	.05	.01
☐ 67T Scott Scudder	.10	.05	.01
☐ 68T Tom Candiotti	.10	.05	.01
☐ 69T Hubie Brooks	.10	.05	.01
☐ 70T Kal Daniels	.10	.05	.01
☐ 71T Bruce Ruffin	.10	.05	.01
☐ 72T Billy Hatcher	.10	.05	.01
☐ 73T Bob Melvin	.10	.05	.01
☐ 74T Lee Guetterman	.10	.05	.01
☐ 75T Rene Gonzales	.10	.05	.01
☐ 76T Kevin Bass	.10	.05	.01
☐ 77T Tom Bolton	.10	.05	.01
☐ 78T John Wetteland	.10	.05	.01
☐ 79T Bip Roberts	.10	.05	.01
☐ 80T Pat Listach	.40	.18	.05
☐ 81T John Doherty	.30	.14	.04
☐ 82T Sam Militello	.10	.05	.01
☐ 83T Brian Jordan	.60	.25	.08
☐ 84T Jeff Kent	2.00	.90	.25
☐ 85T Dave Fleming	.15	.07	.02
☐ 86T Jeff Tackett	.10	.05	.01
☐ 87T Chad Curtis	1.00	.45	.13
☐ 88T Eric Fox	.15	.07	.02
☐ 89T Denny Neagle	.10	.05	.01
☐ 90T Donovan Osborne	.10	.05	.01
☐ 91T Carlos Hernandez	.10	.05	.01
☐ 92T Tim Wakefield	.10	.05	.01
☐ 93T Tim Salmon	6.00	2.70	.75
☐ 94T Dave Nilsson	1.25	.55	.16
☐ 95T Mike Perez	.10	.05	.01
☐ 96T Pat Hentgen	1.25	.55	.16
☐ 97T Frank Seminara	.10	.05	.01
☐ 98T Ruben Amaro Jr.	.10	.05	.01
☐ 99T Archi Cianfrocco	.10	.05	.01
☐ 100T Andy Stankiewicz	.10	.05	.01
☐ 101T Jim Bullinger	.10	.05	.01
☐ 102T Pat Mahomes	.75	.35	.09
☐ 103T Hipolito Pichardo	.10	.05	.01
☐ 104T Bret Boone	1.50	.65	.19
☐ 105T John Vander Wal	.15	.07	.02
☐ 106T Vince Horsman	.15	.07	.02
☐ 107T James Austin	.10	.05	.01
☐ 108T Brian Williams	.40	.18	.05
☐ 109T Dan Walters	.15	.07	.02
☐ 110T Wil Cordero	1.50	.65	.19

1993 Score

The 1993 Score baseball set consists of 660 cards, each measuring the standard size (2 1/2" by 3 1/2"). The fronts feature

color action player photos surrounded by white borders. The player's name appears in the bottom white border, while the team name and position appear in a team color-coded stripe that edges the left side of the picture. The backs carry a close-up color photo, biography, and team logo on the top portion; full career statistics and player profile appear on the bottom portion on a pastel color panel. Topical subsets featured are Rookie (221-222, 224-255, 257-260, 262-312, 314-316, 318-322, 324-330, 458, 561, 565, 569, 573, 586), Award Winners (481-486), Draft Picks (487-501), All-Star Caricature (502-512 [AL], 522-531 [NL]), Highlight (513-519), World Series Highlight (520-521), and Dream Team (532-542). The cards are numbered on the back. Rookie Cards in this set include Derek Jeter, Jason Kendall and J.T. Snow.

	MINT	EXC	G-VG
COMPLETE SET (660)	40.00	18.00	5.00
COMMON CARD (1-660)	.05	.02	.01
☐ 1 Ken Griffey Jr.	2.00	.90	.25
☐ 2 Gary Sheffield	.10	.05	.01
☐ 3 Frank Thomas	2.00	.90	.25
☐ 4 Ryne Sandberg	.60	.25	.08
☐ 5 Larry Walker	.10	.05	.01
☐ 6 Cal Ripken Jr.	1.50	.65	.19
☐ 7 Roger Clemens	.50	.23	.06
☐ 8 Bobby Bonilla	.10	.05	.01
☐ 9 Carlos Baerga	.30	.14	.04
☐ 10 Darren Daulton	.10	.05	.01
☐ 11 Travis Fryman	.15	.07	.02
☐ 12 Andy Van Slyke	.10	.05	.01
☐ 13 Jose Canseco	.30	.14	.04
☐ 14 Roberto Alomar	.40	.18	.05
☐ 15 Tom Glavine	.10	.05	.01
☐ 16 Barry Larkin	.10	.05	.01
☐ 17 Gregg Jefferies	.10	.05	.01
☐ 18 Craig Biggio	.08	.04	.01
☐ 19 Shane Mack	.08	.04	.01
☐ 20 Brett Butler	.08	.04	.01
☐ 21 Dennis Eckersley	.10	.05	.01
☐ 22 Will Clark	.30	.14	.04
☐ 23 Don Mattingly	.75	.35	.09
☐ 24 Tony Gwynn	.50	.23	.06
☐ 25 Ivan Rodriguez	.10	.05	.01
☐ 26 Shawon Dunston	.05	.02	.01
☐ 27 Mike Mussina	.40	.18	.05
☐ 28 Marquis Grissom	.10	.05	.01
☐ 29 Charles Nagy	.05	.02	.01
☐ 30 Len Dykstra	.10	.05	.01
☐ 31 Cecil Fielder	.10	.05	.01
☐ 32 Jay Bell	.08	.04	.01
☐ 33 B.J. Surhoff	.05	.02	.01
☐ 34 Bob Tewksbury	.05	.02	.01
☐ 35 Danny Tartabull	.08	.04	.01
☐ 36 Terry Pendleton	.10	.05	.01
☐ 37 Jack Morris	.10	.05	.01
☐ 38 Hal Morris	.08	.04	.01
☐ 39 Luis Polonia	.05	.02	.01
☐ 40 Ken Caminiti	.08	.04	.01
☐ 41 Robin Ventura	.10	.05	.01
☐ 42 Darryl Strawberry	.08	.04	.01
☐ 43 Wally Joyner	.08	.04	.01
☐ 44 Fred McGriff	.30	.14	.04
☐ 45 Kevin Tapani	.05	.02	.01
☐ 46 Matt Williams	.30	.14	.04
☐ 47 Robin Yount	.30	.14	.04
☐ 48 Ken Hill	.08	.04	.01
☐ 49 Edgar Martinez	.05	.02	.01
☐ 50 Mark Grace	.10	.05	.01
☐ 51 Juan Gonzalez	.60	.25	.08
☐ 52 Curt Schilling	.08	.04	.01
☐ 53 Dwight Gooden	.05	.02	.01
☐ 54 Chris Hoiles	.08	.04	.01
☐ 55 Frank Viola	.08	.04	.01
☐ 56 Ray Lankford	.10	.05	.01
☐ 57 George Brett	.75	.35	.09
☐ 58 Kenny Lofton	.50	.23	.06
☐ 59 Nolan Ryan	2.00	.90	.25
☐ 60 Mickey Tettleton	.08	.04	.01
☐ 61 John Smoltz	.08	.04	.01
☐ 62 Howard Johnson	.05	.02	.01
☐ 63 Eric Karros	.08	.04	.01
☐ 64 Rick Aguilera	.08	.04	.01
☐ 65 Steve Finley	.05	.02	.01
☐ 66 Mark Langston	.10	.05	.01
☐ 67 Bill Swift	.08	.04	.01
☐ 68 John Olerud	.10	.05	.01
☐ 69 Kevin McReynolds	.05	.02	.01
☐ 70 Jack McDowell	.10	.05	.01
☐ 71 Rickey Henderson	.10	.05	.01
☐ 72 Brian Harper	.05	.02	.01
☐ 73 Mike Morgan	.05	.02	.01
☐ 74 Rafael Palmeiro	.10	.05	.01
☐ 75 Dennis Martinez	.08	.04	.01
☐ 76 Tino Martinez	.08	.04	.01
☐ 77 Eddie Murray	.10	.05	.01
☐ 78 Ellis Burks	.08	.04	.01
☐ 79 John Kruk	.10	.05	.01
☐ 80 Gregg Olson	.05	.02	.01
☐ 81 Bernard Gilkey	.05	.02	.01
☐ 82 Milt Cuyler	.05	.02	.01
☐ 83 Mike LaValliere	.05	.02	.01
☐ 84 Albert Belle	.60	.25	.08
☐ 85 Bip Roberts	.05	.02	.01
☐ 86 Melido Perez	.05	.02	.01
☐ 87 Otis Nixon	.05	.02	.01
☐ 88 Bill Spiers	.05	.02	.01
☐ 89 Jeff Bagwell	1.00	.45	.13
☐ 90 Orel Hershiser	.08	.04	.01
☐ 91 Andy Benes	.08	.04	.01
☐ 92 Devon White	.08	.04	.01
☐ 93 Willie McGee	.08	.04	.01
☐ 94 Ozzie Guillen	.05	.02	.01
☐ 95 Ivan Calderon	.05	.02	.01
☐ 96 Keith Miller	.05	.02	.01
☐ 97 Steve Buechele	.05	.02	.01
☐ 98 Kent Hrbek	.08	.04	.01
☐ 99 Dave Hollins	.10	.05	.01
☐ 100 Mike Bordick	.05	.02	.01
☐ 101 Randy Tomlin	.05	.02	.01
☐ 102 Omar Vizquel	.05	.02	.01
☐ 103 Lee Smith	.10	.05	.01
☐ 104 Leo Gomez	.05	.02	.01
☐ 105 Jose Rijo	.08	.04	.01
☐ 106 Mark Whiten	.08	.04	.01
☐ 107 David Justice	.30	.14	.04
☐ 108 Eddie Taubensee	.05	.02	.01
☐ 109 Lance Johnson	.05	.02	.01
☐ 110 Felix Jose	.05	.02	.01
☐ 111 Mike Harkey	.05	.02	.01
☐ 112 Randy Milligan	.05	.02	.01
☐ 113 Anthony Young	.05	.02	.01
☐ 114 Rico Brogna	.05	.02	.01
☐ 115 Bret Saberhagen	.08	.04	.01
☐ 116 Sandy Alomar	.08	.04	.01
☐ 117 Terry Mulholland	.05	.02	.01
☐ 118 Darryl Hamilton	.05	.02	.01
☐ 119 Todd Zeile	.08	.04	.01
☐ 120 Bernie Williams	.08	.04	.01
☐ 121 Zane Smith	.05	.02	.01

☐ 122	Derek Bell	.08	.04	.01
☐ 123	Deion Sanders	.40	.18	.05
☐ 124	Luis Sojo	.05	.02	.01
☐ 125	Joe Oliver	.05	.02	.01
☐ 126	Craig Grebeck	.05	.02	.01
☐ 127	Andujar Cedeno	.08	.04	.01
☐ 128	Brian McRae	.10	.05	.01
☐ 129	Jose Offerman	.05	.02	.01
☐ 130	Pedro Munoz	.05	.02	.01
☐ 131	Bud Black	.05	.02	.01
☐ 132	Mo Vaughn	.10	.05	.01
☐ 133	Bruce Hurst	.05	.02	.01
☐ 134	Dave Henderson	.05	.02	.01
☐ 135	Tom Pagnozzi	.05	.02	.01
☐ 136	Erik Hanson	.05	.02	.01
☐ 137	Orlando Merced	.08	.04	.01
☐ 138	Dean Palmer	.08	.04	.01
☐ 139	John Franco	.05	.02	.01
☐ 140	Brady Anderson	.08	.04	.01
☐ 141	Ricky Jordan	.05	.02	.01
☐ 142	Jeff Blauser	.08	.04	.01
☐ 143	Sammy Sosa	.10	.05	.01
☐ 144	Bob Walk	.05	.02	.01
☐ 145	Delino DeShields	.08	.04	.01
☐ 146	Kevin Brown	.05	.02	.01
☐ 147	Mark Lemke	.05	.02	.01
☐ 148	Chuck Knoblauch	.10	.05	.01
☐ 149	Chris Sabo	.08	.04	.01
☐ 150	Bobby Witt	.05	.02	.01
☐ 151	Luis Gonzalez	.08	.04	.01
☐ 152	Ron Karkovice	.05	.02	.01
☐ 153	Jeff Brantley	.05	.02	.01
☐ 154	Kevin Appier	.08	.04	.01
☐ 155	Darrin Jackson	.05	.02	.01
☐ 156	Kelly Gruber	.05	.02	.01
☐ 157	Royce Clayton	.08	.04	.01
☐ 158	Chuck Finley	.05	.02	.01
☐ 159	Jeff King	.05	.02	.01
☐ 160	Greg Vaughn	.08	.04	.01
☐ 161	Geronimo Pena	.05	.02	.01
☐ 162	Steve Farr	.05	.02	.01
☐ 163	Jose Oquendo	.05	.02	.01
☐ 164	Mark Lewis	.05	.02	.01
☐ 165	John Wetteland	.05	.02	.01
☐ 166	Mike Henneman	.05	.02	.01
☐ 167	Todd Hundley	.05	.02	.01
☐ 168	Wes Chamberlain	.05	.02	.01
☐ 169	Steve Avery	.10	.05	.01
☐ 170	Mike Devereaux	.08	.04	.01
☐ 171	Reggie Sanders	.10	.05	.01
☐ 172	Jay Buhner	.08	.04	.01
☐ 173	Eric Anthony	.05	.02	.01
☐ 174	John Burkett	.08	.04	.01
☐ 175	Tom Candiotti	.05	.02	.01
☐ 176	Phil Plantier	.10	.05	.01
☐ 177	Doug Henry	.05	.02	.01
☐ 178	Scott Leius	.05	.02	.01
☐ 179	Kirt Manwaring	.05	.02	.01
☐ 180	Jeff Parrett	.05	.02	.01
☐ 181	Don Slaught	.05	.02	.01
☐ 182	Scott Radinsky	.05	.02	.01
☐ 183	Luis Alicea	.05	.02	.01
☐ 184	Tom Gordon	.05	.02	.01
☐ 185	Rick Wilkins	.05	.02	.01
☐ 186	Todd Stottlemyre	.05	.02	.01
☐ 187	Moises Alou	.10	.05	.01
☐ 188	Joe Grahe	.05	.02	.01
☐ 189	Jeff Kent	.10	.05	.01
☐ 190	Bill Wegman	.05	.02	.01
☐ 191	Kim Batiste	.05	.02	.01
☐ 192	Matt Nokes	.05	.02	.01
☐ 193	Mark Wohlers	.05	.02	.01
☐ 194	Paul Sorrento	.05	.02	.01
☐ 195	Chris Hammond	.05	.02	.01
☐ 196	Scott Livingstone	.05	.02	.01
☐ 197	Doug Jones	.05	.02	.01
☐ 198	Scott Cooper	.08	.04	.01
☐ 199	Ramon Martinez	.08	.04	.01
☐ 200	Dave Valle	.05	.02	.01
☐ 201	Mariano Duncan	.05	.02	.01
☐ 202	Ben McDonald	.08	.04	.01
☐ 203	Darren Lewis	.05	.02	.01
☐ 204	Kenny Rogers	.05	.02	.01
☐ 205	Manny Lee	.05	.02	.01
☐ 206	Scott Erickson	.05	.02	.01
☐ 207	Dan Gladden	.05	.02	.01
☐ 208	Bob Welch	.05	.02	.01
☐ 209	Greg Olson	.05	.02	.01
☐ 210	Dan Pasqua	.05	.02	.01
☐ 211	Tim Wallach	.05	.02	.01
☐ 212	Jeff Montgomery	.08	.04	.01
☐ 213	Derrick May	.08	.04	.01
☐ 214	Ed Sprague	.05	.02	.01
☐ 215	David Haas	.05	.02	.01
☐ 216	Darrin Fletcher	.05	.02	.01
☐ 217	Brian Jordan	.08	.04	.01
☐ 218	Jaime Navarro	.05	.02	.01
☐ 219	Randy Velarde	.05	.02	.01
☐ 220	Ron Gant	.08	.04	.01
☐ 221	Paul Quantrill	.05	.02	.01
☐ 222	Damion Easley	.08	.04	.01
☐ 223	Charlie Hough	.08	.04	.01
☐ 224	Brad Brink	.05	.02	.01
☐ 225	Barry Manuel	.05	.02	.01
☐ 226	Kevin Koslofski	.05	.02	.01
☐ 227	Ryan Thompson	.10	.05	.01
☐ 228	Mike Munoz	.05	.02	.01
☐ 229	Dan Wilson	.05	.02	.01
☐ 230	Peter Hoy	.05	.02	.01
☐ 231	Pedro Astacio	.08	.04	.01
☐ 232	Matt Stairs	.05	.02	.01
☐ 233	Jeff Reboulet	.05	.02	.01
☐ 234	Manny Alexander	.05	.02	.01
☐ 235	Willie Banks	.05	.02	.01
☐ 236	John Jaha	.08	.04	.01
☐ 237	Scooter Tucker	.05	.02	.01
☐ 238	Russ Springer	.05	.02	.01
☐ 239	Paul Miller	.05	.02	.01
☐ 240	Dan Peltier	.05	.02	.01
☐ 241	Ozzie Canseco	.05	.02	.01
☐ 242	Ben Rivera	.05	.02	.01
☐ 243	John Valentin	.08	.04	.01
☐ 244	Henry Rodriguez	.05	.02	.01
☐ 245	Derek Parks	.05	.02	.01
☐ 246	Carlos Garcia	.08	.04	.01
☐ 247	Tim Pugh	.05	.02	.01
☐ 248	Melvin Nieves	.10	.05	.01
☐ 249	Rich Amaral	.05	.02	.01
☐ 250	Willie Greene	.08	.04	.01
☐ 251	Tim Scott	.05	.02	.01
☐ 252	Dave Silvestri	.05	.02	.01
☐ 253	Rob Mallicoat	.05	.02	.01
☐ 254	Donald Harris	.05	.02	.01
☐ 255	Craig Colbert	.05	.02	.01
☐ 256	Jose Guzman	.05	.02	.01
☐ 257	Domingo Martinez	.05	.02	.01
☐ 258	William Suero	.05	.02	.01
☐ 259	Juan Guerrero	.05	.02	.01
☐ 260	J.T. Snow	.15	.07	.02
☐ 261	Tony Pena	.05	.02	.01
☐ 262	Tim Fortugno	.05	.02	.01
☐ 263	Tom Marsh	.05	.02	.01
☐ 264	Kurt Knudsen	.05	.02	.01
☐ 265	Tim Costo	.05	.02	.01
☐ 266	Steve Shifflett	.05	.02	.01
☐ 267	Billy Ashley	.35	.16	.04

☐ 268	Jerry Nielsen	.05	.02	.01
☐ 269	Pete Young	.05	.02	.01
☐ 270	Johnny Guzman	.05	.02	.01
☐ 271	Greg Colbrunn	.05	.02	.01
☐ 272	Jeff Nelson	.05	.02	.01
☐ 273	Kevin Young	.05	.02	.01
☐ 274	Jeff Frye	.05	.02	.01
☐ 275	J.T. Bruett	.05	.02	.01
☐ 276	Todd Pratt	.05	.02	.01
☐ 277	Mike Butcher	.05	.02	.01
☐ 278	John Flaherty	.05	.02	.01
☐ 279	John Patterson	.05	.02	.01
☐ 280	Eric Hillman	.05	.02	.01
☐ 281	Bien Figueroa	.05	.02	.01
☐ 282	Shane Reynolds	.08	.04	.01
☐ 283	Rich Rowland	.05	.02	.01
☐ 284	Steve Foster	.05	.02	.01
☐ 285	Dave Mlicki	.05	.02	.01
☐ 286	Mike Piazza	2.00	.90	.25
☐ 287	Mike Trombley	.05	.02	.01
☐ 288	Jim Pena	.05	.02	.01
☐ 289	Bob Ayrault	.05	.02	.01
☐ 290	Henry Mercedes	.05	.02	.01
☐ 291	Bob Wickman	.05	.02	.01
☐ 292	Jacob Brumfield	.05	.02	.01
☐ 293	David Hulse	.05	.02	.01
☐ 294	Ryan Klesko	.60	.25	.08
☐ 295	Doug Linton	.05	.02	.01
☐ 296	Steve Cooke	.05	.02	.01
☐ 297	Eddie Zosky	.05	.02	.01
☐ 298	Gerald Williams	.05	.02	.01
☐ 299	Jonathan Hurst	.05	.02	.01
☐ 300	Larry Carter	.05	.02	.01
☐ 301	William Pennyfeather	.05	.02	.01
☐ 302	Cesar Hernandez	.05	.02	.01
☐ 303	Steve Hosey	.05	.02	.01
☐ 304	Blas Minor	.05	.02	.01
☐ 305	Jeff Grotewald	.05	.02	.01
☐ 306	Bernardo Brito	.05	.02	.01
☐ 307	Rafael Bournigal	.08	.04	.01
☐ 308	Jeff Branson	.05	.02	.01
☐ 309	Tom Quinlan	.05	.02	.01
☐ 310	Pat Gomez	.05	.02	.01
☐ 311	Sterling Hitchcock	.15	.07	.02
☐ 312	Kent Bottenfield	.05	.02	.01
☐ 313	Alan Trammell	.10	.05	.01
☐ 314	Cris Colon	.05	.02	.01
☐ 315	Paul Wagner	.05	.02	.01
☐ 316	Matt Maysey	.05	.02	.01
☐ 317	Mike Stanton	.05	.02	.01
☐ 318	Rick Trlicek	.05	.02	.01
☐ 319	Kevin Rogers	.05	.02	.01
☐ 320	Mark Clark	.08	.04	.01
☐ 321	Pedro Martinez	.10	.05	.01
☐ 322	Al Martin	.08	.04	.01
☐ 323	Mike Macfarlane	.05	.02	.01
☐ 324	Rey Sanchez	.05	.02	.01
☐ 325	Roger Pavlik	.08	.04	.01
☐ 326	Troy Neel	.08	.04	.01
☐ 327	Kerry Woodson	.05	.02	.01
☐ 328	Wayne Kirby	.05	.02	.01
☐ 329	Ken Ryan	.20	.09	.03
☐ 330	Jesse Levis	.05	.02	.01
☐ 331	James Austin	.05	.02	.01
☐ 332	Dan Walters	.05	.02	.01
☐ 333	Brian Williams	.05	.02	.01
☐ 334	Wil Cordero	.10	.05	.01
☐ 335	Bret Boone	.10	.05	.01
☐ 336	Hipolito Pichardo	.05	.02	.01
☐ 337	Pat Mahomes	.05	.02	.01
☐ 338	Andy Stankiewicz	.05	.02	.01
☐ 339	Jim Bullinger	.05	.02	.01
☐ 340	Archi Cianfrocco	.05	.02	.01
☐ 341	Ruben Amaro Jr.	.05	.02	.01
☐ 342	Frank Seminara	.05	.02	.01
☐ 343	Pat Hentgen	.08	.04	.01
☐ 344	Dave Nilsson	.08	.04	.01
☐ 345	Mike Perez	.05	.02	.01
☐ 346	Tim Salmon	.40	.18	.05
☐ 347	Tim Wakefield	.05	.02	.01
☐ 348	Carlos Hernandez	.05	.02	.01
☐ 349	Donovan Osborne	.05	.02	.01
☐ 350	Denny Neagle	.05	.02	.01
☐ 351	Sam Militello	.05	.02	.01
☐ 352	Eric Fox	.05	.02	.01
☐ 353	John Doherty	.05	.02	.01
☐ 354	Chad Curtis	.08	.04	.01
☐ 355	Jeff Tackett	.05	.02	.01
☐ 356	Dave Fleming	.08	.04	.01
☐ 357	Pat Listach	.08	.04	.01
☐ 358	Kevin Wickander	.05	.02	.01
☐ 359	John Vander Wal	.05	.02	.01
☐ 360	Arthur Rhodes	.05	.02	.01
☐ 361	Bob Scanlan	.05	.02	.01
☐ 362	Bob Zupcic	.05	.02	.01
☐ 363	Mel Rojas	.05	.02	.01
☐ 364	Jim Thome	.25	.11	.03
☐ 365	Bill Pecota	.05	.02	.01
☐ 366	Mark Carreon	.05	.02	.01
☐ 367	Mitch Williams	.08	.04	.01
☐ 368	Cal Eldred	.08	.04	.01
☐ 369	Stan Belinda	.05	.02	.01
☐ 370	Pat Kelly	.05	.02	.01
☐ 371	Rheal Cormier	.05	.02	.01
☐ 372	Juan Guzman	.08	.04	.01
☐ 373	Damon Berryhill	.05	.02	.01
☐ 374	Gary DiSarcina	.05	.02	.01
☐ 375	Norm Charlton	.05	.02	.01
☐ 376	Roberto Hernandez	.05	.02	.01
☐ 377	Scott Kamieniecki	.05	.02	.01
☐ 378	Rusty Meacham	.05	.02	.01
☐ 379	Kurt Stillwell	.05	.02	.01
☐ 380	Lloyd McClendon	.05	.02	.01
☐ 381	Mark Leonard	.05	.02	.01
☐ 382	Jerry Browne	.05	.02	.01
☐ 383	Glenn Davis	.05	.02	.01
☐ 384	Randy Johnson	.10	.05	.01
☐ 385	Mike Greenwell	.08	.04	.01
☐ 386	Scott Chiamparino	.05	.02	.01
☐ 387	George Bell	.08	.04	.01
☐ 388	Steve Olin	.05	.02	.01
☐ 389	Chuck McElroy	.05	.02	.01
☐ 390	Mark Gardner	.05	.02	.01
☐ 391	Rod Beck	.10	.05	.01
☐ 392	Dennis Rasmussen	.05	.02	.01
☐ 393	Charlie Leibrandt	.05	.02	.01
☐ 394	Julio Franco	.08	.04	.01
☐ 395	Pete Harnisch	.05	.02	.01
☐ 396	Sid Bream	.05	.02	.01
☐ 397	Milt Thompson	.05	.02	.01
☐ 398	Glenallen Hill	.05	.02	.01
☐ 399	Chico Walker	.05	.02	.01
☐ 400	Alex Cole	.05	.02	.01
☐ 401	Trevor Wilson	.05	.02	.01
☐ 402	Jeff Conine	.10	.05	.01
☐ 403	Kyle Abbott	.05	.02	.01
☐ 404	Tom Browning	.05	.02	.01
☐ 405	Jerald Clark	.05	.02	.01
☐ 406	Vince Horsman	.05	.02	.01
☐ 407	Kevin Mitchell	.08	.04	.01
☐ 408	Pete Smith	.05	.02	.01
☐ 409	Jeff Innis	.05	.02	.01
☐ 410	Mike Timlin	.05	.02	.01
☐ 411	Charlie Hayes	.08	.04	.01
☐ 412	Alex Fernandez	.10	.05	.01
☐ 413	Jeff Russell	.05	.02	.01

☐ 414 Jody Reed	.05	.02	.01
☐ 415 Mickey Morandini	.05	.02	.01
☐ 416 Darnell Coles	.05	.02	.01
☐ 417 Xavier Hernandez	.05	.02	.01
☐ 418 Steve Sax	.05	.02	.01
☐ 419 Joe Girardi	.05	.02	.01
☐ 420 Mike Fetters	.05	.02	.01
☐ 421 Danny Jackson	.05	.02	.01
☐ 422 Jim Gott	.05	.02	.01
☐ 423 Tim Belcher	.05	.02	.01
☐ 424 Jose Mesa	.05	.02	.01
☐ 425 Junior Felix	.05	.02	.01
☐ 426 Thomas Howard	.05	.02	.01
☐ 427 Julio Valera	.05	.02	.01
☐ 428 Dante Bichette	.10	.05	.01
☐ 429 Mike Sharperson	.05	.02	.01
☐ 430 Darryl Kile	.08	.04	.01
☐ 431 Lonnie Smith	.05	.02	.01
☐ 432 Monty Fariss	.05	.02	.01
☐ 433 Reggie Jefferson	.05	.02	.01
☐ 434 Bob McClure	.05	.02	.01
☐ 435 Craig Lefferts	.05	.02	.01
☐ 436 Duane Ward	.08	.04	.01
☐ 437 Shawn Abner	.05	.02	.01
☐ 438 Roberto Kelly	.08	.04	.01
☐ 439 Paul O'Neill	.08	.04	.01
☐ 440 Alan Mills	.05	.02	.01
☐ 441 Roger Mason	.05	.02	.01
☐ 442 Gary Pettis	.05	.02	.01
☐ 443 Steve Lake	.05	.02	.01
☐ 444 Gene Larkin	.05	.02	.01
☐ 445 Larry Andersen	.05	.02	.01
☐ 446 Doug Dascenzo	.05	.02	.01
☐ 447 Daryl Boston	.05	.02	.01
☐ 448 John Candelaria	.05	.02	.01
☐ 449 Storm Davis	.05	.02	.01
☐ 450 Tom Edens	.05	.02	.01
☐ 451 Mike Maddux	.05	.02	.01
☐ 452 Tim Naehring	.05	.02	.01
☐ 453 John Orton	.05	.02	.01
☐ 454 Joey Cora	.05	.02	.01
☐ 455 Chuck Crim	.05	.02	.01
☐ 456 Dan Plesac	.05	.02	.01
☐ 457 Mike Bielecki	.05	.02	.01
☐ 458 Terry Jorgensen	.05	.02	.01
☐ 459 John Habyan	.05	.02	.01
☐ 460 Pete O'Brien	.05	.02	.01
☐ 461 Jeff Treadway	.05	.02	.01
☐ 462 Frank Castillo	.05	.02	.01
☐ 463 Jimmy Jones	.05	.02	.01
☐ 464 Tommy Greene	.08	.04	.01
☐ 465 Tracy Woodson	.05	.02	.01
☐ 466 Rich Rodriguez	.05	.02	.01
☐ 467 Joe Hesketh	.05	.02	.01
☐ 468 Greg Myers	.05	.02	.01
☐ 469 Kirk McCaskill	.05	.02	.01
☐ 470 Ricky Bones	.05	.02	.01
☐ 471 Lenny Webster	.05	.02	.01
☐ 472 Francisco Cabrera	.05	.02	.01
☐ 473 Turner Ward	.05	.02	.01
☐ 474 Dwayne Henry	.05	.02	.01
☐ 475 Al Osuna	.05	.02	.01
☐ 476 Craig Wilson	.05	.02	.01
☐ 477 Chris Nabholz	.05	.02	.01
☐ 478 Rafael Belliard	.05	.02	.01
☐ 479 Terry Leach	.05	.02	.01
☐ 480 Tim Teufel	.05	.02	.01
☐ 481 Dennis Eckersley AW	.08	.04	.01
☐ 482 Barry Bonds AW	.40	.18	.05
☐ 483 Dennis Eckersley AW	.08	.04	.01
☐ 484 Greg Maddux AW	.20	.09	.03
☐ 485 Pat Listach AW	.05	.02	.01
☐ 486 Eric Karros AW	.08	.04	.01
☐ 487 Jamie Arnold DP	.15	.07	.02
☐ 488 B.J. Wallace DP	.10	.05	.01
☐ 489 Derek Jeter DP	2.00	.90	.25
☐ 490 Jason Kendall DP	.60	.25	.08
☐ 491 Rick Helling DP	.15	.07	.02
☐ 492 Derek Wallace DP	.10	.05	.01
☐ 493 Sean Lowe DP	.20	.09	.03
☐ 494 Shannon Stewart DP	.25	.11	.03
☐ 495 Benji Grigsby DP	.15	.07	.02
☐ 496 Todd Steverson DP	.20	.09	.03
☐ 497 Dan Serafini DP	.25	.11	.03
☐ 498 Michael Tucker DP	.25	.11	.03
☐ 499 Chris Roberts DP	.15	.07	.02
☐ 500 Pete Janicki DP	.10	.05	.01
☐ 501 Jeff Schmidt DP	.10	.05	.01
☐ 502 Edgar Martinez AS	.05	.02	.01
☐ 503 Omar Vizquel AS	.05	.02	.01
☐ 504 Ken Griffey Jr. AS	1.00	.45	.13
☐ 505 Kirby Puckett AS	.40	.18	.05
☐ 506 Joe Carter AS	.15	.07	.02
☐ 507 Ivan Rodriguez AS	.08	.04	.01
☐ 508 Jack Morris AS	.08	.04	.01
☐ 509 Dennis Eckersley AS	.08	.04	.01
☐ 510 Frank Thomas AS	1.00	.45	.13
☐ 511 Roberto Alomar AS	.20	.09	.03
☐ 512 Mickey Morandini AS	.05	.02	.01
☐ 513 Dennis Eckersley HL	.08	.04	.01
☐ 514 Jeff Reardon HL	.08	.04	.01
☐ 515 Danny Tartabull HL	.08	.04	.01
☐ 516 Bip Roberts HL	.05	.02	.01
☐ 517 George Brett HL	.40	.18	.05
☐ 518 Robin Yount HL	.15	.07	.02
☐ 519 Kevin Gross HL	.05	.02	.01
☐ 520 Ed Sprague WS	.05	.02	.01
☐ 521 Dave Winfield WS	.08	.04	.01
☐ 522 Ozzie Smith AS	.20	.09	.03
☐ 523 Barry Bonds AS	.40	.18	.05
☐ 524 Andy Van Slyke AS	.08	.04	.01
☐ 525 Tony Gwynn AS	.25	.11	.03
☐ 526 Darren Daulton AS	.08	.04	.01
☐ 527 Greg Maddux AS	.25	.11	.03
☐ 528 Fred McGriff AS	.15	.07	.02
☐ 529 Lee Smith AS	.08	.04	.01
☐ 530 Ryne Sandberg AS	.30	.14	.04
☐ 531 Gary Sheffield AS	.08	.04	.01
☐ 532 Ozzie Smith DT	.20	.09	.03
☐ 533 Kirby Puckett DT	.40	.18	.05
☐ 534 Gary Sheffield DT	.08	.04	.01
☐ 535 Andy Van Slyke DT	.08	.04	.01
☐ 536 Ken Griffey Jr. DT	1.00	.45	.13
☐ 537 Ivan Rodriguez DT	.08	.04	.01
☐ 538 Charles Nagy DT	.05	.02	.01
☐ 539 Tom Glavine DT	.08	.04	.01
☐ 540 Dennis Eckersley DT	.08	.04	.01
☐ 541 Frank Thomas DT	1.00	.45	.13
☐ 542 Roberto Alomar DT	.25	.11	.03
☐ 543 Sean Berry	.05	.02	.01
☐ 544 Mike Schooler	.05	.02	.01
☐ 545 Chuck Carr	.05	.02	.01
☐ 546 Lenny Harris	.05	.02	.01
☐ 547 Gary Scott	.05	.02	.01
☐ 548 Derek Lilliquist	.05	.02	.01
☐ 549 Brian Hunter	.05	.02	.01
☐ 550 Kirby Puckett MOY	.40	.18	.05
☐ 551 Jim Eisenreich	.05	.02	.01
☐ 552 Andre Dawson	.10	.05	.01
☐ 553 David Nied	.10	.05	.01
☐ 554 Spike Owen	.05	.02	.01
☐ 555 Greg Gagne	.05	.02	.01
☐ 556 Sid Fernandez	.05	.02	.01
☐ 557 Mark McGwire	.10	.05	.01
☐ 558 Bryan Harvey	.08	.04	.01
☐ 559 Harold Reynolds	.05	.02	.01

☐ 560	Barry Bonds	.75	.35	.09
☐ 561	Eric Wedge	.05	.02	.01
☐ 562	Ozzie Smith	.40	.18	.05
☐ 563	Rick Sutcliffe	.08	.04	.01
☐ 564	Jeff Reardon	.08	.04	.01
☐ 565	Alex Arias	.05	.02	.01
☐ 566	Greg Swindell	.05	.02	.01
☐ 567	Brook Jacoby	.05	.02	.01
☐ 568	Pete Incaviglia	.05	.02	.01
☐ 569	Butch Henry	.05	.02	.01
☐ 570	Eric Davis	.05	.02	.01
☐ 571	Kevin Seitzer	.05	.02	.01
☐ 572	Tony Fernandez	.05	.02	.01
☐ 573	Steve Reed	.08	.04	.01
☐ 574	Cory Snyder	.05	.02	.01
☐ 575	Joe Carter	.30	.14	.04
☐ 576	Greg Maddux	.40	.18	.05
☐ 577	Bert Blyleven UER (Should say 3701 career strikeouts)	.10	.05	.01
☐ 578	Kevin Bass	.05	.02	.01
☐ 579	Carlton Fisk	.10	.05	.01
☐ 580	Doug Drabek	.10	.05	.01
☐ 581	Mark Gubicza	.05	.02	.01
☐ 582	Bobby Thigpen	.05	.02	.01
☐ 583	Chili Davis	.08	.04	.01
☐ 584	Scott Bankhead	.05	.02	.01
☐ 585	Harold Baines	.08	.04	.01
☐ 586	Eric Young	.08	.04	.01
☐ 587	Lance Parrish	.08	.04	.01
☐ 588	Juan Bell	.05	.02	.01
☐ 589	Bob Ojeda	.05	.02	.01
☐ 590	Joe Orsulak	.05	.02	.01
☐ 591	Benito Santiago	.05	.02	.01
☐ 592	Wade Boggs	.10	.05	.01
☐ 593	Robby Thompson	.05	.02	.01
☐ 594	Eric Plunk	.05	.02	.01
☐ 595	Hensley Meulens	.05	.02	.01
☐ 596	Lou Whitaker	.10	.05	.01
☐ 597	Dale Murphy	.10	.05	.01
☐ 598	Paul Molitor	.30	.14	.04
☐ 599	Greg W. Harris	.05	.02	.01
☐ 600	Darren Holmes	.05	.02	.01
☐ 601	Dave Martinez	.05	.02	.01
☐ 602	Tom Henke	.08	.04	.01
☐ 603	Mike Benjamin	.05	.02	.01
☐ 604	Rene Gonzales	.05	.02	.01
☐ 605	Roger McDowell	.05	.02	.01
☐ 606	Kirby Puckett	.75	.35	.09
☐ 607	Randy Myers	.08	.04	.01
☐ 608	Ruben Sierra	.10	.05	.01
☐ 609	Wilson Alvarez	.10	.05	.01
☐ 610	David Segui	.05	.02	.01
☐ 611	Juan Samuel	.05	.02	.01
☐ 612	Tom Brunansky	.05	.02	.01
☐ 613	Willie Randolph	.08	.04	.01
☐ 614	Tony Phillips	.05	.02	.01
☐ 615	Candy Maldonado	.05	.02	.01
☐ 616	Chris Bosio	.05	.02	.01
☐ 617	Bret Barberie	.05	.02	.01
☐ 618	Scott Sanderson	.05	.02	.01
☐ 619	Ron Darling	.05	.02	.01
☐ 620	Dave Winfield	.10	.05	.01
☐ 621	Mike Felder	.05	.02	.01
☐ 622	Greg Hibbard	.05	.02	.01
☐ 623	Mike Scioscia	.05	.02	.01
☐ 624	John Smiley	.05	.02	.01
☐ 625	Alejandro Pena	.05	.02	.01
☐ 626	Terry Steinbach	.08	.04	.01
☐ 627	Freddie Benavides	.05	.02	.01
☐ 628	Kevin Reimer	.05	.02	.01
☐ 629	Braulio Castillo	.05	.02	.01
☐ 630	Dave Stieb	.05	.02	.01
☐ 631	Dave Magadan	.05	.02	.01
☐ 632	Scott Fletcher	.05	.02	.01
☐ 633	Cris Carpenter	.05	.02	.01
☐ 634	Kevin Maas	.05	.02	.01
☐ 635	Todd Worrell	.05	.02	.01
☐ 636	Rob Deer	.05	.02	.01
☐ 637	Dwight Smith	.05	.02	.01
☐ 638	Chito Martinez	.05	.02	.01
☐ 639	Jimmy Key	.08	.04	.01
☐ 640	Greg A. Harris	.05	.02	.01
☐ 641	Mike Moore	.05	.02	.01
☐ 642	Pat Borders	.05	.02	.01
☐ 643	Bill Gullickson	.05	.02	.01
☐ 644	Gary Gaetti	.05	.02	.01
☐ 645	David Howard	.05	.02	.01
☐ 646	Jim Abbott	.10	.05	.01
☐ 647	Willie Wilson	.05	.02	.01
☐ 648	David Wells	.05	.02	.01
☐ 649	Andres Galarraga	.10	.05	.01
☐ 650	Vince Coleman	.05	.02	.01
☐ 651	Rob Dibble	.05	.02	.01
☐ 652	Frank Tanana	.05	.02	.01
☐ 653	Steve Decker	.05	.02	.01
☐ 654	David Cone	.10	.05	.01
☐ 655	Jack Armstrong	.05	.02	.01
☐ 656	Dave Stewart	.08	.04	.01
☐ 657	Billy Hatcher	.05	.02	.01
☐ 658	Tim Raines	.10	.05	.01
☐ 659	Walt Weiss	.05	.02	.01
☐ 660	Jose Lind	.05	.02	.01

1993 Score Boys of Summer

Randomly inserted in 1993 Score 35-card super packs only, this standard-size (2 1/2" by 3 1/2") set features 30 rookies expected to be the best in their class. The fronts are borderless with a color action player photo superimposed over an illustration of the sun. The player's name appears in cursive lettering within a greenish stripe across the bottom. The back carries a posed color player photo in the upper left that is also superimposed over an illustration of the sun. The player's name, profile, and team logo appear within the greenish area beneath the photo. According to Score, the odds of finding one of these cards are at least one in every four super packs. The cards are numbered on the back.

	MINT	EXC	G-VG
COMPLETE SET (30)	60.00	27.00	7.50

	MINT	EXC	G-VG
COMMON CARD (1-30)	.60	.25	.08
☐ 1 Billy Ashley	5.00	2.30	.60
☐ 2 Tim Salmon	7.00	3.10	.85
☐ 3 Pedro Martinez	2.50	1.15	.30
☐ 4 Luis Mercedes	.60	.25	.08
☐ 5 Mike Piazza	30.00	13.50	3.80
☐ 6 Troy Neel	1.00	.45	.13
☐ 7 Melvin Nieves	.60	.25	.08
☐ 8 Ryan Klesko	10.00	4.50	1.25
☐ 9 Ryan Thompson	2.00	.90	.25
☐ 10 Kevin Young	.60	.25	.08
☐ 11 Gerald Williams	.60	.25	.08
☐ 12 Willie Greene	1.00	.45	.13
☐ 13 John Patterson	.60	.25	.08
☐ 14 Carlos Garcia	1.00	.45	.13
☐ 15 Ed Zosky	.60	.25	.08
☐ 16 Sean Berry	.60	.25	.08
☐ 17 Rico Brogna	1.00	.45	.13
☐ 18 Larry Carter	.60	.25	.08
☐ 19 Bobby Ayala	2.00	.90	.25
☐ 20 Alan Embree	.60	.25	.08
☐ 21 Donald Harris	.60	.25	.08
☐ 22 Sterling Hitchcock	.60	.25	.08
☐ 23 David Nied	.60	.25	.08
☐ 24 Henry Mercedes	.60	.25	.08
☐ 25 Ozzie Canseco	.60	.25	.08
☐ 26 David Hulse	.60	.25	.08
☐ 27 Al Martin	.60	.25	.08
☐ 28 Dan Wilson	.60	.25	.08
☐ 29 Paul Miller	.60	.25	.08
☐ 30 Rich Rowland	.60	.25	.08

	MINT	EXC	G-VG
COMPLETE SET (28)	125.00	57.50	15.50
COMMON CARD (1-28)	2.00	.90	.25
☐ 1 Cal Ripken	25.00	11.50	3.10
☐ 2 Roger Clemens	9.00	4.00	1.15
☐ 3 Mark Langston	2.00	.90	.25
☐ 4 Frank Thomas	35.00	16.00	4.40
☐ 5 Carlos Baerga	5.00	2.30	.60
☐ 6 Cecil Fielder	3.50	1.55	.45
☐ 7 Gregg Jefferies	2.50	1.15	.30
☐ 8 Robin Yount	5.00	2.30	.60
☐ 9 Kirby Puckett	15.00	6.75	1.90
☐ 10 Don Mattingly	15.00	6.75	1.90
☐ 11 Dennis Eckersley	2.50	1.15	.30
☐ 12 Ken Griffey Jr.	35.00	16.00	4.40
☐ 13 Juan Gonzalez	12.00	5.50	1.50
☐ 14 Roberto Alomar	9.00	4.00	1.15
☐ 15 Terry Pendleton	2.00	.90	.25
☐ 16 Ryne Sandberg	12.00	5.50	1.50
☐ 17 Barry Larkin	2.50	1.15	.30
☐ 18 Jeff Bagwell	18.00	8.00	2.30
☐ 19 Brett Butler	2.00	.90	.25
☐ 20 Larry Walker	2.50	1.15	.30
☐ 21 Bobby Bonilla	2.00	.90	.25
☐ 22 Darren Daulton	2.50	1.15	.30
☐ 23 Andy Van Slyke	2.00	.90	.25
☐ 24 Ray Lankford	2.50	1.15	.30
☐ 25 Gary Sheffield	2.50	1.15	.30
☐ 26 Will Clark	5.00	2.30	.60
☐ 27 Bryan Harvey	2.00	.90	.25
☐ 28 David Nied	2.50	1.15	.30

1993 Score Franchise

This 28-card set honors the top player on each of the 28 teams. These cards were randomly inserted in 16-card count goods packs. According to Score, the chances of finding one of these cards is not less than one in 24 packs. The full-bleed, color action photos on the fronts have the background darkened so that the player stands out. His name appears in white lettering within a team color-coded bar near the bottom, which conjoins with the set logo in the lower left. The back features a borderless color posed player photo. His name and team appear within a darkened rectangle near the bottom, within which is a white rectangle that carries a player profile. The cards are numbered on the back.

1993 Score Gold Dream Team

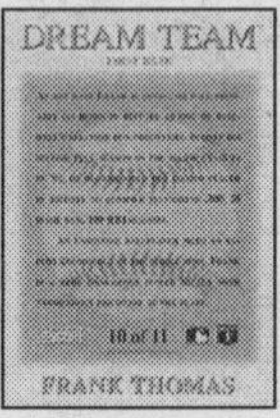

This 12-card standard-size (2 1/2" by 3 1/2") set features sepia tone photos of the players out of uniform, with the exception of Griffey's card. The photo edges are rounded with an airbrush effect. The words "Dream Team" are printed in gold lettering at the top. The player's name is printed in sepia tones on the bottom edge. The backs contain a career summary printed in brown over a ghosted baseball picture in soft brown. The cards are numbered on the back.

	MINT	EXC	G-VG
COMPLETE SET (12)	8.00	3.60	1.00
COMMON CARD (1-11)	.50	.23	.06

#	Card	MINT	EXC	G-VG
☐ 1	Ozzie Smith	.75	.35	.09
☐ 2	Kirby Puckett	1.50	.65	.19
☐ 3	Gary Sheffield	.50	.23	.06
☐ 4	Andy Van Slyke	.50	.23	.06
☐ 5	Ken Griffey Jr.	4.00	1.80	.50
☐ 6	Ivan Rodriguez	.50	.23	.06
☐ 7	Charles Nagy	.50	.23	.06
☐ 8	Tom Glavine	.50	.23	.06
☐ 9	Dennis Eckersley	.50	.23	.06
☐ 10	Frank Thomas	4.00	1.80	.50
☐ 11	Roberto Alomar	1.00	.45	.13
☐ NNO	Header Card	.50	.23	.06

1994 Score

The 1994 Score set of 660 cards was issued in two series of 330. The cards are standard size. The navy blue bordered fronts feature color action photos with the player's name and team name appearing on two team color-coded stripes across the bottom. The horizontal back features a narrow-cropped color player close-up shot on the left side. On a team color-coded stripe at the top are the player's name and position, and below are the team logo, biography, player profile, and career statistics. Among the subsets are American League stadiums (317-330) and National League stadiums (647-660). The cards are numbered on the back. Rookie Cards include Brian Anderson, Brooks Kieschnick, Derrek Lee, Trot Nixon and Kirk Presley.

	MINT	EXC	G-VG
COMPLETE SET (660)	30.00	13.50	3.80
COMPLETE SERIES 1 (330)	15.00	6.75	1.90
COMPLETE SERIES 2 (330)	15.00	6.75	1.90
COMMON CARD (1-330)	.05	.02	.01
COMMON CARD (331-660)	.05	.02	.01

#	Card	MINT	EXC	G-VG
☐ 1	Barry Bonds	.75	.35	.09
☐ 2	John Olerud	.10	.05	.01
☐ 3	Ken Griffey Jr.	2.00	.90	.25
☐ 4	Jeff Bagwell	1.00	.45	.13
☐ 5	John Burkett	.08	.04	.01
☐ 6	Jack McDowell	.10	.05	.01
☐ 7	Albert Belle	.60	.25	.08
☐ 8	Andres Galarraga	.10	.05	.01
☐ 9	Mike Mussina	.30	.14	.04
☐ 10	Will Clark	.30	.14	.04
☐ 11	Travis Fryman	.15	.07	.02
☐ 12	Tony Gwynn	.50	.23	.06
☐ 13	Robin Yount	.30	.14	.04
☐ 14	Dave Magadan	.05	.02	.01
☐ 15	Paul O'Neill	.08	.04	.01
☐ 16	Ray Lankford	.10	.05	.01
☐ 17	Damion Easley	.05	.02	.01
☐ 18	Andy Van Slyke	.10	.05	.01
☐ 19	Brian McRae	.08	.04	.01
☐ 20	Ryne Sandberg	.60	.25	.08
☐ 21	Kirby Puckett	.75	.35	.09
☐ 22	Dwight Gooden	.05	.02	.01
☐ 23	Don Mattingly	.75	.35	.09
☐ 24	Kevin Mitchell	.08	.04	.01
☐ 25	Roger Clemens	.50	.23	.06
☐ 26	Eric Karros	.08	.04	.01
☐ 27	Juan Gonzalez	.60	.25	.08
☐ 28	John Kruk	.10	.05	.01
☐ 29	Gregg Jefferies	.10	.05	.01
☐ 30	Tom Glavine	.10	.05	.01
☐ 31	Ivan Rodriguez	.10	.05	.01
☐ 32	Jay Bell	.08	.04	.01
☐ 33	Randy Johnson	.10	.05	.01
☐ 34	Darren Daulton	.10	.05	.01
☐ 35	Rickey Henderson	.10	.05	.01
☐ 36	Eddie Murray	.10	.05	.01
☐ 37	Brian Harper	.05	.02	.01
☐ 38	Delino DeShields	.08	.04	.01
☐ 39	Jose Lind	.05	.02	.01
☐ 40	Benito Santiago	.05	.02	.01
☐ 41	Frank Thomas	2.00	.90	.25
☐ 42	Mark Grace	.10	.05	.01
☐ 43	Roberto Alomar	.50	.23	.06
☐ 44	Andy Benes	.08	.04	.01
☐ 45	Luis Polonia	.05	.02	.01
☐ 46	Brett Butler	.08	.04	.01
☐ 47	Terry Steinbach	.08	.04	.01
☐ 48	Craig Biggio	.08	.04	.01
☐ 49	Greg Vaughn	.08	.04	.01
☐ 50	Charlie Hayes	.08	.04	.01
☐ 51	Mickey Tettleton	.08	.04	.01
☐ 52	Jose Rijo	.08	.04	.01
☐ 53	Carlos Baerga	.30	.14	.04
☐ 54	Jeff Blauser	.08	.04	.01
☐ 55	Leo Gomez	.05	.02	.01
☐ 56	Bob Tewksbury	.05	.02	.01
☐ 57	Mo Vaughn	.10	.05	.01
☐ 58	Orlando Merced	.08	.04	.01
☐ 59	Tino Martinez	.05	.02	.01
☐ 60	Lenny Dykstra	.10	.05	.01
☐ 61	Jose Canseco	.30	.14	.04
☐ 62	Tony Fernandez	.05	.02	.01
☐ 63	Donovan Osborne	.05	.02	.01
☐ 64	Ken Hill	.08	.04	.01
☐ 65	Kent Hrbek	.08	.04	.01
☐ 66	Bryan Harvey	.08	.04	.01
☐ 67	Wally Joyner	.08	.04	.01
☐ 68	Derrick May	.05	.02	.01
☐ 69	Lance Johnson	.05	.02	.01
☐ 70	Willie McGee	.05	.02	.01
☐ 71	Mark Langston	.10	.05	.01
☐ 72	Terry Pendleton	.10	.05	.01
☐ 73	Joe Carter	.30	.14	.04
☐ 74	Barry Larkin	.10	.05	.01
☐ 75	Jimmy Key	.08	.04	.01
☐ 76	Joe Girardi	.05	.02	.01
☐ 77	B.J. Surhoff	.05	.02	.01
☐ 78	Pete Harnisch	.05	.02	.01
☐ 79	Lou Whitaker UER (Milt Cuyler pictured on front)	.10	.05	.01
☐ 80	Cory Snyder	.05	.02	.01
☐ 81	Kenny Lofton	.50	.23	.06
☐ 82	Fred McGriff	.30	.14	.04
☐ 83	Mike Greenwell	.08	.04	.01
☐ 84	Mike Perez	.05	.02	.01

☐	85 Cal Ripken	1.25	.55	.16
☐	86 Don Slaught	.05	.02	.01
☐	87 Omar Vizquel	.05	.02	.01
☐	88 Curt Schilling	.05	.02	.01
☐	89 Chuck Knoblauch	.10	.05	.01
☐	90 Moises Alou	.10	.05	.01
☐	91 Greg Gagne	.05	.02	.01
☐	92 Bret Saberhagen	.08	.04	.01
☐	93 Ozzie Guillen	.05	.02	.01
☐	94 Matt Williams	.40	.18	.05
☐	95 Chad Curtis	.08	.04	.01
☐	96 Mike Harkey	.05	.02	.01
☐	97 Devon White	.08	.04	.01
☐	98 Walt Weiss	.05	.02	.01
☐	99 Kevin Brown	.05	.02	.01
☐	100 Gary Sheffield	.10	.05	.01
☐	101 Wade Boggs	.10	.05	.01
☐	102 Orel Hershiser	.08	.04	.01
☐	103 Tony Phillips	.05	.02	.01
☐	104 Andujar Cedeno	.05	.02	.01
☐	105 Bill Spiers	.05	.02	.01
☐	106 Otis Nixon	.05	.02	.01
☐	107 Felix Fermin	.05	.02	.01
☐	108 Bip Roberts	.05	.02	.01
☐	109 Dennis Eckersley	.10	.05	.01
☐	110 Dante Bichette	.10	.05	.01
☐	111 Ben McDonald	.08	.04	.01
☐	112 Jim Poole	.05	.02	.01
☐	113 John Dopson	.05	.02	.01
☐	114 Rob Dibble	.05	.02	.01
☐	115 Jeff Treadway	.05	.02	.01
☐	116 Ricky Jordan	.05	.02	.01
☐	117 Mike Henneman	.05	.02	.01
☐	118 Willie Blair	.05	.02	.01
☐	119 Doug Henry	.05	.02	.01
☐	120 Gerald Perry	.05	.02	.01
☐	121 Greg Myers	.05	.02	.01
☐	122 John Franco	.05	.02	.01
☐	123 Roger Mason	.05	.02	.01
☐	124 Chris Hammond	.05	.02	.01
☐	125 Hubie Brooks	.05	.02	.01
☐	126 Kent Mercker	.05	.02	.01
☐	127 Jim Abbott	.10	.05	.01
☐	128 Kevin Bass	.05	.02	.01
☐	129 Rick Aguilera	.08	.04	.01
☐	130 Mitch Webster	.05	.02	.01
☐	131 Eric Plunk	.05	.02	.01
☐	132 Mark Carreon	.05	.02	.01
☐	133 Dave Stewart	.08	.04	.01
☐	134 Willie Wilson	.05	.02	.01
☐	135 Dave Fleming	.05	.02	.01
☐	136 Jeff Tackett	.05	.02	.01
☐	137 Geno Petralli	.05	.02	.01
☐	138 Gene Harris	.05	.02	.01
☐	139 Scott Bankhead	.05	.02	.01
☐	140 Trevor Wilson	.05	.02	.01
☐	141 Alvaro Espinoza	.05	.02	.01
☐	142 Ryan Bowen	.05	.02	.01
☐	143 Mike Moore	.05	.02	.01
☐	144 Bill Pecota	.05	.02	.01
☐	145 Jaime Navarro	.05	.02	.01
☐	146 Jack Daugherty	.05	.02	.01
☐	147 Bob Wickman	.05	.02	.01
☐	148 Chris Jones	.05	.02	.01
☐	149 Todd Stottlemyre	.05	.02	.01
☐	150 Brian Williams	.05	.02	.01
☐	151 Chuck Finley	.05	.02	.01
☐	152 Lenny Harris	.05	.02	.01
☐	153 Alex Fernandez	.10	.05	.01
☐	154 Candy Maldonado	.05	.02	.01
☐	155 Jeff Montgomery	.08	.04	.01
☐	156 David West	.05	.02	.01
☐	157 Mark Williamson	.05	.02	.01
☐	158 Milt Thompson	.05	.02	.01
☐	159 Ron Darling	.05	.02	.01
☐	160 Stan Belinda	.05	.02	.01
☐	161 Henry Cotto	.05	.02	.01
☐	162 Mel Rojas	.05	.02	.01
☐	163 Doug Strange	.05	.02	.01
☐	164 Rene Arocha	.08	.04	.01
☐	165 Tim Hulett	.05	.02	.01
☐	166 Steve Avery	.10	.05	.01
☐	167 Jim Thome	.10	.05	.01
☐	168 Tom Browning	.05	.02	.01
☐	169 Mario Diaz	.05	.02	.01
☐	170 Steve Reed	.05	.02	.01
☐	171 Scott Livingstone	.05	.02	.01
☐	172 Chris Donnels	.05	.02	.01
☐	173 John Jaha	.05	.02	.01
☐	174 Carlos Hernandez	.05	.02	.01
☐	175 Dion James	.05	.02	.01
☐	176 Bud Black	.05	.02	.01
☐	177 Tony Castillo	.05	.02	.01
☐	178 Jose Guzman	.05	.02	.01
☐	179 Torey Lovullo	.05	.02	.01
☐	180 John Vander Wal	.05	.02	.01
☐	181 Mike LaValliere	.05	.02	.01
☐	182 Sid Fernandez	.05	.02	.01
☐	183 Brent Mayne	.05	.02	.01
☐	184 Terry Mulholland	.05	.02	.01
☐	185 Willie Banks	.05	.02	.01
☐	186 Steve Cooke	.05	.02	.01
☐	187 Brent Gates	.10	.05	.01
☐	188 Erik Pappas	.05	.02	.01
☐	189 Bill Haselman	.05	.02	.01
☐	190 Fernando Valenzuela	.05	.02	.01
☐	191 Gary Redus	.05	.02	.01
☐	192 Danny Darwin	.05	.02	.01
☐	193 Mark Portugal	.05	.02	.01
☐	194 Derek Lilliquist	.05	.02	.01
☐	195 Charlie O'Brien	.05	.02	.01
☐	196 Matt Nokes	.05	.02	.01
☐	197 Danny Sheaffer	.05	.02	.01
☐	198 Bill Gullickson	.05	.02	.01
☐	199 Alex Arias	.05	.02	.01
☐	200 Mike Fetters	.05	.02	.01
☐	201 Brian Jordan	.08	.04	.01
☐	202 Joe Grahe	.05	.02	.01
☐	203 Tom Candiotti	.05	.02	.01
☐	204 Jeremy Hernandez	.05	.02	.01
☐	205 Mike Stanton	.05	.02	.01
☐	206 David Howard	.05	.02	.01
☐	207 Darren Holmes	.05	.02	.01
☐	208 Rick Honeycutt	.05	.02	.01
☐	209 Danny Jackson	.05	.02	.01
☐	210 Rich Amaral	.05	.02	.01
☐	211 Blas Minor	.05	.02	.01
☐	212 Kenny Rogers	.05	.02	.01
☐	213 Jim Leyritz	.05	.02	.01
☐	214 Mike Morgan	.05	.02	.01
☐	215 Dan Gladden	.05	.02	.01
☐	216 Randy Velarde	.05	.02	.01
☐	217 Mitch Williams	.05	.02	.01
☐	218 Hipolito Pichardo	.05	.02	.01
☐	219 Dave Burba	.05	.02	.01
☐	220 Wilson Alvarez	.10	.05	.01
☐	221 Bob Zupcic	.05	.02	.01
☐	222 Francisco Cabrera	.05	.02	.01
☐	223 Julio Valera	.05	.02	.01
☐	224 Paul Assenmacher	.05	.02	.01
☐	225 Jeff Branson	.05	.02	.01
☐	226 Todd Frohwirth	.05	.02	.01
☐	227 Armando Reynoso	.05	.02	.01
☐	228 Rich Rowland	.05	.02	.01
☐	229 Freddie Benavides	.05	.02	.01
☐	230 Wayne Kirby	.05	.02	.01

	No.	Player			
☐	231	Darryl Kile	.08	.04	.01
☐	232	Skeeter Barnes	.05	.02	.01
☐	233	Ramon Martinez	.08	.04	.01
☐	234	Tom Gordon	.05	.02	.01
☐	235	Dave Gallagher	.05	.02	.01
☐	236	Ricky Bones	.05	.02	.01
☐	237	Larry Andersen	.05	.02	.01
☐	238	Pat Meares	.05	.02	.01
☐	239	Zane Smith	.05	.02	.01
☐	240	Tim Leary	.05	.02	.01
☐	241	Phil Clark	.05	.02	.01
☐	242	Danny Cox	.05	.02	.01
☐	243	Mike Jackson	.05	.02	.01
☐	244	Mike Gallego	.05	.02	.01
☐	245	Lee Smith	.10	.05	.01
☐	246	Todd Jones	.05	.02	.01
☐	247	Steve Bedrosian	.05	.02	.01
☐	248	Troy Neel	.08	.04	.01
☐	249	Jose Bautista	.05	.02	.01
☐	250	Steve Frey	.05	.02	.01
☐	251	Jeff Reardon	.08	.04	.01
☐	252	Stan Javier	.05	.02	.01
☐	253	Mo Sanford	.05	.02	.01
☐	254	Steve Sax	.05	.02	.01
☐	255	Luis Aquino	.05	.02	.01
☐	256	Domingo Jean	.05	.02	.01
☐	257	Scott Servais	.05	.02	.01
☐	258	Brad Pennington	.05	.02	.01
☐	259	Dave Hansen	.05	.02	.01
☐	260	Goose Gossage	.10	.05	.01
☐	261	Jeff Fassero	.05	.02	.01
☐	262	Junior Ortiz	.05	.02	.01
☐	263	Anthony Young	.05	.02	.01
☐	264	Chris Bosio	.05	.02	.01
☐	265	Ruben Amaro Jr.	.05	.02	.01
☐	266	Mark Eichhorn	.05	.02	.01
☐	267	Dave Clark	.05	.02	.01
☐	268	Gary Thurman	.05	.02	.01
☐	269	Les Lancaster	.05	.02	.01
☐	270	Jamie Moyer	.05	.02	.01
☐	271	Ricky Gutierrez	.05	.02	.01
☐	272	Greg A.Harris	.05	.02	.01
☐	273	Mike Benjamin	.05	.02	.01
☐	274	Gene Nelson	.05	.02	.01
☐	275	Damon Berryhill	.05	.02	.01
☐	276	Scott Radinsky	.05	.02	.01
☐	277	Mike Aldrete	.05	.02	.01
☐	278	Jerry DiPoto	.08	.04	.01
☐	279	Chris Haney	.05	.02	.01
☐	280	Richie Lewis	.05	.02	.01
☐	281	Jarvis Brown	.05	.02	.01
☐	282	Juan Bell	.05	.02	.01
☐	283	Joe Klink	.05	.02	.01
☐	284	Graeme Lloyd	.05	.02	.01
☐	285	Casey Candaele	.05	.02	.01
☐	286	Bob MacDonald	.05	.02	.01
☐	287	Mike Sharperson	.05	.02	.01
☐	288	Gene Larkin	.05	.02	.01
☐	289	Brian Barnes	.05	.02	.01
☐	290	David McCarty	.08	.04	.01
☐	291	Jeff Innis	.05	.02	.01
☐	292	Bob Patterson	.05	.02	.01
☐	293	Ben Rivera	.05	.02	.01
☐	294	John Habyan	.05	.02	.01
☐	295	Rich Rodriguez	.05	.02	.01
☐	296	Edwin Nunez	.05	.02	.01
☐	297	Rod Brewer	.05	.02	.01
☐	298	Mike Timlin	.05	.02	.01
☐	299	Jesse Orosco	.05	.02	.01
☐	300	Gary Gaetti	.05	.02	.01
☐	301	Todd Benzinger	.05	.02	.01
☐	302	Jeff Nelson	.05	.02	.01
☐	303	Rafael Belliard	.05	.02	.01

	No.	Player			
☐	304	Matt Whiteside	.05	.02	.01
☐	305	Vinny Castilla	.10	.05	.01
☐	306	Matt Turner	.10	.05	.01
☐	307	Eduardo Perez	.10	.05	.01
☐	308	Joel Johnston	.10	.05	.01
☐	309	Chris Gomez	.15	.07	.02
☐	310	Pat Rapp	.10	.05	.01
☐	311	Jim Tatum	.10	.05	.01
☐	312	Kirk Rueter	.10	.05	.01
☐	313	John Flaherty	.10	.05	.01
☐	314	Tom Kramer	.10	.05	.01
☐	315	Mark Whiten	.10	.05	.01
☐	316	Chris Bosio	.10	.05	.01
☐	317	Baltimore Orioles CL	.10	.05	.01
☐	318	Boston Red Sox CL UER (Viola listed as 316; should be 331)	.10	.05	.01
☐	319	California Angels CL	.10	.05	.01
☐	320	Chicago White Sox CL	.10	.05	.01
☐	321	Cleveland Indians CL	.10	.05	.01
☐	322	Detroit Tigers CL	.10	.05	.01
☐	323	Kansas City Royals CL	.10	.05	.01
☐	324	Milwaukee Brewers CL	.10	.05	.01
☐	325	Minnesota Twins CL	.10	.05	.01
☐	326	New York Yankees CL	.10	.05	.01
☐	327	Oakland Athletics CL	.10	.05	.01
☐	328	Seattle Mariners CL	.10	.05	.01
☐	329	Texas Rangers CL	.10	.05	.01
☐	330	Toronto Blue Jays CL	.10	.05	.01
☐	331	Frank Viola	.05	.02	.01
☐	332	Ron Gant	.08	.04	.01
☐	333	Charles Nagy	.05	.02	.01
☐	334	Roberto Kelly	.05	.02	.01
☐	335	Brady Anderson	.08	.04	.01
☐	336	Alex Cole	.05	.02	.01
☐	337	Alan Trammell	.10	.05	.01
☐	338	Derek Bell	.08	.04	.01
☐	339	Bernie Williams	.08	.04	.01
☐	340	Jose Offerman	.05	.02	.01
☐	341	Bill Wegman	.05	.02	.01
☐	342	Ken Caminiti	.08	.04	.01
☐	343	Pat Borders	.05	.02	.01
☐	344	Kirt Manwaring	.05	.02	.01
☐	345	Chili Davis	.08	.04	.01
☐	346	Steve Buechele	.05	.02	.01
☐	347	Robin Ventura	.08	.04	.01
☐	348	Teddy Higuera	.05	.02	.01
☐	349	Jerry Browne	.05	.02	.01
☐	350	Scott Kamieniecki	.05	.02	.01
☐	351	Kevin Tapani	.05	.02	.01
☐	352	Marquis Grissom	.10	.05	.01
☐	353	Jay Buhner	.08	.04	.01
☐	354	Dave Hollins	.10	.05	.01
☐	355	Dan Wilson	.05	.02	.01
☐	356	Bob Walk	.05	.02	.01
☐	357	Chris Hoiles	.08	.04	.01
☐	358	Todd Zeile	.08	.04	.01
☐	359	Kevin Appier	.08	.04	.01
☐	360	Chris Sabo	.05	.02	.01
☐	361	David Segui	.05	.02	.01
☐	362	Jerald Clark	.05	.02	.01
☐	363	Tony Pena	.05	.02	.01
☐	364	Steve Finley	.05	.02	.01
☐	365	Roger Pavlik	.05	.02	.01
☐	366	John Smoltz	.08	.04	.01
☐	367	Scott Fletcher	.05	.02	.01
☐	368	Jody Reed	.05	.02	.01
☐	369	David Wells	.05	.02	.01
☐	370	Jose Vizcaino	.05	.02	.01
☐	371	Pat Listach	.05	.02	.01
☐	372	Orestes Destrade	.05	.02	.01
☐	373	Danny Tartabull	.08	.04	.01
☐	374	Greg W. Harris	.05	.02	.01

	No.	Player			
☐	375	Juan Guzman	.08	.04	.01
☐	376	Larry Walker	.10	.05	.01
☐	377	Gary DiSarcina	.05	.02	.01
☐	378	Bobby Bonilla	.10	.05	.01
☐	379	Tim Raines	.10	.05	.01
☐	380	Tommy Greene	.05	.02	.01
☐	381	Chris Gwynn	.05	.02	.01
☐	382	Jeff King	.05	.02	.01
☐	383	Shane Mack	.08	.04	.01
☐	384	Ozzie Smith	.40	.18	.05
☐	385	Eddie Zambrano	.05	.02	.01
☐	386	Mike Devereaux	.08	.04	.01
☐	387	Erik Hanson	.05	.02	.01
☐	388	Scott Cooper	.08	.04	.01
☐	389	Dean Palmer	.08	.04	.01
☐	390	John Wetteland	.05	.02	.01
☐	391	Reggie Jefferson	.05	.02	.01
☐	392	Mark Lemke	.05	.02	.01
☐	393	Cecil Fielder	.10	.05	.01
☐	394	Reggie Sanders	.08	.04	.01
☐	395	Darryl Hamilton	.05	.02	.01
☐	396	Daryl Boston	.05	.02	.01
☐	397	Pat Kelly	.05	.02	.01
☐	398	Joe Orsulak	.05	.02	.01
☐	399	Ed Sprague	.05	.02	.01
☐	400	Eric Anthony	.05	.02	.01
☐	401	Scott Sanderson	.05	.02	.01
☐	402	Jim Gott	.05	.02	.01
☐	403	Ron Karkovice	.05	.02	.01
☐	404	Phil Plantier	.08	.04	.01
☐	405	David Cone	.10	.05	.01
☐	406	Robby Thompson	.05	.02	.01
☐	407	Dave Winfield	.10	.05	.01
☐	408	Dwight Smith	.05	.02	.01
☐	409	Ruben Sierra	.10	.05	.01
☐	410	Jack Armstrong	.05	.02	.01
☐	411	Mike Felder	.05	.02	.01
☐	412	Wil Cordero	.10	.05	.01
☐	413	Julio Franco	.08	.04	.01
☐	414	Howard Johnson	.05	.02	.01
☐	415	Mark McLemore	.05	.02	.01
☐	416	Pete Incaviglia	.05	.02	.01
☐	417	John Valentin	.08	.04	.01
☐	418	Tim Wakefield	.05	.02	.01
☐	419	Jose Mesa	.05	.02	.01
☐	420	Bernard Gilkey	.05	.02	.01
☐	421	Kirk Gibson	.08	.04	.01
☐	422	David Justice	.30	.14	.04
☐	423	Tom Brunansky	.05	.02	.01
☐	424	John Smiley	.05	.02	.01
☐	425	Kevin Maas	.05	.02	.01
☐	426	Doug Drabek	.10	.05	.01
☐	427	Paul Molitor	.30	.14	.04
☐	428	Darryl Strawberry	.08	.04	.01
☐	429	Tim Naehring	.05	.02	.01
☐	430	Bill Swift	.05	.02	.01
☐	431	Ellis Burks	.08	.04	.01
☐	432	Greg Hibbard	.05	.02	.01
☐	433	Felix Jose	.05	.02	.01
☐	434	Bret Barberie	.05	.02	.01
☐	435	Pedro Munoz	.05	.02	.01
☐	436	Darrin Fletcher	.05	.02	.01
☐	437	Bobby Witt	.05	.02	.01
☐	438	Wes Chamberlain	.05	.02	.01
☐	439	Mackey Sasser	.05	.02	.01
☐	440	Mark Whiten	.08	.04	.01
☐	441	Harold Reynolds	.05	.02	.01
☐	442	Greg Olson	.05	.02	.01
☐	443	Billy Hatcher	.05	.02	.01
☐	444	Joe Oliver	.05	.02	.01
☐	445	Sandy Alomar Jr.	.08	.04	.01
☐	446	Tim Wallach	.05	.02	.01
☐	447	Karl Rhodes	.05	.02	.01
☐	448	Royce Clayton	.08	.04	.01
☐	449	Cal Eldred	.08	.04	.01
☐	450	Rick Wilkins	.05	.02	.01
☐	451	Mike Stanley	.05	.02	.01
☐	452	Charlie Hough	.08	.04	.01
☐	453	Jack Morris	.10	.05	.01
☐	454	Jon Ratliff	.15	.07	.02
☐	455	Rene Gonzales	.05	.02	.01
☐	456	Eddie Taubensee	.05	.02	.01
☐	457	Roberto Hernandez	.05	.02	.01
☐	458	Todd Hundley	.05	.02	.01
☐	459	Mike Macfarlane	.05	.02	.01
☐	460	Mickey Morandini	.05	.02	.01
☐	461	Scott Erickson	.05	.02	.01
☐	462	Lonnie Smith	.05	.02	.01
☐	463	Dave Henderson	.05	.02	.01
☐	464	Ryan Klesko	.30	.14	.04
☐	465	Edgar Martinez	.05	.02	.01
☐	466	Tom Pagnozzi	.05	.02	.01
☐	467	Charlie Leibrandt	.05	.02	.01
☐	468	Brian Anderson	.50	.23	.06
☐	469	Harold Baines	.08	.04	.01
☐	470	Tim Belcher	.05	.02	.01
☐	471	Andre Dawson	.10	.05	.01
☐	472	Eric Young	.08	.04	.01
☐	473	Paul Sorrento	.05	.02	.01
☐	474	Luis Gonzalez	.05	.02	.01
☐	475	Rob Deer	.05	.02	.01
☐	476	Mike Piazza	1.00	.45	.13
☐	477	Kevin Reimer	.05	.02	.01
☐	478	Jeff Gardner	.05	.02	.01
☐	479	Melido Perez	.05	.02	.01
☐	480	Darren Lewis	.05	.02	.01
☐	481	Duane Ward	.05	.02	.01
☐	482	Rey Sanchez	.05	.02	.01
☐	483	Mark Lewis	.05	.02	.01
☐	484	Jeff Conine	.10	.05	.01
☐	485	Joey Cora	.05	.02	.01
☐	486	Trot Nixon	.50	.23	.06
☐	487	Kevin McReynolds	.05	.02	.01
☐	488	Mike Lansing	.08	.04	.01
☐	489	Mike Pagliarulo	.05	.02	.01
☐	490	Mariano Duncan	.05	.02	.01
☐	491	Mike Bordick	.05	.02	.01
☐	492	Kevin Young	.05	.02	.01
☐	493	Dave Valle	.05	.02	.01
☐	494	Wayne Gomes	.15	.07	.02
☐	495	Rafael Palmeiro	.10	.05	.01
☐	496	Deion Sanders	.35	.16	.04
☐	497	Rick Sutcliffe	.08	.04	.01
☐	498	Randy Milligan	.05	.02	.01
☐	499	Carlos Quintana	.05	.02	.01
☐	500	Chris Turner	.05	.02	.01
☐	501	Thomas Howard	.05	.02	.01
☐	502	Greg Swindell	.05	.02	.01
☐	503	Chad Kreuter	.05	.02	.01
☐	504	Eric Davis	.05	.02	.01
☐	505	Dickie Thon	.05	.02	.01
☐	506	Matt Drews	.35	.16	.04
☐	507	Spike Owen	.05	.02	.01
☐	508	Rod Beck	.08	.04	.01
☐	509	Pat Hentgen	.08	.04	.01
☐	510	Sammy Sosa	.10	.05	.01
☐	511	J.T. Snow	.08	.04	.01
☐	512	Chuck Carr	.05	.02	.01
☐	513	Bo Jackson	.10	.05	.01
☐	514	Dennis Martinez	.08	.04	.01
☐	515	Phil Hiatt	.05	.02	.01
☐	516	Jeff Kent	.08	.04	.01
☐	517	Brooks Kieschnick	.60	.25	.08
☐	518	Kirk Presley	.50	.23	.06
☐	519	Kevin Seitzer	.05	.02	.01
☐	520	Carlos Garcia	.05	.02	.01

- ☐ 521 Mike Blowers .05 .02 .01
- ☐ 522 Luis Alicea .05 .02 .01
- ☐ 523 David Hulse .05 .02 .01
- ☐ 524 Greg Maddux UER .40 .18 .05 (career strikeout totals listed as 113; should be 1134)
- ☐ 525 Gregg Olson .05 .02 .01
- ☐ 526 Hal Morris .08 .04 .01
- ☐ 527 Daron Kirkreit .05 .02 .01
- ☐ 528 David Nied .10 .05 .01
- ☐ 529 Jeff Russell .05 .02 .01
- ☐ 530 Kevin Gross .05 .02 .01
- ☐ 531 John Doherty .05 .02 .01
- ☐ 532 Matt Brunson .20 .09 .03
- ☐ 533 Dave Nilsson .05 .02 .01
- ☐ 534 Randy Myers .05 .02 .01
- ☐ 535 Steve Farr .05 .02 .01
- ☐ 536 Billy Wagner .40 .18 .05
- ☐ 537 Darnell Coles .05 .02 .01
- ☐ 538 Frank Tanana .05 .02 .01
- ☐ 539 Tim Salmon .30 .14 .04
- ☐ 540 Kim Batiste .05 .02 .01
- ☐ 541 George Bell .05 .02 .01
- ☐ 542 Tom Henke .05 .02 .01
- ☐ 543 Sam Horn .05 .02 .01
- ☐ 544 Doug Jones .05 .02 .01
- ☐ 545 Scott Leius .05 .02 .01
- ☐ 546 Al Martin .05 .02 .01
- ☐ 547 Bob Welch .05 .02 .01
- ☐ 548 Scott Christmas .20 .09 .03
- ☐ 549 Norm Charlton .05 .02 .01
- ☐ 550 Mark McGwire .10 .05 .01
- ☐ 551 Greg McMichael .08 .04 .01
- ☐ 552 Tim Costo .05 .02 .01
- ☐ 553 Rodney Bolton .05 .02 .01
- ☐ 554 Pedro Martinez .10 .05 .01
- ☐ 555 Marc Valdes .05 .02 .01
- ☐ 556 Darrell Whitmore .08 .04 .01
- ☐ 557 Tim Bogar .05 .02 .01
- ☐ 558 Steve Karsay .05 .02 .01
- ☐ 559 Danny Bautista .08 .04 .01
- ☐ 560 Jeffrey Hammonds .25 .11 .03
- ☐ 561 Aaron Sele .15 .07 .02
- ☐ 562 Russ Springer .05 .02 .01
- ☐ 563 Jason Bere .25 .11 .03
- ☐ 564 Billy Brewer .05 .02 .01
- ☐ 565 Sterling Hitchcock .08 .04 .01
- ☐ 566 Bobby Munoz .05 .02 .01
- ☐ 567 Craig Paquette .05 .02 .01
- ☐ 568 Bret Boone .10 .05 .01
- ☐ 569 Dan Peltier .05 .02 .01
- ☐ 570 Jeromy Burnitz .08 .04 .01
- ☐ 571 John Wasdin .40 .18 .05
- ☐ 572 Chipper Jones .25 .11 .03
- ☐ 573 Jamey Wright .25 .11 .03
- ☐ 574 Jeff Granger .08 .04 .01
- ☐ 575 Jay Powell .20 .09 .03
- ☐ 576 Ryan Thompson .08 .04 .01
- ☐ 577 Lou Frazier .05 .02 .01
- ☐ 578 Paul Wagner .05 .02 .01
- ☐ 579 Brad Ausmus .05 .02 .01
- ☐ 580 Jack Voigt .05 .02 .01
- ☐ 581 Kevin Rogers .05 .02 .01
- ☐ 582 Damon Buford .05 .02 .01
- ☐ 583 Paul Quantrill .05 .02 .01
- ☐ 584 Marc Newfield .10 .05 .01
- ☐ 585 Derrek Lee .50 .23 .06
- ☐ 586 Shane Reynolds .05 .02 .01
- ☐ 587 Cliff Floyd .30 .14 .04
- ☐ 588 Jeff Schwarz .05 .02 .01
- ☐ 589 Ross Powell .05 .02 .01
- ☐ 590 Gerald Williams .05 .02 .01
- ☐ 591 Mike Trombley .05 .02 .01
- ☐ 592 Ken Ryan .05 .02 .01
- ☐ 593 John O'Donoghue .05 .02 .01
- ☐ 594 Rod Correia .05 .02 .01
- ☐ 595 Darrell Sherman .05 .02 .01
- ☐ 596 Steve Scarsone .05 .02 .01
- ☐ 597 Sherman Obando .05 .02 .01
- ☐ 598 Kurt Abbott .20 .09 .03
- ☐ 599 Dave Telgheder .05 .02 .01
- ☐ 600 Rick Trlicek .05 .02 .01
- ☐ 601 Carl Everett .08 .04 .01
- ☐ 602 Luis Ortiz .05 .02 .01
- ☐ 603 Larry Luebbers .05 .02 .01
- ☐ 604 Kevin Roberson .05 .02 .01
- ☐ 605 Butch Huskey .05 .02 .01
- ☐ 606 Benji Gil .08 .04 .01
- ☐ 607 Todd Van Poppel .08 .04 .01
- ☐ 608 Mark Hutton .05 .02 .01
- ☐ 609 Chip Hale .05 .02 .01
- ☐ 610 Matt Maysey .05 .02 .01
- ☐ 611 Scott Ruffcorn .10 .05 .01
- ☐ 612 Hilly Hathaway .05 .02 .01
- ☐ 613 Allen Watson .05 .02 .01
- ☐ 614 Carlos Delgado .30 .14 .04
- ☐ 615 Roberto Mejia .08 .04 .01
- ☐ 616 Turk Wendell .05 .02 .01
- ☐ 617 Tony Tarasco .10 .05 .01
- ☐ 618 Raul Mondesi .75 .35 .09
- ☐ 619 Kevin Stocker .08 .04 .01
- ☐ 620 Javy Lopez .20 .09 .03
- ☐ 621 Keith Kessinger .05 .02 .01
- ☐ 622 Bob Hamelin .10 .05 .01
- ☐ 623 John Roper .08 .04 .01
- ☐ 624 Lenny Dykstra WS .10 .05 .01
- ☐ 625 Joe Carter WS .15 .07 .02
- ☐ 626 Jim Abbott HL .10 .05 .01
- ☐ 627 Lee Smith HL .10 .05 .01
- ☐ 628 Ken Griffey Jr. HL 1.00 .45 .13
- ☐ 629 Dave Winfield HL .15 .07 .02
- ☐ 630 Darryl Kile HL .10 .05 .01
- ☐ 631 Frank Thomas AL MVP 1.00 .45 .13
- ☐ 632 Barry Bonds NL MVP .40 .18 .05
- ☐ 633 Jack McDowell AL CY .10 .05 .01
- ☐ 634 Greg Maddux NL CY .20 .09 .03
- ☐ 635 Tim Salmon AL ROY .15 .07 .02
- ☐ 636 Mike Piazza NL ROY .50 .23 .06
- ☐ 637 Brian Turang .05 .02 .01
- ☐ 638 Rondell White .20 .09 .03
- ☐ 639 Nigel Wilson .08 .04 .01
- ☐ 640 Torii Hunter .20 .09 .03
- ☐ 641 Salomon Torres .08 .04 .01
- ☐ 642 Kevin Higgins .05 .02 .01
- ☐ 643 Eric Wedge .05 .02 .01
- ☐ 644 Roger Salkeld .05 .02 .01
- ☐ 645 Manny Ramirez .40 .18 .05
- ☐ 646 Jeff McNeely .05 .02 .01
- ☐ 647 Checklist .10 .05 .01 Atlanta Braves
- ☐ 648 Checklist .10 .05 .01 Chicago Cubs
- ☐ 649 Checklist .10 .05 .01 Cincinnati Reds
- ☐ 650 Checklist .10 .05 .01 Colorado Rockies
- ☐ 651 Checklist .10 .05 .01 Florida Marlins
- ☐ 652 Checklist .10 .05 .01 Houston Astros
- ☐ 653 Checklist .10 .05 .01 Los Angeles Dodgers
- ☐ 654 Checklist .10 .05 .01 Montreal Expos
- ☐ 655 Checklist .10 .05 .01 New York Mets

		MINT	EXC	G-VG
☐ 656	Checklist .... Philadelphia Phillies	.10	.05	.01
☐ 657	Checklist .... Pittsburgh Pirates	.10	.05	.01
☐ 658	Checklist .... St. Louis Cardinals	.10	.05	.01
☐ 659	Checklist .... San Diego Padres	.10	.05	.01
☐ 660	Checklist .... San Francisco Giants	.10	.05	.01

1994 Score Gold Rush

This 660-card set is parallel to the basic Score issue. This standard-size set features metallicized and gold-bordered fronts. The Gold Rush logo is prominent on the back. Gold Rush cards come one per 14-card pack (13 regular issue and one Gold Rush) and were inserted into both hobby and retail packs. Since 4,875 cases of 1994 Score baseball were printed for the hobby, it appears that roughly 3.5 million Gold Rush cards were distributed in hobby cases alone.

	MINT	EXC	G-VG
COMPLETE SET (660)	225.00	100.00	28.00
COMPLETE SERIES 1 (330).	115.00	52.50	14.50
COMPLETE SERIES 2 (330).	115.00	52.50	14.50
COMMON CARD (1-330)	.25	.11	.03
COMMON CARD (331-660)	.25	.11	.03

*VETERAN STARS: 4X to 7X BASIC CARDS
*YOUNG STARS: 3X to 6X BASIC CARDS
*RCs: 2X to 4X BASIC CARDS

1994 Score Boys of Summer

Randomly inserted in super packs at a rate of one in four, this 60-card set features top young stars and hopefuls. The set was issued in two series of 30 cards. The fronts have a color player photo that is outlined by what resembles static electricity. The backgrounds are blurred and the player's name and Boys of Summer logo appear up the right-hand side. An orange back contains a player photo and text.

	MINT	EXC	G-VG
COMPLETE SET (60)	120.00	55.00	15.00
COMPLETE SERIES 1 (30).....	60.00	27.00	7.50
COMPLETE SERIES 2 (30).....	60.00	27.00	7.50
COMMON CARD (1-30)	1.50	.65	.19
COMMON CARD (31-60)	1.50	.65	.19

		MINT	EXC	G-VG
☐ 1	Jeff Conine	1.50	.65	.19
☐ 2	Aaron Sele	3.50	1.55	.45
☐ 3	Kevin Stocker	1.75	.80	.22
☐ 4	Pat Meares	1.50	.65	.19
☐ 5	Jeromy Burnitz	1.50	.65	.19
☐ 6	Mike Piazza	20.00	9.00	2.50
☐ 7	Allen Watson	1.50	.65	.19
☐ 8	Jeffrey Hammonds	4.00	1.80	.50
☐ 9	Kevin Roberson	1.50	.65	.19
☐ 10	Hilly Hathaway	1.50	.65	.19
☐ 11	Kirk Rueter	1.75	.80	.22
☐ 12	Eduardo Perez	1.75	.80	.22
☐ 13	Ricky Gutierrez	1.50	.65	.19
☐ 14	Domingo Jean	1.50	.65	.19
☐ 15	David Nied	2.00	.90	.25
☐ 16	Wayne Kirby	1.50	.65	.19
☐ 17	Mike Lansing	1.50	.65	.19
☐ 18	Jason Bere	5.00	2.30	.60
☐ 19	Brent Gates	2.00	.90	.25
☐ 20	Javy Lopez	4.00	1.80	.50
☐ 21	Greg McMichael	1.50	.65	.19
☐ 22	David Hulse	1.50	.65	.19
☐ 23	Roberto Mejia	1.75	.80	.22
☐ 24	Tim Salmon	6.00	2.70	.75
☐ 25	Rene Arocha	1.50	.65	.19
☐ 26	Bret Boone	2.00	.90	.25
☐ 27	David McCarty	1.50	.65	.19
☐ 28	Todd Van Poppel	1.75	.80	.22
☐ 29	Lance Painter	1.50	.65	.19
☐ 30	Erik Pappas	1.50	.65	.19
☐ 31	Chuck Carr	1.50	.65	.19
☐ 32	Mark Hutton	1.50	.65	.19
☐ 33	Jeff McNeely	1.50	.65	.19
☐ 34	Willie Greene	1.75	.80	.22
☐ 35	Nigel Wilson	1.75	.80	.22
☐ 36	Rondell White	4.00	1.80	.50
☐ 37	Brian Turang	1.50	.65	.19
☐ 38	Manny Ramirez	8.00	3.60	1.00
☐ 39	Salomon Torres	1.50	.65	.19
☐ 40	Melvin Nieves	2.00	.90	.25
☐ 41	Ryan Klesko	7.00	3.10	.85
☐ 42	Keith Kessinger	1.50	.65	.19
☐ 43	Brad Ausmus	1.50	.65	.19
☐ 44	Bob Hamelin	4.00	1.80	.50
☐ 45	Carlos Delgado	6.00	2.70	.75
☐ 46	Marc Newfield	1.50	.65	.19
☐ 47	Raul Mondesi	14.00	6.25	1.75

☐ 48	Tim Costo	1.50	.65	.19
☐ 49	Pedro Martinez	2.00	.90	.25
☐ 50	Steve Karsay	2.00	.90	.25
☐ 51	Danny Bautista	1.50	.65	.19
☐ 52	Butch Huskey	1.50	.65	.19
☐ 53	Kurt Abbott	2.00	.90	.25
☐ 54	Darrell Sherman	1.50	.65	.19
☐ 55	Damon Buford	1.50	.65	.19
☐ 56	Ross Powell	1.50	.65	.19
☐ 57	Darrell Whitmore	1.50	.65	.19
☐ 58	Chipper Jones	5.00	2.30	.60
☐ 59	Jeff Granger	1.50	.65	.19
☐ 60	Cliff Floyd	6.00	2.70	.75

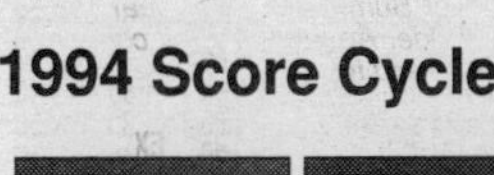

1994 Score Cycle

This 20-card set was randomly inserted in second series foil and jumbo packs at a rate of one in 90. The set is arranged according to players with the most singles (1-5), doubles (6-10), triples (11-15) and home runs (16-20). The front contains an oval player photo with "The Cycle" at top and the players name at the bottom. Also at the bottom, is the number of of that particular base hit the player accumulated in 1993. A small baseball diamond appears beneath the oval photo. The back lists the top five of the given base hit category. A dark blue border surrounds both sides. The cards are number with a TC prefix.

	MINT	EXC	G-VG
COMPLETE SET (20)	300.00	135.00	38.00
COMMON CARD (TC1-TC20)	5.00	2.30	.60

☐ TC1	Brett Butler	5.00	2.30	.60
☐ TC2	Kenny Lofton	20.00	9.00	2.50
☐ TC3	Paul Molitor	12.00	5.50	1.50
☐ TC4	Carlos Baerga	12.00	5.50	1.50
☐ TC5	Gregg Jefferies Tony Phillips	7.00	3.10	.85
☐ TC6	John Olerud	7.00	3.10	.85
☐ TC7	Charlie Hayes	5.00	2.30	.60
☐ TC8	Lenny Dykstra	7.00	3.10	.85
☐ TC9	Dante Bichette	7.00	3.10	.85
☐ TC10	Devon White	7.00	3.10	.85
☐ TC11	Lance Johnson	5.00	2.30	.60
☐ TC12	Joey Cora Steve Finley	5.00	2.30	.60
☐ TC13	Tony Fernandez	5.00	2.30	.60
☐ TC14	David Hulse Brett Butler	5.00	2.30	.60
☐ TC15	Jay Bell Brian McRae Mickey Morandini	5.00	2.30	.60
☐ TC16	Juan Gonzalez Barry Bonds	30.00	13.50	3.80
☐ TC17	Ken Griffey Jr.	75.00	34.00	9.50
☐ TC18	Frank Thomas	75.00	34.00	9.50
☐ TC19	David Justice	12.00	5.50	1.50
☐ TC20	Matt Williams	20.00	9.00	2.50

1994 Score Dream Team

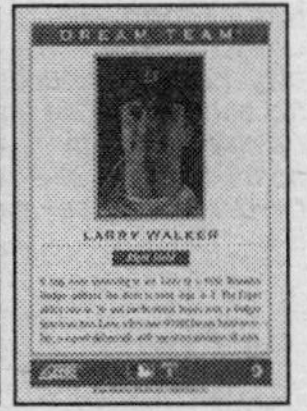

Randomly inserted in first series foil and jumbo packs at a rate of one in 72, this ten-card set feature's baseball's Dream Team as selected by Pinnacle Brands. Banded by forest green stripes above and below, the player photos on the fronts feature ten of baseball's best players sporting historical team uniforms from the 1930's. The set title and player's name appear in gold foil lettering on black bars above and below the picture. The backs carry a color head shot and brief player profile.

	MINT	EXC	G-VG
COMPLETE SET (10)	125.00	57.50	15.50
COMMON CARD (1-10)	4.00	1.80	.50

☐ 1	Mike Mussina	12.00	5.50	1.50
☐ 2	Tom Glavine	6.00	2.70	.75
☐ 3	Don Mattingly	30.00	13.50	3.80
☐ 4	Carlos Baerga	12.00	5.50	1.50
☐ 5	Barry Larkin	6.00	2.70	.75
☐ 6	Matt Williams	15.00	6.75	1.90
☐ 7	Juan Gonzalez	25.00	11.50	3.10
☐ 8	Andy Van Slyke	4.00	1.80	.50
☐ 9	Larry Walker	6.00	2.70	.75
☐ 10	Mike Stanley	4.00	1.80	.50

1994 Score Gold Stars

Randomly inserted at a rate of one in every 18 hobby packs, this 60-card set features National and American stars. Split into two series of 30 cards, the first series (1-30)

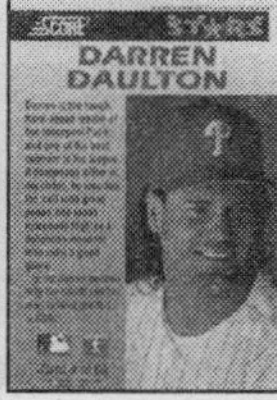

comprises of National League players and the second series (31-60) American Leaguers. The fronts feature a color action player photo cut out and superimposed on a foil background. At the bottom, a navy blue triangle carries the set title and the player's name appears in a white bar. The backs have a color close-up shot and a player profile.

	MINT	EXC	G-VG
COMPLETE SET (60)	375.00	170.00	47.50
COMPLETE NL SERIES (30)	160.00	70.00	20.00
COMPLETE AL SERIES (30)	215.00	95.00	27.00
COMMON CARD (1-30)	2.00	.90	.25
COMMON CARD (31-60)	2.00	.90	.25

	MINT	EXC	G-VG
☐ 1 Barry Bonds	20.00	9.00	2.50
☐ 2 Orlando Merced	2.00	.90	.25
☐ 3 Mark Grace	3.00	1.35	.40
☐ 4 Darren Daulton	4.00	1.80	.50
☐ 5 Jeff Blauser	2.00	.90	.25
☐ 6 Deion Sanders	10.00	4.50	1.25
☐ 7 John Kruk	3.00	1.35	.40
☐ 8 Jeff Bagwell	25.00	11.50	3.10
☐ 9 Gregg Jefferies	4.00	1.80	.50
☐ 10 Matt Williams	10.00	4.50	1.25
☐ 11 Andres Galarraga	4.00	1.80	.50
☐ 12 Jay Bell	2.00	.90	.25
☐ 13 Mike Piazza	25.00	11.50	3.10
☐ 14 Ron Gant	2.00	.90	.25
☐ 15 Barry Larkin	4.00	1.80	.50
☐ 16 Tom Glavine	4.00	1.80	.50
☐ 17 Lenny Dykstra	4.00	1.80	.50
☐ 18 Fred McGriff	8.00	3.60	1.00
☐ 19 Andy Van Slyke	3.00	1.35	.40
☐ 20 Gary Sheffield	4.00	1.80	.50
☐ 21 John Burkett	2.00	.90	.25
☐ 22 Dante Bichette	4.00	1.80	.50
☐ 23 Tony Gwynn	12.00	5.50	1.50
☐ 24 David Justice	8.00	3.60	1.00
☐ 25 Marquis Grissom	4.00	1.80	.50
☐ 26 Bobby Bonilla	3.00	1.35	.40
☐ 27 Larry Walker	4.00	1.80	.50
☐ 28 Brett Butler	2.00	.90	.25
☐ 29 Robby Thompson	2.00	.90	.25
☐ 30 Jeff Conine	4.00	1.80	.50
☐ 31 Joe Carter	8.00	3.60	1.00
☐ 32 Ken Griffey Jr.	50.00	23.00	6.25
☐ 33 Juan Gonzalez	18.00	8.00	2.30
☐ 34 Rickey Henderson	4.00	1.80	.50
☐ 35 Bo Jackson	4.00	1.80	.50
☐ 36 Cal Ripken	40.00	18.00	5.00
☐ 37 John Olerud	4.00	1.80	.50
☐ 38 Carlos Baerga	8.00	3.60	1.00
☐ 39 Jack McDowell	4.00	1.80	.50
☐ 40 Cecil Fielder	4.00	1.80	.50
☐ 41 Kenny Lofton	12.00	5.50	1.50
☐ 42 Roberto Alomar	12.00	5.50	1.50
☐ 43 Randy Johnson	4.00	1.80	.50
☐ 44 Tim Salmon	8.00	3.60	1.00
☐ 45 Frank Thomas	50.00	23.00	6.25
☐ 46 Albert Belle	18.00	8.00	2.30
☐ 47 Greg Vaughn	2.00	.90	.25
☐ 48 Travis Fryman	5.00	2.30	.60
☐ 49 Don Mattingly	20.00	9.00	2.50
☐ 50 Wade Boggs	4.00	1.80	.50
☐ 51 Mo Vaughn	4.00	1.80	.50
☐ 52 Kirby Puckett	20.00	9.00	2.50
☐ 53 Devon White	3.00	1.35	.40
☐ 54 Tony Phillips	2.00	.90	.25
☐ 55 Brian Harper	2.00	.90	.25
☐ 56 Chad Curtis	2.00	.90	.25
☐ 57 Paul Molitor	8.00	3.60	1.00
☐ 58 Ivan Rodriguez	3.00	1.35	.40
☐ 59 Rafael Palmeiro	4.00	1.80	.50
☐ 60 Brian McRae	3.00	1.35	.40

1994 Score Rookie/Traded

The 1994 Score Rookie and Traded set consists of 165 standard-size cards featuring rookie standouts, traded players, and new young prospects. Each foil pack contained one Gold Rush card. The cards are numbered on the back with an "RT" prefix. A special unnumbered September Call-Up Redemption card could be exchanged for an Alex Rodriguez card. The expiration date was January 31, 1995. Odds of finding a redemption card are approximately one in 240 retail and hobby packs. Rookie Cards include John Hudek and Chan Ho Park.

	MINT	EXC	G-VG
COMPLETE SET (165)	10.00	4.50	1.25
COMMON CARD (RT1-RT165)	.05	.02	.01

	MINT	EXC	G-VG
☐ RT1 Will Clark	.30	.14	.04
☐ RT2 Lee Smith	.10	.05	.01
☐ RT3 Bo Jackson	.10	.05	.01
☐ RT4 Ellis Burks	.08	.04	.01
☐ RT5 Eddie Murray	.10	.05	.01
☐ RT6 Delino DeShields	.08	.04	.01
☐ RT7 Erik Hanson	.05	.02	.01
☐ RT8 Rafael Palmeiro	.10	.05	.01
☐ RT9 Luis Polonia	.05	.02	.01
☐ RT10 Omar Vizquel	.05	.02	.01
☐ RT11 Kurt Abbott	.15	.07	.02

☐	RT12 Vince Coleman	.05	.02	.01
☐	RT13 Rickey Henderson	.10	.05	.01
☐	RT14 Terry Mulholland	.05	.02	.01
☐	RT15 Greg Hibbard	.05	.02	.01
☐	RT16 Walt Weiss	.05	.02	.01
☐	RT17 Chris Sabo	.05	.02	.01
☐	RT18 Dave Henderson	.05	.02	.01
☐	RT19 Rick Sutcliffe	.08	.04	.01
☐	RT20 Harold Reynolds	.05	.02	.01
☐	RT21 Jack Morris	.10	.05	.01
☐	RT22 Dan Wilson	.05	.02	.01
☐	RT23 Dave Magadan	.05	.02	.01
☐	RT24 Dennis Martinez	.08	.04	.01
☐	RT25 Wes Chamberlain	.05	.02	.01
☐	RT26 Otis Nixon	.05	.02	.01
☐	RT27 Eric Anthony	.05	.02	.01
☐	RT28 Randy Milligan	.05	.02	.01
☐	RT29 Julio Franco	.08	.04	.01
☐	RT30 Kevin McReynolds	.05	.02	.01
☐	RT31 Anthony Young	.05	.02	.01
☐	RT32 Brian Harper	.05	.02	.01
☐	RT33 Gene Harris	.05	.02	.01
☐	RT34 Eddie Taubensee	.05	.02	.01
☐	RT35 David Segui	.05	.02	.01
☐	RT36 Stan Javier	.05	.02	.01
☐	RT37 Felix Fermin	.05	.02	.01
☐	RT38 Darrin Jackson	.05	.02	.01
☐	RT39 Tony Fernandez	.05	.02	.01
☐	RT40 Jose Vizcaino	.05	.02	.01
☐	RT41 Willie Banks	.05	.02	.01
☐	RT42 Brian Hunter	.05	.02	.01
☐	RT43 Reggie Jefferson	.05	.02	.01
☐	RT44 Junior Felix	.05	.02	.01
☐	RT45 Jack Armstrong	.05	.02	.01
☐	RT46 Bip Roberts	.05	.02	.01
☐	RT47 Jerry Browne	.05	.02	.01
☐	RT48 Marvin Freeman	.05	.02	.01
☐	RT49 Jody Reed	.05	.02	.01
☐	RT50 Alex Cole	.05	.02	.01
☐	RT51 Sid Fernandez	.05	.02	.01
☐	RT52 Pete Smith	.05	.02	.01
☐	RT53 Xavier Hernandez	.05	.02	.01
☐	RT54 Scott Sanderson	.05	.02	.01
☐	RT55 Turner Ward	.05	.02	.01
☐	RT56 Rex Hudler	.05	.02	.01
☐	RT57 Deion Sanders	.35	.16	.04
☐	RT58 Sid Bream	.05	.02	.01
☐	RT59 Tony Pena	.05	.02	.01
☐	RT60 Bret Boone	.10	.05	.01
☐	RT61 Bobby Ayala	.05	.02	.01
☐	RT62 Pedro Martinez	.10	.05	.01
☐	RT63 Howard Johnson	.05	.02	.01
☐	RT64 Mark Portugal	.05	.02	.01
☐	RT65 Roberto Kelly	.05	.02	.01
☐	RT66 Spike Owen	.05	.02	.01
☐	RT67 Jeff Treadway	.05	.02	.01
☐	RT68 Mike Harkey	.05	.02	.01
☐	RT69 Doug Jones	.05	.02	.01
☐	RT70 Steve Farr	.05	.02	.01
☐	RT71 Billy Taylor	.05	.02	.01
☐	RT72 Manny Ramirez	.40	.18	.05
☐	RT73 Bob Hamelin	.10	.05	.01
☐	RT74 Steve Karsay	.05	.02	.01
☐	RT75 Ryan Klesko	.30	.14	.04
☐	RT76 Cliff Floyd	.30	.14	.04
☐	RT77 Jeffrey Hammonds	.25	.11	.03
☐	RT78 Javy Lopez	.20	.09	.03
☐	RT79 Roger Salkeld	.05	.02	.01
☐	RT80 Hector Carrasco	.05	.02	.01
☐	RT81 Gerald Williams	.05	.02	.01
☐	RT82 Raul Mondesi	.75	.35	.09
☐	RT83 Sterling Hitchcock	.08	.04	.01
☐	RT84 Danny Bautista	.08	.04	.01
☐	RT85 Chris Turner	.05	.02	.01
☐	RT86 Shane Reynolds	.05	.02	.01
☐	RT87 Rondell White	.20	.09	.03
☐	RT88 Salomon Torres	.08	.04	.01
☐	RT89 Turk Wendell	.05	.02	.01
☐	RT90 Tony Tarasco	.10	.05	.01
☐	RT91 Shawn Green	.10	.05	.01
☐	RT92 Greg Colbrunn	.05	.02	.01
☐	RT93 Eddie Zambrano	.05	.02	.01
☐	RT94 Rich Becker	.08	.04	.01
☐	RT95 Chris Gomez	.10	.05	.01
☐	RT96 John Patterson	.05	.02	.01
☐	RT97 Derek Parks	.05	.02	.01
☐	RT98 Rich Rowland	.05	.02	.01
☐	RT99 James Mouton	.10	.05	.01
☐	RT100 Tim Hyers	.20	.09	.03
☐	RT101 Jose Valentin	.05	.02	.01
☐	RT102 Carlos Delgado	.30	.14	.04
☐	RT103 Robert Eenhoorn	.05	.02	.01
☐	RT104 John Hudek	.50	.23	.06
☐	RT105 Domingo Cedeno	.05	.02	.01
☐	RT106 Denny Hocking	.05	.02	.01
☐	RT107 Greg Pirkl	.05	.02	.01
☐	RT108 Mark Smith	.05	.02	.01
☐	RT109 Paul Shuey	.08	.04	.01
☐	RT110 Jorge Fabregas	.05	.02	.01
☐	RT111 Rikkert Faneyte	.05	.02	.01
☐	RT112 Rob Butler	.05	.02	.01
☐	RT113 Darren Oliver	.05	.02	.01
☐	RT114 Troy O'Leary	.05	.02	.01
☐	RT115 Scott Brow	.05	.02	.01
☐	RT116 Tony Eusebio	.05	.02	.01
☐	RT117 Carlos Reyes	.05	.02	.01
☐	RT118 J.R. Phillips	.10	.05	.01
☐	RT119 Alex Diaz	.05	.02	.01
☐	RT120 Charles Johnson	.20	.09	.03
☐	RT121 Nate Minchey	.08	.04	.01
☐	RT122 Scott Sanders	.05	.02	.01
☐	RT123 Daryl Boston	.05	.02	.01
☐	RT124 Joey Hamilton	.35	.16	.04
☐	RT125 Brian Anderson	.25	.11	.03
☐	RT126 Dan Miceli	.05	.02	.01
☐	RT127 Tom Brunansky	.05	.02	.01
☐	RT128 Dave Staton	.05	.02	.01
☐	RT129 Mike Oquist	.05	.02	.01
☐	RT130 John Mabry	.25	.11	.03
☐	RT131 Norberto Martin	.05	.02	.01
☐	RT132 Hector Fajardo	.05	.02	.01
☐	RT133 Mark Hutton	.05	.02	.01
☐	RT134 Fernando Vina	.05	.02	.01
☐	RT135 Lee Tinsley	.05	.02	.01
☐	RT136 Chan Ho Park	.75	.35	.09
☐	RT137 Paul Spoljaric	.05	.02	.01
☐	RT138 Matias Carillo	.15	.07	.02
☐	RT139 Mark Kiefer	.05	.02	.01
☐	RT140 Stan Royer	.05	.02	.01
☐	RT141 Bryan Eversgerd	.05	.02	.01
☐	RT142 Bryan Hunter	.35	.16	.04
☐	RT143 Joe Hall	.05	.02	.01
☐	RT144 Johnny Ruffin	.05	.02	.01
☐	RT145 Alex Gonzalez	.20	.09	.03
☐	RT146 Keith Lockhart	.05	.02	.01
☐	RT147 Tom Marsh	.05	.02	.01
☐	RT148 Tony Longmire	.05	.02	.01
☐	RT149 Keith Mitchell	.05	.02	.01
☐	RT150 Melvin Nieves	.10	.05	.01
☐	RT151 Kelly Stinnett	.05	.02	.01
☐	RT152 Miguel Jimenez	.08	.04	.01
☐	RT153 Jeff Juden	.05	.02	.01
☐	RT154 Matt Walbeck	.05	.02	.01
☐	RT155 Marc Newfield	.10	.05	.01
☐	RT156 Matt Mieske	.05	.02	.01
☐	RT157 Marcus Moore	.05	.02	.01

☐ RT158 Jose Lima	.25	.11	.03
☐ RT159 Mike Kelly	.08	.04	.01
☐ RT160 Jim Edmonds	.05	.02	.01
☐ RT161 Steve Trachsel	.25	.11	.03
☐ RT162 Greg Blosser	.05	.02	.01
☐ RT163 Marc Acre	.15	.07	.02
☐ RT164 AL Checklist	.05	.02	.01
☐ RT165 NL Checklist	.05	.02	.01
☐ NNO Sept. Call-Up Expired	5.00	2.30	.60

1994 Score R/T Gold Rush

Issued one per pack, these cards are a gold foil version of the 165-card Rookie/Traded set. The differences between the basic card and Gold Rush version are the gold foil borders that surround a metallicized player photo. The only difference on back is Gold Rush logo.

	MINT	EXC	G-VG
COMPLETE SET (165)	50.00	23.00	6.25
COMMON CARD (1-165)	.25	.11	.03

*VETERAN STARS: 3X to 6X BASIC CARDS
*YOUNG STARS: 2.5X to 5X BASIC CARDS
*RCs: 1.5X to 3X BASIC CARDS

1994 Score R/T Changing Places

Randomly inserted in both retail and hobby packs at a rate of one in 36 Rookie/Traded packs, this 10-card standard-size set focuses on ten veteran superstar players who were traded prior to or during the 1994 season. Cards fronts feature a color photo with a slanted design. The backs have a short write-up and a distorted photo.

	MINT	EXC	G-VG
COMPLETE SET (10)	35.00	16.00	4.40
COMMON CARD (CP1-CP10)	2.00	.90	.25

☐ CP1 Will Clark	8.00	3.60	1.00
☐ CP2 Rafael Palmeiro	4.00	1.80	.50
☐ CP3 Roberto Kelly	2.00	.90	.25
☐ CP4 Bo Jackson	4.00	1.80	.50
☐ CP5 Otis Nixon	2.00	.90	.25
☐ CP6 Rickey Henderson	5.00	2.30	.60
☐ CP7 Ellis Burks	2.00	.90	.25
☐ CP8 Lee Smith	2.00	.90	.25
☐ CP9 Delino DeShields	2.00	.90	.25
☐ CP10 Deion Sanders	10.00	4.50	1.25

1994 Score R/T Super Rookies

Randomly inserted in hobby packs at a rate of one in 36, this 18-card standard-size set focuses on top rookies of 1994. Odds of finding one of these cards is approximately one in 36 hobby packs. Designed much like the Gold Rush, the cards have an all-foil design. The fronts have a player photo and the backs have a photo that serves as background to the Super Rookies logo and text.

	MINT	EXC	G-VG
COMPLETE SET (18)	75.00	34.00	9.50
COMMON CARD (SU1-SU18)	1.50	.65	.19

☐ SU1 Carlos Delgado	8.00	3.60	1.00
☐ SU2 Manny Ramirez	10.00	4.50	1.25
☐ SU3 Ryan Klesko	8.00	3.60	1.00
☐ SU4 Raul Mondesi	18.00	8.00	2.30
☐ SU5 Bob Hamelin	5.00	2.30	.60
☐ SU6 Steve Karsay	2.00	.90	.25
☐ SU7 Jeffrey Hammonds	4.00	1.80	.50
☐ SU8 Cliff Floyd	8.00	3.60	1.00
☐ SU9 Kurt Abbott	2.00	.90	.25
☐ SU10 Marc Newfield	1.50	.65	.19
☐ SU11 Javy Lopez	5.00	2.30	.60
☐ SU12 Rich Becker	2.00	.90	.25
☐ SU13 Greg Pirkl	1.50	.65	.19

		MINT	EXC	G-VG
☐ SU14	Rondell White	5.00	2.30	.60
☐ SU15	James Mouton	2.00	.90	.25
☐ SU16	Tony Tarasco	2.00	.90	.25
☐ SU17	Brian Anderson	5.00	2.30	.60
☐ SU18	Jim Edmonds	1.50	.65	.19

1995 Score

The 1995 Score first series consists of 330 standard-size cards. The horizontal and vertical fronts feature color action player shots with irregular dark green and sand brown borders. The player's name, position and the team logo appear in a blue bar under the photo. The horizontal backs have the same design as the fronts. They carry another small color headshot on the left, with the player's name, short biography, career highlights and statistics on the right. Topical subsets featured are Rookies (277-312), Season Highlights (313-316).

	MINT	EXC	G-VG
COMPLETE SERIES 1 (330)	15.00	6.75	1.90
COMMON CARD (1-330)	.05	.02	.01

		MINT	EXC	G-VG
☐ 1	Ken Griffey Jr.	2.00	.90	.25
☐ 2	Roberto Alomar	.40	.18	.05
☐ 3	Cal Ripken	1.25	.55	.16
☐ 4	Jose Canseco	.30	.14	.04
☐ 5	Matt Williams	.40	.18	.05
☐ 6	Esteban Beltre	.05	.02	.01
☐ 7	Domingo Cedeno	.05	.02	.01
☐ 8	John Valentin	.08	.04	.01
☐ 9	Glenallen Hill	.05	.02	.01
☐ 10	Rafael Belliard	.05	.02	.01
☐ 11	Randy Myers	.05	.02	.01
☐ 12	Mo Vaughn	.10	.05	.01
☐ 13	Hector Carrasco	.05	.02	.01
☐ 14	Chili Davis	.08	.04	.01
☐ 15	Dante Bichette	.10	.05	.01
☐ 16	Darrin Jackson	.05	.02	.01
☐ 17	Mike Piazza	.75	.35	.09
☐ 18	Junior Felix	.05	.02	.01
☐ 19	Moises Alou	.10	.05	.01
☐ 20	Mark Gubicza	.05	.02	.01
☐ 21	Bret Saberhagen	.08	.04	.01
☐ 22	Lenny Dykstra	.10	.05	.01
☐ 23	Steve Howe	.05	.02	.01
☐ 24	Mark Dewey	.05	.02	.01
☐ 25	Brian Harper	.05	.02	.01
☐ 26	Ozzie Smith	.40	.18	.05
☐ 27	Scott Erickson	.05	.02	.01
☐ 28	Tony Gwynn	.40	.18	.05
☐ 29	Bob Welch	.05	.02	.01
☐ 30	Barry Bonds	.75	.35	.09
☐ 31	Leo Gomez	.05	.02	.01
☐ 32	Greg Maddux	.40	.18	.05
☐ 33	Mike Greenwell	.08	.04	.01
☐ 34	Sammy Sosa	.10	.05	.01
☐ 35	Darnell Coles	.05	.02	.01
☐ 36	Tommy Greene	.05	.02	.01
☐ 37	Will Clark	.30	.14	.04
☐ 38	Steve Ontiveros	.05	.02	.01
☐ 39	Stan Javier	.05	.02	.01
☐ 40	Bip Roberts	.05	.02	.01
☐ 41	Paul O'Neill	.08	.04	.01
☐ 42	Bill Haselman	.05	.02	.01
☐ 43	Shane Mack	.08	.04	.01
☐ 44	Orlando Merced	.05	.02	.01
☐ 45	Kevin Seitzer	.05	.02	.01
☐ 46	Trevor Hoffman	.05	.02	.01
☐ 47	Greg Gagne	.05	.02	.01
☐ 48	Jeff Kent	.08	.04	.01
☐ 49	Tony Phillips	.05	.02	.01
☐ 50	Ken Hill	.08	.04	.01
☐ 51	Carlos Baerga	.30	.14	.04
☐ 52	Henry Rodriguez	.05	.02	.01
☐ 53	Scott Sanderson	.05	.02	.01
☐ 54	Jeff Conine	.10	.05	.01
☐ 55	Chris Turner	.05	.02	.01
☐ 56	Ken Caminiti	.08	.04	.01
☐ 57	Harold Baines	.08	.04	.01
☐ 58	Charlie Hayes	.08	.04	.01
☐ 59	Roberto Kelly	.05	.02	.01
☐ 60	John Olerud	.10	.05	.01
☐ 61	Tim Davis	.05	.02	.01
☐ 62	Rich Rowland	.05	.02	.01
☐ 63	Rey Sanchez	.05	.02	.01
☐ 64	Junior Ortiz	.05	.02	.01
☐ 65	Ricky Gutierrez	.05	.02	.01
☐ 66	Rex Hudler	.05	.02	.01
☐ 67	Johnny Ruffin	.05	.02	.01
☐ 68	Jay Buhner	.08	.04	.01
☐ 69	Tom Pagnozzi	.05	.02	.01
☐ 70	Julio Franco	.08	.04	.01
☐ 71	Eric Young	.08	.04	.01
☐ 72	Mike Bordick	.05	.02	.01
☐ 73	Don Slaught	.05	.02	.01
☐ 74	Goose Gossage	.10	.05	.01
☐ 75	Lonnie Smith	.05	.02	.01
☐ 76	Jimmy Key	.08	.04	.01
☐ 77	Dave Hollins	.10	.05	.01
☐ 78	Mickey Tettleton	.08	.04	.01
☐ 79	Luis Gonzalez	.05	.02	.01
☐ 80	Dave Winfield	.10	.05	.01
☐ 81	Ryan Thompson	.08	.04	.01
☐ 82	Felix Jose	.05	.02	.01
☐ 83	Rusty Meacham	.05	.02	.01
☐ 84	Darryl Hamilton	.05	.02	.01
☐ 85	John Wetteland	.05	.02	.01
☐ 86	Tom Brunansky	.05	.02	.01
☐ 87	Mark Lemke	.05	.02	.01
☐ 88	Spike Owen	.05	.02	.01
☐ 89	Shawon Dunston	.05	.02	.01
☐ 90	Wilson Alvarez	.10	.05	.01
☐ 91	Lee Smith	.10	.05	.01
☐ 92	Scott Kamieniecki	.05	.02	.01
☐ 93	Jacob Brumfield	.05	.02	.01
☐ 94	Kirk Gibson	.08	.04	.01
☐ 95	Joe Girardi	.05	.02	.01
☐ 96	Mike Macfarlane	.05	.02	.01
☐ 97	Greg Colbrunn	.05	.02	.01
☐ 98	Ricky Bones	.05	.02	.01
☐ 99	Delino DeShields	.08	.04	.01
☐ 100	Pat Meares	.05	.02	.01
☐ 101	Jeff Fassero	.05	.02	.01

☐	102 Jim Leyritz	.05	.02	.01
☐	103 Gary Redus	.05	.02	.01
☐	104 Terry Steinbach	.08	.04	.01
☐	105 Kevin McReynolds	.05	.02	.01
☐	106 Felix Fermin	.05	.02	.01
☐	107 Danny Jackson	.05	.02	.01
☐	108 Chris James	.05	.02	.01
☐	109 Jeff King	.05	.02	.01
☐	110 Pat Hentgen	.08	.04	.01
☐	111 Gerald Perry	.05	.02	.01
☐	112 Tim Raines	.10	.05	.01
☐	113 Eddie Williams	.05	.02	.01
☐	114 Jamie Moyer	.05	.02	.01
☐	115 Bud Black	.05	.02	.01
☐	116 Chris Gomez	.08	.04	.01
☐	117 Luis Lopez	.05	.02	.01
☐	118 Roger Clemens	.40	.18	.05
☐	119 Javy Lopez	.05	.02	.01
☐	120 Dave Nilsson	.05	.02	.01
☐	121 Karl Rhodes	.05	.02	.01
☐	122 Rick Aguilera	.08	.04	.01
☐	123 Tony Fernandez	.05	.02	.01
☐	124 Bernie Williams	.08	.04	.01
☐	125 James Mouton	.05	.02	.01
☐	126 Mark Langston	.10	.05	.01
☐	127 Mike Lansing	.05	.02	.01
☐	128 Tino Martinez	.05	.02	.01
☐	129 Joe Orsulak	.05	.02	.01
☐	130 David Hulse	.05	.02	.01
☐	131 Pete Incaviglia	.05	.02	.01
☐	132 Mark Clark	.05	.02	.01
☐	133 Tony Eusebio	.05	.02	.01
☐	134 Chuck Finley	.05	.02	.01
☐	135 Lou Frazier	.05	.02	.01
☐	136 Craig Grebeck	.05	.02	.01
☐	137 Kelly Stinnett	.05	.02	.01
☐	138 Paul Shuey	.08	.04	.01
☐	139 David Nied	.10	.05	.01
☐	140 Billy Brewer	.05	.02	.01
☐	141 Dave Weathers	.05	.02	.01
☐	142 Scott Leius	.05	.02	.01
☐	143 Brian Jordan	.08	.04	.01
☐	144 Melido Perez	.05	.02	.01
☐	145 Tony Tarasco	.08	.04	.01
☐	146 Dan Wilson	.05	.02	.01
☐	147 Rondell White	.10	.05	.01
☐	148 Mike Henneman	.05	.02	.01
☐	149 Brian Johnson	.05	.02	.01
☐	150 Tom Henke	.05	.02	.01
☐	151 John Patterson	.05	.02	.01
☐	152 Bobby Witt	.05	.02	.01
☐	153 Eddie Taubensee	.05	.02	.01
☐	154 Pat Borders	.05	.02	.01
☐	155 Ramon Martinez	.08	.04	.01
☐	156 Mike Kingery	.05	.02	.01
☐	157 Zane Smith	.05	.02	.01
☐	158 Benito Santiago	.05	.02	.01
☐	159 Matias Carrillo	.05	.02	.01
☐	160 Scott Brosius	.05	.02	.01
☐	161 Dave Clark	.05	.02	.01
☐	162 Mark McLemore	.05	.02	.01
☐	163 Curt Schilling	.05	.02	.01
☐	164 J.T. Snow	.05	.02	.01
☐	165 Rod Beck	.08	.04	.01
☐	166 Scott Fletcher	.05	.02	.01
☐	167 Bob Tewksbury	.05	.02	.01
☐	168 Mike LaValliere	.05	.02	.01
☐	169 Dave Hansen	.05	.02	.01
☐	170 Pedro Martinez	.10	.05	.01
☐	171 Kirk Rueter	.05	.02	.01
☐	172 Jose Lind	.05	.02	.01
☐	173 Luis Alicea	.05	.02	.01
☐	174 Mike Moore	.05	.02	.01
☐	175 Andy Ashby	.05	.02	.01
☐	176 Jody Reed	.05	.02	.01
☐	177 Darryl Kile	.08	.04	.01
☐	178 Carl Willis	.05	.02	.01
☐	179 Jeromy Burnitz	.05	.02	.01
☐	180 Mike Gallego	.05	.02	.01
☐	181 Will VanLandingham	.05	.02	.01
☐	182 Sid Fernandez	.05	.02	.01
☐	183 Kim Batiste	.05	.02	.01
☐	184 Greg Myers	.05	.02	.01
☐	185 Steve Avery	.10	.05	.01
☐	186 Steve Farr	.05	.02	.01
☐	187 Robb Nen	.05	.02	.01
☐	188 Dan Pasqua	.05	.02	.01
☐	189 Bruce Ruffin	.05	.02	.01
☐	190 Jose Valentin	.05	.02	.01
☐	191 Willie Banks	.05	.02	.01
☐	192 Mike Aldrete	.05	.02	.01
☐	193 Randy Milligan	.05	.02	.01
☐	194 Steve Karsay	.05	.02	.01
☐	195 Mike Stanley	.05	.02	.01
☐	196 Jose Mesa	.05	.02	.01
☐	197 Tom Browning	.05	.02	.01
☐	198 John Vander Wal	.05	.02	.01
☐	199 Kevin Brown	.05	.02	.01
☐	200 Mike Oquist	.05	.02	.01
☐	201 Greg Swindell	.05	.02	.01
☐	202 Eddie Zambrano	.05	.02	.01
☐	203 Joe Boever	.05	.02	.01
☐	204 Gary Varsho	.05	.02	.01
☐	205 Chris Gwynn	.05	.02	.01
☐	206 David Howard	.05	.02	.01
☐	207 Jerome Walton	.05	.02	.01
☐	208 Danny Darwin	.05	.02	.01
☐	209 Darryl Strawberry	.08	.04	.01
☐	210 Todd Van Poppel	.08	.04	.01
☐	211 Scott Livingstone	.05	.02	.01
☐	212 Dave Fleming	.05	.02	.01
☐	213 Todd Worrell	.05	.02	.01
☐	214 Carlos Delgado	.25	.11	.03
☐	215 Bill Pecota	.05	.02	.01
☐	216 Jim Lindeman	.05	.02	.01
☐	217 Rick White	.05	.02	.01
☐	218 Jose Oquendo	.05	.02	.01
☐	219 Tony Castillo	.05	.02	.01
☐	220 Fernando Vina	.05	.02	.01
☐	221 Jeff Bagwell	1.00	.45	.13
☐	222 Randy Johnson	.10	.05	.01
☐	223 Albert Belle	.60	.25	.08
☐	224 Chuck Carr	.05	.02	.01
☐	225 Mark Leiter	.05	.02	.01
☐	226 Hal Morris	.08	.04	.01
☐	227 Robin Ventura	.08	.04	.01
☐	228 Mike Munoz	.05	.02	.01
☐	229 Jim Thome	.10	.05	.01
☐	230 Mario Diaz	.05	.02	.01
☐	231 John Doherty	.05	.02	.01
☐	232 Bobby Jones	.10	.05	.01
☐	233 Raul Mondesi	.50	.23	.06
☐	234 Ricky Jordan	.05	.02	.01
☐	235 John Jaha	.05	.02	.01
☐	236 Carlos Garcia	.05	.02	.01
☐	237 Kirby Puckett	.75	.35	.09
☐	238 Orel Hershiser	.08	.04	.01
☐	239 Don Mattingly	.75	.35	.09
☐	240 Sid Bream	.05	.02	.01
☐	241 Brent Gates	.10	.05	.01
☐	242 Tony Longmire	.05	.02	.01
☐	243 Robby Thompson	.05	.02	.01
☐	244 Rick Sutcliffe	.08	.04	.01
☐	245 Dean Palmer	.08	.04	.01
☐	246 Marquis Grissom	.10	.05	.01
☐	247 Paul Molitor	.30	.14	.04

☐ 248	Mark Carreon	.05	.02	.01
☐ 249	Jack Voigt	.05	.02	.01
☐ 250	Greg McMichael	.05	.02	.01
☐ 251	Damon Berryhill	.05	.02	.01
☐ 252	Brian Dorsett	.05	.02	.01
☐ 253	Jim Edmonds	.05	.02	.01
☐ 254	Barry Larkin	.10	.05	.01
☐ 255	Jack McDowell	.10	.05	.01
☐ 256	Wally Joyner	.08	.04	.01
☐ 257	Eddie Murray	.10	.05	.01
☐ 258	Lenny Webster	.05	.02	.01
☐ 259	Milt Cuyler	.05	.02	.01
☐ 260	Todd Benzinger	.05	.02	.01
☐ 261	Vince Coleman	.05	.02	.01
☐ 262	Todd Stottlemyre	.05	.02	.01
☐ 263	Turner Ward	.05	.02	.01
☐ 264	Ray Lankford	.10	.05	.01
☐ 265	Matt Walbeck	.05	.02	.01
☐ 266	Deion Sanders	.35	.16	.04
☐ 267	Gerald Williams	.05	.02	.01
☐ 268	Jim Gott	.05	.02	.01
☐ 269	Jeff Frye	.05	.02	.01
☐ 270	Jose Rijo	.08	.04	.01
☐ 271	David Justice	.30	.14	.04
☐ 272	Ismael Valdes	.05	.02	.01
☐ 273	Ben McDonald	.08	.04	.01
☐ 274	Darren Lewis	.05	.02	.01
☐ 275	Graeme Lloyd	.05	.02	.01
☐ 276	Luis Ortiz	.05	.02	.01
☐ 277	Julian Tavarez	.05	.02	.01
☐ 278	Mark Dalesandro	.05	.02	.01
☐ 279	Brett Merriman	.05	.02	.01
☐ 280	Ricky Bottalico	.05	.02	.01
☐ 281	Robert Eenhoorn	.05	.02	.01
☐ 282	Rikkert Faneyte	.05	.02	.01
☐ 283	Mike Kelly	.08	.04	.01
☐ 284	Mark Smith	.05	.02	.01
☐ 285	Turk Wendell	.05	.02	.01
☐ 286	Greg Blosser	.05	.02	.01
☐ 287	Garey Ingram	.05	.02	.01
☐ 288	Jorge Fabregas	.05	.02	.01
☐ 289	Blaise Ilsley	.05	.02	.01
☐ 290	Joe Hall	.05	.02	.01
☐ 291	Orlando Miller	.08	.04	.01
☐ 292	Jose Lima	.05	.02	.01
☐ 293	Greg O'Halloran	.15	.07	.02
☐ 294	Mark Kiefer	.05	.02	.01
☐ 295	Jose Oliva	.10	.05	.01
☐ 296	Rich Becker	.08	.04	.01
☐ 297	Brian L. Hunter	.05	.02	.01
☐ 298	Dave Silvestri	.05	.02	.01
☐ 299	Armando Benitez	.05	.02	.01
☐ 300	Darren Dreifort	.05	.02	.01
☐ 301	John Mabry	.05	.02	.01
☐ 302	Greg Pirkl	.05	.02	.01
☐ 303	J.R. Phillips	.10	.05	.01
☐ 304	Shawn Green	.10	.05	.01
☐ 305	Roberto Petagine	.08	.04	.01
☐ 306	Keith Lockhart	.05	.02	.01
☐ 307	Jonathan Hurst	.05	.02	.01
☐ 308	Paul Spoljaric	.05	.02	.01
☐ 309	Mike Lieberthal	.05	.02	.01
☐ 310	Garret Anderson	.08	.04	.01
☐ 311	John Johnstone	.05	.02	.01
☐ 312	Alex Rodriguez	.75	.35	.09
☐ 313	Kent Mercker	.05	.02	.01
☐ 314	John Valentin	.08	.04	.01
☐ 315	Kenny Rogers	.05	.02	.01
☐ 316	Fred McGriff	.30	.14	.04
☐ 317	Braves/Orioles CL	.05	.02	.01
☐ 318	Red Sox/Cubs CL	.05	.02	.01
☐ 319	Angels/Reds CL	.05	.02	.01
☐ 320	White Sox/Colorado CL	.05	.02	.01
☐ 321	Indians/Marlins CL	.05	.02	.01
☐ 322	Tigers/Astros CL	.05	.02	.01
☐ 323	Royals/Dodgers CL	.05	.02	.01
☐ 324	Brewers/Expos CL	.05	.02	.01
☐ 325	Twins/Mets CL	.05	.02	.01
☐ 326	Yankees/Phillies CL	.05	.02	.01
☐ 327	Athletics/Pirates CL	.05	.02	.01
☐ 328	Mariners/Padres CL	.05	.02	.01
☐ 329	Rangers/Giants CL	.05	.02	.01
☐ 330	Blue Jays/Cardinals CL	.05	.02	.01
☐ RG1	Ryan Klesko Rookie Greatness	20.00	9.00	2.50
☐ SG1	Ryan Klesko AU/6100	40.00	18.00	5.00

1995 Score Gold Rush

Parallel to the basic Score issue, these cards were inserted one per foil pack and two per jumbo pack. The fronts were printed in gold foil and the backs contain the Gold Rush logo. As part of the Gold Rush program, one Platinum Team Redemption card was randomly inserted in Score packs at a rate of one in 36. This redemption card and up to four Gold Rush team sets (and $2) could be redeemed for platinum versions of the team set(s). The Gold Rush sets that were sent in would be returned with a stamp indicating they were already used for redemption purposes. Only 4,950 of each platinum team set was produced. The offer is good through 7/13/95.

	MINT	EXC	G-VG
COMPLETE SERIES 1 (330)	120.00	55.00	15.00
COMMON CARD (1-330)	.30	.14	.04

*VETERAN STARS: 4X to 8X BASIC CARDS
*YOUNG STARS: 3X to 6X BASIC CARDS

☐ NNO	Platinum Team Redemption	4.00	1.80	.50

1995 Score Draft Picks

Randomly inserted in hobby packs at a rate of one in 36, this 18-card set takes a look at top picks selected in June of 1994.

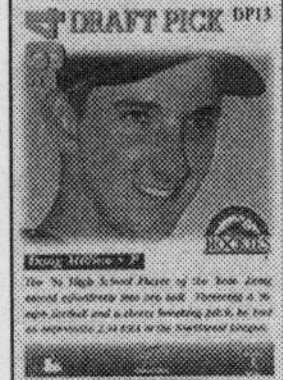

Horizontal fronts have two player photos on a white background. Vertical backs have a player photo and 1994 season's highlights. The cards are numbered with a DP prefix.

	MINT	EXC	G-VG
COMPLETE SET (18)	60.00	27.00	7.50
COMMON CARD (DP1-DP18)	3.00	1.35	.40

	MINT	EXC	G-VG
☐ DP1 McKay Christensen	3.00	1.35	.40
☐ DP2 Brett Wagner	4.00	1.80	.50
☐ DP3 Paul Wilson	6.00	2.70	.75
☐ DP4 C.J. Nitkowski	4.00	1.80	.50
☐ DP5 Josh Booty	9.00	4.00	1.15
☐ DP6 Antone Williamson	4.00	1.80	.50
☐ DP7 Paul Konerko	4.00	1.80	.50
☐ DP8 Scott Elarton	4.00	1.80	.50
☐ DP9 Jacob Shumate	3.00	1.35	.40
☐ DP10 Terrance Long	6.00	2.70	.75
☐ DP11 Mark Johnson	3.00	1.35	.40
☐ DP12 Ben Grieve	9.00	4.00	1.15
☐ DP13 Doug Million	5.00	2.30	.60
☐ DP14 Jayson Peterson	3.00	1.35	.40
☐ DP15 Dustin Hermanson	4.00	1.80	.50
☐ DP16 Matt Smith	3.00	1.35	.40
☐ DP17 Kevin Witt	3.00	1.35	.40
☐ DP18 Brian Buchanan	3.00	1.35	.40

1995 Score Dream Team

Randomly inserted in hobby and retail packs at a rate of one in 72 packs, this 12-card hologram set showcases top performers from the 1994 season. The holographic fronts have two player images. The horizontal backs are not holographic. They are multi-colored with a small player close-up and a brief write-up. The cards are numbered with a DG prefix.

	MINT	EXC	G-VG
COMPLETE SET (12)	130.00	57.50	16.50
COMMON CARD (DG1-DG12)	3.00	1.35	.40

	MINT	EXC	G-VG
☐ DG1 Frank Thomas	35.00	16.00	4.40
☐ DG2 Roberto Alomar	9.00	4.00	1.15
☐ DG3 Cal Ripken	25.00	11.50	3.10
☐ DG4 Matt Williams	7.00	3.10	.85
☐ DG5 Mike Piazza	15.00	6.75	1.90
☐ DG6 Albert Belle	12.00	5.50	1.50
☐ DG7 Ken Griffey Jr.	35.00	16.00	4.40
☐ DG8 Tony Gwynn	9.00	4.00	1.15
☐ DG9 Paul Molitor	5.00	2.30	.60
☐ DG10 Jimmy Key	3.00	1.35	.40
☐ DG11 Greg Maddux	9.00	4.00	1.15
☐ DG12 Lee Smith	3.00	1.35	.40

1995 Score Hall of Gold

Randomly inserted in packs at a rate one in six, this 55-card set is collection of top stars and young hopefuls. Metallic fronts are presented in shades of silver and gold that overlay a player photo. The Hall of Gold logo appears in the upper right-hand corner. Black backs contain a brief write-up and a player photo. The cards are numbered with an HG prefix.

	MINT	EXC	G-VG
COMPLETE SET (55)	65.00	29.00	8.25
COMMON CARD (HG1-HG55)	.60	.25	.08

	MINT	EXC	G-VG
☐ HG1 Ken Griffey Jr.	12.00	5.50	1.50
☐ HG2 Matt Williams	2.50	1.15	.30
☐ HG3 Roberto Alomar	3.00	1.35	.40
☐ HG4 Jeff Bagwell	6.00	2.70	.75
☐ HG5 David Justice	2.00	.90	.25
☐ HG6 Cal Ripken	9.00	4.00	1.15
☐ HG7 Randy Johnson	1.00	.45	.13
☐ HG8 Barry Larkin	1.00	.45	.13
☐ HG9 Albert Belle	4.00	1.80	.50
☐ HG10 Mike Piazza	5.00	2.30	.60
☐ HG11 Kirby Puckett	5.00	2.30	.60
☐ HG12 Moises Alou	.75	.35	.09
☐ HG13 Jose Canseco	2.00	.90	.25
☐ HG14 Tony Gwynn	3.00	1.35	.40
☐ HG15 Roger Clemens	3.00	1.35	.40

☐ HG16 Barry Bonds	5.00	2.30	.60
☐ HG17 Mo Vaughn	1.00	.45	.13
☐ HG18 Greg Maddux	3.00	1.35	.40
☐ HG19 Dante Bichette	1.00	.45	.13
☐ HG20 Will Clark	2.00	.90	.25
☐ HG21 Lenny Dykstra	1.00	.45	.13
☐ HG22 Don Mattingly	5.00	2.30	.60
☐ HG23 Carlos Baerga	2.00	.90	.25
☐ HG24 Ozzie Smith	2.50	1.15	.30
☐ HG25 Paul Molitor	2.00	.90	.25
☐ HG26 Paul O'Neill	.75	.35	.09
☐ HG27 Deion Sanders	2.50	1.15	.30
☐ HG28 Jeff Conine	1.00	.45	.13
☐ HG29 John Olerud	1.00	.45	.13
☐ HG30 Jose Rijo	.75	.35	.09
☐ HG31 Sammy Sosa	.75	.35	.09
☐ HG32 Robin Ventura	1.00	.45	.13
☐ HG33 Raul Mondesi	3.00	1.35	.40
☐ HG34 Eddie Murray	1.00	.45	.13
☐ HG35 Marquis Grissom	1.00	.45	.13
☐ HG36 Darryl Strawberry	.60	.25	.08
☐ HG37 Dave Nilsson	.60	.25	.08
☐ HG38 Manny Ramirez	2.00	.90	.25
☐ HG39 Delino DeShields	.60	.25	.08
☐ HG40 Lee Smith	.75	.35	.09
☐ HG41 Alex Rodriguez	6.00	2.70	.75
☐ HG42 Julio Franco	.60	.25	.08
☐ HG43 Bret Saberhagen	1.00	.45	.13
☐ HG44 Ken Hill	.75	.35	.09
☐ HG45 Roberto Kelly	.60	.25	.08
☐ HG46 Hal Morris	.60	.25	.08
☐ HG47 Jimmy Key	.75	.35	.09
☐ HG48 Terry Steinbach	.60	.25	.08
☐ HG49 Mickey Tettleton	.60	.25	.08
☐ HG50 Tony Phillips	.60	.25	.08
☐ HG51 Carlos Garcia	.60	.25	.08
☐ HG52 Jim Edmonds	.60	.25	.08
☐ HG53 Rod Beck	.75	.35	.09
☐ HG54 Shane Mack	.60	.25	.08
☐ HG55 Ken Caminiti	.75	.35	.09

1993 Select

Seeking a niche in the premium, mid-price market, Score produced a new 405-card baseball set. The set includes regular players, rookies, and draft picks, and was sold in 15-card packs and 28-card super packs. Themed Chase Cards (24 in all) were randomly inserted into the 15-card packs. The cards measure the standard size (2 1/2" by 3 1/2"). The front photos, composed either horizontally or vertically, are ultra-violet coated while the two-toned green borders received a matte finish. The player's name appears in mustard-colored lettering in the bottom border. The backs carry a second color photo as well as 1992 statistics, career totals, and an in-depth player profile, all on a two-toned green background. The cards are numbered on the back. The set includes Draft Pick (291, 297, 303, 310, 352-360) and Rookie (271-290, 292-296, 298-302, 304-309, 311-351, 383, 385, 391, 394, 400-405) subsets. Rookie Cards in this set include Derek Jeter, Jason Kendall and J.T. Snow.

	MINT	EXC	G-VG
COMPLETE SET (405)	35.00	16.00	4.40
COMMON CARD (1-405)	.10	.05	.01
☐ 1 Barry Bonds	1.25	.55	.16
☐ 2 Ken Griffey Jr.	3.00	1.35	.40
☐ 3 Will Clark	.40	.18	.05
☐ 4 Kirby Puckett	1.25	.55	.16
☐ 5 Tony Gwynn	.75	.35	.09
☐ 6 Frank Thomas	3.00	1.35	.40
☐ 7 Tom Glavine	.20	.09	.03
☐ 8 Roberto Alomar	.75	.35	.09
☐ 9 Andre Dawson	.20	.09	.03
☐ 10 Ron Darling	.10	.05	.01
☐ 11 Bobby Bonilla	.20	.09	.03
☐ 12 Danny Tartabull	.15	.07	.02
☐ 13 Darren Daulton	.20	.09	.03
☐ 14 Roger Clemens	.75	.35	.09
☐ 15 Ozzie Smith	.60	.25	.08
☐ 16 Mark McGwire	.20	.09	.03
☐ 17 Terry Pendleton	.20	.09	.03
☐ 18 Cal Ripken	2.00	.90	.25
☐ 19 Fred McGriff	.40	.18	.05
☐ 20 Cecil Fielder	.20	.09	.03
☐ 21 Darryl Strawberry	.15	.07	.02
☐ 22 Robin Yount	.40	.18	.05
☐ 23 Barry Larkin	.20	.09	.03
☐ 24 Don Mattingly	1.25	.55	.16
☐ 25 Craig Biggio	.15	.07	.02
☐ 26 Sandy Alomar Jr.	.15	.07	.02
☐ 27 Larry Walker	.20	.09	.03
☐ 28 Junior Felix	.10	.05	.01
☐ 29 Eddie Murray	.20	.09	.03
☐ 30 Robin Ventura	.20	.09	.03
☐ 31 Greg Maddux	.60	.25	.08
☐ 32 Dave Winfield	.20	.09	.03
☐ 33 John Kruk	.20	.09	.03
☐ 34 Wally Joyner	.15	.07	.02
☐ 35 Andy Van Slyke	.20	.09	.03
☐ 36 Chuck Knoblauch	.20	.09	.03
☐ 37 Tom Pagnozzi	.10	.05	.01
☐ 38 Dennis Eckersley	.20	.09	.03
☐ 39 David Justice	.40	.18	.05
☐ 40 Juan Gonzalez	1.00	.45	.13
☐ 41 Gary Sheffield	.20	.09	.03
☐ 42 Paul Molitor	.40	.18	.05
☐ 43 Delino DeShields	.15	.07	.02
☐ 44 Travis Fryman	.25	.11	.03
☐ 45 Hal Morris	.15	.07	.02
☐ 46 Greg Olson	.15	.07	.02
☐ 47 Ken Caminiti	.15	.07	.02
☐ 48 Wade Boggs	.20	.09	.03
☐ 49 Orel Hershiser	.15	.07	.02
☐ 50 Albert Belle	1.00	.45	.13
☐ 51 Bill Swift	.15	.07	.02
☐ 52 Mark Langston	.20	.09	.03
☐ 53 Joe Girardi	.10	.05	.01
☐ 54 Keith Miller	.10	.05	.01
☐ 55 Gary Carter	.20	.09	.03

	Player			
☐	56 Brady Anderson	.15	.07	.02
☐	57 Dwight Gooden	.10	.05	.01
☐	58 Julio Franco	.15	.07	.02
☐	59 Lenny Dykstra	.20	.09	.03
☐	60 Mickey Tettleton	.15	.07	.02
☐	61 Randy Tomlin	.10	.05	.01
☐	62 B.J. Surhoff	.10	.05	.01
☐	63 Todd Zeile	.15	.07	.02
☐	64 Roberto Kelly	.15	.07	.02
☐	65 Rob Dibble	.10	.05	.01
☐	66 Leo Gomez	.10	.05	.01
☐	67 Doug Jones	.10	.05	.01
☐	68 Ellis Burks	.15	.07	.02
☐	69 Mike Scioscia	.10	.05	.01
☐	70 Charles Nagy	.10	.05	.01
☐	71 Cory Snyder	.10	.05	.01
☐	72 Devon White	.15	.07	.02
☐	73 Mark Grace	.20	.09	.03
☐	74 Luis Polonia	.10	.05	.01
☐	75 John Smiley 2X	.15	.07	.02
☐	76 Carlton Fisk	.20	.09	.03
☐	77 Luis Sojo	.10	.05	.01
☐	78 George Brett	1.25	.55	.16
☐	79 Mitch Williams	.15	.07	.02
☐	80 Kent Hrbek	.15	.07	.02
☐	81 Jay Bell	.15	.07	.02
☐	82 Edgar Martinez	.10	.05	.01
☐	83 Lee Smith	.20	.09	.03
☐	84 Deion Sanders	.60	.25	.08
☐	85 Bill Gullickson	.10	.05	.01
☐	86 Paul O'Neill	.15	.07	.02
☐	87 Kevin Seitzer	.15	.07	.02
☐	88 Steve Finley	.10	.05	.01
☐	89 Mel Hall	.10	.05	.01
☐	90 Nolan Ryan	3.00	1.35	.40
☐	91 Eric Davis	.10	.05	.01
☐	92 Mike Mussina	.60	.25	.08
☐	93 Tony Fernandez	.15	.07	.02
☐	94 Frank Viola	.15	.07	.02
☐	95 Matt Williams	.50	.23	.06
☐	96 Joe Carter	.40	.18	.05
☐	97 Ryne Sandberg	1.00	.45	.13
☐	98 Jim Abbott	.20	.09	.03
☐	99 Marquis Grissom	.20	.09	.03
☐	100 George Bell	.15	.07	.02
☐	101 Howard Johnson	.10	.05	.01
☐	102 Kevin Appier	.15	.07	.02
☐	103 Dale Murphy	.20	.09	.03
☐	104 Shane Mack	.15	.07	.02
☐	105 Jose Lind	.10	.05	.01
☐	106 Rickey Henderson	.20	.09	.03
☐	107 Bob Tewksbury	.10	.05	.01
☐	108 Kevin Mitchell	.15	.07	.02
☐	109 Steve Avery	.20	.09	.03
☐	110 Candy Maldonado	.10	.05	.01
☐	111 Bip Roberts	.15	.07	.02
☐	112 Lou Whitaker	.20	.09	.03
☐	113 Jeff Bagwell	1.50	.65	.19
☐	114 Dante Bichette	.20	.09	.03
☐	115 Brett Butler	.15	.07	.02
☐	116 Melido Perez	.10	.05	.01
☐	117 Andy Benes	.15	.07	.02
☐	118 Randy Johnson	.20	.09	.03
☐	119 Willie McGee	.15	.07	.02
☐	120 Jody Reed	.10	.05	.01
☐	121 Shawon Dunston	.10	.05	.01
☐	122 Carlos Baerga	.40	.18	.05
☐	123 Bret Saberhagen	.15	.07	.02
☐	124 John Olerud	.20	.09	.03
☐	125 Ivan Calderon	.10	.05	.01
☐	126 Bryan Harvey	.15	.07	.02
☐	127 Terry Mulholland	.10	.05	.01
☐	128 Ozzie Guillen	.10	.05	.01
☐	129 Steve Buechele	.10	.05	.01
☐	130 Kevin Tapani	.10	.05	.01
☐	131 Felix Jose	.10	.05	.01
☐	132 Terry Steinbach	.15	.07	.02
☐	133 Ron Gant	.15	.07	.02
☐	134 Harold Reynolds	.10	.05	.01
☐	135 Chris Sabo	.15	.07	.02
☐	136 Ivan Rodriguez	.20	.09	.03
☐	137 Eric Anthony	.10	.05	.01
☐	138 Mike Henneman	.10	.05	.01
☐	139 Robby Thompson	.10	.05	.01
☐	140 Scott Fletcher	.10	.05	.01
☐	141 Bruce Hurst	.10	.05	.01
☐	142 Kevin Maas	.15	.07	.02
☐	143 Tom Candiotti	.10	.05	.01
☐	144 Chris Hoiles	.15	.07	.02
☐	145 Mike Morgan	.10	.05	.01
☐	146 Mark Whiten	.15	.07	.02
☐	147 Dennis Martinez	.15	.07	.02
☐	148 Tony Pena	.10	.05	.01
☐	149 Dave Magadan	.10	.05	.01
☐	150 Mark Lewis	.10	.05	.01
☐	151 Mariano Duncan	.10	.05	.01
☐	152 Gregg Jefferies	.20	.09	.03
☐	153 Doug Drabek	.20	.09	.03
☐	154 Brian Harper	.10	.05	.01
☐	155 Ray Lankford	.20	.09	.03
☐	156 Carney Lansford	.15	.07	.02
☐	157 Mike Sharperson	.10	.05	.01
☐	158 Jack Morris	.20	.09	.03
☐	159 Otis Nixon	.10	.05	.01
☐	160 Steve Sax	.10	.05	.01
☐	161 Mark Lemke	.10	.05	.01
☐	162 Rafael Palmeiro	.20	.09	.03
☐	163 Jose Rijo	.15	.07	.02
☐	164 Omar Vizquel	.10	.05	.01
☐	165 Sammy Sosa	.20	.09	.03
☐	166 Milt Cuyler	.10	.05	.01
☐	167 John Franco	.10	.05	.01
☐	168 Darryl Hamilton	.10	.05	.01
☐	169 Ken Hill	.15	.07	.02
☐	170 Mike Devereaux	.15	.07	.02
☐	171 Don Slaught	.10	.05	.01
☐	172 Steve Farr	.10	.05	.01
☐	173 Bernard Gilkey	.10	.05	.01
☐	174 Mike Fetters	.10	.05	.01
☐	175 Vince Coleman	.10	.05	.01
☐	176 Kevin McReynolds	.10	.05	.01
☐	177 John Smoltz	.15	.07	.02
☐	178 Greg Gagne	.10	.05	.01
☐	179 Greg Swindell	.10	.05	.01
☐	180 Juan Guzman	.15	.07	.02
☐	181 Kal Daniels	.10	.05	.01
☐	182 Rick Sutcliffe	.15	.07	.02
☐	183 Orlando Merced	.15	.07	.02
☐	184 Bill Wegman	.10	.05	.01
☐	185 Mark Gardner	.10	.05	.01
☐	186 Rob Deer	.10	.05	.01
☐	187 Dave Hollins	.20	.09	.03
☐	188 Jack Clark	.15	.07	.02
☐	189 Brian Hunter	.15	.07	.02
☐	190 Tim Wallach	.10	.05	.01
☐	191 Tim Belcher	.10	.05	.01
☐	192 Walt Weiss	.10	.05	.01
☐	193 Kurt Stillwell	.10	.05	.01
☐	194 Charlie Hayes	.15	.07	.02
☐	195 Willie Randolph	.15	.07	.02
☐	196 Jack McDowell	.20	.09	.03
☐	197 Jose Offerman	.10	.05	.01
☐	198 Chuck Finley	.10	.05	.01
☐	199 Darrin Jackson	.10	.05	.01
☐	200 Kelly Gruber	.10	.05	.01
☐	201 John Wetteland	.10	.05	.01

	#	Player			
☐	202	Jay Buhner	.15	.07	.02
☐	203	Mike LaValliere	.10	.05	.01
☐	204	Kevin Brown	.10	.05	.01
☐	205	Luis Gonzalez	.15	.07	.02
☐	206	Rick Aguilera	.15	.07	.02
☐	207	Norm Charlton	.10	.05	.01
☐	208	Mike Bordick	.15	.07	.02
☐	209	Charlie Leibrandt	.10	.05	.01
☐	210	Tom Brunansky	.10	.05	.01
☐	211	Tom Henke	.15	.07	.02
☐	212	Randy Milligan	.10	.05	.01
☐	213	Ramon Martinez	.15	.07	.02
☐	214	Mo Vaughn	.20	.09	.03
☐	215	Randy Myers	.15	.07	.02
☐	216	Greg Hibbard	.10	.05	.01
☐	217	Wes Chamberlain	.10	.05	.01
☐	218	Tony Phillips	.10	.05	.01
☐	219	Pete Harnisch	.10	.05	.01
☐	220	Mike Gallego	.10	.05	.01
☐	221	Bud Black	.10	.05	.01
☐	222	Greg Vaughn	.15	.07	.02
☐	223	Milt Thompson	.10	.05	.01
☐	224	Ben McDonald	.15	.07	.02
☐	225	Billy Hatcher	.10	.05	.01
☐	226	Paul Sorrento	.10	.05	.01
☐	227	Mark Gubicza	.10	.05	.01
☐	228	Mike Greenwell	.15	.07	.02
☐	229	Curt Schilling	.15	.07	.02
☐	230	Alan Trammell	.20	.09	.03
☐	231	Zane Smith	.10	.05	.01
☐	232	Bobby Thigpen	.10	.05	.01
☐	233	Greg Olson	.10	.05	.01
☐	234	Joe Orsulak	.10	.05	.01
☐	235	Joe Oliver	.10	.05	.01
☐	236	Tim Raines	.20	.09	.03
☐	237	Juan Samuel	.10	.05	.01
☐	238	Chili Davis	.15	.07	.02
☐	239	Spike Owen	.10	.05	.01
☐	240	Dave Stewart	.15	.07	.02
☐	241	Jim Eisenreich	.10	.05	.01
☐	242	Phil Plantier	.20	.09	.03
☐	243	Sid Fernandez	.10	.05	.01
☐	244	Dan Gladden	.10	.05	.01
☐	245	Mickey Morandini	.10	.05	.01
☐	246	Tino Martinez	.15	.07	.02
☐	247	Kirt Manwaring	.10	.05	.01
☐	248	Dean Palmer	.15	.07	.02
☐	249	Tom Browning	.10	.05	.01
☐	250	Brian McRae	.20	.09	.03
☐	251	Scott Leius	.10	.05	.01
☐	252	Bert Blyleven	.20	.09	.03
☐	253	Scott Erickson	.10	.05	.01
☐	254	Bob Welch	.10	.05	.01
☐	255	Pat Kelly	.10	.05	.01
☐	256	Felix Fermin	.10	.05	.01
☐	257	Harold Baines	.15	.07	.02
☐	258	Duane Ward	.15	.07	.02
☐	259	Bill Spiers	.10	.05	.01
☐	260	Jaime Navarro	.15	.07	.02
☐	261	Scott Sanderson	.10	.05	.01
☐	262	Gary Gaetti	.10	.05	.01
☐	263	Bob Ojeda	.10	.05	.01
☐	264	Jeff Montgomery	.15	.07	.02
☐	265	Scott Bankhead	.10	.05	.01
☐	266	Lance Johnson	.10	.05	.01
☐	267	Rafael Belliard	.10	.05	.01
☐	268	Kevin Reimer	.10	.05	.01
☐	269	Benito Santiago	.10	.05	.01
☐	270	Mike Moore	.10	.05	.01
☐	271	Dave Fleming	.15	.07	.02
☐	272	Moises Alou	.20	.09	.03
☐	273	Pat Listach	.15	.07	.02
☐	274	Reggie Sanders	.20	.09	.03
☐	275	Kenny Lofton	.75	.35	.09
☐	276	Donovan Osborne	.10	.05	.01
☐	277	Rusty Meacham	.10	.05	.01
☐	278	Eric Karros	.15	.07	.02
☐	279	Andy Stankiewicz	.10	.05	.01
☐	280	Brian Jordan	.15	.07	.02
☐	281	Gary DiSarcina	.10	.05	.01
☐	282	Mark Wohlers	.10	.05	.01
☐	283	Dave Nilsson	.15	.07	.02
☐	284	Anthony Young	.15	.07	.02
☐	285	Jim Bullinger	.10	.05	.01
☐	286	Derek Bell	.15	.07	.02
☐	287	Brian Williams	.10	.05	.01
☐	288	Julio Valera	.10	.05	.01
☐	289	Dan Walters	.10	.05	.01
☐	290	Chad Curtis	.15	.07	.02
☐	291	Michael Tucker DP	.40	.18	.05
☐	292	Bob Zupcic	.10	.05	.01
☐	293	Todd Hundley	.10	.05	.01
☐	294	Jeff Tackett	.10	.05	.01
☐	295	Greg Colbrunn	.10	.05	.01
☐	296	Cal Eldred	.15	.07	.02
☐	297	Chris Roberts DP	.20	.09	.03
☐	298	John Doherty	.10	.05	.01
☐	299	Denny Neagle	.10	.05	.01
☐	300	Arthur Rhodes	.10	.05	.01
☐	301	Mark Clark	.15	.07	.02
☐	302	Scott Cooper	.15	.07	.02
☐	303	Jamie Arnold DP	.25	.11	.03
☐	304	Jim Thome	.40	.18	.05
☐	305	Frank Seminara	.10	.05	.01
☐	306	Kurt Knudsen	.10	.05	.01
☐	307	Tim Wakefield	.10	.05	.01
☐	308	John Jaha	.15	.07	.02
☐	309	Pat Hentgen	.15	.07	.02
☐	310	B.J. Wallace DP	.10	.05	.01
☐	311	Roberto Hernandez	.10	.05	.01
☐	312	Hipolito Pichardo	.10	.05	.01
☐	313	Eric Fox	.10	.05	.01
☐	314	Willie Banks	.10	.05	.01
☐	315	Sam Militello	.10	.05	.01
☐	316	Vince Horsman	.10	.05	.01
☐	317	Carlos Hernandez	.10	.05	.01
☐	318	Jeff Kent	.20	.09	.03
☐	319	Mike Perez	.10	.05	.01
☐	320	Scott Livingstone	.10	.05	.01
☐	321	Jeff Conine	.20	.09	.03
☐	322	James Austin	.10	.05	.01
☐	323	John Vander Wal	.10	.05	.01
☐	324	Pat Mahomes	.10	.05	.01
☐	325	Pedro Astacio	.15	.07	.02
☐	326	Bret Boone UER (Misspelled Brett)	.20	.09	.03
☐	327	Matt Stairs	.10	.05	.01
☐	328	Damion Easley	.15	.07	.02
☐	329	Ben Rivera	.10	.05	.01
☐	330	Reggie Jefferson	.10	.05	.01
☐	331	Luis Mercedes	.15	.07	.02
☐	332	Kyle Abbott	.10	.05	.01
☐	333	Eddie Taubensee	.10	.05	.01
☐	334	Tim McIntosh	.10	.05	.01
☐	335	Phil Clark	.10	.05	.01
☐	336	Wil Cordero	.20	.09	.03
☐	337	Russ Springer	.10	.05	.01
☐	338	Craig Colbert	.10	.05	.01
☐	339	Tim Salmon	.50	.23	.06
☐	340	Braulio Castillo	.10	.05	.01
☐	341	Donald Harris	.10	.05	.01
☐	342	Eric Young	.15	.07	.02
☐	343	Bob Wickman	.10	.05	.01
☐	344	John Valentin	.15	.07	.02
☐	345	Dan Wilson	.10	.05	.01
☐	346	Steve Hosey	.10	.05	.01

	No.	Player	MINT	EXC	G-VG
☐	347	Mike Piazza	3.00	1.35	.40
☐	348	Willie Greene	.15	.07	.02
☐	349	Tom Goodwin	.10	.05	.01
☐	350	Eric Hillman	.10	.05	.01
☐	351	Steve Reed	.15	.07	.02
☐	352	Dan Serafini DP	.40	.18	.05
☐	353	Todd Steverson DP	.30	.14	.04
☐	354	Benji Grigsby DP	.20	.09	.03
☐	355	Shannon Stewart DP	.40	.18	.05
☐	356	Sean Lowe DP	.30	.14	.04
☐	357	Derek Wallace DP	.10	.05	.01
☐	358	Rick Helling DP	.15	.07	.02
☐	359	Jason Kendall DP	1.00	.45	.13
☐	360	Derek Jeter DP	3.00	1.35	.40
☐	361	David Cone	.20	.09	.03
☐	362	Jeff Reardon	.15	.07	.02
☐	363	Bobby Witt	.10	.05	.01
☐	364	Jose Canseco	.40	.18	.05
☐	365	Jeff Russell	.10	.05	.01
☐	366	Ruben Sierra	.20	.09	.03
☐	367	Alan Mills	.10	.05	.01
☐	368	Matt Nokes	.10	.05	.01
☐	369	Pat Borders	.10	.05	.01
☐	370	Pedro Munoz	.10	.05	.01
☐	371	Danny Jackson	.10	.05	.01
☐	372	Geronimo Pena	.10	.05	.01
☐	373	Craig Lefferts	.10	.05	.01
☐	374	Joe Grahe	.10	.05	.01
☐	375	Roger McDowell	.10	.05	.01
☐	376	Jimmy Key	.15	.07	.02
☐	377	Steve Olin	.10	.05	.01
☐	378	Glenn Davis	.10	.05	.01
☐	379	Rene Gonzales	.10	.05	.01
☐	380	Manny Lee	.10	.05	.01
☐	381	Ron Karkovice	.10	.05	.01
☐	382	Sid Bream	.10	.05	.01
☐	383	Gerald Williams	.10	.05	.01
☐	384	Lenny Harris	.10	.05	.01
☐	385	J.T. Snow	.15	.07	.02
☐	386	Dave Stieb	.10	.05	.01
☐	387	Kirk McCaskill	.10	.05	.01
☐	388	Lance Parrish	.15	.07	.02
☐	389	Craig Grebeck	.10	.05	.01
☐	390	Rick Wilkins	.10	.05	.01
☐	391	Manny Alexander	.10	.05	.01
☐	392	Mike Schooler	.10	.05	.01
☐	393	Bernie Williams	.15	.07	.02
☐	394	Kevin Koslofski	.10	.05	.01
☐	395	Willie Wilson	.10	.05	.01
☐	396	Jeff Parrett	.10	.05	.01
☐	397	Mike Harkey	.10	.05	.01
☐	398	Frank Tanana	.10	.05	.01
☐	399	Doug Henry	.10	.05	.01
☐	400	Royce Clayton	.15	.07	.02
☐	401	Eric Wedge	.10	.05	.01
☐	402	Derrick May	.15	.07	.02
☐	403	Carlos Garcia	.15	.07	.02
☐	404	Henry Rodriguez	.15	.07	.02
☐	405	Ryan Klesko	1.00	.45	.13

1993 Select Aces

This 24-card set of the top starting pitchers in both leagues was randomly inserted in 1993 Score Select 28-card super packs. According to Score, the chances of finding an Ace card are not less than one in eight packs. The fronts display an action player pose cut out and superimposed on a metallic variegated red and silver diamond design. The diamond itself rests on a background consisting of silver metallic streaks that emanate from the center of the card. In imitation of playing card design, the fronts have a large "A" for Ace in upper left and lower right corners. The player's name in the upper right corner rounds out the card face. On a red background, the horizontal backs have a white "Ace" playing card with a color head shot emanating from a diamond, team logo, and player profile. The cards are numbered on the back.

	MINT	EXC	G-VG
COMPLETE SET (24)	70.00	32.00	8.75
COMMON CARD (1-24)	3.00	1.35	.40

	No.	Player	MINT	EXC	G-VG
☐	1	Roger Clemens	12.00	5.50	1.50
☐	2	Tom Glavine	4.00	1.80	.50
☐	3	Jack McDowell	4.00	1.80	.50
☐	4	Greg Maddux	12.00	5.50	1.50
☐	5	Jack Morris	4.00	1.80	.50
☐	6	Dennis Martinez	3.00	1.35	.40
☐	7	Kevin Brown	3.00	1.35	.40
☐	8	Dwight Gooden	3.00	1.35	.40
☐	9	Kevin Appier	3.50	1.55	.45
☐	10	Mike Morgan	3.00	1.35	.40
☐	11	Juan Guzman	3,50	1.55	.45
☐	12	Charles Nagy	3.00	1.35	.40
☐	13	John Smiley	3.00	1.35	.40
☐	14	Ken Hill	3.50	1.55	.45
☐	15	Bob Tewksbury	3.00	1.35	.40
☐	16	Doug Drabek	3.50	1.55	.45
☐	17	John Smoltz	3.50	1.55	.45
☐	18	Greg Swindell	3.00	1.35	.40
☐	19	Bruce Hurst	3.00	1.35	.40
☐	20	Mike Mussina	10.00	4.50	1.25
☐	21	Cal Eldred	3.50	1.55	.45
☐	22	Melido Perez	3.00	1.35	.40
☐	23	Dave Fleming	3.00	1.35	.40
☐	24	Kevin Tapani	3.00	1.35	.40

1993 Select Chase Rookies

This 21-card set showcases rookies. The cards were randomly inserted in hobby packs only with at least two cards per box of 36 15-card packs. The fronts exhibit Score's "dufex" printing process, in which a color photo is printed on a metallic base creating an unusual, three-dimensional look. The pictures are tilted slightly to the left and edged on the left and bottom by red metallic borders. On a two-toned red back-

ground, the backs present a color headshot in a triangular design and player profile. The cards are numbered on the back at the bottom center.

	MINT	EXC	G-VG
COMPLETE SET (21)	150.00	70.00	19.00
COMMON CARD (1-21)	4.00	1.80	.50
☐ 1 Pat Listach	4.00	1.80	.50
☐ 2 Moises Alou	15.00	6.75	1.90
☐ 3 Reggie Sanders	10.00	4.50	1.25
☐ 4 Kenny Lofton	50.00	23.00	6.25
☐ 5 Eric Karros	4.00	1.80	.50
☐ 6 Brian Williams	4.00	1.80	.50
☐ 7 Donovan Osborne	4.00	1.80	.50
☐ 8 Sam Militello	4.00	1.80	.50
☐ 9 Chad Curtis	7.00	3.10	.85
☐ 10 Bob Zupcic	4.00	1.80	.50
☐ 11 Tim Salmon	30.00	13.50	3.80
☐ 12 Jeff Conine	12.00	5.50	1.50
☐ 13 Pedro Astacio	7.00	3.10	.85
☐ 14 Arthur Rhodes	7.00	3.10	.85
☐ 15 Cal Eldred	7.00	3.10	.85
☐ 16 Tim Wakefield	4.00	1.80	.50
☐ 17 Andy Stankiewicz	4.00	1.80	.50
☐ 18 Wil Cordero	10.00	4.50	1.25
☐ 19 Todd Hundley	4.00	1.80	.50
☐ 20 Dave Fleming	4.00	1.80	.50
☐ 21 Bret Boone	10.00	4.50	1.25

1993 Select Chase Stars

This 24-card set showcases the top players in Major League Baseball. The cards were randomly inserted in retail packs only with at least two cards per box of 36 15-card packs. The fronts exhibit Score's "dufex" printing process, in which a color photo is printed on a metallic base creating an unusual, three-dimensional look. The pictures are tilted slightly to the left and edged on the left and bottom by green metallic borders. On a two-toned green background, the backs present a color headshot in a triangular design and player profile. The cards are numbered on the back at the bottom center.

	MINT	EXC	G-VG
COMPLETE SET (24)	175.00	80.00	22.00
COMMON CARD (1-24)	4.00	1.80	.50
☐ 1 Fred McGriff	8.00	3.60	1.00
☐ 2 Ryne Sandberg	18.00	8.00	2.30
☐ 3 Ozzie Smith	10.00	4.50	1.25
☐ 4 Gary Sheffield	5.00	2.30	.60
☐ 5 Darren Daulton	5.00	2.30	.60
☐ 6 Andy Van Slyke	4.00	1.80	.50
☐ 7 Barry Bonds	20.00	9.00	2.50
☐ 8 Tony Gwynn	12.00	5.50	1.50
☐ 9 Greg Maddux	12.00	5.50	1.50
☐ 10 Tom Glavine	5.00	2.30	.60
☐ 11 John Franco	4.00	1.80	.50
☐ 12 Lee Smith	5.00	2.30	.60
☐ 13 Cecil Fielder	5.00	2.30	.60
☐ 14 Roberto Alomar	12.00	5.50	1.50
☐ 15 Cal Ripken	35.00	16.00	4.40
☐ 16 Edgar Martinez	4.00	1.80	.50
☐ 17 Ivan Rodriguez	5.00	2.30	.60
☐ 18 Kirby Puckett	20.00	9.00	2.50
☐ 19 Ken Griffey Jr.	60.00	27.00	7.50
☐ 20 Joe Carter	8.00	3.60	1.00
☐ 21 Roger Clemens	12.00	5.50	1.50
☐ 22 Dave Fleming	4.00	1.80	.50
☐ 23 Paul Molitor	8.00	3.60	1.00
☐ 24 Dennis Eckersley	5.00	2.30	.60

1993 Select Stat Leaders

Featuring 45 cards from each league, these 90 Stat Leaders were inserted one per 1993 Score pack in every regular pack and super pack. The fronts feature color player action photos that are borderless on the sides and have oblique green borders at the top and bottom. The player's name appears within an oblique orange stripe across the

bottom of the photo. The player's league appears within the top border, and the set's title appears within the bottom border. The same oblique green border design appears on the back, and between the borders, a green rectangle within an orange-colored area carries a chart highlighting the player's statistical league standings. The cards are numbered on the back.

	MINT	EXC	G-VG
COMPLETE SET (90)	12.00	5.50	1.50
COMMON CARD (1-90)	.10	.05	.01
☐ 1 Edgar Martinez	.10	.05	.01
☐ 2 Kirby Puckett	.75	.35	.09
☐ 3 Frank Thomas	2.00	.90	.25
☐ 4 Gary Sheffield	.15	.07	.02
☐ 5 Andy Van Slyke	.12	.05	.02
☐ 6 John Kruk	.15	.07	.02
☐ 7 Kirby Puckett	.75	.35	.09
☐ 8 Carlos Baerga	.30	.14	.04
☐ 9 Paul Molitor	.30	.14	.04
☐ 10 Terry Pendleton Andy Van Slyke	.12	.05	.02
☐ 11 Ryne Sandberg	.60	.25	.08
☐ 12 Mark Grace	.15	.07	.02
☐ 13 Frank Thomas Edgar Martinez	1.00	.45	.13
☐ 14 Don Mattingly Robin Yount	.25	.11	.03
☐ 15 Ken Griffey Jr.	2.00	.90	.25
☐ 16 Andy Van Slyke	.12	.05	.02
☐ 17 Mariano Duncan Will Clark Ray Lankford	.15	.07	.02
☐ 18 Marquis Grissom Terry Pendleton	.12	.05	.02
☐ 19 Lance Johnson	.10	.05	.01
☐ 20 Mike Devereaux	.10	.05	.01
☐ 21 Brady Anderson	.10	.05	.01
☐ 22 Deion Sanders	.40	.18	.05
☐ 23 Steve Finley	.10	.05	.01
☐ 24 Andy Van Slyke	.12	.05	.02
☐ 25 Juan Gonzalez	.60	.25	.08
☐ 26 Mark McGwire	.12	.05	.02
☐ 27 Cecil Fielder	.15	.07	.02
☐ 28 Fred McGriff	.30	.14	.04
☐ 29 Barry Bonds	.75	.35	.09
☐ 30 Gary Sheffield	.15	.07	.02
☐ 31 Cecil Fielder	.15	.07	.02
☐ 32 Joe Carter	.30	.14	.04
☐ 33 Frank Thomas	2.00	.90	.25
☐ 34 Darren Daulton	.15	.07	.02
☐ 35 Terry Pendleton	.10	.05	.01
☐ 36 Fred McGriff	.30	.14	.04
☐ 37 Tony Phillips	.10	.05	.01
☐ 38 Frank Thomas	2.00	.90	.25
☐ 39 Roberto Alomar	.50	.23	.06
☐ 40 Barry Bonds	.75	.35	.09
☐ 41 Dave Hollins	.10	.05	.01
☐ 42 Andy Van Slyke	.12	.05	.02
☐ 43 Mark McGwire	.12	.05	.02
☐ 44 Edgar Martinez	.10	.05	.01
☐ 45 Frank Thomas	2.00	.90	.25
☐ 46 Barry Bonds	.75	.35	.09
☐ 47 Gary Sheffield	.15	.07	.02
☐ 48 Fred McGriff	.30	.14	.04
☐ 49 Frank Thomas	2.00	.90	.25
☐ 50 Danny Tartabull	.10	.05	.01
☐ 51 Roberto Alomar	.50	.23	.06
☐ 52 Barry Bonds	.75	.35	.09
☐ 53 John Kruk	.15	.07	.02
☐ 54 Brett Butler	.10	.05	.01
☐ 55 Kenny Lofton	.50	.23	.06
☐ 56 Pat Listach	.10	.05	.01
☐ 57 Brady Anderson	.10	.05	.01
☐ 58 Marquis Grissom	.15	.07	.02
☐ 59 Delino DeShields	.10	.05	.01
☐ 60 Bip Roberts Steve Finley	.10	.05	.01
☐ 61 Jack McDowell	.15	.07	.02
☐ 62 Kevin Brown Roger Clemens	.25	.11	.03
☐ 63 Charles Nagy Melido Perez	.10	.05	.01
☐ 64 Terry Mulholland	.10	.05	.01
☐ 65 Curt Schilling Doug Drabek	.10	.05	.01
☐ 66 Greg Maddux John Smoltz	.25	.11	.03
☐ 67 Dennis Eckersley	.15	.07	.02
☐ 68 Rick Aguilera	.10	.05	.01
☐ 69 Jeff Montgomery	.10	.05	.01
☐ 70 Lee Smith	.15	.07	.02
☐ 71 Randy Myers	.10	.05	.01
☐ 72 John Wetteland	.10	.05	.01
☐ 73 Randy Johnson	.15	.07	.02
☐ 74 Melido Perez	.10	.05	.01
☐ 75 Roger Clemens	.50	.23	.06
☐ 76 John Smoltz	.12	.05	.02
☐ 77 David Cone	.15	.07	.02
☐ 78 Greg Maddux	.50	.23	.06
☐ 79 Roger Clemens	.50	.23	.06
☐ 80 Kevin Appier	.12	.05	.02
☐ 81 Mike Mussina	.40	.18	.05
☐ 82 Bill Swift	.10	.05	.01
☐ 83 Bob Tewksbury	.10	.05	.01
☐ 84 Greg Maddux	.50	.23	.06
☐ 85 Jack Morris Kevin Brown	.12	.05	.02
☐ 86 Jack McDowell	.15	.07	.02
☐ 87 Roger Clemens Mike Mussina	.40	.18	.05
☐ 88 Tom Glavine Greg Maddux	.25	.11	.03
☐ 89 Ken Hill Bob Tewksbury	.10	.05	.01
☐ 90 Mike Morgan Dennis Martinez	.10	.05	.01

1993 Select Triple Crown

Honoring Triple Crown winners, this 3-card set was randomly inserted in hobby packs

only with at least two cards per box of 36 15-card packs. The fronts exhibit Score's "dufex" printing process, in which a color photo is printed on a metallic base creating an unusual, three-dimensional look. The color player photos on the fronts have a forest green metallic border. The player's name and the year he won the Triple Crown appear above the picture, while the words "Triple Crown" are written in script beneath it. On a forest green background, the backs carry a black and white close-up photo of the player wearing a crown and a summary of the player's award winning performance. The cards are numbered on the back "X of 3" at the lower right corner.

	MINT	EXC	G-VG
COMPLETE SET (3)	110.00	50.00	14.00
COMMON CARD (1-3)	20.00	9.00	2.50
☐ 1 Mickey Mantle	75.00	34.00	9.50
☐ 2 Carl Yastrzemski	20.00	9.00	2.50
☐ 3 Frank Robinson	20.00	9.00	2.50

1993 Select Rookie/Traded

These 150 standard-size (2 1/2" by 3 1/2") cards feature rookies and traded veteran players. The production run comprised 1,950 individually numbered cases. A ten-card All-Star Rookies subset, a two-card Rookie of the Year subset, and a Nolan Ryan Tribute card were randomly inserted in the foil packs. The chances of finding a Nolan Ryan card was listed at not less than one per 288 packs. The two-card set of ROY's featuring American League Rookie of the Year, Tim Salmon and National League Rookie of the Year, Mike Piazza was reportedly randomly inserted at a rate of not less than one in 576 foil packs of 1993 Select Rookie and Traded. The set has horizontal and vertical fronts that carry glossy color player photos, some action, others posed. These photos are borderless on their top and right sides, and have oblique blue-and-black borders set off by gold-foil lines on their bottom and left sides. The player's name is stamped in gold foil and rests in the lower right. The blue-and-black back carries another obliquely bordered color player photo in the upper right. His career highlights appear in white lettering alongside on the left, and his stats and team logo appear below. The cards are numbered on the back with a "T" suffix. Rookie Cards Chris Gomez and Kirk Reuter.

	MINT	EXC	G-VG
COMPLETE SET (150)	30.00	13.50	3.80
COMMON CARD (1T-150T)	.15	.07	.02
☐ 1T Rickey Henderson	.40	.18	.05
☐ 2T Rob Deer	.15	.07	.02
☐ 3T Tim Belcher	.15	.07	.02
☐ 4T Gary Sheffield	.30	.14	.04
☐ 5T Fred McGriff	1.25	.55	.16
☐ 6T Mark Whiten	.25	.11	.03
☐ 7T Jeff Russell	.15	.07	.02
☐ 8T Harold Baines	.25	.11	.03
☐ 9T Dave Winfield	.50	.23	.06
☐ 10T Ellis Burks	.25	.11	.03
☐ 11T Andre Dawson	.30	.14	.04
☐ 12T Gregg Jefferies	.30	.14	.04
☐ 13T Jimmy Key	.25	.11	.03
☐ 14T Harold Reynolds	.15	.07	.02
☐ 15T Tom Henke	.25	.11	.03
☐ 16T Paul Molitor	1.50	.65	.19
☐ 17T Wade Boggs	.60	.25	.08
☐ 18T David Cone	.30	.14	.04
☐ 19T Tony Fernandez	.15	.07	.02
☐ 20T Roberto Kelly	.25	.11	.03
☐ 21T Paul O'Neill	.25	.11	.03
☐ 22T Jose Lind	.15	.07	.02
☐ 23T Barry Bonds	4.00	1.80	.50
☐ 24T Dave Stewart	.25	.11	.03
☐ 25T Randy Myers	.25	.11	.03
☐ 26T Benito Santiago	.15	.07	.02
☐ 27T Tim Wallach	.15	.07	.02
☐ 28T Greg Gagne	.15	.07	.02
☐ 29T Kevin Mitchell	.25	.11	.03
☐ 30T Jim Abbott	.30	.14	.04
☐ 31T Lee Smith	.30	.14	.04
☐ 32T Bobby Munoz	.15	.07	.02
☐ 33T Mo Sanford	.15	.07	.02
☐ 34T John Roper	.50	.23	.06
☐ 35T David Hulse	.15	.07	.02
☐ 36T Pedro Martinez	.75	.35	.09
☐ 37T Chuck Carr	.15	.07	.02
☐ 38T Armando Reynoso	.15	.07	.02
☐ 39T Ryan Thompson	.50	.23	.06
☐ 40T Carlos Garcia	.25	.11	.03
☐ 41T Matt Whiteside	.15	.07	.02
☐ 42T Benji Gil	.50	.23	.06
☐ 43T Rodney Bolton	.15	.07	.02
☐ 44T J.T. Snow	.50	.23	.06
☐ 45T David McCarty	.15	.07	.02
☐ 46T Paul Quantrill	.15	.07	.02
☐ 47T Al Martin	.40	.18	.05
☐ 48T Lance Painter	.15	.07	.02
☐ 49T Lou Frazier	.25	.11	.03
☐ 50T Eduardo Perez	.50	.23	.06
☐ 51T Kevin Young	.15	.07	.02
☐ 52T Mike Trombley	.15	.07	.02
☐ 53T Sterling Hitchcock	.50	.23	.06
☐ 54T Tim Bogar	.15	.07	.02
☐ 55T Hilly Hathaway	.15	.07	.02
☐ 56T Wayne Kirby	.15	.07	.02
☐ 57T Craig Paquette	.15	.07	.02
☐ 58T Bret Boone	.60	.25	.08
☐ 59T Greg McMichael	.50	.23	.06
☐ 60T Mike Lansing	1.00	.45	.13
☐ 61T Brent Gates	.60	.25	.08

☐ 62T Rene Arocha .60 .25 .08
☐ 63T Ricky Gutierrez .15 .07 .02
☐ 64T Kevin Rogers .15 .07 .02
☐ 65T Ken Ryan 1.00 .45 .13
☐ 66T Phil Hiatt .15 .07 .02
☐ 67T Pat Meares .60 .25 .08
☐ 68T Troy Neel .25 .11 .03
☐ 69T Steve Cooke .15 .07 .02
☐ 70T Sherman Obando .60 .25 .08
☐ 71T Blas Minor .15 .07 .02
☐ 72T Angel Miranda .15 .07 .02
☐ 73T Tom Kramer .15 .07 .02
☐ 74T Chip Hale .15 .07 .02
☐ 75T Brad Pennington .15 .07 .02
☐ 76T Graeme Lloyd .15 .07 .02
☐ 77T Darrell Whitmore .60 .25 .08
☐ 78T David Nied .75 .35 .09
☐ 79T Todd Van Poppel .25 .11 .03
☐ 80T Chris Gomez 2.00 .90 .25
☐ 81T Jason Bere 3.00 1.35 .40
☐ 82T Jeffrey Hammonds 2.00 .90 .25
☐ 83T Brad Ausmus .15 .07 .02
☐ 84T Kevin Stocker .60 .25 .08
☐ 85T Jeromy Burnitz .15 .07 .02
☐ 86T Aaron Sele 1.50 .65 .19
☐ 87T Roberto Mejia .50 .23 .06
☐ 88T Kirk Rueter 1.00 .45 .13
☐ 89T Kevin Roberson .15 .07 .02
☐ 90T Allen Watson .40 .18 .05
☐ 91T Charlie Leibrandt .15 .07 .02
☐ 92T Eric Davis .15 .07 .02
☐ 93T Jody Reed .15 .07 .02
☐ 94T Danny Jackson .15 .07 .02
☐ 95T Gary Gaetti .15 .07 .02
☐ 96T Norm Charlton .15 .07 .02
☐ 97T Doug Drabek .30 .14 .04
☐ 98T Scott Fletcher .15 .07 .02
☐ 99T Greg Swindell .15 .07 .02
☐ 100T John Smiley .15 .07 .02
☐ 101T Kevin Reimer .15 .07 .02
☐ 102T Andres Galarraga .40 .18 .05
☐ 103T Greg Hibbard .15 .07 .02
☐ 104T Chris Hammond .15 .07 .02
☐ 105T Darnell Coles .15 .07 .02
☐ 106T Mike Felder .15 .07 .02
☐ 107T Jose Guzman .15 .07 .02
☐ 108T Chris Bosio .15 .07 .02
☐ 109T Spike Owen .15 .07 .02
☐ 110T Felix Jose .15 .07 .02
☐ 111T Cory Snyder .15 .07 .02
☐ 112T Craig Lefferts .15 .07 .02
☐ 113T David Wells .15 .07 .02
☐ 114T Pete Incaviglia .15 .07 .02
☐ 115T Mike Pagliarulo .15 .07 .02
☐ 116T Dave Magadan .15 .07 .02
☐ 117T Charlie Hough .25 .11 .03
☐ 118T Ivan Calderon .15 .07 .02
☐ 119T Manny Lee .15 .07 .02
☐ 120T Bob Patterson .15 .07 .02
☐ 121T Bob Ojeda .15 .07 .02
☐ 122T Scott Bankhead .15 .07 .02
☐ 123T Greg Maddux 2.00 .90 .25
☐ 124T Chili Davis .25 .11 .03
☐ 125T Milt Thompson .15 .07 .02
☐ 126T Dave Martinez .15 .07 .02
☐ 127T Frank Tanana .15 .07 .02
☐ 128T Phil Plantier .15 .07 .02
☐ 129T Juan Samuel .15 .07 .02
☐ 130T Eric Young .25 .11 .03
☐ 131T Joe Orsulak .15 .07 .02
☐ 132T Derek Bell .25 .11 .03
☐ 133T Darrin Jackson .15 .07 .02
☐ 134T Tom Brunansky .15 .07 .02
☐ 135T Jeff Reardon .25 .11 .03
☐ 136T Kevin Higgins .25 .11 .03
☐ 137T Joel Johnston .15 .07 .02
☐ 138T Rick Trlicek .15 .07 .02
☐ 139T Richie Lewis .15 .07 .02
☐ 140T Jeff Gardner .15 .07 .02
☐ 141T Jack Voigt .25 .11 .03
☐ 142T Rod Correia .25 .11 .03
☐ 143T Billy Brewer .25 .11 .03
☐ 144T Terry Jorgensen .15 .07 .02
☐ 145T Rich Amaral .15 .07 .02
☐ 146T Sean Berry .15 .07 .02
☐ 147T Dan Peltier .15 .07 .02
☐ 148T Paul Wagner .15 .07 .02
☐ 149T Damon Buford .15 .07 .02
☐ 150T Wil Cordero .50 .23 .06
☐ NR1 Nolan Ryan Tribute 125.00 57.50 15.50
☐ ROY1 Tim Salmon AL ROY 25.00 11.50 3.10
☐ ROY2 Mike Piazza NL ROY 100.00 45.00 12.50

1993 Select R/T All-Star Rookies

This ten-card set was randomly inserted in foil packs of 1993 Select Rookie and Traded. The insertion rate was reportedly not less than one in 36 packs. The cards measure the standard size (2 1/2" by 3 1/2") and feature on their fronts color player action shots that have a grainy metallic appearance. These photos are borderless, except at the top, where the silver-colored player's name is displayed upon red and blue metallic stripes. The set's title appears within a metallic silver-colored stripe near the bottom, which has a star-and-baseball icon emblazoned over its center. This combination of the set's title, stripe, and star-and-baseball icon reappears at the top of the non-metallic back, but in a red, white, and blue design. The player's name, position, and team logo are shown on the red-colored right half of the card. His career highlights appear in white lettering on the blue-colored left half. The cards are numbered on the back.

	MINT	EXC	G-VG
COMPLETE SET (10)	175.00	80.00	22.00
COMMON CARD (1-10)	7.00	3.10	.85

☐ 1 Jeff Conine 12.00 5.50 1.50
☐ 2 Brent Gates 7.00 3.10 .85

☐ 3 Mike Lansing	7.00	3.10	.85
☐ 4 Kevin Stocker	7.00	3.10	.85
☐ 5 Mike Piazza	100.00	45.00	12.50
☐ 6 Jeffrey Hammonds	20.00	9.00	2.50
☐ 7 David Hulse	7.00	3.10	.85
☐ 8 Tim Salmon	25.00	11.50	3.10
☐ 9 Rene Arocha	7.00	3.10	.85
☐ 10 Greg McMichael	7.00	3.10	.85

1994 Select

Measuring the standard size, the 1994 Select set consists of 420 cards that were issued in two series of 210. The horizontal fronts feature a color player action photo and a duo-tone player shot. The backs are vertical and contain a photo, 1993 and career statistics and highlights. Special Dave Winfield and Cal Ripken cards were insertd in first series packs. A Paul Molitor MVP card and a Carlos Delgado Rookie of the Year card were inserted in second series packs. The insertion rate for ech card was one in 360 packs. Rookie Cards include Brian Anderson, John Hudek and Chan Ho Park.

	MINT	EXC	G-VG
COMPLETE SET (420)	35.00	16.00	4.40
COMPLETE SERIES 1 (210)	20.00	9.00	2.50
COMPLETE SERIES 2 (210)	15.00	6.75	1.90
COMMON CARD (1-210)	.10	.05	.01
COMMON CARD (211-420)	.10	.05	.01

☐ 1 Ken Griffey Jr.	3.00	1.35	.40
☐ 2 Greg Maddux	.60	.25	.08
☐ 3 Paul Molitor	.40	.18	.05
☐ 4 Mike Piazza	1.50	.65	.19
☐ 5 Jay Bell	.15	.07	.02
☐ 6 Frank Thomas	3.00	1.35	.40
☐ 7 Barry Larkin	.20	.09	.03
☐ 8 Paul O'Neill	.15	.07	.02
☐ 9 Darren Daulton	.20	.09	.03
☐ 10 Mike Greenwell	.15	.07	.02
☐ 11 Chuck Carr	.10	.05	.01
☐ 12 Joe Carter	.40	.18	.05
☐ 13 Lance Johnson	.10	.05	.01
☐ 14 Jeff Blauser	.15	.07	.02
☐ 15 Chris Hoiles	.15	.07	.02
☐ 16 Rick Wilkins	.10	.05	.01
☐ 17 Kirby Puckett	1.25	.55	.16
☐ 18 Larry Walker	.20	.09	.03
☐ 19 Randy Johnson	.20	.09	.03
☐ 20 Bernard Gilkey	.10	.05	.01
☐ 21 Devon White	.10	.05	.01
☐ 22 Randy Myers	.10	.05	.01
☐ 23 Don Mattingly	1.25	.55	.16
☐ 24 John Kruk	.20	.09	.03
☐ 25 Ozzie Guillen	.10	.05	.01
☐ 26 Jeff Conine	.20	.09	.03
☐ 27 Mike Macfarlane	.10	.05	.01
☐ 28 Dave Hollins	.20	.09	.03
☐ 29 Chuck Knoblauch	.20	.09	.03
☐ 30 Ozzie Smith	.60	.25	.08
☐ 31 Harold Baines	.15	.07	.02
☐ 32 Ryne Sandberg	1.00	.45	.13
☐ 33 Ron Karkovice	.10	.05	.01
☐ 34 Terry Pendleton	.10	.05	.01
☐ 35 Wally Joyner	.15	.07	.02
☐ 36 Mike Mussina	.40	.18	.05
☐ 37 Felix Jose	.10	.05	.01
☐ 38 Derrick May	.10	.05	.01
☐ 39 Scott Cooper	.15	.07	.02
☐ 40 Jose Rijo	.15	.07	.02
☐ 41 Robin Ventura	.15	.07	.02
☐ 42 Charlie Hayes	.15	.07	.02
☐ 43 Jimmy Key	.15	.07	.02
☐ 44 Eric Karros	.15	.07	.02
☐ 45 Ruben Sierra	.20	.09	.03
☐ 46 Ryan Thompson	.15	.07	.02
☐ 47 Brian McRae	.15	.07	.02
☐ 48 Pat Hentgen	.15	.07	.02
☐ 49 John Valentin	.15	.07	.02
☐ 50 Al Martin	.10	.05	.01
☐ 51 Jose Lind	.10	.05	.01
☐ 52 Kevin Stocker	.15	.07	.02
☐ 53 Mike Gallego	.10	.05	.01
☐ 54 Dwight Gooden	.10	.05	.01
☐ 55 Brady Anderson	.15	.07	.02
☐ 56 Jeff King	.10	.05	.01
☐ 57 Mark McGwire	.20	.09	.03
☐ 58 Sammy Sosa	.20	.09	.03
☐ 59 Ryan Bowen	.10	.05	.01
☐ 60 Mark Lemke	.10	.05	.01
☐ 61 Roger Clemens	.75	.35	.09
☐ 62 Brian Jordan	.15	.07	.02
☐ 63 Andres Galarraga	.20	.09	.03
☐ 64 Kevin Appier	.15	.07	.02
☐ 65 Don Slaught	.10	.05	.01
☐ 66 Mike Blowers	.10	.05	.01
☐ 67 Wes Chamberlain	.10	.05	.01
☐ 68 Troy Neel	.15	.07	.02
☐ 69 John Wetteland	.10	.05	.01
☐ 70 Joe Girardi	.10	.05	.01
☐ 71 Reggie Sanders	.15	.07	.02
☐ 72 Edgar Martinez	.10	.05	.01
☐ 73 Todd Hundley	.10	.05	.01
☐ 74 Pat Borders	.10	.05	.01
☐ 75 Roberto Mejia	.15	.07	.02
☐ 76 David Cone	.20	.09	.03
☐ 77 Tony Gwynn	.75	.35	.09
☐ 78 Jim Abbott	.20	.09	.03
☐ 79 Jay Buhner	.15	.07	.02
☐ 80 Mark McLemore	.10	.05	.01
☐ 81 Wil Cordero	.20	.09	.03
☐ 82 Pedro Astacio	.15	.07	.02
☐ 83 Bob Tewksbury	.10	.05	.01
☐ 84 Dave Winfield	.20	.09	.03
☐ 85 Jeff Kent	.15	.07	.02
☐ 86 Todd Van Poppel	.15	.07	.02
☐ 87 Steve Avery	.20	.09	.03
☐ 88 Mike Lansing	.15	.07	.02
☐ 89 Lenny Dykstra	.20	.09	.03
☐ 90 Jose Guzman	.10	.05	.01
☐ 91 Brian R. Hunter	.10	.05	.01
☐ 92 Tim Raines	.20	.09	.03
☐ 93 Andre Dawson	.20	.09	.03

	#	Player			
☐	94	Joe Orsulak	.10	.05	.01
☐	95	Ricky Jordan	.10	.05	.01
☐	96	Billy Hatcher	.10	.05	.01
☐	97	Jack McDowell	.20	.09	.03
☐	98	Tom Pagnozzi	.10	.05	.01
☐	99	Darryl Strawberry	.15	.07	.02
☐	100	Mike Stanley	.10	.05	.01
☐	101	Bret Saberhagen	.15	.07	.02
☐	102	Willie Greene	.15	.07	.02
☐	103	Bryan Harvey	.15	.07	.02
☐	104	Tim Bogar	.10	.05	.01
☐	105	Jack Voigt	.10	.05	.01
☐	106	Brad Ausmus	.10	.05	.01
☐	107	Ramon Martinez	.15	.07	.02
☐	108	Mike Perez	.10	.05	.01
☐	109	Jeff Montgomery	.15	.07	.02
☐	110	Danny Darwin	.10	.05	.01
☐	111	Wilson Alvarez	.20	.09	.03
☐	112	Kevin Mitchell	.15	.07	.02
☐	113	David Nied	.20	.09	.03
☐	114	Rich Amaral	.10	.05	.01
☐	115	Stan Javier	.10	.05	.01
☐	116	Mo Vaughn	.20	.09	.03
☐	117	Ben McDonald	.15	.07	.02
☐	118	Tom Gordon	.10	.05	.01
☐	119	Carlos Garcia	.10	.05	.01
☐	120	Phil Plantier	.15	.07	.02
☐	121	Mike Morgan	.10	.05	.01
☐	122	Pat Meares	.10	.05	.01
☐	123	Kevin Young	.10	.05	.01
☐	124	Jeff Fassero	.10	.05	.01
☐	125	Gene Harris	.10	.05	.01
☐	126	Bob Welch	.10	.05	.01
☐	127	Walt Weiss	.10	.05	.01
☐	128	Bobby Witt	.10	.05	.01
☐	129	Andy Van Slyke	.20	.09	.03
☐	130	Steve Cooke	.10	.05	.01
☐	131	Mike Devereaux	.15	.07	.02
☐	132	Joey Cora	.10	.05	.01
☐	133	Bret Barberie	.10	.05	.01
☐	134	Orel Hershiser	.15	.07	.02
☐	135	Ed Sprague	.10	.05	.01
☐	136	Shawon Dunston	.10	.05	.01
☐	137	Alex Arias	.10	.05	.01
☐	138	Archi Cianfrocco	.10	.05	.01
☐	139	Tim Wallach	.10	.05	.01
☐	140	Bernie Williams	.15	.07	.02
☐	141	Karl Rhodes	.10	.05	.01
☐	142	Pat Kelly	.10	.05	.01
☐	143	Dave Magadan	.10	.05	.01
☐	144	Kevin Tapani	.10	.05	.01
☐	145	Eric Young	.15	.07	.02
☐	146	Derek Bell	.15	.07	.02
☐	147	Dante Bichette	.20	.09	.03
☐	148	Geronimo Pena	.10	.05	.01
☐	149	Joe Oliver	.10	.05	.01
☐	150	Orestes Destrade	.10	.05	.01
☐	151	Tim Naehring	.10	.05	.01
☐	152	Ray Lankford	.20	.09	.03
☐	153	Phil Clark	.10	.05	.01
☐	154	David McCarty	.15	.07	.02
☐	155	Tommy Greene	.10	.05	.01
☐	156	Wade Boggs	.20	.09	.03
☐	157	Kevin Gross	.10	.05	.01
☐	158	Hal Morris	.15	.07	.02
☐	159	Moises Alou	.20	.09	.03
☐	160	Rick Aguilera	.15	.07	.02
☐	161	Curt Schilling	.10	.05	.01
☐	162	Chip Hale	.10	.05	.01
☐	163	Tino Martinez	.10	.05	.01
☐	164	Mark Whiten	.15	.07	.02
☐	165	Dave Stewart	.15	.07	.02
☐	166	Steve Buechele	.10	.05	.01
☐	167	Bobby Jones	.25	.11	.03
☐	168	Darrin Fletcher	.10	.05	.01
☐	169	John Smiley	.10	.05	.01
☐	170	Cory Snyder	.10	.05	.01
☐	171	Scott Erickson	.10	.05	.01
☐	172	Kirk Rueter	.10	.05	.01
☐	173	Dave Fleming	.10	.05	.01
☐	174	John Smoltz	.15	.07	.02
☐	175	Ricky Gutierrez	.10	.05	.01
☐	176	Mike Bordick	.10	.05	.01
☐	177	Chan Ho Park	1.25	.55	.16
☐	178	Alex Gonzalez	.30	.14	.04
☐	179	Steve Karsay	.10	.05	.01
☐	180	Jeffrey Hammonds	.30	.14	.04
☐	181	Manny Ramirez	.60	.25	.08
☐	182	Salomon Torres	.15	.07	.02
☐	183	Raul Mondesi	1.00	.45	.13
☐	184	James Mouton	.20	.09	.03
☐	185	Cliff Floyd	.50	.23	.06
☐	186	Danny Bautista	.15	.07	.02
☐	187	Kurt Abbott	.30	.14	.04
☐	188	Javy Lopez	.30	.14	.04
☐	189	John Patterson	.10	.05	.01
☐	190	Greg Blosser	.10	.05	.01
☐	191	Bob Hamelin	.20	.09	.03
☐	192	Tony Eusebio	.10	.05	.01
☐	193	Carlos Delgado	.50	.23	.06
☐	194	Chris Gomez	.20	.09	.03
☐	195	Kelly Stinnett	.10	.05	.01
☐	196	Shane Reynolds	.10	.05	.01
☐	197	Ryan Klesko	.50	.23	.06
☐	198	Jim Edmonds	.10	.05	.01
☐	199	James Hurst	.10	.05	.01
☐	200	Dave Staton	.10	.05	.01
☐	201	Rondell White	.30	.14	.04
☐	202	Keith Mitchell	.10	.05	.01
☐	203	Darren Oliver	.10	.05	.01
☐	204	Mike Matheny	.10	.05	.01
☐	205	Chris Turner	.10	.05	.01
☐	206	Matt Mieske	.10	.05	.01
☐	207	NL Team Checklist	.10	.05	.01
☐	208	NL Team Checklist	.10	.05	.01
☐	209	AL Team Checklist	.10	.05	.01
☐	210	AL Team Checklist	.10	.05	.01
☐	211	Barry Bonds	1.25	.55	.16
☐	212	Juan Gonzalez	1.00	.45	.13
☐	213	Jim Eisenreich	.10	.05	.01
☐	214	Ivan Rodriguez	.20	.09	.03
☐	215	Tony Phillips	.10	.05	.01
☐	216	John Jaha	.10	.05	.01
☐	217	Lee Smith	.20	.09	.03
☐	218	Bip Roberts	.10	.05	.01
☐	219	Dave Hansen	.10	.05	.01
☐	220	Pat Listach	.10	.05	.01
☐	221	Willie McGee	.10	.05	.01
☐	222	Damion Easley	.10	.05	.01
☐	223	Dean Palmer	.15	.07	.02
☐	224	Mike Moore	.10	.05	.01
☐	225	Brian Harper	.10	.05	.01
☐	226	Gary DiSarcina	.10	.05	.01
☐	227	Delino DeShields	.15	.07	.02
☐	228	Otis Nixon	.10	.05	.01
☐	229	Roberto Alomar	.75	.35	.09
☐	230	Mark Grace	.20	.09	.03
☐	231	Kenny Lofton	.75	.35	.09
☐	232	Gregg Jefferies	.20	.09	.03
☐	233	Cecil Fielder	.20	.09	.03
☐	234	Jeff Bagwell	1.50	.65	.19
☐	235	Albert Belle	1.00	.45	.13
☐	236	David Justice	.40	.18	.05
☐	237	Tom Henke	.10	.05	.01
☐	238	Bobby Bonilla	.20	.09	.03
☐	239	John Olerud	.20	.09	.03

	No.	Player			
☐	240	Robby Thompson	.10	.05	.01
☐	241	Dave Valle	.10	.05	.01
☐	242	Marquis Grissom	.20	.09	.03
☐	243	Greg Swindell	.10	.05	.01
☐	244	Todd Zeile	.15	.07	.02
☐	245	Dennis Eckersley	.20	.09	.03
☐	246	Jose Offerman	.10	.05	.01
☐	247	Greg McMichael	.15	.07	.02
☐	248	Tim Belcher	.10	.05	.01
☐	249	Cal Ripken	2.25	1.00	.30
☐	250	Tom Glavine	.20	.09	.03
☐	251	Luis Polonia	.10	.05	.01
☐	252	Bill Swift	.10	.05	.01
☐	253	Juan Guzman	.15	.07	.02
☐	254	Rickey Henderson	.20	.09	.03
☐	255	Terry Mulholland	.10	.05	.01
☐	256	Gary Sheffield	.20	.09	.03
☐	257	Terry Steinbach	.15	.07	.02
☐	258	Brett Butler	.15	.07	.02
☐	259	Jason Bere	.40	.18	.05
☐	260	Doug Strange	.10	.05	.01
☐	261	Kent Hrbek	.15	.07	.02
☐	262	Graeme Lloyd	.10	.05	.01
☐	263	Lou Frazier	.10	.05	.01
☐	264	Charles Nagy	.10	.05	.01
☐	265	Bret Boone	.20	.09	.03
☐	266	Kirk Gibson	.15	.07	.02
☐	267	Kevin Brown	.10	.05	.01
☐	268	Fred McGriff	.40	.18	.05
☐	269	Matt Williams	.50	.23	.06
☐	270	Greg Gagne	.10	.05	.01
☐	271	Mariano Duncan	.10	.05	.01
☐	272	Jeff Russell	.10	.05	.01
☐	273	Eric Davis	.10	.05	.01
☐	274	Shane Mack	.15	.07	.02
☐	275	Jose Vizcaino	.10	.05	.01
☐	276	Jose Canseco	.40	.18	.05
☐	277	Roberto Hernandez	.10	.05	.01
☐	278	Royce Clayton	.15	.07	.02
☐	279	Carlos Baerga	.40	.18	.05
☐	280	Pete Incaviglia	.10	.05	.01
☐	281	Brent Gates	.20	.09	.03
☐	282	Jeromy Burnitz	.15	.07	.02
☐	283	Chili Davis	.15	.07	.02
☐	284	Pete Harnisch	.10	.05	.01
☐	285	Alan Trammell	.20	.09	.03
☐	286	Eric Anthony	.10	.05	.01
☐	287	Ellis Burks	.15	.07	.02
☐	288	Julio Franco	.15	.07	.02
☐	289	Jack Morris	.20	.09	.03
☐	290	Erik Hanson	.10	.05	.01
☐	291	Chuck Finley	.10	.05	.01
☐	292	Reggie Jefferson	.10	.05	.01
☐	293	Kevin McReynolds	.10	.05	.01
☐	294	Greg Hibbard	.10	.05	.01
☐	295	Travis Fryman	.25	.11	.03
☐	296	Craig Biggio	.15	.07	.02
☐	297	Kenny Rogers	.10	.05	.01
☐	298	Dave Henderson	.10	.05	.01
☐	299	Jim Thome	.20	.09	.03
☐	300	Rene Arocha	.15	.07	.02
☐	301	Pedro Munoz	.10	.05	.01
☐	302	David Hulse	.10	.05	.01
☐	303	Greg Vaughn	.15	.07	.02
☐	304	Darren Lewis	.10	.05	.01
☐	305	Deion Sanders	.50	.23	.06
☐	306	Danny Tartabull	.15	.07	.02
☐	307	Darryl Hamilton	.10	.05	.01
☐	308	Andujar Cedeno	.10	.05	.01
☐	309	Tim Salmon	.40	.18	.05
☐	310	Tony Fernandez	.10	.05	.01
☐	311	Alex Fernandez	.20	.09	.03
☐	312	Roberto Kelly	.10	.05	.01
☐	313	Harold Reynolds	.10	.05	.01
☐	314	Chris Sabo	.10	.05	.01
☐	315	Howard Johnson	.10	.05	.01
☐	316	Mark Portugal	.10	.05	.01
☐	317	Rafael Palmeiro	.20	.09	.03
☐	318	Pete Smith	.10	.05	.01
☐	319	Will Clark	.40	.18	.05
☐	320	Henry Rodriguez	.10	.05	.01
☐	321	Omar Vizquel	.10	.05	.01
☐	322	David Segui	.10	.05	.01
☐	323	Lou Whitaker	.20	.09	.03
☐	324	Felix Fermin	.10	.05	.01
☐	325	Spike Owen	.10	.05	.01
☐	326	Darryl Kile	.15	.07	.02
☐	327	Chad Kreuter	.10	.05	.01
☐	328	Rod Beck	.15	.07	.02
☐	329	Eddie Murray	.20	.09	.03
☐	330	B.J. Surhoff	.10	.05	.01
☐	331	Mickey Tettleton	.15	.07	.02
☐	332	Pedro Martinez	.20	.09	.03
☐	333	Roger Pavlik	.10	.05	.01
☐	334	Eddie Taubensee	.10	.05	.01
☐	335	John Doherty	.10	.05	.01
☐	336	Jody Reed	.10	.05	.01
☐	337	Aaron Sele	.30	.14	.04
☐	338	Leo Gomez	.10	.05	.01
☐	339	Dave Nilsson	.10	.05	.01
☐	340	Rob Dibble	.10	.05	.01
☐	341	John Burkett	.15	.07	.02
☐	342	Wayne Kirby	.10	.05	.01
☐	343	Dan Wilson	.10	.05	.01
☐	344	Armando Reynoso	.10	.05	.01
☐	345	Chad Curtis	.15	.07	.02
☐	346	Dennis Martinez	.15	.07	.02
☐	347	Cal Eldred	.15	.07	.02
☐	348	Luis Gonzalez	.10	.05	.01
☐	349	Doug Drabek	.20	.09	.03
☐	350	Jim Leyritz	.10	.05	.01
☐	351	Mark Langston	.20	.09	.03
☐	352	Darrin Jackson	.10	.05	.01
☐	353	Sid Fernandez	.10	.05	.01
☐	354	Benito Santiago	.10	.05	.01
☐	355	Kevin Seitzer	.10	.05	.01
☐	356	Bo Jackson	.20	.09	.03
☐	357	David Wells	.10	.05	.01
☐	358	Paul Sorrento	.10	.05	.01
☐	359	Ken Caminiti	.15	.07	.02
☐	360	Eduardo Perez	.15	.07	.02
☐	361	Orlando Merced	.15	.07	.02
☐	362	Steve Finley	.10	.05	.01
☐	363	Andy Benes	.15	.07	.02
☐	364	Manny Lee	.10	.05	.01
☐	365	Todd Benzinger	.10	.05	.01
☐	366	Sandy Alomar Jr.	.15	.07	.02
☐	367	Rex Hudler	.10	.05	.01
☐	368	Mike Henneman	.10	.05	.01
☐	369	Vince Coleman	.10	.05	.01
☐	370	Kirt Manwaring	.10	.05	.01
☐	371	Ken Hill	.15	.07	.02
☐	372	Glenallen Hill	.10	.05	.01
☐	373	Sean Berry	.10	.05	.01
☐	374	Geronimo Berroa	.10	.05	.01
☐	375	Duane Ward	.10	.05	.01
☐	376	Allen Watson	.10	.05	.01
☐	377	Marc Newfield	.20	.09	.03
☐	378	Dan Miceli	.10	.05	.01
☐	379	Denny Hocking	.10	.05	.01
☐	380	Mark Kiefer	.10	.05	.01
☐	381	Tony Tarasco	.20	.09	.03
☐	382	Tony Longmire	.10	.05	.01
☐	383	Brian Anderson	.75	.35	.09
☐	384	Fernando Vina	.10	.05	.01
☐	385	Hector Carrasco	.10	.05	.01

		MINT	EXC	G-VG
☐ 386	Mike Kelly	.15	.07	.02
☐ 387	Greg Colbrunn	.10	.05	.01
☐ 388	Roger Salkeld	.10	.05	.01
☐ 389	Steve Trachsel	.40	.18	.05
☐ 390	Rich Becker	.15	.07	.02
☐ 391	Billy Taylor	.10	.05	.01
☐ 392	Rich Rowland	.10	.05	.01
☐ 393	Carl Everett	.15	.07	.02
☐ 394	Johnny Ruffin	.10	.05	.01
☐ 395	Keith Lockhart	.10	.05	.01
☐ 396	J.R. Phillips	.20	.09	.03
☐ 397	Sterling Hitchcock	.15	.07	.02
☐ 398	Jorge Fabregas	.10	.05	.01
☐ 399	Jeff Granger	.15	.07	.02
☐ 400	Eddie Zambrano	.10	.05	.01
☐ 401	Rikkert Faneyte	.10	.05	.01
☐ 402	Gerald Williams	.10	.05	.01
☐ 403	Joey Hamilton	.60	.25	.08
☐ 404	Joe Hall	.10	.05	.01
☐ 405	John Hudek	.75	.35	.09
☐ 406	Roberto Petagine	.15	.07	.02
☐ 407	Charles Johnson	.30	.14	.04
☐ 408	Mark Smith	.10	.05	.01
☐ 409	Jeff Juden	.10	.05	.01
☐ 410	Carlos Pulido	.15	.07	.02
☐ 411	Paul Shuey	.15	.07	.02
☐ 412	Rob Butler	.10	.05	.01
☐ 413	Mark Acre	.20	.09	.03
☐ 414	Greg Pirkl	.10	.05	.01
☐ 415	Melvin Nieves	.20	.09	.03
☐ 416	Tim Hyers	.20	.09	.03
☐ 417	NL Checklist	.10	.05	.01
☐ 418	NL Checklist	.10	.05	.01
☐ 419	AL Checklist	.10	.05	.01
☐ 420	AL Checklist	.10	.05	.01
☐ MVP1	Paul Molitor MVP	30.00	13.50	3.80
☐ RY1	Carlos Delgado ROY	25.00	11.50	3.10
☐ SS1	Cal Ripken Salute	100.00	45.00	12.50
☐ SS2	Dave Winfield Salute	20.00	9.00	2.50

1994 Select Crown Contenders

This ten-card set showcases top contenders for various awards such as batting champion, Cy Young Award winner and Most Valuable Player. The cards were inserted in packs at a rate of one in 24 and measure the standard size. The horizontal fronts feature color action player shots on a holographic gold foil background. The backs carry a color player close-up photo and highlights. The cards are numbered on the back with a CC prefix.

	MINT	EXC	G-VG
COMPLETE SET (10)	150.00	70.00	19.00
COMMON CARD (CC1-CC10)	5.00	2.30	.60

		MINT	EXC	G-VG
☐ CC1	Lenny Dykstra	5.00	2.30	.60
☐ CC2	Greg Maddux	10.00	4.50	1.25
☐ CC3	Roger Clemens	10.00	4.50	1.25
☐ CC4	Randy Johnson	5.00	2.30	.60
☐ CC5	Frank Thomas	40.00	18.00	5.00
☐ CC6	Barry Bonds	15.00	6.75	1.90
☐ CC7	Juan Gonzalez	12.00	5.50	1.50
☐ CC8	John Olerud	5.00	2.30	.60
☐ CC9	Mike Piazza	20.00	9.00	2.50
☐ CC10	Ken Griffey Jr.	40.00	18.00	5.00

1994 Select Rookie Surge

This 18-card set showcased potential top rookies for 1994. The set was divided into two series of nine cards. The cards were randomly inserted in packs at a rate of one in 48. The fronts exhibit Score's "dufex" printing process, in which a color photo is printed on a metallic base creating an unusual, three-dimensional look. On a multi-colored background, the horizontal backs present a color player headshot. The cards are numbered on the back with an RS prefix.

	MINT	EXC	G-VG
COMPLETE SET (18)	275.00	125.00	34.00
COMPLETE SERIES 1 (9)	140.00	65.00	17.50
COMPLETE SERIES 2 (9)	140.00	65.00	17.50
COMMON CARD (RS1-RS9)	6.00	2.70	.75
COMMON CARD (RS10-RS18)	6.00	2.70	.75

		MINT	EXC	G-VG
☐ RS1	Cliff Floyd	25.00	11.50	3.10
☐ RS2	Bob Hamelin	15.00	6.75	1.90
☐ RS3	Ryan Klesko	25.00	11.50	3.10
☐ RS4	Carlos Delgado	25.00	11.50	3.10
☐ RS5	Jeffrey Hammonds	15.00	6.75	1.90
☐ RS6	Rondell White	15.00	6.75	1.90
☐ RS7	Salomon Torres	6.00	2.70	.75
☐ RS8	Steve Karsay	6.00	2.70	.75
☐ RS9	Javy Lopez	15.00	6.75	1.90
☐ RS10	Manny Ramirez	30.00	13.50	3.80
☐ RS11	Tony Tarasco	6.00	2.70	.75
☐ RS12	Kurt Abbott	6.00	2.70	.75

		MINT	EXC	G-VG
☐ RS13	Chan Ho Park	30.00	13.50	3.80
☐ RS14	Rich Becker	6.00	2.70	.75
☐ RS15	James Mouton	6.00	2.70	.75
☐ RS16	Alex Gonzalez	10.00	4.50	1.25
☐ RS17	Raul Mondesi	50.00	23.00	6.25
☐ RS18	Steve Trachsel	10.00	4.50	1.25

1994 Select Skills

This 10-card standard-size set takes an up close look at the leagues top statistical leaders. The cards were randomly inserted in second series packs at a rate of approximately one in 24. A foil front has a holographic appearance that allows the player to stand out. The bottom of the front notes the player as being the best at something. For example, the front of Barry Bonds' card notes, "Select's Best Run Producer". The back has a small photo with text. The cards are numbered with an "SK" prefix.

	MINT	EXC	G-VG
COMPLETE SET (10)	70.00	32.00	8.75
COMMON CARD (SK1-SK10)	2.50	1.15	.30

		MINT	EXC	G-VG
☐ SK1	Randy Johnson	2.50	1.15	.30
☐ SK2	Barry Larkin	2.50	1.15	.30
☐ SK3	Lenny Dykstra	2.50	1.15	.30
☐ SK4	Kenny Lofton	12.00	5.50	1.50
☐ SK5	Juan Gonzalez	18.00	8.00	2.30
☐ SK6	Barry Bonds	20.00	9.00	2.50
☐ SK7	Marquis Grissom	2.50	1.15	.30
☐ SK8	Ivan Rodriguez	2.50	1.15	.30
☐ SK9	Larry Walker	2.50	1.15	.30
☐ SK10	Travis Fryman	4.50	2.00	.55

1994 Signature Rookies Draft Picks

The 1994 Signature Rookies Draft Picks set consists of 100 standard-size cards. The fronts feature full-bleed color action shots. Marbleized green stripes accent the pictures on the left and bottom. In these green stripes appear the production figures ("of 7,750") and the player's name, both in gold foil. On a background consisting of a ghosted version of the front photo, the backs have a color headshot in the upper left corner, with the remainder of the back filled with biography, statistics, and player profile.

	MINT	EXC	G-VG
COMPLETE SET (100)	20.00	9.00	2.50
COMMON CARD (1-100)	.15	.07	.02

		MINT	EXC	G-VG
☐ 1	Josh Booty	1.50	.65	.19
☐ 2	Paul Wilson	1.00	.45	.13
☐ 3	Ben Grieve	2.00	.90	.25
☐ 4	Dustin Hermanson	.60	.25	.08
☐ 5	Antone Williamson	.75	.35	.09
☐ 6	McKay Christensen	.40	.18	.05
☐ 7	Doug Million	1.00	.45	.13
☐ 8	Todd Walker	1.50	.65	.19
☐ 9	C.J. Nitkowski	.60	.25	.08
☐ 10	Jaret Wright	.40	.18	.05
☐ 11	Mark Farris	.50	.23	.06
☐ 12	Nomar Garciaparra	.50	.23	.06
☐ 13	Paul Konerko	.75	.35	.09
☐ 14	Jason Varitek	.40	.18	.05
☐ 15	Jayson Peterson	.50	.23	.06
☐ 16	Matt Smith	.50	.23	.06
☐ 17	Ramon Castro	.50	.23	.06
☐ 18	Cade Gaspar	.40	.18	.05
☐ 19	Bret Wagner	.60	.25	.08
☐ 20	Terrence Long	1.00	.45	.13
☐ 21	Hiram Bocachica	.40	.18	.05
☐ 22	Dante Powell	1.25	.55	.16
☐ 23	Brian Buchanan	.50	.23	.06
☐ 24	Scott Elarton	.75	.35	.09
☐ 25	Mark Johnson	.50	.23	.06
☐ 26	Jacob Shumate	.50	.23	.06
☐ 27	Kevin Witt	.50	.23	.06
☐ 28	Jay Payton	1.00	.45	.13
☐ 29	Mike Thurman	.30	.14	.04
☐ 30	Jacob Cruz	.40	.18	.05
☐ 31	Chris Clemons	.15	.07	.02
☐ 32	Travis Miller	.50	.23	.06
☐ 33	Sean Johnston	.15	.07	.02
☐ 34	Brad Rigby	.40	.18	.05
☐ 35	Doug Webb	.15	.07	.02
☐ 36	John Ambrose	.15	.07	.02
☐ 37	Cletus Davidson	.15	.07	.02
☐ 38	Tony Terry	.15	.07	.02
☐ 39	Jason Camilli	.15	.07	.02
☐ 40	Roger Goedde	.15	.07	.02
☐ 41	Corey Pointer	.25	.11	.03
☐ 42	Trey Moore	.15	.07	.02
☐ 43	Brian Stephenson	.15	.07	.02
☐ 44	Dan Lock	.15	.07	.02
☐ 45	Mike Darr	.15	.07	.02
☐ 46	Carl Dale	.15	.07	.02
☐ 47	Tommy Davis	.30	.14	.04
☐ 48	Kevin Brown	.40	.18	.05
☐ 49	Ryan Nye	.30	.14	.04

☐ 50 Rodriguez Smith	.15	.07	.02
☐ 51 Andy Taulbee	.30	.14	.04
☐ 52 Jerry Whittaker	.30	.14	.04
☐ 53 John Crowther	.15	.07	.02
☐ 54 Bryon Gainey	.15	.07	.02
☐ 55 Bill King	.15	.07	.02
☐ 56 Heath Murray	.25	.11	.03
☐ 57 Larry Barnes	.15	.07	.02
☐ 58 Todd Cady	.15	.07	.02
☐ 59 Paul Failla	.15	.07	.02
☐ 60 Brian Meadows	.15	.07	.02
☐ 61 A.J. Pierzynski	.15	.07	.02
☐ 62 Aaron Boone	.75	.35	.09
☐ 63 Mike Metcalfe	.15	.07	.02
☐ 64 Matt Wagner	.25	.11	.03
☐ 65 Jaime Bluma	.30	.14	.04
☐ 66 Oscar Robles	.15	.07	.02
☐ 67 Greg Whiteman	.15	.07	.02
☐ 68 Roger Worley	.15	.07	.02
☐ 69 Paul Ottavinia	.15	.07	.02
☐ 70 Joe Giuliano	.15	.07	.02
☐ 71 Chris McBride	.15	.07	.02
☐ 72 Jason Beverlin	.15	.07	.02
☐ 73 Gordon Amerson	.15	.07	.02
☐ 74 Tom Mott	.15	.07	.02
☐ 75 Rob Welch	.15	.07	.02
☐ 76 Jason Kelley	.15	.07	.02
☐ 77 Matt Treanor	.15	.07	.02
☐ 78 Jason Sikes	.15	.07	.02
☐ 79 Steve Shoemaker	.15	.07	.02
☐ 80 Troy Brohawn	.15	.07	.02
☐ 81 Jeff Abbott	1.25	.55	.16
☐ 82 Steve Woodard	.15	.07	.02
☐ 83 Greg Morris	.15	.07	.02
☐ 84 John Slamka	.15	.07	.02
☐ 85 John Schroeder	.15	.07	.02
☐ 86 Clay Caruthers	.15	.07	.02
☐ 87 Eddie Brooks	.15	.07	.02
☐ 88 Tim Byrdak	.15	.07	.02
☐ 89 Bob Howry	.15	.07	.02
☐ 90 Midre Cummings	.30	.14	.04
☐ 91 John Dettmer	.25	.11	.03
☐ 92 Gar Finnvold	.15	.07	.02
☐ 93 Dwayne Hosey	.25	.11	.03
☐ 94 Jason Jacome	.40	.18	.05
☐ 95 Doug Jennings	.15	.07	.02
☐ 96 Luis Lopez	.15	.07	.02
☐ 97 John Mabry	.25	.11	.03
☐ 98 Rondell White	.40	.18	.05
☐ 99 J.T. Snow	.15	.07	.02
☐ 100 Vic Darensbourg	.30	.14	.04

1994 Signature Rookies Draft Picks Signature

The 1994 Signature Rookies Draft Picks Signature set consists of 100 standard-size cards. An autographed card or a trade coupon was seeded in each pack. The trade coupon could be mailed in and redeemed for an autograph card. The card design is identical to the regular issue series. These cards differ in that an autograph in blue ink is inscribed across the picture and the cards are individually numbered out "of 7,750."

	MINT	EXC	G-VG
COMPLETE SET (100)	350.00	160.00	45.00
COMMON CARD (1-100)	3.00	1.35	.40
☐ 1 Josh Booty	12.00	5.50	1.50
☐ 2 Paul Wilson	9.00	4.00	1.15
☐ 3 Ben Grieve	18.00	8.00	2.30
☐ 4 Dustin Hermanson	6.00	2.70	.75
☐ 5 Antone Williamson	7.00	3.10	.85
☐ 6 McKay Christensen	3.00	1.35	.40
☐ 7 Doug Million	9.00	4.00	1.15
☐ 8 Todd Walker	12.00	5.50	1.50
☐ 9 C.J. Nitkowski	6.00	2.70	.75
☐ 10 Jaret Wright	5.00	2.30	.60
☐ 11 Mark Farris	5.00	2.30	.60
☐ 12 Nomar Garciaparra	5.00	2.30	.60
☐ 13 Paul Konerko	7.00	3.10	.85
☐ 14 Jason Varitek	5.00	2.30	.60
☐ 15 Jayson Peterson	5.00	2.30	.60
☐ 16 Matt Smith	5.00	2.30	.60
☐ 17 Ramon Castro	5.00	2.30	.60
☐ 18 Cade Gaspar	3.00	1.35	.40
☐ 19 Bret Wagner	6.00	2.70	.75
☐ 20 Terrence Long	9.00	4.00	1.15
☐ 21 Hiram Bocachica	5.00	2.30	.60
☐ 22 Dante Powell	10.00	4.50	1.25
☐ 23 Brian Buchanan	5.00	2.30	.60
☐ 24 Scott Elarton	7.00	3.10	.85
☐ 25 Mark Johnson	5.00	2.30	.60
☐ 26 Jacob Shumate	3.00	1.35	.40
☐ 27 Kevin Witt	5.00	2.30	.60
☐ 28 Jay Payton	9.00	4.00	1.15
☐ 29 Mike Thurman	3.00	1.35	.40
☐ 30 Jacob Cruz	3.00	1.35	.40
☐ 31 Chris Clemons	3.00	1.35	.40
☐ 32 Travis Miller	3.00	1.35	.40
☐ 33 Sean Johnston	3.00	1.35	.40
☐ 34 Brad Rigby	3.00	1.35	.40
☐ 35 Doug Webb	3.00	1.35	.40
☐ 36 John Ambrose	3.00	1.35	.40
☐ 37 Cletus Davidson	3.00	1.35	.40
☐ 38 Tony Terry	3.00	1.35	.40
☐ 39 Jason Camilli	3.00	1.35	.40
☐ 40 Roger Goedde	3.00	1.35	.40
☐ 41 Corey Pointer	4.00	1.80	.50
☐ 42 Trey Moore	3.00	1.35	.40
☐ 43 Brian Stephenson	3.00	1.35	.40
☐ 44 Dan Lock	3.00	1.35	.40
☐ 45 Mike Darr	3.00	1.35	.40
☐ 46 Carl Dale	3.00	1.35	.40
☐ 47 Tommy Davis	3.00	1.35	.40
☐ 48 Kevin Brown	5.00	2.30	.60
☐ 49 Ryan Nye	3.00	1.35	.40
☐ 50 Rodriguez Smith	3.00	1.35	.40
☐ 51 Andy Taulbee	3.00	1.35	.40
☐ 52 Jerry Whittaker	3.00	1.35	.40
☐ 53 John Crowther	3.00	1.35	.40
☐ 54 Bryon Gainey	3.00	1.35	.40

☐ 55 Bill King	3.00	1.35	.40
☐ 56 Heath Murray	4.00	1.80	.50
☐ 57 Larry Barnes	3.00	1.35	.40
☐ 58 Todd Cady	3.00	1.35	.40
☐ 59 Paul Failla	3.00	1.35	.40
☐ 60 Brian Meadows	3.00	1.35	.40
☐ 61 A.J. Pierzynski	3.00	1.35	.40
☐ 62 Aaron Boone	7.00	3.10	.85
☐ 63 Mike Metcalfe	3.00	1.35	.40
☐ 64 Matt Wagner	4.00	1.80	.50
☐ 65 Jaime Bluma	3.00	1.35	.40
☐ 66 Oscar Robles	3.00	1.35	.40
☐ 67 Greg Whiteman	3.00	1.35	.40
☐ 68 Roger Worley	3.00	1.35	.40
☐ 69 Paul Ottavinia	3.00	1.35	.40
☐ 70 Joe Giuliano	3.00	1.35	.40
☐ 71 Chris McBride	3.00	1.35	.40
☐ 72 Jason Beverlin	3.00	1.35	.40
☐ 73 Gordon Amerson	3.00	1.35	.40
☐ 74 Tom Mott	3.00	1.35	.40
☐ 75 Rob Welch	3.00	1.35	.40
☐ 76 Jason Kelley	3.00	1.35	.40
☐ 77 Matt Treanor	3.00	1.35	.40
☐ 78 Jason Sikes	3.00	1.35	.40
☐ 79 Steve Shoemaker	3.00	1.35	.40
☐ 80 Troy Brohawn	3.00	1.35	.40
☐ 81 Jeff Abbott	9.00	4.00	1.15
☐ 82 Steve Woodard	3.00	1.35	.40
☐ 83 Greg Morris	3.00	1.35	.40
☐ 84 John Slamka	3.00	1.35	.40
☐ 85 John Schroeder	3.00	1.35	.40
☐ 86 Clay Caruthers	3.00	1.35	.40
☐ 87 Eddie Brooks	3.00	1.35	.40
☐ 88 Tim Byrdak	3.00	1.35	.40
☐ 89 Bob Howry	3.00	1.35	.40
☐ 90 Midre Cummings	5.00	2.30	.60
☐ 91 John Dettmer	4.00	1.80	.50
☐ 92 Gar Finnvold	3.00	1.35	.40
☐ 93 Dwayne Hosey	4.00	1.80	.50
☐ 94 Jason Jacome	5.00	2.30	.60
☐ 95 Doug Jennings	3.00	1.35	.40
☐ 96 Luis Lopez	3.00	1.35	.40
☐ 97 John Mabry	4.00	1.80	.50
☐ 98 Rondell White	5.00	2.30	.60
☐ 99 J.T. Snow	3.00	1.35	.40
☐ 100 Vic Darensbourg	3.00	1.35	.40

1994 Signature Rookies Bonus Signature

Randomly inserted in packs, this 10-card standard-size set features on its fronts full-bleed color action shots. Marbleized green stripes accent the pictures on the left and bottom. In these green stripes appear the production figures ("of 3,250") and the player's name, both in gold foil. The autograph is inscribed across the picture in blue ink. On a background consisting of a ghosted version of the front photo, the backs have a color headshot in the upper left corner, with the remainder of the back filled with biography, statistics, and player profile.

	MINT	EXC	G-VG
COMPLETE SET (10)	70.00	32.00	8.75
COMMON CARD (1-10)	6.00	2.70	.75
☐ 1 Matt Beaumont	10.00	4.50	1.25
☐ 2 Yates Hall	6.00	2.70	.75
☐ 3 Jed Hansen	6.00	2.70	.75
☐ 4 Ryan Helms	12.00	5.50	1.50
☐ 5 Russ Johnson	12.00	5.50	1.50
☐ 6 Carlton Loewer	8.00	3.60	1.00
☐ 7 Darrell Nicholas	7.00	3.10	.85
☐ 8 Paul O'Malley	7.00	3.10	.85
☐ 9 Jeremy Powell	10.00	4.50	1.25
☐ 10 Scott Shores	7.00	3.10	.85

1994 Signature Rookies Flip Cards

Randomly inserted in packs, this 5-card standard-size set features full-bleed color action shots on both sides. Marbleized green stripes accent the pictures on the left and bottom. In these green stripes appear the production figures ("1 of 15,000") and the player's name, both in gold foil. The cards are unnumbered and checklisted below alphabetically according to the first player listed.

	MINT	EXC	G-VG
COMPLETE SET (5)	20.00	9.00	2.50
COMMON CARD (1-5)	2.00	.90	.25
☐ 1 Craig Griffey Ken Griffey Sr.	2.50	1.15	.30
☐ 2 Craig Griffey Ken Griffey Jr.	6.00	2.70	.75
☐ 3 Ken Griffey Jr. Ken Griffey Sr.	2.00	.90	.25
☐ 4 Reid Ryan Nolan Ryan	6.00	2.70	.75
☐ 5 Paul Wilson Phil Nevin	7.00	3.10	.85

1994 Signature Rookies Flip Cards Signature

Randomly inserted in Signature Rookie Draft Picks baseball packs, this 9-card standard-size, autograph set features full-bleed color action shots on both sides. Marbleized green stripes accent the pictures on the left and bottom. In these green stripes appear the production figures ("1 of 15,000") and the player's name, both in gold foil. Individual autographs appear across the photo. Instead of inserting an autographed card, a individually numbered certificate was inserted to be redeemed for those cards featuring the autographs of Nolan Ryan and Ken Griffey Jr. Ryan signed 1,000 of the Nolan/Reid cards and Ken Jr. signed 500 picturing him with Ken Sr. and 500 with brother Craig. Phil Nevin signed 1,050 cards, Reid Ryan 2,100, Craig Griffey signed 2,000 (1000 with Ken Jr. and 1000 with Ken Sr.) and Ken Sr. signed 2000 (1000 with Craig and 1000 with Ken Jr.). The cards are unnumbered and checklisted below alphabetically according to the first player listed.

	MINT	EXC	G-VG
COMPLETE SET (9)	900.00	400.00	115.00
COMMON CARD (1-9)	18.00	8.00	2.30
☐ AU1 Craig Griffey AU Ken Griffey Sr.	18.00	8.00	2.30
☐ AU2 Craig Griffey AU Ken Griffey Jr.	20.00	9.00	2.50
☐ AU3 Ken Griffey Sr. AU Craig Griffey	20.00	9.00	2.50
☐ AU4 Ken Griffey Sr. AU Ken Griffey Jr.	25.00	11.50	3.10
☐ AU5 Ken Griffey Jr. AU Craig Griffey	300.00	135.00	38.00
☐ AU6 Ken Griffey Jr. AU Ken Griffey Sr.	300.00	135.00	38.00
☐ AU7 Nolan Ryan AU Reid Ryan	350.00	160.00	45.00
☐ AU8 Reid Ryan AU Nolan Ryan	30.00	13.50	3.80
☐ AU9 Phil Nevin AU Paul Wilson	35.00	16.00	4.40

1994 Signature Rookies Top Prospects

Randomly inserted in packs, this 5-card standard-size set features on its fronts full-bleed color action shots. Marbleized green stripes accent the pictures on the left and bottom. In these green stripes appear the production figures ("1 of 20,000") and the player's name, both in gold foil. On a background consisting of a ghosted version of the front photo, the backs have a color headshot in the upper left corner, with the remainder of the back filled with biography, statistics, and player profile. In production, numbering errors occurred, resulting in each players' cards having two different numbers (T1/T6; T2/T7; T3/T8; T4/T9; T5/T10). There is no added premium to any of the errors.

	MINT	EXC	G-VG
COMPLETE SET (5)	12.00	5.50	1.50
COMMON CARD (T1-T5)	1.50	.65	.19
☐ T1 Scott Ruffcorn	1.50	.65	.19
☐ T2 Brad Woodall	1.50	.65	.19
☐ T3 Andrew Lorraine	2.50	1.15	.30
☐ T4 LaTroy Hawkins	3.00	1.35	.40
☐ T5 Alan Benes	4.00	1.80	.50

1994 Signature Rookies Top Prospects Signature

Randomly inserted in packs, this 5-card standard-size set features on its fronts full-bleed color action shots. Marbleized green stripes accent the pictures on the left and bottom. In these green stripes appear the production figures ("1 of 2,100") and the player's name, both in gold foil. The autograph is inscribed across the picture in blue ink. On a background consisting of a ghosted version of the front photo, the backs have a color headshot in the upper left corner, with the remainder of the back filled with biography, statistics, and player profile.

	MINT	EXC	G-VG
COMPLETE SET (5)	100.00	45.00	12.50
COMMON CARD (T1-T5)	20.00	9.00	2.50
☐ T1 Scott Ruffcorn	20.00	9.00	2.50
☐ T2 Brad Woodall	20.00	9.00	2.50
☐ T3 Andrew Lorraine	25.00	11.50	3.10
☐ T4 LaTroy Hawkins	30.00	13.50	3.80
☐ T5 Alan Benes	40.00	18.00	5.00

1994 Sportflics

Each of the 193 "Magic Motion" cards features two images, which alternate when the card is viewed from different angles and creates the illusion of movement. Cards 176-193 are Starflics featuring top stars. The two commemorative cards, featuring Cliff Floyd and Paul Molitor, were inserted at a rate of one in every 360 packs.

	MINT	EXC	G-VG
COMPLETE SET (193)	25.00	11.50	3.10
COMMON CARD (1-193)	.10	.05	.01
☐ 1 Lenny Dykstra	.20	.09	.03
☐ 2 Mike Stanley	.10	.05	.01
☐ 3 Alex Fernandez	.20	.09	.03
☐ 4 Mark McGwire UER (name spelled McGuire on front)	.20	.09	.03
☐ 5 Eric Karros	.15	.07	.02
☐ 6 David Justice	.40	.18	.05
☐ 7 Jeff Bagwell	1.50	.65	.19
☐ 8 Darren Lewis	.10	.05	.01
☐ 9 David McCarty	.15	.07	.02
☐ 10 Albert Belle	1.00	.45	.13
☐ 11 Ben McDonald	.15	.07	.02
☐ 12 Joe Carter	.40	.18	.05
☐ 13 Benito Santiago	.10	.05	.01
☐ 14 Rob Dibble	.10	.05	.01
☐ 15 Roger Clemens	.60	.25	.08
☐ 16 Travis Fryman	.25	.11	.03
☐ 17 Doug Drabek	.20	.09	.03
☐ 18 Jay Buhner	.15	.07	.02
☐ 19 Orlando Merced	.15	.07	.02
☐ 20 Ryan Klesko	.50	.23	.06
☐ 21 Chuck Finley	.10	.05	.01
☐ 22 Dante Bichette	.20	.09	.03
☐ 23 Wally Joyner	.15	.07	.02
☐ 24 Robin Yount	.40	.18	.05
☐ 25 Tony Gwynn	.60	.25	.08
☐ 26 Allen Watson	.10	.05	.01
☐ 27 Rick Wilkins	.10	.05	.01
☐ 28 Gary Sheffield	.20	.09	.03
☐ 29 John Burkett	.15	.07	.02
☐ 30 Randy Johnson	.20	.09	.03
☐ 31 Roberto Alomar	.60	.25	.08
☐ 32 Fred McGriff	.40	.18	.05
☐ 33 Ozzie Guillen	.10	.05	.01
☐ 34 Jimmy Key	.15	.07	.02
☐ 35 Juan Gonzalez	1.00	.45	.13
☐ 36 Wil Cordero	.20	.09	.03
☐ 37 Aaron Sele	.25	.11	.03
☐ 38 Mark Langston	.20	.09	.03
☐ 39 David Cone	.20	.09	.03
☐ 40 John Jaha	.10	.05	.01
☐ 41 Ozzie Smith	.60	.25	.08
☐ 42 Kirby Puckett	1.25	.55	.16
☐ 43 Kenny Lofton	.75	.35	.09
☐ 44 Mike Mussina	.40	.18	.05
☐ 45 Ryne Sandberg	1.00	.45	.13
☐ 46 Robby Thompson	.10	.05	.01
☐ 47 Bryan Harvey	.15	.07	.02
☐ 48 Marquis Grissom	.20	.09	.03
☐ 49 Bobby Bonilla	.20	.09	.03
☐ 50 Dennis Eckersley	.20	.09	.03
☐ 51 Curt Schilling	.10	.05	.01
☐ 52 Andy Benes	.15	.07	.02
☐ 53 Greg Maddux	.60	.25	.08
☐ 54 Bill Swift	.10	.05	.01
☐ 55 Andres Galarraga	.20	.09	.03
☐ 56 Tony Phillips	.10	.05	.01
☐ 57 Darryl Hamilton	.10	.05	.01
☐ 58 Duane Ward	.10	.05	.01
☐ 59 Bernie Williams	.15	.07	.02
☐ 60 Steve Avery	.20	.09	.03
☐ 61 Eduardo Perez	.15	.07	.02
☐ 62 Jeff Conine	.20	.09	.03
☐ 63 Dave Winfield	.20	.09	.03
☐ 64 Phil Plantier	.15	.07	.02
☐ 65 Ray Lankford	.20	.09	.03
☐ 66 Robin Ventura	.15	.07	.02
☐ 67 Mike Piazza	1.50	.65	.19
☐ 68 Jason Bere	.40	.18	.05
☐ 69 Cal Ripken	2.25	1.00	.30
☐ 70 Frank Thomas	3.00	1.35	.40
☐ 71 Carlos Baerga	.40	.18	.05
☐ 72 Darryl Kile	.15	.07	.02
☐ 73 Ruben Sierra	.20	.09	.03
☐ 74 Gregg Jefferies	.20	.09	.03
☐ 75 John Olerud	.20	.09	.03
☐ 76 Andy Van Slyke	.20	.09	.03
☐ 77 Larry Walker	.20	.09	.03
☐ 78 Cecil Fielder	.20	.09	.03
☐ 79 Andre Dawson	.20	.09	.03
☐ 80 Tom Glavine	.20	.09	.03
☐ 81 Sammy Sosa	.20	.09	.03
☐ 82 Charlie Hayes	.15	.07	.02
☐ 83 Chuck Knoblauch	.20	.09	.03
☐ 84 Kevin Appier	.15	.07	.02
☐ 85 Dean Palmer	.15	.07	.02
☐ 86 Royce Clayton	.15	.07	.02
☐ 87 Moises Alou	.20	.09	.03
☐ 88 Ivan Rodriguez	.20	.09	.03
☐ 89 Tim Salmon	.40	.18	.05
☐ 90 Ron Gant	.15	.07	.02
☐ 91 Barry Bonds	1.25	.55	.16
☐ 92 Jack McDowell	.20	.09	.03
☐ 93 Alan Trammell	.20	.09	.03
☐ 94 Dwight Gooden	.10	.05	.01
☐ 95 Jay Bell	.15	.07	.02
☐ 96 Devon White	.10	.05	.01
☐ 97 Wilson Alvarez	.20	.09	.03
☐ 98 Jim Thome	.20	.09	.03
☐ 99 Ramon Martinez	.15	.07	.02
☐ 100 Kent Hrbek	.15	.07	.02
☐ 101 John Kruk	.10	.05	.01
☐ 102 Wade Boggs	.20	.09	.03
☐ 103 Greg Vaughn	.15	.07	.02
☐ 104 Tom Henke	.10	.05	.01
☐ 105 Brian Jordan	.15	.07	.02
☐ 106 Paul Molitor	.40	.18	.05
☐ 107 Cal Eldred	.15	.07	.02
☐ 108 Deion Sanders	.50	.23	.06
☐ 109 Barry Larkin	.20	.09	.03
☐ 110 Mike Greenwell	.15	.07	.02
☐ 111 Jeff Blauser	.15	.07	.02
☐ 112 Jose Rijo	.15	.07	.02
☐ 113 Pete Harnisch	.10	.05	.01

☐ 114 Chris Hoiles	.15	.07	.02
☐ 115 Edgar Martinez	.10	.05	.01
☐ 116 Juan Guzman	.15	.07	.02
☐ 117 Todd Zeile	.15	.07	.02
☐ 118 Danny Tartabull	.15	.07	.02
☐ 119 Chad Curtis	.15	.07	.02
☐ 120 Mark Grace	.20	.09	.03
☐ 121 J.T. Snow	.15	.07	.02
☐ 122 Mo Vaughn	.20	.09	.03
☐ 123 Lance Johnson	.10	.05	.01
☐ 124 Eric Davis	.10	.05	.01
☐ 125 Orel Hershiser	.15	.07	.02
☐ 126 Kevin Mitchell	.15	.07	.02
☐ 127 Don Mattingly	1.25	.55	.16
☐ 128 Darren Daulton	.20	.09	.03
☐ 129 Rod Beck	.15	.07	.02
☐ 130 Charles Nagy	.10	.05	.01
☐ 131 Mickey Tettleton	.15	.07	.02
☐ 132 Kevin Brown	.10	.05	.01
☐ 133 Pat Hentgen	.15	.07	.02
☐ 134 Terry Mulholland	.10	.05	.01
☐ 135 Steve Finley	.10	.05	.01
☐ 136 John Smoltz	.15	.07	.02
☐ 137 Frank Viola	.10	.05	.01
☐ 138 Jim Abbott	.20	.09	.03
☐ 139 Matt Williams	.50	.23	.06
☐ 140 Bernard Gilkey	.10	.05	.01
☐ 141 Jose Canseco	.40	.18	.05
☐ 142 Mark Whiten	.15	.07	.02
☐ 143 Ken Griffey Jr.	3.00	1.35	.40
☐ 144 Rafael Palmeiro	.20	.09	.03
☐ 145 Dave Hollins	.20	.09	.03
☐ 146 Will Clark	.40	.18	.05
☐ 147 Paul O'Neill	.15	.07	.02
☐ 148 Bobby Jones	.25	.11	.03
☐ 149 Butch Huskey	.10	.05	.01
☐ 150 Jeffrey Hammonds	.30	.14	.04
☐ 151 Manny Ramirez	.60	.25	.08
☐ 152 Bob Hamelin	.20	.09	.03
☐ 153 Kurt Abbott	.30	.14	.04
☐ 154 Scott Stahoviak	.10	.05	.01
☐ 155 Steve Hosey	.10	.05	.01
☐ 156 Salomon Torres	.15	.07	.02
☐ 157 Sterling Hitchcock	.15	.07	.02
☐ 158 Nigel Wilson	.15	.07	.02
☐ 159 Luis Lopez	.10	.05	.01
☐ 160 Chipper Jones	.40	.18	.05
☐ 161 Norberto Martin	.10	.05	.01
☐ 162 Raul Mondesi	1.00	.45	.13
☐ 163 Steve Karsay	.10	.05	.01
☐ 164 J.R. Phillips	.20	.09	.03
☐ 165 Marc Newfield	.20	.09	.03
☐ 166 Mark Hutton	.10	.05	.01
☐ 167 Curtis Pride	.30	.14	.04
☐ 168 Carl Everett	.15	.07	.02
☐ 169 Scott Ruffcorn	.20	.09	.03
☐ 170 Turk Wendell	.10	.05	.01
☐ 171 Jeff McNeely	.10	.05	.01
☐ 172 Javy Lopez	.30	.14	.04
☐ 173 Cliff Floyd	.50	.23	.06
☐ 174 Rondell White	.30	.14	.04
☐ 175 Scott Lydy	.10	.05	.01
☐ 176 Frank Thomas SF	1.50	.65	.19
☐ 177 Roberto Alomar SF	.30	.14	.04
☐ 178 Travis Fryman SF	.20	.09	.03
☐ 179 Cal Ripken SF	1.00	.45	.13
☐ 180 Chris Hoiles SF	.10	.05	.01
☐ 181 Ken Griffey Jr. SF	1.50	.65	.19
☐ 182 Juan Gonzalez SF	.50	.23	.06
☐ 183 Joe Carter SF	.20	.09	.03
☐ 184 Jack McDowell SF	.15	.07	.02
☐ 185 Fred McGriff SF	.15	.07	.02
☐ 186 Robby Thompson SF	.10	.05	.01
☐ 187 Matt Williams SF	.30	.14	.04
☐ 188 Jay Bell SF	.10	.05	.01
☐ 189 Mike Piazza SF	.75	.35	.09
☐ 190 Barry Bonds SF	.60	.25	.08
☐ 191 Lenny Dykstra SF	.15	.07	.02
☐ 192 David Justice SF	.15	.07	.02
☐ 193 Greg Maddux SF	.30	.14	.04
☐ NNO Cliff Floyd Special	35.00	16.00	4.40
☐ NNO Paul Molitor Special	35.00	16.00	4.40

1994 Sportflics Movers

These 12 standard-size chase cards were randomly inserted in retail foil packs and picture the game's top veterans. The insertion rate was one in every 24 packs. Fronts feature the dual image effect with the player's name appearing in dual image. The name "Movers" appears in a circular design off to the left of the player's name.

	MINT	EXC	G-VG
COMPLETE SET (12)	75.00	34.00	9.50
COMMON CARD (MM1-MM12)	2.50	1.15	.30
☐ MM1 Gregg Jefferies	2.50	1.15	.30
☐ MM2 Ryne Sandberg	13.00	5.75	1.65
☐ MM3 Cecil Fielder	2.50	1.15	.30
☐ MM4 Kirby Puckett	15.00	6.75	1.90
☐ MM5 Tony Gwynn	10.00	4.50	1.25
☐ MM6 Andres Galarraga	2.50	1.15	.30
☐ MM7 Sammy Sosa	2.50	1.15	.30
☐ MM8 Rickey Henderson	2.50	1.15	.30
☐ MM9 Don Mattingly	15.00	6.75	1.90
☐ MM10 Joe Carter	6.00	2.70	.75
☐ MM11 Carlos Baerga	6.00	2.70	.75
☐ MM12 Lenny Dykstra	2.50	1.15	.30

1994 Sportflics Shakers

These 12 standard-size chase cards were randomly inserted in hobby foil packs and picture baseball's elite young players. The insertion rate was one in every 24 packs. Fronts feature the dual image effect with the

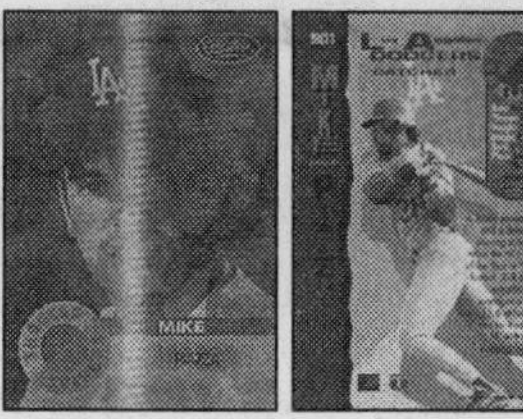

player's name also appearing as dual image. The name "Shakers" appears in a circular design off to the left of the player's name.

	MINT	EXC	G-VG
COMPLETE SET (12)	75.00	34.00	9.50
COMMON CARD (SH1-SH12)	2.00	.90	.25

	MINT	EXC	G-VG
☐ SH1 Kenny Lofton	10.00	4.50	1.25
☐ SH2 Tim Salmon	6.00	2.70	.75
☐ SH3 Jeff Bagwell	20.00	9.00	2.50
☐ SH4 Jason Bere	5.00	2.30	.60
☐ SH5 Salomon Torres	2.00	.90	.25
☐ SH6 Rondell White	4.00	1.80	.50
☐ SH7 Javy Lopez	4.00	1.80	.50
☐ SH8 Dean Palmer	2.00	.90	.25
☐ SH9 Jim Thome	3.00	1.35	.40
☐ SH10 J.T. Snow	2.00	.90	.25
☐ SH11 Mike Piazza	20.00	9.00	2.50
☐ SH12 Manny Ramirez	8.00	3.60	1.00

1991 Stadium Club

This 600-card standard size (2 1/2" by 3 1/2") set marked Topps first entry into the mass market with a premium quality set. The set features borderless full-color action photos on the front with the name of the player and the Topps Stadium club logo on the bottom of the card, while the back of the card has the basic biographical information as well as making use of the Fastball BARS system and an inset photo of the player's Topps rookie card. The set was issued in two series of 300 cards each. The cards are numbered on the back. Series II cards were also available at McDonald's restaurants in the Northeast at three cards per pack. Rookie Cards include Steve Avery, Juan Gonzalez, Ken Griffey Jr., Dave Justice, Nolan Ryan, Frank Thomas, Jeff Bagwell, Jeff Conine, Luis Gonzalez, Brian McRae, Pedro Munoz, and Phil Plantier.

	MINT	EXC	G-VG
COMPLETE SET (600)	150.00	70.00	19.00
COMPLETE SERIES 1 (300)	100.00	45.00	12.50
COMPLETE SERIES 2 (300)	50.00	23.00	6.25
COMMON CARD (1-300)	.15	.07	.02
COMMON CARD (301-600)	.15	.07	.02

	MINT	EXC	G-VG
☐ 1 Dave Stewart TUX	.20	.09	.03
☐ 2 Wally Joyner	.20	.09	.03
☐ 3 Shawon Dunston	.15	.07	.02
☐ 4 Darren Daulton	.50	.23	.06
☐ 5 Will Clark	2.00	.90	.25
☐ 6 Sammy Sosa	2.00	.90	.25
☐ 7 Dan Plesac	.15	.07	.02
☐ 8 Marquis Grissom	2.00	.90	.25
☐ 9 Erik Hanson	.15	.07	.02
☐ 10 Geno Petralli	.15	.07	.02
☐ 11 Jose Rijo	.20	.09	.03
☐ 12 Carlos Quintana	.15	.07	.02
☐ 13 Junior Ortiz	.15	.07	.02
☐ 14 Bob Walk	.15	.07	.02
☐ 15 Mike Macfarlane	.15	.07	.02
☐ 16 Eric Yelding	.15	.07	.02
☐ 17 Bryn Smith	.15	.07	.02
☐ 18 Bip Roberts	.15	.07	.02
☐ 19 Mike Scioscia	.15	.07	.02
☐ 20 Mark Williamson	.15	.07	.02
☐ 21 Don Mattingly	2.50	1.15	.30
☐ 22 John Franco	.20	.09	.03
☐ 23 Chet Lemon	.15	.07	.02
☐ 24 Tom Henke	.20	.09	.03
☐ 25 Jerry Browne	.15	.07	.02
☐ 26 David Justice	3.50	1.55	.45
☐ 27 Mark Langston	.30	.14	.04
☐ 28 Damon Berryhill	.15	.07	.02
☐ 29 Kevin Bass	.15	.07	.02
☐ 30 Scott Fletcher	.15	.07	.02
☐ 31 Moises Alou	3.00	1.35	.40
☐ 32 Dave Valle	.15	.07	.02
☐ 33 Jody Reed	.15	.07	.02
☐ 34 Dave West	.15	.07	.02
☐ 35 Kevin McReynolds	.15	.07	.02
☐ 36 Pat Combs	.15	.07	.02
☐ 37 Eric Davis	.20	.09	.03
☐ 38 Bret Saberhagen	.20	.09	.03
☐ 39 Stan Javier	.15	.07	.02
☐ 40 Chuck Cary	.15	.07	.02
☐ 41 Tony Phillips	.20	.09	.03
☐ 42 Lee Smith	.30	.14	.04
☐ 43 Tim Teufel	.15	.07	.02
☐ 44 Lance Dickson	.15	.07	.02
☐ 45 Greg Litton	.15	.07	.02
☐ 46 Teddy Higuera	.15	.07	.02
☐ 47 Edgar Martinez	.15	.07	.02
☐ 48 Steve Avery	2.50	1.15	.30
☐ 49 Walt Weiss	.15	.07	.02
☐ 50 David Segui	.15	.07	.02
☐ 51 Andy Benes	.50	.23	.06
☐ 52 Karl Rhodes	.15	.07	.02
☐ 53 Neal Heaton	.15	.07	.02
☐ 54 Danny Gladden	.15	.07	.02
☐ 55 Luis Rivera	.15	.07	.02
☐ 56 Kevin Brown	.15	.07	.02
☐ 57 Frank Thomas	24.00	11.00	3.00
☐ 58 Terry Mulholland	.15	.07	.02
☐ 59 Dick Schofield	.15	.07	.02
☐ 60 Ron Darling	.15	.07	.02

□ 61 Sandy Alomar Jr. .20 .09 .03
□ 62 Dave Stieb .20 .09 .03
□ 63 Alan Trammell .30 .14 .04
□ 64 Matt Nokes .15 .07 .02
□ 65 Lenny Harris .15 .07 .02
□ 66 Milt Thompson .15 .07 .02
□ 67 Storm Davis .15 .07 .02
□ 68 Joe Oliver .15 .07 .02
□ 69 Andres Galarraga .75 .35 .09
□ 70 Ozzie Guillen .15 .07 .02
□ 71 Ken Howell .15 .07 .02
□ 72 Garry Templeton .15 .07 .02
□ 73 Derrick May .20 .09 .03
□ 74 Xavier Hernandez .15 .07 .02
□ 75 Dave Parker .30 .14 .04
□ 76 Rick Aguilera .20 .09 .03
□ 77 Robby Thompson .20 .09 .03
□ 78 Pete Incaviglia .15 .07 .02
□ 79 Bob Welch .15 .07 .02
□ 80 Randy Milligan .15 .07 .02
□ 81 Chuck Finley .20 .09 .03
□ 82 Alvin Davis .15 .07 .02
□ 83 Tim Naehring .20 .09 .03
□ 84 Jay Bell .20 .09 .03
□ 85 Joe Magrane .15 .07 .02
□ 86 Howard Johnson .20 .09 .03
□ 87 Jack McDowell .75 .35 .09
□ 88 Kevin Seitzer .15 .07 .02
□ 89 Bruce Ruffin .15 .07 .02
□ 90 Fernando Valenzuela .15 .07 .02
□ 91 Terry Kennedy .15 .07 .02
□ 92 Barry Larkin .50 .23 .06
□ 93 Larry Walker 2.00 .90 .25
□ 94 Luis Salazar .15 .07 .02
□ 95 Gary Sheffield 1.50 .65 .19
□ 96 Bobby Witt .15 .07 .02
□ 97 Lonnie Smith .15 .07 .02
□ 98 Bryan Harvey .20 .09 .03
□ 99 Mookie Wilson .15 .07 .02
□ 100 Dwight Gooden .20 .09 .03
□ 101 Lou Whitaker .30 .14 .04
□ 102 Ron Karkovice .15 .07 .02
□ 103 Jesse Barfield .15 .07 .02
□ 104 Jose DeJesus .15 .07 .02
□ 105 Benito Santiago .20 .09 .03
□ 106 Brian Holman .15 .07 .02
□ 107 Rafael Ramirez .15 .07 .02
□ 108 Ellis Burks .20 .09 .03
□ 109 Mike Bielecki .15 .07 .02
□ 110 Kirby Puckett 2.50 1.15 .30
□ 111 Terry Shumpert .15 .07 .02
□ 112 Chuck Crim .15 .07 .02
□ 113 Todd Benzinger .15 .07 .02
□ 114 Brian Barnes .15 .07 .02
□ 115 Carlos Baerga 4.00 1.80 .50
□ 116 Kal Daniels .15 .07 .02
□ 117 Dave Johnson .15 .07 .02
□ 118 Andy Van Slyke .30 .14 .04
□ 119 John Burkett .75 .35 .09
□ 120 Rickey Henderson .75 .35 .09
□ 121 Tim Jones .15 .07 .02
□ 122 Daryl Irvine .15 .07 .02
□ 123 Ruben Sierra .75 .35 .09
□ 124 Jim Abbott .75 .35 .09
□ 125 Daryl Boston .15 .07 .02
□ 126 Greg Maddux 3.00 1.35 .40
□ 127 Von Hayes .15 .07 .02
□ 128 Mike Fitzgerald .15 .07 .02
□ 129 Wayne Edwards .15 .07 .02
□ 130 Greg Briley .15 .07 .02
□ 131 Rob Dibble .15 .07 .02
□ 132 Gene Larkin .15 .07 .02
□ 133 David Wells .15 .07 .02
□ 134 Steve Balboni .15 .07 .02
□ 135 Greg Vaughn .60 .25 .08
□ 136 Mark Davis .15 .07 .02
□ 137 Dave Rhode .15 .07 .02
□ 138 Eric Show .15 .07 .02
□ 139 Bobby Bonilla .50 .23 .06
□ 140 Dana Kiecker .15 .07 .02
□ 141 Gary Pettis .15 .07 .02
□ 142 Dennis Boyd .15 .07 .02
□ 143 Mike Benjamin .15 .07 .02
□ 144 Luis Polonia .20 .09 .03
□ 145 Doug Jones .15 .07 .02
□ 146 Al Newman .15 .07 .02
□ 147 Alex Fernandez 3.00 1.35 .40
□ 148 Bill Doran .15 .07 .02
□ 149 Kevin Elster .15 .07 .02
□ 150 Len Dykstra .60 .25 .08
□ 151 Mike Gallego .15 .07 .02
□ 152 Tim Belcher .15 .07 .02
□ 153 Jay Buhner .50 .23 .06
□ 154 Ozzie Smith UER 1.00 .45 .13
(Rookie card is 1979,
but card back says '78)
□ 155 Jose Canseco 2.00 .90 .25
□ 156 Gregg Olson .20 .09 .03
□ 157 Charlie O'Brien .15 .07 .02
□ 158 Frank Tanana .15 .07 .02
□ 159 George Brett 2.50 1.15 .30
□ 160 Jeff Huson .15 .07 .02
□ 161 Kevin Tapani .15 .07 .02
□ 162 Jerome Walton .15 .07 .02
□ 163 Charlie Hayes .20 .09 .03
□ 164 Chris Bosio .15 .07 .02
□ 165 Chris Sabo .20 .09 .03
□ 166 Lance Parrish .20 .09 .03
□ 167 Don Robinson .15 .07 .02
□ 168 Manny Lee .15 .07 .02
□ 169 Dennis Rasmussen .15 .07 .02
□ 170 Wade Boggs 1.00 .45 .13
□ 171 Bob Geren .15 .07 .02
□ 172 Mackey Sasser .15 .07 .02
□ 173 Julio Franco .20 .09 .03
□ 174 Otis Nixon .20 .09 .03
□ 175 Bert Blyleven .30 .14 .04
□ 176 Craig Biggio .50 .23 .06
□ 177 Eddie Murray .60 .25 .08
□ 178 Randy Tomlin .15 .07 .02
□ 179 Tino Martinez .20 .09 .03
□ 180 Carlton Fisk .50 .23 .06
□ 181 Dwight Smith .15 .07 .02
□ 182 Scott Garrelts .15 .07 .02
□ 183 Jim Gantner .15 .07 .02
□ 184 Dickie Thon .15 .07 .02
□ 185 John Farrell .15 .07 .02
□ 186 Cecil Fielder 1.00 .45 .13
□ 187 Glenn Braggs .15 .07 .02
□ 188 Allan Anderson .15 .07 .02
□ 189 Kurt Stillwell .15 .07 .02
□ 190 Jose Oquendo .15 .07 .02
□ 191 Joe Orsulak .15 .07 .02
□ 192 Ricky Jordan .15 .07 .02
□ 193 Kelly Downs .15 .07 .02
□ 194 Delino DeShields .75 .35 .09
□ 195 Omar Vizquel .15 .07 .02
□ 196 Mark Carreon .15 .07 .02
□ 197 Mike Harkey .15 .07 .02
□ 198 Jack Howell .15 .07 .02
□ 199 Lance Johnson .20 .09 .03
□ 200 Nolan Ryan TUX 12.00 5.50 1.50
□ 201 John Marzano .15 .07 .02
□ 202 Doug Drabek .30 .14 .04
□ 203 Mark Lemke .15 .07 .02
□ 204 Steve Sax .15 .07 .02

☐ 205 Greg Harris	.15	.07	.02
☐ 206 B.J. Surhoff	.15	.07	.02
☐ 207 Todd Burns	.15	.07	.02
☐ 208 Jose Gonzalez	.15	.07	.02
☐ 209 Mike Scott	.15	.07	.02
☐ 210 Dave Magadan	.15	.07	.02
☐ 211 Dante Bichette	1.50	.65	.19
☐ 212 Trevor Wilson	.15	.07	.02
☐ 213 Hector Villanueva	.15	.07	.02
☐ 214 Dan Pasqua	.15	.07	.02
☐ 215 Greg Colbrunn	.20	.09	.03
☐ 216 Mike Jeffcoat	.15	.07	.02
☐ 217 Harold Reynolds	.15	.07	.02
☐ 218 Paul O'Neill	.30	.14	.04
☐ 219 Mark Guthrie	.15	.07	.02
☐ 220 Barry Bonds	3.50	1.55	.45
☐ 221 Jimmy Key	.40	.18	.05
☐ 222 Billy Ripken	.15	.07	.02
☐ 223 Tom Pagnozzi	.15	.07	.02
☐ 224 Bo Jackson	1.50	.65	.19
☐ 225 Sid Fernandez	.20	.09	.03
☐ 226 Mike Marshall	.15	.07	.02
☐ 227 John Kruk	.40	.18	.05
☐ 228 Mike Fetters	.15	.07	.02
☐ 229 Eric Anthony	.20	.09	.03
☐ 230 Ryne Sandberg	2.00	.90	.25
☐ 231 Carney Lansford	.20	.09	.03
☐ 232 Melido Perez	.15	.07	.02
☐ 233 Jose Lind	.15	.07	.02
☐ 234 Darryl Hamilton	.20	.09	.03
☐ 235 Tom Browning	.15	.07	.02
☐ 236 Spike Owen	.15	.07	.02
☐ 237 Juan Gonzalez	10.00	4.50	1.25
☐ 238 Felix Fermin	.15	.07	.02
☐ 239 Keith Miller	.15	.07	.02
☐ 240 Mark Gubicza	.15	.07	.02
☐ 241 Kent Anderson	.15	.07	.02
☐ 242 Alvaro Espinoza	.15	.07	.02
☐ 243 Dale Murphy	.15	.07	.02
☐ 244 Orel Hershiser	.20	.09	.03
☐ 245 Paul Molitor	1.00	.45	.13
☐ 246 Eddie Whitson	.15	.07	.02
☐ 247 Joe Girardi	.15	.07	.02
☐ 248 Kent Hrbek	.20	.09	.03
☐ 249 Bill Sampen	.15	.07	.02
☐ 250 Kevin Mitchell	.20	.09	.03
☐ 251 Mariano Duncan	.15	.07	.02
☐ 252 Scott Bradley	.15	.07	.02
☐ 253 Mike Greenwell	.20	.09	.03
☐ 254 Tom Gordon	.20	.09	.03
☐ 255 Todd Zeile	.15	.07	.02
☐ 256 Bobby Thigpen	.15	.07	.02
☐ 257 Gregg Jefferies	1.00	.45	.13
☐ 258 Kenny Rogers	.15	.07	.02
☐ 259 Shane Mack	.20	.09	.03
☐ 260 Zane Smith	.15	.07	.02
☐ 261 Mitch Williams	.20	.09	.03
☐ 262 Jim Deshaies	.15	.07	.02
☐ 263 Dave Winfield	1.00	.45	.13
☐ 264 Ben McDonald	1.25	.55	.16
☐ 265 Randy Ready	.15	.07	.02
☐ 266 Pat Borders	.15	.07	.02
☐ 267 Jose Uribe	.15	.07	.02
☐ 268 Derek Lilliquist	.15	.07	.02
☐ 269 Greg Brock	.15	.07	.02
☐ 270 Ken Griffey Jr.	20.00	9.00	2.50
☐ 271 Jeff Gray	.15	.07	.02
☐ 272 Danny Tartabull	.20	.09	.03
☐ 273 Denny Martinez	.20	.09	.03
☐ 274 Robin Ventura	1.50	.65	.19
☐ 275 Randy Myers	.20	.09	.03
☐ 276 Jack Daugherty	.15	.07	.02
☐ 277 Greg Gagne	.15	.07	.02
☐ 278 Jay Howell	.15	.07	.02
☐ 279 Mike LaValliere	.15	.07	.02
☐ 280 Rex Hudler	.15	.07	.02
☐ 281 Mike Simms	.15	.07	.02
☐ 282 Kevin Maas	.15	.07	.02
☐ 283 Jeff Ballard	.15	.07	.02
☐ 284 Dave Henderson	.15	.07	.02
☐ 285 Pete O'Brien	.15	.07	.02
☐ 286 Brook Jacoby	.15	.07	.02
☐ 287 Mike Henneman	.15	.07	.02
☐ 288 Greg Olson	.15	.07	.02
☐ 289 Greg Myers	.15	.07	.02
☐ 290 Mark Grace	.75	.35	.09
☐ 291 Shawn Abner	.15	.07	.02
☐ 292 Frank Viola	.20	.09	.03
☐ 293 Lee Stevens	.15	.07	.02
☐ 294 Jason Grimsley	.15	.07	.02
☐ 295 Matt Williams	2.50	1.15	.30
☐ 296 Ron Robinson	.15	.07	.02
☐ 297 Tom Brunansky	.15	.07	.02
☐ 298 Checklist 1-100	.15	.07	.02
☐ 299 Checklist 101-200	.15	.07	.02
☐ 300 Checklist 201-300	.15	.07	.02
☐ 301 Darryl Strawberry	.30	.14	.04
☐ 302 Bud Black	.15	.07	.02
☐ 303 Harold Baines	.20	.09	.03
☐ 304 Roberto Alomar	2.50	1.15	.30
☐ 305 Norm Charlton	.15	.07	.02
☐ 306 Gary Thurman	.15	.07	.02
☐ 307 Mike Felder	.15	.07	.02
☐ 308 Tony Gwynn	2.00	.90	.25
☐ 309 Roger Clemens	2.00	.90	.25
☐ 310 Andre Dawson	.50	.23	.06
☐ 311 Scott Radinsky	.15	.07	.02
☐ 312 Bob Melvin	.15	.07	.02
☐ 313 Kirk McCaskill	.15	.07	.02
☐ 314 Pedro Guerrero	.20	.09	.03
☐ 315 Walt Terrell	.15	.07	.02
☐ 316 Sam Horn	.15	.07	.02
☐ 317 Wes Chamberlain UER (Card listed as 1989 Debut card, should be 1990)	.15	.07	.02
☐ 318 Pedro Munoz	.40	.18	.05
☐ 319 Roberto Kelly	.40	.18	.05
☐ 320 Mark Portugal	.15	.07	.02
☐ 321 Tim McIntosh	.15	.07	.02
☐ 322 Jesse Orosco	.15	.07	.02
☐ 323 Gary Green	.15	.07	.02
☐ 324 Greg Harris	.15	.07	.02
☐ 325 Hubie Brooks	.15	.07	.02
☐ 326 Chris Nabholz	.15	.07	.02
☐ 327 Terry Pendleton	.15	.07	.02
☐ 328 Eric King	.15	.07	.02
☐ 329 Chili Davis	.20	.09	.03
☐ 330 Anthony Telford	.15	.07	.02
☐ 331 Kelly Gruber	.15	.07	.02
☐ 332 Dennis Eckersley	.30	.14	.04
☐ 333 Mel Hall	.15	.07	.02
☐ 334 Bob Kipper	.15	.07	.02
☐ 335 Willie McGee	.20	.09	.03
☐ 336 Steve Olin	.15	.07	.02
☐ 337 Steve Buechele	.15	.07	.02
☐ 338 Scott Leius	.15	.07	.02
☐ 339 Hal Morris	.20	.09	.03
☐ 340 Jose Offerman	.20	.09	.03
☐ 341 Kent Mercker	1.00	.45	.13
☐ 342 Ken Griffey	.20	.09	.03
☐ 343 Pete Harnisch	.20	.09	.03
☐ 344 Kirk Gibson	.20	.09	.03
☐ 345 Dave Smith	.15	.07	.02
☐ 346 Dave Martinez	.15	.07	.02
☐ 347 Atlee Hammaker	.15	.07	.02
☐ 348 Brian Downing	.15	.07	.02

☐ 349 Todd Hundley .... .20 .09 .03
☐ 350 Candy Maldonado .... .15 .07 .02
☐ 351 Dwight Evans .... .20 .09 .03
☐ 352 Steve Searcy .... .15 .07 .02
☐ 353 Gary Gaetti .... .15 .07 .02
☐ 354 Jeff Reardon .... .20 .09 .03
☐ 355 Travis Fryman .... 5.00 2.30 .60
☐ 356 Dave Righetti .... .15 .07 .02
☐ 357 Fred McGriff .... 1.50 .65 .19
☐ 358 Don Slaught .... .15 .07 .02
☐ 359 Gene Nelson .... .15 .07 .02
☐ 360 Billy Spiers .... .15 .07 .02
☐ 361 Lee Guetterman .... .15 .07 .02
☐ 362 Darren Lewis .... .20 .09 .03
☐ 363 Duane Ward .... .20 .09 .03
☐ 364 Lloyd Moseby .... .15 .07 .02
☐ 365 John Smoltz .... .50 .23 .06
☐ 366 Felix Jose .... .20 .09 .03
☐ 367 David Cone .... .60 .25 .08
☐ 368 Wally Backman .... .15 .07 .02
☐ 369 Jeff Montgomery .... .20 .09 .03
☐ 370 Rich Garces .... .15 .07 .02
☐ 371 Billy Hatcher .... .15 .07 .02
☐ 372 Bill Swift .... .20 .09 .03
☐ 373 Jim Eisenreich .... .15 .07 .02
☐ 374 Rob Ducey .... .15 .07 .02
☐ 375 Tim Crews .... .15 .07 .02
☐ 376 Steve Finley .... .15 .07 .02
☐ 377 Jeff Blauser .... .20 .09 .03
☐ 378 Willie Wilson .... .15 .07 .02
☐ 379 Gerald Perry .... .15 .07 .02
☐ 380 Jose Mesa .... .15 .07 .02
☐ 381 Pat Kelly .... .40 .18 .05
☐ 382 Matt Merullo .... .15 .07 .02
☐ 383 Ivan Calderon .... .15 .07 .02
☐ 384 Scott Chiamparino .... .15 .07 .02
☐ 385 Lloyd McClendon .... .15 .07 .02
☐ 386 Dave Bergman .... .15 .07 .02
☐ 387 Ed Sprague .... .15 .07 .02
☐ 388 Jeff Bagwell 15.00 6.75 1.90
☐ 389 Brett Butler .... .20 .09 .03
☐ 390 Larry Andersen .... .15 .07 .02
☐ 391 Glenn Davis .... .15 .07 .02
☐ 392 Alex Cole UER .... .15 .07 .02
(Front photo actually
Otis Nixon)
☐ 393 Mike Heath .... .15 .07 .02
☐ 394 Danny Darwin .... .15 .07 .02
☐ 395 Steve Lake .... .15 .07 .02
☐ 396 Tim Layana .... .15 .07 .02
☐ 397 Terry Leach .... .15 .07 .02
☐ 398 Bill Wegman .... .15 .07 .02
☐ 399 Mark McGwire .... .75 .35 .09
☐ 400 Mike Boddicker .... .15 .07 .02
☐ 401 Steve Howe .... .15 .07 .02
☐ 402 Bernard Gilkey .... .20 .09 .03
☐ 403 Thomas Howard .... .15 .07 .02
☐ 404 Rafael Belliard .... .15 .07 .02
☐ 405 Tom Candiotti .... .15 .07 .02
☐ 406 Rene Gonzales .... .15 .07 .02
☐ 407 Chuck McElroy .... .15 .07 .02
☐ 408 Paul Sorrento .... .20 .09 .03
☐ 409 Randy Johnson .... 1.50 .65 .19
☐ 410 Brady Anderson .... .20 .09 .03
☐ 411 Dennis Cook .... .15 .07 .02
☐ 412 Mickey Tettleton .... .20 .09 .03
☐ 413 Mike Stanton .... .15 .07 .02
☐ 414 Ken Oberkfell .... .15 .07 .02
☐ 415 Rick Honeycutt .... .15 .07 .02
☐ 416 Nelson Santovenia .... .15 .07 .02
☐ 417 Bob Tewksbury .... .20 .09 .03
☐ 418 Brent Mayne .... .15 .07 .02
☐ 419 Steve Farr .... .15 .07 .02
☐ 420 Phil Stephenson .... .15 .07 .02
☐ 421 Jeff Russell .... .15 .07 .02
☐ 422 Chris James .... .15 .07 .02
☐ 423 Tim Leary .... .15 .07 .02
☐ 424 Gary Carter .... .30 .14 .04
☐ 425 Glenallen Hill .... .15 .07 .02
☐ 426 Matt Young UER .... .15 .07 .02
(Card mentions 83T/Tr
as RC, but 84T shown)
☐ 427 Sid Bream .... .15 .07 .02
☐ 428 Greg Swindell .... .15 .07 .02
☐ 429 Scott Aldred .... .15 .07 .02
☐ 430 Cal Ripken .... 4.00 1.80 .50
☐ 431 Bill Landrum .... .15 .07 .02
☐ 432 Earnest Riles .... .15 .07 .02
☐ 433 Danny Jackson .... .15 .07 .02
☐ 434 Casey Candaele .... .15 .07 .02
☐ 435 Ken Hill .... .75 .35 .09
☐ 436 Jaime Navarro .... .15 .07 .02
☐ 437 Lance Blankenship .... .15 .07 .02
☐ 438 Randy Velarde .... .15 .07 .02
☐ 439 Frank DiPino .... .15 .07 .02
☐ 440 Carl Nichols .... .15 .07 .02
☐ 441 Jeff M. Robinson .... .15 .07 .02
☐ 442 Deion Sanders .... 2.00 .90 .25
☐ 443 Vicente Palacios .... .15 .07 .02
☐ 444 Devon White .... .20 .09 .03
☐ 445 John Cerutti .... .15 .07 .02
☐ 446 Tracy Jones .... .15 .07 .02
☐ 447 Jack Morris .... .30 .14 .04
☐ 448 Mitch Webster .... .15 .07 .02
☐ 449 Bob Ojeda .... .15 .07 .02
☐ 450 Oscar Azocar .... .15 .07 .02
☐ 451 Luis Aquino .... .15 .07 .02
☐ 452 Mark Whiten .... .30 .14 .04
☐ 453 Stan Belinda .... .15 .07 .02
☐ 454 Ron Gant .... .60 .25 .08
☐ 455 Jose DeLeon .... .15 .07 .02
☐ 456 Mark Salas UER .... .15 .07 .02
(Back has 85T photo,
but calls it 86T)
☐ 457 Junior Felix .... .15 .07 .02
☐ 458 Wally Whitehurst .... .15 .07 .02
☐ 459 Phil Plantier .... 2.00 .90 .25
☐ 460 Juan Berenguer .... .15 .07 .02
☐ 461 Franklin Stubbs .... .15 .07 .02
☐ 462 Joe Boever .... .15 .07 .02
☐ 463 Tim Wallach .... .15 .07 .02
☐ 464 Mike Moore .... .15 .07 .02
☐ 465 Albert Belle .... 6.00 2.70 .75
☐ 466 Mike Witt .... .15 .07 .02
☐ 467 Craig Worthington .... .15 .07 .02
☐ 468 Jerald Clark .... .15 .07 .02
☐ 469 Scott Terry .... .15 .07 .02
☐ 470 Milt Cuyler .... .15 .07 .02
☐ 471 John Smiley .... .15 .07 .02
☐ 472 Charles Nagy .... .50 .23 .06
☐ 473 Alan Mills .... .15 .07 .02
☐ 474 John Russell .... .15 .07 .02
☐ 475 Bruce Hurst .... .15 .07 .02
☐ 476 Andujar Cedeno .... .75 .35 .09
☐ 477 Dave Eiland .... .15 .07 .02
☐ 478 Brian McRae .... 2.00 .90 .25
☐ 479 Mike LaCoss .... .15 .07 .02
☐ 480 Chris Gwynn .... .15 .07 .02
☐ 481 Jamie Moyer .... .15 .07 .02
☐ 482 John Olerud .... 2.00 .90 .25
☐ 483 Efrain Valdez .... .15 .07 .02
☐ 484 Sil Campusano .... .15 .07 .02
☐ 485 Pascual Perez .... .15 .07 .02
☐ 486 Gary Redus .... .15 .07 .02
☐ 487 Andy Hawkins .... .15 .07 .02
☐ 488 Cory Snyder .... .15 .07 .02

	No.	Player			
☐	489	Chris Hoiles	.75	.35	.09
☐	490	Ron Hassey	.15	.07	.02
☐	491	Gary Wayne	.15	.07	.02
☐	492	Mark Lewis	.15	.07	.02
☐	493	Scott Coolbaugh	.15	.07	.02
☐	494	Gerald Young	.15	.07	.02
☐	495	Juan Samuel	.15	.07	.02
☐	496	Willie Fraser	.15	.07	.02
☐	497	Jeff Treadway	.15	.07	.02
☐	498	Vince Coleman	.15	.07	.02
☐	499	Cris Carpenter	.15	.07	.02
☐	500	Jack Clark	.20	.09	.03
☐	501	Kevin Appier	1.25	.55	.16
☐	502	Rafael Palmeiro	1.25	.55	.16
☐	503	Hensley Meulens	.15	.07	.02
☐	504	George Bell	.20	.09	.03
☐	505	Tony Pena	.15	.07	.02
☐	506	Roger McDowell	.15	.07	.02
☐	507	Luis Sojo	.15	.07	.02
☐	508	Mike Schooler	.15	.07	.02
☐	509	Robin Yount	1.00	.45	.13
☐	510	Jack Armstrong	.15	.07	.02
☐	511	Rick Cerone	.15	.07	.02
☐	512	Curt Wilkerson	.15	.07	.02
☐	513	Joe Carter	1.50	.65	.19
☐	514	Tim Burke	.15	.07	.02
☐	515	Tony Fernandez	.20	.09	.03
☐	516	Ramon Martinez	.50	.23	.06
☐	517	Tim Hulett	.15	.07	.02
☐	518	Terry Steinbach	.20	.09	.03
☐	519	Pete Smith	.15	.07	.02
☐	520	Ken Caminiti	.20	.09	.03
☐	521	Shawn Boskie	.15	.07	.02
☐	522	Mike Pagliarulo	.15	.07	.02
☐	523	Tim Raines	.30	.14	.04
☐	524	Alfredo Griffin	.15	.07	.02
☐	525	Henry Cotto	.15	.07	.02
☐	526	Mike Stanley	.15	.07	.02
☐	527	Charlie Leibrandt	.15	.07	.02
☐	528	Jeff King	.20	.09	.03
☐	529	Eric Plunk	.15	.07	.02
☐	530	Tom Lampkin	.15	.07	.02
☐	531	Steve Bedrosian	.15	.07	.02
☐	532	Tom Herr	.15	.07	.02
☐	533	Craig Lefferts	.15	.07	.02
☐	534	Jeff Reed	.15	.07	.02
☐	535	Mickey Morandini	.15	.07	.02
☐	536	Greg Cadaret	.15	.07	.02
☐	537	Ray Lankford	2.00	.90	.25
☐	538	John Candelaria	.15	.07	.02
☐	539	Rob Deer	.15	.07	.02
☐	540	Brad Arnsberg	.15	.07	.02
☐	541	Mike Sharperson	.15	.07	.02
☐	542	Jeff D. Robinson	.15	.07	.02
☐	543	Mo Vaughn	5.00	2.30	.60
☐	544	Jeff Parrett	.15	.07	.02
☐	545	Willie Randolph	.20	.09	.03
☐	546	Herm Winningham	.15	.07	.02
☐	547	Jeff Innis	.15	.07	.02
☐	548	Chuck Knoblauch	3.00	1.35	.40
☐	549	Tommy Greene UER (Born in North Carolina, not South Carolina)	.20	.09	.03
☐	550	Jeff Hamilton	.15	.07	.02
☐	551	Barry Jones	.15	.07	.02
☐	552	Ken Dayley	.15	.07	.02
☐	553	Rick Dempsey	.15	.07	.02
☐	554	Greg Smith	.15	.07	.02
☐	555	Mike Devereaux	.20	.09	.03
☐	556	Keith Comstock	.15	.07	.02
☐	557	Paul Faries	.15	.07	.02
☐	558	Tom Glavine	1.00	.45	.13
☐	559	Craig Grebeck	.15	.07	.02
☐	560	Scott Erickson	.20	.09	.03
☐	561	Joel Skinner	.15	.07	.02
☐	562	Mike Morgan	.15	.07	.02
☐	563	Dave Gallagher	.15	.07	.02
☐	564	Todd Stottlemyre	.15	.07	.02
☐	565	Rich Rodriguez	.15	.07	.02
☐	566	Craig Wilson	.15	.07	.02
☐	567	Jeff Brantley	.15	.07	.02
☐	568	Scott Kamieniecki	.15	.07	.02
☐	569	Steve Decker	.15	.07	.02
☐	570	Juan Agosto	.15	.07	.02
☐	571	Tommy Gregg	.15	.07	.02
☐	572	Kevin Wickander	.15	.07	.02
☐	573	Jamie Quirk UER (Rookie card is 1976, but card back is 1990)	.15	.07	.02
☐	574	Jerry Don Gleaton	.15	.07	.02
☐	575	Chris Hammond	.20	.09	.03
☐	576	Luis Gonzalez	1.25	.55	.16
☐	577	Russ Swan	.15	.07	.02
☐	578	Jeff Conine	3.00	1.35	.40
☐	579	Charlie Hough	.20	.09	.03
☐	580	Jeff Kunkel	.15	.07	.02
☐	581	Darrel Akerfelds	.15	.07	.02
☐	582	Jeff Manto	.15	.07	.02
☐	583	Alejandro Pena	.15	.07	.02
☐	584	Mark Davidson	.15	.07	.02
☐	585	Bob MacDonald	.15	.07	.02
☐	586	Paul Assenmacher	.15	.07	.02
☐	587	Dan Wilson	.15	.07	.02
☐	588	Tom Bolton	.15	.07	.02
☐	589	Brian Harper	.15	.07	.02
☐	590	John Habyan	.15	.07	.02
☐	591	John Orton	.15	.07	.02
☐	592	Mark Gardner	.15	.07	.02
☐	593	Turner Ward	.50	.23	.06
☐	594	Bob Patterson	.15	.07	.02
☐	595	Ed Nunez	.15	.07	.02
☐	596	Gary Scott UER (Major League Batting Record should be Minor League)	.15	.07	.02
☐	597	Scott Bankhead	.15	.07	.02
☐	598	Checklist 301-400	.15	.07	.02
☐	599	Checklist 401-500	.15	.07	.02
☐	600	Checklist 501-600	.15	.07	.02

1992 Stadium Club

The 1992 Topps Stadium Club baseball card set consists of 900 standard-size (2 1/2" by 3 1/2") cards issued in three series of 300 cards each. The glossy color player photos on the fronts are full-bleed.

The "Topps Stadium Club" logo is superimposed at the bottom of the card face, with the player's name appearing immediately below the logo. Some cards in the set have the Stadium Club logo printed upside down. The backs display a mini reprint of the player's rookie card and "BARS" (Baseball Analysis and Reporting System) statistics. A card-like application form for membership in Topps Stadium Club was inserted in each wax pack. The cards are numbered on the back. Card numbers 591-600 in the second series form a "Members Choice" subset. The only noteworthy Rookie Card in the second series is Rob Maurer. Card numbers 601-610 in the third series form a "Members Choice" subset. Rookie Cards include Pat Listach and Bill Pulsipher.

	MINT	EXC	G-VG
COMPLETE SET (900)	60.00	27.00	7.50
COMPLETE SERIES 1 (300)	20.00	9.00	2.50
COMPLETE SERIES 2 (300)	20.00	9.00	2.50
COMPLETE SERIES 3 (300)	20.00	9.00	2.50
COMMON CARD (1-300)	.10	.05	.01
COMMON CARD (301-600)	.10	.05	.01
COMMON CARD (601-900)	.10	.05	.01

Card	MINT	EXC	G-VG
☐ 1 Cal Ripken UER (Misspelled Ripkin on card back)	1.25	.55	.16
☐ 2 Eric Yelding	.10	.05	.01
☐ 3 Geno Petralli	.10	.05	.01
☐ 4 Wally Backman	.10	.05	.01
☐ 5 Milt Cuyler	.10	.05	.01
☐ 6 Kevin Bass	.10	.05	.01
☐ 7 Dante Bichette	.25	.11	.03
☐ 8 Ray Lankford	.25	.11	.03
☐ 9 Mel Hall	.10	.05	.01
☐ 10 Joe Carter	.50	.23	.06
☐ 11 Juan Samuel	.10	.05	.01
☐ 12 Jeff Montgomery	.15	.07	.02
☐ 13 Glenn Braggs	.10	.05	.01
☐ 14 Henry Cotto	.10	.05	.01
☐ 15 Deion Sanders	.50	.23	.06
☐ 16 Dick Schofield	.10	.05	.01
☐ 17 David Cone	.25	.11	.03
☐ 18 Chili Davis	.15	.07	.02
☐ 19 Tom Foley	.10	.05	.01
☐ 20 Ozzie Guillen	.10	.05	.01
☐ 21 Luis Salazar	.10	.05	.01
☐ 22 Terry Steinbach	.15	.07	.02
☐ 23 Chris James	.10	.05	.01
☐ 24 Jeff King	.10	.05	.01
☐ 25 Carlos Quintana	.10	.05	.01
☐ 26 Mike Maddux	.10	.05	.01
☐ 27 Tommy Greene	.15	.07	.02
☐ 28 Jeff Russell	.10	.05	.01
☐ 29 Steve Finley	.10	.05	.01
☐ 30 Mike Flanagan	.10	.05	.01
☐ 31 Darren Lewis	.15	.07	.02
☐ 32 Mark Lee	.10	.05	.01
☐ 33 Willie Fraser	.10	.05	.01
☐ 34 Mike Henneman	.10	.05	.01
☐ 35 Kevin Maas	.10	.05	.01
☐ 36 Dave Hansen	.10	.05	.01
☐ 37 Erik Hanson	.10	.05	.01
☐ 38 Bill Doran	.10	.05	.01
☐ 39 Mike Boddicker	.10	.05	.01
☐ 40 Vince Coleman	.10	.05	.01
☐ 41 Devon White	.15	.07	.02
☐ 42 Mark Gardner	.10	.05	.01
☐ 43 Scott Lewis	.10	.05	.01
☐ 44 Juan Berenguer	.10	.05	.01
☐ 45 Carney Lansford	.15	.07	.02
☐ 46 Curt Wilkerson	.10	.05	.01
☐ 47 Shane Mack	.15	.07	.02
☐ 48 Bip Roberts	.10	.05	.01
☐ 49 Greg A. Harris	.10	.05	.01
☐ 50 Ryne Sandberg	.75	.35	.09
☐ 51 Mark Whiten	.15	.07	.02
☐ 52 Jack McDowell	.25	.11	.03
☐ 53 Jimmy Jones	.10	.05	.01
☐ 54 Steve Lake	.10	.05	.01
☐ 55 Bud Black	.10	.05	.01
☐ 56 Dave Valle	.10	.05	.01
☐ 57 Kevin Reimer	.10	.05	.01
☐ 58 Rich Gedman UER (Wrong BARS chart used)	.10	.05	.01
☐ 59 Travis Fryman	.50	.23	.06
☐ 60 Steve Avery	.30	.14	.04
☐ 61 Francisco de la Rosa	.10	.05	.01
☐ 62 Scott Hemond	.10	.05	.01
☐ 63 Hal Morris	.15	.07	.02
☐ 64 Hensley Meulens	.10	.05	.01
☐ 65 Frank Castillo	.10	.05	.01
☐ 66 Gene Larkin	.10	.05	.01
☐ 67 Jose DeLeon	.10	.05	.01
☐ 68 Al Osuna	.10	.05	.01
☐ 69 Dave Cochrane	.10	.05	.01
☐ 70 Robin Ventura	.30	.14	.04
☐ 71 John Cerutti	.10	.05	.01
☐ 72 Kevin Gross	.10	.05	.01
☐ 73 Ivan Calderon	.10	.05	.01
☐ 74 Mike Macfarlane	.10	.05	.01
☐ 75 Stan Belinda	.10	.05	.01
☐ 76 Shawn Hillegas	.10	.05	.01
☐ 77 Pat Borders	.10	.05	.01
☐ 78 Jim Vatcher	.10	.05	.01
☐ 79 Bobby Rose	.10	.05	.01
☐ 80 Roger Clemens	.75	.35	.09
☐ 81 Craig Worthington	.10	.05	.01
☐ 82 Jeff Treadway	.10	.05	.01
☐ 83 Jamie Quirk	.10	.05	.01
☐ 84 Randy Bush	.10	.05	.01
☐ 85 Anthony Young	.10	.05	.01
☐ 86 Trevor Wilson	.10	.05	.01
☐ 87 Jaime Navarro	.10	.05	.01
☐ 88 Les Lancaster	.10	.05	.01
☐ 89 Pat Kelly	.15	.07	.02
☐ 90 Alvin Davis	.10	.05	.01
☐ 91 Larry Andersen	.10	.05	.01
☐ 92 Rob Deer	.10	.05	.01
☐ 93 Mike Sharperson	.10	.05	.01
☐ 94 Lance Parrish	.15	.07	.02
☐ 95 Cecil Espy	.10	.05	.01
☐ 96 Tim Spehr	.10	.05	.01
☐ 97 Dave Stieb	.15	.07	.02
☐ 98 Terry Mulholland	.10	.05	.01
☐ 99 Dennis Boyd	.10	.05	.01
☐ 100 Barry Larkin	.25	.11	.03
☐ 101 Ryan Bowen	.10	.05	.01
☐ 102 Felix Fermin	.10	.05	.01
☐ 103 Luis Alicea	.10	.05	.01
☐ 104 Tim Hulett	.10	.05	.01
☐ 105 Rafael Belliard	.10	.05	.01
☐ 106 Mike Gallego	.10	.05	.01
☐ 107 Dave Righetti	.10	.05	.01
☐ 108 Jeff Schaefer	.10	.05	.01
☐ 109 Ricky Bones	.15	.07	.02
☐ 110 Scott Erickson	.10	.05	.01
☐ 111 Matt Nokes	.10	.05	.01
☐ 112 Bob Scanlan	.10	.05	.01
☐ 113 Tom Candiotti	.10	.05	.01
☐ 114 Sean Berry	.15	.07	.02
☐ 115 Kevin Morton	.10	.05	.01

☐ 116 Scott Fletcher	.10	.05	.01
☐ 117 B.J. Surhoff	.10	.05	.01
☐ 118 Dave Magadan UER (Born Tampa, not Tamps)	.10	.05	.01
☐ 119 Bill Gullickson	.10	.05	.01
☐ 120 Marquis Grissom	.25	.11	.03
☐ 121 Lenny Harris	.10	.05	.01
☐ 122 Wally Joyner	.15	.07	.02
☐ 123 Kevin Brown	.15	.07	.02
☐ 124 Braulio Castillo	.10	.05	.01
☐ 125 Eric King	.10	.05	.01
☐ 126 Mark Portugal	.10	.05	.01
☐ 127 Calvin Jones	.10	.05	.01
☐ 128 Mike Heath	.10	.05	.01
☐ 129 Todd Van Poppel	.25	.11	.03
☐ 130 Benny Santiago	.10	.05	.01
☐ 131 Gary Thurman	.10	.05	.01
☐ 132 Joe Girardi	.10	.05	.01
☐ 133 Dave Eiland	.10	.05	.01
☐ 134 Orlando Merced	.15	.07	.02
☐ 135 Joe Orsulak	.10	.05	.01
☐ 136 John Burkett	.15	.07	.02
☐ 137 Ken Dayley	.10	.05	.01
☐ 138 Ken Hill	.15	.07	.02
☐ 139 Walt Terrell	.10	.05	.01
☐ 140 Mike Scioscia	.10	.05	.01
☐ 141 Junior Felix	.10	.05	.01
☐ 142 Ken Caminiti	.15	.07	.02
☐ 143 Carlos Baerga	.50	.23	.06
☐ 144 Tony Fossas	.10	.05	.01
☐ 145 Craig Grebeck	.10	.05	.01
☐ 146 Scott Bradley	.10	.05	.01
☐ 147 Kent Mercker	.10	.05	.01
☐ 148 Derrick May	.15	.07	.02
☐ 149 Jerald Clark	.10	.05	.01
☐ 150 George Brett	1.00	.45	.13
☐ 151 Luis Quinones	.10	.05	.01
☐ 152 Mike Pagliarulo	.10	.05	.01
☐ 153 Jose Guzman	.10	.05	.01
☐ 154 Charlie O'Brien	.10	.05	.01
☐ 155 Darren Holmes	.10	.05	.01
☐ 156 Joe Boever	.10	.05	.01
☐ 157 Rich Monteleone	.10	.05	.01
☐ 158 Reggie Harris	.10	.05	.01
☐ 159 Roberto Alomar	.50	.23	.06
☐ 160 Robby Thompson	.10	.05	.01
☐ 161 Chris Hoiles	.25	.11	.03
☐ 162 Tom Pagnozzi	.10	.05	.01
☐ 163 Omar Vizquel	.10	.05	.01
☐ 164 John Candelaria	.10	.05	.01
☐ 165 Terry Shumpert	.10	.05	.01
☐ 166 Andy Mota	.10	.05	.01
☐ 167 Scott Bailes	.10	.05	.01
☐ 168 Jeff Blauser	.15	.07	.02
☐ 169 Steve Olin	.10	.05	.01
☐ 170 Doug Drabek	.25	.11	.03
☐ 171 Dave Bergman	.10	.05	.01
☐ 172 Eddie Whitson	.10	.05	.01
☐ 173 Gilberto Reyes	.10	.05	.01
☐ 174 Mark Grace	.25	.11	.03
☐ 175 Paul O'Neill	.15	.07	.02
☐ 176 Greg Cadaret	.10	.05	.01
☐ 177 Mark Williamson	.10	.05	.01
☐ 178 Casey Candaele	.10	.05	.01
☐ 179 Candy Maldonado	.10	.05	.01
☐ 180 Lee Smith	.25	.11	.03
☐ 181 Harold Reynolds	.10	.05	.01
☐ 182 David Justice	.50	.23	.06
☐ 183 Lenny Webster	.10	.05	.01
☐ 184 Donn Pall	.10	.05	.01
☐ 185 Gerald Alexander	.10	.05	.01
☐ 186 Jack Clark	.15	.07	.02
☐ 187 Stan Javier	.10	.05	.01
☐ 188 Ricky Jordan	.10	.05	.01
☐ 189 Franklin Stubbs	.10	.05	.01
☐ 190 Dennis Eckersley	.25	.11	.03
☐ 191 Danny Tartabull	.15	.07	.02
☐ 192 Pete O'Brien	.10	.05	.01
☐ 193 Mark Lewis	.15	.07	.02
☐ 194 Mike Felder	.10	.05	.01
☐ 195 Mickey Tettleton	.15	.07	.02
☐ 196 Dwight Smith	.10	.05	.01
☐ 197 Shawn Abner	.10	.05	.01
☐ 198 Jim Leyritz UER (Career totals less than 1991 totals)	.10	.05	.01
☐ 199 Mike Devereaux	.15	.07	.02
☐ 200 Craig Biggio	.15	.07	.02
☐ 201 Kevin Elster	.10	.05	.01
☐ 202 Rance Mulliniks	.10	.05	.01
☐ 203 Tony Fernandez	.15	.07	.02
☐ 204 Allan Anderson	.10	.05	.01
☐ 205 Herm Winningham	.10	.05	.01
☐ 206 Tim Jones	.10	.05	.01
☐ 207 Ramon Martinez	.15	.07	.02
☐ 208 Teddy Higuera	.10	.05	.01
☐ 209 John Kruk	.25	.11	.03
☐ 210 Jim Abbott	.25	.11	.03
☐ 211 Dean Palmer	.15	.07	.02
☐ 212 Mark Davis	.10	.05	.01
☐ 213 Jay Buhner	.15	.07	.02
☐ 214 Jesse Barfield	.10	.05	.01
☐ 215 Kevin Mitchell	.15	.07	.02
☐ 216 Mike LaValliere	.10	.05	.01
☐ 217 Mark Wohlers	.15	.07	.02
☐ 218 Dave Henderson	.10	.05	.01
☐ 219 Dave Smith	.10	.05	.01
☐ 220 Albert Belle	1.25	.55	.16
☐ 221 Spike Owen	.10	.05	.01
☐ 222 Jeff Gray	.10	.05	.01
☐ 223 Paul Gibson	.10	.05	.01
☐ 224 Bobby Thigpen	.10	.05	.01
☐ 225 Mike Mussina	.75	.35	.09
☐ 226 Darrin Jackson	.10	.05	.01
☐ 227 Luis Gonzalez	.15	.07	.02
☐ 228 Greg Briley	.10	.05	.01
☐ 229 Brent Mayne	.10	.05	.01
☐ 230 Paul Molitor	.35	.16	.04
☐ 231 Al Leiter	.10	.05	.01
☐ 232 Andy Van Slyke	.25	.11	.03
☐ 233 Ron Tingley	.10	.05	.01
☐ 234 Bernard Gilkey	.15	.07	.02
☐ 235 Kent Hrbek	.15	.07	.02
☐ 236 Eric Karros	.25	.11	.03
☐ 237 Randy Velarde	.10	.05	.01
☐ 238 Andy Allanson	.10	.05	.01
☐ 239 Willie McGee	.15	.07	.02
☐ 240 Juan Gonzalez	1.25	.55	.16
☐ 241 Karl Rhodes	.10	.05	.01
☐ 242 Luis Mercedes	.10	.05	.01
☐ 243 Billy Swift	.15	.07	.02
☐ 244 Tommy Gregg	.10	.05	.01
☐ 245 David Howard	.10	.05	.01
☐ 246 Dave Hollins	.25	.11	.03
☐ 247 Kip Gross	.10	.05	.01
☐ 248 Walt Weiss	.10	.05	.01
☐ 249 Mackey Sasser	.10	.05	.01
☐ 250 Cecil Fielder	.35	.16	.04
☐ 251 Jerry Browne	.10	.05	.01
☐ 252 Doug Dascenzo	.10	.05	.01
☐ 253 Darryl Hamilton	.15	.07	.02
☐ 254 Dann Bilardello	.10	.05	.01
☐ 255 Luis Rivera	.10	.05	.01
☐ 256 Larry Walker	.25	.11	.03
☐ 257 Ron Karkovice	.10	.05	.01
☐ 258 Bob Tewksbury	.10	.05	.01

☐ 259 Jimmy Key .15 .07 .02
☐ 260 Bernie Williams .15 .07 .02
☐ 261 Gary Wayne .10 .05 .01
☐ 262 Mike Simms UER .10 .05 .01
(Reversed negative)
☐ 263 John Orton .10 .05 .01
☐ 264 Marvin Freeman .10 .05 .01
☐ 265 Mike Jeffcoat .10 .05 .01
☐ 266 Roger Mason .10 .05 .01
☐ 267 Edgar Martinez .15 .07 .02
☐ 268 Henry Rodriguez .15 .07 .02
☐ 269 Sam Horn .10 .05 .01
☐ 270 Brian McRae .25 .11 .03
☐ 271 Kirt Manwaring .10 .05 .01
☐ 272 Mike Bordick .10 .05 .01
☐ 273 Chris Sabo .15 .07 .02
☐ 274 Jim Olander .10 .05 .01
☐ 275 Greg W. Harris .10 .05 .01
☐ 276 Dan Gakeler .10 .05 .01
☐ 277 Bill Sampen .10 .05 .01
☐ 278 Joel Skinner .10 .05 .01
☐ 279 Curt Schilling .15 .07 .02
☐ 280 Dale Murphy .25 .11 .03
☐ 281 Lee Stevens .10 .05 .01
☐ 282 Lonnie Smith .10 .05 .01
☐ 283 Manny Lee .10 .05 .01
☐ 284 Shawn Boskie .10 .05 .01
☐ 285 Kevin Seitzer .10 .05 .01
☐ 286 Stan Royer .10 .05 .01
☐ 287 John Dopson .10 .05 .01
☐ 288 Scott Bullett .10 .05 .01
☐ 289 Ken Patterson .10 .05 .01
☐ 290 Todd Hundley .10 .05 .01
☐ 291 Tim Leary .10 .05 .01
☐ 292 Brett Butler .15 .07 .02
☐ 293 Gregg Olson .10 .05 .01
☐ 294 Jeff Brantley .10 .05 .01
☐ 295 Brian Holman .10 .05 .01
☐ 296 Brian Harper .10 .05 .01
☐ 297 Brian Bohanon .10 .05 .01
☐ 298 Checklist 1-100 .10 .05 .01
☐ 299 Checklist 101-200 .10 .05 .01
☐ 300 Checklist 201-300 .10 .05 .01
☐ 301 Frank Thomas 4.00 1.80 .50
☐ 302 Lloyd McClendon .10 .05 .01
☐ 303 Brady Anderson .15 .07 .02
☐ 304 Julio Valera .10 .05 .01
☐ 305 Mike Aldrete .10 .05 .01
☐ 306 Joe Oliver .10 .05 .01
☐ 307 Todd Stottlemyre .10 .05 .01
☐ 308 Rey Sanchez .15 .07 .02
☐ 309 Gary Sheffield UER .25 .11 .03
(Listed as 5'1",
should be 5'11")
☐ 310 Andujar Cedeno .15 .07 .02
☐ 311 Kenny Rogers .10 .05 .01
☐ 312 Bruce Hurst .10 .05 .01
☐ 313 Mike Schooler .10 .05 .01
☐ 314 Mike Benjamin .10 .05 .01
☐ 315 Chuck Finley .10 .05 .01
☐ 316 Mark Lemke .10 .05 .01
☐ 317 Scott Livingstone .10 .05 .01
☐ 318 Chris Nabholz .10 .05 .01
☐ 319 Mike Humphreys .15 .07 .02
☐ 320 Pedro Guerrero .15 .07 .02
☐ 321 Willie Banks .10 .05 .01
☐ 322 Tom Goodwin .10 .05 .01
☐ 323 Hector Wagner .10 .05 .01
☐ 324 Wally Ritchie .10 .05 .01
☐ 325 Mo Vaughn .50 .23 .06
☐ 326 Joe Klink .10 .05 .01
☐ 327 Cal Eldred .15 .07 .02
☐ 328 Daryl Boston .10 .05 .01
☐ 329 Mike Huff .10 .05 .01
☐ 330 Jeff Bagwell 2.00 .90 .25
☐ 331 Bob Milacki .10 .05 .01
☐ 332 Tom Prince .10 .05 .01
☐ 333 Pat Tabler .10 .05 .01
☐ 334 Ced Landrum .10 .05 .01
☐ 335 Reggie Jefferson .10 .05 .01
☐ 336 Mo Sanford .10 .05 .01
☐ 337 Kevin Ritz .10 .05 .01
☐ 338 Gerald Perry .10 .05 .01
☐ 339 Jeff Hamilton .10 .05 .01
☐ 340 Tim Wallach .10 .05 .01
☐ 341 Jeff Huson .10 .05 .01
☐ 342 Jose Melendez .10 .05 .01
☐ 343 Willie Wilson .10 .05 .01
☐ 344 Mike Stanton .10 .05 .01
☐ 345 Joel Johnston .10 .05 .01
☐ 346 Lee Guetterman .10 .05 .01
☐ 347 Francisco Oliveras .10 .05 .01
☐ 348 Dave Burba .10 .05 .01
☐ 349 Tim Crews .10 .05 .01
☐ 350 Scott Leius .10 .05 .01
☐ 351 Danny Cox .10 .05 .01
☐ 352 Wayne Housie .15 .07 .02
☐ 353 Chris Donnels .10 .05 .01
☐ 354 Chris George .10 .05 .01
☐ 355 Gerald Young .10 .05 .01
☐ 356 Roberto Hernandez .15 .07 .02
☐ 357 Neal Heaton .10 .05 .01
☐ 358 Todd Frohwirth .10 .05 .01
☐ 359 Jose Vizcaino .10 .05 .01
☐ 360 Jim Thome 1.00 .45 .13
☐ 361 Craig Wilson .10 .05 .01
☐ 362 Dave Haas .10 .05 .01
☐ 363 Billy Hatcher .10 .05 .01
☐ 364 John Barfield .10 .05 .01
☐ 365 Luis Aquino .10 .05 .01
☐ 366 Charlie Leibrandt .10 .05 .01
☐ 367 Howard Farmer .10 .05 .01
☐ 368 Bryn Smith .10 .05 .01
☐ 369 Mickey Morandini .10 .05 .01
☐ 370 Jose Canseco .60 .25 .08
(See also 597)
☐ 371 Jose Uribe .10 .05 .01
☐ 372 Bob MacDonald .10 .05 .01
☐ 373 Luis Sojo .10 .05 .01
☐ 374 Craig Shipley .15 .07 .02
☐ 375 Scott Bankhead .10 .05 .01
☐ 376 Greg Gagne .10 .05 .01
☐ 377 Scott Cooper .10 .05 .01
☐ 378 Jose Offerman .10 .05 .01
☐ 379 Billy Spiers .10 .05 .01
☐ 380 John Smiley .10 .05 .01
☐ 381 Jeff Carter .10 .05 .01
☐ 382 Heathcliff Slocumb .10 .05 .01
☐ 383 Jeff Tackett .10 .05 .01
☐ 384 John Kiely .10 .05 .01
☐ 385 John Vander Wal .15 .07 .02
☐ 386 Omar Olivares .10 .05 .01
☐ 387 Ruben Sierra .25 .11 .03
☐ 388 Tom Gordon .10 .05 .01
☐ 389 Charles Nagy .10 .05 .01
☐ 390 Dave Stewart .15 .07 .02
☐ 391 Pete Harnisch .15 .07 .02
☐ 392 Tim Burke .10 .05 .01
☐ 393 Roberto Kelly .15 .07 .02
☐ 394 Freddie Benavides .10 .05 .01
☐ 395 Tom Glavine .25 .11 .03
☐ 396 Wes Chamberlain .10 .05 .01
☐ 397 Eric Gunderson .10 .05 .01
☐ 398 Dave West .10 .05 .01
☐ 399 Ellis Burks .15 .07 .02
☐ 400 Ken Griffey Jr. 4.00 1.80 .50

	No.	Player			
☐	401	Thomas Howard	.10	.05	.01
☐	402	Juan Guzman	.15	.07	.02
☐	403	Mitch Webster	.10	.05	.01
☐	404	Matt Merullo	.10	.05	.01
☐	405	Steve Buechele	.10	.05	.01
☐	406	Danny Jackson	.10	.05	.01
☐	407	Felix Jose	.15	.07	.02
☐	408	Doug Piatt	.10	.05	.01
☐	409	Jim Eisenreich	.10	.05	.01
☐	410	Bryan Harvey	.15	.07	.02
☐	411	Jim Austin	.10	.05	.01
☐	412	Jim Poole	.10	.05	.01
☐	413	Glenallen Hill	.10	.05	.01
☐	414	Gene Nelson	.10	.05	.01
☐	415	Ivan Rodriguez	.30	.14	.04
☐	416	Frank Tanana	.10	.05	.01
☐	417	Steve Decker	.10	.05	.01
☐	418	Jason Grimsley	.10	.05	.01
☐	419	Tim Layana	.10	.05	.01
☐	420	Don Mattingly	1.00	.45	.13
☐	421	Jerome Walton	.10	.05	.01
☐	422	Rob Ducey	.10	.05	.01
☐	423	Andy Benes	.15	.07	.02
☐	424	John Marzano	.10	.05	.01
☐	425	Gene Harris	.10	.05	.01
☐	426	Tim Raines	.25	.11	.03
☐	427	Bret Barberie	.10	.05	.01
☐	428	Harvey Pulliam	.10	.05	.01
☐	429	Cris Carpenter	.10	.05	.01
☐	430	Howard Johnson	.15	.07	.02
☐	431	Orel Hershiser	.15	.07	.02
☐	432	Brian Hunter	.10	.05	.01
☐	433	Kevin Tapani	.10	.05	.01
☐	434	Rick Reed	.10	.05	.01
☐	435	Ron Witmeyer	.10	.05	.01
☐	436	Gary Gaetti	.10	.05	.01
☐	437	Alex Cole	.10	.05	.01
☐	438	Chito Martinez	.10	.05	.01
☐	439	Greg Litton	.10	.05	.01
☐	440	Julio Franco	.15	.07	.02
☐	441	Mike Munoz	.10	.05	.01
☐	442	Erik Pappas	.10	.05	.01
☐	443	Pat Combs	.10	.05	.01
☐	444	Lance Johnson	.10	.05	.01
☐	445	Ed Sprague	.15	.07	.02
☐	446	Mike Greenwell	.15	.07	.02
☐	447	Milt Thompson	.10	.05	.01
☐	448	Mike Magnante	.10	.05	.01
☐	449	Chris Haney	.10	.05	.01
☐	450	Robin Yount	.30	.14	.04
☐	451	Rafael Ramirez	.10	.05	.01
☐	452	Gino Minutelli	.10	.05	.01
☐	453	Tom Lampkin	.10	.05	.01
☐	454	Tony Perezchica	.10	.05	.01
☐	455	Dwight Gooden	.15	.07	.02
☐	456	Mark Guthrie	.10	.05	.01
☐	457	Jay Howell	.10	.05	.01
☐	458	Gary DiSarcina	.10	.05	.01
☐	459	John Smoltz	.15	.07	.02
☐	460	Will Clark	.50	.23	.06
☐	461	Dave Otto	.10	.05	.01
☐	462	Rob Maurer	.15	.07	.02
☐	463	Dwight Evans	.15	.07	.02
☐	464	Tom Brunansky	.10	.05	.01
☐	465	Shawn Hare	.15	.07	.02
☐	466	Geronimo Pena	.10	.05	.01
☐	467	Alex Fernandez	.30	.14	.04
☐	468	Greg Myers	.10	.05	.01
☐	469	Jeff Fassero	.10	.05	.01
☐	470	Len Dykstra	.25	.11	.03
☐	471	Jeff Johnson	.10	.05	.01
☐	472	Russ Swan	.10	.05	.01
☐	473	Archie Corbin	.15	.07	.02
☐	474	Chuck McElroy	.10	.05	.01
☐	475	Mark McGwire	.25	.11	.03
☐	476	Wally Whitehurst	.10	.05	.01
☐	477	Tim McIntosh	.10	.05	.01
☐	478	Sid Bream	.10	.05	.01
☐	479	Jeff Juden	.15	.07	.02
☐	480	Carlton Fisk	.25	.11	.03
☐	481	Jeff Plympton	.15	.07	.02
☐	482	Carlos Martinez	.10	.05	.01
☐	483	Jim Gott	.10	.05	.01
☐	484	Bob McClure	.10	.05	.01
☐	485	Tim Teufel	.10	.05	.01
☐	486	Vicente Palacios	.10	.05	.01
☐	487	Jeff Reed	.10	.05	.01
☐	488	Tony Phillips	.10	.05	.01
☐	489	Mel Rojas	.10	.05	.01
☐	490	Ben McDonald	.15	.07	.02
☐	491	Andres Santana	.10	.05	.01
☐	492	Chris Beasley	.10	.05	.01
☐	493	Mike Timlin	.10	.05	.01
☐	494	Brian Downing	.10	.05	.01
☐	495	Kirk Gibson	.15	.07	.02
☐	496	Scott Sanderson	.10	.05	.01
☐	497	Nick Esasky	.10	.05	.01
☐	498	Johnny Guzman	.10	.05	.01
☐	499	Mitch Williams	.15	.07	.02
☐	500	Kirby Puckett	1.00	.45	.13
☐	501	Mike Harkey	.10	.05	.01
☐	502	Jim Gantner	.10	.05	.01
☐	503	Bruce Egloff	.10	.05	.01
☐	504	Josias Manzanillo	.15	.07	.02
☐	505	Delino DeShields	.25	.11	.03
☐	506	Rheal Cormier	.10	.05	.01
☐	507	Jay Bell	.15	.07	.02
☐	508	Rich Rowland	.10	.05	.01
☐	509	Scott Servais	.10	.05	.01
☐	510	Terry Pendleton	.25	.11	.03
☐	511	Rich DeLucia	.10	.05	.01
☐	512	Warren Newson	.10	.05	.01
☐	513	Paul Faries	.10	.05	.01
☐	514	Kal Daniels	.10	.05	.01
☐	515	Jarvis Brown	.15	.07	.02
☐	516	Rafael Palmeiro	.30	.14	.04
☐	517	Kelly Downs	.10	.05	.01
☐	518	Steve Chitren	.10	.05	.01
☐	519	Moises Alou	.30	.14	.04
☐	520	Wade Boggs	.25	.11	.03
☐	521	Pete Schourek	.15	.07	.02
☐	522	Scott Terry	.10	.05	.01
☐	523	Kevin Appier	.15	.07	.02
☐	524	Gary Redus	.10	.05	.01
☐	525	George Bell	.15	.07	.02
☐	526	Jeff Kaiser	.10	.05	.01
☐	527	Alvaro Espinoza	.10	.05	.01
☐	528	Luis Polonia	.10	.05	.01
☐	529	Darren Daulton	.25	.11	.03
☐	530	Norm Charlton	.10	.05	.01
☐	531	John Olerud	.25	.11	.03
☐	532	Dan Plesac	.10	.05	.01
☐	533	Billy Ripken	.10	.05	.01
☐	534	Rod Nichols	.10	.05	.01
☐	535	Joey Cora	.10	.05	.01
☐	536	Harold Baines	.15	.07	.02
☐	537	Bob Ojeda	.10	.05	.01
☐	538	Mark Leonard	.10	.05	.01
☐	539	Danny Darwin	.10	.05	.01
☐	540	Shawon Dunston	.10	.05	.01
☐	541	Pedro Munoz	.15	.07	.02
☐	542	Mark Gubicza	.10	.05	.01
☐	543	Kevin Baez	.15	.07	.02
☐	544	Todd Zeile	.15	.07	.02
☐	545	Don Slaught	.10	.05	.01
☐	546	Tony Eusebio	.15	.07	.02

☐ 547	Alonzo Powell	.10	.05	.01
☐ 548	Gary Pettis	.10	.05	.01
☐ 549	Brian Barnes	.10	.05	.01
☐ 550	Lou Whitaker	.25	.11	.03
☐ 551	Keith Mitchell	.10	.05	.01
☐ 552	Oscar Azocar	.10	.05	.01
☐ 553	Stu Cole	.10	.05	.01
☐ 554	Steve Wapnick	.10	.05	.01
☐ 555	Derek Bell	.15	.07	.02
☐ 556	Luis Lopez	.10	.05	.01
☐ 557	Anthony Telford	.10	.05	.01
☐ 558	Tim Mauser	.15	.07	.02
☐ 559	Glen Sutko	.10	.05	.01
☐ 560	Darryl Strawberry	.15	.07	.02
☐ 561	Tom Bolton	.10	.05	.01
☐ 562	Cliff Young	.10	.05	.01
☐ 563	Bruce Walton	.10	.05	.01
☐ 564	Chico Walker	.10	.05	.01
☐ 565	John Franco	.10	.05	.01
☐ 566	Paul McClellan	.10	.05	.01
☐ 567	Paul Abbott	.10	.05	.01
☐ 568	Gary Varsho	.10	.05	.01
☐ 569	Carlos Maldonado	.10	.05	.01
☐ 570	Kelly Gruber	.10	.05	.01
☐ 571	Jose Oquendo	.10	.05	.01
☐ 572	Steve Frey	.10	.05	.01
☐ 573	Tino Martinez	.15	.07	.02
☐ 574	Bill Haselman	.10	.05	.01
☐ 575	Eric Anthony	.10	.05	.01
☐ 576	John Habyan	.10	.05	.01
☐ 577	Jeff McNeely	.10	.05	.01
☐ 578	Chris Bosio	.10	.05	.01
☐ 579	Joe Grahe	.10	.05	.01
☐ 580	Fred McGriff	.50	.23	.06
☐ 581	Rick Honeycutt	.10	.05	.01
☐ 582	Matt Williams	.50	.23	.06
☐ 583	Cliff Brantley	.15	.07	.02
☐ 584	Rob Dibble	.10	.05	.01
☐ 585	Skeeter Barnes	.10	.05	.01
☐ 586	Greg Hibbard	.10	.05	.01
☐ 587	Randy Milligan	.10	.05	.01
☐ 588	Checklist 301-400	.10	.05	.01
☐ 589	Checklist 401-500	.10	.05	.01
☐ 590	Checklist 501-600	.10	.05	.01
☐ 591	Frank Thomas MC	2.00	.90	.25
☐ 592	David Justice MC	.25	.11	.03
☐ 593	Roger Clemens MC	.40	.18	.05
☐ 594	Steve Avery MC	.25	.11	.03
☐ 595	Cal Ripken MC	.75	.35	.09
☐ 596	Barry Larkin MC UER (Ranked in AL, should be NL)	.25	.11	.03
☐ 597	Jose Canseco MC UER (Mistakenly numbered 370 on card back)	.30	.14	.04
☐ 598	Will Clark MC	.30	.14	.04
☐ 599	Cecil Fielder MC	.20	.09	.03
☐ 600	Ryne Sandberg MC	.50	.23	.06
☐ 601	Chuck Knoblauch MC	.20	.09	.03
☐ 602	Dwight Gooden MC	.15	.07	.02
☐ 603	Ken Griffey Jr. MC	2.50	1.15	.30
☐ 604	Barry Bonds MC	.60	.25	.08
☐ 605	Nolan Ryan MC	1.50	.65	.19
☐ 606	Jeff Bagwell MC	1.00	.45	.13
☐ 607	Robin Yount MC	.25	.11	.03
☐ 608	Bobby Bonilla MC	.25	.11	.03
☐ 609	George Brett MC	.50	.23	.06
☐ 610	Howard Johnson MC	.15	.07	.02
☐ 611	Esteban Beltre	.15	.07	.02
☐ 612	Mike Christopher	.10	.05	.01
☐ 613	Troy Afenir	.10	.05	.01
☐ 614	Mariano Duncan	.10	.05	.01
☐ 615	Doug Henry	.10	.05	.01
☐ 616	Doug Jones	.10	.05	.01
☐ 617	Alvin Davis	.10	.05	.01
☐ 618	Craig Lefferts	.10	.05	.01
☐ 619	Kevin McReynolds	.10	.05	.01
☐ 620	Barry Bonds	1.25	.55	.16
☐ 621	Turner Ward	.10	.05	.01
☐ 622	Joe Magrane	.10	.05	.01
☐ 623	Mark Parent	.10	.05	.01
☐ 624	Tom Browning	.10	.05	.01
☐ 625	John Smiley	.10	.05	.01
☐ 626	Steve Wilson	.10	.05	.01
☐ 627	Mike Gallego	.10	.05	.01
☐ 628	Sammy Sosa	.25	.11	.03
☐ 629	Rico Rossy	.10	.05	.01
☐ 630	Royce Clayton	.25	.11	.03
☐ 631	Clay Parker	.10	.05	.01
☐ 632	Pete Smith	.10	.05	.01
☐ 633	Jeff McKnight	.10	.05	.01
☐ 634	Jack Daugherty	.10	.05	.01
☐ 635	Steve Sax	.10	.05	.01
☐ 636	Joe Hesketh	.10	.05	.01
☐ 637	Vince Horsman	.15	.07	.02
☐ 638	Eric King	.10	.05	.01
☐ 639	Joe Boever	.10	.05	.01
☐ 640	Jack Morris	.25	.11	.03
☐ 641	Arthur Rhodes	.15	.07	.02
☐ 642	Bob Melvin	.10	.05	.01
☐ 643	Rick Wilkins	.15	.07	.02
☐ 644	Scott Scudder	.10	.05	.01
☐ 645	Bip Roberts	.10	.05	.01
☐ 646	Julio Valera	.10	.05	.01
☐ 647	Kevin Campbell	.10	.05	.01
☐ 648	Steve Searcy	.10	.05	.01
☐ 649	Scott Kamieniecki	.10	.05	.01
☐ 650	Kurt Stillwell	.10	.05	.01
☐ 651	Bob Welch	.10	.05	.01
☐ 652	Andres Galarraga	.25	.11	.03
☐ 653	Mike Jackson	.10	.05	.01
☐ 654	Bo Jackson	.25	.11	.03
☐ 655	Sid Fernandez	.15	.07	.02
☐ 656	Mike Bielecki	.10	.05	.01
☐ 657	Jeff Reardon	.15	.07	.02
☐ 658	Wayne Rosenthal	.10	.05	.01
☐ 659	Eric Bullock	.10	.05	.01
☐ 660	Eric Davis	.10	.05	.01
☐ 661	Randy Tomlin	.10	.05	.01
☐ 662	Tom Edens	.10	.05	.01
☐ 663	Rob Murphy	.10	.05	.01
☐ 664	Leo Gomez	.10	.05	.01
☐ 665	Greg Maddux	.50	.23	.06
☐ 666	Greg Vaughn	.15	.07	.02
☐ 667	Wade Taylor	.10	.05	.01
☐ 668	Brad Arnsberg	.10	.05	.01
☐ 669	Mike Moore	.10	.05	.01
☐ 670	Mark Langston	.25	.11	.03
☐ 671	Barry Jones	.10	.05	.01
☐ 672	Bill Landrum	.10	.05	.01
☐ 673	Greg Swindell	.10	.05	.01
☐ 674	Wayne Edwards	.10	.05	.01
☐ 675	Greg Olson	.10	.05	.01
☐ 676	Bill Pulsipher	2.00	.90	.25
☐ 677	Bobby Witt	.10	.05	.01
☐ 678	Mark Carreon	.10	.05	.01
☐ 679	Patrick Lennon	.10	.05	.01
☐ 680	Ozzie Smith	.40	.18	.05
☐ 681	John Briscoe	.10	.05	.01
☐ 682	Matt Young	.10	.05	.01
☐ 683	Jeff Conine	.25	.11	.03
☐ 684	Phil Stephenson	.10	.05	.01
☐ 685	Ron Darling	.10	.05	.01
☐ 686	Bryan Hickerson	.10	.05	.01
☐ 687	Dale Sveum	.10	.05	.01
☐ 688	Kirk McCaskill	.10	.05	.01

☐ 689 Rich Amaral .10 .05 .01
☐ 690 Danny Tartabull .15 .07 .02
☐ 691 Donald Harris .10 .05 .01
☐ 692 Doug Davis .10 .05 .01
☐ 693 John Farrell .10 .05 .01
☐ 694 Paul Gibson .10 .05 .01
☐ 695 Kenny Lofton 2.50 1.15 .30
☐ 696 Mike Fetters .10 .05 .01
☐ 697 Rosario Rodriguez .10 .05 .01
☐ 698 Chris Jones .10 .05 .01
☐ 699 Jeff Manto .10 .05 .01
☐ 700 Rick Sutcliffe .15 .07 .02
☐ 701 Scott Bankhead .10 .05 .01
☐ 702 Donnie Hill .10 .05 .01
☐ 703 Todd Worrell .10 .05 .01
☐ 704 Rene Gonzales .10 .05 .01
☐ 705 Rick Cerone .10 .05 .01
☐ 706 Tony Pena .10 .05 .01
☐ 707 Paul Sorrento .10 .05 .01
☐ 708 Gary Scott .10 .05 .01
☐ 709 Junior Noboa .10 .05 .01
☐ 710 Wally Joyner .15 .07 .02
☐ 711 Charlie Hayes .15 .07 .02
☐ 712 Rich Rodriguez .10 .05 .01
☐ 713 Rudy Seanez .15 .07 .02
☐ 714 Jim Bullinger .10 .05 .01
☐ 715 Jeff M. Robinson .10 .05 .01
☐ 716 Jeff Branson .10 .05 .01
☐ 717 Andy Ashby .10 .05 .01
☐ 718 Dave Burba .10 .05 .01
☐ 719 Rich Gossage .25 .11 .03
☐ 720 Randy Johnson .25 .11 .03
☐ 721 David Wells .10 .05 .01
☐ 722 Paul Kilgus .10 .05 .01
☐ 723 Dave Martinez .10 .05 .01
☐ 724 Denny Neagle .10 .05 .01
☐ 725 Andy Stankiewicz .10 .05 .01
☐ 726 Rick Aguilera .15 .07 .02
☐ 727 Junior Ortiz .10 .05 .01
☐ 728 Storm Davis .10 .05 .01
☐ 729 Don Robinson .10 .05 .01
☐ 730 Ron Gant .15 .07 .02
☐ 731 Paul Assenmacher .10 .05 .01
☐ 732 Mike Gardiner .10 .05 .01
☐ 733 Milt Hill .15 .07 .02
☐ 734 Jeremy Hernandez .15 .07 .02
☐ 735 Ken Hill .15 .07 .02
☐ 736 Xavier Hernandez .10 .05 .01
☐ 737 Gregg Jefferies .30 .14 .04
☐ 738 Dick Schofield .10 .05 .01
☐ 739 Ron Robinson .10 .05 .01
☐ 740 Sandy Alomar .15 .07 .02
☐ 741 Mike Stanley .10 .05 .01
☐ 742 Butch Henry .20 .09 .03
☐ 743 Floyd Bannister .10 .05 .01
☐ 744 Brian Drahman .10 .05 .01
☐ 745 Dave Winfield .35 .16 .04
☐ 746 Bob Walk .10 .05 .01
☐ 747 Chris James .10 .05 .01
☐ 748 Don Prybylinski .10 .05 .01
☐ 749 Dennis Rasmussen .10 .05 .01
☐ 750 Rickey Henderson .25 .11 .03
☐ 751 Chris Hammond .10 .05 .01
☐ 752 Bob Kipper .10 .05 .01
☐ 753 Dave Rohde .10 .05 .01
☐ 754 Hubie Brooks .10 .05 .01
☐ 755 Bret Saberhagen .15 .07 .02
☐ 756 Jeff D. Robinson .10 .05 .01
☐ 757 Pat Listach .20 .09 .03
☐ 758 Bill Wegman .10 .05 .01
☐ 759 John Wetteland .10 .05 .01
☐ 760 Phil Plantier .25 .11 .03
☐ 761 Wilson Alvarez .30 .14 .04
☐ 762 Scott Aldred .10 .05 .01
☐ 763 Armando Reynoso .10 .05 .01
☐ 764 Todd Benzinger .10 .05 .01
☐ 765 Kevin Mitchell .15 .07 .02
☐ 766 Gary Sheffield .25 .11 .03
☐ 767 Allan Anderson .10 .05 .01
☐ 768 Rusty Meacham .10 .05 .01
☐ 769 Rick Parker .10 .05 .01
☐ 770 Nolan Ryan 3.00 1.35 .40
☐ 771 Jeff Ballard .10 .05 .01
☐ 772 Cory Snyder .10 .05 .01
☐ 773 Denis Boucher .10 .05 .01
☐ 774 Jose Gonzalez .10 .05 .01
☐ 775 Juan Guerrero .15 .07 .02
☐ 776 Ed Nunez .10 .05 .01
☐ 777 Scott Ruskin .10 .05 .01
☐ 778 Terry Leach .10 .05 .01
☐ 779 Carl Willis .10 .05 .01
☐ 780 Bobby Bonilla .25 .11 .03
☐ 781 Duane Ward .15 .07 .02
☐ 782 Joe Slusarski .10 .05 .01
☐ 783 David Segui .10 .05 .01
☐ 784 Kirk Gibson .15 .07 .02
☐ 785 Frank Viola .15 .07 .02
☐ 786 Keith Miller .10 .05 .01
☐ 787 Mike Morgan .10 .05 .01
☐ 788 Kim Batiste .10 .05 .01
☐ 789 Sergio Valdez .10 .05 .01
☐ 790 Eddie Taubensee .10 .05 .01
☐ 791 Jack Armstrong .10 .05 .01
☐ 792 Scott Fletcher .10 .05 .01
☐ 793 Steve Farr .10 .05 .01
☐ 794 Dan Pasqua .10 .05 .01
☐ 795 Eddie Murray .25 .11 .03
☐ 796 John Morris .10 .05 .01
☐ 797 Francisco Cabrera .10 .05 .01
☐ 798 Mike Perez .10 .05 .01
☐ 799 Ted Wood .10 .05 .01
☐ 800 Jose Rijo .15 .07 .02
☐ 801 Danny Gladden .10 .05 .01
☐ 802 Archi Cianfrocco .10 .05 .01
☐ 803 Monty Fariss .10 .05 .01
☐ 804 Roger McDowell .10 .05 .01
☐ 805 Randy Myers .15 .07 .02
☐ 806 Kirk Dressendorfer .10 .05 .01
☐ 807 Zane Smith .10 .05 .01
☐ 808 Glenn Davis .10 .05 .01
☐ 809 Torey Lovullo .10 .05 .01
☐ 810 Andre Dawson .25 .11 .03
☐ 811 Bill Pecota .10 .05 .01
☐ 812 Ted Power .10 .05 .01
☐ 813 Willie Blair .10 .05 .01
☐ 814 Dave Fleming .15 .07 .02
☐ 815 Chris Gwynn .10 .05 .01
☐ 816 Jody Reed .10 .05 .01
☐ 817 Mark Dewey .10 .05 .01
☐ 818 Kyle Abbott .10 .05 .01
☐ 819 Tom Henke .15 .07 .02
☐ 820 Kevin Seitzer .10 .05 .01
☐ 821 Al Newman .10 .05 .01
☐ 822 Tim Sherrill .10 .05 .01
☐ 823 Chuck Crim .10 .05 .01
☐ 824 Darren Reed .10 .05 .01
☐ 825 Tony Gwynn .60 .25 .08
☐ 826 Steve Foster .15 .07 .02
☐ 827 Steve Howe .10 .05 .01
☐ 828 Brook Jacoby .10 .05 .01
☐ 829 Rodney McCray .10 .05 .01
☐ 830 Chuck Knoblauch .30 .14 .04
☐ 831 John Wehner .10 .05 .01
☐ 832 Scott Garrelts .10 .05 .01
☐ 833 Alejandro Pena .10 .05 .01
☐ 834 Jeff Parrett UER .10 .05 .01

	(Kentucy)			
☐ 835	Juan Bell	.10	.05	.01
☐ 836	Lance Dickson	.15	.07	.02
☐ 837	Darryl Kile	.15	.07	.02
☐ 838	Efrain Valdez	.10	.05	.01
☐ 839	Bob Zupcic	.15	.07	.02
☐ 840	George Bell	.15	.07	.02
☐ 841	Dave Gallagher	.10	.05	.01
☐ 842	Tim Belcher	.10	.05	.01
☐ 843	Jeff Shaw	.10	.05	.01
☐ 844	Mike Fitzgerald	.10	.05	.01
☐ 845	Gary Carter	.25	.11	.03
☐ 846	John Russell	.10	.05	.01
☐ 847	Eric Hillman	.10	.05	.01
☐ 848	Mike Witt	.10	.05	.01
☐ 849	Curt Wilkerson	.10	.05	.01
☐ 850	Alan Trammell	.25	.11	.03
☐ 851	Rex Hudler	.10	.05	.01
☐ 852	Mike Walkden	.10	.05	.01
☐ 853	Kevin Ward	.10	.05	.01
☐ 854	Tim Naehring	.10	.05	.01
☐ 855	Bill Swift	.15	.07	.02
☐ 856	Damon Berryhill	.10	.05	.01
☐ 857	Mark Eichhorn	.10	.05	.01
☐ 858	Hector Villanueva	.10	.05	.01
☐ 859	Jose Lind	.10	.05	.01
☐ 860	Denny Martinez	.15	.07	.02
☐ 861	Bill Krueger	.10	.05	.01
☐ 862	Mike Kingery	.10	.05	.01
☐ 863	Jeff Innis	.10	.05	.01
☐ 864	Derek Lilliquist	.10	.05	.01
☐ 865	Reggie Sanders	.50	.23	.06
☐ 866	Ramon Garcia	.10	.05	.01
☐ 867	Bruce Ruffin	.10	.05	.01
☐ 868	Dickie Thon	.10	.05	.01
☐ 869	Melido Perez	.10	.05	.01
☐ 870	Ruben Amaro	.10	.05	.01
☐ 871	Alan Mills	.10	.05	.01
☐ 872	Matt Sinatro	.10	.05	.01
☐ 873	Eddie Zosky	.10	.05	.01
☐ 874	Pete Incaviglia	.10	.05	.01
☐ 875	Tom Candiotti	.10	.05	.01
☐ 876	Bob Patterson	.10	.05	.01
☐ 877	Neal Heaton	.10	.05	.01
☐ 878	Terrel Hansen	.15	.07	.02
☐ 879	Dave Eiland	.10	.05	.01
☐ 880	Von Hayes	.10	.05	.01
☐ 881	Tim Scott	.15	.07	.02
☐ 882	Otis Nixon	.10	.05	.01
☐ 883	Herm Winningham	.10	.05	.01
☐ 884	Dion James	.10	.05	.01
☐ 885	Dave Wainhouse	.10	.05	.01
☐ 886	Frank DiPino	.10	.05	.01
☐ 887	Dennis Cook	.10	.05	.01
☐ 888	Jose Mesa	.10	.05	.01
☐ 889	Mark Leiter	.10	.05	.01
☐ 890	Willie Randolph	.15	.07	.02
☐ 891	Craig Colbert	.10	.05	.01
☐ 892	Dwayne Henry	.10	.05	.01
☐ 893	Jim Lindeman	.10	.05	.01
☐ 894	Charlie Hough	.15	.07	.02
☐ 895	Gil Heredia	.15	.07	.02
☐ 896	Scott Chiamparino	.10	.05	.01
☐ 897	Lance Blankenship	.10	.05	.01
☐ 898	Checklist 601-700	.10	.05	.01
☐ 899	Checklist 701-800	.10	.05	.01
☐ 900	Checklist 801-900	.10	.05	.01

1992 Stadium Club First Draft Picks

This three-card subset, featuring Major League Baseball's Number 1 draft pick for 1990, 1991, and 1992, was randomly inserted into 1992 Topps Stadium Club Series III packs. Topps estimated that one of these cards can be found in every 72 packs. One card also was mailed to each member of Topps Stadium Club. The cards measure the standard size (2 1/2" by 3 1/2") and feature on the fronts full-bleed posed color player photos. The player's draft year is printed on an orange circle in the upper right corner and is accented by gold foil stripes of varying lengths that run vertically down the right edge of the card. The player's name appears on the Stadium Club logo at the bottom. The number "1" is gold-foil stamped in a black diamond at the lower left and is followed by a red stripe gold-foil stamped with the words "Draft Pick of the '90s". The back design features color photos on a black and red background with the player's signature gold-foil stamped across the bottom of the photo and gold foil bars running down the right edge of the picture. The team name and biographical information is included in a yellow and white box. The cards are numbered on the back.

	MINT	EXC	G-VG
COMPLETE SET (3)	12.00	5.50	1.50
COMMON CARD (1-3)	2.00	.90	.25
☐ 1 Chipper Jones	8.00	3.60	1.00
☐ 2 Brien Taylor	2.00	.90	.25
☐ 3 Phil Nevin	2.50	1.15	.30

1992 Stadium Club Dome

The 1992 Topps Stadium Club Special Stadium set features 100 top draft picks, 56 1991 All-Star Game cards, 25 1991 Team U.S.A. cards, and 19 1991 Championship and World Series cards, all packaged in a set box inside a molded-plastic SkyDome

display. Topps actually references this set as a 1991 set and the copyright lines on the card backs say 1991, but the set was released well into 1992. The standard-size (2 1/2" by 3 1/2" cards display full-bleed glossy player photos on the fronts. The player's name appears in an sky-blue stripe that is accented by parallel gold stripes. These stripes intersect the Topps Stadium Club logo. The horizontally oriented backs present biography, statistics, or highlights on a colorful artwork background depicting some aspect of baseball. The cards are numbered on the back. Rookie Cards in this set include Brian Barber, Cliff Floyd, Brent Gates, Benji Gil, Tyler Green, Tyrone Hill, Todd Hollandsworth, Bobby Jones, Manny Ramirez, Scott Ruffcorn, Aaron Sele, Kevin Stocker, Brien Taylor, and Allen Watson.

	MINT	EXC	G-VG
COMPLETE FACT.SET (200) ..	30.00	13.50	3.80
COMMON CARD (1-200)	.10	.05	.01
□ 1 Terry Adams	.15	.07	.02
□ 2 Tommy Adams	.10	.05	.01
□ 3 Rick Aguilera	.12	.05	.02
□ 4 Ron Allen	.15	.07	.02
□ 5 Roberto Alomar	.40	.18	.05
□ 6 Sandy Alomar	.12	.05	.02
□ 7 Greg Anthony	.10	.05	.01
□ 8 James Austin	.10	.05	.01
□ 9 Steve Avery	.20	.09	.03
□ 10 Harold Baines	.12	.05	.02
□ 11 Brian Barber	.20	.09	.03
□ 12 Jon Barnes	.15	.07	.02
□ 13 George Bell	.12	.05	.02
□ 14 Doug Bennett	.10	.05	.01
□ 15 Sean Bergman	.25	.11	.03
□ 16 Craig Biggio	.12	.05	.02
□ 17 Bill Bliss	.10	.05	.01
□ 18 Wade Boggs	.15	.07	.02
□ 19 Bobby Bonilla	.15	.07	.02
□ 20 Russell Brock	.25	.11	.03
□ 21 Tarrik Brock	.20	.09	.03
□ 22 Tom Browning	.10	.05	.01
□ 23 Brett Butler	.12	.05	.02
□ 24 Ivan Calderon	.10	.05	.01
□ 25 Joe Carter	.25	.11	.03
□ 26 Joe Caruso	.15	.07	.02
□ 27 Dan Cholowsky	.10	.05	.01
□ 28 Will Clark	.25	.11	.03
□ 29 Roger Clemens	.35	.16	.04
□ 30 Shawn Curran	.10	.05	.01
□ 31 Chris Curtis	.15	.07	.02
□ 32 Chili Davis	.12	.05	.02
□ 33 Andre Dawson	.15	.07	.02
□ 34 Joe DeBerry	.10	.05	.01
□ 35 John Dettmer	.50	.23	.06
□ 36 Rob Dibble	.10	.05	.01
□ 37 John Donati	.20	.09	.03
□ 38 Dave Doorneweerd	.15	.07	.02
□ 39 Darren Dreifort	.50	.23	.06
□ 40 Mike Durant	.15	.07	.02
□ 41 Chris Durkin	.15	.07	.02
□ 42 Dennis Eckersley	.15	.07	.02
□ 43 Brian Edmondson	.20	.09	.03
□ 44 Vaughn Eshelman	.20	.09	.03
□ 45 Shawn Estes	.15	.07	.02
□ 46 Jorge Fabregas	.15	.07	.02
□ 47 Jon Farrell	.15	.07	.02
□ 48 Cecil Fielder	.15	.07	.02
□ 49 Carlton Fisk	.15	.07	.02
□ 50 Tim Flannelly	.15	.07	.02
□ 51 Cliff Floyd	3.00	1.35	.40
□ 52 Julio Franco	.12	.05	.02
□ 53 Greg Gagne	.10	.05	.01
□ 54 Chris Gambs	.15	.07	.02
□ 55 Ron Gant	.12	.05	.02
□ 56 Brent Gates	.60	.25	.08
□ 57 Dwayne Gerald	.10	.05	.01
□ 58 Jason Giambi	.60	.25	.08
□ 59 Benji Gil	.50	.23	.06
□ 60 Mark Gipner	.10	.05	.01
□ 61 Danny Gladden	.10	.05	.01
□ 62 Tom Glavine	.15	.07	.02
□ 63 Jimmy Gonzalez	.10	.05	.01
□ 64 Jeff Granger	.50	.23	.06
□ 65 Dan Grapenthien	.10	.05	.01
□ 66 Dennis Gray	.10	.05	.01
□ 67 Shawn Green	2.00	.90	.25
□ 68 Tyler Green	.20	.09	.03
□ 69 Todd Greene	1.25	.55	.16
□ 70 Ken Griffey Jr.	2.50	1.15	.30
□ 71 Kelly Gruber	.10	.05	.01
□ 72 Ozzie Guillen	.10	.05	.01
□ 73 Tony Gwynn	.35	.16	.04
□ 74 Shane Halter	.15	.07	.02
□ 75 Jeffrey Hammonds	1.50	.65	.19
□ 76 Larry Hanlon	.15	.07	.02
□ 77 Pete Harnisch	.12	.05	.02
□ 78 Mike Harrison	.10	.05	.01
□ 79 Bryan Harvey	.12	.05	.02
□ 80 Scott Hatteberg	.15	.07	.02
□ 81 Rick Helling	.40	.18	.05
□ 82 Dave Henderson	.10	.05	.01
□ 83 Rickey Henderson	.20	.09	.03
□ 84 Tyrone Hill	.20	.09	.03
□ 85 Todd Hollandsworth	2.00	.90	.25
□ 86 Brian Holliday	.10	.05	.01
□ 87 Terry Horn	.10	.05	.01
□ 88 Jeff Hostetler	.15	.07	.02
□ 89 Kent Hrbek	.12	.05	.02
□ 90 Mark Hubbard	.20	.09	.03
□ 91 Charles Johnson	1.50	.65	.19
□ 92 Howard Johnson	.12	.05	.02
□ 93 Todd Johnson	.20	.09	.03
□ 94 Bobby Jones	1.00	.45	.13
□ 95 Dan Jones	.10	.05	.01
□ 96 Felix Jose	.12	.05	.02
□ 97 David Justice	.25	.11	.03
□ 98 Jimmy Key	.12	.05	.02
□ 99 Marc Kroon	.30	.14	.04
□ 100 John Kruk	.10	.05	.01
□ 101 Mark Langston	.15	.07	.02
□ 102 Barry Larkin	.15	.07	.02
□ 103 Mike LaValliere	.10	.05	.01
□ 104 Scott Leius	.10	.05	.01
□ 105 Mark Lemke	.10	.05	.01
□ 106 Donnie Leshnock	.10	.05	.01

☐ 107	Jimmy Lewis	.15	.07	.02
☐ 108	Shane Livesy	.10	.05	.01
☐ 109	Ryan Long	.15	.07	.02
☐ 110	Trevor Mallory	.20	.09	.03
☐ 111	Denny Martinez	.12	.05	.02
☐ 112	Justin Mashore	.15	.07	.02
☐ 113	Jason McDonald	.20	.09	.03
☐ 114	Jack McDowell	.15	.07	.02
☐ 115	Tom McKinnon	.10	.05	.01
☐ 116	Billy McMillon	.20	.09	.03
☐ 117	Buck McNabb	.20	.09	.03
☐ 118	Jim Mecir	.20	.09	.03
☐ 119	Dan Melendez	.10	.05	.01
☐ 120	Shawn Miller	.20	.09	.03
☐ 121	Trever Miller	.10	.05	.01
☐ 122	Paul Molitor	.25	.11	.03
☐ 123	Vincent Moore	.20	.09	.03
☐ 124	Mike Morgan	.10	.05	.01
☐ 125	Jack Morris WS	.15	.07	.02
☐ 126	Jack Morris AS	.15	.07	.02
☐ 127	Sean Mulligan	.40	.18	.05
☐ 128	Eddie Murray	.15	.07	.02
☐ 129	Mike Neill	.15	.07	.02
☐ 130	Phil Nevin	.60	.25	.08
☐ 131	Mark O'Brien	.15	.07	.02
☐ 132	Alex Ochoa	1.00	.45	.13
☐ 133	Chad Ogea	.40	.18	.05
☐ 134	Greg Olson	.10	.05	.01
☐ 135	Paul O'Neill	.12	.05	.02
☐ 136	Jared Osentowski	.15	.07	.02
☐ 137	Mike Pagliarulo	.10	.05	.01
☐ 138	Rafael Palmeiro	.20	.09	.03
☐ 139	Rodney Pedraza	.15	.07	.02
☐ 140	Tony Phillips (P)	.15	.07	.02
☐ 141	Scott Pisciotta	.20	.09	.03
☐ 142	Christopher Pritchett	.15	.07	.02
☐ 143	Jason Pruitt	.10	.05	.01
☐ 144	Kirby Puckett WS UER (Championship series AB and BA is wrong)	.50	.23	.06
☐ 145	Kirby Puckett AS	.50	.23	.06
☐ 146	Manny Ramirez	4.00	1.80	.50
☐ 147	Eddie Ramos	.15	.07	.02
☐ 148	Mark Ratekin	.20	.09	.03
☐ 149	Jeff Reardon	.12	.05	.02
☐ 150	Sean Rees	.20	.09	.03
☐ 151	Calvin Reese	.40	.18	.05
☐ 152	Desmond Relaford	.60	.25	.08
☐ 153	Eric Richardson	.15	.07	.02
☐ 154	Cal Ripken	.60	.25	.08
☐ 155	Chris Roberts	.50	.23	.06
☐ 156	Mike Robertson	.15	.07	.02
☐ 157	Steve Rodriguez	.10	.05	.01
☐ 158	Mike Rossiter	.10	.05	.01
☐ 159	Scott Ruffcorn	.75	.35	.09
☐ 160	Chris Sabo	.12	.05	.02
☐ 161	Juan Samuel	.10	.05	.01
☐ 162	Ryne Sandberg UER (On 5th line, prior misspelled as prilor)	.50	.23	.06
☐ 163	Scott Sanderson	.10	.05	.01
☐ 164	Benny Santiago	.10	.05	.01
☐ 165	Gene Schall	.60	.25	.08
☐ 166	Chad Schoenvogel	.15	.07	.02
☐ 167	Chris Seelbach	.30	.14	.04
☐ 168	Aaron Sele	1.50	.65	.19
☐ 169	Basil Shabazz	.15	.07	.02
☐ 170	Al Shirley	.20	.09	.03
☐ 171	Paul Shuey	.60	.25	.08
☐ 172	Ruben Sierra	.15	.07	.02
☐ 173	John Smiley	.10	.05	.01
☐ 174	Lee Smith	.15	.07	.02
☐ 175	Ozzie Smith	.25	.11	.03
☐ 176	Tim Smith	.15	.07	.02
☐ 177	Zane Smith	.10	.05	.01
☐ 178	John Smoltz	.12	.05	.02
☐ 179	Scott Stahoviak	.20	.09	.03
☐ 180	Kennie Steenstra	.40	.18	.05
☐ 181	Kevin Stocker	.50	.23	.06
☐ 182	Chris Stynes	.30	.14	.04
☐ 183	Danny Tartabull	.12	.05	.02
☐ 184	Brien Taylor	.50	.23	.06
☐ 185	Todd Taylor	.10	.05	.01
☐ 186	Larry Thomas	.20	.09	.03
☐ 187	Ozzie Timmons (See also 188)	.60	.25	.08
☐ 188	David Tuttle UER (Mistakenly numbered as 187 on card)	.10	.05	.01
☐ 189	Andy Van Slyke	.15	.07	.02
☐ 190	Frank Viola	.12	.05	.02
☐ 191	Michael Walkden	.10	.05	.01
☐ 192	Jeff Ware	.10	.05	.01
☐ 193	Allen Watson	.30	.14	.04
☐ 194	Steve Whitaker	.30	.14	.04
☐ 195	Jerry Willard	.10	.05	.01
☐ 196	Craig Wilson	.10	.05	.01
☐ 197	Chris Wimmer	.15	.07	.02
☐ 198	Steve Wojciechowski	.20	.09	.03
☐ 199	Joel Wolfe	.10	.05	.01
☐ 200	Ivan Zweig	.10	.05	.01

1993 Stadium Club

The 1993 Stadium Club baseball set consists of 750 cards issued in three series of 300, 300, and 150 cards respectively. Randomly inserted throughout first series packs were a Stadium Club Master Photo winner card (redeemable for three master photos), a 1st Day Production card, and four special bonus cards featuring the newest members of the 3,000 Hit Club (Robin Yount and George Brett) and the Number One Expansion Draft Picks of the Florida Marlins and Colorado Rockies (Nigel Wilson and David Nied). Fewer than 2,000 of each card were imprinted with a special foil First Day Production logo. According to Topps, one of these insert cards were to be found in approximately one in every 24 packs. Also every hobby box contained a Stadium Club Master Photo. The cards measure the standard size (2 1/2" by 3 1/2"). The fronts display full-bleed glossy color player photos. A red stripe carrying the player's name and edged on the bottom by a gold stripe cuts across

the bottom of the picture. A white baseball icon with gold motion streaks rounds out the front. Award Winner and League Leader cards are studded with gold foil stars. On a background consisting of an artistic drawing of a baseball player's arm extended with ball in glove, the backs carry a second color action photo, biographical information, 1992 Stats Player Profile, the player's ranking (either on his team and/or the AL or NL), statistics, and a miniature reproduction of his Topps rookie card. Each series closes with a Members Choice subset (291-300, 591-600, and 746-750. The cards are numbered on the back. Rookie Cards in this set include Roberto Mejia, J.T. Snow, Tony Tarasco, and Darrell Whitmore. A 1993 Stadium Club "Members Only" set was also issued as a direct-mail offer to members of Topps Stadium Club. Also issued in three series, this set is identical to the regular 750-set, except that each card has in its upper corner a gold foil "Members Only" seal. With the third and final shipment, the collector received a certificate of authenticity registering the set serial number out of a production run of 12,000 sets.

	MINT	EXC	G-VG
COMPLETE SET (750)	60.00	27.00	7.50
COMPLETE SERIES 1 (300)	20.00	9.00	2.50
COMPLETE SERIES 2 (300)	25.00	11.50	3.10
COMPLETE SERIES 3 (150)	15.00	6.75	1.90
COMMON CARD (1-300)	.10	.05	.01
COMMON CARD (301-600)	.10	.05	.01
COMMON CARD (601-750)	.10	.05	.01

Card	MINT	EXC	G-VG
☐ 1 Pat Borders	.10	.05	.01
☐ 2 Greg Maddux	.75	.35	.09
☐ 3 Daryl Boston	.10	.05	.01
☐ 4 Bob Ayrault	.10	.05	.01
☐ 5 Tony Phillips IF	.10	.05	.01
☐ 6 Damion Easley	.15	.07	.02
☐ 7 Kip Gross	.10	.05	.01
☐ 8 Jim Thome	.40	.18	.05
☐ 9 Tim Belcher	.10	.05	.01
☐ 10 Gary Wayne	.10	.05	.01
☐ 11 Sam Militello	.10	.05	.01
☐ 12 Mike Magnante	.10	.05	.01
☐ 13 Tim Wakefield	.10	.05	.01
☐ 14 Tim Hulett	.10	.05	.01
☐ 15 Rheal Cormier	.10	.05	.01
☐ 16 Juan Guerrero	.10	.05	.01
☐ 17 Rich Gossage	.20	.09	.03
☐ 18 Tim Laker	.10	.05	.01
☐ 19 Darrin Jackson	.10	.05	.01
☐ 20 Jack Clark	.10	.05	.01
☐ 21 Roberto Hernandez	.10	.05	.01
☐ 22 Dean Palmer	.15	.07	.02
☐ 23 Harold Reynolds	.10	.05	.01
☐ 24 Dan Plesac	.10	.05	.01
☐ 25 Brent Mayne	.10	.05	.01
☐ 26 Pat Hentgen	.15	.07	.02
☐ 27 Luis Sojo	.10	.05	.01
☐ 28 Ron Gant	.15	.07	.02
☐ 29 Paul Gibson	.10	.05	.01
☐ 30 Bip Roberts	.10	.05	.01
☐ 31 Mickey Tettleton	.15	.07	.02
☐ 32 Randy Velarde	.10	.05	.01
☐ 33 Brian McRae	.10	.05	.01
☐ 34 Wes Chamberlain	.10	.05	.01
☐ 35 Wayne Kirby	.10	.05	.01
☐ 36 Rey Sanchez	.10	.05	.01
☐ 37 Jesse Orosco	.10	.05	.01
☐ 38 Mike Stanton	.10	.05	.01
☐ 39 Royce Clayton	.15	.07	.02
☐ 40 Cal Ripken UER (Place of birth Havre de Grave; should be Havre de Grace)	2.25	1.00	.30
☐ 41 John Dopson	.10	.05	.01
☐ 42 Gene Larkin	.10	.05	.01
☐ 43 Tim Raines	.20	.09	.03
☐ 44 Randy Myers	.15	.07	.02
☐ 45 Clay Parker	.10	.05	.01
☐ 46 Mike Scioscia	.10	.05	.01
☐ 47 Pete Incaviglia	.10	.05	.01
☐ 48 Todd Van Poppel	.15	.07	.02
☐ 49 Ray Lankford	.20	.09	.03
☐ 50 Eddie Murray	.20	.09	.03
☐ 51A Barry Bonds ERR (Missing four stars over name to indicate NL MVP)	1.25	.55	.16
☐ 51B Barry Bonds COR	1.25	.55	.16
☐ 52 Gary Thurman	.10	.05	.01
☐ 53 Bob Wickman	.10	.05	.01
☐ 54 Joey Cora	.10	.05	.01
☐ 55 Kenny Rogers	.10	.05	.01
☐ 56 Mike Devereaux	.15	.07	.02
☐ 57 Kevin Seitzer	.10	.05	.01
☐ 58 Rafael Belliard	.10	.05	.01
☐ 59 David Wells	.10	.05	.01
☐ 60 Mark Clark	.15	.07	.02
☐ 61 Carlos Baerga	.40	.18	.05
☐ 62 Scott Brosius	.10	.05	.01
☐ 63 Jeff Grotewold	.10	.05	.01
☐ 64 Rick Wrona	.10	.05	.01
☐ 65 Kurt Knudsen	.10	.05	.01
☐ 66 Lloyd McClendon	.10	.05	.01
☐ 67 Omar Vizquel	.10	.05	.01
☐ 68 Jose Vizcaino	.10	.05	.01
☐ 69 Rob Ducey	.10	.05	.01
☐ 70 Casey Candaele	.10	.05	.01
☐ 71 Ramon Martinez	.15	.07	.02
☐ 72 Todd Hundley	.10	.05	.01
☐ 73 John Marzano	.10	.05	.01
☐ 74 Derek Parks	.10	.05	.01
☐ 75 Jack McDowell	.20	.09	.03
☐ 76 Tim Scott	.10	.05	.01
☐ 77 Mike Mussina	.60	.25	.08
☐ 78 Delino DeShields	.15	.07	.02
☐ 79 Chris Bosio	.10	.05	.01
☐ 80 Mike Bordick	.10	.05	.01
☐ 81 Rod Beck	.20	.09	.03
☐ 82 Ted Power	.10	.05	.01
☐ 83 John Kruk	.20	.09	.03
☐ 84 Steve Shifflett	.10	.05	.01
☐ 85 Danny Tartabull	.15	.07	.02
☐ 86 Mike Greenwell	.15	.07	.02
☐ 87 Jose Melendez	.10	.05	.01
☐ 88 Craig Wilson	.10	.05	.01
☐ 89 Melvin Nieves	.20	.09	.03
☐ 90 Ed Sprague	.10	.05	.01
☐ 91 Willie McGee	.15	.07	.02
☐ 92 Joe Orsulak	.10	.05	.01
☐ 93 Jeff King	.10	.05	.01
☐ 94 Dan Pasqua	.10	.05	.01
☐ 95 Brian Harper	.10	.05	.01
☐ 96 Joe Oliver	.10	.05	.01
☐ 97 Shane Turner	.10	.05	.01
☐ 98 Lenny Harris	.10	.05	.01
☐ 99 Jeff Parrett	.10	.05	.01
☐ 100 Luis Polonia	.10	.05	.01
☐ 101 Kent Bottenfield	.10	.05	.01
☐ 102 Albert Belle	1.00	.45	.13
☐ 103 Mike Maddux	.10	.05	.01
☐ 104 Randy Tomlin	.10	.05	.01

□ 105 Andy Stankiewicz .... .10 .05 .01
□ 106 Rico Rossy .... .10 .05 .01
□ 107 Joe Hesketh .... .10 .05 .01
□ 108 Dennis Powell .... .10 .05 .01
□ 109 Derrick May .... .15 .07 .02
□ 110 Pete Harnisch .... .10 .05 .01
□ 111 Kent Mercker .... .10 .05 .01
□ 112 Scott Fletcher .... .10 .05 .01
□ 113 Rex Hudler .... .10 .05 .01
□ 114 Chico Walker .... .10 .05 .01
□ 115 Rafael Palmeiro .... .20 .09 .03
□ 116 Mark Leiter .... .10 .05 .01
□ 117 Pedro Munoz .... .10 .05 .01
□ 118 Jim Bullinger .... .10 .05 .01
□ 119 Ivan Calderon .... .10 .05 .01
□ 120 Mike Timlin .... .10 .05 .01
□ 121 Rene Gonzales .... .10 .05 .01
□ 122 Greg Vaughn .... .15 .07 .02
□ 123 Mike Flanagan .... .10 .05 .01
□ 124 Mike Hartley .... .10 .05 .01
□ 125 Jeff Montgomery .... .15 .07 .02
□ 126 Mike Gallego .... .10 .05 .01
□ 127 Don Slaught .... .10 .05 .01
□ 128 Charlie O'Brien .... .10 .05 .01
□ 129 Jose Offerman .... .10 .05 .01
(Can be found with home town missing on back)
□ 130 Mark Wohlers .... .10 .05 .01
□ 131 Eric Fox .... .10 .05 .01
□ 132 Doug Strange .... .10 .05 .01
□ 133 Jeff Frye .... .10 .05 .01
□ 134 Wade Boggs UER .... .20 .09 .03
(Redundantly lists lefty breakdown)
□ 135 Lou Whitaker .... .20 .09 .03
□ 136 Craig Grebeck .... .10 .05 .01
□ 137 Rich Rodriguez .... .10 .05 .01
□ 138 Jay Bell .... .15 .07 .02
□ 139 Felix Fermin .... .10 .05 .01
□ 140 Denny Martinez .... .15 .07 .02
□ 141 Eric Anthony .... .10 .05 .01
□ 142 Roberto Alomar .... .75 .35 .09
□ 143 Darren Lewis .... .10 .05 .01
□ 144 Mike Blowers .... .10 .05 .01
□ 145 Scott Bankhead .... .10 .05 .01
□ 146 Jeff Reboulet .... .10 .05 .01
□ 147 Frank Viola .... .15 .07 .02
□ 148 Bill Pecota .... .10 .05 .01
□ 149 Carlos Hernandez .... .10 .05 .01
□ 150 Bobby Witt .... .10 .05 .01
□ 151 Sid Bream .... .10 .05 .01
□ 152 Todd Zeile .... .15 .07 .02
□ 153 Dennis Cook .... .10 .05 .01
□ 154 Brian Bohanon .... .10 .05 .01
□ 155 Pat Kelly .... .10 .05 .01
□ 156 Milt Cuyler .... .10 .05 .01
□ 157 Juan Bell .... .10 .05 .01
□ 158 Randy Milligan .... .10 .05 .01
□ 159 Mark Gardner .... .10 .05 .01
□ 160 Pat Tabler .... .10 .05 .01
□ 161 Jeff Reardon .... .15 .07 .02
□ 162 Ken Patterson .... .10 .05 .01
□ 163 Bobby Bonilla .... .20 .09 .03
□ 164 Tony Pena .... .10 .05 .01
□ 165 Greg Swindell .... .10 .05 .01
□ 166 Kirk McCaskill .... .10 .05 .01
□ 167 Doug Drabek .... .20 .09 .03
□ 168 Franklin Stubbs .... .10 .05 .01
□ 169 Ron Tingley .... .10 .05 .01
□ 170 Willie Banks .... .10 .05 .01
□ 171 Sergio Valdez .... .10 .05 .01
□ 172 Mark Lemke .... .10 .05 .01
□ 173 Robin Yount .... .40 .18 .05
□ 174 Storm Davis .... .10 .05 .01
□ 175 Dan Walters .... .10 .05 .01
□ 176 Steve Farr .... .10 .05 .01
□ 177 Curt Wilkerson .... .10 .05 .01
□ 178 Luis Alicea .... .10 .05 .01
□ 179 Russ Swan .... .10 .05 .01
□ 180 Mitch Williams .... .15 .07 .02
□ 181 Wilson Alvarez .... .20 .09 .03
□ 182 Carl Willis .... .10 .05 .01
□ 183 Craig Biggio .... .15 .07 .02
□ 184 Sean Berry .... .10 .05 .01
□ 185 Trevor Wilson .... .10 .05 .01
□ 186 Jeff Tackett .... .10 .05 .01
□ 187 Ellis Burks .... .15 .07 .02
□ 188 Jeff Branson .... .10 .05 .01
□ 189 Matt Nokes .... .10 .05 .01
□ 190 John Smiley .... .10 .05 .01
□ 191 Danny Gladden .... .10 .05 .01
□ 192 Mike Boddicker .... .10 .05 .01
□ 193 Roger Pavlik .... .15 .07 .02
□ 194 Paul Sorrento .... .10 .05 .01
□ 195 Vince Coleman .... .10 .05 .01
□ 196 Gary DiSarcina .... .10 .05 .01
□ 197 Rafael Bournigal .... .15 .07 .02
□ 198 Mike Schooler .... .10 .05 .01
□ 199 Scott Ruskin .... .10 .05 .01
□ 200 Frank Thomas .... 3.00 1.35 .40
□ 201 Kyle Abbott .... .10 .05 .01
□ 202 Mike Perez .... .10 .05 .01
□ 203 Andre Dawson .... .20 .09 .03
□ 204 Bill Swift .... .15 .07 .02
□ 205 Alejandro Pena .... .10 .05 .01
□ 206 Dave Winfield .... .20 .09 .03
□ 207 Andujar Cedeno .... .15 .07 .02
□ 208 Terry Steinbach .... .15 .07 .02
□ 209 Chris Hammond .... .10 .05 .01
□ 210 Todd Burns .... .10 .05 .01
□ 211 Hipolito Pichardo .... .10 .05 .01
□ 212 John Kiely .... .10 .05 .01
□ 213 Tim Teufel .... .10 .05 .01
□ 214 Lee Guetterman .... .10 .05 .01
□ 215 Geronimo Pena .... .10 .05 .01
□ 216 Brett Butler .... .15 .07 .02
□ 217 Bryan Hickerson .... .10 .05 .01
□ 218 Rick Trlicek .... .10 .05 .01
□ 219 Lee Stevens .... .10 .05 .01
□ 220 Roger Clemens .... .75 .35 .09
□ 221 Carlton Fisk .... .20 .09 .03
□ 222 Chili Davis .... .15 .07 .02
□ 223 Walt Terrell .... .10 .05 .01
□ 224 Jim Eisenreich .... .10 .05 .01
□ 225 Ricky Bones .... .10 .05 .01
□ 226 Henry Rodriguez .... .10 .05 .01
□ 227 Ken Hill .... .15 .07 .02
□ 228 Rick Wilkins .... .10 .05 .01
□ 229 Ricky Jordan .... .10 .05 .01
□ 230 Bernard Gilkey .... .10 .05 .01
□ 231 Tim Fortugno .... .10 .05 .01
□ 232 Geno Petralli .... .10 .05 .01
□ 233 Jose Rijo .... .15 .07 .02
□ 234 Jim Leyritz .... .10 .05 .01
□ 235 Kevin Campbell .... .10 .05 .01
□ 236 Al Osuna .... .10 .05 .01
□ 237 Pete Smith .... .10 .05 .01
□ 238 Pete Schourek .... .10 .05 .01
□ 239 Moises Alou .... .20 .09 .03
□ 240 Donn Pall .... .10 .05 .01
□ 241 Denny Neagle .... .10 .05 .01
□ 242 Dan Peltier .... .10 .05 .01
□ 243 Scott Scudder .... .10 .05 .01
□ 244 Juan Guzman .... .15 .07 .02
□ 245 Dave Burba .... .10 .05 .01
□ 246 Rick Sutcliffe .... .15 .07 .02

☐ 247	Tony Fossas	.10	.05	.01
☐ 248	Mike Munoz	.10	.05	.01
☐ 249	Tim Salmon	.50	.23	.06
☐ 250	Rob Murphy	.10	.05	.01
☐ 251	Roger McDowell	.10	.05	.01
☐ 252	Lance Parrish	.15	.07	.02
☐ 253	Cliff Brantley	.10	.05	.01
☐ 254	Scott Leius	.10	.05	.01
☐ 255	Carlos Martinez	.10	.05	.01
☐ 256	Vince Horsman	.10	.05	.01
☐ 257	Oscar Azocar	.10	.05	.01
☐ 258	Craig Shipley	.10	.05	.01
☐ 259	Ben McDonald	.15	.07	.02
☐ 260	Jeff Brantley	.10	.05	.01
☐ 261	Damon Berryhill	.10	.05	.01
☐ 262	Joe Grahe	.10	.05	.01
☐ 263	Dave Hansen	.10	.05	.01
☐ 264	Rich Amaral	.10	.05	.01
☐ 265	Tim Pugh	.10	.05	.01
☐ 266	Dion James	.10	.05	.01
☐ 267	Frank Tanana	.10	.05	.01
☐ 268	Stan Belinda	.10	.05	.01
☐ 269	Jeff Kent	.20	.09	.03
☐ 270	Bruce Ruffin	.10	.05	.01
☐ 271	Xavier Hernandez	.10	.05	.01
☐ 272	Darrin Fletcher	.10	.05	.01
☐ 273	Tino Martinez	.15	.07	.02
☐ 274	Benny Santiago	.10	.05	.01
☐ 275	Scott Radinsky	.10	.05	.01
☐ 276	Mariano Duncan	.10	.05	.01
☐ 277	Kenny Lofton	.75	.35	.09
☐ 278	Dwight Smith	.10	.05	.01
☐ 279	Joe Carter	.40	.18	.05
☐ 280	Tim Jones	.10	.05	.01
☐ 281	Jeff Huson	.10	.05	.01
☐ 282	Phil Plantier	.20	.09	.03
☐ 283	Kirby Puckett	1.25	.55	.16
☐ 284	Johnny Guzman	.10	.05	.01
☐ 285	Mike Morgan	.10	.05	.01
☐ 286	Chris Sabo	.15	.07	.02
☐ 287	Matt Williams	.50	.23	.06
☐ 288	Checklist 1-100	.10	.05	.01
☐ 289	Checklist 101-200	.10	.05	.01
☐ 290	Checklist 201-300	.10	.05	.01
☐ 291	Dennis Eckersley MC	.10	.05	.01
☐ 292	Eric Karros MC	.15	.07	.02
☐ 293	Pat Listach MC	.15	.07	.02
☐ 294	Andy Van Slyke MC	.20	.09	.03
☐ 295	Robin Ventura MC	.20	.09	.03
☐ 296	Tom Glavine MC	.20	.09	.03
☐ 297	Juan Gonzalez MC UER (Misspelled Gonzales)	.60	.25	.08
☐ 298	Travis Fryman MC	.15	.07	.02
☐ 299	Larry Walker MC	.15	.07	.02
☐ 300	Gary Sheffield MC	.20	.09	.03
☐ 301	Chuck Finley	.10	.05	.01
☐ 302	Luis Gonzalez	.15	.07	.02
☐ 303	Darryl Hamilton	.10	.05	.01
☐ 304	Bien Figueroa	.10	.05	.01
☐ 305	Ron Darling	.10	.05	.01
☐ 306	Jonathan Hurst	.10	.05	.01
☐ 307	Mike Sharperson	.10	.05	.01
☐ 308	Mike Christopher	.10	.05	.01
☐ 309	Marvin Freeman	.10	.05	.01
☐ 310	Jay Buhner	.15	.07	.02
☐ 311	Butch Henry	.10	.05	.01
☐ 312	Greg W. Harris	.10	.05	.01
☐ 313	Darren Daulton	.20	.09	.03
☐ 314	Chuck Knoblauch	.20	.09	.03
☐ 315	Greg A. Harris	.10	.05	.01
☐ 316	John Franco	.10	.05	.01
☐ 317	John Wehner	.10	.05	.01
☐ 318	Donald Harris	.10	.05	.01
☐ 319	Benny Santiago	.10	.05	.01
☐ 320	Larry Walker	.20	.09	.03
☐ 321	Randy Knorr	.10	.05	.01
☐ 322	Ramon Martinez	.10	.05	.01
☐ 323	Mike Stanley	.10	.05	.01
☐ 324	Bill Wegman	.10	.05	.01
☐ 325	Tom Candiotti	.10	.05	.01
☐ 326	Glenn Davis	.10	.05	.01
☐ 327	Chuck Crim	.10	.05	.01
☐ 328	Scott Livingstone	.10	.05	.01
☐ 329	Eddie Taubensee	.10	.05	.01
☐ 330	George Bell	.15	.07	.02
☐ 331	Edgar Martinez	.10	.05	.01
☐ 332	Paul Assenmacher	.10	.05	.01
☐ 333	Steve Hosey	.10	.05	.01
☐ 334	Mo Vaughn	.20	.09	.03
☐ 335	Bret Saberhagen	.15	.07	.02
☐ 336	Mike Trombley	.10	.05	.01
☐ 337	Mark Lewis	.10	.05	.01
☐ 338	Terry Pendleton	.20	.09	.03
☐ 339	Dave Hollins	.20	.09	.03
☐ 340	Jeff Conine	.20	.09	.03
☐ 341	Bob Tewksbury	.10	.05	.01
☐ 342	Billy Ashley	.50	.23	.06
☐ 343	Zane Smith	.10	.05	.01
☐ 344	John Wetteland	.10	.05	.01
☐ 345	Chris Hoiles	.15	.07	.02
☐ 346	Frank Castillo	.10	.05	.01
☐ 347	Bruce Hurst	.10	.05	.01
☐ 348	Kevin McReynolds	.10	.05	.01
☐ 349	Dave Henderson	.10	.05	.01
☐ 350	Ryan Bowen	.10	.05	.01
☐ 351	Sid Fernandez	.10	.05	.01
☐ 352	Mark Whiten	.15	.07	.02
☐ 353	Nolan Ryan	3.00	1.35	.40
☐ 354	Rick Aguilera	.15	.07	.02
☐ 355	Mark Langston	.20	.09	.03
☐ 356	Jack Morris	.20	.09	.03
☐ 357	Rob Deer	.10	.05	.01
☐ 358	Dave Fleming	.15	.07	.02
☐ 359	Lance Johnson	.10	.05	.01
☐ 360	Joe Millette	.10	.05	.01
☐ 361	Wil Cordero	.20	.09	.03
☐ 362	Chito Martinez	.10	.05	.01
☐ 363	Scott Servais	.10	.05	.01
☐ 364	Bernie Williams	.15	.07	.02
☐ 365	Pedro Martinez	.20	.09	.03
☐ 366	Ryne Sandberg	1.00	.45	.13
☐ 367	Brad Ausmus	.10	.05	.01
☐ 368	Scott Cooper	.15	.07	.02
☐ 369	Rob Dibble	.10	.05	.01
☐ 370	Walt Weiss	.10	.05	.01
☐ 371	Mark Davis	.10	.05	.01
☐ 372	Orlando Merced	.15	.07	.02
☐ 373	Mike Jackson	.10	.05	.01
☐ 374	Kevin Appier	.15	.07	.02
☐ 375	Esteban Beltre	.10	.05	.01
☐ 376	Joe Slusarski	.10	.05	.01
☐ 377	William Suero	.10	.05	.01
☐ 378	Pete O'Brien	.10	.05	.01
☐ 379	Alan Embree	.10	.05	.01
☐ 380	Lenny Webster	.10	.05	.01
☐ 381	Eric Davis	.10	.05	.01
☐ 382	Duane Ward	.15	.07	.02
☐ 383	John Habyan	.10	.05	.01
☐ 384	Jeff Bagwell	1.50	.65	.19
☐ 385	Ruben Amaro	.10	.05	.01
☐ 386	Julio Valera	.10	.05	.01
☐ 387	Robin Ventura	.20	.09	.03
☐ 388	Archi Cianfrocco	.10	.05	.01
☐ 389	Skeeter Barnes	.10	.05	.01
☐ 390	Tim Costo	.10	.05	.01
☐ 391	Luis Mercedes	.10	.05	.01

☐ 392 Jeremy Hernandez .... .10 .05 .01
☐ 393 Shawon Dunston .... .10 .05 .01
☐ 394 Andy Van Slyke .... .20 .09 .03
☐ 395 Kevin Maas .... .10 .05 .01
☐ 396 Kevin Brown .... .10 .05 .01
☐ 397 J.T. Bruett.................... .10 .05 .01
☐ 398 Darryl Strawberry .... .15 .07 .02
☐ 399 Tom Pagnozzi .... .10 .05 .01
☐ 400 Sandy Alomar Jr. .... .10 .05 .01
☐ 401 Keith Miller .... .10 .05 .01
☐ 402 Rich DeLucia................ .10 .05 .01
☐ 403 Shawn Abner .... .10 .05 .01
☐ 404 Howard Johnson.......... .10 .05 .01
☐ 405 Mike Benjamin .... .10 .05 .01
☐ 406 Roberto Mejia .... .15 .07 .02
☐ 407 Mike Butcher................ .10 .05 .01
☐ 408 Deion Sanders UER ..... .50 .23 .06
(Braves on front and Yankees on back)
☐ 409 Todd Stottlemyre .... .10 .05 .01
☐ 410 Scott Kamieniecki .... .10 .05 .01
☐ 411 Doug Jones................... .10 .05 .01
☐ 412 John Burkett .... .15 .07 .02
☐ 413 Lance Blankenship....... .10 .05 .01
☐ 414 Jeff Parrett................... .10 .05 .01
☐ 415 Barry Larkin .... .20 .09 .03
☐ 416 Alan Trammell.............. .20 .09 .03
☐ 417 Mark Kiefer .... .10 .05 .01
☐ 418 Gregg Olson................. .10 .05 .01
☐ 419 Mark Grace .... .20 .09 .03
☐ 420 Shane Mack .... .15 .07 .02
☐ 421 Bob Walk .... .10 .05 .01
☐ 422 Curt Schilling .... .15 .07 .02
☐ 423 Erik Hanson .... .10 .05 .01
☐ 424 George Brett .... 1.25 .55 .16
☐ 425 Reggie Jefferson.......... .10 .05 .01
☐ 426 Mark Portugal............... .10 .05 .01
☐ 427 Ron Karkovice.............. .10 .05 .01
☐ 428 Matt Young................... .10 .05 .01
☐ 429 Troy Neel .... .15 .07 .02
☐ 430 Hector Fajardo .... .10 .05 .01
☐ 431 Dave Righetti .... .10 .05 .01
☐ 432 Pat Listach.................... .15 .07 .02
☐ 433 Jeff Innis....................... .10 .05 .01
☐ 434 Bob MacDonald .... .10 .05 .01
☐ 435 Brian Jordan .... .15 .07 .02
☐ 436 Jeff Blauser.................. .15 .07 .02
☐ 437 Mike Myers................... .10 .05 .01
☐ 438 Frank Seminara............ .10 .05 .01
☐ 439 Rusty Meacham .... .10 .05 .01
☐ 440 Greg Briley................... .10 .05 .01
☐ 441 Derek Lilliquist............. .10 .05 .01
☐ 442 John Vander Wal .... .10 .05 .01
☐ 443 Scott Erickson.............. .10 .05 .01
☐ 444 Bob Scanlan................. .10 .05 .01
☐ 445 Todd Frohwirth .... .10 .05 .01
☐ 446 Tom Goodwin .... .10 .05 .01
☐ 447 William Pennyfeather... .10 .05 .01
☐ 448 Travis Fryman.............. .25 .11 .03
☐ 449 Mickey Morandini .... .10 .05 .01
☐ 450 Greg Olson................... .10 .05 .01
☐ 451 Trevor Hoffman............ .10 .05 .01
☐ 452 Dave Magadan .... .10 .05 .01
☐ 453 Shawn Jeter................. .10 .05 .01
☐ 454 Andres Galarraga .... .20 .09 .03
☐ 455 Ted Wood .... .10 .05 .01
☐ 456 Freddie Benavides........ .10 .05 .01
☐ 457 Junior Felix .... .10 .05 .01
☐ 458 Alex Cole...................... .10 .05 .01
☐ 459 John Orton.................... .10 .05 .01
☐ 460 Eddie Zosky .... .10 .05 .01
☐ 461 Dennis Eckersley.......... .20 .09 .03
☐ 462 Lee Smith .... .20 .09 .03
☐ 463 John Smoltz.................. .15 .07 .02
☐ 464 Ken Caminiti .... .15 .07 .02
☐ 465 Melido Perez................ .10 .05 .01
☐ 466 Tom Marsh .... .10 .05 .01
☐ 467 Jeff Nelson................... .10 .05 .01
☐ 468 Jesse Levis .... .10 .05 .01
☐ 469 Chris Nabholz .... .10 .05 .01
☐ 470 Mike Macfarlane .... .10 .05 .01
☐ 471 Reggie Sanders............ .20 .09 .03
☐ 472 Chuck McElroy............. .10 .05 .01
☐ 473 Kevin Gross.................. .10 .05 .01
☐ 474 Matt Whiteside............. .10 .05 .01
☐ 475 Cal Eldred .... .15 .07 .02
☐ 476 Dave Gallagher............. .10 .05 .01
☐ 477 Len Dykstra.................. .20 .09 .03
☐ 478 Mark McGwire .... .20 .09 .03
☐ 479 David Segui.................. .10 .05 .01
☐ 480 Mike Henneman............ .10 .05 .01
☐ 481 Bret Barberie................ .10 .05 .01
☐ 482 Steve Sax..................... .10 .05 .01
☐ 483 Dave Valle .... .10 .05 .01
☐ 484 Danny Darwin .... .10 .05 .01
☐ 485 Devon White .... .15 .07 .02
☐ 486 Eric Plunk .... .10 .05 .01
☐ 487 Jim Gott......................... .10 .05 .01
☐ 488 Scooter Tucker .... .10 .05 .01
☐ 489 Omar Olivares .... .10 .05 .01
☐ 490 Greg Myers .... .10 .05 .01
☐ 491 Brian Hunter .... .10 .05 .01
☐ 492 Kevin Tapani .... .10 .05 .01
☐ 493 Rich Monteleone.......... .10 .05 .01
☐ 494 Steve Buechele .... .10 .05 .01
☐ 495 Bo Jackson .... .20 .09 .03
☐ 496 Mike LaValliere .... .10 .05 .01
☐ 497 Mark Leonard .... .10 .05 .01
☐ 498 Daryl Boston .... .10 .05 .01
☐ 499 Jose Canseco.............. .40 .18 .05
☐ 500 Brian Barnes .... .10 .05 .01
☐ 501 Randy Johnson............ .20 .09 .03
☐ 502 Tim McIntosh .... .10 .05 .01
☐ 503 Cecil Fielder .... .25 .11 .03
☐ 504 Derek Bell .... .15 .07 .02
☐ 505 Kevin Koslofski .... .10 .05 .01
☐ 506 Darren Holmes............. .10 .05 .01
☐ 507 Brady Anderson .... .15 .07 .02
☐ 508 John Valentin................ .15 .07 .02
☐ 509 Jerry Browne .... .10 .05 .01
☐ 510 Fred McGriff.................. .40 .18 .05
☐ 511 Pedro Astacio .... .15 .07 .02
☐ 512 Gary Gaetti.................... .10 .05 .01
☐ 513 John Burke .... .20 .09 .03
☐ 514 Dwight Gooden .... .10 .05 .01
☐ 515 Thomas Howard .... .10 .05 .01
☐ 516 Darrell Whitmore UER . .20 .09 .03
(11 games played in 1992; should be 121)
☐ 517 Ozzie Guillen .... .10 .05 .01
☐ 518 Darryl Kile..................... .15 .07 .02
☐ 519 Rich Rowland .... .10 .05 .01
☐ 520 Carlos Delgado .... 1.00 .45 .13
☐ 521 Doug Henry................... .10 .05 .01
☐ 522 Greg Colbrunn .... .10 .05 .01
☐ 523 Tom Gordon .... .10 .05 .01
☐ 524 Ivan Rodriguez............. .20 .09 .03
☐ 525 Kent Hrbek.................... .15 .07 .02
☐ 526 Eric Young .... .15 .07 .02
☐ 527 Rod Brewer................... .10 .05 .01
☐ 528 Eric Karros.................... .15 .07 .02
☐ 529 Marquis Grissom .... .20 .09 .03
☐ 530 Rico Brogna.................. .10 .05 .01
☐ 531 Sammy Sosa................. .20 .09 .03
☐ 532 Bret Boone.................... .20 .09 .03
☐ 533 Luis Rivera.................... .10 .05 .01
☐ 534 Hal Morris...................... .15 .07 .02

☐ 535 Monty Fariss	.10	.05	.01
☐ 536 Leo Gomez	.10	.05	.01
☐ 537 Wally Joyner	.15	.07	.02
☐ 538 Tony Gwynn	.75	.35	.09
☐ 539 Mike Williams	.10	.05	.01
☐ 540 Juan Gonzalez	1.00	.45	.13
☐ 541 Ryan Klesko	1.00	.45	.13
☐ 542 Ryan Thompson	.20	.09	.03
☐ 543 Chad Curtis	.15	.07	.02
☐ 544 Orel Hershiser	.15	.07	.02
☐ 545 Carlos Garcia	.15	.07	.02
☐ 546 Bob Welch	.10	.05	.01
☐ 547 Vinny Castilla	.10	.05	.01
☐ 548 Ozzie Smith	.60	.25	.08
☐ 549 Luis Salazar	.10	.05	.01
☐ 550 Mark Guthrie	.10	.05	.01
☐ 551 Charles Nagy	.10	.05	.01
☐ 552 Alex Fernandez	.20	.09	.03
☐ 553 Mel Rojas	.10	.05	.01
☐ 554 Orestes Destrade	.10	.05	.01
☐ 555 Mark Gubicza	.10	.05	.01
☐ 556 Steve Finley	.10	.05	.01
☐ 557 Don Mattingly	1.25	.55	.16
☐ 558 Rickey Henderson	.20	.09	.03
☐ 559 Tommy Greene	.15	.07	.02
☐ 560 Arthur Rhodes	.10	.05	.01
☐ 561 Alfredo Griffin	.10	.05	.01
☐ 562 Will Clark	.40	.18	.05
☐ 563 Bob Zupcic	.10	.05	.01
☐ 564 Chuck Carr	.10	.05	.01
☐ 565 Henry Cotto	.10	.05	.01
☐ 566 Billy Spiers	.10	.05	.01
☐ 567 Jack Armstrong	.10	.05	.01
☐ 568 Kurt Stillwell	.10	.05	.01
☐ 569 David McCarty	.15	.07	.02
☐ 570 Joe Vitiello	1.00	.45	.13
☐ 571 Gerald Williams	.10	.05	.01
☐ 572 Dale Murphy	.20	.09	.03
☐ 573 Scott Aldred	.10	.05	.01
☐ 574 Bill Gullickson	.10	.05	.01
☐ 575 Bobby Thigpen	.10	.05	.01
☐ 576 Glenallen Hill	.10	.05	.01
☐ 577 Dwayne Henry	.10	.05	.01
☐ 578 Calvin Jones	.10	.05	.01
☐ 579 Al Martin	.15	.07	.02
☐ 580 Ruben Sierra	.20	.09	.03
☐ 581 Andy Benes	.15	.07	.02
☐ 582 Anthony Young	.10	.05	.01
☐ 583 Shawn Boskie	.10	.05	.01
☐ 584 Scott Pose	.10	.05	.01
☐ 585 Mike Piazza	3.00	1.35	.40
☐ 586 Donovan Osborne	.10	.05	.01
☐ 587 James Austin	.10	.05	.01
☐ 588 Checklist 301-400	.10	.05	.01
☐ 589 Checklist 401-500	.10	.05	.01
☐ 590 Checklist 501-600	.10	.05	.01
☐ 591 Ken Griffey Jr. MC	1.50	.65	.19
☐ 592 Ivan Rodriguez MC	.20	.09	.03
☐ 593 Carlos Baerga MC	.20	.09	.03
☐ 594 Fred McGriff MC	.20	.09	.03
☐ 595 Mark McGwire MC	.15	.07	.02
☐ 596 Roberto Alomar MC	.40	.18	.05
☐ 597 Kirby Puckett MC	.60	.25	.08
☐ 598 Marquis Grissom MC	.20	.09	.03
☐ 599 John Smoltz MC	.15	.07	.02
☐ 600 Ryne Sandberg MC	.60	.25	.08
☐ 601 Wade Boggs	.20	.09	.03
☐ 602 Jeff Reardon	.15	.07	.02
☐ 603 Billy Ripken	.10	.05	.01
☐ 604 Bryan Harvey	.15	.07	.02
☐ 605 Carlos Quintana	.10	.05	.01
☐ 606 Greg Hibbard	.10	.05	.01
☐ 607 Ellis Burks	.15	.07	.02
☐ 608 Greg Swindell	.10	.05	.01
☐ 609 Dave Winfield	.20	.09	.03
☐ 610 Charlie Hough	.15	.07	.02
☐ 611 Chili Davis	.15	.07	.02
☐ 612 Jody Reed	.10	.05	.01
☐ 613 Mark Williamson	.10	.05	.01
☐ 614 Phil Plantier	.20	.09	.03
☐ 615 Jim Abbott	.20	.09	.03
☐ 616 Dante Bichette	.20	.09	.03
☐ 617 Mark Eichhorn	.10	.05	.01
☐ 618 Gary Sheffield	.20	.09	.03
☐ 619 Richie Lewis	.10	.05	.01
☐ 620 Joe Girardi	.10	.05	.01
☐ 621 Jaime Navarro	.10	.05	.01
☐ 622 Willie Wilson	.10	.05	.01
☐ 623 Scott Fletcher	.10	.05	.01
☐ 624 Bud Black	.10	.05	.01
☐ 625 Tom Brunansky	.10	.05	.01
☐ 626 Steve Avery	.20	.09	.03
☐ 627 Paul Molitor	.40	.18	.05
☐ 628 Gregg Jefferies	.20	.09	.03
☐ 629 Dave Stewart	.15	.07	.02
☐ 630 Javy Lopez	.60	.25	.08
☐ 631 Greg Gagne	.10	.05	.01
☐ 632 Roberto Kelly	.15	.07	.02
☐ 633 Mike Fetters	.10	.05	.01
☐ 634 Ozzie Canseco	.10	.05	.01
☐ 635 Jeff Russell	.10	.05	.01
☐ 636 Pete Incaviglia	.10	.05	.01
☐ 637 Tom Henke	.15	.07	.02
☐ 638 Chipper Jones	.75	.35	.09
☐ 639 Jimmy Key	.15	.07	.02
☐ 640 Dave Martinez	.10	.05	.01
☐ 641 Dave Stieb	.10	.05	.01
☐ 642 Milt Thompson	.10	.05	.01
☐ 643 Alan Mills	.10	.05	.01
☐ 644 Tony Fernandez	.10	.05	.01
☐ 645 Randy Bush	.10	.05	.01
☐ 646 Joe Magrane	.10	.05	.01
☐ 647 Ivan Calderon	.10	.05	.01
☐ 648 Jose Guzman	.10	.05	.01
☐ 649 John Olerud	.20	.09	.03
☐ 650 Tom Glavine	.20	.09	.03
☐ 651 Julio Franco	.15	.07	.02
☐ 652 Armando Reynoso	.10	.05	.01
☐ 653 Felix Jose	.10	.05	.01
☐ 654 Ben Rivera	.10	.05	.01
☐ 655 Andre Dawson	.20	.09	.03
☐ 656 Mike Harkey	.10	.05	.01
☐ 657 Kevin Seitzer	.10	.05	.01
☐ 658 Lonnie Smith	.10	.05	.01
☐ 659 Norm Charlton	.10	.05	.01
☐ 660 David Justice	.40	.18	.05
☐ 661 Fernando Valenzuela	.10	.05	.01
☐ 662 Dan Wilson	.10	.05	.01
☐ 663 Mark Gardner	.10	.05	.01
☐ 664 Doug Dascenzo	.10	.05	.01
☐ 665 Greg Maddux	.75	.35	.09
☐ 666 Harold Baines	.15	.07	.02
☐ 667 Randy Myers	.15	.07	.02
☐ 668 Harold Reynolds	.10	.05	.01
☐ 669 Candy Maldonado	.10	.05	.01
☐ 670 Al Leiter	.10	.05	.01
☐ 671 Jerald Clark	.10	.05	.01
☐ 672 Doug Drabek	.20	.09	.03
☐ 673 Kirk Gibson	.15	.07	.02
☐ 674 Steve Reed	.15	.07	.02
☐ 675 Mike Felder	.10	.05	.01
☐ 676 Ricky Gutierrez	.10	.05	.01
☐ 677 Spike Owen	.10	.05	.01
☐ 678 Otis Nixon	.10	.05	.01
☐ 679 Scott Sanderson	.10	.05	.01
☐ 680 Mark Carreon	.10	.05	.01

☐ 681 Troy Percival .10 .05 .01
☐ 682 Kevin Stocker .15 .07 .02
☐ 683 Jim Converse .15 .07 .02
☐ 684 Barry Bonds 1.25 .55 .16
☐ 685 Greg Gohr .10 .05 .01
☐ 686 Tim Wallach .10 .05 .01
☐ 687 Matt Mieske .15 .07 .02
☐ 688 Robby Thompson .10 .05 .01
☐ 689 Brien Taylor .20 .09 .03
☐ 690 Kirt Manwaring .10 .05 .01
☐ 691 Mike Lansing .30 .14 .04
☐ 692 Steve Decker .10 .05 .01
☐ 693 Mike Moore .10 .05 .01
☐ 694 Kevin Mitchell .15 .07 .02
☐ 695 Phil Hiatt .10 .05 .01
☐ 696 Tony Tarasco .40 .18 .05
☐ 697 Benji Gil .15 .07 .02
☐ 698 Jeff Juden .10 .05 .01
☐ 699 Kevin Reimer .10 .05 .01
☐ 700 Andy Ashby .10 .05 .01
☐ 701 John Jaha .15 .07 .02
☐ 702 Tim Bogar .10 .05 .01
☐ 703 David Cone .20 .09 .03
☐ 704 Willie Greene .15 .07 .02
☐ 705 David Hulse .10 .05 .01
☐ 706 Cris Carpenter .10 .05 .01
☐ 707 Ken Griffey Jr. 3.00 1.35 .40
☐ 708 Steve Bedrosian .10 .05 .01
☐ 709 Dave Nilsson .15 .07 .02
☐ 710 Paul Wagner .10 .05 .01
☐ 711 B.J. Surhoff .10 .05 .01
☐ 712 Rene Arocha .20 .09 .03
☐ 713 Manny Lee .10 .05 .01
☐ 714 Brian Williams .10 .05 .01
☐ 715 Sherman Obando .20 .09 .03
☐ 716 Terry Mulholland .10 .05 .01
☐ 717 Paul O'Neill .15 .07 .02
☐ 718 David Nied .20 .09 .03
☐ 719 J.T. Snow .15 .07 .02
☐ 720 Nigel Wilson .20 .09 .03
☐ 721 Mike Bielecki .10 .05 .01
☐ 722 Kevin Young .10 .05 .01
☐ 723 Charlie Leibrandt .10 .05 .01
☐ 724 Frank Bolick .10 .05 .01
☐ 725 Jon Shave .10 .05 .01
☐ 726 Steve Cooke .10 .05 .01
☐ 727 Domingo Martinez .10 .05 .01
☐ 728 Todd Worrell .10 .05 .01
☐ 729 Jose Lind .10 .05 .01
☐ 730 Jim Tatum .10 .05 .01
☐ 731 Mike Hampton .10 .05 .01
☐ 732 Mike Draper .10 .05 .01
☐ 733 Henry Mercedes .10 .05 .01
☐ 734 John Johnstone .10 .05 .01
☐ 735 Mitch Webster .10 .05 .01
☐ 736 Russ Springer .10 .05 .01
☐ 737 Rob Natal .10 .05 .01
☐ 738 Steve Howe .10 .05 .01
☐ 739 Darrell Sherman .10 .05 .01
☐ 740 Pat Mahomes .10 .05 .01
☐ 741 Alex Arias .10 .05 .01
☐ 742 Damon Buford .10 .05 .01
☐ 743 Charlie Hayes .15 .07 .02
☐ 744 Guillermo Velasquez .10 .05 .01
☐ 745 Checklist 601-750 UER .10 .05 .01
(650 Tom Glavin)
☐ 746 Frank Thomas MC 1.50 .65 .19
☐ 747 Barry Bonds MC .60 .25 .08
☐ 748 Roger Clemens MC .40 .18 .05
☐ 749 Joe Carter MC .20 .09 .03
☐ 750 Greg Maddux MC .40 .18 .05

1993 Stadium Club First Day Issue

Two thousand of each 1993 Stadium Club baseball card were produced on the first day and then randomly inserted in packs. These standard-size (2 1/2" by 3 1/2") cards are identical to the regular-issue 1993 Stadium Club cards, except for the embossed prismatic-foil "1st Day Production" logo stamped in an upper corner. The fronts feature unbordered color player action shots and carry the player's name in gold foil backed by a red stripe near the bottom. A baseball icon appears in the lower right with gold-foil motion-streaking. The back carries another color player action photo in the upper left. His name appears in white lettering upon a black stripe alongside on the right. Beneath are the player's team, biography, and 1992 stats. Further below are a picture of the player's first Topps card, his ranking, and career stats. All the back's design elements are superposed upon a ghosted and grainy photo of a player's gloved hand holding a baseball. The cards are numbered on the back.

	MINT	EXC	G-VG
COMPLETE SET (750)	4800.00	2200.00	600.00
COMPLETE SERIES 1 (300)	1800.00	800.00	230.00
COMPLETE SERIES 2 (300)	2000.00	900.00	250.00
COMPLETE SERIES 3 (150)	1000.00	450.00	125.00
COMMON FDI (1-300)	2.00	.90	.25
COMMON FDI (301-600)	2.00	.90	.25
COMMON FDI (601-750)	2.00	.90	.25

*UNLISTED VETERAN STARS: 30X TO 60X BASIC CARDS
*UNLISTED YOUNG STARS: 25X TO 50X BASIC CARDS
*UNLISTED RCs: 15X to 30X BASIC CARDS

☐ 40 Cal Ripken 150.00 70.00 19.00
☐ 51 Barry Bonds 60.00 27.00 7.50
☐ 200 Frank Thomas 150.00 70.00 19.00
☐ 283 Kirby Puckett 60.00 27.00 7.50
☐ 353 Nolan Ryan 300.00 135.00 38.00
☐ 366 Ryne Sandberg 50.00 23.00 6.25
☐ 384 Jeff Bagwell 75.00 34.00 9.50
☐ 424 George Brett 100.00 45.00 12.50
☐ 540 Juan Gonzalez 50.00 23.00 6.25
☐ 557 Don Mattingly 60.00 27.00 7.50
☐ 585 Mike Piazza 90.00 40.00 11.50
☐ 591 Ken Griffey Jr. MC 75.00 34.00 9.50

☐ 684 Barry Bonds	60.00	27.00	7.50
☐ 707 Ken Griffey Jr.	150.00	70.00	19.00
☐ 746 Frank Thomas MC	75.00	34.00	9.50

1993 Stadium Club Inserts I

Randomly inserted in first series packs, these four standard-size (2 1/2" by 3 1/2") cards feature borderless color player action shots on their fronts. The player's name appears in gold foil upon the blue diamond below the Stadium Club logo in a lower corner. The horizontal back carries the player's accomplishment in large gold-foil lettering. A narrow-cropped color player photo appears at the top, and the player's name and date of his accomplishment are printed in gold foil upon the picture of a baseball bat across the bottom. The cards are numbered on the back.

	MINT	EXC	G-VG
COMPLETE SET (4)	6.00	2.70	.75
COMMON CARD (1-4)	.60	.25	.08
☐ 1 Robin Yount 3000 Hit Club	1.50	.65	.19
☐ 2 George Brett 3000 Hit Club	4.00	1.80	.50
☐ 3 David Nied 1st DP Rockies	.60	.25	.08
☐ 4 Nigel Wilson 1st DP Marlins	.60	.25	.08

1993 Stadium Club Inserts II

Issued as unnumbered random inserts in second series packs, these four cards feature borderless color player action photos on both sides, each with the card's title stamped in gold foil near the top. The first and last cards below are titled "Pacific Terrific;" the second, "Broadway Stars;" and the third, "Second City Sluggers." Players' names appear below the Stadium Club logo near the bottom of each side, gold-foil stamped over a blue diamond.

	MINT	EXC	G-VG
COMPLETE SET (4)	12.00	5.50	1.50
COMMON CARD (1-4)	1.00	.45	.13
☐ 1 Will Clark Mark McGwire Pacific Terrific	1.00	.45	.13
☐ 2 Dwight Gooden Don Mattingly Broadway Stars NY	1.50	.65	.19
☐ 3 Ryne Sandberg Frank Thomas Second City Sluggers	6.00	2.70	.75
☐ 4 Darryl Strawberry Ken Griffey Jr. Pacific Terrific	4.00	1.80	.50

1993 Stadium Club Inserts III

Randomly inserted in third series packs, these two horizontally designed, standard-size (2 1/2" by 3 1/2") cards celebrate the "Firsts" of the Rockies and Marlins and feature borderless color photos of David Nied and Charlie Hough on their fronts. The player's name appears in gold foil upon the blue diamond below the Stadium Club logo in the lower left. The horizontal back carries the team's name in gold foil upon a black stripe near the top. Below are listed the team's firsts in black lettering upon a slightly ghosted photo of the ballpark where those firsts occurred. The cards are numbered on the back.

	MINT	EXC	G-VG
COMPLETE SET (2)	2.00	.90	.25
COMMON CARD (1-2)	1.00	.45	.13

☐ 1 David Nied UER Colorado Rockies Firsts (Misspelled pitch- hitter on back)	1.50	.65	.19
☐ 2 Charlie Hough Florida Marlins Firsts	1.00	.45	.13

1993 Stadium Club Master Photos

Each of the three Stadium Club series features Master Photos, uncropped versions of the regular Stadium Club cards. Each Master Photo is inlaid in a 5" by 7" white frame and bordered with a prismatic foil trim. The Master Photos were made available to the public in two ways. First, one in every 24 packs included a Master Photo winner card redeemable for a group of three Master Photos. Second, each hobby dealer box contained one Master Photo. The cards are unnumbered and checklisted below in alphabetical order within series I (1-12), II (13-24), and III (25-30). Two different versions of these master photos were issued, one with and one without the "Members Only" gold foil seal at the upper right corner. The "Members Only" Master Photos were only available with the direct-mail solicited 750-card Stadium Club Members Only set.

	MINT	EXC	G-VG
COMPLETE SET (30)	25.00	11.50	3.10
COMPLETE SERIES 1 (12)	7.00	3.10	.85
COMPLETE SERIES 2 (12)	10.00	4.50	1.25
COMPLETE SERIES 3 (6)	8.00	3.60	1.00
COMMON CARD (1-12)	.30	.14	.04
COMMON CARD (13-24)	.30	.14	.04
COMMON CARD (25-30)	.30	.14	.04

*WINNER CARDS SAME VALUE AS PLAYER SHOWN

☐ 1 Carlos Baerga	.75	.35	.09
☐ 2 Delino DeShields	.30	.14	.04
☐ 3 Brian McRae	.50	.23	.06
☐ 4 Sam Militello	.30	.14	.04
☐ 5 Joe Oliver	.30	.14	.04
☐ 6 Kirby Puckett	2.00	.90	.25
☐ 7 Cal Ripken	4.00	1.80	.50
☐ 8 Bip Roberts	.30	.14	.04
☐ 9 Mike Scioscia	.30	.14	.04
☐ 10 Rick Sutcliffe	.30	.14	.04
☐ 11 Danny Tartabull	.30	.14	.04
☐ 12 Tim Wakefield	.30	.14	.04
☐ 13 George Brett	2.00	.90	.25
☐ 14 Jose Canseco	.75	.35	.09
☐ 15 Will Clark	.75	.35	.09
☐ 16 Travis Fryman	.50	.23	.06
☐ 17 Dwight Gooden	.30	.14	.04
☐ 18 Mark Grace	.30	.14	.04
☐ 19 Rickey Henderson	.50	.23	.06
☐ 20 Mark McGwire MC	.30	.14	.04
☐ 21 Nolan Ryan	5.00	2.30	.60
☐ 22 Ruben Sierra	.50	.23	.06
☐ 23 Darryl Strawberry	.30	.14	.04
☐ 24 Larry Walker	.50	.23	.06
☐ 25 Barry Bonds	2.00	.90	.25
☐ 26 Ken Griffey Jr.	5.00	2.30	.60
☐ 27 Greg Maddux	1.25	.55	.16
☐ 28 David Nied	.50	.23	.06
☐ 29 J.T. Snow	.30	.14	.04
☐ 30 Brien Taylor	.30	.14	.04

1993 Stadium Club Murphy

This 200-card boxed set features 1992 All-Star Game cards, 1992 Team USA cards, and 1992 Championship and World Series cards. Topps actually refers to this set as a 1992 issue, but the set was released in 1993. The standard-size (2 1/2" by 3 1/2") cards display full-bleed posed and action color player shots on the fronts. The player's name appears below the Topps Stadium Club logo in the lower right with parallel gold foil stripes intersecting the logo. The horizontal back presents the player's biography, statistics, and highlights on a ghosted photo. The cards are numbered on the back. This 200-card set is housed in a replica of San Diego's Jack Murphy Stadium, site of the 1992 All-Star Game. Production was limited to 8,000 cases, with 16 boxes per case. The set includes 100 Draft Pick cards, 56 All-Star cards, 25 Team USA cards, and 19 cards commemorating the 1992 National and American League Championship Series and the World Series. Rookie Cards in this set include Trey Beamon, Derek Jeter, Jason Kendall, Jon Lieber, Michael Moore, Chad Mottola, Benji Simonton and Preston Wilson.

	MINT	EXC	G-VG
COMPLETE FACT.SET (212)	30.00	13.50	3.80
COMPLETE SET (200)	25.00	11.50	3.10
COMMON CARD (1-200)	.10	.05	.01

	MINT	EXC	G-VG
☐ 1 Dave Winfield	.20	.09	.03
☐ 2 Juan Guzman	.15	.07	.02
☐ 3 Tony Gwynn	.75	.35	.09
☐ 4 Chris Roberts	.20	.09	.03
☐ 5 Benny Santiago	.10	.05	.01
☐ 6 Sherard Clinkscales	.15	.07	.02
☐ 7 Jon Nunnally	.50	.23	.06
☐ 8 Chuck Knoblauch	.20	.09	.03
☐ 9 Bob Wolcott	.30	.14	.04
☐ 10 Steve Rodriguez	.10	.05	.01
☐ 11 Mark Williams	.15	.07	.02
☐ 12 Danny Clyburn	1.00	.45	.13
☐ 13 Darren Dreifort	.25	.11	.03
☐ 14 Andy Van Slyke	.20	.09	.03
☐ 15 Wade Boggs	.20	.09	.03
☐ 16 Scott Patton	.15	.07	.02
☐ 17 Gary Sheffield	.10	.05	.01
☐ 18 Ron Villone	.20	.09	.03
☐ 19 Roberto Alomar	.75	.35	.09
☐ 20 Marc Valdes	.50	.23	.06
☐ 21 Daron Kirkreit	.40	.18	.05
☐ 22 Jeff Granger	.30	.14	.04
☐ 23 Levon Largusa	.10	.05	.01
☐ 24 Jimmy Key	.15	.07	.02
☐ 25 Kevin Pearson	.15	.07	.02
☐ 26 Michael Moore	.30	.14	.04
☐ 27 Preston Wilson	.40	.18	.05
☐ 28 Kirby Puckett	1.25	.55	.16
☐ 29 Tim Crabtree	.10	.05	.01
☐ 30 Bip Roberts	.10	.05	.01
☐ 31 Kelly Gruber	.10	.05	.01
☐ 32 Tony Fernandez	.10	.05	.01
☐ 33 Jason Angel	.15	.07	.02
☐ 34 Calvin Murray	.10	.05	.01
☐ 35 Chad McConnell	.10	.05	.01
☐ 36 Jason Moler	.40	.18	.05
☐ 37 Mark Lemke	.10	.05	.01
☐ 38 Tom Knauss	.15	.07	.02
☐ 39 Larry Mitchell	.15	.07	.02
☐ 40 Doug Mirabelli	.10	.05	.01
☐ 41 Everett Stull II	.35	.16	.04
☐ 42 Chris Wimmer	.10	.05	.01
☐ 43 Dan Serafini	.40	.18	.05
☐ 44 Ryne Sandberg	1.00	.45	.13
☐ 45 Steve Lyons	.15	.07	.02
☐ 46 Ryan Freeburg	.10	.05	.01
☐ 47 Ruben Sierra	.20	.09	.03
☐ 48 David Mysel	.15	.07	.02
☐ 49 Joe Hamilton	.15	.07	.02
☐ 50 Steve Rodriguez	.10	.05	.01
☐ 51 Tim Wakefield	.10	.05	.01
☐ 52 Scott Gentile	.25	.11	.03
☐ 53 Doug Jones	.10	.05	.01
☐ 54 Willie Brown	.25	.11	.03
☐ 55 Chad Mottola	.30	.14	.04
☐ 56 Ken Griffey Jr.	3.00	1.35	.40
☐ 57 Jon Lieber	.75	.35	.09
☐ 58 Denny Martinez	.15	.07	.02
☐ 59 Joe Petcka	.10	.05	.01
☐ 60 Benji Simonton	1.00	.45	.13
☐ 61 Brett Backlund	.10	.05	.01
☐ 62 Damon Berryhill	.10	.05	.01
☐ 63 Juan Guzman	.15	.07	.02
☐ 64 Doug Hecker	.25	.11	.03
☐ 65 Jamie Arnold	.25	.11	.03
☐ 66 Bob Tewksbury	.10	.05	.01
☐ 67 Tim Leger	.15	.07	.02
☐ 68 Todd Etler	.20	.09	.03
☐ 69 Lloyd McClendon	.10	.05	.01
☐ 70 Kurt Ehmann	.10	.05	.01
☐ 71 Rick Magdaleno	.25	.11	.03
☐ 72 Tom Pagnozzi	.10	.05	.01
☐ 73 Jeffrey Hammonds	.60	.25	.08
☐ 74 Joe Carter	.40	.18	.05
☐ 75 Chris Holt	.50	.23	.06
☐ 76 Charles Johnson	.60	.25	.08
☐ 77 Bob Walk	.10	.05	.01
☐ 78 Fred McGriff	.40	.18	.05
☐ 79 Tom Evans	.25	.11	.03
☐ 80 Scott Klingenbeck	.30	.14	.04
☐ 81 Chad McConnell	.10	.05	.01
☐ 82 Chris Eddy	.15	.07	.02
☐ 83 Phil Nevin	.25	.11	.03
☐ 84 John Kruk	.20	.09	.03
☐ 85 Tony Sheffield	.15	.07	.02
☐ 86 John Smoltz	.15	.07	.02
☐ 87 Trevor Humphry	.15	.07	.02
☐ 88 Charles Nagy	.10	.05	.01
☐ 89 Sean Runyan	.15	.07	.02
☐ 90 Mike Gulan	.15	.07	.02
☐ 91 Darren Daulton	.20	.09	.03
☐ 92 Otis Nixon	.10	.05	.01
☐ 93 Nomar Garciaparra	1.00	.45	.13
☐ 94 Larry Walker	.20	.09	.03
☐ 95 Hut Smith	.15	.07	.02
☐ 96 Rick Helling	.15	.07	.02
☐ 97 Roger Clemens	.75	.35	.09
☐ 98 Ron Gant	.15	.07	.02
☐ 99 Kenny Felder	.30	.14	.04
☐ 100 Steve Murphy	.10	.05	.01
☐ 101 Mike Smith	.40	.18	.05
☐ 102 Terry Pendleton	.10	.05	.01
☐ 103 Tim Davis	.40	.18	.05
☐ 104 Jeff Patzke	.15	.07	.02
☐ 105 Craig Wilson	.10	.05	.01
☐ 106 Tom Glavine	.20	.09	.03
☐ 107 Mark Langston	.20	.09	.03
☐ 108 Mark Thompson	.25	.11	.03
☐ 109 Eric Owens	.20	.09	.03
☐ 110 Keith Johnson	.10	.05	.01
☐ 111 Robin Ventura	.20	.09	.03
☐ 112 Ed Sprague	.10	.05	.01
☐ 113 Jeff Schmidt	.10	.05	.01
☐ 114 Don Wengert	.10	.05	.01
☐ 115 Craig Biggio	.15	.07	.02
☐ 116 Kenny Carlyle	.15	.07	.02
☐ 117 Derek Jeter	3.00	1.35	.40
☐ 118 Manny Lee	.10	.05	.01
☐ 119 Jeff Haas	.10	.05	.01
☐ 120 Roger Bailey	.20	.09	.03
☐ 121 Sean Lowe	.30	.14	.04
☐ 122 Rick Aguilera	.10	.05	.01
☐ 123 Sandy Alomar	.15	.07	.02
☐ 124 Derek Wallace	.10	.05	.01
☐ 125 B.J. Wallace	.10	.05	.01
☐ 126 Greg Maddux	.75	.35	.09
☐ 127 Tim Moore	.20	.09	.03
☐ 128 Lee Smith	.20	.09	.03
☐ 129 Todd Steverson	.30	.14	.04
☐ 130 Chris Widger	.25	.11	.03
☐ 131 Paul Molitor	.40	.18	.05
☐ 132 Chris Smith	.20	.09	.03
☐ 133 Chris Gomez	.60	.25	.08
☐ 134 Jimmy Baron	.15	.07	.02
☐ 135 John Smoltz	.15	.07	.02
☐ 136 Pat Borders	.10	.05	.01
☐ 137 Donnie Leshnock	.10	.05	.01
☐ 138 Gus Gandarillos	.20	.09	.03
☐ 139 Will Clark	.10	.05	.01
☐ 140 Ryan Luzinski	.25	.11	.03
☐ 141 Cal Ripken	2.00	.90	.25

☐ 142	B.J. Wallace	.10	.05	.01
☐ 143	Trey Beamon	1.50	.65	.19
☐ 144	Norm Charlton	.10	.05	.01
☐ 145	Mike Mussina	.60	.25	.08
☐ 146	Billy Owens	.40	.18	.05
☐ 147	Ozzie Smith	.60	.25	.08
☐ 148	Jason Kendall	1.00	.45	.13
☐ 149	Mike Matthews	.20	.09	.03
☐ 150	David Spykstra	.15	.07	.02
☐ 151	Benji Grigsby	.20	.09	.03
☐ 152	Sean Smith	.15	.07	.02
☐ 153	Mark McGwire	.10	.05	.01
☐ 154	David Cone	.20	.09	.03
☐ 155	Shon Walker	.25	.11	.03
☐ 156	Jason Giambi	.30	.14	.04
☐ 157	Jack McDowell	.20	.09	.03
☐ 158	Paxton Briley	.10	.05	.01
☐ 159	Edgar Martinez	.10	.05	.01
☐ 160	Brian Sackinsky	.30	.14	.04
☐ 161	Barry Bonds	1.25	.55	.16
☐ 162	Roberto Kelly	.15	.07	.02
☐ 163	Jeff Alkire	.25	.11	.03
☐ 164	Mike Sharperson	.10	.05	.01
☐ 165	Jamie Taylor	.10	.05	.01
☐ 166	John Saffer	.20	.09	.03
☐ 167	Jerry Browne	.10	.05	.01
☐ 168	Travis Fryman	.20	.09	.03
☐ 169	Brady Anderson	.15	.07	.02
☐ 170	Chris Roberts	.20	.09	.03
☐ 171	Lloyd Peever	.20	.09	.03
☐ 172	Francisco Cabrera	.10	.05	.01
☐ 173	Ramiro Martinez	.25	.11	.03
☐ 174	Jeff Alkire	.25	.11	.03
☐ 175	Ivan Rodriguez	.20	.09	.03
☐ 176	Kevin Brown	.10	.05	.01
☐ 177	Chad Roper	.25	.11	.03
☐ 178	Rod Henderson	.30	.14	.04
☐ 179	Dennis Eckersley	.20	.09	.03
☐ 180	Shannon Stewart	.40	.18	.05
☐ 181	DeShawn Warren	.20	.09	.03
☐ 182	Lonnie Smith	.10	.05	.01
☐ 183	Willie Adams	.40	.18	.05
☐ 184	Jeff Montgomery	.15	.07	.02
☐ 185	Damon Hollins	.60	.25	.08
☐ 186	Byron Mathews	.10	.05	.01
☐ 187	Harold Baines	.15	.07	.02
☐ 188	Rick Greene	.15	.07	.02
☐ 189	Carlos Baerga	.40	.18	.05
☐ 190	Brandon Cromer	.15	.07	.02
☐ 191	Roberto Alomar	.75	.35	.09
☐ 192	Rich Ireland	.15	.07	.02
☐ 193	Steve Montgomery	.15	.07	.02
☐ 194	Brant Brown	.40	.18	.05
☐ 195	Ritchie Moody	.10	.05	.01
☐ 196	Michael Tucker	.40	.18	.05
☐ 197	Jason Varitek	1.00	.45	.13
☐ 198	David Manning	.15	.07	.02
☐ 199	Marquis Riley	.20	.09	.03
☐ 200	Jason Giambi	.30	.14	.04

1993 Stadium Club Murphy Master Photos

Each of these uncropped Murphy Master Photos is inlaid in a 5" by 7" white frame and bordered with a prismatic foil trim. One Murphy Master Photo was included in each 1993 Stadium Club Murphy Special factory set. The photos are unnumbered and checklisted below in alphabetical order.

	MINT	EXC	G-VG
COMPLETE SET (12)	5.00	2.30	.60
COMMON CARD (1-12)	.30	.14	.04

☐ 1	Sandy Alomar AS	.30	.14	.04
☐ 2	Tom Glavine AS	.50	.23	.06
☐ 3	Ken Griffey Jr. AS	3.00	1.35	.40
☐ 4	Tony Gwynn AS	.75	.35	.09
☐ 5	Chuck Knoblauch AS	.50	.23	.06
☐ 6	Chad Mottola '92	.30	.14	.04
☐ 7	Kirby Puckett AS	1.25	.55	.16
☐ 8	Chris Roberts USA	.30	.14	.04
☐ 9	Ryne Sandberg AS	1.00	.45	.13
☐ 10	Gary Sheffield AS	.50	.23	.06
☐ 11	Larry Walker AS	.50	.23	.06
☐ 12	Preston Wilson '92	.30	.14	.04

1994 Stadium Club

The 720 standard-size cards comprising this set were issued two series of 270 and a third series of 180. Card fronts feature borderless color player action photos. The player's last name appears in white lettering within a red-foil-stamped rectangle at the bottom. His first name appears alongside in black "typewritten" lettering within a division color-coded "tearaway." The red-foil-stamped Stadium Club logo appears in an upper corner. The back carries a color player action cutout superimposed upon a blue and black background. The player's name, team, biography, career highlights and statistics appear in lettering of several different colors and typefaces. There are a number

of subsets including Home Run Club (258-268), Tale of Two Players (525/526), Division Leaders (527-532), Quick Starts (533-538), Career Contributors (541-543), Rookie Rocker (626-630), Rookie Rocket (631-634) and Fantastic Finishes (714-719). Rookie Cards include Brian Anderson, Chan Ho Park and Julian Tavarez.

	MINT	EXC	G-VG
COMPLETE SET (720)	55.00	25.00	7.00
COMPLETE SERIES 1 (270)	20.00	9.00	2.50
COMPLETE SERIES 2 (270)	20.00	9.00	2.50
COMPLETE SERIES 3 (180)	15.00	6.75	1.90
COMMON CARD (1-270)	.10	.05	.01
COMMON CARD (271-540)	.10	.05	.01
COMMON CARD (541-720)	.10	.05	.01

Card	MINT	EXC	G-VG
☐ 1 Robin Yount	.40	.18	.05
☐ 2 Rick Wilkins	.10	.05	.01
☐ 3 Steve Scarsone	.10	.05	.01
☐ 4 Gary Sheffield	.20	.09	.03
☐ 5 George Brett UER (birthdate listed as 1963; should be 1953)	1.25	.55	.16
☐ 6 Al Martin	.10	.05	.01
☐ 7 Joe Oliver	.10	.05	.01
☐ 8 Stan Belinda	.10	.05	.01
☐ 9 Denny Hocking	.10	.05	.01
☐ 10 Roberto Alomar	.75	.35	.09
☐ 11 Luis Polonia	.10	.05	.01
☐ 12 Scott Hemond	.10	.05	.01
☐ 13 Jody Reed	.10	.05	.01
☐ 14 Mel Rojas	.10	.05	.01
☐ 15 Junior Ortiz	.10	.05	.01
☐ 16 Harold Baines	.15	.07	.02
☐ 17 Brad Pennington	.10	.05	.01
☐ 18 Jay Bell	.15	.07	.02
☐ 19 Tom Henke	.10	.05	.01
☐ 20 Jeff Branson	.10	.05	.01
☐ 21 Roberto Mejia	.15	.07	.02
☐ 22 Pedro Munoz	.10	.05	.01
☐ 23 Matt Nokes	.10	.05	.01
☐ 24 Jack McDowell	.20	.09	.03
☐ 25 Cecil Fielder	.20	.09	.03
☐ 26 Tony Fossas	.10	.05	.01
☐ 27 Jim Eisenreich	.10	.05	.01
☐ 28 Anthony Young	.10	.05	.01
☐ 29 Chuck Carr	.10	.05	.01
☐ 30 Jeff Treadway	.10	.05	.01
☐ 31 Chris Nabholz	.10	.05	.01
☐ 32 Tom Candiotti	.10	.05	.01
☐ 33 Mike Maddux	.10	.05	.01
☐ 34 Nolan Ryan	3.00	1.35	.40
☐ 35 Luis Gonzalez	.10	.05	.01
☐ 36 Tim Salmon	.40	.18	.05
☐ 37 Mark Whiten	.15	.07	.02
☐ 38 Roger McDowell	.10	.05	.01
☐ 39 Royce Clayton	.15	.07	.02
☐ 40 Troy Neel	.15	.07	.02
☐ 41 Mike Harkey	.10	.05	.01
☐ 42 Darrin Fletcher	.10	.05	.01
☐ 43 Wayne Kirby	.15	.07	.02
☐ 44 Rich Amaral	.10	.05	.01
☐ 45 Robb Nen UER (Nenn on back)	.10	.05	.01
☐ 46 Tim Teufel	.10	.05	.01
☐ 47 Steve Cooke	.10	.05	.01
☐ 48 Jeff McNeely	.10	.05	.01
☐ 49 Jeff Montgomery	.15	.07	.02
☐ 50 Skeeter Barnes	.10	.05	.01
☐ 51 Scott Stahoviak	.10	.05	.01
☐ 52 Pat Kelly	.10	.05	.01
☐ 53 Brady Anderson	.15	.07	.02
☐ 54 Mariano Duncan	.10	.05	.01
☐ 55 Brian Bohanon	.10	.05	.01
☐ 56 Jerry Spradlin	.10	.05	.01
☐ 57 Ron Karkovice	.10	.05	.01
☐ 58 Jeff Gardner	.10	.05	.01
☐ 59 Bobby Bonilla	.20	.09	.03
☐ 60 Tino Martinez	.10	.05	.01
☐ 61 Todd Benzinger	.10	.05	.01
☐ 62 Steve Trachsel	.40	.18	.05
☐ 63 Brian Jordan	.15	.07	.02
☐ 64 Steve Bedrosian	.10	.05	.01
☐ 65 Brent Gates	.20	.09	.03
☐ 66 Shawn Green	.20	.09	.03
☐ 67 Sean Berry	.10	.05	.01
☐ 68 Joe Klink	.10	.05	.01
☐ 69 Fernando Valenzuela	.10	.05	.01
☐ 70 Andy Tomberlin	.10	.05	.01
☐ 71 Tony Pena	.10	.05	.01
☐ 72 Eric Young	.15	.07	.02
☐ 73 Chris Gomez	.20	.09	.03
☐ 74 Paul O'Neill	.15	.07	.02
☐ 75 Ricky Gutierrez	.10	.05	.01
☐ 76 Brad Holman	.10	.05	.01
☐ 77 Lance Painter	.10	.05	.01
☐ 78 Mike Butcher	.10	.05	.01
☐ 79 Sid Bream	.10	.05	.01
☐ 80 Sammy Sosa	.20	.09	.03
☐ 81 Felix Fermin	.10	.05	.01
☐ 82 Todd Hundley	.10	.05	.01
☐ 83 Kevin Higgins	.10	.05	.01
☐ 84 Todd Pratt	.10	.05	.01
☐ 85 Ken Griffey Jr.	3.00	1.35	.40
☐ 86 John O'Donoghue	.15	.07	.02
☐ 87 Rick Renteria	.10	.05	.01
☐ 88 John Burkett	.15	.07	.02
☐ 89 Jose Vizcaino	.10	.05	.01
☐ 90 Kevin Seitzer	.10	.05	.01
☐ 91 Bobby Witt	.10	.05	.01
☐ 92 Chris Turner	.10	.05	.01
☐ 93 Omar Vizquel	.10	.05	.01
☐ 94 David Justice	.40	.18	.05
☐ 95 David Segui	.10	.05	.01
☐ 96 Dave Hollins	.20	.09	.03
☐ 97 Doug Strange	.10	.05	.01
☐ 98 Jerald Clark	.10	.05	.01
☐ 99 Mike Moore	.10	.05	.01
☐ 100 Joey Cora	.10	.05	.01
☐ 101 Scott Kamieniecki	.10	.05	.01
☐ 102 Andy Benes	.15	.07	.02
☐ 103 Chris Bosio	.10	.05	.01
☐ 104 Rey Sanchez	.10	.05	.01
☐ 105 John Jaha	.10	.05	.01
☐ 106 Otis Nixon	.10	.05	.01
☐ 107 Rickey Henderson	.20	.09	.03
☐ 108 Jeff Bagwell	1.50	.65	.19
☐ 109 Gregg Jefferies	.20	.09	.03
☐ 110 Blue Jays Trio (Roberto Alomar/Paul Molitor/ John Olerud)	.20	.09	.03
☐ 111 Braves Trio (Ron Gant/David Justice/ Fred McGriff)	.10	.05	.01
☐ 112 Rangers Trio (Juan Gonzalez/Rafael Palmeiro/ Dean Palmer)	.10	.05	.01
☐ 113 Greg Swindell	.10	.05	.01
☐ 114 Bill Haselman	.10	.05	.01
☐ 115 Phil Plantier	.15	.07	.02
☐ 116 Ivan Rodriguez	.20	.09	.03
☐ 117 Kevin Tapani	.10	.05	.01
☐ 118 Mike LaValliere	.10	.05	.01
☐ 119 Tim Costo	.10	.05	.01

☐ 120 Mickey Morandini .... .10 .05 .01
☐ 121 Brett Butler .... .15 .07 .02
☐ 122 Tom Pagnozzi .... .10 .05 .01
☐ 123 Ron Gant...................... .15 .07 .02
☐ 124 Damion Easley .... .10 .05 .01
☐ 125 Dennis Eckersley.......... .20 .09 .03
☐ 126 Matt Mieske .... .10 .05 .01
☐ 127 Cliff Floyd..................... .50 .23 .06
☐ 128 Julian Tavarez.............. .60 .25 .08
☐ 129 Arthur Rhodes .... .10 .05 .01
☐ 130 Dave West..................... .10 .05 .01
☐ 131 Tim Naehring .... .10 .05 .01
☐ 132 Freddie Benavides........ .10 .05 .01
☐ 133 Paul Assenmacher .... .10 .05 .01
☐ 134 David McCarty .... .15 .07 .02
☐ 135 Jose Lind .... .10 .05 .01
☐ 136 Reggie Sanders............ .15 .07 .02
☐ 137 Don Slaught.................. .10 .05 .01
☐ 138 Andujar Cedeno .... .10 .05 .01
☐ 139 Rob Deer....................... .10 .05 .01
☐ 140 Mike Piazza UER .... 1.50 .65 .19
(listed as outfielder)
☐ 141 Moises Alou .... .20 .09 .03
☐ 142 Tom Foley..................... .10 .05 .01
☐ 143 Benito Santiago............ .10 .05 .01
☐ 144 Sandy Alomar .... .15 .07 .02
☐ 145 Carlos Hernandez......... .10 .05 .01
☐ 146 Luis Alicea .... .10 .05 .01
☐ 147 Tom Lampkin................ .10 .05 .01
☐ 148 Ryan Klesko .... .50 .23 .06
☐ 149 Juan Guzman .... .15 .07 .02
☐ 150 Scott Servais................ .10 .05 .01
☐ 151 Tony Gwynn.................. .75 .35 .09
☐ 152 Tim Wakefield .... .10 .05 .01
☐ 153 David Nied .... .20 .09 .03
☐ 154 Chris Haney .... .10 .05 .01
☐ 155 Danny Bautista............. .15 .07 .02
☐ 156 Randy Velarde.............. .10 .05 .01
☐ 157 Darrin Jackson............. .10 .05 .01
☐ 158 J.R. Phillips.................. .20 .09 .03
☐ 159 Greg Gagne.................. .10 .05 .01
☐ 160 Luis Aquino................... .10 .05 .01
☐ 161 John Vander Wal .... .10 .05 .01
☐ 162 Randy Myers................ .10 .05 .01
☐ 163 Ted Power..................... .10 .05 .01
☐ 164 Scott Brosius .... .10 .05 .01
☐ 165 Len Dykstra.................. .20 .09 .03
☐ 166 Jacob Brumfield........... .10 .05 .01
☐ 167 Bo Jackson .... .20 .09 .03
☐ 168 Eddie Taubensee.......... .10 .05 .01
☐ 169 Carlos Baerga .... .40 .18 .05
☐ 170 Tim Bogar..................... .10 .05 .01
☐ 171 Jose Canseco............... .40 .18 .05
☐ 172 Greg Blosser UER .... .10 .05 .01
(Gregg on front)
☐ 173 Chili Davis.................... .15 .07 .02
☐ 174 Randy Knorr .... .10 .05 .01
☐ 175 Mike Perez.................... .10 .05 .01
☐ 176 Henry Rodriguez.......... .10 .05 .01
☐ 177 Brian Turang................ .10 .05 .01
☐ 178 Roger Pavlik .... .20 .09 .03
☐ 179 Aaron Sele .... .25 .11 .03
☐ 180 Fred McGriff................. .20 .09 .03
Gary Sheffield
Tale of 2 Players
☐ 181 J.T. Snow...................... .20 .09 .03
Tim Salmon
Tale of 2 Players
☐ 182 Roberto Hernandez...... .10 .05 .01
☐ 183 Jeff Reboulet................ .10 .05 .01
☐ 184 John Doherty................ .10 .05 .01
☐ 185 Danny Sheaffer .... .10 .05 .01
☐ 186 Bip Roberts................... .10 .05 .01
☐ 187 Denny Martinez............ .15 .07 .02
☐ 188 Darryl Hamilton............ .10 .05 .01
☐ 189 Eduardo Perez.............. .15 .07 .02
☐ 190 Pete Harnisch .... .10 .05 .01
☐ 191 Rich Gossage............... .20 .09 .03
☐ 192 Mickey Tettleton .... .15 .07 .02
☐ 193 Lenny Webster............. .10 .05 .01
☐ 194 Lance Johnson .... .10 .05 .01
☐ 195 Don Mattingly .... 1.25 .55 .16
☐ 196 Gregg Olson................. .10 .05 .01
☐ 197 Mark Gubicza............... .10 .05 .01
☐ 198 Scott Fletcher............... .10 .05 .01
☐ 199 Jon Shave..................... .10 .05 .01
☐ 200 Tim Mauser................... .10 .05 .01
☐ 201 Jeromy Burnitz .... .15 .07 .02
☐ 202 Rob Dibble.................... .10 .05 .01
☐ 203 Will Clark .... .40 .18 .05
☐ 204 Steve Buechele .... .10 .05 .01
☐ 205 Brian Williams.............. .10 .05 .01
☐ 206 Carlos Garcia .... .10 .05 .01
☐ 207 Mark Clark .... .10 .05 .01
☐ 208 Rafael Palmeiro............ .20 .09 .03
☐ 209 Eric Davis..................... .10 .05 .01
☐ 210 Pat Meares.................... .10 .05 .01
☐ 211 Chuck Finley .... .10 .05 .01
☐ 212 Jason Bere................... .40 .18 .05
☐ 213 Gary DiSarcina............. .10 .05 .01
☐ 214 Tony Fernandez............ .10 .05 .01
☐ 215 B.J. Surhoff.................. .10 .05 .01
☐ 216 Lee Guetterman .... .10 .05 .01
☐ 217 Tim Wallach.................. .10 .05 .01
☐ 218 Kirt Manwaring .... .10 .05 .01
☐ 219 Albert Belle .... 1.00 .45 .13
☐ 220 Dwight Gooden............ .10 .05 .01
☐ 221 Archi Cianfrocco .... .10 .05 .01
☐ 222 Terry Mulholland.......... .15 .07 .02
☐ 223 Hipolito Pichardo .... .10 .05 .01
☐ 224 Kent Hrbek................... .15 .07 .02
☐ 225 Craig Grebeck .... .10 .05 .01
☐ 226 Todd Jones................... .10 .05 .01
☐ 227 Mike Bordick................. .10 .05 .01
☐ 228 John Olerud.................. .20 .09 .03
☐ 229 Jeff Blauser.................. .15 .07 .02
☐ 230 Alex Arias..................... .10 .05 .01
☐ 231 Bernard Gilkey .... .10 .05 .01
☐ 232 Denny Neagle.............. .10 .05 .01
☐ 233 Pedro Borbon .... .10 .05 .01
☐ 234 Dick Schofield.............. .10 .05 .01
☐ 235 Matias Carrillo.............. .10 .05 .01
☐ 236 Juan Bell....................... .10 .05 .01
☐ 237 Mike Hampton .... .10 .05 .01
☐ 238 Barry Bonds.............. 1.25 .55 .16
☐ 239 Cris Carpenter.............. .10 .05 .01
☐ 240 Eric Karros................... .15 .07 .02
☐ 241 Greg McMichael........... .15 .07 .02
☐ 242 Pat Hentgen .... .15 .07 .02
☐ 243 Tim Pugh .... .20 .09 .03
☐ 244 Vinny Castilla .... .10 .05 .01
☐ 245 Charlie Hough .... .15 .07 .02
☐ 246 Bobby Munoz............... .10 .05 .01
☐ 247 Kevin Baez................... .10 .05 .01
☐ 248 Todd Frohwirth .... .10 .05 .01
☐ 249 Charlie Hayes............... .15 .07 .02
☐ 250 Mike Macfarlane .... .10 .05 .01
☐ 251 Danny Darwin .... .10 .05 .01
☐ 252 Ben Rivera .... .10 .05 .01
☐ 253 Dave Henderson .... .10 .05 .01
☐ 254 Steve Avery.................. .20 .09 .03
☐ 255 Tim Belcher.................. .10 .05 .01
☐ 256 Dan Plesac................... .10 .05 .01
☐ 257 Jim Thome................... .20 .09 .03
☐ 258 Albert Belle 35 HR........ .50 .23 .06
☐ 259 Barry Bonds 35 HR ...... .60 .25 .08

☐ 260 Ron Gant 35 HR .15 .07 .02
☐ 261 Juan Gonzalez 35 HR .50 .23 .06
☐ 262 Ken Griffey Jr. 35 HR 1.50 .65 .19
☐ 263 David Justice 35 HR .20 .09 .03
☐ 264 Fred McGriff 35 HR .20 .09 .03
☐ 265 Rafael Palmeiro 35 HR .20 .09 .03
☐ 266 Mike Piazza 35 HR .75 .35 .09
☐ 267 Frank Thomas 35 HR 1.50 .65 .19
☐ 268 Matt Williams 35 HR .30 .14 .04
☐ 269 Checklist 1-135 .10 .05 .01
☐ 270 Checklist 136-270 .10 .05 .01
☐ 271 Mike Stanley .10 .05 .01
☐ 272 Tony Tarasco .20 .09 .03
☐ 273 Teddy Higuera .10 .05 .01
☐ 274 Ryan Thompson .15 .07 .02
☐ 275 Rick Aguilera .15 .07 .02
☐ 276 Ramon Martinez .15 .07 .02
☐ 277 Orlando Merced .15 .07 .02
☐ 278 Guillermo Velasquez .10 .05 .01
☐ 279 Mark Hutton .10 .05 .01
☐ 280 Larry Walker .20 .09 .03
☐ 281 Kevin Gross .10 .05 .01
☐ 282 Jose Offerman .10 .05 .01
☐ 283 Jim Leyritz .10 .05 .01
☐ 284 Jamie Moyer .10 .05 .01
☐ 285 Frank Thomas 3.00 1.35 .40
☐ 286 Derek Bell .15 .07 .02
☐ 287 Derrick May .10 .05 .01
☐ 288 Dave Winfield .20 .09 .03
☐ 289 Curt Schilling .10 .05 .01
☐ 290 Carlos Quintana .10 .05 .01
☐ 291 Bob Natal .10 .05 .01
☐ 292 David Cone .20 .09 .03
☐ 293 Al Osuna .10 .05 .01
☐ 294 Bob Hamelin .20 .09 .03
☐ 295 Chad Curtis .15 .07 .02
☐ 296 Danny Jackson .10 .05 .01
☐ 297 Bob Welch .10 .05 .01
☐ 298 Felix Jose .10 .05 .01
☐ 299 Jay Buhner .15 .07 .02
☐ 300 Joe Carter .40 .18 .05
☐ 301 Kenny Lofton .75 .35 .09
☐ 302 Kirk Rueter .10 .05 .01
☐ 303 Kim Batiste .10 .05 .01
☐ 304 Mike Morgan .10 .05 .01
☐ 305 Pat Borders .10 .05 .01
☐ 306 Rene Arocha .15 .07 .02
☐ 307 Ruben Sierra .20 .09 .03
☐ 308 Steve Finley .10 .05 .01
☐ 309 Travis Fryman .25 .11 .03
☐ 310 Zane Smith .10 .05 .01
☐ 311 Willie Wilson .10 .05 .01
☐ 312 Trevor Hoffman .10 .05 .01
☐ 313 Terry Pendleton .10 .05 .01
☐ 314 Salomon Torres .15 .07 .02
☐ 315 Robin Ventura .15 .07 .02
☐ 316 Randy Tomlin .10 .05 .01
☐ 317 Dave Stewart .15 .07 .02
☐ 318 Mike Benjamin .10 .05 .01
☐ 319 Matt Turner .10 .05 .01
☐ 320 Manny Ramirez .60 .25 .08
☐ 321 Kevin Young .10 .05 .01
☐ 322 Ken Caminiti .15 .07 .02
☐ 323 Joe Girardi .10 .05 .01
☐ 324 Jeff McKnight .10 .05 .01
☐ 325 Gene Harris .10 .05 .01
☐ 326 Devon White .10 .05 .01
☐ 327 Darryl Kile .15 .07 .02
☐ 328 Craig Paquette .10 .05 .01
☐ 329 Cal Eldred .15 .07 .02
☐ 330 Bill Swift .10 .05 .01
☐ 331 Alan Trammell .20 .09 .03
☐ 332 Armando Reynoso .10 .05 .01
☐ 333 Brent Mayne .10 .05 .01
☐ 334 Chris Donnels .10 .05 .01
☐ 335 Darryl Strawberry .15 .07 .02
☐ 336 Dean Palmer .15 .07 .02
☐ 337 Frank Castillo .10 .05 .01
☐ 338 Jeff King .10 .05 .01
☐ 339 John Franco .10 .05 .01
☐ 340 Kevin Appier .15 .07 .02
☐ 341 Lance Blankenship .10 .05 .01
☐ 342 Mark McLemore .10 .05 .01
☐ 343 Pedro Astacio .15 .07 .02
☐ 344 Rich Batchelor .10 .05 .01
☐ 345 Ryan Bowen .10 .05 .01
☐ 346 Terry Steinbach .15 .07 .02
☐ 347 Troy O'Leary .10 .05 .01
☐ 348 Willie Blair .10 .05 .01
☐ 349 Wade Boggs .20 .09 .03
☐ 350 Tim Raines .20 .09 .03
☐ 351 Scott Livingstone .10 .05 .01
☐ 352 Rod Correia .10 .05 .01
☐ 353 Ray Lankford .20 .09 .03
☐ 354 Pat Listach .10 .05 .01
☐ 355 Milt Thompson .10 .05 .01
☐ 356 Miguel Jimenez .15 .07 .02
☐ 357 Marc Newfield .20 .09 .03
☐ 358 Mark McGwire .20 .09 .03
☐ 359 Kirby Puckett 1.25 .55 .16
☐ 360 Kent Mercker .10 .05 .01
☐ 361 John Kruk .20 .09 .03
☐ 362 Jeff Kent .15 .07 .02
☐ 363 Hal Morris .15 .07 .02
☐ 364 Edgar Martinez .10 .05 .01
☐ 365 Dave Magadan .10 .05 .01
☐ 366 Dante Bichette .20 .09 .03
☐ 367 Chris Hammond .10 .05 .01
☐ 368 Bret Saberhagen .15 .07 .02
☐ 369 Billy Ripken .10 .05 .01
☐ 370 Bill Gullickson .10 .05 .01
☐ 371 Andre Dawson .20 .09 .03
☐ 372 Roberto Kelly .10 .05 .01
☐ 373 Cal Ripken 2.25 1.00 .30
☐ 374 Craig Biggio .15 .07 .02
☐ 375 Dan Pasqua .10 .05 .01
☐ 376 Dave Nilsson .10 .05 .01
☐ 377 Duane Ward .10 .05 .01
☐ 378 Greg Vaughn .15 .07 .02
☐ 379 Jeff Fassero .10 .05 .01
☐ 380 Jerry DiPoto .10 .05 .01
☐ 381 John Patterson .10 .05 .01
☐ 382 Kevin Brown .10 .05 .01
☐ 383 Kevin Roberson .10 .05 .01
☐ 384 Joe Orsulak .10 .05 .01
☐ 385 Hilly Hathaway .10 .05 .01
☐ 386 Mike Greenwell .15 .07 .02
☐ 387 Orestes Destrade .10 .05 .01
☐ 388 Mike Gallego .10 .05 .01
☐ 389 Ozzie Guillen .10 .05 .01
☐ 390 Raul Mondesi 1.00 .45 .13
☐ 391 Scott Lydy .10 .05 .01
☐ 392 Tom Urbani .10 .05 .01
☐ 393 Wil Cordero .20 .09 .03
☐ 394 Tony Longmire .10 .05 .01
☐ 395 Todd Zeile .15 .07 .02
☐ 396 Scott Cooper .15 .07 .02
☐ 397 Ryne Sandberg 1.00 .45 .13
☐ 398 Ricky Bones .10 .05 .01
☐ 399 Phil Clark .10 .05 .01
☐ 400 Orel Hershiser .15 .07 .02
☐ 401 Mike Henneman .10 .05 .01
☐ 402 Mark Lemke .10 .05 .01
☐ 403 Mark Grace .20 .09 .03
☐ 404 Ken Ryan .10 .05 .01
☐ 405 John Smoltz .15 .07 .02

No.	Player			
☐ 406	Jeff Conine	.20	.09	.03
☐ 407	Greg Harris	.10	.05	.01
☐ 408	Doug Drabek	.20	.09	.03
☐ 409	Dave Fleming	.10	.05	.01
☐ 410	Danny Tartabull	.15	.07	.02
☐ 411	Chad Kreuter	.10	.05	.01
☐ 412	Brad Ausmus	.10	.05	.01
☐ 413	Ben McDonald	.15	.07	.02
☐ 414	Barry Larkin	.20	.09	.03
☐ 415	Bret Barberie	.10	.05	.01
☐ 416	Chuck Knoblauch	.20	.09	.03
☐ 417	Ozzie Smith	.60	.25	.08
☐ 418	Ed Sprague	.10	.05	.01
☐ 419	Matt Williams	.60	.25	.08
☐ 420	Jeremy Hernandez	.10	.05	.01
☐ 421	Jose Bautista	.10	.05	.01
☐ 422	Kevin Mitchell	.15	.07	.02
☐ 423	Manny Lee	.10	.05	.01
☐ 424	Mike Devereaux	.15	.07	.02
☐ 425	Omar Olivares	.10	.05	.01
☐ 426	Rafael Belliard	.10	.05	.01
☐ 427	Richie Lewis	.10	.05	.01
☐ 428	Ron Darling	.10	.05	.01
☐ 429	Shane Mack	.15	.07	.02
☐ 430	Tim Hulett	.10	.05	.01
☐ 431	Wally Joyner	.15	.07	.02
☐ 432	Wes Chamberlain	.10	.05	.01
☐ 433	Tom Browning	.10	.05	.01
☐ 434	Scott Radinsky	.10	.05	.01
☐ 435	Rondell White	.30	.14	.04
☐ 436	Rod Beck	.15	.07	.02
☐ 437	Rheal Cormier	.10	.05	.01
☐ 438	Randy Johnson	.20	.09	.03
☐ 439	Pete Schourek	.10	.05	.01
☐ 440	Mo Vaughn	.20	.09	.03
☐ 441	Mike Timlin	.10	.05	.01
☐ 442	Mark Langston	.20	.09	.03
☐ 443	Lou Whitaker	.20	.09	.03
☐ 444	Kevin Stocker	.15	.07	.02
☐ 445	Ken Hill	.15	.07	.02
☐ 446	John Wetteland	.10	.05	.01
☐ 447	J.T. Snow	.15	.07	.02
☐ 448	Erik Pappas	.10	.05	.01
☐ 449	David Hulse	.10	.05	.01
☐ 450	Darren Daulton	.20	.09	.03
☐ 451	Chris Hoiles	.15	.07	.02
☐ 452	Bryan Harvey	.15	.07	.02
☐ 453	Darren Lewis	.10	.05	.01
☐ 454	Andres Galarraga	.20	.09	.03
☐ 455	Joe Hesketh	.10	.05	.01
☐ 456	Jose Valentin	.10	.05	.01
☐ 457	Dan Peltier	.10	.05	.01
☐ 458	Joe Boever	.10	.05	.01
☐ 459	Kevin Rogers	.10	.05	.01
☐ 460	Craig Shipley	.10	.05	.01
☐ 461	Alvaro Espinoza	.10	.05	.01
☐ 462	Wilson Alvarez	.20	.09	.03
☐ 463	Cory Snyder	.10	.05	.01
☐ 464	Candy Maldonado	.10	.05	.01
☐ 465	Blas Minor	.10	.05	.01
☐ 466	Rod Bolton	.10	.05	.01
☐ 467	Kenny Rogers	.10	.05	.01
☐ 468	Greg Myers	.10	.05	.01
☐ 469	Jimmy Key	.15	.07	.02
☐ 470	Tony Castillo	.10	.05	.01
☐ 471	Mike Stanton	.10	.05	.01
☐ 472	Deion Sanders	.50	.23	.06
☐ 473	Tito Navarro	.10	.05	.01
☐ 474	Mike Gardiner	.10	.05	.01
☐ 475	Steve Reed	.10	.05	.01
☐ 476	John Roper	.15	.07	.02
☐ 477	Mike Trombley	.10	.05	.01
☐ 478	Charles Nagy	.10	.05	.01
☐ 479	Larry Casian	.10	.05	.01
☐ 480	Eric Hillman	.10	.05	.01
☐ 481	Bill Wertz	.10	.05	.01
☐ 482	Jeff Schwarz	.10	.05	.01
☐ 483	John Valentin	.15	.07	.02
☐ 484	Carl Willis	.10	.05	.01
☐ 485	Gary Gaetti	.10	.05	.01
☐ 486	Bill Pecota	.10	.05	.01
☐ 487	John Smiley	.10	.05	.01
☐ 488	Mike Mussina	.40	.18	.05
☐ 489	Mike Ignasiak	.10	.05	.01
☐ 490	Billy Brewer	.10	.05	.01
☐ 491	Jack Voigt	.10	.05	.01
☐ 492	Mike Munoz	.10	.05	.01
☐ 493	Lee Tinsley	.10	.05	.01
☐ 494	Bob Wickman	.10	.05	.01
☐ 495	Roger Salkeld	.10	.05	.01
☐ 496	Thomas Howard	.10	.05	.01
☐ 497	Mark Davis	.10	.05	.01
☐ 498	Dave Clark	.10	.05	.01
☐ 499	Turk Wendell	.10	.05	.01
☐ 500	Rafael Bournigal	.10	.05	.01
☐ 501	Chip Hale	.10	.05	.01
☐ 502	Matt Whiteside	.10	.05	.01
☐ 503	Brian Koelling	.10	.05	.01
☐ 504	Jeff Reed	.10	.05	.01
☐ 505	Paul Wagner	.10	.05	.01
☐ 506	Torey Lovullo	.10	.05	.01
☐ 507	Curtis Leskanic	.10	.05	.01
☐ 508	Derek Lilliquist	.10	.05	.01
☐ 509	Joe Magrane	.10	.05	.01
☐ 510	Mackey Sasser	.10	.05	.01
☐ 511	Lloyd McClendon	.10	.05	.01
☐ 512	Jayhawk Owens	.10	.05	.01
☐ 513	Woody Williams	.10	.05	.01
☐ 514	Gary Redus	.10	.05	.01
☐ 515	Tim Spehr	.10	.05	.01
☐ 516	Jim Abbott	.20	.09	.03
☐ 517	Lou Frazier	.10	.05	.01
☐ 518	Erik Plantenberg	.10	.05	.01
☐ 519	Tim Worrell	.10	.05	.01
☐ 520	Brian McRae	.15	.07	.02
☐ 521	Chan Ho Park	1.25	.55	.16
☐ 522	Mark Wohlers	.10	.05	.01
☐ 523	Geronimo Pena	.10	.05	.01
☐ 524	Andy Ashby	.10	.05	.01
☐ 525	Tim Raines TALE	.15	.07	.02
☐ 526	Paul Molitor TALE	.20	.09	.03
☐ 527	Joe Carter DL	.20	.09	.03
☐ 528	Frank Thomas DL UER (listed as third in RBI in 1993; was actually second)	1.50	.65	.19
☐ 529	Ken Griffey Jr. DL	1.50	.65	.19
☐ 530	David Justice DL	.15	.07	.02
☐ 531	Gregg Jefferies DL	.15	.07	.02
☐ 532	Barry Bonds DL	.60	.25	.08
☐ 533	John Kruk QS	.15	.07	.02
☐ 534	Roger Clemens QS	.40	.18	.05
☐ 535	Cecil Fielder QS	.15	.07	.02
☐ 536	Ruben Sierra QS	.15	.07	.02
☐ 537	Tony Gwynn QS	.40	.18	.05
☐ 538	Tom Glavine QS	.15	.07	.02
☐ 539	Checklist 271-405 UER (number on back is 269)	.10	.05	.01
☐ 540	Checklist 406-540 UER (numbered 270 on back)	.10	.05	.01
☐ 541	Ozzie Smith CC	.30	.14	.04
☐ 542	Eddie Murray CC	.20	.09	.03
☐ 543	Lee Smith CC	.20	.09	.03
☐ 544	Greg Maddux	.60	.25	.08
☐ 545	Denis Boucher	.10	.05	.01
☐ 546	Mark Gardner	.10	.05	.01
☐ 547	Bo Jackson	.20	.09	.03

	No.	Player			
☐	548	Eric Anthony	.10	.05	.01
☐	549	Delino DeShields	.15	.07	.02
☐	550	Turner Ward	.10	.05	.01
☐	551	Scott Sanderson	.10	.05	.01
☐	552	Hector Carrasco	.10	.05	.01
☐	553	Tony Phillips	.10	.05	.01
☐	554	Melido Perez	.10	.05	.01
☐	555	Mike Felder	.10	.05	.01
☐	556	Jack Morris	.20	.09	.03
☐	557	Rafael Palmeiro	.20	.09	.03
☐	558	Shane Reynolds	.10	.05	.01
☐	559	Pete Incaviglia	.10	.05	.01
☐	560	Greg Harris	.10	.05	.01
☐	561	Matt Walbeck	.10	.05	.01
☐	562	Todd Van Poppel	.15	.07	.02
☐	563	Todd Stottlemyre	.10	.05	.01
☐	564	Ricky Bones	.10	.05	.01
☐	565	Mike Jackson	.10	.05	.01
☐	566	Kevin McReynolds	.10	.05	.01
☐	567	Melvin Nieves	.20	.09	.03
☐	568	Juan Gonzalez	1.00	.45	.13
☐	569	Frank Viola	.10	.05	.01
☐	570	Vince Coleman	.10	.05	.01
☐	571	Brian Anderson	.75	.35	.09
☐	572	Omar Vizquel	.10	.05	.01
☐	573	Bernie Williams	.15	.07	.02
☐	574	Tom Glavine	.20	.09	.03
☐	575	Mitch Williams	.10	.05	.01
☐	576	Shawon Dunston	.10	.05	.01
☐	577	Mike Lansing	.15	.07	.02
☐	578	Greg Pirkl	.10	.05	.01
☐	579	Sid Fernandez	.10	.05	.01
☐	580	Doug Jones	.10	.05	.01
☐	581	Walt Weiss	.10	.05	.01
☐	582	Tim Belcher	.10	.05	.01
☐	583	Alex Fernandez	.20	.09	.03
☐	584	Alex Cole	.10	.05	.01
☐	585	Greg Cadaret	.10	.05	.01
☐	586	Bob Tewksbury	.10	.05	.01
☐	587	Dave Hansen	.10	.05	.01
☐	588	Kurt Abbott	.30	.14	.04
☐	589	Rick White	.10	.05	.01
☐	590	Kevin Bass	.10	.05	.01
☐	591	Geronimo Berroa	.10	.05	.01
☐	592	Jaime Navarro	.10	.05	.01
☐	593	Steve Farr	.10	.05	.01
☐	594	Jack Armstrong	.10	.05	.01
☐	595	Steve Howe	.10	.05	.01
☐	596	Jose Rijo	.15	.07	.02
☐	597	Otis Nixon	.10	.05	.01
☐	598	Robby Thompson	.10	.05	.01
☐	599	Kelly Stinnett	.10	.05	.01
☐	600	Carlos Delgado	.50	.23	.06
☐	601	Brian Johnson	.10	.05	.01
☐	602	Gregg Olson	.10	.05	.01
☐	603	Jim Edmonds	.10	.05	.01
☐	604	Mike Blowers	.10	.05	.01
☐	605	Lee Smith	.20	.09	.03
☐	606	Pat Rapp	.10	.05	.01
☐	607	Mike Magnante	.10	.05	.01
☐	608	Karl Rhodes	.10	.05	.01
☐	609	Jeff Juden	.10	.05	.01
☐	610	Rusty Meacham	.10	.05	.01
☐	611	Pedro Martinez	.20	.09	.03
☐	612	Todd Worrell	.10	.05	.01
☐	613	Stan Javier	.10	.05	.01
☐	614	Mike Hampton	.10	.05	.01
☐	615	Jose Guzman	.10	.05	.01
☐	616	Xavier Hernandez	.10	.05	.01
☐	617	David Wells	.10	.05	.01
☐	618	John Habyan	.10	.05	.01
☐	619	Chris Nabholz	.10	.05	.01
☐	620	Bobby Jones	.25	.11	.03
☐	621	Chris James	.10	.05	.01
☐	622	Ellis Burks	.15	.07	.02
☐	623	Erik Hanson	.10	.05	.01
☐	624	Pat Meares	.10	.05	.01
☐	625	Harold Reynolds	.10	.05	.01
☐	626	Bob Hamelin RR	.20	.09	.03
☐	627	Manny Ramirez RR	.30	.14	.04
☐	628	Ryan Klesko RR	.25	.11	.03
☐	629	Carlos Delgado RR	.25	.11	.03
☐	630	Javy Lopez RR	.20	.09	.03
☐	631	Steve Karsay RR	.10	.05	.01
☐	632	Rick Helling RR	.10	.05	.01
☐	633	Steve Trachsel RR	.20	.09	.03
☐	634	Hector Carrasco RR	.10	.05	.01
☐	635	Andy Stankiewicz	.10	.05	.01
☐	636	Paul Sorrento	.10	.05	.01
☐	637	Scott Erickson	.10	.05	.01
☐	638	Chipper Jones	.40	.18	.05
☐	639	Luis Polonia	.10	.05	.01
☐	640	Howard Johnson	.10	.05	.01
☐	641	John Dopson	.10	.05	.01
☐	642	Jody Reed	.10	.05	.01
☐	643	Lonnie Smith UER (No. 543 on back)	.10	.05	.01
☐	644	Mark Portugal	.10	.05	.01
☐	645	Paul Molitor	.40	.18	.05
☐	646	Paul Assenmacher	.10	.05	.01
☐	647	Hubie Brooks	.10	.05	.01
☐	648	Gary Wayne	.10	.05	.01
☐	649	Sean Berry	.10	.05	.01
☐	650	Roger Clemens	.75	.35	.09
☐	651	Brian Hunter	.10	.05	.01
☐	652	Wally Whitehurst	.10	.05	.01
☐	653	Allen Watson	.10	.05	.01
☐	654	Rickey Henderson	.20	.09	.03
☐	655	Sid Bream	.10	.05	.01
☐	656	Dan Wilson	.10	.05	.01
☐	657	Ricky Jordan	.10	.05	.01
☐	658	Sterling Hitchcock	.15	.07	.02
☐	659	Darrin Jackson	.10	.05	.01
☐	660	Junior Felix	.10	.05	.01
☐	661	Tom Brunansky	.10	.05	.01
☐	662	Jose Vizcaino	.10	.05	.01
☐	663	Mark Leiter	.10	.05	.01
☐	664	Gil Heredia	.10	.05	.01
☐	665	Fred McGriff	.40	.18	.05
☐	666	Will Clark	.40	.18	.05
☐	667	Al Leiter	.10	.05	.01
☐	668	James Mouton	.20	.09	.03
☐	669	Billy Bean	.10	.05	.01
☐	670	Scott Leius	.10	.05	.01
☐	671	Bret Boone	.20	.09	.03
☐	672	Darren Holmes	.10	.05	.01
☐	673	Dave Weathers	.10	.05	.01
☐	674	Eddie Murray	.20	.09	.03
☐	675	Felix Fermin	.10	.05	.01
☐	676	Chris Sabo	.10	.05	.01
☐	677	Billy Spiers	.10	.05	.01
☐	678	Aaron Sele	.25	.11	.03
☐	679	Juan Samuel	.10	.05	.01
☐	680	Julio Franco	.15	.07	.02
☐	681	Heathcliff Slocumb	.10	.05	.01
☐	682	Denny Martinez	.15	.07	.02
☐	683	Jerry Browne	.10	.05	.01
☐	684	Pedro Martinez	.20	.09	.03
☐	685	Rex Hudler	.10	.05	.01
☐	686	Willie McGee	.10	.05	.01
☐	687	Andy Van Slyke	.20	.09	.03
☐	688	Pat Mahomes	.10	.05	.01
☐	689	Dave Henderson	.10	.05	.01
☐	690	Tony Eusebio	.10	.05	.01
☐	691	Rick Sutcliffe	.15	.07	.02
☐	692	Willie Banks	.10	.05	.01

	#	Player	MINT	EXC	G-VG
☐	693	Alan Mills	.10	.05	.01
☐	694	Jeff Treadway	.10	.05	.01
☐	695	Alex Gonzalez	.30	.14	.04
☐	696	David Segui	.10	.05	.01
☐	697	Rick Helling	.10	.05	.01
☐	698	Bip Roberts	.10	.05	.01
☐	699	Jeff Cirillo	.25	.11	.03
☐	700	Terry Mulholland	.10	.05	.01
☐	701	Marvin Freeman	.10	.05	.01
☐	702	Jason Bere	.40	.18	.05
☐	703	Javy Lopez	.30	.14	.04
☐	704	Greg Hibbard	.10	.05	.01
☐	705	Tommy Greene	.10	.05	.01
☐	706	Marquis Grissom	.20	.09	.03
☐	707	Brian Harper	.10	.05	.01
☐	708	Steve Karsay	.10	.05	.01
☐	709	Jeff Brantley	.10	.05	.01
☐	710	Jeff Russell	.10	.05	.01
☐	711	Bryan Hickerson	.10	.05	.01
☐	712	Jim Pittsley	.30	.14	.04
☐	713	Bobby Ayala	.10	.05	.01
☐	714	John Smoltz FAN	.15	.07	.02
☐	715	Jose Rijo FAN	.15	.07	.02
☐	716	Greg Maddux FAN	.30	.14	.04
☐	717	Matt Williams FAN	.30	.14	.04
☐	718	Frank Thomas FAN	1.50	.65	.19
☐	719	Ryne Sandberg FAN	.50	.23	.06
☐	720	Checklist 541-720	.10	.05	.01

1994 Stadium Club First Day Issue

Randomly inserted in one of every 24 packs, these First Day Production cards are identical to the regular issues except for a special 1st Day foil stamp engraved on the front of each card. No more than 2,000 of each Stadium Club card was issued as First Day Issue.

	MINT	EXC	G-VG
COMPLETE SET (720)	3000.00	1350.00	375.00
COMPLETE SERIES 1 (270)	1300.00	575.00	160.00
COMPLETE SERIES 2 (270)	1200.00	550.00	150.00
COMPLETE SERIES 3 (180)	500.00	230.00	65.00
COMMON CARD (1-270)	2.00	.90	.25
COMMON CARD (271-540)	2.00	.90	.25
COMMON CARD (541-720)	2.00	.90	.25

*UNLISTED VETERAN STARS: 30X TO 60X BASIC CARDS
*UNLISTED YOUNG STARS: 20X TO 40X BASIC CARDS
*UNLISTED RCs: 15X TO 30X BASIC CARDS

	#	Player	MINT	EXC	G-VG
☐	5	George Brett	60.00	27.00	7.50
☐	34	Nolan Ryan	150.00	70.00	19.00
☐	85	Ken Grifey Jr.	100.00	45.00	12.50
☐	108	Jeff Bagwell	50.00	23.00	6.25
☐	140	Mike Piazza	50.00	23.00	6.25
☐	195	Don Mattingly	40.00	18.00	5.00
☐	238	Barry Bonds	40.00	18.00	5.00
☐	262	Ken Griffey Jr. HR	50.00	23.00	6.25
☐	267	Frank Thomas HR	50.00	23.00	6.25
☐	285	Frank Thomas HR	100.00	45.00	12.50
☐	359	Frank Thomas	40.00	18.00	5.00
☐	373	Kirby Puckett	70.00	32.00	8.75
☐	390	Raul Mondesi	35.00	16.00	4.40
☐	397	Ryne Sandberg	35.00	16.00	4.40
☐	528	Frank Thomas DL	50.00	23.00	6.25
☐	529	Ken Griffey Jr. DL	50.00	23.00	6.25
☐	718	Frank Thomas FAN	50.00	23.00	6.25

1994 Stadium Club Golden Rainbow

Parallel to the basic Stadium Club set, Golden Rainbows differ in that the player's last name on front has gold refracting foil over it. The cards were inserted one per Stadium Club foil pack and two per jumbo.

	MINT	EXC	G-VG
COMPLETE SET (720)	190.00	85.00	24.00
COMPLETE SERIES 1 (270)	70.00	32.00	8.75
COMPLETE SERIES 2 (270)	70.00	32.00	8.75
COMPLETE SERIES 3 (180)	50.00	23.00	6.25
COMMON CARD (1-270)	.25	.11	.03
COMMON CARD (271-540)	.25	.11	.03
COMMON CARD (541-720)	.25	.11	.03

*VETERAN STARS: 2X to 4X BASIC CARDS
*YOUNG STARS: 1.5X to 3X BASIC CARDS
*RCs: 1.25X to 2.5X BASIC CARDS

1994 Stadium Club Dugout Dirt

Randomly inserted at a rate of one per six packs, these standard-size cards feature some of baseball's most popular and colorful players by sports cartoonists Daniel Guidera and Steve Benson. The cards

resemble basic Stadium Club cards except for a Dugout Dirt logo at the bottom. Backs contain a cartoon. Cards 1-4 were found in first series packs with cards 5-8 and 9-12 were inserted in second series and third series packs respectively.

	MINT	EXC	G-VG
COMPLETE SET (12)	12.00	5.50	1.50
COMPLETE SERIES 1 (4)	4.00	1.80	.50
COMPLETE SERIES 2 (4)	4.00	1.80	.50
COMPLETE SERIES 3 (4)	4.00	1.80	.50
COMMON CARD (1-4)	.25	.11	.03
COMMON CARD (5-8)	.25	.11	.03
COMMON CARD (9-12)	.25	.11	.03
☐ 1 Mike Piazza	1.50	.65	.19
☐ 2 Dave Winfield	.45	.20	.06
☐ 3 John Kruk	.25	.11	.03
☐ 4 Cal Ripken	2.25	1.00	.30
☐ 5 Kirby Puckett	.25	.11	.03
☐ 6 Barry Bonds	1.25	.55	.16
☐ 7 Ken Griffey Jr.	3.00	1.35	.40
☐ 8 Tim Salmon	.60	.25	.08
☐ 9 Frank Thomas	3.00	1.35	.40
☐ 10 Jeff Kent	.25	.11	.03
☐ 11 Randy Johnson	.25	.11	.03
☐ 12 Darren Daulton	.45	.20	.06

1994 Stadium Club Finest Inserts

This set contains 10 standard-size metallic cards of top players. They were randomly inserted one in 24 third series packs. The fronts feature a color player photo with a red and yellow background. Backs contain a color player photo with 1993 and career statistics.

	MINT	EXC	G-VG
COMPLETE SET (10)	35.00	16.00	4.40
COMMON CARD (1-10)	1.50	.65	.19
☐ 1 Jeff Bagwell	5.00	2.30	.60
☐ 2 Albert Belle	3.50	1.55	.45
☐ 3 Barry Bonds	4.00	1.80	.50
☐ 4 Juan Gonzalez	3.50	1.55	.45
☐ 5 Ken Griffey Jr.	10.00	4.50	1.25
☐ 6 Marquis Grissom	1.50	.65	.19
☐ 7 David Justice	1.50	.65	.19
☐ 8 Mike Piazza	5.00	2.30	.60
☐ 9 Tim Salmon	2.50	1.15	.30
☐ 10 Frank Thomas	10.00	4.50	1.25

1994 Stadium Club Super Teams

Randomly inserted at a rate of one per 24 first series packs only, this 28-card standard-size features one card for each of the 28 MLB teams. Collectors holding team cards could redeem them for special prizes if those teams won a division title, a league championship, or the World Series. But, since the strike affected the 1994 season, Topps postponed the promotion until the 1995 season. The expiration was pushed back to January 31, 1996.

	MINT	EXC	G-VG
COMPLETE SET (28)	175.00	80.00	22.00
COMMON TEAM (1-28)	2.00	.90	.25
☐ 1 Atlanta Braves	15.00	6.75	1.90
☐ 2 Chicago Cubs	2.00	.90	.25
☐ 3 Cincinnati Reds	10.00	4.50	1.25
☐ 4 Colorado Rockies	4.00	1.80	.50
☐ 5 Florida Marlins	2.00	.90	.25
☐ 6 Houston Astros	10.00	4.50	1.25
☐ 7 Los Angeles Dodgers	10.00	4.50	1.25
☐ 8 Montreal Expos	15.00	6.75	1.90
☐ 9 New York Mets	2.00	.90	.25
☐ 10 Philadelphia Phillies	5.00	2.30	.60
☐ 11 Pittsburgh Pirates	2.00	.90	.25
☐ 12 St. Louis Cardinals	4.00	1.80	.50
☐ 13 San Diego Padres	4.00	1.80	.50
☐ 14 San Francisco Giants	10.00	4.50	1.25
☐ 15 Baltimore Orioles	10.00	4.50	1.25
☐ 16 Boston Red Sox	4.00	1.80	.50
☐ 17 California Angels	4.00	1.80	.50
☐ 18 Chicago White Sox	15.00	6.75	1.90
☐ 19 Cleveland Indians	15.00	6.75	1.90

		MINT	EXC	G-VG
☐ 20	Detroit Tigers	2.00	.90	.25
☐ 21	Kansas City Royals	5.00	2.30	.60
☐ 22	Milwaukee Brewers	2.00	.90	.25
☐ 23	Minnesota Twins	2.00	.90	.25
☐ 24	New York Yankees	15.00	6.75	1.90
☐ 25	Oakland Athletics	6.00	2.70	.75
☐ 26	Seattle Mariners	5.00	2.30	.60
☐ 27	Texas Rangers	8.00	3.60	1.00
☐ 28	Toronto Blue Jays	10.00	4.50	1.25

1994 Stadium Club Draft Picks

This 90-card standard-size set features 90 players chosen in the June 1994 MLB draft and photographed in their major league uniforms. Each 24-pack box included four First Day Issue Draft Pick cards randomly packed, one in every six packs. The fronts display full-bleed color player photos. A "'94 Draft Pick" emblem in the shape of a home plate appears in an upper corner. The player's name is printed vertically in gold foil on a line extending down from this emblem. On a colorful screened background, the horizontal backs present a color closeup cutout, biography, scouting report, and a short list of other first round draft picks.

		MINT	EXC	G-VG
COMPLETE SET (90)		16.00	7.25	2.00
COMMON CARD (1-90)		.15	.07	.02
☐ 1	Jacob Shumate	.50	.23	.06
☐ 2	C.J. Nitkowski	.60	.25	.08
☐ 3	Doug Million	1.00	.45	.13
☐ 4	Matt Smith	.50	.23	.06
☐ 5	Kevin Lovinger	.15	.07	.02
☐ 6	Alberto Castillo	.15	.07	.02
☐ 7	Mike Russell	.15	.07	.02
☐ 8	Dan Lock	.15	.07	.02
☐ 9	Tom Szimanski	.15	.07	.02
☐ 10	Aaron Boone	.75	.35	.09
☐ 11	Jayson Peterson	.50	.23	.06
☐ 12	Mark Johnson	.50	.23	.06
☐ 13	Cade Gaspar	.40	.18	.05
☐ 14	George Lombard	.15	.07	.02
☐ 15	Russ Johnson	.50	.23	.06
☐ 16	Travis Miller	.50	.23	.06
☐ 17	Jay Payton	1.00	.45	.13
☐ 18	Brian Buchanan	.50	.23	.06
☐ 19	Jacob Cruz	.40	.18	.05
☐ 20	Gary Rath	.15	.07	.02
☐ 21	Ramon Castro	.50	.23	.06
☐ 22	Tommy Davis	.30	.14	.04
☐ 23	Tony Terry	.15	.07	.02
☐ 24	Jerry Whittaker	.30	.14	.04
☐ 25	Mike Darr	.15	.07	.02
☐ 26	Doug Webb	.15	.07	.02
☐ 27	Jason Camilli	.15	.07	.02
☐ 28	Brad Rigby	.40	.18	.05
☐ 29	Ryan Nye	.30	.14	.04
☐ 30	Carl Dale	.15	.07	.02
☐ 31	Andy Taulbee	.30	.14	.04
☐ 32	Trey Moore	.15	.07	.02
☐ 33	John Crowther	.15	.07	.02
☐ 34	Joe Giuliano	.15	.07	.02
☐ 35	Brian Rose	.15	.07	.02
☐ 36	Paul Failla	.15	.07	.02
☐ 37	Brian Meadows	.15	.07	.02
☐ 38	Oscar Robles	.15	.07	.02
☐ 39	Mike Metcalfe	.15	.07	.02
☐ 40	Larry Barnes	.15	.07	.02
☐ 41	Paul Ottavinia	.15	.07	.02
☐ 42	Chris McBride	.15	.07	.02
☐ 43	Ricky Stone	.15	.07	.02
☐ 44	Billy Blythe	.15	.07	.02
☐ 45	Eddie Priest	.30	.14	.04
☐ 46	Scott Forster	.15	.07	.02
☐ 47	Eric Pickett	.15	.07	.02
☐ 48	Matt Beaumont	.40	.18	.05
☐ 49	Darrell Nicholas UER (Name misspelled Nicolas on back)	.15	.07	.02
☐ 50	Mike Hampton	.15	.07	.02
☐ 51	Paul O'Malley	.15	.07	.02
☐ 52	Steve Shoemaker	.15	.07	.02
☐ 53	Jason Sikes	.15	.07	.02
☐ 54	Bryan Farson	.15	.07	.02
☐ 55	Yates Hall	.15	.07	.02
☐ 56	Troy Brohawn	.15	.07	.02
☐ 57	Dan Hower	.15	.07	.02
☐ 58	Clay Caruthers	.15	.07	.02
☐ 59	Pepe McNeal	.15	.07	.02
☐ 60	Ray Ricken	.15	.07	.02
☐ 61	Scott Shores	.15	.07	.02
☐ 62	Eddie Brooks	.15	.07	.02
☐ 63	Dave Kauflin	.15	.07	.02
☐ 64	David Meyer	.15	.07	.02
☐ 65	Geoff Blum	.30	.14	.04
☐ 66	Roy Marsh	.15	.07	.02
☐ 67	Ryan Beeney	.15	.07	.02
☐ 68	Derek Dukart	.15	.07	.02
☐ 69	Nomar Garciaparra	.50	.23	.06
☐ 70	Jason Kelley	.15	.07	.02
☐ 71	Jesse Ibarra	.15	.07	.02
☐ 72	Bucky Buckles	.40	.18	.05
☐ 73	Mark Little	.15	.07	.02
☐ 74	Heath Murray	.25	.11	.03
☐ 75	Greg Morris	.15	.07	.02
☐ 76	Mike Halperlin	.15	.07	.02
☐ 77	Wes Helms	.25	.11	.03
☐ 78	Ray Brown	.75	.35	.09
☐ 79	Kevin Brown	.40	.18	.05
☐ 80	Paul Konerko	.75	.35	.09
☐ 81	Mike Thurman	.30	.14	.04
☐ 82	Paul Wilson	1.00	.45	.13
☐ 83	Terrence Long	1.00	.45	.13
☐ 84	Ben Grieve	2.00	.90	.25
☐ 85	Mark Farris	.50	.23	.06
☐ 86	Bret Wagner	.60	.25	.08
☐ 87	Dustin Hermanson	.60	.25	.08
☐ 88	Kevin Witt	.50	.23	.06
☐ 89	Corey Pointer	.25	.11	.03
☐ 90	Tim Grieve	.50	.23	.06

1994 Stadium Club Draft Picks First Day Issue

Randomly inserted in packs, this 90-card standard-size set is identical in design with the regular Stadium Club Draft Picks cards except for a holographic "1st Day Issue" emblem on the fronts.

	MINT	EXC	G-VG
COMPLETE SET (90)	300.00	135.00	38.00
COMMON CARD (1-90)	3.00	1.35	.40

*STARS: 10X TO 20X BASIC CARDS

1991 Studio Previews

This 18-card preview set was issued (four at a time) within 1991 (specially marked) Donruss retail factory sets in order to show dealers and collectors the look of their new Studio cards. The standard-size (2 1/2" by 3 1/2") cards are exactly the same style as those in the Studio series, with black and white player photos bordered in mauve and player information on the backs. The cards are numbered on the back.

	MINT	EXC	G-VG
COMPLETE SET (18)	30.00	13.50	3.80
COMMON CARD (1-17)	1.00	.45	.13
☐ 1 Juan Bell	1.00	.45	.13
☐ 2 Roger Clemens	7.00	3.10	.85
☐ 3 Dave Parker	1.50	.65	.19
☐ 4 Tim Raines	1.50	.65	.19
☐ 5 Kevin Seitzer	1.00	.45	.13
☐ 6 Ted Higuera	1.00	.45	.13
☐ 7 Bernie Williams	2.00	.90	.25
☐ 8 Harold Baines	1.50	.65	.19
☐ 9 Gary Pettis	1.00	.45	.13
☐ 10 David Justice	7.00	3.10	.85
☐ 11 Eric Davis	1.00	.45	.13
☐ 12 Andujar Cedeno	1.50	.65	.19
☐ 13 Tom Foley	1.00	.45	.13
☐ 14 Dwight Gooden	1.00	.45	.13
☐ 15 Doug Drabek	1.50	.65	.19
☐ 16 Steve Decker	1.00	.45	.13
☐ 17 Joe Torre MG	1.00	.45	.13
☐ NNO Title card	1.00	.45	.13

1991 Studio

The 1991 Leaf Studio set contains 264 cards and a puzzle of recently inducted Hall of Famer Rod Carew. The Carew puzzle was issued on twenty-one 2 1/2" by 3 1/2" cards, with 3 puzzle pieces per card, for a total of 63 pieces. The player cards measure the standard-size (2 1/2" by 3 1/2"), and the fronts feature posed black and white head-and-shoulders player photos with mauve borders. The team logo, player's name, and position appear along the bottom of the card face. The backs are printed in black and white and have four categories of information: personal, career, hobbies and interests, and heroes. The cards are numbered on the back. The cards are checklisted below alphabetically within and according to teams for each league as follows: Baltimore Orioles (1-10), Boston Red Sox (11-20), California Angels (21-30), Chicago White Sox (31-40), Cleveland Indians (41-50), Detroit Tigers (51-60), Kansas City Royals (61-70), Milwaukee Brewers (71-80), Minnesota Twins (81-90), New York Yankees (91-100), Oakland Athletics (101-110), Seattle Mariners (111-120), Texas Rangers (121-130), Toronto Blue Jays (131-140), Atlanta Braves (141-150), Chicago Cubs (151-160), Cincinnati Reds (161-170), Houston Astros (171-180), Los Angeles Dodgers (181-190), Montreal Expos (191-200), New York Mets (201-210), Philadelphia Phillies (211-220), Pittsburgh Pirates (221-230), St. Louis Cardinals (231-240), San Diego Padres (241-250), and San Francisco Giants (251-

260). Rookie Cards in the set include Jeff Bagwell, Wes Chamberlain, Jeff Conine, Brian McRae, Phil Plantier, and Todd Van Poppel. Among the other notable cards are Frank Thomas and Dave Justice.

	MINT	EXC	G-VG
COMPLETE SET (264)	15.00	6.75	1.90
COMMON CARD (1-263)	.05	.02	.01

	MINT	EXC	G-VG
☐ 1 Glenn Davis	.05	.02	.01
☐ 2 Dwight Evans	.10	.05	.01
☐ 3 Leo Gomez	.10	.05	.01
☐ 4 Chris Hoiles	.20	.09	.03
☐ 5 Sam Horn	.05	.02	.01
☐ 6 Ben McDonald	.20	.09	.03
☐ 7 Randy Milligan	.05	.02	.01
☐ 8 Gregg Olson	.10	.05	.01
☐ 9 Cal Ripken	.75	.35	.09
☐ 10 David Segui	.05	.02	.01
☐ 11 Wade Boggs	.20	.09	.03
☐ 12 Ellis Burks	.10	.05	.01
☐ 13 Jack Clark	.10	.05	.01
☐ 14 Roger Clemens	.50	.23	.06
☐ 15 Mike Greenwell	.10	.05	.01
☐ 16 Tim Naehring	.05	.02	.01
☐ 17 Tony Pena	.05	.02	.01
☐ 18 Phil Plantier	.50	.23	.06
☐ 19 Jeff Reardon	.10	.05	.01
☐ 20 Mo Vaughn	.75	.35	.09
☐ 21 Jimmy Reese CO	.25	.11	.03
☐ 22 Jim Abbott UER (Born in 1967, not 1969)	.20	.09	.03
☐ 23 Bert Blyleven	.20	.09	.03
☐ 24 Chuck Finley	.10	.05	.01
☐ 25 Gary Gaetti	.05	.02	.01
☐ 26 Wally Joyner	.10	.05	.01
☐ 27 Mark Langston	.20	.09	.03
☐ 28 Kirk McCaskill	.05	.02	.01
☐ 29 Lance Parrish	.10	.05	.01
☐ 30 Dave Winfield	.30	.14	.04
☐ 31 Alex Fernandez	.50	.23	.06
☐ 32 Carlton Fisk	.20	.09	.03
☐ 33 Scott Fletcher	.05	.02	.01
☐ 34 Greg Hibbard	.05	.02	.01
☐ 35 Charlie Hough	.10	.05	.01
☐ 36 Jack McDowell	.20	.09	.03
☐ 37 Tim Raines	.20	.09	.03
☐ 38 Sammy Sosa	.35	.16	.04
☐ 39 Bobby Thigpen	.05	.02	.01
☐ 40 Frank Thomas	4.00	1.80	.50
☐ 41 Sandy Alomar Jr.	.10	.05	.01
☐ 42 John Farrell	.05	.02	.01
☐ 43 Glenallen Hill	.05	.02	.01
☐ 44 Brook Jacoby	.05	.02	.01
☐ 45 Chris James	.05	.02	.01
☐ 46 Doug Jones	.05	.02	.01
☐ 47 Eric King	.05	.02	.01
☐ 48 Mark Lewis	.10	.05	.01
☐ 49 Greg Swindell UER (Photo actually Turner Ward)	.05	.02	.01
☐ 50 Mark Whiten	.20	.09	.03
☐ 51 Milt Cuyler	.10	.05	.01
☐ 52 Rob Deer	.05	.02	.01
☐ 53 Cecil Fielder	.35	.16	.04
☐ 54 Travis Fryman	1.00	.45	.13
☐ 55 Bill Gullickson	.05	.02	.01
☐ 56 Lloyd Moseby	.05	.02	.01
☐ 57 Frank Tanana	.05	.02	.01
☐ 58 Mickey Tettleton	.10	.05	.01
☐ 59 Alan Trammell	.20	.09	.03
☐ 60 Lou Whitaker	.20	.09	.03
☐ 61 Mike Boddicker	.05	.02	.01
☐ 62 George Brett	.60	.25	.08
☐ 63 Jeff Conine	.75	.35	.09
☐ 64 Warren Cromartie	.05	.02	.01
☐ 65 Storm Davis	.05	.02	.01
☐ 66 Kirk Gibson	.10	.05	.01
☐ 67 Mark Gubicza	.05	.02	.01
☐ 68 Brian McRae	.50	.23	.06
☐ 69 Bret Saberhagen	.10	.05	.01
☐ 70 Kurt Stillwell	.05	.02	.01
☐ 71 Tim McIntosh	.05	.02	.01
☐ 72 Candy Maldonado	.05	.02	.01
☐ 73 Paul Molitor	.30	.14	.04
☐ 74 Willie Randolph	.10	.05	.01
☐ 75 Ron Robinson	.05	.02	.01
☐ 76 Gary Sheffield	.35	.16	.04
☐ 77 Franklin Stubbs	.05	.02	.01
☐ 78 B.J. Surhoff	.05	.02	.01
☐ 79 Greg Vaughn	.10	.05	.01
☐ 80 Robin Yount	.30	.14	.04
☐ 81 Rick Aguilera	.10	.05	.01
☐ 82 Steve Bedrosian	.05	.02	.01
☐ 83 Scott Erickson	.05	.02	.01
☐ 84 Greg Gagne	.05	.02	.01
☐ 85 Dan Gladden	.05	.02	.01
☐ 86 Brian Harper	.05	.02	.01
☐ 87 Kent Hrbek	.10	.05	.01
☐ 88 Shane Mack	.10	.05	.01
☐ 89 Jack Morris	.20	.09	.03
☐ 90 Kirby Puckett	.75	.35	.09
☐ 91 Jesse Barfield	.05	.02	.01
☐ 92 Steve Farr	.05	.02	.01
☐ 93 Steve Howe	.05	.02	.01
☐ 94 Roberto Kelly	.10	.05	.01
☐ 95 Tim Leary	.05	.02	.01
☐ 96 Kevin Maas	.05	.02	.01
☐ 97 Don Mattingly	.75	.35	.09
☐ 98 Hensley Meulens	.05	.02	.01
☐ 99 Scott Sanderson	.05	.02	.01
☐ 100 Steve Sax	.05	.02	.01
☐ 101 Jose Canseco	.50	.23	.06
☐ 102 Dennis Eckersley	.20	.09	.03
☐ 103 Dave Henderson	.05	.02	.01
☐ 104 Rickey Henderson	.30	.14	.04
☐ 105 Rick Honeycutt	.05	.02	.01
☐ 106 Mark McGwire	.20	.09	.03
☐ 107 Dave Stewart UER (No-hitter against Toronto, not Texas)	.10	.05	.01
☐ 108 Eric Show	.05	.02	.01
☐ 109 Todd Van Poppel	.30	.14	.04
☐ 110 Bob Welch	.05	.02	.01
☐ 111 Alvin Davis	.05	.02	.01
☐ 112 Ken Griffey Jr.	3.50	1.55	.45
☐ 113 Ken Griffey	.10	.05	.01
☐ 114 Erik Hanson UER (Misspelled Eric)	.05	.02	.01
☐ 115 Brian Holman	.05	.02	.01
☐ 116 Randy Johnson	.25	.11	.03
☐ 117 Edgar Martinez	.10	.05	.01
☐ 118 Tino Martinez	.10	.05	.01
☐ 119 Harold Reynolds	.05	.02	.01
☐ 120 David Valle	.05	.02	.01
☐ 121 Kevin Belcher	.05	.02	.01
☐ 122 Scott Chiamparino	.05	.02	.01
☐ 123 Julio Franco	.10	.05	.01
☐ 124 Juan Gonzalez	2.00	.90	.25
☐ 125 Rich Gossage	.20	.09	.03
☐ 126 Jeff Kunkel	.05	.02	.01
☐ 127 Rafael Palmeiro	.35	.16	.04
☐ 128 Nolan Ryan	1.50	.65	.19
☐ 129 Ruben Sierra	.20	.09	.03
☐ 130 Bobby Witt	.05	.02	.01

☐ 131	Roberto Alomar	1.00	.45	.13
☐ 132	Tom Candiotti	.05	.02	.01
☐ 133	Joe Carter	.40	.18	.05
☐ 134	Ken Dayley	.05	.02	.01
☐ 135	Kelly Gruber	.05	.02	.01
☐ 136	John Olerud	.30	.14	.04
☐ 137	Dave Stieb	.10	.05	.01
☐ 138	Turner Ward	.15	.07	.02
☐ 139	Devon White	.10	.05	.01
☐ 140	Mookie Wilson	.05	.02	.01
☐ 141	Steve Avery	.40	.18	.05
☐ 142	Sid Bream	.05	.02	.01
☐ 143	Nick Esasky UER (Homers abbreviated RH)	.05	.02	.01
☐ 144	Ron Gant	.10	.05	.01
☐ 145	Tom Glavine	.75	.35	.09
☐ 146	David Justice	.60	.25	.08
☐ 147	Kelly Mann	.05	.02	.01
☐ 148	Terry Pendleton	.20	.09	.03
☐ 149	John Smoltz	.20	.09	.03
☐ 150	Jeff Treadway	.05	.02	.01
☐ 151	George Bell	.10	.05	.01
☐ 152	Shawn Boskie	.05	.02	.01
☐ 153	Andre Dawson	.20	.09	.03
☐ 154	Lance Dickson	.05	.02	.01
☐ 155	Shawon Dunston	.05	.02	.01
☐ 156	Joe Girardi	.05	.02	.01
☐ 157	Mark Grace	.20	.09	.03
☐ 158	Ryne Sandberg	.75	.35	.09
☐ 159	Gary Scott	.05	.02	.01
☐ 160	Dave Smith	.05	.02	.01
☐ 161	Tom Browning	.05	.02	.01
☐ 162	Eric Davis	.10	.05	.01
☐ 163	Rob Dibble	.05	.02	.01
☐ 164	Mariano Duncan	.05	.02	.01
☐ 165	Chris Hammond	.10	.05	.01
☐ 166	Billy Hatcher	.05	.02	.01
☐ 167	Barry Larkin	.20	.09	.03
☐ 168	Hal Morris	.10	.05	.01
☐ 169	Paul O'Neill	.10	.05	.01
☐ 170	Chris Sabo	.10	.05	.01
☐ 171	Eric Anthony	.10	.05	.01
☐ 172	Jeff Bagwell	4.00	1.80	.50
☐ 173	Craig Biggio	.20	.09	.03
☐ 174	Ken Caminiti	.10	.05	.01
☐ 175	Jim Deshaies	.05	.02	.01
☐ 176	Steve Finley	.05	.02	.01
☐ 177	Pete Harnisch	.10	.05	.01
☐ 178	Darryl Kile	.20	.09	.03
☐ 179	Curt Schilling	.10	.05	.01
☐ 180	Mike Scott	.05	.02	.01
☐ 181	Brett Butler	.10	.05	.01
☐ 182	Gary Carter	.20	.09	.03
☐ 183	Orel Hershiser	.10	.05	.01
☐ 184	Ramon Martinez	.10	.05	.01
☐ 185	Eddie Murray	.20	.09	.03
☐ 186	Jose Offerman	.10	.05	.01
☐ 187	Bob Ojeda	.05	.02	.01
☐ 188	Juan Samuel	.05	.02	.01
☐ 189	Mike Scioscia	.05	.02	.01
☐ 190	Darryl Strawberry	.20	.09	.03
☐ 191	Moises Alou	.50	.23	.06
☐ 192	Brian Barnes	.05	.02	.01
☐ 193	Oil Can Boyd	.05	.02	.01
☐ 194	Ivan Calderon	.05	.02	.01
☐ 195	Delino DeShields	.20	.09	.03
☐ 196	Mike Fitzgerald	.05	.02	.01
☐ 197	Andres Galarraga	.20	.09	.03
☐ 198	Marquis Grissom	.30	.14	.04
☐ 199	Bill Sampen	.05	.02	.01
☐ 200	Tim Wallach	.05	.02	.01
☐ 201	Daryl Boston	.05	.02	.01
☐ 202	Vince Coleman	.05	.02	.01
☐ 203	John Franco	.10	.05	.01
☐ 204	Dwight Gooden	.10	.05	.01
☐ 205	Tom Herr	.05	.02	.01
☐ 206	Gregg Jefferies	.35	.16	.04
☐ 207	Howard Johnson	.10	.05	.01
☐ 208	Dave Magadan UER (Born 1862, should be 1962)	.05	.02	.01
☐ 209	Kevin McReynolds	.05	.02	.01
☐ 210	Frank Viola	.10	.05	.01
☐ 211	Wes Chamberlain	.05	.02	.01
☐ 212	Darren Daulton	.20	.09	.03
☐ 213	Len Dykstra	.20	.09	.03
☐ 214	Charlie Hayes	.10	.05	.01
☐ 215	Ricky Jordan	.05	.02	.01
☐ 216	Steve Lake (Pictured with parrot on his shoulder)	.05	.02	.01
☐ 217	Roger McDowell	.05	.02	.01
☐ 218	Mickey Morandini	.05	.02	.01
☐ 219	Terry Mulholland	.05	.02	.01
☐ 220	Dale Murphy	.20	.09	.03
☐ 221	Jay Bell	.10	.05	.01
☐ 222	Barry Bonds	1.00	.45	.13
☐ 223	Bobby Bonilla	.20	.09	.03
☐ 224	Doug Drabek	.20	.09	.03
☐ 225	Bill Landrum	.05	.02	.01
☐ 226	Mike LaValliere	.05	.02	.01
☐ 227	Jose Lind	.05	.02	.01
☐ 228	Don Slaught	.05	.02	.01
☐ 229	John Smiley	.05	.02	.01
☐ 230	Andy Van Slyke	.20	.09	.03
☐ 231	Bernard Gilkey	.10	.05	.01
☐ 232	Pedro Guerrero	.10	.05	.01
☐ 233	Rex Hudler	.05	.02	.01
☐ 234	Ray Lankford	.40	.18	.05
☐ 235	Joe Magrane	.05	.02	.01
☐ 236	Jose Oquendo	.05	.02	.01
☐ 237	Lee Smith	.20	.09	.03
☐ 238	Ozzie Smith	.25	.11	.03
☐ 239	Milt Thompson	.05	.02	.01
☐ 240	Todd Zeile	.10	.05	.01
☐ 241	Larry Andersen	.05	.02	.01
☐ 242	Andy Benes	.20	.09	.03
☐ 243	Paul Faries	.05	.02	.01
☐ 244	Tony Fernandez	.10	.05	.01
☐ 245	Tony Gwynn	.50	.23	.06
☐ 246	Atlee Hammaker	.05	.02	.01
☐ 247	Fred McGriff	.40	.18	.05
☐ 248	Bip Roberts	.05	.02	.01
☐ 249	Bentio Santiago	.05	.02	.01
☐ 250	Ed Whitson	.05	.02	.01
☐ 251	Dave Anderson	.05	.02	.01
☐ 252	Mike Benjamin	.05	.02	.01
☐ 253	John Burkett UER (Front photo actually Trevor Wilson)	.10	.05	.01
☐ 254	Will Clark	.60	.25	.08
☐ 255	Scott Garrelts	.05	.02	.01
☐ 256	Willie McGee	.10	.05	.01
☐ 257	Kevin Mitchell	.10	.05	.01
☐ 258	Dave Righetti	.05	.02	.01
☐ 259	Matt Williams	.35	.16	.04
☐ 260	Black and Decker Bud Black Steve Decker	.05	.02	.01
☐ 261	Checklist Card 1-88 Sparky Anderson MG	.05	.02	.01
☐ 262	Checklist Card 89-176 Tom Lasorda MG	.05	.02	.01
☐ 263	Checklist Card 177-263 Tony LaRussa MG	.05	.02	.01
☐ NNO	Title Card	.05	.02	.01

1992 Studio

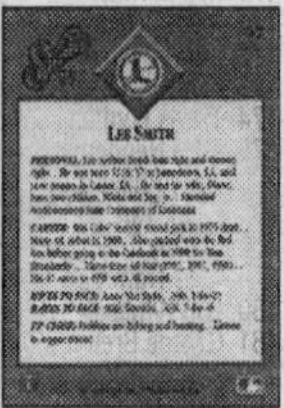

The 1992 Leaf Studio set consists of ten players from each of the 26 major league teams, three checklists, and an introduction card for a total of 264 cards. A Heritage series eight-card subset, featuring today's star players dressed in vintage uniforms, was randomly inserted in 12-card foil packs. Six additional Heritage cards were featured only in 28-card jumbo packs. The cards measure the standard size (2 1/2" by 3 1/2"). Inside champagne color metallic borders, the fronts carry a color close-up shot superimposed on a black and white action player photo. The backs focus on the personal side of each player by providing an up-close look, and unusual statistics show the batter or pitcher each player "Loves to Face" or "Hates to Face". The cards are numbered on the back. The key Rookie Cards in this set are Chad Curtis and Pat Mahomes.

	MINT	EXC	G-VG
COMPLETE SET (264)	15.00	6.75	1.90
COMMON CARD (1-264)	.05	.02	.01

	MINT	EXC	G-VG
☐ 1 Steve Avery	.20	.09	.03
☐ 2 Sid Bream	.05	.02	.01
☐ 3 Ron Gant	.10	.05	.01
☐ 4 Tom Glavine	.20	.09	.03
☐ 5 David Justice	.30	.14	.04
☐ 6 Mark Lemke	.05	.02	.01
☐ 7 Greg Olson	.05	.02	.01
☐ 8 Terry Pendleton	.20	.09	.03
☐ 9 Deion Sanders	.30	.14	.04
☐ 10 John Smoltz	.10	.05	.01
☐ 11 Doug Dascenzo	.05	.02	.01
☐ 12 Andre Dawson	.20	.09	.03
☐ 13 Joe Girardi	.05	.02	.01
☐ 14 Mark Grace	.20	.09	.03
☐ 15 Greg Maddux	.30	.14	.04
☐ 16 Chuck McElroy	.05	.02	.01
☐ 17 Mike Morgan	.05	.02	.01
☐ 18 Ryne Sandberg	.50	.23	.06
☐ 19 Gary Scott	.05	.02	.01
☐ 20 Sammy Sosa	.20	.09	.03
☐ 21 Norm Charlton	.05	.02	.01
☐ 22 Rob Dibble	.05	.02	.01
☐ 23 Barry Larkin	.20	.09	.03
☐ 24 Hal Morris	.10	.05	.01
☐ 25 Paul O'Neill	.10	.05	.01
☐ 26 Jose Rijo	.10	.05	.01
☐ 27 Bip Roberts	.05	.02	.01
☐ 28 Chris Sabo	.10	.05	.01
☐ 29 Reggie Sanders	.30	.14	.04
☐ 30 Greg Swindell	.05	.02	.01
☐ 31 Jeff Bagwell	1.25	.55	.16
☐ 32 Craig Biggio	.10	.05	.01
☐ 33 Ken Caminiti	.10	.05	.01
☐ 34 Andujar Cedeno	.10	.05	.01
☐ 35 Steve Finley	.05	.02	.01
☐ 36 Pete Harnisch	.10	.05	.01
☐ 37 Butch Henry	.15	.07	.02
☐ 38 Doug Jones	.05	.02	.01
☐ 39 Darryl Kile	.10	.05	.01
☐ 40 Eddie Taubensee	.05	.02	.01
☐ 41 Brett Butler	.10	.05	.01
☐ 42 Tom Candiotti	.05	.02	.01
☐ 43 Eric Davis	.05	.02	.01
☐ 44 Orel Hershiser	.10	.05	.01
☐ 45 Eric Karros	.20	.09	.03
☐ 46 Ramon Martinez	.10	.05	.01
☐ 47 Jose Offerman	.05	.02	.01
☐ 48 Mike Scioscia	.05	.02	.01
☐ 49 Mike Sharperson	.05	.02	.01
☐ 50 Darryl Strawberry	.10	.05	.01
☐ 51 Bret Barberie	.05	.02	.01
☐ 52 Ivan Calderon	.05	.02	.01
☐ 53 Gary Carter	.20	.09	.03
☐ 54 Delino DeShields	.20	.09	.03
☐ 55 Marquis Grissom	.20	.09	.03
☐ 56 Ken Hill	.10	.05	.01
☐ 57 Dennis Martinez	.10	.05	.01
☐ 58 Spike Owen	.05	.02	.01
☐ 59 Larry Walker	.20	.09	.03
☐ 60 Tim Wallach	.05	.02	.01
☐ 61 Bobby Bonilla	.20	.09	.03
☐ 62 Tim Burke	.05	.02	.01
☐ 63 Vince Coleman	.05	.02	.01
☐ 64 John Franco	.05	.02	.01
☐ 65 Dwight Gooden	.10	.05	.01
☐ 66 Todd Hundley	.05	.02	.01
☐ 67 Howard Johnson	.10	.05	.01
☐ 68 Eddie Murray UER (He's not all-time switch homer leader, but he has most games with homers from both sides)	.20	.09	.03
☐ 69 Bret Saberhagen	.10	.05	.01
☐ 70 Anthony Young	.05	.02	.01
☐ 71 Kim Batiste	.05	.02	.01
☐ 72 Wes Chamberlain	.05	.02	.01
☐ 73 Darren Daulton	.20	.09	.03
☐ 74 Mariano Duncan	.05	.02	.01
☐ 75 Len Dykstra	.20	.09	.03
☐ 76 John Kruk	.20	.09	.03
☐ 77 Mickey Morandini	.05	.02	.01
☐ 78 Terry Mulholland	.05	.02	.01
☐ 79 Dale Murphy	.20	.09	.03
☐ 80 Mitch Williams	.10	.05	.01
☐ 81 Jay Bell	.10	.05	.01
☐ 82 Barry Bonds	.60	.25	.08
☐ 83 Steve Buechele	.05	.02	.01
☐ 84 Doug Drabek	.20	.09	.03
☐ 85 Mike LaValliere	.05	.02	.01
☐ 86 Jose Lind	.05	.02	.01
☐ 87 Denny Neagle	.05	.02	.01
☐ 88 Randy Tomlin	.05	.02	.01
☐ 89 Andy Van Slyke	.20	.09	.03
☐ 90 Gary Varsho	.05	.02	.01
☐ 91 Pedro Guerrero	.10	.05	.01
☐ 92 Rex Hudler	.05	.02	.01
☐ 93 Brian Jordan	.15	.07	.02

☐ 94	Felix Jose	.10	.05	.01
☐ 95	Donovan Osborne	.05	.02	.01
☐ 96	Tom Pagnozzi	.05	.02	.01
☐ 97	Lee Smith	.20	.09	.03
☐ 98	Ozzie Smith	.25	.11	.03
☐ 99	Todd Worrell	.05	.02	.01
☐ 100	Todd Zeile	.10	.05	.01
☐ 101	Andy Benes	.10	.05	.01
☐ 102	Jerald Clark	.05	.02	.01
☐ 103	Tony Fernandez	.10	.05	.01
☐ 104	Tony Gwynn	.35	.16	.04
☐ 105	Greg W. Harris	.05	.02	.01
☐ 106	Fred McGriff	.30	.14	.04
☐ 107	Benito Santiago	.05	.02	.01
☐ 108	Gary Sheffield	.20	.09	.03
☐ 109	Kurt Stillwell	.05	.02	.01
☐ 110	Tim Teufel	.05	.02	.01
☐ 111	Kevin Bass	.05	.02	.01
☐ 112	Jeff Brantley	.05	.02	.01
☐ 113	John Burkett	.10	.05	.01
☐ 114	Will Clark	.30	.14	.04
☐ 115	Royce Clayton	.20	.09	.03
☐ 116	Mike Jackson	.05	.02	.01
☐ 117	Darren Lewis	.10	.05	.01
☐ 118	Bill Swift	.10	.05	.01
☐ 119	Robby Thompson	.05	.02	.01
☐ 120	Matt Williams	.30	.14	.04
☐ 121	Brady Anderson	.10	.05	.01
☐ 122	Glenn Davis	.05	.02	.01
☐ 123	Mike Devereaux	.10	.05	.01
☐ 124	Chris Hoiles	.20	.09	.03
☐ 125	Sam Horn	.05	.02	.01
☐ 126	Ben McDonald	.10	.05	.01
☐ 127	Mike Mussina	.50	.23	.06
☐ 128	Gregg Olson	.05	.02	.01
☐ 129	Cal Ripken	.60	.25	.08
☐ 130	Rick Sutcliffe	.10	.05	.01
☐ 131	Wade Boggs	.20	.09	.03
☐ 132	Roger Clemens	.35	.16	.04
☐ 133	Greg A. Harris	.05	.02	.01
☐ 134	Tim Naehring	.05	.02	.01
☐ 135	Tony Pena	.05	.02	.01
☐ 136	Phil Plantier	.20	.09	.03
☐ 137	Jeff Reardon	.10	.05	.01
☐ 138	Jody Reed	.05	.02	.01
☐ 139	Mo Vaughn	.30	.14	.04
☐ 140	Frank Viola	.10	.05	.01
☐ 141	Jim Abbott	.20	.09	.03
☐ 142	Hubie Brooks	.05	.02	.01
☐ 143	Chad Curtis	.25	.11	.03
☐ 144	Gary DiSarcina	.05	.02	.01
☐ 145	Chuck Finley	.05	.02	.01
☐ 146	Bryan Harvey	.10	.05	.01
☐ 147	Von Hayes	.05	.02	.01
☐ 148	Mark Langston	.20	.09	.03
☐ 149	Lance Parrish	.10	.05	.01
☐ 150	Lee Stevens	.05	.02	.01
☐ 151	George Bell	.10	.05	.01
☐ 152	Alex Fernandez	.20	.09	.03
☐ 153	Greg Hibbard	.05	.02	.01
☐ 154	Lance Johnson	.05	.02	.01
☐ 155	Kirk McCaskill	.05	.02	.01
☐ 156	Tim Raines	.20	.09	.03
☐ 157	Steve Sax	.05	.02	.01
☐ 158	Bobby Thigpen	.05	.02	.01
☐ 159	Frank Thomas	2.50	1.15	.30
☐ 160	Robin Ventura	.20	.09	.03
☐ 161	Sandy Alomar Jr.	.10	.05	.01
☐ 162	Jack Armstrong	.05	.02	.01
☐ 163	Carlos Baerga	.30	.14	.04
☐ 164	Albert Belle	.60	.25	.08
☐ 165	Alex Cole	.05	.02	.01
☐ 166	Glenallen Hill	.05	.02	.01
☐ 167	Mark Lewis	.10	.05	.01
☐ 168	Kenny Lofton	2.00	.90	.25
☐ 169	Paul Sorrento	.05	.02	.01
☐ 170	Mark Whiten	.10	.05	.01
☐ 171	Milt Cuyler	.05	.02	.01
☐ 172	Rob Deer	.05	.02	.01
☐ 173	Cecil Fielder	.25	.11	.03
☐ 174	Travis Fryman	.30	.14	.04
☐ 175	Mike Henneman	.05	.02	.01
☐ 176	Tony Phillips	.05	.02	.01
☐ 177	Frank Tanana	.05	.02	.01
☐ 178	Mickey Tettleton	.10	.05	.01
☐ 179	Alan Trammell	.20	.09	.03
☐ 180	Lou Whitaker	.20	.09	.03
☐ 181	George Brett	.50	.23	.06
☐ 182	Tom Gordon	.05	.02	.01
☐ 183	Mark Gubicza	.05	.02	.01
☐ 184	Gregg Jefferies	.15	.07	.02
☐ 185	Wally Joyner	.10	.05	.01
☐ 186	Brent Mayne	.05	.02	.01
☐ 187	Brian McRae	.20	.09	.03
☐ 188	Kevin McReynolds	.05	.02	.01
☐ 189	Keith Miller	.05	.02	.01
☐ 190	Jeff Montgomery	.10	.05	.01
☐ 191	Dante Bichette	.20	.09	.03
☐ 192	Ricky Bones	.10	.05	.01
☐ 193	Scott Fletcher	.05	.02	.01
☐ 194	Paul Molitor	.25	.11	.03
☐ 195	Jaime Navarro	.05	.02	.01
☐ 196	Franklin Stubbs	.05	.02	.01
☐ 197	B.J. Surhoff	.05	.02	.01
☐ 198	Greg Vaughn	.10	.05	.01
☐ 199	Bill Wegman	.05	.02	.01
☐ 200	Robin Yount	.20	.09	.03
☐ 201	Rick Aguilera	.10	.05	.01
☐ 202	Scott Erickson	.05	.02	.01
☐ 203	Greg Gagne	.05	.02	.01
☐ 204	Brian Harper	.05	.02	.01
☐ 205	Kent Hrbek	.10	.05	.01
☐ 206	Scott Leius	.05	.02	.01
☐ 207	Shane Mack	.10	.05	.01
☐ 208	Pat Mahomes	.20	.09	.03
☐ 209	Kirby Puckett	.50	.23	.06
☐ 210	John Smiley	.05	.02	.01
☐ 211	Mike Gallego	.05	.02	.01
☐ 212	Charlie Hayes	.10	.05	.01
☐ 213	Pat Kelly	.10	.05	.01
☐ 214	Roberto Kelly	.10	.05	.01
☐ 215	Kevin Maas	.05	.02	.01
☐ 216	Don Mattingly	.50	.23	.06
☐ 217	Matt Nokes	.05	.02	.01
☐ 218	Melido Perez	.05	.02	.01
☐ 219	Scott Sanderson	.05	.02	.01
☐ 220	Danny Tartabull	.10	.05	.01
☐ 221	Harold Baines	.10	.05	.01
☐ 222	Jose Canseco	.30	.14	.04
☐ 223	Dennis Eckersley	.20	.09	.03
☐ 224	Dave Henderson	.05	.02	.01
☐ 225	Carney Lansford	.10	.05	.01
☐ 226	Mark McGwire	.20	.09	.03
☐ 227	Mike Moore	.05	.02	.01
☐ 228	Randy Ready	.05	.02	.01
☐ 229	Terry Steinbach	.10	.05	.01
☐ 230	Dave Stewart	.10	.05	.01
☐ 231	Jay Buhner	.10	.05	.01
☐ 232	Ken Griffey Jr.	2.50	1.15	.30
☐ 233	Erik Hanson	.05	.02	.01
☐ 234	Randy Johnson	.20	.09	.03
☐ 235	Edgar Martinez	.10	.05	.01
☐ 236	Tino Martinez	.10	.05	.01
☐ 237	Kevin Mitchell	.10	.05	.01
☐ 238	Pete O'Brien	.05	.02	.01
☐ 239	Harold Reynolds	.05	.02	.01

☐ 240	David Valle	.05	.02	.01
☐ 241	Julio Franco	.10	.05	.01
☐ 242	Juan Gonzalez	.90	.40	.11
☐ 243	Jose Guzman	.05	.02	.01
☐ 244	Rafael Palmeiro	.20	.09	.03
☐ 245	Dean Palmer	.10	.05	.01
☐ 246	Ivan Rodriguez	.20	.09	.03
☐ 247	Jeff Russell	.05	.02	.01
☐ 248	Nolan Ryan	1.50	.65	.19
☐ 249	Ruben Sierra	.20	.09	.03
☐ 250	Dickie Thon	.05	.02	.01
☐ 251	Roberto Alomar	.35	.16	.04
☐ 252	Derek Bell	.10	.05	.01
☐ 253	Pat Borders	.05	.02	.01
☐ 254	Joe Carter	.30	.14	.04
☐ 255	Kelly Gruber	.05	.02	.01
☐ 256	Juan Guzman	.10	.05	.01
☐ 257	Jack Morris	.20	.09	.03
☐ 258	John Olerud	.20	.09	.03
☐ 259	Devon White	.10	.05	.01
☐ 260	Dave Winfield	.20	.09	.03
☐ 261	Checklist	.10	.02	.01
☐ 262	Checklist	.10	.02	.01
☐ 263	Checklist	.10	.02	.01
☐ 264	History Card	.05	.02	.01

1992 Studio Heritage

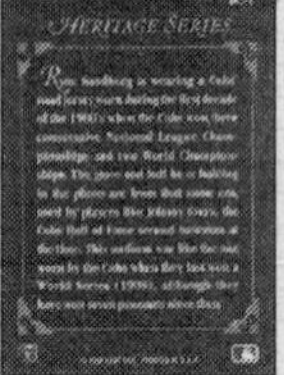

The 1992 Leaf Studio Heritage series subset presents today's star players dressed in vintage uniforms. Cards numbered 1-8 were randomly inserted in 12-card Leaf Studio foil packs while cards numbered 9-14 were inserted one per pack in 28-card Leaf Studio jumbo packs. The cards measure the standard size (2 1/2" by 3 1/2"). The fronts display sepia-toned portraits of the players dressed in vintage uniforms of their current teams. The pictures are bordered by dark turquoise and have bronze foil picture holders at each corner. The set title "Heritage Series" also appears in bronze foil lettering above the pictures. Within a bronze picture frame design on dark turquoise, the backs give a brief history of the team with special reference to the year of the vintage uniform. The cards are numbered on the back with a "BC" prefix.

	MINT	EXC	G-VG
COMPLETE SET (14)	25.00	11.50	3.10
COMPLETE FOIL SET (8)	15.00	6.75	1.90
COMPLETE JUMBO SET (6)	10.00	4.50	1.25
COMMON CARD (BC1-BC8)	1.00	.45	.13
COMMON CARD (BC9-BC14)	1.00	.45	.13

☐ BC1	Ryne Sandberg 1908 Cubs	4.00	1.80	.50
☐ BC2	Carlton Fisk 1917 White Sox	1.50	.65	.19
☐ BC3	Wade Boggs 1918 Red Sox	1.50	.65	.19
☐ BC4	Jose Canseco 1929 Athletics	2.50	1.15	.30
☐ BC5	Don Mattingly 1939 Yankees	4.00	1.80	.50
☐ BC6	Darryl Strawberry 1944 Dodgers	1.00	.45	.13
☐ BC7	Cal Ripken 1951 Browns	6.00	2.70	.75
☐ BC8	Will Clark 1951 Giants	2.50	1.15	.30
☐ BC9	Andre Dawson 1944 Cubs	1.50	.65	.19
☐ BC10	Andy Van Slyke 1960 Pirates	1.00	.45	.13
☐ BC11	Paul Molitor 1969 Pilots	2.50	1.15	.30
☐ BC12	Jeff Bagwell 1962 Colt 45s	6.00	2.70	.75
☐ BC13	Darren Daulton 1945 Phillies	1.50	.65	.19
☐ BC14	Kirby Puckett 1960 Senators	4.00	1.80	.50

1993 Studio

The 220 standard-size (2 1/2" by 3 1/2") cards comprising this set feature borderless fronts with posed color player photos that are cut out and superposed upon a closeup of an embroidered team logo. A facsimile player autograph appears in prismatic gold foil across the lower portion of the photo. The borderless black backs carry another posed color player photo shunted to the right side, with the player's name, position, team, biography, and personal profile appearing in white lettering on the left side. The cards are numbered on the back. The key Rookie Card in this set is J.T. Snow.

	MINT	EXC	G-VG
COMPLETE SET (220)	20.00	9.00	2.50
COMMON CARD (1-220)	.10	.05	.01

☐ 1	Dennis Eckersley	.15	.07	.02

☐	2 Chad Curtis	.12	.05	.02
☐	3 Eric Anthony	.10	.05	.01
☐	4 Roberto Alomar	.60	.25	.08
☐	5 Steve Avery	.15	.07	.02
☐	6 Cal Eldred	.12	.05	.02
☐	7 Bernard Gilkey	.10	.05	.01
☐	8 Steve Buechele	.10	.05	.01
☐	9 Brett Butler	.12	.05	.02
☐	10 Terry Mulholland	.10	.05	.01
☐	11 Moises Alou	.15	.07	.02
☐	12 Barry Bonds	1.00	.45	.13
☐	13 Sandy Alomar Jr.	.12	.05	.02
☐	14 Chris Bosio	.10	.05	.01
☐	15 Scott Sanderson	.10	.05	.01
☐	16 Bobby Bonilla	.15	.07	.02
☐	17 Brady Anderson	.12	.05	.02
☐	18 Derek Bell	.12	.05	.02
☐	19 Wes Chamberlain	.10	.05	.01
☐	20 Jay Bell	.12	.05	.02
☐	21 Kevin Brown	.10	.05	.01
☐	22 Roger Clemens	.60	.25	.08
☐	23 Roberto Kelly	.12	.05	.02
☐	24 Dante Bichette	.15	.07	.02
☐	25 George Brett	1.00	.45	.13
☐	26 Rob Deer	.10	.05	.01
☐	27 Brian Harper	.10	.05	.01
☐	28 George Bell	.12	.05	.02
☐	29 Jim Abbott	.15	.07	.02
☐	30 Dave Henderson	.10	.05	.01
☐	31 Wade Boggs	.15	.07	.02
☐	32 Chili Davis	.12	.05	.02
☐	33 Ellis Burks	.12	.05	.02
☐	34 Jeff Bagwell	1.25	.55	.16
☐	35 Kent Hrbek	.12	.05	.02
☐	36 Pat Borders	.10	.05	.01
☐	37 Cecil Fielder	.20	.09	.03
☐	38 Sid Bream	.10	.05	.01
☐	39 Greg Gagne	.10	.05	.01
☐	40 Darryl Hamilton	.10	.05	.01
☐	41 Jerald Clark	.10	.05	.01
☐	42 Mark Grace	.15	.07	.02
☐	43 Barry Larkin	.15	.07	.02
☐	44 John Burkett	.12	.05	.02
☐	45 Scott Cooper	.12	.05	.02
☐	46 Mike Lansing	.25	.11	.03
☐	47 Jose Canseco	.40	.18	.05
☐	48 Will Clark	.40	.18	.05
☐	49 Carlos Garcia	.12	.05	.02
☐	50 Carlos Baerga	.40	.18	.05
☐	51 Darren Daulton	.15	.07	.02
☐	52 Jay Buhner	.12	.05	.02
☐	53 Andy Benes	.12	.05	.02
☐	54 Jeff Conine	.15	.07	.02
☐	55 Mike Devereaux	.12	.05	.02
☐	56 Vince Coleman	.10	.05	.01
☐	57 Terry Steinbach	.12	.05	.02
☐	58 J.T. Snow	.15	.07	.02
☐	59 Greg Swindell	.10	.05	.01
☐	60 Devon White	.12	.05	.02
☐	61 John Smoltz	.12	.05	.02
☐	62 Todd Zeile	.12	.05	.02
☐	63 Rick Wilkins	.10	.05	.01
☐	64 Tim Wallach	.10	.05	.01
☐	65 John Wetteland	.10	.05	.01
☐	66 Matt Williams	.40	.18	.05
☐	67 Paul Sorrento	.10	.05	.01
☐	68 David Valle	.10	.05	.01
☐	69 Walt Weiss	.10	.05	.01
☐	70 John Franco	.10	.05	.01
☐	71 Nolan Ryan	2.50	1.15	.30
☐	72 Frank Viola	.10	.05	.01
☐	73 Chris Sabo	.12	.05	.02
☐	74 David Nied	.15	.07	.02
☐	75 Kevin McReynolds	.10	.05	.01
☐	76 Lou Whitaker	.15	.07	.02
☐	77 Dave Winfield	.15	.07	.02
☐	78 Robin Ventura	.15	.07	.02
☐	79 Spike Owen	.10	.05	.01
☐	80 Cal Ripken	1.50	.65	.19
☐	81 Dan Walters	.10	.05	.01
☐	82 Mitch Williams	.12	.05	.02
☐	83 Tim Wakefield	.10	.05	.01
☐	84 Rickey Henderson	.15	.07	.02
☐	85 Gary DiSarcina	.10	.05	.01
☐	86 Craig Biggio	.12	.05	.02
☐	87 Joe Carter	.40	.18	.05
☐	88 Ron Gant	.12	.05	.02
☐	89 John Jaha	.12	.05	.02
☐	90 Gregg Jefferies	.15	.07	.02
☐	91 Jose Guzman	.10	.05	.01
☐	92 Eric Karros	.12	.05	.02
☐	93 Wil Cordero	.15	.07	.02
☐	94 Royce Clayton	.12	.05	.02
☐	95 Albert Belle	.75	.35	.09
☐	96 Ken Griffey Jr.	2.50	1.15	.30
☐	97 Orestes Destrade	.10	.05	.01
☐	98 Tony Fernandez	.10	.05	.01
☐	99 Leo Gomez	.10	.05	.01
☐	100 Tony Gwynn	.60	.25	.08
☐	101 Len Dykstra	.15	.07	.02
☐	102 Jeff King	.10	.05	.01
☐	103 Julio Franco	.12	.05	.02
☐	104 Andre Dawson	.15	.07	.02
☐	105 Randy Milligan	.10	.05	.01
☐	106 Alex Cole	.10	.05	.01
☐	107 Phil Hiatt	.10	.05	.01
☐	108 Travis Fryman	.20	.09	.03
☐	109 Chuck Knoblauch	.15	.07	.02
☐	110 Bo Jackson	.15	.07	.02
☐	111 Pat Kelly	.10	.05	.01
☐	112 Bret Saberhagen	.12	.05	.02
☐	113 Ruben Sierra	.15	.07	.02
☐	114 Tim Salmon	.50	.23	.06
☐	115 Doug Jones	.10	.05	.01
☐	116 Ed Sprague	.10	.05	.01
☐	117 Terry Pendleton	.15	.07	.02
☐	118 Robin Yount	.40	.18	.05
☐	119 Mark Whiten	.12	.05	.02
☐	120 Checklist 1-110	.10	.05	.01
☐	121 Sammy Sosa	.15	.07	.02
☐	122 Darryl Strawberry	.12	.05	.02
☐	123 Larry Walker	.15	.07	.02
☐	124 Robby Thompson	.10	.05	.01
☐	125 Carlos Martinez	.10	.05	.01
☐	126 Edgar Martinez	.10	.05	.01
☐	127 Benito Santiago	.10	.05	.01
☐	128 Howard Johnson	.10	.05	.01
☐	129 Harold Reynolds	.10	.05	.01
☐	130 Craig Shipley	.10	.05	.01
☐	131 Curt Schilling	.12	.05	.02
☐	132 Andy Van Slyke	.15	.07	.02
☐	133 Ivan Rodriguez	.15	.07	.02
☐	134 Mo Vaughn	.15	.07	.02
☐	135 Bip Roberts	.10	.05	.01
☐	136 Charlie Hayes	.12	.05	.02
☐	137 Brian McRae	.15	.07	.02
☐	138 Mickey Tettleton	.12	.05	.02
☐	139 Frank Thomas	2.50	1.15	.30
☐	140 Paul O'Neill	.12	.05	.02
☐	141 Mark McGwire	.15	.07	.02
☐	142 Damion Easley	.12	.05	.02
☐	143 Ken Caminiti	.12	.05	.02
☐	144 Juan Guzman	.12	.05	.02
☐	145 Tom Glavine	.15	.07	.02
☐	146 Pat Listach	.12	.05	.02
☐	147 Lee Smith	.15	.07	.02

☐ 148 Derrick May	.12	.05	.02
☐ 149 Ramon Martinez	.12	.05	.02
☐ 150 Delino DeShields	.12	.05	.02
☐ 151 Kirt Manwaring	.10	.05	.01
☐ 152 Reggie Jefferson	.10	.05	.01
☐ 153 Randy Johnson	.15	.07	.02
☐ 154 Dave Magadan	.10	.05	.01
☐ 155 Dwight Gooden	.10	.05	.01
☐ 156 Chris Hoiles	.12	.05	.02
☐ 157 Fred McGriff	.40	.18	.05
☐ 158 Dave Hollins	.15	.07	.02
☐ 159 Al Martin	.12	.05	.02
☐ 160 Juan Gonzalez	1.00	.45	.13
☐ 161 Mike Greenwell	.12	.05	.02
☐ 162 Kevin Mitchell	.12	.05	.02
☐ 163 Andres Galarraga	.15	.07	.02
☐ 164 Wally Joyner	.12	.05	.02
☐ 165 Kirk Gibson	.12	.05	.02
☐ 166 Pedro Munoz	.10	.05	.01
☐ 167 Ozzie Guillen	.10	.05	.01
☐ 168 Jimmy Key	.12	.05	.02
☐ 169 Kevin Seitzer	.10	.05	.01
☐ 170 Luis Polonia	.10	.05	.01
☐ 171 Luis Gonzalez	.12	.05	.02
☐ 172 Paul Molitor	.40	.18	.05
☐ 173 David Justice	.40	.18	.05
☐ 174 B.J. Surhoff	.10	.05	.01
☐ 175 Ray Lankford	.15	.07	.02
☐ 176 Ryne Sandberg	.75	.35	.09
☐ 177 Jody Reed	.10	.05	.01
☐ 178 Marquis Grissom	.15	.07	.02
☐ 179 Willie McGee	.12	.05	.02
☐ 180 Kenny Lofton	.60	.25	.08
☐ 181 Junior Felix	.10	.05	.01
☐ 182 Jose Offerman	.10	.05	.01
☐ 183 John Kruk	.15	.07	.02
☐ 184 Orlando Merced	.12	.05	.02
☐ 185 Rafael Palmeiro	.15	.07	.02
☐ 186 Billy Hatcher	.10	.05	.01
☐ 187 Joe Oliver	.10	.05	.01
☐ 188 Joe Girardi	.10	.05	.01
☐ 189 Jose Lind	.10	.05	.01
☐ 190 Harold Baines	.12	.05	.02
☐ 191 Mike Pagliarulo	.10	.05	.01
☐ 192 Lance Johnson	.10	.05	.01
☐ 193 Don Mattingly	1.00	.45	.13
☐ 194 Doug Drabek	.15	.07	.02
☐ 195 John Olerud	.15	.07	.02
☐ 196 Greg Maddux	.60	.25	.08
☐ 197 Greg Vaughn	.12	.05	.02
☐ 198 Tom Pagnozzi	.10	.05	.01
☐ 199 Willie Wilson	.10	.05	.01
☐ 200 Jack McDowell	.15	.07	.02
☐ 201 Mike Piazza	2.50	1.15	.30
☐ 202 Mike Mussina	.50	.23	.06
☐ 203 Charles Nagy	.10	.05	.01
☐ 204 Tino Martinez	.12	.05	.02
☐ 205 Charlie Hough	.12	.05	.02
☐ 206 Todd Hundley	.10	.05	.01
☐ 207 Gary Sheffield	.15	.07	.02
☐ 208 Mickey Morandini	.10	.05	.01
☐ 209 Don Slaught	.10	.05	.01
☐ 210 Dean Palmer	.12	.05	.02
☐ 211 Jose Rijo	.12	.05	.02
☐ 212 Vinny Castilla	.10	.05	.01
☐ 213 Tony Phillips	.10	.05	.01
☐ 214 Kirby Puckett	1.00	.45	.13
☐ 215 Tim Raines	.15	.07	.02
☐ 216 Otis Nixon	.10	.05	.01
☐ 217 Ozzie Smith	.40	.18	.05
☐ 218 Jose Vizcaino	.10	.05	.01
☐ 219 Randy Tomlin	.10	.05	.01
☐ 220 Checklist 111-220	.10	.05	.01

1993 Studio Heritage

This 12-card set was randomly inserted in all 1993 Leaf Studio foil packs, measures the standard size (2 1/2" by 3 1/2"), and features sepia-toned portraits of current players in vintage team uniforms. The pictures are bordered in turquoise blue and have bronze-foil simulated picture holders at each corner. The set title appears in white lettering above the picture, and the player's name is printed in white below. The horizontal and turquoise-blue-bordered back shades from beige to red from top to bottom, and carries a posed sepia-toned player picture on the right within an oval set off by red and black lines. His name appears in white lettering at the top within a black arc. A brief story of the team represented by the player's vintage uniform follows below. The cards are numbered on the back.

	MINT	EXC	G-VG
COMPLETE SET (12)	30.00	13.50	3.80
COMMON CARD (1-12)	1.00	.45	.13
☐ 1 George Brett	6.00	2.70	.75
☐ 2 Juan Gonzalez	5.00	2.30	.60
☐ 3 Roger Clemens	4.00	1.80	.50
☐ 4 Mark McGwire	1.00	.45	.13
☐ 5 Mark Grace	1.50	.65	.19
☐ 6 Ozzie Smith	3.00	1.35	.40
☐ 7 Barry Larkin	1.50	.65	.19
☐ 8 Frank Thomas	15.00	6.75	1.90
☐ 9 Carlos Baerga	2.25	1.00	.30
☐ 10 Eric Karros	1.00	.45	.13
☐ 11 J.T. Snow	1.00	.45	.13
☐ 12 John Kruk	1.50	.65	.19

1993 Studio Silhouettes

One 1993 Leaf Studio Silhouettes card was inserted in each 20-card Leaf Studio jumbo pack. The ten-card set measures the standard size (2 1/2" by 3 1/2"). Full-bleed grayish fronts display posed color photos of star

players against action silhouettes. The set's title is printed across the top and the player's name appears along the bottom in copper foil within a darker gray area. The borderless and grayish back features a color player action photo on one side and a personal profile on the other. The cards are numbered on the back.

	MINT	EXC	G-VG
COMPLETE SET (10)	25.00	11.50	3.10
COMMON CARD (1-10)	.60	.25	.08
☐ 1 Frank Thomas	8.00	3.60	1.00
☐ 2 Barry Bonds	3.00	1.35	.40
☐ 3 Jeff Bagwell	4.00	1.80	.50
☐ 4 Juan Gonzalez	3.00	1.35	.40
☐ 5 Travis Fryman	1.00	.45	.13
☐ 6 J.T. Snow	.85	.40	.11
☐ 7 John Kruk	.85	.40	.11
☐ 8 Jeff Blauser	.60	.25	.08
☐ 9 Mike Piazza	6.00	2.70	.75
☐ 10 Nolan Ryan	8.00	3.60	1.00

1993 Studio Superstars on Canvas

This ten-card set was randomly inserted in 1993 Leaf Studio hobby and retail foil packs. The cards measure the standard size (2 1/2" by 3 1/2") and feature players in gray-bordered portraits that blend photography and artwork. The design of each front simulates a canvas painting of a player displayed on an artist's easel. The player's name appears in copper foil across the easel's base near the bottom. The set's title appears in white lettering beneath. The horizontal back carries a cutout color action player photo on one side and the player's name and career highlights within a black rectangle on the other, all superposed upon an abstract team color-coded design. The cards are numbered on the back.

	MINT	EXC	G-VG
COMPLETE SET (10)	35.00	16.00	4.40
COMMON CARD (1-10)	1.50	.65	.19
☐ 1 Ken Griffey Jr.	15.00	6.75	1.90
☐ 2 Jose Canseco	2.50	1.15	.30
☐ 3 Mark McGwire	1.50	.65	.19
☐ 4 Mike Mussina	3.00	1.35	.40
☐ 5 Joe Carter	2.25	1.00	.30
☐ 6 Frank Thomas	15.00	6.75	1.90
☐ 7 Darren Daulton	2.00	.90	.25
☐ 8 Mark Grace	2.00	.90	.25
☐ 9 Andres Galarraga	2.00	.90	.25
☐ 10 Barry Bonds	6.00	2.70	.75

1993 Studio Frank Thomas

The 1993 Leaf Studio Frank Thomas set was randomly inserted in all 1993 Leaf Studio foil packs. The five-card set measures the standard size (2 1/2" by 3 1/2"). The fronts feature posed black-and-white portraits of the Chicago White Sox slugging first baseman, which are borderless, except along the bottom edge, which has a white border that carries the Studio logo and the set's title. The white back carries another posed black-and-white photo of Thomas on the left side, beneath the blue-lettered subject of Thomas' reflections that appear alongside on the right. The cards are numbered on the back.

	MINT	EXC	G-VG
COMPLETE SET (5)	30.00	13.50	3.80
COMMON THOMAS (1-5)	6.00	2.70	.75
☐ 1 Frank Thomas Childhood	6.00	2.70	.75
☐ 2 Frank Thomas Baseball Memories	6.00	2.70	.75
☐ 3 Frank Thomas	6.00	2.70	.75

Family			
☐ 4 Frank Thomas	6.00	2.70	.75
Performance			
☐ 5 Frank Thomas	6.00	2.70	.75
Role Model			

1994 Studio

The 1994 Studio set consists of 220 full-bleed, standard-size cards. Card fronts offer a player photo with his jersey hanging in a locker room setting in the background. Backs contain statistics and a small photo. The set is grouped by team as follows: Oakland Athletics (1-7), California Angels (8-15), Houston Astros (16-23), Toronto Blue Jays (24-32), Atlanta Braves (33-41), Milwaukee Brewers (42-49), St. Louis Cardinals (50-57), Chicago Cubs (58-65), Los Angeles Dodgers (66-73), Montreal Expos (74-81), San Francisco Giants (82-89), Cleveland Indians (90-97), Seattle Mariners (98-104), Florida Marlins (105-112), New York Mets (113-120), Baltimore Orioles (121-128), San Diego Padres (129-135), Philadelphia Phillies (136-143), Pittsburgh Pirates (144-150), Texas Rangers (151-158), Boston Red Sox (159-166), Cincinnati Reds (167-174), Colorado Rockies (175-181), Kansas City Royals (182-188), Detroit Tigers (189-195), Minnesota Twins (196-202), Chicago White Sox (203-210), and New York Yankees (211-218).

	MINT	EXC	G-VG
COMPLETE SET (220)	15.00	6.75	1.90
COMMON CARD (1-220)	.10	.05	.01

☐ 1 Dennis Eckersley	.20	.09	.03
☐ 2 Brent Gates	.20	.09	.03
☐ 3 Rickey Henderson	.20	.09	.03
☐ 4 Mark McGwire	.20	.09	.03
☐ 5 Troy Neel	.15	.07	.02
☐ 6 Ruben Sierra	.20	.09	.03
☐ 7 Terry Steinbach	.15	.07	.02
☐ 8 Chad Curtis	.15	.07	.02
☐ 9 Chili Davis	.15	.07	.02
☐ 10 Gary DiSarcina	.10	.05	.01
☐ 11 Damion Easley	.10	.05	.01
☐ 12 Bo Jackson	.20	.09	.03
☐ 13 Mark Langston	.20	.09	.03
☐ 14 Eduardo Perez	.15	.07	.02
☐ 15 Tim Salmon	.40	.18	.05
☐ 16 Jeff Bagwell	1.50	.65	.19
☐ 17 Craig Biggio	.15	.07	.02
☐ 18 Ken Caminiti	.15	.07	.02
☐ 19 Andujar Cedeno	.10	.05	.01
☐ 20 Doug Drabek	.20	.09	.03
☐ 21 Steve Finley	.10	.05	.01
☐ 22 Luis Gonzalez	.10	.05	.01
☐ 23 Darryl Kile	.15	.07	.02
☐ 24 Roberto Alomar	.75	.35	.09
☐ 25 Pat Borders	.10	.05	.01
☐ 26 Joe Carter	.40	.18	.05
☐ 27 Carlos Delgado	.50	.23	.06
☐ 28 Pat Hentgen	.15	.07	.02
☐ 29 Paul Molitor	.40	.18	.05
☐ 30 John Olerud	.20	.09	.03
☐ 31 Ed Sprague	.10	.05	.01
☐ 32 Devon White	.10	.05	.01
☐ 33 Steve Avery	.20	.09	.03
☐ 34 Tom Glavine	.20	.09	.03
☐ 35 David Justice	.40	.18	.05
☐ 36 Roberto Kelly	.10	.05	.01
☐ 37 Ryan Klesko	.50	.23	.06
☐ 38 Javy Lopez	.30	.14	.04
☐ 39 Greg Maddux	.60	.25	.08
☐ 40 Fred McGriff	.40	.18	.05
☐ 41 Terry Pendleton	.10	.05	.01
☐ 42 Ricky Bones	.10	.05	.01
☐ 43 Darryl Hamilton	.10	.05	.01
☐ 44 Brian Harper	.10	.05	.01
☐ 45 John Jaha	.10	.05	.01
☐ 46 Dave Nilsson	.10	.05	.01
☐ 47 Kevin Seitzer	.10	.05	.01
☐ 48 Greg Vaughn	.15	.07	.02
☐ 49 Turner Ward	.10	.05	.01
☐ 50 Bernard Gilkey	.10	.05	.01
☐ 51 Gregg Jefferies	.20	.09	.03
☐ 52 Ray Lankford	.20	.09	.03
☐ 53 Tom Pagnozzi	.10	.05	.01
☐ 54 Ozzie Smith	.60	.25	.08
☐ 55 Bob Tewksbury	.10	.05	.01
☐ 56 Mark Whiten	.15	.07	.02
☐ 57 Todd Zeile	.15	.07	.02
☐ 58 Steve Buechele	.10	.05	.01
☐ 59 Shawon Dunston	.10	.05	.01
☐ 60 Mark Grace	.20	.09	.03
☐ 61 Derrick May	.10	.05	.01
☐ 62 Karl Rhodes	.10	.05	.01
☐ 63 Ryne Sandberg	1.00	.45	.13
☐ 64 Sammy Sosa	.20	.09	.03
☐ 65 Rick Wilkins	.10	.05	.01
☐ 66 Brett Butler	.15	.07	.02
☐ 67 Delino DeShields	.15	.07	.02
☐ 68 Orel Hershiser	.15	.07	.02
☐ 69 Eric Karros	.15	.07	.02
☐ 70 Raul Mondesi	1.00	.45	.13
☐ 71 Jose Offerman	.10	.05	.01
☐ 72 Mike Piazza	1.50	.65	.19
☐ 73 Tim Wallach	.10	.05	.01
☐ 74 Moises Alou	.20	.09	.03
☐ 75 Sean Berry	.10	.05	.01
☐ 76 Wil Cordero	.20	.09	.03
☐ 77 Cliff Floyd	.50	.23	.06
☐ 78 Marquis Grissom	.20	.09	.03
☐ 79 Ken Hill	.15	.07	.02
☐ 80 Larry Walker	.20	.09	.03
☐ 81 John Wetteland	.10	.05	.01
☐ 82 Rod Beck	.15	.07	.02
☐ 83 Barry Bonds	1.25	.55	.16
☐ 84 Royce Clayton	.15	.07	.02
☐ 85 Darren Lewis	.10	.05	.01
☐ 86 Willie McGee	.10	.05	.01
☐ 87 Bill Swift	.10	.05	.01
☐ 88 Robby Thompson	.10	.05	.01
☐ 89 Matt Williams	.60	.25	.08

No.	Player			
☐ 90	Sandy Alomar Jr.	.15	.07	.02
☐ 91	Carlos Baerga	.40	.18	.05
☐ 92	Albert Belle	1.00	.45	.13
☐ 93	Kenny Lofton	.75	.35	.09
☐ 94	Eddie Murray	.20	.09	.03
☐ 95	Manny Ramirez	.60	.25	.08
☐ 96	Paul Sorrento	.10	.05	.01
☐ 97	Jim Thome	.20	.09	.03
☐ 98	Rich Amaral	.10	.05	.01
☐ 99	Eric Anthony	.10	.05	.01
☐ 100	Jay Buhner	.15	.07	.02
☐ 101	Ken Griffey Jr.	3.00	1.35	.40
☐ 102	Randy Johnson	.20	.09	.03
☐ 103	Edgar Martinez	.10	.05	.01
☐ 104	Tino Martinez	.10	.05	.01
☐ 105	Kurt Abbott	.30	.14	.04
☐ 106	Bret Barberie	.10	.05	.01
☐ 107	Chuck Carr	.10	.05	.01
☐ 108	Jeff Conine	.20	.09	.03
☐ 109	Chris Hammond	.10	.05	.01
☐ 110	Bryan Harvey	.15	.07	.02
☐ 111	Benito Santiago	.10	.05	.01
☐ 112	Gary Sheffield	.20	.09	.03
☐ 113	Bobby Bonilla	.20	.09	.03
☐ 114	Dwight Gooden	.10	.05	.01
☐ 115	Todd Hundley	.10	.05	.01
☐ 116	Bobby Jones	.25	.11	.03
☐ 117	Jeff Kent	.15	.07	.02
☐ 118	Kevin McReynolds	.10	.05	.01
☐ 119	Bret Saberhagen	.15	.07	.02
☐ 120	Ryan Thompson	.15	.07	.02
☐ 121	Harold Baines	.15	.07	.02
☐ 122	Mike Devereaux	.15	.07	.02
☐ 123	Jeffrey Hammonds	.30	.14	.04
☐ 124	Ben McDonald	.15	.07	.02
☐ 125	Mike Mussina	.40	.18	.05
☐ 126	Rafael Palmeiro	.20	.09	.03
☐ 127	Cal Ripken	2.25	1.00	.30
☐ 128	Lee Smith	.20	.09	.03
☐ 129	Brad Ausmus	.10	.05	.01
☐ 130	Derek Bell	.15	.07	.02
☐ 131	Andy Benes	.15	.07	.02
☐ 132	Tony Gwynn	.75	.35	.09
☐ 133	Trevor Hoffman	.10	.05	.01
☐ 134	Scott Livingstone	.10	.05	.01
☐ 135	Phil Plantier	.15	.07	.02
☐ 136	Darren Daulton	.20	.09	.03
☐ 137	Mariano Duncan	.10	.05	.01
☐ 138	Lenny Dykstra	.20	.09	.03
☐ 139	Dave Hollins	.20	.09	.03
☐ 140	Pete Incaviglia	.10	.05	.01
☐ 141	Danny Jackson	.10	.05	.01
☐ 142	John Kruk	.20	.09	.03
☐ 143	Kevin Stocker	.15	.07	.02
☐ 144	Jay Bell	.15	.07	.02
☐ 145	Carlos Garcia	.10	.05	.01
☐ 146	Jeff King	.10	.05	.01
☐ 147	Al Martin	.10	.05	.01
☐ 148	Orlando Merced	.15	.07	.02
☐ 149	Don Slaught	.10	.05	.01
☐ 150	Andy Van Slyke	.20	.09	.03
☐ 151	Kevin Brown	.10	.05	.01
☐ 152	Jose Canseco	.40	.18	.05
☐ 153	Will Clark	.40	.18	.05
☐ 154	Juan Gonzalez	1.00	.45	.13
☐ 155	David Hulse	.10	.05	.01
☐ 156	Dean Palmer	.15	.07	.02
☐ 157	Ivan Rodriguez	.20	.09	.03
☐ 158	Kenny Rogers	.10	.05	.01
☐ 159	Roger Clemens	.75	.35	.09
☐ 160	Scott Cooper	.15	.07	.02
☐ 161	Andre Dawson	.20	.09	.03
☐ 162	Mike Greenwell	.15	.07	.02
☐ 163	Otis Nixon	.10	.05	.01
☐ 164	Aaron Sele	.25	.11	.03
☐ 165	John Valentin	.15	.07	.02
☐ 166	Mo Vaughn	.20	.09	.03
☐ 167	Bret Boone	.20	.09	.03
☐ 168	Barry Larkin	.20	.09	.03
☐ 169	Kevin Mitchell	.15	.07	.02
☐ 170	Hal Morris	.15	.07	.02
☐ 171	Jose Rijo	.15	.07	.02
☐ 172	Deion Sanders	.50	.23	.06
☐ 173	Reggie Sanders	.15	.07	.02
☐ 174	John Smiley	.10	.05	.01
☐ 175	Dante Bichette	.20	.09	.03
☐ 176	Ellis Burks	.15	.07	.02
☐ 177	Andres Galarraga	.20	.09	.03
☐ 178	Joe Girardi	.10	.05	.01
☐ 179	Charlie Hayes	.15	.07	.02
☐ 180	Roberto Mejia	.15	.07	.02
☐ 181	Walt Weiss	.10	.05	.01
☐ 182	David Cone	.20	.09	.03
☐ 183	Gary Gaetti	.10	.05	.01
☐ 184	Greg Gagne	.10	.05	.01
☐ 185	Felix Jose	.10	.05	.01
☐ 186	Wally Joyner	.15	.07	.02
☐ 187	Mike Macfarlane	.10	.05	.01
☐ 188	Brian McRae	.15	.07	.02
☐ 189	Eric Davis	.10	.05	.01
☐ 190	Cecil Fielder	.20	.09	.03
☐ 191	Travis Fryman	.25	.11	.03
☐ 192	Tony Phillips	.10	.05	.01
☐ 193	Mickey Tettleton	.15	.07	.02
☐ 194	Alan Trammell	.20	.09	.03
☐ 195	Lou Whitaker	.20	.09	.03
☐ 196	Kent Hrbek	.15	.07	.02
☐ 197	Chuck Knoblauch	.20	.09	.03
☐ 198	Shane Mack	.15	.07	.02
☐ 199	Pat Meares	.10	.05	.01
☐ 200	Kirby Puckett	1.25	.55	.16
☐ 201	Matt Walbeck	.10	.05	.01
☐ 202	Dave Winfield	.20	.09	.03
☐ 203	Wilson Alvarez	.20	.09	.03
☐ 204	Alex Fernandez	.20	.09	.03
☐ 205	Julio Franco	.15	.07	.02
☐ 206	Ozzie Guillen	.10	.05	.01
☐ 207	Jack McDowell	.20	.09	.03
☐ 208	Tim Raines	.20	.09	.03
☐ 209	Frank Thomas	3.00	1.35	.40
☐ 210	Robin Ventura	.15	.07	.02
☐ 211	Jim Abbott	.20	.09	.03
☐ 212	Wade Boggs	.20	.09	.03
☐ 213	Pat Kelly	.10	.05	.01
☐ 214	Jimmy Key	.15	.07	.02
☐ 215	Don Mattingly	1.25	.55	.16
☐ 216	Paul O'Neill	.15	.07	.02
☐ 217	Mike Stanley	.10	.05	.01
☐ 218	Danny Tartabull	.15	.07	.02
☐ 219	Checklist 1-110	.10	.05	.01
☐ 220	Checklist 111-220	.10	.05	.01

1994 Studio Editor's Choice

This eight-card set was randomly inserted in foil packs at a rate of one in 36. These standard-size cards are acetate and were designed much like a film strip with black borders. The fronts have various stop-action shots of the player and no back.

	MINT	EXC	G-VG
COMPLETE SET (8)	60.00	27.00	7.50
COMMON CARD (1-8)	2.00	.90	.25
☐ 1 Barry Bonds	8.00	3.60	1.00
☐ 2 Frank Thomas	20.00	9.00	2.50
☐ 3 Ken Griffey Jr.	20.00	9.00	2.50
☐ 4 Andres Galarraga	2.00	.90	.25
☐ 5 Juan Gonzalez	7.00	3.10	.85
☐ 6 Tim Salmon	4.00	1.80	.50
☐ 7 Paul O'Neill	2.00	.90	.25
☐ 8 Mike Piazza	10.00	4.50	1.25

1994 Studio Heritage

Each player in this eight-card insert set (randomly inserted in foil packs at a rate of one in nine) is modelling a vintage uniform of his team. The year of the uniform is noted in gold lettering at the top with a gold Heritage Collection logo at the bottom. A black and white photo of the stadium that the team used from the era of the depicted uniform serves as background. The back has a small photo a team highlight from that year.

	MINT	EXC	G-VG
COMPLETE SET (8)	25.00	11.50	3.10
COMMON CARD (1-8)	1.25	.55	.16
☐ 1 Barry Bonds	4.00	1.80	.50
☐ 2 Frank Thomas	10.00	4.50	1.25
☐ 3 Joe Carter	1.25	.55	.16
☐ 4 Don Mattingly	4.00	1.80	.50
☐ 5 Ryne Sandberg	3.50	1.55	.45
☐ 6 Javy Lopez	1.25	.55	.16
☐ 7 Gregg Jefferies	1.25	.55	.16
☐ 8 Mike Mussina	2.50	1.15	.30

1994 Studio Series Stars

This 10-card acetate set showcases top stars and was limited to 10,000 of each card. They were randomly inserted in foil packs at a rate of one in 60. The player cutout is surrounded by a small circle of stars with the player's name at the top. The team name, limited edition notation and the Series Stars logo are at the bottom. The back of the cutout contains a photo. Gold versions of this set were more difficult to obtain in packs (one in 120, 5,000 total) and are valued at twice the prices below.

	MINT	EXC	G-VG
COMPLETE SILVER SET (10)	275.00	125.00	34.00
COMMON SILVER (1-10)	10.00	4.50	1.25
*GOLD VERSIONS: 2X VALUES BELOW			
☐ 1 Tony Gwynn	18.00	8.00	2.30
☐ 2 Barry Bonds	25.00	11.50	3.10
☐ 3 Frank Thomas	60.00	27.00	7.50
☐ 4 Ken Griffey Jr.	60.00	27.00	7.50
☐ 5 Joe Carter	10.00	4.50	1.25
☐ 6 Mike Piazza	30.00	13.50	3.80
☐ 7 Cal Ripken	45.00	20.00	5.75
☐ 8 Greg Maddux	18.00	8.00	2.30
☐ 9 Juan Gonzalez	20.00	9.00	2.50
☐ 10 Don Mattingly	25.00	11.50	3.10

1951 Topps Blue Backs

The cards in this 52-card set measure approximately 2" by 2 5/8". The 1951 Topps series of blue-backed baseball cards could be used to play a baseball game by shuffling the cards and drawing them from a pile. These cards were marketed with a piece of caramel candy, which often melted or was squashed in such a way as to dam-

age the card and wrapper (despite the fact that a paper shield was inserted between candy and card). Blue Backs are more difficult to obtain than the similarly styled Red Backs. The set is denoted on the cards as "Set B" and the Red Back set is correspondingly Set A. The only notable Rookie Card in the set is Billy Pierce.

	NRMT	VG-E	GOOD
COMPLETE SET (52)	1800.00	800.00	230.00
COMMON CARD (1-52)	30.00	13.50	3.80
☐ 1 Eddie Yost	60.00	18.00	6.00
☐ 2 Hank Majeski	30.00	13.50	3.80
☐ 3 Richie Ashburn	200.00	90.00	25.00
☐ 4 Del Ennis	35.00	16.00	4.40
☐ 5 Johnny Pesky	35.00	16.00	4.40
☐ 6 Red Schoendienst	100.00	45.00	12.50
☐ 7 Gerry Staley	30.00	13.50	3.80
☐ 8 Dick Sisler	30.00	13.50	3.80
☐ 9 Johnny Sain	45.00	20.00	5.75
☐ 10 Joe Page	30.00	13.50	3.80
☐ 11 Johnny Groth	30.00	13.50	3.80
☐ 12 Sam Jethroe	35.00	16.00	4.40
☐ 13 Mickey Vernon	30.00	13.50	3.80
☐ 14 Red Munger	30.00	13.50	3.80
☐ 15 Eddie Joost	30.00	13.50	3.80
☐ 16 Murry Dickson	30.00	13.50	3.80
☐ 17 Roy Smalley	30.00	13.50	3.80
☐ 18 Ned Garver	30.00	13.50	3.80
☐ 19 Phil Masi	30.00	13.50	3.80
☐ 20 Ralph Branca	45.00	20.00	5.75
☐ 21 Billy Johnson	30.00	13.50	3.80
☐ 22 Bob Kuzava	30.00	13.50	3.80
☐ 23 Dizzy Trout	35.00	16.00	4.40
☐ 24 Sherman Lollar	35.00	16.00	4.40
☐ 25 Sam Mele	30.00	13.50	3.80
☐ 26 Chico Carrasquel	38.00	17.00	4.70
☐ 27 Andy Pafko	35.00	16.00	4.40
☐ 28 Harry Brecheen	35.00	16.00	4.40
☐ 29 Granville Hamner	30.00	13.50	3.80
☐ 30 Enos Slaughter	110.00	50.00	14.00
☐ 31 Lou Brissie	30.00	13.50	3.80
☐ 32 Bob Elliott	35.00	16.00	4.40
☐ 33 Don Lenhardt	30.00	13.50	3.80
☐ 34 Earl Torgeson	30.00	13.50	3.80
☐ 35 Tommy Byrne	30.00	13.50	3.80
☐ 36 Cliff Fannin	30.00	13.50	3.80
☐ 37 Bobby Doerr	100.00	45.00	12.50
☐ 38 Irv Noren	35.00	16.00	4.40
☐ 39 Ed Lopat	40.00	18.00	5.00
☐ 40 Vic Wertz	35.00	16.00	4.40
☐ 41 Johnny Schmitz	30.00	13.50	3.80
☐ 42 Bruce Edwards	30.00	13.50	3.80
☐ 43 Willie Jones	30.00	13.50	3.80
☐ 44 Johnny Wyrostek	30.00	13.50	3.80
☐ 45 Billy Pierce	50.00	23.00	6.25
☐ 46 Gerry Priddy	30.00	13.50	3.80
☐ 47 Herman Wehmeier	30.00	13.50	3.80
☐ 48 Billy Cox	30.00	13.50	3.80
☐ 49 Hank Sauer	30.00	13.50	3.80
☐ 50 Johnny Mize	150.00	70.00	19.00
☐ 51 Eddie Waitkus	30.00	13.50	3.80
☐ 52 Sam Chapman	42.00	13.50	3.80

1951 Topps Red Backs

The cards in this 52-card set measure approximately 2" by 2 5/8". The 1951 Topps Red Back set is identical in style to the Blue Back set of the same year. The cards have rounded corners and were designed to be used as a baseball game. Zernial, number 36, is listed with either the White Sox or Athletics, and Holmes, number 52, with either the Braves or Hartford. The set is denoted on the cards as "Set A" and the Blue Back set is correspondingly Set B. The only notable Rookie Card in the set is Monte Irvin.

	NRMT	VG-E	GOOD
COMPLETE SET (54)	850.00	375.00	105.00
COMMON CARD (1-52)	10.00	4.50	1.25
☐ 1 Yogi Berra	125.00	45.00	10.00
☐ 2 Sid Gordon	10.00	4.50	1.25
☐ 3 Ferris Fain	12.00	5.50	1.50
☐ 4 Vern Stephens	12.00	5.50	1.50
☐ 5 Phil Rizzuto	55.00	25.00	7.00
☐ 6 Allie Reynolds	16.00	7.25	2.00
☐ 7 Howie Pollet	10.00	4.50	1.25
☐ 8 Early Wynn	25.00	11.50	3.10
☐ 9 Roy Sievers	12.00	5.50	1.50
☐ 10 Mel Parnell	12.00	5.50	1.50
☐ 11 Gene Hermanski	10.00	4.50	1.25
☐ 12 Jim Hegan	12.00	5.50	1.50
☐ 13 Dale Mitchell	12.00	5.50	1.50
☐ 14 Wayne Terwilliger	10.00	4.50	1.25
☐ 15 Ralph Kiner	35.00	16.00	4.40
☐ 16 Preacher Roe	12.00	5.50	1.50
☐ 17 Gus Bell	12.00	5.50	1.50
☐ 18 Jerry Coleman	12.00	5.50	1.50
☐ 19 Dick Kokos	10.00	4.50	1.25
☐ 20 Dom DiMaggio	16.00	7.25	2.00
☐ 21 Larry Jansen	12.00	5.50	1.50
☐ 22 Bob Feller	60.00	27.00	7.50
☐ 23 Ray Boone	12.00	5.50	1.50
☐ 24 Hank Bauer	15.00	6.75	1.90
☐ 25 Cliff Chambers	10.00	4.50	1.25
☐ 26 Luke Easter	12.00	5.50	1.50

		NRMT	VG-E	GOOD
☐ 27	Wally Westlake	10.00	4.50	1.25
☐ 28	Elmer Valo	10.00	4.50	1.25
☐ 29	Bob Kennedy	12.00	5.50	1.50
☐ 30	Warren Spahn	60.00	27.00	7.50
☐ 31	Gil Hodges	40.00	18.00	5.00
☐ 32	Henry Thompson	12.00	5.50	1.50
☐ 33	William Werle	10.00	4.50	1.25
☐ 34	Grady Hatton	10.00	4.50	1.25
☐ 35	Al Rosen	15.00	6.75	1.90
☐ 36A	Gus Zernial (Chicago)	40.00	18.00	5.00
☐ 36B	Gus Zernial (Philadelphia)	20.00	9.00	2.50
☐ 37	Wes Westrum	12.00	5.50	1.50
☐ 38	Duke Snider	80.00	36.00	10.00
☐ 39	Ted Kluszewski	20.00	9.00	2.50
☐ 40	Mike Garcia	12.00	5.50	1.50
☐ 41	Whitey Lockman	12.00	5.50	1.50
☐ 42	Ray Scarborough	10.00	4.50	1.25
☐ 43	Maurice McDermott	10.00	4.50	1.25
☐ 44	Sid Hudson	10.00	4.50	1.25
☐ 45	Andy Seminick	10.00	4.50	1.25
☐ 46	Billy Goodman	12.00	5.50	1.50
☐ 47	Tommy Glaviano	10.00	4.50	1.25
☐ 48	Eddie Stanky	12.00	5.50	1.50
☐ 49	Al Zarilla	10.00	4.50	1.25
☐ 50	Monte Irvin	40.00	18.00	5.00
☐ 51	Eddie Robinson	10.00	4.50	1.25
☐ 52A	Tommy Holmes (Boston)	40.00	12.00	4.00
☐ 52B	Tommy Holmes (Hartford)	25.00	7.50	2.50

1952 Topps

The cards in this 407-card set measure approximately 2 5/8" by 3 3/4". The 1952 Topps set is Topps' first truly major set. Card numbers 1 to 80 were issued with red or black backs, both of which are less plentiful than card numbers 81 to 250. In fact, the first series is considered the most difficult with respect to finding perfect condition cards. Card number 48 (Joe Page) and number 49 (Johnny Sain) can be found with each other's write-up on their back. Card numbers 251 to 310 are somewhat scarce and numbers 311 to 407 are quite scarce. Cards 281-300 were single printed compared to the other cards in the next to last series. Cards 311-313 were double printed on the last high number printing sheet. The key card in the set is obviously Mickey Mantle, number 311, Mickey's first of many Topps cards. Although rarely seen, there exist salesman sample panels of three cards containing the fronts of regular cards with ad information on the back. Two such panels seen are Bob Mahoney/Robin Roberts/Sid Hudson . and Wally Westlake/Dizzy Trout/Irv Noren. The key Rookie Cards in this set are Billy Martin, Eddie Mathews (the last card in the set), and Hoyt Wilhelm.

		NRMT	VG-E	GOOD
	COMPLETE SET (407)	65000.	29300.	8100.
	COMMON CARD (1-80)	50.00	23.00	6.25
	COMMON CARD (81-130)	25.00	11.50	3.10
	COMMON CARD (131-190)	25.00	11.50	3.10
	COMMON CARD (191-250)	25.00	11.50	3.10
	COMMON CARD (251-280)	50.00	23.00	6.25
	COMMON CARD (281-300)	50.00	23.00	6.25
	COMMON CARD (301-310)	50.00	23.00	6.25
	COMMON CARD (311-407)	250.00	115.00	31.00
☐ 1	Andy Pafko	1200.00	120.00	36.00
☐ 2	Pete Runnels	65.00	29.00	8.25
☐ 3	Hank Thompson	55.00	25.00	7.00
☐ 4	Don Lenhardt	50.00	23.00	6.25
☐ 5	Larry Jansen	55.00	25.00	7.00
☐ 6	Grady Hatton	50.00	23.00	6.25
☐ 7	Wayne Terwilliger	55.00	25.00	7.00
☐ 8	Fred Marsh	50.00	23.00	6.25
☐ 9	Robert Hogue	50.00	23.00	6.25
☐ 10	Al Rosen	70.00	32.00	8.75
☐ 11	Phil Rizzuto	225.00	100.00	28.00
☐ 12	Monty Basgall	50.00	23.00	6.25
☐ 13	Johnny Wyrostek	50.00	23.00	6.25
☐ 14	Bob Elliott	55.00	25.00	7.00
☐ 15	Johnny Pesky	55.00	25.00	7.00
☐ 16	Gene Hermanski	50.00	23.00	6.25
☐ 17	Jim Hegan	55.00	25.00	7.00
☐ 18	Merrill Combs	50.00	23.00	6.25
☐ 19	Johnny Bucha	50.00	23.00	6.25
☐ 20	Billy Loes	100.00	45.00	12.50
☐ 21	Ferris Fain	55.00	25.00	7.00
☐ 22	Dom DiMaggio	90.00	40.00	11.50
☐ 23	Billy Goodman	55.00	25.00	7.00
☐ 24	Luke Easter	55.00	25.00	7.00
☐ 25	Johnny Groth	50.00	23.00	6.25
☐ 26	Monte Irvin	90.00	40.00	11.50
☐ 27	Sam Jethroe	55.00	25.00	7.00
☐ 28	Jerry Priddy	50.00	23.00	6.25
☐ 29	Ted Kluszewski	90.00	40.00	11.50
☐ 30	Mel Parnell	55.00	25.00	7.00
☐ 31	Gus Zernial	70.00	32.00	8.75
☐ 32	Eddie Robinson	50.00	23.00	6.25
☐ 33	Warren Spahn	210.00	95.00	26.00
☐ 34	Elmer Valo	50.00	23.00	6.25
☐ 35	Hank Sauer	65.00	29.00	8.25
☐ 36	Gil Hodges	140.00	65.00	17.50
☐ 37	Duke Snider	275.00	125.00	34.00
☐ 38	Wally Westlake	50.00	23.00	6.25
☐ 39	Dizzy Trout	55.00	25.00	7.00
☐ 40	Irv Noren	55.00	25.00	7.00
☐ 41	Bob Wellman	50.00	23.00	6.25
☐ 42	Lou Kretlow	50.00	23.00	6.25
☐ 43	Ray Scarborough	50.00	23.00	6.25
☐ 44	Con Dempsey	50.00	23.00	6.25
☐ 45	Eddie Joost	50.00	23.00	6.25
☐ 46	Gordon Goldsberry	50.00	23.00	6.25
☐ 47	Willie Jones	50.00	23.00	6.25
☐ 48A	Joe Page COR	75.00	34.00	9.50
☐ 48B	Joe Page ERR (Bio for Sain)	300.00	135.00	38.00
☐ 49A	Johnny Sain COR	90.00	40.00	11.50
☐ 49B	Johnny Sain ERR	300.00	135.00	38.00

	(Bio for Page)			
☐ 50	Marv Rickert	50.00	23.00	6.25
☐ 51	Jim Russell	50.00	23.00	6.25
☐ 52	Don Mueller	55.00	25.00	7.00
☐ 53	Chris Van Cuyk	50.00	23.00	6.25
☐ 54	Leo Kiely	50.00	23.00	6.25
☐ 55	Ray Boone	55.00	25.00	7.00
☐ 56	Tommy Glaviano	50.00	23.00	6.25
☐ 57	Ed Lopat	90.00	40.00	11.50
☐ 58	Bob Mahoney	50.00	23.00	6.25
☐ 59	Robin Roberts	150.00	70.00	19.00
☐ 60	Sid Hudson	50.00	23.00	6.25
☐ 61	Tookie Gilbert	50.00	23.00	6.25
☐ 62	Chuck Stobbs	50.00	23.00	6.25
☐ 63	Howie Pollet	50.00	23.00	6.25
☐ 64	Roy Sievers	55.00	25.00	7.00
☐ 65	Enos Slaughter	125.00	57.50	15.50
☐ 66	Preacher Roe	90.00	40.00	11.50
☐ 67	Allie Reynolds	90.00	40.00	11.50
☐ 68	Cliff Chambers	50.00	23.00	6.25
☐ 69	Virgil Stallcup	50.00	23.00	6.25
☐ 70	Al Zarilla	50.00	23.00	6.25
☐ 71	Tom Upton	50.00	23.00	6.25
☐ 72	Karl Olson	50.00	23.00	6.25
☐ 73	Bill Werle	50.00	23.00	6.25
☐ 74	Andy Hansen	50.00	23.00	6.25
☐ 75	Wes Westrum	55.00	25.00	7.00
☐ 76	Eddie Stanky	65.00	29.00	8.25
☐ 77	Bob Kennedy	55.00	25.00	7.00
☐ 78	Ellis Kinder	50.00	23.00	6.25
☐ 79	Gerry Staley	50.00	23.00	6.25
☐ 80	Herman Wehmeier	50.00	23.00	6.25
☐ 81	Vernon Law	25.00	11.50	3.10
☐ 82	Duane Pillette	25.00	11.50	3.10
☐ 83	Billy Johnson	25.00	11.50	3.10
☐ 84	Vern Stephens	28.00	12.50	3.50
☐ 85	Bob Kuzava	28.00	12.50	3.50
☐ 86	Ted Gray	25.00	11.50	3.10
☐ 87	Dale Coogan	25.00	11.50	3.10
☐ 88	Bob Feller	150.00	70.00	19.00
☐ 89	Johnny Lipon	25.00	11.50	3.10
☐ 90	Mickey Grasso	25.00	11.50	3.10
☐ 91	Red Schoendienst	80.00	36.00	10.00
☐ 92	Dale Mitchell	28.00	12.50	3.50
☐ 93	Al Sima	25.00	11.50	3.10
☐ 94	Sam Mele	25.00	11.50	3.10
☐ 95	Ken Holcombe	25.00	11.50	3.10
☐ 96	Willard Marshall	25.00	11.50	3.10
☐ 97	Earl Torgeson	25.00	11.50	3.10
☐ 98	Billy Pierce	25.00	11.50	3.10
☐ 99	Gene Woodling	50.00	23.00	6.25
☐ 100	Del Rice	25.00	11.50	3.10
☐ 101	Max Lanier	25.00	11.50	3.10
☐ 102	Bill Kennedy	25.00	11.50	3.10
☐ 103	Cliff Mapes	25.00	11.50	3.10
☐ 104	Don Kolloway	25.00	11.50	3.10
☐ 105	Johnny Pramesa	25.00	11.50	3.10
☐ 106	Mickey Vernon	30.00	13.50	3.80
☐ 107	Connie Ryan	25.00	11.50	3.10
☐ 108	Jim Konstanty	35.00	16.00	4.40
☐ 109	Ted Wilks	25.00	11.50	3.10
☐ 110	Dutch Leonard	25.00	11.50	3.10
☐ 111	Peanuts Lowrey	25.00	11.50	3.10
☐ 112	Hank Majeski	25.00	11.50	3.10
☐ 113	Dick Sisler	28.00	12.50	3.50
☐ 114	Willard Ramsdell	25.00	11.50	3.10
☐ 115	Red Munger	25.00	11.50	3.10
☐ 116	Carl Scheib	25.00	11.50	3.10
☐ 117	Sherm Lollar	28.00	12.50	3.50
☐ 118	Ken Raffensberger	25.00	11.50	3.10
☐ 119	Mickey McDermott	25.00	11.50	3.10
☐ 120	Bob Chakales	25.00	11.50	3.10
☐ 121	Gus Niarhos	25.00	11.50	3.10
☐ 122	Jackie Jensen	70.00	32.00	8.75
☐ 123	Eddie Yost	28.00	12.50	3.50
☐ 124	Monte Kennedy	25.00	11.50	3.10
☐ 125	Bill Rigney	25.00	11.50	3.10
☐ 126	Fred Hutchinson	28.00	12.50	3.50
☐ 127	Paul Minner	25.00	11.50	3.10
☐ 128	Don Bollweg	25.00	11.50	3.10
☐ 129	Johnny Mize	110.00	50.00	14.00
☐ 130	Sheldon Jones	25.00	11.50	3.10
☐ 131	Morrie Martin	25.00	11.50	3.10
☐ 132	Clyde Kluttz	25.00	11.50	3.10
☐ 133	Al Widmar	25.00	11.50	3.10
☐ 134	Joe Tipton	25.00	11.50	3.10
☐ 135	Dixie Howell	25.00	11.50	3.10
☐ 136	Johnny Schmitz	25.00	11.50	3.10
☐ 137	Roy McMillan	35.00	16.00	4.40
☐ 138	Bill MacDonald	25.00	11.50	3.10
☐ 139	Ken Wood	25.00	11.50	3.10
☐ 140	Johnny Antonelli	28.00	12.50	3.50
☐ 141	Clint Hartung	25.00	11.50	3.10
☐ 142	Harry Perkowski	25.00	11.50	3.10
☐ 143	Les Moss	25.00	11.50	3.10
☐ 144	Ed Blake	25.00	11.50	3.10
☐ 145	Joe Haynes	25.00	11.50	3.10
☐ 146	Frank House	25.00	11.50	3.10
☐ 147	Bob Young	25.00	11.50	3.10
☐ 148	Johnny Klippstein	25.00	11.50	3.10
☐ 149	Dick Kryhoski	25.00	11.50	3.10
☐ 150	Ted Beard	25.00	11.50	3.10
☐ 151	Wally Post	35.00	16.00	4.40
☐ 152	Al Evans	25.00	11.50	3.10
☐ 153	Bob Rush	25.00	11.50	3.10
☐ 154	Joe Muir	25.00	11.50	3.10
☐ 155	Frank Overmire	25.00	11.50	3.10
☐ 156	Frank Hiller	25.00	11.50	3.10
☐ 157	Bob Usher	25.00	11.50	3.10
☐ 158	Eddie Waitkus	25.00	11.50	3.10
☐ 159	Saul Rogovin	25.00	11.50	3.10
☐ 160	Owen Friend	25.00	11.50	3.10
☐ 161	Bud Byerly	25.00	11.50	3.10
☐ 162	Del Crandall	28.00	12.50	3.50
☐ 163	Stan Rojek	25.00	11.50	3.10
☐ 164	Walt Dubiel	25.00	11.50	3.10
☐ 165	Eddie Kazak	25.00	11.50	3.10
☐ 166	Paul LaPalme	25.00	11.50	3.10
☐ 167	Bill Howerton	25.00	11.50	3.10
☐ 168	Charlie Silvera	35.00	16.00	4.40
☐ 169	Howie Judson	25.00	11.50	3.10
☐ 170	Gus Bell	28.00	12.50	3.50
☐ 171	Ed Erautt	25.00	11.50	3.10
☐ 172	Eddie Miksis	25.00	11.50	3.10
☐ 173	Roy Smalley	25.00	11.50	3.10
☐ 174	Clarence Marshall	25.00	11.50	3.10
☐ 175	Billy Martin	250.00	115.00	31.00
☐ 176	Hank Edwards	25.00	11.50	3.10
☐ 177	Bill Wight	25.00	11.50	3.10
☐ 178	Cass Michaels	25.00	11.50	3.10
☐ 179	Frank Smith	25.00	11.50	3.10
☐ 180	Charlie Maxwell	35.00	16.00	4.40
☐ 181	Bob Swift	25.00	11.50	3.10
☐ 182	Billy Hitchcock	25.00	11.50	3.10
☐ 183	Erv Dusak	25.00	11.50	3.10
☐ 184	Bob Ramazzotti	25.00	11.50	3.10
☐ 185	Bill Nicholson	28.00	12.50	3.50
☐ 186	Walt Masterson	25.00	11.50	3.10
☐ 187	Bob Miller	25.00	11.50	3.10
☐ 188	Clarence Podbielan	25.00	11.50	3.10
☐ 189	Pete Reiser	30.00	13.50	3.80
☐ 190	Don Johnson	25.00	11.50	3.10
☐ 191	Yogi Berra	375.00	170.00	47.50
☐ 192	Myron Ginsberg	25.00	11.50	3.10
☐ 193	Harry Simpson	28.00	12.50	3.50
☐ 194	Joe Hatton	25.00	11.50	3.10

	No.	Player			
☐	195	Minnie Minoso	150.00	70.00	19.00
☐	196	Solly Hemus	35.00	16.00	4.40
☐	197	George Strickland	25.00	11.50	3.10
☐	198	Phil Haugstad	25.00	11.50	3.10
☐	199	George Zuverink	25.00	11.50	3.10
☐	200	Ralph Houk	70.00	32.00	8.75
☐	201	Alex Kellner	25.00	11.50	3.10
☐	202	Joe Collins	40.00	18.00	5.00
☐	203	Curt Simmons	30.00	13.50	3.80
☐	204	Ron Northey	25.00	11.50	3.10
☐	205	Clyde King	28.00	12.50	3.50
☐	206	Joe Ostrowski	25.00	11.50	3.10
☐	207	Mickey Harris	25.00	11.50	3.10
☐	208	Marlin Stuart	25.00	11.50	3.10
☐	209	Howie Fox	25.00	11.50	3.10
☐	210	Dick Fowler	25.00	11.50	3.10
☐	211	Ray Coleman	25.00	11.50	3.10
☐	212	Ned Garver	25.00	11.50	3.10
☐	213	Nippy Jones	25.00	11.50	3.10
☐	214	Johnny Hopp	28.00	12.50	3.50
☐	215	Hank Bauer	65.00	29.00	8.25
☐	216	Richie Ashburn	125.00	57.50	15.50
☐	217	Snuffy Stirnweiss	28.00	12.50	3.50
☐	218	Clyde McCullough	25.00	11.50	3.10
☐	219	Bobby Shantz	40.00	18.00	5.00
☐	220	Joe Presko	25.00	11.50	3.10
☐	221	Granny Hamner	25.00	11.50	3.10
☐	222	Hoot Evers	25.00	11.50	3.10
☐	223	Del Ennis	28.00	12.50	3.50
☐	224	Bruce Edwards	25.00	11.50	3.10
☐	225	Frank Baumholtz	25.00	11.50	3.10
☐	226	Dave Philley	25.00	11.50	3.10
☐	227	Joe Garagiola	80.00	36.00	10.00
☐	228	Al Brazle	25.00	11.50	3.10
☐	229	Gene Bearden UER (Misspelled Beardon)	25.00	11.50	3.10
☐	230	Matt Batts	25.00	11.50	3.10
☐	231	Sam Zoldak	25.00	11.50	3.10
☐	232	Billy Cox	25.00	11.50	3.10
☐	233	Bob Friend	50.00	23.00	6.25
☐	234	Steve Souchock	25.00	11.50	3.10
☐	235	Walt Dropo	25.00	11.50	3.10
☐	236	Ed Fitzgerald	25.00	11.50	3.10
☐	237	Jerry Coleman	35.00	16.00	4.40
☐	238	Art Houtteman	25.00	11.50	3.10
☐	239	Rocky Bridges	28.00	12.50	3.50
☐	240	Jack Phillips	25.00	11.50	3.10
☐	241	Tommy Byrne	25.00	11.50	3.10
☐	242	Tom Poholsky	25.00	11.50	3.10
☐	243	Larry Doby	65.00	29.00	8.25
☐	244	Vic Wertz	28.00	12.50	3.50
☐	245	Sherry Robertson	25.00	11.50	3.10
☐	246	George Kell	70.00	32.00	8.75
☐	247	Randy Gumpert	25.00	11.50	3.10
☐	248	Frank Shea	25.00	11.50	3.10
☐	249	Bobby Adams	25.00	11.50	3.10
☐	250	Carl Erskine	80.00	36.00	10.00
☐	251	Chico Carrasquel	50.00	23.00	6.25
☐	252	Vern Bickford	50.00	23.00	6.25
☐	253	Johnny Berardino	60.00	27.00	7.50
☐	254	Joe Dobson	50.00	23.00	6.25
☐	255	Clyde Vollmer	50.00	23.00	6.25
☐	256	Pete Suder	50.00	23.00	6.25
☐	257	Bobby Avila	55.00	25.00	7.00
☐	258	Steve Gromek	50.00	23.00	6.25
☐	259	Bob Addis	50.00	23.00	6.25
☐	260	Pete Castiglione	50.00	23.00	6.25
☐	261	Willie Mays	2800.00	1250.00	350.00
☐	262	Virgil Trucks	60.00	27.00	7.50
☐	263	Harry Brecheen	55.00	25.00	7.00
☐	264	Roy Hartsfield	50.00	23.00	6.25
☐	265	Chuck Diering	50.00	23.00	6.25
☐	266	Murry Dickson	50.00	23.00	6.25
☐	267	Sid Gordon	50.00	23.00	6.25
☐	268	Bob Lemon	140.00	65.00	17.50
☐	269	Willard Nixon	50.00	23.00	6.25
☐	270	Lou Brissie	50.00	23.00	6.25
☐	271	Jim Delsing	50.00	23.00	6.25
☐	272	Mike Garcia	55.00	25.00	7.00
☐	273	Erv Palica	50.00	23.00	6.25
☐	274	Ralph Branca	90.00	40.00	11.50
☐	275	Pat Mullin	50.00	23.00	6.25
☐	276	Jim Wilson	50.00	23.00	6.25
☐	277	Early Wynn	150.00	70.00	19.00
☐	278	Allie Clark	50.00	23.00	6.25
☐	279	Eddie Stewart	50.00	23.00	6.25
☐	280	Cloyd Boyer	55.00	25.00	7.00
☐	281	Tommy Brown SP	50.00	23.00	6.25
☐	282	Birdie Tebbetts SP	55.00	25.00	7.00
☐	283	Phil Masi SP	50.00	23.00	6.25
☐	284	Hank Arft SP	50.00	23.00	6.25
☐	285	Cliff Fannin SP	50.00	23.00	6.25
☐	286	Joe DeMaestri SP	50.00	23.00	6.25
☐	287	Steve Bilko SP	50.00	23.00	6.25
☐	288	Chet Nichols SP	50.00	23.00	6.25
☐	289	Tommy Holmes SP	60.00	27.00	7.50
☐	290	Joe Astroth SP	50.00	23.00	6.25
☐	291	Gil Coan SP	50.00	23.00	6.25
☐	292	Floyd Baker SP	50.00	23.00	6.25
☐	293	Sibby Sisti SP	50.00	23.00	6.25
☐	294	Walker Cooper SP	50.00	23.00	6.25
☐	295	Phil Cavarretta SP	60.00	27.00	7.50
☐	296	Red Rolfe MG SP	60.00	27.00	7.50
☐	297	Andy Seminick SP	50.00	23.00	6.25
☐	298	Bob Ross SP	50.00	23.00	6.25
☐	299	Ray Murray SP	50.00	23.00	6.25
☐	300	Barney McCosky SP	50.00	23.00	6.25
☐	301	Bob Porterfield	50.00	23.00	6.25
☐	302	Max Surkont	50.00	23.00	6.25
☐	303	Harry Dorish	50.00	23.00	6.25
☐	304	Sam Dente	50.00	23.00	6.25
☐	305	Paul Richards MG	55.00	25.00	7.00
☐	306	Lou Sleater	50.00	23.00	6.25
☐	307	Frank Campos	50.00	23.00	6.25
☐	308	Luis Aloma	50.00	23.00	6.25
☐	309	Jim Busby	50.00	23.00	6.25
☐	310	George Metkovich	60.00	27.00	7.50
☐	311	Mickey Mantle DP	25000.	7500.	2500.
☐	312	Jackie Robinson DP	1400.	650.00	180.00
☐	313	Bobby Thomson DP	275.00	125.00	34.00
☐	314	Roy Campanella	2100.00	950.00	275.00
☐	315	Leo Durocher MG	400.00	180.00	50.00
☐	316	Dave Williams	275.00	125.00	34.00
☐	317	Conrado Marrero	275.00	125.00	34.00
☐	318	Harold Gregg	250.00	115.00	31.00
☐	319	Al Walker	250.00	115.00	31.00
☐	320	John Rutherford	275.00	125.00	34.00
☐	321	Joe Black	300.00	135.00	38.00
☐	322	Randy Jackson	250.00	115.00	31.00
☐	323	Bubba Church	250.00	115.00	31.00
☐	324	Warren Hacker	250.00	115.00	31.00
☐	325	Bill Serena	250.00	115.00	31.00
☐	326	George Shuba	300.00	135.00	38.00
☐	327	Al Wilson	250.00	115.00	31.00
☐	328	Bob Borkowski	250.00	115.00	31.00
☐	329	Ike Delock	250.00	115.00	31.00
☐	330	Turk Lown	250.00	115.00	31.00
☐	331	Tom Morgan	250.00	115.00	31.00
☐	332	Anthony Bartirome	250.00	115.00	31.00
☐	333	Pee Wee Reese	1200.00	550.00	150.00
☐	334	Wilmer Mizell	275.00	125.00	34.00
☐	335	Ted Lepcio	250.00	115.00	31.00
☐	336	Dave Koslo	250.00	115.00	31.00
☐	337	Jim Hearn	250.00	115.00	31.00
☐	338	Sal Yvars	250.00	115.00	31.00
☐	339	Russ Meyer	250.00	115.00	31.00

☐	340 Bob Hooper	250.00	115.00	31.00
☐	341 Hal Jeffcoat	250.00	115.00	31.00
☐	342 Clem Labine	300.00	135.00	38.00
☐	343 Dick Gernert	250.00	115.00	31.00
☐	344 Ewell Blackwell	300.00	135.00	38.00
☐	345 Sammy White	250.00	115.00	31.00
☐	346 George Spencer	250.00	115.00	31.00
☐	347 Joe Adcock	300.00	135.00	38.00
☐	348 Robert Kelly	250.00	115.00	31.00
☐	349 Bob Cain	250.00	115.00	31.00
☐	350 Cal Abrams	250.00	115.00	31.00
☐	351 Alvin Dark	300.00	135.00	38.00
☐	352 Karl Drews	250.00	115.00	31.00
☐	353 Bobby Del Greco	250.00	115.00	31.00
☐	354 Fred Hatfield	250.00	115.00	31.00
☐	355 Bobby Morgan	250.00	115.00	31.00
☐	356 Toby Atwell	250.00	115.00	31.00
☐	357 Smoky Burgess	300.00	135.00	38.00
☐	358 John Kucab	250.00	115.00	31.00
☐	359 Dee Fondy	250.00	115.00	31.00
☐	360 George Crowe	275.00	125.00	34.00
☐	361 William Posedel CO	250.00	115.00	31.00
☐	362 Ken Heintzelman	250.00	115.00	31.00
☐	363 Dick Rozek	250.00	115.00	31.00
☐	364 Clyde Sukeforth CO	250.00	115.00	31.00
☐	365 Cookie Lavagetto CO	275.00	125.00	34.00
☐	366 Dave Madison	250.00	115.00	31.00
☐	367 Ben Thorpe	250.00	115.00	31.00
☐	368 Ed Wright	250.00	115.00	31.00
☐	369 Dick Groat	375.00	170.00	47.50
☐	370 Billy Hoeft	275.00	125.00	34.00
☐	371 Bobby Hofman	250.00	115.00	31.00
☐	372 Gil McDougald	350.00	160.00	45.00
☐	373 Jim Turner CO	300.00	135.00	38.00
☐	374 John Benton	250.00	115.00	31.00
☐	375 John Merson	250.00	115.00	31.00
☐	376 Faye Throneberry	250.00	115.00	31.00
☐	377 Chuck Dressen MG	250.00	115.00	31.00
☐	378 Leroy Fusselman	250.00	115.00	31.00
☐	379 Joe Rossi	250.00	115.00	31.00
☐	380 Clem Koshorek	250.00	115.00	31.00
☐	381 Milton Stock CO	250.00	115.00	31.00
☐	382 Sam Jones	300.00	135.00	38.00
☐	383 Del Wilber	250.00	115.00	31.00
☐	384 Frank Crosetti CO	300.00	135.00	38.00
☐	385 Herman Franks CO	250.00	115.00	31.00
☐	386 John Yuhas	250.00	115.00	31.00
☐	387 Billy Meyer MG	250.00	115.00	31.00
☐	388 Bob Chipman	250.00	115.00	31.00
☐	389 Ben Wade	250.00	115.00	31.00
☐	390 Glenn Nelson	250.00	115.00	31.00
☐	391 Ben Chapman UER CO (Photo actually Sam Chapman)	250.00	115.00	31.00
☐	392 Hoyt Wilhelm	700.00	325.00	90.00
☐	393 Ebba St.Claire	250.00	115.00	31.00
☐	394 Billy Herman CO	325.00	145.00	40.00
☐	395 Jake Pitler CO	250.00	115.00	31.00
☐	396 Dick Williams	325.00	145.00	40.00
☐	397 Forrest Main	250.00	115.00	31.00
☐	398 Hal Rice	250.00	115.00	31.00
☐	399 Jim Fridley	250.00	115.00	31.00
☐	400 Bill Dickey CO	700.00	325.00	90.00
☐	401 Bob Schultz	250.00	115.00	31.00
☐	402 Earl Harrist	250.00	115.00	31.00
☐	403 Bill Miller	250.00	115.00	31.00
☐	404 Dick Brodowski	250.00	115.00	31.00
☐	405 Eddie Pellagrini	250.00	115.00	31.00
☐	406 Joe Nuxhall	325.00	145.00	40.00
☐	407 Eddie Mathews	2500.00	650.00	200.00

1953 Topps

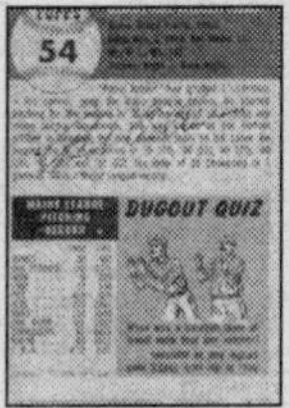

The cards in this 274-card set measure 2 5/8" by 3 3/4". Although the last card is numbered 280, there are only 274 cards in the set since numbers 253, 261, 267, 268, 271, and 275 were never issued. The 1953 Topps series contains line drawings of players in full color. The name and team panel at the card base is easily damaged, making it very difficult to complete a mint set. The high number series, 221 to 280, was produced in shorter supply late in the year and hence is more difficult to complete than the lower numbers. The key cards in the set are Mickey Mantle (82) and Willie Mays (244). The key Rookie Cards in this set are Roy Face, Jim Gilliam, and Johnny Podres, all from the last series. There are a number of double-printed cards (actually not double but 50 percent more of each of these numbers were printed compared to the other cards in the series) indicated by DP in the checklist below. There were five players (10 Smoky Burgess, 44 Ellis Kinder, 61 Early Wynn, 72 Fred Hutchinson, and 81 Joe Black) held out of the first run of 1-85 (but printed in with numbers 86-165), who are each marked by SP in the checklist below. In addition, there are five numbers which were printed with the more plentiful series 166-220; these cards (94, 107, 131, 145, and 156) are also indicated by DP in the checklist below. There were some three-card advertising panels produced by Topps; the players include Johnny Mize/Clem Koshorek/Toby Atwell and Mickey Mantle/Johnny Wyrostek/Sal Yvars. When cut apart, these advertising cards are distinguished by the non-standard card back, i.e., part of an advertisement for the 1953 Topps set instead of the typical statistics and biographical information about the player pictured.

		NRMT	VG-E	GOOD
	COMPLETE SET (274)	13500.	6100.	1700.
	COMMON CARD (1-165)	25.00	11.50	3.10
	COMMON CARD (166-220)	20.00	9.00	2.50
	COMMON CARD (221-280)	90.00	40.00	11.50
☐	1 Jackie Robinson DP	500.00	125.00	40.00
☐	2 Luke Easter DP	18.00	8.00	2.30
☐	3 George Crowe	25.00	11.50	3.10
☐	4 Ben Wade	25.00	11.50	3.10
☐	5 Joe Dobson	25.00	11.50	3.10

☐ 6	Sam Jones	28.00	12.50	3.50
☐ 7	Bob Borkowski DP	16.00	7.25	2.00
☐ 8	Clem Koshorek DP	16.00	7.25	2.00
☐ 9	Joe Collins	35.00	16.00	4.40
☐ 10	Smoky Burgess SP	60.00	27.00	7.50
☐ 11	Sal Yvars	25.00	11.50	3.10
☐ 12	Howie Judson DP	16.00	7.25	2.00
☐ 13	Conrado Marrero DP	16.00	7.25	2.00
☐ 14	Clem Labine DP	16.00	7.25	2.00
☐ 15	Bobo Newsom DP	24.00	11.00	3.00
☐ 16	Peanuts Lowrey DP	16.00	7.25	2.00
☐ 17	Billy Hitchcock	25.00	11.50	3.10
☐ 18	Ted Lepcio DP	16.00	7.25	2.00
☐ 19	Mel Parnell DP	18.00	8.00	2.30
☐ 20	Hank Thompson	28.00	12.50	3.50
☐ 21	Billy Johnson	25.00	11.50	3.10
☐ 22	Howie Fox	25.00	11.50	3.10
☐ 23	Toby Atwell DP	16.00	7.25	2.00
☐ 24	Ferris Fain	28.00	12.50	3.50
☐ 25	Ray Boone	28.00	12.50	3.50
☐ 26	Dale Mitchell DP	18.00	8.00	2.30
☐ 27	Roy Campanella DP	200.00	90.00	25.00
☐ 28	Eddie Pellagrini	25.00	11.50	3.10
☐ 29	Hal Jeffcoat	25.00	11.50	3.10
☐ 30	Willard Nixon	25.00	11.50	3.10
☐ 31	Ewell Blackwell	50.00	23.00	6.25
☐ 32	Clyde Vollmer	25.00	11.50	3.10
☐ 33	Bob Kennedy DP	18.00	8.00	2.30
☐ 34	George Shuba	28.00	12.50	3.50
☐ 35	Irv Noren DP	18.00	8.00	2.30
☐ 36	Johnny Groth DP	16.00	7.25	2.00
☐ 37	Eddie Mathews DP	110.00	50.00	14.00
☐ 38	Jim Hearn DP	16.00	7.25	2.00
☐ 39	Eddie Miksis	25.00	11.50	3.10
☐ 40	John Lipon	25.00	11.50	3.10
☐ 41	Enos Slaughter	80.00	36.00	10.00
☐ 42	Gus Zernial DP	16.00	7.25	2.00
☐ 43	Gil McDougald	55.00	25.00	7.00
☐ 44	Ellis Kinder SP	35.00	16.00	4.40
☐ 45	Grady Hatton DP	16.00	7.25	2.00
☐ 46	Johnny Klippstein DP	16.00	7.25	2.00
☐ 47	Bubba Church DP	16.00	7.25	2.00
☐ 48	Bob Del Greco DP	16.00	7.25	2.00
☐ 49	Faye Throneberry DP	16.00	7.25	2.00
☐ 50	Chuck Dressen MG DP	24.00	11.00	3.00
☐ 51	Frank Campos DP	16.00	7.25	2.00
☐ 52	Ted Gray DP	16.00	7.25	2.00
☐ 53	Sherm Lollar DP	18.00	8.00	2.30
☐ 54	Bob Feller DP	90.00	40.00	11.50
☐ 55	Maurice McDermott DP	16.00	7.25	2.00
☐ 56	Gerry Staley DP	16.00	7.25	2.00
☐ 57	Carl Scheib	25.00	11.50	3.10
☐ 58	George Metkovich	25.00	11.50	3.10
☐ 59	Karl Drews DP	16.00	7.25	2.00
☐ 60	Cloyd Boyer DP	16.00	7.25	2.00
☐ 61	Early Wynn SP	100.00	45.00	12.50
☐ 62	Monte Irvin DP	40.00	18.00	5.00
☐ 63	Gus Niarhos DP	16.00	7.25	2.00
☐ 64	Dave Philley	25.00	11.50	3.10
☐ 65	Earl Harrist	25.00	11.50	3.10
☐ 66	Minnie Minoso	50.00	23.00	6.25
☐ 67	Roy Sievers DP	18.00	8.00	2.30
☐ 68	Del Rice	25.00	11.50	3.10
☐ 69	Dick Brodowski	25.00	11.50	3.10
☐ 70	Ed Yuhas	25.00	11.50	3.10
☐ 71	Tony Bartirome	25.00	11.50	3.10
☐ 72	Fred Hutchinson MG SP	40.00	18.00	5.00
☐ 73	Eddie Robinson	25.00	11.50	3.10
☐ 74	Joe Rossi	25.00	11.50	3.10
☐ 75	Mike Garcia	28.00	12.50	3.50
☐ 76	Pee Wee Reese	165.00	75.00	21.00
☐ 77	Johnny Mize DP	65.00	29.00	8.25
☐ 78	Red Schoendienst	65.00	29.00	8.25
☐ 79	Johnny Wyrostek	25.00	11.50	3.10
☐ 80	Jim Hegan	28.00	12.50	3.50
☐ 81	Joe Black SP	60.00	27.00	7.50
☐ 82	Mickey Mantle	3400.00	1200.00	350.00
☐ 83	Howie Pollet	25.00	11.50	3.10
☐ 84	Bob Hooper DP	16.00	7.25	2.00
☐ 85	Bobby Morgan DP	16.00	7.25	2.00
☐ 86	Billy Martin	135.00	60.00	17.00
☐ 87	Ed Lopat	40.00	18.00	5.00
☐ 88	Willie Jones DP	16.00	7.25	2.00
☐ 89	Chuck Stobbs DP	16.00	7.25	2.00
☐ 90	Hank Edwards DP	16.00	7.25	2.00
☐ 91	Ebba St.Claire DP	16.00	7.25	2.00
☐ 92	Paul Minner DP	16.00	7.25	2.00
☐ 93	Hal Rice DP	16.00	7.25	2.00
☐ 94	Bill Kennedy DP	16.00	7.25	2.00
☐ 95	Willard Marshall DP	16.00	7.25	2.00
☐ 96	Virgil Trucks	28.00	12.50	3.50
☐ 97	Don Kolloway DP	16.00	7.25	2.00
☐ 98	Cal Abrams DP	16.00	7.25	2.00
☐ 99	Dave Madison	25.00	11.50	3.10
☐ 100	Bill Miller	25.00	11.50	3.10
☐ 101	Ted Wilks	25.00	11.50	3.10
☐ 102	Connie Ryan DP	16.00	7.25	2.00
☐ 103	Joe Astroth DP	16.00	7.25	2.00
☐ 104	Yogi Berra	225.00	100.00	28.00
☐ 105	Joe Nuxhall DP	18.00	8.00	2.30
☐ 106	Johnny Antonelli	25.00	11.50	3.10
☐ 107	Danny O'Connell DP	16.00	7.25	2.00
☐ 108	Bob Porterfield DP	16.00	7.25	2.00
☐ 109	Alvin Dark	35.00	16.00	4.40
☐ 110	Herman Wehmeier DP	16.00	7.25	2.00
☐ 111	Hank Sauer DP	18.00	8.00	2.30
☐ 112	Ned Garver DP	16.00	7.25	2.00
☐ 113	Jerry Priddy	25.00	11.50	3.10
☐ 114	Phil Rizzuto	150.00	70.00	19.00
☐ 115	George Spencer	25.00	11.50	3.10
☐ 116	Frank Smith DP	16.00	7.25	2.00
☐ 117	Sid Gordon DP	16.00	7.25	2.00
☐ 118	Gus Bell DP	18.00	8.00	2.30
☐ 119	Johnny Sain SP	50.00	23.00	6.25
☐ 120	Davey Williams	28.00	12.50	3.50
☐ 121	Walt Dropo	28.00	12.50	3.50
☐ 122	Elmer Valo	25.00	11.50	3.10
☐ 123	Tommy Byrne DP	16.00	7.25	2.00
☐ 124	Sibby Sisti DP	16.00	7.25	2.00
☐ 125	Dick Williams DP	18.00	8.00	2.30
☐ 126	Bill Connelly DP	16.00	7.25	2.00
☐ 127	Clint Courtney DP	16.00	7.25	2.00
☐ 128	Wilmer Mizell DP (Inconsistent design, logo on front with black birds)	18.00	8.00	2.30
☐ 129	Keith Thomas	25.00	11.50	3.10
☐ 130	Turk Lown DP	16.00	7.25	2.00
☐ 131	Harry Byrd DP	16.00	7.25	2.00
☐ 132	Tom Morgan	25.00	11.50	3.10
☐ 133	Gil Coan	25.00	11.50	3.10
☐ 134	Rube Walker	28.00	12.50	3.50
☐ 135	Al Rosen DP	30.00	13.50	3.80
☐ 136	Ken Heintzelman DP	16.00	7.25	2.00
☐ 137	John Rutherford DP	16.00	7.25	2.00
☐ 138	George Kell	50.00	23.00	6.25
☐ 139	Sammy White	25.00	11.50	3.10
☐ 140	Tommy Glaviano	25.00	11.50	3.10
☐ 141	Allie Reynolds DP	30.00	13.50	3.80
☐ 142	Vic Wertz	28.00	12.50	3.50
☐ 143	Billy Pierce	35.00	16.00	4.40
☐ 144	Bob Schultz DP	16.00	7.25	2.00
☐ 145	Harry Dorish DP	16.00	7.25	2.00
☐ 146	Granny Hamner	25.00	11.50	3.10
☐ 147	Warren Spahn	150.00	70.00	19.00
☐ 148	Mickey Grasso	25.00	11.50	3.10

☐ 149 Dom DiMaggio DP ... 35.00 16.00 4.40
☐ 150 Harry Simpson DP ... 16.00 7.25 2.00
☐ 151 Hoyt Wilhelm ... 75.00 34.00 9.50
☐ 152 Bob Adams DP ... 16.00 7.25 2.00
☐ 153 Andy Seminick DP ... 16.00 7.25 2.00
☐ 154 Dick Groat ... 35.00 16.00 4.40
☐ 155 Dutch Leonard ... 25.00 11.50 3.10
☐ 156 Jim Rivera DP ... 18.00 8.00 2.30
☐ 157 Bob Addis DP ... 16.00 7.25 2.00
☐ 158 Johnny Logan ... 35.00 16.00 4.40
☐ 159 Wayne Terwilliger DP 16.00 7.25 2.00
☐ 160 Bob Young ... 25.00 11.50 3.10
☐ 161 Vern Bickford DP ... 16.00 7.25 2.00
☐ 162 Ted Kluszewski ... 50.00 23.00 6.25
☐ 163 Fred Hatfield DP ... 16.00 7.25 2.00
☐ 164 Frank Shea DP ... 16.00 7.25 2.00
☐ 165 Billy Hoeft ... 25.00 11.50 3.10
☐ 166 Billy Hunter ... 20.00 9.00 2.50
☐ 167 Art Schult ... 20.00 9.00 2.50
☐ 168 Willard Schmidt ... 20.00 9.00 2.50
☐ 169 Dizzy Trout ... 22.50 10.00 2.80
☐ 170 Bill Werle ... 20.00 9.00 2.50
☐ 171 Bill Glynn ... 20.00 9.00 2.50
☐ 172 Rip Repulski ... 20.00 9.00 2.50
☐ 173 Preston Ward ... 20.00 9.00 2.50
☐ 174 Billy Loes ... 35.00 16.00 4.40
☐ 175 Ron Kline ... 20.00 9.00 2.50
☐ 176 Don Hoak ... 28.00 12.50 3.50
☐ 177 Jim Dyck ... 20.00 9.00 2.50
☐ 178 Jim Waugh ... 20.00 9.00 2.50
☐ 179 Gene Hermanski ... 20.00 9.00 2.50
☐ 180 Virgil Stallcup ... 20.00 9.00 2.50
☐ 181 Al Zarilla ... 20.00 9.00 2.50
☐ 182 Bobby Hofman ... 20.00 9.00 2.50
☐ 183 Stu Miller ... 25.00 11.50 3.10
☐ 184 Hal Brown ... 20.00 9.00 2.50
☐ 185 Jim Pendleton ... 20.00 9.00 2.50
☐ 186 Charlie Bishop ... 20.00 9.00 2.50
☐ 187 Jim Fridley ... 20.00 9.00 2.50
☐ 188 Andy Carey ... 35.00 16.00 4.40
☐ 189 Ray Jablonski ... 20.00 9.00 2.50
☐ 190 Dixie Walker CO ... 22.50 10.00 2.80
☐ 191 Ralph Kiner ... 70.00 32.00 8.75
☐ 192 Wally Westlake ... 20.00 9.00 2.50
☐ 193 Mike Clark ... 20.00 9.00 2.50
☐ 194 Eddie Kazak ... 20.00 9.00 2.50
☐ 195 Ed McGhee ... 20.00 9.00 2.50
☐ 196 Bob Keegan ... 20.00 9.00 2.50
☐ 197 Del Crandall ... 22.50 10.00 2.80
☐ 198 Forrest Main ... 20.00 9.00 2.50
☐ 199 Marion Fricano ... 20.00 9.00 2.50
☐ 200 Gordon Goldsberry ... 20.00 9.00 2.50
☐ 201 Paul LaPalme ... 20.00 9.00 2.50
☐ 202 Carl Sawatski ... 20.00 9.00 2.50
☐ 203 Cliff Fannin ... 20.00 9.00 2.50
☐ 204 Dick Bokelman ... 20.00 9.00 2.50
☐ 205 Vern Benson ... 20.00 9.00 2.50
☐ 206 Ed Bailey ... 20.00 9.00 2.50
☐ 207 Whitey Ford ... 115.00 52.50 14.50
☐ 208 Jim Wilson ... 20.00 9.00 2.50
☐ 209 Jim Greengrass ... 20.00 9.00 2.50
☐ 210 Bob Cerv ... 30.00 13.50 3.80
☐ 211 J.W. Porter ... 20.00 9.00 2.50
☐ 212 Jack Dittmer ... 20.00 9.00 2.50
☐ 213 Ray Scarborough ... 20.00 9.00 2.50
☐ 214 Bill Bruton ... 25.00 11.50 3.10
☐ 215 Gene Conley ... 25.00 11.50 3.10
☐ 216 Jim Hughes ... 20.00 9.00 2.50
☐ 217 Murray Wall ... 20.00 9.00 2.50
☐ 218 Les Fusselman ... 20.00 9.00 2.50
☐ 219 Pete Runnels UER ... 22.50 10.00 2.80
(Photo actually
Don Johnson)
☐ 220 Satchel Paige UER . 425.00 190.00 52.50
(Misspelled Satchell
on card front)
☐ 221 Bob Milliken ... 90.00 40.00 11.50
☐ 222 Vic Janowicz DP ... 60.00 27.00 7.50
☐ 223 Johnny O'Brien DP .. 55.00 25.00 7.00
☐ 224 Lou Sleater DP ... 50.00 23.00 6.25
☐ 225 Bobby Shantz ... 90.00 40.00 11.50
☐ 226 Ed Erautt ... 90.00 40.00 11.50
☐ 227 Morrie Martin ... 90.00 40.00 11.50
☐ 228 Hal Newhouser ... 150.00 70.00 19.00
☐ 229 Rocky Krsnich ... 90.00 40.00 11.50
☐ 230 Johnny Lindell DP ... 50.00 23.00 6.25
☐ 231 Solly Hemus DP ... 50.00 23.00 6.25
☐ 232 Dick Kokos ... 90.00 40.00 11.50
☐ 233 Al Aber ... 90.00 40.00 11.50
☐ 234 Ray Murray DP ... 50.00 23.00 6.25
☐ 235 John Hetki DP ... 50.00 23.00 6.25
☐ 236 Harry Perkowski DP . 50.00 23.00 6.25
☐ 237 Bud Podbielan DP ... 50.00 23.00 6.25
☐ 238 Cal Hogue DP ... 50.00 23.00 6.25
☐ 239 Jim Delsing ... 90.00 40.00 11.50
☐ 240 Fred Marsh ... 90.00 40.00 11.50
☐ 241 Al Sima DP ... 50.00 23.00 6.25
☐ 242 Charlie Silvera ... 90.00 40.00 11.50
☐ 243 Carlos Bernier DP ... 50.00 23.00 6.25
☐ 244 Willie Mays ... 3300.00 1000.00 325.00
☐ 245 Bill Norman CO ... 90.00 40.00 11.50
☐ 246 Roy Face DP ... 75.00 34.00 9.50
☐ 247 Mike Sandlock DP ... 50.00 23.00 6.25
☐ 248 Gene Stephens DP ... 50.00 23.00 6.25
☐ 249 Eddie O'Brien ... 90.00 40.00 11.50
☐ 250 Bob Wilson ... 90.00 40.00 11.50
☐ 251 Sid Hudson ... 90.00 40.00 11.50
☐ 252 Hank Foiles ... 90.00 40.00 11.50
☐ 253 Does not exist ... .00 .00 .00
☐ 254 Preacher Roe DP ... 75.00 34.00 9.50
☐ 255 Dixie Howell ... 90.00 40.00 11.50
☐ 256 Les Peden ... 90.00 40.00 11.50
☐ 257 Bob Boyd ... 90.00 40.00 11.50
☐ 258 Jim Gilliam ... 275.00 125.00 34.00
☐ 259 Roy McMillan DP ... 55.00 25.00 7.00
☐ 260 Sam Calderone ... 90.00 40.00 11.50
☐ 261 Does not exist ... .00 .00 .00
☐ 262 Bob Oldis ... 90.00 40.00 11.50
☐ 263 Johnny Podres ... 275.00 125.00 34.00
☐ 264 Gene Woodling DP ... 50.00 23.00 6.25
☐ 265 Jackie Jensen ... 110.00 50.00 14.00
☐ 266 Bob Cain ... 90.00 40.00 11.50
☐ 267 Does not exist ... .00 .00 .00
☐ 268 Does not exist ... .00 .00 .00
☐ 269 Duane Pillette ... 90.00 40.00 11.50
☐ 270 Vern Stephens ... 100.00 45.00 12.50
☐ 271 Does not exist ... .00 .00 .00
☐ 272 Bill Antonello ... 90.00 40.00 11.50
☐ 273 Harvey Haddix ... 125.00 57.50 15.50
☐ 274 John Riddle CO ... 90.00 40.00 11.50
☐ 275 Does not exist ... .00 .00 .00
☐ 276 Ken Raffensberger ... 90.00 40.00 11.50
☐ 277 Don Lund ... 90.00 40.00 11.50
☐ 278 Willie Miranda ... 90.00 40.00 11.50
☐ 279 Joe Coleman DP ... 50.00 23.00 6.25
☐ 280 Milt Bolling ... 325.00 65.00 19.50

1954 Topps

The cards in this 250-card set measure approximately 2 5/8" by 3 3/4". Each of the cards in the 1954 Topps set contains a

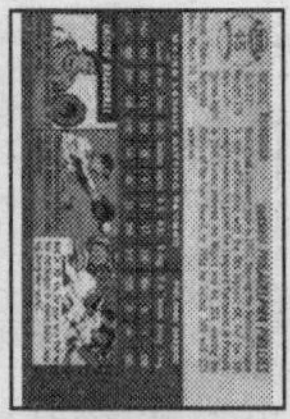

large "head" shot of the player in color plus a smaller full-length photo in black and white set against a color background. This series contains the Rookie Cards of Hank Aaron, Ernie Banks, and Al Kaline and two separate cards of Ted Williams (number 1 and number 250). Conspicuous by his absence is Mickey Mantle who apparently was the exclusive property of Bowman during 1954 (and 1955). The first two issues of Sports Illustrated magazine contained "card" inserts on regular paper stock. The first issue showed actual cards in the set in color, while the second issue showed some created cards of New York Yankees players in black and white, including Mickey Mantle.

	NRMT	VG-E	GOOD
COMPLETE SET (250)	7500.00	3400.00	950.00
COMMON CARD (1-50)	15.00	6.75	1.90
COMMON CARD (51-75)	25.00	11.50	3.10
COMMON CARD (76-125)	15.00	6.75	1.90
COMMON CARD (126-250)	15.00	6.75	1.90

	NRMT	VG-E	GOOD
□ 1 Ted Williams	650.00	200.00	65.00
□ 2 Gus Zernial	18.00	8.00	2.30
□ 3 Monte Irvin	38.00	17.00	4.70
□ 4 Hank Sauer	18.00	8.00	2.30
□ 5 Ed Lopat	20.00	9.00	2.50
□ 6 Pete Runnels	18.00	8.00	2.30
□ 7 Ted Kluszewski	35.00	16.00	4.40
□ 8 Bob Young	15.00	6.75	1.90
□ 9 Harvey Haddix	18.00	8.00	2.30
□ 10 Jackie Robinson	250.00	115.00	31.00
□ 11 Paul Leslie Smith	15.00	6.75	1.90
□ 12 Del Crandall	18.00	8.00	2.30
□ 13 Billy Martin	60.00	27.00	7.50
□ 14 Preacher Roe	20.00	9.00	2.50
□ 15 Al Rosen	20.00	9.00	2.50
□ 16 Vic Janowicz	20.00	9.00	2.50
□ 17 Phil Rizzuto	85.00	38.00	10.50
□ 18 Walt Dropo	18.00	8.00	2.30
□ 19 Johnny Lipon	15.00	6.75	1.90
□ 20 Warren Spahn	75.00	34.00	9.50
□ 21 Bobby Shantz	18.00	8.00	2.30
□ 22 Jim Greengrass	15.00	6.75	1.90
□ 23 Luke Easter	18.00	8.00	2.30
□ 24 Granny Hamner	15.00	6.75	1.90
□ 25 Harvey Kuenn	40.00	18.00	5.00
□ 26 Ray Jablonski	15.00	6.75	1.90
□ 27 Ferris Fain	18.00	8.00	2.30
□ 28 Paul Minner	15.00	6.75	1.90
□ 29 Jim Hegan	18.00	8.00	2.30
□ 30 Eddie Mathews	75.00	34.00	9.50
□ 31 Johnny Klippstein	15.00	6.75	1.90
□ 32 Duke Snider	125.00	57.50	15.50
□ 33 Johnny Schmitz	15.00	6.75	1.90
□ 34 Jim Rivera	15.00	6.75	1.90
□ 35 Jim Gilliam	30.00	13.50	3.80
□ 36 Hoyt Wilhelm	50.00	23.00	6.25
□ 37 Whitey Ford	90.00	40.00	11.50
□ 38 Eddie Stanky MG	18.00	8.00	2.30
□ 39 Sherm Lollar	18.00	8.00	2.30
□ 40 Mel Parnell	18.00	8.00	2.30
□ 41 Willie Jones	15.00	6.75	1.90
□ 42 Don Mueller	18.00	8.00	2.30
□ 43 Dick Groat	20.00	9.00	2.50
□ 44 Ned Garver	15.00	6.75	1.90
□ 45 Richie Ashburn	50.00	23.00	6.25
□ 46 Ken Raffensberger	15.00	6.75	1.90
□ 47 Ellis Kinder	15.00	6.75	1.90
□ 48 Billy Hunter	18.00	8.00	2.30
□ 49 Ray Murray	15.00	6.75	1.90
□ 50 Yogi Berra	200.00	90.00	25.00
□ 51 Johnny Lindell	28.00	12.50	3.50
□ 52 Vic Power	30.00	13.50	3.80
□ 53 Jack Dittmer	25.00	11.50	3.10
□ 54 Vern Stephens	28.00	12.50	3.50
□ 55 Phil Cavarretta MG	28.00	12.50	3.50
□ 56 Willie Miranda	25.00	11.50	3.10
□ 57 Luis Aloma	25.00	11.50	3.10
□ 58 Bob Wilson	25.00	11.50	3.10
□ 59 Gene Conley	28.00	12.50	3.50
□ 60 Frank Baumholtz	25.00	11.50	3.10
□ 61 Bob Cain	25.00	11.50	3.10
□ 62 Eddie Robinson	25.00	11.50	3.10
□ 63 Johnny Pesky	25.00	11.50	3.10
□ 64 Hank Thompson	28.00	12.50	3.50
□ 65 Bob Swift CO	25.00	11.50	3.10
□ 66 Ted Lepcio	25.00	11.50	3.10
□ 67 Jim Willis	25.00	11.50	3.10
□ 68 Sam Calderone	25.00	11.50	3.10
□ 69 Bud Podbielan	25.00	11.50	3.10
□ 70 Larry Doby	70.00	32.00	8.75
□ 71 Frank Smith	25.00	11.50	3.10
□ 72 Preston Ward	25.00	11.50	3.10
□ 73 Wayne Terwilliger	25.00	11.50	3.10
□ 74 Bill Taylor	25.00	11.50	3.10
□ 75 Fred Haney MG	25.00	11.50	3.10
□ 76 Bob Scheffing CO	15.00	6.75	1.90
□ 77 Ray Boone	18.00	8.00	2.30
□ 78 Ted Kazanski	15.00	6.75	1.90
□ 79 Andy Pafko	18.00	8.00	2.30
□ 80 Jackie Jensen	20.00	9.00	2.50
□ 81 Dave Hoskins	15.00	6.75	1.90
□ 82 Milt Bolling	15.00	6.75	1.90
□ 83 Joe Collins	15.00	6.75	1.90
□ 84 Dick Cole	15.00	6.75	1.90
□ 85 Bob Turley	35.00	16.00	4.40
□ 86 Billy Herman CO	25.00	11.50	3.10
□ 87 Roy Face	18.00	8.00	2.30
□ 88 Matt Batts	15.00	6.75	1.90
□ 89 Howie Pollet	15.00	6.75	1.90
□ 90 Willie Mays	525.00	240.00	65.00
□ 91 Bob Oldis	15.00	6.75	1.90
□ 92 Wally Westlake	15.00	6.75	1.90
□ 93 Sid Hudson	15.00	6.75	1.90
□ 94 Ernie Banks	800.00	350.00	100.00
□ 95 Hal Rice	15.00	6.75	1.90
□ 96 Charlie Silvera	18.00	8.00	2.30
□ 97 Jerald Hal Lane	15.00	6.75	1.90
□ 98 Joe Black	25.00	11.50	3.10
□ 99 Bobby Hofman	15.00	6.75	1.90
□ 100 Bob Keegan	15.00	6.75	1.90
□ 101 Gene Woodling	25.00	11.50	3.10
□ 102 Gil Hodges	90.00	40.00	11.50
□ 103 Jim Lemon	15.00	6.75	1.90
□ 104 Mike Sandlock	15.00	6.75	1.90
□ 105 Andy Carey	15.00	6.75	1.90
□ 106 Dick Kokos	15.00	6.75	1.90
□ 107 Duane Pillette	15.00	6.75	1.90

	No.	Player			
☐	108	Thornton Kipper	15.00	6.75	1.90
☐	109	Bill Bruton	18.00	8.00	2.30
☐	110	Harry Dorish	15.00	6.75	1.90
☐	111	Jim Delsing	15.00	6.75	1.90
☐	112	Bill Renna	15.00	6.75	1.90
☐	113	Bob Boyd	15.00	6.75	1.90
☐	114	Dean Stone	15.00	6.75	1.90
☐	115	Rip Repulski	15.00	6.75	1.90
☐	116	Steve Bilko	15.00	6.75	1.90
☐	117	Solly Hemus	15.00	6.75	1.90
☐	118	Carl Scheib	15.00	6.75	1.90
☐	119	Johnny Antonelli	18.00	8.00	2.30
☐	120	Roy McMillan	18.00	8.00	2.30
☐	121	Clem Labine	15.00	6.75	1.90
☐	122	Johnny Logan	18.00	8.00	2.30
☐	123	Bobby Adams	15.00	6.75	1.90
☐	124	Marion Fricano	15.00	6.75	1.90
☐	125	Harry Perkowski	15.00	6.75	1.90
☐	126	Ben Wade	15.00	6.75	1.90
☐	127	Steve O'Neill MG	15.00	6.75	1.90
☐	128	Hank Aaron	1500.00	700.00	190.00
☐	129	Forrest Jacobs	15.00	6.75	1.90
☐	130	Hank Bauer	35.00	16.00	4.40
☐	131	Reno Bertoia	15.00	6.75	1.90
☐	132	Tom Lasorda	125.00	57.50	15.50
☐	133	Dave Baker CO	15.00	6.75	1.90
☐	134	Cal Hogue	15.00	6.75	1.90
☐	135	Joe Presko	15.00	6.75	1.90
☐	136	Connie Ryan	15.00	6.75	1.90
☐	137	Wally Moon	35.00	16.00	4.40
☐	138	Bob Borkowski	15.00	6.75	1.90
☐	139	The O'Briens Johnny O'Brien Eddie O'Brien	40.00	18.00	5.00
☐	140	Tom Wright	15.00	6.75	1.90
☐	141	Joey Jay	15.00	6.75	1.90
☐	142	Tom Poholsky	15.00	6.75	1.90
☐	143	Rollie Hemsley CO	15.00	6.75	1.90
☐	144	Bill Werle	15.00	6.75	1.90
☐	145	Elmer Valo	15.00	6.75	1.90
☐	146	Don Johnson	15.00	6.75	1.90
☐	147	Johnny Riddle CO	15.00	6.75	1.90
☐	148	Bob Trice	15.00	6.75	1.90
☐	149	Al Robertson	15.00	6.75	1.90
☐	150	Dick Kryhoski	15.00	6.75	1.90
☐	151	Alex Grammas	15.00	6.75	1.90
☐	152	Michael Blyzka	15.00	6.75	1.90
☐	153	Al Walker	15.00	6.75	1.90
☐	154	Mike Fornieles	15.00	6.75	1.90
☐	155	Bob Kennedy	18.00	8.00	2.30
☐	156	Joe Coleman	15.00	6.75	1.90
☐	157	Don Lenhardt	15.00	6.75	1.90
☐	158	Peanuts Lowrey	15.00	6.75	1.90
☐	159	Dave Philley	15.00	6.75	1.90
☐	160	Ralph Kress CO	15.00	6.75	1.90
☐	161	John Hetki	15.00	6.75	1.90
☐	162	Herman Wehmeier	15.00	6.75	1.90
☐	163	Frank House	15.00	6.75	1.90
☐	164	Stu Miller	18.00	8.00	2.30
☐	165	Jim Pendleton	15.00	6.75	1.90
☐	166	Johnny Podres	30.00	13.50	3.80
☐	167	Don Lund	15.00	6.75	1.90
☐	168	Morrie Martin	15.00	6.75	1.90
☐	169	Jim Hughes	15.00	6.75	1.90
☐	170	James(Dusty) Rhodes	20.00	9.00	2.50
☐	171	Leo Kiely	15.00	6.75	1.90
☐	172	Harold Brown	15.00	6.75	1.90
☐	173	Jack Harshman	15.00	6.75	1.90
☐	174	Tom Qualters	15.00	6.75	1.90
☐	175	Frank Leja	25.00	11.50	3.10
☐	176	Robert Keely CO	15.00	6.75	1.90
☐	177	Bob Milliken	15.00	6.75	1.90
☐	178	Bill Glynn	15.00	6.75	1.90
☐	179	Gair Allie	15.00	6.75	1.90
☐	180	Wes Westrum	18.00	8.00	2.30
☐	181	Mel Roach	15.00	6.75	1.90
☐	182	Chuck Harmon	15.00	6.75	1.90
☐	183	Earle Combs CO	25.00	11.50	3.10
☐	184	Ed Bailey	15.00	6.75	1.90
☐	185	Chuck Stobbs	15.00	6.75	1.90
☐	186	Karl Olson	15.00	6.75	1.90
☐	187	Heinie Manush CO	25.00	11.50	3.10
☐	188	Dave Jolly	15.00	6.75	1.90
☐	189	Bob Ross	15.00	6.75	1.90
☐	190	Ray Herbert	15.00	6.75	1.90
☐	191	John(Dick) Schofield	20.00	9.00	2.50
☐	192	Ellis Deal CO	15.00	6.75	1.90
☐	193	Johnny Hopp CO	18.00	8.00	2.30
☐	194	Bill Sarni	15.00	6.75	1.90
☐	195	Billy Consolo	15.00	6.75	1.90
☐	196	Stan Jok	15.00	6.75	1.90
☐	197	Lynwood Rowe CO ("Schoolboy")	18.00	8.00	2.30
☐	198	Carl Sawatski	15.00	6.75	1.90
☐	199	Glenn(Rocky) Nelson	15.00	6.75	1.90
☐	200	Larry Jansen	18.00	8.00	2.30
☐	201	Al Kaline	750.00	350.00	95.00
☐	202	Bob Purkey	20.00	9.00	2.50
☐	203	Harry Brecheen CO	18.00	8.00	2.30
☐	204	Angel Scull	15.00	6.75	1.90
☐	205	Johnny Sain	30.00	13.50	3.80
☐	206	Ray Crone	15.00	6.75	1.90
☐	207	Tom Oliver CO	15.00	6.75	1.90
☐	208	Grady Hatton	15.00	6.75	1.90
☐	209	Chuck Thompson	15.00	6.75	1.90
☐	210	Bob Buhl	20.00	9.00	2.50
☐	211	Don Hoak	15.00	6.75	1.90
☐	212	Bob Micelotta	15.00	6.75	1.90
☐	213	Johnny Fitzpatrick CO	15.00	6.75	1.90
☐	214	Arnie Portocarrero	15.00	6.75	1.90
☐	215	Ed McGhee	15.00	6.75	1.90
☐	216	Al Sima	15.00	6.75	1.90
☐	217	Paul Schreiber CO	15.00	6.75	1.90
☐	218	Fred Marsh	15.00	6.75	1.90
☐	219	Chuck Kress	15.00	6.75	1.90
☐	220	Ruben Gomez	18.00	8.00	2.30
☐	221	Dick Brodowski	15.00	6.75	1.90
☐	222	Bill Wilson	15.00	6.75	1.90
☐	223	Joe Haynes CO	15.00	6.75	1.90
☐	224	Dick Weik	15.00	6.75	1.90
☐	225	Don Liddle	15.00	6.75	1.90
☐	226	Jehosie Heard	15.00	6.75	1.90
☐	227	Colonel Mills CO	15.00	6.75	1.90
☐	228	Gene Hermanski	15.00	6.75	1.90
☐	229	Bob Talbot	15.00	6.75	1.90
☐	230	Bob Kuzava	18.00	8.00	2.30
☐	231	Roy Smalley	15.00	6.75	1.90
☐	232	Lou Limmer	15.00	6.75	1.90
☐	233	Augie Galan CO	15.00	6.75	1.90
☐	234	Jerry Lynch	15.00	6.75	1.90
☐	235	Vernon Law	18.00	8.00	2.30
☐	236	Paul Penson	15.00	6.75	1.90
☐	237	Mike Ryba CO	15.00	6.75	1.90
☐	238	Al Aber	15.00	6.75	1.90
☐	239	Bill Skowron	90.00	40.00	11.50
☐	240	Sam Mele	18.00	8.00	2.30
☐	241	Robert Miller	15.00	6.75	1.90
☐	242	Curt Roberts	15.00	6.75	1.90
☐	243	Ray Blades CO	15.00	6.75	1.90
☐	244	Leroy Wheat	15.00	6.75	1.90
☐	245	Roy Sievers	15.00	6.75	1.90
☐	246	Howie Fox	15.00	6.75	1.90
☐	247	Ed Mayo CO	15.00	6.75	1.90
☐	248	Al Smith	20.00	9.00	2.50
☐	249	Wilmer Mizell	18.00	8.00	2.30
☐	250	Ted Williams	700.00	210.00	70.00

1955 Topps

The cards in this 206-card set measure approximately 2 5/8" by 3 3/4". Both the large "head" shot and the smaller full-length photos used on each card of the 1955 Topps set are in color. The card fronts were designed horizontally for the first time in Topps' history. The first card features Dusty Rhodes, hitting star for the Giants' 1954 World Series sweep over the Indians. A "high" series, 161 to 210, is more difficult to find than cards 1 to 160. Numbers 175, 186, 203, and 209 were never issued. To fill in for the four cards not issued in the high number series, Topps double printed four players, those appearing on cards 170, 172, 184, and 188. Although rarely seen, there exist salesman sample panels of three cards containing the fronts of regular cards with ad information for the 1955 Topps regular and the 1955 Topps Doubleheaders on the back. One such ad panel depicts (from top to bottom) Danny Schell, Jake Thies, and Howie Pollet. The key Rookie Cards in this set are Ken Boyer, Roberto Clemente, Harmon Killebrew, and Sandy Koufax.

	NRMT	VG-E	GOOD
COMPLETE SET (206)	7500.00	3400.00	950.00
COMMON CARD (1-150)	12.00	5.50	1.50
COMMON CARD (151-160)	20.00	9.00	2.50
COMMON CARD (161-210)	30.00	13.50	3.80

Card	NRMT	VG-E	GOOD
☐ 1 Dusty Rhodes	45.00	9.00	2.70
☐ 2 Ted Williams	425.00	190.00	52.50
☐ 3 Art Fowler	14.00	6.25	1.75
☐ 4 Al Kaline	180.00	80.00	23.00
☐ 5 Jim Gilliam	16.00	7.25	2.00
☐ 6 Stan Hack MG	14.00	6.25	1.75
☐ 7 Jim Hegan	14.00	6.25	1.75
☐ 8 Harold Smith	12.00	5.50	1.50
☐ 9 Robert Miller	12.00	5.50	1.50
☐ 10 Bob Keegan	12.00	5.50	1.50
☐ 11 Ferris Fain	14.00	6.25	1.75
☐ 12 Vernon(Jake) Thies	12.00	5.50	1.50
☐ 13 Fred Marsh	12.00	5.50	1.50
☐ 14 Jim Finigan	12.00	5.50	1.50
☐ 15 Jim Pendleton	12.00	5.50	1.50
☐ 16 Roy Sievers	14.00	6.25	1.75
☐ 17 Bobby Hofman	12.00	5.50	1.50
☐ 18 Russ Kemmerer	12.00	5.50	1.50
☐ 19 Billy Herman CO	14.00	6.25	1.75
☐ 20 Andy Carey	13.00	5.75	1.65
☐ 21 Alex Grammas	12.00	5.50	1.50
☐ 22 Bill Skowron	20.00	9.00	2.50
☐ 23 Jack Parks	12.00	5.50	1.50
☐ 24 Hal Newhouser	20.00	9.00	2.50
☐ 25 Johnny Podres	20.00	9.00	2.50
☐ 26 Dick Groat	14.00	6.25	1.75
☐ 27 Billy Gardner	14.00	6.25	1.75
☐ 28 Ernie Banks	180.00	80.00	23.00
☐ 29 Herman Wehmeier	12.00	5.50	1.50
☐ 30 Vic Power	14.00	6.25	1.75
☐ 31 Warren Spahn	80.00	36.00	10.00
☐ 32 Warren McGhee	12.00	5.50	1.50
☐ 33 Tom Qualters	12.00	5.50	1.50
☐ 34 Wayne Terwilliger	12.00	5.50	1.50
☐ 35 Dave Jolly	12.00	5.50	1.50
☐ 36 Leo Kiely	12.00	5.50	1.50
☐ 37 Joe Cunningham	14.00	6.25	1.75
☐ 38 Bob Turley	16.00	7.25	2.00
☐ 39 Bill Glynn	12.00	5.50	1.50
☐ 40 Don Hoak	14.00	6.25	1.75
☐ 41 Chuck Stobbs	12.00	5.50	1.50
☐ 42 John(Windy) McCall	12.00	5.50	1.50
☐ 43 Harvey Haddix	14.00	6.25	1.75
☐ 44 Harold Valentine	12.00	5.50	1.50
☐ 45 Hank Sauer	14.00	6.25	1.75
☐ 46 Ted Kazanski	12.00	5.50	1.50
☐ 47 Hank Aaron UER (Birth incorrectly listed as 2/10)	350.00	160.00	45.00
☐ 48 Bob Kennedy	14.00	6.25	1.75
☐ 49 J.W. Porter	12.00	5.50	1.50
☐ 50 Jackie Robinson	250.00	115.00	31.00
☐ 51 Jim Hughes	14.00	6.25	1.75
☐ 52 Bill Tremel	12.00	5.50	1.50
☐ 53 Bill Taylor	12.00	5.50	1.50
☐ 54 Lou Limmer	12.00	5.50	1.50
☐ 55 Rip Repulski	12.00	5.50	1.50
☐ 56 Ray Jablonski	12.00	5.50	1.50
☐ 57 Billy O'Dell	12.00	5.50	1.50
☐ 58 Jim Rivera	12.00	5.50	1.50
☐ 59 Gair Allie	12.00	5.50	1.50
☐ 60 Dean Stone	12.00	5.50	1.50
☐ 61 Forrest Jacobs	12.00	5.50	1.50
☐ 62 Thornton Kipper	12.00	5.50	1.50
☐ 63 Joe Collins	14.00	6.25	1.75
☐ 64 Gus Triandos	14.00	6.25	1.75
☐ 65 Ray Boone	14.00	6.25	1.75
☐ 66 Ron Jackson	12.00	5.50	1.50
☐ 67 Wally Moon	14.00	6.25	1.75
☐ 68 Jim Davis	12.00	5.50	1.50
☐ 69 Ed Bailey	14.00	6.25	1.75
☐ 70 Al Rosen	15.00	6.75	1.90
☐ 71 Ruben Gomez	12.00	5.50	1.50
☐ 72 Karl Olson	12.00	5.50	1.50
☐ 73 Jack Shepard	12.00	5.50	1.50
☐ 74 Bob Borkowski	12.00	5.50	1.50
☐ 75 Sandy Amoros	30.00	13.50	3.80
☐ 76 Howie Pollet	12.00	5.50	1.50
☐ 77 Arnie Portocarrero	12.00	5.50	1.50
☐ 78 Gordon Jones	12.00	5.50	1.50
☐ 79 Clyde(Danny) Schell	12.00	5.50	1.50
☐ 80 Bob Grim	15.00	6.75	1.90
☐ 81 Gene Conley	14.00	6.25	1.75
☐ 82 Chuck Harmon	12.00	5.50	1.50
☐ 83 Tom Brewer	12.00	5.50	1.50
☐ 84 Camilo Pascual	18.00	8.00	2.30
☐ 85 Don Mossi	18.00	8.00	2.30
☐ 86 Bill Wilson	12.00	5.50	1.50
☐ 87 Frank House	12.00	5.50	1.50
☐ 88 Bob Skinner	15.00	6.75	1.90
☐ 89 Joe Frazier	14.00	6.25	1.75
☐ 90 Karl Spooner	14.00	6.25	1.75
☐ 91 Milt Bolling	12.00	5.50	1.50
☐ 92 Don Zimmer	30.00	13.50	3.80
☐ 93 Steve Bilko	12.00	5.50	1.50

☐ 94 Reno Bertoia 12.00 5.50 1.50
☐ 95 Preston Ward 12.00 5.50 1.50
☐ 96 Chuck Bishop 12.00 5.50 1.50
☐ 97 Carlos Paula 12.00 5.50 1.50
☐ 98 John Riddle CO 12.00 5.50 1.50
☐ 99 Frank Leja 12.00 5.50 1.50
☐ 100 Monte Irvin 30.00 13.50 3.80
☐ 101 Johnny Gray 12.00 5.50 1.50
☐ 102 Wally Westlake 12.00 5.50 1.50
☐ 103 Chuck White 12.00 5.50 1.50
☐ 104 Jack Harshman 12.00 5.50 1.50
☐ 105 Chuck Diering 12.00 5.50 1.50
☐ 106 Frank Sullivan 12.00 5.50 1.50
☐ 107 Curt Roberts 12.00 5.50 1.50
☐ 108 Al Walker 14.00 6.25 1.75
☐ 109 Ed Lopat 15.00 6.75 1.90
☐ 110 Gus Zernial 14.00 6.25 1.75
☐ 111 Bob Milliken 14.00 6.25 1.75
☐ 112 Nelson King 12.00 5.50 1.50
☐ 113 Harry Brecheen CO 14.00 6.25 1.75
☐ 114 Louis Ortiz 12.00 5.50 1.50
☐ 115 Ellis Kinder 12.00 5.50 1.50
☐ 116 Tom Hurd 12.00 5.50 1.50
☐ 117 Mel Roach 12.00 5.50 1.50
☐ 118 Bob Purkey 12.00 5.50 1.50
☐ 119 Bob Lennon 12.00 5.50 1.50
☐ 120 Ted Kluszewski 28.00 12.50 3.50
☐ 121 Bill Renna 12.00 5.50 1.50
☐ 122 Carl Sawatski 12.00 5.50 1.50
☐ 123 Sandy Koufax 950.00 425.00 120.00
☐ 124 Harmon Killebrew 275.00 125.00 34.00
☐ 125 Ken Boyer 70.00 32.00 8.75
☐ 126 Dick Hall 12.00 5.50 1.50
☐ 127 Dale Long 14.00 6.25 1.75
☐ 128 Ted Lepcio 12.00 5.50 1.50
☐ 129 Elvin Tappe 12.00 5.50 1.50
☐ 130 Mayo Smith MG 12.00 5.50 1.50
☐ 131 Grady Hatton 12.00 5.50 1.50
☐ 132 Bob Trice 12.00 5.50 1.50
☐ 133 Dave Hoskins 12.00 5.50 1.50
☐ 134 Joey Jay 14.00 6.25 1.75
☐ 135 Johnny O'Brien 14.00 6.25 1.75
☐ 136 Veston(Bunky) Stewart 12.00 5.50 1.50
☐ 137 Harry Elliott 12.00 5.50 1.50
☐ 138 Ray Herbert 12.00 5.50 1.50
☐ 139 Steve Kraly 12.00 5.50 1.50
☐ 140 Mel Parnell 14.00 6.25 1.75
☐ 141 Tom Wright 12.00 5.50 1.50
☐ 142 Jerry Lynch 14.00 6.25 1.75
☐ 143 John(Dick) Schofield 14.00 6.25 1.75
☐ 144 John(Joe) Amalfitano 12.00 5.50 1.50
☐ 145 Elmer Valo 12.00 5.50 1.50
☐ 146 Dick Donovan 12.00 5.50 1.50
☐ 147 Hugh Pepper 12.00 5.50 1.50
☐ 148 Hector Brown 12.00 5.50 1.50
☐ 149 Ray Crone 12.00 5.50 1.50
☐ 150 Mike Higgins MG 12.00 5.50 1.50
☐ 151 Ralph Kress CO 20.00 9.00 2.50
☐ 152 Harry Agganis 60.00 27.00 7.50
☐ 153 Bud Podbielan 20.00 9.00 2.50
☐ 154 Willie Miranda 20.00 9.00 2.50
☐ 155 Eddie Mathews 90.00 40.00 11.50
☐ 156 Joe Black 35.00 16.00 4.40
☐ 157 Robert Miller 20.00 9.00 2.50
☐ 158 Tommy Carroll 20.00 9.00 2.50
☐ 159 Johnny Schmitz 20.00 9.00 2.50
☐ 160 Ray Narleski 30.00 13.50 3.80
☐ 161 Chuck Tanner 32.00 14.50 4.00
☐ 162 Joe Coleman 30.00 13.50 3.80
☐ 163 Faye Throneberry 30.00 13.50 3.80
☐ 164 Roberto Clemente 2100.00 950.00 275.00
☐ 165 Don Johnson 30.00 13.50 3.80
☐ 166 Hank Bauer 35.00 16.00 4.40
☐ 167 Thomas Casagrande 30.00 13.50 3.80
☐ 168 Duane Pillette 30.00 13.50 3.80
☐ 169 Bob Oldis 30.00 13.50 3.80
☐ 170 Jim Pearce DP 15.00 6.75 1.90
☐ 171 Dick Brodowski 30.00 13.50 3.80
☐ 172 Frank Baumholtz DP 15.00 6.75 1.90
☐ 173 Bob Kline 30.00 13.50 3.80
☐ 174 Rudy Minarcin 30.00 13.50 3.80
☐ 175 Does not exist .00 .00 .00
☐ 176 Norm Zauchin 30.00 13.50 3.80
☐ 177 Al Robertson 30.00 13.50 3.80
☐ 178 Bobby Adams 30.00 13.50 3.80
☐ 179 Jim Bolger 30.00 13.50 3.80
☐ 180 Clem Labine 35.00 16.00 4.40
☐ 181 Roy McMillan 35.00 16.00 4.40
☐ 182 Humberto Robinson 30.00 13.50 3.80
☐ 183 Anthony Jacobs 30.00 13.50 3.80
☐ 184 Harry Perkowski DP 15.00 6.75 1.90
☐ 185 Don Ferrarese 30.00 13.50 3.80
☐ 186 Does not exist .00 .00 .00
☐ 187 Gil Hodges 135.00 60.00 17.00
☐ 188 Charlie Silvera DP 15.00 6.75 1.90
☐ 189 Phil Rizzuto 135.00 60.00 17.00
☐ 190 Gene Woodling 30.00 13.50 3.80
☐ 191 Eddie Stanky MG 30.00 13.50 3.80
☐ 192 Jim Delsing 30.00 13.50 3.80
☐ 193 Johnny Sain 45.00 20.00 5.75
☐ 194 Willie Mays 475.00 210.00 60.00
☐ 195 Ed Roebuck 35.00 16.00 4.40
☐ 196 Gale Wade 30.00 13.50 3.80
☐ 197 Al Smith 35.00 16.00 4.40
☐ 198 Yogi Berra 225.00 100.00 28.00
☐ 199 Odbert Hamric 35.00 16.00 4.40
☐ 200 Jackie Jensen 35.00 16.00 4.40
☐ 201 Sherm Lollar 35.00 16.00 4.40
☐ 202 Jim Owens 30.00 13.50 3.80
☐ 203 Does not exist .00 .00 .00
☐ 204 Frank Smith 30.00 13.50 3.80
☐ 205 Gene Freese 30.00 13.50 3.80
☐ 206 Pete Daley 30.00 13.50 3.80
☐ 207 Billy Consolo 30.00 13.50 3.80
☐ 208 Ray Moore 30.00 13.50 3.80
☐ 209 Does not exist .00 .00 .00
☐ 210 Duke Snider 475.00 120.00 38.00

1956 Topps

The cards in this 340-card set measure approximately 2 5/8" by 3 3/4". Following up with another horizontally oriented card in 1956, Topps improved the format by layering the color "head" shot onto an actual action sequence involving the player. Cards 1 to 180 come with either white or gray

backs: in the 1 to 100 sequence, gray backs are less common (worth about 10 percent more) and in the 101 to 180 sequence, white backs are less common (worth 30 percent more). The team cards, used for the first time in a regular set by Topps, are found dated 1955, or undated, with the team name appearing on either side. The dated team cards in the first series were not printed on the gray stock. The two unnumbered checklist cards are highly prized (must be unmarked to qualify as excellent or mint). The complete set price below does not include the unnumbered checklist cards or any of the variations. The key Rookie Cards in this set are Walt Alston, Luis Aparicio, and Roger Craig. There are ten double-printed cards in the first series as evidenced by the discovery of an uncut sheet of 110 cards (10 by 11); these DP's are listed below.

	NRMT	VG-E	GOOD
COMPLETE SET (340)	7000.00	3200.00	900.00
COMMON CARD (1-100)	10.00	4.50	1.25
COMMON CARD (101-180)	12.00	5.50	1.50
COMMON CARD (181-260)	15.00	6.75	1.90
COMMON CARD (261-340)	12.00	5.50	1.50

	NRMT	VG-E	GOOD
☐ 1 William Harridge (AL President)	90.00	23.00	7.25
☐ 2 Warren Giles (NL President)	20.00	9.00	2.50
☐ 3 Elmer Valo	10.00	4.50	1.25
☐ 4 Carlos Paula	10.00	4.50	1.25
☐ 5 Ted Williams	300.00	135.00	38.00
☐ 6 Ray Boone	12.00	5.50	1.50
☐ 7 Ron Negray	10.00	4.50	1.25
☐ 8 Walter Alston MG	42.00	19.00	5.25
☐ 9 Ruben Gomez DP	8.50	3.80	1.05
☐ 10 Warren Spahn	65.00	29.00	8.25
☐ 11A Chicago Cubs (Centered)	30.00	13.50	3.80
☐ 11B Cubs Team (Dated 1955)	75.00	34.00	9.50
☐ 11C Cubs Team (Name at far left)	30.00	13.50	3.80
☐ 12 Andy Carey	12.00	5.50	1.50
☐ 13 Roy Face	10.00	4.50	1.25
☐ 14 Ken Boyer DP	16.00	7.25	2.00
☐ 15 Ernie Banks DP	80.00	36.00	10.00
☐ 16 Hector Lopez	14.00	6.25	1.75
☐ 17 Gene Conley	12.00	5.50	1.50
☐ 18 Dick Donovan	10.00	4.50	1.25
☐ 19 Chuck Diering	10.00	4.50	1.25
☐ 20 Al Kaline	100.00	45.00	12.50
☐ 21 Joe Collins DP	10.00	4.50	1.25
☐ 22 Jim Finigan	10.00	4.50	1.25
☐ 23 Fred Marsh	10.00	4.50	1.25
☐ 24 Dick Groat	14.00	6.25	1.75
☐ 25 Ted Kluszewski	30.00	13.50	3.80
☐ 26 Grady Hatton	10.00	4.50	1.25
☐ 27 Nelson Burbrink	10.00	4.50	1.25
☐ 28 Bobby Hofman	10.00	4.50	1.25
☐ 29 Jack Harshman	10.00	4.50	1.25
☐ 30 Jackie Robinson DP	160.00	70.00	20.00
☐ 31 Hank Aaron UER (Small photo actually Willie Mays)	260.00	115.00	33.00
☐ 32 Frank House	10.00	4.50	1.25
☐ 33 Roberto Clemente	425.00	190.00	52.50
☐ 34 Tom Brewer	10.00	4.50	1.25
☐ 35 Al Rosen	15.00	6.75	1.90
☐ 36 Rudy Minarcin	10.00	4.50	1.25
☐ 37 Alex Grammas	10.00	4.50	1.25
☐ 38 Bob Kennedy	12.00	5.50	1.50
☐ 39 Don Mossi	12.00	5.50	1.50
☐ 40 Bob Turley	14.00	6.25	1.75
☐ 41 Hank Sauer	12.00	5.50	1.50
☐ 42 Sandy Amoros	14.00	6.25	1.75
☐ 43 Ray Moore	10.00	4.50	1.25
☐ 44 Windy McCall	10.00	4.50	1.25
☐ 45 Gus Zernial	12.00	5.50	1.50
☐ 46 Gene Freese DP	8.50	3.80	1.05
☐ 47 Art Fowler	10.00	4.50	1.25
☐ 48 Jim Hegan	12.00	5.50	1.50
☐ 49 Pedro Ramos	10.00	4.50	1.25
☐ 50 Dusty Rhodes	12.00	5.50	1.50
☐ 51 Ernie Oravetz	10.00	4.50	1.25
☐ 52 Bob Grim	12.00	5.50	1.50
☐ 53 Arnie Portocarrero	10.00	4.50	1.25
☐ 54 Bob Keegan	10.00	4.50	1.25
☐ 55 Wally Moon	12.00	5.50	1.50
☐ 56 Dale Long	12.00	5.50	1.50
☐ 57 Duke Maas	10.00	4.50	1.25
☐ 58 Ed Roebuck	12.00	5.50	1.50
☐ 59 Jose Santiago	10.00	4.50	1.25
☐ 60 Mayo Smith MG DP	8.50	3.80	1.05
☐ 61 Bill Skowron	18.00	8.00	2.30
☐ 62 Hal Smith	10.00	4.50	1.25
☐ 63 Roger Craig	20.00	9.00	2.50
☐ 64 Luis Arroyo	10.00	4.50	1.25
☐ 65 Johnny O'Brien	12.00	5.50	1.50
☐ 66 Bob Speake	10.00	4.50	1.25
☐ 67 Vic Power	12.00	5.50	1.50
☐ 68 Chuck Stobbs	10.00	4.50	1.25
☐ 69 Chuck Tanner	10.00	4.50	1.25
☐ 70 Jim Rivera	10.00	4.50	1.25
☐ 71 Frank Sullivan	10.00	4.50	1.25
☐ 72A Phillies Team (Centered)	30.00	13.50	3.80
☐ 72B Phillies Team (Dated 1955)	75.00	34.00	9.50
☐ 72C Phillies Team (Name at far left)	30.00	13.50	3.80
☐ 73 Wayne Terwilliger	10.00	4.50	1.25
☐ 74 Jim King	10.00	4.50	1.25
☐ 75 Roy Sievers DP	10.00	4.50	1.25
☐ 76 Ray Crone	10.00	4.50	1.25
☐ 77 Harvey Haddix	12.00	5.50	1.50
☐ 78 Herman Wehmeier	10.00	4.50	1.25
☐ 79 Sandy Koufax	325.00	145.00	40.00
☐ 80 Gus Triandos DP	10.00	4.50	1.25
☐ 81 Wally Westlake	10.00	4.50	1.25
☐ 82 Bill Renna	10.00	4.50	1.25
☐ 83 Karl Spooner	12.00	5.50	1.50
☐ 84 Babe Birrer	10.00	4.50	1.25
☐ 85A Cleveland Indians (Centered)	30.00	13.50	3.80
☐ 85B Indians Team (Dated 1955)	75.00	34.00	9.50
☐ 85C Indians Team (Name at far left)	30.00	13.50	3.80
☐ 86 Ray Jablonski DP	8.50	3.80	1.05
☐ 87 Dean Stone	10.00	4.50	1.25
☐ 88 Johnny Kucks	10.00	4.50	1.25
☐ 89 Norm Zauchin	10.00	4.50	1.25
☐ 90A Cincinnati Redlegs Team (Centered)	30.00	13.50	3.80
☐ 90B Reds Team (Dated 1955)	75.00	34.00	9.50
☐ 90C Reds Team (Name at far left)	30.00	13.50	3.80
☐ 91 Gail Harris	10.00	4.50	1.25
☐ 92 Bob(Red) Wilson	10.00	4.50	1.25
☐ 93 George Susce	10.00	4.50	1.25

☐ 94 Ron Kline 10.00 4.50 1.25
☐ 95A Milwaukee Braves 42.00 19.00 5.25
Team (Centered)
☐ 95B Braves Team 75.00 34.00 9.50
(Dated 1955)
☐ 95C Braves Team 42.00 19.00 5.25
(Name at far left)
☐ 96 Bill Tremel 10.00 4.50 1.25
☐ 97 Jerry Lynch 12.00 5.50 1.50
☐ 98 Camilo Pascual 12.00 5.50 1.50
☐ 99 Don Zimmer 14.00 6.25 1.75
☐ 100A Baltimore Orioles ... 35.00 16.00 4.40
Team (centered)
☐ 100B Orioles Team 75.00 34.00 9.50
(Dated 1955)
☐ 100C Orioles Team 35.00 16.00 4.40
(Name at far left)
☐ 101 Roy Campanella 150.00 70.00 19.00
☐ 102 Jim Davis 12.00 5.50 1.50
☐ 103 Willie Miranda 12.00 5.50 1.50
☐ 104 Bob Lennon 12.00 5.50 1.50
☐ 105 Al Smith 12.00 5.50 1.50
☐ 106 Joe Astroth 12.00 5.50 1.50
☐ 107 Eddie Mathews 55.00 25.00 7.00
☐ 108 Laurin Pepper 12.00 5.50 1.50
☐ 109 Enos Slaughter 38.00 17.00 4.70
☐ 110 Yogi Berra 125.00 57.50 15.50
☐ 111 Boston Red Sox 35.00 16.00 4.40
Team Card
☐ 112 Dee Fondy 12.00 5.50 1.50
☐ 113 Phil Rizzuto 80.00 36.00 10.00
☐ 114 Jim Owens 12.00 5.50 1.50
☐ 115 Jackie Jensen 15.00 6.75 1.90
☐ 116 Eddie O'Brien 12.00 5.50 1.50
☐ 117 Virgil Trucks 14.00 6.25 1.75
☐ 118 Nellie Fox 35.00 16.00 4.40
☐ 119 Larry Jackson 12.00 5.50 1.50
☐ 120 Richie Ashburn 40.00 18.00 5.00
☐ 121 Pittsburgh Pirates 35.00 16.00 4.40
Team Card
☐ 122 Willard Nixon 12.00 5.50 1.50
☐ 123 Roy McMillan 14.00 6.25 1.75
☐ 124 Don Kaiser 12.00 5.50 1.50
☐ 125 Minnie Minoso 25.00 11.50 3.10
☐ 126 Jim Brady 12.00 5.50 1.50
☐ 127 Willie Jones 12.00 5.50 1.50
☐ 128 Eddie Yost 14.00 6.25 1.75
☐ 129 Jake Martin 12.00 5.50 1.50
☐ 130 Willie Mays 375.00 170.00 47.50
☐ 131 Bob Roselli 12.00 5.50 1.50
☐ 132 Bobby Avila 12.00 5.50 1.50
☐ 133 Ray Narleski 12.00 5.50 1.50
☐ 134 St. Louis Cardinals ... 35.00 16.00 4.40
Team Card
☐ 135 Mickey Mantle 1200.00 550.00 150.00
☐ 136 Johnny Logan 14.00 6.25 1.75
☐ 137 Al Silvera 12.00 5.50 1.50
☐ 138 Johnny Antonelli 14.00 6.25 1.75
☐ 139 Tommy Carroll 12.00 5.50 1.50
☐ 140 Herb Score 50.00 23.00 6.25
☐ 141 Joe Frazier 12.00 5.50 1.50
☐ 142 Gene Baker 12.00 5.50 1.50
☐ 143 Jim Piersall 15.00 6.75 1.90
☐ 144 Leroy Powell 12.00 5.50 1.50
☐ 145 Gil Hodges 50.00 23.00 6.25
☐ 146 Washington Nationals 35.00 16.00 4.40
Team Card
☐ 147 Earl Torgeson 12.00 5.50 1.50
☐ 148 Alvin Dark 14.00 6.25 1.75
☐ 149 Dixie Howell 12.00 5.50 1.50
☐ 150 Duke Snider 120.00 55.00 15.00
☐ 151 Spook Jacobs 14.00 6.25 1.75
☐ 152 Billy Hoeft 14.00 6.25 1.75
☐ 153 Frank Thomas 12.00 5.50 1.50
☐ 154 Dave Pope 12.00 5.50 1.50
☐ 155 Harvey Kuenn 20.00 9.00 2.50
☐ 156 Wes Westrum 14.00 6.25 1.75
☐ 157 Dick Brodowski 12.00 5.50 1.50
☐ 158 Wally Post 14.00 6.25 1.75
☐ 159 Clint Courtney 12.00 5.50 1.50
☐ 160 Billy Pierce 12.00 5.50 1.50
☐ 161 Joe DeMaestri 12.00 5.50 1.50
☐ 162 Dave(Gus) Bell 14.00 6.25 1.75
☐ 163 Gene Woodling 12.00 5.50 1.50
☐ 164 Harmon Killebrew .. 110.00 50.00 14.00
☐ 165 Red Schoendienst 25.00 11.50 3.10
☐ 166 Brooklyn Dodgers .. 175.00 80.00 22.00
Team Card
☐ 167 Harry Dorish 12.00 5.50 1.50
☐ 168 Sammy White 12.00 5.50 1.50
☐ 169 Bob Nelson 12.00 5.50 1.50
☐ 170 Bill Virdon 14.00 6.25 1.75
☐ 171 Jim Wilson 12.00 5.50 1.50
☐ 172 Frank Torre 12.00 5.50 1.50
☐ 173 Johnny Podres 18.00 8.00 2.30
☐ 174 Glen Gorbous 12.00 5.50 1.50
☐ 175 Del Crandall 14.00 6.25 1.75
☐ 176 Alex Kellner 12.00 5.50 1.50
☐ 177 Hank Bauer 16.00 7.25 2.00
☐ 178 Joe Black 12.00 5.50 1.50
☐ 179 Harry Chiti 12.00 5.50 1.50
☐ 180 Robin Roberts 40.00 18.00 5.00
☐ 181 Billy Martin 55.00 25.00 7.00
☐ 182 Paul Minner 15.00 6.75 1.90
☐ 183 Stan Lopata 15.00 6.75 1.90
☐ 184 Don Bessent 15.00 6.75 1.90
☐ 185 Bill Bruton 18.00 8.00 2.30
☐ 186 Ron Jackson 15.00 6.75 1.90
☐ 187 Early Wynn 40.00 18.00 5.00
☐ 188 Chicago White Sox ... 40.00 18.00 5.00
Team Card
☐ 189 Ned Garver 15.00 6.75 1.90
☐ 190 Carl Furillo 25.00 11.50 3.10
☐ 191 Frank Lary 20.00 9.00 2.50
☐ 192 Smoky Burgess 18.00 8.00 2.30
☐ 193 Wilmer Mizell 18.00 8.00 2.30
☐ 194 Monte Irvin 35.00 16.00 4.40
☐ 195 George Kell 35.00 16.00 4.40
☐ 196 Tom Poholsky 15.00 6.75 1.90
☐ 197 Granny Hamner 15.00 6.75 1.90
☐ 198 Ed Fitzgerald 15.00 6.75 1.90
☐ 199 Hank Thompson 18.00 8.00 2.30
☐ 200 Bob Feller 100.00 45.00 12.50
☐ 201 Rip Repulski 15.00 6.75 1.90
☐ 202 Jim Hearn 15.00 6.75 1.90
☐ 203 Bill Tuttle 15.00 6.75 1.90
☐ 204 Art Swanson 15.00 6.75 1.90
☐ 205 Whitey Lockman 18.00 8.00 2.30
☐ 206 Erv Palica 15.00 6.75 1.90
☐ 207 Jim Small 15.00 6.75 1.90
☐ 208 Elston Howard 55.00 25.00 7.00
☐ 209 Max Surkont 15.00 6.75 1.90
☐ 210 Mike Garcia 18.00 8.00 2.30
☐ 211 Murry Dickson 15.00 6.75 1.90
☐ 212 Johnny Temple 15.00 6.75 1.90
☐ 213 Detroit Tigers 55.00 25.00 7.00
Team Card
☐ 214 Bob Rush 15.00 6.75 1.90
☐ 215 Tommy Byrne 15.00 6.75 1.90
☐ 216 Jerry Schoonmaker .. 15.00 6.75 1.90
☐ 217 Billy Klaus 15.00 6.75 1.90
☐ 218 Joe Nuxhall UER 18.00 8.00 2.30
(Misspelled Nuxall)
☐ 219 Lew Burdette 15.00 6.75 1.90
☐ 220 Del Ennis 18.00 8.00 2.30
☐ 221 Bob Friend 18.00 8.00 2.30

☐ 222	Dave Philley	15.00	6.75	1.90
☐ 223	Randy Jackson	15.00	6.75	1.90
☐ 224	Bud Podbielan	15.00	6.75	1.90
☐ 225	Gil McDougald	30.00	13.50	3.80
☐ 226	New York Giants Team Card	70.00	32.00	8.75
☐ 227	Russ Meyer	15.00	6.75	1.90
☐ 228	Mickey Vernon	18.00	8.00	2.30
☐ 229	Harry Brecheen CO	18.00	8.00	2.30
☐ 230	Chico Carrasquel	15.00	6.75	1.90
☐ 231	Bob Hale	15.00	6.75	1.90
☐ 232	Toby Atwell	15.00	6.75	1.90
☐ 233	Carl Erskine	30.00	13.50	3.80
☐ 234	Pete Runnels	18.00	8.00	2.30
☐ 235	Don Newcombe	50.00	23.00	6.25
☐ 236	Kansas City Athletics Team Card	35.00	16.00	4.40
☐ 237	Jose Valdivielso	15.00	6.75	1.90
☐ 238	Walt Dropo	18.00	8.00	2.30
☐ 239	Harry Simpson	15.00	6.75	1.90
☐ 240	Whitey Ford	110.00	50.00	14.00
☐ 241	Don Mueller UER (6" tall)	18.00	8.00	2.30
☐ 242	Hershell Freeman	15.00	6.75	1.90
☐ 243	Sherm Lollar	18.00	8.00	2.30
☐ 244	Bob Buhl	18.00	8.00	2.30
☐ 245	Billy Goodman	18.00	8.00	2.30
☐ 246	Tom Gorman	15.00	6.75	1.90
☐ 247	Bill Sarni	15.00	6.75	1.90
☐ 248	Bob Porterfield	15.00	6.75	1.90
☐ 249	Johnny Klippstein	15.00	6.75	1.90
☐ 250	Larry Doby	32.00	14.50	4.00
☐ 251	New York Yankees Team Card UER (Don Larsen misspelled as Larson on front)	200.00	90.00	25.00
☐ 252	Vern Law	18.00	8.00	2.30
☐ 253	Irv Noren	15.00	6.75	1.90
☐ 254	George Crowe	15.00	6.75	1.90
☐ 255	Bob Lemon	35.00	16.00	4.40
☐ 256	Tom Hurd	15.00	6.75	1.90
☐ 257	Bobby Thomson	28.00	12.50	3.50
☐ 258	Art Ditmar	15.00	6.75	1.90
☐ 259	Sam Jones	18.00	8.00	2.30
☐ 260	Pee Wee Reese	120.00	55.00	15.00
☐ 261	Bobby Shantz	14.00	6.25	1.75
☐ 262	Howie Pollet	12.00	5.50	1.50
☐ 263	Bob Miller	12.00	5.50	1.50
☐ 264	Ray Monzant	12.00	5.50	1.50
☐ 265	Sandy Consuegra	12.00	5.50	1.50
☐ 266	Don Ferrarese	12.00	5.50	1.50
☐ 267	Bob Nieman	12.00	5.50	1.50
☐ 268	Dale Mitchell	18.00	8.00	2.30
☐ 269	Jack Meyer	12.00	5.50	1.50
☐ 270	Billy Loes	14.00	6.25	1.75
☐ 271	Foster Castleman	12.00	5.50	1.50
☐ 272	Danny O'Connell	12.00	5.50	1.50
☐ 273	Walker Cooper	12.00	5.50	1.50
☐ 274	Frank Baumholtz	12.00	5.50	1.50
☐ 275	Jim Greengrass	12.00	5.50	1.50
☐ 276	George Zuverink	12.00	5.50	1.50
☐ 277	Daryl Spencer	12.00	5.50	1.50
☐ 278	Chet Nichols	12.00	5.50	1.50
☐ 279	Johnny Groth	12.00	5.50	1.50
☐ 280	Jim Gilliam	20.00	9.00	2.50
☐ 281	Art Houtteman	12.00	5.50	1.50
☐ 282	Warren Hacker	12.00	5.50	1.50
☐ 283	Hal Smith	12.00	5.50	1.50
☐ 284	Ike Delock	12.00	5.50	1.50
☐ 285	Eddie Miksis	12.00	5.50	1.50
☐ 286	Bill Wight	12.00	5.50	1.50
☐ 287	Bobby Adams	12.00	5.50	1.50
☐ 288	Bob Cerv	25.00	11.50	3.10
☐ 289	Hal Jeffcoat	12.00	5.50	1.50
☐ 290	Curt Simmons	14.00	6.25	1.75
☐ 291	Frank Kellert	12.00	5.50	1.50
☐ 292	Luis Aparicio	125.00	57.50	15.50
☐ 293	Stu Miller	12.00	5.50	1.50
☐ 294	Ernie Johnson	14.00	6.25	1.75
☐ 295	Clem Labine	12.00	5.50	1.50
☐ 296	Andy Seminick	12.00	5.50	1.50
☐ 297	Bob Skinner	14.00	6.25	1.75
☐ 298	Johnny Schmitz	12.00	5.50	1.50
☐ 299	Charlie Neal	30.00	13.50	3.80
☐ 300	Vic Wertz	14.00	6.25	1.75
☐ 301	Marv Grissom	12.00	5.50	1.50
☐ 302	Eddie Robinson	12.00	5.50	1.50
☐ 303	Jim Dyck	12.00	5.50	1.50
☐ 304	Frank Malzone	20.00	9.00	2.50
☐ 305	Brooks Lawrence	12.00	5.50	1.50
☐ 306	Curt Roberts	12.00	5.50	1.50
☐ 307	Hoyt Wilhelm	35.00	16.00	4.40
☐ 308	Chuck Harmon	12.00	5.50	1.50
☐ 309	Don Blasingame	12.00	5.50	1.50
☐ 310	Steve Gromek	12.00	5.50	1.50
☐ 311	Hal Naragon	12.00	5.50	1.50
☐ 312	Andy Pafko	14.00	6.25	1.75
☐ 313	Gene Stephens	12.00	5.50	1.50
☐ 314	Hobie Landrith	12.00	5.50	1.50
☐ 315	Milt Bolling	12.00	5.50	1.50
☐ 316	Jerry Coleman	12.00	5.50	1.50
☐ 317	Al Aber	12.00	5.50	1.50
☐ 318	Fred Hatfield	12.00	5.50	1.50
☐ 319	Jack Crimian	12.00	5.50	1.50
☐ 320	Joe Adcock	14.00	6.25	1.75
☐ 321	Jim Konstanty	14.00	6.25	1.75
☐ 322	Karl Olson	12.00	5.50	1.50
☐ 323	Willard Schmidt	12.00	5.50	1.50
☐ 324	Rocky Bridges	12.00	5.50	1.50
☐ 325	Don Liddle	12.00	5.50	1.50
☐ 326	Connie Johnson	12.00	5.50	1.50
☐ 327	Bob Wiesler	12.00	5.50	1.50
☐ 328	Preston Ward	12.00	5.50	1.50
☐ 329	Lou Berberet	12.00	5.50	1.50
☐ 330	Jim Busby	12.00	5.50	1.50
☐ 331	Dick Hall	12.00	5.50	1.50
☐ 332	Don Larsen	60.00	27.00	7.50
☐ 333	Rube Walker	12.00	5.50	1.50
☐ 334	Bob Miller	12.00	5.50	1.50
☐ 335	Don Hoak	14.00	6.25	1.75
☐ 336	Ellis Kinder	12.00	5.50	1.50
☐ 337	Bobby Morgan	12.00	5.50	1.50
☐ 338	Jim Delsing	12.00	5.50	1.50
☐ 339	Rance Pless	12.00	5.50	1.50
☐ 340	Mickey McDermott	50.00	10.00	3.00
☐ NNO	Checklist 1/3	280.00	42.50	14.00
☐ NNO	Checklist 2/4	280.00	42.50	14.00

1957 Topps

The cards in this 407-card set measure 2 1/2" by 3 1/2". In 1957, Topps returned to the vertical obverse, adopted what we now call the standard card size, and used a large, uncluttered color photo for the first time since 1952. Cards in the series 265 to 352 and the unnumbered checklist cards are scarcer than other cards in the set. However within this scarce series (265-352) there are 22 cards which were printed in double the quantity of the other cards in the series; these 22 double prints are indicated

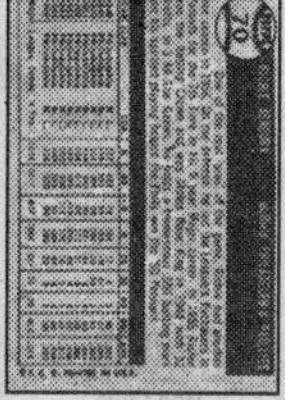

by DP in the checklist below. The first star combination cards, cards 400 and 407, are quite popular with collectors. They feature the big stars of the previous season's World Series teams, the Dodgers (Furillo, Hodges, Campanella, and Snider) and Yankees (Berra and Mantle). The complete set price below does not include the unnumbered checklist cards. The key Rookie Cards in this set are Jim Bunning, Rocky Colavito, Don Drysdale, Whitey Herzog, Tony Kubek, Bobby Richardson, Brooks Robinson, and Frank Robinson.

	NRMT	VG-E	GOOD
COMPLETE SET (407)	7250.00	3300.00	900.00
COMMON CARD (1-88)	9.00	4.00	1.15
COMMON CARD (89-176)	8.00	3.60	1.00
COMMON CARD (177-264)	7.00	3.10	.85
COMMON CARD (265-352)	20.00	9.00	2.50
COMMON CARD (353-407)	8.00	3.60	1.00

		NRMT	VG-E	GOOD
☐ 1	Ted Williams	500.00	150.00	50.00
☐ 2	Yogi Berra	120.00	55.00	15.00
☐ 3	Dale Long	10.00	4.50	1.25
☐ 4	Johnny Logan	10.00	4.50	1.25
☐ 5	Sal Maglie	14.00	6.25	1.75
☐ 6	Hector Lopez	10.00	4.50	1.25
☐ 7	Luis Aparicio	40.00	18.00	5.00
☐ 8	Don Mossi	10.00	4.50	1.25
☐ 9	Johnny Temple	10.00	4.50	1.25
☐ 10	Willie Mays	225.00	100.00	28.00
☐ 11	George Zuverink	9.00	4.00	1.15
☐ 12	Dick Groat	10.00	4.50	1.25
☐ 13	Wally Burnette	9.00	4.00	1.15
☐ 14	Bob Nieman	9.00	4.00	1.15
☐ 15	Robin Roberts	25.00	11.50	3.10
☐ 16	Walt Moryn	9.00	4.00	1.15
☐ 17	Billy Gardner	9.00	4.00	1.15
☐ 18	Don Drysdale	210.00	95.00	26.00
☐ 19	Bob Wilson	9.00	4.00	1.15
☐ 20	Hank Aaron UER (Reverse negative photo on front)	250.00	115.00	31.00
☐ 21	Frank Sullivan	9.00	4.00	1.15
☐ 22	Jerry Snyder UER (Photo actually Ed Fitzgerald)	9.00	4.00	1.15
☐ 23	Sherm Lollar	10.00	4.50	1.25
☐ 24	Bill Mazeroski	75.00	34.00	9.50
☐ 25	Whitey Ford	60.00	27.00	7.50
☐ 26	Bob Boyd	9.00	4.00	1.15
☐ 27	Ted Kazanski	9.00	4.00	1.15
☐ 28	Gene Conley	10.00	4.50	1.25
☐ 29	Whitey Herzog	25.00	11.50	3.10
☐ 30	Pee Wee Reese	60.00	27.00	7.50
☐ 31	Ron Northey	9.00	4.00	1.15
☐ 32	Hershell Freeman	9.00	4.00	1.15
☐ 33	Jim Small	9.00	4.00	1.15
☐ 34	Tom Sturdivant	9.00	4.00	1.15
☐ 35	Frank Robinson	225.00	100.00	28.00
☐ 36	Bob Grim	9.00	4.00	1.15
☐ 37	Frank Torre	10.00	4.50	1.25
☐ 38	Nellie Fox	25.00	11.50	3.10
☐ 39	Al Worthington	9.00	4.00	1.15
☐ 40	Early Wynn	25.00	11.50	3.10
☐ 41	Hal W. Smith	9.00	4.00	1.15
☐ 42	Dee Fondy	9.00	4.00	1.15
☐ 43	Connie Johnson	9.00	4.00	1.15
☐ 44	Joe DeMaestri	9.00	4.00	1.15
☐ 45	Carl Furillo	20.00	9.00	2.50
☐ 46	Robert J. Miller	9.00	4.00	1.15
☐ 47	Don Blasingame	9.00	4.00	1.15
☐ 48	Bill Bruton	9.00	4.00	1.15
☐ 49	Daryl Spencer	9.00	4.00	1.15
☐ 50	Herb Score	20.00	9.00	2.50
☐ 51	Clint Courtney	9.00	4.00	1.15
☐ 52	Lee Walls	9.00	4.00	1.15
☐ 53	Clem Labine	9.00	4.00	1.15
☐ 54	Elmer Valo	9.00	4.00	1.15
☐ 55	Ernie Banks	125.00	57.50	15.50
☐ 56	Dave Sisler	9.00	4.00	1.15
☐ 57	Jim Lemon	10.00	4.50	1.25
☐ 58	Ruben Gomez	9.00	4.00	1.15
☐ 59	Dick Williams	10.00	4.50	1.25
☐ 60	Billy Hoeft	10.00	4.50	1.25
☐ 61	James(Dusty) Rhodes	10.00	4.50	1.25
☐ 62	Billy Martin	40.00	18.00	5.00
☐ 63	Ike Delock	9.00	4.00	1.15
☐ 64	Pete Runnels	10.00	4.50	1.25
☐ 65	Wally Moon	10.00	4.50	1.25
☐ 66	Brooks Lawrence	9.00	4.00	1.15
☐ 67	Chico Carrasquel	9.00	4.00	1.15
☐ 68	Ray Crone	9.00	4.00	1.15
☐ 69	Roy McMillan	10.00	4.50	1.25
☐ 70	Richie Ashburn	25.00	11.50	3.10
☐ 71	Murry Dickson	9.00	4.00	1.15
☐ 72	Bill Tuttle	9.00	4.00	1.15
☐ 73	George Crowe	9.00	4.00	1.15
☐ 74	Vito Valentinetti	9.00	4.00	1.15
☐ 75	Jim Piersall	12.00	5.50	1.50
☐ 76	Roberto Clemente	250.00	115.00	31.00
☐ 77	Paul Foytack	9.00	4.00	1.15
☐ 78	Vic Wertz	10.00	4.50	1.25
☐ 79	Lindy McDaniel	15.00	6.75	1.90
☐ 80	Gil Hodges	50.00	23.00	6.25
☐ 81	Herman Wehmeier	9.00	4.00	1.15
☐ 82	Elston Howard	20.00	9.00	2.50
☐ 83	Lou Skizas	9.00	4.00	1.15
☐ 84	Moe Drabowsky	10.00	4.50	1.25
☐ 85	Larry Doby	12.00	5.50	1.50
☐ 86	Bill Sarni	9.00	4.00	1.15
☐ 87	Tom Gorman	9.00	4.00	1.15
☐ 88	Harvey Kuenn	12.00	5.50	1.50
☐ 89	Roy Sievers	9.00	4.00	1.15
☐ 90	Warren Spahn	65.00	29.00	8.25
☐ 91	Mack Burk	8.00	3.60	1.00
☐ 92	Mickey Vernon	9.00	4.00	1.15
☐ 93	Hal Jeffcoat	8.00	3.60	1.00
☐ 94	Bobby Del Greco	8.00	3.60	1.00
☐ 95	Mickey Mantle	1100.00	325.00	110.00
☐ 96	Hank Aguirre	8.00	3.60	1.00
☐ 97	New York Yankees Team Card	65.00	29.00	8.25
☐ 98	Alvin Dark	9.00	4.00	1.15
☐ 99	Bob Keegan	8.00	3.60	1.00
☐ 100	League Presidents Warren Giles Will Harridge	14.00	6.25	1.75
☐ 101	Chuck Stobbs	8.00	3.60	1.00
☐ 102	Ray Boone	9.00	4.00	1.15
☐ 103	Joe Nuxhall	9.00	4.00	1.15

☐ 104 Hank Foiles 8.00 3.60 1.00
☐ 105 Johnny Antonelli 9.00 4.00 1.15
☐ 106 Ray Moore 8.00 3.60 1.00
☐ 107 Jim Rivera 8.00 3.60 1.00
☐ 108 Tommy Byrne 8.00 3.60 1.00
☐ 109 Hank Thompson 9.00 4.00 1.15
☐ 110 Bill Virdon 8.00 3.60 1.00
☐ 111 Hal R. Smith 8.00 3.60 1.00
☐ 112 Tom Brewer 8.00 3.60 1.00
☐ 113 Wilmer Mizell 9.00 4.00 1.15
☐ 114 Milwaukee Braves 20.00 9.00 2.50
Team Card
☐ 115 Jim Gilliam 12.00 5.50 1.50
☐ 116 Mike Fornieles 8.00 3.60 1.00
☐ 117 Joe Adcock 9.00 4.00 1.15
☐ 118 Bob Porterfield 8.00 3.60 1.00
☐ 119 Stan Lopata 8.00 3.60 1.00
☐ 120 Bob Lemon 25.00 11.50 3.10
☐ 121 Clete Boyer 27.00 12.00 3.40
☐ 122 Ken Boyer 15.00 6.75 1.90
☐ 123 Steve Ridzik 8.00 3.60 1.00
☐ 124 Dave Philley 8.00 3.60 1.00
☐ 125 Al Kaline 85.00 38.00 10.50
☐ 126 Bob Wiesler 8.00 3.60 1.00
☐ 127 Bob Buhl 9.00 4.00 1.15
☐ 128 Ed Bailey 9.00 4.00 1.15
☐ 129 Saul Rogovin 8.00 3.60 1.00
☐ 130 Don Newcombe 15.00 6.75 1.90
☐ 131 Milt Bolling 8.00 3.60 1.00
☐ 132 Art Ditmar 9.00 4.00 1.15
☐ 133 Del Crandall 9.00 4.00 1.15
☐ 134 Don Kaiser 8.00 3.60 1.00
☐ 135 Bill Skowron 16.00 7.25 2.00
☐ 136 Jim Hegan 9.00 4.00 1.15
☐ 137 Bob Rush 8.00 3.60 1.00
☐ 138 Minnie Minoso 16.00 7.25 2.00
☐ 139 Lou Kretlow 8.00 3.60 1.00
☐ 140 Frank Thomas 9.00 4.00 1.15
☐ 141 Al Aber 8.00 3.60 1.00
☐ 142 Charley Thompson 8.00 3.60 1.00
☐ 143 Andy Pafko 9.00 4.00 1.15
☐ 144 Ray Narleski 8.00 3.60 1.00
☐ 145 Al Smith 8.00 3.60 1.00
☐ 146 Don Ferrarese 8.00 3.60 1.00
☐ 147 Al Walker 8.00 3.60 1.00
☐ 148 Don Mueller 9.00 4.00 1.15
☐ 149 Bob Kennedy 9.00 4.00 1.15
☐ 150 Bob Friend 9.00 4.00 1.15
☐ 151 Willie Miranda 8.00 3.60 1.00
☐ 152 Jack Harshman 8.00 3.60 1.00
☐ 153 Karl Olson 8.00 3.60 1.00
☐ 154 Red Schoendienst 20.00 9.00 2.50
☐ 155 Jim Brosnan 9.00 4.00 1.15
☐ 156 Gus Triandos 9.00 4.00 1.15
☐ 157 Wally Post 9.00 4.00 1.15
☐ 158 Curt Simmons 9.00 4.00 1.15
☐ 159 Solly Drake 8.00 3.60 1.00
☐ 160 Billy Pierce 8.00 3.60 1.00
☐ 161 Pittsburgh Pirates 15.00 6.75 1.90
Team Card
☐ 162 Jack Meyer 8.00 3.60 1.00
☐ 163 Sammy White 8.00 3.60 1.00
☐ 164 Tommy Carroll 8.00 3.60 1.00
☐ 165 Ted Kluszewski 45.00 20.00 5.75
☐ 166 Roy Face 10.00 4.50 1.25
☐ 167 Vic Power 9.00 4.00 1.15
☐ 168 Frank Lary 9.00 4.00 1.15
☐ 169 Herb Plews 8.00 3.60 1.00
☐ 170 Duke Snider 90.00 40.00 11.50
☐ 171 Boston Red Sox 15.00 6.75 1.90
Team Card
☐ 172 Gene Woodling 9.00 4.00 1.15
☐ 173 Roger Craig 16.00 7.25 2.00
☐ 174 Willie Jones 8.00 3.60 1.00
☐ 175 Don Larsen 20.00 9.00 2.50
☐ 176A Gene Baker ERR .. 350.00 160.00 45.00
(Misspelled Bakep
on card back)
☐ 176B Gene Baker COR 8.00 3.60 1.00
☐ 177 Eddie Yost 8.00 3.60 1.00
☐ 178 Don Bessent .... 7.00 3.10 .85
☐ 179 Ernie Oravetz .... 7.00 3.10 .85
☐ 180 Gus Bell 8.00 3.60 1.00
☐ 181 Dick Donovan .... 7.00 3.10 .85
☐ 182 Hobie Landrith .... 7.00 3.10 .85
☐ 183 Chicago Cubs 15.00 6.75 1.90
Team Card
☐ 184 Tito Francona .... 7.00 3.10 .85
☐ 185 Johnny Kucks .... 7.00 3.10 .85
☐ 186 Jim King .... 7.00 3.10 .85
☐ 187 Virgil Trucks 8.00 3.60 1.00
☐ 188 Felix Mantilla .... 7.00 3.10 .85
☐ 189 Willard Nixon .... 7.00 3.10 .85
☐ 190 Randy Jackson .... 7.00 3.10 .85
☐ 191 Joe Margoneri .... 7.00 3.10 .85
☐ 192 Jerry Coleman 8.00 3.60 1.00
☐ 193 Del Rice .... 7.00 3.10 .85
☐ 194 Hal Brown .... 7.00 3.10 .85
☐ 195 Bobby Avila .... 7.00 3.10 .85
☐ 196 Larry Jackson 8.00 3.60 1.00
☐ 197 Hank Sauer 8.00 3.60 1.00
☐ 198 Detroit Tigers 15.00 6.75 1.90
Team Card
☐ 199 Vern Law 8.00 3.60 1.00
☐ 200 Gil McDougald 16.00 7.25 2.00
☐ 201 Sandy Amoros 9.00 4.00 1.15
☐ 202 Dick Gernert .... 7.00 3.10 .85
☐ 203 Hoyt Wilhelm 20.00 9.00 2.50
☐ 204 Kansas City Athletics 15.00 6.75 1.90
Team Card
☐ 205 Charlie Maxwell 8.00 3.60 1.00
☐ 206 Willard Schmidt .... 7.00 3.10 .85
☐ 207 Gordon(Billy) Hunter.. 7.00 3.10 .85
☐ 208 Lou Burdette .... 7.00 3.10 .85
☐ 209 Bob Skinner 8.00 3.60 1.00
☐ 210 Roy Campanella 125.00 57.50 15.50
☐ 211 Camilo Pascual 8.00 3.60 1.00
☐ 212 Rocky Colavito 150.00 70.00 19.00
☐ 213 Les Moss .... 7.00 3.10 .85
☐ 214 Philadelphia Phillies. 15.00 6.75 1.90
Team Card
☐ 215 Enos Slaughter 25.00 11.50 3.10
☐ 216 Marv Grissom .... 7.00 3.10 .85
☐ 217 Gene Stephens .... 7.00 3.10 .85
☐ 218 Ray Jablonski .... 7.00 3.10 .85
☐ 219 Tom Acker .... 7.00 3.10 .85
☐ 220 Jackie Jensen 10.00 4.50 1.25
☐ 221 Dixie Howell .... 7.00 3.10 .85
☐ 222 Alex Grammas .... 7.00 3.10 .85
☐ 223 Frank House .... 7.00 3.10 .85
☐ 224 Marv Blaylock .... 7.00 3.10 .85
☐ 225 Harry Simpson .... 7.00 3.10 .85
☐ 226 Preston Ward .... 7.00 3.10 .85
☐ 227 Gerry Staley .... 7.00 3.10 .85
☐ 228 Smoky Burgess UER.. 8.00 3.60 1.00
(Misspelled Smokey
on card back)
☐ 229 George Susce .... 7.00 3.10 .85
☐ 230 George Kell 20.00 9.00 2.50
☐ 231 Solly Hemus .... 7.00 3.10 .85
☐ 232 Whitey Lockman 8.00 3.60 1.00
☐ 233 Art Fowler .... 7.00 3.10 .85
☐ 234 Dick Cole .... 7.00 3.10 .85
☐ 235 Tom Poholsky .... 7.00 3.10 .85
☐ 236 Joe Ginsberg .... 7.00 3.10 .85
☐ 237 Foster Castleman .... 7.00 3.10 .85

☐ 238 Eddie Robinson.......... 7.00 3.10 .85
☐ 239 Tom Morgan.......... 7.00 3.10 .85
☐ 240 Hank Bauer.......... 16.00 7.25 2.00
☐ 241 Joe Lonnett.......... 7.00 3.10 .85
☐ 242 Charlie Neal.......... 8.00 3.60 1.00
☐ 243 St. Louis Cardinals... 15.00 6.75 1.90
Team Card
☐ 244 Billy Loes.......... 8.00 3.60 1.00
☐ 245 Rip Repulski.......... 7.00 3.10 .85
☐ 246 Jose Valdivielso.......... 7.00 3.10 .85
☐ 247 Turk Lown.......... 7.00 3.10 .85
☐ 248 Jim Finigan.......... 7.00 3.10 .85
☐ 249 Dave Pope.......... 7.00 3.10 .85
☐ 250 Eddie Mathews.......... 38.00 17.00 4.70
☐ 251 Baltimore Orioles..... 15.00 6.75 1.90
Team Card
☐ 252 Carl Erskine.......... 12.00 5.50 1.50
☐ 253 Gus Zernial.......... 8.00 3.60 1.00
☐ 254 Ron Negray.......... 7.00 3.10 .85
☐ 255 Charlie Silvera.......... 8.00 3.60 1.00
☐ 256 Ron Kline.......... 7.00 3.10 .85
☐ 257 Walt Dropo.......... 7.00 3.10 .85
☐ 258 Steve Gromek.......... 7.00 3.10 .85
☐ 259 Eddie O'Brien.......... 7.00 3.10 .85
☐ 260 Del Ennis.......... 8.00 3.60 1.00
☐ 261 Bob Chakales.......... 7.00 3.10 .85
☐ 262 Bobby Thomson...... 12.00 5.50 1.50
☐ 263 George Strickland...... 7.00 3.10 .85
☐ 264 Bob Turley.......... 15.00 6.75 1.90
☐ 265 Harvey Haddix DP.... 14.00 6.25 1.75
☐ 266 Ken Kuhn DP.......... 13.00 5.75 1.65
☐ 267 Danny Kravitz.......... 20.00 9.00 2.50
☐ 268 Jack Collum.......... 20.00 9.00 2.50
☐ 269 Bob Cerv.......... 22.00 10.00 2.80
☐ 270 Washington Senators 60.00 27.00 7.50
Team Card
☐ 271 Danny O'Connell DP 13.00 5.75 1.65
☐ 272 Bobby Shantz.......... 25.00 11.50 3.10
☐ 273 Jim Davis.......... 20.00 9.00 2.50
☐ 274 Don Hoak.......... 22.00 10.00 2.80
☐ 275 Cleveland Indians..... 60.00 27.00 7.50
Team Card UER
(Text on back credits Tribe
with winning AL title in '28.
The Yankees won that year.)
☐ 276 Jim Pyburn.......... 20.00 9.00 2.50
☐ 277 Johnny Podres DP... 45.00 20.00 5.75
☐ 278 Fred Hatfield DP....... 13.00 5.75 1.65
☐ 279 Bob Thurman.......... 20.00 9.00 2.50
☐ 280 Alex Kellner.......... 20.00 9.00 2.50
☐ 281 Gail Harris.......... 20.00 9.00 2.50
☐ 282 Jack Dittmer DP....... 13.00 5.75 1.65
☐ 283 Wes Covington DP... 15.00 6.75 1.90
☐ 284 Don Zimmer.......... 25.00 11.50 3.10
☐ 285 Ned Garver.......... 20.00 9.00 2.50
☐ 286 Bobby Richardson . 125.00 57.50 15.50
☐ 287 Sam Jones.......... 22.00 10.00 2.80
☐ 288 Ted Lepcio.......... 20.00 9.00 2.50
☐ 289 Jim Bolger DP.......... 13.00 5.75 1.65
☐ 290 Andy Carey DP.......... 15.00 6.75 1.90
☐ 291 Windy McCall.......... 20.00 9.00 2.50
☐ 292 Billy Klaus.......... 20.00 9.00 2.50
☐ 293 Ted Abernathy.......... 20.00 9.00 2.50
☐ 294 Rocky Bridges DP.... 13.00 5.75 1.65
☐ 295 Joe Collins DP.......... 15.00 6.75 1.90
☐ 296 Johnny Klippstein.... 20.00 9.00 2.50
☐ 297 Jack Crimian.......... 20.00 9.00 2.50
☐ 298 Irv Noren DP.......... 13.00 5.75 1.65
☐ 299 Chuck Harmon.......... 20.00 9.00 2.50
☐ 300 Mike Garcia.......... 22.00 10.00 2.80
☐ 301 Sammy Esposito DP 13.00 5.75 1.65
☐ 302 Sandy Koufax DP... 275.00 125.00 34.00
☐ 303 Billy Goodman.......... 22.00 10.00 2.80
☐ 304 Joe Cunningham...... 22.00 10.00 2.80
☐ 305 Chico Fernandez...... 20.00 9.00 2.50
☐ 306 Darrell Johnson DP.. 15.00 6.75 1.90
☐ 307 Jack D. Phillips DP... 13.00 5.75 1.65
☐ 308 Dick Hall.......... 20.00 9.00 2.50
☐ 309 Jim Busby DP.......... 13.00 5.75 1.65
☐ 310 Max Surkont DP....... 13.00 5.75 1.65
☐ 311 Al Pilarcik DP.......... 13.00 5.75 1.65
☐ 312 Tony Kubek DP.......... 80.00 36.00 10.00
☐ 313 Mel Parnell.......... 22.00 10.00 2.80
☐ 314 Ed Bouchee DP.......... 13.00 5.75 1.65
☐ 315 Lou Berberet DP...... 13.00 5.75 1.65
☐ 316 Billy O'Dell.......... 20.00 9.00 2.50
☐ 317 New York Giants...... 70.00 32.00 8.75
Team Card
☐ 318 Mickey McDermott.. 20.00 9.00 2.50
☐ 319 Gino Cimoli.......... 20.00 9.00 2.50
☐ 320 Neil Chrisley.......... 20.00 9.00 2.50
☐ 321 John(Red) Murff...... 20.00 9.00 2.50
☐ 322 Cincinnati Reds........ 70.00 32.00 8.75
Team Card
☐ 323 Wes Westrum.......... 22.00 10.00 2.80
☐ 324 Brooklyn Dodgers.. 125.00 57.50 15.50
Team Card
☐ 325 Frank Bolling.......... 20.00 9.00 2.50
☐ 326 Pedro Ramos.......... 20.00 9.00 2.50
☐ 327 Jim Pendleton.......... 20.00 9.00 2.50
☐ 328 Brooks Robinson... 350.00 160.00 45.00
☐ 329 Chicago White Sox... 60.00 27.00 7.50
Team Card
☐ 330 Jim Wilson.......... 20.00 9.00 2.50
☐ 331 Ray Katt.......... 20.00 9.00 2.50
☐ 332 Bob Bowman.......... 20.00 9.00 2.50
☐ 333 Ernie Johnson.......... 22.00 10.00 2.80
☐ 334 Jerry Schoonmaker.. 20.00 9.00 2.50
☐ 335 Granny Hamner........ 20.00 9.00 2.50
☐ 336 Haywood Sullivan.... 20.00 9.00 2.50
☐ 337 Rene Valdes.......... 20.00 9.00 2.50
☐ 338 Jim Bunning.......... 135.00 60.00 17.00
☐ 339 Bob Speake.......... 20.00 9.00 2.50
☐ 340 Bill Wight.......... 20.00 9.00 2.50
☐ 341 Don Gross.......... 20.00 9.00 2.50
☐ 342 Gene Mauch.......... 22.00 10.00 2.80
☐ 343 Taylor Phillips.......... 20.00 9.00 2.50
☐ 344 Paul LaPalme.......... 20.00 9.00 2.50
☐ 345 Paul Smith.......... 20.00 9.00 2.50
☐ 346 Dick Littlefield.......... 20.00 9.00 2.50
☐ 347 Hal Naragon.......... 20.00 9.00 2.50
☐ 348 Jim Hearn.......... 20.00 9.00 2.50
☐ 349 Nellie King.......... 20.00 9.00 2.50
☐ 350 Eddie Miksis.......... 20.00 9.00 2.50
☐ 351 Dave Hillman.......... 20.00 9.00 2.50
☐ 352 Ellis Kinder.......... 20.00 9.00 2.50
☐ 353 Cal Neeman.......... 8.00 3.60 1.00
☐ 354 W. (Rip) Coleman...... 8.00 3.60 1.00
☐ 355 Frank Malzone.......... 9.00 4.00 1.15
☐ 356 Faye Throneberry....... 8.00 3.60 1.00
☐ 357 Earl Torgeson.......... 8.00 3.60 1.00
☐ 358 Jerry Lynch.......... 9.00 4.00 1.15
☐ 359 Tom Cheney.......... 9.00 4.00 1.15
☐ 360 Johnny Groth.......... 8.00 3.60 1.00
☐ 361 Curt Barclay.......... 8.00 3.60 1.00
☐ 362 Roman Mejias.......... 9.00 4.00 1.15
☐ 363 Eddie Kasko.......... 8.00 3.60 1.00
☐ 364 Cal McLish.......... 9.00 4.00 1.15
☐ 365 Ozzie Virgil.......... 8.00 3.60 1.00
☐ 366 Ken Lehman.......... 8.00 3.60 1.00
☐ 367 Ed Fitzgerald.......... 8.00 3.60 1.00
☐ 368 Bob Purkey.......... 8.00 3.60 1.00
☐ 369 Milt Graff.......... 8.00 3.60 1.00
☐ 370 Warren Hacker.......... 8.00 3.60 1.00
☐ 371 Bob Lennon.......... 8.00 3.60 1.00
☐ 372 Norm Zauchin.......... 8.00 3.60 1.00

Card			
☐ 373 Pete Whisenant	8.00	3.60	1.00
☐ 374 Don Cardwell	8.00	3.60	1.00
☐ 375 Jim Landis	9.00	4.00	1.15
☐ 376 Don Elston	8.00	3.60	1.00
☐ 377 Andre Rodgers	8.00	3.60	1.00
☐ 378 Elmer Singleton	8.00	3.60	1.00
☐ 379 Don Lee	8.00	3.60	1.00
☐ 380 Walker Cooper	8.00	3.60	1.00
☐ 381 Dean Stone	8.00	3.60	1.00
☐ 382 Jim Brideweser	8.00	3.60	1.00
☐ 383 Juan Pizarro	8.00	3.60	1.00
☐ 384 Bobby G. Smith	8.00	3.60	1.00
☐ 385 Art Houtteman	8.00	3.60	1.00
☐ 386 Lyle Luttrell	8.00	3.60	1.00
☐ 387 Jack Sanford	11.00	4.90	1.40
☐ 388 Pete Daley	8.00	3.60	1.00
☐ 389 Dave Jolly	8.00	3.60	1.00
☐ 390 Reno Bertoia	8.00	3.60	1.00
☐ 391 Ralph Terry	11.00	4.90	1.40
☐ 392 Chuck Tanner	9.00	4.00	1.15
☐ 393 Raul Sanchez	8.00	3.60	1.00
☐ 394 Luis Arroyo	9.00	4.00	1.15
☐ 395 Bubba Phillips	8.00	3.60	1.00
☐ 396 Casey Wise	8.00	3.60	1.00
☐ 397 Roy Smalley	8.00	3.60	1.00
☐ 398 Al Cicotte	9.00	4.00	1.15
☐ 399 Billy Consolo	8.00	3.60	1.00
☐ 400 Dodgers' Sluggers	250.00	115.00	31.00
Carl Furillo			
Gil Hodges			
Roy Campanella			
Duke Snider			
☐ 401 Earl Battey	14.00	6.25	1.75
☐ 402 Jim Pisoni	8.00	3.60	1.00
☐ 403 Dick Hyde	8.00	3.60	1.00
☐ 404 Harry Anderson	8.00	3.60	1.00
☐ 405 Duke Maas	8.00	3.60	1.00
☐ 406 Bob Hale	8.00	3.60	1.00
☐ 407 Yankee Power Hitters	450.00	135.00	45.00
Mickey Mantle			
Yogi Berra			
☐ NNO1 Checklist 1/2	250.00	38.00	12.50
☐ NNO2 Checklist 2/3	400.00	60.00	20.00
☐ NNO3 Checklist 3/4	750.00	115.00	38.00
☐ NNO4 Checklist 4/5	900.00	135.00	45.00
☐ NNO5 Saturday, May 4th	40.00	10.00	3.00
Boston Red Sox			
vs. Cincinnati Redlegs			
Cleveland Indians			
vs. New York Giants			
☐ NNO6 Sat., May 25th	50.00	12.50	4.00
☐ NNO7 Sat., June 22nd	70.00	17.50	5.75
Brooklyn Dodgers			
vs. Chicago White Sox			
St. Louis Cardinals			
vs. New York Yankees			
☐ NNO8 Sat., July 19th	80.00	20.00	6.50
Milwaukee Braves			
vs. New York Giants			
Baltimore Orioles			
vs. Kansas City Athletics			
☐ NNO9 Lucky Penny	40.00	10.00	3.00
Charm and Key Chain offer card			

1958 Topps

The cards in this 494-card set measure 2 1/2" by 3 1/2". Although the last card is numbered 495, number 145 was not issued, bringing the set total to 494 cards. The 1958 Topps set contains the first Sport Magazine All-Star Selection series (475-495) and expanded use of combination cards. The team cards carried series checklists on back (Milwaukee, Detroit, Baltimore, and Cincinnati are also found with players listed alphabetically). Cards with the scarce yellow name (YL) or team (YT) lettering, as opposed to the common white lettering, are noted in the checklist. In the last series, cards of Stan Musial and Mickey Mantle were triple printed; the cards they replaced (443, 446, 450, and 462) on the printing sheet were hence printed in shorter supply than other cards in the last series and are marked with an SP in the list below. Technically the New York Giants team card (19) is an error as the Giants had already moved to San Francisco. The key Rookie Cards in this set are Orlando Cepeda, Curt Flood, Roger Maris, and Vada Pinson.

	NRMT	VG-E	GOOD
COMPLETE SET (494)	5000.00	2300.00	650.00
COMMON CARD (1-110)	10.00	4.50	1.25
COMMON CARD (111-198)	7.00	3.10	.85
COMMON CARD (199-352)	5.50	2.50	.70
COMMON CARD (353-440)	5.00	2.30	.60
COMMON CARD (441-474)	4.00	1.80	.50
COMMON AS (475-495)	5.00	2.30	.60

Card	NRMT	VG-E	GOOD
☐ 1 Ted Williams	400.00	120.00	40.00
☐ 2A Bob Lemon	28.00	12.50	3.50
☐ 2B Bob Lemon YT	60.00	27.00	7.50
☐ 3 Alex Kellner	10.00	4.50	1.25
☐ 4 Hank Foiles	10.00	4.50	1.25
☐ 5 Willie Mays	225.00	100.00	28.00
☐ 6 George Zuverink	10.00	4.50	1.25
☐ 7 Dale Long	11.00	4.90	1.40
☐ 8A Eddie Kasko	10.00	4.50	1.25
☐ 8B Eddie Kasko YL	45.00	20.00	5.75
☐ 9 Hank Bauer	15.00	6.75	1.90
☐ 10 Lou Burdette	11.00	4.90	1.40
☐ 11A Jim Rivera	10.00	4.50	1.25
☐ 11B Jim Rivera YT	40.00	18.00	5.00
☐ 12 George Crowe	10.00	4.50	1.25
☐ 13A Billy Hoeft	10.00	4.50	1.25
☐ 13B Billy Hoeft YL	45.00	20.00	5.75
☐ 14 Rip Repulski	10.00	4.50	1.25
☐ 15 Jim Lemon	11.00	4.90	1.40
☐ 16 Charlie Neal	11.00	4.90	1.40
☐ 17 Felix Mantilla	10.00	4.50	1.25
☐ 18 Frank Sullivan	10.00	4.50	1.25
☐ 19 New York Giants Team Card	35.00	16.00	4.40

(Checklist on back)			
☐ 20A Gil McDougald	16.00	7.25	2.00
☐ 20B Gil McDougald YL	55.00	25.00	7.00
☐ 21 Curt Barclay	10.00	4.50	1.25
☐ 22 Hal Naragon	10.00	4.50	1.25
☐ 23A Bill Tuttle	10.00	4.50	1.25
☐ 23B Bill Tuttle YL	45.00	20.00	5.75
☐ 24A Hobie Landrith	10.00	4.50	1.25
☐ 24B Hobie Landrith YL	45.00	20.00	5.75
☐ 25 Don Drysdale	70.00	32.00	8.75
☐ 26 Ron Jackson	10.00	4.50	1.25
☐ 27 Bud Freeman	10.00	4.50	1.25
☐ 28 Jim Busby	10.00	4.50	1.25
☐ 29 Ted Lepcio	10.00	4.50	1.25
☐ 30A Hank Aaron	225.00	100.00	28.00
☐ 30B Hank Aaron YL	425.00	190.00	52.50
☐ 31 Tex Clevenger	10.00	4.50	1.25
☐ 32A J.W. Porter	10.00	4.50	1.25
☐ 32B J.W. Porter YL	45.00	20.00	5.75
☐ 33A Cal Neeman	10.00	4.50	1.25
☐ 33B Cal Neeman YT	40.00	18.00	5.00
☐ 34 Bob Thurman	10.00	4.50	1.25
☐ 35A Don Mossi	11.00	4.90	1.40
☐ 35B Don Mossi YT	40.00	18.00	5.00
☐ 36 Ted Kazanski	10.00	4.50	1.25
☐ 37 Mike McCormick UER (Photo actually Ray Monzant)	12.00	5.50	1.50
☐ 38 Dick Gernert	10.00	4.50	1.25
☐ 39 Bob Martyn	10.00	4.50	1.25
☐ 40 George Kell	16.00	7.25	2.00
☐ 41 Dave Hillman	10.00	4.50	1.25
☐ 42 John Roseboro	20.00	9.00	2.50
☐ 43 Sal Maglie	11.00	4.90	1.40
☐ 44 Washington Senators Team Card (Checklist on back)	20.00	9.00	2.50
☐ 45 Dick Groat	11.00	4.90	1.40
☐ 46A Lou Sleater	10.00	4.50	1.25
☐ 46B Lou Sleater YL	45.00	20.00	5.75
☐ 47 Roger Maris	450.00	200.00	57.50
☐ 48 Chuck Harmon	10.00	4.50	1.25
☐ 49 Smoky Burgess	11.00	4.90	1.40
☐ 50A Billy Pierce	11.00	4.90	1.40
☐ 50B Billy Pierce YT	45.00	20.00	5.75
☐ 51 Del Rice	10.00	4.50	1.25
☐ 52A Bob Clemente	225.00	100.00	28.00
☐ 52B Bob Clemente YT	425.00	190.00	52.50
☐ 53A Morrie Martin	10.00	4.50	1.25
☐ 53B Morrie Martin YL	45.00	20.00	5.75
☐ 54 Norm Siebern	10.00	4.50	1.25
☐ 55 Chico Carrasquel	10.00	4.50	1.25
☐ 56 Bill Fischer	10.00	4.50	1.25
☐ 57A Tim Thompson	10.00	4.50	1.25
☐ 57B Tim Thompson YL	45.00	20.00	5.75
☐ 58A Art Schult	10.00	4.50	1.25
☐ 58B Art Schult YT	40.00	18.00	5.00
☐ 59 Dave Sisler	10.00	4.50	1.25
☐ 60A Del Ennis	11.00	4.90	1.40
☐ 60B Del Ennis YL	45.00	20.00	5.75
☐ 61A Darrell Johnson	11.00	4.90	1.40
☐ 61B Darrell Johnson YL	45.00	20.00	5.75
☐ 62 Joe DeMaestri	10.00	4.50	1.25
☐ 63 Joe Nuxhall	11.00	4.90	1.40
☐ 64 Joe Lonnett	10.00	4.50	1.25
☐ 65A Von McDaniel	10.00	4.50	1.25
☐ 65B Von McDaniel YL	45.00	20.00	5.75
☐ 66 Lee Walls	10.00	4.50	1.25
☐ 67 Joe Ginsberg	10.00	4.50	1.25
☐ 68 Daryl Spencer	10.00	4.50	1.25
☐ 69 Wally Burnette	10.00	4.50	1.25
☐ 70A Al Kaline	85.00	38.00	10.50
☐ 70B Al Kaline YL	175.00	80.00	22.00
☐ 71 Dodgers Team (Checklist on back)	50.00	23.00	6.25
☐ 72 Bud Byerly	10.00	4.50	1.25
☐ 73 Pete Daley	10.00	4.50	1.25
☐ 74 Roy Face	11.00	4.90	1.40
☐ 75 Gus Bell	11.00	4.90	1.40
☐ 76A Dick Farrell	11.00	4.90	1.40
☐ 76B Dick Farrell YT	40.00	18.00	5.00
☐ 77A Don Zimmer	10.00	4.50	1.25
☐ 77B Don Zimmer YT	40.00	18.00	5.00
☐ 78A Ernie Johnson	11.00	4.90	1.40
☐ 78B Ernie Johnson YL	45.00	20.00	5.75
☐ 79A Dick Williams	10.00	4.50	1.25
☐ 79B Dick Williams YT	40.00	18.00	5.00
☐ 80 Dick Drott	10.00	4.50	1.25
☐ 81A Steve Boros	10.00	4.50	1.25
☐ 81B Steve Boros YT	40.00	18.00	5.00
☐ 82 Ron Kline	10.00	4.50	1.25
☐ 83 Bob Hazle	12.00	5.50	1.50
☐ 84 Billy O'Dell	10.00	4.50	1.25
☐ 85A Luis Aparicio	30.00	13.50	3.80
☐ 85B Luis Aparicio YT	70.00	32.00	8.75
☐ 86 Valmy Thomas	10.00	4.50	1.25
☐ 87 Johnny Kucks	10.00	4.50	1.25
☐ 88 Duke Snider	70.00	32.00	8.75
☐ 89 Billy Klaus	10.00	4.50	1.25
☐ 90 Robin Roberts	27.00	12.00	3.40
☐ 91 Chuck Tanner	11.00	4.90	1.40
☐ 92A Clint Courtney	10.00	4.50	1.25
☐ 92B Clint Courtney YL	45.00	20.00	5.75
☐ 93 Sandy Amoros	11.00	4.90	1.40
☐ 94 Bob Skinner	11.00	4.90	1.40
☐ 95 Frank Bolling	10.00	4.50	1.25
☐ 96 Joe Durham	10.00	4.50	1.25
☐ 97A Larry Jackson	11.00	4.90	1.40
☐ 97B Larry Jackson YL	45.00	20.00	5.75
☐ 98A Billy Hunter	10.00	4.50	1.25
☐ 98B Billy Hunter YL	45.00	20.00	5.75
☐ 99 Bobby Adams	10.00	4.50	1.25
☐ 100A Early Wynn	24.00	11.00	3.00
☐ 100B Early Wynn YT	60.00	27.00	7.50
☐ 101A Bobby Richardson	20.00	9.00	2.50
☐ 101B Bobby RichardsonYL	60.00	27.00	7.50
☐ 102 George Strickland	10.00	4.50	1.25
☐ 103 Jerry Lynch	11.00	4.90	1.40
☐ 104 Jim Pendleton	10.00	4.50	1.25
☐ 105 Billy Gardner	10.00	4.50	1.25
☐ 106 Dick Schofield	11.00	4.90	1.40
☐ 107 Ossie Virgil	10.00	4.50	1.25
☐ 108A Jim Landis	10.00	4.50	1.25
☐ 108B Jim Landis YT	40.00	18.00	5.00
☐ 109 Herb Plews	10.00	4.50	1.25
☐ 110 Johnny Logan	11.00	4.90	1.40
☐ 111 Stu Miller	9.00	4.00	1.15
☐ 112 Gus Zernial	7.50	3.40	.95
☐ 113 Jerry Walker	7.00	3.10	.85
☐ 114 Irv Noren	7.50	3.40	.95
☐ 115 Jim Bunning	24.00	11.00	3.00
☐ 116 Dave Philley	7.00	3.10	.85
☐ 117 Frank Torre	7.50	3.40	.95
☐ 118 Harvey Haddix	7.50	3.40	.95
☐ 119 Harry Chiti	7.00	3.10	.85
☐ 120 Johnny Podres	9.00	4.00	1.15
☐ 121 Eddie Miksis	7.00	3.10	.85
☐ 122 Walt Moryn	7.00	3.10	.85
☐ 123 Dick Tomanek	7.00	3.10	.85
☐ 124 Bobby Usher	7.00	3.10	.85
☐ 125 Alvin Dark	7.50	3.40	.95
☐ 126 Stan Palys	7.00	3.10	.85
☐ 127 Tom Sturdivant	7.50	3.40	.95
☐ 128 Willie Kirkland	7.50	3.40	.95
☐ 129 Jim Derrington	7.00	3.10	.85
☐ 130 Jackie Jensen	10.00	4.50	1.25

☐ 131 Bob Henrich 7.00 3.10 .85
☐ 132 Vern Law 7.50 3.40 .95
☐ 133 Russ Nixon 7.00 3.10 .85
☐ 134 Philadelphia Phillies 15.00 6.75 1.90
Team Card
(Checklist on back)
☐ 135 Mike(Moe) Drabowsky 7.50 3.40 .95
☐ 136 Jim Finigan 7.00 3.10 .85
☐ 137 Russ Kemmerer 7.00 3.10 .85
☐ 138 Earl Torgeson 7.00 3.10 .85
☐ 139 George Brunet 7.00 3.10 .85
☐ 140 Wes Covington 7.50 3.40 .95
☐ 141 Ken Lehman 7.00 3.10 .85
☐ 142 Enos Slaughter 20.00 9.00 2.50
☐ 143 Billy Muffett 7.00 3.10 .85
☐ 144 Bobby Morgan 7.00 3.10 .85
☐ 145 Never issued .00 .00 .00
☐ 146 Dick Gray 7.00 3.10 .85
☐ 147 Don McMahon 7.00 3.10 .85
☐ 148 Billy Consolo 7.00 3.10 .85
☐ 149 Tom Acker 7.00 3.10 .85
☐ 150 Mickey Mantle 775.00 350.00 95.00
☐ 151 Buddy Pritchard 7.00 3.10 .85
☐ 152 Johnny Antonelli 7.50 3.40 .95
☐ 153 Les Moss 7.00 3.10 .85
☐ 154 Harry Byrd 7.00 3.10 .85
☐ 155 Hector Lopez 7.50 3.40 .95
☐ 156 Dick Hyde 7.00 3.10 .85
☐ 157 Dee Fondy 7.00 3.10 .85
☐ 158 Cleveland Indians 15.00 6.75 1.90
Team Card
(Checklist on back)
☐ 159 Taylor Phillips 7.00 3.10 .85
☐ 160 Don Hoak 7.50 3.40 .95
☐ 161 Don Larsen 15.00 6.75 1.90
☐ 162 Gil Hodges 27.00 12.00 3.40
☐ 163 Jim Wilson 7.00 3.10 .85
☐ 164 Bob Taylor 7.00 3.10 .85
☐ 165 Bob Nieman 7.00 3.10 .85
☐ 166 Danny O'Connell 7.00 3.10 .85
☐ 167 Frank Baumann 7.00 3.10 .85
☐ 168 Joe Cunningham 7.50 3.40 .95
☐ 169 Ralph Terry 7.50 3.40 .95
☐ 170 Vic Wertz 7.50 3.40 .95
☐ 171 Harry Anderson 7.00 3.10 .85
☐ 172 Don Gross 7.00 3.10 .85
☐ 173 Eddie Yost 7.50 3.40 .95
☐ 174 Athletics Team 15.00 6.75 1.90
(Checklist on back)
☐ 175 Marv Throneberry 13.00 5.75 1.65
☐ 176 Bob Buhl 7.50 3.40 .95
☐ 177 Al Smith 7.00 3.10 .85
☐ 178 Ted Kluszewski 14.00 6.25 1.75
☐ 179 Willie Miranda 7.00 3.10 .85
☐ 180 Lindy McDaniel 7.50 3.40 .95
☐ 181 Willie Jones 7.00 3.10 .85
☐ 182 Joe Caffie 7.00 3.10 .85
☐ 183 Dave Jolly 7.00 3.10 .85
☐ 184 Elvin Tappe 7.00 3.10 .85
☐ 185 Ray Boone 7.50 3.40 .95
☐ 186 Jack Meyer 7.00 3.10 .85
☐ 187 Sandy Koufax 200.00 90.00 25.00
☐ 188 Milt Bolling UER 7.00 3.10 .85
(Photo actually
Lou Berberet)
☐ 189 George Susce 7.00 3.10 .85
☐ 190 Red Schoendienst 18.00 8.00 2.30
☐ 191 Art Ceccarelli 7.00 3.10 .85
☐ 192 Milt Graff 7.00 3.10 .85
☐ 193 Jerry Lumpe 7.00 3.10 .85
☐ 194 Roger Craig 10.00 4.50 1.25
☐ 195 Whitey Lockman 7.50 3.40 .95
☐ 196 Mike Garcia 7.50 3.40 .95
☐ 197 Haywood Sullivan 7.50 3.40 .95
☐ 198 Bill Virdon 7.00 3.10 .85
☐ 199 Don Blasingame 5.50 2.50 .70
☐ 200 Bob Keegan 5.50 2.50 .70
☐ 201 Jim Bolger 5.50 2.50 .70
☐ 202 Woody Held 5.50 2.50 .70
☐ 203 Al Walker 5.50 2.50 .70
☐ 204 Leo Kiely 5.50 2.50 .70
☐ 205 Johnny Temple 6.00 2.70 .75
☐ 206 Bob Shaw 5.50 2.50 .70
☐ 207 Solly Hemus 5.50 2.50 .70
☐ 208 Cal McLish 5.50 2.50 .70
☐ 209 Bob Anderson 5.50 2.50 .70
☐ 210 Wally Moon 6.00 2.70 .75
☐ 211 Pete Burnside 5.50 2.50 .70
☐ 212 Bubba Phillips 5.50 2.50 .70
☐ 213 Red Wilson 5.50 2.50 .70
☐ 214 Willard Schmidt 5.50 2.50 .70
☐ 215 Jim Gilliam 10.00 4.50 1.25
☐ 216 St. Louis Cardinals 15.00 6.75 1.90
Team Card
(Checklist on back)
☐ 217 Jack Harshman 5.50 2.50 .70
☐ 218 Dick Rand 5.50 2.50 .70
☐ 219 Camilo Pascual 6.00 2.70 .75
☐ 220 Tom Brewer 5.50 2.50 .70
☐ 221 Jerry Kindall 5.50 2.50 .70
☐ 222 Bud Daley 5.50 2.50 .70
☐ 223 Andy Pafko 6.00 2.70 .75
☐ 224 Bob Grim 6.00 2.70 .75
☐ 225 Billy Goodman 6.00 2.70 .75
☐ 226 Bob Smith 5.50 2.50 .70
☐ 227 Gene Stephens 5.50 2.50 .70
☐ 228 Duke Maas 5.50 2.50 .70
☐ 229 Frank Zupo 5.50 2.50 .70
☐ 230 Richie Ashburn 20.00 9.00 2.50
☐ 231 Lloyd Merritt 5.50 2.50 .70
☐ 232 Reno Bertoia 5.50 2.50 .70
☐ 233 Mickey Vernon 6.00 2.70 .75
☐ 234 Carl Sawatski 5.50 2.50 .70
☐ 235 Tom Gorman 5.50 2.50 .70
☐ 236 Ed Fitzgerald 5.50 2.50 .70
☐ 237 Bill Wight 5.50 2.50 .70
☐ 238 Bill Mazeroski 20.00 9.00 2.50
☐ 239 Chuck Stobbs 5.50 2.50 .70
☐ 240 Bill Skowron 16.00 7.25 2.00
☐ 241 Dick Littlefield 5.50 2.50 .70
☐ 242 Johnny Klippstein 5.50 2.50 .70
☐ 243 Larry Raines 5.50 2.50 .70
☐ 244 Don Demeter 5.50 2.50 .70
☐ 245 Frank Lary 6.00 2.70 .75
☐ 246 New York Yankees 55.00 25.00 7.00
Team Card
(Checklist on back)
☐ 247 Casey Wise 5.50 2.50 .70
☐ 248 Herman Wehmeier 5.50 2.50 .70
☐ 249 Ray Moore 5.50 2.50 .70
☐ 250 Roy Sievers 6.00 2.70 .75
☐ 251 Warren Hacker 5.50 2.50 .70
☐ 252 Bob Trowbridge 5.50 2.50 .70
☐ 253 Don Mueller 6.00 2.70 .75
☐ 254 Alex Grammas 5.50 2.50 .70
☐ 255 Bob Turley 10.00 4.50 1.25
☐ 256 Chicago White Sox 15.00 6.75 1.90
Team Card
(Checklist on back)
☐ 257 Hal Smith 5.50 2.50 .70
☐ 258 Carl Erskine 10.00 4.50 1.25
☐ 259 Al Pilarcik 5.50 2.50 .70
☐ 260 Frank Malzone 6.00 2.70 .75
☐ 261 Turk Lown 5.50 2.50 .70
☐ 262 Johnny Groth 5.50 2.50 .70
☐ 263 Eddie Bressoud 6.00 2.70 .75

☐ 264	Jack Sanford	6.00	2.70	.75
☐ 265	Pete Runnels	6.00	2.70	.75
☐ 266	Connie Johnson	5.50	2.50	.70
☐ 267	Sherm Lollar	6.00	2.70	.75
☐ 268	Granny Hamner	5.50	2.50	.70
☐ 269	Paul Smith	5.50	2.50	.70
☐ 270	Warren Spahn	50.00	23.00	6.25
☐ 271	Billy Martin	18.00	8.00	2.30
☐ 272	Ray Crone	5.50	2.50	.70
☐ 273	Hal Smith	5.50	2.50	.70
☐ 274	Rocky Bridges	5.50	2.50	.70
☐ 275	Elston Howard	15.00	6.75	1.90
☐ 276	Bobby Avila	5.50	2.50	.70
☐ 277	Virgil Trucks	6.00	2.70	.75
☐ 278	Mack Burk	5.50	2.50	.70
☐ 279	Bob Boyd	5.50	2.50	.70
☐ 280	Jim Piersall	6.00	2.70	.75
☐ 281	Sammy Taylor	5.50	2.50	.70
☐ 282	Paul Foytack	5.50	2.50	.70
☐ 283	Ray Shearer	5.50	2.50	.70
☐ 284	Ray Katt	5.50	2.50	.70
☐ 285	Frank Robinson	100.00	45.00	12.50
☐ 286	Gino Cimoli	5.50	2.50	.70
☐ 287	Sam Jones	6.00	2.70	.75
☐ 288	Harmon Killebrew	90.00	40.00	11.50
☐ 289	Series Hurling Rivals Lou Burdette Bobby Shantz	5.50	2.50	.70
☐ 290	Dick Donovan	5.50	2.50	.70
☐ 291	Don Landrum	5.50	2.50	.70
☐ 292	Ned Garver	5.50	2.50	.70
☐ 293	Gene Freese	5.50	2.50	.70
☐ 294	Hal Jeffcoat	5.50	2.50	.70
☐ 295	Minnie Minoso	10.00	4.50	1.25
☐ 296	Ryne Duren	16.00	7.25	2.00
☐ 297	Don Buddin	5.50	2.50	.70
☐ 298	Jim Hearn	5.50	2.50	.70
☐ 299	Harry Simpson	5.50	2.50	.70
☐ 300	League Presidents Will Harridge Warren Giles	10.00	4.50	1.25
☐ 301	Randy Jackson	5.50	2.50	.70
☐ 302	Mike Baxes	5.50	2.50	.70
☐ 303	Neil Chrisley	5.50	2.50	.70
☐ 304	Tigers' Big Bats Harvey Kuenn Al Kaline	20.00	9.00	2.50
☐ 305	Clem Labine	6.00	2.70	.75
☐ 306	Whammy Douglas	5.50	2.50	.70
☐ 307	Brooks Robinson	110.00	50.00	14.00
☐ 308	Paul Giel	6.00	2.70	.75
☐ 309	Gail Harris	5.50	2.50	.70
☐ 310	Ernie Banks	100.00	45.00	12.50
☐ 311	Bob Purkey	5.50	2.50	.70
☐ 312	Boston Red Sox Team Card (Checklist on back)	15.00	6.75	1.90
☐ 313	Bob Rush	5.50	2.50	.70
☐ 314	Dodgers' Boss and Power: Duke Snider Walt Alston MG	25.00	11.50	3.10
☐ 315	Bob Friend	6.00	2.70	.75
☐ 316	Tito Francona	6.00	2.70	.75
☐ 317	Albie Pearson	6.00	2.70	.75
☐ 318	Frank House	5.50	2.50	.70
☐ 319	Lou Skizas	5.50	2.50	.70
☐ 320	Whitey Ford	42.00	19.00	5.25
☐ 321	Sluggers Supreme Ted Kluszewski Ted Williams	55.00	25.00	7.00
☐ 322	Harding Peterson	6.00	2.70	.75
☐ 323	Elmer Valo	5.50	2.50	.70
☐ 324	Hoyt Wilhelm	20.00	9.00	2.50
☐ 325	Joe Adcock	6.00	2.70	.75
☐ 326	Bob Miller	5.50	2.50	.70
☐ 327	Chicago Cubs Team Card (Checklist on back)	15.00	6.75	1.90
☐ 328	Ike Delock	5.50	2.50	.70
☐ 329	Bob Cerv	6.00	2.70	.75
☐ 330	Ed Bailey	6.00	2.70	.75
☐ 331	Pedro Ramos	5.50	2.50	.70
☐ 332	Jim King	5.50	2.50	.70
☐ 333	Andy Carey	6.00	2.70	.75
☐ 334	Mound Aces Bob Friend Billy Pierce	6.00	2.70	.75
☐ 335	Ruben Gomez	5.50	2.50	.70
☐ 336	Bert Hamric	5.50	2.50	.70
☐ 337	Hank Aguirre	5.50	2.50	.70
☐ 338	Walt Dropo	6.00	2.70	.75
☐ 339	Fred Hatfield	5.50	2.50	.70
☐ 340	Don Newcombe	10.00	4.50	1.25
☐ 341	Pittsburgh Pirates Team Card (Checklist on back)	15.00	6.75	1.90
☐ 342	Jim Brosnan	6.00	2.70	.75
☐ 343	Orlando Cepeda	100.00	45.00	12.50
☐ 344	Bob Porterfield	5.50	2.50	.70
☐ 345	Jim Hegan	6.00	2.70	.75
☐ 346	Steve Bilko	5.50	2.50	.70
☐ 347	Don Rudolph	5.50	2.50	.70
☐ 348	Chico Fernandez	5.50	2.50	.70
☐ 349	Murry Dickson	5.50	2.50	.70
☐ 350	Ken Boyer	15.00	6.75	1.90
☐ 351	Braves Fence Busters Del Crandall Eddie Mathews Hank Aaron Joe Adcock	35.00	16.00	4.40
☐ 352	Herb Score	14.00	6.25	1.75
☐ 353	Stan Lopata	5.00	2.30	.60
☐ 354	Art Ditmar	5.50	2.50	.70
☐ 355	Bill Bruton	5.50	2.50	.70
☐ 356	Bob Malkmus	5.00	2.30	.60
☐ 357	Danny McDevitt	5.00	2.30	.60
☐ 358	Gene Baker	5.00	2.30	.60
☐ 359	Billy Loes	5.50	2.50	.70
☐ 360	Roy McMillan	5.50	2.50	.70
☐ 361	Mike Fornieles	5.00	2.30	.60
☐ 362	Ray Jablonski	5.00	2.30	.60
☐ 363	Don Elston	5.00	2.30	.60
☐ 364	Earl Battey	5.00	2.30	.60
☐ 365	Tom Morgan	5.00	2.30	.60
☐ 366	Gene Green	5.00	2.30	.60
☐ 367	Jack Urban	5.00	2.30	.60
☐ 368	Rocky Colavito	50.00	23.00	6.25
☐ 369	Ralph Lumenti	5.00	2.30	.60
☐ 370	Yogi Berra	85.00	38.00	10.50
☐ 371	Marty Keough	5.00	2.30	.60
☐ 372	Don Cardwell	5.00	2.30	.60
☐ 373	Joe Pignatano	5.00	2.30	.60
☐ 374	Brooks Lawrence	5.00	2.30	.60
☐ 375	Pee Wee Reese	55.00	25.00	7.00
☐ 376	Charley Rabe	5.00	2.30	.60
☐ 377A	Milwaukee Braves Team Card (Alphabetical)	15.00	6.75	1.90
☐ 377B	Milwaukee Team numerical checklist	90.00	40.00	11.50
☐ 378	Hank Sauer	5.50	2.50	.70
☐ 379	Ray Herbert	5.00	2.30	.60
☐ 380	Charlie Maxwell	5.50	2.50	.70
☐ 381	Hal Brown	5.00	2.30	.60
☐ 382	Al Cicotte	5.00	2.30	.60
☐ 383	Lou Berberet	5.00	2.30	.60

☐ 384 John Goryl .... 5.00 2.30 .60
☐ 385 Wilmer Mizell .... 5.50 2.50 .70
☐ 386 Birdie's Sluggers 12.00 5.50 1.50
Ed Bailey
Birdie Tebbetts MG
Frank Robinson
☐ 387 Wally Post .... 5.50 2.50 .70
☐ 388 Billy Moran .... 5.00 2.30 .60
☐ 389 Bill Taylor .... 5.00 2.30 .60
☐ 390 Del Crandall .... 5.50 2.50 .70
☐ 391 Dave Melton .... 5.00 2.30 .60
☐ 392 Bennie Daniels .... 5.00 2.30 .60
☐ 393 Tony Kubek 18.00 8.00 2.30
☐ 394 Jim Grant .... 5.00 2.30 .60
☐ 395 Willard Nixon .... 5.00 2.30 .60
☐ 396 Dutch Dotterer .... 5.00 2.30 .60
☐ 397A Detroit Tigers 15.00 6.75 1.90
Team Card
(Alphabetical)
☐ 397B Detroit Team 90.00 40.00 11.50
numerical checklist
☐ 398 Gene Woodling .... 5.50 2.50 .70
☐ 399 Marv Grissom .... 5.00 2.30 .60
☐ 400 Nellie Fox 15.00 6.75 1.90
☐ 401 Don Bessent .... 5.00 2.30 .60
☐ 402 Bobby Gene Smith ..... 5.00 2.30 .60
☐ 403 Steve Korcheck .... 5.00 2.30 .60
☐ 404 Curt Simmons .... 5.50 2.50 .70
☐ 405 Ken Aspromonte .... 5.00 2.30 .60
☐ 406 Vic Power .... 5.50 2.50 .70
☐ 407 Carlton Willey .... 5.50 2.50 .70
☐ 408A Baltimore Orioles ... 15.00 6.75 1.90
Team Card
(Alphabetical)
☐ 408B Baltimore Team 90.00 40.00 11.50
numerical checklist
☐ 409 Frank Thomas .... 5.50 2.50 .70
☐ 410 Murray Wall .... 5.00 2.30 .60
☐ 411 Tony Taylor 9.00 4.00 1.15
☐ 412 Gerry Staley .... 5.00 2.30 .60
☐ 413 Jim Davenport .... 5.00 2.30 .60
☐ 414 Sammy White .... 5.00 2.30 .60
☐ 415 Bob Bowman .... 5.00 2.30 .60
☐ 416 Foster Castleman .... 5.00 2.30 .60
☐ 417 Carl Furillo 10.00 4.50 1.25
☐ 418 World Series Batting 175.00 80.00 22.00
Foes: Mickey Mantle
Hank Aaron
☐ 419 Bobby Shantz .... 5.50 2.50 .70
☐ 420 Vada Pinson 38.00 17.00 4.70
☐ 421 Dixie Howell .... 5.00 2.30 .60
☐ 422 Norm Zauchin .... 5.00 2.30 .60
☐ 423 Phil Clark .... 5.00 2.30 .60
☐ 424 Larry Doby 8.00 3.60 1.00
☐ 425 Sammy Esposito .... 5.00 2.30 .60
☐ 426 Johnny O'Brien .... 5.50 2.50 .70
☐ 427 Al Worthington .... 5.00 2.30 .60
☐ 428A Cincinnati Reds 15.00 6.75 1.90
Team Card
(Alphabetical)
☐ 428B Cincinnati Team 90.00 40.00 11.50
numerical checklist
☐ 429 Gus Triandos .... 5.50 2.50 .70
☐ 430 Bobby Thomson 8.00 3.60 1.00
☐ 431 Gene Conley .... 5.50 2.50 .70
☐ 432 John Powers .... 5.00 2.30 .60
☐ 433A Pancho Herrer ERR 650.00 300.00 80.00
☐ 433B Pancho Herrera COR 5.00 2.30 .60
☐ 434 Harvey Kuenn 8.00 3.60 1.00
☐ 435 Ed Roebuck .... 5.50 2.50 .70
☐ 436 Rival Fence Busters . 70.00 32.00 8.75
Willie Mays
Duke Snider
☐ 437 Bob Speake .... 5.00 2.30 .60
☐ 438 Whitey Herzog 9.00 4.00 1.15
☐ 439 Ray Narleski .... 5.00 2.30 .60
☐ 440 Eddie Mathews 35.00 16.00 4.40
☐ 441 Jim Marshall .... 4.50 2.00 .55
☐ 442 Phil Paine .... 4.00 1.80 .50
☐ 443 Billy Harrell SP 20.00 9.00 2.50
☐ 444 Danny Kravitz .... 4.00 1.80 .50
☐ 445 Bob Smith .... 4.00 1.80 .50
☐ 446 Carroll Hardy SP 20.00 9.00 2.50
☐ 447 Ray Monzant .... 4.00 1.80 .50
☐ 448 Charlie Lau 8.00 3.60 1.00
☐ 449 Gene Fodge .... 4.00 1.80 .50
☐ 450 Preston Ward SP 20.00 9.00 2.50
☐ 451 Joe Taylor .... 4.00 1.80 .50
☐ 452 Roman Mejias .... 4.00 1.80 .50
☐ 453 Tom Qualters .... 4.00 1.80 .50
☐ 454 Harry Hanebrink .... 4.00 1.80 .50
☐ 455 Hal Griggs .... 4.00 1.80 .50
☐ 456 Dick Brown .... 4.00 1.80 .50
☐ 457 Milt Pappas 8.00 3.60 1.00
☐ 458 Julio Becquer .... 4.00 1.80 .50
☐ 459 Ron Blackburn .... 4.00 1.80 .50
☐ 460 Chuck Essegian .... 4.00 1.80 .50
☐ 461 Ed Mayer .... 4.00 1.80 .50
☐ 462 Gary Geiger SP 20.00 9.00 2.50
☐ 463 Vito Valentinetti .... 4.00 1.80 .50
☐ 464 Curt Flood 25.00 11.50 3.10
☐ 465 Arnie Portocarrero ..... 4.00 1.80 .50
☐ 466 Pete Whisenant .... 4.00 1.80 .50
☐ 467 Glen Hobbie .... 4.00 1.80 .50
☐ 468 Bob Schmidt .... 4.00 1.80 .50
☐ 469 Don Ferrarese .... 4.00 1.80 .50
☐ 470 R.C. Stevens .... 4.00 1.80 .50
☐ 471 Lenny Green .... 4.00 1.80 .50
☐ 472 Joey Jay .... 4.50 2.00 .55
☐ 473 Bill Renna .... 4.00 1.80 .50
☐ 474 Roman Semproch ...... 4.00 1.80 .50
☐ 475 Fred Haney AS MG and 20.00 9.00 2.50
Casey Stengel AS MG
(Checklist back)
☐ 476 Stan Musial AS TP ... 40.00 18.00 5.00
☐ 477 Bill Skowron AS 9.00 4.00 1.15
☐ 478 Johnny Temple AS ..... 5.00 2.30 .60
☐ 479 Nellie Fox AS 9.00 4.00 1.15
☐ 480 Eddie Mathews AS ... 15.00 6.75 1.90
☐ 481 Frank Malzone AS ...... 5.00 2.30 .60
☐ 482 Ernie Banks AS 30.00 13.50 3.80
☐ 483 Luis Aparicio AS 16.00 7.25 2.00
☐ 484 Frank Robinson AS .. 25.00 11.50 3.10
☐ 485 Ted Williams AS 100.00 45.00 12.50
☐ 486 Willie Mays AS 50.00 23.00 6.25
☐ 487 Mickey Mantle AS TP 125.00 57.50 15.50
☐ 488 Hank Aaron AS 50.00 23.00 6.25
☐ 489 Jackie Jensen AS .... 5.50 2.50 .70
☐ 490 Ed Bailey AS .... 5.00 2.30 .60
☐ 491 Sherm Lollar AS .... 5.00 2.30 .60
☐ 492 Bob Friend AS .... 5.00 2.30 .60
☐ 493 Bob Turley AS .... 5.50 2.50 .70
☐ 494 Warren Spahn AS 20.00 9.00 2.50
☐ 495 Herb Score AS .... 15.00 3.00 .90
☐ xx Contest Cards 30.00 7.25 2.40

1959 Topps

The cards in this 572-card set measure 2 1/2" by 3 1/2". The 1959 Topps set contains bust pictures of the players in a colored circle. Card numbers 551 to 572 are Sporting News All-Star Selections. High numbers 507 to 572 have the card number

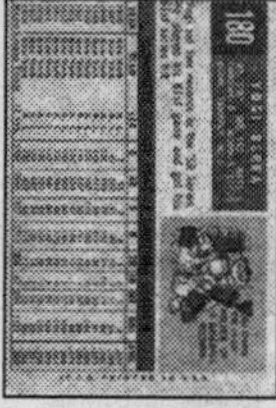

in a black background on the reverse rather than a green background as in the lower numbers. The high numbers are more difficult to obtain. Several cards in the 300s exist with or without an extra traded or option line on the back of the card. Cards 199 to 286 exist with either white or gray backs. Cards 461 to 470 contain "Highlights" while cards 116 to 146 give an alphabetically ordered listing of "Rookie Prospects." These Rookie Prospects (RP) were Topps' first organized inclusion of untested "Rookie" cards. Card 440 features Lew Burdette erroneously posing as a left-handed pitcher. There were some three-card advertising panels produced by Topps; the players included are from the first series. One advertising panel shows Don McMahon, Red Wilson and Bob Boyd on the front with Ted Kluszewski's card back on the back of the panel. Other panels are: Joe Pignatano, Sam Jones and Jack Urban also with Kluszewski's card back on back, Billy Hunter, Chuck Stobbs and Carl Sawatski on the front with the back of Nellie Fox's card on the back, Vito Valentinetti, Ken Lehman and Ed Bouchee on the front with Fox's card back on back and Mel Roach, Brooks Lawrence and Warren Spahn also with Fox on back. When separated, these advertising cards are distinguished by the non-standard card back, i.e., part of an advertisement for the 1959 Topps set instead of the typical statistics and biographical information about the player pictured. The key Rookie Cards in this set are Felipe Alou, Sparky Anderson, Bob Gibson, and Bill White.

	NRMT	VG-E	GOOD
COMPLETE SET (572)	4500.00	2000.00	575.00
COMMON CARD (1-110)	5.00	2.30	.60
COMMON CARD (111-198)	4.00	1.80	.50
COMMON CARD (199-286)	4.00	1.80	.50
COMMON CARD (287-506)	4.00	1.80	.50
COMMON CARD (507-550)	15.00	6.75	1.90
COMMON AS (551-572)	15.00	6.75	1.90

	NRMT	VG-E	GOOD
☐ 1 Ford Frick COMM	55.00	11.00	3.30
☐ 2 Eddie Yost	6.00	2.70	.75
☐ 3 Don McMahon	6.00	2.70	.75
☐ 4 Albie Pearson	6.00	2.70	.75
☐ 5 Dick Donovan	6.00	2.70	.75
☐ 6 Alex Grammas	5.00	2.30	.60
☐ 7 Al Pilarcik	5.00	2.30	.60
☐ 8 Phillies Team (Checklist on back)	60.00	12.00	3.60
☐ 9 Paul Giel	6.00	2.70	.75
☐ 10 Mickey Mantle	550.00	250.00	70.00
☐ 11 Billy Hunter	8.50	3.80	1.05
☐ 12 Vern Law	9.00	4.00	1.15
☐ 13 Dick Gernert	5.00	2.30	.60
☐ 14 Pete Whisenant	5.00	2.30	.60
☐ 15 Dick Drott	5.00	2.30	.60
☐ 16 Joe Pignatano	5.00	2.30	.60
☐ 17 Danny's Stars Frank Thomas Danny Murtaugh MG Ted Kluszewski	6.00	2.70	.75
☐ 18 Jack Urban	5.00	2.30	.60
☐ 19 Eddie Bressoud	5.00	2.30	.60
☐ 20 Duke Snider	50.00	23.00	6.25
☐ 21 Connie Johnson	5.00	2.30	.60
☐ 22 Al Smith	6.00	2.70	.75
☐ 23 Murry Dickson	6.00	2.70	.75
☐ 24 Red Wilson	5.00	2.30	.60
☐ 25 Don Hoak	6.00	2.70	.75
☐ 26 Chuck Stobbs	5.00	2.30	.60
☐ 27 Andy Pafko	6.00	2.70	.75
☐ 28 Al Worthington	5.00	2.30	.60
☐ 29 Jim Bolger	5.00	2.30	.60
☐ 30 Nellie Fox	15.00	6.75	1.90
☐ 31 Ken Lehman	5.00	2.30	.60
☐ 32 Don Buddin	5.00	2.30	.60
☐ 33 Ed Fitzgerald	5.00	2.30	.60
☐ 34 Pitchers Beware Al Kaline Charley Maxwell	15.00	6.75	1.90
☐ 35 Ted Kluszewski	15.00	6.75	1.90
☐ 36 Hank Aguirre	5.00	2.30	.60
☐ 37 Gene Green	5.00	2.30	.60
☐ 38 Morrie Martin	5.00	2.30	.60
☐ 39 Ed Bouchee	5.00	2.30	.60
☐ 40A Warren Spahn ERR (Born 1931)	85.00	38.00	10.50
☐ 40B Warren Spahn ERR (Born 1931, but three is partially obscured)	110.00	50.00	14.00
☐ 40C Warren Spahn COR (Born 1921)	55.00	25.00	7.00
☐ 41 Bob Martyn	5.00	2.30	.60
☐ 42 Murray Wall	5.00	2.30	.60
☐ 43 Steve Bilko	5.00	2.30	.60
☐ 44 Vito Valentinetti	5.00	2.30	.60
☐ 45 Andy Carey	6.00	2.70	.75
☐ 46 Bill R. Henry	5.00	2.30	.60
☐ 47 Jim Finigan	5.00	2.30	.60
☐ 48 Orioles Team (Checklist on back)	24.00	4.80	1.45
☐ 49 Bill Hall	5.00	2.30	.60
☐ 50 Willie Mays	150.00	70.00	19.00
☐ 51 Rip Coleman	5.00	2.30	.60
☐ 52 Coot Veal	5.00	2.30	.60
☐ 53 Stan Williams	10.00	4.50	1.25
☐ 54 Mel Roach	5.00	2.30	.60
☐ 55 Tom Brewer	5.00	2.30	.60
☐ 56 Carl Sawatski	5.00	2.30	.60
☐ 57 Al Cicotte	5.00	2.30	.60
☐ 58 Eddie Miksis	5.00	2.30	.60
☐ 59 Irv Noren	6.00	2.70	.75
☐ 60 Bob Turley	10.00	4.50	1.25
☐ 61 Dick Brown	5.00	2.30	.60
☐ 62 Tony Taylor	6.00	2.70	.75
☐ 63 Jim Hearn	5.00	2.30	.60
☐ 64 Joe DeMaestri	5.00	2.30	.60
☐ 65 Frank Torre	6.00	2.70	.75
☐ 66 Joe Ginsberg	5.00	2.30	.60
☐ 67 Brooks Lawrence	5.00	2.30	.60
☐ 68 Dick Schofield	6.00	2.70	.75
☐ 69 Giants Team (Checklist on back)	24.00	4.80	1.45
☐ 70 Harvey Kuenn	10.00	4.50	1.25

- ☐ 71 Don Bessent .... 5.00 2.30 .60
- ☐ 72 Bill Renna .... 5.00 2.30 .60
- ☐ 73 Ron Jackson .... 6.00 2.70 .75
- ☐ 74 Directing Power .... 6.00 2.70 .75
  Jim Lemon
  Cookie Lavagetto MG
  Roy Sievers
- ☐ 75 Sam Jones .... 6.00 2.70 .75
- ☐ 76 Bobby Richardson 20.00 9.00 2.50
- ☐ 77 John Goryl .... 5.00 2.30 .60
- ☐ 78 Pedro Ramos .... 5.00 2.30 .60
- ☐ 79 Harry Chiti .... 5.00 2.30 .60
- ☐ 80 Minnie Minoso 10.00 4.50 1.25
- ☐ 81 Hal Jeffcoat .... 5.00 2.30 .60
- ☐ 82 Bob Boyd .... 5.00 2.30 .60
- ☐ 83 Bob Smith .... 5.00 2.30 .60
- ☐ 84 Reno Bertoia .... 5.00 2.30 .60
- ☐ 85 Harry Anderson .... 5.00 2.30 .60
- ☐ 86 Bob Keegan .... 6.00 2.70 .75
- ☐ 87 Danny O'Connell .... 5.00 2.30 .60
- ☐ 88 Herb Score 10.00 4.50 1.25
- ☐ 89 Billy Gardner .... 5.00 2.30 .60
- ☐ 90 Bill Skowron 15.00 6.75 1.90
- ☐ 91 Herb Moford .... 5.00 2.30 .60
- ☐ 92 Dave Philley .... 5.00 2.30 .60
- ☐ 93 Julio Becquer .... 5.00 2.30 .60
- ☐ 94 White Sox Team 30.00 6.00 1.80
  (Checklist on back)
- ☐ 95 Carl Willey .... 5.00 2.30 .60
- ☐ 96 Lou Berberet .... 5.00 2.30 .60
- ☐ 97 Jerry Lynch .... 6.00 2.70 .75
- ☐ 98 Arnie Portocarrero .... 5.00 2.30 .60
- ☐ 99 Ted Kazanski .... 5.00 2.30 .60
- ☐ 100 Bob Cerv .... 6.00 2.70 .75
- ☐ 101 Alex Kellner .... 5.00 2.30 .60
- ☐ 102 Felipe Alou 38.00 17.00 4.70
- ☐ 103 Billy Goodman .... 6.00 2.70 .75
- ☐ 104 Del Rice 8.50 3.80 1.05
- ☐ 105 Lee Walls .... 5.00 2.30 .60
- ☐ 106 Hal Woodeshick .... 5.00 2.30 .60
- ☐ 107 Norm Larker .... 6.00 2.70 .75
- ☐ 108 Zack Monroe .... 6.00 2.70 .75
- ☐ 109 Bob Schmidt .... 5.00 2.30 .60
- ☐ 110 George Witt .... 6.00 2.70 .75
- ☐ 111 Redlegs Team .... 15.00 3.00 .90
  (Checklist on back)
- ☐ 112 Billy Consolo .... 4.00 1.80 .50
- ☐ 113 Taylor Phillips .... 4.00 1.80 .50
- ☐ 114 Earl Battey .... 5.00 2.30 .60
- ☐ 115 Mickey Vernon .... 5.00 2.30 .60
- ☐ 116 Bob Allison RP 10.00 4.50 1.25
- ☐ 117 John Blanchard RP 10.00 4.50 1.25
- ☐ 118 John Buzhardt RP .... 4.50 2.00 .55
- ☐ 119 John Callison RP 12.00 5.50 1.50
- ☐ 120 Chuck Coles RP .... 4.50 2.00 .55
- ☐ 121 Bob Conley RP .... 4.50 2.00 .55
- ☐ 122 Bennie Daniels RP .... 4.50 2.00 .55
- ☐ 123 Don Dillard RP .... 4.50 2.00 .55
- ☐ 124 Dan Dobbek RP .... 4.50 2.00 .55
- ☐ 125 Ron Fairly RP 9.00 4.00 1.15
- ☐ 126 Ed Haas RP .... 5.50 2.50 .70
- ☐ 127 Kent Hadley RP .... 4.50 2.00 .55
- ☐ 128 Bob Hartman RP .... 4.50 2.00 .55
- ☐ 129 Frank Herrera RP .... 4.50 2.00 .55
- ☐ 130 Lou Jackson RP .... 5.50 2.50 .70
- ☐ 131 Deron Johnson RP 9.00 4.00 1.15
- ☐ 132 Don Lee RP .... 4.50 2.00 .55
- ☐ 133 Bob Lillis RP .... 4.50 2.00 .55
- ☐ 134 Jim McDaniel RP .... 4.50 2.00 .55
- ☐ 135 Gene Oliver RP .... 4.50 2.00 .55
- ☐ 136 Jim O'Toole RP .... 4.50 2.00 .55
- ☐ 137 Dick Ricketts RP .... 5.50 2.50 .70
- ☐ 138 John Romano RP .... 4.50 2.00 .55
- ☐ 139 Ed Sadowski RP .... 4.50 2.00 .55
- ☐ 140 Charlie Secrest RP .... 4.50 2.00 .55
- ☐ 141 Joe Shipley RP .... 4.50 2.00 .55
- ☐ 142 Dick Stigman RP .... 4.50 2.00 .55
- ☐ 143 Willie Tasby RP .... 4.50 2.00 .55
- ☐ 144 Jerry Walker RP .... 5.50 2.50 .70
- ☐ 145 Dom Zanni RP .... 4.50 2.00 .55
- ☐ 146 Jerry Zimmerman RP. 4.50 2.00 .55
- ☐ 147 Cubs Clubbers 18.00 8.00 2.30
  Dale Long
  Ernie Banks
  Walt Moryn
- ☐ 148 Mike McCormick .... 5.00 2.30 .60
- ☐ 149 Jim Bunning 15.00 6.75 1.90
- ☐ 150 Stan Musial 125.00 57.50 15.50
- ☐ 151 Bob Malkmus .... 4.00 1.80 .50
- ☐ 152 Johnny Klippstein .... 4.00 1.80 .50
- ☐ 153 Jim Marshall .... 4.00 1.80 .50
- ☐ 154 Ray Herbert .... 4.00 1.80 .50
- ☐ 155 Enos Slaughter 17.00 7.75 2.10
- ☐ 156 Ace Hurlers 8.00 3.60 1.00
  Billy Pierce
  Robin Roberts
- ☐ 157 Felix Mantilla .... 4.00 1.80 .50
- ☐ 158 Walt Dropo .... 4.00 1.80 .50
- ☐ 159 Bob Shaw .... 5.00 2.30 .60
- ☐ 160 Dick Groat .... 5.00 2.30 .60
- ☐ 161 Frank Baumann .... 4.00 1.80 .50
- ☐ 162 Bobby G. Smith .... 4.00 1.80 .50
- ☐ 163 Sandy Koufax 140.00 65.00 17.50
- ☐ 164 Johnny Groth .... 4.00 1.80 .50
- ☐ 165 Bill Bruton .... 4.00 1.80 .50
- ☐ 166 Destruction Crew 12.00 5.50 1.50
  Minnie Minoso
  Rocky Colavito
  (Misspelled Colovito
  on card back)
  Larry Doby
- ☐ 167 Duke Maas .... 4.00 1.80 .50
- ☐ 168 Carroll Hardy .... 4.00 1.80 .50
- ☐ 169 Ted Abernathy .... 4.00 1.80 .50
- ☐ 170 Gene Woodling .... 5.00 2.30 .60
- ☐ 171 Willard Schmidt .... 4.00 1.80 .50
- ☐ 172 Athletics Team .... 15.00 3.00 .90
  (Checklist on back)
- ☐ 173 Bill Monbouquette .... 5.00 2.30 .60
- ☐ 174 Jim Pendleton .... 4.00 1.80 .50
- ☐ 175 Dick Farrell .... 5.00 2.30 .60
- ☐ 176 Preston Ward .... 4.00 1.80 .50
- ☐ 177 John Briggs .... 4.00 1.80 .50
- ☐ 178 Ruben Amaro .... 4.00 1.80 .50
- ☐ 179 Don Rudolph .... 4.00 1.80 .50
- ☐ 180 Yogi Berra 70.00 32.00 8.75
- ☐ 181 Bob Porterfield .... 4.00 1.80 .50
- ☐ 182 Milt Graff .... 4.00 1.80 .50
- ☐ 183 Stu Miller .... 5.00 2.30 .60
- ☐ 184 Harvey Haddix .... 5.00 2.30 .60
- ☐ 185 Jim Busby .... 4.00 1.80 .50
- ☐ 186 Mudcat Grant .... 5.00 2.30 .60
- ☐ 187 Bubba Phillips .... 5.00 2.30 .60
- ☐ 188 Juan Pizarro .... 4.00 1.80 .50
- ☐ 189 Neil Chrisley .... 4.00 1.80 .50
- ☐ 190 Bill Virdon .... 4.00 1.80 .50
- ☐ 191 Russ Kemmerer .... 4.00 1.80 .50
- ☐ 192 Charlie Beamon .... 4.00 1.80 .50
- ☐ 193 Sammy Taylor .... 4.00 1.80 .50
- ☐ 194 Jim Brosnan .... 5.00 2.30 .60
- ☐ 195 Rip Repulski .... 4.00 1.80 .50
- ☐ 196 Billy Moran .... 4.00 1.80 .50
- ☐ 197 Ray Semproch .... 4.00 1.80 .50
- ☐ 198 Jim Davenport .... 5.00 2.30 .60
- ☐ 199 Leo Kiely .... 4.00 1.80 .50
- ☐ 200 Warren Giles .... 7.00 3.10 .85

(NL President)
☐ 201 Tom Acker .... 4.00 1.80 .50
☐ 202 Roger Maris 100.00 45.00 12.50
☐ 203 Ossie Virgil .... 4.00 1.80 .50
☐ 204 Casey Wise .... 4.00 1.80 .50
☐ 205 Don Larsen .... 6.00 2.70 .75
☐ 206 Carl Furillo .... 6.00 2.70 .75
☐ 207 George Strickland .... 4.00 1.80 .50
☐ 208 Willie Jones .... 4.00 1.80 .50
☐ 209 Lenny Green .... 4.00 1.80 .50
☐ 210 Ed Bailey .... 4.00 1.80 .50
☐ 211 Bob Blaylock .... 4.00 1.80 .50
☐ 212 Fence Busters 65.00 29.00 8.25
Hank Aaron
Eddie Mathews
☐ 213 Jim Rivera .... 5.00 2.30 .60
☐ 214 Marcelino Solis .... 4.00 1.80 .50
☐ 215 Jim Lemon .... 5.00 2.30 .60
☐ 216 Andre Rodgers .... 4.00 1.80 .50
☐ 217 Carl Erskine .... 5.00 2.30 .60
☐ 218 Roman Mejias .... 4.00 1.80 .50
☐ 219 George Zuverink .... 4.00 1.80 .50
☐ 220 Frank Malzone .... 5.00 2.30 .60
☐ 221 Bob Bowman .... 4.00 1.80 .50
☐ 222 Bobby Shantz .... 4.00 1.80 .50
☐ 223 Cardinals Team .... 15.00 3.00 .90
(Checklist on back)
☐ 224 Claude Osteen 9.00 4.00 1.15
☐ 225 Johnny Logan .... 5.00 2.30 .60
☐ 226 Art Ceccarelli .... 4.00 1.80 .50
☐ 227 Hal W. Smith .... 4.00 1.80 .50
☐ 228 Don Gross .... 4.00 1.80 .50
☐ 229 Vic Power .... 5.00 2.30 .60
☐ 230 Bill Fischer .... 4.00 1.80 .50
☐ 231 Ellis Burton .... 4.00 1.80 .50
☐ 232 Eddie Kasko .... 4.00 1.80 .50
☐ 233 Paul Foytack .... 4.00 1.80 .50
☐ 234 Chuck Tanner .... 5.00 2.30 .60
☐ 235 Valmy Thomas .... 4.00 1.80 .50
☐ 236 Ted Bowsfield .... 4.00 1.80 .50
☐ 237 Run Preventers 12.00 5.50 1.50
Gil McDougald
Bob Turley
Bobby Richardson
☐ 238 Gene Baker .... 4.00 1.80 .50
☐ 239 Bob Trowbridge .... 4.00 1.80 .50
☐ 240 Hank Bauer .... 4.00 1.80 .50
☐ 241 Billy Muffett .... 4.00 1.80 .50
☐ 242 Ron Samford .... 4.00 1.80 .50
☐ 243 Marv Grissom .... 4.00 1.80 .50
☐ 244 Ted Gray .... 4.00 1.80 .50
☐ 245 Ned Garver .... 4.00 1.80 .50
☐ 246 J.W. Porter .... 4.00 1.80 .50
☐ 247 Don Ferrarese .... 4.00 1.80 .50
☐ 248 Red Sox Team .... 15.00 3.00 .90
(Checklist on back)
☐ 249 Bobby Adams .... 4.00 1.80 .50
☐ 250 Billy O'Dell .... 4.00 1.80 .50
☐ 251 Clete Boyer .... 6.00 2.70 .75
☐ 252 Ray Boone .... 5.00 2.30 .60
☐ 253 Seth Morehead .... 4.00 1.80 .50
☐ 254 Zeke Bella .... 4.00 1.80 .50
☐ 255 Del Ennis .... 5.00 2.30 .60
☐ 256 Jerry Davie .... 4.00 1.80 .50
☐ 257 Leon Wagner 9.00 4.00 1.15
☐ 258 Fred Kipp .... 4.00 1.80 .50
☐ 259 Jim Pisoni .... 4.00 1.80 .50
☐ 260 Early Wynn UER 15.00 6.75 1.90
(1957 Cleeveland)
☐ 261 Gene Stephens .... 4.00 1.80 .50
☐ 262 Hitters' Foes 14.00 6.25 1.75
Johnny Podres
Clem Labine
Don Drysdale

☐ 263 Bud Daley .... 4.00 1.80 .50
☐ 264 Chico Carrasquel .... 4.00 1.80 .50
☐ 265 Ron Kline .... 4.00 1.80 .50
☐ 266 Woody Held .... 4.00 1.80 .50
☐ 267 John Romonosky .... 4.00 1.80 .50
☐ 268 Tito Francona .... 5.00 2.30 .60
☐ 269 Jack Meyer .... 4.00 1.80 .50
☐ 270 Gil Hodges 20.00 9.00 2.50
☐ 271 Orlando Pena .... 4.00 1.80 .50
☐ 272 Jerry Lumpe .... 4.00 1.80 .50
☐ 273 Joey Jay .... 5.00 2.30 .60
☐ 274 Jerry Kindall .... 5.00 2.30 .60
☐ 275 Jack Sanford .... 5.00 2.30 .60
☐ 276 Pete Daley .... 4.00 1.80 .50
☐ 277 Turk Lown .... 5.00 2.30 .60
☐ 278 Chuck Essegian .... 4.00 1.80 .50
☐ 279 Ernie Johnson .... 5.00 2.30 .60
☐ 280 Frank Bolling .... 4.00 1.80 .50
☐ 281 Walt Craddock .... 4.00 1.80 .50
☐ 282 R.C. Stevens .... 4.00 1.80 .50
☐ 283 Russ Heman .... 4.00 1.80 .50
☐ 284 Steve Korcheck .... 4.00 1.80 .50
☐ 285 Joe Cunningham .... 5.00 2.30 .60
☐ 286 Dean Stone .... 4.00 1.80 .50
☐ 287 Don Zimmer .... 5.00 2.30 .60
☐ 288 Dutch Dotterer .... 4.00 1.80 .50
☐ 289 Johnny Kucks .... 4.00 1.80 .50
☐ 290 Wes Covington .... 5.00 2.30 .60
☐ 291 Pitching Partners .... 5.00 2.30 .60
Pedro Ramos
Camilo Pascual
☐ 292 Dick Williams .... 5.00 2.30 .60
☐ 293 Ray Moore .... 4.00 1.80 .50
☐ 294 Hank Foiles .... 4.00 1.80 .50
☐ 295 Billy Martin 15.00 6.75 1.90
☐ 296 Ernie Broglio .... 4.00 1.80 .50
☐ 297 Jackie Brandt .... 4.00 1.80 .50
☐ 298 Tex Clevenger .... 4.00 1.80 .50
☐ 299 Billy Klaus .... 4.00 1.80 .50
☐ 300 Richie Ashburn 15.00 6.75 1.90
☐ 301 Earl Averill .... 4.00 1.80 .50
☐ 302 Don Mossi .... 5.00 2.30 .60
☐ 303 Marty Keough .... 4.00 1.80 .50
☐ 304 Cubs Team .... 15.00 3.00 .90
(Checklist on back)
☐ 305 Curt Raydon .... 4.00 1.80 .50
☐ 306 Jim Gilliam .... 7.00 3.10 .85
☐ 307 Curt Barclay .... 4.00 1.80 .50
☐ 308 Norm Siebern .... 4.00 1.80 .50
☐ 309 Sal Maglie .... 5.00 2.30 .60
☐ 310 Luis Aparicio 20.00 9.00 2.50
☐ 311 Norm Zauchin .... 4.00 1.80 .50
☐ 312 Don Newcombe .... 5.00 2.30 .60
☐ 313 Frank House .... 4.00 1.80 .50
☐ 314 Don Cardwell .... 4.00 1.80 .50
☐ 315 Joe Adcock .... 5.00 2.30 .60
☐ 316A Ralph Lumenti UER . 4.00 1.80 .50
(Option)
(Photo actually
Camilo Pascual)
☐ 316B Ralph Lumenti UER 80.00 36.00 10.00
(No option)
(Photo actually
Camilo Pascual)
☐ 317 Hitting Kings 40.00 18.00 5.00
Willie Mays
Richie Ashburn
☐ 318 Rocky Bridges .... 4.00 1.80 .50
☐ 319 Dave Hillman .... 4.00 1.80 .50
☐ 320 Bob Skinner .... 5.00 2.30 .60
☐ 321A Bob Giallombardo .... 4.00 1.80 .50
(Option)
☐ 321B Bob Giallombardo .. 80.00 36.00 10.00

No.	Player			
	(No option)			
☐ 322A	Harry Hanebrink	4.00	1.80	.50
	(Traded)			
☐ 322B	Harry Hanebrink	80.00	36.00	10.00
	(No trade)			
☐ 323	Frank Sullivan	4.00	1.80	.50
☐ 324	Don Demeter	4.00	1.80	.50
☐ 325	Ken Boyer	10.00	4.50	1.25
☐ 326	Marv Throneberry	6.00	2.70	.75
☐ 327	Gary Bell	4.00	1.80	.50
☐ 328	Lou Skizas	4.00	1.80	.50
☐ 329	Tigers Team	15.00	3.00	.90
	(Checklist on back)			
☐ 330	Gus Triandos	5.00	2.30	.60
☐ 331	Steve Boros	4.00	1.80	.50
☐ 332	Ray Monzant	4.00	1.80	.50
☐ 333	Harry Simpson	4.00	1.80	.50
☐ 334	Glen Hobbie	4.00	1.80	.50
☐ 335	Johnny Temple	5.00	2.30	.60
☐ 336A	Billy Loes	5.00	2.30	.60
	(With traded line)			
☐ 336B	Billy Loes	80.00	36.00	10.00
	(No trade)			
☐ 337	George Crowe	4.00	1.80	.50
☐ 338	Sparky Anderson	75.00	34.00	9.50
☐ 339	Roy Face	4.00	1.80	.50
☐ 340	Roy Sievers	5.00	2.30	.60
☐ 341	Tom Qualters	4.00	1.80	.50
☐ 342	Ray Jablonski	4.00	1.80	.50
☐ 343	Billy Hoeft	4.00	1.80	.50
☐ 344	Russ Nixon	4.00	1.80	.50
☐ 345	Gil McDougald	8.00	3.60	1.00
☐ 346	Batter Bafflers	4.00	1.80	.50
	Dave Sisler			
	Tom Brewer			
☐ 347	Bob Buhl	5.00	2.30	.60
☐ 348	Ted Lepcio	4.00	1.80	.50
☐ 349	Hoyt Wilhelm	15.00	6.75	1.90
☐ 350	Ernie Banks	70.00	32.00	8.75
☐ 351	Earl Torgeson	4.00	1.80	.50
☐ 352	Robin Roberts	18.00	8.00	2.30
☐ 353	Curt Flood	6.50	2.90	.80
☐ 354	Pete Burnside	4.00	1.80	.50
☐ 355	Jim Piersall	5.00	2.30	.60
☐ 356	Bob Mabe	4.00	1.80	.50
☐ 357	Dick Stuart	7.00	3.10	.85
☐ 358	Ralph Terry	5.00	2.30	.60
☐ 359	Bill White	25.00	11.50	3.10
☐ 360	Al Kaline	65.00	29.00	8.25
☐ 361	Willard Nixon	4.00	1.80	.50
☐ 362A	Dolan Nichols	4.00	1.80	.50
	(With option line)			
☐ 362B	Dolan Nichols	80.00	36.00	10.00
	(No option)			
☐ 363	Bobby Avila	4.00	1.80	.50
☐ 364	Danny McDevitt	4.00	1.80	.50
☐ 365	Gus Bell	5.00	2.30	.60
☐ 366	Humberto Robinson	4.00	1.80	.50
☐ 367	Cal Neeman	4.00	1.80	.50
☐ 368	Don Mueller	5.00	2.30	.60
☐ 369	Dick Tomanek	4.00	1.80	.50
☐ 370	Pete Runnels	5.00	2.30	.60
☐ 371	Dick Brodowski	4.00	1.80	.50
☐ 372	Jim Hegan	5.00	2.30	.60
☐ 373	Herb Plews	4.00	1.80	.50
☐ 374	Art Ditmar	4.00	1.80	.50
☐ 375	Bob Nieman	4.00	1.80	.50
☐ 376	Hal Naragon	4.00	1.80	.50
☐ 377	John Antonelli	5.00	2.30	.60
☐ 378	Gail Harris	4.00	1.80	.50
☐ 379	Bob Miller	4.00	1.80	.50
☐ 380	Hank Aaron	125.00	57.50	15.50
☐ 381	Mike Baxes	4.00	1.80	.50
☐ 382	Curt Simmons	5.00	2.30	.60
☐ 383	Words of Wisdom	10.00	4.50	1.25
	Don Larsen			
	Casey Stengel MG			
☐ 384	Dave Sisler	4.00	1.80	.50
☐ 385	Sherm Lollar	5.00	2.30	.60
☐ 386	Jim Delsing	4.00	1.80	.50
☐ 387	Don Drysdale	35.00	16.00	4.40
☐ 388	Bob Will	4.00	1.80	.50
☐ 389	Joe Nuxhall	5.00	2.30	.60
☐ 390	Orlando Cepeda	18.00	8.00	2.30
☐ 391	Milt Pappas	5.00	2.30	.60
☐ 392	Whitey Herzog	6.00	2.70	.75
☐ 393	Frank Lary	5.00	2.30	.60
☐ 394	Randy Jackson	4.00	1.80	.50
☐ 395	Elston Howard	9.00	4.00	1.15
☐ 396	Bob Rush	4.00	1.80	.50
☐ 397	Senators Team	15.00	3.00	.90
	(Checklist on back)			
☐ 398	Wally Post	5.00	2.30	.60
☐ 399	Larry Jackson	4.00	1.80	.50
☐ 400	Jackie Jensen	5.00	2.30	.60
☐ 401	Ron Blackburn	4.00	1.80	.50
☐ 402	Hector Lopez	5.00	2.30	.60
☐ 403	Clem Labine	5.00	2.30	.60
☐ 404	Hank Sauer	5.00	2.30	.60
☐ 405	Roy McMillan	5.00	2.30	.60
☐ 406	Solly Drake	4.00	1.80	.50
☐ 407	Moe Drabowsky	5.00	2.30	.60
☐ 408	Keystone Combo	12.00	5.50	1.50
	Nellie Fox			
	Luis Aparicio			
☐ 409	Gus Zernial	5.00	2.30	.60
☐ 410	Billy Pierce	5.00	2.30	.60
☐ 411	Whitey Lockman	5.00	2.30	.60
☐ 412	Stan Lopata	4.00	1.80	.50
☐ 413	Camilo Pascual UER	5.00	2.30	.60
	(Listed as Camillo on front and Pasqual on back)			
☐ 414	Dale Long	5.00	2.30	.60
☐ 415	Bill Mazeroski	12.00	5.50	1.50
☐ 416	Haywood Sullivan	5.00	2.30	.60
☐ 417	Virgil Trucks	5.00	2.30	.60
☐ 418	Gino Cimoli	4.00	1.80	.50
☐ 419	Braves Team	15.00	3.00	.90
	(Checklist on back)			
☐ 420	Rocky Colavito	25.00	11.50	3.10
☐ 421	Herman Wehmeier	4.00	1.80	.50
☐ 422	Hobie Landrith	4.00	1.80	.50
☐ 423	Bob Grim	5.00	2.30	.60
☐ 424	Ken Aspromonte	4.00	1.80	.50
☐ 425	Del Crandall	5.00	2.30	.60
☐ 426	Gerry Staley	5.00	2.30	.60
☐ 427	Charlie Neal	5.00	2.30	.60
☐ 428	Buc Hill Aces	5.00	2.30	.60
	Ron Kline			
	Bob Friend			
	Vernon Law			
	Roy Face			
☐ 429	Bobby Thomson	4.00	1.80	.50
☐ 430	Whitey Ford	40.00	18.00	5.00
☐ 431	Whammy Douglas	4.00	1.80	.50
☐ 432	Smoky Burgess	5.00	2.30	.60
☐ 433	Billy Harrell	4.00	1.80	.50
☐ 434	Hal Griggs	4.00	1.80	.50
☐ 435	Frank Robinson	50.00	23.00	6.25
☐ 436	Granny Hamner	4.00	1.80	.50
☐ 437	Ike Delock	4.00	1.80	.50
☐ 438	Sammy Esposito	4.00	1.80	.50
☐ 439	Brooks Robinson	50.00	23.00	6.25
☐ 440	Lou Burdette	7.50	3.40	.95
	(Posing as if			

lefthanded)
☐ 441 John Roseboro .... 5.00 2.30 .60
☐ 442 Ray Narleski.............. 4.00 1.80 .50
☐ 443 Daryl Spencer .... 4.00 1.80 .50
☐ 444 Ron Hansen .... 7.00 3.10 .85
☐ 445 Cal McLish................. 4.00 1.80 .50
☐ 446 Rocky Nelson............ 4.00 1.80 .50
☐ 447 Bob Anderson .... 4.00 1.80 .50
☐ 448 Vada Pinson UER....... 9.00 4.00 1.15
(Born: 8/8/38,
should be 8/11/38)
☐ 449 Tom Gorman............. 4.00 1.80 .50
☐ 450 Eddie Mathews 28.00 12.50 3.50
☐ 451 Jimmy Constable ...... 4.00 1.80 .50
☐ 452 Chico Fernandez .... 4.00 1.80 .50
☐ 453 Les Moss .... 4.00 1.80 .50
☐ 454 Phil Clark .... 4.00 1.80 .50
☐ 455 Larry Doby................. 6.00 2.70 .75
☐ 456 Jerry Casale .... 4.00 1.80 .50
☐ 457 Dodgers Team 25.00 5.00 1.50
(Checklist on back)
☐ 458 Gordon Jones .... 4.00 1.80 .50
☐ 459 Bill Tuttle.................... 4.00 1.80 .50
☐ 460 Bob Friend .... 5.00 2.30 .60
☐ 461 Mickey Mantle Hits .. 75.00 34.00 9.50
Homer
☐ 462 Rocky Colavito's 12.00 5.50 1.50
Catch
☐ 463 Al Kaline Batting....... 18.00 8.00 2.30
Champ
☐ 464 Willie Mays' Series .. 35.00 16.00 4.40
Catch
☐ 465 Roy Sievers Sets Mark 5.00 2.30 .60
☐ 466 Billy Pierce All-Star .... 5.00 2.30 .60
☐ 467 Hank Aaron Clubs 30.00 13.50 3.80
Homer
☐ 468 Duke Snider's Play... 18.00 8.00 2.30
☐ 469 Hustler Ernie Banks . 18.00 8.00 2.30
☐ 470 Stan Musial's 3000th 20.00 9.00 2.50
Hit
☐ 471 Tom Sturdivant.......... 4.00 1.80 .50
☐ 472 Gene Freese .... 4.00 1.80 .50
☐ 473 Mike Fornieles........... 4.00 1.80 .50
☐ 474 Moe Thacker .... 4.00 1.80 .50
☐ 475 Jack Harshman .... 4.00 1.80 .50
☐ 476 Indians Team .... 15.00 3.00 .90
(Checklist on back)
☐ 477 Barry Latman .... 4.00 1.80 .50
☐ 478 Bob Clemente 135.00 60.00 17.00
☐ 479 Lindy McDaniel.......... 5.00 2.30 .60
☐ 480 Red Schoendienst.... 14.00 6.25 1.75
☐ 481 Charlie Maxwell.......... 5.00 2.30 .60
☐ 482 Russ Meyer................ 4.00 1.80 .50
☐ 483 Clint Courtney .... 4.00 1.80 .50
☐ 484 Willie Kirkland .... 4.00 1.80 .50
☐ 485 Ryne Duren................ 7.00 3.10 .85
☐ 486 Sammy White .... 4.00 1.80 .50
☐ 487 Hal Brown .... 4.00 1.80 .50
☐ 488 Walt Moryn .... 4.00 1.80 .50
☐ 489 John Powers.............. 4.00 1.80 .50
☐ 490 Frank Thomas .... 5.00 2.30 .60
☐ 491 Don Blasingame......... 4.00 1.80 .50
☐ 492 Gene Conley.............. 5.00 2.30 .60
☐ 493 Jim Landis .... 5.00 2.30 .60
☐ 494 Don Pavletich............ 4.00 1.80 .50
☐ 495 Johnny Podres............ 5.00 2.30 .60
☐ 496 Wayne Terwilliger UER 4.00 1.80 .50
(Athlftics on front)
☐ 497 Hal R. Smith .... 4.00 1.80 .50
☐ 498 Dick Hyde .... 4.00 1.80 .50
☐ 499 Johnny O'Brien .... 5.00 2.30 .60
☐ 500 Vic Wertz .... 5.00 2.30 .60
☐ 501 Bob Tiefenauer.......... 4.00 1.80 .50
☐ 502 Alvin Dark .... 5.00 2.30 .60
☐ 503 Jim Owens.................. 4.00 1.80 .50
☐ 504 Ossie Alvarez .... 4.00 1.80 .50
☐ 505 Tony Kubek.............. 11.00 4.90 1.40
☐ 506 Bob Purkey .... 4.00 1.80 .50
☐ 507 Bob Hale 15.00 6.75 1.90
☐ 508 Art Fowler 15.00 6.75 1.90
☐ 509 Norm Cash............... 60.00 27.00 7.50
☐ 510 Yankees Team.......... 90.00 18.00 5.50
(Checklist on back)
☐ 511 George Susce 15.00 6.75 1.90
☐ 512 George Altman......... 15.00 6.75 1.90
☐ 513 Tommy Carroll......... 15.00 6.75 1.90
☐ 514 Bob Gibson 300.00 135.00 38.00
☐ 515 Harmon Killebrew .. 125.00 57.50 15.50
☐ 516 Mike Garcia............. 18.00 8.00 2.30
☐ 517 Joe Koppe............... 15.00 6.75 1.90
☐ 518 Mike Cueller UER..... 30.00 13.50 3.80
(Sic, Cuellar)
☐ 519 Infield Power............ 18.00 8.00 2.30
Pete Runnels
Dick Gernert
Frank Malzone
☐ 520 Don Elston 15.00 6.75 1.90
☐ 521 Gary Geiger............. 15.00 6.75 1.90
☐ 522 Gene Snyder 15.00 6.75 1.90
☐ 523 Harry Bright 15.00 6.75 1.90
☐ 524 Larry Osborne.......... 15.00 6.75 1.90
☐ 525 Jim Coates 15.00 6.75 1.90
☐ 526 Bob Speake.............. 15.00 6.75 1.90
☐ 527 Solly Hemus 15.00 6.75 1.90
☐ 528 Pirates Team............ 55.00 11.00 3.30
(Checklist on back)
☐ 529 George Bamberger... 20.00 9.00 2.50
☐ 530 Wally Moon.............. 18.00 8.00 2.30
☐ 531 Ray Webster 15.00 6.75 1.90
☐ 532 Mark Freeman.......... 15.00 6.75 1.90
☐ 533 Darrell Johnson 18.00 8.00 2.30
☐ 534 Faye Throneberry..... 15.00 6.75 1.90
☐ 535 Ruben Gomez 15.00 6.75 1.90
☐ 536 Danny Kravitz........... 15.00 6.75 1.90
☐ 537 Rudolph Arias 15.00 6.75 1.90
☐ 538 Chick King................ 15.00 6.75 1.90
☐ 539 Gary Blaylock........... 15.00 6.75 1.90
☐ 540 Willie Miranda.......... 15.00 6.75 1.90
☐ 541 Bob Thurman 15.00 6.75 1.90
☐ 542 Jim Perry 30.00 13.50 3.80
☐ 543 Corsair Trio........... 100.00 45.00 12.50
Bob Skinner
Bill Virdon
Roberto Clemente
☐ 544 Lee Tate 15.00 6.75 1.90
☐ 545 Tom Morgan 15.00 6.75 1.90
☐ 546 Al Schroll................. 15.00 6.75 1.90
☐ 547 Jim Baxes 15.00 6.75 1.90
☐ 548 Elmer Singleton 15.00 6.75 1.90
☐ 549 Howie Nunn 15.00 6.75 1.90
☐ 550 Roy Campanella..... 175.00 80.00 22.00
(Symbol of Courage)
☐ 551 Fred Haney AS MG... 15.00 6.75 1.90
☐ 552 Casey Stengel AS MG 35.00 16.00 4.40
☐ 553 Orlando Cepeda AS.. 25.00 11.50 3.10
☐ 554 Bill Skowron AS 25.00 11.50 3.10
☐ 555 Bill Mazeroski AS 25.00 11.50 3.10
☐ 556 Nellie Fox AS............ 25.00 11.50 3.10
☐ 557 Ken Boyer AS............ 25.00 11.50 3.10
☐ 558 Frank Malzone AS 15.00 6.75 1.90
☐ 559 Ernie Banks AS 60.00 27.00 7.50
☐ 560 Luis Aparicio AS 30.00 13.50 3.80
☐ 561 Hank Aaron AS....... 125.00 57.50 15.50
☐ 562 Al Kaline AS 60.00 27.00 7.50
☐ 563 Willie Mays AS....... 125.00 57.50 15.50
☐ 564 Mickey Mantle AS .. 285.00 130.00 36.00

	NRMT	VG-E	GOOD
☐ 565 Wes Covington AS	15.00	6.75	1.90
☐ 566 Roy Sievers AS	15.00	6.75	1.90
☐ 567 Del Crandall AS	15.00	6.75	1.90
☐ 568 Gus Triandos AS	15.00	6.75	1.90
☐ 569 Bob Friend AS	15.00	6.75	1.90
☐ 570 Bob Turley AS	15.00	6.75	1.90
☐ 571 Warren Spahn AS	35.00	16.00	4.40
☐ 572 Billy Pierce AS	30.00	9.00	3.00

1960 Topps

The cards in this 572-card set measure 2 1/2" by 3 1/2". The 1960 Topps set is the only Topps standard size issue to use a horizontally oriented front. World Series cards appeared for the first time (385 to 391), and there is a Rookie Prospect (RP) series (117-148), the most famous of which is Carl Yastrzemski, and a Sport Magazine All-Star Selection (AS) series (553-572). There are 16 manager cards listed alphabetically from 212 through 227. The 1959 Topps All-Rookie team is featured on cards 316-325. The coaching staff of each team was also afforded their own card in a 16-card subset (455-470). Cards 375 to 440 come with either gray or white backs, and the high series (507-572) were printed on a more limited basis than the rest of the set. The team cards have series checklists on the reverse. The key Rookie Cards in this set are Willie McCovey and Carl Yastrzemski.

	NRMT	VG-E	GOOD
COMPLETE SET (572)	3600.00	1600.00	450.00
COMMON CARD (1-110)	4.00	1.80	.50
COMMON CARD (111-198)	4.00	1.80	.50
COMMON CARD (199-286)	4.00	1.80	.50
COMMON CARD (287-440)	4.00	1.80	.50
COMMON CARD (441-506)	6.00	2.70	.75
COMMON CARD (507-552)	15.00	6.75	1.90
COMMON AS (553-572)	15.00	6.75	1.90

	NRMT	VG-E	GOOD
☐ 1 Early Wynn	30.00	7.50	2.40
☐ 2 Roman Mejias	4.00	1.80	.50
☐ 3 Joe Adcock	4.50	2.00	.55
☐ 4 Bob Purkey	4.00	1.80	.50
☐ 5 Wally Moon	4.50	2.00	.55
☐ 6 Lou Berberet	4.00	1.80	.50
☐ 7 Master and Mentor	20.00	9.00	2.50
Willie Mays			
Bill Rigney MG			
☐ 8 Bud Daley	4.00	1.80	.50
☐ 9 Faye Throneberry	4.00	1.80	.50
☐ 10 Ernie Banks	45.00	20.00	5.75
☐ 11 Norm Siebern	4.00	1.80	.50
☐ 12 Milt Pappas	4.50	2.00	.55
☐ 13 Wally Post	4.50	2.00	.55
☐ 14 Jim Grant	4.50	2.00	.55
☐ 15 Pete Runnels	4.50	2.00	.55
☐ 16 Ernie Broglio	4.50	2.00	.55
☐ 17 Johnny Callison	4.00	1.80	.50
☐ 18 Dodgers Team	32.00	8.00	2.60
(Checklist on back)			
☐ 19 Felix Mantilla	4.00	1.80	.50
☐ 20 Roy Face	4.50	2.00	.55
☐ 21 Dutch Dotterer	4.00	1.80	.50
☐ 22 Rocky Bridges	4.00	1.80	.50
☐ 23 Eddie Fisher	4.00	1.80	.50
☐ 24 Dick Gray	4.00	1.80	.50
☐ 25 Roy Sievers	4.50	2.00	.55
☐ 26 Wayne Terwilliger	4.00	1.80	.50
☐ 27 Dick Drott	4.00	1.80	.50
☐ 28 Brooks Robinson	45.00	20.00	5.75
☐ 29 Clem Labine	4.50	2.00	.55
☐ 30 Tito Francona	4.00	1.80	.50
☐ 31 Sammy Esposito	4.00	1.80	.50
☐ 32 Sophomore Stalwarts	4.00	1.80	.50
Jim O'Toole			
Vada Pinson			
☐ 33 Tom Morgan	4.00	1.80	.50
☐ 34 Sparky Anderson	20.00	9.00	2.50
☐ 35 Whitey Ford	40.00	18.00	5.00
☐ 36 Russ Nixon	4.00	1.80	.50
☐ 37 Bill Bruton	4.00	1.80	.50
☐ 38 Jerry Casale	4.00	1.80	.50
☐ 39 Earl Averill	4.00	1.80	.50
☐ 40 Joe Cunningham	4.50	2.00	.55
☐ 41 Barry Latman	4.00	1.80	.50
☐ 42 Hobie Landrith	4.00	1.80	.50
☐ 43 Senators Team	9.00	2.30	.70
(Checklist on back)			
☐ 44 Bobby Locke	4.00	1.80	.50
☐ 45 Roy McMillan	4.50	2.00	.55
☐ 46 Jerry Fisher	4.00	1.80	.50
☐ 47 Don Zimmer	4.50	2.00	.55
☐ 48 Hal W. Smith	4.00	1.80	.50
☐ 49 Curt Raydon	4.00	1.80	.50
☐ 50 Al Kaline	40.00	18.00	5.00
☐ 51 Jim Coates	4.00	1.80	.50
☐ 52 Dave Philley	4.00	1.80	.50
☐ 53 Jackie Brandt	4.00	1.80	.50
☐ 54 Mike Fornieles	4.00	1.80	.50
☐ 55 Bill Mazeroski	10.00	4.50	1.25
☐ 56 Steve Korcheck	4.00	1.80	.50
☐ 57 Win Savers	4.00	1.80	.50
Turk Lown			
Gerry Staley			
☐ 58 Gino Cimoli	4.00	1.80	.50
☐ 59 Juan Pizarro	4.00	1.80	.50
☐ 60 Gus Triandos	4.50	2.00	.55
☐ 61 Eddie Kasko	4.00	1.80	.50
☐ 62 Roger Craig	4.00	1.80	.50
☐ 63 George Strickland	4.00	1.80	.50
☐ 64 Jack Meyer	4.00	1.80	.50
☐ 65 Elston Howard	7.00	3.10	.85
☐ 66 Bob Trowbridge	4.00	1.80	.50
☐ 67 Jose Pagan	4.00	1.80	.50
☐ 68 Dave Hillman	4.00	1.80	.50
☐ 69 Billy Goodman	4.50	2.00	.55
☐ 70 Lew Burdette	4.00	1.80	.50
☐ 71 Marty Keough	4.00	1.80	.50
☐ 72 Tigers Team	16.00	4.00	1.30
(Checklist on back)			
☐ 73 Bob Gibson	50.00	23.00	6.25
☐ 74 Walt Moryn	4.00	1.80	.50

☐ 75 Vic Power 4.50 2.00 .55
☐ 76 Bill Fischer 4.00 1.80 .50
☐ 77 Hank Foiles 4.00 1.80 .50
☐ 78 Bob Grim 4.00 1.80 .50
☐ 79 Walt Dropo 4.00 1.80 .50
☐ 80 Johnny Antonelli 4.50 2.00 .55
☐ 81 Russ Snyder 4.00 1.80 .50
☐ 82 Ruben Gomez 4.00 1.80 .50
☐ 83 Tony Kubek 8.00 3.60 1.00
☐ 84 Hal R. Smith 4.00 1.80 .50
☐ 85 Frank Lary 4.50 2.00 .55
☐ 86 Dick Gernert 4.00 1.80 .50
☐ 87 John Romonosky 4.00 1.80 .50
☐ 88 John Roseboro 4.50 2.00 .55
☐ 89 Hal Brown 4.00 1.80 .50
☐ 90 Bobby Avila 4.00 1.80 .50
☐ 91 Bennie Daniels 4.00 1.80 .50
☐ 92 Whitey Herzog 4.50 2.00 .55
☐ 93 Art Schult 4.00 1.80 .50
☐ 94 Leo Kiely 4.00 1.80 .50
☐ 95 Frank Thomas 4.50 2.00 .55
☐ 96 Ralph Terry 4.50 2.00 .55
☐ 97 Ted Lepcio 4.00 1.80 .50
☐ 98 Gordon Jones 4.00 1.80 .50
☐ 99 Lenny Green 4.00 1.80 .50
☐ 100 Nellie Fox 9.00 4.00 1.15
☐ 101 Bob Miller 4.00 1.80 .50
☐ 102 Kent Hadley 4.00 1.80 .50
☐ 103 Dick Farrell 4.50 2.00 .55
☐ 104 Dick Schofield 4.50 2.00 .55
☐ 105 Larry Sherry 8.00 3.60 1.00
☐ 106 Billy Gardner 4.00 1.80 .50
☐ 107 Carlton Willey 4.00 1.80 .50
☐ 108 Pete Daley 4.00 1.80 .50
☐ 109 Clete Boyer 4.50 2.00 .55
☐ 110 Cal McLish 4.00 1.80 .50
☐ 111 Vic Wertz 4.50 2.00 .55
☐ 112 Jack Harshman 4.00 1.80 .50
☐ 113 Bob Skinner 4.50 2.00 .55
☐ 114 Ken Aspromonte 4.00 1.80 .50
☐ 115 Fork and Knuckler 6.00 2.70 .75
Roy Face
Hoyt Wilhelm
☐ 116 Jim Rivera 4.00 1.80 .50
☐ 117 Tom Borland RP 4.00 1.80 .50
☐ 118 Bob Bruce RP 4.00 1.80 .50
☐ 119 Chico Cardenas RP 4.50 2.00 .55
☐ 120 Duke Carmel RP 4.00 1.80 .50
☐ 121 Camilo Carreon RP 4.00 1.80 .50
☐ 122 Don Dillard RP 4.00 1.80 .50
☐ 123 Dan Dobbek RP 4.00 1.80 .50
☐ 124 Jim Donohue RP 4.00 1.80 .50
☐ 125 Dick Ellsworth RP 4.00 1.80 .50
☐ 126 Chuck Estrada RP 4.00 1.80 .50
☐ 127 Ron Hansen RP 4.50 2.00 .55
☐ 128 Bill Harris RP 4.00 1.80 .50
☐ 129 Bob Hartman RP 4.00 1.80 .50
☐ 130 Frank Herrera RP 4.00 1.80 .50
☐ 131 Ed Hobaugh RP 4.00 1.80 .50
☐ 132 Frank Howard RP 20.00 9.00 2.50
☐ 133 Manuel Javier RP 6.00 2.70 .75
(Sic, Julian)
☐ 134 Deron Johnson RP 4.50 2.00 .55
☐ 135 Ken Johnson RP 4.50 2.00 .55
☐ 136 Jim Kaat RP 40.00 18.00 5.00
☐ 137 Lou Klimchock RP 4.00 1.80 .50
☐ 138 Art Mahaffey RP 4.00 1.80 .50
☐ 139 Carl Mathias RP 4.00 1.80 .50
☐ 140 Julio Navarro RP 4.00 1.80 .50
☐ 141 Jim Proctor RP 4.00 1.80 .50
☐ 142 Bill Short RP 4.00 1.80 .50
☐ 143 Al Spangler RP 4.00 1.80 .50
☐ 144 Al Stieglitz RP 4.00 1.80 .50
☐ 145 Jim Umbricht RP 4.00 1.80 .50
☐ 146 Ted Wieand RP 4.00 1.80 .50
☐ 147 Bob Will RP 4.00 1.80 .50
☐ 148 Carl Yastrzemski RP 150.00 70.00 19.00
☐ 149 Bob Nieman 4.00 1.80 .50
☐ 150 Billy Pierce 4.50 2.00 .55
☐ 151 Giants Team 9.00 2.30 .70
(Checklist on back)
☐ 152 Gail Harris 4.00 1.80 .50
☐ 153 Bobby Thomson 4.50 2.00 .55
☐ 154 Jim Davenport 4.50 2.00 .55
☐ 155 Charlie Neal 4.50 2.00 .55
☐ 156 Art Ceccarelli 4.00 1.80 .50
☐ 157 Rocky Nelson 4.00 1.80 .50
☐ 158 Wes Covington 4.50 2.00 .55
☐ 159 Jim Piersall 4.00 1.80 .50
☐ 160 Rival All-Stars 70.00 32.00 8.75
Mickey Mantle
Ken Boyer
☐ 161 Ray Narleski 4.00 1.80 .50
☐ 162 Sammy Taylor 4.00 1.80 .50
☐ 163 Hector Lopez 4.50 2.00 .55
☐ 164 Reds Team 9.00 2.30 .70
(Checklist on back)
☐ 165 Jack Sanford 4.50 2.00 .55
☐ 166 Chuck Essegian 4.00 1.80 .50
☐ 167 Valmy Thomas 4.00 1.80 .50
☐ 168 Alex Grammas 4.00 1.80 .50
☐ 169 Jake Striker 4.00 1.80 .50
☐ 170 Del Crandall 4.50 2.00 .55
☐ 171 Johnny Groth 4.00 1.80 .50
☐ 172 Willie Kirkland 4.00 1.80 .50
☐ 173 Billy Martin 10.00 4.50 1.25
☐ 174 Indians Team 9.00 2.30 .70
(Checklist on back)
☐ 175 Pedro Ramos 4.00 1.80 .50
☐ 176 Vada Pinson 6.00 2.70 .75
☐ 177 Johnny Kucks 4.00 1.80 .50
☐ 178 Woody Held 4.00 1.80 .50
☐ 179 Rip Coleman 4.00 1.80 .50
☐ 180 Harry Simpson 4.00 1.80 .50
☐ 181 Billy Loes 4.50 2.00 .55
☐ 182 Glen Hobbie 4.00 1.80 .50
☐ 183 Eli Grba 4.00 1.80 .50
☐ 184 Gary Geiger 4.00 1.80 .50
☐ 185 Jim Owens 4.00 1.80 .50
☐ 186 Dave Sisler 4.00 1.80 .50
☐ 187 Jay Hook 4.00 1.80 .50
☐ 188 Dick Williams 4.50 2.00 .55
☐ 189 Don McMahon 4.00 1.80 .50
☐ 190 Gene Woodling 4.50 2.00 .55
☐ 191 Johnny Klippstein 4.00 1.80 .50
☐ 192 Danny O'Connell 4.00 1.80 .50
☐ 193 Dick Hyde 4.00 1.80 .50
☐ 194 Bobby Gene Smith 4.00 1.80 .50
☐ 195 Lindy McDaniel 4.50 2.00 .55
☐ 196 Andy Carey 4.50 2.00 .55
☐ 197 Ron Kline 4.00 1.80 .50
☐ 198 Jerry Lynch 4.50 2.00 .55
☐ 199 Dick Donovan 4.50 2.00 .55
☐ 200 Willie Mays 100.00 45.00 12.50
☐ 201 Larry Osborne 4.00 1.80 .50
☐ 202 Fred Kipp 4.00 1.80 .50
☐ 203 Sammy White 4.00 1.80 .50
☐ 204 Ryne Duren 4.00 1.80 .50
☐ 205 Johnny Logan 4.50 2.00 .55
☐ 206 Claude Osteen 4.50 2.00 .55
☐ 207 Bob Boyd 4.00 1.80 .50
☐ 208 White Sox Team 9.00 2.30 .70
(Checklist on back)
☐ 209 Ron Blackburn 4.00 1.80 .50
☐ 210 Harmon Killebrew 25.00 11.50 3.10
☐ 211 Taylor Phillips 4.00 1.80 .50

	No.	Card			
☐	212	Walt Alston MG	12.00	5.50	1.50
☐	213	Chuck Dressen MG	4.50	2.00	.55
☐	214	Jimmy Dykes MG	4.50	2.00	.55
☐	215	Bob Elliott MG	4.50	2.00	.55
☐	216	Joe Gordon MG	4.50	2.00	.55
☐	217	Charlie Grimm MG	4.50	2.00	.55
☐	218	Solly Hemus MG	4.00	1.80	.50
☐	219	Fred Hutchinson MG	4.50	2.00	.55
☐	220	Billy Jurges MG	4.00	1.80	.50
☐	221	Cookie Lavagetto MG	4.00	1.80	.50
☐	222	Al Lopez MG	6.00	2.70	.75
☐	223	Danny Murtaugh MG	4.00	1.80	.50
☐	224	Paul Richards MG	4.50	2.00	.55
☐	225	Bill Rigney MG	4.00	1.80	.50
☐	226	Eddie Sawyer MG	4.00	1.80	.50
☐	227	Casey Stengel MG	16.00	7.25	2.00
☐	228	Ernie Johnson	4.50	2.00	.55
☐	229	Joe M. Morgan	4.00	1.80	.50
☐	230	Mound Magicians Lou Burdette Warren Spahn Bob Buhl	10.00	4.50	1.25
☐	231	Hal Naragon	4.00	1.80	.50
☐	232	Jim Busby	4.00	1.80	.50
☐	233	Don Elston	4.00	1.80	.50
☐	234	Don Demeter	4.00	1.80	.50
☐	235	Gus Bell	4.50	2.00	.55
☐	236	Dick Ricketts	4.00	1.80	.50
☐	237	Elmer Valo	4.00	1.80	.50
☐	238	Danny Kravitz	4.00	1.80	.50
☐	239	Joe Shipley	4.00	1.80	.50
☐	240	Luis Aparicio	14.00	6.25	1.75
☐	241	Albie Pearson	4.50	2.00	.55
☐	242	Cardinals Team (Checklist on back)	9.00	2.30	.70
☐	243	Bubba Phillips	4.00	1.80	.50
☐	244	Hal Griggs	4.00	1.80	.50
☐	245	Eddie Yost	4.50	2.00	.55
☐	246	Lee Maye	4.50	2.00	.55
☐	247	Gil McDougald	6.00	2.70	.75
☐	248	Del Rice	4.00	1.80	.50
☐	249	Earl Wilson	5.00	2.30	.60
☐	250	Stan Musial	100.00	45.00	12.50
☐	251	Bob Malkmus	4.00	1.80	.50
☐	252	Ray Herbert	4.00	1.80	.50
☐	253	Eddie Bressoud	4.00	1.80	.50
☐	254	Arnie Portocarrero	4.00	1.80	.50
☐	255	Jim Gilliam	4.50	2.00	.55
☐	256	Dick Brown	4.00	1.80	.50
☐	257	Gordy Coleman	4.00	1.80	.50
☐	258	Dick Groat	5.00	2.30	.60
☐	259	George Altman	4.00	1.80	.50
☐	260	Power Plus Rocky Colavito Tito Francona	7.50	3.40	.95
☐	261	Pete Burnside	4.00	1.80	.50
☐	262	Hank Bauer	4.00	1.80	.50
☐	263	Darrell Johnson	4.00	1.80	.50
☐	264	Robin Roberts	14.00	6.25	1.75
☐	265	Rip Repulski	4.00	1.80	.50
☐	266	Joey Jay	4.50	2.00	.55
☐	267	Jim Marshall	4.00	1.80	.50
☐	268	Al Worthington	4.00	1.80	.50
☐	269	Gene Green	4.00	1.80	.50
☐	270	Bob Turley	4.00	1.80	.50
☐	271	Julio Becquer	4.00	1.80	.50
☐	272	Fred Green	4.00	1.80	.50
☐	273	Neil Chrisley	4.00	1.80	.50
☐	274	Tom Acker	4.00	1.80	.50
☐	275	Curt Flood	5.00	2.30	.60
☐	276	Ken McBride	4.00	1.80	.50
☐	277	Harry Bright	4.00	1.80	.50
☐	278	Stan Williams	4.50	2.00	.55
☐	279	Chuck Tanner	4.50	2.00	.55
☐	280	Frank Sullivan	4.00	1.80	.50
☐	281	Ray Boone	4.50	2.00	.55
☐	282	Joe Nuxhall	4.50	2.00	.55
☐	283	John Blanchard	4.00	1.80	.50
☐	284	Don Gross	4.00	1.80	.50
☐	285	Harry Anderson	4.00	1.80	.50
☐	286	Ray Semproch	4.00	1.80	.50
☐	287	Felipe Alou	8.00	3.60	1.00
☐	288	Bob Mabe	4.00	1.80	.50
☐	289	Willie Jones	4.00	1.80	.50
☐	290	Jerry Lumpe	4.00	1.80	.50
☐	291	Bob Keegan	4.00	1.80	.50
☐	292	Dodger Backstops Joe Pignatano John Roseboro	4.50	2.00	.55
☐	293	Gene Conley	4.50	2.00	.55
☐	294	Tony Taylor	4.50	2.00	.55
☐	295	Gil Hodges	16.00	7.25	2.00
☐	296	Nelson Chittum	4.00	1.80	.50
☐	297	Reno Bertoia	4.00	1.80	.50
☐	298	George Witt	4.00	1.80	.50
☐	299	Earl Torgeson	4.00	1.80	.50
☐	300	Hank Aaron	100.00	45.00	12.50
☐	301	Jerry Davie	4.00	1.80	.50
☐	302	Phillies Team (Checklist on back)	9.00	2.30	.70
☐	303	Billy O'Dell	4.00	1.80	.50
☐	304	Joe Ginsberg	4.00	1.80	.50
☐	305	Richie Ashburn	10.00	4.50	1.25
☐	306	Frank Baumann	4.00	1.80	.50
☐	307	Gene Oliver	4.00	1.80	.50
☐	308	Dick Hall	4.00	1.80	.50
☐	309	Bob Hale	4.00	1.80	.50
☐	310	Frank Malzone	4.50	2.00	.55
☐	311	Raul Sanchez	4.00	1.80	.50
☐	312	Charley Lau	4.50	2.00	.55
☐	313	Turk Lown	4.00	1.80	.50
☐	314	Chico Fernandez	4.00	1.80	.50
☐	315	Bobby Shantz	4.50	2.00	.55
☐	316	Willie McCovey	150.00	70.00	19.00
☐	317	Pumpsie Green	5.50	2.50	.70
☐	318	Jim Baxes	5.00	2.30	.60
☐	319	Joe Koppe	5.00	2.30	.60
☐	320	Bob Allison	5.50	2.50	.70
☐	321	Ron Fairly	5.50	2.50	.70
☐	322	Willie Tasby	5.00	2.30	.60
☐	323	John Romano	5.00	2.30	.60
☐	324	Jim Perry	6.00	2.70	.75
☐	325	Jim O'Toole	5.50	2.50	.70
☐	326	Bob Clemente	135.00	60.00	17.00
☐	327	Ray Sadecki	4.00	1.80	.50
☐	328	Earl Battey	4.00	1.80	.50
☐	329	Zack Monroe	4.00	1.80	.50
☐	330	Harvey Kuenn	5.00	2.30	.60
☐	331	Henry Mason	4.00	1.80	.50
☐	332	Yankees Team (Checklist on back)	36.00	9.00	2.90
☐	333	Danny McDevitt	4.00	1.80	.50
☐	334	Ted Abernathy	4.00	1.80	.50
☐	335	Red Schoendienst	12.00	5.50	1.50
☐	336	Ike Delock	4.00	1.80	.50
☐	337	Cal Neeman	4.00	1.80	.50
☐	338	Ray Monzant	4.00	1.80	.50
☐	339	Harry Chiti	4.00	1.80	.50
☐	340	Harvey Haddix	4.50	2.00	.55
☐	341	Carroll Hardy	4.00	1.80	.50
☐	342	Casey Wise	4.00	1.80	.50
☐	343	Sandy Koufax	100.00	45.00	12.50
☐	344	Clint Courtney	4.00	1.80	.50
☐	345	Don Newcombe	4.50	2.00	.55
☐	346	J.C. Martin UER (Face actually	4.50	2.00	.55

Gary Peters)
- ☐ 347 Ed Bouchee .... 4.00 1.80 .50
- ☐ 348 Barry Shetrone .... 4.00 1.80 .50
- ☐ 349 Moe Drabowsky .... 4.50 2.00 .55
- ☐ 350 Mickey Mantle 450.00 200.00 57.50
- ☐ 351 Don Nottebart .... 4.00 1.80 .50
- ☐ 352 Cincy Clouters 8.00 3.60 1.00
  Gus Bell
  Frank Robinson
  Jerry Lynch
- ☐ 353 Don Larsen .... 5.00 2.30 .60
- ☐ 354 Bob Lillis .... 4.00 1.80 .50
- ☐ 355 Bill White .... 7.50 3.40 .95
- ☐ 356 Joe Amalfitano .... 4.00 1.80 .50
- ☐ 357 Al Schroll .... 4.00 1.80 .50
- ☐ 358 Joe DeMaestri .... 4.00 1.80 .50
- ☐ 359 Buddy Gilbert .... 4.00 1.80 .50
- ☐ 360 Herb Score .... 6.00 2.70 .75
- ☐ 361 Bob Oldis .... 4.00 1.80 .50
- ☐ 362 Russ Kemmerer .... 4.00 1.80 .50
- ☐ 363 Gene Stephens .... 4.00 1.80 .50
- ☐ 364 Paul Foytack .... 4.00 1.80 .50
- ☐ 365 Minnie Minoso .... 6.00 2.70 .75
- ☐ 366 Dallas Green 9.00 4.00 1.15
- ☐ 367 Bill Tuttle .... 4.00 1.80 .50
- ☐ 368 Daryl Spencer .... 4.00 1.80 .50
- ☐ 369 Billy Hoeft .... 4.00 1.80 .50
- ☐ 370 Bill Skowron 8.00 3.60 1.00
- ☐ 371 Bud Byerly .... 4.00 1.80 .50
- ☐ 372 Frank House .... 4.00 1.80 .50
- ☐ 373 Don Hoak .... 4.50 2.00 .55
- ☐ 374 Bob Buhl .... 4.50 2.00 .55
- ☐ 375 Dale Long .... 4.50 2.00 .55
- ☐ 376 John Briggs .... 4.00 1.80 .50
- ☐ 377 Roger Maris 100.00 45.00 12.50
- ☐ 378 Stu Miller .... 4.50 2.00 .55
- ☐ 379 Red Wilson .... 4.00 1.80 .50
- ☐ 380 Bob Shaw .... 4.00 1.80 .50
- ☐ 381 Braves Team .... 9.00 2.30 .70
  (Checklist on back)
- ☐ 382 Ted Bowsfield .... 4.00 1.80 .50
- ☐ 383 Leon Wagner .... 4.00 1.80 .50
- ☐ 384 Don Cardwell .... 4.00 1.80 .50
- ☐ 385 World Series Game 1. 7.00 3.10 .85
  Charlie Neal
  Steals Second
- ☐ 386 World Series Game 2. 7.00 3.10 .85
  Charlie Neal
  Belts Second Homer
- ☐ 387 World Series Game 3. 7.00 3.10 .85
  Carl Furillo
  Breaks Game
- ☐ 388 World Series Game 4 10.00 4.50 1.25
  Gil Hodges' Homer
- ☐ 389 World Series Game 5 10.00 4.50 1.25
  Luis Aparicio
  Swipes Base
  (Maury Wills
  applies late tag)
- ☐ 390 World Series Game 6. 7.00 3.10 .85
  Scrambling After Ball
- ☐ 391 World Series Summary 7.00 3.10 .85
  The Champs Celebrate
- ☐ 392 Tex Clevenger .... 4.00 1.80 .50
- ☐ 393 Smoky Burgess .... 4.50 2.00 .55
- ☐ 394 Norm Larker .... 4.50 2.00 .55
- ☐ 395 Hoyt Wilhelm 12.00 5.50 1.50
- ☐ 396 Steve Bilko .... 4.00 1.80 .50
- ☐ 397 Don Blasingame .... 4.00 1.80 .50
- ☐ 398 Mike Cuellar .... 4.50 2.00 .55
- ☐ 399 Young Hill Stars .... 4.50 2.00 .55
  Milt Pappas
  Jack Fisher
  Jerry Walker
- ☐ 400 Rocky Colavito 14.00 6.25 1.75
- ☐ 401 Bob Duliba .... 4.00 1.80 .50
- ☐ 402 Dick Stuart .... 4.50 2.00 .55
- ☐ 403 Ed Sadowski .... 4.00 1.80 .50
- ☐ 404 Bob Rush .... 4.00 1.80 .50
- ☐ 405 Bobby Richardson ... 14.00 6.25 1.75
- ☐ 406 Billy Klaus .... 4.00 1.80 .50
- ☐ 407 Gary Peters UER .... 6.00 2.70 .75
  (Face actually
  J.C. Martin)
- ☐ 408 Carl Furillo .... 6.00 2.70 .75
- ☐ 409 Ron Samford .... 4.00 1.80 .50
- ☐ 410 Sam Jones .... 4.50 2.00 .55
- ☐ 411 Ed Bailey .... 4.00 1.80 .50
- ☐ 412 Bob Anderson .... 4.00 1.80 .50
- ☐ 413 Athletics Team .... 9.00 2.30 .70
  (Checklist on back)
- ☐ 414 Don Williams .... 4.00 1.80 .50
- ☐ 415 Bob Cerv .... 4.00 1.80 .50
- ☐ 416 Humberto Robinson .. 4.00 1.80 .50
- ☐ 417 Chuck Cottier .... 4.00 1.80 .50
- ☐ 418 Don Mossi .... 4.50 2.00 .55
- ☐ 419 George Crowe .... 4.00 1.80 .50
- ☐ 420 Eddie Mathews 24.00 11.00 3.00
- ☐ 421 Duke Maas .... 4.00 1.80 .50
- ☐ 422 John Powers .... 4.00 1.80 .50
- ☐ 423 Ed Fitzgerald .... 4.00 1.80 .50
- ☐ 424 Pete Whisenant .... 4.00 1.80 .50
- ☐ 425 Johnny Podres .... 5.00 2.30 .60
- ☐ 426 Ron Jackson .... 4.00 1.80 .50
- ☐ 427 Al Grunwald .... 4.00 1.80 .50
- ☐ 428 Al Smith .... 4.00 1.80 .50
- ☐ 429 AL Kings .... 6.50 2.90 .80
  Nellie Fox
  Harvey Kuenn
- ☐ 430 Art Ditmar .... 4.00 1.80 .50
- ☐ 431 Andre Rodgers .... 4.00 1.80 .50
- ☐ 432 Chuck Stobbs .... 4.00 1.80 .50
- ☐ 433 Irv Noren .... 4.00 1.80 .50
- ☐ 434 Brooks Lawrence .... 4.00 1.80 .50
- ☐ 435 Gene Freese .... 4.00 1.80 .50
- ☐ 436 Marv Throneberry .... 5.00 2.30 .60
- ☐ 437 Bob Friend .... 4.50 2.00 .55
- ☐ 438 Jim Coker .... 4.00 1.80 .50
- ☐ 439 Tom Brewer .... 4.00 1.80 .50
- ☐ 440 Jim Lemon .... 4.50 2.00 .55
- ☐ 441 Gary Bell .... 6.00 2.70 .75
- ☐ 442 Joe Pignatano .... 6.00 2.70 .75
- ☐ 443 Charlie Maxwell .... 6.50 2.90 .80
- ☐ 444 Jerry Kindall .... 6.50 2.90 .80
- ☐ 445 Warren Spahn 40.00 18.00 5.00
- ☐ 446 Ellis Burton .... 6.00 2.70 .75
- ☐ 447 Ray Moore .... 6.00 2.70 .75
- ☐ 448 Jim Gentile 18.00 8.00 2.30
- ☐ 449 Jim Brosnan .... 6.50 2.90 .80
- ☐ 450 Orlando Cepeda 20.00 9.00 2.50
- ☐ 451 Curt Simmons .... 6.50 2.90 .80
- ☐ 452 Ray Webster .... 6.00 2.70 .75
- ☐ 453 Vern Law 8.00 3.60 1.00
- ☐ 454 Hal Woodeshick .... 6.00 2.70 .75
- ☐ 455 Baltimore Coaches .... 7.00 3.10 .85
  Eddie Robinson
  Harry Brecheen
  Luman Harris
- ☐ 456 Red Sox Coaches 8.50 3.80 1.05
  Rudy York
  Billy Herman
  Sal Maglie
  Del Baker
- ☐ 457 Cubs Coaches .... 7.00 3.10 .85
  Charlie Root
  Lou Klein
  Elvin Tappe

☐	458 White Sox Coaches	7.00	3.10	.85
	Johnny Cooney Don Gutteridge Tony Cuccinello Ray Berres			
☐	459 Reds Coaches	7.00	3.10	.85
	Reggie Otero Cot Deal Wally Moses			
☐	460 Indians Coaches	8.50	3.80	1.05
	Mel Harder Jo-Jo White Bob Lemon Ralph(Red) Kress			
☐	461 Tigers Coaches	8.50	3.80	1.05
	Tom Ferrick Luke Appling Billy Hitchcock			
☐	462 Athletics Coaches	7.00	3.10	.85
	Fred Fitzsimmons Don Heffner Walker Cooper			
☐	463 Dodgers Coaches	8.00	3.60	1.00
	Bobby Bragan Pete Reiser Joe Becker Greg Mulleavy			
☐	464 Braves Coaches	7.00	3.10	.85
	Bob Scheffing Whitlow Wyatt Andy Pafko George Myatt			
☐	465 Yankees Coaches	14.00	6.25	1.75
	Bill Dickey Ralph Houk Frank Crosetti Ed Lopat			
☐	466 Phillies Coaches	7.00	3.10	.85
	Ken Silvestri Dick Carter Andy Cohen			
☐	467 Pirates Coaches	7.00	3.10	.85
	Mickey Vernon Frank Oceak Sam Narron Bill Burwell			
☐	468 Cardinals Coaches	7.00	3.10	.85
	Johnny Keane Howie Pollet Ray Katt Harry Walker			
☐	469 Giants Coaches	7.00	3.10	.85
	Wes Westrum Salty Parker Bill Posedel			
☐	470 Senators Coaches	7.00	3.10	.85
	Bob Swift Ellis Clary Sam Mele			
☐	471 Ned Garver	6.00	2.70	.75
☐	472 Alvin Dark	7.00	3.10	.85
☐	473 Al Cicotte	6.00	2.70	.75
☐	474 Haywood Sullivan	7.00	3.10	.85
☐	475 Don Drysdale	40.00	18.00	5.00
☐	476 Lou Johnson	6.00	2.70	.75
☐	477 Don Ferrarese	6.00	2.70	.75
☐	478 Frank Torre	7.00	3.10	.85
☐	479 Georges Maranda	6.00	2.70	.75
☐	480 Yogi Berra	70.00	32.00	8.75
☐	481 Wes Stock	7.00	3.10	.85
☐	482 Frank Bolling	6.00	2.70	.75
☐	483 Camilo Pascual	7.00	3.10	.85
☐	484 Pirates Team (Checklist on back)	35.00	8.75	2.80
☐	485 Ken Boyer	12.00	5.50	1.50
☐	486 Bobby Del Greco	6.00	2.70	.75
☐	487 Tom Sturdivant	6.00	2.70	.75
☐	488 Norm Cash	14.00	6.25	1.75
☐	489 Steve Ridzik	6.00	2.70	.75
☐	490 Frank Robinson	45.00	20.00	5.75
☐	491 Mel Roach	6.00	2.70	.75
☐	492 Larry Jackson	6.00	2.70	.75
☐	493 Duke Snider	50.00	23.00	6.25
☐	494 Orioles Team (Checklist on back)	16.00	4.00	1.30
☐	495 Sherm Lollar	7.00	3.10	.85
☐	496 Bill Virdon	8.50	3.80	1.05
☐	497 John Tsitouris	6.00	2.70	.75
☐	498 Al Pilarcik	6.00	2.70	.75
☐	499 Johnny James	6.00	2.70	.75
☐	500 Johnny Temple	7.00	3.10	.85
☐	501 Bob Schmidt	6.00	2.70	.75
☐	502 Jim Bunning	14.00	6.25	1.75
☐	503 Don Lee	6.00	2.70	.75
☐	504 Seth Morehead	6.00	2.70	.75
☐	505 Ted Kluszewski	15.00	6.75	1.90
☐	506 Lee Walls	6.00	2.70	.75
☐	507 Dick Stigman	17.00	7.75	2.10
☐	508 Billy Consolo	15.00	6.75	1.90
☐	509 Tommy Davis	27.00	12.00	3.40
☐	510 Gerry Staley	15.00	6.75	1.90
☐	511 Ken Walters	15.00	6.75	1.90
☐	512 Joe Gibbon	15.00	6.75	1.90
☐	513 Chicago Cubs Team Card (Checklist on back)	30.00	7.50	2.40
☐	514 Steve Barber	18.00	8.00	2.30
☐	515 Stan Lopata	15.00	6.75	1.90
☐	516 Marty Kutyna	15.00	6.75	1.90
☐	517 Charlie James	15.00	6.75	1.90
☐	518 Tony Gonzalez	17.00	7.75	2.10
☐	519 Ed Roebuck	15.00	6.75	1.90
☐	520 Don Buddin	15.00	6.75	1.90
☐	521 Mike Lee	15.00	6.75	1.90
☐	522 Ken Hunt	15.00	6.75	1.90
☐	523 Clay Dalrymple	15.00	6.75	1.90
☐	524 Bill Henry	15.00	6.75	1.90
☐	525 Marv Breeding	15.00	6.75	1.90
☐	526 Paul Giel	17.00	7.75	2.10
☐	527 Jose Valdivielso	15.00	6.75	1.90
☐	528 Ben Johnson	15.00	6.75	1.90
☐	529 Norm Sherry	18.00	8.00	2.30
☐	530 Mike McCormick	17.00	7.75	2.10
☐	531 Sandy Amoros	17.00	7.75	2.10
☐	532 Mike Garcia	17.00	7.75	2.10
☐	533 Lu Clinton	15.00	6.75	1.90
☐	534 Ken MacKenzie	15.00	6.75	1.90
☐	535 Whitey Lockman	17.00	7.75	2.10
☐	536 Wynn Hawkins	15.00	6.75	1.90
☐	537 Boston Red Sox Team Card (Checklist on back)	30.00	7.50	2.40
☐	538 Frank Barnes	15.00	6.75	1.90
☐	539 Gene Baker	15.00	6.75	1.90
☐	540 Jerry Walker	15.00	6.75	1.90
☐	541 Tony Curry	15.00	6.75	1.90
☐	542 Ken Hamlin	15.00	6.75	1.90
☐	543 Elio Chacon	15.00	6.75	1.90
☐	544 Bill Monbouquette	15.00	6.75	1.90
☐	545 Carl Sawatski	15.00	6.75	1.90
☐	546 Hank Aguirre	15.00	6.75	1.90
☐	547 Bob Aspromonte	15.00	6.75	1.90
☐	548 Don Mincher	17.00	7.75	2.10
☐	549 John Buzhardt	15.00	6.75	1.90
☐	550 Jim Landis	15.00	6.75	1.90
☐	551 Ed Rakow	15.00	6.75	1.90

☐	552 Walt Bond	15.00	6.75	1.90
☐	553 Bill Skowron AS	15.00	6.75	1.90
☐	554 Willie McCovey AS	50.00	23.00	6.25
☐	555 Nellie Fox AS	22.00	10.00	2.80
☐	556 Charlie Neal AS	15.00	6.75	1.90
☐	557 Frank Malzone AS	15.00	6.75	1.90
☐	558 Eddie Mathews AS	30.00	13.50	3.80
☐	559 Luis Aparicio AS	25.00	11.50	3.10
☐	560 Ernie Banks AS	60.00	27.00	7.50
☐	561 Al Kaline AS	60.00	27.00	7.50
☐	562 Joe Cunningham AS	15.00	6.75	1.90
☐	563 Mickey Mantle AS	300.00	135.00	38.00
☐	564 Willie Mays AS	125.00	57.50	15.50
☐	565 Roger Maris AS	100.00	45.00	12.50
☐	566 Hank Aaron AS	125.00	57.50	15.50
☐	567 Sherm Lollar AS	15.00	6.75	1.90
☐	568 Del Crandall AS	15.00	6.75	1.90
☐	569 Camilo Pascual AS	15.00	6.75	1.90
☐	570 Don Drysdale AS	30.00	13.50	3.80
☐	571 Billy Pierce AS	15.00	6.75	1.90
☐	572 Johnny Antonelli AS	24.00	7.25	2.40

1961 Topps

The cards in this 587-card set measure 2 1/2" by 3 1/2". In 1961, Topps returned to the vertical obverse format. Introduced for the first time were "League Leaders" (41 to 50) and separate, numbered checklist cards. Two number 463s exist: the Braves team card carrying that number was meant to be number 426. There are three versions of the second series checklist card number 98; the variations are distinguished by the color of the "CHECKLIST" headline on the front of the card, the color of the printing of the card number on the bottom of the reverse, and the presence of the copyright notice running vertically on the card back. There are two groups of managers (131-139 and 219-226) as well as separate series of World Series cards (306-313), Baseball Thrills (401 to 410), previous MVP's (AL 471-478 and NL 479-486) and Sporting News All-Stars (566 to 589). The usual last series scarcity (523 to 589) exists. The set actually totals 587 cards since numbers 587 and 588 were never issued. The key Rookie Cards in this set are Juan Marichal, Ron Santo and Billy Williams.

	NRMT	VG-E	GOOD
COMPLETE SET (587)	5200.00	2300.00	650.00
COMMON CARD (1-109)	3.00	1.35	.40
COMMON CARD (110-370)	3.00	1.35	.40
COMMON CARD (371-446)	4.00	1.80	.50
COMMON CARD (447-522)	6.00	2.70	.75
COMMON CARD (523-565)	30.00	13.50	3.80
COMMON AS (566-589)	30.00	13.50	3.80

☐	1 Dick Groat	20.00	4.00	1.20
☐	2 Roger Maris	160.00	70.00	20.00
☐	3 John Buzhardt	3.00	1.35	.40
☐	4 Lenny Green	3.00	1.35	.40
☐	5 John Romano	3.00	1.35	.40
☐	6 Ed Roebuck	3.00	1.35	.40
☐	7 White Sox Team	7.50	3.40	.95
☐	8 Dick Williams	3.50	1.55	.45
☐	9 Bob Purkey	3.00	1.35	.40
☐	10 Brooks Robinson	30.00	13.50	3.80
☐	11 Curt Simmons	3.50	1.55	.45
☐	12 Moe Thacker	3.00	1.35	.40
☐	13 Chuck Cottier	3.00	1.35	.40
☐	14 Don Mossi	3.50	1.55	.45
☐	15 Willie Kirkland	3.00	1.35	.40
☐	16 Billy Muffett	3.00	1.35	.40
☐	17 Checklist 1	10.00	2.00	.60
☐	18 Jim Grant	3.50	1.55	.45
☐	19 Clete Boyer	5.00	2.30	.60
☐	20 Robin Roberts	12.00	5.50	1.50
☐	21 Zorro Versalles UER (First name should be Zoilo)	4.50	2.00	.55
☐	22 Clem Labine	3.50	1.55	.45
☐	23 Don Demeter	3.00	1.35	.40
☐	24 Ken Johnson	3.00	1.35	.40
☐	25 Reds' Heavy Artillery Vada Pinson Gus Bell Frank Robinson	8.00	3.60	1.00
☐	26 Wes Stock	3.00	1.35	.40
☐	27 Jerry Kindall	3.00	1.35	.40
☐	28 Hector Lopez	3.00	1.35	.40
☐	29 Don Nottebart	3.00	1.35	.40
☐	30 Nellie Fox	8.00	3.60	1.00
☐	31 Bob Schmidt	3.00	1.35	.40
☐	32 Ray Sadecki	3.00	1.35	.40
☐	33 Gary Geiger	3.00	1.35	.40
☐	34 Wynn Hawkins	3.00	1.35	.40
☐	35 Ron Santo	60.00	27.00	7.50
☐	36 Jack Kralick	3.00	1.35	.40
☐	37 Charley Maxwell	3.50	1.55	.45
☐	38 Bob Lillis	3.00	1.35	.40
☐	39 Leo Posada	3.00	1.35	.40
☐	40 Bob Turley	3.50	1.55	.45
☐	41 NL Batting Leaders Dick Groat Norm Larker Willie Mays Roberto Clemente	14.00	6.25	1.75
☐	42 AL Batting Leaders Pete Runnels Al Smith Minnie Minoso Bill Skowron	8.00	3.60	1.00
☐	43 NL Home Run Leaders Ernie Banks Hank Aaron Ed Mathews Ken Boyer	16.00	7.25	2.00
☐	44 AL Home Run Leaders Mickey Mantle Roger Maris Jim Lemon Rocky Colavito	60.00	27.00	7.50
☐	45 NL ERA Leaders Mike McCormick	8.00	3.60	1.00

	Ernie Broglio Don Drysdale Bob Friend Stan Williams			
☐ 46	AL ERA Leaders Frank Baumann Jim Bunning Art Ditmar Hal Brown	8.00	3.60	1.00
☐ 47	NL Pitching Leaders Ernie Broglio Warren Spahn Vern Law Lou Burdette	8.00	3.60	1.00
☐ 48	AL Pitching Leaders Chuck Estrada Jim Perry UER (Listed as an Oriole) Bud Daley Art Ditmar Frank Lary Milt Pappas	7.00	3.10	.85
☐ 49	NL Strikeout Leaders Don Drysdale Sandy Koufax Sam Jones Ernie Broglio	14.00	6.25	1.75
☐ 50	AL Strikeout Leaders Jim Bunning Pedro Ramos Early Wynn Frank Lary	8.00	3.60	1.00
☐ 51	Detroit Tigers Team Card	7.50	3.40	.95
☐ 52	George Crowe	3.00	1.35	.40
☐ 53	Russ Nixon	3.00	1.35	.40
☐ 54	Earl Francis	3.00	1.35	.40
☐ 55	Jim Davenport	3.50	1.55	.45
☐ 56	Russ Kemmerer	3.00	1.35	.40
☐ 57	Marv Throneberry	4.00	1.80	.50
☐ 58	Joe Schaffernoth	3.00	1.35	.40
☐ 59	Jim Woods	3.00	1.35	.40
☐ 60	Woody Held	3.00	1.35	.40
☐ 61	Ron Piche	3.00	1.35	.40
☐ 62	Al Pilarcik	3.00	1.35	.40
☐ 63	Jim Kaat	9.00	4.00	1.15
☐ 64	Alex Grammas	3.00	1.35	.40
☐ 65	Ted Kluszewski	6.00	2.70	.75
☐ 66	Bill Henry	3.00	1.35	.40
☐ 67	Ossie Virgil	3.00	1.35	.40
☐ 68	Deron Johnson	3.50	1.55	.45
☐ 69	Earl Wilson	3.50	1.55	.45
☐ 70	Bill Virdon	3.50	1.55	.45
☐ 71	Jerry Adair	3.00	1.35	.40
☐ 72	Stu Miller	3.50	1.55	.45
☐ 73	Al Spangler	3.00	1.35	.40
☐ 74	Joe Pignatano	3.00	1.35	.40
☐ 75	Lindy Shows Larry Lindy McDaniel Larry Jackson	3.50	1.55	.45
☐ 76	Harry Anderson	3.00	1.35	.40
☐ 77	Dick Stigman	3.00	1.35	.40
☐ 78	Lee Walls	3.00	1.35	.40
☐ 79	Joe Ginsberg	3.00	1.35	.40
☐ 80	Harmon Killebrew	20.00	9.00	2.50
☐ 81	Tracy Stallard	3.00	1.35	.40
☐ 82	Joe Christopher	3.00	1.35	.40
☐ 83	Bob Bruce	3.00	1.35	.40
☐ 84	Lee Maye	3.00	1.35	.40
☐ 85	Jerry Walker	3.00	1.35	.40
☐ 86	Los Angeles Dodgers Team Card	7.50	3.40	.95
☐ 87	Joe Amalfitano	3.00	1.35	.40
☐ 88	Richie Ashburn	8.00	3.60	1.00
☐ 89	Billy Martin	7.00	3.10	.85
☐ 90	Gerry Staley	3.00	1.35	.40
☐ 91	Walt Moryn	3.00	1.35	.40
☐ 92	Hal Naragon	3.00	1.35	.40
☐ 93	Tony Gonzalez	3.00	1.35	.40
☐ 94	Johnny Kucks	3.00	1.35	.40
☐ 95	Norm Cash	7.50	3.40	.95
☐ 96	Billy O'Dell	3.00	1.35	.40
☐ 97	Jerry Lynch	3.50	1.55	.45
☐ 98A	Checklist 2 (Red "Checklist", 98 black on white)	10.00	2.00	.60
☐ 98B	Checklist 2 (Yellow "Checklist", 98 black on white)	10.00	2.00	.60
☐ 98C	Checklist 2 (Yellow "Checklist", 98 white on black, no copyright)	10.00	2.00	.60
☐ 99	Don Buddin UER (66 HR's)	3.00	1.35	.40
☐ 100	Harvey Haddix	3.50	1.55	.45
☐ 101	Bubba Phillips	3.00	1.35	.40
☐ 102	Gene Stephens	3.00	1.35	.40
☐ 103	Ruben Amaro	3.00	1.35	.40
☐ 104	John Blanchard	3.50	1.55	.45
☐ 105	Carl Willey	3.00	1.35	.40
☐ 106	Whitey Herzog	3.00	1.35	.40
☐ 107	Seth Morehead	3.00	1.35	.40
☐ 108	Dan Dobbek	3.00	1.35	.40
☐ 109	Johnny Podres	3.50	1.55	.45
☐ 110	Vada Pinson	5.00	2.30	.60
☐ 111	Jack Meyer	3.00	1.35	.40
☐ 112	Chico Fernandez	3.00	1.35	.40
☐ 113	Mike Fornieles	3.00	1.35	.40
☐ 114	Hobie Landrith	3.00	1.35	.40
☐ 115	Johnny Antonelli	3.50	1.55	.45
☐ 116	Joe DeMaestri	3.00	1.35	.40
☐ 117	Dale Long	3.50	1.55	.45
☐ 118	Chris Cannizzaro	3.00	1.35	.40
☐ 119	A's Big Armor Norm Siebern Hank Bauer Jerry Lumpe	3.50	1.55	.45
☐ 120	Eddie Mathews	24.00	11.00	3.00
☐ 121	Eli Grba	3.50	1.55	.45
☐ 122	Chicago Cubs Team Card	7.50	3.40	.95
☐ 123	Billy Gardner	3.00	1.35	.40
☐ 124	J.C. Martin	3.00	1.35	.40
☐ 125	Steve Barber	3.00	1.35	.40
☐ 126	Dick Stuart	3.50	1.55	.45
☐ 127	Ron Kline	3.00	1.35	.40
☐ 128	Rip Repulski	3.00	1.35	.40
☐ 129	Ed Hobaugh	3.00	1.35	.40
☐ 130	Norm Larker	3.00	1.35	.40
☐ 131	Paul Richards MG	4.00	1.80	.50
☐ 132	Al Lopez MG	5.00	2.30	.60
☐ 133	Ralph Houk MG	5.00	2.30	.60
☐ 134	Mickey Vernon MG	4.00	1.80	.50
☐ 135	Fred Hutchinson MG	4.00	1.80	.50
☐ 136	Walt Alston MG	6.00	2.70	.75
☐ 137	Chuck Dressen MG	4.00	1.80	.50
☐ 138	Danny Murtaugh MG	3.50	1.55	.45
☐ 139	Solly Hemus MG	3.50	1.55	.45
☐ 140	Gus Triandos	3.50	1.55	.45
☐ 141	Billy Williams	80.00	36.00	10.00
☐ 142	Luis Arroyo	3.50	1.55	.45
☐ 143	Russ Snyder	3.00	1.35	.40
☐ 144	Jim Coker	3.00	1.35	.40
☐ 145	Bob Buhl	3.50	1.55	.45
☐ 146	Marty Keough	3.00	1.35	.40

	No.	Card			
☐	147	Ed Rakow	3.00	1.35	.40
☐	148	Julian Javier	3.50	1.55	.45
☐	149	Bob Oldis	3.00	1.35	.40
☐	150	Willie Mays	110.00	50.00	14.00
☐	151	Jim Donohue	3.00	1.35	.40
☐	152	Earl Torgeson	3.00	1.35	.40
☐	153	Don Lee	3.00	1.35	.40
☐	154	Bobby Del Greco	3.00	1.35	.40
☐	155	Johnny Temple	3.50	1.55	.45
☐	156	Ken Hunt	3.50	1.55	.45
☐	157	Cal McLish	3.00	1.35	.40
☐	158	Pete Daley	3.00	1.35	.40
☐	159	Orioles Team	7.50	3.40	.95
☐	160	Whitey Ford UER	40.00	18.00	5.00
		(Incorrectly listed			
		as 5'0" tall)			
☐	161	Sherman Jones UER	3.00	1.35	.40
		(Photo actually			
		Eddie Fisher)			
☐	162	Jay Hook	3.00	1.35	.40
☐	163	Ed Sadowski	3.00	1.35	.40
☐	164	Felix Mantilla	3.00	1.35	.40
☐	165	Gino Cimoli	3.00	1.35	.40
☐	166	Danny Kravitz	3.00	1.35	.40
☐	167	San Francisco Giants	7.50	3.40	.95
		Team Card			
☐	168	Tommy Davis	7.00	3.10	.85
☐	169	Don Elston	3.00	1.35	.40
☐	170	Al Smith	3.00	1.35	.40
☐	171	Paul Foytack	3.00	1.35	.40
☐	172	Don Dillard	3.00	1.35	.40
☐	173	Beantown Bombers	3.50	1.55	.45
		Frank Malzone			
		Vic Wertz			
		Jackie Jensen			
☐	174	Ray Semproch	3.00	1.35	.40
☐	175	Gene Freese	3.00	1.35	.40
☐	176	Ken Aspromonte	3.00	1.35	.40
☐	177	Don Larsen	5.00	2.30	.60
☐	178	Bob Nieman	3.00	1.35	.40
☐	179	Joe Koppe	3.00	1.35	.40
☐	180	Bobby Richardson	14.00	6.25	1.75
☐	181	Fred Green	3.00	1.35	.40
☐	182	Dave Nicholson	3.00	1.35	.40
☐	183	Andre Rodgers	3.00	1.35	.40
☐	184	Steve Bilko	3.50	1.55	.45
☐	185	Herb Score	5.00	2.30	.60
☐	186	Elmer Valo	3.50	1.55	.45
☐	187	Billy Klaus	3.00	1.35	.40
☐	188	Jim Marshall	3.00	1.35	.40
☐	189A	Checklist 3	10.00	2.00	.60
		(Copyright symbol			
		almost adjacent to			
		263 Ken Hamlin)			
☐	189B	Checklist 3	10.00	2.00	.60
		(Copyright symbol			
		adjacent to			
		264 Glen Hobbie)			
☐	190	Stan Williams	3.50	1.55	.45
☐	191	Mike de la Hoz	3.00	1.35	.40
☐	192	Dick Brown	3.00	1.35	.40
☐	193	Gene Conley	3.50	1.55	.45
☐	194	Gordy Coleman	3.50	1.55	.45
☐	195	Jerry Casale	3.00	1.35	.40
☐	196	Ed Bouchee	3.00	1.35	.40
☐	197	Dick Hall	3.00	1.35	.40
☐	198	Carl Sawatski	3.00	1.35	.40
☐	199	Bob Boyd	3.00	1.35	.40
☐	200	Warren Spahn	30.00	13.50	3.80
☐	201	Pete Whisenant	3.00	1.35	.40
☐	202	Al Neiger	3.00	1.35	.40
☐	203	Eddie Bressoud	3.00	1.35	.40
☐	204	Bob Skinner	3.50	1.55	.45
☐	205	Billy Pierce	3.50	1.55	.45
☐	206	Gene Green	3.00	1.35	.40
☐	207	Dodger Southpaws	25.00	11.50	3.10
		Sandy Koufax			
		Johnny Podres			
☐	208	Larry Osborne	3.00	1.35	.40
☐	209	Ken McBride	3.00	1.35	.40
☐	210	Pete Runnels	3.50	1.55	.45
☐	211	Bob Gibson	40.00	18.00	5.00
☐	212	Haywood Sullivan	3.50	1.55	.45
☐	213	Bill Stafford	3.00	1.35	.40
☐	214	Danny Murphy	3.00	1.35	.40
☐	215	Gus Bell	3.50	1.55	.45
☐	216	Ted Bowsfield	3.00	1.35	.40
☐	217	Mel Roach	3.00	1.35	.40
☐	218	Hal Brown	3.00	1.35	.40
☐	219	Gene Mauch MG	4.00	1.80	.50
☐	220	Alvin Dark MG	4.00	1.80	.50
☐	221	Mike Higgins MG	3.50	1.55	.45
☐	222	Jimmy Dykes MG	3.50	1.55	.45
☐	223	Bob Scheffing MG	3.50	1.55	.45
☐	224	Joe Gordon MG	3.50	1.55	.45
☐	225	Bill Rigney MG	4.00	1.80	.50
☐	226	Cookie Lavagetto MG	3.50	1.55	.45
☐	227	Juan Pizarro	3.00	1.35	.40
☐	228	New York Yankees	40.00	18.00	5.00
		Team Card			
☐	229	Rudy Hernandez	3.00	1.35	.40
☐	230	Don Hoak	3.50	1.55	.45
☐	231	Dick Drott	3.00	1.35	.40
☐	232	Bill White	7.00	3.10	.85
☐	233	Joey Jay	3.50	1.55	.45
☐	234	Ted Lepcio	3.00	1.35	.40
☐	235	Camilo Pascual	3.50	1.55	.45
☐	236	Don Gile	3.00	1.35	.40
☐	237	Billy Loes	3.50	1.55	.45
☐	238	Jim Gilliam	3.50	1.55	.45
☐	239	Dave Sisler	3.00	1.35	.40
☐	240	Ron Hansen	3.00	1.35	.40
☐	241	Al Cicotte	3.00	1.35	.40
☐	242	Hal Smith	3.00	1.35	.40
☐	243	Frank Lary	3.50	1.55	.45
☐	244	Chico Cardenas	3.50	1.55	.45
☐	245	Joe Adcock	3.50	1.55	.45
☐	246	Bob Davis	3.00	1.35	.40
☐	247	Billy Goodman	3.50	1.55	.45
☐	248	Ed Keegan	3.00	1.35	.40
☐	249	Cincinnati Reds	7.50	3.40	.95
		Team Card			
☐	250	Buc Hill Aces	3.50	1.55	.45
		Vern Law			
		Roy Face			
☐	251	Bill Bruton	3.00	1.35	.40
☐	252	Bill Short	3.00	1.35	.40
☐	253	Sammy Taylor	3.00	1.35	.40
☐	254	Ted Sadowski	3.00	1.35	.40
☐	255	Vic Power	3.50	1.55	.45
☐	256	Billy Hoeft	3.00	1.35	.40
☐	257	Carroll Hardy	3.00	1.35	.40
☐	258	Jack Sanford	3.50	1.55	.45
☐	259	John Schaive	3.00	1.35	.40
☐	260	Don Drysdale	30.00	13.50	3.80
☐	261	Charlie Lau	3.50	1.55	.45
☐	262	Tony Curry	3.00	1.35	.40
☐	263	Ken Hamlin	3.00	1.35	.40
☐	264	Glen Hobbie	3.00	1.35	.40
☐	265	Tony Kubek	12.00	5.50	1.50
☐	266	Lindy McDaniel	3.50	1.55	.45
☐	267	Norm Siebern	3.00	1.35	.40
☐	268	Ike Delock	3.00	1.35	.40
☐	269	Harry Chiti	3.00	1.35	.40
☐	270	Bob Friend	3.50	1.55	.45
☐	271	Jim Landis	3.00	1.35	.40

☐ 272 Tom Morgan .... 3.00 1.35 .40
☐ 273A Checklist 4 .... 15.00 3.00 .90
(Copyright symbol adjacent to 336 Don Mincher)
☐ 273B Checklist 4 .... 10.00 2.00 .60
(Copyright symbol adjacent to 339 Gene Baker)
☐ 274 Gary Bell .... 3.00 1.35 .40
☐ 275 Gene Woodling .... 3.50 1.55 .45
☐ 276 Ray Rippelmeyer .... 3.00 1.35 .40
☐ 277 Hank Foiles .... 3.00 1.35 .40
☐ 278 Don McMahon .... 3.00 1.35 .40
☐ 279 Jose Pagan .... 3.00 1.35 .40
☐ 280 Frank Howard 8.00 3.60 1.00
☐ 281 Frank Sullivan .... 3.00 1.35 .40
☐ 282 Faye Throneberry .... 3.00 1.35 .40
☐ 283 Bob Anderson .... 3.00 1.35 .40
☐ 284 Dick Gernert .... 3.00 1.35 .40
☐ 285 Sherm Lollar .... 3.50 1.55 .45
☐ 286 George Witt .... 3.00 1.35 .40
☐ 287 Carl Yastrzemski 65.00 29.00 8.25
☐ 288 Albie Pearson .... 3.50 1.55 .45
☐ 289 Ray Moore .... 3.00 1.35 .40
☐ 290 Stan Musial 100.00 45.00 12.50
☐ 291 Tex Clevenger .... 3.00 1.35 .40
☐ 292 Jim Baumer .... 3.00 1.35 .40
☐ 293 Tom Sturdivant .... 3.00 1.35 .40
☐ 294 Don Blasingame .... 3.00 1.35 .40
☐ 295 Milt Pappas .... 3.50 1.55 .45
☐ 296 Wes Covington .... 3.50 1.55 .45
☐ 297 Athletics Team .... 7.50 3.40 .95
☐ 298 Jim Golden .... 3.00 1.35 .40
☐ 299 Clay Dalrymple .... 3.00 1.35 .40
☐ 300 Mickey Mantle 450.00 200.00 57.50
☐ 301 Chet Nichols .... 3.00 1.35 .40
☐ 302 Al Heist .... 3.00 1.35 .40
☐ 303 Gary Peters .... 3.50 1.55 .45
☐ 304 Rocky Nelson .... 3.00 1.35 .40
☐ 305 Mike McCormick .... 3.50 1.55 .45
☐ 306 World Series Game 1 . 8.00 3.60 1.00
Bill Virdon Saves Game
☐ 307 World Series Game 2 55.00 25.00 7.00
Mickey Mantle
Two Homers
☐ 308 World Series Game 3 . 9.00 4.00 1.15
Bobby Richardson
Is Hero
☐ 309 World Series Game 4 . 8.00 3.60 1.00
Gino Cimoli Safe
☐ 310 World Series Game 5 . 8.00 3.60 1.00
Roy Face Saves Day
☐ 311 World Series Game 6 15.00 6.75 1.90
Whitey Ford
Second Shutout
☐ 312 World Series Game 7 18.00 8.00 2.30
Bill Mazeroski's Homer
☐ 313 World Series Summary 14.00 6.25 1.75
Pirates Celebrate
☐ 314 Bob Miller .... 3.00 1.35 .40
☐ 315 Earl Battey .... 3.50 1.55 .45
☐ 316 Bobby Gene Smith .... 3.00 1.35 .40
☐ 317 Jim Brewer .... 3.00 1.35 .40
☐ 318 Danny O'Connell .... 3.00 1.35 .40
☐ 319 Valmy Thomas .... 3.00 1.35 .40
☐ 320 Lou Burdette .... 3.50 1.55 .45
☐ 321 Marv Breeding .... 3.00 1.35 .40
☐ 322 Bill Kunkel .... 3.50 1.55 .45
☐ 323 Sammy Esposito .... 3.00 1.35 .40
☐ 324 Hank Aguirre .... 3.00 1.35 .40
☐ 325 Wally Moon .... 3.50 1.55 .45
☐ 326 Dave Hillman .... 3.00 1.35 .40
☐ 327 Matty Alou 10.00 4.50 1.25
☐ 328 Jim O'Toole .... 3.50 1.55 .45
☐ 329 Julio Becquer .... 3.00 1.35 .40
☐ 330 Rocky Colavito 18.00 8.00 2.30
☐ 331 Ned Garver .... 3.00 1.35 .40
☐ 332 Dutch Dotterer UER ..... 3.00 1.35 .40
(Photo actually Tommy Dotterer, Dutch's brother)
☐ 333 Fritz Brickell .... 3.00 1.35 .40
☐ 334 Walt Bond .... 3.00 1.35 .40
☐ 335 Frank Bolling .... 3.00 1.35 .40
☐ 336 Don Mincher .... 3.50 1.55 .45
☐ 337 Al's Aces .... 5.50 2.50 .70
Early Wynn
Al Lopez
Herb Score
☐ 338 Don Landrum .... 3.00 1.35 .40
☐ 339 Gene Baker .... 3.00 1.35 .40
☐ 340 Vic Wertz .... 3.50 1.55 .45
☐ 341 Jim Owens .... 3.00 1.35 .40
☐ 342 Clint Courtney .... 3.00 1.35 .40
☐ 343 Earl Robinson .... 3.00 1.35 .40
☐ 344 Sandy Koufax 85.00 38.00 10.50
☐ 345 Jim Piersall .... 3.50 1.55 .45
☐ 346 Howie Nunn .... 3.00 1.35 .40
☐ 347 St. Louis Cardinals .... 7.50 3.40 .95
Team Card
☐ 348 Steve Boros .... 3.00 1.35 .40
☐ 349 Danny McDevitt .... 3.00 1.35 .40
☐ 350 Ernie Banks 40.00 18.00 5.00
☐ 351 Jim King .... 3.00 1.35 .40
☐ 352 Bob Shaw .... 3.00 1.35 .40
☐ 353 Howie Bedell .... 3.00 1.35 .40
☐ 354 Billy Harrell .... 3.00 1.35 .40
☐ 355 Bob Allison .... 3.50 1.55 .45
☐ 356 Ryne Duren .... 3.00 1.35 .40
☐ 357 Daryl Spencer .... 3.00 1.35 .40
☐ 358 Earl Averill .... 3.50 1.55 .45
☐ 359 Dallas Green .... 3.00 1.35 .40
☐ 360 Frank Robinson 45.00 20.00 5.75
☐ 361A Checklist 5 .... 10.00 2.00 .60
(No ad on back)
☐ 361B Checklist 5 .... 15.00 3.00 .90
(Special Feature ad on back)
☐ 362 Frank Funk .... 3.00 1.35 .40
☐ 363 John Roseboro .... 3.50 1.55 .45
☐ 364 Moe Drabowsky .... 3.50 1.55 .45
☐ 365 Jerry Lumpe .... 3.00 1.35 .40
☐ 366 Eddie Fisher .... 3.00 1.35 .40
☐ 367 Jim Rivera .... 3.00 1.35 .40
☐ 368 Bennie Daniels .... 3.00 1.35 .40
☐ 369 Dave Philley .... 3.00 1.35 .40
☐ 370 Roy Face .... 4.00 1.80 .50
☐ 371 Bill Skowron SP 55.00 25.00 7.00
☐ 372 Bob Hendley .... 4.00 1.80 .50
☐ 373 Boston Red Sox 9.00 4.00 1.15
Team Card
☐ 374 Paul Giel .... 4.50 2.00 .55
☐ 375 Ken Boyer 9.00 4.00 1.15
☐ 376 Mike Roarke .... 4.00 1.80 .50
☐ 377 Ruben Gomez .... 4.00 1.80 .50
☐ 378 Wally Post .... 4.50 2.00 .55
☐ 379 Bobby Shantz .... 4.00 1.80 .50
☐ 380 Minnie Minoso .... 7.00 3.10 .85
☐ 381 Dave Wickersham .... 4.00 1.80 .50
☐ 382 Frank Thomas .... 5.00 2.30 .60
☐ 383 Frisco First Liners .... 4.50 2.00 .55
Mike McCormick
Jack Sanford
Billy O'Dell
☐ 384 Chuck Essegian .... 4.00 1.80 .50

☐ 385 Jim Perry .... 6.00 2.70 .75
☐ 386 Joe Hicks .... 4.00 1.80 .50
☐ 387 Duke Maas .... 4.00 1.80 .50
☐ 388 Bob Clemente 110.00 50.00 14.00
☐ 389 Ralph Terry .... 5.00 2.30 .60
☐ 390 Del Crandall .... 5.00 2.30 .60
☐ 391 Winston Brown .... 4.00 1.80 .50
☐ 392 Reno Bertoia .... 4.00 1.80 .50
☐ 393 Batter Bafflers .... 4.00 1.80 .50
Don Cardwell
Glen Hobbie
☐ 394 Ken Walters .... 4.00 1.80 .50
☐ 395 Chuck Estrada .... 4.50 2.00 .55
☐ 396 Bob Aspromonte .... 4.00 1.80 .50
☐ 397 Hal Woodeshick .... 4.00 1.80 .50
☐ 398 Hank Bauer .... 4.00 1.80 .50
☐ 399 Cliff Cook .... 4.00 1.80 .50
☐ 400 Vern Law .... 5.00 2.30 .60
☐ 401 Babe Ruth 60th Homer 38.00 17.00 4.70
☐ 402 Don Larsen SP 20.00 9.00 2.50
Perfect Game
☐ 403 26 Inning Tie .... 6.00 2.70 .75
☐ 404 Rogers Hornsby .424. 9.00 4.00 1.15
Average
☐ 405 Lou Gehrig's Streak. 35.00 16.00 4.40
☐ 406 Mickey Mantle 565... 50.00 23.00 6.25
Foot Homer
☐ 407 Jack Chesbro Wins 41 6.00 2.70 .75
☐ 408 Christy Mathewson SP 20.00 9.00 2.50
Fans 267
☐ 409 Walter Johnson 12.00 5.50 1.50
Shutouts
☐ 410 Harvey Haddix 12....... 7.00 3.10 .85
Perfect Innings
☐ 411 Tony Taylor .... 4.50 2.00 .55
☐ 412 Larry Sherry .... 4.50 2.00 .55
☐ 413 Eddie Yost .... 4.50 2.00 .55
☐ 414 Dick Donovan .... 4.50 2.00 .55
☐ 415 Hank Aaron 110.00 50.00 14.00
☐ 416 Dick Howser 10.00 4.50 1.25
☐ 417 Juan Marichal SP ... 125.00 57.50 15.50
☐ 418 Ed Bailey .... 4.50 2.00 .55
☐ 419 Tom Borland .... 4.00 1.80 .50
☐ 420 Ernie Broglio .... 4.50 2.00 .55
☐ 421 Ty Cline SP 16.00 7.25 2.00
☐ 422 Bud Daley .... 4.00 1.80 .50
☐ 423 Charlie Neal SP 16.00 7.25 2.00
☐ 424 Turk Lown .... 4.00 1.80 .50
☐ 425 Yogi Berra 70.00 32.00 8.75
☐ 426 Milwaukee Braves 12.00 5.50 1.50
Team Card
(Back numbered 463)
☐ 427 Dick Ellsworth .... 4.50 2.00 .55
☐ 428 Ray Barker SP 16.00 7.25 2.00
☐ 429 Al Kaline 40.00 18.00 5.00
☐ 430 Bill Mazeroski SP 55.00 25.00 7.00
☐ 431 Chuck Stobbs .... 4.00 1.80 .50
☐ 432 Coot Veal .... 4.50 2.00 .55
☐ 433 Art Mahaffey .... 4.00 1.80 .50
☐ 434 Tom Brewer .... 4.00 1.80 .50
☐ 435 Orlando Cepeda UER 14.00 6.25 1.75
(San Francis on
card front)
☐ 436 Jim Maloney 20.00 9.00 2.50
☐ 437A Checklist 6 .... 15.00 3.00 .90
440 Louis Aparicio
☐ 437B Checklist 6 .... 15.00 3.00 .90
440 Luis Aparicio
☐ 438 Curt Flood .... 6.00 2.70 .75
☐ 439 Phil Regan .... 6.00 2.70 .75
☐ 440 Luis Aparicio 15.00 6.75 1.90
☐ 441 Dick Bertell .... 4.00 1.80 .50
☐ 442 Gordon Jones .... 4.00 1.80 .50
☐ 443 Duke Snider 40.00 18.00 5.00
☐ 444 Joe Nuxhall .... 5.00 2.30 .60
☐ 445 Frank Malzone .... 4.50 2.00 .55
☐ 446 Bob Taylor .... 4.00 1.80 .50
☐ 447 Harry Bright .... 6.50 2.90 .80
☐ 448 Del Rice .... 6.50 2.90 .80
☐ 449 Bob Bolin .... 6.00 2.70 .75
☐ 450 Jim Lemon .... 6.50 2.90 .80
☐ 451 Power for Ernie .... 7.00 3.10 .85
Daryl Spencer
Bill White
Ernie Broglio
☐ 452 Bob Allen .... 6.00 2.70 .75
☐ 453 Dick Schofield .... 6.50 2.90 .80
☐ 454 Pumpsie Green .... 6.50 2.90 .80
☐ 455 Early Wynn 15.00 6.75 1.90
☐ 456 Hal Bevan .... 6.00 2.70 .75
☐ 457 Johnny James .... 6.50 2.90 .80
(Listed as Angel,
but wearing Yankee
uniform and cap)
☐ 458 Willie Tasby .... 6.50 2.90 .80
☐ 459 Terry Fox .... 6.00 2.70 .75
☐ 460 Gil Hodges 15.00 6.75 1.90
☐ 461 Smoky Burgess .... 7.00 3.10 .85
☐ 462 Lou Klimchock .... 6.00 2.70 .75
☐ 463 Jack Fisher .... 6.50 2.90 .80
(See also 426)
☐ 464 Lee Thomas 8.00 3.60 1.00
(Pictured with Yankee
cap but listed as
Los Angeles Angel)
☐ 465 Roy McMillan .... 6.50 2.90 .80
☐ 466 Ron Moeller .... 6.50 2.90 .80
☐ 467 Cleveland Indians 9.00 4.00 1.15
Team Card
☐ 468 John Callison .... 7.00 3.10 .85
☐ 469 Ralph Lumenti .... 6.50 2.90 .80
☐ 470 Roy Sievers .... 6.50 2.90 .80
☐ 471 Phil Rizzuto MVP 16.00 7.25 2.00
☐ 472 Yogi Berra MVP SP .. 50.00 23.00 6.25
☐ 473 Bob Shantz MVP .... 6.00 2.70 .75
☐ 474 Al Rosen MVP .... 6.00 2.70 .75
☐ 475 Mickey Mantle MVP 135.00 60.00 17.00
☐ 476 Jackie Jensen MVP .... 6.00 2.70 .75
☐ 477 Nellie Fox MVP 9.00 4.00 1.15
☐ 478 Roger Maris MVP 45.00 20.00 5.75
☐ 479 Jim Konstanty MVP ... 6.00 2.70 .75
☐ 480 Roy Campanella MVP 35.00 16.00 4.40
☐ 481 Hank Sauer MVP .... 6.00 2.70 .75
☐ 482 Willie Mays MVP 50.00 23.00 6.25
☐ 483 Don Newcombe MVP. 6.00 2.70 .75
☐ 484 Hank Aaron MVP 50.00 23.00 6.25
☐ 485 Ernie Banks MVP 30.00 13.50 3.80
☐ 486 Dick Groat MVP .... 6.00 2.70 .75
☐ 487 Gene Oliver .... 6.00 2.70 .75
☐ 488 Joe McClain .... 6.50 2.90 .80
☐ 489 Walt Dropo .... 6.00 2.70 .75
☐ 490 Jim Bunning 12.00 5.50 1.50
☐ 491 Philadelphia Phillies ... 9.00 4.00 1.15
Team Card
☐ 492 Ron Fairly .... 6.50 2.90 .80
☐ 493 Don Zimmer UER .... 6.00 2.70 .75
(Brooklyn A.L.)
☐ 494 Tom Cheney .... 6.00 2.70 .75
☐ 495 Elston Howard 12.00 5.50 1.50
☐ 496 Ken MacKenzie .... 6.00 2.70 .75
☐ 497 Willie Jones .... 6.00 2.70 .75
☐ 498 Ray Herbert .... 6.00 2.70 .75
☐ 499 Chuck Schilling .... 6.00 2.70 .75
☐ 500 Harvey Kuenn .... 7.00 3.10 .85
☐ 501 John DeMerit .... 6.00 2.70 .75
☐ 502 Clarence Coleman 8.00 3.60 1.00

☐	503 Tito Francona	6.00	2.70	.75
☐	504 Billy Consolo	6.00	2.70	.75
☐	505 Red Schoendienst	14.00	6.25	1.75
☐	506 Willie Davis	18.00	8.00	2.30
☐	507 Pete Burnside	6.50	2.90	.80
☐	508 Rocky Bridges	6.50	2.90	.80
☐	509 Camilo Carreon	6.00	2.70	.75
☐	510 Art Ditmar	6.00	2.70	.75
☐	511 Joe M. Morgan	6.50	2.90	.80
☐	512 Bob Will	6.00	2.70	.75
☐	513 Jim Brosnan	7.00	3.10	.85
☐	514 Jake Wood	6.00	2.70	.75
☐	515 Jackie Brandt	6.00	2.70	.75
☐	516 Checklist 7	15.00	3.00	.90
☐	517 Willie McCovey	50.00	23.00	6.25
☐	518 Andy Carey	6.50	2.90	.80
☐	519 Jim Pagliaroni	6.50	2.90	.80
☐	520 Joe Cunningham	6.50	2.90	.80
☐	521 Brother Battery Norm Sherry Larry Sherry	6.50	2.90	.80
☐	522 Dick Farrell UER (Phillies cap, but listed on Dodgers)	6.50	2.90	.80
☐	523 Joe Gibbon	30.00	13.50	3.80
☐	524 Johnny Logan	30.00	13.50	3.80
☐	525 Ron Perranoski	40.00	18.00	5.00
☐	526 R.C. Stevens	32.00	14.50	4.00
☐	527 Gene Leek	32.00	14.50	4.00
☐	528 Pedro Ramos	32.00	14.50	4.00
☐	529 Bob Roselli	30.00	13.50	3.80
☐	530 Bob Malkmus	30.00	13.50	3.80
☐	531 Jim Coates	30.00	13.50	3.80
☐	532 Bob Hale	30.00	13.50	3.80
☐	533 Jack Curtis	30.00	13.50	3.80
☐	534 Eddie Kasko	30.00	13.50	3.80
☐	535 Larry Jackson	30.00	13.50	3.80
☐	536 Bill Tuttle	32.00	14.50	4.00
☐	537 Bobby Locke	30.00	13.50	3.80
☐	538 Chuck Hiller	30.00	13.50	3.80
☐	539 Johnny Klippstein	32.00	14.50	4.00
☐	540 Jackie Jensen	40.00	18.00	5.00
☐	541 Roland Sheldon	38.00	17.00	4.70
☐	542 Minnesota Twins Team Card	70.00	32.00	8.75
☐	543 Roger Craig	30.00	13.50	3.80
☐	544 George Thomas	30.00	13.50	3.80
☐	545 Hoyt Wilhelm	50.00	23.00	6.25
☐	546 Marty Kutyna	32.00	14.50	4.00
☐	547 Leon Wagner	32.00	14.50	4.00
☐	548 Ted Wills	30.00	13.50	3.80
☐	549 Hal R. Smith	30.00	13.50	3.80
☐	550 Frank Baumann	30.00	13.50	3.80
☐	551 George Altman	30.00	13.50	3.80
☐	552 Jim Archer	30.00	13.50	3.80
☐	553 Bill Fischer	30.00	13.50	3.80
☐	554 Pittsburgh Pirates Team Card	70.00	32.00	8.75
☐	555 Sam Jones	32.00	14.50	4.00
☐	556 Ken R. Hunt	30.00	13.50	3.80
☐	557 Jose Valdivielso	32.00	14.50	4.00
☐	558 Don Ferrarese	30.00	13.50	3.80
☐	559 Jim Gentile	50.00	23.00	6.25
☐	560 Barry Latman	30.00	13.50	3.80
☐	561 Charley James	30.00	13.50	3.80
☐	562 Bill Monbouquette	30.00	13.50	3.80
☐	563 Bob Cerv	38.00	17.00	4.70
☐	564 Don Cardwell	30.00	13.50	3.80
☐	565 Felipe Alou	50.00	23.00	6.25
☐	566 Paul Richards AS MG	30.00	13.50	3.80
☐	567 Danny Murtaugh AS MG	30.00	13.50	3.80
☐	568 Bill Skowron AS	35.00	16.00	4.40
☐	569 Frank Herrera AS	30.00	13.50	3.80
☐	570 Nellie Fox AS	35.00	16.00	4.40
☐	571 Bill Mazeroski AS	35.00	16.00	4.40
☐	572 Brooks Robinson AS	90.00	40.00	11.50
☐	573 Ken Boyer AS	35.00	16.00	4.40
☐	574 Luis Aparicio AS	50.00	23.00	6.25
☐	575 Ernie Banks AS	90.00	40.00	11.50
☐	576 Roger Maris AS	165.00	75.00	21.00
☐	577 Hank Aaron AS	175.00	80.00	22.00
☐	578 Mickey Mantle AS	425.00	190.00	52.50
☐	579 Willie Mays AS	175.00	80.00	22.00
☐	580 Al Kaline AS	90.00	40.00	11.50
☐	581 Frank Robinson AS	90.00	40.00	11.50
☐	582 Earl Battey AS	30.00	13.50	3.80
☐	583 Del Crandall AS	30.00	13.50	3.80
☐	584 Jim Perry AS	30.00	13.50	3.80
☐	585 Bob Friend AS	30.00	13.50	3.80
☐	586 Whitey Ford AS	90.00	40.00	11.50
☐	587 Does not exist	.00	.00	.00
☐	588 Does not exist	.00	.00	.00
☐	589 Warren Spahn AS	110.00	33.00	8.75

1962 Topps

The cards in this 598-card set measure 2 1/2" by 3 1/2". The 1962 Topps set contains a mini-series spotlighting Babe Ruth (135-144). Other subsets in the set include League Leaders (51-60), World Series cards (232-237), In Action cards (311-319), NL All Stars (390-399), AL All Stars (466-475), and Rookie Prospects (591-598). The All-Star selections were again provided by Sport Magazine, as in 1958 and 1960. The second series had two distinct printings which are distinguishable by numerous color and pose variations. Those cards with a distinctive "green tint" are valued at a slight premuim as they are basically the result of a flawed printing process occurring early in the second series run. Card number 139 exists as A: Babe Ruth Special card, B: Hal Reniff with arms over head, or C: Hal Reniff in the same pose as card number 159. In addition, two poses exist for players depicted on card numbers 129, 132, 134, 147, 174, 176, and 190. The high number series, 523 to 598, is somewhat more difficult to obtain than other cards in the set. Within the last series (523-598) there are 43 cards which were printed in lesser quantities; these are marked SP in the checklist below. In particular, the Rookie Parade subset (591-598) of this last series is even more difficult. This was the first year Topps

produced multi-player Rookie Cards. The set price listed does not include the pose variations (see checklist below for individual values). The key Rookie Cards in this set are Lou Brock, Tim McCarver, Gaylord Perry, and Bob Uecker.

	NRMT	VG-E	GOOD
COMPLETE SET (598)	4800.00	2200.00	600.00
COMMON CARD (1-109)	4.50	2.00	.55
COMMON CARD (110-196)	4.50	2.00	.55
COMMON CARD (197-283)	4.50	2.00	.55
COMMON CARD (284-370)	4.50	2.00	.55
COMMON CARD (371-446)	6.00	2.70	.75
COMMON CARD (447-522)	12.00	5.50	1.50
COMMON CARD (523-590)	20.00	9.00	2.50
COMMON ROOKIES (591-598)	40.00	18.00	5.00
□ 1 Roger Maris	200.00	50.00	16.00
□ 2 Jim Brosnan	4.50	2.00	.55
□ 3 Pete Runnels	5.00	2.30	.60
□ 4 John DeMerit	4.50	2.00	.55
□ 5 Sandy Koufax UER (Struck ou 18)	125.00	57.50	15.50
□ 6 Marv Breeding	4.50	2.00	.55
□ 7 Frank Thomas	5.00	2.30	.60
□ 8 Ray Herbert	4.50	2.00	.55
□ 9 Jim Davenport	5.00	2.30	.60
□ 10 Bob Clemente	135.00	60.00	17.00
□ 11 Tom Morgan	4.50	2.00	.55
□ 12 Harry Craft MG	4.50	2.00	.55
□ 13 Dick Howser	5.00	2.30	.60
□ 14 Bill White	6.00	2.70	.75
□ 15 Dick Donovan	4.50	2.00	.55
□ 16 Darrell Johnson	4.50	2.00	.55
□ 17 John Callison	5.00	2.30	.60
□ 18 Managers' Dream Mickey Mantle Willie Mays	150.00	70.00	19.00
□ 19 Ray Washburn	4.50	2.00	.55
□ 20 Rocky Colavito	14.00	6.25	1.75
□ 21 Jim Kaat	8.00	3.60	1.00
□ 22A Checklist 1 ERR (121-176 on back)	12.00	1.80	.60
□ 22B Checklist 1 COR	12.00	1.80	.60
□ 23 Norm Larker	4.50	2.00	.55
□ 24 Tigers Team	7.00	3.10	.85
□ 25 Ernie Banks	45.00	20.00	5.75
□ 26 Chris Cannizzaro	5.00	2.30	.60
□ 27 Chuck Cottier	4.50	2.00	.55
□ 28 Minnie Minoso	6.00	2.70	.75
□ 29 Casey Stengel MG	20.00	9.00	2.50
□ 30 Eddie Mathews	18.00	8.00	2.30
□ 31 Tom Tresh	18.00	8.00	2.30
□ 32 John Roseboro	5.00	2.30	.60
□ 33 Don Larsen	5.00	2.30	.60
□ 34 Johnny Temple	5.00	2.30	.60
□ 35 Don Schwall	5.00	2.30	.60
□ 36 Don Leppert	4.50	2.00	.55
□ 37 Tribe Hill Trio Barry Latman Dick Stigman Jim Perry	5.00	2.30	.60
□ 38 Gene Stephens	4.50	2.00	.55
□ 39 Joe Koppe	4.50	2.00	.55
□ 40 Orlando Cepeda	14.00	6.25	1.75
□ 41 Cliff Cook	4.50	2.00	.55
□ 42 Jim King	4.50	2.00	.55
□ 43 Los Angeles Dodgers Team Card	7.00	3.10	.85
□ 44 Don Taussig	4.50	2.00	.55
□ 45 Brooks Robinson	35.00	16.00	4.40
□ 46 Jack Baldschun	4.50	2.00	.55
□ 47 Bob Will	4.50	2.00	.55
□ 48 Ralph Terry	5.00	2.30	.60
□ 49 Hal Jones	4.50	2.00	.55
□ 50 Stan Musial	90.00	40.00	11.50
□ 51 AL Batting Leaders Norm Cash Jim Piersall Al Kaline Elston Howard	7.00	3.10	.85
□ 52 NL Batting Leaders Bob Clemente Vada Pinson Ken Boyer Wally Moon	12.00	5.50	1.50
□ 53 AL Home Run Leaders Roger Maris Mickey Mantle Jim Gentile Harmon Killebrew	60.00	27.00	7.50
□ 54 NL Home Run Leaders Orlando Cepeda Willie Mays Frank Robinson	12.00	5.50	1.50
□ 55 AL ERA Leaders Dick Donovan Bill Stafford Don Mossi Milt Pappas	6.50	2.90	.80
□ 56 NL ERA Leaders Warren Spahn Jim O'Toole Curt Simmons Mike McCormick	7.00	3.10	.85
□ 57 AL Wins Leaders Whitey Ford Frank Lary Steve Barber Jim Bunning	7.00	3.10	.85
□ 58 NL Wins Leaders Warren Spahn Joe Jay Jim O'Toole	7.00	3.10	.85
□ 59 AL Strikeout Leaders Camilo Pascual Whitey Ford Jim Bunning Juan Pizzaro	7.00	3.10	.85
□ 60 NL Strikeout Leaders Sandy Koufax Stan Williams Don Drysdale Jim O'Toole	12.00	5.50	1.50
□ 61 Cardinals Team	7.00	3.10	.85
□ 62 Steve Boros	4.50	2.00	.55
□ 63 Tony Cloninger	6.00	2.70	.75
□ 64 Russ Snyder	4.50	2.00	.55
□ 65 Bobby Richardson	12.00	5.50	1.50
□ 66 Cuno Barragan	4.50	2.00	.55
□ 67 Harvey Haddix	5.00	2.30	.60
□ 68 Ken Hunt	4.50	2.00	.55
□ 69 Phil Ortega	4.50	2.00	.55
□ 70 Harmon Killebrew	20.00	9.00	2.50
□ 71 Dick LeMay	4.50	2.00	.55
□ 72 Bob's Pupils Steve Boros Bob Scheffing MG Jake Wood	4.50	2.00	.55
□ 73 Nellie Fox	10.00	4.50	1.25
□ 74 Bob Lillis	5.00	2.30	.60
□ 75 Milt Pappas	5.00	2.30	.60
□ 76 Howie Bedell	4.50	2.00	.55
□ 77 Tony Taylor	5.00	2.30	.60
□ 78 Gene Green	4.50	2.00	.55

☐ 79 Ed Hobaugh .... 4.50 2.00 .55
☐ 80 Vada Pinson .... 6.00 2.70 .75
☐ 81 Jim Pagliaroni .... 4.50 2.00 .55
☐ 82 Deron Johnson .... 5.00 2.30 .60
☐ 83 Larry Jackson .... 4.50 2.00 .55
☐ 84 Lenny Green .... 4.50 2.00 .55
☐ 85 Gil Hodges 15.00 6.75 1.90
☐ 86 Donn Clendenon .... 6.00 2.70 .75
☐ 87 Mike Roarke .... 4.50 2.00 .55
☐ 88 Ralph Houk MG .... 4.50 2.00 .55
(Berra in background)
☐ 89 Barney Schultz .... 4.50 2.00 .55
☐ 90 Jim Piersall .... 4.50 2.00 .55
☐ 91 J.C. Martin .... 4.50 2.00 .55
☐ 92 Sam Jones .... 4.50 2.00 .55
☐ 93 John Blanchard .... 5.00 2.30 .60
☐ 94 Jay Hook .... 5.00 2.30 .60
☐ 95 Don Hoak .... 5.00 2.30 .60
☐ 96 Eli Grba .... 4.50 2.00 .55
☐ 97 Tito Francona .... 4.50 2.00 .55
☐ 98 Checklist 2 .... 12.00 1.80 .60
☐ 99 John (Boog) Powell ... 32.00 14.50 4.00
☐ 100 Warren Spahn 30.00 13.50 3.80
☐ 101 Carroll Hardy .... 4.50 2.00 .55
☐ 102 Al Schroll .... 4.50 2.00 .55
☐ 103 Don Blasingame .... 4.50 2.00 .55
☐ 104 Ted Savage .... 4.50 2.00 .55
☐ 105 Don Mossi .... 5.00 2.30 .60
☐ 106 Carl Sawatski .... 4.50 2.00 .55
☐ 107 Mike McCormick .... 5.00 2.30 .60
☐ 108 Willie Davis .... 4.50 2.00 .55
☐ 109 Bob Shaw .... 4.50 2.00 .55
☐ 110 Bill Skowron .... 6.00 2.70 .75
☐ 111 Dallas Green .... 5.50 2.50 .70
☐ 112 Hank Foiles .... 5.00 2.30 .60
☐ 113 Chicago White Sox..... 7.00 3.10 .85
Team Card
☐ 114 Howie Koplitz .... 5.00 2.30 .60
☐ 115 Bob Skinner .... 5.50 2.50 .70
☐ 116 Herb Score .... 5.00 2.30 .60
☐ 117 Gary Geiger .... 5.00 2.30 .60
☐ 118 Julian Javier .... 5.50 2.50 .70
☐ 119 Danny Murphy .... 5.00 2.30 .60
☐ 120 Bob Purkey .... 5.00 2.30 .60
☐ 121 Billy Hitchcock MG..... 5.00 2.30 .60
☐ 122 Norm Bass .... 5.00 2.30 .60
☐ 123 Mike de la Hoz .... 5.00 2.30 .60
☐ 124 Bill Pleis .... 5.00 2.30 .60
☐ 125 Gene Woodling .... 5.50 2.50 .70
☐ 126 Al Cicotte .... 5.00 2.30 .60
☐ 127 Pride of A's .... 5.50 2.50 .70
Norm Siebern
Hank Bauer MG
Jerry Lumpe
☐ 128 Art Fowler .... 5.00 2.30 .60
☐ 129A Lee Walls .... 5.00 2.30 .60
(Facing right)
☐ 129B Lee Walls 30.00 13.50 3.80
(Facing left)
☐ 130 Frank Bolling .... 5.00 2.30 .60
☐ 131 Pete Richert .... 5.00 2.30 .60
☐ 132A Angels Team .... 7.00 3.10 .85
(Without photo)
☐ 132B Angels Team 30.00 13.50 3.80
(With photo)
☐ 133 Felipe Alou .... 6.00 2.70 .75
☐ 134A Billy Hoeft .... 5.00 2.30 .60
(Facing right)
☐ 134B Billy Hoeft 30.00 13.50 3.80
(Facing straight)
☐ 135 Babe Ruth Special 1. 20.00 9.00 2.50
Babe as a Boy
☐ 136 Babe Ruth Special 2. 20.00 9.00 2.50
Babe Joins Yanks
☐ 137 Babe Ruth Special 3. 20.00 9.00 2.50
With Miller Huggins
☐ 138 Babe Ruth Special 4. 20.00 9.00 2.50
Famous Slugger
☐ 139A Babe Ruth Special 5 27.00 12.00 3.40
Babe Hits 60
☐ 139B Hal Reniff PORT..... 12.00 5.50 1.50
☐ 139C Hal Reniff 65.00 29.00 8.25
(Pitching)
☐ 140 Babe Ruth Special 6. 40.00 18.00 5.00
With Lou Gehrig
☐ 141 Babe Ruth Special 7. 20.00 9.00 2.50
Twilight Years
☐ 142 Babe Ruth Special 8. 20.00 9.00 2.50
Coaching Dodgers
☐ 143 Babe Ruth Special 9. 20.00 9.00 2.50
Greatest Sports Hero
☐ 144 Babe Ruth Special 10 20.00 9.00 2.50
Farewell Speech
☐ 145 Barry Latman .... 5.00 2.30 .60
☐ 146 Don Demeter .... 5.00 2.30 .60
☐ 147A Bill Kunkel PORT ..... 5.00 2.30 .60
☐ 147B Bill Kunkel 30.00 13.50 3.80
(Pitching pose)
☐ 148 Wally Post .... 5.50 2.50 .70
☐ 149 Bob Duliba .... 5.00 2.30 .60
☐ 150 Al Kaline 35.00 16.00 4.40
☐ 151 Johnny Klippstein ...... 5.00 2.30 .60
☐ 152 Mickey Vernon MG .... 5.50 2.50 .70
☐ 153 Pumpsie Green .... 5.50 2.50 .70
☐ 154 Lee Thomas .... 5.50 2.50 .70
☐ 155 Stu Miller .... 5.50 2.50 .70
☐ 156 Merritt Ranew .... 5.00 2.30 .60
☐ 157 Wes Covington .... 5.50 2.50 .70
☐ 158 Braves Team .... 7.00 3.10 .85
☐ 159 Hal Reniff .... 6.00 2.70 .75
☐ 160 Dick Stuart .... 5.50 2.50 .70
☐ 161 Frank Baumann .... 5.00 2.30 .60
☐ 162 Sammy Drake .... 5.00 2.30 .60
☐ 163 Hot Corner Guard...... 5.50 2.50 .70
Billy Gardner
Cletis Boyer
☐ 164 Hal Naragon .... 5.00 2.30 .60
☐ 165 Jackie Brandt .... 5.00 2.30 .60
☐ 166 Don Lee .... 5.00 2.30 .60
☐ 167 Tim McCarver 30.00 13.50 3.80
☐ 168 Leo Posada .... 5.00 2.30 .60
☐ 169 Bob Cerv .... 5.50 2.50 .70
☐ 170 Ron Santo 14.00 6.25 1.75
☐ 171 Dave Sisler .... 5.00 2.30 .60
☐ 172 Fred Hutchinson MG.. 5.50 2.50 .70
☐ 173 Chico Fernandez .... 5.00 2.30 .60
☐ 174A Carl Willey .... 5.00 2.30 .60
(Capless)
☐ 174B Carl Willey 30.00 13.50 3.80
(With cap)
☐ 175 Frank Howard .... 6.00 2.70 .75
☐ 176A Eddie Yost PORT ..... 5.50 2.50 .70
☐ 176B Eddie Yost BATTING 30.00 13.50 3.80
☐ 177 Bobby Shantz .... 5.50 2.50 .70
☐ 178 Camilo Carreon .... 5.00 2.30 .60
☐ 179 Tom Sturdivant .... 5.00 2.30 .60
☐ 180 Bob Allison .... 5.50 2.50 .70
☐ 181 Paul Brown .... 5.00 2.30 .60
☐ 182 Bob Nieman .... 5.00 2.30 .60
☐ 183 Roger Craig .... 5.50 2.50 .70
☐ 184 Haywood Sullivan ...... 5.50 2.50 .70
☐ 185 Roland Sheldon .... 5.00 2.30 .60
☐ 186 Mack Jones .... 5.00 2.30 .60
☐ 187 Gene Conley .... 5.50 2.50 .70
☐ 188 Chuck Hiller .... 5.00 2.30 .60
☐ 189 Dick Hall .... 5.00 2.30 .60

	Card	Price	Price	Price
☐ 190A	Wally Moon PORT	5.50	2.50	.70
☐ 190B	Wally Moon BATTING	30.00	13.50	3.80
☐ 191	Jim Brewer	5.00	2.30	.60
☐ 192A	Checklist 3 (Without comma)	12.00	1.80	.60
☐ 192B	Checklist 3 (Comma after Checklist)	12.00	1.80	.60
☐ 193	Eddie Kasko	5.00	2.30	.60
☐ 194	Dean Chance	6.00	2.70	.75
☐ 195	Joe Cunningham	5.50	2.50	.70
☐ 196	Terry Fox	5.00	2.30	.60
☐ 197	Daryl Spencer	4.50	2.00	.55
☐ 198	Johnny Keane MG	5.00	2.30	.60
☐ 199	Gaylord Perry	100.00	45.00	12.50
☐ 200	Mickey Mantle	525.00	240.00	65.00
☐ 201	Ike Delock	4.50	2.00	.55
☐ 202	Carl Warwick	4.50	2.00	.55
☐ 203	Jack Fisher	4.50	2.00	.55
☐ 204	Johnny Weekly	4.50	2.00	.55
☐ 205	Gene Freese	4.50	2.00	.55
☐ 206	Senators Team	7.00	3.10	.85
☐ 207	Pete Burnside	4.50	2.00	.55
☐ 208	Billy Martin	10.00	4.50	1.25
☐ 209	Jim Fregosi	15.00	6.75	1.90
☐ 210	Roy Face	6.50	2.90	.80
☐ 211	Midway Masters Frank Bolling Roy McMillan	5.00	2.30	.60
☐ 212	Jim Owens	4.50	2.00	.55
☐ 213	Richie Ashburn	14.00	6.25	1.75
☐ 214	Dom Zanni	4.50	2.00	.55
☐ 215	Woody Held	4.50	2.00	.55
☐ 216	Ron Kline	4.50	2.00	.55
☐ 217	Walt Alston MG	6.00	2.70	.75
☐ 218	Joe Torre	30.00	13.50	3.80
☐ 219	Al Downing	6.50	2.90	.80
☐ 220	Roy Sievers	5.00	2.30	.60
☐ 221	Bill Short	4.50	2.00	.55
☐ 222	Jerry Zimmerman	4.50	2.00	.55
☐ 223	Alex Grammas	4.50	2.00	.55
☐ 224	Don Rudolph	4.50	2.00	.55
☐ 225	Frank Malzone	5.00	2.30	.60
☐ 226	San Francisco Giants Team Card	7.00	3.10	.85
☐ 227	Bob Tiefenauer	4.50	2.00	.55
☐ 228	Dale Long	5.00	2.30	.60
☐ 229	Jesus McFarlane	4.50	2.00	.55
☐ 230	Camilo Pascual	5.00	2.30	.60
☐ 231	Ernie Bowman	4.50	2.00	.55
☐ 232	World Series Game 1. Yanks win opener	6.00	2.70	.75
☐ 233	World Series Game 2. Joey Jay ties it up	6.00	2.70	.75
☐ 234	World Series Game 3 Roger Maris wins in 9th	20.00	9.00	2.50
☐ 235	World Series Game 4 Whitey Ford sets new mark	10.00	4.50	1.25
☐ 236	World Series Game 5. Yanks crush Reds	6.00	2.70	.75
☐ 237	World Series Summary Yanks celebrate	6.00	2.70	.75
☐ 238	Norm Sherry	5.00	2.30	.60
☐ 239	Cecil Butler	4.50	2.00	.55
☐ 240	George Altman	4.50	2.00	.55
☐ 241	Johnny Kucks	4.50	2.00	.55
☐ 242	Mel McGaha MG	4.50	2.00	.55
☐ 243	Robin Roberts	14.00	6.25	1.75
☐ 244	Don Gile	4.50	2.00	.55
☐ 245	Ron Hansen	4.50	2.00	.55
☐ 246	Art Ditmar	4.50	2.00	.55
☐ 247	Joe Pignatano	4.50	2.00	.55
☐ 248	Bob Aspromonte	5.00	2.30	.60
☐ 249	Ed Keegan	4.50	2.00	.55
☐ 250	Norm Cash	8.00	3.60	1.00
☐ 251	New York Yankees Team Card	32.00	14.50	4.00
☐ 252	Earl Francis	4.50	2.00	.55
☐ 253	Harry Chiti MG	4.50	2.00	.55
☐ 254	Gordon Windhorn	4.50	2.00	.55
☐ 255	Juan Pizarro	4.50	2.00	.55
☐ 256	Elio Chacon	5.00	2.30	.60
☐ 257	Jack Spring	4.50	2.00	.55
☐ 258	Marty Keough	4.50	2.00	.55
☐ 259	Lou Klimchock	4.50	2.00	.55
☐ 260	Billy Pierce	5.00	2.30	.60
☐ 261	George Alusik	4.50	2.00	.55
☐ 262	Bob Schmidt	4.50	2.00	.55
☐ 263	The Right Pitch Bob Purkey Jim Turner CO Joe Jay	5.00	2.30	.60
☐ 264	Dick Ellsworth	5.00	2.30	.60
☐ 265	Joe Adcock	5.00	2.30	.60
☐ 266	John Anderson	4.50	2.00	.55
☐ 267	Dan Dobbek	4.50	2.00	.55
☐ 268	Ken McBride	4.50	2.00	.55
☐ 269	Bob Oldis	4.50	2.00	.55
☐ 270	Dick Groat	6.50	2.90	.80
☐ 271	Ray Rippelmeyer	4.50	2.00	.55
☐ 272	Earl Robinson	4.50	2.00	.55
☐ 273	Gary Bell	4.50	2.00	.55
☐ 274	Sammy Taylor	4.50	2.00	.55
☐ 275	Norm Siebern	4.50	2.00	.55
☐ 276	Hal Kolstad	4.50	2.00	.55
☐ 277	Checklist 4	12.00	1.80	.60
☐ 278	Ken Johnson	5.00	2.30	.60
☐ 279	Hobie Landrith UER (Wrong birthdate)	5.00	2.30	.60
☐ 280	Johnny Podres	5.00	2.30	.60
☐ 281	Jake Gibbs	5.00	2.30	.60
☐ 282	Dave Hillman	4.50	2.00	.55
☐ 283	Charlie Smith	4.50	2.00	.55
☐ 284	Ruben Amaro	4.50	2.00	.55
☐ 285	Curt Simmons	5.00	2.30	.60
☐ 286	Al Lopez MG	5.50	2.50	.70
☐ 287	George Witt	4.50	2.00	.55
☐ 288	Billy Williams	30.00	13.50	3.80
☐ 289	Mike Krsnich	4.50	2.00	.55
☐ 290	Jim Gentile	5.00	2.30	.60
☐ 291	Hal Stowe	4.50	2.00	.55
☐ 292	Jerry Kindall	4.50	2.00	.55
☐ 293	Bob Miller	5.00	2.30	.60
☐ 294	Phillies Team	8.00	3.60	1.00
☐ 295	Vern Law	5.00	2.30	.60
☐ 296	Ken Hamlin	4.50	2.00	.55
☐ 297	Ron Perranoski	5.00	2.30	.60
☐ 298	Bill Tuttle	4.50	2.00	.55
☐ 299	Don Wert	4.50	2.00	.55
☐ 300	Willie Mays	135.00	60.00	17.00
☐ 301	Galen Cisco	4.50	2.00	.55
☐ 302	Johnny Edwards	4.50	2.00	.55
☐ 303	Frank Torre	5.00	2.30	.60
☐ 304	Dick Farrell	5.00	2.30	.60
☐ 305	Jerry Lumpe	4.50	2.00	.55
☐ 306	Redbird Rippers Lindy McDaniel Larry Jackson	5.00	2.30	.60
☐ 307	Jim Grant	5.00	2.30	.60
☐ 308	Neil Chrisley	5.00	2.30	.60
☐ 309	Moe Morhardt	4.50	2.00	.55
☐ 310	Whitey Ford	35.00	16.00	4.40
☐ 311	Tony Kubek IA	7.50	3.40	.95
☐ 312	Warren Spahn IA	14.00	6.25	1.75

☐ 313 Roger Maris IA 32.00 14.50 4.00
☐ 314 Rocky Colavito IA 12.00 5.50 1.50
☐ 315 Whitey Ford IA 14.00 6.25 1.75
☐ 316 Harmon Killebrew IA 14.00 6.25 1.75
☐ 317 Stan Musial IA 20.00 9.00 2.50
☐ 318 Mickey Mantle IA 80.00 36.00 10.00
☐ 319 Mike McCormick IA 5.00 2.30 .60
☐ 320 Hank Aaron 150.00 70.00 19.00
☐ 321 Lee Stange 4.50 2.00 .55
☐ 322 Alvin Dark MG 5.00 2.30 .60
☐ 323 Don Landrum 4.50 2.00 .55
☐ 324 Joe McClain 4.50 2.00 .55
☐ 325 Luis Aparicio 16.00 7.25 2.00
☐ 326 Tom Parsons 4.50 2.00 .55
☐ 327 Ozzie Virgil 4.50 2.00 .55
☐ 328 Ken Walters 4.50 2.00 .55
☐ 329 Bob Bolin 4.50 2.00 .55
☐ 330 John Romano 4.50 2.00 .55
☐ 331 Moe Drabowsky 5.00 2.30 .60
☐ 332 Don Buddin 4.50 2.00 .55
☐ 333 Frank Cipriani 4.50 2.00 .55
☐ 334 Boston Red Sox 8.00 3.60 1.00
Team Card
☐ 335 Bill Bruton 4.50 2.00 .55
☐ 336 Billy Muffett 4.50 2.00 .55
☐ 337 Jim Marshall 5.00 2.30 .60
☐ 338 Billy Gardner 4.50 2.00 .55
☐ 339 Jose Valdivielso 4.50 2.00 .55
☐ 340 Don Drysdale 40.00 18.00 5.00
☐ 341 Mike Hershberger 4.50 2.00 .55
☐ 342 Ed Rakow 4.50 2.00 .55
☐ 343 Albie Pearson 5.00 2.30 .60
☐ 344 Ed Bauta 4.50 2.00 .55
☐ 345 Chuck Schilling 4.50 2.00 .55
☐ 346 Jack Kralick 4.50 2.00 .55
☐ 347 Chuck Hinton 4.50 2.00 .55
☐ 348 Larry Burright 4.50 2.00 .55
☐ 349 Paul Foytack 4.50 2.00 .55
☐ 350 Frank Robinson 50.00 23.00 6.25
☐ 351 Braves' Backstops 7.00 3.10 .85
Joe Torre
Del Crandall
☐ 352 Frank Sullivan 4.50 2.00 .55
☐ 353 Bill Mazeroski 10.00 4.50 1.25
☐ 354 Roman Mejias 5.00 2.30 .60
☐ 355 Steve Barber 4.50 2.00 .55
☐ 356 Tom Haller 4.50 2.00 .55
☐ 357 Jerry Walker 4.50 2.00 .55
☐ 358 Tommy Davis 7.00 3.10 .85
☐ 359 Bobby Locke 4.50 2.00 .55
☐ 360 Yogi Berra 85.00 38.00 10.50
☐ 361 Bob Hendley 4.50 2.00 .55
☐ 362 Ty Cline 4.50 2.00 .55
☐ 363 Bob Roselli 4.50 2.00 .55
☐ 364 Ken Hunt 4.50 2.00 .55
☐ 365 Charlie Neal 6.00 2.70 .75
☐ 366 Phil Regan 5.00 2.30 .60
☐ 367 Checklist 5 12.00 1.80 .60
☐ 368 Bob Tillman 4.50 2.00 .55
☐ 369 Ted Bowsfield 4.50 2.00 .55
☐ 370 Ken Boyer 7.00 3.10 .85
☐ 371 Earl Battey 6.00 2.70 .75
☐ 372 Jack Curtis 6.00 2.70 .75
☐ 373 Al Heist 6.00 2.70 .75
☐ 374 Gene Mauch MG 8.00 3.60 1.00
☐ 375 Ron Fairly 8.00 3.60 1.00
☐ 376 Bud Daley 6.00 2.70 .75
☐ 377 John Orsino 6.00 2.70 .75
☐ 378 Bennie Daniels 6.00 2.70 .75
☐ 379 Chuck Essegian 6.00 2.70 .75
☐ 380 Lou Burdette 6.00 2.70 .75
☐ 381 Chico Cardenas 8.00 3.60 1.00
☐ 382 Dick Williams 8.00 3.60 1.00
☐ 383 Ray Sadecki 6.00 2.70 .75
☐ 384 K.C. Athletics 12.00 5.50 1.50
Team Card
☐ 385 Early Wynn 18.00 8.00 2.30
☐ 386 Don Mincher 8.00 3.60 1.00
☐ 387 Lou Brock 150.00 70.00 19.00
☐ 388 Ryne Duren 6.00 2.70 .75
☐ 389 Smoky Burgess 8.00 3.60 1.00
☐ 390 Orlando Cepeda AS 10.00 4.50 1.25
☐ 391 Bill Mazeroski AS 10.00 4.50 1.25
☐ 392 Ken Boyer AS 9.00 4.00 1.15
☐ 393 Roy McMillan AS 6.50 2.90 .80
☐ 394 Hank Aaron AS 50.00 23.00 6.25
☐ 395 Willie Mays AS 50.00 23.00 6.25
☐ 396 Frank Robinson AS 16.00 7.25 2.00
☐ 397 John Roseboro AS 6.50 2.90 .80
☐ 398 Don Drysdale AS 16.00 7.25 2.00
☐ 399 Warren Spahn AS 16.00 7.25 2.00
☐ 400 Elston Howard 10.00 4.50 1.25
☐ 401 AL/NL Homer Kings 50.00 23.00 6.25
Roger Maris
Orlando Cepeda
☐ 402 Gino Cimoli 6.00 2.70 .75
☐ 403 Chet Nichols 6.00 2.70 .75
☐ 404 Tim Harkness 6.00 2.70 .75
☐ 405 Jim Perry 6.00 2.70 .75
☐ 406 Bob Taylor 6.00 2.70 .75
☐ 407 Hank Aguirre 6.00 2.70 .75
☐ 408 Gus Bell 8.00 3.60 1.00
☐ 409 Pittsburgh Pirates 12.00 5.50 1.50
Team Card
☐ 410 Al Smith 6.00 2.70 .75
☐ 411 Danny O'Connell 6.00 2.70 .75
☐ 412 Charlie James 6.00 2.70 .75
☐ 413 Matty Alou 6.00 2.70 .75
☐ 414 Joe Gaines 6.00 2.70 .75
☐ 415 Bill Virdon 8.00 3.60 1.00
☐ 416 Bob Scheffing MG 6.00 2.70 .75
☐ 417 Joe Azcue 6.00 2.70 .75
☐ 418 Andy Carey 6.00 2.70 .75
☐ 419 Bob Bruce 8.00 3.60 1.00
☐ 420 Gus Triandos 8.00 3.60 1.00
☐ 421 Ken MacKenzie 8.00 3.60 1.00
☐ 422 Steve Bilko 6.00 2.70 .75
☐ 423 Rival League 8.00 3.60 1.00
Relief Aces:
Roy Face
Hoyt Wilhelm
☐ 424 Al McBean 6.00 2.70 .75
☐ 425 Carl Yastrzemski 150.00 70.00 19.00
☐ 426 Bob Farley 6.00 2.70 .75
☐ 427 Jake Wood 6.00 2.70 .75
☐ 428 Joe Hicks 6.00 2.70 .75
☐ 429 Billy O'Dell 6.00 2.70 .75
☐ 430 Tony Kubek 12.00 5.50 1.50
☐ 431 Bob Rodgers 8.00 3.60 1.00
☐ 432 Jim Pendleton 6.00 2.70 .75
☐ 433 Jim Archer 6.00 2.70 .75
☐ 434 Clay Dalrymple 6.00 2.70 .75
☐ 435 Larry Sherry 8.00 3.60 1.00
☐ 436 Felix Mantilla 8.00 3.60 1.00
☐ 437 Ray Moore 6.00 2.70 .75
☐ 438 Dick Brown 6.00 2.70 .75
☐ 439 Jerry Buchek 6.00 2.70 .75
☐ 440 Joey Jay 6.00 2.70 .75
☐ 441 Checklist 6 16.00 2.40 .80
☐ 442 Wes Stock 6.00 2.70 .75
☐ 443 Del Crandall 8.00 3.60 1.00
☐ 444 Ted Wills 6.00 2.70 .75
☐ 445 Vic Power 8.00 3.60 1.00
☐ 446 Don Elston 6.00 2.70 .75
☐ 447 Willie Kirkland 12.00 5.50 1.50
☐ 448 Joe Gibbon 12.00 5.50 1.50

☐ 449	Jerry Adair	12.00	5.50	1.50
☐ 450	Jim O'Toole	14.00	6.25	1.75
☐ 451	Jose Tartabull	14.00	6.25	1.75
☐ 452	Earl Averill Jr.	12.00	5.50	1.50
☐ 453	Cal McLish	12.00	5.50	1.50
☐ 454	Floyd Robinson	12.00	5.50	1.50
☐ 455	Luis Arroyo	14.00	6.25	1.75
☐ 456	Joe Amalfitano	14.00	6.25	1.75
☐ 457	Lou Clinton	12.00	5.50	1.50
☐ 458A	Bob Buhl (Braves emblem on cap)	14.00	6.25	1.75
☐ 458B	Bob Buhl (No emblem on cap)	55.00	25.00	7.00
☐ 459	Ed Bailey	12.00	5.50	1.50
☐ 460	Jim Bunning	13.00	5.75	1.65
☐ 461	Ken Hubbs	30.00	13.50	3.80
☐ 462A	Willie Tasby (Senators emblem on cap)	12.00	5.50	1.50
☐ 462B	Willie Tasby (No emblem on cap)	55.00	25.00	7.00
☐ 463	Hank Bauer MG	14.00	6.25	1.75
☐ 464	Al Jackson	14.00	6.25	1.75
☐ 465	Reds Team	16.00	7.25	2.00
☐ 466	Norm Cash AS	14.00	6.25	1.75
☐ 467	Chuck Schilling AS	12.00	5.50	1.50
☐ 468	Brooks Robinson AS	20.00	9.00	2.50
☐ 469	Luis Aparicio AS	15.00	6.75	1.90
☐ 470	Al Kaline AS	20.00	9.00	2.50
☐ 471	Mickey Mantle AS	150.00	70.00	19.00
☐ 472	Rocky Colavito AS	14.00	6.25	1.75
☐ 473	Elston Howard AS	14.00	6.25	1.75
☐ 474	Frank Lary AS	12.00	5.50	1.50
☐ 475	Whitey Ford AS	16.00	7.25	2.00
☐ 476	Orioles Team	16.00	7.25	2.00
☐ 477	Andre Rodgers	12.00	5.50	1.50
☐ 478	Don Zimmer (Shown with Mets cap, but listed as with Cincinnati)	14.00	6.25	1.75
☐ 479	Joel Horlen	12.00	5.50	1.50
☐ 480	Harvey Kuenn	14.00	6.25	1.75
☐ 481	Vic Wertz	14.00	6.25	1.75
☐ 482	Sam Mele MG	12.00	5.50	1.50
☐ 483	Don McMahon	12.00	5.50	1.50
☐ 484	Dick Schofield	12.00	5.50	1.50
☐ 485	Pedro Ramos	12.00	5.50	1.50
☐ 486	Jim Gilliam	14.00	6.25	1.75
☐ 487	Jerry Lynch	12.00	5.50	1.50
☐ 488	Hal Brown	12.00	5.50	1.50
☐ 489	Julio Gotay	12.00	5.50	1.50
☐ 490	Clete Boyer	14.00	6.25	1.75
☐ 491	Leon Wagner	12.00	5.50	1.50
☐ 492	Hal W. Smith	14.00	6.25	1.75
☐ 493	Danny McDevitt	12.00	5.50	1.50
☐ 494	Sammy White	12.00	5.50	1.50
☐ 495	Don Cardwell	12.00	5.50	1.50
☐ 496	Wayne Causey	12.00	5.50	1.50
☐ 497	Ed Bouchee	14.00	6.25	1.75
☐ 498	Jim Donohue	12.00	5.50	1.50
☐ 499	Zoilo Versalles	14.00	6.25	1.75
☐ 500	Duke Snider	50.00	23.00	6.25
☐ 501	Claude Osteen	14.00	6.25	1.75
☐ 502	Hector Lopez	14.00	6.25	1.75
☐ 503	Danny Murtaugh MG	14.00	6.25	1.75
☐ 504	Eddie Bressoud	12.00	5.50	1.50
☐ 505	Juan Marichal	40.00	18.00	5.00
☐ 506	Charlie Maxwell	14.00	6.25	1.75
☐ 507	Ernie Broglio	14.00	6.25	1.75
☐ 508	Gordy Coleman	14.00	6.25	1.75
☐ 509	Dave Giusti	14.00	6.25	1.75
☐ 510	Jim Lemon	12.00	5.50	1.50
☐ 511	Bubba Phillips	12.00	5.50	1.50
☐ 512	Mike Fornieles	12.00	5.50	1.50
☐ 513	Whitey Herzog	14.00	6.25	1.75
☐ 514	Sherm Lollar	14.00	6.25	1.75
☐ 515	Stan Williams	14.00	6.25	1.75
☐ 516	Checklist 7	16.00	4.00	1.30
☐ 517	Dave Wickersham	12.00	5.50	1.50
☐ 518	Lee Maye	12.00	5.50	1.50
☐ 519	Bob Johnson	12.00	5.50	1.50
☐ 520	Bob Friend	14.00	6.25	1.75
☐ 521	Jacke Davis UER (Listed as OF on front and P on back)	12.00	5.50	1.50
☐ 522	Lindy McDaniel	14.00	6.25	1.75
☐ 523	Russ Nixon SP	30.00	13.50	3.80
☐ 524	Howie Nunn SP	30.00	13.50	3.80
☐ 525	George Thomas	20.00	9.00	2.50
☐ 526	Hal Woodeshick SP	32.00	14.50	4.00
☐ 527	Dick McAuliffe	24.00	11.00	3.00
☐ 528	Turk Lown	20.00	9.00	2.50
☐ 529	John Schaive SP	30.00	13.50	3.80
☐ 530	Bob Gibson SP	160.00	70.00	20.00
☐ 531	Bobby G. Smith	20.00	9.00	2.50
☐ 532	Dick Stigman	20.00	9.00	2.50
☐ 533	Charley Lau SP	32.00	14.50	4.00
☐ 534	Tony Gonzalez SP	30.00	13.50	3.80
☐ 535	Ed Roebuck	20.00	9.00	2.50
☐ 536	Dick Gernert	22.00	10.00	2.80
☐ 537	Cleveland Indians Team Card	45.00	20.00	5.75
☐ 538	Jack Sanford	22.00	10.00	2.80
☐ 539	Billy Moran	20.00	9.00	2.50
☐ 540	Jim Landis SP	30.00	13.50	3.80
☐ 541	Don Nottebart SP	30.00	13.50	3.80
☐ 542	Dave Philley	20.00	9.00	2.50
☐ 543	Bob Allen SP	30.00	13.50	3.80
☐ 544	Willie McCovey SP	125.00	57.50	15.50
☐ 545	Hoyt Wilhelm SP	50.00	23.00	6.25
☐ 546	Moe Thacker SP	30.00	13.50	3.80
☐ 547	Don Ferrarese	20.00	9.00	2.50
☐ 548	Bobby Del Greco	20.00	9.00	2.50
☐ 549	Bill Rigney MG SP	30.00	13.50	3.80
☐ 550	Art Mahaffey SP	30.00	13.50	3.80
☐ 551	Harry Bright	20.00	9.00	2.50
☐ 552	Chicago Cubs SP Team Card	50.00	23.00	6.25
☐ 553	Jim Coates	20.00	9.00	2.50
☐ 554	Bubba Morton SP	30.00	13.50	3.80
☐ 555	John Buzhardt SP	30.00	13.50	3.80
☐ 556	Al Spangler	22.00	10.00	2.80
☐ 557	Bob Anderson SP	30.00	13.50	3.80
☐ 558	John Goryl	20.00	9.00	2.50
☐ 559	Mike Higgins MG	20.00	9.00	2.50
☐ 560	Chuck Estrada SP	30.00	13.50	3.80
☐ 561	Gene Oliver SP	30.00	13.50	3.80
☐ 562	Bill Henry	20.00	9.00	2.50
☐ 563	Ken Aspromonte	20.00	9.00	2.50
☐ 564	Bob Grim	20.00	9.00	2.50
☐ 565	Jose Pagan	20.00	9.00	2.50
☐ 566	Marty Kutyna SP	30.00	13.50	3.80
☐ 567	Tracy Stallard SP	30.00	13.50	3.80
☐ 568	Jim Golden	22.00	10.00	2.80
☐ 569	Ed Sadowski SP	30.00	13.50	3.80
☐ 570	Bill Stafford SP	30.00	13.50	3.80
☐ 571	Billy Klaus SP	30.00	13.50	3.80
☐ 572	Bob G. Miller SP	35.00	16.00	4.40
☐ 573	Johnny Logan	22.00	10.00	2.80
☐ 574	Dean Stone	22.00	10.00	2.80
☐ 575	Red Schoendienst SP	45.00	20.00	5.75
☐ 576	Russ Kemmerer SP	30.00	13.50	3.80
☐ 577	Dave Nicholson SP	30.00	13.50	3.80
☐ 578	Jim Duffalo	20.00	9.00	2.50
☐ 579	Jim Schaffer SP	30.00	13.50	3.80

- ☐ 580 Bill Monbouquette.... 20.00 9.00 2.50
- ☐ 581 Mel Roach................ 20.00 9.00 2.50
- ☐ 582 Ron Piche 20.00 9.00 2.50
- ☐ 583 Larry Osborne.......... 20.00 9.00 2.50
- ☐ 584 Minnesota Twins SP 50.00 23.00 6.25
  Team Card
- ☐ 585 Glen Hobbie SP........ 30.00 13.50 3.80
- ☐ 586 Sammy Esposito SP 30.00 13.50 3.80
- ☐ 587 Frank Funk SP.......... 30.00 13.50 3.80
- ☐ 588 Birdie Tebbetts MG.. 22.00 10.00 2.80
- ☐ 589 Bob Turley 20.00 9.00 2.50
- ☐ 590 Curt Flood................ 25.00 11.50 3.10
- ☐ 591 Rookie Pitchers SP .. 70.00 32.00 8.75
  Sam McDowell
  Ron Taylor
  Ron Nischwitz
  Art Quirk
  Dick Radatz
- ☐ 592 Rookie Pitchers SP .. 70.00 32.00 8.75
  Dan Pfister
  Bo Belinsky
  Dave Stenhouse
  Jim Bouton
  Joe Bonikowski
- ☐ 593 Rookie Pitchers SP .. 42.50 19.00 5.25
  Jack Lamabe
  Craig Anderson
  Jack Hamilton
  Bob Moorhead
  Bob Veale
- ☐ 594 Rookie Catchers SP . 70.00 32.00 8.75
  Doc Edwards
  Ken Retzer
  Bob Uecker
  Doug Camilli
  Don Pavletich
- ☐ 595 Rookie Infielders SP 40.00 18.00 5.00
  Bob Sadowski
  Felix Torres
  Marlan Coughtry
  Ed Charles
- ☐ 596 Rookie Infielders SP 70.00 32.00 8.75
  Bernie Allen
  Joe Pepitone
  Phil Linz
  Rich Rollins
- ☐ 597 Rookie Infielders SP 45.00 20.00 5.75
  Jim McKnight
  Rod Kanehl
  Amado Samuel
  Denis Menke
- ☐ 598 Rookie Outfielders SP 70.00 21.00 5.50
  Al Luplow
  Manny Jimenez
  Howie Goss
  Jim Hickman
  Ed Olivares

1963 Topps

The cards in this 576-card set measure 2 1/2" by 3 1/2". The sharp color photographs of the 1963 set are a vivid contrast to the drab pictures of 1962. In addition to the "League Leaders" series (1-10) and World Series cards (142-148), the seventh and last series of cards (523-576) contains seven rookie cards (each depicting four players). There were some three-card

advertising panels produced by Topps; the players included are from the first series; one panel shows Hoyt Wilhelm, Don Lock, and Bob Duliba on the front with a Stan Musial ad/endorsement on one of the backs. This set has gained special prominence in recent years since it contains the Rookie Card of Pete Rose (537). Other key Rookie Cards in this set are Bill Freehan, Tony Oliva, Willie Stargell, and Rusty Staub.

	NRMT	VG-E	GOOD
COMPLETE SET (576)	5000.00	2300.00	650.00
COMMON CARD (1-109)	3.00	1.35	.40
COMMON CARD (110-196)	3.00	1.35	.40
COMMON CARD (197-283)	4.00	1.80	.50
COMMON CARD (284-370)	4.50	2.00	.55
COMMON CARD (371-446)	5.00	2.30	.60
COMMON CARD (447-522) ...	16.00	7.25	2.00
COMMON CARD (523-576) ...	12.00	5.50	1.50

- ☐ 1 NL Batting Leaders 34.00 6.75 2.00
  Tommy Davis
  Frank Robinson
  Stan Musial
  Hank Aaron
  Bill White
- ☐ 2 AL Batting Leaders....... 28.00 12.50 3.50
  Pete Runnels
  Mickey Mantle
  Floyd Robinson
  Norm Siebern
  Chuck Hinton
- ☐ 3 NL Home Run Leaders. 28.00 12.50 3.50
  Willie Mays
  Hank Aaron
  Frank Robinson
  Orlando Cepeda
  Ernie Banks
- ☐ 4 AL Home Run Leaders. 12.00 5.50 1.50
  Harmon Killebrew
  Norm Cash
  Rocky Colavito
  Roger Maris
  Jim Gentile
  Leon Wagner
- ☐ 5 NL ERA Leaders.......... 18.00 8.00 2.30
  Sandy Koufax
  Bob Shaw
  Bob Purkey
  Bob Gibson
  Don Drysdale
- ☐ 6 AL ERA Leaders............ 7.00 3.10 .85
  Hank Aguirre
  Robin Roberts
  Whitey Ford
  Eddie Fisher

	No.	Card			
		Dean Chance			
☐	7	NL Pitching Leaders	7.00	3.10	.85
		Don Drysdale			
		Jack Sanford			
		Bob Purkey			
		Billy O'Dell			
		Art Mahaffey			
		Joe Jay			
☐	8	AL Pitching Leaders	6.00	2.70	.75
		Ralph Terry			
		Dick Donovan			
		Ray Herbert			
		Jim Bunning			
		Camilo Pascual			
☐	9	NL Strikeout Leaders	16.00	7.25	2.00
		Don Drysdale			
		Sandy Koufax			
		Bob Gibson			
		Billy O'Dell			
		Dick Farrell			
☐	10	AL Strikeout Leaders	6.00	2.70	.75
		Camilo Pascual			
		Jim Bunning			
		Ralph Terry			
		Juan Pizarro			
		Jim Kaat			
☐	11	Lee Walls	3.00	1.35	.40
☐	12	Steve Barber	3.00	1.35	.40
☐	13	Philadelphia Phillies	5.00	2.30	.60
		Team Card			
☐	14	Pedro Ramos	3.00	1.35	.40
☐	15	Ken Hubbs UER	6.00	2.70	.75
		(No position listed on front of card)			
☐	16	Al Smith	3.00	1.35	.40
☐	17	Ryne Duren	3.50	1.55	.45
☐	18	Buc Blasters	28.00	12.50	3.50
		Smoky Burgess			
		Dick Stuart			
		Bob Clemente			
		Bob Skinner			
☐	19	Pete Burnside	3.00	1.35	.40
☐	20	Tony Kubek	5.00	2.30	.60
☐	21	Marty Keough	3.00	1.35	.40
☐	22	Curt Simmons	3.50	1.55	.45
☐	23	Ed Lopat MG	3.50	1.55	.45
☐	24	Bob Bruce	3.00	1.35	.40
☐	25	Al Kaline	35.00	16.00	4.40
☐	26	Ray Moore	3.00	1.35	.40
☐	27	Choo Choo Coleman	3.00	1.35	.40
☐	28	Mike Fornieles	3.00	1.35	.40
☐	29A	1962 Rookie Stars	6.00	2.70	.75
		Sammy Ellis			
		Ray Culp			
		John Boozer			
		Jesse Gonder			
☐	29B	1963 Rookie Stars	3.00	1.35	.40
		Sammy Ellis			
		Ray Culp			
		John Boozer			
		Jesse Gonder			
☐	30	Harvey Kuenn	3.50	1.55	.45
☐	31	Cal Koonce	3.00	1.35	.40
☐	32	Tony Gonzalez	3.00	1.35	.40
☐	33	Bo Belinsky	3.50	1.55	.45
☐	34	Dick Schofield	3.00	1.35	.40
☐	35	John Buzhardt	3.00	1.35	.40
☐	36	Jerry Kindall	3.00	1.35	.40
☐	37	Jerry Lynch	3.00	1.35	.40
☐	38	Bud Daley	3.00	1.35	.40
☐	39	Angels Team	5.00	2.30	.60
☐	40	Vic Power	3.50	1.55	.45
☐	41	Charley Lau	3.50	1.55	.45
☐	42	Stan Williams	3.50	1.55	.45
		(Listed as Yankee on card but LA cap)			
☐	43	Veteran Masters	5.00	2.30	.60
		Casey Stengel MG			
		Gene Woodling			
☐	44	Terry Fox	3.00	1.35	.40
☐	45	Bob Aspromonte	3.00	1.35	.40
☐	46	Tommie Aaron	4.50	2.00	.55
☐	47	Don Lock	3.00	1.35	.40
☐	48	Birdie Tebbetts MG	3.50	1.55	.45
☐	49	Dal Maxvill	4.50	2.00	.55
☐	50	Billy Pierce	3.50	1.55	.45
☐	51	George Alusik	3.00	1.35	.40
☐	52	Chuck Schilling	3.00	1.35	.40
☐	53	Joe Moeller	3.00	1.35	.40
☐	54A	1962 Rookie Stars	18.00	8.00	2.30
		Nelson Mathews			
		Harry Fanok			
		Jack Cullen			
		Dave DeBusschere			
☐	54B	1963 Rookie Stars	7.00	3.10	.85
		Nelson Mathews			
		Harry Fanok			
		Jack Cullen			
		Dave DeBusschere			
☐	55	Bill Virdon	3.50	1.55	.45
☐	56	Dennis Bennett	3.00	1.35	.40
☐	57	Billy Moran	3.00	1.35	.40
☐	58	Bob Will	3.00	1.35	.40
☐	59	Craig Anderson	3.00	1.35	.40
☐	60	Elston Howard	6.00	2.70	.75
☐	61	Ernie Bowman	3.00	1.35	.40
☐	62	Bob Hendley	3.00	1.35	.40
☐	63	Reds Team	5.00	2.30	.60
☐	64	Dick McAuliffe	3.50	1.55	.45
☐	65	Jackie Brandt	3.00	1.35	.40
☐	66	Mike Joyce	3.00	1.35	.40
☐	67	Ed Charles	3.00	1.35	.40
☐	68	Friendly Foes	15.00	6.75	1.90
		Duke Snider			
		Gil Hodges			
☐	69	Bud Zipfel	3.00	1.35	.40
☐	70	Jim O'Toole	3.50	1.55	.45
☐	71	Bobby Wine	3.50	1.55	.45
☐	72	Johnny Romano	3.00	1.35	.40
☐	73	Bobby Bragan MG	4.50	2.00	.55
☐	74	Denny Lemaster	3.00	1.35	.40
☐	75	Bob Allison	3.50	1.55	.45
☐	76	Earl Wilson	3.50	1.55	.45
☐	77	Al Spangler	3.00	1.35	.40
☐	78	Marv Throneberry	3.00	1.35	.40
☐	79	Checklist 1	10.00	1.50	.50
☐	80	Jim Gilliam	3.00	1.35	.40
☐	81	Jim Schaffer	3.00	1.35	.40
☐	82	Ed Rakow	3.00	1.35	.40
☐	83	Charley James	3.00	1.35	.40
☐	84	Ron Kline	3.00	1.35	.40
☐	85	Tom Haller	3.50	1.55	.45
☐	86	Charley Maxwell	3.50	1.55	.45
☐	87	Bob Veale	3.50	1.55	.45
☐	88	Ron Hansen	3.00	1.35	.40
☐	89	Dick Stigman	3.00	1.35	.40
☐	90	Gordy Coleman	3.50	1.55	.45
☐	91	Dallas Green	3.50	1.55	.45
☐	92	Hector Lopez	3.50	1.55	.45
☐	93	Galen Cisco	3.00	1.35	.40
☐	94	Bob Schmidt	3.00	1.35	.40
☐	95	Larry Jackson	3.00	1.35	.40
☐	96	Lou Clinton	3.00	1.35	.40
☐	97	Bob Duliba	3.00	1.35	.40
☐	98	George Thomas	3.00	1.35	.40
☐	99	Jim Umbricht	3.00	1.35	.40

☐ 100 Joe Cunningham........ 3.00 1.35 .40
☐ 101 Joe Gibbon .... 3.00 1.35 .40
☐ 102A Checklist 2............. 10.00 1.50 .50
(Red on yellow)
☐ 102B Checklist 2............. 10.00 1.50 .50
(White on red)
☐ 103 Chuck Essegian.......... 3.00 1.35 .40
☐ 104 Lew Krausse .... 3.00 1.35 .40
☐ 105 Ron Fairly .... 3.50 1.55 .45
☐ 106 Bobby Bolin .... 3.00 1.35 .40
☐ 107 Jim Hickman............... 3.50 1.55 .45
☐ 108 Hoyt Wilhelm............. 9.00 4.00 1.15
☐ 109 Lee Maye .... 3.00 1.35 .40
☐ 110 Rich Rollins .... 3.50 1.55 .45
☐ 111 Al Jackson .... 3.00 1.35 .40
☐ 112 Dick Brown .... 3.00 1.35 .40
☐ 113 Don Landrum UER..... 3.00 1.35 .40
(Photo actually
Ron Santo)
☐ 114 Dan Osinski................ 3.00 1.35 .40
☐ 115 Carl Yastrzemski...... 45.00 20.00 5.75
☐ 116 Jim Brosnan .... 3.50 1.55 .45
☐ 117 Jacke Davis................ 3.00 1.35 .40
☐ 118 Sherm Lollar.............. 3.00 1.35 .40
☐ 119 Bob Lillis................... 3.00 1.35 .40
☐ 120 Roger Maris............. 50.00 23.00 6.25
☐ 121 Jim Hannan................ 3.00 1.35 .40
☐ 122 Julio Gotay................ 3.00 1.35 .40
☐ 123 Frank Howard .... 4.50 2.00 .55
☐ 124 Dick Howser .... 3.50 1.55 .45
☐ 125 Robin Roberts.......... 12.00 5.50 1.50
☐ 126 Bob Uecker 10.00 4.50 1.25
☐ 127 Bill Tuttle................... 3.00 1.35 .40
☐ 128 Matty Alou .... 3.50 1.55 .45
☐ 129 Gary Bell .... 3.00 1.35 .40
☐ 130 Dick Groat.................. 6.00 2.70 .75
☐ 131 Washington Senators 5.00 2.30 .60
Team Card
☐ 132 Jack Hamilton............ 3.00 1.35 .40
☐ 133 Gene Freese.............. 3.00 1.35 .40
☐ 134 Bob Scheffing MG...... 3.00 1.35 .40
☐ 135 Richie Ashburn 10.00 4.50 1.25
☐ 136 Ike Delock.................. 3.00 1.35 .40
☐ 137 Mack Jones................ 3.00 1.35 .40
☐ 138 Pride of NL.............. 50.00 23.00 6.25
Willie Mays
Stan Musial
☐ 139 Earl Averill................. 3.00 1.35 .40
☐ 140 Frank Lary.................. 3.50 1.55 .45
☐ 141 Manny Mota............... 7.00 3.10 .85
☐ 142 World Series Game 1. 8.00 3.60 1.00
Whitey Ford wins
series opener
☐ 143 World Series Game 2. 6.00 2.70 .75
Jack Sanford flashes
shutout magic
☐ 144 World Series Game 3 12.00 5.50 1.50
Roger Maris sparks
Yankee rally
☐ 145 World Series Game 4. 6.00 2.70 .75
Chuck Hiller blasts
grand slammer
☐ 146 World Series Game 5. 6.00 2.70 .75
Tom Tresh's homer
defeats Giants
☐ 147 World Series Game 6. 6.00 2.70 .75
Billy Pierce stars in
3 hit victory
☐ 148 World Series Game 7. 6.00 2.70 .75
Yanks celebrate
as Ralph Terry wins
☐ 149 Marv Breeding .... 3.00 1.35 .40
☐ 150 Johnny Podres........... 3.50 1.55 .45
☐ 151 Pirates Team............. 5.00 2.30 .60
☐ 152 Ron Nischwitz........... 3.00 1.35 .40
☐ 153 Hal Smith.................. 3.00 1.35 .40
☐ 154 Walt Alston MG......... 5.00 2.30 .60
☐ 155 Bill Stafford.............. 3.00 1.35 .40
☐ 156 Roy McMillan............ 3.50 1.55 .45
☐ 157 Diego Segui .... 4.50 2.00 .55
☐ 158 Rookie Stars .... 5.00 2.30 .60
Rogelio Alvares
Dave Roberts
Tommy Harper
Bob Saverine
☐ 159 Jim Pagliaroni........... 3.00 1.35 .40
☐ 160 Juan Pizarro.............. 3.00 1.35 .40
☐ 161 Frank Torre .... 3.50 1.55 .45
☐ 162 Twins Team .... 5.00 2.30 .60
☐ 163 Don Larsen .... 3.50 1.55 .45
☐ 164 Bubba Morton............ 3.00 1.35 .40
☐ 165 Jim Kaat.................... 6.00 2.70 .75
☐ 166 Johnny Keane MG...... 3.00 1.35 .40
☐ 167 Jim Fregosi............... 6.00 2.70 .75
☐ 168 Russ Nixon .... 3.00 1.35 .40
☑ 169 Rookie Stars 25.00 11.50 3.10
Dick Egan
Julio Navarro
Tommie Sisk
Gaylord Perry
☐ 170 Joe Adcock .... 3.00 1.35 .40
☐ 171 Steve Hamilton .... 3.00 1.35 .40
☐ 172 Gene Oliver............... 3.00 1.35 .40
☐ 173A Bombers' Best......... 3.00 1.35 .40
Tom Tresh
Mickey Mantle
Bobby Richardson
(Bat knob showing)
☐ 173B Bombers' Best....... 90.00 40.00 11.50
Tom Tresh
Mickey Mantle
Bobby Richardson
(Bat knob airbrushed out)
☐ 174 Larry Burright........... 3.00 1.35 .40
☐ 175 Bob Buhl.................. 3.50 1.55 .45
☐ 176 Jim King .... 3.00 1.35 .40
☐ 177 Bubba Phillips........... 3.00 1.35 .40
☐ 178 Johnny Edwards .... 3.00 1.35 .40
☐ 179 Ron Piche.................. 3.00 1.35 .40
☐ 180 Bill Skowron .... 4.50 2.00 .55
☐ 181 Sammy Esposito........ 3.00 1.35 .40
☐ 182 Albie Pearson............ 3.50 1.55 .45
☐ 183 Joe Pepitone............. 4.50 2.00 .55
☐ 184 Vern Law................... 3.50 1.55 .45
☐ 185 Chuck Hiller .... 3.00 1.35 .40
☐ 186 Jerry Zimmerman ...... 3.00 1.35 .40
☐ 187 Willie Kirkland........... 3.00 1.35 .40
☐ 188 Eddie Bressoud.......... 3.00 1.35 .40
☐ 189 Dave Giusti .... 3.50 1.55 .45
☐ 190 Minnie Minoso........... 4.50 2.00 .55
☐ 191 Checklist 3.............. 10.00 1.50 .50
☐ 192 Clay Dalrymple.......... 3.00 1.35 .40
☐ 193 Andre Rodgers........... 3.00 1.35 .40
☐ 194 Joe Nuxhall............... 3.50 1.55 .45
☐ 195 Manny Jimenez.......... 3.00 1.35 .40
☐ 196 Doug Camilli .... 3.00 1.35 .40
☐ 197 Roger Craig............... 4.00 1.80 .50
☐ 198 Lenny Green .... 4.00 1.80 .50
☐ 199 Joe Amalfitano........... 4.00 1.80 .50
☐ 200 Mickey Mantle........ 500.00 230.00 65.00
☐ 201 Cecil Butler .... 4.00 1.80 .50
☐ 202 Boston Red Sox......... 6.00 2.70 .75
Team Card
☐ 203 Chico Cardenas.......... 4.50 2.00 .55
☐ 204 Don Nottebart .... 4.00 1.80 .50
☐ 205 Luis Aparicio........... 15.00 6.75 1.90

☐ 206 Ray Washburn .... 4.00 1.80 .50
☐ 207 Ken Hunt .... 4.00 1.80 .50
☐ 208 Rookie Stars .... 4.00 1.80 .50
Ron Herbel
John Miller
Wally Wolf
Ron Taylor
☐ 209 Hobie Landrith .... 4.00 1.80 .50
☐ 210 Sandy Koufax 135.00 60.00 17.00
☐ 211 Fred Whitfield .... 4.00 1.80 .50
☐ 212 Glen Hobbie .... 4.00 1.80 .50
☐ 213 Billy Hitchcock MG .... 4.00 1.80 .50
☐ 214 Orlando Pena .... 4.00 1.80 .50
☐ 215 Bob Skinner .... 4.50 2.00 .55
☐ 216 Gene Conley .... 4.50 2.00 .55
☐ 217 Joe Christopher .... 4.00 1.80 .50
☐ 218 Tiger Twirlers .... 4.50 2.00 .55
Frank Lary
Don Mossi
Jim Bunning
☐ 219 Chuck Cottier .... 4.00 1.80 .50
☐ 220 Camilo Pascual .... 4.50 2.00 .55
☐ 221 Cookie Rojas .... 5.50 2.50 .70
☐ 222 Cubs Team .... 6.00 2.70 .75
☐ 223 Eddie Fisher .... 4.00 1.80 .50
☐ 224 Mike Roarke .... 4.00 1.80 .50
☐ 225 Joey Jay .... 4.00 1.80 .50
☐ 226 Julian Javier .... 4.50 2.00 .55
☐ 227 Jim Grant .... 4.50 2.00 .55
☐ 228 Rookie Stars 45.00 20.00 5.75
Max Alvis
Bob Bailey
Tony Oliva
(Listed as Pedro)
Ed Kranepool
☐ 229 Willie Davis .... 4.50 2.00 .55
☐ 230 Pete Runnels .... 4.50 2.00 .55
☐ 231 Eli Grba UER .... 4.00 1.80 .50
(Large photo is
Ryne Duren)
☐ 232 Frank Malzone .... 4.50 2.00 .55
☐ 233 Casey Stengel MG 16.00 7.25 2.00
☐ 234 Dave Nicholson .... 4.00 1.80 .50
☐ 235 Billy O'Dell .... 4.00 1.80 .50
☐ 236 Bill Bryan .... 4.00 1.80 .50
☐ 237 Jim Coates .... 4.00 1.80 .50
☐ 238 Lou Johnson .... 4.50 2.00 .55
☐ 239 Harvey Haddix .... 4.50 2.00 .55
☐ 240 Rocky Colavito 15.00 6.75 1.90
☐ 241 Bob Smith .... 4.00 1.80 .50
☐ 242 Power Plus 50.00 23.00 6.25
Ernie Banks
Hank Aaron
☐ 243 Don Leppert .... 4.00 1.80 .50
☐ 244 John Tsitouris .... 4.00 1.80 .50
☐ 245 Gil Hodges 18.00 8.00 2.30
☐ 246 Lee Stange .... 4.00 1.80 .50
☐ 247 Yankees Team 24.00 11.00 3.00
☐ 248 Tito Francona .... 4.00 1.80 .50
☐ 249 Leo Burke .... 4.00 1.80 .50
☐ 250 Stan Musial 110.00 50.00 14.00
☐ 251 Jack Lamabe .... 4.00 1.80 .50
☐ 252 Ron Santo 8.00 3.60 1.00
☐ 253 Rookie Stars .... 4.50 2.00 .55
Len Gabrielson
Pete Jernigan
John Wojcik
Deacon Jones
☐ 254 Mike Hershberger .... 4.00 1.80 .50
☐ 255 Bob Shaw .... 4.00 1.80 .50
☐ 256 Jerry Lumpe .... 4.00 1.80 .50
☐ 257 Hank Aguirre .... 4.00 1.80 .50
☐ 258 Alvin Dark MG .... 4.50 2.00 .55
☐ 259 Johnny Logan .... 4.50 2.00 .55
☐ 260 Jim Gentile .... 4.50 2.00 .55
☐ 261 Bob Miller .... 4.00 1.80 .50
☐ 262 Ellis Burton .... 4.00 1.80 .50
☐ 263 Dave Stenhouse .... 4.00 1.80 .50
☐ 264 Phil Linz .... 4.50 2.00 .55
☐ 265 Vada Pinson .... 6.00 2.70 .75
☐ 266 Bob Allen .... 4.00 1.80 .50
☐ 267 Carl Sawatski .... 4.00 1.80 .50
☐ 268 Don Demeter .... 4.00 1.80 .50
☐ 269 Don Mincher .... 4.00 1.80 .50
☐ 270 Felipe Alou .... 6.00 2.70 .75
☐ 271 Dean Stone .... 4.00 1.80 .50
☐ 272 Danny Murphy .... 4.00 1.80 .50
☐ 273 Sammy Taylor .... 4.00 1.80 .50
☐ 274 Checklist 4 .... 10.00 1.75 .50
☐ 275 Eddie Mathews 20.00 9.00 2.50
☐ 276 Barry Shetrone .... 4.00 1.80 .50
☐ 277 Dick Farrell .... 4.00 1.80 .50
☐ 278 Chico Fernandez .... 4.00 1.80 .50
☐ 279 Wally Moon .... 4.50 2.00 .55
☐ 280 Bob Rodgers .... 4.00 1.80 .50
☐ 281 Tom Sturdivant .... 4.00 1.80 .50
☐ 282 Bobby Del Greco .... 4.00 1.80 .50
☐ 283 Roy Sievers .... 4.50 2.00 .55
☐ 284 Dave Sisler .... 4.50 2.00 .55
☐ 285 Dick Stuart .... 5.00 2.30 .60
☐ 286 Stu Miller .... 5.00 2.30 .60
☐ 287 Dick Bertell .... 4.50 2.00 .55
☐ 288 Chicago White Sox... 10.00 4.50 1.25
Team Card
☐ 289 Hal Brown .... 4.50 2.00 .55
☐ 290 Bill White .... 6.50 2.90 .80
☐ 291 Don Rudolph .... 4.50 2.00 .55
☐ 292 Pumpsie Green .... 5.00 2.30 .60
☐ 293 Bill Pleis .... 4.50 2.00 .55
☐ 294 Bill Rigney MG .... 4.50 2.00 .55
☐ 295 Ed Roebuck .... 4.50 2.00 .55
☐ 296 Doc Edwards .... 4.50 2.00 .55
☐ 297 Jim Golden .... 4.50 2.00 .55
☐ 298 Don Dillard .... 4.50 2.00 .55
☐ 299 Rookie Stars .... 5.00 2.30 .60
Dave Morehead
Bob Dustal
Tom Butters
Dan Schneider
☐ 300 Willie Mays 140.00 65.00 17.50
☐ 301 Bill Fischer .... 4.50 2.00 .55
☐ 302 Whitey Herzog .... 7.00 3.10 .85
☐ 303 Earl Francis .... 4.50 2.00 .55
☐ 304 Harry Bright .... 4.50 2.00 .55
☐ 305 Don Hoak .... 5.00 2.30 .60
☐ 306 Star Receivers .... 6.00 2.70 .75
Earl Battey
Elston Howard
☐ 307 Chet Nichols .... 4.50 2.00 .55
☐ 308 Camilo Carreon .... 4.50 2.00 .55
☐ 309 Jim Brewer .... 4.50 2.00 .55
☐ 310 Tommy Davis .... 7.00 3.10 .85
☐ 311 Joe McClain .... 4.50 2.00 .55
☐ 312 Houston Colts 20.00 9.00 2.50
Team Card
☐ 313 Ernie Broglio .... 5.00 2.30 .60
☐ 314 John Goryl .... 4.50 2.00 .55
☐ 315 Ralph Terry .... 5.00 2.30 .60
☐ 316 Norm Sherry .... 5.00 2.30 .60
☐ 317 Sam McDowell .... 7.50 3.40 .95
☐ 318 Gene Mauch MG .... 5.00 2.30 .60
☐ 319 Joe Gaines .... 4.50 2.00 .55
☐ 320 Warren Spahn 40.00 18.00 5.00
☐ 321 Gino Cimoli .... 4.50 2.00 .55
☐ 322 Bob Turley .... 5.00 2.30 .60
☐ 323 Bill Mazeroski 8.00 3.60 1.00

□ 324 Rookie Stars .... 7.50 3.40 .95
George Williams
Pete Ward
Phil Roof
Vic Davalillo
□ 325 Jack Sanford .... 4.50 2.00 .55
□ 326 Hank Foiles .... 4.50 2.00 .55
□ 327 Paul Foytack .... 4.50 2.00 .55
□ 328 Dick Williams .... 5.00 2.30 .60
□ 329 Lindy McDaniel .... 5.00 2.30 .60
□ 330 Chuck Hinton .... 4.50 2.00 .55
□ 331 Series Foes .... 5.00 2.30 .60
Bill Stafford
Bill Pierce
□ 332 Joel Horlen .... 5.00 2.30 .60
□ 333 Carl Warwick .... 4.50 2.00 .55
□ 334 Wynn Hawkins .... 4.50 2.00 .55
□ 335 Leon Wagner .... 4.50 2.00 .55
□ 336 Ed Bauta .... 4.50 2.00 .55
□ 337 Dodgers Team 20.00 9.00 2.50
□ 338 Russ Kemmerer .... 4.50 2.00 .55
□ 339 Ted Bowsfield .... 4.50 2.00 .55
□ 340 Yogi Berra P/CO 70.00 32.00 8.75
□ 341 Jack Baldschun .... 4.50 2.00 .55
□ 342 Gene Woodling .... 5.00 2.30 .60
□ 343 Johnny Pesky MG .... 5.00 2.30 .60
□ 344 Don Schwall .... 5.00 2.30 .60
□ 345 Brooks Robinson 50.00 23.00 6.25
□ 346 Billy Hoeft .... 4.50 2.00 .55
□ 347 Joe Torre 10.00 4.50 1.25
□ 348 Vic Wertz .... 5.00 2.30 .60
□ 349 Zoilo Versalles .... 5.00 2.30 .60
□ 350 Bob Purkey .... 4.50 2.00 .55
□ 351 Al Luplow .... 4.50 2.00 .55
□ 352 Ken Johnson .... 4.50 2.00 .55
□ 353 Billy Williams 28.00 12.50 3.50
□ 354 Dom Zanni .... 4.50 2.00 .55
□ 355 Dean Chance .... 4.50 2.00 .55
□ 356 John Schaive .... 4.50 2.00 .55
□ 357 George Altman .... 4.50 2.00 .55
□ 358 Milt Pappas .... 5.00 2.30 .60
□ 359 Haywood Sullivan .... 5.00 2.30 .60
□ 360 Don Drysdale 42.00 19.00 5.25
□ 361 Clete Boyer .... 7.00 3.10 .85
□ 362 Checklist 5 .... 10.00 1.80 .50
□ 363 Dick Radatz .... 7.50 3.40 .95
□ 364 Howie Goss .... 4.50 2.00 .55
□ 365 Jim Bunning 12.00 5.50 1.50
□ 366 Tony Taylor .... 5.00 2.30 .60
□ 367 Tony Cloninger .... 4.50 2.00 .55
□ 368 Ed Bailey .... 4.50 2.00 .55
□ 369 Jim Lemon .... 4.50 2.00 .55
□ 370 Dick Donovan .... 4.50 2.00 .55
□ 371 Rod Kanehl .... 5.00 2.30 .60
□ 372 Don Lee .... 5.00 2.30 .60
□ 373 Jim Campbell .... 5.00 2.30 .60
□ 374 Claude Osteen .... 5.50 2.50 .70
□ 375 Ken Boyer 8.00 3.60 1.00
□ 376 John Wyatt .... 5.00 2.30 .60
□ 377 Baltimore Orioles 10.00 4.50 1.25
Team Card
□ 378 Bill Henry .... 5.00 2.30 .60
□ 379 Bob Anderson .... 5.00 2.30 .60
□ 380 Ernie Banks UER 65.00 29.00 8.25
(Back has career Major
and Minor, but he
never played in Minors)
□ 381 Frank Baumann .... 5.00 2.30 .60
□ 382 Ralph Houk MG .... 5.00 2.30 .60
□ 383 Pete Richert .... 5.00 2.30 .60
□ 384 Bob Tillman .... 5.00 2.30 .60
□ 385 Art Mahaffey .... 5.00 2.30 .60
□ 386 Rookie Stars .... 5.00 2.30 .60
Ed Kirkpatrick
John Bateman
Larry Bearnarth
Garry Roggenburk
□ 387 Al McBean .... 5.00 2.30 .60
□ 388 Jim Davenport .... 5.50 2.50 .70
□ 389 Frank Sullivan .... 5.00 2.30 .60
□ 390 Hank Aaron 135.00 60.00 17.00
□ 391 Bill Dailey .... 5.00 2.30 .60
□ 392 Tribe Thumpers .... 5.00 2.30 .60
Johnny Romano
Tito Francona
□ 393 Ken MacKenzie .... 5.00 2.30 .60
□ 394 Tim McCarver 14.00 6.25 1.75
□ 395 Don McMahon .... 5.00 2.30 .60
□ 396 Joe Koppe .... 5.00 2.30 .60
□ 397 Kansas City Athletics 10.00 4.50 1.25
Team Card
□ 398 Boog Powell 27.00 12.00 3.40
□ 399 Dick Ellsworth .... 5.50 2.50 .70
□ 400 Frank Robinson 50.00 23.00 6.25
□ 401 Jim Bouton 10.00 4.50 1.25
□ 402 Mickey Vernon MG .... 5.50 2.50 .70
□ 403 Ron Perranoski .... 5.50 2.50 .70
□ 404 Bob Oldis .... 5.00 2.30 .60
□ 405 Floyd Robinson .... 5.00 2.30 .60
□ 406 Howie Koplitz .... 5.00 2.30 .60
□ 407 Rookie Stars .... 5.00 2.30 .60
Frank Kostro
Chico Ruiz
Larry Elliot
Dick Simpson
□ 408 Billy Gardner .... 5.00 2.30 .60
□ 409 Roy Face 8.00 3.60 1.00
□ 410 Earl Battey .... 5.00 2.30 .60
□ 411 Jim Constable .... 5.00 2.30 .60
□ 412 Dodger Big Three 40.00 18.00 5.00
Johnny Podres
Don Drysdale
Sandy Koufax
□ 413 Jerry Walker .... 5.00 2.30 .60
□ 414 Ty Cline .... 5.00 2.30 .60
□ 415 Bob Gibson 50.00 23.00 6.25
□ 416 Alex Grammas .... 5.00 2.30 .60
□ 417 Giants Team 10.00 4.50 1.25
□ 418 John Orsino .... 5.00 2.30 .60
□ 419 Tracy Stallard .... 5.00 2.30 .60
□ 420 Bobby Richardson ... 14.00 6.25 1.75
□ 421 Tom Morgan .... 5.00 2.30 .60
□ 422 Fred Hutchinson MG .. 5.50 2.50 .70
□ 423 Ed Hobaugh .... 5.00 2.30 .60
□ 424 Charlie Smith .... 5.00 2.30 .60
□ 425 Smoky Burgess .... 5.50 2.50 .70
□ 426 Barry Latman .... 5.00 2.30 .60
□ 427 Bernie Allen .... 5.00 2.30 .60
□ 428 Carl Boles .... 5.00 2.30 .60
□ 429 Lou Burdette .... 5.00 2.30 .60
□ 430 Norm Siebern .... 5.00 2.30 .60
□ 431A Checklist 6 .... 10.00 2.30 .60
(White on red)
□ 431B Checklist 6 .... 18.00 2.70 .90
(Black on orange)
□ 432 Roman Mejias .... 5.00 2.30 .60
□ 433 Denis Menke .... 5.00 2.30 .60
□ 434 John Callison .... 5.50 2.50 .70
□ 435 Woody Held .... 5.00 2.30 .60
□ 436 Tim Harkness .... 5.00 2.30 .60
□ 437 Bill Bruton .... 5.00 2.30 .60
□ 438 Wes Stock .... 5.00 2.30 .60
□ 439 Don Zimmer .... 5.00 2.30 .60
□ 440 Juan Marichal 30.00 13.50 3.80
□ 441 Lee Thomas .... 5.50 2.50 .70
□ 442 J.C. Hartman .... 5.00 2.30 .60

□ 443 Jim Piersall 6.00 2.70 .75
□ 444 Jim Maloney 5.00 2.30 .60
□ 445 Norm Cash 8.00 3.60 1.00
□ 446 Whitey Ford 40.00 18.00 5.00
□ 447 Felix Mantilla 16.00 7.25 2.00
□ 448 Jack Kralick 16.00 7.25 2.00
□ 449 Jose Tartabull 16.00 7.25 2.00
□ 450 Bob Friend 19.00 8.50 2.40
□ 451 Indians Team 40.00 18.00 5.00
□ 452 Barney Schultz 16.00 7.25 2.00
□ 453 Jake Wood 16.00 7.25 2.00
□ 454A Art Fowler 16.00 7.25 2.00
(Card number on white background)
□ 454B Art Fowler 30.00 13.50 3.80
(Card number on orange background)
□ 455 Ruben Amaro 16.00 7.25 2.00
□ 456 Jim Coker 16.00 7.25 2.00
□ 457 Tex Clevenger 16.00 7.25 2.00
□ 458 Al Lopez MG 20.00 9.00 2.50
□ 459 Dick LeMay 16.00 7.25 2.00
□ 460 Del Crandall 20.00 9.00 2.50
□ 461 Norm Bass 16.00 7.25 2.00
□ 462 Wally Post 20.00 9.00 2.50
□ 463 Joe Schaffernoth 16.00 7.25 2.00
□ 464 Ken Aspromonte 16.00 7.25 2.00
□ 465 Chuck Estrada 16.00 7.25 2.00
□ 466 Rookie Stars SP 70.00 32.00 8.75
Nate Oliver
Tony Martinez
Bill Freehan
Jerry Robinson
□ 467 Phil Ortega 16.00 7.25 2.00
□ 468 Carroll Hardy 18.00 8.00 2.30
□ 469 Jay Hook 16.00 7.25 2.00
□ 470 Tom Tresh SP 60.00 27.00 7.50
□ 471 Ken Retzer 16.00 7.25 2.00
□ 472 Lou Brock 110.00 50.00 14.00
□ 473 New York Mets 100.00 45.00 12.50
Team Card
□ 474 Jack Fisher 16.00 7.25 2.00
□ 475 Gus Triandos 20.00 9.00 2.50
□ 476 Frank Funk 16.00 7.25 2.00
□ 477 Donn Clendenon 20.00 9.00 2.50
□ 478 Paul Brown 16.00 7.25 2.00
□ 479 Ed Brinkman 16.00 7.25 2.00
□ 480 Bill Monbouquette 16.00 7.25 2.00
□ 481 Bob Taylor 16.00 7.25 2.00
□ 482 Felix Torres 16.00 7.25 2.00
□ 483 Jim Owens UER 16.00 7.25 2.00
(Stat column for Wins has an R instead)
□ 484 Dale Long SP 24.00 11.00 3.00
□ 485 Jim Landis 16.00 7.25 2.00
□ 486 Ray Sadecki 16.00 7.25 2.00
□ 487 John Roseboro 20.00 9.00 2.50
□ 488 Jerry Adair 16.00 7.25 2.00
□ 489 Paul Toth 16.00 7.25 2.00
□ 490 Willie McCovey 125.00 57.50 15.50
□ 491 Harry Craft MG 16.00 7.25 2.00
□ 492 Dave Wickersham 16.00 7.25 2.00
□ 493 Walt Bond 16.00 7.25 2.00
□ 494 Phil Regan 20.00 9.00 2.50
□ 495 Frank Thomas SP 25.00 11.50 3.10
□ 496 Rookie Stars 18.00 8.00 2.30
Steve Dalkowski
Fred Newman
Jack Smith
Carl Bouldin
□ 497 Bennie Daniels 16.00 7.25 2.00
□ 498 Eddie Kasko 16.00 7.25 2.00
□ 499 J.C. Martin 16.00 7.25 2.00
□ 500 Harmon Killebrew SP 135.00 60.00 17.00
□ 501 Joe Azcue 16.00 7.25 2.00
□ 502 Daryl Spencer 16.00 7.25 2.00
□ 503 Braves Team 40.00 18.00 5.00
□ 504 Bob Johnson 16.00 7.25 2.00
□ 505 Curt Flood 20.00 9.00 2.50
□ 506 Gene Green 16.00 7.25 2.00
□ 507 Roland Sheldon 16.00 7.25 2.00
□ 508 Ted Savage 16.00 7.25 2.00
□ 509A Checklist 7 18.00 6.00 1.60
(Copyright centered)
□ 509B Checklist 7 18.00 6.00 1.60
(Copyright to right)
□ 510 Ken McBride 16.00 7.25 2.00
□ 511 Charlie Neal 20.00 9.00 2.50
□ 512 Cal McLish 16.00 7.25 2.00
□ 513 Gary Geiger 16.00 7.25 2.00
□ 514 Larry Osborne 16.00 7.25 2.00
□ 515 Don Elston 16.00 7.25 2.00
□ 516 Purnell Goldy 16.00 7.25 2.00
□ 517 Hal Woodeshick 16.00 7.25 2.00
□ 518 Don Blasingame 16.00 7.25 2.00
□ 519 Claude Raymond 16.00 7.25 2.00
□ 520 Orlando Cepeda 27.00 12.00 3.40
□ 521 Dan Pfister 16.00 7.25 2.00
□ 522 Rookie Stars 20.00 9.00 2.50
Mel Nelson
Gary Peters
Jim Roland
Art Quirk
□ 523 Bill Kunkel 12.00 5.50 1.50
□ 524 Cardinals Team 30.00 13.50 3.80
□ 525 Nellie Fox 27.00 12.00 3.40
□ 526 Dick Hall 12.00 5.50 1.50
□ 527 Ed Sadowski 12.00 5.50 1.50
□ 528 Carl Willey 12.00 5.50 1.50
□ 529 Wes Covington 15.00 6.75 1.90
□ 530 Don Mossi 15.00 6.75 1.90
□ 531 Sam Mele MG 12.00 5.50 1.50
□ 532 Steve Boros 12.00 5.50 1.50
□ 533 Bobby Shantz 12.00 5.50 1.50
□ 534 Ken Walters 12.00 5.50 1.50
□ 535 Jim Perry 12.00 5.50 1.50
□ 536 Norm Larker 12.00 5.50 1.50
□ 537 Rookie Stars 1000.00 450.00 125.00
Pedro Gonzalez
Ken McMullen
Al Weis
Pete Rose
□ 538 George Brunet 12.00 5.50 1.50
□ 539 Wayne Causey 12.00 5.50 1.50
□ 540 Bob Clemente 300.00 135.00 38.00
□ 541 Ron Moeller 12.00 5.50 1.50
□ 542 Lou Klimchock 12.00 5.50 1.50
□ 543 Russ Snyder 12.00 5.50 1.50
□ 544 Rookie Stars 45.00 20.00 5.75
Duke Carmel
Bill Haas
Rusty Staub
Dick Phillips
□ 545 Jose Pagan 12.00 5.50 1.50
□ 546 Hal Reniff 12.00 5.50 1.50
□ 547 Gus Bell 15.00 6.75 1.90
□ 548 Tom Satriano 12.00 5.50 1.50
□ 549 Rookie Stars 12.00 5.50 1.50
Marcelino Lopez
Pete Lovrich
Paul Ratliff
Elmo Plaskett
□ 550 Duke Snider 70.00 32.00 8.75
□ 551 Billy Klaus 12.00 5.50 1.50
□ 552 Detroit Tigers 38.00 17.00 4.70
Team Card

		NRMT	VG-E	GOOD
☐	553 Rookie Stars	125.00	57.50	15.50
	Brock Davis			
	Jim Gosger			
	Willie Stargell			
	John Herrnstein			
☐	554 Hank Fischer	12.00	5.50	1.50
☐	555 John Blanchard	15.00	6.75	1.90
☐	556 Al Worthington	12.00	5.50	1.50
☐	557 Cuno Barragan	12.00	5.50	1.50
☐	558 Rookie Stars	16.00	7.25	2.00
	Bill Faul			
	Ron Hunt			
	Al Moran			
	Bob Lipski			
☐	559 Danny Murtaugh MG	15.00	6.75	1.90
☐	560 Ray Herbert	12.00	5.50	1.50
☐	561 Mike De La Hoz	12.00	5.50	1.50
☐	562 Rookie Stars	24.00	11.00	3.00
	Randy Cardinal			
	Dave McNally			
	Ken Rowe			
	Don Rowe			
☐	563 Mike McCormick	15.00	6.75	1.90
☐	564 George Banks	12.00	5.50	1.50
☐	565 Larry Sherry	15.00	6.75	1.90
☐	566 Cliff Cook	12.00	5.50	1.50
☐	567 Jim Duffalo	12.00	5.50	1.50
☐	568 Bob Sadowski	12.00	5.50	1.50
☐	569 Luis Arroyo	15.00	6.75	1.90
☐	570 Frank Bolling	12.00	5.50	1.50
☐	571 Johnny Klippstein	12.00	5.50	1.50
☐	572 Jack Spring	12.00	5.50	1.50
☐	573 Coot Veal	12.00	5.50	1.50
☐	574 Hal Kolstad	12.00	5.50	1.50
☐	575 Don Cardwell	12.00	5.50	1.50
☐	576 Johnny Temple	20.00	5.50	1.50

1964 Topps

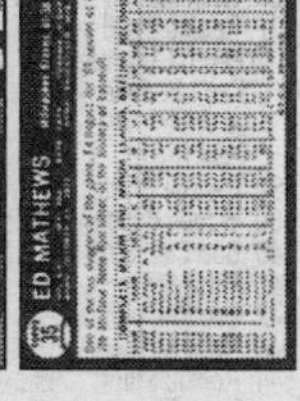

The cards in this 587-card set measure 2 1/2" by 3 1/2". Players in the 1964 Topps baseball series were easy to sort by team due to the giant block lettering found at the top of each card. The name and position of the player are found underneath the picture, and the card is numbered in a ball design on the orange-colored back. The usual last series scarcity holds for this set (523 to 587). Subsets within this set include League Leaders (1-12) and World Series cards (136-140). There were some three-card advertising panels produced by Topps; the players included are from the first series; one panel shows Walt Alston, Bill Henry, and Vada Pinson on the front with a Mickey Mantle card back on one of the backs. Another panel shows Carl Willey, White Sox Rookies, and Bob Friend on the front with a Mickey Mantle card back on one of the backs. The key Rookie Cards in this set are Richie Allen, Tommy John, Tony LaRussa, Lou Piniella, and Phil Niekro.

		NRMT	VG-E	GOOD
	COMPLETE SET (587)	3000.00	1350.00	375.00
	COMMON CARD (1-109)	3.00	1.35	.40
	COMMON CARD (110-196)	3.00	1.35	.40
	COMMON CARD (197-283)	3.50	1.55	.45
	COMMON CARD (284-370)	3.50	1.55	.45
	COMMON CARD (371-446)	7.50	3.40	.95
	COMMON CARD (447-522)	7.50	3.40	.95
	COMMON CARD (523-587)	12.00	5.50	1.50
☐	1 NL ERA Leaders	22.00	5.50	1.75
	Sandy Koufax			
	Dick Ellsworth			
	Bob Friend			
☐	2 AL ERA Leaders	6.00	2.70	.75
	Gary Peters			
	Juan Pizarro			
	Camilo Pascual			
☐	3 NL Pitching Leaders	15.00	6.75	1.90
	Sandy Koufax			
	Juan Marichal			
	Warren Spahn			
	Jim Maloney			
☐	4 AL Pitching Leaders	7.50	3.40	.95
	Whitey Ford			
	Camilo Pascual			
	Jim Bouton			
☐	5 NL Strikeout Leaders	12.00	5.50	1.50
	Sandy Koufax			
	Jim Maloney			
	Don Drysdale			
☐	6 AL Strikeout Leaders	6.00	2.70	.75
	Camilo Pascual			
	Jim Bunning			
	Dick Stigman			
☐	7 NL Batting Leaders	14.00	6.25	1.75
	Tommy Davis			
	Bob Clemente			
	Dick Groat			
	Hank Aaron			
☐	8 AL Batting Leaders	10.00	4.50	1.25
	Carl Yastrzemski			
	Al Kaline			
	Rich Rollins			
☐	9 NL Home Run Leaders	25.00	11.50	3.10
	Hank Aaron			
	Willie McCovey			
	Willie Mays			
	Orlando Cepeda			
☐	10 AL Home Run Leaders	7.00	3.10	.85
	Harmon Killebrew			
	Dick Stuart			
	Bob Allison			
☐	11 NL RBI Leaders	10.00	4.50	1.25
	Hank Aaron			
	Ken Boyer			
	Bill White			
☐	12 AL RBI Leaders	7.50	3.40	.95
	Dick Stuart			
	Al Kaline			
	Harmon Killebrew			
☐	13 Hoyt Wilhelm	9.00	4.00	1.15
☐	14 Dodgers Rookies	3.00	1.35	.40
	Dick Nen			

Nick Willhite
- ☐ 15 Zoilo Versalles .... 3.50 1.55 .45
- ☐ 16 John Boozer.................. 3.00 1.35 .40
- ☐ 17 Willie Kirkland............. 3.00 1.35 .40
- ☐ 18 Billy O'Dell .... 3.00 1.35 .40
- ☐ 19 Don Wert .... 3.00 1.35 .40
- ☐ 20 Bob Friend .... 3.50 1.55 .45
- ☐ 21 Yogi Berra MG 32.00 14.50 4.00
- ☐ 22 Jerry Adair .... 3.00 1.35 .40
- ☐ 23 Chris Zachary.............. 3.00 1.35 .40
- ☐ 24 Carl Sawatski .... 3.00 1.35 .40
- ☐ 25 Bill Monbouquette........ 3.00 1.35 .40
- ☐ 26 Gino Cimoli.................. 3.00 1.35 .40
- ☐ 27 New York Mets .... 7.00 3.10 .85
  Team Card
- ☐ 28 Claude Osteen.............. 3.50 1.55 .45
- ☐ 29 Lou Brock 35.00 16.00 4.40
- ☐ 30 Ron Perranoski .... 3.50 1.55 .45
- ☐ 31 Dave Nicholson............ 3.00 1.35 .40
- ☐ 32 Dean Chance............... 4.50 2.00 .55
- ☐ 33 Reds Rookies............... 3.50 1.55 .45
  Sammy Ellis
  Mel Queen
- ☐ 34 Jim Perry .... 3.50 1.55 .45
- ☐ 35 Eddie Mathews 20.00 9.00 2.50
- ☐ 36 Hal Reniff..................... 3.00 1.35 .40
- ☐ 37 Smoky Burgess........... 3.50 1.55 .45
- ☐ 38 Jim Wynn 8.00 3.60 1.00
- ☐ 39 Hank Aguirre............... 3.00 1.35 .40
- ☐ 40 Dick Groat................... 3.50 1.55 .45
- ☐ 41 Friendly Foes................ 7.50 3.40 .95
  Willie McCovey
  Leon Wagner
- ☐ 42 Moe Drabowsky........... 3.50 1.55 .45
- ☐ 43 Roy Sievers.................. 3.50 1.55 .45
- ☐ 44 Duke Carmel .... 3.00 1.35 .40
- ☐ 45 Milt Pappas.................. 3.50 1.55 .45
- ☐ 46 Ed Brinkman .... 3.00 1.35 .40
- ☐ 47 Giants Rookies............. 5.50 2.50 .70
  Jesus Alou
  Ron Herbel
- ☐ 48 Bob Perry..................... 3.00 1.35 .40
- ☐ 49 Bill Henry..................... 3.00 1.35 .40
- ☐ 50 Mickey Mantle.......... 275.00 125.00 34.00
- ☐ 51 Pete Richert .... 3.00 1.35 .40
- ☐ 52 Chuck Hinton .... 3.00 1.35 .40
- ☐ 53 Denis Menke................. 3.00 1.35 .40
- ☐ 54 Sam Mele MG .... 3.00 1.35 .40
- ☐ 55 Ernie Banks............... 35.00 16.00 4.40
- ☐ 56 Hal Brown .... 3.00 1.35 .40
- ☐ 57 Tim Harkness............... 3.00 1.35 .40
- ☐ 58 Don Demeter................ 3.00 1.35 .40
- ☐ 59 Ernie Broglio .... 3.00 1.35 .40
- ☐ 60 Frank Malzone.............. 3.50 1.55 .45
- ☐ 61 Angel Backstops .... 3.50 1.55 .45
  Bob Rodgers
  Ed Sadowski
- ☐ 62 Ted Savage .... 3.00 1.35 .40
- ☐ 63 John Orsino .... 3.00 1.35 .40
- ☐ 64 Ted Abernathy.............. 3.00 1.35 .40
- ☐ 65 Felipe Alou .... 4.50 2.00 .55
- ☐ 66 Eddie Fisher .... 3.00 1.35 .40
- ☐ 67 Tigers Team .... 5.00 2.30 .60
- ☐ 68 Willie Davis .... 3.50 1.55 .45
- ☐ 69 Clete Boyer .... 3.00 1.35 .40
- ☐ 70 Joe Torre .... 5.00 2.30 .60
- ☐ 71 Jack Spring................... 3.00 1.35 .40
- ☐ 72 Chico Cardenas............. 3.50 1.55 .45
- ☐ 73 Jimmie Hall................... 3.50 1.55 .45
- ☐ 74 Pirates Rookies............. 3.00 1.35 .40
  Bob Priddy
  Tom Butters
- ☐ 75 Wayne Causey .... 3.00 1.35 .40
- ☐ 76 Checklist 1 .... 10.00 1.50 .50
- ☐ 77 Jerry Walker .... 3.00 1.35 .40
- ☐ 78 Merritt Ranew .... 3.00 1.35 .40
- ☐ 79 Bob Heffner.................. 3.00 1.35 .40
- ☐ 80 Vada Pinson................. 4.00 1.80 .50
- ☐ 81 All-Star Vets.................. 7.50 3.40 .95
  Nellie Fox
  Harmon Killebrew
- ☐ 82 Jim Davenport .... 3.50 1.55 .45
- ☐ 83 Gus Triandos .... 3.50 1.55 .45
- ☐ 84 Carl Willey.................... 3.00 1.35 .40
- ☐ 85 Pete Ward .... 3.00 1.35 .40
- ☐ 86 Al Downing .... 3.00 1.35 .40
- ☐ 87 St. Louis Cardinals....... 5.00 2.30 .60
  Team Card
- ☐ 88 John Roseboro .... 3.50 1.55 .45
- ☐ 89 Boog Powell.................. 6.50 2.90 .80
- ☐ 90 Earl Battey.................... 3.00 1.35 .40
- ☐ 91 Bob Bailey..................... 3.50 1.55 .45
- ☐ 92 Steve Ridzik .... 3.00 1.35 .40
- ☐ 93 Gary Geiger.................. 3.00 1.35 .40
- ☐ 94 Braves Rookies .... 3.00 1.35 .40
  Jim Britton
  Larry Maxie
- ☐ 95 George Altman............. 3.00 1.35 .40
- ☐ 96 Bob Buhl....................... 3.50 1.55 .45
- ☐ 97 Jim Fregosi .... 3.50 1.55 .45
- ☐ 98 Bill Bruton.................... 3.00 1.35 .40
- ☐ 99 Al Stanek...................... 3.00 1.35 .40
- ☐ 100 Elston Howard .... 5.00 2.30 .60
- ☐ 101 Walt Alston MG........... 4.50 2.00 .55
- ☐ 102 Checklist 2 .... 10.00 1.50 .50
- ☐ 103 Curt Flood .... 4.00 1.80 .50
- ☐ 104 Art Mahaffey .... 3.50 1.55 .45
- ☐ 105 Woody Held .... 3.00 1.35 .40
- ☐ 106 Joe Nuxhall .... 3.50 1.55 .45
- ☐ 107 White Sox Rookies...... 3.00 1.35 .40
  Bruce Howard
  Frank Kreutzer
- ☐ 108 John Wyatt .... 3.00 1.35 .40
- ☐ 109 Rusty Staub 9.00 4.00 1.15
- ☐ 110 Albie Pearson............. 3.50 1.55 .45
- ☐ 111 Don Elston .... 3.00 1.35 .40
- ☐ 112 Bob Tillman................. 3.00 1.35 .40
- ☐ 113 Grover Powell .... 3.00 1.35 .40
- ☐ 114 Don Lock .... 3.00 1.35 .40
- ☐ 115 Frank Bolling.............. 3.00 1.35 .40
- ☐ 116 Twins Rookies 14.00 6.25 1.75
  Jay Ward
  Tony Oliva
- ☐ 117 Earl Francis .... 3.00 1.35 .40
- ☐ 118 John Blanchard .... 3.50 1.55 .45
- ☐ 119 Gary Kolb................... 3.00 1.35 .40
- ☐ 120 Don Drysdale 20.00 9.00 2.50
- ☐ 121 Pete Runnels.............. 3.50 1.55 .45
- ☐ 122 Don McMahon .... 3.00 1.35 .40
- ☐ 123 Jose Pagan .... 3.00 1.35 .40
- ☐ 124 Orlando Pena .... 3.00 1.35 .40
- ☐ 125 Pete Rose 125.00 57.50 15.50
- ☐ 126 Russ Snyder .... 3.00 1.35 .40
- ☐ 127 Angels Rookies .... 3.00 1.35 .40
  Aubrey Gatewood
  Dick Simpson
- ☐ 128 Mickey Lolich........... 24.00 11.00 3.00
- ☐ 129 Amado Samuel .... 3.00 1.35 .40
- ☐ 130 Gary Peters................ 3.50 1.55 .45
- ☐ 131 Steve Boros .... 3.00 1.35 .40
- ☐ 132 Braves Team .... 5.00 2.30 .60
- ☐ 133 Jim Grant.................... 3.50 1.55 .45
- ☐ 134 Don Zimmer................ 3.50 1.55 .45
- ☐ 135 Johnny Callison .... 3.50 1.55 .45
- ☐ 136 World Series Game 1 16.00 7.25 2.00
  Sandy Koufax

strikes out 15
☐ 137 World Series Game 2. 6.00 2.70 .75
Tommy Davis
sparks rally
☐ 138 World Series Game 3. 6.00 2.70 .75
LA Three Straight
(Ron Fairly)
☐ 139 World Series Game 4. 6.00 2.70 .75
Sealing Yanks doom
(Frank Howard)
☐ 140 World Series Summary 6.00 2.70 .75
Dodgers celebrate
☐ 141 Danny Murtaugh MG . 3.50 1.55 .45
☐ 142 John Bateman 3.00 1.35 .40
☐ 143 Bubba Phillips 3.00 1.35 .40
☐ 144 Al Worthington 3.00 1.35 .40
☐ 145 Norm Siebern 3.00 1.35 .40
☐ 146 Indians Rookies 35.00 16.00 4.40
Tommy John
Bob Chance
☐ 147 Ray Sadecki 3.00 1.35 .40
☐ 148 J.C. Martin 3.00 1.35 .40
☐ 149 Paul Foytack 3.00 1.35 .40
☐ 150 Willie Mays 85.00 38.00 10.50
☐ 151 Athletics Team 5.00 2.30 .60
☐ 152 Denny Lemaster 3.00 1.35 .40
☐ 153 Dick Williams 3.50 1.55 .45
☐ 154 Dick Tracewski 3.50 1.55 .45
☐ 155 Duke Snider 28.00 12.50 3.50
☐ 156 Bill Dailey 3.00 1.35 .40
☐ 157 Gene Mauch MG 3.50 1.55 .45
☐ 158 Ken Johnson 3.00 1.35 .40
☐ 159 Charlie Dees 3.00 1.35 .40
☐ 160 Ken Boyer 6.00 2.70 .75
☐ 161 Dave McNally 3.50 1.55 .45
☐ 162 Hitting Area 3.50 1.55 .45
Dick Sisler CO
Vada Pinson
☐ 163 Donn Clendenon 3.50 1.55 .45
☐ 164 Bud Daley 3.00 1.35 .40
☐ 165 Jerry Lumpe 3.00 1.35 .40
☐ 166 Marty Keough 3.00 1.35 .40
☐ 167 Senators Rookies 30.00 13.50 3.80
Mike Brumley
Lou Piniella
☐ 168 Al Weis 3.00 1.35 .40
☐ 169 Del Crandall 3.50 1.55 .45
☐ 170 Dick Radatz 3.50 1.55 .45
☐ 171 Ty Cline 3.00 1.35 .40
☐ 172 Indians Team 5.00 2.30 .60
☐ 173 Ryne Duren 3.50 1.55 .45
☐ 174 Doc Edwards 3.00 1.35 .40
☐ 175 Billy Williams 14.00 6.25 1.75
☐ 176 Tracy Stallard 3.00 1.35 .40
☐ 177 Harmon Killebrew 20.00 9.00 2.50
☐ 178 Hank Bauer MG 3.50 1.55 .45
☐ 179 Carl Warwick 3.00 1.35 .40
☐ 180 Tommy Davis 3.00 1.35 .40
☐ 181 Dave Wickersham 3.00 1.35 .40
☐ 182 Sox Sockers 14.00 6.25 1.75
Carl Yastrzemski
Chuck Schilling
☐ 183 Ron Taylor 3.00 1.35 .40
☐ 184 Al Luplow 3.00 1.35 .40
☐ 185 Jim O'Toole 3.50 1.55 .45
☐ 186 Roman Mejias 3.00 1.35 .40
☐ 187 Ed Roebuck 3.00 1.35 .40
☐ 188 Checklist 3 10.00 1.50 .50
☐ 189 Bob Hendley 3.00 1.35 .40
☐ 190 Bobby Richardson 8.00 3.60 1.00
☐ 191 Clay Dalrymple 3.50 1.55 .45
☐ 192 Cubs Rookies 3.00 1.35 .40
John Boccabella
Billy Cowan
☐ 193 Jerry Lynch 3.00 1.35 .40
☐ 194 John Goryl 3.00 1.35 .40
☐ 195 Floyd Robinson 3.00 1.35 .40
☐ 196 Jim Gentile 3.00 1.35 .40
☐ 197 Frank Lary 4.00 1.80 .50
☐ 198 Len Gabrielson 3.50 1.55 .45
☐ 199 Joe Azcue 3.50 1.55 .45
☐ 200 Sandy Koufax 100.00 45.00 12.50
☐ 201 Orioles Rookies 4.00 1.80 .50
Sam Bowens
Wally Bunker
☐ 202 Galen Cisco 4.00 1.80 .50
☐ 203 John Kennedy 4.00 1.80 .50
☐ 204 Matty Alou 3.50 1.55 .45
☐ 205 Nellie Fox 7.00 3.10 .85
☐ 206 Steve Hamilton 3.50 1.55 .45
☐ 207 Fred Hutchinson MG 4.00 1.80 .50
☐ 208 Wes Covington 4.00 1.80 .50
☐ 209 Bob Allen 3.50 1.55 .45
☐ 210 Carl Yastrzemski 40.00 18.00 5.00
☐ 211 Jim Coker 3.50 1.55 .45
☐ 212 Pete Lovrich 3.50 1.55 .45
☐ 213 Angels Team 6.00 2.70 .75
☐ 214 Ken McMullen 4.00 1.80 .50
☐ 215 Ray Herbert 3.50 1.55 .45
☐ 216 Mike de la Hoz 3.50 1.55 .45
☐ 217 Jim King 3.50 1.55 .45
☐ 218 Hank Fischer 3.50 1.55 .45
☐ 219 Young Aces 5.00 2.30 .60
Al Downing
Jim Bouton
☐ 220 Dick Ellsworth 4.00 1.80 .50
☐ 221 Bob Saverine 3.50 1.55 .45
☐ 222 Billy Pierce 4.00 1.80 .50
☐ 223 George Banks 3.50 1.55 .45
☐ 224 Tommie Sisk 3.50 1.55 .45
☐ 225 Roger Maris 60.00 27.00 7.50
☐ 226 Colts Rookies 7.00 3.10 .85
Jerry Grote
Larry Yellen
☐ 227 Barry Latman 3.50 1.55 .45
☐ 228 Felix Mantilla 3.50 1.55 .45
☐ 229 Charley Lau 4.00 1.80 .50
☐ 230 Brooks Robinson 38.00 17.00 4.70
☐ 231 Dick Calmus 3.50 1.55 .45
☐ 232 Al Lopez MG 5.00 2.30 .60
☐ 233 Hal Smith 3.50 1.55 .45
☐ 234 Gary Bell 3.50 1.55 .45
☐ 235 Ron Hunt 3.50 1.55 .45
☐ 236 Bill Faul 3.50 1.55 .45
☐ 237 Cubs Team 6.00 2.70 .75
☐ 238 Roy McMillan 4.00 1.80 .50
☐ 239 Herm Starrette 3.50 1.55 .45
☐ 240 Bill White 5.00 2.30 .60
☐ 241 Jim Owens 3.50 1.55 .45
☐ 242 Harvey Kuenn 4.00 1.80 .50
☐ 243 Phillies Rookies 35.00 16.00 4.40
Richie Allen
John Herrnstein
☐ 244 Tony LaRussa 30.00 13.50 3.80
☐ 245 Dick Stigman 3.50 1.55 .45
☐ 246 Manny Mota 3.50 1.55 .45
☐ 247 Dave DeBusschere 5.50 2.50 .70
☐ 248 Johnny Pesky MG 4.00 1.80 .50
☐ 249 Doug Camilli 3.50 1.55 .45
☐ 250 Al Kaline 38.00 17.00 4.70
☐ 251 Choo Choo Coleman 3.50 1.55 .45
☐ 252 Ken Aspromonte 3.50 1.55 .45
☐ 253 Wally Post 4.00 1.80 .50
☐ 254 Don Hoak 4.00 1.80 .50
☐ 255 Lee Thomas 4.00 1.80 .50
☐ 256 Johnny Weekly 3.50 1.55 .45
☐ 257 San Francisco Giants 6.00 2.70 .75

	No.	Card			
		Team Card			
☐	258	Garry Roggenburk	3.50	1.55	.45
☐	259	Harry Bright	3.50	1.55	.45
☐	260	Frank Robinson	32.00	14.50	4.00
☐	261	Jim Hannan	3.50	1.55	.45
☐	262	Cards Rookies	8.00	3.60	1.00
		Mike Shannon			
		Harry Fanok			
☐	263	Chuck Estrada	3.50	1.55	.45
☐	264	Jim Landis	3.50	1.55	.45
☐	265	Jim Bunning	7.50	3.40	.95
☐	266	Gene Freese	3.50	1.55	.45
☐	267	Wilbur Wood	8.00	3.60	1.00
☐	268	Bill's Got It	4.00	1.80	.50
		Danny Murtaugh MG			
		Bill Virdon			
☐	269	Ellis Burton	3.50	1.55	.45
☐	270	Rich Rollins	4.00	1.80	.50
☐	271	Bob Sadowski	3.50	1.55	.45
☐	272	Jake Wood	3.50	1.55	.45
☐	273	Mel Nelson	3.50	1.55	.45
☐	274	Checklist 4	10.00	1.50	.50
☐	275	John Tsitouris	3.50	1.55	.45
☐	276	Jose Tartabull	4.00	1.80	.50
☐	277	Ken Retzer	3.50	1.55	.45
☐	278	Bobby Shantz	4.00	1.80	.50
☐	279	Joe Koppe UER	4.00	1.80	.50
		(Glove on wrong hand)			
☐	280	Juan Marichal	15.00	6.75	1.90
☐	281	Yankees Rookies	4.00	1.80	.50
		Jake Gibbs			
		Tom Metcalf			
☐	282	Bob Bruce	3.50	1.55	.45
☐	283	Tom McCraw	3.50	1.55	.45
☐	284	Dick Schofield	3.50	1.55	.45
☐	285	Robin Roberts	14.00	6.25	1.75
☐	286	Don Landrum	3.50	1.55	.45
☐	287	Red Sox Rookies	45.00	20.00	5.75
		Tony Conigliaro			
		Bill Spanswick			
☐	288	Al Moran	3.50	1.55	.45
☐	289	Frank Funk	3.50	1.55	.45
☐	290	Bob Allison	4.00	1.80	.50
☐	291	Phil Ortega	3.50	1.55	.45
☐	292	Mike Roarke	3.50	1.55	.45
☐	293	Phillies Team	6.00	2.70	.75
☐	294	Ken L. Hunt	3.50	1.55	.45
☐	295	Roger Craig	4.00	1.80	.50
☐	296	Ed Kirkpatrick	3.50	1.55	.45
☐	297	Ken MacKenzie	3.50	1.55	.45
☐	298	Harry Craft MG	3.50	1.55	.45
☐	299	Bill Stafford	3.50	1.55	.45
☐	300	Hank Aaron	100.00	45.00	12.50
☐	301	Larry Brown	3.50	1.55	.45
☐	302	Dan Pfister	3.50	1.55	.45
☐	303	Jim Campbell	3.50	1.55	.45
☐	304	Bob Johnson	3.50	1.55	.45
☐	305	Jack Lamabe	3.50	1.55	.45
☐	306	Giant Gunners	32.00	14.50	4.00
		Willie Mays			
		Orlando Cepeda			
☐	307	Joe Gibbon	3.50	1.55	.45
☐	308	Gene Stephens	3.50	1.55	.45
☐	309	Paul Toth	3.50	1.55	.45
☐	310	Jim Gilliam	3.50	1.55	.45
☐	311	Tom Brown	4.00	1.80	.50
☐	312	Tigers Rookies	3.50	1.55	.45
		Fritz Fisher			
		Fred Gladding			
☐	313	Chuck Hiller	3.50	1.55	.45
☐	314	Jerry Buchek	3.50	1.55	.45
☐	315	Bo Belinsky	4.00	1.80	.50
☐	316	Gene Oliver	3.50	1.55	.45
☐	317	Al Smith	3.50	1.55	.45
☐	318	Minnesota Twins	6.00	2.70	.75
		Team Card			
☐	319	Paul Brown	3.50	1.55	.45
☐	320	Rocky Colavito	12.00	5.50	1.50
☐	321	Bob Lillis	3.50	1.55	.45
☐	322	George Brunet	3.50	1.55	.45
☐	323	John Buzhardt	3.50	1.55	.45
☐	324	Casey Stengel MG	16.00	7.25	2.00
☐	325	Hector Lopez	4.00	1.80	.50
☐	326	Ron Brand	3.50	1.55	.45
☐	327	Don Blasingame	3.50	1.55	.45
☐	328	Bob Shaw	3.50	1.55	.45
☐	329	Russ Nixon	3.50	1.55	.45
☐	330	Tommy Harper	4.00	1.80	.50
☐	331	AL Bombers	125.00	57.50	15.50
		Roger Maris			
		Norm Cash			
		Mickey Mantle			
		Al Kaline			
☐	332	Ray Washburn	3.50	1.55	.45
☐	333	Billy Moran	3.50	1.55	.45
☐	334	Lew Krausse	3.50	1.55	.45
☐	335	Don Mossi	4.00	1.80	.50
☐	336	Andre Rodgers	3.50	1.55	.45
☐	337	Dodgers Rookies	8.00	3.60	1.00
		Al Ferrara			
		Jeff Torborg			
☐	338	Jack Kralick	3.50	1.55	.45
☐	339	Walt Bond	3.50	1.55	.45
☐	340	Joe Cunningham	3.50	1.55	.45
☐	341	Jim Roland	3.50	1.55	.45
☐	342	Willie Stargell	30.00	13.50	3.80
☐	343	Senators Team	6.00	2.70	.75
☐	344	Phil Linz	4.00	1.80	.50
☐	345	Frank Thomas	4.00	1.80	.50
☐	346	Joey Jay	3.50	1.55	.45
☐	347	Bobby Wine	4.00	1.80	.50
☐	348	Ed Lopat MG	4.00	1.80	.50
☐	349	Art Fowler	3.50	1.55	.45
☐	350	Willie McCovey	20.00	9.00	2.50
☐	351	Dan Schneider	3.50	1.55	.45
☐	352	Eddie Bressoud	3.50	1.55	.45
☐	353	Wally Moon	4.00	1.80	.50
☐	354	Dave Giusti	3.50	1.55	.45
☐	355	Vic Power	4.00	1.80	.50
☐	356	Reds Rookies	4.00	1.80	.50
		Bill McCool			
		Chico Ruiz			
☐	357	Charley James	3.50	1.55	.45
☐	358	Ron Kline	3.50	1.55	.45
☐	359	Jim Schaffer	3.50	1.55	.45
☐	360	Joe Pepitone	7.00	3.10	.85
☐	361	Jay Hook	3.50	1.55	.45
☐	362	Checklist 5	10.00	1.50	.50
☐	363	Dick McAuliffe	4.00	1.80	.50
☐	364	Joe Gaines	3.50	1.55	.45
☐	365	Cal McLish	4.00	1.80	.50
☐	366	Nelson Mathews	3.50	1.55	.45
☐	367	Fred Whitfield	3.50	1.55	.45
☐	368	White Sox Rookies	7.00	3.10	.85
		Fritz Ackley			
		Don Buford			
☐	369	Jerry Zimmerman	3.50	1.55	.45
☐	370	Hal Woodeshick	3.50	1.55	.45
☐	371	Frank Howard	9.50	4.30	1.20
☐	372	Howie Koplitz	7.50	3.40	.95
☐	373	Pirates Team	12.00	5.50	1.50
☐	374	Bobby Bolin	7.50	3.40	.95
☐	375	Ron Santo	9.00	4.00	1.15
☐	376	Dave Morehead	7.50	3.40	.95
☐	377	Bob Skinner	8.00	3.60	1.00
☐	378	Braves Rookies	8.00	3.60	1.00

	No.	Card			
		Woody Woodward			
		Jack Smith			
☐	379	Tony Gonzalez	8.00	3.60	1.00
☐	380	Whitey Ford	30.00	13.50	3.80
☐	381	Bob Taylor	7.50	3.40	.95
☐	382	Wes Stock	7.50	3.40	.95
☐	383	Bill Rigney MG	7.50	3.40	.95
☐	384	Ron Hansen	7.50	3.40	.95
☐	385	Curt Simmons	8.00	3.60	1.00
☐	386	Lenny Green	7.50	3.40	.95
☐	387	Terry Fox	7.50	3.40	.95
☐	388	A's Rookies	8.00	3.60	1.00
		John O'Donoghue			
		George Williams			
☐	389	Jim Umbricht	8.00	3.60	1.00
		(Card back mentions his death)			
☐	390	Orlando Cepeda	9.00	4.00	1.15
☐	391	Sam McDowell	8.00	3.60	1.00
☐	392	Jim Pagliaroni	7.50	3.40	.95
☐	393	Casey Teaches	8.00	3.60	1.00
		Casey Stengel MG			
		Ed Kranepool			
☐	394	Bob Miller	7.50	3.40	.95
☐	395	Tom Tresh	8.00	3.60	1.00
☐	396	Dennis Bennett	7.50	3.40	.95
☐	397	Chuck Cottier	7.50	3.40	.95
☐	398	Mets Rookies	7.50	3.40	.95
		Bill Haas			
		Dick Smith			
☐	399	Jackie Brandt	7.50	3.40	.95
☐	400	Warren Spahn	40.00	18.00	5.00
☐	401	Charlie Maxwell	8.00	3.60	1.00
☐	402	Tom Sturdivant	7.50	3.40	.95
☐	403	Reds Team	12.00	5.50	1.50
☐	404	Tony Martinez	7.50	3.40	.95
☐	405	Ken McBride	7.50	3.40	.95
☐	406	Al Spangler	7.50	3.40	.95
☐	407	Bill Freehan	9.00	4.00	1.15
☐	408	Cubs Rookies	7.50	3.40	.95
		Jim Stewart			
		Fred Burdette			
☐	409	Bill Fischer	7.50	3.40	.95
☐	410	Dick Stuart	8.00	3.60	1.00
☐	411	Lee Walls	7.50	3.40	.95
☐	412	Ray Culp	8.00	3.60	1.00
☐	413	Johnny Keane MG	7.50	3.40	.95
☐	414	Jack Sanford	7.50	3.40	.95
☐	415	Tony Kubek	8.00	3.60	1.00
☐	416	Lee Maye	7.50	3.40	.95
☐	417	Don Cardwell	7.50	3.40	.95
☐	418	Orioles Rookies	8.00	3.60	1.00
		Darold Knowles			
		Les Narum			
☐	419	Ken Harrelson	14.00	6.25	1.75
☐	420	Jim Maloney	8.00	3.60	1.00
☐	421	Camilo Carreon	7.50	3.40	.95
☐	422	Jack Fisher	7.50	3.40	.95
☐	423	Tops in NL	125.00	57.50	15.50
		Hank Aaron			
		Willie Mays			
☐	424	Dick Bertell	7.50	3.40	.95
☐	425	Norm Cash	8.00	3.60	1.00
☐	426	Bob Rodgers	8.00	3.60	1.00
☐	427	Don Rudolph	7.50	3.40	.95
☐	428	Red Sox Rookies	7.50	3.40	.95
		Archie Skeen			
		Pete Smith			
		(Back states Archie has retired)			
☐	429	Tim McCarver	10.00	4.50	1.25
☐	430	Juan Pizarro	7.50	3.40	.95
☐	431	George Alusik	7.50	3.40	.95
☐	432	Ruben Amaro	8.00	3.60	1.00
☐	433	Yankees Team	20.00	9.00	2.50
☐	434	Don Nottebart	7.50	3.40	.95
☐	435	Vic Davalillo	7.50	3.40	.95
☐	436	Charlie Neal	8.00	3.60	1.00
☐	437	Ed Bailey	7.50	3.40	.95
☐	438	Checklist 6	16.00	3.20	.80
☐	439	Harvey Haddix	8.00	3.60	1.00
☐	440	Bob Clemente UER.	200.00	90.00	25.00
		(1960 Pittsburfh)			
☐	441	Bob Duliba	7.50	3.40	.95
☐	442	Pumpsie Green	8.00	3.60	1.00
☐	443	Chuck Dressen MG	8.00	3.60	1.00
☐	444	Larry Jackson	7.50	3.40	.95
☐	445	Bill Skowron	8.00	3.60	1.00
☐	446	Julian Javier	8.00	3.60	1.00
☐	447	Ted Bowsfield	7.50	3.40	.95
☐	448	Cookie Rojas	8.00	3.60	1.00
☐	449	Deron Johnson	8.00	3.60	1.00
☐	450	Steve Barber	7.50	3.40	.95
☐	451	Joe Amalfitano	7.50	3.40	.95
☐	452	Giants Rookies	9.00	4.00	1.15
		Gil Garrido			
		Jim Ray Hart			
☐	453	Frank Baumann	7.50	3.40	.95
☐	454	Tommie Aaron	8.00	3.60	1.00
☐	455	Bernie Allen	7.50	3.40	.95
☐	456	Dodgers Rookies	9.00	4.00	1.15
		Wes Parker			
		John Werhas			
☐	457	Jesse Gonder	7.50	3.40	.95
☐	458	Ralph Terry	8.00	3.60	1.00
☐	459	Red Sox Rookies	7.50	3.40	.95
		Pete Charton			
		Dalton Jones			
☐	460	Bob Gibson	40.00	18.00	5.00
☐	461	George Thomas	7.50	3.40	.95
☐	462	Birdie Tebbetts MG	8.00	3.60	1.00
☐	463	Don Leppert	7.50	3.40	.95
☐	464	Dallas Green	8.00	3.60	1.00
☐	465	Mike Hershberger	7.50	3.40	.95
☐	466	A's Rookies	8.00	3.60	1.00
		Dick Green			
		Aurelio Monteagudo			
☐	467	Bob Aspromonte	7.50	3.40	.95
☐	468	Gaylord Perry	35.00	16.00	4.40
☐	469	Cubs Rookies	8.00	3.60	1.00
		Fred Norman			
		Sterling Slaughter			
☐	470	Jim Bouton	9.00	4.00	1.15
☐	471	Gates Brown	10.00	4.50	1.25
☐	472	Vern Law	8.00	3.60	1.00
☐	473	Baltimore Orioles	12.00	5.50	1.50
		Team Card			
☐	474	Larry Sherry	8.00	3.60	1.00
☐	475	Ed Charles	7.50	3.40	.95
☐	476	Braves Rookies	12.00	5.50	1.50
		Rico Carty			
		Dick Kelley			
☐	477	Mike Joyce	7.50	3.40	.95
☐	478	Dick Howser	8.00	3.60	1.00
☐	479	Cardinals Rookies	7.50	3.40	.95
		Dave Bakenhaster			
		Johnny Lewis			
☐	480	Bob Purkey	7.50	3.40	.95
☐	481	Chuck Schilling	7.50	3.40	.95
☐	482	Phillies Rookies	8.00	3.60	1.00
		John Briggs			
		Danny Cater			
☐	483	Fred Valentine	7.50	3.40	.95
☐	484	Bill Pleis	7.50	3.40	.95
☐	485	Tom Haller	8.00	3.60	1.00
☐	486	Bob Kennedy MG	8.00	3.60	1.00

☐ 487 Mike McCormick........ 8.00 3.60 1.00
☐ 488 Yankees Rookies........ 8.00 3.60 1.00
Pete Mikkelsen
Bob Meyer
☐ 489 Julio Navarro .... 7.50 3.40 .95
☐ 490 Ron Fairly 8.00 3.60 1.00
☐ 491 Ed Rakow.................. 7.50 3.40 .95
☐ 492 Colts Rookies............ 7.50 3.40 .95
Jim Beauchamp
Mike White
☐ 493 Don Lee .... 7.50 3.40 .95
☐ 494 Al Jackson .... 7.50 3.40 .95
☐ 495 Bill Virdon 8.00 3.60 1.00
☐ 496 White Sox Team....... 12.00 5.50 1.50
☐ 497 Jeoff Long................ 7.50 3.40 .95
☐ 498 Dave Stenhouse......... 7.50 3.40 .95
☐ 499 Indians Rookies......... 8.00 3.60 1.00
Chico Salmon
Gordon Seyfried
☐ 500 Camilo Pascual 8.00 3.60 1.00
☐ 501 Bob Veale.................. 8.00 3.60 1.00
☐ 502 Angels Rookies.......... 7.50 3.40 .95
Bobby Knoop
Bob Lee
☐ 503 Earl Wilson 8.00 3.60 1.00
☐ 504 Claude Raymond........ 8.00 3.60 1.00
☐ 505 Stan Williams............ 8.00 3.60 1.00
☐ 506 Bobby Bragan MG...... 7.50 3.40 .95
☐ 507 Johnny Edwards .... 7.50 3.40 .95
☐ 508 Diego Segui .... 7.50 3.40 .95
☐ 509 Pirates Rookies........ 10.00 4.50 1.25
Gene Alley
Orlando McFarlane
☐ 510 Lindy McDaniel.......... 8.00 3.60 1.00
☐ 511 Lou Jackson 8.00 3.60 1.00
☐ 512 Tigers Rookies......... 15.00 6.75 1.90
Willie Horton
Joe Sparma
☐ 513 Don Larsen .... 7.50 3.40 .95
☐ 514 Jim Hickman.............. 8.00 3.60 1.00
☐ 515 Johnny Romano .... 7.50 3.40 .95
☐ 516 Twins Rookies .... 7.50 3.40 .95
Jerry Arrigo
Dwight Siebler
☐ 517A Checklist 7 ERR..... 25.00 3.80 1.25
(Incorrect numbering
sequence on back)
☐ 517B Checklist 7 COR..... 16.00 3.20 .80
(Correct numbering
on back)
☐ 518 Carl Bouldin.............. 7.50 3.40 .95
☐ 519 Charlie Smith............. 7.50 3.40 .95
☐ 520 Jack Baldschun.......... 8.00 3.60 1.00
☐ 521 Tom Satriano .... 7.50 3.40 .95
☐ 522 Bob Tiefenauer........... 7.50 3.40 .95
☐ 523 Lou Burdette UER 12.00 5.50 1.50
(Pitching lefty)
☐ 524 Reds Rookies........... 12.00 5.50 1.50
Jim Dickson
Bobby Klaus
☐ 525 Al McBean............... 12.00 5.50 1.50
☐ 526 Lou Clinton 12.00 5.50 1.50
☐ 527 Larry Bearnarth........ 12.00 5.50 1.50
☐ 528 A's Rookies............. 14.00 6.25 1.75
Dave Duncan
Tommie Reynolds
☐ 529 Alvin Dark MG.......... 14.00 6.25 1.75
☐ 530 Leon Wagner 12.00 5.50 1.50
☐ 531 Los Angeles Dodgers 26.00 11.50 3.30
Team Card
☐ 532 Twins Rookies 14.00 6.25 1.75
Bud Bloomfield
(Bloomfield photo
actually Jay Ward)
Joe Nossek
☐ 533 Johnny Klippstein 12.00 5.50 1.50
☐ 534 Gus Bell 14.00 6.25 1.75
☐ 535 Phil Regan 14.00 6.25 1.75
☐ 536 Mets Rookies........... 12.00 5.50 1.50
Larry Elliot
John Stephenson
☐ 537 Dan Osinski............. 12.00 5.50 1.50
☐ 538 Minnie Minoso......... 14.00 6.25 1.75
☐ 539 Roy Face.................. 14.00 6.25 1.75
☐ 540 Luis Aparicio............ 20.00 9.00 2.50
☐ 541 Braves Rookies...... 100.00 45.00 12.50
Phil Roof
Phil Niekro
☐ 542 Don Mincher............ 12.00 5.50 1.50
☐ 543 Bob Uecker 35.00 16.00 4.40
☐ 544 Colts Rookies........... 14.00 6.25 1.75
Steve Hertz
Joe Hoerner
☐ 545 Max Alvis 12.00 5.50 1.50
☐ 546 Joe Christopher 12.00 5.50 1.50
☐ 547 Gil Hodges MG......... 16.00 7.25 2.00
☐ 548 NL Rookies 12.00 5.50 1.50
Wayne Schurr
Paul Speckenbach
☐ 549 Joe Moeller 12.00 5.50 1.50
☐ 550 Ken Hubbs MEM...... 30.00 13.50 3.80
☐ 551 Billy Hoeft 12.00 5.50 1.50
☐ 552 Indians Rookies 14.00 6.25 1.75
Tom Kelley
Sonny Siebert
☐ 553 Jim Brewer 12.00 5.50 1.50
☐ 554 Hank Foiles 12.00 5.50 1.50
☐ 555 Lee Stange.............. 12.00 5.50 1.50
☐ 556 Mets Rookies........... 12.00 5.50 1.50
Steve Dillon
Ron Locke
☐ 557 Leo Burke 12.00 5.50 1.50
☐ 558 Don Schwall............ 12.00 5.50 1.50
☐ 559 Dick Phillips 12.00 5.50 1.50
☐ 560 Dick Farrell.............. 12.00 5.50 1.50
☐ 561 Phillies Rookies UER 20.00 9.00 2.50
Dave Bennett
(19 ... is 18)
Rick Wise
☐ 562 Pedro Ramos........... 12.00 5.50 1.50
☐ 563 Dal Maxvill 14.00 6.25 1.75
☐ 564 AL Rookies 12.00 5.50 1.50
Joe McCabe
Jerry McNertney
☐ 565 Stu Miller 14.00 6.25 1.75
☐ 566 Ed Kranepool 14.00 6.25 1.75
☐ 567 Jim Kaat.................. 18,00 8.00 2.30
☐ 568 NL Rookies 12.00 5.50 1.50
Phil Gagliano
Cap Peterson
☐ 569 Fred Newman........... 12.00 5.50 1.50
☐ 570 Bill Mazeroski 15.00 6.75 1.90
☐ 571 Gene Conley............ 14.00 6.25 1.75
☐ 572 AL Rookies 12.00 5.50 1.50
Dave Gray
Dick Egan
☐ 573 Jim Duffalo 12.00 5.50 1.50
☐ 574 Manny Jimenez........ 12.00 5.50 1.50
☐ 575 Tony Cloninger 12.00 5.50 1.50
☐ 576 Mets Rookies........... 12.00 5.50 1.50
Jerry Hinsley
Bill Wakefield
☐ 577 Gordy Coleman 14.00 6.25 1.75
☐ 578 Glen Hobbie 12.00 5.50 1.50
☐ 579 Red Sox Team 24.00 11.00 3.00
☐ 580 Johnny Podres......... 14.00 6.25 1.75

☐ 581	Yankees Rookies	12.00	5.50	1.50
	Pedro Gonzalez			
	Archie Moore			
☐ 582	Rod Kanehl	12.00	5.50	1.50
☐ 583	Tito Francona	12.00	5.50	1.50
☐ 584	Joel Horlen	14.00	6.25	1.75
☐ 585	Tony Taylor	14.00	6.25	1.75
☐ 586	Jim Piersall	15.00	6.75	1.90
☐ 587	Bennie Daniels	14.00	5.50	1.75

1965 Topps

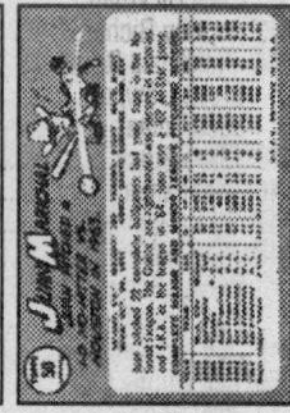

The cards in this 598-card set measure 2 1/2" by 3 1/2". The cards comprising the 1965 Topps set have team names located within a distinctive pennant design below the picture. The cards have blue borders on the reverse and were issued by series. Cards 523 to 598 are more difficult to obtain than all other series. Within this last series there are 44 cards that were printed in lesser quantities than the other cards in that series; these shorter-printed cards are marked by SP in the checklist below. In addition, the sixth series (447-522) is more difficult to obtain than series one through five. Featured subsets within this set include League Leaders (1-12) and World Series cards (132-139). Key cards in this set include Steve Carlton's Rookie Card, Mickey Mantle, and Pete Rose. Other key Rookie Cards in this set are Jim Hunter, Joe Morgan, and Tony Perez.

	NRMT	VG-E	GOOD
COMPLETE SET (598)	3400.00	1500.00	425.00
COMMON CARD (1-109)	2.00	.90	.25
COMMON CARD (110-196)	2.00	.90	.25
COMMON CARD (197-283)	2.50	1.15	.30
COMMON CARD (284-370)	3.50	1.55	.45
COMMON CARD (371-446)	6.50	2.90	.80
COMMON CARD (447-522)	7.00	3.10	.85
COMMON CARD (523-598)	6.50	2.90	.80

☐ 1	AL Batting Leaders	18.00	5.50	1.80
	Tony Oliva			
	Elston Howard			
	Brooks Robinson			
☐ 2	NL Batting Leaders	16.00	7.25	2.00
	Bob Clemente			
	Hank Aaron			
	Rico Carty			
☐ 3	AL Home Run Leaders	30.00	13.50	3.80
	Harmon Killebrew			
	Mickey Mantle			
	Boog Powell			
☐ 4	NL Home Run Leaders	12.00	5.50	1.50
	Willie Mays			
	Billy Williams			
	Jim Ray Hart			
	Orlando Cepeda			
	Johnny Callison			
☐ 5	AL RBI Leaders	30.00	13.50	3.80
	Brooks Robinson			
	Harmon Killebrew			
	Mickey Mantle			
	Dick Stuart			
☐ 6	NL RBI Leaders	7.00	3.10	.85
	Ken Boyer			
	Willie Mays			
	Ron Santo			
☐ 7	AL ERA Leaders	4.00	1.80	.50
	Dean Chance			
	Joel Horlen			
☐ 8	NL ERA Leaders	20.00	9.00	2.50
	Sandy Koufax			
	Don Drysdale			
☐ 9	AL Pitching Leaders	4.00	1.80	.50
	Dean Chance			
	Gary Peters			
	Dave Wickersham			
	Juan Pizarro			
	Wally Bunker			
☐ 10	NL Pitching Leaders	4.00	1.80	.50
	Larry Jackson			
	Ray Sadecki			
	Juan Marichal			
☐ 11	AL Strikeout Leaders	4.00	1.80	.50
	Al Downing			
	Dean Chance			
	Camilo Pascual			
☐ 12	NL Strikeout Leaders	7.00	3.10	.85
	Bob Veale			
	Don Drysdale			
	Bob Gibson			
☐ 13	Pedro Ramos	2.00	.90	.25
☐ 14	Len Gabrielson	2.00	.90	.25
☐ 15	Robin Roberts	12.00	5.50	1.50
☐ 16	Houston Rookies	80.00	36.00	10.00
	Joe Morgan			
	Sonny Jackson			
☐ 17	Johnny Romano	2.00	.90	.25
☐ 18	Bill McCool	2.00	.90	.25
☐ 19	Gates Brown	2.50	1.15	.30
☐ 20	Jim Bunning	5.00	2.30	.60
☐ 21	Don Blasingame	2.00	.90	.25
☐ 22	Charlie Smith	2.00	.90	.25
☐ 23	Bob Tiefenauer	2.00	.90	.25
☐ 24	Minnesota Twins Team Card	4.00	1.80	.50
☐ 25	Al McBean	2.00	.90	.25
☐ 26	Bobby Knoop	2.00	.90	.25
☐ 27	Dick Bertell	2.00	.90	.25
☐ 28	Barney Schultz	2.00	.90	.25
☐ 29	Felix Mantilla	2.00	.90	.25
☐ 30	Jim Bouton	4.50	2.00	.55
☐ 31	Mike White	2.00	.90	.25
☐ 32	Herman Franks MG	2.00	.90	.25
☐ 33	Jackie Brandt	2.00	.90	.25
☐ 34	Cal Koonce	2.00	.90	.25
☐ 35	Ed Charles	2.00	.90	.25
☐ 36	Bobby Wine	2.00	.90	.25
☐ 37	Fred Gladding	2.00	.90	.25
☐ 38	Jim King	2.00	.90	.25
☐ 39	Gerry Arrigo	2.00	.90	.25
☐ 40	Frank Howard	3.00	1.35	.40
☐ 41	White Sox Rookies	2.00	.90	.25
	Bruce Howard			

	No.	Card			
		Marv Staehle			
☐	42	Earl Wilson	2.50	1.15	.30
☐	43	Mike Shannon	2.50	1.15	.30
		(Name in red, other Cardinals in yellow)			
☐	44	Wade Blasingame	2.00	.90	.25
☐	45	Roy McMillan	2.50	1.15	.30
☐	46	Bob Lee	2.00	.90	.25
☐	47	Tommy Harper	2.50	1.15	.30
☐	48	Claude Raymond	2.50	1.15	.30
☐	49	Orioles Rookies	3.50	1.55	.45
		Curt Blefary			
		John Miller			
☐	50	Juan Marichal	12.00	5.50	1.50
☐	51	Bill Bryan	2.00	.90	.25
☐	52	Ed Roebuck	2.00	.90	.25
☐	53	Dick McAuliffe	2.50	1.15	.30
☐	54	Joe Gibbon	2.00	.90	.25
☐	55	Tony Conigliaro	15.00	6.75	1.90
☐	56	Ron Kline	2.00	.90	.25
☐	57	Cardinals Team	4.00	1.80	.50
☐	58	Fred Talbot	2.00	.90	.25
☐	59	Nate Oliver	2.00	.90	.25
☐	60	Jim O'Toole	2.50	1.15	.30
☐	61	Chris Cannizzaro	2.00	.90	.25
☐	62	Jim Kaat UER	5.00	2.30	.60
		(Misspelled Katt)			
☐	63	Ty Cline	2.00	.90	.25
☐	64	Lou Burdette	2.50	1.15	.30
☐	65	Tony Kubek	5.00	2.30	.60
☐	66	Bill Rigney MG	2.00	.90	.25
☐	67	Harvey Haddix	2.50	1.15	.30
☐	68	Del Crandall	2.50	1.15	.30
☐	69	Bill Virdon	2.50	1.15	.30
☐	70	Bill Skowron	2.50	1.15	.30
☐	71	John O'Donoghue	2.00	.90	.25
☐	72	Tony Gonzalez	2.00	.90	.25
☐	73	Dennis Ribant	2.00	.90	.25
☐	74	Red Sox Rookies	12.00	5.50	1.50
		Rico Petrocelli			
		Jerry Stephenson			
☐	75	Deron Johnson	2.50	1.15	.30
☐	76	Sam McDowell	2.50	1.15	.30
☐	77	Doug Camilli	2.00	.90	.25
☐	78	Dal Maxvill	2.00	.90	.25
☐	79A	Checklist 1	10.00	1.50	.50
		(61 Cannizzaro)			
☐	79B	Checklist 1	10.00	1.50	.50
		(61 C.Cannizzaro)			
☐	80	Turk Farrell	2.00	.90	.25
☐	81	Don Buford	2.50	1.15	.30
☐	82	Braves Rookies	6.50	2.90	.80
		Santos Alomar			
		John Braun			
☐	83	George Thomas	2.00	.90	.25
☐	84	Ron Herbel	2.00	.90	.25
☐	85	Willie Smith	2.00	.90	.25
☐	86	Les Narum	2.00	.90	.25
☐	87	Nelson Mathews	2.00	.90	.25
☐	88	Jack Lamabe	2.00	.90	.25
☐	89	Mike Hershberger	2.00	.90	.25
☐	90	Rich Rollins	2.50	1.15	.30
☐	91	Cubs Team	4.00	1.80	.50
☐	92	Dick Howser	2.50	1.15	.30
☐	93	Jack Fisher	2.00	.90	.25
☐	94	Charlie Lau	2.50	1.15	.30
☐	95	Bill Mazeroski	4.50	2.00	.55
☐	96	Sonny Siebert	2.50	1.15	.30
☐	97	Pedro Gonzalez	2.00	.90	.25
☐	98	Bob Miller	2.00	.90	.25
☐	99	Gil Hodges MG	7.00	3.10	.85
☐	100	Ken Boyer	4.50	2.00	.55
☐	101	Fred Newman	2.00	.90	.25
☐	102	Steve Boros	2.00	.90	.25
☐	103	Harvey Kuenn	2.50	1.15	.30
☐	104	Checklist 2	10.00	1.50	.50
☐	105	Chico Salmon	2.00	.90	.25
☐	106	Gene Oliver	2.00	.90	.25
☐	107	Phillies Rookies	3.50	1.55	.45
		Pat Corrales			
		Costen Shockley			
☐	108	Don Mincher	2.00	.90	.25
☐	109	Walt Bond	2.00	.90	.25
☐	110	Ron Santo	4.50	2.00	.55
☐	111	Lee Thomas	2.50	1.15	.30
☐	112	Derrell Griffith	2.00	.90	.25
☐	113	Steve Barber	2.00	.90	.25
☐	114	Jim Hickman	2.50	1.15	.30
☐	115	Bobby Richardson	5.00	2.30	.60
☐	116	Cardinals Rookies	4.00	1.80	.50
		Dave Dowling			
		Bob Tolan			
☐	117	Wes Stock	2.00	.90	.25
☐	118	Hal Lanier	2.50	1.15	.30
☐	119	John Kennedy	2.00	.90	.25
☐	120	Frank Robinson	27.00	12.00	3.40
☐	121	Gene Alley	2.50	1.15	.30
☐	122	Bill Pleis	2.00	.90	.25
☐	123	Frank Thomas	2.50	1.15	.30
☐	124	Tom Satriano	2.00	.90	.25
☐	125	Juan Pizarro	2.00	.90	.25
☐	126	Dodgers Team	5.00	2.30	.60
☐	127	Frank Lary	2.00	.90	.25
☐	128	Vic Davalillo	2.00	.90	.25
☐	129	Bennie Daniels	2.00	.90	.25
☐	130	Al Kaline	30.00	13.50	3.80
☐	131	Johnny Keane MG	2.00	.90	.25
☐	132	World Series Game 1.	4.00	1.80	.50
		Cards take opener (Mike Shannon)			
☐	133	World Series Game 2.	4.00	1.80	.50
		Mel Stottlemyre wins			
☐	134	World Series Game 3	50.00	23.00	6.25
		Mickey Mantle's homer			
☐	135	World Series Game 4.	4.00	1.80	.50
		Ken Boyer's grand-slam			
☐	136	World Series Game 5.	4.00	1.80	.50
		10th inning triumph (Tim McCarver being greeted at home)			
☐	137	World Series Game 6.	4.00	1.80	.50
		Jim Bouton wins again			
☐	138	World Series Game 7	11.00	4.90	1.40
		Bob Gibson wins finale			
☐	139	World Series Summary	4.00	1.80	.50
		Cards celebrate			
☐	140	Dean Chance	2.50	1.15	.30
☐	141	Charlie James	2.00	.90	.25
☐	142	Bill Monbouquette	2.00	.90	.25
☐	143	Pirates Rookies	2.00	.90	.25
		John Gelnar			
		Jerry May			
☐	144	Ed Kranepool	2.50	1.15	.30
☐	145	Luis Tiant	25.00	11.50	3.10
☐	146	Ron Hansen	2.00	.90	.25
☐	147	Dennis Bennett	2.00	.90	.25
☐	148	Willie Kirkland	2.00	.90	.25
☐	149	Wayne Schurr	2.00	.90	.25
☐	150	Brooks Robinson	27.00	12.00	3.40
☐	151	Athletics Team	4.00	1.80	.50
☐	152	Phil Ortega	2.00	.90	.25
☐	153	Norm Cash	6.00	2.70	.75
☐	154	Bob Humphreys	2.00	.90	.25
☐	155	Roger Maris	45.00	20.00	5.75
☐	156	Bob Sadowski	2.00	.90	.25
☐	157	Zoilo Versalles	4.00	1.80	.50

☐ 158 Dick Sisler .... 2.00 .90 .25
☐ 159 Jim Duffalo .... 2.00 .90 .25
☐ 160 Bob Clemente UER... 80.00 36.00 10.00
(1960 Pittsburfh)
☐ 161 Frank Baumann .... 2.00 .90 .25
☐ 162 Russ Nixon .... 2.00 .90 .25
☐ 163 Johnny Briggs .... 2.00 .90 .25
☐ 164 Al Spangler .... 2.00 .90 .25
☐ 165 Dick Ellsworth .... 2.00 .90 .25
☐ 166 Indians Rookies .... 5.50 2.50 .70
George Culver
Tommie Agee
☐ 167 Bill Wakefield .... 2.00 .90 .25
☐ 168 Dick Green .... 2.00 .90 .25
☐ 169 Dave Vineyard .... 2.00 .90 .25
☐ 170 Hank Aaron 80.00 36.00 10.00
☐ 171 Jim Roland .... 2.00 .90 .25
☐ 172 Jim Piersall .... 2.50 1.15 .30
☐ 173 Detroit Tigers .... 4.00 1.80 .50
Team Card
☐ 174 Joey Jay .... 2.00 .90 .25
☐ 175 Bob Aspromonte .... 2.00 .90 .25
☐ 176 Willie McCovey 20.00 9.00 2.50
☐ 177 Pete Mikkelsen .... 2.00 .90 .25
☐ 178 Dalton Jones .... 2.00 .90 .25
☐ 179 Hal Woodeshick .... 2.00 .90 .25
☐ 180 Bob Allison .... 2.50 1.15 .30
☐ 181 Senators Rookies .... 2.00 .90 .25
Don Loun
Joe McCabe
☐ 182 Mike de la Hoz .... 2.00 .90 .25
☐ 183 Dave Nicholson .... 2.00 .90 .25
☐ 184 John Boozer .... 2.00 .90 .25
☐ 185 Max Alvis .... 2.00 .90 .25
☐ 186 Billy Cowan .... 2.00 .90 .25
☐ 187 Casey Stengel MG 15.00 6.75 1.90
☐ 188 Sam Bowens .... 2.00 .90 .25
☐ 189 Checklist 3 .... 10.00 1.50 .50
☐ 190 Bill White .... 4.00 1.80 .50
☐ 191 Phil Regan .... 2.50 1.15 .30
☐ 192 Jim Coker .... 2.00 .90 .25
☐ 193 Gaylord Perry 18.00 8.00 2.30
☐ 194 Rookie Stars .... 2.00 .90 .25
Bill Kelso
Rick Reichardt
☐ 195 Bob Veale .... 2.50 1.15 .30
☐ 196 Ron Fairly .... 2.00 .90 .25
☐ 197 Diego Segui .... 2.50 1.15 .30
☐ 198 Smoky Burgess .... 3.00 1.35 .40
☐ 199 Bob Heffner .... 2.50 1.15 .30
☐ 200 Joe Torre .... 5.00 2.30 .60
☐ 201 Twins Rookies .... 4.00 1.80 .50
Sandy Valdespino
Cesar Tovar
☐ 202 Leo Burke .... 2.50 1.15 .30
☐ 203 Dallas Green .... 2.50 1.15 .30
☐ 204 Russ Snyder .... 2.50 1.15 .30
☐ 205 Warren Spahn 30.00 13.50 3.80
☐ 206 Willie Horton .... 5.50 2.50 .70
☐ 207 Pete Rose 125.00 57.50 15.50
☐ 208 Tommy John 13.00 5.75 1.65
☐ 209 Pirates Team .... 4.50 2.00 .55
☐ 210 Jim Fregosi .... 3.00 1.35 .40
☐ 211 Steve Ridzik .... 2.50 1.15 .30
☐ 212 Ron Brand .... 2.50 1.15 .30
☐ 213 Jim Davenport .... 2.50 1.15 .30
☐ 214 Bob Purkey .... 2.50 1.15 .30
☐ 215 Pete Ward .... 2.50 1.15 .30
☐ 216 Al Worthington .... 2.50 1.15 .30
☐ 217 Walt Alston MG .... 4.00 1.80 .50
☐ 218 Dick Schofield .... 2.50 1.15 .30
☐ 219 Bob Meyer .... 2.50 1.15 .30
☐ 220 Billy Williams 10.00 4.50 1.25

☐ 221 John Tsitouris .... 2.50 1.15 .30
☐ 222 Bob Tillman .... 2.50 1.15 .30
☐ 223 Dan Osinski .... 2.50 1.15 .30
☐ 224 Bob Chance .... 2.50 1.15 .30
☐ 225 Bo Belinsky .... 3.00 1.35 .40
☐ 226 Yankees Rookies .... 2.50 1.15 .30
Elvio Jimenez
Jake Gibbs
☐ 227 Bobby Klaus .... 2.50 1.15 .30
☐ 228 Jack Sanford .... 2.50 1.15 .30
☐ 229 Lou Clinton .... 2.50 1.15 .30
☐ 230 Ray Sadecki .... 2.50 1.15 .30
☐ 231 Jerry Adair .... 2.50 1.15 .30
☐ 232 Steve Blass .... 4.00 1.80 .50
☐ 233 Don Zimmer .... 3.00 1.35 .40
☐ 234 White Sox Team .... 4.50 2.00 .55
☐ 235 Chuck Hinton .... 2.50 1.15 .30
☐ 236 Denny McLain 32.00 14.50 4.00
☐ 237 Bernie Allen .... 2.50 1.15 .30
☐ 238 Joe Moeller .... 2.50 1.15 .30
☐ 239 Doc Edwards .... 2.50 1.15 .30
☐ 240 Bob Bruce .... 2.50 1.15 .30
☐ 241 Mack Jones .... 2.50 1.15 .30
☐ 242 George Brunet .... 2.50 1.15 .30
☐ 243 Reds Rookies .... 5.50 2.50 .70
Ted Davidson
Tommy Helms
☐ 244 Lindy McDaniel .... 3.00 1.35 .40
☐ 245 Joe Pepitone .... 3.00 1.35 .40
☐ 246 Tom Butters .... 2.50 1.15 .30
☐ 247 Wally Moon .... 3.00 1.35 .40
☐ 248 Gus Triandos .... 3.00 1.35 .40
☐ 249 Dave McNally .... 3.50 1.55 .45
☐ 250 Willie Mays 110.00 50.00 14.00
☐ 251 Billy Herman MG .... 3.50 1.55 .45
☐ 252 Pete Richert .... 2.50 1.15 .30
☐ 253 Danny Cater .... 2.50 1.15 .30
☐ 254 Roland Sheldon .... 2.50 1.15 .30
☐ 255 Camilo Pascual .... 3.00 1.35 .40
☐ 256 Tito Francona .... 2.50 1.15 .30
☐ 257 Jim Wynn .... 3.50 1.55 .45
☐ 258 Larry Bearnarth .... 2.50 1.15 .30
☐ 259 Tigers Rookies .... 7.00 3.10 .85
Jim Northrup
Ray Oyler
☐ 260 Don Drysdale 18.00 8.00 2.30
☐ 261 Duke Carmel .... 2.50 1.15 .30
☐ 262 Bud Daley .... 2.50 1.15 .30
☐ 263 Marty Keough .... 2.50 1.15 .30
☐ 264 Bob Buhl .... 3.00 1.35 .40
☐ 265 Jim Pagliaroni .... 2.50 1.15 .30
☐ 266 Bert Campaneris 12.00 5.50 1.50
☐ 267 Senators Team .... 4.50 2.00 .55
☐ 268 Ken McBride .... 2.50 1.15 .30
☐ 269 Frank Bolling .... 2.50 1.15 .30
☐ 270 Milt Pappas .... 3.00 1.35 .40
☐ 271 Don Wert .... 2.50 1.15 .30
☐ 272 Chuck Schilling .... 2.50 1.15 .30
☐ 273 Checklist 4 .... 10.00 1.50 .50
☐ 274 Lum Harris MG .... 2.50 1.15 .30
☐ 275 Dick Groat .... 3.50 1.55 .45
☐ 276 Hoyt Wilhelm 10.00 4.50 1.25
☐ 277 Johnny Lewis .... 2.50 1.15 .30
☐ 278 Ken Retzer .... 2.50 1.15 .30
☐ 279 Dick Tracewski .... 2.50 1.15 .30
☐ 280 Dick Stuart .... 3.00 1.35 .40
☐ 281 Bill Stafford .... 2.50 1.15 .30
☐ 282 Giants Rookies 18.00 8.00 2.30
Dick Estelle
Masanori Murakami
☐ 283 Fred Whitfield .... 2.50 1.15 .30
☐ 284 Nick Willhite .... 3.50 1.55 .45
☐ 285 Ron Hunt .... 3.50 1.55 .45

	No.	Card			
☐	286	Athletics Rookies	3.50	1.55	.45
		Jim Dickson			
		Aurelio Monteagudo			
☐	287	Gary Kolb	3.50	1.55	.45
☐	288	Jack Hamilton	3.50	1.55	.45
☐	289	Gordy Coleman	4.00	1.80	.50
☐	290	Wally Bunker	4.00	1.80	.50
☐	291	Jerry Lynch	3.50	1.55	.45
☐	292	Larry Yellen	3.50	1.55	.45
☐	293	Angels Team	7.00	3.10	.85
☐	294	Tim McCarver	7.00	3.10	.85
☐	295	Dick Radatz	4.00	1.80	.50
☐	296	Tony Taylor	3.50	1.55	.45
☐	297	Dave DeBusschere	5.50	2.50	.70
☐	298	Jim Stewart	3.50	1.55	.45
☐	299	Jerry Zimmerman	3.50	1.55	.45
☐	300	Sandy Koufax	110.00	50.00	14.00
☐	301	Birdie Tebbetts MG	4.00	1.80	.50
☐	302	Al Stanek	3.50	1.55	.45
☐	303	John Orsino	3.50	1.55	.45
☐	304	Dave Stenhouse	3.50	1.55	.45
☐	305	Rico Carty	6.00	2.70	.75
☐	306	Bubba Phillips	3.50	1.55	.45
☐	307	Barry Latman	3.50	1.55	.45
☐	308	Mets Rookies	10.00	4.50	1.25
		Cleon Jones			
		Tom Parsons			
☐	309	Steve Hamilton	3.50	1.55	.45
☐	310	Johnny Callison	4.00	1.80	.50
☐	311	Orlando Pena	3.50	1.55	.45
☐	312	Joe Nuxhall	4.00	1.80	.50
☐	313	Jim Schaffer	3.50	1.55	.45
☐	314	Sterling Slaughter	3.50	1.55	.45
☐	315	Frank Malzone	4.00	1.80	.50
☐	316	Reds Team	7.00	3.10	.85
☐	317	Don McMahon	3.50	1.55	.45
☐	318	Matty Alou	4.00	1.80	.50
☐	319	Ken McMullen	3.50	1.55	.45
☐	320	Bob Gibson	35.00	16.00	4.40
☐	321	Rusty Staub	7.00	3.10	.85
☐	322	Rick Wise	4.00	1.80	.50
☐	323	Hank Bauer MG	4.00	1.80	.50
☐	324	Bobby Locke	3.50	1.55	.45
☐	325	Donn Clendenon	4.00	1.80	.50
☐	326	Dwight Siebler	3.50	1.55	.45
☐	327	Denis Menke	3.50	1.55	.45
☐	328	Eddie Fisher	3.50	1.55	.45
☐	329	Hawk Taylor	3.50	1.55	.45
☐	330	Whitey Ford	30.00	13.50	3.80
☐	331	Dodgers Rookies	4.00	1.80	.50
		Al Ferrara			
		John Purdin			
☐	332	Ted Abernathy	3.50	1.55	.45
☐	333	Tom Reynolds	3.50	1.55	.45
☐	334	Vic Roznovsky	3.50	1.55	.45
☐	335	Mickey Lolich	7.50	3.40	.95
☐	336	Woody Held	3.50	1.55	.45
☐	337	Mike Cuellar	4.00	1.80	.50
☐	338	Philadelphia Phillies	7.00	3.10	.85
		Team Card			
☐	339	Ryne Duren	4.00	1.80	.50
☐	340	Tony Oliva	16.00	7.25	2.00
☐	341	Bob Bolin	3.50	1.55	.45
☐	342	Bob Rodgers	4.00	1.80	.50
☐	343	Mike McCormick	4.00	1.80	.50
☐	344	Wes Parker	4.00	1.80	.50
☐	345	Floyd Robinson	3.50	1.55	.45
☐	346	Bobby Bragan MG	3.50	1.55	.45
☐	347	Roy Face	4.50	2.00	.55
☐	348	George Banks	3.50	1.55	.45
☐	349	Larry Miller	3.50	1.55	.45
☐	350	Mickey Mantle	550.00	250.00	70.00
☐	351	Jim Perry	4.00	1.80	.50

	No.	Card			
☐	352	Alex Johnson	5.00	2.30	.60
☐	353	Jerry Lumpe	3.50	1.55	.45
☐	354	Cubs Rookies	3.50	1.55	.45
		Billy Ott			
		Jack Warner			
☐	355	Vada Pinson	4.50	2.00	.55
☐	356	Bill Spanswick	3.50	1.55	.45
☐	357	Carl Warwick	3.50	1.55	.45
☐	358	Albie Pearson	4.00	1.80	.50
☐	359	Ken Johnson	3.50	1.55	.45
☐	360	Orlando Cepeda	10.00	4.50	1.25
☐	361	Checklist 5	12.00	1.80	.60
☐	362	Don Schwall	3.50	1.55	.45
☐	363	Bob Johnson	3.50	1.55	.45
☐	364	Galen Cisco	3.50	1.55	.45
☐	365	Jim Gentile	4.00	1.80	.50
☐	366	Dan Schneider	3.50	1.55	.45
☐	367	Leon Wagner	3.50	1.55	.45
☐	368	White Sox Rookies	4.00	1.80	.50
		Ken Berry			
		Joel Gibson			
☐	369	Phil Linz	4.00	1.80	.50
☐	370	Tommy Davis	4.00	1.80	.50
☐	371	Frank Kreutzer	6.50	2.90	.80
☐	372	Clay Dalrymple	6.50	2.90	.80
☐	373	Curt Simmons	7.00	3.10	.85
☐	374	Angels Rookies	8.00	3.60	1.00
		Jose Cardenal			
		Dick Simpson			
☐	375	Dave Wickersham	6.50	2.90	.80
☐	376	Jim Landis	6.50	2.90	.80
☐	377	Willie Stargell	30.00	13.50	3.80
☐	378	Chuck Estrada	6.50	2.90	.80
☐	379	Giants Team	10.00	4.50	1.25
☐	380	Rocky Colavito	15.00	6.75	1.90
☐	381	Al Jackson	6.50	2.90	.80
☐	382	J.C. Martin	6.50	2.90	.80
☐	383	Felipe Alou	8.00	3.60	1.00
☐	384	Johnny Klippstein	6.50	2.90	.80
☐	385	Carl Yastrzemski	75.00	34.00	9.50
☐	386	Cubs Rookies	6.50	2.90	.80
		Paul Jaeckel			
		Fred Norman			
☐	387	Johnny Podres	7.00	3.10	.85
☐	388	John Blanchard	6.50	2.90	.80
☐	389	Don Larsen	7.00	3.10	.85
☐	390	Bill Freehan	8.00	3.60	1.00
☐	391	Mel McGaha MG	6.50	2.90	.80
☐	392	Bob Friend	7.00	3.10	.85
☐	393	Ed Kirkpatrick	6.50	2.90	.80
☐	394	Jim Hannan	6.50	2.90	.80
☐	395	Jim Ray Hart	7.00	3.10	.85
☐	396	Frank Bertaina	6.50	2.90	.80
☐	397	Jerry Buchek	6.50	2.90	.80
☐	398	Reds Rookies	7.00	3.10	.85
		Dan Neville			
		Art Shamsky			
☐	399	Ray Herbert	6.50	2.90	.80
☐	400	Harmon Killebrew	35.00	16.00	4.40
☐	401	Carl Willey	6.50	2.90	.80
☐	402	Joe Amalfitano	6.50	2.90	.80
☐	403	Boston Red Sox	10.00	4.50	1.25
		Team Card			
☐	404	Stan Williams	7.00	3.10	.85
		(Listed as Indian			
		but Yankee cap)			
☐	405	John Roseboro	7.00	3.10	.85
☐	406	Ralph Terry	7.00	3.10	.85
☐	407	Lee Maye	6.50	2.90	.80
☐	408	Larry Sherry	7.00	3.10	.85
☐	409	Astros Rookies	8.00	3.60	1.00
		Jim Beauchamp			
		Larry Dierker			

□ 410 Luis Aparicio........... 10.00 4.50 1.25
□ 411 Roger Craig............... 7.00 3.10 .85
□ 412 Bob Bailey.................. 7.00 3.10 .85
□ 413 Hal Reniff..................... 6.50 2.90 .80
□ 414 Al Lopez MG.............. 8.00 3.60 1.00
□ 415 Curt Flood.................. 8.00 3.60 1.00
□ 416 Jim Brewer.................. 6.50 2.90 .80
□ 417 Ed Brinkman.............. 6.50 2.90 .80
□ 418 Johnny Edwards........ 6.50 2.90 .80
□ 419 Ruben Amaro............ 6.50 2.90 .80
□ 420 Larry Jackson........... 6.50 2.90 .80
□ 421 Twins Rookies........... 6.50 2.90 .80
Gary Dotter
Jay Ward
□ 422 Aubrey Gatewood...... 6.50 2.90 .80
□ 423 Jesse Gonder............ 6.50 2.90 .80
□ 424 Gary Bell.................... 6.50 2.90 .80
□ 425 Wayne Causey........... 6.50 2.90 .80
□ 426 Braves Team........... 10.00 4.50 1.25
□ 427 Bob Saverine............ 6.50 2.90 .80
□ 428 Bob Shaw.................. 6.50 2.90 .80
□ 429 Don Demeter............. 6.50 2.90 .80
□ 430 Gary Peters............... 6.50 2.90 .80
□ 431 Cards Rookies........... 8.00 3.60 1.00
Nelson Briles
Wayne Spiezio
□ 432 Jim Grant.................. 7.00 3.10 .85
□ 433 John Bateman........... 6.50 2.90 .80
□ 434 Dave Morehead.......... 6.50 2.90 .80
□ 435 Willie Davis............... 7.00 3.10 .85
□ 436 Don Elston................ 6.50 2.90 .80
□ 437 Chico Cardenas.......... 7.00 3.10 .85
□ 438 Harry Walker MG....... 6.50 2.90 .80
□ 439 Moe Drabowsky......... 7.00 3.10 .85
□ 440 Tom Tresh................ 6.50 2.90 .80
□ 441 Denny Lemaster......... 6.50 2.90 .80
□ 442 Vic Power.................. 7.00 3.10 .85
□ 443 Checklist 6.............. 12.00 3.00 .95
□ 444 Bob Hendley.............. 6.50 2.90 .80
□ 445 Don Lock.................. 6.50 2.90 .80
□ 446 Art Mahaffey............. 6.50 2.90 .80
□ 447 Julian Javier............. 7.50 3.40 .95
□ 448 Lee Stange................ 7.00 3.10 .85
□ 449 Mets Rookies............ 7.00 3.10 .85
Jerry Hinsley
Gary Kroll
□ 450 Elston Howard.......... 8.00 3.60 1.00
□ 451 Jim Owens................ 7.00 3.10 .85
□ 452 Gary Geiger............... 7.00 3.10 .85
□ 453 Dodgers Rookies....... 7.50 3.40 .95
Willie Crawford
John Werhas
□ 454 Ed Rakow.................. 7.00 3.10 .85
□ 455 Norm Siebern........... 7.00 3.10 .85
□ 456 Bill Henry.................. 7.00 3.10 .85
□ 457 Bob Kennedy MG....... 7.50 3.40 .95
□ 458 John Buzhardt........... 7.00 3.10 .85
□ 459 Frank Kostro............. 7.00 3.10 .85
□ 460 Richie Allen............. 40.00 18.00 5.00
□ 461 Braves Rookies........ 48.00 22.00 6.00
Clay Carroll
Phil Niekro
□ 462 Lew Krausse UER...... 7.50 3.40 .95
(Photo actually
Pete Lovrich)
□ 463 Manny Mota.............. 8.00 3.60 1.00
□ 464 Ron Piche.................. 7.00 3.10 .85
□ 465 Tom Haller................ 8.00 3.60 1.00
□ 466 Senators Rookies....... 7.00 3.10 .85
Pete Craig
Dick Nen
□ 467 Ray Washburn........... 7.00 3.10 .85
□ 468 Larry Brown.............. 7.00 3.10 .85

□ 469 Don Nottebart............ 7.00 3.10 .85
□ 470 Yogi Berra P/CO....... 50.00 23.00 6.25
□ 471 Billy Hoeft.................. 7.00 3.10 .85
□ 472 Don Pavletich............ 7.00 3.10 .85
□ 473 Orioles Rookies........ 14.00 6.25 1.75
Paul Blair
Dave Johnson
□ 474 Cookie Rojas............. 8.00 3.60 1.00
□ 475 Clete Boyer............... 8.00 3.60 1.00
□ 476 Billy O'Dell................ 7.00 3.10 .85
□ 477 Cards Rookies........ 350.00 160.00 45.00
Fritz Ackley
Steve Carlton
□ 478 Wilbur Wood............. 8.00 3.60 1.00
□ 479 Ken Harrelson........... 8.00 3.60 1.00
□ 480 Joel Horlen............... 7.00 3.10 .85
□ 481 Cleveland Indians..... 12.00 5.50 1.50
Team Card
□ 482 Bob Priddy................ 7.00 3.10 .85
□ 483 George Smith............ 7.00 3.10 .85
□ 484 Ron Perranoski.......... 8.00 3.60 1.00
□ 485 Nellie Fox P/CO........ 14.00 6.25 1.75
□ 486 Angels Rookies.......... 7.00 3.10 .85
Tom Egan
Pat Rogan
□ 487 Woody Woodward..... 7.50 3.40 .95
□ 488 Ted Wills.................... 7.00 3.10 .85
□ 489 Gene Mauch MG........ 7.50 3.40 .95
□ 490 Earl Battey................. 7.00 3.10 .85
□ 491 Tracy Stallard............ 7.00 3.10 .85
□ 492 Gene Freese.............. 7.00 3.10 .85
□ 493 Tigers Rookies.......... 7.00 3.10 .85
Bill Roman
Bruce Brubaker
□ 494 Jay Ritchie................. 7.00 3.10 .85
□ 495 Joe Christopher......... 7.00 3.10 .85
□ 496 Joe Cunningham........ 7.00 3.10 .85
□ 497 Giants Rookies.......... 7.50 3.40 .95
Ken Henderson
Jack Hiatt
□ 498 Gene Stephens........... 7.00 3.10 .85
□ 499 Stu Miller................... 7.50 3.40 .95
□ 500 Eddie Mathews........ 32.00 14.50 4.00
□ 501 Indians Rookies......... 7.00 3.10 .85
Ralph Gagliano
Jim Rittwage
□ 502 Don Cardwell............. 7.00 3.10 .85
□ 503 Phil Gagliano............. 7.00 3.10 .85
□ 504 Jerry Grote................ 7.00 3.10 .85
□ 505 Ray Culp.................... 7.00 3.10 .85
□ 506 Sam Mele MG............ 7.00 3.10 .85
□ 507 Sammy Ellis............... 7.00 3.10 .85
□ 508 Checklist 7.............. 12.00 3.00 .95
□ 509 Red Sox Rookies....... 7.00 3.10 .85
Bob Guindon
Gerry Vezendy
□ 510 Ernie Banks............. 75.00 34.00 9.50
□ 511 Ron Locke.................. 7.00 3.10 .85
□ 512 Cap Peterson............. 7.00 3.10 .85
□ 513 New York Yankees... 25.00 11.50 3.10
Team Card
□ 514 Joe Azcue.................. 7.00 3.10 .85
□ 515 Vern Law.................... 8.00 3.60 1.00
□ 516 Al Weis...................... 7.00 3.10 .85
□ 517 Angels Rookies.......... 7.50 3.40 .95
Paul Schaal
Jack Warner
□ 518 Ken Rowe.................. 7.00 3.10 .85
□ 519 Bob Uecker UER...... 30.00 13.50 3.80
(Posing as a left-
handed batter)
□ 520 Tony Cloninger.......... 7.00 3.10 .85
□ 521 Phillies Rookies......... 7.00 3.10 .85

	Dave Bennett			
	Morrie Stevens			
☐ 522	Hank Aguirre	7.00	3.10	.85
☐ 523	Mike Brumley SP	11.00	4.90	1.40
☐ 524	Dave Giusti SP	11.00	4.90	1.40
☐ 525	Eddie Bressoud	6.50	2.90	.80
☐ 526	Athletics Rookies SP	100.00	45.00	12.50
	Rene Lachemann			
	Johnny Odom			
	Jim Hunter UER			
	("Tim" on back)			
	Skip Lockwood			
☐ 527	Jeff Torborg SP	16.00	7.25	2.00
☐ 528	George Altman	6.50	2.90	.80
☐ 529	Jerry Fosnow SP	11.00	4.90	1.40
☐ 530	Jim Maloney	7.50	3.40	.95
☐ 531	Chuck Hiller	6.50	2.90	.80
☐ 532	Hector Lopez	7.00	3.10	.85
☐ 533	Mets Rookies SP	28.00	12.50	3.50
	Dan Napoleon			
	Ron Swoboda			
	Tug McGraw			
	Jim Bethke			
☐ 534	John Herrnstein	6.50	2.90	.80
☐ 535	Jack Kralick SP	11.00	4.90	1.40
☐ 536	Andre Rodgers SP	11.00	4.90	1.40
☐ 537	Angels Rookies	6.50	2.90	.80
	Marcelino Lopez			
	Phil Roof			
	Rudy May			
☐ 538	Chuck Dressen SP MG	12.00	5.50	1.50
☐ 539	Herm Starrette	6.50	2.90	.80
☐ 540	Lou Brock SP	50.00	23.00	6.25
☐ 541	White Sox Rookies	6.50	2.90	.80
	Greg Bollo			
	Bob Locker			
☐ 542	Lou Klimchock	6.50	2.90	.80
☐ 543	Ed Connolly SP	11.00	4.90	1.40
☐ 544	Howie Reed	6.50	2.90	.80
☐ 545	Jesus Alou SP	11.00	4.90	1.40
☐ 546	Indians Rookies	6.50	2.90	.80
	Bill Davis			
	Mike Hedlund			
	Ray Barker			
	Floyd Weaver			
☐ 547	Jake Wood SP	11.00	4.90	1.40
☐ 548	Dick Stigman	6.50	2.90	.80
☐ 549	Cubs Rookies SP	20.00	9.00	2.50
	Roberto Pena			
	Glenn Beckert			
☐ 550	Mel Stottlemyre SP	32.00	14.50	4.00
☐ 551	New York Mets SP	35.00	16.00	4.40
	Team Card			
☐ 552	Julio Gotay	6.50	2.90	.80
☐ 553	Astros Rookies	6.50	2.90	.80
	Dan Coombs			
	Gene Ratliff			
	Jack McClure			
☐ 554	Chico Ruiz SP	11.00	4.90	1.40
☐ 555	Jack Baldschun SP	11.00	4.90	1.40
☐ 556	Red Schoendienst	20.00	9.00	2.50
	SP MG			
☐ 557	Jose Santiago	6.50	2.90	.80
☐ 558	Tommie Sisk	6.50	2.90	.80
☐ 559	Ed Bailey SP	11.00	4.90	1.40
☐ 560	Boog Powell SP	22.00	10.00	2.80
☐ 561	Dodgers Rookies	12.00	5.50	1.50
	Dennis Daboll			
	Mike Kekich			
	Hector Valle			
	Jim Lefebvre			
☐ 562	Billy Moran	6.50	2.90	.80
☐ 563	Julio Navarro	6.50	2.90	.80
☐ 564	Mel Nelson	6.50	2.90	.80
☐ 565	Ernie Broglio SP	11.00	4.90	1.40
☐ 566	Yankees Rookies SP	11.00	4.90	1.40
	Gil Blanco			
	Ross Moschitto			
	Art Lopez			
☐ 567	Tommie Aaron	7.50	3.40	.95
☐ 568	Ron Taylor SP	11.00	4.90	1.40
☐ 569	Gino Cimoli SP	11.00	4.90	1.40
☐ 570	Claude Osteen SP	11.00	4.90	1.40
☐ 571	Ossie Virgil SP	11.00	4.90	1.40
☐ 572	Baltimore Orioles SP	30.00	13.50	3.80
	Team Card			
☐ 573	Red Sox Rookies SP	22.00	10.00	2.80
	Jim Lonborg			
	Gerry Moses			
	Bill Schlesinger			
	Mike Ryan			
☐ 574	Roy Sievers	7.50	3.40	.95
☐ 575	Jose Pagan	6.50	2.90	.80
☐ 576	Terry Fox SP	11.00	4.90	1.40
☐ 577	AL Rookie Stars SP	13.00	5.75	1.65
	Darold Knowles			
	Don Buschhorn			
	Richie Scheinblum			
☐ 578	Camilo Carreon SP	11.00	4.90	1.40
☐ 579	Dick Smith SP	11.00	4.90	1.40
☐ 580	Jimmie Hall SP	11.00	4.90	1.40
☐ 581	NL Rookie Stars SP	100.00	45.00	12.50
	Tony Perez			
	Dave Ricketts			
	Kevin Collins			
☐ 582	Bob Schmidt SP	11.00	4.90	1.40
☐ 583	Wes Covington SP	11.00	4.90	1.40
☐ 584	Harry Bright	6.50	2.90	.80
☐ 585	Hank Fischer	6.50	2.90	.80
☐ 586	Tom McCraw SP	11.00	4.90	1.40
☐ 587	Joe Sparma	6.50	2.90	.80
☐ 588	Lenny Green	6.50	2.90	.80
☐ 589	Giants Rookies SP	11.00	4.90	1.40
	Frank Linzy			
	Bob Schroder			
☐ 590	John Wyatt	6.50	2.90	.80
☐ 591	Bob Skinner SP	13.00	5.75	1.65
☐ 592	Frank Bork SP	11.00	4.90	1.40
☐ 593	Tigers Rookies SP	11.00	4.90	1.40
	Jackie Moore			
	John Sullivan			
☐ 594	Joe Gaines	6.50	2.90	.80
☐ 595	Don Lee	6.50	2.90	.80
☐ 596	Don Landrum SP	11.00	4.90	1.40
☐ 597	Twins Rookies	6.50	2.90	.80
	Joe Nossek			
	John Sevcik			
	Dick Reese			
☐ 598	Al Downing SP	20.00	6.00	2.00

1966 Topps

The cards in this 598-card set measure 2 1/2" by 3 1/2". There are the same number of cards as in the 1965 set. Once again, the seventh series cards (523 to 598) are considered more difficult to obtain than the cards of any other series in the set. Within this last series there are 43 cards that were printed in lesser quantities than the other cards in that series; these shorter-printed cards are marked by SP in the checklist

below. The only featured subset within this set is League Leaders (215-226). Noteworthy Rookie Cards in the set include Jim Palmer (126), Ferguson Jenkins (254), and Don Sutton (288). Jim Palmer is described in the bio (on his card back) as a left-hander.

	NRMT	VG-E	GOOD
COMPLETE SET (598)	4000.00	1800.00	500.00
COMMON CARD (1-109)	1.50	.65	.19
COMMON CARD (110-196)	2.00	.90	.25
COMMON CARD (197-283)	2.00	.90	.25
COMMON CARD (284-370)	2.50	1.15	.30
COMMON CARD (371-446)	4.50	2.00	.55
COMMON CARD (447-522)	9.00	4.00	1.15
COMMON CARD (523-598)	16.00	7.25	2.00

Card	NRMT	VG-E	GOOD
☐ 1 Willie Mays	130.00	39.00	13.00
☐ 2 Ted Abernathy	1.50	.65	.19
☐ 3 Sam Mele MG	1.50	.65	.19
☐ 4 Ray Culp	1.50	.65	.19
☐ 5 Jim Fregosi	2.00	.90	.25
☐ 6 Chuck Schilling	1.50	.65	.19
☐ 7 Tracy Stallard	1.50	.65	.19
☐ 8 Floyd Robinson	1.50	.65	.19
☐ 9 Clete Boyer	2.00	.90	.25
☐ 10 Tony Cloninger	1.50	.65	.19
☐ 11 Senators Rookies Brant Alyea Pete Craig	1.50	.65	.19
☐ 12 John Tsitouris	1.50	.65	.19
☐ 13 Lou Johnson	2.00	.90	.25
☐ 14 Norm Siebern	1.50	.65	.19
☐ 15 Vern Law	2.00	.90	.25
☐ 16 Larry Brown	1.50	.65	.19
☐ 17 John Stephenson	1.50	.65	.19
☐ 18 Roland Sheldon	1.50	.65	.19
☐ 19 San Francisco Giants Team Card	3.50	1.55	.45
☐ 20 Willie Horton	2.00	.90	.25
☐ 21 Don Nottebart	1.50	.65	.19
☐ 22 Joe Nossek	1.50	.65	.19
☐ 23 Jack Sanford	1.50	.65	.19
☐ 24 Don Kessinger	5.50	2.50	.70
☐ 25 Pete Ward	1.50	.65	.19
☐ 26 Ray Sadecki	1.50	.65	.19
☐ 27 Orioles Rookies Darold Knowles Andy Etchebarren	1.50	.65	.19
☐ 28 Phil Niekro	20.00	9.00	2.50
☐ 29 Mike Brumley	1.50	.65	.19
☐ 30 Pete Rose DP	45.00	20.00	5.75
☐ 31 Jack Cullen	1.50	.65	.19
☐ 32 Adolfo Phillips	1.50	.65	.19
☐ 33 Jim Pagliaroni	1.50	.65	.19
☐ 34 Checklist 1	8.00	1.20	.40
☐ 35 Ron Swoboda	1.50	.65	.19
☐ 36 Jim Hunter UER (Stats say 1963 and 1964, should be 1963 and 1964)	20.00	9.00	2.50
☐ 37 Billy Herman MG	2.50	1.15	.30
☐ 38 Ron Nischwitz	1.50	.65	.19
☐ 39 Ken Henderson	1.50	.65	.19
☐ 40 Jim Grant	1.50	.65	.19
☐ 41 Don LeJohn	1.50	.65	.19
☐ 42 Aubrey Gatewood	1.50	.65	.19
☐ 43A Don Landrum (Dark button on pants showing)	2.00	.90	.25
☐ 43B Don Landrum (Button on pants partially airbrushed)	2.00	.90	.25
☐ 43C Don Landrum (Button on pants not showing)	2.00	.90	.25
☐ 44 Indians Rookies Bill Davis Tom Kelley	1.50	.65	.19
☐ 45 Jim Gentile	2.00	.90	.25
☐ 46 Howie Koplitz	1.50	.65	.19
☐ 47 J.C. Martin	1.50	.65	.19
☐ 48 Paul Blair	2.00	.90	.25
☐ 49 Woody Woodward	2.00	.90	.25
☐ 50 Mickey Mantle DP	200.00	90.00	25.00
☐ 51 Gordon Richardson	1.50	.65	.19
☐ 52 Power Plus Wes Covington Johnny Callison	2.00	.90	.25
☐ 53 Bob Duliba	1.50	.65	.19
☐ 54 Jose Pagan	1.50	.65	.19
☐ 55 Ken Harrelson	2.00	.90	.25
☐ 56 Sandy Valdespino	1.50	.65	.19
☐ 57 Jim Lefebvre	1.50	.65	.19
☐ 58 Dave Wickersham	1.50	.65	.19
☐ 59 Reds Team	3.50	1.55	.45
☐ 60 Curt Flood	2.50	1.15	.30
☐ 61 Bob Bolin	1.50	.65	.19
☐ 62A Merritt Ranew (With sold line)	1.50	.65	.19
☐ 62B Merritt Ranew (Without sold line)	36.00	16.00	4.50
☐ 63 Jim Stewart	1.50	.65	.19
☐ 64 Bob Bruce	1.50	.65	.19
☐ 65 Leon Wagner	1.50	.65	.19
☐ 66 Al Weis	1.50	.65	.19
☐ 67 Mets Rookies Cleon Jones Dick Selma	2.00	.90	.25
☐ 68 Hal Reniff	1.50	.65	.19
☐ 69 Ken Hamlin	1.50	.65	.19
☐ 70 Carl Yastrzemski	32.00	14.50	4.00
☐ 71 Frank Carpin	1.50	.65	.19
☐ 72 Tony Perez	30.00	13.50	3.80
☐ 73 Jerry Zimmerman	1.50	.65	.19
☐ 74 Don Mossi	2.00	.90	.25
☐ 75 Tommy Davis	2.00	.90	.25
☐ 76 Red Schoendienst MG	4.00	1.80	.50
☐ 77 John Orsino	1.50	.65	.19
☐ 78 Frank Linzy	1.50	.65	.19
☐ 79 Joe Pepitone	2.00	.90	.25
☐ 80 Richie Allen	6.00	2.70	.75
☐ 81 Ray Oyler	1.50	.65	.19
☐ 82 Bob Hendley	1.50	.65	.19
☐ 83 Albie Pearson	2.00	.90	.25
☐ 84 Braves Rookies Jim Beauchamp Dick Kelley	1.50	.65	.19
☐ 85 Eddie Fisher	1.50	.65	.19
☐ 86 John Bateman	1.50	.65	.19

☐ 87 Dan Napoleon .... 1.50 .65 .19
☐ 88 Fred Whitfield .... 1.50 .65 .19
☐ 89 Ted Davidson .... 1.50 .65 .19
☐ 90 Luis Aparicio .... 7.00 3.10 .85
☐ 91A Bob Uecker TR 10.00 4.50 1.25
☐ 91B Bob Uecker NTR 38.00 17.00 4.70
☐ 92 Yankees Team .... 5.00 2.30 .60
☐ 93 Jim Lonborg .... 1.50 .65 .19
☐ 94 Matty Alou .... 2.00 .90 .25
☐ 95 Pete Richert .... 1.50 .65 .19
☐ 96 Felipe Alou .... 3.00 1.35 .40
☐ 97 Jim Merritt .... 1.50 .65 .19
☐ 98 Don Demeter .... 1.50 .65 .19
☐ 99 Buc Belters .... 5.50 2.50 .70
Willie Stargell
Donn Clendenon
☐ 100 Sandy Koufax 80.00 36.00 10.00
☐ 101A Checklist 2 .... 16.00 2.40 .80
(115 W. Spahn) ERR
☐ 101B Checklist 2 .... 10.00 1.50 .50
(115 Bill Henry) COR
☐ 102 Ed Kirkpatrick .... 1.50 .65 .19
☐ 103A Dick Groat TR .... 2.00 .90 .25
☐ 103B Dick Groat NTR 36.00 16.00 4.50
☐ 104A Alex Johnson TR .... 2.00 .90 .25
☐ 104B Alex Johnson NTR. 36.00 16.00 4.50
☐ 105 Milt Pappas .... 2.00 .90 .25
☐ 106 Rusty Staub .... 4.50 2.00 .55
☐ 107 A's Rookies .... 1.50 .65 .19
Larry Stahl
Ron Tompkins
☐ 108 Bobby Klaus .... 1.50 .65 .19
☐ 109 Ralph Terry .... 2.00 .90 .25
☐ 110 Ernie Banks 25.00 11.50 3.10
☐ 111 Gary Peters .... 2.00 .90 .25
☐ 112 Manny Mota .... 2.50 1.15 .30
☐ 113 Hank Aguirre .... 2.00 .90 .25
☐ 114 Jim Gosger .... 2.00 .90 .25
☐ 115 Bill Henry .... 2.00 .90 .25
☐ 116 Walt Alston MG .... 4.00 1.80 .50
☐ 117 Jake Gibbs .... 2.50 1.15 .30
☐ 118 Mike McCormick .... 2.50 1.15 .30
☐ 119 Art Shamsky .... 2.00 .90 .25
☐ 120 Harmon Killebrew 18.00 8.00 2.30
☐ 121 Ray Herbert .... 2.00 .90 .25
☐ 122 Joe Gaines .... 2.00 .90 .25
☐ 123 Pirates Rookies .... 2.00 .90 .25
Frank Bork
Jerry May
☐ 124 Tug McGraw .... 6.00 2.70 .75
☐ 125 Lou Brock 20.00 9.00 2.50
☐ 126 Jim Palmer UER 135.00 60.00 17.00
(Described as a
lefthander on
card back)
☐ 127 Ken Berry .... 2.00 .90 .25
☐ 128 Jim Landis .... 2.00 .90 .25
☐ 129 Jack Kralick .... 2.00 .90 .25
☐ 130 Joe Torre .... 4.50 2.00 .55
☐ 131 Angels Team .... 4.50 2.00 .55
☐ 132 Orlando Cepeda .... 6.00 2.70 .75
☐ 133 Don McMahon .... 2.00 .90 .25
☐ 134 Wes Parker .... 2.50 1.15 .30
☐ 135 Dave Morehead .... 2.00 .90 .25
☐ 136 Woody Held .... 2.00 .90 .25
☐ 137 Pat Corrales .... 2.50 1.15 .30
☐ 138 Roger Repoz .... 2.00 .90 .25
☐ 139 Cubs Rookies .... 2.00 .90 .25
Byron Browne
Don Young
☐ 140 Jim Maloney .... 2.50 1.15 .30
☐ 141 Tom McCraw .... 2.00 .90 .25
☐ 142 Don Dennis .... 2.00 .90 .25
☐ 143 Jose Tartabull .... 2.50 1.15 .30
☐ 144 Don Schwall .... 2.00 .90 .25
☐ 145 Bill Freehan .... 3.50 1.55 .45
☐ 146 George Altman .... 2.00 .90 .25
☐ 147 Lum Harris MG .... 2.00 .90 .25
☐ 148 Bob Johnson .... 2.00 .90 .25
☐ 149 Dick Nen .... 2.00 .90 .25
☐ 150 Rocky Colavito 8.00 3.60 1.00
☐ 151 Gary Wagner .... 2.00 .90 .25
☐ 152 Frank Malzone .... 2.50 1.15 .30
☐ 153 Rico Carty .... 2.50 1.15 .30
☐ 154 Chuck Hiller .... 2.00 .90 .25
☐ 155 Marcelino Lopez .... 2.00 .90 .25
☐ 156 Double Play Combo ... 2.00 .90 .25
Dick Schofield
Hal Lanier
☐ 157 Rene Lachemann .... 2.50 1.15 .30
☐ 158 Jim Brewer .... 2.00 .90 .25
☐ 159 Chico Ruiz .... 2.00 .90 .25
☐ 160 Whitey Ford 25.00 11.50 3.10
☐ 161 Jerry Lumpe .... 2.00 .90 .25
☐ 162 Lee Maye .... 2.00 .90 .25
☐ 163 Tito Francona .... 2.00 .90 .25
☐ 164 White Sox Rookies .... 2.50 1.15 .30
Tommie Agee
Marv Staehle
☐ 165 Don Lock .... 2.00 .90 .25
☐ 166 Chris Krug .... 2.00 .90 .25
☐ 167 Boog Powell .... 5.00 2.30 .60
☐ 168 Dan Osinski .... 2.00 .90 .25
☐ 169 Duke Sims .... 2.00 .90 .25
☐ 170 Cookie Rojas .... 2.50 1.15 .30
☐ 171 Nick Willhite .... 2.00 .90 .25
☐ 172 Mets Team .... 4.50 2.00 .55
☐ 173 Al Spangler .... 2.00 .90 .25
☐ 174 Ron Taylor .... 2.00 .90 .25
☐ 175 Bert Campaneris .... 2.50 1.15 .30
☐ 176 Jim Davenport .... 2.00 .90 .25
☐ 177 Hector Lopez .... 2.00 .90 .25
☐ 178 Bob Tillman .... 2.00 .90 .25
☐ 179 Cards Rookies .... 2.50 1.15 .30
Dennis Aust
Bob Tolan
☐ 180 Vada Pinson .... 3.50 1.55 .45
☐ 181 Al Worthington .... 2.00 .90 .25
☐ 182 Jerry Lynch .... 2.00 .90 .25
☐ 183A Checklist 3 .... 8.00 1.20 .40
(Large print
on front)
☐ 183B Checklist 3 .... 8.00 1.20 .40
(Small print
on front)
☐ 184 Denis Menke .... 2.00 .90 .25
☐ 185 Bob Buhl .... 2.50 1.15 .30
☐ 186 Ruben Amaro .... 2.00 .90 .25
☐ 187 Chuck Dressen MG .... 2.50 1.15 .30
☐ 188 Al Luplow .... 2.00 .90 .25
☐ 189 John Roseboro .... 2.50 1.15 .30
☐ 190 Jimmie Hall .... 2.00 .90 .25
☐ 191 Darrell Sutherland .... 2.00 .90 .25
☐ 192 Vic Power .... 2.50 1.15 .30
☐ 193 Dave McNally .... 2.50 1.15 .30
☐ 194 Senators Team .... 4.50 2.00 .55
☐ 195 Joe Morgan 16.00 7.25 2.00
☐ 196 Don Pavletich .... 2.00 .90 .25
☐ 197 Sonny Siebert .... 2.00 .90 .25
☐ 198 Mickey Stanley .... 4.50 2.00 .55
☐ 199 Chisox Clubbers .... 2.50 1.15 .30
Bill Skowron
Johnny Romano
Floyd Robinson
☐ 200 Eddie Mathews 14.00 6.25 1.75
☐ 201 Jim Dickson .... 2.00 .90 .25

☐ 202 Clay Dalrymple........... 2.00 .90 .25
☐ 203 Jose Santiago........... 2.00 .90 .25
☐ 204 Cubs Team................ 5.00 2.30 .60
☐ 205 Tom Tresh................. 2.00 .90 .25
☐ 206 Al Jackson................. 2.00 .90 .25
☐ 207 Frank Quilici............... 2.00 .90 .25
☐ 208 Bob Miller.................. 2.00 .90 .25
☐ 209 Tigers Rookies.......... 3.50 1.55 .45
Fritz Fisher
John Hiller
☐ 210 Bill Mazeroski........... 5.00 2.30 .60
☐ 211 Frank Kreutzer........... 2.00 .90 .25
☐ 212 Ed Kranepool............ 2.50 1.15 .30
☐ 213 Fred Newman............ 2.00 .90 .25
☐ 214 Tommy Harper........... 2.50 1.15 .30
☐ 215 NL Batting Leaders.. 36.00 16.00 4.50
Bob Clemente
Hank Aaron
Willie Mays
☐ 216 AL Batting Leaders..... 6.00 2.70 .75
Tony Oliva
Carl Yastrzemski
Vic Davalillo
☐ 217 NL Home Run Leaders 20.00 9.00 2.50
Willie Mays
Willie McCovey
Billy Williams
☐ 218 AL Home Run Leaders 5.00 2.30 .60
Tony Conigliaro
Norm Cash
Willie Horton
☐ 219 NL RBI Leaders........ 10.00 4.50 1.25
Deron Johnson
Frank Robinson
Willie Mays
☐ 220 AL RBI Leaders.......... 5.00 2.30 .60
Rocky Colavito
Willie Horton
Tony Oliva
☐ 221 NL ERA Leaders....... 10.00 4.50 1.25
Sandy Koufax
Juan Marichal
Vern Law
☐ 222 AL ERA Leaders......... 5.00 2.30 .60
Sam McDowell
Eddie Fisher
Sonny Siebert
☐ 223 NL Pitching Leaders. 12.00 5.50 1.50
Sandy Koufax
Tony Cloninger
Don Drysdale
☐ 224 AL Pitching Leaders... 5.00 2.30 .60
Jim Grant
Mel Stottlemyre
Jim Kaat
☐ 225 NL Strikeout Leaders 10.00 4.50 1.25
Sandy Koufax
Bob Veale
Bob Gibson
☐ 226 AL Strikeout Leaders. 5.00 2.30 .60
Sam McDowell
Mickey Lolich
Dennis McLain
Sonny Siebert
☐ 227 Russ Nixon............... 2.00 .90 .25
☐ 228 Larry Dierker............. 2.00 .90 .25
☐ 229 Hank Bauer MG.......... 2.50 1.15 .30
☐ 230 Johnny Callison......... 2.50 1.15 .30
☐ 231 Floyd Weaver............ 2.00 .90 .25
☐ 232 Glenn Beckert........... 2.50 1.15 .30
☐ 233 Dom Zanni................ 2.00 .90 .25
☐ 234 Yankees Rookies...... 10.00 4.50 1.25
Rich Beck
Roy White
☐ 235 Don Cardwell............ 2.00 .90 .25
☐ 236 Mike Hershberger...... 2.00 .90 .25
☐ 237 Billy O'Dell................ 2.00 .90 .25
☐ 238 Dodgers Team........... 5.00 2.30 .60
☐ 239 Orlando Pena............ 2.00 .90 .25
☐ 240 Earl Battey................ 2.00 .90 .25
☐ 241 Dennis Ribant............ 2.00 .90 .25
☐ 242 Jesus Alou................ 2.00 .90 .25
☐ 243 Nelson Briles............. 2.50 1.15 .30
☐ 244 Astros Rookies.......... 2.00 .90 .25
Chuck Harrison
Sonny Jackson
☐ 245 John Buzhardt............ 2.00 .90 .25
☐ 246 Ed Bailey.................. 2.00 .90 .25
☐ 247 Carl Warwick............. 2.00 .90 .25
☐ 248 Pete Mikkelsen........... 2.00 .90 .25
☐ 249 Bill Rigney MG........... 2.00 .90 .25
☐ 250 Sammy Ellis.............. 2.00 .90 .25
☐ 251 Ed Brinkman.............. 2.00 .90 .25
☐ 252 Denny Lemaster......... 2.00 .90 .25
☐ 253 Don Wert.................. 2.00 .90 .25
☐ 254 Phillies Rookies....... 90.00 40.00 11.50
Ferguson Jenkins
Bill Sorrell
☐ 255 Willie Stargell.......... 20.00 9.00 2.50
☐ 256 Lew Krausse............. 2.00 .90 .25
☐ 257 Jeff Torborg............. 2.50 1.15 .30
☐ 258 Dave Giusti.............. 2.00 .90 .25
☐ 259 Boston Red Sox......... 5.00 2.30 .60
Team Card
☐ 260 Bob Shaw................. 2.00 .90 .25
☐ 261 Ron Hansen.............. 2.00 .90 .25
☐ 262 Jack Hamilton........... 2.00 .90 .25
☐ 263 Tom Egan................. 2.00 .90 .25
☐ 264 Twins Rookies........... 2.00 .90 .25
Andy Kosco
Ted Uhlaender
☐ 265 Stu Miller.................. 2.50 1.15 .30
☐ 266 Pedro Gonzalez UER.. 2.00 .90 .25
(Misspelled Gonzales
on card back)
☐ 267 Joe Sparma............... 2.00 .90 .25
☐ 268 John Blanchard.......... 2.00 .90 .25
☐ 269 Don Heffner MG......... 2.00 .90 .25
☐ 270 Claude Osteen........... 2.50 1.15 .30
☐ 271 Hal Lanier................. 2.00 .90 .25
☐ 272 Jack Baldschun.......... 2.00 .90 .25
☐ 273 Astro Aces................ 2.50 1.15 .30
Bob Aspromonte
Rusty Staub
☐ 274 Buster Narum............ 2.00 .90 .25
☐ 275 Tim McCarver............ 5.00 2.30 .60
☐ 276 Jim Bouton............... 4.50 2.00 .55
☐ 277 George Thomas......... 2.00 .90 .25
☐ 278 Cal Koonce............... 2.00 .90 .25
☐ 279A Checklist 4............ 8.00 1.20 .40
(Player's cap black)
☐ 279B Checklist 4............ 8.00 1.20 .40
(Player's cap red)
☐ 280 Bobby Knoop............ 2.00 .90 .25
☐ 281 Bruce Howard........... 2.00 .90 .25
☐ 282 Johnny Lewis............ 2.00 .90 .25
☐ 283 Jim Perry................. 2.50 1.15 .30
☐ 284 Bobby Wine.............. 3.00 1.35 .40
☐ 285 Luis Tiant................. 6.50 2.90 .80
☐ 286 Gary Geiger.............. 2.50 1.15 .30
☐ 287 Jack Aker................. 2.50 1.15 .30
☐ 288 Dodgers Rookies..... 90.00 40.00 11.50
Bill Singer
Don Sutton
☐ 289 Larry Sherry.............. 3.00 1.35 .40
☐ 290 Ron Santo................. 6.00 2.70 .75

☐ 291 Moe Drabowsky .... 3.00 1.35 .40
☐ 292 Jim Coker .... 2.50 1.15 .30
☐ 293 Mike Shannon .... 3.00 1.35 .40
☐ 294 Steve Ridzik .... 2.50 1.15 .30
☐ 295 Jim Ray Hart .... 3.00 1.35 .40
☐ 296 Johnny Keane MG ...... 2.50 1.15 .30
☐ 297 Jim Owens .... 2.50 1.15 .30
☐ 298 Rico Petrocelli .... 2.50 1.15 .30
☐ 299 Lou Burdette .... 3.00 1.35 .40
☐ 300 Bob Clemente 110.00 50.00 14.00
☐ 301 Greg Bollo .... 2.50 1.15 .30
☐ 302 Ernie Bowman .... 2.50 1.15 .30
☐ 303 Cleveland Indians .... 5.00 2.30 .60
Team Card
☐ 304 John Herrnstein .... 2.50 1.15 .30
☐ 305 Camilo Pascual .... 3.00 1.35 .40
☐ 306 Ty Cline .... 2.50 1.15 .30
☐ 307 Clay Carroll .... 3.00 1.35 .40
☐ 308 Tom Haller .... 3.00 1.35 .40
☐ 309 Diego Segui .... 2.50 1.15 .30
☐ 310 Frank Robinson 38.00 17.00 4.70
☐ 311 Reds Rookies .... 3.00 1.35 .40
Tommy Helms
Dick Simpson
☐ 312 Bob Saverine .... 2.50 1.15 .30
☐ 313 Chris Zachary .... 2.50 1.15 .30
☐ 314 Hector Valle .... 2.50 1.15 .30
☐ 315 Norm Cash .... 5.00 2.30 .60
☐ 316 Jack Fisher .... 2.50 1.15 .30
☐ 317 Dalton Jones .... 2.50 1.15 .30
☐ 318 Harry Walker MG .... 2.50 1.15 .30
☐ 319 Gene Freese .... 2.50 1.15 .30
☐ 320 Bob Gibson 27.00 12.00 3.40
☐ 321 Rick Reichardt .... 2.50 1.15 .30
☐ 322 Bill Faul .... 2.50 1.15 .30
☐ 323 Ray Barker .... 2.50 1.15 .30
☐ 324 John Boozer .... 2.50 1.15 .30
☐ 325 Vic Davalillo .... 2.50 1.15 .30
☐ 326 Braves Team .... 5.00 2.30 .60
☐ 327 Bernie Allen .... 2.50 1.15 .30
☐ 328 Jerry Grote .... 2.50 1.15 .30
☐ 329 Pete Charton .... 2.50 1.15 .30
☐ 330 Ron Fairly .... 3.00 1.35 .40
☐ 331 Ron Herbel .... 2.50 1.15 .30
☐ 332 Bill Bryan .... 2.50 1.15 .30
☐ 333 Senators Rookies .... 2.50 1.15 .30
Joe Coleman
Jim French
☐ 334 Marty Keough .... 2.50 1.15 .30
☐ 335 Juan Pizarro .... 2.50 1.15 .30
☐ 336 Gene Alley .... 3.00 1.35 .40
☐ 337 Fred Gladding .... 2.50 1.15 .30
☐ 338 Dal Maxvill .... 2.50 1.15 .30
☐ 339 Del Crandall .... 3.00 1.35 .40
☐ 340 Dean Chance .... 3.00 1.35 .40
☐ 341 Wes Westrum MG ..... 3.00 1.35 .40
☐ 342 Bob Humphreys .... 2.50 1.15 .30
☐ 343 Joe Christopher .... 2.50 1.15 .30
☐ 344 Steve Blass .... 3.00 1.35 .40
☐ 345 Bob Allison .... 3.00 1.35 .40
☐ 346 Mike de la Hoz .... 2.50 1.15 .30
☐ 347 Phil Regan .... 3.00 1.35 .40
☐ 348 Orioles Team .... 7.00 3.10 .85
☐ 349 Cap Peterson .... 2.50 1.15 .30
☐ 350 Mel Stottlemyre .... 5.00 2.30 .60
☐ 351 Fred Valentine .... 2.50 1.15 .30
☐ 352 Bob Aspromonte .... 2.50 1.15 .30
☐ 353 Al McBean .... 2.50 1.15 .30
☐ 354 Smoky Burgess .... 3.00 1.35 .40
☐ 355 Wade Blasingame ...... 2.50 1.15 .30
☐ 356 Red Sox Rookies .... 2.50 1.15 .30
Owen Johnson
Ken Sanders

☐ 357 Gerry Arrigo .... 2.50 1.15 .30
☐ 358 Charlie Smith .... 2.50 1.15 .30
☐ 359 Johnny Briggs .... 2.50 1.15 .30
☐ 360 Ron Hunt .... 2.50 1.15 .30
☐ 361 Tom Satriano .... 2.50 1.15 .30
☐ 362 Gates Brown .... 3.00 1.35 .40
☐ 363 Checklist 5 .... 10.00 1.50 .50
☐ 364 Nate Oliver .... 2.50 1.15 .30
☐ 365 Roger Maris 45.00 20.00 5.75
☐ 366 Wayne Causey .... 2.50 1.15 .30
☐ 367 Mel Nelson .... 2.50 1.15 .30
☐ 368 Charlie Lau .... 3.00 1.35 .40
☐ 369 Jim King .... 2.50 1.15 .30
☐ 370 Chico Cardenas .... 2.50 1.15 .30
☐ 371 Lee Stange .... 4.50 2.00 .55
☐ 372 Harvey Kuenn .... 5.00 2.30 .60
☐ 373 Giants Rookies .... 5.00 2.30 .60
Jack Hiatt
Dick Estelle
☐ 374 Bob Locker .... 4.50 2.00 .55
☐ 375 Donn Clendenon .... 5.00 2.30 .60
☐ 376 Paul Schaal .... 4.50 2.00 .55
☐ 377 Turk Farrell .... 4.50 2.00 .55
☐ 378 Dick Tracewski .... 4.50 2.00 .55
☐ 379 Cardinal Team 10.00 4.50 1.25
☐ 380 Tony Conigliaro 12.00 5.50 1.50
☐ 381 Hank Fischer .... 4.50 2.00 .55
☐ 382 Phil Roof .... 4.50 2.00 .55
☐ 383 Jackie Brandt .... 4.50 2.00 .55
☐ 384 Al Downing .... 5.00 2.30 .60
☐ 385 Ken Boyer .... 5.00 2.30 .60
☐ 386 Gil Hodges MG 8.00 3.60 1.00
☐ 387 Howie Reed .... 4.50 2.00 .55
☐ 388 Don Mincher .... 4.50 2.00 .55
☐ 389 Jim O'Toole .... 5.00 2.30 .60
☐ 390 Brooks Robinson 38.00 17.00 4.70
☐ 391 Chuck Hinton .... 4.50 2.00 .55
☐ 392 Cubs Rookies .... 6.00 2.70 .75
Bill Hands
Randy Hundley
☐ 393 George Brunet .... 4.50 2.00 .55
☐ 394 Ron Brand .... 4.50 2.00 .55
☐ 395 Len Gabrielson .... 4.50 2.00 .55
☐ 396 Jerry Stephenson .... 4.50 2.00 .55
☐ 397 Bill White .... 6.00 2.70 .75
☐ 398 Danny Cater .... 4.50 2.00 .55
☐ 399 Ray Washburn .... 4.50 2.00 .55
☐ 400 Zoilo Versalles .... 4.50 2.00 .55
☐ 401 Ken McMullen .... 4.50 2.00 .55
☐ 402 Jim Hickman .... 4.50 2.00 .55
☐ 403 Fred Talbot .... 4.50 2.00 .55
☐ 404 Pittsburgh Pirates 10.00 4.50 1.25
Team Card
☐ 405 Elston Howard .... 6.00 2.70 .75
☐ 406 Joey Jay .... 4.50 2.00 .55
☐ 407 John Kennedy .... 4.50 2.00 .55
☐ 408 Lee Thomas .... 5.00 2.30 .60
☐ 409 Billy Hoeft .... 4.50 2.00 .55
☐ 410 Al Kaline 32.00 14.50 4.00
☐ 411 Gene Mauch MG .... 5.00 2.30 .60
☐ 412 Sam Bowens .... 4.50 2.00 .55
☐ 413 Johnny Romano .... 4.50 2.00 .55
☐ 414 Dan Coombs .... 4.50 2.00 .55
☐ 415 Max Alvis .... 4.50 2.00 .55
☐ 416 Phil Ortega .... 4.50 2.00 .55
☐ 417 Angels Rookies .... 5.00 2.30 .60
Jim McGlothlin
Ed Sukla
☐ 418 Phil Gagliano .... 4.50 2.00 .55
☐ 419 Mike Ryan .... 4.50 2.00 .55
☐ 420 Juan Marichal 12.00 5.50 1.50
☐ 421 Roy McMillan .... 5.00 2.30 .60
☐ 422 Ed Charles .... 4.50 2.00 .55

☐ 423 Ernie Broglio .... 4.50 2.00 .55
☐ 424 Reds Rookies 10.00 4.50 1.25
Lee May
Darrell Osteen
☐ 425 Bob Veale .... 5.00 2.30 .60
☐ 426 White Sox Team 10.00 4.50 1.25
☐ 427 John Miller .... 4.50 2.00 .55
☐ 428 Sandy Alomar .... 5.00 2.30 .60
☐ 429 Bill Monbouquette ...... 4.50 2.00 .55
☐ 430 Don Drysdale 20.00 9.00 2.50
☐ 431 Walt Bond .... 4.50 2.00 .55
☐ 432 Bob Heffner .... 4.50 2.00 .55
☐ 433 Alvin Dark MG .... 5.00 2.30 .60
☐ 434 Willie Kirkland .... 4.50 2.00 .55
☐ 435 Jim Bunning 12.00 5.50 1.50
☐ 436 Julian Javier .... 5.00 2.30 .60
☐ 437 Al Stanek .... 4.50 2.00 .55
☐ 438 Willie Smith .... 4.50 2.00 .55
☐ 439 Pedro Ramos .... 4.50 2.00 .55
☐ 440 Deron Johnson .... 5.00 2.30 .60
☐ 441 Tommie Sisk .... 4.50 2.00 .55
☐ 442 Orioles Rookies .... 4.50 2.00 .55
Ed Barnowski
Eddie Watt
☐ 443 Bill Wakefield .... 4.50 2.00 .55
☐ 444 Checklist 6 .... 10.00 1.80 .50
☐ 445 Jim Kaat 10.00 4.50 1.25
☐ 446 Mack Jones .... 4.50 2.00 .55
☐ 447 Dick Ellsworth UER .. 10.00 4.50 1.25
(Photo actually
Ken Hubbs)
☐ 448 Eddie Stanky MG 10.00 4.50 1.25
☐ 449 Joe Moeller 9.00 4.00 1.15
☐ 450 Tony Oliva 12.00 5.50 1.50
☐ 451 Barry Latman 9.00 4.00 1.15
☐ 452 Joe Azcue 9.00 4.00 1.15
☐ 453 Ron Kline 9.00 4.00 1.15
☐ 454 Jerry Buchek 9.00 4.00 1.15
☐ 455 Mickey Lolich 10.00 4.50 1.25
☐ 456 Red Sox Rookies 9.00 4.00 1.15
Darrell Brandon
Joe Foy
☐ 457 Joe Gibbon 9.00 4.00 1.15
☐ 458 Manny Jiminez 9.00 4.00 1.15
☐ 459 Bill McCool 9.00 4.00 1.15
☐ 460 Curt Blefary 9.00 4.00 1.15
☐ 461 Roy Face 10.00 4.50 1.25
☐ 462 Bob Rodgers 10.00 4.50 1.25
☐ 463 Philadelphia Phillies . 14.00 6.25 1.75
Team Card
☐ 464 Larry Bearnarth 9.00 4.00 1.15
☐ 465 Don Buford 10.00 4.50 1.25
☐ 466 Ken Johnson 9.00 4.00 1.15
☐ 467 Vic Roznovsky 9.00 4.00 1.15
☐ 468 Johnny Podres 10.00 4.50 1.25
☐ 469 Yankees Rookies 30.00 13.50 3.80
Bobby Murcer
Dooley Womack
☐ 470 Sam McDowell 10.00 4.50 1.25
☐ 471 Bob Skinner 10.00 4.50 1.25
☐ 472 Terry Fox 9.00 4.00 1.15
☐ 473 Rich Rollins 9.00 4.00 1.15
☐ 474 Dick Schofield 9.00 4.00 1.15
☐ 475 Dick Radatz 10.00 4.50 1.25
☐ 476 Bobby Bragan MG 9.00 4.00 1.15
☐ 477 Steve Barber 9.00 4.00 1.15
☐ 478 Tony Gonzalez 9.00 4.00 1.15
☐ 479 Jim Hannan 9.00 4.00 1.15
☐ 480 Dick Stuart 10.00 4.50 1.25
☐ 481 Bob Lee 9.00 4.00 1.15
☐ 482 Cubs Rookies 9.00 4.00 1.15
John Boccabella
Dave Dowling
☐ 483 Joe Nuxhall 10.00 4.50 1.25
☐ 484 Wes Covington 9.00 4.00 1.15
☐ 485 Bob Bailey 10.00 4.50 1.25
☐ 486 Tommy John 14.00 6.25 1.75
☐ 487 Al Ferrara 9.00 4.00 1.15
☐ 488 George Banks 9.00 4.00 1.15
☐ 489 Curt Simmons 10.00 4.50 1.25
☐ 490 Bobby Richardson ... 14.00 6.25 1.75
☐ 491 Dennis Bennett 9.00 4.00 1.15
☐ 492 Athletics Team 14.00 6.25 1.75
☐ 493 Johnny Klippstein 9.00 4.00 1.15
☐ 494 Gordy Coleman 10.00 4.50 1.25
☐ 495 Dick McAuliffe 10.00 4.50 1.25
☐ 496 Lindy McDaniel 10.00 4.50 1.25
☐ 497 Chris Cannizzaro 9.00 4.00 1.15
☐ 498 Pirates Rookies 10.00 4.50 1.25
Luke Walker
Woody Fryman
☐ 499 Wally Bunker 9.00 4.00 1.15
☐ 500 Hank Aaron 125.00 57.50 15.50
☐ 501 John O'Donoghue 9.00 4.00 1.15
☐ 502 Lenny Green UER 9.00 4.00 1.15
(Born: aJn. 6, 1933)
☐ 503 Steve Hamilton 9.00 4.00 1.15
☐ 504 Grady Hatton MG 9.00 4.00 1.15
☐ 505 Jose Cardenal 10.00 4.50 1.25
☐ 506 Bo Belinsky 10.00 4.50 1.25
☐ 507 Johnny Edwards 9.00 4.00 1.15
☐ 508 Steve Hargan 9.00 4.00 1.15
☐ 509 Jake Wood 9.00 4.00 1.15
☐ 510 Hoyt Wilhelm 15.00 6.75 1.90
☐ 511 Giants Rookies 9.00 4.00 1.15
Bob Barton
Tito Fuentes
☐ 512 Dick Stigman 9.00 4.00 1.15
☐ 513 Camilo Carreon 9.00 4.00 1.15
☐ 514 Hal Woodeshick 9.00 4.00 1.15
☐ 515 Frank Howard 12.00 5.50 1.50
☐ 516 Eddie Bressoud 9.00 4.00 1.15
☐ 517A Checklist 7 .... 16.00 3.50 1.30
529 White Sox Rookies
544 Cardinals Rookies
☐ 517B Checklist 7 .... 16.00 3.50 1.30
529 W. Sox Rookies
544 Cards Rookies
☐ 518 Braves Rookies 9.00 4.00 1.15
Herb Hippauf
Arnie Umbach
☐ 519 Bob Friend 10.00 4.50 1.25
☐ 520 Jim Wynn 10.00 4.50 1.25
☐ 521 John Wyatt 9.00 4.00 1.15
☐ 522 Phil Linz 10.00 4.50 1.25
☐ 523 Bob Sadowski 18.00 8.00 2.30
☐ 524 Giants Rookies SP ... 28.00 12.50 3.50
Ollie Brown
Don Mason
☐ 525 Gary Bell SP 28.00 12.50 3.50
☐ 526 Twins Team SP 65.00 29.00 8.25
☐ 527 Julio Navarro 16.00 7.25 2.00
☐ 528 Jesse Gonder SP 28.00 12.50 3.50
☐ 529 White Sox Rookies ... 18.00 8.00 2.30
Lee Elia
Dennis Higgins
Bill Voss
☐ 530 Robin Roberts 50.00 23.00 6.25
☐ 531 Joe Cunningham 16.00 7.25 2.00
☐ 532 Aurelio Monteagudo SP 28.0012.50 3.50
☐ 533 Jerry Adair SP 28.00 12.50 3.50
☐ 534 Mets Rookies 16.00 7.25 2.00
Dave Eilers
Rob Gardner
☐ 535 Willie Davis SP 45.00 20.00 5.75
☐ 536 Dick Egan 16.00 7.25 2.00

☐ 537 Herman Franks MG.. 16.00 7.25 2.00
☐ 538 Bob Allen SP............ 28.00 12.50 3.50
☐ 539 Astros Rookies 16.00 7.25 2.00
Bill Heath
Carroll Sembera
☐ 540 Denny McLain SP 75.00 34.00 9.50
☐ 541 Gene Oliver SP......... 28.00 12.50 3.50
☐ 542 George Smith........... 16.00 7.25 2.00
☐ 543 Roger Craig SP 30.00 13.50 3.80
☐ 544 Cardinals Rookies SP 28.00 12.50 3.50
Joe Hoerner
George Kernek
Jimy Williams UER
(Misspelled Jimmy
on card)
☐ 545 Dick Green SP.......... 28.00 12.50 3.50
☐ 546 Dwight Siebler 16.00 7.25 2.00
☐ 547 Horace Clarke SP..... 32.00 14.50 4.00
☐ 548 Gary Kroll SP 28.00 12.50 3.50
☐ 549 Senators Rookies..... 16.00 7.25 2.00
Al Closter
Casey Cox
☐ 550 Willie McCovey SP. 100.00 45.00 12.50
☐ 551 Bob Purkey SP......... 28.00 12.50 3.50
☐ 552 Birdie Tebbetts......... 28.00 12.50 3.50
MG SP
☐ 553 Rookie Stars 16.00 7.25 2.00
Pat Garrett
Jackie Warner
☐ 554 Jim Northrup SP...... 28.00 12.50 3.50
☐ 555 Ron Perranoski SP... 28.00 12.50 3.50
☐ 556 Mel Queen SP.......... 28.00 12.50 3.50
☐ 557 Felix Mantilla SP 28.00 12.50 3.50
☐ 558 Red Sox Rookies 24.00 11.00 3.00
Guido Grilli
Pete Magrini
George Scott
☐ 559 Roberto Pena SP 28.00 12.50 3.50
☐ 560 Joel Horlen 16.00 7.25 2.00
☐ 561 ChooChoo Coleman SP 30.00 13.50 3.80
☐ 562 Russ Snyder 16.00 7.25 2.00
☐ 563 Twins Rookies 16.00 7.25 2.00
Pete Cimino
Cesar Tovar
☐ 564 Bob Chance SP......... 28.00 12.50 3.50
☐ 565 Jim Piersall SP......... 35.00 16.00 4.40
☐ 566 Mike Cuellar SP 30.00 13.50 3.80
☐ 567 Dick Howser SP........ 32.00 14.50 4.00
☐ 568 Athletics Rookies..... 18.00 8.00 2.30
Paul Lindblad
Ron Stone
☐ 569 Orlando McFarlane SP 28.00 12.50 3.50
☐ 570 Art Mahaffey SP....... 28.00 12.50 3.50
☐ 571 Dave Roberts SP...... 28.00 12.50 3.50
☐ 572 Bob Priddy............... 16.00 7.25 2.00
☐ 573 Derrell Griffith.......... 16.00 7.25 2.00
☐ 574 Mets Rookies........... 16.00 7.25 2.00
Bill Hepler
Bill Murphy
☐ 575 Earl Wilson 18.00 8.00 2.30
☐ 576 Dave Nicholson SP .. 28.00 12.50 3.50
☐ 577 Jack Lamabe SP 28.00 12.50 3.50
☐ 578 Chi Chi Olivo SP....... 28.00 12.50 3.50
☐ 579 Orioles Rookies........ 20.00 9.00 2.50
Frank Bertaina
Gene Brabender
Dave Johnson
☐ 580 Billy Williams SP...... 65.00 29.00 8.25
☐ 581 Tony Martinez.......... 16.00 7.25 2.00
☐ 582 Garry Roggenburk ... 16.00 7.25 2.00
☐ 583 Tigers Team SP UER 125.00 57.50 15.50
(Text on back states Tigers
finished third in 1966 instead
of fourth.)
☐ 584 Yankees Rookies...... 16.00 7.25 2.00
Frank Fernandez
Fritz Peterson
☐ 585 Tony Taylor............. 16.00 7.25 2.00
☐ 586 Claude Raymond SP 28.00 12.50 3.50
☐ 587 Dick Bertell 16.00 7.25 2.00
☐ 588 Athletics Rookies..... 16.00 7.25 2.00
Chuck Dobson
Ken Suarez
☐ 589 Lou Klimchock SP ... 28.00 12.50 3.50
☐ 590 Bill Skowron SP....... 35.00 16.00 4.40
☐ 591 NL Rookies SP......... 35.00 16.00 4.40
Bart Shirley
Grant Jackson
☐ 592 Andre Rodgers......... 16.00 7.25 2.00
☐ 593 Doug Camilli SP....... 28.00 12.50 3.50
☐ 594 Chico Salmon 16.00 7.25 2.00
☐ 595 Larry Jackson 16.00 7.25 2.00
☐ 596 Astros Rookies SP... 30.00 13.50 3.80
Nate Colbert
Greg Sims
☐ 597 John Sullivan........... 16.00 7.25 2.00
☐ 598 Gaylord Perry SP ... 175.00 45.00 8.75

1967 Topps

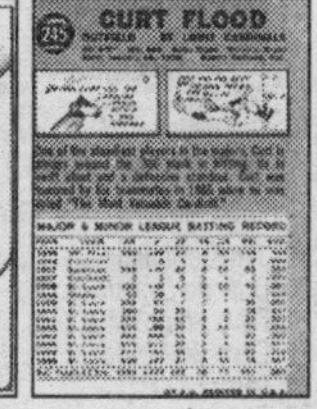

The cards in this 609-card set measure 2 1/2" by 3 1/2". The 1967 Topps series is considered by some collectors to be one of the company's finest accomplishments in baseball card production. Excellent color photographs are combined with easy-to-read backs. Cards 458 to 533 are slightly harder to find than numbers 1 to 457, and the inevitable (difficult to find) high series (534 to 609) exists. Each checklist card features a small circular picture of a popular player included in that series. Printing discrepancies resulted in some high series cards being in shorter supply. The checklist below identifies (by DP) 22 double-printed high numbers; of the 76 cards in the last series, 54 cards were short printed and the other 22 cards are much more plentiful. Featured subsets within this set include World Series cards (151-155) and League Leaders (233-244). Although there are several relatively expensive cards in this popular set, the key cards in the set are undoubtedly the Tom Seaver Rookie Card (581) and the Rod Carew Rookie Card (569). Although rarely seen, there exists a salesman's sample panel of three cards that pictures Earl Battey, Manny Mota, and

Gene Brabender with ad information on the back about the "new" Topps cards.

	NRMT	VG-E	GOOD
COMPLETE SET (609)	4600.00	2100.00	575.00
COMMON CARD (1-109)	1.50	.65	.19
COMMON CARD (110-196)	2.00	.90	.25
COMMON CARD (197-283)	2.00	.90	.25
COMMON CARD (284-370)	2.50	1.15	.30
COMMON CARD (371-457)	4.00	1.80	.50
COMMON CARD (458-533)	6.00	2.70	.75
COMMON CARD (534-609)	15.00	6.75	1.90

Card	NRMT	VG-E	GOOD
□ 1 The Champs DP	20.00	6.00	2.00
Frank Robinson			
Hank Bauer MG			
Brooks Robinson			
□ 2 Jack Hamilton	1.50	.65	.19
□ 3 Duke Sims	1.50	.65	.19
□ 4 Hal Lanier	1.50	.65	.19
□ 5 Whitey Ford UER	20.00	9.00	2.50
(1953 listed as			
1933 in stats on back)			
□ 6 Dick Simpson	1.50	.65	.19
□ 7 Don McMahon	1.50	.65	.19
□ 8 Chuck Harrison	1.50	.65	.19
□ 9 Ron Hansen	1.50	.65	.19
□ 10 Matty Alou	2.00	.90	.25
□ 11 Barry Moore	1.50	.65	.19
□ 12 Dodgers Rookies	2.00	.90	.25
Jim Campanis			
Bill Singer			
□ 13 Joe Sparma	1.50	.65	.19
□ 14 Phil Linz	2.00	.90	.25
□ 15 Earl Battey	1.50	.65	.19
□ 16 Bill Hands	1.50	.65	.19
□ 17 Jim Gosger	1.50	.65	.19
□ 18 Gene Oliver	1.50	.65	.19
□ 19 Jim McGlothlin	1.50	.65	.19
□ 20 Orlando Cepeda	7.50	3.40	.95
□ 21 Dave Bristol MG	1.50	.65	.19
□ 22 Gene Brabender	1.50	.65	.19
□ 23 Larry Elliot	1.50	.65	.19
□ 24 Bob Allen	1.50	.65	.19
□ 25 Elston Howard	4.00	1.80	.50
□ 26A Bob Priddy NTR	30.00	13.50	3.80
□ 26B Bob Priddy TR	1.50	.65	.19
□ 27 Bob Saverine	1.50	.65	.19
□ 28 Barry Latman	1.50	.65	.19
□ 29 Tom McCraw	1.50	.65	.19
□ 30 Al Kaline DP	18.00	8.00	2.30
□ 31 Jim Brewer	1.50	.65	.19
□ 32 Bob Bailey	2.00	.90	.25
□ 33 Athletic Rookies	5.00	2.30	.60
Sal Bando			
Randy Schwartz			
□ 34 Pete Cimino	1.50	.65	.19
□ 35 Rico Carty	2.00	.90	.25
□ 36 Bob Tillman	1.50	.65	.19
□ 37 Rick Wise	2.00	.90	.25
□ 38 Bob Johnson	1.50	.65	.19
□ 39 Curt Simmons	2.00	.90	.25
□ 40 Rick Reichardt	1.50	.65	.19
□ 41 Joe Hoerner	1.50	.65	.19
□ 42 Mets Team	6.00	2.70	.75
□ 43 Chico Salmon	1.50	.65	.19
□ 44 Joe Nuxhall	2.00	.90	.25
□ 45 Roger Maris	40.00	18.00	5.00
□ 46 Lindy McDaniel	2.00	.90	.25
□ 47 Ken McMullen	1.50	.65	.19
□ 48 Bill Freehan	2.00	.90	.25
□ 49 Roy Face	2.00	.90	.25
□ 50 Tony Oliva	5.00	2.30	.60
□ 51 Astros Rookies	1.50	.65	.19
Dave Adlesh			
Wes Bales			
□ 52 Dennis Higgins	1.50	.65	.19
□ 53 Clay Dalrymple	1.50	.65	.19
□ 54 Dick Green	1.50	.65	.19
□ 55 Don Drysdale	15.00	6.75	1.90
□ 56 Jose Tartabull	2.00	.90	.25
□ 57 Pat Jarvis	1.50	.65	.19
□ 58 Paul Schaal	1.50	.65	.19
□ 59 Ralph Terry	2.00	.90	.25
□ 60 Luis Aparicio	7.00	3.10	.85
□ 61 Gordy Coleman	2.00	.90	.25
□ 62 Checklist 1	7.00	2.10	.70
Frank Robinson			
□ 63 Cards' Clubbers	8.00	3.60	1.00
Lou Brock			
Curt Flood			
□ 64 Fred Valentine	1.50	.65	.19
□ 65 Tom Haller	2.00	.90	.25
□ 66 Manny Mota	2.00	.90	.25
□ 67 Ken Berry	1.50	.65	.19
□ 68 Bob Buhl	2.00	.90	.25
□ 69 Vic Davalillo	1.50	.65	.19
□ 70 Ron Santo	4.50	2.00	.55
□ 71 Camilo Pascual	2.00	.90	.25
□ 72 Tigers Rookies	1.50	.65	.19
George Korince			
(Photo actually			
James Murray Brown)			
John (Tom) Matchick			
□ 73 Rusty Staub	4.00	1.80	.50
□ 74 Wes Stock	1.50	.65	.19
□ 75 George Scott	2.00	.90	.25
□ 76 Jim Barbieri	1.50	.65	.19
□ 77 Dooley Womack	1.50	.65	.19
□ 78 Pat Corrales	2.00	.90	.25
□ 79 Bubba Morton	1.50	.65	.19
□ 80 Jim Maloney	2.00	.90	.25
□ 81 Eddie Stanky MG	2.00	.90	.25
□ 82 Steve Barber	1.50	.65	.19
□ 83 Ollie Brown	1.50	.65	.19
□ 84 Tommie Sisk	1.50	.65	.19
□ 85 Johnny Callison	2.00	.90	.25
□ 86A Mike McCormick NTR	30.00	13.50	3.80
(Senators on front			
and Senators on back)			
□ 86B Mike McCormick TR	2.00	.90	.25
(Traded line			
at end of bio;			
Senators on front,			
but Giants on back)			
□ 87 George Altman	1.50	.65	.19
□ 88 Mickey Lolich	6.00	2.70	.75
□ 89 Felix Millan	2.00	.90	.25
□ 90 Jim Nash	1.50	.65	.19
□ 91 Johnny Lewis	1.50	.65	.19
□ 92 Ray Washburn	1.50	.65	.19
□ 93 Yankees Rookies	4.50	2.00	.55
Stan Bahnsen			
Bobby Murcer			
□ 94 Ron Fairly	2.00	.90	.25
□ 95 Sonny Siebert	1.50	.65	.19
□ 96 Art Shamsky	1.50	.65	.19
□ 97 Mike Cuellar	2.00	.90	.25
□ 98 Rich Rollins	1.50	.65	.19
□ 99 Lee Stange	1.50	.65	.19
□ 100 Frank Robinson DP	15.00	6.75	1.90
□ 101 Ken Johnson	1.50	.65	.19
□ 102 Philadelphia Phillies	3.00	1.35	.40
Team Card			
□ 103 Checklist 2	12.00	3.60	1.20
Mickey Mantle			

☐ 104 Minnie Rojas 1.50 .65 .19
☐ 105 Ken Boyer 3.00 1.35 .40
☐ 106 Randy Hundley 2.00 .90 .25
☐ 107 Joel Horlen 1.50 .65 .19
☐ 108 Alex Johnson 2.00 .90 .25
☐ 109 Tribe Thumpers 4.00 1.80 .50
Rocky Colavito
Leon Wagner
☐ 110 Jack Aker 2.50 1.15 .30
☐ 111 John Kennedy 2.00 .90 .25
☐ 112 Dave Wickersham 2.00 .90 .25
☐ 113 Dave Nicholson 2.00 .90 .25
☐ 114 Jack Baldschun 2.00 .90 .25
☐ 115 Paul Casanova 2.00 .90 .25
☐ 116 Herman Franks MG 2.00 .90 .25
☐ 117 Darrell Brandon 2.00 .90 .25
☐ 118 Bernie Allen 2.00 .90 .25
☐ 119 Wade Blasingame 2.00 .90 .25
☐ 120 Floyd Robinson 2.00 .90 .25
☐ 121 Eddie Bressoud 2.00 .90 .25
☐ 122 George Brunet 2.00 .90 .25
☐ 123 Pirates Rookies 2.00 .90 .25
Jim Price
Luke Walker
☐ 124 Jim Stewart 2.00 .90 .25
☐ 125 Moe Drabowsky 2.50 1.15 .30
☐ 126 Tony Taylor 2.00 .90 .25
☐ 127 John O'Donoghue 2.00 .90 .25
☐ 128 Ed Spiezio 2.00 .90 .25
☐ 129 Phil Roof 2.00 .90 .25
☐ 130 Phil Regan 2.50 1.15 .30
☐ 131 Yankees Team 5.00 2.30 .60
☐ 132 Ozzie Virgil 2.00 .90 .25
☐ 133 Ron Kline 2.00 .90 .25
☐ 134 Gates Brown 2.50 1.15 .30
☐ 135 Deron Johnson 2.50 1.15 .30
☐ 136 Carroll Sembera 2.00 .90 .25
☐ 137 Twins Rookies 2.00 .90 .25
Ron Clark
Jim Ollum
☐ 138 Dick Kelley 2.00 .90 .25
☐ 139 Dalton Jones 2.50 1.15 .30
☐ 140 Willie Stargell 20.00 9.00 2.50
☐ 141 John Miller 2.00 .90 .25
☐ 142 Jackie Brandt 2.00 .90 .25
☐ 143 Sox Sockers 2.00 .90 .25
Pete Ward
Don Buford
☐ 144 Bill Hepler 2.00 .90 .25
☐ 145 Larry Brown 2.00 .90 .25
☐ 146 Steve Carlton 90.00 40.00 11.50
☐ 147 Tom Egan 2.00 .90 .25
☐ 148 Adolfo Phillips 2.00 .90 .25
☐ 149 Joe Moeller 2.00 .90 .25
☐ 150 Mickey Mantle 300.00 135.00 38.00
☐ 151 World Series Game 1. 4.00 1.80 .50
Moe mows down 11
(Moe Drabowsky)
☐ 152 World Series Game 2. 7.50 3.40 .95
Jim Palmer blanks
Dodgers
☐ 153 World Series Game 3. 4.00 1.80 .50
Paul Blair's homer
defeats L.A.
☐ 154 World Series Game 4. 4.00 1.80 .50
Orioles 4 straight
(Brooks Robinson
and Dave McNally)
☐ 155 World Series Summary 4.00 1.80 .50
Winners celebrate
☐ 156 Ron Herbel 2.00 .90 .25
☐ 157 Danny Cater 2.00 .90 .25
☐ 158 Jimmie Coker 2.00 .90 .25
☐ 159 Bruce Howard 2.00 .90 .25
☐ 160 Willie Davis 2.50 1.15 .30
☐ 161 Dick Williams MG 2.50 1.15 .30
☐ 162 Billy O'Dell 2.00 .90 .25
☐ 163 Vic Roznovsky 2.00 .90 .25
☐ 164 Dwight Siebler UER 2.00 .90 .25
(Last line of stats
shows 1960 Minnesota)
☐ 165 Cleon Jones 2.50 1.15 .30
☐ 166 Eddie Mathews 14.00 6.25 1.75
☐ 167 Senators Rookies 2.00 .90 .25
Joe Coleman
Tim Cullen
☐ 168 Ray Culp 2.00 .90 .25
☐ 169 Horace Clarke 2.00 .90 .25
☐ 170 Dick McAuliffe 2.50 1.15 .30
☐ 171 Cal Koonce 2.00 .90 .25
☐ 172 Bill Heath 2.00 .90 .25
☐ 173 St. Louis Cardinals 4.00 1.80 .50
Team Card
☐ 174 Dick Radatz 2.50 1.15 .30
☐ 175 Bobby Knoop 2.00 .90 .25
☐ 176 Sammy Ellis 2.00 .90 .25
☐ 177 Tito Fuentes 2.00 .90 .25
☐ 178 John Buzhardt 2.00 .90 .25
☐ 179 Braves Rookies 2.00 .90 .25
Charles Vaughan
Cecil Upshaw
☐ 180 Curt Blefary 2.00 .90 .25
☐ 181 Terry Fox 2.00 .90 .25
☐ 182 Ed Charles 2.00 .90 .25
☐ 183 Jim Pagliaroni 2.00 .90 .25
☐ 184 George Thomas 2.00 .90 .25
☐ 185 Ken Holtzman 5.50 2.50 .70
☐ 186 Mets Maulers 2.50 1.15 .30
Ed Kranepool
Ron Swoboda
☐ 187 Pedro Ramos 2.00 .90 .25
☐ 188 Ken Harrelson 2.50 1.15 .30
☐ 189 Chuck Hinton 2.00 .90 .25
☐ 190 Turk Farrell 2.00 .90 .25
☐ 191A Checklist 3 8.00 2.40 .80
(214 Tom Kelley)
(Willie Mays)
☐ 191B Checklist 3 12.00 3.60 1.20
(214 Dick Kelley)
(Willie Mays)
☐ 192 Fred Gladding 2.00 .90 .25
☐ 193 Jose Cardenal 2.50 1.15 .30
☐ 194 Bob Allison 2.50 1.15 .30
☐ 195 Al Jackson 2.00 .90 .25
☐ 196 Johnny Romano 2.00 .90 .25
☐ 197 Ron Perranoski 2.50 1.15 .30
☐ 198 Chuck Hiller 2.00 .90 .25
☐ 199 Billy Hitchcock MG 2.00 .90 .25
☐ 200 Willie Mays UER 90.00 40.00 11.50
('63 Sna Francisco
on card back stats)
☐ 201 Hal Reniff 2.00 .90 .25
☐ 202 Johnny Edwards 2.00 .90 .25
☐ 203 Al McBean 2.00 .90 .25
☐ 204 Orioles Rookies 2.50 1.15 .30
Mike Epstein
Tom Phoebus
☐ 205 Dick Groat 2.50 1.15 .30
☐ 206 Dennis Bennett 2.00 .90 .25
☐ 207 John Orsino 2.00 .90 .25
☐ 208 Jack Lamabe 2.00 .90 .25
☐ 209 Joe Nossek 2.00 .90 .25
☐ 210 Bob Gibson 20.00 9.00 2.50
☐ 211 Twins Team 4.00 1.80 .50
☐ 212 Chris Zachary 2.00 .90 .25
☐ 213 Jay Johnstone 4.50 2.00 .55

☐ 214 Dick Kelley .... 2.00 .90 .25
☐ 215 Ernie Banks 20.00 9.00 2.50
☐ 216 Bengal Belters 8.00 3.60 1.00
Norm Cash
Al Kaline
☐ 217 Rob Gardner .... 2.00 .90 .25
☐ 218 Wes Parker .... 2.50 1.15 .30
☐ 219 Clay Carroll .... 2.50 1.15 .30
☐ 220 Jim Ray Hart .... 2.50 1.15 .30
☐ 221 Woodie Fryman .... 2.50 1.15 .30
☐ 222 Reds Rookies .... 2.00 .90 .25
Darrell Osteen
Lee May
☐ 223 Mike Ryan .... 2.00 .90 .25
☐ 224 Walt Bond .... 2.00 .90 .25
☐ 225 Mel Stottlemyre .... 4.00 1.80 .50
☐ 226 Julian Javier .... 2.50 1.15 .30
☐ 227 Paul Lindblad .... 2.00 .90 .25
☐ 228 Gil Hodges MG .... 5.00 2.30 .60
☐ 229 Larry Jackson .... 2.00 .90 .25
☐ 230 Boog Powell .... 5.00 2.30 .60
☐ 231 John Bateman .... 2.00 .90 .25
☐ 232 Don Buford .... 2.00 .90 .25
☐ 233 AL ERA Leaders .... 4.00 1.80 .50
Gary Peters
Joel Horlen
Steve Hargan
☐ 234 NL ERA Leaders 15.00 6.75 1.90
Sandy Koufax
Mike Cuellar
Juan Marichal
☐ 235 AL Pitching Leaders ... 4.50 2.00 .55
Jim Kaat
Denny McLain
Earl Wilson
☐ 236 NL Pitching Leaders. 25.00 11.50 3.10
Sandy Koufax
Juan Marichal
Bob Gibson
Gaylord Perry
☐ 237 AL Strikeout Leaders . 4.50 2.00 .55
Sam McDowell
Jim Kaat
Earl Wilson
☐ 238 NL Strikeout Leaders 12.00 5.50 1.50
Sandy Koufax
Jim Bunning
Bob Veale
☐ 239 AL Batting Leaders 9.00 4.00 1.15
Frank Robinson
Tony Oliva
Al Kaline
☐ 240 NL Batting Leaders .... 4.50 2.00 .55
Matty Alou
Felipe Alou
Rico Carty
☐ 241 AL RBI Leaders 9.00 4.00 1.15
Frank Robinson
Harmon Killebrew
Boog Powell
☐ 242 NL RBI Leaders 18.00 8.00 2.30
Hank Aaron
Bob Clemente
Richie Allen
☐ 243 AL Home Run Leaders 9.00 4.00 1.15
Frank Robinson
Harmon Killebrew
Boog Powell
☐ 244 NL Home Run Leaders 18.00 8.00 2.30
Hank Aaron
Richie Allen
Willie Mays
☐ 245 Curt Flood .... 3.00 1.35 .40
☐ 246 Jim Perry .... 2.50 1.15 .30
☐ 247 Jerry Lumpe .... 2.00 .90 .25
☐ 248 Gene Mauch MG .... 2.50 1.15 .30
☐ 249 Nick Willhite .... 2.00 .90 .25
☐ 250 Hank Aaron UER 85.00 38.00 10.50
(Second 1961 in stats
should be 1962)
☐ 251 Woody Held .... 2.00 .90 .25
☐ 252 Bob Bolin .... 2.00 .90 .25
☐ 253 Indians Rookies .... 2.00 .90 .25
Bill Davis
Gus Gil
☐ 254 Milt Pappas .... 2.50 1.15 .30
(No facsimile auto-
graph on card front)
☐ 255 Frank Howard .... 4.50 2.00 .55
☐ 256 Bob Hendley .... 2.00 .90 .25
☐ 257 Charlie Smith .... 2.00 .90 .25
☐ 258 Lee Maye .... 2.00 .90 .25
☐ 259 Don Dennis .... 2.00 .90 .25
☐ 260 Jim Lefebvre .... 2.50 1.15 .30
☐ 261 John Wyatt .... 2.00 .90 .25
☐ 262 Athletics Team .... 4.00 1.80 .50
☐ 263 Hank Aguirre .... 2.00 .90 .25
☐ 264 Ron Swoboda .... 2.50 1.15 .30
☐ 265 Lou Burdette .... 2.50 1.15 .30
☐ 266 Pitt Power .... 5.00 2.30 .60
Willie Stargell
Donn Clendenon
☐ 267 Don Schwall .... 2.00 .90 .25
☐ 268 Johnny Briggs .... 2.00 .90 .25
☐ 269 Don Nottebart .... 2.00 .90 .25
☐ 270 Zoilo Versalles .... 2.00 .90 .25
☐ 271 Eddie Watt .... 2.00 .90 .25
☐ 272 Cubs Rookies .... 2.00 .90 .25
Bill Connors
Dave Dowling
☐ 273 Dick Lines .... 2.00 .90 .25
☐ 274 Bob Aspromonte .... 2.00 .90 .25
☐ 275 Fred Whitfield .... 2.00 .90 .25
☐ 276 Bruce Brubaker .... 2.00 .90 .25
☐ 277 Steve Whitaker .... 2.00 .90 .25
☐ 278 Checklist 4 .... 7.00 2.10 .70
Jim Kaat
☐ 279 Frank Linzy .... 2.00 .90 .25
☐ 280 Tony Conigliaro 12.00 5.50 1.50
☐ 281 Bob Rodgers .... 2.50 1.15 .30
☐ 282 John Odom .... 2.00 .90 .25
☐ 283 Gene Alley .... 2.50 1.15 .30
☐ 284 Johnny Podres .... 3.00 1.35 .40
☐ 285 Lou Brock 20.00 9.00 2.50
☐ 286 Wayne Causey .... 2.50 1.15 .30
☐ 287 Mets Rookies .... 2.50 1.15 .30
Greg Goossen
Bart Shirley
☐ 288 Denny Lemaster .... 2.50 1.15 .30
☐ 289 Tom Tresh .... 3.00 1.35 .40
☐ 290 Bill White .... 4.00 1.80 .50
☐ 291 Jim Hannan .... 2.50 1.15 .30
☐ 292 Don Pavletich .... 2.50 1.15 .30
☐ 293 Ed Kirkpatrick .... 2.50 1.15 .30
☐ 294 Walt Alston MG .... 4.00 1.80 .50
☐ 295 Sam McDowell .... 3.00 1.35 .40
☐ 296 Glenn Beckert .... 3.00 1.35 .40
☐ 297 Dave Morehead .... 2.50 1.15 .30
☐ 298 Ron Davis .... 2.50 1.15 .30
☐ 299 Norm Siebern .... 2.50 1.15 .30
☐ 300 Jim Kaat .... 6.00 2.70 .75
☐ 301 Jesse Gonder .... 2.50 1.15 .30
☐ 302 Orioles Team .... 6.00 2.70 .75
☐ 303 Gil Blanco .... 2.50 1.15 .30
☐ 304 Phil Gagliano .... 2.50 1.15 .30
☐ 305 Earl Wilson .... 3.00 1.35 .40

☐ 306 Bud Harrelson 6.00 2.70 .75
☐ 307 Jim Beauchamp 2.50 1.15 .30
☐ 308 Al Downing 3.00 1.35 .40
☐ 309 Hurlers Beware 3.00 1.35 .40
Johnny Callison
Richie Allen
☐ 310 Gary Peters 2.50 1.15 .30
☐ 311 Ed Brinkman 2.50 1.15 .30
☐ 312 Don Mincher 2.50 1.15 .30
☐ 313 Bob Lee 2.50 1.15 .30
☐ 314 Red Sox Rookies 9.00 4.00 1.15
Mike Andrews
Reggie Smith
☐ 315 Billy Williams 12.00 5.50 1.50
☐ 316 Jack Kralick 2.50 1.15 .30
☐ 317 Cesar Tovar 3.00 1.35 .40
☐ 318 Dave Giusti 2.50 1.15 .30
☐ 319 Paul Blair 3.00 1.35 .40
☐ 320 Gaylord Perry 14.00 6.25 1.75
☐ 321 Mayo Smith MG 2.50 1.15 .30
☐ 322 Jose Pagan 2.50 1.15 .30
☐ 323 Mike Hershberger 2.50 1.15 .30
☐ 324 Hal Woodeshick 2.50 1.15 .30
☐ 325 Chico Cardenas 3.00 1.35 .40
☐ 326 Bob Uecker 10.00 4.50 1.25
☐ 327 California Angels 6.00 2.70 .75
Team Card
☐ 328 Clete Boyer UER 3.00 1.35 .40
(Stats only go up
through 1965)
☐ 329 Charlie Lau 3.00 1.35 .40
☐ 330 Claude Osteen 3.00 1.35 .40
☐ 331 Joe Foy 3.00 1.35 .40
☐ 332 Jesus Alou 2.50 1.15 .30
☐ 333 Fergie Jenkins 24.00 11.00 3.00
☐ 334 Twin Terrors 6.50 2.90 .80
Bob Allison
Harmon Killebrew
☐ 335 Bob Veale 3.00 1.35 .40
☐ 336 Joe Azcue 2.50 1.15 .30
☐ 337 Joe Morgan 14.00 6.25 1.75
☐ 338 Bob Locker 2.50 1.15 .30
☐ 339 Chico Ruiz 2.50 1.15 .30
☐ 340 Joe Pepitone 3.00 1.35 .40
☐ 341 Giants Rookies 2.50 1.15 .30
Dick Dietz
Bill Sorrell
☐ 342 Hank Fischer 2.50 1.15 .30
☐ 343 Tom Satriano 2.50 1.15 .30
☐ 344 Ossie Chavarria 2.50 1.15 .30
☐ 345 Stu Miller 3.00 1.35 .40
☐ 346 Jim Hickman 2.50 1.15 .30
☐ 347 Grady Hatton MG 2.50 1.15 .30
☐ 348 Tug McGraw 5.00 2.30 .60
☐ 349 Bob Chance 2.50 1.15 .30
☐ 350 Joe Torre 5.00 2.30 .60
☐ 351 Vern Law 3.00 1.35 .40
☐ 352 Ray Oyler 2.50 1.15 .30
☐ 353 Bill McCool 2.50 1.15 .30
☐ 354 Cubs Team 6.00 2.70 .75
☐ 355 Carl Yastrzemski 45.00 20.00 5.75
☐ 356 Larry Jaster 2.50 1.15 .30
☐ 357 Bill Skowron 3.00 1.35 .40
☐ 358 Ruben Amaro 2.50 1.15 .30
☐ 359 Dick Ellsworth 2.50 1.15 .30
☐ 360 Leon Wagner 2.50 1.15 .30
☐ 361 Checklist 5 10.00 3.00 1.00
Roberto Clemente
☐ 362 Darold Knowles 2.50 1.15 .30
☐ 363 Dave Johnson 3.00 1.35 .40
☐ 364 Claude Raymond 2.50 1.15 .30
☐ 365 John Roseboro 3.00 1.35 .40
☐ 366 Andy Kosco 2.50 1.15 .30
☐ 367 Angels Rookies 2.50 1.15 .30
Bill Kelso
Don Wallace
☐ 368 Jack Hiatt 2.50 1.15 .30
☐ 369 Jim Hunter 18.00 8.00 2.30
☐ 370 Tommy Davis 3.00 1.35 .40
☐ 371 Jim Lonborg 6.50 2.90 .80
☐ 372 Mike de la Hoz 4.00 1.80 .50
☐ 373 White Sox Rookies DP 4.00 1.80 .50
Duane Josephson
Fred Klages
☐ 374A Mel Queen ERR DP 4.00 1.80 .50
(Incomplete stat
line on back)
☐ 374B Mel Queen COR DP 4.00 1.80 .50
(Complete stat
line on back)
☐ 375 Jake Gibbs 4.00 1.80 .50
☐ 376 Don Lock DP 4.00 1.80 .50
☐ 377 Luis Tiant 7.50 3.40 .95
☐ 378 Detroit Tigers 8.00 3.60 1.00
Team Card UER
(Willie Horton with
262 RBI's in 1966)
☐ 379 Jerry May DP 4.00 1.80 .50
☐ 380 Dean Chance DP 4.00 1.80 .50
☐ 381 Dick Schofield DP 4.00 1.80 .50
☐ 382 Dave McNally 4.50 2.00 .55
☐ 383 Ken Henderson DP 4.00 1.80 .50
☐ 384 Cardinals Rookies 4.00 1.80 .50
Jim Cosman
Dick Hughes
☐ 385 Jim Fregosi 4.50 2.00 .55
(Batting wrong)
☐ 386 Dick Selma DP 4.00 1.80 .50
☐ 387 Cap Peterson DP 4.00 1.80 .50
☐ 388 Arnold Earley DP 4.00 1.80 .50
☐ 389 Alvin Dark MG DP 4.50 2.00 .55
☐ 390 Jim Wynn DP 4.50 2.00 .55
☐ 391 Wilbur Wood DP 4.50 2.00 .55
☐ 392 Tommy Harper DP 4.50 2.00 .55
☐ 393 Jim Bouton DP 4.50 2.00 .55
☐ 394 Jake Wood DP 4.00 1.80 .50
☐ 395 Chris Short 4.50 2.00 .55
☐ 396 Atlanta Aces 4.00 1.80 .50
Denis Menke
Tony Cloninger
☐ 397 Willie Smith DP 4.00 1.80 .50
☐ 398 Jeff Torborg 4.50 2.00 .55
☐ 399 Al Worthington DP 4.00 1.80 .50
☐ 400 Bob Clemente DP 70.00 32.00 8.75
☐ 401 Jim Coates 4.00 1.80 .50
☐ 402 Phillies Rookies DP 4.50 2.00 .55
Grant Jackson
Billy Wilson
☐ 403 Dick Nen 4.00 1.80 .50
☐ 404 Nelson Briles 4.50 2.00 .55
☐ 405 Russ Snyder 4.00 1.80 .50
☐ 406 Lee Elia DP 4.00 1.80 .50
☐ 407 Reds Team 8.00 3.60 1.00
☐ 408 Jim Northrup DP 4.50 2.00 .55
☐ 409 Ray Sadecki 4.00 1.80 .50
☐ 410 Lou Johnson DP 4.00 1.80 .50
☐ 411 Dick Howser DP 4.50 2.00 .55
☐ 412 Astros Rookies 5.00 2.30 .60
Norm Miller
Doug Rader
☐ 413 Jerry Grote 4.00 1.80 .50
☐ 414 Casey Cox 4.00 1.80 .50
☐ 415 Sonny Jackson 4.00 1.80 .50
☐ 416 Roger Repoz 4.00 1.80 .50
☐ 417A Bob Bruce ERR DP 30.00 13.50 3.80
(RBAVES on back)

☐ 417B Bob Bruce COR DP .. 4.00 1.80 .50
☐ 418 Sam Mele MG .... 4.00 1.80 .50
☐ 419 Don Kessinger DP ...... 4.50 2.00 .55
☐ 420 Denny McLain .... 7.50 3.40 .95
☐ 421 Dal Maxvill DP .... 4.00 1.80 .50
☐ 422 Hoyt Wilhelm 8.00 3.60 1.00
☐ 423 Fence Busters DP 25.00 11.50 3.10
Willie Mays
Willie McCovey
☐ 424 Pedro Gonzalez .... 4.00 1.80 .50
☐ 425 Pete Mikkelsen .... 4.00 1.80 .50
☐ 426 Lou Clinton .... 4.00 1.80 .50
☐ 427A Ruben Gomez ERR DP 4.00 1.80 .50
(Incomplete stat
line on back)
☐ 427B Ruben Gomez COR DP 4.00 1.80 .50
(Complete stat
line on back)
☐ 428 Dodgers Rookies DP .. 5.00 2.30 .60
Tom Hutton
Gene Michael
☐ 429 Garry Roggenburk DP 4.00 1.80 .50
☐ 430 Pete Rose 75.00 34.00 9.50
☐ 431 Ted Uhlaender .... 4.00 1.80 .50
☐ 432 Jimmie Hall DP .... 4.00 1.80 .50
☐ 433 Al Luplow DP .... 4.00 1.80 .50
☐ 434 Eddie Fisher DP .... 4.00 1.80 .50
☐ 435 Mack Jones DP .... 4.00 1.80 .50
☐ 436 Pete Ward .... 4.00 1.80 .50
☐ 437 Senators Team 8.00 3.60 1.00
☐ 438 Chuck Dobson .... 4.00 1.80 .50
☐ 439 Byron Browne .... 4.00 1.80 .50
☐ 440 Steve Hargan .... 4.00 1.80 .50
☐ 441 Jim Davenport .... 4.00 1.80 .50
☐ 442 Yankees Rookies DP .. 4.00 1.80 .50
Bill Robinson
Joe Verbanic
☐ 443 Tito Francona DP .... 4.00 1.80 .50
☐ 444 George Smith .... 4.00 1.80 .50
☐ 445 Don Sutton 25.00 11.50 3.10
☐ 446 Russ Nixon DP .... 4.00 1.80 .50
☐ 447A Bo Belinsky ERR DP 4.50 2.00 .55
(Incomplete stat
line on back)
☐ 447B Bo Belinsky COR DP 4.50 2.00 .55
(Complete stat
line on back)
☐ 448 Harry Walker DP MG .. 4.00 1.80 .50
☐ 449 Orlando Pena .... 4.00 1.80 .50
☐ 450 Richie Allen 8.00 3.60 1.00
☐ 451 Fred Newman DP .... 4.00 1.80 .50
☐ 452 Ed Kranepool .... 4.50 2.00 .55
☐ 453 Aurelio Monteagudo DP 4.00 1.80 .50
☐ 454A Checklist 6 DP .... 8.00 2.40 .80
Juan Marichal
(Missing left ear)
☐ 454B Checklist 6 DP .... 8.00 2.40 .80
Juan Marichal
(left ear showing)
☐ 455 Tommie Agee .... 4.50 2.00 .55
☐ 456 Phil Niekro 15.00 6.75 1.90
☐ 457 Andy Etchebarren DP. 4.50 2.00 .55
☐ 458 Lee Thomas .... 7.00 3.10 .85
☐ 459 Senators Rookies .... 6.00 2.70 .75
Dick Bosman
Pete Craig
☐ 460 Harmon Killebrew 50.00 23.00 6.25
☐ 461 Bob Miller .... 6.00 2.70 .75
☐ 462 Bob Barton .... 6.00 2.70 .75
☐ 463 Hill Aces .... 7.00 3.10 .85
Sam McDowell
Sonny Siebert
☐ 464 Dan Coombs .... 6.00 2.70 .75
☐ 465 Willie Horton .... 7.00 3.10 .85
☐ 466 Bobby Wine .... 6.00 2.70 .75
☐ 467 Jim O'Toole .... 7.00 3.10 .85
☐ 468 Ralph Houk MG .... 7.00 3.10 .85
☐ 469 Len Gabrielson .... 6.00 2.70 .75
☐ 470 Bob Shaw .... 6.00 2.70 .75
☐ 471 Rene Lachemann ...... 7.00 3.10 .85
☐ 472 Rookies Pirates .... 6.00 2.70 .75
John Gelnar
George Spriggs
☐ 473 Jose Santiago .... 7.00 3.10 .85
☐ 474 Bob Tolan .... 7.00 3.10 .85
☐ 475 Jim Palmer 100.00 45.00 12.50
☐ 476 Tony Perez SP 70.00 32.00 8.75
☐ 477 Braves Team 15.00 6.75 1.90
☐ 478 Bob Humphreys .... 6.00 2.70 .75
☐ 479 Gary Bell .... 6.00 2.70 .75
☐ 480 Willie McCovey 38.00 17.00 4.70
☐ 481 Leo Durocher MG 15.00 6.75 1.90
☐ 482 Bill Monbouquette ...... 6.00 2.70 .75
☐ 483 Jim Landis .... 6.00 2.70 .75
☐ 484 Jerry Adair .... 6.00 2.70 .75
☐ 485 Tim McCarver 24.00 11.00 3.00
☐ 486 Twins Rookies .... 6.00 2.70 .75
Rich Reese
Bill Whitby
☐ 487 Tommie Reynolds ...... 6.00 2.70 .75
☐ 488 Gerry Arrigo .... 6.00 2.70 .75
☐ 489 Doug Clemens .... 6.00 2.70 .75
☐ 490 Tony Cloninger .... 6.00 2.70 .75
☐ 491 Sam Bowens .... 6.00 2.70 .75
☐ 492 Pittsburgh Pirates 15.00 6.75 1.90
Team Card
☐ 493 Phil Ortega .... 6.00 2.70 .75
☐ 494 Bill Rigney MG .... 6.00 2.70 .75
☐ 495 Fritz Peterson .... 6.00 2.70 .75
☐ 496 Orlando McFarlane ..... 6.00 2.70 .75
☐ 497 Ron Campbell .... 6.00 2.70 .75
☐ 498 Larry Dierker .... 6.00 2.70 .75
☐ 499 Indians Rookies .... 6.00 2.70 .75
George Culver
Jose Vidal
☐ 500 Juan Marichal 25.00 11.50 3.10
☐ 501 Jerry Zimmerman ...... 6.00 2.70 .75
☐ 502 Derrell Griffith .... 6.00 2.70 .75
☐ 503 Los Angeles Dodgers 15.00 6.75 1.90
Team Card
☐ 504 Orlando Martinez .... 6.00 2.70 .75
☐ 505 Tommy Helms 8.00 3.60 1.00
☐ 506 Smoky Burgess .... 7.00 3.10 .85
☐ 507 Orioles Rookies .... 6.00 2.70 .75
Ed Barnowski
Larry Haney
☐ 508 Dick Hall .... 6.00 2.70 .75
☐ 509 Jim King .... 6.00 2.70 .75
☐ 510 Bill Mazeroski 12.00 5.50 1.50
☐ 511 Don Wert .... 6.00 2.70 .75
☐ 512 Red Schoendienst MG 12.00 5.50 1.50
☐ 513 Marcelino Lopez .... 6.00 2.70 .75
☐ 514 John Werhas .... 6.00 2.70 .75
☐ 515 Bert Campaneris 9.00 4.00 1.15
☐ 516 Giants Team 15.00 6.75 1.90
☐ 517 Fred Talbot .... 6.00 2.70 .75
☐ 518 Denis Menke .... 6.00 2.70 .75
☐ 519 Ted Davidson .... 6.00 2.70 .75
☐ 520 Max Alvis .... 6.00 2.70 .75
☐ 521 Bird Bombers .... 7.00 3.10 .85
Boog Powell
Curt Blefary
☐ 522 John Stephenson .... 6.00 2.70 .75
☐ 523 Jim Merritt .... 6.00 2.70 .75
☐ 524 Felix Mantilla .... 6.00 2.70 .75
☐ 525 Ron Hunt .... 6.00 2.70 .75

☐ 526 Tigers Rookies........... 6.00 2.70 .75
Pat Dobson
George Korince
(See 67T-72)
☐ 527 Dennis Ribant............ 6.00 2.70 .75
☐ 528 Rico Petrocelli.......... 10.00 4.50 1.25
☐ 529 Gary Wagner.............. 6.00 2.70 .75
☐ 530 Felipe Alou............... 12.00 5.50 1.50
☐ 531 Checklist 7.............. 12.00 3.60 1.20
Brooks Robinson
☐ 532 Jim Hicks.................. 6.00 2.70 .75
☐ 533 Jack Fisher................ 6.00 2.70 .75
☐ 534 Hank Bauer MG DP.... 9.00 4.00 1.15
☐ 535 Donn Clendenon...... 18.00 8.00 2.30
☐ 536 Cubs Rookies........... 35.00 16.00 4.40
Joe Niekro
Paul Popovich
☐ 537 Chuck Estrada DP...... 9.00 4.00 1.15
☐ 538 J.C. Martin............... 15.00 6.75 1.90
☐ 539 Dick Egan DP............ 9.00 4.00 1.15
☐ 540 Norm Cash............... 40.00 18.00 5.00
☐ 541 Joe Gibbon............... 15.00 6.75 1.90
☐ 542 Athletics Rookies DP 15.00 6.75 1.90
Rick Monday
Tony Pierce
☐ 543 Dan Schneider......... 15.00 6.75 1.90
☐ 544 Cleveland Indians..... 30.00 13.50 3.80
Team Card
☐ 545 Jim Grant................. 15.00 6.75 1.90
☐ 546 Woody Woodward... 18.00 8.00 2.30
☐ 547 Red Sox Rookies DP 12.00 5.50 1.50
Russ Gibson
Bill Rohr
☐ 548 Tony Gonzalez DP...... 9.00 4.00 1.15
☐ 549 Jack Sanford............ 15.00 6.75 1.90
☐ 550 Vada Pinson DP....... 12.00 5.50 1.50
☐ 551 Doug Camilli DP......... 9.00 4.00 1.15
☐ 552 Ted Savage.............. 15.00 6.75 1.90
☐ 553 Yankees Rookies...... 25.00 11.50 3.10
Mike Hegan
Thad Tillotson
☐ 554 Andre Rodgers DP..... 9.00 4.00 1.15
☐ 555 Don Cardwell........... 15.00 6.75 1.90
☐ 556 Al Weis DP................ 9.00 4.00 1.15
☐ 557 Al Ferrara................ 15.00 6.75 1.90
☐ 558 Orioles Rookies........ 50.00 23.00 6.25
Mark Belanger
Bill Dillman
☐ 559 Dick Tracewski DP..... 9.00 4.00 1.15
☐ 560 Jim Bunning............ 50.00 23.00 6.25
☐ 561 Sandy Alomar.......... 18.00 8.00 2.30
☐ 562 Steve Blass DP......... 12.00 5.50 1.50
☐ 563 Joe Adcock............. 20.00 9.00 2.50
☐ 564 Astros Rookies DP... 12.00 5.50 1.50
Alonzo Harris
Aaron Pointer
☐ 565 Lew Krausse............ 15.00 6.75 1.90
☐ 566 Gary Geiger DP.......... 9.00 4.00 1.15
☐ 567 Steve Hamilton........ 15.00 6.75 1.90
☐ 568 John Sullivan........... 15.00 6.75 1.90
☐ 569 AL Rookies DP....... 250.00 115.00 31.00
Rod Carew
Hank Allen
☐ 570 Maury Wills............. 85.00 38.00 10.50
☐ 571 Larry Sherry............ 15.00 6.75 1.90
☐ 572 Don Demeter............ 15.00 6.75 1.90
☐ 573 Chicago White Sox... 30.00 13.50 3.80
Team Card UER
(Indians team
stats on back)
☐ 574 Jerry Buchek............ 15.00 6.75 1.90
☐ 575 Dave Boswell........... 15.00 6.75 1.90
☐ 576 NL Rookies.............. 15.00 6.75 1.90
Ramon Hernandez
Norm Gigon
☐ 577 Bill Short.................. 15.00 6.75 1.90
☐ 578 John Boccabella....... 15.00 6.75 1.90
☐ 579 Bill Henry................ 15.00 6.75 1.90
☐ 580 Rocky Colavito......... 85.00 38.00 10.50
☐ 581 Mets Rookies......... 800.00 350.00 100.00
Bill Denehy
Tom Seaver
☐ 582 Jim Owens DP........... 9.00 4.00 1.15
☐ 583 Ray Barker............... 15.00 6.75 1.90
☐ 584 Jim Piersall............. 25.00 11.50 3.10
☐ 585 Wally Bunker........... 15.00 6.75 1.90
☐ 586 Manny Jimenez........ 15.00 6.75 1.90
☐ 587 NL Rookies.............. 25.00 11.50 3.10
Don Shaw
Gary Sutherland
☐ 588 Johnny Klippstein DP. 9.00 4.00 1.15
☐ 589 Dave Ricketts DP....... 9.00 4.00 1.15
☐ 590 Pete Richert............ 15.00 6.75 1.90
☐ 591 Ty Cline................... 15.00 6.75 1.90
☐ 592 NL Rookies.............. 15.00 6.75 1.90
Jim Shellenback
Ron Willis
☐ 593 Wes Westrum MG... 18.00 8.00 2.30
☐ 594 Dan Osinski............. 18.00 8.00 2.30
☐ 595 Cookie Rojas........... 18.00 8.00 2.30
☐ 596 Galen Cisco DP........ 12.00 5.50 1.50
☐ 597 Ted Abernathy.......... 15.00 6.75 1.90
☐ 598 White Sox Rookies... 18.00 8.00 2.30
Walt Williams
Ed Stroud
☐ 599 Bob Duliba DP........... 9.00 4.00 1.15
☐ 600 Brooks Robinson... 250.00 115.00 31.00
☐ 601 Bill Bryan DP............. 9.00 4.00 1.15
☐ 602 Juan Pizarro............ 15.00 6.75 1.90
☐ 603 Athletics Rookies..... 15.00 6.75 1.90
Tim Talton
Ramon Webster
☐ 604 Red Sox Team....... 100.00 45.00 12.50
☐ 605 Mike Shannon.......... 50.00 23.00 6.25
☐ 606 Ron Taylor............... 15.00 6.75 1.90
☐ 607 Mickey Stanley......... 35.00 16.00 4.40
☐ 608 Cubs Rookies DP....... 9.00 4.00 1.15
Rich Nye
John Upham
☐ 609 Tommy John............ 70.00 17.50 5.50

1968 Topps

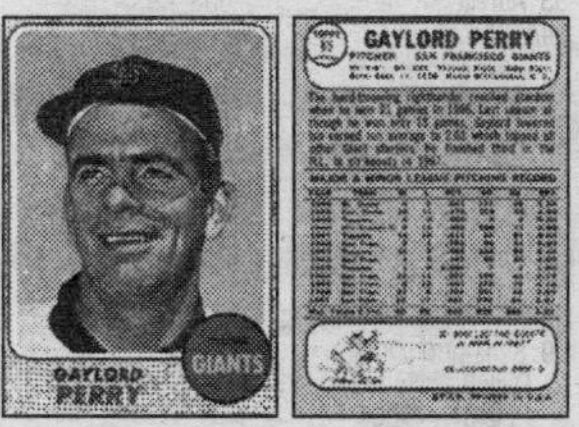

The cards in this 598-card set measure 2 1/2" by 3 1/2". The 1968 Topps set includes Sporting News All-Star Selections as card numbers 361 to 380. Other subsets in the set include League Leaders (1-12)

and World Series cards (151-158). The front of each checklist card features a picture of a popular player inside a circle. High numbers 534 to 598 are slightly more difficult to obtain. The first series looks different from the other series, as it has a lighter, wider mesh background on the card front. The later series all had a much darker, finer mesh pattern. Key cards in the set are the Rookie Cards of Johnny Bench (247) and Nolan Ryan (177).

	NRMT	EXC	G-VG
COMPLETE SET (598)	3000.00	1350.00	375.00
COMMON CARD (1-109)	1.75	.80	.22
COMMON CARD (110-196)	1.75	.80	.22
COMMON CARD (197-283)	1.75	.80	.22
COMMON CARD (284-370)	1.75	.80	.22
COMMON CARD (371-457)	1.75	.80	.22
COMMON CARD (458-533)	3.00	1.35	.40
COMMON CARD (534-598)	4.00	1.80	.50

	NRMT	EXC	G-VG
☐ 1 NL Batting Leaders Bob Clemente Tony Gonzalez Matty Alou	20.00	6.00	1.60
☐ 2 AL Batting Leaders Carl Yastrzemski Frank Robinson Al Kaline	12.50	5.75	1.55
☐ 3 NL RBI Leaders Orlando Cepeda Bob Clemente Hank Aaron	14.00	6.25	1.75
☐ 4 AL RBI Leaders Carl Yastrzemski Harmon Killebrew Frank Robinson	11.00	4.90	1.40
☐ 5 NL Home Run Leaders Hank Aaron Jim Wynn Ron Santo Willie McCovey	8.00	3.60	1.00
☐ 6 AL Home Run Leaders Carl Yastrzemski Harmon Killebrew Frank Howard	8.00	3.60	1.00
☐ 7 NL ERA Leaders Phil Niekro Jim Bunning Chris Short	4.00	1.80	.50
☐ 8 AL ERA Leaders Joel Horlen Gary Peters Sonny Siebert	3.50	1.55	.45
☐ 9 NL Pitching Leaders Mike McCormick Ferguson Jenkins Jim Bunning Claude Osteen	4.00	1.80	.50
☐ 10A AL Pitching Leaders Jim Lonborg ERR (Misspelled Lonberg on card back) Earl Wilson Dean Chance	4.00	1.80	.50
☐ 10B AL Pitching Leaders Jim Lonborg COR Earl Wilson Dean Chance	4.00	1.80	.50
☐ 11 NL Strikeout Leaders Jim Bunning Ferguson Jenkins Gaylord Perry	4.50	2.00	.55
☐ 12 AL Strikeout Leaders Jim Lonborg UER (Misspelled Longberg on card back) Sam McDowell Dean Chance	3.50	1.55	.45
☐ 13 Chuck Hartenstein	1.75	.80	.22
☐ 14 Jerry McNertney	1.75	.80	.22
☐ 15 Ron Hunt	1.75	.80	.22
☐ 16 Indians Rookies Lou Piniella Richie Scheinblum	5.00	2.30	.60
☐ 17 Dick Hall	1.75	.80	.22
☐ 18 Mike Hershberger	1.75	.80	.22
☐ 19 Juan Pizarro	1.75	.80	.22
☐ 20 Brooks Robinson	25.00	11.50	3.10
☐ 21 Ron Davis	1.75	.80	.22
☐ 22 Pat Dobson	2.25	1.00	.30
☐ 23 Chico Cardenas	2.25	1.00	.30
☐ 24 Bobby Locke	1.75	.80	.22
☐ 25 Julian Javier	2.25	1.00	.30
☐ 26 Darrell Brandon	1.75	.80	.22
☐ 27 Gil Hodges MG	8.00	3.60	1.00
☐ 28 Ted Uhlaender	1.75	.80	.22
☐ 29 Joe Verbanic	1.75	.80	.22
☐ 30 Joe Torre	4.00	1.80	.50
☐ 31 Ed Stroud	1.75	.80	.22
☐ 32 Joe Gibbon	1.75	.80	.22
☐ 33 Pete Ward	1.75	.80	.22
☐ 34 Al Ferrara	1.75	.80	.22
☐ 35 Steve Hargan	1.75	.80	.22
☐ 36 Pirates Rookies Bob Moose Bob Robertson	2.25	1.00	.30
☐ 37 Billy Williams	10.00	4.50	1.25
☐ 38 Tony Pierce	1.75	.80	.22
☐ 39 Cookie Rojas	2.25	1.00	.30
☐ 40 Denny McLain	10.00	4.50	1.25
☐ 41 Julio Gotay	1.75	.80	.22
☐ 42 Larry Haney	1.75	.80	.22
☐ 43 Gary Bell	1.75	.80	.22
☐ 44 Frank Kostro	1.75	.80	.22
☐ 45 Tom Seaver	75.00	34.00	9.50
☐ 46 Dave Ricketts	1.75	.80	.22
☐ 47 Ralph Houk MG	2.25	1.00	.30
☐ 48 Ted Davidson	1.75	.80	.22
☐ 49A Eddie Brinkman (White team name)	1.75	.80	.22
☐ 49B Eddie Brinkman (Yellow team name)	50.00	23.00	6.25
☐ 50 Willie Mays	75.00	34.00	9.50
☐ 51 Bob Locker	1.75	.80	.22
☐ 52 Hawk Taylor	1.75	.80	.22
☐ 53 Gene Alley	2.25	1.00	.30
☐ 54 Stan Williams	2.25	1.00	.30
☐ 55 Felipe Alou	2.50	1.15	.30
☐ 56 Orioles Rookies Dave Leonhard Dave May	1.75	.80	.22
☐ 57 Dan Schneider	1.75	.80	.22
☐ 58 Eddie Mathews	14.00	6.25	1.75
☐ 59 Don Lock	1.75	.80	.22
☐ 60 Ken Holtzman	2.25	1.00	.30
☐ 61 Reggie Smith	3.00	1.35	.40
☐ 62 Chuck Dobson	1.75	.80	.22
☐ 63 Dick Kenworthy	1.75	.80	.22
☐ 64 Jim Merritt	1.75	.80	.22
☐ 65 John Roseboro	2.25	1.00	.30
☐ 66A Casey Cox (White team name)	1.75	.80	.22
☐ 66B Casey Cox (Yellow team name)	110.00	50.00	14.00

☐ 67 Checklist 1 .... 6.00 1.50 .50
Jim Kaat
☐ 68 Ron Willis .... 1.75 .80 .22
☐ 69 Tom Tresh .... 2.25 1.00 .30
☐ 70 Bob Veale .... 2.25 1.00 .30
☐ 71 Vern Fuller .... 1.75 .80 .22
☐ 72 Tommy John .... 5.00 2.30 .60
☐ 73 Jim Ray Hart .... 2.25 1.00 .30
☐ 74 Milt Pappas .... 2.25 1.00 .30
☐ 75 Don Mincher .... 1.75 .80 .22
☐ 76 Braves Rookies .... 2.25 1.00 .30
Jim Britton
Ron Reed
☐ 77 Don Wilson .... 2.25 1.00 .30
☐ 78 Jim Northrup .... 2.50 1.15 .30
☐ 79 Ted Kubiak .... 1.75 .80 .22
☐ 80 Rod Carew 70.00 32.00 8.75
☐ 81 Larry Jackson .... 1.75 .80 .22
☐ 82 Sam Bowens .... 1.75 .80 .22
☐ 83 John Stephenson .... 1.75 .80 .22
☐ 84 Bob Tolan .... 2.25 1.00 .30
☐ 85 Gaylord Perry 8.00 3.60 1.00
☐ 86 Willie Stargell 12.00 5.50 1.50
☐ 87 Dick Williams MG .... 2.25 1.00 .30
☐ 88 Phil Regan .... 2.25 1.00 .30
☐ 89 Jake Gibbs .... 1.75 .80 .22
☐ 90 Vada Pinson .... 2.50 1.15 .30
☐ 91 Jim Ollom .... 1.75 .80 .22
☐ 92 Ed Kranepool .... 2.25 1.00 .30
☐ 93 Tony Cloninger .... 1.75 .80 .22
☐ 94 Lee Maye .... 1.75 .80 .22
☐ 95 Bob Aspromonte .... 1.75 .80 .22
☐ 96 Senator Rookies .... 1.75 .80 .22
Frank Coggins
Dick Nold
☐ 97 Tom Phoebus .... 1.75 .80 .22
☐ 98 Gary Sutherland .... 1.75 .80 .22
☐ 99 Rocky Colavito .... 5.00 2.30 .60
☐ 100 Bob Gibson 25.00 11.50 3.10
☐ 101 Glenn Beckert .... 2.25 1.00 .30
☐ 102 Jose Cardenal .... 2.25 1.00 .30
☐ 103 Don Sutton 10.00 4.50 1.25
☐ 104 Dick Dietz .... 1.75 .80 .22
☐ 105 Al Downing .... 2.25 1.00 .30
☐ 106 Dalton Jones .... 1.75 .80 .22
☐ 107A Checklist 2 .... 6.00 1.50 .50
Juan Marichal
(Tan wide mesh)
☐ 107B Checklist 2 .... 6.00 1.50 .50
Juan Marichal
(Brown fine mesh)
☐ 108 Don Pavletich .... 1.75 .80 .22
☐ 109 Bert Campaneris .... 2.25 1.00 .30
☐ 110 Hank Aaron 75.00 34.00 9.50
☐ 111 Rich Reese .... 1.75 .80 .22
☐ 112 Woodie Fryman .... 1.75 .80 .22
☐ 113 Tigers Rookies .... 1.75 .80 .22
Tom Matchick
Daryl Patterson
☐ 114 Ron Swoboda .... 2.25 1.00 .30
☐ 115 Sam McDowell .... 2.25 1.00 .30
☐ 116 Ken McMullen .... 1.75 .80 .22
☐ 117 Larry Jaster .... 1.75 .80 .22
☐ 118 Mark Belanger .... 2.25 1.00 .30
☐ 119 Ted Savage .... 1.75 .80 .22
☐ 120 Mel Stottlemyre .... 3.00 1.35 .40
☐ 121 Jimmie Hall .... 1.75 .80 .22
☐ 122 Gene Mauch MG .... 2.25 1.00 .30
☐ 123 Jose Santiago .... 1.75 .80 .22
☐ 124 Nate Oliver .... 1.75 .80 .22
☐ 125 Joel Horlen .... 1.75 .80 .22
☐ 126 Bobby Etheridge .... 1.75 .80 .22
☐ 127 Paul Lindblad .... 1.75 .80 .22
☐ 128 Astros Rookies .... 1.75 .80 .22
Tom Dukes
Alonzo Harris
☐ 129 Mickey Stanley .... 3.50 1.55 .45
☐ 130 Tony Perez 10.00 4.50 1.25
☐ 131 Frank Bertaina .... 1.75 .80 .22
☐ 132 Bud Harrelson .... 2.25 1.00 .30
☐ 133 Fred Whitfield .... 1.75 .80 .22
☐ 134 Pat Jarvis .... 1.75 .80 .22
☐ 135 Paul Blair .... 2.25 1.00 .30
☐ 136 Randy Hundley .... 2.25 1.00 .30
☐ 137 Twins Team .... 3.00 1.35 .40
☐ 138 Ruben Amaro .... 1.75 .80 .22
☐ 139 Chris Short .... 1.75 .80 .22
☐ 140 Tony Conigliaro 8.00 3.60 1.00
☐ 141 Dal Maxvill .... 1.75 .80 .22
☐ 142 White Sox Rookies .... 1.75 .80 .22
Buddy Bradford
Bill Voss
☐ 143 Pete Cimino .... 1.75 .80 .22
☐ 144 Joe Morgan 12.00 5.50 1.50
☐ 145 Don Drysdale 12.00 5.50 1.50
☐ 146 Sal Bando .... 2.25 1.00 .30
☐ 147 Frank Linzy .... 1.75 .80 .22
☐ 148 Dave Bristol MG .... 1.75 .80 .22
☐ 149 Bob Saverine .... 1.75 .80 .22
☐ 150 Bob Clemente 55.00 25.00 7.00
☐ 151 World Series Game 1 10.00 4.50 1.25
Lou Brock socks 4
hits in opener
☐ 152 World Series Game 2 10.00 4.50 1.25
Carl Yastrzemski
smashes 2 homers
☐ 153 World Series Game 3. 4.50 2.00 .55
Nellie Briles
cools Boston
☐ 154 World Series Game 4. 8.00 3.60 1.00
Bob Gibson hurls
shutout
☐ 155 World Series Game 5. 4.50 2.00 .55
Jim Lonborg wins
again
☐ 156 World Series Game 6. 4.50 2.00 .55
Rico Petrocelli
two homers
☐ 157 World Series Game 7. 4.50 2.00 .55
St. Louis wins it
☐ 158 World Series Summary 4.50 2.00 .55
Cardinals celebrate
☐ 159 Don Kessinger .... 2.25 1.00 .30
☐ 160 Earl Wilson .... 2.25 1.00 .30
☐ 161 Norm Miller .... 1.75 .80 .22
☐ 162 Cards Rookies .... 2.25 1.00 .30
Hal Gilson
Mike Torrez
☐ 163 Gene Brabender .... 1.75 .80 .22
☐ 164 Ramon Webster .... 1.75 .80 .22
☐ 165 Tony Oliva .... 4.00 1.80 .50
☐ 166 Claude Raymond .... 1.75 .80 .22
☐ 167 Elston Howard .... 3.00 1.35 .40
☐ 168 Dodgers Team .... 3.00 1.35 .40
☐ 169 Bob Bolin .... 1.75 .80 .22
☐ 170 Jim Fregosi .... 2.25 1.00 .30
☐ 171 Don Nottebart .... 1.75 .80 .22
☐ 172 Walt Williams .... 1.75 .80 .22
☐ 173 John Boozer .... 1.75 .80 .22
☐ 174 Bob Tillman .... 1.75 .80 .22
☐ 175 Maury Wills .... 5.00 2.30 .60
☐ 176 Bob Allen .... 1.75 .80 .22
☐ 177 Mets Rookies 1200.00 550.00 150.00
Jerry Koosman
Nolan Ryan
☐ 178 Don Wert .... 2.25 1.00 .30

☐ 179 Bill Stoneman .... 1.75 .80 .22
☐ 180 Curt Flood .... 2.75 1.25 .35
☐ 181 Jerry Zimmerman ...... 1.75 .80 .22
☐ 182 Dave Giusti .... 1.75 .80 .22
☐ 183 Bob Kennedy MG .... 2.25 1.00 .30
☐ 184 Lou Johnson .... 2.25 1.00 .30
☐ 185 Tom Haller .... 1.75 .80 .22
☐ 186 Eddie Watt .... 1.75 .80 .22
☐ 187 Sonny Jackson .... 1.75 .80 .22
☐ 188 Cap Peterson .... 1.75 .80 .22
☐ 189 Bill Landis .... 1.75 .80 .22
☐ 190 Bill White .... 2.50 1.15 .30
☐ 191 Dan Frisella .... 1.75 .80 .22
☐ 192A Checklist 3 .... 7.50 1.90 .60
Carl Yastrzemski
(Special Baseball
Playing Card)
☐ 192B Checklist 3 .... 7.50 1.90 .60
Carl Yastrzemski
(Special Baseball
Playing Card Game)
☐ 193 Jack Hamilton .... 1.75 .80 .22
☐ 194 Don Buford .... 1.75 .80 .22
☐ 195 Joe Pepitone .... 2.25 1.00 .30
☐ 196 Gary Nolan .... 2.25 1.00 .30
☐ 197 Larry Brown .... 1.75 .80 .22
☐ 198 Roy Face .... 2.25 1.00 .30
☐ 199 A's Rookies .... 1.75 .80 .22
Roberto Rodriquez
Darrell Osteen
☐ 200 Orlando Cepeda .... 5.00 2.30 .60
☐ 201 Mike Marshall .... 6.00 2.70 .75
☐ 202 Adolfo Phillips .... 1.75 .80 .22
☐ 203 Dick Kelley .... 1.75 .80 .22
☐ 204 Andy Etchebarren ...... 1.75 .80 .22
☐ 205 Juan Marichal 10.00 4.50 1.25
☐ 206 Cal Ermer MG .... 1.75 .80 .22
☐ 207 Carroll Sembera .... 1.75 .80 .22
☐ 208 Willie Davis .... 2.25 1.00 .30
☐ 209 Tim Cullen .... 1.75 .80 .22
☐ 210 Gary Peters .... 1.75 .80 .22
☐ 211 J.C. Martin .... 1.75 .80 .22
☐ 212 Dave Morehead .... 1.75 .80 .22
☐ 213 Chico Ruiz .... 1.75 .80 .22
☐ 214 Yankees Rookies .... 2.25 1.00 .30
Stan Bahnsen
Frank Fernandez
☐ 215 Jim Bunning .... 4.50 2.00 .55
☐ 216 Bubba Morton .... 1.75 .80 .22
☐ 217 Dick Farrell .... 1.75 .80 .22
☐ 218 Ken Suarez .... 1.75 .80 .22
☐ 219 Rob Gardner .... 1.75 .80 .22
☐ 220 Harmon Killebrew 14.00 6.25 1.75
☐ 221 Braves Team .... 3.00 1.35 .40
☐ 222 Jim Hardin .... 1.75 .80 .22
☐ 223 Ollie Brown .... 1.75 .80 .22
☐ 224 Jack Aker .... 1.75 .80 .22
☐ 225 Richie Allen .... 4.50 2.00 .55
☐ 226 Jimmie Price .... 1.75 .80 .22
☐ 227 Joe Hoerner .... 1.75 .80 .22
☐ 228 Dodgers Rookies .... 2.25 1.00 .30
Jack Billingham
Jim Fairey
☐ 229 Fred Klages .... 1.75 .80 .22
☐ 230 Pete Rose 40.00 18.00 5.00
☐ 231 Dave Baldwin .... 1.75 .80 .22
☐ 232 Denis Menke .... 1.75 .80 .22
☐ 233 George Scott .... 2.25 1.00 .30
☐ 234 Bill Monbouquette ...... 1.75 .80 .22
☐ 235 Ron Santo .... 4.50 2.00 .55
☐ 236 Tug McGraw .... 3.00 1.35 .40
☐ 237 Alvin Dark MG .... 2.25 1.00 .30
☐ 238 Tom Satriano .... 1.75 .80 .22
☐ 239 Bill Henry .... 1.75 .80 .22
☐ 240 Al Kaline 25.00 11.50 3.10
☐ 241 Felix Millan .... 1.75 .80 .22
☐ 242 Moe Drabowsky .... 2.25 1.00 .30
☐ 243 Rich Rollins .... 1.75 .80 .22
☐ 244 John Donaldson .... 1.75 .80 .22
☐ 245 Tony Gonzalez .... 1.75 .80 .22
☐ 246 Fritz Peterson .... 1.75 .80 .22
☐ 247 Reds Rookies 175.00 80.00 22.00
Johnny Bench
Ron Tompkins
☐ 248 Fred Valentine .... 1.75 .80 .22
☐ 249 Bill Singer .... 1.75 .80 .22
☐ 250 Carl Yastrzemski 35.00 16.00 4.40
☐ 251 Manny Sanguillen ...... 6.50 2.90 .80
☐ 252 Angels Team .... 3.00 1.35 .40
☐ 253 Dick Hughes .... 1.75 .80 .22
☐ 254 Cleon Jones .... 2.25 1.00 .30
☐ 255 Dean Chance .... 2.25 1.00 .30
☐ 256 Norm Cash .... 6.00 2.70 .75
☐ 257 Phil Niekro 9.00 4.00 1.15
☐ 258 Cubs Rookies .... 1.75 .80 .22
Jose Arcia
Bill Schlesinger
☐ 259 Ken Boyer .... 2.50 1.15 .30
☐ 260 Jim Wynn .... 2.25 1.00 .30
☐ 261 Dave Duncan .... 2.25 1.00 .30
☐ 262 Rick Wise .... 2.25 1.00 .30
☐ 263 Horace Clarke .... 1.75 .80 .22
☐ 264 Ted Abernathy .... 1.75 .80 .22
☐ 265 Tommy Davis .... 2.25 1.00 .30
☐ 266 Paul Popovich .... 1.75 .80 .22
☐ 267 Herman Franks MG .... 1.75 .80 .22
☐ 268 Bob Humphreys .... 1.75 .80 .22
☐ 269 Bob Tiefenauer .... 1.75 .80 .22
☐ 270 Matty Alou .... 2.25 1.00 .30
☐ 271 Bobby Knoop .... 1.75 .80 .22
☐ 272 Ray Culp .... 1.75 .80 .22
☐ 273 Dave Johnson .... 2.25 1.00 .30
☐ 274 Mike Cuellar .... 2.25 1.00 .30
☐ 275 Tim McCarver .... 4.00 1.80 .50
☐ 276 Jim Roland .... 1.75 .80 .22
☐ 277 Jerry Buchek .... 1.75 .80 .22
☐ 278 Checklist 4 .... 6.00 1.50 .50
Orlando Cepeda
☐ 279 Bill Hands .... 1.75 .80 .22
☐ 280 Mickey Mantle 250.00 115.00 31.00
☐ 281 Jim Campanis .... 1.75 .80 .22
☐ 282 Rick Monday .... 2.25 1.00 .30
☐ 283 Mel Queen .... 1.75 .80 .22
☐ 284 Johnny Briggs .... 1.75 .80 .22
☐ 285 Dick McAuliffe .... 2.50 1.15 .30
☐ 286 Cecil Upshaw .... 1.75 .80 .22
☐ 287 White Sox Rookies ..... 1.75 .80 .22
Mickey Abarbanel
Cisco Carlos
☐ 288 Dave Wickersham ...... 1.75 .80 .22
☐ 289 Woody Held .... 1.75 .80 .22
☐ 290 Willie McCovey 12.00 5.50 1.50
☐ 291 Dick Lines .... 1.75 .80 .22
☐ 292 Art Shamsky .... 1.75 .80 .22
☐ 293 Bruce Howard .... 1.75 .80 .22
☐ 294 Red Schoendienst MG 4.50 2.00 .55
☐ 295 Sonny Siebert .... 1.75 .80 .22
☐ 296 Byron Browne .... 1.75 .80 .22
☐ 297 Russ Gibson .... 1.75 .80 .22
☐ 298 Jim Brewer .... 1.75 .80 .22
☐ 299 Gene Michael .... 2.25 1.00 .30
☐ 300 Rusty Staub .... 3.50 1.55 .45
☐ 301 Twins Rookies .... 1.75 .80 .22
George Mitterwald
Rick Renick
☐ 302 Gerry Arrigo .... 1.75 .80 .22

	Card			
☐ 303	Dick Green	2.25	1.00	.30
☐ 304	Sandy Valdespino	1.75	.80	.22
☐ 305	Minnie Rojas	1.75	.80	.22
☐ 306	Mike Ryan	1.75	.80	.22
☐ 307	John Hiller	2.25	1.00	.30
☐ 308	Pirates Team	3.00	1.35	.40
☐ 309	Ken Henderson	1.75	.80	.22
☐ 310	Luis Aparicio	6.00	2.70	.75
☐ 311	Jack Lamabe	1.75	.80	.22
☐ 312	Curt Blefary	1.75	.80	.22
☐ 313	Al Weis	1.75	.80	.22
☐ 314	Red Sox Rookies Bill Rohr George Spriggs	1.75	.80	.22
☐ 315	Zoilo Versalles	1.75	.80	.22
☐ 316	Steve Barber	1.75	.80	.22
☐ 317	Ron Brand	1.75	.80	.22
☐ 318	Chico Salmon	1.75	.80	.22
☐ 319	George Culver	1.75	.80	.22
☐ 320	Frank Howard	3.50	1.55	.45
☐ 321	Leo Durocher MG	4.50	2.00	.55
☐ 322	Dave Boswell	1.75	.80	.22
☐ 323	Deron Johnson	2.25	1.00	.30
☐ 324	Jim Nash	1.75	.80	.22
☐ 325	Manny Mota	2.25	1.00	.30
☐ 326	Dennis Ribant	1.75	.80	.22
☐ 327	Tony Taylor	1.75	.80	.22
☐ 328	Angels Rookies Chuck Vinson Jim Weaver	1.75	.80	.22
☐ 329	Duane Josephson	1.75	.80	.22
☐ 330	Roger Maris	30.00	13.50	3.80
☐ 331	Dan Osinski	1.75	.80	.22
☐ 332	Doug Rader	2.25	1.00	.30
☐ 333	Ron Herbel	1.75	.80	.22
☐ 334	Orioles Team	3.00	1.35	.40
☐ 335	Bob Allison	2.25	1.00	.30
☐ 336	John Purdin	1.75	.80	.22
☐ 337	Bill Robinson	2.25	1.00	.30
☐ 338	Bob Johnson	1.75	.80	.22
☐ 339	Rich Nye	1.75	.80	.22
☐ 340	Max Alvis	1.75	.80	.22
☐ 341	Jim Lemon MG	1.75	.80	.22
☐ 342	Ken Johnson	1.75	.80	.22
☐ 343	Jim Gosger	1.75	.80	.22
☐ 344	Donn Clendenon	2.25	1.00	.30
☐ 345	Bob Hendley	1.75	.80	.22
☐ 346	Jerry Adair	1.75	.80	.22
☐ 347	George Brunet	1.75	.80	.22
☐ 348	Phillies Rookies Larry Colton Dick Thoenen	1.75	.80	.22
☐ 349	Ed Spiezio	1.75	.80	.22
☐ 350	Hoyt Wilhelm	7.00	3.10	.85
☐ 351	Bob Barton	1.75	.80	.22
☐ 352	Jackie Hernandez	1.75	.80	.22
☐ 353	Mack Jones	1.75	.80	.22
☐ 354	Pete Richert	1.75	.80	.22
☐ 355	Ernie Banks	25.00	11.50	3.10
☐ 356A	Checklist 5 Ken Holtzman (Head centered within circle)	6.00	1.50	.50
☐ 356B	Checklist 5 Ken Holtzman (Head shifted right within circle)	6.00	1.50	.50
☐ 357	Len Gabrielson	1.75	.80	.22
☐ 358	Mike Epstein	1.75	.80	.22
☐ 359	Joe Moeller	1.75	.80	.22
☐ 360	Willie Horton	4.50	2.00	.55
☐ 361	Harmon Killebrew AS	8.00	3.60	1.00
☐ 362	Orlando Cepeda AS	3.00	1.35	.40
☐ 363	Rod Carew AS	8.00	3.60	1.00
☐ 364	Joe Morgan AS	8.00	3.60	1.00
☐ 365	Brooks Robinson AS	8.00	3.60	1.00
☐ 366	Ron Santo AS	4.00	1.80	.50
☐ 367	Jim Fregosi AS	2.50	1.15	.30
☐ 368	Gene Alley AS	2.50	1.15	.30
☐ 369	Carl Yastrzemski AS	12.00	5.50	1.50
☐ 370	Hank Aaron AS	15.00	6.75	1.90
☐ 371	Tony Oliva AS	3.00	1.35	.40
☐ 372	Lou Brock AS	8.00	3.60	1.00
☐ 373	Frank Robinson AS	8.00	3.60	1.00
☐ 374	Bob Clemente AS	18.00	8.00	2.30
☐ 375	Bill Freehan AS	3.00	1.35	.40
☐ 376	Tim McCarver AS	3.00	1.35	.40
☐ 377	Joel Horlen AS	2.50	1.15	.30
☐ 378	Bob Gibson AS	8.00	3.60	1.00
☐ 379	Gary Peters AS	2.50	1.15	.30
☐ 380	Ken Holtzman AS	2.50	1.15	.30
☐ 381	Boog Powell	4.00	1.80	.50
☐ 382	Ramon Hernandez	1.75	.80	.22
☐ 383	Steve Whitaker	1.75	.80	.22
☐ 384	Reds Rookies Bill Henry Hal McRae	10.00	4.50	1.25
☐ 385	Jim Hunter	14.00	6.25	1.75
☐ 386	Greg Goossen	1.75	.80	.22
☐ 387	Joe Foy	1.75	.80	.22
☐ 388	Ray Washburn	1.75	.80	.22
☐ 389	Jay Johnstone	2.25	1.00	.30
☐ 390	Bill Mazeroski	4.00	1.80	.50
☐ 391	Bob Priddy	1.75	.80	.22
☐ 392	Grady Hatton MG	1.75	.80	.22
☐ 393	Jim Perry	2.25	1.00	.30
☐ 394	Tommie Aaron	2.25	1.00	.30
☐ 395	Camilo Pascual	2.25	1.00	.30
☐ 396	Bobby Wine	1.75	.80	.22
☐ 397	Vic Davalillo	1.75	.80	.22
☐ 398	Jim Grant	1.75	.80	.22
☐ 399	Ray Oyler	2.25	1.00	.30
☐ 400A	Mike McCormick (Yellow letters)	2.25	1.00	.30
☐ 400B	Mike McCormick (Team name in white letters)	125.00	57.50	15.50
☐ 401	Mets Team	3.00	1.35	.40
☐ 402	Mike Hegan	1.75	.80	.22
☐ 403	John Buzhardt	1.75	.80	.22
☐ 404	Floyd Robinson	1.75	.80	.22
☐ 405	Tommy Helms	2.25	1.00	.30
☐ 406	Dick Ellsworth	1.75	.80	.22
☐ 407	Gary Kolb	1.75	.80	.22
☐ 408	Steve Carlton	40.00	18.00	5.00
☐ 409	Orioles Rookies Frank Peters Ron Stone	1.75	.80	.22
☐ 410	Fergie Jenkins	14.00	6.25	1.75
☐ 411	Ron Hansen	1.75	.80	.22
☐ 412	Clay Carroll	2.25	1.00	.30
☐ 413	Tom McCraw	1.75	.80	.22
☐ 414	Mickey Lolich	7.00	3.10	.85
☐ 415	Johnny Callison	2.25	1.00	.30
☐ 416	Bill Rigney MG	1.75	.80	.22
☐ 417	Willie Crawford	1.75	.80	.22
☐ 418	Eddie Fisher	1.75	.80	.22
☐ 419	Jack Hiatt	1.75	.80	.22
☐ 420	Cesar Tovar	1.75	.80	.22
☐ 421	Ron Taylor	1.75	.80	.22
☐ 422	Rene Lachemann	2.25	1.00	.30
☐ 423	Fred Gladding	1.75	.80	.22
☐ 424	Chicago White Sox Team Card	3.00	1.35	.40
☐ 425	Jim Maloney	2.25	1.00	.30
☐ 426	Hank Allen	1.75	.80	.22

☐ 427 Dick Calmus 1.75 .80 .22
☐ 428 Vic Roznovsky 1.75 .80 .22
☐ 429 Tommie Sisk 1.75 .80 .22
☐ 430 Rico Petrocelli 2.25 1.00 .30
☐ 431 Dooley Womack 1.75 .80 .22
☐ 432 Indians Rookies 1.75 .80 .22
Bill Davis
Jose Vidal
☐ 433 Bob Rodgers 2.25 1.00 .30
☐ 434 Ricardo Joseph 1.75 .80 .22
☐ 435 Ron Perranoski 2.25 1.00 .30
☐ 436 Hal Lanier 1.75 .80 .22
☐ 437 Don Cardwell 1.75 .80 .22
☐ 438 Lee Thomas 2.25 1.00 .30
☐ 439 Lum Harris MG 1.75 .80 .22
☐ 440 Claude Osteen 2.25 1.00 .30
☐ 441 Alex Johnson 2.25 1.00 .30
☐ 442 Dick Bosman 1.75 .80 .22
☐ 443 Joe Azcue 1.75 .80 .22
☐ 444 Jack Fisher 1.75 .80 .22
☐ 445 Mike Shannon 2.25 1.00 .30
☐ 446 Ron Kline 1.75 .80 .22
☐ 447 Tigers Rookies 1.75 .80 .22
George Korince
Fred Lasher
☐ 448 Gary Wagner 1.75 .80 .22
☐ 449 Gene Oliver 1.75 .80 .22
☐ 450 Jim Kaat 5.00 2.30 .60
☐ 451 Al Spangler 1.75 .80 .22
☐ 452 Jesus Alou 1.75 .80 .22
☐ 453 Sammy Ellis 1.75 .80 .22
☐ 454A Checklist 6 7.50 1.90 .60
Frank Robinson
(Cap complete
within circle)
☐ 454B Checklist 6 7.50 1.90 .60
Frank Robinson
(Cap partially
within circle)
☐ 455 Rico Carty 2.25 1.00 .30
☐ 456 John O'Donoghue 1.75 .80 .22
☐ 457 Jim Lefebvre 2.25 1.00 .30
☐ 458 Lew Krausse 3.50 1.55 .45
☐ 459 Dick Simpson 3.00 1.35 .40
☐ 460 Jim Lonborg 5.00 2.30 .60
☐ 461 Chuck Hiller 3.00 1.35 .40
☐ 462 Barry Moore 3.00 1.35 .40
☐ 463 Jim Schaffer 3.00 1.35 .40
☐ 464 Don McMahon 3.00 1.35 .40
☐ 465 Tommie Agee 3.50 1.55 .45
☐ 466 Bill Dillman 3.00 1.35 .40
☐ 467 Dick Howser 3.50 1.55 .45
☐ 468 Larry Sherry 3.00 1.35 .40
☐ 469 Ty Cline 3.00 1.35 .40
☐ 470 Bill Freehan 6.00 2.70 .75
☐ 471 Orlando Pena 3.00 1.35 .40
☐ 472 Walt Alston MG 4.50 2.00 .55
☐ 473 Al Worthington 3.00 1.35 .40
☐ 474 Paul Schaal 3.00 1.35 .40
☐ 475 Joe Niekro 3.00 1.35 .40
☐ 476 Woody Woodward 3.50 1.55 .45
☐ 477 Philadelphia Phillies 6.50 2.90 .80
Team Card
☐ 478 Dave McNally 3.50 1.55 .45
☐ 479 Phil Gagliano 3.00 1.35 .40
☐ 480 Manager's Dream 50.00 23.00 6.25
Tony Oliva
Chico Cardenas
Bob Clemente
☐ 481 John Wyatt 3.00 1.35 .40
☐ 482 Jose Pagan 3.00 1.35 .40
☐ 483 Darold Knowles 3.00 1.35 .40
☐ 484 Phil Roof 3.50 1.55 .45
☐ 485 Ken Berry 3.00 1.35 .40
☐ 486 Cal Koonce 3.00 1.35 .40
☐ 487 Lee May 3.50 1.55 .45
☐ 488 Dick Tracewski 5.00 2.30 .60
☐ 489 Wally Bunker 3.00 1.35 .40
☐ 490 Super Stars 125.00 57.50 15.50
Harmon Killebrew
Willie Mays
Mickey Mantle
☐ 491 Denny Lemaster 3.00 1.35 .40
☐ 492 Jeff Torborg 3.50 1.55 .45
☐ 493 Jim McGlothlin 3.00 1.35 .40
☐ 494 Ray Sadecki 3.00 1.35 .40
☐ 495 Leon Wagner 3.00 1.35 .40
☐ 496 Steve Hamilton 3.00 1.35 .40
☐ 497 Cardinals Team 6.50 2.90 .80
☐ 498 Bill Bryan 3.00 1.35 .40
☐ 499 Steve Blass 3.50 1.55 .45
☐ 500 Frank Robinson 30.00 13.50 3.80
☐ 501 John Odom 3.50 1.55 .45
☐ 502 Mike Andrews 3.00 1.35 .40
☐ 503 Al Jackson 3.00 1.35 .40
☐ 504 Russ Snyder 3.00 1.35 .40
☐ 505 Joe Sparma 8.00 3.60 1.00
☐ 506 Clarence Jones 3.00 1.35 .40
☐ 507 Wade Blasingame 3.00 1.35 .40
☐ 508 Duke Sims 3.00 1.35 .40
☐ 509 Dennis Higgins 3.00 1.35 .40
☐ 510 Ron Fairly 3.50 1.55 .45
☐ 511 Bill Kelso 3.00 1.35 .40
☐ 512 Grant Jackson 3.00 1.35 .40
☐ 513 Hank Bauer MG 3.50 1.55 .45
☐ 514 Al McBean 3.00 1.35 .40
☐ 515 Russ Nixon 3.00 1.35 .40
☐ 516 Pete Mikkelsen 3.00 1.35 .40
☐ 517 Diego Segui 3.50 1.55 .45
☐ 518A Checklist 7 ERR 12.00 3.00 .95
(539 AL Rookies)
(Clete Boyer)
☐ 518B Checklist 7 COR 12.00 3.00 .95
(539 ML Rookies)
(Clete Boyer)
☐ 519 Jerry Stephenson 3.00 1.35 .40
☐ 520 Lou Brock 25.00 11.50 3.10
☐ 521 Don Shaw 3.00 1.35 .40
☐ 522 Wayne Causey 3.00 1.35 .40
☐ 523 John Tsitouris 3.00 1.35 .40
☐ 524 Andy Kosco 3.00 1.35 .40
☐ 525 Jim Davenport 3.00 1.35 .40
☐ 526 Bill Denehy 3.00 1.35 .40
☐ 527 Tito Francona 3.00 1.35 .40
☐ 528 Tigers Team 70.00 32.00 8.75
☐ 529 Bruce Von Hoff 3.00 1.35 .40
☐ 530 Bird Belters 28.00 12.50 3.50
Brooks Robinson
Frank Robinson
☐ 531 Chuck Hinton 3.00 1.35 .40
☐ 532 Luis Tiant 6.00 2.70 .75
☐ 533 Wes Parker 3.50 1.55 .45
☐ 534 Bob Miller 4.00 1.80 .50
☐ 535 Danny Cater 5.00 2.30 .60
☐ 536 Bill Short 4.00 1.80 .50
☐ 537 Norm Siebern 4.00 1.80 .50
☐ 538 Manny Jimenez 4.00 1.80 .50
☐ 539 Major League Rookies 4.00 1.80 .50
Jim Ray
Mike Ferraro
☐ 540 Nelson Briles 5.00 2.30 .60
☐ 541 Sandy Alomar 5.00 2.30 .60
☐ 542 John Boccabella 4.00 1.80 .50
☐ 543 Bob Lee 4.00 1.80 .50
☐ 544 Mayo Smith MG 7.50 3.40 .95
☐ 545 Lindy McDaniel 5.00 2.30 .60

	NRMT	EXC	G-VG
☐ 546 Roy White	5.00	2.30	.60
☐ 547 Dan Coombs	4.00	1.80	.50
☐ 548 Bernie Allen	4.00	1.80	.50
☐ 549 Orioles Rookies	4.00	1.80	.50
Curt Motton			
Roger Nelson			
☐ 550 Clete Boyer	5.00	2.30	.60
☐ 551 Darrell Sutherland	4.00	1.80	.50
☐ 552 Ed Kirkpatrick	4.00	1.80	.50
☐ 553 Hank Aguirre	4.00	1.80	.50
☐ 554 A's Team	8.00	3.60	1.00
☐ 555 Jose Tartabull	5.00	2.30	.60
☐ 556 Dick Selma	4.00	1.80	.50
☐ 557 Frank Quilici	4.00	1.80	.50
☐ 558 Johnny Edwards	4.00	1.80	.50
☐ 559 Pirates Rookies	4.00	1.80	.50
Carl Taylor			
Luke Walker			
☐ 560 Paul Casanova	4.00	1.80	.50
☐ 561 Lee Elia	4.50	2.00	.55
☐ 562 Jim Bouton	7.00	3.10	.85
☐ 563 Ed Charles	4.00	1.80	.50
☐ 564 Eddie Stanky MG	5.00	2.30	.60
☐ 565 Larry Dierker	4.50	2.00	.55
☐ 566 Ken Harrelson	5.00	2.30	.60
☐ 567 Clay Dalrymple	4.00	1.80	.50
☐ 568 Willie Smith	4.00	1.80	.50
☐ 569 NL Rookies	4.00	1.80	.50
Ivan Murrell			
Les Rohr			
☐ 570 Rick Reichardt	4.00	1.80	.50
☐ 571 Tony LaRussa	10.00	4.50	1.25
☐ 572 Don Bosch	4.00	1.80	.50
☐ 573 Joe Coleman	4.00	1.80	.50
☐ 574 Cincinnati Reds	8.00	3.60	1.00
Team Card			
☐ 575 Jim Palmer	45.00	20.00	5.75
☐ 576 Dave Adlesh	4.00	1.80	.50
☐ 577 Fred Talbot	4.00	1.80	.50
☐ 578 Orlando Martinez	4.00	1.80	.50
☐ 579 NL Rookies	8.00	3.60	1.00
Larry Hisle			
Mike Lum			
☐ 580 Bob Bailey	4.00	1.80	.50
☐ 581 Garry Roggenburk	4.00	1.80	.50
☐ 582 Jerry Grote	4.00	1.80	.50
☐ 583 Gates Brown	7.00	3.10	.85
☐ 584 Larry Shepard MG	4.00	1.80	.50
☐ 585 Wilbur Wood	5.00	2.30	.60
☐ 586 Jim Pagliaroni	5.00	2.30	.60
☐ 587 Roger Repoz	4.00	1.80	.50
☐ 588 Dick Schofield	4.00	1.80	.50
☐ 589 Twins Rookies	4.00	1.80	.50
Ron Clark			
Moe Ogier			
☐ 590 Tommy Harper	5.00	2.30	.60
☐ 591 Dick Nen	4.00	1.80	.50
☐ 592 John Bateman	4.00	1.80	.50
☐ 593 Lee Stange	4.00	1.80	.50
☐ 594 Phil Linz	5.00	2.30	.60
☐ 595 Phil Ortega	4.00	1.80	.50
☐ 596 Charlie Smith	4.00	1.80	.50
☐ 597 Bill McCool	4.00	1.80	.50
☐ 598 Jerry May	5.00	1.70	.50

1969 Topps

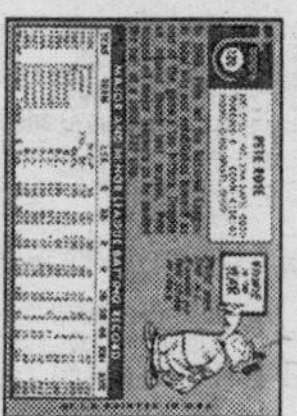

The cards in this 664-card set measure 2 1/2" by 3 1/2". The 1969 Topps set includes Sporting News All-Star Selections as card numbers 416 to 435. Other popular subsets within this set include League Leaders (1-12) and World Series cards (162-169). The fifth series contains several variations; the more difficult variety consists of cards with the player's first name, last name, and/or position in white letters instead of lettering in some other color. These are designated in the checklist below by WL (white letters). Each checklist card features a different popular player's picture inside a circle on the front of the checklist card. Two different team identifications of Clay Dalrymple and Donn Clendenon exist, as indicated in the checklist. The key Rookie Cards in this set are Rollie Fingers, Reggie Jackson, and Graig Nettles. This was the last year that Topps issued multi-player special star cards, ending a 13-year tradition, which they had begun in 1957. There were cropping differences in checklist cards 57, 214, and 412, due to their each being printed with two different series. The differences are difficult to explain and have not been greatly sought by collectors; hence they are not listed explicitly in the list below. The All-Star cards 426-435, when turned over and placed together, form a puzzle back of Pete Rose.

	NRMT	EXC	G-VG
COMPLETE SET (664)	2400.00	1100.00	300.00
COMMON CARD (1-109)	1.50	.65	.19
COMMON CARD (110-218)	1.50	.65	.19
COMMON CARD (219-327)	2.50	1.15	.30
COMMON CARD (328-425)	1.50	.65	.19
COMMON CARD (426-512)	1.50	.65	.19
COMMON CARD (513-588)	2.00	.90	.25
COMMON CARD (589-664)	3.00	1.35	.40
☐ 1 AL Batting Leaders	13.00	3.90	1.30
Carl Yastrzemski			
Danny Cater			
Tony Oliva			
☐ 2 NL Batting Leaders	7.00	3.10	.85
Pete Rose			
Matty Alou			
Felipe Alou			
☐ 3 AL RBI Leaders	3.50	1.55	.45
Ken Harrelson			
Frank Howard			
Jim Northrup			
☐ 4 NL RBI Leaders	6.00	2.70	.75
Willie McCovey			
Ron Santo			
Billy Williams			
☐ 5 AL Home Run Leaders	3.50	1.55	.45

Card			
Frank Howard			
Willie Horton			
Ken Harrelson			
☐ 6 NL Home Run Leaders	6.00	2.70	.75
Willie McCovey			
Richie Allen			
Ernie Banks			
☐ 7 AL ERA Leaders	3.50	1.55	.45
Luis Tiant			
Sam McDowell			
Dave McNally			
☐ 8 NL ERA Leaders	4.50	2.00	.55
Bob Gibson			
Bobby Bolin			
Bob Veale			
☐ 9 AL Pitching Leaders	3.50	1.55	.45
Denny McLain			
Dave McNally			
Luis Tiant			
Mel Stottlemyre			
☐ 10 NL Pitching Leaders	6.50	2.90	.80
Juan Marichal			
Bob Gibson			
Fergie Jenkins			
☐ 11 AL Strikeout Leaders	3.50	1.55	.45
Sam McDowell			
Denny McLain			
Luis Tiant			
☐ 12 NL Strikeout Leaders	4.00	1.80	.50
Bob Gibson			
Fergie Jenkins			
Bill Singer			
☐ 13 Mickey Stanley	2.00	.90	.25
☐ 14 Al McBean	1.50	.65	.19
☐ 15 Boog Powell	3.50	1.55	.45
☐ 16 Giants Rookies	1.50	.65	.19
Cesar Gutierrez			
Rich Robertson			
☐ 17 Mike Marshall	2.00	.90	.25
☐ 18 Dick Schofield	1.50	.65	.19
☐ 19 Ken Suarez	1.50	.65	.19
☐ 20 Ernie Banks	20.00	9.00	2.50
☐ 21 Jose Santiago	1.50	.65	.19
☐ 22 Jesus Alou	2.00	.90	.25
☐ 23 Lew Krausse	1.50	.65	.19
☐ 24 Walt Alston MG	2.50	1.15	.30
☐ 25 Roy White	2.00	.90	.25
☐ 26 Clay Carroll	2.00	.90	.25
☐ 27 Bernie Allen	1.50	.65	.19
☐ 28 Mike Ryan	1.50	.65	.19
☐ 29 Dave Morehead	1.50	.65	.19
☐ 30 Bob Allison	2.00	.90	.25
☐ 31 Mets Rookies	3.00	1.35	.40
Gary Gentry			
Amos Otis			
☐ 32 Sammy Ellis	1.50	.65	.19
☐ 33 Wayne Causey	1.50	.65	.19
☐ 34 Gary Peters	1.50	.65	.19
☐ 35 Joe Morgan	10.00	4.50	1.25
☐ 36 Luke Walker	1.50	.65	.19
☐ 37 Curt Motton	1.50	.65	.19
☐ 38 Zoilo Versalles	1.50	.65	.19
☐ 39 Dick Hughes	1.50	.65	.19
☐ 40 Mayo Smith MG	1.50	.65	.19
☐ 41 Bob Barton	1.50	.65	.19
☐ 42 Tommy Harper	2.00	.90	.25
☐ 43 Joe Niekro	1.50	.65	.19
☐ 44 Danny Cater	1.50	.65	.19
☐ 45 Maury Wills	3.00	1.35	.40
☐ 46 Fritz Peterson	1.50	.65	.19
☐ 47A Paul Popovich	1.50	.65	.19
(No helmet emblem)			
☐ 47B Paul Popovich	25.00	11.50	3.10
(C emblem on helmet)			
☐ 48 Brant Alyea	1.50	.65	.19
☐ 49A Royals Rookies ERR	1.50	.65	.19
Steve Jones			
E. Rodriguez "q"			
☐ 49B Royals Rookies COR	25.00	11.50	3.10
Steve Jones			
E. Rodriguez "g"			
☐ 50 Bob Clemente UER	50.00	23.00	6.25
(Bats Right listed twice)			
☐ 51 Woodie Fryman	1.50	.65	.19
☐ 52 Mike Andrews	1.50	.65	.19
☐ 53 Sonny Jackson	1.50	.65	.19
☐ 54 Cisco Carlos	1.50	.65	.19
☐ 55 Jerry Grote	2.00	.90	.25
☐ 56 Rich Reese	1.50	.65	.19
☐ 57 Checklist 1	6.00	1.50	.50
Denny McLain			
☐ 58 Fred Gladding	1.50	.65	.19
☐ 59 Jay Johnstone	2.00	.90	.25
☐ 60 Nelson Briles	2.00	.90	.25
☐ 61 Jimmie Hall	1.50	.65	.19
☐ 62 Chico Salmon	1.50	.65	.19
☐ 63 Jim Hickman	2.00	.90	.25
☐ 64 Bill Monbouquette	1.50	.65	.19
☐ 65 Willie Davis	2.00	.90	.25
☐ 66 Orioles Rookies	1.50	.65	.19
Mike Adamson			
Merv Rettenmund			
☐ 67 Bill Stoneman	2.00	.90	.25
☐ 68 Dave Duncan	2.00	.90	.25
☐ 69 Steve Hamilton	1.50	.65	.19
☐ 70 Tommy Helms	2.00	.90	.25
☐ 71 Steve Whitaker	1.50	.65	.19
☐ 72 Ron Taylor	1.50	.65	.19
☐ 73 Johnny Briggs	1.50	.65	.19
☐ 74 Preston Gomez MG	2.00	.90	.25
☐ 75 Luis Aparicio	5.00	2.30	.60
☐ 76 Norm Miller	1.50	.65	.19
☐ 77A Ron Perranoski	2.00	.90	.25
(No emblem on cap)			
☐ 77B Ron Perranoski	25.00	11.50	3.10
(LA on cap)			
☐ 78 Tom Satriano	1.50	.65	.19
☐ 79 Milt Pappas	2.00	.90	.25
☐ 80 Norm Cash	3.00	1.35	.40
☐ 81 Mel Queen	1.50	.65	.19
☐ 82 Pirates Rookies	15.00	6.75	1.90
Rich Hebner			
Al Oliver			
☐ 83 Mike Ferraro	2.00	.90	.25
☐ 84 Bob Humphreys	1.50	.65	.19
☐ 85 Lou Brock	18.00	8.00	2.30
☐ 86 Pete Richert	1.50	.65	.19
☐ 87 Horace Clarke	1.50	.65	.19
☐ 88 Rich Nye	1.50	.65	.19
☐ 89 Russ Gibson	1.50	.65	.19
☐ 90 Jerry Koosman	6.00	2.70	.75
☐ 91 Alvin Dark MG	2.00	.90	.25
☐ 92 Jack Billingham	2.00	.90	.25
☐ 93 Joe Foy	1.50	.65	.19
☐ 94 Hank Aguirre	1.50	.65	.19
☐ 95 Johnny Bench	70.00	32.00	8.75
☐ 96 Denny Lemaster	1.50	.65	.19
☐ 97 Buddy Bradford	1.50	.65	.19
☐ 98 Dave Giusti	1.50	.65	.19
☐ 99A Twins Rookies	24.00	11.00	3.00
Danny Morris			
Graig Nettles			
(No loop)			
☐ 99B Twins Rookies	24.00	11.00	3.00
Danny Morris			
Graig Nettles			

(Errant loop in
upper left corner
of obverse)
□ 100 Hank Aaron 50.00 23.00 6.25
□ 101 Daryl Patterson .... 1.50 .65 .19
□ 102 Jim Davenport .... 1.50 .65 .19
□ 103 Roger Repoz .... 1.50 .65 .19
□ 104 Steve Blass .... 2.00 .90 .25
□ 105 Rick Monday .... 2.00 .90 .25
□ 106 Jim Hannan .... 1.50 .65 .19
□ 107A Checklist 2 ERR .... 6.00 1.50 .50
(161 Jim Purdin)
(Bob Gibson)
□ 107B Checklist 2 COR .... 7.50 1.90 .60
(161 John Purdin)
(Bob Gibson)
□ 108 Tony Taylor .... 1.50 .65 .19
□ 109 Jim Lonborg .... 2.00 .90 .25
□ 110 Mike Shannon .... 2.00 .90 .25
□ 111 Johnny Morris .... 1.50 .65 .19
□ 112 J.C. Martin .... 1.50 .65 .19
□ 113 Dave May .... 1.50 .65 .19
□ 114 Yankees Rookies .... 1.50 .65 .19
Alan Closter
John Cumberland
□ 115 Bill Hands .... 1.50 .65 .19
□ 116 Chuck Harrison .... 1.50 .65 .19
□ 117 Jim Fairey .... 1.50 .65 .19
□ 118 Stan Williams .... 1.50 .65 .19
□ 119 Doug Rader .... 2.00 .90 .25
□ 120 Pete Rose 30.00 13.50 3.80
□ 121 Joe Grzenda .... 1.50 .65 .19
□ 122 Ron Fairly .... 2.00 .90 .25
□ 123 Wilbur Wood .... 2.00 .90 .25
□ 124 Hank Bauer MG .... 2.00 .90 .25
□ 125 Ray Sadecki .... 1.50 .65 .19
□ 126 Dick Tracewski .... 1.50 .65 .19
□ 127 Kevin Collins .... 2.00 .90 .25
□ 128 Tommie Aaron .... 2.00 .90 .25
□ 129 Bill McCool .... 1.50 .65 .19
□ 130 Carl Yastrzemski 20.00 9.00 2.50
□ 131 Chris Cannizzaro .... 1.50 .65 .19
□ 132 Dave Baldwin .... 1.50 .65 .19
□ 133 Johnny Callison .... 2.00 .90 .25
□ 134 Jim Weaver .... 1.50 .65 .19
□ 135 Tommy Davis .... 2.00 .90 .25
□ 136 Cards Rookies .... 1.50 .65 .19
Steve Huntz
Mike Torrez
□ 137 Wally Bunker .... 1.50 .65 .19
□ 138 John Bateman .... 1.50 .65 .19
□ 139 Andy Kosco .... 1.50 .65 .19
□ 140 Jim Lefebvre .... 2.00 .90 .25
□ 141 Bill Dillman .... 1.50 .65 .19
□ 142 Woody Woodward ..... 2.00 .90 .25
□ 143 Joe Nossek .... 1.50 .65 .19
□ 144 Bob Hendley .... 1.50 .65 .19
□ 145 Max Alvis .... 1.50 .65 .19
□ 146 Jim Perry .... 2.00 .90 .25
□ 147 Leo Durocher MG ...... 3.50 1.55 .45
□ 148 Lee Stange .... 1.50 .65 .19
□ 149 Ollie Brown .... 2.00 .90 .25
□ 150 Denny McLain .... 6.00 2.70 .75
□ 151A Clay Dalrymple .... 1.50 .65 .19
(Portrait, Orioles)
□ 151B Clay Dalrymple 16.00 7.25 2.00
(Catching, Phillies)
□ 152 Tommie Sisk .... 1.50 .65 .19
□ 153 Ed Brinkman .... 1.50 .65 .19
□ 154 Jim Britton .... 1.50 .65 .19
□ 155 Pete Ward .... 1.50 .65 .19
□ 156 Houston Rookies .... 1.50 .65 .19
Hal Gilson
Leon McFadden
□ 157 Bob Rodgers .... 2.00 .90 .25
□ 158 Joe Gibbon .... 1.50 .65 .19
□ 159 Jerry Adair .... 1.50 .65 .19
□ 160 Vada Pinson .... 2.50 1.15 .30
□ 161 John Purdin .... 1.50 .65 .19
□ 162 World Series Game 1. 7.00 3.10 .85
Bob Gibson fans 17
□ 163 World Series Game 2. 4.50 2.00 .55
Tiger homers
deck the Cards
(Willie Horton)
□ 164 World Series Game 3. 7.00 3.10 .85
Tim McCarver's homer
□ 165 World Series Game 4. 7.50 3.40 .95
Lou Brock lead-off
homer
□ 166 World Series Game 5. 8.00 3.60 1.00
Al Kaline's key hit
□ 167 World Series Game 6. 4.50 2.00 .55
Jim Northrup grandslam
□ 168 World Series Game 7. 7.50 3.40 .95
Mickey Lolich outduels
Bob Gibson
□ 169 World Series Summary 4.50 2.00 .55
Tigers celebrate
(Dick McAuliffe,
Denny McLain, and
Willie Horton)
□ 170 Frank Howard .... 3.50 1.55 .45
□ 171 Glenn Beckert .... 2.00 .90 .25
□ 172 Jerry Stephenson .... 1.50 .65 .19
□ 173 White Sox Rookies ..... 1.50 .65 .19
Bob Christian
Gerry Nyman
□ 174 Grant Jackson .... 1.50 .65 .19
□ 175 Jim Bunning .... 4.50 2.00 .55
□ 176 Joe Azcue .... 1.50 .65 .19
□ 177 Ron Reed .... 1.50 .65 .19
□ 178 Ray Oyler .... 2.00 .90 .25
□ 179 Don Pavletich .... 1.50 .65 .19
□ 180 Willie Horton .... 2.00 .90 .25
□ 181 Mel Nelson .... 1.50 .65 .19
□ 182 Bill Rigney MG .... 1.50 .65 .19
□ 183 Don Shaw .... 1.50 .65 .19
□ 184 Roberto Pena .... 1.50 .65 .19
□ 185 Tom Phoebus .... 1.50 .65 .19
□ 186 Johnny Edwards .... 1.50 .65 .19
□ 187 Leon Wagner .... 1.50 .65 .19
□ 188 Rick Wise .... 2.00 .90 .25
□ 189 Red Sox Rookies .... 1.50 .65 .19
Joe Lahoud
John Thibodeau
□ 190 Willie Mays 50.00 23.00 6.25
□ 191 Lindy McDaniel .... 2.00 .90 .25
□ 192 Jose Pagan .... 1.50 .65 .19
□ 193 Don Cardwell .... 1.50 .65 .19
□ 194 Ted Uhlaender .... 1.50 .65 .19
□ 195 John Odom .... 1.50 .65 .19
□ 196 Lum Harris MG .... 1.50 .65 .19
□ 197 Dick Selma .... 1.50 .65 .19
□ 198 Willie Smith .... 1.50 .65 .19
□ 199 Jim French .... 1.50 .65 .19
□ 200 Bob Gibson 14.00 6.25 1.75
□ 201 Russ Snyder .... 1.50 .65 .19
□ 202 Don Wilson .... 2.00 .90 .25
□ 203 Dave Johnson .... 2.00 .90 .25
□ 204 Jack Hiatt .... 1.50 .65 .19
□ 205 Rick Reichardt .... 1.50 .65 .19
□ 206 Phillies Rookies .... 2.00 .90 .25
Larry Hisle
Barry Lersch
□ 207 Roy Face .... 2.00 .90 .25
□ 208A Donn Clendenon ...... 2.00 .90 .25

(Houston)
(On back, some cards have the last "N" of last name backwards)
- ☐ 208B Donn Clendenon 16.00 7.25 2.00
(Expos)
- ☐ 209 Larry Haney UER .... 1.50 .65 .19
(Reverse negative)
- ☐ 210 Felix Millan .... 1.50 .65 .19
- ☐ 211 Galen Cisco .... 1.50 .65 .19
- ☐ 212 Tom Tresh .... 1.50 .65 .19
- ☐ 213 Gerry Arrigo .... 1.50 .65 .19
- ☐ 214 Checklist 3 .... 6.00 1.50 .50
With 69T deckle CL on back (no player)
- ☐ 215 Rico Petrocelli .... 2.00 .90 .25
- ☐ 216 Don Sutton .... 7.00 3.10 .85
- ☐ 217 John Donaldson .... 1.50 .65 .19
- ☐ 218 John Roseboro .... 2.00 .90 .25
- ☐ 219 Freddie Patek .... 4.50 2.00 .55
- ☐ 220 Sam McDowell .... 3.00 1.35 .40
- ☐ 221 Art Shamsky .... 3.00 1.35 .40
- ☐ 222 Duane Josephson ...... 2.50 1.15 .30
- ☐ 223 Tom Dukes .... 3.00 1.35 .40
- ☐ 224 Angels Rookies .... 2.50 1.15 .30
Bill Harrelson
Steve Kealey
- ☐ 225 Don Kessinger .... 3.00 1.35 .40
- ☐ 226 Bruce Howard .... 2.50 1.15 .30
- ☐ 227 Frank Johnson .... 2.50 1.15 .30
- ☐ 228 Dave Leonhard .... 2.50 1.15 .30
- ☐ 229 Don Lock .... 2.50 1.15 .30
- ☐ 230 Rusty Staub .... 5.00 2.30 .60
- ☐ 231 Pat Dobson .... 3.00 1.35 .40
- ☐ 232 Dave Ricketts .... 2.50 1.15 .30
- ☐ 233 Steve Barber .... 3.00 1.35 .40
- ☐ 234 Dave Bristol MG .... 2.50 1.15 .30
- ☐ 235 Jim Hunter 12.00 5.50 1.50
- ☐ 236 Manny Mota .... 3.00 1.35 .40
- ☐ 237 Bobby Cox 8.00 3.60 1.00
- ☐ 238 Ken Johnson .... 2.50 1.15 .30
- ☐ 239 Bob Taylor .... 3.00 1.35 .40
- ☐ 240 Ken Harrelson .... 3.00 1.35 .40
- ☐ 241 Jim Brewer .... 2.50 1.15 .30
- ☐ 242 Frank Kostro .... 2.50 1.15 .30
- ☐ 243 Ron Kline .... 2.50 1.15 .30
- ☐ 244 Indians Rookies .... 6.50 2.90 .80
Ray Fosse
George Woodson
- ☐ 245 Ed Charles .... 3.00 1.35 .40
- ☐ 246 Joe Coleman .... 2.50 1.15 .30
- ☐ 247 Gene Oliver .... 2.50 1.15 .30
- ☐ 248 Bob Priddy .... 2.50 1.15 .30
- ☐ 249 Ed Spiezio .... 3.00 1.35 .40
- ☐ 250 Frank Robinson 33.00 15.00 4.10
- ☐ 251 Ron Herbel .... 2.50 1.15 .30
- ☐ 252 Chuck Cottier .... 2.50 1.15 .30
- ☐ 253 Jerry Johnson .... 2.50 1.15 .30
- ☐ 254 Joe Schultz MG .... 3.00 1.35 .40
- ☐ 255 Steve Carlton 40.00 18.00 5.00
- ☐ 256 Gates Brown .... 3.00 1.35 .40
- ☐ 257 Jim Ray .... 2.50 1.15 .30
- ☐ 258 Jackie Hernandez .... 3.00 1.35 .40
- ☐ 259 Bill Short .... 2.50 1.15 .30
- ☐ 260 Reggie Jackson 425.00 190.00 52.50
- ☐ 261 Bob Johnson .... 2.50 1.15 .30
- ☐ 262 Mike Kekich .... 2.50 1.15 .30
- ☐ 263 Jerry May .... 2.50 1.15 .30
- ☐ 264 Bill Landis .... 2.50 1.15 .30
- ☐ 265 Chico Cardenas .... 3.00 1.35 .40
- ☐ 266 Dodger Rookies .... 2.50 1.15 .30
Tom Hutton
Alan Foster
- ☐ 267 Vicente Romo .... 2.50 1.15 .30
- ☐ 268 Al Spangler .... 2.50 1.15 .30
- ☐ 269 Al Weis .... 3.00 1.35 .40
- ☐ 270 Mickey Lolich .... 5.50 2.50 .70
- ☐ 271 Larry Stahl .... 3.00 1.35 .40
- ☐ 272 Ed Stroud .... 2.50 1.15 .30
- ☐ 273 Ron Willis .... 2.50 1.15 .30
- ☐ 274 Clyde King MG .... 2.50 1.15 .30
- ☐ 275 Vic Davalillo .... 2.50 1.15 .30
- ☐ 276 Gary Wagner .... 2.50 1.15 .30
- ☐ 277 Elrod Hendricks .... 2.50 1.15 .30
- ☐ 278 Gary Geiger UER .... 2.50 1.15 .30
(Batting wrong)
- ☐ 279 Roger Nelson .... 3.00 1.35 .40
- ☐ 280 Alex Johnson .... 3.00 1.35 .40
- ☐ 281 Ted Kubiak .... 2.50 1.15 .30
- ☐ 282 Pat Jarvis .... 2.50 1.15 .30
- ☐ 283 Sandy Alomar .... 3.00 1.35 .40
- ☐ 284 Expos Rookies .... 3.00 1.35 .40
Jerry Robertson
Mike Wegener
- ☐ 285 Don Mincher .... 3.00 1.35 .40
- ☐ 286 Dock Ellis .... 5.00 2.30 .60
- ☐ 287 Jose Tartabull .... 3.00 1.35 .40
- ☐ 288 Ken Holtzman .... 3.00 1.35 .40
- ☐ 289 Bart Shirley .... 2.50 1.15 .30
- ☐ 290 Jim Kaat .... 5.00 2.30 .60
- ☐ 291 Vern Fuller .... 2.50 1.15 .30
- ☐ 292 Al Downing .... 3.00 1.35 .40
- ☐ 293 Dick Dietz .... 2.50 1.15 .30
- ☐ 294 Jim Lemon MG .... 2.50 1.15 .30
- ☐ 295 Tony Perez 14.00 6.25 1.75
- ☐ 296 Andy Messersmith ..... 4.50 2.00 .55
- ☐ 297 Deron Johnson .... 2.50 1.15 .30
- ☐ 298 Dave Nicholson .... 3.00 1.35 .40
- ☐ 299 Mark Belanger .... 3.00 1.35 .40
- ☐ 300 Felipe Alou .... 5.50 2.50 .70
- ☐ 301 Darrell Brandon .... 3.00 1.35 .40
- ☐ 302 Jim Pagliaroni .... 2.50 1.15 .30
- ☐ 303 Cal Koonce .... 3.00 1.35 .40
- ☐ 304 Padres Rookies 15.00 6.75 1.90
Bill Davis
Clarence Gaston
- ☐ 305 Dick McAuliffe .... 3.00 1.35 .40
- ☐ 306 Jim Grant .... 3.00 1.35 .40
- ☐ 307 Gary Kolb .... 2.50 1.15 .30
- ☐ 308 Wade Blasingame ...... 2.50 1.15 .30
- ☐ 309 Walt Williams .... 2.50 1.15 .30
- ☐ 310 Tom Haller .... 2.50 1.15 .30
- ☐ 311 Sparky Lyle 20.00 9.00 2.50
- ☐ 312 Lee Elia .... 3.00 1.35 .40
- ☐ 313 Bill Robinson .... 3.00 1.35 .40
- ☐ 314 Checklist 4 .... 6.00 1.50 .50
Don Drysdale
- ☐ 315 Eddie Fisher .... 2.50 1.15 .30
- ☐ 316 Hal Lanier .... 2.50 1.15 .30
- ☐ 317 Bruce Look .... 2.50 1.15 .30
- ☐ 318 Jack Fisher .... 2.50 1.15 .30
- ☐ 319 Ken McMullen UER .... 2.50 1.15 .30
(Headings on back are for a pitcher)
- ☐ 320 Dal Maxvill .... 2.50 1.15 .30
- ☐ 321 Jim McAndrew .... 3.00 1.35 .40
- ☐ 322 Jose Vidal .... 3.00 1.35 .40
- ☐ 323 Larry Miller .... 2.50 1.15 .30
- ☐ 324 Tiger Rookies .... 2.50 1.15 .30
Les Cain
Dave Campbell
- ☐ 325 Jose Cardenal .... 3.00 1.35 .40
- ☐ 326 Gary Sutherland .... 3.00 1.35 .40
- ☐ 327 Willie Crawford .... 2.50 1.15 .30
- ☐ 328 Joel Horlen .... 1.50 .65 .19
- ☐ 329 Rick Joseph .... 1.50 .65 .19
- ☐ 330 Tony Conigliaro .... 6.00 2.70 .75

	No.	Player			
☐	331	Braves Rookies	1.50	.65	.19
		Gil Garrido			
		Tom House			
☐	332	Fred Talbot	1.50	.65	.19
☐	333	Ivan Murrell	1.50	.65	.19
☐	334	Phil Roof	1.50	.65	.19
☐	335	Bill Mazeroski	3.50	1.55	.45
☐	336	Jim Roland	1.50	.65	.19
☐	337	Marty Martinez	1.50	.65	.19
☐	338	Del Unser	1.50	.65	.19
☐	339	Reds Rookies	1.50	.65	.19
		Steve Mingori			
		Jose Pena			
☐	340	Dave McNally	2.00	.90	.25
☐	341	Dave Adlesh	1.50	.65	.19
☐	342	Bubba Morton	1.50	.65	.19
☐	343	Dan Frisella	1.50	.65	.19
☐	344	Tom Matchick	1.50	.65	.19
☐	345	Frank Linzy	1.50	.65	.19
☐	346	Wayne Comer	1.50	.65	.19
☐	347	Randy Hundley	1.50	.65	.19
☐	348	Steve Hargan	1.50	.65	.19
☐	349	Dick Williams MG	2.00	.90	.25
☐	350	Richie Allen	4.00	1.80	.50
☐	351	Carroll Sembera	1.50	.65	.19
☐	352	Paul Schaal	2.00	.90	.25
☐	353	Jeff Torborg	2.00	.90	.25
☐	354	Nate Oliver	1.50	.65	.19
☐	355	Phil Niekro	7.00	3.10	.85
☐	356	Frank Quilici	1.50	.65	.19
☐	357	Carl Taylor	1.50	.65	.19
☐	358	Athletics Rookies	1.50	.65	.19
		George Lauzerique			
		Roberto Rodriquez			
☐	359	Dick Kelley	1.50	.65	.19
☐	360	Jim Wynn	2.00	.90	.25
☐	361	Gary Holman	1.50	.65	.19
☐	362	Jim Maloney	2.00	.90	.25
☐	363	Russ Nixon	1.50	.65	.19
☐	364	Tommie Agee	2.00	.90	.25
☐	365	Jim Fregosi	2.00	.90	.25
☐	366	Bo Belinsky	2.00	.90	.25
☐	367	Lou Johnson	2.00	.90	.25
☐	368	Vic Roznovsky	1.50	.65	.19
☐	369	Bob Skinner	2.00	.90	.25
☐	370	Juan Marichal	8.00	3.60	1.00
☐	371	Sal Bando	2.00	.90	.25
☐	372	Adolfo Phillips	1.50	.65	.19
☐	373	Fred Lasher	1.50	.65	.19
☐	374	Bob Tillman	1.50	.65	.19
☐	375	Harmon Killebrew	18.00	8.00	2.30
☐	376	Royals Rookies	1.50	.65	.19
		Mike Fiore			
		Jim Rooker			
☐	377	Gary Bell	2.00	.90	.25
☐	378	Jose Herrera	1.50	.65	.19
☐	379	Ken Boyer	3.00	1.35	.40
☐	380	Stan Bahnsen	1.50	.65	.19
☐	381	Ed Kranepool	2.00	.90	.25
☐	382	Pat Corrales	2.00	.90	.25
☐	383	Casey Cox	1.50	.65	.19
☐	384	Larry Shepard MG	1.50	.65	.19
☐	385	Orlando Cepeda	3.50	1.55	.45
☐	386	Jim McGlothlin	1.50	.65	.19
☐	387	Bobby Klaus	1.50	.65	.19
☐	388	Tom McCraw	1.50	.65	.19
☐	389	Dan Coombs	1.50	.65	.19
☐	390	Bill Freehan	3.50	1.55	.45
☐	391	Ray Culp	1.50	.65	.19
☐	392	Bob Burda	1.50	.65	.19
☐	393	Gene Brabender	1.50	.65	.19
☐	394	Pilots Rookies	5.00	2.30	.60
		Lou Piniella			
		Marv Staehle			
☐	395	Chris Short	1.50	.65	.19
☐	396	Jim Campanis	1.50	.65	.19
☐	397	Chuck Dobson	1.50	.65	.19
☐	398	Tito Francona	1.50	.65	.19
☐	399	Bob Bailey	2.00	.90	.25
☐	400	Don Drysdale	14.00	6.25	1.75
☐	401	Jake Gibbs	1.50	.65	.19
☐	402	Ken Boswell	2.00	.90	.25
☐	403	Bob Miller	1.50	.65	.19
☐	404	Cubs Rookies	1.50	.65	.19
		Vic LaRose			
		Gary Ross			
☐	405	Lee May	2.00	.90	.25
☐	406	Phil Ortega	1.50	.65	.19
☐	407	Tom Egan	1.50	.65	.19
☐	408	Nate Colbert	1.50	.65	.19
☐	409	Bob Moose	1.50	.65	.19
☐	410	Al Kaline	20.00	9.00	2.50
☐	411	Larry Dierker	1.50	.65	.19
☐	412	Checklist 5 DP	10.00	2.50	.80
		Mickey Mantle			
☐	413	Roland Sheldon	1.50	.65	.19
☐	414	Duke Sims	1.50	.65	.19
☐	415	Ray Washburn	1.50	.65	.19
☐	416	Willie McCovey AS	7.00	3.10	.85
☐	417	Ken Harrelson AS	2.50	1.15	.30
☐	418	Tommy Helms AS	2.50	1.15	.30
☐	419	Rod Carew AS	10.00	4.50	1.25
☐	420	Ron Santo AS	3.00	1.35	.40
☐	421	Brooks Robinson AS	7.00	3.10	.85
☐	422	Don Kessinger AS	2.50	1.15	.30
☐	423	Bert Campaneris AS	2.50	1.15	.30
☐	424	Pete Rose AS	14.00	6.25	1.75
☐	425	Carl Yastrzemski AS	10.00	4.50	1.25
☐	426	Curt Flood AS	3.00	1.35	.40
☐	427	Tony Oliva AS	3.00	1.35	.40
☐	428	Lou Brock AS	6.00	2.70	.75
☐	429	Willie Horton AS	2.50	1.15	.30
☐	430	Johnny Bench AS	10.00	4.50	1.25
☐	431	Bill Freehan AS	3.00	1.35	.40
☐	432	Bob Gibson AS	5.50	2.50	.70
☐	433	Denny McLain AS	2.50	1.15	.30
☐	434	Jerry Koosman AS	3.00	1.35	.40
☐	435	Sam McDowell AS	2.50	1.15	.30
☐	436	Gene Alley	2.00	.90	.25
☐	437	Luis Alcaraz	1.50	.65	.19
☐	438	Gary Waslewski	1.50	.65	.19
☐	439	White Sox Rookies	1.50	.65	.19
		Ed Herrmann			
		Dan Lazar			
☐	440A	Willie McCovey	18.00	8.00	2.30
☐	440B	Willie McCovey WL	100.00	45.00	12.50
		(McCovey white)			
☐	441A	Dennis Higgins	1.50	.65	.19
☐	441B	Dennis Higgins WL	20.00	9.00	2.50
		(Higgins white)			
☐	442	Ty Cline	1.50	.65	.19
☐	443	Don Wert	1.50	.65	.19
☐	444A	Joe Moeller	1.50	.65	.19
☐	444B	Joe Moeller WL	20.00	9.00	2.50
		(Moeller white)			
☐	445	Bobby Knoop	1.50	.65	.19
☐	446	Claude Raymond	1.50	.65	.19
☐	447A	Ralph Houk MG	2.00	.90	.25
☐	447B	Ralph Houk WL	20.00	9.00	2.50
		MG (Houk white)			
☐	448	Bob Tolan	2.00	.90	.25
☐	449	Paul Lindblad	1.50	.65	.19
☐	450	Billy Williams	6.00	2.70	.75
☐	451A	Rich Rollins	2.00	.90	.25
☐	451B	Rich Rollins WL	20.00	9.00	2.50
		(Rich and 3B white)			

☐ 452A Al Ferrara .... 1.50 .65 .19
☐ 452B Al Ferrara WL 20.00 9.00 2.50
(Al and OF white)
☐ 453 Mike Cuellar .... 2.50 1.15 .30
☐ 454A Phillies Rookies .... 2.00 .90 .25
Larry Colton
Don Money
☐ 454B Phillies Rookies WL 20.00 9.00 2.50
Larry Colton
Don Money
(Names in white)
☐ 455 Sonny Siebert .... 1.50 .65 .19
☐ 456 Bud Harrelson .... 2.00 .90 .25
☐ 457 Dalton Jones .... 1.50 .65 .19
☐ 458 Curt Blefary .... 1.50 .65 .19
☐ 459 Dave Boswell .... 1.50 .65 .19
☐ 460 Joe Torre .... 3.50 1.55 .45
☐ 461A Mike Epstein .... 1.50 .65 .19
☐ 461B Mike Epstein WL 20.00 9.00 2.50
(Epstein white)
☐ 462 Red Schoendienst ...... 2.50 1.15 .30
MG
☐ 463 Dennis Ribant .... 1.50 .65 .19
☐ 464A Dave Marshall .... 1.50 .65 .19
☐ 464B Dave Marshall WL . 20.00 9.00 2.50
(Marshall white)
☐ 465 Tommy John .... 4.00 1.80 .50
☐ 466 John Boccabella .... 2.00 .90 .25
☐ 467 Tommie Reynolds ...... 1.50 .65 .19
☐ 468A Pirates Rookies .... 1.50 .65 .19
Bruce Dal Canton
Bob Robertson
☐ 468B Pirates Rookies WL 20.00 9.00 2.50
Bruce Dal Canton
Bob Robertson
(Names in white)
☐ 469 Chico Ruiz .... 1.50 .65 .19
☐ 470A Mel Stottlemyre .... 2.50 1.15 .30
☐ 470B Mel Stottlemyre WL 30.00 13.50 3.80
(Stottlemyre white)
☐ 471A Ted Savage .... 1.50 .65 .19
☐ 471B Ted Savage WL 20.00 9.00 2.50
(Savage white)
☐ 472 Jim Price .... 1.50 .65 .19
☐ 473A Jose Arcia .... 1.50 .65 .19
☐ 473B Jose Arcia WL 20.00 9.00 2.50
(Jose and 2B white)
☐ 474 Tom Murphy .... 1.50 .65 .19
☐ 475 Tim McCarver .... 3.00 1.35 .40
☐ 476A Boston Rookies .... 3.00 1.35 .40
Ken Brett
Gerry Moses
☐ 476B Boston Rookies WL 28.00 12.50 3.50
Ken Brett
Gerry Moses
(Names in white)
☐ 477 Jeff James .... 1.50 .65 .19
☐ 478 Don Buford .... 1.50 .65 .19
☐ 479 Richie Scheinblum ..... 1.50 .65 .19
☐ 480 Tom Seaver 85.00 38.00 10.50
☐ 481 Bill Melton .... 2.00 .90 .25
☐ 482A Jim Gosger .... 1.50 .65 .19
☐ 482B Jim Gosger WL 20.00 9.00 2.50
(Jim and OF white)
☐ 483 Ted Abernathy .... 1.50 .65 .19
☐ 484 Joe Gordon MG .... 2.00 .90 .25
☐ 485A Gaylord Perry 10.00 4.50 1.25
☐ 485B Gaylord Perry WL .. 85.00 38.00 10.50
(Perry white)
☐ 486A Paul Casanova .... 1.50 .65 .19
☐ 486B Paul Casanova WL. 20.00 9.00 2.50
(Casanova white)
☐ 487 Denis Menke .... 1.50 .65 .19
☐ 488 Joe Sparma .... 1.50 .65 .19
☐ 489 Clete Boyer .... 2.00 .90 .25
☐ 490 Matty Alou .... 2.00 .90 .25
☐ 491A Twins Rookies .... 1.50 .65 .19
Jerry Crider
George Mitterwald
☐ 491B Twins Rookies WL. 20.00 9.00 2.50
Jerry Crider
George Mitterwald
(Names in white)
☐ 492 Tony Cloninger .... 1.50 .65 .19
☐ 493A Wes Parker .... 2.00 .90 .25
☐ 493B Wes Parker WL 20.00 9.00 2.50
(Parker white)
☐ 494 Ken Berry .... 1.50 .65 .19
☐ 495 Bert Campaneris .... 2.00 .90 .25
☐ 496 Larry Jaster .... 1.50 .65 .19
☐ 497 Julian Javier .... 2.00 .90 .25
☐ 498 Juan Pizarro .... 2.00 .90 .25
☐ 499 Astro Rookies .... 1.50 .65 .19
Don Bryant
Steve Shea
☐ 500A Mickey Mantle UER 350.00 160.00 45.00
(No Topps copy-
right on card back)
☐ 500B Mickey Mantle WL 825.00 375.00 105.00
(Mantle in white;
no Topps copyright
on card back) UER
☐ 501A Tony Gonzalez .... 2.00 .90 .25
☐ 501B Tony Gonzalez WL. 20.00 9.00 2.50
(Tony and OF white)
☐ 502 Minnie Rojas .... 1.50 .65 .19
☐ 503 Larry Brown .... 1.50 .65 .19
☐ 504 Checklist 6 .... 7.50 1.90 .60
Brooks Robinson
☐ 505A Bobby Bolin .... 1.50 .65 .19
☐ 505B Bobby Bolin WL 20.00 9.00 2.50
(Bolin white)
☐ 506 Paul Blair .... 2.00 .90 .25
☐ 507 Cookie Rojas .... 2.00 .90 .25
☐ 508 Moe Drabowsky .... 2.00 .90 .25
☐ 509 Manny Sanguillen ...... 2.00 .90 .25
☐ 510 Rod Carew 40.00 18.00 5.00
☐ 511A Diego Segui .... 2.00 .90 .25
☐ 511B Diego Segui WL 20.00 9.00 2.50
(Diego and P white)
☐ 512 Cleon Jones .... 2.00 .90 .25
☐ 513 Camilo Pascual .... 2.50 1.15 .30
☐ 514 Mike Lum .... 2.00 .90 .25
☐ 515 Dick Green .... 2.00 .90 .25
☐ 516 Earl Weaver MG 16.00 7.25 2.00
☐ 517 Mike McCormick .... 2.50 1.15 .30
☐ 518 Fred Whitfield .... 2.00 .90 .25
☐ 519 Yankees Rookies .... 2.00 .90 .25
Jerry Kenney
Len Boehmer
☐ 520 Bob Veale .... 2.50 1.15 .30
☐ 521 George Thomas .... 2.00 .90 .25
☐ 522 Joe Hoerner .... 2.00 .90 .25
☐ 523 Bob Chance .... 2.00 .90 .25
☐ 524 Expos Rookies .... 2.50 1.15 .30
Jose Laboy
Floyd Wicker
☐ 525 Earl Wilson .... 2.50 1.15 .30
☐ 526 Hector Torres .... 2.00 .90 .25
☐ 527 Al Lopez MG .... 3.50 1.55 .45
☐ 528 Claude Osteen .... 2.50 1.15 .30
☐ 529 Ed Kirkpatrick .... 2.50 1.15 .30
☐ 530 Cesar Tovar .... 2.00 .90 .25
☐ 531 Dick Farrell .... 2.00 .90 .25
☐ 532 Bird Hill Aces .... 2.50 1.15 .30
Tom Phoebus

Jim Hardin
Dave McNally
Mike Cuellar
☐ 533 Nolan Ryan 475.00 210.00 60.00
☐ 534 Jerry McNertney 2.50 1.15 .30
☐ 535 Phil Regan 2.50 1.15 .30
☐ 536 Padres Rookies 2.00 .90 .25
Danny Breeden
Dave Roberts
☐ 537 Mike Paul 2.00 .90 .25
☐ 538 Charlie Smith 2.00 .90 .25
☐ 539 Ted Shows How 8.00 3.60 1.00
Mike Epstein
Ted Williams MG
☐ 540 Curt Flood 3.00 1.35 .40
☐ 541 Joe Verbanic 2.00 .90 .25
☐ 542 Bob Aspromonte 2.00 .90 .25
☐ 543 Fred Newman 2.00 .90 .25
☐ 544 Tigers Rookies 2.00 .90 .25
Mike Kilkenny
Ron Woods
☐ 545 Willie Stargell 14.00 6.25 1.75
☐ 546 Jim Nash 2.00 .90 .25
☐ 547 Billy Martin MG 6.00 2.70 .75
☐ 548 Bob Locker 2.00 .90 .25
☐ 549 Ron Brand 2.00 .90 .25
☐ 550 Brooks Robinson 30.00 13.50 3.80
☐ 551 Wayne Granger 2.00 .90 .25
☐ 552 Dodgers Rookies 5.00 2.30 .60
Ted Sizemore
Bill Sudakis
☐ 553 Ron Davis 2.00 .90 .25
☐ 554 Frank Bertaina 2.00 .90 .25
☐ 555 Jim Ray Hart 2.50 1.15 .30
☐ 556 A's Stars 2.50 1.15 .30
Sal Bando
Bert Campaneris
Danny Cater
☐ 557 Frank Fernandez 2.00 .90 .25
☐ 558 Tom Burgmeier 2.50 1.15 .30
☐ 559 Cardinals Rookies 2.00 .90 .25
Joe Hague
Jim Hicks
☐ 560 Luis Tiant 5.00 2.30 .60
☐ 561 Ron Clark 2.00 .90 .25
☐ 562 Bob Watson 7.00 3.10 .85
☐ 563 Marty Pattin 2.50 1.15 .30
☐ 564 Gil Hodges MG 10.00 4.50 1.25
☐ 565 Hoyt Wilhelm 7.00 3.10 .85
☐ 566 Ron Hansen 2.00 .90 .25
☐ 567 Pirates Rookies 2.00 .90 .25
Elvio Jimenez
Jim Shellenback
☐ 568 Cecil Upshaw 2.00 .90 .25
☐ 569 Billy Harris 2.00 .90 .25
☐ 570 Ron Santo 7.00 3.10 .85
☐ 571 Cap Peterson 2.00 .90 .25
☐ 572 Giants Heroes 15.00 6.75 1.90
Willie McCovey
Juan Marichal
☐ 573 Jim Palmer 40.00 18.00 5.00
☐ 574 George Scott 2.50 1.15 .30
☐ 575 Bill Singer 2.50 1.15 .30
☐ 576 Phillies Rookies 2.00 .90 .25
Ron Stone
Bill Wilson
☐ 577 Mike Hegan 2.50 1.15 .30
☐ 578 Don Bosch 2.00 .90 .25
☐ 579 Dave Nelson 2.00 .90 .25
☐ 580 Jim Northrup 2.50 1.15 .30
☐ 581 Gary Nolan 2.50 1.15 .30
☐ 582A Checklist 7 6.00 1.50 .50
(White circle on back)
(Tony Oliva)

☐ 582B Checklist 7 7.50 1.90 .60
(Red circle on back)
(Tony Oliva)
☐ 583 Clyde Wright 2.00 .90 .25
☐ 584 Don Mason 2.00 .90 .25
☐ 585 Ron Swoboda 2.50 1.15 .30
☐ 586 Tim Cullen 2.00 .90 .25
☐ 587 Joe Rudi 7.00 3.10 .85
☐ 588 Bill White 3.00 1.35 .40
☐ 589 Joe Pepitone 4.50 2.00 .55
☐ 590 Rico Carty 3.50 1.55 .45
☐ 591 Mike Hedlund 3.00 1.35 .40
☐ 592 Padres Rookies 3.50 1.55 .45
Rafael Robles
Al Santorini
☐ 593 Don Nottebart 3.00 1.35 .40
☐ 594 Dooley Womack 3.00 1.35 .40
☐ 595 Lee Maye 3.00 1.35 .40
☐ 596 Chuck Hartenstein 3.00 1.35 .40
☐ 597 A.L. Rookies 70.00 32.00 8.75
Bob Floyd
Larry Burchart
Rollie Fingers
☐ 598 Ruben Amaro 3.00 1.35 .40
☐ 599 John Boozer 3.00 1.35 .40
☐ 600 Tony Oliva 7.00 3.10 .85
☐ 601 Tug McGraw 7.50 3.40 .95
☐ 602 Cubs Rookies 3.00 1.35 .40
Alec Distaso
Don Young
Jim Qualls
☐ 603 Joe Keough 3.00 1.35 .40
☐ 604 Bobby Etheridge 3.00 1.35 .40
☐ 605 Dick Ellsworth 3.00 1.35 .40
☐ 606 Gene Mauch MG 3.50 1.55 .45
☐ 607 Dick Bosman 3.00 1.35 .40
☐ 608 Dick Simpson 3.00 1.35 .40
☐ 609 Phil Gagliano 3.00 1.35 .40
☐ 610 Jim Hardin 3.00 1.35 .40
☐ 611 Braves Rookies 5.00 2.30 .60
Bob Didier
Walt Hriniak
Gary Neibauer
☐ 612 Jack Aker 3.50 1.55 .45
☐ 613 Jim Beauchamp 3.00 1.35 .40
☐ 614 Houston Rookies 3.00 1.35 .40
Tom Griffin
Skip Guinn
☐ 615 Len Gabrielson 3.00 1.35 .40
☐ 616 Don McMahon 3.00 1.35 .40
☐ 617 Jesse Gonder 3.00 1.35 .40
☐ 618 Ramon Webster 3.00 1.35 .40
☐ 619 Royals Rookies 3.50 1.55 .45
Bill Butler
Pat Kelly
Juan Rios
☐ 620 Dean Chance 3.50 1.55 .45
☐ 621 Bill Voss 3.00 1.35 .40
☐ 622 Dan Osinski 3.00 1.35 .40
☐ 623 Hank Allen 3.00 1.35 .40
☐ 624 NL Rookies 4.00 1.80 .50
Darrel Chaney
Duffy Dyer
Terry Harmon
☐ 625 Mack Jones UER 3.50 1.55 .45
(Batting wrong)
☐ 626 Gene Michael 3.50 1.55 .45
☐ 627 George Stone 3.00 1.35 .40
☐ 628 Red Sox Rookies 5.00 2.30 .60
Bill Conigliaro
Syd O'Brien
Fred Wenz
☐ 629 Jack Hamilton 3.00 1.35 .40

	#	Player			
☐	630	Bobby Bonds	35.00	16.00	4.40
☐	631	John Kennedy	3.50	1.55	.45
☐	632	Jon Warden	3.00	1.35	.40
☐	633	Harry Walker MG	3.00	1.35	.40
☐	634	Andy Etchebarren	3.00	1.35	.40
☐	635	George Culver	3.00	1.35	.40
☐	636	Woody Held	3.00	1.35	.40
☐	637	Padres Rookies	3.50	1.55	.45
		Jerry DaVanon			
		Frank Reberger			
		Clay Kirby			
☐	638	Ed Sprague	3.00	1.35	.40
☐	639	Barry Moore	3.00	1.35	.40
☐	640	Fergie Jenkins	18.00	8.00	2.30
☐	641	NL Rookies	3.50	1.55	.45
		Bobby Darwin			
		John Miller			
		Tommy Dean			
☐	642	John Hiller	3.00	1.35	.40
☐	643	Billy Cowan	3.00	1.35	.40
☐	644	Chuck Hinton	3.00	1.35	.40
☐	645	George Brunet	3.00	1.35	.40
☐	646	Expos Rookies	3.50	1.55	.45
		Dan McGinn			
		Carl Morton			
☐	647	Dave Wickersham	3.00	1.35	.40
☐	648	Bobby Wine	3.50	1.55	.45
☐	649	Al Jackson	3.00	1.35	.40
☐	650	Ted Williams MG	15.00	6.75	1.90
☐	651	Gus Gil	3.50	1.55	.45
☐	652	Eddie Watt	3.00	1.35	.40
☐	653	Aurelio Rodriguez UER	6.00	2.70	.75
		(Photo actually			
		Angels' batboy)			
☐	654	White Sox Rookies	5.00	2.30	.60
		Carlos May			
		Don Secrist			
		Rich Morales			
☐	655	Mike Hershberger	3.00	1.35	.40
☐	656	Dan Schneider	3.00	1.35	.40
☐	657	Bobby Murcer	6.00	2.70	.75
☐	658	AL Rookies	3.50	1.55	.45
		Tom Hall			
		Bill Burbach			
		Jim Miles			
☐	659	Johnny Podres	3.50	1.55	.45
☐	660	Reggie Smith	6.50	2.90	.80
☐	661	Jim Merritt	3.00	1.35	.40
☐	662	Royals Rookies	3.50	1.55	.45
		Dick Drago			
		George Spriggs			
		Bob Oliver			
☐	663	Dick Radatz	3.50	1.55	.45
☐	664	Ron Hunt	5.00	1.55	.45

1970 Topps

The cards in this 720-card set measure 2 1/2" by 3 1/2". The Topps set for 1970 has color photos surrounded by white frame lines and gray borders. The backs have a blue biographical section and a yellow record section. All-Star selections are featured on cards 450 to 469. Other topical subsets within this set include League Leaders (61-72), Playoffs cards (195-202), and World Series cards (305-310). There are graduations of scarcity, terminating in the high series (634-720), which are outlined in the value summary. The key Rookie Card in this set is Thurman Munson.

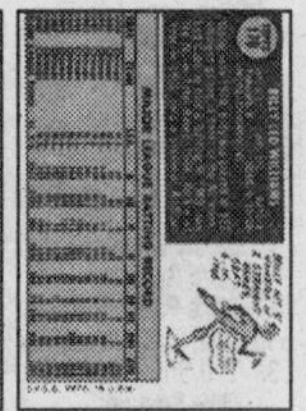

	NRMT	EXC	G-VG
COMPLETE SET (720)	1800.01	800.00	230.00
COMMON CARD (1-132)	1.00	.45	.13
COMMON CARD (133-263)	1.00	.45	.13
COMMON CARD (264-372)	1.00	.45	.13
COMMON CARD (373-459)	1.25	.55	.16
COMMON CARD (460-546)	1.50	.65	.19
COMMON CARD (547-633)	3.00	1.35	.40
COMMON CARD (634-720)	8.00	3.60	1.00

	#	Player	NRMT	EXC	G-VG
☐	1	New York Mets	15.00	3.00	.90
		Team Card			
☐	2	Diego Segui	1.25	.55	.16
☐	3	Darrel Chaney	1.00	.45	.13
☐	4	Tom Egan	1.00	.45	.13
☐	5	Wes Parker	1.25	.55	.16
☐	6	Grant Jackson	1.00	.45	.13
☐	7	Indians Rookies	1.00	.45	.13
		Gary Boyd			
		Russ Nagelson			
☐	8	Jose Martinez	1.00	.45	.13
☐	9	Checklist 1	10.00	1.00	.30
☐	10	Carl Yastrzemski	16.00	7.25	2.00
☐	11	Nate Colbert	1.00	.45	.13
☐	12	John Hiller	1.25	.55	.16
☐	13	Jack Hiatt	1.00	.45	.13
☐	14	Hank Allen	1.00	.45	.13
☐	15	Larry Dierker	1.00	.45	.13
☐	16	Charlie Metro MG	1.00	.45	.13
☐	17	Hoyt Wilhelm	4.00	1.80	.50
☐	18	Carlos May	1.25	.55	.16
☐	19	John Boccabella	1.00	.45	.13
☐	20	Dave McNally	1.25	.55	.16
☐	21	A's Rookies	7.00	3.10	.85
		Vida Blue			
		Gene Tenace			
☐	22	Ray Washburn	1.00	.45	.13
☐	23	Bill Robinson	1.25	.55	.16
☐	24	Dick Selma	1.00	.45	.13
☐	25	Cesar Tovar	1.00	.45	.13
☐	26	Tug McGraw	1.50	.65	.19
☐	27	Chuck Hinton	1.00	.45	.13
☐	28	Billy Wilson	1.00	.45	.13
☐	29	Sandy Alomar	1.25	.55	.16
☐	30	Matty Alou	1.25	.55	.16
☐	31	Marty Pattin	1.25	.55	.16
☐	32	Harry Walker MG	1.00	.45	.13
☐	33	Don Wert	1.00	.45	.13
☐	34	Willie Crawford	1.00	.45	.13
☐	35	Joel Horlen	1.00	.45	.13
☐	36	Red Rookies	1.25	.55	.16
		Danny Breeden			
		Bernie Carbo			
☐	37	Dick Drago	1.00	.45	.13

☐ 38 Mack Jones 1.00 .45 .13
☐ 39 Mike Nagy 1.00 .45 .13
☐ 40 Rich Allen 2.00 .90 .25
☐ 41 George Lauzerique 1.00 .45 .13
☐ 42 Tito Fuentes 1.00 .45 .13
☐ 43 Jack Aker 1.00 .45 .13
☐ 44 Roberto Pena 1.00 .45 .13
☐ 45 Dave Johnson 1.25 .55 .16
☐ 46 Ken Rudolph 1.00 .45 .13
☐ 47 Bob Miller 1.00 .45 .13
☐ 48 Gil Garrido 1.00 .45 .13
☐ 49 Tim Cullen 1.00 .45 .13
☐ 50 Tommie Agee 1.25 .55 .16
☐ 51 Bob Christian 1.00 .45 .13
☐ 52 Bruce Dal Canton 1.00 .45 .13
☐ 53 John Kennedy 1.00 .45 .13
☐ 54 Jeff Torborg 1.25 .55 .16
☐ 55 John Odom 1.00 .45 .13
☐ 56 Phillies Rookies 1.00 .45 .13
  Joe Lis
  Scott Reid
☐ 57 Pat Kelly 1.00 .45 .13
☐ 58 Dave Marshall 1.00 .45 .13
☐ 59 Dick Ellsworth 1.00 .45 .13
☐ 60 Jim Wynn 1.25 .55 .16
☐ 61 NL Batting Leaders 8.00 3.60 1.00
  Pete Rose
  Bob Clemente
  Cleon Jones
☐ 62 AL Batting Leaders 3.50 1.55 .45
  Rod Carew
  Reggie Smith
  Tony Oliva
☐ 63 NL RBI Leaders 4.00 1.80 .50
  Willie McCovey
  Ron Santo
  Tony Perez
☐ 64 AL RBI Leaders 5.50 2.50 .70
  Harmon Killebrew
  Boog Powell
  Reggie Jackson
☐ 65 NL Home Run Leaders. 5.00 2.30 .60
  Willie McCovey
  Hank Aaron
  Lee May
☐ 66 AL Home Run Leaders. 5.50 2.50 .70
  Harmon Killebrew
  Frank Howard
  Reggie Jackson
☐ 67 NL ERA Leaders 6.50 2.90 .80
  Juan Marichal
  Steve Carlton
  Bob Gibson
☐ 68 AL ERA Leaders 3.00 1.35 .40
  Dick Bosman
  Jim Palmer
  Mike Cuellar
☐ 69 NL Pitching Leaders 6.50 2.90 .80
  Tom Seaver
  Phil Niekro
  Fergie Jenkins
  Juan Marichal
☐ 70 AL Pitching Leaders 2.00 .90 .25
  Dennis McLain
  Mike Cuellar
  Dave Boswell
  Dave McNally
  Jim Perry
  Mel Stottlemyre
☐ 71 NL Strikeout Leaders 4.00 1.80 .50
  Fergie Jenkins
  Bob Gibson
  Bill Singer
☐ 72 AL Strikeout Leaders 2.00 .90 .25
  Sam McDowell
  Mickey Lolich
  Andy Messersmith
☐ 73 Wayne Granger 1.00 .45 .13
☐ 74 Angels Rookies 1.00 .45 .13
  Greg Washburn
  Wally Wolf
☐ 75 Jim Kaat 2.00 .90 .25
☐ 76 Carl Taylor 1.00 .45 .13
☐ 77 Frank Linzy 1.00 .45 .13
☐ 78 Joe Lahoud 1.00 .45 .13
☐ 79 Clay Kirby 1.00 .45 .13
☐ 80 Don Kessinger 1.25 .55 .16
☐ 81 Dave May 1.00 .45 .13
☐ 82 Frank Fernandez 1.00 .45 .13
☐ 83 Don Cardwell 1.00 .45 .13
☐ 84 Paul Casanova 1.00 .45 .13
☐ 85 Max Alvis 1.00 .45 .13
☐ 86 Lum Harris MG 1.00 .45 .13
☐ 87 Steve Renko 1.00 .45 .13
☐ 88 Pilots Rookies 1.00 .45 .13
  Miguel Fuentes
  Dick Baney
☐ 89 Juan Rios 1.00 .45 .13
☐ 90 Tim McCarver 1.50 .65 .19
☐ 91 Rich Morales 1.00 .45 .13
☐ 92 George Culver 1.00 .45 .13
☐ 93 Rick Renick 1.00 .45 .13
☐ 94 Freddie Patek 1.25 .55 .16
☐ 95 Earl Wilson 1.25 .55 .16
☐ 96 Cardinals Rookies 4.00 1.80 .50
  Leron Lee
  Jerry Reuss
☐ 97 Joe Moeller 1.00 .45 .13
☐ 98 Gates Brown 1.25 .55 .16
☐ 99 Bobby Pfeil 1.00 .45 .13
☐ 100 Mel Stottlemyre 1.25 .55 .16
☐ 101 Bobby Floyd 1.00 .45 .13
☐ 102 Joe Rudi 1.25 .55 .16
☐ 103 Frank Reberger 1.00 .45 .13
☐ 104 Gerry Moses 1.00 .45 .13
☐ 105 Tony Gonzalez 1.00 .45 .13
☐ 106 Darold Knowles 1.00 .45 .13
☐ 107 Bobby Etheridge 1.00 .45 .13
☐ 108 Tom Burgmeier 1.00 .45 .13
☐ 109 Expos Rookies 1.00 .45 .13
  Garry Jestadt
  Carl Morton
☐ 110 Bob Moose 1.00 .45 .13
☐ 111 Mike Hegan 1.25 .55 .16
☐ 112 Dave Nelson 1.00 .45 .13
☐ 113 Jim Ray 1.00 .45 .13
☐ 114 Gene Michael 1.25 .55 .16
☐ 115 Alex Johnson 1.25 .55 .16
☐ 116 Sparky Lyle 1.50 .65 .19
☐ 117 Don Young 1.00 .45 .13
☐ 118 George Mitterwald 1.00 .45 .13
☐ 119 Chuck Taylor 1.00 .45 .13
☐ 120 Sal Bando 1.25 .55 .16
☐ 121 Orioles Rookies 1.00 .45 .13
  Fred Beene
  Terry Crowley
☐ 122 George Stone 1.00 .45 .13
☐ 123 Don Gutteridge MG 1.00 .45 .13
☐ 124 Larry Jaster 1.00 .45 .13
☐ 125 Deron Johnson 1.00 .45 .13
☐ 126 Marty Martinez 1.00 .45 .13
☐ 127 Joe Coleman 1.00 .45 .13
☐ 128A Checklist 2 ERR 6.00 .60 .18
  (226 R Perranoski)
☐ 128B Checklist 2 COR 6.00 .60 .18
  (226 R. Perranoski)

☐	129	Jimmie Price	1.00	.45	.13
☐	130	Ollie Brown	1.00	.45	.13
☐	131	Dodgers Rookies	1.00	.45	.13
		Ray Lamb			
		Bob Stinson			
☐	132	Jim McGlothlin	1.00	.45	.13
☐	133	Clay Carroll	1.00	.45	.13
☐	134	Danny Walton	1.00	.45	.13
☐	135	Dick Dietz	1.00	.45	.13
☐	136	Steve Hargan	1.00	.45	.13
☐	137	Art Shamsky	1.00	.45	.13
☐	138	Joe Foy	1.00	.45	.13
☐	139	Rich Nye	1.00	.45	.13
☐	140	Reggie Jackson	75.00	34.00	9.50
☐	141	Pirates Rookies	1.25	.55	.16
		Dave Cash			
		Johnny Jeter			
☐	142	Fritz Peterson	1.00	.45	.13
☐	143	Phil Gagliano	1.00	.45	.13
☐	144	Ray Culp	1.00	.45	.13
☐	145	Rico Carty	1.25	.55	.16
☐	146	Danny Murphy	1.00	.45	.13
☐	147	Angel Hermoso	1.00	.45	.13
☐	148	Earl Weaver MG	4.00	1.80	.50
☐	149	Billy Champion	1.00	.45	.13
☐	150	Harmon Killebrew	10.00	4.50	1.25
☐	151	Dave Roberts	1.00	.45	.13
☐	152	Ike Brown	1.00	.45	.13
☐	153	Gary Gentry	1.00	.45	.13
☐	154	Senators Rookies	1.00	.45	.13
		Jim Miles			
		Jan Dukes			
☐	155	Denis Menke	1.00	.45	.13
☐	156	Eddie Fisher	1.00	.45	.13
☐	157	Manny Mota	1.25	.55	.16
☐	158	Jerry McNertney	1.25	.55	.16
☐	159	Tommy Helms	1.25	.55	.16
☐	160	Phil Niekro	5.00	2.30	.60
☐	161	Richie Scheinblum	1.00	.45	.13
☐	162	Jerry Johnson	1.00	.45	.13
☐	163	Syd O'Brien	1.00	.45	.13
☐	164	Ty Cline	1.00	.45	.13
☐	165	Ed Kirkpatrick	1.00	.45	.13
☐	166	Al Oliver	3.00	1.35	.40
☐	167	Bill Burbach	1.00	.45	.13
☐	168	Dave Watkins	1.00	.45	.13
☐	169	Tom Hall	1.00	.45	.13
☐	170	Billy Williams	6.00	2.70	.75
☐	171	Jim Nash	1.00	.45	.13
☐	172	Braves Rookies	3.00	1.35	.40
		Garry Hill			
		Ralph Garr			
☐	173	Jim Hicks	1.00	.45	.13
☐	174	Ted Sizemore	1.25	.55	.16
☐	175	Dick Bosman	1.00	.45	.13
☐	176	Jim Ray Hart	1.25	.55	.16
☐	177	Jim Northrup	1.25	.55	.16
☐	178	Denny Lemaster	1.00	.45	.13
☐	179	Ivan Murrell	1.00	.45	.13
☐	180	Tommy John	3.00	1.35	.40
☐	181	Sparky Anderson MG	4.50	2.00	.55
☐	182	Dick Hall	1.00	.45	.13
☐	183	Jerry Grote	1.00	.45	.13
☐	184	Ray Fosse	1.00	.45	.13
☐	185	Don Mincher	1.25	.55	.16
☐	186	Rick Joseph	1.00	.45	.13
☐	187	Mike Hedlund	1.00	.45	.13
☐	188	Manny Sanguillen	1.25	.55	.16
☐	189	Yankees Rookies	80.00	36.00	10.00
		Thurman Munson			
		Dave McDonald			
☐	190	Joe Torre	2.50	1.15	.30
☐	191	Vicente Romo	1.00	.45	.13

☐	192	Jim Qualls	1.00	.45	.13
☐	193	Mike Wegener	1.00	.45	.13
☐	194	Chuck Manuel	1.00	.45	.13
☐	195	NL Playoff Game 1	15.00	6.75	1.90
		Tom Seaver wins opener			
☐	196	NL Playoff Game 2	2.25	1.00	.30
		Mets show muscle			
		(Ken Boswell)			
☐	197	NL Playoff Game 3	30.00	13.50	3.80
		Nolan Ryan saves			
		the day			
☐	198	NL Playoff Summary	16.00	7.25	2.00
		Mets celebrate			
		(Nolan Ryan)			
☐	199	AL Playoff Game 1	2.25	1.00	.30
		Orioles win squeaker			
		(Mike Cuellar)			
☐	200	AL Playoff Game 2	2.25	1.00	.30
		Boog Powell scores			
		winning run			
☐	201	AL Playoff Game 3	2.25	1.00	.30
		Birds wrap it up			
		(Boog Powell and			
		Andy Etchebarren)			
☐	202	AL Playoff Summary	2.25	1.00	.30
		Orioles celebrate			
☐	203	Rudy May	1.00	.45	.13
☐	204	Len Gabrielson	1.00	.45	.13
☐	205	Bert Campaneris	1.25	.55	.16
☐	206	Clete Boyer	1.25	.55	.16
☐	207	Tigers Rookies	1.00	.45	.13
		Norman McRae			
		Bob Reed			
☐	208	Fred Gladding	1.00	.45	.13
☐	209	Ken Suarez	1.00	.45	.13
☐	210	Juan Marichal	6.50	2.90	.80
☐	211	Ted Williams MG	12.00	5.50	1.50
☐	212	Al Santorini	1.00	.45	.13
☐	213	Andy Etchebarren	1.00	.45	.13
☐	214	Ken Boswell	1.00	.45	.13
☐	215	Reggie Smith	2.50	1.15	.30
☐	216	Chuck Hartenstein	1.00	.45	.13
☐	217	Ron Hansen	1.00	.45	.13
☐	218	Ron Stone	1.00	.45	.13
☐	219	Jerry Kenney	1.00	.45	.13
☐	220	Steve Carlton	22.00	10.00	2.80
☐	221	Ron Brand	1.00	.45	.13
☐	222	Jim Rooker	1.25	.55	.16
☐	223	Nate Oliver	1.00	.45	.13
☐	224	Steve Barber	1.25	.55	.16
☐	225	Lee May	1.25	.55	.16
☐	226	Ron Perranoski	1.25	.55	.16
☐	227	Astros Rookies	2.00	.90	.25
		John Mayberry			
		Bob Watkins			
☐	228	Aurelio Rodriguez	1.25	.55	.16
☐	229	Rich Robertson	1.00	.45	.13
☐	230	Brooks Robinson	12.00	5.50	1.50
☐	231	Luis Tiant	2.00	.90	.25
☐	232	Bob Didier	1.00	.45	.13
☐	233	Lew Krausse	1.00	.45	.13
☐	234	Tommy Dean	1.00	.45	.13
☐	235	Mike Epstein	1.00	.45	.13
☐	236	Bob Veale	1.25	.55	.16
☐	237	Russ Gibson	1.00	.45	.13
☐	238	Jose Laboy	1.00	.45	.13
☐	239	Ken Berry	1.00	.45	.13
☐	240	Fergie Jenkins	8.00	3.60	1.00
☐	241	Royals Rookies	1.00	.45	.13
		Al Fitzmorris			
		Scott Northey			
☐	242	Walter Alston MG	2.00	.90	.25
☐	243	Joe Sparma	1.00	.45	.13

	No.	Card			
☐	244A	Checklist 3	6.00	.60	.18
		(Red bat on front)			
☐	244B	Checklist 3	6.00	.60	.18
		(Brown bat on front)			
☐	245	Leo Cardenas	1.00	.45	.13
☐	246	Jim McAndrew	1.00	.45	.13
☐	247	Lou Klimchock	1.00	.45	.13
☐	248	Jesus Alou	1.00	.45	.13
☐	249	Bob Locker	1.00	.45	.13
☐	250	Willie McCovey UER	9.00	4.00	1.15
		(1963 San Francisci)			
☐	251	Dick Schofield	1.00	.45	.13
☐	252	Lowell Palmer	1.00	.45	.13
☐	253	Ron Woods	1.00	.45	.13
☐	254	Camilo Pascual	1.25	.55	.16
☐	255	Jim Spencer	1.00	.45	.13
☐	256	Vic Davalillo	1.00	.45	.13
☐	257	Dennis Higgins	1.00	.45	.13
☐	258	Paul Popovich	1.00	.45	.13
☐	259	Tommie Reynolds	1.00	.45	.13
☐	260	Claude Osteen	1.25	.55	.16
☐	261	Curt Motton	1.00	.45	.13
☐	262	Padres Rookies	1.00	.45	.13
		Jerry Morales			
		Jim Williams			
☐	263	Duane Josephson	1.25	.55	.16
☐	264	Rich Hebner	1.25	.55	.16
☐	265	Randy Hundley	1.00	.45	.13
☐	266	Wally Bunker	1.00	.45	.13
☐	267	Twins Rookies	1.00	.45	.13
		Herman Hill			
		Paul Ratliff			
☐	268	Claude Raymond	1.00	.45	.13
☐	269	Cesar Gutierrez	1.00	.45	.13
☐	270	Chris Short	1.00	.45	.13
☐	271	Greg Goossen	1.00	.45	.13
☐	272	Hector Torres	1.00	.45	.13
☐	273	Ralph Houk MG	1.25	.55	.16
☐	274	Gerry Arrigo	1.00	.45	.13
☐	275	Duke Sims	1.00	.45	.13
☐	276	Ron Hunt	1.00	.45	.13
☐	277	Paul Doyle	1.00	.45	.13
☐	278	Tommie Aaron	1.25	.55	.16
☐	279	Bill Lee	2.00	.90	.25
☐	280	Donn Clendenon	1.25	.55	.16
☐	281	Casey Cox	1.00	.45	.13
☐	282	Steve Huntz	1.00	.45	.13
☐	283	Angel Bravo	1.00	.45	.13
☐	284	Jack Baldschun	1.00	.45	.13
☐	285	Paul Blair	1.25	.55	.16
☐	286	Dodgers Rookies	7.00	3.10	.85
		Jack Jenkins			
		Bill Buckner			
☐	287	Fred Talbot	1.00	.45	.13
☐	288	Larry Hisle	1.25	.55	.16
☐	289	Gene Brabender	1.00	.45	.13
☐	290	Rod Carew	20.00	9.00	2.50
☐	291	Leo Durocher MG	2.50	1.15	.30
☐	292	Eddie Leon	1.00	.45	.13
☐	293	Bob Bailey	1.00	.45	.13
☐	294	Jose Azcue	1.00	.45	.13
☐	295	Cecil Upshaw	1.00	.45	.13
☐	296	Woody Woodward	1.25	.55	.16
☐	297	Curt Blefary	1.00	.45	.13
☐	298	Ken Henderson	1.00	.45	.13
☐	299	Buddy Bradford	1.00	.45	.13
☐	300	Tom Seaver	45.00	20.00	5.75
☐	301	Chico Salmon	1.00	.45	.13
☐	302	Jeff James	1.00	.45	.13
☐	303	Brant Alyea	1.00	.45	.13
☐	304	Bill Russell	5.00	2.30	.60
☐	305	World Series Game 1.	3.00	1.35	.40
		Don Buford leadoff			
		homer			
☐	306	World Series Game 2.	3.00	1.35	.40
		Donn Clendenon's			
		homer breaks ice			
☐	307	World Series Game 3.	3.00	1.35	.40
		Tommie Agee's catch			
		saves the day			
☐	308	World Series Game 4.	3.00	1.35	.40
		J.C. Martin's bunt			
		ends deadlock			
☐	309	World Series Game 5.	3.25	1.45	.40
		Jerry Koosman			
		shuts door			
☐	310	World Series Summary	5.00	2.30	.60
		(Mets whoop it up;			
		Tug McGraw, Ed Kranepool)			
☐	311	Dick Green	1.00	.45	.13
☐	312	Mike Torrez	1.25	.55	.16
☐	313	Mayo Smith MG	1.00	.45	.13
☐	314	Bill McCool	1.00	.45	.13
☐	315	Luis Aparicio	5.00	2.30	.60
☐	316	Skip Guinn	1.00	.45	.13
☐	317	Red Sox Rookies	1.25	.55	.16
		Billy Conigliaro			
		Luis Alvarado			
☐	318	Willie Smith	1.00	.45	.13
☐	319	Clay Dalrymple	1.00	.45	.13
☐	320	Jim Maloney	1.25	.55	.16
☐	321	Lou Piniella	3.00	1.35	.40
☐	322	Luke Walker	1.00	.45	.13
☐	323	Wayne Comer	1.00	.45	.13
☐	324	Tony Taylor	1.00	.45	.13
☐	325	Dave Boswell	1.00	.45	.13
☐	326	Bill Voss	1.00	.45	.13
☐	327	Hal King	1.00	.45	.13
☐	328	George Brunet	1.00	.45	.13
☐	329	Chris Cannizzaro	1.00	.45	.13
☐	330	Lou Brock	10.00	4.50	1.25
☐	331	Chuck Dobson	1.00	.45	.13
☐	332	Bobby Wine	1.00	.45	.13
☐	333	Bobby Murcer	2.00	.90	.25
☐	334	Phil Regan	1.25	.55	.16
☐	335	Bill Freehan	1.25	.55	.16
☐	336	Del Unser	1.00	.45	.13
☐	337	Mike McCormick	1.25	.55	.16
☐	338	Paul Schaal	1.00	.45	.13
☐	339	Johnny Edwards	1.00	.45	.13
☐	340	Tony Conigliaro	3.00	1.35	.40
☐	341	Bill Sudakis	1.00	.45	.13
☐	342	Wilbur Wood	1.25	.55	.16
☐	343A	Checklist 4	6.00	.60	.18
		(Red bat on front)			
☐	343B	Checklist 4	6.00	.60	.18
		(Brown bat on front)			
☐	344	Marcelino Lopez	1.00	.45	.13
☐	345	Al Ferrara	1.00	.45	.13
☐	346	Red Schoendienst MG	2.00	.90	.25
☐	347	Russ Snyder	1.00	.45	.13
☐	348	Mets Rookies	1.50	.65	.19
		Mike Jorgensen			
		Jesse Hudson			
☐	349	Steve Hamilton	1.00	.45	.13
☐	350	Roberto Clemente	55.00	25.00	7.00
☐	351	Tom Murphy	1.00	.45	.13
☐	352	Bob Barton	1.00	.45	.13
☐	353	Stan Williams	1.00	.45	.13
☐	354	Amos Otis	1.25	.55	.16
☐	355	Doug Rader	1.25	.55	.16
☐	356	Fred Lasher	1.00	.45	.13
☐	357	Bob Burda	1.00	.45	.13
☐	358	Pedro Borbon	1.50	.65	.19
☐	359	Phil Roof	1.00	.45	.13
☐	360	Curt Flood	1.50	.65	.19

☐ 361 Ray Jarvis 1.00 .45 .13
☐ 362 Joe Hague 1.00 .45 .13
☐ 363 Tom Shopay 1.00 .45 .13
☐ 364 Dan McGinn 1.00 .45 .13
☐ 365 Zoilo Versalles 1.00 .45 .13
☐ 366 Barry Moore 1.00 .45 .13
☐ 367 Mike Lum 1.00 .45 .13
☐ 368 Ed Herrmann 1.00 .45 .13
☐ 369 Alan Foster 1.00 .45 .13
☐ 370 Tommy Harper 1.25 .55 .16
☐ 371 Rod Gaspar 1.00 .45 .13
☐ 372 Dave Giusti 1.25 .55 .16
☐ 373 Roy White 1.50 .65 .19
☐ 374 Tommie Sisk 1.25 .55 .16
☐ 375 Johnny Callison 1.50 .65 .19
☐ 376 Lefty Phillips MG 1.25 .55 .16
☐ 377 Bill Butler 1.25 .55 .16
☐ 378 Jim Davenport 1.25 .55 .16
☐ 379 Tom Tischinski 1.25 .55 .16
☐ 380 Tony Perez 8.00 3.60 1.00
☐ 381 Athletics Rookies 1.25 .55 .16
Bobby Brooks
Mike Olivo
☐ 382 Jack DiLauro 1.25 .55 .16
☐ 383 Mickey Stanley 1.50 .65 .19
☐ 384 Gary Neibauer 1.25 .55 .16
☐ 385 George Scott 1.50 .65 .19
☐ 386 Bill Dillman 1.25 .55 .16
☐ 387 Baltimore Orioles 2.50 1.15 .30
Team Card
☐ 388 Byron Browne 1.25 .55 .16
☐ 389 Jim Shellenback 1.25 .55 .16
☐ 390 Willie Davis 1.50 .65 .19
☐ 391 Larry Brown 1.25 .55 .16
☐ 392 Walt Hriniak 1.25 .55 .16
☐ 393 John Gelnar 1.25 .55 .16
☐ 394 Gil Hodges MG 4.00 1.80 .50
☐ 395 Walt Williams 1.25 .55 .16
☐ 396 Steve Blass 1.50 .65 .19
☐ 397 Roger Repoz 1.25 .55 .16
☐ 398 Bill Stoneman 1.25 .55 .16
☐ 399 New York Yankees 2.50 1.15 .30
Team Card
☐ 400 Denny McLain 2.50 1.15 .30
☐ 401 Giants Rookies 1.25 .55 .16
John Harrell
Bernie Williams
☐ 402 Ellie Rodriguez 1.25 .55 .16
☐ 403 Jim Bunning 2.50 1.15 .30
☐ 404 Rich Reese 1.25 .55 .16
☐ 405 Bill Hands 1.25 .55 .16
☐ 406 Mike Andrews 1.25 .55 .16
☐ 407 Bob Watson 1.50 .65 .19
☐ 408 Paul Lindblad 1.25 .55 .16
☐ 409 Bob Tolan 1.50 .65 .19
☐ 410 Boog Powell 4.50 2.00 .55
☐ 411 Los Angeles Dodgers 2.50 1.15 .30
Team Card
☐ 412 Larry Burchart 1.25 .55 .16
☐ 413 Sonny Jackson 1.25 .55 .16
☐ 414 Paul Edmondson 1.25 .55 .16
☐ 415 Julian Javier 1.50 .65 .19
☐ 416 Joe Verbanic 1.25 .55 .16
☐ 417 John Bateman 1.25 .55 .16
☐ 418 John Donaldson 1.25 .55 .16
☐ 419 Ron Taylor 1.25 .55 .16
☐ 420 Ken McMullen 1.50 .65 .19
☐ 421 Pat Dobson 1.50 .65 .19
☐ 422 Royals Team 2.50 1.15 .30
☐ 423 Jerry May 1.25 .55 .16
☐ 424 Mike Kilkenny 1.25 .55 .16
(Inconsistent design,
card number in
white circle)
☐ 425 Bobby Bonds 7.00 3.10 .85
☐ 426 Bill Rigney MG 1.25 .55 .16
☐ 427 Fred Norman 1.25 .55 .16
☐ 428 Don Buford 1.25 .55 .16
☐ 429 Cubs Rookies 1.25 .55 .16
Randy Bobb
Jim Cosman
☐ 430 Andy Messersmith 1.50 .65 .19
☐ 431 Ron Swoboda 1.50 .65 .19
☐ 432A Checklist 5 6.00 .90 .30
("Baseball" in
yellow letters)
☐ 432B Checklist 5 6.00 .90 .30
("Baseball" in
white letters)
☐ 433 Ron Bryant 1.25 .55 .16
☐ 434 Felipe Alou 2.00 .90 .25
☐ 435 Nelson Briles 1.50 .65 .19
☐ 436 Philadelphia Phillies 2.50 1.15 .30
Team Card
☐ 437 Danny Cater 1.25 .55 .16
☐ 438 Pat Jarvis 1.25 .55 .16
☐ 439 Lee Maye 1.25 .55 .16
☐ 440 Bill Mazeroski 3.00 1.35 .40
☐ 441 John O'Donoghue 1.25 .55 .16
☐ 442 Gene Mauch MG 1.50 .65 .19
☐ 443 Al Jackson 1.25 .55 .16
☐ 444 White Sox Rookies 1.25 .55 .16
Billy Farmer
John Matias
☐ 445 Vada Pinson 1.75 .80 .22
☐ 446 Billy Grabarkewitz 1.25 .55 .16
☐ 447 Lee Stange 1.25 .55 .16
☐ 448 Houston Astros 2.50 1.15 .30
Team Card
☐ 449 Jim Palmer 15.00 6.75 1.90
☐ 450 Willie McCovey AS 7.00 3.10 .85
☐ 451 Boog Powell AS 1.75 .80 .22
☐ 452 Felix Millan AS 1.75 .80 .22
☐ 453 Rod Carew AS 7.00 3.10 .85
☐ 454 Ron Santo AS 2.00 .90 .25
☐ 455 Brooks Robinson AS 6.00 2.70 .75
☐ 456 Don Kessinger AS 1.75 .80 .22
☐ 457 Rico Petrocelli AS 1.75 .80 .22
☐ 458 Pete Rose AS 12.00 5.50 1.50
☐ 459 Reggie Jackson AS 12.00 5.50 1.50
☐ 460 Matty Alou AS 2.25 1.00 .30
☐ 461 Carl Yastrzemski AS 10.00 4.50 1.25
☐ 462 Hank Aaron AS 14.00 6.25 1.75
☐ 463 Frank Robinson AS 7.50 3.40 .95
☐ 464 Johnny Bench AS 12.00 5.50 1.50
☐ 465 Bill Freehan AS 2.75 1.25 .35
☐ 466 Juan Marichal AS 4.50 2.00 .55
☐ 467 Denny McLain AS 2.25 1.00 .30
☐ 468 Jerry Koosman AS 2.75 1.25 .35
☐ 469 Sam McDowell AS 2.25 1.00 .30
☐ 470 Willie Stargell 10.00 4.50 1.25
☐ 471 Chris Zachary 1.50 .65 .19
☐ 472 Braves Team 3.00 1.35 .40
☐ 473 Don Bryant 1.50 .65 .19
☐ 474 Dick Kelley 1.50 .65 .19
☐ 475 Dick McAuliffe 2.00 .90 .25
☐ 476 Don Shaw 1.50 .65 .19
☐ 477 Orioles Rookies 1.50 .65 .19
Al Severinsen
Roger Freed
☐ 478 Bobby Heise 1.50 .65 .19
☐ 479 Dick Woodson 1.50 .65 .19
☐ 480 Glenn Beckert 2.00 .90 .25
☐ 481 Jose Tartabull 2.00 .90 .25
☐ 482 Tom Hilgendorf 1.50 .65 .19
☐ 483 Gail Hopkins 1.50 .65 .19

☐ 484 Gary Nolan .... 2.00 .90 .25
☐ 485 Jay Johnstone .... 2.00 .90 .25
☐ 486 Terry Harmon .... 1.50 .65 .19
☐ 487 Cisco Carlos .... 1.50 .65 .19
☐ 488 J.C. Martin .... 1.50 .65 .19
☐ 489 Eddie Kasko MG .... 1.50 .65 .19
☐ 490 Bill Singer .... 2.00 .90 .25
☐ 491 Graig Nettles .... 7.00 3.10 .85
☐ 492 Astros Rookies .... 1.50 .65 .19
Keith Lampard
Scipio Spinks
☐ 493 Lindy McDaniel .... 2.00 .90 .25
☐ 494 Larry Stahl .... 1.50 .65 .19
☐ 495 Dave Morehead .... 1.50 .65 .19
☐ 496 Steve Whitaker .... 1.50 .65 .19
☐ 497 Eddie Watt .... 1.50 .65 .19
☐ 498 Al Weis .... 1.50 .65 .19
☐ 499 Skip Lockwood .... 1.50 .65 .19
☐ 500 Hank Aaron 55.00 25.00 7.00
☐ 501 Chicago White Sox .... 3.00 1.35 .40
Team Card
☐ 502 Rollie Fingers 12.00 5.50 1.50
☐ 503 Dal Maxvill .... 1.50 .65 .19
☐ 504 Don Pavletich .... 1.50 .65 .19
☐ 505 Ken Holtzman .... 2.00 .90 .25
☐ 506 Ed Stroud .... 1.50 .65 .19
☐ 507 Pat Corrales .... 2.00 .90 .25
☐ 508 Joe Niekro .... 2.00 .90 .25
☐ 509 Montreal Expos .... 3.00 1.35 .40
Team Card
☐ 510 Tony Oliva .... 3.00 1.35 .40
☐ 511 Joe Hoerner .... 1.50 .65 .19
☐ 512 Billy Harris .... 1.50 .65 .19
☐ 513 Preston Gomez MG .... 1.50 .65 .19
☐ 514 Steve Hovley .... 1.50 .65 .19
☐ 515 Don Wilson .... 2.00 .90 .25
☐ 516 Yankees Rookies .... 1.50 .65 .19
John Ellis
Jim Lyttle
☐ 517 Joe Gibbon .... 1.50 .65 .19
☐ 518 Bill Melton .... 1.50 .65 .19
☐ 519 Don McMahon .... 1.50 .65 .19
☐ 520 Willie Horton .... 2.00 .90 .25
☐ 521 Cal Koonce .... 1.50 .65 .19
☐ 522 Angels Team .... 3.00 1.35 .40
☐ 523 Jose Pena .... 1.50 .65 .19
☐ 524 Alvin Dark MG .... 2.00 .90 .25
☐ 525 Jerry Adair .... 1.50 .65 .19
☐ 526 Ron Herbel .... 1.50 .65 .19
☐ 527 Don Bosch .... 1.50 .65 .19
☐ 528 Elrod Hendricks .... 1.50 .65 .19
☐ 529 Bob Aspromonte .... 1.50 .65 .19
☐ 530 Bob Gibson 12.00 5.50 1.50
☐ 531 Ron Clark .... 1.50 .65 .19
☐ 532 Danny Murtaugh MG . 2.00 .90 .25
☐ 533 Buzz Stephen .... 1.50 .65 .19
☐ 534 Minnesota Twins .... 3.00 1.35 .40
Team Card
☐ 535 Andy Kosco .... 1.50 .65 .19
☐ 536 Mike Kekich .... 1.50 .65 .19
☐ 537 Joe Morgan 10.00 4.50 1.25
☐ 538 Bob Humphreys .... 1.50 .65 .19
☐ 539 Phillies Rookies .... 7.50 3.40 .95
Denny Doyle
Larry Bowa
☐ 540 Gary Peters .... 1.50 .65 .19
☐ 541 Bill Heath .... 1.50 .65 .19
☐ 542 Checklist 6 .... 6.00 .90 .30
☐ 543 Clyde Wright .... 1.50 .65 .19
☐ 544 Cincinnati Reds .... 3.00 1.35 .40
Team Card
☐ 545 Ken Harrelson .... 2.00 .90 .25
☐ 546 Ron Reed .... 1.50 .65 .19
☐ 547 Rick Monday .... 3.50 1.55 .45
☐ 548 Howie Reed .... 3.00 1.35 .40
☐ 549 St. Louis Cardinals .... 6.00 2.70 .75
Team Card
☐ 550 Frank Howard .... 4.50 2.00 .55
☐ 551 Dock Ellis .... 3.50 1.55 .45
☐ 552 Royals Rookies .... 3.00 1.35 .40
Don O'Riley
Dennis Paepke
Fred Rico
☐ 553 Jim Lefebvre .... 3.50 1.55 .45
☐ 554 Tom Timmermann .... 3.00 1.35 .40
☐ 555 Orlando Cepeda .... 6.00 2.70 .75
☐ 556 Dave Bristol MG .... 3.50 1.55 .45
☐ 557 Ed Kranepool .... 3.50 1.55 .45
☐ 558 Vern Fuller .... 3.00 1.35 .40
☐ 559 Tommy Davis .... 3.50 1.55 .45
☐ 560 Gaylord Perry 10.00 4.50 1.25
☐ 561 Tom McCraw .... 3.00 1.35 .40
☐ 562 Ted Abernathy .... 3.00 1.35 .40
☐ 563 Boston Red Sox .... 6.00 2.70 .75
Team Card
☐ 564 Johnny Briggs .... 3.00 1.35 .40
☐ 565 Jim Hunter 10.00 4.50 1.25
☐ 566 Gene Alley .... 3.50 1.55 .45
☐ 567 Bob Oliver .... 3.00 1.35 .40
☐ 568 Stan Bahnsen .... 3.50 1.55 .45
☐ 569 Cookie Rojas .... 3.50 1.55 .45
☐ 570 Jim Fregosi .... 3.50 1.55 .45
☐ 571 Jim Brewer .... 3.00 1.35 .40
☐ 572 Frank Quilici MG .... 3.00 1.35 .40
☐ 573 Padres Rookies .... 3.00 1.35 .40
Mike Corkins
Rafael Robles
Ron Slocum
☐ 574 Bobby Bolin .... 3.50 1.55 .45
☐ 575 Cleon Jones .... 3.50 1.55 .45
☐ 576 Milt Pappas .... 3.50 1.55 .45
☐ 577 Bernie Allen .... 3.00 1.35 .40
☐ 578 Tom Griffin .... 3.00 1.35 .40
☐ 579 Detroit Tigers .... 6.00 2.70 .75
Team Card
☐ 580 Pete Rose 55.00 25.00 7.00
☐ 581 Tom Satriano .... 3.00 1.35 .40
☐ 582 Mike Paul .... 3.00 1.35 .40
☐ 583 Hal Lanier .... 3.00 1.35 .40
☐ 584 Al Downing .... 3.50 1.55 .45
☐ 585 Rusty Staub .... 4.50 2.00 .55
☐ 586 Rickey Clark .... 3.00 1.35 .40
☐ 587 Jose Arcia .... 3.00 1.35 .40
☐ 588A Checklist 7 ERR .... 8.00 1.60 .50
(666 Adolfo)
☐ 588B Checklist 7 COR .... 6.00 1.65 .60
(666 Adolpho)
☐ 589 Joe Keough .... 3.00 1.35 .40
☐ 590 Mike Cuellar .... 3.50 1.55 .45
☐ 591 Mike Ryan UER .... 3.00 1.35 .40
(Pitching Record
header on card back)
☐ 592 Daryl Patterson .... 3.00 1.35 .40
☐ 593 Chicago Cubs .... 6.00 2.70 .75
Team Card
☐ 594 Jake Gibbs .... 3.00 1.35 .40
☐ 595 Maury Wills .... 4.50 2.00 .55
☐ 596 Mike Hershberger .... 3.50 1.55 .45
☐ 597 Sonny Siebert .... 3.00 1.35 .40
☐ 598 Joe Pepitone .... 3.50 1.55 .45
☐ 599 Senators Rookies .... 3.00 1.35 .40
Dick Stelmaszek
Gene Martin
Dick Such
☐ 600 Willie Mays 75.00 34.00 9.50
☐ 601 Pete Richert .... 3.00 1.35 .40

☐ 602 Ted Savage .... 3.00 1.35 .40
☐ 603 Ray Oyler .... 3.00 1.35 .40
☐ 604 Clarence Gaston.......... 4.50 2.00 .55
☐ 605 Rick Wise.................... 3.50 1.55 .45
☐ 606 Chico Ruiz.................. 3.00 1.35 .40
☐ 607 Gary Waslewski .... 3.00 1.35 .40
☐ 608 Pittsburgh Pirates...... 6.00 2.70 .75
Team Card
☐ 609 Buck Martinez............ 4.50 2.00 .55
(Inconsistent design,
card number in
white circle)
☐ 610 Jerry Koosman .... 4.50 2.00 .55
☐ 611 Norm Cash.................. 5.50 2.50 .70
☐ 612 Jim Hickman............... 3.50 1.55 .45
☐ 613 Dave Baldwin.............. 3.50 1.55 .45
☐ 614 Mike Shannon............. 3.50 1.55 .45
☐ 615 Mark Belanger............. 3.50 1.55 .45
☐ 616 Jim Merritt.................. 3.00 1.35 .40
☐ 617 Jim French.................. 3.00 1.35 .40
☐ 618 Billy Wynne................. 3.00 1.35 .40
☐ 619 Norm Miller................. 3.00 1.35 .40
☐ 620 Jim Perry .... 5.00 2.30 .60
☐ 621 Braves Rookies 14.00 6.25 1.75
Mike McQueen
Darrell Evans
Rick Kester
☐ 622 Don Sutton 14.00 6.25 1.75
☐ 623 Horace Clarke .... 3.00 1.35 .40
☐ 624 Clyde King MG .... 3.00 1.35 .40
☐ 625 Dean Chance.............. 3.00 1.35 .40
☐ 626 Dave Ricketts............. 3.00 1.35 .40
☐ 627 Gary Wagner.............. 3.00 1.35 .40
☐ 628 Wayne Garrett............ 3.00 1.35 .40
☐ 629 Merv Rettenmund...... 3.00 1.35 .40
☐ 630 Ernie Banks.............. 45.00 20.00 5.75
☐ 631 Oakland Athletics .... 6.00 2.70 .75
Team Card
☐ 632 Gary Sutherland......... 3.00 1.35 .40
☐ 633 Roger Nelson............. 3.00 1.35 .40
☐ 634 Bud Harrelson............ 8.50 3.80 1.05
☐ 635 Bob Allison 8.50 3.80 1.05
☐ 636 Jim Stewart................ 8.00 3.60 1.00
☐ 637 Cleveland Indians..... 12.00 5.50 1.50
Team Card
☐ 638 Frank Bertaina............ 8.00 3.60 1.00
☐ 639 Dave Campbell........... 8.00 3.60 1.00
☐ 640 Al Kaline.................. 50.00 23.00 6.25
☐ 641 Al McBean.................. 8.00 3.60 1.00
☐ 642 Angels Rookies 8.00 3.60 1.00
Greg Garrett
Gordon Lund
Jarvis Tatum
☐ 643 Jose Pagan 8.00 3.60 1.00
☐ 644 Gerry Nyman............. 8.00 3.60 1.00
☐ 645 Don Money 9.00 4.00 1.15
☐ 646 Jim Britton................. 8.00 3.60 1.00
☐ 647 Tom Matchick............ 8.00 3.60 1.00
☐ 648 Larry Haney 8.00 3.60 1.00
☐ 649 Jimmie Hall................ 8.00 3.60 1.00
☐ 650 Sam McDowell........... 9.00 4.00 1.15
☐ 651 Jim Gosger 8.00 3.60 1.00
☐ 652 Rich Rollins 9.00 4.00 1.15
☐ 653 Moe Drabowsky......... 8.00 3.60 1.00
☐ 654 NL Rookies 10.00 4.50 1.25
Oscar Gamble
Boots Day
Angel Mangual
☐ 655 John Roseboro 9.00 4.00 1.15
☐ 656 Jim Hardin 8.00 3.60 1.00
☐ 657 San Diego Padres 12.00 5.50 1.50
Team Card
☐ 658 Ken Tatum 8.00 3.60 1.00
☐ 659 Pete Ward 8.00 3.60 1.00
☐ 660 Johnny Bench 100.00 45.00 12.50
☐ 661 Jerry Robertson 8.00 3.60 1.00
☐ 662 Frank Lucchesi MG 8.00 3.60 1.00
☐ 663 Tito Francona 8.00 3.60 1.00
☐ 664 Bob Robertson........... 8.00 3.60 1.00
☐ 665 Jim Lonborg 9.00 4.00 1.15
☐ 666 Adolpho Phillips......... 8.00 3.60 1.00
☐ 667 Bob Meyer 9.00 4.00 1.15
☐ 668 Bob Tillman................ 8.00 3.60 1.00
☐ 669 White Sox Rookies..... 9.00 4.00 1.15
Bart Johnson
Dan Lazar
Mickey Scott
☐ 670 Ron Santo.................. 9.00 4.00 1.15
☐ 671 Jim Campanis 8.00 3.60 1.00
☐ 672 Leon McFadden 8.00 3.60 1.00
☐ 673 Ted Uhlaender............ 8.00 3.60 1.00
☐ 674 Dave Leonhard........... 8.00 3.60 1.00
☐ 675 Jose Cardenal 9.00 4.00 1.15
☐ 676 Washington Senators 12.00 5.50 1.50
Team Card
☐ 677 Woodie Fryman.......... 8.00 3.60 1.00
☐ 678 Dave Duncan.............. 9.00 4.00 1.15
☐ 679 Ray Sadecki 8.00 3.60 1.00
☐ 680 Rico Petrocelli............ 9.00 4.00 1.15
☐ 681 Bob Garibaldi 8.00 3.60 1.00
☐ 682 Dalton Jones.............. 8.00 3.60 1.00
☐ 683 Reds Rookies............ 8.00 3.60 1.00
Vern Geishert
Hal McRae
Wayne Simpson
☐ 684 Jack Fisher................. 8.00 3.60 1.00
☐ 685 Tom Haller 8.00 3.60 1.00
☐ 686 Jackie Hernandez....... 8.00 3.60 1.00
☐ 687 Bob Priddy................. 8.00 3.60 1.00
☐ 688 Ted Kubiak................. 9.00 4.00 1.15
☐ 689 Frank Tepedino 8.00 3.60 1.00
☐ 690 Ron Fairly 9.00 4.00 1.15
☐ 691 Joe Grzenda............... 8.00 3.60 1.00
☐ 692 Duffy Dyer.................. 8.00 3.60 1.00
☐ 693 Bob Johnson.............. 8.00 3.60 1.00
☐ 694 Gary Ross 8.00 3.60 1.00
☐ 695 Bobby Knoop 8.00 3.60 1.00
☐ 696 San Francisco Giants 12.00 5.50 1.50
Team Card
☐ 697 Jim Hannan................ 8.00 3.60 1.00
☐ 698 Tom Tresh 9.00 4.00 1.15
☐ 699 Hank Aguirre.............. 8.00 3.60 1.00
☐ 700 Frank Robinson........ 50.00 23.00 6.25
☐ 701 Jack Billingham.......... 8.00 3.60 1.00
☐ 702 AL Rookies 8.00 3.60 1.00
Bob Johnson
Ron Klimkowski
Bill Zepp
☐ 703 Lou Marone 8.00 3.60 1.00
☐ 704 Frank Baker................ 8.00 3.60 1.00
☐ 705 Tony Cloninger UER... 8.00 3.60 1.00
(Batter headings
on card back)
☐ 706 John McNamara MG.. 8.00 3.60 1.00
☐ 707 Kevin Collins 8.00 3.60 1.00
☐ 708 Jose Santiago 8.00 3.60 1.00
☐ 709 Mike Fiore 8.00 3.60 1.00
☐ 710 Felix Millan................. 8.00 3.60 1.00
☐ 711 Ed Brinkman 8.00 3.60 1.00
☐ 712 Nolan Ryan 500.00 230.00 65.00
☐ 713 Seattle Pilots............ 24.00 11.00 3.00
Team Card
☐ 714 Al Spangler 8.00 3.60 1.00
☐ 715 Mickey Lolich............. 9.00 4.00 1.15
☐ 716 Cardinals Rookies 9.00 4.00 1.15
Sal Campisi

	Card	NRMT	EXC	G-VG
	Reggie Cleveland			
	Santiago Guzman			
☐ 717	Tom Phoebus	8.00	3.60	1.00
☐ 718	Ed Spiezio	8.00	3.60	1.00
☐ 719	Jim Roland	8.00	3.60	1.00
☐ 720	Rick Reichardt	9.00	3.70	1.05

1971 Topps

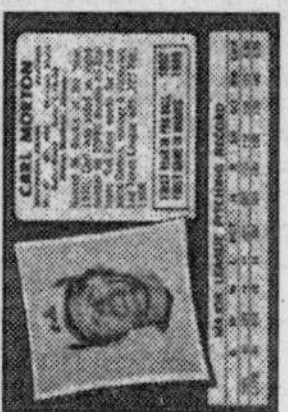

The cards in this 752-card set measure 2 1/2" by 3 1/2". The 1971 Topps set is a challenge to complete in strict mint condition because the black obverse border is easily scratched and damaged. An unusual feature of this set is that the player is also pictured in black and white on the back of the card. Featured subsets within this set include League Leaders (61-72), Playoffs cards (195-202), and World Series cards (327-332). Cards 524-643 and the last series (644-752) are somewhat scarce. The last series was printed in two sheets of 132. On the printing sheets 44 cards were printed in 50 percent greater quantity than the other 66 cards. These 66 (slightly) shorter-printed numbers are identified in the checklist below by SP. The key Rookie Cards in this set are the multi-player Rookie Card of Dusty Baker and Don Baylor and the individual cards of Bert Blyleven, Dave Concepcion, Steve Garvey, and Ted Simmons.

	NRMT	EXC	G-VG
COMPLETE SET (752)	2100.00	950.00	275.00
COMMON CARD (1-132)	1.50	.65	.19
COMMON CARD (133-263)	1.50	.65	.19
COMMON CARD (264-393)	1.50	.65	.19
COMMON CARD (394-523)	2.00	.90	.25
COMMON CARD (524-643)	4.00	1.80	.50
COMMON CARD (644-752)	7.00	3.10	.85

	Card	NRMT	EXC	G-VG
☐ 1	Baltimore Orioles	14.00	2.80	.85
	Team Card			
☐ 2	Dock Ellis	1.75	.80	.22
☐ 3	Dick McAuliffe	1.75	.80	.22
☐ 4	Vic Davalillo	1.50	.65	.19
☐ 5	Thurman Munson	36.00	16.00	4.50
☐ 6	Ed Spiezio	1.50	.65	.19
☐ 7	Jim Holt	1.50	.65	.19
☐ 8	Mike McQueen	1.50	.65	.19
☐ 9	George Scott	1.75	.80	.22
☐ 10	Claude Osteen	1.75	.80	.22
☐ 11	Elliott Maddox	1.75	.80	.22
☐ 12	Johnny Callison	1.75	.80	.22
☐ 13	White Sox Rookies	1.50	.65	.19
	Charlie Brinkman			
	Dick Moloney			
☐ 14	Dave Concepcion	25.00	11.50	3.10
☐ 15	Andy Messersmith	1.75	.80	.22
☐ 16	Ken Singleton	5.00	2.30	.60
☐ 17	Billy Sorrell	1.50	.65	.19
☐ 18	Norm Miller	1.50	.65	.19
☐ 19	Skip Pitlock	1.50	.65	.19
☐ 20	Reggie Jackson	50.00	23.00	6.25
☐ 21	Dan McGinn	1.50	.65	.19
☐ 22	Phil Roof	1.50	.65	.19
☐ 23	Oscar Gamble	1.75	.80	.22
☐ 24	Rich Hand	1.50	.65	.19
☐ 25	Clarence Gaston	3.50	1.55	.45
☐ 26	Bert Blyleven	30.00	13.50	3.80
☐ 27	Pirates Rookies	1.50	.65	.19
	Fred Cambria			
	Gene Clines			
☐ 28	Ron Klimkowski	1.50	.65	.19
☐ 29	Don Buford	1.50	.65	.19
☐ 30	Phil Niekro	5.00	2.30	.60
☐ 31	Eddie Kasko MG	1.50	.65	.19
☐ 32	Jerry DaVanon	1.50	.65	.19
☐ 33	Del Unser	1.50	.65	.19
☐ 34	Sandy Vance	1.50	.65	.19
☐ 35	Lou Piniella	2.00	.90	.25
☐ 36	Dean Chance	1.50	.65	.19
☐ 37	Rich McKinney	1.50	.65	.19
☐ 38	Jim Colborn	1.50	.65	.19
☐ 39	Tiger Rookies	2.50	1.15	.30
	Lerrin LaGrow			
	Gene Lamont			
☐ 40	Lee May	1.75	.80	.22
☐ 41	Rick Austin	1.50	.65	.19
☐ 42	Boots Day	1.50	.65	.19
☐ 43	Steve Kealey	1.50	.65	.19
☐ 44	Johnny Edwards	1.50	.65	.19
☐ 45	Jim Hunter	7.00	3.10	.85
☐ 46	Dave Campbell	1.50	.65	.19
☐ 47	Johnny Jeter	1.50	.65	.19
☐ 48	Dave Baldwin	1.50	.65	.19
☐ 49	Don Money	1.50	.65	.19
☐ 50	Willie McCovey	10.00	4.50	1.25
☐ 51	Steve Kline	1.50	.65	.19
☐ 52	Braves Rookies	1.50	.65	.19
	Oscar Brown			
	Earl Williams			
☐ 53	Paul Blair	1.75	.80	.22
☐ 54	Checklist 1	6.00	.60	.19
☐ 55	Steve Carlton	24.00	11.00	3.00
☐ 56	Duane Josephson	1.50	.65	.19
☐ 57	Von Joshua	1.50	.65	.19
☐ 58	Bill Lee	1.75	.80	.22
☐ 59	Gene Mauch MG	1.75	.80	.22
☐ 60	Dick Bosman	1.50	.65	.19
☐ 61	AL Batting Leaders	3.50	1.55	.45
	Alex Johnson			
	Carl Yastrzemski			
	Tony Oliva			
☐ 62	NL Batting Leaders	2.50	1.15	.30
	Rico Carty			
	Joe Torre			
	Manny Sanguillen			
☐ 63	AL RBI Leaders	2.50	1.15	.30
	Frank Howard			
	Tony Conigliaro			
	Boog Powell			
☐ 64	NL RBI Leaders	5.00	2.30	.60
	Johnny Bench			
	Tony Perez			
	Billy Williams			

☐	65 AL HR Leaders	4.50	2.00	.55
	Frank Howard			
	Harmon Killebrew			
	Carl Yastrzemski			
☐	66 NL HR Leaders	6.00	2.70	.75
	Johnny Bench			
	Billy Williams			
	Tony Perez			
☐	67 AL ERA Leaders	3.50	1.55	.45
	Diego Segui			
	Jim Palmer			
	Clyde Wright			
☐	68 NL ERA Leaders	3.50	1.55	.45
	Tom Seaver			
	Wayne Simpson			
	Luke Walker			
☐	69 AL Pitching Leaders	2.50	1.15	.30
	Mike Cuellar			
	Dave McNally			
	Jim Perry			
☐	70 NL Pitching Leaders	6.00	2.70	.75
	Bob Gibson			
	Gaylord Perry			
	Fergie Jenkins			
☐	71 AL Strikeout Leaders	2.50	1.15	.30
	Sam McDowell			
	Mickey Lolich			
	Bob Johnson			
☐	72 NL Strikeout Leaders	6.50	2.90	.80
	Tom Seaver			
	Bob Gibson			
	Fergie Jenkins			
☐	73 George Brunet	1.50	.65	.19
☐	74 Twins Rookies	1.50	.65	.19
	Pete Hamm			
	Jim Nettles			
☐	75 Gary Nolan	1.75	.80	.22
☐	76 Ted Savage	1.50	.65	.19
☐	77 Mike Compton	1.50	.65	.19
☐	78 Jim Spencer	1.50	.65	.19
☐	79 Wade Blasingame	1.50	.65	.19
☐	80 Bill Melton	1.50	.65	.19
☐	81 Felix Millan	1.50	.65	.19
☐	82 Casey Cox	1.50	.65	.19
☐	83 Met Rookies	1.50	.65	.19
	Tim Foli			
	Randy Bobb			
☐	84 Marcel Lachemann	2.00	.90	.25
☐	85 Billy Grabarkewitz	1.50	.65	.19
☐	86 Mike Kilkenny	1.50	.65	.19
☐	87 Jack Heidemann	1.50	.65	.19
☐	88 Hal King	1.50	.65	.19
☐	89 Ken Brett	1.50	.65	.19
☐	90 Joe Pepitone	1.75	.80	.22
☐	91 Bob Lemon MG	2.00	.90	.25
☐	92 Fred Wenz	1.50	.65	.19
☐	93 Senators Rookies	1.50	.65	.19
	Norm McRae			
	Denny Riddleberger			
☐	94 Don Hahn	1.50	.65	.19
☐	95 Luis Tiant	2.00	.90	.25
☐	96 Joe Hague	1.50	.65	.19
☐	97 Floyd Wicker	1.50	.65	.19
☐	98 Joe Decker	1.50	.65	.19
☐	99 Mark Belanger	1.75	.80	.22
☐	100 Pete Rose	50.00	23.00	6.25
☐	101 Les Cain	1.50	.65	.19
☐	102 Astros Rookies	1.75	.80	.22
	Ken Forsch			
	Larry Howard			
☐	103 Rich Severson	1.50	.65	.19
☐	104 Dan Frisella	1.50	.65	.19
☐	105 Tony Conigliaro	3.50	1.55	.45
☐	106 Tom Dukes	1.50	.65	.19
☐	107 Roy Foster	1.50	.65	.19
☐	108 John Cumberland	1.50	.65	.19
☐	109 Steve Hovley	1.50	.65	.19
☐	110 Bill Mazeroski	2.50	1.15	.30
☐	111 Yankee Rookies	1.50	.65	.19
	Loyd Colson			
	Bobby Mitchell			
☐	112 Manny Mota	1.75	.80	.22
☐	113 Jerry Crider	1.50	.65	.19
☐	114 Billy Conigliaro	1.75	.80	.22
☐	115 Donn Clendenon	1.75	.80	.22
☐	116 Ken Sanders	1.50	.65	.19
☐	117 Ted Simmons	24.00	11.00	3.00
☐	118 Cookie Rojas	1.75	.80	.22
☐	119 Frank Lucchesi MG	1.50	.65	.19
☐	120 Willie Horton	1.75	.80	.22
☐	121 Cubs Rookies	1.50	.65	.19
	Jim Dunegan			
	Roe Skidmore			
☐	122 Eddie Watt	1.50	.65	.19
☐	123A Checklist 2	6.00	.60	.19
	(Card number at bottom right)			
☐	123B Checklist 2	6.00	.60	.19
	(Card number centered)			
☐	124 Don Gullett	2.00	.90	.25
☐	125 Ray Fosse	1.75	.80	.22
☐	126 Danny Coombs	1.50	.65	.19
☐	127 Danny Thompson	1.75	.80	.22
☐	128 Frank Johnson	1.50	.65	.19
☐	129 Aurelio Monteagudo	1.50	.65	.19
☐	130 Denis Menke	1.50	.65	.19
☐	131 Curt Blefary	1.50	.65	.19
☐	132 Jose Laboy	1.50	.65	.19
☐	133 Mickey Lolich	2.00	.90	.25
☐	134 Jose Arcia	1.50	.65	.19
☐	135 Rick Monday	1.75	.80	.22
☐	136 Duffy Dyer	1.50	.65	.19
☐	137 Marcelino Lopez	1.50	.65	.19
☐	138 Phillies Rookies	1.75	.80	.22
	Joe Lis			
	Willie Montanez			
☐	139 Paul Casanova	1.50	.65	.19
☐	140 Gaylord Perry	8.00	3.60	1.00
☐	141 Frank Quilici	1.50	.65	.19
☐	142 Mack Jones	1.50	.65	.19
☐	143 Steve Blass	1.75	.80	.22
☐	144 Jackie Hernandez	1.50	.65	.19
☐	145 Bill Singer	1.75	.80	.22
☐	146 Ralph Houk MG	1.75	.80	.22
☐	147 Bob Priddy	1.50	.65	.19
☐	148 John Mayberry	1.75	.80	.22
☐	149 Mike Hershberger	1.50	.65	.19
☐	150 Sam McDowell	1.75	.80	.22
☐	151 Tommy Davis	1.75	.80	.22
☐	152 Angels Rookies	1.50	.65	.19
	Lloyd Allen			
	Winston Llenas			
☐	153 Gary Ross	1.50	.65	.19
☐	154 Cesar Gutierrez	1.50	.65	.19
☐	155 Ken Henderson	1.50	.65	.19
☐	156 Bart Johnson	1.50	.65	.19
☐	157 Bob Bailey	1.50	.65	.19
☐	158 Jerry Reuss	2.00	.90	.25
☐	159 Jarvis Tatum	1.50	.65	.19
☐	160 Tom Seaver	40.00	18.00	5.00
☐	161 Coin Checklist	6.00	.60	.19
☐	162 Jack Billingham	1.50	.65	.19
☐	163 Buck Martinez	1.50	.65	.19
☐	164 Reds Rookies	1.75	.80	.22
	Frank Duffy			

	Card			
		Milt Wilcox		
☐	165	Cesar Tovar	1.50	.65	.19
☐	166	Joe Hoerner	1.50	.65	.19
☐	167	Tom Grieve	2.00	.90	.25
☐	168	Bruce Dal Canton	1.50	.65	.19
☐	169	Ed Herrmann	1.50	.65	.19
☐	170	Mike Cuellar	1.75	.80	.22
☐	171	Bobby Wine	1.50	.65	.19
☐	172	Duke Sims	1.50	.65	.19
☐	173	Gil Garrido	1.50	.65	.19
☐	174	Dave LaRoche	1.50	.65	.19
☐	175	Jim Hickman	1.50	.65	.19
☐	176	Red Sox Rookies	1.50	.65	.19
		Bob Montgomery			
		Doug Griffin			
☐	177	Hal McRae	1.75	.80	.22
☐	178	Dave Duncan	1.50	.65	.19
☐	179	Mike Corkins	1.50	.65	.19
☐	180	Al Kaline UER	20.00	9.00	2.50
		(Home instead			
		of Birth)			
☐	181	Hal Lanier	1.50	.65	.19
☐	182	Al Downing	1.75	.80	.22
☐	183	Gil Hodges MG	5.00	2.30	.60
☐	184	Stan Bahnsen	1.50	.65	.19
☐	185	Julian Javier	1.75	.80	.22
☐	186	Bob Spence	1.50	.65	.19
☐	187	Ted Abernathy	1.50	.65	.19
☐	188	Dodgers Rookies	3.50	1.55	.45
		Bob Valentine			
		Mike Strahler			
☐	189	George Mitterwald	1.50	.65	.19
☐	190	Bob Tolan	1.75	.80	.22
☐	191	Mike Andrews	1.50	.65	.19
☐	192	Billy Wilson	1.50	.65	.19
☐	193	Bob Grich	6.00	2.70	.75
☐	194	Mike Lum	1.50	.65	.19
☐	195	AL Playoff Game 1	2.50	1.15	.30
		Boog Powell muscles			
		Twins			
☐	196	AL Playoff Game 2	2.50	1.15	.30
		Dave McNally makes			
		it two straight			
☐	197	AL Playoff Game 3	4.00	1.80	.50
		Jim Palmer mows'em down			
☐	198	AL Playoff Summary	2.50	1.15	.30
		Orioles celebrate			
☐	199	NL Playoff Game 1	2.50	1.15	.30
		Ty Cline pinch-triple			
		decides it			
☐	200	NL Playoff Game 2	2.50	1.15	.30
		Bobby Tolan scores			
		for third time			
☐	201	NL Playoff Game 3	2.50	1.15	.30
		Ty Cline scores			
		winning run			
☐	202	NL Playoff Summary	2.50	1.15	.30
		Reds celebrate			
☐	203	Larry Gura	1.50	.65	.19
☐	204	Brewers Rookies	1.50	.65	.19
		Bernie Smith			
		George Kopacz			
☐	205	Gerry Moses	1.50	.65	.19
☐	206	Checklist 3	6.00	.60	.19
☐	207	Alan Foster	1.50	.65	.19
☐	208	Billy Martin MG	4.00	1.80	.50
☐	209	Steve Renko	1.50	.65	.19
☐	210	Rod Carew	24.00	11.00	3.00
☐	211	Phil Hennigan	1.50	.65	.19
☐	212	Rich Hebner	1.75	.80	.22
☐	213	Frank Baker	1.50	.65	.19
☐	214	Al Ferrara	1.50	.65	.19
☐	215	Diego Segui	1.50	.65	.19
☐	216	Cards Rookies	1.50	.65	.19
		Reggie Cleveland			
		Luis Melendez			
☐	217	Ed Stroud	1.50	.65	.19
☐	218	Tony Cloninger	1.50	.65	.19
☐	219	Elrod Hendricks	1.50	.65	.19
☐	220	Ron Santo	2.50	1.15	.30
☐	221	Dave Morehead	1.50	.65	.19
☐	222	Bob Watson	1.75	.80	.22
☐	223	Cecil Upshaw	1.50	.65	.19
☐	224	Alan Gallagher	1.50	.65	.19
☐	225	Gary Peters	1.50	.65	.19
☐	226	Bill Russell	3.50	1.55	.45
☐	227	Floyd Weaver	1.50	.65	.19
☐	228	Wayne Garrett	1.50	.65	.19
☐	229	Jim Hannan	1.50	.65	.19
☐	230	Willie Stargell	8.00	3.60	1.00
☐	231	Indians Rookies	1.50	.65	.19
		Vince Colbert			
		John Lowenstein			
☐	232	John Strohmayer	1.50	.65	.19
☐	233	Larry Bowa	2.00	.90	.25
☐	234	Jim Lyttle	1.50	.65	.19
☐	235	Nate Colbert	1.50	.65	.19
☐	236	Bob Humphreys	1.50	.65	.19
☐	237	Cesar Cedeno	4.50	2.00	.55
☐	238	Chuck Dobson	1.50	.65	.19
☐	239	Red Schoendienst MG	2.00	.90	.25
☐	240	Clyde Wright	1.50	.65	.19
☐	241	Dave Nelson	1.50	.65	.19
☐	242	Jim Ray	1.50	.65	.19
☐	243	Carlos May	1.75	.80	.22
☐	244	Bob Tillman	1.50	.65	.19
☐	245	Jim Kaat	3.00	1.35	.40
☐	246	Tony Taylor	1.50	.65	.19
☐	247	Royals Rookies	1.50	.65	.19
		Jerry Cram			
		Paul Splittorff			
☐	248	Hoyt Wilhelm	4.00	1.80	.50
☐	249	Chico Salmon	1.50	.65	.19
☐	250	Johnny Bench	30.00	13.50	3.80
☐	251	Frank Reberger	1.50	.65	.19
☐	252	Eddie Leon	1.50	.65	.19
☐	253	Bill Sudakis	1.50	.65	.19
☐	254	Cal Koonce	1.50	.65	.19
☐	255	Bob Robertson	1.75	.80	.22
☐	256	Tony Gonzalez	1.50	.65	.19
☐	257	Nelson Briles	1.50	.65	.19
☐	258	Dick Green	1.50	.65	.19
☐	259	Dave Marshall	1.50	.65	.19
☐	260	Tommy Harper	1.75	.80	.22
☐	261	Darold Knowles	1.50	.65	.19
☐	262	Padres Rookies	1.50	.65	.19
		Jim Williams			
		Dave Robinson			
☐	263	John Ellis	1.75	.80	.22
☐	264	Joe Morgan	7.50	3.40	.95
☐	265	Jim Northrup	1.75	.80	.22
☐	266	Bill Stoneman	1.50	.65	.19
☐	267	Rich Morales	1.50	.65	.19
☐	268	Philadelphia Phillies	2.50	1.15	.30
		Team Card			
☐	269	Gail Hopkins	1.50	.65	.19
☐	270	Rico Carty	1.75	.80	.22
☐	271	Bill Zepp	1.50	.65	.19
☐	272	Tommy Helms	1.75	.80	.22
☐	273	Pete Richert	1.50	.65	.19
☐	274	Ron Slocum	1.50	.65	.19
☐	275	Vada Pinson	2.00	.90	.25
☐	276	Giants Rookies	9.00	4.00	1.15
		Mike Davison			
		George Foster			
☐	277	Gary Waslewski	1.50	.65	.19

	No.	Card			
☐	278	Jerry Grote	1.50	.65	.19
☐	279	Lefty Phillips MG	1.50	.65	.19
☐	280	Fergie Jenkins	8.00	3.60	1.00
☐	281	Danny Walton	1.50	.65	.19
☐	282	Jose Pagan	1.50	.65	.19
☐	283	Dick Such	1.50	.65	.19
☐	284	Jim Gosger	1.50	.65	.19
☐	285	Sal Bando	1.75	.80	.22
☐	286	Jerry McNertney	1.50	.65	.19
☐	287	Mike Fiore	1.50	.65	.19
☐	288	Joe Moeller	1.50	.65	.19
☐	289	Chicago White Sox Team Card	2.50	1.15	.30
☐	290	Tony Oliva	3.00	1.35	.40
☐	291	George Culver	1.50	.65	.19
☐	292	Jay Johnstone	1.75	.80	.22
☐	293	Pat Corrales	1.75	.80	.22
☐	294	Steve Dunning	1.50	.65	.19
☐	295	Bobby Bonds	5.00	2.30	.60
☐	296	Tom Timmermann	1.50	.65	.19
☐	297	Johnny Briggs	1.50	.65	.19
☐	298	Jim Nelson	1.50	.65	.19
☐	299	Ed Kirkpatrick	1.50	.65	.19
☐	300	Brooks Robinson	20.00	9.00	2.50
☐	301	Earl Wilson	1.50	.65	.19
☐	302	Phil Gagliano	1.50	.65	.19
☐	303	Lindy McDaniel	1.75	.80	.22
☐	304	Ron Brand	1.50	.65	.19
☐	305	Reggie Smith	3.50	1.55	.45
☐	306	Jim Nash	1.50	.65	.19
☐	307	Don Wert	1.50	.65	.19
☐	308	St. Louis Cardinals Team Card	2.50	1.15	.30
☐	309	Dick Ellsworth	1.50	.65	.19
☐	310	Tommie Agee	1.75	.80	.22
☐	311	Lee Stange	1.50	.65	.19
☐	312	Harry Walker MG	1.50	.65	.19
☐	313	Tom Hall	1.50	.65	.19
☐	314	Jeff Torborg	1.75	.80	.22
☐	315	Ron Fairly	1.75	.80	.22
☐	316	Fred Scherman	1.50	.65	.19
☐	317	Athletic Rookies Jim Driscoll Angel Mangual	1.50	.65	.19
☐	318	Rudy May	1.50	.65	.19
☐	319	Ty Cline	1.50	.65	.19
☐	320	Dave McNally	1.75	.80	.22
☐	321	Tom Matchick	1.50	.65	.19
☐	322	Jim Beauchamp	1.50	.65	.19
☐	323	Billy Champion	1.50	.65	.19
☐	324	Graig Nettles	3.50	1.55	.45
☐	325	Juan Marichal	6.00	2.70	.75
☐	326	Richie Scheinblum	1.50	.65	.19
☐	327	World Series Game 1. Boog Powell homers to opposite field	2.50	1.15	.30
☐	328	World Series Game 2. (Don Buford)	2.50	1.15	.30
☐	329	World Series Game 3. Frank Robinson shows muscle	4.50	2.00	.55
☐	330	World Series Game 4. Reds stay alive	2.50	1.15	.30
☐	331	World Series Game 5. Brooks Robinson commits robbery	5.00	2.30	.60
☐	332	World Series Summary Orioles celebrate	2.50	1.15	.30
☐	333	Clay Kirby	1.50	.65	.19
☐	334	Roberto Pena	1.50	.65	.19
☐	335	Jerry Koosman	3.00	1.35	.40
☐	336	Detroit Tigers Team Card	2.50	1.15	.30
☐	337	Jesus Alou	1.50	.65	.19
☐	338	Gene Tenace	1.75	.80	.22
☐	339	Wayne Simpson	1.50	.65	.19
☐	340	Rico Petrocelli	1.75	.80	.22
☐	341	Steve Garvey	45.00	20.00	5.75
☐	342	Frank Tepedino	1.50	.65	.19
☐	343	Pirates Rookies Ed Acosta Milt May	1.50	.65	.19
☐	344	Ellie Rodriguez	1.50	.65	.19
☐	345	Joel Horlen	1.50	.65	.19
☐	346	Lum Harris MG	1.50	.65	.19
☐	347	Ted Uhlaender	1.50	.65	.19
☐	348	Fred Norman	1.50	.65	.19
☐	349	Rich Reese	1.50	.65	.19
☐	350	Billy Williams	6.00	2.70	.75
☐	351	Jim Shellenback	1.50	.65	.19
☐	352	Denny Doyle	1.50	.65	.19
☐	353	Carl Taylor	1.50	.65	.19
☐	354	Don McMahon	1.50	.65	.19
☐	355	Bud Harrelson (Nolan Ryan in photo)	3.00	1.35	.40
☐	356	Bob Locker	1.50	.65	.19
☐	357	Cincinnati Reds Team Card	2.50	1.15	.30
☐	358	Danny Cater	1.50	.65	.19
☐	359	Ron Reed	1.50	.65	.19
☐	360	Jim Fregosi	1.75	.80	.22
☐	361	Don Sutton	8.00	3.60	1.00
☐	362	Orioles Rookies Mike Adamson Roger Freed	1.50	.65	.19
☐	363	Mike Nagy	1.50	.65	.19
☐	364	Tommy Dean	1.50	.65	.19
☐	365	Bob Johnson	1.50	.65	.19
☐	366	Ron Stone	1.50	.65	.19
☐	367	Dalton Jones	1.50	.65	.19
☐	368	Bob Veale	1.75	.80	.22
☐	369	Checklist 4	6.00	.60	.19
☐	370	Joe Torre	4.00	1.80	.50
☐	371	Jack Hiatt	1.50	.65	.19
☐	372	Lew Krausse	1.50	.65	.19
☐	373	Tom McCraw	1.50	.65	.19
☐	374	Clete Boyer	1.75	.80	.22
☐	375	Steve Hargan	1.50	.65	.19
☐	376	Expos Rookies Clyde Mashore Ernie McAnally	1.50	.65	.19
☐	377	Greg Garrett	1.50	.65	.19
☐	378	Tito Fuentes	1.50	.65	.19
☐	379	Wayne Granger	1.50	.65	.19
☐	380	Ted Williams MG	12.00	5.50	1.50
☐	381	Fred Gladding	1.50	.65	.19
☐	382	Jake Gibbs	1.50	.65	.19
☐	383	Rod Gaspar	1.50	.65	.19
☐	384	Rollie Fingers	9.00	4.00	1.15
☐	385	Maury Wills	3.00	1.35	.40
☐	386	Boston Red Sox Team Card	2.50	1.15	.30
☐	387	Ron Herbel	1.50	.65	.19
☐	388	Al Oliver	3.50	1.55	.45
☐	389	Ed Brinkman	1.50	.65	.19
☐	390	Glenn Beckert	1.75	.80	.22
☐	391	Twins Rookies Steve Brye Cotton Nash	1.50	.65	.19
☐	392	Grant Jackson	1.50	.65	.19
☐	393	Merv Rettenmund	1.75	.80	.22
☐	394	Clay Carroll	2.50	1.15	.30
☐	395	Roy White	2.50	1.15	.30
☐	396	Dick Schofield	2.00	.90	.25
☐	397	Alvin Dark MG	2.50	1.15	.30
☐	398	Howie Reed	2.00	.90	.25

	#	Player			
☐	399	Jim French	2.00	.90	.25
☐	400	Hank Aaron	55.00	25.00	7.00
☐	401	Tom Murphy	2.00	.90	.25
☐	402	Los Angeles Dodgers. Team Card	4.00	1.80	.50
☐	403	Joe Coleman	2.00	.90	.25
☐	404	Astros Rookies Buddy Harris Roger Metzger	2.00	.90	.25
☐	405	Leo Cardenas	2.00	.90	.25
☐	406	Ray Sadecki	2.00	.90	.25
☐	407	Joe Rudi	2.50	1.15	.30
☐	408	Rafael Robles	2.00	.90	.25
☐	409	Don Pavletich	2.00	.90	.25
☐	410	Ken Holtzman	2.50	1.15	.30
☐	411	George Spriggs	2.00	.90	.25
☐	412	Jerry Johnson	2.00	.90	.25
☐	413	Pat Kelly	2.50	1.15	.30
☐	414	Woodie Fryman	2.50	1.15	.30
☐	415	Mike Hegan	2.00	.90	.25
☐	416	Gene Alley	2.00	.90	.25
☐	417	Dick Hall	2.00	.90	.25
☐	418	Adolfo Phillips	2.00	.90	.25
☐	419	Ron Hansen	2.00	.90	.25
☐	420	Jim Merritt	2.00	.90	.25
☐	421	John Stephenson	2.00	.90	.25
☐	422	Frank Bertaina	2.00	.90	.25
☐	423	Tigers Rookies Dennis Saunders Tim Marting	2.00	.90	.25
☐	424	Roberto Rodriquez	2.00	.90	.25
☐	425	Doug Rader	2.50	1.15	.30
☐	426	Chris Cannizzaro	2.00	.90	.25
☐	427	Bernie Allen	2.00	.90	.25
☐	428	Jim McAndrew	2.00	.90	.25
☐	429	Chuck Hinton	2.00	.90	.25
☐	430	Wes Parker	2.50	1.15	.30
☐	431	Tom Burgmeier	2.00	.90	.25
☐	432	Bob Didier	2.00	.90	.25
☐	433	Skip Lockwood	2.00	.90	.25
☐	434	Gary Sutherland	2.00	.90	.25
☐	435	Jose Cardenal	2.50	1.15	.30
☐	436	Wilbur Wood	2.50	1.15	.30
☐	437	Danny Murtaugh MG	2.50	1.15	.30
☐	438	Mike McCormick	2.50	1.15	.30
☐	439	Phillies Rookies Greg Luzinski Scott Reid	6.50	2.90	.80
☐	440	Bert Campaneris	2.50	1.15	.30
☐	441	Milt Pappas	2.50	1.15	.30
☐	442	California Angels Team Card	4.00	1.80	.50
☐	443	Rich Robertson	2.00	.90	.25
☐	444	Jimmie Price	2.00	.90	.25
☐	445	Art Shamsky	2.00	.90	.25
☐	446	Bobby Bolin	2.00	.90	.25
☐	447	Cesar Geronimo	2.50	1.15	.30
☐	448	Dave Roberts	2.00	.90	.25
☐	449	Brant Alyea	2.00	.90	.25
☐	450	Bob Gibson	18.00	8.00	2.30
☐	451	Joe Keough	2.00	.90	.25
☐	452	John Boccabella	2.00	.90	.25
☐	453	Terry Crowley	2.00	.90	.25
☐	454	Mike Paul	2.00	.90	.25
☐	455	Don Kessinger	2.50	1.15	.30
☐	456	Bob Meyer	2.00	.90	.25
☐	457	Willie Smith	2.00	.90	.25
☐	458	White Sox Rookies Ron Lolich Dave Lemonds	2.00	.90	.25
☐	459	Jim Lefebvre	2.00	.90	.25
☐	460	Fritz Peterson	2.00	.90	.25
☐	461	Jim Ray Hart	2.50	1.15	.30
☐	462	Washington Senators Team Card	4.00	1.80	.50
☐	463	Tom Kelley	2.00	.90	.25
☐	464	Aurelio Rodriguez	2.00	.90	.25
☐	465	Tim McCarver	3.00	1.35	.40
☐	466	Ken Berry	2.00	.90	.25
☐	467	Al Santorini	2.00	.90	.25
☐	468	Frank Fernandez	2.00	.90	.25
☐	469	Bob Aspromonte	2.00	.90	.25
☐	470	Bob Oliver	2.00	.90	.25
☐	471	Tom Griffin	2.00	.90	.25
☐	472	Ken Rudolph	2.00	.90	.25
☐	473	Gary Wagner	2.00	.90	.25
☐	474	Jim Fairey	2.00	.90	.25
☐	475	Ron Perranoski	2.50	1.15	.30
☐	476	Dal Maxvill	2.00	.90	.25
☐	477	Earl Weaver MG	4.00	1.80	.50
☐	478	Bernie Carbo	2.00	.90	.25
☐	479	Dennis Higgins	2.00	.90	.25
☐	480	Manny Sanguillen	2.50	1.15	.30
☐	481	Daryl Patterson	2.00	.90	.25
☐	482	San Diego Padres Team Card	4.00	1.80	.50
☐	483	Gene Michael	2.50	1.15	.30
☐	484	Don Wilson	2.50	1.15	.30
☐	485	Ken McMullen	2.00	.90	.25
☐	486	Steve Huntz	2.00	.90	.25
☐	487	Paul Schaal	2.00	.90	.25
☐	488	Jerry Stephenson	2.00	.90	.25
☐	489	Luis Alvarado	2.00	.90	.25
☐	490	Deron Johnson	2.00	.90	.25
☐	491	Jim Hardin	2.00	.90	.25
☐	492	Ken Boswell	2.00	.90	.25
☐	493	Dave May	2.00	.90	.25
☐	494	Braves Rookies Ralph Garr Rick Kester	2.50	1.15	.30
☐	495	Felipe Alou	3.00	1.35	.40
☐	496	Woody Woodward	2.50	1.15	.30
☐	497	Horacio Pina	2.00	.90	.25
☐	498	John Kennedy	2.00	.90	.25
☐	499	Checklist 5	6.00	1.10	.30
☐	500	Jim Perry	2.50	1.15	.30
☐	501	Andy Etchebarren	2.00	.90	.25
☐	502	Chicago Cubs Team Card	4.00	1.80	.50
☐	503	Gates Brown	2.50	1.15	.30
☐	504	Ken Wright	2.00	.90	.25
☐	505	Ollie Brown	2.00	.90	.25
☐	506	Bobby Knoop	2.00	.90	.25
☐	507	George Stone	2.00	.90	.25
☐	508	Roger Repoz	2.00	.90	.25
☐	509	Jim Grant	2.00	.90	.25
☐	510	Ken Harrelson	2.50	1.15	.30
☐	511	Chris Short (Pete Rose leading off second)	3.00	1.35	.40
☐	512	Red Sox Rookies Dick Mills Mike Garman	2.00	.90	.25
☐	513	Nolan Ryan	250.00	115.00	31.00
☐	514	Ron Woods	2.00	.90	.25
☐	515	Carl Morton	2.00	.90	.25
☐	516	Ted Kubiak	2.00	.90	.25
☐	517	Charlie Fox MG	2.00	.90	.25
☐	518	Joe Grzenda	2.00	.90	.25
☐	519	Willie Crawford	2.00	.90	.25
☐	520	Tommy John	5.00	2.30	.60
☐	521	Leron Lee	2.00	.90	.25
☐	522	Minnesota Twins Team Card	4.00	1.80	.50
☐	523	John Odom	2.00	.90	.25
☐	524	Mickey Stanley	4.50	2.00	.55
☐	525	Ernie Banks	45.00	20.00	5.75

☐ 526 Ray Jarvis .... 4.00 1.80 .50
☐ 527 Cleon Jones .... 4.50 2.00 .55
☐ 528 Wally Bunker .... 4.00 1.80 .50
☐ 529 NL Rookie Infielders .. 5.00 2.30 .60
Enzo Hernandez
Bill Buckner
Marty Perez
☐ 530 Carl Yastrzemski 40.00 18.00 5.00
☐ 531 Mike Torrez .... 4.50 2.00 .55
☐ 532 Bill Rigney MG .... 4.00 1.80 .50
☐ 533 Mike Ryan .... 4.00 1.80 .50
☐ 534 Luke Walker .... 4.00 1.80 .50
☐ 535 Curt Flood .... 4.50 2.00 .55
☐ 536 Claude Raymond .... 5.00 2.30 .60
☐ 537 Tom Egan .... 4.00 1.80 .50
☐ 538 Angel Bravo .... 4.00 1.80 .50
☐ 539 Larry Brown .... 4.00 1.80 .50
☐ 540 Larry Dierker .... 4.00 1.80 .50
☐ 541 Bob Burda .... 4.00 1.80 .50
☐ 542 Bob Miller .... 4.00 1.80 .50
☐ 543 New York Yankees 8.00 3.60 1.00
Team Card
☐ 544 Vida Blue .... 7.00 3.10 .85
☐ 545 Dick Dietz .... 4.00 1.80 .50
☐ 546 John Matias .... 4.00 1.80 .50
☐ 547 Pat Dobson .... 4.50 2.00 .55
☐ 548 Don Mason .... 4.00 1.80 .50
☐ 549 Jim Brewer .... 5.00 2.30 .60
☐ 550 Harmon Killebrew 28.00 12.50 3.50
☐ 551 Frank Linzy .... 4.00 1.80 .50
☐ 552 Buddy Bradford .... 4.00 1.80 .50
☐ 553 Kevin Collins .... 4.50 2.00 .55
☐ 554 Lowell Palmer .... 4.00 1.80 .50
☐ 555 Walt Williams .... 4.00 1.80 .50
☐ 556 Jim McGlothlin .... 4.00 1.80 .50
☐ 557 Tom Satriano .... 4.00 1.80 .50
☐ 558 Hector Torres .... 4.00 1.80 .50
☐ 559 AL Rookie Pitchers .... 4.00 1.80 .50
Terry Cox
Bill Gogolewski
Gary Jones
☐ 560 Rusty Staub .... 5.00 2.30 .60
☐ 561 Syd O'Brien .... 4.00 1.80 .50
☐ 562 Dave Giusti .... 4.00 1.80 .50
☐ 563 San Francisco Giants . 8.00 3.60 1.00
Team Card
☐ 564 Al Fitzmorris .... 4.00 1.80 .50
☐ 565 Jim Wynn .... 4.50 2.00 .55
☐ 566 Tim Cullen .... 4.00 1.80 .50
☐ 567 Walt Alston MG .... 5.00 2.30 .60
☐ 568 Sal Campisi .... 4.00 1.80 .50
☐ 569 Ivan Murrell .... 4.00 1.80 .50
☐ 570 Jim Palmer 35.00 16.00 4.40
☐ 571 Ted Sizemore .... 4.00 1.80 .50
☐ 572 Jerry Kenney .... 4.00 1.80 .50
☐ 573 Ed Kranepool .... 4.50 2.00 .55
☐ 574 Jim Bunning .... 6.00 2.70 .75
☐ 575 Bill Freehan .... 4.50 2.00 .55
☐ 576 Cubs Rookies .... 4.00 1.80 .50
Adrian Garrett
Brock Davis
Garry Jestadt
☐ 577 Jim Lonborg .... 4.50 2.00 .55
☐ 578 Ron Hunt .... 4.00 1.80 .50
☐ 579 Marty Pattin .... 4.00 1.80 .50
☐ 580 Tony Perez 18.00 8.00 2.30
☐ 581 Roger Nelson .... 4.00 1.80 .50
☐ 582 Dave Cash .... 5.00 2.30 .60
☐ 583 Ron Cook .... 4.00 1.80 .50
☐ 584 Cleveland Indians 8.00 3.60 1.00
Team Card
☐ 585 Willie Davis .... 5.00 2.30 .60
☐ 586 Dick Woodson .... 4.00 1.80 .50
☐ 587 Sonny Jackson .... 4.00 1.80 .50
☐ 588 Tom Bradley .... 4.00 1.80 .50
☐ 589 Bob Barton .... 4.00 1.80 .50
☐ 590 Alex Johnson .... 4.50 2.00 .55
☐ 591 Jackie Brown .... 4.00 1.80 .50
☐ 592 Randy Hundley .... 4.00 1.80 .50
☐ 593 Jack Aker .... 4.00 1.80 .50
☐ 594 Cards Rookies .... 6.00 2.70 .75
Bob Chlupsa
Bob Stinson
Al Hrabosky
☐ 595 Dave Johnson .... 4.50 2.00 .55
☐ 596 Mike Jorgensen .... 4.00 1.80 .50
☐ 597 Ken Suarez .... 4.00 1.80 .50
☐ 598 Rick Wise .... 4.50 2.00 .55
☐ 599 Norm Cash .... 6.00 2.70 .75
☐ 600 Willie Mays 100.00 45.00 12.50
☐ 601 Ken Tatum .... 4.00 1.80 .50
☐ 602 Marty Martinez .... 4.00 1.80 .50
☐ 603 Pittsburgh Pirates 8.00 3.60 1.00
Team Card
☐ 604 John Gelnar .... 4.00 1.80 .50
☐ 605 Orlando Cepeda .... 6.00 2.70 .75
☐ 606 Chuck Taylor .... 4.00 1.80 .50
☐ 607 Paul Ratliff .... 4.00 1.80 .50
☐ 608 Mike Wegener .... 4.00 1.80 .50
☐ 609 Leo Durocher MG ...... 7.00 3.10 .85
☐ 610 Amos Otis .... 4.50 2.00 .55
☐ 611 Tom Phoebus .... 4.00 1.80 .50
☐ 612 Indians Rookies .... 4.00 1.80 .50
Lou Camilli
Ted Ford
Steve Mingori
☐ 613 Pedro Borbon .... 4.00 1.80 .50
☐ 614 Billy Cowan .... 4.00 1.80 .50
☐ 615 Mel Stottlemyre .... 6.00 2.70 .75
☐ 616 Larry Hisle .... 4.50 2.00 .55
☐ 617 Clay Dalrymple .... 4.00 1.80 .50
☐ 618 Tug McGraw .... 6.00 2.70 .75
☐ 619A Checklist 6 ERR .... 6.00 2.20 .60
(No copyright)
☐ 619B Checklist 6 COR ..... 10.00 1.80 .50
(Copyright on back)
☐ 620 Frank Howard .... 5.00 2.30 .60
☐ 621 Ron Bryant .... 4.00 1.80 .50
☐ 622 Joe Lahoud .... 4.00 1.80 .50
☐ 623 Pat Jarvis .... 4.00 1.80 .50
☐ 624 Oakland Athletics 8.00 3.60 1.00
Team Card
☐ 625 Lou Brock 30.00 13.50 3.80
☐ 626 Freddie Patek .... 4.50 2.00 .55
☐ 627 Steve Hamilton .... 4.00 1.80 .50
☐ 628 John Bateman .... 4.00 1.80 .50
☐ 629 John Hiller .... 4.50 2.00 .55
☐ 630 Roberto Clemente 85.00 38.00 10.50
☐ 631 Eddie Fisher .... 4.00 1.80 .50
☐ 632 Darrel Chaney .... 4.00 1.80 .50
☐ 633 AL Rookie Outfielders 4.00 1.80 .50
Bobby Brooks
Pete Koegel
Scott Northey
☐ 634 Phil Regan .... 4.50 2.00 .55
☐ 635 Bobby Murcer .... 7.00 3.10 .85
☐ 636 Denny Lemaster .... 4.00 1.80 .50
☐ 637 Dave Bristol MG .... 4.00 1.80 .50
☐ 638 Stan Williams .... 4.00 1.80 .50
☐ 639 Tom Haller .... 4.00 1.80 .50
☐ 640 Frank Robinson 40.00 18.00 5.00
☐ 641 New York Mets 14.00 6.25 1.75
Team Card
☐ 642 Jim Roland .... 4.00 1.80 .50
☐ 643 Rick Reichardt .... 5.00 2.30 .60
☐ 644 Jim Stewart SP 11.00 4.90 1.40

☐ 645 Jim Maloney SP....... 12.00 5.50 1.50
☐ 646 Bobby Floyd SP....... 11.00 4.90 1.40
☐ 647 Juan Pizarro.............. 7.00 3.10 .85
☐ 648 Mets Rookies SP..... 20.00 9.00 2.50
Rich Folkers
Ted Martinez
John Matlack
☐ 649 Sparky Lyle SP........ 20.00 9.00 2.50
☐ 650 Rich Allen SP.......... 30.00 13.50 3.80
☐ 651 Jerry Robertson SP. 11.00 4.90 1.40
☐ 652 Atlanta Braves.......... 12.00 5.50 1.50
Team Card
☐ 653 Russ Snyder SP....... 11.00 4.90 1.40
☐ 654 Don Shaw SP.......... 11.00 4.90 1.40
☐ 655 Mike Epstein SP....... 11.00 4.90 1.40
☐ 656 Gerry Nyman SP...... 11.00 4.90 1.40
☐ 657 Jose Azcue................ 7.00 3.10 .85
☐ 658 Paul Lindblad SP..... 11.00 4.90 1.40
☐ 659 Byron Browne SP..... 11.00 4.90 1.40
☐ 660 Ray Culp.................... 7.00 3.10 .85
☐ 661 Chuck Tanner MG SP 11.00 4.90 1.40
☐ 662 Mike Hedlund SP..... 11.00 4.90 1.40
☐ 663 Marv Staehle............. 7.00 3.10 .85
☐ 664 Rookie Pitchers SP.. 11.00 4.90 1.40
Archie Reynolds
Bob Reynolds
Ken Reynolds
☐ 665 Ron Swoboda SP..... 15.00 6.75 1.90
☐ 666 Gene Brabender SP.. 11.00 4.90 1.40
☐ 667 Pete Ward.................. 7.00 3.10 .85
☐ 668 Gary Neibauer........... 7.00 3.10 .85
☐ 669 Ike Brown SP........... 11.00 4.90 1.40
☐ 670 Bill Hands.................. 7.00 3.10 .85
☐ 671 Bill Voss SP............ 11.00 4.90 1.40
☐ 672 Ed Crosby SP.......... 11.00 4.90 1.40
☐ 673 Gerry Janeski SP..... 11.00 4.90 1.40
☐ 674 Montreal Expos........ 12.00 5.50 1.50
Team Card
☐ 675 Dave Boswell............ 7.00 3.10 .85
☐ 676 Tommie Reynolds...... 7.00 3.10 .85
☐ 677 Jack DiLauro SP...... 11.00 4.90 1.40
☐ 678 George Thomas......... 7.00 3.10 .85
☐ 679 Don O'Riley............... 7.00 3.10 .85
☐ 680 Don Mincher SP....... 11.00 4.90 1.40
☐ 681 Bill Butler.................. 7.00 3.10 .85
☐ 682 Terry Harmon........... 7.00 3.10 .85
☐ 683 Bill Burbach SP........ 11.00 4.90 1.40
☐ 684 Curt Motton............... 7.00 3.10 .85
☐ 685 Moe Drabowsky......... 7.00 3.10 .85
☐ 686 Chico Ruiz SP.......... 11.00 4.90 1.40
☐ 687 Ron Taylor SP.......... 11.00 4.90 1.40
☐ 688 Sparky Anderson MG SP 35.00 16.00 4.40
☐ 689 Frank Baker............... 7.00 3.10 .85
☐ 690 Bob Moose................ 7.00 3.10 .85
☐ 691 Bobby Heise.............. 7.00 3.10 .85
☐ 692 AL Rookie Pitchers SP 11.00 4.90 1.40
Hal Haydel
Rogelio Moret
Wayne Twitchell
☐ 693 Jose Pena SP.......... 11.00 4.90 1.40
☐ 694 Rick Renick SP........ 11.00 4.90 1.40
☐ 695 Joe Niekro................. 7.50 3.40 .95
☐ 696 Jerry Morales............ 7.00 3.10 .85
☐ 697 Rickey Clark SP....... 11.00 4.90 1.40
☐ 698 Milwaukee Brewers SP 20.00 9.00 2.50
Team Card
☐ 699 Jim Britton................ 7.00 3.10 .85
☐ 700 Boog Powell SP....... 26.00 11.50 3.30
☐ 701 Bob Garibaldi............ 7.00 3.10 .85
☐ 702 Milt Ramirez............. 7.00 3.10 .85
☐ 703 Mike Kekich.............. 7.00 3.10 .85
☐ 704 J.C. Martin SP......... 11.00 4.90 1.40
☐ 705 Dick Selma SP......... 11.00 4.90 1.40
☐ 706 Joe Foy SP.............. 11.00 4.90 1.40
☐ 707 Fred Lasher............... 7.00 3.10 .85
☐ 708 Russ Nagelson SP... 11.00 4.90 1.40
☐ 709 Rookie Outfielders SP 100.00 45.00 12.50
Dusty Baker
Don Baylor
Tom Paciorek
☐ 710 Sonny Siebert........... 7.00 3.10 .85
☐ 711 Larry Stahl SP......... 11.00 4.90 1.40
☐ 712 Jose Martinez........... 7.00 3.10 .85
☐ 713 Mike Marshall SP..... 11.00 4.90 1.40
☐ 714 Dick Williams MG SP 11.00 4.90 1.40
☐ 715 Horace Clarke SP..... 11.00 4.90 1.40
☐ 716 Dave Leonhard.......... 7.00 3.10 .85
☐ 717 Tommie Aaron SP.... 11.00 4.90 1.40
☐ 718 Billy Wynne............... 7.00 3.10 .85
☐ 719 Jerry May SP.......... 11.00 4.90 1.40
☐ 720 Matty Alou................ 7.50 3.40 .95
☐ 721 John Morris.............. 7.00 3.10 .85
☐ 722 Houston Astros SP.. 20.00 9.00 2.50
Team Card
☐ 723 Vicente Romo SP..... 11.00 4.90 1.40
☐ 724 Tom Tischinski SP... 11.00 4.90 1.40
☐ 725 Gary Gentry SP........ 11.00 4.90 1.40
☐ 726 Paul Popovich........... 7.00 3.10 .85
☐ 727 Ray Lamb SP........... 11.00 4.90 1.40
☐ 728 NL Rookie Outfielders 7.00 3.10 .85
Wayne Redmond
Keith Lampard
Bernie Williams
☐ 729 Dick Billings.............. 7.00 3.10 .85
☐ 730 Jim Rooker............... 7.00 3.10 .85
☐ 731 Jim Qualls SP.......... 11.00 4.90 1.40
☐ 732 Bob Reed.................. 7.00 3.10 .85
☐ 733 Lee Maye SP........... 11.00 4.90 1.40
☐ 734 Rob Gardner SP....... 11.00 4.90 1.40
☐ 735 Mike Shannon SP.... 11.00 4.90 1.40
☐ 736 Mel Queen SP.......... 11.00 4.90 1.40
☐ 737 Preston Gomez SP MG 11.00 4.90 1.40
☐ 738 Russ Gibson SP....... 11.00 4.90 1.40
☐ 739 Barry Lersch SP....... 11.00 4.90 1.40
☐ 740 Luis Aparicio SP UER 25.00 11.50 3.10
(Led AL in steals
from 1965 to 1964,
should be 1956 to 1964)
☐ 741 Skip Guinn................ 7.00 3.10 .85
☐ 742 Kansas City Royals.. 12.00 5.50 1.50
Team Card
☐ 743 John O'Donoghue SP 11.00 4.90 1.40
☐ 744 Chuck Manuel SP..... 11.00 4.90 1.40
☐ 745 Sandy Alomar SP..... 11.00 4.90 1.40
☐ 746 Andy Kosco............... 7.00 3.10 .85
☐ 747 NL Rookie Pitchers.... 7.00 3.10 .85
Al Severinsen
Scipio Spinks
Balor Moore
☐ 748 John Purdin SP........ 11.00 4.90 1.40
☐ 749 Ken Szotkiewicz........ 7.00 3.10 .85
☐ 750 Denny McLain SP.... 20.00 9.00 2.50
☐ 751 Al Weis SP.............. 14.00 6.25 1.75
☐ 752 Dick Drago................ 8.00 2.40 .80

1972 Topps

The cards in this 787-card set measure 2 1/2" by 3 1/2". The 1972 Topps set contained the most cards ever for a Topps set to that point in time. Features appearing for the first time were "Boyhood Photos"

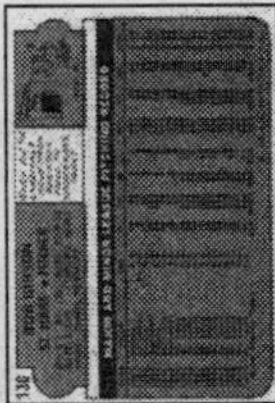

(KP: 341-348 and 491-498), Awards and Trophy cards (621-626), "In Action" (distributed throughout the set), and "Traded Cards" (TR: 751-757). Other subsets included League Leaders (85-96), Playoffs cards (221-222), and World Series cards (223-230). The curved lines of the color picture are a departure from the rectangular designs of other years. There is a series of intermediate scarcity (526-656) and the usual high numbers (657-787). The key Rookie Card in this set is Carlton Fisk.

	NRMT	EXC	G-VG
COMPLETE SET (787)	1800.00	800.00	230.00
COMMON CARD (1-132)	.50	.23	.06
COMMON CARD (133-263)	.75	.35	.09
COMMON CARD (264-394)	1.00	.45	.13
COMMON CARD (395-525)	1.50	.65	.19
COMMON CARD (526-656)	3.50	1.55	.45
COMMON CARD (657-787)	9.00	4.00	1.15

No.	Card	NRMT	EXC	G-VG
☐ 1	Pittsburgh Pirates	6.00	1.20	.35
	Team Card			
☐ 2	Ray Culp	.50	.23	.06
☐ 3	Bob Tolan	.50	.23	.06
☐ 4	Checklist 1-132	4.00	.40	.12
☐ 5	John Bateman	.50	.23	.06
☐ 6	Fred Scherman	.50	.23	.06
☐ 7	Enzo Hernandez	.50	.23	.06
☐ 8	Ron Swoboda	.75	.35	.09
☐ 9	Stan Williams	.50	.23	.06
☐ 10	Amos Otis	.75	.35	.09
☐ 11	Bobby Valentine	.50	.23	.06
☐ 12	Jose Cardenal	.50	.23	.06
☐ 13	Joe Grzenda	.50	.23	.06
☐ 14	Phillies Rookies	.50	.23	.06
	Pete Koegel			
	Mike Anderson			
	Wayne Twitchell			
☐ 15	Walt Williams	.50	.23	.06
☐ 16	Mike Jorgensen	.50	.23	.06
☐ 17	Dave Duncan	.50	.23	.06
☐ 18A	Juan Pizarro	.50	.23	.06
	(Yellow underline C and S of Cubs)			
☐ 18B	Juan Pizarro	5.00	2.30	.60
	(Green underline C and S of Cubs)			
☐ 19	Billy Cowan	.50	.23	.06
☐ 20	Don Wilson	.50	.23	.06
☐ 21	Atlanta Braves	1.50	.65	.19
	Team Card			
☐ 22	Rob Gardner	.50	.23	.06
☐ 23	Ted Kubiak	.50	.23	.06
☐ 24	Ted Ford	.50	.23	.06
☐ 25	Bill Singer	.50	.23	.06
☐ 26	Andy Etchebarren	.50	.23	.06
☐ 27	Bob Johnson	.50	.23	.06
☐ 28	Twins Rookies	.50	.23	.06
	Bob Gebhard			
	Steve Brye			
	Hal Haydel			
☐ 29A	Bill Bonham	.50	.23	.06
	(Yellow underline C and S of Cubs)			
☐ 29B	Bill Bonham	5.00	2.30	.60
	(Green underline C and S of Cubs)			
☐ 30	Rico Petrocelli	.75	.35	.09
☐ 31	Cleon Jones	.75	.35	.09
☐ 32	Cleon Jones IA	.50	.23	.06
☐ 33	Billy Martin MG	4.00	1.80	.50
☐ 34	Billy Martin IA	2.00	.90	.25
☐ 35	Jerry Johnson	.50	.23	.06
☐ 36	Jerry Johnson IA	.50	.23	.06
☐ 37	Carl Yastrzemski	12.00	5.50	1.50
☐ 38	Carl Yastrzemski IA	6.00	2.70	.75
☐ 39	Bob Barton	.50	.23	.06
☐ 40	Bob Barton IA	.50	.23	.06
☐ 41	Tommy Davis	.75	.35	.09
☐ 42	Tommy Davis IA	.50	.23	.06
☐ 43	Rick Wise	.75	.35	.09
☐ 44	Rick Wise IA	.50	.23	.06
☐ 45A	Glenn Beckert	.75	.35	.09
	(Yellow underline C and S of Cubs)			
☐ 45B	Glenn Beckert	5.00	2.30	.60
	(Green underline C and S of Cubs)			
☐ 46	Glenn Beckert IA	.50	.23	.06
☐ 47	John Ellis	.50	.23	.06
☐ 48	John Ellis IA	.50	.23	.06
☐ 49	Willie Mays	20.00	9.00	2.50
☐ 50	Willie Mays IA	10.00	4.50	1.25
☐ 51	Harmon Killebrew	6.00	2.70	.75
☐ 52	Harmon Killebrew IA	3.00	1.35	.40
☐ 53	Bud Harrelson	.75	.35	.09
☐ 54	Bud Harrelson IA	.50	.23	.06
☐ 55	Clyde Wright	.50	.23	.06
☐ 56	Rich Chiles	.50	.23	.06
☐ 57	Bob Oliver	.50	.23	.06
☐ 58	Ernie McAnally	.50	.23	.06
☐ 59	Fred Stanley	.50	.23	.06
☐ 60	Manny Sanguillen	.75	.35	.09
☐ 61	Cubs Rookies	1.50	.65	.19
	Burt Hooton			
	Gene Hiser			
	Earl Stephenson			
☐ 62	Angel Mangual	.50	.23	.06
☐ 63	Duke Sims	.50	.23	.06
☐ 64	Pete Broberg	.50	.23	.06
☐ 65	Cesar Cedeno	1.50	.65	.19
☐ 66	Ray Corbin	.50	.23	.06
☐ 67	Red Schoendienst MG	1.50	.65	.19
☐ 68	Jim York	.50	.23	.06
☐ 69	Roger Freed	.50	.23	.06
☐ 70	Mike Cuellar	.75	.35	.09
☐ 71	California Angels	1.50	.65	.19
	Team Card			
☐ 72	Bruce Kison	.50	.23	.06
☐ 73	Steve Huntz	.50	.23	.06
☐ 74	Cecil Upshaw	.50	.23	.06
☐ 75	Bert Campaneris	.75	.35	.09
☐ 76	Don Carrithers	.50	.23	.06
☐ 77	Ron Theobald	.50	.23	.06
☐ 78	Steve Arlin	.50	.23	.06
☐ 79	Red Sox Rookies	75.00	34.00	9.50
	Mike Garman			
	Cecil Cooper			

	Carlton Fisk			
☐ 80	Tony Perez	4.50	2.00	.55
☐ 81	Mike Hedlund	.50	.23	.06
☐ 82	Ron Woods	.50	.23	.06
☐ 83	Dalton Jones	.50	.23	.06
☐ 84	Vince Colbert	.50	.23	.06
☐ 85	NL Batting Leaders	1.75	.80	.22
	Joe Torre Ralph Garr Glenn Beckert			
☐ 86	AL Batting Leaders	1.75	.80	.22
	Tony Oliva Bobby Murcer Merv Rettenmund			
☐ 87	NL RBI Leaders	3.50	1.55	.45
	Joe Torre Willie Stargell Hank Aaron			
☐ 88	AL RBI Leaders	3.00	1.35	.40
	Harmon Killebrew Frank Robinson Reggie Smith			
☐ 89	NL Home Run Leaders	3.00	1.35	.40
	Willie Stargell Hank Aaron Lee May			
☐ 90	AL Home Run Leaders	2.50	1.15	.30
	Bill Melton Norm Cash Reggie Jackson			
☐ 91	NL ERA Leaders	2.50	1.15	.30
	Tom Seaver Dave Roberts UER (Photo actually Danny Coombs) Don Wilson			
☐ 92	AL ERA Leaders	2.50	1.15	.30
	Vida Blue Wilbur Wood Jim Palmer			
☐ 93	NL Pitching Leaders	4.00	1.80	.50
	Fergie Jenkins Steve Carlton Al Downing Tom Seaver			
☐ 94	AL Pitching Leaders	1.75	.80	.22
	Mickey Lolich Vida Blue Wilbur Wood			
☐ 95	NL Strikeout Leaders	3.00	1.35	.40
	Tom Seaver Fergie Jenkins Bill Stoneman			
☐ 96	AL Strikeout Leaders	1.75	.80	.22
	Mickey Lolich Vida Blue Joe Coleman			
☐ 97	Tom Kelley	.50	.23	.06
☐ 98	Chuck Tanner MG	.75	.35	.09
☐ 99	Ross Grimsley	.50	.23	.06
☐ 100	Frank Robinson	7.50	3.40	.95
☐ 101	Astros Rookies	3.00	1.35	.40
	Bill Greif J.R. Richard Ray Busse			
☐ 102	Lloyd Allen	.50	.23	.06
☐ 103	Checklist 133-263	4.00	.40	.12
☐ 104	Toby Harrah	2.00	.90	.25
☐ 105	Gary Gentry	.50	.23	.06
☐ 106	Milwaukee Brewers Team Card	1.50	.65	.19
☐ 107	Jose Cruz	2.50	1.15	.30
☐ 108	Gary Waslewski	.50	.23	.06
☐ 109	Jerry May	.50	.23	.06
☐ 110	Ron Hunt	.50	.23	.06
☐ 111	Jim Grant	.50	.23	.06
☐ 112	Greg Luzinski	2.00	.90	.25
☐ 113	Rogelio Moret	.50	.23	.06
☐ 114	Bill Buckner	2.00	.90	.25
☐ 115	Jim Fregosi	.75	.35	.09
☐ 116	Ed Farmer	.50	.23	.06
☐ 117A	Cleo James	.50	.23	.06
	(Yellow underline C and S of Cubs)			
☐ 117B	Cleo James	5.00	2.30	.60
	(Green underline C and S of Cubs)			
☐ 118	Skip Lockwood	.50	.23	.06
☐ 119	Marty Perez	.50	.23	.06
☐ 120	Bill Freehan	.75	.35	.09
☐ 121	Ed Sprague	.50	.23	.06
☐ 122	Larry Biittner	.50	.23	.06
☐ 123	Ed Acosta	.50	.23	.06
☐ 124	Yankees Rookies	.50	.23	.06
	Alan Closter Rusty Torres Roger Hambright			
☐ 125	Dave Cash	.75	.35	.09
☐ 126	Bart Johnson	.50	.23	.06
☐ 127	Duffy Dyer	.50	.23	.06
☐ 128	Eddie Watt	.50	.23	.06
☐ 129	Charlie Fox MG	.50	.23	.06
☐ 130	Bob Gibson	7.50	3.40	.95
☐ 131	Jim Nettles	.50	.23	.06
☐ 132	Joe Morgan	5.00	2.30	.60
☐ 133	Joe Keough	.75	.35	.09
☐ 134	Carl Morton	.75	.35	.09
☐ 135	Vada Pinson	1.25	.55	.16
☐ 136	Darrel Chaney	.75	.35	.09
☐ 137	Dick Williams MG	1.00	.45	.13
☐ 138	Mike Kekich	.75	.35	.09
☐ 139	Tim McCarver	1.00	.45	.13
☐ 140	Pat Dobson	1.00	.45	.13
☐ 141	Mets Rookies	1.00	.45	.13
	Buzz Capra Lee Stanton Jon Matlack			
☐ 142	Chris Chambliss	6.00	2.70	.75
☐ 143	Garry Jestadt	.75	.35	.09
☐ 144	Marty Pattin	.75	.35	.09
☐ 145	Don Kessinger	1.00	.45	.13
☐ 146	Steve Kealey	.75	.35	.09
☐ 147	Dave Kingman	6.00	2.70	.75
☐ 148	Dick Billings	.75	.35	.09
☐ 149	Gary Neibauer	.75	.35	.09
☐ 150	Norm Cash	1.25	.55	.16
☐ 151	Jim Brewer	.75	.35	.09
☐ 152	Gene Clines	.75	.35	.09
☐ 153	Rick Auerbach	.75	.35	.09
☐ 154	Ted Simmons	3.50	1.55	.45
☐ 155	Larry Dierker	.75	.35	.09
☐ 156	Minnesota Twins Team Card	1.50	.65	.19
☐ 157	Don Gullett	.75	.35	.09
☐ 158	Jerry Kenney	.75	.35	.09
☐ 159	John Boccabella	.75	.35	.09
☐ 160	Andy Messersmith	1.00	.45	.13
☐ 161	Brock Davis	.75	.35	.09
☐ 162	Brewers Rookies UER	1.25	.55	.16
	Jerry Bell Darrell Porter Bob Reynolds (Porter and Bell photos switched)			
☐ 163	Tug McGraw	1.50	.65	.19
☐ 164	McGraw In Action	1.00	.45	.13

	No.	Card			
☐	165	Chris Speier	1.25	.55	.16
☐	166	Speier In Action	1.00	.45	.13
☐	167	Deron Johnson	.75	.35	.09
☐	168	Johnson In Action	.75	.35	.09
☐	169	Vida Blue	1.50	.65	.19
☐	170	Blue In Action	1.00	.45	.13
☐	171	Darrell Evans	2.00	.90	.25
☐	172	Evans In Action	1.00	.45	.13
☐	173	Clay Kirby	.75	.35	.09
☐	174	Kirby In Action	.75	.35	.09
☐	175	Tom Haller	.75	.35	.09
☐	176	Haller In Action	.75	.35	.09
☐	177	Paul Schaal	.75	.35	.09
☐	178	Schaal In Action	.75	.35	.09
☐	179	Dock Ellis	.75	.35	.09
☐	180	Ellis In Action	.75	.35	.09
☐	181	Ed Kranepool	.75	.35	.09
☐	182	Kranepool In Action	.75	.35	.09
☐	183	Bill Melton	.75	.35	.09
☐	184	Melton In Action	.75	.35	.09
☐	185	Ron Bryant	.75	.35	.09
☐	186	Bryant In Action	.75	.35	.09
☐	187	Gates Brown	1.00	.45	.13
☐	188	Frank Lucchesi MG	.75	.35	.09
☐	189	Gene Tenace	1.00	.45	.13
☐	190	Dave Giusti	.75	.35	.09
☐	191	Jeff Burroughs	1.50	.65	.19
☐	192	Chicago Cubs	1.50	.65	.19
		Team Card			
☐	193	Kurt Bevacqua	.75	.35	.09
☐	194	Fred Norman	.75	.35	.09
☐	195	Orlando Cepeda	3.50	1.55	.45
☐	196	Mel Queen	.75	.35	.09
☐	197	Johnny Briggs	.75	.35	.09
☐	198	Dodgers Rookies	8.00	3.60	1.00
		Charlie Hough			
		Bob O'Brien			
		Mike Strahler			
☐	199	Mike Fiore	.75	.35	.09
☐	200	Lou Brock	6.00	2.70	.75
☐	201	Phil Roof	.75	.35	.09
☐	202	Scipio Spinks	.75	.35	.09
☐	203	Ron Blomberg	.75	.35	.09
☐	204	Tommy Helms	.75	.35	.09
☐	205	Dick Drago	.75	.35	.09
☐	206	Dal Maxvill	.75	.35	.09
☐	207	Tom Egan	.75	.35	.09
☐	208	Milt Pappas	1.00	.45	.13
☐	209	Joe Rudi	1.00	.45	.13
☐	210	Denny McLain	1.50	.65	.19
☐	211	Gary Sutherland	.75	.35	.09
☐	212	Grant Jackson	.75	.35	.09
☐	213	Angels Rookies	.75	.35	.09
		Billy Parker			
		Art Kusnyer			
		Tom Silverio			
☐	214	Mike McQueen	.75	.35	.09
☐	215	Alex Johnson	1.00	.45	.13
☐	216	Joe Niekro	1.00	.45	.13
☐	217	Roger Metzger	.75	.35	.09
☐	218	Eddie Kasko MG	.75	.35	.09
☐	219	Rennie Stennett	1.00	.45	.13
☐	220	Jim Perry	1.00	.45	.13
☐	221	NL Playoffs	1.50	.65	.19
		Bucs champs			
☐	222	AL Playoffs	2.50	1.15	.30
		Orioles champs			
		(Brooks Robinson)			
☐	223	World Series Game 1	1.75	.80	.22
		(Dave McNally pitching)			
☐	224	World Series Game 2	1.75	.80	.22
		(Dave Johnson and			
		Mark Belanger)			
☐	225	World Series Game 3	1.75	.80	.22
		(Manny Sanguillen			
		scoring)			
☐	226	World Series Game 4	5.00	2.30	.60
		(Roberto Clemente			
		on second)			
☐	227	World Series Game 5	1.75	.80	.22
		(Nellie Briles			
		pitching)			
☐	228	World Series Game 6	1.75	.80	.22
		(Frank Robinson and			
		Manny Sanguillen)			
☐	229	World Series Game 7	1.75	.80	.22
		(Steve Blass pitching)			
☐	230	World Series Summary	1.75	.80	.22
		(Pirates celebrate)			
☐	231	Casey Cox	.75	.35	.09
☐	232	Giants Rookies	.75	.35	.09
		Chris Arnold			
		Jim Barr			
		Dave Rader			
☐	233	Jay Johnstone	1.00	.45	.13
☐	234	Ron Taylor	.75	.35	.09
☐	235	Merv Rettenmund	.75	.35	.09
☐	236	Jim McGlothlin	.75	.35	.09
☐	237	New York Yankees	1.50	.65	.19
		Team Card			
☐	238	Leron Lee	.75	.35	.09
☐	239	Tom Timmermann	.75	.35	.09
☐	240	Rich Allen	3.00	1.35	.40
☐	241	Rollie Fingers	6.50	2.90	.80
☐	242	Don Mincher	1.00	.45	.13
☐	243	Frank Linzy	.75	.35	.09
☐	244	Steve Braun	.75	.35	.09
☐	245	Tommie Agee	1.00	.45	.13
☐	246	Tom Burgmeier	.75	.35	.09
☐	247	Milt May	.75	.35	.09
☐	248	Tom Bradley	.75	.35	.09
☐	249	Harry Walker MG	.75	.35	.09
☐	250	Boog Powell	2.00	.90	.25
☐	251	Checklist 264-394	4.00	.40	.12
☐	252	Ken Reynolds	.75	.35	.09
☐	253	Sandy Alomar	1.00	.45	.13
☐	254	Boots Day	.75	.35	.09
☐	255	Jim Lonborg	1.00	.45	.13
☐	256	George Foster	2.50	1.15	.30
☐	257	Tigers Rookies	.75	.35	.09
		Jim Foor			
		Tim Hosley			
		Paul Jata			
☐	258	Randy Hundley	.75	.35	.09
☐	259	Sparky Lyle	1.00	.45	.13
☐	260	Ralph Garr	1.00	.45	.13
☐	261	Steve Mingori	.75	.35	.09
☐	262	San Diego Padres	1.50	.65	.19
		Team Card			
☐	263	Felipe Alou	1.50	.65	.19
☐	264	Tommy John	2.50	1.15	.30
☐	265	Wes Parker	1.25	.55	.16
☐	266	Bobby Bolin	1.00	.45	.13
☐	267	Dave Concepcion	4.00	1.80	.50
☐	268	A's Rookies	1.00	.45	.13
		Dwain Anderson			
		Chris Floethe			
☐	269	Don Hahn	1.00	.45	.13
☐	270	Jim Palmer	12.00	5.50	1.50
☐	271	Ken Rudolph	1.00	.45	.13
☐	272	Mickey Rivers	2.00	.90	.25
☐	273	Bobby Floyd	1.00	.45	.13
☐	274	Al Severinsen	1.00	.45	.13
☐	275	Cesar Tovar	1.00	.45	.13
☐	276	Gene Mauch MG	1.25	.55	.16
☐	277	Elliott Maddox	1.00	.45	.13

□ 278 Dennis Higgins .... 1.00 .45 .13
□ 279 Larry Brown .... 1.00 .45 .13
□ 280 Willie McCovey .... 6.50 2.90 .80
□ 281 Bill Parsons .... 1.00 .45 .13
□ 282 Houston Astros .... 2.00 .90 .25
Team Card
□ 283 Darrell Brandon .... 1.00 .45 .13
□ 284 Ike Brown .... 1.00 .45 .13
□ 285 Gaylord Perry .... 6.00 2.70 .75
□ 286 Gene Alley .... 1.25 .55 .16
□ 287 Jim Hardin .... 1.00 .45 .13
□ 288 Johnny Jeter .... 1.00 .45 .13
□ 289 Syd O'Brien .... 1.00 .45 .13
□ 290 Sonny Siebert .... 1.00 .45 .13
□ 291 Hal McRae .... 1.00 .45 .13
□ 292 Hal McRae IA .... 1.00 .45 .13
□ 293 Dan Frisella .... 1.00 .45 .13
□ 294 Dan Frisella IA .... 1.00 .45 .13
□ 295 Dick Dietz .... 1.00 .45 .13
□ 296 Dick Dietz IA .... 1.00 .45 .13
□ 297 Claude Osteen .... 1.25 .55 .16
□ 298 Claude Osteen IA .... 1.00 .45 .13
□ 299 Hank Aaron 36.00 16.00 4.50
□ 300 Hank Aaron IA 18.00 8.00 2.30
□ 301 George Mitterwald ..... 1.00 .45 .13
□ 302 George Mitterwald IA. 1.00 .45 .13
□ 303 Joe Pepitone .... 1.25 .55 .16
□ 304 Joe Pepitone IA .... 1.00 .45 .13
□ 305 Ken Boswell .... 1.00 .45 .13
□ 306 Ken Boswell IA .... 1.00 .45 .13
□ 307 Steve Renko .... 1.00 .45 .13
□ 308 Steve Renko IA .... 1.00 .45 .13
□ 309 Roberto Clemente 36.00 16.00 4.50
□ 310 Roberto Clemente IA 18.00 8.00 2.30
□ 311 Clay Carroll .... 1.00 .45 .13
□ 312 Clay Carroll IA .... 1.00 .45 .13
□ 313 Luis Aparicio .... 3.00 1.35 .40
□ 314 Luis Aparicio IA .... 1.50 .65 .19
□ 315 Paul Splittorff .... 1.00 .45 .13
□ 316 Cardinals Rookies ...... 1.25 .55 .16
Jim Bibby
Jorge Roque
Santiago Guzman
□ 317 Rich Hand .... 1.00 .45 .13
□ 318 Sonny Jackson .... 1.00 .45 .13
□ 319 Aurelio Rodriguez ...... 1.00 .45 .13
□ 320 Steve Blass .... 1.25 .55 .16
□ 321 Joe Lahoud .... 1.00 .45 .13
□ 322 Jose Pena .... 1.00 .45 .13
□ 323 Earl Weaver MG .... 2.00 .90 .25
□ 324 Mike Ryan .... 1.00 .45 .13
□ 325 Mel Stottlemyre .... 1.25 .55 .16
□ 326 Pat Kelly .... 1.00 .45 .13
□ 327 Steve Stone .... 3.50 1.55 .45
□ 328 Boston Red Sox .... 2.00 .90 .25
Team Card
□ 329 Roy Foster .... 1.00 .45 .13
□ 330 Jim Hunter .... 5.00 2.30 .60
□ 331 Stan Swanson .... 1.00 .45 .13
□ 332 Buck Martinez .... 1.00 .45 .13
□ 333 Steve Barber .... 1.00 .45 .13
□ 334 Rangers Rookies .... 1.00 .45 .13
Bill Fahey
Jim Mason
Tom Ragland
□ 335 Bill Hands .... 1.00 .45 .13
□ 336 Marty Martinez .... 1.00 .45 .13
□ 337 Mike Kilkenny .... 1.00 .45 .13
□ 338 Bob Grich .... 2.50 1.15 .30
□ 339 Ron Cook .... 1.00 .45 .13
□ 340 Roy White .... 1.25 .55 .16
□ 341 Joe Torre KP .... 1.25 .55 .16
□ 342 Wilbur Wood KP .... 1.25 .55 .16
□ 343 Willie Stargell KP .... 1.50 .65 .19
□ 344 Dave McNally KP .... 1.25 .55 .16
□ 345 Rick Wise KP .... 1.25 .55 .16
□ 346 Jim Fregosi KP .... 1.25 .55 .16
□ 347 Tom Seaver KP .... 3.00 1.35 .40
□ 348 Sal Bando KP .... 1.25 .55 .16
□ 349 Al Fitzmorris .... 1.00 .45 .13
□ 350 Frank Howard .... 1.50 .65 .19
□ 351 Braves Rookies .... 1.25 .55 .16
Tom House
Rick Kester
Jimmy Britton
□ 352 Dave LaRoche .... 1.00 .45 .13
□ 353 Art Shamsky .... 1.00 .45 .13
□ 354 Tom Murphy .... 1.00 .45 .13
□ 355 Bob Watson .... 1.25 .55 .16
□ 356 Gerry Moses .... 1.00 .45 .13
□ 357 Woodie Fryman .... 1.00 .45 .13
□ 358 Sparky Anderson MG. 2.50 1.15 .30
□ 359 Don Pavletich .... 1.00 .45 .13
□ 360 Dave Roberts .... 1.00 .45 .13
□ 361 Mike Andrews .... 1.00 .45 .13
□ 362 New York Mets .... 2.00 .90 .25
Team Card
□ 363 Ron Klimkowski .... 1.00 .45 .13
□ 364 Johnny Callison .... 1.25 .55 .16
□ 365 Dick Bosman .... 1.25 .55 .16
□ 366 Jimmy Rosario .... 1.00 .45 .13
□ 367 Ron Perranoski .... 1.25 .55 .16
□ 368 Danny Thompson ...... 1.00 .45 .13
□ 369 Jim Lefebvre .... 1.25 .55 .16
□ 370 Don Buford .... 1.00 .45 .13
□ 371 Denny Lemaster .... 1.00 .45 .13
□ 372 Royals Rookies .... 1.00 .45 .13
Lance Clemons
Monty Montgomery
□ 373 John Mayberry .... 1.25 .55 .16
□ 374 Jack Heidemann .... 1.00 .45 .13
□ 375 Reggie Cleveland ...... 1.00 .45 .13
□ 376 Andy Kosco .... 1.00 .45 .13
□ 377 Terry Harmon .... 1.00 .45 .13
□ 378 Checklist 395-525 ...... 4.00 .45 .13
□ 379 Ken Berry .... 1.00 .45 .13
□ 380 Earl Williams .... 1.00 .45 .13
□ 381 Chicago White Sox ..... 2.00 .90 .25
Team Card
□ 382 Joe Gibbon .... 1.00 .45 .13
□ 383 Brant Alyea .... 1.00 .45 .13
□ 384 Dave Campbell .... 1.00 .45 .13
□ 385 Mickey Stanley .... 1.25 .55 .16
□ 386 Jim Colborn .... 1.00 .45 .13
□ 387 Horace Clarke .... 1.00 .45 .13
□ 388 Charlie Williams .... 1.00 .45 .13
□ 389 Bill Rigney MG .... 1.00 .45 .13
□ 390 Willie Davis .... 1.25 .55 .16
□ 391 Ken Sanders .... 1.00 .45 .13
□ 392 Pirates Rookies .... 1.00 .45 .13
Fred Cambria
Richie Zisk
□ 393 Curt Motton .... 1.00 .45 .13
□ 394 Ken Forsch .... 1.25 .55 .16
□ 395 Matty Alou .... 1.75 .80 .22
□ 396 Paul Lindblad .... 1.50 .65 .19
□ 397 Philadelphia Phillies ... 3.00 1.35 .40
Team Card
□ 398 Larry Hisle .... 1.75 .80 .22
□ 399 Milt Wilcox .... 1.50 .65 .19
□ 400 Tony Oliva .... 2.50 1.15 .30
□ 401 Jim Nash .... 1.50 .65 .19
□ 402 Bobby Heise .... 1.50 .65 .19
□ 403 John Cumberland ...... 1.50 .65 .19
□ 404 Jeff Torborg .... 1.75 .80 .22
□ 405 Ron Fairly .... 1.75 .80 .22

☐ 406	George Hendrick	2.00	.90	.25
☐ 407	Chuck Taylor	1.50	.65	.19
☐ 408	Jim Northrup	1.75	.80	.22
☐ 409	Frank Baker	1.50	.65	.19
☐ 410	Fergie Jenkins	7.00	3.10	.85
☐ 411	Bob Montgomery	1.50	.65	.19
☐ 412	Dick Kelley	1.50	.65	.19
☐ 413	White Sox Rookies	1.50	.65	.19
	Don Eddy			
	Dave Lemonds			
☐ 414	Bob Miller	1.50	.65	.19
☐ 415	Cookie Rojas	1.75	.80	.22
☐ 416	Johnny Edwards	1.50	.65	.19
☐ 417	Tom Hall	1.50	.65	.19
☐ 418	Tom Shopay	1.50	.65	.19
☐ 419	Jim Spencer	1.50	.65	.19
☐ 420	Steve Carlton	20.00	9.00	2.50
☐ 421	Ellie Rodriguez	1.50	.65	.19
☐ 422	Ray Lamb	1.50	.65	.19
☐ 423	Oscar Gamble	1.75	.80	.22
☐ 424	Bill Gogolewski	1.50	.65	.19
☐ 425	Ken Singleton	2.50	1.15	.30
☐ 426	Ken Singleton IA	1.50	.65	.19
☐ 427	Tito Fuentes	1.50	.65	.19
☐ 428	Tito Fuentes IA	1.50	.65	.19
☐ 429	Bob Robertson	1.50	.65	.19
☐ 430	Bob Robertson IA	1.50	.65	.19
☐ 431	Clarence Gaston	4.00	1.80	.50
☐ 432	Clarence Gaston IA	2.00	.90	.25
☐ 433	Johnny Bench	30.00	13.50	3.80
☐ 434	Johnny Bench IA	15.00	6.75	1.90
☐ 435	Reggie Jackson	30.00	13.50	3.80
☐ 436	Reggie Jackson IA	15.00	6.75	1.90
☐ 437	Maury Wills	2.50	1.15	.30
☐ 438	Maury Wills IA	1.50	.65	.19
☐ 439	Billy Williams	5.00	2.30	.60
☐ 440	Billy Williams IA	2.50	1.15	.30
☐ 441	Thurman Munson	20.00	9.00	2.50
☐ 442	THurman Munson IA	10.00	4.50	1.25
☐ 443	Ken Henderson	1.50	.65	.19
☐ 444	Ken Henderson IA	1.50	.65	.19
☐ 445	Tom Seaver	28.00	12.50	3.50
☐ 446	Tom Seaver IA	14.00	6.25	1.75
☐ 447	Willie Stargell	6.00	2.70	.75
☐ 448	Willie Stargell IA	3.00	1.35	.40
☐ 449	Bob Lemon MG	1.50	.65	.19
☐ 450	Mickey Lolich	3.00	1.35	.40
☐ 451	Tony LaRussa	3.00	1.35	.40
☐ 452	Ed Herrmann	1.50	.65	.19
☐ 453	Barry Lersch	1.50	.65	.19
☐ 454	Oakland A's	3.00	1.35	.40
	Team Card			
☐ 455	Tommy Harper	1.75	.80	.22
☐ 456	Mark Belanger	1.75	.80	.22
☐ 457	Padres Rookies	1.50	.65	.19
	Darcy Fast			
	Derrel Thomas			
	Mike Ivie			
☐ 458	Aurelio Monteagudo	1.50	.65	.19
☐ 459	Rick Renick	1.50	.65	.19
☐ 460	Al Downing	1.50	.65	.19
☐ 461	Tim Cullen	1.50	.65	.19
☐ 462	Rickey Clark	1.50	.65	.19
☐ 463	Bernie Carbo	1.50	.65	.19
☐ 464	Jim Roland	1.50	.65	.19
☐ 465	Gil Hodges MG	4.50	2.00	.55
☐ 466	Norm Miller	1.50	.65	.19
☐ 467	Steve Kline	1.50	.65	.19
☐ 468	Richie Scheinblum	1.50	.65	.19
☐ 469	Ron Herbel	1.50	.65	.19
☐ 470	Ray Fosse	1.50	.65	.19
☐ 471	Luke Walker	1.50	.65	.19
☐ 472	Phil Gagliano	1.50	.65	.19

☐ 473	Dan McGinn	1.50	.65	.19
☐ 474	Orioles Rookies	15.00	6.75	1.90
	Don Baylor			
	Roric Harrison			
	Johnny Oates			
☐ 475	Gary Nolan	1.75	.80	.22
☐ 476	Lee Richard	1.50	.65	.19
☐ 477	Tom Phoebus	1.50	.65	.19
☐ 478	Checklist 526-656	4.00	.65	.19
☐ 479	Don Shaw	1.50	.65	.19
☐ 480	Lee May	1.75	.80	.22
☐ 481	Billy Conigliaro	1.75	.80	.22
☐ 482	Joe Hoerner	1.50	.65	.19
☐ 483	Ken Suarez	1.50	.65	.19
☐ 484	Lum Harris MG	1.50	.65	.19
☐ 485	Phil Regan	1.75	.80	.22
☐ 486	John Lowenstein	1.50	.65	.19
☐ 487	Detroit Tigers	3.00	1.35	.40
	Team Card			
☐ 488	Mike Nagy	1.50	.65	.19
☐ 489	Expos Rookies	1.50	.65	.19
	Terry Humphrey			
	Keith Lampard			
☐ 490	Dave McNally	1.75	.80	.22
☐ 491	Lou Piniella KP	2.00	.90	.25
☐ 492	Mel Stottlemyre KP	1.75	.80	.22
☐ 493	Bob Bailey KP	1.75	.80	.22
☐ 494	Willie Horton KP	1.75	.80	.22
☐ 495	Bill Melton KP	1.75	.80	.22
☐ 496	Bud Harrelson KP	1.75	.80	.22
☐ 497	Jim Perry KP	1.75	.80	.22
☐ 498	Brooks Robinson KP	3.00	1.35	.40
☐ 499	Vicente Romo	1.50	.65	.19
☐ 500	Joe Torre	2.50	1.15	.30
☐ 501	Pete Hamm	1.50	.65	.19
☐ 502	Jackie Hernandez	1.50	.65	.19
☐ 503	Gary Peters	1.50	.65	.19
☐ 504	Ed Spiezio	1.50	.65	.19
☐ 505	Mike Marshall	1.75	.80	.22
☐ 506	Indians Rookies	1.50	.65	.19
	Terry Ley			
	Jim Moyer			
	Dick Tidrow			
☐ 507	Fred Gladding	1.50	.65	.19
☐ 508	Elrod Hendricks	1.50	.65	.19
☐ 509	Don McMahon	1.50	.65	.19
☐ 510	Ted Williams MG	10.00	4.50	1.25
☐ 511	Tony Taylor	1.50	.65	.19
☐ 512	Paul Popovich	1.50	.65	.19
☐ 513	Lindy McDaniel	1.75	.80	.22
☐ 514	Ted Sizemore	1.50	.65	.19
☐ 515	Bert Blyleven	7.00	3.10	.85
☐ 516	Oscar Brown	1.50	.65	.19
☐ 517	Ken Brett	1.50	.65	.19
☐ 518	Wayne Garrett	1.50	.65	.19
☐ 519	Ted Abernathy	1.50	.65	.19
☐ 520	Larry Bowa	3.00	1.35	.40
☐ 521	Alan Foster	1.50	.65	.19
☐ 522	Los Angeles Dodgers	3.00	1.35	.40
	Team Card			
☐ 523	Chuck Dobson	1.50	.65	.19
☐ 524	Reds Rookies	1.50	.65	.19
	Ed Armbrister			
	Mel Behney			
☐ 525	Carlos May	1.75	.80	.22
☐ 526	Bob Bailey	4.00	1.80	.50
☐ 527	Dave Leonhard	3.50	1.55	.45
☐ 528	Ron Stone	3.50	1.55	.45
☐ 529	Dave Nelson	4.00	1.80	.50
☐ 530	Don Sutton	7.00	3.10	.85
☐ 531	Freddie Patek	4.00	1.80	.50
☐ 532	Fred Kendall	3.50	1.55	.45
☐ 533	Ralph Houk MG	4.00	1.80	.50

	No.	Player			
☐	534	Jim Hickman	4.00	1.80	.50
☐	535	Ed Brinkman	3.50	1.55	.45
☐	536	Doug Rader	4.00	1.80	.50
☐	537	Bob Locker	3.50	1.55	.45
☐	538	Charlie Sands	3.50	1.55	.45
☐	539	Terry Forster	4.00	1.80	.50
☐	540	Felix Millan	3.50	1.55	.45
☐	541	Roger Repoz	3.50	1.55	.45
☐	542	Jack Billingham	3.50	1.55	.45
☐	543	Duane Josephson	3.50	1.55	.45
☐	544	Ted Martinez	3.50	1.55	.45
☐	545	Wayne Granger	3.50	1.55	.45
☐	546	Joe Hague	3.50	1.55	.45
☐	547	Cleveland Indians Team Card	6.50	2.90	.80
☐	548	Frank Reberger	3.50	1.55	.45
☐	549	Dave May	3.50	1.55	.45
☐	550	Brooks Robinson	20.00	9.00	2.50
☐	551	Ollie Brown	3.50	1.55	.45
☐	552	Ollie Brown IA	3.50	1.55	.45
☐	553	Wilbur Wood	4.00	1.80	.50
☐	554	Wilbur Wood IA	3.50	1.55	.45
☐	555	Ron Santo	5.00	2.30	.60
☐	556	Ron Santo IA	4.00	1.80	.50
☐	557	John Odom	3.50	1.55	.45
☐	558	John Odom IA	3.50	1.55	.45
☐	559	Pete Rose	40.00	18.00	5.00
☐	560	Pete Rose IA	20.00	9.00	2.50
☐	561	Leo Cardenas	3.50	1.55	.45
☐	562	Leo Cardenas IA	3.50	1.55	.45
☐	563	Ray Sadecki	3.50	1.55	.45
☐	564	Ray Sadecki IA	3.50	1.55	.45
☐	565	Reggie Smith	3.75	1.70	.45
☐	566	Reggie Smith IA	3.50	1.55	.45
☐	567	Juan Marichal	8.00	3.60	1.00
☐	568	Juan Marichal IA	4.00	1.80	.50
☐	569	Ed Kirkpatrick	3.50	1.55	.45
☐	570	Ed Kirkpatrick IA	3.50	1.55	.45
☐	571	Nate Colbert	3.50	1.55	.45
☐	572	Nate Colbert IA	3.50	1.55	.45
☐	573	Fritz Peterson	3.50	1.55	.45
☐	574	Fritz Peterson IA	3.50	1.55	.45
☐	575	Al Oliver	4.50	2.00	.55
☐	576	Leo Durocher MG	5.00	2.30	.60
☐	577	Mike Paul	4.00	1.80	.50
☐	578	Billy Grabarkewitz	3.50	1.55	.45
☐	579	Doyle Alexander	4.00	1.80	.50
☐	580	Lou Piniella	5.00	2.30	.60
☐	581	Wade Blasingame	3.50	1.55	.45
☐	582	Montreal Expos Team Card	6.50	2.90	.80
☐	583	Darold Knowles	3.50	1.55	.45
☐	584	Jerry McNertney	3.50	1.55	.45
☐	585	George Scott	4.00	1.80	.50
☐	586	Denis Menke	3.50	1.55	.45
☐	587	Billy Wilson	3.50	1.55	.45
☐	588	Jim Holt	3.50	1.55	.45
☐	589	Hal Lanier	3.50	1.55	.45
☐	590	Graig Nettles	6.00	2.70	.75
☐	591	Paul Casanova	3.50	1.55	.45
☐	592	Lew Krausse	3.50	1.55	.45
☐	593	Rich Morales	3.50	1.55	.45
☐	594	Jim Beauchamp	3.50	1.55	.45
☐	595	Nolan Ryan	250.00	115.00	31.00
☐	596	Manny Mota	4.00	1.80	.50
☐	597	Jim Magnuson	3.50	1.55	.45
☐	598	Hal King	4.00	1.80	.50
☐	599	Billy Champion	3.50	1.55	.45
☐	600	Al Kaline	25.00	11.50	3.10
☐	601	George Stone	3.50	1.55	.45
☐	602	Dave Bristol MG	3.50	1.55	.45
☐	603	Jim Ray	3.50	1.55	.45
☐	604A	Checklist 657-787 (Copyright on back bottom right)	9.00	1.35	.40
☐	604B	Checklist 657-787 (Copyright on back bottom left)	9.00	1.35	.40
☐	605	Nelson Briles	4.00	1.80	.50
☐	606	Luis Melendez	3.50	1.55	.45
☐	607	Frank Duffy	3.50	1.55	.45
☐	608	Mike Corkins	3.50	1.55	.45
☐	609	Tom Grieve	4.00	1.80	.50
☐	610	Bill Stoneman	3.50	1.55	.45
☐	611	Rich Reese	3.50	1.55	.45
☐	612	Joe Decker	3.50	1.55	.45
☐	613	Mike Ferraro	3.50	1.55	.45
☐	614	Ted Uhlaender	3.50	1.55	.45
☐	615	Steve Hargan	3.50	1.55	.45
☐	616	Joe Ferguson	4.00	1.80	.50
☐	617	Kansas City Royals Team Card	6.50	2.90	.80
☐	618	Rich Robertson	3.50	1.55	.45
☐	619	Rich McKinney	3.50	1.55	.45
☐	620	Phil Niekro	9.00	4.00	1.15
☐	621	Commissioners Award	4.50	2.00	.55
☐	622	MVP Award	4.50	2.00	.55
☐	623	Cy Young Award	4.50	2.00	.55
☐	624	Minor League Player of the Year	4.50	2.00	.55
☐	625	Rookie of the Year	4.50	2.00	.55
☐	626	Babe Ruth Award	4.50	2.00	.55
☐	627	Moe Drabowsky	3.50	1.55	.45
☐	628	Terry Crowley	3.50	1.55	.45
☐	629	Paul Doyle	3.50	1.55	.45
☐	630	Rich Hebner	4.00	1.80	.50
☐	631	John Strohmayer	3.50	1.55	.45
☐	632	Mike Hegan	3.50	1.55	.45
☐	633	Jack Hiatt	3.50	1.55	.45
☐	634	Dick Woodson	3.50	1.55	.45
☐	635	Don Money	4.00	1.80	.50
☐	636	Bill Lee	4.00	1.80	.50
☐	637	Preston Gomez MG	3.50	1.55	.45
☐	638	Ken Wright	3.50	1.55	.45
☐	639	J.C. Martin	3.50	1.55	.45
☐	640	Joe Coleman	3.50	1.55	.45
☐	641	Mike Lum	3.50	1.55	.45
☐	642	Dennis Riddleberger	3.50	1.55	.45
☐	643	Russ Gibson	3.50	1.55	.45
☐	644	Bernie Allen	3.50	1.55	.45
☐	645	Jim Maloney	4.00	1.80	.50
☐	646	Chico Salmon	3.50	1.55	.45
☐	647	Bob Moose	3.50	1.55	.45
☐	648	Jim Lyttle	3.50	1.55	.45
☐	649	Pete Richert	3.50	1.55	.45
☐	650	Sal Bando	4.00	1.80	.50
☐	651	Cincinnati Reds Team Card	6.50	2.90	.80
☐	652	Marcelino Lopez	3.50	1.55	.45
☐	653	Jim Fairey	3.50	1.55	.45
☐	654	Horacio Pina	4.00	1.80	.50
☐	655	Jerry Grote	3.50	1.55	.45
☐	656	Rudy May	3.50	1.55	.45
☐	657	Bobby Wine	9.00	4.00	1.15
☐	658	Steve Dunning	9.00	4.00	1.15
☐	659	Bob Aspromonte	9.00	4.00	1.15
☐	660	Paul Blair	10.00	4.50	1.25
☐	661	Bill Virdon MG	10.00	4.50	1.25
☐	662	Stan Bahnsen	9.00	4.00	1.15
☐	663	Fran Healy	10.00	4.50	1.25
☐	664	Bobby Knoop	9.00	4.00	1.15
☐	665	Chris Short	9.00	4.00	1.15
☐	666	Hector Torres	9.00	4.00	1.15
☐	667	Ray Newman	9.00	4.00	1.15
☐	668	Texas Rangers Team Card	22.00	10.00	2.80

☐ 669 Willie Crawford 9.00 4.00 1.15
☐ 670 Ken Holtzman 10.00 4.50 1.25
☐ 671 Donn Clendenon 10.00 4.50 1.25
☐ 672 Archie Reynolds......... 9.00 4.00 1.15
☐ 673 Dave Marshall 9.00 4.00 1.15
☐ 674 John Kennedy............ 9.00 4.00 1.15
☐ 675 Pat Jarvis................... 9.00 4.00 1.15
☐ 676 Danny Cater 9.00 4.00 1.15
☐ 677 Ivan Murrell 9.00 4.00 1.15
☐ 678 Steve Luebber............ 9.00 4.00 1.15
☐ 679 Astros Rookies 9.00 4.00 1.15
Bob Fenwick
Bob Stinson
☐ 680 Dave Johnson 10.00 4.50 1.25
☐ 681 Bobby Pfeil 9.00 4.00 1.15
☐ 682 Mike McCormick...... 10.00 4.50 1.25
☐ 683 Steve Hovley 9.00 4.00 1.15
☐ 684 Hal Breeden 9.00 4.00 1.15
☐ 685 Joel Horlen 9.00 4.00 1.15
☐ 686 Steve Garvey........... 45.00 20.00 5.75
☐ 687 Del Unser.................. 9.00 4.00 1.15
☐ 688 St. Louis Cardinals... 15.00 6.75 1.90
Team Card
☐ 689 Eddie Fisher 9.00 4.00 1.15
☐ 690 Willie Montanez 10.00 4.50 1.25
☐ 691 Curt Blefary............... 9.00 4.00 1.15
☐ 692 Curt Blefary IA 9.00 4.00 1.15
☐ 693 Alan Gallagher........... 9.00 4.00 1.15
☐ 694 Alan Gallagher IA 9.00 4.00 1.15
☐ 695 Rod Carew 70.00 32.00 8.75
☐ 696 Rod Carew IA........... 35.00 16.00 4.40
☐ 697 Jerry Koosman 16.00 7.25 2.00
☐ 698 Jerry Koosman IA.... 12.00 5.50 1.50
☐ 699 Bobby Murcer........... 16.00 7.25 2.00
☐ 700 Bobby Murcer IA...... 12.00 5.50 1.50
☐ 701 Jose Pagan 9.00 4.00 1.15
☐ 702 Jose Pagan IA........... 9.00 4.00 1.15
☐ 703 Doug Griffin 9.00 4.00 1.15
☐ 704 Doug Griffin IA........... 9.00 4.00 1.15
☐ 705 Pat Corrales 10.00 4.50 1.25
☐ 706 Pat Corrales IA.......... 9.00 4.00 1.15
☐ 707 Tim Foli...................... 9.00 4.00 1.15
☐ 708 Tim Foli IA 9.00 4.00 1.15
☐ 709 Jim Kaat.................. 16.00 7.25 2.00
☐ 710 Jim Kaat IA 12.00 5.50 1.50
☐ 711 Bobby Bonds 18.00 8.00 2.30
☐ 712 Bobby Bonds IA....... 14.00 6.25 1.75
☐ 713 Gene Michael 9.00 4.00 1.15
☐ 714 Gene Michael IA......... 9.00 4.00 1.15
☐ 715 Mike Epstein 9.00 4.00 1.15
☐ 716 Jesus Alou 9.00 4.00 1.15
☐ 717 Bruce Dal Canton 9.00 4.00 1.15
☐ 718 Del Rice MG............... 9.00 4.00 1.15
☐ 719 Cesar Geronimo......... 9.00 4.00 1.15
☐ 720 Sam McDowell......... 10.00 4.50 1.25
☐ 721 Eddie Leon 9.00 4.00 1.15
☐ 722 Bill Sudakis 9.00 4.00 1.15
☐ 723 Al Santorini 9.00 4.00 1.15
☐ 724 AL Rookie Pitchers 9.00 4.00 1.15
John Curtis
Rich Hinton
Mickey Scott
☐ 725 Dick McAuliffe.......... 10.00 4.50 1.25
☐ 726 Dick Selma................ 9.00 4.00 1.15
☐ 727 Jose Laboy 9.00 4.00 1.15
☐ 728 Gail Hopkins 9.00 4.00 1.15
☐ 729 Bob Veale................ 10.00 4.50 1.25
☐ 730 Rick Monday........... 10.00 4.50 1.25
☐ 731 Baltimore Orioles 15.00 6.75 1.90
Team Card
☐ 732 George Culver........... 9.00 4.00 1.15
☐ 733 Jim Ray Hart........... 10.00 4.50 1.25
☐ 734 Bob Burda.................. 9.00 4.00 1.15
☐ 735 Diego Segui 9.00 4.00 1.15
☐ 736 Bill Russell.............. 12.00 5.50 1.50
☐ 737 Len Randle.............. 10.00 4.50 1.25
☐ 738 Jim Merritt................ 9.00 4.00 1.15
☐ 739 Don Mason 9.00 4.00 1.15
☐ 740 Rico Carty 10.00 4.50 1.25
☐ 741 Rookie First Basemen 14.00 6.25 1.75
Tom Hutton
John Milner
Rick Miller
☐ 742 Jim Rooker 9.00 4.00 1.15
☐ 743 Cesar Gutierrez 9.00 4.00 1.15
☐ 744 Jim Slaton.................. 9.00 4.00 1.15
☐ 745 Julian Javier............ 10.00 4.50 1.25
☐ 746 Lowell Palmer 9.00 4.00 1.15
☐ 747 Jim Stewart................ 9.00 4.00 1.15
☐ 748 Phil Hennigan 9.00 4.00 1.15
☐ 749 Walter Alston MG..... 14.00 6.25 1.75
☐ 750 Willie Horton........... 10.00 4.50 1.25
☐ 751 Steve Carlton TR...... 65.00 29.00 8.25
☐ 752 Joe Morgan TR 50.00 23.00 6.25
☐ 753 Denny McLain TR 18.00 8.00 2.30
☐ 754 Frank Robinson TR .. 38.00 17.00 4.70
☐ 755 Jim Fregosi TR......... 10.00 4.50 1.25
☐ 756 Rick Wise TR 10.00 4.50 1.25
☐ 757 Jose Cardenal TR..... 10.00 4.50 1.25
☐ 758 Gil Garrido 9.00 4.00 1.15
☐ 759 Chris Cannizzaro 9.00 4.00 1.15
☐ 760 Bill Mazeroski 16.00 7.25 2.00
☐ 761 Rookie Outfielders ... 25.00 11.50 3.10
Ben Oglivie
Ron Cey
Bernie Williams
☐ 762 Wayne Simpson......... 9.00 4.00 1.15
☐ 763 Ron Hansen 9.00 4.00 1.15
☐ 764 Dusty Baker 20.00 9.00 2.50
☐ 765 Ken McMullen............ 9.00 4.00 1.15
☐ 766 Steve Hamilton 9.00 4.00 1.15
☐ 767 Tom McCraw 10.00 4.50 1.25
☐ 768 Denny Doyle 9.00 4.00 1.15
☐ 769 Jack Aker................... 9.00 4.00 1.15
☐ 770 Jim Wynn 10.00 4.50 1.25
☐ 771 San Francisco Giants 15.00 6.75 1.90
Team Card
☐ 772 Ken Tatum 9.00 4.00 1.15
☐ 773 Ron Brand.................. 9.00 4.00 1.15
☐ 774 Luis Alvarado............. 9.00 4.00 1.15
☐ 775 Jerry Reuss............. 10.00 4.50 1.25
☐ 776 Bill Voss..................... 9.00 4.00 1.15
☐ 777 Hoyt Wilhelm 20.00 9.00 2.50
☐ 778 Twins Rookies 18.00 8.00 2.30
Vic Albury
Rick Dempsey
Jim Strickland
☐ 779 Tony Cloninger 9.00 4.00 1.15
☐ 780 Dick Green 9.00 4.00 1.15
☐ 781 Jim McAndrew........... 9.00 4.00 1.15
☐ 782 Larry Stahl 9.00 4.00 1.15
☐ 783 Les Cain..................... 9.00 4.00 1.15
☐ 784 Ken Aspromonte 9.00 4.00 1.15
☐ 785 Vic Davalillo 9.00 4.00 1.15
☐ 786 Chuck Brinkman 9.00 4.00 1.15
☐ 787 Ron Reed................ 12.00 4.80 1.30

1973 Topps

The cards in this 660-card set measure 2 1/2" by 3 1/2". The 1973 Topps set marked the last year in which Topps

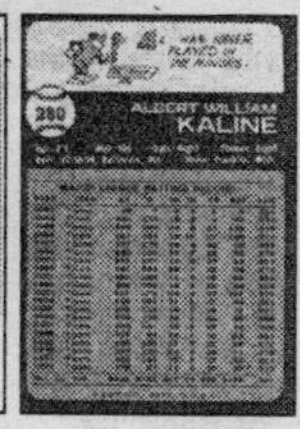

marketed baseball cards in consecutive series. The last series (529-660) is more difficult to obtain. In some parts of the country, however, all five series were distributed together. Beginning in 1974, all Topps cards were printed at the same time, thus eliminating the "high number" factor. The set features team leader cards with small individual pictures of the coaching staff members and a larger picture of the manager. The "background" variations below with respect to these leader cards are subtle and are best understood after a side-by-side comparison of the two varieties. An "All-Time Leaders" series (471-478) appeared for the first time in this set. Kid Pictures appeared again for the second year in a row (341-346). Other topical subsets within the set included League Leaders (61-68), Playoffs cards (201-202), World Series cards (203-210), and Rookie Prospects (601-616). The key Rookie Cards in this set are all in the Rookie Prospect series: Bob Boone, Dwight Evans, and Mike Schmidt.

	NRMT	EXC	G-VG
COMPLETE SET (660)	850.00	375.00	105.00
COMMON CARD (1-132)	.50	.23	.06
COMMON CARD (133-264)	.50	.23	.06
COMMON CARD (265-396)	.75	.35	.09
COMMON CARD (397-528)	1.25	.55	.16
COMMON CARD (529-660)	3.50	1.55	.45

☐ 1 All-Time HR Leaders	35.00	8.75	2.80
Babe Ruth 714			
Hank Aaron 673			
Willie Mays 654			
☐ 2 Rich Hebner	.75	.35	.09
☐ 3 Jim Lonborg	.75	.35	.09
☐ 4 John Milner	.50	.23	.06
☐ 5 Ed Brinkman	.50	.23	.06
☐ 6 Mac Scarce	.50	.23	.06
☐ 7 Texas Rangers	1.25	.55	.16
Team Card			
☐ 8 Tom Hall	.50	.23	.06
☐ 9 Johnny Oates	.50	.23	.06
☐ 10 Don Sutton	2.50	1.15	.30
☐ 11 Chris Chambliss	1.75	.80	.22
☐ 12A Padres Leaders	.75	.35	.09
Don Zimmer MG			
Dave Garcia CO			
Johnny Podres CO			
Bob Skinner CO			
Whitey Wietelmann CO			
(Podres no right ear)			
☐ 12B Padres Leaders	1.50	.65	.19
(Podres has right ear)			
☐ 13 George Hendrick	.75	.35	.09
☐ 14 Sonny Siebert	.50	.23	.06
☐ 15 Ralph Garr	.75	.35	.09
☐ 16 Steve Braun	.50	.23	.06
☐ 17 Fred Gladding	.50	.23	.06
☐ 18 Leroy Stanton	.50	.23	.06
☐ 19 Tim Foli	.50	.23	.06
☐ 20 Stan Bahnsen	.50	.23	.06
☐ 21 Randy Hundley	.50	.23	.06
☐ 22 Ted Abernathy	.50	.23	.06
☐ 23 Dave Kingman	1.50	.65	.19
☐ 24 Al Santorini	.50	.23	.06
☐ 25 Roy White	.75	.35	.09
☐ 26 Pittsburgh Pirates	1.25	.55	.16
Team Card			
☐ 27 Bill Gogolewski	.50	.23	.06
☐ 28 Hal McRae	1.50	.65	.19
☐ 29 Tony Taylor	.50	.23	.06
☐ 30 Tug McGraw	1.25	.55	.16
☐ 31 Buddy Bell	4.00	1.80	.50
☐ 32 Fred Norman	.50	.23	.06
☐ 33 Jim Breazeale	.50	.23	.06
☐ 34 Pat Dobson	.50	.23	.06
☐ 35 Willie Davis	.75	.35	.09
☐ 36 Steve Barber	.50	.23	.06
☐ 37 Bill Robinson	.75	.35	.09
☐ 38 Mike Epstein	.50	.23	.06
☐ 39 Dave Roberts	.50	.23	.06
☐ 40 Reggie Smith	.75	.35	.09
☐ 41 Tom Walker	.50	.23	.06
☐ 42 Mike Andrews	.50	.23	.06
☐ 43 Randy Moffitt	.50	.23	.06
☐ 44 Rick Monday	.75	.35	.09
☐ 45 Ellie Rodriguez UER	.50	.23	.06
(Photo actually			
John Felske)			
☐ 46 Lindy McDaniel	.75	.35	.09
☐ 47 Luis Melendez	.50	.23	.06
☐ 48 Paul Splittorff	.50	.23	.06
☐ 49A Twins Leaders	.75	.35	.09
Frank Quilici MG			
Vern Morgan CO			
Bob Rodgers CO			
Ralph Rowe CO			
Al Worthington CO			
(Solid backgrounds)			
☐ 49B Twins Leaders	1.50	.65	.19
(Natural backgrounds)			
☐ 50 Roberto Clemente	40.00	18.00	5.00
☐ 51 Chuck Seelbach	.50	.23	.06
☐ 52 Denis Menke	.50	.23	.06
☐ 53 Steve Dunning	.50	.23	.06
☐ 54 Checklist 1-132	3.00	.30	.09
☐ 55 Jon Matlack	.75	.35	.09
☐ 56 Merv Rettenmund	.50	.23	.06
☐ 57 Derrel Thomas	.50	.23	.06
☐ 58 Mike Paul	.50	.23	.06
☐ 59 Steve Yeager	1.50	.65	.19
☐ 60 Ken Holtzman	.75	.35	.09
☐ 61 Batting Leaders	3.00	1.35	.40
Billy Williams			
Rod Carew			
☐ 62 Home Run Leaders	2.50	1.15	.30
Johnny Bench			
Dick Allen			
☐ 63 RBI Leaders	2.50	1.15	.30
Johnny Bench			
Dick Allen			
☐ 64 Stolen Base Leaders	2.00	.90	.25
Lou Brock			
Bert Campaneris			
☐ 65 ERA Leaders	2.00	.90	.25
Steve Carlton			

	Luis Tiant			
☐ 66	Victory Leaders	2.00	.90	.25
	Steve Carlton			
	Gaylord Perry			
	Wilbur Wood			
☐ 67	Strikeout Leaders	28.00	12.50	3.50
	Steve Carlton			
	Nolan Ryan			
☐ 68	Leading Firemen	1.00	.45	.13
	Clay Carroll			
	Sparky Lyle			
☐ 69	Phil Gagliano	.50	.23	.06
☐ 70	Milt Pappas	.75	.35	.09
☐ 71	Johnny Briggs	.50	.23	.06
☐ 72	Ron Reed	.50	.23	.06
☐ 73	Ed Herrmann	.50	.23	.06
☐ 74	Billy Champion	.50	.23	.06
☐ 75	Vada Pinson	1.00	.45	.13
☐ 76	Doug Rader	.50	.23	.06
☐ 77	Mike Torrez	.75	.35	.09
☐ 78	Richie Scheinblum	.50	.23	.06
☐ 79	Jim Willoughby	.50	.23	.06
☐ 80	Tony Oliva UER	1.50	.65	.19
	(Minnseota on front)			
☐ 81A	Cubs Leaders	1.25	.55	.16
	Whitey Lockman MG			
	Hank Aguirre CO			
	Ernie Banks CO			
	Larry Jansen CO			
	Pete Reiser CO			
	(Solid backgrounds)			
☐ 81B	Cubs Leaders	2.00	.90	.25
	(Natural backgrounds)			
☐ 82	Fritz Peterson	.50	.23	.06
☐ 83	Leron Lee	.50	.23	.06
☐ 84	Rollie Fingers	5.00	2.30	.60
☐ 85	Ted Simmons	2.50	1.15	.30
☐ 86	Tom McCraw	.50	.23	.06
☐ 87	Ken Boswell	.50	.23	.06
☐ 88	Mickey Stanley	.75	.35	.09
☐ 89	Jack Billingham	.50	.23	.06
☐ 90	Brooks Robinson	8.50	3.80	1.05
☐ 91	Los Angeles Dodgers	1.25	.55	.16
	Team Card			
☐ 92	Jerry Bell	.50	.23	.06
☐ 93	Jesus Alou	.50	.23	.06
☐ 94	Dick Billings	.50	.23	.06
☐ 95	Steve Blass	.75	.35	.09
☐ 96	Doug Griffin	.50	.23	.06
☐ 97	Willie Montanez	.75	.35	.09
☐ 98	Dick Woodson	.50	.23	.06
☐ 99	Carl Taylor	.50	.23	.06
☐ 100	Hank Aaron	30.00	13.50	3.80
☐ 101	Ken Henderson	.50	.23	.06
☐ 102	Rudy May	.50	.23	.06
☐ 103	Celerino Sanchez	.50	.23	.06
☐ 104	Reggie Cleveland	.50	.23	.06
☐ 105	Carlos May	.50	.23	.06
☐ 106	Terry Humphrey	.50	.23	.06
☐ 107	Phil Hennigan	.50	.23	.06
☐ 108	Bill Russell	.75	.35	.09
☐ 109	Doyle Alexander	.75	.35	.09
☐ 110	Bob Watson	.75	.35	.09
☐ 111	Dave Nelson	.50	.23	.06
☐ 112	Gary Ross	.50	.23	.06
☐ 113	Jerry Grote	.50	.23	.06
☐ 114	Lynn McGlothen	.50	.23	.06
☐ 115	Ron Santo	1.00	.45	.13
☐ 116A	Yankees Leaders	.75	.35	.09
	Ralph Houk MG			
	Jim Hegan CO			
	Elston Howard CO			
	Dick Howser CO			
	Jim Turner CO			
	(Solid backgrounds)			
☐ 116B	Yankees Leaders	1.50	.65	.19
	(Natural backgrounds)			
☐ 117	Ramon Hernandez	.50	.23	.06
☐ 118	John Mayberry	.75	.35	.09
☐ 119	Larry Bowa	1.25	.55	.16
☐ 120	Joe Coleman	.50	.23	.06
☐ 121	Dave Rader	.50	.23	.06
☐ 122	Jim Strickland	.50	.23	.06
☐ 123	Sandy Alomar	.75	.35	.09
☐ 124	Jim Hardin	.50	.23	.06
☐ 125	Ron Fairly	.50	.23	.06
☐ 126	Jim Brewer	.50	.23	.06
☐ 127	Milwaukee Brewers	1.25	.55	.16
	Team Card			
☐ 128	Ted Sizemore	.50	.23	.06
☐ 129	Terry Forster	.75	.35	.09
☐ 130	Pete Rose	22.00	10.00	2.80
☐ 131A	Red Sox Leaders	.75	.35	.09
	Eddie Kasko MG			
	Doug Camilli CO			
	Don Lenhardt CO			
	Eddie Popowski CO			
	(No right ear)			
	Lee Stange CO			
☐ 131B	Red Sox Leaders	1.50	.65	.19
	(Popowski has right ear showing)			
☐ 132	Matty Alou	.75	.35	.09
☐ 133	Dave Roberts	.50	.23	.06
☐ 134	Milt Wilcox	.50	.23	.06
☐ 135	Lee May UER	.75	.35	.09
	(Career average .000)			
☐ 136A	Orioles Leaders	1.25	.55	.16
	Earl Weaver MG			
	George Bamberger CO			
	Jim Frey CO			
	Billy Hunter CO			
	George Staller CO			
	(Orange backgrounds)			
☐ 136B	Orioles Leaders	2.00	.90	.25
	(Dark pale backgrounds)			
☐ 137	Jim Beauchamp	.50	.23	.06
☐ 138	Horacio Pina	.50	.23	.06
☐ 139	Carmen Fanzone	.50	.23	.06
☐ 140	Lou Piniella	1.25	.55	.16
☐ 141	Bruce Kison	.50	.23	.06
☐ 142	Thurman Munson	10.00	4.50	1.25
☐ 143	John Curtis	.50	.23	.06
☐ 144	Marty Perez	.50	.23	.06
☐ 145	Bobby Bonds	2.50	1.15	.30
☐ 146	Woodie Fryman	.50	.23	.06
☐ 147	Mike Anderson	.50	.23	.06
☐ 148	Dave Goltz	.50	.23	.06
☐ 149	Ron Hunt	.50	.23	.06
☐ 150	Wilbur Wood	.75	.35	.09
☐ 151	Wes Parker	.75	.35	.09
☐ 152	Dave May	.50	.23	.06
☐ 153	Al Hrabosky	.75	.35	.09
☐ 154	Jeff Torborg	.75	.35	.09
☐ 155	Sal Bando	.75	.35	.09
☐ 156	Cesar Geronimo	.50	.23	.06
☐ 157	Denny Riddleberger	.50	.23	.06
☐ 158	Houston Astros	1.25	.55	.16
	Team Card			
☐ 159	Clarence Gaston	1.25	.55	.16
☐ 160	Jim Palmer	8.00	3.60	1.00
☐ 161	Ted Martinez	.50	.23	.06
☐ 162	Pete Broberg	.50	.23	.06
☐ 163	Vic Davalillo	.50	.23	.06
☐ 164	Monty Montgomery	.50	.23	.06
☐ 165	Luis Aparicio	3.00	1.35	.40

☐ 166 Terry Harmon .... .50 .23 .06
☐ 167 Steve Stone.................. .75 .35 .09
☐ 168 Jim Northrup .... .75 .35 .09
☐ 169 Ron Schueler .... .50 .23 .06
☐ 170 Harmon Killebrew ...... 5.00 2.30 .60
☐ 171 Bernie Carbo .... .50 .23 .06
☐ 172 Steve Kline................... .50 .23 .06
☐ 173 Hal Breeden .... .50 .23 .06
☐ 174 Rich Gossage........... 14.00 6.25 1.75
☐ 175 Frank Robinson.......... 6.00 2.70 .75
☐ 176 Chuck Taylor............... .50 .23 .06
☐ 177 Bill Plummer................ .50 .23 .06
☐ 178 Don Rose..................... .50 .23 .06
☐ 179A A's Leaders................ .75 .35 .09
Dick Williams MG
Jerry Adair CO
Vern Hoscheit CO
Irv Noren CO
Wes Stock CO
(Hoscheit left ear showing)
☐ 179B A's Leaders............. 1.50 .65 .19
(Hoscheit left ear not showing)
☐ 180 Fergie Jenkins........... 5.00 2.30 .60
☐ 181 Jack Brohamer............ .50 .23 .06
☐ 182 Mike Caldwell.............. .50 .23 .06
☐ 183 Don Buford .... .50 .23 .06
☐ 184 Jerry Koosman .... .75 .35 .09
☐ 185 Jim Wynn .... .75 .35 .09
☐ 186 Bill Fahey .... .50 .23 .06
☐ 187 Luke Walker................. .50 .23 .06
☐ 188 Cookie Rojas................ .75 .35 .09
☐ 189 Greg Luzinski............ 1.50 .65 .19
☐ 190 Bob Gibson............... 7.00 3.10 .85
☐ 191 Detroit Tigers............ 1.25 .55 .16
Team Card
☐ 192 Pat Jarvis..................... .50 .23 .06
☐ 193 Carlton Fisk............. 30.00 13.50 3.80
☐ 194 Jorge Orta.................... .50 .23 .06
☐ 195 Clay Carroll.................. .50 .23 .06
☐ 196 Ken McMullen.............. .50 .23 .06
☐ 197 Ed Goodson .... .50 .23 .06
☐ 198 Horace Clarke .... .50 .23 .06
☐ 199 Bert Blyleven............ 4.00 1.80 .50
☐ 200 Billy Williams............ 4.00 1.80 .50
☐ 201 A.L. Playoffs .... 1.00 .45 .13
A's over Tigers;
George Hendrick scores winning run
☐ 202 N.L. Playoffs .... 1.00 .45 .13
Reds over Pirates
George Foster's run decides
☐ 203 World Series Game 1. 1.00 .45 .13
Gene Tenace the Menace
☐ 204 World Series Game 2. 1.00 .45 .13
A's two straight
☐ 205 World Series Game 3. 1.00 .45 .13
Reds win squeeker
(Tony Perez)
☐ 206 World Series Game 4. 1.00 .45 .13
Gene Tenace singles in ninth
☐ 207 World Series Game 5. 1.00 .45 .13
Blue Moon Odom out at plate
☐ 208 World Series Game 6. 1.00 .45 .13
Reds' slugging ties series
(Johnny Bench)
☐ 209 World Series Game 7. 1.00 .45 .13
Bert Campaneris starts winning rally
☐ 210 World Series Summary 1.00 .45 .13
World champions:
A's Win
☐ 211 Balor Moore................. .50 .23 .06
☐ 212 Joe Lahoud .... .50 .23 .06
☐ 213 Steve Garvey............. 9.00 4.00 1.15
☐ 214 Steve Hamilton .... .50 .23 .06
☐ 215 Dusty Baker .... 2.50 1.15 .30
☐ 216 Toby Harrah................. .75 .35 .09
☐ 217 Don Wilson................... .50 .23 .06
☐ 218 Aurelio Rodriguez .... .50 .23 .06
☐ 219 St. Louis Cardinals..... 1.25 .55 .16
Team Card
☐ 220 Nolan Ryan 100.00 45.00 12.50
☐ 221 Fred Kendall................ .50 .23 .06
☐ 222 Rob Gardner .... .50 .23 .06
☐ 223 Bud Harrelson.............. .75 .35 .09
☐ 224 Bill Lee......................... .75 .35 .09
☐ 225 Al Oliver.................... 1.50 .65 .19
☐ 226 Ray Fosse .... .50 .23 .06
☐ 227 Wayne Twitchell........... .50 .23 .06
☐ 228 Bobby Darwin .... .50 .23 .06
☐ 229 Roric Harrison .... .50 .23 .06
☐ 230 Joe Morgan............... 6.50 2.90 .80
☐ 231 Bill Parsons.................. .50 .23 .06
☐ 232 Ken Singleton .... .75 .35 .09
☐ 233 Ed Kirkpatrick .... .50 .23 .06
☐ 234 Bill North...................... .50 .23 .06
☐ 235 Jim Hunter................. 4.00 1.80 .50
☐ 236 Tito Fuentes................. .50 .23 .06
☐ 237A Braves Leaders........ 1.50 .65 .19
Eddie Mathews MG
Lew Burdette CO
Jim Busby CO
Roy Hartsfield CO
Ken Silvestri CO
(Burdette right ear showing)
☐ 237B Braves Leaders........ 3.00 1.35 .40
(Burdette right ear not showing)
☐ 238 Tony Muser................... .50 .23 .06
☐ 239 Pete Richert................. .50 .23 .06
☐ 240 Bobby Murcer .... 1.00 .45 .13
☐ 241 Dwain Anderson .... .50 .23 .06
☐ 242 George Culver.............. .50 .23 .06
☐ 243 California Angels........ 1.25 .55 .16
Team Card
☐ 244 Ed Acosta..................... .50 .23 .06
☐ 245 Carl Yastrzemski...... 14.00 6.25 1.75
☐ 246 Ken Sanders .... .50 .23 .06
☐ 247 Del Unser..................... .50 .23 .06
☐ 248 Jerry Johnson.............. .50 .23 .06
☐ 249 Larry Biittner................ .50 .23 .06
☐ 250 Manny Sanguillen .... .75 .35 .09
☐ 251 Roger Nelson............... .50 .23 .06
☐ 252A Giants Leaders........... .75 .35 .09
Charlie Fox MG
Joe Amalfitano CO
Andy Gilbert CO
Don McMahon CO
John McNamara CO
(Orange backgrounds)
☐ 252B Giants Leaders......... 1.50 .65 .19
(Dark pale backgrounds)
☐ 253 Mark Belanger.............. .75 .35 .09
☐ 254 Bill Stoneman .... .50 .23 .06
☐ 255 Reggie Jackson........ 25.00 11.50 3.10
☐ 256 Chris Zachary............... .50 .23 .06
☐ 257A Mets Leaders........... 2.50 1.15 .30
Yogi Berra MG
Roy McMillan CO

No.	Card			
	Joe Pignatano CO			
	Rube Walker CO			
	Eddie Yost CO			
	(Orange backgrounds)			
☐ 257B	Mets Leaders	5.00	2.30	.60
	(Dark pale backgrounds)			
☐ 258	Tommy John	1.50	.65	.19
☐ 259	Jim Holt	.50	.23	.06
☐ 260	Gary Nolan	.75	.35	.09
☐ 261	Pat Kelly	.50	.23	.06
☐ 262	Jack Aker	.50	.23	.06
☐ 263	George Scott	.75	.35	.09
☐ 264	Checklist 133-264	3.00	.30	.09
☐ 265	Gene Michael	1.00	.45	.13
☐ 266	Mike Lum	.75	.35	.09
☐ 267	Lloyd Allen	.75	.35	.09
☐ 268	Jerry Morales	.75	.35	.09
☐ 269	Tim McCarver	1.00	.45	.13
☐ 270	Luis Tiant	1.00	.45	.13
☐ 271	Tom Hutton	.75	.35	.09
☐ 272	Ed Farmer	.75	.35	.09
☐ 273	Chris Speier	.75	.35	.09
☐ 274	Darold Knowles	.75	.35	.09
☐ 275	Tony Perez	4.00	1.80	.50
☐ 276	Joe Lovitto	.75	.35	.09
☐ 277	Bob Miller	.75	.35	.09
☐ 278	Baltimore Orioles Team Card	1.50	.65	.19
☐ 279	Mike Strahler	.75	.35	.09
☐ 280	Al Kaline	6.50	2.90	.80
☐ 281	Mike Jorgensen	.75	.35	.09
☐ 282	Steve Hovley	.75	.35	.09
☐ 283	Ray Sadecki	.75	.35	.09
☐ 284	Glenn Borgmann	.75	.35	.09
☐ 285	Don Kessinger	1.00	.45	.13
☐ 286	Frank Linzy	.75	.35	.09
☐ 287	Eddie Leon	.75	.35	.09
☐ 288	Gary Gentry	.75	.35	.09
☐ 289	Bob Oliver	.75	.35	.09
☐ 290	Cesar Cedeno	1.00	.45	.13
☐ 291	Rogelio Moret	.75	.35	.09
☐ 292	Jose Cruz	1.50	.65	.19
☐ 293	Bernie Allen	.75	.35	.09
☐ 294	Steve Arlin	.75	.35	.09
☐ 295	Bert Campaneris	1.00	.45	.13
☐ 296	Reds Leaders	2.00	.90	.25
	Sparky Anderson MG			
	Alex Grammas CO			
	Ted Kluszewski CO			
	George Scherger CO			
	Larry Shepard CO			
☐ 297	Walt Williams	.75	.35	.09
☐ 298	Ron Bryant	.75	.35	.09
☐ 299	Ted Ford	.75	.35	.09
☐ 300	Steve Carlton	10.00	4.50	1.25
☐ 301	Billy Grabarkewitz	.75	.35	.09
☐ 302	Terry Crowley	.75	.35	.09
☐ 303	Nelson Briles	1.00	.45	.13
☐ 304	Duke Sims	.75	.35	.09
☐ 305	Willie Mays	40.00	18.00	5.00
☐ 306	Tom Burgmeier	.75	.35	.09
☐ 307	Boots Day	.75	.35	.09
☐ 308	Skip Lockwood	.75	.35	.09
☐ 309	Paul Popovich	.75	.35	.09
☐ 310	Dick Allen	1.75	.80	.22
☐ 311	Joe Decker	.75	.35	.09
☐ 312	Oscar Brown	.75	.35	.09
☐ 313	Jim Ray	.75	.35	.09
☐ 314	Ron Swoboda	1.00	.45	.13
☐ 315	John Odom	.75	.35	.09
☐ 316	San Diego Padres Team Card	1.50	.65	.19
☐ 317	Danny Cater	.75	.35	.09
☐ 318	Jim McGlothlin	.75	.35	.09
☐ 319	Jim Spencer	.75	.35	.09
☐ 320	Lou Brock	6.00	2.70	.75
☐ 321	Rich Hinton	.75	.35	.09
☐ 322	Garry Maddox	2.50	1.15	.30
☐ 323	Tigers Leaders	1.50	.65	.19
	Billy Martin MG			
	Art Fowler CO			
	Charlie Silvera CO			
	Dick Tracewski CO			
☐ 324	Al Downing	.75	.35	.09
☐ 325	Boog Powell	1.00	.45	.13
☐ 326	Darrell Brandon	.75	.35	.09
☐ 327	John Lowenstein	.75	.35	.09
☐ 328	Bill Bonham	.75	.35	.09
☐ 329	Ed Kranepool	.75	.35	.09
☐ 330	Rod Carew	7.00	3.10	.85
☐ 331	Carl Morton	.75	.35	.09
☐ 332	John Felske	.75	.35	.09
☐ 333	Gene Clines	.75	.35	.09
☐ 334	Freddie Patek	1.00	.45	.13
☐ 335	Bob Tolan	.75	.35	.09
☐ 336	Tom Bradley	.75	.35	.09
☐ 337	Dave Duncan	.75	.35	.09
☐ 338	Checklist 265-396	3.00	.30	.09
☐ 339	Dick Tidrow	.75	.35	.09
☐ 340	Nate Colbert	.75	.35	.09
☐ 341	Jim Palmer KP	1.50	.65	.19
☐ 342	Sam McDowell KP	.75	.35	.09
☐ 343	Bobby Murcer KP	.75	.35	.09
☐ 344	Jim Hunter KP	1.50	.65	.19
☐ 345	Chris Speier KP	.75	.35	.09
☐ 346	Gaylord Perry KP	1.50	.65	.19
☐ 347	Kansas City Royals Team Card	1.50	.65	.19
☐ 348	Rennie Stennett	.75	.35	.09
☐ 349	Dick McAuliffe	1.00	.45	.13
☐ 350	Tom Seaver	14.00	6.25	1.75
☐ 351	Jimmy Stewart	.75	.35	.09
☐ 352	Don Stanhouse	.75	.35	.09
☐ 353	Steve Brye	.75	.35	.09
☐ 354	Billy Parker	.75	.35	.09
☐ 355	Mike Marshall	1.00	.45	.13
☐ 356	White Sox Leaders	.75	.35	.09
	Chuck Tanner MG			
	Joe Lonnett CO			
	Jim Mahoney CO			
	Al Monchak CO			
	Johnny Sain CO			
☐ 357	Ross Grimsley	.75	.35	.09
☐ 358	Jim Nettles	.75	.35	.09
☐ 359	Cecil Upshaw	.75	.35	.09
☐ 360	Joe Rudi UER	1.00	.45	.13
	(Photo actually Gene Tenace)			
☐ 361	Fran Healy	.75	.35	.09
☐ 362	Eddie Watt	.75	.35	.09
☐ 363	Jackie Hernandez	.75	.35	.09
☐ 364	Rick Wise	.75	.35	.09
☐ 365	Rico Petrocelli	1.00	.45	.13
☐ 366	Brock Davis	.75	.35	.09
☐ 367	Burt Hooton	1.00	.45	.13
☐ 368	Bill Buckner	1.00	.45	.13
☐ 369	Lerrin LaGrow	.75	.35	.09
☐ 370	Willie Stargell	5.00	2.30	.60
☐ 371	Mike Kekich	.75	.35	.09
☐ 372	Oscar Gamble	1.00	.45	.13
☐ 373	Clyde Wright	.75	.35	.09
☐ 374	Darrell Evans	1.00	.45	.13
☐ 375	Larry Dierker	.75	.35	.09
☐ 376	Frank Duffy	.75	.35	.09
☐ 377	Expos Leaders	.75	.35	.09

Gene Mauch MG
Dave Bristol CO
Larry Doby CO
Cal McLish CO
Jerry Zimmerman CO

	No.	Card			
☐	378	Len Randle	.75	.35	.09
☐	379	Cy Acosta	.75	.35	.09
☐	380	Johnny Bench	14.00	6.25	1.75
☐	381	Vicente Romo	.75	.35	.09
☐	382	Mike Hegan	.75	.35	.09
☐	383	Diego Segui	.75	.35	.09
☐	384	Don Baylor	4.00	1.80	.50
☐	385	Jim Perry	1.00	.45	.13
☐	386	Don Money	1.00	.45	.13
☐	387	Jim Barr	.75	.35	.09
☐	388	Ben Oglivie	1.00	.45	.13
☐	389	New York Mets Team Card	3.50	1.55	.45
☐	390	Mickey Lolich	1.00	.45	.13
☐	391	Lee Lacy	.75	.35	.09
☐	392	Dick Drago	.75	.35	.09
☐	393	Jose Cardenal	.75	.35	.09
☐	394	Sparky Lyle	1.00	.45	.13
☐	395	Roger Metzger	.75	.35	.09
☐	396	Grant Jackson	1.00	.45	.13
☐	397	Dave Cash	1.50	.65	.19
☐	398	Rich Hand	1.25	.55	.16
☐	399	George Foster	2.00	.90	.25
☐	400	Gaylord Perry	5.00	2.30	.60
☐	401	Clyde Mashore	1.25	.55	.16
☐	402	Jack Hiatt	1.25	.55	.16
☐	403	Sonny Jackson	1.25	.55	.16
☐	404	Chuck Brinkman	1.25	.55	.16
☐	405	Cesar Tovar	1.25	.55	.16
☐	406	Paul Lindblad	1.25	.55	.16
☐	407	Felix Millan	1.25	.55	.16
☐	408	Jim Colborn	1.25	.55	.16
☐	409	Ivan Murrell	1.25	.55	.16
☐	410	Willie McCovey (Bench behind plate)	6.00	2.70	.75
☐	411	Ray Corbin	1.25	.55	.16
☐	412	Manny Mota	1.75	.80	.22
☐	413	Tom Timmermann	1.25	.55	.16
☐	414	Ken Rudolph	1.25	.55	.16
☐	415	Marty Pattin	1.25	.55	.16
☐	416	Paul Schaal	1.25	.55	.16
☐	417	Scipio Spinks	1.25	.55	.16
☐	418	Bob Grich	1.75	.80	.22
☐	419	Casey Cox	1.25	.55	.16
☐	420	Tommie Agee	1.50	.65	.19
☐	421A	Angels Leaders Bobby Winkles MG Tom Morgan CO Salty Parker CO Jimmie Reese CO John Roseboro CO (Orange backgrounds)	1.50	.65	.19
☐	421B	Angels Leaders (Dark pale backgrounds)	3.00	1.35	.40
☐	422	Bob Robertson	1.25	.55	.16
☐	423	Johnny Jeter	1.25	.55	.16
☐	424	Denny Doyle	1.25	.55	.16
☐	425	Alex Johnson	1.50	.65	.19
☐	426	Dave LaRoche	1.25	.55	.16
☐	427	Rick Auerbach	1.25	.55	.16
☐	428	Wayne Simpson	1.25	.55	.16
☐	429	Jim Fairey	1.25	.55	.16
☐	430	Vida Blue	1.75	.80	.22
☐	431	Gerry Moses	1.25	.55	.16
☐	432	Dan Frisella	1.25	.55	.16
☐	433	Willie Horton	1.75	.80	.22
☐	434	San Francisco Giants Team Card	2.50	1.15	.30
☐	435	Rico Carty	1.75	.80	.22
☐	436	Jim McAndrew	1.25	.55	.16
☐	437	John Kennedy	1.25	.55	.16
☐	438	Enzo Hernandez	1.25	.55	.16
☐	439	Eddie Fisher	1.25	.55	.16
☐	440	Glenn Beckert	1.50	.65	.19
☐	441	Gail Hopkins	1.25	.55	.16
☐	442	Dick Dietz	1.25	.55	.16
☐	443	Danny Thompson	1.25	.55	.16
☐	444	Ken Brett	1.25	.55	.16
☐	445	Ken Berry	1.25	.55	.16
☐	446	Jerry Reuss	1.50	.65	.19
☐	447	Joe Hague	1.25	.55	.16
☐	448	John Hiller	1.50	.65	.19
☐	449A	Indians Leaders Ken Aspromonte MG Rocky Colavito CO Joe Lutz CO Warren Spahn CO (Spahn's right ear pointed)	2.00	.90	.25
☐	449B	Indians Leaders (Spahn's right ear round)	4.00	1.80	.50
☐	450	Joe Torre	2.00	.90	.25
☐	451	John Vukovich	1.25	.55	.16
☐	452	Paul Casanova	1.25	.55	.16
☐	453	Checklist 397-528	3.00	.45	.13
☐	454	Tom Haller	1.25	.55	.16
☐	455	Bill Melton	1.25	.55	.16
☐	456	Dick Green	1.25	.55	.16
☐	457	John Strohmayer	1.25	.55	.16
☐	458	Jim Mason	1.25	.55	.16
☐	459	Jimmy Howarth	1.25	.55	.16
☐	460	Bill Freehan	1.75	.80	.22
☐	461	Mike Corkins	1.25	.55	.16
☐	462	Ron Blomberg	1.25	.55	.16
☐	463	Ken Tatum	1.25	.55	.16
☐	464	Chicago Cubs Team Card	2.50	1.15	.30
☐	465	Dave Giusti	1.25	.55	.16
☐	466	Jose Arcia	1.25	.55	.16
☐	467	Mike Ryan	1.25	.55	.16
☐	468	Tom Griffin	1.25	.55	.16
☐	469	Dan Monzon	1.25	.55	.16
☐	470	Mike Cuellar	1.50	.65	.19
☐	471	Ty Cobb ATL 4191 Hits	7.50	3.40	.95
☐	472	Lou Gehrig ATL 23 Grand Slams	9.00	4.00	1.15
☐	473	Hank Aaron ATL 6172 Total Bases	9.00	4.00	1.15
☐	474	Babe Ruth ATL 2209 RBI	14.00	6.25	1.75
☐	475	Ty Cobb ATL .367 Batting Average	7.00	3.10	.85
☐	476	Walter Johnson ATL 113 Shutouts	3.00	1.35	.40
☐	477	Cy Young ATL 511 Victories	3.00	1.35	.40
☐	478	Walter Johnson ATL 3508 Strikeouts	3.00	1.35	.40
☐	479	Hal Lanier	1.25	.55	.16
☐	480	Juan Marichal	5.00	2.30	.60
☐	481	Chicago White Sox Team Card	2.50	1.15	.30
☐	482	Rick Reuschel	3.00	1.35	.40
☐	483	Dal Maxvill	1.25	.55	.16
☐	484	Ernie McAnally	1.25	.55	.16
☐	485	Norm Cash	1.75	.80	.22
☐	486A	Phillies Leaders Danny Ozark MG Carroll Beringer CO	1.50	.65	.19

	Billy DeMars CO			
	Ray Rippelmeyer CO			
	Bobby Wine CO			
	(Orange backgrounds)			
☐ 486B	Phillies Leaders	3.00	1.35	.40
	(Dark pale backgrounds)			
☐ 487	Bruce Dal Canton	1.25	.55	.16
☐ 488	Dave Campbell	1.25	.55	.16
☐ 489	Jeff Burroughs	1.50	.65	.19
☐ 490	Claude Osteen	1.50	.65	.19
☐ 491	Bob Montgomery	1.25	.55	.16
☐ 492	Pedro Borbon	1.25	.55	.16
☐ 493	Duffy Dyer	1.25	.55	.16
☐ 494	Rich Morales	1.25	.55	.16
☐ 495	Tommy Helms	1.25	.55	.16
☐ 496	Ray Lamb	1.25	.55	.16
☐ 497A	Cardinals Leaders	2.00	.90	.25
	Red Schoendienst MG			
	Vern Benson CO			
	George Kissell CO			
	Barney Schultz CO			
	(Orange backgrounds)			
☐ 497B	Cardinals Leaders	4.00	1.80	.50
	(Dark pale backgrounds)			
☐ 498	Graig Nettles	3.00	1.35	.40
☐ 499	Bob Moose	1.25	.55	.16
☐ 500	Oakland A's	2.50	1.15	.30
	Team Card			
☐ 501	Larry Gura	1.50	.65	.19
☐ 502	Bobby Valentine	1.75	.80	.22
☐ 503	Phil Niekro	5.00	2.30	.60
☐ 504	Earl Williams	1.25	.55	.16
☐ 505	Bob Bailey	1.25	.55	.16
☐ 506	Bart Johnson	1.25	.55	.16
☐ 507	Darrel Chaney	1.25	.55	.16
☐ 508	Gates Brown	1.25	.55	.16
☐ 509	Jim Nash	1.25	.55	.16
☐ 510	Amos Otis	1.75	.80	.22
☐ 511	Sam McDowell	1.50	.65	.19
☐ 512	Dalton Jones	1.25	.55	.16
☐ 513	Dave Marshall	1.25	.55	.16
☐ 514	Jerry Kenney	1.25	.55	.16
☐ 515	Andy Messersmith	1.50	.65	.19
☐ 516	Danny Walton	1.25	.55	.16
☐ 517A	Pirates Leaders	1.50	.65	.19
	Bill Virdon MG			
	Don Leppert CO			
	Bill Mazeroski CO			
	Dave Ricketts CO			
	Mel Wright CO			
	(Mazeroski has no right ear)			
☐ 517B	Pirates Leaders	3.00	1.35	.40
	(Mazeroski has right ear)			
☐ 518	Bob Veale	1.50	.65	.19
☐ 519	Johnny Edwards	1.25	.55	.16
☐ 520	Mel Stottlemyre	1.75	.80	.22
☐ 521	Atlanta Braves	2.50	1.15	.30
	Team Card			
☐ 522	Leo Cardenas	1.25	.55	.16
☐ 523	Wayne Granger	1.25	.55	.16
☐ 524	Gene Tenace	1.50	.65	.19
☐ 525	Jim Fregosi	1.75	.80	.22
☐ 526	Ollie Brown	1.25	.55	.16
☐ 527	Dan McGinn	1.25	.55	.16
☐ 528	Paul Blair	1.50	.65	.19
☐ 529	Milt May	4.00	1.80	.50
☐ 530	Jim Kaat	5.00	2.30	.60
☐ 531	Ron Woods	3.50	1.55	.45
☐ 532	Steve Mingori	3.50	1.55	.45
☐ 533	Larry Stahl	3.50	1.55	.45
☐ 534	Dave Lemonds	3.50	1.55	.45
☐ 535	Johnny Callison	4.00	1.80	.50
☐ 536	Philadelphia Phillies	6.00	2.70	.75
	Team Card			
☐ 537	Bill Slayback	3.50	1.55	.45
☐ 538	Jim Ray Hart	4.00	1.80	.50
☐ 539	Tom Murphy	3.50	1.55	.45
☐ 540	Cleon Jones	4.00	1.80	.50
☐ 541	Bob Bolin	3.50	1.55	.45
☐ 542	Pat Corrales	4.00	1.80	.50
☐ 543	Alan Foster	3.50	1.55	.45
☐ 544	Von Joshua	3.50	1.55	.45
☐ 545	Orlando Cepeda	5.00	2.30	.60
☐ 546	Jim York	3.50	1.55	.45
☐ 547	Bobby Heise	3.50	1.55	.45
☐ 548	Don Durham	3.50	1.55	.45
☐ 549	Rangers Leaders	5.00	2.30	.60
	Whitey Herzog MG			
	Chuck Estrada CO			
	Chuck Hiller CO			
	Jackie Moore CO			
☐ 550	Dave Johnson	4.00	1.80	.50
☐ 551	Mike Kilkenny	3.50	1.55	.45
☐ 552	J.C. Martin	3.50	1.55	.45
☐ 553	Mickey Scott	3.50	1.55	.45
☐ 554	Dave Concepcion	5.00	2.30	.60
☐ 555	Bill Hands	3.50	1.55	.45
☐ 556	New York Yankees	7.50	3.40	.95
	Team Card			
☐ 557	Bernie Williams	3.50	1.55	.45
☐ 558	Jerry May	3.50	1.55	.45
☐ 559	Barry Lersch	3.50	1.55	.45
☐ 560	Frank Howard	5.00	2.30	.60
☐ 561	Jim Geddes	3.50	1.55	.45
☐ 562	Wayne Garrett	3.50	1.55	.45
☐ 563	Larry Haney	3.50	1.55	.45
☐ 564	Mike Thompson	3.50	1.55	.45
☐ 565	Jim Hickman	3.50	1.55	.45
☐ 566	Lew Krausse	3.50	1.55	.45
☐ 567	Bob Fenwick	3.50	1.55	.45
☐ 568	Ray Newman	3.50	1.55	.45
☐ 569	Dodgers Leaders	5.00	2.30	.60
	Walt Alston MG			
	Red Adams CO			
	Monty Basgall CO			
	Jim Gilliam CO			
	Tom Lasorda CO			
☐ 570	Bill Singer	4.00	1.80	.50
☐ 571	Rusty Torres	3.50	1.55	.45
☐ 572	Gary Sutherland	3.50	1.55	.45
☐ 573	Fred Beene	3.50	1.55	.45
☐ 574	Bob Didier	3.50	1.55	.45
☐ 575	Dock Ellis	3.50	1.55	.45
☐ 576	Montreal Expos	6.00	2.70	.75
	Team Card			
☐ 577	Eric Soderholm	3.50	1.55	.45
☐ 578	Ken Wright	3.50	1.55	.45
☐ 579	Tom Grieve	4.00	1.80	.50
☐ 580	Joe Pepitone	4.00	1.80	.50
☐ 581	Steve Kealey	3.50	1.55	.45
☐ 582	Darrell Porter	4.00	1.80	.50
☐ 583	Bill Grief	3.50	1.55	.45
☐ 584	Chris Arnold	3.50	1.55	.45
☐ 585	Joe Niekro	4.00	1.80	.50
☐ 586	Bill Sudakis	3.50	1.55	.45
☐ 587	Rich McKinney	3.50	1.55	.45
☐ 588	Checklist 529-660	24.00	2.40	.70
☐ 589	Ken Forsch	3.50	1.55	.45
☐ 590	Deron Johnson	3.50	1.55	.45
☐ 591	Mike Hedlund	3.50	1.55	.45
☐ 592	John Boccabella	3.50	1.55	.45
☐ 593	Royals Leaders	3.50	1.55	.45

Jack McKeon MG
Galen Cisco CO
Harry Dunlop CO
Charlie Lau CO

☐ 594	Vic Harris	3.50	1.55	.45
☐ 595	Don Gullett	4.00	1.80	.50
☐ 596	Boston Red Sox Team Card	6.00	2.70	.75
☐ 597	Mickey Rivers	4.00	1.80	.50
☐ 598	Phil Roof	3.50	1.55	.45
☐ 599	Ed Crosby	3.50	1.55	.45
☐ 600	Dave McNally	4.00	1.80	.50
☐ 601	Rookie Catchers Sergio Robles George Pena Rick Stelmaszek	4.00	1.80	.50
☐ 602	Rookie Pitchers Mel Behney Ralph Garcia Doug Rau	4.00	1.80	.50
☐ 603	Rookie 3rd Basemen Terry Hughes Bill McNulty Ken Reitz	4.00	1.80	.50
☐ 604	Rookie Pitchers Jesse Jefferson Dennis O'Toole Bob Strampe	4.00	1.80	.50
☐ 605	Rookie 1st Basemen Enos Cabell Pat Bourque Gonzalo Marquez	5.00	2.30	.60
☐ 606	Rookie Outfielders Gary Matthews Tom Paciorek Jorge Roque	6.00	2.70	.75
☐ 607	Rookie Shortstops Pepe Frias Ray Busse Mario Guerrero	4.00	1.80	.50
☐ 608	Rookie Pitchers Steve Busby Dick Colpaert George Medich	6.00	2.70	.75
☐ 609	Rookie 2nd Basemen Larvell Blanks Pedro Garcia Dave Lopes	7.00	3.10	.85
☐ 610	Rookie Pitchers Jimmy Freeman Charlie Hough Hank Webb	7.00	3.10	.85
☐ 611	Rookie Outfielders Rich Coggins Jim Wohlford Richie Zisk	4.00	1.80	.50
☐ 612	Rookie Pitchers Steve Lawson Bob Reynolds Brent Strom	4.00	1.80	.50
☐ 613	Rookie Catchers Bob Boone Skip Jutze Mike Ivie	30.00	13.50	3.80
☐ 614	Rookie Outfielders Al Bumbry Dwight Evans Charlie Spikes	30.00	13.50	3.80
☐ 615	Rookie 3rd Basemen Ron Cey John Hilton Mike Schmidt	375.00	170.00	47.50
☐ 616	Rookie Pitchers Norm Angelini Steve Blateric Mike Garman	4.00	1.80	.50
☐ 617	Rich Chiles	3.50	1.55	.45
☐ 618	Andy Etchebarren	3.50	1.55	.45
☐ 619	Billy Wilson	3.50	1.55	.45
☐ 620	Tommy Harper	4.00	1.80	.50
☐ 621	Joe Ferguson	4.00	1.80	.50
☐ 622	Larry Hisle	4.00	1.80	.50
☐ 623	Steve Renko	3.50	1.55	.45
☐ 624	Astros Leaders Leo Durocher MG Preston Gomez CO Grady Hatton CO Hub Kittle CO Jim Owens CO	6.00	2.70	.75
☐ 625	Angel Mangual	3.50	1.55	.45
☐ 626	Bob Barton	3.50	1.55	.45
☐ 627	Luis Alvarado	3.50	1.55	.45
☐ 628	Jim Slaton	3.50	1.55	.45
☐ 629	Cleveland Indians Team Card	6.00	2.70	.75
☐ 630	Denny McLain	5.00	2.30	.60
☐ 631	Tom Matchick	3.50	1.55	.45
☐ 632	Dick Selma	3.50	1.55	.45
☐ 633	Ike Brown	3.50	1.55	.45
☐ 634	Alan Closter	3.50	1.55	.45
☐ 635	Gene Alley	4.00	1.80	.50
☐ 636	Rickey Clark	3.50	1.55	.45
☐ 637	Norm Miller	3.50	1.55	.45
☐ 638	Ken Reynolds	3.50	1.55	.45
☐ 639	Willie Crawford	3.50	1.55	.45
☐ 640	Dick Bosman	3.50	1.55	.45
☐ 641	Cincinnati Reds Team Card	6.00	2.70	.75
☐ 642	Jose Laboy	3.50	1.55	.45
☐ 643	Al Fitzmorris	3.50	1.55	.45
☐ 644	Jack Heidemann	3.50	1.55	.45
☐ 645	Bob Locker	3.50	1.55	.45
☐ 646	Brewers Leaders Del Crandall MG Harvey Kuenn CO Joe Nossek CO Bob Shaw CO Jim Walton CO	3.50	1.55	.45
☐ 647	George Stone	3.50	1.55	.45
☐ 648	Tom Egan	3.50	1.55	.45
☐ 649	Rich Folkers	3.50	1.55	.45
☐ 650	Felipe Alou	5.00	2.30	.60
☐ 651	Don Carrithers	3.50	1.55	.45
☐ 652	Ted Kubiak	3.50	1.55	.45
☐ 653	Joe Hoerner	3.50	1.55	.45
☐ 654	Minnesota Twins Team Card	6.00	2.70	.75
☐ 655	Clay Kirby	3.50	1.55	.45
☐ 656	John Ellis	3.50	1.55	.45
☐ 657	Bob Johnson	3.50	1.55	.45
☐ 658	Elliott Maddox	3.50	1.55	.45
☐ 659	Jose Pagan	3.50	1.55	.45
☐ 660	Fred Scherman	4.00	1.55	.45

1974 Topps

The cards in this 660-card set measure 2 1/2" by 3 1/2". This year marked the first time Topps issued all the cards of its baseball set at the same time rather than in series. Some interesting variations were created by the rumored move of the San Diego Padres to Washington. Fifteen cards

(13 players, the team card, and the rookie card (599) of the Padres were printed either as "San Diego" (SD) or "Washington." The latter are the scarcer variety and are denoted in the checklist below by WAS. Each team's manager and his coaches again have a combined card with small pictures of each coach below the larger photo of the team's manager. The first six cards in the set (1-6) feature Hank Aaron and his illustrious career. Other topical subsets included in the set are League Leaders (201-208), All-Star selections (331-339), Playoffs cards (470-471), World Series cards (472-479), and Rookie Prospects (596-608). The card backs for the All-Stars (331-339) have no statistics, but form a picture puzzle of Bobby Bonds, the 1973 All-Star Game MVP. The key Rookie Cards in this set are Ken Griffey Sr., Dave Parker, and Dave Winfield.)

	NRMT-MT	EXC	G-VG
COMPLETE SET (660)	650.00	300.00	80.00
COMPLETE FACT.SET (660)	650.00	300.00	80.00
COMMON CARD (1-660)	.50	.23	.06
☐ 1 Hank Aaron All-Time Home Run King (Complete ML record)	35.00	8.75	2.80
☐ 2 Aaron Special 54-57 (Records on back)	6.50	2.90	.80
☐ 3 Aaron Special 58-61 (Memorable homers)	6.50	2.90	.80
☐ 4 Aaron Special 62-65 (Life in ML's 1954-63)	6.50	2.90	.80
☐ 5 Aaron Special 66-69 (Life in ML's 1964-73)	6.50	2.90	.80
☐ 6 Aaron Special 70-73 (Milestone homers)	6.50	2.90	.80
☐ 7 Jim Hunter	4.50	2.00	.55
☐ 8 George Theodore	.50	.23	.06
☐ 9 Mickey Lolich	.60	.25	.08
☐ 10 Johnny Bench	14.00	6.25	1.75
☐ 11 Jim Bibby	.50	.23	.06
☐ 12 Dave May	.50	.23	.06
☐ 13 Tom Hilgendorf	.50	.23	.06
☐ 14 Paul Popovich	.50	.23	.06
☐ 15 Joe Torre	1.00	.45	.13
☐ 16 Baltimore Orioles Team Card	1.50	.65	.19
☐ 17 Doug Bird	.50	.23	.06
☐ 18 Gary Thomasson	.50	.23	.06
☐ 19 Gerry Moses	.50	.23	.06
☐ 20 Nolan Ryan	80.00	36.00	10.00
☐ 21 Bob Gallagher	.50	.23	.06
☐ 22 Cy Acosta	.50	.23	.06
☐ 23 Craig Robinson	.50	.23	.06
☐ 24 John Hiller	.60	.25	.08
☐ 25 Ken Singleton	.60	.25	.08
☐ 26 Bill Campbell	.50	.23	.06
☐ 27 George Scott	.60	.25	.08
☐ 28 Manny Sanguillen	.60	.25	.08
☐ 29 Phil Niekro	3.50	1.55	.45
☐ 30 Bobby Bonds	2.00	.90	.25
☐ 31 Astros Leaders Preston Gomez MG Roger Craig CO Hub Kittle CO Grady Hatton CO Bob Lillis CO	.60	.25	.08
☐ 32A Johnny Grubb SD	.60	.25	.08
☐ 32B Johnny Grubb WAS	7.00	3.10	.85
☐ 33 Don Newhauser	.50	.23	.06
☐ 34 Andy Kosco	.50	.23	.06
☐ 35 Gaylord Perry	3.50	1.55	.45
☐ 36 St. Louis Cardinals Team Card	1.50	.65	.19
☐ 37 Dave Sells	.50	.23	.06
☐ 38 Don Kessinger	.60	.25	.08
☐ 39 Ken Suarez	.50	.23	.06
☐ 40 Jim Palmer	8.00	3.60	1.00
☐ 41 Bobby Floyd	.50	.23	.06
☐ 42 Claude Osteen	.60	.25	.08
☐ 43 Jim Wynn	.60	.25	.08
☐ 44 Mel Stottlemyre	.60	.25	.08
☐ 45 Dave Johnson	.60	.25	.08
☐ 46 Pat Kelly	.50	.23	.06
☐ 47 Dick Ruthven	.50	.23	.06
☐ 48 Dick Sharon	.50	.23	.06
☐ 49 Steve Renko	.50	.23	.06
☐ 50 Rod Carew	7.00	3.10	.85
☐ 51 Bobby Heise	.50	.23	.06
☐ 52 Al Oliver	.50	.23	.06
☐ 53A Fred Kendall SD	.60	.25	.08
☐ 53B Fred Kendall WAS	7.00	3.10	.85
☐ 54 Elias Sosa	.50	.23	.06
☐ 55 Frank Robinson	5.50	2.50	.70
☐ 56 New York Mets Team Card	1.50	.65	.19
☐ 57 Darold Knowles	.50	.23	.06
☐ 58 Charlie Spikes	.50	.23	.06
☐ 59 Ross Grimsley	.50	.23	.06
☐ 60 Lou Brock	6.00	2.70	.75
☐ 61 Luis Aparicio	3.00	1.35	.40
☐ 62 Bob Locker	.50	.23	.06
☐ 63 Bill Sudakis	.50	.23	.06
☐ 64 Doug Rau	.50	.23	.06
☐ 65 Amos Otis	.60	.25	.08
☐ 66 Sparky Lyle	.50	.23	.06
☐ 67 Tommy Helms	.50	.23	.06
☐ 68 Grant Jackson	.50	.23	.06
☐ 69 Del Unser	.50	.23	.06
☐ 70 Dick Allen	1.00	.45	.13
☐ 71 Dan Frisella	.50	.23	.06
☐ 72 Aurelio Rodriguez	.50	.23	.06
☐ 73 Mike Marshall	.50	.23	.06
☐ 74 Minnesota Twins Team Card	1.50	.65	.19
☐ 75 Jim Colborn	.50	.23	.06
☐ 76 Mickey Rivers	.60	.25	.08
☐ 77A Rich Troedson SD	.60	.25	.08
☐ 77B Rich Troedson WAS	7.00	3.10	.85
☐ 78 Giants Leaders Charlie Fox MG John McNamara CO Joe Amalfitano CO Andy Gilbert CO Don McMahon CO	.60	.25	.08
☐ 79 Gene Tenace	.60	.25	.08
☐ 80 Tom Seaver	14.00	6.25	1.75

☐ 81 Frank Duffy .50 .23 .06
☐ 82 Dave Giusti .50 .23 .06
☐ 83 Orlando Cepeda 1.50 .65 .19
☐ 84 Rick Wise .50 .23 .06
☐ 85 Joe Morgan 6.00 2.70 .75
☐ 86 Joe Ferguson .60 .25 .08
☐ 87 Fergie Jenkins 4.00 1.80 .50
☐ 88 Freddie Patek .60 .25 .08
☐ 89 Jackie Brown .50 .23 .06
☐ 90 Bobby Murcer .50 .23 .06
☐ 91 Ken Forsch .50 .23 .06
☐ 92 Paul Blair .60 .25 .08
☐ 93 Rod Gilbreath .50 .23 .06
☐ 94 Detroit Tigers 1.50 .65 .19
Team Card
☐ 95 Steve Carlton 10.00 4.50 1.25
☐ 96 Jerry Hairston .50 .23 .06
☐ 97 Bob Bailey .50 .23 .06
☐ 98 Bert Blyleven 2.00 .90 .25
☐ 99 Brewers Leaders .60 .25 .08
Del Crandall MG
Harvey Kuenn CO
Joe Nossek CO
Jim Walton CO
Al Widmar CO
☐ 100 Willie Stargell 4.00 1.80 .50
☐ 101 Bobby Valentine .60 .25 .08
☐ 102A Bill Greif SD .60 .25 .08
☐ 102B Bill Greif WAS 7.00 3.10 .85
☐ 103 Sal Bando .60 .25 .08
☐ 104 Ron Bryant .50 .23 .06
☐ 105 Carlton Fisk 17.00 7.75 2.10
☐ 106 Harry Parker .50 .23 .06
☐ 107 Alex Johnson .50 .23 .06
☐ 108 Al Hrabosky .60 .25 .08
☐ 109 Bob Grich .60 .25 .08
☐ 110 Billy Williams 4.00 1.80 .50
☐ 111 Clay Carroll .50 .23 .06
☐ 112 Dave Lopes 1.00 .45 .13
☐ 113 Dick Drago .50 .23 .06
☐ 114 Angels Team 1.50 .65 .19
☐ 115 Willie Horton .60 .25 .08
☐ 116 Jerry Reuss .60 .25 .08
☐ 117 Ron Blomberg .50 .23 .06
☐ 118 Bill Lee .60 .25 .08
☐ 119 Phillies Leaders .60 .25 .08
Danny Ozark MG
Ray Ripplemeyer CO
Bobby Wine CO
Carroll Beringer CO
Billy DeMars CO
☐ 120 Wilbur Wood .50 .23 .06
☐ 121 Larry Lintz .50 .23 .06
☐ 122 Jim Holt .50 .23 .06
☐ 123 Nelson Briles .60 .25 .08
☐ 124 Bobby Coluccio .50 .23 .06
☐ 125A Nate Colbert SD .60 .25 .08
☐ 125B Nate Colbert WAS 7.00 3.10 .85
☐ 126 Checklist 1-132 2.50 .25 .08
☐ 127 Tom Paciorek .60 .25 .08
☐ 128 John Ellis .50 .23 .06
☐ 129 Chris Speier .50 .23 .06
☐ 130 Reggie Jackson 22.00 10.00 2.80
☐ 131 Bob Boone 2.50 1.15 .30
☐ 132 Felix Millan .50 .23 .06
☐ 133 David Clyde .60 .25 .08
☐ 134 Denis Menke .50 .23 .06
☐ 135 Roy White .60 .25 .08
☐ 136 Rick Reuschel .50 .23 .06
☐ 137 Al Bumbry .60 .25 .08
☐ 138 Eddie Brinkman .50 .23 .06
☐ 139 Aurelio Monteagudo .50 .23 .06
☐ 140 Darrell Evans .60 .25 .08
☐ 141 Pat Bourque .50 .23 .06
☐ 142 Pedro Garcia .50 .23 .06
☐ 143 Dick Woodson .50 .23 .06
☐ 144 Dodgers Leaders 1.25 .55 .16
Walter Alston MG
Tom Lasorda CO
Jim Gilliam CO
Red Adams CO
Monty Basgall CO
☐ 145 Dock Ellis .50 .23 .06
☐ 146 Ron Fairly .50 .23 .06
☐ 147 Bart Johnson .50 .23 .06
☐ 148A Dave Hilton SD .60 .25 .08
☐ 148B Dave Hilton WAS 7.00 3.10 .85
☐ 149 Mac Scarce .50 .23 .06
☐ 150 John Mayberry .60 .25 .08
☐ 151 Diego Segui .50 .23 .06
☐ 152 Oscar Gamble .60 .25 .08
☐ 153 Jon Matlack .60 .25 .08
☐ 154 Houston Astros 1.50 .65 .19
Team Card
☐ 155 Bert Campaneris .60 .25 .08
☐ 156 Randy Moffitt .50 .23 .06
☐ 157 Vic Harris .50 .23 .06
☐ 158 Jack Billingham .50 .23 .06
☐ 159 Jim Ray Hart .60 .25 .08
☐ 160 Brooks Robinson 7.00 3.10 .85
☐ 161 Ray Burris UER .60 .25 .08
(Card number is
printed sideways)
☐ 162 Bill Freehan .60 .25 .08
☐ 163 Ken Berry .50 .23 .06
☐ 164 Tom House .50 .23 .06
☐ 165 Willie Davis .60 .25 .08
☐ 166 Royals Leaders .60 .25 .08
Jack McKeon MG
Charlie Lau CO
Harry Dunlop CO
Galen Cisco CO
☐ 167 Luis Tiant .60 .25 .08
☐ 168 Danny Thompson .50 .23 .06
☐ 169 Steve Rogers .60 .25 .08
☐ 170 Bill Melton .50 .23 .06
☐ 171 Eduardo Rodriguez .50 .23 .06
☐ 172 Gene Clines .50 .23 .06
☐ 173A Randy Jones SD 1.00 .45 .13
☐ 173B Randy Jones WAS 10.00 4.50 1.25
☐ 174 Bill Robinson .60 .25 .08
☐ 175 Reggie Cleveland .50 .23 .06
☐ 176 John Lowenstein .50 .23 .06
☐ 177 Dave Roberts .50 .23 .06
☐ 178 Garry Maddox .60 .25 .08
☐ 179 Mets Leaders 2.00 .90 .25
Yogi Berra MG
Rube Walker CO
Eddie Yost CO
Roy McMillan CO
Joe Pignatano CO
☐ 180 Ken Holtzman .60 .25 .08
☐ 181 Cesar Geronimo .50 .23 .06
☐ 182 Lindy McDaniel .60 .25 .08
☐ 183 Johnny Oates .60 .25 .08
☐ 184 Texas Rangers 1.50 .65 .19
Team Card
☐ 185 Jose Cardenal .50 .23 .06
☐ 186 Fred Scherman .50 .23 .06
☐ 187 Don Baylor 3.50 1.55 .45
☐ 188 Rudy Meoli .50 .23 .06
☐ 189 Jim Brewer .50 .23 .06
☐ 190 Tony Oliva 1.50 .65 .19
☐ 191 Al Fitzmorris .50 .23 .06
☐ 192 Mario Guerrero .50 .23 .06
☐ 193 Tom Walker .50 .23 .06

☐ 194 Darrell Porter .60 .25 .08
☐ 195 Carlos May .50 .23 .06
☐ 196 Jim Fregosi .60 .25 .08
☐ 197A Vicente Romo SD .60 .25 .08
☐ 197B Vicente Romo WAS . 7.00 3.10 .85
☐ 198 Dave Cash .50 .23 .06
☐ 199 Mike Kekich .50 .23 .06
☐ 200 Cesar Cedeno .60 .25 .08
☐ 201 Batting Leaders 5.00 2.30 .60
Rod Carew
Pete Rose
☐ 202 Home Run Leaders 5.00 2.30 .60
Reggie Jackson
Willie Stargell
☐ 203 RBI Leaders 5.00 2.30 .60
Reggie Jackson
Willie Stargell
☐ 204 Stolen Base Leaders 1.25 .55 .16
Tommy Harper
Lou Brock
☐ 205 Victory Leaders 1.00 .45 .13
Wilbur Wood
Ron Bryant
☐ 206 ERA Leaders 5.00 2.30 .60
Jim Palmer
Tom Seaver
☐ 207 Strikeout Leaders 20.00 9.00 2.50
Nolan Ryan
Tom Seaver
☐ 208 Leading Firemen 1.00 .45 .13
John Hiller
Mike Marshall
☐ 209 Ted Sizemore .50 .23 .06
☐ 210 Bill Singer .50 .23 .06
☐ 211 Chicago Cubs Team 1.50 .65 .19
☐ 212 Rollie Fingers 4.00 1.80 .50
☐ 213 Dave Rader .50 .23 .06
☐ 214 Billy Grabarkewitz .50 .23 .06
☐ 215 Al Kaline UER 6.00 2.70 .75
(No copyright on back)
☐ 216 Ray Sadecki .50 .23 .06
☐ 217 Tim Foli .50 .23 .06
☐ 218 Johnny Briggs .50 .23 .06
☐ 219 Doug Griffin .50 .23 .06
☐ 220 Don Sutton 3.50 1.55 .45
☐ 221 White Sox Leaders .60 .25 .08
Chuck Tanner MG
Jim Mahoney CO
Alex Monchak CO
Johnny Sain CO
Joe Lonnett CO
☐ 222 Ramon Hernandez .50 .23 .06
☐ 223 Jeff Burroughs .60 .25 .08
☐ 224 Roger Metzger .50 .23 .06
☐ 225 Paul Splittorff .50 .23 .06
☐ 226A Padres Team SD 1.50 .65 .19
☐ 226B Padres Team WAS 9.00 4.00 1.15
☐ 227 Mike Lum .50 .23 .06
☐ 228 Ted Kubiak .50 .23 .06
☐ 229 Fritz Peterson .50 .23 .06
☐ 230 Tony Perez 3.00 1.35 .40
☐ 231 Dick Tidrow .50 .23 .06
☐ 232 Steve Brye .50 .23 .06
☐ 233 Jim Barr .50 .23 .06
☐ 234 John Milner .50 .23 .06
☐ 235 Dave McNally .60 .25 .08
☐ 236 Cardinals Leaders .50 .23 .06
Red Schoendienst MG
Barney Schultz CO
George Kissell CO
Johnny Lewis CO
Vern Benson CO
☐ 237 Ken Brett .50 .23 .06
☐ 238 Fran Healy HOR .60 .25 .08
(Munson sliding
in background)
☐ 239 Bill Russell .60 .25 .08
☐ 240 Joe Coleman .50 .23 .06
☐ 241A Glenn Beckert SD .60 .25 .08
☐ 241B Glenn Beckert WAS . 7.00 3.10 .85
☐ 242 Bill Gogolewski .50 .23 .06
☐ 243 Bob Oliver .50 .23 .06
☐ 244 Carl Morton .50 .23 .06
☐ 245 Cleon Jones .60 .25 .08
☐ 246 Oakland Athletics 1.25 .55 .16
Team Card
☐ 247 Rick Miller .50 .23 .06
☐ 248 Tom Hall .50 .23 .06
☐ 249 George Mitterwald .50 .23 .06
☐ 250A Willie McCovey SD 6.00 2.70 .75
☐ 250B Willie McCovey WAS 30.00 13.50 3.80
☐ 251 Graig Nettles 2.00 .90 .25
☐ 252 Dave Parker 17.00 7.75 2.10
☐ 253 John Boccabella .50 .23 .06
☐ 254 Stan Bahnsen .50 .23 .06
☐ 255 Larry Bowa 1.00 .45 .13
☐ 256 Tom Griffin .50 .23 .06
☐ 257 Buddy Bell .50 .23 .06
☐ 258 Jerry Morales .50 .23 .06
☐ 259 Bob Reynolds .50 .23 .06
☐ 260 Ted Simmons 2.00 .90 .25
☐ 261 Jerry Bell .50 .23 .06
☐ 262 Ed Kirkpatrick .50 .23 .06
☐ 263 Checklist 133-264 2.50 .25 .08
☐ 264 Joe Rudi .60 .25 .08
☐ 265 Tug McGraw 1.00 .45 .13
☐ 266 Jim Northrup .60 .25 .08
☐ 267 Andy Messersmith .60 .25 .08
☐ 268 Tom Grieve .60 .25 .08
☐ 269 Bob Johnson .50 .23 .06
☐ 270 Ron Santo 1.00 .45 .13
☐ 271 Bill Hands .50 .23 .06
☐ 272 Paul Casanova .50 .23 .06
☐ 273 Checklist 265-396 2.50 .25 .08
☐ 274 Fred Beene .50 .23 .06
☐ 275 Ron Hunt .50 .23 .06
☐ 276 Angels Leaders .60 .25 .08
Bobby Winkles MG
John Roseboro CO
Tom Morgan CO
Jimmie Reese CO
Salty Parker CO
☐ 277 Gary Nolan .60 .25 .08
☐ 278 Cookie Rojas .60 .25 .08
☐ 279 Jim Crawford .50 .23 .06
☐ 280 Carl Yastrzemski 7.00 3.10 .85
☐ 281 San Francisco Giants . 1.50 .65 .19
Team Card
☐ 282 Doyle Alexander .60 .25 .08
☐ 283 Mike Schmidt 75.00 34.00 9.50
☐ 284 Dave Duncan .50 .23 .06
☐ 285 Reggie Smith .60 .25 .08
☐ 286 Tony Muser .50 .23 .06
☐ 287 Clay Kirby .50 .23 .06
☐ 288 Gorman Thomas 1.50 .65 .19
☐ 289 Rick Auerbach .50 .23 .06
☐ 290 Vida Blue .60 .25 .08
☐ 291 Don Hahn .50 .23 .06
☐ 292 Chuck Seelbach .50 .23 .06
☐ 293 Milt May .50 .23 .06
☐ 294 Steve Foucault .50 .23 .06
☐ 295 Rick Monday .60 .25 .08
☐ 296 Ray Corbin .50 .23 .06
☐ 297 Hal Breeden .50 .23 .06
☐ 298 Roric Harrison .50 .23 .06
☐ 299 Gene Michael .60 .25 .08

	#	Player			
☐	300	Pete Rose	15.00	6.75	1.90
☐	301	Bob Montgomery	.50	.23	.06
☐	302	Rudy May	.50	.23	.06
☐	303	George Hendrick	.60	.25	.08
☐	304	Don Wilson	.50	.23	.06
☐	305	Tito Fuentes	.50	.23	.06
☐	306	Orioles Leaders Earl Weaver MG Jim Frey CO George Bamberger CO Billy Hunter CO George Staller CO	1.25	.55	.16
☐	307	Luis Melendez	.50	.23	.06
☐	308	Bruce Dal Canton	.50	.23	.06
☐	309A	Dave Roberts SD	.60	.25	.08
☐	309B	Dave Roberts WAS	9.00	4.00	1.15
☐	310	Terry Forster	.60	.25	.08
☐	311	Jerry Grote	.50	.23	.06
☐	312	Deron Johnson	.50	.23	.06
☐	313	Barry Lersch	.50	.23	.06
☐	314	Milwaukee Brewers Team Card	1.50	.65	.19
☐	315	Ron Cey	1.50	.65	.19
☐	316	Jim Perry	.60	.25	.08
☐	317	Richie Zisk	.60	.25	.08
☐	318	Jim Merritt	.50	.23	.06
☐	319	Randy Hundley	.50	.23	.06
☐	320	Dusty Baker	2.00	.90	.25
☐	321	Steve Braun	.50	.23	.06
☐	322	Ernie McAnally	.50	.23	.06
☐	323	Richie Scheinblum	.50	.23	.06
☐	324	Steve Kline	.50	.23	.06
☐	325	Tommy Harper	.60	.25	.08
☐	326	Reds Leaders Sparky Anderson MG Larry Shepard CO George Scherger CO Alex Grammas CO Ted Kluszewski CO	2.00	.90	.25
☐	327	Tom Timmermann	.50	.23	.06
☐	328	Skip Jutze	.50	.23	.06
☐	329	Mark Belanger	.60	.25	.08
☐	330	Juan Marichal	3.00	1.35	.40
☐	331	All-Star Catchers Carlton Fisk Johnny Bench	7.00	3.10	.85
☐	332	All-Star 1B Dick Allen Hank Aaron	5.00	2.30	.60
☐	333	All-Star 2B Rod Carew Joe Morgan	3.00	1.35	.40
☐	334	All-Star 3B Brooks Robinson Ron Santo	2.50	1.15	.30
☐	335	All-Star SS Bert Campaneris Chris Speier	.75	.35	.09
☐	336	All-Star LF Bobby Murcer Pete Rose	3.00	1.35	.40
☐	337	All-Star CF Amos Otis Cesar Cedeno	.75	.35	.09
☐	338	All-Star RF Reggie Jackson Billy Williams	5.00	2.30	.60
☐	339	All-Star Pitchers Jim Hunter Rick Wise	1.25	.55	.16
☐	340	Thurman Munson	9.00	4.00	1.15
☐	341	Dan Driessen	1.00	.45	.13
☐	342	Jim Lonborg	.60	.25	.08
☐	343	Royals Team	1.50	.65	.19
☐	344	Mike Caldwell	.50	.23	.06
☐	345	Bill North	.50	.23	.06
☐	346	Ron Reed	.50	.23	.06
☐	347	Sandy Alomar	.60	.25	.08
☐	348	Pete Richert	.50	.23	.06
☐	349	John Vukovich	.50	.23	.06
☐	350	Bob Gibson	6.00	2.70	.75
☐	351	Dwight Evans	4.00	1.80	.50
☐	352	Bill Stoneman	.50	.23	.06
☐	353	Rich Coggins	.50	.23	.06
☐	354	Cubs Leaders Whitey Lockman MG J.C. Martin CO Hank Aguirre CO Al Spangler CO Jim Marshall CO	.60	.25	.08
☐	355	Dave Nelson	.50	.23	.06
☐	356	Jerry Koosman	.60	.25	.08
☐	357	Buddy Bradford	.50	.23	.06
☐	358	Dal Maxvill	.50	.23	.06
☐	359	Brent Strom	.50	.23	.06
☐	360	Greg Luzinski	1.25	.55	.16
☐	361	Don Carrithers	.50	.23	.06
☐	362	Hal King	.50	.23	.06
☐	363	New York Yankees Team Card	1.50	.65	.19
☐	364A	Cito Gaston SD	1.25	.55	.16
☐	364B	Cito Gaston WAS	14.00	6.25	1.75
☐	365	Steve Busby	.60	.25	.08
☐	366	Larry Hisle	.60	.25	.08
☐	367	Norm Cash	.75	.35	.09
☐	368	Manny Mota	.60	.25	.08
☐	369	Paul Lindblad	.50	.23	.06
☐	370	Bob Watson	.60	.25	.08
☐	371	Jim Slaton	.50	.23	.06
☐	372	Ken Reitz	.50	.23	.06
☐	373	John Curtis	.50	.23	.06
☐	374	Marty Perez	.50	.23	.06
☐	375	Earl Williams	.50	.23	.06
☐	376	Jorge Orta	.50	.23	.06
☐	377	Ron Woods	.50	.23	.06
☐	378	Burt Hooton	.60	.25	.08
☐	379	Rangers Leaders Billy Martin MG Frank Lucchesi CO Art Fowler CO Charlie Silvera CO Jackie Moore CO	1.25	.55	.16
☐	380	Bud Harrelson	.60	.25	.08
☐	381	Charlie Sands	.50	.23	.06
☐	382	Bob Moose	.50	.23	.06
☐	383	Philadelphia Phillies Team Card	1.50	.65	.19
☐	384	Chris Chambliss	.60	.25	.08
☐	385	Don Gullett	.60	.25	.08
☐	386	Gary Matthews	.60	.25	.08
☐	387A	Rich Morales SD	.60	.25	.08
☐	387B	Rich Morales WAS	9.00	4.00	1.15
☐	388	Phil Roof	.50	.23	.06
☐	389	Gates Brown	.50	.23	.06
☐	390	Lou Piniella	1.25	.55	.16
☐	391	Billy Champion	.50	.23	.06
☐	392	Dick Green	.50	.23	.06
☐	393	Orlando Pena	.50	.23	.06
☐	394	Ken Henderson	.50	.23	.06
☐	395	Doug Rader	.50	.23	.06
☐	396	Tommy Davis	.60	.25	.08
☐	397	George Stone	.50	.23	.06
☐	398	Duke Sims	.50	.23	.06
☐	399	Mike Paul	.50	.23	.06
☐	400	Harmon Killebrew	5.00	2.30	.60
☐	401	Elliott Maddox	.50	.23	.06

	No.	Card			
☐	402	Jim Rooker	.50	.23	.06
☐	403	Red Sox Leaders	.60	.25	.08
		Darrell Johnson MG			
		Eddie Popowski CO			
		Lee Stange CO			
		Don Zimmer CO			
		Don Bryant CO			
☐	404	Jim Howarth	.50	.23	.06
☐	405	Ellie Rodriguez	.50	.23	.06
☐	406	Steve Arlin	.50	.23	.06
☐	407	Jim Wohlford	.50	.23	.06
☐	408	Charlie Hough	2.00	.90	.25
☐	409	Ike Brown	.50	.23	.06
☐	410	Pedro Borbon	.50	.23	.06
☐	411	Frank Baker	.50	.23	.06
☐	412	Chuck Taylor	.50	.23	.06
☐	413	Don Money	.60	.25	.08
☐	414	Checklist 397-528	2.50	.25	.08
☐	415	Gary Gentry	.50	.23	.06
☐	416	Chicago White Sox	1.50	.65	.19
		Team Card			
☐	417	Rich Folkers	.50	.23	.06
☐	418	Walt Williams	.50	.23	.06
☐	419	Wayne Twitchell	.50	.23	.06
☐	420	Ray Fosse	.50	.23	.06
☐	421	Dan Fife	.50	.23	.06
☐	422	Gonzalo Marquez	.50	.23	.06
☐	423	Fred Stanley	.50	.23	.06
☐	424	Jim Beauchamp	.50	.23	.06
☐	425	Pete Broberg	.50	.23	.06
☐	426	Rennie Stennett	.50	.23	.06
☐	427	Bobby Bolin	.50	.23	.06
☐	428	Gary Sutherland	.50	.23	.06
☐	429	Dick Lange	.50	.23	.06
☐	430	Matty Alou	.60	.25	.08
☐	431	Gene Garber	.50	.23	.06
☐	432	Chris Arnold	.50	.23	.06
☐	433	Lerrin LaGrow	.50	.23	.06
☐	434	Ken McMullen	.50	.23	.06
☐	435	Dave Concepcion	3.00	1.35	.40
☐	436	Don Hood	.50	.23	.06
☐	437	Jim Lyttle	.50	.23	.06
☐	438	Ed Herrmann	.50	.23	.06
☐	439	Norm Miller	.50	.23	.06
☐	440	Jim Kaat	1.50	.65	.19
☐	441	Tom Ragland	.50	.23	.06
☐	442	Alan Foster	.50	.23	.06
☐	443	Tom Hutton	.50	.23	.06
☐	444	Vic Davalillo	.50	.23	.06
☐	445	George Medich	.50	.23	.06
☐	446	Len Randle	.50	.23	.06
☐	447	Twins Leaders	.60	.25	.08
		Frank Quilici MG			
		Ralph Rowe CO			
		Bob Rodgers CO			
		Vern Morgan CO			
☐	448	Ron Hodges	.50	.23	.06
☐	449	Tom McCraw	.50	.23	.06
☐	450	Rich Hebner	.60	.25	.08
☐	451	Tommy John	2.00	.90	.25
☐	452	Gene Hiser	.50	.23	.06
☐	453	Balor Moore	.50	.23	.06
☐	454	Kurt Bevacqua	.50	.23	.06
☐	455	Tom Bradley	.50	.23	.06
☐	456	Dave Winfield	200.00	90.00	25.00
☐	457	Chuck Goggin	.50	.23	.06
☐	458	Jim Ray	.50	.23	.06
☐	459	Cincinnati Reds	1.50	.65	.19
		Team Card			
☐	460	Boog Powell	1.00	.45	.13
☐	461	John Odom	.50	.23	.06
☐	462	Luis Alvarado	.50	.23	.06
☐	463	Pat Dobson	.50	.23	.06
☐	464	Jose Cruz	.60	.25	.08
☐	465	Dick Bosman	.50	.23	.06
☐	466	Dick Billings	.50	.23	.06
☐	467	Winston Llenas	.50	.23	.06
☐	468	Pepe Frias	.50	.23	.06
☐	469	Joe Decker	.50	.23	.06
☐	470	AL Playoffs	6.00	2.70	.75
		A's over Orioles			
		(Reggie Jackson)			
☐	471	NL Playoffs	1.00	.45	.13
		Mets over Reds			
		(Jon Matlack pitching)			
☐	472	World Series Game 1	1.00	.45	.13
		(Darold Knowles			
		pitching)			
☐	473	World Series Game 2	7.00	3.10	.85
		(Willie Mays batting)			
☐	474	World Series Game 3	1.00	.45	.13
		(Bert Campaneris			
		stealing)			
☐	475	World Series Game 4	1.00	.45	.13
		(Rusty Staub batting)			
☐	476	World Series Game 5	1.00	.45	.13
		(Cleon Jones scoring)			
☐	477	World Series Game 6	6.00	2.70	.75
		(Reggie Jackson)			
☐	478	World Series Game 7	1.00	.45	.13
		(Bert Campaneris			
		batting)			
☐	479	World Series Summary	1.00	.45	.13
		A's celebrate; win			
		2nd consecutive			
		championship			
☐	480	Willie Crawford	.50	.23	.06
☐	481	Jerry Terrell	.50	.23	.06
☐	482	Bob Didier	.50	.23	.06
☐	483	Atlanta Braves	1.50	.65	.19
		Team Card			
☐	484	Carmen Fanzone	.50	.23	.06
☐	485	Felipe Alou	1.25	.55	.16
☐	486	Steve Stone	.60	.25	.08
☐	487	Ted Martinez	.50	.23	.06
☐	488	Andy Etchebarren	.50	.23	.06
☐	489	Pirates Leaders	.75	.35	.09
		Danny Murtaugh MG			
		Don Osborn CO			
		Don Leppert CO			
		Bill Mazeroski CO			
		Bob Skinner CO			
☐	490	Vada Pinson	.75	.35	.09
☐	491	Roger Nelson	.50	.23	.06
☐	492	Mike Rogodzinski	.50	.23	.06
☐	493	Joe Hoerner	.50	.23	.06
☐	494	Ed Goodson	.50	.23	.06
☐	495	Dick McAuliffe	.60	.25	.08
☐	496	Tom Murphy	.50	.23	.06
☐	497	Bobby Mitchell	.50	.23	.06
☐	498	Pat Corrales	.60	.25	.08
☐	499	Rusty Torres	.50	.23	.06
☐	500	Lee May	.60	.25	.08
☐	501	Eddie Leon	.50	.23	.06
☐	502	Dave LaRoche	.50	.23	.06
☐	503	Eric Soderholm	.50	.23	.06
☐	504	Joe Niekro	.60	.25	.08
☐	505	Bill Buckner	.75	.35	.09
☐	506	Ed Farmer	.50	.23	.06
☐	507	Larry Stahl	.50	.23	.06
☐	508	Montreal Expos	1.50	.65	.19
		Team Card			
☐	509	Jesse Jefferson	.50	.23	.06
☐	510	Wayne Garrett	.50	.23	.06
☐	511	Toby Harrah	.60	.25	.08
☐	512	Joe Lahoud	.50	.23	.06

	No.	Player			
☐	513	Jim Campanis	.50	.23	.06
☐	514	Paul Schaal	.50	.23	.06
☐	515	Willie Montanez	.50	.23	.06
☐	516	Horacio Pina	.50	.23	.06
☐	517	Mike Hegan	.50	.23	.06
☐	518	Derrel Thomas	.50	.23	.06
☐	519	Bill Sharp	.50	.23	.06
☐	520	Tim McCarver	.75	.35	.09
☐	521	Indians Leaders Ken Aspromonte MG Clay Bryant CO Tony Pacheco CO	.60	.25	.08
☐	522	J.R. Richard	.60	.25	.08
☐	523	Cecil Cooper	1.50	.65	.19
☐	524	Bill Plummer	.50	.23	.06
☐	525	Clyde Wright	.50	.23	.06
☐	526	Frank Tepedino	.50	.23	.06
☐	527	Bobby Darwin	.50	.23	.06
☐	528	Bill Bonham	.50	.23	.06
☐	529	Horace Clarke	.50	.23	.06
☐	530	Mickey Stanley	.60	.25	.08
☐	531	Expos Leaders Gene Mauch MG Dave Bristol CO Cal McLish CO Larry Doby CO Jerry Zimmerman CO	.60	.25	.08
☐	532	Skip Lockwood	.50	.23	.06
☐	533	Mike Phillips	.50	.23	.06
☐	534	Eddie Watt	.50	.23	.06
☐	535	Bob Tolan	.50	.23	.06
☐	536	Duffy Dyer	.50	.23	.06
☐	537	Steve Mingori	.50	.23	.06
☐	538	Cesar Tovar	.50	.23	.06
☐	539	Lloyd Allen	.50	.23	.06
☐	540	Bob Robertson	.50	.23	.06
☐	541	Cleveland Indians Team Card	1.50	.65	.19
☐	542	Rich Gossage	3.00	1.35	.40
☐	543	Danny Cater	.50	.23	.06
☐	544	Ron Schueler	.50	.23	.06
☐	545	Billy Conigliaro	.60	.25	.08
☐	546	Mike Corkins	.50	.23	.06
☐	547	Glenn Borgmann	.50	.23	.06
☐	548	Sonny Siebert	.50	.23	.06
☐	549	Mike Jorgensen	.50	.23	.06
☐	550	Sam McDowell	.60	.25	.08
☐	551	Von Joshua	.50	.23	.06
☐	552	Denny Doyle	.50	.23	.06
☐	553	Jim Willoughby	.50	.23	.06
☐	554	Tim Johnson	.50	.23	.06
☐	555	Woodie Fryman	.50	.23	.06
☐	556	Dave Campbell	.50	.23	.06
☐	557	Jim McGlothlin	.50	.23	.06
☐	558	Bill Fahey	.50	.23	.06
☐	559	Darrel Chaney	.50	.23	.06
☐	560	Mike Cuellar	.60	.25	.08
☐	561	Ed Kranepool	.50	.23	.06
☐	562	Jack Aker	.50	.23	.06
☐	563	Hal McRae	1.50	.65	.19
☐	564	Mike Ryan	.50	.23	.06
☐	565	Milt Wilcox	.50	.23	.06
☐	566	Jackie Hernandez	.50	.23	.06
☐	567	Boston Red Sox Team Card	1.50	.65	.19
☐	568	Mike Torrez	.60	.25	.08
☐	569	Rick Dempsey	.50	.23	.06
☐	570	Ralph Garr	.60	.25	.08
☐	571	Rich Hand	.50	.23	.06
☐	572	Enzo Hernandez	.50	.23	.06
☐	573	Mike Adams	.50	.23	.06
☐	574	Bill Parsons	.50	.23	.06
☐	575	Steve Garvey	6.00	2.70	.75
☐	576	Scipio Spinks	.50	.23	.06
☐	577	Mike Sadek	.50	.23	.06
☐	578	Ralph Houk MG	.60	.25	.08
☐	579	Cecil Upshaw	.50	.23	.06
☐	580	Jim Spencer	.50	.23	.06
☐	581	Fred Norman	.50	.23	.06
☐	582	Bucky Dent	2.00	.90	.25
☐	583	Marty Pattin	.50	.23	.06
☐	584	Ken Rudolph	.50	.23	.06
☐	585	Merv Rettenmund	.50	.23	.06
☐	586	Jack Brohamer	.50	.23	.06
☐	587	Larry Christenson	.50	.23	.06
☐	588	Hal Lanier	.50	.23	.06
☐	589	Boots Day	.50	.23	.06
☐	590	Roger Moret	.50	.23	.06
☐	591	Sonny Jackson	.50	.23	.06
☐	592	Ed Bane	.50	.23	.06
☐	593	Steve Yeager	.60	.25	.08
☐	594	Leroy Stanton	.50	.23	.06
☐	595	Steve Blass	.60	.25	.08
☐	596	Rookie Pitchers Wayne Garland Fred Holdsworth Mark Littell Dick Pole	.60	.25	.08
☐	597	Rookie Shortstops Dave Chalk John Gamble Pete MacKanin Manny Trillo	.60	.25	.08
☐	598	Rookie Outfielders Dave Augustine Ken Griffey Steve Ontiveros Jim Tyrone	20.00	9.00	2.50
☐	599A	Rookie Pitchers WAS Ron Diorio Dave Freisleben Frank Riccelli Greg Shanahan	1.25	.55	.16
☐	599B	Rookie Pitchers SD (SD in large print)	4.00	1.80	.50
☐	599C	Rookie Pitchers SD (SD in small print)	6.00	2.70	.75
☐	600	Rookie Infielders Ron Cash Jim Cox Bill Madlock Reggie Sanders	5.00	2.30	.60
☐	601	Rookie Outfielders Ed Armbrister Rich Bladt Brian Downing Bake McBride	4.00	1.80	.50
☐	602	Rookie Pitchers Glen Abbott Rick Henninger Craig Swan Dan Vossler	.75	.35	.09
☐	603	Rookie Catchers Barry Foote Tom Lundstedt Charlie Moore Sergio Robles	.60	.25	.08
☐	604	Rookie Infielders Terry Hughes John Knox Andre Thornton Frank White	6.00	2.70	.75
☐	605	Rookie Pitchers Vic Albury Ken Frailing Kevin Kobel	6.00	2.70	.75

Frank Tanana
☐ 606 Rookie Outfielders .... .60 .25 .08
Jim Fuller
Wilbur Howard
Tommy Smith
Otto Velez
☐ 607 Rookie Shortstops .... .60 .25 .08
Leo Foster
Tom Heintzelman
Dave Rosello
Frank Taveras
☐ 608A Rookie Pitchers: ERR 2.00 .90 .25
Bob Apodaco (sic)
Dick Baney
John D'Acquisto
Mike Wallace
☐ 608B Rookie Pitchers: COR .60 .25 .08
Bob Apodaca
Dick Baney
John D'Acquisto
Mike Wallace
☐ 609 Rico Petrocelli.............. .60 .25 .08
☐ 610 Dave Kingman........... 1.00 .45 .13
☐ 611 Rich Stelmaszek .... .50 .23 .06
☐ 612 Luke Walker................. .50 .23 .06
☐ 613 Dan Monzon .... .50 .23 .06
☐ 614 Adrian Devine .... .50 .23 .06
☐ 615 Johnny Jeter UER........ .50 .23 .06
(Misspelled Johnnie
on card back)
☐ 616 Larry Gura..................... .50 .23 .06
☐ 617 Ted Ford .... .50 .23 .06
☐ 618 Jim Mason..................... .50 .23 .06
☐ 619 Mike Anderson.............. .50 .23 .06
☐ 620 Al Downing .... .50 .23 .06
☐ 621 Bernie Carbo .... .50 .23 .06
☐ 622 Phil Gagliano................. .50 .23 .06
☐ 623 Celerino Sanchez .... .50 .23 .06
☐ 624 Bob Miller .... .50 .23 .06
☐ 625 Ollie Brown .... .50 .23 .06
☐ 626 Pittsburgh Pirates...... 1.50 .65 .19
Team Card
☐ 627 Carl Taylor .... .50 .23 .06
☐ 628 Ivan Murrell .... .50 .23 .06
☐ 629 Rusty Staub .... 1.00 .45 .13
☐ 630 Tommie Agee................ .60 .25 .08
☐ 631 Steve Barber .... .50 .23 .06
☐ 632 George Culver............... .50 .23 .06
☐ 633 Dave Hamilton .... .50 .23 .06
☐ 634 Braves Leaders .... 1.25 .55 .16
Eddie Mathews MG
Herm Starrette CO
Connie Ryan CO
Jim Busby CO
Ken Silvestri CO
☐ 635 Johnny Edwards .... .50 .23 .06
☐ 636 Dave Goltz.................... .50 .23 .06
☐ 637 Checklist 529-660...... 2.50 .25 .08
☐ 638 Ken Sanders .... .50 .23 .06
☐ 639 Joe Lovitto..................... .50 .23 .06
☐ 640 Milt Pappas.................... .60 .25 .08
☐ 641 Chuck Brinkman .... .50 .23 .06
☐ 642 Terry Harmon .... .50 .23 .06
☐ 643 Dodgers Team .... 1.50 .65 .19
☐ 644 Wayne Granger............. .50 .23 .06
☐ 645 Ken Boswell .... .50 .23 .06
☐ 646 George Foster .... 1.75 .80 .22
☐ 647 Juan Beniquez............... .50 .23 .06
☐ 648 Terry Crowley .... .50 .23 .06
☐ 649 Fernando Gonzalez....... .50 .23 .06
☐ 650 Mike Epstein .... .50 .23 .06
☐ 651 Leron Lee....................... .50 .23 .06
☐ 652 Gail Hopkins .... .50 .23 .06
☐ 653 Bob Stinson.................. .50 .23 .06
☐ 654A Jesus Alou ERR.......... .60 .25 .08
(No position)
☐ 654B Jesus Alou COR....... 7.00 3.10 .85
(Outfield)
☐ 655 Mike Tyson .... .50 .23 .06
☐ 656 Adrian Garrett .... .50 .23 .06
☐ 657 Jim Shellenback........... .50 .23 .06
☐ 658 Lee Lacy .... .50 .23 .06
☐ 659 Joe Lis........................... .50 .23 .06
☐ 660 Larry Dierker.............. 1.00 .23 .06

1974 Topps Traded

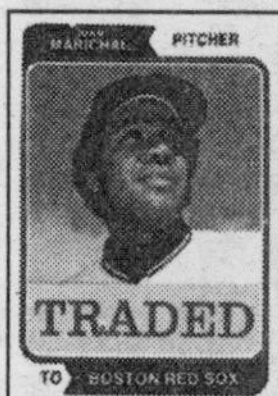

The cards in this 44-card set measure 2 1/2" by 3 1/2". The 1974 Topps Traded set contains 43 player cards and one unnumbered checklist card. The fronts have the word "traded" in block letters and the backs are designed in newspaper style. Card numbers are the same as in the regular set except they are followed by a "T." No known scarcities exist for this set. The cards were inserted in wax packs toward the end of the production run. They were produced in large enough quantity that they are no scarcer than the regular Topps cards.

	NRMT	VG-E	GOOD
COMPLETE SET (44)	15.00	6.75	1.90
COMMON CARD	.50	.23	.06

☐ 23T Craig Robinson .... .50 .23 .06
☐ 42T Claude Osteen............. .60 .25 .08
☐ 43T Jim Wynn .... .60 .25 .08
☐ 51T Bobby Heise................. .50 .23 .06
☐ 59T Ross Grimsley .... .50 .23 .06
☐ 62T Bob Locker .... .50 .23 .06
☐ 63T Bill Sudakis.................. .50 .23 .06
☐ 73T Mike Marshall .... .50 .23 .06
☐ 123T Nelson Briles.............. .60 .25 .08
☐ 139T Aurelio Monteagudo .. .50 .23 .06
☐ 151T Diego Segui .... .50 .23 .06
☐ 165T Willie Davis................ .60 .25 .08
☐ 175T Reggie Cleveland .... .50 .23 .06
☐ 182T Lindy McDaniel........... .60 .25 .08
☐ 186T Fred Scherman .... .50 .23 .06
☐ 249T George Mitterwald ..... .50 .23 .06
☐ 262T Ed Kirkpatrick .... .50 .23 .06
☐ 269T Bob Johnson.............. .50 .23 .06
☐ 270T Ron Santo.............. 1.00 .45 .13
☐ 313T Barry Lersch .... .50 .23 .06
☐ 319T Randy Hundley .... .50 .23 .06
☐ 330T Juan Marichal .... 2.00 .90 .25

		NRMT-MT	EXC	G-VG
☐ 348T	Pete Richert	.50	.23	.06
☐ 373T	John Curtis	.50	.23	.06
☐ 390T	Lou Piniella	1.00	.45	.13
☐ 428T	Gary Sutherland	.50	.23	.06
☐ 454T	Kurt Bevacqua	.50	.23	.06
☐ 458T	Jim Ray	.50	.23	.06
☐ 485T	Felipe Alou	1.25	.55	.16
☐ 486T	Steve Stone	1.00	.45	.13
☐ 496T	Tom Murphy	.50	.23	.06
☐ 516T	Horacio Pina	.50	.23	.06
☐ 534T	Eddie Watt	.50	.23	.06
☐ 538T	Cesar Tovar	.50	.23	.06
☐ 544T	Ron Schueler	.50	.23	.06
☐ 579T	Cecil Upshaw	.50	.23	.06
☐ 585T	Merv Rettenmund	.50	.23	.06
☐ 612T	Luke Walker	.50	.23	.06
☐ 616T	Larry Gura	.60	.25	.08
☐ 618T	Jim Mason	.50	.23	.06
☐ 630T	Tommie Agee	.60	.25	.08
☐ 648T	Terry Crowley	.50	.23	.06
☐ 649T	Fernando Gonzalez	.50	.23	.06
☐ NNO	Traded Checklist	1.50	.23	.06

1975 Topps

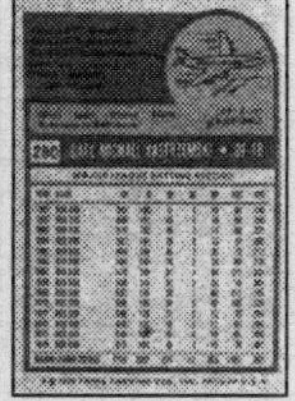

The cards in the 1975 Topps set were issued in two different sizes: a regular standard size (2 1/2" by 3 1/2") and a mini size (2 1/2" by 3 1/8") which was issued as a test in certain areas of the country. The 660-card Topps baseball set for 1975 was radically different in appearance from sets of the preceding years. The most prominent change was the use of a two-color frame surrounding the picture area rather than a single, subdued color. A facsimile autograph appears on the picture, and the backs are printed in red and green on gray. Cards 189-212 depict the MVP's of both leagues from 1951 through 1974. The first seven cards (1-7) feature players (listed in alphabetical order) breaking records or achieving milestones during the previous season. Cards 306-313 picture league leaders in various statistical categories. Cards 459-466 depict the results of post-season action. Team cards feature a checklist back for players on that team and show a small inset photo of the manager on the front. The following players' regular issue cards are explicitly denoted as All-Stars, 1, 50, 80, 140, 170, 180, 260, 320, 350, 390, 400, 420, 440, 470, 530, 570, and 600. This set is quite popular with collectors, at least in part due to the fact that the Rookie Cards of Robin Yount, George Brett, Gary Carter, Jim Rice, Fred Lynn, and Keith Hernandez are all in the set. Topps minis have the same checklist and are valued from approximately 1.25 times to 1.75 times the prices listed below.

	NRMT-MT	EXC	G-VG
COMPLETE SET (660)	850.00	375.00	105.00
COMMON CARD (1-132)	.50	.23	.06
COMMON CARD (133-264)	.50	.23	.06
COMMON CARD (265-660)	.50	.23	.06
*MINI's: 1X to 1.75X VALUES BELOW			

		NRMT-MT	EXC	G-VG
☐ 1	RB: Hank Aaron Sets Homer Mark	28.00	7.00	2.20
☐ 2	RB: Lou Brock 118 Stolen Bases	3.00	1.35	.40
☐ 3	RB: Bob Gibson 3000th Strikeout	3.00	1.35	.40
☐ 4	RB: Al Kaline 3000 Hit Club	4.00	1.80	.50
☐ 5	RB: Nolan Ryan Fans 300 for 3rd Year in a Row	30.00	13.50	3.80
☐ 6	RB: Mike Marshall Hurls 106 Games	.75	.35	.09
☐ 7	No Hitters Steve Busby Dick Bosman Nolan Ryan	12.00	5.50	1.50
☐ 8	Rogelio Moret	.50	.23	.06
☐ 9	Frank Tepedino	.50	.23	.06
☐ 10	Willie Davis	.60	.25	.08
☐ 11	Bill Melton	.50	.23	.06
☐ 12	David Clyde	.50	.23	.06
☐ 13	Gene Locklear	1.00	.45	.13
☐ 14	Milt Wilcox	.50	.23	.06
☐ 15	Jose Cardenal	.50	.23	.06
☐ 16	Frank Tanana	2.00	.90	.25
☐ 17	Dave Concepcion	2.50	1.15	.30
☐ 18	Tigers: Team/Mgr. Ralph Houk (Checklist back)	2.25	.45	.23
☐ 19	Jerry Koosman	.60	.25	.08
☐ 20	Thurman Munson	8.00	3.60	1.00
☐ 21	Rollie Fingers	4.00	1.80	.50
☐ 22	Dave Cash	.50	.23	.06
☐ 23	Bill Russell	.60	.25	.08
☐ 24	Al Fitzmorris	.50	.23	.06
☐ 25	Lee May	.60	.25	.08
☐ 26	Dave McNally	.60	.25	.08
☐ 27	Ken Reitz	.50	.23	.06
☐ 28	Tom Murphy	.50	.23	.06
☐ 29	Dave Parker	5.00	2.30	.60
☐ 30	Bert Blyleven	2.00	.90	.25
☐ 31	Dave Rader	.50	.23	.06
☐ 32	Reggie Cleveland	.50	.23	.06
☐ 33	Dusty Baker	2.00	.90	.25
☐ 34	Steve Renko	.50	.23	.06
☐ 35	Ron Santo	1.00	.45	.13
☐ 36	Joe Lovitto	.50	.23	.06
☐ 37	Dave Freisleben	.50	.23	.06
☐ 38	Buddy Bell	.75	.35	.09
☐ 39	Andre Thornton	.60	.25	.08
☐ 40	Bill Singer	.50	.23	.06
☐ 41	Cesar Geronimo	.60	.25	.08
☐ 42	Joe Coleman	.50	.23	.06
☐ 43	Cleon Jones	.60	.25	.08
☐ 44	Pat Dobson	.50	.23	.06
☐ 45	Joe Rudi	.60	.25	.08
☐ 46	Phillies: Team/Mgr.	2.25	.45	.23

Danny Ozark UER
(Checklist back)
(Terry Harmon listed as 339
instead of 399)

	#	Player			
☐	47	Tommy John	1.75	.80	.22
☐	48	Freddie Patek	.60	.25	.08
☐	49	Larry Dierker	.50	.23	.06
☐	50	Brooks Robinson	7.00	3.10	.85
☐	51	Bob Forsch	.50	.23	.06
☐	52	Darrell Porter	.60	.25	.08
☐	53	Dave Giusti	.50	.23	.06
☐	54	Eric Soderholm	.50	.23	.06
☐	55	Bobby Bonds	2.00	.90	.25
☐	56	Rick Wise	.60	.25	.08
☐	57	Dave Johnson	.60	.25	.08
☐	58	Chuck Taylor	.50	.23	.06
☐	59	Ken Henderson	.50	.23	.06
☐	60	Fergie Jenkins	4.00	1.80	.50
☐	61	Dave Winfield	70.00	32.00	8.75
☐	62	Fritz Peterson	.50	.23	.06
☐	63	Steve Swisher	.50	.23	.06
☐	64	Dave Chalk	.50	.23	.06
☐	65	Don Gullett	.60	.25	.08
☐	66	Willie Horton	.60	.25	.08
☐	67	Tug McGraw	1.00	.45	.13
☐	68	Ron Blomberg	.50	.23	.06
☐	69	John Odom	.50	.23	.06
☐	70	Mike Schmidt	55.00	25.00	7.00
☐	71	Charlie Hough	1.75	.80	.22
☐	72	Royals: Team/Mgr. Jack McKeon (Checklist back)	2.25	.45	.23
☐	73	J.R. Richard	.60	.25	.08
☐	74	Mark Belanger	.60	.25	.08
☐	75	Ted Simmons	1.50	.65	.19
☐	76	Ed Sprague	.50	.23	.06
☐	77	Richie Zisk	.60	.25	.08
☐	78	Ray Corbin	.50	.23	.06
☐	79	Gary Matthews	.60	.25	.08
☐	80	Carlton Fisk	18.00	8.00	2.30
☐	81	Ron Reed	.50	.23	.06
☐	82	Pat Kelly	.50	.23	.06
☐	83	Jim Merritt	.50	.23	.06
☐	84	Enzo Hernandez	.50	.23	.06
☐	85	Bill Bonham	.50	.23	.06
☐	86	Joe Lis	.50	.23	.06
☐	87	George Foster	1.75	.80	.22
☐	88	Tom Egan	.50	.23	.06
☐	89	Jim Ray	.50	.23	.06
☐	90	Rusty Staub	1.00	.45	.13
☐	91	Dick Green	.50	.23	.06
☐	92	Cecil Upshaw	.50	.23	.06
☐	93	Dave Lopes	1.00	.45	.13
☐	94	Jim Lonborg	.60	.25	.08
☐	95	John Mayberry	.60	.25	.08
☐	96	Mike Cosgrove	.50	.23	.06
☐	97	Earl Williams	.50	.23	.06
☐	98	Rich Folkers	.50	.23	.06
☐	99	Mike Hegan	.50	.23	.06
☐	100	Willie Stargell	4.00	1.80	.50
☐	101	Expos: Team/Mgr. Gene Mauch (Checklist back)	2.25	.45	.23
☐	102	Joe Decker	.50	.23	.06
☐	103	Rick Miller	.50	.23	.06
☐	104	Bill Madlock	1.00	.45	.13
☐	105	Buzz Capra	.50	.23	.06
☐	106	Mike Hargrove	2.00	.90	.25
☐	107	Jim Barr	.50	.23	.06
☐	108	Tom Hall	.50	.23	.06
☐	109	George Hendrick	.60	.25	.08
☐	110	Wilbur Wood	.50	.23	.06
☐	111	Wayne Garrett	.50	.23	.06
☐	112	Larry Hardy	.50	.23	.06
☐	113	Elliott Maddox	.50	.23	.06
☐	114	Dick Lange	.50	.23	.06
☐	115	Joe Ferguson	.50	.23	.06
☐	116	Lerrin LaGrow	.50	.23	.06
☐	117	Orioles: Team/Mgr. Earl Weaver (Checklist back)	2.25	.45	.23
☐	118	Mike Anderson	.50	.23	.06
☐	119	Tommy Helms	.50	.23	.06
☐	120	Steve Busby UER (Photo actually Fran Healy)	.60	.25	.08
☐	121	Bill North	.50	.23	.06
☐	122	Al Hrabosky	.60	.25	.08
☐	123	Johnny Briggs	.50	.23	.06
☐	124	Jerry Reuss	.60	.25	.08
☐	125	Ken Singleton	.60	.25	.08
☐	126	Checklist 1-132	2.25	.23	.07
☐	127	Glenn Borgmann	.50	.23	.06
☐	128	Bill Lee	.60	.25	.08
☐	129	Rick Monday	.60	.25	.08
☐	130	Phil Niekro	3.50	1.55	.45
☐	131	Toby Harrah	.60	.25	.08
☐	132	Randy Moffitt	.50	.23	.06
☐	133	Dan Driessen	.60	.25	.08
☐	134	Ron Hodges	.50	.23	.06
☐	135	Charlie Spikes	.50	.23	.06
☐	136	Jim Mason	.50	.23	.06
☐	137	Terry Forster	.60	.25	.08
☐	138	Del Unser	.50	.23	.06
☐	139	Horacio Pina	.50	.23	.06
☐	140	Steve Garvey	6.00	2.70	.75
☐	141	Mickey Stanley	.60	.25	.08
☐	142	Bob Reynolds	.50	.23	.06
☐	143	Cliff Johnson	.60	.25	.08
☐	144	Jim Wohlford	.50	.23	.06
☐	145	Ken Holtzman	.60	.25	.08
☐	146	Padres: Team/Mgr. John McNamara (Checklist back)	2.25	.45	.23
☐	147	Pedro Garcia	.50	.23	.06
☐	148	Jim Rooker	.50	.23	.06
☐	149	Tim Foli	.50	.23	.06
☐	150	Bob Gibson	6.00	2.70	.75
☐	151	Steve Brye	.50	.23	.06
☐	152	Mario Guerrero	.50	.23	.06
☐	153	Rick Reuschel	.60	.25	.08
☐	154	Mike Lum	.50	.23	.06
☐	155	Jim Bibby	.50	.23	.06
☐	156	Dave Kingman	1.00	.45	.13
☐	157	Pedro Borbon	.60	.25	.08
☐	158	Jerry Grote	.50	.23	.06
☐	159	Steve Arlin	.50	.23	.06
☐	160	Graig Nettles	2.00	.90	.25
☐	161	Stan Bahnsen	.50	.23	.06
☐	162	Willie Montanez	.50	.23	.06
☐	163	Jim Brewer	.50	.23	.06
☐	164	Mickey Rivers	.60	.25	.08
☐	165	Doug Rader	.60	.25	.08
☐	166	Woodie Fryman	.50	.23	.06
☐	167	Rich Coggins	.50	.23	.06
☐	168	Bill Greif	.50	.23	.06
☐	169	Cookie Rojas	.60	.25	.08
☐	170	Bert Campaneris	.60	.25	.08
☐	171	Ed Kirkpatrick	.50	.23	.06
☐	172	Red Sox: Team/Mgr. Darrell Johnson (Checklist back)	2.25	.45	.23
☐	173	Steve Rogers	.60	.25	.08
☐	174	Bake McBride	.60	.25	.08
☐	175	Don Money	.60	.25	.08
☐	176	Burt Hooton	.60	.25	.08

☐ 177 Vic Correll .50 .23 .06
☐ 178 Cesar Tovar .50 .23 .06
☐ 179 Tom Bradley .50 .23 .06
☐ 180 Joe Morgan 7.00 3.10 .85
☐ 181 Fred Beene .50 .23 .06
☐ 182 Don Hahn .50 .23 .06
☐ 183 Mel Stottlemyre .60 .25 .08
☐ 184 Jorge Orta .50 .23 .06
☐ 185 Steve Carlton 10.00 4.50 1.25
☐ 186 Willie Crawford .50 .23 .06
☐ 187 Denny Doyle .50 .23 .06
☐ 188 Tom Griffin .50 .23 .06
☐ 189 1951 MVP's 3.50 1.55 .45
Larry (Yogi) Berra
Roy Campanella
(Campy never issued)
☐ 190 1952 MVP's 1.00 .45 .13
Bobby Shantz
Hank Sauer
☐ 191 1953 MVP's 1.75 .80 .22
Al Rosen
Roy Campanella
☐ 192 1954 MVP's 3.50 1.55 .45
Yogi Berra
Willie Mays
☐ 193 1955 MVP's UER 3.50 1.55 .45
Yogi Berra
Roy Campanella
(Campy card never
issued, pictured
with LA cap, sic)
☐ 194 1956 MVP's 8.00 3.60 1.00
Mickey Mantle
Don Newcombe
☐ 195 1957 MVP's 15.00 6.75 1.90
Mickey Mantle
Hank Aaron
☐ 196 1958 MVP's 1.25 .55 .16
Jackie Jensen
Ernie Banks
☐ 197 1959 MVP's 1.50 .65 .19
Nellie Fox
Ernie Banks
☐ 198 1960 MVP's 1.25 .55 .16
Roger Maris
Dick Groat
☐ 199 1961 MVP's 3.00 1.35 .40
Roger Maris
Frank Robinson
☐ 200 1962 MVP's 10.00 4.50 1.25
Mickey Mantle
Maury Wills
(Wills never issued)
☐ 201 1963 MVP's 1.50 .65 .19
Elston Howard
Sandy Koufax
☐ 202 1964 MVP's 1.50 .65 .19
Brooks Robinson
Ken Boyer
☐ 203 1965 MVP's 1.50 .65 .19
Zoilo Versalles
Willie Mays
☐ 204 1966 MVP's 5.00 2.30 .60
Frank Robinson
Bob Clemente
☐ 205 1967 MVP's 1.50 .65 .19
Carl Yastrzemski
Orlando Cepeda
☐ 206 1968 MVP's 1.50 .65 .19
Denny McLain
Bob Gibson
☐ 207 1969 MVP's 1.50 .65 .19
Harmon Killebrew
Willie McCovey
☐ 208 1970 MVP's 1.50 .65 .19
Boog Powell
Johnny Bench
☐ 209 1971 MVP's 1.00 .45 .13
Vida Blue
Joe Torre
☐ 210 1972 MVP's 1.50 .65 .19
Rich Allen
Johnny Bench
☐ 211 1973 MVP's 6.00 2.70 .75
Reggie Jackson
Pete Rose
☐ 212 1974 MVP's 1.00 .45 .13
Jeff Burroughs
Steve Garvey
☐ 213 Oscar Gamble .60 .25 .08
☐ 214 Harry Parker .50 .23 .06
☐ 215 Bobby Valentine .50 .23 .06
☐ 216 Giants: Team/Mgr. 2.25 .45 .23
Wes Westrum
(Checklist back)
☐ 217 Lou Piniella 1.25 .55 .16
☐ 218 Jerry Johnson .50 .23 .06
☐ 219 Ed Herrmann .50 .23 .06
☐ 220 Don Sutton 3.50 1.55 .45
☐ 221 Aurelio Rodriguez .50 .23 .06
☐ 222 Dan Spillner .50 .23 .06
☐ 223 Robin Yount 150.00 70.00 19.00
☐ 224 Ramon Hernandez .50 .23 .06
☐ 225 Bob Grich .60 .25 .08
☐ 226 Bill Campbell .50 .23 .06
☐ 227 Bob Watson .60 .25 .08
☐ 228 George Brett 225.00 100.00 28.00
☐ 229 Barry Foote .50 .23 .06
☐ 230 Jim Hunter 4.00 1.80 .50
☐ 231 Mike Tyson .50 .23 .06
☐ 232 Diego Segui .50 .23 .06
☐ 233 Billy Grabarkewitz .50 .23 .06
☐ 234 Tom Grieve .60 .25 .08
☐ 235 Jack Billingham .60 .25 .08
☐ 236 Angels: Team/Mgr. 2.25 .45 .23
Dick Williams
(Checklist back)
☐ 237 Carl Morton .50 .23 .06
☐ 238 Dave Duncan .50 .23 .06
☐ 239 George Stone .50 .23 .06
☐ 240 Garry Maddox .60 .25 .08
☐ 241 Dick Tidrow .50 .23 .06
☐ 242 Jay Johnstone .60 .25 .08
☐ 243 Jim Kaat 1.25 .55 .16
☐ 244 Bill Buckner .60 .25 .08
☐ 245 Mickey Lolich .60 .25 .08
☐ 246 Cardinals: Team/Mgr. 2.25 .45 .23
Red Schoendienst
(Checklist back)
☐ 247 Enos Cabell .50 .23 .06
☐ 248 Randy Jones .60 .25 .08
☐ 249 Danny Thompson .50 .23 .06
☐ 250 Ken Brett .50 .23 .06
☐ 251 Fran Healy .50 .23 .06
☐ 252 Fred Scherman .50 .23 .06
☐ 253 Jesus Alou .50 .23 .06
☐ 254 Mike Torrez .60 .25 .08
☐ 255 Dwight Evans 3.00 1.35 .40
☐ 256 Billy Champion .50 .23 .06
☐ 257 Checklist: 133-264 2.25 .23 .07
☐ 258 Dave LaRoche .50 .23 .06
☐ 259 Len Randle .50 .23 .06
☐ 260 Johnny Bench 15.00 6.75 1.90
☐ 261 Andy Hassler .50 .23 .06
☐ 262 Rowland Office .50 .23 .06
☐ 263 Jim Perry .60 .25 .08

	No.	Card			
☐	264	John Milner	.50	.23	.06
☐	265	Ron Bryant	.50	.23	.06
☐	266	Sandy Alomar	.60	.25	.08
☐	267	Dick Ruthven	.50	.23	.06
☐	268	Hal McRae	1.50	.65	.19
☐	269	Doug Rau	.50	.23	.06
☐	270	Ron Fairly	.50	.23	.06
☐	271	Gerry Moses	.50	.23	.06
☐	272	Lynn McGlothen	.50	.23	.06
☐	273	Steve Braun	.50	.23	.06
☐	274	Vicente Romo	.50	.23	.06
☐	275	Paul Blair	.60	.25	.08
☐	276	White Sox Team/Mgr. Chuck Tanner (Checklist back)	2.25	.45	.23
☐	277	Frank Taveras	.50	.23	.06
☐	278	Paul Lindblad	.50	.23	.06
☐	279	Milt May	.50	.23	.06
☐	280	Carl Yastrzemski	7.00	3.10	.85
☐	281	Jim Slaton	.50	.23	.06
☐	282	Jerry Morales	.50	.23	.06
☐	283	Steve Foucault	.50	.23	.06
☐	284	Ken Griffey	5.00	2.30	.60
☐	285	Ellie Rodriguez	.50	.23	.06
☐	286	Mike Jorgensen	.50	.23	.06
☐	287	Roric Harrison	.50	.23	.06
☐	288	Bruce Ellingsen	.50	.23	.06
☐	289	Ken Rudolph	.50	.23	.06
☐	290	Jon Matlack	.50	.23	.06
☐	291	Bill Sudakis	.50	.23	.06
☐	292	Ron Schueler	.50	.23	.06
☐	293	Dick Sharon	.50	.23	.06
☐	294	Geoff Zahn	.50	.23	.06
☐	295	Vada Pinson	.75	.35	.09
☐	296	Alan Foster	.50	.23	.06
☐	297	Craig Kusick	.50	.23	.06
☐	298	Johnny Grubb	.50	.23	.06
☐	299	Bucky Dent	.60	.25	.08
☐	300	Reggie Jackson	22.00	10.00	2.80
☐	301	Dave Roberts	.50	.23	.06
☐	302	Rick Burleson	.75	.35	.09
☐	303	Grant Jackson	.50	.23	.06
☐	304	Pirates: Team/Mgr. Danny Murtaugh (Checklist back)	2.25	.45	.23
☐	305	Jim Colborn	.50	.23	.06
☐	306	Batting Leaders Rod Carew Ralph Garr	1.50	.65	.19
☐	307	Home Run Leaders Dick Allen Mike Schmidt	3.00	1.35	.40
☐	308	RBI Leaders Jeff Burroughs Johnny Bench	1.50	.65	.19
☐	309	Stolen Base Leaders Bill North Lou Brock	1.50	.65	.19
☐	310	Victory Leaders Jim Hunter Fergie Jenkins Andy Messersmith Phil Niekro	1.50	.65	.19
☐	311	ERA Leaders Jim Hunter Buzz Capra	1.50	.65	.19
☐	312	Strikeout Leaders Nolan Ryan Steve Carlton	20.00	9.00	2.50
☐	313	Leading Firemen Terry Forster Mike Marshall	1.00	.45	.13
☐	314	Buck Martinez	.50	.23	.06
☐	315	Don Kessinger	.60	.25	.08
☐	316	Jackie Brown	.50	.23	.06
☐	317	Joe Lahoud	.50	.23	.06
☐	318	Ernie McAnally	.50	.23	.06
☐	319	Johnny Oates	.60	.25	.08
☐	320	Pete Rose	20.00	9.00	2.50
☐	321	Rudy May	.50	.23	.06
☐	322	Ed Goodson	.50	.23	.06
☐	323	Fred Holdsworth	.50	.23	.06
☐	324	Ed Kranepool	.50	.23	.06
☐	325	Tony Oliva	1.25	.55	.16
☐	326	Wayne Twitchell	.50	.23	.06
☐	327	Jerry Hairston	.50	.23	.06
☐	328	Sonny Siebert	.50	.23	.06
☐	329	Ted Kubiak	.50	.23	.06
☐	330	Mike Marshall	.60	.25	.08
☐	331	Indians: Team/Mgr. Frank Robinson (Checklist back)	2.25	.45	.23
☐	332	Fred Kendall	.50	.23	.06
☐	333	Dick Drago	.50	.23	.06
☐	334	Greg Gross	.50	.23	.06
☐	335	Jim Palmer	8.00	3.60	1.00
☐	336	Rennie Stennett	.50	.23	.06
☐	337	Kevin Kobel	.50	.23	.06
☐	338	Rich Stelmaszek	.50	.23	.06
☐	339	Jim Fregosi	.60	.25	.08
☐	340	Paul Splittorff	.50	.23	.06
☐	341	Hal Breeden	.50	.23	.06
☐	342	Leroy Stanton	.50	.23	.06
☐	343	Danny Frisella	.50	.23	.06
☐	344	Ben Oglivie	.60	.25	.08
☐	345	Clay Carroll	.60	.25	.08
☐	346	Bobby Darwin	.50	.23	.06
☐	347	Mike Caldwell	.50	.23	.06
☐	348	Tony Muser	.50	.23	.06
☐	349	Ray Sadecki	.50	.23	.06
☐	350	Bobby Murcer	.75	.35	.09
☐	351	Bob Boone	1.50	.65	.19
☐	352	Darold Knowles	.50	.23	.06
☐	353	Luis Melendez	.50	.23	.06
☐	354	Dick Bosman	.50	.23	.06
☐	355	Chris Cannizzaro	.50	.23	.06
☐	356	Rico Petrocelli	.60	.25	.08
☐	357	Ken Forsch	.50	.23	.06
☐	358	Al Bumbry	.60	.25	.08
☐	359	Paul Popovich	.50	.23	.06
☐	360	George Scott	.60	.25	.08
☐	361	Dodgers: Team/Mgr. Walter Alston (Checklist back)	2.25	.45	.23
☐	362	Steve Hargan	.50	.23	.06
☐	363	Carmen Fanzone	.50	.23	.06
☐	364	Doug Bird	.50	.23	.06
☐	365	Bob Bailey	.50	.23	.06
☐	366	Ken Sanders	.50	.23	.06
☐	367	Craig Robinson	.50	.23	.06
☐	368	Vic Albury	.50	.23	.06
☐	369	Merv Rettenmund	.50	.23	.06
☐	370	Tom Seaver	15.00	6.75	1.90
☐	371	Gates Brown	.50	.23	.06
☐	372	John D'Acquisto	.50	.23	.06
☐	373	Bill Sharp	.50	.23	.06
☐	374	Eddie Watt	.50	.23	.06
☐	375	Roy White	.60	.25	.08
☐	376	Steve Yeager	.60	.25	.08
☐	377	Tom Hilgendorf	.50	.23	.06
☐	378	Derrel Thomas	.50	.23	.06
☐	379	Bernie Carbo	.50	.23	.06
☐	380	Sal Bando	.60	.25	.08
☐	381	John Curtis	.50	.23	.06
☐	382	Don Baylor	3.00	1.35	.40
☐	383	Jim York	.50	.23	.06

□	384 Brewers: Team/Mgr. .. Del Crandall (Checklist back)	2.25	.45	.23
□	385 Dock Ellis	.50	.23	.06
□	386 Checklist: 265-396	2.25	.23	.07
□	387 Jim Spencer	.50	.23	.06
□	388 Steve Stone	.60	.25	.08
□	389 Tony Solaita	.50	.23	.06
□	390 Ron Cey	1.00	.45	.13
□	391 Don DeMola	.50	.23	.06
□	392 Bruce Bochte	.50	.23	.06
□	393 Gary Gentry	.50	.23	.06
□	394 Larvell Blanks	.50	.23	.06
□	395 Bud Harrelson	.60	.25	.08
□	396 Fred Norman	.60	.25	.08
□	397 Bill Freehan	.60	.25	.08
□	398 Elias Sosa	.50	.23	.06
□	399 Terry Harmon	.50	.23	.06
□	400 Dick Allen	1.00	.45	.13
□	401 Mike Wallace	.50	.23	.06
□	402 Bob Tolan	.50	.23	.06
□	403 Tom Buskey	.50	.23	.06
□	404 Ted Sizemore	.50	.23	.06
□	405 John Montague	.50	.23	.06
□	406 Bob Gallagher	.50	.23	.06
□	407 Herb Washington	1.00	.45	.13
□	408 Clyde Wright	.50	.23	.06
□	409 Bob Robertson	.50	.23	.06
□	410 Mike Cueller UER (Sic, Cuellar)	.60	.25	.08
□	411 George Mitterwald	.50	.23	.06
□	412 Bill Hands	.50	.23	.06
□	413 Marty Pattin	.50	.23	.06
□	414 Manny Mota	.60	.25	.08
□	415 John Hiller	.60	.25	.08
□	416 Larry Lintz	.50	.23	.06
□	417 Skip Lockwood	.50	.23	.06
□	418 Leo Foster	.50	.23	.06
□	419 Dave Goltz	.50	.23	.06
□	420 Larry Bowa	1.00	.45	.13
□	421 Mets: Team/Mgr. Yogi Berra (Checklist back)	2.25	.45	.23
□	422 Brian Downing	1.00	.45	.13
□	423 Clay Kirby	.50	.23	.06
□	424 John Lowenstein	.50	.23	.06
□	425 Tito Fuentes	.50	.23	.06
□	426 George Medich	.50	.23	.06
□	427 Clarence Gaston	.60	.25	.08
□	428 Dave Hamilton	.50	.23	.06
□	429 Jim Dwyer	.50	.23	.06
□	430 Luis Tiant	.60	.25	.08
□	431 Rod Gilbreath	.50	.23	.06
□	432 Ken Berry	.50	.23	.06
□	433 Larry Demery	.50	.23	.06
□	434 Bob Locker	.50	.23	.06
□	435 Dave Nelson	.50	.23	.06
□	436 Ken Frailing	.50	.23	.06
□	437 Al Cowens	.60	.25	.08
□	438 Don Carrithers	.50	.23	.06
□	439 Ed Brinkman	.50	.23	.06
□	440 Andy Messersmith	.60	.25	.08
□	441 Bobby Heise	.50	.23	.06
□	442 Maximino Leon	.50	.23	.06
□	443 Twins: Team/Mgr. Frank Quilici (Checklist back)	2.25	.45	.23
□	444 Gene Garber	.60	.25	.08
□	445 Felix Millan	.50	.23	.06
□	446 Bart Johnson	.50	.23	.06
□	447 Terry Crowley	.50	.23	.06
□	448 Frank Duffy	.50	.23	.06
□	449 Charlie Williams	.50	.23	.06

□	450 Willie McCovey	5.00	2.30	.60
□	451 Rick Dempsey	.60	.25	.08
□	452 Angel Mangual	.50	.23	.06
□	453 Claude Osteen	.60	.25	.08
□	454 Doug Griffin	.50	.23	.06
□	455 Don Wilson	.50	.23	.06
□	456 Bob Coluccio	.50	.23	.06
□	457 Mario Mendoza	.50	.23	.06
□	458 Ross Grimsley	.50	.23	.06
□	459 1974 AL Champs A's over Orioles (Second base action pictured)	1.00	.45	.13
□	460 1974 NL Champs Dodgers over Pirates (Frank Taveras and Steve Garvey at second)	1.50	.65	.19
□	461 World Series Game 1. (Reggie Jackson)	4.00	1.80	.50
□	462 World Series Game 2. (Dodger dugout)	1.00	.45	.13
□	463 World Series Game 3. (Rollie Fingers pitching)	1.25	.55	.16
□	464 World Series Game 4. (A's batter)	1.00	.45	.13
□	465 World Series Game 5. (Joe Rudi rounding third)	1.00	.45	.13
□	466 World Series Summary A's do it again; win third straight (A's group picture)	1.50	.65	.19
□	467 Ed Halicki	.50	.23	.06
□	468 Bobby Mitchell	.50	.23	.06
□	469 Tom Dettore	.50	.23	.06
□	470 Jeff Burroughs	.60	.25	.08
□	471 Bob Stinson	.50	.23	.06
□	472 Bruce Dal Canton	.50	.23	.06
□	473 Ken McMullen	.50	.23	.06
□	474 Luke Walker	.50	.23	.06
□	475 Darrell Evans	.60	.25	.08
□	476 Ed Figueroa	.50	.23	.06
□	477 Tom Hutton	.50	.23	.06
□	478 Tom Burgmeier	.50	.23	.06
□	479 Ken Boswell	.50	.23	.06
□	480 Carlos May	.50	.23	.06
□	481 Will McEnaney	.60	.25	.08
□	482 Tom McCraw	.50	.23	.06
□	483 Steve Ontiveros	.50	.23	.06
□	484 Glenn Beckert	.60	.25	.08
□	485 Sparky Lyle	.75	.35	.09
□	486 Ray Fosse	.50	.23	.06
□	487 Astros: Team/Mgr. Preston Gomez (Checklist back)	2.25	.45	.23
□	488 Bill Travers	.50	.23	.06
□	489 Cecil Cooper	1.00	.45	.13
□	490 Reggie Smith	.60	.25	.08
□	491 Doyle Alexander	.60	.25	.08
□	492 Rich Hebner	.60	.25	.08
□	493 Don Stanhouse	.50	.23	.06
□	494 Pete LaCock	.50	.23	.06
□	495 Nelson Briles	.60	.25	.08
□	496 Pepe Frias	.50	.23	.06
□	497 Jim Nettles	.50	.23	.06
□	498 Al Downing	.50	.23	.06
□	499 Marty Perez	.50	.23	.06
□	500 Nolan Ryan	80.00	36.00	10.00
□	501 Bill Robinson	.60	.25	.08
□	502 Pat Bourque	.50	.23	.06
□	503 Fred Stanley	.50	.23	.06
□	504 Buddy Bradford	.50	.23	.06

	No.	Card			
☐	505	Chris Speier	.50	.23	.06
☐	506	Leron Lee	.50	.23	.06
☐	507	Tom Carroll	.50	.23	.06
☐	508	Bob Hansen	.50	.23	.06
☐	509	Dave Hilton	.50	.23	.06
☐	510	Vida Blue	.60	.25	.08
☐	511	Rangers: Team/Mgr.	2.25	.45	.23
		Billy Martin			
		(Checklist back)			
☐	512	Larry Milbourne	.50	.23	.06
☐	513	Dick Pole	.50	.23	.06
☐	514	Jose Cruz	.60	.25	.08
☐	515	Manny Sanguillen	.60	.25	.08
☐	516	Don Hood	.50	.23	.06
☐	517	Checklist: 397-528	2.25	.23	.07
☐	518	Leo Cardenas	.50	.23	.06
☐	519	Jim Todd	.50	.23	.06
☐	520	Amos Otis	.60	.25	.08
☐	521	Dennis Blair	.50	.23	.06
☐	522	Gary Sutherland	.50	.23	.06
☐	523	Tom Paciorek	.60	.25	.08
☐	524	John Doherty	.50	.23	.06
☐	525	Tom House	.50	.23	.06
☐	526	Larry Hisle	.60	.25	.08
☐	527	Mac Scarce	.50	.23	.06
☐	528	Eddie Leon	.50	.23	.06
☐	529	Gary Thomasson	.50	.23	.06
☐	530	Gaylord Perry	3.50	1.55	.45
☐	531	Reds: Team/Mgr.	3.00	.60	.30
		Sparky Anderson			
		(Checklist back)			
☐	532	Gorman Thomas	.60	.25	.08
☐	533	Rudy Meoli	.50	.23	.06
☐	534	Alex Johnson	.50	.23	.06
☐	535	Gene Tenace	.60	.25	.08
☐	536	Bob Moose	.50	.23	.06
☐	537	Tommy Harper	.60	.25	.08
☐	538	Duffy Dyer	.50	.23	.06
☐	539	Jesse Jefferson	.50	.23	.06
☐	540	Lou Brock	5.00	2.30	.60
☐	541	Roger Metzger	.50	.23	.06
☐	542	Pete Broberg	.50	.23	.06
☐	543	Larry Biittner	.50	.23	.06
☐	544	Steve Mingori	.50	.23	.06
☐	545	Billy Williams	3.50	1.55	.45
☐	546	John Knox	.50	.23	.06
☐	547	Von Joshua	.50	.23	.06
☐	548	Charlie Sands	.50	.23	.06
☐	549	Bill Butler	.50	.23	.06
☐	550	Ralph Garr	.60	.25	.08
☐	551	Larry Christenson	.50	.23	.06
☐	552	Jack Brohamer	.50	.23	.06
☐	553	John Boccabella	.50	.23	.06
☐	554	Rich Gossage	2.50	1.15	.30
☐	555	Al Oliver	.75	.35	.09
☐	556	Tim Johnson	.50	.23	.06
☐	557	Larry Gura	.50	.23	.06
☐	558	Dave Roberts	.50	.23	.06
☐	559	Bob Montgomery	.50	.23	.06
☐	560	Tony Perez	3.50	1.55	.45
☐	561	A's: Team/Mgr.	2.25	.45	.23
		Alvin Dark			
		(Checklist back)			
☐	562	Gary Nolan	.60	.25	.08
☐	563	Wilbur Howard	.50	.23	.06
☐	564	Tommy Davis	.60	.25	.08
☐	565	Joe Torre	1.00	.45	.13
☐	566	Ray Burris	.50	.23	.06
☐	567	Jim Sundberg	1.25	.55	.16
☐	568	Dale Murray	.50	.23	.06
☐	569	Frank White	1.00	.45	.13
☐	570	Jim Wynn	.60	.25	.08
☐	571	Dave Lemanczyk	.50	.23	.06

	No.	Card			
☐	572	Roger Nelson	.50	.23	.06
☐	573	Orlando Pena	.50	.23	.06
☐	574	Tony Taylor	.50	.23	.06
☐	575	Gene Clines	.50	.23	.06
☐	576	Phil Roof	.50	.23	.06
☐	577	John Morris	.50	.23	.06
☐	578	Dave Tomlin	.50	.23	.06
☐	579	Skip Pitlock	.50	.23	.06
☐	580	Frank Robinson	5.00	2.30	.60
☐	581	Darrel Chaney	.50	.23	.06
☐	582	Eduardo Rodriguez	.50	.23	.06
☐	583	Andy Etchebarren	.50	.23	.06
☐	584	Mike Garman	.50	.23	.06
☐	585	Chris Chambliss	.60	.25	.08
☐	586	Tim McCarver	.75	.35	.09
☐	587	Chris Ward	.50	.23	.06
☐	588	Rick Auerbach	.50	.23	.06
☐	589	Braves: Team/Mgr.	2.25	.45	.23
		Clyde King			
		(Checklist back)			
☐	590	Cesar Cedeno	.60	.25	.08
☐	591	Glenn Abbott	.50	.23	.06
☐	592	Balor Moore	.50	.23	.06
☐	593	Gene Lamont	.50	.23	.06
☐	594	Jim Fuller	.50	.23	.06
☐	595	Joe Niekro	.60	.25	.08
☐	596	Ollie Brown	.50	.23	.06
☐	597	Winston Llenas	.50	.23	.06
☐	598	Bruce Kison	.50	.23	.06
☐	599	Nate Colbert	.50	.23	.06
☐	600	Rod Carew	7.00	3.10	.85
☐	601	Juan Beniquez	.50	.23	.06
☐	602	John Vukovich	.50	.23	.06
☐	603	Lew Krausse	.50	.23	.06
☐	604	Oscar Zamora	.50	.23	.06
☐	605	John Ellis	.50	.23	.06
☐	606	Bruce Miller	.50	.23	.06
☐	607	Jim Holt	.50	.23	.06
☐	608	Gene Michael	.60	.25	.08
☐	609	Elrod Hendricks	.50	.23	.06
☐	610	Ron Hunt	.50	.23	.06
☐	611	Yankees: Team/Mgr.	2.25	.45	.23
		Bill Virdon			
		(Checklist back)			
☐	612	Terry Hughes	.50	.23	.06
☐	613	Bill Parsons	.50	.23	.06
☐	614	Rookie Pitchers	.75	.35	.09
		Jack Kucek			
		Dyar Miller			
		Vern Ruhle			
		Paul Siebert			
☐	615	Rookie Pitchers	1.00	.45	.13
		Pat Darcy			
		Dennis Leonard			
		Tom Underwood			
		Hank Webb			
☐	616	Rookie Outfielders	16.00	7.25	2.00
		Dave Augustine			
		Pepe Mangual			
		Jim Rice			
		John Scott			
☐	617	Rookie Infielders	2.50	1.15	.30
		Mike Cubbage			
		Doug DeCinces			
		Reggie Sanders			
		Manny Trillo			
☐	618	Rookie Pitchers	1.00	.45	.13
		Jamie Easterly			
		Tom Johnson			
		Scott McGregor			
		Rick Rhoden			
☐	619	Rookie Outfielders	.75	.35	.09
		Benny Ayala			

		NRMT-MT	EXC	G-VG
	Nyls Nyman Tommy Smith Jerry Turner			
☐ 620	Rookie Catcher/OF...	35.00	16.00	4.40
	Gary Carter Marc Hill Danny Meyer Leon Roberts			
☐ 621	Rookie Pitchers..........	1.00	.45	.13
	John Denny Rawly Eastwick Jim Kern Juan Veintidos			
☐ 622	Rookie Outfielders ...	10.00	4.50	1.25
	Ed Armbrister Fred Lynn Tom Poquette Terry Whitfield UER (Listed as Ney York)			
☐ 623	Rookie Infielders......	10.00	4.50	1.25
	Phil Garner Keith Hernandez UER (Sic, bats right) Bob Sheldon Tom Veryzer			
☐ 624	Rookie Pitchers............	.75	.35	.09
	Doug Konieczny Gary Lavelle Jim Otten Eddie Solomon			
☐ 625	Boog Powell..............	1.00	.45	.13
☐ 626	Larry Haney UER .... (Photo actually Dave Duncan)	.50	.23	.06
☐ 627	Tom Walker	.50	.23	.06
☐ 628	Ron LeFlore	1.00	.45	.13
☐ 629	Joe Hoerner..................	.50	.23	.06
☐ 630	Greg Luzinski.............	1.00	.45	.13
☐ 631	Lee Lacy	.50	.23	.06
☐ 632	Morris Nettles..............	.50	.23	.06
☐ 633	Paul Casanova	.50	.23	.06
☐ 634	Cy Acosta.....................	.50	.23	.06
☐ 635	Chuck Dobson	.50	.23	.06
☐ 636	Charlie Moore	.50	.23	.06
☐ 637	Ted Martinez................	.50	.23	.06
☐ 638	Cubs: Team/Mgr.	2.25	.45	.23
	Jim Marshall (Checklist back)			
☐ 639	Steve Kline...................	.50	.23	.06
☐ 640	Harmon Killebrew	5.00	2.30	.60
☐ 641	Jim Northrup	.50	.23	.06
☐ 642	Mike Phillips	.50	.23	.06
☐ 643	Brent Strom	.50	.23	.06
☐ 644	Bill Fahey	.50	.23	.06
☐ 645	Danny Cater.................	.50	.23	.06
☐ 646	Checklist: 529-660.....	2.25	.23	.07
☐ 647	Claudell Washington..	1.00	.45	.13
☐ 648	Dave Pagan..................	.50	.23	.06
☐ 649	Jack Heidemann	.50	.23	.06
☐ 650	Dave May.....................	.50	.23	.06
☐ 651	John Morlan	.50	.23	.06
☐ 652	Lindy McDaniel............	.60	.25	.08
☐ 653	Lee Richard UER.......... (Listed as Richards on card front)	.50	.23	.06
☐ 654	Jerry Terrell	.50	.23	.06
☐ 655	Rico Carty....................	.60	.25	.08
☐ 656	Bill Plummer................	.50	.23	.06
☐ 657	Bob Oliver....................	.50	.23	.06
☐ 658	Vic Harris.....................	.50	.23	.06
☐ 659	Bob Apodaca................	.50	.23	.06
☐ 660	Hank Aaron	30.00	7.50	2.40

1976 Topps

The 1976 Topps set of 660 cards (measuring 2 1/2" by 3 1/2") is known for its sharp color photographs and interesting presentation of subjects. Team cards feature a checklist back for players on that team and show a small inset photo of the manager on the front. A "Father and Son" series (66-70) spotlights five Major Leaguers whose fathers also made the "Big Show." Other subseries include "All Time All Stars" (341-350), "Record Breakers" from the previous season (1-6), League Leaders (191-205), Post-season cards (461-462), and Rookie Prospects (589-599). The following players' regular issue cards are explicitly denoted as All-Stars, 10, 48, 60, 140, 150, 165, 169, 240, 300, 370, 380, 395, 400, 420, 475, 500, 580, and 650. The key Rookie Cards in this set are Dennis Eckersley, Ron Guidry, and Willie Randolph.

	NRMT-MT	EXC	G-VG
COMPLETE SET (660)	400.00	180.00	50.00
COMMON CARD (1-660)	.30	.14	.04

		NRMT-MT	EXC	G-VG
☐ 1	RB: Hank Aaron .... Most RBI's, 2262	16.00	4.00	1.30
☐ 2	RB: Bobby Bonds........... Most leadoff HR's 32; plus three seasons 30 homers/30 steals	1.00	.45	.13
☐ 3	RB: Mickey Lolich............ Lefthander, Most Strikeouts, 2679	.75	.35	.09
☐ 4	RB: Dave Lopes .... Most Consecutive SB attempts, 38	.75	.35	.09
☐ 5	RB: Tom Seaver............ Most Cons. seasons with 200 SO's, 8	5.00	2.30	.60
☐ 6	RB: Rennie Stennett......... Most Hits in a 9 inning game, 7	.60	.25	.08
☐ 7	Jim Umbarger...................	.30	.14	.04
☐ 8	Tito Fuentes	.30	.14	.04
☐ 9	Paul Lindblad....................	.30	.14	.04
☐ 10	Lou Brock	5.00	2.30	.60
☐ 11	Jim Hughes.....................	.30	.14	.04
☐ 12	Richie Zisk.....................	.40	.18	.05
☐ 13	John Wockenfuss	.30	.14	.04
☐ 14	Gene Garber....................	.30	.14	.04
☐ 15	George Scott....................	.40	.18	.05
☐ 16	Bob Apodaca....................	.30	.14	.04
☐ 17	New York Yankees .... Team Card;	1.50	.30	.15

Card			
Billy Martin MG (Checklist back)			
☐ 18 Dale Murray	.30	.14	.04
☐ 19 George Brett	65.00	29.00	8.25
☐ 20 Bob Watson	.40	.18	.05
☐ 21 Dave LaRoche	.30	.14	.04
☐ 22 Bill Russell	.40	.18	.05
☐ 23 Brian Downing	.30	.14	.04
☐ 24 Cesar Geronimo	.40	.18	.05
☐ 25 Mike Torrez	.40	.18	.05
☐ 26 Andre Thornton	.40	.18	.05
☐ 27 Ed Figueroa	.30	.14	.04
☐ 28 Dusty Baker	1.50	.65	.19
☐ 29 Rick Burleson	.40	.18	.05
☐ 30 John Montefusco	.40	.18	.05
☐ 31 Len Randle	.30	.14	.04
☐ 32 Danny Frisella	.30	.14	.04
☐ 33 Bill North	.30	.14	.04
☐ 34 Mike Garman	.30	.14	.04
☐ 35 Tony Oliva	1.00	.45	.13
☐ 36 Frank Taveras	.30	.14	.04
☐ 37 John Hiller	.40	.18	.05
☐ 38 Garry Maddox	.40	.18	.05
☐ 39 Pete Broberg	.30	.14	.04
☐ 40 Dave Kingman	.60	.25	.08
☐ 41 Tippy Martinez	.50	.23	.06
☐ 42 Barry Foote	.30	.14	.04
☐ 43 Paul Splittorff	.30	.14	.04
☐ 44 Doug Rader	.40	.18	.05
☐ 45 Boog Powell	.75	.35	.09
☐ 46 Los Angeles Dodgers Team Card; Walter Alston MG (Checklist back)	1.50	.30	.15
☐ 47 Jesse Jefferson	.30	.14	.04
☐ 48 Dave Concepcion	1.75	.80	.22
☐ 49 Dave Duncan	.30	.14	.04
☐ 50 Fred Lynn	1.75	.80	.22
☐ 51 Ray Burris	.30	.14	.04
☐ 52 Dave Chalk	.30	.14	.04
☐ 53 Mike Beard	.30	.14	.04
☐ 54 Dave Rader	.30	.14	.04
☐ 55 Gaylord Perry	3.00	1.35	.40
☐ 56 Bob Tolan	.30	.14	.04
☐ 57 Phil Garner	1.00	.45	.13
☐ 58 Ron Reed	.30	.14	.04
☐ 59 Larry Hisle	.40	.18	.05
☐ 60 Jerry Reuss	.40	.18	.05
☐ 61 Ron LeFlore	.40	.18	.05
☐ 62 Johnny Oates	.40	.18	.05
☐ 63 Bobby Darwin	.30	.14	.04
☐ 64 Jerry Koosman	.40	.18	.05
☐ 65 Chris Chambliss	.40	.18	.05
☐ 66 Father and Son Gus Bell Buddy Bell	.50	.23	.06
☐ 67 Father and Son Ray Boone Bob Boone	.60	.25	.08
☐ 68 Father and Son Joe Coleman Joe Coleman Jr.	.50	.23	.06
☐ 69 Father and Son Jim Hegan Mike Hegan	.50	.23	.06
☐ 70 Father and Son Roy Smalley Roy Smalley Jr.	.50	.23	.06
☐ 71 Steve Rogers	.40	.18	.05
☐ 72 Hal McRae	.75	.35	.09
☐ 73 Baltimore Orioles Team Card; Earl Weaver MG (Checklist back)	1.50	.30	.15
☐ 74 Oscar Gamble	.40	.18	.05
☐ 75 Larry Dierker	.30	.14	.04
☐ 76 Willie Crawford	.30	.14	.04
☐ 77 Pedro Borbon	.40	.18	.05
☐ 78 Cecil Cooper	.40	.18	.05
☐ 79 Jerry Morales	.30	.14	.04
☐ 80 Jim Kaat	.75	.35	.09
☐ 81 Darrell Evans	.40	.18	.05
☐ 82 Von Joshua	.30	.14	.04
☐ 83 Jim Spencer	.30	.14	.04
☐ 84 Brent Strom	.30	.14	.04
☐ 85 Mickey Rivers	.40	.18	.05
☐ 86 Mike Tyson	.30	.14	.04
☐ 87 Tom Burgmeier	.30	.14	.04
☐ 88 Duffy Dyer	.30	.14	.04
☐ 89 Vern Ruhle	.30	.14	.04
☐ 90 Sal Bando	.40	.18	.05
☐ 91 Tom Hutton	.30	.14	.04
☐ 92 Eduardo Rodriguez	.30	.14	.04
☐ 93 Mike Phillips	.30	.14	.04
☐ 94 Jim Dwyer	.30	.14	.04
☐ 95 Brooks Robinson	6.00	2.70	.75
☐ 96 Doug Bird	.30	.14	.04
☐ 97 Wilbur Howard	.30	.14	.04
☐ 98 Dennis Eckersley	45.00	20.00	5.75
☐ 99 Lee Lacy	.30	.14	.04
☐ 100 Jim Hunter	3.50	1.55	.45
☐ 101 Pete LaCock	.30	.14	.04
☐ 102 Jim Willoughby	.30	.14	.04
☐ 103 Biff Pocoroba	.30	.14	.04
☐ 104 Cincinnati Reds Team Card; Sparky Anderson MG (Checklist back)	2.50	.50	.25
☐ 105 Gary Lavelle	.30	.14	.04
☐ 106 Tom Grieve	.40	.18	.05
☐ 107 Dave Roberts	.30	.14	.04
☐ 108 Don Kirkwood	.30	.14	.04
☐ 109 Larry Lintz	.30	.14	.04
☐ 110 Carlos May	.30	.14	.04
☐ 111 Danny Thompson	.30	.14	.04
☐ 112 Kent Tekulve	1.50	.65	.19
☐ 113 Gary Sutherland	.30	.14	.04
☐ 114 Jay Johnstone	.40	.18	.05
☐ 115 Ken Holtzman	.40	.18	.05
☐ 116 Charlie Moore	.30	.14	.04
☐ 117 Mike Jorgensen	.30	.14	.04
☐ 118 Boston Red Sox Team Card; Darrell Johnson MG (Checklist back)	1.50	.30	.15
☐ 119 Checklist 1-132	1.50	.15	.05
☐ 120 Rusty Staub	.40	.18	.05
☐ 121 Tony Solaita	.30	.14	.04
☐ 122 Mike Cosgrove	.30	.14	.04
☐ 123 Walt Williams	.30	.14	.04
☐ 124 Doug Rau	.30	.14	.04
☐ 125 Don Baylor	2.00	.90	.25
☐ 126 Tom Dettore	.30	.14	.04
☐ 127 Larvell Blanks	.30	.14	.04
☐ 128 Ken Griffey	2.50	1.15	.30
☐ 129 Andy Etchebarren	.30	.14	.04
☐ 130 Luis Tiant	.40	.18	.05
☐ 131 Bill Stein	.30	.14	.04
☐ 132 Don Hood	.30	.14	.04
☐ 133 Gary Matthews	.40	.18	.05
☐ 134 Mike Ivie	.30	.14	.04
☐ 135 Bake McBride	.40	.18	.05
☐ 136 Dave Goltz	.30	.14	.04
☐ 137 Bill Robinson	.40	.18	.05
☐ 138 Lerrin LaGrow	.30	.14	.04
☐ 139 Gorman Thomas	.40	.18	.05
☐ 140 Vida Blue	.40	.18	.05

☐ 141 Larry Parrish .... 1.00 .45 .13
☐ 142 Dick Drago .... .30 .14 .04
☐ 143 Jerry Grote .... .30 .14 .04
☐ 144 Al Fitzmorris .... .30 .14 .04
☐ 145 Larry Bowa .... .30 .14 .04
☐ 146 George Medich .... .30 .14 .04
☐ 147 Houston Astros .... 1.50 .30 .15
Team Card;
Bill Virdon MG
(Checklist back)
☐ 148 Stan Thomas .... .30 .14 .04
☐ 149 Tommy Davis .... .40 .18 .05
☐ 150 Steve Garvey .... 4.50 2.00 .55
☐ 151 Bill Bonham .... .30 .14 .04
☐ 152 Leroy Stanton .... .30 .14 .04
☐ 153 Buzz Capra .... .30 .14 .04
☐ 154 Bucky Dent .... .30 .14 .04
☐ 155 Jack Billingham .... .40 .18 .05
☐ 156 Rico Carty .... .40 .18 .05
☐ 157 Mike Caldwell .... .30 .14 .04
☐ 158 Ken Reitz .... .30 .14 .04
☐ 159 Jerry Terrell .... .30 .14 .04
☐ 160 Dave Winfield 35.00 16.00 4.40
☐ 161 Bruce Kison .... .30 .14 .04
☐ 162 Jack Pierce .... .30 .14 .04
☐ 163 Jim Slaton .... .30 .14 .04
☐ 164 Pepe Mangual .... .30 .14 .04
☐ 165 Gene Tenace .... .40 .18 .05
☐ 166 Skip Lockwood .... .30 .14 .04
☐ 167 Freddie Patek .... .40 .18 .05
☐ 168 Tom Hilgendorf .... .30 .14 .04
☐ 169 Graig Nettles .... 1.25 .55 .16
☐ 170 Rick Wise .... .30 .14 .04
☐ 171 Greg Gross .... .30 .14 .04
☐ 172 Texas Rangers .... 1.50 .30 .15
Team Card;
Frank Lucchesi MG
(Checklist back)
☐ 173 Steve Swisher .... .30 .14 .04
☐ 174 Charlie Hough .... 1.00 .45 .13
☐ 175 Ken Singleton .... .40 .18 .05
☐ 176 Dick Lange .... .30 .14 .04
☐ 177 Marty Perez .... .30 .14 .04
☐ 178 Tom Buskey .... .30 .14 .04
☐ 179 George Foster .... 1.00 .45 .13
☐ 180 Rich Gossage .... 2.00 .90 .25
☐ 181 Willie Montanez .... .30 .14 .04
☐ 182 Harry Rasmussen .... .30 .14 .04
☐ 183 Steve Braun .... .30 .14 .04
☐ 184 Bill Greif .... .30 .14 .04
☐ 185 Dave Parker .... 2.00 .90 .25
☐ 186 Tom Walker .... .30 .14 .04
☐ 187 Pedro Garcia .... .30 .14 .04
☐ 188 Fred Scherman .... .30 .14 .04
☐ 189 Claudell Washington .... .40 .18 .05
☐ 190 Jon Matlack .... .30 .14 .04
☐ 191 NL Batting Leaders .... .75 .35 .09
Bill Madlock
Ted Simmons
Manny Sanguillen
☐ 192 AL Batting Leaders .... 3.00 1.35 .40
Rod Carew
Fred Lynn
Thurman Munson
☐ 193 NL Home Run Leaders 2.50 1.15 .30
Mike Schmidt
Dave Kingman
Greg Luzinski
☐ 194 AL Home Run Leaders 2.50 1.15 .30
Reggie Jackson
George Scott
John Mayberry
☐ 195 NL RBI Leaders .... 1.50 .65 .19
Greg Luzinski
Johnny Bench
Tony Perez
☐ 196 AL RBI Leaders .... .75 .35 .09
George Scott
John Mayberry
Fred Lynn
☐ 197 NL Steals Leaders .... 1.50 .65 .19
Dave Lopes
Joe Morgan
Lou Brock
☐ 198 AL Steals Leaders .... .75 .35 .09
Mickey Rivers
Claudell Washington
Amos Otis
☐ 199 NL Victory Leaders .... 1.50 .65 .19
Tom Seaver
Randy Jones
Andy Messersmith
☐ 200 AL Victory Leaders .... 1.50 .65 .19
Jim Hunter
Jim Palmer
Vida Blue
☐ 201 NL ERA Leaders .... 1.50 .65 .19
Randy Jones
Andy Messersmith
Tom Seaver
☐ 202 AL ERA Leaders .... 5.00 2.30 .60
Jim Palmer
Jim Hunter
Dennis Eckersley
☐ 203 NL Strikeout Leaders . 1.50 .65 .19
Tom Seaver
John Montefusco
Andy Messersmith
☐ 204 AL Strikeout Leaders . 1.00 .45 .13
Frank Tanana
Bert Blyleven
Gaylord Perry
☐ 205 Leading Firemen .... .75 .35 .09
Al Hrabosky
Rich Gossage
☐ 206 Manny Trillo .... .30 .14 .04
☐ 207 Andy Hassler .... .30 .14 .04
☐ 208 Mike Lum .... .30 .14 .04
☐ 209 Alan Ashby .... .40 .18 .05
☐ 210 Lee May .... .40 .18 .05
☐ 211 Clay Carroll .... .40 .18 .05
☐ 212 Pat Kelly .... .30 .14 .04
☐ 213 Dave Heaverlo .... .30 .14 .04
☐ 214 Eric Soderholm .... .30 .14 .04
☐ 215 Reggie Smith .... .40 .18 .05
☐ 216 Montreal Expos .... 1.50 .30 .15
Team Card;
Karl Kuehl MG
(Checklist back)
☐ 217 Dave Freisleben .... .30 .14 .04
☐ 218 John Knox .... .30 .14 .04
☐ 219 Tom Murphy .... .30 .14 .04
☐ 220 Manny Sanguillen .... .40 .18 .05
☐ 221 Jim Todd .... .30 .14 .04
☐ 222 Wayne Garrett .... .30 .14 .04
☐ 223 Ollie Brown .... .30 .14 .04
☐ 224 Jim York .... .30 .14 .04
☐ 225 Roy White .... .40 .18 .05
☐ 226 Jim Sundberg .... .40 .18 .05
☐ 227 Oscar Zamora .... .30 .14 .04
☐ 228 John Hale .... .30 .14 .04
☐ 229 Jerry Remy .... .30 .14 .04
☐ 230 Carl Yastrzemski .... 6.00 2.70 .75
☐ 231 Tom House .... .30 .14 .04
☐ 232 Frank Duffy .... .30 .14 .04
☐ 233 Grant Jackson .... .30 .14 .04

☐ 234 Mike Sadek .30 .14 .04
☐ 235 Bert Blyleven 1.50 .65 .19
☐ 236 Kansas City Royals 1.50 .30 .15
Team Card;
Whitey Herzog MG
(Checklist back)
☐ 237 Dave Hamilton .30 .14 .04
☐ 238 Larry Biittner .30 .14 .04
☐ 239 John Curtis .30 .14 .04
☐ 240 Pete Rose 14.00 6.25 1.75
☐ 241 Hector Torres .30 .14 .04
☐ 242 Dan Meyer .30 .14 .04
☐ 243 Jim Rooker .30 .14 .04
☐ 244 Bill Sharp .30 .14 .04
☐ 245 Felix Millan .30 .14 .04
☐ 246 Cesar Tovar .30 .14 .04
☐ 247 Terry Harmon .30 .14 .04
☐ 248 Dick Tidrow .30 .14 .04
☐ 249 Cliff Johnson .40 .18 .05
☐ 250 Fergie Jenkins 3.00 1.35 .40
☐ 251 Rick Monday .40 .18 .05
☐ 252 Tim Nordbrook .30 .14 .04
☐ 253 Bill Buckner .40 .18 .05
☐ 254 Rudy Meoli .30 .14 .04
☐ 255 Fritz Peterson .30 .14 .04
☐ 256 Rowland Office .30 .14 .04
☐ 257 Ross Grimsley .30 .14 .04
☐ 258 Nyls Nyman .30 .14 .04
☐ 259 Darrel Chaney .30 .14 .04
☐ 260 Steve Busby .30 .14 .04
☐ 261 Gary Thomasson .30 .14 .04
☐ 262 Checklist 133-264 1.50 .15 .05
☐ 263 Lyman Bostock 1.00 .45 .13
☐ 264 Steve Renko .30 .14 .04
☐ 265 Willie Davis .40 .18 .05
☐ 266 Alan Foster .30 .14 .04
☐ 267 Aurelio Rodriguez .30 .14 .04
☐ 268 Del Unser .30 .14 .04
☐ 269 Rick Austin .30 .14 .04
☐ 270 Willie Stargell 3.00 1.35 .40
☐ 271 Jim Lonborg .40 .18 .05
☐ 272 Rick Dempsey .40 .18 .05
☐ 273 Joe Niekro .40 .18 .05
☐ 274 Tommy Harper .40 .18 .05
☐ 275 Rick Manning .30 .14 .04
☐ 276 Mickey Scott .30 .14 .04
☐ 277 Chicago Cubs 1.50 .30 .15
Team Card;
Jim Marshall MG
(Checklist back)
☐ 278 Bernie Carbo .30 .14 .04
☐ 279 Roy Howell .30 .14 .04
☐ 280 Burt Hooton .40 .18 .05
☐ 281 Dave May .30 .14 .04
☐ 282 Dan Osborn .30 .14 .04
☐ 283 Merv Rettenmund .30 .14 .04
☐ 284 Steve Ontiveros .30 .14 .04
(Mike Schmidt in background)
☐ 285 Mike Cuellar .40 .18 .05
☐ 286 Jim Wohlford .30 .14 .04
☐ 287 Pete Mackanin .30 .14 .04
☐ 288 Bill Campbell .30 .14 .04
☐ 289 Enzo Hernandez .30 .14 .04
☐ 290 Ted Simmons 1.00 .45 .13
☐ 291 Ken Sanders .30 .14 .04
☐ 292 Leon Roberts .30 .14 .04
☐ 293 Bill Castro .30 .14 .04
☐ 294 Ed Kirkpatrick .30 .14 .04
☐ 295 Dave Cash .30 .14 .04
☐ 296 Pat Dobson .30 .14 .04
☐ 297 Roger Metzger .30 .14 .04
☐ 298 Dick Bosman .30 .14 .04
☐ 299 Champ Summers .30 .14 .04
☐ 300 Johnny Bench 10.00 4.50 1.25
☐ 301 Jackie Brown .30 .14 .04
☐ 302 Rick Miller .30 .14 .04
☐ 303 Steve Foucault .30 .14 .04
☐ 304 California Angels 1.50 .30 .15
Team Card;
Dick Williams MG
(Checklist back)
☐ 305 Andy Messersmith .40 .18 .05
☐ 306 Rod Gilbreath .30 .14 .04
☐ 307 Al Bumbry .40 .18 .05
☐ 308 Jim Barr .30 .14 .04
☐ 309 Bill Melton .30 .14 .04
☐ 310 Randy Jones .40 .18 .05
☐ 311 Cookie Rojas .40 .18 .05
☐ 312 Don Carrithers .30 .14 .04
☐ 313 Dan Ford .30 .14 .04
☐ 314 Ed Kranepool .30 .14 .04
☐ 315 Al Hrabosky .40 .18 .05
☐ 316 Robin Yount 45.00 20.00 5.75
☐ 317 John Candelaria 2.00 .90 .25
☐ 318 Bob Boone 1.00 .45 .13
☐ 319 Larry Gura .30 .14 .04
☐ 320 Willie Horton .40 .18 .05
☐ 321 Jose Cruz .40 .18 .05
☐ 322 Glenn Abbott .30 .14 .04
☐ 323 Rob Sperring .30 .14 .04
☐ 324 Jim Bibby .30 .14 .04
☐ 325 Tony Perez 2.00 .90 .25
☐ 326 Dick Pole .30 .14 .04
☐ 327 Dave Moates .30 .14 .04
☐ 328 Carl Morton .30 .14 .04
☐ 329 Joe Ferguson .30 .14 .04
☐ 330 Nolan Ryan 75.00 34.00 9.50
☐ 331 San Diego Padres 1.50 .30 .15
Team Card;
John McNamara MG
(Checklist back)
☐ 332 Charlie Williams .30 .14 .04
☐ 333 Bob Coluccio .30 .14 .04
☐ 334 Dennis Leonard .40 .18 .05
☐ 335 Bob Grich .40 .18 .05
☐ 336 Vic Albury .30 .14 .04
☐ 337 Bud Harrelson .40 .18 .05
☐ 338 Bob Bailey .30 .14 .04
☐ 339 John Denny .40 .18 .05
☐ 340 Jim Rice 5.00 2.30 .60
☐ 341 Lou Gehrig 8.00 3.60 1.00
All-Time 1B
☐ 342 Rogers Hornsby 3.00 1.35 .40
All-Time 2B
☐ 343 Pie Traynor 1.00 .45 .13
All-Time 3B
☐ 344 Honus Wagner 5.00 2.30 .60
All-Time SS
☐ 345 Babe Ruth 12.00 5.50 1.50
All-Time OF
☐ 346 Ty Cobb 8.00 3.60 1.00
All-Time OF
☐ 347 Ted Williams 10.00 4.50 1.25
All-Time OF
☐ 348 Mickey Cochrane 1.00 .45 .13
All-Time C
☐ 349 Walter Johnson 3.00 1.35 .40
All-Time RHP
☐ 350 Lefty Grove 1.00 .45 .13
All-Time LHP
☐ 351 Randy Hundley .30 .14 .04
☐ 352 Dave Giusti .30 .14 .04
☐ 353 Sixto Lezcano .40 .18 .05
☐ 354 Ron Blomberg .30 .14 .04
☐ 355 Steve Carlton 7.50 3.40 .95
☐ 356 Ted Martinez .30 .14 .04

☐ 357	Ken Forsch	.30	.14	.04
☐ 358	Buddy Bell	.40	.18	.05
☐ 359	Rick Reuschel	.40	.18	.05
☐ 360	Jeff Burroughs	.40	.18	.05
☐ 361	Detroit Tigers Team Card; Ralph Houk MG (Checklist back)	1.50	.30	.15
☐ 362	Will McEnaney	.40	.18	.05
☐ 363	Dave Collins	.75	.35	.09
☐ 364	Elias Sosa	.30	.14	.04
☐ 365	Carlton Fisk	10.00	4.50	1.25
☐ 366	Bobby Valentine	.30	.14	.04
☐ 367	Bruce Miller	.30	.14	.04
☐ 368	Wilbur Wood	.30	.14	.04
☐ 369	Frank White	.40	.18	.05
☐ 370	Ron Cey	.40	.18	.05
☐ 371	Elrod Hendricks	.30	.14	.04
☐ 372	Rick Baldwin	.30	.14	.04
☐ 373	Johnny Briggs	.30	.14	.04
☐ 374	Dan Warthen	.30	.14	.04
☐ 375	Ron Fairly	.30	.14	.04
☐ 376	Rich Hebner	.40	.18	.05
☐ 377	Mike Hegan	.30	.14	.04
☐ 378	Steve Stone	.40	.18	.05
☐ 379	Ken Boswell	.30	.14	.04
☐ 380	Bobby Bonds	1.75	.80	.22
☐ 381	Denny Doyle	.30	.14	.04
☐ 382	Matt Alexander	.30	.14	.04
☐ 383	John Ellis	.30	.14	.04
☐ 384	Philadelphia Phillies Team Card; Danny Ozark MG (Checklist back)	1.50	.30	.15
☐ 385	Mickey Lolich	.40	.18	.05
☐ 386	Ed Goodson	.30	.14	.04
☐ 387	Mike Miley	.30	.14	.04
☐ 388	Stan Perzanowski	.30	.14	.04
☐ 389	Glenn Adams	.30	.14	.04
☐ 390	Don Gullett	.40	.18	.05
☐ 391	Jerry Hairston	.30	.14	.04
☐ 392	Checklist 265-396	1.50	.15	.05
☐ 393	Paul Mitchell	.30	.14	.04
☐ 394	Fran Healy	.30	.14	.04
☐ 395	Jim Wynn	.40	.18	.05
☐ 396	Bill Lee	.30	.14	.04
☐ 397	Tim Foli	.30	.14	.04
☐ 398	Dave Tomlin	.30	.14	.04
☐ 399	Luis Melendez	.30	.14	.04
☐ 400	Rod Carew	5.00	2.30	.60
☐ 401	Ken Brett	.30	.14	.04
☐ 402	Don Money	.40	.18	.05
☐ 403	Geoff Zahn	.30	.14	.04
☐ 404	Enos Cabell	.30	.14	.04
☐ 405	Rollie Fingers	3.00	1.35	.40
☐ 406	Ed Herrmann	.30	.14	.04
☐ 407	Tom Underwood	.30	.14	.04
☐ 408	Charlie Spikes	.30	.14	.04
☐ 409	Dave Lemanczyk	.30	.14	.04
☐ 410	Ralph Garr	.40	.18	.05
☐ 411	Bill Singer	.30	.14	.04
☐ 412	Toby Harrah	.40	.18	.05
☐ 413	Pete Varney	.30	.14	.04
☐ 414	Wayne Garland	.30	.14	.04
☐ 415	Vada Pinson	.50	.23	.06
☐ 416	Tommy John	1.25	.55	.16
☐ 417	Gene Clines	.30	.14	.04
☐ 418	Jose Morales	.30	.14	.04
☐ 419	Reggie Cleveland	.30	.14	.04
☐ 420	Joe Morgan	6.00	2.70	.75
☐ 421	Oakland A's Team Card; (No MG on front; checklist back)	1.50	.30	.15
☐ 422	Johnny Grubb	.30	.14	.04
☐ 423	Ed Halicki	.30	.14	.04
☐ 424	Phil Roof	.30	.14	.04
☐ 425	Rennie Stennett	.30	.14	.04
☐ 426	Bob Forsch	.30	.14	.04
☐ 427	Kurt Bevacqua	.30	.14	.04
☐ 428	Jim Crawford	.30	.14	.04
☐ 429	Fred Stanley	.30	.14	.04
☐ 430	Jose Cardenal	.30	.14	.04
☐ 431	Dick Ruthven	.30	.14	.04
☐ 432	Tom Veryzer	.30	.14	.04
☐ 433	Rick Waits	.30	.14	.04
☐ 434	Morris Nettles	.30	.14	.04
☐ 435	Phil Niekro	2.50	1.15	.30
☐ 436	Bill Fahey	.30	.14	.04
☐ 437	Terry Forster	.30	.14	.04
☐ 438	Doug DeCinces	.30	.14	.04
☐ 439	Rick Rhoden	.40	.18	.05
☐ 440	John Mayberry	.40	.18	.05
☐ 441	Gary Carter	8.00	3.60	1.00
☐ 442	Hank Webb	.30	.14	.04
☐ 443	San Francisco Giants Team Card; (No MG on front; checklist back)	1.50	.30	.15
☐ 444	Gary Nolan	.40	.18	.05
☐ 445	Rico Petrocelli	.40	.18	.05
☐ 446	Larry Haney	.30	.14	.04
☐ 447	Gene Locklear	.30	.14	.04
☐ 448	Tom Johnson	.30	.14	.04
☐ 449	Bob Robertson	.30	.14	.04
☐ 450	Jim Palmer	6.50	2.90	.80
☐ 451	Buddy Bradford	.30	.14	.04
☐ 452	Tom Hausman	.30	.14	.04
☐ 453	Lou Piniella	1.00	.45	.13
☐ 454	Tom Griffin	.30	.14	.04
☐ 455	Dick Allen	.75	.35	.09
☐ 456	Joe Coleman	.30	.14	.04
☐ 457	Ed Crosby	.30	.14	.04
☐ 458	Earl Williams	.30	.14	.04
☐ 459	Jim Brewer	.30	.14	.04
☐ 460	Cesar Cedeno	.40	.18	.05
☐ 461	NL and AL Champs Reds sweep Bucs, Bosox surprise A's	.75	.35	.09
☐ 462	'75 World Series Reds Champs	.75	.35	.09
☐ 463	Steve Hargan	.30	.14	.04
☐ 464	Ken Henderson	.30	.14	.04
☐ 465	Mike Marshall	.40	.18	.05
☐ 466	Bob Stinson	.30	.14	.04
☐ 467	Woodie Fryman	.30	.14	.04
☐ 468	Jesus Alou	.30	.14	.04
☐ 469	Rawly Eastwick	.40	.18	.05
☐ 470	Bobby Murcer	.30	.14	.04
☐ 471	Jim Burton	.30	.14	.04
☐ 472	Bob Davis	.30	.14	.04
☐ 473	Paul Blair	.40	.18	.05
☐ 474	Ray Corbin	.30	.14	.04
☐ 475	Joe Rudi	.40	.18	.05
☐ 476	Bob Moose	.30	.14	.04
☐ 477	Cleveland Indians Team Card; Frank Robinson MG (Checklist back)	1.50	.30	.15
☐ 478	Lynn McGlothen	.30	.14	.04
☐ 479	Bobby Mitchell	.30	.14	.04
☐ 480	Mike Schmidt	25.00	11.50	3.10
☐ 481	Rudy May	.30	.14	.04
☐ 482	Tim Hosley	.30	.14	.04
☐ 483	Mickey Stanley	.30	.14	.04
☐ 484	Eric Raich	.30	.14	.04

	No.	Card			
☐	485	Mike Hargrove	.40	.18	.05
☐	486	Bruce Dal Canton	.30	.14	.04
☐	487	Leron Lee	.30	.14	.04
☐	488	Claude Osteen	.40	.18	.05
☐	489	Skip Jutze	.30	.14	.04
☐	490	Frank Tanana	1.00	.45	.13
☐	491	Terry Crowley	.30	.14	.04
☐	492	Marty Pattin	.30	.14	.04
☐	493	Derrel Thomas	.30	.14	.04
☐	494	Craig Swan	.40	.18	.05
☐	495	Nate Colbert	.30	.14	.04
☐	496	Juan Beniquez	.30	.14	.04
☐	497	Joe McIntosh	.30	.14	.04
☐	498	Glenn Borgmann	.30	.14	.04
☐	499	Mario Guerrero	.30	.14	.04
☐	500	Reggie Jackson	18.00	8.00	2.30
☐	501	Billy Champion	.30	.14	.04
☐	502	Tim McCarver	.40	.18	.05
☐	503	Elliott Maddox	.30	.14	.04
☐	504	Pittsburgh Pirates	1.50	.30	.15
		Team Card;			
		Danny Murtaugh MG			
		(Checklist back)			
☐	505	Mark Belanger	.40	.18	.05
☐	506	George Mitterwald	.30	.14	.04
☐	507	Ray Bare	.30	.14	.04
☐	508	Duane Kuiper	.30	.14	.04
☐	509	Bill Hands	.30	.14	.04
☐	510	Amos Otis	.40	.18	.05
☐	511	Jamie Easterley	.30	.14	.04
☐	512	Ellie Rodriguez	.30	.14	.04
☐	513	Bart Johnson	.30	.14	.04
☐	514	Dan Driessen	.40	.18	.05
☐	515	Steve Yeager	.40	.18	.05
☐	516	Wayne Granger	.30	.14	.04
☐	517	John Milner	.30	.14	.04
☐	518	Doug Flynn	.30	.14	.04
☐	519	Steve Brye	.30	.14	.04
☐	520	Willie McCovey	4.00	1.80	.50
☐	521	Jim Colborn	.30	.14	.04
☐	522	Ted Sizemore	.30	.14	.04
☐	523	Bob Montgomery	.30	.14	.04
☐	524	Pete Falcone	.30	.14	.04
☐	525	Billy Williams	3.00	1.35	.40
☐	526	Checklist 397-528	1.50	.15	.05
☐	527	Mike Anderson	.30	.14	.04
☐	528	Dock Ellis	.30	.14	.04
☐	529	Deron Johnson	.30	.14	.04
☐	530	Don Sutton	2.50	1.15	.30
☐	531	New York Mets	1.50	.30	.15
		Team Card;			
		Joe Frazier MG			
		(Checklist back)			
☐	532	Milt May	.30	.14	.04
☐	533	Lee Richard	.30	.14	.04
☐	534	Stan Bahnsen	.30	.14	.04
☐	535	Dave Nelson	.30	.14	.04
☐	536	Mike Thompson	.30	.14	.04
☐	537	Tony Muser	.30	.14	.04
☐	538	Pat Darcy	.30	.14	.04
☐	539	John Balaz	.30	.14	.04
☐	540	Bill Freehan	.40	.18	.05
☐	541	Steve Mingori	.30	.14	.04
☐	542	Keith Hernandez	1.75	.80	.22
☐	543	Wayne Twitchell	.30	.14	.04
☐	544	Pepe Frias	.30	.14	.04
☐	545	Sparky Lyle	.30	.14	.04
☐	546	Dave Rosello	.30	.14	.04
☐	547	Roric Harrison	.30	.14	.04
☐	548	Manny Mota	.40	.18	.05
☐	549	Randy Tate	.30	.14	.04
☐	550	Hank Aaron	24.00	11.00	3.00
☐	551	Jerry DaVanon	.30	.14	.04
☐	552	Terry Humphrey	.30	.14	.04
☐	553	Randy Moffitt	.30	.14	.04
☐	554	Ray Fosse	.30	.14	.04
☐	555	Dyar Miller	.30	.14	.04
☐	556	Minnesota Twins	1.50	.30	.15
		Team Card;			
		Gene Mauch MG			
		(Checklist back)			
☐	557	Dan Spillner	.30	.14	.04
☐	558	Clarence Gaston	.40	.18	.05
☐	559	Clyde Wright	.30	.14	.04
☐	560	Jorge Orta	.30	.14	.04
☐	561	Tom Carroll	.30	.14	.04
☐	562	Adrian Garrett	.30	.14	.04
☐	563	Larry Demery	.30	.14	.04
☐	564	Bubble Gum Champ	.75	.35	.09
		Kurt Bevacqua			
☐	565	Tug McGraw	.40	.18	.05
☐	566	Ken McMullen	.30	.14	.04
☐	567	George Stone	.30	.14	.04
☐	568	Rob Andrews	.30	.14	.04
☐	569	Nelson Briles	.40	.18	.05
☐	570	George Hendrick	.40	.18	.05
☐	571	Don DeMola	.30	.14	.04
☐	572	Rich Coggins	.30	.14	.04
☐	573	Bill Travers	.30	.14	.04
☐	574	Don Kessinger	.40	.18	.05
☐	575	Dwight Evans	2.00	.90	.25
☐	576	Maximino Leon	.30	.14	.04
☐	577	Marc Hill	.30	.14	.04
☐	578	Ted Kubiak	.30	.14	.04
☐	579	Clay Kirby	.30	.14	.04
☐	580	Bert Campaneris	.40	.18	.05
☐	581	St. Louis Cardinals	1.50	.30	.15
		Team Card;			
		Red Schoendienst MG			
		(Checklist back)			
☐	582	Mike Kekich	.30	.14	.04
☐	583	Tommy Helms	.30	.14	.04
☐	584	Stan Wall	.30	.14	.04
☐	585	Joe Torre	.60	.25	.08
☐	586	Ron Schueler	.30	.14	.04
☐	587	Leo Cardenas	.30	.14	.04
☐	588	Kevin Kobel	.30	.14	.04
☐	589	Rookie Pitchers	1.75	.80	.22
		Santo Alcala			
		Mike Flanagan			
		Joe Pactwa			
		Pablo Torrealba			
☐	590	Rookie Outfielders	.75	.35	.09
		Henry Cruz			
		Chet Lemon			
		Ellis Valentine			
		Terry Whitfield			
☐	591	Rookie Pitchers	.40	.18	.05
		Steve Grilli			
		Craig Mitchell			
		Jose Sosa			
		George Throop			
☐	592	Rookie Infielders	7.00	3.10	.85
		Willie Randolph			
		Dave McKay			
		Jerry Royster			
		Roy Staiger			
☐	593	Rookie Pitchers	.40	.18	.05
		Larry Anderson			
		Ken Crosby			
		Mark Littell			
		Butch Metzger			
☐	594	Rookie Catchers/OF	.40	.18	.05
		Andy Merchant			
		Ed Ott			
		Royle Stillman			

Jerry White
☐ 595 Rookie Pitchers .... .40 .18 .05
Art DeFillipis
Randy Lerch
Sid Monge
Steve Barr
☐ 596 Rookie Infielders .... .40 .18 .05
Craig Reynolds
Lamar Johnson
Johnnie LeMaster
Jerry Manuel
☐ 597 Rookie Pitchers .... .40 .18 .05
Don Aase
Jack Kucek
Frank LaCorte
Mike Pazik
☐ 598 Rookie Outfielders .... .40 .18 .05
Hector Cruz
Jamie Quirk
Jerry Turner
Joe Wallis
☐ 599 Rookie Pitchers .... 7.00 3.10 .85
Rob Dressler
Ron Guidry
Bob McClure
Pat Zachry
☐ 600 Tom Seaver 9.00 4.00 1.15
☐ 601 Ken Rudolph .... .30 .14 .04
☐ 602 Doug Konieczny .... .30 .14 .04
☐ 603 Jim Holt .... .30 .14 .04
☐ 604 Joe Lovitto .... .30 .14 .04
☐ 605 Al Downing .... .30 .14 .04
☐ 606 Milwaukee Brewers .... 1.50 .30 .15
Team Card;
Alex Grammas MG
(Checklist back)
☐ 607 Rich Hinton .... .30 .14 .04
☐ 608 Vic Correll .... .30 .14 .04
☐ 609 Fred Norman .... .40 .18 .05
☐ 610 Greg Luzinski .... .30 .14 .04
☐ 611 Rich Folkers .... .30 .14 .04
☐ 612 Joe Lahoud .... .30 .14 .04
☐ 613 Tim Johnson .... .30 .14 .04
☐ 614 Fernando Arroyo .... .30 .14 .04
☐ 615 Mike Cubbage .... .30 .14 .04
☐ 616 Buck Martinez .... .30 .14 .04
☐ 617 Darold Knowles .... .30 .14 .04
☐ 618 Jack Brohamer .... .30 .14 .04
☐ 619 Bill Butler .... .30 .14 .04
☐ 620 Al Oliver .... .40 .18 .05
☐ 621 Tom Hall .... .30 .14 .04
☐ 622 Rick Auerbach .... .30 .14 .04
☐ 623 Bob Allietta .... .30 .14 .04
☐ 624 Tony Taylor .... .30 .14 .04
☐ 625 J.R. Richard .... .40 .18 .05
☐ 626 Bob Sheldon .... .30 .14 .04
☐ 627 Bill Plummer .... .30 .14 .04
☐ 628 John D'Acquisto .... .30 .14 .04
☐ 629 Sandy Alomar .... .40 .18 .05
☐ 630 Chris Speier .... .30 .14 .04
☐ 631 Atlanta Braves .... 1.50 .30 .15
Team Card;
Dave Bristol MG
(Checklist back)
☐ 632 Rogelio Moret .... .30 .14 .04
☐ 633 John Stearns .... .30 .14 .04
☐ 634 Larry Christenson .... .30 .14 .04
☐ 635 Jim Fregosi .... .40 .18 .05
☐ 636 Joe Decker .... .30 .14 .04
☐ 637 Bruce Bochte .... .30 .14 .04
☐ 638 Doyle Alexander .... .40 .18 .05
☐ 639 Fred Kendall .... .30 .14 .04
☐ 640 Bill Madlock .... .75 .35 .09
☐ 641 Tom Paciorek .... .40 .18 .05
☐ 642 Dennis Blair .... .30 .14 .04
☐ 643 Checklist 529-660 ...... 1.50 .15 .05
☐ 644 Tom Bradley .... .30 .14 .04
☐ 645 Darrell Porter .... .40 .18 .05
☐ 646 John Lowenstein .... .30 .14 .04
☐ 647 Ramon Hernandez .... .30 .14 .04
☐ 648 Al Cowens .... .30 .14 .04
☐ 649 Dave Roberts .... .30 .14 .04
☐ 650 Thurman Munson ...... 6.00 2.70 .75
☐ 651 John Odom .... .30 .14 .04
☐ 652 Ed Armbrister .... .30 .14 .04
☐ 653 Mike Norris .... .30 .14 .04
☐ 654 Doug Griffin .... .30 .14 .04
☐ 655 Mike Vail .... .30 .14 .04
☐ 656 Chicago White Sox ..... 1.50 .30 .15
Team Card;
Chuck Tanner MG
(Checklist back)
☐ 657 Roy Smalley .... .30 .14 .04
☐ 658 Jerry Johnson .... .30 .14 .04
☐ 659 Ben Oglivie .... .40 .18 .05
☐ 660 Dave Lopes .... .75 .14 .04

1976 Topps Traded

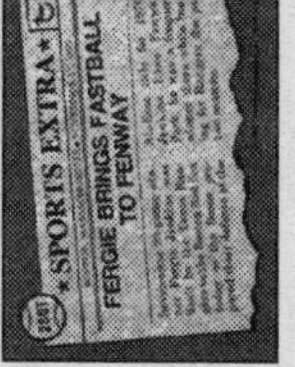

The cards in this 44-card set measure 2 1/2" by 3 1/2". The 1976 Topps Traded set contains 43 players and one unnumbered checklist card. The individuals pictured were traded after the Topps regular set was printed. A "Sports Extra" heading design is found on each picture and is also used to introduce the biographical section of the reverse. Each card is numbered according to the player's regular 1976 card with the addition of "T" to indicate his new status. As in 1974, the cards were inserted in wax packs toward the end of the production run. Because they were produced in large quantities, they are no scarcer than the basic cards.

	NRMT	VG-E	GOOD
COMPLETE SET (44)	15.00	6.75	1.90
COMMON CARD	.30	.14	.04

☐ 27T Ed Figueroa .... .30 .14 .04
☐ 28T Dusty Baker .... 1.00 .45 .13
☐ 44T Doug Rader .... .50 .23 .06
☐ 58T Ron Reed .... .30 .14 .04
☐ 74T Oscar Gamble .... .75 .35 .09
☐ 80T Jim Kaat .... .75 .35 .09
☐ 83T Jim Spencer .... .30 .14 .04

☐ 85T Mickey Rivers	.50	.23	.06
☐ 99T Lee Lacy	.30	.14	.04
☐ 120T Rusty Staub	.50	.23	.06
☐ 127T Larvell Blanks	.30	.14	.04
☐ 146T George Medich	.30	.14	.04
☐ 158T Ken Reitz	.30	.14	.04
☐ 208T Mike Lum	.30	.14	.04
☐ 211T Clay Carroll	.30	.14	.04
☐ 231T Tom House	.30	.14	.04
☐ 250T Fergie Jenkins	3.00	1.35	.40
☐ 259T Darrel Chaney	.30	.14	.04
☐ 292T Leon Roberts	.30	.14	.04
☐ 296T Pat Dobson	.30	.14	.04
☐ 309T Bill Melton	.30	.14	.04
☐ 338T Bob Bailey	.30	.14	.04
☐ 380T Bobby Bonds	1.50	.65	.19
☐ 383T John Ellis	.30	.14	.04
☐ 385T Mickey Lolich	.30	.14	.04
☐ 401T Ken Brett	.30	.14	.04
☐ 410T Ralph Garr	.50	.23	.06
☐ 411T Bill Singer	.30	.14	.04
☐ 428T Jim Crawford	.30	.14	.04
☐ 434T Morris Nettles	.30	.14	.04
☐ 464T Ken Henderson	.30	.14	.04
☐ 497T Joe McIntosh	.30	.14	.04
☐ 524T Pete Falcone	.30	.14	.04
☐ 527T Mike Anderson	.30	.14	.04
☐ 528T Dock Ellis	.30	.14	.04
☐ 532T Milt May	.30	.14	.04
☐ 554T Ray Fosse	.30	.14	.04
☐ 579T Clay Kirby	.30	.14	.04
☐ 583T Tommy Helms	.30	.14	.04
☐ 592T Willie Randolph	4.50	2.00	.55
☐ 618T Jack Brohamer	.30	.14	.04
☐ 632T Rogelio Moret	.30	.14	.04
☐ 649T Dave Roberts	.30	.14	.04
☐ NNO Traded Checklist	1.25	.14	.04

1977 Topps

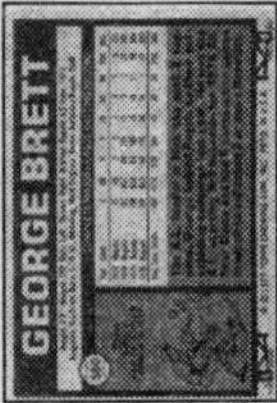

The cards in this 660-card set measure 2 1/2" by 3 1/2". In 1977 for the fifth consecutive year, Topps produced a 660-card baseball set. The player's name, team affiliation, and his position are compactly arranged over the picture area and a facsimile autograph appears on the photo. Team cards feature a checklist of that team's players in the set and a small picture of the manager on the front of the card. Appearing for the first time are the series "Brothers" (631-634) and "Turn Back the Clock" (433-437). Other subseries in the set are League Leaders (1-8), Record Breakers (231-234), Playoffs cards (276-277), World Series cards (411-413), and Rookie Prospects (472-479 and 487-494). The following players' regular issue cards are explicitly denoted as All-Stars, 30, 70, 100, 120, 170, 210, 240, 265, 301, 347, 400, 420, 450, 500, 521, 550, 560, and 580. The key cards in the set are the Rookie Cards of Dale Murphy (476) and Andre Dawson (473). Other notable Rookie Cards in the set include Jack Clark, Dennis Martinez, and Bruce Sutter. Cards numbered 23 or lower, that feature Yankees and do not follow the numbering checklisted below, are not necessarily error cards. They are undoubtedly Burger King cards, a separate set with its own pricing and mass distribution. Burger King cards are indistinguishable from the corresponding Topps cards except for the card numbering difference and the fact that Burger King cards do not have a printing sheet designation (such as A through F like the regular Topps) anywhere on the card back in very small print. There was an aluminum version of the Dale Murphy rookie card number 476 produced (legally) in the early '80s; proceeds from the sales (originally priced at 10.00) of this "card" went to the Huntington's Disease Foundation.

	NRMT-MT	EXC	G-VG
COMPLETE SET (660)	400.00	180.00	50.00
COMMON CARD (1-660)	.25	.11	.03
☐ 1 Batting Leaders George Brett Bill Madlock	6.50	1.65	.50
☐ 2 Home Run Leaders Graig Nettles Mike Schmidt	1.75	.80	.22
☐ 3 RBI Leaders Lee May George Foster	.50	.23	.06
☐ 4 Stolen Base Leaders Bill North Dave Lopes	.50	.23	.06
☐ 5 Victory Leaders Jim Palmer Randy Jones	.75	.35	.09
☐ 6 Strikeout Leaders Nolan Ryan Tom Seaver	15.00	6.75	1.90
☐ 7 ERA Leaders Mark Fidrych John Denny	.50	.23	.06
☐ 8 Leading Firemen Bill Campbell Rawly Eastwick	.50	.23	.06
☐ 9 Doug Rader	.25	.11	.03
☐ 10 Reggie Jackson	14.00	6.25	1.75
☐ 11 Rob Dressler	.25	.11	.03
☐ 12 Larry Haney	.25	.11	.03
☐ 13 Luis Gomez	.25	.11	.03
☐ 14 Tommy Smith	.25	.11	.03
☐ 15 Don Gullett	.35	.16	.04
☐ 16 Bob Jones	.25	.11	.03
☐ 17 Steve Stone	.35	.16	.04
☐ 18 Indians Team/Mgr. Frank Robinson (Checklist back)	1.25	.25	.13
☐ 19 John D'Acquisto	.25	.11	.03
☐ 20 Graig Nettles	.75	.35	.09

☐	21 Ken Forsch	.25	.11	.03
☐	22 Bill Freehan	.35	.16	.04
☐	23 Dan Driessen	.25	.11	.03
☐	24 Carl Morton	.25	.11	.03
☐	25 Dwight Evans	1.50	.65	.19
☐	26 Ray Sadecki	.25	.11	.03
☐	27 Bill Buckner	.35	.16	.04
☐	28 Woodie Fryman	.25	.11	.03
☐	29 Bucky Dent	.25	.11	.03
☐	30 Greg Luzinski	.50	.23	.06
☐	31 Jim Todd	.25	.11	.03
☐	32 Checklist 1-132	1.25	.13	.04
☐	33 Wayne Garland	.25	.11	.03
☐	34 Angels Team/Mgr. Norm Sherry (Checklist back)	1.25	.25	.13
☐	35 Rennie Stennett	.25	.11	.03
☐	36 John Ellis	.25	.11	.03
☐	37 Steve Hargan	.25	.11	.03
☐	38 Craig Kusick	.25	.11	.03
☐	39 Tom Griffin	.25	.11	.03
☐	40 Bobby Murcer	.35	.16	.04
☐	41 Jim Kern	.25	.11	.03
☐	42 Jose Cruz	.35	.16	.04
☐	43 Ray Bare	.25	.11	.03
☐	44 Bud Harrelson	.35	.16	.04
☐	45 Rawly Eastwick	.25	.11	.03
☐	46 Buck Martinez	.25	.11	.03
☐	47 Lynn McGlothen	.25	.11	.03
☐	48 Tom Paciorek	.35	.16	.04
☐	49 Grant Jackson	.25	.11	.03
☐	50 Ron Cey	.25	.11	.03
☐	51 Brewers Team/Mgr. Alex Grammas (Checklist back)	1.25	.25	.13
☐	52 Ellis Valentine	.25	.11	.03
☐	53 Paul Mitchell	.25	.11	.03
☐	54 Sandy Alomar	.35	.16	.04
☐	55 Jeff Burroughs	.35	.16	.04
☐	56 Rudy May	.25	.11	.03
☐	57 Marc Hill	.25	.11	.03
☐	58 Chet Lemon	.35	.16	.04
☐	59 Larry Christenson	.25	.11	.03
☐	60 Jim Rice	4.00	1.80	.50
☐	61 Manny Sanguillen	.35	.16	.04
☐	62 Eric Raich	.25	.11	.03
☐	63 Tito Fuentes	.25	.11	.03
☐	64 Larry Biittner	.25	.11	.03
☐	65 Skip Lockwood	.25	.11	.03
☐	66 Roy Smalley	.35	.16	.04
☐	67 Joaquin Andujar	.50	.23	.06
☐	68 Bruce Bochte	.25	.11	.03
☐	69 Jim Crawford	.25	.11	.03
☐	70 Johnny Bench	8.00	3.60	1.00
☐	71 Dock Ellis	.25	.11	.03
☐	72 Mike Anderson	.25	.11	.03
☐	73 Charlie Williams	.25	.11	.03
☐	74 A's Team/Mgr. Jack McKeon (Checklist back)	1.25	.25	.13
☐	75 Dennis Leonard	.35	.16	.04
☐	76 Tim Foli	.25	.11	.03
☐	77 Dyar Miller	.25	.11	.03
☐	78 Bob Davis	.25	.11	.03
☐	79 Don Money	.35	.16	.04
☐	80 Andy Messersmith	.35	.16	.04
☐	81 Juan Beniquez	.25	.11	.03
☐	82 Jim Rooker	.25	.11	.03
☐	83 Kevin Bell	.25	.11	.03
☐	84 Ollie Brown	.25	.11	.03
☐	85 Duane Kuiper	.25	.11	.03
☐	86 Pat Zachry	.25	.11	.03
☐	87 Glenn Borgmann	.25	.11	.03
☐	88 Stan Wall	.25	.11	.03
☐	89 Butch Hobson	1.00	.45	.13
☐	90 Cesar Cedeno	.35	.16	.04
☐	91 John Verhoeven	.25	.11	.03
☐	92 Dave Rosello	.25	.11	.03
☐	93 Tom Poquette	.25	.11	.03
☐	94 Craig Swan	.25	.11	.03
☐	95 Keith Hernandez	1.00	.45	.13
☐	96 Lou Piniella	.75	.35	.09
☐	97 Dave Heaverlo	.25	.11	.03
☐	98 Milt May	.25	.11	.03
☐	99 Tom Hausman	.25	.11	.03
☐	100 Joe Morgan	5.00	2.30	.60
☐	101 Dick Bosman	.25	.11	.03
☐	102 Jose Morales	.25	.11	.03
☐	103 Mike Bacsik	.25	.11	.03
☐	104 Omar Moreno	.35	.16	.04
☐	105 Steve Yeager	.35	.16	.04
☐	106 Mike Flanagan	.25	.11	.03
☐	107 Bill Melton	.25	.11	.03
☐	108 Alan Foster	.25	.11	.03
☐	109 Jorge Orta	.25	.11	.03
☐	110 Steve Carlton	6.50	2.90	.80
☐	111 Rico Petrocelli	.35	.16	.04
☐	112 Bill Greif	.25	.11	.03
☐	113 Blue Jays Leaders Roy Hartsfield MG Don Leppert CO Bob Miller CO Jackie Moore CO Harry Warner CO (Checklist back)	1.25	.25	.13
☐	114 Bruce Dal Canton	.25	.11	.03
☐	115 Rick Manning	.25	.11	.03
☐	116 Joe Niekro	.35	.16	.04
☐	117 Frank White	.35	.16	.04
☐	118 Rick Jones	.25	.11	.03
☐	119 John Stearns	.25	.11	.03
☐	120 Rod Carew	4.50	2.00	.55
☐	121 Gary Nolan	.25	.11	.03
☐	122 Ben Oglivie	.35	.16	.04
☐	123 Fred Stanley	.25	.11	.03
☐	124 George Mitterwald	.25	.11	.03
☐	125 Bill Travers	.25	.11	.03
☐	126 Rod Gilbreath	.25	.11	.03
☐	127 Ron Fairly	.25	.11	.03
☐	128 Tommy John	1.00	.45	.13
☐	129 Mike Sadek	.25	.11	.03
☐	130 Al Oliver	.25	.11	.03
☐	131 Orlando Ramirez	.25	.11	.03
☐	132 Chip Lang	.25	.11	.03
☐	133 Ralph Garr	.35	.16	.04
☐	134 Padres Team/Mgr. John McNamara (Checklist back)	1.25	.25	.13
☐	135 Mark Belanger	.35	.16	.04
☐	136 Jerry Mumphrey	.25	.11	.03
☐	137 Jeff Terpko	.25	.11	.03
☐	138 Bob Stinson	.25	.11	.03
☐	139 Fred Norman	.25	.11	.03
☐	140 Mike Schmidt	15.00	6.75	1.90
☐	141 Mark Littell	.25	.11	.03
☐	142 Steve Dillard	.25	.11	.03
☐	143 Ed Herrmann	.25	.11	.03
☐	144 Bruce Sutter	4.00	1.80	.50
☐	145 Tom Veryzer	.25	.11	.03
☐	146 Dusty Baker	.50	.23	.06
☐	147 Jackie Brown	.25	.11	.03
☐	148 Fran Healy	.25	.11	.03
☐	149 Mike Cubbage	.25	.11	.03
☐	150 Tom Seaver	8.00	3.60	1.00
☐	151 Johnny LeMaster	.25	.11	.03
☐	152 Gaylord Perry	2.50	1.15	.30

	No.	Card			
☐	153	Ron Jackson	.25	.11	.03
☐	154	Dave Giusti	.25	.11	.03
☐	155	Joe Rudi	.35	.16	.04
☐	156	Pete Mackanin	.25	.11	.03
☐	157	Ken Brett	.25	.11	.03
☐	158	Ted Kubiak	.25	.11	.03
☐	159	Bernie Carbo	.25	.11	.03
☐	160	Will McEnaney	.25	.11	.03
☐	161	Garry Templeton	1.00	.45	.13
☐	162	Mike Cuellar	.35	.16	.04
☐	163	Dave Hilton	.25	.11	.03
☐	164	Tug McGraw	.35	.16	.04
☐	165	Jim Wynn	.35	.16	.04
☐	166	Bill Campbell	.25	.11	.03
☐	167	Rich Hebner	.35	.16	.04
☐	168	Charlie Spikes	.25	.11	.03
☐	169	Darold Knowles	.25	.11	.03
☐	170	Thurman Munson	5.00	2.30	.60
☐	171	Ken Sanders	.25	.11	.03
☐	172	John Milner	.25	.11	.03
☐	173	Chuck Scrivener	.25	.11	.03
☐	174	Nelson Briles	.35	.16	.04
☐	175	Butch Wynegar	.25	.11	.03
☐	176	Bob Robertson	.25	.11	.03
☐	177	Bart Johnson	.25	.11	.03
☐	178	Bombo Rivera	.25	.11	.03
☐	179	Paul Hartzell	.25	.11	.03
☐	180	Dave Lopes	.35	.16	.04
☐	181	Ken McMullen	.25	.11	.03
☐	182	Dan Spillner	.25	.11	.03
☐	183	Cardinals Team/Mgr. Vern Rapp (Checklist back)	1.25	.25	.13
☐	184	Bo McLaughlin	.25	.11	.03
☐	185	Sixto Lezcano	.25	.11	.03
☐	186	Doug Flynn	.25	.11	.03
☐	187	Dick Pole	.25	.11	.03
☐	188	Bob Tolan	.25	.11	.03
☐	189	Rick Dempsey	.35	.16	.04
☐	190	Ray Burris	.25	.11	.03
☐	191	Doug Griffin	.25	.11	.03
☐	192	Clarence Gaston	.35	.16	.04
☐	193	Larry Gura	.25	.11	.03
☐	194	Gary Matthews	.35	.16	.04
☐	195	Ed Figueroa	.25	.11	.03
☐	196	Len Randle	.25	.11	.03
☐	197	Ed Ott	.25	.11	.03
☐	198	Wilbur Wood	.25	.11	.03
☐	199	Pepe Frias	.25	.11	.03
☐	200	Frank Tanana	.75	.35	.09
☐	201	Ed Kranepool	.25	.11	.03
☐	202	Tom Johnson	.25	.11	.03
☐	203	Ed Armbrister	.25	.11	.03
☐	204	Jeff Newman	.25	.11	.03
☐	205	Pete Falcone	.25	.11	.03
☐	206	Boog Powell	.35	.16	.04
☐	207	Glenn Abbott	.25	.11	.03
☐	208	Checklist 133-264	1.25	.13	.04
☐	209	Rob Andrews	.25	.11	.03
☐	210	Fred Lynn	1.25	.55	.16
☐	211	Giants Team/Mgr. Joe Altobelli (Checklist back)	1.25	.25	.13
☐	212	Jim Mason	.25	.11	.03
☐	213	Maximino Leon	.25	.11	.03
☐	214	Darrell Porter	.35	.16	.04
☐	215	Butch Metzger	.25	.11	.03
☐	216	Doug DeCinces	.35	.16	.04
☐	217	Tom Underwood	.25	.11	.03
☐	218	John Wathan	.25	.11	.03
☐	219	Joe Coleman	.25	.11	.03
☐	220	Chris Chambliss	.35	.16	.04
☐	221	Bob Bailey	.25	.11	.03
☐	222	Francisco Barrios	.25	.11	.03
☐	223	Earl Williams	.25	.11	.03
☐	224	Rusty Torres	.25	.11	.03
☐	225	Bob Apodaca	.25	.11	.03
☐	226	Leroy Stanton	.35	.16	.04
☐	227	Joe Sambito	.25	.11	.03
☐	228	Twins Team/Mgr. Gene Mauch (Checklist back)	1.25	.25	.13
☐	229	Don Kessinger	.35	.16	.04
☐	230	Vida Blue	.35	.16	.04
☐	231	RB: George Brett Most cons. games with 3 or more hits	12.00	5.50	1.50
☐	232	RB: Minnie Minoso Oldest to hit safely	.50	.23	.06
☐	233	RB: Jose Morales, Most pinch-hits, season	.40	.18	.05
☐	234	RB: Nolan Ryan Most seasons, 300 or more strikeouts	18.00	8.00	2.30
☐	235	Cecil Cooper	.25	.11	.03
☐	236	Tom Buskey	.25	.11	.03
☐	237	Gene Clines	.25	.11	.03
☐	238	Tippy Martinez	.35	.16	.04
☐	239	Bill Plummer	.25	.11	.03
☐	240	Ron LeFlore	.35	.16	.04
☐	241	Dave Tomlin	.25	.11	.03
☐	242	Ken Henderson	.25	.11	.03
☐	243	Ron Reed	.25	.11	.03
☐	244	John Mayberry (Cartoon mentions T206 Wagner)	.50	.23	.06
☐	245	Rick Rhoden	.35	.16	.04
☐	246	Mike Vail	.25	.11	.03
☐	247	Chris Knapp	.25	.11	.03
☐	248	Wilbur Howard	.25	.11	.03
☐	249	Pete Redfern	.25	.11	.03
☐	250	Bill Madlock	.35	.16	.04
☐	251	Tony Muser	.25	.11	.03
☐	252	Dale Murray	.25	.11	.03
☐	253	John Hale	.25	.11	.03
☐	254	Doyle Alexander	.25	.11	.03
☐	255	George Scott	.35	.16	.04
☐	256	Joe Hoerner	.25	.11	.03
☐	257	Mike Miley	.25	.11	.03
☐	258	Luis Tiant	.35	.16	.04
☐	259	Mets Team/Mgr. Joe Frazier (Checklist back)	1.25	.25	.13
☐	260	J.R. Richard	.35	.16	.04
☐	261	Phil Garner	.35	.16	.04
☐	262	Al Cowens	.25	.11	.03
☐	263	Mike Marshall	.35	.16	.04
☐	264	Tom Hutton	.25	.11	.03
☐	265	Mark Fidrych	5.00	2.30	.60
☐	266	Derrel Thomas	.25	.11	.03
☐	267	Ray Fosse	.25	.11	.03
☐	268	Rick Sawyer	.25	.11	.03
☐	269	Joe Lis	.25	.11	.03
☐	270	Dave Parker	2.00	.90	.25
☐	271	Terry Forster	.25	.11	.03
☐	272	Lee Lacy	.25	.11	.03
☐	273	Eric Soderholm	.25	.11	.03
☐	274	Don Stanhouse	.25	.11	.03
☐	275	Mike Hargrove	.35	.16	.04
☐	276	AL Champs Chris Chambliss' homer decides it	.50	.23	.06
☐	277	NL Champs Reds sweep Phillies	2.00	.90	.25
☐	278	Danny Frisella	.25	.11	.03
☐	279	Joe Wallis	.25	.11	.03

	#	Player			
☐	280	Jim Hunter	3.00	1.35	.40
☐	281	Roy Staiger	.25	.11	.03
☐	282	Sid Monge	.25	.11	.03
☐	283	Jerry DaVanon	.25	.11	.03
☐	284	Mike Norris	.25	.11	.03
☐	285	Brooks Robinson	5.00	2.30	.60
☐	286	Johnny Grubb	.25	.11	.03
☐	287	Reds Team/Mgr. Sparky Anderson (Checklist back)	1.25	.25	.13
☐	288	Bob Montgomery	.25	.11	.03
☐	289	Gene Garber	.25	.11	.03
☐	290	Amos Otis	.35	.16	.04
☐	291	Jason Thompson	.25	.11	.03
☐	292	Rogelio Moret	.25	.11	.03
☐	293	Jack Brohamer	.25	.11	.03
☐	294	George Medich	.25	.11	.03
☐	295	Gary Carter	5.00	2.30	.60
☐	296	Don Hood	.25	.11	.03
☐	297	Ken Reitz	.25	.11	.03
☐	298	Charlie Hough	.75	.35	.09
☐	299	Otto Velez	.35	.16	.04
☐	300	Jerry Koosman	.35	.16	.04
☐	301	Toby Harrah	.35	.16	.04
☐	302	Mike Garman	.25	.11	.03
☐	303	Gene Tenace	.35	.16	.04
☐	304	Jim Hughes	.25	.11	.03
☐	305	Mickey Rivers	.35	.16	.04
☐	306	Rick Waits	.25	.11	.03
☐	307	Gary Sutherland	.25	.11	.03
☐	308	Gene Pentz	.25	.11	.03
☐	309	Red Sox Team/Mgr. Don Zimmer (Checklist back)	1.25	.25	.13
☐	310	Larry Bowa	.50	.23	.06
☐	311	Vern Ruhle	.25	.11	.03
☐	312	Rob Belloir	.25	.11	.03
☐	313	Paul Blair	.35	.16	.04
☐	314	Steve Mingori	.25	.11	.03
☐	315	Dave Chalk	.25	.11	.03
☐	316	Steve Rogers	.25	.11	.03
☐	317	Kurt Bevacqua	.25	.11	.03
☐	318	Duffy Dyer	.25	.11	.03
☐	319	Rich Gossage	1.25	.55	.16
☐	320	Ken Griffey	1.50	.65	.19
☐	321	Dave Goltz	.25	.11	.03
☐	322	Bill Russell	.35	.16	.04
☐	323	Larry Lintz	.25	.11	.03
☐	324	John Curtis	.25	.11	.03
☐	325	Mike Ivie	.25	.11	.03
☐	326	Jesse Jefferson	.25	.11	.03
☐	327	Astros Team/Mgr. Bill Virdon (Checklist back)	1.25	.25	.13
☐	328	Tommy Boggs	.25	.11	.03
☐	329	Ron Hodges	.25	.11	.03
☐	330	George Hendrick	.35	.16	.04
☐	331	Jim Colborn	.25	.11	.03
☐	332	Elliott Maddox	.25	.11	.03
☐	333	Paul Reuschel	.25	.11	.03
☐	334	Bill Stein	.25	.11	.03
☐	335	Bill Robinson	.35	.16	.04
☐	336	Denny Doyle	.25	.11	.03
☐	337	Ron Schueler	.25	.11	.03
☐	338	Dave Duncan	.25	.11	.03
☐	339	Adrian Devine	.25	.11	.03
☐	340	Hal McRae	.50	.23	.06
☐	341	Joe Kerrigan	.25	.11	.03
☐	342	Jerry Remy	.25	.11	.03
☐	343	Ed Halicki	.25	.11	.03
☐	344	Brian Downing	.35	.16	.04
☐	345	Reggie Smith	.35	.16	.04
☐	346	Bill Singer	.25	.11	.03
☐	347	George Foster	.75	.35	.09
☐	348	Brent Strom	.25	.11	.03
☐	349	Jim Holt	.25	.11	.03
☐	350	Larry Dierker	.25	.11	.03
☐	351	Jim Sundberg	.35	.16	.04
☐	352	Mike Phillips	.25	.11	.03
☐	353	Stan Thomas	.25	.11	.03
☐	354	Pirates Team/Mgr. Chuck Tanner (Checklist back)	1.25	.25	.13
☐	355	Lou Brock	4.00	1.80	.50
☐	356	Checklist 265-396	1.25	.13	.04
☐	357	Tim McCarver	.35	.16	.04
☐	358	Tom House	.25	.11	.03
☐	359	Willie Randolph	2.00	.90	.25
☐	360	Rick Monday	.35	.16	.04
☐	361	Eduardo Rodriguez	.25	.11	.03
☐	362	Tommy Davis	.35	.16	.04
☐	363	Dave Roberts	.25	.11	.03
☐	364	Vic Correll	.25	.11	.03
☐	365	Mike Torrez	.35	.16	.04
☐	366	Ted Sizemore	.25	.11	.03
☐	367	Dave Hamilton	.25	.11	.03
☐	368	Mike Jorgensen	.25	.11	.03
☐	369	Terry Humphrey	.25	.11	.03
☐	370	John Montefusco	.25	.11	.03
☐	371	Royals Team/Mgr. Whitey Herzog (Checklist back)	1.25	.25	.13
☐	372	Rich Folkers	.25	.11	.03
☐	373	Bert Campaneris	.35	.16	.04
☐	374	Kent Tekulve	.50	.23	.06
☐	375	Larry Hisle	.35	.16	.04
☐	376	Nino Espinosa	.25	.11	.03
☐	377	Dave McKay	.25	.11	.03
☐	378	Jim Umbarger	.25	.11	.03
☐	379	Larry Cox	.25	.11	.03
☐	380	Lee May	.35	.16	.04
☐	381	Bob Forsch	.25	.11	.03
☐	382	Charlie Moore	.25	.11	.03
☐	383	Stan Bahnsen	.25	.11	.03
☐	384	Darrel Chaney	.25	.11	.03
☐	385	Dave LaRoche	.25	.11	.03
☐	386	Manny Mota	.35	.16	.04
☐	387	Yankees Team/Mgr. Billy Martin (Checklist back)	1.75	.35	.18
☐	388	Terry Harmon	.25	.11	.03
☐	389	Ken Kravec	.25	.11	.03
☐	390	Dave Winfield	25.00	11.50	3.10
☐	391	Dan Warthen	.25	.11	.03
☐	392	Phil Roof	.25	.11	.03
☐	393	John Lowenstein	.25	.11	.03
☐	394	Bill Laxton	.25	.11	.03
☐	395	Manny Trillo	.25	.11	.03
☐	396	Tom Murphy	.25	.11	.03
☐	397	Larry Herndon	.25	.11	.03
☐	398	Tom Burgmeier	.25	.11	.03
☐	399	Bruce Boisclair	.25	.11	.03
☐	400	Steve Garvey	3.50	1.55	.45
☐	401	Mickey Scott	.25	.11	.03
☐	402	Tommy Helms	.25	.11	.03
☐	403	Tom Grieve	.35	.16	.04
☐	404	Eric Rasmussen	.25	.11	.03
☐	405	Claudell Washington	.35	.16	.04
☐	406	Tim Johnson	.25	.11	.03
☐	407	Dave Freisleben	.25	.11	.03
☐	408	Cesar Tovar	.25	.11	.03
☐	409	Pete Broberg	.25	.11	.03
☐	410	Willie Montanez	.25	.11	.03
☐	411	W.S. Games 1 and 2 Joe Morgan homers in opener;	1.75	.80	.22

Johnny Bench stars as
Reds take 2nd game
☐ 412 W.S. Games 3 and 4.. 1.75 .80 .22
Reds stop Yankees;
Johnny Bench's two
homers wrap it up
☐ 413 World Series Summary .50 .23 .06
Cincy wins 2nd
straight series
☐ 414 Tommy Harper............. .35 .16 .04
☐ 415 Jay Johnstone.............. .35 .16 .04
☐ 416 Chuck Hartenstein........ .25 .11 .03
☐ 417 Wayne Garrett.............. .25 .11 .03
☐ 418 White Sox Team/Mgr. 1.25 .25 .13
Bob Lemon
(Checklist back)
☐ 419 Steve Swisher............. .25 .11 .03
☐ 420 Rusty Staub................. .50 .23 .06
☐ 421 Doug Rau...................... .25 .11 .03
☐ 422 Freddie Patek.............. .35 .16 .04
☐ 423 Gary Lavelle................ .25 .11 .03
☐ 424 Steve Brye................... .25 .11 .03
☐ 425 Joe Torre...................... .35 .16 .04
☐ 426 Dick Drago.................. .25 .11 .03
☐ 427 Dave Rader.................. .25 .11 .03
☐ 428 Rangers Team/Mgr.... 1.25 .25 .13
Frank Lucchesi
(Checklist back)
☐ 429 Ken Boswell................. .25 .11 .03
☐ 430 Fergie Jenkins............ 2.50 1.15 .30
☐ 431 Dave Collins UER......... .35 .16 .04
(Photo actually
Bobby Jones)
☐ 432 Buzz Capra.................. .25 .11 .03
☐ 433 Nate Colbert TBC '72 ... .40 .18 .05
(5 HR, 13 RBI)
☐ 434 Carl Yastrzemski TBC. 1.50 .65 .19
'67 Triple Crown
☐ 435 Maury Wills TBC '62.... .40 .18 .05
104 steals
☐ 436 Bob Keegan TBC '57.... .40 .18 .05
Majors' only no-hitter
☐ 437 Ralph Kiner TBC '52..... .50 .23 .06
Leads NL in HR's
7th straight year
☐ 438 Marty Perez................. .25 .11 .03
☐ 439 Gorman Thomas.......... .35 .16 .04
☐ 440 Jon Matlack................ .25 .11 .03
☐ 441 Larvell Blanks .... .25 .11 .03
☐ 442 Braves Team/Mgr. ...... 1.25 .25 .13
Dave Bristol
(Checklist back)
☐ 443 Lamar Johnson............ .25 .11 .03
☐ 444 Wayne Twitchell.......... .25 .11 .03
☐ 445 Ken Singleton .... .35 .16 .04
☐ 446 Bill Bonham .... .25 .11 .03
☐ 447 Jerry Turner................ .25 .11 .03
☐ 448 Ellie Rodriguez............ .25 .11 .03
☐ 449 Al Fitzmorris .... .25 .11 .03
☐ 450 Pete Rose 10.00 4.50 1.25
☐ 451 Checklist 397-528...... 1.25 .13 .04
☐ 452 Mike Caldwell.............. .25 .11 .03
☐ 453 Pedro Garcia............... .25 .11 .03
☐ 454 Andy Etchebarren .... .25 .11 .03
☐ 455 Rick Wise..................... .25 .11 .03
☐ 456 Leon Roberts.............. .25 .11 .03
☐ 457 Steve Luebber............. .25 .11 .03
☐ 458 Leo Foster................... .25 .11 .03
☐ 459 Steve Foucault .... .25 .11 .03
☐ 460 Willie Stargell............ 2.50 1.15 .30
☐ 461 Dick Tidrow................. .25 .11 .03
☐ 462 Don Baylor................. 1.50 .65 .19
☐ 463 Jamie Quirk.................. .25 .11 .03
☐ 464 Randy Moffitt.............. .25 .11 .03
☐ 465 Rico Carty.................... .35 .16 .04
☐ 466 Fred Holdsworth .... .25 .11 .03
☐ 467 Phillies Team/Mgr...... 1.25 .25 .13
Danny Ozark
(Checklist back)
☐ 468 Ramon Hernandez .... .25 .11 .03
☐ 469 Pat Kelly...................... .25 .11 .03
☐ 470 Ted Simmons .... .25 .11 .03
☐ 471 Del Unser..................... .25 .11 .03
☐ 472 Rookie Pitchers............ .25 .11 .03
Don Aase
Bob McClure
Gil Patterson
Dave Wehrmeister
☐ 473 Rookie Outfielders ... 70.00 32.00 8.75
Andre Dawson
Gene Richards
John Scott
Denny Walling
☐ 474 Rookie Shortstops .... .25 .11 .03
Bob Bailor
Kiko Garcia
Craig Reynolds
Alex Taveras
☐ 475 Rookie Pitchers............ .35 .16 .04
Chris Batton
Rick Camp
Scott McGregor
Manny Sarmiento
☐ 476 Rookie Catchers....... 25.00 11.50 3.10
Gary Alexander
Rick Cerone
Dale Murphy
Kevin Pasley
☐ 477 Rookie Infielders.......... .35 .16 .04
Doug Ault
Rich Dauer
Orlando Gonzalez
Phil Mankowski
☐ 478 Rookie Pitchers............ .25 .11 .03
Jim Gideon
Leon Hooten
Dave Johnson
Mark Lemongello
☐ 479 Rookie Outfielders .... .35 .16 .04
Brian Asselstine
Wayne Gross
Sam Mejias
Alvis Woods
☐ 480 Carl Yastrzemski........ 5.00 2.30 .60
☐ 481 Roger Metzger............ .25 .11 .03
☐ 482 Tony Solaita................ .25 .11 .03
☐ 483 Richie Zisk.................. .25 .11 .03
☐ 484 Burt Hooton................. .35 .16 .04
☐ 485 Roy White.................... .35 .16 .04
☐ 486 Ed Bane........................ .25 .11 .03
☐ 487 Rookie Pitchers............ .25 .11 .03
Larry Anderson
Ed Glynn
Joe Henderson
Greg Terlecky
☐ 488 Rookie Outfielders ..... 5.00 2.30 .60
Jack Clark
Ruppert Jones
Lee Mazzilli
Dan Thomas
☐ 489 Rookie Pitchers............ .25 .11 .03
Len Barker
Randy Lerch
Greg Minton
Mike Overy
☐ 490 Rookie Shortstops .... .25 .11 .03

Billy Almon
Mickey Klutts
Tommy McMillan
Mark Wagner
☐ 491 Rookie Pitchers 9.00 4.00 1.15
Mike Dupree
Dennis Martinez
Craig Mitchell
Bob Sykes
☐ 492 Rookie Outfielders .... .75 .35 .09
Tony Armas
Steve Kemp
Carlos Lopez
Gary Woods
☐ 493 Rookie Pitchers .... .25 .11 .03
Mike Krukow
Jim Otten
Gary Wheelock
Mike Willis
☐ 494 Rookie Infielders .... 2.00 .90 .25
Juan Bernhardt
Mike Champion
Jim Gantner
Bump Wills
☐ 495 Al Hrabosky .... .25 .11 .03
☐ 496 Gary Thomasson .... .25 .11 .03
☐ 497 Clay Carroll .... .25 .11 .03
☐ 498 Sal Bando .... .35 .16 .04
☐ 499 Pablo Torrealba .... .25 .11 .03
☐ 500 Dave Kingman .... .35 .16 .04
☐ 501 Jim Bibby .... .25 .11 .03
☐ 502 Randy Hundley .... .25 .11 .03
☐ 503 Bill Lee .... .25 .11 .03
☐ 504 Dodgers Team/Mgr. .... 1.25 .25 .13
Tom Lasorda
(Checklist back)
☐ 505 Oscar Gamble .... .35 .16 .04
☐ 506 Steve Grilli .... .25 .11 .03
☐ 507 Mike Hegan .... .25 .11 .03
☐ 508 Dave Pagan .... .25 .11 .03
☐ 509 Cookie Rojas .... .35 .16 .04
☐ 510 John Candelaria .... .25 .11 .03
☐ 511 Bill Fahey .... .25 .11 .03
☐ 512 Jack Billingham .... .25 .11 .03
☐ 513 Jerry Terrell .... .25 .11 .03
☐ 514 Cliff Johnson .... .25 .11 .03
☐ 515 Chris Speier .... .25 .11 .03
☐ 516 Bake McBride .... .35 .16 .04
☐ 517 Pete Vuckovich .... .35 .16 .04
☐ 518 Cubs Team/Mgr. .... 1.25 .25 .13
Herman Franks
(Checklist back)
☐ 519 Don Kirkwood .... .25 .11 .03
☐ 520 Garry Maddox .... .25 .11 .03
☐ 521 Bob Grich .... .35 .16 .04
☐ 522 Enzo Hernandez .... .25 .11 .03
☐ 523 Rollie Fingers .... 2.50 1.15 .30
☐ 524 Rowland Office .... .25 .11 .03
☐ 525 Dennis Eckersley 8.00 3.60 1.00
☐ 526 Larry Parrish .... .35 .16 .04
☐ 527 Dan Meyer .... .35 .16 .04
☐ 528 Bill Castro .... .25 .11 .03
☐ 529 Jim Essian .... .25 .11 .03
☐ 530 Rick Reuschel .... .35 .16 .04
☐ 531 Lyman Bostock .... .35 .16 .04
☐ 532 Jim Willoughby .... .25 .11 .03
☐ 533 Mickey Stanley .... .25 .11 .03
☐ 534 Paul Splittorff .... .25 .11 .03
☐ 535 Cesar Geronimo .... .25 .11 .03
☐ 536 Vic Albury .... .25 .11 .03
☐ 537 Dave Roberts .... .25 .11 .03
☐ 538 Frank Taveras .... .25 .11 .03
☐ 539 Mike Wallace .... .25 .11 .03
☐ 540 Bob Watson .... .35 .16 .04
☐ 541 John Denny .... .35 .16 .04
☐ 542 Frank Duffy .... .25 .11 .03
☐ 543 Ron Blomberg .... .25 .11 .03
☐ 544 Gary Ross .... .25 .11 .03
☐ 545 Bob Boone .... .75 .35 .09
☐ 546 Orioles Team/Mgr. ...... 1.25 .25 .13
Earl Weaver
(Checklist back)
☐ 547 Willie McCovey .... 3.50 1.55 .45
☐ 548 Joel Youngblood .... .25 .11 .03
☐ 549 Jerry Royster .... .25 .11 .03
☐ 550 Randy Jones .... .25 .11 .03
☐ 551 Bill North .... .25 .11 .03
☐ 552 Pepe Mangual .... .25 .11 .03
☐ 553 Jack Heidemann .... .25 .11 .03
☐ 554 Bruce Kimm .... .25 .11 .03
☐ 555 Dan Ford .... .25 .11 .03
☐ 556 Doug Bird .... .25 .11 .03
☐ 557 Jerry White .... .25 .11 .03
☐ 558 Elias Sosa .... .25 .11 .03
☐ 559 Alan Bannister .... .25 .11 .03
☐ 560 Dave Concepcion .... 1.25 .55 .16
☐ 561 Pete LaCock .... .25 .11 .03
☐ 562 Checklist 529-660 ...... 1.25 .13 .04
☐ 563 Bruce Kison .... .25 .11 .03
☐ 564 Alan Ashby .... .35 .16 .04
☐ 565 Mickey Lolich .... .35 .16 .04
☐ 566 Rick Miller .... .25 .11 .03
☐ 567 Enos Cabell .... .25 .11 .03
☐ 568 Carlos May .... .25 .11 .03
☐ 569 Jim Lonborg .... .35 .16 .04
☐ 570 Bobby Bonds .... 1.25 .55 .16
☐ 571 Darrell Evans .... .35 .16 .04
☐ 572 Ross Grimsley .... .25 .11 .03
☐ 573 Joe Ferguson .... .25 .11 .03
☐ 574 Aurelio Rodriguez .... .25 .11 .03
☐ 575 Dick Ruthven .... .25 .11 .03
☐ 576 Fred Kendall .... .25 .11 .03
☐ 577 Jerry Augustine .... .25 .11 .03
☐ 578 Bob Randall .... .25 .11 .03
☐ 579 Don Carrithers .... .25 .11 .03
☐ 580 George Brett 40.00 18.00 5.00
☐ 581 Pedro Borbon .... .25 .11 .03
☐ 582 Ed Kirkpatrick .... .25 .11 .03
☐ 583 Paul Lindblad .... .25 .11 .03
☐ 584 Ed Goodson .... .25 .11 .03
☐ 585 Rick Burleson .... .35 .16 .04
☐ 586 Steve Renko .... .25 .11 .03
☐ 587 Rick Baldwin .... .25 .11 .03
☐ 588 Dave Moates .... .25 .11 .03
☐ 589 Mike Cosgrove .... .25 .11 .03
☐ 590 Buddy Bell .... .35 .16 .04
☐ 591 Chris Arnold .... .25 .11 .03
☐ 592 Dan Briggs .... .25 .11 .03
☐ 593 Dennis Blair .... .25 .11 .03
☐ 594 Biff Pocoroba .... .25 .11 .03
☐ 595 John Hiller .... .25 .11 .03
☐ 596 Jerry Martin .... .25 .11 .03
☐ 597 Mariners Leaders .... 1.25 .25 .13
Darrell Johnson MG
Don Bryant CO
Jim Busby CO
Vada Pinson CO
Wes Stock CO
(Checklist back)
☐ 598 Sparky Lyle .... .35 .16 .04
☐ 599 Mike Tyson .... .25 .11 .03
☐ 600 Jim Palmer .... 6.00 2.70 .75
☐ 601 Mike Lum .... .25 .11 .03
☐ 602 Andy Hassler .... .25 .11 .03
☐ 603 Willie Davis .... .35 .16 .04
☐ 604 Jim Slaton .... .25 .11 .03

☐ 605	Felix Millan	.25	.11	.03
☐ 606	Steve Braun	.25	.11	.03
☐ 607	Larry Demery	.25	.11	.03
☐ 608	Roy Howell	.25	.11	.03
☐ 609	Jim Barr	.25	.11	.03
☐ 610	Jose Cardenal	.25	.11	.03
☐ 611	Dave Lemanczyk	.25	.11	.03
☐ 612	Barry Foote	.25	.11	.03
☐ 613	Reggie Cleveland	.25	.11	.03
☐ 614	Greg Gross	.25	.11	.03
☐ 615	Phil Niekro	2.00	.90	.25
☐ 616	Tommy Sandt	.25	.11	.03
☐ 617	Bobby Darwin	.25	.11	.03
☐ 618	Pat Dobson	.25	.11	.03
☐ 619	Johnny Oates	.25	.11	.03
☐ 620	Don Sutton	2.00	.90	.25
☐ 621	Tigers Team/Mgr. Ralph Houk (Checklist back)	1.25	.25	.13
☐ 622	Jim Wohlford	.25	.11	.03
☐ 623	Jack Kucek	.25	.11	.03
☐ 624	Hector Cruz	.25	.11	.03
☐ 625	Ken Holtzman	.35	.16	.04
☐ 626	Al Bumbry	.35	.16	.04
☐ 627	Bob Myrick	.25	.11	.03
☐ 628	Mario Guerrero	.25	.11	.03
☐ 629	Bobby Valentine	.25	.11	.03
☐ 630	Bert Blyleven	1.00	.45	.13
☐ 631	Big League Brothers George Brett Ken Brett	8.00	3.60	1.00
☐ 632	Big League Brothers Bob Forsch Ken Forsch	.35	.16	.04
☐ 633	Big League Brothers Lee May Carlos May	.35	.16	.04
☐ 634	Big League Brothers Paul Reuschel Rick Reuschel UER (Photos switched)	.35	.16	.04
☐ 635	Robin Yount	25.00	11.50	3.10
☐ 636	Santo Alcala	.25	.11	.03
☐ 637	Alex Johnson	.25	.11	.03
☐ 638	Jim Kaat	.75	.35	.09
☐ 639	Jerry Morales	.25	.11	.03
☐ 640	Carlton Fisk	8.00	3.60	1.00
☐ 641	Dan Larson	.25	.11	.03
☐ 642	Willie Crawford	.25	.11	.03
☐ 643	Mike Pazik	.25	.11	.03
☐ 644	Matt Alexander	.25	.11	.03
☐ 645	Jerry Reuss	.35	.16	.04
☐ 646	Andres Mora	.25	.11	.03
☐ 647	Expos Team/Mgr. Dick Williams (Checklist back)	1.25	.25	.13
☐ 648	Jim Spencer	.25	.11	.03
☐ 649	Dave Cash	.25	.11	.03
☐ 650	Nolan Ryan	50.00	23.00	6.25
☐ 651	Von Joshua	.25	.11	.03
☐ 652	Tom Walker	.25	.11	.03
☐ 653	Diego Segui	.35	.16	.04
☐ 654	Ron Pruitt	.25	.11	.03
☐ 655	Tony Perez	1.50	.65	.19
☐ 656	Ron Guidry	1.50	.65	.19
☐ 657	Mick Kelleher	.25	.11	.03
☐ 658	Marty Pattin	.25	.11	.03
☐ 659	Merv Rettenmund	.25	.11	.03
☐ 660	Willie Horton	.50	.11	.03

1978 Topps

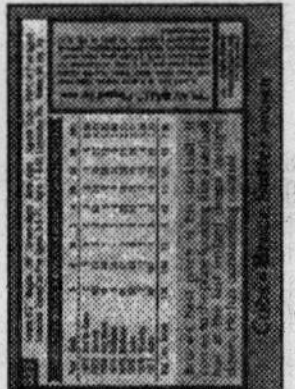

The cards in this 726-card set measure 2 1/2" by 3 1/2". The 1978 Topps set experienced an increase in number of cards from the previous five regular issue sets of 660. Card numbers 1 through 7 feature Record Breakers (RB) of the 1977 season. Other subsets within this set include League Leaders (201-208), Post-season cards (411-413), and Rookie Prospects (701-711). The key Rookie Cards in this set are the multi-player Rookie Card of Paul Molitor and Alan Trammell, Jack Morris, Eddie Murray, Lance Parrish, and Lou Whitaker. The manager cards in the set feature a "then and now" format on the card front showing the manager as he looked many years before, e.g., during his playing days. While no scarcities exist, 66 of the cards are more abundant in supply, as they were "double printed." These 66 double-printed cards are noted in the checklist by DP. Team cards again feature a checklist of that team's players in the set on the back. Cards numbered 23 or lower, that feature Astros, Rangers, Tigers, or Yankees and do not follow the numbering checklisted below, are not necessarily error cards. They are undoubtedly Burger King cards, a separate set with its own pricing and mass distribution. Burger King cards are indistinguishable from the corresponding Topps cards except for the card numbering difference and the fact that Burger King cards do not have a printing sheet designation (such as A through F like the regular Topps) anywhere on the card back in very small print.

	NRMT-MT	EXC	G-VG
COMPLETE SET (726)	300.00	135.00	38.00
COMMON CARD (1-726)	.25	.11	.03
COMMON CARD DP	.15	.07	.02

☐ 1	RB: Lou Brock Most steals, lifetime	3.00	.75	.24
☐ 2	RB: Sparky Lyle Most games, pure relief, lifetime	.35	.16	.04
☐ 3	RB: Willie McCovey Most times, 2 HR's in inning, lifetime	1.50	.65	.19
☐ 4	RB: Brooks Robinson Most consecutive seasons with one club	2.00	.90	.25
☐ 5	RB: Pete Rose Most hits, switch	3.50	1.55	.45

hitter, lifetime
☐ 6 RB: Nolan Ryan 15.00 6.75 1.90
Most games with
10 or more
strikeouts, lifetime
☐ 7 RB: Reggie Jackson .... 4.00 1.80 .50
Most homers,
one World Series
☐ 8 Mike Sadek .... .25 .11 .03
☐ 9 Doug DeCinces .... .35 .16 .04
☐ 10 Phil Niekro .... 1.50 .65 .19
☐ 11 Rick Manning .... .25 .11 .03
☐ 12 Don Aase .... .25 .11 .03
☐ 13 Art Howe .... .35 .16 .04
☐ 14 Lerrin LaGrow .... .25 .11 .03
☐ 15 Tony Perez DP .... .75 .35 .09
☐ 16 Roy White .... .35 .16 .04
☐ 17 Mike Krukow .... .25 .11 .03
☐ 18 Bob Grich .... .35 .16 .04
☐ 19 Darrell Porter .... .35 .16 .04
☐ 20 Pete Rose DP .... 5.00 2.30 .60
☐ 21 Steve Kemp .... .25 .11 .03
☐ 22 Charlie Hough .... .35 .16 .04
☐ 23 Bump Wills .... .25 .11 .03
☐ 24 Don Money DP .... .15 .07 .02
☐ 25 Jon Matlack .... .25 .11 .03
☐ 26 Rich Hebner .... .25 .11 .03
☐ 27 Geoff Zahn .... .25 .11 .03
☐ 28 Ed Ott .... .25 .11 .03
☐ 29 Bob Lacey .... .25 .11 .03
☐ 30 George Hendrick .... .35 .16 .04
☐ 31 Glenn Abbott .... .25 .11 .03
☐ 32 Garry Templeton .... .40 .18 .05
☐ 33 Dave Lemanczyk .... .25 .11 .03
☐ 34 Willie McCovey .... 3.00 1.35 .40
☐ 35 Sparky Lyle .... .35 .16 .04
☐ 36 Eddie Murray 85.00 38.00 10.50
☐ 37 Rick Waits .... .25 .11 .03
☐ 38 Willie Montanez .... .25 .11 .03
☐ 39 Floyd Bannister .... .25 .11 .03
☐ 40 Carl Yastrzemski .... 4.00 1.80 .50
☐ 41 Burt Hooton .... .35 .16 .04
☐ 42 Jorge Orta .... .25 .11 .03
☐ 43 Bill Atkinson .... .25 .11 .03
☐ 44 Toby Harrah .... .35 .16 .04
☐ 45 Mark Fidrych .... 1.25 .55 .16
☐ 46 Al Cowens .... .25 .11 .03
☐ 47 Jack Billingham .... .25 .11 .03
☐ 48 Don Baylor .... 1.00 .45 .13
☐ 49 Ed Kranepool .... .25 .11 .03
☐ 50 Rick Reuschel .... .35 .16 .04
☐ 51 Charlie Moore DP .... .15 .07 .02
☐ 52 Jim Lonborg .... .25 .11 .03
☐ 53 Phil Garner DP .... .25 .11 .03
☐ 54 Tom Johnson .... .25 .11 .03
☐ 55 Mitchell Page .... .25 .11 .03
☐ 56 Randy Jones .... .25 .11 .03
☐ 57 Dan Meyer .... .25 .11 .03
☐ 58 Bob Forsch .... .25 .11 .03
☐ 59 Otto Velez .... .25 .11 .03
☐ 60 Thurman Munson .... 4.00 1.80 .50
☐ 61 Larvell Blanks .... .25 .11 .03
☐ 62 Jim Barr .... .25 .11 .03
☐ 63 Don Zimmer MG .... .35 .16 .04
☐ 64 Gene Pentz .... .25 .11 .03
☐ 65 Ken Singleton .... .35 .16 .04
☐ 66 Chicago White Sox .... 1.25 .25 .13
Team Card
(Checklist back)
☐ 67 Claudell Washington ...... .35 .16 .04
☐ 68 Steve Foucault DP .... .15 .07 .02
☐ 69 Mike Vail .... .25 .11 .03
☐ 70 Rich Gossage .... 1.00 .45 .13
☐ 71 Terry Humphrey .... .25 .11 .03
☐ 72 Andre Dawson 16.00 7.25 2.00
☐ 73 Andy Hassler .... .25 .11 .03
☐ 74 Checklist 1-121 .... 1.25 .13 .04
☐ 75 Dick Ruthven .... .25 .11 .03
☐ 76 Steve Ontiveros .... .25 .11 .03
☐ 77 Ed Kirkpatrick .... .25 .11 .03
☐ 78 Pablo Torrealba .... .25 .11 .03
☐ 79 Darrell Johnson DP MG . .15 .07 .02
☐ 80 Ken Griffey .... 1.00 .45 .13
☐ 81 Pete Redfern .... .25 .11 .03
☐ 82 San Francisco Giants ... 1.25 .25 .13
Team Card
(Checklist back)
☐ 83 Bob Montgomery .... .25 .11 .03
☐ 84 Kent Tekulve .... .35 .16 .04
☐ 85 Ron Fairly .... .25 .11 .03
☐ 86 Dave Tomlin .... .25 .11 .03
☐ 87 John Lowenstein .... .25 .11 .03
☐ 88 Mike Phillips .... .25 .11 .03
☐ 89 Ken Clay .... .25 .11 .03
☐ 90 Larry Bowa .... .40 .18 .05
☐ 91 Oscar Zamora .... .25 .11 .03
☐ 92 Adrian Devine .... .25 .11 .03
☐ 93 Bobby Cox DP .... .15 .07 .02
☐ 94 Chuck Scrivener .... .25 .11 .03
☐ 95 Jamie Quirk .... .25 .11 .03
☐ 96 Baltimore Orioles .... 1.25 .25 .13
Team Card
(Checklist back)
☐ 97 Stan Bahnsen .... .25 .11 .03
☐ 98 Jim Essian .... .35 .16 .04
☐ 99 Willie Hernandez .... .50 .23 .06
☐ 100 George Brett 25.00 11.50 3.10
☐ 101 Sid Monge .... .25 .11 .03
☐ 102 Matt Alexander .... .25 .11 .03
☐ 103 Tom Murphy .... .25 .11 .03
☐ 104 Lee Lacy .... .25 .11 .03
☐ 105 Reggie Cleveland .... .25 .11 .03
☐ 106 Bill Plummer .... .25 .11 .03
☐ 107 Ed Halicki .... .25 .11 .03
☐ 108 Von Joshua .... .25 .11 .03
☐ 109 Joe Torre MG .... .25 .11 .03
☐ 110 Richie Zisk .... .25 .11 .03
☐ 111 Mike Tyson .... .25 .11 .03
☐ 112 Houston Astros .... 1.25 .25 .13
Team Card
(Checklist back)
☐ 113 Don Carrithers .... .25 .11 .03
☐ 114 Paul Blair .... .35 .16 .04
☐ 115 Gary Nolan .... .25 .11 .03
☐ 116 Tucker Ashford .... .25 .11 .03
☐ 117 John Montague .... .25 .11 .03
☐ 118 Terry Harmon .... .25 .11 .03
☐ 119 Dennis Martinez .... 3.00 1.35 .40
☐ 120 Gary Carter .... 3.50 1.55 .45
☐ 121 Alvis Woods .... .25 .11 .03
☐ 122 Dennis Eckersley .... 4.50 2.00 .55
☐ 123 Manny Trillo .... .25 .11 .03
☐ 124 Dave Rozema .... .25 .11 .03
☐ 125 George Scott .... .35 .16 .04
☐ 126 Paul Moskau .... .25 .11 .03
☐ 127 Chet Lemon .... .35 .16 .04
☐ 128 Bill Russell .... .35 .16 .04
☐ 129 Jim Colborn .... .25 .11 .03
☐ 130 Jeff Burroughs .... .35 .16 .04
☐ 131 Bert Blyleven .... .60 .25 .08
☐ 132 Enos Cabell .... .25 .11 .03
☐ 133 Jerry Augustine .... .25 .11 .03
☐ 134 Steve Henderson .... .25 .11 .03
☐ 135 Ron Guidry DP .... .75 .35 .09
☐ 136 Ted Sizemore .... .25 .11 .03
☐ 137 Craig Kusick .... .25 .11 .03

☐ 138 Larry Demery .25 .11 .03
☐ 139 Wayne Gross .25 .11 .03
☐ 140 Rollie Fingers 1.75 .80 .22
☐ 141 Ruppert Jones .25 .11 .03
☐ 142 John Montefusco .25 .11 .03
☐ 143 Keith Hernandez .75 .35 .09
☐ 144 Jesse Jefferson .25 .11 .03
☐ 145 Rick Monday .35 .16 .04
☐ 146 Doyle Alexander .25 .11 .03
☐ 147 Lee Mazzilli .25 .11 .03
☐ 148 Andre Thornton .35 .16 .04
☐ 149 Dale Murray .25 .11 .03
☐ 150 Bobby Bonds .75 .35 .09
☐ 151 Milt Wilcox .25 .11 .03
☐ 152 Ivan DeJesus .25 .11 .03
☐ 153 Steve Stone .35 .16 .04
☐ 154 Cecil Cooper DP .25 .11 .03
☐ 155 Butch Hobson .40 .18 .05
☐ 156 Andy Messersmith .35 .16 .04
☐ 157 Pete LaCock DP .15 .07 .02
☐ 158 Joaquin Andujar .35 .16 .04
☐ 159 Lou Piniella .25 .11 .03
☐ 160 Jim Palmer 4.00 1.80 .50
☐ 161 Bob Boone .25 .11 .03
☐ 162 Paul Thormodsgard .25 .11 .03
☐ 163 Bill North .25 .11 .03
☐ 164 Bob Owchinko .25 .11 .03
☐ 165 Rennie Stennett .25 .11 .03
☐ 166 Carlos Lopez .25 .11 .03
☐ 167 Tim Foli .25 .11 .03
☐ 168 Reggie Smith .35 .16 .04
☐ 169 Jerry Johnson .25 .11 .03
☐ 170 Lou Brock 3.50 1.55 .45
☐ 171 Pat Zachry .25 .11 .03
☐ 172 Mike Hargrove .35 .16 .04
☐ 173 Robin Yount UER 16.00 7.25 2.00
(Played for Newark
in 1973, not 1971)
☐ 174 Wayne Garland .25 .11 .03
☐ 175 Jerry Morales .25 .11 .03
☐ 176 Milt May .25 .11 .03
☐ 177 Gene Garber DP .15 .07 .02
☐ 178 Dave Chalk .25 .11 .03
☐ 179 Dick Tidrow .25 .11 .03
☐ 180 Dave Concepcion 1.00 .45 .13
☐ 181 Ken Forsch .25 .11 .03
☐ 182 Jim Spencer .25 .11 .03
☐ 183 Doug Bird .25 .11 .03
☐ 184 Checklist 122-242 1.25 .13 .04
☐ 185 Ellis Valentine .25 .11 .03
☐ 186 Bob Stanley DP .30 .14 .04
☐ 187 Jerry Royster DP .15 .07 .02
☐ 188 Al Bumbry .35 .16 .04
☐ 189 Tom Lasorda MG .60 .25 .08
☐ 190 John Candelaria .35 .16 .04
☐ 191 Rodney Scott .25 .11 .03
☐ 192 San Diego Padres 1.25 .25 .13
Team Card
(Checklist back)
☐ 193 Rich Chiles .25 .11 .03
☐ 194 Derrel Thomas .25 .11 .03
☐ 195 Larry Dierker .25 .11 .03
☐ 196 Bob Bailor .25 .11 .03
☐ 197 Nino Espinosa .25 .11 .03
☐ 198 Ron Pruitt .25 .11 .03
☐ 199 Craig Reynolds .25 .11 .03
☐ 200 Reggie Jackson 12.00 5.50 1.50
☐ 201 Batting Leaders 1.00 .45 .13
Dave Parker
Rod Carew
☐ 202 Home Run Leaders DP .35 .16 .04
George Foster
Jim Rice
☐ 203 RBI Leaders .40 .18 .05
George Foster
Larry Hisle
☐ 204 Steals Leaders DP .25 .11 .03
Frank Taveras
Freddie Patek
☐ 205 Victory Leaders 1.50 .65 .19
Steve Carlton
Dave Goltz
Dennis Leonard
Jim Palmer
☐ 206 Strikeout Leaders DP 5.00 2.30 .60
Phil Niekro
Nolan Ryan
☐ 207 ERA Leaders DP .25 .11 .03
John Candelaria
Frank Tanana
☐ 208 Top Firemen .75 .35 .09
Rollie Fingers
Bill Campbell
☐ 209 Dock Ellis .25 .11 .03
☐ 210 Jose Cardenal .25 .11 .03
☐ 211 Earl Weaver MG DP .25 .11 .03
☐ 212 Mike Caldwell .25 .11 .03
☐ 213 Alan Bannister .25 .11 .03
☐ 214 California Angels 1.25 .25 .13
Team Card
(Checklist back)
☐ 215 Darrell Evans .40 .18 .05
☐ 216 Mike Paxton .25 .11 .03
☐ 217 Rod Gilbreath .25 .11 .03
☐ 218 Marty Pattin .25 .11 .03
☐ 219 Mike Cubbage .25 .11 .03
☐ 220 Pedro Borbon .25 .11 .03
☐ 221 Chris Speier .25 .11 .03
☐ 222 Jerry Martin .25 .11 .03
☐ 223 Bruce Kison .25 .11 .03
☐ 224 Jerry Tabb .25 .11 .03
☐ 225 Don Gullett DP .25 .11 .03
☐ 226 Joe Ferguson .25 .11 .03
☐ 227 Al Fitzmorris .25 .11 .03
☐ 228 Manny Mota DP .15 .07 .02
☐ 229 Leo Foster .25 .11 .03
☐ 230 Al Hrabosky .25 .11 .03
☐ 231 Wayne Nordhagen .25 .11 .03
☐ 232 Mickey Stanley .25 .11 .03
☐ 233 Dick Pole .25 .11 .03
☐ 234 Herman Franks MG .25 .11 .03
☐ 235 Tim McCarver .35 .16 .04
☐ 236 Terry Whitfield .25 .11 .03
☐ 237 Rich Dauer .25 .11 .03
☐ 238 Juan Beniquez .25 .11 .03
☐ 239 Dyar Miller .25 .11 .03
☐ 240 Gene Tenace .35 .16 .04
☐ 241 Pete Vuckovich .35 .16 .04
☐ 242 Barry Bonnell DP .15 .07 .02
☐ 243 Bob McClure .25 .11 .03
☐ 244 Montreal Expos .75 .15 .08
Team Card DP
(Checklist back)
☐ 245 Rick Burleson .35 .16 .04
☐ 246 Dan Driessen .25 .11 .03
☐ 247 Larry Christenson .25 .11 .03
☐ 248 Frank White DP .25 .11 .03
☐ 249 Dave Goltz DP .15 .07 .02
☐ 250 Graig Nettles DP .25 .11 .03
☐ 251 Don Kirkwood .25 .11 .03
☐ 252 Steve Swisher DP .15 .07 .02
☐ 253 Jim Kern .25 .11 .03
☐ 254 Dave Collins .35 .16 .04
☐ 255 Jerry Reuss .35 .16 .04
☐ 256 Joe Altobelli MG .25 .11 .03
☐ 257 Hector Cruz .25 .11 .03

☐ 258 John Hiller	.25	.11	.03
☐ 259 Los Angeles Dodgers. Team Card (Checklist back)	1.25	.25	.13
☐ 260 Bert Campaneris	.35	.16	.04
☐ 261 Tim Hosley	.25	.11	.03
☐ 262 Rudy May	.25	.11	.03
☐ 263 Danny Walton	.25	.11	.03
☐ 264 Jamie Easterly	.25	.11	.03
☐ 265 Sal Bando DP	.25	.11	.03
☐ 266 Bob Shirley	.25	.11	.03
☐ 267 Doug Ault	.25	.11	.03
☐ 268 Gil Flores	.25	.11	.03
☐ 269 Wayne Twitchell	.25	.11	.03
☐ 270 Carlton Fisk	6.00	2.70	.75
☐ 271 Randy Lerch DP	.15	.07	.02
☐ 272 Royle Stillman	.25	.11	.03
☐ 273 Fred Norman	.25	.11	.03
☐ 274 Freddie Patek	.35	.16	.04
☐ 275 Dan Ford	.25	.11	.03
☐ 276 Bill Bonham DP	.15	.07	.02
☐ 277 Bruce Boisclair	.25	.11	.03
☐ 278 Enrique Romo	.25	.11	.03
☐ 279 Bill Virdon MG	.25	.11	.03
☐ 280 Buddy Bell	.35	.16	.04
☐ 281 Eric Rasmussen DP	.15	.07	.02
☐ 282 New York Yankees Team Card (Checklist back)	1.50	.30	.15
☐ 283 Omar Moreno	.25	.11	.03
☐ 284 Randy Moffitt	.25	.11	.03
☐ 285 Steve Yeager DP	.25	.11	.03
☐ 286 Ben Oglivie	.35	.16	.04
☐ 287 Kiko Garcia	.25	.11	.03
☐ 288 Dave Hamilton	.25	.11	.03
☐ 289 Checklist 243-363	1.25	.13	.04
☐ 290 Willie Horton	.35	.16	.04
☐ 291 Gary Ross	.25	.11	.03
☐ 292 Gene Richards	.25	.11	.03
☐ 293 Mike Willis	.25	.11	.03
☐ 294 Larry Parrish	.35	.16	.04
☐ 295 Bill Lee	.25	.11	.03
☐ 296 Biff Pocoroba	.25	.11	.03
☐ 297 Warren Brusstar DP	.15	.07	.02
☐ 298 Tony Armas	.35	.16	.04
☐ 299 Whitey Herzog MG	.35	.16	.04
☐ 300 Joe Morgan	3.50	1.55	.45
☐ 301 Buddy Schultz	.25	.11	.03
☐ 302 Chicago Cubs Team Card (Checklist back)	1.25	.25	.13
☐ 303 Sam Hinds	.25	.11	.03
☐ 304 John Milner	.25	.11	.03
☐ 305 Rico Carty	.35	.16	.04
☐ 306 Joe Niekro	.35	.16	.04
☐ 307 Glenn Borgmann	.25	.11	.03
☐ 308 Jim Rooker	.25	.11	.03
☐ 309 Cliff Johnson	.25	.11	.03
☐ 310 Don Sutton	1.50	.65	.19
☐ 311 Jose Baez DP	.15	.07	.02
☐ 312 Greg Minton	.25	.11	.03
☐ 313 Andy Etchebarren	.25	.11	.03
☐ 314 Paul Lindblad	.25	.11	.03
☐ 315 Mark Belanger	.35	.16	.04
☐ 316 Henry Cruz DP	.15	.07	.02
☐ 317 Dave Johnson	.25	.11	.03
☐ 318 Tom Griffin	.25	.11	.03
☐ 319 Alan Ashby	.25	.11	.03
☐ 320 Fred Lynn	1.00	.45	.13
☐ 321 Santo Alcala	.25	.11	.03
☐ 322 Tom Paciorek	.35	.16	.04
☐ 323 Jim Fregosi DP	.25	.11	.03
☐ 324 Vern Rapp MG	.25	.11	.03
☐ 325 Bruce Sutter	.75	.35	.09
☐ 326 Mike Lum DP	.15	.07	.02
☐ 327 Rick Langford DP	.15	.07	.02
☐ 328 Milwaukee Brewers Team Card (Checklist back)	1.25	.25	.13
☐ 329 John Verhoeven	.25	.11	.03
☐ 330 Bob Watson	.35	.16	.04
☐ 331 Mark Littell	.25	.11	.03
☐ 332 Duane Kuiper	.25	.11	.03
☐ 333 Jim Todd	.25	.11	.03
☐ 334 John Stearns	.25	.11	.03
☐ 335 Bucky Dent	.25	.11	.03
☐ 336 Steve Busby	.25	.11	.03
☐ 337 Tom Grieve	.35	.16	.04
☐ 338 Dave Heaverlo	.25	.11	.03
☐ 339 Mario Guerrero	.25	.11	.03
☐ 340 Bake McBride	.35	.16	.04
☐ 341 Mike Flanagan	.25	.11	.03
☐ 342 Aurelio Rodriguez	.25	.11	.03
☐ 343 John Wathan DP	.15	.07	.02
☐ 344 Sam Ewing	.25	.11	.03
☐ 345 Luis Tiant	.35	.16	.04
☐ 346 Larry Biittner	.25	.11	.03
☐ 347 Terry Forster	.25	.11	.03
☐ 348 Del Unser	.25	.11	.03
☐ 349 Rick Camp DP	.15	.07	.02
☐ 350 Steve Garvey	2.00	.90	.25
☐ 351 Jeff Torborg	.35	.16	.04
☐ 352 Tony Scott	.25	.11	.03
☐ 353 Doug Bair	.25	.11	.03
☐ 354 Cesar Geronimo	.25	.11	.03
☐ 355 Bill Travers	.25	.11	.03
☐ 356 New York Mets Team Card (Checklist back)	1.25	.25	.13
☐ 357 Tom Poquette	.25	.11	.03
☐ 358 Mark Lemongello	.25	.11	.03
☐ 359 Marc Hill	.25	.11	.03
☐ 360 Mike Schmidt	12.00	5.50	1.50
☐ 361 Chris Knapp	.25	.11	.03
☐ 362 Dave May	.25	.11	.03
☐ 363 Bob Randall	.25	.11	.03
☐ 364 Jerry Turner	.25	.11	.03
☐ 365 Ed Figueroa	.25	.11	.03
☐ 366 Larry Milbourne DP	.15	.07	.02
☐ 367 Rick Dempsey	.35	.16	.04
☐ 368 Balor Moore	.25	.11	.03
☐ 369 Tim Nordbrook	.25	.11	.03
☐ 370 Rusty Staub	.40	.18	.05
☐ 371 Ray Burris	.25	.11	.03
☐ 372 Brian Asselstine	.25	.11	.03
☐ 373 Jim Willoughby	.25	.11	.03
☐ 374 Jose Morales	.25	.11	.03
☐ 375 Tommy John	.75	.35	.09
☐ 376 Jim Wohlford	.25	.11	.03
☐ 377 Manny Sarmiento	.25	.11	.03
☐ 378 Bobby Winkles MG	.25	.11	.03
☐ 379 Skip Lockwood	.25	.11	.03
☐ 380 Ted Simmons	.25	.11	.03
☐ 381 Philadelphia Phillies Team Card (Checklist back)	1.25	.25	.13
☐ 382 Joe Lahoud	.25	.11	.03
☐ 383 Mario Mendoza	.25	.11	.03
☐ 384 Jack Clark	.75	.35	.09
☐ 385 Tito Fuentes	.25	.11	.03
☐ 386 Bob Gorinski	.25	.11	.03
☐ 387 Ken Holtzman	.25	.11	.03
☐ 388 Bill Fahey DP	.15	.07	.02
☐ 389 Julio Gonzalez	.25	.11	.03
☐ 390 Oscar Gamble	.35	.16	.04
☐ 391 Larry Haney	.25	.11	.03

☐ 392 Billy Almon .... .25 .11 .03
☐ 393 Tippy Martinez .... .35 .16 .04
☐ 394 Roy Howell DP............. .15 .07 .02
☐ 395 Jim Hughes.................. .25 .11 .03
☐ 396 Bob Stinson DP .... .15 .07 .02
☐ 397 Greg Gross .... .25 .11 .03
☐ 398 Don Hood .... .25 .11 .03
☐ 399 Pete Mackanin .... .25 .11 .03
☐ 400 Nolan Ryan 40.00 18.00 5.00
☐ 401 Sparky Anderson MG... .35 .16 .04
☐ 402 Dave Campbell............. .25 .11 .03
☐ 403 Bud Harrelson.............. .25 .11 .03
☐ 404 Detroit Tigers............ 1.25 .25 .13
Team Card
(Checklist back)
☐ 405 Rawly Eastwick............ .25 .11 .03
☐ 406 Mike Jorgensen .... .25 .11 .03
☐ 407 Odell Jones.................. .25 .11 .03
☐ 408 Joe Zdeb .... .25 .11 .03
☐ 409 Ron Schueler .... .25 .11 .03
☐ 410 Bill Madlock.................. .35 .16 .04
☐ 411 AL Champs .... .50 .23 .06
Yankees rally to
defeat Royals
(Willie Randolph sliding)
☐ 412 NL Champs .... .50 .23 .06
Dodgers overpower
Phillies in four
☐ 413 World Series .... 3.50 1.55 .45
Reggie Jackson and
Yankees reign supreme
(Davey Lopes batting)
☐ 414 Darold Knowles DP...... .15 .07 .02
☐ 415 Ray Fosse .... .25 .11 .03
☐ 416 Jack Brohamer............. .25 .11 .03
☐ 417 Mike Garman DP.......... .15 .07 .02
☐ 418 Tony Muser.................. .25 .11 .03
☐ 419 Jerry Garvin .... .25 .11 .03
☐ 420 Greg Luzinski............... .40 .18 .05
☐ 421 Junior Moore .... .25 .11 .03
☐ 422 Steve Braun .... .25 .11 .03
☐ 423 Dave Rosello................ .25 .11 .03
☐ 424 Boston Red Sox......... 1.25 .25 .13
Team Card
(Checklist back)
☐ 425 Steve Rogers DP.......... .15 .07 .02
☐ 426 Fred Kendall................. .25 .11 .03
☐ 427 Mario Soto.................... .40 .18 .05
☐ 428 Joel Youngblood.......... .25 .11 .03
☐ 429 Mike Barlow.................. .25 .11 .03
☐ 430 Al Oliver........................ .35 .16 .04
☐ 431 Butch Metzger............. .25 .11 .03
☐ 432 Terry Bulling .... .25 .11 .03
☐ 433 Fernando Gonzalez....... .25 .11 .03
☐ 434 Mike Norris................... .25 .11 .03
☐ 435 Checklist 364-484...... 1.25 .13 .04
☐ 436 Vic Harris DP .... .15 .07 .02
☐ 437 Bo McLaughlin............. .25 .11 .03
☐ 438 John Ellis .... .25 .11 .03
☐ 439 Ken Kravec................... .25 .11 .03
☐ 440 Dave Lopes.................. .35 .16 .04
☐ 441 Larry Gura.................... .25 .11 .03
☐ 442 Elliott Maddox.............. .25 .11 .03
☐ 443 Darrel Chaney.............. .25 .11 .03
☐ 444 Roy Hartsfield MG .... .25 .11 .03
☐ 445 Mike Ivie .... .25 .11 .03
☐ 446 Tug McGraw .... .35 .16 .04
☐ 447 Leroy Stanton .... .25 .11 .03
☐ 448 Bill Castro .... .25 .11 .03
☐ 449 Tim Blackwell DP .... .15 .07 .02
☐ 450 Tom Seaver............... 4.50 2.00 .55
☐ 451 Minnesota Twins........ 1.25 .25 .13
Team Card
(Checklist back)
☐ 452 Jerry Mumphrey .... .25 .11 .03
☐ 453 Doug Flynn .... .25 .11 .03
☐ 454 Dave LaRoche.............. .25 .11 .03
☐ 455 Bill Robinson .... .35 .16 .04
☐ 456 Vern Ruhle.................... .25 .11 .03
☐ 457 Bob Bailey.................... .25 .11 .03
☐ 458 Jeff Newman................ .25 .11 .03
☐ 459 Charlie Spikes .... .25 .11 .03
☐ 460 Jim Hunter .... 2.00 .90 .25
☐ 461 Rob Andrews DP .... .15 .07 .02
☐ 462 Rogelio Moret.............. .25 .11 .03
☐ 463 Kevin Bell..................... .25 .11 .03
☐ 464 Jerry Grote................... .25 .11 .03
☐ 465 Hal McRae .... .40 .18 .05
☐ 466 Dennis Blair .... .25 .11 .03
☐ 467 Alvin Dark MG.............. .25 .11 .03
☐ 468 Warren Cromartie .... .40 .18 .05
☐ 469 Rick Cerone .... .35 .16 .04
☐ 470 J.R. Richard................. .35 .16 .04
☐ 471 Roy Smalley................. .35 .16 .04
☐ 472 Ron Reed..................... .25 .11 .03
☐ 473 Bill Buckner.................. .40 .18 .05
☐ 474 Jim Slaton.................... .25 .11 .03
☐ 475 Gary Matthews............. .35 .16 .04
☐ 476 Bill Stein .... .25 .11 .03
☐ 477 Doug Capilla .... .25 .11 .03
☐ 478 Jerry Remy .... .25 .11 .03
☐ 479 St. Louis Cardinals..... 1.25 .25 .13
Team Card
(Checklist back)
☐ 480 Ron LeFlore .... .35 .16 .04
☐ 481 Jackson Todd .... .25 .11 .03
☐ 482 Rick Miller..................... .25 .11 .03
☐ 483 Ken Macha.................... .25 .11 .03
☐ 484 Jim Norris..................... .25 .11 .03
☐ 485 Chris Chambliss........... .35 .16 .04
☐ 486 John Curtis .... .25 .11 .03
☐ 487 Jim Tyrone.................... .25 .11 .03
☐ 488 Dan Spillner .... .25 .11 .03
☐ 489 Rudy Meoli .... .25 .11 .03
☐ 490 Amos Otis .... .35 .16 .04
☐ 491 Scott McGregor .... .35 .16 .04
☐ 492 Jim Sundberg .... .35 .16 .04
☐ 493 Steve Renko................. .25 .11 .03
☐ 494 Chuck Tanner MG .... .35 .16 .04
☐ 495 Dave Cash.................... .25 .11 .03
☐ 496 Jim Clancy DP .... .15 .07 .02
☐ 497 Glenn Adams .... .25 .11 .03
☐ 498 Joe Sambito................. .25 .11 .03
☐ 499 Seattle Mariners......... 1.25 .25 .13
Team Card
(Checklist back)
☐ 500 George Foster .... .60 .25 .08
☐ 501 Dave Roberts .... .25 .11 .03
☐ 502 Pat Rockett .... .25 .11 .03
☐ 503 Ike Hampton .... .25 .11 .03
☐ 504 Roger Freed .... .25 .11 .03
☐ 505 Felix Millan.................. .25 .11 .03
☐ 506 Ron Blomberg.............. .25 .11 .03
☐ 507 Willie Crawford .... .25 .11 .03
☐ 508 Johnny Oates............... .25 .11 .03
☐ 509 Brent Strom .... .25 .11 .03
☐ 510 Willie Stargell............. 2.00 .90 .25
☐ 511 Frank Duffy .... .25 .11 .03
☐ 512 Larry Herndon.............. .25 .11 .03
☐ 513 Barry Foote .... .25 .11 .03
☐ 514 Rob Sperring .... .25 .11 .03
☐ 515 Tim Corcoran............... .25 .11 .03
☐ 516 Gary Beare .... .25 .11 .03
☐ 517 Andres Mora................ .25 .11 .03
☐ 518 Tommy Boggs DP........ .15 .07 .02
☐ 519 Brian Downing .... .35 .16 .04

	#	Player			
☐	520	Larry Hisle	.25	.11	.03
☐	521	Steve Staggs	.25	.11	.03
☐	522	Dick Williams MG	.35	.16	.04
☐	523	Donnie Moore	.25	.11	.03
☐	524	Bernie Carbo	.25	.11	.03
☐	525	Jerry Terrell	.25	.11	.03
☐	526	Cincinnati Reds Team Card (Checklist back)	1.25	.25	.13
☐	527	Vic Correll	.25	.11	.03
☐	528	Rob Picciolo	.25	.11	.03
☐	529	Paul Hartzell	.25	.11	.03
☐	530	Dave Winfield	18.00	8.00	2.30
☐	531	Tom Underwood	.25	.11	.03
☐	532	Skip Jutze	.25	.11	.03
☐	533	Sandy Alomar	.35	.16	.04
☐	534	Wilbur Howard	.25	.11	.03
☐	535	Checklist 485-605	1.25	.13	.04
☐	536	Roric Harrison	.25	.11	.03
☐	537	Bruce Bochte	.25	.11	.03
☐	538	Johnny LeMaster	.25	.11	.03
☐	539	Vic Davalillo DP	.15	.07	.02
☐	540	Steve Carlton	4.50	2.00	.55
☐	541	Larry Cox	.25	.11	.03
☐	542	Tim Johnson	.25	.11	.03
☐	543	Larry Harlow DP	.15	.07	.02
☐	544	Len Randle DP	.15	.07	.02
☐	545	Bill Campbell	.25	.11	.03
☐	546	Ted Martinez	.25	.11	.03
☐	547	John Scott	.25	.11	.03
☐	548	Billy Hunter DP MG	.15	.07	.02
☐	549	Joe Kerrigan	.25	.11	.03
☐	550	John Mayberry	.35	.16	.04
☐	551	Atlanta Braves Team Card (Checklist back)	1.25	.25	.13
☐	552	Francisco Barrios	.25	.11	.03
☐	553	Terry Puhl	.40	.18	.05
☐	554	Joe Coleman	.25	.11	.03
☐	555	Butch Wynegar	.25	.11	.03
☐	556	Ed Armbrister	.25	.11	.03
☐	557	Tony Solaita	.25	.11	.03
☐	558	Paul Mitchell	.25	.11	.03
☐	559	Phil Mankowski	.25	.11	.03
☐	560	Dave Parker	1.50	.65	.19
☐	561	Charlie Williams	.25	.11	.03
☐	562	Glenn Burke	.25	.11	.03
☐	563	Dave Rader	.25	.11	.03
☐	564	Mick Kelleher	.25	.11	.03
☐	565	Jerry Koosman	.35	.16	.04
☐	566	Merv Rettenmund	.25	.11	.03
☐	567	Dick Drago	.25	.11	.03
☐	568	Tom Hutton	.25	.11	.03
☐	569	Lary Sorensen	.25	.11	.03
☐	570	Dave Kingman	.35	.16	.04
☐	571	Buck Martinez	.25	.11	.03
☐	572	Rick Wise	.25	.11	.03
☐	573	Luis Gomez	.25	.11	.03
☐	574	Bob Lemon MG	.35	.16	.04
☐	575	Pat Dobson	.25	.11	.03
☐	576	Sam Mejias	.25	.11	.03
☐	577	Oakland A's Team Card (Checklist back)	1.25	.25	.13
☐	578	Buzz Capra	.25	.11	.03
☐	579	Rance Mulliniks	.25	.11	.03
☐	580	Rod Carew	3.50	1.55	.45
☐	581	Lynn McGlothen	.25	.11	.03
☐	582	Fran Healy	.25	.11	.03
☐	583	George Medich	.25	.11	.03
☐	584	John Hale	.25	.11	.03
☐	585	Woodie Fryman DP	.15	.07	.02
☐	586	Ed Goodson	.25	.11	.03
☐	587	John Urrea	.25	.11	.03
☐	588	Jim Mason	.25	.11	.03
☐	589	Bob Knepper	.25	.11	.03
☐	590	Bobby Murcer	.35	.16	.04
☐	591	George Zeber	.25	.11	.03
☐	592	Bob Apodaca	.25	.11	.03
☐	593	Dave Skaggs	.25	.11	.03
☐	594	Dave Freisleben	.25	.11	.03
☐	595	Sixto Lezcano	.25	.11	.03
☐	596	Gary Wheelock	.25	.11	.03
☐	597	Steve Dillard	.25	.11	.03
☐	598	Eddie Solomon	.25	.11	.03
☐	599	Gary Woods	.25	.11	.03
☐	600	Frank Tanana	.25	.11	.03
☐	601	Gene Mauch MG	.35	.16	.04
☐	602	Eric Soderholm	.25	.11	.03
☐	603	Will McEnaney	.25	.11	.03
☐	604	Earl Williams	.25	.11	.03
☐	605	Rick Rhoden	.35	.16	.04
☐	606	Pittsburgh Pirates Team Card (Checklist back)	1.25	.25	.13
☐	607	Fernando Arroyo	.25	.11	.03
☐	608	Johnny Grubb	.25	.11	.03
☐	609	John Denny	.25	.11	.03
☐	610	Garry Maddox	.35	.16	.04
☐	611	Pat Scanlon	.25	.11	.03
☐	612	Ken Henderson	.25	.11	.03
☐	613	Marty Perez	.25	.11	.03
☐	614	Joe Wallis	.25	.11	.03
☐	615	Clay Carroll	.25	.11	.03
☐	616	Pat Kelly	.25	.11	.03
☐	617	Joe Nolan	.25	.11	.03
☐	618	Tommy Helms	.25	.11	.03
☐	619	Thad Bosley DP	.15	.07	.02
☐	620	Willie Randolph	.75	.35	.09
☐	621	Craig Swan DP	.15	.07	.02
☐	622	Champ Summers	.25	.11	.03
☐	623	Eduardo Rodriguez	.25	.11	.03
☐	624	Gary Alexander DP	.15	.07	.02
☐	625	Jose Cruz	.35	.16	.04
☐	626	Toronto Blue Jays Team Card DP (Checklist back)	.75	.15	.08
☐	627	David Johnson	.25	.11	.03
☐	628	Ralph Garr	.25	.11	.03
☐	629	Don Stanhouse	.25	.11	.03
☐	630	Ron Cey	.40	.18	.05
☐	631	Danny Ozark MG	.25	.11	.03
☐	632	Rowland Office	.25	.11	.03
☐	633	Tom Veryzer	.25	.11	.03
☐	634	Len Barker	.25	.11	.03
☐	635	Joe Rudi	.35	.16	.04
☐	636	Jim Bibby	.25	.11	.03
☐	637	Duffy Dyer	.25	.11	.03
☐	638	Paul Splittorff	.25	.11	.03
☐	639	Gene Clines	.25	.11	.03
☐	640	Lee May DP	.25	.11	.03
☐	641	Doug Rau	.25	.11	.03
☐	642	Denny Doyle	.25	.11	.03
☐	643	Tom House	.25	.11	.03
☐	644	Jim Dwyer	.25	.11	.03
☐	645	Mike Torrez	.35	.16	.04
☐	646	Rick Auerbach DP	.15	.07	.02
☐	647	Steve Dunning	.25	.11	.03
☐	648	Gary Thomasson	.25	.11	.03
☐	649	Moose Haas	.25	.11	.03
☐	650	Cesar Cedeno	.35	.16	.04
☐	651	Doug Rader	.25	.11	.03
☐	652	Checklist 606-726	1.25	.13	.04
☐	653	Ron Hodges DP	.15	.07	.02
☐	654	Pepe Frias	.25	.11	.03
☐	655	Lyman Bostock	.35	.16	.04

☐ 656 Dave Garcia MG .... .25 .11 .03
☐ 657 Bombo Rivera .... .25 .11 .03
☐ 658 Manny Sanguillen .... .35 .16 .04
☐ 659 Texas Rangers .... 1.25 .25 .13
Team Card
(Checklist back)
☐ 660 Jason Thompson .... .35 .16 .04
☐ 661 Grant Jackson .... .25 .11 .03
☐ 662 Paul Dade .... .25 .11 .03
☐ 663 Paul Reuschel .... .25 .11 .03
☐ 664 Fred Stanley .... .25 .11 .03
☐ 665 Dennis Leonard .... .35 .16 .04
☐ 666 Billy Smith .... .25 .11 .03
☐ 667 Jeff Byrd .... .25 .11 .03
☐ 668 Dusty Baker .... .40 .18 .05
☐ 669 Pete Falcone .... .25 .11 .03
☐ 670 Jim Rice .... 2.50 1.15 .30
☐ 671 Gary Lavelle .... .25 .11 .03
☐ 672 Don Kessinger .... .35 .16 .04
☐ 673 Steve Brye .... .25 .11 .03
☐ 674 Ray Knight .... 2.50 1.15 .30
☐ 675 Jay Johnstone .... .40 .18 .05
☐ 676 Bob Myrick .... .25 .11 .03
☐ 677 Ed Herrmann .... .25 .11 .03
☐ 678 Tom Burgmeier .... .25 .11 .03
☐ 679 Wayne Garrett .... .25 .11 .03
☐ 680 Vida Blue .... .35 .16 .04
☐ 681 Rob Belloir .... .25 .11 .03
☐ 682 Ken Brett .... .25 .11 .03
☐ 683 Mike Champion .... .25 .11 .03
☐ 684 Ralph Houk MG .... .35 .16 .04
☐ 685 Frank Taveras .... .25 .11 .03
☐ 686 Gaylord Perry .... 1.50 .65 .19
☐ 687 Julio Cruz .... .25 .11 .03
☐ 688 George Mitterwald .... .25 .11 .03
☐ 689 Cleveland Indians .... 1.25 .25 .13
Team Card
(Checklist back)
☐ 690 Mickey Rivers .... .35 .16 .04
☐ 691 Ross Grimsley .... .25 .11 .03
☐ 692 Ken Reitz .... .25 .11 .03
☐ 693 Lamar Johnson .... .25 .11 .03
☐ 694 Elias Sosa .... .25 .11 .03
☐ 695 Dwight Evans .... 1.00 .45 .13
☐ 696 Steve Mingori .... .25 .11 .03
☐ 697 Roger Metzger .... .25 .11 .03
☐ 698 Juan Bernhardt .... .25 .11 .03
☐ 699 Jackie Brown .... .25 .11 .03
☐ 700 Johnny Bench .... 4.50 2.00 .55
☐ 701 Rookie Pitchers .... .25 .11 .03
Tom Hume
Larry Landreth
Steve McCatty
Bruce Taylor
☐ 702 Rookie Catchers .... .25 .11 .03
Bill Nahorodny
Kevin Pasley
Rick Sweet
Don Werner
☐ 703 Rookie Pitchers DP .... 7.00 3.10 .85
Larry Andersen
Tim Jones
Mickey Mahler
Jack Morris
☐ 704 Rookie 2nd Basemen 24.00 11.00 3.00
Garth Iorg
Dave Oliver
Sam Perlozzo
Lou Whitaker
☐ 705 Rookie Outfielders .... .40 .18 .05
Dave Bergman
Miguel Dilone
Clint Hurdle
Willie Norwood
☐ 706 Rookie 1st Basemen .... .25 .11 .03
Wayne Cage
Ted Cox
Pat Putnam
Dave Revering
☐ 707 Rookie Shortstops ... 90.00 40.00 11.50
Mickey Klutts
Paul Molitor
Alan Trammell
U.L. Washington
☐ 708 Rookie Catchers 10.00 4.50 1.25
Bo Diaz
Dale Murphy
Lance Parrish
Ernie Whitt
☐ 709 Rookie Pitchers .... .25 .11 .03
Steve Burke
Matt Keough
Lance Rautzhan
Dan Schatzeder
☐ 710 Rookie Outfielders .... .75 .35 .09
Dell Alston
Rick Bosetti
Mike Easler
Keith Smith
☐ 711 Rookie Pitchers DP ...... .15 .07 .02
Cardell Camper
Dennis Lamp
Craig Mitchell
Roy Thomas
☐ 712 Bobby Valentine .... .25 .11 .03
☐ 713 Bob Davis .... .25 .11 .03
☐ 714 Mike Anderson .... .25 .11 .03
☐ 715 Jim Kaat .... .50 .23 .06
☐ 716 Clarence Gaston .... .35 .16 .04
☐ 717 Nelson Briles .... .25 .11 .03
☐ 718 Ron Jackson .... .25 .11 .03
☐ 719 Randy Elliott .... .25 .11 .03
☐ 720 Fergie Jenkins .... 1.50 .65 .19
☐ 721 Billy Martin MG .... .50 .23 .06
☐ 722 Pete Broberg .... .25 .11 .03
☐ 723 John Wockenfuss .... .25 .11 .03
☐ 724 Kansas City Royals .... 1.25 .25 .13
Team Card
(Checklist back)
☐ 725 Kurt Bevacqua .... .25 .11 .03
☐ 726 Wilbur Wood .... .50 .11 .03

1979 Topps

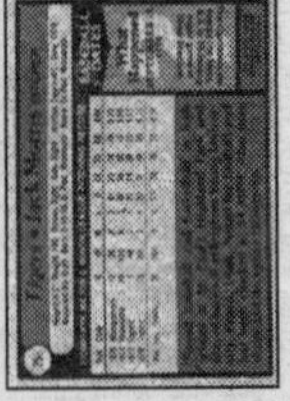

The cards in this 726-card set measure 2 1/2" by 3 1/2". Topps continued with the same number of cards as in 1978. Various series spotlight League Leaders (1-8),

"Season and Career Record Holders" (411-418), "Record Breakers of 1978" (201-206), and one "Prospects" card for each team (701-726). Team cards feature a checklist on back of that team's players in the set and a small picture of the manager on the front of the card. There are 66 cards that were double printed and these are noted in the checklist by the abbreviation DP. Bump Wills (369) was initially depicted in a Ranger uniform but with a Blue Jays affiliation; later printings correctly labeled him with Texas. The set price listed does not include the scarcer Wills (Rangers) card. The key Rookie Cards in this set are Pedro Guerrero, Carney Lansford, Ozzie Smith, and Bob Welch. Cards numbered 23 or lower, which feature Phillies or Yankees and do not follow the numbering checklisted below, are not necessarily error cards. They are undoubtedly Burger King cards, separate sets for each team each with its own pricing and mass distribution. Burger King cards are indistinguishable from the corresponding Topps cards except for the card numbering difference and the fact that Burger King cards do not have a printing sheet designation (such as A through F like the regular Topps) anywhere on the card back in very small print.

	NRMT-MT	EXC	G-VG
COMPLETE SET (726)	225.00	100.00	28.00
COMMON CARD (1-726)	.20	.09	.03
COMMON CARD DP	.10	.05	.01
☐ 1 Batting Leaders Rod Carew Dave Parker	2.50	.50	.15
☐ 2 Home Run Leaders Jim Rice George Foster	.40	.18	.05
☐ 3 RBI Leaders Jim Rice George Foster	.40	.18	.05
☐ 4 Stolen Base Leaders Ron LeFlore Omar Moreno	.35	.16	.04
☐ 5 Victory Leaders Ron Guidry Gaylord Perry	.35	.16	.04
☐ 6 Strikeout Leaders Nolan Ryan J.R. Richard	6.00	2.70	.75
☐ 7 ERA Leaders Ron Guidry Craig Swan	.35	.16	.04
☐ 8 Leading Firemen Rich Gossage Rollie Fingers	.50	.23	.06
☐ 9 Dave Campbell	.20	.09	.03
☐ 10 Lee May	.30	.14	.04
☐ 11 Marc Hill	.20	.09	.03
☐ 12 Dick Drago	.20	.09	.03
☐ 13 Paul Dade	.20	.09	.03
☐ 14 Rafael Landestoy	.20	.09	.03
☐ 15 Ross Grimsley	.20	.09	.03
☐ 16 Fred Stanley	.20	.09	.03
☐ 17 Donnie Moore	.20	.09	.03
☐ 18 Tony Solaita	.20	.09	.03
☐ 19 Larry Gura DP	.10	.05	.01
☐ 20 Joe Morgan DP	1.00	.45	.13
☐ 21 Kevin Kobel	.20	.09	.03
☐ 22 Mike Jorgensen	.20	.09	.03
☐ 23 Terry Forster	.20	.09	.03
☐ 24 Paul Molitor	35.00	16.00	4.40
☐ 25 Steve Carlton	4.00	1.80	.50
☐ 26 Jamie Quirk	.20	.09	.03
☐ 27 Dave Goltz	.20	.09	.03
☐ 28 Steve Brye	.20	.09	.03
☐ 29 Rick Langford	.20	.09	.03
☐ 30 Dave Winfield	12.00	5.50	1.50
☐ 31 Tom House DP	.10	.05	.01
☐ 32 Jerry Mumphrey	.20	.09	.03
☐ 33 Dave Rozema	.20	.09	.03
☐ 34 Rob Andrews	.20	.09	.03
☐ 35 Ed Figueroa	.20	.09	.03
☐ 36 Alan Ashby	.20	.09	.03
☐ 37 Joe Kerrigan DP	.10	.05	.01
☐ 38 Bernie Carbo	.20	.09	.03
☐ 39 Dale Murphy	5.00	2.30	.60
☐ 40 Dennis Eckersley	2.50	1.15	.30
☐ 41 Twins Team/Mgr. Gene Mauch (Checklist back)	1.00	.15	.05
☐ 42 Ron Blomberg	.20	.09	.03
☐ 43 Wayne Twitchell	.20	.09	.03
☐ 44 Kurt Bevacqua	.20	.09	.03
☐ 45 Al Hrabosky	.20	.09	.03
☐ 46 Ron Hodges	.20	.09	.03
☐ 47 Fred Norman	.20	.09	.03
☐ 48 Merv Rettenmund	.20	.09	.03
☐ 49 Vern Ruhle	.20	.09	.03
☐ 50 Steve Garvey DP	1.00	.45	.13
☐ 51 Ray Fosse DP	.10	.05	.01
☐ 52 Randy Lerch	.20	.09	.03
☐ 53 Mick Kelleher	.20	.09	.03
☐ 54 Dell Alston DP	.10	.05	.01
☐ 55 Willie Stargell	2.50	1.15	.30
☐ 56 John Hale	.20	.09	.03
☐ 57 Eric Rasmussen	.20	.09	.03
☐ 58 Bob Randall DP	.10	.05	.01
☐ 59 John Denny DP	.10	.05	.01
☐ 60 Mickey Rivers	.30	.14	.04
☐ 61 Bo Diaz	.20	.09	.03
☐ 62 Randy Moffitt	.20	.09	.03
☐ 63 Jack Brohamer	.20	.09	.03
☐ 64 Tom Underwood	.20	.09	.03
☐ 65 Mark Belanger	.30	.14	.04
☐ 66 Tigers Team/Mgr. Les Moss (Checklist back)	1.00	.15	.05
☐ 67 Jim Mason DP	.10	.05	.01
☐ 68 Joe Niekro DP	.20	.09	.03
☐ 69 Elliott Maddox	.20	.09	.03
☐ 70 John Candelaria	.30	.14	.04
☐ 71 Brian Downing	.30	.14	.04
☐ 72 Steve Mingori	.20	.09	.03
☐ 73 Ken Henderson	.20	.09	.03
☐ 74 Shane Rawley	.20	.09	.03
☐ 75 Steve Yeager	.30	.14	.04
☐ 76 Warren Cromartie	.30	.14	.04
☐ 77 Dan Briggs DP	.10	.05	.01
☐ 78 Elias Sosa	.20	.09	.03
☐ 79 Ted Cox	.20	.09	.03
☐ 80 Jason Thompson	.30	.14	.04
☐ 81 Roger Erickson	.20	.09	.03
☐ 82 Mets Team/Mgr. Joe Torre (Checklist back)	1.00	.15	.05
☐ 83 Fred Kendall	.20	.09	.03
☐ 84 Greg Minton	.20	.09	.03
☐ 85 Gary Matthews	.30	.14	.04
☐ 86 Rodney Scott	.20	.09	.03
☐ 87 Pete Falcone	.20	.09	.03
☐ 88 Bob Molinaro	.20	.09	.03

☐ 89 Dick Tidrow .20 .09 .03
☐ 90 Bob Boone .20 .09 .03
☐ 91 Terry Crowley .20 .09 .03
☐ 92 Jim Bibby .20 .09 .03
☐ 93 Phil Mankowski .20 .09 .03
☐ 94 Len Barker .20 .09 .03
☐ 95 Robin Yount 10.00 4.50 1.25
☐ 96 Indians Team/Mgr. 1.00 .15 .05
Jeff Torborg
(Checklist back)
☐ 97 Sam Mejias .20 .09 .03
☐ 98 Ray Burris .20 .09 .03
☐ 99 John Wathan .30 .14 .04
☐ 100 Tom Seaver DP 3.00 1.35 .40
☐ 101 Roy Howell .20 .09 .03
☐ 102 Mike Anderson .20 .09 .03
☐ 103 Jim Todd .20 .09 .03
☐ 104 Johnny Oates DP .10 .05 .01
☐ 105 Rick Camp DP .10 .05 .01
☐ 106 Frank Duffy .20 .09 .03
☐ 107 Jesus Alou DP .10 .05 .01
☐ 108 Eduardo Rodriguez .20 .09 .03
☐ 109 Joel Youngblood .20 .09 .03
☐ 110 Vida Blue .30 .14 .04
☐ 111 Roger Freed .20 .09 .03
☐ 112 Phillies Team/Mgr. 1.00 .15 .05
Danny Ozark
(Checklist back)
☐ 113 Pete Redfern .20 .09 .03
☐ 114 Cliff Johnson .20 .09 .03
☐ 115 Nolan Ryan 30.00 13.50 3.80
☐ 116 Ozzie Smith 90.00 40.00 11.50
☐ 117 Grant Jackson .20 .09 .03
☐ 118 Bud Harrelson .20 .09 .03
☐ 119 Don Stanhouse .20 .09 .03
☐ 120 Jim Sundberg .30 .14 .04
☐ 121 Checklist 1-121 DP .60 .08 .02
☐ 122 Mike Paxton .20 .09 .03
☐ 123 Lou Whitaker 10.00 4.50 1.25
☐ 124 Dan Schatzeder .20 .09 .03
☐ 125 Rick Burleson .20 .09 .03
☐ 126 Doug Bair .20 .09 .03
☐ 127 Thad Bosley .20 .09 .03
☐ 128 Ted Martinez .20 .09 .03
☐ 129 Marty Pattin DP .10 .05 .01
☐ 130 Bob Watson DP .20 .09 .03
☐ 131 Jim Clancy .20 .09 .03
☐ 132 Rowland Office .20 .09 .03
☐ 133 Bill Castro .20 .09 .03
☐ 134 Alan Bannister .20 .09 .03
☐ 135 Bobby Murcer .30 .14 .04
☐ 136 Jim Kaat .30 .14 .04
☐ 137 Larry Wolfe DP .10 .05 .01
☐ 138 Mark Lee .20 .09 .03
☐ 139 Luis Pujols .20 .09 .03
☐ 140 Don Gullett .30 .14 .04
☐ 141 Tom Paciorek .30 .14 .04
☐ 142 Charlie Williams .20 .09 .03
☐ 143 Tony Scott .20 .09 .03
☐ 144 Sandy Alomar .30 .14 .04
☐ 145 Rick Rhoden .20 .09 .03
☐ 146 Duane Kuiper .20 .09 .03
☐ 147 Dave Hamilton .20 .09 .03
☐ 148 Bruce Boisclair .20 .09 .03
☐ 149 Manny Sarmiento .20 .09 .03
☐ 150 Wayne Cage .20 .09 .03
☐ 151 John Hiller .20 .09 .03
☐ 152 Rick Cerone .20 .09 .03
☐ 153 Dennis Lamp .20 .09 .03
☐ 154 Jim Gantner DP .20 .09 .03
☐ 155 Dwight Evans .75 .35 .09
☐ 156 Buddy Solomon .20 .09 .03
☐ 157 U.L. Washington UER .20 .09 .03
(Sic, bats left,
should be right)
☐ 158 Joe Sambito .20 .09 .03
☐ 159 Roy White .30 .14 .04
☐ 160 Mike Flanagan .40 .18 .05
☐ 161 Barry Foote .20 .09 .03
☐ 162 Tom Johnson .20 .09 .03
☐ 163 Glenn Burke .20 .09 .03
☐ 164 Mickey Lolich .30 .14 .04
☐ 165 Frank Taveras .20 .09 .03
☐ 166 Leon Roberts .20 .09 .03
☐ 167 Roger Metzger DP .10 .05 .01
☐ 168 Dave Freisleben .20 .09 .03
☐ 169 Bill Nahorodny .20 .09 .03
☐ 170 Don Sutton 1.00 .45 .13
☐ 171 Gene Clines .20 .09 .03
☐ 172 Mike Bruhert .20 .09 .03
☐ 173 John Lowenstein .20 .09 .03
☐ 174 Rick Auerbach .20 .09 .03
☐ 175 George Hendrick .30 .14 .04
☐ 176 Aurelio Rodriguez .20 .09 .03
☐ 177 Ron Reed .20 .09 .03
☐ 178 Alvis Woods .20 .09 .03
☐ 179 Jim Beattie DP .10 .05 .01
☐ 180 Larry Hisle .20 .09 .03
☐ 181 Mike Garman .20 .09 .03
☐ 182 Tim Johnson .20 .09 .03
☐ 183 Paul Splittorff .20 .09 .03
☐ 184 Darrel Chaney .20 .09 .03
☐ 185 Mike Torrez .30 .14 .04
☐ 186 Eric Soderholm .20 .09 .03
☐ 187 Mark Lemongello .20 .09 .03
☐ 188 Pat Kelly .20 .09 .03
☐ 189 Eddie Whitson .20 .09 .03
☐ 190 Ron Cey .30 .14 .04
☐ 191 Mike Norris .20 .09 .03
☐ 192 Cardinals Team/Mgr. 1.00 .15 .05
Ken Boyer
(Checklist back)
☐ 193 Glenn Adams .20 .09 .03
☐ 194 Randy Jones .20 .09 .03
☐ 195 Bill Madlock .30 .14 .04
☐ 196 Steve Kemp DP .10 .05 .01
☐ 197 Bob Apodaca .20 .09 .03
☐ 198 Johnny Grubb .20 .09 .03
☐ 199 Larry Milbourne .20 .09 .03
☐ 200 Johnny Bench DP 2.50 1.15 .30
☐ 201 RB: Mike Edwards .20 .09 .03
Most unassisted DP's,
second basemen
☐ 202 RB: Ron Guidry, Most .30 .14 .04
strikeouts, lefthander,
nine inning game
☐ 203 RB: J.R. Richard .20 .09 .03
Most strikeouts,
season, righthander
☐ 204 RB: Pete Rose 2.00 .90 .25
Most consecutive
games batting safely
☐ 205 RB: John Stearns .20 .09 .03
Most SB's by
catcher, season
☐ 206 RB: Sammy Stewart .20 .09 .03
7 straight SO's,
first ML game
☐ 207 Dave Lemanczyk .20 .09 .03
☐ 208 Clarence Gaston .30 .14 .04
☐ 209 Reggie Cleveland .20 .09 .03
☐ 210 Larry Bowa .30 .14 .04
☐ 211 Denny Martinez 1.75 .80 .22
☐ 212 Carney Lansford 2.50 1.15 .30
☐ 213 Bill Travers .20 .09 .03
☐ 214 Red Sox Team/Mgr. 1.00 .15 .05
Don Zimmer

No.	Player			
	(Checklist back)			
☐ 215	Willie McCovey	2.50	1.15	.30
☐ 216	Wilbur Wood	.20	.09	.03
☐ 217	Steve Dillard	.20	.09	.03
☐ 218	Dennis Leonard	.30	.14	.04
☐ 219	Roy Smalley	.30	.14	.04
☐ 220	Cesar Geronimo	.20	.09	.03
☐ 221	Jesse Jefferson	.20	.09	.03
☐ 222	Bob Beall	.20	.09	.03
☐ 223	Kent Tekulve	.30	.14	.04
☐ 224	Dave Revering	.20	.09	.03
☐ 225	Rich Gossage	.60	.25	.08
☐ 226	Ron Pruitt	.20	.09	.03
☐ 227	Steve Stone	.30	.14	.04
☐ 228	Vic Davalillo	.20	.09	.03
☐ 229	Doug Flynn	.20	.09	.03
☐ 230	Bob Forsch	.20	.09	.03
☐ 231	John Wockenfuss	.20	.09	.03
☐ 232	Jimmy Sexton	.20	.09	.03
☐ 233	Paul Mitchell	.20	.09	.03
☐ 234	Toby Harrah	.30	.14	.04
☐ 235	Steve Rogers	.20	.09	.03
☐ 236	Jim Dwyer	.20	.09	.03
☐ 237	Billy Smith	.20	.09	.03
☐ 238	Balor Moore	.20	.09	.03
☐ 239	Willie Horton	.30	.14	.04
☐ 240	Rick Reuschel	.30	.14	.04
☐ 241	Checklist 122-242 DP	.60	.08	.02
☐ 242	Pablo Torrealba	.20	.09	.03
☐ 243	Buck Martinez DP	.10	.05	.01
☐ 244	Pirates Team/Mgr. Chuck Tanner (Checklist back)	1.20	.18	.06
☐ 245	Jeff Burroughs	.20	.09	.03
☐ 246	Darrell Jackson	.20	.09	.03
☐ 247	Tucker Ashford DP	.10	.05	.01
☐ 248	Pete LaCock	.20	.09	.03
☐ 249	Paul Thormodsgard	.20	.09	.03
☐ 250	Willie Randolph	.60	.25	.08
☐ 251	Jack Morris	3.00	1.35	.40
☐ 252	Bob Stinson	.20	.09	.03
☐ 253	Rick Wise	.20	.09	.03
☐ 254	Luis Gomez	.20	.09	.03
☐ 255	Tommy John	.40	.18	.05
☐ 256	Mike Sadek	.20	.09	.03
☐ 257	Adrian Devine	.20	.09	.03
☐ 258	Mike Phillips	.20	.09	.03
☐ 259	Reds Team/Mgr. Sparky Anderson (Checklist back)	1.00	.15	.05
☐ 260	Richie Zisk	.20	.09	.03
☐ 261	Mario Guerrero	.20	.09	.03
☐ 262	Nelson Briles	.20	.09	.03
☐ 263	Oscar Gamble	.30	.14	.04
☐ 264	Don Robinson	.20	.09	.03
☐ 265	Don Money	.20	.09	.03
☐ 266	Jim Willoughby	.20	.09	.03
☐ 267	Joe Rudi	.30	.14	.04
☐ 268	Julio Gonzalez	.20	.09	.03
☐ 269	Woodie Fryman	.20	.09	.03
☐ 270	Butch Hobson	.30	.14	.04
☐ 271	Rawly Eastwick	.20	.09	.03
☐ 272	Tim Corcoran	.20	.09	.03
☐ 273	Jerry Terrell	.20	.09	.03
☐ 274	Willie Norwood	.20	.09	.03
☐ 275	Junior Moore	.20	.09	.03
☐ 276	Jim Colborn	.20	.09	.03
☐ 277	Tom Grieve	.30	.14	.04
☐ 278	Andy Messersmith	.30	.14	.04
☐ 279	Jerry Grote DP	.10	.05	.01
☐ 280	Andre Thornton	.30	.14	.04
☐ 281	Vic Correll DP	.10	.05	.01
☐ 282	Blue Jays Team/Mgr. Roy Hartsfield (Checklist back)	1.00	.15	.05
☐ 283	Ken Kravec	.20	.09	.03
☐ 284	Johnnie LeMaster	.20	.09	.03
☐ 285	Bobby Bonds	.50	.23	.06
☐ 286	Duffy Dyer	.20	.09	.03
☐ 287	Andres Mora	.20	.09	.03
☐ 288	Milt Wilcox	.20	.09	.03
☐ 289	Jose Cruz	.30	.14	.04
☐ 290	Dave Lopes	.30	.14	.04
☐ 291	Tom Griffin	.20	.09	.03
☐ 292	Don Reynolds	.20	.09	.03
☐ 293	Jerry Garvin	.20	.09	.03
☐ 294	Pepe Frias	.20	.09	.03
☐ 295	Mitchell Page	.20	.09	.03
☐ 296	Preston Hanna	.20	.09	.03
☐ 297	Ted Sizemore	.20	.09	.03
☐ 298	Rich Gale	.20	.09	.03
☐ 299	Steve Ontiveros	.20	.09	.03
☐ 300	Rod Carew	3.00	1.35	.40
☐ 301	Tom Hume	.20	.09	.03
☐ 302	Braves Team/Mgr. Bobby Cox (Checklist back)	1.00	.15	.05
☐ 303	Lary Sorensen DP	.10	.05	.01
☐ 304	Steve Swisher	.20	.09	.03
☐ 305	Willie Montanez	.20	.09	.03
☐ 306	Floyd Bannister	.20	.09	.03
☐ 307	Larvell Blanks	.20	.09	.03
☐ 308	Bert Blyleven	.50	.23	.06
☐ 309	Ralph Garr	.20	.09	.03
☐ 310	Thurman Munson	3.00	1.35	.40
☐ 311	Gary Lavelle	.20	.09	.03
☐ 312	Bob Robertson	.20	.09	.03
☐ 313	Dyar Miller	.20	.09	.03
☐ 314	Larry Harlow	.20	.09	.03
☐ 315	Jon Matlack	.20	.09	.03
☐ 316	Milt May	.20	.09	.03
☐ 317	Jose Cardenal	.20	.09	.03
☐ 318	Bob Welch	2.50	1.15	.30
☐ 319	Wayne Garrett	.20	.09	.03
☐ 320	Carl Yastrzemski	3.00	1.35	.40
☐ 321	Gaylord Perry	1.00	.45	.13
☐ 322	Danny Goodwin	.20	.09	.03
☐ 323	Lynn McGlothen	.20	.09	.03
☐ 324	Mike Tyson	.20	.09	.03
☐ 325	Cecil Cooper	.30	.14	.04
☐ 326	Pedro Borbon	.20	.09	.03
☐ 327	Art Howe DP	.10	.05	.01
☐ 328	Oakland A's Team/Mgr. Jack McKeon (Checklist back)	1.00	.15	.05
☐ 329	Joe Coleman	.20	.09	.03
☐ 330	George Brett	20.00	9.00	2.50
☐ 331	Mickey Mahler	.20	.09	.03
☐ 332	Gary Alexander	.20	.09	.03
☐ 333	Chet Lemon	.30	.14	.04
☐ 334	Craig Swan	.20	.09	.03
☐ 335	Chris Chambliss	.30	.14	.04
☐ 336	Bobby Thompson	.20	.09	.03
☐ 337	John Montague	.20	.09	.03
☐ 338	Vic Harris	.20	.09	.03
☐ 339	Ron Jackson	.20	.09	.03
☐ 340	Jim Palmer	3.00	1.35	.40
☐ 341	Willie Upshaw	.30	.14	.04
☐ 342	Dave Roberts	.20	.09	.03
☐ 343	Ed Glynn	.20	.09	.03
☐ 344	Jerry Royster	.20	.09	.03
☐ 345	Tug McGraw	.30	.14	.04
☐ 346	Bill Buckner	.30	.14	.04
☐ 347	Doug Rau	.20	.09	.03
☐ 348	Andre Dawson	9.00	4.00	1.15
☐ 349	Jim Wright	.20	.09	.03
☐ 350	Garry Templeton	.30	.14	.04

- ☐ 351 Wayne Nordhagen DP .. .10 .05 .01
- ☐ 352 Steve Renko .20 .09 .03
- ☐ 353 Checklist 243-363 1.00 .10 .03
- ☐ 354 Bill Bonham .20 .09 .03
- ☐ 355 Lee Mazzilli .20 .09 .03
- ☐ 356 Giants Team/Mgr. 1.00 .15 .05
  Joe Altobelli
  (Checklist back)
- ☐ 357 Jerry Augustine .20 .09 .03
- ☐ 358 Alan Trammell 15.00 6.75 1.90
- ☐ 359 Dan Spillner DP .10 .05 .01
- ☐ 360 Amos Otis .30 .14 .04
- ☐ 361 Tom Dixon .20 .09 .03
- ☐ 362 Mike Cubbage .20 .09 .03
- ☐ 363 Craig Skok .20 .09 .03
- ☐ 364 Gene Richards .20 .09 .03
- ☐ 365 Sparky Lyle .30 .14 .04
- ☐ 366 Juan Bernhardt .20 .09 .03
- ☐ 367 Dave Skaggs .20 .09 .03
- ☐ 368 Don Aase .20 .09 .03
- ☐ 369A Bump Wills ERR 3.00 1.35 .40
  (Blue Jays)
- ☐ 369B Bump Wills COR 3.00 1.35 .40
  (Rangers)
- ☐ 370 Dave Kingman .30 .14 .04
- ☐ 371 Jeff Holly .20 .09 .03
- ☐ 372 Lamar Johnson .20 .09 .03
- ☐ 373 Lance Rautzhan .20 .09 .03
- ☐ 374 Ed Herrmann .20 .09 .03
- ☐ 375 Bill Campbell .20 .09 .03
- ☐ 376 Gorman Thomas .30 .14 .04
- ☐ 377 Paul Moskau .20 .09 .03
- ☐ 378 Rob Picciolo DP .10 .05 .01
- ☐ 379 Dale Murray .20 .09 .03
- ☐ 380 John Mayberry .30 .14 .04
- ☐ 381 Astros Team/Mgr. 1.00 .15 .05
  Bill Virdon
  (Checklist back)
- ☐ 382 Jerry Martin .20 .09 .03
- ☐ 383 Phil Garner .30 .14 .04
- ☐ 384 Tommy Boggs .20 .09 .03
- ☐ 385 Dan Ford .20 .09 .03
- ☐ 386 Francisco Barrios .20 .09 .03
- ☐ 387 Gary Thomasson .20 .09 .03
- ☐ 388 Jack Billingham .20 .09 .03
- ☐ 389 Joe Zdeb .20 .09 .03
- ☐ 390 Rollie Fingers 1.00 .45 .13
- ☐ 391 Al Oliver .30 .14 .04
- ☐ 392 Doug Ault .20 .09 .03
- ☐ 393 Scott McGregor .30 .14 .04
- ☐ 394 Randy Stein .20 .09 .03
- ☐ 395 Dave Cash .20 .09 .03
- ☐ 396 Bill Plummer .20 .09 .03
- ☐ 397 Sergio Ferrer .20 .09 .03
- ☐ 398 Ivan DeJesus .20 .09 .03
- ☐ 399 David Clyde .20 .09 .03
- ☐ 400 Jim Rice 1.50 .65 .19
- ☐ 401 Ray Knight .50 .23 .06
- ☐ 402 Paul Hartzell .20 .09 .03
- ☐ 403 Tim Foli .20 .09 .03
- ☐ 404 White Sox Team/Mgr. 1.00 .15 .05
  Don Kessinger
  (Checklist back)
- ☐ 405 Butch Wynegar DP .10 .05 .01
- ☐ 406 Joe Wallis DP .10 .05 .01
- ☐ 407 Pete Vuckovich .30 .14 .04
- ☐ 408 Charlie Moore DP .10 .05 .01
- ☐ 409 Willie Wilson 2.00 .90 .25
- ☐ 410 Darrell Evans .40 .18 .05
- ☐ 411 Hits Record .60 .25 .08
  Season: George Sisler
  Career: Ty Cobb
- ☐ 412 RBI Record .75 .35 .09
  Season: Hack Wilson
  Career: Hank Aaron
- ☐ 413 Home Run Record 1.50 .65 .19
  Season: Roger Maris
  Career: Hank Aaron
- ☐ 414 Batting Record 1.00 .45 .13
  Season: Rogers Hornsby
  Career: Ty Cobb
- ☐ 415 Steals Record .50 .23 .06
  Season: Lou Brock
  Career: Lou Brock
- ☐ 416 Wins Record .35 .16 .04
  Season: Jack Chesbro
  Career: Cy Young
- ☐ 417 Strikeout Record DP .. 4.50 2.00 .55
  Season: Nolan Ryan
  Career: Walter Johnson
- ☐ 418 ERA Record DP .20 .09 .03
  Season: Dutch Leonard
  Career: Walter Johnson
- ☐ 419 Dick Ruthven .20 .09 .03
- ☐ 420 Ken Griffey .75 .35 .09
- ☐ 421 Doug DeCinces .30 .14 .04
- ☐ 422 Ruppert Jones .20 .09 .03
- ☐ 423 Bob Montgomery .20 .09 .03
- ☐ 424 Angels Team/Mgr. 1.00 .15 .05
  Jim Fregosi
  (Checklist back)
- ☐ 425 Rick Manning .20 .09 .03
- ☐ 426 Chris Speier .20 .09 .03
- ☐ 427 Andy Replogle .20 .09 .03
- ☐ 428 Bobby Valentine .20 .09 .03
- ☐ 429 John Urrea DP .10 .05 .01
- ☐ 430 Dave Parker 1.25 .55 .16
- ☐ 431 Glenn Borgmann .20 .09 .03
- ☐ 432 Dave Heaverlo .20 .09 .03
- ☐ 433 Larry Biittner .20 .09 .03
- ☐ 434 Ken Clay .20 .09 .03
- ☐ 435 Gene Tenace .30 .14 .04
- ☐ 436 Hector Cruz .20 .09 .03
- ☐ 437 Rick Williams .20 .09 .03
- ☐ 438 Horace Speed .20 .09 .03
- ☐ 439 Frank White .30 .14 .04
- ☐ 440 Rusty Staub .40 .18 .05
- ☐ 441 Lee Lacy .20 .09 .03
- ☐ 442 Doyle Alexander .20 .09 .03
- ☐ 443 Bruce Bochte .20 .09 .03
- ☐ 444 Aurelio Lopez .20 .09 .03
- ☐ 445 Steve Henderson .20 .09 .03
- ☐ 446 Jim Lonborg .20 .09 .03
- ☐ 447 Manny Sanguillen .30 .14 .04
- ☐ 448 Moose Haas .20 .09 .03
- ☐ 449 Bombo Rivera .20 .09 .03
- ☐ 450 Dave Concepcion .60 .25 .08
- ☐ 451 Royals Team/Mgr. 1.00 .15 .05
  Whitey Herzog
  (Checklist back)
- ☐ 452 Jerry Morales .20 .09 .03
- ☐ 453 Chris Knapp .20 .09 .03
- ☐ 454 Len Randle .20 .09 .03
- ☐ 455 Bill Lee DP .10 .05 .01
- ☐ 456 Chuck Baker .20 .09 .03
- ☐ 457 Bruce Sutter .50 .23 .06
- ☐ 458 Jim Essian .20 .09 .03
- ☐ 459 Sid Monge .20 .09 .03
- ☐ 460 Graig Nettles .30 .14 .04
- ☐ 461 Jim Barr DP .10 .05 .01
- ☐ 462 Otto Velez .20 .09 .03
- ☐ 463 Steve Comer .20 .09 .03
- ☐ 464 Joe Nolan .20 .09 .03
- ☐ 465 Reggie Smith .30 .14 .04
- ☐ 466 Mark Littell .20 .09 .03
- ☐ 467 Don Kessinger DP .10 .05 .01

	#	Player			
☐	468	Stan Bahnsen DP	.10	.05	.01
☐	469	Lance Parrish	1.50	.65	.19
☐	470	Garry Maddox DP	.10	.05	.01
☐	471	Joaquin Andujar	.30	.14	.04
☐	472	Craig Kusick	.20	.09	.03
☐	473	Dave Roberts	.20	.09	.03
☐	474	Dick Davis	.20	.09	.03
☐	475	Dan Driessen	.20	.09	.03
☐	476	Tom Poquette	.20	.09	.03
☐	477	Bob Grich	.30	.14	.04
☐	478	Juan Beniquez	.20	.09	.03
☐	479	Padres Team/Mgr. Roger Craig (Checklist back)	1.00	.15	.05
☐	480	Fred Lynn	.75	.35	.09
☐	481	Skip Lockwood	.20	.09	.03
☐	482	Craig Reynolds	.20	.09	.03
☐	483	Checklist 364-484 DP	.60	.08	.02
☐	484	Rick Waits	.20	.09	.03
☐	485	Bucky Dent	.30	.14	.04
☐	486	Bob Knepper	.20	.09	.03
☐	487	Miguel Dilone	.20	.09	.03
☐	488	Bob Owchinko	.20	.09	.03
☐	489	Larry Cox UER (Photo actually Dave Rader)	.20	.09	.03
☐	490	Al Cowens	.20	.09	.03
☐	491	Tippy Martinez	.30	.14	.04
☐	492	Bob Bailor	.20	.09	.03
☐	493	Larry Christenson	.20	.09	.03
☐	494	Jerry White	.20	.09	.03
☐	495	Tony Perez	1.00	.45	.13
☐	496	Barry Bonnell DP	.10	.05	.01
☐	497	Glenn Abbott	.20	.09	.03
☐	498	Rich Chiles	.20	.09	.03
☐	499	Rangers Team/Mgr. Pat Corrales (Checklist back)	1.00	.15	.05
☐	500	Ron Guidry	.50	.23	.06
☐	501	Junior Kennedy	.20	.09	.03
☐	502	Steve Braun	.20	.09	.03
☐	503	Terry Humphrey	.20	.09	.03
☐	504	Larry McWilliams	.20	.09	.03
☐	505	Ed Kranepool	.20	.09	.03
☐	506	John D'Acquisto	.20	.09	.03
☐	507	Tony Armas	.20	.09	.03
☐	508	Charlie Hough	.30	.14	.04
☐	509	Mario Mendoza UER (Career BA .278, should say .204)	.20	.09	.03
☐	510	Ted Simmons	.20	.09	.03
☐	511	Paul Reuschel DP	.10	.05	.01
☐	512	Jack Clark	.50	.23	.06
☐	513	Dave Johnson	.20	.09	.03
☐	514	Mike Proly	.20	.09	.03
☐	515	Enos Cabell	.20	.09	.03
☐	516	Champ Summers DP	.10	.05	.01
☐	517	Al Bumbry	.30	.14	.04
☐	518	Jim Umbarger	.20	.09	.03
☐	519	Ben Oglivie	.30	.14	.04
☐	520	Gary Carter	3.00	1.35	.40
☐	521	Sam Ewing	.20	.09	.03
☐	522	Ken Holtzman	.20	.09	.03
☐	523	John Milner	.20	.09	.03
☐	524	Tom Burgmeier	.20	.09	.03
☐	525	Freddie Patek	.20	.09	.03
☐	526	Dodgers Team/Mgr. Tom Lasorda (Checklist back)	1.00	.15	.05
☐	527	Lerrin LaGrow	.20	.09	.03
☐	528	Wayne Gross DP	.10	.05	.01
☐	529	Brian Asselstine	.20	.09	.03
☐	530	Frank Tanana	.20	.09	.03

	#	Player			
☐	531	Fernando Gonzalez	.20	.09	.03
☐	532	Buddy Schultz	.20	.09	.03
☐	533	Leroy Stanton	.20	.09	.03
☐	534	Ken Forsch	.20	.09	.03
☐	535	Ellis Valentine	.20	.09	.03
☐	536	Jerry Reuss	.30	.14	.04
☐	537	Tom Veryzer	.20	.09	.03
☐	538	Mike Ivie DP	.10	.05	.01
☐	539	John Ellis	.20	.09	.03
☐	540	Greg Luzinski	.30	.14	.04
☐	541	Jim Slaton	.20	.09	.03
☐	542	Rick Bosetti	.20	.09	.03
☐	543	Kiko Garcia	.20	.09	.03
☐	544	Fergie Jenkins	1.00	.45	.13
☐	545	John Stearns	.20	.09	.03
☐	546	Bill Russell	.30	.14	.04
☐	547	Clint Hurdle	.20	.09	.03
☐	548	Enrique Romo	.20	.09	.03
☐	549	Bob Bailey	.20	.09	.03
☐	550	Sal Bando	.30	.14	.04
☐	551	Cubs Team/Mgr. Herman Franks (Checklist back)	1.00	.15	.05
☐	552	Jose Morales	.20	.09	.03
☐	553	Denny Walling	.20	.09	.03
☐	554	Matt Keough	.20	.09	.03
☐	555	Biff Pocoroba	.20	.09	.03
☐	556	Mike Lum	.20	.09	.03
☐	557	Ken Brett	.20	.09	.03
☐	558	Jay Johnstone	.30	.14	.04
☐	559	Greg Pryor	.20	.09	.03
☐	560	John Montefusco	.20	.09	.03
☐	561	Ed Ott	.20	.09	.03
☐	562	Dusty Baker	.40	.18	.05
☐	563	Roy Thomas	.20	.09	.03
☐	564	Jerry Turner	.20	.09	.03
☐	565	Rico Carty	.30	.14	.04
☐	566	Nino Espinosa	.20	.09	.03
☐	567	Richie Hebner	.20	.09	.03
☐	568	Carlos Lopez	.20	.09	.03
☐	569	Bob Sykes	.20	.09	.03
☐	570	Cesar Cedeno	.30	.14	.04
☐	571	Darrell Porter	.20	.09	.03
☐	572	Rod Gilbreath	.20	.09	.03
☐	573	Jim Kern	.20	.09	.03
☐	574	Claudell Washington	.30	.14	.04
☐	575	Luis Tiant	.30	.14	.04
☐	576	Mike Parrott	.20	.09	.03
☐	577	Brewers Team/Mgr. George Bamberger (Checklist back)	1.00	.15	.05
☐	578	Pete Broberg	.20	.09	.03
☐	579	Greg Gross	.20	.09	.03
☐	580	Ron Fairly	.20	.09	.03
☐	581	Darold Knowles	.20	.09	.03
☐	582	Paul Blair	.30	.14	.04
☐	583	Julio Cruz	.20	.09	.03
☐	584	Jim Rooker	.20	.09	.03
☐	585	Hal McRae	.40	.18	.05
☐	586	Bob Horner	1.00	.45	.13
☐	587	Ken Reitz	.20	.09	.03
☐	588	Tom Murphy	.20	.09	.03
☐	589	Terry Whitfield	.20	.09	.03
☐	590	J.R. Richard	.30	.14	.04
☐	591	Mike Hargrove	.30	.14	.04
☐	592	Mike Krukow	.20	.09	.03
☐	593	Rick Dempsey	.30	.14	.04
☐	594	Bob Shirley	.20	.09	.03
☐	595	Phil Niekro	1.00	.45	.13
☐	596	Jim Wohlford	.20	.09	.03
☐	597	Bob Stanley	.20	.09	.03
☐	598	Mark Wagner	.20	.09	.03
☐	599	Jim Spencer	.20	.09	.03

	No.	Card			
☐	600	George Foster	.30	.14	.04
☐	601	Dave LaRoche	.20	.09	.03
☐	602	Checklist 485-605	1.00	.10	.03
☐	603	Rudy May	.20	.09	.03
☐	604	Jeff Newman	.20	.09	.03
☐	605	Rick Monday DP	.10	.05	.01
☐	606	Expos Team/Mgr. Dick Williams (Checklist back)	1.00	.15	.05
☐	607	Omar Moreno	.20	.09	.03
☐	608	Dave McKay	.20	.09	.03
☐	609	Silvio Martinez	.20	.09	.03
☐	610	Mike Schmidt	7.50	3.40	.95
☐	611	Jim Norris	.20	.09	.03
☐	612	Rick Honeycutt	.60	.25	.08
☐	613	Mike Edwards	.20	.09	.03
☐	614	Willie Hernandez	.30	.14	.04
☐	615	Ken Singleton	.30	.14	.04
☐	616	Billy Almon	.20	.09	.03
☐	617	Terry Puhl	.30	.14	.04
☐	618	Jerry Remy	.20	.09	.03
☐	619	Ken Landreaux	.30	.14	.04
☐	620	Bert Campaneris	.30	.14	.04
☐	621	Pat Zachry	.20	.09	.03
☐	622	Dave Collins	.30	.14	.04
☐	623	Bob McClure	.20	.09	.03
☐	624	Larry Herndon	.20	.09	.03
☐	625	Mark Fidrych	.50	.23	.06
☐	626	Yankees Team/Mgr. Bob Lemon (Checklist back)	1.00	.15	.05
☐	627	Gary Serum	.20	.09	.03
☐	628	Del Unser	.20	.09	.03
☐	629	Gene Garber	.20	.09	.03
☐	630	Bake McBride	.30	.14	.04
☐	631	Jorge Orta	.20	.09	.03
☐	632	Don Kirkwood	.20	.09	.03
☐	633	Rob Wilfong DP	.10	.05	.01
☐	634	Paul Lindblad	.20	.09	.03
☐	635	Don Baylor	.75	.35	.09
☐	636	Wayne Garland	.20	.09	.03
☐	637	Bill Robinson	.30	.14	.04
☐	638	Al Fitzmorris	.20	.09	.03
☐	639	Manny Trillo	.20	.09	.03
☐	640	Eddie Murray	25.00	11.50	3.10
☐	641	Bobby Castillo	.20	.09	.03
☐	642	Wilbur Howard DP	.10	.05	.01
☐	643	Tom Hausman	.20	.09	.03
☐	644	Manny Mota	.30	.14	.04
☐	645	George Scott DP	.10	.05	.01
☐	646	Rick Sweet	.20	.09	.03
☐	647	Bob Lacey	.20	.09	.03
☐	648	Lou Piniella	.20	.09	.03
☐	649	John Curtis	.20	.09	.03
☐	650	Pete Rose	5.00	2.30	.60
☐	651	Mike Caldwell	.20	.09	.03
☐	652	Stan Papi	.20	.09	.03
☐	653	Warren Brusstar DP	.10	.05	.01
☐	654	Rick Miller	.20	.09	.03
☐	655	Jerry Koosman	.30	.14	.04
☐	656	Hosken Powell	.20	.09	.03
☐	657	George Medich	.20	.09	.03
☐	658	Taylor Duncan	.20	.09	.03
☐	659	Mariners Team/Mgr. Darrell Johnson (Checklist back)	1.00	.15	.05
☐	660	Ron LeFlore DP	.10	.05	.01
☐	661	Bruce Kison	.20	.09	.03
☐	662	Kevin Bell	.20	.09	.03
☐	663	Mike Vail	.20	.09	.03
☐	664	Doug Bird	.20	.09	.03
☐	665	Lou Brock	3.00	1.35	.40
☐	666	Rich Dauer	.20	.09	.03
☐	667	Don Hood	.20	.09	.03
☐	668	Bill North	.20	.09	.03
☐	669	Checklist 606-726	1.00	.10	.03
☐	670	Jim Hunter DP	.75	.35	.09
☐	671	Joe Ferguson DP	.10	.05	.01
☐	672	Ed Halicki	.20	.09	.03
☐	673	Tom Hutton	.20	.09	.03
☐	674	Dave Tomlin	.20	.09	.03
☐	675	Tim McCarver	.20	.09	.03
☐	676	Johnny Sutton	.30	.14	.04
☐	677	Larry Parrish	.30	.14	.04
☐	678	Geoff Zahn	.20	.09	.03
☐	679	Derrel Thomas	.20	.09	.03
☐	680	Carlton Fisk	4.50	2.00	.55
☐	681	John Henry Johnson	.20	.09	.03
☐	682	Dave Chalk	.20	.09	.03
☐	683	Dan Meyer DP	.10	.05	.01
☐	684	Jamie Easterly DP	.10	.05	.01
☐	685	Sixto Lezcano	.20	.09	.03
☐	686	Ron Schueler DP	.10	.05	.01
☐	687	Rennie Stennett	.20	.09	.03
☐	688	Mike Willis	.20	.09	.03
☐	689	Orioles Team/Mgr. Earl Weaver (Checklist back)	1.00	.15	.05
☐	690	Buddy Bell DP	.20	.09	.03
☐	691	Dock Ellis DP	.10	.05	.01
☐	692	Mickey Stanley	.20	.09	.03
☐	693	Dave Rader	.20	.09	.03
☐	694	Burt Hooton	.30	.14	.04
☐	695	Keith Hernandez	.60	.25	.08
☐	696	Andy Hassler	.20	.09	.03
☐	697	Dave Bergman	.20	.09	.03
☐	698	Bill Stein	.20	.09	.03
☐	699	Hal Dues	.20	.09	.03
☐	700	Reggie Jackson DP	2.25	1.00	.30
☐	701	Orioles Prospects Mark Corey, John Flinn, Sammy Stewart	.20	.09	.03
☐	702	Red Sox Prospects Joel Finch, Garry Hancock, Allen Ripley	.20	.09	.03
☐	703	Angels Prospects Jim Anderson, Dave Frost, Bob Slater	.20	.09	.03
☐	704	White Sox Prospects Ross Baumgarten, Mike Colbern, Mike Squires	.20	.09	.03
☐	705	Indians Prospects Alfredo Griffin, Tim Norrid, Dave Oliver	.20	.09	.03
☐	706	Tigers Prospects Dave Stegman, Dave Tobik, Kip Young	.20	.09	.03
☐	707	Royals Prospects Randy Bass, Jim Gaudet, Randy McGilberry	.20	.09	.03
☐	708	Brewers Prospects Kevin Bass, Eddie Romero, Ned Yost	1.00	.45	.13
☐	709	Twins Prospects Sam Perlozzo, Rick Sofield, Kevin Stanfield	.20	.09	.03
☐	710	Yankees Prospects	.30	.14	.04

		NRMT-MT	EXC	G-VG
	Brian Doyle Mike Heath Dave Rajsich			
☐ 711	A's Prospects	.20	.09	.03
	Dwayne Murphy Bruce Robinson Alan Wirth			
☐ 712	Mariners Prospects	.20	.09	.03
	Bud Anderson Greg Biercevicz Byron McLaughlin			
☐ 713	Rangers Prospects	1.50	.65	.19
	Danny Darwin Pat Putnam Billy Sample			
☐ 714	Blue Jays Prospects	.20	.09	.03
	Victor Cruz Pat Kelly Ernie Whitt			
☐ 715	Braves Prospects	.20	.09	.03
	Bruce Benedict Glenn Hubbard Larry Whisenton			
☐ 716	Cubs Prospects	.20	.09	.03
	Dave Geisel Karl Pagel Scot Thompson			
☐ 717	Reds Prospects	.20	.09	.03
	Mike LaCoss Ron Oester Harry Spilman			
☐ 718	Astros Prospects	.20	.09	.03
	Bruce Bochy Mike Fischlin Don Pisker			
☐ 719	Dodgers Prospects	2.50	1.15	.30
	Pedro Guerrero Rudy Law Joe Simpson			
☐ 720	Expos Prospects	1.00	.45	.13
	Jerry Fry Jerry Pirtle Scott Sanderson			
☐ 721	Mets Prospects	.30	.14	.04
	Juan Berenguer Dwight Bernard Dan Norman			
☐ 722	Phillies Prospects	1.00	.45	.13
	Jim Morrison Lonnie Smith Jim Wright			
☐ 723	Pirates Prospects	.20	.09	.03
	Dale Berra Eugenio Cotes Ben Wiltbank			
☐ 724	Cardinals Prospects	.50	.23	.06
	Tom Bruno George Frazier Terry Kennedy			
☐ 725	Padres Prospects	.20	.09	.03
	Jim Beswick Steve Mura Broderick Perkins			
☐ 726	Giants Prospects	.35	.09	.03
	Greg Johnston Joe Strain John Tamargo			

1980 Topps

The cards in this 726-card set measure 2 1/2" by 3 1/2". In 1980 Topps released another set of the same size and number of cards as the previous two years. As with those sets, Topps again has produced 66 double-printed cards in the set; they are noted by DP in the checklist below. The player's name appears over the picture and his position and team are found in pennant design. Every card carries a facsimile autograph. Team cards feature a team checklist of players in the set on the back and the manager's name on the front. Cards 1-6 show Highlights (HL) of the 1979 season, cards 201-207 are League Leaders, and cards 661-686 feature American and National League rookie "Future Stars," one card for each team showing three young prospects. The key Rookie Card in this set is Rickey Henderson; other Rookie Cards included in this set are Dave Stieb and Rick Sutcliffe.

	NRMT-MT	EXC	G-VG
COMPLETE SET (726)	200.00	90.00	25.00
COMMON CARD (1-726)	.20	.09	.03
COMMON CARD DP	.10	.05	.01

		NRMT-MT	EXC	G-VG
☐ 1	Lou Brock and Carl Yastrzemski HL Enter 3000 hit circle	3.00	.60	.18
☐ 2	Willie McCovey HL 512th homer sets new mark for NL lefties	1.00	.45	.13
☐ 3	Manny Mota HL All-time pinch-hits, 145	.25	.11	.03
☐ 4	Pete Rose HL Career Record 10th season with 200 or more hits	2.00	.90	.25
☐ 5	Garry Templeton HL First with 100 hits from each side of plate	.25	.11	.03
☐ 6	Del Unser HL Third consecutive pinch homer sets new ML standard	.25	.11	.03
☐ 7	Mike Lum	.20	.09	.03
☐ 8	Craig Swan	.20	.09	.03
☐ 9	Steve Braun	.20	.09	.03
☐ 10	Dennis Martinez	1.00	.45	.13
☐ 11	Jimmy Sexton	.20	.09	.03
☐ 12	John Curtis DP	.10	.05	.01
☐ 13	Ron Pruitt	.20	.09	.03
☐ 14	Dave Cash	.20	.09	.03

	No.	Player			
☐	15	Bill Campbell	.20	.09	.03
☐	16	Jerry Narron	.20	.09	.03
☐	17	Bruce Sutter	.25	.11	.03
☐	18	Ron Jackson	.20	.09	.03
☐	19	Balor Moore	.20	.09	.03
☐	20	Dan Ford	.20	.09	.03
☐	21	Manny Sarmiento	.20	.09	.03
☐	22	Pat Putnam	.20	.09	.03
☐	23	Derrel Thomas	.20	.09	.03
☐	24	Jim Slaton	.20	.09	.03
☐	25	Lee Mazzilli	.20	.09	.03
☐	26	Marty Pattin	.20	.09	.03
☐	27	Del Unser	.20	.09	.03
☐	28	Bruce Kison	.20	.09	.03
☐	29	Mark Wagner	.20	.09	.03
☐	30	Vida Blue	.25	.11	.03
☐	31	Jay Johnstone	.25	.11	.03
☐	32	Julio Cruz DP	.10	.05	.01
☐	33	Tony Scott	.20	.09	.03
☐	34	Jeff Newman DP	.10	.05	.01
☐	35	Luis Tiant	.25	.11	.03
☐	36	Rusty Torres	.20	.09	.03
☐	37	Kiko Garcia	.20	.09	.03
☐	38	Dan Spillner DP	.10	.05	.01
☐	39	Rowland Office	.20	.09	.03
☐	40	Carlton Fisk	3.50	1.55	.45
☐	41	Rangers Team/Mgr. Pat Corrales (Checklist back)	.75	.19	.06
☐	42	David Palmer	.20	.09	.03
☐	43	Bombo Rivera	.20	.09	.03
☐	44	Bill Fahey	.20	.09	.03
☐	45	Frank White	.25	.11	.03
☐	46	Rico Carty	.25	.11	.03
☐	47	Bill Bonham DP	.10	.05	.01
☐	48	Rick Miller	.20	.09	.03
☐	49	Mario Guerrero	.20	.09	.03
☐	50	J.R. Richard	.25	.11	.03
☐	51	Joe Ferguson DP	.10	.05	.01
☐	52	Warren Brusstar	.20	.09	.03
☐	53	Ben Oglivie	.25	.11	.03
☐	54	Dennis Lamp	.20	.09	.03
☐	55	Bill Madlock	.25	.11	.03
☐	56	Bobby Valentine	.20	.09	.03
☐	57	Pete Vuckovich	.25	.11	.03
☐	58	Doug Flynn	.20	.09	.03
☐	59	Eddy Putman	.20	.09	.03
☐	60	Bucky Dent	.25	.11	.03
☐	61	Gary Serum	.20	.09	.03
☐	62	Mike Ivie	.20	.09	.03
☐	63	Bob Stanley	.20	.09	.03
☐	64	Joe Nolan	.20	.09	.03
☐	65	Al Bumbry	.25	.11	.03
☐	66	Royals Team/Mgr. Jim Frey (Checklist back)	.75	.19	.06
☐	67	Doyle Alexander	.20	.09	.03
☐	68	Larry Harlow	.20	.09	.03
☐	69	Rick Williams	.20	.09	.03
☐	70	Gary Carter	2.00	.90	.25
☐	71	John Milner DP	.10	.05	.01
☐	72	Fred Howard DP	.10	.05	.01
☐	73	Dave Collins	.20	.09	.03
☐	74	Sid Monge	.20	.09	.03
☐	75	Bill Russell	.25	.11	.03
☐	76	John Stearns	.20	.09	.03
☐	77	Dave Stieb	1.50	.65	.19
☐	78	Ruppert Jones	.20	.09	.03
☐	79	Bob Owchinko	.20	.09	.03
☐	80	Ron LeFlore	.25	.11	.03
☐	81	Ted Sizemore	.20	.09	.03
☐	82	Astros Team/Mgr. Bill Virdon (Checklist back)	.75	.19	.06
☐	83	Steve Trout	.20	.09	.03
☐	84	Gary Lavelle	.20	.09	.03
☐	85	Ted Simmons	.25	.11	.03
☐	86	Dave Hamilton	.20	.09	.03
☐	87	Pepe Frias	.20	.09	.03
☐	88	Ken Landreaux	.20	.09	.03
☐	89	Don Hood	.20	.09	.03
☐	90	Manny Trillo	.20	.09	.03
☐	91	Rick Dempsey	.25	.11	.03
☐	92	Rick Rhoden	.20	.09	.03
☐	93	Dave Roberts DP	.10	.05	.01
☐	94	Neil Allen	.20	.09	.03
☐	95	Cecil Cooper	.25	.11	.03
☐	96	A's Team/Mgr. Jim Marshall (Checklist back)	.75	.19	.06
☐	97	Bill Lee	.20	.09	.03
☐	98	Jerry Terrell	.20	.09	.03
☐	99	Victor Cruz	.20	.09	.03
☐	100	Johnny Bench	3.00	1.35	.40
☐	101	Aurelio Lopez	.20	.09	.03
☐	102	Rich Dauer	.20	.09	.03
☐	103	Bill Caudill	.20	.09	.03
☐	104	Manny Mota	.25	.11	.03
☐	105	Frank Tanana	.30	.14	.04
☐	106	Jeff Leonard	.40	.18	.05
☐	107	Francisco Barrios	.20	.09	.03
☐	108	Bob Horner	.25	.11	.03
☐	109	Bill Travers	.20	.09	.03
☐	110	Fred Lynn DP	.15	.07	.02
☐	111	Bob Knepper	.20	.09	.03
☐	112	White Sox Team/Mgr. Tony LaRussa (Checklist back)	.75	.19	.06
☐	113	Geoff Zahn	.20	.09	.03
☐	114	Juan Beniquez	.20	.09	.03
☐	115	Sparky Lyle	.25	.11	.03
☐	116	Larry Cox	.20	.09	.03
☐	117	Dock Ellis	.20	.09	.03
☐	118	Phil Garner	.25	.11	.03
☐	119	Sammy Stewart	.20	.09	.03
☐	120	Greg Luzinski	.25	.11	.03
☐	121	Checklist 1-121	.75	.09	.03
☐	122	Dave Rosello DP	.10	.05	.01
☐	123	Lynn Jones	.20	.09	.03
☐	124	Dave Lemanczyk	.20	.09	.03
☐	125	Tony Perez	.75	.35	.09
☐	126	Dave Tomlin	.20	.09	.03
☐	127	Gary Thomasson	.20	.09	.03
☐	128	Tom Burgmeier	.20	.09	.03
☐	129	Craig Reynolds	.20	.09	.03
☐	130	Amos Otis	.25	.11	.03
☐	131	Paul Mitchell	.20	.09	.03
☐	132	Biff Pocoroba	.20	.09	.03
☐	133	Jerry Turner	.20	.09	.03
☐	134	Matt Keough	.20	.09	.03
☐	135	Bill Buckner	.25	.11	.03
☐	136	Dick Ruthven	.20	.09	.03
☐	137	John Castino	.20	.09	.03
☐	138	Ross Baumgarten	.20	.09	.03
☐	139	Dane Iorg	.20	.09	.03
☐	140	Rich Gossage	.50	.23	.06
☐	141	Gary Alexander	.20	.09	.03
☐	142	Phil Huffman	.20	.09	.03
☐	143	Bruce Bochte DP	.10	.05	.01
☐	144	Steve Comer	.20	.09	.03
☐	145	Darrell Evans	.25	.11	.03
☐	146	Bob Welch	.50	.23	.06
☐	147	Terry Puhl	.20	.09	.03
☐	148	Manny Sanguillen	.25	.11	.03
☐	149	Tom Hume	.20	.09	.03
☐	150	Jason Thompson	.25	.11	.03

	No.	Player			
☐	151	Tom Hausman DP	.10	.05	.01
☐	152	John Fulgham	.20	.09	.03
☐	153	Tim Blackwell	.20	.09	.03
☐	154	Lary Sorensen	.20	.09	.03
☐	155	Jerry Remy	.20	.09	.03
☐	156	Tony Brizzolara	.20	.09	.03
☐	157	Willie Wilson DP	.20	.09	.03
☐	158	Rob Picciolo DP	.10	.05	.01
☐	159	Ken Clay	.20	.09	.03
☐	160	Eddie Murray	15.00	6.75	1.90
☐	161	Larry Christenson	.20	.09	.03
☐	162	Bob Randall	.20	.09	.03
☐	163	Steve Swisher	.20	.09	.03
☐	164	Greg Pryor	.20	.09	.03
☐	165	Omar Moreno	.20	.09	.03
☐	166	Glenn Abbott	.20	.09	.03
☐	167	Jack Clark	.20	.09	.03
☐	168	Rick Waits	.20	.09	.03
☐	169	Luis Gomez	.20	.09	.03
☐	170	Burt Hooton	.25	.11	.03
☐	171	Fernando Gonzalez	.20	.09	.03
☐	172	Ron Hodges	.20	.09	.03
☐	173	John Henry Johnson	.20	.09	.03
☐	174	Ray Knight	.25	.11	.03
☐	175	Rick Reuschel	.25	.11	.03
☐	176	Champ Summers	.20	.09	.03
☐	177	Dave Heaverlo	.20	.09	.03
☐	178	Tim McCarver	.30	.14	.04
☐	179	Ron Davis	.20	.09	.03
☐	180	Warren Cromartie	.20	.09	.03
☐	181	Moose Haas	.20	.09	.03
☐	182	Ken Reitz	.20	.09	.03
☐	183	Jim Anderson DP	.10	.05	.01
☐	184	Steve Renko DP	.10	.05	.01
☐	185	Hal McRae	.30	.14	.04
☐	186	Junior Moore	.20	.09	.03
☐	187	Alan Ashby	.20	.09	.03
☐	188	Terry Crowley	.20	.09	.03
☐	189	Kevin Kobel	.20	.09	.03
☐	190	Buddy Bell	.25	.11	.03
☐	191	Ted Martinez	.20	.09	.03
☐	192	Braves Team/Mgr.	.75	.19	.06
		Bobby Cox			
		(Checklist back)			
☐	193	Dave Goltz	.20	.09	.03
☐	194	Mike Easler	.20	.09	.03
☐	195	John Montefusco	.20	.09	.03
☐	196	Lance Parrish	.50	.23	.06
☐	197	Byron McLaughlin	.20	.09	.03
☐	198	Dell Alston DP	.10	.05	.01
☐	199	Mike LaCoss	.20	.09	.03
☐	200	Jim Rice	1.00	.45	.13
☐	201	Batting Leaders	.30	.14	.04
		Keith Hernandez			
		Fred Lynn			
☐	202	Home Run Leaders	.30	.14	.04
		Dave Kingman			
		Gorman Thomas			
☐	203	RBI Leaders	1.25	.55	.16
		Dave Winfield			
		Don Baylor			
☐	204	Stolen Base Leaders	.30	.14	.04
		Omar Moreno			
		Willie Wilson			
☐	205	Victory Leaders	.30	.14	.04
		Joe Niekro			
		Phil Niekro			
		Mike Flanagan			
☐	206	Strikeout Leaders	4.00	1.80	.50
		J.R. Richard			
		Nolan Ryan			
☐	207	ERA Leaders	.30	.14	.04
		J.R. Richard			
		Ron Guidry			
☐	208	Wayne Cage	.20	.09	.03
☐	209	Von Joshua	.20	.09	.03
☐	210	Steve Carlton	3.00	1.35	.40
☐	211	Dave Skaggs DP	.10	.05	.01
☐	212	Dave Roberts	.20	.09	.03
☐	213	Mike Jorgensen DP	.10	.05	.01
☐	214	Angels Team/Mgr.	.75	.19	.06
		Jim Fregosi			
		(Checklist back)			
☐	215	Sixto Lezcano	.20	.09	.03
☐	216	Phil Mankowski	.20	.09	.03
☐	217	Ed Halicki	.20	.09	.03
☐	218	Jose Morales	.20	.09	.03
☐	219	Steve Mingori	.20	.09	.03
☐	220	Dave Concepcion	.50	.23	.06
☐	221	Joe Cannon	.20	.09	.03
☐	222	Ron Hassey	.20	.09	.03
☐	223	Bob Sykes	.20	.09	.03
☐	224	Willie Montanez	.20	.09	.03
☐	225	Lou Piniella	.20	.09	.03
☐	226	Bill Stein	.20	.09	.03
☐	227	Len Barker	.20	.09	.03
☐	228	Johnny Oates	.20	.09	.03
☐	229	Jim Bibby	.20	.09	.03
☐	230	Dave Winfield	8.00	3.60	1.00
☐	231	Steve McCatty	.20	.09	.03
☐	232	Alan Trammell	7.00	3.10	.85
☐	233	LaRue Washington	.20	.09	.03
☐	234	Vern Ruhle	.20	.09	.03
☐	235	Andre Dawson	7.00	3.10	.85
☐	236	Marc Hill	.20	.09	.03
☐	237	Scott McGregor	.25	.11	.03
☐	238	Rob Wilfong	.20	.09	.03
☐	239	Don Aase	.20	.09	.03
☐	240	Dave Kingman	.25	.11	.03
☐	241	Checklist 122-242	.75	.09	.03
☐	242	Lamar Johnson	.20	.09	.03
☐	243	Jerry Augustine	.20	.09	.03
☐	244	Cardinals Team/Mgr.	.75	.19	.06
		Ken Boyer			
		(Checklist back)			
☐	245	Phil Niekro	.75	.35	.09
☐	246	Tim Foli DP	.10	.05	.01
☐	247	Frank Riccelli	.20	.09	.03
☐	248	Jamie Quirk	.20	.09	.03
☐	249	Jim Clancy	.20	.09	.03
☐	250	Jim Kaat	.30	.14	.04
☐	251	Kip Young	.20	.09	.03
☐	252	Ted Cox	.20	.09	.03
☐	253	John Montague	.20	.09	.03
☐	254	Paul Dade DP	.10	.05	.01
☐	255	Dusty Baker DP	.20	.09	.03
☐	256	Roger Erickson	.20	.09	.03
☐	257	Larry Herndon	.20	.09	.03
☐	258	Paul Moskau	.20	.09	.03
☐	259	Mets Team/Mgr.	.75	.19	.06
		Joe Torre			
		(Checklist back)			
☐	260	Al Oliver	.30	.14	.04
☐	261	Dave Chalk	.20	.09	.03
☐	262	Benny Ayala	.20	.09	.03
☐	263	Dave LaRoche DP	.10	.05	.01
☐	264	Bill Robinson	.25	.11	.03
☐	265	Robin Yount	9.00	4.00	1.15
☐	266	Bernie Carbo	.20	.09	.03
☐	267	Dan Schatzeder	.20	.09	.03
☐	268	Rafael Landestoy	.20	.09	.03
☐	269	Dave Tobik	.20	.09	.03
☐	270	Mike Schmidt DP	3.00	1.35	.40
☐	271	Dick Drago DP	.10	.05	.01
☐	272	Ralph Garr	.20	.09	.03
☐	273	Eduardo Rodriguez	.20	.09	.03

☐ 274 Dale Murphy .... 3.00 1.35 .40
☐ 275 Jerry Koosman .... .25 .11 .03
☐ 276 Tom Veryzer .... .20 .09 .03
☐ 277 Rick Bosetti.................. .20 .09 .03
☐ 278 Jim Spencer.................. .20 .09 .03
☐ 279 Rob Andrews .... .20 .09 .03
☐ 280 Gaylord Perry............... .75 .35 .09
☐ 281 Paul Blair .... .25 .11 .03
☐ 282 Mariners Team/Mgr. ..... .75 .19 .06
Darrell Johnson
(Checklist back)
☐ 283 John Ellis .... .20 .09 .03
☐ 284 Larry Murray DP .... .10 .05 .01
☐ 285 Don Baylor.................... .50 .23 .06
☐ 286 Darold Knowles DP...... .10 .05 .01
☐ 287 John Lowenstein.......... .20 .09 .03
☐ 288 Dave Rozema............... .20 .09 .03
☐ 289 Bruce Bochy .... .20 .09 .03
☐ 290 Steve Garvey............. 1.25 .55 .16
☐ 291 Randy Scarberry.......... .20 .09 .03
☐ 292 Dale Berra..................... .20 .09 .03
☐ 293 Elias Sosa..................... .20 .09 .03
☐ 294 Charlie Spikes.............. .20 .09 .03
☐ 295 Larry Gura..................... .20 .09 .03
☐ 296 Dave Rader .... .20 .09 .03
☐ 297 Tim Johnson.................. .20 .09 .03
☐ 298 Ken Holtzman .... .20 .09 .03
☐ 299 Steve Henderson.......... .20 .09 .03
☐ 300 Ron Guidry .... .25 .11 .03
☐ 301 Mike Edwards............... .20 .09 .03
☐ 302 Dodgers Team/Mgr...... .75 .19 .06
Tom Lasorda
(Checklist back)
☐ 303 Bill Castro .... .20 .09 .03
☐ 304 Butch Wynegar .... .20 .09 .03
☐ 305 Randy Jones................. .20 .09 .03
☐ 306 Denny Walling.............. .20 .09 .03
☐ 307 Rick Honeycutt .... .25 .11 .03
☐ 308 Mike Hargrove .... .25 .11 .03
☐ 309 Larry McWilliams......... .20 .09 .03
☐ 310 Dave Parker .... .75 .35 .09
☐ 311 Roger Metzger .... .20 .09 .03
☐ 312 Mike Barlow.................. .20 .09 .03
☐ 313 Johnny Grubb.............. .20 .09 .03
☐ 314 Tim Stoddard................ .20 .09 .03
☐ 315 Steve Kemp.................. .20 .09 .03
☐ 316 Bob Lacey..................... .20 .09 .03
☐ 317 Mike Anderson DP .... .10 .05 .01
☐ 318 Jerry Reuss.................. .25 .11 .03
☐ 319 Chris Speier.................. .20 .09 .03
☐ 320 Dennis Eckersley........ 2.00 .90 .25
☐ 321 Keith Hernandez........... .60 .25 .08
☐ 322 Claudell Washington.... .25 .11 .03
☐ 323 Mick Kelleher................ .20 .09 .03
☐ 324 Tom Underwood........... .20 .09 .03
☐ 325 Dan Driessen .... .20 .09 .03
☐ 326 Bo McLaughlin.............. .20 .09 .03
☐ 327 Ray Fosse DP............... .10 .05 .01
☐ 328 Twins Team/Mgr........... .75 .19 .06
Gene Mauch
(Checklist back)
☐ 329 Bert Roberge................. .20 .09 .03
☐ 330 Al Cowens..................... .20 .09 .03
☐ 331 Richie Hebner .... .20 .09 .03
☐ 332 Enrique Romo............... .20 .09 .03
☐ 333 Jim Norris DP .... .10 .05 .01
☐ 334 Jim Beattie.................... .20 .09 .03
☐ 335 Willie McCovey .... 2.00 .90 .25
☐ 336 George Medich .... .20 .09 .03
☐ 337 Carney Lansford .... .50 .23 .06
☐ 338 John Wockenfuss .... .20 .09 .03
☐ 339 John D'Acquisto .... .20 .09 .03
☐ 340 Ken Singleton .... .25 .11 .03
☐ 341 Jim Essian .... .20 .09 .03
☐ 342 Odell Jones................... .20 .09 .03
☐ 343 Mike Vail........................ .20 .09 .03
☐ 344 Randy Lerch .... .20 .09 .03
☐ 345 Larry Parrish................. .25 .11 .03
☐ 346 Buddy Solomon .... .20 .09 .03
☐ 347 Harry Chappas .... .20 .09 .03
☐ 348 Checklist 243-363........ .75 .09 .03
☐ 349 Jack Brohamer.............. .20 .09 .03
☐ 350 George Hendrick .... .25 .11 .03
☐ 351 Bob Davis .... .20 .09 .03
☐ 352 Dan Briggs.................... .20 .09 .03
☐ 353 Andy Hassler................ .20 .09 .03
☐ 354 Rick Auerbach.............. .20 .09 .03
☐ 355 Gary Matthews............. .25 .11 .03
☐ 356 Padres Team/Mgr. .... .75 .19 .06
Jerry Coleman
(Checklist back)
☐ 357 Bob McClure................. .20 .09 .03
☐ 358 Lou Whitaker .... 5.00 2.30 .60
☐ 359 Randy Moffitt............... .20 .09 .03
☐ 360 Darrell Porter DP .... .10 .05 .01
☐ 361 Wayne Garland .... .20 .09 .03
☐ 362 Danny Goodwin .... .20 .09 .03
☐ 363 Wayne Gross .... .20 .09 .03
☐ 364 Ray Burris..................... .20 .09 .03
☐ 365 Bobby Murcer............... .25 .11 .03
☐ 366 Rob Dressler................. .20 .09 .03
☐ 367 Billy Smith .... .20 .09 .03
☐ 368 Willie Aikens .... .25 .11 .03
☐ 369 Jim Kern .... .20 .09 .03
☐ 370 Cesar Cedeno.............. .25 .11 .03
☐ 371 Jack Morris.............. 1.25 .55 .16
☐ 372 Joel Youngblood.......... .20 .09 .03
☐ 373 Dan Petry DP .... .20 .09 .03
☐ 374 Jim Gantner.................. .25 .11 .03
☐ 375 Ross Grimsley .... .20 .09 .03
☐ 376 Gary Allenson .... .20 .09 .03
☐ 377 Junior Kennedy............ .20 .09 .03
☐ 378 Jerry Mumphrey .... .20 .09 .03
☐ 379 Kevin Bell...................... .20 .09 .03
☐ 380 Garry Maddox............... .20 .09 .03
☐ 381 Cubs Team/Mgr. .... .75 .19 .06
Preston Gomez
(Checklist back)
☐ 382 Dave Freisleben............ .20 .09 .03
☐ 383 Ed Ott............................ .20 .09 .03
☐ 384 Joey McLaughlin.......... .20 .09 .03
☐ 385 Enos Cabell.................. .20 .09 .03
☐ 386 Darrell Jackson .... .20 .09 .03
☐ 387A Fred Stanley............ 2.00 .90 .25
(Yellow name on front)
☐ 387B Fred Stanley.............. .20 .09 .03
(Red name on front)
☐ 388 Mike Paxton.................. .20 .09 .03
☐ 389 Pete LaCock................. .20 .09 .03
☐ 390 Fergie Jenkins........... 1.00 .45 .13
☐ 391 Tony Armas DP............ .10 .05 .01
☐ 392 Milt Wilcox.................... .20 .09 .03
☐ 393 Ozzie Smith............ 18.00 8.00 2.30
☐ 394 Reggie Cleveland .... .20 .09 .03
☐ 395 Ellis Valentine .... .20 .09 .03
☐ 396 Dan Meyer .... .20 .09 .03
☐ 397 Roy Thomas DP........... .10 .05 .01
☐ 398 Barry Foote.................. .20 .09 .03
☐ 399 Mike Proly DP .... .10 .05 .01
☐ 400 George Foster .... .20 .09 .03
☐ 401 Pete Falcone .... .20 .09 .03
☐ 402 Merv Rettenmund .... .20 .09 .03
☐ 403 Pete Redfern DP .... .10 .05 .01
☐ 404 Orioles Team/Mgr. .... .75 .19 .06
Earl Weaver
(Checklist back)

☐ 405 Dwight Evans .50 .23 .06
☐ 406 Paul Molitor 18.00 8.00 2.30
☐ 407 Tony Solaita .20 .09 .03
☐ 408 Bill North .20 .09 .03
☐ 409 Paul Splittorff .20 .09 .03
☐ 410 Bobby Bonds .30 .14 .04
☐ 411 Frank LaCorte .20 .09 .03
☐ 412 Thad Bosley .20 .09 .03
☐ 413 Allen Ripley .20 .09 .03
☐ 414 George Scott .25 .11 .03
☐ 415 Bill Atkinson .20 .09 .03
☐ 416 Tom Brookens .20 .09 .03
☐ 417 Craig Chamberlain DP .10 .05 .01
☐ 418 Roger Freed DP .10 .05 .01
☐ 419 Vic Correll .20 .09 .03
☐ 420 Butch Hobson .25 .11 .03
☐ 421 Doug Bird .20 .09 .03
☐ 422 Larry Milbourne .20 .09 .03
☐ 423 Dave Frost .20 .09 .03
☐ 424 Yankees Team/Mgr. .75 .19 .06
Dick Howser
(Checklist back)
☐ 425 Mark Belanger .25 .11 .03
☐ 426 Grant Jackson .20 .09 .03
☐ 427 Tom Hutton DP .10 .05 .01
☐ 428 Pat Zachry .20 .09 .03
☐ 429 Duane Kuiper .20 .09 .03
☐ 430 Larry Hisle DP .10 .05 .01
☐ 431 Mike Krukow .20 .09 .03
☐ 432 Willie Norwood .20 .09 .03
☐ 433 Rich Gale .20 .09 .03
☐ 434 Johnnie LeMaster .20 .09 .03
☐ 435 Don Gullett .25 .11 .03
☐ 436 Billy Almon .20 .09 .03
☐ 437 Joe Niekro .25 .11 .03
☐ 438 Dave Revering .20 .09 .03
☐ 439 Mike Phillips .20 .09 .03
☐ 440 Don Sutton .75 .35 .09
☐ 441 Eric Soderholm .20 .09 .03
☐ 442 Jorge Orta .20 .09 .03
☐ 443 Mike Parrott .20 .09 .03
☐ 444 Alvis Woods .20 .09 .03
☐ 445 Mark Fidrych .25 .11 .03
☐ 446 Duffy Dyer .20 .09 .03
☐ 447 Nino Espinosa .20 .09 .03
☐ 448 Jim Wohlford .20 .09 .03
☐ 449 Doug Bair .20 .09 .03
☐ 450 George Brett 16.00 7.25 2.00
☐ 451 Indians Team/Mgr. .75 .19 .06
Dave Garcia
(Checklist back)
☐ 452 Steve Dillard .20 .09 .03
☐ 453 Mike Bacsik .20 .09 .03
☐ 454 Tom Donohue .20 .09 .03
☐ 455 Mike Torrez .20 .09 .03
☐ 456 Frank Taveras .20 .09 .03
☐ 457 Bert Blyleven .30 .14 .04
☐ 458 Billy Sample .20 .09 .03
☐ 459 Mickey Lolich DP .15 .07 .02
☐ 460 Willie Randolph .25 .11 .03
☐ 461 Dwayne Murphy .20 .09 .03
☐ 462 Mike Sadek DP .10 .05 .01
☐ 463 Jerry Royster .20 .09 .03
☐ 464 John Denny .20 .09 .03
☐ 465 Rick Monday .25 .11 .03
☐ 466 Mike Squires .20 .09 .03
☐ 467 Jesse Jefferson .20 .09 .03
☐ 468 Aurelio Rodriguez .20 .09 .03
☐ 469 Randy Niemann DP .10 .05 .01
☐ 470 Bob Boone .20 .09 .03
☐ 471 Hosken Powell DP .10 .05 .01
☐ 472 Willie Hernandez .25 .11 .03
☐ 473 Bump Wills .20 .09 .03
☐ 474 Steve Busby .20 .09 .03
☐ 475 Cesar Geronimo .20 .09 .03
☐ 476 Bob Shirley .20 .09 .03
☐ 477 Buck Martinez .20 .09 .03
☐ 478 Gil Flores .20 .09 .03
☐ 479 Expos Team/Mgr. .75 .19 .06
Dick Williams
(Checklist back)
☐ 480 Bob Watson .25 .11 .03
☐ 481 Tom Paciorek .25 .11 .03
☐ 482 Rickey Henderson UER 70.00 32.00 8.75
(7 steals at Modesto,
should be at Fresno)
☐ 483 Bo Diaz .20 .09 .03
☐ 484 Checklist 364-484 .75 .09 .03
☐ 485 Mickey Rivers .25 .11 .03
☐ 486 Mike Tyson DP .10 .05 .01
☐ 487 Wayne Nordhagen .20 .09 .03
☐ 488 Roy Howell .20 .09 .03
☐ 489 Preston Hanna DP .10 .05 .01
☐ 490 Lee May .25 .11 .03
☐ 491 Steve Mura DP .10 .05 .01
☐ 492 Todd Cruz .20 .09 .03
☐ 493 Jerry Martin .20 .09 .03
☐ 494 Craig Minetto .20 .09 .03
☐ 495 Bake McBride .25 .11 .03
☐ 496 Silvio Martinez .20 .09 .03
☐ 497 Jim Mason .20 .09 .03
☐ 498 Danny Darwin .20 .09 .03
☐ 499 Giants Team/Mgr. .75 .19 .06
Dave Bristol
(Checklist back)
☐ 500 Tom Seaver 3.50 1.55 .45
☐ 501 Rennie Stennett .20 .09 .03
☐ 502 Rich Wortham DP .10 .05 .01
☐ 503 Mike Cubbage .20 .09 .03
☐ 504 Gene Garber .20 .09 .03
☐ 505 Bert Campaneris .25 .11 .03
☐ 506 Tom Buskey .20 .09 .03
☐ 507 Leon Roberts .20 .09 .03
☐ 508 U.L. Washington .20 .09 .03
☐ 509 Ed Glynn .20 .09 .03
☐ 510 Ron Cey .25 .11 .03
☐ 511 Eric Wilkins .20 .09 .03
☐ 512 Jose Cardenal .20 .09 .03
☐ 513 Tom Dixon DP .10 .05 .01
☐ 514 Steve Ontiveros .20 .09 .03
☐ 515 Mike Caldwell UER .20 .09 .03
(1979 loss total reads
96 instead of 6)
☐ 516 Hector Cruz .20 .09 .03
☐ 517 Don Stanhouse .20 .09 .03
☐ 518 Nelson Norman .20 .09 .03
☐ 519 Steve Nicosia .20 .09 .03
☐ 520 Steve Rogers .20 .09 .03
☐ 521 Ken Brett .20 .09 .03
☐ 522 Jim Morrison .20 .09 .03
☐ 523 Ken Henderson .20 .09 .03
☐ 524 Jim Wright DP .10 .05 .01
☐ 525 Clint Hurdle .20 .09 .03
☐ 526 Phillies Team/Mgr. .85 .21 .07
Dallas Green
(Checklist back)
☐ 527 Doug Rau DP .10 .05 .01
☐ 528 Adrian Devine .20 .09 .03
☐ 529 Jim Barr .20 .09 .03
☐ 530 Jim Sundberg DP .15 .07 .02
☐ 531 Eric Rasmussen .20 .09 .03
☐ 532 Willie Horton .25 .11 .03
☐ 533 Checklist 485-605 .75 .09 .03
☐ 534 Andre Thornton .25 .11 .03
☐ 535 Bob Forsch .20 .09 .03
☐ 536 Lee Lacy .20 .09 .03

- ☐ 537 Alex Trevino .20 .09 .03
- ☐ 538 Joe Strain .20 .09 .03
- ☐ 539 Rudy May .20 .09 .03
- ☐ 540 Pete Rose 4.50 2.00 .55
- ☐ 541 Miguel Dilone .20 .09 .03
- ☐ 542 Joe Coleman .20 .09 .03
- ☐ 543 Pat Kelly .20 .09 .03
- ☐ 544 Rick Sutcliffe 2.00 .90 .25
- ☐ 545 Jeff Burroughs .20 .09 .03
- ☐ 546 Rick Langford .20 .09 .03
- ☐ 547 John Wathan .20 .09 .03
- ☐ 548 Dave Rajsich .20 .09 .03
- ☐ 549 Larry Wolfe .20 .09 .03
- ☐ 550 Ken Griffey .60 .25 .08
- ☐ 551 Pirates Team/Mgr. .75 .19 .06
  Chuck Tanner
  (Checklist back)
- ☐ 552 Bill Nahorodny .20 .09 .03
- ☐ 553 Dick Davis .20 .09 .03
- ☐ 554 Art Howe .25 .11 .03
- ☐ 555 Ed Figueroa .20 .09 .03
- ☐ 556 Joe Rudi .25 .11 .03
- ☐ 557 Mark Lee .20 .09 .03
- ☐ 558 Alfredo Griffin .20 .09 .03
- ☐ 559 Dale Murray .20 .09 .03
- ☐ 560 Dave Lopes .25 .11 .03
- ☐ 561 Eddie Whitson .20 .09 .03
- ☐ 562 Joe Wallis .20 .09 .03
- ☐ 563 Will McEnaney .20 .09 .03
- ☐ 564 Rick Manning .20 .09 .03
- ☐ 565 Dennis Leonard .25 .11 .03
- ☐ 566 Bud Harrelson .20 .09 .03
- ☐ 567 Skip Lockwood .20 .09 .03
- ☐ 568 Gary Roenicke .20 .09 .03
- ☐ 569 Terry Kennedy .25 .11 .03
- ☐ 570 Roy Smalley .25 .11 .03
- ☐ 571 Joe Sambito .20 .09 .03
- ☐ 572 Jerry Morales DP .10 .05 .01
- ☐ 573 Kent Tekulve .25 .11 .03
- ☐ 574 Scot Thompson .20 .09 .03
- ☐ 575 Ken Kravec .20 .09 .03
- ☐ 576 Jim Dwyer .20 .09 .03
- ☐ 577 Blue Jays Team/Mgr. .75 .19 .06
  Bobby Mattick
  (Checklist back)
- ☐ 578 Scott Sanderson .50 .23 .06
- ☐ 579 Charlie Moore .20 .09 .03
- ☐ 580 Nolan Ryan 22.00 10.00 2.80
- ☐ 581 Bob Bailor .20 .09 .03
- ☐ 582 Brian Doyle .20 .09 .03
- ☐ 583 Bob Stinson .20 .09 .03
- ☐ 584 Kurt Bevacqua .20 .09 .03
- ☐ 585 Al Hrabosky .20 .09 .03
- ☐ 586 Mitchell Page .20 .09 .03
- ☐ 587 Garry Templeton .25 .11 .03
- ☐ 588 Greg Minton .20 .09 .03
- ☐ 589 Chet Lemon .25 .11 .03
- ☐ 590 Jim Palmer 2.50 1.15 .30
- ☐ 591 Rick Cerone .20 .09 .03
- ☐ 592 Jon Matlack .20 .09 .03
- ☐ 593 Jesus Alou .20 .09 .03
- ☐ 594 Dick Tidrow .20 .09 .03
- ☐ 595 Don Money .20 .09 .03
- ☐ 596 Rick Matula .20 .09 .03
- ☐ 597 Tom Poquette .20 .09 .03
- ☐ 598 Fred Kendall DP .10 .05 .01
- ☐ 599 Mike Norris .20 .09 .03
- ☐ 600 Reggie Jackson 7.00 3.10 .85
- ☐ 601 Buddy Schultz .20 .09 .03
- ☐ 602 Brian Downing .25 .11 .03
- ☐ 603 Jack Billingham DP .10 .05 .01
- ☐ 604 Glenn Adams .20 .09 .03
- ☐ 605 Terry Forster .20 .09 .03
- ☐ 606 Reds Team/Mgr. .75 .19 .06
  John McNamara
  (Checklist back)
- ☐ 607 Woodie Fryman .20 .09 .03
- ☐ 608 Alan Bannister .20 .09 .03
- ☐ 609 Ron Reed .20 .09 .03
- ☐ 610 Willie Stargell 1.50 .65 .19
- ☐ 611 Jerry Garvin DP .10 .05 .01
- ☐ 612 Cliff Johnson .20 .09 .03
- ☐ 613 Randy Stein .20 .09 .03
- ☐ 614 John Hiller .20 .09 .03
- ☐ 615 Doug DeCinces .25 .11 .03
- ☐ 616 Gene Richards .20 .09 .03
- ☐ 617 Joaquin Andujar .25 .11 .03
- ☐ 618 Bob Montgomery DP .10 .05 .01
- ☐ 619 Sergio Ferrer .20 .09 .03
- ☐ 620 Richie Zisk .20 .09 .03
- ☐ 621 Bob Grich .25 .11 .03
- ☐ 622 Mario Soto .20 .09 .03
- ☐ 623 Gorman Thomas .25 .11 .03
- ☐ 624 Lerrin LaGrow .20 .09 .03
- ☐ 625 Chris Chambliss .25 .11 .03
- ☐ 626 Tigers Team/Mgr. .75 .19 .06
  Sparky Anderson
  (Checklist back)
- ☐ 627 Pedro Borbon .20 .09 .03
- ☐ 628 Doug Capilla .20 .09 .03
- ☐ 629 Jim Todd .20 .09 .03
- ☐ 630 Larry Bowa .25 .11 .03
- ☐ 631 Mark Littell .20 .09 .03
- ☐ 632 Barry Bonnell .20 .09 .03
- ☐ 633 Bob Apodaca .20 .09 .03
- ☐ 634 Glenn Borgmann DP .10 .05 .01
- ☐ 635 John Candelaria .25 .11 .03
- ☐ 636 Toby Harrah .25 .11 .03
- ☐ 637 Joe Simpson .20 .09 .03
- ☐ 638 Mark Clear .20 .09 .03
- ☐ 639 Larry Biittner .20 .09 .03
- ☐ 640 Mike Flanagan .25 .11 .03
- ☐ 641 Ed Kranepool .20 .09 .03
- ☐ 642 Ken Forsch DP .10 .05 .01
- ☐ 643 John Mayberry .20 .09 .03
- ☐ 644 Charlie Hough .25 .11 .03
- ☐ 645 Rick Burleson .20 .09 .03
- ☐ 646 Checklist 606-726 .75 .09 .03
- ☐ 647 Milt May .20 .09 .03
- ☐ 648 Roy White .25 .11 .03
- ☐ 649 Tom Griffin .20 .09 .03
- ☐ 650 Joe Morgan 2.00 .90 .25
- ☐ 651 Rollie Fingers 1.00 .45 .13
- ☐ 652 Mario Mendoza .20 .09 .03
- ☐ 653 Stan Bahnsen .20 .09 .03
- ☐ 654 Bruce Boisclair DP .10 .05 .01
- ☐ 655 Tug McGraw .25 .11 .03
- ☐ 656 Larvell Blanks .20 .09 .03
- ☐ 657 Dave Edwards .20 .09 .03
- ☐ 658 Chris Knapp .20 .09 .03
- ☐ 659 Brewers Team/Mgr. .75 .19 .06
  George Bamberger
  (Checklist back)
- ☐ 660 Rusty Staub .25 .11 .03
- ☐ 661 Orioles Rookies .20 .09 .03
  Mark Corey
  Dave Ford
  Wayne Krenchicki
- ☐ 662 Red Sox Rookies .20 .09 .03
  Joel Finch
  Mike O'Berry
  Chuck Rainey
- ☐ 663 Angels Rookies .75 .35 .09
  Ralph Botting
  Bob Clark
  Dickie Thon

- ☐ 664 White Sox Rookies....... .20 .09 .03
  Mike Colbern
  Guy Hoffman
  Dewey Robinson
- ☐ 665 Indians Rookies .... .25 .11 .03
  Larry Andersen
  Bobby Cuellar
  Sandy Wihtol
- ☐ 666 Tigers Rookies .... .20 .09 .03
  Mike Chris
  Al Greene
  Bruce Robbins
- ☐ 667 Royals Rookies .... 2.50 1.15 .30
  Renie Martin
  Bill Paschall
  Dan Quisenberry
- ☐ 668 Brewers Rookies.......... .20 .09 .03
  Danny Boitano
  Willie Mueller
  Lenn Sakata
- ☐ 669 Twins Rookies .... .20 .09 .03
  Dan Graham
  Rick Sofield
  Gary Ward
- ☐ 670 Yankees Rookies.......... .20 .09 .03
  Bobby Brown
  Brad Gulden
  Darryl Jones
- ☐ 671 A's Rookies............... 1.00 .45 .13
  Derek Bryant
  Brian Kingman
  Mike Morgan
- ☐ 672 Mariners Rookies......... .20 .09 .03
  Charlie Beamon
  Rodney Craig
  Rafael Vasquez
- ☐ 673 Rangers Rookies.......... .20 .09 .03
  Brian Allard
  Jerry Don Gleaton
  Greg Mahlberg
- ☐ 674 Blue Jays Rookies........ .20 .09 .03
  Butch Edge
  Pat Kelly
  Ted Wilborn
- ☐ 675 Braves Rookies .... .20 .09 .03
  Bruce Benedict
  Larry Bradford
  Eddie Miller
- ☐ 676 Cubs Rookies................ .20 .09 .03
  Dave Geisel
  Steve Macko
  Karl Pagel
- ☐ 677 Reds Rookies............... .20 .09 .03
  Art DeFreites
  Frank Pastore
  Harry Spilman
- ☐ 678 Astros Rookies .... .20 .09 .03
  Reggie Baldwin
  Alan Knicely
  Pete Ladd
- ☐ 679 Dodgers Rookies .... .25 .11 .03
  Joe Beckwith
  Mickey Hatcher
  Dave Patterson
- ☐ 680 Expos Rookies............. .25 .11 .03
  Tony Bernazard
  Randy Miller
  John Tamargo
- ☐ 681 Mets Rookies............. 1.50 .65 .19
  Dan Norman
  Jesse Orosco
  Mike Scott
- ☐ 682 Phillies Rookies .... .20 .09 .03
  Ramon Aviles
  Dickie Noles
  Kevin Saucier
- ☐ 683 Pirates Rookies............ .20 .09 .03
  Dorian Boyland
  Alberto Lois
  Harry Saferight
- ☐ 684 Cardinals Rookies .... .50 .23 .06
  George Frazier
  Tom Herr
  Dan O'Brien
- ☐ 685 Padres Rookies............ .20 .09 .03
  Tim Flannery
  Brian Greer
  Jim Wilhelm
- ☐ 686 Giants Rookies............ .20 .09 .03
  Greg Johnston
  Dennis Littlejohn
  Phil Nastu
- ☐ 687 Mike Heath DP .... .10 .05 .01
- ☐ 688 Steve Stone.................. .20 .09 .03
- ☐ 689 Red Sox Team/Mgr....... .75 .19 .06
  Don Zimmer
  (Checklist back)
- ☐ 690 Tommy John................ .30 .14 .04
- ☐ 691 Ivan DeJesus .... .20 .09 .03
- ☐ 692 Rawly Eastwick DP .... .10 .05 .01
- ☐ 693 Craig Kusick................. .20 .09 .03
- ☐ 694 Jim Rooker .... .20 .09 .03
- ☐ 695 Reggie Smith .... .25 .11 .03
- ☐ 696 Julio Gonzalez.............. .20 .09 .03
- ☐ 697 David Clyde.................. .20 .09 .03
- ☐ 698 Oscar Gamble .... .25 .11 .03
- ☐ 699 Floyd Bannister............ .20 .09 .03
- ☐ 700 Rod Carew DP .... 1.50 .65 .19
- ☐ 701 Ken Oberkfell .... .20 .09 .03
- ☐ 702 Ed Farmer .... .20 .09 .03
- ☐ 703 Otto Velez .... .20 .09 .03
- ☐ 704 Gene Tenace .... .25 .11 .03
- ☐ 705 Freddie Patek .... .20 .09 .03
- ☐ 706 Tippy Martinez .... .25 .11 .03
- ☐ 707 Elliott Maddox............... .20 .09 .03
- ☐ 708 Bob Tolan .... .20 .09 .03
- ☐ 709 Pat Underwood .... .20 .09 .03
- ☐ 710 Graig Nettles .... .25 .11 .03
- ☐ 711 Bob Galasso................. .20 .09 .03
- ☐ 712 Rodney Scott .... .20 .09 .03
- ☐ 713 Terry Whitfield .... .20 .09 .03
- ☐ 714 Fred Norman................. .20 .09 .03
- ☐ 715 Sal Bando .... .25 .11 .03
- ☐ 716 Lynn McGlothen .... .20 .09 .03
- ☐ 717 Mickey Klutts DP .... .10 .05 .01
- ☐ 718 Greg Gross .... .20 .09 .03
- ☐ 719 Don Robinson............... .25 .11 .03
- ☐ 720 Carl Yastrzemski DP .. 1.50 .65 .19
- ☐ 721 Paul Hartzell................. .20 .09 .03
- ☐ 722 Jose Cruz..................... .25 .11 .03
- ☐ 723 Shane Rawley .... .20 .09 .03
- ☐ 724 Jerry White .... .20 .09 .03
- ☐ 725 Rick Wise...................... .20 .09 .03
- ☐ 726 Steve Yeager................ .35 .10 .03

1981 Topps

The cards in this 726-card set measure 2 1/2" by 3 1/2". League Leaders (1-8), Record Breakers (201-208), and Post-season cards (401-404) are topical subsets found in this set marketed by Topps in

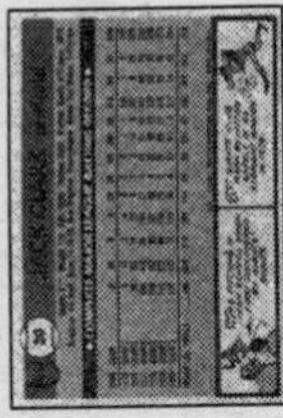

1981. The team cards are all grouped together (661-686) and feature team checklist backs and a very small photo of the team's manager in the upper right corner of the obverse. The obverses carry the player's position and team in a baseball cap design, and the company name is printed in a small baseball. The backs are red and gray. The 66 double-printed cards are noted in the checklist by DP. The more notable Rookie Cards in the set include Harold Baines, Kirk Gibson, Bruce Hurst, Tim Raines, Jeff Reardon, and Fernando Valenzuela. Other Rookie Cards in the set are Mike Boddicker, Hubie Brooks, Bill Gullickson, Charlie Leibrandt, Lloyd Moseby, Tony Pena, and John Tudor.

	NRMT-MT	EXC	G-VG
COMPLETE SET (726)	70.00	32.00	8.75
COMMON CARD (1-726)	.10	.05	.01
COMMON CARD DP	.05	.02	.01
☐ 1 Batting Leaders	2.50	.50	.15
George Brett			
Bill Buckner			
☐ 2 Home Run Leaders	1.00	.45	.13
Reggie Jackson			
Ben Oglivie			
Mike Schmidt			
☐ 3 RBI Leaders	.50	.23	.06
Cecil Cooper			
Mike Schmidt			
☐ 4 Stolen Base Leaders	1.50	.65	.19
Rickey Henderson			
Ron LeFlore			
☐ 5 Victory Leaders	.40	.18	.05
Steve Stone			
Steve Carlton			
☐ 6 Strikeout Leaders	.40	.18	.05
Len Barker			
Steve Carlton			
☐ 7 ERA Leaders	.20	.09	.03
Rudy May			
Don Sutton			
☐ 8 Leading Firemen	.35	.16	.04
Dan Quisenberry			
Rollie Fingers			
Tom Hume			
☐ 9 Pete LaCock DP	.05	.02	.01
☐ 10 Mike Flanagan	.15	.07	.02
☐ 11 Jim Wohlford DP	.05	.02	.01
☐ 12 Mark Clear	.10	.05	.01
☐ 13 Joe Charboneau	.75	.35	.09
☐ 14 John Tudor	.50	.23	.06
☐ 15 Larry Parrish	.10	.05	.01
☐ 16 Ron Davis	.10	.05	.01
☐ 17 Cliff Johnson	.10	.05	.01
☐ 18 Glenn Adams	.10	.05	.01
☐ 19 Jim Clancy	.10	.05	.01
☐ 20 Jeff Burroughs	.10	.05	.01
☐ 21 Ron Oester	.10	.05	.01
☐ 22 Danny Darwin	.15	.07	.02
☐ 23 Alex Trevino	.10	.05	.01
☐ 24 Don Stanhouse	.10	.05	.01
☐ 25 Sixto Lezcano	.10	.05	.01
☐ 26 U.L. Washington	.10	.05	.01
☐ 27 Champ Summers DP	.05	.02	.01
☐ 28 Enrique Romo	.10	.05	.01
☐ 29 Gene Tenace	.10	.05	.01
☐ 30 Jack Clark	.15	.07	.02
☐ 31 Checklist 1-121 DP	.15	.02	.01
☐ 32 Ken Oberkfell	.10	.05	.01
☐ 33 Rick Honeycutt	.10	.05	.01
☐ 34 Aurelio Rodriguez	.10	.05	.01
☐ 35 Mitchell Page	.10	.05	.01
☐ 36 Ed Farmer	.10	.05	.01
☐ 37 Gary Roenicke	.10	.05	.01
☐ 38 Win Remmerswaal	.10	.05	.01
☐ 39 Tom Veryzer	.10	.05	.01
☐ 40 Tug McGraw	.15	.07	.02
☐ 41 Ranger Rookies	.10	.05	.01
Bob Babcock			
John Butcher			
Jerry Don Gleaton			
☐ 42 Jerry White DP	.05	.02	.01
☐ 43 Jose Morales	.10	.05	.01
☐ 44 Larry McWilliams	.10	.05	.01
☐ 45 Enos Cabell	.10	.05	.01
☐ 46 Rick Bosetti	.10	.05	.01
☐ 47 Ken Brett	.10	.05	.01
☐ 48 Dave Skaggs	.10	.05	.01
☐ 49 Bob Shirley	.10	.05	.01
☐ 50 Dave Lopes	.15	.07	.02
☐ 51 Bill Robinson DP	.10	.05	.01
☐ 52 Hector Cruz	.10	.05	.01
☐ 53 Kevin Saucier	.10	.05	.01
☐ 54 Ivan DeJesus	.10	.05	.01
☐ 55 Mike Norris	.10	.05	.01
☐ 56 Buck Martinez	.10	.05	.01
☐ 57 Dave Roberts	.10	.05	.01
☐ 58 Joel Youngblood	.10	.05	.01
☐ 59 Dan Petry	.15	.07	.02
☐ 60 Willie Randolph	.15	.07	.02
☐ 61 Butch Wynegar	.10	.05	.01
☐ 62 Joe Pettini	.10	.05	.01
☐ 63 Steve Renko DP	.05	.02	.01
☐ 64 Brian Asselstine	.10	.05	.01
☐ 65 Scott McGregor	.10	.05	.01
☐ 66 Royals Rookies	.10	.05	.01
Manny Castillo			
Tim Ireland			
Mike Jones			
☐ 67 Ken Kravec	.10	.05	.01
☐ 68 Matt Alexander DP	.05	.02	.01
☐ 69 Ed Halicki	.10	.05	.01
☐ 70 Al Oliver DP	.10	.05	.01
☐ 71 Hal Dues	.10	.05	.01
☐ 72 Barry Evans DP	.05	.02	.01
☐ 73 Doug Bair	.10	.05	.01
☐ 74 Mike Hargrove	.15	.07	.02
☐ 75 Reggie Smith	.15	.07	.02
☐ 76 Mario Mendoza	.10	.05	.01
☐ 77 Mike Barlow	.10	.05	.01
☐ 78 Steve Dillard	.10	.05	.01
☐ 79 Bruce Robbins	.10	.05	.01
☐ 80 Rusty Staub	.15	.07	.02
☐ 81 Dave Stapleton	.10	.05	.01
☐ 82 Astros Rookies DP	.10	.05	.01
Danny Heep			
Alan Knicely			
Bobby Sprowl			

☐ 83 Mike Proly	.10	.05	.01
☐ 84 Johnnie LeMaster	.10	.05	.01
☐ 85 Mike Caldwell	.10	.05	.01
☐ 86 Wayne Gross	.10	.05	.01
☐ 87 Rick Camp	.10	.05	.01
☐ 88 Joe Lefebvre	.10	.05	.01
☐ 89 Darrell Jackson	.10	.05	.01
☐ 90 Bake McBride	.10	.05	.01
☐ 91 Tim Stoddard DP	.05	.02	.01
☐ 92 Mike Easler	.10	.05	.01
☐ 93 Ed Glynn DP	.10	.05	.01
☐ 94 Harry Spilman DP	.05	.02	.01
☐ 95 Jim Sundberg	.15	.07	.02
☐ 96 A's Rookies Dave Beard Ernie Camacho Pat Dempsey	.10	.05	.01
☐ 97 Chris Speier	.10	.05	.01
☐ 98 Clint Hurdle	.10	.05	.01
☐ 99 Eric Wilkins	.10	.05	.01
☐ 100 Rod Carew	2.00	.90	.25
☐ 101 Benny Ayala	.10	.05	.01
☐ 102 Dave Tobik	.10	.05	.01
☐ 103 Jerry Martin	.10	.05	.01
☐ 104 Terry Forster	.10	.05	.01
☐ 105 Jose Cruz	.15	.07	.02
☐ 106 Don Money	.10	.05	.01
☐ 107 Rich Wortham	.10	.05	.01
☐ 108 Bruce Benedict	.10	.05	.01
☐ 109 Mike Scott	.10	.05	.01
☐ 110 Carl Yastrzemski	2.00	.90	.25
☐ 111 Greg Minton	.10	.05	.01
☐ 112 White Sox Rookies Rusty Kuntz Fran Mullins Leo Sutherland	.10	.05	.01
☐ 113 Mike Phillips	.10	.05	.01
☐ 114 Tom Underwood	.10	.05	.01
☐ 115 Roy Smalley	.10	.05	.01
☐ 116 Joe Simpson	.10	.05	.01
☐ 117 Pete Falcone	.10	.05	.01
☐ 118 Kurt Bevacqua	.10	.05	.01
☐ 119 Tippy Martinez	.15	.07	.02
☐ 120 Larry Bowa	.15	.07	.02
☐ 121 Larry Harlow	.10	.05	.01
☐ 122 John Denny	.10	.05	.01
☐ 123 Al Cowens	.10	.05	.01
☐ 124 Jerry Garvin	.10	.05	.01
☐ 125 Andre Dawson	2.50	1.15	.30
☐ 126 Charlie Leibrandt	.50	.23	.06
☐ 127 Rudy Law	.10	.05	.01
☐ 128 Gary Allenson DP	.05	.02	.01
☐ 129 Art Howe	.15	.07	.02
☐ 130 Larry Gura	.10	.05	.01
☐ 131 Keith Moreland	.15	.07	.02
☐ 132 Tommy Boggs	.10	.05	.01
☐ 133 Jeff Cox	.10	.05	.01
☐ 134 Steve Mura	.10	.05	.01
☐ 135 Gorman Thomas	.15	.07	.02
☐ 136 Doug Capilla	.10	.05	.01
☐ 137 Hosken Powell	.10	.05	.01
☐ 138 Rich Dotson DP	.05	.02	.01
☐ 139 Oscar Gamble	.10	.05	.01
☐ 140 Bob Forsch	.10	.05	.01
☐ 141 Miguel Dilone	.10	.05	.01
☐ 142 Jackson Todd	.10	.05	.01
☐ 143 Dan Meyer	.10	.05	.01
☐ 144 Allen Ripley	.10	.05	.01
☐ 145 Mickey Rivers	.15	.07	.02
☐ 146 Bobby Castillo	.10	.05	.01
☐ 147 Dale Berra	.10	.05	.01
☐ 148 Randy Niemann	.10	.05	.01
☐ 149 Joe Nolan	.10	.05	.01
☐ 150 Mark Fidrych	.15	.07	.02
☐ 151 Claudell Washington	.10	.05	.01
☐ 152 John Urrea	.10	.05	.01
☐ 153 Tom Poquette	.10	.05	.01
☐ 154 Rick Langford	.10	.05	.01
☐ 155 Chris Chambliss	.15	.07	.02
☐ 156 Bob McClure	.10	.05	.01
☐ 157 John Wathan	.10	.05	.01
☐ 158 Fergie Jenkins	.75	.35	.09
☐ 159 Brian Doyle	.10	.05	.01
☐ 160 Garry Maddox	.10	.05	.01
☐ 161 Dan Graham	.10	.05	.01
☐ 162 Doug Corbett	.10	.05	.01
☐ 163 Bill Almon	.10	.05	.01
☐ 164 LaMarr Hoyt	.15	.07	.02
☐ 165 Tony Scott	.10	.05	.01
☐ 166 Floyd Bannister	.10	.05	.01
☐ 167 Terry Whitfield	.10	.05	.01
☐ 168 Don Robinson DP	.05	.02	.01
☐ 169 John Mayberry	.10	.05	.01
☐ 170 Ross Grimsley	.10	.05	.01
☐ 171 Gene Richards	.10	.05	.01
☐ 172 Gary Woods	.10	.05	.01
☐ 173 Bump Wills	.10	.05	.01
☐ 174 Doug Rau	.10	.05	.01
☐ 175 Dave Collins	.10	.05	.01
☐ 176 Mike Krukow	.10	.05	.01
☐ 177 Rick Peters	.10	.05	.01
☐ 178 Jim Essian DP	.05	.02	.01
☐ 179 Rudy May	.10	.05	.01
☐ 180 Pete Rose	3.50	1.55	.45
☐ 181 Elias Sosa	.10	.05	.01
☐ 182 Bob Grich	.15	.07	.02
☐ 183 Dick Davis DP	.05	.02	.01
☐ 184 Jim Dwyer	.10	.05	.01
☐ 185 Dennis Leonard	.10	.05	.01
☐ 186 Wayne Nordhagen	.10	.05	.01
☐ 187 Mike Parrott	.10	.05	.01
☐ 188 Doug DeCinces	.15	.07	.02
☐ 189 Craig Swan	.10	.05	.01
☐ 190 Cesar Cedeno	.15	.07	.02
☐ 191 Rick Sutcliffe	.40	.18	.05
☐ 192 Braves Rookies Terry Harper Ed Miller Rafael Ramirez	.15	.07	.02
☐ 193 Pete Vuckovich	.15	.07	.02
☐ 194 Rod Scurry	.10	.05	.01
☐ 195 Rich Murray	.10	.05	.01
☐ 196 Duffy Dyer	.10	.05	.01
☐ 197 Jim Kern	.10	.05	.01
☐ 198 Jerry Dybzinski	.10	.05	.01
☐ 199 Chuck Rainey	.10	.05	.01
☐ 200 George Foster	.15	.07	.02
☐ 201 Johnny Bench RB Most homers, lifetime, catcher	1.00	.45	.13
☐ 202 Steve Carlton RB Most strikeouts, lefthander, lifetime	1.00	.45	.13
☐ 203 Bill Gullickson RB Most strikeouts, game, rookie	.25	.11	.03
☐ 204 Ron LeFlore and Rodney Scott RB Most stolen bases, teammates, season	.20	.09	.03
☐ 205 Pete Rose RB Most cons. seasons 600 or more at-bats	1.50	.65	.19
☐ 206 Mike Schmidt RB Most homers, third baseman, season	1.50	.65	.19

☐ 207 Ozzie Smith RB .... 2.00 .90 .25
Most assists,
season, shortstop
☐ 208 Willie Wilson RB .... .20 .09 .03
Most at-bats, season
☐ 209 Dickie Thon DP .... .10 .05 .01
☐ 210 Jim Palmer .... 2.00 .90 .25
☐ 211 Derrel Thomas .... .10 .05 .01
☐ 212 Steve Nicosia .... .10 .05 .01
☐ 213 Al Holland .... .10 .05 .01
☐ 214 Angels Rookies .... .10 .05 .01
Ralph Botting
Jim Dorsey
John Harris
☐ 215 Larry Hisle .... .10 .05 .01
☐ 216 John Henry Johnson .... .10 .05 .01
☐ 217 Rich Hebner .... .10 .05 .01
☐ 218 Paul Splittorff .... .10 .05 .01
☐ 219 Ken Landreaux .... .10 .05 .01
☐ 220 Tom Seaver .... 2.25 1.00 .30
☐ 221 Bob Davis .... .10 .05 .01
☐ 222 Jorge Orta .... .10 .05 .01
☐ 223 Roy Lee Jackson .... .10 .05 .01
☐ 224 Pat Zachry .... .10 .05 .01
☐ 225 Ruppert Jones .... .10 .05 .01
☐ 226 Manny Sanguillen DP .... .05 .02 .01
☐ 227 Fred Martinez .... .10 .05 .01
☐ 228 Tom Paciorek .... .15 .07 .02
☐ 229 Rollie Fingers .... .75 .35 .09
☐ 230 George Hendrick .... .15 .07 .02
☐ 231 Joe Beckwith .... .10 .05 .01
☐ 232 Mickey Klutts .... .10 .05 .01
☐ 233 Skip Lockwood .... .10 .05 .01
☐ 234 Lou Whitaker .... 1.50 .65 .19
☐ 235 Scott Sanderson .... .15 .07 .02
☐ 236 Mike Ivie .... .10 .05 .01
☐ 237 Charlie Moore .... .10 .05 .01
☐ 238 Willie Hernandez .... .15 .07 .02
☐ 239 Rick Miller DP .... .05 .02 .01
☐ 240 Nolan Ryan 12.00 5.50 1.50
☐ 241 Checklist 122-242 DP .... .15 .02 .01
☐ 242 Chet Lemon .... .10 .05 .01
☐ 243 Sal Butera .... .10 .05 .01
☐ 244 Cardinals Rookies .... .10 .05 .01
Tito Landrum
Al Olmsted
Andy Rincon
☐ 245 Ed Figueroa .... .10 .05 .01
☐ 246 Ed Ott DP .... .05 .02 .01
☐ 247 Glenn Hubbard DP .... .05 .02 .01
☐ 248 Joey McLaughlin .... .10 .05 .01
☐ 249 Larry Cox .... .10 .05 .01
☐ 250 Ron Guidry .... .15 .07 .02
☐ 251 Tom Brookens .... .10 .05 .01
☐ 252 Victor Cruz .... .10 .05 .01
☐ 253 Dave Bergman .... .10 .05 .01
☐ 254 Ozzie Smith .... 5.00 2.30 .60
☐ 255 Mark Littell .... .10 .05 .01
☐ 256 Bombo Rivera .... .10 .05 .01
☐ 257 Rennie Stennett .... .10 .05 .01
☐ 258 Joe Price .... .10 .05 .01
☐ 259 Mets Rookies .... .90 .40 .11
Juan Berenguer
Hubie Brooks
Mookie Wilson
☐ 260 Ron Cey .... .15 .07 .02
☐ 261 Rickey Henderson 12.00 5.50 1.50
☐ 262 Sammy Stewart .... .10 .05 .01
☐ 263 Brian Downing .... .15 .07 .02
☐ 264 Jim Norris .... .10 .05 .01
☐ 265 John Candelaria .... .15 .07 .02
☐ 266 Tom Herr .... .15 .07 .02
☐ 267 Stan Bahnsen .... .10 .05 .01
☐ 268 Jerry Royster .... .10 .05 .01
☐ 269 Ken Forsch .... .10 .05 .01
☐ 270 Greg Luzinski .... .15 .07 .02
☐ 271 Bill Castro .... .10 .05 .01
☐ 272 Bruce Kimm .... .10 .05 .01
☐ 273 Stan Papi .... .10 .05 .01
☐ 274 Craig Chamberlain .... .10 .05 .01
☐ 275 Dwight Evans .... .20 .09 .03
☐ 276 Dan Spillner .... .10 .05 .01
☐ 277 Alfredo Griffin .... .10 .05 .01
☐ 278 Rick Sofield .... .10 .05 .01
☐ 279 Bob Knepper .... .10 .05 .01
☐ 280 Ken Griffey .... .10 .05 .01
☐ 281 Fred Stanley .... .10 .05 .01
☐ 282 Mariners Rookies .... .10 .05 .01
Rick Anderson
Greg Biercevicz
Rodney Craig
☐ 283 Billy Sample .... .10 .05 .01
☐ 284 Brian Kingman .... .10 .05 .01
☐ 285 Jerry Turner .... .10 .05 .01
☐ 286 Dave Frost .... .10 .05 .01
☐ 287 Lenn Sakata .... .10 .05 .01
☐ 288 Bob Clark .... .10 .05 .01
☐ 289 Mickey Hatcher .... .10 .05 .01
☐ 290 Bob Boone DP .... .10 .05 .01
☐ 291 Aurelio Lopez .... .10 .05 .01
☐ 292 Mike Squires .... .10 .05 .01
☐ 293 Charlie Lea .... .10 .05 .01
☐ 294 Mike Tyson DP .... .05 .02 .01
☐ 295 Hal McRae .... .20 .09 .03
☐ 296 Bill Nahorodny DP .... .05 .02 .01
☐ 297 Bob Bailor .... .10 .05 .01
☐ 298 Buddy Solomon .... .10 .05 .01
☐ 299 Elliott Maddox .... .10 .05 .01
☐ 300 Paul Molitor .... 5.00 2.30 .60
☐ 301 Matt Keough .... .10 .05 .01
☐ 302 Dodgers Rookies .... 3.00 1.35 .40
Jack Perconte
Mike Scioscia
Fernando Valenzuela
☐ 303 Johnny Oates .... .10 .05 .01
☐ 304 John Castino .... .10 .05 .01
☐ 305 Ken Clay .... .10 .05 .01
☐ 306 Juan Beniquez DP .... .05 .02 .01
☐ 307 Gene Garber .... .10 .05 .01
☐ 308 Rick Manning .... .10 .05 .01
☐ 309 Luis Salazar .... .10 .05 .01
☐ 310 Vida Blue DP .... .05 .02 .01
☐ 311 Freddie Patek .... .10 .05 .01
☐ 312 Rick Rhoden .... .10 .05 .01
☐ 313 Luis Pujols .... .10 .05 .01
☐ 314 Rich Dauer .... .10 .05 .01
☐ 315 Kirk Gibson .... 5.00 2.30 .60
☐ 316 Craig Minetto .... .10 .05 .01
☐ 317 Lonnie Smith .... .10 .05 .01
☐ 318 Steve Yeager .... .10 .05 .01
☐ 319 Rowland Office .... .10 .05 .01
☐ 320 Tom Burgmeier .... .10 .05 .01
☐ 321 Leon Durham .... .15 .07 .02
☐ 322 Neil Allen .... .10 .05 .01
☐ 323 Jim Morrison DP .... .05 .02 .01
☐ 324 Mike Willis .... .10 .05 .01
☐ 325 Ray Knight .... .15 .07 .02
☐ 326 Biff Pocoroba .... .10 .05 .01
☐ 327 Moose Haas .... .10 .05 .01
☐ 328 Twins Rookies .... .10 .05 .01
Dave Engle
Greg Johnston
Gary Ward
☐ 329 Joaquin Andujar .... .15 .07 .02
☐ 330 Frank White .... .15 .07 .02
☐ 331 Dennis Lamp .... .10 .05 .01

☐ 581 Roy Howell	.10	.05	.01
☐ 582 Gaylord Perry	.75	.35	.09
☐ 583 Larry Milbourne	.10	.05	.01
☐ 584 Randy Lerch	.10	.05	.01
☐ 585 Amos Otis	.15	.07	.02
☐ 586 Silvio Martinez	.10	.05	.01
☐ 587 Jeff Newman	.10	.05	.01
☐ 588 Gary Lavelle	.10	.05	.01
☐ 589 Lamar Johnson	.10	.05	.01
☐ 590 Bruce Sutter	.15	.07	.02
☐ 591 John Lowenstein	.10	.05	.01
☐ 592 Steve Comer	.10	.05	.01
☐ 593 Steve Kemp	.10	.05	.01
☐ 594 Preston Hanna DP	.05	.02	.01
☐ 595 Butch Hobson	.15	.07	.02
☐ 596 Jerry Augustine	.10	.05	.01
☐ 597 Rafael Landestoy	.10	.05	.01
☐ 598 George Vukovich DP	.05	.02	.01
☐ 599 Dennis Kinney	.10	.05	.01
☐ 600 Johnny Bench	2.50	1.15	.30
☐ 601 Don Aase	.10	.05	.01
☐ 602 Bobby Murcer	.15	.07	.02
☐ 603 John Verhoeven	.10	.05	.01
☐ 604 Rob Picciolo	.10	.05	.01
☐ 605 Don Sutton	.75	.35	.09
☐ 606 Reds Rookies DP	.10	.05	.01
Bruce Berenyi			
Geoff Combe			
Paul Householder			
☐ 607 David Palmer	.10	.05	.01
☐ 608 Greg Pryor	.10	.05	.01
☐ 609 Lynn McGlothen	.10	.05	.01
☐ 610 Darrell Porter	.10	.05	.01
☐ 611 Rick Matula DP	.05	.02	.01
☐ 612 Duane Kuiper	.10	.05	.01
☐ 613 Jim Anderson	.10	.05	.01
☐ 614 Dave Rozema	.10	.05	.01
☐ 615 Rick Dempsey	.15	.07	.02
☐ 616 Rick Wise	.10	.05	.01
☐ 617 Craig Reynolds	.10	.05	.01
☐ 618 John Milner	.10	.05	.01
☐ 619 Steve Henderson	.10	.05	.01
☐ 620 Dennis Eckersley	1.25	.55	.16
☐ 621 Tom Donohue	.10	.05	.01
☐ 622 Randy Moffitt	.10	.05	.01
☐ 623 Sal Bando	.15	.07	.02
☐ 624 Bob Welch	.15	.07	.02
☐ 625 Bill Buckner	.15	.07	.02
☐ 626 Tigers Rookies	.10	.05	.01
Dave Steffen			
Jerry Ujdur			
Roger Weaver			
☐ 627 Luis Tiant	.15	.07	.02
☐ 628 Vic Correll	.10	.05	.01
☐ 629 Tony Armas	.15	.07	.02
☐ 630 Steve Carlton	2.25	1.00	.30
☐ 631 Ron Jackson	.10	.05	.01
☐ 632 Alan Bannister	.10	.05	.01
☐ 633 Bill Lee	.10	.05	.01
☐ 634 Doug Flynn	.10	.05	.01
☐ 635 Bobby Bonds	.15	.07	.02
☐ 636 Al Hrabosky	.10	.05	.01
☐ 637 Jerry Narron	.10	.05	.01
☐ 638 Checklist 606-726	.30	.05	.01
☐ 639 Carney Lansford	.15	.07	.02
☐ 640 Dave Parker	.20	.09	.03
☐ 641 Mark Belanger	.15	.07	.02
☐ 642 Vern Ruhle	.10	.05	.01
☐ 643 Lloyd Moseby	.15	.07	.02
☐ 644 Ramon Aviles DP	.05	.02	.01
☐ 645 Rick Reuschel	.15	.07	.02
☐ 646 Marvis Foley	.10	.05	.01
☐ 647 Dick Drago	.10	.05	.01
☐ 648 Darrell Evans	.15	.07	.02
☐ 649 Manny Sarmiento	.10	.05	.01
☐ 650 Bucky Dent	.15	.07	.02
☐ 651 Pedro Guerrero	.10	.05	.01
☐ 652 John Montague	.10	.05	.01
☐ 653 Bill Fahey	.10	.05	.01
☐ 654 Ray Burris	.10	.05	.01
☐ 655 Dan Driessen	.10	.05	.01
☐ 656 Jon Matlack	.10	.05	.01
☐ 657 Mike Cubbage DP	.05	.02	.01
☐ 658 Milt Wilcox	.10	.05	.01
☐ 659 Brewers Rookies	.10	.05	.01
John Flinn			
Ed Romero			
Ned Yost			
☐ 660 Gary Carter	1.00	.45	.13
☐ 661 Orioles Team/Mgr.	.30	.10	.05
Earl Weaver			
(Checklist back)			
☐ 662 Red Sox Team/Mgr.	.30	.10	.05
Ralph Houk			
(Checklist back)			
☐ 663 Angels Team/Mgr.	.30	.10	.05
Jim Fregosi			
(Checklist back)			
☐ 664 White Sox Team/Mgr.	.30	.10	.05
Tony LaRussa			
(Checklist back)			
☐ 665 Indians Team/Mgr.	.30	.10	.05
Dave Garcia			
(Checklist back)			
☐ 666 Tigers Team/Mgr.	.30	.10	.05
Sparky Anderson			
(Checklist back)			
☐ 667 Royals Team/Mgr.	.30	.10	.05
Jim Frey			
(Checklist back)			
☐ 668 Brewers Team/Mgr.	.30	.10	.05
Bob Rodgers			
(Checklist back)			
☐ 669 Twins Team/Mgr.	.30	.10	.05
John Goryl			
(Checklist back)			
☐ 670 Yankees Team/Mgr.	.30	.10	.05
Gene Michael			
(Checklist back)			
☐ 671 A's Team/Mgr.	.30	.10	.05
Billy Martin			
(Checklist back)			
☐ 672 Mariners Team/Mgr.	.30	.10	.05
Maury Wills			
(Checklist back)			
☐ 673 Rangers Team/Mgr.	.30	.10	.05
Don Zimmer			
(Checklist back)			
☐ 674 Blue Jays Team/Mgr.	.30	.10	.05
Bobby Mattick			
(Checklist back)			
☐ 675 Braves Team/Mgr.	.30	.10	.05
Bobby Cox			
(Checklist back)			
☐ 676 Cubs Team/Mgr.	.30	.10	.05
Joe Amalfitano			
(Checklist back)			
☐ 677 Reds Team/Mgr.	.30	.10	.05
John McNamara			
(Checklist back)			
☐ 678 Astros Team/Mgr.	.30	.10	.05
Bill Virdon			
(Checklist back)			
☐ 679 Dodgers Team/Mgr.	.30	.10	.05
Tom Lasorda			
(Checklist back)			

□ 680 Expos Team/Mgr. Dick Williams (Checklist back)	.30	.10	.05
□ 681 Mets Team/Mgr. Joe Torre (Checklist back)	.30	.10	.05
□ 682 Phillies Team/Mgr. Dallas Green (Checklist back)	.30	.10	.05
□ 683 Pirates Team/Mgr. Chuck Tanner (Checklist back)	.30	.10	.05
□ 684 Cardinals Team/Mgr. Whitey Herzog (Checklist back)	.30	.10	.05
□ 685 Padres Team/Mgr. Frank Howard (Checklist back)	.30	.10	.05
□ 686 Giants Team/Mgr. Dave Bristol (Checklist back)	.30	.10	.05
□ 687 Jeff Jones	.10	.05	.01
□ 688 Kiko Garcia	.10	.05	.01
□ 689 Red Sox Rookies Bruce Hurst Keith MacWhorter Reid Nichols	.75	.35	.09
□ 690 Bob Watson	.15	.07	.02
□ 691 Dick Ruthven	.10	.05	.01
□ 692 Lenny Randle	.10	.05	.01
□ 693 Steve Howe	.15	.07	.02
□ 694 Bud Harrelson DP	.05	.02	.01
□ 695 Kent Tekulve	.15	.07	.02
□ 696 Alan Ashby	.10	.05	.01
□ 697 Rick Waits	.10	.05	.01
□ 698 Mike Jorgensen	.10	.05	.01
□ 699 Glenn Abbott	.10	.05	.01
□ 700 George Brett	6.00	2.70	.75
□ 701 Joe Rudi	.15	.07	.02
□ 702 George Medich	.10	.05	.01
□ 703 Alvis Woods	.10	.05	.01
□ 704 Bill Travers DP	.05	.02	.01
□ 705 Ted Simmons	.15	.07	.02
□ 706 Dave Ford	.10	.05	.01
□ 707 Dave Cash	.10	.05	.01
□ 708 Doyle Alexander	.10	.05	.01
□ 709 Alan Trammell DP	1.75	.80	.22
□ 710 Ron LeFlore DP	.05	.02	.01
□ 711 Joe Ferguson	.10	.05	.01
□ 712 Bill Bonham	.10	.05	.01
□ 713 Bill North	.10	.05	.01
□ 714 Pete Redfern	.10	.05	.01
□ 715 Bill Madlock	.15	.07	.02
□ 716 Glenn Borgmann	.10	.05	.01
□ 717 Jim Barr DP	.05	.02	.01
□ 718 Larry Biittner	.10	.05	.01
□ 719 Sparky Lyle	.15	.07	.02
□ 720 Fred Lynn	.15	.07	.02
□ 721 Toby Harrah	.15	.07	.02
□ 722 Joe Niekro	.15	.07	.02
□ 723 Bruce Bochte	.10	.05	.01
□ 724 Lou Piniella	.15	.07	.02
□ 725 Steve Rogers	.10	.05	.01
□ 726 Rick Monday	.25	.07	.02

1981 Topps Traded

The cards in this 132-card set measure 2 1/2" by 3 1/2". For the first time since 1976, Topps issued a "traded" set in 1981. Unlike the small traded sets of 1974 and 1976, this set contains a larger number of cards and was sequentially numbered, alphabetically, from 727 to 858. Thus, this set gives the impression it is a continuation of their regular issue of this year. The sets were issued only through hobby card dealers and were boxed in complete sets of 132 cards. There are no key Rookie Cards in this set although Tim Raines, Jeff Reardon, and Fernando Valenzuela are depicted in their rookie year for cards. The key extended Rookie Card in the set is Danny Ainge.

	NRMT-MT	EXC	G-VG
COMPLETE SET (132)	35.00	16.00	4.40
COMPLETE FACT.SET (132)	40.00	18.00	5.00
COMMON CARD (727-858)	.25	.11	.03
□ 727 Danny Ainge	8.00	3.60	1.00
□ 728 Doyle Alexander	.25	.11	.03
□ 729 Gary Alexander	.25	.11	.03
□ 730 Bill Almon	.25	.11	.03
□ 731 Joaquin Andujar	.35	.16	.04
□ 732 Bob Bailor	.25	.11	.03
□ 733 Juan Beniquez	.25	.11	.03
□ 734 Dave Bergman	.25	.11	.03
□ 735 Tony Bernazard	.25	.11	.03
□ 736 Larry Biittner	.25	.11	.03
□ 737 Doug Bird	.25	.11	.03
□ 738 Bert Blyleven	.50	.23	.06
□ 739 Mark Bomback	.25	.11	.03
□ 740 Bobby Bonds	.50	.23	.06
□ 741 Rick Bosetti	.25	.11	.03
□ 742 Hubie Brooks	.75	.35	.09
□ 743 Rick Burleson	.25	.11	.03
□ 744 Ray Burris	.25	.11	.03
□ 745 Jeff Burroughs	.25	.11	.03
□ 746 Enos Cabell	.25	.11	.03
□ 747 Ken Clay	.25	.11	.03
□ 748 Mark Clear	.25	.11	.03
□ 749 Larry Cox	.25	.11	.03
□ 750 Hector Cruz	.25	.11	.03
□ 751 Victor Cruz	.25	.11	.03
□ 752 Mike Cubbage	.25	.11	.03
□ 753 Dick Davis	.25	.11	.03
□ 754 Brian Doyle	.25	.11	.03
□ 755 Dick Drago	.25	.11	.03
□ 756 Leon Durham	.35	.16	.04
□ 757 Jim Dwyer	.25	.11	.03
□ 758 Dave Edwards	.25	.11	.03
□ 759 Jim Essian	.25	.11	.03
□ 760 Bill Fahey	.25	.11	.03
□ 761 Rollie Fingers	2.00	.90	.25
□ 762 Carlton Fisk	5.00	2.30	.60
□ 763 Barry Foote	.25	.11	.03
□ 764 Ken Forsch	.25	.11	.03

Card			
☐ 765 Kiko Garcia	.25	.11	.03
☐ 766 Cesar Geronimo	.25	.11	.03
☐ 767 Gary Gray	.25	.11	.03
☐ 768 Mickey Hatcher	.25	.11	.03
☐ 769 Steve Henderson	.25	.11	.03
☐ 770 Marc Hill	.25	.11	.03
☐ 771 Butch Hobson	.35	.16	.04
☐ 772 Rick Honeycutt	.25	.11	.03
☐ 773 Roy Howell	.25	.11	.03
☐ 774 Mike Ivie	.25	.11	.03
☐ 775 Roy Lee Jackson	.25	.11	.03
☐ 776 Cliff Johnson	.25	.11	.03
☐ 777 Randy Jones	.25	.11	.03
☐ 778 Ruppert Jones	.25	.11	.03
☐ 779 Mick Kelleher	.25	.11	.03
☐ 780 Terry Kennedy	.25	.11	.03
☐ 781 Dave Kingman	.35	.16	.04
☐ 782 Bob Knepper	.25	.11	.03
☐ 783 Ken Kravec	.25	.11	.03
☐ 784 Bob Lacey	.25	.11	.03
☐ 785 Dennis Lamp	.25	.11	.03
☐ 786 Rafael Landestoy	.25	.11	.03
☐ 787 Ken Landreaux	.25	.11	.03
☐ 788 Carney Lansford	.50	.23	.06
☐ 789 Dave LaRoche	.25	.11	.03
☐ 790 Joe Lefebvre	.25	.11	.03
☐ 791 Ron LeFlore	.35	.16	.04
☐ 792 Randy Lerch	.25	.11	.03
☐ 793 Sixto Lezcano	.25	.11	.03
☐ 794 John Littlefield	.25	.11	.03
☐ 795 Mike Lum	.25	.11	.03
☐ 796 Greg Luzinski	.35	.16	.04
☐ 797 Fred Lynn	.35	.16	.04
☐ 798 Jerry Martin	.25	.11	.03
☐ 799 Buck Martinez	.25	.11	.03
☐ 800 Gary Matthews	.35	.16	.04
☐ 801 Mario Mendoza	.25	.11	.03
☐ 802 Larry Milbourne	.25	.11	.03
☐ 803 Rick Miller	.25	.11	.03
☐ 804 John Montefusco	.25	.11	.03
☐ 805 Jerry Morales	.25	.11	.03
☐ 806 Jose Morales	.25	.11	.03
☐ 807 Joe Morgan	3.00	1.35	.40
☐ 808 Jerry Mumphrey	.25	.11	.03
☐ 809 Gene Nelson	.25	.11	.03
☐ 810 Ed Ott	.25	.11	.03
☐ 811 Bob Owchinko	.25	.11	.03
☐ 812 Gaylord Perry	2.00	.90	.25
☐ 813 Mike Phillips	.25	.11	.03
☐ 814 Darrell Porter	.25	.11	.03
☐ 815 Mike Proly	.25	.11	.03
☐ 816 Tim Raines	12.00	5.50	1.50
☐ 817 Lenny Randle	.25	.11	.03
☐ 818 Doug Rau	.25	.11	.03
☐ 819 Jeff Reardon	4.00	1.80	.50
☐ 820 Ken Reitz	.25	.11	.03
☐ 821 Steve Renko	.25	.11	.03
☐ 822 Rick Reuschel	.35	.16	.04
☐ 823 Dave Revering	.25	.11	.03
☐ 824 Dave Roberts	.25	.11	.03
☐ 825 Leon Roberts	.25	.11	.03
☐ 826 Joe Rudi	.35	.16	.04
☐ 827 Kevin Saucier	.25	.11	.03
☐ 828 Tony Scott	.25	.11	.03
☐ 829 Bob Shirley	.25	.11	.03
☐ 830 Ted Simmons	.35	.16	.04
☐ 831 Lary Sorensen	.25	.11	.03
☐ 832 Jim Spencer	.25	.11	.03
☐ 833 Harry Spilman	.25	.11	.03
☐ 834 Fred Stanley	.25	.11	.03
☐ 835 Rusty Staub	.35	.16	.04
☐ 836 Bill Stein	.25	.11	.03
☐ 837 Joe Strain	.25	.11	.03
☐ 838 Bruce Sutter	.35	.16	.04
☐ 839 Don Sutton	1.50	.65	.19
☐ 840 Steve Swisher	.25	.11	.03
☐ 841 Frank Tanana	.35	.16	.04
☐ 842 Gene Tenace	.25	.11	.03
☐ 843 Jason Thompson	.25	.11	.03
☐ 844 Dickie Thon	.35	.16	.04
☐ 845 Bill Travers	.25	.11	.03
☐ 846 Tom Underwood	.25	.11	.03
☐ 847 John Urrea	.25	.11	.03
☐ 848 Mike Vail	.25	.11	.03
☐ 849 Ellis Valentine	.25	.11	.03
☐ 850 Fernando Valenzuela	2.50	1.15	.30
☐ 851 Pete Vuckovich	.35	.16	.04
☐ 852 Mark Wagner	.25	.11	.03
☐ 853 Bob Walk	.25	.11	.03
☐ 854 Claudell Washington	.25	.11	.03
☐ 855 Dave Winfield	8.00	3.60	1.00
☐ 856 Geoff Zahn	.25	.11	.03
☐ 857 Richie Zisk	.25	.11	.03
☐ 858 Checklist 727-858	.25	.11	.03

1982 Topps

The cards in this 792-card set measure 2 1/2" by 3 1/2". The 1982 baseball series was the first of the largest sets Topps issued at one printing. The 66-card increase from the previous year's total eliminated the "double print" practice, that had occurred in every regular issue since 1978. Cards 1-6 depict Highlights (HL) of the 1981 season, cards 161-168 picture League Leaders, and there are mini-series of AL (547-557) and NL (337-347) All-Stars (AS). The abbreviation "SA" in the checklist is given for the 40 "Super Action" cards introduced in this set. The team cards are actually Team Leader (TL) cards picturing the batting (BA: batting average) and pitching leader for that team with a checklist back. All 26 cards were available from Topps on a perforated sheet through an offer on wax pack wrappers. The key Rookie Cards in this set are Steve Bedrosian, George Bell, Brett Butler, Chili Davis, Kent Hrbek, Cal Ripken, Steve Sax, Lee Smith, and Dave Stewart.

	NRMT-MT	EXC	G-VG
COMPLETE SET (792)	125.00	57.50	15.50
COMMON CARD (1-792)	.10	.05	.01
☐ 1 Steve Carlton HL Sets new NL	1.00	.25	.08

strikeout record
☐ 2 Ron Davis HL .15 .07 .02
Fans 8 straight
in relief
☐ 3 Tim Raines HL .75 .35 .09
Swipes 71 bases
as rookie
☐ 4 Pete Rose HL 1.00 .45 .13
Sets NL career
hits mark
☐ 5 Nolan Ryan HL 4.00 1.80 .50
Pitches fifth
career no-hitter
☐ 6 Fernando Valenzuela HL .20 .09 .03
8 shutouts as rookie
☐ 7 Scott Sanderson .15 .07 .02
☐ 8 Rich Dauer .10 .05 .01
☐ 9 Ron Guidry .15 .07 .02
☐ 10 Ron Guidry SA .10 .05 .01
☐ 11 Gary Alexander .10 .05 .01
☐ 12 Moose Haas .10 .05 .01
☐ 13 Lamar Johnson .10 .05 .01
☐ 14 Steve Howe .10 .05 .01
☐ 15 Ellis Valentine .10 .05 .01
☐ 16 Steve Comer .10 .05 .01
☐ 17 Darrell Evans .15 .07 .02
☐ 18 Fernando Arroyo .10 .05 .01
☐ 19 Ernie Whitt .10 .05 .01
☐ 20 Garry Maddox .10 .05 .01
☐ 21 Orioles Rookies 65.00 29.00 8.25
Bob Bonner
Cal Ripken
Jeff Schneider
☐ 22 Jim Beattie .10 .05 .01
☐ 23 Willie Hernandez .15 .07 .02
☐ 24 Dave Frost .10 .05 .01
☐ 25 Jerry Remy .10 .05 .01
☐ 26 Jorge Orta .10 .05 .01
☐ 27 Tom Herr .15 .07 .02
☐ 28 John Urrea .10 .05 .01
☐ 29 Dwayne Murphy .10 .05 .01
☐ 30 Tom Seaver 2.00 .90 .25
☐ 31 Tom Seaver SA 1.00 .45 .13
☐ 32 Gene Garber .10 .05 .01
☐ 33 Jerry Morales .10 .05 .01
☐ 34 Joe Sambito .10 .05 .01
☐ 35 Willie Aikens .10 .05 .01
☐ 36 Rangers TL .20 .07 .02
BA: Al Oliver
Pitching: Doc Medich
(Checklist on back)
☐ 37 Dan Graham .10 .05 .01
☐ 38 Charlie Lea .10 .05 .01
☐ 39 Lou Whitaker 1.00 .45 .13
☐ 40 Dave Parker .20 .09 .03
☐ 41 Dave Parker SA .15 .07 .02
☐ 42 Rick Sofield .10 .05 .01
☐ 43 Mike Cubbage .10 .05 .01
☐ 44 Britt Burns .10 .05 .01
☐ 45 Rick Cerone .10 .05 .01
☐ 46 Jerry Augustine .10 .05 .01
☐ 47 Jeff Leonard .10 .05 .01
☐ 48 Bobby Castillo .10 .05 .01
☐ 49 Alvis Woods .10 .05 .01
☐ 50 Buddy Bell .15 .07 .02
☐ 51 Cubs Rookies .40 .18 .05
Jay Howell
Carlos Lezcano
Ty Waller
☐ 52 Larry Andersen .10 .05 .01
☐ 53 Greg Gross .10 .05 .01
☐ 54 Ron Hassey .10 .05 .01
☐ 55 Rick Burleson .10 .05 .01
☐ 56 Mark Littell .10 .05 .01
☐ 57 Craig Reynolds .10 .05 .01
☐ 58 John D'Acquisto .10 .05 .01
☐ 59 Rich Gedman .10 .05 .01
☐ 60 Tony Armas .10 .05 .01
☐ 61 Tommy Boggs .10 .05 .01
☐ 62 Mike Tyson .10 .05 .01
☐ 63 Mario Soto .10 .05 .01
☐ 64 Lynn Jones .10 .05 .01
☐ 65 Terry Kennedy .10 .05 .01
☐ 66 Astros TL 1.50 .23 .08
BA: Art Howe
Pitching: Nolan Ryan
(Checklist on back)
☐ 67 Rich Gale .10 .05 .01
☐ 68 Roy Howell .10 .05 .01
☐ 69 Al Williams .10 .05 .01
☐ 70 Tim Raines 3.00 1.35 .40
☐ 71 Roy Lee Jackson .10 .05 .01
☐ 72 Rick Auerbach .10 .05 .01
☐ 73 Buddy Solomon .10 .05 .01
☐ 74 Bob Clark .10 .05 .01
☐ 75 Tommy John .20 .09 .03
☐ 76 Greg Pryor .10 .05 .01
☐ 77 Miguel Dilone .10 .05 .01
☐ 78 George Medich .10 .05 .01
☐ 79 Bob Bailor .10 .05 .01
☐ 80 Jim Palmer 1.50 .65 .19
☐ 81 Jim Palmer SA .75 .35 .09
☐ 82 Bob Welch .15 .07 .02
☐ 83 Yankees Rookies .20 .09 .03
Steve Balboni
Andy McGaffigan
Andre Robertson
☐ 84 Rennie Stennett .10 .05 .01
☐ 85 Lynn McGlothen .10 .05 .01
☐ 86 Dane Iorg .10 .05 .01
☐ 87 Matt Keough .10 .05 .01
☐ 88 Biff Pocoroba .10 .05 .01
☐ 89 Steve Henderson .10 .05 .01
☐ 90 Nolan Ryan 10.00 4.50 1.25
☐ 91 Carney Lansford .15 .07 .02
☐ 92 Brad Havens .10 .05 .01
☐ 93 Larry Hisle .10 .05 .01
☐ 94 Andy Hassler .10 .05 .01
☐ 95 Ozzie Smith 4.00 1.80 .50
☐ 96 Royals TL .60 .09 .03
BA: George Brett
Pitching: Larry Gura
(Checklist on back)
☐ 97 Paul Moskau .10 .05 .01
☐ 98 Terry Bulling .10 .05 .01
☐ 99 Barry Bonnell .10 .05 .01
☐ 100 Mike Schmidt 3.00 1.35 .40
☐ 101 Mike Schmidt SA 1.50 .65 .19
☐ 102 Dan Briggs .10 .05 .01
☐ 103 Bob Lacey .10 .05 .01
☐ 104 Rance Mulliniks .10 .05 .01
☐ 105 Kirk Gibson 1.50 .65 .19
☐ 106 Enrique Romo .10 .05 .01
☐ 107 Wayne Krenchicki .10 .05 .01
☐ 108 Bob Sykes .10 .05 .01
☐ 109 Dave Revering .10 .05 .01
☐ 110 Carlton Fisk 2.00 .90 .25
☐ 111 Carlton Fisk SA 1.00 .45 .13
☐ 112 Billy Sample .10 .05 .01
☐ 113 Steve McCatty .10 .05 .01
☐ 114 Ken Landreaux .10 .05 .01
☐ 115 Gaylord Perry .60 .25 .08
☐ 116 Jim Wohlford .10 .05 .01
☐ 117 Rawly Eastwick .10 .05 .01
☐ 118 Expos Rookies .15 .07 .02
Terry Francona

Brad Mills
Bryn Smith
☐ 119 Joe Pittman .10 .05 .01
☐ 120 Gary Lucas .10 .05 .01
☐ 121 Ed Lynch .10 .05 .01
☐ 122 Jamie Easterly UER .10 .05 .01
(Photo actually
Reggie Cleveland)
☐ 123 Danny Goodwin .10 .05 .01
☐ 124 Reid Nichols .10 .05 .01
☐ 125 Danny Ainge 3.00 1.35 .40
☐ 126 Braves TL .20 .07 .02
BA: Claudell Washington
Pitching: Rick Mahler
(Checklist on back)
☐ 127 Lonnie Smith .15 .07 .02
☐ 128 Frank Pastore .10 .05 .01
☐ 129 Checklist 1-132 .20 .05 .01
☐ 130 Julio Cruz .10 .05 .01
☐ 131 Stan Bahnsen .10 .05 .01
☐ 132 Lee May .15 .07 .02
☐ 133 Pat Underwood .10 .05 .01
☐ 134 Dan Ford .10 .05 .01
☐ 135 Andy Rincon .10 .05 .01
☐ 136 Lenn Sakata .10 .05 .01
☐ 137 George Cappuzzello .10 .05 .01
☐ 138 Tony Pena .15 .07 .02
☐ 139 Jeff Jones .10 .05 .01
☐ 140 Ron LeFlore .15 .07 .02
☐ 141 Indians Rookies .15 .07 .02
Chris Bando
Tom Brennan
Von Hayes
☐ 142 Dave LaRoche .10 .05 .01
☐ 143 Mookie Wilson .15 .07 .02
☐ 144 Fred Breining .10 .05 .01
☐ 145 Bob Horner .15 .07 .02
☐ 146 Mike Griffin .10 .05 .01
☐ 147 Denny Walling .10 .05 .01
☐ 148 Mickey Klutts .10 .05 .01
☐ 149 Pat Putnam .10 .05 .01
☐ 150 Ted Simmons .15 .07 .02
☐ 151 Dave Edwards .10 .05 .01
☐ 152 Ramon Aviles .10 .05 .01
☐ 153 Roger Erickson .10 .05 .01
☐ 154 Dennis Werth .10 .05 .01
☐ 155 Otto Velez .10 .05 .01
☐ 156 Oakland A's TL .75 .11 .04
BA: Rickey Henderson
Pitching: Steve McCatty
(Checklist on back)
☐ 157 Steve Crawford .10 .05 .01
☐ 158 Brian Downing .15 .07 .02
☐ 159 Larry Biittner .10 .05 .01
☐ 160 Luis Tiant .15 .07 .02
☐ 161 Batting Leaders .15 .07 .02
Bill Madlock
Carney Lansford
☐ 162 Home Run Leaders .75 .35 .09
Mike Schmidt
Tony Armas
Dwight Evans
Bobby Grich
Eddie Murray
☐ 163 RBI Leaders .75 .35 .09
Mike Schmidt
Eddie Murray
☐ 164 Stolen Base Leaders 1.50 .65 .19
Tim Raines
Rickey Henderson
☐ 165 Victory Leaders .60 .25 .08
Tom Seaver
Denny Martinez
Steve McCatty
Jack Morris
Pete Vuckovich
☐ 166 Strikeout Leaders .15 .07 .02
Fernando Valenzuela
Len Barker
☐ 167 ERA Leaders 2.50 1.15 .30
Nolan Ryan
Steve McCatty
☐ 168 Leading Firemen .25 .11 .03
Bruce Sutter
Rollie Fingers
☐ 169 Charlie Leibrandt .15 .07 .02
☐ 170 Jim Bibby .10 .05 .01
☐ 171 Giants Rookies 3.00 1.35 .40
Bob Brenly
Chili Davis
Bob Tufts
☐ 172 Bill Gullickson .15 .07 .02
☐ 173 Jamie Quirk .10 .05 .01
☐ 174 Dave Ford .10 .05 .01
☐ 175 Jerry Mumphrey .10 .05 .01
☐ 176 Dewey Robinson .10 .05 .01
☐ 177 John Ellis .10 .05 .01
☐ 178 Dyar Miller .10 .05 .01
☐ 179 Steve Garvey .75 .35 .09
☐ 180 Steve Garvey SA .35 .16 .04
☐ 181 Silvio Martinez .10 .05 .01
☐ 182 Larry Herndon .10 .05 .01
☐ 183 Mike Proly .10 .05 .01
☐ 184 Mick Kelleher .10 .05 .01
☐ 185 Phil Niekro .60 .25 .08
☐ 186 Cardinals TL .20 .07 .02
BA: Keith Hernandez
Pitching: Bob Forsch
(Checklist on back)
☐ 187 Jeff Newman .10 .05 .01
☐ 188 Randy Martz .10 .05 .01
☐ 189 Glenn Hoffman .10 .05 .01
☐ 190 J.R. Richard .15 .07 .02
☐ 191 Tim Wallach 2.50 1.15 .30
☐ 192 Broderick Perkins .10 .05 .01
☐ 193 Darrell Jackson .10 .05 .01
☐ 194 Mike Vail .10 .05 .01
☐ 195 Paul Molitor 4.00 1.80 .50
☐ 196 Willie Upshaw .10 .05 .01
☐ 197 Shane Rawley .10 .05 .01
☐ 198 Chris Speier .10 .05 .01
☐ 199 Don Aase .10 .05 .01
☐ 200 George Brett 5.00 2.30 .60
☐ 201 George Brett SA 2.50 1.15 .30
☐ 202 Rick Manning .10 .05 .01
☐ 203 Blue Jays Rookies .50 .23 .06
Jesse Barfield
Brian Milner
Boomer Wells
☐ 204 Gary Roenicke .10 .05 .01
☐ 205 Neil Allen .10 .05 .01
☐ 206 Tony Bernazard .10 .05 .01
☐ 207 Rod Scurry .10 .05 .01
☐ 208 Bobby Murcer .15 .07 .02
☐ 209 Gary Lavelle .10 .05 .01
☐ 210 Keith Hernandez .20 .09 .03
☐ 211 Dan Petry .10 .05 .01
☐ 212 Mario Mendoza .10 .05 .01
☐ 213 Dave Stewart 3.00 1.35 .40
☐ 214 Brian Asselstine .10 .05 .01
☐ 215 Mike Krukow .10 .05 .01
☐ 216 White Sox TL .20 .07 .02
BA: Chet Lemon
Pitching: Dennis Lamp
(Checklist on back)
☐ 217 Bo McLaughlin .10 .05 .01
☐ 218 Dave Roberts .10 .05 .01

☐ 219 John Curtis	.10	.05	.01
☐ 220 Manny Trillo	.10	.05	.01
☐ 221 Jim Slaton	.10	.05	.01
☐ 222 Butch Wynegar	.10	.05	.01
☐ 223 Lloyd Moseby	.10	.05	.01
☐ 224 Bruce Bochte	.10	.05	.01
☐ 225 Mike Torrez	.10	.05	.01
☐ 226 Checklist 133-264	.20	.05	.01
☐ 227 Ray Burris	.10	.05	.01
☐ 228 Sam Mejias	.10	.05	.01
☐ 229 Geoff Zahn	.10	.05	.01
☐ 230 Willie Wilson	.15	.07	.02
☐ 231 Phillies Rookies Mark Davis Bob Dernier Ozzie Virgil	.30	.14	.04
☐ 232 Terry Crowley	.10	.05	.01
☐ 233 Duane Kuiper	.10	.05	.01
☐ 234 Ron Hodges	.10	.05	.01
☐ 235 Mike Easler	.10	.05	.01
☐ 236 John Martin	.10	.05	.01
☐ 237 Rusty Kuntz	.10	.05	.01
☐ 238 Kevin Saucier	.10	.05	.01
☐ 239 Jon Matlack	.10	.05	.01
☐ 240 Bucky Dent	.15	.07	.02
☐ 241 Bucky Dent SA	.10	.05	.01
☐ 242 Milt May	.10	.05	.01
☐ 243 Bob Owchinko	.10	.05	.01
☐ 244 Rufino Linares	.10	.05	.01
☐ 245 Ken Reitz	.10	.05	.01
☐ 246 New York Mets TL BA: Hubie Brooks Pitching: Mike Scott (Checklist on back)	.20	.07	.02
☐ 247 Pedro Guerrero	.15	.07	.02
☐ 248 Frank LaCorte	.10	.05	.01
☐ 249 Tim Flannery	.10	.05	.01
☐ 250 Tug McGraw	.15	.07	.02
☐ 251 Fred Lynn	.15	.07	.02
☐ 252 Fred Lynn SA	.10	.05	.01
☐ 253 Chuck Baker	.10	.05	.01
☐ 254 George Bell	2.50	1.15	.30
☐ 255 Tony Perez	.50	.23	.06
☐ 256 Tony Perez SA	.25	.11	.03
☐ 257 Larry Harlow	.10	.05	.01
☐ 258 Bo Diaz	.10	.05	.01
☐ 259 Rodney Scott	.10	.05	.01
☐ 260 Bruce Sutter	.15	.07	.02
☐ 261 Tigers Rookies UER Howard Bailey Marty Castillo Dave Rucker (Rucker photo actually Roger Weaver)	.10	.05	.01
☐ 262 Doug Bair	.10	.05	.01
☐ 263 Victor Cruz	.10	.05	.01
☐ 264 Dan Quisenberry	.15	.07	.02
☐ 265 Al Bumbry	.15	.07	.02
☐ 266 Rick Leach	.10	.05	.01
☐ 267 Kurt Bevacqua	.10	.05	.01
☐ 268 Rickey Keeton	.10	.05	.01
☐ 269 Jim Essian	.10	.05	.01
☐ 270 Rusty Staub	.15	.07	.02
☐ 271 Larry Bradford	.10	.05	.01
☐ 272 Bump Wills	.10	.05	.01
☐ 273 Doug Bird	.10	.05	.01
☐ 274 Bob Ojeda	.60	.25	.08
☐ 275 Bob Watson	.15	.07	.02
☐ 276 Angels TL BA: Rod Carew Pitching: Ken Forsch (Checklist on back)	.30	.10	.02
☐ 277 Terry Puhl	.10	.05	.01
☐ 278 John Littlefield	.10	.05	.01
☐ 279 Bill Russell	.15	.07	.02
☐ 280 Ben Oglivie	.15	.07	.02
☐ 281 John Verhoeven	.10	.05	.01
☐ 282 Ken Macha	.10	.05	.01
☐ 283 Brian Allard	.10	.05	.01
☐ 284 Bob Grich	.15	.07	.02
☐ 285 Sparky Lyle	.15	.07	.02
☐ 286 Bill Fahey	.10	.05	.01
☐ 287 Alan Bannister	.10	.05	.01
☐ 288 Garry Templeton	.15	.07	.02
☐ 289 Bob Stanley	.10	.05	.01
☐ 290 Ken Singleton	.15	.07	.02
☐ 291 Pirates Rookies Vance Law Bob Long Johnny Ray	.15	.07	.02
☐ 292 David Palmer	.10	.05	.01
☐ 293 Rob Picciolo	.10	.05	.01
☐ 294 Mike LaCoss	.10	.05	.01
☐ 295 Jason Thompson	.10	.05	.01
☐ 296 Bob Walk	.10	.05	.01
☐ 297 Clint Hurdle	.10	.05	.01
☐ 298 Danny Darwin	.10	.05	.01
☐ 299 Steve Trout	.10	.05	.01
☐ 300 Reggie Jackson	2.50	1.15	.30
☐ 301 Reggie Jackson SA	1.25	.55	.16
☐ 302 Doug Flynn	.10	.05	.01
☐ 303 Bill Caudill	.10	.05	.01
☐ 304 Johnnie LeMaster	.10	.05	.01
☐ 305 Don Sutton	.60	.25	.08
☐ 306 Don Sutton SA	.30	.14	.04
☐ 307 Randy Bass	.35	.16	.04
☐ 308 Charlie Moore	.10	.05	.01
☐ 309 Pete Redfern	.10	.05	.01
☐ 310 Mike Hargrove	.15	.07	.02
☐ 311 Dodgers TL BA: Dusty Baker Pitching: Burt Hooton (Checklist on back)	.25	.08	.02
☐ 312 Lenny Randle	.10	.05	.01
☐ 313 John Harris	.10	.05	.01
☐ 314 Buck Martinez	.10	.05	.01
☐ 315 Burt Hooton	.10	.05	.01
☐ 316 Steve Braun	.10	.05	.01
☐ 317 Dick Ruthven	.10	.05	.01
☐ 318 Mike Heath	.10	.05	.01
☐ 319 Dave Rozema	.10	.05	.01
☐ 320 Chris Chambliss	.15	.07	.02
☐ 321 Chris Chambliss SA	.10	.05	.01
☐ 322 Garry Hancock	.10	.05	.01
☐ 323 Bill Lee	.10	.05	.01
☐ 324 Steve Dillard	.10	.05	.01
☐ 325 Jose Cruz	.15	.07	.02
☐ 326 Pete Falcone	.10	.05	.01
☐ 327 Joe Nolan	.10	.05	.01
☐ 328 Ed Farmer	.10	.05	.01
☐ 329 U.L. Washington	.10	.05	.01
☐ 330 Rick Wise	.10	.05	.01
☐ 331 Benny Ayala	.10	.05	.01
☐ 332 Don Robinson	.10	.05	.01
☐ 333 Brewers Rookies Frank DiPino Marshall Edwards Chuck Porter	.10	.05	.01
☐ 334 Aurelio Rodriguez	.10	.05	.01
☐ 335 Jim Sundberg	.15	.07	.02
☐ 336 Mariners TL BA: Tom Paciorek Pitching: Glenn Abbott (Checklist on back)	.20	.07	.02
☐ 337 Pete Rose AS	1.00	.45	.13
☐ 338 Dave Lopes AS	.15	.07	.02

☐ 339 Mike Schmidt AS .... .75 .35 .09
☐ 340 Dave Concepcion AS.... .15 .07 .02
☐ 341 Andre Dawson AS .... .75 .35 .09
☐ 342A George Foster AS....... .15 .07 .02
(With autograph)
☐ 342B George Foster AS..... 1.00 .45 .13
(W/o autograph)
☐ 343 Dave Parker AS .... .20 .09 .03
☐ 344 Gary Carter AS .... .35 .16 .04
☐ 345 Fernando Valenzuela AS .20 .09 .03
☐ 346A Tom Seaver AS ERR 1.25 .55 .16
("t ed")
☐ 346B Tom Seaver AS COR.. .75 .35 .09
("tied")
☐ 347 Bruce Sutter AS .... .15 .07 .02
☐ 348 Derrel Thomas .... .10 .05 .01
☐ 349 George Frazier.............. .10 .05 .01
☐ 350 Thad Bosley .... .10 .05 .01
☐ 351 Reds Rookies............... .10 .05 .01
Scott Brown
Geoff Combe
Paul Householder
☐ 352 Dick Davis..................... .10 .05 .01
☐ 353 Jack O'Connor .... .10 .05 .01
☐ 354 Roberto Ramos............ .10 .05 .01
☐ 355 Dwight Evans .... .20 .09 .03
☐ 356 Denny Lewallyn............ .10 .05 .01
☐ 357 Butch Hobson .... .15 .07 .02
☐ 358 Mike Parrott.................. .10 .05 .01
☐ 359 Jim Dwyer...................... .10 .05 .01
☐ 360 Len Barker .... .10 .05 .01
☐ 361 Rafael Landestoy .... .10 .05 .01
☐ 362 Jim Wright UER .... .10 .05 .01
(Wrong Jim Wright
pictured)
☐ 363 Bob Molinaro .... .10 .05 .01
☐ 364 Doyle Alexander........... .10 .05 .01
☐ 365 Bill Madlock .... .15 .07 .02
☐ 366 Padres TL .... .20 .07 .02
BA: Luis Salazar
Pitching: Juan
Eichelberger
(Checklist on back)
☐ 367 Jim Kaat........................ .15 .07 .02
☐ 368 Alex Trevino .... .10 .05 .01
☐ 369 Champ Summers.......... .10 .05 .01
☐ 370 Mike Norris .... .10 .05 .01
☐ 371 Jerry Don Gleaton........ .10 .05 .01
☐ 372 Luis Gomez.................... .10 .05 .01
☐ 373 Gene Nelson .... .10 .05 .01
☐ 374 Tim Blackwell................ .10 .05 .01
☐ 375 Dusty Baker .... .20 .09 .03
☐ 376 Chris Welsh .... .10 .05 .01
☐ 377 Kiko Garcia .... .10 .05 .01
☐ 378 Mike Caldwell................ .10 .05 .01
☐ 379 Rob Wilfong.................. .10 .05 .01
☐ 380 Dave Stieb.................... .15 .07 .02
☐ 381 Red Sox Rookies .... .15 .07 .02
Bruce Hurst
Dave Schmidt
Julio Valdez
☐ 382 Joe Simpson................. .10 .05 .01
☐ 383A Pascual Perez ERR 10.00 4.50 1.25
(No position
on front)
☐ 383B Pascual Perez COR .... .15 .07 .02
☐ 384 Keith Moreland .... .10 .05 .01
☐ 385 Ken Forsch.................... .10 .05 .01
☐ 386 Jerry White .... .10 .05 .01
☐ 387 Tom Veryzer .... .10 .05 .01
☐ 388 Joe Rudi .... .10 .05 .01
☐ 389 George Vukovich.......... .10 .05 .01
☐ 390 Eddie Murray .... 3.00 1.35 .40
☐ 391 Dave Tobik..................... .10 .05 .01
☐ 392 Rick Bosetti.................... .10 .05 .01
☐ 393 Al Hrabosky .... .10 .05 .01
☐ 394 Checklist 265-396......... .20 .05 .01
☐ 395 Omar Moreno .... .10 .05 .01
☐ 396 Twins TL......................... .20 .07 .02
BA: John Castino
Pitching: Fernando
Arroyo
(Checklist on back)
☐ 397 Ken Brett........................ .10 .05 .01
☐ 398 Mike Squires.................. .10 .05 .01
☐ 399 Pat Zachry...................... .10 .05 .01
☐ 400 Johnny Bench .... 1.75 .80 .22
☐ 401 Johnny Bench SA......... .75 .35 .09
☐ 402 Bill Stein .... .10 .05 .01
☐ 403 Jim Tracy........................ .10 .05 .01
☐ 404 Dickie Thon.................... .10 .05 .01
☐ 405 Rick Reuschel .... .15 .07 .02
☐ 406 Al Holland .... .10 .05 .01
☐ 407 Danny Boone .... .10 .05 .01
☐ 408 Ed Romero...................... .10 .05 .01
☐ 409 Don Cooper.................... .10 .05 .01
☐ 410 Ron Cey .... .15 .07 .02
☐ 411 Ron Cey SA.................... .10 .05 .01
☐ 412 Luis Leal .... .10 .05 .01
☐ 413 Dan Meyer .... .10 .05 .01
☐ 414 Elias Sosa .... .10 .05 .01
☐ 415 Don Baylor .... .20 .09 .03
☐ 416 Marty Bystrom............... .10 .05 .01
☐ 417 Pat Kelly......................... .10 .05 .01
☐ 418 Rangers Rookies........... .10 .05 .01
John Butcher
Bobby Johnson
Dave Schmidt
☐ 419 Steve Stone.................... .15 .07 .02
☐ 420 George Hendrick .... .15 .07 .02
☐ 421 Mark Clear .... .10 .05 .01
☐ 422 Cliff Johnson.................. .10 .05 .01
☐ 423 Stan Papi .... .10 .05 .01
☐ 424 Bruce Benedict.............. .10 .05 .01
☐ 425 John Candelaria .... .10 .05 .01
☐ 426 Orioles TL .... .40 .10 .03
BA: Eddie Murray
Pitching: Sammy Stewart
(Checklist on back)
☐ 427 Ron Oester..................... .10 .05 .01
☐ 428 LaMarr Hoyt.................. .10 .05 .01
☐ 429 John Wathan.................. .10 .05 .01
☐ 430 Vida Blue........................ .15 .07 .02
☐ 431 Vida Blue SA .... .10 .05 .01
☐ 432 Mike Scott....................... .15 .07 .02
☐ 433 Alan Ashby..................... .10 .05 .01
☐ 434 Joe Lefebvre .... .10 .05 .01
☐ 435 Robin Yount.............. 2.50 1.15 .30
☐ 436 Joe Strain .... .10 .05 .01
☐ 437 Juan Berenguer............. .10 .05 .01
☐ 438 Pete Mackanin .... .10 .05 .01
☐ 439 Dave Righetti .... .60 .25 .08
☐ 440 Jeff Burroughs............... .10 .05 .01
☐ 441 Astros Rookies .... .10 .05 .01
Danny Heep
Billy Smith
Bobby Sprowl
☐ 442 Bruce Kison .... .10 .05 .01
☐ 443 Mark Wagner .... .10 .05 .01
☐ 444 Terry Forster.................. .10 .05 .01
☐ 445 Larry Parrish.................. .10 .05 .01
☐ 446 Wayne Garland .... .10 .05 .01
☐ 447 Darrell Porter .... .10 .05 .01
☐ 448 Darrell Porter SA.......... .10 .05 .01
☐ 449 Luis Aguayo................... .10 .05 .01
☐ 450 Jack Morris.................... .75 .35 .09

	No.	Player			
☐	451	Ed Miller	.10	.05	.01
☐	452	Lee Smith	12.00	5.50	1.50
☐	453	Art Howe	.10	.05	.01
☐	454	Rick Langford	.10	.05	.01
☐	455	Tom Burgmeier	.10	.05	.01
☐	456	Chicago Cubs TL	.20	.07	.02
		BA: Bill Buckner			
		Pitching: Randy Martz			
		(Checklist on back)			
☐	457	Tim Stoddard	.10	.05	.01
☐	458	Willie Montanez	.10	.05	.01
☐	459	Bruce Berenyi	.10	.05	.01
☐	460	Jack Clark	.15	.07	.02
☐	461	Rich Dotson	.10	.05	.01
☐	462	Dave Chalk	.10	.05	.01
☐	463	Jim Kern	.10	.05	.01
☐	464	Juan Bonilla	.10	.05	.01
☐	465	Lee Mazzilli	.10	.05	.01
☐	466	Randy Lerch	.10	.05	.01
☐	467	Mickey Hatcher	.10	.05	.01
☐	468	Floyd Bannister	.10	.05	.01
☐	469	Ed Ott	.10	.05	.01
☐	470	John Mayberry	.10	.05	.01
☐	471	Royals Rookies	.10	.05	.01
		Atlee Hammaker			
		Mike Jones			
		Darryl Motley			
☐	472	Oscar Gamble	.10	.05	.01
☐	473	Mike Stanton	.10	.05	.01
☐	474	Ken Oberkfell	.10	.05	.01
☐	475	Alan Trammell	1.50	.65	.19
☐	476	Brian Kingman	.10	.05	.01
☐	477	Steve Yeager	.10	.05	.01
☐	478	Ray Searage	.10	.05	.01
☐	479	Rowland Office	.10	.05	.01
☐	480	Steve Carlton	1.50	.65	.19
☐	481	Steve Carlton SA	.75	.35	.09
☐	482	Glenn Hubbard	.10	.05	.01
☐	483	Gary Woods	.10	.05	.01
☐	484	Ivan DeJesus	.10	.05	.01
☐	485	Kent Tekulve	.15	.07	.02
☐	486	Yankees TL	.25	.08	.02
		BA: Jerry Mumphrey			
		Pitching: Tommy John			
		(Checklist on back)			
☐	487	Bob McClure	.10	.05	.01
☐	488	Ron Jackson	.10	.05	.01
☐	489	Rick Dempsey	.15	.07	.02
☐	490	Dennis Eckersley	1.00	.45	.13
☐	491	Checklist 397-528	.20	.05	.01
☐	492	Joe Price	.10	.05	.01
☐	493	Chet Lemon	.10	.05	.01
☐	494	Hubie Brooks	.15	.07	.02
☐	495	Dennis Leonard	.10	.05	.01
☐	496	Johnny Grubb	.10	.05	.01
☐	497	Jim Anderson	.10	.05	.01
☐	498	Dave Bergman	.10	.05	.01
☐	499	Paul Mirabella	.10	.05	.01
☐	500	Rod Carew	1.25	.55	.16
☐	501	Rod Carew SA	.60	.25	.08
☐	502	Braves Rookies	4.00	1.80	.50
		Steve Bedrosian UER			
		(Photo actually			
		Larry Owen)			
		Brett Butler			
		Larry Owen			
☐	503	Julio Gonzalez	.10	.05	.01
☐	504	Rick Peters	.10	.05	.01
☐	505	Graig Nettles	.15	.07	.02
☐	506	Graig Nettles SA	.10	.05	.01
☐	507	Terry Harper	.10	.05	.01
☐	508	Jody Davis	.10	.05	.01
☐	509	Harry Spilman	.10	.05	.01
☐	510	Fernando Valenzuela	.30	.14	.04
☐	511	Ruppert Jones	.10	.05	.01
☐	512	Jerry Dybzinski	.10	.05	.01
☐	513	Rick Rhoden	.10	.05	.01
☐	514	Joe Ferguson	.10	.05	.01
☐	515	Larry Bowa	.15	.07	.02
☐	516	Larry Bowa SA	.10	.05	.01
☐	517	Mark Brouhard	.10	.05	.01
☐	518	Garth Iorg	.10	.05	.01
☐	519	Glenn Adams	.10	.05	.01
☐	520	Mike Flanagan	.15	.07	.02
☐	521	Bill Almon	.10	.05	.01
☐	522	Chuck Rainey	.10	.05	.01
☐	523	Gary Gray	.10	.05	.01
☐	524	Tom Hausman	.10	.05	.01
☐	525	Ray Knight	.15	.07	.02
☐	526	Expos TL	.20	.07	.02
		BA: Warren Cromartie			
		Pitching: Bill Gullickson			
		(Checklist on back)			
☐	527	John Henry Johnson	.10	.05	.01
☐	528	Matt Alexander	.10	.05	.01
☐	529	Allen Ripley	.10	.05	.01
☐	530	Dickie Noles	.10	.05	.01
☐	531	A's Rookies	.10	.05	.01
		Rich Bordi			
		Mark Budaska			
		Kelvin Moore			
☐	532	Toby Harrah	.15	.07	.02
☐	533	Joaquin Andujar	.15	.07	.02
☐	534	Dave McKay	.10	.05	.01
☐	535	Lance Parrish	.20	.09	.03
☐	536	Rafael Ramirez	.10	.05	.01
☐	537	Doug Capilla	.10	.05	.01
☐	538	Lou Piniella	.15	.07	.02
☐	539	Vern Ruhle	.10	.05	.01
☐	540	Andre Dawson	2.00	.90	.25
☐	541	Barry Evans	.10	.05	.01
☐	542	Ned Yost	.10	.05	.01
☐	543	Bill Robinson	.15	.07	.02
☐	544	Larry Christenson	.10	.05	.01
☐	545	Reggie Smith	.15	.07	.02
☐	546	Reggie Smith SA	.10	.05	.01
☐	547	Rod Carew AS	.50	.23	.06
☐	548	Willie Randolph AS	.15	.07	.02
☐	549	George Brett AS	2.50	1.15	.30
☐	550	Bucky Dent AS	.15	.07	.02
☐	551	Reggie Jackson AS	1.00	.45	.13
☐	552	Ken Singleton AS	.15	.07	.02
☐	553	Dave Winfield AS	1.50	.65	.19
☐	554	Carlton Fisk AS	.60	.25	.08
☐	555	Scott McGregor AS	.15	.07	.02
☐	556	Jack Morris AS	.30	.14	.04
☐	557	Rich Gossage AS	.20	.09	.03
☐	558	John Tudor	.15	.07	.02
☐	559	Indians TL	.25	.08	.02
		BA: Mike Hargrove			
		Pitching: Bert Blyleven			
		(Checklist on back)			
☐	560	Doug Corbett	.10	.05	.01
☐	561	Cardinals Rookies	.10	.05	.01
		Glenn Brummer			
		Luis DeLeon			
		Gene Roof			
☐	562	Mike O'Berry	.10	.05	.01
☐	563	Ross Baumgarten	.10	.05	.01
☐	564	Doug DeCinces	.15	.07	.02
☐	565	Jackson Todd	.10	.05	.01
☐	566	Mike Jorgensen	.10	.05	.01
☐	567	Bob Babcock	.10	.05	.01
☐	568	Joe Pettini	.10	.05	.01
☐	569	Willie Randolph	.15	.07	.02
☐	570	Willie Randolph SA	.10	.05	.01

	#	Player			
☐	571	Glenn Abbott	.10	.05	.01
☐	572	Juan Beniquez	.10	.05	.01
☐	573	Rick Waits	.10	.05	.01
☐	574	Mike Ramsey	.10	.05	.01
☐	575	Al Cowens	.10	.05	.01
☐	576	Giants TL BA: Milt May Pitching: Vida Blue (Checklist on back)	.20	.07	.02
☐	577	Rick Monday	.10	.05	.01
☐	578	Shooty Babitt	.10	.05	.01
☐	579	Rick Mahler	.10	.05	.01
☐	580	Bobby Bonds	.15	.07	.02
☐	581	Ron Reed	.15	.07	.02
☐	582	Luis Pujols	.10	.05	.01
☐	583	Tippy Martinez	.10	.05	.01
☐	584	Hosken Powell	.10	.05	.01
☐	585	Rollie Fingers	.60	.25	.08
☐	586	Rollie Fingers SA	.30	.14	.04
☐	587	Tim Lollar	.10	.05	.01
☐	588	Dale Berra	.10	.05	.01
☐	589	Dave Stapleton	.10	.05	.01
☐	590	Al Oliver	.15	.07	.02
☐	591	Al Oliver SA	.10	.05	.01
☐	592	Craig Swan	.10	.05	.01
☐	593	Billy Smith	.10	.05	.01
☐	594	Renie Martin	.10	.05	.01
☐	595	Dave Collins	.10	.05	.01
☐	596	Damaso Garcia	.10	.05	.01
☐	597	Wayne Nordhagen	.10	.05	.01
☐	598	Bob Galasso	.10	.05	.01
☐	599	White Sox Rookies Jay Loviglio Reggie Patterson Leo Sutherland	.10	.05	.01
☐	600	Dave Winfield	3.00	1.35	.40
☐	601	Sid Monge	.10	.05	.01
☐	602	Freddie Patek	.10	.05	.01
☐	603	Rich Hebner	.10	.05	.01
☐	604	Orlando Sanchez	.10	.05	.01
☐	605	Steve Rogers	.10	.05	.01
☐	606	Blue Jays TL BA: John Mayberry Pitching: Dave Stieb (Checklist on back)	.20	.07	.02
☐	607	Leon Durham	.10	.05	.01
☐	608	Jerry Royster	.10	.05	.01
☐	609	Rick Sutcliffe	.15	.07	.02
☐	610	Rickey Henderson	5.00	2.30	.60
☐	611	Joe Niekro	.15	.07	.02
☐	612	Gary Ward	.10	.05	.01
☐	613	Jim Gantner	.15	.07	.02
☐	614	Juan Eichelberger	.10	.05	.01
☐	615	Bob Boone	.15	.07	.02
☐	616	Bob Boone SA	.10	.05	.01
☐	617	Scott McGregor	.10	.05	.01
☐	618	Tim Foli	.10	.05	.01
☐	619	Bill Campbell	.10	.05	.01
☐	620	Ken Griffey	.15	.07	.02
☐	621	Ken Griffey SA	.10	.05	.01
☐	622	Dennis Lamp	.10	.05	.01
☐	623	Mets Rookies Ron Gardenhire Terry Leach Tim Leary	.35	.16	.04
☐	624	Fergie Jenkins	.60	.25	.08
☐	625	Hal McRae	.20	.09	.03
☐	626	Randy Jones	.10	.05	.01
☐	627	Enos Cabell	.10	.05	.01
☐	628	Bill Travers	.10	.05	.01
☐	629	John Wockenfuss	.10	.05	.01
☐	630	Joe Charboneau	.15	.07	.02
☐	631	Gene Tenace	.10	.05	.01
☐	632	Bryan Clark	.10	.05	.01
☐	633	Mitchell Page	.10	.05	.01
☐	634	Checklist 529-660	.20	.05	.01
☐	635	Ron Davis	.10	.05	.01
☐	636	Phillies TL BA: Pete Rose Pitching: Steve Carlton (Checklist on back)	.40	.06	.02
☐	637	Rick Camp	.10	.05	.01
☐	638	John Milner	.10	.05	.01
☐	639	Ken Kravec	.10	.05	.01
☐	640	Cesar Cedeno	.15	.07	.02
☐	641	Steve Mura	.10	.05	.01
☐	642	Mike Scioscia	.15	.07	.02
☐	643	Pete Vuckovich	.15	.07	.02
☐	644	John Castino	.10	.05	.01
☐	645	Frank White	.15	.07	.02
☐	646	Frank White SA	.10	.05	.01
☐	647	Warren Brusstar	.10	.05	.01
☐	648	Jose Morales	.10	.05	.01
☐	649	Ken Clay	.10	.05	.01
☐	650	Carl Yastrzemski	1.50	.65	.19
☐	651	Carl Yastrzemski SA	.75	.35	.09
☐	652	Steve Nicosia	.10	.05	.01
☐	653	Angels Rookies Tom Brunansky Luis Sanchez Daryl Sconiers	.75	.35	.09
☐	654	Jim Morrison	.10	.05	.01
☐	655	Joel Youngblood	.10	.05	.01
☐	656	Eddie Whitson	.10	.05	.01
☐	657	Tom Poquette	.10	.05	.01
☐	658	Tito Landrum	.10	.05	.01
☐	659	Fred Martinez	.10	.05	.01
☐	660	Dave Concepcion	.15	.07	.02
☐	661	Dave Concepcion SA	.10	.05	.01
☐	662	Luis Salazar	.10	.05	.01
☐	663	Hector Cruz	.10	.05	.01
☐	664	Dan Spillner	.10	.05	.01
☐	665	Jim Clancy	.10	.05	.01
☐	666	Tigers TL BA: Steve Kemp Pitching: Dan Petry (Checklist on back)	.20	.07	.02
☐	667	Jeff Reardon	.75	.35	.09
☐	668	Dale Murphy	1.00	.45	.13
☐	669	Larry Milbourne	.10	.05	.01
☐	670	Steve Kemp	.10	.05	.01
☐	671	Mike Davis	.10	.05	.01
☐	672	Bob Knepper	.10	.05	.01
☐	673	Keith Drumwright	.10	.05	.01
☐	674	Dave Goltz	.10	.05	.01
☐	675	Cecil Cooper	.15	.07	.02
☐	676	Sal Butera	.10	.05	.01
☐	677	Alfredo Griffin	.10	.05	.01
☐	678	Tom Paciorek	.15	.07	.02
☐	679	Sammy Stewart	.10	.05	.01
☐	680	Gary Matthews	.15	.07	.02
☐	681	Dodgers Rookies Mike Marshall Ron Roenicke Steve Sax	1.50	.65	.19
☐	682	Jesse Jefferson	.10	.05	.01
☐	683	Phil Garner	.15	.07	.02
☐	684	Harold Baines	1.00	.45	.13
☐	685	Bert Blyleven	.20	.09	.03
☐	686	Gary Allenson	.10	.05	.01
☐	687	Greg Minton	.10	.05	.01
☐	688	Leon Roberts	.10	.05	.01
☐	689	Lary Sorensen	.10	.05	.01
☐	690	Dave Kingman	.15	.07	.02
☐	691	Dan Schatzeder	.10	.05	.01
☐	692	Wayne Gross	.10	.05	.01

☐ 693 Cesar Geronimo .10 .05 .01
☐ 694 Dave Wehrmeister .10 .05 .01
☐ 695 Warren Cromartie .10 .05 .01
☐ 696 Pirates TL .20 .07 .02
BA: Bill Madlock
Pitching: Eddie Solomon
(Checklist on back)
☐ 697 John Montefusco .10 .05 .01
☐ 698 Tony Scott .10 .05 .01
☐ 699 Dick Tidrow .10 .05 .01
☐ 700 George Foster .15 .07 .02
☐ 701 George Foster SA .10 .05 .01
☐ 702 Steve Renko .10 .05 .01
☐ 703 Brewers TL .20 .07 .02
BA: Cecil Cooper
Pitching: Pete Vuckovich
(Checklist on back)
☐ 704 Mickey Rivers .10 .05 .01
☐ 705 Mickey Rivers SA .10 .05 .01
☐ 706 Barry Foote .10 .05 .01
☐ 707 Mark Bomback .10 .05 .01
☐ 708 Gene Richards .10 .05 .01
☐ 709 Don Money .10 .05 .01
☐ 710 Jerry Reuss .10 .05 .01
☐ 711 Mariners Rookies .75 .35 .09
Dave Edler
Dave Henderson
Reggie Walton
☐ 712 Dennis Martinez .15 .07 .02
☐ 713 Del Unser .10 .05 .01
☐ 714 Jerry Koosman .15 .07 .02
☐ 715 Willie Stargell 1.00 .45 .13
☐ 716 Willie Stargell SA .50 .23 .06
☐ 717 Rick Miller .10 .05 .01
☐ 718 Charlie Hough .15 .07 .02
☐ 719 Jerry Narron .10 .05 .01
☐ 720 Greg Luzinski .15 .07 .02
☐ 721 Greg Luzinski SA .10 .05 .01
☐ 722 Jerry Martin .10 .05 .01
☐ 723 Junior Kennedy .10 .05 .01
☐ 724 Dave Rosello .10 .05 .01
☐ 725 Amos Otis .15 .07 .02
☐ 726 Amos Otis SA .10 .05 .01
☐ 727 Sixto Lezcano .10 .05 .01
☐ 728 Aurelio Lopez .10 .05 .01
☐ 729 Jim Spencer .10 .05 .01
☐ 730 Gary Carter .75 .35 .09
☐ 731 Padres Rookies .10 .05 .01
Mike Armstrong
Doug Gwosdz
Fred Kuhaulua
☐ 732 Mike Lum .10 .05 .01
☐ 733 Larry McWilliams .10 .05 .01
☐ 734 Mike Ivie .10 .05 .01
☐ 735 Rudy May .10 .05 .01
☐ 736 Jerry Turner .10 .05 .01
☐ 737 Reggie Cleveland .10 .05 .01
☐ 738 Dave Engle .10 .05 .01
☐ 739 Joey McLaughlin .10 .05 .01
☐ 740 Dave Lopes .15 .07 .02
☐ 741 Dave Lopes SA .10 .05 .01
☐ 742 Dick Drago .10 .05 .01
☐ 743 John Stearns .10 .05 .01
☐ 744 Mike Witt .10 .05 .01
☐ 745 Bake McBride .10 .05 .01
☐ 746 Andre Thornton .15 .07 .02
☐ 747 John Lowenstein .10 .05 .01
☐ 748 Marc Hill .10 .05 .01
☐ 749 Bob Shirley .10 .05 .01
☐ 750 Jim Rice .20 .09 .03
☐ 751 Rick Honeycutt .10 .05 .01
☐ 752 Lee Lacy .10 .05 .01
☐ 753 Tom Brookens .10 .05 .01
☐ 754 Joe Morgan .90 .40 .11
☐ 755 Joe Morgan SA .40 .18 .05
☐ 756 Reds TL .30 .08 .02
BA: Ken Griffey
Pitching: Tom Seaver
(Checklist on back)
☐ 757 Tom Underwood .10 .05 .01
☐ 758 Claudell Washington .10 .05 .01
☐ 759 Paul Splittorff .10 .05 .01
☐ 760 Bill Buckner .15 .07 .02
☐ 761 Dave Smith .10 .05 .01
☐ 762 Mike Phillips .10 .05 .01
☐ 763 Tom Hume .10 .05 .01
☐ 764 Steve Swisher .10 .05 .01
☐ 765 Gorman Thomas .15 .07 .02
☐ 766 Twins Rookies 3.00 1.35 .40
Lenny Faedo
Kent Hrbek
Tim Laudner
☐ 767 Roy Smalley .10 .05 .01
☐ 768 Jerry Garvin .10 .05 .01
☐ 769 Richie Zisk .10 .05 .01
☐ 770 Rich Gossage .20 .09 .03
☐ 771 Rich Gossage SA .15 .07 .02
☐ 772 Bert Campaneris .15 .07 .02
☐ 773 John Denny .10 .05 .01
☐ 774 Jay Johnstone .15 .07 .02
☐ 775 Bob Forsch .10 .05 .01
☐ 776 Mark Belanger .15 .07 .02
☐ 777 Tom Griffin .10 .05 .01
☐ 778 Kevin Hickey .10 .05 .01
☐ 779 Grant Jackson .10 .05 .01
☐ 780 Pete Rose 2.50 1.15 .30
☐ 781 Pete Rose SA 1.00 .45 .13
☐ 782 Frank Taveras .10 .05 .01
☐ 783 Greg Harris .10 .05 .01
☐ 784 Milt Wilcox .10 .05 .01
☐ 785 Dan Driessen .10 .05 .01
☐ 786 Red Sox TL .20 .07 .02
BA: Carney Lansford
Pitching: Mike Torrez
(Checklist on back)
☐ 787 Fred Stanley .10 .05 .01
☐ 788 Woodie Fryman .10 .05 .01
☐ 789 Checklist 661-792 .20 .05 .01
☐ 790 Larry Gura .10 .05 .01
☐ 791 Bobby Brown .10 .05 .01
☐ 792 Frank Tanana .15 .07 .02

1982 Topps Traded

The cards in this 132-card set measure 2 1/2" by 3 1/2". The 1982 Topps Traded or extended series is distinguished by a "T" printed after the number (located on the reverse). This was the first time Topps began a tradition of newly numbering (and alphabetizing) their traded series from 1T to 132T. Of the total cards, 70 players represent the American League and 61 represent the National League, with the remaining card a numbered checklist (132T). The Cubs lead the pack with 12 changes, while the Red Sox are the only team in either league to have no new additions. All 131 player photos used in the set are completely new. Of this total, 112 individuals are seen in the uniform of their new team, 11 others have been elevated to single card status from "Future Stars" cards, and eight more are entirely new to the 1982 Topps lineup. The backs are almost completely red in color with black print. There are no key rookie cards in this set. Although the Cal Ripken card is this set's most valuable card, it is not his Rookie Card since he had already been included in the 1982 regular set, albeit on a multi-player card.

	NRMT-MT	EXC	G-VG
COMPLETE FACT.SET (132)	260.00	115.00	33.00
COMMON CARD (1T-132T)	.35	.16	.04

	NRMT-MT	EXC	G-VG
☐ 1T Doyle Alexander	.35	.16	.04
☐ 2T Jesse Barfield	.75	.35	.09
☐ 3T Ross Baumgarten	.35	.16	.04
☐ 4T Steve Bedrosian	.75	.35	.09
☐ 5T Mark Belanger	.35	.16	.04
☐ 6T Kurt Bevacqua	.35	.16	.04
☐ 7T Tim Blackwell	.35	.16	.04
☐ 8T Vida Blue	.50	.23	.06
☐ 9T Bob Boone	.50	.23	.06
☐ 10T Larry Bowa	.50	.23	.06
☐ 11T Dan Briggs	.35	.16	.04
☐ 12T Bobby Brown	.35	.16	.04
☐ 13T Tom Brunansky	1.00	.45	.13
☐ 14T Jeff Burroughs	.35	.16	.04
☐ 15T Enos Cabell	.35	.16	.04
☐ 16T Bill Campbell	.35	.16	.04
☐ 17T Bobby Castillo	.35	.16	.04
☐ 18T Bill Caudill	.35	.16	.04
☐ 19T Cesar Cedeno	.50	.23	.06
☐ 20T Dave Collins	.35	.16	.04
☐ 21T Doug Corbett	.35	.16	.04
☐ 22T Al Cowens	.35	.16	.04
☐ 23T Chili Davis	5.00	2.30	.60
☐ 24T Dick Davis	.35	.16	.04
☐ 25T Ron Davis	.35	.16	.04
☐ 26T Doug DeCinces	.50	.23	.06
☐ 27T Ivan DeJesus	.35	.16	.04
☐ 28T Bob Dernier	.35	.16	.04
☐ 29T Bo Diaz	.35	.16	.04
☐ 30T Roger Erickson	.35	.16	.04
☐ 31T Jim Essian	.35	.16	.04
☐ 32T Ed Farmer	.35	.16	.04
☐ 33T Doug Flynn	.35	.16	.04
☐ 34T Tim Foli	.35	.16	.04
☐ 35T Dan Ford	.35	.16	.04
☐ 36T George Foster	.50	.23	.06
☐ 37T Dave Frost	.35	.16	.04
☐ 38T Rich Gale	.35	.16	.04
☐ 39T Ron Gardenhire	.35	.16	.04
☐ 40T Ken Griffey	.60	.25	.08
☐ 41T Greg Harris	.35	.16	.04
☐ 42T Von Hayes	.50	.23	.06
☐ 43T Larry Herndon	.35	.16	.04
☐ 44T Kent Hrbek	5.00	2.30	.60
☐ 45T Mike Ivie	.35	.16	.04
☐ 46T Grant Jackson	.35	.16	.04
☐ 47T Reggie Jackson	14.00	6.25	1.75
☐ 48T Ron Jackson	.35	.16	.04
☐ 49T Fergie Jenkins	2.00	.90	.25
☐ 50T Lamar Johnson	.35	.16	.04
☐ 51T Randy Johnson	.35	.16	.04
☐ 52T Jay Johnstone	.50	.23	.06
☐ 53T Mick Kelleher	.35	.16	.04
☐ 54T Steve Kemp	.35	.16	.04
☐ 55T Junior Kennedy	.35	.16	.04
☐ 56T Jim Kern	.35	.16	.04
☐ 57T Ray Knight	.50	.23	.06
☐ 58T Wayne Krenchicki	.35	.16	.04
☐ 59T Mike Krukow	.35	.16	.04
☐ 60T Duane Kuiper	.35	.16	.04
☐ 61T Mike LaCoss	.35	.16	.04
☐ 62T Chet Lemon	.35	.16	.04
☐ 63T Sixto Lezcano	.35	.16	.04
☐ 64T Dave Lopes	.50	.23	.06
☐ 65T Jerry Martin	.35	.16	.04
☐ 66T Renie Martin	.35	.16	.04
☐ 67T John Mayberry	.35	.16	.04
☐ 68T Lee Mazzilli	.35	.16	.04
☐ 69T Bake McBride	.35	.16	.04
☐ 70T Dan Meyer	.35	.16	.04
☐ 71T Larry Milbourne	.35	.16	.04
☐ 72T Eddie Milner	.35	.16	.04
☐ 73T Sid Monge	.35	.16	.04
☐ 74T John Montefusco	.35	.16	.04
☐ 75T Jose Morales	.35	.16	.04
☐ 76T Keith Moreland	.35	.16	.04
☐ 77T Jim Morrison	.35	.16	.04
☐ 78T Rance Mulliniks	.35	.16	.04
☐ 79T Steve Mura	.35	.16	.04
☐ 80T Gene Nelson	.35	.16	.04
☐ 81T Joe Nolan	.35	.16	.04
☐ 82T Dickie Noles	.35	.16	.04
☐ 83T Al Oliver	.50	.23	.06
☐ 84T Jorge Orta	.35	.16	.04
☐ 85T Tom Paciorek	.50	.23	.06
☐ 86T Larry Parrish	.35	.16	.04
☐ 87T Jack Perconte	.35	.16	.04
☐ 88T Gaylord Perry	1.50	.65	.19
☐ 89T Rob Picciolo	.35	.16	.04
☐ 90T Joe Pittman	.35	.16	.04
☐ 91T Hosken Powell	.35	.16	.04
☐ 92T Mike Proly	.35	.16	.04
☐ 93T Greg Pryor	.35	.16	.04
☐ 94T Charlie Puleo	.35	.16	.04
☐ 95T Shane Rawley	.35	.16	.04
☐ 96T Johnny Ray	.50	.23	.06
☐ 97T Dave Revering	.35	.16	.04
☐ 98T Cal Ripken	225.00	100.00	28.00
☐ 99T Allen Ripley	.35	.16	.04
☐ 100T Bill Robinson	.50	.23	.06
☐ 101T Aurelio Rodriguez	.35	.16	.04
☐ 102T Joe Rudi	.35	.16	.04
☐ 103T Steve Sax	2.00	.90	.25
☐ 104T Dan Schatzeder	.35	.16	.04
☐ 105T Bob Shirley	.35	.16	.04
☐ 106T Eric Show	.50	.23	.06
☐ 107T Roy Smalley	.35	.16	.04
☐ 108T Lonnie Smith	.50	.23	.06
☐ 109T Ozzie Smith	25.00	11.50	3.10
☐ 110T Reggie Smith	.50	.23	.06
☐ 111T Lary Sorensen	.35	.16	.04
☐ 112T Elias Sosa	.35	.16	.04
☐ 113T Mike Stanton	.35	.16	.04
☐ 114T Steve Stroughter	.35	.16	.04
☐ 115T Champ Summers	.35	.16	.04
☐ 116T Rick Sutcliffe	.50	.23	.06
☐ 117T Frank Tanana	.50	.23	.06

☐ 118T Frank Taveras	.35	.16	.04
☐ 119T Garry Templeton	.50	.23	.06
☐ 120T Alex Trevino	.35	.16	.04
☐ 121T Jerry Turner	.35	.16	.04
☐ 122T Ed VandeBerg	.35	.16	.04
☐ 123T Tom Veryzer	.35	.16	.04
☐ 124T Ron Washington	.35	.16	.04
☐ 125T Bob Watson	.50	.23	.06
☐ 126T Dennis Werth	.35	.16	.04
☐ 127T Eddie Whitson	.35	.16	.04
☐ 128T Rob Wilfong	.35	.16	.04
☐ 129T Bump Wills	.35	.16	.04
☐ 130T Gary Woods	.35	.16	.04
☐ 131T Butch Wynegar	.35	.16	.04
☐ 132T Checklist: 1-132	.35	.16	.04

1983 Topps

The cards in this 792-card set measure 2 1/2" by 3 1/2". Each regular card of the Topps set for 1983 features a large action shot of a player with a small cameo portrait at bottom right. There are special series for AL and NL All Stars (386-407), League Leaders (701-708), and Record Breakers (1-6). In addition, there are 34 "Super Veteran" (SV) cards and six numbered checklist cards. The Super Veteran cards are oriented horizontally and show two pictures of the featured player, a recent picture and a picture showing the player as a rookie when he broke in. The cards are numbered on the reverse at the upper left corner. The team cards are actually Team Leader (TL) cards picturing the batting (BA: batting average) and pitching leader for that team with a checklist back. The key Rookie Cards in this set are Wade Boggs, Tony Gwynn, Willie McGee, Ryne Sandberg, and Frank Viola.

	NRMT-MT	EXC	G-VG
COMPLETE SET (792)	130.00	57.50	16.50
COMMON CARD (1-792)	.10	.05	.01

☐ 1 Tony Armas RB	.15	.07	.02
11 putouts by rightfielder			
☐ 2 Rickey Henderson RB	1.50	.65	.19
Sets modern record for steals, season			
☐ 3 Greg Minton RB	.15	.07	.02
269 1/3 homerless innings streak			
☐ 4 Lance Parrish RB	.20	.09	.03
Threw out three baserunners in All-Star game			
☐ 5 Manny Trillo RB	.15	.07	.02
479 consecutive errorless chances, second baseman			
☐ 6 John Wathan RB	.15	.07	.02
ML steals record for catchers, 31			
☐ 7 Gene Richards	.10	.05	.01
☐ 8 Steve Balboni	.10	.05	.01
☐ 9 Joey McLaughlin	.10	.05	.01
☐ 10 Gorman Thomas	.10	.05	.01
☐ 11 Billy Gardner MG	.10	.05	.01
☐ 12 Paul Mirabella	.10	.05	.01
☐ 13 Larry Herndon	.10	.05	.01
☐ 14 Frank LaCorte	.10	.05	.01
☐ 15 Ron Cey	.15	.07	.02
☐ 16 George Vukovich	.10	.05	.01
☐ 17 Kent Tekulve	.15	.07	.02
☐ 18 Kent Tekulve SV	.10	.05	.01
☐ 19 Oscar Gamble	.10	.05	.01
☐ 20 Carlton Fisk	1.50	.65	.19
☐ 21 Baltimore Orioles TL	.40	.12	.02
BA: Eddie Murray ERA: Jim Palmer (Checklist on back)			
☐ 22 Randy Martz	.10	.05	.01
☐ 23 Mike Heath	.10	.05	.01
☐ 24 Steve Mura	.10	.05	.01
☐ 25 Hal McRae	.20	.09	.03
☐ 26 Jerry Royster	.10	.05	.01
☐ 27 Doug Corbett	.10	.05	.01
☐ 28 Bruce Bochte	.10	.05	.01
☐ 29 Randy Jones	.10	.05	.01
☐ 30 Jim Rice	.20	.09	.03
☐ 31 Bill Gullickson	.15	.07	.02
☐ 32 Dave Bergman	.10	.05	.01
☐ 33 Jack O'Connor	.10	.05	.01
☐ 34 Paul Householder	.10	.05	.01
☐ 35 Rollie Fingers	.50	.23	.06
☐ 36 Rollie Fingers SV	.25	.11	.03
☐ 37 Darrell Johnson MG	.10	.05	.01
☐ 38 Tim Flannery	.10	.05	.01
☐ 39 Terry Puhl	.10	.05	.01
☐ 40 Fernando Valenzuela	.15	.07	.02
☐ 41 Jerry Turner	.10	.05	.01
☐ 42 Dale Murray	.10	.05	.01
☐ 43 Bob Dernier	.10	.05	.01
☐ 44 Don Robinson	.10	.05	.01
☐ 45 John Mayberry	.10	.05	.01
☐ 46 Richard Dotson	.10	.05	.01
☐ 47 Dave McKay	.10	.05	.01
☐ 48 Lary Sorensen	.10	.05	.01
☐ 49 Willie McGee	2.50	1.15	.30
☐ 50 Bob Horner UER	.15	.07	.02
('82 RBI total 7)			
☐ 51 Chicago Cubs TL	.20	.06	.01
BA: Leon Durham ERA: Fergie Jenkins (Checklist on back)			
☐ 52 Onix Concepcion	.10	.05	.01
☐ 53 Mike Witt	.10	.05	.01
☐ 54 Jim Maler	.10	.05	.01
☐ 55 Mookie Wilson	.15	.07	.02
☐ 56 Chuck Rainey	.10	.05	.01
☐ 57 Tim Blackwell	.10	.05	.01
☐ 58 Al Holland	.10	.05	.01
☐ 59 Benny Ayala	.10	.05	.01
☐ 60 Johnny Bench	1.50	.65	.19
☐ 61 Johnny Bench SV	.75	.35	.09

	#	Player			
☐	62	Bob McClure	.10	.05	.01
☐	63	Rick Monday	.10	.05	.01
☐	64	Bill Stein	.10	.05	.01
☐	65	Jack Morris	.50	.23	.06
☐	66	Bob Lillis MG	.10	.05	.01
☐	67	Sal Butera	.10	.05	.01
☐	68	Eric Show	.15	.07	.02
☐	69	Lee Lacy	.10	.05	.01
☐	70	Steve Carlton	1.25	.55	.16
☐	71	Steve Carlton SV	.75	.35	.09
☐	72	Tom Paciorek	.15	.07	.02
☐	73	Allen Ripley	.10	.05	.01
☐	74	Julio Gonzalez	.10	.05	.01
☐	75	Amos Otis	.15	.07	.02
☐	76	Rick Mahler	.10	.05	.01
☐	77	Hosken Powell	.10	.05	.01
☐	78	Bill Caudill	.10	.05	.01
☐	79	Mick Kelleher	.10	.05	.01
☐	80	George Foster	.15	.07	.02
☐	81	Yankees TL BA: Jerry Mumphrey ERA: Dave Righetti (Checklist on back)	.15	.05	.01
☐	82	Bruce Hurst	.15	.07	.02
☐	83	Ryne Sandberg	35.00	16.00	4.40
☐	84	Milt May	.10	.05	.01
☐	85	Ken Singleton	.15	.07	.02
☐	86	Tom Hume	.10	.05	.01
☐	87	Joe Rudi	.10	.05	.01
☐	88	Jim Gantner	.15	.07	.02
☐	89	Leon Roberts	.10	.05	.01
☐	90	Jerry Reuss	.10	.05	.01
☐	91	Larry Milbourne	.10	.05	.01
☐	92	Mike LaCoss	.10	.05	.01
☐	93	John Castino	.10	.05	.01
☐	94	Dave Edwards	.10	.05	.01
☐	95	Alan Trammell	1.50	.65	.19
☐	96	Dick Howser MG	.10	.05	.01
☐	97	Ross Baumgarten	.10	.05	.01
☐	98	Vance Law	.10	.05	.01
☐	99	Dickie Noles	.10	.05	.01
☐	100	Pete Rose	2.00	.90	.25
☐	101	Pete Rose SV	1.00	.45	.13
☐	102	Dave Beard	.10	.05	.01
☐	103	Darrell Porter	.10	.05	.01
☐	104	Bob Walk	.10	.05	.01
☐	105	Don Baylor	.20	.09	.03
☐	106	Gene Nelson	.10	.05	.01
☐	107	Mike Jorgensen	.10	.05	.01
☐	108	Glenn Hoffman	.10	.05	.01
☐	109	Luis Leal	.10	.05	.01
☐	110	Ken Griffey	.15	.07	.02
☐	111	Montreal Expos TL BA: Al Oliver ERA: Steve Rogers (Checklist on back)	.15	.05	.01
☐	112	Bob Shirley	.10	.05	.01
☐	113	Ron Roenicke	.10	.05	.01
☐	114	Jim Slaton	.10	.05	.01
☐	115	Chili Davis	1.25	.55	.16
☐	116	Dave Schmidt	.10	.05	.01
☐	117	Alan Knicely	.10	.05	.01
☐	118	Chris Welsh	.10	.05	.01
☐	119	Tom Brookens	.10	.05	.01
☐	120	Len Barker	.10	.05	.01
☐	121	Mickey Hatcher	.10	.05	.01
☐	122	Jimmy Smith	.10	.05	.01
☐	123	George Frazier	.10	.05	.01
☐	124	Marc Hill	.10	.05	.01
☐	125	Leon Durham	.10	.05	.01
☐	126	Joe Torre MG	.15	.07	.02
☐	127	Preston Hanna	.10	.05	.01
☐	128	Mike Ramsey	.10	.05	.01
☐	129	Checklist: 1-132	.15	.05	.01
☐	130	Dave Stieb	.15	.07	.02
☐	131	Ed Ott	.10	.05	.01
☐	132	Todd Cruz	.10	.05	.01
☐	133	Jim Barr	.10	.05	.01
☐	134	Hubie Brooks	.15	.07	.02
☐	135	Dwight Evans	.15	.07	.02
☐	136	Willie Aikens	.10	.05	.01
☐	137	Woodie Fryman	.10	.05	.01
☐	138	Rick Dempsey	.15	.07	.02
☐	139	Bruce Berenyi	.10	.05	.01
☐	140	Willie Randolph	.15	.07	.02
☐	141	Indians TL BA: Toby Harrah ERA: Rick Sutcliffe (Checklist on back)	.15	.05	.01
☐	142	Mike Caldwell	.10	.05	.01
☐	143	Joe Pettini	.10	.05	.01
☐	144	Mark Wagner	.10	.05	.01
☐	145	Don Sutton	.50	.23	.06
☐	146	Don Sutton SV	.25	.11	.03
☐	147	Rick Leach	.10	.05	.01
☐	148	Dave Roberts	.10	.05	.01
☐	149	Johnny Ray	.10	.05	.01
☐	150	Bruce Sutter	.15	.07	.02
☐	151	Bruce Sutter SV	.10	.05	.01
☐	152	Jay Johnstone	.15	.07	.02
☐	153	Jerry Koosman	.15	.07	.02
☐	154	Johnnie LeMaster	.10	.05	.01
☐	155	Dan Quisenberry	.15	.07	.02
☐	156	Billy Martin MG	.15	.07	.02
☐	157	Steve Bedrosian	.15	.07	.02
☐	158	Rob Wilfong	.10	.05	.01
☐	159	Mike Stanton	.10	.05	.01
☐	160	Dave Kingman	.15	.07	.02
☐	161	Dave Kingman SV	.10	.05	.01
☐	162	Mark Clear	.10	.05	.01
☐	163	Cal Ripken	20.00	9.00	2.50
☐	164	David Palmer	.10	.05	.01
☐	165	Dan Driessen	.10	.05	.01
☐	166	John Pacella	.10	.05	.01
☐	167	Mark Brouhard	.10	.05	.01
☐	168	Juan Eichelberger	.10	.05	.01
☐	169	Doug Flynn	.10	.05	.01
☐	170	Steve Howe	.10	.05	.01
☐	171	Giants TL BA: Joe Morgan ERA: Bill Laskey (Checklist on back)	.25	.08	.01
☐	172	Vern Ruhle	.10	.05	.01
☐	173	Jim Morrison	.10	.05	.01
☐	174	Jerry Ujdur	.10	.05	.01
☐	175	Bo Diaz	.10	.05	.01
☐	176	Dave Righetti	.15	.07	.02
☐	177	Harold Baines	.75	.35	.09
☐	178	Luis Tiant	.15	.07	.02
☐	179	Luis Tiant SV	.10	.05	.01
☐	180	Rickey Henderson	3.50	1.55	.45
☐	181	Terry Felton	.10	.05	.01
☐	182	Mike Fischlin	.10	.05	.01
☐	183	Ed VandeBerg	.10	.05	.01
☐	184	Bob Clark	.10	.05	.01
☐	185	Tim Lollar	.10	.05	.01
☐	186	Whitey Herzog MG	.15	.07	.02
☐	187	Terry Leach	.10	.05	.01
☐	188	Rick Miller	.10	.05	.01
☐	189	Dan Schatzeder	.10	.05	.01
☐	190	Cecil Cooper	.15	.07	.02
☐	191	Joe Price	.10	.05	.01
☐	192	Floyd Rayford	.10	.05	.01
☐	193	Harry Spilman	.10	.05	.01
☐	194	Cesar Geronimo	.10	.05	.01
☐	195	Bob Stoddard	.10	.05	.01

- ☐ 196 Bill Fahey .10 .05 .01
- ☐ 197 Jim Eisenreich 1.75 .80 .22
- ☐ 198 Kiko Garcia .10 .05 .01
- ☐ 199 Marty Bystrom .10 .05 .01
- ☐ 200 Rod Carew 1.00 .45 .13
- ☐ 201 Rod Carew SV .50 .23 .06
- ☐ 202 Blue Jays TL .15 .05 .01
  BA: Damaso Garcia
  ERA: Dave Stieb
  (Checklist on back)
- ☐ 203 Mike Morgan .10 .05 .01
- ☐ 204 Junior Kennedy .10 .05 .01
- ☐ 205 Dave Parker .20 .09 .03
- ☐ 206 Ken Oberkfell .10 .05 .01
- ☐ 207 Rick Camp .10 .05 .01
- ☐ 208 Dan Meyer .10 .05 .01
- ☐ 209 Mike Moore .75 .35 .09
- ☐ 210 Jack Clark .15 .07 .02
- ☐ 211 John Denny .10 .05 .01
- ☐ 212 John Stearns .10 .05 .01
- ☐ 213 Tom Burgmeier .10 .05 .01
- ☐ 214 Jerry White .10 .05 .01
- ☐ 215 Mario Soto .10 .05 .01
- ☐ 216 Tony LaRussa MG .15 .07 .02
- ☐ 217 Tim Stoddard .10 .05 .01
- ☐ 218 Roy Howell .10 .05 .01
- ☐ 219 Mike Armstrong .10 .05 .01
- ☐ 220 Dusty Baker .20 .09 .03
- ☐ 221 Joe Niekro .15 .07 .02
- ☐ 222 Damaso Garcia .10 .05 .01
- ☐ 223 John Montefusco .10 .05 .01
- ☐ 224 Mickey Rivers .10 .05 .01
- ☐ 225 Enos Cabell .10 .05 .01
- ☐ 226 Enrique Romo .10 .05 .01
- ☐ 227 Chris Bando .10 .05 .01
- ☐ 228 Joaquin Andujar .10 .05 .01
- ☐ 229 Phillies TL .25 .08 .01
  BA: Bo Diaz
  ERA: Steve Carlton
  (Checklist on back)
- ☐ 230 Fergie Jenkins .50 .23 .06
- ☐ 231 Fergie Jenkins SV .30 .14 .04
- ☐ 232 Tom Brunansky .15 .07 .02
- ☐ 233 Wayne Gross .10 .05 .01
- ☐ 234 Larry Andersen .10 .05 .01
- ☐ 235 Claudell Washington .10 .05 .01
- ☐ 236 Steve Renko .10 .05 .01
- ☐ 237 Dan Norman .10 .05 .01
- ☐ 238 Bud Black .60 .25 .08
- ☐ 239 Dave Stapleton .10 .05 .01
- ☐ 240 Rich Gossage .20 .09 .03
- ☐ 241 Rich Gossage SV .20 .09 .03
- ☐ 242 Joe Nolan .10 .05 .01
- ☐ 243 Duane Walker .10 .05 .01
- ☐ 244 Dwight Bernard .10 .05 .01
- ☐ 245 Steve Sax .15 .07 .02
- ☐ 246 George Bamberger MG .10 .05 .01
- ☐ 247 Dave Smith .10 .05 .01
- ☐ 248 Bake McBride .10 .05 .01
- ☐ 249 Checklist: 133-264 .15 .05 .01
- ☐ 250 Bill Buckner .15 .07 .02
- ☐ 251 Alan Wiggins .10 .05 .01
- ☐ 252 Luis Aguayo .10 .05 .01
- ☐ 253 Larry McWilliams .10 .05 .01
- ☐ 254 Rick Cerone .10 .05 .01
- ☐ 255 Gene Garber .10 .05 .01
- ☐ 256 Gene Garber SV .10 .05 .01
- ☐ 257 Jesse Barfield .15 .07 .02
- ☐ 258 Manny Castillo .10 .05 .01
- ☐ 259 Jeff Jones .10 .05 .01
- ☐ 260 Steve Kemp .10 .05 .01
- ☐ 261 Tigers TL .15 .05 .01
  BA: Larry Herndon
  ERA: Dan Petry
  (Checklist on back)
- ☐ 262 Ron Jackson .10 .05 .01
- ☐ 263 Renie Martin .10 .05 .01
- ☐ 264 Jamie Quirk .10 .05 .01
- ☐ 265 Joel Youngblood .10 .05 .01
- ☐ 266 Paul Boris .10 .05 .01
- ☐ 267 Terry Francona .10 .05 .01
- ☐ 268 Storm Davis .10 .05 .01
- ☐ 269 Ron Oester .10 .05 .01
- ☐ 270 Dennis Eckersley .75 .35 .09
- ☐ 271 Ed Romero .10 .05 .01
- ☐ 272 Frank Tanana .15 .07 .02
- ☐ 273 Mark Belanger .10 .05 .01
- ☐ 274 Terry Kennedy .10 .05 .01
- ☐ 275 Ray Knight .15 .07 .02
- ☐ 276 Gene Mauch MG .10 .05 .01
- ☐ 277 Rance Mulliniks .10 .05 .01
- ☐ 278 Kevin Hickey .10 .05 .01
- ☐ 279 Greg Gross .10 .05 .01
- ☐ 280 Bert Blyleven .20 .09 .03
- ☐ 281 Andre Robertson .10 .05 .01
- ☐ 282 Reggie Smith .50 .23 .06
  (Ryne Sandberg
  ducking back)
- ☐ 283 Reggie Smith SV .10 .05 .01
- ☐ 284 Jeff Lahti .10 .05 .01
- ☐ 285 Lance Parrish .15 .07 .02
- ☐ 286 Rick Langford .10 .05 .01
- ☐ 287 Bobby Brown .10 .05 .01
- ☐ 288 Joe Cowley .10 .05 .01
- ☐ 289 Jerry Dybzinski .10 .05 .01
- ☐ 290 Jeff Reardon .40 .18 .05
- ☐ 291 Pirates TL .15 .05 .01
  BA: Bill Madlock
  ERA: John Candelaria
  (Checklist on back)
- ☐ 292 Craig Swan .10 .05 .01
- ☐ 293 Glenn Gulliver .10 .05 .01
- ☐ 294 Dave Engle .10 .05 .01
- ☐ 295 Jerry Remy .10 .05 .01
- ☐ 296 Greg Harris .10 .05 .01
- ☐ 297 Ned Yost .10 .05 .01
- ☐ 298 Floyd Chiffer .10 .05 .01
- ☐ 299 George Wright .10 .05 .01
- ☐ 300 Mike Schmidt 2.00 .90 .25
- ☐ 301 Mike Schmidt SV 1.00 .45 .13
- ☐ 302 Ernie Whitt .10 .05 .01
- ☐ 303 Miguel Dilone .10 .05 .01
- ☐ 304 Dave Rucker .10 .05 .01
- ☐ 305 Larry Bowa .15 .07 .02
- ☐ 306 Tom Lasorda MG .15 .07 .02
- ☐ 307 Lou Piniella .15 .07 .02
- ☐ 308 Jesus Vega .10 .05 .01
- ☐ 309 Jeff Leonard .10 .05 .01
- ☐ 310 Greg Luzinski .15 .07 .02
- ☐ 311 Glenn Brummer .10 .05 .01
- ☐ 312 Brian Kingman .10 .05 .01
- ☐ 313 Gary Gray .10 .05 .01
- ☐ 314 Ken Dayley .10 .05 .01
- ☐ 315 Rick Burleson .10 .05 .01
- ☐ 316 Paul Splittorff .10 .05 .01
- ☐ 317 Gary Rajsich .10 .05 .01
- ☐ 318 John Tudor .15 .07 .02
- ☐ 319 Lenn Sakata .10 .05 .01
- ☐ 320 Steve Rogers .10 .05 .01
- ☐ 321 Brewers TL .40 .12 .02
  BA: Robin Yount
  ERA: Pete Vuckovich
  (Checklist on back)
- ☐ 322 Dave Van Gorder .10 .05 .01
- ☐ 323 Luis DeLeon .10 .05 .01
- ☐ 324 Mike Marshall .10 .05 .01

	No.	Player			
☐	325	Von Hayes	.15	.07	.02
☐	326	Garth Iorg	.10	.05	.01
☐	327	Bobby Castillo	.10	.05	.01
☐	328	Craig Reynolds	.10	.05	.01
☐	329	Randy Niemann	.10	.05	.01
☐	330	Buddy Bell	.15	.07	.02
☐	331	Mike Krukow	.10	.05	.01
☐	332	Glenn Wilson	.15	.07	.02
☐	333	Dave LaRoche	.10	.05	.01
☐	334	Dave LaRoche SV	.10	.05	.01
☐	335	Steve Henderson	.10	.05	.01
☐	336	Rene Lachemann MG	.10	.05	.01
☐	337	Tito Landrum	.10	.05	.01
☐	338	Bob Owchinko	.10	.05	.01
☐	339	Terry Harper	.10	.05	.01
☐	340	Larry Gura	.10	.05	.01
☐	341	Doug DeCinces	.15	.07	.02
☐	342	Atlee Hammaker	.10	.05	.01
☐	343	Bob Bailor	.10	.05	.01
☐	344	Roger LaFrancois	.10	.05	.01
☐	345	Jim Clancy	.10	.05	.01
☐	346	Joe Pittman	.10	.05	.01
☐	347	Sammy Stewart	.10	.05	.01
☐	348	Alan Bannister	.10	.05	.01
☐	349	Checklist: 265-396	.15	.05	.01
☐	350	Robin Yount	2.50	1.15	.30
☐	351	Reds TL	.15	.05	.01
		BA: Cesar Cedeno			
		ERA: Mario Soto			
		(Checklist on back)			
☐	352	Mike Scioscia	.15	.07	.02
☐	353	Steve Comer	.10	.05	.01
☐	354	Randy Johnson	.10	.05	.01
☐	355	Jim Bibby	.10	.05	.01
☐	356	Gary Woods	.10	.05	.01
☐	357	Len Matuszek	.10	.05	.01
☐	358	Jerry Garvin	.10	.05	.01
☐	359	Dave Collins	.10	.05	.01
☐	360	Nolan Ryan	10.00	4.50	1.25
☐	361	Nolan Ryan SV	5.00	2.30	.60
☐	362	Bill Almon	.10	.05	.01
☐	363	John Stuper	.10	.05	.01
☐	364	Brett Butler	1.00	.45	.13
☐	365	Dave Lopes	.15	.07	.02
☐	366	Dick Williams MG	.10	.05	.01
☐	367	Bud Anderson	.10	.05	.01
☐	368	Richie Zisk	.10	.05	.01
☐	369	Jesse Orosco	.10	.05	.01
☐	370	Gary Carter	.75	.35	.09
☐	371	Mike Richardt	.10	.05	.01
☐	372	Terry Crowley	.10	.05	.01
☐	373	Kevin Saucier	.10	.05	.01
☐	374	Wayne Krenchicki	.10	.05	.01
☐	375	Pete Vuckovich	.10	.05	.01
☐	376	Ken Landreaux	.10	.05	.01
☐	377	Lee May	.15	.07	.02
☐	378	Lee May SV	.10	.05	.01
☐	379	Guy Sularz	.10	.05	.01
☐	380	Ron Davis	.10	.05	.01
☐	381	Red Sox TL	.20	.06	.01
		BA: Jim Rice			
		ERA: Bob Stanley			
		(Checklist on back)			
☐	382	Bob Knepper	.10	.05	.01
☐	383	Ozzie Virgil	.10	.05	.01
☐	384	Dave Dravecky	.75	.35	.09
☐	385	Mike Easler	.10	.05	.01
☐	386	Rod Carew AS	.40	.18	.05
☐	387	Bob Grich AS	.12	.05	.02
☐	388	George Brett AS	2.00	.90	.25
☐	389	Robin Yount AS	1.25	.55	.16
☐	390	Reggie Jackson AS	.75	.35	.09
☐	391	Rickey Henderson AS	1.25	.55	.16
☐	392	Fred Lynn AS	.12	.05	.02
☐	393	Carlton Fisk AS	.50	.23	.06
☐	394	Pete Vuckovich AS	.12	.05	.02
☐	395	Larry Gura AS	.12	.05	.02
☐	396	Dan Quisenberry AS	.12	.05	.02
☐	397	Pete Rose AS	1.00	.45	.13
☐	398	Manny Trillo AS	.12	.05	.02
☐	399	Mike Schmidt AS	1.00	.45	.13
☐	400	Dave Concepcion AS	.12	.05	.02
☐	401	Dale Murphy AS	.35	.16	.04
☐	402	Andre Dawson AS	.60	.25	.08
☐	403	Tim Raines AS	.50	.23	.06
☐	404	Gary Carter AS	.25	.11	.03
☐	405	Steve Rogers AS	.12	.05	.02
☐	406	Steve Carlton AS	.75	.35	.09
☐	407	Bruce Sutter AS	.12	.05	.02
☐	408	Rudy May	.10	.05	.01
☐	409	Marvis Foley	.10	.05	.01
☐	410	Phil Niekro	.50	.23	.06
☐	411	Phil Niekro SV	.25	.11	.03
☐	412	Rangers TL	.15	.05	.01
		BA: Buddy Bell			
		ERA: Charlie Hough			
		(Checklist on back)			
☐	413	Matt Keough	.10	.05	.01
☐	414	Julio Cruz	.10	.05	.01
☐	415	Bob Forsch	.10	.05	.01
☐	416	Joe Ferguson	.10	.05	.01
☐	417	Tom Hausman	.10	.05	.01
☐	418	Greg Pryor	.10	.05	.01
☐	419	Steve Crawford	.10	.05	.01
☐	420	Al Oliver	.15	.07	.02
☐	421	Al Oliver SV	.10	.05	.01
☐	422	George Cappuzzello	.10	.05	.01
☐	423	Tom Lawless	.10	.05	.01
☐	424	Jerry Augustine	.10	.05	.01
☐	425	Pedro Guerrero	.15	.07	.02
☐	426	Earl Weaver MG	.15	.07	.02
☐	427	Roy Lee Jackson	.10	.05	.01
☐	428	Champ Summers	.10	.05	.01
☐	429	Eddie Whitson	.10	.05	.01
☐	430	Kirk Gibson	1.25	.55	.16
☐	431	Gary Gaetti	1.00	.45	.13
☐	432	Porfirio Altamirano	.10	.05	.01
☐	433	Dale Berra	.10	.05	.01
☐	434	Dennis Lamp	.10	.05	.01
☐	435	Tony Armas	.10	.05	.01
☐	436	Bill Campbell	.10	.05	.01
☐	437	Rick Sweet	.10	.05	.01
☐	438	Dave LaPoint	.10	.05	.01
☐	439	Rafael Ramirez	.10	.05	.01
☐	440	Ron Guidry	.15	.07	.02
☐	441	Astros TL	.15	.05	.01
		BA: Ray Knight			
		ERA: Joe Niekro			
		(Checklist on back)			
☐	442	Brian Downing	.15	.07	.02
☐	443	Don Hood	.10	.05	.01
☐	444	Wally Backman	.10	.05	.01
☐	445	Mike Flanagan	.15	.07	.02
☐	446	Reid Nichols	.10	.05	.01
☐	447	Bryn Smith	.10	.05	.01
☐	448	Darrell Evans	.15	.07	.02
☐	449	Eddie Milner	.10	.05	.01
☐	450	Ted Simmons	.15	.07	.02
☐	451	Ted Simmons SV	.10	.05	.01
☐	452	Lloyd Moseby	.10	.05	.01
☐	453	Lamar Johnson	.10	.05	.01
☐	454	Bob Welch	.15	.07	.02
☐	455	Sixto Lezcano	.10	.05	.01
☐	456	Lee Elia MG	.10	.05	.01
☐	457	Milt Wilcox	.10	.05	.01
☐	458	Ron Washington	.10	.05	.01

☐	459 Ed Farmer	.10	.05	.01
☐	460 Roy Smalley	.10	.05	.01
☐	461 Steve Trout	.10	.05	.01
☐	462 Steve Nicosia	.10	.05	.01
☐	463 Gaylord Perry	.50	.23	.06
☐	464 Gaylord Perry SV	.25	.11	.03
☐	465 Lonnie Smith	.15	.07	.02
☐	466 Tom Underwood	.10	.05	.01
☐	467 Rufino Linares	.10	.05	.01
☐	468 Dave Goltz	.10	.05	.01
☐	469 Ron Gardenhire	.10	.05	.01
☐	470 Greg Minton	.10	.05	.01
☐	471 Kansas City Royals TL BA: Willie Wilson ERA: Vida Blue (Checklist on back)	.15	.05	.01
☐	472 Gary Allenson	.10	.05	.01
☐	473 John Lowenstein	.10	.05	.01
☐	474 Ray Burris	.10	.05	.01
☐	475 Cesar Cedeno	.15	.07	.02
☐	476 Rob Picciolo	.10	.05	.01
☐	477 Tom Niedenfuer	.10	.05	.01
☐	478 Phil Garner	.15	.07	.02
☐	479 Charlie Hough	.15	.07	.02
☐	480 Toby Harrah	.10	.05	.01
☐	481 Scot Thompson	.10	.05	.01
☐	482 Tony Gwynn UER (No Topps logo under card number on back)	35.00	16.00	4.40
☐	483 Lynn Jones	.10	.05	.01
☐	484 Dick Ruthven	.10	.05	.01
☐	485 Omar Moreno	.10	.05	.01
☐	486 Clyde King MG	.10	.05	.01
☐	487 Jerry Hairston	.10	.05	.01
☐	488 Alfredo Griffin	.10	.05	.01
☐	489 Tom Herr	.15	.07	.02
☐	490 Jim Palmer	1.00	.45	.13
☐	491 Jim Palmer SV	.50	.23	.06
☐	492 Paul Serna	.10	.05	.01
☐	493 Steve McCatty	.10	.05	.01
☐	494 Bob Brenly	.10	.05	.01
☐	495 Warren Cromartie	.10	.05	.01
☐	496 Tom Veryzer	.10	.05	.01
☐	497 Rick Sutcliffe	.15	.07	.02
☐	498 Wade Boggs	25.00	11.50	3.10
☐	499 Jeff Little	.10	.05	.01
☐	500 Reggie Jackson	1.75	.80	.22
☐	501 Reggie Jackson SV	.75	.35	.09
☐	502 Atlanta Braves TL BA: Dale Murphy ERA: Phil Niekro (Checklist on back)	.25	.08	.01
☐	503 Moose Haas	.10	.05	.01
☐	504 Don Werner	.10	.05	.01
☐	505 Garry Templeton	.10	.05	.01
☐	506 Jim Gott	.40	.18	.05
☐	507 Tony Scott	.10	.05	.01
☐	508 Tom Filer	.10	.05	.01
☐	509 Lou Whitaker	.75	.35	.09
☐	510 Tug McGraw	.15	.07	.02
☐	511 Tug McGraw SV	.10	.05	.01
☐	512 Doyle Alexander	.10	.05	.01
☐	513 Fred Stanley	.10	.05	.01
☐	514 Rudy Law	.10	.05	.01
☐	515 Gene Tenace	.10	.05	.01
☐	516 Bill Virdon MG	.10	.05	.01
☐	517 Gary Ward	.10	.05	.01
☐	518 Bill Laskey	.10	.05	.01
☐	519 Terry Bulling	.10	.05	.01
☐	520 Fred Lynn	.15	.07	.02
☐	521 Bruce Benedict	.10	.05	.01
☐	522 Pat Zachry	.10	.05	.01
☐	523 Carney Lansford	.15	.07	.02
☐	524 Tom Brennan	.10	.05	.01
☐	525 Frank White	.15	.07	.02
☐	526 Checklist: 397-528	.15	.05	.01
☐	527 Larry Biittner	.10	.05	.01
☐	528 Jamie Easterly	.10	.05	.01
☐	529 Tim Laudner	.10	.05	.01
☐	530 Eddie Murray	2.50	1.15	.30
☐	531 Oakland A's TL BA: Rickey Henderson ERA: Rick Langford (Checklist on back)	.40	.12	.02
☐	532 Dave Stewart	.75	.35	.09
☐	533 Luis Salazar	.10	.05	.01
☐	534 John Butcher	.10	.05	.01
☐	535 Manny Trillo	.10	.05	.01
☐	536 John Wockenfuss	.10	.05	.01
☐	537 Rod Scurry	.10	.05	.01
☐	538 Danny Heep	.10	.05	.01
☐	539 Roger Erickson	.10	.05	.01
☐	540 Ozzie Smith	3.00	1.35	.40
☐	541 Britt Burns	.10	.05	.01
☐	542 Jody Davis	.10	.05	.01
☐	543 Alan Fowlkes	.10	.05	.01
☐	544 Larry Whisenton	.10	.05	.01
☐	545 Floyd Bannister	.10	.05	.01
☐	546 Dave Garcia MG	.10	.05	.01
☐	547 Geoff Zahn	.10	.05	.01
☐	548 Brian Giles	.10	.05	.01
☐	549 Charlie Puleo	.10	.05	.01
☐	550 Carl Yastrzemski	1.25	.55	.16
☐	551 Carl Yastrzemski SV	.60	.25	.08
☐	552 Tim Wallach	.20	.09	.03
☐	553 Dennis Martinez	.15	.07	.02
☐	554 Mike Vail	.10	.05	.01
☐	555 Steve Yeager	.10	.05	.01
☐	556 Willie Upshaw	.10	.05	.01
☐	557 Rick Honeycutt	.10	.05	.01
☐	558 Dickie Thon	.10	.05	.01
☐	559 Pete Redfern	.10	.05	.01
☐	560 Ron LeFlore	.15	.07	.02
☐	561 Cardinals TL BA: Lonnie Smith ERA: Joaquin Andujar (Checklist on back)	.15	.05	.01
☐	562 Dave Rozema	.10	.05	.01
☐	563 Juan Bonilla	.10	.05	.01
☐	564 Sid Monge	.10	.05	.01
☐	565 Bucky Dent	.15	.07	.02
☐	566 Manny Sarmiento	.10	.05	.01
☐	567 Joe Simpson	.10	.05	.01
☐	568 Willie Hernandez	.15	.07	.02
☐	569 Jack Perconte	.10	.05	.01
☐	570 Vida Blue	.15	.07	.02
☐	571 Mickey Klutts	.10	.05	.01
☐	572 Bob Watson	.15	.07	.02
☐	573 Andy Hassler	.10	.05	.01
☐	574 Glenn Adams	.10	.05	.01
☐	575 Neil Allen	.10	.05	.01
☐	576 Frank Robinson MG	.30	.14	.04
☐	577 Luis Aponte	.10	.05	.01
☐	578 David Green	.10	.05	.01
☐	579 Rich Dauer	.10	.05	.01
☐	580 Tom Seaver	1.50	.65	.19
☐	581 Tom Seaver SV	.75	.35	.09
☐	582 Marshall Edwards	.10	.05	.01
☐	583 Terry Forster	.10	.05	.01
☐	584 Dave Hostetler	.10	.05	.01
☐	585 Jose Cruz	.15	.07	.02
☐	586 Frank Viola	2.50	1.15	.30
☐	587 Ivan DeJesus	.10	.05	.01
☐	588 Pat Underwood	.10	.05	.01
☐	589 Alvis Woods	.10	.05	.01
☐	590 Tony Pena	.15	.07	.02

☐	591	White Sox TL BA: Greg Luzinski ERA: LaMarr Hoyt (Checklist on back)	.15	.05	.01
☐	592	Shane Rawley	.10	.05	.01
☐	593	Broderick Perkins	.10	.05	.01
☐	594	Eric Rasmussen	.10	.05	.01
☐	595	Tim Raines	1.25	.55	.16
☐	596	Randy Johnson	.10	.05	.01
☐	597	Mike Proly	.10	.05	.01
☐	598	Dwayne Murphy	.10	.05	.01
☐	599	Don Aase	.10	.05	.01
☐	600	George Brett	4.00	1.80	.50
☐	601	Ed Lynch	.10	.05	.01
☐	602	Rich Gedman	.10	.05	.01
☐	603	Joe Morgan	.75	.35	.09
☐	604	Joe Morgan SV	.35	.16	.04
☐	605	Gary Roenicke	.10	.05	.01
☐	606	Bobby Cox MG	.10	.05	.01
☐	607	Charlie Leibrandt	.15	.07	.02
☐	608	Don Money	.10	.05	.01
☐	609	Danny Darwin	.10	.05	.01
☐	610	Steve Garvey	.50	.23	.06
☐	611	Bert Roberge	.10	.05	.01
☐	612	Steve Swisher	.10	.05	.01
☐	613	Mike Ivie	.10	.05	.01
☐	614	Ed Glynn	.10	.05	.01
☐	615	Garry Maddox	.10	.05	.01
☐	616	Bill Nahorodny	.10	.05	.01
☐	617	Butch Wynegar	.10	.05	.01
☐	618	LaMarr Hoyt	.10	.05	.01
☐	619	Keith Moreland	.10	.05	.01
☐	620	Mike Norris	.10	.05	.01
☐	621	New York Mets TL BA: Mookie Wilson ERA: Craig Swan (Checklist on back)	.15	.05	.01
☐	622	Dave Edler	.10	.05	.01
☐	623	Luis Sanchez	.10	.05	.01
☐	624	Glenn Hubbard	.10	.05	.01
☐	625	Ken Forsch	.10	.05	.01
☐	626	Jerry Martin	.10	.05	.01
☐	627	Doug Bair	.10	.05	.01
☐	628	Julio Valdez	.10	.05	.01
☐	629	Charlie Lea	.10	.05	.01
☐	630	Paul Molitor	3.00	1.35	.40
☐	631	Tippy Martinez	.10	.05	.01
☐	632	Alex Trevino	.10	.05	.01
☐	633	Vicente Romo	.10	.05	.01
☐	634	Max Venable	.10	.05	.01
☐	635	Graig Nettles	.15	.07	.02
☐	636	Graig Nettles SV	.10	.05	.01
☐	637	Pat Corrales MG	.10	.05	.01
☐	638	Dan Petry	.10	.05	.01
☐	639	Art Howe	.10	.05	.01
☐	640	Andre Thornton	.10	.05	.01
☐	641	Billy Sample	.10	.05	.01
☐	642	Checklist: 529-660	.15	.05	.01
☐	643	Bump Wills	.10	.05	.01
☐	644	Joe Lefebvre	.10	.05	.01
☐	645	Bill Madlock	.15	.07	.02
☐	646	Jim Essian	.10	.05	.01
☐	647	Bobby Mitchell	.10	.05	.01
☐	648	Jeff Burroughs	.10	.05	.01
☐	649	Tommy Boggs	.10	.05	.01
☐	650	George Hendrick	.10	.05	.01
☐	651	Angels TL BA: Rod Carew ERA: Mike Witt (Checklist on back)	.20	.06	.01
☐	652	Butch Hobson	.15	.07	.02
☐	653	Ellis Valentine	.10	.05	.01
☐	654	Bob Ojeda	.15	.07	.02
☐	655	Al Bumbry	.15	.07	.02
☐	656	Dave Frost	.10	.05	.01
☐	657	Mike Gates	.10	.05	.01
☐	658	Frank Pastore	.10	.05	.01
☐	659	Charlie Moore	.10	.05	.01
☐	660	Mike Hargrove	.15	.07	.02
☐	661	Bill Russell	.15	.07	.02
☐	662	Joe Sambito	.10	.05	.01
☐	663	Tom O'Malley	.10	.05	.01
☐	664	Bob Molinaro	.10	.05	.01
☐	665	Jim Sundberg	.15	.07	.02
☐	666	Sparky Anderson MG	.15	.07	.02
☐	667	Dick Davis	.10	.05	.01
☐	668	Larry Christenson	.10	.05	.01
☐	669	Mike Squires	.10	.05	.01
☐	670	Jerry Mumphrey	.10	.05	.01
☐	671	Lenny Faedo	.10	.05	.01
☐	672	Jim Kaat	.15	.07	.02
☐	673	Jim Kaat SV	.10	.05	.01
☐	674	Kurt Bevacqua	.10	.05	.01
☐	675	Jim Beattie	.10	.05	.01
☐	676	Biff Pocoroba	.10	.05	.01
☐	677	Dave Revering	.10	.05	.01
☐	678	Juan Beniquez	.10	.05	.01
☐	679	Mike Scott	.15	.07	.02
☐	680	Andre Dawson	2.00	.90	.25
☐	681	Dodgers Leaders BA: Pedro Guerrero ERA: Fernando Valenzuela (Checklist on back)	.15	.05	.01
☐	682	Bob Stanley	.10	.05	.01
☐	683	Dan Ford	.10	.05	.01
☐	684	Rafael Landestoy	.10	.05	.01
☐	685	Lee Mazzilli	.10	.05	.01
☐	686	Randy Lerch	.10	.05	.01
☐	687	U.L. Washington	.10	.05	.01
☐	688	Jim Wohlford	.10	.05	.01
☐	689	Ron Hassey	.10	.05	.01
☐	690	Kent Hrbek	.75	.35	.09
☐	691	Dave Tobik	.10	.05	.01
☐	692	Denny Walling	.10	.05	.01
☐	693	Sparky Lyle	.15	.07	.02
☐	694	Sparky Lyle SV	.10	.05	.01
☐	695	Ruppert Jones	.10	.05	.01
☐	696	Chuck Tanner MG	.10	.05	.01
☐	697	Barry Foote	.10	.05	.01
☐	698	Tony Bernazard	.10	.05	.01
☐	699	Lee Smith	3.00	1.35	.40
☐	700	Keith Hernandez	.20	.09	.03
☐	701	Batting Leaders AL: Willie Wilson NL: Al Oliver	.20	.09	.03
☐	702	Home Run Leaders AL: Reggie Jackson AL: Gorman Thomas NL: Dave Kingman	.35	.16	.04
☐	703	RBI Leaders AL: Hal McRae NL: Dale Murphy NL: Al Oliver	.25	.11	.03
☐	704	SB Leaders AL: Rickey Henderson NL: Tim Raines	1.00	.45	.13
☐	705	Victory Leaders AL: LaMarr Hoyt NL: Steve Carlton	.25	.11	.03
☐	706	Strikeout Leaders AL: Floyd Bannister NL: Steve Carlton	.25	.11	.03
☐	707	ERA Leaders AL: Rick Sutcliffe NL: Steve Rogers	.20	.09	.03
☐	708	Leading Firemen	.20	.09	.03

	AL: Dan Quisenberry NL: Bruce Sutter			
☐ 709	Jimmy Sexton	.10	.05	.01
☐ 710	Willie Wilson	.15	.07	.02
☐ 711	Mariners TL BA: Bruce Bochte ERA: Jim Beattie (Checklist on back)	.15	.05	.01
☐ 712	Bruce Kison	.10	.05	.01
☐ 713	Ron Hodges	.10	.05	.01
☐ 714	Wayne Nordhagen	.10	.05	.01
☐ 715	Tony Perez	.20	.09	.03
☐ 716	Tony Perez SV	.15	.07	.02
☐ 717	Scott Sanderson	.10	.05	.01
☐ 718	Jim Dwyer	.10	.05	.01
☐ 719	Rich Gale	.10	.05	.01
☐ 720	Dave Concepcion	.15	.07	.02
☐ 721	John Martin	.10	.05	.01
☐ 722	Jorge Orta	.10	.05	.01
☐ 723	Randy Moffitt	.10	.05	.01
☐ 724	Johnny Grubb	.10	.05	.01
☐ 725	Dan Spillner	.10	.05	.01
☐ 726	Harvey Kuenn MG	.15	.07	.02
☐ 727	Chet Lemon	.10	.05	.01
☐ 728	Ron Reed	.10	.05	.01
☐ 729	Jerry Morales	.10	.05	.01
☐ 730	Jason Thompson	.10	.05	.01
☐ 731	Al Williams	.10	.05	.01
☐ 732	Dave Henderson	.15	.07	.02
☐ 733	Buck Martinez	.10	.05	.01
☐ 734	Steve Braun	.10	.05	.01
☐ 735	Tommy John	.20	.09	.03
☐ 736	Tommy John SV	.15	.07	.02
☐ 737	Mitchell Page	.10	.05	.01
☐ 738	Tim Foli	.10	.05	.01
☐ 739	Rick Ownbey	.10	.05	.01
☐ 740	Rusty Staub	.15	.07	.02
☐ 741	Rusty Staub SV	.10	.05	.01
☐ 742	Padres TL BA: Terry Kennedy ERA: Tim Lollar (Checklist on back)	.15	.05	.01
☐ 743	Mike Torrez	.10	.05	.01
☐ 744	Brad Mills	.10	.05	.01
☐ 745	Scott McGregor	.10	.05	.01
☐ 746	John Wathan	.10	.05	.01
☐ 747	Fred Breining	.10	.05	.01
☐ 748	Derrel Thomas	.10	.05	.01
☐ 749	Jon Matlack	.10	.05	.01
☐ 750	Ben Oglivie	.10	.05	.01
☐ 751	Brad Havens	.10	.05	.01
☐ 752	Luis Pujols	.10	.05	.01
☐ 753	Elias Sosa	.10	.05	.01
☐ 754	Bill Robinson	.15	.07	.02
☐ 755	John Candelaria	.10	.05	.01
☐ 756	Russ Nixon MG	.10	.05	.01
☐ 757	Rick Manning	.10	.05	.01
☐ 758	Aurelio Rodriguez	.10	.05	.01
☐ 759	Doug Bird	.10	.05	.01
☐ 760	Dale Murphy	1.00	.45	.13
☐ 761	Gary Lucas	.10	.05	.01
☐ 762	Cliff Johnson	.10	.05	.01
☐ 763	Al Cowens	.10	.05	.01
☐ 764	Pete Falcone	.10	.05	.01
☐ 765	Bob Boone	.15	.07	.02
☐ 766	Barry Bonnell	.10	.05	.01
☐ 767	Duane Kuiper	.10	.05	.01
☐ 768	Chris Speier	.10	.05	.01
☐ 769	Checklist: 661-792	.15	.05	.01
☐ 770	Dave Winfield	2.50	1.15	.30
☐ 771	Twins TL BA: Kent Hrbek ERA: Bobby Castillo (Checklist on back)	.20	.06	.01
☐ 772	Jim Kern	.10	.05	.01
☐ 773	Larry Hisle	.10	.05	.01
☐ 774	Alan Ashby	.10	.05	.01
☐ 775	Burt Hooton	.10	.05	.01
☐ 776	Larry Parrish	.10	.05	.01
☐ 777	John Curtis	.10	.05	.01
☐ 778	Rich Hebner	.10	.05	.01
☐ 779	Rick Waits	.10	.05	.01
☐ 780	Gary Matthews	.15	.07	.02
☐ 781	Rick Rhoden	.10	.05	.01
☐ 782	Bobby Murcer	.15	.07	.02
☐ 783	Bobby Murcer SV	.10	.05	.01
☐ 784	Jeff Newman	.10	.05	.01
☐ 785	Dennis Leonard	.10	.05	.01
☐ 786	Ralph Houk MG	.10	.05	.01
☐ 787	Dick Tidrow	.10	.05	.01
☐ 788	Dane Iorg	.10	.05	.01
☐ 789	Bryan Clark	.10	.05	.01
☐ 790	Bob Grich	.15	.07	.02
☐ 791	Gary Lavelle	.10	.05	.01
☐ 792	Chris Chambliss	.15	.07	.02

1983 Topps Traded

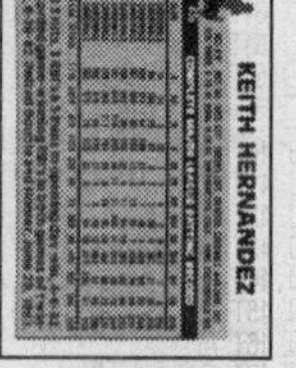

The cards in this 132-card set measure 2 1/2" by 3 1/2". For the third year in a row, Topps issued a 132-card Traded (or extended) set featuring some of the year's top rookies and players who had changed teams during the year, but were featured with their old team in the Topps regular issue of 1983. The cards were available through hobby dealers only and were printed in Ireland by the Topps affiliate in that country. The set is numbered alphabetically by the last name of the player of the card. The Darryl Strawberry card number 108 can be found with either one or two asterisks (in the lower left corner of the reverse). The key (extended) Rookie Cards in this set are Tony Phillips and Darryl Strawberry. Also noteworthy is Julio Franco's first Topps (extended) card.

		NRMT-MT	EXC	G-VG
COMPLETE FACT.SET (132)		50.00	23.00	6.25
COMMON CARD (1T-132T)		.25	.11	.03
☐ 1T	Neil Allen	.25	.11	.03
☐ 2T	Bill Almon	.25	.11	.03
☐ 3T	Joe Altobelli MG	.25	.11	.03
☐ 4T	Tony Armas	.25	.11	.03
☐ 5T	Doug Bair	.25	.11	.03
☐ 6T	Steve Baker	.25	.11	.03

☐ 7T Floyd Bannister .25 .11 .03
☐ 8T Don Baylor .50 .23 .06
☐ 9T Tony Bernazard .25 .11 .03
☐ 10T Larry Biittner .25 .11 .03
☐ 11T Dann Bilardello .25 .11 .03
☐ 12T Doug Bird .25 .11 .03
☐ 13T Steve Boros MG .25 .11 .03
☐ 14T Greg Brock .25 .11 .03
☐ 15T Mike C. Brown .25 .11 .03
☐ 16T Tom Burgmeier .25 .11 .03
☐ 17T Randy Bush .25 .11 .03
☐ 18T Bert Campaneris .35 .16 .04
☐ 19T Ron Cey .35 .16 .04
☐ 20T Chris Codiroli .25 .11 .03
☐ 21T Dave Collins .25 .11 .03
☐ 22T Terry Crowley .25 .11 .03
☐ 23T Julio Cruz .25 .11 .03
☐ 24T Mike Davis .25 .11 .03
☐ 25T Frank DiPino .25 .11 .03
☐ 26T Bill Doran .50 .23 .06
☐ 27T Jerry Dybzinski .25 .11 .03
☐ 28T Jamie Easterly .25 .11 .03
☐ 29T Juan Eichelberger .25 .11 .03
☐ 30T Jim Essian .25 .11 .03
☐ 31T Pete Falcone .25 .11 .03
☐ 32T Mike Ferraro MG .25 .11 .03
☐ 33T Terry Forster .25 .11 .03
☐ 34T Julio Franco 7.00 3.10 .85
☐ 35T Rich Gale .25 .11 .03
☐ 36T Kiko Garcia .25 .11 .03
☐ 37T Steve Garvey 1.00 .45 .13
☐ 38T Johnny Grubb .25 .11 .03
☐ 39T Mel Hall .50 .23 .06
☐ 40T Von Hayes .35 .16 .04
☐ 41T Danny Heep .25 .11 .03
☐ 42T Steve Henderson .25 .11 .03
☐ 43T Keith Hernandez .50 .23 .06
☐ 44T Leo Hernandez .25 .11 .03
☐ 45T Willie Hernandez .35 .16 .04
☐ 46T Al Holland .25 .11 .03
☐ 47T Frank Howard MG .35 .16 .04
☐ 48T Bobby Johnson .25 .11 .03
☐ 49T Cliff Johnson .25 .11 .03
☐ 50T Odell Jones .25 .11 .03
☐ 51T Mike Jorgensen .25 .11 .03
☐ 52T Bob Kearney .25 .11 .03
☐ 53T Steve Kemp .25 .11 .03
☐ 54T Matt Keough .25 .11 .03
☐ 55T Ron Kittle .40 .18 .05
☐ 56T Mickey Klutts .25 .11 .03
☐ 57T Alan Knicely .25 .11 .03
☐ 58T Mike Krukow .25 .11 .03
☐ 59T Rafael Landestoy .25 .11 .03
☐ 60T Carney Lansford .35 .16 .04
☐ 61T Joe Lefebvre .25 .11 .03
☐ 62T Bryan Little .25 .11 .03
☐ 63T Aurelio Lopez .25 .11 .03
☐ 64T Mike Madden .25 .11 .03
☐ 65T Rick Manning .25 .11 .03
☐ 66T Billy Martin MG .35 .16 .04
☐ 67T Lee Mazzilli .25 .11 .03
☐ 68T Andy McGaffigan .25 .11 .03
☐ 69T Craig McMurtry .25 .11 .03
☐ 70T John McNamara MG .25 .11 .03
☐ 71T Orlando Mercado .25 .11 .03
☐ 72T Larry Milbourne .25 .11 .03
☐ 73T Randy Moffitt .25 .11 .03
☐ 74T Sid Monge .25 .11 .03
☐ 75T Jose Morales .25 .11 .03
☐ 76T Omar Moreno .25 .11 .03
☐ 77T Joe Morgan 2.00 .90 .25
☐ 78T Mike Morgan .25 .11 .03
☐ 79T Dale Murray .25 .11 .03
☐ 80T Jeff Newman .25 .11 .03
☐ 81T Pete O'Brien .50 .23 .06
☐ 82T Jorge Orta .25 .11 .03
☐ 83T Alejandro Pena .50 .23 .06
☐ 84T Pascual Perez .25 .11 .03
☐ 85T Tony Perez 1.00 .45 .13
☐ 86T Broderick Perkins .25 .11 .03
☐ 87T Tony Phillips 6.00 2.70 .75
☐ 88T Charlie Puleo .25 .11 .03
☐ 89T Pat Putnam .25 .11 .03
☐ 90T Jamie Quirk .25 .11 .03
☐ 91T Doug Rader MG .25 .11 .03
☐ 92T Chuck Rainey .25 .11 .03
☐ 93T Bobby Ramos .25 .11 .03
☐ 94T Gary Redus .50 .23 .06
☐ 95T Steve Renko .25 .11 .03
☐ 96T Leon Roberts .25 .11 .03
☐ 97T Aurelio Rodriguez .25 .11 .03
☐ 98T Dick Ruthven .25 .11 .03
☐ 99T Daryl Sconiers .25 .11 .03
☐ 100T Mike Scott .35 .16 .04
☐ 101T Tom Seaver 8.00 3.60 1.00
☐ 102T John Shelby .25 .11 .03
☐ 103T Bob Shirley .25 .11 .03
☐ 104T Joe Simpson .25 .11 .03
☐ 105T Doug Sisk .25 .11 .03
☐ 106T Mike Smithson .25 .11 .03
☐ 107T Elias Sosa .25 .11 .03
☐ 108T Darryl Strawberry 20.00 9.00 2.50
☐ 109T Tom Tellmann .25 .11 .03
☐ 110T Gene Tenace .25 .11 .03
☐ 111T Gorman Thomas .25 .11 .03
☐ 112T Dick Tidrow .25 .11 .03
☐ 113T Dave Tobik .25 .11 .03
☐ 114T Wayne Tolleson .25 .11 .03
☐ 115T Mike Torrez .25 .11 .03
☐ 116T Manny Trillo .25 .11 .03
☐ 117T Steve Trout .25 .11 .03
☐ 118T Lee Tunnell .25 .11 .03
☐ 119T Mike Vail .25 .11 .03
☐ 120T Ellis Valentine .25 .11 .03
☐ 121T Tom Veryzer .25 .11 .03
☐ 122T George Vukovich .25 .11 .03
☐ 123T Rick Waits .25 .11 .03
☐ 124T Greg Walker .25 .11 .03
☐ 125T Chris Welsh .25 .11 .03
☐ 126T Len Whitehouse .25 .11 .03
☐ 127T Eddie Whitson .25 .11 .03
☐ 128T Jim Wohlford .25 .11 .03
☐ 129T Matt Young .25 .11 .03
☐ 130T Joel Youngblood .25 .11 .03
☐ 131T Pat Zachry .25 .11 .03
☐ 132T Checklist 1T-132T .25 .11 .03

1984 Topps

The cards in this 792-card set measure 2 1/2" by 3 1/2". For the second year in a row, Topps utilized a dual picture on the front of the card. A portrait is shown in a square insert and an action shot is featured in the main photo. Card numbers 1-6 feature 1983 Highlights (HL), cards 131-138 depict League Leaders, card numbers 386-407 feature All-Stars, and card numbers 701-718 feature active Major League career leaders in various statistical categories. Each team leader (TL) card features the team's leading hitter and pitcher pictured on

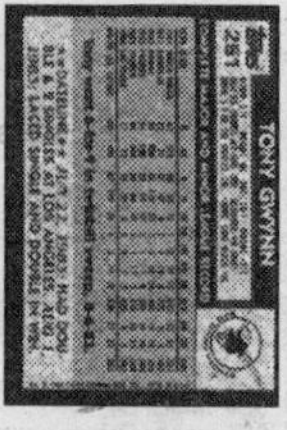

the front with a team checklist back. There are six numerical checklist cards in the set. The player cards feature team logos in the upper right corner of the reverse. The key Rookie Cards in this set are Don Mattingly, Darryl Strawberry, and Andy Van Slyke. Topps also produced a specially boxed "glossy" edition, frequently referred to as the Topps Tiffany set. There were supposedly only 10,000 sets of the Tiffany cards produced; they were marketed to hobby dealers. The checklist of cards (792 regular and 132 Traded) is identical to that of the normal non-glossy cards. There are two primary distinguishing features of the Tiffany cards, white card stock reverses and high gloss obverses. These Tiffany cards are valued approximately from five to ten times the values listed below. Topps tested a special send-in offer in Michigan and a few other states whereby collectors could obtain direct from Topps ten cards of their choice. Needless to say most people ordered the key (most valuable) players necessitating the printing of a special sheet to keep up with the demand. The special sheet had five cards of Darryl Strawberry, three cards of Don Mattingly, etc. The test was apparently a failure in Topps' eyes as they have never tried it again.

	NRMT-MT	EXC	G-VG
COMPLETE SET (792)	60.00	27.00	7.50
COMMON CARD (1-792)	.08	.04	.01
□ 1 Steve Carlton HL 300th win and all-time SO king	.60	.12	.04
□ 2 Rickey Henderson HL 100 stolen bases, three times	1.00	.45	.13
□ 3 Dan Quisenberry HL Sets save record	.12	.05	.02
□ 4 Nolan Ryan, Steve Carlton, and Gaylord Perry HL (All surpass Johnson)	1.00	.45	.13
□ 5 Dave Righetti, Bob Forsch, and Mike Warren HL (All pitch no-hitters)	.12	.05	.02
□ 6 Johnny Bench, Gaylord Perry, and Carl Yastrzemski HL (Superstars retire)	.50	.23	.06
□ 7 Gary Lucas	.08	.04	.01
□ 8 Don Mattingly	14.00	6.25	1.75
□ 9 Jim Gott	.08	.04	.01
□ 10 Robin Yount	1.25	.55	.16
□ 11 Minnesota Twins TL Kent Hrbek Ken Schrom (Checklist on back)	.12	.05	.02
□ 12 Billy Sample	.08	.04	.01
□ 13 Scott Holman	.08	.04	.01
□ 14 Tom Brookens	.08	.04	.01
□ 15 Burt Hooton	.08	.04	.01
□ 16 Omar Moreno	.08	.04	.01
□ 17 John Denny	.08	.04	.01
□ 18 Dale Berra	.08	.04	.01
□ 19 Ray Fontenot	.08	.04	.01
□ 20 Greg Luzinski	.12	.05	.02
□ 21 Joe Altobelli MG	.08	.04	.01
□ 22 Bryan Clark	.08	.04	.01
□ 23 Keith Moreland	.08	.04	.01
□ 24 John Martin	.08	.04	.01
□ 25 Glenn Hubbard	.08	.04	.01
□ 26 Bud Black	.08	.04	.01
□ 27 Daryl Sconiers	.08	.04	.01
□ 28 Frank Viola	.35	.16	.04
□ 29 Danny Heep	.08	.04	.01
□ 30 Wade Boggs	3.50	1.55	.45
□ 31 Andy McGaffigan	.08	.04	.01
□ 32 Bobby Ramos	.08	.04	.01
□ 33 Tom Burgmeier	.08	.04	.01
□ 34 Eddie Milner	.08	.04	.01
□ 35 Don Sutton	.25	.11	.03
□ 36 Denny Walling	.08	.04	.01
□ 37 Texas Rangers TL Buddy Bell Rick Honeycutt (Checklist on back)	.12	.05	.02
□ 38 Luis DeLeon	.08	.04	.01
□ 39 Garth Iorg	.08	.04	.01
□ 40 Dusty Baker	.15	.07	.02
□ 41 Tony Bernazard	.08	.04	.01
□ 42 Johnny Grubb	.08	.04	.01
□ 43 Ron Reed	.08	.04	.01
□ 44 Jim Morrison	.08	.04	.01
□ 45 Jerry Mumphrey	.08	.04	.01
□ 46 Ray Smith	.08	.04	.01
□ 47 Rudy Law	.08	.04	.01
□ 48 Julio Franco	1.00	.45	.13
□ 49 John Stuper	.08	.04	.01
□ 50 Chris Chambliss	.12	.05	.02
□ 51 Jim Frey MG	.08	.04	.01
□ 52 Paul Splittorff	.08	.04	.01
□ 53 Juan Beniquez	.08	.04	.01
□ 54 Jesse Orosco	.08	.04	.01
□ 55 Dave Concepcion	.12	.05	.02
□ 56 Gary Allenson	.08	.04	.01
□ 57 Dan Schatzeder	.08	.04	.01
□ 58 Max Venable	.08	.04	.01
□ 59 Sammy Stewart	.08	.04	.01
□ 60 Paul Molitor UER ('83 stats .272, 613, 167; should be .270, 608, 164)	1.50	.65	.19
□ 61 Chris Codiroli	.08	.04	.01
□ 62 Dave Hostetler	.08	.04	.01
□ 63 Ed VandeBerg	.08	.04	.01
□ 64 Mike Scioscia	.12	.05	.02
□ 65 Kirk Gibson	.40	.18	.05
□ 66 Houston Astros TL Jose Cruz Nolan Ryan (Checklist on back)	.75	.35	.09
□ 67 Gary Ward	.08	.04	.01
□ 68 Luis Salazar	.08	.04	.01
□ 69 Rod Scurry	.08	.04	.01
□ 70 Gary Matthews	.12	.05	.02

	No.	Player			
☐	71	Leo Hernandez	.08	.04	.01
☐	72	Mike Squires	.08	.04	.01
☐	73	Jody Davis	.08	.04	.01
☐	74	Jerry Martin	.08	.04	.01
☐	75	Bob Forsch	.08	.04	.01
☐	76	Alfredo Griffin	.08	.04	.01
☐	77	Brett Butler	.30	.14	.04
☐	78	Mike Torrez	.08	.04	.01
☐	79	Rob Wilfong	.08	.04	.01
☐	80	Steve Rogers	.08	.04	.01
☐	81	Billy Martin MG	.12	.05	.02
☐	82	Doug Bird	.08	.04	.01
☐	83	Richie Zisk	.08	.04	.01
☐	84	Lenny Faedo	.08	.04	.01
☐	85	Atlee Hammaker	.08	.04	.01
☐	86	John Shelby	.08	.04	.01
☐	87	Frank Pastore	.08	.04	.01
☐	88	Rob Picciolo	.08	.04	.01
☐	89	Mike Smithson	.08	.04	.01
☐	90	Pedro Guerrero	.12	.05	.02
☐	91	Dan Spillner	.08	.04	.01
☐	92	Lloyd Moseby	.08	.04	.01
☐	93	Bob Knepper	.08	.04	.01
☐	94	Mario Ramirez	.08	.04	.01
☐	95	Aurelio Lopez	.08	.04	.01
☐	96	Kansas City Royals TL	.15	.07	.02
		Hal McRae			
		Larry Gura			
		(Checklist on back)			
☐	97	LaMarr Hoyt	.08	.04	.01
☐	98	Steve Nicosia	.08	.04	.01
☐	99	Craig Lefferts	.08	.04	.01
☐	100	Reggie Jackson	1.00	.45	.13
☐	101	Porfirio Altamirano	.08	.04	.01
☐	102	Ken Oberkfell	.08	.04	.01
☐	103	Dwayne Murphy	.08	.04	.01
☐	104	Ken Dayley	.08	.04	.01
☐	105	Tony Armas	.08	.04	.01
☐	106	Tim Stoddard	.08	.04	.01
☐	107	Ned Yost	.08	.04	.01
☐	108	Randy Moffitt	.08	.04	.01
☐	109	Brad Wellman	.08	.04	.01
☐	110	Ron Guidry	.12	.05	.02
☐	111	Bill Virdon MG	.08	.04	.01
☐	112	Tom Niedenfuer	.08	.04	.01
☐	113	Kelly Paris	.08	.04	.01
☐	114	Checklist 1-132	.12	.04	.01
☐	115	Andre Thornton	.08	.04	.01
☐	116	George Bjorkman	.08	.04	.01
☐	117	Tom Veryzer	.08	.04	.01
☐	118	Charlie Hough	.12	.05	.02
☐	119	John Wockenfuss	.08	.04	.01
☐	120	Keith Hernandez	.15	.07	.02
☐	121	Pat Sheridan	.08	.04	.01
☐	122	Cecilio Guante	.08	.04	.01
☐	123	Butch Wynegar	.08	.04	.01
☐	124	Damaso Garcia	.08	.04	.01
☐	125	Britt Burns	.08	.04	.01
☐	126	Atlanta Braves TL	.15	.07	.02
		Dale Murphy			
		Craig McMurtry			
		(Checklist on back)			
☐	127	Mike Madden	.08	.04	.01
☐	128	Rick Manning	.08	.04	.01
☐	129	Bill Laskey	.08	.04	.01
☐	130	Ozzie Smith	1.25	.55	.16
☐	131	Batting Leaders	.60	.25	.08
		Bill Madlock			
		Wade Boggs			
☐	132	Home Run Leaders	.35	.16	.04
		Mike Schmidt			
		Jim Rice			
☐	133	RBI Leaders	.20	.09	.03
		Dale Murphy			
		Cecil Cooper			
		Jim Rice			
☐	134	Stolen Base Leaders	.75	.35	.09
		Tim Raines			
		Rickey Henderson			
☐	135	Victory Leaders	.15	.07	.02
		John Denny			
		LaMarr Hoyt			
☐	136	Strikeout Leaders	.30	.14	.04
		Steve Carlton			
		Jack Morris			
☐	137	ERA Leaders	.15	.07	.02
		Atlee Hammaker			
		Rick Honeycutt			
☐	138	Leading Firemen	.15	.07	.02
		Al Holland			
		Dan Quisenberry			
☐	139	Bert Campaneris	.12	.05	.02
☐	140	Storm Davis	.08	.04	.01
☐	141	Pat Corrales MG	.08	.04	.01
☐	142	Rich Gale	.08	.04	.01
☐	143	Jose Morales	.08	.04	.01
☐	144	Brian Harper	.75	.35	.09
☐	145	Gary Lavelle	.08	.04	.01
☐	146	Ed Romero	.08	.04	.01
☐	147	Dan Petry	.08	.04	.01
☐	148	Joe Lefebvre	.08	.04	.01
☐	149	Jon Matlack	.08	.04	.01
☐	150	Dale Murphy	.50	.23	.06
☐	151	Steve Trout	.08	.04	.01
☐	152	Glenn Brummer	.08	.04	.01
☐	153	Dick Tidrow	.08	.04	.01
☐	154	Dave Henderson	.12	.05	.02
☐	155	Frank White	.12	.05	.02
☐	156	Oakland A's TL	.25	.11	.03
		Rickey Henderson			
		Tim Conroy			
		(Checklist on back)			
☐	157	Gary Gaetti	.12	.05	.02
☐	158	John Curtis	.08	.04	.01
☐	159	Darryl Cias	.08	.04	.01
☐	160	Mario Soto	.08	.04	.01
☐	161	Junior Ortiz	.08	.04	.01
☐	162	Bob Ojeda	.12	.05	.02
☐	163	Lorenzo Gray	.08	.04	.01
☐	164	Scott Sanderson	.08	.04	.01
☐	165	Ken Singleton	.12	.05	.02
☐	166	Jamie Nelson	.08	.04	.01
☐	167	Marshall Edwards	.08	.04	.01
☐	168	Juan Bonilla	.08	.04	.01
☐	169	Larry Parrish	.08	.04	.01
☐	170	Jerry Reuss	.08	.04	.01
☐	171	Frank Robinson MG	.20	.09	.03
☐	172	Frank DiPino	.08	.04	.01
☐	173	Marvell Wynne	.08	.04	.01
☐	174	Juan Berenguer	.08	.04	.01
☐	175	Graig Nettles	.12	.05	.02
☐	176	Lee Smith	1.00	.45	.13
☐	177	Jerry Hairston	.08	.04	.01
☐	178	Bill Krueger	.08	.04	.01
☐	179	Buck Martinez	.08	.04	.01
☐	180	Manny Trillo	.08	.04	.01
☐	181	Roy Thomas	.08	.04	.01
☐	182	Darryl Strawberry	3.50	1.55	.45
☐	183	Al Williams	.08	.04	.01
☐	184	Mike O'Berry	.08	.04	.01
☐	185	Sixto Lezcano	.08	.04	.01
☐	186	Cardinal TL	.12	.05	.02
		Lonnie Smith			
		John Stuper			
		(Checklist on back)			
☐	187	Luis Aponte	.08	.04	.01

☐ 188 Bryan Little .08 .04 .01
☐ 189 Tim Conroy .08 .04 .01
☐ 190 Ben Oglivie .08 .04 .01
☐ 191 Mike Boddicker .08 .04 .01
☐ 192 Nick Esasky .08 .04 .01
☐ 193 Darrell Brown .08 .04 .01
☐ 194 Domingo Ramos .08 .04 .01
☐ 195 Jack Morris .40 .18 .05
☐ 196 Don Slaught .08 .04 .01
☐ 197 Garry Hancock .08 .04 .01
☐ 198 Bill Doran .20 .09 .03
☐ 199 Willie Hernandez .12 .05 .02
☐ 200 Andre Dawson 1.00 .45 .13
☐ 201 Bruce Kison .08 .04 .01
☐ 202 Bobby Cox MG .08 .04 .01
☐ 203 Matt Keough .08 .04 .01
☐ 204 Bobby Meacham .08 .04 .01
☐ 205 Greg Minton .08 .04 .01
☐ 206 Andy Van Slyke 1.50 .65 .19
☐ 207 Donnie Moore .08 .04 .01
☐ 208 Jose Oquendo .15 .07 .02
☐ 209 Manny Sarmiento .08 .04 .01
☐ 210 Joe Morgan .40 .18 .05
☐ 211 Rick Sweet .08 .04 .01
☐ 212 Broderick Perkins .08 .04 .01
☐ 213 Bruce Hurst .12 .05 .02
☐ 214 Paul Householder .08 .04 .01
☐ 215 Tippy Martinez .08 .04 .01
☐ 216 White Sox TL .15 .07 .02
Carlton Fisk
Richard Dotson
(Checklist on back)
☐ 217 Alan Ashby .08 .04 .01
☐ 218 Rick Waits .08 .04 .01
☐ 219 Joe Simpson .08 .04 .01
☐ 220 Fernando Valenzuela .12 .05 .02
☐ 221 Cliff Johnson .08 .04 .01
☐ 222 Rick Honeycutt .08 .04 .01
☐ 223 Wayne Krenchicki .08 .04 .01
☐ 224 Sid Monge .08 .04 .01
☐ 225 Lee Mazzilli .08 .04 .01
☐ 226 Juan Eichelberger .08 .04 .01
☐ 227 Steve Braun .08 .04 .01
☐ 228 John Rabb .08 .04 .01
☐ 229 Paul Owens MG .08 .04 .01
☐ 230 Rickey Henderson 2.00 .90 .25
☐ 231 Gary Woods .08 .04 .01
☐ 232 Tim Wallach .12 .05 .02
☐ 233 Checklist 133-264 .12 .04 .01
☐ 234 Rafael Ramirez .08 .04 .01
☐ 235 Matt Young .08 .04 .01
☐ 236 Ellis Valentine .08 .04 .01
☐ 237 John Castino .08 .04 .01
☐ 238 Reid Nichols .08 .04 .01
☐ 239 Jay Howell .12 .05 .02
☐ 240 Eddie Murray 1.50 .65 .19
☐ 241 Bill Almon .08 .04 .01
☐ 242 Alex Trevino .08 .04 .01
☐ 243 Pete Ladd .08 .04 .01
☐ 244 Candy Maldonado .08 .04 .01
☐ 245 Rick Sutcliffe .12 .05 .02
☐ 246 New York Mets TL .25 .11 .03
Mookie Wilson
Tom Seaver
(Checklist on back)
☐ 247 Onix Concepcion .08 .04 .01
☐ 248 Bill Dawley .08 .04 .01
☐ 249 Jay Johnstone .12 .05 .02
☐ 250 Bill Madlock .12 .05 .02
☐ 251 Tony Gwynn 5.00 2.30 .60
☐ 252 Larry Christenson .08 .04 .01
☐ 253 Jim Wohlford .08 .04 .01
☐ 254 Shane Rawley .08 .04 .01
☐ 255 Bruce Benedict .08 .04 .01
☐ 256 Dave Geisel .08 .04 .01
☐ 257 Julio Cruz .08 .04 .01
☐ 258 Luis Sanchez .08 .04 .01
☐ 259 Sparky Anderson MG .12 .05 .02
☐ 260 Scott McGregor .08 .04 .01
☐ 261 Bobby Brown .08 .04 .01
☐ 262 Tom Candiotti .50 .23 .06
☐ 263 Jack Fimple .08 .04 .01
☐ 264 Doug Frobel .08 .04 .01
☐ 265 Donnie Hill .08 .04 .01
☐ 266 Steve Lubratich .08 .04 .01
☐ 267 Carmelo Martinez .08 .04 .01
☐ 268 Jack O'Connor .08 .04 .01
☐ 269 Aurelio Rodriguez .08 .04 .01
☐ 270 Jeff Russell .35 .16 .04
☐ 271 Moose Haas .08 .04 .01
☐ 272 Rick Dempsey .12 .05 .02
☐ 273 Charlie Puleo .08 .04 .01
☐ 274 Rick Monday .08 .04 .01
☐ 275 Len Matuszek .08 .04 .01
☐ 276 Angels TL .15 .07 .02
Rod Carew
Geoff Zahn
(Checklist on back)
☐ 277 Eddie Whitson .08 .04 .01
☐ 278 George Bell .35 .16 .04
☐ 279 Ivan DeJesus .08 .04 .01
☐ 280 Floyd Bannister .08 .04 .01
☐ 281 Larry Milbourne .08 .04 .01
☐ 282 Jim Barr .08 .04 .01
☐ 283 Larry Biittner .08 .04 .01
☐ 284 Howard Bailey .08 .04 .01
☐ 285 Darrell Porter .08 .04 .01
☐ 286 Lary Sorensen .08 .04 .01
☐ 287 Warren Cromartie .08 .04 .01
☐ 288 Jim Beattie .08 .04 .01
☐ 289 Randy Johnson .08 .04 .01
☐ 290 Dave Dravecky .08 .01 .00
☐ 291 Chuck Tanner MG .08 .04 .01
☐ 292 Tony Scott .08 .04 .01
☐ 293 Ed Lynch .08 .04 .01
☐ 294 U.L. Washington .08 .04 .01
☐ 295 Mike Flanagan .08 .04 .01
☐ 296 Jeff Newman .08 .04 .01
☐ 297 Bruce Berenyi .08 .04 .01
☐ 298 Jim Gantner .12 .05 .02
☐ 299 John Butcher .08 .04 .01
☐ 300 Pete Rose 1.25 .55 .16
☐ 301 Frank LaCorte .08 .04 .01
☐ 302 Barry Bonnell .08 .04 .01
☐ 303 Marty Castillo .08 .04 .01
☐ 304 Warren Brusstar .08 .04 .01
☐ 305 Roy Smalley .08 .04 .01
☐ 306 Dodgers TL .12 .05 .02
Pedro Guerrero
Bob Welch
(Checklist on back)
☐ 307 Bobby Mitchell .08 .04 .01
☐ 308 Ron Hassey .08 .04 .01
☐ 309 Tony Phillips 1.50 .65 .19
☐ 310 Willie McGee .25 .11 .03
☐ 311 Jerry Koosman .12 .05 .02
☐ 312 Jorge Orta .08 .04 .01
☐ 313 Mike Jorgensen .08 .04 .01
☐ 314 Orlando Mercado .08 .04 .01
☐ 315 Bob Grich .12 .05 .02
☐ 316 Mark Bradley .08 .04 .01
☐ 317 Greg Pryor .08 .04 .01
☐ 318 Bill Gullickson .12 .05 .02
☐ 319 Al Bumbry .12 .05 .02
☐ 320 Bob Stanley .08 .04 .01
☐ 321 Harvey Kuenn MG .12 .01 .00

	#	Player			
☐	322	Ken Schrom	.08	.04	.01
☐	323	Alan Knicely	.08	.04	.01
☐	324	Alejandro Pena	.20	.09	.03
☐	325	Darrell Evans	.12	.05	.02
☐	326	Bob Kearney	.08	.04	.01
☐	327	Ruppert Jones	.08	.04	.01
☐	328	Vern Ruhle	.08	.04	.01
☐	329	Pat Tabler	.08	.04	.01
☐	330	John Candelaria	.08	.04	.01
☐	331	Bucky Dent	.12	.05	.02
☐	332	Kevin Gross	.20	.09	.03
☐	333	Larry Herndon	.08	.04	.01
☐	334	Chuck Rainey	.08	.04	.01
☐	335	Don Baylor	.15	.07	.02
☐	336	Seattle Mariners TL	.12	.05	.02
		Pat Putnam			
		Matt Young			
		(Checklist on back)			
☐	337	Kevin Hagen	.08	.04	.01
☐	338	Mike Warren	.08	.04	.01
☐	339	Roy Lee Jackson	.08	.04	.01
☐	340	Hal McRae	.15	.07	.02
☐	341	Dave Tobik	.08	.04	.01
☐	342	Tim Foli	.08	.04	.01
☐	343	Mark Davis	.08	.04	.01
☐	344	Rick Miller	.08	.04	.01
☐	345	Kent Hrbek	.25	.11	.03
☐	346	Kurt Bevacqua	.08	.04	.01
☐	347	Allan Ramirez	.08	.04	.01
☐	348	Toby Harrah	.08	.04	.01
☐	349	Bob L. Gibson	.08	.04	.01
☐	350	George Foster	.12	.05	.02
☐	351	Russ Nixon MG	.08	.04	.01
☐	352	Dave Stewart	.15	.07	.02
☐	353	Jim Anderson	.08	.04	.01
☐	354	Jeff Burroughs	.08	.04	.01
☐	355	Jason Thompson	.08	.04	.01
☐	356	Glenn Abbott	.08	.04	.01
☐	357	Ron Cey	.12	.05	.02
☐	358	Bob Dernier	.08	.04	.01
☐	359	Jim Acker	.08	.04	.01
☐	360	Willie Randolph	.12	.05	.02
☐	361	Dave Smith	.08	.04	.01
☐	362	David Green	.08	.04	.01
☐	363	Tim Laudner	.08	.04	.01
☐	364	Scott Fletcher	.08	.04	.01
☐	365	Steve Bedrosian	.12	.05	.02
☐	366	Padres TL	.12	.05	.02
		Terry Kennedy			
		Dave Dravecky			
		(Checklist on back)			
☐	367	Jamie Easterly	.08	.04	.01
☐	368	Hubie Brooks	.12	.05	.02
☐	369	Steve McCatty	.08	.04	.01
☐	370	Tim Raines	.60	.25	.08
☐	371	Dave Gumpert	.08	.04	.01
☐	372	Gary Roenicke	.08	.04	.01
☐	373	Bill Scherrer	.08	.04	.01
☐	374	Don Money	.08	.04	.01
☐	375	Dennis Leonard	.08	.04	.01
☐	376	Dave Anderson	.08	.04	.01
☐	377	Danny Darwin	.08	.04	.01
☐	378	Bob Brenly	.08	.04	.01
☐	379	Checklist 265-396	.12	.04	.01
☐	380	Steve Garvey	.35	.16	.04
☐	381	Ralph Houk MG	.12	.05	.02
☐	382	Chris Nyman	.08	.04	.01
☐	383	Terry Puhl	.08	.04	.01
☐	384	Lee Tunnell	.08	.04	.01
☐	385	Tony Perez	.15	.07	.02
☐	386	George Hendrick AS	.12	.05	.02
☐	387	Johnny Ray AS	.12	.05	.02
☐	388	Mike Schmidt AS	.50	.23	.06
☐	389	Ozzie Smith AS	.60	.25	.08
☐	390	Tim Raines AS	.30	.14	.04
☐	391	Dale Murphy AS	.30	.14	.04
☐	392	Andre Dawson AS	.50	.23	.06
☐	393	Gary Carter AS	.20	.09	.03
☐	394	Steve Rogers AS	.12	.05	.02
☐	395	Steve Carlton AS	.50	.23	.06
☐	396	Jesse Orosco AS	.12	.05	.02
☐	397	Eddie Murray AS	.50	.23	.06
☐	398	Lou Whitaker AS	.20	.09	.03
☐	399	George Brett AS	1.00	.45	.13
☐	400	Cal Ripken AS	2.00	.90	.25
☐	401	Jim Rice AS	.15	.07	.02
☐	402	Dave Winfield AS	.60	.25	.08
☐	403	Lloyd Moseby AS	.12	.05	.02
☐	404	Ted Simmons AS	.12	.05	.02
☐	405	LaMarr Hoyt AS	.12	.05	.02
☐	406	Ron Guidry AS	.12	.05	.02
☐	407	Dan Quisenberry AS	.12	.05	.02
☐	408	Lou Piniella	.12	.05	.02
☐	409	Juan Agosto	.08	.04	.01
☐	410	Claudell Washington	.08	.04	.01
☐	411	Houston Jimenez	.08	.04	.01
☐	412	Doug Rader MG	.08	.04	.01
☐	413	Spike Owen	.15	.07	.02
☐	414	Mitchell Page	.08	.04	.01
☐	415	Tommy John	.15	.07	.02
☐	416	Dane Iorg	.08	.04	.01
☐	417	Mike Armstrong	.08	.04	.01
☐	418	Ron Hodges	.08	.04	.01
☐	419	John Henry Johnson	.08	.04	.01
☐	420	Cecil Cooper	.12	.05	.02
☐	421	Charlie Lea	.08	.04	.01
☐	422	Jose Cruz	.12	.05	.02
☐	423	Mike Morgan	.12	.05	.02
☐	424	Dann Bilardello	.08	.04	.01
☐	425	Steve Howe	.08	.04	.01
☐	426	Orioles TL	1.00	.45	.13
		Cal Ripken			
		Mike Boddicker			
		(Checklist on back)			
☐	427	Rick Leach	.08	.04	.01
☐	428	Fred Breining	.08	.04	.01
☐	429	Randy Bush	.08	.04	.01
☐	430	Rusty Staub	.12	.05	.02
☐	431	Chris Bando	.08	.04	.01
☐	432	Charles Hudson	.08	.04	.01
☐	433	Rich Hebner	.08	.04	.01
☐	434	Harold Baines	.25	.11	.03
☐	435	Neil Allen	.08	.04	.01
☐	436	Rick Peters	.08	.04	.01
☐	437	Mike Proly	.08	.04	.01
☐	438	Biff Pocoroba	.08	.04	.01
☐	439	Bob Stoddard	.08	.04	.01
☐	440	Steve Kemp	.08	.04	.01
☐	441	Bob Lillis MG	.08	.04	.01
☐	442	Byron McLaughlin	.08	.04	.01
☐	443	Benny Ayala	.08	.04	.01
☐	444	Steve Renko	.08	.04	.01
☐	445	Jerry Remy	.08	.04	.01
☐	446	Luis Pujols	.08	.04	.01
☐	447	Tom Brunansky	.12	.05	.02
☐	448	Ben Hayes	.08	.04	.01
☐	449	Joe Pettini	.08	.04	.01
☐	450	Gary Carter	.35	.16	.04
☐	451	Bob Jones	.08	.04	.01
☐	452	Chuck Porter	.08	.04	.01
☐	453	Willie Upshaw	.08	.04	.01
☐	454	Joe Beckwith	.08	.04	.01
☐	455	Terry Kennedy	.08	.04	.01
☐	456	Chicago Cubs TL	.15	.07	.02
		Keith Moreland			
		Fergie Jenkins			

(Checklist on back)

	#	Player			
☐	457	Dave Rozema	.08	.04	.01
☐	458	Kiko Garcia	.08	.04	.01
☐	459	Kevin Hickey	.08	.04	.01
☐	460	Dave Winfield	1.00	.45	.13
☐	461	Jim Maler	.08	.04	.01
☐	462	Lee Lacy	.08	.04	.01
☐	463	Dave Engle	.08	.04	.01
☐	464	Jeff A. Jones	.08	.04	.01
☐	465	Mookie Wilson	.12	.05	.02
☐	466	Gene Garber	.08	.04	.01
☐	467	Mike Ramsey	.08	.04	.01
☐	468	Geoff Zahn	.08	.04	.01
☐	469	Tom O'Malley	.08	.04	.01
☐	470	Nolan Ryan	6.00	2.70	.75
☐	471	Dick Howser MG	.08	.04	.01
☐	472	Mike G. Brown	.08	.04	.01
☐	473	Jim Dwyer	.08	.04	.01
☐	474	Greg Bargar	.08	.04	.01
☐	475	Gary Redus	.15	.07	.02
☐	476	Tom Tellmann	.08	.04	.01
☐	477	Rafael Landestoy	.08	.04	.01
☐	478	Alan Bannister	.08	.04	.01
☐	479	Frank Tanana	.12	.05	.02
☐	480	Ron Kittle	.08	.04	.01
☐	481	Mark Thurmond	.08	.04	.01
☐	482	Enos Cabell	.08	.04	.01
☐	483	Fergie Jenkins	.25	.11	.03
☐	484	Ozzie Virgil	.08	.04	.01
☐	485	Rick Rhoden	.08	.04	.01
☐	486	N.Y. Yankees TL Don Baylor Ron Guidry (Checklist on back)	.15	.07	.02
☐	487	Ricky Adams	.08	.04	.01
☐	488	Jesse Barfield	.12	.05	.02
☐	489	Dave Von Ohlen	.08	.04	.01
☐	490	Cal Ripken	6.00	2.70	.75
☐	491	Bobby Castillo	.08	.04	.01
☐	492	Tucker Ashford	.08	.04	.01
☐	493	Mike Norris	.08	.04	.01
☐	494	Chili Davis	.25	.11	.03
☐	495	Rollie Fingers	.30	.14	.04
☐	496	Terry Francona	.08	.04	.01
☐	497	Bud Anderson	.08	.04	.01
☐	498	Rich Gedman	.08	.04	.01
☐	499	Mike Witt	.08	.04	.01
☐	500	George Brett	2.50	1.15	.30
☐	501	Steve Henderson	.08	.04	.01
☐	502	Joe Torre MG	.12	.05	.02
☐	503	Elias Sosa	.08	.04	.01
☐	504	Mickey Rivers	.08	.04	.01
☐	505	Pete Vuckovich	.08	.04	.01
☐	506	Ernie Whitt	.08	.04	.01
☐	507	Mike LaCoss	.08	.04	.01
☐	508	Mel Hall	.12	.05	.02
☐	509	Brad Havens	.08	.04	.01
☐	510	Alan Trammell	.60	.25	.08
☐	511	Marty Bystrom	.08	.04	.01
☐	512	Oscar Gamble	.08	.04	.01
☐	513	Dave Beard	.08	.04	.01
☐	514	Floyd Rayford	.08	.04	.01
☐	515	Gorman Thomas	.08	.04	.01
☐	516	Montreal Expos TL Al Oliver Charlie Lea (Checklist on back)	.12	.05	.02
☐	517	John Moses	.08	.04	.01
☐	518	Greg Walker	.08	.04	.01
☐	519	Ron Davis	.08	.04	.01
☐	520	Bob Boone	.12	.05	.02
☐	521	Pete Falcone	.08	.04	.01
☐	522	Dave Bergman	.08	.04	.01
☐	523	Glenn Hoffman	.08	.04	.01
☐	524	Carlos Diaz	.08	.04	.01
☐	525	Willie Wilson	.12	.05	.02
☐	526	Ron Oester	.08	.04	.01
☐	527	Checklist 397-528	.12	.04	.01
☐	528	Mark Brouhard	.08	.04	.01
☐	529	Keith Atherton	.08	.04	.01
☐	530	Dan Ford	.08	.04	.01
☐	531	Steve Boros MG	.08	.04	.01
☐	532	Eric Show	.08	.04	.01
☐	533	Ken Landreaux	.08	.04	.01
☐	534	Pete O'Brien	.15	.07	.02
☐	535	Bo Diaz	.08	.04	.01
☐	536	Doug Bair	.08	.04	.01
☐	537	Johnny Ray	.08	.04	.01
☐	538	Kevin Bass	.08	.04	.01
☐	539	George Frazier	.08	.04	.01
☐	540	George Hendrick	.08	.04	.01
☐	541	Dennis Lamp	.08	.04	.01
☐	542	Duane Kuiper	.08	.04	.01
☐	543	Craig McMurtry	.08	.04	.01
☐	544	Cesar Geronimo	.08	.04	.01
☐	545	Bill Buckner	.12	.05	.02
☐	546	Indians TL Mike Hargrove Lary Sorensen (Checklist on back)	.12	.05	.02
☐	547	Mike Moore	.12	.05	.02
☐	548	Ron Jackson	.08	.04	.01
☐	549	Walt Terrell	.08	.04	.01
☐	550	Jim Rice	.15	.07	.02
☐	551	Scott Ullger	.08	.04	.01
☐	552	Ray Burris	.08	.04	.01
☐	553	Joe Nolan	.08	.04	.01
☐	554	Ted Power	.08	.04	.01
☐	555	Greg Brock	.08	.04	.01
☐	556	Joey McLaughlin	.08	.04	.01
☐	557	Wayne Tolleson	.08	.04	.01
☐	558	Mike Davis	.08	.04	.01
☐	559	Mike Scott	.12	.05	.02
☐	560	Carlton Fisk	1.00	.45	.13
☐	561	Whitey Herzog MG	.12	.05	.02
☐	562	Manny Castillo	.08	.04	.01
☐	563	Glenn Wilson	.08	.04	.01
☐	564	Al Holland	.08	.04	.01
☐	565	Leon Durham	.08	.04	.01
☐	566	Jim Bibby	.08	.04	.01
☐	567	Mike Heath	.08	.04	.01
☐	568	Pete Filson	.08	.04	.01
☐	569	Bake McBride	.08	.04	.01
☐	570	Dan Quisenberry	.12	.05	.02
☐	571	Bruce Bochy	.08	.04	.01
☐	572	Jerry Royster	.08	.04	.01
☐	573	Dave Kingman	.12	.05	.02
☐	574	Brian Downing	.12	.05	.02
☐	575	Jim Clancy	.08	.04	.01
☐	576	Giants TL Jeff Leonard Atlee Hammaker (Checklist on back)	.12	.05	.02
☐	577	Mark Clear	.08	.04	.01
☐	578	Lenn Sakata	.08	.04	.01
☐	579	Bob James	.08	.04	.01
☐	580	Lonnie Smith	.12	.05	.02
☐	581	Jose DeLeon	.12	.05	.02
☐	582	Bob McClure	.08	.04	.01
☐	583	Derrel Thomas	.08	.04	.01
☐	584	Dave Schmidt	.08	.04	.01
☐	585	Dan Driessen	.08	.04	.01
☐	586	Joe Niekro	.12	.05	.02
☐	587	Von Hayes	.08	.04	.01
☐	588	Milt Wilcox	.08	.04	.01
☐	589	Mike Easler	.08	.04	.01

☐ 590	Dave Stieb	.12	.05	.02
☐ 591	Tony LaRussa MG	.12	.05	.02
☐ 592	Andre Robertson	.08	.04	.01
☐ 593	Jeff Lahti	.08	.04	.01
☐ 594	Gene Richards	.08	.04	.01
☐ 595	Jeff Reardon	.20	.09	.03
☐ 596	Ryne Sandberg	5.00	2.30	.60
☐ 597	Rick Camp	.08	.04	.01
☐ 598	Rusty Kuntz	.08	.04	.01
☐ 599	Doug Sisk	.08	.04	.01
☐ 600	Rod Carew	.75	.35	.09
☐ 601	John Tudor	.12	.05	.02
☐ 602	John Wathan	.08	.04	.01
☐ 603	Renie Martin	.08	.04	.01
☐ 604	John Lowenstein	.08	.04	.01
☐ 605	Mike Caldwell	.08	.04	.01
☐ 606	Blue Jays TL Lloyd Moseby Dave Stieb (Checklist on back)	.12	.05	.02
☐ 607	Tom Hume	.08	.04	.01
☐ 608	Bobby Johnson	.08	.04	.01
☐ 609	Dan Meyer	.08	.04	.01
☐ 610	Steve Sax	.12	.05	.02
☐ 611	Chet Lemon	.08	.04	.01
☐ 612	Harry Spilman	.08	.04	.01
☐ 613	Greg Gross	.08	.04	.01
☐ 614	Len Barker	.08	.04	.01
☐ 615	Garry Templeton	.08	.04	.01
☐ 616	Don Robinson	.08	.04	.01
☐ 617	Rick Cerone	.08	.04	.01
☐ 618	Dickie Noles	.08	.04	.01
☐ 619	Jerry Dybzinski	.08	.04	.01
☐ 620	Al Oliver	.12	.05	.02
☐ 621	Frank Howard MG	.12	.05	.02
☐ 622	Al Cowens	.08	.04	.01
☐ 623	Ron Washington	.08	.04	.01
☐ 624	Terry Harper	.08	.04	.01
☐ 625	Larry Gura	.08	.04	.01
☐ 626	Bob Clark	.08	.04	.01
☐ 627	Dave LaPoint	.08	.04	.01
☐ 628	Ed Jurak	.08	.04	.01
☐ 629	Rick Langford	.08	.04	.01
☐ 630	Ted Simmons	.12	.05	.02
☐ 631	Dennis Martinez	.12	.05	.02
☐ 632	Tom Foley	.08	.04	.01
☐ 633	Mike Krukow	.08	.04	.01
☐ 634	Mike Marshall	.08	.04	.01
☐ 635	Dave Righetti	.12	.05	.02
☐ 636	Pat Putnam	.08	.04	.01
☐ 637	Phillies TL Gary Matthews John Denny (Checklist on back)	.12	.05	.02
☐ 638	George Vukovich	.08	.04	.01
☐ 639	Rick Lysander	.08	.04	.01
☐ 640	Lance Parrish	.12	.05	.02
☐ 641	Mike Richardt	.08	.04	.01
☐ 642	Tom Underwood	.08	.04	.01
☐ 643	Mike C. Brown	.08	.04	.01
☐ 644	Tim Lollar	.08	.04	.01
☐ 645	Tony Pena	.12	.05	.02
☐ 646	Checklist 529-660	.12	.04	.01
☐ 647	Ron Roenicke	.08	.04	.01
☐ 648	Len Whitehouse	.08	.04	.01
☐ 649	Tom Herr	.12	.05	.02
☐ 650	Phil Niekro	.30	.14	.04
☐ 651	John McNamara MG	.08	.04	.01
☐ 652	Rudy May	.08	.04	.01
☐ 653	Dave Stapleton	.08	.04	.01
☐ 654	Bob Bailor	.08	.04	.01
☐ 655	Amos Otis	.12	.05	.02
☐ 656	Bryn Smith	.08	.04	.01

☐ 657	Thad Bosley	.08	.04	.01
☐ 658	Jerry Augustine	.08	.04	.01
☐ 659	Duane Walker	.08	.04	.01
☐ 660	Ray Knight	.12	.05	.02
☐ 661	Steve Yeager	.08	.04	.01
☐ 662	Tom Brennan	.08	.04	.01
☐ 663	Johnnie LeMaster	.08	.04	.01
☐ 664	Dave Stegman	.08	.04	.01
☐ 665	Buddy Bell	.12	.05	.02
☐ 666	Detroit Tigers TL Lou Whitaker Jack Morris (Checklist on back)	.20	.09	.03
☐ 667	Vance Law	.08	.04	.01
☐ 668	Larry McWilliams	.08	.04	.01
☐ 669	Dave Lopes	.12	.05	.02
☐ 670	Rich Gossage	.15	.07	.02
☐ 671	Jamie Quirk	.08	.04	.01
☐ 672	Ricky Nelson	.08	.04	.01
☐ 673	Mike Walters	.08	.04	.01
☐ 674	Tim Flannery	.08	.04	.01
☐ 675	Pascual Perez	.08	.04	.01
☐ 676	Brian Giles	.08	.04	.01
☐ 677	Doyle Alexander	.08	.04	.01
☐ 678	Chris Speier	.08	.04	.01
☐ 679	Art Howe	.08	.04	.01
☐ 680	Fred Lynn	.12	.05	.02
☐ 681	Tom Lasorda MG	.12	.05	.02
☐ 682	Dan Morogiello	.08	.04	.01
☐ 683	Marty Barrett	.12	.05	.02
☐ 684	Bob Shirley	.08	.04	.01
☐ 685	Willie Aikens	.08	.04	.01
☐ 686	Joe Price	.08	.04	.01
☐ 687	Roy Howell	.08	.04	.01
☐ 688	George Wright	.08	.04	.01
☐ 689	Mike Fischlin	.08	.04	.01
☐ 690	Jack Clark	.12	.05	.02
☐ 691	Steve Lake	.08	.04	.01
☐ 692	Dickie Thon	.08	.04	.01
☐ 693	Alan Wiggins	.08	.04	.01
☐ 694	Mike Stanton	.08	.04	.01
☐ 695	Lou Whitaker	.50	.23	.06
☐ 696	Pirates TL Bill Madlock Rick Rhoden (Checklist on back)	.12	.05	.02
☐ 697	Dale Murray	.08	.04	.01
☐ 698	Marc Hill	.08	.04	.01
☐ 699	Dave Rucker	.08	.04	.01
☐ 700	Mike Schmidt	2.00	.90	.25
☐ 701	NL Active Batting Bill Madlock Pete Rose Dave Parker	.25	.11	.03
☐ 702	NL Active Hits Pete Rose Rusty Staub Tony Perez	.25	.11	.03
☐ 703	NL Active Home Run Mike Schmidt Tony Perez Dave Kingman	.25	.11	.03
☐ 704	NL Active RBI Tony Perez Rusty Staub Al Oliver	.15	.07	.02
☐ 705	NL Active Steals Joe Morgan Cesar Cedeno Larry Bowa	.15	.07	.02
☐ 706	NL Active Victory Steve Carlton Fergie Jenkins	.40	.18	.05

Tom Seaver
- ☐ 707 NL Active Strikeout .... 1.75 .80 .22
  Steve Carlton
  Nolan Ryan
  Tom Seaver
- ☐ 708 NL Active ERA .... .35 .16 .04
  Tom Seaver
  Steve Carlton
  Steve Rogers
- ☐ 709 NL Active Save .... .12 .05 .02
  Bruce Sutter
  Tug McGraw
  Gene Garber
- ☐ 710 AL Active Batting .... .30 .14 .04
  Rod Carew
  George Brett
  Cecil Cooper
- ☐ 711 AL Active Hits .... .25 .11 .03
  Rod Carew
  Bert Campaneris
  Reggie Jackson
- ☐ 712 AL Active Home Run.... .25 .11 .03
  Reggie Jackson
  Graig Nettles
  Greg Luzinski
- ☐ 713 AL Active RBI .... .25 .11 .03
  Reggie Jackson
  Ted Simmons
  Graig Nettles
- ☐ 714 AL Active Steals .... .12 .05 .02
  Bert Campaneris
  Dave Lopes
  Omar Moreno
- ☐ 715 AL Active Victory .... .15 .07 .02
  Jim Palmer
  Don Sutton
  Tommy John
- ☐ 716 AL Active Strikeout .... .15 .07 .02
  Don Sutton
  Bert Blyleven
  Jerry Koosman
- ☐ 717 AL Active ERA .... .15 .07 .02
  Jim Palmer
  Rollie Fingers
  Ron Guidry
- ☐ 718 AL Active Save .... .15 .07 .02
  Rollie Fingers
  Rich Gossage
  Dan Quisenberry
- ☐ 719 Andy Hassler .... .08 .04 .01
- ☐ 720 Dwight Evans .... .12 .05 .02
- ☐ 721 Del Crandall MG .... .08 .04 .01
- ☐ 722 Bob Welch .... .12 .05 .02
- ☐ 723 Rich Dauer .... .08 .04 .01
- ☐ 724 Eric Rasmussen .... .08 .04 .01
- ☐ 725 Cesar Cedeno .... .12 .05 .02
- ☐ 726 Brewers TL .... .12 .05 .02
  Ted Simmons
  Moose Haas
  (Checklist on back)
- ☐ 727 Joel Youngblood .... .08 .04 .01
- ☐ 728 Tug McGraw .... .12 .05 .02
- ☐ 729 Gene Tenace .... .08 .04 .01
- ☐ 730 Bruce Sutter .... .12 .05 .02
- ☐ 731 Lynn Jones .... .08 .04 .01
- ☐ 732 Terry Crowley .... .08 .04 .01
- ☐ 733 Dave Collins .... .08 .04 .01
- ☐ 734 Odell Jones .... .08 .04 .01
- ☐ 735 Rick Burleson .... .08 .04 .01
- ☐ 736 Dick Ruthven .... .08 .04 .01
- ☐ 737 Jim Essian .... .08 .04 .01
- ☐ 738 Bill Schroeder .... .08 .04 .01
- ☐ 739 Bob Watson .... .12 .05 .02
- ☐ 740 Tom Seaver .... 1.00 .45 .13
- ☐ 741 Wayne Gross .... .08 .04 .01
- ☐ 742 Dick Williams MG .... .08 .04 .01
- ☐ 743 Don Hood .... .08 .04 .01
- ☐ 744 Jamie Allen .... .08 .04 .01
- ☐ 745 Dennis Eckersley .... .60 .25 .08
- ☐ 746 Mickey Hatcher .... .08 .04 .01
- ☐ 747 Pat Zachry .... .08 .04 .01
- ☐ 748 Jeff Leonard .... .08 .04 .01
- ☐ 749 Doug Flynn .... .08 .04 .01
- ☐ 750 Jim Palmer .... .75 .35 .09
- ☐ 751 Charlie Moore .... .08 .04 .01
- ☐ 752 Phil Garner .... .12 .05 .02
- ☐ 753 Doug Gwosdz .... .08 .04 .01
- ☐ 754 Kent Tekulve .... .12 .05 .02
- ☐ 755 Garry Maddox .... .08 .04 .01
- ☐ 756 Reds TL .... .12 .05 .02
  Ron Oester
  Mario Soto
  (Checklist on back)
- ☐ 757 Larry Bowa .... .12 .05 .02
- ☐ 758 Bill Stein .... .08 .04 .01
- ☐ 759 Richard Dotson .... .08 .04 .01
- ☐ 760 Bob Horner .... .12 .05 .02
- ☐ 761 John Montefusco .... .08 .04 .01
- ☐ 762 Rance Mulliniks .... .08 .04 .01
- ☐ 763 Craig Swan .... .08 .04 .01
- ☐ 764 Mike Hargrove .... .12 .05 .02
- ☐ 765 Ken Forsch .... .08 .04 .01
- ☐ 766 Mike Vail .... .08 .04 .01
- ☐ 767 Carney Lansford .... .12 .05 .02
- ☐ 768 Champ Summers .... .08 .04 .01
- ☐ 769 Bill Caudill .... .08 .04 .01
- ☐ 770 Ken Griffey .... .12 .05 .02
- ☐ 771 Billy Gardner MG .... .08 .04 .01
- ☐ 772 Jim Slaton .... .08 .04 .01
- ☐ 773 Todd Cruz .... .08 .04 .01
- ☐ 774 Tom Gorman .... .08 .04 .01
- ☐ 775 Dave Parker .... .15 .07 .02
- ☐ 776 Craig Reynolds .... .08 .04 .01
- ☐ 777 Tom Paciorek .... .12 .05 .02
- ☐ 778 Andy Hawkins .... .08 .04 .01
- ☐ 779 Jim Sundberg .... .12 .05 .02
- ☐ 780 Steve Carlton .... 1.00 .45 .13
- ☐ 781 Checklist 661-792 .... .12 .04 .01
- ☐ 782 Steve Balboni .... .08 .04 .01
- ☐ 783 Luis Leal .... .08 .04 .01
- ☐ 784 Leon Roberts .... .08 .04 .01
- ☐ 785 Joaquin Andujar .... .08 .04 .01
- ☐ 786 Red Sox TL .... .50 .23 .06
  Wade Boggs
  Bob Ojeda
  (Checklist on back)
- ☐ 787 Bill Campbell .... .08 .04 .01
- ☐ 788 Milt May .... .08 .04 .01
- ☐ 789 Bert Blyleven .... .15 .07 .02
- ☐ 790 Doug DeCinces .... .08 .04 .01
- ☐ 791 Terry Forster .... .08 .04 .01
- ☐ 792 Bill Russell .... .12 .05 .02

1984 Topps Traded

The cards in this 132-card set measure 2 1/2" by 3 1/2". In its now standard procedure, Topps issued its Traded (or extended) set for the fourth year in a row. Because all photos and statistics of its regular set for the year were developed during the fall and winter months of the preceding year,

players who changed teams during the fall, winter, and spring months are portrayed with the teams they were with in 1983. The Traded set updates the shortcomings of the regular set by presenting the players with their proper teams for the current year. Several of 1984's top rookies not contained in the regular set are pictured in the Traded set. The (extended) rookie cards in this set are Alvin Davis, Dwight Gooden, Jimmy Key, Mark Langston, Jose Rijo, and Bret Saberhagen. Again this year, the Topps affiliate in Ireland printed the cards, and the cards were available through hobby channels only. Topps also produced a specially boxed "glossy" edition, frequently referred to as the Topps Traded Tiffany set. There were supposedly only 10,000 sets of the Tiffany cards produced; they were marketed to hobby dealers. The checklist of cards is identical to that of the normal non-glossy cards. There are two primary distinguishing features of the Tiffany cards, white card stock reverses and high gloss obverses. These Tiffany cards are valued approximately from five to ten times the values listed below. The set numbering is in alphabetical order by player's name.

	NRMT-MT	EXC	G-VG
COMPLETE FACT.SET (132)	70.00	32.00	8.75
COMMON CARD (1T-132T)	.25	.11	.03
☐ 1T Willie Aikens	.25	.11	.03
☐ 2T Luis Aponte	.25	.11	.03
☐ 3T Mike Armstrong	.25	.11	.03
☐ 4T Bob Bailor	.25	.11	.03
☐ 5T Dusty Baker	.40	.18	.05
☐ 6T Steve Balboni	.25	.11	.03
☐ 7T Alan Bannister	.25	.11	.03
☐ 8T Dave Beard	.25	.11	.03
☐ 9T Joe Beckwith	.25	.11	.03
☐ 10T Bruce Berenyi	.25	.11	.03
☐ 11T Dave Bergman	.25	.11	.03
☐ 12T Tony Bernazard	.25	.11	.03
☐ 13T Yogi Berra MG	.75	.35	.09
☐ 14T Barry Bonnell	.25	.11	.03
☐ 15T Phil Bradley	.30	.14	.04
☐ 16T Fred Breining	.25	.11	.03
☐ 17T Bill Buckner	.30	.14	.04
☐ 18T Ray Burris	.25	.11	.03
☐ 19T John Butcher	.25	.11	.03
☐ 20T Brett Butler	.75	.35	.09
☐ 21T Enos Cabell	.25	.11	.03
☐ 22T Bill Campbell	.25	.11	.03
☐ 23T Bill Caudill	.25	.11	.03
☐ 24T Bob Clark	.25	.11	.03
☐ 25T Bryan Clark	.25	.11	.03
☐ 26T Jaime Cocanower	.25	.11	.03
☐ 27T Ron Darling	1.00	.45	.13
☐ 28T Alvin Davis	.50	.23	.06
☐ 29T Ken Dayley	.25	.11	.03
☐ 30T Jeff Dedmon	.25	.11	.03
☐ 31T Bob Dernier	.25	.11	.03
☐ 32T Carlos Diaz	.25	.11	.03
☐ 33T Mike Easler	.25	.11	.03
☐ 34T Dennis Eckersley	4.00	1.80	.50
☐ 35T Jim Essian	.25	.11	.03
☐ 36T Darrell Evans	.30	.14	.04
☐ 37T Mike Fitzgerald	.25	.11	.03
☐ 38T Tim Foli	.25	.11	.03
☐ 39T George Frazier	.25	.11	.03
☐ 40T Rich Gale	.25	.11	.03
☐ 41T Barbaro Garbey	.25	.11	.03
☐ 42T Dwight Gooden	4.00	1.80	.50
☐ 43T Rich Gossage	.40	.18	.05
☐ 44T Wayne Gross	.25	.11	.03
☐ 45T Mark Gubicza	1.00	.45	.13
☐ 46T Jackie Gutierrez	.25	.11	.03
☐ 47T Mel Hall	.30	.14	.04
☐ 48T Toby Harrah	.25	.11	.03
☐ 49T Ron Hassey	.25	.11	.03
☐ 50T Rich Hebner	.25	.11	.03
☐ 51T Willie Hernandez	.30	.14	.04
☐ 52T Ricky Horton	.25	.11	.03
☐ 53T Art Howe	.25	.11	.03
☐ 54T Dane Iorg	.25	.11	.03
☐ 55T Brook Jacoby	.30	.14	.04
☐ 56T Mike Jeffcoat	.25	.11	.03
☐ 57T Dave Johnson MG	.30	.14	.04
☐ 58T Lynn Jones	.25	.11	.03
☐ 59T Ruppert Jones	.25	.11	.03
☐ 60T Mike Jorgensen	.25	.11	.03
☐ 61T Bob Kearney	.25	.11	.03
☐ 62T Jimmy Key	16.00	7.25	2.00
☐ 63T Dave Kingman	.30	.14	.04
☐ 64T Jerry Koosman	.30	.14	.04
☐ 65T Wayne Krenchicki	.25	.11	.03
☐ 66T Rusty Kuntz	.25	.11	.03
☐ 67T Rene Lachemann MG	.25	.11	.03
☐ 68T Frank LaCorte	.25	.11	.03
☐ 69T Dennis Lamp	.25	.11	.03
☐ 70T Mark Langston	7.00	3.10	.85
☐ 71T Rick Leach	.25	.11	.03
☐ 72T Craig Lefferts	.30	.14	.04
☐ 73T Gary Lucas	.25	.11	.03
☐ 74T Jerry Martin	.25	.11	.03
☐ 75T Carmelo Martinez	.25	.11	.03
☐ 76T Mike Mason	.25	.11	.03
☐ 77T Gary Matthews	.30	.14	.04
☐ 78T Andy McGaffigan	.25	.11	.03
☐ 79T Larry Milbourne	.25	.11	.03
☐ 80T Sid Monge	.25	.11	.03
☐ 81T Jackie Moore MG	.25	.11	.03
☐ 82T Joe Morgan	3.00	1.35	.40
☐ 83T Graig Nettles	.30	.14	.04
☐ 84T Phil Niekro	1.25	.55	.16
☐ 85T Ken Oberkfell	.25	.11	.03
☐ 86T Mike O'Berry	.25	.11	.03
☐ 87T Al Oliver	.30	.14	.04
☐ 88T Jorge Orta	.25	.11	.03
☐ 89T Amos Otis	.30	.14	.04
☐ 90T Dave Parker	.40	.18	.05
☐ 91T Tony Perez	1.00	.45	.13
☐ 92T Gerald Perry	.30	.14	.04
☐ 93T Gary Pettis	.25	.11	.03
☐ 94T Rob Picciolo	.25	.11	.03
☐ 95T Vern Rapp MG	.25	.11	.03
☐ 96T Floyd Rayford	.25	.11	.03
☐ 97T Randy Ready	.25	.11	.03
☐ 98T Ron Reed	.25	.11	.03

☐ 99T	Gene Richards	.25	.11	.03
☐ 100T	Jose Rijo	10.00	4.50	1.25
☐ 101T	Jeff D. Robinson	.25	.11	.03
☐ 102T	Ron Romanick	.25	.11	.03
☐ 103T	Pete Rose	10.00	4.50	1.25
☐ 104T	Bret Saberhagen	10.00	4.50	1.25
☐ 105T	Juan Samuel	.50	.23	.06
☐ 106T	Scott Sanderson	.25	.11	.03
☐ 107T	Dick Schofield	.40	.18	.05
☐ 108T	Tom Seaver	6.00	2.70	.75
☐ 109T	Jim Slaton	.25	.11	.03
☐ 110T	Mike Smithson	.25	.11	.03
☐ 111T	Lary Sorensen	.25	.11	.03
☐ 112T	Tim Stoddard	.25	.11	.03
☐ 113T	Champ Summers	.25	.11	.03
☐ 114T	Jim Sundberg	.30	.14	.04
☐ 115T	Rick Sutcliffe	.30	.14	.04
☐ 116T	Craig Swan	.25	.11	.03
☐ 117T	Tim Teufel	.25	.11	.03
☐ 118T	Derrel Thomas	.25	.11	.03
☐ 119T	Gorman Thomas	.25	.11	.03
☐ 120T	Alex Trevino	.25	.11	.03
☐ 121T	Manny Trillo	.25	.11	.03
☐ 122T	John Tudor	.30	.14	.04
☐ 123T	Tom Underwood	.25	.11	.03
☐ 124T	Mike Vail	.25	.11	.03
☐ 125T	Tom Waddell	.25	.11	.03
☐ 126T	Gary Ward	.25	.11	.03
☐ 127T	Curt Wilkerson	.25	.11	.03
☐ 128T	Frank Williams	.25	.11	.03
☐ 129T	Glenn Wilson	.25	.11	.03
☐ 130T	John Wockenfuss	.25	.11	.03
☐ 131T	Ned Yost	.25	.11	.03
☐ 132T	Checklist 1T-132T	.25	.11	.03

1985 Topps

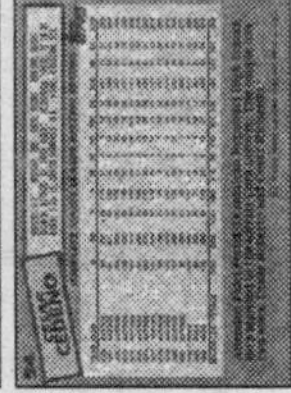

The cards in this 792-card set measure 2 1/2" by 3 1/2". The 1985 Topps set contains full color cards. The fronts feature both the Topps and team logos along with the team name, player's name, and his position. The backs feature player statistics with ink colors of light green and maroon on a gray stock. A trivia quiz is included on the lower portion of the backs. The first ten cards (1-10) are Record Breakers (RB), cards 131-143 are Father and Son (FS) cards, and cards 701 to 722 portray All-Star selections (AS). Cards 271 to 282 represent "First Draft Picks" still active in professional baseball and cards 389-404 feature the coach and eligible (not returning to college) players on the 1984 U.S. Olympic Baseball Team. The manager cards in the set are important in that they contain the checklist of that team's players on the back. The key Rookie Cards in this set are Roger Clemens, Eric Davis, Shawon Dunston, Dwight Gooden, Orel Hershiser, Jimmy Key, Mark Langston, Shane Mack, Mark McGwire, Terry Pendleton, Kirby Puckett, Jose Rijo, Bret Saberhagen, and Bill Swift. Topps also produced a specially boxed "glossy" edition, frequently referred to as the Topps Tiffany set. There were supposedly only 8,000 sets of the Tiffany cards produced; they were marketed to hobby dealers. The checklist of cards (792 regular and 132 Traded) is identical to that of the normal non-glossy cards. There are two primary distinguishing features of the Tiffany cards, white card stock reverses and high gloss obverses. These Tiffany cards are valued approximately from five to ten times the values listed below.

	NRMT-MT	EXC	G-VG
COMPLETE SET (792)	60.00	27.00	7.50
COMMON CARD (1-792)	.08	.04	.01
☐ 1 Carlton Fisk RB Longest game by catcher	.35	.09	.03
☐ 2 Steve Garvey RB Consecutive error-less games, 1B	.15	.07	.02
☐ 3 Dwight Gooden RB Most strikeouts, rookie, season	.25	.11	.03
☐ 4 Cliff Johnson RB Most pinch homers, lifetime	.10	.05	.01
☐ 5 Joe Morgan RB Most homers, 2B, lifetime	.15	.07	.02
☐ 6 Pete Rose RB Most singles, lifetime	.40	.18	.05
☐ 7 Nolan Ryan RB Most strikeouts, lifetime	1.50	.65	.19
☐ 8 Juan Samuel RB Most stolen bases, rookie, season	.10	.05	.01
☐ 9 Bruce Sutter RB Most saves, season, NL	.10	.05	.01
☐ 10 Don Sutton RB Most seasons, 100 or more K's	.12	.05	.02
☐ 11 Ralph Houk MG (Checklist back)	.10	.05	.01
☐ 12 Dave Lopes (Now with Cubs on card front)	.10	.05	.01
☐ 13 Tim Lollar	.08	.04	.01
☐ 14 Chris Bando	.08	.04	.01
☐ 15 Jerry Koosman	.10	.05	.01
☐ 16 Bobby Meacham	.08	.04	.01
☐ 17 Mike Scott	.10	.05	.01
☐ 18 Mickey Hatcher	.08	.04	.01
☐ 19 George Frazier	.08	.04	.01
☐ 20 Chet Lemon	.08	.04	.01
☐ 21 Lee Tunnell	.08	.04	.01
☐ 22 Duane Kuiper	.08	.04	.01
☐ 23 Bret Saberhagen	1.50	.65	.19

☐ 24	Jesse Barfield	.08	.04	.01
☐ 25	Steve Bedrosian	.08	.04	.01
☐ 26	Roy Smalley	.08	.04	.01
☐ 27	Bruce Berenyi	.08	.04	.01
☐ 28	Dann Bilardello	.08	.04	.01
☐ 29	Odell Jones	.08	.04	.01
☐ 30	Cal Ripken	3.00	1.35	.40
☐ 31	Terry Whitfield	.08	.04	.01
☐ 32	Chuck Porter	.08	.04	.01
☐ 33	Tito Landrum	.08	.04	.01
☐ 34	Ed Nunez	.08	.04	.01
☐ 35	Graig Nettles	.10	.05	.01
☐ 36	Fred Breining	.08	.04	.01
☐ 37	Reid Nichols	.08	.04	.01
☐ 38	Jackie Moore MG (Checklist back)	.10	.05	.01
☐ 39	John Wockenfuss	.08	.04	.01
☐ 40	Phil Niekro	.15	.07	.02
☐ 41	Mike Fischlin	.08	.04	.01
☐ 42	Luis Sanchez	.08	.04	.01
☐ 43	Andre David	.08	.04	.01
☐ 44	Dickie Thon	.08	.04	.01
☐ 45	Greg Minton	.08	.04	.01
☐ 46	Gary Woods	.08	.04	.01
☐ 47	Dave Rozema	.08	.04	.01
☐ 48	Tony Fernandez	.40	.18	.05
☐ 49	Butch Davis	.08	.04	.01
☐ 50	John Candelaria	.08	.04	.01
☐ 51	Bob Watson	.10	.05	.01
☐ 52	Jerry Dybzinski	.08	.04	.01
☐ 53	Tom Gorman	.08	.04	.01
☐ 54	Cesar Cedeno	.10	.05	.01
☐ 55	Frank Tanana	.10	.05	.01
☐ 56	Jim Dwyer	.08	.04	.01
☐ 57	Pat Zachry	.08	.04	.01
☐ 58	Orlando Mercado	.08	.04	.01
☐ 59	Rick Waits	.08	.04	.01
☐ 60	George Hendrick	.08	.04	.01
☐ 61	Curt Kaufman	.08	.04	.01
☐ 62	Mike Ramsey	.08	.04	.01
☐ 63	Steve McCatty	.08	.04	.01
☐ 64	Mark Bailey	.08	.04	.01
☐ 65	Bill Buckner	.10	.05	.01
☐ 66	Dick Williams MG (Checklist back)	.10	.05	.01
☐ 67	Rafael Santana	.08	.04	.01
☐ 68	Von Hayes	.08	.04	.01
☐ 69	Jim Winn	.08	.04	.01
☐ 70	Don Baylor	.15	.07	.02
☐ 71	Tim Laudner	.08	.04	.01
☐ 72	Rick Sutcliffe	.10	.05	.01
☐ 73	Rusty Kuntz	.08	.04	.01
☐ 74	Mike Krukow	.08	.04	.01
☐ 75	Willie Upshaw	.08	.04	.01
☐ 76	Alan Bannister	.08	.04	.01
☐ 77	Joe Beckwith	.08	.04	.01
☐ 78	Scott Fletcher	.08	.04	.01
☐ 79	Rick Mahler	.08	.04	.01
☐ 80	Keith Hernandez	.15	.07	.02
☐ 81	Lenn Sakata	.08	.04	.01
☐ 82	Joe Price	.08	.04	.01
☐ 83	Charlie Moore	.08	.04	.01
☐ 84	Spike Owen	.08	.04	.01
☐ 85	Mike Marshall	.08	.04	.01
☐ 86	Don Aase	.08	.04	.01
☐ 87	David Green	.08	.04	.01
☐ 88	Bryn Smith	.08	.04	.01
☐ 89	Jackie Gutierrez	.08	.04	.01
☐ 90	Rich Gossage	.15	.07	.02
☐ 91	Jeff Burroughs	.08	.04	.01
☐ 92	Paul Owens MG (Checklist back)	.10	.05	.01
☐ 93	Don Schulze	.08	.04	.01
☐ 94	Toby Harrah	.08	.04	.01
☐ 95	Jose Cruz	.10	.05	.01
☐ 96	Johnny Ray	.08	.04	.01
☐ 97	Pete Filson	.08	.04	.01
☐ 98	Steve Lake	.08	.04	.01
☐ 99	Milt Wilcox	.08	.04	.01
☐ 100	George Brett	1.50	.65	.19
☐ 101	Jim Acker	.08	.04	.01
☐ 102	Tommy Dunbar	.08	.04	.01
☐ 103	Randy Lerch	.08	.04	.01
☐ 104	Mike Fitzgerald	.08	.04	.01
☐ 105	Ron Kittle	.08	.04	.01
☐ 106	Pascual Perez	.08	.04	.01
☐ 107	Tom Foley	.08	.04	.01
☐ 108	Darnell Coles	.08	.04	.01
☐ 109	Gary Roenicke	.08	.04	.01
☐ 110	Alejandro Pena	.08	.04	.01
☐ 111	Doug DeCinces	.08	.04	.01
☐ 112	Tom Tellmann	.08	.04	.01
☐ 113	Tom Herr	.10	.05	.01
☐ 114	Bob James	.08	.04	.01
☐ 115	Rickey Henderson	1.00	.45	.13
☐ 116	Dennis Boyd	.08	.04	.01
☐ 117	Greg Gross	.08	.04	.01
☐ 118	Eric Show	.08	.04	.01
☐ 119	Pat Corrales MG (Checklist back)	.10	.05	.01
☐ 120	Steve Kemp	.08	.04	.01
☐ 121	Checklist: 1-132	.12	.03	.01
☐ 122	Tom Brunansky	.10	.05	.01
☐ 123	Dave Smith	.08	.04	.01
☐ 124	Rich Hebner	.08	.04	.01
☐ 125	Kent Tekulve	.08	.04	.01
☐ 126	Ruppert Jones	.08	.04	.01
☐ 127	Mark Gubicza	.25	.11	.03
☐ 128	Ernie Whitt	.08	.04	.01
☐ 129	Gene Garber	.08	.04	.01
☐ 130	Al Oliver	.10	.05	.01
☐ 131	Buddy/Gus Bell FS	.12	.05	.02
☐ 132	Dale/Yogi Berra FS	.15	.07	.02
☐ 133	Bob/Ray Boone FS	.12	.05	.02
☐ 134	Terry/Tito Francona FS	.10	.05	.01
☐ 135	Terry/Bob Kennedy FS	.10	.05	.01
☐ 136	Jeff/Bill Kunkel FS	.10	.05	.01
☐ 137	Vance/Vern Law FS	.10	.05	.01
☐ 138	Dick/Dick Schofield FS	.10	.05	.01
☐ 139	Joel/Bob Skinner FS	.10	.05	.01
☐ 140	Roy/Roy Smalley FS	.10	.05	.01
☐ 141	Mike/Dave Stenhouse FS	.10	.05	.01
☐ 142	Steve/Dizzy Trout FS	.10	.05	.01
☐ 143	Ozzie/Ossie Virgil FS	.10	.05	.01
☐ 144	Ron Gardenhire	.08	.04	.01
☐ 145	Alvin Davis	.12	.05	.02
☐ 146	Gary Redus	.08	.04	.01
☐ 147	Bill Swaggerty	.08	.04	.01
☐ 148	Steve Yeager	.08	.04	.01
☐ 149	Dickie Noles	.08	.04	.01
☐ 150	Jim Rice	.15	.07	.02
☐ 151	Moose Haas	.08	.04	.01
☐ 152	Steve Braun	.08	.04	.01
☐ 153	Frank LaCorte	.08	.04	.01
☐ 154	Argenis Salazar	.08	.04	.01
☐ 155	Yogi Berra MG (Checklist back)	.15	.07	.02
☐ 156	Craig Reynolds	.08	.04	.01
☐ 157	Tug McGraw	.10	.05	.01
☐ 158	Pat Tabler	.08	.04	.01
☐ 159	Carlos Diaz	.08	.04	.01
☐ 160	Lance Parrish	.10	.05	.01
☐ 161	Ken Schrom	.08	.04	.01
☐ 162	Benny Distefano	.08	.04	.01
☐ 163	Dennis Eckersley	.25	.11	.03
☐ 164	Jorge Orta	.08	.04	.01

☐ 165 Dusty Baker .15 .07 .02
☐ 166 Keith Atherton .08 .04 .01
☐ 167 Rufino Linares .08 .04 .01
☐ 168 Garth Iorg .08 .04 .01
☐ 169 Dan Spillner .08 .04 .01
☐ 170 George Foster .10 .05 .01
☐ 171 Bill Stein .08 .04 .01
☐ 172 Jack Perconte .08 .04 .01
☐ 173 Mike Young .08 .04 .01
☐ 174 Rick Honeycutt .08 .04 .01
☐ 175 Dave Parker .15 .07 .02
☐ 176 Bill Schroeder .08 .04 .01
☐ 177 Dave Von Ohlen .08 .04 .01
☐ 178 Miguel Dilone .08 .04 .01
☐ 179 Tommy John .15 .07 .02
☐ 180 Dave Winfield .75 .35 .09
☐ 181 Roger Clemens 14.00 6.25 1.75
☐ 182 Tim Flannery .08 .04 .01
☐ 183 Larry McWilliams .08 .04 .01
☐ 184 Carmen Castillo .08 .04 .01
☐ 185 Al Holland .08 .04 .01
☐ 186 Bob Lillis MG .10 .05 .01
(Checklist back)
☐ 187 Mike Walters .08 .04 .01
☐ 188 Greg Pryor .08 .04 .01
☐ 189 Warren Brusstar .08 .04 .01
☐ 190 Rusty Staub .10 .05 .01
☐ 191 Steve Nicosia .08 .04 .01
☐ 192 Howard Johnson .30 .14 .04
☐ 193 Jimmy Key 2.50 1.15 .30
☐ 194 Dave Stegman .08 .04 .01
☐ 195 Glenn Hubbard .08 .04 .01
☐ 196 Pete O'Brien .10 .05 .01
☐ 197 Mike Warren .08 .04 .01
☐ 198 Eddie Milner .08 .04 .01
☐ 199 Dennis Martinez .10 .05 .01
☐ 200 Reggie Jackson .60 .25 .08
☐ 201 Burt Hooton .08 .04 .01
☐ 202 Gorman Thomas .08 .04 .01
☐ 203 Bob McClure .08 .04 .01
☐ 204 Art Howe .08 .04 .01
☐ 205 Steve Rogers .08 .04 .01
☐ 206 Phil Garner .10 .05 .01
☐ 207 Mark Clear .08 .04 .01
☐ 208 Champ Summers .08 .04 .01
☐ 209 Bill Campbell .08 .04 .01
☐ 210 Gary Matthews .08 .04 .01
☐ 211 Clay Christiansen .08 .04 .01
☐ 212 George Vukovich .08 .04 .01
☐ 213 Billy Gardner MG .10 .05 .01
(Checklist back)
☐ 214 John Tudor .10 .05 .01
☐ 215 Bob Brenly .08 .04 .01
☐ 216 Jerry Don Gleaton .08 .04 .01
☐ 217 Leon Roberts .08 .04 .01
☐ 218 Doyle Alexander .08 .04 .01
☐ 219 Gerald Perry .08 .04 .01
☐ 220 Fred Lynn .10 .05 .01
☐ 221 Ron Reed .08 .04 .01
☐ 222 Hubie Brooks .10 .05 .01
☐ 223 Tom Hume .08 .04 .01
☐ 224 Al Cowens .08 .04 .01
☐ 225 Mike Boddicker .08 .04 .01
☐ 226 Juan Beniquez .08 .04 .01
☐ 227 Danny Darwin .08 .04 .01
☐ 228 Dion James .08 .04 .01
☐ 229 Dave LaPoint .08 .04 .01
☐ 230 Gary Carter .20 .09 .03
☐ 231 Dwayne Murphy .08 .04 .01
☐ 232 Dave Beard .08 .04 .01
☐ 233 Ed Jurak .08 .04 .01
☐ 234 Jerry Narron .08 .04 .01
☐ 235 Garry Maddox .08 .04 .01
☐ 236 Mark Thurmond .08 .04 .01
☐ 237 Julio Franco .30 .14 .04
☐ 238 Jose Rijo 1.50 .65 .19
☐ 239 Tim Teufel .08 .04 .01
☐ 240 Dave Stieb .10 .05 .01
☐ 241 Jim Frey MG .10 .05 .01
(Checklist back)
☐ 242 Greg Harris .08 .04 .01
☐ 243 Barbaro Garbey .08 .04 .01
☐ 244 Mike Jones .08 .04 .01
☐ 245 Chili Davis .10 .05 .01
☐ 246 Mike Norris .08 .04 .01
☐ 247 Wayne Tolleson .08 .04 .01
☐ 248 Terry Forster .08 .04 .01
☐ 249 Harold Baines .15 .07 .02
☐ 250 Jesse Orosco .08 .04 .01
☐ 251 Brad Gulden .08 .04 .01
☐ 252 Dan Ford .08 .04 .01
☐ 253 Sid Bream .25 .11 .03
☐ 254 Pete Vuckovich .08 .04 .01
☐ 255 Lonnie Smith .08 .04 .01
☐ 256 Mike Stanton .08 .04 .01
☐ 257 Bryan Little .08 .04 .01
☐ 258 Mike C. Brown .08 .04 .01
☐ 259 Gary Allenson .08 .04 .01
☐ 260 Dave Righetti .10 .05 .01
☐ 261 Checklist: 133-264 .12 .03 .01
☐ 262 Greg Booker .08 .04 .01
☐ 263 Mel Hall .08 .04 .01
☐ 264 Joe Sambito .08 .04 .01
☐ 265 Juan Samuel .08 .04 .01
☐ 266 Frank Viola .10 .05 .01
☐ 267 Henry Cotto .08 .04 .01
☐ 268 Chuck Tanner MG .10 .05 .01
(Checklist back)
☐ 269 Doug Baker .08 .04 .01
☐ 270 Dan Quisenberry .10 .05 .01
☐ 271 Tim Foli FDP68 .10 .05 .01
☐ 272 Jeff Burroughs FDP69 .10 .05 .01
☐ 273 Bill Almon FDP74 .10 .05 .01
☐ 274 Floyd Bannister FDP76 .10 .05 .01
☐ 275 Harold Baines FDP77 .15 .07 .02
☐ 276 Bob Horner FDP78 .10 .05 .01
☐ 277 Al Chambers FDP79 .10 .05 .01
☐ 278 Darryl Strawberry .30 .14 .04
FDP80
☐ 279 Mike Moore FDP81 .10 .05 .01
☐ 280 Shawon Dunston FDP82 .50 .23 .06
☐ 281 Tim Belcher FDP83 .50 .23 .06
☐ 282 Shawn Abner FDP84 .10 .05 .01
☐ 283 Fran Mullins .08 .04 .01
☐ 284 Marty Bystrom .08 .04 .01
☐ 285 Dan Driessen .08 .04 .01
☐ 286 Rudy Law .08 .04 .01
☐ 287 Walt Terrell .08 .04 .01
☐ 288 Jeff Kunkel .08 .04 .01
☐ 289 Tom Underwood .08 .04 .01
☐ 290 Cecil Cooper .10 .05 .01
☐ 291 Bob Welch .10 .05 .01
☐ 292 Brad Komminsk .08 .04 .01
☐ 293 Curt Young .08 .04 .01
☐ 294 Tom Nieto .08 .04 .01
☐ 295 Joe Niekro .10 .05 .01
☐ 296 Ricky Nelson .08 .04 .01
☐ 297 Gary Lucas .08 .04 .01
☐ 298 Marty Barrett .08 .04 .01
☐ 299 Andy Hawkins .08 .04 .01
☐ 300 Rod Carew .50 .23 .06
☐ 301 John Montefusco .08 .04 .01
☐ 302 Tim Corcoran .08 .04 .01
☐ 303 Mike Jeffcoat .08 .04 .01
☐ 304 Gary Gaetti .10 .05 .01
☐ 305 Dale Berra .08 .04 .01

- ☐ 306 Rick Reuschel .10 .05 .01
- ☐ 307 Sparky Anderson MG .15 .07 .02 (Checklist back)
- ☐ 308 John Wathan .08 .04 .01
- ☐ 309 Mike Witt .08 .04 .01
- ☐ 310 Manny Trillo .08 .04 .01
- ☐ 311 Jim Gott .08 .04 .01
- ☐ 312 Marc Hill .08 .04 .01
- ☐ 313 Dave Schmidt .08 .04 .01
- ☐ 314 Ron Oester .08 .04 .01
- ☐ 315 Doug Sisk .08 .04 .01
- ☐ 316 John Lowenstein .08 .04 .01
- ☐ 317 Jack Lazorko .08 .04 .01
- ☐ 318 Ted Simmons .10 .05 .01
- ☐ 319 Jeff Jones .08 .04 .01
- ☐ 320 Dale Murphy .25 .11 .03
- ☐ 321 Ricky Horton .08 .04 .01
- ☐ 322 Dave Stapleton .08 .04 .01
- ☐ 323 Andy McGaffigan .08 .04 .01
- ☐ 324 Bruce Bochy .08 .04 .01
- ☐ 325 John Denny .08 .04 .01
- ☐ 326 Kevin Bass .08 .04 .01
- ☐ 327 Brook Jacoby .08 .04 .01
- ☐ 328 Bob Shirley .08 .04 .01
- ☐ 329 Ron Washington .08 .04 .01
- ☐ 330 Leon Durham .08 .04 .01
- ☐ 331 Bill Laskey .08 .04 .01
- ☐ 332 Brian Harper .10 .05 .01
- ☐ 333 Willie Hernandez .08 .04 .01
- ☐ 334 Dick Howser MG .10 .05 .01 (Checklist back)
- ☐ 335 Bruce Benedict .08 .04 .01
- ☐ 336 Rance Mulliniks .08 .04 .01
- ☐ 337 Billy Sample .08 .04 .01
- ☐ 338 Britt Burns .08 .04 .01
- ☐ 339 Danny Heep .08 .04 .01
- ☐ 340 Robin Yount .75 .35 .09
- ☐ 341 Floyd Rayford .08 .04 .01
- ☐ 342 Ted Power .08 .04 .01
- ☐ 343 Bill Russell .10 .05 .01
- ☐ 344 Dave Henderson .10 .05 .01
- ☐ 345 Charlie Lea .08 .04 .01
- ☐ 346 Terry Pendleton 1.00 .45 .13
- ☐ 347 Rick Langford .08 .04 .01
- ☐ 348 Bob Boone .10 .05 .01
- ☐ 349 Domingo Ramos .08 .04 .01
- ☐ 350 Wade Boggs 1.50 .65 .19
- ☐ 351 Juan Agosto .08 .04 .01
- ☐ 352 Joe Morgan .25 .11 .03
- ☐ 353 Julio Solano .08 .04 .01
- ☐ 354 Andre Robertson .08 .04 .01
- ☐ 355 Bert Blyleven .15 .07 .02
- ☐ 356 Dave Meier .08 .04 .01
- ☐ 357 Rich Bordi .08 .04 .01
- ☐ 358 Tony Pena .08 .04 .01
- ☐ 359 Pat Sheridan .08 .04 .01
- ☐ 360 Steve Carlton .50 .23 .06
- ☐ 361 Alfredo Griffin .08 .04 .01
- ☐ 362 Craig McMurtry .08 .04 .01
- ☐ 363 Ron Hodges .08 .04 .01
- ☐ 364 Richard Dotson .08 .04 .01
- ☐ 365 Danny Ozark MG .10 .05 .01 (Checklist back)
- ☐ 366 Todd Cruz .08 .04 .01
- ☐ 367 Keefe Cato .08 .04 .01
- ☐ 368 Dave Bergman .08 .04 .01
- ☐ 369 R.J. Reynolds .08 .04 .01
- ☐ 370 Bruce Sutter .10 .05 .01
- ☐ 371 Mickey Rivers .08 .04 .01
- ☐ 372 Roy Howell .08 .04 .01
- ☐ 373 Mike Moore .10 .05 .01
- ☐ 374 Brian Downing .10 .05 .01
- ☐ 375 Jeff Reardon .15 .07 .02
- ☐ 376 Jeff Newman .08 .04 .01
- ☐ 377 Checklist: 265-396 .12 .03 .01
- ☐ 378 Alan Wiggins .08 .04 .01
- ☐ 379 Charles Hudson .08 .04 .01
- ☐ 380 Ken Griffey .10 .05 .01
- ☐ 381 Roy Smith .08 .04 .01
- ☐ 382 Denny Walling .08 .04 .01
- ☐ 383 Rick Lysander .08 .04 .01
- ☐ 384 Jody Davis .08 .04 .01
- ☐ 385 Jose DeLeon .08 .04 .01
- ☐ 386 Dan Gladden .25 .11 .03
- ☐ 387 Buddy Biancalana .08 .04 .01
- ☐ 388 Bert Roberge .08 .04 .01
- ☐ 389 Rod Dedeaux OLY CO .12 .05 .02
- ☐ 390 Sid Akins OLY .12 .05 .02
- ☐ 391 Flavio Alfaro OLY .12 .05 .02
- ☐ 392 Don August OLY .14 .06 .02
- ☐ 393 Scott Bankhead OLY .12 .05 .02
- ☐ 394 Bob Caffrey OLY .12 .05 .02
- ☐ 395 Mike Dunne OLY .12 .05 .02
- ☐ 396 Gary Green OLY .12 .05 .02
- ☐ 397 John Hoover OLY .12 .05 .02
- ☐ 398 Shane Mack OLY 1.50 .65 .19
- ☐ 399 John Marzano OLY .12 .05 .02
- ☐ 400 Oddibe McDowell OLY .30 .14 .04
- ☐ 401 Mark McGwire OLY 8.00 3.60 1.00
- ☐ 402 Pat Pacillo OLY .12 .05 .02
- ☐ 403 Cory Snyder OLY 1.00 .45 .13
- ☐ 404 Billy Swift OLY 2.00 .90 .25
- ☐ 405 Tom Veryzer .08 .04 .01
- ☐ 406 Len Whitehouse .08 .04 .01
- ☐ 407 Bobby Ramos .08 .04 .01
- ☐ 408 Sid Monge .08 .04 .01
- ☐ 409 Brad Wellman .08 .04 .01
- ☐ 410 Bob Horner .08 .04 .01
- ☐ 411 Bobby Cox MG .10 .05 .01 (Checklist back)
- ☐ 412 Bud Black .08 .04 .01
- ☐ 413 Vance Law .08 .04 .01
- ☐ 414 Gary Ward .08 .04 .01
- ☐ 415 Ron Darling UER .10 .05 .01 (No trivia answer)
- ☐ 416 Wayne Gross .08 .04 .01
- ☐ 417 John Franco .50 .23 .06
- ☐ 418 Ken Landreaux .08 .04 .01
- ☐ 419 Mike Caldwell .08 .04 .01
- ☐ 420 Andre Dawson .60 .25 .08
- ☐ 421 Dave Rucker .08 .04 .01
- ☐ 422 Carney Lansford .10 .05 .01
- ☐ 423 Barry Bonnell .08 .04 .01
- ☐ 424 Al Nipper .08 .04 .01
- ☐ 425 Mike Hargrove .10 .05 .01
- ☐ 426 Vern Ruhle .08 .04 .01
- ☐ 427 Mario Ramirez .08 .04 .01
- ☐ 428 Larry Andersen .08 .04 .01
- ☐ 429 Rick Cerone .08 .04 .01
- ☐ 430 Ron Davis .08 .04 .01
- ☐ 431 U.L. Washington .08 .04 .01
- ☐ 432 Thad Bosley .08 .04 .01
- ☐ 433 Jim Morrison .08 .04 .01
- ☐ 434 Gene Richards .08 .04 .01
- ☐ 435 Dan Petry .08 .04 .01
- ☐ 436 Willie Aikens .08 .04 .01
- ☐ 437 Al Jones .08 .04 .01
- ☐ 438 Joe Torre MG .10 .05 .01 (Checklist back)
- ☐ 439 Junior Ortiz .08 .04 .01
- ☐ 440 Fernando Valenzuela .10 .05 .01
- ☐ 441 Duane Walker .08 .04 .01
- ☐ 442 Ken Forsch .08 .04 .01
- ☐ 443 George Wright .08 .04 .01
- ☐ 444 Tony Phillips .10 .05 .01
- ☐ 445 Tippy Martinez .08 .04 .01

	No.	Player			
☐	446	Jim Sundberg	.10	.05	.01
☐	447	Jeff Lahti	.08	.04	.01
☐	448	Derrel Thomas	.08	.04	.01
☐	449	Phil Bradley	.10	.05	.01
☐	450	Steve Garvey	.15	.07	.02
☐	451	Bruce Hurst	.10	.05	.01
☐	452	John Castino	.08	.04	.01
☐	453	Tom Waddell	.08	.04	.01
☐	454	Glenn Wilson	.08	.04	.01
☐	455	Bob Knepper	.08	.04	.01
☐	456	Tim Foli	.08	.04	.01
☐	457	Cecilio Guante	.08	.04	.01
☐	458	Randy Johnson	.08	.04	.01
☐	459	Charlie Leibrandt	.08	.04	.01
☐	460	Ryne Sandberg	2.50	1.15	.30
☐	461	Marty Castillo	.08	.04	.01
☐	462	Gary Lavelle	.08	.04	.01
☐	463	Dave Collins	.08	.04	.01
☐	464	Mike Mason	.08	.04	.01
☐	465	Bob Grich	.10	.05	.01
☐	466	Tony LaRussa MG (Checklist back)	.15	.07	.02
☐	467	Ed Lynch	.08	.04	.01
☐	468	Wayne Krenchicki	.08	.04	.01
☐	469	Sammy Stewart	.08	.04	.01
☐	470	Steve Sax	.10	.05	.01
☐	471	Pete Ladd	.08	.04	.01
☐	472	Jim Essian	.08	.04	.01
☐	473	Tim Wallach	.10	.05	.01
☐	474	Kurt Kepshire	.08	.04	.01
☐	475	Andre Thornton	.08	.04	.01
☐	476	Jeff Stone	.08	.04	.01
☐	477	Bob Ojeda	.10	.05	.01
☐	478	Kurt Bevacqua	.08	.04	.01
☐	479	Mike Madden	.08	.04	.01
☐	480	Lou Whitaker	.30	.14	.04
☐	481	Dale Murray	.08	.04	.01
☐	482	Harry Spilman	.08	.04	.01
☐	483	Mike Smithson	.08	.04	.01
☐	484	Larry Bowa	.10	.05	.01
☐	485	Matt Young	.08	.04	.01
☐	486	Steve Balboni	.08	.04	.01
☐	487	Frank Williams	.08	.04	.01
☐	488	Joel Skinner	.08	.04	.01
☐	489	Bryan Clark	.08	.04	.01
☐	490	Jason Thompson	.08	.04	.01
☐	491	Rick Camp	.08	.04	.01
☐	492	Dave Johnson MG (Checklist back)	.10	.05	.01
☐	493	Orel Hershiser	1.25	.55	.16
☐	494	Rich Dauer	.08	.04	.01
☐	495	Mario Soto	.08	.04	.01
☐	496	Donnie Scott	.08	.04	.01
☐	497	Gary Pettis UER (Photo actually Gary's little brother, Lynn)	.08	.04	.01
☐	498	Ed Romero	.08	.04	.01
☐	499	Danny Cox	.08	.04	.01
☐	500	Mike Schmidt	1.00	.45	.13
☐	501	Dan Schatzeder	.08	.04	.01
☐	502	Rick Miller	.08	.04	.01
☐	503	Tim Conroy	.08	.04	.01
☐	504	Jerry Willard	.08	.04	.01
☐	505	Jim Beattie	.08	.04	.01
☐	506	Franklin Stubbs	.08	.04	.01
☐	507	Ray Fontenot	.08	.04	.01
☐	508	John Shelby	.08	.04	.01
☐	509	Milt May	.08	.04	.01
☐	510	Kent Hrbek	.10	.05	.01
☐	511	Lee Smith	.35	.16	.04
☐	512	Tom Brookens	.08	.04	.01
☐	513	Lynn Jones	.08	.04	.01
☐	514	Jeff Cornell	.08	.04	.01
☐	515	Dave Concepcion	.10	.05	.01
☐	516	Roy Lee Jackson	.08	.04	.01
☐	517	Jerry Martin	.08	.04	.01
☐	518	Chris Chambliss	.10	.05	.01
☐	519	Doug Rader MG (Checklist back)	.10	.05	.01
☐	520	LaMarr Hoyt	.08	.04	.01
☐	521	Rick Dempsey	.08	.04	.01
☐	522	Paul Molitor	1.00	.45	.13
☐	523	Candy Maldonado	.08	.04	.01
☐	524	Rob Wilfong	.08	.04	.01
☐	525	Darrell Porter	.08	.04	.01
☐	526	David Palmer	.08	.04	.01
☐	527	Checklist: 397-528	.12	.03	.01
☐	528	Bill Krueger	.08	.04	.01
☐	529	Rich Gedman	.08	.04	.01
☐	530	Dave Dravecky	.10	.05	.01
☐	531	Joe Lefebvre	.08	.04	.01
☐	532	Frank DiPino	.08	.04	.01
☐	533	Tony Bernazard	.08	.04	.01
☐	534	Brian Dayett	.08	.04	.01
☐	535	Pat Putnam	.08	.04	.01
☐	536	Kirby Puckett	16.00	7.25	2.00
☐	537	Don Robinson	.08	.04	.01
☐	538	Keith Moreland	.08	.04	.01
☐	539	Aurelio Lopez	.08	.04	.01
☐	540	Claudell Washington	.08	.04	.01
☐	541	Mark Davis	.08	.04	.01
☐	542	Don Slaught	.08	.04	.01
☐	543	Mike Squires	.08	.04	.01
☐	544	Bruce Kison	.08	.04	.01
☐	545	Lloyd Moseby	.08	.04	.01
☐	546	Brent Gaff	.08	.04	.01
☐	547	Pete Rose MG (Checklist back)	.50	.23	.06
☐	548	Larry Parrish	.08	.04	.01
☐	549	Mike Scioscia	.08	.04	.01
☐	550	Scott McGregor	.08	.04	.01
☐	551	Andy Van Slyke	.35	.16	.04
☐	552	Chris Codiroli	.08	.04	.01
☐	553	Bob Clark	.08	.04	.01
☐	554	Doug Flynn	.08	.04	.01
☐	555	Bob Stanley	.08	.04	.01
☐	556	Sixto Lezcano	.08	.04	.01
☐	557	Len Barker	.08	.04	.01
☐	558	Carmelo Martinez	.08	.04	.01
☐	559	Jay Howell	.10	.05	.01
☐	560	Bill Madlock	.10	.05	.01
☐	561	Darryl Motley	.08	.04	.01
☐	562	Houston Jimenez	.08	.04	.01
☐	563	Dick Ruthven	.08	.04	.01
☐	564	Alan Ashby	.08	.04	.01
☐	565	Kirk Gibson	.15	.07	.02
☐	566	Ed VandeBerg	.08	.04	.01
☐	567	Joel Youngblood	.08	.04	.01
☐	568	Cliff Johnson	.08	.04	.01
☐	569	Ken Oberkfell	.08	.04	.01
☐	570	Darryl Strawberry	.35	.16	.04
☐	571	Charlie Hough	.10	.05	.01
☐	572	Tom Paciorek	.10	.05	.01
☐	573	Jay Tibbs	.08	.04	.01
☐	574	Joe Altobelli MG (Checklist back)	.10	.05	.01
☐	575	Pedro Guerrero	.10	.05	.01
☐	576	Jaime Cocanower	.08	.04	.01
☐	577	Chris Speier	.08	.04	.01
☐	578	Terry Francona	.08	.04	.01
☐	579	Ron Romanick	.08	.04	.01
☐	580	Dwight Evans	.10	.05	.01
☐	581	Mark Wagner	.08	.04	.01
☐	582	Ken Phelps	.08	.04	.01
☐	583	Bobby Brown	.08	.04	.01

☐ 584 Kevin Gross .08 .04 .01
☐ 585 Butch Wynegar .08 .04 .01
☐ 586 Bill Scherrer .08 .04 .01
☐ 587 Doug Frobel .08 .04 .01
☐ 588 Bobby Castillo .08 .04 .01
☐ 589 Bob Dernier .08 .04 .01
☐ 590 Ray Knight .10 .05 .01
☐ 591 Larry Herndon .08 .04 .01
☐ 592 Jeff D. Robinson .08 .04 .01
☐ 593 Rick Leach .08 .04 .01
☐ 594 Curt Wilkerson .08 .04 .01
☐ 595 Larry Gura .08 .04 .01
☐ 596 Jerry Hairston .08 .04 .01
☐ 597 Brad Lesley .08 .04 .01
☐ 598 Jose Oquendo .08 .04 .01
☐ 599 Storm Davis .08 .04 .01
☐ 600 Pete Rose .75 .35 .09
☐ 601 Tom Lasorda MG .15 .07 .02
(Checklist back)
☐ 602 Jeff Dedmon .08 .04 .01
☐ 603 Rick Manning .08 .04 .01
☐ 604 Daryl Sconiers .08 .04 .01
☐ 605 Ozzie Smith 1.00 .45 .13
☐ 606 Rich Gale .08 .04 .01
☐ 607 Bill Almon .08 .04 .01
☐ 608 Craig Lefferts .10 .05 .01
☐ 609 Broderick Perkins .08 .04 .01
☐ 610 Jack Morris .25 .11 .03
☐ 611 Ozzie Virgil .08 .04 .01
☐ 612 Mike Armstrong .08 .04 .01
☐ 613 Terry Puhl .08 .04 .01
☐ 614 Al Williams .08 .04 .01
☐ 615 Marvell Wynne .08 .04 .01
☐ 616 Scott Sanderson .08 .04 .01
☐ 617 Willie Wilson .10 .05 .01
☐ 618 Pete Falcone .08 .04 .01
☐ 619 Jeff Leonard .08 .04 .01
☐ 620 Dwight Gooden .75 .35 .09
☐ 621 Marvis Foley .08 .04 .01
☐ 622 Luis Leal .08 .04 .01
☐ 623 Greg Walker .08 .04 .01
☐ 624 Benny Ayala .08 .04 .01
☐ 625 Mark Langston 1.25 .55 .16
☐ 626 German Rivera .08 .04 .01
☐ 627 Eric Davis 1.00 .45 .13
☐ 628 Rene Lachemann MG .10 .05 .01
(Checklist back)
☐ 629 Dick Schofield .08 .04 .01
☐ 630 Tim Raines .25 .11 .03
☐ 631 Bob Forsch .08 .04 .01
☐ 632 Bruce Bochte .08 .04 .01
☐ 633 Glenn Hoffman .08 .04 .01
☐ 634 Bill Dawley .08 .04 .01
☐ 635 Terry Kennedy .08 .04 .01
☐ 636 Shane Rawley .08 .04 .01
☐ 637 Brett Butler .15 .07 .02
☐ 638 Mike Pagliarulo .08 .04 .01
☐ 639 Ed Hodge .08 .04 .01
☐ 640 Steve Henderson .08 .04 .01
☐ 641 Rod Scurry .08 .04 .01
☐ 642 Dave Owen .08 .04 .01
☐ 643 Johnny Grubb .08 .04 .01
☐ 644 Mark Huismann .08 .04 .01
☐ 645 Damaso Garcia .08 .04 .01
☐ 646 Scot Thompson .08 .04 .01
☐ 647 Rafael Ramirez .08 .04 .01
☐ 648 Bob Jones .08 .04 .01
☐ 649 Sid Fernandez .25 .11 .03
☐ 650 Greg Luzinski .10 .05 .01
☐ 651 Jeff Russell .10 .05 .01
☐ 652 Joe Nolan .08 .04 .01
☐ 653 Mark Brouhard .08 .04 .01
☐ 654 Dave Anderson .08 .04 .01
☐ 655 Joaquin Andujar .08 .04 .01
☐ 656 Chuck Cottier MG .10 .05 .01
(Checklist back)
☐ 657 Jim Slaton .08 .04 .01
☐ 658 Mike Stenhouse .08 .04 .01
☐ 659 Checklist: 529-660 .12 .03 .01
☐ 660 Tony Gwynn 2.00 .90 .25
☐ 661 Steve Crawford .08 .04 .01
☐ 662 Mike Heath .08 .04 .01
☐ 663 Luis Aguayo .08 .04 .01
☐ 664 Steve Farr .30 .14 .04
☐ 665 Don Mattingly 3.00 1.35 .40
☐ 666 Mike LaCoss .08 .04 .01
☐ 667 Dave Engle .08 .04 .01
☐ 668 Steve Trout .08 .04 .01
☐ 669 Lee Lacy .08 .04 .01
☐ 670 Tom Seaver .50 .23 .06
☐ 671 Dane Iorg .08 .04 .01
☐ 672 Juan Berenguer .08 .04 .01
☐ 673 Buck Martinez .08 .04 .01
☐ 674 Atlee Hammaker .08 .04 .01
☐ 675 Tony Perez .15 .07 .02
☐ 676 Albert Hall .08 .04 .01
☐ 677 Wally Backman .08 .04 .01
☐ 678 Joey McLaughlin .08 .04 .01
☐ 679 Bob Kearney .08 .04 .01
☐ 680 Jerry Reuss .08 .04 .01
☐ 681 Ben Oglivie .08 .04 .01
☐ 682 Doug Corbett .08 .04 .01
☐ 683 Whitey Herzog MG .12 .05 .02
(Checklist back)
☐ 684 Bill Doran .08 .04 .01
☐ 685 Bill Caudill .08 .04 .01
☐ 686 Mike Easler .08 .04 .01
☐ 687 Bill Gullickson .10 .05 .01
☐ 688 Len Matuszek .08 .04 .01
☐ 689 Luis DeLeon .08 .04 .01
☐ 690 Alan Trammell .30 .14 .04
☐ 691 Dennis Rasmussen .08 .04 .01
☐ 692 Randy Bush .08 .04 .01
☐ 693 Tim Stoddard .08 .04 .01
☐ 694 Joe Carter 5.00 2.30 .60
☐ 695 Rick Rhoden .08 .04 .01
☐ 696 John Rabb .08 .04 .01
☐ 697 Onix Concepcion .08 .04 .01
☐ 698 George Bell .15 .07 .02
☐ 699 Donnie Moore .08 .04 .01
☐ 700 Eddie Murray .75 .35 .09
☐ 701 Eddie Murray AS .35 .16 .04
☐ 702 Damaso Garcia AS .10 .05 .01
☐ 703 George Brett AS .75 .35 .09
☐ 704 Cal Ripken AS 1.50 .65 .19
☐ 705 Dave Winfield AS .35 .16 .04
☐ 706 Rickey Henderson AS .35 .16 .04
☐ 707 Tony Armas AS .10 .05 .01
☐ 708 Lance Parrish AS .10 .05 .01
☐ 709 Mike Boddicker AS .10 .05 .01
☐ 710 Frank Viola AS .10 .05 .01
☐ 711 Dan Quisenberry AS .10 .05 .01
☐ 712 Keith Hernandez AS .10 .05 .01
☐ 713 Ryne Sandberg AS .75 .35 .09
☐ 714 Mike Schmidt AS .35 .16 .04
☐ 715 Ozzie Smith AS .50 .23 .06
☐ 716 Dale Murphy AS .15 .07 .02
☐ 717 Tony Gwynn AS .75 .35 .09
☐ 718 Jeff Leonard AS .10 .05 .01
☐ 719 Gary Carter AS .15 .07 .02
☐ 720 Rick Sutcliffe AS .10 .05 .01
☐ 721 Bob Knepper AS .10 .05 .01
☐ 722 Bruce Sutter AS .10 .05 .01
☐ 723 Dave Stewart .15 .07 .02
☐ 724 Oscar Gamble .08 .04 .01
☐ 725 Floyd Bannister .08 .04 .01

☐	726 Al Bumbry	.10	.05	.01
☐	727 Frank Pastore	.08	.04	.01
☐	728 Bob Bailor	.08	.04	.01
☐	729 Don Sutton	.15	.07	.02
☐	730 Dave Kingman	.10	.05	.01
☐	731 Neil Allen	.08	.04	.01
☐	732 John McNamara MG (Checklist back)	.10	.05	.01
☐	733 Tony Scott	.08	.04	.01
☐	734 John Henry Johnson	.08	.04	.01
☐	735 Garry Templeton	.08	.04	.01
☐	736 Jerry Mumphrey	.08	.04	.01
☐	737 Bo Diaz	.08	.04	.01
☐	738 Omar Moreno	.08	.04	.01
☐	739 Ernie Camacho	.08	.04	.01
☐	740 Jack Clark	.10	.05	.01
☐	741 John Butcher	.08	.04	.01
☐	742 Ron Hassey	.08	.04	.01
☐	743 Frank White	.10	.05	.01
☐	744 Doug Bair	.08	.04	.01
☐	745 Buddy Bell	.10	.05	.01
☐	746 Jim Clancy	.08	.04	.01
☐	747 Alex Trevino	.08	.04	.01
☐	748 Lee Mazzilli	.08	.04	.01
☐	749 Julio Cruz	.08	.04	.01
☐	750 Rollie Fingers	.15	.07	.02
☐	751 Kelvin Chapman	.08	.04	.01
☐	752 Bob Owchinko	.08	.04	.01
☐	753 Greg Brock	.08	.04	.01
☐	754 Larry Milbourne	.08	.04	.01
☐	755 Ken Singleton	.10	.05	.01
☐	756 Rob Picciolo	.08	.04	.01
☐	757 Willie McGee	.10	.05	.01
☐	758 Ray Burris	.08	.04	.01
☐	759 Jim Fanning MG (Checklist back)	.10	.05	.01
☐	760 Nolan Ryan	4.00	1.80	.50
☐	761 Jerry Remy	.08	.04	.01
☐	762 Eddie Whitson	.08	.04	.01
☐	763 Kiko Garcia	.08	.04	.01
☐	764 Jamie Easterly	.08	.04	.01
☐	765 Willie Randolph	.10	.05	.01
☐	766 Paul Mirabella	.08	.04	.01
☐	767 Darrell Brown	.08	.04	.01
☐	768 Ron Cey	.10	.05	.01
☐	769 Joe Cowley	.08	.04	.01
☐	770 Carlton Fisk	.60	.25	.08
☐	771 Geoff Zahn	.08	.04	.01
☐	772 Johnnie LeMaster	.08	.04	.01
☐	773 Hal McRae	.15	.07	.02
☐	774 Dennis Lamp	.08	.04	.01
☐	775 Mookie Wilson	.10	.05	.01
☐	776 Jerry Royster	.08	.04	.01
☐	777 Ned Yost	.08	.04	.01
☐	778 Mike Davis	.08	.04	.01
☐	779 Nick Esasky	.08	.04	.01
☐	780 Mike Flanagan	.08	.04	.01
☐	781 Jim Gantner	.08	.04	.01
☐	782 Tom Niedenfuer	.08	.04	.01
☐	783 Mike Jorgensen	.08	.04	.01
☐	784 Checklist: 661-792	.12	.03	.01
☐	785 Tony Armas	.08	.04	.01
☐	786 Enos Cabell	.08	.04	.01
☐	787 Jim Wohlford	.08	.04	.01
☐	788 Steve Comer	.08	.04	.01
☐	789 Luis Salazar	.08	.04	.01
☐	790 Ron Guidry	.10	.05	.01
☐	791 Ivan DeJesus	.08	.04	.01
☐	792 Darrell Evans	.10	.05	.01

1985 Topps Traded

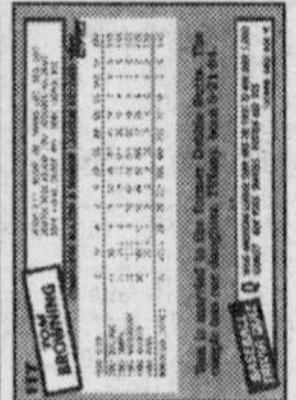

The cards in this 132-card set measure 2 1/2" by 3 1/2". In its now standard procedure, Topps issued its Traded (or extended) set for the fifth year in a row. Topps did however test on a limited basis the issuance of these Traded cards in wax packs. Because all photos and statistics of its regular set for the year were developed during the fall and winter months of the preceding year, players who changed teams during the fall, winter, and spring months are portrayed in the 1985 regular issue set with the teams they were with in 1984. The Traded set updates the shortcomings of the regular set by presenting the players with their proper teams for the current year. Most of 1985's top rookies not contained in the regular set are picked up in the Traded set. The key (extended) Rookie Cards in this set are Vince Coleman, Mariano Duncan, Ozzie Guillen, and Mickey Tettleton. Again this year, the Topps affiliate in Ireland printed the cards, and the cards were available through hobby channels only. Topps also produced a specially boxed "glossy" edition, frequently referred to as the Topps Traded Tiffany set. There were supposedly only 8,000 sets of the Tiffany cards produced; they were marketed to hobby dealers. The checklist of cards is identical to that of the normal non-glossy cards. There are two primary distinguishing features of the Tiffany cards, white card stock reverses and high gloss obverses. These Tiffany cards are valued from approximately five to ten times the values listed below. The set numbering is in alphabetical order by player's name.

		NRMT-MT	EXC	G-VG
	COMPLETE FACT.SET (132)	18.00	8.00	2.30
	COMMON CARD (1T-132T)	.15	.07	.02
☐	1T Don Aase	.15	.07	.02
☐	2T Bill Almon	.15	.07	.02
☐	3T Benny Ayala	.15	.07	.02
☐	4T Dusty Baker	.25	.11	.03
☐	5T George Bamberger MG	.15	.07	.02
☐	6T Dale Berra	.15	.07	.02
☐	7T Rich Bordi	.15	.07	.02
☐	8T Daryl Boston	.30	.14	.04
☐	9T Hubie Brooks	.20	.09	.03
☐	10T Chris Brown	.15	.07	.02
☐	11T Tom Browning	.50	.23	.06

☐ 12T	Al Bumbry	.15	.07	.02
☐ 13T	Ray Burris	.15	.07	.02
☐ 14T	Jeff Burroughs	.15	.07	.02
☐ 15T	Bill Campbell	.15	.07	.02
☐ 16T	Don Carman	.15	.07	.02
☐ 17T	Gary Carter	.35	.16	.04
☐ 18T	Bobby Castillo	.15	.07	.02
☐ 19T	Bill Caudill	.15	.07	.02
☐ 20T	Rick Cerone	.15	.07	.02
☐ 21T	Bryan Clark	.15	.07	.02
☐ 22T	Jack Clark	.20	.09	.03
☐ 23T	Pat Clements	.15	.07	.02
☐ 24T	Vince Coleman	1.00	.45	.13
☐ 25T	Dave Collins	.15	.07	.02
☐ 26T	Danny Darwin	.15	.07	.02
☐ 27T	Jim Davenport MG	.15	.07	.02
☐ 28T	Jerry Davis	.15	.07	.02
☐ 29T	Brian Dayett	.15	.07	.02
☐ 30T	Ivan DeJesus	.15	.07	.02
☐ 31T	Ken Dixon	.15	.07	.02
☐ 32T	Mariano Duncan	1.00	.45	.13
☐ 33T	John Felske MG	.15	.07	.02
☐ 34T	Mike Fitzgerald	.15	.07	.02
☐ 35T	Ray Fontenot	.15	.07	.02
☐ 36T	Greg Gagne	.40	.18	.05
☐ 37T	Oscar Gamble	.15	.07	.02
☐ 38T	Scott Garrelts	.15	.07	.02
☐ 39T	Bob L. Gibson	.15	.07	.02
☐ 40T	Jim Gott	.15	.07	.02
☐ 41T	David Green	.15	.07	.02
☐ 42T	Alfredo Griffin	.15	.07	.02
☐ 43T	Ozzie Guillen	2.00	.90	.25
☐ 44T	Eddie Haas MG	.15	.07	.02
☐ 45T	Terry Harper	.15	.07	.02
☐ 46T	Toby Harrah	.15	.07	.02
☐ 47T	Greg Harris	.15	.07	.02
☐ 48T	Ron Hassey	.15	.07	.02
☐ 49T	Rickey Henderson	2.50	1.15	.30
☐ 50T	Steve Henderson	.15	.07	.02
☐ 51T	George Hendrick	.15	.07	.02
☐ 52T	Joe Hesketh	.15	.07	.02
☐ 53T	Teddy Higuera	.25	.11	.03
☐ 54T	Donnie Hill	.15	.07	.02
☐ 55T	Al Holland	.15	.07	.02
☐ 56T	Burt Hooton	.15	.07	.02
☐ 57T	Jay Howell	.15	.07	.02
☐ 58T	Ken Howell	.15	.07	.02
☐ 59T	LaMarr Hoyt	.15	.07	.02
☐ 60T	Tim Hulett	.30	.14	.04
☐ 61T	Bob James	.15	.07	.02
☐ 62T	Steve Jeltz	.15	.07	.02
☐ 63T	Cliff Johnson	.15	.07	.02
☐ 64T	Howard Johnson	.40	.18	.05
☐ 65T	Ruppert Jones	.15	.07	.02
☐ 66T	Steve Kemp	.15	.07	.02
☐ 67T	Bruce Kison	.15	.07	.02
☐ 68T	Alan Knicely	.15	.07	.02
☐ 69T	Mike LaCoss	.15	.07	.02
☐ 70T	Lee Lacy	.15	.07	.02
☐ 71T	Dave LaPoint	.15	.07	.02
☐ 72T	Gary Lavelle	.15	.07	.02
☐ 73T	Vance Law	.15	.07	.02
☐ 74T	Johnnie LeMaster	.15	.07	.02
☐ 75T	Sixto Lezcano	.15	.07	.02
☐ 76T	Tim Lollar	.15	.07	.02
☐ 77T	Fred Lynn	.20	.09	.03
☐ 78T	Billy Martin MG	.20	.09	.03
☐ 79T	Ron Mathis	.15	.07	.02
☐ 80T	Len Matuszek	.15	.07	.02
☐ 81T	Gene Mauch MG	.15	.07	.02
☐ 82T	Oddibe McDowell	.15	.07	.02
☐ 83T	Roger McDowell	.40	.18	.05
☐ 84T	John McNamara MG	.15	.07	.02
☐ 85T	Donnie Moore	.15	.07	.02
☐ 86T	Gene Nelson	.15	.07	.02
☐ 87T	Steve Nicosia	.15	.07	.02
☐ 88T	Al Oliver	.20	.09	.03
☐ 89T	Joe Orsulak	.50	.23	.06
☐ 90T	Rob Picciolo	.15	.07	.02
☐ 91T	Chris Pittaro	.15	.07	.02
☐ 92T	Jim Presley	.15	.07	.02
☐ 93T	Rick Reuschel	.20	.09	.03
☐ 94T	Bert Roberge	.15	.07	.02
☐ 95T	Bob Rodgers MG	.15	.07	.02
☐ 96T	Jerry Royster	.15	.07	.02
☐ 97T	Dave Rozema	.15	.07	.02
☐ 98T	Dave Rucker	.15	.07	.02
☐ 99T	Vern Ruhle	.15	.07	.02
☐ 100T	Paul Runge	.15	.07	.02
☐ 101T	Mark Salas	.15	.07	.02
☐ 102T	Luis Salazar	.15	.07	.02
☐ 103T	Joe Sambito	.15	.07	.02
☐ 104T	Rick Schu	.15	.07	.02
☐ 105T	Donnie Scott	.15	.07	.02
☐ 106T	Larry Sheets	.15	.07	.02
☐ 107T	Don Slaught	.15	.07	.02
☐ 108T	Roy Smalley	.15	.07	.02
☐ 109T	Lonnie Smith	.15	.07	.02
☐ 110T	Nate Snell UER (Headings on back for a batter)	.15	.07	.02
☐ 111T	Chris Speier	.15	.07	.02
☐ 112T	Mike Stenhouse	.15	.07	.02
☐ 113T	Tim Stoddard	.15	.07	.02
☐ 114T	Jim Sundberg	.20	.09	.03
☐ 115T	Bruce Sutter	.15	.07	.02
☐ 116T	Don Sutton	.25	.11	.03
☐ 117T	Kent Tekulve	.15	.07	.02
☐ 118T	Tom Tellmann	.15	.07	.02
☐ 119T	Walt Terrell	.15	.07	.02
☐ 120T	Mickey Tettleton	5.00	2.30	.60
☐ 121T	Derrel Thomas	.15	.07	.02
☐ 122T	Rich Thompson	.15	.07	.02
☐ 123T	Alex Trevino	.15	.07	.02
☐ 124T	John Tudor	.20	.09	.03
☐ 125T	Jose Uribe	.15	.07	.02
☐ 126T	Bobby Valentine MG	.15	.07	.02
☐ 127T	Dave Von Ohlen	.15	.07	.02
☐ 128T	U.L. Washington	.15	.07	.02
☐ 129T	Earl Weaver MG	.20	.09	.03
☐ 130T	Eddie Whitson	.15	.07	.02
☐ 131T	Herm Winningham	.15	.07	.02
☐ 132T	Checklist 1-132	.15	.07	.02

1986 Topps

The cards in this 792-card set are standard-size (2 1/2" by 3 1/2"). The first seven cards

are a tribute to Pete Rose and his career. Card numbers 2-7 show small photos of Pete's Topps cards of the given years on the front with biographical information pertaining to those years on the back. The team leader cards were done differently with a simple player action shot on a white background; the player pictured is dubbed the "Dean" of that team, i.e., the player with the longest continuous service with that team. Topps again features a "Turn Back the Clock" series (401-405). Record breakers of the previous year are acknowledged on card numbers 201 to 207. Card numbers 701-722 feature All-Star selections from each league. Manager cards feature the team checklist on the reverse. Ryne Sandberg (690) is the only player card in the set without a Topps logo on the front of the card; this omission was never corrected by Topps. There are two other uncorrected errors involving misnumbered cards; see card numbers 51, 57, 141, and 171 in the checklist below. The backs of all the cards have a distinctive red background. The key Rookie Cards in this set are Vince Coleman, Darren Daulton, Len Dykstra, Cecil Fielder, and Mickey Tettleton. Topps also produced a specially boxed "glossy" edition, frequently referred to as the Topps Tiffany set. There were supposedly only 5,000 sets of the Tiffany cards produced; they were marketed to hobby dealers. The checklist of cards (792 regular and 132 Traded) is identical to that of the normal non-glossy cards. There are two primary distinguishing features of the Tiffany cards, white card stock reverses and high gloss obverses. These Tiffany cards are valued approximately from five to ten times the values listed below.

	MINT	EXC	G-VG
COMPLETE SET (792)	28.00	12.50	3.50
COMPLETE FACT.SET (792)	30.00	13.50	3.80
COMMON CARD (1-792)	.06	.03	.01

	Card	MINT	EXC	G-VG
☐ 1	Pete Rose	1.00	.25	.08
☐ 2	Rose Special: '63-'66	.30	.14	.04
☐ 3	Rose Special: '67-'70	.30	.14	.04
☐ 4	Rose Special: '71-'74	.30	.14	.04
☐ 5	Rose Special: '75-'78	.30	.14	.04
☐ 6	Rose Special: '79-'82	.30	.14	.04
☐ 7	Rose Special: '83-'85	.30	.14	.04
☐ 8	Dwayne Murphy	.06	.03	.01
☐ 9	Roy Smith	.06	.03	.01
☐ 10	Tony Gwynn	1.00	.45	.13
☐ 11	Bob Ojeda	.10	.05	.01
☐ 12	Jose Uribe	.06	.03	.01
☐ 13	Bob Kearney	.06	.03	.01
☐ 14	Julio Cruz	.06	.03	.01
☐ 15	Eddie Whitson	.06	.03	.01
☐ 16	Rick Schu	.06	.03	.01
☐ 17	Mike Stenhouse	.06	.03	.01
☐ 18	Brent Gaff	.06	.03	.01
☐ 19	Rich Hebner	.06	.03	.01
☐ 20	Lou Whitaker	.15	.07	.02
☐ 21	George Bamberger MG (Checklist back)	.08	.04	.01
☐ 22	Duane Walker	.06	.03	.01
☐ 23	Manny Lee	.06	.03	.01
☐ 24	Len Barker	.06	.03	.01
☐ 25	Willie Wilson	.06	.03	.01
☐ 26	Frank DiPino	.06	.03	.01
☐ 27	Ray Knight	.10	.05	.01
☐ 28	Eric Davis	.20	.09	.03
☐ 29	Tony Phillips	.10	.05	.01
☐ 30	Eddie Murray	.40	.18	.05
☐ 31	Jamie Easterly	.06	.03	.01
☐ 32	Steve Yeager	.06	.03	.01
☐ 33	Jeff Lahti	.06	.03	.01
☐ 34	Ken Phelps	.06	.03	.01
☐ 35	Jeff Reardon	.15	.07	.02
☐ 36	Tigers Leaders Lance Parrish	.08	.04	.01
☐ 37	Mark Thurmond	.06	.03	.01
☐ 38	Glenn Hoffman	.06	.03	.01
☐ 39	Dave Rucker	.06	.03	.01
☐ 40	Ken Griffey	.10	.05	.01
☐ 41	Brad Wellman	.06	.03	.01
☐ 42	Geoff Zahn	.06	.03	.01
☐ 43	Dave Engle	.06	.03	.01
☐ 44	Lance McCullers	.06	.03	.01
☐ 45	Damaso Garcia	.06	.03	.01
☐ 46	Billy Hatcher	.10	.05	.01
☐ 47	Juan Berenguer	.06	.03	.01
☐ 48	Bill Almon	.06	.03	.01
☐ 49	Rick Manning	.06	.03	.01
☐ 50	Dan Quisenberry	.10	.05	.01
☐ 51	Bobby Wine MG ERR (Checklist back) (Number of card on back is actually 57)	.08	.04	.01
☐ 52	Chris Welsh	.06	.03	.01
☐ 53	Len Dykstra	1.50	.65	.19
☐ 54	John Franco	.10	.05	.01
☐ 55	Fred Lynn	.10	.05	.01
☐ 56	Tom Niedenfuer	.06	.03	.01
☐ 57	Bill Doran (See also 51)	.06	.03	.01
☐ 58	Bill Krueger	.06	.03	.01
☐ 59	Andre Thornton	.06	.03	.01
☐ 60	Dwight Evans	.10	.05	.01
☐ 61	Karl Best	.06	.03	.01
☐ 62	Bob Boone	.10	.05	.01
☐ 63	Ron Roenicke	.06	.03	.01
☐ 64	Floyd Bannister	.06	.03	.01
☐ 65	Dan Driessen	.06	.03	.01
☐ 66	Cardinals Leaders Bob Forsch	.08	.04	.01
☐ 67	Carmelo Martinez	.06	.03	.01
☐ 68	Ed Lynch	.06	.03	.01
☐ 69	Luis Aguayo	.06	.03	.01
☐ 70	Dave Winfield	.40	.18	.05
☐ 71	Ken Schrom	.06	.03	.01
☐ 72	Shawon Dunston	.10	.05	.01
☐ 73	Randy O'Neal	.06	.03	.01
☐ 74	Rance Mulliniks	.06	.03	.01
☐ 75	Jose DeLeon	.06	.03	.01
☐ 76	Dion James	.06	.03	.01
☐ 77	Charlie Leibrandt	.06	.03	.01
☐ 78	Bruce Benedict	.06	.03	.01
☐ 79	Dave Schmidt	.06	.03	.01
☐ 80	Darryl Strawberry	.25	.11	.03
☐ 81	Gene Mauch MG (Checklist back)	.08	.04	.01
☐ 82	Tippy Martinez	.06	.03	.01
☐ 83	Phil Garner	.10	.05	.01
☐ 84	Curt Young	.06	.03	.01
☐ 85	Tony Perez (Eric Davis also shown on card)	.15	.07	.02
☐ 86	Tom Waddell	.06	.03	.01
☐ 87	Candy Maldonado	.06	.03	.01
☐ 88	Tom Nieto	.06	.03	.01
☐ 89	Randy St.Claire	.06	.03	.01

90	Garry Templeton	.06	.03	.01
91	Steve Crawford	.06	.03	.01
92	Al Cowens	.06	.03	.01
93	Scot Thompson	.06	.03	.01
94	Rich Bordi	.06	.03	.01
95	Ozzie Virgil	.06	.03	.01
96	Blue Jays Leaders	.08	.04	.01
	Jim Clancy			
97	Gary Gaetti	.06	.03	.01
98	Dick Ruthven	.06	.03	.01
99	Buddy Biancalana	.06	.03	.01
100	Nolan Ryan	2.50	1.15	.30
101	Dave Bergman	.06	.03	.01
102	Joe Orsulak	.15	.07	.02
103	Luis Salazar	.06	.03	.01
104	Sid Fernandez	.10	.05	.01
105	Gary Ward	.06	.03	.01
106	Ray Burris	.06	.03	.01
107	Rafael Ramirez	.06	.03	.01
108	Ted Power	.06	.03	.01
109	Len Matuszek	.06	.03	.01
110	Scott McGregor	.06	.03	.01
111	Roger Craig MG	.08	.04	.01
	(Checklist back)			
112	Bill Campbell	.06	.03	.01
113	U.L. Washington	.06	.03	.01
114	Mike C. Brown	.06	.03	.01
115	Jay Howell	.06	.03	.01
116	Brook Jacoby	.06	.03	.01
117	Bruce Kison	.06	.03	.01
118	Jerry Royster	.06	.03	.01
119	Barry Bonnell	.06	.03	.01
120	Steve Carlton	.40	.18	.05
121	Nelson Simmons	.06	.03	.01
122	Pete Filson	.06	.03	.01
123	Greg Walker	.06	.03	.01
124	Luis Sanchez	.06	.03	.01
125	Dave Lopes	.10	.05	.01
126	Mets Leaders	.08	.04	.01
	Mookie Wilson			
127	Jack Howell	.06	.03	.01
128	John Wathan	.06	.03	.01
129	Jeff Dedmon	.06	.03	.01
130	Alan Trammell	.15	.07	.02
131	Checklist: 1-132	.10	.03	.01
132	Razor Shines	.06	.03	.01
133	Andy McGaffigan	.06	.03	.01
134	Carney Lansford	.10	.05	.01
135	Joe Niekro	.10	.05	.01
136	Mike Hargrove	.10	.05	.01
137	Charlie Moore	.06	.03	.01
138	Mark Davis	.06	.03	.01
139	Daryl Boston	.06	.03	.01
140	John Candelaria	.06	.03	.01
141	Chuck Cottier MG	.08	.04	.01
	(Checklist back)			
	(See also 171)			
142	Bob Jones	.06	.03	.01
143	Dave Van Gorder	.06	.03	.01
144	Doug Sisk	.06	.03	.01
145	Pedro Guerrero	.10	.05	.01
146	Jack Perconte	.06	.03	.01
147	Larry Sheets	.06	.03	.01
148	Mike Heath	.06	.03	.01
149	Brett Butler	.10	.05	.01
150	Joaquin Andujar	.06	.03	.01
151	Dave Stapleton	.06	.03	.01
152	Mike Morgan	.06	.03	.01
153	Ricky Adams	.06	.03	.01
154	Bert Roberge	.06	.03	.01
155	Bob Grich	.10	.05	.01
156	White Sox Leaders	.08	.04	.01
	Richard Dotson			

157	Ron Hassey	.06	.03	.01
158	Derrel Thomas	.06	.03	.01
159	Orel Hershiser UER	.20	.09	.03
	(82 Alburquerque)			
160	Chet Lemon	.06	.03	.01
161	Lee Tunnell	.06	.03	.01
162	Greg Gagne	.10	.05	.01
163	Pete Ladd	.06	.03	.01
164	Steve Balboni	.06	.03	.01
165	Mike Davis	.06	.03	.01
166	Dickie Thon	.06	.03	.01
167	Zane Smith	.06	.03	.01
168	Jeff Burroughs	.06	.03	.01
169	George Wright	.06	.03	.01
170	Gary Carter	.15	.07	.02
171	Bob Rodgers MG ERR	.08	.04	.01
	(Checklist back)			
	(Number of card on back actually 141)			
172	Jerry Reed	.06	.03	.01
173	Wayne Gross	.06	.03	.01
174	Brian Snyder	.06	.03	.01
175	Steve Sax	.06	.03	.01
176	Jay Tibbs	.06	.03	.01
177	Joel Youngblood	.06	.03	.01
178	Ivan DeJesus	.06	.03	.01
179	Stu Cliburn	.06	.03	.01
180	Don Mattingly	1.00	.45	.13
181	Al Nipper	.06	.03	.01
182	Bobby Brown	.06	.03	.01
183	Larry Andersen	.06	.03	.01
184	Tim Laudner	.06	.03	.01
185	Rollie Fingers	.15	.07	.02
186	Astros Leaders	.08	.04	.01
	Jose Cruz			
187	Scott Fletcher	.06	.03	.01
188	Bob Dernier	.06	.03	.01
189	Mike Mason	.06	.03	.01
190	George Hendrick	.06	.03	.01
191	Wally Backman	.06	.03	.01
192	Milt Wilcox	.06	.03	.01
193	Daryl Sconiers	.06	.03	.01
194	Craig McMurtry	.06	.03	.01
195	Dave Concepcion	.10	.05	.01
196	Doyle Alexander	.06	.03	.01
197	Enos Cabell	.06	.03	.01
198	Ken Dixon	.06	.03	.01
199	Dick Howser MG	.08	.04	.01
	(Checklist back)			
200	Mike Schmidt	.40	.18	.05
201	Vince Coleman RB	.12	.05	.02
	Most stolen bases, season, rookie			
202	Dwight Gooden RB	.12	.05	.02
	Youngest 20 game winner			
203	Keith Hernandez RB	.08	.04	.01
	Most game-winning RBI's			
204	Phil Niekro RB	.12	.05	.02
	Oldest shutout pitcher			
205	Tony Perez RB	.12	.05	.02
	Oldest grand slammer			
206	Pete Rose RB	.35	.16	.04
	Most hits, lifetime			
207	Fernando Valenzuela RB	.08	.04	.01
	Most cons. innings, start of season, no earned runs			
208	Ramon Romero	.06	.03	.01
209	Randy Ready	.06	.03	.01
210	Calvin Schiraldi	.06	.03	.01
211	Ed Wojna	.06	.03	.01

☐ 212	Chris Speier	.06	.03	.01
☐ 213	Bob Shirley	.06	.03	.01
☐ 214	Randy Bush	.06	.03	.01
☐ 215	Frank White	.10	.05	.01
☐ 216	A's Leaders Dwayne Murphy	.08	.04	.01
☐ 217	Bill Scherrer	.06	.03	.01
☐ 218	Randy Hunt	.06	.03	.01
☐ 219	Dennis Lamp	.06	.03	.01
☐ 220	Bob Horner	.06	.03	.01
☐ 221	Dave Henderson	.10	.05	.01
☐ 222	Craig Gerber	.06	.03	.01
☐ 223	Atlee Hammaker	.06	.03	.01
☐ 224	Cesar Cedeno	.10	.05	.01
☐ 225	Ron Darling	.10	.05	.01
☐ 226	Lee Lacy	.06	.03	.01
☐ 227	Al Jones	.06	.03	.01
☐ 228	Tom Lawless	.06	.03	.01
☐ 229	Bill Gullickson	.10	.05	.01
☐ 230	Terry Kennedy	.06	.03	.01
☐ 231	Jim Frey MG (Checklist back)	.08	.04	.01
☐ 232	Rick Rhoden	.06	.03	.01
☐ 233	Steve Lyons	.06	.03	.01
☐ 234	Doug Corbett	.06	.03	.01
☐ 235	Butch Wynegar	.06	.03	.01
☐ 236	Frank Eufemia	.06	.03	.01
☐ 237	Ted Simmons	.10	.05	.01
☐ 238	Larry Parrish	.06	.03	.01
☐ 239	Joel Skinner	.06	.03	.01
☐ 240	Tommy John	.15	.07	.02
☐ 241	Tony Fernandez	.10	.05	.01
☐ 242	Rich Thompson	.06	.03	.01
☐ 243	Johnny Grubb	.06	.03	.01
☐ 244	Craig Lefferts	.06	.03	.01
☐ 245	Jim Sundberg	.06	.03	.01
☐ 246	Phillies Leaders Steve Carlton	.12	.05	.02
☐ 247	Terry Harper	.06	.03	.01
☐ 248	Spike Owen	.06	.03	.01
☐ 249	Rob Deer	.10	.05	.01
☐ 250	Dwight Gooden	.25	.11	.03
☐ 251	Rich Dauer	.06	.03	.01
☐ 252	Bobby Castillo	.06	.03	.01
☐ 253	Dann Bilardello	.06	.03	.01
☐ 254	Ozzie Guillen	.30	.14	.04
☐ 255	Tony Armas	.06	.03	.01
☐ 256	Kurt Kepshire	.06	.03	.01
☐ 257	Doug DeCinces	.06	.03	.01
☐ 258	Tim Burke	.06	.03	.01
☐ 259	Dan Pasqua	.06	.03	.01
☐ 260	Tony Pena	.06	.03	.01
☐ 261	Bobby Valentine MG (Checklist back)	.08	.04	.01
☐ 262	Mario Ramirez	.06	.03	.01
☐ 263	Checklist: 133-264	.10	.03	.01
☐ 264	Darren Daulton	1.50	.65	.19
☐ 265	Ron Davis	.06	.03	.01
☐ 266	Keith Moreland	.06	.03	.01
☐ 267	Paul Molitor	.60	.25	.08
☐ 268	Mike Scott	.06	.03	.01
☐ 269	Dane Iorg	.06	.03	.01
☐ 270	Jack Morris	.15	.07	.02
☐ 271	Dave Collins	.06	.03	.01
☐ 272	Tim Tolman	.06	.03	.01
☐ 273	Jerry Willard	.06	.03	.01
☐ 274	Ron Gardenhire	.06	.03	.01
☐ 275	Charlie Hough	.10	.05	.01
☐ 276	Yankees Leaders Willie Randolph	.08	.04	.01
☐ 277	Jaime Cocanower	.06	.03	.01
☐ 278	Sixto Lezcano	.06	.03	.01
☐ 279	Al Pardo	.06	.03	.01
☐ 280	Tim Raines	.15	.07	.02
☐ 281	Steve Mura	.06	.03	.01
☐ 282	Jerry Mumphrey	.06	.03	.01
☐ 283	Mike Fischlin	.06	.03	.01
☐ 284	Brian Dayett	.06	.03	.01
☐ 285	Buddy Bell	.10	.05	.01
☐ 286	Luis DeLeon	.06	.03	.01
☐ 287	John Christensen	.06	.03	.01
☐ 288	Don Aase	.06	.03	.01
☐ 289	Johnnie LeMaster	.06	.03	.01
☐ 290	Carlton Fisk	.40	.18	.05
☐ 291	Tom Lasorda MG (Checklist back)	.12	.05	.02
☐ 292	Chuck Porter	.06	.03	.01
☐ 293	Chris Chambliss	.10	.05	.01
☐ 294	Danny Cox	.06	.03	.01
☐ 295	Kirk Gibson	.10	.05	.01
☐ 296	Geno Petralli	.06	.03	.01
☐ 297	Tim Lollar	.06	.03	.01
☐ 298	Craig Reynolds	.06	.03	.01
☐ 299	Bryn Smith	.06	.03	.01
☐ 300	George Brett	1.00	.45	.13
☐ 301	Dennis Rasmussen	.06	.03	.01
☐ 302	Greg Gross	.06	.03	.01
☐ 303	Curt Wardle	.06	.03	.01
☐ 304	Mike Gallego	.15	.07	.02
☐ 305	Phil Bradley	.06	.03	.01
☐ 306	Padres Leaders Terry Kennedy	.08	.04	.01
☐ 307	Dave Sax	.06	.03	.01
☐ 308	Ray Fontenot	.06	.03	.01
☐ 309	John Shelby	.06	.03	.01
☐ 310	Greg Minton	.06	.03	.01
☐ 311	Dick Schofield	.06	.03	.01
☐ 312	Tom Filer	.06	.03	.01
☐ 313	Joe DeSa	.06	.03	.01
☐ 314	Frank Pastore	.06	.03	.01
☐ 315	Mookie Wilson	.10	.05	.01
☐ 316	Sammy Khalifa	.06	.03	.01
☐ 317	Ed Romero	.06	.03	.01
☐ 318	Terry Whitfield	.06	.03	.01
☐ 319	Rick Camp	.06	.03	.01
☐ 320	Jim Rice	.15	.07	.02
☐ 321	Earl Weaver MG (Checklist back)	.12	.05	.02
☐ 322	Bob Forsch	.06	.03	.01
☐ 323	Jerry Davis	.06	.03	.01
☐ 324	Dan Schatzeder	.06	.03	.01
☐ 325	Juan Beniquez	.06	.03	.01
☐ 326	Kent Tekulve	.06	.03	.01
☐ 327	Mike Pagliarulo	.06	.03	.01
☐ 328	Pete O'Brien	.06	.03	.01
☐ 329	Kirby Puckett	3.00	1.35	.40
☐ 330	Rick Sutcliffe	.10	.05	.01
☐ 331	Alan Ashby	.06	.03	.01
☐ 332	Darryl Motley	.06	.03	.01
☐ 333	Tom Henke	.10	.05	.01
☐ 334	Ken Oberkfell	.06	.03	.01
☐ 335	Don Sutton	.15	.07	.02
☐ 336	Indians Leaders Andre Thornton	.08	.04	.01
☐ 337	Darnell Coles	.06	.03	.01
☐ 338	George Bell	.10	.05	.01
☐ 339	Bruce Berenyi	.06	.03	.01
☐ 340	Cal Ripken	2.00	.90	.25
☐ 341	Frank Williams	.06	.03	.01
☐ 342	Gary Redus	.06	.03	.01
☐ 343	Carlos Diaz	.06	.03	.01
☐ 344	Jim Wohlford	.06	.03	.01
☐ 345	Donnie Moore	.06	.03	.01
☐ 346	Bryan Little	.06	.03	.01
☐ 347	Teddy Higuera	.10	.05	.01
☐ 348	Cliff Johnson	.06	.03	.01

	No.	Player			
☐	349	Mark Clear	.06	.03	.01
☐	350	Jack Clark	.10	.05	.01
☐	351	Chuck Tanner MG	.08	.04	.01
		(Checklist back)			
☐	352	Harry Spilman	.06	.03	.01
☐	353	Keith Atherton	.06	.03	.01
☐	354	Tony Bernazard	.06	.03	.01
☐	355	Lee Smith	.25	.11	.03
☐	356	Mickey Hatcher	.06	.03	.01
☐	357	Ed VandeBerg	.06	.03	.01
☐	358	Rick Dempsey	.06	.03	.01
☐	359	Mike LaCoss	.06	.03	.01
☐	360	Lloyd Moseby	.06	.03	.01
☐	361	Shane Rawley	.06	.03	.01
☐	362	Tom Paciorek	.10	.05	.01
☐	363	Terry Forster	.06	.03	.01
☐	364	Reid Nichols	.06	.03	.01
☐	365	Mike Flanagan	.06	.03	.01
☐	366	Reds Leaders	.08	.04	.01
		Dave Concepcion			
☐	367	Aurelio Lopez	.06	.03	.01
☐	368	Greg Brock	.06	.03	.01
☐	369	Al Holland	.06	.03	.01
☐	370	Vince Coleman	.25	.11	.03
☐	371	Bill Stein	.06	.03	.01
☐	372	Ben Oglivie	.06	.03	.01
☐	373	Urbano Lugo	.06	.03	.01
☐	374	Terry Francona	.06	.03	.01
☐	375	Rich Gedman	.06	.03	.01
☐	376	Bill Dawley	.06	.03	.01
☐	377	Joe Carter	1.50	.65	.19
☐	378	Bruce Bochte	.06	.03	.01
☐	379	Bobby Meacham	.06	.03	.01
☐	380	LaMarr Hoyt	.06	.03	.01
☐	381	Ray Miller MG	.08	.04	.01
		(Checklist back)			
☐	382	Ivan Calderon	.15	.07	.02
☐	383	Chris Brown	.06	.03	.01
☐	384	Steve Trout	.06	.03	.01
☐	385	Cecil Cooper	.10	.05	.01
☐	386	Cecil Fielder	4.00	1.80	.50
☐	387	Steve Kemp	.06	.03	.01
☐	388	Dickie Noles	.06	.03	.01
☐	389	Glenn Davis	.06	.03	.01
☐	390	Tom Seaver	.40	.18	.05
☐	391	Julio Franco	.20	.09	.03
☐	392	John Russell	.06	.03	.01
☐	393	Chris Pittaro	.06	.03	.01
☐	394	Checklist: 265-396	.10	.03	.01
☐	395	Scott Garrelts	.06	.03	.01
☐	396	Red Sox Leaders	.08	.04	.01
		Dwight Evans			
☐	397	Steve Buechele	.25	.11	.03
☐	398	Earnie Riles	.06	.03	.01
☐	399	Bill Swift	.25	.11	.03
☐	400	Rod Carew	.25	.11	.03
☐	401	Fernando Valenzuela	.08	.04	.01
		TBC '81			
☐	402	Tom Seaver TBC '76	.20	.09	.03
☐	403	Willie Mays TBC '71	.25	.11	.03
☐	404	Frank Robinson	.08	.04	.01
		TBC '66			
☐	405	Roger Maris TBC '61	.15	.07	.02
☐	406	Scott Sanderson	.06	.03	.01
☐	407	Sal Butera	.06	.03	.01
☐	408	Dave Smith	.06	.03	.01
☐	409	Paul Runge	.06	.03	.01
☐	410	Dave Kingman	.10	.05	.01
☐	411	Sparky Anderson MG	.12	.05	.02
		(Checklist back)			
☐	412	Jim Clancy	.06	.03	.01
☐	413	Tim Flannery	.06	.03	.01
☐	414	Tom Gorman	.06	.03	.01
☐	415	Hal McRae	.15	.07	.02
☐	416	Dennis Martinez	.10	.05	.01
☐	417	R.J. Reynolds	.06	.03	.01
☐	418	Alan Knicely	.06	.03	.01
☐	419	Frank Wills	.06	.03	.01
☐	420	Von Hayes	.06	.03	.01
☐	421	David Palmer	.06	.03	.01
☐	422	Mike Jorgensen	.06	.03	.01
☐	423	Dan Spillner	.06	.03	.01
☐	424	Rick Miller	.06	.03	.01
☐	425	Larry McWilliams	.06	.03	.01
☐	426	Brewers Leaders	.08	.04	.01
		Charlie Moore			
☐	427	Joe Cowley	.06	.03	.01
☐	428	Max Venable	.06	.03	.01
☐	429	Greg Booker	.06	.03	.01
☐	430	Kent Hrbek	.10	.05	.01
☐	431	George Frazier	.06	.03	.01
☐	432	Mark Bailey	.06	.03	.01
☐	433	Chris Codiroli	.06	.03	.01
☐	434	Curt Wilkerson	.06	.03	.01
☐	435	Bill Caudill	.06	.03	.01
☐	436	Doug Flynn	.06	.03	.01
☐	437	Rick Mahler	.06	.03	.01
☐	438	Clint Hurdle	.06	.03	.01
☐	439	Rick Honeycutt	.06	.03	.01
☐	440	Alvin Davis	.06	.03	.01
☐	441	Whitey Herzog MG	.12	.05	.02
		(Checklist back)			
☐	442	Ron Robinson	.06	.03	.01
☐	443	Bill Buckner	.10	.05	.01
☐	444	Alex Trevino	.06	.03	.01
☐	445	Bert Blyleven	.15	.07	.02
☐	446	Lenn Sakata	.06	.03	.01
☐	447	Jerry Don Gleaton	.06	.03	.01
☐	448	Herm Winningham	.06	.03	.01
☐	449	Rod Scurry	.06	.03	.01
☐	450	Graig Nettles	.10	.05	.01
☐	451	Mark Brown	.06	.03	.01
☐	452	Bob Clark	.06	.03	.01
☐	453	Steve Jeltz	.06	.03	.01
☐	454	Burt Hooton	.06	.03	.01
☐	455	Willie Randolph	.10	.05	.01
☐	456	Braves Leaders	.12	.05	.02
		Dale Murphy			
☐	457	Mickey Tettleton	1.00	.45	.13
☐	458	Kevin Bass	.06	.03	.01
☐	459	Luis Leal	.06	.03	.01
☐	460	Leon Durham	.06	.03	.01
☐	461	Walt Terrell	.06	.03	.01
☐	462	Domingo Ramos	.06	.03	.01
☐	463	Jim Gott	.06	.03	.01
☐	464	Ruppert Jones	.06	.03	.01
☐	465	Jesse Orosco	.06	.03	.01
☐	466	Tom Foley	.06	.03	.01
☐	467	Bob James	.06	.03	.01
☐	468	Mike Scioscia	.06	.03	.01
☐	469	Storm Davis	.06	.03	.01
☐	470	Bill Madlock	.10	.05	.01
☐	471	Bobby Cox MG	.08	.04	.01
		(Checklist back)			
☐	472	Joe Hesketh	.06	.03	.01
☐	473	Mark Brouhard	.06	.03	.01
☐	474	John Tudor	.10	.05	.01
☐	475	Juan Samuel	.06	.03	.01
☐	476	Ron Mathis	.06	.03	.01
☐	477	Mike Easler	.06	.03	.01
☐	478	Andy Hawkins	.06	.03	.01
☐	479	Bob Melvin	.06	.03	.01
☐	480	Oddibe McDowell	.06	.03	.01
☐	481	Scott Bradley	.06	.03	.01
☐	482	Rick Lysander	.06	.03	.01
☐	483	George Vukovich	.06	.03	.01

☐ 484 Donnie Hill .06 .03 .01
☐ 485 Gary Matthews .06 .03 .01
☐ 486 Angels Leaders .08 .04 .01
Bobby Grich
☐ 487 Bret Saberhagen .25 .11 .03
☐ 488 Lou Thornton .06 .03 .01
☐ 489 Jim Winn .06 .03 .01
☐ 490 Jeff Leonard .06 .03 .01
☐ 491 Pascual Perez .06 .03 .01
☐ 492 Kelvin Chapman .06 .03 .01
☐ 493 Gene Nelson .06 .03 .01
☐ 494 Gary Roenicke .06 .03 .01
☐ 495 Mark Langston .25 .11 .03
☐ 496 Jay Johnstone .10 .05 .01
☐ 497 John Stuper .06 .03 .01
☐ 498 Tito Landrum .06 .03 .01
☐ 499 Bob L. Gibson .06 .03 .01
☐ 500 Rickey Henderson .75 .35 .09
☐ 501 Dave Johnson MG .08 .04 .01
(Checklist back)
☐ 502 Glen Cook .06 .03 .01
☐ 503 Mike Fitzgerald .06 .03 .01
☐ 504 Denny Walling .06 .03 .01
☐ 505 Jerry Koosman .10 .05 .01
☐ 506 Bill Russell .10 .05 .01
☐ 507 Steve Ontiveros .06 .03 .01
☐ 508 Alan Wiggins .06 .03 .01
☐ 509 Ernie Camacho .06 .03 .01
☐ 510 Wade Boggs .75 .35 .09
☐ 511 Ed Nunez .06 .03 .01
☐ 512 Thad Bosley .06 .03 .01
☐ 513 Ron Washington .06 .03 .01
☐ 514 Mike Jones .06 .03 .01
☐ 515 Darrell Evans .10 .05 .01
☐ 516 Giants Leaders .08 .04 .01
Greg Minton
☐ 517 Milt Thompson .15 .07 .02
☐ 518 Buck Martinez .06 .03 .01
☐ 519 Danny Darwin .06 .03 .01
☐ 520 Keith Hernandez .15 .07 .02
☐ 521 Nate Snell .06 .03 .01
☐ 522 Bob Bailor .06 .03 .01
☐ 523 Joe Price .06 .03 .01
☐ 524 Darrell Miller .06 .03 .01
☐ 525 Marvell Wynne .06 .03 .01
☐ 526 Charlie Lea .06 .03 .01
☐ 527 Checklist: 397-528 .10 .03 .01
☐ 528 Terry Pendleton .40 .18 .05
☐ 529 Marc Sullivan .06 .03 .01
☐ 530 Rich Gossage .15 .07 .02
☐ 531 Tony LaRussa MG .12 .05 .02
(Checklist back)
☐ 532 Don Carman .06 .03 .01
☐ 533 Billy Sample .06 .03 .01
☐ 534 Jeff Calhoun .06 .03 .01
☐ 535 Toby Harrah .06 .03 .01
☐ 536 Jose Rijo .25 .11 .03
☐ 537 Mark Salas .06 .03 .01
☐ 538 Dennis Eckersley .20 .09 .03
☐ 539 Glenn Hubbard .06 .03 .01
☐ 540 Dan Petry .06 .03 .01
☐ 541 Jorge Orta .06 .03 .01
☐ 542 Don Schulze .06 .03 .01
☐ 543 Jerry Narron .06 .03 .01
☐ 544 Eddie Milner .06 .03 .01
☐ 545 Jimmy Key .30 .14 .04
☐ 546 Mariners Leaders .08 .04 .01
Dave Henderson
☐ 547 Roger McDowell .12 .05 .02
☐ 548 Mike Young .06 .03 .01
☐ 549 Bob Welch .10 .05 .01
☐ 550 Tom Herr .06 .03 .01
☐ 551 Dave LaPoint .06 .03 .01
☐ 552 Marc Hill .06 .03 .01
☐ 553 Jim Morrison .06 .03 .01
☐ 554 Paul Householder .06 .03 .01
☐ 555 Hubie Brooks .06 .03 .01
☐ 556 John Denny .06 .03 .01
☐ 557 Gerald Perry .06 .03 .01
☐ 558 Tim Stoddard .06 .03 .01
☐ 559 Tommy Dunbar .06 .03 .01
☐ 560 Dave Righetti .10 .05 .01
☐ 561 Bob Lillis MG .08 .04 .01
(Checklist back)
☐ 562 Joe Beckwith .06 .03 .01
☐ 563 Alejandro Sanchez .06 .03 .01
☐ 564 Warren Brusstar .06 .03 .01
☐ 565 Tom Brunansky .10 .05 .01
☐ 566 Alfredo Griffin .06 .03 .01
☐ 567 Jeff Barkley .06 .03 .01
☐ 568 Donnie Scott .06 .03 .01
☐ 569 Jim Acker .06 .03 .01
☐ 570 Rusty Staub .10 .05 .01
☐ 571 Mike Jeffcoat .06 .03 .01
☐ 572 Paul Zuvella .06 .03 .01
☐ 573 Tom Hume .06 .03 .01
☐ 574 Ron Kittle .06 .03 .01
☐ 575 Mike Boddicker .06 .03 .01
☐ 576 Expos Leaders .12 .05 .02
Andre Dawson
☐ 577 Jerry Reuss .06 .03 .01
☐ 578 Lee Mazzilli .06 .03 .01
☐ 579 Jim Slaton .06 .03 .01
☐ 580 Willie McGee .10 .05 .01
☐ 581 Bruce Hurst .10 .05 .01
☐ 582 Jim Gantner .06 .03 .01
☐ 583 Al Bumbry .06 .03 .01
☐ 584 Brian Fisher .06 .03 .01
☐ 585 Garry Maddox .06 .03 .01
☐ 586 Greg Harris .06 .03 .01
☐ 587 Rafael Santana .06 .03 .01
☐ 588 Steve Lake .06 .03 .01
☐ 589 Sid Bream .10 .05 .01
☐ 590 Bob Knepper .06 .03 .01
☐ 591 Jackie Moore MG .08 .04 .01
(Checklist back)
☐ 592 Frank Tanana .10 .05 .01
☐ 593 Jesse Barfield .06 .03 .01
☐ 594 Chris Bando .06 .03 .01
☐ 595 Dave Parker .15 .07 .02
☐ 596 Onix Concepcion .06 .03 .01
☐ 597 Sammy Stewart .06 .03 .01
☐ 598 Jim Presley .06 .03 .01
☐ 599 Rick Aguilera .50 .23 .06
☐ 600 Dale Murphy .15 .07 .02
☐ 601 Gary Lucas .06 .03 .01
☐ 602 Mariano Duncan .25 .11 .03
☐ 603 Bill Laskey .06 .03 .01
☐ 604 Gary Pettis .06 .03 .01
☐ 605 Dennis Boyd .06 .03 .01
☐ 606 Royals Leaders .12 .05 .02
Hal McRae
☐ 607 Ken Dayley .06 .03 .01
☐ 608 Bruce Bochy .06 .03 .01
☐ 609 Barbaro Garbey .06 .03 .01
☐ 610 Ron Guidry .10 .05 .01
☐ 611 Gary Woods .06 .03 .01
☐ 612 Richard Dotson .06 .03 .01
☐ 613 Roy Smalley .06 .03 .01
☐ 614 Rick Waits .06 .03 .01
☐ 615 Johnny Ray .06 .03 .01
☐ 616 Glenn Brummer .06 .03 .01
☐ 617 Lonnie Smith .06 .03 .01
☐ 618 Jim Pankovits .06 .03 .01
☐ 619 Danny Heep .06 .03 .01
☐ 620 Bruce Sutter .10 .05 .01

☐ 621 John Felske MG .... .08 .04 .01
(Checklist back)
☐ 622 Gary Lavelle .... .06 .03 .01
☐ 623 Floyd Rayford .... .06 .03 .01
☐ 624 Steve McCatty .... .06 .03 .01
☐ 625 Bob Brenly .... .06 .03 .01
☐ 626 Roy Thomas .... .06 .03 .01
☐ 627 Ron Oester .... .06 .03 .01
☐ 628 Kirk McCaskill .... .15 .07 .02
☐ 629 Mitch Webster .... .06 .03 .01
☐ 630 Fernando Valenzuela .... .10 .05 .01
☐ 631 Steve Braun .... .06 .03 .01
☐ 632 Dave Von Ohlen .... .06 .03 .01
☐ 633 Jackie Gutierrez .... .06 .03 .01
☐ 634 Roy Lee Jackson .... .06 .03 .01
☐ 635 Jason Thompson .... .06 .03 .01
☐ 636 Cubs Leaders .... .12 .05 .02
Lee Smith
☐ 637 Rudy Law .... .06 .03 .01
☐ 638 John Butcher .... .06 .03 .01
☐ 639 Bo Diaz .... .06 .03 .01
☐ 640 Jose Cruz .... .06 .03 .01
☐ 641 Wayne Tolleson .... .06 .03 .01
☐ 642 Ray Searage .... .06 .03 .01
☐ 643 Tom Brookens .... .06 .03 .01
☐ 644 Mark Gubicza .... .10 .05 .01
☐ 645 Dusty Baker .... .15 .07 .02
☐ 646 Mike Moore .... .06 .03 .01
☐ 647 Mel Hall .... .06 .03 .01
☐ 648 Steve Bedrosian .... .06 .03 .01
☐ 649 Ronn Reynolds .... .06 .03 .01
☐ 650 Dave Stieb .... .10 .05 .01
☐ 651 Billy Martin MG .... .12 .05 .02
(Checklist back)
☐ 652 Tom Browning .... .10 .05 .01
☐ 653 Jim Dwyer .... .06 .03 .01
☐ 654 Ken Howell .... .06 .03 .01
☐ 655 Manny Trillo .... .06 .03 .01
☐ 656 Brian Harper .... .10 .05 .01
☐ 657 Juan Agosto .... .06 .03 .01
☐ 658 Rob Wilfong .... .06 .03 .01
☐ 659 Checklist: 529-660 .... .10 .03 .01
☐ 660 Steve Garvey .... .15 .07 .02
☐ 661 Roger Clemens .... 2.50 1.15 .30
☐ 662 Bill Schroeder .... .06 .03 .01
☐ 663 Neil Allen .... .06 .03 .01
☐ 664 Tim Corcoran .... .06 .03 .01
☐ 665 Alejandro Pena .... .06 .03 .01
☐ 666 Rangers Leaders .... .08 .04 .01
Charlie Hough
☐ 667 Tim Teufel .... .06 .03 .01
☐ 668 Cecilio Guante .... .06 .03 .01
☐ 669 Ron Cey .... .10 .05 .01
☐ 670 Willie Hernandez .... .06 .03 .01
☐ 671 Lynn Jones .... .06 .03 .01
☐ 672 Rob Picciolo .... .06 .03 .01
☐ 673 Ernie Whitt .... .06 .03 .01
☐ 674 Pat Tabler .... .06 .03 .01
☐ 675 Claudell Washington .... .06 .03 .01
☐ 676 Matt Young .... .06 .03 .01
☐ 677 Nick Esasky .... .06 .03 .01
☐ 678 Dan Gladden .... .06 .03 .01
☐ 679 Britt Burns .... .06 .03 .01
☐ 680 George Foster .... .10 .05 .01
☐ 681 Dick Williams MG .... .08 .04 .01
(Checklist back)
☐ 682 Junior Ortiz .... .06 .03 .01
☐ 683 Andy Van Slyke .... .15 .07 .02
☐ 684 Bob McClure .... .06 .03 .01
☐ 685 Tim Wallach .... .10 .05 .01
☐ 686 Jeff Stone .... .06 .03 .01
☐ 687 Mike Trujillo .... .06 .03 .01
☐ 688 Larry Herndon .... .06 .03 .01
☐ 689 Dave Stewart .... .15 .07 .02
☐ 690 Ryne Sandberg UER .. 1.50 .65 .19
(No Topps logo
on front)
☐ 691 Mike Madden .... .06 .03 .01
☐ 692 Dale Berra .... .06 .03 .01
☐ 693 Tom Tellmann .... .06 .03 .01
☐ 694 Garth Iorg .... .06 .03 .01
☐ 695 Mike Smithson .... .06 .03 .01
☐ 696 Dodgers Leaders .... .08 .04 .01
Bill Russell
☐ 697 Bud Black .... .06 .03 .01
☐ 698 Brad Komminsk .... .06 .03 .01
☐ 699 Pat Corrales MG .... .08 .04 .01
(Checklist back)
☐ 700 Reggie Jackson .... .50 .23 .06
☐ 701 Keith Hernandez AS .... .12 .05 .02
☐ 702 Tom Herr AS .... .08 .04 .01
☐ 703 Tim Wallach AS .... .08 .04 .01
☐ 704 Ozzie Smith AS .... .20 .09 .03
☐ 705 Dale Murphy AS .... .12 .05 .02
☐ 706 Pedro Guerrero AS .... .08 .04 .01
☐ 707 Willie McGee AS .... .08 .04 .01
☐ 708 Gary Carter AS .... .12 .05 .02
☐ 709 Dwight Gooden AS .... .12 .05 .02
☐ 710 John Tudor AS .... .08 .04 .01
☐ 711 Jeff Reardon AS .... .12 .05 .02
☐ 712 Don Mattingly AS .... .50 .23 .06
☐ 713 Damaso Garcia AS .... .08 .04 .01
☐ 714 George Brett AS .... .40 .18 .05
☐ 715 Cal Ripken AS .... .75 .35 .09
☐ 716 Rickey Henderson AS .. .30 .14 .04
☐ 717 Dave Winfield AS .... .20 .09 .03
☐ 718 George Bell AS .... .08 .04 .01
☐ 719 Carlton Fisk AS .... .20 .09 .03
☐ 720 Bret Saberhagen AS .... .12 .05 .02
☐ 721 Ron Guidry AS .... .08 .04 .01
☐ 722 Dan Quisenberry AS .... .08 .04 .01
☐ 723 Marty Bystrom .... .06 .03 .01
☐ 724 Tim Hulett .... .06 .03 .01
☐ 725 Mario Soto .... .06 .03 .01
☐ 726 Orioles Leaders .... .08 .04 .01
Rick Dempsey
☐ 727 David Green .... .06 .03 .01
☐ 728 Mike Marshall .... .06 .03 .01
☐ 729 Jim Beattie .... .06 .03 .01
☐ 730 Ozzie Smith .... .50 .23 .06
☐ 731 Don Robinson .... .06 .03 .01
☐ 732 Floyd Youmans .... .06 .03 .01
☐ 733 Ron Romanick .... .06 .03 .01
☐ 734 Marty Barrett .... .06 .03 .01
☐ 735 Dave Dravecky .... .10 .05 .01
☐ 736 Glenn Wilson .... .06 .03 .01
☐ 737 Pete Vuckovich .... .06 .03 .01
☐ 738 Andre Robertson .... .06 .03 .01
☐ 739 Dave Rozema .... .06 .03 .01
☐ 740 Lance Parrish .... .10 .05 .01
☐ 741 Pete Rose MG .... .40 .18 .05
(Checklist back)
☐ 742 Frank Viola .... .10 .05 .01
☐ 743 Pat Sheridan .... .06 .03 .01
☐ 744 Lary Sorensen .... .06 .03 .01
☐ 745 Willie Upshaw .... .06 .03 .01
☐ 746 Denny Gonzalez .... .06 .03 .01
☐ 747 Rick Cerone .... .06 .03 .01
☐ 748 Steve Henderson .... .06 .03 .01
☐ 749 Ed Jurak .... .06 .03 .01
☐ 750 Gorman Thomas .... .06 .03 .01
☐ 751 Howard Johnson .... .10 .05 .01
☐ 752 Mike Krukow .... .06 .03 .01
☐ 753 Dan Ford .... .06 .03 .01
☐ 754 Pat Clements .... .06 .03 .01
☐ 755 Harold Baines .... .10 .05 .01

☐ 756	Pirates Leaders Rick Rhoden	.08	.04	.01
☐ 757	Darrell Porter	.06	.03	.01
☐ 758	Dave Anderson	.06	.03	.01
☐ 759	Moose Haas	.06	.03	.01
☐ 760	Andre Dawson	.35	.16	.04
☐ 761	Don Slaught	.06	.03	.01
☐ 762	Eric Show	.06	.03	.01
☐ 763	Terry Puhl	.06	.03	.01
☐ 764	Kevin Gross	.06	.03	.01
☐ 765	Don Baylor	.15	.07	.02
☐ 766	Rick Langford	.06	.03	.01
☐ 767	Jody Davis	.06	.03	.01
☐ 768	Vern Ruhle	.06	.03	.01
☐ 769	Harold Reynolds	.20	.09	.03
☐ 770	Vida Blue	.10	.05	.01
☐ 771	John McNamara MG (Checklist back)	.08	.04	.01
☐ 772	Brian Downing	.10	.05	.01
☐ 773	Greg Pryor	.06	.03	.01
☐ 774	Terry Leach	.06	.03	.01
☐ 775	Al Oliver	.10	.05	.01
☐ 776	Gene Garber	.06	.03	.01
☐ 777	Wayne Krenchicki	.06	.03	.01
☐ 778	Jerry Hairston	.06	.03	.01
☐ 779	Rick Reuschel	.06	.03	.01
☐ 780	Robin Yount	.40	.18	.05
☐ 781	Joe Nolan	.06	.03	.01
☐ 782	Ken Landreaux	.06	.03	.01
☐ 783	Ricky Horton	.06	.03	.01
☐ 784	Alan Bannister	.06	.03	.01
☐ 785	Bob Stanley	.06	.03	.01
☐ 786	Twins Leaders Mickey Hatcher	.08	.04	.01
☐ 787	Vance Law	.06	.03	.01
☐ 788	Marty Castillo	.06	.03	.01
☐ 789	Kurt Bevacqua	.06	.03	.01
☐ 790	Phil Niekro	.15	.07	.02
☐ 791	Checklist: 661-792	.10	.03	.01
☐ 792	Charles Hudson	.10	.04	.01

1986 Topps Traded

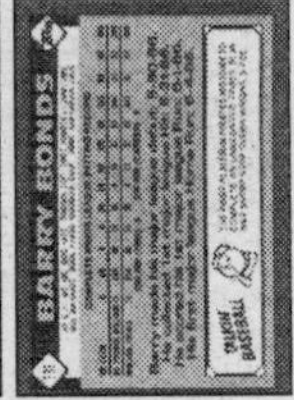

This 132-card Traded or extended set was distributed by Topps to dealers in a special red and white box as a complete set. The card fronts are identical in style to the Topps regular issue and are also 2 1/2" by 3 1/2". The backs are printed in red and black on white card stock. Cards are numbered (with a T suffix) alphabetically according to the name of the player. The key (extended) Rookie Cards in this set are Barry Bonds, Bobby Bonilla, Jose Canseco, Will Clark, Andres Galarraga, Bo Jackson, Wally Joyner, John Kruk, Kevin Mitchell, and Robby Thompson. Topps also produced a specially boxed "glossy" edition frequently referred to as the Topps Traded Tiffany set. There were supposedly only 5,000 sets of the Tiffany cards produced; they were marketed to hobby dealers. The checklist of cards is identical to that of the normal non-glossy cards. There are two primary distinguishing features of the Tiffany cards, white card stock reverses and high gloss obverses. These Tiffany cards are valued approximately from five to ten times the values listed below.

		MINT	EXC	G-VG
COMPLETE FACT.SET (132)		20.00	9.00	2.50
COMMON CARD (1T-132T)		.08	.04	.01
☐ 1T	Andy Allanson	.08	.04	.01
☐ 2T	Neil Allen	.08	.04	.01
☐ 3T	Joaquin Andujar	.08	.04	.01
☐ 4T	Paul Assenmacher	.08	.04	.01
☐ 5T	Scott Bailes	.08	.04	.01
☐ 6T	Don Baylor	.15	.07	.02
☐ 7T	Steve Bedrosian	.08	.04	.01
☐ 8T	Juan Beniquez	.08	.04	.01
☐ 9T	Juan Berenguer	.08	.04	.01
☐ 10T	Mike Bielecki	.08	.04	.01
☐ 11T	Barry Bonds	6.00	2.70	.75
☐ 12T	Bobby Bonilla	1.50	.65	.19
☐ 13T	Juan Bonilla	.08	.04	.01
☐ 14T	Rich Bordi	.08	.04	.01
☐ 15T	Steve Boros MG	.08	.04	.01
☐ 16T	Rick Burleson	.08	.04	.01
☐ 17T	Bill Campbell	.08	.04	.01
☐ 18T	Tom Candiotti	.10	.05	.01
☐ 19T	John Cangelosi	.08	.04	.01
☐ 20T	Jose Canseco	3.50	1.55	.45
☐ 21T	Carmen Castillo	.08	.04	.01
☐ 22T	Rick Cerone	.08	.04	.01
☐ 23T	John Cerutti	.08	.04	.01
☐ 24T	Will Clark	3.50	1.55	.45
☐ 25T	Mark Clear	.08	.04	.01
☐ 26T	Darnell Coles	.08	.04	.01
☐ 27T	Dave Collins	.08	.04	.01
☐ 28T	Tim Conroy	.08	.04	.01
☐ 29T	Joe Cowley	.08	.04	.01
☐ 30T	Joel Davis	.08	.04	.01
☐ 31T	Rob Deer	.10	.05	.01
☐ 32T	John Denny	.08	.04	.01
☐ 33T	Mike Easler	.08	.04	.01
☐ 34T	Mark Eichhorn	.08	.04	.01
☐ 35T	Steve Farr	.10	.05	.01
☐ 36T	Scott Fletcher	.08	.04	.01
☐ 37T	Terry Forster	.08	.04	.01
☐ 38T	Terry Francona	.08	.04	.01
☐ 39T	Jim Fregosi MG	.08	.04	.01
☐ 40T	Andres Galarraga	2.00	.90	.25
☐ 41T	Ken Griffey	.15	.07	.02
☐ 42T	Bill Gullickson	.10	.05	.01
☐ 43T	Jose Guzman	.25	.11	.03
☐ 44T	Moose Haas	.08	.04	.01
☐ 45T	Billy Hatcher	.10	.05	.01
☐ 46T	Mike Heath	.08	.04	.01
☐ 47T	Tom Hume	.08	.04	.01
☐ 48T	Pete Incaviglia	.40	.18	.05
☐ 49T	Dane Iorg	.08	.04	.01
☐ 50T	Bo Jackson	2.00	.90	.25
☐ 51T	Wally Joyner	.50	.23	.06
☐ 52T	Charlie Kerfeld	.08	.04	.01
☐ 53T	Eric King	.08	.04	.01

☐ 54T	Bob Kipper	.08	.04	.01
☐ 55T	Wayne Krenchicki	.08	.04	.01
☐ 56T	John Kruk	1.50	.65	.19
☐ 57T	Mike LaCoss	.08	.04	.01
☐ 58T	Pete Ladd	.08	.04	.01
☐ 59T	Mike Laga	.08	.04	.01
☐ 60T	Hal Lanier MG	.08	.04	.01
☐ 61T	Dave LaPoint	.08	.04	.01
☐ 62T	Rudy Law	.08	.04	.01
☐ 63T	Rick Leach	.08	.04	.01
☐ 64T	Tim Leary	.08	.04	.01
☐ 65T	Dennis Leonard	.08	.04	.01
☐ 66T	Jim Leyland MG	.20	.09	.03
☐ 67T	Steve Lyons	.08	.04	.01
☐ 68T	Mickey Mahler	.08	.04	.01
☐ 69T	Candy Maldonado	.08	.04	.01
☐ 70T	Roger Mason	.08	.04	.01
☐ 71T	Bob McClure	.08	.04	.01
☐ 72T	Andy McGaffigan	.08	.04	.01
☐ 73T	Gene Michael MG	.08	.04	.01
☐ 74T	Kevin Mitchell	1.00	.45	.13
☐ 75T	Omar Moreno	.08	.04	.01
☐ 76T	Jerry Mumphrey	.08	.04	.01
☐ 77T	Phil Niekro	.15	.07	.02
☐ 78T	Randy Niemann	.08	.04	.01
☐ 79T	Juan Nieves	.08	.04	.01
☐ 80T	Otis Nixon	.50	.23	.06
☐ 81T	Bob Ojeda	.10	.05	.01
☐ 82T	Jose Oquendo	.08	.04	.01
☐ 83T	Tom Paciorek	.10	.05	.01
☐ 84T	David Palmer	.08	.04	.01
☐ 85T	Frank Pastore	.08	.04	.01
☐ 86T	Lou Piniella MG	.10	.05	.01
☐ 87T	Dan Plesac	.08	.04	.01
☐ 88T	Darrell Porter	.08	.04	.01
☐ 89T	Rey Quinones	.08	.04	.01
☐ 90T	Gary Redus	.08	.04	.01
☐ 91T	Bip Roberts	.30	.14	.04
☐ 92T	Billy Joe Robidoux	.08	.04	.01
☐ 93T	Jeff D. Robinson	.08	.04	.01
☐ 94T	Gary Roenicke	.08	.04	.01
☐ 95T	Ed Romero	.08	.04	.01
☐ 96T	Argenis Salazar	.08	.04	.01
☐ 97T	Joe Sambito	.08	.04	.01
☐ 98T	Billy Sample	.08	.04	.01
☐ 99T	Dave Schmidt	.08	.04	.01
☐ 100T	Ken Schrom	.08	.04	.01
☐ 101T	Tom Seaver	.50	.23	.06
☐ 102T	Ted Simmons	.10	.05	.01
☐ 103T	Sammy Stewart	.08	.04	.01
☐ 104T	Kurt Stillwell	.08	.04	.01
☐ 105T	Franklin Stubbs	.08	.04	.01
☐ 106T	Dale Sveum	.08	.04	.01
☐ 107T	Chuck Tanner MG	.08	.04	.01
☐ 108T	Danny Tartabull	.50	.23	.06
☐ 109T	Tim Teufel	.08	.04	.01
☐ 110T	Bob Tewksbury	.30	.14	.04
☐ 111T	Andres Thomas	.08	.04	.01
☐ 112T	Milt Thompson	.10	.05	.01
☐ 113T	Robby Thompson	.50	.23	.06
☐ 114T	Jay Tibbs	.08	.04	.01
☐ 115T	Wayne Tolleson	.08	.04	.01
☐ 116T	Alex Trevino	.08	.04	.01
☐ 117T	Manny Trillo	.08	.04	.01
☐ 118T	Ed VandeBerg	.08	.04	.01
☐ 119T	Ozzie Virgil	.08	.04	.01
☐ 120T	Bob Walk	.08	.04	.01
☐ 121T	Gene Walter	.08	.04	.01
☐ 122T	Claudell Washington	.08	.04	.01
☐ 123T	Bill Wegman	.15	.07	.02
☐ 124T	Dick Williams MG	.08	.04	.01
☐ 125T	Mitch Williams	.30	.14	.04
☐ 126T	Bobby Witt	.20	.09	.03
☐ 127T	Todd Worrell	.15	.07	.02
☐ 128T	George Wright	.08	.04	.01
☐ 129T	Ricky Wright	.08	.04	.01
☐ 130T	Steve Yeager	.08	.04	.01
☐ 131T	Paul Zuvella	.08	.04	.01
☐ 132T	Checklist 1T-132T	.08	.04	.01

1987 Topps

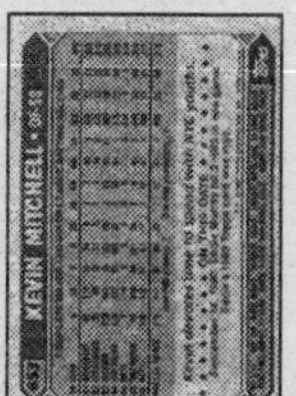

This 792-card set is reminiscent of the 1962 Topps baseball cards with their simulated wood grain borders. The backs are printed in yellow and blue on gray card stock. The manager cards contain a checklist of the respective team's players on the back. Subsets in the set include Record Breakers (1-7), Turn Back the Clock (311-315), and All-Star selections (595-616). The Team Leader cards typically show players conferring on the mound inside a white cloud. The wax pack wrapper gives details of "Spring Fever Baseball" where a lucky collector can win a trip for four to Spring Training. The key Rookie Cards in this set are Barry Bonds, Bobby Bonilla, Will Clark, Doug Drabek, Mike Greenwell, Bo Jackson, Wally Joyner, John Kruk, Barry Larkin, Dave Magadan, Kevin Mitchell, Rafael Palmiero, Ruben Sierra, Duane Ward, and Devon White. Topps also produced a specially boxed "glossy" edition, frequently referred to as the Topps Tiffany set. This year Topps did not disclose the number of sets they produced or sold. It is apparent from the availability that there were many more sets produced this year compared to the 1984-86 Tiffany sets, perhaps 30,000 sets, more than three times as many. The checklist of cards (792 regular and 132 Traded) is identical to that of the normal non-glossy cards. There are two primary distinguishing features of the Tiffany cards, white card stock reverses and high gloss obverses. These Tiffany cards are valued approximately from three to five times the values listed below.

	MINT	EXC	G-VG
COMPLETE SET (792)	15.00	6.75	1.90
COMPLETE FACT.SET (792)	20.00	9.00	2.50
COMMON CARD (1-792)	.05	.02	.01

☐ 1 Roger Clemens RB Most strikeouts, nine inning game	.40	.10	.03

☐ 2 Jim Deshaies RB .05 .02 .01
Most cons. K's,
start of game
☐ 3 Dwight Evans RB .05 .02 .01
Earliest home run,
season
☐ 4 Davey Lopes RB .05 .02 .01
Most steals, season,
40-year-old
☐ 5 Dave Righetti RB .05 .02 .01
Most saves, season
☐ 6 Ruben Sierra RB .20 .09 .03
Youngest player to
switch hit homers
in game
☐ 7 Todd Worrell RB .05 .02 .01
Most saves,
season, rookie
☐ 8 Terry Pendleton .05 .02 .01
☐ 9 Jay Tibbs .05 .02 .01
☐ 10 Cecil Cooper .10 .05 .01
☐ 11 Indians Team .05 .02 .01
(Mound conference)
☐ 12 Jeff Sellers .05 .02 .01
☐ 13 Nick Esasky .05 .02 .01
☐ 14 Dave Stewart .15 .07 .02
☐ 15 Claudell Washington .05 .02 .01
☐ 16 Pat Clements .05 .02 .01
☐ 17 Pete O'Brien .05 .02 .01
☐ 18 Dick Howser MG .06 .03 .01
(Checklist back)
☐ 19 Matt Young .05 .02 .01
☐ 20 Gary Carter .15 .07 .02
☐ 21 Mark Davis .05 .02 .01
☐ 22 Doug DeCinces .05 .02 .01
☐ 23 Lee Smith .15 .07 .02
☐ 24 Tony Walker .05 .02 .01
☐ 25 Bert Blyleven .15 .07 .02
☐ 26 Greg Brock .05 .02 .01
☐ 27 Joe Cowley .05 .02 .01
☐ 28 Rick Dempsey .05 .02 .01
☐ 29 Jimmy Key .20 .09 .03
☐ 30 Tim Raines .15 .07 .02
☐ 31 Braves Team .05 .02 .01
(Glenn Hubbard and
Rafael Ramirez)
☐ 32 Tim Leary .05 .02 .01
☐ 33 Andy Van Slyke .15 .07 .02
☐ 34 Jose Rijo .15 .07 .02
☐ 35 Sid Bream .05 .02 .01
☐ 36 Eric King .05 .02 .01
☐ 37 Marvell Wynne .05 .02 .01
☐ 38 Dennis Leonard .05 .02 .01
☐ 39 Marty Barrett .05 .02 .01
☐ 40 Dave Righetti .10 .05 .01
☐ 41 Bo Diaz .05 .02 .01
☐ 42 Gary Redus .05 .02 .01
☐ 43 Gene Michael MG .06 .03 .01
(Checklist back)
☐ 44 Greg Harris .05 .02 .01
☐ 45 Jim Presley .05 .02 .01
☐ 46 Dan Gladden .05 .02 .01
☐ 47 Dennis Powell .05 .02 .01
☐ 48 Wally Backman .05 .02 .01
☐ 49 Terry Harper .05 .02 .01
☐ 50 Dave Smith .05 .02 .01
☐ 51 Mel Hall .05 .02 .01
☐ 52 Keith Atherton .05 .02 .01
☐ 53 Ruppert Jones .05 .02 .01
☐ 54 Bill Dawley .05 .02 .01
☐ 55 Tim Wallach .10 .05 .01
☐ 56 Brewers Team .05 .02 .01
(Mound conference)
☐ 57 Scott Nielsen .05 .02 .01
☐ 58 Thad Bosley .05 .02 .01
☐ 59 Ken Dayley .05 .02 .01
☐ 60 Tony Pena .05 .02 .01
☐ 61 Bobby Thigpen .05 .02 .01
☐ 62 Bobby Meacham .05 .02 .01
☐ 63 Fred Toliver .05 .02 .01
☐ 64 Harry Spilman .05 .02 .01
☐ 65 Tom Browning .05 .02 .01
☐ 66 Marc Sullivan .05 .02 .01
☐ 67 Bill Swift .10 .05 .01
☐ 68 Tony LaRussa MG .10 .05 .01
(Checklist back)
☐ 69 Lonnie Smith .05 .02 .01
☐ 70 Charlie Hough .10 .05 .01
☐ 71 Mike Aldrete .05 .02 .01
☐ 72 Walt Terrell .05 .02 .01
☐ 73 Dave Anderson .05 .02 .01
☐ 74 Dan Pasqua .05 .02 .01
☐ 75 Ron Darling .10 .05 .01
☐ 76 Rafael Ramirez .05 .02 .01
☐ 77 Bryan Oelkers .05 .02 .01
☐ 78 Tom Foley .05 .02 .01
☐ 79 Juan Nieves .05 .02 .01
☐ 80 Wally Joyner .50 .23 .06
☐ 81 Padres Team .05 .02 .01
(Andy Hawkins and
Terry Kennedy)
☐ 82 Rob Murphy .05 .02 .01
☐ 83 Mike Davis .05 .02 .01
☐ 84 Steve Lake .05 .02 .01
☐ 85 Kevin Bass .05 .02 .01
☐ 86 Nate Snell .05 .02 .01
☐ 87 Mark Salas .05 .02 .01
☐ 88 Ed Wojna .05 .02 .01
☐ 89 Ozzie Guillen .10 .05 .01
☐ 90 Dave Stieb .10 .05 .01
☐ 91 Harold Reynolds .05 .02 .01
☐ 92A Urbano Lugo .30 .14 .04
ERR (no trademark)
☐ 92B Urbano Lugo COR .05 .02 .01
☐ 93 Jim Leyland MG .15 .07 .02
(Checklist back)
☐ 94 Calvin Schiraldi .05 .02 .01
☐ 95 Oddibe McDowell .05 .02 .01
☐ 96 Frank Williams .05 .02 .01
☐ 97 Glenn Wilson .05 .02 .01
☐ 98 Bill Scherrer .05 .02 .01
☐ 99 Darryl Motley .05 .02 .01
(Now with Braves
on card front)
☐ 100 Steve Garvey .15 .07 .02
☐ 101 Carl Willis .05 .02 .01
☐ 102 Paul Zuvella .05 .02 .01
☐ 103 Rick Aguilera .10 .05 .01
☐ 104 Billy Sample .05 .02 .01
☐ 105 Floyd Youmans .05 .02 .01
☐ 106 Blue Jays Team .05 .02 .01
(George Bell and
Jesse Barfield)
☐ 107 John Butcher .05 .02 .01
☐ 108 Jim Gantner UER .05 .02 .01
(Brewers logo
reversed)
☐ 109 R.J. Reynolds .05 .02 .01
☐ 110 John Tudor .05 .02 .01
☐ 111 Alfredo Griffin .05 .02 .01
☐ 112 Alan Ashby .05 .02 .01
☐ 113 Neil Allen .05 .02 .01
☐ 114 Billy Beane .05 .02 .01
☐ 115 Donnie Moore .05 .02 .01
☐ 116 Bill Russell .10 .05 .01
☐ 117 Jim Beattie .05 .02 .01

No.	Card			
☐ 118	Bobby Valentine MG (Checklist back)	.06	.03	.01
☐ 119	Ron Robinson	.05	.02	.01
☐ 120	Eddie Murray	.25	.11	.03
☐ 121	Kevin Romine	.05	.02	.01
☐ 122	Jim Clancy	.05	.02	.01
☐ 123	John Kruk	.50	.23	.06
☐ 124	Ray Fontenot	.05	.02	.01
☐ 125	Bob Brenly	.05	.02	.01
☐ 126	Mike Loynd	.05	.02	.01
☐ 127	Vance Law	.05	.02	.01
☐ 128	Checklist 1-132	.06	.02	.01
☐ 129	Rick Cerone	.05	.02	.01
☐ 130	Dwight Gooden	.10	.05	.01
☐ 131	Pirates Team (Sid Bream and Tony Pena)	.05	.02	.01
☐ 132	Paul Assenmacher	.05	.02	.01
☐ 133	Jose Oquendo	.05	.02	.01
☐ 134	Rich Yett	.05	.02	.01
☐ 135	Mike Easler	.05	.02	.01
☐ 136	Ron Romanick	.05	.02	.01
☐ 137	Jerry Willard	.05	.02	.01
☐ 138	Roy Lee Jackson	.05	.02	.01
☐ 139	Devon White	.50	.23	.06
☐ 140	Bret Saberhagen	.20	.09	.03
☐ 141	Herm Winningham	.05	.02	.01
☐ 142	Rick Sutcliffe	.10	.05	.01
☐ 143	Steve Boros MG (Checklist back)	.06	.03	.01
☐ 144	Mike Scioscia	.05	.02	.01
☐ 145	Charlie Kerfeld	.05	.02	.01
☐ 146	Tracy Jones	.05	.02	.01
☐ 147	Randy Niemann	.05	.02	.01
☐ 148	Dave Collins	.05	.02	.01
☐ 149	Ray Searage	.05	.02	.01
☐ 150	Wade Boggs	.40	.18	.05
☐ 151	Mike LaCoss	.05	.02	.01
☐ 152	Toby Harrah	.05	.02	.01
☐ 153	Duane Ward	.50	.23	.06
☐ 154	Tom O'Malley	.05	.02	.01
☐ 155	Eddie Whitson	.05	.02	.01
☐ 156	Mariners Team (Mound conference)	.05	.02	.01
☐ 157	Danny Darwin	.05	.02	.01
☐ 158	Tim Teufel	.05	.02	.01
☐ 159	Ed Olwine	.05	.02	.01
☐ 160	Julio Franco	.15	.07	.02
☐ 161	Steve Ontiveros	.05	.02	.01
☐ 162	Mike LaValliere	.05	.02	.01
☐ 163	Kevin Gross	.05	.02	.01
☐ 164	Sammy Khalifa	.05	.02	.01
☐ 165	Jeff Reardon	.15	.07	.02
☐ 166	Bob Boone	.10	.05	.01
☐ 167	Jim Deshaies	.15	.07	.02
☐ 168	Lou Piniella MG (Checklist back)	.10	.05	.01
☐ 169	Ron Washington	.05	.02	.01
☐ 170	Bo Jackson	1.00	.45	.13
☐ 171	Chuck Cary	.05	.02	.01
☐ 172	Ron Oester	.05	.02	.01
☐ 173	Alex Trevino	.05	.02	.01
☐ 174	Henry Cotto	.05	.02	.01
☐ 175	Bob Stanley	.05	.02	.01
☐ 176	Steve Buechele	.10	.05	.01
☐ 177	Keith Moreland	.05	.02	.01
☐ 178	Cecil Fielder	.50	.23	.06
☐ 179	Bill Wegman	.05	.02	.01
☐ 180	Chris Brown	.05	.02	.01
☐ 181	Cardinals Team (Mound conference)	.05	.02	.01
☐ 182	Lee Lacy	.05	.02	.01
☐ 183	Andy Hawkins	.05	.02	.01
☐ 184	Bobby Bonilla	.60	.25	.08
☐ 185	Roger McDowell	.05	.02	.01
☐ 186	Bruce Benedict	.05	.02	.01
☐ 187	Mark Huismann	.05	.02	.01
☐ 188	Tony Phillips	.10	.05	.01
☐ 189	Joe Hesketh	.05	.02	.01
☐ 190	Jim Sundberg	.05	.02	.01
☐ 191	Charles Hudson	.05	.02	.01
☐ 192	Cory Snyder	.10	.05	.01
☐ 193	Roger Craig MG (Checklist back)	.06	.03	.01
☐ 194	Kirk McCaskill	.05	.02	.01
☐ 195	Mike Pagliarulo	.05	.02	.01
☐ 196	Randy O'Neal UER (Wrong ML career W-L totals)	.05	.02	.01
☐ 197	Mark Bailey	.05	.02	.01
☐ 198	Lee Mazzilli	.05	.02	.01
☐ 199	Mariano Duncan	.05	.02	.01
☐ 200	Pete Rose	.30	.14	.04
☐ 201	John Cangelosi	.05	.02	.01
☐ 202	Ricky Wright	.05	.02	.01
☐ 203	Mike Kingery	.10	.05	.01
☐ 204	Sammy Stewart	.05	.02	.01
☐ 205	Graig Nettles	.10	.05	.01
☐ 206	Twins Team (Frank Viola and Tim Laudner)	.05	.02	.01
☐ 207	George Frazier	.05	.02	.01
☐ 208	John Shelby	.05	.02	.01
☐ 209	Rick Schu	.05	.02	.01
☐ 210	Lloyd Moseby	.05	.02	.01
☐ 211	John Morris	.05	.02	.01
☐ 212	Mike Fitzgerald	.05	.02	.01
☐ 213	Randy Myers	.35	.16	.04
☐ 214	Omar Moreno	.05	.02	.01
☐ 215	Mark Langston	.15	.07	.02
☐ 216	B.J. Surhoff	.12	.05	.02
☐ 217	Chris Codiroli	.05	.02	.01
☐ 218	Sparky Anderson MG (Checklist back)	.10	.05	.01
☐ 219	Cecilio Guante	.05	.02	.01
☐ 220	Joe Carter	.50	.23	.06
☐ 221	Vern Ruhle	.05	.02	.01
☐ 222	Denny Walling	.05	.02	.01
☐ 223	Charlie Leibrandt	.05	.02	.01
☐ 224	Wayne Tolleson	.05	.02	.01
☐ 225	Mike Smithson	.05	.02	.01
☐ 226	Max Venable	.05	.02	.01
☐ 227	Jamie Moyer	.12	.05	.02
☐ 228	Curt Wilkerson	.05	.02	.01
☐ 229	Mike Birkbeck	.05	.02	.01
☐ 230	Don Baylor	.15	.07	.02
☐ 231	Giants Team (Bob Brenly and Jim Gott)	.05	.02	.01
☐ 232	Reggie Williams	.05	.02	.01
☐ 233	Russ Morman	.05	.02	.01
☐ 234	Pat Sheridan	.05	.02	.01
☐ 235	Alvin Davis	.05	.02	.01
☐ 236	Tommy John	.15	.07	.02
☐ 237	Jim Morrison	.05	.02	.01
☐ 238	Bill Krueger	.05	.02	.01
☐ 239	Juan Espino	.05	.02	.01
☐ 240	Steve Balboni	.05	.02	.01
☐ 241	Danny Heep	.05	.02	.01
☐ 242	Rick Mahler	.05	.02	.01
☐ 243	Whitey Herzog MG (Checklist back)	.11	.05	.01
☐ 244	Dickie Noles	.05	.02	.01
☐ 245	Willie Upshaw	.05	.02	.01
☐ 246	Jim Dwyer	.05	.02	.01
☐ 247	Jeff Reed	.05	.02	.01

☐ 248	Gene Walter	.05	.02	.01
☐ 249	Jim Pankovits	.05	.02	.01
☐ 250	Teddy Higuera	.05	.02	.01
☐ 251	Rob Wilfong	.05	.02	.01
☐ 252	Dennis Martinez	.10	.05	.01
☐ 253	Eddie Milner	.05	.02	.01
☐ 254	Bob Tewksbury	.25	.11	.03
☐ 255	Juan Samuel	.05	.02	.01
☐ 256	Royals Team (George Brett and Frank White)	.10	.05	.01
☐ 257	Bob Forsch	.05	.02	.01
☐ 258	Steve Yeager	.05	.02	.01
☐ 259	Mike Greenwell	.50	.23	.06
☐ 260	Vida Blue	.10	.05	.01
☐ 261	Ruben Sierra	1.00	.45	.13
☐ 262	Jim Winn	.05	.02	.01
☐ 263	Stan Javier	.10	.05	.01
☐ 264	Checklist 133-264	.06	.02	.01
☐ 265	Darrell Evans	.10	.05	.01
☐ 266	Jeff Hamilton	.05	.02	.01
☐ 267	Howard Johnson	.10	.05	.01
☐ 268	Pat Corrales MG (Checklist back)	.06	.03	.01
☐ 269	Cliff Speck	.05	.02	.01
☐ 270	Jody Davis	.05	.02	.01
☐ 271	Mike G. Brown	.05	.02	.01
☐ 272	Andres Galarraga	.60	.25	.08
☐ 273	Gene Nelson	.05	.02	.01
☐ 274	Jeff Hearron UER (Duplicate 1986 stat line on back)	.05	.02	.01
☐ 275	LaMarr Hoyt	.05	.02	.01
☐ 276	Jackie Gutierrez	.05	.02	.01
☐ 277	Juan Agosto	.05	.02	.01
☐ 278	Gary Pettis	.05	.02	.01
☐ 279	Dan Plesac	.05	.02	.01
☐ 280	Jeff Leonard	.05	.02	.01
☐ 281	Reds Team (Pete Rose, Bo Diaz, and Bill Gullickson)	.10	.05	.01
☐ 282	Jeff Calhoun	.05	.02	.01
☐ 283	Doug Drabek	.50	.23	.06
☐ 284	John Moses	.05	.02	.01
☐ 285	Dennis Boyd	.05	.02	.01
☐ 286	Mike Woodard	.05	.02	.01
☐ 287	Dave Von Ohlen	.05	.02	.01
☐ 288	Tito Landrum	.05	.02	.01
☐ 289	Bob Kipper	.05	.02	.01
☐ 290	Leon Durham	.05	.02	.01
☐ 291	Mitch Williams	.25	.11	.03
☐ 292	Franklin Stubbs	.05	.02	.01
☐ 293	Bob Rodgers MG (Checklist back, inconsistent design on card back)	.06	.03	.01
☐ 294	Steve Jeltz	.05	.02	.01
☐ 295	Len Dykstra	.25	.11	.03
☐ 296	Andres Thomas	.05	.02	.01
☐ 297	Don Schulze	.05	.02	.01
☐ 298	Larry Herndon	.05	.02	.01
☐ 299	Joel Davis	.05	.02	.01
☐ 300	Reggie Jackson	.30	.14	.04
☐ 301	Luis Aquino UER (No trademark, never corrected)	.05	.02	.01
☐ 302	Bill Schroeder	.05	.02	.01
☐ 303	Juan Berenguer	.05	.02	.01
☐ 304	Phil Garner	.10	.05	.01
☐ 305	John Franco	.10	.05	.01
☐ 306	Red Sox Team (Tom Seaver, John McNamara MG, and Rich Gedman)	.10	.05	.01
☐ 307	Lee Guetterman	.05	.02	.01
☐ 308	Don Slaught	.05	.02	.01
☐ 309	Mike Young	.05	.02	.01
☐ 310	Frank Viola	.10	.05	.01
☐ 311	Rickey Henderson TBC '82	.20	.09	.03
☐ 312	Reggie Jackson TBC '77	.10	.05	.01
☐ 313	Roberto Clemente TBC '72	.20	.09	.03
☐ 314	Carl Yastrzemski UER TBC '67 (Sic, 112 RBI's on back)	.10	.05	.01
☐ 315	Maury Wills TBC '62	.05	.02	.01
☐ 316	Brian Fisher	.05	.02	.01
☐ 317	Clint Hurdle	.05	.02	.01
☐ 318	Jim Fregosi MG (Checklist back)	.06	.03	.01
☐ 319	Greg Swindell	.30	.14	.04
☐ 320	Barry Bonds	3.00	1.35	.40
☐ 321	Mike Laga	.05	.02	.01
☐ 322	Chris Bando	.05	.02	.01
☐ 323	Al Newman	.05	.02	.01
☐ 324	David Palmer	.05	.02	.01
☐ 325	Garry Templeton	.05	.02	.01
☐ 326	Mark Gubicza	.05	.02	.01
☐ 327	Dale Sveum	.05	.02	.01
☐ 328	Bob Welch	.10	.05	.01
☐ 329	Ron Roenicke	.05	.02	.01
☐ 330	Mike Scott	.05	.02	.01
☐ 331	Mets Team (Gary Carter and Darryl Strawberry)	.15	.07	.02
☐ 332	Joe Price	.05	.02	.01
☐ 333	Ken Phelps	.05	.02	.01
☐ 334	Ed Correa	.05	.02	.01
☐ 335	Candy Maldonado	.05	.02	.01
☐ 336	Allan Anderson	.05	.02	.01
☐ 337	Darrell Miller	.05	.02	.01
☐ 338	Tim Conroy	.05	.02	.01
☐ 339	Donnie Hill	.05	.02	.01
☐ 340	Roger Clemens	.75	.35	.09
☐ 341	Mike C. Brown	.05	.02	.01
☐ 342	Bob James	.05	.02	.01
☐ 343	Hal Lanier MG (Checklist back)	.06	.03	.01
☐ 344A	Joe Niekro (Copyright inside righthand border)	.10	.05	.01
☐ 344B	Joe Niekro (Copyright outside righthand border)	.30	.14	.04
☐ 345	Andre Dawson	.25	.11	.03
☐ 346	Shawon Dunston	.10	.05	.01
☐ 347	Mickey Brantley	.05	.02	.01
☐ 348	Carmelo Martinez	.05	.02	.01
☐ 349	Storm Davis	.05	.02	.01
☐ 350	Keith Hernandez	.10	.05	.01
☐ 351	Gene Garber	.05	.02	.01
☐ 352	Mike Felder	.05	.02	.01
☐ 353	Ernie Camacho	.05	.02	.01
☐ 354	Jamie Quirk	.05	.02	.01
☐ 355	Don Carman	.05	.02	.01
☐ 356	White Sox Team (Mound conference)	.05	.02	.01
☐ 357	Steve Fireovid	.05	.02	.01
☐ 358	Sal Butera	.05	.02	.01
☐ 359	Doug Corbett	.05	.02	.01
☐ 360	Pedro Guerrero	.10	.05	.01
☐ 361	Mark Thurmond	.05	.02	.01
☐ 362	Luis Quinones	.05	.02	.01
☐ 363	Jose Guzman	.10	.05	.01

☐	364	Randy Bush	.05	.02	.01
☐	365	Rick Rhoden	.05	.02	.01
☐	366	Mark McGwire	.75	.35	.09
☐	367	Jeff Lahti	.05	.02	.01
☐	368	John McNamara MG	.06	.03	.01
		(Checklist back)			
☐	369	Brian Dayett	.05	.02	.01
☐	370	Fred Lynn	.10	.05	.01
☐	371	Mark Eichhorn	.05	.02	.01
☐	372	Jerry Mumphrey	.05	.02	.01
☐	373	Jeff Dedmon	.05	.02	.01
☐	374	Glenn Hoffman	.05	.02	.01
☐	375	Ron Guidry	.10	.05	.01
☐	376	Scott Bradley	.05	.02	.01
☐	377	John Henry Johnson	.05	.02	.01
☐	378	Rafael Santana	.05	.02	.01
☐	379	John Russell	.05	.02	.01
☐	380	Rich Gossage	.15	.07	.02
☐	381	Expos Team	.05	.02	.01
		(Mound conference)			
☐	382	Rudy Law	.05	.02	.01
☐	383	Ron Davis	.05	.02	.01
☐	384	Johnny Grubb	.05	.02	.01
☐	385	Orel Hershiser	.10	.05	.01
☐	386	Dickie Thon	.05	.02	.01
☐	387	T.R. Bryden	.05	.02	.01
☐	388	Geno Petralli	.05	.02	.01
☐	389	Jeff D. Robinson	.05	.02	.01
☐	390	Gary Matthews	.05	.02	.01
☐	391	Jay Howell	.05	.02	.01
☐	392	Checklist 265-396	.06	.02	.01
☐	393	Pete Rose MG	.25	.11	.03
		(Checklist back)			
☐	394	Mike Bielecki	.05	.02	.01
☐	395	Damaso Garcia	.05	.02	.01
☐	396	Tim Lollar	.05	.02	.01
☐	397	Greg Walker	.05	.02	.01
☐	398	Brad Havens	.05	.02	.01
☐	399	Curt Ford	.05	.02	.01
☐	400	George Brett	.50	.23	.06
☐	401	Billy Joe Robidoux	.05	.02	.01
☐	402	Mike Trujillo	.05	.02	.01
☐	403	Jerry Royster	.05	.02	.01
☐	404	Doug Sisk	.05	.02	.01
☐	405	Brook Jacoby	.05	.02	.01
☐	406	Yankees Team	.20	.09	.03
		(Rickey Henderson and			
		Don Mattingly)			
☐	407	Jim Acker	.05	.02	.01
☐	408	John Mizerock	.05	.02	.01
☐	409	Milt Thompson	.10	.05	.01
☐	410	Fernando Valenzuela	.05	.02	.01
☐	411	Darnell Coles	.05	.02	.01
☐	412	Eric Davis	.15	.07	.02
☐	413	Moose Haas	.05	.02	.01
☐	414	Joe Orsulak	.05	.02	.01
☐	415	Bobby Witt	.15	.07	.02
☐	416	Tom Nieto	.05	.02	.01
☐	417	Pat Perry	.05	.02	.01
☐	418	Dick Williams MG	.06	.03	.01
		(Checklist back)			
☐	419	Mark Portugal	.30	.14	.04
☐	420	Will Clark	1.50	.65	.19
☐	421	Jose DeLeon	.05	.02	.01
☐	422	Jack Howell	.05	.02	.01
☐	423	Jaime Cocanower	.05	.02	.01
☐	424	Chris Speier	.05	.02	.01
☐	425	Tom Seaver	.25	.11	.03
☐	426	Floyd Rayford	.05	.02	.01
☐	427	Edwin Nunez	.05	.02	.01
☐	428	Bruce Bochy	.05	.02	.01
☐	429	Tim Pyznarski	.05	.02	.01
☐	430	Mike Schmidt	.35	.16	.04
☐	431	Dodgers Team	.05	.02	.01
		(Mound conference)			
☐	432	Jim Slaton	.05	.02	.01
☐	433	Ed Hearn	.05	.02	.01
☐	434	Mike Fischlin	.05	.02	.01
☐	435	Bruce Sutter	.10	.05	.01
☐	436	Andy Allanson	.05	.02	.01
☐	437	Ted Power	.05	.02	.01
☐	438	Kelly Downs	.05	.02	.01
☐	439	Karl Best	.05	.02	.01
☐	440	Willie McGee	.10	.05	.01
☐	441	Dave Leiper	.05	.02	.01
☐	442	Mitch Webster	.05	.02	.01
☐	443	John Felske MG	.06	.03	.01
		(Checklist back)			
☐	444	Jeff Russell	.05	.02	.01
☐	445	Dave Lopes	.10	.05	.01
☐	446	Chuck Finley	.30	.14	.04
☐	447	Bill Almon	.05	.02	.01
☐	448	Chris Bosio	.15	.07	.02
☐	449	Pat Dodson	.05	.02	.01
☐	450	Kirby Puckett	1.00	.45	.13
☐	451	Joe Sambito	.05	.02	.01
☐	452	Dave Henderson	.10	.05	.01
☐	453	Scott Terry	.05	.02	.01
☐	454	Luis Salazar	.05	.02	.01
☐	455	Mike Boddicker	.05	.02	.01
☐	456	A's Team	.05	.02	.01
		(Mound conference)			
☐	457	Len Matuszek	.05	.02	.01
☐	458	Kelly Gruber	.05	.02	.01
☐	459	Dennis Eckersley	.15	.07	.02
☐	460	Darryl Strawberry	.15	.07	.02
☐	461	Craig McMurtry	.05	.02	.01
☐	462	Scott Fletcher	.05	.02	.01
☐	463	Tom Candiotti	.10	.05	.01
☐	464	Butch Wynegar	.05	.02	.01
☐	465	Todd Worrell	.10	.05	.01
☐	466	Kal Daniels	.05	.02	.01
☐	467	Randy St.Claire	.05	.02	.01
☐	468	George Bamberger MG	.06	.03	.01
		(Checklist back)			
☐	469	Mike Diaz	.05	.02	.01
☐	470	Dave Dravecky	.10	.05	.01
☐	471	Ronn Reynolds	.05	.02	.01
☐	472	Bill Doran	.05	.02	.01
☐	473	Steve Farr	.05	.02	.01
☐	474	Jerry Narron	.05	.02	.01
☐	475	Scott Garrelts	.05	.02	.01
☐	476	Danny Tartabull	.25	.11	.03
☐	477	Ken Howell	.05	.02	.01
☐	478	Tim Laudner	.05	.02	.01
☐	479	Bob Sebra	.05	.02	.01
☐	480	Jim Rice	.15	.07	.02
☐	481	Phillies Team	.05	.02	.01
		(Glenn Wilson,			
		Juan Samuel, and			
		Von Hayes)			
☐	482	Daryl Boston	.05	.02	.01
☐	483	Dwight Lowry	.05	.02	.01
☐	484	Jim Traber	.05	.02	.01
☐	485	Tony Fernandez	.10	.05	.01
☐	486	Otis Nixon	.05	.02	.01
☐	487	Dave Gumpert	.05	.02	.01
☐	488	Ray Knight	.10	.05	.01
☐	489	Bill Gullickson	.05	.02	.01
☐	490	Dale Murphy	.15	.07	.02
☐	491	Ron Karkovice	.15	.07	.02
☐	492	Mike Heath	.05	.02	.01
☐	493	Tom Lasorda MG	.10	.05	.01
		(Checklist back)			
☐	494	Barry Jones	.05	.02	.01
☐	495	Gorman Thomas	.05	.02	.01

☐	496	Bruce Bochte	.05	.02	.01
☐	497	Dale Mohorcic	.05	.02	.01
☐	498	Bob Kearney	.05	.02	.01
☐	499	Bruce Ruffin	.10	.05	.01
☐	500	Don Mattingly	.50	.23	.06
☐	501	Craig Lefferts	.05	.02	.01
☐	502	Dick Schofield	.05	.02	.01
☐	503	Larry Andersen	.05	.02	.01
☐	504	Mickey Hatcher	.05	.02	.01
☐	505	Bryn Smith	.05	.02	.01
☐	506	Orioles Team (Mound conference)	.05	.02	.01
☐	507	Dave L. Stapleton	.05	.02	.01
☐	508	Scott Bankhead	.05	.02	.01
☐	509	Enos Cabell	.05	.02	.01
☐	510	Tom Henke	.10	.05	.01
☐	511	Steve Lyons	.05	.02	.01
☐	512	Dave Magadan	.15	.07	.02
☐	513	Carmen Castillo	.05	.02	.01
☐	514	Orlando Mercado	.05	.02	.01
☐	515	Willie Hernandez	.05	.02	.01
☐	516	Ted Simmons	.10	.05	.01
☐	517	Mario Soto	.05	.02	.01
☐	518	Gene Mauch MG (Checklist back)	.06	.03	.01
☐	519	Curt Young	.05	.02	.01
☐	520	Jack Clark	.10	.05	.01
☐	521	Rick Reuschel	.05	.02	.01
☐	522	Checklist 397-528	.06	.02	.01
☐	523	Earnie Riles	.05	.02	.01
☐	524	Bob Shirley	.05	.02	.01
☐	525	Phil Bradley	.05	.02	.01
☐	526	Roger Mason	.05	.02	.01
☐	527	Jim Wohlford	.05	.02	.01
☐	528	Ken Dixon	.05	.02	.01
☐	529	Alvaro Espinoza	.05	.02	.01
☐	530	Tony Gwynn	.50	.23	.06
☐	531	Astros Team (Yogi Berra conference)	.10	.05	.01
☐	532	Jeff Stone	.05	.02	.01
☐	533	Argenis Salazar	.05	.02	.01
☐	534	Scott Sanderson	.05	.02	.01
☐	535	Tony Armas	.05	.02	.01
☐	536	Terry Mulholland	.35	.16	.04
☐	537	Rance Mulliniks	.05	.02	.01
☐	538	Tom Niedenfuer	.05	.02	.01
☐	539	Reid Nichols	.05	.02	.01
☐	540	Terry Kennedy	.05	.02	.01
☐	541	Rafael Belliard	.05	.02	.01
☐	542	Ricky Horton	.05	.02	.01
☐	543	Dave Johnson MG (Checklist back)	.06	.03	.01
☐	544	Zane Smith	.05	.02	.01
☐	545	Buddy Bell	.10	.05	.01
☐	546	Mike Morgan	.05	.02	.01
☐	547	Rob Deer	.05	.02	.01
☐	548	Bill Mooneyham	.05	.02	.01
☐	549	Bob Melvin	.05	.02	.01
☐	550	Pete Incaviglia	.25	.11	.03
☐	551	Frank Wills	.05	.02	.01
☐	552	Larry Sheets	.05	.02	.01
☐	553	Mike Maddux	.05	.02	.01
☐	554	Buddy Biancalana	.05	.02	.01
☐	555	Dennis Rasmussen	.05	.02	.01
☐	556	Angels Team (Rene Lachemann CO, Mike Witt, and Bob Boone)	.05	.02	.01
☐	557	John Cerutti	.05	.02	.01
☐	558	Greg Gagne	.10	.05	.01
☐	559	Lance McCullers	.05	.02	.01
☐	560	Glenn Davis	.05	.02	.01
☐	561	Rey Quinones	.05	.02	.01
☐	562	Bryan Clutterbuck	.05	.02	.01
☐	563	John Stefero	.05	.02	.01
☐	564	Larry McWilliams	.05	.02	.01
☐	565	Dusty Baker	.15	.07	.02
☐	566	Tim Hulett	.05	.02	.01
☐	567	Greg Mathews	.05	.02	.01
☐	568	Earl Weaver MG (Checklist back)	.10	.05	.01
☐	569	Wade Rowdon	.05	.02	.01
☐	570	Sid Fernandez	.10	.05	.01
☐	571	Ozzie Virgil	.05	.02	.01
☐	572	Pete Ladd	.05	.02	.01
☐	573	Hal McRae	.15	.07	.02
☐	574	Manny Lee	.05	.02	.01
☐	575	Pat Tabler	.05	.02	.01
☐	576	Frank Pastore	.05	.02	.01
☐	577	Dann Bilardello	.05	.02	.01
☐	578	Billy Hatcher	.10	.05	.01
☐	579	Rick Burleson	.05	.02	.01
☐	580	Mike Krukow	.05	.02	.01
☐	581	Cubs Team (Ron Cey and Steve Trout)	.05	.02	.01
☐	582	Bruce Berenyi	.05	.02	.01
☐	583	Junior Ortiz	.05	.02	.01
☐	584	Ron Kittle	.05	.02	.01
☐	585	Scott Bailes	.05	.02	.01
☐	586	Ben Oglivie	.05	.02	.01
☐	587	Eric Plunk	.05	.02	.01
☐	588	Wallace Johnson	.05	.02	.01
☐	589	Steve Crawford	.05	.02	.01
☐	590	Vince Coleman	.10	.05	.01
☐	591	Spike Owen	.05	.02	.01
☐	592	Chris Welsh	.05	.02	.01
☐	593	Chuck Tanner MG (Checklist back)	.06	.03	.01
☐	594	Rick Anderson	.05	.02	.01
☐	595	Keith Hernandez AS	.05	.02	.01
☐	596	Steve Sax AS	.05	.02	.01
☐	597	Mike Schmidt AS	.25	.11	.03
☐	598	Ozzie Smith AS	.10	.05	.01
☐	599	Tony Gwynn AS	.25	.11	.03
☐	600	Dave Parker AS	.05	.02	.01
☐	601	Darryl Strawberry AS	.10	.05	.01
☐	602	Gary Carter AS	.10	.05	.01
☐	603A	Dwight Gooden AS ERR (no trademark)	.30	.14	.04
☐	603B	Dwight Gooden AS COR	.10	.05	.01
☐	604	Fernando Valenzuela AS	.05	.02	.01
☐	605	Todd Worrell AS	.05	.02	.01
☐	606A	Don Mattingly AS ERR (no trademark)	.75	.35	.09
☐	606B	Don Mattingly AS COR	.25	.11	.03
☐	607	Tony Bernazard AS	.05	.02	.01
☐	608	Wade Boggs AS	.25	.11	.03
☐	609	Cal Ripken AS	.50	.23	.06
☐	610	Jim Rice AS	.10	.05	.01
☐	611	Kirby Puckett AS	.35	.16	.04
☐	612	George Bell AS	.05	.02	.01
☐	613	Lance Parrish AS UER (Pitcher heading on back)	.05	.02	.01
☐	614	Roger Clemens AS	.25	.11	.03
☐	615	Teddy Higuera AS	.05	.02	.01
☐	616	Dave Righetti AS	.05	.02	.01
☐	617	Al Nipper	.05	.02	.01
☐	618	Tom Kelly MG (Checklist back)	.06	.03	.01
☐	619	Jerry Reed	.05	.02	.01
☐	620	Jose Canseco	1.25	.55	.16
☐	621	Danny Cox	.05	.02	.01
☐	622	Glenn Braggs	.05	.02	.01
☐	623	Kurt Stillwell	.05	.02	.01

	No.	Player			
☐	624	Tim Burke	.05	.02	.01
☐	625	Mookie Wilson	.10	.05	.01
☐	626	Joel Skinner	.05	.02	.01
☐	627	Ken Oberkfell	.05	.02	.01
☐	628	Bob Walk	.05	.02	.01
☐	629	Larry Parrish	.05	.02	.01
☐	630	John Candelaria	.05	.02	.01
☐	631	Tigers Team (Mound conference)	.05	.02	.01
☐	632	Rob Woodward	.05	.02	.01
☐	633	Jose Uribe	.05	.02	.01
☐	634	Rafael Palmeiro	1.50	.65	.19
☐	635	Ken Schrom	.05	.02	.01
☐	636	Darren Daulton	.25	.11	.03
☐	637	Bip Roberts	.20	.09	.03
☐	638	Rich Bordi	.05	.02	.01
☐	639	Gerald Perry	.05	.02	.01
☐	640	Mark Clear	.05	.02	.01
☐	641	Domingo Ramos	.05	.02	.01
☐	642	Al Pulido	.05	.02	.01
☐	643	Ron Shepherd	.05	.02	.01
☐	644	John Denny	.05	.02	.01
☐	645	Dwight Evans	.10	.05	.01
☐	646	Mike Mason	.05	.02	.01
☐	647	Tom Lawless	.05	.02	.01
☐	648	Barry Larkin	.75	.35	.09
☐	649	Mickey Tettleton	.10	.05	.01
☐	650	Hubie Brooks	.05	.02	.01
☐	651	Benny Distefano	.05	.02	.01
☐	652	Terry Forster	.05	.02	.01
☐	653	Kevin Mitchell	.50	.23	.06
☐	654	Checklist 529-660	.06	.02	.01
☐	655	Jesse Barfield	.05	.02	.01
☐	656	Rangers Team (Bobby Valentine MG and Ricky Wright)	.05	.02	.01
☐	657	Tom Waddell	.05	.02	.01
☐	658	Robby Thompson	.25	.11	.03
☐	659	Aurelio Lopez	.05	.02	.01
☐	660	Bob Horner	.05	.02	.01
☐	661	Lou Whitaker	.15	.07	.02
☐	662	Frank DiPino	.05	.02	.01
☐	663	Cliff Johnson	.05	.02	.01
☐	664	Mike Marshall	.05	.02	.01
☐	665	Rod Scurry	.05	.02	.01
☐	666	Von Hayes	.05	.02	.01
☐	667	Ron Hassey	.05	.02	.01
☐	668	Juan Bonilla	.05	.02	.01
☐	669	Bud Black	.05	.02	.01
☐	670	Jose Cruz	.05	.02	.01
☐	671A	Ray Soff ERR (No D* before copyright line)	.05	.02	.01
☐	671B	Ray Soff COR (D* before copyright line)	.05	.02	.01
☐	672	Chili Davis	.10	.05	.01
☐	673	Don Sutton	.15	.07	.02
☐	674	Bill Campbell	.05	.02	.01
☐	675	Ed Romero	.05	.02	.01
☐	676	Charlie Moore	.05	.02	.01
☐	677	Bob Grich	.10	.05	.01
☐	678	Carney Lansford	.10	.05	.01
☐	679	Kent Hrbek	.10	.05	.01
☐	680	Ryne Sandberg	.40	.18	.05
☐	681	George Bell	.10	.05	.01
☐	682	Jerry Reuss	.05	.02	.01
☐	683	Gary Roenicke	.05	.02	.01
☐	684	Kent Tekulve	.05	.02	.01
☐	685	Jerry Hairston	.05	.02	.01
☐	686	Doyle Alexander	.05	.02	.01
☐	687	Alan Trammell	.15	.07	.02
☐	688	Juan Beniquez	.05	.02	.01
☐	689	Darrell Porter	.05	.02	.01
☐	690	Dane Iorg	.05	.02	.01
☐	691	Dave Parker	.15	.07	.02
☐	692	Frank White	.10	.05	.01
☐	693	Terry Puhl	.05	.02	.01
☐	694	Phil Niekro	.15	.07	.02
☐	695	Chico Walker	.05	.02	.01
☐	696	Gary Lucas	.05	.02	.01
☐	697	Ed Lynch	.05	.02	.01
☐	698	Ernie Whitt	.05	.02	.01
☐	699	Ken Landreaux	.05	.02	.01
☐	700	Dave Bergman	.05	.02	.01
☐	701	Willie Randolph	.10	.05	.01
☐	702	Greg Gross	.05	.02	.01
☐	703	Dave Schmidt	.05	.02	.01
☐	704	Jesse Orosco	.05	.02	.01
☐	705	Bruce Hurst	.05	.02	.01
☐	706	Rick Manning	.05	.02	.01
☐	707	Bob McClure	.05	.02	.01
☐	708	Scott McGregor	.05	.02	.01
☐	709	Dave Kingman	.10	.05	.01
☐	710	Gary Gaetti	.05	.02	.01
☐	711	Ken Griffey	.10	.05	.01
☐	712	Don Robinson	.05	.02	.01
☐	713	Tom Brookens	.05	.02	.01
☐	714	Dan Quisenberry	.10	.05	.01
☐	715	Bob Dernier	.05	.02	.01
☐	716	Rick Leach	.05	.02	.01
☐	717	Ed VandeBerg	.05	.02	.01
☐	718	Steve Carlton	.25	.11	.03
☐	719	Tom Hume	.05	.02	.01
☐	720	Richard Dotson	.05	.02	.01
☐	721	Tom Herr	.05	.02	.01
☐	722	Bob Knepper	.05	.02	.01
☐	723	Brett Butler	.10	.05	.01
☐	724	Greg Minton	.05	.02	.01
☐	725	George Hendrick	.05	.02	.01
☐	726	Frank Tanana	.05	.02	.01
☐	727	Mike Moore	.05	.02	.01
☐	728	Tippy Martinez	.05	.02	.01
☐	729	Tom Paciorek	.10	.05	.01
☐	730	Eric Show	.05	.02	.01
☐	731	Dave Concepcion	.10	.05	.01
☐	732	Manny Trillo	.05	.02	.01
☐	733	Bill Caudill	.05	.02	.01
☐	734	Bill Madlock	.10	.05	.01
☐	735	Rickey Henderson	.25	.11	.03
☐	736	Steve Bedrosian	.05	.02	.01
☐	737	Floyd Bannister	.05	.02	.01
☐	738	Jorge Orta	.05	.02	.01
☐	739	Chet Lemon	.05	.02	.01
☐	740	Rich Gedman	.05	.02	.01
☐	741	Paul Molitor	.25	.11	.03
☐	742	Andy McGaffigan	.05	.02	.01
☐	743	Dwayne Murphy	.05	.02	.01
☐	744	Roy Smalley	.05	.02	.01
☐	745	Glenn Hubbard	.05	.02	.01
☐	746	Bob Ojeda	.05	.02	.01
☐	747	Johnny Ray	.05	.02	.01
☐	748	Mike Flanagan	.05	.02	.01
☐	749	Ozzie Smith	.35	.16	.04
☐	750	Steve Trout	.05	.02	.01
☐	751	Garth Iorg	.05	.02	.01
☐	752	Dan Petry	.05	.02	.01
☐	753	Rick Honeycutt	.05	.02	.01
☐	754	Dave LaPoint	.05	.02	.01
☐	755	Luis Aguayo	.05	.02	.01
☐	756	Carlton Fisk	.25	.11	.03
☐	757	Nolan Ryan	1.00	.45	.13
☐	758	Tony Bernazard	.05	.02	.01
☐	759	Joel Youngblood	.05	.02	.01
☐	760	Mike Witt	.05	.02	.01
☐	761	Greg Pryor	.05	.02	.01

☐ 762	Gary Ward	.05	.02	.01
☐ 763	Tim Flannery	.05	.02	.01
☐ 764	Bill Buckner	.10	.05	.01
☐ 765	Kirk Gibson	.10	.05	.01
☐ 766	Don Aase	.05	.02	.01
☐ 767	Ron Cey	.10	.05	.01
☐ 768	Dennis Lamp	.05	.02	.01
☐ 769	Steve Sax	.05	.02	.01
☐ 770	Dave Winfield	.25	.11	.03
☐ 771	Shane Rawley	.05	.02	.01
☐ 772	Harold Baines	.10	.05	.01
☐ 773	Robin Yount	.25	.11	.03
☐ 774	Wayne Krenchicki	.05	.02	.01
☐ 775	Joaquin Andujar	.05	.02	.01
☐ 776	Tom Brunansky	.05	.02	.01
☐ 777	Chris Chambliss	.10	.05	.01
☐ 778	Jack Morris	.15	.07	.02
☐ 779	Craig Reynolds	.05	.02	.01
☐ 780	Andre Thornton	.05	.02	.01
☐ 781	Atlee Hammaker	.05	.02	.01
☐ 782	Brian Downing	.05	.02	.01
☐ 783	Willie Wilson	.05	.02	.01
☐ 784	Cal Ripken	.75	.35	.09
☐ 785	Terry Francona	.05	.02	.01
☐ 786	Jimy Williams MG (Checklist back)	.06	.03	.01
☐ 787	Alejandro Pena	.05	.02	.01
☐ 788	Tim Stoddard	.05	.02	.01
☐ 789	Dan Schatzeder	.05	.02	.01
☐ 790	Julio Cruz	.05	.02	.01
☐ 791	Lance Parrish UER (No trademark, never corrected)	.10	.05	.01
☐ 792	Checklist 661-792	.06	.02	.01

This year Topps did not disclose the number of sets they produced or sold. It is apparent from the availability that there were many more sets produced this year compared to the 1984-86 Tiffany sets, perhaps 30,000 sets, more than three times as many. The checklist of cards is identical to that of the normal non-glossy cards. There are two primary distinguishing features of the Tiffany cards, white card stock reverses and high gloss obverses. These Tiffany cards are valued approximately from three to five times the values listed below.

	MINT	EXC	G-VG
COMPLETE FACT.SET (132)	8.00	3.60	1.00
COMMON CARD (1T-132T)	.05	.02	.01

☐ 1T	Bill Almon	.05	.02	.01
☐ 2T	Scott Bankhead	.05	.02	.01
☐ 3T	Eric Bell	.05	.02	.01
☐ 4T	Juan Beniquez	.05	.02	.01
☐ 5T	Juan Berenguer	.05	.02	.01
☐ 6T	Greg Booker	.05	.02	.01
☐ 7T	Thad Bosley	.05	.02	.01
☐ 8T	Larry Bowa MG	.08	.04	.01
☐ 9T	Greg Brock	.05	.02	.01
☐ 10T	Bob Brower	.05	.02	.01
☐ 11T	Jerry Browne	.08	.04	.01
☐ 12T	Ralph Bryant	.05	.02	.01
☐ 13T	DeWayne Buice	.05	.02	.01
☐ 14T	Ellis Burks	.75	.35	.09
☐ 15T	Ivan Calderon	.05	.02	.01
☐ 16T	Jeff Calhoun	.05	.02	.01
☐ 17T	Casey Candaele	.05	.02	.01
☐ 18T	John Cangelosi	.05	.02	.01
☐ 19T	Steve Carlton	.25	.11	.03
☐ 20T	Juan Castillo	.05	.02	.01
☐ 21T	Rick Cerone	.05	.02	.01
☐ 22T	Ron Cey	.08	.04	.01
☐ 23T	John Christensen	.05	.02	.01
☐ 24T	David Cone	1.25	.55	.16
☐ 25T	Chuck Crim	.05	.02	.01
☐ 26T	Storm Davis	.05	.02	.01
☐ 27T	Andre Dawson	.25	.11	.03
☐ 28T	Rick Dempsey	.05	.02	.01
☐ 29T	Doug Drabek	.40	.18	.05
☐ 30T	Mike Dunne	.05	.02	.01
☐ 31T	Dennis Eckersley	.10	.05	.01
☐ 32T	Lee Elia MG	.05	.02	.01
☐ 33T	Brian Fisher	.05	.02	.01
☐ 34T	Terry Francona	.05	.02	.01
☐ 35T	Willie Fraser	.05	.02	.01
☐ 36T	Billy Gardner MG	.05	.02	.01
☐ 37T	Ken Gerhart	.05	.02	.01
☐ 38T	Dan Gladden	.05	.02	.01
☐ 39T	Jim Gott	.05	.02	.01
☐ 40T	Cecilio Guante	.05	.02	.01
☐ 41T	Albert Hall	.05	.02	.01
☐ 42T	Terry Harper	.05	.02	.01
☐ 43T	Mickey Hatcher	.05	.02	.01
☐ 44T	Brad Havens	.05	.02	.01
☐ 45T	Neal Heaton	.05	.02	.01
☐ 46T	Mike Henneman	.25	.11	.03
☐ 47T	Donnie Hill	.05	.02	.01
☐ 48T	Guy Hoffman	.05	.02	.01
☐ 49T	Brian Holton	.05	.02	.01
☐ 50T	Charles Hudson	.05	.02	.01
☐ 51T	Danny Jackson	.08	.04	.01
☐ 52T	Reggie Jackson	.35	.16	.04
☐ 53T	Chris James	.05	.02	.01
☐ 54T	Dion James	.05	.02	.01
☐ 55T	Stan Jefferson	.05	.02	.01

1987 Topps Traded

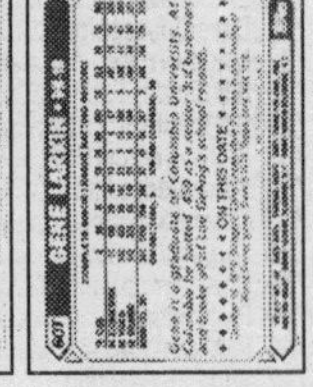

This 132-card Traded or extended set was distributed by Topps to dealers in a special green and white box as a complete set. The card fronts are identical in style to the Topps regular issue and are also 2 1/2" by 3 1/2". The backs are printed in yellow and blue on white card stock. Cards are numbered (with a T suffix) alphabetically according to the name of the player. The key (extended) Rookie Cards in this set (without any prior cards) are Ellis Burks and Matt Williams. Extended Rookie Cards in this set (with prior cards but not from Topps) are David Cone, Greg Maddux, and Fred McGriff. Topps also produced a specially boxed "glossy" edition, frequently referred to as the Topps Traded Tiffany set.

☐ 56T	Joe Johnson	.05	.02	.01
☐ 57T	Terry Kennedy	.05	.02	.01
☐ 58T	Mike Kingery	.08	.04	.01
☐ 59T	Ray Knight	.08	.04	.01
☐ 60T	Gene Larkin	.05	.02	.01
☐ 61T	Mike LaValliere	.05	.02	.01
☐ 62T	Jack Lazorko	.05	.02	.01
☐ 63T	Terry Leach	.05	.02	.01
☐ 64T	Tim Leary	.05	.02	.01
☐ 65T	Jim Lindeman	.05	.02	.01
☐ 66T	Steve Lombardozzi	.05	.02	.01
☐ 67T	Bill Long	.05	.02	.01
☐ 68T	Barry Lyons	.05	.02	.01
☐ 69T	Shane Mack	.35	.16	.04
☐ 70T	Greg Maddux	3.50	1.55	.45
☐ 71T	Bill Madlock	.08	.04	.01
☐ 72T	Joe Magrane	.12	.05	.02
☐ 73T	Dave Martinez	.15	.07	.02
☐ 74T	Fred McGriff	2.50	1.15	.30
☐ 75T	Mark McLemore	.20	.09	.03
☐ 76T	Kevin McReynolds	.08	.04	.01
☐ 77T	Dave Meads	.05	.02	.01
☐ 78T	Eddie Milner	.05	.02	.01
☐ 79T	Greg Minton	.05	.02	.01
☐ 80T	John Mitchell	.05	.02	.01
☐ 81T	Kevin Mitchell	.25	.11	.03
☐ 82T	Charlie Moore	.05	.02	.01
☐ 83T	Jeff Musselman	.05	.02	.01
☐ 84T	Gene Nelson	.05	.02	.01
☐ 85T	Graig Nettles	.08	.04	.01
☐ 86T	Al Newman	.05	.02	.01
☐ 87T	Reid Nichols	.05	.02	.01
☐ 88T	Tom Niedenfuer	.05	.02	.01
☐ 89T	Joe Niekro	.08	.04	.01
☐ 90T	Tom Nieto	.05	.02	.01
☐ 91T	Matt Nokes	.20	.09	.03
☐ 92T	Dickie Noles	.05	.02	.01
☐ 93T	Pat Pacillo	.05	.02	.01
☐ 94T	Lance Parrish	.08	.04	.01
☐ 95T	Tony Pena	.05	.02	.01
☐ 96T	Luis Polonia	.40	.18	.05
☐ 97T	Randy Ready	.05	.02	.01
☐ 98T	Jeff Reardon	.10	.05	.01
☐ 99T	Gary Redus	.05	.02	.01
☐ 100T	Jeff Reed	.05	.02	.01
☐ 101T	Rick Rhoden	.05	.02	.01
☐ 102T	Cal Ripken Sr. MG	.08	.04	.01
☐ 103T	Wally Ritchie	.05	.02	.01
☐ 104T	Jeff M. Robinson	.05	.02	.01
☐ 105T	Gary Roenicke	.05	.02	.01
☐ 106T	Jerry Royster	.05	.02	.01
☐ 107T	Mark Salas	.05	.02	.01
☐ 108T	Luis Salazar	.05	.02	.01
☐ 109T	Benito Santiago	.20	.09	.03
☐ 110T	Dave Schmidt	.05	.02	.01
☐ 111T	Kevin Seitzer	.15	.07	.02
☐ 112T	John Shelby	.05	.02	.01
☐ 113T	Steve Shields	.05	.02	.01
☐ 114T	John Smiley	.30	.14	.04
☐ 115T	Chris Speier	.05	.02	.01
☐ 116T	Mike Stanley	.35	.16	.04
☐ 117T	Terry Steinbach	.30	.14	.04
☐ 118T	Les Straker	.05	.02	.01
☐ 119T	Jim Sundberg	.05	.02	.01
☐ 120T	Danny Tartabull	.20	.09	.03
☐ 121T	Tom Trebelhorn MG	.05	.02	.01
☐ 122T	Dave Valle	.05	.02	.01
☐ 123T	Ed VandeBerg	.05	.02	.01
☐ 124T	Andy Van Slyke	.10	.05	.01
☐ 125T	Gary Ward	.05	.02	.01
☐ 126T	Alan Wiggins	.05	.02	.01
☐ 127T	Bill Wilkinson	.05	.02	.01
☐ 128T	Frank Williams	.05	.02	.01
☐ 129T	Matt Williams	2.50	1.15	.30
☐ 130T	Jim Winn	.05	.02	.01
☐ 131T	Matt Young	.05	.02	.01
☐ 132T	Checklist 1T-132T	.05	.02	.01

1988 Topps

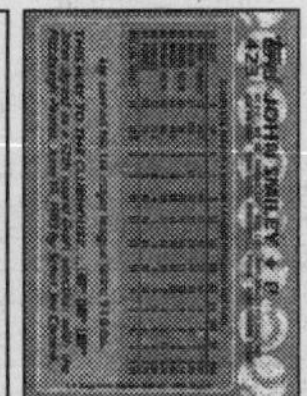

This 792-card set features backs that are printed in orange and black on light gray card stock. The manager cards contain a checklist of the respective team's players on the back. Subsets in the set include Record Breakers (1-7), Turn Back the Clock (661-665), and All-Star selections (386-407). The Team Leader cards typically show two players together inside a white cloud. The key Rookie Cards in this set are Ellis Burks, Tom Glavine, Jeff Montgomery, and Matt Williams. Topps also produced a specially boxed "glossy" edition, frequently referred to as the Topps Tiffany set. This year, again, Topps did not disclose the number of Tiffany sets they produced or sold. It is apparent from the availability that there were many more sets produced this year compared to the 1984-86 Tiffany sets, perhaps 25,000 sets. The checklist of cards (792 regular and 132 Traded) is identical to that of the normal non-glossy cards. There are two primary distinguishing features of the Tiffany cards, white card stock reverses and high gloss obverses. These Tiffany cards are valued approximately from three to five times the values listed below.

	MINT	EXC	G-VG
COMPLETE SET (792)	15.00	6.75	1.90
COMPLETE FACT.SET (792)	15.00	6.75	1.90
COMMON CARD (1-792)	.05	.02	.01

☐ 1	Vince Coleman RB 100 Steals for Third Cons. Season	.10	.05	.01
☐ 2	Don Mattingly RB Six Grand Slams	.15	.07	.02
☐ 3A	Mark McGwire RB Rookie Homer Record (White spot behind left foot)	.25	.11	.03
☐ 3B	Mark McGwire RB Rookie Homer Record (No white spot)	.10	.05	.01
☐ 4A	Eddie Murray RB Switch Home Runs,	.30	.14	.04

	No.	Card			
		Two Straight Games (Caption in box on card front)			
☐	4B	Eddie Murray RB	.10	.05	.01
		Switch Home Runs, Two Straight Games (No caption on front)			
☐	5	Phil/Joe Niekro RB	.05	.02	.01
		Brothers Win Record			
☐	6	Nolan Ryan RB	.40	.18	.05
		11th Season with 200 Strikeouts			
☐	7	Benito Santiago RB	.05	.02	.01
		34-Game Hitting Streak, Rookie Record			
☐	8	Kevin Elster	.05	.02	.01
☐	9	Andy Hawkins	.05	.02	.01
☐	10	Ryne Sandberg	.50	.23	.06
☐	11	Mike Young	.05	.02	.01
☐	12	Bill Schroeder	.05	.02	.01
☐	13	Andres Thomas	.05	.02	.01
☐	14	Sparky Anderson MG	.10	.05	.01
		(Checklist back)			
☐	15	Chili Davis	.10	.05	.01
☐	16	Kirk McCaskill	.05	.02	.01
☐	17	Ron Oester	.05	.02	.01
☐	18A	Al Leiter ERR	.25	.11	.03
		(Photo actually Steve George, right ear visible)			
☐	18B	Al Leiter COR	.15	.07	.02
		(Left ear visible)			
☐	19	Mark Davidson	.05	.02	.01
☐	20	Kevin Gross	.05	.02	.01
☐	21	Red Sox TL	.10	.05	.01
		Wade Boggs and Spike Owen			
☐	22	Greg Swindell	.10	.05	.01
☐	23	Ken Landreaux	.05	.02	.01
☐	24	Jim Deshaies	.05	.02	.01
☐	25	Andres Galarraga	.25	.11	.03
☐	26	Mitch Williams	.10	.05	.01
☐	27	R.J. Reynolds	.05	.02	.01
☐	28	Jose Nunez	.05	.02	.01
☐	29	Argenis Salazar	.05	.02	.01
☐	30	Sid Fernandez	.10	.05	.01
☐	31	Bruce Bochy	.05	.02	.01
☐	32	Mike Morgan	.05	.02	.01
☐	33	Rob Deer	.05	.02	.01
☐	34	Ricky Horton	.05	.02	.01
☐	35	Harold Baines	.10	.05	.01
☐	36	Jamie Moyer	.05	.02	.01
☐	37	Ed Romero	.05	.02	.01
☐	38	Jeff Calhoun	.05	.02	.01
☐	39	Gerald Perry	.05	.02	.01
☐	40	Orel Hershiser	.10	.05	.01
☐	41	Bob Melvin	.05	.02	.01
☐	42	Bill Landrum	.05	.02	.01
☐	43	Dick Schofield	.05	.02	.01
☐	44	Lou Piniella MG	.05	.02	.01
		(Checklist back)			
☐	45	Kent Hrbek	.10	.05	.01
☐	46	Darnell Coles	.05	.02	.01
☐	47	Joaquin Andujar	.05	.02	.01
☐	48	Alan Ashby	.05	.02	.01
☐	49	Dave Clark	.05	.02	.01
☐	50	Hubie Brooks	.05	.02	.01
☐	51	Orioles TL	.25	.11	.03
		Eddie Murray and Cal Ripken			
☐	52	Don Robinson	.05	.02	.01
☐	53	Curt Wilkerson	.05	.02	.01
☐	54	Jim Clancy	.05	.02	.01
☐	55	Phil Bradley	.05	.02	.01
☐	56	Ed Hearn	.05	.02	.01
☐	57	Tim Crews	.10	.05	.01
☐	58	Dave Magadan	.10	.05	.01
☐	59	Danny Cox	.05	.02	.01
☐	60	Rickey Henderson	.25	.11	.03
☐	61	Mark Knudson	.05	.02	.01
☐	62	Jeff Hamilton	.05	.02	.01
☐	63	Jimmy Jones	.05	.02	.01
☐	64	Ken Caminiti	.50	.23	.06
☐	65	Leon Durham	.05	.02	.01
☐	66	Shane Rawley	.05	.02	.01
☐	67	Ken Oberkfell	.05	.02	.01
☐	68	Dave Dravecky	.10	.05	.01
☐	69	Mike Hart	.05	.02	.01
☐	70	Roger Clemens	.40	.18	.05
☐	71	Gary Pettis	.05	.02	.01
☐	72	Dennis Eckersley	.15	.07	.02
☐	73	Randy Bush	.05	.02	.01
☐	74	Tom Lasorda MG	.10	.05	.01
		(Checklist back)			
☐	75	Joe Carter	.30	.14	.04
☐	76	Dennis Martinez	.10	.05	.01
☐	77	Tom O'Malley	.05	.02	.01
☐	78	Dan Petry	.05	.02	.01
☐	79	Ernie Whitt	.05	.02	.01
☐	80	Mark Langston	.15	.07	.02
☐	81	Reds TL	.05	.02	.01
		Ron Robinson and John Franco			
☐	82	Darrel Akerfelds	.05	.02	.01
☐	83	Jose Oquendo	.05	.02	.01
☐	84	Cecilio Guante	.05	.02	.01
☐	85	Howard Johnson	.10	.05	.01
☐	86	Ron Karkovice	.05	.02	.01
☐	87	Mike Mason	.05	.02	.01
☐	88	Earnie Riles	.05	.02	.01
☐	89	Gary Thurman	.05	.02	.01
☐	90	Dale Murphy	.15	.07	.02
☐	91	Joey Cora	.15	.07	.02
☐	92	Len Matuszek	.05	.02	.01
☐	93	Bob Sebra	.05	.02	.01
☐	94	Chuck Jackson	.05	.02	.01
☐	95	Lance Parrish	.10	.05	.01
☐	96	Todd Benzinger	.10	.05	.01
☐	97	Scott Garrelts	.05	.02	.01
☐	98	Rene Gonzales	.05	.02	.01
☐	99	Chuck Finley	.10	.05	.01
☐	100	Jack Clark	.10	.05	.01
☐	101	Allan Anderson	.05	.02	.01
☐	102	Barry Larkin	.20	.09	.03
☐	103	Curt Young	.05	.02	.01
☐	104	Dick Williams MG	.05	.02	.01
		(Checklist back)			
☐	105	Jesse Orosco	.05	.02	.01
☐	106	Jim Walewander	.05	.02	.01
☐	107	Scott Bailes	.05	.02	.01
☐	108	Steve Lyons	.05	.02	.01
☐	109	Joel Skinner	.05	.02	.01
☐	110	Teddy Higuera	.05	.02	.01
☐	111	Expos TL	.05	.02	.01
		Hubie Brooks and Vance Law			
☐	112	Les Lancaster	.05	.02	.01
☐	113	Kelly Gruber	.05	.02	.01
☐	114	Jeff Russell	.05	.02	.01
☐	115	Johnny Ray	.05	.02	.01
☐	116	Jerry Don Gleaton	.05	.02	.01
☐	117	James Steels	.05	.02	.01
☐	118	Bob Welch	.10	.05	.01
☐	119	Robbie Wine	.05	.02	.01
☐	120	Kirby Puckett	.50	.23	.06
☐	121	Checklist 1-132	.06	.02	.01

Card			
☐ 122 Tony Bernazard	.05	.02	.01
☐ 123 Tom Candiotti	.05	.02	.01
☐ 124 Ray Knight	.10	.05	.01
☐ 125 Bruce Hurst	.05	.02	.01
☐ 126 Steve Jeltz	.05	.02	.01
☐ 127 Jim Gott	.05	.02	.01
☐ 128 Johnny Grubb	.05	.02	.01
☐ 129 Greg Minton	.05	.02	.01
☐ 130 Buddy Bell	.10	.05	.01
☐ 131 Don Schulze	.05	.02	.01
☐ 132 Donnie Hill	.05	.02	.01
☐ 133 Greg Mathews	.05	.02	.01
☐ 134 Chuck Tanner MG	.05	.02	.01
(Checklist back)			
☐ 135 Dennis Rasmussen	.05	.02	.01
☐ 136 Brian Dayett	.05	.02	.01
☐ 137 Chris Bosio	.10	.05	.01
☐ 138 Mitch Webster	.05	.02	.01
☐ 139 Jerry Browne	.05	.02	.01
☐ 140 Jesse Barfield	.05	.02	.01
☐ 141 Royals TL	.12	.05	.02
George Brett and			
Bret Saberhagen			
☐ 142 Andy Van Slyke	.15	.07	.02
☐ 143 Mickey Tettleton	.10	.05	.01
☐ 144 Don Gordon	.05	.02	.01
☐ 145 Bill Madlock	.10	.05	.01
☐ 146 Donell Nixon	.05	.02	.01
☐ 147 Bill Buckner	.10	.05	.01
☐ 148 Carmelo Martinez	.05	.02	.01
☐ 149 Ken Howell	.05	.02	.01
☐ 150 Eric Davis	.10	.05	.01
☐ 151 Bob Knepper	.05	.02	.01
☐ 152 Jody Reed	.15	.07	.02
☐ 153 John Habyan	.05	.02	.01
☐ 154 Jeff Stone	.05	.02	.01
☐ 155 Bruce Sutter	.10	.05	.01
☐ 156 Gary Matthews	.05	.02	.01
☐ 157 Atlee Hammaker	.05	.02	.01
☐ 158 Tim Hulett	.05	.02	.01
☐ 159 Brad Arnsberg	.05	.02	.01
☐ 160 Willie McGee	.10	.05	.01
☐ 161 Bryn Smith	.05	.02	.01
☐ 162 Mark McLemore	.05	.02	.01
☐ 163 Dale Mohorcic	.05	.02	.01
☐ 164 Dave Johnson MG	.05	.02	.01
(Checklist back)			
☐ 165 Robin Yount	.20	.09	.03
☐ 166 Rick Rodriquez	.05	.02	.01
☐ 167 Rance Mulliniks	.05	.02	.01
☐ 168 Barry Jones	.05	.02	.01
☐ 169 Ross Jones	.05	.02	.01
☐ 170 Rich Gossage	.15	.07	.02
☐ 171 Cubs TL	.05	.02	.01
Shawon Dunston			
and Manny Trillo			
☐ 172 Lloyd McClendon	.05	.02	.01
☐ 173 Eric Plunk	.05	.02	.01
☐ 174 Phil Garner	.10	.05	.01
☐ 175 Kevin Bass	.05	.02	.01
☐ 176 Jeff Reed	.05	.02	.01
☐ 177 Frank Tanana	.05	.02	.01
☐ 178 Dwayne Henry	.05	.02	.01
☐ 179 Charlie Puleo	.05	.02	.01
☐ 180 Terry Kennedy	.05	.02	.01
☐ 181 David Cone	.35	.16	.04
☐ 182 Ken Phelps	.05	.02	.01
☐ 183 Tom Lawless	.05	.02	.01
☐ 184 Ivan Calderon	.10	.05	.01
☐ 185 Rick Rhoden	.05	.02	.01
☐ 186 Rafael Palmeiro	.50	.23	.06
☐ 187 Steve Kiefer	.05	.02	.01
☐ 188 John Russell	.05	.02	.01
☐ 189 Wes Gardner	.05	.02	.01
☐ 190 Candy Maldonado	.05	.02	.01
☐ 191 John Cerutti	.05	.02	.01
☐ 192 Devon White	.15	.07	.02
☐ 193 Brian Fisher	.05	.02	.01
☐ 194 Tom Kelly MG	.05	.02	.01
(Checklist back)			
☐ 195 Dan Quisenberry	.10	.05	.01
☐ 196 Dave Engle	.05	.02	.01
☐ 197 Lance McCullers	.05	.02	.01
☐ 198 Franklin Stubbs	.05	.02	.01
☐ 199 Dave Meads	.05	.02	.01
☐ 200 Wade Boggs	.25	.11	.03
☐ 201 Rangers TL	.05	.02	.01
Bobby Valentine MG,			
Pete O'Brien,			
Pete Incaviglia, and			
Steve Buechele			
☐ 202 Glenn Hoffman	.05	.02	.01
☐ 203 Fred Toliver	.05	.02	.01
☐ 204 Paul O'Neill	.25	.11	.03
☐ 205 Nelson Liriano	.05	.02	.01
☐ 206 Domingo Ramos	.05	.02	.01
☐ 207 John Mitchell	.05	.02	.01
☐ 208 Steve Lake	.05	.02	.01
☐ 209 Richard Dotson	.05	.02	.01
☐ 210 Willie Randolph	.10	.05	.01
☐ 211 Frank DiPino	.05	.02	.01
☐ 212 Greg Brock	.05	.02	.01
☐ 213 Albert Hall	.05	.02	.01
☐ 214 Dave Schmidt	.05	.02	.01
☐ 215 Von Hayes	.05	.02	.01
☐ 216 Jerry Reuss	.05	.02	.01
☐ 217 Harry Spilman	.05	.02	.01
☐ 218 Dan Schatzeder	.05	.02	.01
☐ 219 Mike Stanley	.10	.05	.01
☐ 220 Tom Henke	.10	.05	.01
☐ 221 Rafael Belliard	.05	.02	.01
☐ 222 Steve Farr	.05	.02	.01
☐ 223 Stan Jefferson	.05	.02	.01
☐ 224 Tom Trebelhorn MG	.05	.02	.01
(Checklist back)			
☐ 225 Mike Scioscia	.05	.02	.01
☐ 226 Dave Lopes	.10	.05	.01
☐ 227 Ed Correa	.05	.02	.01
☐ 228 Wallace Johnson	.05	.02	.01
☐ 229 Jeff Musselman	.05	.02	.01
☐ 230 Pat Tabler	.05	.02	.01
☐ 231 Pirates TL	.15	.07	.02
Barry Bonds and			
Bobby Bonilla			
☐ 232 Bob James	.05	.02	.01
☐ 233 Rafael Santana	.05	.02	.01
☐ 234 Ken Dayley	.05	.02	.01
☐ 235 Gary Ward	.05	.02	.01
☐ 236 Ted Power	.05	.02	.01
☐ 237 Mike Heath	.05	.02	.01
☐ 238 Luis Polonia	.25	.11	.03
☐ 239 Roy Smalley	.05	.02	.01
☐ 240 Lee Smith	.15	.07	.02
☐ 241 Damaso Garcia	.05	.02	.01
☐ 242 Tom Niedenfuer	.05	.02	.01
☐ 243 Mark Ryal	.05	.02	.01
☐ 244 Jeff D. Robinson	.05	.02	.01
☐ 245 Rich Gedman	.05	.02	.01
☐ 246 Mike Campbell	.05	.02	.01
☐ 247 Thad Bosley	.05	.02	.01
☐ 248 Storm Davis	.05	.02	.01
☐ 249 Mike Marshall	.05	.02	.01
☐ 250 Nolan Ryan	.75	.35	.09
☐ 251 Tom Foley	.05	.02	.01
☐ 252 Bob Brower	.05	.02	.01
☐ 253 Checklist 133-264	.06	.02	.01

☐ 254 Lee Elia MG .05 .02 .01
(Checklist back)
☐ 255 Mookie Wilson .10 .05 .01
☐ 256 Ken Schrom .05 .02 .01
☐ 257 Jerry Royster .05 .02 .01
☐ 258 Ed Nunez .05 .02 .01
☐ 259 Ron Kittle .05 .02 .01
☐ 260 Vince Coleman .10 .05 .01
☐ 261 Giants TL .05 .02 .01
(Five players)
☐ 262 Drew Hall .05 .02 .01
☐ 263 Glenn Braggs .05 .02 .01
☐ 264 Les Straker .05 .02 .01
☐ 265 Bo Diaz .05 .02 .01
☐ 266 Paul Assenmacher .05 .02 .01
☐ 267 Billy Bean .05 .02 .01
☐ 268 Bruce Ruffin .05 .02 .01
☐ 269 Ellis Burks .40 .18 .05
☐ 270 Mike Witt .05 .02 .01
☐ 271 Ken Gerhart .05 .02 .01
☐ 272 Steve Ontiveros .05 .02 .01
☐ 273 Garth Iorg .05 .02 .01
☐ 274 Junior Ortiz .05 .02 .01
☐ 275 Kevin Seitzer .10 .05 .01
☐ 276 Luis Salazar .05 .02 .01
☐ 277 Alejandro Pena .05 .02 .01
☐ 278 Jose Cruz .05 .02 .01
☐ 279 Randy St.Claire .05 .02 .01
☐ 280 Pete Incaviglia .10 .05 .01
☐ 281 Jerry Hairston .05 .02 .01
☐ 282 Pat Perry .05 .02 .01
☐ 283 Phil Lombardi .05 .02 .01
☐ 284 Larry Bowa MG .10 .05 .01
(Checklist back)
☐ 285 Jim Presley .05 .02 .01
☐ 286 Chuck Crim .05 .02 .01
☐ 287 Manny Trillo .05 .02 .01
☐ 288 Pat Pacillo .05 .02 .01
(Chris Sabo in
background of photo)
☐ 289 Dave Bergman .05 .02 .01
☐ 290 Tony Fernandez .10 .05 .01
☐ 291 Astros TL .05 .02 .01
Billy Hatcher
and Kevin Bass
☐ 292 Carney Lansford .10 .05 .01
☐ 293 Doug Jones .30 .14 .04
☐ 294 Al Pedrique .05 .02 .01
☐ 295 Bert Blyleven .15 .07 .02
☐ 296 Floyd Rayford .05 .02 .01
☐ 297 Zane Smith .05 .02 .01
☐ 298 Milt Thompson .05 .02 .01
☐ 299 Steve Crawford .05 .02 .01
☐ 300 Don Mattingly .40 .18 .05
☐ 301 Bud Black .05 .02 .01
☐ 302 Jose Uribe .05 .02 .01
☐ 303 Eric Show .05 .02 .01
☐ 304 George Hendrick .05 .02 .01
☐ 305 Steve Sax .05 .02 .01
☐ 306 Billy Hatcher .05 .02 .01
☐ 307 Mike Trujillo .05 .02 .01
☐ 308 Lee Mazzilli .05 .02 .01
☐ 309 Bill Long .05 .02 .01
☐ 310 Tom Herr .05 .02 .01
☐ 311 Scott Sanderson .05 .02 .01
☐ 312 Joey Meyer .05 .02 .01
☐ 313 Bob McClure .05 .02 .01
☐ 314 Jimy Williams MG .05 .02 .01
(Checklist back)
☐ 315 Dave Parker .15 .07 .02
☐ 316 Jose Rijo .15 .07 .02
☐ 317 Tom Nieto .05 .02 .01
☐ 318 Mel Hall .05 .02 .01
☐ 319 Mike Loynd .05 .02 .01
☐ 320 Alan Trammell .15 .07 .02
☐ 321 White Sox TL .10 .05 .01
Harold Baines and
Carlton Fisk
☐ 322 Vicente Palacios .05 .02 .01
☐ 323 Rick Leach .05 .02 .01
☐ 324 Danny Jackson .05 .02 .01
☐ 325 Glenn Hubbard .05 .02 .01
☐ 326 Al Nipper .05 .02 .01
☐ 327 Larry Sheets .05 .02 .01
☐ 328 Greg Cadaret .05 .02 .01
☐ 329 Chris Speier .05 .02 .01
☐ 330 Eddie Whitson .05 .02 .01
☐ 331 Brian Downing .05 .02 .01
☐ 332 Jerry Reed .05 .02 .01
☐ 333 Wally Backman .05 .02 .01
☐ 334 Dave LaPoint .05 .02 .01
☐ 335 Claudell Washington .05 .02 .01
☐ 336 Ed Lynch .05 .02 .01
☐ 337 Jim Gantner .05 .02 .01
☐ 338 Brian Holton UER .05 .02 .01
(1987 ERA .389,
should be 3.89)
☐ 339 Kurt Stillwell .05 .02 .01
☐ 340 Jack Morris .15 .07 .02
☐ 341 Carmen Castillo .05 .02 .01
☐ 342 Larry Andersen .05 .02 .01
☐ 343 Greg Gagne .05 .02 .01
☐ 344 Tony LaRussa MG .10 .05 .01
(Checklist back)
☐ 345 Scott Fletcher .05 .02 .01
☐ 346 Vance Law .05 .02 .01
☐ 347 Joe Johnson .05 .02 .01
☐ 348 Jim Eisenreich .10 .05 .01
☐ 349 Bob Walk .05 .02 .01
☐ 350 Will Clark .40 .18 .05
☐ 351 Cardinals TL .05 .02 .01
Red Schoendienst CO
and Tony Pena
☐ 352 Billy Ripken .05 .02 .01
☐ 353 Ed Olwine .05 .02 .01
☐ 354 Marc Sullivan .05 .02 .01
☐ 355 Roger McDowell .05 .02 .01
☐ 356 Luis Aguayo .05 .02 .01
☐ 357 Floyd Bannister .05 .02 .01
☐ 358 Rey Quinones .05 .02 .01
☐ 359 Tim Stoddard .05 .02 .01
☐ 360 Tony Gwynn .35 .16 .04
☐ 361 Greg Maddux 1.25 .55 .16
☐ 362 Juan Castillo .05 .02 .01
☐ 363 Willie Fraser .05 .02 .01
☐ 364 Nick Esasky .05 .02 .01
☐ 365 Floyd Youmans .05 .02 .01
☐ 366 Chet Lemon .05 .02 .01
☐ 367 Tim Leary .05 .02 .01
☐ 368 Gerald Young .05 .02 .01
☐ 369 Greg Harris .05 .02 .01
☐ 370 Jose Canseco .50 .23 .06
☐ 371 Joe Hesketh .05 .02 .01
☐ 372 Matt Williams 2.00 .90 .25
☐ 373 Checklist 265-396 .06 .02 .01
☐ 374 Doc Edwards MG .05 .02 .01
(Checklist back)
☐ 375 Tom Brunansky .05 .02 .01
☐ 376 Bill Wilkinson .05 .02 .01
☐ 377 Sam Horn .05 .02 .01
☐ 378 Todd Frohwirth .05 .02 .01
☐ 379 Rafael Ramirez .05 .02 .01
☐ 380 Joe Magrane .10 .05 .01
☐ 381 Angels TL .05 .02 .01
Wally Joyner and
Jack Howell

☐ 382	Keith A. Miller	.05	.02	.01
☐ 383	Eric Bell	.05	.02	.01
☐ 384	Neil Allen	.05	.02	.01
☐ 385	Carlton Fisk	.15	.07	.02
☐ 386	Don Mattingly AS	.20	.09	.03
☐ 387	Willie Randolph AS	.05	.02	.01
☐ 388	Wade Boggs AS	.05	.02	.01
☐ 389	Alan Trammell AS	.10	.05	.01
☐ 390	George Bell AS	.05	.02	.01
☐ 391	Kirby Puckett AS	.25	.11	.03
☐ 392	Dave Winfield AS	.15	.07	.02
☐ 393	Matt Nokes AS	.05	.02	.01
☐ 394	Roger Clemens AS	.20	.09	.03
☐ 395	Jimmy Key AS	.05	.02	.01
☐ 396	Tom Henke AS	.05	.02	.01
☐ 397	Jack Clark AS	.05	.02	.01
☐ 398	Juan Samuel AS	.05	.02	.01
☐ 399	Tim Wallach AS	.05	.02	.01
☐ 400	Ozzie Smith AS	.10	.05	.01
☐ 401	Andre Dawson AS	.10	.05	.01
☐ 402	Tony Gwynn AS	.15	.07	.02
☐ 403	Tim Raines AS	.10	.05	.01
☐ 404	Benny Santiago AS	.05	.02	.01
☐ 405	Dwight Gooden AS	.10	.05	.01
☐ 406	Shane Rawley AS	.05	.02	.01
☐ 407	Steve Bedrosian AS	.05	.02	.01
☐ 408	Dion James	.05	.02	.01
☐ 409	Joel McKeon	.05	.02	.01
☐ 410	Tony Pena	.05	.02	.01
☐ 411	Wayne Tolleson	.05	.02	.01
☐ 412	Randy Myers	.10	.05	.01
☐ 413	John Christensen	.05	.02	.01
☐ 414	John McNamara MG	.05	.02	.01
	(Checklist back)			
☐ 415	Don Carman	.05	.02	.01
☐ 416	Keith Moreland	.05	.02	.01
☐ 417	Mark Ciardi	.05	.02	.01
☐ 418	Joel Youngblood	.05	.02	.01
☐ 419	Scott McGregor	.05	.02	.01
☐ 420	Wally Joyner	.10	.05	.01
☐ 421	Ed VandeBerg	.05	.02	.01
☐ 422	Dave Concepcion	.10	.05	.01
☐ 423	John Smiley	.25	.11	.03
☐ 424	Dwayne Murphy	.05	.02	.01
☐ 425	Jeff Reardon	.15	.07	.02
☐ 426	Randy Ready	.05	.02	.01
☐ 427	Paul Kilgus	.05	.02	.01
☐ 428	John Shelby	.05	.02	.01
☐ 429	Tigers TL	.10	.05	.01
	Alan Trammell and			
	Kirk Gibson			
☐ 430	Glenn Davis	.05	.02	.01
☐ 431	Casey Candaele	.05	.02	.01
☐ 432	Mike Moore	.05	.02	.01
☐ 433	Bill Pecota	.05	.02	.01
☐ 434	Rick Aguilera	.10	.05	.01
☐ 435	Mike Pagliarulo	.05	.02	.01
☐ 436	Mike Bielecki	.05	.02	.01
☐ 437	Fred Manrique	.05	.02	.01
☐ 438	Rob Ducey	.05	.02	.01
☐ 439	Dave Martinez	.05	.02	.01
☐ 440	Steve Bedrosian	.05	.02	.01
☐ 441	Rick Manning	.05	.02	.01
☐ 442	Tom Bolton	.05	.02	.01
☐ 443	Ken Griffey	.10	.05	.01
☐ 444	Cal Ripken, Sr. MG	.05	.02	.01
	(Checklist back)			
	UER (two copyrights)			
☐ 445	Mike Krukow	.05	.02	.01
☐ 446	Doug DeCinces	.05	.02	.01
	(Now with Cardinals			
	on card front)			
☐ 447	Jeff Montgomery	.40	.18	.05
☐ 448	Mike Davis	.05	.02	.01
☐ 449	Jeff M. Robinson	.05	.02	.01
☐ 450	Barry Bonds	.75	.35	.09
☐ 451	Keith Atherton	.05	.02	.01
☐ 452	Willie Wilson	.05	.02	.01
☐ 453	Dennis Powell	.05	.02	.01
☐ 454	Marvell Wynne	.05	.02	.01
☐ 455	Shawn Hillegas	.05	.02	.01
☐ 456	Dave Anderson	.05	.02	.01
☐ 457	Terry Leach	.05	.02	.01
☐ 458	Ron Hassey	.05	.02	.01
☐ 459	Yankees TL	.10	.05	.01
	Dave Winfield and			
	Willie Randolph			
☐ 460	Ozzie Smith	.30	.14	.04
☐ 461	Danny Darwin	.05	.02	.01
☐ 462	Don Slaught	.05	.02	.01
☐ 463	Fred McGriff	.50	.23	.06
☐ 464	Jay Tibbs	.05	.02	.01
☐ 465	Paul Molitor	.25	.11	.03
☐ 466	Jerry Mumphrey	.05	.02	.01
☐ 467	Don Aase	.05	.02	.01
☐ 468	Darren Daulton	.15	.07	.02
☐ 469	Jeff Dedmon	.05	.02	.01
☐ 470	Dwight Evans	.10	.05	.01
☐ 471	Donnie Moore	.05	.02	.01
☐ 472	Robby Thompson	.10	.05	.01
☐ 473	Joe Niekro	.10	.05	.01
☐ 474	Tom Brookens	.05	.02	.01
☐ 475	Pete Rose MG	.20	.09	.03
	(Checklist back)			
☐ 476	Dave Stewart	.10	.05	.01
☐ 477	Jamie Quirk	.05	.02	.01
☐ 478	Sid Bream	.05	.02	.01
☐ 479	Brett Butler	.10	.05	.01
☐ 480	Dwight Gooden	.10	.05	.01
☐ 481	Mariano Duncan	.05	.02	.01
☐ 482	Mark Davis	.05	.02	.01
☐ 483	Rod Booker	.05	.02	.01
☐ 484	Pat Clements	.05	.02	.01
☐ 485	Harold Reynolds	.05	.02	.01
☐ 486	Pat Keedy	.05	.02	.01
☐ 487	Jim Pankovits	.05	.02	.01
☐ 488	Andy McGaffigan	.05	.02	.01
☐ 489	Dodgers TL	.05	.02	.01
	Pedro Guerrero and			
	Fernando Valenzuela			
☐ 490	Larry Parrish	.05	.02	.01
☐ 491	B.J. Surhoff	.10	.05	.01
☐ 492	Doyle Alexander	.05	.02	.01
☐ 493	Mike Greenwell	.15	.07	.02
☐ 494	Wally Ritchie	.05	.02	.01
☐ 495	Eddie Murray	.20	.09	.03
☐ 496	Guy Hoffman	.05	.02	.01
☐ 497	Kevin Mitchell	.15	.07	.02
☐ 498	Bob Boone	.10	.05	.01
☐ 499	Eric King	.05	.02	.01
☐ 500	Andre Dawson	.15	.07	.02
☐ 501	Tim Birtsas	.05	.02	.01
☐ 502	Dan Gladden	.05	.02	.01
☐ 503	Junior Noboa	.05	.02	.01
☐ 504	Bob Rodgers MG	.05	.02	.01
	(Checklist back)			
☐ 505	Willie Upshaw	.05	.02	.01
☐ 506	John Cangelosi	.05	.02	.01
☐ 507	Mark Gubicza	.05	.02	.01
☐ 508	Tim Teufel	.05	.02	.01
☐ 509	Bill Dawley	.05	.02	.01
☐ 510	Dave Winfield	.20	.09	.03
☐ 511	Joel Davis	.05	.02	.01
☐ 512	Alex Trevino	.05	.02	.01
☐ 513	Tim Flannery	.05	.02	.01
☐ 514	Pat Sheridan	.05	.02	.01

☐ 515	Juan Nieves	.05	.02	.01
☐ 516	Jim Sundberg	.05	.02	.01
☐ 517	Ron Robinson	.05	.02	.01
☐ 518	Greg Gross	.05	.02	.01
☐ 519	Mariners TL	.05	.02	.01
	Harold Reynolds and			
	Phil Bradley			
☐ 520	Dave Smith	.05	.02	.01
☐ 521	Jim Dwyer	.05	.02	.01
☐ 522	Bob Patterson	.05	.02	.01
☐ 523	Gary Roenicke	.05	.02	.01
☐ 524	Gary Lucas	.05	.02	.01
☐ 525	Marty Barrett	.05	.02	.01
☐ 526	Juan Berenguer	.05	.02	.01
☐ 527	Steve Henderson	.05	.02	.01
☐ 528A	Checklist 397-528	.25	.02	.01
	ERR (455 S. Carlton)			
☐ 528B	Checklist 397-528	.06	.02	.01
	COR (455 S. Hillegas)			
☐ 529	Tim Burke	.05	.02	.01
☐ 530	Gary Carter	.15	.07	.02
☐ 531	Rich Yett	.05	.02	.01
☐ 532	Mike Kingery	.05	.02	.01
☐ 533	John Farrell	.05	.02	.01
☐ 534	John Wathan MG	.05	.02	.01
	(Checklist back)			
☐ 535	Ron Guidry	.10	.05	.01
☐ 536	John Morris	.05	.02	.01
☐ 537	Steve Buechele	.05	.02	.01
☐ 538	Bill Wegman	.05	.02	.01
☐ 539	Mike LaValliere	.05	.02	.01
☐ 540	Bret Saberhagen	.15	.07	.02
☐ 541	Juan Beniquez	.05	.02	.01
☐ 542	Paul Noce	.05	.02	.01
☐ 543	Kent Tekulve	.05	.02	.01
☐ 544	Jim Traber	.05	.02	.01
☐ 545	Don Baylor	.15	.07	.02
☐ 546	John Candelaria	.05	.02	.01
☐ 547	Felix Fermin	.05	.02	.01
☐ 548	Shane Mack	.10	.05	.01
☐ 549	Braves TL	.05	.02	.01
	Albert Hall,			
	Dale Murphy,			
	Ken Griffey,			
	and Dion James			
☐ 550	Pedro Guerrero	.10	.05	.01
☐ 551	Terry Steinbach	.10	.05	.01
☐ 552	Mark Thurmond	.05	.02	.01
☐ 553	Tracy Jones	.05	.02	.01
☐ 554	Mike Smithson	.05	.02	.01
☐ 555	Brook Jacoby	.05	.02	.01
☐ 556	Stan Clarke	.05	.02	.01
☐ 557	Craig Reynolds	.05	.02	.01
☐ 558	Bob Ojeda	.05	.02	.01
☐ 559	Ken Williams	.05	.02	.01
☐ 560	Tim Wallach	.10	.05	.01
☐ 561	Rick Cerone	.05	.02	.01
☐ 562	Jim Lindeman	.05	.02	.01
☐ 563	Jose Guzman	.10	.05	.01
☐ 564	Frank Lucchesi MG	.05	.02	.01
	(Checklist back)			
☐ 565	Lloyd Moseby	.05	.02	.01
☐ 566	Charlie O'Brien	.05	.02	.01
☐ 567	Mike Diaz	.05	.02	.01
☐ 568	Chris Brown	.05	.02	.01
☐ 569	Charlie Leibrandt	.05	.02	.01
☐ 570	Jeffrey Leonard	.05	.02	.01
☐ 571	Mark Williamson	.05	.02	.01
☐ 572	Chris James	.05	.02	.01
☐ 573	Bob Stanley	.05	.02	.01
☐ 574	Graig Nettles	.10	.05	.01
☐ 575	Don Sutton	.15	.07	.02
☐ 576	Tommy Hinzo	.05	.02	.01
☐ 577	Tom Browning	.05	.02	.01
☐ 578	Gary Gaetti	.05	.02	.01
☐ 579	Mets TL	.10	.05	.01
	Gary Carter and			
	Kevin McReynolds			
☐ 580	Mark McGwire	.35	.16	.04
☐ 581	Tito Landrum	.05	.02	.01
☐ 582	Mike Henneman	.20	.09	.03
☐ 583	Dave Valle	.05	.02	.01
☐ 584	Steve Trout	.05	.02	.01
☐ 585	Ozzie Guillen	.10	.05	.01
☐ 586	Bob Forsch	.05	.02	.01
☐ 587	Terry Puhl	.05	.02	.01
☐ 588	Jeff Parrett	.05	.02	.01
☐ 589	Geno Petralli	.05	.02	.01
☐ 590	George Bell	.10	.05	.01
☐ 591	Doug Drabek	.15	.07	.02
☐ 592	Dale Sveum	.05	.02	.01
☐ 593	Bob Tewksbury	.10	.05	.01
☐ 594	Bobby Valentine MG	.05	.02	.01
	(Checklist back)			
☐ 595	Frank White	.10	.05	.01
☐ 596	John Kruk	.15	.07	.02
☐ 597	Gene Garber	.05	.02	.01
☐ 598	Lee Lacy	.05	.02	.01
☐ 599	Calvin Schiraldi	.05	.02	.01
☐ 600	Mike Schmidt	.25	.11	.03
☐ 601	Jack Lazorko	.05	.02	.01
☐ 602	Mike Aldrete	.05	.02	.01
☐ 603	Rob Murphy	.05	.02	.01
☐ 604	Chris Bando	.05	.02	.01
☐ 605	Kirk Gibson	.10	.05	.01
☐ 606	Moose Haas	.05	.02	.01
☐ 607	Mickey Hatcher	.05	.02	.01
☐ 608	Charlie Kerfeld	.05	.02	.01
☐ 609	Twins TL	.05	.02	.01
	Gary Gaetti and			
	Kent Hrbek			
☐ 610	Keith Hernandez	.10	.05	.01
☐ 611	Tommy John	.15	.07	.02
☐ 612	Curt Ford	.05	.02	.01
☐ 613	Bobby Thigpen	.05	.02	.01
☐ 614	Herm Winningham	.05	.02	.01
☐ 615	Jody Davis	.05	.02	.01
☐ 616	Jay Aldrich	.05	.02	.01
☐ 617	Oddibe McDowell	.05	.02	.01
☐ 618	Cecil Fielder	.30	.14	.04
☐ 619	Mike Dunne	.05	.02	.01
	(Inconsistent design,			
	black name on front)			
☐ 620	Cory Snyder	.05	.02	.01
☐ 621	Gene Nelson	.05	.02	.01
☐ 622	Kal Daniels	.05	.02	.01
☐ 623	Mike Flanagan	.05	.02	.01
☐ 624	Jim Leyland MG	.05	.02	.01
	(Checklist back)			
☐ 625	Frank Viola	.10	.05	.01
☐ 626	Glenn Wilson	.05	.02	.01
☐ 627	Joe Boever	.05	.02	.01
☐ 628	Dave Henderson	.10	.05	.01
☐ 629	Kelly Downs	.05	.02	.01
☐ 630	Darrell Evans	.10	.05	.01
☐ 631	Jack Howell	.05	.02	.01
☐ 632	Steve Shields	.05	.02	.01
☐ 633	Barry Lyons	.05	.02	.01
☐ 634	Jose DeLeon	.05	.02	.01
☐ 635	Terry Pendleton	.15	.07	.02
☐ 636	Charles Hudson	.05	.02	.01
☐ 637	Jay Bell	.50	.23	.06
☐ 638	Steve Balboni	.05	.02	.01
☐ 639	Brewers TL	.05	.02	.01
	Glenn Braggs			
	and Tony Muser CO			

☐ 640 Garry Templeton .... .05 .02 .01
(Inconsistent design, green border)
☐ 641 Rick Honeycutt .... .05 .02 .01
☐ 642 Bob Dernier .... .05 .02 .01
☐ 643 Rocky Childress .... .05 .02 .01
☐ 644 Terry McGriff .... .05 .02 .01
☐ 645 Matt Nokes .... .15 .07 .02
☐ 646 Checklist 529-660 .... .06 .02 .01
☐ 647 Pascual Perez .... .05 .02 .01
☐ 648 Al Newman .... .05 .02 .01
☐ 649 DeWayne Buice .... .05 .02 .01
☐ 650 Cal Ripken .... .60 .25 .08
☐ 651 Mike Jackson .... .10 .05 .01
☐ 652 Bruce Benedict .... .05 .02 .01
☐ 653 Jeff Sellers .... .05 .02 .01
☐ 654 Roger Craig MG .... .05 .02 .01
(Checklist back)
☐ 655 Len Dykstra .... .25 .11 .03
☐ 656 Lee Guetterman .... .05 .02 .01
☐ 657 Gary Redus .... .05 .02 .01
☐ 658 Tim Conroy .... .05 .02 .01
(Inconsistent design, name in white)
☐ 659 Bobby Meacham .... .05 .02 .01
☐ 660 Rick Reuschel .... .05 .02 .01
☐ 661 Nolan Ryan TBC '83 .... .35 .16 .04
☐ 662 Jim Rice TBC '78 .... .15 .07 .02
☐ 663 Ron Blomberg TBC '73 .05 .02 .01
☐ 664 Bob Gibson TBC '68 .... .15 .07 .02
☐ 665 Stan Musial TBC '63 .... .10 .05 .01
☐ 666 Mario Soto .... .05 .02 .01
☐ 667 Luis Quinones .... .05 .02 .01
☐ 668 Walt Terrell .... .05 .02 .01
☐ 669 Phillies TL .... .05 .02 .01
Lance Parrish and Mike Ryan CO
☐ 670 Dan Plesac .... .05 .02 .01
☐ 671 Tim Laudner .... .05 .02 .01
☐ 672 John Davis .... .05 .02 .01
☐ 673 Tony Phillips .... .10 .05 .01
☐ 674 Mike Fitzgerald .... .05 .02 .01
☐ 675 Jim Rice .... .15 .07 .02
☐ 676 Ken Dixon .... .05 .02 .01
☐ 677 Eddie Milner .... .05 .02 .01
☐ 678 Jim Acker .... .05 .02 .01
☐ 679 Darrell Miller .... .05 .02 .01
☐ 680 Charlie Hough .... .10 .05 .01
☐ 681 Bobby Bonilla .... .20 .09 .03
☐ 682 Jimmy Key .... .15 .07 .02
☐ 683 Julio Franco .... .10 .05 .01
☐ 684 Hal Lanier MG .... .05 .02 .01
(Checklist back)
☐ 685 Ron Darling .... .10 .05 .01
☐ 686 Terry Francona .... .05 .02 .01
☐ 687 Mickey Brantley .... .05 .02 .01
☐ 688 Jim Winn .... .05 .02 .01
☐ 689 Tom Pagnozzi .... .20 .09 .03
☐ 690 Jay Howell .... .05 .02 .01
☐ 691 Dan Pasqua .... .05 .02 .01
☐ 692 Mike Birkbeck .... .05 .02 .01
☐ 693 Benito Santiago .... .10 .05 .01
☐ 694 Eric Nolte .... .05 .02 .01
☐ 695 Shawon Dunston .... .10 .05 .01
☐ 696 Duane Ward .... .10 .05 .01
☐ 697 Steve Lombardozzi .... .05 .02 .01
☐ 698 Brad Havens .... .05 .02 .01
☐ 699 Padres TL .... .10 .05 .01
Benito Santiago and Tony Gwynn
☐ 700 George Brett .... .40 .18 .05
☐ 701 Sammy Stewart .... .05 .02 .01
☐ 702 Mike Gallego .... .05 .02 .01
☐ 703 Bob Brenly .... .05 .02 .01
☐ 704 Dennis Boyd .... .05 .02 .01
☐ 705 Juan Samuel .... .05 .02 .01
☐ 706 Rick Mahler .... .05 .02 .01
☐ 707 Fred Lynn .... .10 .05 .01
☐ 708 Gus Polidor .... .05 .02 .01
☐ 709 George Frazier .... .05 .02 .01
☐ 710 Darryl Strawberry .... .15 .07 .02
☐ 711 Bill Gullickson .... .05 .02 .01
☐ 712 John Moses .... .05 .02 .01
☐ 713 Willie Hernandez .... .05 .02 .01
☐ 714 Jim Fregosi MG .... .05 .02 .01
(Checklist back)
☐ 715 Todd Worrell .... .05 .02 .01
☐ 716 Lenn Sakata .... .05 .02 .01
☐ 717 Jay Baller .... .05 .02 .01
☐ 718 Mike Felder .... .05 .02 .01
☐ 719 Denny Walling .... .05 .02 .01
☐ 720 Tim Raines .... .15 .07 .02
☐ 721 Pete O'Brien .... .05 .02 .01
☐ 722 Manny Lee .... .05 .02 .01
☐ 723 Bob Kipper .... .05 .02 .01
☐ 724 Danny Tartabull .... .10 .05 .01
☐ 725 Mike Boddicker .... .05 .02 .01
☐ 726 Alfredo Griffin .... .05 .02 .01
☐ 727 Greg Booker .... .05 .02 .01
☐ 728 Andy Allanson .... .05 .02 .01
☐ 729 Blue Jays TL .... .15 .07 .02
George Bell and Fred McGriff
☐ 730 John Franco .... .10 .05 .01
☐ 731 Rick Schu .... .05 .02 .01
☐ 732 David Palmer .... .05 .02 .01
☐ 733 Spike Owen .... .05 .02 .01
☐ 734 Craig Lefferts .... .05 .02 .01
☐ 735 Kevin McReynolds .... .10 .05 .01
☐ 736 Matt Young .... .05 .02 .01
☐ 737 Butch Wynegar .... .05 .02 .01
☐ 738 Scott Bankhead .... .05 .02 .01
☐ 739 Daryl Boston .... .05 .02 .01
☐ 740 Rick Sutcliffe .... .10 .05 .01
☐ 741 Mike Easler .... .05 .02 .01
☐ 742 Mark Clear .... .05 .02 .01
☐ 743 Larry Herndon .... .05 .02 .01
☐ 744 Whitey Herzog MG .... .10 .05 .01
(Checklist back)
☐ 745 Bill Doran .... .05 .02 .01
☐ 746 Gene Larkin .... .05 .02 .01
☐ 747 Bobby Witt .... .10 .05 .01
☐ 748 Reid Nichols .... .05 .02 .01
☐ 749 Mark Eichhorn .... .05 .02 .01
☐ 750 Bo Jackson .... .25 .11 .03
☐ 751 Jim Morrison .... .05 .02 .01
☐ 752 Mark Grant .... .05 .02 .01
☐ 753 Danny Heep .... .05 .02 .01
☐ 754 Mike LaCoss .... .05 .02 .01
☐ 755 Ozzie Virgil .... .05 .02 .01
☐ 756 Mike Maddux .... .05 .02 .01
☐ 757 John Marzano .... .05 .02 .01
☐ 758 Eddie Williams .... .15 .07 .02
☐ 759 A's TL UER .... .25 .11 .03
Mark McGwire and Jose Canseco (two copyrights)
☐ 760 Mike Scott .... .05 .02 .01
☐ 761 Tony Armas .... .05 .02 .01
☐ 762 Scott Bradley .... .05 .02 .01
☐ 763 Doug Sisk .... .05 .02 .01
☐ 764 Greg Walker .... .05 .02 .01
☐ 765 Neal Heaton .... .05 .02 .01
☐ 766 Henry Cotto .... .05 .02 .01
☐ 767 Jose Lind .... .15 .07 .02
☐ 768 Dickie Noles .... .05 .02 .01

		MINT	EXC	G-VG
	(Now with Tigers on card front)			
☐ 769	Cecil Cooper	.10	.05	.01
☐ 770	Lou Whitaker	.15	.07	.02
☐ 771	Ruben Sierra	.25	.11	.03
☐ 772	Sal Butera	.05	.02	.01
☐ 773	Frank Williams	.05	.02	.01
☐ 774	Gene Mauch MG (Checklist back)	.05	.02	.01
☐ 775	Dave Stieb	.10	.05	.01
☐ 776	Checklist 661-792	.06	.02	.01
☐ 777	Lonnie Smith	.05	.02	.01
☐ 778A	Keith Comstock ERR (White "Padres")	2.50	1.15	.30
☐ 778B	Keith Comstock COR (Blue "Padres")	.05	.02	.01
☐ 779	Tom Glavine	1.25	.55	.16
☐ 780	Fernando Valenzuela	.05	.02	.01
☐ 781	Keith Hughes	.05	.02	.01
☐ 782	Jeff Ballard	.05	.02	.01
☐ 783	Ron Roenicke	.05	.02	.01
☐ 784	Joe Sambito	.05	.02	.01
☐ 785	Alvin Davis	.05	.02	.01
☐ 786	Joe Price (Inconsistent design, orange team name)	.05	.02	.01
☐ 787	Bill Almon	.05	.02	.01
☐ 788	Ray Searage	.05	.02	.01
☐ 789	Indians' TL Joe Carter and Cory Snyder	.15	.07	.02
☐ 790	Dave Righetti	.05	.02	.01
☐ 791	Ted Simmons	.10	.05	.01
☐ 792	John Tudor	.05	.02	.01

1988 Topps Traded

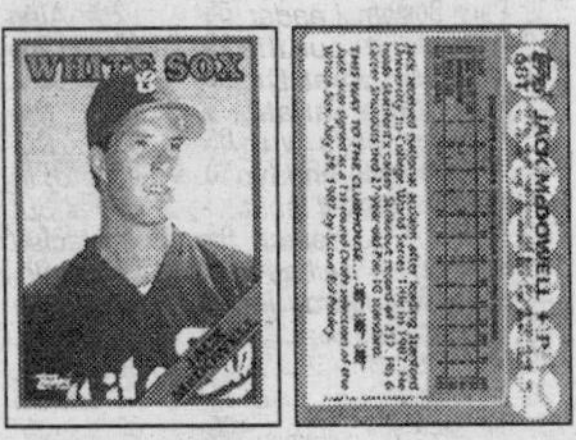

This 132-card Traded or extended set was distributed by Topps to dealers in a special blue and white box as a complete set. The card fronts are identical in style to the Topps regular issue and are also 2 1/2" by 3 1/2". The backs are printed in orange and black on white card stock. Cards are numbered (with a T suffix) alphabetically according to the name of the player. This set has generated additional interest due to the inclusion of the 1988 U.S. Olympic baseball team members. These Olympians are indicated in the checklist below by OLY. The key (extended) Rookie Cards in this set are Jim Abbott, Roberto Alomar, Brady Anderson, Andy Benes, Jay Buhner, Ron Gant, Mark Grace, Bryan Harvey, Roberto Kelly, Tino Martinez, Jack McDowell, Charles Nagy, Chris Sabo, Robin Ventura, and Walt Weiss. Topps also produced a specially boxed "glossy" edition, frequently referred to as the Topps Traded Tiffany set. This year, again, Topps did not disclose the number of Tiffany sets they produced or sold. It is apparent from the availability that there were many more sets produced this year compared to the 1984-86 Tiffany sets, perhaps 25,000 sets. The checklist of cards is identical to that of the normal non-glossy cards. There are two primary distinguishing features of the Tiffany cards, white card stock reverses and high gloss obverses. These Tiffany cards are valued approximately from three to five times the values listed below.

		MINT	EXC	G-VG
	COMPLETE FACT.SET (132)	18.00	8.00	2.30
	COMMON CARD (1T-132T)	.05	.02	.01
☐ 1T	Jim Abbott OLY	2.00	.90	.25
☐ 2T	Juan Agosto	.05	.02	.01
☐ 3T	Luis Alicea	.05	.02	.01
☐ 4T	Roberto Alomar	4.00	1.80	.50
☐ 5T	Brady Anderson	1.00	.45	.13
☐ 6T	Jack Armstrong	.05	.02	.01
☐ 7T	Don August	.05	.02	.01
☐ 8T	Floyd Bannister	.05	.02	.01
☐ 9T	Bret Barberie OLY	.30	.14	.04
☐ 10T	Jose Bautista	.05	.02	.01
☐ 11T	Don Baylor	.10	.05	.01
☐ 12T	Tim Belcher	.05	.02	.01
☐ 13T	Buddy Bell	.08	.04	.01
☐ 14T	Andy Benes OLY	1.50	.65	.19
☐ 15T	Damon Berryhill	.15	.07	.02
☐ 16T	Bud Black	.05	.02	.01
☐ 17T	Pat Borders	.40	.18	.05
☐ 18T	Phil Bradley	.05	.02	.01
☐ 19T	Jeff Branson OLY	.08	.04	.01
☐ 20T	Tom Brunansky	.05	.02	.01
☐ 21T	Jay Buhner	1.00	.45	.13
☐ 22T	Brett Butler	.08	.04	.01
☐ 23T	Jim Campanis OLY	.05	.02	.01
☐ 24T	Sil Campusano	.05	.02	.01
☐ 25T	John Candelaria	.05	.02	.01
☐ 26T	Jose Cecena	.05	.02	.01
☐ 27T	Rick Cerone	.05	.02	.01
☐ 28T	Jack Clark	.08	.04	.01
☐ 29T	Kevin Coffman	.05	.02	.01
☐ 30T	Pat Combs OLY	.05	.02	.01
☐ 31T	Henry Cotto	.05	.02	.01
☐ 32T	Chili Davis	.08	.04	.01
☐ 33T	Mike Davis	.05	.02	.01
☐ 34T	Jose DeLeon	.05	.02	.01
☐ 35T	Richard Dotson	.05	.02	.01
☐ 36T	Cecil Espy	.05	.02	.01
☐ 37T	Tom Filer	.05	.02	.01
☐ 38T	Mike Fiore OLY	.05	.02	.01
☐ 39T	Ron Gant	1.50	.65	.19
☐ 40T	Kirk Gibson	.08	.04	.01
☐ 41T	Rich Gossage	.10	.05	.01
☐ 42T	Mark Grace	1.25	.55	.16
☐ 43T	Alfredo Griffin	.05	.02	.01
☐ 44T	Ty Griffin OLY	.05	.02	.01
☐ 45T	Bryan Harvey	1.00	.45	.13
☐ 46T	Ron Hassey	.05	.02	.01
☐ 47T	Ray Hayward	.05	.02	.01
☐ 48T	Dave Henderson	.08	.04	.01
☐ 49T	Tom Herr	.05	.02	.01
☐ 50T	Bob Horner	.05	.02	.01
☐ 51T	Ricky Horton	.05	.02	.01

☐ 52T Jay Howell	.05	.02	.01
☐ 53T Glenn Hubbard	.05	.02	.01
☐ 54T Jeff Innis	.05	.02	.01
☐ 55T Danny Jackson	.05	.02	.01
☐ 56T Darrin Jackson	.25	.11	.03
☐ 57T Roberto Kelly	.75	.35	.09
☐ 58T Ron Kittle	.05	.02	.01
☐ 59T Ray Knight	.08	.04	.01
☐ 60T Vance Law	.05	.02	.01
☐ 61T Jeffrey Leonard	.05	.02	.01
☐ 62T Mike Macfarlane	.50	.23	.06
☐ 63T Scotti Madison	.05	.02	.01
☐ 64T Kirt Manwaring	.05	.02	.01
☐ 65T Mark Marquess OLY CO	.05	.02	.01
☐ 66T Tino Martinez OLY	.50	.23	.06
☐ 67T Billy Masse OLY	.05	.02	.01
☐ 68T Jack McDowell	1.00	.45	.13
☐ 69T Jack McKeon MG	.05	.02	.01
☐ 70T Larry McWilliams	.05	.02	.01
☐ 71T Mickey Morandini OLY.	.40	.18	.05
☐ 72T Keith Moreland	.05	.02	.01
☐ 73T Mike Morgan	.05	.02	.01
☐ 74T Charles Nagy OLY	.60	.25	.08
☐ 75T Al Nipper	.05	.02	.01
☐ 76T Russ Nixon MG	.05	.02	.01
☐ 77T Jesse Orosco	.05	.02	.01
☐ 78T Joe Orsulak	.05	.02	.01
☐ 79T Dave Palmer	.05	.02	.01
☐ 80T Mark Parent	.05	.02	.01
☐ 81T Dave Parker	.10	.05	.01
☐ 82T Dan Pasqua	.05	.02	.01
☐ 83T Melido Perez	.25	.11	.03
☐ 84T Steve Peters	.05	.02	.01
☐ 85T Dan Petry	.05	.02	.01
☐ 86T Gary Pettis	.05	.02	.01
☐ 87T Jeff Pico	.05	.02	.01
☐ 88T Jim Poole OLY	.15	.07	.02
☐ 89T Ted Power	.05	.02	.01
☐ 90T Rafael Ramirez	.05	.02	.01
☐ 91T Dennis Rasmussen	.05	.02	.01
☐ 92T Jose Rijo	.10	.05	.01
☐ 93T Ernest Riles	.05	.02	.01
☐ 94T Luis Rivera	.05	.02	.01
☐ 95T Doug Robbins OLY	.05	.02	.01
☐ 96T Frank Robinson MG	.08	.04	.01
☐ 97T Cookie Rojas MG	.05	.02	.01
☐ 98T Chris Sabo	.50	.23	.06
☐ 99T Mark Salas	.05	.02	.01
☐ 100T Luis Salazar	.05	.02	.01
☐ 101T Rafael Santana	.05	.02	.01
☐ 102T Nelson Santovenia	.05	.02	.01
☐ 103T Mackey Sasser	.05	.02	.01
☐ 104T Calvin Schiraldi	.05	.02	.01
☐ 105T Mike Schooler	.05	.02	.01
☐ 106T Scott Servais OLY	.20	.09	.03
☐ 107T Dave Silvestri OLY	.05	.02	.01
☐ 108T Don Slaught	.05	.02	.01
☐ 109T Joe Slusarski OLY	.05	.02	.01
☐ 110T Lee Smith	.10	.05	.01
☐ 111T Pete Smith	.25	.11	.03
☐ 112T Jim Snyder MG	.05	.02	.01
☐ 113T Ed Sprague OLY	.50	.23	.06
☐ 114T Pete Stanicek	.05	.02	.01
☐ 115T Kurt Stillwell	.05	.02	.01
☐ 116T Todd Stottlemyre	.25	.11	.03
☐ 117T Bill Swift	.08	.04	.01
☐ 118T Pat Tabler	.05	.02	.01
☐ 119T Scott Terry	.05	.02	.01
☐ 120T Mickey Tettleton	.08	.04	.01
☐ 121T Dickie Thon	.05	.02	.01
☐ 122T Jeff Treadway	.05	.02	.01
☐ 123T Willie Upshaw	.05	.02	.01
☐ 124T Robin Ventura OLY	3.50	1.55	.45
☐ 125T Ron Washington	.05	.02	.01
☐ 126T Walt Weiss	.25	.11	.03
☐ 127T Bob Welch	.08	.04	.01
☐ 128T David Wells	.25	.11	.03
☐ 129T Glenn Wilson	.05	.02	.01
☐ 130T Ted Wood OLY	.05	.02	.01
☐ 131T Don Zimmer MG	.08	.04	.01
☐ 132T Checklist 1T-132T	.05	.02	.01

1989 Topps

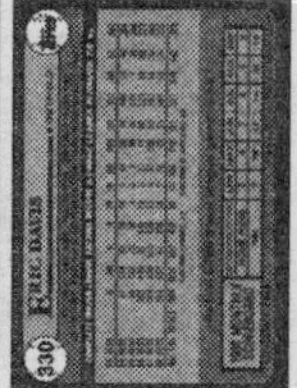

This 792-card set features backs that are printed in pink and black on gray card stock. The manager cards contain a checklist of the respective team's players on the back. Subsets in the set include Record Breakers (1-7), Turn Back the Clock (661-665), and All-Star selections (386-407). The bonus cards distributed throughout the set, which are indicated on the Topps checklist cards, are actually Team Leader (TL) cards. Also sprinkled throughout the set are Future Stars (FS) and First Draft Picks (FDP). There are subtle variations found in the Future Stars cards with respect to the placement of photo and type on the card; in fact, each card has at least two varieties but they are difficult to detect (requiring precise measurement) as well as difficult to explain. The key Rookie Cards in this set are Jim Abbott, Sandy Alomar Jr., Brady Anderson, Steve Avery, Andy Benes, Craig Biggio, Bryan Harvey, Randy Johnson, Ramon Martinez, Gregg Olson, Gary Sheffield, John Smoltz, and Robin Ventura. Topps also produced a specially boxed "glossy" edition, frequently referred to as the Topps Tiffany set. This year, again, Topps did not disclose the number of Tiffany sets they produced or sold but it seems that production quantities were roughly similar (or slightly smaller, approximately 15,000 sets) to the previous two years. The checklist of cards (792 regular and 132 Traded) is identical to that of the normal non-glossy cards. There are two primary distinguishing features of the Tiffany cards, white card stock reverses and high gloss obverses. These Tiffany cards are valued approximately from three to five times the values listed below.

	MINT	EXC	G-VG
COMPLETE SET (792)	15.00	6.75	1.90
COMPLETE FACT.SET (792)	15.00	6.75	1.90

COMMON CARD (1-792) .05 .02 .01

☐ 1 George Bell RB .10 .05 .01
Slams 3 HR on
Opening Day
☐ 2 Wade Boggs RB .15 .07 .02
Gets 200 Hits
6th Straight Season
☐ 3 Gary Carter RB .10 .05 .01
Sets Record for
Career Putouts
☐ 4 Andre Dawson RB .10 .05 .01
Logs Double Figures
in HR and SB
☐ 5 Orel Hershiser RB .10 .05 .01
Pitches 59
Scoreless Innings
☐ 6 Doug Jones RB UER .05 .02 .01
Earns His 15th
Straight Save
(Photo actually
Chris Codiroli)
☐ 7 Kevin McReynolds RB .05 .02 .01
Steals 21 Without
Being Caught
☐ 8 Dave Eiland .05 .02 .01
☐ 9 Tim Teufel .05 .02 .01
☐ 10 Andre Dawson .15 .07 .02
☐ 11 Bruce Sutter .10 .05 .01
☐ 12 Dale Sveum .05 .02 .01
☐ 13 Doug Sisk .05 .02 .01
☐ 14 Tom Kelly MG .05 .02 .01
(Team checklist back)
☐ 15 Robby Thompson .10 .05 .01
☐ 16 Ron Robinson .05 .02 .01
☐ 17 Brian Downing .05 .02 .01
☐ 18 Rick Rhoden .05 .02 .01
☐ 19 Greg Gagne .05 .02 .01
☐ 20 Steve Bedrosian .05 .02 .01
☐ 21 Chicago White Sox TL .05 .02 .01
Greg Walker
☐ 22 Tim Crews .05 .02 .01
☐ 23 Mike Fitzgerald .05 .02 .01
☐ 24 Larry Andersen .05 .02 .01
☐ 25 Frank White .10 .05 .01
☐ 26 Dale Mohorcic .05 .02 .01
☐ 27A Orestes Destrade .05 .02 .01
(F* next to copyright)
☐ 27B Orestes Destrade .05 .02 .01
(E*F* next to
copyright)
☐ 28 Mike Moore .05 .02 .01
☐ 29 Kelly Gruber .05 .02 .01
☐ 30 Dwight Gooden .10 .05 .01
☐ 31 Terry Francona .05 .02 .01
☐ 32 Dennis Rasmussen .05 .02 .01
☐ 33 B.J. Surhoff .05 .02 .01
☐ 34 Ken Williams .05 .02 .01
☐ 35 John Tudor UER .05 .02 .01
(With Red Sox in '84,should be Pirates)
☐ 36 Mitch Webster .05 .02 .01
☐ 37 Bob Stanley .05 .02 .01
☐ 38 Paul Runge .05 .02 .01
☐ 39 Mike Maddux .05 .02 .01
☐ 40 Steve Sax .05 .02 .01
☐ 41 Terry Mulholland .10 .05 .01
☐ 42 Jim Eppard .05 .02 .01
☐ 43 Guillermo Hernandez .05 .02 .01
☐ 44 Jim Snyder MG .05 .02 .01
(Team checklist back)
☐ 45 Kal Daniels .05 .02 .01
☐ 46 Mark Portugal .10 .05 .01
☐ 47 Carney Lansford .10 .05 .01
☐ 48 Tim Burke .05 .02 .01
☐ 49 Craig Biggio .60 .25 .08
☐ 50 George Bell .10 .05 .01
☐ 51 California Angels TL .05 .02 .01
Mark McLemore
☐ 52 Bob Brenly .05 .02 .01
☐ 53 Ruben Sierra .25 .11 .03
☐ 54 Steve Trout .05 .02 .01
☐ 55 Julio Franco .10 .05 .01
☐ 56 Pat Tabler .05 .02 .01
☐ 57 Alejandro Pena .05 .02 .01
☐ 58 Lee Mazzilli .05 .02 .01
☐ 59 Mark Davis .05 .02 .01
☐ 60 Tom Brunansky .05 .02 .01
☐ 61 Neil Allen .05 .02 .01
☐ 62 Alfredo Griffin .05 .02 .01
☐ 63 Mark Clear .05 .02 .01
☐ 64 Alex Trevino .05 .02 .01
☐ 65 Rick Reuschel .05 .02 .01
☐ 66 Manny Trillo .05 .02 .01
☐ 67 Dave Palmer .05 .02 .01
☐ 68 Darrell Miller .05 .02 .01
☐ 69 Jeff Ballard .05 .02 .01
☐ 70 Mark McGwire .15 .07 .02
☐ 71 Mike Boddicker .05 .02 .01
☐ 72 John Moses .05 .02 .01
☐ 73 Pascual Perez .05 .02 .01
☐ 74 Nick Leyva MG .05 .02 .01
(Team checklist back)
☐ 75 Tom Henke .10 .05 .01
☐ 76 Terry Blocker .05 .02 .01
☐ 77 Doyle Alexander .05 .02 .01
☐ 78 Jim Sundberg .05 .02 .01
☐ 79 Scott Bankhead .05 .02 .01
☐ 80 Cory Snyder .05 .02 .01
☐ 81 Montreal Expos TL .10 .05 .01
Tim Raines
☐ 82 Dave Leiper .05 .02 .01
☐ 83 Jeff Blauser .15 .07 .02
☐ 84 Bill Bene FDP .05 .02 .01
☐ 85 Kevin McReynolds .10 .05 .01
☐ 86 Al Nipper .05 .02 .01
☐ 87 Larry Owen .05 .02 .01
☐ 88 Darryl Hamilton .25 .11 .03
☐ 89 Dave LaPoint .05 .02 .01
☐ 90 Vince Coleman UER .10 .05 .01
(Wrong birth year)
☐ 91 Floyd Youmans .05 .02 .01
☐ 92 Jeff Kunkel .05 .02 .01
☐ 93 Ken Howell .05 .02 .01
☐ 94 Chris Speier .05 .02 .01
☐ 95 Gerald Young .05 .02 .01
☐ 96 Rick Cerone .05 .02 .01
(Ellis Burks in
background of photo)
☐ 97 Greg Mathews .05 .02 .01
☐ 98 Larry Sheets .05 .02 .01
☐ 99 Sherman Corbett .05 .02 .01
☐ 100 Mike Schmidt .25 .11 .03
☐ 101 Les Straker .05 .02 .01
☐ 102 Mike Gallego .05 .02 .01
☐ 103 Tim Birtsas .05 .02 .01
☐ 104 Dallas Green MG .05 .02 .01
(Team checklist back)
☐ 105 Ron Darling .10 .05 .01
☐ 106 Willie Upshaw .05 .02 .01
☐ 107 Jose DeLeon .05 .02 .01
☐ 108 Fred Manrique .05 .02 .01
☐ 109 Hipolito Pena .05 .02 .01
☐ 110 Paul Molitor .25 .11 .03
☐ 111 Cincinnati Reds TL .10 .05 .01
Eric Davis
(Swinging bat)

☐ 112 Jim Presley .05 .02 .01
☐ 113 Lloyd Moseby .05 .02 .01
☐ 114 Bob Kipper .05 .02 .01
☐ 115 Jody Davis .05 .02 .01
☐ 116 Jeff Montgomery .10 .05 .01
☐ 117 Dave Anderson .05 .02 .01
☐ 118 Checklist 1-132 .05 .02 .01
☐ 119 Terry Puhl .05 .02 .01
☐ 120 Frank Viola .10 .05 .01
☐ 121 Garry Templeton .05 .02 .01
☐ 122 Lance Johnson .10 .05 .01
☐ 123 Spike Owen .05 .02 .01
☐ 124 Jim Traber .05 .02 .01
☐ 125 Mike Krukow .05 .02 .01
☐ 126 Sid Bream .05 .02 .01
☐ 127 Walt Terrell .05 .02 .01
☐ 128 Milt Thompson .05 .02 .01
☐ 129 Terry Clark .05 .02 .01
☐ 130 Gerald Perry .05 .02 .01
☐ 131 Dave Otto .05 .02 .01
☐ 132 Curt Ford .05 .02 .01
☐ 133 Bill Long .05 .02 .01
☐ 134 Don Zimmer MG .05 .02 .01
(Team checklist back)
☐ 135 Jose Rijo .15 .07 .02
☐ 136 Joey Meyer .05 .02 .01
☐ 137 Geno Petralli .05 .02 .01
☐ 138 Wallace Johnson .05 .02 .01
☐ 139 Mike Flanagan .05 .02 .01
☐ 140 Shawon Dunston .10 .05 .01
☐ 141 Cleveland Indians TL .05 .02 .01
Brook Jacoby
☐ 142 Mike Diaz .05 .02 .01
☐ 143 Mike Campbell .05 .02 .01
☐ 144 Jay Bell .15 .07 .02
☐ 145 Dave Stewart .10 .05 .01
☐ 146 Gary Pettis .05 .02 .01
☐ 147 DeWayne Buice .05 .02 .01
☐ 148 Bill Pecota .05 .02 .01
☐ 149 Doug Dascenzo .05 .02 .01
☐ 150 Fernando Valenzuela .05 .02 .01
☐ 151 Terry McGriff .05 .02 .01
☐ 152 Mark Thurmond .05 .02 .01
☐ 153 Jim Pankovits .05 .02 .01
☐ 154 Don Carman .05 .02 .01
☐ 155 Marty Barrett .05 .02 .01
☐ 156 Dave Gallagher .05 .02 .01
☐ 157 Tom Glavine .40 .18 .05
☐ 158 Mike Aldrete .05 .02 .01
☐ 159 Pat Clements .05 .02 .01
☐ 160 Jeffrey Leonard .05 .02 .01
☐ 161 Gregg Olson FDP UER . .25 .11 .03
(Born Scribner, NE,
should be Omaha, NE)
☐ 162 John Davis .05 .02 .01
☐ 163 Bob Forsch .05 .02 .01
☐ 164 Hal Lanier MG .05 .02 .01
(Team checklist back)
☐ 165 Mike Dunne .05 .02 .01
☐ 166 Doug Jennings .05 .02 .01
☐ 167 Steve Searcy FS .05 .02 .01
☐ 168 Willie Wilson .05 .02 .01
☐ 169 Mike Jackson .05 .02 .01
☐ 170 Tony Fernandez .10 .05 .01
☐ 171 Atlanta Braves TL .05 .02 .01
Andres Thomas
☐ 172 Frank Williams .05 .02 .01
☐ 173 Mel Hall .05 .02 .01
☐ 174 Todd Burns .05 .02 .01
☐ 175 John Shelby .05 .02 .01
☐ 176 Jeff Parrett .05 .02 .01
☐ 177 Monty Fariss FDP .05 .02 .01
☐ 178 Mark Grant .05 .02 .01
☐ 179 Ozzie Virgil .05 .02 .01
☐ 180 Mike Scott .05 .02 .01
☐ 181 Craig Worthington .05 .02 .01
☐ 182 Bob McClure .05 .02 .01
☐ 183 Oddibe McDowell .05 .02 .01
☐ 184 John Costello .05 .02 .01
☐ 185 Claudell Washington .05 .02 .01
☐ 186 Pat Perry .05 .02 .01
☐ 187 Darren Daulton .15 .07 .02
☐ 188 Dennis Lamp .05 .02 .01
☐ 189 Kevin Mitchell .15 .07 .02
☐ 190 Mike Witt .05 .02 .01
☐ 191 Sil Campusano .05 .02 .01
☐ 192 Paul Mirabella .05 .02 .01
☐ 193 Sparky Anderson MG .10 .05 .01
(Team checklist back)
UER (553 Salazer)
☐ 194 Greg W. Harris .05 .02 .01
☐ 195 Ozzie Guillen .10 .05 .01
☐ 196 Denny Walling .05 .02 .01
☐ 197 Neal Heaton .05 .02 .01
☐ 198 Danny Heep .05 .02 .01
☐ 199 Mike Schooler .05 .02 .01
☐ 200 George Brett .35 .16 .04
☐ 201 Blue Jays TL .05 .02 .01
Kelly Gruber
☐ 202 Brad Moore .05 .02 .01
☐ 203 Rob Ducey .05 .02 .01
☐ 204 Brad Havens .05 .02 .01
☐ 205 Dwight Evans .10 .05 .01
☐ 206 Roberto Alomar .75 .35 .09
☐ 207 Terry Leach .05 .02 .01
☐ 208 Tom Pagnozzi .05 .02 .01
☐ 209 Jeff Bittiger .05 .02 .01
☐ 210 Dale Murphy .15 .07 .02
☐ 211 Mike Pagliarulo .05 .02 .01
☐ 212 Scott Sanderson .05 .02 .01
☐ 213 Rene Gonzales .05 .02 .01
☐ 214 Charlie O'Brien .05 .02 .01
☐ 215 Kevin Gross .05 .02 .01
☐ 216 Jack Howell .05 .02 .01
☐ 217 Joe Price .05 .02 .01
☐ 218 Mike LaValliere .05 .02 .01
☐ 219 Jim Clancy .05 .02 .01
☐ 220 Gary Gaetti .05 .02 .01
☐ 221 Cecil Espy .05 .02 .01
☐ 222 Mark Lewis FDP .20 .09 .03
☐ 223 Jay Buhner .20 .09 .03
☐ 224 Tony LaRussa MG .10 .05 .01
(Team checklist back)
☐ 225 Ramon Martinez .50 .23 .06
☐ 226 Bill Doran .05 .02 .01
☐ 227 John Farrell .05 .02 .01
☐ 228 Nelson Santovenia .05 .02 .01
☐ 229 Jimmy Key .15 .07 .02
☐ 230 Ozzie Smith .30 .14 .04
☐ 231 San Diego Padres TL ... .15 .07 .02
Roberto Alomar
(Gary Carter at plate)
☐ 232 Ricky Horton .05 .02 .01
☐ 233 Gregg Jefferies FS .35 .16 .04
☐ 234 Tom Browning .05 .02 .01
☐ 235 John Kruk .15 .07 .02
☐ 236 Charles Hudson .05 .02 .01
☐ 237 Glenn Hubbard .05 .02 .01
☐ 238 Eric King .05 .02 .01
☐ 239 Tim Laudner .05 .02 .01
☐ 240 Greg Maddux .35 .16 .04
☐ 241 Brett Butler .10 .05 .01
☐ 242 Ed VandeBerg .05 .02 .01
☐ 243 Bob Boone .10 .05 .01
☐ 244 Jim Acker .05 .02 .01
☐ 245 Jim Rice .15 .07 .02

	No.	Player			
☐	246	Rey Quinones	.05	.02	.01
☐	247	Shawn Hillegas	.05	.02	.01
☐	248	Tony Phillips	.10	.05	.01
☐	249	Tim Leary	.05	.02	.01
☐	250	Cal Ripken	.50	.23	.06
☐	251	John Dopson	.05	.02	.01
☐	252	Billy Hatcher	.05	.02	.01
☐	253	Jose Alvarez	.05	.02	.01
☐	254	Tom Lasorda MG	.10	.05	.01
		(Team checklist back)			
☐	255	Ron Guidry	.10	.05	.01
☐	256	Benny Santiago	.10	.05	.01
☐	257	Rick Aguilera	.10	.05	.01
☐	258	Checklist 133-264	.05	.02	.01
☐	259	Larry McWilliams	.05	.02	.01
☐	260	Dave Winfield	.20	.09	.03
☐	261	St.Louis Cardinals TL	.05	.02	.01
		Tom Brunansky			
		(With Luis Alicea)			
☐	262	Jeff Pico	.05	.02	.01
☐	263	Mike Felder	.05	.02	.01
☐	264	Rob Dibble	.20	.09	.03
☐	265	Kent Hrbek	.10	.05	.01
☐	266	Luis Aquino	.05	.02	.01
☐	267	Jeff M. Robinson	.05	.02	.01
☐	268	N. Keith Miller	.05	.02	.01
☐	269	Tom Bolton	.05	.02	.01
☐	270	Wally Joyner	.10	.05	.01
☐	271	Jay Tibbs	.05	.02	.01
☐	272	Ron Hassey	.05	.02	.01
☐	273	Jose Lind	.05	.02	.01
☐	274	Mark Eichhorn	.05	.02	.01
☐	275	Danny Tartabull UER	.10	.05	.01
		(Born San Juan, PR			
		should be Miami, FL)			
☐	276	Paul Kilgus	.05	.02	.01
☐	277	Mike Davis	.05	.02	.01
☐	278	Andy McGaffigan	.05	.02	.01
☐	279	Scott Bradley	.05	.02	.01
☐	280	Bob Knepper	.05	.02	.01
☐	281	Gary Redus	.05	.02	.01
☐	282	Cris Carpenter	.05	.02	.01
☐	283	Andy Allanson	.05	.02	.01
☐	284	Jim Leyland MG	.05	.02	.01
		(Team checklist back)			
☐	285	John Candelaria	.05	.02	.01
☐	286	Darrin Jackson	.10	.05	.01
☐	287	Juan Nieves	.05	.02	.01
☐	288	Pat Sheridan	.05	.02	.01
☐	289	Ernie Whitt	.05	.02	.01
☐	290	John Franco	.10	.05	.01
☐	291	New York Mets TL	.10	.05	.01
		Darryl Strawberry			
		(With Keith Hernandez			
		and Kevin McReynolds)			
☐	292	Jim Corsi	.05	.02	.01
☐	293	Glenn Wilson	.05	.02	.01
☐	294	Juan Berenguer	.05	.02	.01
☐	295	Scott Fletcher	.05	.02	.01
☐	296	Ron Gant	.25	.11	.03
☐	297	Oswald Peraza	.05	.02	.01
☐	298	Chris James	.05	.02	.01
☐	299	Steve Ellsworth	.05	.02	.01
☐	300	Darryl Strawberry	.15	.07	.02
☐	301	Charlie Leibrandt	.05	.02	.01
☐	302	Gary Ward	.05	.02	.01
☐	303	Felix Fermin	.05	.02	.01
☐	304	Joel Youngblood	.05	.02	.01
☐	305	Dave Smith	.05	.02	.01
☐	306	Tracy Woodson	.05	.02	.01
☐	307	Lance McCullers	.05	.02	.01
☐	308	Ron Karkovice	.05	.02	.01
☐	309	Mario Diaz	.05	.02	.01
☐	310	Rafael Palmeiro	.25	.11	.03
☐	311	Chris Bosio	.05	.02	.01
☐	312	Tom Lawless	.05	.02	.01
☐	313	Dennis Martinez	.10	.05	.01
☐	314	Bobby Valentine MG	.05	.02	.01
		(Team checklist back)			
☐	315	Greg Swindell	.10	.05	.01
☐	316	Walt Weiss	.05	.02	.01
☐	317	Jack Armstrong	.05	.02	.01
☐	318	Gene Larkin	.05	.02	.01
☐	319	Greg Booker	.05	.02	.01
☐	320	Lou Whitaker	.15	.07	.02
☐	321	Boston Red Sox TL	.05	.02	.01
		Jody Reed			
☐	322	John Smiley	.05	.02	.01
☐	323	Gary Thurman	.05	.02	.01
☐	324	Bob Milacki	.05	.02	.01
☐	325	Jesse Barfield	.05	.02	.01
☐	326	Dennis Boyd	.05	.02	.01
☐	327	Mark Lemke	.15	.07	.02
☐	328	Rick Honeycutt	.05	.02	.01
☐	329	Bob Melvin	.05	.02	.01
☐	330	Eric Davis	.10	.05	.01
☐	331	Curt Wilkerson	.05	.02	.01
☐	332	Tony Armas	.05	.02	.01
☐	333	Bob Ojeda	.05	.02	.01
☐	334	Steve Lyons	.05	.02	.01
☐	335	Dave Righetti	.05	.02	.01
☐	336	Steve Balboni	.05	.02	.01
☐	337	Calvin Schiraldi	.05	.02	.01
☐	338	Jim Adduci	.05	.02	.01
☐	339	Scott Bailes	.05	.02	.01
☐	340	Kirk Gibson	.10	.05	.01
☐	341	Jim Deshaies	.05	.02	.01
☐	342	Tom Brookens	.05	.02	.01
☐	343	Gary Sheffield FS	1.00	.45	.13
☐	344	Tom Trebelhorn MG	.05	.02	.01
		(Team checklist back)			
☐	345	Charlie Hough	.10	.05	.01
☐	346	Rex Hudler	.05	.02	.01
☐	347	John Cerutti	.05	.02	.01
☐	348	Ed Hearn	.05	.02	.01
☐	349	Ron Jones	.05	.02	.01
☐	350	Andy Van Slyke	.15	.07	.02
☐	351	San Fran. Giants TL	.05	.02	.01
		Bob Melvin			
		(With Bill Fahey CO)			
☐	352	Rick Schu	.05	.02	.01
☐	353	Marvell Wynne	.05	.02	.01
☐	354	Larry Parrish	.05	.02	.01
☐	355	Mark Langston	.15	.07	.02
☐	356	Kevin Elster	.05	.02	.01
☐	357	Jerry Reuss	.05	.02	.01
☐	358	Ricky Jordan	.05	.02	.01
☐	359	Tommy John	.15	.07	.02
☐	360	Ryne Sandberg	.40	.18	.05
☐	361	Kelly Downs	.05	.02	.01
☐	362	Jack Lazorko	.05	.02	.01
☐	363	Rich Yett	.05	.02	.01
☐	364	Rob Deer	.05	.02	.01
☐	365	Mike Henneman	.10	.05	.01
☐	366	Herm Winningham	.05	.02	.01
☐	367	Johnny Paredes	.05	.02	.01
☐	368	Brian Holton	.05	.02	.01
☐	369	Ken Caminiti	.15	.07	.02
☐	370	Dennis Eckersley	.15	.07	.02
☐	371	Manny Lee	.05	.02	.01
☐	372	Craig Lefferts	.05	.02	.01
☐	373	Tracy Jones	.05	.02	.01
☐	374	John Wathan MG	.05	.02	.01
		(Team checklist back)			
☐	375	Terry Pendleton	.15	.07	.02
☐	376	Steve Lombardozzi	.05	.02	.01

☐ 377 Mike Smithson .05 .02 .01
☐ 378 Checklist 265-396 .05 .02 .01
☐ 379 Tim Flannery .05 .02 .01
☐ 380 Rickey Henderson .15 .07 .02
☐ 381 Baltimore Orioles TL .05 .02 .01
Larry Sheets
☐ 382 John Smoltz .40 .18 .05
☐ 383 Howard Johnson .10 .05 .01
☐ 384 Mark Salas .05 .02 .01
☐ 385 Von Hayes .05 .02 .01
☐ 386 Andres Galarraga AS .10 .05 .01
☐ 387 Ryne Sandberg AS .20 .09 .03
☐ 388 Bobby Bonilla AS .10 .05 .01
☐ 389 Ozzie Smith AS .10 .05 .01
☐ 390 Darryl Strawberry AS .10 .05 .01
☐ 391 Andre Dawson AS .10 .05 .01
☐ 392 Andy Van Slyke AS .05 .02 .01
☐ 393 Gary Carter AS .10 .05 .01
☐ 394 Orel Hershiser AS .05 .02 .01
☐ 395 Danny Jackson AS .05 .02 .01
☐ 396 Kirk Gibson AS .10 .05 .01
☐ 397 Don Mattingly AS .20 .09 .03
☐ 398 Julio Franco AS .05 .02 .01
☐ 399 Wade Boggs AS .10 .05 .01
☐ 400 Alan Trammell AS .10 .05 .01
☐ 401 Jose Canseco AS .15 .07 .02
☐ 402 Mike Greenwell AS .05 .02 .01
☐ 403 Kirby Puckett AS .20 .09 .03
☐ 404 Bob Boone AS .05 .02 .01
☐ 405 Roger Clemens AS .15 .07 .02
☐ 406 Frank Viola AS .05 .02 .01
☐ 407 Dave Winfield AS .10 .05 .01
☐ 408 Greg Walker .05 .02 .01
☐ 409 Ken Dayley .05 .02 .01
☐ 410 Jack Clark .10 .05 .01
☐ 411 Mitch Williams .10 .05 .01
☐ 412 Barry Lyons .05 .02 .01
☐ 413 Mike Kingery .05 .02 .01
☐ 414 Jim Fregosi MG .05 .02 .01
(Team checklist back)
☐ 415 Rich Gossage .15 .07 .02
☐ 416 Fred Lynn .10 .05 .01
☐ 417 Mike LaCoss .05 .02 .01
☐ 418 Bob Dernier .05 .02 .01
☐ 419 Tom Filer .05 .02 .01
☐ 420 Joe Carter .25 .11 .03
☐ 421 Kirk McCaskill .05 .02 .01
☐ 422 Bo Diaz .05 .02 .01
☐ 423 Brian Fisher .05 .02 .01
☐ 424 Luis Polonia UER .10 .05 .01
(Wrong birthdate)
☐ 425 Jay Howell .05 .02 .01
☐ 426 Dan Gladden .05 .02 .01
☐ 427 Eric Show .05 .02 .01
☐ 428 Craig Reynolds .05 .02 .01
☐ 429 Minnesota Twins TL .05 .02 .01
Greg Gagne
(Taking throw at 2nd)
☐ 430 Mark Gubicza .05 .02 .01
☐ 431 Luis Rivera .05 .02 .01
☐ 432 Chad Kreuter .15 .07 .02
☐ 433 Albert Hall .05 .02 .01
☐ 434 Ken Patterson .05 .02 .01
☐ 435 Len Dykstra .15 .07 .02
☐ 436 Bobby Meacham .05 .02 .01
☐ 437 Andy Benes FDP .50 .23 .06
☐ 438 Greg Gross .05 .02 .01
☐ 439 Frank DiPino .05 .02 .01
☐ 440 Bobby Bonilla .15 .07 .02
☐ 441 Jerry Reed .05 .02 .01
☐ 442 Jose Oquendo .05 .02 .01
☐ 443 Rod Nichols .05 .02 .01
☐ 444 Moose Stubing MG .05 .02 .01
(Team checklist back)
☐ 445 Matt Nokes .05 .02 .01
☐ 446 Rob Murphy .05 .02 .01
☐ 447 Donell Nixon .05 .02 .01
☐ 448 Eric Plunk .05 .02 .01
☐ 449 Carmelo Martinez .05 .02 .01
☐ 450 Roger Clemens .35 .16 .04
☐ 451 Mark Davidson .05 .02 .01
☐ 452 Israel Sanchez .05 .02 .01
☐ 453 Tom Prince .05 .02 .01
☐ 454 Paul Assenmacher .05 .02 .01
☐ 455 Johnny Ray .05 .02 .01
☐ 456 Tim Belcher .05 .02 .01
☐ 457 Mackey Sasser .05 .02 .01
☐ 458 Donn Pall .05 .02 .01
☐ 459 Seattle Mariners TL .05 .02 .01
Dave Valle
☐ 460 Dave Stieb .10 .05 .01
☐ 461 Buddy Bell .10 .05 .01
☐ 462 Jose Guzman .10 .05 .01
☐ 463 Steve Lake .05 .02 .01
☐ 464 Bryn Smith .05 .02 .01
☐ 465 Mark Grace .50 .23 .06
☐ 466 Chuck Crim .05 .02 .01
☐ 467 Jim Walewander .05 .02 .01
☐ 468 Henry Cotto .05 .02 .01
☐ 469 Jose Bautista .05 .02 .01
☐ 470 Lance Parrish .10 .05 .01
☐ 471 Steve Curry .05 .02 .01
☐ 472 Brian Harper .10 .05 .01
☐ 473 Don Robinson .05 .02 .01
☐ 474 Bob Rodgers MG .05 .02 .01
(Team checklist back)
☐ 475 Dave Parker .15 .07 .02
☐ 476 Jon Perlman .05 .02 .01
☐ 477 Dick Schofield .05 .02 .01
☐ 478 Doug Drabek .15 .07 .02
☐ 479 Mike Macfarlane .10 .05 .01
☐ 480 Keith Hernandez .10 .05 .01
☐ 481 Chris Brown .05 .02 .01
☐ 482 Steve Peters .05 .02 .01
☐ 483 Mickey Hatcher .05 .02 .01
☐ 484 Steve Shields .05 .02 .01
☐ 485 Hubie Brooks .05 .02 .01
☐ 486 Jack McDowell .30 .14 .04
☐ 487 Scott Lusader .05 .02 .01
☐ 488 Kevin Coffman .05 .02 .01
("Now with Cubs")
☐ 489 Phila. Phillies TL .10 .05 .01
Mike Schmidt
☐ 490 Chris Sabo .25 .11 .03
☐ 491 Mike Birkbeck .05 .02 .01
☐ 492 Alan Ashby .05 .02 .01
☐ 493 Todd Benzinger .05 .02 .01
☐ 494 Shane Rawley .05 .02 .01
☐ 495 Candy Maldonado .05 .02 .01
☐ 496 Dwayne Henry .05 .02 .01
☐ 497 Pete Stanicek .05 .02 .01
☐ 498 Dave Valle .05 .02 .01
☐ 499 Don Heinkel .05 .02 .01
☐ 500 Jose Canseco .30 .14 .04
☐ 501 Vance Law .05 .02 .01
☐ 502 Duane Ward .10 .05 .01
☐ 503 Al Newman .05 .02 .01
☐ 504 Bob Walk .05 .02 .01
☐ 505 Pete Rose MG .20 .09 .03
(Team checklist back)
☐ 506 Kirt Manwaring .05 .02 .01
☐ 507 Steve Farr .05 .02 .01
☐ 508 Wally Backman .05 .02 .01
☐ 509 Bud Black .05 .02 .01
☐ 510 Bob Horner .05 .02 .01
☐ 511 Richard Dotson .05 .02 .01

	No.	Player			
☐	512	Donnie Hill	.05	.02	.01
☐	513	Jesse Orosco	.05	.02	.01
☐	514	Chet Lemon	.05	.02	.01
☐	515	Barry Larkin	.15	.07	.02
☐	516	Eddie Whitson	.05	.02	.01
☐	517	Greg Brock	.05	.02	.01
☐	518	Bruce Ruffin	.05	.02	.01
☐	519	New York Yankees TL	.05	.02	.01
		Willie Randolph			
☐	520	Rick Sutcliffe	.10	.05	.01
☐	521	Mickey Tettleton	.10	.05	.01
☐	522	Randy Kramer	.05	.02	.01
☐	523	Andres Thomas	.05	.02	.01
☐	524	Checklist 397-528	.05	.02	.01
☐	525	Chili Davis	.10	.05	.01
☐	526	Wes Gardner	.05	.02	.01
☐	527	Dave Henderson	.05	.02	.01
☐	528	Luis Medina	.05	.02	.01
		(Lower left front			
		has white triangle)			
☐	529	Tom Foley	.05	.02	.01
☐	530	Nolan Ryan	.75	.35	.09
☐	531	Dave Hengel	.05	.02	.01
☐	532	Jerry Browne	.05	.02	.01
☐	533	Andy Hawkins	.05	.02	.01
☐	534	Doc Edwards MG	.05	.02	.01
		(Team checklist back)			
☐	535	Todd Worrell UER	.10	.05	.01
		(4 wins in '88,			
		should be 5)			
☐	536	Joel Skinner	.05	.02	.01
☐	537	Pete Smith	.05	.02	.01
☐	538	Juan Castillo	.05	.02	.01
☐	539	Barry Jones	.05	.02	.01
☐	540	Bo Jackson	.25	.11	.03
☐	541	Cecil Fielder	.25	.11	.03
☐	542	Todd Frohwirth	.05	.02	.01
☐	543	Damon Berryhill	.05	.02	.01
☐	544	Jeff Sellers	.05	.02	.01
☐	545	Mookie Wilson	.10	.05	.01
☐	546	Mark Williamson	.05	.02	.01
☐	547	Mark McLemore	.05	.02	.01
☐	548	Bobby Witt	.10	.05	.01
☐	549	Chicago Cubs TL	.05	.02	.01
		Jamie Moyer			
		(Pitching)			
☐	550	Orel Hershiser	.10	.05	.01
☐	551	Randy Ready	.05	.02	.01
☐	552	Greg Cadaret	.05	.02	.01
☐	553	Luis Salazar	.05	.02	.01
☐	554	Nick Esasky	.05	.02	.01
☐	555	Bert Blyleven	.15	.07	.02
☐	556	Bruce Fields	.05	.02	.01
☐	557	Keith A. Miller	.05	.02	.01
☐	558	Dan Pasqua	.05	.02	.01
☐	559	Juan Agosto	.05	.02	.01
☐	560	Tim Raines	.15	.07	.02
☐	561	Luis Aguayo	.05	.02	.01
☐	562	Danny Cox	.05	.02	.01
☐	563	Bill Schroeder	.05	.02	.01
☐	564	Russ Nixon MG	.05	.02	.01
		(Team checklist back)			
☐	565	Jeff Russell	.05	.02	.01
☐	566	Al Pedrique	.05	.02	.01
☐	567	David Wells UER	.05	.02	.01
		(Complete Pitching			
		Recor)			
☐	568	Mickey Brantley	.05	.02	.01
☐	569	German Jimenez	.05	.02	.01
☐	570	Tony Gwynn UER	.30	.14	.04
		('88 average should			
		be italicized as			
		league leader)			
☐	571	Billy Ripken	.05	.02	.01
☐	572	Atlee Hammaker	.05	.02	.01
☐	573	Jim Abbott FDP	.60	.25	.08
☐	574	Dave Clark	.05	.02	.01
☐	575	Juan Samuel	.05	.02	.01
☐	576	Greg Minton	.05	.02	.01
☐	577	Randy Bush	.05	.02	.01
☐	578	John Morris	.05	.02	.01
☐	579	Houston Astros TL	.05	.02	.01
		Glenn Davis			
		(Batting stance)			
☐	580	Harold Reynolds	.05	.02	.01
☐	581	Gene Nelson	.05	.02	.01
☐	582	Mike Marshall	.05	.02	.01
☐	583	Paul Gibson	.05	.02	.01
☐	584	Randy Velarde UER	.05	.02	.01
		(Signed 1935,			
		should be 1985)			
☐	585	Harold Baines	.10	.05	.01
☐	586	Joe Boever	.05	.02	.01
☐	587	Mike Stanley	.10	.05	.01
☐	588	Luis Alicea	.05	.02	.01
☐	589	Dave Meads	.05	.02	.01
☐	590	Andres Galarraga	.15	.07	.02
☐	591	Jeff Musselman	.05	.02	.01
☐	592	John Cangelosi	.05	.02	.01
☐	593	Drew Hall	.05	.02	.01
☐	594	Jimy Williams MG	.05	.02	.01
		(Team checklist back)			
☐	595	Teddy Higuera	.05	.02	.01
☐	596	Kurt Stillwell	.05	.02	.01
☐	597	Terry Taylor	.05	.02	.01
☐	598	Ken Gerhart	.05	.02	.01
☐	599	Tom Candiotti	.05	.02	.01
☐	600	Wade Boggs	.20	.09	.03
☐	601	Dave Dravecky	.10	.05	.01
☐	602	Devon White	.10	.05	.01
☐	603	Frank Tanana	.05	.02	.01
☐	604	Paul O'Neill	.15	.07	.02
☐	605A	Bob Welch ERR	2.25	1.00	.30
		(Missing line on back,			
		"Complete M.L.			
		Pitching Record")			
☐	605B	Bob Welch COR	.10	.05	.01
☐	606	Rick Dempsey	.05	.02	.01
☐	607	Willie Ansley FDP	.10	.05	.01
☐	608	Phil Bradley	.05	.02	.01
☐	609	Detroit Tigers TL	.05	.02	.01
		Frank Tanana			
		(With Alan Trammell			
		and Mike Heath)			
☐	610	Randy Myers	.10	.05	.01
☐	611	Don Slaught	.05	.02	.01
☐	612	Dan Quisenberry	.10	.05	.01
☐	613	Gary Varsho	.05	.02	.01
☐	614	Joe Hesketh	.05	.02	.01
☐	615	Robin Yount	.20	.09	.03
☐	616	Steve Rosenberg	.05	.02	.01
☐	617	Mark Parent	.05	.02	.01
☐	618	Rance Mulliniks	.05	.02	.01
☐	619	Checklist 529-660	.05	.02	.01
☐	620	Barry Bonds	.60	.25	.08
☐	621	Rick Mahler	.05	.02	.01
☐	622	Stan Javier	.05	.02	.01
☐	623	Fred Toliver	.05	.02	.01
☐	624	Jack McKeon MG	.05	.02	.01
		(Team checklist back)			
☐	625	Eddie Murray	.15	.07	.02
☐	626	Jeff Reed	.05	.02	.01
☐	627	Greg A. Harris	.05	.02	.01
☐	628	Matt Williams	.40	.18	.05
☐	629	Pete O'Brien	.05	.02	.01
☐	630	Mike Greenwell	.10	.05	.01

☐ 631 Dave Bergman .05 .02 .01
☐ 632 Bryan Harvey .25 .11 .03
☐ 633 Daryl Boston .05 .02 .01
☐ 634 Marvin Freeman .05 .02 .01
☐ 635 Willie Randolph .10 .05 .01
☐ 636 Bill Wilkinson .05 .02 .01
☐ 637 Carmen Castillo .05 .02 .01
☐ 638 Floyd Bannister .05 .02 .01
☐ 639 Oakland A's TL .05 .02 .01
Walt Weiss
☐ 640 Willie McGee .10 .05 .01
☐ 641 Curt Young .05 .02 .01
☐ 642 Argenis Salazar .05 .02 .01
☐ 643 Louie Meadows .05 .02 .01
☐ 644 Lloyd McClendon .05 .02 .01
☐ 645 Jack Morris .15 .07 .02
☐ 646 Kevin Bass .05 .02 .01
☐ 647 Randy Johnson .75 .35 .09
☐ 648 Sandy Alomar FS .25 .11 .03
☐ 649 Stewart Cliburn .05 .02 .01
☐ 650 Kirby Puckett .50 .23 .06
☐ 651 Tom Niedenfuer .05 .02 .01
☐ 652 Rich Gedman .05 .02 .01
☐ 653 Tommy Barrett .05 .02 .01
☐ 654 Whitey Herzog MG .10 .05 .01
(Team checklist back)
☐ 655 Dave Magadan .05 .02 .01
☐ 656 Ivan Calderon .05 .02 .01
☐ 657 Joe Magrane .05 .02 .01
☐ 658 R.J. Reynolds .05 .02 .01
☐ 659 Al Leiter .05 .02 .01
☐ 660 Will Clark .40 .18 .05
☐ 661 Dwight Gooden TBC84. .05 .02 .01
☐ 662 Lou Brock TBC79 .10 .05 .01
☐ 663 Hank Aaron TBC74 .20 .09 .03
☐ 664 Gil Hodges TBC69 .10 .05 .01
☐ 665A Tony Oliva TBC64 2.00 .90 .25
ERR (fabricated card is enlarged version of Oliva's 64T card; Topps copyright missing)
☐ 665B Tony Oliva TBC64 .10 .05 .01
COR (fabricated card)
☐ 666 Randy St.Claire .05 .02 .01
☐ 667 Dwayne Murphy .05 .02 .01
☐ 668 Mike Bielecki .05 .02 .01
☐ 669 L.A. Dodgers TL .05 .02 .01
Orel Hershiser
(Mound conference with Mike Scioscia)
☐ 670 Kevin Seitzer .05 .02 .01
☐ 671 Jim Gantner .05 .02 .01
☐ 672 Allan Anderson .05 .02 .01
☐ 673 Don Baylor .15 .07 .02
☐ 674 Otis Nixon .10 .05 .01
☐ 675 Bruce Hurst .05 .02 .01
☐ 676 Ernest Riles .05 .02 .01
☐ 677 Dave Schmidt .05 .02 .01
☐ 678 Dion James .05 .02 .01
☐ 679 Willie Fraser .05 .02 .01
☐ 680 Gary Carter .15 .07 .02
☐ 681 Jeff D. Robinson .05 .02 .01
☐ 682 Rick Leach .05 .02 .01
☐ 683 Jose Cecena .05 .02 .01
☐ 684 Dave Johnson MG .05 .02 .01
(Team checklist back)
☐ 685 Jeff Treadway .05 .02 .01
☐ 686 Scott Terry .05 .02 .01
☐ 687 Alvin Davis .05 .02 .01
☐ 688 Zane Smith .05 .02 .01
☐ 689A Stan Jefferson .05 .02 .01
(Pink triangle on front bottom left)
☐ 689B Stan Jefferson .05 .02 .01
(Violet triangle on front bottom left)
☐ 690 Doug Jones .10 .05 .01
☐ 691 Roberto Kelly UER .20 .09 .03
(83 Oneonita)
☐ 692 Steve Ontiveros .05 .02 .01
☐ 693 Pat Borders .25 .11 .03
☐ 694 Les Lancaster .05 .02 .01
☐ 695 Carlton Fisk .15 .07 .02
☐ 696 Don August .05 .02 .01
☐ 697A Franklin Stubbs .05 .02 .01
(Team name on front in white)
☐ 697B Franklin Stubbs .05 .02 .01
(Team name on front in gray)
☐ 698 Keith Atherton .05 .02 .01
☐ 699 Pittsburgh Pirates TL .05 .02 .01
Al Pedrique
(Tony Gwynn sliding)
☐ 700 Don Mattingly .40 .18 .05
☐ 701 Storm Davis .05 .02 .01
☐ 702 Jamie Quirk .05 .02 .01
☐ 703 Scott Garrelts .05 .02 .01
☐ 704 Carlos Quintana .05 .02 .01
☐ 705 Terry Kennedy .05 .02 .01
☐ 706 Pete Incaviglia .10 .05 .01
☐ 707 Steve Jeltz .05 .02 .01
☐ 708 Chuck Finley .10 .05 .01
☐ 709 Tom Herr .05 .02 .01
☐ 710 David Cone .20 .09 .03
☐ 711 Candy Sierra .05 .02 .01
☐ 712 Bill Swift .10 .05 .01
☐ 713 Ty Griffin FDP .05 .02 .01
☐ 714 Joe Morgan MG .05 .02 .01
(Team checklist back)
☐ 715 Tony Pena .05 .02 .01
☐ 716 Wayne Tolleson .05 .02 .01
☐ 717 Jamie Moyer .05 .02 .01
☐ 718 Glenn Braggs .05 .02 .01
☐ 719 Danny Darwin .05 .02 .01
☐ 720 Tim Wallach .05 .02 .01
☐ 721 Ron Tingley .05 .02 .01
☐ 722 Todd Stottlemyre .10 .05 .01
☐ 723 Rafael Belliard .05 .02 .01
☐ 724 Jerry Don Gleaton .05 .02 .01
☐ 725 Terry Steinbach .10 .05 .01
☐ 726 Dickie Thon .05 .02 .01
☐ 727 Joe Orsulak .05 .02 .01
☐ 728 Charlie Puleo .05 .02 .01
☐ 729 Texas Rangers TL .05 .02 .01
Steve Buechele
(Inconsistent design, team name on front surrounded by black, should be white)
☐ 730 Danny Jackson .05 .02 .01
☐ 731 Mike Young .05 .02 .01
☐ 732 Steve Buechele .05 .02 .01
☐ 733 Randy Bockus .05 .02 .01
☐ 734 Jody Reed .05 .02 .01
☐ 735 Roger McDowell .05 .02 .01
☐ 736 Jeff Hamilton .05 .02 .01
☐ 737 Norm Charlton .15 .07 .02
☐ 738 Darnell Coles .05 .02 .01
☐ 739 Brook Jacoby .05 .02 .01
☐ 740 Dan Plesac .05 .02 .01
☐ 741 Ken Phelps .05 .02 .01
☐ 742 Mike Harkey FS .05 .02 .01
☐ 743 Mike Heath .05 .02 .01

	No.	Player	Mint	Exc	G-VG
□	744	Roger Craig MG (Team checklist back)	.05	.02	.01
□	745	Fred McGriff	.25	.11	.03
□	746	German Gonzalez UER (Wrong birthdate)	.05	.02	.01
□	747	Wil Tejada	.05	.02	.01
□	748	Jimmy Jones	.05	.02	.01
□	749	Rafael Ramirez	.05	.02	.01
□	750	Bret Saberhagen	.10	.05	.01
□	751	Ken Oberkfell	.05	.02	.01
□	752	Jim Gott	.05	.02	.01
□	753	Jose Uribe	.05	.02	.01
□	754	Bob Brower	.05	.02	.01
□	755	Mike Scioscia	.05	.02	.01
□	756	Scott Medvin	.05	.02	.01
□	757	Brady Anderson	.40	.18	.05
□	758	Gene Walter	.05	.02	.01
□	759	Milwaukee Brewers TL. Rob Deer	.05	.02	.01
□	760	Lee Smith	.15	.07	.02
□	761	Dante Bichette	.75	.35	.09
□	762	Bobby Thigpen	.05	.02	.01
□	763	Dave Martinez	.05	.02	.01
□	764	Robin Ventura FDP	1.00	.45	.13
□	765	Glenn Davis	.05	.02	.01
□	766	Cecilio Guante	.05	.02	.01
□	767	Mike Capel	.05	.02	.01
□	768	Bill Wegman	.05	.02	.01
□	769	Junior Ortiz	.05	.02	.01
□	770	Alan Trammell	.15	.07	.02
□	771	Ron Kittle	.05	.02	.01
□	772	Ron Oester	.05	.02	.01
□	773	Keith Moreland	.05	.02	.01
□	774	Frank Robinson MG (Team checklist back)	.05	.02	.01
□	775	Jeff Reardon	.15	.07	.02
□	776	Nelson Liriano	.05	.02	.01
□	777	Ted Power	.05	.02	.01
□	778	Bruce Benedict	.05	.02	.01
□	779	Craig McMurtry	.05	.02	.01
□	780	Pedro Guerrero	.10	.05	.01
□	781	Greg Briley	.05	.02	.01
□	782	Checklist 661-792	.05	.02	.01
□	783	Trevor Wilson	.05	.02	.01
□	784	Steve Avery FDP	1.00	.45	.13
□	785	Ellis Burks	.10	.05	.01
□	786	Melido Perez	.05	.02	.01
□	787	Dave West	.10	.05	.01
□	788	Mike Morgan	.05	.02	.01
□	789	Kansas City Royals TL. Bo Jackson (Throwing)	.10	.05	.01
□	790	Sid Fernandez	.10	.05	.01
□	791	Jim Lindeman	.05	.02	.01
□	792	Rafael Santana	.05	.02	.01

1989 Topps Traded

The 1989 Topps Traded set contains 132 standard-size (2 1/2" by 3 1/2") cards. The fronts have white borders; the horizontally oriented backs are red and pink. From the front the cards' style is indistinguishable from the 1989 Topps regular issue. The cards were distributed as a boxed set. Rookie Cards in this set include Ken Griffey Jr., Ken Hill, Deion Sanders, and Jerome Walton. Topps also produced a specially boxed "glossy" edition frequently referred to

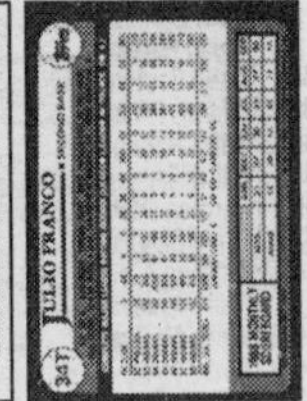

as the Topps Traded Tiffany set. This year, again, Topps did not disclose the number of Tiffany sets they produced or sold but it seems that production quantities were roughly similar (or slightly smaller, 15,000 sets) to the previous two years. The checklist of cards is identical to that of the normal non-glossy cards. There are two primary distinguishing features of the Tiffany cards, white card stock reverses and high gloss obverses. These Tiffany cards are valued approximately from three to five times the values listed below.

			MINT	EXC	G-VG
		COMPLETE FACT.SET (132)	6.00	2.70	.75
		COMMON CARD (1T-132T)	.05	.02	.01
□	1T	Don Aase	.05	.02	.01
□	2T	Jim Abbott	.60	.25	.08
□	3T	Kent Anderson	.05	.02	.01
□	4T	Keith Atherton	.05	.02	.01
□	5T	Wally Backman	.05	.02	.01
□	6T	Steve Balboni	.05	.02	.01
□	7T	Jesse Barfield	.05	.02	.01
□	8T	Steve Bedrosian	.05	.02	.01
□	9T	Todd Benzinger	.05	.02	.01
□	10T	Geronimo Berroa	.25	.11	.03
□	11T	Bert Blyleven	.10	.05	.01
□	12T	Bob Boone	.08	.04	.01
□	13T	Phil Bradley	.05	.02	.01
□	14T	Jeff Brantley	.05	.02	.01
□	15T	Kevin Brown	.08	.04	.01
□	16T	Jerry Browne	.05	.02	.01
□	17T	Chuck Cary	.05	.02	.01
□	18T	Carmen Castillo	.05	.02	.01
□	19T	Jim Clancy	.05	.02	.01
□	20T	Jack Clark	.08	.04	.01
□	21T	Bryan Clutterbuck	.05	.02	.01
□	22T	Jody Davis	.05	.02	.01
□	23T	Mike Devereaux	.08	.04	.01
□	24T	Frank DiPino	.05	.02	.01
□	25T	Benny Distefano	.05	.02	.01
□	26T	John Dopson	.05	.02	.01
□	27T	Len Dykstra	.10	.05	.01
□	28T	Jim Eisenreich	.05	.02	.01
□	29T	Nick Esasky	.05	.02	.01
□	30T	Alvaro Espinoza	.05	.02	.01
□	31T	Darrell Evans UER (Stat headings on back are for a pitcher)	.08	.04	.01
□	32T	Junior Felix	.20	.09	.03
□	33T	Felix Fermin	.05	.02	.01
□	34T	Julio Franco	.08	.04	.01
□	35T	Terry Francona	.05	.02	.01
□	36T	Cito Gaston MG	.08	.04	.01
□	37T	Bob Geren UER	.05	.02	.01

(Photo actually
Mike Fennell)

☐ 38T	Tom Gordon	.20	.09	.03
☐ 39T	Tommy Gregg	.05	.02	.01
☐ 40T	Ken Griffey	.08	.04	.01
☐ 41T	Ken Griffey Jr.	4.00	1.80	.50
☐ 42T	Kevin Gross	.05	.02	.01
☐ 43T	Lee Guetterman	.05	.02	.01
☐ 44T	Mel Hall	.05	.02	.01
☐ 45T	Erik Hanson	.25	.11	.03
☐ 46T	Gene Harris	.10	.05	.01
☐ 47T	Andy Hawkins	.05	.02	.01
☐ 48T	Rickey Henderson	.25	.11	.03
☐ 49T	Tom Herr	.05	.02	.01
☐ 50T	Ken Hill	.60	.25	.08
☐ 51T	Brian Holman	.05	.02	.01
☐ 52T	Brian Holton	.05	.02	.01
☐ 53T	Art Howe MG	.05	.02	.01
☐ 54T	Ken Howell	.05	.02	.01
☐ 55T	Bruce Hurst	.05	.02	.01
☐ 56T	Chris James	.05	.02	.01
☐ 57T	Randy Johnson	.75	.35	.09
☐ 58T	Jimmy Jones	.05	.02	.01
☐ 59T	Terry Kennedy	.05	.02	.01
☐ 60T	Paul Kilgus	.05	.02	.01
☐ 61T	Eric King	.05	.02	.01
☐ 62T	Ron Kittle	.05	.02	.01
☐ 63T	John Kruk	.10	.05	.01
☐ 64T	Randy Kutcher	.05	.02	.01
☐ 65T	Steve Lake	.05	.02	.01
☐ 66T	Mark Langston	.10	.05	.01
☐ 67T	Dave LaPoint	.05	.02	.01
☐ 68T	Rick Leach	.05	.02	.01
☐ 69T	Terry Leach	.05	.02	.01
☐ 70T	Jim Lefebvre MG	.05	.02	.01
☐ 71T	Al Leiter	.05	.02	.01
☐ 72T	Jeffrey Leonard	.05	.02	.01
☐ 73T	Derek Lilliquist	.05	.02	.01
☐ 74T	Rick Mahler	.05	.02	.01
☐ 75T	Tom McCarthy	.05	.02	.01
☐ 76T	Lloyd McClendon	.05	.02	.01
☐ 77T	Lance McCullers	.05	.02	.01
☐ 78T	Oddibe McDowell	.05	.02	.01
☐ 79T	Roger McDowell	.05	.02	.01
☐ 80T	Larry McWilliams	.05	.02	.01
☐ 81T	Randy Milligan	.05	.02	.01
☐ 82T	Mike Moore	.05	.02	.01
☐ 83T	Keith Moreland	.05	.02	.01
☐ 84T	Mike Morgan	.05	.02	.01
☐ 85T	Jamie Moyer	.05	.02	.01
☐ 86T	Rob Murphy	.05	.02	.01
☐ 87T	Eddie Murray	.25	.11	.03
☐ 88T	Pete O'Brien	.05	.02	.01
☐ 89T	Gregg Olson	.20	.09	.03
☐ 90T	Steve Ontiveros	.05	.02	.01
☐ 91T	Jesse Orosco	.05	.02	.01
☐ 92T	Spike Owen	.05	.02	.01
☐ 93T	Rafael Palmeiro	.30	.14	.04
☐ 94T	Clay Parker	.05	.02	.01
☐ 95T	Jeff Parrett	.05	.02	.01
☐ 96T	Lance Parrish	.08	.04	.01
☐ 97T	Dennis Powell	.05	.02	.01
☐ 98T	Rey Quinones	.05	.02	.01
☐ 99T	Doug Rader MG	.05	.02	.01
☐ 100T	Willie Randolph	.08	.04	.01
☐ 101T	Shane Rawley	.05	.02	.01
☐ 102T	Randy Ready	.05	.02	.01
☐ 103T	Bip Roberts	.08	.04	.01
☐ 104T	Kenny Rogers	.35	.16	.04
☐ 105T	Ed Romero	.05	.02	.01
☐ 106T	Nolan Ryan	1.25	.55	.16
☐ 107T	Luis Salazar	.05	.02	.01
☐ 108T	Juan Samuel	.05	.02	.01
☐ 109T	Alex Sanchez	.05	.02	.01
☐ 110T	Deion Sanders	1.50	.65	.19
☐ 111T	Steve Sax	.05	.02	.01
☐ 112T	Rick Schu	.05	.02	.01
☐ 113T	Dwight Smith	.15	.07	.02
☐ 114T	Lonnie Smith	.05	.02	.01
☐ 115T	Billy Spiers	.05	.02	.01
☐ 116T	Kent Tekulve	.05	.02	.01
☐ 117T	Walt Terrell	.05	.02	.01
☐ 118T	Milt Thompson	.05	.02	.01
☐ 119T	Dickie Thon	.05	.02	.01
☐ 120T	Jeff Torborg MG	.05	.02	.01
☐ 121T	Jeff Treadway	.05	.02	.01
☐ 122T	Omar Vizquel	.20	.09	.03
☐ 123T	Jerome Walton	.05	.02	.01
☐ 124T	Gary Ward	.05	.02	.01
☐ 125T	Claudell Washington	.05	.02	.01
☐ 126T	Curt Wilkerson	.05	.02	.01
☐ 127T	Eddie Williams	.05	.02	.01
☐ 128T	Frank Williams	.05	.02	.01
☐ 129T	Ken Williams	.05	.02	.01
☐ 130T	Mitch Williams	.08	.04	.01
☐ 131T	Steve Wilson	.05	.02	.01
☐ 132T	Checklist 1T-132T	.05	.02	.01

1990 Topps

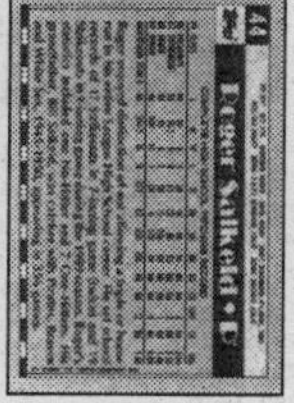

The 1990 Topps set contains 792 standard-size (2 1/2" by 3 1/2") cards. The front borders are various colors with the player's name at the bottom and team name at top. The horizontally oriented backs are yellowish green and contain statistics and highlights. Subsets include All-Stars (385-407) and Turn Back the Clock (661-665). The checklist cards are oriented alphabetically by team name and player name. The key Rookie Cards in this set are Delino DeShields, Juan Gonzalez, Marquis Grissom, Ben McDonald, Sammy Sosa, Frank Thomas, and Larry Walker. The Thomas card (414A) was printed without his name on front creating a scarce variation. The card is rarely seen and, for a newer issue, has experienced unprecedented growth as far as value. Topps also produced a specially boxed "glossy" edition frequently referred to as the Topps Tiffany set. This year, again, Topps did not disclose the number of Tiffany sets they produced or sold but it seems that production quantities were roughly similar (approximately 15,000 sets) to the previous year. The checklist of cards is identical to that of the normal non-

glossy cards. There are two primary distinguishing features of the Tiffany cards, white card stock reverses and high gloss obverses. These Tiffany cards are valued approximately from three to five times the values listed below.

	MINT	EXC	G-VG
COMPLETE SET (792)	15.00	6.75	1.90
COMPLETE FACT.SET (792)	15.00	6.75	1.90
COMMON CARD (1-792)	.05	.02	.01

	Card	MINT	EXC	G-VG
☐ 1	Nolan Ryan	.75	.35	.09
☐ 2	Nolan Ryan Salute New York Mets	.25	.11	.03
☐ 3	Nolan Ryan Salute California Angels	.25	.11	.03
☐ 4	Nolan Ryan Salute Houston Astros	.25	.11	.03
☐ 5	Nolan Ryan Salute Texas Rangers UER (Says Texas Stadium rather than Arlington Stadium)	.25	.11	.03
☐ 6	Vince Coleman RB (50 consecutive stolen bases)	.05	.02	.01
☐ 7	Rickey Henderson RB (40 career leadoff home runs)	.10	.05	.01
☐ 8	Cal Ripken RB (20 or more homers for 8 consecutive years, record for shortstops)	.25	.11	.03
☐ 9	Eric Plunk	.05	.02	.01
☐ 10	Barry Larkin	.15	.07	.02
☐ 11	Paul Gibson	.05	.02	.01
☐ 12	Joe Girardi	.05	.02	.01
☐ 13	Mark Williamson	.05	.02	.01
☐ 14	Mike Fetters	.05	.02	.01
☐ 15	Teddy Higuera	.05	.02	.01
☐ 16	Kent Anderson	.05	.02	.01
☐ 17	Kelly Downs	.05	.02	.01
☐ 18	Carlos Quintana	.05	.02	.01
☐ 19	Al Newman	.05	.02	.01
☐ 20	Mark Gubicza	.05	.02	.01
☐ 21	Jeff Torborg MG	.05	.02	.01
☐ 22	Bruce Ruffin	.05	.02	.01
☐ 23	Randy Velarde	.05	.02	.01
☐ 24	Joe Hesketh	.05	.02	.01
☐ 25	Willie Randolph	.10	.05	.01
☐ 26	Don Slaught	.05	.02	.01
☐ 27	Rick Leach	.05	.02	.01
☐ 28	Duane Ward	.10	.05	.01
☐ 29	John Cangelosi	.05	.02	.01
☐ 30	David Cone	.15	.07	.02
☐ 31	Henry Cotto	.05	.02	.01
☐ 32	John Farrell	.05	.02	.01
☐ 33	Greg Walker	.05	.02	.01
☐ 34	Tony Fossas	.05	.02	.01
☐ 35	Benito Santiago	.10	.05	.01
☐ 36	John Costello	.05	.02	.01
☐ 37	Domingo Ramos	.05	.02	.01
☐ 38	Wes Gardner	.05	.02	.01
☐ 39	Curt Ford	.05	.02	.01
☐ 40	Jay Howell	.05	.02	.01
☐ 41	Matt Williams	.25	.11	.03
☐ 42	Jeff M. Robinson	.05	.02	.01
☐ 43	Dante Bichette	.20	.09	.03
☐ 44	Roger Salkeld FDP	.15	.07	.02
☐ 45	Dave Parker UER (Born in Jackson, not Calhoun)	.15	.07	.02
☐ 46	Rob Dibble	.10	.05	.01
☐ 47	Brian Harper	.10	.05	.01
☐ 48	Zane Smith	.05	.02	.01
☐ 49	Tom Lawless	.05	.02	.01
☐ 50	Glenn Davis	.05	.02	.01
☐ 51	Doug Rader MG	.05	.02	.01
☐ 52	Jack Daugherty	.05	.02	.01
☐ 53	Mike LaCoss	.05	.02	.01
☐ 54	Joel Skinner	.05	.02	.01
☐ 55	Darrell Evans UER (HR total should be 414, not 424)	.10	.05	.01
☐ 56	Franklin Stubbs	.05	.02	.01
☐ 57	Greg Vaughn	.20	.09	.03
☐ 58	Keith Miller	.05	.02	.01
☐ 59	Ted Power	.05	.02	.01
☐ 60	George Brett	.30	.14	.04
☐ 61	Deion Sanders	.50	.23	.06
☐ 62	Ramon Martinez	.10	.05	.01
☐ 63	Mike Pagliarulo	.05	.02	.01
☐ 64	Danny Darwin	.05	.02	.01
☐ 65	Devon White	.10	.05	.01
☐ 66	Greg Litton	.05	.02	.01
☐ 67	Scott Sanderson	.05	.02	.01
☐ 68	Dave Henderson	.05	.02	.01
☐ 69	Todd Frohwirth	.05	.02	.01
☐ 70	Mike Greenwell	.10	.05	.01
☐ 71	Allan Anderson	.05	.02	.01
☐ 72	Jeff Huson	.05	.02	.01
☐ 73	Bob Milacki	.05	.02	.01
☐ 74	Jeff Jackson FDP	.05	.02	.01
☐ 75	Doug Jones	.05	.02	.01
☐ 76	Dave Valle	.05	.02	.01
☐ 77	Dave Bergman	.05	.02	.01
☐ 78	Mike Flanagan	.05	.02	.01
☐ 79	Ron Kittle	.05	.02	.01
☐ 80	Jeff Russell	.05	.02	.01
☐ 81	Bob Rodgers MG	.05	.02	.01
☐ 82	Scott Terry	.05	.02	.01
☐ 83	Hensley Meulens	.05	.02	.01
☐ 84	Ray Searage	.05	.02	.01
☐ 85	Juan Samuel	.05	.02	.01
☐ 86	Paul Kilgus	.05	.02	.01
☐ 87	Rick Luecken	.05	.02	.01
☐ 88	Glenn Braggs	.05	.02	.01
☐ 89	Clint Zavaras	.05	.02	.01
☐ 90	Jack Clark	.10	.05	.01
☐ 91	Steve Frey	.05	.02	.01
☐ 92	Mike Stanley	.05	.02	.01
☐ 93	Shawn Hillegas	.05	.02	.01
☐ 94	Herm Winningham	.05	.02	.01
☐ 95	Todd Worrell	.05	.02	.01
☐ 96	Jody Reed	.05	.02	.01
☐ 97	Curt Schilling	.10	.05	.01
☐ 98	Jose Gonzalez	.05	.02	.01
☐ 99	Rich Monteleone	.05	.02	.01
☐ 100	Will Clark	.25	.11	.03
☐ 101	Shane Rawley	.05	.02	.01
☐ 102	Stan Javier	.05	.02	.01
☐ 103	Marvin Freeman	.05	.02	.01
☐ 104	Bob Knepper	.05	.02	.01
☐ 105	Randy Myers	.10	.05	.01
☐ 106	Charlie O'Brien	.05	.02	.01
☐ 107	Fred Lynn	.10	.05	.01
☐ 108	Rod Nichols	.05	.02	.01
☐ 109	Roberto Kelly	.10	.05	.01
☐ 110	Tommy Helms MG	.05	.02	.01
☐ 111	Ed Whited	.05	.02	.01
☐ 112	Glenn Wilson	.05	.02	.01
☐ 113	Manny Lee	.05	.02	.01
☐ 114	Mike Bielecki	.05	.02	.01
☐ 115	Tony Pena	.05	.02	.01
☐ 116	Floyd Bannister	.05	.02	.01

☐ 117 Mike Sharperson .05 .02 .01
☐ 118 Erik Hanson .10 .05 .01
☐ 119 Billy Hatcher .05 .02 .01
☐ 120 John Franco .10 .05 .01
☐ 121 Robin Ventura .50 .23 .06
☐ 122 Shawn Abner .05 .02 .01
☐ 123 Rich Gedman .05 .02 .01
☐ 124 Dave Dravecky .10 .05 .01
☐ 125 Kent Hrbek .10 .05 .01
☐ 126 Randy Kramer .05 .02 .01
☐ 127 Mike Devereaux .10 .05 .01
☐ 128 Checklist 1 .05 .02 .01
☐ 129 Ron Jones .05 .02 .01
☐ 130 Bert Blyleven .15 .07 .02
☐ 131 Matt Nokes .05 .02 .01
☐ 132 Lance Blankenship .05 .02 .01
☐ 133 Ricky Horton .05 .02 .01
☐ 134 Earl Cunningham FDP .05 .02 .01
☐ 135 Dave Magadan .05 .02 .01
☐ 136 Kevin Brown .10 .05 .01
☐ 137 Marty Pevey .05 .02 .01
☐ 138 Al Leiter .05 .02 .01
☐ 139 Greg Brock .05 .02 .01
☐ 140 Andre Dawson .15 .07 .02
☐ 141 John Hart MG .05 .02 .01
☐ 142 Jeff Wetherby .05 .02 .01
☐ 143 Rafael Belliard .05 .02 .01
☐ 144 Bud Black .05 .02 .01
☐ 145 Terry Steinbach .10 .05 .01
☐ 146 Rob Richie .05 .02 .01
☐ 147 Chuck Finley .10 .05 .01
☐ 148 Edgar Martinez .10 .05 .01
☐ 149 Steve Farr .05 .02 .01
☐ 150 Kirk Gibson .10 .05 .01
☐ 151 Rick Mahler .05 .02 .01
☐ 152 Lonnie Smith .05 .02 .01
☐ 153 Randy Milligan .05 .02 .01
☐ 154 Mike Maddux .05 .02 .01
☐ 155 Ellis Burks .10 .05 .01
☐ 156 Ken Patterson .05 .02 .01
☐ 157 Craig Biggio .15 .07 .02
☐ 158 Craig Lefferts .05 .02 .01
☐ 159 Mike Felder .05 .02 .01
☐ 160 Dave Righetti .05 .02 .01
☐ 161 Harold Reynolds .05 .02 .01
☐ 162 Todd Zeile .15 .07 .02
☐ 163 Phil Bradley .05 .02 .01
☐ 164 Jeff Juden FDP .15 .07 .02
☐ 165 Walt Weiss .05 .02 .01
☐ 166 Bobby Witt .05 .02 .01
☐ 167 Kevin Appier .30 .14 .04
☐ 168 Jose Lind .05 .02 .01
☐ 169 Richard Dotson .05 .02 .01
☐ 170 George Bell .10 .05 .01
☐ 171 Russ Nixon MG .05 .02 .01
☐ 172 Tom Lampkin .05 .02 .01
☐ 173 Tim Belcher .05 .02 .01
☐ 174 Jeff Kunkel .05 .02 .01
☐ 175 Mike Moore .05 .02 .01
☐ 176 Luis Quinones .05 .02 .01
☐ 177 Mike Henneman .05 .02 .01
☐ 178 Chris James .05 .02 .01
☐ 179 Brian Holton .05 .02 .01
☐ 180 Tim Raines .15 .07 .02
☐ 181 Juan Agosto .05 .02 .01
☐ 182 Mookie Wilson .05 .02 .01
☐ 183 Steve Lake .05 .02 .01
☐ 184 Danny Cox .05 .02 .01
☐ 185 Ruben Sierra .10 .05 .01
☐ 186 Dave LaPoint .05 .02 .01
☐ 187 Rick Wrona .05 .02 .01
☐ 188 Mike Smithson .05 .02 .01
☐ 189 Dick Schofield .05 .02 .01
☐ 190 Rick Reuschel .05 .02 .01
☐ 191 Pat Borders .10 .05 .01
☐ 192 Don August .05 .02 .01
☐ 193 Andy Benes .15 .07 .02
☐ 194 Glenallen Hill .05 .02 .01
☐ 195 Tim Burke .05 .02 .01
☐ 196 Gerald Young .05 .02 .01
☐ 197 Doug Drabek .15 .07 .02
☐ 198 Mike Marshall .05 .02 .01
☐ 199 Sergio Valdez .05 .02 .01
☐ 200 Don Mattingly .35 .16 .04
☐ 201 Cito Gaston MG .10 .05 .01
☐ 202 Mike Macfarlane .05 .02 .01
☐ 203 Mike Roesler .05 .02 .01
☐ 204 Bob Dernier .05 .02 .01
☐ 205 Mark Davis .05 .02 .01
☐ 206 Nick Esasky .05 .02 .01
☐ 207 Bob Ojeda .05 .02 .01
☐ 208 Brook Jacoby .05 .02 .01
☐ 209 Greg Mathews .05 .02 .01
☐ 210 Ryne Sandberg .35 .16 .04
☐ 211 John Cerutti .05 .02 .01
☐ 212 Joe Orsulak .05 .02 .01
☐ 213 Scott Bankhead .05 .02 .01
☐ 214 Terry Francona .05 .02 .01
☐ 215 Kirk McCaskill .05 .02 .01
☐ 216 Ricky Jordan .05 .02 .01
☐ 217 Don Robinson .05 .02 .01
☐ 218 Wally Backman .05 .02 .01
☐ 219 Donn Pall .05 .02 .01
☐ 220 Barry Bonds .50 .23 .06
☐ 221 Gary Mielke .05 .02 .01
☐ 222 Kurt Stillwell UER .05 .02 .01
(Graduate misspelled as gradute)
☐ 223 Tommy Gregg .05 .02 .01
☐ 224 Delino DeShields .20 .09 .03
☐ 225 Jim Deshaies .05 .02 .01
☐ 226 Mickey Hatcher .05 .02 .01
☐ 227 Kevin Tapani .20 .09 .03
☐ 228 Dave Martinez .05 .02 .01
☐ 229 David Wells .05 .02 .01
☐ 230 Keith Hernandez .10 .05 .01
☐ 231 Jack McKeon MG .05 .02 .01
☐ 232 Darnell Coles .05 .02 .01
☐ 233 Ken Hill .15 .07 .02
☐ 234 Mariano Duncan .05 .02 .01
☐ 235 Jeff Reardon .15 .07 .02
☐ 236 Hal Morris .10 .05 .01
☐ 237 Kevin Ritz .05 .02 .01
☐ 238 Felix Jose .10 .05 .01
☐ 239 Eric Show .05 .02 .01
☐ 240 Mark Grace .20 .09 .03
☐ 241 Mike Krukow .05 .02 .01
☐ 242 Fred Manrique .05 .02 .01
☐ 243 Barry Jones .05 .02 .01
☐ 244 Bill Schroeder .05 .02 .01
☐ 245 Roger Clemens .30 .14 .04
☐ 246 Jim Eisenreich .05 .02 .01
☐ 247 Jerry Reed .05 .02 .01
☐ 248 Dave Anderson .05 .02 .01
☐ 249 Mike(Texas) Smith .05 .02 .01
☐ 250 Jose Canseco .30 .14 .04
☐ 251 Jeff Blauser .10 .05 .01
☐ 252 Otis Nixon .10 .05 .01
☐ 253 Mark Portugal .05 .02 .01
☐ 254 Francisco Cabrera .05 .02 .01
☐ 255 Bobby Thigpen .05 .02 .01
☐ 256 Marvell Wynne .05 .02 .01
☐ 257 Jose DeLeon .05 .02 .01
☐ 258 Barry Lyons .05 .02 .01
☐ 259 Lance McCullers .05 .02 .01
☐ 260 Eric Davis .10 .05 .01

☐ 261	Whitey Herzog MG	.10	.05	.01
☐ 262	Checklist 2	.05	.02	.01
☐ 263	Mel Stottlemyre Jr.	.05	.02	.01
☐ 264	Bryan Clutterbuck	.05	.02	.01
☐ 265	Pete O'Brien	.05	.02	.01
☐ 266	German Gonzalez	.05	.02	.01
☐ 267	Mark Davidson	.05	.02	.01
☐ 268	Rob Murphy	.05	.02	.01
☐ 269	Dickie Thon	.05	.02	.01
☐ 270	Dave Stewart	.10	.05	.01
☐ 271	Chet Lemon	.05	.02	.01
☐ 272	Bryan Harvey	.10	.05	.01
☐ 273	Bobby Bonilla	.15	.07	.02
☐ 274	Mauro Gozzo	.05	.02	.01
☐ 275	Mickey Tettleton	.10	.05	.01
☐ 276	Gary Thurman	.05	.02	.01
☐ 277	Lenny Harris	.05	.02	.01
☐ 278	Pascual Perez	.05	.02	.01
☐ 279	Steve Buechele	.05	.02	.01
☐ 280	Lou Whitaker	.15	.07	.02
☐ 281	Kevin Bass	.05	.02	.01
☐ 282	Derek Lilliquist	.05	.02	.01
☐ 283	Joey Belle	1.50	.65	.19
☐ 284	Mark Gardner	.05	.02	.01
☐ 285	Willie McGee	.10	.05	.01
☐ 286	Lee Guetterman	.05	.02	.01
☐ 287	Vance Law	.05	.02	.01
☐ 288	Greg Briley	.05	.02	.01
☐ 289	Norm Charlton	.10	.05	.01
☐ 290	Robin Yount	.20	.09	.03
☐ 291	Dave Johnson MG	.10	.05	.01
☐ 292	Jim Gott	.05	.02	.01
☐ 293	Mike Gallego	.05	.02	.01
☐ 294	Craig McMurtry	.05	.02	.01
☐ 295	Fred McGriff	.30	.14	.04
☐ 296	Jeff Ballard	.05	.02	.01
☐ 297	Tommy Herr	.05	.02	.01
☐ 298	Dan Gladden	.05	.02	.01
☐ 299	Adam Peterson	.05	.02	.01
☐ 300	Bo Jackson	.15	.07	.02
☐ 301	Don Aase	.05	.02	.01
☐ 302	Marcus Lawton	.05	.02	.01
☐ 303	Rick Cerone	.05	.02	.01
☐ 304	Marty Clary	.05	.02	.01
☐ 305	Eddie Murray	.15	.07	.02
☐ 306	Tom Niedenfuer	.05	.02	.01
☐ 307	Bip Roberts	.10	.05	.01
☐ 308	Jose Guzman	.05	.02	.01
☐ 309	Eric Yelding	.05	.02	.01
☐ 310	Steve Bedrosian	.05	.02	.01
☐ 311	Dwight Smith	.05	.02	.01
☐ 312	Dan Quisenberry	.10	.05	.01
☐ 313	Gus Polidor	.05	.02	.01
☐ 314	Donald Harris FDP	.05	.02	.01
☐ 315	Bruce Hurst	.05	.02	.01
☐ 316	Carney Lansford	.10	.05	.01
☐ 317	Mark Guthrie	.05	.02	.01
☐ 318	Wallace Johnson	.05	.02	.01
☐ 319	Dion James	.05	.02	.01
☐ 320	Dave Stieb	.10	.05	.01
☐ 321	Joe Morgan MG	.05	.02	.01
☐ 322	Junior Ortiz	.05	.02	.01
☐ 323	Willie Wilson	.05	.02	.01
☐ 324	Pete Harnisch	.10	.05	.01
☐ 325	Robby Thompson	.10	.05	.01
☐ 326	Tom McCarthy	.05	.02	.01
☐ 327	Ken Williams	.05	.02	.01
☐ 328	Curt Young	.05	.02	.01
☐ 329	Oddibe McDowell	.05	.02	.01
☐ 330	Ron Darling	.05	.02	.01
☐ 331	Juan Gonzalez	2.00	.90	.25
☐ 332	Paul O'Neill	.10	.05	.01
☐ 333	Bill Wegman	.05	.02	.01
☐ 334	Johnny Ray	.05	.02	.01
☐ 335	Andy Hawkins	.05	.02	.01
☐ 336	Ken Griffey Jr.	2.50	1.15	.30
☐ 337	Lloyd McClendon	.05	.02	.01
☐ 338	Dennis Lamp	.05	.02	.01
☐ 339	Dave Clark	.05	.02	.01
☐ 340	Fernando Valenzuela	.05	.02	.01
☐ 341	Tom Foley	.05	.02	.01
☐ 342	Alex Trevino	.05	.02	.01
☐ 343	Frank Tanana	.05	.02	.01
☐ 344	George Canale	.05	.02	.01
☐ 345	Harold Baines	.10	.05	.01
☐ 346	Jim Presley	.05	.02	.01
☐ 347	Junior Felix	.05	.02	.01
☐ 348	Gary Wayne	.05	.02	.01
☐ 349	Steve Finley	.10	.05	.01
☐ 350	Bret Saberhagen	.10	.05	.01
☐ 351	Roger Craig MG	.05	.02	.01
☐ 352	Bryn Smith	.05	.02	.01
☐ 353	Sandy Alomar Jr. (Not listed as Jr. on card front)	.15	.07	.02
☐ 354	Stan Belinda	.05	.02	.01
☐ 355	Marty Barrett	.05	.02	.01
☐ 356	Randy Ready	.05	.02	.01
☐ 357	Dave West	.05	.02	.01
☐ 358	Andres Thomas	.05	.02	.01
☐ 359	Jimmy Jones	.05	.02	.01
☐ 360	Paul Molitor	.20	.09	.03
☐ 361	Randy McCament	.05	.02	.01
☐ 362	Damon Berryhill	.05	.02	.01
☐ 363	Dan Petry	.05	.02	.01
☐ 364	Rolando Roomes	.05	.02	.01
☐ 365	Ozzie Guillen	.05	.02	.01
☐ 366	Mike Heath	.05	.02	.01
☐ 367	Mike Morgan	.05	.02	.01
☐ 368	Bill Doran	.05	.02	.01
☐ 369	Todd Burns	.05	.02	.01
☐ 370	Tim Wallach	.05	.02	.01
☐ 371	Jimmy Key	.10	.05	.01
☐ 372	Terry Kennedy	.05	.02	.01
☐ 373	Alvin Davis	.05	.02	.01
☐ 374	Steve Cummings	.05	.02	.01
☐ 375	Dwight Evans	.10	.05	.01
☐ 376	Checklist 3 UER (Higuera misalphabetized in Brewer list)	.05	.02	.01
☐ 377	Mickey Weston	.05	.02	.01
☐ 378	Luis Salazar	.05	.02	.01
☐ 379	Steve Rosenberg	.05	.02	.01
☐ 380	Dave Winfield	.15	.07	.02
☐ 381	Frank Robinson MG	.10	.05	.01
☐ 382	Jeff Musselman	.05	.02	.01
☐ 383	John Morris	.05	.02	.01
☐ 384	Pat Combs	.05	.02	.01
☐ 385	Fred McGriff AS	.12	.05	.02
☐ 386	Julio Franco AS	.08	.04	.01
☐ 387	Wade Boggs AS	.10	.05	.01
☐ 388	Cal Ripken AS	.25	.11	.03
☐ 389	Robin Yount AS	.10	.05	.01
☐ 390	Ruben Sierra AS	.10	.05	.01
☐ 391	Kirby Puckett AS	.20	.09	.03
☐ 392	Carlton Fisk AS	.10	.05	.01
☐ 393	Bret Saberhagen AS	.10	.05	.01
☐ 394	Jeff Ballard AS	.08	.04	.01
☐ 395	Jeff Russell AS	.08	.04	.01
☐ 396	A.Bartlett Giamatti COMM MEM	.20	.09	.03
☐ 397	Will Clark AS	.15	.07	.02
☐ 398	Ryne Sandberg AS	.20	.09	.03
☐ 399	Howard Johnson AS	.08	.04	.01
☐ 400	Ozzie Smith AS	.10	.05	.01
☐ 401	Kevin Mitchell AS	.10	.05	.01

☐ 402 Eric Davis AS .08 .04 .01
☐ 403 Tony Gwynn AS .15 .07 .02
☐ 404 Craig Biggio AS .10 .05 .01
☐ 405 Mike Scott AS .08 .04 .01
☐ 406 Joe Magrane AS .08 .04 .01
☐ 407 Mark Davis AS .08 .04 .01
☐ 408 Trevor Wilson .05 .02 .01
☐ 409 Tom Brunansky .05 .02 .01
☐ 410 Joe Boever .05 .02 .01
☐ 411 Ken Phelps .05 .02 .01
☐ 412 Jamie Moyer .05 .02 .01
☐ 413 Brian DuBois .05 .02 .01
☐ 414A Frank Thomas FDP 1200.00 350.00 100.00
ERR (Name missing
on card front)
☐ 414B Frank Thomas FDP COR 4.00 1.80 .50
☐ 415 Shawon Dunston .05 .02 .01
☐ 416 Dave Johnson (P) .05 .02 .01
☐ 417 Jim Gantner .05 .02 .01
☐ 418 Tom Browning .05 .02 .01
☐ 419 Beau Allred .05 .02 .01
☐ 420 Carlton Fisk .15 .07 .02
☐ 421 Greg Minton .05 .02 .01
☐ 422 Pat Sheridan .05 .02 .01
☐ 423 Fred Toliver .05 .02 .01
☐ 424 Jerry Reuss .05 .02 .01
☐ 425 Bill Landrum .05 .02 .01
☐ 426 Jeff Hamilton UER .05 .02 .01
(Stats say he fanned
197 times in 1987, but
he only had 147 at bats)
☐ 427 Carmen Castillo .05 .02 .01
☐ 428 Steve Davis .05 .02 .01
☐ 429 Tom Kelly MG .05 .02 .01
☐ 430 Pete Incaviglia .05 .02 .01
☐ 431 Randy Johnson .20 .09 .03
☐ 432 Damaso Garcia .05 .02 .01
☐ 433 Steve Olin .10 .05 .01
☐ 434 Mark Carreon .05 .02 .01
☐ 435 Kevin Seitzer .05 .02 .01
☐ 436 Mel Hall .05 .02 .01
☐ 437 Les Lancaster .05 .02 .01
☐ 438 Greg Myers .05 .02 .01
☐ 439 Jeff Parrett .05 .02 .01
☐ 440 Alan Trammell .15 .07 .02
☐ 441 Bob Kipper .05 .02 .01
☐ 442 Jerry Browne .05 .02 .01
☐ 443 Cris Carpenter .05 .02 .01
☐ 444 Kyle Abbott FDP .05 .02 .01
☐ 445 Danny Jackson .05 .02 .01
☐ 446 Dan Pasqua .05 .02 .01
☐ 447 Atlee Hammaker .05 .02 .01
☐ 448 Greg Gagne .05 .02 .01
☐ 449 Dennis Rasmussen .05 .02 .01
☐ 450 Rickey Henderson .15 .07 .02
☐ 451 Mark Lemke .10 .05 .01
☐ 452 Luis DeLosSantos .05 .02 .01
☐ 453 Jody Davis .05 .02 .01
☐ 454 Jeff King UER .10 .05 .01
(Card number, Topps logo,
name and bio are shaded
in yellow instead of black)
☐ 455 Jeffrey Leonard .05 .02 .01
☐ 456 Chris Gwynn .05 .02 .01
☐ 457 Gregg Jefferies .25 .11 .03
☐ 458 Bob McClure .05 .02 .01
☐ 459 Jim Lefebvre MG .05 .02 .01
☐ 460 Mike Scott .05 .02 .01
☐ 461 Carlos Martinez .05 .02 .01
☐ 462 Denny Walling .05 .02 .01
☐ 463 Drew Hall .05 .02 .01
☐ 464 Jerome Walton .05 .02 .01
☐ 465 Kevin Gross .05 .02 .01

☐ 466 Rance Mulliniks .05 .02 .01
☐ 467 Juan Nieves .05 .02 .01
☐ 468 Bill Ripken .05 .02 .01
☐ 469 John Kruk .15 .07 .02
☐ 470 Frank Viola .10 .05 .01
☐ 471 Mike Brumley .05 .02 .01
☐ 472 Jose Uribe .05 .02 .01
☐ 473 Joe Price .05 .02 .01
☐ 474 Rich Thompson .05 .02 .01
☐ 475 Bob Welch .05 .02 .01
☐ 476 Brad Komminsk .05 .02 .01
☐ 477 Willie Fraser .05 .02 .01
☐ 478 Mike LaValliere .05 .02 .01
☐ 479 Frank White .10 .05 .01
☐ 480 Sid Fernandez .10 .05 .01
☐ 481 Garry Templeton .05 .02 .01
☐ 482 Steve Carter .05 .02 .01
☐ 483 Alejandro Pena .05 .02 .01
☐ 484 Mike Fitzgerald .05 .02 .01
☐ 485 John Candelaria .05 .02 .01
☐ 486 Jeff Treadway .05 .02 .01
☐ 487 Steve Searcy .05 .02 .01
☐ 488 Ken Oberkfell .05 .02 .01
☐ 489 Nick Leyva MG .05 .02 .01
☐ 490 Dan Plesac .05 .02 .01
☐ 491 Dave Cochrane .05 .02 .01
☐ 492 Ron Oester .05 .02 .01
☐ 493 Jason Grimsley .05 .02 .01
☐ 494 Terry Puhl .05 .02 .01
☐ 495 Lee Smith .15 .07 .02
☐ 496 Cecil Espy UER .05 .02 .01
('88 stats have 3
SB's, should be 33)
☐ 497 Dave Schmidt .05 .02 .01
☐ 498 Rick Schu .05 .02 .01
☐ 499 Bill Long .05 .02 .01
☐ 500 Kevin Mitchell .10 .05 .01
☐ 501 Matt Young .05 .02 .01
☐ 502 Mitch Webster .05 .02 .01
☐ 503 Randy St.Claire .05 .02 .01
☐ 504 Tom O'Malley .05 .02 .01
☐ 505 Kelly Gruber .05 .02 .01
☐ 506 Tom Glavine .25 .11 .03
☐ 507 Gary Redus .05 .02 .01
☐ 508 Terry Leach .05 .02 .01
☐ 509 Tom Pagnozzi .05 .02 .01
☐ 510 Dwight Gooden .10 .05 .01
☐ 511 Clay Parker .05 .02 .01
☐ 512 Gary Pettis .05 .02 .01
☐ 513 Mark Eichhorn .05 .02 .01
☐ 514 Andy Allanson .05 .02 .01
☐ 515 Len Dykstra .15 .07 .02
☐ 516 Tim Leary .05 .02 .01
☐ 517 Roberto Alomar .40 .18 .05
☐ 518 Bill Krueger .05 .02 .01
☐ 519 Bucky Dent MG .05 .02 .01
☐ 520 Mitch Williams .10 .05 .01
☐ 521 Craig Worthington .05 .02 .01
☐ 522 Mike Dunne .05 .02 .01
☐ 523 Jay Bell .10 .05 .01
☐ 524 Daryl Boston .05 .02 .01
☐ 525 Wally Joyner .10 .05 .01
☐ 526 Checklist 4 .05 .02 .01
☐ 527 Ron Hassey .05 .02 .01
☐ 528 Kevin Wickander UER .05 .02 .01
(Monthly scoreboard
strikeout total was 2.2,
that was his innings
pitched total)
☐ 529 Greg A. Harris .05 .02 .01
☐ 530 Mark Langston .15 .07 .02
☐ 531 Ken Caminiti .10 .05 .01
☐ 532 Cecilio Guante .05 .02 .01

No.	Player			
533	Tim Jones	.05	.02	.01
534	Louie Meadows	.05	.02	.01
535	John Smoltz	.15	.07	.02
536	Bob Geren	.05	.02	.01
537	Mark Grant	.05	.02	.01
538	Bill Spiers UER (Photo actually George Canale)	.05	.02	.01
539	Neal Heaton	.05	.02	.01
540	Danny Tartabull	.10	.05	.01
541	Pat Perry	.05	.02	.01
542	Darren Daulton	.15	.07	.02
543	Nelson Liriano	.05	.02	.01
544	Dennis Boyd	.05	.02	.01
545	Kevin McReynolds	.05	.02	.01
546	Kevin Hickey	.05	.02	.01
547	Jack Howell	.05	.02	.01
548	Pat Clements	.05	.02	.01
549	Don Zimmer MG	.05	.02	.01
550	Julio Franco	.10	.05	.01
551	Tim Crews	.05	.02	.01
552	Mike(Miss.) Smith	.05	.02	.01
553	Scott Scudder UER (Cedar Rap1ds)	.05	.02	.01
554	Jay Buhner	.15	.07	.02
555	Jack Morris	.15	.07	.02
556	Gene Larkin	.05	.02	.01
557	Jeff Innis	.05	.02	.01
558	Rafael Ramirez	.05	.02	.01
559	Andy McGaffigan	.05	.02	.01
560	Steve Sax	.05	.02	.01
561	Ken Dayley	.05	.02	.01
562	Chad Kreuter	.05	.02	.01
563	Alex Sanchez	.05	.02	.01
564	Tyler Houston FDP	.05	.02	.01
565	Scott Fletcher	.05	.02	.01
566	Mark Knudson	.05	.02	.01
567	Ron Gant	.20	.09	.03
568	John Smiley	.05	.02	.01
569	Ivan Calderon	.05	.02	.01
570	Cal Ripken	.40	.18	.05
571	Brett Butler	.10	.05	.01
572	Greg W. Harris	.05	.02	.01
573	Danny Heep	.05	.02	.01
574	Bill Swift	.10	.05	.01
575	Lance Parrish	.10	.05	.01
576	Mike Dyer	.05	.02	.01
577	Charlie Hayes	.10	.05	.01
578	Joe Magrane	.05	.02	.01
579	Art Howe MG	.05	.02	.01
580	Joe Carter	.25	.11	.03
581	Ken Griffey	.10	.05	.01
582	Rick Honeycutt	.05	.02	.01
583	Bruce Benedict	.05	.02	.01
584	Phil Stephenson	.05	.02	.01
585	Kal Daniels	.05	.02	.01
586	Edwin Nunez	.05	.02	.01
587	Lance Johnson	.10	.05	.01
588	Rick Rhoden	.05	.02	.01
589	Mike Aldrete	.05	.02	.01
590	Ozzie Smith	.25	.11	.03
591	Todd Stottlemyre	.10	.05	.01
592	R.J. Reynolds	.05	.02	.01
593	Scott Bradley	.05	.02	.01
594	Luis Sojo	.05	.02	.01
595	Greg Swindell	.10	.05	.01
596	Jose DeJesus	.05	.02	.01
597	Chris Bosio	.05	.02	.01
598	Brady Anderson	.10	.05	.01
599	Frank Williams	.05	.02	.01
600	Darryl Strawberry	.15	.07	.02
601	Luis Rivera	.05	.02	.01
602	Scott Garrelts	.05	.02	.01
603	Tony Armas	.05	.02	.01
604	Ron Robinson	.05	.02	.01
605	Mike Scioscia	.05	.02	.01
606	Storm Davis	.05	.02	.01
607	Steve Jeltz	.05	.02	.01
608	Eric Anthony	.15	.07	.02
609	Sparky Anderson MG	.10	.05	.01
610	Pedro Guerrero	.10	.05	.01
611	Walt Terrell	.05	.02	.01
612	Dave Gallagher	.05	.02	.01
613	Jeff Pico	.05	.02	.01
614	Nelson Santovenia	.05	.02	.01
615	Rob Deer	.05	.02	.01
616	Brian Holman	.05	.02	.01
617	Geronimo Berroa	.10	.05	.01
618	Ed Whitson	.05	.02	.01
619	Rob Ducey	.15	.07	.02
620	Tony Castillo	.05	.02	.01
621	Melido Perez	.05	.02	.01
622	Sid Bream	.05	.02	.01
623	Jim Corsi	.05	.02	.01
624	Darrin Jackson	.05	.02	.01
625	Roger McDowell	.05	.02	.01
626	Bob Melvin	.05	.02	.01
627	Jose Rijo	.10	.05	.01
628	Candy Maldonado	.05	.02	.01
629	Eric Hetzel	.05	.02	.01
630	Gary Gaetti	.05	.02	.01
631	John Wetteland	.10	.05	.01
632	Scott Lusader	.05	.02	.01
633	Dennis Cook	.05	.02	.01
634	Luis Polonia	.10	.05	.01
635	Brian Downing	.05	.02	.01
636	Jesse Orosco	.05	.02	.01
637	Craig Reynolds	.05	.02	.01
638	Jeff Montgomery	.10	.05	.01
639	Tony LaRussa MG	.10	.05	.01
640	Rick Sutcliffe	.10	.05	.01
641	Doug Strange	.05	.02	.01
642	Jack Armstrong	.05	.02	.01
643	Alfredo Griffin	.05	.02	.01
644	Paul Assenmacher	.05	.02	.01
645	Jose Oquendo	.05	.02	.01
646	Checklist 5	.05	.02	.01
647	Rex Hudler	.05	.02	.01
648	Jim Clancy	.05	.02	.01
649	Dan Murphy	.05	.02	.01
650	Mike Witt	.05	.02	.01
651	Rafael Santana	.05	.02	.01
652	Mike Boddicker	.05	.02	.01
653	John Moses	.05	.02	.01
654	Paul Coleman FDP	.05	.02	.01
655	Gregg Olson	.10	.05	.01
656	Mackey Sasser	.05	.02	.01
657	Terry Mulholland	.10	.05	.01
658	Donell Nixon	.05	.02	.01
659	Greg Cadaret	.05	.02	.01
660	Vince Coleman	.10	.05	.01
661	Dick Howser TBC'85 UER (Seaver's 300th on 7/11/85, should be 8/4/85)	.05	.02	.01
662	Mike Schmidt TBC'80	.10	.05	.01
663	Fred Lynn TBC'75	.05	.02	.01
664	Johnny Bench TBC'70	.08	.04	.01
665	Sandy Koufax TBC'65	.08	.04	.01
666	Brian Fisher	.05	.02	.01
667	Curt Wilkerson	.05	.02	.01
668	Joe Oliver	.05	.02	.01
669	Tom Lasorda MG	.10	.05	.01
670	Dennis Eckersley	.15	.07	.02
671	Bob Boone	.10	.05	.01
672	Roy Smith	.05	.02	.01

☐ 673 Joey Meyer	.05	.02	.01
☐ 674 Spike Owen	.05	.02	.01
☐ 675 Jim Abbott	.15	.07	.02
☐ 676 Randy Kutcher	.05	.02	.01
☐ 677 Jay Tibbs	.05	.02	.01
☐ 678 Kirt Manwaring UER ('88 Phoenix stats repeated)	.05	.02	.01
☐ 679 Gary Ward	.05	.02	.01
☐ 680 Howard Johnson	.10	.05	.01
☐ 681 Mike Schooler	.05	.02	.01
☐ 682 Dann Bilardello	.05	.02	.01
☐ 683 Kenny Rogers	.05	.02	.01
☐ 684 Julio Machado	.05	.02	.01
☐ 685 Tony Fernandez	.10	.05	.01
☐ 686 Carmelo Martinez	.05	.02	.01
☐ 687 Tim Birtsas	.05	.02	.01
☐ 688 Milt Thompson	.05	.02	.01
☐ 689 Rich Yett	.05	.02	.01
☐ 690 Mark McGwire	.15	.07	.02
☐ 691 Chuck Cary	.05	.02	.01
☐ 692 Sammy Sosa	.50	.23	.06
☐ 693 Calvin Schiraldi	.05	.02	.01
☐ 694 Mike Stanton	.05	.02	.01
☐ 695 Tom Henke	.10	.05	.01
☐ 696 B.J. Surhoff	.05	.02	.01
☐ 697 Mike Davis	.05	.02	.01
☐ 698 Omar Vizquel	.05	.02	.01
☐ 699 Jim Leyland MG	.05	.02	.01
☐ 700 Kirby Puckett	.35	.16	.04
☐ 701 Bernie Williams	.25	.11	.03
☐ 702 Tony Phillips	.10	.05	.01
☐ 703 Jeff Brantley	.05	.02	.01
☐ 704 Chip Hale	.05	.02	.01
☐ 705 Claudell Washington	.05	.02	.01
☐ 706 Geno Petralli	.05	.02	.01
☐ 707 Luis Aquino	.05	.02	.01
☐ 708 Larry Sheets	.05	.02	.01
☐ 709 Juan Berenguer	.05	.02	.01
☐ 710 Von Hayes	.05	.02	.01
☐ 711 Rick Aguilera	.10	.05	.01
☐ 712 Todd Benzinger	.05	.02	.01
☐ 713 Tim Drummond	.05	.02	.01
☐ 714 Marquis Grissom	.50	.23	.06
☐ 715 Greg Maddux	.30	.14	.04
☐ 716 Steve Balboni	.05	.02	.01
☐ 717 Ron Karkovice	.05	.02	.01
☐ 718 Gary Sheffield	.30	.14	.04
☐ 719 Wally Whitehurst	.05	.02	.01
☐ 720 Andres Galarraga	.15	.07	.02
☐ 721 Lee Mazzilli	.05	.02	.01
☐ 722 Felix Fermin	.05	.02	.01
☐ 723 Jeff D. Robinson	.05	.02	.01
☐ 724 Juan Bell	.05	.02	.01
☐ 725 Terry Pendleton	.15	.07	.02
☐ 726 Gene Nelson	.05	.02	.01
☐ 727 Pat Tabler	.05	.02	.01
☐ 728 Jim Acker	.05	.02	.01
☐ 729 Bobby Valentine MG	.05	.02	.01
☐ 730 Tony Gwynn	.25	.11	.03
☐ 731 Don Carman	.05	.02	.01
☐ 732 Ernest Riles	.05	.02	.01
☐ 733 John Dopson	.05	.02	.01
☐ 734 Kevin Elster	.05	.02	.01
☐ 735 Charlie Hough	.10	.05	.01
☐ 736 Rick Dempsey	.05	.02	.01
☐ 737 Chris Sabo	.10	.05	.01
☐ 738 Gene Harris	.05	.02	.01
☐ 739 Dale Sveum	.05	.02	.01
☐ 740 Jesse Barfield	.05	.02	.01
☐ 741 Steve Wilson	.05	.02	.01
☐ 742 Ernie Whitt	.05	.02	.01
☐ 743 Tom Candiotti	.05	.02	.01

☐ 744 Kelly Mann	.05	.02	.01
☐ 745 Hubie Brooks	.05	.02	.01
☐ 746 Dave Smith	.05	.02	.01
☐ 747 Randy Bush	.05	.02	.01
☐ 748 Doyle Alexander	.05	.02	.01
☐ 749 Mark Parent UER ('87 BA .80, should be .080)	.05	.02	.01
☐ 750 Dale Murphy	.15	.07	.02
☐ 751 Steve Lyons	.05	.02	.01
☐ 752 Tom Gordon	.10	.05	.01
☐ 753 Chris Speier	.05	.02	.01
☐ 754 Bob Walk	.05	.02	.01
☐ 755 Rafael Palmeiro	.15	.07	.02
☐ 756 Ken Howell	.05	.02	.01
☐ 757 Larry Walker	.50	.23	.06
☐ 758 Mark Thurmond	.05	.02	.01
☐ 759 Tom Trebelhorn MG	.05	.02	.01
☐ 760 Wade Boggs	.20	.09	.03
☐ 761 Mike Jackson	.05	.02	.01
☐ 762 Doug Dascenzo	.05	.02	.01
☐ 763 Dennis Martinez	.10	.05	.01
☐ 764 Tim Teufel	.05	.02	.01
☐ 765 Chili Davis	.10	.05	.01
☐ 766 Brian Meyer	.05	.02	.01
☐ 767 Tracy Jones	.05	.02	.01
☐ 768 Chuck Crim	.05	.02	.01
☐ 769 Greg Hibbard	.05	.02	.01
☐ 770 Cory Snyder	.05	.02	.01
☐ 771 Pete Smith	.05	.02	.01
☐ 772 Jeff Reed	.05	.02	.01
☐ 773 Dave Leiper	.05	.02	.01
☐ 774 Ben McDonald	.40	.18	.05
☐ 775 Andy Van Slyke	.15	.07	.02
☐ 776 Charlie Leibrandt	.05	.02	.01
☐ 777 Tim Laudner	.05	.02	.01
☐ 778 Mike Jeffcoat	.05	.02	.01
☐ 779 Lloyd Moseby	.05	.02	.01
☐ 780 Orel Hershiser	.10	.05	.01
☐ 781 Mario Diaz	.05	.02	.01
☐ 782 Jose Alvarez	.05	.02	.01
☐ 783 Checklist 6	.05	.02	.01
☐ 784 Scott Bailes	.05	.02	.01
☐ 785 Jim Rice	.15	.07	.02
☐ 786 Eric King	.05	.02	.01
☐ 787 Rene Gonzales	.05	.02	.01
☐ 788 Frank DiPino	.05	.02	.01
☐ 789 John Wathan MG	.05	.02	.01
☐ 790 Gary Carter	.15	.07	.02
☐ 791 Alvaro Espinoza	.05	.02	.01
☐ 792 Gerald Perry	.05	.02	.01

1990 Topps Traded

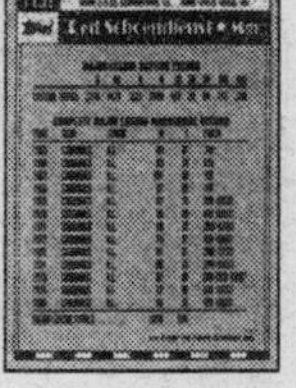

The 1990 Topps Traded Set was the tenth consecutive year Topps issued a set at the

end of the year. This 132-card standard size (2 1/2" by 3 1/2") set was arranged alphabetically by player and includes a mix of traded players and rookies for whom Topps did not include a card in the regular set. The key Rookie Cards in this set are Carlos Baerga, Scott Erickson, Travis Fryman, Dave Hollins, Dave Justice, Kevin Maas, and John Olerud. Also for the first time, Topps not only issued the set in a special collector boxes (made in Ireland) but distributed (on a significant basis) the set via their own wax packs. The wax pack cards were produced Topps' Duryea, Pennsylvania plant. There were seven cards in the packs and the wrapper highlighted the set as containing promising rookies, players who changed teams, and new managers. The cards differ in that the Irish-made cards have the whiter-type backs typical of the cards made in Ireland while the American cards have the typical Topps gray-type card stock on the back. Topps also produced a specially boxed "glossy" edition frequently referred to as the Topps Traded Tiffany set. This year, again, Topps did not disclose the number of Tiffany sets they produced or sold but it seems that production quantities were roughly similar (approximately 15,000 sets) to the previous year. The checklist of cards is identical to that of the normal non-glossy cards. There are two primary distinguishing features of the Tiffany cards, white card stock reverses and high gloss obverses. These Tiffany cards are valued approximately from three to five times the values listed below.

	MINT	EXC	G-VG
COMPLETE SET (132)	5.00	2.30	.60
COMPLETE FACT.SET (132)	5.00	2.30	.60
COMMON CARD (1T-132T)	.05	.02	.01

*GRAY AND WHITE BACKS: SAME VALUE

	Card	MINT	EXC	G-VG
☐ 1T	Darrel Akerfelds	.05	.02	.01
☐ 2T	Sandy Alomar Jr.	.08	.04	.01
☐ 3T	Brad Arnsberg	.05	.02	.01
☐ 4T	Steve Avery	.40	.18	.05
☐ 5T	Wally Backman	.05	.02	.01
☐ 6T	Carlos Baerga	1.00	.45	.13
☐ 7T	Kevin Bass	.05	.02	.01
☐ 8T	Willie Blair	.05	.02	.01
☐ 9T	Mike Blowers	.05	.02	.01
☐ 10T	Shawn Boskie	.05	.02	.01
☐ 11T	Daryl Boston	.05	.02	.01
☐ 12T	Dennis Boyd	.05	.02	.01
☐ 13T	Glenn Braggs	.05	.02	.01
☐ 14T	Hubie Brooks	.05	.02	.01
☐ 15T	Tom Brunansky	.05	.02	.01
☐ 16T	John Burkett	.25	.11	.03
☐ 17T	Casey Candaele	.05	.02	.01
☐ 18T	John Candelaria	.05	.02	.01
☐ 19T	Gary Carter	.10	.05	.01
☐ 20T	Joe Carter	.30	.14	.04
☐ 21T	Rick Cerone	.05	.02	.01
☐ 22T	Scott Coolbaugh	.05	.02	.01
☐ 23T	Bobby Cox MG	.05	.02	.01
☐ 24T	Mark Davis	.05	.02	.01
☐ 25T	Storm Davis	.05	.02	.01
☐ 26T	Edgar Diaz	.05	.02	.01
☐ 27T	Wayne Edwards	.05	.02	.01
☐ 28T	Mark Eichhorn	.05	.02	.01
☐ 29T	Scott Erickson	.20	.09	.03
☐ 30T	Nick Esasky	.05	.02	.01
☐ 31T	Cecil Fielder	.20	.09	.03
☐ 32T	John Franco	.08	.04	.01
☐ 33T	Travis Fryman	1.00	.45	.13
☐ 34T	Bill Gullickson	.05	.02	.01
☐ 35T	Darryl Hamilton	.08	.04	.01
☐ 36T	Mike Harkey	.05	.02	.01
☐ 37T	Bud Harrelson MG	.05	.02	.01
☐ 38T	Billy Hatcher	.05	.02	.01
☐ 39T	Keith Hernandez	.08	.04	.01
☐ 40T	Joe Hesketh	.05	.02	.01
☐ 41T	Dave Hollins	.25	.11	.03
☐ 42T	Sam Horn	.05	.02	.01
☐ 43T	Steve Howard	.05	.02	.01
☐ 44T	Todd Hundley	.20	.09	.03
☐ 45T	Jeff Huson	.05	.02	.01
☐ 46T	Chris James	.05	.02	.01
☐ 47T	Stan Javier	.05	.02	.01
☐ 48T	David Justice	1.00	.45	.13
☐ 49T	Jeff Kaiser	.05	.02	.01
☐ 50T	Dana Kiecker	.05	.02	.01
☐ 51T	Joe Klink	.05	.02	.01
☐ 52T	Brent Knackert	.05	.02	.01
☐ 53T	Brad Komminsk	.05	.02	.01
☐ 54T	Mark Langston	.10	.05	.01
☐ 55T	Tim Layana	.05	.02	.01
☐ 56T	Rick Leach	.05	.02	.01
☐ 57T	Terry Leach	.05	.02	.01
☐ 58T	Tim Leary	.05	.02	.01
☐ 59T	Craig Lefferts	.05	.02	.01
☐ 60T	Charlie Leibrandt	.05	.02	.01
☐ 61T	Jim Leyritz	.15	.07	.02
☐ 62T	Fred Lynn	.08	.04	.01
☐ 63T	Kevin Maas	.05	.02	.01
☐ 64T	Shane Mack	.08	.04	.01
☐ 65T	Candy Maldonado	.05	.02	.01
☐ 66T	Fred Manrique	.05	.02	.01
☐ 67T	Mike Marshall	.05	.02	.01
☐ 68T	Carmelo Martinez	.05	.02	.01
☐ 69T	John Marzano	.05	.02	.01
☐ 70T	Ben McDonald	.30	.14	.04
☐ 71T	Jack McDowell	.20	.09	.03
☐ 72T	John McNamara MG	.05	.02	.01
☐ 73T	Orlando Mercado	.05	.02	.01
☐ 74T	Stump Merrill MG	.05	.02	.01
☐ 75T	Alan Mills	.05	.02	.01
☐ 76T	Hal Morris	.08	.04	.01
☐ 77T	Lloyd Moseby	.05	.02	.01
☐ 78T	Randy Myers	.08	.04	.01
☐ 79T	Tim Naehring	.20	.09	.03
☐ 80T	Junior Noboa	.05	.02	.01
☐ 81T	Matt Nokes	.05	.02	.01
☐ 82T	Pete O'Brien	.05	.02	.01
☐ 83T	John Olerud	.60	.25	.08
☐ 84T	Greg Olson	.05	.02	.01
☐ 85T	Junior Ortiz	.05	.02	.01
☐ 86T	Dave Parker	.10	.05	.01
☐ 87T	Rick Parker	.05	.02	.01
☐ 88T	Bob Patterson	.05	.02	.01
☐ 89T	Alejandro Pena	.05	.02	.01
☐ 90T	Tony Pena	.05	.02	.01
☐ 91T	Pascual Perez	.05	.02	.01
☐ 92T	Gerald Perry	.05	.02	.01
☐ 93T	Dan Petry	.05	.02	.01
☐ 94T	Gary Pettis	.05	.02	.01
☐ 95T	Tony Phillips	.08	.04	.01
☐ 96T	Lou Piniella MG	.08	.04	.01
☐ 97T	Luis Polonia	.08	.04	.01
☐ 98T	Jim Presley	.05	.02	.01
☐ 99T	Scott Radinsky	.05	.02	.01
☐ 100T	Willie Randolph	.08	.04	.01
☐ 101T	Jeff Reardon	.10	.05	.01

☐ 102T	Greg Riddoch MG	.05	.02	.01
☐ 103T	Jeff Robinson	.05	.02	.01
☐ 104T	Ron Robinson	.05	.02	.01
☐ 105T	Kevin Romine	.05	.02	.01
☐ 106T	Scott Ruskin	.05	.02	.01
☐ 107T	John Russell	.05	.02	.01
☐ 108T	Bill Sampen	.05	.02	.01
☐ 109T	Juan Samuel	.05	.02	.01
☐ 110T	Scott Sanderson	.05	.02	.01
☐ 111T	Jack Savage	.05	.02	.01
☐ 112T	Dave Schmidt	.05	.02	.01
☐ 113T	Red Schoendienst MG	.08	.04	.01
☐ 114T	Terry Shumpert	.05	.02	.01
☐ 115T	Matt Sinatro	.05	.02	.01
☐ 116T	Don Slaught	.05	.02	.01
☐ 117T	Bryn Smith	.05	.02	.01
☐ 118T	Lee Smith	.10	.05	.01
☐ 119T	Paul Sorrento	.15	.07	.02
☐ 120T	Franklin Stubbs UER ('84 says '99 and has the same stats as '89, '83 stats are missing)	.05	.02	.01
☐ 121T	Russ Swan	.05	.02	.01
☐ 122T	Bob Tewksbury	.08	.04	.01
☐ 123T	Wayne Tolleson	.05	.02	.01
☐ 124T	John Tudor	.05	.02	.01
☐ 125T	Randy Veres	.05	.02	.01
☐ 126T	Hector Villanueva	.05	.02	.01
☐ 127T	Mitch Webster	.05	.02	.01
☐ 128T	Ernie Whitt	.05	.02	.01
☐ 129T	Frank Wills	.05	.02	.01
☐ 130T	Dave Winfield	.10	.05	.01
☐ 131T	Matt Young	.05	.02	.01
☐ 132T	Checklist 1T-132T	.05	.02	.01

1991 Topps

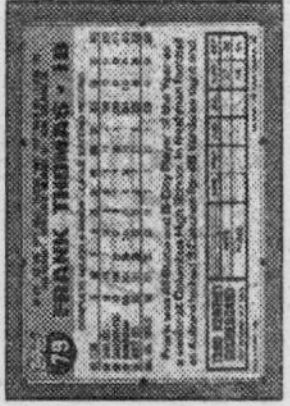

The 1991 Topps Set consists of 792 cards in the now standard size of 2 1/2" by 3 1/2". This set marks Topps tenth consecutive year of issuing a 792-card set. Topps also commemorated their fortieth anniversary by including a "Topps 40" logo on the front and back of each card. Virtually all of the cards have been discovered without the 40th logo on the back. As a special promotion Topps inserted (randomly) into their wax packs one of every previous card they ever issued. Topps again issued their checklists in team order (and alphabetically within team) and included a special 22-card All-Star set (386-407). There are five players listed as Future Stars, 114 Lance Dickson, 211 Brian Barnes, 561 Tim McIntosh, 587 Jose Offerman, and 594 Rich Garces. There are nine players listed as First Draft Picks, 74 Shane Andrews, 103 Tim Costo, 113 Carl Everett, 278 Alex Fernandez, 471 Mike Lieberthal, 491 Kurt Miller, 529 Marc Newfield, 596 Ronnie Walden, and 767 Dan Wilson. The key Rookie Cards in this set are Wes Chamberlain, Carl Everett, Chipper Jones, Brian McRae, Marc Newfield, and Phil Plantier. The complete 1991 Topps set was also issued as a factory set of micro baseball cards with cards measuring approximately one-fourth the size of the regular size cards but identical in other respects. The micro set and its cards are valued at approximately half the values listed below for the regular size cards. The set was also issued with a gold "Operation Desert Shield" emblem stamped on the cards. It has been reported that Topps sent wax cases (equivalent to 6,313 sets) as gifts to U.S. troops stationed in the Persian Gulf. These Desert Shield cards are quite valuable in comparison to the regular issue of Topps; but one must be careful as counterfeits of these cards are known. These counterfeit Desert Shield cards can typically be detected by the shape of the gold shield stamped on the card. The bottom of the shield on the original is rounded, almost flat; the known forgeries come to a point. Due to the scarcity of these Desert Shield cards, they are usually sold at one hundred times the value of the corresponding regular card. Topps also produced a specially boxed glossy edition frequently referred to as the Topps Tiffany set. This year, again, Topps did not disclose the number of Tiffany sets they produced or sold. The checklist of cards is identical to that of the normal non-glossy cards. There are two primary distinguishing features of the Tiffany cards, white card stock reverses and high gloss obverses. These Tiffany cards are valued approximately from three to five times the values listed below.

	MINT	EXC	G-VG
COMPLETE SET (792)	15.00	6.75	1.90
COMPLETE FACT.SET (792)	18.00	8.00	2.30
COMMON CARD (1-792)	.05	.02	.01

☐ 1	Nolan Ryan	.75	.35	.09
☐ 2	George Brett RB	.15	.07	.02
☐ 3	Carlton Fisk RB	.10	.05	.01
☐ 4	Kevin Maas RB	.05	.02	.01
☐ 5	Cal Ripken RB	.20	.09	.03
☐ 6	Nolan Ryan RB	.35	.16	.04
☐ 7	Ryne Sandberg RB	.15	.07	.02
☐ 8	Bobby Thigpen RB	.05	.02	.01
☐ 9	Darrin Fletcher	.05	.02	.01
☐ 10	Gregg Olson	.10	.05	.01
☐ 11	Roberto Kelly	.10	.05	.01
☐ 12	Paul Assenmacher	.05	.02	.01
☐ 13	Mariano Duncan	.05	.02	.01
☐ 14	Dennis Lamp	.05	.02	.01
☐ 15	Von Hayes	.05	.02	.01
☐ 16	Mike Heath	.05	.02	.01
☐ 17	Jeff Brantley	.05	.02	.01
☐ 18	Nelson Liriano	.05	.02	.01
☐ 19	Jeff D. Robinson	.05	.02	.01
☐ 20	Pedro Guerrero	.10	.05	.01

- ☐ 21 Joe Morgan MG .05 .02 .01
- ☐ 22 Storm Davis .05 .02 .01
- ☐ 23 Jim Gantner .05 .02 .01
- ☐ 24 Dave Martinez .05 .02 .01
- ☐ 25 Tim Belcher .05 .02 .01
- ☐ 26 Luis Sojo UER .05 .02 .01
  (Born in Barquisimento, not Carquis)
- ☐ 27 Bobby Witt .05 .02 .01
- ☐ 28 Alvaro Espinoza .05 .02 .01
- ☐ 29 Bob Walk .05 .02 .01
- ☐ 30 Gregg Jefferies .15 .07 .02
- ☐ 31 Colby Ward .05 .02 .01
- ☐ 32 Mike Simms .05 .02 .01
- ☐ 33 Barry Jones .05 .02 .01
- ☐ 34 Atlee Hammaker .05 .02 .01
- ☐ 35 Greg Maddux .25 .11 .03
- ☐ 36 Donnie Hill .05 .02 .01
- ☐ 37 Tom Bolton .05 .02 .01
- ☐ 38 Scott Bradley .05 .02 .01
- ☐ 39 Jim Neidlinger .05 .02 .01
- ☐ 40 Kevin Mitchell .10 .05 .01
- ☐ 41 Ken Dayley .05 .02 .01
- ☐ 42 Chris Hoiles .15 .07 .02
- ☐ 43 Roger McDowell .05 .02 .01
- ☐ 44 Mike Felder .05 .02 .01
- ☐ 45 Chris Sabo .10 .05 .01
- ☐ 46 Tim Drummond .05 .02 .01
- ☐ 47 Brook Jacoby .05 .02 .01
- ☐ 48 Dennis Boyd .05 .02 .01
- ☐ 49A Pat Borders ERR .25 .11 .03
  (40 steals at Kinston in '86)
- ☐ 49B Pat Borders COR .05 .02 .01
  (0 steals at Kinston in '86)
- ☐ 50 Bob Welch .05 .02 .01
- ☐ 51 Art Howe MG .05 .02 .01
- ☐ 52 Francisco Oliveras .05 .02 .01
- ☐ 53 Mike Sharperson UER .05 .02 .01
  (Born in 1961, not 1960)
- ☐ 54 Gary Mielke .05 .02 .01
- ☐ 55 Jeffrey Leonard .05 .02 .01
- ☐ 56 Jeff Parrett .05 .02 .01
- ☐ 57 Jack Howell .05 .02 .01
- ☐ 58 Mel Stottlemyre Jr. .05 .02 .01
- ☐ 59 Eric Yelding .05 .02 .01
- ☐ 60 Frank Viola .10 .05 .01
- ☐ 61 Stan Javier .05 .02 .01
- ☐ 62 Lee Guetterman .05 .02 .01
- ☐ 63 Milt Thompson .05 .02 .01
- ☐ 64 Tom Herr .05 .02 .01
- ☐ 65 Bruce Hurst .05 .02 .01
- ☐ 66 Terry Kennedy .05 .02 .01
- ☐ 67 Rick Honeycutt .05 .02 .01
- ☐ 68 Gary Sheffield .15 .07 .02
- ☐ 69 Steve Wilson .05 .02 .01
- ☐ 70 Ellis Burks .10 .05 .01
- ☐ 71 Jim Acker .05 .02 .01
- ☐ 72 Junior Ortiz .05 .02 .01
- ☐ 73 Craig Worthington .05 .02 .01
- ☐ 74 Shane Andrews .20 .09 .03
- ☐ 75 Jack Morris .15 .07 .02
- ☐ 76 Jerry Browne .05 .02 .01
- ☐ 77 Drew Hall .05 .02 .01
- ☐ 78 Geno Petralli .05 .02 .01
- ☐ 79 Frank Thomas 2.00 .90 .25
- ☐ 80A Fernando Valenzuela .25 .11 .03
  ERR (104 earned runs in '90 tied for league lead)
- ☐ 80B Fernando Valenzuela .05 .02 .01
  COR (104 earned runs in '90 led league, 20 CG's in 1986 now italicized)
- ☐ 81 Cito Gaston MG .05 .02 .01
- ☐ 82 Tom Glavine .20 .09 .03
- ☐ 83 Daryl Boston .05 .02 .01
- ☐ 84 Bob McClure .05 .02 .01
- ☐ 85 Jesse Barfield .05 .02 .01
- ☐ 86 Les Lancaster .05 .02 .01
- ☐ 87 Tracy Jones .05 .02 .01
- ☐ 88 Bob Tewksbury .10 .05 .01
- ☐ 89 Darren Daulton .15 .07 .02
- ☐ 90 Danny Tartabull .10 .05 .01
- ☐ 91 Greg Colbrunn .15 .07 .02
- ☐ 92 Danny Jackson .05 .02 .01
- ☐ 93 Ivan Calderon .05 .02 .01
- ☐ 94 John Dopson .05 .02 .01
- ☐ 95 Paul Molitor .15 .07 .02
- ☐ 96 Trevor Wilson .05 .02 .01
- ☐ 97A Brady Anderson ERR .25 .11 .03
  (September, 2 RBI and 3 hits, should be 3 RBI and 14 hits
- ☐ 97B Brady Anderson COR .10 .05 .01
- ☐ 98 Sergio Valdez .05 .02 .01
- ☐ 99 Chris Gwynn .05 .02 .01
- ☐ 100A Don Mattingly ERR .50 .23 .06
  (10 hits in 1990)
- ☐ 100B Don Mattingly COR .30 .14 .04
  (101 hits in 1990)
- ☐ 101 Rob Ducey .05 .02 .01
- ☐ 102 Gene Larkin .05 .02 .01
- ☐ 103 Tim Costo .05 .02 .01
- ☐ 104 Don Robinson .05 .02 .01
- ☐ 105 Kevin McReynolds .05 .02 .01
- ☐ 106 Ed Nunez .05 .02 .01
- ☐ 107 Luis Polonia .05 .02 .01
- ☐ 108 Matt Young .05 .02 .01
- ☐ 109 Greg Riddoch MG .05 .02 .01
- ☐ 110 Tom Henke .10 .05 .01
- ☐ 111 Andres Thomas .05 .02 .01
- ☐ 112 Frank DiPino .05 .02 .01
- ☐ 113 Carl Everett .15 .07 .02
- ☐ 114 Lance Dickson .05 .02 .01
- ☐ 115 Hubie Brooks .05 .02 .01
- ☐ 116 Mark Davis .05 .02 .01
- ☐ 117 Dion James .05 .02 .01
- ☐ 118 Tom Edens .05 .02 .01
- ☐ 119 Carl Nichols .05 .02 .01
- ☐ 120 Joe Carter .20 .09 .03
- ☐ 121 Eric King .05 .02 .01
- ☐ 122 Paul O'Neill .10 .05 .01
- ☐ 123 Greg A. Harris .05 .02 .01
- ☐ 124 Randy Bush .05 .02 .01
- ☐ 125 Steve Bedrosian .05 .02 .01
- ☐ 126 Bernard Gilkey .10 .05 .01
- ☐ 127 Joe Price .05 .02 .01
- ☐ 128 Travis Fryman .40 .18 .05
  (Front has SS, back has SS-3B)
- ☐ 129 Mark Eichhorn .05 .02 .01
- ☐ 130 Ozzie Smith .20 .09 .03
- ☐ 131A Checklist 1 ERR .15 .02 .01
  727 Phil Bradley
- ☐ 131B Checklist 1 COR .05 .02 .01
  717 Phil Bradley
- ☐ 132 Jamie Quirk .05 .02 .01
- ☐ 133 Greg Briley .05 .02 .01
- ☐ 134 Kevin Elster .05 .02 .01
- ☐ 135 Jerome Walton .05 .02 .01
- ☐ 136 Dave Schmidt .05 .02 .01
- ☐ 137 Randy Ready .05 .02 .01
- ☐ 138 Jamie Moyer .05 .02 .01

☐ 139 Jeff Treadway .05 .02 .01
☐ 140 Fred McGriff .20 .09 .03
☐ 141 Nick Leyva MG .05 .02 .01
☐ 142 Curt Wilkerson .05 .02 .01
☐ 143 John Smiley .05 .02 .01
☐ 144 Dave Henderson .05 .02 .01
☐ 145 Lou Whitaker .15 .07 .02
☐ 146 Dan Plesac .05 .02 .01
☐ 147 Carlos Baerga .30 .14 .04
☐ 148 Rey Palacios .05 .02 .01
☐ 149 Al Osuna UER .05 .02 .01
(Shown throwing right, but bio says lefty)
☐ 150 Cal Ripken .35 .16 .04
☐ 151 Tom Browning .05 .02 .01
☐ 152 Mickey Hatcher .05 .02 .01
☐ 153 Bryan Harvey .10 .05 .01
☐ 154 Jay Buhner .10 .05 .01
☐ 155A Dwight Evans ERR .30 .14 .04
(Led league with 162 games in '82)
☐ 155B Dwight Evans COR .10 .05 .01
(Tied for lead with 162 games in '82)
☐ 156 Carlos Martinez .05 .02 .01
☐ 157 John Smoltz .15 .07 .02
☐ 158 Jose Uribe .05 .02 .01
☐ 159 Joe Boever .05 .02 .01
☐ 160 Vince Coleman UER .05 .02 .01
(Wrong birth year, born 9/22/60)
☐ 161 Tim Leary .05 .02 .01
☐ 162 Ozzie Canseco .05 .02 .01
☐ 163 Dave Johnson .05 .02 .01
☐ 164 Edgar Diaz .05 .02 .01
☐ 165 Sandy Alomar Jr. .10 .05 .01
☐ 166 Harold Baines .10 .05 .01
☐ 167A Randy Tomlin ERR .25 .11 .03
(Harriburg)
☐ 167B Randy Tomlin COR .05 .02 .01
(Harrisburg)
☐ 168 John Olerud .15 .07 .02
☐ 169 Luis Aquino .05 .02 .01
☐ 170 Carlton Fisk .15 .07 .02
☐ 171 Tony LaRussa MG .10 .05 .01
☐ 172 Pete Incaviglia .05 .02 .01
☐ 173 Jason Grimsley .05 .02 .01
☐ 174 Ken Caminiti .10 .05 .01
☐ 175 Jack Armstrong .05 .02 .01
☐ 176 John Orton .05 .02 .01
☐ 177 Reggie Harris .05 .02 .01
☐ 178 Dave Valle .05 .02 .01
☐ 179 Pete Harnisch .10 .05 .01
☐ 180 Tony Gwynn .25 .11 .03
☐ 181 Duane Ward .10 .05 .01
☐ 182 Junior Noboa .05 .02 .01
☐ 183 Clay Parker .05 .02 .01
☐ 184 Gary Green .05 .02 .01
☐ 185 Joe Magrane .05 .02 .01
☐ 186 Rod Booker .05 .02 .01
☐ 187 Greg Cadaret .05 .02 .01
☐ 188 Damon Berryhill .05 .02 .01
☐ 189 Daryl Irvine .05 .02 .01
☐ 190 Matt Williams .20 .09 .03
☐ 191 Willie Blair .05 .02 .01
☐ 192 Rob Deer .05 .02 .01
☐ 193 Felix Fermin .05 .02 .01
☐ 194 Xavier Hernandez .05 .02 .01
☐ 195 Wally Joyner .10 .05 .01
☐ 196 Jim Vatcher .05 .02 .01
☐ 197 Chris Nabholz .05 .02 .01
☐ 198 R.J. Reynolds .05 .02 .01
☐ 199 Mike Hartley .05 .02 .01
☐ 200 Darryl Strawberry .15 .07 .02
☐ 201 Tom Kelly MG .05 .02 .01
☐ 202 Jim Leyritz .05 .02 .01
☐ 203 Gene Harris .05 .02 .01
☐ 204 Herm Winningham .05 .02 .01
☐ 205 Mike Perez .05 .02 .01
☐ 206 Carlos Quintana .05 .02 .01
☐ 207 Gary Wayne .05 .02 .01
☐ 208 Willie Wilson .05 .02 .01
☐ 209 Ken Howell .05 .02 .01
☐ 210 Lance Parrish .10 .05 .01
☐ 211 Brian Barnes .05 .02 .01
☐ 212 Steve Finley .05 .02 .01
☐ 213 Frank Wills .05 .02 .01
☐ 214 Joe Girardi .05 .02 .01
☐ 215 Dave Smith .05 .02 .01
☐ 216 Greg Gagne .05 .02 .01
☐ 217 Chris Bosio .05 .02 .01
☐ 218 Rick Parker .05 .02 .01
☐ 219 Jack McDowell .15 .07 .02
☐ 220 Tim Wallach .05 .02 .01
☐ 221 Don Slaught .05 .02 .01
☐ 222 Brian McRae .30 .14 .04
☐ 223 Allan Anderson .05 .02 .01
☐ 224 Juan Gonzalez 1.00 .45 .13
☐ 225 Randy Johnson .15 .07 .02
☐ 226 Alfredo Griffin .05 .02 .01
☐ 227 Steve Avery UER .15 .07 .02
(Pitched 13 games for Durham in 1989, not 2)
☐ 228 Rex Hudler .05 .02 .01
☐ 229 Rance Mulliniks .05 .02 .01
☐ 230 Sid Fernandez .10 .05 .01
☐ 231 Doug Rader MG .05 .02 .01
☐ 232 Jose DeJesus .05 .02 .01
☐ 233 Al Leiter .05 .02 .01
☐ 234 Scott Erickson .05 .02 .01
☐ 235 Dave Parker .15 .07 .02
☐ 236A Frank Tanana ERR .25 .11 .03
(Tied for lead with 269 K's in '75)
☐ 236B Frank Tanana COR .05 .02 .01
(Led league with 269 K's in '75)
☐ 237 Rick Cerone .05 .02 .01
☐ 238 Mike Dunne .05 .02 .01
☐ 239 Darren Lewis .10 .05 .01
☐ 240 Mike Scott .05 .02 .01
☐ 241 Dave Clark UER .05 .02 .01
(Career totals 19 HR and 5 3B, should be 22 and 3)
☐ 242 Mike LaCoss .05 .02 .01
☐ 243 Lance Johnson .05 .02 .01
☐ 244 Mike Jeffcoat .05 .02 .01
☐ 245 Kal Daniels .05 .02 .01
☐ 246 Kevin Wickander .05 .02 .01
☐ 247 Jody Reed .05 .02 .01
☐ 248 Tom Gordon .10 .05 .01
☐ 249 Bob Melvin .05 .02 .01
☐ 250 Dennis Eckersley .15 .07 .02
☐ 251 Mark Lemke .05 .02 .01
☐ 252 Mel Rojas .05 .02 .01
☐ 253 Garry Templeton .05 .02 .01
☐ 254 Shawn Boskie .05 .02 .01
☐ 255 Brian Downing .05 .02 .01
☐ 256 Greg Hibbard .05 .02 .01
☐ 257 Tom O'Malley .05 .02 .01
☐ 258 Chris Hammond .10 .05 .01
☐ 259 Hensley Meulens .05 .02 .01
☐ 260 Harold Reynolds .05 .02 .01
☐ 261 Bud Harrelson MG .05 .02 .01
☐ 262 Tim Jones .05 .02 .01

☐ 263 Checklist 2	.05	.02	.01
☐ 264 Dave Hollins	.15	.07	.02
☐ 265 Mark Gubicza	.05	.02	.01
☐ 266 Carmelo Castillo	.05	.02	.01
☐ 267 Mark Knudson	.05	.02	.01
☐ 268 Tom Brookens	.05	.02	.01
☐ 269 Joe Hesketh	.05	.02	.01
☐ 270A Mark McGwire ERR (1987 Slugging Pctg. listed as 618)	.25	.11	.03
☐ 270B Mark McGwire COR (1987 Slugging Pctg. listed as .618)	.15	.07	.02
☐ 271 Omar Olivares	.05	.02	.01
☐ 272 Jeff King	.05	.02	.01
☐ 273 Johnny Ray	.05	.02	.01
☐ 274 Ken Williams	.05	.02	.01
☐ 275 Alan Trammell	.15	.07	.02
☐ 276 Bill Swift	.10	.05	.01
☐ 277 Scott Coolbaugh	.05	.02	.01
☐ 278 Alex Fernandez UER (No '90 White Sox stats)	.25	.11	.03
☐ 279A Jose Gonzalez ERR (Photo actually Billy Bean)	.25	.11	.03
☐ 279B Jose Gonzalez COR	.05	.02	.01
☐ 280 Bret Saberhagen	.10	.05	.01
☐ 281 Larry Sheets	.05	.02	.01
☐ 282 Don Carman	.05	.02	.01
☐ 283 Marquis Grissom	.15	.07	.02
☐ 284 Billy Spiers	.05	.02	.01
☐ 285 Jim Abbott	.15	.07	.02
☐ 286 Ken Oberkfell	.05	.02	.01
☐ 287 Mark Grant	.05	.02	.01
☐ 288 Derrick May	.10	.05	.01
☐ 289 Tim Birtsas	.05	.02	.01
☐ 290 Steve Sax	.05	.02	.01
☐ 291 John Wathan MG	.05	.02	.01
☐ 292 Bud Black	.05	.02	.01
☐ 293 Jay Bell	.10	.05	.01
☐ 294 Mike Moore	.05	.02	.01
☐ 295 Rafael Palmeiro	.15	.07	.02
☐ 296 Mark Williamson	.05	.02	.01
☐ 297 Manny Lee	.05	.02	.01
☐ 298 Omar Vizquel	.05	.02	.01
☐ 299 Scott Radinsky	.05	.02	.01
☐ 300 Kirby Puckett	.30	.14	.04
☐ 301 Steve Farr	.05	.02	.01
☐ 302 Tim Teufel	.05	.02	.01
☐ 303 Mike Boddicker	.05	.02	.01
☐ 304 Kevin Reimer	.05	.02	.01
☐ 305 Mike Scioscia	.05	.02	.01
☐ 306A Lonnie Smith ERR (136 games in '90)	.25	.11	.03
☐ 306B Lonnie Smith COR (135 games in '90)	.05	.02	.01
☐ 307 Andy Benes	.15	.07	.02
☐ 308 Tom Pagnozzi	.05	.02	.01
☐ 309 Norm Charlton	.05	.02	.01
☐ 310 Gary Carter	.15	.07	.02
☐ 311 Jeff Pico	.05	.02	.01
☐ 312 Charlie Hayes	.10	.05	.01
☐ 313 Ron Robinson	.05	.02	.01
☐ 314 Gary Pettis	.05	.02	.01
☐ 315 Roberto Alomar	.25	.11	.03
☐ 316 Gene Nelson	.05	.02	.01
☐ 317 Mike Fitzgerald	.05	.02	.01
☐ 318 Rick Aguilera	.10	.05	.01
☐ 319 Jeff McKnight	.05	.02	.01
☐ 320 Tony Fernandez	.10	.05	.01
☐ 321 Bob Rodgers MG	.05	.02	.01
☐ 322 Terry Shumpert	.05	.02	.01
☐ 323 Cory Snyder	.05	.02	.01
☐ 324A Ron Kittle ERR (Set another standard ...)	.25	.11	.03
☐ 324B Ron Kittle COR (Tied another standard ...)	.05	.02	.01
☐ 325 Brett Butler	.10	.05	.01
☐ 326 Ken Patterson	.05	.02	.01
☐ 327 Ron Hassey	.05	.02	.01
☐ 328 Walt Terrell	.05	.02	.01
☐ 329 David Justice UER (Drafted third round on card, should say fourth pick)	.35	.16	.04
☐ 330 Dwight Gooden	.10	.05	.01
☐ 331 Eric Anthony	.10	.05	.01
☐ 332 Kenny Rogers	.05	.02	.01
☐ 333 Chipper Jones FDP	1.25	.55	.16
☐ 334 Todd Benzinger	.05	.02	.01
☐ 335 Mitch Williams	.10	.05	.01
☐ 336 Matt Nokes	.05	.02	.01
☐ 337A Keith Comstock ERR (Cubs logo on front)	.25	.11	.03
☐ 337B Keith Comstock COR (Mariners logo on front)	.05	.02	.01
☐ 338 Luis Rivera	.05	.02	.01
☐ 339 Larry Walker	.15	.07	.02
☐ 340 Ramon Martinez	.10	.05	.01
☐ 341 John Moses	.05	.02	.01
☐ 342 Mickey Morandini	.05	.02	.01
☐ 343 Jose Oquendo	.05	.02	.01
☐ 344 Jeff Russell	.05	.02	.01
☐ 345 Len Dykstra	.15	.07	.02
☐ 346 Jesse Orosco	.05	.02	.01
☐ 347 Greg Vaughn	.10	.05	.01
☐ 348 Todd Stottlemyre	.05	.02	.01
☐ 349 Dave Gallagher	.05	.02	.01
☐ 350 Glenn Davis	.05	.02	.01
☐ 351 Joe Torre MG	.10	.05	.01
☐ 352 Frank White	.10	.05	.01
☐ 353 Tony Castillo	.05	.02	.01
☐ 354 Sid Bream	.05	.02	.01
☐ 355 Chili Davis	.10	.05	.01
☐ 356 Mike Marshall	.05	.02	.01
☐ 357 Jack Savage	.05	.02	.01
☐ 358 Mark Parent	.05	.02	.01
☐ 359 Chuck Cary	.05	.02	.01
☐ 360 Tim Raines	.15	.07	.02
☐ 361 Scott Garrelts	.05	.02	.01
☐ 362 Hector Villenueva	.05	.02	.01
☐ 363 Rick Mahler	.05	.02	.01
☐ 364 Dan Pasqua	.05	.02	.01
☐ 365 Mike Schooler	.05	.02	.01
☐ 366A Checklist 3 ERR 19 Carl Nichols	.15	.02	.01
☐ 366B Checklist 3 COR 119 Carl Nichols	.05	.02	.01
☐ 367 Dave Walsh	.05	.02	.01
☐ 368 Felix Jose	.10	.05	.01
☐ 369 Steve Searcy	.05	.02	.01
☐ 370 Kelly Gruber	.05	.02	.01
☐ 371 Jeff Montgomery	.10	.05	.01
☐ 372 Spike Owen	.05	.02	.01
☐ 373 Darrin Jackson	.05	.02	.01
☐ 374 Larry Casian	.05	.02	.01
☐ 375 Tony Pena	.05	.02	.01
☐ 376 Mike Harkey	.05	.02	.01
☐ 377 Rene Gonzales	.05	.02	.01
☐ 378A Wilson Alvarez ERR ('89 Port Charlotte and '90 Birmingham stat lines omitted)	1.00	.45	.13
☐ 378B Wilson Alvarez COR	.25	.11	.03

(Text still says 143 K's in 1988, whereas stats say 134)

☐ 379 Randy Velarde .05 .02 .01
☐ 380 Willie McGee .10 .05 .01
☐ 381 Jim Leyland MG .05 .02 .01
☐ 382 Mackey Sasser .05 .02 .01
☐ 383 Pete Smith .05 .02 .01
☐ 384 Gerald Perry .05 .02 .01
☐ 385 Mickey Tettleton .10 .05 .01
☐ 386 Cecil Fielder AS .10 .05 .01
☐ 387 Julio Franco AS .05 .02 .01
☐ 388 Kelly Gruber AS .05 .02 .01
☐ 389 Alan Trammell AS .10 .05 .01
☐ 390 Jose Canseco AS .15 .07 .02
☐ 391 Rickey Henderson AS .10 .05 .01
☐ 392 Ken Griffey Jr. AS .75 .35 .09
☐ 393 Carlton Fisk AS .10 .05 .01
☐ 394 Bob Welch AS .05 .02 .01
☐ 395 Chuck Finley AS .05 .02 .01
☐ 396 Bobby Thigpen AS .05 .02 .01
☐ 397 Eddie Murray AS .10 .05 .01
☐ 398 Ryne Sandberg AS .15 .07 .02
☐ 399 Matt Williams AS .10 .05 .01
☐ 400 Barry Larkin AS .10 .05 .01
☐ 401 Barry Bonds AS .25 .11 .03
☐ 402 Darryl Strawbery AS .10 .05 .01
☐ 403 Bobby Bonilla AS .10 .05 .01
☐ 404 Mike Scioscia AS .05 .02 .01
☐ 405 Doug Drabek AS .10 .05 .01
☐ 406 Frank Viola AS .05 .02 .01
☐ 407 John Franco AS .05 .02 .01
☐ 408 Earnie Riles .05 .02 .01
☐ 409 Mike Stanley .05 .02 .01
☐ 410 Dave Righetti .05 .02 .01
☐ 411 Lance Blankenship .05 .02 .01
☐ 412 Dave Bergman .05 .02 .01
☐ 413 Terry Mulholland .05 .02 .01
☐ 414 Sammy Sosa .15 .07 .02
☐ 415 Rick Sutcliffe .10 .05 .01
☐ 416 Randy Milligan .05 .02 .01
☐ 417 Bill Krueger .05 .02 .01
☐ 418 Nick Esasky .05 .02 .01
☐ 419 Jeff Reed .05 .02 .01
☐ 420 Bobby Thigpen .05 .02 .01
☐ 421 Alex Cole .05 .02 .01
☐ 422 Rick Reuschel .05 .02 .01
☐ 423 Rafael Ramirez UER .05 .02 .01
(Born 1959, not 1958)
☐ 424 Calvin Schiraldi .05 .02 .01
☐ 425 Andy Van Slyke .15 .07 .02
☐ 426 Joe Grahe .05 .02 .01
☐ 427 Rick Dempsey .05 .02 .01
☐ 428 John Barfield .05 .02 .01
☐ 429 Stump Merrill MG .05 .02 .01
☐ 430 Gary Gaetti .05 .02 .01
☐ 431 Paul Gibson .05 .02 .01
☐ 432 Delino DeShields .15 .07 .02
☐ 433 Pat Tabler .05 .02 .01
☐ 434 Julio Machado .05 .02 .01
☐ 435 Kevin Maas .05 .02 .01
☐ 436 Scott Bankhead .05 .02 .01
☐ 437 Doug Dascenzo .05 .02 .01
☐ 438 Vicente Palacios .05 .02 .01
☐ 439 Dickie Thon .05 .02 .01
☐ 440 George Bell .10 .05 .01
☐ 441 Zane Smith .05 .02 .01
☐ 442 Charlie O'Brien .05 .02 .01
☐ 443 Jeff Innis .05 .02 .01
☐ 444 Glenn Braggs .05 .02 .01
☐ 445 Greg Swindell .05 .02 .01
☐ 446 Craig Grebeck .05 .02 .01
☐ 447 John Burkett .10 .05 .01
☐ 448 Craig Lefferts .05 .02 .01
☐ 449 Juan Berenguer .05 .02 .01
☐ 450 Wade Boggs .15 .07 .02
☐ 451 Neal Heaton .05 .02 .01
☐ 452 Bill Schroeder .05 .02 .01
☐ 453 Lenny Harris .05 .02 .01
☐ 454A Kevin Appier ERR .30 .14 .04
('90 Omaha stat line omitted)
☐ 454B Kevin Appier COR .10 .05 .01
☐ 455 Walt Weiss .05 .02 .01
☐ 456 Charlie Leibrandt .05 .02 .01
☐ 457 Todd Hundley .10 .05 .01
☐ 458 Brian Holman .05 .02 .01
☐ 459 Tom Trebelhorn MG UER .05 .02 .01
(Pitching and batting columns switched)
☐ 460 Dave Stieb .10 .05 .01
☐ 461 Robin Ventura .20 .09 .03
☐ 462 Steve Frey .05 .02 .01
☐ 463 Dwight Smith .05 .02 .01
☐ 464 Steve Buechele .05 .02 .01
☐ 465 Ken Griffey .10 .05 .01
☐ 466 Charles Nagy .10 .05 .01
☐ 467 Dennis Cook .05 .02 .01
☐ 468 Tim Hulett .05 .02 .01
☐ 469 Chet Lemon .05 .02 .01
☐ 470 Howard Johnson .10 .05 .01
☐ 471 Mike Lieberthal .10 .05 .01
☐ 472 Kirt Manwaring .05 .02 .01
☐ 473 Curt Young .05 .02 .01
☐ 474 Phil Plantier .30 .14 .04
☐ 475 Teddy Higuera .05 .02 .01
☐ 476 Glenn Wilson .05 .02 .01
☐ 477 Mike Fetters .05 .02 .01
☐ 478 Kurt Stillwell .05 .02 .01
☐ 479 Bob Patterson UER .05 .02 .01
(Has a decimal point between 7 and 9)
☐ 480 Dave Magadan .05 .02 .01
☐ 481 Eddie Whitson .05 .02 .01
☐ 482 Tino Martinez .10 .05 .01
☐ 483 Mike Aldrete .05 .02 .01
☐ 484 Dave LaPoint .05 .02 .01
☐ 485 Terry Pendleton .15 .07 .02
☐ 486 Tommy Greene .10 .05 .01
☐ 487 Rafael Belliard .05 .02 .01
☐ 488 Jeff Manto .05 .02 .01
☐ 489 Bobby Valentine MG .05 .02 .01
☐ 490 Kirk Gibson .10 .05 .01
☐ 491 Kurt Miller .05 .02 .01
☐ 492 Ernie Whitt .05 .02 .01
☐ 493 Jose Rijo .10 .05 .01
☐ 494 Chris James .05 .02 .01
☐ 495 Charlie Hough .10 .05 .01
☐ 496 Marty Barrett .05 .02 .01
☐ 497 Ben McDonald .15 .07 .02
☐ 498 Mark Salas .05 .02 .01
☐ 499 Melido Perez .05 .02 .01
☐ 500 Will Clark .20 .09 .03
☐ 501 Mike Bielecki .05 .02 .01
☐ 502 Carney Lansford .10 .05 .01
☐ 503 Roy Smith .05 .02 .01
☐ 504 Julio Valera .05 .02 .01
☐ 505 Chuck Finley .10 .05 .01
☐ 506 Darnell Coles .05 .02 .01
☐ 507 Steve Jeltz .05 .02 .01
☐ 508 Mike York .05 .02 .01
☐ 509 Glenallen Hill .05 .02 .01
☐ 510 John Franco .10 .05 .01
☐ 511 Steve Balboni .05 .02 .01
☐ 512 Jose Mesa .05 .02 .01
☐ 513 Jerald Clark .05 .02 .01

- ☐ 514 Mike Stanton .05 .02 .01
- ☐ 515 Alvin Davis .05 .02 .01
- ☐ 516 Karl Rhodes .05 .02 .01
- ☐ 517 Joe Oliver .05 .02 .01
- ☐ 518 Cris Carpenter .05 .02 .01
- ☐ 519 Sparky Anderson MG .10 .05 .01
- ☐ 520 Mark Grace .15 .07 .02
- ☐ 521 Joe Orsulak .05 .02 .01
- ☐ 522 Stan Belinda .05 .02 .01
- ☐ 523 Rodney McCray .05 .02 .01
- ☐ 524 Darrel Akerfelds .05 .02 .01
- ☐ 525 Willie Randolph .10 .05 .01
- ☐ 526A Moises Alou ERR 1.00 .45 .13 (37 runs in 2 games for '90 Pirates)
- ☐ 526B Moises Alou COR .25 .11 .03 (0 runs in 2 games for '90 Pirates)
- ☐ 527A Checklist 4 ERR .15 .02 .01 105 Keith Miller 719 Kevin McReynolds
- ☐ 527B Checklist 4 COR .05 .02 .01 105 Kevin McReynolds 719 Keith Miller
- ☐ 528 Denny Martinez .10 .05 .01
- ☐ 529 Marc Newfield .50 .23 .06
- ☐ 530 Roger Clemens .25 .11 .03
- ☐ 531 Dave Rohde .05 .02 .01
- ☐ 532 Kirk McCaskill .05 .02 .01
- ☐ 533 Oddibe McDowell .05 .02 .01
- ☐ 534 Mike Jackson .05 .02 .01
- ☐ 535 Ruben Sierra UER .15 .07 .02 (Back reads 100 Runs amd 100 RBI's)
- ☐ 536 Mike Witt .05 .02 .01
- ☐ 537 Jose Lind .05 .02 .01
- ☐ 538 Bip Roberts .05 .02 .01
- ☐ 539 Scott Terry .05 .02 .01
- ☐ 540 George Brett .30 .14 .04
- ☐ 541 Domingo Ramos .05 .02 .01
- ☐ 542 Rob Murphy .05 .02 .01
- ☐ 543 Junior Felix .05 .02 .01
- ☐ 544 Alejandro Pena .05 .02 .01
- ☐ 545 Dale Murphy .15 .07 .02
- ☐ 546 Jeff Ballard .05 .02 .01
- ☐ 547 Mike Pagliarulo .05 .02 .01
- ☐ 548 Jaime Navarro .05 .02 .01
- ☐ 549 John McNamara MG .05 .02 .01
- ☐ 550 Eric Davis .10 .05 .01
- ☐ 551 Bob Kipper .05 .02 .01
- ☐ 552 Jeff Hamilton .05 .02 .01
- ☐ 553 Joe Klink .05 .02 .01
- ☐ 554 Brian Harper .05 .02 .01
- ☐ 555 Turner Ward .15 .07 .02
- ☐ 556 Gary Ward .05 .02 .01
- ☐ 557 Wally Whitehurst .05 .02 .01
- ☐ 558 Otis Nixon .10 .05 .01
- ☐ 559 Adam Peterson .05 .02 .01
- ☐ 560 Greg Smith .05 .02 .01
- ☐ 561 Tim McIntosh .05 .02 .01
- ☐ 562 Jeff Kunkel .05 .02 .01
- ☐ 563 Brent Knackert .05 .02 .01
- ☐ 564 Dante Bichette .15 .07 .02
- ☐ 565 Craig Biggio .15 .07 .02
- ☐ 566 Craig Wilson .05 .02 .01
- ☐ 567 Dwayne Henry .05 .02 .01
- ☐ 568 Ron Karkovice .05 .02 .01
- ☐ 569 Curt Schilling .10 .05 .01
- ☐ 570 Barry Bonds .40 .18 .05
- ☐ 571 Pat Combs .05 .02 .01
- ☐ 572 Dave Anderson .05 .02 .01
- ☐ 573 Rich Rodriguez UER .05 .02 .01 (Stats say drafted 4th, but bio says 9th round)
- ☐ 574 John Marzano .05 .02 .01
- ☐ 575 Robin Yount .15 .07 .02
- ☐ 576 Jeff Kaiser .05 .02 .01
- ☐ 577 Bill Doran .05 .02 .01
- ☐ 578 Dave West .05 .02 .01
- ☐ 579 Roger Craig MG .05 .02 .01
- ☐ 580 Dave Stewart .10 .05 .01
- ☐ 581 Luis Quinones .05 .02 .01
- ☐ 582 Marty Clary .05 .02 .01
- ☐ 583 Tony Phillips .05 .02 .01
- ☐ 584 Kevin Brown .10 .05 .01
- ☐ 585 Pete O'Brien .05 .02 .01
- ☐ 586 Fred Lynn .10 .05 .01
- ☐ 587 Jose Offerman UER .10 .05 .01 (Text says he signed 7/24/86, but bio says 1988)
- ☐ 588 Mark Whiten .15 .07 .02
- ☐ 589 Scott Ruskin .05 .02 .01
- ☐ 590 Eddie Murray .15 .07 .02
- ☐ 591 Ken Hill .15 .07 .02
- ☐ 592 B.J. Surhoff .05 .02 .01
- ☐ 593A Mike Walker ERR .25 .11 .03 ('90 Canton-Akron stat line omitted)
- ☐ 593B Mike Walker COR .05 .02 .01
- ☐ 594 Rich Garces .05 .02 .01
- ☐ 595 Bill Landrum .05 .02 .01
- ☐ 596 Ronnie Walden .05 .02 .01
- ☐ 597 Jerry Don Gleaton .05 .02 .01
- ☐ 598 Sam Horn .05 .02 .01
- ☐ 599A Greg Myers ERR .25 .11 .03 ('90 Syracuse stat line omitted)
- ☐ 599B Greg Myers COR .05 .02 .01
- ☐ 600 Bo Jackson .15 .07 .02
- ☐ 601 Bob Ojeda .05 .02 .01
- ☐ 602 Casey Candaele .05 .02 .01
- ☐ 603A Wes Chamberlain ERR .50 .23 .06 (Photo actually Louie Meadows)
- ☐ 603B Wes Chamberlain COR .05 .02 .01
- ☐ 604 Billy Hatcher .05 .02 .01
- ☐ 605 Jeff Reardon .10 .05 .01
- ☐ 606 Jim Gott .05 .02 .01
- ☐ 607 Edgar Martinez .10 .05 .01
- ☐ 608 Todd Burns .05 .02 .01
- ☐ 609 Jeff Torborg MG .05 .02 .01
- ☐ 610 Andres Galarraga .15 .07 .02
- ☐ 611 Dave Eiland .05 .02 .01
- ☐ 612 Steve Lyons .05 .02 .01
- ☐ 613 Eric Show .05 .02 .01
- ☐ 614 Luis Salazar .05 .02 .01
- ☐ 615 Bert Blyleven .15 .07 .02
- ☐ 616 Todd Zeile .10 .05 .01
- ☐ 617 Bill Wegman .05 .02 .01
- ☐ 618 Sil Campusano .05 .02 .01
- ☐ 619 David Wells .05 .02 .01
- ☐ 620 Ozzie Guillen .05 .02 .01
- ☐ 621 Ted Power .05 .02 .01
- ☐ 622 Jack Daugherty .05 .02 .01
- ☐ 623 Jeff Blauser .10 .05 .01
- ☐ 624 Tom Candiotti .05 .02 .01
- ☐ 625 Terry Steinbach .10 .05 .01
- ☐ 626 Gerald Young .05 .02 .01
- ☐ 627 Tim Layana .05 .02 .01
- ☐ 628 Greg Litton .05 .02 .01
- ☐ 629 Wes Gardner .05 .02 .01
- ☐ 630 Dave Winfield .15 .07 .02
- ☐ 631 Mike Morgan .05 .02 .01
- ☐ 632 Lloyd Moseby .05 .02 .01
- ☐ 633 Kevin Tapani .10 .05 .01

☐ 634 Henry Cotto .05 .02 .01
☐ 635 Andy Hawkins .05 .02 .01
☐ 636 Geronimo Pena .05 .02 .01
☐ 637 Bruce Ruffin .05 .02 .01
☐ 638 Mike Macfarlane .05 .02 .01
☐ 639 Frank Robinson MG .05 .02 .01
☐ 640 Andre Dawson .15 .07 .02
☐ 641 Mike Henneman .05 .02 .01
☐ 642 Hal Morris .10 .05 .01
☐ 643 Jim Presley .05 .02 .01
☐ 644 Chuck Crim .05 .02 .01
☐ 645 Juan Samuel .05 .02 .01
☐ 646 Andujar Cedeno .10 .05 .01
☐ 647 Mark Portugal .05 .02 .01
☐ 648 Lee Stevens .05 .02 .01
☐ 649 Bill Sampen .05 .02 .01
☐ 650 Jack Clark .10 .05 .01
☐ 651 Alan Mills .05 .02 .01
☐ 652 Kevin Romine .05 .02 .01
☐ 653 Anthony Telford .05 .02 .01
☐ 654 Paul Sorrento .10 .05 .01
☐ 655 Erik Hanson .05 .02 .01
☐ 656A Checklist 5 ERR .15 .02 .01
348 Vicente Palacios
381 Jose Lind
537 Mike LaValliere
665 Jim Leyland
☐ 656B Checklist 5 ERR .15 .02 .01
433 Vicente Palacios
(Palacios should be 438)
537 Jose Lind
665 Mike LaValliere
381 Jim Leyland
☐ 656C Checklist 5 COR .15 .02 .01
438 Vicente Palacios
537 Jose Lind
665 Mike LaValliere
381 Jim Leyland
☐ 657 Mike Kingery .05 .02 .01
☐ 658 Scott Aldred .05 .02 .01
☐ 659 Oscar Azocar .05 .02 .01
☐ 660 Lee Smith .15 .07 .02
☐ 661 Steve Lake .05 .02 .01
☐ 662 Ron Dibble .05 .02 .01
☐ 663 Greg Brock .05 .02 .01
☐ 664 John Farrell .05 .02 .01
☐ 665 Mike LaValliere .05 .02 .01
☐ 666 Danny Darwin .05 .02 .01
☐ 667 Kent Anderson .05 .02 .01
☐ 668 Bill Long .05 .02 .01
☐ 669 Lou Piniella MG .05 .02 .01
☐ 670 Rickey Henderson .15 .07 .02
☐ 671 Andy McGaffigan .05 .02 .01
☐ 672 Shane Mack .10 .05 .01
☐ 673 Greg Olson UER .05 .02 .01
(6 RBI in '88 at Tidewater and 2 RBI in '87, should be 48 and 15)
☐ 674A Kevin Gross ERR .25 .11 .03
(89 BB with Phillies in '88 tied for league lead)
☐ 674B Kevin Gross COR .05 .02 .01
(89 BB with Phillies in '88 led league)
☐ 675 Tom Brunansky .05 .02 .01
☐ 676 Scott Chiamparino .05 .02 .01
☐ 677 Billy Ripken .05 .02 .01
☐ 678 Mark Davidson .05 .02 .01
☐ 679 Bill Bathe .05 .02 .01
☐ 680 David Cone .15 .07 .02
☐ 681 Jeff Schaefer .05 .02 .01
☐ 682 Ray Lankford .15 .07 .02
☐ 683 Derek Lilliquist .05 .02 .01
☐ 684 Milt Cuyler .05 .02 .01
☐ 685 Doug Drabek .15 .07 .02
☐ 686 Mike Gallego .05 .02 .01
☐ 687A John Cerutti ERR .25 .11 .03
(4.46 ERA in '90)
☐ 687B John Cerutti COR .05 .02 .01
(4.76 ERA in '90)
☐ 688 Rosario Rodriguez .05 .02 .01
☐ 689 John Kruk .15 .07 .02
☐ 690 Orel Hershiser .10 .05 .01
☐ 691 Mike Blowers .05 .02 .01
☐ 692A Efrain Valdez ERR .25 .11 .03
(Born 6/11/66)
☐ 692B Efrain Valdez COR .05 .02 .01
(Born 7/11/66 and two lines of text added)
☐ 693 Francisco Cabrera .05 .02 .01
☐ 694 Randy Veres .05 .02 .01
☐ 695 Kevin Seitzer .05 .02 .01
☐ 696 Steve Olin .05 .02 .01
☐ 697 Shawn Abner .05 .02 .01
☐ 698 Mark Guthrie .05 .02 .01
☐ 699 Jim Lefebvre MG .05 .02 .01
☐ 700 Jose Canseco .20 .09 .03
☐ 701 Pascual Perez .05 .02 .01
☐ 702 Tim Naehring .05 .02 .01
☐ 703 Juan Agosto .05 .02 .01
☐ 704 Devon White .10 .05 .01
☐ 705 Robby Thompson .05 .02 .01
☐ 706A Brad Arnsberg ERR .25 .11 .03
(68.2 IP in '90)
☐ 706B Brad Arnsberg COR .05 .02 .01
(62.2 IP in '90)
☐ 707 Jim Eisenreich .05 .02 .01
☐ 708 John Mitchell .05 .02 .01
☐ 709 Matt Sinatro .05 .02 .01
☐ 710 Kent Hrbek .10 .05 .01
☐ 711 Jose DeLeon .05 .02 .01
☐ 712 Ricky Jordan .05 .02 .01
☐ 713 Scott Scudder .05 .02 .01
☐ 714 Marvell Wynne .05 .02 .01
☐ 715 Tim Burke .05 .02 .01
☐ 716 Bob Geren .05 .02 .01
☐ 717 Phil Bradley .05 .02 .01
☐ 718 Steve Crawford .05 .02 .01
☐ 719 Keith Miller .05 .02 .01
☐ 720 Cecil Fielder .15 .07 .02
☐ 721 Mark Lee .05 .02 .01
☐ 722 Wally Backman .05 .02 .01
☐ 723 Candy Maldonado .05 .02 .01
☐ 724 David Segui .05 .02 .01
☐ 725 Ron Gant .10 .05 .01
☐ 726 Phil Stephenson .05 .02 .01
☐ 727 Mookie Wilson .05 .02 .01
☐ 728 Scott Sanderson .05 .02 .01
☐ 729 Don Zimmer MG .05 .02 .01
☐ 730 Barry Larkin .15 .07 .02
☐ 731 Jeff Gray .05 .02 .01
☐ 732 Franklin Stubbs .05 .02 .01
☐ 733 Kelly Downs .05 .02 .01
☐ 734 John Russell .05 .02 .01
☐ 735 Ron Darling .05 .02 .01
☐ 736 Dick Schofield .05 .02 .01
☐ 737 Tim Crews .05 .02 .01
☐ 738 Mel Hall .05 .02 .01
☐ 739 Russ Swan .05 .02 .01
☐ 740 Ryne Sandberg .25 .11 .03
☐ 741 Jimmy Key .10 .05 .01
☐ 742 Tommy Gregg .05 .02 .01
☐ 743 Bryn Smith .05 .02 .01
☐ 744 Nelson Santovenia .05 .02 .01
☐ 745 Doug Jones .05 .02 .01

	No.	Player	MINT	EXC	G-VG
☐	746	John Shelby	.05	.02	.01
☐	747	Tony Fossas	.05	.02	.01
☐	748	Al Newman	.05	.02	.01
☐	749	Greg W. Harris	.05	.02	.01
☐	750	Bobby Bonilla	.15	.07	.02
☐	751	Wayne Edwards	.05	.02	.01
☐	752	Kevin Bass	.05	.02	.01
☐	753	Paul Marak UER (Stats say drafted in Jan., but bio says May)	.05	.02	.01
☐	754	Bill Pecota	.05	.02	.01
☐	755	Mark Langston	.15	.07	.02
☐	756	Jeff Huson	.05	.02	.01
☐	757	Mark Gardner	.05	.02	.01
☐	758	Mike Devereaux	.10	.05	.01
☐	759	Bobby Cox MG	.05	.02	.01
☐	760	Benny Santiago	.05	.02	.01
☐	761	Larry Andersen	.05	.02	.01
☐	762	Mitch Webster	.05	.02	.01
☐	763	Dana Kiecker	.05	.02	.01
☐	764	Mark Carreon	.05	.02	.01
☐	765	Shawon Dunston	.05	.02	.01
☐	766	Jeff Robinson	.05	.02	.01
☐	767	Dan Wilson	.05	.02	.01
☐	768	Don Pall	.05	.02	.01
☐	769	Tim Sherrill	.05	.02	.01
☐	770	Jay Howell	.05	.02	.01
☐	771	Gary Redus UER (Born in Tanner, should say Athens)	.05	.02	.01
☐	772	Kent Mercker (Born in Indianapolis, should say Dublin, Ohio)	.10	.05	.01
☐	773	Tom Foley	.05	.02	.01
☐	774	Dennis Rasmussen	.05	.02	.01
☐	775	Julio Franco	.10	.05	.01
☐	776	Brent Mayne	.05	.02	.01
☐	777	John Candelaria	.05	.02	.01
☐	778	Dan Gladden	.05	.02	.01
☐	779	Carmelo Martinez	.05	.02	.01
☐	780A	Randy Myers ERR (15 career losses)	.25	.11	.03
☐	780B	Randy Myers COR (19 career losses)	.10	.05	.01
☐	781	Darryl Hamilton	.10	.05	.01
☐	782	Jim Deshaies	.05	.02	.01
☐	783	Joel Skinner	.05	.02	.01
☐	784	Willie Fraser	.05	.02	.01
☐	785	Scott Fletcher	.05	.02	.01
☐	786	Eric Plunk	.05	.02	.01
☐	787	Checklist 6	.05	.02	.01
☐	788	Bob Milacki	.05	.02	.01
☐	789	Tom Lasorda MG	.10	.05	.01
☐	790	Ken Griffey Jr.	1.50	.65	.19
☐	791	Mike Benjamin	.05	.02	.01
☐	792	Mike Greenwell	.10	.05	.01

1991 Topps Traded

The 1991 Topps Traded set contains 132 cards measuring the standard size (2 1/2 by 3 1/2"). The set includes a Team U.S.A. subset, featuring 25 of America's top collegiate players; these players are indicated in the checklist below by USA. The cards were sold in wax packs as well as factory sets. The cards in the wax packs (gray backs) and collated factory sets (white backs) are from different card stock. The fronts have

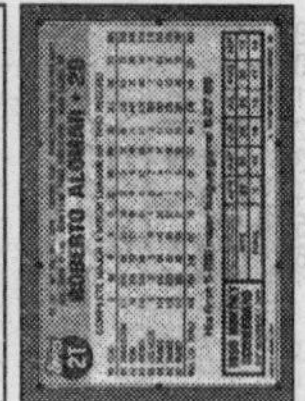

color action player photos, with two different color borders on a white card face. The player's position and name are given in the thicker border below the picture. In blue print on a pink and gray background, the horizontally oriented backs have biographical information and statistics. The cards are numbered on the back in the upper left corner; the set numbering corresponds to alphabetical order. The key Rookie Cards in this set are Jeff Bagwell, Darren Dreifort, Todd Greene, Jeffrey Hammonds, Charles Johnson, Phil Nevin, and Ivan Rodriguez.

	MINT	EXC	G-VG
COMPLETE SET (132)	8.00	3.60	1.00
COMPLETE FACT.SET (132)	8.00	3.60	1.00
COMMON CARD (1T-132T)	.05	.02	.01

*GRAY AND WHITE BACKS: SAME VALUE

	No.	Player	MINT	EXC	G-VG
☐	1T	Juan Agosto	.05	.02	.01
☐	2T	Roberto Alomar	.25	.11	.03
☐	3T	Wally Backman	.05	.02	.01
☐	4T	Jeff Bagwell	3.00	1.35	.40
☐	5T	Skeeter Barnes	.05	.02	.01
☐	6T	Steve Bedrosian	.05	.02	.01
☐	7T	Derek Bell	.08	.04	.01
☐	8T	George Bell	.08	.04	.01
☐	9T	Rafael Belliard	.05	.02	.01
☐	10T	Dante Bichette	.10	.05	.01
☐	11T	Bud Black	.05	.02	.01
☐	12T	Mike Boddicker	.05	.02	.01
☐	13T	Sid Bream	.05	.02	.01
☐	14T	Hubie Brooks	.05	.02	.01
☐	15T	Brett Butler	.08	.04	.01
☐	16T	Ivan Calderon	.05	.02	.01
☐	17T	John Candelaria	.05	.02	.01
☐	18T	Tom Candiotti	.05	.02	.01
☐	19T	Gary Carter	.10	.05	.01
☐	20T	Joe Carter	.20	.09	.03
☐	21T	Rick Cerone	.05	.02	.01
☐	22T	Jack Clark	.08	.04	.01
☐	23T	Vince Coleman	.05	.02	.01
☐	24T	Scott Coolbaugh	.05	.02	.01
☐	25T	Danny Cox	.05	.02	.01
☐	26T	Danny Darwin	.05	.02	.01
☐	27T	Chili Davis	.08	.04	.01
☐	28T	Glenn Davis	.05	.02	.01
☐	29T	Steve Decker	.05	.02	.01
☐	30T	Rob Deer	.05	.02	.01
☐	31T	Rich DeLucia	.05	.02	.01
☐	32T	John Dettmer USA	.30	.14	.04
☐	33T	Brian Downing	.05	.02	.01
☐	34T	Darren Dreifort USA	.30	.14	.04
☐	35T	Kirk Dressendorfer	.05	.02	.01
☐	36T	Jim Essian MG	.05	.02	.01
☐	37T	Dwight Evans	.08	.04	.01
☐	38T	Steve Farr	.05	.02	.01

☐	39T Jeff Fassero	.20	.09	.03
☐	40T Junior Felix	.05	.02	.01
☐	41T Tony Fernandez	.08	.04	.01
☐	42T Steve Finley	.05	.02	.01
☐	43T Jim Fregosi MG	.05	.02	.01
☐	44T Gary Gaetti	.05	.02	.01
☐	45T Jason Giambi USA	.40	.18	.05
☐	46T Kirk Gibson	.08	.04	.01
☐	47T Leo Gomez	.08	.04	.01
☐	48T Luis Gonzalez	.25	.11	.03
☐	49T Jeff Granger USA	.40	.18	.05
☐	50T Todd Greene USA	.75	.35	.09
☐	51T Jeffrey Hammonds USA	1.00	.45	.13
☐	52T Mike Hargrove MG	.05	.02	.01
☐	53T Pete Harnisch	.08	.04	.01
☐	54T Rick Helling USA UER (Misspelled Hellings on card back)	.25	.11	.03
☐	55T Glenallen Hill	.05	.02	.01
☐	56T Charlie Hough	.08	.04	.01
☐	57T Pete Incaviglia	.05	.02	.01
☐	58T Bo Jackson	.10	.05	.01
☐	59T Danny Jackson	.05	.02	.01
☐	60T Reggie Jefferson	.08	.04	.01
☐	61T Charles Johnson USA	1.00	.45	.13
☐	62T Jeff Johnson	.05	.02	.01
☐	63T Todd Johnson USA	.15	.07	.02
☐	64T Barry Jones	.05	.02	.01
☐	65T Chris Jones	.05	.02	.01
☐	66T Scott Kamieniecki	.05	.02	.01
☐	67T Pat Kelly	.15	.07	.02
☐	68T Darryl Kile	.10	.05	.01
☐	69T Chuck Knoblauch	.25	.11	.03
☐	70T Bill Krueger	.05	.02	.01
☐	71T Scott Leius	.05	.02	.01
☐	72T Donnie Leshnock USA	.05	.02	.01
☐	73T Mark Lewis	.08	.04	.01
☐	74T Candy Maldonado	.05	.02	.01
☐	75T Jason McDonald USA	.15	.07	.02
☐	76T Willie McGee	.08	.04	.01
☐	77T Fred McGriff	.20	.09	.03
☐	78T Billy McMillon USA	.15	.07	.02
☐	79T Hal McRae MG	.05	.02	.01
☐	80T Dan Melendez USA	.05	.02	.01
☐	81T Orlando Merced	.25	.11	.03
☐	82T Jack Morris	.10	.05	.01
☐	83T Phil Nevin USA	.50	.23	.06
☐	84T Otis Nixon	.08	.04	.01
☐	85T Johnny Oates MG	.05	.02	.01
☐	86T Bob Ojeda	.05	.02	.01
☐	87T Mike Pagliarulo	.05	.02	.01
☐	88T Dean Palmer	.08	.04	.01
☐	89T Dave Parker	.10	.05	.01
☐	90T Terry Pendleton	.10	.05	.01
☐	91T Tony Phillips (P) USA	.15	.07	.02
☐	92T Doug Piatt	.05	.02	.01
☐	93T Ron Polk USA CO	.05	.02	.01
☐	94T Tim Raines	.10	.05	.01
☐	95T Willie Randolph	.08	.04	.01
☐	96T Dave Righetti	.05	.02	.01
☐	97T Ernest Riles	.05	.02	.01
☐	98T Chris Roberts USA	.40	.18	.05
☐	99T Jeff D. Robinson	.05	.02	.01
☐	100T Jeff M. Robinson	.05	.02	.01
☐	101T Ivan Rodriguez	.50	.23	.06
☐	102T Steve Rodriguez USA	.05	.02	.01
☐	103T Tom Runnells MG	.05	.02	.01
☐	104T Scott Sanderson	.05	.02	.01
☐	105T Bob Scanlan	.05	.02	.01
☐	106T Pete Schourek	.05	.02	.01
☐	107T Gary Scott	.05	.02	.01
☐	108T Paul Shuey USA	.40	.18	.05
☐	109T Doug Simons	.05	.02	.01
☐	110T Dave Smith	.05	.02	.01
☐	111T Cory Snyder	.05	.02	.01
☐	112T Luis Sojo	.05	.02	.01
☐	113T Kennie Steenstra USA	.25	.11	.03
☐	114T Darryl Strawberry	.10	.05	.01
☐	115T Franklin Stubbs	.05	.02	.01
☐	116T Todd Taylor USA	.05	.02	.01
☐	117T Wade Taylor	.05	.02	.01
☐	118T Garry Templeton	.05	.02	.01
☐	119T Mickey Tettleton	.08	.04	.01
☐	120T Tim Teufel	.05	.02	.01
☐	121T Mike Timlin	.05	.02	.01
☐	122T David Tuttle USA	.05	.02	.01
☐	123T Mo Vaughn	.40	.18	.05
☐	124T Jeff Ware USA	.05	.02	.01
☐	125T Devon White	.08	.04	.01
☐	126T Mark Whiten	.10	.05	.01
☐	127T Mitch Williams	.08	.04	.01
☐	128T Craig Wilson USA	.05	.02	.01
☐	129T Willie Wilson	.05	.02	.01
☐	130T Chris Wimmer	.15	.07	.02
☐	131T Ivan Zweig USA	.05	.02	.01
☐	132T Checklist 1T-132T	.05	.02	.01

1992 Topps

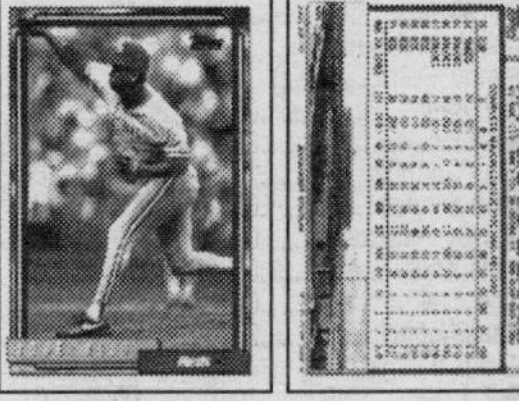

The 1992 Topps set contains 792 cards measuring the standard size (2 1/2" by 3 1/2"). The fronts have either posed or action color player photos on a white card face. Different color stripes frame the pictures, and the player's name and team name appear in two short color stripes respectively at the bottom. In a horizontal format, the backs have biography and complete career batting or pitching record. In addition, some of the cards have a picture of a baseball field and stadium on the back. Special subsets included are Record Breakers (2-5), Prospects (58, 126, 179, 473, 551, 591, 618, 656, 676), and All-Stars (386-407). The cards are numbered on the back. These cards were not issued with bubble gum and feature white card stock. The key Rookie Cards in this set are Cliff Floyd, Shawn Green, Manny Ramirez, Aaron Sele, and Brien Taylor. The complete 1992 Topps set was also issued as a factory set of micro baseball cards with cards measuring approximately one-fourth the size of the regular size cards but identical in other respects. The micro set and its cards are valued at approximately half the values listed below for the regular size cards.

	MINT	EXC	G-VG
COMPLETE SET (792)	20.00	9.00	2.50
COMPLETE FACT.SET (802)	30.00	13.50	3.80
COMPLETE HOLIDAY SET (811)	35.00	16.00	4.40
COMMON CARD (1-792)	.05	.02	.01
☐ 1 Nolan Ryan	1.00	.45	.13
☐ 2 Ricky Henderson RB (Some cards have print marks that show 1.991 on the front)	.10	.05	.01
☐ 3 Jeff Reardon RB	.05	.02	.01
☐ 4 Nolan Ryan RB	.50	.23	.06
☐ 5 Dave Winfield RB	.10	.05	.01
☐ 6 Brien Taylor	.25	.11	.03
☐ 7 Jim Olander	.05	.02	.01
☐ 8 Bryan Hickerson	.05	.02	.01
☐ 9 Jon Farrell	.15	.07	.02
☐ 10 Wade Boggs	.15	.07	.02
☐ 11 Jack McDowell	.15	.07	.02
☐ 12 Luis Gonzalez	.10	.05	.01
☐ 13 Mike Scioscia	.05	.02	.01
☐ 14 Wes Chamberlain	.10	.05	.01
☐ 15 Dennis Martinez	.10	.05	.01
☐ 16 Jeff Montgomery	.10	.05	.01
☐ 17 Randy Milligan	.05	.02	.01
☐ 18 Greg Cadaret	.05	.02	.01
☐ 19 Jamie Quirk	.05	.02	.01
☐ 20 Bip Roberts	.05	.02	.01
☐ 21 Buck Rogers MG	.05	.02	.01
☐ 22 Bill Wegman	.05	.02	.01
☐ 23 Chuck Knoblauch	.15	.07	.02
☐ 24 Randy Myers	.10	.05	.01
☐ 25 Ron Gant	.10	.05	.01
☐ 26 Mike Bielecki	.05	.02	.01
☐ 27 Juan Gonzalez	.60	.25	.08
☐ 28 Mike Schooler	.05	.02	.01
☐ 29 Mickey Tettleton	.10	.05	.01
☐ 30 John Kruk	.15	.07	.02
☐ 31 Bryn Smith	.05	.02	.01
☐ 32 Chris Nabholz	.05	.02	.01
☐ 33 Carlos Baerga	.20	.09	.03
☐ 34 Jeff Juden	.10	.05	.01
☐ 35 Dave Righetti	.05	.02	.01
☐ 36 Scott Ruffcorn	.25	.11	.03
☐ 37 Luis Polonia	.05	.02	.01
☐ 38 Tom Candiotti	.05	.02	.01
☐ 39 Greg Olson	.05	.02	.01
☐ 40 Cal Ripken	.40	.18	.05
☐ 41 Craig Lefferts	.05	.02	.01
☐ 42 Mike Macfarlane	.05	.02	.01
☐ 43 Jose Lind	.05	.02	.01
☐ 44 Rick Aguilera	.10	.05	.01
☐ 45 Gary Carter	.15	.07	.02
☐ 46 Steve Farr	.05	.02	.01
☐ 47 Rex Hudler	.05	.02	.01
☐ 48 Scott Scudder	.05	.02	.01
☐ 49 Damon Berryhill	.05	.02	.01
☐ 50 Ken Griffey Jr.	1.50	.65	.19
☐ 51 Tom Runnells MG	.05	.02	.01
☐ 52 Juan Bell	.05	.02	.01
☐ 53 Tommy Gregg	.05	.02	.01
☐ 54 David Wells	.05	.02	.01
☐ 55 Rafael Palmeiro	.15	.07	.02
☐ 56 Charlie O'Brien	.05	.02	.01
☐ 57 Donn Pall	.05	.02	.01
☐ 58 1992 Prospects C: Brad Ausmus, Jim Campanis Jr., Dave Nilsson, Doug Robbins	.15	.07	.02
☐ 59 Mo Vaughn	.20	.09	.03
☐ 60 Tony Fernandez	.10	.05	.01
☐ 61 Paul O'Neill	.10	.05	.01
☐ 62 Gene Nelson	.05	.02	.01
☐ 63 Randy Ready	.05	.02	.01
☐ 64 Bob Kipper	.05	.02	.01
☐ 65 Willie McGee	.10	.05	.01
☐ 66 Scott Stahoviak	.15	.07	.02
☐ 67 Luis Salazar	.05	.02	.01
☐ 68 Marvin Freeman	.05	.02	.01
☐ 69 Kenny Lofton	1.00	.45	.13
☐ 70 Gary Gaetti	.05	.02	.01
☐ 71 Erik Hanson	.05	.02	.01
☐ 72 Eddie Zosky	.10	.05	.01
☐ 73 Brian Barnes	.05	.02	.01
☐ 74 Scott Leius	.05	.02	.01
☐ 75 Bret Saberhagen	.10	.05	.01
☐ 76 Mike Gallego	.05	.02	.01
☐ 77 Jack Armstrong	.05	.02	.01
☐ 78 Ivan Rodriguez	.15	.07	.02
☐ 79 Jesse Orosco	.05	.02	.01
☐ 80 David Justice	.20	.09	.03
☐ 81 Ced Landrum	.05	.02	.01
☐ 82 Doug Simons	.05	.02	.01
☐ 83 Tommy Greene	.10	.05	.01
☐ 84 Leo Gomez	.05	.02	.01
☐ 85 Jose DeLeon	.05	.02	.01
☐ 86 Steve Finley	.05	.02	.01
☐ 87 Bob MacDonald	.05	.02	.01
☐ 88 Darrin Jackson	.05	.02	.01
☐ 89 Neal Heaton	.05	.02	.01
☐ 90 Robin Yount	.20	.09	.03
☐ 91 Jeff Reed	.05	.02	.01
☐ 92 Lenny Harris	.05	.02	.01
☐ 93 Reggie Jefferson	.05	.02	.01
☐ 94 Sammy Sosa	.15	.07	.02
☐ 95 Scott Bailes	.05	.02	.01
☐ 96 Tom McKinnon	.05	.02	.01
☐ 97 Luis Rivera	.05	.02	.01
☐ 98 Mike Harkey	.05	.02	.01
☐ 99 Jeff Treadway	.05	.02	.01
☐ 100 Jose Canseco	.20	.09	.03
☐ 101 Omar Vizquel	.05	.02	.01
☐ 102 Scott Kamieniecki	.05	.02	.01
☐ 103 Ricky Jordan	.05	.02	.01
☐ 104 Jeff Ballard	.05	.02	.01
☐ 105 Felix Jose	.10	.05	.01
☐ 106 Mike Boddicker	.05	.02	.01
☐ 107 Dan Pasqua	.05	.02	.01
☐ 108 Mike Timlin	.05	.02	.01
☐ 109 Roger Craig MG	.05	.02	.01
☐ 110 Ryne Sandberg	.30	.14	.04
☐ 111 Mark Carreon	.05	.02	.01
☐ 112 Oscar Azocar	.05	.02	.01
☐ 113 Mike Greenwell	.10	.05	.01
☐ 114 Mark Portugal	.05	.02	.01
☐ 115 Terry Pendleton	.15	.07	.02
☐ 116 Willie Randolph	.10	.05	.01
☐ 117 Scott Terry	.05	.02	.01
☐ 118 Chili Davis	.10	.05	.01
☐ 119 Mark Gardner	.05	.02	.01
☐ 120 Alan Trammell	.15	.07	.02
☐ 121 Derek Bell	.10	.05	.01
☐ 122 Gary Varsho	.05	.02	.01
☐ 123 Bob Ojeda	.05	.02	.01
☐ 124 Shawn Livsey	.05	.02	.01
☐ 125 Chris Hoiles	.15	.07	.02
☐ 126 1992 Prospects 1B: Ryan Klesko, John Jaha, Rico Brogna, Dave Staton	1.00	.45	.13
☐ 127 Carlos Quintana	.05	.02	.01
☐ 128 Kurt Stillwell	.05	.02	.01
☐ 129 Melido Perez	.05	.02	.01

☐ 130 Alvin Davis .05 .02 .01
☐ 131 Checklist 1-132 .05 .02 .01
☐ 132 Eric Show .05 .02 .01
☐ 133 Rance Mulliniks .05 .02 .01
☐ 134 Darryl Kile .10 .05 .01
☐ 135 Von Hayes .05 .02 .01
☐ 136 Bill Doran .05 .02 .01
☐ 137 Jeff D. Robinson .05 .02 .01
☐ 138 Monty Fariss .05 .02 .01
☐ 139 Jeff Innis .05 .02 .01
☐ 140 Mark Grace UER .15 .07 .02
(Home Calie., should
be Calif.)
☐ 141 Jim Leyland MG UER .05 .02 .01
(No closed parenthesis
after East in 1991)
☐ 142 Todd Van Poppel .15 .07 .02
☐ 143 Paul Gibson .05 .02 .01
☐ 144 Bill Swift .10 .05 .01
☐ 145 Danny Tartabull .10 .05 .01
☐ 146 Al Newman .05 .02 .01
☐ 147 Cris Carpenter .05 .02 .01
☐ 148 Anthony Young .10 .05 .01
☐ 149 Brian Bohanon .05 .02 .01
☐ 150 Roger Clemens UER .25 .11 .03
(League leading ERA in
1990 not italicized)
☐ 151 Jeff Hamilton .05 .02 .01
☐ 152 Charlie Leibrandt .05 .02 .01
☐ 153 Ron Karkovice .05 .02 .01
☐ 154 Hensley Meulens .05 .02 .01
☐ 155 Scott Bankhead .05 .02 .01
☐ 156 Manny Ramirez 1.50 .65 .19
☐ 157 Keith Miller .05 .02 .01
☐ 158 Todd Frohwirth .05 .02 .01
☐ 159 Darrin Fletcher .05 .02 .01
☐ 160 Bobby Bonilla .15 .07 .02
☐ 161 Casey Candaele .05 .02 .01
☐ 162 Paul Faries .05 .02 .01
☐ 163 Dana Kiecker .05 .02 .01
☐ 164 Shane Mack .10 .05 .01
☐ 165 Mark Langston .15 .07 .02
☐ 166 Geronimo Pena .05 .02 .01
☐ 167 Andy Allanson .05 .02 .01
☐ 168 Dwight Smith .05 .02 .01
☐ 169 Chuck Crim .05 .02 .01
☐ 170 Alex Cole .05 .02 .01
☐ 171 Bill Plummer MG .05 .02 .01
☐ 172 Juan Berenguer .05 .02 .01
☐ 173 Brian Downing .05 .02 .01
☐ 174 Steve Frey .05 .02 .01
☐ 175 Orel Hershiser .10 .05 .01
☐ 176 Ramon Garcia .05 .02 .01
☐ 177 Dan Gladden .05 .02 .01
☐ 178 Jim Acker .05 .02 .01
☐ 179 1992 Prospects 2B .05 .02 .01
Bobby DeJardin
Cesar Bernhardt
Armando Moreno
Andy Stankiewicz
☐ 180 Kevin Mitchell .10 .05 .01
☐ 181 Hector Villanueva .05 .02 .01
☐ 182 Jeff Reardon .10 .05 .01
☐ 183 Brent Mayne .05 .02 .01
☐ 184 Jimmy Jones .05 .02 .01
☐ 185 Benito Santiago .05 .02 .01
☐ 186 Cliff Floyd 1.25 .55 .16
☐ 187 Ernest Riles .05 .02 .01
☐ 188 Jose Guzman .05 .02 .01
☐ 189 Junior Felix .05 .02 .01
☐ 190 Glenn Davis .05 .02 .01
☐ 191 Charlie Hough .10 .05 .01
☐ 192 Dave Fleming .10 .05 .01
☐ 193 Omar Olivares .05 .02 .01
☐ 194 Eric Karros .15 .07 .02
☐ 195 David Cone .15 .07 .02
☐ 196 Frank Castillo .05 .02 .01
☐ 197 Glenn Braggs .05 .02 .01
☐ 198 Scott Aldred .05 .02 .01
☐ 199 Jeff Blauser .10 .05 .01
☐ 200 Len Dykstra .15 .07 .02
☐ 201 Buck Showalter MG .05 .02 .01
☐ 202 Rick Honeycutt .05 .02 .01
☐ 203 Greg Myers .05 .02 .01
☐ 204 Trevor Wilson .05 .02 .01
☐ 205 Jay Howell .05 .02 .01
☐ 206 Luis Sojo .05 .02 .01
☐ 207 Jack Clark .10 .05 .01
☐ 208 Julio Machado .05 .02 .01
☐ 209 Lloyd McClendon .05 .02 .01
☐ 210 Ozzie Guillen .05 .02 .01
☐ 211 Jeremy Hernandez .10 .05 .01
☐ 212 Randy Velarde .05 .02 .01
☐ 213 Les Lancaster .05 .02 .01
☐ 214 Andy Mota .05 .02 .01
☐ 215 Rich Gossage .15 .07 .02
☐ 216 Brent Gates .25 .11 .03
☐ 217 Brian Harper .05 .02 .01
☐ 218 Mike Flanagan .05 .02 .01
☐ 219 Jerry Browne .05 .02 .01
☐ 220 Jose Rijo .10 .05 .01
☐ 221 Skeeter Barnes .05 .02 .01
☐ 222 Jaime Navarro .05 .02 .01
☐ 223 Mel Hall .05 .02 .01
☐ 224 Bret Barberie .05 .02 .01
☐ 225 Roberto Alomar .25 .11 .03
☐ 226 Pete Smith .05 .02 .01
☐ 227 Daryl Boston .05 .02 .01
☐ 228 Eddie Whitson .05 .02 .01
☐ 229 Shawn Boskie .05 .02 .01
☐ 230 Dick Schofield .05 .02 .01
☐ 231 Brian Drahman .05 .02 .01
☐ 232 John Smiley .05 .02 .01
☐ 233 Mitch Webster .05 .02 .01
☐ 234 Terry Steinbach .10 .05 .01
☐ 235 Jack Morris .15 .07 .02
☐ 236 Bill Pecota .05 .02 .01
☐ 237 Jose Hernandez .05 .02 .01
☐ 238 Greg Litton .05 .02 .01
☐ 239 Brian Holman .05 .02 .01
☐ 240 Andres Galarraga .15 .07 .02
☐ 241 Gerald Young .05 .02 .01
☐ 242 Mike Mussina .30 .14 .04
☐ 243 Alvaro Espinoza .05 .02 .01
☐ 244 Darren Daulton .15 .07 .02
☐ 245 John Smoltz .10 .05 .01
☐ 246 Jason Pruitt .05 .02 .01
☐ 247 Chuck Finley .05 .02 .01
☐ 248 Jim Gantner .05 .02 .01
☐ 249 Tony Fossas .05 .02 .01
☐ 250 Ken Griffey .10 .05 .01
☐ 251 Kevin Elster .05 .02 .01
☐ 252 Dennis Rasmussen .05 .02 .01
☐ 253 Terry Kennedy .05 .02 .01
☐ 254 Ryan Bowen .05 .02 .01
☐ 255 Robin Ventura .15 .07 .02
☐ 256 Mike Aldrete .05 .02 .01
☐ 257 Jeff Russell .05 .02 .01
☐ 258 Jim Lindeman .05 .02 .01
☐ 259 Ron Darling .05 .02 .01
☐ 260 Devon White .10 .05 .01
☐ 261 Tom Lasorda MG .10 .05 .01
☐ 262 Terry Lee .05 .02 .01
☐ 263 Bob Patterson .05 .02 .01
☐ 264 Checklist 133-264 .05 .02 .01
☐ 265 Teddy Higuera .05 .02 .01

☐	266 Roberto Kelly	.10	.05	.01
☐	267 Steve Bedrosian	.05	.02	.01
☐	268 Brady Anderson	.10	.05	.01
☐	269 Ruben Amaro Jr.	.05	.02	.01
☐	270 Tony Gwynn	.25	.11	.03
☐	271 Tracy Jones	.05	.02	.01
☐	272 Jerry Don Gleaton	.05	.02	.01
☐	273 Craig Grebeck	.05	.02	.01
☐	274 Bob Scanlan	.05	.02	.01
☐	275 Todd Zeile	.10	.05	.01
☐	276 Shawn Green	.75	.35	.09
☐	277 Scott Chiamparino	.05	.02	.01
☐	278 Darryl Hamilton	.10	.05	.01
☐	279 Jim Clancy	.05	.02	.01
☐	280 Carlos Martinez	.05	.02	.01
☐	281 Kevin Appier	.10	.05	.01
☐	282 John Wehner	.05	.02	.01
☐	283 Reggie Sanders	.20	.09	.03
☐	284 Gene Larkin	.05	.02	.01
☐	285 Bob Welch	.05	.02	.01
☐	286 Gilberto Reyes	.05	.02	.01
☐	287 Pete Schourek	.10	.05	.01
☐	288 Andujar Cedeno	.10	.05	.01
☐	289 Mike Morgan	.05	.02	.01
☐	290 Bo Jackson	.15	.07	.02
☐	291 Phil Garner MG	.05	.02	.01
☐	292 Ray Lankford	.15	.07	.02
☐	293 Mike Henneman	.05	.02	.01
☐	294 Dave Valle	.05	.02	.01
☐	295 Alonzo Powell	.05	.02	.01
☐	296 Tom Brunansky	.05	.02	.01
☐	297 Kevin Brown	.10	.05	.01
☐	298 Kelly Gruber	.05	.02	.01
☐	299 Charles Nagy	.05	.02	.01
☐	300 Don Mattingly	.30	.14	.04
☐	301 Kirk McCaskill	.05	.02	.01
☐	302 Joey Cora	.05	.02	.01
☐	303 Dan Plesac	.05	.02	.01
☐	304 Joe Oliver	.05	.02	.01
☐	305 Tom Glavine	.15	.07	.02
☐	306 Al Shirley	.20	.09	.03
☐	307 Bruce Ruffin	.05	.02	.01
☐	308 Craig Shipley	.10	.05	.01
☐	309 Dave Martinez	.05	.02	.01
☐	310 Jose Mesa	.05	.02	.01
☐	311 Henry Cotto	.05	.02	.01
☐	312 Mike LaValliere	.05	.02	.01
☐	313 Kevin Tapani	.05	.02	.01
☐	314 Jeff Huson (Shows Jose Canseco sliding into second)	.05	.02	.01
☐	315 Juan Samuel	.05	.02	.01
☐	316 Curt Schilling	.10	.05	.01
☐	317 Mike Bordick	.05	.02	.01
☐	318 Steve Howe	.05	.02	.01
☐	319 Tony Phillips	.05	.02	.01
☐	320 George Bell	.10	.05	.01
☐	321 Lou Piniella MG	.05	.02	.01
☐	322 Tim Burke	.05	.02	.01
☐	323 Milt Thompson	.05	.02	.01
☐	324 Danny Darwin	.05	.02	.01
☐	325 Joe Orsulak	.05	.02	.01
☐	326 Eric King	.05	.02	.01
☐	327 Jay Buhner	.10	.05	.01
☐	328 Joel Johnston	.05	.02	.01
☐	329 Franklin Stubbs	.05	.02	.01
☐	330 Will Clark	.20	.09	.03
☐	331 Steve Lake	.05	.02	.01
☐	332 Chris Jones	.05	.02	.01
☐	333 Pat Tabler	.05	.02	.01
☐	334 Kevin Gross	.05	.02	.01
☐	335 Dave Henderson	.05	.02	.01
☐	336 Greg Anthony	.05	.02	.01
☐	337 Alejandro Pena	.05	.02	.01
☐	338 Shawn Abner	.05	.02	.01
☐	339 Tom Browning	.05	.02	.01
☐	340 Otis Nixon	.10	.05	.01
☐	341 Bob Geren	.05	.02	.01
☐	342 Tim Spehr	.05	.02	.01
☐	343 John Vander Wal	.10	.05	.01
☐	344 Jack Daugherty	.05	.02	.01
☐	345 Zane Smith	.05	.02	.01
☐	346 Rheal Cormier	.05	.02	.01
☐	347 Kent Hrbek	.10	.05	.01
☐	348 Rick Wilkins	.10	.05	.01
☐	349 Steve Lyons	.05	.02	.01
☐	350 Gregg Olson	.05	.02	.01
☐	351 Greg Riddoch MG	.05	.02	.01
☐	352 Ed Nunez	.05	.02	.01
☐	353 Braulio Castillo	.05	.02	.01
☐	354 Dave Bergman	.05	.02	.01
☐	355 Warren Newson	.05	.02	.01
☐	356 Luis Quinones	.05	.02	.01
☐	357 Mike Witt	.05	.02	.01
☐	358 Ted Wood	.05	.02	.01
☐	359 Mike Moore	.05	.02	.01
☐	360 Lance Parrish	.10	.05	.01
☐	361 Barry Jones	.05	.02	.01
☐	362 Javier Ortiz	.05	.02	.01
☐	363 John Candelaria	.05	.02	.01
☐	364 Glenallen Hill	.05	.02	.01
☐	365 Duane Ward	.10	.05	.01
☐	366 Checklist 265-396	.05	.02	.01
☐	367 Rafael Belliard	.05	.02	.01
☐	368 Bill Krueger	.05	.02	.01
☐	369 Steve Whitaker	.15	.07	.02
☐	370 Shawon Dunston	.05	.02	.01
☐	371 Dante Bichette	.15	.07	.02
☐	372 Kip Gross	.10	.05	.01
☐	373 Don Robinson	.05	.02	.01
☐	374 Bernie Williams	.10	.05	.01
☐	375 Bert Blyleven	.15	.07	.02
☐	376 Chris Donnels	.05	.02	.01
☐	377 Bob Zupcic	.10	.05	.01
☐	378 Joel Skinner	.05	.02	.01
☐	379 Steve Chitren	.05	.02	.01
☐	380 Barry Bonds	.40	.18	.05
☐	381 Sparky Anderson MG	.10	.05	.01
☐	382 Sid Fernandez	.10	.05	.01
☐	383 Dave Hollins	.15	.07	.02
☐	384 Mark Lee	.05	.02	.01
☐	385 Tim Wallach	.05	.02	.01
☐	386 Will Clark AS	.10	.05	.01
☐	387 Ryne Sandberg AS	.20	.09	.03
☐	388 Howard Johnson AS	.05	.02	.01
☐	389 Barry Larkin AS	.10	.05	.01
☐	390 Barry Bonds AS	.25	.11	.03
☐	391 Ron Gant AS	.10	.05	.01
☐	392 Bobby Bonilla AS	.10	.05	.01
☐	393 Craig Biggio AS	.05	.02	.01
☐	394 Dennis Martinez AS	.05	.02	.01
☐	395 Tom Glavine AS	.10	.05	.01
☐	396 Lee Smith AS	.10	.05	.01
☐	397 Cecil Fielder AS	.10	.05	.01
☐	398 Julio Franco AS	.05	.02	.01
☐	399 Wade Boggs AS	.10	.05	.01
☐	400 Cal Ripken AS	.20	.09	.03
☐	401 Jose Canseco AS	.10	.05	.01
☐	402 Joe Carter AS	.10	.05	.01
☐	403 Ruben Sierra AS	.10	.05	.01
☐	404 Matt Nokes AS	.05	.02	.01
☐	405 Roger Clemens AS	.15	.07	.02
☐	406 Jim Abbott AS	.10	.05	.01
☐	407 Bryan Harvey AS	.05	.02	.01
☐	408 Bob Milacki	.05	.02	.01
☐	409 Geno Petralli	.05	.02	.01

☐ 410 Dave Stewart .10 .05 .01
☐ 411 Mike Jackson .05 .02 .01
☐ 412 Luis Aquino .05 .02 .01
☐ 413 Tim Teufel .05 .02 .01
☐ 414 Jeff Ware .05 .02 .01
☐ 415 Jim Deshaies .05 .02 .01
☐ 416 Ellis Burks .10 .05 .01
☐ 417 Allan Anderson .05 .02 .01
☐ 418 Alfredo Griffin .05 .02 .01
☐ 419 Wally Whitehurst .05 .02 .01
☐ 420 Sandy Alomar Jr. .10 .05 .01
☐ 421 Juan Agosto .05 .02 .01
☐ 422 Sam Horn .05 .02 .01
☐ 423 Jeff Fassero .05 .02 .01
☐ 424 Paul McClellan .05 .02 .01
☐ 425 Cecil Fielder .15 .07 .02
☐ 426 Tim Raines .15 .07 .02
☐ 427 Eddie Taubensee .05 .02 .01
☐ 428 Dennis Boyd .05 .02 .01
☐ 429 Tony LaRussa MG .10 .05 .01
☐ 430 Steve Sax .05 .02 .01
☐ 431 Tom Gordon .05 .02 .01
☐ 432 Billy Hatcher .05 .02 .01
☐ 433 Cal Eldred .10 .05 .01
☐ 434 Wally Backman .05 .02 .01
☐ 435 Mark Eichhorn .05 .02 .01
☐ 436 Mookie Wilson .05 .02 .01
☐ 437 Scott Servais .05 .02 .01
☐ 438 Mike Maddux .05 .02 .01
☐ 439 Chico Walker .05 .02 .01
☐ 440 Doug Drabek .15 .07 .02
☐ 441 Rob Deer .05 .02 .01
☐ 442 Dave West .05 .02 .01
☐ 443 Spike Owen .05 .02 .01
☐ 444 Tyrone Hill .15 .07 .02
☐ 445 Matt Williams .20 .09 .03
☐ 446 Mark Lewis .10 .05 .01
☐ 447 David Segui .05 .02 .01
☐ 448 Tom Pagnozzi .05 .02 .01
☐ 449 Jeff Johnson .05 .02 .01
☐ 450 Mark McGwire .15 .07 .02
☐ 451 Tom Henke .10 .05 .01
☐ 452 Wilson Alvarez .15 .07 .02
☐ 453 Gary Redus .05 .02 .01
☐ 454 Darren Holmes .05 .02 .01
☐ 455 Pete O'Brien .05 .02 .01
☐ 456 Pat Combs .05 .02 .01
☐ 457 Hubie Brooks .05 .02 .01
☐ 458 Frank Tanana .05 .02 .01
☐ 459 Tom Kelly MG .05 .02 .01
☐ 460 Andre Dawson .15 .07 .02
☐ 461 Doug Jones .05 .02 .01
☐ 462 Rich Rodriguez .05 .02 .01
☐ 463 Mike Simms .05 .02 .01
☐ 464 Mike Jeffcoat .05 .02 .01
☐ 465 Barry Larkin .15 .07 .02
☐ 466 Stan Belinda .05 .02 .01
☐ 467 Lonnie Smith .05 .02 .01
☐ 468 Greg Harris .05 .02 .01
☐ 469 Jim Eisenreich .05 .02 .01
☐ 470 Pedro Guerrero .10 .05 .01
☐ 471 Jose DeJesus .05 .02 .01
☐ 472 Rich Rowland .05 .02 .01
☐ 473 1992 Prospects 3B UER .05 .02 .01
Frank Bolick
Craig Paquette
Tom Redington
Paul Russo
(Line around top border)
☐ 474 Mike Rossiter .05 .02 .01
☐ 475 Robby Thompson .05 .02 .01
☐ 476 Randy Bush .05 .02 .01
☐ 477 Greg Hibbard .05 .02 .01
☐ 478 Dale Sveum .05 .02 .01
☐ 479 Chito Martinez .05 .02 .01
☐ 480 Scott Sanderson .05 .02 .01
☐ 481 Tino Martinez .10 .05 .01
☐ 482 Jimmy Key .10 .05 .01
☐ 483 Terry Shumpert .05 .02 .01
☐ 484 Mike Hartley .05 .02 .01
☐ 485 Chris Sabo .10 .05 .01
☐ 486 Bob Walk .05 .02 .01
☐ 487 John Cerutti .05 .02 .01
☐ 488 Scott Cooper .10 .05 .01
☐ 489 Bobby Cox MG .05 .02 .01
☐ 490 Julio Franco .10 .05 .01
☐ 491 Jeff Brantley .05 .02 .01
☐ 492 Mike Devereaux .10 .05 .01
☐ 493 Jose Offerman .05 .02 .01
☐ 494 Gary Thurman .05 .02 .01
☐ 495 Carney Lansford .10 .05 .01
☐ 496 Joe Grahe .05 .02 .01
☐ 497 Andy Ashby .05 .02 .01
☐ 498 Gerald Perry .05 .02 .01
☐ 499 Dave Otto .05 .02 .01
☐ 500 Vince Coleman .05 .02 .01
☐ 501 Rob Mallicoat .05 .02 .01
☐ 502 Greg Briley .05 .02 .01
☐ 503 Pascual Perez .05 .02 .01
☐ 504 Aaron Sele .60 .25 .08
☐ 505 Bobby Thigpen .05 .02 .01
☐ 506 Todd Benzinger .05 .02 .01
☐ 507 Candy Maldonado .05 .02 .01
☐ 508 Bill Gullickson .05 .02 .01
☐ 509 Doug Dascenzo .05 .02 .01
☐ 510 Frank Viola .10 .05 .01
☐ 511 Kenny Rogers .05 .02 .01
☐ 512 Mike Heath .05 .02 .01
☐ 513 Kevin Bass .05 .02 .01
☐ 514 Kim Batiste .05 .02 .01
☐ 515 Delino DeShields .15 .07 .02
☐ 516 Ed Sprague Jr. .10 .05 .01
☐ 517 Jim Gott .05 .02 .01
☐ 518 Jose Melendez .05 .02 .01
☐ 519 Hal McRae MG .05 .02 .01
☐ 520 Jeff Bagwell .75 .35 .09
☐ 521 Joe Hesketh .05 .02 .01
☐ 522 Milt Cuyler .05 .02 .01
☐ 523 Shawn Hillegas .05 .02 .01
☐ 524 Don Slaught .05 .02 .01
☐ 525 Randy Johnson .15 .07 .02
☐ 526 Doug Piatt .05 .02 .01
☐ 527 Checklist 397-528 .05 .02 .01
☐ 528 Steve Foster .10 .05 .01
☐ 529 Joe Girardi .05 .02 .01
☐ 530 Jim Abbott .15 .07 .02
☐ 531 Larry Walker .15 .07 .02
☐ 532 Mike Huff .05 .02 .01
☐ 533 Mackey Sasser .05 .02 .01
☐ 534 Benji Gil .20 .09 .03
☐ 535 Dave Stieb .10 .05 .01
☐ 536 Willie Wilson .05 .02 .01
☐ 537 Mark Leiter .05 .02 .01
☐ 538 Jose Uribe .05 .02 .01
☐ 539 Thomas Howard .05 .02 .01
☐ 540 Ben McDonald .10 .05 .01
☐ 541 Jose Tolentino .05 .02 .01
☐ 542 Keith Mitchell .10 .05 .01
☐ 543 Jerome Walton .05 .02 .01
☐ 544 Cliff Brantley .10 .05 .01
☐ 545 Andy Van Slyke .15 .07 .02
☐ 546 Paul Sorrento .05 .02 .01
☐ 547 Herm Winningham .05 .02 .01
☐ 548 Mark Guthrie .05 .02 .01
☐ 549 Joe Torre MG .05 .02 .01
☐ 550 Darryl Strawberry .10 .05 .01

☐ 551 1992 Prospects SS UER .60 .25 .08
Wilfredo Cordero
Chipper Jones
Manny Alexander
Alex Arias
(No line around
top border)
☐ 552 Dave Gallagher............ .05 .02 .01
☐ 553 Edgar Martinez............ .10 .05 .01
☐ 554 Donald Harris.............. .05 .02 .01
☐ 555 Frank Thomas........... 1.50 .65 .19
☐ 556 Storm Davis................ .05 .02 .01
☐ 557 Dickie Thon................. .05 .02 .01
☐ 558 Scott Garrelts.............. .05 .02 .01
☐ 559 Steve Olin .... .05 .02 .01
☐ 560 Rickey Henderson........ .15 .07 .02
☐ 561 Jose Vizcaino.............. .05 .02 .01
☐ 562 Wade Taylor................ .05 .02 .01
☐ 563 Pat Borders................. .05 .02 .01
☐ 564 Jimmy Gonzalez.......... .05 .02 .01
☐ 565 Lee Smith .... .15 .07 .02
☐ 566 Bill Sampen.................. .05 .02 .01
☐ 567 Dean Palmer .... .10 .05 .01
☐ 568 Bryan Harvey .... .10 .05 .01
☐ 569 Tony Pena.................... .05 .02 .01
☐ 570 Lou Whitaker .... .15 .07 .02
☐ 571 Randy Tomlin .... .05 .02 .01
☐ 572 Greg Vaughn................ .10 .05 .01
☐ 573 Kelly Downs................. .05 .02 .01
☐ 574 Steve Avery UER.......... .15 .07 .02
(Should be 13 games
for Durham in 1989)
☐ 575 Kirby Puckett .... .35 .16 .04
☐ 576 Heathcliff Slocumb ...... .05 .02 .01
☐ 577 Kevin Seitzer............... .05 .02 .01
☐ 578 Lee Guetterman........... .05 .02 .01
☐ 579 Johnny Oates MG........ .05 .02 .01
☐ 580 Greg Maddux............... .20 .09 .03
☐ 581 Stan Javier.................. .05 .02 .01
☐ 582 Vicente Palacios........... .05 .02 .01
☐ 583 Mel Rojas..................... .05 .02 .01
☐ 584 Wayne Rosenthal......... .05 .02 .01
☐ 585 Lenny Webster............. .05 .02 .01
☐ 586 Rod Nichols.................. .05 .02 .01
☐ 587 Mickey Morandini .... .05 .02 .01
☐ 588 Russ Swan.................... .05 .02 .01
☐ 589 Mariano Duncan .... .05 .02 .01
☐ 590 Howard Johnson.......... .10 .05 .01
☐ 591 1992 Prospects OF ...... .10 .05 .01
Jeromy Burnitz
Jacob Brumfield
Alan Cockrell
D.J. Dozier
☐ 592 Denny Neagle.............. .05 .02 .01
☐ 593 Steve Decker............... .05 .02 .01
☐ 594 Brian Barber................ .15 .07 .02
☐ 595 Bruce Hurst................. .05 .02 .01
☐ 596 Kent Mercker .... .05 .02 .01
☐ 597 Mike Magnante .... .05 .02 .01
☐ 598 Jody Reed.................... .05 .02 .01
☐ 599 Steve Searcy .... .05 .02 .01
☐ 600 Paul Molitor................. .20 .09 .03
☐ 601 Dave Smith .... .05 .02 .01
☐ 602 Mike Fetters................. .05 .02 .01
☐ 603 Luis Mercedes .... .10 .05 .01
☐ 604 Chris Gwynn .... .05 .02 .01
☐ 605 Scott Erickson.............. .05 .02 .01
☐ 606 Brook Jacoby............... .05 .02 .01
☐ 607 Todd Stottlemyre .... .05 .02 .01
☐ 608 Scott Bradley .... .05 .02 .01
☐ 609 Mike Hargrove MG....... .05 .02 .01
☐ 610 Eric Davis..................... .05 .02 .01
☐ 611 Brian Hunter .... .05 .02 .01
☐ 612 Pat Kelly...................... .10 .05 .01
☐ 613 Pedro Munoz .... .10 .05 .01
☐ 614 Al Osuna .... .05 .02 .01
☐ 615 Matt Merullo .... .05 .02 .01
☐ 616 Larry Andersen .... .05 .02 .01
☐ 617 Junior Ortiz.................. .05 .02 .01
☐ 618 1992 Prospects OF ...... .05 .02 .01
Cesar Hernandez
Steve Hosey
Jeff McNeely
Dan Peltier
☐ 619 Danny Jackson .... .05 .02 .01
☐ 620 George Brett .... .30 .14 .04
☐ 621 Dan Gakeler .... .05 .02 .01
☐ 622 Steve Buechele .... .05 .02 .01
☐ 623 Bob Tewksbury............. .05 .02 .01
☐ 624 Shawn Estes .... .15 .07 .02
☐ 625 Kevin McReynolds .... .05 .02 .01
☐ 626 Chris Haney .... .05 .02 .01
☐ 627 Mike Sharperson.......... .05 .02 .01
☐ 628 Mark Williamson.......... .05 .02 .01
☐ 629 Wally Joyner................ .10 .05 .01
☐ 630 Carlton Fisk.................. .15 .07 .02
☐ 631 Armando Reynoso .... .05 .02 .01
☐ 632 Felix Fermin .... .05 .02 .01
☐ 633 Mitch Williams............. .10 .05 .01
☐ 634 Manny Lee .... .05 .02 .01
☐ 635 Harold Baines .... .10 .05 .01
☐ 636 Greg Harris .... .05 .02 .01
☐ 637 Orlando Merced........... .10 .05 .01
☐ 638 Chris Bosio .... .05 .02 .01
☐ 639 Wayne Housie.............. .10 .05 .01
☐ 640 Xavier Hernandez......... .05 .02 .01
☐ 641 David Howard .... .05 .02 .01
☐ 642 Tim Crews.................... .05 .02 .01
☐ 643 Rick Cerone .... .05 .02 .01
☐ 644 Terry Leach.................. .05 .02 .01
☐ 645 Deion Sanders .... .25 .11 .03
☐ 646 Craig Wilson .... .05 .02 .01
☐ 647 Marquis Grissom .... .15 .07 .02
☐ 648 Scott Fletcher............... .05 .02 .01
☐ 649 Norm Charlton .... .05 .02 .01
☐ 650 Jesse Barfield .... .05 .02 .01
☐ 651 Joe Slusarski .... .05 .02 .01
☐ 652 Bobby Rose .... .05 .02 .01
☐ 653 Dennis Lamp................ .05 .02 .01
☐ 654 Allen Watson................ .15 .07 .02
☐ 655 Brett Butler .... .10 .05 .01
☐ 656 1992 Prospects OF ...... .15 .07 .02
Rudy Pemberton
Henry Rodriguez
Lee Tinsley
Gerald Williams
☐ 657 Dave Johnson .... .05 .02 .01
☐ 658 Checklist 529-660........ .05 .02 .01
☐ 659 Brian McRae .... .15 .07 .02
☐ 660 Fred McGriff................. .20 .09 .03
☐ 661 Bill Landrum .... .05 .02 .01
☐ 662 Juan Guzman .... .10 .05 .01
☐ 663 Greg Gagne.................. .05 .02 .01
☐ 664 Ken Hill .... .10 .05 .01
☐ 665 Dave Haas.................... .05 .02 .01
☐ 666 Tom Foley .... .05 .02 .01
☐ 667 Roberto Hernandez ...... .10 .05 .01
☐ 668 Dwayne Henry.............. .05 .02 .01
☐ 669 Jim Fregosi MG .... .05 .02 .01
☐ 670 Harold Reynolds .... .05 .02 .01
☐ 671 Mark Whiten .... .10 .05 .01
☐ 672 Eric Plunk .... .05 .02 .01
☐ 673 Todd Hundley .... .05 .02 .01
☐ 674 Mo Sanford.................. .05 .02 .01
☐ 675 Bobby Witt................... .05 .02 .01
☐ 676 1992 Prospects P .... .15 .07 .02

Sam Militello
Pat Mahomes
Turk Wendell
Roger Salkeld

☐ 677 John Marzano .05 .02 .01
☐ 678 Joe Klink .05 .02 .01
☐ 679 Pete Incaviglia .05 .02 .01
☐ 680 Dale Murphy .15 .07 .02
☐ 681 Rene Gonzales .05 .02 .01
☐ 682 Andy Benes .10 .05 .01
☐ 683 Jim Poole .05 .02 .01
☐ 684 Trever Miller .05 .02 .01
☐ 685 Scott Livingstone .05 .02 .01
☐ 686 Rich DeLucia .05 .02 .01
☐ 687 Harvey Pulliam .05 .02 .01
☐ 688 Tim Belcher .05 .02 .01
☐ 689 Mark Lemke .05 .02 .01
☐ 690 John Franco .05 .02 .01
☐ 691 Walt Weiss .05 .02 .01
☐ 692 Scott Ruskin .05 .02 .01
☐ 693 Jeff King .05 .02 .01
☐ 694 Mike Gardiner .05 .02 .01
☐ 695 Gary Sheffield .15 .07 .02
☐ 696 Joe Boever .05 .02 .01
☐ 697 Mike Felder .05 .02 .01
☐ 698 John Habyan .05 .02 .01
☐ 699 Cito Gaston MG .05 .02 .01
☐ 700 Ruben Sierra .15 .07 .02
☐ 701 Scott Radinsky .05 .02 .01
☐ 702 Lee Stevens .05 .02 .01
☐ 703 Mark Wohlers .10 .05 .01
☐ 704 Curt Young .05 .02 .01
☐ 705 Dwight Evans .10 .05 .01
☐ 706 Rob Murphy .05 .02 .01
☐ 707 Gregg Jefferies .15 .07 .02
☐ 708 Tom Bolton .05 .02 .01
☐ 709 Chris James .05 .02 .01
☐ 710 Kevin Maas .05 .02 .01
☐ 711 Ricky Bones .10 .05 .01
☐ 712 Curt Wilkerson .05 .02 .01
☐ 713 Roger McDowell .05 .02 .01
☐ 714 Calvin Reese .20 .09 .03
☐ 715 Craig Biggio .10 .05 .01
☐ 716 Kirk Dressendorfer .05 .02 .01
☐ 717 Ken Dayley .05 .02 .01
☐ 718 B.J. Surhoff .05 .02 .01
☐ 719 Terry Mulholland .05 .02 .01
☐ 720 Kirk Gibson .10 .05 .01
☐ 721 Mike Pagliarulo .05 .02 .01
☐ 722 Walt Terrell .05 .02 .01
☐ 723 Jose Oquendo .05 .02 .01
☐ 724 Kevin Morton .05 .02 .01
☐ 725 Dwight Gooden .10 .05 .01
☐ 726 Kirt Manwaring .05 .02 .01
☐ 727 Chuck McElroy .05 .02 .01
☐ 728 Dave Burba .05 .02 .01
☐ 729 Art Howe MG .05 .02 .01
☐ 730 Ramon Martinez .10 .05 .01
☐ 731 Donnie Hill .05 .02 .01
☐ 732 Nelson Santovenia .05 .02 .01
☐ 733 Bob Melvin .05 .02 .01
☐ 734 Scott Hatteberg .15 .07 .02
☐ 735 Greg Swindell .05 .02 .01
☐ 736 Lance Johnson .05 .02 .01
☐ 737 Kevin Reimer .05 .02 .01
☐ 738 Dennis Eckersley .15 .07 .02
☐ 739 Rob Ducey .05 .02 .01
☐ 740 Ken Caminiti .10 .05 .01
☐ 741 Mark Gubicza .05 .02 .01
☐ 742 Billy Spiers .05 .02 .01
☐ 743 Darren Lewis .10 .05 .01
☐ 744 Chris Hammond .05 .02 .01
☐ 745 Dave Magadan .05 .02 .01
☐ 746 Bernard Gilkey .10 .05 .01
☐ 747 Willie Banks .05 .02 .01
☐ 748 Matt Nokes .05 .02 .01
☐ 749 Jerald Clark .05 .02 .01
☐ 750 Travis Fryman .20 .09 .03
☐ 751 Steve Wilson .05 .02 .01
☐ 752 Billy Ripken .05 .02 .01
☐ 753 Paul Assenmacher .05 .02 .01
☐ 754 Charlie Hayes .10 .05 .01
☐ 755 Alex Fernandez .15 .07 .02
☐ 756 Gary Pettis .05 .02 .01
☐ 757 Rob Dibble .05 .02 .01
☐ 758 Tim Naehring .05 .02 .01
☐ 759 Jeff Torborg MG .05 .02 .01
☐ 760 Ozzie Smith .20 .09 .03
☐ 761 Mike Fitzgerald .05 .02 .01
☐ 762 John Burkett .10 .05 .01
☐ 763 Kyle Abbott .05 .02 .01
☐ 764 Tyler Green .15 .07 .02
☐ 765 Pete Harnisch .10 .05 .01
☐ 766 Mark Davis .05 .02 .01
☐ 767 Kal Daniels .05 .02 .01
☐ 768 Jim Thome .40 .18 .05
☐ 769 Jack Howell .05 .02 .01
☐ 770 Sid Bream .05 .02 .01
☐ 771 Arthur Rhodes .10 .05 .01
☐ 772 Garry Templeton UER .05 .02 .01
(Stat heading is for pitchers)
☐ 773 Hal Morris .10 .05 .01
☐ 774 Bud Black .05 .02 .01
☐ 775 Ivan Calderon .05 .02 .01
☐ 776 Doug Henry .05 .02 .01
☐ 777 John Olerud .15 .07 .02
☐ 778 Tim Leary .05 .02 .01
☐ 779 Jay Bell .10 .05 .01
☐ 780 Eddie Murray .15 .07 .02
☐ 781 Paul Abbott .05 .02 .01
☐ 782 Phil Plantier .15 .07 .02
☐ 783 Joe Magrane .05 .02 .01
☐ 784 Ken Patterson .05 .02 .01
☐ 785 Albert Belle .40 .18 .05
☐ 786 Royce Clayton .15 .07 .02
☐ 787 Checklist 661-792 .05 .02 .01
☐ 788 Mike Stanton .05 .02 .01
☐ 789 Bobby Valentine MG .05 .02 .01
☐ 790 Joe Carter .20 .09 .03
☐ 791 Danny Cox .05 .02 .01
☐ 792 Dave Winfield .15 .07 .02

1992 Topps Gold

Topps produced a 792-card Topps Gold factory set packaged in a foil display box. Only this set contained an additional card of

Brien Taylor, numbered 793 and hand signed by him. The production run was 12,000 sets. The Topps Gold cards were also available in regular series packs. According to Topps, on average collectors would find one Topps Gold card in every 36 wax packs, one in every 18 cello packs, one in every 12 rak packs, five per Vending box, one in every six jumbo packs, and ten per regular factory set. The packs also featured "Match-the-Stats" game cards in which the consumer could save "Runs". For 2.00 and every 100 Runs saved in this game, the consumer could receive through a mail-in offer ten Topps Gold cards. These particular Topps Gold cards carry the word "Winner" in gold foil on the card front. The checklist cards in the regular set were replaced with six individual Rookie player cards (131, 264, 366, 527, 658, 787) in the gold set. There were a number of uncorrected errors in the Gold set. Steve Finley (86) has gold band indicating he is Mark Davidson of the Astros. Andujar Cedeno (288) is listed as a member of the New York Yankees. Mike Huff (532) is listed as a member of the Boston Red Sox. Barry Larkin (465) is listed as a member of the Houston Astros but is correctly listed as a member of the Cincinnati Reds on his Gold Winners cards. Typically the individual cards are sold at a multiple of the player's respective value in the regular set.

	MINT	EXC	G-VG
COMPLETE SET (792)	200.00	90.00	25.00
COMPLETE FACT.SET (793)	250.00	115.00	31.00
COMMON CARD (1-792)	.25	.11	.03

*UNLISTED VETERAN STARS: 10X TO 20X BASIC CARDS
*UNLISTED YOUNG STARS: 6X TO 12 X BASIC CARDS
*UNLISTED RCs: 4X to 8X BASIC CARDS

	MINT	EXC	G-VG
☐ 1 Nolan Ryan	20.00	9.00	2.50
☐ 4 Nolan Ryan RB............	10.00	4.50	1.25
☐ 40 Cal Ripken..................	15.00	6.75	1.90
☐ 50 Ken Griffey Jr.............	20.00	9.00	2.50
☐ 86 Steve Finley UER............ (Gold band has Mark Davidson, Astros)	.50	.23	.06
☐ 131 Terry Mathews............. (Replaces Checklist 1)	.75	.35	.09
☐ 264 Rod Beck .... (Replaces Checklist 2)	3.00	1.35	.40
☐ 288 Andujar Cedeno UER . (Listed on Yankees)	1.00	.45	.13
☐ 366 Tony Perezchica........... (Replaces Checklist 3)	.75	.35	.09
☐ 400 Cal Ripken AS	6.00	2.70	.75
☐ 465 Barry Larkin UER .... (Listed on Astros)	2.00	.90	.25
☐ 520 Jeff Bagwell	12.00	5.50	1.50
☐ 527 Terry McDaniel .... (Replaces Checklist 4)	.75	.35	.09
☐ 532 Mike Huff UER .... (Listed on Red Sox)	.50	.23	.06
☐ 555 Frank Thomas	20.00	9.00	2.50
☐ 658 John Ramos .... (Replaces Checklist 5)	.75	.35	.09
☐ 787 Brian Williams........... (Replaces Checklist 6)	1.00	.45	.13
☐ 793 Brien Taylor AU/12000	35.00	16.00	4.40

1992 Topps Gold Winners

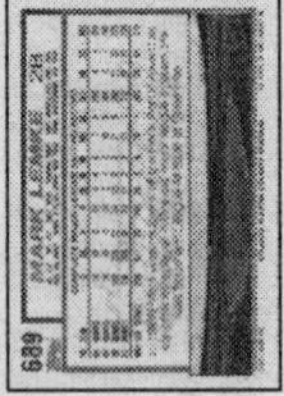

The 1992 Topps baseball card packs featured "Match-the-Stats" game cards in which the consumer could save "Runs". For 2.00 and every 100 Runs saved in this game, the consumer could receive through a mail-in offer ten Topps Gold cards. These particular Topps Gold cards carry the word "Winner" in gold foil on the card front. The checklist cards in the regular set were replaced with six individual Rookie player cards (131, 264, 366, 527, 658, 787) in the gold set. Typically the individual cards are sold at a multiple of the player's respective value in the regular set.

	MINT	EXC	G-VG
COMPLETE SET (792)	70.00	32.00	8.75
COMMON CARD (1-792)	.10	.05	.01

*UNLISTED VETERAN STARS: 4X TO 8X BASIC CARDS
*UNLISTED YOUNG STARS: 2X TO 4X BASIC CARDS
*UNLISTED RCs: 1.25X to 2.5X BASIC CARDS

	MINT	EXC	G-VG
☐ 1 Nolan Ryan	8.00	3.60	1.00
☐ 4 Nolan Ryan RB...............	4.00	1.80	.50
☐ 40 Cal Ripken....................	4.00	1.80	.50
☐ 50 Ken Griffey Jr...............	8.00	3.60	1.00
☐ 264 Rod Beck .... (Replaces Checklist 2)	1.50	.65	.19
☐ 400 Cal Ripken AS	1.50	.65	.19
☐ 520 Jeff Bagwell	3.00	1.35	.40
☐ 555 Frank Thomas............	8.00	3.60	1.00
☐ 787 Brian Williams.............. (Replaces Checklist 6)	.50	.23	.06

1992 Topps Traded

The 1992 Topps Traded set comprises 132 cards, each measuring the standard size (2 1/2" by 3 1/2"). As in past editions, the set focuses on promising rookies, new managers, and players who changed teams. The set also includes a Team U.S.A. subset, featuring 25 of America's top college players and the Team U.S.A. coach. Inside a white outer border, the fronts display color action photos that have two-color (white

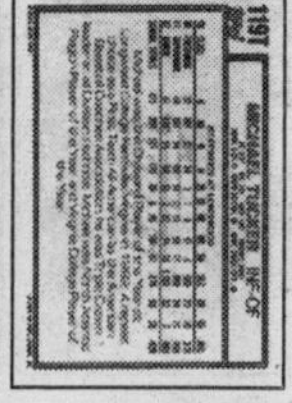

and another color) picture frames. The player's name appears in a short color bar at the lower left corner while the team name is given in a different color bar at the lower right corner. In a horizontal format, the backs carry biography, statistics, player summary, or a small color picture of the team's stadium . The cards are arranged in alphabetical order by player's last name and numbered on the back. The key Rookie Cards in this set are Jeff Alkire, Chad Curtis, Tim Davis, Nomar Garciaparra, Pat Listach, Jason Moler, Calvin Murray, Michael Tucker, Jason Varitek, and B.J. Wallace.

	MINT	EXC	G-VG
COMPLETE FACT.SET (132)	20.00	9.00	2.50
COMMON CARD (1T-132T)	.10	.05	.01

	MINT	EXC	G-VG
☐ 1T Willie Adams USA	.50	.23	.06
☐ 2T Jeff Alkire USA	.30	.14	.04
☐ 3T Felipe Alou MG	.10	.05	.01
☐ 4T Moises Alou	.30	.14	.04
☐ 5T Ruben Amaro	.10	.05	.01
☐ 6T Jack Armstrong	.10	.05	.01
☐ 7T Scott Bankhead	.10	.05	.01
☐ 8T Tim Belcher	.10	.05	.01
☐ 9T George Bell	.15	.07	.02
☐ 10T Freddie Benavides	.10	.05	.01
☐ 11T Todd Benzinger	.10	.05	.01
☐ 12T Joe Boever	.10	.05	.01
☐ 13T Ricky Bones	.15	.07	.02
☐ 14T Bobby Bonilla	.20	.09	.03
☐ 15T Hubie Brooks	.10	.05	.01
☐ 16T Jerry Browne	.10	.05	.01
☐ 17T Jim Bullinger	.10	.05	.01
☐ 18T Dave Burba	.10	.05	.01
☐ 19T Kevin Campbell	.15	.07	.02
☐ 20T Tom Candiotti	.10	.05	.01
☐ 21T Mark Carreon	.10	.05	.01
☐ 22T Gary Carter	.20	.09	.03
☐ 23T Archi Cianfrocco	.10	.05	.01
☐ 24T Phil Clark	.10	.05	.01
☐ 25T Chad Curtis	.35	.16	.04
☐ 26T Eric Davis	.10	.05	.01
☐ 27T Tim Davis USA	.40	.18	.05
☐ 28T Gary DiSarcina	.10	.05	.01
☐ 29T Darren Dreifort USA	.50	.23	.06
☐ 30T Mariano Duncan	.10	.05	.01
☐ 31T Mike Fitzgerald	.10	.05	.01
☐ 32T John Flaherty	.15	.07	.02
☐ 33T Darrin Fletcher	.10	.05	.01
☐ 34T Scott Fletcher	.10	.05	.01
☐ 35T Ron Fraser CO USA	.10	.05	.01
☐ 36T Andres Galarraga	.20	.09	.03
☐ 37T Dave Gallagher	.10	.05	.01
☐ 38T Mike Gallego	.10	.05	.01
☐ 39T Nomar Garciaparra USA	1.25	.55	.16
☐ 40T Jason Giambi USA	.60	.25	.08
☐ 41T Danny Gladden	.10	.05	.01
☐ 42T Rene Gonzales	.10	.05	.01
☐ 43T Jeff Granger USA	.50	.23	.06
☐ 44T Rick Greene USA	.15	.07	.02
☐ 45T Jeffrey Hammonds USA	1.50	.65	.19
☐ 46T Charlie Hayes	.15	.07	.02
☐ 47T Von Hayes	.10	.05	.01
☐ 48T Rick Helling USA	.50	.23	.06
☐ 49T Butch Henry	.15	.07	.02
☐ 50T Carlos Hernandez	.10	.05	.01
☐ 51T Ken Hill	.15	.07	.02
☐ 52T Butch Hobson	.10	.05	.01
☐ 53T Vince Horsman	.15	.07	.02
☐ 54T Pete Incaviglia	.10	.05	.01
☐ 55T Gregg Jefferies	.25	.11	.03
☐ 56T Charles Johnson USA	1.50	.65	.19
☐ 57T Doug Jones	.10	.05	.01
☐ 58T Brian Jordan	.20	.09	.03
☐ 59T Wally Joyner	.15	.07	.02
☐ 60T Daron Kirkreit USA	.50	.23	.06
☐ 61T Bill Krueger	.10	.05	.01
☐ 62T Gene Lamont MG	.10	.05	.01
☐ 63T Jim Lefebvre MG	.10	.05	.01
☐ 64T Danny Leon	.15	.07	.02
☐ 65T Pat Listach	.20	.09	.03
☐ 66T Kenny Lofton	2.50	1.15	.30
☐ 67T Dave Martinez	.10	.05	.01
☐ 68T Derrick May	.15	.07	.02
☐ 69T Kirk McCaskill	.10	.05	.01
☐ 70T Chad McConnell USA	.20	.09	.03
☐ 71T Kevin McReynolds	.10	.05	.01
☐ 72T Rusty Meacham	.10	.05	.01
☐ 73T Keith Miller	.10	.05	.01
☐ 74T Kevin Mitchell	.15	.07	.02
☐ 75T Jason Moler USA	.50	.23	.06
☐ 76T Mike Morgan	.10	.05	.01
☐ 77T Jack Morris	.20	.09	.03
☐ 78T Calvin Murray USA	.20	.09	.03
☐ 79T Eddie Murray	.20	.09	.03
☐ 80T Randy Myers	.15	.07	.02
☐ 81T Denny Neagle	.10	.05	.01
☐ 82T Phil Nevin USA	.60	.25	.08
☐ 83T Dave Nilsson	.40	.18	.05
☐ 84T Junior Ortiz	.10	.05	.01
☐ 85T Donovan Osborne	.10	.05	.01
☐ 86T Bill Pecota	.10	.05	.01
☐ 87T Melido Perez	.10	.05	.01
☐ 88T Mike Perez	.10	.05	.01
☐ 89T Hipolito Pichardo	.10	.05	.01
☐ 90T Willie Randolph	.15	.07	.02
☐ 91T Darren Reed	.10	.05	.01
☐ 92T Bip Roberts	.10	.05	.01
☐ 93T Chris Roberts USA	.50	.23	.06
☐ 94T Steve Rodriguez USA	.10	.05	.01
☐ 95T Bruce Ruffin	.10	.05	.01
☐ 96T Scott Ruskin	.10	.05	.01
☐ 97T Bret Saberhagen	.15	.07	.02
☐ 98T Rey Sanchez	.15	.07	.02
☐ 99T Steve Sax	.10	.05	.01
☐ 100T Curt Schilling	.15	.07	.02
☐ 101T Dick Schofield	.10	.05	.01
☐ 102T Gary Scott	.10	.05	.01
☐ 103T Kevin Seitzer	.10	.05	.01
☐ 104T Frank Seminara	.10	.05	.01
☐ 105T Gary Sheffield	.25	.11	.03
☐ 106T John Smiley	.10	.05	.01
☐ 107T Cory Snyder	.10	.05	.01
☐ 108T Paul Sorrento	.10	.05	.01
☐ 109T Sammy Sosa	.20	.09	.03
☐ 110T Matt Stairs	.10	.05	.01
☐ 111T Andy Stankiewicz	.10	.05	.01

☐ 112T	Kurt Stillwell	.10	.05	.01
☐ 113T	Rick Sutcliffe	.15	.07	.02
☐ 114T	Bill Swift	.15	.07	.02
☐ 115T	Jeff Tackett	.10	.05	.01
☐ 116T	Danny Tartabull	.15	.07	.02
☐ 117T	Eddie Taubensee	.10	.05	.01
☐ 118T	Dickie Thon	.10	.05	.01
☐ 119T	Michael Tucker USA	1.00	.45	.13
☐ 120T	Scooter Tucker	.15	.07	.02
☐ 121T	Marc Valdes USA	.75	.35	.09
☐ 122T	Julio Valera	.15	.07	.02
☐ 123T	Jason Varitek USA	1.25	.55	.16
☐ 124T	Ron Villone USA	.30	.14	.04
☐ 125T	Frank Viola	.15	.07	.02
☐ 126T	B.J. Wallace USA	.30	.14	.04
☐ 127T	Dan Walters	.15	.07	.02
☐ 128T	Craig Wilson USA	.10	.05	.01
☐ 129T	Chris Wimmer USA	.15	.07	.02
☐ 130T	Dave Winfield	.30	.14	.04
☐ 131T	Herm Winningham	.10	.05	.01
☐ 132T	Checklist 1T-132T	.10	.05	.01

1992 Topps Traded Gold

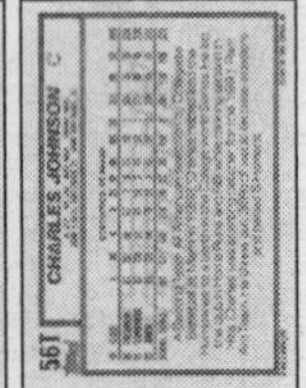

Topps also produced a "ToppsGold" version of their 1992 Topps Traded set. The card design is identical to the regular issue, except for the gold-foil bars on the fronts carrying the player's name and team name. Just 6,000 of these sets were produced. The only difference in the listing is the replacement of the checklist card by a player card. The cards are numbered on the back.

	MINT	EXC	G-VG
COMPLETE FACT.SET (132)	35.00	16.00	4.40
COMMON CARD (1T-132T)	.15	.07	.02

*STARS: 1.25X to 2X BASIC CARDS

1993 Topps

The 1993 Topps baseball set consists of two series of 396 and 429 cards measuring the standard size (2 1/2" by 3 1/2"). A Topps Gold card was inserted in every 15-card pack, and Topps Black Gold cards were randomly inserted throughout the packs. The fronts feature color action player photos with white borders. The player's name appears in a stripe at the bottom of the picture, and this stripe and two short diagonal stripes at the bottom corners of the picture are team color-coded. The backs are colorful and carry a color head shot, biography, complete statistical information, with a career highlight if space permitted. The cards are numbered on the back. Cards 401-411 comprise an All-Star subset. Rookie Cards in this set include Derek Jeter, Chad Mottola, J.T. Snow, and Preston Wilson. For the Colorado Rockies and the Florida Marlins, Topps also produced cards gold-foil stamped factory complete sets on the front with the inaugural team's logo. Five thousand complete factory sets with the Rockies' logo and four thousand complete factory sets with the Marlins' logo were initially printed, and each team has the option of having a maximum of 10,000 special sets produced. The Rockies' sets were distributed through the four team-owned stores and at Mile High Stadium. The Marlins' sets were distributed through FMI and Joe Robbie Stadium. The complete 1993 Topps set was also issued as a factory set of micro baseball cards with cards measuring approximately one-fourth the size of the regular size cards but identical in other respects. The micro set and its cards are valued at approximately half the values listed below for the regular size cards.

	MINT	EXC	G-VG
COMPLETE SET (825)	30.00	13.50	3.80
COMPLETE RETAIL SET (838)	40.00	18.00	5.00
COMPLETE HOBBY SET (847)	45.00	20.00	5.75
COMP.1994 PREPROD. (9)	7.00	3.10	.85
COMPLETE SERIES 1 (396)	15.00	6.75	1.90
COMPLETE SERIES 2 (429)	15.00	6.75	1.90
COMMON CARD (1-396)	.05	.02	.01
COMMON CARD (397-825)	.05	.02	.01

☐ 1	Robin Yount	.30	.14	.04
☐ 2	Barry Bonds	.75	.35	.09
☐ 3	Ryne Sandberg	.60	.25	.08
☐ 4	Roger Clemens	.50	.23	.06
☐ 5	Tony Gwynn	.50	.23	.06
☐ 6	Jeff Tackett	.05	.02	.01
☐ 7	Pete Incaviglia	.05	.02	.01
☐ 8	Mark Wohlers	.05	.02	.01
☐ 9	Kent Hrbek	.08	.04	.01
☐ 10	Will Clark	.30	.14	.04
☐ 11	Eric Karros	.08	.04	.01
☐ 12	Lee Smith	.10	.05	.01

☐	13	Esteban Beltre	.05	.02	.01
☐	14	Greg Briley	.05	.02	.01
☐	15	Marquis Grissom	.10	.05	.01
☐	16	Dan Plesac	.05	.02	.01
☐	17	Dave Hollins	.10	.05	.01
☐	18	Terry Steinbach	.08	.04	.01
☐	19	Ed Nunez	.05	.02	.01
☐	20	Tim Salmon	.40	.18	.05
☐	21	Luis Salazar	.05	.02	.01
☐	22	Jim Eisenreich	.05	.02	.01
☐	23	Todd Stottlemyre	.05	.02	.01
☐	24	Tim Naehring	.05	.02	.01
☐	25	John Franco	.05	.02	.01
☐	26	Skeeter Barnes	.05	.02	.01
☐	27	Carlos Garcia	.08	.04	.01
☐	28	Joe Orsulak	.05	.02	.01
☐	29	Dwayne Henry	.05	.02	.01
☐	30	Fred McGriff	.30	.14	.04
☐	31	Derek Lilliquist	.05	.02	.01
☐	32	Don Mattingly	.75	.35	.09
☐	33	B.J. Wallace	.05	.02	.01
☐	34	Juan Gonzalez	.60	.25	.08
☐	35	John Smoltz	.08	.04	.01
☐	36	Scott Servais	.05	.02	.01
☐	37	Lenny Webster	.05	.02	.01
☐	38	Chris James	.05	.02	.01
☐	39	Roger McDowell	.05	.02	.01
☐	40	Ozzie Smith	.40	.18	.05
☐	41	Alex Fernandez	.10	.05	.01
☐	42	Spike Owen	.05	.02	.01
☐	43	Ruben Amaro	.05	.02	.01
☐	44	Kevin Seitzer	.05	.02	.01
☐	45	Dave Fleming	.08	.04	.01
☐	46	Eric Fox	.05	.02	.01
☐	47	Bob Scanlan	.05	.02	.01
☐	48	Bert Blyleven	.10	.05	.01
☐	49	Brian McRae	.10	.05	.01
☐	50	Roberto Alomar	.40	.18	.05
☐	51	Mo Vaughn	.10	.05	.01
☐	52	Bobby Bonilla	.10	.05	.01
☐	53	Frank Tanana	.05	.02	.01
☐	54	Mike LaValliere	.05	.02	.01
☐	55	Mark McLemore	.05	.02	.01
☐	56	Chad Mottola	.20	.09	.03
☐	57	Norm Charlton	.05	.02	.01
☐	58	Jose Melendez	.05	.02	.01
☐	59	Carlos Martinez	.05	.02	.01
☐	60	Roberto Kelly	.08	.04	.01
☐	61	Gene Larkin	.05	.02	.01
☐	62	Rafael Belliard	.05	.02	.01
☐	63	Al Osuna	.05	.02	.01
☐	64	Scott Chiamparino	.05	.02	.01
☐	65	Brett Butler	.08	.04	.01
☐	66	John Burkett	.08	.04	.01
☐	67	Felix Jose	.05	.02	.01
☐	68	Omar Vizquel	.05	.02	.01
☐	69	John Vander Wal	.05	.02	.01
☐	70	Roberto Hernandez	.05	.02	.01
☐	71	Ricky Bones	.05	.02	.01
☐	72	Jeff Grotewold	.05	.02	.01
☐	73	Mike Moore	.05	.02	.01
☐	74	Steve Buechele	.05	.02	.01
☐	75	Juan Guzman	.08	.04	.01
☐	76	Kevin Appier	.08	.04	.01
☐	77	Junior Felix	.05	.02	.01
☐	78	Greg W. Harris	.05	.02	.01
☐	79	Dick Schofield	.05	.02	.01
☐	80	Cecil Fielder	.10	.05	.01
☐	81	Lloyd McClendon	.05	.02	.01
☐	82	David Segui	.05	.02	.01
☐	83	Reggie Sanders	.10	.05	.01
☐	84	Kurt Stillwell	.05	.02	.01
☐	85	Sandy Alomar	.08	.04	.01
☐	86	John Habyan	.05	.02	.01
☐	87	Kevin Reimer	.05	.02	.01
☐	88	Mike Stanton	.05	.02	.01
☐	89	Eric Anthony	.05	.02	.01
☐	90	Scott Erickson	.05	.02	.01
☐	91	Craig Colbert	.05	.02	.01
☐	92	Tom Pagnozzi	.05	.02	.01
☐	93	Pedro Astacio	.08	.04	.01
☐	94	Lance Johnson	.05	.02	.01
☐	95	Larry Walker	.10	.05	.01
☐	96	Russ Swan	.05	.02	.01
☐	97	Scott Fletcher	.05	.02	.01
☐	98	Derek Jeter	2.00	.90	.25
☐	99	Mike Williams	.05	.02	.01
☐	100	Mark McGwire	.10	.05	.01
☐	101	Jim Bullinger	.05	.02	.01
☐	102	Brian Hunter	.08	.04	.01
☐	103	Jody Reed	.05	.02	.01
☐	104	Mike Butcher	.05	.02	.01
☐	105	Gregg Jefferies	.10	.05	.01
☐	106	Howard Johnson	.05	.02	.01
☐	107	John Kiely	.05	.02	.01
☐	108	Jose Lind	.05	.02	.01
☐	109	Sam Horn	.05	.02	.01
☐	110	Barry Larkin	.10	.05	.01
☐	111	Bruce Hurst	.05	.02	.01
☐	112	Brian Barnes	.05	.02	.01
☐	113	Thomas Howard	.05	.02	.01
☐	114	Mel Hall	.05	.02	.01
☐	115	Robby Thompson	.05	.02	.01
☐	116	Mark Lemke	.05	.02	.01
☐	117	Eddie Taubensee	.05	.02	.01
☐	118	David Hulse	.05	.02	.01
☐	119	Pedro Munoz	.05	.02	.01
☐	120	Ramon Martinez	.08	.04	.01
☐	121	Todd Worrell	.05	.02	.01
☐	122	Joey Cora	.05	.02	.01
☐	123	Moises Alou	.10	.05	.01
☐	124	Franklin Stubbs	.05	.02	.01
☐	125	Pete O'Brien	.05	.02	.01
☐	126	Bob Ayrault	.05	.02	.01
☐	127	Carney Lansford	.08	.04	.01
☐	128	Kal Daniels	.05	.02	.01
☐	129	Joe Grahe	.05	.02	.01
☐	130	Jeff Montgomery	.08	.04	.01
☐	131	Dave Winfield	.10	.05	.01
☐	132	Preston Wilson	.25	.11	.03
☐	133	Steve Wilson	.05	.02	.01
☐	134	Lee Guetterman	.05	.02	.01
☐	135	Mickey Tettleton	.08	.04	.01
☐	136	Jeff King	.05	.02	.01
☐	137	Alan Mills	.05	.02	.01
☐	138	Joe Oliver	.05	.02	.01
☐	139	Gary Gaetti	.05	.02	.01
☐	140	Gary Sheffield	.10	.05	.01
☐	141	Dennis Cook	.05	.02	.01
☐	142	Charlie Hayes	.08	.04	.01
☐	143	Jeff Huson	.05	.02	.01
☐	144	Kent Mercker	.05	.02	.01
☐	145	Eric Young	.08	.04	.01
☐	146	Scott Leius	.05	.02	.01
☐	147	Bryan Hickerson	.05	.02	.01
☐	148	Steve Finley	.05	.02	.01
☐	149	Rheal Cormier	.05	.02	.01
☐	150	Frank Thomas UER (Categories leading league are italicized but not printed in red)	2.00	.90	.25
☐	151	Archi Cianfrocco	.05	.02	.01
☐	152	Rich DeLucia	.05	.02	.01
☐	153	Greg Vaughn	.08	.04	.01
☐	154	Wes Chamberlain	.05	.02	.01
☐	155	Dennis Eckersley	.10	.05	.01

☐ 156 Sammy Sosa	.10	.05	.01
☐ 157 Gary DiSarcina	.05	.02	.01
☐ 158 Kevin Koslofski	.05	.02	.01
☐ 159 Doug Linton	.05	.02	.01
☐ 160 Lou Whitaker	.10	.05	.01
☐ 161 Chad McConnell	.05	.02	.01
☐ 162 Joe Hesketh	.05	.02	.01
☐ 163 Tim Wakefield	.05	.02	.01
☐ 164 Leo Gomez	.05	.02	.01
☐ 165 Jose Rijo	.08	.04	.01
☐ 166 Tim Scott	.05	.02	.01
☐ 167 Steve Olin UER (Born 10/4/65, should say 10/10/65)	.05	.02	.01
☐ 168 Kevin Maas	.05	.02	.01
☐ 169 Kenny Rogers	.05	.02	.01
☐ 170 David Justice	.30	.14	.04
☐ 171 Doug Jones	.05	.02	.01
☐ 172 Jeff Reboulet	.05	.02	.01
☐ 173 Andres Galarraga	.10	.05	.01
☐ 174 Randy Velarde	.05	.02	.01
☐ 175 Kirk McCaskill	.05	.02	.01
☐ 176 Darren Lewis	.05	.02	.01
☐ 177 Lenny Harris	.05	.02	.01
☐ 178 Jeff Fassero	.05	.02	.01
☐ 179 Ken Griffey Jr.	2.00	.90	.25
☐ 180 Darren Daulton	.10	.05	.01
☐ 181 John Jaha	.08	.04	.01
☐ 182 Ron Darling	.05	.02	.01
☐ 183 Greg Maddux	.40	.18	.05
☐ 184 Damion Easley	.08	.04	.01
☐ 185 Jack Morris	.10	.05	.01
☐ 186 Mike Magnante	.05	.02	.01
☐ 187 John Dopson	.05	.02	.01
☐ 188 Sid Fernandez	.05	.02	.01
☐ 189 Tony Phillips	.08	.04	.01
☐ 190 Doug Drabek	.10	.05	.01
☐ 191 Sean Lowe	.20	.09	.03
☐ 192 Bob Milacki	.05	.02	.01
☐ 193 Steve Foster	.05	.02	.01
☐ 194 Jerald Clark	.05	.02	.01
☐ 195 Pete Harnisch	.05	.02	.01
☐ 196 Pat Kelly	.05	.02	.01
☐ 197 Jeff Frye	.05	.02	.01
☐ 198 Alejandro Pena	.05	.02	.01
☐ 199 Junior Ortiz	.05	.02	.01
☐ 200 Kirby Puckett	.75	.35	.09
☐ 201 Jose Uribe	.05	.02	.01
☐ 202 Mike Scioscia	.05	.02	.01
☐ 203 Bernard Gilkey	.05	.02	.01
☐ 204 Dan Pasqua	.05	.02	.01
☐ 205 Gary Carter	.10	.05	.01
☐ 206 Henry Cotto	.05	.02	.01
☐ 207 Paul Molitor	.30	.14	.04
☐ 208 Mike Hartley	.05	.02	.01
☐ 209 Jeff Parrett	.05	.02	.01
☐ 210 Mark Langston	.10	.05	.01
☐ 211 Doug Dascenzo	.05	.02	.01
☐ 212 Rick Reed	.05	.02	.01
☐ 213 Candy Maldonado	.05	.02	.01
☐ 214 Danny Darwin	.05	.02	.01
☐ 215 Pat Howell	.05	.02	.01
☐ 216 Mark Leiter	.05	.02	.01
☐ 217 Kevin Mitchell	.08	.04	.01
☐ 218 Ben McDonald	.08	.04	.01
☐ 219 Bip Roberts	.05	.02	.01
☐ 220 Benny Santiago	.05	.02	.01
☐ 221 Carlos Baerga	.30	.14	.04
☐ 222 Bernie Williams	.08	.04	.01
☐ 223 Roger Pavlik	.08	.04	.01
☐ 224 Sid Bream	.05	.02	.01
☐ 225 Matt Williams	.30	.14	.04
☐ 226 Willie Banks	.05	.02	.01
☐ 227 Jeff Bagwell	1.00	.45	.13
☐ 228 Tom Goodwin	.05	.02	.01
☐ 229 Mike Perez	.05	.02	.01
☐ 230 Carlton Fisk	.10	.05	.01
☐ 231 John Wetteland	.05	.02	.01
☐ 232 Tino Martinez	.08	.04	.01
☐ 233 Rick Greene	.08	.04	.01
☐ 234 Tim McIntosh	.05	.02	.01
☐ 235 Mitch Williams	.08	.04	.01
☐ 236 Kevin Campbell	.05	.02	.01
☐ 237 Jose Vizcaino	.05	.02	.01
☐ 238 Chris Donnels	.05	.02	.01
☐ 239 Mike Boddicker	.05	.02	.01
☐ 240 John Olerud	.10	.05	.01
☐ 241 Mike Gardiner	.05	.02	.01
☐ 242 Charlie O'Brien	.05	.02	.01
☐ 243 Rob Deer	.05	.02	.01
☐ 244 Denny Neagle	.05	.02	.01
☐ 245 Chris Sabo	.08	.04	.01
☐ 246 Gregg Olson	.05	.02	.01
☐ 247 Frank Seminara UER (Acquired 12/3/98)	.05	.02	.01
☐ 248 Scott Scudder	.05	.02	.01
☐ 249 Tim Burke	.05	.02	.01
☐ 250 Chuck Knoblauch	.10	.05	.01
☐ 251 Mike Bielecki	.05	.02	.01
☐ 252 Xavier Hernandez	.05	.02	.01
☐ 253 Jose Guzman	.05	.02	.01
☐ 254 Cory Snyder	.05	.02	.01
☐ 255 Orel Hershiser	.08	.04	.01
☐ 256 Wil Cordero	.10	.05	.01
☐ 257 Luis Alicea	.05	.02	.01
☐ 258 Mike Schooler	.05	.02	.01
☐ 259 Craig Grebeck	.05	.02	.01
☐ 260 Duane Ward	.08	.04	.01
☐ 261 Bill Wegman	.05	.02	.01
☐ 262 Mickey Morandini	.05	.02	.01
☐ 263 Vince Horsman	.05	.02	.01
☐ 264 Paul Sorrento	.05	.02	.01
☐ 265 Andre Dawson	.10	.05	.01
☐ 266 Rene Gonzales	.05	.02	.01
☐ 267 Keith Miller	.05	.02	.01
☐ 268 Derek Bell	.08	.04	.01
☐ 269 Todd Steverson	.20	.09	.03
☐ 270 Frank Viola	.08	.04	.01
☐ 271 Wally Whitehurst	.05	.02	.01
☐ 272 Kurt Knudsen	.05	.02	.01
☐ 273 Dan Walters	.05	.02	.01
☐ 274 Rick Sutcliffe	.08	.04	.01
☐ 275 Andy Van Slyke	.10	.05	.01
☐ 276 Paul O'Neill	.08	.04	.01
☐ 277 Mark Whiten	.08	.04	.01
☐ 278 Chris Nabholz	.05	.02	.01
☐ 279 Todd Burns	.05	.02	.01
☐ 280 Tom Glavine	.10	.05	.01
☐ 281 Butch Henry	.05	.02	.01
☐ 282 Shane Mack	.08	.04	.01
☐ 283 Mike Jackson	.05	.02	.01
☐ 284 Henry Rodriguez	.08	.04	.01
☐ 285 Bob Tewksbury	.05	.02	.01
☐ 286 Ron Karkovice	.05	.02	.01
☐ 287 Mike Gallego	.05	.02	.01
☐ 288 Dave Cochrane	.05	.02	.01
☐ 289 Jesse Orosco	.05	.02	.01
☐ 290 Dave Stewart	.08	.04	.01
☐ 291 Tommy Greene	.08	.04	.01
☐ 292 Rey Sanchez	.05	.02	.01
☐ 293 Rob Ducey	.05	.02	.01
☐ 294 Brent Mayne	.05	.02	.01
☐ 295 Dave Stieb	.08	.04	.01
☐ 296 Luis Rivera	.05	.02	.01
☐ 297 Jeff Innis	.05	.02	.01
☐ 298 Scott Livingstone	.05	.02	.01

	No.	Player			
☐	299	Bob Patterson	.05	.02	.01
☐	300	Cal Ripken	1.50	.65	.19
☐	301	Cesar Hernandez	.05	.02	.01
☐	302	Randy Myers	.08	.04	.01
☐	303	Brook Jacoby	.05	.02	.01
☐	304	Melido Perez	.05	.02	.01
☐	305	Rafael Palmeiro	.10	.05	.01
☐	306	Damon Berryhill	.05	.02	.01
☐	307	Dan Serafini	.25	.11	.03
☐	308	Darryl Kile	.08	.04	.01
☐	309	J.T. Bruett	.05	.02	.01
☐	310	Dave Righetti	.05	.02	.01
☐	311	Jay Howell	.05	.02	.01
☐	312	Geronimo Pena	.05	.02	.01
☐	313	Greg Hibbard	.05	.02	.01
☐	314	Mark Gardner	.05	.02	.01
☐	315	Edgar Martinez	.05	.02	.01
☐	316	Dave Nilsson	.08	.04	.01
☐	317	Kyle Abbott	.05	.02	.01
☐	318	Willie Wilson	.05	.02	.01
☐	319	Paul Assenmacher	.05	.02	.01
☐	320	Tim Fortugno	.05	.02	.01
☐	321	Rusty Meacham	.05	.02	.01
☐	322	Pat Borders	.05	.02	.01
☐	323	Mike Greenwell	.08	.04	.01
☐	324	Willie Randolph	.08	.04	.01
☐	325	Bill Gullickson	.05	.02	.01
☐	326	Gary Varsho	.05	.02	.01
☐	327	Tim Hulett	.05	.02	.01
☐	328	Scott Ruskin	.05	.02	.01
☐	329	Mike Maddux	.05	.02	.01
☐	330	Danny Tartabull	.08	.04	.01
☐	331	Kenny Lofton	.50	.23	.06
☐	332	Geno Petralli	.05	.02	.01
☐	333	Otis Nixon	.05	.02	.01
☐	334	Jason Kendall	.60	.25	.08
☐	335	Mark Portugal	.05	.02	.01
☐	336	Mike Pagliarulo	.05	.02	.01
☐	337	Kirt Manwaring	.05	.02	.01
☐	338	Bob Ojeda	.05	.02	.01
☐	339	Mark Clark	.08	.04	.01
☐	340	John Kruk	.10	.05	.01
☐	341	Mel Rojas	.05	.02	.01
☐	342	Erik Hanson	.05	.02	.01
☐	343	Doug Henry	.05	.02	.01
☐	344	Jack McDowell	.10	.05	.01
☐	345	Harold Baines	.08	.04	.01
☐	346	Chuck McElroy	.05	.02	.01
☐	347	Luis Sojo	.05	.02	.01
☐	348	Andy Stankiewicz	.05	.02	.01
☐	349	Hipolito Pichardo	.05	.02	.01
☐	350	Joe Carter	.30	.14	.04
☐	351	Ellis Burks	.08	.04	.01
☐	352	Pete Schourek	.08	.04	.01
☐	353	Bubby Groom	.05	.02	.01
☐	354	Jay Bell	.08	.04	.01
☐	355	Brady Anderson	.08	.04	.01
☐	356	Freddie Benavides	.05	.02	.01
☐	357	Phil Stephenson	.05	.02	.01
☐	358	Kevin Wickander	.05	.02	.01
☐	359	Mike Stanley	.05	.02	.01
☐	360	Ivan Rodriguez	.10	.05	.01
☐	361	Scott Bankhead	.05	.02	.01
☐	362	Luis Gonzalez	.08	.04	.01
☐	363	John Smiley	.05	.02	.01
☐	364	Trevor Wilson	.05	.02	.01
☐	365	Tom Candiotti	.05	.02	.01
☐	366	Craig Wilson	.05	.02	.01
☐	367	Steve Sax	.05	.02	.01
☐	368	Delino DeShields	.08	.04	.01
☐	369	Jaime Navarro	.05	.02	.01
☐	370	Dave Valle	.05	.02	.01
☐	371	Mariano Duncan	.05	.02	.01
☐	372	Rod Nichols	.05	.02	.01
☐	373	Mike Morgan	.05	.02	.01
☐	374	Julio Valera	.05	.02	.01
☐	375	Wally Joyner	.08	.04	.01
☐	376	Tom Henke	.08	.04	.01
☐	377	Herm Winningham	.05	.02	.01
☐	378	Orlando Merced	.08	.04	.01
☐	379	Mike Munoz	.05	.02	.01
☐	380	Todd Hundley	.05	.02	.01
☐	381	Mike Flanagan	.05	.02	.01
☐	382	Tim Belcher	.05	.02	.01
☐	383	Jerry Browne	.05	.02	.01
☐	384	Mike Benjamin	.05	.02	.01
☐	385	Jim Leyritz	.05	.02	.01
☐	386	Ray Lankford	.10	.05	.01
☐	387	Devon White	.08	.04	.01
☐	388	Jeremy Hernandez	.05	.02	.01
☐	389	Brian Harper	.05	.02	.01
☐	390	Wade Boggs	.10	.05	.01
☐	391	Derrick May	.08	.04	.01
☐	392	Travis Fryman	.15	.07	.02
☐	393	Ron Gant	.08	.04	.01
☐	394	Checklist 1-132	.05	.02	.01
☐	395	Checklist 133-264 UER (Eckerlsey)	.05	.02	.01
☐	396	Checklist 265-396	.05	.02	.01
☐	397	George Brett	.75	.35	.09
☐	398	Bobby Witt	.05	.02	.01
☐	399	Daryl Boston	.05	.02	.01
☐	400	Bo Jackson	.10	.05	.01
☐	401	Fred McGriff Frank Thomas	.50	.23	.06
☐	402	Ryne Sandberg Carlos Baerga	.15	.07	.02
☐	403	Gary Sheffield Edgar Martinez	.08	.04	.01
☐	404	Barry Larkin Travis Fryman	.08	.04	.01
☐	405	Andy Van Slyke Ken Griffey Jr.	.50	.23	.06
☐	406	Larry Walker Kirby Puckett	.15	.07	.02
☐	407	Barry Bonds Joe Carter	.15	.07	.02
☐	408	Darren Daulton Brian Harper	.08	.04	.01
☐	409	Greg Maddux Roger Clemens	.15	.07	.02
☐	410	Tom Glavine Dave Fleming	.08	.04	.01
☐	411	Lee Smith Dennis Eckersley	.10	.05	.01
☐	412	Jamie McAndrew	.05	.02	.01
☐	413	Pete Smith	.05	.02	.01
☐	414	Juan Guerrero	.05	.02	.01
☐	415	Todd Frohwirth	.05	.02	.01
☐	416	Randy Tomlin	.05	.02	.01
☐	417	B.J. Surhoff	.05	.02	.01
☐	418	Jim Gott	.05	.02	.01
☐	419	Mark Thompson	.15	.07	.02
☐	420	Kevin Tapani	.05	.02	.01
☐	421	Curt Schilling	.08	.04	.01
☐	422	J.T. Snow	.15	.07	.02
☐	423	1993 Prospects Ryan Klesko Ivan Cruz Bubba Smith Larry Sutton	.60	.25	.08
☐	424	John Valentin	.08	.04	.01
☐	425	Joe Girardi	.05	.02	.01
☐	426	Nigel Wilson	.10	.05	.01
☐	427	Bob MacDonald	.05	.02	.01
☐	428	Todd Zeile	.08	.04	.01

- ☐ 429 Milt Cuyler .05 .02 .01
- ☐ 430 Eddie Murray .10 .05 .01
- ☐ 431 Rich Amaral .05 .02 .01
- ☐ 432 Pete Young .05 .02 .01
- ☐ 433 Roger Bailey and .15 .07 .02
  Tom Schmidt
- ☐ 434 Jack Armstrong .05 .02 .01
- ☐ 435 Willie McGee .08 .04 .01
- ☐ 436 Greg W. Harris .05 .02 .01
- ☐ 437 Chris Hammond .05 .02 .01
- ☐ 438 Ritchie Moody .05 .02 .01
- ☐ 439 Bryan Harvey .08 .04 .01
- ☐ 440 Ruben Sierra .10 .05 .01
- ☐ 441 Don Lemon and .15 .07 .02
  Todd Pridy
- ☐ 442 Kevin McReynolds .05 .02 .01
- ☐ 443 Terry Leach .05 .02 .01
- ☐ 444 David Nied .10 .05 .01
- ☐ 445 Dale Murphy .10 .05 .01
- ☐ 446 Luis Mercedes .05 .02 .01
- ☐ 447 Keith Shepherd .05 .02 .01
- ☐ 448 Ken Caminiti .08 .04 .01
- ☐ 449 James Austin .05 .02 .01
- ☐ 450 Darryl Strawberry .08 .04 .01
- ☐ 451 1993 Prospects .15 .07 .02
  Ramon Caraballo
  Jon Shave
  Brent Gates
  Quinton McCracken
- ☐ 452 Bob Wickman .05 .02 .01
- ☐ 453 Victor Cole .05 .02 .01
- ☐ 454 John Johnstone .05 .02 .01
- ☐ 455 Chili Davis .08 .04 .01
- ☐ 456 Scott Taylor .05 .02 .01
- ☐ 457 Tracy Woodson .05 .02 .01
- ☐ 458 David Wells .05 .02 .01
- ☐ 459 Derek Wallace .05 .02 .01
- ☐ 460 Randy Johnson .10 .05 .01
- ☐ 461 Steve Reed .08 .04 .01
- ☐ 462 Felix Fermin .05 .02 .01
- ☐ 463 Scott Aldred .05 .02 .01
- ☐ 464 Greg Colbrunn .05 .02 .01
- ☐ 465 Tony Fernandez .05 .02 .01
- ☐ 466 Mike Felder .05 .02 .01
- ☐ 467 Lee Stevens .05 .02 .01
- ☐ 468 Matt Whiteside .05 .02 .01
- ☐ 469 Dave Hansen .05 .02 .01
- ☐ 470 Rob Dibble .05 .02 .01
- ☐ 471 Dave Gallagher .05 .02 .01
- ☐ 472 Chris Gwynn .05 .02 .01
- ☐ 473 Dave Henderson .05 .02 .01
- ☐ 474 Ozzie Guillen .05 .02 .01
- ☐ 475 Jeff Reardon .08 .04 .01
- ☐ 476 Mark Voisard and .15 .07 .02
  Will Scalzitti
- ☐ 477 Jimmy Jones .05 .02 .01
- ☐ 478 Greg Cadaret .05 .02 .01
- ☐ 479 Todd Pratt .05 .02 .01
- ☐ 480 Pat Listach .08 .04 .01
- ☐ 481 Ryan Luzinski .15 .07 .02
- ☐ 482 Darren Reed .05 .02 .01
- ☐ 483 Brian Griffiths .05 .02 .01
- ☐ 484 John Wehner .05 .02 .01
- ☐ 485 Glenn Davis .05 .02 .01
- ☐ 486 Eric Wedge .05 .02 .01
- ☐ 487 Jesse Hollins .05 .02 .01
- ☐ 488 Manny Lee .05 .02 .01
- ☐ 489 Scott Fredrickson .08 .04 .01
- ☐ 490 Omar Olivares .05 .02 .01
- ☐ 491 Shawn Hare .05 .02 .01
- ☐ 492 Tom Lampkin .05 .02 .01
- ☐ 493 Jeff Nelson .05 .02 .01
- ☐ 494 1993 Prospects .15 .07 .02
  Kevin Young
  Adell Davenport
  Eduardo Perez
  Lou Lucca
- ☐ 495 Ken Hill .08 .04 .01
- ☐ 496 Reggie Jefferson .05 .02 .01
- ☐ 497 Matt Petersen and .15 .07 .02
  Willie Brown
- ☐ 498 Bud Black .05 .02 .01
- ☐ 499 Chuck Crim .05 .02 .01
- ☐ 500 Jose Canseco .30 .14 .04
- ☐ 501 Johnny Oates MG .05 .02 .01
  Bobby Cox MG
- ☐ 502 Butch Hobson MG .05 .02 .01
  Jim Lefebvre MG
- ☐ 503 Buck Rodgers MG .08 .04 .01
  Tony Perez MG
- ☐ 504 Gene Lamont MG .08 .04 .01
  Don Baylor MG
- ☐ 505 Mike Hargrove MG .08 .04 .01
  Rene Lachemann MG
- ☐ 506 Sparky Anderson MG .08 .04 .01
  Art Howe MG
- ☐ 507 Hal McRae MG .08 .04 .01
  Tom Lasorda MG
- ☐ 508 Phil Garner MG .05 .02 .01
  Felipe Alou MG
- ☐ 509 Tom Kelly MG .05 .02 .01
  Jeff Torborg MG
- ☐ 510 Buck Showalter MG .05 .02 .01
  Jim Fregosi MG
- ☐ 511 Tony LaRussa MG .08 .04 .01
  Jim Leyland MG
- ☐ 512 Lou Piniella MG .08 .04 .01
  Joe Torre MG
- ☐ 513 Kevin Kennedy MG .05 .02 .01
  Jim Riggleman MG
- ☐ 514 Cito Gaston MG .08 .04 .01
  Dusty Baker MG
- ☐ 515 Greg Swindell .05 .02 .01
- ☐ 516 Alex Arias .05 .02 .01
- ☐ 517 Bill Pecota .05 .02 .01
- ☐ 518 Benji Grigsby UER .15 .07 .02
  (Misspelled Bengi
  on card front)
- ☐ 519 David Howard .05 .02 .01
- ☐ 520 Charlie Hough .08 .04 .01
- ☐ 521 Kevin Flora .05 .02 .01
- ☐ 522 Shane Reynolds .08 .04 .01
- ☐ 523 Doug Bochtler .05 .02 .01
- ☐ 524 Chris Hoiles .08 .04 .01
- ☐ 525 Scott Sanderson .05 .02 .01
- ☐ 526 Mike Sharperson .05 .02 .01
- ☐ 527 Mike Fetters .05 .02 .01
- ☐ 528 Paul Quantrill .05 .02 .01
- ☐ 529 1993 Prospects .50 .23 .06
  Dave Silvestri
  Chipper Jones
  Benji Gil
  Jeff Patzke
- ☐ 530 Sterling Hitchcock .15 .07 .02
- ☐ 531 Joe Millette .05 .02 .01
- ☐ 532 Tom Brunansky .05 .02 .01
- ☐ 533 Frank Castillo .05 .02 .01
- ☐ 534 Randy Knorr .05 .02 .01
- ☐ 535 Jose Oquendo .05 .02 .01
- ☐ 536 Dave Haas .05 .02 .01
- ☐ 537 Jason Hutchins and .05 .02 .01
  Ryan Turner
- ☐ 538 Jimmy Baron .15 .07 .02
- ☐ 539 Kerry Woodson .05 .02 .01
- ☐ 540 Ivan Calderon .05 .02 .01
- ☐ 541 Denis Boucher .05 .02 .01

☐ 542 Royce Clayton .08 .04 .01
☐ 543 Reggie Williams .05 .02 .01
☐ 544 Steve Decker .05 .02 .01
☐ 545 Dean Palmer .08 .04 .01
☐ 546 Hal Morris .08 .04 .01
☐ 547 Ryan Thompson .10 .05 .01
☐ 548 Lance Blankenship .05 .02 .01
☐ 549 Hensley Meulens .05 .02 .01
☐ 550 Scott Radinsky .05 .02 .01
☐ 551 Eric Young .08 .04 .01
☐ 552 Jeff Blauser .08 .04 .01
☐ 553 Andujar Cedeno .08 .04 .01
☐ 554 Arthur Rhodes .05 .02 .01
☐ 555 Terry Mulholland .05 .02 .01
☐ 556 Darryl Hamilton .05 .02 .01
☐ 557 Pedro Martinez .10 .05 .01
☐ 558 Ryan Whitman and .15 .07 .02
Mark Skeels
☐ 559 Jamie Arnold .15 .07 .02
☐ 560 Zane Smith .05 .02 .01
☐ 561 Matt Nokes .05 .02 .01
☐ 562 Bob Zupcic .05 .02 .01
☐ 563 Shawn Boskie .05 .02 .01
☐ 564 Mike Timlin .05 .02 .01
☐ 565 Jerald Clark .05 .02 .01
☐ 566 Rod Brewer .05 .02 .01
☐ 567 Mark Carreon .05 .02 .01
☐ 568 Andy Benes .08 .04 .01
☐ 569 Shawn Barton .08 .04 .01
☐ 570 Tim Wallach .05 .02 .01
☐ 571 Dave Mlicki .05 .02 .01
☐ 572 Trevor Hoffman .05 .02 .01
☐ 573 John Patterson .05 .02 .01
☐ 574 De Shawn Warren .20 .09 .03
☐ 575 Monty Fariss .05 .02 .01
☐ 576 1993 Prospects .50 .23 .06
Darrell Sherman
Damon Buford
Cliff Floyd
Michael Moore
☐ 577 Tim Costo .05 .02 .01
☐ 578 Dave Magadan .05 .02 .01
☐ 579 Neil Garret and .20 .09 .03
Jason Bates
☐ 580 Walt Weiss .05 .02 .01
☐ 581 Chris Haney .05 .02 .01
☐ 582 Shawn Abner .05 .02 .01
☐ 583 Marvin Freeman .05 .02 .01
☐ 584 Casey Candaele .05 .02 .01
☐ 585 Ricky Jordan .05 .02 .01
☐ 586 Jeff Tabaka .05 .02 .01
☐ 587 Manny Alexander .05 .02 .01
☐ 588 Mike Trombley .05 .02 .01
☐ 589 Carlos Hernandez .05 .02 .01
☐ 590 Cal Eldred .08 .04 .01
☐ 591 Alex Cole .05 .02 .01
☐ 592 Phil Plantier .10 .05 .01
☐ 593 Brett Merriman .05 .02 .01
☐ 594 Jerry Nielsen .05 .02 .01
☐ 595 Shawon Dunston .05 .02 .01
☐ 596 Jimmy Key .08 .04 .01
☐ 597 Gerald Perry .05 .02 .01
☐ 598 Rico Brogna .05 .02 .01
☐ 599 Clemente Nunez and .05 .02 .01
Daniel Robinson
☐ 600 Bret Saberhagen .08 .04 .01
☐ 601 Craig Shipley .05 .02 .01
☐ 602 Henry Mercedes .05 .02 .01
☐ 603 Jim Thome .25 .11 .03
☐ 604 Rod Beck .10 .05 .01
☐ 605 Chuck Finley .05 .02 .01
☐ 606 J. Owens .05 .02 .01
☐ 607 Dan Smith .05 .02 .01
☐ 608 Bill Doran .05 .02 .01
☐ 609 Lance Parrish .08 .04 .01
☐ 610 Denny Martinez .08 .04 .01
☐ 611 Tom Gordon .05 .02 .01
☐ 612 Byron Mathews .05 .02 .01
☐ 613 Joel Adamson .05 .02 .01
☐ 614 Brian Williams .05 .02 .01
☐ 615 Steve Avery .10 .05 .01
☐ 616 1993 Prospects .60 .25 .08
Matt Mieske
Tracy Sanders
Midre Cummings
Ryan Freeburg
☐ 617 Craig Lefferts .05 .02 .01
☐ 618 Tony Pena .05 .02 .01
☐ 619 Billy Spiers .05 .02 .01
☐ 620 Todd Benzinger .05 .02 .01
☐ 621 Mike Kotarski and .15 .07 .02
Greg Boyd
☐ 622 Ben Rivera .05 .02 .01
☐ 623 Al Martin .08 .04 .01
☐ 624 Sam Militello UER .05 .02 .01
(Profile says drafted
in 1988, bio says
drafted in 1990)
☐ 625 Rick Aguilera .08 .04 .01
☐ 626 Dan Gladden .05 .02 .01
☐ 627 Andres Berumen .15 .07 .02
☐ 628 Kelly Gruber .05 .02 .01
☐ 629 Cris Carpenter .05 .02 .01
☐ 630 Mark Grace .10 .05 .01
☐ 631 Jeff Brantley .05 .02 .01
☐ 632 Chris Widger .15 .07 .02
☐ 633 Three Russians UER .05 .02 .01
(Ilya Bogatyrev is
shortstop, but he has
pitching stats header)
☐ 634 Mo Sanford .05 .02 .01
☐ 635 Albert Belle .60 .25 .08
☐ 636 Tim Teufel .05 .02 .01
☐ 637 Greg Myers .05 .02 .01
☐ 638 Brian Bohanon .05 .02 .01
☐ 639 Mike Bordick .05 .02 .01
☐ 640 Dwight Gooden .05 .02 .01
☐ 641 Pat Leahy and .20 .09 .03
Gavin Baugh
☐ 642 Milt Hill .05 .02 .01
☐ 643 Luis Aquino .05 .02 .01
☐ 644 Dante Bichette .10 .05 .01
☐ 645 Bobby Thigpen .05 .02 .01
☐ 646 Rich Scheid .05 .02 .01
☐ 647 Brian Sackinsky .20 .09 .03
☐ 648 Ryan Hawblitzel .05 .02 .01
☐ 649 Tom Marsh .05 .02 .01
☐ 650 Terry Pendleton .10 .05 .01
☐ 651 Rafael Bournigal .08 .04 .01
☐ 652 Dave West .05 .02 .01
☐ 653 Steve Hosey .05 .02 .01
☐ 654 Gerald Williams .05 .02 .01
☐ 655 Scott Cooper .08 .04 .01
☐ 656 Gary Scott .05 .02 .01
☐ 657 Mike Harkey .05 .02 .01
☐ 658 1993 Prospects .15 .07 .02
Jeromy Burnitz
Melvin Nieves
Rich Becker
Shon Walker
☐ 659 Ed Sprague .05 .02 .01
☐ 660 Alan Trammell .10 .05 .01
☐ 661 Garvin Alston and .15 .07 .02
Michael Case
☐ 662 Donovan Osborne .05 .02 .01
☐ 663 Jeff Gardner .05 .02 .01

	No.	Player			
☐	664	Calvin Jones	.05	.02	.01
☐	665	Darrin Fletcher	.05	.02	.01
☐	666	Glenallen Hill	.05	.02	.01
☐	667	Jim Rosenbohm	.15	.07	.02
☐	668	Scott Lewis	.05	.02	.01
☐	669	Kip Yaughn	.05	.02	.01
☐	670	Julio Franco	.08	.04	.01
☐	671	Dave Martinez	.05	.02	.01
☐	672	Kevin Bass	.05	.02	.01
☐	673	Todd Van Poppel	.08	.04	.01
☐	674	Mark Gubicza	.05	.02	.01
☐	675	Tim Raines	.10	.05	.01
☐	676	Rudy Seanez	.05	.02	.01
☐	677	Charlie Leibrandt	.05	.02	.01
☐	678	Randy Milligan	.05	.02	.01
☐	679	Kim Batiste	.05	.02	.01
☐	680	Craig Biggio	.08	.04	.01
☐	681	Darren Holmes	.05	.02	.01
☐	682	John Candelaria	.05	.02	.01
☐	683	Jerry Stafford and Eddie Christian	.15	.07	.02
☐	684	Pat Mahomes	.05	.02	.01
☐	685	Bob Walk	.05	.02	.01
☐	686	Russ Springer	.05	.02	.01
☐	687	Tony Sheffield	.15	.07	.02
☐	688	Dwight Smith	.05	.02	.01
☐	689	Eddie Zosky	.05	.02	.01
☐	690	Bien Figueroa	.05	.02	.01
☐	691	Jim Tatum	.05	.02	.01
☐	692	Chad Kreuter	.05	.02	.01
☐	693	Rich Rodriguez	.05	.02	.01
☐	694	Shane Turner	.05	.02	.01
☐	695	Kent Bottenfield	.05	.02	.01
☐	696	Jose Mesa	.05	.02	.01
☐	697	Darrell Whitmore	.15	.07	.02
☐	698	Ted Wood	.05	.02	.01
☐	699	Chad Curtis	.08	.04	.01
☐	700	Nolan Ryan	2.00	.90	.25
☐	701	1993 Prospects Mike Piazza Brook Fordyce Carlos Delgado Donnie Leshnock	2.50	1.15	.30
☐	702	Tim Pugh	.05	.02	.01
☐	703	Jeff Kent	.10	.05	.01
☐	704	Jon Goodrich and Danny Figueroa	.15	.07	.02
☐	705	Bob Welch	.05	.02	.01
☐	706	Sherard Clinkscales	.15	.07	.02
☐	707	Donn Pall	.05	.02	.01
☐	708	Greg Olson	.05	.02	.01
☐	709	Jeff Juden	.05	.02	.01
☐	710	Mike Mussina	.40	.18	.05
☐	711	Scott Chiamparino	.05	.02	.01
☐	712	Stan Javier	.05	.02	.01
☐	713	John Doherty	.05	.02	.01
☐	714	Kevin Gross	.05	.02	.01
☐	715	Greg Gagne	.05	.02	.01
☐	716	Steve Cooke	.05	.02	.01
☐	717	Steve Farr	.05	.02	.01
☐	718	Jay Buhner	.08	.04	.01
☐	719	Butch Henry	.05	.02	.01
☐	720	David Cone	.10	.05	.01
☐	721	Rick Wilkins	.05	.02	.01
☐	722	Chuck Carr	.05	.02	.01
☐	723	Kenny Felder	.15	.07	.02
☐	724	Guillermo Velasquez	.05	.02	.01
☐	725	Billy Hatcher	.05	.02	.01
☐	726	Mike Veneziale and Ken Kendrena	.15	.07	.02
☐	727	Jonathan Hurst	.05	.02	.01
☐	728	Steve Frey	.05	.02	.01
☐	729	Mark Leonard	.05	.02	.01
☐	730	Charles Nagy	.05	.02	.01
☐	731	Donald Harris	.05	.02	.01
☐	732	Travis Buckley	.05	.02	.01
☐	733	Tom Browning	.05	.02	.01
☐	734	Anthony Young	.05	.02	.01
☐	735	Steve Shifflett	.05	.02	.01
☐	736	Jeff Russell	.05	.02	.01
☐	737	Wilson Alvarez	.10	.05	.01
☐	738	Lance Painter	.05	.02	.01
☐	739	Dave Weathers	.08	.04	.01
☐	740	Len Dykstra	.10	.05	.01
☐	741	Mike Devereaux	.08	.04	.01
☐	742	1993 Prospects Rene Arocha Alan Embree Brien Taylor Tim Crabtree	.15	.07	.02
☐	743	Dave Landaker	.15	.07	.02
☐	744	Chris George	.05	.02	.01
☐	745	Eric Davis	.05	.02	.01
☐	746	Mark Strittmatter and Lamarr Rogers	.15	.07	.02
☐	747	Carl Willis	.05	.02	.01
☐	748	Stan Belinda	.05	.02	.01
☐	749	Scott Kamieniecki	.05	.02	.01
☐	750	Rickey Henderson	.10	.05	.01
☐	751	Eric Hillman	.05	.02	.01
☐	752	Pat Hentgen	.08	.04	.01
☐	753	Jim Corsi	.05	.02	.01
☐	754	Brian Jordan	.08	.04	.01
☐	755	Bill Swift	.08	.04	.01
☐	756	Mike Henneman	.05	.02	.01
☐	757	Harold Reynolds	.05	.02	.01
☐	758	Sean Berry	.05	.02	.01
☐	759	Charlie Hayes	.08	.04	.01
☐	760	Luis Polonia	.05	.02	.01
☐	761	Darrin Jackson	.05	.02	.01
☐	762	Mark Lewis	.05	.02	.01
☐	763	Rob Maurer	.05	.02	.01
☐	764	Willie Greene	.08	.04	.01
☐	765	Vince Coleman	.05	.02	.01
☐	766	Todd Revenig	.05	.02	.01
☐	767	Rich Ireland	.15	.07	.02
☐	768	Mike Macfarlane	.05	.02	.01
☐	769	Francisco Cabrera	.05	.02	.01
☐	770	Robin Ventura	.10	.05	.01
☐	771	Kevin Ritz	.05	.02	.01
☐	772	Chito Martinez	.05	.02	.01
☐	773	Cliff Brantley	.05	.02	.01
☐	774	Curtis Leskanic	.05	.02	.01
☐	775	Chris Bosio	.05	.02	.01
☐	776	Jose Offerman	.05	.02	.01
☐	777	Mark Guthrie	.05	.02	.01
☐	778	Don Slaught	.05	.02	.01
☐	779	Rich Monteleone	.05	.02	.01
☐	780	Jim Abbott	.10	.05	.01
☐	781	Jack Clark	.05	.02	.01
☐	782	Reynol Mendoza and Dan Roman	.05	.02	.01
☐	783	Heathcliff Slocumb	.05	.02	.01
☐	784	Jeff Branson	.05	.02	.01
☐	785	Kevin Brown	.05	.02	.01
☐	786	1993 Prospects Mike Christopher Ken Ryan Aaron Taylor Gus Gandarillas	.20	.09	.03
☐	787	Mike Matthews	.15	.07	.02
☐	788	Mackey Sasser	.05	.02	.01
☐	789	Jeff Conine UER (No inclusion of 1990 stats in career total)	.10	.05	.01
☐	790	George Bell	.08	.04	.01

☐ 791	Pat Rapp	.08	.04	.01
☐ 792	Joe Boever	.05	.02	.01
☐ 793	Jim Poole	.05	.02	.01
☐ 794	Andy Ashby	.05	.02	.01
☐ 795	Deion Sanders	.40	.18	.05
☐ 796	Scott Brosius	.05	.02	.01
☐ 797	Brad Pennington	.05	.02	.01
☐ 798	Greg Blosser	.05	.02	.01
☐ 799	Jim Edmonds	.30	.14	.04
☐ 800	Shawn Jeter	.05	.02	.01
☐ 801	Jesse Levis	.05	.02	.01
☐ 802	Phil Clark UER (Word "a" is missing in sentence beginning with "In 1992 ...)	.05	.02	.01
☐ 803	Ed Pierce	.05	.02	.01
☐ 804	Jose Valentin	.30	.14	.04
☐ 805	Terry Jorgensen	.05	.02	.01
☐ 806	Mark Hutton	.05	.02	.01
☐ 807	Troy Neel	.08	.04	.01
☐ 808	Bret Boone	.10	.05	.01
☐ 809	Cris Colon	.05	.02	.01
☐ 810	Domingo Martinez	.05	.02	.01
☐ 811	Javy Lopez	.40	.18	.05
☐ 812	Matt Walbeck	.05	.02	.01
☐ 813	Dan Wilson	.05	.02	.01
☐ 814	Scooter Tucker	.05	.02	.01
☐ 815	Billy Ashley	.35	.16	.04
☐ 816	Tim Laker	.05	.02	.01
☐ 817	Bobby Jones	.30	.14	.04
☐ 818	Brad Brink	.05	.02	.01
☐ 819	William Pennyfeather	.05	.02	.01
☐ 820	Stan Royer	.05	.02	.01
☐ 821	Doug Brocail	.05	.02	.01
☐ 822	Kevin Rogers	.05	.02	.01
☐ 823	Checklist 397-540	.05	.02	.01
☐ 824	Checklist 541-691	.05	.02	.01
☐ 825	Checklist 692-825	.05	.02	.01

1993 Topps Gold

Several insertion schemes were devised for these 825 standard-size (2 1/2" by 3 1/2") cards. Gold cards were inserted one per wax pack, three per rack pack, five per jumbo pack, and ten per factory set. The cards are identical to the regular-issue 1993 Topps baseball cards except that the gold-foil Topps Gold logo appears in an upper corner, and the team color-coded stripe at the bottom of the front, which carried the player's name, has been replaced with an embossed gold-foil stripe. The white-bordered front features a color action player photo; the white-bordered back carries a posed color player photo within an oblique rectangle near the upper left. The player's name and position appear above in white lettering within a colored banner. His biography appears alongside. Beneath are the player's stats and career highlights. All design elements of the back are superposed upon a colorful, oblique, and textured pattern. The cards are numbered on the back, and the checklist cards (394-396, 823-825) have been replaced by player cards.

	MINT	EXC	G-VG
COMPLETE GOLD SET (825)	100.00	45.00	12.50
COMPLETE SERIES 1 (396)	50.00	23.00	6.25
COMPLETE SERIES 2 (429)	50.00	23.00	6.25
COMMON CARD (1G-396G)	.10	.05	.01
COMMON CARD (397G-825G)	.10	.05	.01

*VETERAN STARS: 2X to 4X BASIC CARDS
*YOUNG STARS: 1.5X to 3X BASIC CARDS
*RCs: 1.25X to 2.5X BASIC CARDS

1993 Topps Black Gold

Topps Black Gold cards 1-22 were randomly inserted in series I wax packs while card numbers 23-44 were featured in series II packs. Hobbyists could obtain the set by collecting individual random insert cards or receive 11, 22, or 44 Black Gold cards by mail when they sent in special "You've Just Won" cards, which were randomly inserted in packs. Series I packs featured three different "You've Just Won" cards, entitling the holder to receive Group A (cards 1-11), Group B (cards 12-22), or Groups A and B (Cards 1-22). In a similar fashion, four "You've Just Won" cards were inserted in series II packs and entitled the holder to receive Group C (23-33), Group D (34-44), Groups C and D (23-44), or Groups A-D (1-44). By returning the "You've Just Won" card with 1.50 for postage and handling, the collector received not only the Black Gold cards won but also a special "You've Just Won" card and a congratulatory letter informing the collector that his/her name has been entered into a drawing for one of 500 uncut sheets of all 44 Topps Black Gold cards in a leatherette frame. These standard-size (2 1/2" by 3 1/2") cards fea-

ture different color player photos than either the 1993 Topps regular issue or the Topps Gold issue. The player pictures are cut out and superimposed on a black gloss background. Inside white borders, gold refractory foil edges the top and bottom of the card face. On a black-and-gray pinstripe pattern inside white borders, the horizontal backs have a a second cut out player photo and a player profile on a blue panel. The player's name appears in gold foil lettering on a blue-and-gray geometric shape. The cards are numbered on the back in the upper left corner. The first 22 cards are National Leaguers while the second 22 cards are American Leaguers. Winner cards C and D were both originally produced erroneously and later corrected; the error versions show the players from Winner A and B on the respective fronts of Winner cards C and D. There is no value difference in the variations at this time.

	MINT	EXC	G-VG
COMPLETE SET (44)	15.00	6.75	1.90
COMPLETE SERIES 1 (22)	5.00	2.30	.60
COMPLETE SERIES 2 (22)	10.00	4.50	1.25
COMMON CARD (1-22)	.25	.11	.03
COMMON CARD (23-44)	.25	.11	.03

	MINT	EXC	G-VG
☐ 1 Barry Bonds	1.25	.55	.16
☐ 2 Will Clark	.40	.18	.05
☐ 3 Darren Daulton	.35	.16	.04
☐ 4 Andre Dawson	.35	.16	.04
☐ 5 Delino DeShields	.25	.11	.03
☐ 6 Tom Glavine	.35	.16	.04
☐ 7 Marquis Grissom	.35	.16	.04
☐ 8 Tony Gwynn	.75	.35	.09
☐ 9 Eric Karros	.25	.11	.03
☐ 10 Ray Lankford	.35	.16	.04
☐ 11 Barry Larkin	.35	.16	.04
☐ 12 Greg Maddux	.75	.35	.09
☐ 13 Fred McGriff	.40	.18	.05
☐ 14 Joe Oliver	.25	.11	.03
☐ 15 Terry Pendleton	.25	.11	.03
☐ 16 Bip Roberts	.25	.11	.03
☐ 17 Ryne Sandberg	1.00	.45	.13
☐ 18 Gary Sheffield	.35	.16	.04
☐ 19 Lee Smith	.25	.11	.03
☐ 20 Ozzie Smith	.60	.25	.08
☐ 21 Andy Van Slyke	.25	.11	.03
☐ 22 Larry Walker	.35	.16	.04
☐ 23 Roberto Alomar	.75	.35	.09
☐ 24 Brady Anderson	.25	.11	.03
☐ 25 Carlos Baerga	.40	.18	.05
☐ 26 Joe Carter	.40	.18	.05
☐ 27 Roger Clemens	.75	.35	.09
☐ 28 Mike Devereaux	.25	.11	.03
☐ 29 Dennis Eckersley	.25	.11	.03
☐ 30 Cecil Fielder	.35	.16	.04
☐ 31 Travis Fryman	.35	.16	.04
☐ 32 Juan Gonzalez UER (No copyright or licensing on card)	1.00	.45	.13
☐ 33 Ken Griffey Jr.	3.00	1.35	.40
☐ 34 Brian Harper	.25	.11	.03
☐ 35 Pat Listach	.25	.11	.03
☐ 36 Kenny Lofton	.75	.35	.09
☐ 37 Edgar Martinez	.25	.11	.03
☐ 38 Jack McDowell	.35	.16	.04
☐ 39 Mark McGwire	.25	.11	.03
☐ 40 Kirby Puckett	1.25	.55	.16
☐ 41 Mickey Tettleton	.25	.11	.03
☐ 42 Frank Thomas UER (No copyright or licensing on card)	3.00	1.35	.40
☐ 43 Robin Ventura	.35	.16	.04
☐ 44 Dave Winfield	.35	.16	.04
☐ A Winner A 1-11	.50	.23	.06
☐ AB Winner AB 1-22 UER (Numbers 10 and 11 have the 1 missing)	1.00	.45	.13
☐ ABCD Winner ABCD 1-44	2.50	1.15	.30
☐ B Winner B 12-22	.50	.23	.06
☐ C Winner C 23-33	.75	.35	.09
☐ CD Winner C/D 23-44	1.50	.65	.19
☐ D Winner D 34-44	.75	.35	.09

1993 Topps Traded

This 132-card set focuses on promising rookies, new managers, free agents, and players who changed teams. The set also includes 22 members of Team USA. The standard-size (2 1/2" by 3 1/2") cards carry the same design on the front as the regular 1993 Topps issue. The backs are also the same design and carry a head shot, biography, stats, and career highlights. The cards are numbered on the back. Rookie Cards in this set include Todd Helton, Dante Powell, Todd Walker and Paul Wilson.

	MINT	EXC	G-VG
COMPLETE FACT.SET (132)	14.00	6.25	1.75
COMMON CARD (1T-132T)	.05	.02	.01

	MINT	EXC	G-VG
☐ 1T Barry Bonds	.75	.35	.09
☐ 2T Rich Renteria	.05	.02	.01
☐ 3T Aaron Sele	.35	.16	.04
☐ 4T Carlton Loewer USA	.30	.14	.04
☐ 5T Erik Pappas	.05	.02	.01
☐ 6T Greg McMichael	.15	.07	.02
☐ 7T Freddie Benavides	.05	.02	.01
☐ 8T Kirk Gibson	.08	.04	.01
☐ 9T Tony Fernandez	.05	.02	.01
☐ 10T Jay Gainer	.05	.02	.01
☐ 11T Orestes Destrade	.05	.02	.01
☐ 12T A.J. Hinch USA	.50	.23	.06
☐ 13T Bobby Munoz	.05	.02	.01
☐ 14T Tom Henke	.08	.04	.01
☐ 15T Rob Butler	.08	.04	.01
☐ 16T Gary Wayne	.05	.02	.01
☐ 17T David McCarty	.08	.04	.01
☐ 18T Walt Weiss	.05	.02	.01
☐ 19T Todd Helton USA	1.50	.65	.19
☐ 20T Mark Whiten	.08	.04	.01
☐ 21T Ricky Gutierrez	.05	.02	.01

	No.	Player			
☐	22T	Dustin Hermanson USA	.75	.35	.09
☐	23T	Sherman Obando	.15	.07	.02
☐	24T	Mike Piazza	2.00	.90	.25
☐	25T	Jeff Russell	.05	.02	.01
☐	26T	Jason Bere	.50	.23	.06
☐	27T	Jack Voigt	.08	.04	.01
☐	28T	Chris Bosio	.05	.02	.01
☐	29T	Phil Hiatt	.05	.02	.01
☐	30T	Matt Beaumont USA	.40	.18	.05
☐	31T	Andres Galarraga	.10	.05	.01
☐	32T	Greg Swindell	.05	.02	.01
☐	33T	Vinny Castilla	.05	.02	.01
☐	34T	Pat Clougherty USA	.25	.11	.03
☐	35T	Greg Briley	.05	.02	.01
☐	36T	Dallas Green MG Davey Johnson MG	.05	.02	.01
☐	37T	Tyler Green	.05	.02	.01
☐	38T	Craig Paquette	.05	.02	.01
☐	39T	Danny Sheaffer	.05	.02	.01
☐	40T	Jim Converse	.15	.07	.02
☐	41T	Terry Harvey USA	.25	.11	.03
☐	42T	Phil Plantier	.10	.05	.01
☐	43T	Doug Saunders	.05	.02	.01
☐	44T	Benny Santiago	.05	.02	.01
☐	45T	Dante Powell USA	1.25	.55	.16
☐	46T	Jeff Parrett	.05	.02	.01
☐	47T	Wade Boggs	.10	.05	.01
☐	48T	Paul Molitor	.30	.14	.04
☐	49T	Turk Wendell	.08	.04	.01
☐	50T	David Wells	.05	.02	.01
☐	51T	Gary Sheffield	.10	.05	.01
☐	52T	Kevin Young	.05	.02	.01
☐	53T	Nelson Liriano	.05	.02	.01
☐	54T	Greg Maddux	.40	.18	.05
☐	55T	Derek Bell	.08	.04	.01
☐	56T	Matt Turner	.08	.04	.01
☐	57T	Charlie Nelson USA	.40	.18	.05
☐	58T	Mike Hampton	.05	.02	.01
☐	59T	Troy O'Leary	.05	.02	.01
☐	60T	Benji Gil	.08	.04	.01
☐	61T	Mitch Lyden	.08	.04	.01
☐	62T	J.T. Snow	.15	.07	.02
☐	63T	Damon Buford	.05	.02	.01
☐	64T	Gene Harris	.05	.02	.01
☐	65T	Randy Myers	.08	.04	.01
☐	66T	Felix Jose	.05	.02	.01
☐	67T	Todd Dunn USA	.25	.11	.03
☐	68T	Jimmy Key	.08	.04	.01
☐	69T	Pedro Castellano	.05	.02	.01
☐	70T	Mark Merila USA	.25	.11	.03
☐	71T	Rich Rodriguez	.05	.02	.01
☐	72T	Matt Mieske	.08	.04	.01
☐	73T	Pete Incaviglia	.05	.02	.01
☐	74T	Carl Everett	.08	.04	.01
☐	75T	Jim Abbott	.10	.05	.01
☐	76T	Luis Aquino	.05	.02	.01
☐	77T	Rene Arocha	.15	.07	.02
☐	78T	Jon Shave	.05	.02	.01
☐	79T	Todd Walker USA	1.50	.65	.19
☐	80T	Jack Armstrong	.05	.02	.01
☐	81T	Jeff Richardson	.05	.02	.01
☐	82T	Blas Minor	.05	.02	.01
☐	83T	Dave Winfield	.10	.05	.01
☐	84T	Paul O'Neill	.08	.04	.01
☐	85T	Steve Reich USA	.25	.11	.03
☐	86T	Chris Hammond	.05	.02	.01
☐	87T	Hilly Hathaway	.05	.02	.01
☐	88T	Fred McGriff	.30	.14	.04
☐	89T	Dave Telgheder	.05	.02	.01
☐	90T	Richie Lewis	.05	.02	.01
☐	91T	Brent Gates	.10	.05	.01
☐	92T	Andre Dawson	.10	.05	.01
☐	93T	Andy Barkett USA	.25	.11	.03
☐	94T	Doug Drabek	.10	.05	.01
☐	95T	Joe Klink	.05	.02	.01
☐	96T	Willie Blair	.05	.02	.01
☐	97T	Danny Graves USA	.30	.14	.04
☐	98T	Pat Meares	.15	.07	.02
☐	99T	Mike Lansing	.20	.09	.03
☐	100T	Marcos Armas	.05	.02	.01
☐	101T	Darren Grass USA	.40	.18	.05
☐	102T	Chris Jones	.05	.02	.01
☐	103T	Ken Ryan	.15	.07	.02
☐	104T	Ellis Burks	.08	.04	.01
☐	105T	Roberto Kelly	.08	.04	.01
☐	106T	Dave Magadan	.05	.02	.01
☐	107T	Paul Wilson USA	1.25	.55	.16
☐	108T	Rob Natal	.05	.02	.01
☐	109T	Paul Wagner	.05	.02	.01
☐	110T	Jeromy Burnitz	.08	.04	.01
☐	111T	Monty Fariss	.05	.02	.01
☐	112T	Kevin Mitchell	.08	.04	.01
☐	113T	Scott Pose	.05	.02	.01
☐	114T	Dave Stewart	.08	.04	.01
☐	115T	Russ Johnson USA	.40	.18	.05
☐	116T	Armando Reynoso	.05	.02	.01
☐	117T	Geronimo Berroa	.05	.02	.01
☐	118T	Woody Williams	.05	.02	.01
☐	119T	Tim Bogar	.05	.02	.01
☐	120T	Bob Scafa USA	.25	.11	.03
☐	121T	Henry Cotto	.05	.02	.01
☐	122T	Gregg Jefferies	.10	.05	.01
☐	123T	Norm Charlton	.05	.02	.01
☐	124T	Bret Wagner USA	.75	.35	.09
☐	125T	David Cone	.10	.05	.01
☐	126T	Daryl Boston	.05	.02	.01
☐	127T	Tim Wallach	.05	.02	.01
☐	128T	Mike Martin USA	.50	.23	.06
☐	129T	John Cummings	.05	.02	.01
☐	130T	Ryan Bowen	.05	.02	.01
☐	131T	John Powell USA	.40	.18	.05
☐	132T	Checklist 1-132	.05	.02	.01

1994 Topps

These 792 standard-size cards were issued in two series of 396. Two types of factory sets were also issued. One features the 792 basic cards, ten Topps Gold, three Black Gold and three Finest Pre-Production cards for a total of 808. The other factory set (Bakers Dozen) includes the 792 basic cards, ten Topps Gold, three Black Gold, ten 1995 Topps Pre-Production cards and a sample pack of three special Topps cards for a total of 818. In each case, one of the Pre-Production cards is a Spectralite ver-

sion of one of the nine players included among the sample. The sample pack consists of three different Topps brand cards (Bowman, Finest, Stadium Club) of the same player. Including those featured in the special packs are Mo Vaughn, Larry Walker, Cliff Floyd, Rafael Palmeiro, David Justice and Ken Griffey Jr. The standard cards feature glossy color player photos with white borders on the fronts. The player's name is in white cursive lettering at the bottom left, with the team name and player's position printed on a team color-coded bar. There is an inner multicolored border along the left side that extends obliquely across the bottom. The horizontal backs carry an action shot of the player with biography, statistics and highlights. Subsets include Draft Picks (201-210/739-762), All-Stars (384-394) and Stat Twins (601-609). Rookie Cards include Alan Benes, Brooks Kieschnick, Kirk Presley and Pat Watkins.

	MINT	EXC	G-VG
COMPLETE SET (792)	40.00	18.00	5.00
COMPLETE FACT.SET (808)	50.00	23.00	6.25
COMP.BAKERS DOZEN (818)	50.00	23.00	6.25
COMPLETE SERIES 1 (396)	20.00	9.00	2.50
COMPLETE SERIES 2 (396)	20.00	9.00	2.50
COMMON CARD (1-396)	.05	.02	.01
COMMON CARD (397-792)	.05	.02	.01

		MINT	EXC	G-VG
☐ 1	Mike Piazza	1.00	.45	.13
☐ 2	Bernie Williams	.08	.04	.01
☐ 3	Kevin Rogers	.05	.02	.01
☐ 4	Paul Carey	.05	.02	.01
☐ 5	Ozzie Guillen	.05	.02	.01
☐ 6	Derrick May	.05	.02	.01
☐ 7	Jose Mesa	.05	.02	.01
☐ 8	Todd Hundley	.05	.02	.01
☐ 9	Chris Haney	.05	.02	.01
☐ 10	John Olerud	.10	.05	.01
☐ 11	Andujar Cedeno	.05	.02	.01
☐ 12	John Smiley	.05	.02	.01
☐ 13	Phil Plantier	.08	.04	.01
☐ 14	Willie Banks	.05	.02	.01
☐ 15	Jay Bell	.08	.04	.01
☐ 16	Doug Henry	.05	.02	.01
☐ 17	Lance Blankenship	.05	.02	.01
☐ 18	Greg W. Harris	.05	.02	.01
☐ 19	Scott Livingstone	.05	.02	.01
☐ 20	Bryan Harvey	.08	.04	.01
☐ 21	Wil Cordero	.10	.05	.01
☐ 22	Roger Pavlik	.05	.02	.01
☐ 23	Mark Lemke	.05	.02	.01
☐ 24	Jeff Nelson	.05	.02	.01
☐ 25	Todd Zeile	.08	.04	.01
☐ 26	Billy Hatcher	.05	.02	.01
☐ 27	Joe Magrane	.05	.02	.01
☐ 28	Tony Longmire	.05	.02	.01
☐ 29	Omar Daal	.05	.02	.01
☐ 30	Kirt Manwaring	.05	.02	.01
☐ 31	Melido Perez	.05	.02	.01
☐ 32	Tim Hulett	.05	.02	.01
☐ 33	Jeff Schwartz	.05	.02	.01
☐ 34	Nolan Ryan	2.00	.90	.25
☐ 35	Jose Guzman	.05	.02	.01
☐ 36	Felix Fermin	.05	.02	.01
☐ 37	Jeff Innis	.05	.02	.01
☐ 38	Brett Mayne	.05	.02	.01
☐ 39	Huck Flener	.05	.02	.01
☐ 40	Jeff Bagwell	1.00	.45	.13
☐ 41	Kevin Wickander	.05	.02	.01
☐ 42	Ricky Gutierrez	.05	.02	.01
☐ 43	Pat Mahomes	.05	.02	.01
☐ 44	Jeff King	.05	.02	.01
☐ 45	Cal Eldred	.08	.04	.01
☐ 46	Craig Paquette	.05	.02	.01
☐ 47	Richie Lewis	.05	.02	.01
☐ 48	Tony Phillips	.05	.02	.01
☐ 49	Armando Reynoso	.05	.02	.01
☐ 50	Moises Alou	.10	.05	.01
☐ 51	Manny Lee	.05	.02	.01
☐ 52	Otis Nixon	.05	.02	.01
☐ 53	Billy Ashley	.10	.05	.01
☐ 54	Mark Whiten	.08	.04	.01
☐ 55	Jeff Russell	.05	.02	.01
☐ 56	Chad Curtis	.08	.04	.01
☐ 57	Kevin Stocker	.08	.04	.01
☐ 58	Mike Jackson	.05	.02	.01
☐ 59	Matt Nokes	.05	.02	.01
☐ 60	Chris Bosio	.05	.02	.01
☐ 61	Damon Buford	.05	.02	.01
☐ 62	Tim Belcher	.05	.02	.01
☐ 63	Glenallen Hill	.05	.02	.01
☐ 64	Bill Wertz	.05	.02	.01
☐ 65	Eddie Murray	.10	.05	.01
☐ 66	Tom Gordon	.05	.02	.01
☐ 67	Alex Gonzalez	.20	.09	.03
☐ 68	Eddie Taubensee	.05	.02	.01
☐ 69	Jacob Brumfield	.05	.02	.01
☐ 70	Andy Benes	.08	.04	.01
☐ 71	Rich Becker	.08	.04	.01
☐ 72	Steve Cooke	.05	.02	.01
☐ 73	Billy Spiers	.05	.02	.01
☐ 74	Scott Brosius	.05	.02	.01
☐ 75	Alan Trammell	.10	.05	.01
☐ 76	Luis Aquino	.05	.02	.01
☐ 77	Jerald Clark	.05	.02	.01
☐ 78	Mel Rojas	.05	.02	.01
☐ 79	Outfield Prospects Billy Masse Stanton Cameron Tim Clark Craig McClure	.40	.18	.05
☐ 80	Jose Canseco	.30	.14	.04
☐ 81	Greg McMichael	.08	.04	.01
☐ 82	Brian Turang	.05	.02	.01
☐ 83	Tom Urbani	.05	.02	.01
☐ 84	Garret Anderson	.08	.04	.01
☐ 85	Tony Pena	.05	.02	.01
☐ 86	Ricky Jordan	.05	.02	.01
☐ 87	Jim Gott	.05	.02	.01
☐ 88	Pat Kelly	.05	.02	.01
☐ 89	Bud Black	.05	.02	.01
☐ 90	Robin Ventura	.08	.04	.01
☐ 91	Rick Sutcliffe	.08	.04	.01
☐ 92	Jose Bautista	.05	.02	.01
☐ 93	Bob Ojeda	.05	.02	.01
☐ 94	Phil Hiatt	.10	.05	.01
☐ 95	Tim Pugh	.05	.02	.01
☐ 96	Randy Knorr	.05	.02	.01
☐ 97	Todd Jones	.05	.02	.01
☐ 98	Ryan Thompson	.08	.04	.01
☐ 99	Tim Mauser	.05	.02	.01
☐ 100	Kirby Puckett	.75	.35	.09
☐ 101	Mark Dewey	.05	.02	.01
☐ 102	B.J. Surhoff	.05	.02	.01
☐ 103	Sterling Hitchcock	.08	.04	.01
☐ 104	Alex Arias	.05	.02	.01
☐ 105	David Wells	.05	.02	.01
☐ 106	Daryl Boston	.05	.02	.01
☐ 107	Mike Stanton	.05	.02	.01
☐ 108	Gary Redus	.05	.02	.01
☐ 109	Delino DeShields	.08	.04	.01
☐ 110	Lee Smith	.10	.05	.01

☐	111	Greg Litton	.05	.02	.01
☐	112	Frankie Rodriguez	.10	.05	.01
☐	113	Russ Springer	.05	.02	.01
☐	114	Mitch Williams	.05	.02	.01
☐	115	Eric Karros	.08	.04	.01
☐	116	Jeff Brantley	.05	.02	.01
☐	117	Jack Voigt	.05	.02	.01
☐	118	Jason Bere	.25	.11	.03
☐	119	Kevin Roberson	.05	.02	.01
☐	120	Jimmy Key	.08	.04	.01
☐	121	Reggie Jefferson	.05	.02	.01
☐	122	Jeromy Burnitz	.08	.04	.01
☐	123	Billy Brewer	.05	.02	.01
☐	124	Willie Canate	.05	.02	.01
☐	125	Greg Swindell	.05	.02	.01
☐	126	Hal Morris	.08	.04	.01
☐	127	Brad Ausmus	.05	.02	.01
☐	128	George Tsamis	.05	.02	.01
☐	129	Denny Neagle	.05	.02	.01
☐	130	Pat Listach	.05	.02	.01
☐	131	Steve Karsay	.05	.02	.01
☐	132	Bret Barberie 3X	.05	.02	.01
		(Jeff Bagwell barrelling in)			
☐	133	Mark Leiter	.05	.02	.01
☐	134	Greg Colbrunn	.05	.02	.01
☐	135	David Nied	.10	.05	.01
☐	136	Dean Palmer	.08	.04	.01
☐	137	Steve Avery	.10	.05	.01
☐	138	Bill Haselman	.05	.02	.01
☐	139	Tripp Cromer	.05	.02	.01
☐	140	Frank Viola	.05	.02	.01
☐	141	Rene Gonzales	.05	.02	.01
☐	142	Curt Schilling	.05	.02	.01
☐	143	Tim Wallach	.05	.02	.01
☐	144	Bobby Munoz	.05	.02	.01
☐	145	Brady Anderson	.08	.04	.01
☐	146	Rod Beck	.08	.04	.01
☐	147	Mike LaValliere	.05	.02	.01
☐	148	Greg Hibbard	.05	.02	.01
☐	149	Kenny Lofton	.50	.23	.06
☐	150	Dwight Gooden	.05	.02	.01
☐	151	Greg Gagne	.05	.02	.01
☐	152	Ray McDavid	.05	.02	.01
☐	153	Chris Donnels	.05	.02	.01
☐	154	Dan Wilson	.05	.02	.01
☐	155	Todd Stottlemyre	.05	.02	.01
☐	156	David McCarty	.08	.04	.01
☐	157	Paul Wagner	.05	.02	.01
☐	158	Shortstop Prospects	.40	.18	.05
		Orlando Miller			
		Brandon Wilson			
		Derek Jeter			
		Mike Neal			
☐	159	Mike Fetters	.05	.02	.01
☐	160	Scott Lydy	.05	.02	.01
☐	161	Darrell Whitmore	.08	.04	.01
☐	162	Bob MacDonald	.05	.02	.01
☐	163	Vinny Castilla	.05	.02	.01
☐	164	Denis Boucher	.05	.02	.01
☐	165	Ivan Rodriguez	.10	.05	.01
☐	166	Ron Gant	.08	.04	.01
☐	167	Tim Davis	.05	.02	.01
☐	168	Steve Dixon	.05	.02	.01
☐	169	Scott Fletcher	.05	.02	.01
☐	170	Terry Mulholland	.05	.02	.01
☐	171	Greg Myers	.05	.02	.01
☐	172	Brett Butler	.08	.04	.01
☐	173	Bob Wickman	.05	.02	.01
☐	174	Dave Martinez	.05	.02	.01
☐	175	Fernando Valenzuela	.05	.02	.01
☐	176	Craig Grebeck	.05	.02	.01
☐	177	Shawn Boskie	.05	.02	.01
☐	178	Albie Lopez	.10	.05	.01
☐	179	Butch Huskey	.05	.02	.01
☐	180	George Brett	.75	.35	.09
☐	181	Juan Guzman	.08	.04	.01
☐	182	Eric Anthony	.05	.02	.01
☐	183	Rob Dibble	.05	.02	.01
☐	184	Craig Shipley	.05	.02	.01
☐	185	Kevin Tapani	.05	.02	.01
☐	186	Marcus Moore	.05	.02	.01
☐	187	Graeme Lloyd	.05	.02	.01
☐	188	Mike Bordick	.05	.02	.01
☐	189	Chris Hammond	.05	.02	.01
☐	190	Cecil Fielder	.10	.05	.01
☐	191	Curtis Leskanic	.05	.02	.01
☐	192	Lou Frazier	.05	.02	.01
☐	193	Steve Dreyer	.15	.07	.02
☐	194	Javy Lopez	.20	.09	.03
☐	195	Edgar Martinez	.05	.02	.01
☐	196	Allen Watson	.05	.02	.01
☐	197	John Flaherty	.05	.02	.01
☐	198	Kurt Stillwell	.05	.02	.01
☐	199	Danny Jackson	.05	.02	.01
☐	200	Cal Ripken	1.50	.65	.19
☐	201	Mike Bell FDP	.25	.11	.03
☐	202	Alan Benes FDP	.60	.25	.08
☐	203	Matt Farner FDP	.25	.11	.03
☐	204	Jeff Granger FDP	.23	.10	.03
☐	205	Brooks Kieschnick FDP	.60	.25	.08
☐	206	Jeremy Lee FDP	.20	.09	.03
☐	207	Charles Peterson FDP	.25	.11	.03
☐	208	Alan Rice FDP	.20	.09	.03
☐	209	Billy Wagner FDP	.40	.18	.05
☐	210	Kelly Wunsch FDP	.30	.14	.04
☐	211	Tom Candiotti	.05	.02	.01
☐	212	Domingo Jean	.05	.02	.01
☐	213	John Burkett	.08	.04	.01
☐	214	George Bell	.08	.04	.01
☐	215	Dan Plesac	.05	.02	.01
☐	216	Manny Ramirez	.40	.18	.05
☐	217	Mike Maddux	.05	.02	.01
☐	218	Kevin McReynolds	.05	.02	.01
☐	219	Pat Borders	.05	.02	.01
☐	220	Doug Drabek	.10	.05	.01
☐	221	Larry Luebbers	.05	.02	.01
☐	222	Trevor Hoffman	.05	.02	.01
☐	223	Pat Meares	.05	.02	.01
☐	224	Danny Miceli	.05	.02	.01
☐	225	Greg Vaughn	.08	.04	.01
☐	226	Scott Hemond	.05	.02	.01
☐	227	Pat Rapp	.05	.02	.01
☐	228	Kirk Gibson	.08	.04	.01
☐	229	Lance Painter	.05	.02	.01
☐	230	Larry Walker	.10	.05	.01
☐	231	Benji Gil	.08	.04	.01
☐	232	Mark Wohlers	.05	.02	.01
☐	233	Rich Amaral	.05	.02	.01
☐	234	Eric Pappas	.05	.02	.01
☐	235	Scott Cooper	.08	.04	.01
☐	236	Mike Butcher	.05	.02	.01
☐	237	Outfield Prospects	.30	.14	.04
		Curtis Pride			
		Shawn Green			
		Mark Sweeney			
		Eddie Davis			
☐	238	Kim Batiste	.05	.02	.01
☐	239	Paul Assenmacher	.05	.02	.01
☐	240	Will Clark	.30	.14	.04
☐	241	Jose Offerman	.08	.04	.01
☐	242	Todd Frohwirth	.05	.02	.01
☐	243	Tim Raines	.10	.05	.01
☐	244	Rick Wilkins	.05	.02	.01
☐	245	Bret Saberhagen	.08	.04	.01
☐	246	Thomas Howard	.05	.02	.01
☐	247	Stan Belinda	.05	.02	.01

	No.	Player			
☐	248	Rickey Henderson	.10	.05	.01
☐	249	Brian Williams	.05	.02	.01
☐	250	Barry Larkin	.10	.05	.01
☐	251	Jose Valentin	.05	.02	.01
☐	252	Lenny Webster	.05	.02	.01
☐	253	Blas Minor	.05	.02	.01
☐	254	Tim Teufel	.05	.02	.01
☐	255	Bobby Witt	.05	.02	.01
☐	256	Walt Weiss	.05	.02	.01
☐	257	Chad Kreuter	.05	.02	.01
☐	258	Roberto Mejia	.08	.04	.01
☐	259	Cliff Floyd	.30	.14	.04
☐	260	Julio Franco	.08	.04	.01
☐	261	Rafael Belliard	.05	.02	.01
☐	262	Marc Newfield	.10	.05	.01
☐	263	Gerald Perry	.05	.02	.01
☐	264	Ken Ryan	.05	.02	.01
☐	265	Chili Davis	.08	.04	.01
☐	266	Dave West	.05	.02	.01
☐	267	Royce Clayton	.08	.04	.01
☐	268	Pedro Martinez	.10	.05	.01
☐	269	Mark Hutton	.05	.02	.01
☐	270	Frank Thomas	2.00	.90	.25
☐	271	Brad Pennington	.05	.02	.01
☐	272	Mike Harkey	.05	.02	.01
☐	273	Sandy Alomar	.08	.04	.01
☐	274	Dave Gallagher	.05	.02	.01
☐	275	Wally Joyner	.08	.04	.01
☐	276	Ricky Trlicek	.05	.02	.01
☐	277	Al Osuna	.05	.02	.01
☐	278	Calvin Reese	.08	.04	.01
☐	279	Kevin Higgins	.05	.02	.01
☐	280	Rick Aguilera	.08	.04	.01
☐	281	Orlando Merced	.08	.04	.01
☐	282	Mike Mohler	.05	.02	.01
☐	283	John Jaha	.05	.02	.01
☐	284	Robb Nen	.05	.02	.01
☐	285	Travis Fryman	.15	.07	.02
☐	286	Mark Thompson	.08	.04	.01
☐	287	Mike Lansing	.08	.04	.01
☐	288	Craig Lefferts	.05	.02	.01
☐	289	Damon Berryhill	.05	.02	.01
☐	290	Randy Johnson	.10	.05	.01
☐	291	Jeff Reed	.05	.02	.01
☐	292	Danny Darwin	.05	.02	.01
☐	293	J.T. Snow	.08	.04	.01
☐	294	Tyler Green	.05	.02	.01
☐	295	Chris Hoiles	.08	.04	.01
☐	296	Roger McDowell	.05	.02	.01
☐	297	Spike Owen	.05	.02	.01
☐	298	Salomon Torres	.08	.04	.01
☐	299	Wilson Alvarez	.10	.05	.01
☐	300	Ryne Sandberg 3X	.60	.25	.08
☐	301	Derek Lilliquist	.05	.02	.01
☐	302	Howard Johnson	.05	.02	.01
☐	303	Greg Cadaret	.05	.02	.01
☐	304	Pat Hentgen	.08	.04	.01
☐	305	Craig Biggio	.08	.04	.01
☐	306	Scott Service	.05	.02	.01
☐	307	Melvin Nieves	.10	.05	.01
☐	308	Mike Trombley	.05	.02	.01
☐	309	Carlos Garcia	.05	.02	.01
☐	310	Robin Yount UER (listed with 111 triples in 1988; should be 11)	.30	.14	.04
☐	311	Marcos Armas	.05	.02	.01
☐	312	Rich Rodriguez	.05	.02	.01
☐	313	Justin Thompson	.05	.02	.01
☐	314	Danny Sheaffer	.05	.02	.01
☐	315	Ken Hill	.08	.04	.01
☐	316	Pitching Prospects	.50	.23	.06
		Chad Ogea			
		Duff Brumley			
		Terrell Wade			
		Chris Michalak			
☐	317	Cris Carpenter	.05	.02	.01
☐	318	Jeff Blauser	.08	.04	.01
☐	319	Ted Power	.05	.02	.01
☐	320	Ozzie Smith	.40	.18	.05
☐	321	John Dopson	.05	.02	.01
☐	322	Chris Turner	.05	.02	.01
☐	323	Pete Incaviglia	.05	.02	.01
☐	324	Alan Mills	.05	.02	.01
☐	325	Jody Reed	.05	.02	.01
☐	326	Rich Monteleone	.05	.02	.01
☐	327	Mark Carreon	.05	.02	.01
☐	328	Donn Pall	.05	.02	.01
☐	329	Matt Walbeck	.05	.02	.01
☐	330	Charley Nagy	.05	.02	.01
☐	331	Jeff McKnight	.05	.02	.01
☐	332	Jose Lind	.05	.02	.01
☐	333	Mike Timlin	.05	.02	.01
☐	334	Doug Jones	.05	.02	.01
☐	335	Kevin Mitchell	.08	.04	.01
☐	336	Luis Lopez	.05	.02	.01
☐	337	Shane Mack	.08	.04	.01
☐	338	Randy Tomlin	.05	.02	.01
☐	339	Matt Mieske	.05	.02	.01
☐	340	Mark McGwire	.10	.05	.01
☐	341	Nigel Wilson	.08	.04	.01
☐	342	Danny Gladden	.05	.02	.01
☐	343	Mo Sanford	.05	.02	.01
☐	344	Sean Berry	.05	.02	.01
☐	345	Kevin Brown	.05	.02	.01
☐	346	Greg Olson	.05	.02	.01
☐	347	Dave Magadan	.05	.02	.01
☐	348	Rene Arocha	.08	.04	.01
☐	349	Carlos Quintana	.05	.02	.01
☐	350	Jim Abbott	.10	.05	.01
☐	351	Gary DiSarcina	.05	.02	.01
☐	352	Ben Rivera	.05	.02	.01
☐	353	Carlos Hernandez	.05	.02	.01
☐	354	Darren Lewis	.05	.02	.01
☐	355	Harold Reynolds	.05	.02	.01
☐	356	Scott Ruffcorn	.10	.05	.01
☐	357	Mark Gubicza	.05	.02	.01
☐	358	Paul Sorrento	.05	.02	.01
☐	359	Anthony Young	.05	.02	.01
☐	360	Mark Grace	.10	.05	.01
☐	361	Rob Butler	.05	.02	.01
☐	362	Kevin Bass	.05	.02	.01
☐	363	Eric Helfand	.05	.02	.01
☐	364	Derek Bell	.08	.04	.01
☐	365	Scott Erickson	.05	.02	.01
☐	366	Al Martin	.05	.02	.01
☐	367	Ricky Bones	.05	.02	.01
☐	368	Jeff Branson	.05	.02	.01
☐	369	Third Base Prospects	.25	.11	.03
		Luis Ortiz			
		David Bell			
		Jason Giambi			
		George Arias			
☐	370	Benito Santiago (See also 379)	.05	.02	.01
☐	371	John Doherty	.05	.02	.01
☐	372	Joe Girardi	.05	.02	.01
☐	373	Tim Scott	.05	.02	.01
☐	374	Marvin Freeman	.05	.02	.01
☐	375	Deion Sanders	.35	.16	.04
☐	376	Roger Salkeld	.05	.02	.01
☐	377	Bernard Gilkey	.05	.02	.01
☐	378	Tony Fossas	.05	.02	.01
☐	379	Mark McLemore UER (Card number is 370)	.05	.02	.01
☐	380	Darren Daulton	.10	.05	.01
☐	381	Chuck Finley	.05	.02	.01

	No.	Player			
☐	382	Mitch Webster	.05	.02	.01
☐	383	Gerald Williams	.05	.02	.01
☐	384	Frank Thomas AS	.50	.23	.06
		Fred McGriff AS			
☐	385	Roberto Alomar AS	.05	.02	.01
		Robby Thompson AS			
☐	386	Wade Boggs AS	.08	.04	.01
		Matt Williams AS			
☐	387	Cal Ripken AS	.35	.16	.04
		Jeff Blauser AS			
☐	388	Ken Griffey Jr. AS	.50	.23	.06
		Len Dykstra AS			
☐	389	Juan Gonzalez AS	.20	.09	.03
		David Justice AS			
☐	390	George Belle AS	.25	.11	.03
		Bobby Bonds AS			
☐	391	Mike Stanley AS	.25	.11	.03
		Mike Piazza AS			
☐	392	Jack McDowell AS	.08	.04	.01
		Greg Maddux AS			
☐	393	Jimmy Key AS	.08	.04	.01
		Tom Glavine AS			
☐	394	Jeff Montgomery AS	.05	.02	.01
		Randy Myers AS			
☐	395	Checklist 1-198	.05	.02	.01
☐	396	Checklist 199-396	.05	.02	.01
☐	397	Tim Salmon	.30	.14	.04
☐	398	Todd Benzinger	.05	.02	.01
☐	399	Frank Castillo	.05	.02	.01
☐	400	Ken Griffey Jr.	2.00	.90	.25
☐	401	John Kruk	.10	.05	.01
☐	402	Dave Telgheder	.05	.02	.01
☐	403	Gary Gaetti	.05	.02	.01
☐	404	Jim Edmonds	.05	.02	.01
☐	405	Don Slaught	.05	.02	.01
☐	406	Jose Oquendo	.05	.02	.01
☐	407	Bruce Ruffin	.05	.02	.01
☐	408	Phil Clark	.05	.02	.01
☐	409	Joe Klink	.05	.02	.01
☐	410	Lou Whitaker	.10	.05	.01
☐	411	Kevin Seitzer	.05	.02	.01
☐	412	Darrin Fletcher	.05	.02	.01
☐	413	Kenny Rogers	.05	.02	.01
☐	414	Bill Pecota	.05	.02	.01
☐	415	Dave Fleming	.05	.02	.01
☐	416	Luis Alicea	.05	.02	.01
☐	417	Paul Quantrill	.05	.02	.01
☐	418	Damion Easley	.05	.02	.01
☐	419	Wes Chamberlain	.05	.02	.01
☐	420	Harold Baines	.08	.04	.01
☐	421	Scott Radinsky	.05	.02	.01
☐	422	Rey Sanchez	.05	.02	.01
☐	423	Junior Ortiz	.05	.02	.01
☐	424	Jeff Kent	.08	.04	.01
☐	425	Brian McRae	.08	.04	.01
☐	426	Ed Sprague	.05	.02	.01
☐	427	Tom Edens	.05	.02	.01
☐	428	Willie Greene	.08	.04	.01
☐	429	Bryan Hickerson	.05	.02	.01
☐	430	Dave Winfield	.10	.05	.01
☐	431	Pedro Astacio	.08	.04	.01
☐	432	Mike Gallego	.05	.02	.01
☐	433	Dave Burba	.05	.02	.01
☐	434	Bob Walk	.05	.02	.01
☐	435	Darryl Hamilton	.05	.02	.01
☐	436	Vince Horsman	.05	.02	.01
☐	437	Bob Natal	.05	.02	.01
☐	438	Mike Henneman	.05	.02	.01
☐	439	Willie Blair	.05	.02	.01
☐	440	Denny Martinez	.08	.04	.01
☐	441	Dan Peltier	.05	.02	.01
☐	442	Tony Tarasco	.10	.05	.01
☐	443	John Cummings	.05	.02	.01
☐	444	Geronimo Pena	.05	.02	.01
☐	445	Aaron Sele	.15	.07	.02
☐	446	Stan Javier	.05	.02	.01
☐	447	Mike Williams	.05	.02	.01
☐	448	First Base Prospects	.15	.07	.02
		Roberto Petagine			
		Greg Pirkl			
		Shawn Wooten			
		D.J. Boston			
☐	449	Jim Poole	.05	.02	.01
☐	450	Carlos Baerga	.30	.14	.04
☐	451	Bob Scanlan	.05	.02	.01
☐	452	Lance Johnson	.05	.02	.01
☐	453	Eric Hillman	.05	.02	.01
☐	454	Keith Miller	.05	.02	.01
☐	455	Dave Stewart	.08	.04	.01
☐	456	Pete Harnisch	.05	.02	.01
☐	457	Roberto Kelly	.05	.02	.01
☐	458	Tim Worrell	.05	.02	.01
☐	459	Pedro Munoz	.05	.02	.01
☐	460	Orel Hershiser	.05	.02	.01
☐	461	Randy Velarde	.05	.02	.01
☐	462	Trevor Wilson	.05	.02	.01
☐	463	Jerry Goff	.05	.02	.01
☐	464	Bill Wegman	.05	.02	.01
☐	465	Dennis Eckersley	.10	.05	.01
☐	466	Jeff Conine	.10	.05	.01
☐	467	Joe Boever	.05	.02	.01
☐	468	Dante Bichette	.10	.05	.01
☐	469	Jeff Shaw	.05	.02	.01
☐	470	Rafael Palmeiro	.10	.05	.01
☐	471	Phil Leftwich	.05	.02	.01
☐	472	Jay Buhner	.08	.04	.01
☐	473	Bob Tewksbury	.05	.02	.01
☐	474	Tim Naehring	.05	.02	.01
☐	475	Tom Glavine	.10	.05	.01
☐	476	Dave Hollins	.10	.05	.01
☐	477	Arthur Rhodes	.05	.02	.01
☐	478	Joey Cora	.05	.02	.01
☐	479	Mike Morgan	.05	.02	.01
☐	480	Albert Belle	.60	.25	.08
☐	481	John Franco	.05	.02	.01
☐	482	Hipolito Pichardo	.05	.02	.01
☐	483	Duane Ward	.05	.02	.01
☐	484	Luis Gonzalez	.05	.02	.01
☐	485	Joe Oliver	.05	.02	.01
☐	486	Wally Whitehurst	.05	.02	.01
☐	487	Mike Benjamin	.05	.02	.01
☐	488	Eric Davis	.05	.02	.01
☐	489	Scott Kamieniecki	.05	.02	.01
☐	490	Kent Hrbek	.08	.04	.01
☐	491	John Hope	.20	.09	.03
☐	492	Jesse Orosco	.05	.02	.01
☐	493	Troy Neel	.08	.04	.01
☐	494	Ryan Bowen	.05	.02	.01
☐	495	Mickey Tettleton	.05	.02	.01
☐	496	Chris Jones	.05	.02	.01
☐	497	John Wetteland	.05	.02	.01
☐	498	David Hulse	.05	.02	.01
☐	499	Greg Maddux	.40	.18	.05
☐	500	Bo Jackson	.10	.05	.01
☐	501	Donovan Osborne	.05	.02	.01
☐	502	Mike Greenwell	.08	.04	.01
☐	503	Steve Frey	.05	.02	.01
☐	504	Jim Eisenreich	.05	.02	.01
☐	505	Robby Thompson	.05	.02	.01
☐	506	Leo Gomez	.05	.02	.01
☐	507	Dave Staton	.05	.02	.01
☐	508	Wayne Kirby	.05	.02	.01
☐	509	Tim Bogar	.05	.02	.01
☐	510	David Cone	.10	.05	.01
☐	511	Devon White	.05	.02	.01
☐	512	Xavier Hernandez	.05	.02	.01

☐ 513 Tim Costo .05 .02 .01
☐ 514 Gene Harris .05 .02 .01
☐ 515 Jack McDowell .10 .05 .01
☐ 516 Kevin Gross .05 .02 .01
☐ 517 Scott Leius .05 .02 .01
☐ 518 Lloyd McClendon .05 .02 .01
☐ 519 Alex Diaz .05 .02 .01
☐ 520 Wade Boggs .10 .05 .01
☐ 521 Bob Welch .05 .02 .01
☐ 522 Henry Cotto .05 .02 .01
☐ 523 Mike Moore .05 .02 .01
☐ 524 Tim Laker .05 .02 .01
☐ 525 Andres Galarraga .10 .05 .01
☐ 526 Jamie Moyer .05 .02 .01
☐ 527 2nd Base Prospects .15 .07 .02
Norberto Martin
Ruben Santana
Jason Hardtke
Chris Sexton
☐ 528 Sid Bream .05 .02 .01
☐ 529 Erik Hanson .05 .02 .01
☐ 530 Ray Lankford .10 .05 .01
☐ 531 Rob Deer .05 .02 .01
☐ 532 Rod Correia .05 .02 .01
☐ 533 Roger Mason .05 .02 .01
☐ 534 Mike Devereaux .08 .04 .01
☐ 535 Jeff Montgomery .08 .04 .01
☐ 536 Dwight Smith .05 .02 .01
☐ 537 Jeremy Hernandez .05 .02 .01
☐ 538 Ellis Burks .08 .04 .01
☐ 539 Bobby Jones .15 .07 .02
☐ 540 Paul Molitor .30 .14 .04
☐ 541 Jeff Juden .05 .02 .01
☐ 542 Chris Sabo .05 .02 .01
☐ 543 Larry Casian .05 .02 .01
☐ 544 Jeff Gardner .05 .02 .01
☐ 545 Ramon Martinez .08 .04 .01
☐ 546 Paul O'Neill .08 .04 .01
☐ 547 Steve Hosey .05 .02 .01
☐ 548 Dave Nilsson .05 .02 .01
☐ 549 Ron Darling .05 .02 .01
☐ 550 Matt Williams .40 .18 .05
☐ 551 Jack Armstrong .05 .02 .01
☐ 552 Bill Krueger .05 .02 .01
☐ 553 Freddie Benavides .05 .02 .01
☐ 554 Jeff Fassero .05 .02 .01
☐ 555 Chuck Knoblauch .10 .05 .01
☐ 556 Guillermo Velasquez .05 .02 .01
☐ 557 Joel Johnston .05 .02 .01
☐ 558 Tom Lampkin .05 .02 .01
☐ 559 Todd Van Poppel .08 .04 .01
☐ 560 Gary Sheffield .10 .05 .01
☐ 561 Skeeter Barnes .05 .02 .01
☐ 562 Darren Holmes .05 .02 .01
☐ 563 John Vander Wal .05 .02 .01
☐ 564 Mike Ignasiak .05 .02 .01
☐ 565 Fred McGriff .30 .14 .04
☐ 566 Luis Polonia .05 .02 .01
☐ 567 Mike Perez .05 .02 .01
☐ 568 John Valentin .08 .04 .01
☐ 569 Mike Felder .05 .02 .01
☐ 570 Tommy Greene .05 .02 .01
☐ 571 David Segui .05 .02 .01
☐ 572 Roberto Hernandez .05 .02 .01
☐ 573 Steve Wilson .05 .02 .01
☐ 574 Willie McGee .05 .02 .01
☐ 575 Randy Myers .05 .02 .01
☐ 576 Darrin Jackson .05 .02 .01
☐ 577 Eric Plunk .05 .02 .01
☐ 578 Mike Macfarlane .05 .02 .01
☐ 579 Doug Brocail .05 .02 .01
☐ 580 Steve Finley .05 .02 .01
☐ 581 John Roper .08 .04 .01
☐ 582 Danny Cox .05 .02 .01
☐ 583 Chip Hale .05 .02 .01
☐ 584 Scott Bullett .05 .02 .01
☐ 585 Kevin Reimer .05 .02 .01
☐ 586 Brent Gates .10 .05 .01
☐ 587 Matt Turner .05 .02 .01
☐ 588 Rich Rowland .05 .02 .01
☐ 589 Kent Bottenfield .05 .02 .01
☐ 590 Marquis Grissom .10 .05 .01
☐ 591 Doug Strange .05 .02 .01
☐ 592 Jay Howell .05 .02 .01
☐ 593 Omar Vizquel .05 .02 .01
☐ 594 Rheal Cormier .05 .02 .01
☐ 595 Andre Dawson .10 .05 .01
☐ 596 Hilly Hathaway .05 .02 .01
☐ 597 Todd Pratt .05 .02 .01
☐ 598 Mike Mussina .30 .14 .04
☐ 599 Alex Fernandez .10 .05 .01
☐ 600 Don Mattingly .75 .35 .09
☐ 601 Frank Thomas ST 1.00 .45 .13
☐ 602 Ryne Sandberg ST .35 .16 .04
☐ 603 Wade Boggs ST .15 .07 .02
☐ 604 Cal Ripken ST .75 .35 .09
☐ 605 Barry Bonds ST .40 .18 .05
☐ 606 Ken Griffey Jr. ST 1.00 .45 .13
☐ 607 Kirby Puckett ST .40 .18 .05
☐ 608 Darren Daulton ST .15 .07 .02
☐ 609 Paul Molitor ST .15 .07 .02
☐ 610 Terry Steinbach .08 .04 .01
☐ 611 Todd Worrell .05 .02 .01
☐ 612 Jim Thome .10 .05 .01
☐ 613 Chuck McElroy .05 .02 .01
☐ 614 John Habyan .05 .02 .01
☐ 615 Sid Fernandez .05 .02 .01
☐ 616 Outfield Prospects .20 .09 .03
Eddie Zambrano
Glenn Murray
Chad Mottola
Jermaine Allensworth
☐ 617 Steve Bedrosian .05 .02 .01
☐ 618 Rob Ducey .05 .02 .01
☐ 619 Tom Browning .05 .02 .01
☐ 620 Tony Gwynn .50 .23 .06
☐ 621 Carl Willis .05 .02 .01
☐ 622 Kevin Young .05 .02 .01
☐ 623 Rafael Novoa .05 .02 .01
☐ 624 Jerry Browne .05 .02 .01
☐ 625 Charlie Hough .08 .04 .01
☐ 626 Chris Gomez .10 .05 .01
☐ 627 Steve Reed .05 .02 .01
☐ 628 Kirk Rueter .05 .02 .01
☐ 629 Matt Whiteside .05 .02 .01
☐ 630 David Justice .30 .14 .04
☐ 631 Brad Holman .05 .02 .01
☐ 632 Brian Jordan .08 .04 .01
☐ 633 Scott Bankhead .05 .02 .01
☐ 634 Torey Lovullo .05 .02 .01
☐ 635 Len Dykstra .10 .05 .01
☐ 636 Ben McDonald .08 .04 .01
☐ 637 Steve Howe .05 .02 .01
☐ 638 Jose Vizcaino .05 .02 .01
☐ 639 Bill Swift .05 .02 .01
☐ 640 Darryl Strawberry .08 .04 .01
☐ 641 Steve Farr .05 .02 .01
☐ 642 Tom Kramer .05 .02 .01
☐ 643 Joe Orsulak .05 .02 .01
☐ 644 Tom Henke .05 .02 .01
☐ 645 Joe Carter .30 .14 .04
☐ 646 Ken Caminiti .08 .04 .01
☐ 647 Reggie Sanders .08 .04 .01
☐ 648 Andy Ashby .05 .02 .01
☐ 649 Derek Parks .05 .02 .01
☐ 650 Andy Van Slyke .10 .05 .01

☐ 651 Juan Bell .05 .02 .01
☐ 652 Roger Smithberg .05 .02 .01
☐ 653 Chuck Carr .05 .02 .01
☐ 654 Bill Gullickson .05 .02 .01
☐ 655 Charlie Hayes .08 .04 .01
☐ 656 Chris Nabholz .05 .02 .01
☐ 657 Karl Rhodes .05 .02 .01
☐ 658 Pete Smith .05 .02 .01
☐ 659 Bret Boone .10 .05 .01
☐ 660 Gregg Jefferies .10 .05 .01
☐ 661 Bob Zupcic .05 .02 .01
☐ 662 Steve Sax .05 .02 .01
☐ 663 Mariano Duncan .05 .02 .01
☐ 664 Jeff Tackett .05 .02 .01
☐ 665 Mark Langston .10 .05 .01
☐ 666 Steve Buechele .05 .02 .01
☐ 667 Candy Maldonado .05 .02 .01
☐ 668 Woody Williams .05 .02 .01
☐ 669 Tim Wakefield .05 .02 .01
☐ 670 Danny Tartabull .08 .04 .01
☐ 671 Charlie O'Brien .05 .02 .01
☐ 672 Felix Jose .05 .02 .01
☐ 673 Bobby Ayala .05 .02 .01
☐ 674 Scott Servais .05 .02 .01
☐ 675 Roberto Alomar .50 .23 .06
☐ 676 Pedro Martinez .10 .05 .01
☐ 677 Eddie Guardado .05 .02 .01
☐ 678 Mark Lewis .05 .02 .01
☐ 679 Jaime Navarro .05 .02 .01
☐ 680 Ruben Sierra .10 .05 .01
☐ 681 Rick Renteria .05 .02 .01
☐ 682 Storm Davis .05 .02 .01
☐ 683 Cory Snyder .05 .02 .01
☐ 684 Ron Karkovice .05 .02 .01
☐ 685 Juan Gonzalez .60 .25 .08
☐ 686 Catching Prospects .30 .14 .04
Paul Bako
Jason Kendall
Chris Howard
Carlos Delgado
☐ 687 John Smoltz .08 .04 .01
☐ 688 Brian Dorsett .05 .02 .01
☐ 689 Omar Olivares .05 .02 .01
☐ 690 Mo Vaughn .10 .05 .01
☐ 691 Joe Grahe .05 .02 .01
☐ 692 Mickey Morandini .05 .02 .01
☐ 693 Tino Martinez .05 .02 .01
☐ 694 Brian Barnes .05 .02 .01
☐ 695 Mike Stanley .05 .02 .01
☐ 696 Mark Clark .05 .02 .01
☐ 697 Dave Hansen .05 .02 .01
☐ 698 Willie Wilson .05 .02 .01
☐ 699 Pete Schourek .05 .02 .01
☐ 700 Barry Bonds .75 .35 .09
☐ 701 Kevin Appier .08 .04 .01
☐ 702 Tony Fernandez .05 .02 .01
☐ 703 Darryl Kile .08 .04 .01
☐ 704 Archi Cianfrocco .05 .02 .01
☐ 705 Jose Rijo .08 .04 .01
☐ 706 Brian Harper .05 .02 .01
☐ 707 Zane Smith .05 .02 .01
☐ 708 Dave Henderson .05 .02 .01
☐ 709 Angel Miranda .05 .02 .01
☐ 710 Orestes Destrade .05 .02 .01
☐ 711 Greg Gohr .05 .02 .01
☐ 712 Eric Young .08 .04 .01
☐ 713 Relief Prospects .15 .07 .02
Todd Williams
Ron Watson
Kirk Bullinger
Mike Welch
☐ 714 Tim Spehr .05 .02 .01
☐ 715 Hank Aaron .50 .23 .06
☐ 716 Nate Minchey .08 .04 .01
☐ 717 Mike Blowers .05 .02 .01
☐ 718 Kent Mercker .05 .02 .01
☐ 719 Tom Pagnozzi .05 .02 .01
☐ 720 Roger Clemens .50 .23 .06
☐ 721 Eduardo Perez .08 .04 .01
☐ 722 Milt Thompson .05 .02 .01
☐ 723 Gregg Olson .05 .02 .01
☐ 724 Kirk McCaskill .05 .02 .01
☐ 725 Sammy Sosa .10 .05 .01
☐ 726 Alvaro Espinoza .05 .02 .01
☐ 727 Henry Rodriguez .05 .02 .01
☐ 728 Jim Leyritz .05 .02 .01
☐ 729 Steve Scarsone .05 .02 .01
☐ 730 Bobby Bonilla .10 .05 .01
☐ 731 Chris Gwynn .05 .02 .01
☐ 732 Al Leiter .05 .02 .01
☐ 733 Bip Roberts UER .05 .02 .01
(Card back says drafted in 1992; should be 1981)
☐ 734 Mark Portugal .05 .02 .01
☐ 735 Terry Pendleton .05 .02 .01
☐ 736 Dave Valle .05 .02 .01
☐ 737 Paul Kilgus .05 .02 .01
☐ 738 Greg A. Harris .05 .02 .01
☐ 739 Jon Ratliff DP .15 .07 .02
☐ 740 Kirk Presley DP .50 .23 .06
☐ 741 Josue Estrada DP .20 .09 .03
☐ 742 Wayne Gomes DP .15 .07 .02
☐ 743 Pat Watkins DP .50 .23 .06
☐ 744 Jamey Wright DP .25 .11 .03
☐ 745 Jay Powell DP .20 .09 .03
☐ 746 Ryan McGuire DP .35 .16 .04
☐ 747 Marc Barcelo DP .30 .14 .04
☐ 748 Sloan Smith DP .20 .09 .03
☐ 749 John Wasdin DP .40 .18 .05
☐ 750 Marc Valdes DP .15 .07 .02
☐ 751 Dan Ehler DP .20 .09 .03
☐ 752 Andre King DP .20 .09 .03
☐ 753 Greg Keagle DP .25 .11 .03
☐ 754 Jason Myers DP .35 .16 .04
☐ 755 Dax Winslett DP .15 .07 .02
☐ 756 Casey Whitten DP .20 .09 .03
☐ 757 Tony Fuduric DP .15 .07 .02
☐ 758 Greg Norton DP .15 .07 .02
☐ 759 Jeff D'Amico DP .20 .09 .03
☐ 760 Ryan Hancock DP .20 .09 .03
☐ 761 David Cooper DP .15 .07 .02
☐ 762 Kevin Orie DP .15 .07 .02
☐ 763 John O'Donoghue .05 .02 .01
Mike Oquist
☐ 764 Cory Bailey .15 .07 .02
Scott Hatteberg
☐ 765 Mark Holzemer .05 .02 .01
Paul Swingle
☐ 766 James Baldwin .30 .14 .04
Rod Bolton
☐ 767 Jerry Di Poto .40 .18 .05
Julian Tavarez
☐ 768 Danny Bautista .08 .04 .01
Sean Bergman
☐ 769 Bob Hamelin .25 .11 .03
Joe Vitiello
☐ 770 Mark Kiefer .05 .02 .01
Troy O'Leary
☐ 771 Denny Hocking .05 .02 .01
Oscar Munoz
☐ 772 Russ Davis .15 .07 .02
Brien Taylor
☐ 773 Kyle Abbott .20 .09 .03
Miguel Jimenez
☐ 774 Kevin King .05 .02 .01
Eric Plantenberg

		MINT	EXC	G-VG
☐ 775	Jon Shave Desi Wilson	.05	.02	.01
☐ 776	Domingo Cedeno Paul Spoljaric	.05	.02	.01
☐ 777	Chipper Jones Ryan Klesko	.50	.23	.06
☐ 778	Steve Trachsel Turk Wendell	.20	.09	.03
☐ 779	Johnny Ruffin Jerry Spradlin	.05	.02	.01
☐ 780	Jason Bates/John Burke	.05	.02	.01
☐ 781	Carl Everett Dave Weathers	.08	.04	.01
☐ 782	Gary Mota James Mouton	.05	.02	.01
☐ 783	Raul Mondesi Ben Van Ryn	.75	.35	.09
☐ 784	Gabe White Rondell White	.20	.09	.03
☐ 785	Brook Fordyce Bill Pulsipher	.40	.18	.05
☐ 786	Kevin Foster Gene Schall	.25	.11	.03
☐ 787	Rich Aude Midre Cummings	.20	.09	.03
☐ 788	Brian Barber Rich Batchelor	.08	.04	.01
☐ 789	Brian Johnson Scott Sanders	.05	.02	.01
☐ 790	Ricky Faneyte J.R. Phillips	.15	.07	.02
☐ 791	Checklist 3	.05	.02	.01
☐ 792	Checklist 4	.05	.02	.01

1994 Topps Gold

The 1994 Topps Gold set is parallel to the basic issue. The cards were inserted in various forms. They were inserted one per wax pack, two per mini jumbo, three per rack pack, four per jumbo, five per jumbo rack and ten per factory set. The only difference between the Gold issue and the basic cards is gold foil on the player's name and the Topps logo.

	MINT	EXC	G-VG
COMPLETE SET (792)	100.00	45.00	12.50
COMPLETE SERIES 1 (396)	50.00	23.00	6.25
COMPLETE SERIES 2 (396)	50.00	23.00	6.25
COMMON CARD (1-396)	.10	.05	.01
COMMON CARD (397-792)	.10	.05	.01

*VETERAN STARS: 2X to 4X BASIC CARDS
*YOUNG STARS: 1.5X to 3X BASIC CARDS
*RCs: 1.25X to 2.5X BASIC CARDS

1994 Topps Black Gold

Randomly inserted one in every 72 packs, this 44-card set was issued in two series of 22. Cards were also issued three per 1994 Topps factory set. Collectors had a chance, through redemption cards to receive all or part of the set. There are seven Winner redemption cards for a total 51 cards associated with this set. The set is considered complete with the 44 player cards. Card fronts feature color player action photos. The player's name at bottom and the team name at top are screened in gold foil. The backs contain a player photo and statistical rankings.

	MINT	EXC	G-VG
COMPLETE SET (44)	30.00	13.50	3.80
COMPLETE SERIES 1 (22)	18.00	8.00	2.30
COMPLETE SERIES 2 (22)	12.00	5.50	1.50
COMMON CARD (1-22)	.25	.11	.03
COMMON CARD (23-44)	.25	.11	.03

		MINT	EXC	G-VG
☐ 1	Roberto Alomar	1.00	.45	.13
☐ 2	Carlos Baerga	.60	.25	.08
☐ 3	Albert Belle	1.25	.55	.16
☐ 4	Joe Carter	.60	.25	.08
☐ 5	Cecil Fielder	.40	.18	.05
☐ 6	Travis Fryman	.50	.23	.06
☐ 7	Juan Gonzalez	1.25	.55	.16
☐ 8	Ken Griffey Jr.	4.00	1.80	.50
☐ 9	Chris Hoiles	.25	.11	.03
☐ 10	Randy Johnson	.40	.18	.05
☐ 11	Kenny Lofton	1.00	.45	.13
☐ 12	Jack McDowell	.40	.18	.05
☐ 13	Paul Molitor	.60	.25	.08
☐ 14	Jeff Montgomery	.25	.11	.03
☐ 15	John Olerud	.40	.18	.05
☐ 16	Rafael Palmeiro	.40	.18	.05
☐ 17	Kirby Puckett	1.50	.65	.19
☐ 18	Cal Ripken	3.00	1.35	.40
☐ 19	Tim Salmon	.60	.25	.08
☐ 20	Mike Stanley	.25	.11	.03
☐ 21	Frank Thomas	4.00	1.80	.50
☐ 22	Robin Ventura	.40	.18	.05
☐ 23	Jeff Bagwell	2.00	.90	.25
☐ 24	Jay Bell	.25	.11	.03
☐ 25	Craig Biggio	.25	.11	.03
☐ 26	Jeff Blauser	.25	.11	.03
☐ 27	Barry Bonds	1.50	.65	.19
☐ 28	Darren Daulton	.40	.18	.05
☐ 29	Len Dykstra	.40	.18	.05
☐ 30	Andres Galarraga	.40	.18	.05

☐ 31 Ron Gant	.25	.11	.03
☐ 32 Tom Glavine	.40	.18	.05
☐ 33 Mark Grace	.25	.11	.03
☐ 34 Marquis Grissom	.40	.18	.05
☐ 35 Gregg Jefferies	.40	.18	.05
☐ 36 David Justice	.60	.25	.08
☐ 37 John Kruk	.25	.11	.03
☐ 38 Greg Maddux	1.00	.45	.13
☐ 39 Fred McGriff	.60	.25	.08
☐ 40 Randy Myers	.25	.11	.03
☐ 41 Mike Piazza	2.00	.90	.25
☐ 42 Sammy Sosa	.25	.11	.03
☐ 43 Robby Thompson	.25	.11	.03
☐ 44 Matt Williams	.75	.35	.09
☐ A Winner A 1-11	3.00	1.35	.40
☐ AB Winner AB 1-22	5.00	2.30	.60
☐ ABCD Winner ABCD 1-44	10.00	4.50	1.25
☐ B Winner B 12-22	3.00	1.35	.40
☐ C Winner C 23-33	3.00	1.35	.40
☐ CD Winner CD 23-44	5.00	2.30	.60
☐ D Winner D 34-44	3.00	1.35	.40

1994 Topps Traded

This set consists of 132 color cards featuring traded players in their new uniforms, rookies and draft choices. Factory sets consisted of 140 cards including a set of eight Topps Finest cards. Card fronts feature a player photo with the player's name, team and position at the bottom. The horizontal backs have a player photo to the left with complete career statisics and highlights. The cards are numbered with a "T" suffix. Rookie Cards include Brian Anderson, John Hudek, Terrance Long, Doug Million, Chan Ho Park, Mac Suzuki and Terrell Wade.

	MINT	EXC	G-VG
COMPLETE FACT.SET (140)	30.00	13.50	3.80
COMPLETE SET (132)	15.00	6.75	1.90
COMMON CARD (1T-132T)	.05	.02	.01

☐ 1T Paul Wilson	.40	.18	.05
☐ 2T Bill Taylor	.05	.02	.01
☐ 3T Dan Wilson	.05	.02	.01
☐ 4T Mark Smith	.05	.02	.01
☐ 5T Toby Borland	.15	.07	.02
☐ 6T Dave Clark	.05	.02	.01
☐ 7T Denny Martinez	.08	.04	.01
☐ 8T Dave Gallagher	.05	.02	.01
☐ 9T Josias Manzanillo	.05	.02	.01
☐ 10T Brian Anderson	.50	.23	.06
☐ 11T Damon Berryhill	.05	.02	.01
☐ 12T Alex Cole	.05	.02	.01
☐ 13T Jacob Shumate	.40	.18	.05
☐ 14T Oddibe McDowell	.05	.02	.01
☐ 15T Willie Banks	.05	.02	.01
☐ 16T Jerry Browne	.05	.02	.01
☐ 17T Donnie Elliott	.05	.02	.01
☐ 18T Ellis Burks	.08	.04	.01
☐ 19T Chuck McElroy	.05	.02	.01
☐ 20T Luis Polonia	.05	.02	.01
☐ 21T Brian Harper	.05	.02	.01
☐ 22T Mark Portugal	.05	.02	.01
☐ 23T Dave Henderson	.05	.02	.01
☐ 24T Mark Acre	.15	.07	.02
☐ 25T Julio Franco	.08	.04	.01
☐ 26T Darren Hall	.05	.02	.01
☐ 27T Eric Anthony	.05	.02	.01
☐ 28T Sid Fernandez	.05	.02	.01
☐ 29T Rusty Greer	.40	.18	.05
☐ 30T Riccardo Ingram	.20	.09	.03
☐ 31T Gabe White	.05	.02	.01
☐ 32T Tim Belcher	.05	.02	.01
☐ 33T Terrence Long	.60	.25	.08
☐ 34T Mark Dalesandro	.15	.07	.02
☐ 35T Mike Kelly	.08	.04	.01
☐ 36T Jack Morris	.10	.05	.01
☐ 37T Jeff Brantley	.05	.02	.01
☐ 38T Larry Barnes	.20	.09	.03
☐ 39T Brian Hunter	.05	.02	.01
☐ 40T Otis Nixon	.05	.02	.01
☐ 41T Bret Wagner	.20	.09	.03
☐ 42T Anatomy of a Trade Pedro Martinez Delino Deshields	.05	.02	.01
☐ 43T Heathcliff Slocumb	.05	.02	.01
☐ 44T Ben Grieve	1.50	.65	.19
☐ 45T John Hudek	.50	.23	.06
☐ 46T Shawon Dunston	.05	.02	.01
☐ 47T Greg Colbrunn	.05	.02	.01
☐ 48T Joey Hamilton	.40	.18	.05
☐ 49T Marvin Freeman	.05	.02	.01
☐ 50T Terry Mulholland	.05	.02	.01
☐ 51T Keith Mitchell	.05	.02	.01
☐ 52T Dwight Smith	.05	.02	.01
☐ 53T Shawn Boskie	.05	.02	.01
☐ 54T Kevin Witt	.30	.14	.04
☐ 55T Ron Gant	.08	.04	.01
☐ 56T 1994 Prospects Trenidad Hubbard Jason Schmidt Larry Sutton Stephen Larkin	.50	.23	.06
☐ 57T Jody Reed	.05	.02	.01
☐ 58T Rick Helling	.05	.02	.01
☐ 59T John Powell	.15	.07	.02
☐ 60T Eddie Murray	.10	.05	.01
☐ 61T Joe Hall	.05	.02	.01
☐ 62T Jorge Fabregas	.05	.02	.01
☐ 63T Mike Mordecai	.15	.07	.02
☐ 64T Ed Vosberg	.05	.02	.01
☐ 65T Rickey Henderson	.10	.05	.01
☐ 66T Tim Grieve	.20	.09	.03
☐ 67T Jon Lieber	.05	.02	.01
☐ 68T Chris Howard	.05	.02	.01
☐ 69T Matt Walbeck	.05	.02	.01
☐ 70T Chan Ho Park	.75	.35	.09
☐ 71T Bryan Eversgerd	.05	.02	.01
☐ 72T John Dettmer	.05	.02	.01
☐ 73T Erik Hanson	.05	.02	.01
☐ 74T Mike Thurman	.25	.11	.03
☐ 75T Bobby Ayala	.05	.02	.01
☐ 76T Rafael Palmeiro	.10	.05	.01
☐ 77T Bret Boone	.10	.05	.01
☐ 78T Paul Shuey	.08	.04	.01

☐ 79T Kevin Foster	.05	.02	.01
☐ 80T Dave Magadan	.05	.02	.01
☐ 81T Bip Roberts	.05	.02	.01
☐ 82T Howard Johnson	.05	.02	.01
☐ 83T Xavier Hernandez	.05	.02	.01
☐ 84T Ross Powell	.05	.02	.01
☐ 85T Doug Million	.60	.25	.08
☐ 86T Geronimo Berroa	.05	.02	.01
☐ 87T Mark Farris	.30	.14	.04
☐ 88T Butch Henry	.05	.02	.01
☐ 89T Junior Felix	.05	.02	.01
☐ 90T Bo Jackson	.10	.05	.01
☐ 91T Hector Carrasco	.05	.02	.01
☐ 92T Charlie O'Brien	.05	.02	.01
☐ 93T Omar Vizquel	.05	.02	.01
☐ 94T David Segui	.05	.02	.01
☐ 95T Dustin Hermanson	.25	.11	.03
☐ 96T Gar Finnvold	.05	.02	.01
☐ 97T Dave Stevens	.05	.02	.01
☐ 98T Corey Pointer	.30	.14	.04
☐ 99T Felix Fermin	.05	.02	.01
☐ 100T Lee Smith	.10	.05	.01
☐ 101T Reid Ryan	.75	.35	.09
☐ 102T Bobby Munoz	.05	.02	.01
☐ 103T Anatomy of a Trade Deion Sanders Roberto Kelly	.25	.11	.03
☐ 104T Turner Ward	.05	.02	.01
☐ 105T Will VanLandingham	.60	.25	.08
☐ 106T Vince Coleman	.05	.02	.01
☐ 107T Stan Javier	.05	.02	.01
☐ 108T Darrin Jackson	.05	.02	.01
☐ 109T C.J. Nitkowski	.50	.23	.06
☐ 110T Anthony Young	.05	.02	.01
☐ 111T Kurt Miller	.05	.02	.01
☐ 112T Paul Konerko	.50	.23	.06
☐ 113T Walt Weiss	.05	.02	.01
☐ 114T Daryl Boston	.05	.02	.01
☐ 115T Will Clark	.30	.14	.04
☐ 116T Matt Smith	.30	.14	.04
☐ 117T Mark Leiter	.05	.02	.01
☐ 118T Gregg Olson	.05	.02	.01
☐ 119T Tony Pena	.05	.02	.01
☐ 120T Jose Vizcaino	.05	.02	.01
☐ 121T Rick White	.05	.02	.01
☐ 122T Rich Rowland	.05	.02	.01
☐ 123T Jeff Reboulet	.05	.02	.01
☐ 124T Greg Hibbard	.05	.02	.01
☐ 125T Chris Sabo	.05	.02	.01
☐ 126T Doug Jones	.05	.02	.01
☐ 127T Tony Fernandez	.05	.02	.01
☐ 128T Carlos Reyes	.05	.02	.01
☐ 129T Kevin Brown	.20	.09	.03
☐ 130T Ryne Sandberg Farewell	1.00	.45	.13
☐ 131T Ryne Sandberg Farewell	1.00	.45	.13
☐ 132T Checklist 1-132	.05	.02	.01

1994 Topps Traded Finest Inserts

Issued one set per Topps Traded factory set, these eight cards showcase top young talent. The metallic cards feature a rainbow colored front with a color player photo and the backs also carry a color player photo with 1994 monthly statistics through July 10.

The backs also have a write-up about the first half of the season. There are six MVP candidate and two Rookie of the Year candidate cards.

	MINT	EXC	G-VG
COMPLETE SET (8)	15.00	6.75	1.90
COMMON CARD (1-8)	1.00	.45	.13
☐ 1 Greg Maddux NL MVP Candidate	1.25	.55	.16
☐ 2 Mike Piazza NL MVP Candidate	2.50	1.15	.30
☐ 3 Matt Williams NL MVP Candidate	1.00	.45	.13
☐ 4 Raul Mondesi NL ROY Candidate	1.75	.80	.22
☐ 5 Ken Griffey Jr. AL MVP Candidate	5.00	2.30	.60
☐ 6 Kenny Lofton AL MVP Candidate	1.25	.55	.16
☐ 7 Frank Thomas AL MVP Candidate	5.00	2.30	.60
☐ 8 Manny Ramirez AL ROY Candidate	1.00	.45	.13

1995 Topps

These 396 standard-size cards feature color action player photos with white borders on the fronts. The player's name in gold-foil appears below the photo, with his position and team name underneath. The horizontal backs carry a color player close-up with a color player cut-out superimposed over it. Player biography, statistics and career highlights complete the backs. One "Own The Game" instant winner card has been inserted in every 120 packs.

	MINT	EXC	G-VG
COMPLETE SERIES 1 (396)	25.00	11.50	3.10
COMMON CARD (1-396)	.10	.05	.01
☐ 1 Frank Thomas	3.00	1.35	.40
☐ 2 Mickey Morandini	.10	.05	.01
☐ 3 Babe Ruth	2.00	.90	.25
☐ 4 Scott Cooper	.10	.05	.01
☐ 5 David Cone	.20	.09	.03
☐ 6 Jacob Shumate	.10	.05	.01
☐ 7 Trevor Hoffman	.10	.05	.01
☐ 8 Shane Mack	.15	.07	.02
☐ 9 Delino DeShields	.15	.07	.02
☐ 10 Matt Williams	.60	.25	.08
☐ 11 Sammy Sosa	.20	.09	.03
☐ 12 Gary DiSarcina	.10	.05	.01
☐ 13 Kenny Rogers	.10	.05	.01
☐ 14 Jose Vizcaino	.10	.05	.01
☐ 15 Lou Whitaker	.20	.09	.03
☐ 16 Ron Darling	.10	.05	.01
☐ 17 Dave Nilsson	.10	.05	.01
☐ 18 Chris Hammond	.10	.05	.01
☐ 19 Sid Bream	.10	.05	.01
☐ 20 Denny Martinez	.15	.07	.02
☐ 21 Orlando Merced	.10	.05	.01
☐ 22 John Wetteland	.10	.05	.01
☐ 23 Mike Devereaux	.15	.07	.02
☐ 24 Rene Arocha	.10	.05	.01
☐ 25 Jay Buhner	.15	.07	.02
☐ 26 Darren Holmes	.10	.05	.01
☐ 27 Hal Morris	.15	.07	.02
☐ 28 Brian Buchanan	.30	.14	.04
☐ 29 Keith Miller	.10	.05	.01
☐ 30 Paul Molitor	.40	.18	.05
☐ 31 Dave West	.10	.05	.01
☐ 32 Tony Tarasco	.15	.07	.02
☐ 33 Scott Sanders	.10	.05	.01
☐ 34 Eddie Zambrano	.10	.05	.01
☐ 35 Ricky Bones	.10	.05	.01
☐ 36 John Valentin	.15	.07	.02
☐ 37 Kevin Tapani	.10	.05	.01
☐ 38 Tim Wallach	.10	.05	.01
☐ 39 Darren Lewis	.10	.05	.01
☐ 40 Travis Fryman	.20	.09	.03
☐ 41 Mark Leiter	.10	.05	.01
☐ 42 Jose Bautista	.10	.05	.01
☐ 43 Pete Smith	.10	.05	.01
☐ 44 Bret Barberie	.10	.05	.01
☐ 45 Dennis Eckersley	.20	.09	.03
☐ 46 Ken Hill	.15	.07	.02
☐ 47 Chad Ogea	.15	.07	.02
☐ 48 Pete Harnisch	.10	.05	.01
☐ 49 James Baldwin	.10	.05	.01
☐ 50 Mike Mussina	.40	.18	.05
☐ 51 Al Martin	.10	.05	.01
☐ 52 Mark Thompson	.15	.07	.02
☐ 53 Matt Smith	.10	.05	.01
☐ 54 Joey Hamilton	.20	.09	.03
☐ 55 Edgar Martinez	.10	.05	.01
☐ 56 John Smiley	.10	.05	.01
☐ 57 Rey Sanchez	.10	.05	.01
☐ 58 Mike Timlin	.10	.05	.01
☐ 59 Ricky Bottalico	.10	.05	.01
☐ 60 Jim Abbott	.20	.09	.03
☐ 61 Mike Kelly	.15	.07	.02
☐ 62 Brian Jordan	.15	.07	.02
☐ 63 Ken Ryan	.10	.05	.01
☐ 64 Matt Mieske	.10	.05	.01
☐ 65 Rick Aguilera	.15	.07	.02
☐ 66 Ismael Valdes	.10	.05	.01
☐ 67 Royce Clayton	.15	.07	.02
☐ 68 Junior Felix	.10	.05	.01
☐ 69 Harold Reynolds	.10	.05	.01
☐ 70 Juan Gonzalez	1.00	.45	.13
☐ 71 Kelly Stinnett	.10	.05	.01
☐ 72 Carlos Reyes	.10	.05	.01
☐ 73 Dave Weathers	.10	.05	.01
☐ 74 Mel Rojas	.10	.05	.01
☐ 75 Doug Drabek	.20	.09	.03
☐ 76 Charles Nagy	.10	.05	.01
☐ 77 Tim Raines	.20	.09	.03
☐ 78 Midre Cummings	.10	.05	.01
☐ 79 First Base Prospects Gene Schall Scott Talanoa Harold Williams Ray Brown	.50	.23	.06
☐ 80 Rafael Palmeiro	.20	.09	.03
☐ 81 Charlie Hayes	.15	.07	.02
☐ 82 Ray Lankford	.20	.09	.03
☐ 83 Tim Davis	.10	.05	.01
☐ 84 C.J. Nitkowski	.10	.05	.01
☐ 85 Andy Ashby	.10	.05	.01
☐ 86 Gerald Williams	.10	.05	.01
☐ 87 Terry Shumpert	.10	.05	.01
☐ 88 Heathcliff Slocumb	.10	.05	.01
☐ 89 Domingo Cedeno	.10	.05	.01
☐ 90 Mark Grace	.20	.09	.03
☐ 91 Brad Woodall	.30	.14	.04
☐ 92 Gar Finnvold	.10	.05	.01
☐ 93 Jaime Navarro	.10	.05	.01
☐ 94 Carlos Hernandez	.10	.05	.01
☐ 95 Mark Langston	.20	.09	.03
☐ 96 Chuck Carr	.10	.05	.01
☐ 97 Mike Gardiner	.10	.05	.01
☐ 98 Dave McCarty	.15	.07	.02
☐ 99 Cris Carpenter	.10	.05	.01
☐ 100 Barry Bonds	1.25	.55	.16
☐ 101 David Segui	.10	.05	.01
☐ 102 Scott Brosius	.10	.05	.01
☐ 103 Mariano Duncan	.10	.05	.01
☐ 104 Kenny Lofton	.75	.35	.09
☐ 105 Ken Caminiti	.15	.07	.02
☐ 106 Darrin Jackson	.10	.05	.01
☐ 107 Jim Poole	.10	.05	.01
☐ 108 Wil Cordero	.15	.07	.02
☐ 109 Danny Miceli	.10	.05	.01
☐ 110 Walt Weiss	.10	.05	.01
☐ 111 Tom Pagnozzi	.10	.05	.01
☐ 112 Terrence Long	.25	.11	.03
☐ 113 Bret Boone	.20	.09	.03
☐ 114 Daryl Boston	.10	.05	.01
☐ 115 Wally Joyner	.15	.07	.02
☐ 116 Rob Butler	.10	.05	.01
☐ 117 Rafael Belliard	.10	.05	.01
☐ 118 Luis Lopez	.10	.05	.01
☐ 119 Tony Fossas	.10	.05	.01
☐ 120 Len Dykstra	.20	.09	.03
☐ 121 Mike Morgan	.10	.05	.01
☐ 122 Denny Hocking	.10	.05	.01
☐ 123 Kevin Gross	.10	.05	.01
☐ 124 Todd Benzinger	.10	.05	.01
☐ 125 John Doherty	.10	.05	.01
☐ 126 Eduardo Perez	.15	.07	.02
☐ 127 Dan Smith	.10	.05	.01
☐ 128 Joe Orsulak	.10	.05	.01
☐ 129 Brent Gates	.20	.09	.03
☐ 130 Jeff Conine	.20	.09	.03
☐ 131 Doug Henry	.10	.05	.01
☐ 132 Paul Sorrento	.10	.05	.01
☐ 133 Mike Hampton	.10	.05	.01
☐ 134 Tim Spehr	.10	.05	.01
☐ 135 Julio Franco	.15	.07	.02
☐ 136 Mike Dyer	.10	.05	.01
☐ 137 Chris Sabo	.10	.05	.01
☐ 138 Rheal Cormier	.10	.05	.01

☐ 139 Paul Konerko	.20	.09	.03
☐ 140 Dante Bichette	.20	.09	.03
☐ 141 Chuck McElroy	.10	.05	.01
☐ 142 Mike Stanley	.10	.05	.01
☐ 143 Bob Hamelin	.20	.09	.03
☐ 144 Tommy Greene	.10	.05	.01
☐ 145 John Smoltz	.15	.07	.02
☐ 146 Ed Sprague	.10	.05	.01
☐ 147 Ray McDavid	.10	.05	.01
☐ 148 Otis Nixon	.10	.05	.01
☐ 149 Turk Wendell	.10	.05	.01
☐ 150 Chris James	.10	.05	.01
☐ 151 Derek Parks	.10	.05	.01
☐ 152 Jose Offerman	.10	.05	.01
☐ 153 Tony Clark	.10	.05	.01
☐ 154 Chad Curtis	.15	.07	.02
☐ 155 Mark Portugal	.10	.05	.01
☐ 156 Bill Pulsipher	.20	.09	.03
☐ 157 Troy Neel	.15	.07	.02
☐ 158 Dave Winfield	.20	.09	.03
☐ 159 Bill Wegman	.10	.05	.01
☐ 160 Benito Santiago	.10	.05	.01
☐ 161 Jose Mesa	.10	.05	.01
☐ 162 Luis Gonzalez	.10	.05	.01
☐ 163 Alex Fernandez	.20	.09	.03
☐ 164 Freddie Benavides	.10	.05	.01
☐ 165 Ben McDonald	.15	.07	.02
☐ 166 Blas Minor	.10	.05	.01
☐ 167 Bret Wagner	.10	.05	.01
☐ 168 Mac Suzuki	.10	.05	.01
☐ 169 Roberto Mejia	.15	.07	.02
☐ 170 Wade Boggs	.20	.09	.03
☐ 171 Calvin Reese	.15	.07	.02
☐ 172 Hipolito Pichardo	.10	.05	.01
☐ 173 Kim Batiste	.10	.05	.01
☐ 174 Darren Hall	.10	.05	.01
☐ 175 Tom Glavine	.20	.09	.03
☐ 176 Phil Plantier	.15	.07	.02
☐ 177 Chris Howard	.10	.05	.01
☐ 178 Karl Rhodes	.10	.05	.01
☐ 179 LaTroy Hawkins	.10	.05	.01
☐ 180 Raul Mondesi	.75	.35	.09
☐ 181 Jeff Reed	.10	.05	.01
☐ 182 Milt Cuyler	.10	.05	.01
☐ 183 Jim Edmonds	.10	.05	.01
☐ 184 Hector Fajardo	.10	.05	.01
☐ 185 Jeff Kent	.15	.07	.02
☐ 186 Wilson Alvarez	.20	.09	.03
☐ 187 Geronimo Berroa	.10	.05	.01
☐ 188 Billy Spiers	.10	.05	.01
☐ 189 Derek Lilliquist	.10	.05	.01
☐ 190 Craig Biggio	.15	.07	.02
☐ 191 Roberto Hernandez	.10	.05	.01
☐ 192 Bob Natal	.10	.05	.01
☐ 193 Bobby Ayala	.10	.05	.01
☐ 194 Travis Miller	.30	.14	.04
☐ 195 Bob Tewksbury	.10	.05	.01
☐ 196 Rondell White	.20	.09	.03
☐ 197 Steve Cooke	.10	.05	.01
☐ 198 Jeff Branson	.10	.05	.01
☐ 199 Derek Jeter	.50	.23	.06
☐ 200 Tim Salmon	.20	.09	.03
☐ 201 Steve Frey	.10	.05	.01
☐ 202 Kent Mercker	.10	.05	.01
☐ 203 Randy Johnson	.20	.09	.03
☐ 204 Todd Worrell	.10	.05	.01
☐ 205 Mo Vaughn	.20	.09	.03
☐ 206 Howard Johnson	.10	.05	.01
☐ 207 John Wasdin	.10	.05	.01
☐ 208 Eddie Williams	.10	.05	.01
☐ 209 Tim Belcher	.10	.05	.01
☐ 210 Jeff Montgomery	.15	.07	.02
☐ 211 Kirt Manwaring	.10	.05	.01
☐ 212 Ben Grieve	.40	.18	.05
☐ 213 Pat Hentgen	.15	.07	.02
☐ 214 Shawon Dunston	.10	.05	.01
☐ 215 Mike Greenwell	.15	.07	.02
☐ 216 Alex Diaz	.10	.05	.01
☐ 217 Pat Mahomes	.10	.05	.01
☐ 218 Dave Hansen	.10	.05	.01
☐ 219 Kevin Rogers	.10	.05	.01
☐ 220 Cecil Fielder	.20	.09	.03
☐ 221 Andrew Lorraine	.10	.05	.01
☐ 222 Jack Armstrong	.10	.05	.01
☐ 223 Todd Hundley	.10	.05	.01
☐ 224 Mark Acre	.10	.05	.01
☐ 225 Darrell Whitmore	.15	.07	.02
☐ 226 Randy Milligan	.10	.05	.01
☐ 227 Wayne Kirby	.10	.05	.01
☐ 228 Darryl Kile	.15	.07	.02
☐ 229 Bob Zupcic	.10	.05	.01
☐ 230 Jay Bell	.15	.07	.02
☐ 231 Dustin Hermanson	.10	.05	.01
☐ 232 Harold Baines	.15	.07	.02
☐ 233 Alan Benes	.25	.11	.03
☐ 234 Felix Fermin	.10	.05	.01
☐ 235 Ellis Burks	.15	.07	.02
☐ 236 Jeff Brantley	.10	.05	.01
☐ 237 Outfield Prospects Brian Hunter Jose Malave Karim Garcia Shane Pullen	.30	.14	.04
☐ 238 Matt Nokes	.10	.05	.01
☐ 239 Ben Rivera	.10	.05	.01
☐ 240 Joe Carter	.40	.18	.05
☐ 241 Jeff Granger	.15	.07	.02
☐ 242 Terry Pendelton	.10	.05	.01
☐ 243 Melvin Nieves	.20	.09	.03
☐ 244 Frankie Rodriguez	.20	.09	.03
☐ 245 Darryl Hamilton	.10	.05	.01
☐ 246 Brooks Kieschnick	.25	.11	.03
☐ 247 Todd Hollandsworth	.10	.05	.01
☐ 248 Joe Rosselli	.10	.05	.01
☐ 249 Bill Gullickson	.10	.05	.01
☐ 250 Chuck Knoblauch	.20	.09	.03
☐ 251 Kurt Miller	.10	.05	.01
☐ 252 Bobby Jones	.20	.09	.03
☐ 253 Lance Blankenship	.10	.05	.01
☐ 254 Matt Whiteside	.10	.05	.01
☐ 255 Darrin Fletcher	.10	.05	.01
☐ 256 Eric Plunk	.10	.05	.01
☐ 257 Shane Reynolds	.10	.05	.01
☐ 258 Norberto Martin	.10	.05	.01
☐ 259 Mike Thurman	.10	.05	.01
☐ 260 Andy Van Slyke	.20	.09	.03
☐ 261 Dwight Smith	.10	.05	.01
☐ 262 Allen Watson	.10	.05	.01
☐ 263 Dan Wilson	.10	.05	.01
☐ 264 Brent Mayne	.10	.05	.01
☐ 265 Bip Roberts	.10	.05	.01
☐ 266 Sterling Hitchcock	.15	.07	.02
☐ 267 Alex Gonzalez	.10	.05	.01
☐ 268 Greg Harris	.10	.05	.01
☐ 269 Ricky Jordan	.10	.05	.01
☐ 270 Johnny Ruffin	.10	.05	.01
☐ 271 Mike Stanton	.10	.05	.01
☐ 272 Rich Rowland	.10	.05	.01
☐ 273 Steve Trachsel	.20	.09	.03
☐ 274 Pedro Munoz	.10	.05	.01
☐ 275 Ramon Martinez	.15	.07	.02
☐ 276 Dave Henderson	.10	.05	.01
☐ 277 Chris Gomez	.15	.07	.02
☐ 278 Joe Grahe	.10	.05	.01
☐ 279 Rusty Greer	.15	.07	.02
☐ 280 John Franco	.10	.05	.01

	No.	Player			
☐	281	Mike Bordick	.10	.05	.01
☐	282	Jeff D'Amico	.10	.05	.01
☐	283	Dave Magadan	.10	.05	.01
☐	284	Tony Pena	.10	.05	.01
☐	285	Greg Swindell	.10	.05	.01
☐	286	Doug Million	.20	.09	.03
☐	287	Gabe White	.10	.05	.01
☐	288	Trey Beamon	.20	.09	.03
☐	289	Arthur Rhodes	.10	.05	.01
☐	290	Juan Guzman	.15	.07	.02
☐	291	Jose Oquendo	.10	.05	.01
☐	292	Willie Blair	.10	.05	.01
☐	293	Eddie Taubensee	.10	.05	.01
☐	294	Steve Howe	.10	.05	.01
☐	295	Greg Maddux	.50	.23	.06
☐	296	Mike Macfarlane	.10	.05	.01
☐	297	Curt Schilling	.10	.05	.01
☐	298	Phil Clark	.10	.05	.01
☐	299	Woody Williams	.10	.05	.01
☐	300	Jose Canseco	.40	.18	.05
☐	301	Aaron Sele	.20	.09	.03
☐	302	Carl Willis	.10	.05	.01
☐	303	Steve Buechele	.10	.05	.01
☐	304	Dave Burba	.10	.05	.01
☐	305	Orel Hershiser	.15	.07	.02
☐	306	Damion Easley	.10	.05	.01
☐	307	Mike Henneman	.10	.05	.01
☐	308	Josias Manzanillo	.10	.05	.01
☐	309	Kevin Seitzer	.10	.05	.01
☐	310	Ruben Sierra	.20	.09	.03
☐	311	Bryan Harvey	.15	.07	.02
☐	312	Jim Thome	.20	.09	.03
☐	313	Ramon Castro	.30	.14	.04
☐	314	Lance Johnson	.10	.05	.01
☐	315	Marquis Grissom	.20	.09	.03
☐	316	Starting Pitcher Prospects Terrell Wade Juan Acevedo Matt Arrandale Eddie Priest	.40	.18	.05
☐	317	Paul Wagner	.10	.05	.01
☐	318	Jamie Moyer	.10	.05	.01
☐	319	Todd Zeile	.15	.07	.02
☐	320	Chris Bosio	.10	.05	.01
☐	321	Steve Reed	.10	.05	.01
☐	322	Erik Hanson	.10	.05	.01
☐	323	Luis Polonia	.10	.05	.01
☐	324	Ryan Klesko	.35	.16	.04
☐	325	Kevin Appier	.15	.07	.02
☐	326	Jim Eisenreich	.10	.05	.01
☐	327	Randy Knorr	.10	.05	.01
☐	328	Craig Shipley	.10	.05	.01
☐	329	Tim Naehring	.10	.05	.01
☐	330	Randy Myers	.10	.05	.01
☐	331	Alex Cole	.10	.05	.01
☐	332	Jim Gott	.10	.05	.01
☐	333	Mike Jackson	.10	.05	.01
☐	334	John Flaherty	.10	.05	.01
☐	335	Chili Davis	.15	.07	.02
☐	336	Benji Gil	.15	.07	.02
☐	337	Jason Jacome	.25	.11	.03
☐	338	Stan Javier	.10	.05	.01
☐	339	Mike Fetters	.10	.05	.01
☐	340	Rich Renteria	.10	.05	.01
☐	341	Kevin Witt	.10	.05	.01
☐	342	Scott Servais	.10	.05	.01
☐	343	Craig Grebeck	.10	.05	.01
☐	344	Kirk Rueter	.10	.05	.01
☐	345	Don Slaught	.10	.05	.01
☐	346	Armando Benitez	.15	.07	.02
☐	347	Ozzie Smith	.50	.23	.06
☐	348	Mike Blowers	.10	.05	.01
☐	349	Armando Reynoso	.10	.05	.01
☐	350	Barry Larkin	.20	.09	.03
☐	351	Mike Williams	.10	.05	.01
☐	352	Scott Kamieniecki	.10	.05	.01
☐	353	Gary Gaetti	.10	.05	.01
☐	354	Todd Stottlemyre	.10	.05	.01
☐	355	Fred McGriff	.35	.16	.04
☐	356	Tim Mauser	.10	.05	.01
☐	357	Chris Gwynn	.10	.05	.01
☐	358	Frank Castillo	.10	.05	.01
☐	359	Jeff Reboulet	.10	.05	.01
☐	360	Roger Clemens	.60	.25	.08
☐	361	Mark Carreon	.10	.05	.01
☐	362	Chad Kreuter	.10	.05	.01
☐	363	Mark Farris	.10	.05	.01
☐	364	Bob Welch	.10	.05	.01
☐	365	Dean Palmer	.15	.07	.02
☐	366	Jeromy Burnitz	.10	.05	.01
☐	367	B.J. Surhoff	.10	.05	.01
☐	368	Mike Butcher	.10	.05	.01
☐	369	Relief Pitcher Prospects Brad Clontz Steve Phoenix Scott Gentile Bucky Buckles	.20	.09	.03
☐	370	Eddie Murray	.20	.09	.03
☐	371	Orlando Miller	.15	.07	.02
☐	372	Ron Karkovice	.10	.05	.01
☐	373	Richie Lewis	.10	.05	.01
☐	374	Lenny Webster	.10	.05	.01
☐	375	Jeff Tackett	.10	.05	.01
☐	376	Tom Urbani	.10	.05	.01
☐	377	Tino Martinez	.10	.05	.01
☐	378	Mark Dewey	.10	.05	.01
☐	379	Charles O'Brien	.10	.05	.01
☐	380	Terry Mulholland	.10	.05	.01
☐	381	Thomas Howard	.10	.05	.01
☐	382	Chris Haney	.10	.05	.01
☐	383	Billy Hatcher	.10	.05	.01
☐	384	Jeff Bagwell AS Frank Thomas AS	.75	.35	.09
☐	385	Bret Boone AS Carlos Baerga AS	.15	.07	.02
☐	386	Matt Williams AS Wade Boggs AS	.20	.09	.03
☐	387	Wil Cordero AS Cal Ripken AS	.40	.18	.05
☐	388	Barry Bonds AS Ken Griffey AS	.50	.23	.06
☐	389	Tony Gwynn AS Albert Belle AS	.30	.14	.04
☐	390	Dante Bichette AS Kirby Puckett AS	.25	.11	.03
☐	391	Mike Piazza AS Mike Stanley AS	.25	.11	.03
☐	392	Greg Maddux AS David Cone AS	.20	.09	.03
☐	393	Danny Jackson AS Jimmy Key AS	.10	.05	.01
☐	394	John Franco AS Lee Smith AS	.10	.05	.01
☐	395	Checklist 1-198	.10	.05	.01
☐	396	Checklist 199-396	.10	.05	.01

1995 Topps Cyberstats

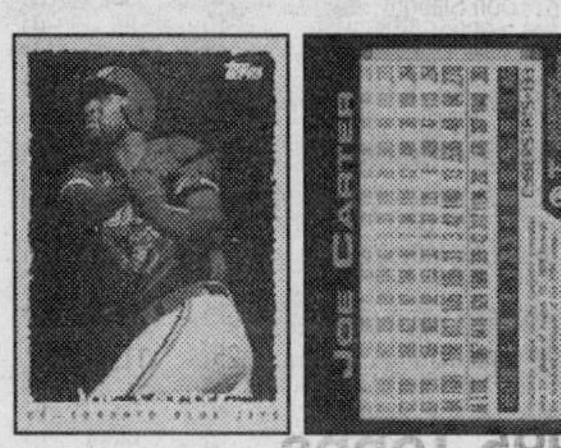

The 198-card Cyberstats insert set was issued one per pack and three per jumbo pack. The idea is to present prorated statistics for the 1994 strike shortened season. The photos on front are the same as the basic issue. The difference is that the photo is given a glossy or metallic finish. The backs contain yearly statistics, including the prorated 1994 numbers. The career statistics include what may have been given a full season.

	MINT	EXC	G-VG
COMPLETE SERIES 1 (198)	90.00	40.00	11.50
COMMON CARD (1-198)	.25	.11	.03
☐ 1 Frank Thomas	10.00	4.50	1.25
☐ 2 Mickey Morandini	.25	.11	.03
☐ 3 Todd Worrell	.25	.11	.03
☐ 4 David Cone	.35	.16	.04
☐ 5 Trevor Hoffman	.25	.11	.03
☐ 6 Shane Mack	.25	.11	.03
☐ 7 Delino DeShields	.25	.11	.03
☐ 8 Matt Williams	2.00	.90	.25
☐ 9 Sammy Sosa	.35	.16	.04
☐ 10 Gary DiSarcina	.25	.11	.03
☐ 11 Kenny Rogers	.25	.11	.03
☐ 12 Jose Vizcaino	.25	.11	.03
☐ 13 Lou Whitaker	.45	.20	.06
☐ 14 Ron Darling	.25	.11	.03
☐ 15 Dave Nilsson	.25	.11	.03
☐ 16 Denny Martinez	.25	.11	.03
☐ 17 Orlando Merced	.25	.11	.03
☐ 18 John Wetteland	.25	.11	.03
☐ 19 Mike Devereaux	.25	.11	.03
☐ 20 Rene Arocha	.25	.11	.03
☐ 21 Jay Buhner	.35	.16	.04
☐ 22 Hal Morris	.25	.11	.03
☐ 23 Paul Molitor	1.50	.65	.19
☐ 24 Dave West	.25	.11	.03
☐ 25 Scott Sanders	.25	.11	.03
☐ 26 Eddie Zambrano	.25	.11	.03
☐ 27 Ricky Bones	.25	.11	.03
☐ 28 John Valentin	.25	.11	.03
☐ 29 Kevin Tapani	.25	.11	.03
☐ 30 Tim Wallach	.25	.11	.03
☐ 31 Darren Lewis	.25	.11	.03
☐ 32 Travis Fryman	1.00	.45	.13
☐ 33 Bret Barberie	.25	.11	.03
☐ 34 Dennis Eckersley	.35	.16	.04
☐ 35 Ken Hill	.35	.16	.04
☐ 36 Pete Harnisch	.25	.11	.03
☐ 37 Mike Mussina	1.50	.65	.19
☐ 38 Dave Winfield	.45	.20	.06
☐ 39 Joey Hamilton	.25	.11	.03
☐ 40 Edgar Martinez	.25	.11	.03
☐ 41 John Smiley	.25	.11	.03
☐ 42 Jim Abbott	.35	.16	.04
☐ 43 Mike Kelly	.35	.16	.04
☐ 44 Brian Jordan	.25	.11	.03
☐ 45 Ken Ryan	.25	.11	.03
☐ 46 Matt Mieske	.25	.11	.03
☐ 47 Rick Aguilera	.25	.11	.03
☐ 48 Ismael Valdes	.25	.11	.03
☐ 49 Royce Clayton	.35	.16	.04
☐ 50 Juan Gonzalez	3.00	1.35	.40
☐ 51 Mel Rojas	.25	.11	.03
☐ 52 Doug Drabek	.35	.16	.04
☐ 53 Charles Nagy	.25	.11	.03
☐ 54 Tim Raines	.35	.16	.04
☐ 55 Midre Cummings	.45	.20	.06
☐ 56 Rafael Palmeiro	.45	.20	.06
☐ 57 Charlie Hayes	.25	.11	.03
☐ 58 Ray Lankford	.35	.16	.04
☐ 59 Tim Davis	.25	.11	.03
☐ 60 Andy Ashby	.25	.11	.03
☐ 61 Mark Grace	.35	.16	.04
☐ 62 Mark Langston	.25	.11	.03
☐ 63 Chuck Carr	.25	.11	.03
☐ 64 Barry Bonds	4.00	1.80	.50
☐ 65 David Segui	.25	.11	.03
☐ 66 Mariano Duncan	.25	.11	.03
☐ 67 Kenny Lofton	2.50	1.15	.30
☐ 68 Ken Caminiti	.25	.11	.03
☐ 69 Darrin Jackson	.25	.11	.03
☐ 70 Wil Cordero	.45	.20	.06
☐ 71 Walt Weiss	.25	.11	.03
☐ 72 Tom Pagnozzi	.25	.11	.03
☐ 73 Bret Boone	.45	.20	.06
☐ 74 Wally Joyner	.25	.11	.03
☐ 75 Luis Lopez	.25	.11	.03
☐ 76 Len Dykstra	.45	.20	.06
☐ 77 Pedro Munoz	.25	.11	.03
☐ 78 Kevin Gross	.25	.11	.03
☐ 79 Eduardo Perez	.25	.11	.03
☐ 80 Brent Gates	.35	.16	.04
☐ 81 Jeff Conine	.45	.20	.06
☐ 82 Paul Sorrento	.25	.11	.03
☐ 83 Julio Franco	.25	.11	.03
☐ 84 Chris Sabo	.25	.11	.03
☐ 85 Dante Bichette	.45	.20	.06
☐ 86 Mike Stanley	.25	.11	.03
☐ 87 Bob Hamelin	.45	.20	.06
☐ 88 Tommy Greene	.25	.11	.03
☐ 89 Jeff Brantley	.25	.11	.03
☐ 90 Ed Sprague	.25	.11	.03
☐ 91 Otis Nixon	.25	.11	.03
☐ 92 Chad Curtis	.25	.11	.03
☐ 93 Chuck McElroy	.25	.11	.03
☐ 94 Troy Neel	.25	.11	.03
☐ 95 Benito Santiago	.25	.11	.03
☐ 96 Jose Mesa	.25	.11	.03
☐ 97 Luis Gonzalez	.25	.11	.03
☐ 98 Alex Fernandez	.45	.20	.06
☐ 99 Ben McDonald	.35	.16	.04
☐ 100 Wade Boggs	.45	.20	.06
☐ 101 Tom Glavine	.45	.20	.06
☐ 102 Phil Plantier	.25	.11	.03
☐ 103 Raul Mondesi	2.50	1.15	.30
☐ 104 Jim Edmonds	.25	.11	.03
☐ 105 Jeff Kent	.25	.11	.03
☐ 106 Wilson Alvarez	.35	.16	.04
☐ 107 Geronimo Berroa	.25	.11	.03
☐ 108 Craig Biggio	.35	.16	.04
☐ 109 Roberto Hernandez	.25	.11	.03

☐ 110 Bobby Ayala .25 .11 .03
☐ 111 Bob Tewksbury .25 .11 .03
☐ 112 Rondell White .45 .20 .06
☐ 113 Steve Cooke .25 .11 .03
☐ 114 Tim Salmon .45 .20 .06
☐ 115 Kent Mercker .25 .11 .03
☐ 116 Randy Johnson .45 .20 .06
☐ 117 Mo Vaughn .45 .20 .06
☐ 118 Eddie Williams .25 .11 .03
☐ 119 Jeff Montgomery .25 .11 .03
☐ 120 Kirt Manwaring .25 .11 .03
☐ 121 Pat Hentgen .35 .16 .04
☐ 122 Shawon Dunston .25 .11 .03
☐ 123 Tim Belcher .25 .11 .03
☐ 124 Cecil Fielder .45 .20 .06
☐ 125 Todd Hundley .25 .11 .03
☐ 126 Mark Acre .25 .11 .03
☐ 127 Darrell Whitmore .25 .11 .03
☐ 128 Darryl Kile .25 .11 .03
☐ 129 Jay Bell .25 .11 .03
☐ 130 Harold Baines .25 .11 .03
☐ 131 Felix Fermin .25 .11 .03
☐ 132 Ellis Burks .25 .11 .03
☐ 133 Joe Carter 1.25 .55 .16
☐ 134 Terry Pendleton .25 .11 .03
☐ 135 Junior Felix .25 .11 .03
☐ 136 Bill Gullickson .25 .11 .03
☐ 137 Melvin Nieves .35 .16 .04
☐ 138 Chuck Knoblauch .45 .20 .06
☐ 139 Bobby Jones .25 .11 .03
☐ 140 Darrin Fletcher .25 .11 .03
☐ 141 Andy Van Slyke .35 .16 .04
☐ 142 Allen Watson .35 .16 .04
☐ 143 Dan Wilson .25 .11 .03
☐ 144 Bip Roberts .25 .11 .03
☐ 145 Sterling Hitchcock .25 .11 .03
☐ 146 Johnny Ruffin .25 .11 .03
☐ 147 Steve Trachsel .45 .20 .06
☐ 148 Ramon Martinez .25 .11 .03
☐ 149 Dave Henderson .25 .11 .03
☐ 150 Chris Gomez .45 .20 .06
☐ 151 Rusty Greer .45 .20 .06
☐ 152 John Franco .25 .11 .03
☐ 153 Mike Bordick .25 .11 .03
☐ 154 Dave Magadan .25 .11 .03
☐ 155 Greg Swindell .25 .11 .03
☐ 156 Arthur Rhodes .25 .11 .03
☐ 157 Juan Guzman .25 .11 .03
☐ 158 Greg Maddux 2.00 .90 .25
☐ 159 Mike Macfarlane .25 .11 .03
☐ 160 Curt Schilling .25 .11 .03
☐ 161 Jose Canseco 1.50 .65 .19
☐ 162 Aaron Sele .45 .20 .06
☐ 163 Steve Buechele .25 .11 .03
☐ 164 Orel Hershiser .25 .11 .03
☐ 165 Mike Henneman .25 .11 .03
☐ 166 Kevin Seitzer .25 .11 .03
☐ 167 Ruben Sierra .45 .20 .06
☐ 168 Alex Cole .25 .11 .03
☐ 169 Jim Thome .45 .20 .06
☐ 170 Lance Johnson .25 .11 .03
☐ 171 Marquis Grissom .45 .20 .06
☐ 172 Jamie Moyer .25 .11 .03
☐ 173 Todd Zeile .35 .16 .04
☐ 174 Chris Bosio .25 .11 .03
☐ 175 Steve Howe .25 .11 .03
☐ 176 Luis Polonia .25 .11 .03
☐ 177 Ryan Klesko 1.25 .55 .16
☐ 178 Kevin Appier .35 .16 .04
☐ 179 Tim Naehring .25 .11 .03
☐ 180 Randy Myers .25 .11 .03
☐ 181 Mike Jackson .25 .11 .03
☐ 182 Chili Davis .25 .11 .03
☐ 183 Jason Jacome .45 .20 .06
☐ 184 Stan Javier .25 .11 .03
☐ 185 Scott Servais .25 .11 .03
☐ 186 Kirk Rueter .25 .11 .03
☐ 187 Don Slaught .25 .11 .03
☐ 188 Ozzie Smith 2.00 .90 .25
☐ 189 Barry Larkin .45 .20 .06
☐ 190 Gary Gaetti .25 .11 .03
☐ 191 Fred McGriff 1.50 .65 .19
☐ 192 Roger Clemens 2.50 1.15 .30
☐ 193 Dean Palmer .35 .16 .04
☐ 194 Jeromy Burnitz .25 .11 .03
☐ 195 Scott Kamieniecki .25 .11 .03
☐ 196 Eddie Murray .45 .20 .06
☐ 197 Ron Karkovice .25 .11 .03
☐ 198 Tino Martinez .25 .11 .03

1995 Topps League Leaders

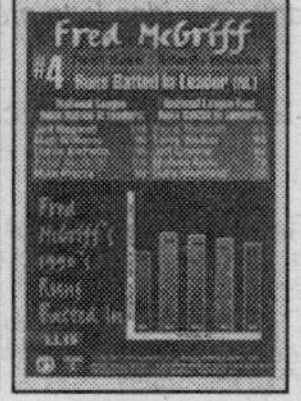

Randomly inserted in jumbo packs at a rate of one in three, this 25-card standard-size set showcases those that were among league leaders in various categories. Card fronts feature a player photo with a black background. The player's name appears in gold foil at the bottom and the category with which he led the league or was among the leaders is in yellow letters up the right side. The backs contain various graphs and where the player placed among the leaders.

	MINT	EXC	G-VG
COMPLETE SET (25)	20.00	9.00	2.50
COMMON CARD (LL1-LL25)	.25	.11	.03

☐ LL1 Albert Belle 1.75 .80 .22
☐ LL2 Kevin Mitchell .25 .11 .03
☐ LL3 Wade Boggs .75 .35 .09
☐ LL4 Tony Gwynn 1.50 .65 .19
☐ LL5 Moises Alou .25 .11 .03
☐ LL6 Andres Galarraga .25 .11 .03
☐ LL7 Matt Williams 1.25 .55 .16
☐ LL8 Barry Bonds 2.00 .90 .25
☐ LL9 Frank Thomas 5.00 2.30 .60
☐ LL10 Jose Canseco 1.00 .45 .13
☐ LL11 Jeff Bagwell 2.50 1.15 .30
☐ LL12 Kirby Puckett 2.00 .90 .25
☐ LL13 Julio Franco .25 .11 .03
☐ LL14 Albert Belle 1.75 .80 .22
☐ LL15 Fred McGriff 1.00 .45 .13
☐ LL16 Kenny Lofton 1.50 .65 .19
☐ LL17 Otis Nixon .25 .11 .03
☐ LL18 Brady Anderson .25 .11 .03
☐ LL19 Deion Sanders 1.50 .65 .19
☐ LL20 Chuck Carr .25 .11 .03

☐ LL21	Pat Hentgen	.25	.11	.03
☐ LL22	Andy Benes	.25	.11	.03
☐ LL23	Roger Clemens	1.50	.65	.19
☐ LL24	Greg Maddux	1.50	.65	.19
☐ LL25	Pedro Martinez	.25	.11	.03

1995 Topps Stadium Club FDI

Randomly inserted in Stadium Club packs at a rate of one in 36, this nine card set serves as a preview of the basic Stadium Club cards. These are the only First Day Issue baseball cards produced for 1994. The full-bleed card fronts have the player's name, First Day Issue logo and Stadium Club logo in gold foil. The team logo is also outlined by gold foil. The backs have various statistical graphs and highlights. The card numbers correspond to those in the basic set.

	MINT	EXC	G-VG
COMPLETE SET (9)	35.00	16.00	4.40
COMMON CARD	2.00	.90	.25

☐ 29F	Shawon Dunston	2.00	.90	.25
☐ 39F	Paul Molitor	5.00	2.30	.60
☐ 79F	Bob Hamelin	3.00	1.35	.40
☐ 96F	Ruben Sierra	3.00	1.35	.40
☐ 131F	Will Clark	5.00	2.30	.60
☐ 149F	Mike Piazza	12.00	5.50	1.50
☐ 153F	Andy Van Slyke	3.00	1.35	.40
☐ 168F	Jeff Tackett	2.00	.90	.25
☐ 197F	Ivan Rodriguez	3.00	1.35	.40

1992 Triple Play

The 1992 Donruss Triple Play set contains 264 cards measuring the standard size (2 1/2" by 3 1/2"). This set was created especially for children ages 5-12, featuring bright color borders, player quotes, fun facts, and a "Little Hotshot" subset (6, 77, 158, 234, 243, 253), picturing some players when they were kids. The Awesome Action subset mostly show more than one player (26, 41, 61, 73, 99, 102, 113, 121, 130, 193, 196). Each 15-card pack included one rub-off game card. Randomly packed Gallery of Stars cards feature the artwork of Dick Perez and capture twelve top players who changed teams in 1992. The color action player photos on the fronts are slightly tilted to the left, and the border alternates shades from red to yellow and back to red again as one moves down the card face. In addition to blue and white print, the backs reflect the same color as the front borders. Player information is displayed inside a home plate or base icon. The cards are numbered on the back and checklisted below accordingly. The only noteworthy Rookie Card in the set is the Phillie Phanatic.

	MINT	EXC	G-VG
COMPLETE SET (264)	10.00	4.50	1.25
COMMON CARD (1-264)	.05	.02	.01

☐ 1	SkyDome	.05	.02	.01
☐ 2	Tom Foley	.05	.02	.01
☐ 3	Scott Erickson	.05	.02	.01
☐ 4	Matt Williams	.20	.09	.03
☐ 5	David Valle	.05	.02	.01
☐ 6	Andy Van Slyke LH	.10	.05	.01
☐ 7	Tom Glavine	.15	.07	.02
☐ 8	Kevin Appier	.10	.05	.01
☐ 9	Pedro Guerrero	.05	.02	.01
☐ 10	Terry Steinbach	.10	.05	.01
☐ 11	Terry Mulholland	.05	.02	.01
☐ 12	Mike Boddicker	.05	.02	.01
☐ 13	Gregg Olson	.05	.02	.01
☐ 14	Tim Burke	.05	.02	.01
☐ 15	Candy Maldonado	.05	.02	.01
☐ 16	Orlando Merced	.10	.05	.01
☐ 17	Robin Ventura	.15	.07	.02
☐ 18	Eric Anthony	.05	.02	.01
☐ 19	Greg Maddux	.20	.09	.03
☐ 20	Erik Hanson	.05	.02	.01
☐ 21	Bobby Ojeda	.05	.02	.01
☐ 22	Nolan Ryan	1.00	.45	.13
☐ 23	Dave Righetti	.05	.02	.01
☐ 24	Reggie Jefferson	.05	.02	.01
☐ 25	Jody Reed	.05	.02	.01
☐ 26	Steve Finley and Gary Carter AA	.05	.02	.01
☐ 27	Chili Davis	.10	.05	.01
☐ 28	Hector Villanueva	.05	.02	.01
☐ 29	Cecil Fielder	.15	.07	.02
☐ 30	Hal Morris	.10	.05	.01
☐ 31	Barry Larkin	.15	.07	.02
☐ 32	Bobby Thigpen	.05	.02	.01
☐ 33	Andy Benes	.10	.05	.01
☐ 34	Harold Baines	.10	.05	.01
☐ 35	David Cone	.15	.07	.02

	#	Player			
☐	36	Mark Langston	.15	.07	.02
☐	37	Bryan Harvey	.10	.05	.01
☐	38	John Kruk	.15	.07	.02
☐	39	Scott Sanderson	.05	.02	.01
☐	40	Lonnie Smith	.05	.02	.01
☐	41	Rex Hudler AA	.05	.02	.01
☐	42	George Bell	.10	.05	.01
☐	43	Steve Finley	.05	.02	.01
☐	44	Mickey Tettleton	.10	.05	.01
☐	45	Robby Thompson	.05	.02	.01
☐	46	Pat Kelly	.10	.05	.01
☐	47	Marquis Grissom	.15	.07	.02
☐	48	Tony Pena	.05	.02	.01
☐	49	Alex Cole	.05	.02	.01
☐	50	Steve Buechele	.05	.02	.01
☐	51	Ivan Rodriguez	.15	.07	.02
☐	52	John Smiley	.05	.02	.01
☐	53	Gary Sheffield	.15	.07	.02
☐	54	Greg Olson	.05	.02	.01
☐	55	Ramon Martinez	.10	.05	.01
☐	56	B.J. Surhoff	.05	.02	.01
☐	57	Bruce Hurst	.05	.02	.01
☐	58	Todd Stottlemyre	.05	.02	.01
☐	59	Brett Butler	.10	.05	.01
☐	60	Glenn Davis	.05	.02	.01
☐	61	Glenn Braggs and Kirt Manwaring AA	.05	.02	.01
☐	62	Lee Smith	.15	.07	.02
☐	63	Rickey Henderson	.15	.07	.02
☐	64	Fun at the Ballpark Dave Cone Jeff Innis John Franco	.05	.02	.01
☐	65	Rick Aguilera	.10	.05	.01
☐	66	Kevin Elster	.05	.02	.01
☐	67	Dwight Evans	.10	.05	.01
☐	68	Andujar Cedeno	.10	.05	.01
☐	69	Brian McRae	.15	.07	.02
☐	70	Benito Santiago	.05	.02	.01
☐	71	Randy Johnson	.15	.07	.02
☐	72	Roberto Kelly	.10	.05	.01
☐	73	Juan Samuel AA	.05	.02	.01
☐	74	Alex Fernandez	.15	.07	.02
☐	75	Felix Jose	.10	.05	.01
☐	76	Brian Harper	.05	.02	.01
☐	77	Scott Sanderson LH	.05	.02	.01
☐	78	Ken Caminiti	.10	.05	.01
☐	79	Mo Vaughn	.20	.09	.03
☐	80	Roger McDowell	.05	.02	.01
☐	81	Robin Yount	.20	.09	.03
☐	82	Dave Magadan	.05	.02	.01
☐	83	Julio Franco	.10	.05	.01
☐	84	Roberto Alomar	.25	.11	.03
☐	85	Steve Avery	.15	.07	.02
☐	86	Travis Fryman	.25	.11	.03
☐	87	Fred McGriff	.20	.09	.03
☐	88	Dave Stewart	.10	.05	.01
☐	89	Larry Walker	.15	.07	.02
☐	90	Chris Sabo	.10	.05	.01
☐	91	Chuck Finley	.05	.02	.01
☐	92	Dennis Martinez	.10	.05	.01
☐	93	Jeff Johnson	.05	.02	.01
☐	94	Len Dykstra	.15	.07	.02
☐	95	Mark Whiten	.10	.05	.01
☐	96	Wade Taylor	.05	.02	.01
☐	97	Lance Dickson	.05	.02	.01
☐	98	Kevin Tapani	.05	.02	.01
☐	99	Luis Polonia and Tony Phillips AA	.05	.02	.01
☐	100	Milt Cuyler	.05	.02	.01
☐	101	Willie McGee	.10	.05	.01
☐	102	Tony Fernandez AA	.05	.02	.01
☐	103	Albert Belle	.35	.16	.04
☐	104	Todd Hundley	.05	.02	.01
☐	105	Ben McDonald	.10	.05	.01
☐	106	Doug Drabek	.15	.07	.02
☐	107	Tim Raines	.15	.07	.02
☐	108	Joe Carter	.20	.09	.03
☐	109	Reggie Sanders	.20	.09	.03
☐	110	John Olerud	.15	.07	.02
☐	111	Darren Lewis	.10	.05	.01
☐	112	Juan Gonzalez	.60	.25	.08
☐	113	Andre Dawson AA	.10	.05	.01
☐	114	Mark Grace	.15	.07	.02
☐	115	George Brett	.30	.14	.04
☐	116	Barry Bonds	.40	.18	.05
☐	117	Lou Whitaker	.15	.07	.02
☐	118	Jose Oquendo	.05	.02	.01
☐	119	Lee Stevens	.05	.02	.01
☐	120	Phil Plantier	.15	.07	.02
☐	121	Matt Merullo AA	.05	.02	.01
☐	122	Greg Vaughn	.10	.05	.01
☐	123	Royce Clayton	.15	.07	.02
☐	124	Bob Welch	.05	.02	.01
☐	125	Juan Samuel	.05	.02	.01
☐	126	Ron Gant	.10	.05	.01
☐	127	Edgar Martinez	.10	.05	.01
☐	128	Andy Ashby	.05	.02	.01
☐	129	Jack McDowell	.15	.07	.02
☐	130	Dave Henderson and Jerry Browne AA	.05	.02	.01
☐	131	Leo Gomez	.05	.02	.01
☐	132	Checklist 1-88	.05	.02	.01
☐	133	Phillie Phanatic	.10	.05	.01
☐	134	Bret Barberie	.05	.02	.01
☐	135	Kent Hrbek	.10	.05	.01
☐	136	Hall of Fame	.05	.02	.01
☐	137	Omar Vizquel	.05	.02	.01
☐	138	The Famous Chicken	.05	.02	.01
☐	139	Terry Pendleton	.15	.07	.02
☐	140	Jim Eisenreich	.05	.02	.01
☐	141	Todd Zeile	.10	.05	.01
☐	142	Todd Van Poppel	.15	.07	.02
☐	143	Darren Daulton	.15	.07	.02
☐	144	Mike Macfarlane	.05	.02	.01
☐	145	Luis Mercedes	.05	.02	.01
☐	146	Trevor Wilson	.05	.02	.01
☐	147	Dave Stieb	.05	.02	.01
☐	148	Andy Van Slyke	.15	.07	.02
☐	149	Carlton Fisk	.15	.07	.02
☐	150	Craig Biggio	.10	.05	.01
☐	151	Joe Girardi	.05	.02	.01
☐	152	Ken Griffey Jr.	1.50	.65	.19
☐	153	Jose Offerman	.05	.02	.01
☐	154	Bobby Witt	.05	.02	.01
☐	155	Will Clark	.20	.09	.03
☐	156	Steve Olin	.05	.02	.01
☐	157	Greg W. Harris	.05	.02	.01
☐	158	Dale Murphy LH	.10	.05	.01
☐	159	Don Mattingly	.35	.16	.04
☐	160	Shawon Dunston	.05	.02	.01
☐	161	Bill Gullickson	.05	.02	.01
☐	162	Paul O'Neill	.10	.05	.01
☐	163	Norm Charlton	.05	.02	.01
☐	164	Bo Jackson	.15	.07	.02
☐	165	Tony Fernandez	.05	.02	.01
☐	166	Dave Henderson	.05	.02	.01
☐	167	Dwight Gooden	.10	.05	.01
☐	168	Junior Felix	.05	.02	.01
☐	169	Lance Parrish	.10	.05	.01
☐	170	Pat Combs	.05	.02	.01
☐	171	Chuck Knoblauch	.15	.07	.02
☐	172	John Smoltz	.10	.05	.01
☐	173	Wrigley Field	.05	.02	.01
☐	174	Andre Dawson	.15	.07	.02
☐	175	Pete Harnisch	.10	.05	.01

☐	176 Alan Trammell	.15	.07	.02
☐	177 Kirk Dressendorfer	.05	.02	.01
☐	178 Matt Nokes	.05	.02	.01
☐	179 Wil Cordero	.20	.09	.03
☐	180 Scott Cooper	.10	.05	.01
☐	181 Glenallen Hill	.05	.02	.01
☐	182 John Franco	.05	.02	.01
☐	183 Rafael Palmeiro	.15	.07	.02
☐	184 Jay Bell	.10	.05	.01
☐	185 Bill Wegman	.05	.02	.01
☐	186 Deion Sanders	.25	.11	.03
☐	187 Darryl Strawberry	.10	.05	.01
☐	188 Jaime Navarro	.05	.02	.01
☐	189 Darrin Jackson	.05	.02	.01
☐	190 Eddie Zosky	.05	.02	.01
☐	191 Mike Scioscia	.05	.02	.01
☐	192 Chito Martinez	.05	.02	.01
☐	193 Pat Kelly and Ron Tingley AA	.05	.02	.01
☐	194 Ray Lankford	.15	.07	.02
☐	195 Dennis Eckersley	.15	.07	.02
☐	196 Ivan Calderon and Mike Maddux AA	.05	.02	.01
☐	197 Shane Mack	.10	.05	.01
☐	198 Checklist 89-176	.05	.02	.01
☐	199 Cal Ripken	.40	.18	.05
☐	200 Jeff Bagwell	.75	.35	.09
☐	201 Dave Howard	.05	.02	.01
☐	202 Kirby Puckett	.35	.16	.04
☐	203 Harold Reynolds	.05	.02	.01
☐	204 Jim Abbott	.15	.07	.02
☐	205 Mark Lewis	.05	.02	.01
☐	206 Frank Thomas	1.50	.65	.19
☐	207 Rex Hudler	.05	.02	.01
☐	208 Vince Coleman	.05	.02	.01
☐	209 Delino DeShields	.15	.07	.02
☐	210 Luis Gonzalez	.10	.05	.01
☐	211 Wade Boggs	.15	.07	.02
☐	212 Orel Hershiser	.10	.05	.01
☐	213 Cal Eldred	.10	.05	.01
☐	214 Jose Canseco	.20	.09	.03
☐	215 Jose Guzman	.05	.02	.01
☐	216 Roger Clemens	.25	.11	.03
☐	217 David Justice	.20	.09	.03
☐	218 Tony Phillips	.05	.02	.01
☐	219 Tony Gwynn	.25	.11	.03
☐	220 Mitch Williams	.10	.05	.01
☐	221 Bill Sampen	.05	.02	.01
☐	222 Billy Hatcher	.05	.02	.01
☐	223 Gary Gaetti	.05	.02	.01
☐	224 Tim Wallach	.05	.02	.01
☐	225 Kevin Maas	.05	.02	.01
☐	226 Kevin Brown	.10	.05	.01
☐	227 Sandy Alomar Jr.	.10	.05	.01
☐	228 John Habyan	.05	.02	.01
☐	229 Ryne Sandberg	.30	.14	.04
☐	230 Greg Gagne	.05	.02	.01
☐	231 Autographs (Mark McGwire)	.05	.02	.01
☐	232 Mike LaValliere	.05	.02	.01
☐	233 Mark Gubicza	.05	.02	.01
☐	234 Lance Parrish LH	.10	.05	.01
☐	235 Carlos Baerga	.20	.09	.03
☐	236 Howard Johnson	.10	.05	.01
☐	237 Mike Mussina	.30	.14	.04
☐	238 Ruben Sierra	.15	.07	.02
☐	239 Lance Johnson	.05	.02	.01
☐	240 Devon White	.05	.02	.01
☐	241 Dan Wilson	.05	.02	.01
☐	242 Kelly Gruber	.05	.02	.01
☐	243 Brett Butler LH	.05	.02	.01
☐	244 Ozzie Smith	.20	.09	.03
☐	245 Chuck McElroy	.05	.02	.01
☐	246 Shawn Boskie	.05	.02	.01
☐	247 Mark Davis	.05	.02	.01
☐	248 Bill Landrum	.05	.02	.01
☐	249 Frank Tanana	.05	.02	.01
☐	250 Darryl Hamilton	.05	.02	.01
☐	251 Gary DiSarcina	.05	.02	.01
☐	252 Mike Greenwell	.10	.05	.01
☐	253 Cal Ripken LH	.20	.09	.03
☐	254 Paul Molitor	.20	.09	.03
☐	255 Tim Teufel	.05	.02	.01
☐	256 Chris Hoiles	.15	.07	.02
☐	257 Rob Dibble	.05	.02	.01
☐	258 Sid Bream	.05	.02	.01
☐	259 Tino Martinez	.10	.05	.01
☐	260 Dale Murphy	.15	.07	.02
☐	261 Greg Hibbard	.05	.02	.01
☐	262 Mark McGwire	.15	.07	.02
☐	263 Oriole Park	.05	.02	.01
☐	264 Checklist 177-264	.05	.02	.01

1992 Triple Play Gallery

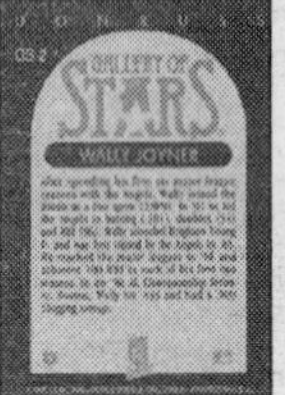

The 1992 Donruss Triple Play Gallery of Stars was an insert subset for the 1992 Donruss Triple Play baseball set. Randomly inserted into foil packs, the first six cards feature six top players who changed teams in 1992 in their new uniforms. The second six cards were randomly inserted one per jumbo pack. The cards measure the standard size (2 1/2" by 3 1/2"). On bright-colored backgrounds, the fronts display color player portraits by noted sports artist Dick Perez. The words "Gallery of Stars" appear in a red and silver-foil stamped banner above the portrait, while the player's name appears in a similarly colored bar between two silver foil stars at the card bottom. The backs are red, white, and gray and carry career summary. The cards are numbered on the back with a "GS" prefix.

	MINT	EXC	G-VG
COMPLETE SET (12)	20.00	9.00	2.50
COMPLETE FOIL SET (6)	2.50	1.15	.30
COMPLETE JUMBO SET (6)	18.00	8.00	2.30
COMMON CARD (GS1-GS6)	.50	.23	.06
COMMON CARD (GS7-GS12)	1.00	.45	.13

☐	GS1 Bobby Bonilla	.50	.23	.06
☐	GS2 Wally Joyner	.50	.23	.06
☐	GS3 Jack Morris	.50	.23	.06
☐	GS4 Steve Sax	.50	.23	.06
☐	GS5 Danny Tartabull	.50	.23	.06

		MINT	EXC	G-VG
☐ GS6	Frank Viola	.50	.23	.06
☐ GS7	Jeff Bagwell	4.00	1.80	.50
☐ GS8	Ken Griffey Jr.	7.00	3.10	.85
☐ GS9	David Justice	1.00	.45	.13
☐ GS10	Ryan Klesko	4.00	1.80	.50
☐ GS11	Cal Ripken	4.00	1.80	.50
☐ GS12	Frank Thomas	7.00	3.10	.85

1993 Triple Play

The 1993 Donruss Triple Play baseball set consists of 264 standard-size (2 1/2" by 3 1/2") cards. Approximately eight players from each of the 28 teams is represented in the set. Eack pack also included one of thirty Triple Play Action Baseball game cards. The fronts display color action player photos inside a red frame on a black card face. The player's last name appears in silver block lettering across the top of the picture. The team logo is placed at the lower right corner. The horizontal backs feature a color close-up photo, biography, and either trivia questions, fun facts, or player quotes. Scattered throughout the set are seven Little Hotshot (11, 77, 97, 143, 209, 229, 245) and eight Awesome Action (12, 61, 64, 68, 144, 193, 196, 200) cards. The cards are numbered on the back. There are no key Rookie Cards in this set, however the set does feature the first card of President Bill Clinton.

	MINT	EXC	G-VG
COMPLETE SET (264)	10.00	4.50	1.25
COMMON CARD (1-264)	.05	.02	.01

		MINT	EXC	G-VG
☐ 1	Ken Griffey Jr.	2.00	.90	.25
☐ 2	Roberto Alomar	.50	.23	.06
☐ 3	Cal Ripken	1.50	.65	.19
☐ 4	Eric Karros	.08	.04	.01
☐ 5	Cecil Fielder	.10	.05	.01
☐ 6	Gary Sheffield	.10	.05	.01
☐ 7	Darren Daulton	.10	.05	.01
☐ 8	Andy Van Slyke	.10	.05	.01
☐ 9	Dennis Eckersley	.10	.05	.01
☐ 10	Ryne Sandberg	.60	.25	.08
☐ 11	Mark Grace LH	.08	.04	.01
☐ 12	David Segui and Luis Polonia AA	.05	.02	.01
☐ 13	Mike Mussina	.40	.18	.05
☐ 14	Vince Coleman	.05	.02	.01
☐ 15	Rafael Belliard	.05	.02	.01
☐ 16	Ivan Rodriguez	.10	.05	.01
☐ 17	Eddie Taubensee	.05	.02	.01
☐ 18	Cal Eldred	.08	.04	.01
☐ 19	Rick Wilkins	.05	.02	.01
☐ 20	Edgar Martinez	.05	.02	.01
☐ 21	Brian McRae	.10	.05	.01
☐ 22	Darren Holmes	.05	.02	.01
☐ 23	Mark Whiten	.08	.04	.01
☐ 24	Todd Zeile	.08	.04	.01
☐ 25	Scott Cooper	.08	.04	.01
☐ 26	Frank Thomas	2.00	.90	.25
☐ 27	Wil Cordero	.10	.05	.01
☐ 28	Juan Guzman	.08	.04	.01
☐ 29	Pedro Astacio	.08	.04	.01
☐ 30	Steve Avery	.10	.05	.01
☐ 31	Barry Larkin	.10	.05	.01
☐ 32	Bill Clinton	1.00	.45	.13
☐ 33	Scott Erickson	.05	.02	.01
☐ 34	Mike Devereaux	.08	.04	.01
☐ 35	Tino Martinez	.08	.04	.01
☐ 36	Brent Mayne	.05	.02	.01
☐ 37	Tim Salmon	.40	.18	.05
☐ 38	Dave Hollins	.10	.05	.01
☐ 39	Royce Clayton	.08	.04	.01
☐ 40	Shawon Dunston	.05	.02	.01
☐ 41	Eddie Murray	.10	.05	.01
☐ 42	Larry Walker	.10	.05	.01
☐ 43	Jeff Bagwell	1.00	.45	.13
☐ 44	Milt Cuyler	.05	.02	.01
☐ 45	Mike Bordick	.05	.02	.01
☐ 46	Mike Greenwell	.08	.04	.01
☐ 47	Steve Sax	.05	.02	.01
☐ 48	Chuck Knoblauch	.10	.05	.01
☐ 49	Charles Nagy	.05	.02	.01
☐ 50	Tim Wakefield	.05	.02	.01
☐ 51	Tony Gwynn	.50	.23	.06
☐ 52	Rob Dibble	.05	.02	.01
☐ 53	Mickey Morandini	.05	.02	.01
☐ 54	Steve Hosey	.05	.02	.01
☐ 55	Mike Piazza	2.00	.90	.25
☐ 56	Bill Wegman	.05	.02	.01
☐ 57	Kevin Maas	.05	.02	.01
☐ 58	Gary DiSarcina	.05	.02	.01
☐ 59	Travis Fryman	.15	.07	.02
☐ 60	Ruben Sierra	.10	.05	.01
☐ 61	Ken Caminiti AA	.05	.02	.01
☐ 62	Brian Jordan	.08	.04	.01
☐ 63	Scott Chiamparino	.05	.02	.01
☐ 64	George Brett and Mike Bordick AA	.40	.18	.05
☐ 65	Carlos Garcia	.08	.04	.01
☐ 66	Checklist	.05	.02	.01
☐ 67	John Smoltz	.08	.04	.01
☐ 68	Mark McGwire and Brian Harper AA	.08	.04	.01
☐ 69	Kurt Stillwell	.05	.02	.01
☐ 70	Chad Curtis	.08	.04	.01
☐ 71	Rafael Palmeiro	.10	.05	.01
☐ 72	Kevin Young	.05	.02	.01
☐ 73	Glenn Davis	.05	.02	.01
☐ 74	Dennis Martinez	.08	.04	.01
☐ 75	Sam Militello	.05	.02	.01
☐ 76	Mike Morgan	.05	.02	.01
☐ 77	Frank Thomas LH	1.00	.45	.13
☐ 78	Staying Fit	.05	.02	.01
☐ 79	Steve Buechele	.05	.02	.01
☐ 80	Carlos Baerga	.30	.14	.04
☐ 81	Robby Thompson	.05	.02	.01
☐ 82	Kirk McCaskill	.05	.02	.01
☐ 83	Lee Smith	.10	.05	.01
☐ 84	Gary Scott	.05	.02	.01
☐ 85	Tony Pena	.05	.02	.01
☐ 86	Howard Johnson	.05	.02	.01
☐ 87	Mark McGwire	.10	.05	.01
☐ 88	Bip Roberts	.05	.02	.01

	Card			
☐	89 Devon White	.05	.02	.01
☐	90 John Franco	.05	.02	.01
☐	91 Tom Browning	.05	.02	.01
☐	92 Mickey Tettleton	.08	.04	.01
☐	93 Jeff Conine	.10	.05	.01
☐	94 Albert Belle	.60	.25	.08
☐	95 Fred McGriff	.30	.14	.04
☐	96 Nolan Ryan	2.00	.90	.25
☐	97 Paul Molitor LH	.15	.07	.02
☐	98 Juan Bell	.05	.02	.01
☐	99 Dave Fleming	.08	.04	.01
☐	100 Craig Biggio	.08	.04	.01
☐	101A Andy Stankiewicz ERR (Name on front in white)	.10	.05	.01
☐	101B Andy Stankiewicz ERR (Name on front in red)	.10	.05	.01
☐	102 Delino DeShields	.08	.04	.01
☐	103 Damion Easley	.08	.04	.01
☐	104 Kevin McReynolds	.05	.02	.01
☐	105 David Nied	.10	.05	.01
☐	106 Rick Sutcliffe	.08	.04	.01
☐	107 Will Clark	.30	.14	.04
☐	108 Tim Raines	.10	.05	.01
☐	109 Eric Anthony	.05	.02	.01
☐	110 Mike LaValliere	.05	.02	.01
☐	111 Dean Palmer	.08	.04	.01
☐	112 Eric Davis	.05	.02	.01
☐	113 Damon Berryhill	.05	.02	.01
☐	114 Felix Jose	.05	.02	.01
☐	115 Ozzie Guillen	.05	.02	.01
☐	116 Pat Listach	.08	.04	.01
☐	117 Tom Glavine	.10	.05	.01
☐	118 Roger Clemens	.50	.23	.06
☐	119 Dave Henderson	.05	.02	.01
☐	120 Don Mattingly	.75	.35	.09
☐	121 Orel Hershiser	.08	.04	.01
☐	122 Ozzie Smith	.40	.18	.05
☐	123 Joe Carter	.30	.14	.04
☐	124 Bret Saberhagen	.08	.04	.01
☐	125 Mitch Williams	.08	.04	.01
☐	126 Jerald Clark	.05	.02	.01
☐	127 Mile High Stadium	.05	.02	.01
☐	128 Kent Hrbek	.08	.04	.01
☐	129 Equipment Curt Schilling	.05	.02	.01
☐	130 Gregg Jefferies	.10	.05	.01
☐	131 John Orton	.05	.02	.01
☐	132 Checklist	.05	.02	.01
☐	133 Bret Boone	.10	.05	.01
☐	134 Pat Borders	.05	.02	.01
☐	135 Gregg Olson	.05	.02	.01
☐	136 Brett Butler	.08	.04	.01
☐	137 Rob Deer	.05	.02	.01
☐	138 Darrin Jackson	.05	.02	.01
☐	139 John Kruk	.10	.05	.01
☐	140 Jay Bell	.08	.04	.01
☐	141 Bobby Witt	.05	.02	.01
☐	142 Dan Plesac Randy Myers Jose Guzman New Cubs	.05	.02	.01
☐	143 Wade Boggs LH	.08	.04	.01
☐	144 Ken Lofton AA	.25	.11	.03
☐	145 Ben McDonald	.08	.04	.01
☐	146 Dwight Gooden	.05	.02	.01
☐	147 Terry Pendleton	.10	.05	.01
☐	148 Julio Franco	.08	.04	.01
☐	149 Ken Caminiti	.08	.04	.01
☐	150 Greg Vaughn	.08	.04	.01
☐	151 Sammy Sosa	.10	.05	.01
☐	152 David Valle	.05	.02	.01
☐	153 Wally Joyner	.08	.04	.01
☐	154 Dante Bichette	.10	.05	.01
☐	155 Mark Lewis	.05	.02	.01
☐	156 Bob Tewksbury	.05	.02	.01
☐	157 Billy Hatcher	.05	.02	.01
☐	158 Jack McDowell	.10	.05	.01
☐	159 Marquis Grissom	.10	.05	.01
☐	160 Jack Morris	.10	.05	.01
☐	161 Ramon Martinez	.08	.04	.01
☐	162 Deion Sanders	.40	.18	.05
☐	163 Tim Belcher	.05	.02	.01
☐	164 Mascots Pirate Parrot	.05	.02	.01
☐	165 Scott Leius	.05	.02	.01
☐	166 Brady Anderson	.08	.04	.01
☐	167 Randy Johnson	.10	.05	.01
☐	168 Mark Gubicza	.05	.02	.01
☐	169 Chuck Finley	.05	.02	.01
☐	170 Terry Mulholland	.05	.02	.01
☐	171 Matt Williams	.40	.18	.05
☐	172 Dwight Smith	.05	.02	.01
☐	173 Bobby Bonilla	.10	.05	.01
☐	174 Ken Hill	.08	.04	.01
☐	175 Doug Jones	.05	.02	.01
☐	176 Tony Phillips	.05	.02	.01
☐	177 Terry Steinbach	.08	.04	.01
☐	178 Frank Viola	.08	.04	.01
☐	179 Robin Ventura	.10	.05	.01
☐	180 Shane Mack	.08	.04	.01
☐	181 Kenny Lofton	.50	.23	.06
☐	182 Jeff King	.05	.02	.01
☐	183 Tim Teufel	.05	.02	.01
☐	184 Chris Sabo	.08	.04	.01
☐	185 Len Dykstra	.10	.05	.01
☐	186 Trevor Wilson	.05	.02	.01
☐	187 Darryl Strawberry	.08	.04	.01
☐	188 Robin Yount	.30	.14	.04
☐	189 Bob Wickman	.05	.02	.01
☐	190 Luis Polonia	.05	.02	.01
☐	191 Alan Trammell	.10	.05	.01
☐	192 Bob Welch	.05	.02	.01
☐	193 Omar Vizquel AA	.05	.02	.01
☐	194 Tom Pagnozzi	.05	.02	.01
☐	195 Bret Barberie	.05	.02	.01
☐	196 Mike Scioscia AA	.05	.02	.01
☐	197 Randy Tomlin	.05	.02	.01
☐	198 Checklist	.05	.02	.01
☐	199 Ron Gant	.08	.04	.01
☐	200 Roberto Alomar AA	.25	.11	.03
☐	201 Andy Benes	.08	.04	.01
☐	202 Six Pirates Playing Pepper	.05	.02	.01
☐	203 Steve Finley	.05	.02	.01
☐	204 Steve Olin	.05	.02	.01
☐	205 Chris Hoiles	.08	.04	.01
☐	206 John Wetteland	.05	.02	.01
☐	207 Danny Tartabull	.08	.04	.01
☐	208 Bernard Gilkey	.05	.02	.01
☐	209 Tom Glavine LH	.08	.04	.01
☐	210 Benito Santiago	.05	.02	.01
☐	211 Mark Grace	.10	.05	.01
☐	212 Glenallen Hill	.05	.02	.01
☐	213 Jeff Brantley	.05	.02	.01
☐	214 George Brett	.75	.35	.09
☐	215 Mark Lemke	.05	.02	.01
☐	216 Ron Karkovice	.05	.02	.01
☐	217 Tom Brunansky	.05	.02	.01
☐	218 Todd Hundley	.05	.02	.01
☐	219 Rickey Henderson	.10	.05	.01
☐	220 Joe Oliver	.05	.02	.01
☐	221 Juan Gonzalez	.60	.25	.08
☐	222 John Olerud	.10	.05	.01
☐	223 Hal Morris	.08	.04	.01
☐	224 Lou Whitaker	.10	.05	.01
☐	225 Bryan Harvey	.08	.04	.01

☐	226 Mike Gallego	.05	.02	.01
☐	227 Willie McGee	.08	.04	.01
☐	228 Jose Oquendo	.05	.02	.01
☐	229 Darren Daulton LH	.08	.04	.01
☐	230 Curt Schilling	.08	.04	.01
☐	231 Jay Buhner	.08	.04	.01
☐	232 Doug Drabek Greg Swindell New Astros	.05	.02	.01
☐	233 Jaime Navarro	.05	.02	.01
☐	234 Kevin Appier	.08	.04	.01
☐	235 Mark Langston	.10	.05	.01
☐	236 Jeff Montgomery	.08	.04	.01
☐	237 Joe Girardi	.05	.02	.01
☐	238 Ed Sprague	.05	.02	.01
☐	239 Dan Walters	.05	.02	.01
☐	240 Kevin Tapani	.05	.02	.01
☐	241 Pete Harnisch	.05	.02	.01
☐	242 Al Martin	.08	.04	.01
☐	243 Jose Canseco	.30	.14	.04
☐	244 Moises Alou	.10	.05	.01
☐	245 Mark McGwire LH	.08	.04	.01
☐	246 Luis Rivera	.05	.02	.01
☐	247 George Bell	.08	.04	.01
☐	248 B.J. Surhoff	.05	.02	.01
☐	249 David Justice	.30	.14	.04
☐	250 Brian Harper	.05	.02	.01
☐	251 Sandy Alomar Jr.	.08	.04	.01
☐	252 Kevin Brown	.05	.02	.01
☐	253 Tim Wallach Todd Worrell Jody Reed New Dodgers	.05	.02	.01
☐	254 Ray Lankford	.10	.05	.01
☐	255 Derek Bell	.08	.04	.01
☐	256 Joe Grahe	.05	.02	.01
☐	257 Charlie Hayes	.08	.04	.01
☐	258 Wade Boggs Jim Abbott New Yankees	.10	.05	.01
☐	259A Joe Robbie Stadium ERR (Misnumbered 129)	.10	.05	.01
☐	259B Joe Robbie Stadium COR	.10	.05	.01
☐	260 Kirby Puckett	.75	.35	.09
☐	261 Jay Bell Fun at the Ballpark	.05	.02	.01
☐	262 Bill Swift	.08	.04	.01
☐	263 Roger McDowell Fun at the Ballpark	.05	.02	.01
☐	264 Checklist	.05	.02	.01

1993 Triple Play Action

The 1993 Triple Play Action set was randomly inserted one per pack of Donruss Triple Play. The cards were designed to serve as a game card with a scratch-off section inside beside a baseball diamond design. The cards are printed on a lighter weight card stock. When unfolded the cards measure approximately 5" by 3 1/2", however when folded they measure standard size (2 1/2" by 3 1/2"). The front of the folded card features a color action player shot with a wide vertical gray border across the top. Within the upper border are the set title

and the words "Action Baseball" printed in black. The player pictured on the card front is not named. Two team logos are superimposed across the photo at the bottom indicating which teams are paired up to play the scratch-off game inside. The inner portion of the card has six game rules printed on the upper left side followed by 32 scratch-off boxes. On the inner right side is a scoreboard printed above a green background baseball diamond. The backs are silver with the Leaf logo printed at the bottom. The cards are numbered on the back.

		MINT	EXC	G-VG
	COMPLETE SET (30)	10.00	4.50	1.25
	COMMON CARD (1-30)	.15	.07	.02
☐	1 Andy Van Slyke	.15	.07	.02
☐	2 Bobby Bonilla	.15	.07	.02
☐	3 Ozzie Smith	.40	.18	.05
☐	4 Ryne Sandberg	.60	.25	.08
☐	5 Darren Daulton	.25	.11	.03
☐	6 Larry Walker	.25	.11	.03
☐	7 Eric Karros	.15	.07	.02
☐	8 Barry Larkin	.25	.11	.03
☐	9 Deion Sanders	.40	.18	.05
☐	10 Gary Sheffield	.25	.11	.03
☐	11 Will Clark	.30	.14	.04
☐	12 Jeff Bagwell	1.00	.45	.13
☐	13 Roberto Alomar	.50	.23	.06
☐	14 Roger Clemens	.50	.23	.06
☐	15 Cecil Fielder	.25	.11	.03
☐	16 Robin Yount	.30	.14	.04
☐	17 Cal Ripken	1.50	.65	.19
☐	18 Carlos Baerga	.30	.14	.04
☐	19 Don Mattingly	.75	.35	.09
☐	20 Kirby Puckett	.75	.35	.09
☐	21 Frank Thomas	2.00	.90	.25
☐	22 Juan Gonzalez	.60	.25	.08
☐	23 Mark McGwire	.15	.07	.02
☐	24 Ken Griffey Jr.	2.00	.90	.25
☐	25 Wally Joyner	.15	.07	.02
☐	26 Chad Curtis	.15	.07	.02
☐	27 Rockies Vs. Marlins	.15	.07	.02
☐	28 Juan Guzman	.15	.07	.02
☐	29 David Justice	.30	.14	.04
☐	30 Joe Carter	.30	.14	.04

1993 Triple Play Gallery

A one per pack insert in 1993 Donruss Triple Play jumbo packs, these ten

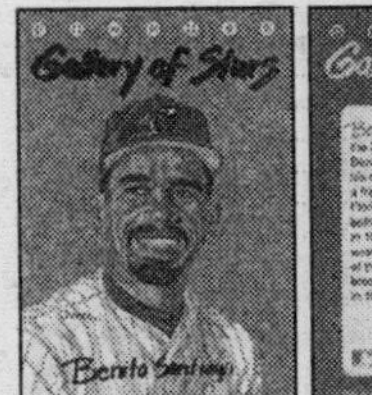

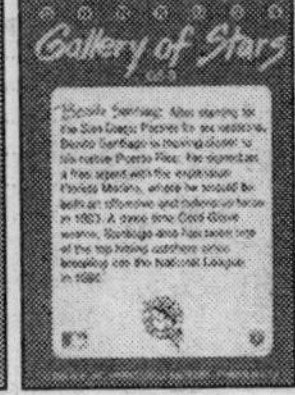

standard-size (2 1/2" by 3 1/2") cards have fronts that feature color player portraits by noted sports artist Dick Perez. The words "Gallery of Stars" printed in gold foil appear near the top, and the player's name, also in gold foil, rests at the bottom. The backs have a gray-bordered, white rectangle with rounded corners that carries the player's career highlights and team logo. The set name appears above in yellow lettering. The cards are numbered on the back with a "GS" prefix.

	MINT	EXC	G-VG
COMPLETE SET (10)	35.00	16.00	4.40
COMMON CARD (GS1-GS10)	1.50	.65	.19
☐ GS1 Barry Bonds	12.00	5.50	1.50
☐ GS2 Andre Dawson	2.00	.90	.25
☐ GS3 Wade Boggs	3.00	1.35	.40
☐ GS4 Greg Maddux	8.00	3.60	1.00
☐ GS5 Dave Winfield	2.50	1.15	.30
☐ GS6 Paul Molitor	4.50	2.00	.55
☐ GS7 Jim Abbott	1.50	.65	.19
☐ GS8 J.T. Snow	2.00	.90	.25
☐ GS9 Benito Santiago	1.50	.65	.19
☐ GS10 David Nied	2.00	.90	.25

1993 Triple Play League Leaders

Randomly inserted in magazine distributor packs only, the six standard-size (2 1/2" by 3 1/2") cards comprising this set feature borderless color action player shots on both sides. A National League leader appears on one side, an American League leader is on the other. The player's league appears in gold-foil lettering across the top. The player's name in white cursive lettering is displayed near the bottom within the set logo, which has a simulated black marble plaque design. The cards are numbered on the American League side with an L prefix.

	MINT	EXC	G-VG
COMPLETE SET (6)	35.00	16.00	4.40
COMMON PAIR (L1-L6)	3.00	1.35	.40
☐ L1 Barry Bonds Dennis Eckersley MVP	12.00	5.50	1.50
☐ L2 Greg Maddux Dennis Eckersley Cy Young	8.00	3.60	1.00
☐ L3 Eric Karros Pat Listach Rookie of the Year	3.00	1.35	.40
☐ L4 Fred McGriff Juan Gonzalez Home Run Crown	12.00	5.50	1.50
☐ L5 Darren Daulton Cecil Fielder RBI Title	4.00	1.80	.50
☐ L6 Gary Sheffield Edgar Martinez Batting Champs	3.00	1.35	.40

1993 Triple Play Nicknames

Randomly inserted in foil packs only, this ten-card standard-size (2 1/2" by 3 1/2") set is a new subset featuring player's nicknames. The borderless fronts feature color player action shots. The player's name appears at the bottom, within an irregular red stripe that simulates a stroke of a paintbrush. His nickname appears in large prismatic-foil lettering at the top of the photo. The white back shades to red near the bottom and carries the player's last name in large purplish letters at the top. His first name appears in smaller white cursive lettering superposed upon his last name. The player's biography, set off by thin black lines, is shown below. A color player action shot appears beneath on the left side, and his career highlights are shown alongside on the right. The player's team logo at the bottom rounds out the card. The cards are numbered on the back.

	MINT	EXC	G-VG
COMPLETE SET (10)	35.00	16.00	4.40
COMMON CARD (1-10)	1.00	.45	.13
☐ 1 Frank Thomas Big Hurt	12.00	5.50	1.50
☐ 2 Roger Clemens Rocket	3.00	1.35	.40
☐ 3 Ryne Sandberg Ryno	4.00	1.80	.50
☐ 4 Will Clark Thrill	1.75	.80	.22
☐ 5 Ken Griffey Jr. Junior	12.00	5.50	1.50
☐ 6 Dwight Gooden Doc	1.00	.45	.13
☐ 7 Nolan Ryan Express	12.00	5.50	1.50
☐ 8 Deion Sanders Prime Time	2.50	1.15	.30
☐ 9 Ozzie Smith Wizard	2.50	1.15	.30
☐ 10 Fred McGriff Crime Dog	1.75	.80	.22

1994 Triple Play

The 1994 Triple Play set consists of 300 standard-size cards, featuring ten players from each team along with a 17-card Rookie Review set. The fronts have color player action shots that are borderless, except at the bottom, where the player's name appears within a colored stripe. The horizontal back carries a posed color player photo on the left side. On the right, beneath the player's name and position, appear biography, statistics, and career highlights on a white background highlighted by his team's ghosted logo. Triple Play game cards, reedemable for various prizes, were inserted one per pack.

	MINT	EXC	G-VG
COMPLETE SET (300)	15.00	6.75	1.90
COMMON CARD (1-300)	.05	.02	.01
☐ 1 Mike Bordick	.05	.02	.01
☐ 2 Dennis Eckersley	.15	.07	.02
☐ 3 Brent Gates	.15	.07	.02
☐ 4 Rickey Henderson	.15	.07	.02
☐ 5 Mark McGwire	.15	.07	.02
☐ 6 Troy Neel	.10	.05	.01
☐ 7 Craig Paquette	.05	.02	.01
☐ 8 Ruben Sierra	.15	.07	.02
☐ 9 Terry Steinbach	.10	.05	.01
☐ 10 Bobby Witt	.05	.02	.01
☐ 11 Chad Curtis	.10	.05	.01
☐ 12 Chili Davis	.10	.05	.01
☐ 13 Gary DiSarcina	.05	.02	.01
☐ 14 Damion Easley	.05	.02	.01
☐ 15 Chuck Finley	.05	.02	.01
☐ 16 Joe Grahe	.05	.02	.01
☐ 17 Mark Langston	.15	.07	.02
☐ 18 Eduardo Perez	.10	.05	.01
☐ 19 Tim Salmon	.30	.14	.04
☐ 20 J.T. Snow	.10	.05	.01
☐ 21 Jeff Bagwell	1.00	.45	.13
☐ 22 Craig Biggio	.10	.05	.01
☐ 23 Ken Caminiti	.10	.05	.01
☐ 24 Andujar Cedeno	.05	.02	.01
☐ 25 Doug Drabek	.15	.07	.02
☐ 26 Steve Finley	.05	.02	.01
☐ 27 Luis Gonzalez	.05	.02	.01
☐ 28 Pete Harnisch	.05	.02	.01
☐ 29 Darryl Kile	.10	.05	.01
☐ 30 Mitch Williams	.05	.02	.01
☐ 31 Roberto Alomar	.50	.23	.06
☐ 32 Joe Carter	.30	.14	.04
☐ 33 Juan Guzman	.10	.05	.01
☐ 34 Pat Hentgen	.10	.05	.01
☐ 35 Paul Molitor	.30	.14	.04
☐ 36 John Olerud	.15	.07	.02
☐ 37 Ed Sprague	.05	.02	.01
☐ 38 Dave Stewart	.10	.05	.01
☐ 39 Duane Ward	.05	.02	.01
☐ 40 Devon White	.05	.02	.01
☐ 41 Steve Avery	.15	.07	.02
☐ 42 Jeff Blauser	.10	.05	.01
☐ 43 Ron Gant	.10	.05	.01
☐ 44 Tom Glavine	.15	.07	.02
☐ 45 David Justice	.30	.14	.04
☐ 46 Greg Maddux	.40	.18	.05
☐ 47 Fred McGriff	.30	.14	.04
☐ 48 Terry Pendleton	.05	.02	.01
☐ 49 Deion Sanders	.35	.16	.04
☐ 50 John Smoltz	.10	.05	.01
☐ 51 Ricky Bones	.05	.02	.01
☐ 52 Cal Eldred	.10	.05	.01
☐ 53 Darryl Hamilton	.05	.02	.01
☐ 54 John Jaha	.05	.02	.01
☐ 55 Pat Listach	.05	.02	.01
☐ 56 Jaime Navarro	.05	.02	.01
☐ 57 Dave Nilsson	.05	.02	.01
☐ 58 B.J. Surhoff	.05	.02	.01
☐ 59 Greg Vaughn	.10	.05	.01
☐ 60 Robin Yount	.30	.14	.04
☐ 61 Bernard Gilkey	.05	.02	.01
☐ 62 Gregg Jefferies	.15	.07	.02
☐ 63 Brian Jordan	.10	.05	.01
☐ 64 Ray Lankford	.15	.07	.02
☐ 65 Tom Pagnozzi	.05	.02	.01
☐ 66 Ozzie Smith	.40	.18	.05
☐ 67 Bob Tewksbury	.05	.02	.01
☐ 68 Allen Watson	.05	.02	.01
☐ 69 Mark Whiten	.10	.05	.01
☐ 70 Todd Zeile	.10	.05	.01
☐ 71 Steve Buechele	.05	.02	.01
☐ 72 Mark Grace	.15	.07	.02
☐ 73 Jose Guzman	.05	.02	.01
☐ 74 Derrick May	.05	.02	.01
☐ 75 Mike Morgan	.05	.02	.01
☐ 76 Randy Myers	.05	.02	.01
☐ 77 Ryne Sandberg	.60	.25	.08
☐ 78 Sammy Sosa	.15	.07	.02
☐ 79 Jose Vizcaino	.05	.02	.01
☐ 80 Rick Wilkins	.05	.02	.01
☐ 81 Pedro Astacio	.10	.05	.01

☐	82 Brett Butler	.10	.05	.01
☐	83 Delino DeShields	.10	.05	.01
☐	84 Orel Hershiser	.10	.05	.01
☐	85 Eric Karros	.10	.05	.01
☐	86 Ramon Martinez	.10	.05	.01
☐	87 Jose Offerman	.05	.02	.01
☐	88 Mike Piazza	1.00	.45	.13
☐	89 Darryl Strawberry	.10	.05	.01
☐	90 Tim Wallach	.05	.02	.01
☐	91 Moises Alou	.15	.07	.02
☐	92 Wil Cordero	.15	.07	.02
☐	93 Jeff Fassero	.05	.02	.01
☐	94 Darrin Fletcher	.05	.02	.01
☐	95 Marquis Grissom	.15	.07	.02
☐	96 Ken Hill	.10	.05	.01
☐	97 Mike Lansing	.10	.05	.01
☐	98 Kirk Rueter	.05	.02	.01
☐	99 Larry Walker	.15	.07	.02
☐	100 John Wetteland	.05	.02	.01
☐	101 Rod Beck	.10	.05	.01
☐	102 Barry Bonds	.75	.35	.09
☐	103 John Burkett	.10	.05	.01
☐	104 Royce Clayton	.10	.05	.01
☐	105 Darren Lewis	.05	.02	.01
☐	106 Kirt Manwaring	.05	.02	.01
☐	107 Willie McGee	.05	.02	.01
☐	108 Bill Swift	.05	.02	.01
☐	109 Robby Thompson	.05	.02	.01
☐	110 Matt Williams	.40	.18	.05
☐	111 Sandy Alomar Jr.	.10	.05	.01
☐	112 Carlos Baerga	.30	.14	.04
☐	113 Albert Belle	.60	.25	.08
☐	114 Wayne Kirby	.05	.02	.01
☐	115 Kenny Lofton	.50	.23	.06
☐	116 Jose Mesa	.05	.02	.01
☐	117 Eddie Murray	.15	.07	.02
☐	118 Charles Nagy	.05	.02	.01
☐	119 Paul Sorrento	.05	.02	.01
☐	120 Jim Thome	.15	.07	.02
☐	121 Rich Amaral	.05	.02	.01
☐	122 Eric Anthony	.05	.02	.01
☐	123 Mike Blowers	.05	.02	.01
☐	124 Chris Bosio	.05	.02	.01
☐	125 Jay Buhner	.10	.05	.01
☐	126 Dave Fleming	.05	.02	.01
☐	127 Ken Griffey Jr.	2.00	.90	.25
☐	128 Randy Johnson	.15	.07	.02
☐	129 Edgar Martinez	.05	.02	.01
☐	130 Tino Martinez	.05	.02	.01
☐	131 Bret Barberie	.05	.02	.01
☐	132 Ryan Bowen	.05	.02	.01
☐	133 Chuck Carr	.05	.02	.01
☐	134 Jeff Conine	.15	.07	.02
☐	135 Orestes Destrade	.05	.02	.01
☐	136 Chris Hammond	.05	.02	.01
☐	137 Bryan Harvey	.10	.05	.01
☐	138 Dave Magadan	.05	.02	.01
☐	139 Benito Santiago	.05	.02	.01
☐	140 Gary Sheffield	.15	.07	.02
☐	141 Bobby Bonilla	.15	.07	.02
☐	142 Jeromy Burnitz	.10	.05	.01
☐	143 Dwight Gooden	.05	.02	.01
☐	144 Todd Hundley	.05	.02	.01
☐	145 Bobby Jones	.15	.07	.02
☐	146 Jeff Kent	.10	.05	.01
☐	147 Joe Orsulak	.05	.02	.01
☐	148 Bret Saberhagen	.10	.05	.01
☐	149 Pete Schourek	.05	.02	.01
☐	150 Ryan Thompson	.10	.05	.01
☐	151 Brady Anderson	.10	.05	.01
☐	152 Harold Baines	.10	.05	.01
☐	153 Mike Devereaux	.10	.05	.01
☐	154 Chris Hoiles	.10	.05	.01
☐	155 Ben McDonald	.10	.05	.01
☐	156 Mark McLemore	.05	.02	.01
☐	157 Mike Mussina	.30	.14	.04
☐	158 Rafael Palmeiro	.15	.07	.02
☐	159 Cal Ripken	1.50	.65	.19
☐	160 Chris Sabo	.05	.02	.01
☐	161 Brad Ausmus	.05	.02	.01
☐	162 Derek Bell	.10	.05	.01
☐	163 Andy Benes	.10	.05	.01
☐	164 Doug Brocail	.05	.02	.01
☐	165 Archi Cianfrocco	.05	.02	.01
☐	166 Ricky Gutierrez	.05	.02	.01
☐	167 Tony Gwynn	.50	.23	.06
☐	168 Gene Harris	.05	.02	.01
☐	169 Pedro Martinez	.15	.07	.02
☐	170 Phil Plantier	.10	.05	.01
☐	171 Darren Daulton	.15	.07	.02
☐	172 Mariano Duncan	.05	.02	.01
☐	173 Lenny Dykstra	.15	.07	.02
☐	174 Tommy Greene	.05	.02	.01
☐	175 Dave Hollins	.15	.07	.02
☐	176 Danny Jackson	.05	.02	.01
☐	177 John Kruk	.15	.07	.02
☐	178 Terry Mulholland	.05	.02	.01
☐	179 Curt Schilling	.05	.02	.01
☐	180 Kevin Stocker	.10	.05	.01
☐	181 Jay Bell	.10	.05	.01
☐	182 Steve Cooke	.05	.02	.01
☐	183 Carlos Garcia	.05	.02	.01
☐	184 Joel Johnston	.05	.02	.01
☐	185 Jeff King	.05	.02	.01
☐	186 Al Martin	.05	.02	.01
☐	187 Orlando Merced	.10	.05	.01
☐	188 Don Slaught	.05	.02	.01
☐	189 Andy Van Slyke	.15	.07	.02
☐	190 Kevin Young	.05	.02	.01
☐	191 Kevin Brown	.05	.02	.01
☐	192 Jose Canseco	.30	.14	.04
☐	193 Will Clark	.30	.14	.04
☐	194 Juan Gonzalez	.60	.25	.08
☐	195 Tom Henke	.05	.02	.01
☐	196 David Hulse	.05	.02	.01
☐	197 Dean Palmer	.10	.05	.01
☐	198 Roger Pavlik	.05	.02	.01
☐	199 Ivan Rodriguez	.15	.07	.02
☐	200 Kenny Rogers	.05	.02	.01
☐	201 Roger Clemens	.50	.23	.06
☐	202 Scott Cooper	.10	.05	.01
☐	203 Andre Dawson	.15	.07	.02
☐	204 Mike Greenwell	.10	.05	.01
☐	205 Billy Hatcher	.05	.02	.01
☐	206 Jeff Russell	.05	.02	.01
☐	207 Aaron Sele	.15	.07	.02
☐	208 John Valentin	.10	.05	.01
☐	209 Mo Vaughn	.15	.07	.02
☐	210 Frank Viola	.05	.02	.01
☐	211 Rob Dibble	.05	.02	.01
☐	212 Willie Greene	.10	.05	.01
☐	213 Roberto Kelly	.05	.02	.01
☐	214 Barry Larkin	.15	.07	.02
☐	215 Kevin Mitchell	.10	.05	.01
☐	216 Hal Morris	.10	.05	.01
☐	217 Joe Oliver	.05	.02	.01
☐	218 Jose Rijo	.10	.05	.01
☐	219 Reggie Sanders	.10	.05	.01
☐	220 John Smiley	.05	.02	.01
☐	221 Dante Bichette	.15	.07	.02
☐	222 Ellis Burks	.10	.05	.01
☐	223 Andres Galarraga	.15	.07	.02
☐	224 Joe Girardi	.05	.02	.01
☐	225 Charlie Hayes	.10	.05	.01
☐	226 Darren Holmes	.05	.02	.01
☐	227 Howard Johnson	.05	.02	.01

	Card	Price 1	Price 2	Price 3
☐	228 Roberto Mejia	.10	.05	.01
☐	229 David Nied	.15	.07	.02
☐	230 Armando Reynoso	.05	.02	.01
☐	231 Kevin Appier	.10	.05	.01
☐	232 David Cone	.15	.07	.02
☐	233 Greg Gagne	.05	.02	.01
☐	234 Tom Gordon	.05	.02	.01
☐	235 Felix Jose	.05	.02	.01
☐	236 Wally Joyner	.10	.05	.01
☐	237 Jose Lind	.05	.02	.01
☐	238 Brian McRae	.10	.05	.01
☐	239 Mike Macfarlane	.05	.02	.01
☐	240 Jeff Montgomery	.10	.05	.01
☐	241 Eric Davis	.05	.02	.01
☐	242 John Doherty	.05	.02	.01
☐	243 Cecil Fielder	.15	.07	.02
☐	244 Travis Fryman	.15	.07	.02
☐	245 Bill Gullickson	.05	.02	.01
☐	246 Mike Henneman	.05	.02	.01
☐	247 Tony Phillips	.05	.02	.01
☐	248 Mickey Tettleton	.10	.05	.01
☐	249 Alan Trammell	.15	.07	.02
☐	250 Lou Whitaker	.15	.07	.02
☐	251 Rick Aguilera	.10	.05	.01
☐	252 Scott Erickson	.05	.02	.01
☐	253 Kent Hrbek	.10	.05	.01
☐	254 Chuck Knoblauch	.15	.07	.02
☐	255 Shane Mack	.10	.05	.01
☐	256 Dave McCarty	.10	.05	.01
☐	257 Pat Meares	.05	.02	.01
☐	258 Kirby Puckett	.75	.35	.09
☐	259 Kevin Tapani	.05	.02	.01
☐	260 Dave Winfield	.15	.07	.02
☐	261 Wilson Alvarez	.15	.07	.02
☐	262 Jason Bere	.25	.11	.03
☐	263 Alex Fernandez	.15	.07	.02
☐	264 Ozzie Guillen	.05	.02	.01
☐	265 Roberto Hernandez	.05	.02	.01
☐	266 Lance Johnson	.05	.02	.01
☐	267 Jack McDowell	.15	.07	.02
☐	268 Tim Raines	.15	.07	.02
☐	269 Frank Thomas	2.00	.90	.25
☐	270 Robin Ventura	.10	.05	.01
☐	271 Jim Abbott	.15	.07	.02
☐	272 Wade Boggs	.15	.07	.02
☐	273 Mike Gallego	.05	.02	.01
☐	274 Pat Kelly	.05	.02	.01
☐	275 Jimmy Key	.10	.05	.01
☐	276 Don Mattingly	.75	.35	.09
☐	277 Paul O'Neill	.10	.05	.01
☐	278 Mike Stanley	.05	.02	.01
☐	279 Danny Tartabull	.10	.05	.01
☐	280 Bernie Williams	.10	.05	.01
☐	281 Chipper Jones	.25	.11	.03
☐	282 Ryan Klesko	.30	.14	.04
☐	283 Javy Lopez	.20	.09	.03
☐	284 Jeffrey Hammonds	.25	.11	.03
☐	285 Jeff McNeely	.05	.02	.01
☐	286 Manny Ramirez	.40	.18	.05
☐	287 Billy Ashley	.15	.07	.02
☐	288 Raul Mondesi	.75	.35	.09
☐	289 Cliff Floyd	.30	.14	.04
☐	290 Rondell White	.20	.09	.03
☐	291 Steve Karsay	.05	.02	.01
☐	292 Midre Cummings	.15	.07	.02
☐	293 Salomon Torres	.10	.05	.01
☐	294 J.R. Phillips	.15	.07	.02
☐	295 Marc Newfield	.15	.07	.02
☐	296 Carlos Delgado	.30	.14	.04
☐	297 Butch Huskey	.05	.02	.01
☐	298 Checklist 1-100 Frank Thomas	.10	.05	.01
☐	299 Checklist 101-200 Barry Bonds	.10	.05	.01
☐	300 Checklist 201-300 Juan Gonzalez	.10	.05	.01

1994 Triple Play Bomb Squad

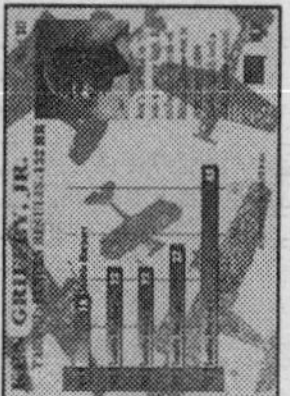

Randomly inserted in regular (one in 18) and jumbo (one in 8) packs, this ten-card standard-size set focuses on the top home run hitters in the majors. Card fronts feature a brown border surrounding a black and white photo. The Bomb Squad logo which includes a pair of wings is at the top. The player's name is at the bottom. Horizontal backs offer more color including a bar graph on yearly home run production with drawings of fighter planes serving as a background.

		MINT	EXC	G-VG
	COMPLETE SET (10)	40.00	18.00	5.00
	COMMON CARD (1-10)	1.00	.45	.13
☐	1 Frank Thomas	12.00	5.50	1.50
☐	2 Cecil Fielder	1.25	.55	.16
☐	3 Juan Gonzalez	4.00	1.80	.50
☐	4 Barry Bonds	5.00	2.30	.60
☐	5 David Justice	1.75	.80	.22
☐	6 Fred McGriff	1.75	.80	.22
☐	7 Ron Gant	1.00	.45	.13
☐	8 Ken Griffey Jr.	12.00	5.50	1.50
☐	9 Albert Belle	4.00	1.80	.50
☐	10 Matt Williams	2.50	1.15	.30

1994 Triple Play Medalists

Randomly inserted in regular (one in 12) and jumbo packs (one in six), this 15-card standard-size set features the top three players in each league at their position. The players included were determined by statistical rankings over the past two seasons. Each card is horizontally designed with gold, silver and bronze foil on front with three player photos. There are also three player photos and brief highlights on back.

	MINT	EXC	G-VG
COMPLETE SET (15)	35.00	16.00	4.40
COMMON TRIO (1-15)	1.00	.45	.13
☐ 1 Chris Hoiles Mickey Tettleton Brian Harper	1.00	.45	.13
☐ 2 Darren Daulton Rick Wilkins Kirt Manwaring	1.00	.45	.13
☐ 3 Frank Thomas Rafael Palmeiro John Olerud	10.00	4.50	1.25
☐ 4 Mark Grace Fred McGriff Jeff Bagwell	5.00	2.30	.60
☐ 5 Roberto Alomar Carlos Baerga Lou Whitaker	3.00	1.35	.40
☐ 6 Ryne Sandberg Craig Biggio Robby Thompson	3.00	1.35	.40
☐ 7 Tony Fernandez Cal Ripken Alan Trammell	6.00	2.70	.75
☐ 8 Barry Larkin Jay Bell Jeff Blauser	1.00	.45	.13
☐ 9 Robin Ventura Travis Fryman Wade Boggs	1.50	.65	.19
☐ 10 Terry Pendleton Dave Hollins Gary Sheffield	1.00	.45	.13
☐ 11 Ken Griffey Jr. Kirby Puckett Albert Belle	10.00	4.50	1.25
☐ 12 Barry Bonds Andy Van Slyke Len Dykstra	3.00	1.35	.40
☐ 13 Jack McDowell Kevin Brown Randy Johnson	1.00	.45	.13
☐ 14 Greg Maddux Jose Rijo Bill Swift	1.50	.65	.19
☐ 15 Paul Molitor Dave Winfield Harold Baines	1.50	.65	.19

1994 Triple Play Nicknames

Randomly inserted in regular (one in 36) and jumbo packs (one in 12), this eight-card standard-size set features players with a photo depicting the team name and mascot in the background. The back of each card describes how the team got its nickname as well as a player photo.

	MINT	EXC	G-VG
COMPLETE SET (8)	35.00	16.00	4.40
COMMON CARD (1-8)	2.00	.90	.25
☐ 1 Cecil Fielder	2.00	.90	.25
☐ 2 Ryne Sandberg	8.00	3.60	1.00
☐ 3 Gary Sheffield	2.00	.90	.25
☐ 4 Joe Carter	3.50	1.55	.45
☐ 5 John Olerud	2.00	.90	.25
☐ 6 Cal Ripken	20.00	9.00	2.50
☐ 7 Mark McGwire	2.00	.90	.25
☐ 8 Gregg Jefferies	2.00	.90	.25

1991 Ultra

This 400-card standard size (2 1/2" by 3 1/2") set marked Fleer's first entry into the high-end premium card market. The set was released in wax packs and features the best players in the majors along with a good mix of young prospects. The cards feature full color action photography on the fronts and three full-color photos on the backs along with 1990 and career statistics.

Fleer claimed in their original press release that there would only be 15 percent of Ultra issued as there was of the regular issue. Fleer also issued the sets in their now traditional alphabetical order as well as the teams in alphabetical order. The card numbering is as follows, Atlanta Braves (1-13), Baltimore Orioles (14-26), Boston Red Sox (27-42), California Angels (43-54), Chicago Cubs (55-71), Chicago White Sox (72-86), Cincinnati Reds (87-103), Cleveland Indians (104-119), Detroit Tigers (120-130), Houston Astros (131-142), Kansas City Royals (143-158), Los Angeles Dodgers (159-171), Milwaukee Brewers (172-184), Minnesota Twins (185-196), Montreal Expos (197-210), New York Mets (211-227), New York Yankees (228-242), Oakland Athletics (243-257), Philadelphia Phillies (258-272), Pittsburgh Pirates (273-287), St. Louis Cardinals (288-299), San Diego Padres (300-313), San Francisco Giants (314-331), Seattle Mariners (332-345), Texas Rangers (346-357), Toronto Blue Jays (358-372), Major League Prospects (373-390), Elite Performance (391-396), and Checklists (397-400). The key Rookie Cards in this set are Wes Chamberlain, Jeff Conine, Carlos Garcia, Eric Karros, Brian McRae, Orlando Merced, Pedro Munoz, and Phil Plantier.

	MINT	EXC	G-VG
COMPLETE SET (400)	20.00	9.00	2.50
COMMON CARD (1-400)	.05	.02	.01
☐ 1 Steve Avery	.40	.18	.05
☐ 2 Jeff Blauser	.10	.05	.01
☐ 3 Francisco Cabrera	.05	.02	.01
☐ 4 Ron Gant	.10	.05	.01
☐ 5 Tom Glavine	.50	.23	.06
☐ 6 Tommy Gregg	.05	.02	.01
☐ 7 David Justice	.60	.25	.08
☐ 8 Oddibe McDowell	.05	.02	.01
☐ 9 Greg Olson	.05	.02	.01
☐ 10 Terry Pendleton	.20	.09	.03
☐ 11 Lonnie Smith	.05	.02	.01
☐ 12 John Smoltz	.20	.09	.03
☐ 13 Jeff Treadway	.05	.02	.01
☐ 14 Glenn Davis	.05	.02	.01
☐ 15 Mike Devereaux	.10	.05	.01
☐ 16 Leo Gomez	.10	.05	.01
☐ 17 Chris Hoiles	.20	.09	.03
☐ 18 Dave Johnson	.05	.02	.01
☐ 19 Ben McDonald	.20	.09	.03
☐ 20 Randy Milligan	.05	.02	.01
☐ 21 Gregg Olson	.10	.05	.01
☐ 22 Joe Orsulak	.05	.02	.01
☐ 23 Bill Ripken	.05	.02	.01
☐ 24 Cal Ripken	.75	.35	.09
☐ 25 David Segui	.05	.02	.01
☐ 26 Craig Worthington	.05	.02	.01
☐ 27 Wade Boggs	.20	.09	.03
☐ 28 Tom Bolton	.05	.02	.01
☐ 29 Tom Brunansky	.05	.02	.01
☐ 30 Ellis Burks	.10	.05	.01
☐ 31 Roger Clemens	.50	.23	.06
☐ 32 Mike Greenwell	.10	.05	.01
☐ 33 Greg A. Harris	.05	.02	.01
☐ 34 Daryl Irvine	.05	.02	.01
☐ 35 Mike Marshall UER (1990 in stats is shown as 990)	.05	.02	.01
☐ 36 Tim Naehring	.05	.02	.01
☐ 37 Tony Pena	.05	.02	.01
☐ 38 Phil Plantier	.50	.23	.06
☐ 39 Carlos Quintana	.05	.02	.01
☐ 40 Jeff Reardon	.10	.05	.01
☐ 41 Jody Reed	.05	.02	.01
☐ 42 Luis Rivera	.05	.02	.01
☐ 43 Jim Abbott	.20	.09	.03
☐ 44 Chuck Finley	.10	.05	.01
☐ 45 Bryan Harvey	.10	.05	.01
☐ 46 Donnie Hill	.05	.02	.01
☐ 47 Jack Howell	.05	.02	.01
☐ 48 Wally Joyner	.10	.05	.01
☐ 49 Mark Langston	.20	.09	.03
☐ 50 Kirk McCaskill	.05	.02	.01
☐ 51 Lance Parrish	.10	.05	.01
☐ 52 Dick Schofield	.05	.02	.01
☐ 53 Lee Stevens	.05	.02	.01
☐ 54 Dave Winfield	.30	.14	.04
☐ 55 George Bell	.10	.05	.01
☐ 56 Damon Berryhill	.05	.02	.01
☐ 57 Mike Bielecki	.05	.02	.01
☐ 58 Andre Dawson	.20	.09	.03
☐ 59 Shawon Dunston	.05	.02	.01
☐ 60 Joe Girardi UER (Bats right, LH hitter shown is Doug Dascenzo)	.05	.02	.01
☐ 61 Mark Grace	.20	.09	.03
☐ 62 Mike Harkey	.05	.02	.01
☐ 63 Les Lancaster	.05	.02	.01
☐ 64 Greg Maddux	.40	.18	.05
☐ 65 Derrick May	.10	.05	.01
☐ 66 Ryne Sandberg	.75	.35	.09
☐ 67 Luis Salazar	.05	.02	.01
☐ 68 Dwight Smith	.05	.02	.01
☐ 69 Hector Villanueva	.05	.02	.01
☐ 70 Jerome Walton	.05	.02	.01
☐ 71 Mitch Williams	.10	.05	.01
☐ 72 Carlton Fisk	.20	.09	.03
☐ 73 Scott Fletcher	.05	.02	.01
☐ 74 Ozzie Guillen	.05	.02	.01
☐ 75 Greg Hibbard	.05	.02	.01
☐ 76 Lance Johnson	.05	.02	.01
☐ 77 Steve Lyons	.05	.02	.01
☐ 78 Jack McDowell	.20	.09	.03
☐ 79 Dan Pasqua	.05	.02	.01
☐ 80 Melido Perez	.05	.02	.01
☐ 81 Tim Raines	.20	.09	.03
☐ 82 Sammy Sosa	.35	.16	.04
☐ 83 Cory Snyder	.05	.02	.01
☐ 84 Bobby Thigpen	.05	.02	.01
☐ 85 Frank Thomas (Card says he is an outfielder)	4.00	1.80	.50
☐ 86 Robin Ventura	.75	.35	.09
☐ 87 Todd Benzinger	.05	.02	.01
☐ 88 Glenn Braggs	.05	.02	.01
☐ 89 Tom Browning UER (Front photo actually Norm Charlton)	.05	.02	.01
☐ 90 Norm Charlton	.05	.02	.01
☐ 91 Eric Davis	.10	.05	.01
☐ 92 Rob Dibble	.05	.02	.01
☐ 93 Bill Doran	.05	.02	.01
☐ 94 Mariano Duncan UER (Right back photo is Billy Hatcher)	.05	.02	.01
☐ 95 Billy Hatcher	.05	.02	.01
☐ 96 Barry Larkin	.20	.09	.03
☐ 97 Randy Myers	.10	.05	.01
☐ 98 Hal Morris	.10	.05	.01
☐ 99 Joe Oliver	.05	.02	.01
☐ 100 Paul O'Neill	.10	.05	.01

☐ 101 Jeff Reed .05 .02 .01
(See also 104)
☐ 102 Jose Rijo .10 .05 .01
☐ 103 Chris Sabo .10 .05 .01
(See also 106)
☐ 104 Beau Allred UER .05 .02 .01
(Card number is 101)
☐ 105 Sandy Alomar Jr. .10 .05 .01
☐ 106 Carlos Baerga UER .60 .25 .08
(Card number is 103)
☐ 107 Albert Belle 1.25 .55 .16
☐ 108 Jerry Browne .05 .02 .01
☐ 109 Tom Candiotti .05 .02 .01
☐ 110 Alex Cole .05 .02 .01
☐ 111 John Farrell .05 .02 .01
(See also 114)
☐ 112 Felix Fermin .05 .02 .01
☐ 113 Brook Jacoby .05 .02 .01
☐ 114 Chris James UER .05 .02 .01
(Card number is 111)
☐ 115 Doug Jones .05 .02 .01
☐ 116 Steve Olin .05 .02 .01
(See also 119)
☐ 117 Greg Swindell .05 .02 .01
☐ 118 Turner Ward .20 .09 .03
☐ 119 Mitch Webster UER .05 .02 .01
(Card number is 116)
☐ 120 Dave Bergman .05 .02 .01
☐ 121 Cecil Fielder .35 .16 .04
☐ 122 Travis Fryman 1.00 .45 .13
☐ 123 Mike Henneman .05 .02 .01
☐ 124 Lloyd Moseby .05 .02 .01
☐ 125 Dan Petry .05 .02 .01
☐ 126 Tony Phillips .05 .02 .01
☐ 127 Mark Salas .05 .02 .01
☐ 128 Frank Tanana .05 .02 .01
☐ 129 Alan Trammell .20 .09 .03
☐ 130 Lou Whitaker .20 .09 .03
☐ 131 Eric Anthony .10 .05 .01
☐ 132 Craig Biggio .20 .09 .03
☐ 133 Ken Caminiti .10 .05 .01
☐ 134 Casey Candaele .05 .02 .01
☐ 135 Andujar Cedeno .10 .05 .01
☐ 136 Mark Davidson .05 .02 .01
☐ 137 Jim Deshaies .05 .02 .01
☐ 138 Mark Portugal .05 .02 .01
☐ 139 Rafael Ramirez .05 .02 .01
☐ 140 Mike Scott .05 .02 .01
☐ 141 Eric Yelding .05 .02 .01
☐ 142 Gerald Young .05 .02 .01
☐ 143 Kevin Appier .10 .05 .01
☐ 144 George Brett .60 .25 .08
☐ 145 Jeff Conine .75 .35 .09
☐ 146 Jim Eisenreich .05 .02 .01
☐ 147 Tom Gordon .10 .05 .01
☐ 148 Mark Gubicza .05 .02 .01
☐ 149 Bo Jackson .25 .11 .03
☐ 150 Brent Mayne .05 .02 .01
☐ 151 Mike Macfarlane .05 .02 .01
☐ 152 Brian McRae .50 .23 .06
☐ 153 Jeff Montgomery .10 .05 .01
☐ 154 Bret Saberhagen .10 .05 .01
☐ 155 Kevin Seitzer .05 .02 .01
☐ 156 Terry Shumpert .05 .02 .01
☐ 157 Kurt Stillwell .05 .02 .01
☐ 158 Danny Tartabull .10 .05 .01
☐ 159 Tim Belcher .05 .02 .01
☐ 160 Kal Daniels .05 .02 .01
☐ 161 Alfredo Griffin .05 .02 .01
☐ 162 Lenny Harris .05 .02 .01
☐ 163 Jay Howell .05 .02 .01
☐ 164 Ramon Martinez .10 .05 .01
☐ 165 Mike Morgan .05 .02 .01
☐ 166 Eddie Murray .20 .09 .03
☐ 167 Jose Offerman .10 .05 .01
☐ 168 Juan Samuel .05 .02 .01
☐ 169 Mike Scioscia .05 .02 .01
☐ 170 Mike Sharperson .05 .02 .01
☐ 171 Darryl Strawberry .20 .09 .03
☐ 172 Greg Brock .05 .02 .01
☐ 173 Chuck Crim .05 .02 .01
☐ 174 Jim Gantner .05 .02 .01
☐ 175 Ted Higuera .05 .02 .01
☐ 176 Mark Knudson .05 .02 .01
☐ 177 Tim McIntosh .05 .02 .01
☐ 178 Paul Molitor .30 .14 .04
☐ 179 Dan Plesac .05 .02 .01
☐ 180 Gary Sheffield .35 .16 .04
☐ 181 Bill Spiers .05 .02 .01
☐ 182 B.J. Surhoff .05 .02 .01
☐ 183 Greg Vaughn .10 .05 .01
☐ 184 Robin Yount .30 .14 .04
☐ 185 Rick Aguilera .10 .05 .01
☐ 186 Greg Gagne .05 .02 .01
☐ 187 Dan Gladden .05 .02 .01
☐ 188 Brian Harper .05 .02 .01
☐ 189 Kent Hrbek .10 .05 .01
☐ 190 Gene Larkin .05 .02 .01
☐ 191 Shane Mack .10 .05 .01
☐ 192 Pedro Munoz .20 .09 .03
☐ 193 Al Newman .05 .02 .01
☐ 194 Junior Ortiz .05 .02 .01
☐ 195 Kirby Puckett .75 .35 .09
☐ 196 Kevin Tapani .10 .05 .01
☐ 197 Dennis Boyd .05 .02 .01
☐ 198 Tim Burke .05 .02 .01
☐ 199 Ivan Calderon .05 .02 .01
☐ 200 Delino DeShields .20 .09 .03
☐ 201 Mike Fitzgerald .05 .02 .01
☐ 202 Steve Frey .05 .02 .01
☐ 203 Andres Galarraga .20 .09 .03
☐ 204 Marquis Grissom .30 .14 .04
☐ 205 Dave Martinez .05 .02 .01
☐ 206 Dennis Martinez .10 .05 .01
☐ 207 Junior Noboa .05 .02 .01
☐ 208 Spike Owen .05 .02 .01
☐ 209 Scott Ruskin .05 .02 .01
☐ 210 Tim Wallach .05 .02 .01
☐ 211 Daryl Boston .05 .02 .01
☐ 212 Vince Coleman .05 .02 .01
☐ 213 David Cone .20 .09 .03
☐ 214 Ron Darling .05 .02 .01
☐ 215 Kevin Elster .05 .02 .01
☐ 216 Sid Fernandez .10 .05 .01
☐ 217 John Franco .10 .05 .01
☐ 218 Dwight Gooden .10 .05 .01
☐ 219 Tom Herr .05 .02 .01
☐ 220 Todd Hundley .10 .05 .01
☐ 221 Gregg Jefferies .35 .16 .04
☐ 222 Howard Johnson .10 .05 .01
☐ 223 Dave Magadan .05 .02 .01
☐ 224 Kevin McReynolds .05 .02 .01
☐ 225 Keith Miller .05 .02 .01
☐ 226 Mackey Sasser .05 .02 .01
☐ 227 Frank Viola .10 .05 .01
☐ 228 Jesse Barfield .05 .02 .01
☐ 229 Greg Cadaret .05 .02 .01
☐ 230 Alvaro Espinoza .05 .02 .01
☐ 231 Bob Geren .05 .02 .01
☐ 232 Lee Guetterman .05 .02 .01
☐ 233 Mel Hall .05 .02 .01
☐ 234 Andy Hawkins UER .05 .02 .01
(Back center photo
is not him)
☐ 235 Roberto Kelly .10 .05 .01
☐ 236 Tim Leary .05 .02 .01

☐ 237 Jim Leyritz .05 .02 .01
☐ 238 Kevin Maas .05 .02 .01
☐ 239 Don Mattingly .75 .35 .09
☐ 240 Hensley Meulens .05 .02 .01
☐ 241 Eric Plunk .05 .02 .01
☐ 242 Steve Sax .05 .02 .01
☐ 243 Todd Burns .05 .02 .01
☐ 244 Jose Canseco .50 .23 .06
☐ 245 Dennis Eckersley .20 .09 .03
☐ 246 Mike Gallego .05 .02 .01
☐ 247 Dave Henderson .05 .02 .01
☐ 248 Rickey Henderson .30 .14 .04
☐ 249 Rick Honeycutt .05 .02 .01
☐ 250 Carney Lansford .10 .05 .01
☐ 251 Mark McGwire .20 .09 .03
☐ 252 Mike Moore .05 .02 .01
☐ 253 Terry Steinbach .10 .05 .01
☐ 254 Dave Stewart .10 .05 .01
☐ 255 Walt Weiss .05 .02 .01
☐ 256 Bob Welch .05 .02 .01
☐ 257 Curt Young .05 .02 .01
☐ 258 Wes Chamberlain .05 .02 .01
☐ 259 Pat Combs .05 .02 .01
☐ 260 Darren Daulton .20 .09 .03
☐ 261 Jose DeJesus .05 .02 .01
☐ 262 Len Dykstra .20 .09 .03
☐ 263 Charlie Hayes .10 .05 .01
☐ 264 Von Hayes .05 .02 .01
☐ 265 Ken Howell .05 .02 .01
☐ 266 John Kruk .20 .09 .03
☐ 267 Roger McDowell .05 .02 .01
☐ 268 Mickey Morandini .05 .02 .01
☐ 269 Terry Mulholland .05 .02 .01
☐ 270 Dale Murphy .20 .09 .03
☐ 271 Randy Ready .05 .02 .01
☐ 272 Dickie Thon .05 .02 .01
☐ 273 Stan Belinda .05 .02 .01
☐ 274 Jay Bell .10 .05 .01
☐ 275 Barry Bonds 1.00 .45 .13
☐ 276 Bobby Bonilla .20 .09 .03
☐ 277 Doug Drabek .20 .09 .03
☐ 278 Carlos Garcia .40 .18 .05
☐ 279 Neal Heaton .05 .02 .01
☐ 280 Jeff King .05 .02 .01
☐ 281 Bill Landrum .05 .02 .01
☐ 282 Mike LaValliere .05 .02 .01
☐ 283 Jose Lind .05 .02 .01
☐ 284 Orlando Merced .40 .18 .05
☐ 285 Gary Redus .05 .02 .01
☐ 286 Don Slaught .05 .02 .01
☐ 287 Andy Van Slyke .20 .09 .03
☐ 288 Jose DeLeon .05 .02 .01
☐ 289 Pedro Guerrero .10 .05 .01
☐ 290 Ray Lankford .40 .18 .05
☐ 291 Joe Magrane .05 .02 .01
☐ 292 Jose Oquendo .05 .02 .01
☐ 293 Tom Pagnozzi .05 .02 .01
☐ 294 Bryn Smith .05 .02 .01
☐ 295 Lee Smith .20 .09 .03
☐ 296 Ozzie Smith UER .25 .11 .03
(Born 12-26, 54,
should have hyphen)
☐ 297 Milt Thompson .05 .02 .01
☐ 298 Craig Wilson .05 .02 .01
☐ 299 Todd Zeile .10 .05 .01
☐ 300 Shawn Abner .05 .02 .01
☐ 301 Andy Benes .20 .09 .03
☐ 302 Paul Faries .05 .02 .01
☐ 303 Tony Gwynn .50 .23 .06
☐ 304 Greg W. Harris .05 .02 .01
☐ 305 Thomas Howard .05 .02 .01
☐ 306 Bruce Hurst .05 .02 .01
☐ 307 Craig Lefferts .05 .02 .01
☐ 308 Fred McGriff .40 .18 .05
☐ 309 Dennis Rasmussen .05 .02 .01
☐ 310 Bip Roberts .05 .02 .01
☐ 311 Benito Santiago .05 .02 .01
☐ 312 Garry Templeton .05 .02 .01
☐ 313 Ed Whitson .05 .02 .01
☐ 314 Dave Anderson .05 .02 .01
☐ 315 Kevin Bass .05 .02 .01
☐ 316 Jeff Brantley .05 .02 .01
☐ 317 John Burkett .10 .05 .01
☐ 318 Will Clark .60 .25 .08
☐ 319 Steve Decker .05 .02 .01
☐ 320 Scott Garrelts .05 .02 .01
☐ 321 Terry Kennedy .05 .02 .01
☐ 322 Mark Leonard .05 .02 .01
☐ 323 Darren Lewis .10 .05 .01
☐ 324 Greg Litton .05 .02 .01
☐ 325 Willie McGee .10 .05 .01
☐ 326 Kevin Mitchell .10 .05 .01
☐ 327 Don Robinson .05 .02 .01
☐ 328 Andres Santana .05 .02 .01
☐ 329 Robby Thompson .05 .02 .01
☐ 330 Jose Uribe .05 .02 .01
☐ 331 Matt Williams .35 .16 .04
☐ 332 Scott Bradley .05 .02 .01
☐ 333 Henry Cotto .05 .02 .01
☐ 334 Alvin Davis .05 .02 .01
☐ 335 Ken Griffey .10 .05 .01
☐ 336 Ken Griffey Jr. 4.00 1.80 .50
☐ 337 Erik Hanson .05 .02 .01
☐ 338 Brian Holman .05 .02 .01
☐ 339 Randy Johnson .30 .14 .04
☐ 340 Edgar Martinez UER .10 .05 .01
(Listed as playing SS)
☐ 341 Tino Martinez .10 .05 .01
☐ 342 Pete O'Brien .05 .02 .01
☐ 343 Harold Reynolds .05 .02 .01
☐ 344 Dave Valle .05 .02 .01
☐ 345 Omar Vizquel .05 .02 .01
☐ 346 Brad Arnsberg .05 .02 .01
☐ 347 Kevin Brown .10 .05 .01
☐ 348 Julio Franco .10 .05 .01
☐ 349 Jeff Huson .05 .02 .01
☐ 350 Rafael Palmeiro .35 .16 .04
☐ 351 Geno Petralli .05 .02 .01
☐ 352 Gary Pettis .05 .02 .01
☐ 353 Kenny Rogers .05 .02 .01
☐ 354 Jeff Russell .05 .02 .01
☐ 355 Nolan Ryan 1.50 .65 .19
☐ 356 Ruben Sierra .20 .09 .03
☐ 357 Bobby Witt .05 .02 .01
☐ 358 Roberto Alomar 1.00 .45 .13
☐ 359 Pat Borders .05 .02 .01
☐ 360 Joe Carter UER .40 .18 .05
(Reverse negative
on back photo)
☐ 361 Kelly Gruber .05 .02 .01
☐ 362 Tom Henke .10 .05 .01
☐ 363 Glenallen Hill .05 .02 .01
☐ 364 Jimmy Key .10 .05 .01
☐ 365 Manny Lee .05 .02 .01
☐ 366 Rance Mulliniks .05 .02 .01
☐ 367 John Olerud UER .30 .14 .04
(Throwing left on card;
back has throws right;
he does throw lefty)
☐ 368 Dave Stieb .10 .05 .01
☐ 369 Duane Ward .10 .05 .01
☐ 370 David Wells .05 .02 .01
☐ 371 Mark Whiten .20 .09 .03
☐ 372 Mookie Wilson .05 .02 .01
☐ 373 Willie Banks MLP .10 .05 .01
☐ 374 Steve Carter MLP .05 .02 .01

		MINT	EXC	G-VG
☐ 375	Scott Chiamparino MLP	.05	.02	.01
☐ 376	Steve Chitren MLP	.05	.02	.01
☐ 377	Darrin Fletcher MLP	.05	.02	.01
☐ 378	Rich Garces MLP	.05	.02	.01
☐ 379	Reggie Jefferson MLP	.10	.05	.01
☐ 380	Eric Karros MLP	.50	.23	.06
☐ 381	Pat Kelly MLP	.25	.11	.03
☐ 382	Chuck Knoblauch MLP	.50	.23	.06
☐ 383	Denny Neagle MLP	.05	.02	.01
☐ 384	Dan Opperman MLP	.05	.02	.01
☐ 385	John Ramos MLP	.05	.02	.01
☐ 386	Henry Rodriguez MLP	.25	.11	.03
☐ 387	Mo Vaughn MLP	.75	.35	.09
☐ 388	Gerald Williams MLP	.05	.02	.01
☐ 389	Mike York MLP	.05	.02	.01
☐ 390	Eddie Zosky MLP	.05	.02	.01
☐ 391	Barry Bonds EP	.35	.16	.04
☐ 392	Cecil Fielder EP	.10	.05	.01
☐ 393	Rickey Henderson EP	.10	.05	.01
☐ 394	David Justice EP	.40	.18	.05
☐ 395	Nolan Ryan EP	.50	.23	.06
☐ 396	Bobby Thigpen EP	.05	.02	.01
☐ 397	Checklist Card Gregg Jefferies	.05	.02	.01
☐ 398	Checklist Card Von Hayes	.05	.02	.01
☐ 399	Checklist Card Terry Kennedy	.05	.02	.01
☐ 400	Checklist Card Nolan Ryan	.20	.09	.03

1991 Ultra Gold

This ten-card set presents Fleer's 1991 Ultra Team. The cards measure the standard size (2 1/2" by 3 1/2"). On a gold background that fades as one moves toward the bottom of the card, the front design has a color head shot, with two cut-out action shots below. Player information is given in a dark blue strip at the bottom of the card face. In blue print on white background with gold borders, the back highlights the player's outstanding achievements. The cards are numbered on the back.

	MINT	EXC	G-VG
COMPLETE SET (10)	10.00	4.50	1.25
COMMON CARD (1-10)	.25	.11	.03

		MINT	EXC	G-VG
☐ 1	Barry Bonds	1.75	.80	.22
☐ 2	Will Clark	1.00	.45	.13
☐ 3	Doug Drabek	.25	.11	.03
☐ 4	Ken Griffey Jr.	6.00	2.70	.75
☐ 5	Rickey Henderson	.75	.35	.09
☐ 6	Bo Jackson	.75	.35	.09
☐ 7	Ramon Martinez	.25	.11	.03
☐ 8	Kirby Puckett UER (Boggs won 1988 batting title, so Puckett didn't win consecutive titles)	1.50	.65	.19
☐ 9	Chris Sabo	.25	.11	.03
☐ 10	Ryne Sandberg UER (Johnson and Hornsby didn't hit 40 homers in 1990, Fielder did hit 51 in '90)	1.50	.65	.19

1991 Ultra Update

The 1991 Fleer Ultra Baseball Update set contains 120 cards and 20 team logo stickers. The set includes the year's hottest rookies and important veteran players traded after the original Ultra series was produced. The cards measure the standard size (2 1/2" by 3 1/2"). The front has a color action shot, while the back has a portrait photo and two full-figure action shots. The cards are numbered (with a U prefix) and checklisted below alphabetically within and according to teams for each league as follow: Baltimore Orioles (1-4), Boston Red Sox (5-7), California Angels (8-12), Chicago White Sox (13-18), Cleveland Indians (19-21), Detroit Tigers (22-24), Kansas City Royals (25-29), Milwaukee Brewers (30-33), Minnesota Twins (34-39), New York Yankees (40-44), Oakland Athletics (45-48), Seattle Mariners (49-53), Texas Rangers (54-58), Toronto Blue Jays (59-64), Atlanta Braves (65-69), Chicago Cubs (70-75), Cincinnati Reds (76-78), Houston Astros (79-84), Los Angeles Dodgers (85-89), Montreal Expos (90-93), New York Mets (94-97), Philadelphia Phillies (98-101), Pittsburgh Pirates (102-104), St. Louis Cardinals (105-109), San Diego Padres (110-114), and San Francisco Giants (115-119). The key Rookie Cards in this set are Jeff Bagwell, Juan Guzman, Mike Mussina, Ivan Rodriguez, and Rick Wilkins.

	MINT	EXC	G-VG
COMPLETE FACT.SET (120)	50.00	23.00	6.25

COMMON CARD (1-120)	.15	.07	.02
☐ 1 Dwight Evans	.20	.09	.03
☐ 2 Chito Martinez	.15	.07	.02
☐ 3 Bob Melvin	.15	.07	.02
☐ 4 Mike Mussina	9.00	4.00	1.15
☐ 5 Jack Clark	.20	.09	.03
☐ 6 Dana Kiecker	.15	.07	.02
☐ 7 Steve Lyons	.15	.07	.02
☐ 8 Gary Gaetti	.15	.07	.02
☐ 9 Dave Gallagher	.15	.07	.02
☐ 10 Dave Parker	.30	.14	.04
☐ 11 Luis Polonia	.15	.07	.02
☐ 12 Luis Sojo	.15	.07	.02
☐ 13 Wilson Alvarez	4.00	1.80	.50
☐ 14 Alex Fernandez	4.00	1.80	.50
☐ 15 Craig Grebeck	.15	.07	.02
☐ 16 Ron Karkovice	.15	.07	.02
☐ 17 Warren Newson	.15	.07	.02
☐ 18 Scott Radinsky	.15	.07	.02
☐ 19 Glenallen Hill	.15	.07	.02
☐ 20 Charles Nagy	.60	.25	.08
☐ 21 Mark Whiten	.30	.14	.04
☐ 22 Milt Cuyler	.15	.07	.02
☐ 23 Paul Gibson	.15	.07	.02
☐ 24 Mickey Tettleton	.20	.09	.03
☐ 25 Todd Benzinger	.15	.07	.02
☐ 26 Storm Davis	.15	.07	.02
☐ 27 Kirk Gibson	.20	.09	.03
☐ 28 Bill Pecota	.15	.07	.02
☐ 29 Gary Thurman	.15	.07	.02
☐ 30 Darryl Hamilton	.15	.07	.02
☐ 31 Jaime Navarro	.15	.07	.02
☐ 32 Willie Randolph	.20	.09	.03
☐ 33 Bill Wegman	.15	.07	.02
☐ 34 Randy Bush	.15	.07	.02
☐ 35 Chili Davis	.20	.09	.03
☐ 36 Scott Erickson	.20	.09	.03
☐ 37 Chuck Knoblauch	4.00	1.80	.50
☐ 38 Scott Leius	.15	.07	.02
☐ 39 Jack Morris	.30	.14	.04
☐ 40 John Habyan	.15	.07	.02
☐ 41 Pat Kelly	.50	.23	.06
☐ 42 Matt Nokes	.15	.07	.02
☐ 43 Scott Sanderson	.15	.07	.02
☐ 44 Bernie Williams	1.25	.55	.16
☐ 45 Harold Baines	.20	.09	.03
☐ 46 Brook Jacoby	.15	.07	.02
☐ 47 Earnest Riles	.15	.07	.02
☐ 48 Willie Wilson	.15	.07	.02
☐ 49 Jay Buhner	.60	.25	.08
☐ 50 Rich DeLucia	.15	.07	.02
☐ 51 Mike Jackson	.15	.07	.02
☐ 52 Bill Krueger	.15	.07	.02
☐ 53 Bill Swift	.20	.09	.03
☐ 54 Brian Downing	.15	.07	.02
☐ 55 Juan Gonzalez	16.00	7.25	2.00
☐ 56 Dean Palmer	2.00	.90	.25
☐ 57 Kevin Reimer	.15	.07	.02
☐ 58 Ivan Rodriguez	3.50	1.55	.45
☐ 59 Tom Candiotti	.15	.07	.02
☐ 60 Juan Guzman	2.00	.90	.25
☐ 61 Bob MacDonald	.15	.07	.02
☐ 62 Greg Myers	.15	.07	.02
☐ 63 Ed Sprague	.15	.07	.02
☐ 64 Devon White	.20	.09	.03
☐ 65 Rafael Belliard	.15	.07	.02
☐ 66 Juan Berenguer	.15	.07	.02
☐ 67 Brian R. Hunter	.60	.25	.08
☐ 68 Kent Mercker	1.50	.65	.19
☐ 69 Otis Nixon	.20	.09	.03
☐ 70 Danny Jackson	.15	.07	.02
☐ 71 Chuck McElroy	.20	.09	.03
☐ 72 Gary Scott	.15	.07	.02
☐ 73 Heathcliff Slocumb	.15	.07	.02
☐ 74 Chico Walker	.15	.07	.02
☐ 75 Rick Wilkins	1.00	.45	.13
☐ 76 Chris Hammond	.20	.09	.03
☐ 77 Luis Quinones	.15	.07	.02
☐ 78 Herm Winningham	.15	.07	.02
☐ 79 Jeff Bagwell	18.00	8.00	2.30
☐ 80 Jim Corsi	.15	.07	.02
☐ 81 Steve Finley	.15	.07	.02
☐ 82 Luis Gonzalez	1.75	.80	.22
☐ 83 Pete Harnisch	.20	.09	.03
☐ 84 Darryl Kile	1.00	.45	.13
☐ 85 Brett Butler	.20	.09	.03
☐ 86 Gary Carter	.30	.14	.04
☐ 87 Tim Crews	.15	.07	.02
☐ 88 Orel Hershiser	.20	.09	.03
☐ 89 Bob Ojeda	.15	.07	.02
☐ 90 Bret Barberie	.40	.18	.05
☐ 91 Barry Jones	.15	.07	.02
☐ 92 Gilberto Reyes	.15	.07	.02
☐ 93 Larry Walker	2.50	1.15	.30
☐ 94 Hubie Brooks	.15	.07	.02
☐ 95 Tim Burke	.15	.07	.02
☐ 96 Rick Cerone	.15	.07	.02
☐ 97 Jeff Innis	.15	.07	.02
☐ 98 Wally Backman	.15	.07	.02
☐ 99 Tommy Greene	.20	.09	.03
☐ 100 Ricky Jordan	.15	.07	.02
☐ 101 Mitch Williams	.20	.09	.03
☐ 102 John Smiley	.15	.07	.02
☐ 103 Randy Tomlin	.15	.07	.02
☐ 104 Gary Varsho	.15	.07	.02
☐ 105 Cris Carpenter	.15	.07	.02
☐ 106 Ken Hill	1.25	.55	.16
☐ 107 Felix Jose	.20	.09	.03
☐ 108 Omar Olivares	.15	.07	.02
☐ 109 Gerald Perry	.15	.07	.02
☐ 110 Jerald Clark	.15	.07	.02
☐ 111 Tony Fernandez	.20	.09	.03
☐ 112 Darrin Jackson	.15	.07	.02
☐ 113 Mike Maddux	.15	.07	.02
☐ 114 Tim Teufel	.15	.07	.02
☐ 115 Bud Black	.15	.07	.02
☐ 116 Kelly Downs	.15	.07	.02
☐ 117 Mike Felder	.15	.07	.02
☐ 118 Willie McGee	.20	.09	.03
☐ 119 Trevor Wilson	.15	.07	.02
☐ 120 Checklist 1-120	.15	.07	.02

1992 Ultra

Consisting of 600 cards, the 1992 Fleer Ultra set was issued in two series of 300 cards. The cards measure the standard size (2 1/2" by 3 1/2"). The glossy color action player photos on the fronts are full-bleed except at the bottom where a diagonal gold-foil stripe edges a green marbleized border. The player's name and team appear on the marble-colored area in bars that are color-coded by team. The horizontally oriented backs display an action and close-up cut-out player photo against a grid shaded with a gradated team color. The grid, team-colored bars containing stats and the player's name, biographical information, and the team logo all rest on a green marbleized background. The cards are numbered on

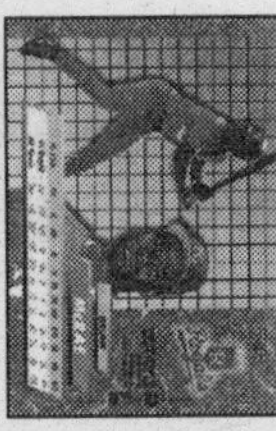

the back and checklisted below alphabetically within and according to teams for each league as follows: Baltimore Orioles (1-11/301-310), Boston Red Sox (12-23/311-320), California Angels (24-31/321-331), Chicago White Sox (32-44/332-343), Cleveland Indians (45-55/344-357), Detroit Tigers (56-65/358-368), Kansas City Royals (66-77/369-377), Milwaukee Brewers (78-87/378-392), Minnesota Twins (88-98/393-403), New York Yankees (99-108/404-417), Oakland Athletics (109-119/418-429), Seattle Mariners (120-130/430-436), Texas Rangers (131-142/437-447), Toronto Blue Jays (143-156/448-454), Atlanta Braves (157-171/455-465), Chicago Cubs (172-184/466-477), Cincinnati Reds (185-197/478-487), Houston Astros (198-208/488-498), Los Angeles Dodgers (209-219/499-510), Montreal Expos (220-226/511-526), New York Mets (227-238/527-539), Philadelphia Phillies (239-249/540-549), Pittsburgh Pirates (250-262/550-561), St. Louis Cardinals (263-273/562-574), San Diego Padres (274-283/575-585) and San Francisco Giants (284-297/586-597). Rookie Cards in the set include Rod Beck, Chad Curtis, Pat Listach, Pat Mahomes, Rey Sanchez, and Brian Williams. Some cards have been found without the word Fleer on the front.

	MINT	EXC	G-VG
COMPLETE SET (600)	40.00	18.00	5.00
COMPLETE SERIES 1 (300)	25.00	11.50	3.10
COMPLETE SERIES 2 (300)	15.00	6.75	1.90
COMMON CARD (1-300)	.10	.05	.01
COMMON CARD (301-600)	.10	.05	.01

	MINT	EXC	G-VG
☐ 1 Glenn Davis	.10	.05	.01
☐ 2 Mike Devereaux	.15	.07	.02
☐ 3 Dwight Evans	.15	.07	.02
☐ 4 Leo Gomez	.10	.05	.01
☐ 5 Chris Hoiles	.25	.11	.03
☐ 6 Sam Horn	.10	.05	.01
☐ 7 Chito Martinez	.10	.05	.01
☐ 8 Randy Milligan	.10	.05	.01
☐ 9 Mike Mussina	.75	.35	.09
☐ 10 Billy Ripken	.10	.05	.01
☐ 11 Cal Ripken	1.25	.55	.16
☐ 12 Tom Brunansky	.10	.05	.01
☐ 13 Ellis Burks	.15	.07	.02
☐ 14 Jack Clark	.15	.07	.02
☐ 15 Roger Clemens	.60	.25	.08
☐ 16 Mike Greenwell	.15	.07	.02
☐ 17 Joe Hesketh	.10	.05	.01
☐ 18 Tony Pena	.10	.05	.01
☐ 19 Carlos Quintana	.10	.05	.01
☐ 20 Jeff Reardon	.15	.07	.02
☐ 21 Jody Reed	.10	.05	.01
☐ 22 Luis Rivera	.10	.05	.01
☐ 23 Mo Vaughn	.50	.23	.06
☐ 24 Gary DiSarcina	.10	.05	.01
☐ 25 Chuck Finley	.10	.05	.01
☐ 26 Gary Gaetti	.10	.05	.01
☐ 27 Bryan Harvey	.15	.07	.02
☐ 28 Lance Parrish	.15	.07	.02
☐ 29 Luis Polonia	.10	.05	.01
☐ 30 Dick Schofield	.10	.05	.01
☐ 31 Luis Sojo	.10	.05	.01
☐ 32 Wilson Alvarez	.30	.14	.04
☐ 33 Carlton Fisk	.25	.11	.03
☐ 34 Craig Grebeck	.10	.05	.01
☐ 35 Ozzie Guillen	.10	.05	.01
☐ 36 Greg Hibbard	.10	.05	.01
☐ 37 Charlie Hough	.15	.07	.02
☐ 38 Lance Johnson	.10	.05	.01
☐ 39 Ron Karkovice	.10	.05	.01
☐ 40 Jack McDowell	.25	.11	.03
☐ 41 Donn Pall	.10	.05	.01
☐ 42 Melido Perez	.10	.05	.01
☐ 43 Tim Raines	.25	.11	.03
☐ 44 Frank Thomas	4.00	1.80	.50
☐ 45 Sandy Alomar Jr.	.15	.07	.02
☐ 46 Carlos Baerga	.50	.23	.06
☐ 47 Albert Belle	1.25	.55	.16
☐ 48 Jerry Browne UER (Reversed negative on card back)	.10	.05	.01
☐ 49 Felix Fermin	.10	.05	.01
☐ 50 Reggie Jefferson UER (Born 1968, not 1966)	.10	.05	.01
☐ 51 Mark Lewis	.15	.07	.02
☐ 52 Carlos Martinez	.10	.05	.01
☐ 53 Steve Olin	.10	.05	.01
☐ 54 Jim Thome	1.00	.45	.13
☐ 55 Mark Whiten	.15	.07	.02
☐ 56 Dave Bergman	.10	.05	.01
☐ 57 Milt Cuyler	.10	.05	.01
☐ 58 Rob Deer	.10	.05	.01
☐ 59 Cecil Fielder	.35	.16	.04
☐ 60 Travis Fryman	.50	.23	.06
☐ 61 Scott Livingstone	.10	.05	.01
☐ 62 Tony Phillips	.10	.05	.01
☐ 63 Mickey Tettleton	.15	.07	.02
☐ 64 Alan Trammell	.25	.11	.03
☐ 65 Lou Whitaker	.25	.11	.03
☐ 66 Kevin Appier	.15	.07	.02
☐ 67 Mike Boddicker	.10	.05	.01
☐ 68 George Brett	1.00	.45	.13
☐ 69 Jim Eisenreich	.10	.05	.01
☐ 70 Mark Gubicza	.10	.05	.01
☐ 71 David Howard	.10	.05	.01
☐ 72 Joel Johnson	.10	.05	.01
☐ 73 Mike Macfarlane	.10	.05	.01
☐ 74 Brent Mayne	.10	.05	.01
☐ 75 Brian McRae	.25	.11	.03
☐ 76 Jeff Montgomery	.15	.07	.02
☐ 77 Danny Tartabull	.15	.07	.02
☐ 78 Don August	.10	.05	.01
☐ 79 Dante Bichette	.25	.11	.03
☐ 80 Ted Higuera	.10	.05	.01
☐ 81 Paul Molitor	.35	.16	.04
☐ 82 Jaime Navarro	.10	.05	.01
☐ 83 Gary Sheffield	.25	.11	.03
☐ 84 Bill Spiers	.10	.05	.01
☐ 85 B.J. Surhoff	.10	.05	.01
☐ 86 Greg Vaughn	.15	.07	.02
☐ 87 Robin Yount	.30	.14	.04
☐ 88 Rick Aguilera	.15	.07	.02
☐ 89 Chili Davis	.15	.07	.02

	No.	Player			
□	90	Scott Erickson	.10	.05	.01
□	91	Brian Harper	.10	.05	.01
□	92	Kent Hrbek	.15	.07	.02
□	93	Chuck Knoblauch	.30	.14	.04
□	94	Scott Leius	.10	.05	.01
□	95	Shane Mack	.15	.07	.02
□	96	Mike Pagliarulo	.10	.05	.01
□	97	Kirby Puckett	1.00	.45	.13
□	98	Kevin Tapani	.10	.05	.01
□	99	Jesse Barfield	.10	.05	.01
□	100	Alvaro Espinoza	.10	.05	.01
□	101	Mel Hall	.10	.05	.01
□	102	Pat Kelly	.15	.07	.02
□	103	Roberto Kelly	.15	.07	.02
□	104	Kevin Maas	.10	.05	.01
□	105	Don Mattingly	1.00	.45	.13
□	106	Hensley Meulens	.10	.05	.01
□	107	Matt Nokes	.10	.05	.01
□	108	Steve Sax	.10	.05	.01
□	109	Harold Baines	.15	.07	.02
□	110	Jose Canseco	.60	.25	.08
□	111	Ron Darling	.10	.05	.01
□	112	Mike Gallego	.10	.05	.01
□	113	Dave Henderson	.10	.05	.01
□	114	Rickey Henderson	.25	.11	.03
□	115	Mark McGwire	.25	.11	.03
□	116	Terry Steinbach	.15	.07	.02
□	117	Dave Stewart	.15	.07	.02
□	118	Todd Van Poppel	.25	.11	.03
□	119	Bob Welch	.10	.05	.01
□	120	Greg Briley	.10	.05	.01
□	121	Jay Buhner	.15	.07	.02
□	122	Rick DeLucia	.10	.05	.01
□	123	Ken Griffey Jr.	4.00	1.80	.50
□	124	Erik Hanson	.10	.05	.01
□	125	Randy Johnson	.25	.11	.03
□	126	Edgar Martinez	.15	.07	.02
□	127	Tino Martinez	.15	.07	.02
□	128	Pete O'Brien	.10	.05	.01
□	129	Harold Reynolds	.10	.05	.01
□	130	Dave Valle	.10	.05	.01
□	131	Julio Franco	.15	.07	.02
□	132	Juan Gonzalez	1.50	.65	.19
□	133	Jeff Huson (Shows Jose Canseco sliding into second)	.10	.05	.01
□	134	Mike Jeffcoat	.10	.05	.01
□	135	Terry Mathews	.10	.05	.01
□	136	Rafael Palmeiro	.30	.14	.04
□	137	Dean Palmer	.15	.07	.02
□	138	Geno Petralli	.10	.05	.01
□	139	Ivan Rodriguez	.30	.14	.04
□	140	Jeff Russell	.10	.05	.01
□	141	Nolan Ryan	3.00	1.35	.40
□	142	Ruben Sierra	.25	.11	.03
□	143	Roberto Alomar	.50	.23	.06
□	144	Pat Borders	.10	.05	.01
□	145	Joe Carter	.50	.23	.06
□	146	Kelly Gruber	.10	.05	.01
□	147	Jimmy Key	.15	.07	.02
□	148	Manny Lee	.10	.05	.01
□	149	Rance Mulliniks	.10	.05	.01
□	150	Greg Myers	.10	.05	.01
□	151	John Olerud	.25	.11	.03
□	152	Dave Stieb	.15	.07	.02
□	153	Todd Stottlemyre	.10	.05	.01
□	154	Duane Ward	.15	.07	.02
□	155	Devon White	.15	.07	.02
□	156	Eddie Zosky	.15	.07	.02
□	157	Steve Avery	.30	.14	.04
□	158	Rafael Belliard	.10	.05	.01
□	159	Jeff Blauser	.15	.07	.02
□	160	Sid Bream	.10	.05	.01
□	161	Ron Gant	.15	.07	.02
□	162	Tom Glavine	.25	.11	.03
□	163	Brian Hunter	.10	.05	.01
□	164	David Justice	.50	.23	.06
□	165	Mark Lemke	.10	.05	.01
□	166	Greg Olson	.10	.05	.01
□	167	Terry Pendleton	.25	.11	.03
□	168	Lonnie Smith	.10	.05	.01
□	169	John Smoltz	.15	.07	.02
□	170	Mike Stanton	.10	.05	.01
□	171	Jeff Treadway	.10	.05	.01
□	172	Paul Assenmacher	.10	.05	.01
□	173	George Bell	.15	.07	.02
□	174	Shawon Dunston	.10	.05	.01
□	175	Mark Grace	.25	.11	.03
□	176	Danny Jackson	.10	.05	.01
□	177	Les Lancaster	.10	.05	.01
□	178	Greg Maddux	.50	.23	.06
□	179	Luis Salazar	.10	.05	.01
□	180	Rey Sanchez	.15	.07	.02
□	181	Ryne Sandberg	.75	.35	.09
□	182	Jose Vizcaino	.10	.05	.01
□	183	Chico Walker	.10	.05	.01
□	184	Jerome Walton	.10	.05	.01
□	185	Glenn Braggs	.10	.05	.01
□	186	Tom Browning	.10	.05	.01
□	187	Rob Dibble	.10	.05	.01
□	188	Bill Doran	.10	.05	.01
□	189	Chris Hammond	.10	.05	.01
□	190	Billy Hatcher	.10	.05	.01
□	191	Barry Larkin	.25	.11	.03
□	192	Hal Morris	.15	.07	.02
□	193	Joe Oliver	.10	.05	.01
□	194	Paul O'Neill	.15	.07	.02
□	195	Jeff Reed	.10	.05	.01
□	196	Jose Rijo	.15	.07	.02
□	197	Chris Sabo	.15	.07	.02
□	198	Jeff Bagwell	2.00	.90	.25
□	199	Craig Biggio	.15	.07	.02
□	200	Ken Caminiti	.15	.07	.02
□	201	Andujar Cedeno	.15	.07	.02
□	202	Steve Finley	.10	.05	.01
□	203	Luis Gonzalez	.15	.07	.02
□	204	Pete Harnisch	.15	.07	.02
□	205	Xavier Hernandez	.10	.05	.01
□	206	Darryl Kile	.15	.07	.02
□	207	Al Osuna	.10	.05	.01
□	208	Curt Schilling	.15	.07	.02
□	209	Brett Butler	.15	.07	.02
□	210	Kal Daniels	.10	.05	.01
□	211	Lenny Harris	.10	.05	.01
□	212	Stan Javier	.10	.05	.01
□	213	Ramon Martinez	.15	.07	.02
□	214	Roger McDowell	.10	.05	.01
□	215	Jose Offerman	.10	.05	.01
□	216	Juan Samuel	.10	.05	.01
□	217	Mike Scioscia	.10	.05	.01
□	218	Mike Sharperson	.10	.05	.01
□	219	Darryl Strawberry	.15	.07	.02
□	220	Delino DeShields	.25	.11	.03
□	221	Tom Foley	.10	.05	.01
□	222	Steve Frey	.10	.05	.01
□	223	Dennis Martinez	.15	.07	.02
□	224	Spike Owen	.10	.05	.01
□	225	Gilberto Reyes	.10	.05	.01
□	226	Tim Wallach	.10	.05	.01
□	227	Daryl Boston	.10	.05	.01
□	228	Tim Burke	.10	.05	.01
□	229	Vince Coleman	.10	.05	.01
□	230	David Cone	.25	.11	.03
□	231	Kevin Elster	.10	.05	.01
□	232	Dwight Gooden	.15	.07	.02
□	233	Todd Hundley	.10	.05	.01

☐ 234 Jeff Innis .10 .05 .01
☐ 235 Howard Johnson .15 .07 .02
☐ 236 Dave Magadan .10 .05 .01
☐ 237 Mackey Sasser .10 .05 .01
☐ 238 Anthony Young .10 .05 .01
☐ 239 Wes Chamberlain .10 .05 .01
☐ 240 Darren Daulton .25 .11 .03
☐ 241 Len Dykstra .25 .11 .03
☐ 242 Tommy Greene .15 .07 .02
☐ 243 Charlie Hayes .15 .07 .02
☐ 244 Dave Hollins .25 .11 .03
☐ 245 Ricky Jordan .10 .05 .01
☐ 246 John Kruk .25 .11 .03
☐ 247 Mickey Morandini .10 .05 .01
☐ 248 Terry Mulholland .10 .05 .01
☐ 249 Dale Murphy .25 .11 .03
☐ 250 Jay Bell .15 .07 .02
☐ 251 Barry Bonds 1.25 .55 .16
☐ 252 Steve Buechele .10 .05 .01
☐ 253 Doug Drabek .25 .11 .03
☐ 254 Mike LaValliere .10 .05 .01
☐ 255 Jose Lind .10 .05 .01
☐ 256 Lloyd McClendon .10 .05 .01
☐ 257 Orlando Merced .15 .07 .02
☐ 258 Don Slaught .10 .05 .01
☐ 259 John Smiley .10 .05 .01
☐ 260 Zane Smith .10 .05 .01
☐ 261 Randy Tomlin .10 .05 .01
☐ 262 Andy Van Slyke .25 .11 .03
☐ 263 Pedro Guerrero .15 .07 .02
☐ 264 Felix Jose .15 .07 .02
☐ 265 Ray Lankford .25 .11 .03
☐ 266 Omar Olivares .10 .05 .01
☐ 267 Jose Oquendo .10 .05 .01
☐ 268 Tom Pagnozzi .10 .05 .01
☐ 269 Bryn Smith .10 .05 .01
☐ 270 Lee Smith UER .25 .11 .03
(1991 record listed
as 61-61)
☐ 271 Ozzie Smith UER .40 .18 .05
(Comma before year of
birth on card back)
☐ 272 Milt Thompson .10 .05 .01
☐ 273 Todd Zeile .15 .07 .02
☐ 274 Andy Benes .15 .07 .02
☐ 275 Jerald Clark .10 .05 .01
☐ 276 Tony Fernandez .15 .07 .02
☐ 277 Tony Gwynn .60 .25 .08
☐ 278 Greg W. Harris .10 .05 .01
☐ 279 Thomas Howard .10 .05 .01
☐ 280 Bruce Hurst .10 .05 .01
☐ 281 Mike Maddux .10 .05 .01
☐ 282 Fred McGriff .50 .23 .06
☐ 283 Benito Santiago .10 .05 .01
☐ 284 Kevin Bass .10 .05 .01
☐ 285 Jeff Brantley .10 .05 .01
☐ 286 John Burkett .15 .07 .02
☐ 287 Will Clark .50 .23 .06
☐ 288 Royce Clayton .25 .11 .03
☐ 289 Steve Decker .10 .05 .01
☐ 290 Kelly Downs .10 .05 .01
☐ 291 Mike Felder .10 .05 .01
☐ 292 Darren Lewis .15 .07 .02
☐ 293 Kirt Manwaring .10 .05 .01
☐ 294 Willie McGee .15 .07 .02
☐ 295 Robby Thompson .10 .05 .01
☐ 296 Matt Williams .50 .23 .06
☐ 297 Trevor Wilson .10 .05 .01
☐ 298 Checklist 1-100 .10 .05 .01
☐ 299 Checklist 101-200 .10 .05 .01
☐ 300 Checklist 201-300 .10 .05 .01
☐ 301 Brady Anderson .15 .07 .02
☐ 302 Todd Frohwirth .10 .05 .01
☐ 303 Ben McDonald .15 .07 .02
☐ 304 Mark McLemore .10 .05 .01
☐ 305 Jose Mesa .10 .05 .01
☐ 306 Bob Milacki .10 .05 .01
☐ 307 Gregg Olson .10 .05 .01
☐ 308 David Segui .10 .05 .01
☐ 309 Rick Sutcliffe .15 .07 .02
☐ 310 Jeff Tackett .10 .05 .01
☐ 311 Wade Boggs .25 .11 .03
☐ 312 Scott Cooper .15 .07 .02
☐ 313 John Flaherty .15 .07 .02
☐ 314 Wayne Housie .15 .07 .02
☐ 315 Peter Hoy .15 .07 .02
☐ 316 John Marzano .10 .05 .01
☐ 317 Tim Naehring .10 .05 .01
☐ 318 Phil Plantier .25 .11 .03
☐ 319 Frank Viola .15 .07 .02
☐ 320 Matt Young .10 .05 .01
☐ 321 Jim Abbott .25 .11 .03
☐ 322 Hubie Brooks .10 .05 .01
☐ 323 Chad Curtis .40 .18 .05
☐ 324 Alvin Davis .10 .05 .01
☐ 325 Junior Felix .10 .05 .01
☐ 326 Von Hayes .10 .05 .01
☐ 327 Mark Langston .25 .11 .03
☐ 328 Scott Lewis .10 .05 .01
☐ 329 Don Robinson .10 .05 .01
☐ 330 Bobby Rose .10 .05 .01
☐ 331 Lee Stevens .10 .05 .01
☐ 332 George Bell .15 .07 .02
☐ 333 Esteban Beltre .15 .07 .02
☐ 334 Joey Cora .10 .05 .01
☐ 335 Alex Fernandez .30 .14 .04
☐ 336 Roberto Hernandez .15 .07 .02
☐ 337 Mike Huff .10 .05 .01
☐ 338 Kirk McCaskill .10 .05 .01
☐ 339 Dan Pasqua .10 .05 .01
☐ 340 Scott Radinsky .10 .05 .01
☐ 341 Steve Sax .10 .05 .01
☐ 342 Bobby Thigpen .10 .05 .01
☐ 343 Robin Ventura .30 .14 .04
☐ 344 Jack Armstrong .10 .05 .01
☐ 345 Alex Cole .10 .05 .01
☐ 346 Dennis Cook .10 .05 .01
☐ 347 Glenallen Hill .10 .05 .01
☐ 348 Thomas Howard .10 .05 .01
☐ 349 Brook Jacoby .10 .05 .01
☐ 350 Kenny Lofton 2.50 1.15 .30
☐ 351 Charles Nagy .10 .05 .01
☐ 352 Rod Nichols .10 .05 .01
☐ 353 Junior Ortiz .10 .05 .01
☐ 354 Dave Otto .10 .05 .01
☐ 355 Tony Perezchica .10 .05 .01
☐ 356 Scott Scudder .10 .05 .01
☐ 357 Paul Sorrento .10 .05 .01
☐ 358 Skeeter Barnes .10 .05 .01
☐ 359 Mark Carreon .10 .05 .01
☐ 360 John Doherty .20 .09 .03
☐ 361 Dan Gladden .10 .05 .01
☐ 362 Bill Gullickson .10 .05 .01
☐ 363 Shawn Hare .15 .07 .02
☐ 364 Mike Henneman .10 .05 .01
☐ 365 Chad Kreuter .10 .05 .01
☐ 366 Mark Leiter .10 .05 .01
☐ 367 Mike Munoz .10 .05 .01
☐ 368 Kevin Ritz .10 .05 .01
☐ 369 Mark Davis .10 .05 .01
☐ 370 Tom Gordon .10 .05 .01
☐ 371 Chris Gwynn .10 .05 .01
☐ 372 Gregg Jefferies .30 .14 .04
☐ 373 Wally Joyner .15 .07 .02
☐ 374 Kevin McReynolds .10 .05 .01
☐ 375 Keith Miller .10 .05 .01

	No.	Player			
☐	376	Rico Rossy	.10	.05	.01
☐	377	Curtis Wilkerson	.10	.05	.01
☐	378	Ricky Bones	.15	.07	.02
☐	379	Chris Bosio	.10	.05	.01
☐	380	Cal Eldred	.15	.07	.02
☐	381	Scott Fletcher	.10	.05	.01
☐	382	Jim Gantner	.10	.05	.01
☐	383	Darryl Hamilton	.15	.07	.02
☐	384	Doug Henry	.10	.05	.01
☐	385	Pat Listach	.20	.09	.03
☐	386	Tim McIntosh	.10	.05	.01
☐	387	Edwin Nunez	.10	.05	.01
☐	388	Dan Plesac	.10	.05	.01
☐	389	Kevin Seitzer	.10	.05	.01
☐	390	Franklin Stubbs	.10	.05	.01
☐	391	William Suero	.10	.05	.01
☐	392	Bill Wegman	.10	.05	.01
☐	393	Willie Banks	.10	.05	.01
☐	394	Jarvis Brown	.15	.07	.02
☐	395	Greg Gagne	.10	.05	.01
☐	396	Mark Guthrie	.10	.05	.01
☐	397	Bill Krueger	.10	.05	.01
☐	398	Pat Mahomes	.25	.11	.03
☐	399	Pedro Munoz	.15	.07	.02
☐	400	John Smiley	.10	.05	.01
☐	401	Gary Wayne	.10	.05	.01
☐	402	Lenny Webster	.10	.05	.01
☐	403	Carl Willis	.10	.05	.01
☐	404	Greg Cadaret	.10	.05	.01
☐	405	Steve Farr	.10	.05	.01
☐	406	Mike Gallego	.10	.05	.01
☐	407	Charlie Hayes	.15	.07	.02
☐	408	Steve Howe	.10	.05	.01
☐	409	Dion James	.10	.05	.01
☐	410	Jeff Johnson	.10	.05	.01
☐	411	Tim Leary	.10	.05	.01
☐	412	Jim Leyritz	.10	.05	.01
☐	413	Melido Perez	.10	.05	.01
☐	414	Scott Sanderson	.10	.05	.01
☐	415	Andy Stankiewicz	.10	.05	.01
☐	416	Mike Stanley	.10	.05	.01
☐	417	Danny Tartabull	.15	.07	.02
☐	418	Lance Blankenship	.10	.05	.01
☐	419	Mike Bordick	.10	.05	.01
☐	420	Scott Brosius	.10	.05	.01
☐	421	Dennis Eckersley	.25	.11	.03
☐	422	Scott Hemond	.10	.05	.01
☐	423	Carney Lansford	.15	.07	.02
☐	424	Henry Mercedes	.10	.05	.01
☐	425	Mike Moore	.10	.05	.01
☐	426	Gene Nelson	.10	.05	.01
☐	427	Randy Ready	.10	.05	.01
☐	428	Bruce Walton	.10	.05	.01
☐	429	Willie Wilson	.10	.05	.01
☐	430	Rich Amaral	.10	.05	.01
☐	431	Dave Cochrane	.10	.05	.01
☐	432	Henry Cotto	.10	.05	.01
☐	433	Calvin Jones	.10	.05	.01
☐	434	Kevin Mitchell	.15	.07	.02
☐	435	Clay Parker	.10	.05	.01
☐	436	Omar Vizquel	.10	.05	.01
☐	437	Floyd Bannister	.10	.05	.01
☐	438	Kevin Brown	.15	.07	.02
☐	439	John Cangelosi	.10	.05	.01
☐	440	Brian Downing	.10	.05	.01
☐	441	Monty Fariss	.10	.05	.01
☐	442	Jose Guzman	.10	.05	.01
☐	443	Donald Harris	.10	.05	.01
☐	444	Kevin Reimer	.10	.05	.01
☐	445	Kenny Rogers	.10	.05	.01
☐	446	Wayne Rosenthal	.10	.05	.01
☐	447	Dickie Thon	.10	.05	.01
☐	448	Derek Bell	.15	.07	.02
☐	449	Juan Guzman	.15	.07	.02
☐	450	Tom Henke	.15	.07	.02
☐	451	Candy Maldonado	.10	.05	.01
☐	452	Jack Morris	.25	.11	.03
☐	453	David Wells	.10	.05	.01
☐	454	Dave Winfield	.30	.14	.04
☐	455	Juan Berenguer	.10	.05	.01
☐	456	Damon Berryhill	.10	.05	.01
☐	457	Mike Bielecki	.10	.05	.01
☐	458	Marvin Freeman	.10	.05	.01
☐	459	Charlie Leibrandt	.10	.05	.01
☐	460	Kent Mercker	.10	.05	.01
☐	461	Otis Nixon	.15	.07	.02
☐	462	Alejandro Pena	.10	.05	.01
☐	463	Ben Rivera	.10	.05	.01
☐	464	Deion Sanders	.50	.23	.06
☐	465	Mark Wohlers	.15	.07	.02
☐	466	Shawn Boskie	.10	.05	.01
☐	467	Frank Castillo	.10	.05	.01
☐	468	Andre Dawson	.25	.11	.03
☐	469	Joe Girardi	.10	.05	.01
☐	470	Chuck McElroy	.10	.05	.01
☐	471	Mike Morgan	.10	.05	.01
☐	472	Ken Patterson	.10	.05	.01
☐	473	Bob Scanlan	.10	.05	.01
☐	474	Gary Scott	.10	.05	.01
☐	475	Dave Smith	.10	.05	.01
☐	476	Sammy Sosa	.25	.11	.03
☐	477	Hector Villanueva	.10	.05	.01
☐	478	Scott Bankhead	.10	.05	.01
☐	479	Tim Belcher	.10	.05	.01
☐	480	Freddie Benavides	.10	.05	.01
☐	481	Jacob Brumfield	.15	.07	.02
☐	482	Norm Charlton	.10	.05	.01
☐	483	Dwayne Henry	.10	.05	.01
☐	484	Dave Martinez	.10	.05	.01
☐	485	Bip Roberts	.10	.05	.01
☐	486	Reggie Sanders	.50	.23	.06
☐	487	Greg Swindell	.10	.05	.01
☐	488	Ryan Bowen	.10	.05	.01
☐	489	Casey Candaele	.10	.05	.01
☐	490	Juan Guerrero	.15	.07	.02
☐	491	Pete Incaviglia	.10	.05	.01
☐	492	Jeff Juden	.15	.07	.02
☐	493	Rob Murphy	.10	.05	.01
☐	494	Mark Portugal	.10	.05	.01
☐	495	Rafael Ramirez	.10	.05	.01
☐	496	Scott Servais	.10	.05	.01
☐	497	Ed Taubensee	.10	.05	.01
☐	498	Brian Williams	.15	.07	.02
☐	499	Todd Benzinger	.10	.05	.01
☐	500	John Candelaria	.10	.05	.01
☐	501	Tom Candiotti	.10	.05	.01
☐	502	Tim Crews	.10	.05	.01
☐	503	Eric Davis	.10	.05	.01
☐	504	Jim Gott	.10	.05	.01
☐	505	Dave Hansen	.10	.05	.01
☐	506	Carlos Hernandez	.10	.05	.01
☐	507	Orel Hershiser	.15	.07	.02
☐	508	Eric Karros	.25	.11	.03
☐	509	Bob Ojeda	.10	.05	.01
☐	510	Steve Wilson	.10	.05	.01
☐	511	Moises Alou	.30	.14	.04
☐	512	Bret Barberie	.10	.05	.01
☐	513	Ivan Calderon	.10	.05	.01
☐	514	Gary Carter	.25	.11	.03
☐	515	Archi Cianfrocco	.10	.05	.01
☐	516	Jeff Fassero	.10	.05	.01
☐	517	Darrin Fletcher	.10	.05	.01
☐	518	Marquis Grissom	.25	.11	.03
☐	519	Chris Haney	.10	.05	.01
☐	520	Ken Hill	.15	.07	.02
☐	521	Chris Nabholz	.10	.05	.01

☐ 522 Bill Sampen	.10	.05	.01
☐ 523 John Vander Wal	.15	.07	.02
☐ 524 Dave Wainhouse	.10	.05	.01
☐ 525 Larry Walker	.25	.11	.03
☐ 526 John Wetteland	.10	.05	.01
☐ 527 Bobby Bonilla	.25	.11	.03
☐ 528 Sid Fernandez	.15	.07	.02
☐ 529 John Franco	.10	.05	.01
☐ 530 Dave Gallagher	.10	.05	.01
☐ 531 Paul Gibson	.10	.05	.01
☐ 532 Eddie Murray	.25	.11	.03
☐ 533 Junior Noboa	.10	.05	.01
☐ 534 Charlie O'Brien	.10	.05	.01
☐ 535 Bill Pecota	.10	.05	.01
☐ 536 Willie Randolph	.15	.07	.02
☐ 537 Bret Saberhagen	.25	.11	.03
☐ 538 Dick Schofield	.10	.05	.01
☐ 539 Pete Schourek	.15	.07	.02
☐ 540 Ruben Amaro	.10	.05	.01
☐ 541 Andy Ashby	.10	.05	.01
☐ 542 Kim Batiste	.10	.05	.01
☐ 543 Cliff Brantley	.15	.07	.02
☐ 544 Mariano Duncan	.10	.05	.01
☐ 545 Jeff Grotewold	.15	.07	.02
☐ 546 Barry Jones	.10	.05	.01
☐ 547 Julio Peguero	.15	.07	.02
☐ 548 Curt Schilling	.15	.07	.02
☐ 549 Mitch Williams	.15	.07	.02
☐ 550 Stan Belinda	.10	.05	.01
☐ 551 Scott Bullett	.10	.05	.01
☐ 552 Cecil Espy	.10	.05	.01
☐ 553 Jeff King	.10	.05	.01
☐ 554 Roger Mason	.10	.05	.01
☐ 555 Paul Miller	.15	.07	.02
☐ 556 Denny Neagle	.10	.05	.01
☐ 557 Vicente Palacios	.10	.05	.01
☐ 558 Bob Patterson	.10	.05	.01
☐ 559 Tom Prince	.10	.05	.01
☐ 560 Gary Redus	.10	.05	.01
☐ 561 Gary Varsho	.10	.05	.01
☐ 562 Juan Agosto	.10	.05	.01
☐ 563 Cris Carpenter	.10	.05	.01
☐ 564 Mark Clark	.30	.14	.04
☐ 565 Jose DeLeon	.10	.05	.01
☐ 566 Rich Gedman	.10	.05	.01
☐ 567 Bernard Gilkey	.15	.07	.02
☐ 568 Rex Hudler	.10	.05	.01
☐ 569 Tim Jones	.10	.05	.01
☐ 570 Donovan Osborne	.10	.05	.01
☐ 571 Mike Perez	.10	.05	.01
☐ 572 Gerald Perry	.10	.05	.01
☐ 573 Bob Tewksbury	.10	.05	.01
☐ 574 Todd Worrell	.10	.05	.01
☐ 575 Dave Eiland	.10	.05	.01
☐ 576 Jeremy Hernandez	.15	.07	.02
☐ 577 Craig Lefferts	.10	.05	.01
☐ 578 Jose Melendez	.10	.05	.01
☐ 579 Randy Myers	.15	.07	.02
☐ 580 Gary Pettis	.10	.05	.01
☐ 581 Rich Rodriguez	.10	.05	.01
☐ 582 Gary Sheffield	.25	.11	.03
☐ 583 Craig Shipley	.15	.07	.02
☐ 584 Kurt Stillwell	.10	.05	.01
☐ 585 Tim Teufel	.10	.05	.01
☐ 586 Rod Beck	.75	.35	.09
☐ 587 Dave Burba	.10	.05	.01
☐ 588 Craig Colbert	.10	.05	.01
☐ 589 Bryan Hickerson	.10	.05	.01
☐ 590 Mike Jackson	.10	.05	.01
☐ 591 Mark Leonard	.10	.05	.01
☐ 592 Jim McNamara	.15	.07	.02
☐ 593 John Patterson	.15	.07	.02
☐ 594 Dave Righetti	.10	.05	.01
☐ 595 Cory Snyder	.10	.05	.01
☐ 596 Bill Swift	.15	.07	.02
☐ 597 Ted Wood	.10	.05	.01
☐ 598 Checklist 301-400	.10	.05	.01
☐ 599 Checklist 401-500	.10	.05	.01
☐ 600 Checklist 501-600	.10	.05	.01

1992 Ultra All-Rookies

This ten-card standard-size (2 1/2" by 3 1/2") set was randomly inserted in 1992 Fleer Ultra II foil packs. The fronts feature borderless color action player photos except at the bottom where they are edged by a marbleized black wedge. The words "All-Rookie Team" in gold foil lettering appear in a black marbleized inverted triangle at the lower right corner, with the player's name on a color banner. On a black marbleized background, the backs present a color headshot inside an inverted triangle and career summary on a gray marbleized panel. The cards are numbered on the back.

	MINT	EXC	G-VG
COMPLETE SET (10)	15.00	6.75	1.90
COMMON CARD (1-10)	.50	.23	.06
☐ 1 Eric Karros	1.50	.65	.19
☐ 2 Andy Stankiewicz	.50	.23	.06
☐ 3 Gary DiSarcina	.50	.23	.06
☐ 4 Archi Cianfrocco	.50	.23	.06
☐ 5 Jim McNamara	.50	.23	.06
☐ 6 Chad Curtis	1.25	.55	.16
☐ 7 Kenny Lofton	10.00	4.50	1.25
☐ 8 Reggie Sanders	2.00	.90	.25
☐ 9 Pat Mahomes	1.00	.45	.13
☐ 10 Donovan Osborne	.50	.23	.06

1992 Ultra All-Stars

Featuring many of the season's current mega-stars, this 20-card standard-size (2 1/2" by 3 1/2") set was randomly inserted in 1992 Fleer Ultra II foil packs. The front design displays color action player photos

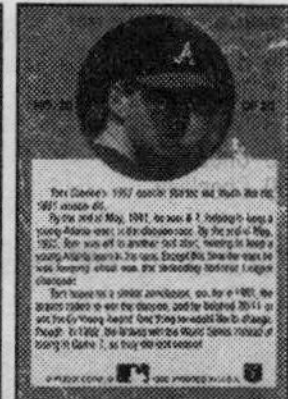

enclosed by black marbleized borders. The word "All-Star" and the player's name are printed in gold foil lettering in the bottom border. On a gray marbleized background, the backs carry a color headshot (in a circular format) and a summary of the player's recent performance in on a pastel yellow panel. The cards are numbered on the back.

	MINT	EXC	G-VG
COMPLETE SET (20)	25.00	11.50	3.10
COMMON CARD (1-20)	.50	.23	.06

	MINT	EXC	G-VG
☐ 1 Mark McGwire	.75	.35	.09
☐ 2 Roberto Alomar	2.50	1.15	.30
☐ 3 Cal Ripken	5.00	2.30	.60
☐ 4 Wade Boggs	1.25	.55	.16
☐ 5 Mickey Tettleton	.50	.23	.06
☐ 6 Ken Griffey Jr.	10.00	4.50	1.25
☐ 7 Roberto Kelly	.50	.23	.06
☐ 8 Kirby Puckett	3.50	1.55	.45
☐ 9 Frank Thomas	10.00	4.50	1.25
☐ 10 Jack McDowell	.75	.35	.09
☐ 11 Will Clark	2.00	.90	.25
☐ 12 Ryne Sandberg	3.50	1.55	.45
☐ 13 Barry Larkin	.75	.35	.09
☐ 14 Gary Sheffield	.75	.35	.09
☐ 15 Tom Pagnozzi	.50	.23	.06
☐ 16 Barry Bonds	3.50	1.55	.45
☐ 17 Deion Sanders	2.00	.90	.25
☐ 18 Darryl Strawberry	.75	.35	.09
☐ 19 David Cone	.75	.35	.09
☐ 20 Tom Glavine	1.00	.45	.13

1992 Ultra Award Winners

This 25-card set features 18 Gold Glove winners, both Cy Young Award winners, both Rookies of the Year, both league MVP's, and the World Series MVP. The cards measure the standard size (2 1/2" by 3 1/2") and were randomly inserted in 1992 Fleer Ultra I packs. The fronts carry full-bleed color player photos that have a diagonal blue marbleized border at the bottom. The player's name appears in this bottom border, and a diamond-shaped gold foil seal signifying the award the player won is superimposed at the lower right corner. The backs also have blue marbleized borders and carry player profile on a tan marbleized panel. A head shot of the player appears in a diamond at the upper right corner, with the words "Award Winners" on orange ribbons extending below the diamond. The cards are numbered on the back.

	MINT	EXC	G-VG
COMPLETE SET (25)	50.00	23.00	6.25
COMMON CARD (1-25)	.75	.35	.09

	MINT	EXC	G-VG
☐ 1 Jack Morris	1.00	.45	.13
☐ 2 Chuck Knoblauch	1.25	.55	.16
☐ 3 Jeff Bagwell	7.00	3.10	.85
☐ 4 Terry Pendleton	1.00	.45	.13
☐ 5 Cal Ripken	7.00	3.10	.85
☐ 6 Roger Clemens	4.00	1.80	.50
☐ 7 Tom Glavine	1.50	.65	.19
☐ 8 Tom Pagnozzi	.75	.35	.09
☐ 9 Ozzie Smith	2.50	1.15	.30
☐ 10 Andy Van Slyke	1.00	.45	.13
☐ 11 Barry Bonds	5.00	2.30	.60
☐ 12 Tony Gwynn	3.00	1.35	.40
☐ 13 Matt Williams	3.00	1.35	.40
☐ 14 Will Clark	3.00	1.35	.40
☐ 15 Robin Ventura	2.00	.90	.25
☐ 16 Mark Langston	1.00	.45	.13
☐ 17 Tony Pena	.75	.35	.09
☐ 18 Devon White	1.00	.45	.13
☐ 19 Don Mattingly	5.00	2.30	.60
☐ 20 Roberto Alomar	4.00	1.80	.50
☐ 21A Cal Ripken ERR (Reversed negative on card back)	6.00	2.70	.75
☐ 21B Cal Ripken COR	6.00	2.70	.75
☐ 22 Ken Griffey Jr.	15.00	6.75	1.90
☐ 23 Kirby Puckett	5.00	2.30	.60
☐ 24 Greg Maddux	3.00	1.35	.40
☐ 25 Ryne Sandberg	5.00	2.30	.60

1992 Ultra Tony Gwynn

Tony Gwynn served as a spokesperson for Fleer Ultra during 1992 and was the exclusive subject of this 12-card set. The first ten-card standard-size (2 1/2" by 3 1/2") series was randomly inserted in 1992 Fleer Ultra I packs. More than 2,000 of these cards were personaly autographed by Gwynn. The fronts display color posed and action shots of Gwynn framed by green marbled borders. The player's name and the words "Commemorative Series" appear

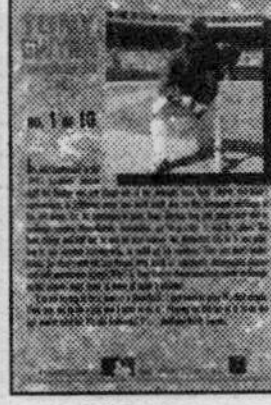

in gold-foil lettering in the bottom border. On a green marbled background, the backs features a color head shot, career summary, and highlights. These insert cards are numbered on the back "No. X of 10." An additional special two-card subset was available through a mail-in offer for ten 1992 Fleer Ultra baseball wrappers plus 1.00 for shipping and handling. This offer was good through October 31st and, according to Fleer, over 100,000 sets were produced. The standard-size (2 1/2" by 3 1/2") cards display action shots of Gwynn framed by green marbled borders. The player's name and the words "Commemorative Series" appear in gold-foil lettering in the bottom border. On a green marbled background, the backs features a color head shot and either a player profile (Special No. 1 on the card back) or Gwynn's comments about other players or the game itself (Special No. 2 on the card back).

	MINT	EXC	G-VG
COMPLETE SET (10)	10.00	4.50	1.25
COMMON GWYNN (1-10)	1.00	.45	.13
COMMON SEND-OFF (S1/S2)	1.00	.45	.13
☐ 1 Tony Gwynn (Leaping and catching ball at outfield wall)	1.00	.45	.13
☐ 2 Tony Gwynn (Batting stance, brown Padres' uniform)	1.00	.45	.13
☐ 3 Tony Gwynn (Awaiting flyball, glove above head)	1.00	.45	.13
☐ 4 Tony Gwynn (Follow-through on swing)	1.00	.45	.13
☐ 5 Tony Gwynn (Leading off base; crouching at the knees)	1.00	.45	.13
☐ 6 Tony Gwynn (Posed with silver bat and Gold Glove trophy)	1.00	.45	.13
☐ 7 Tony Gwynn (Bunting)	1.00	.45	.13
☐ 8 Tony Gwynn (Full body shot; swinging)	1.00	.45	.13
☐ 9 Tony Gwynn (Taking off for first)	1.00	.45	.13
☐ 10 Tony Gwynn (Batting, following through, sun glasses on)	1.00	.45	.13
☐ AU Tony Gwynn AU (Autographed with certified signature)	150.00	70.00	19.00
☐ S1 Tony Gwynn (Batting)	1.00	.45	.13
☐ S2 Tony Gwynn (Fielding)	1.00	.45	.13

1993 Ultra

The 1993 Ultra baseball set was issued in two series and totaled 650 cards. A ten-card Dennis Eckersley subset was randomly inserted in the foil packs. The full-bleed color-enhanced action photos are edged at the bottom by a gold foil stripe and a fawn-colored border that is streaked with white for a marbleized effect. On a dimensionalized ball park background, the horizontal backs have an action shot, a portrait, last season statistics, and the player's entire professional career totals. The cards are numbered on the back, grouped alphabetically within teams, and checklisted below alphabetically according to teams for the National and American Leagues as follows: Atlanta Braves (1-13), Chicago Cubs (14-25), Cincinnati Reds (26-36), Houston Astros (37-48), Los Angeles Dodgers (49-60), Montreal Expos (61-71), New York Mets (72-81), Philadelphia Phillies (82-94), Pittsburgh Pirates (95-105), St. Louis Cardinals (106-115), San Diego Padres (116-125), and San Francisco Giants (126-137), Baltimore Orioles (138-147), Boston Red Sox (148-158), California Angels (159-169), Chicago White Sox (170-181), Cleveland Indians (182-193), Detroit Tigers (194-204), Kansas City Royals (205-216), Milwaukee Brewers (217-227), Minnesota Twins (228-239), New York Yankees (240-252), Oakland Athletics (253-264), Seattle Mariners (265-275), Texas Rangers (276-285), and Toronto Blue Jays (286-297). The first series closes with checklist cards (298-300). The second series features 83 Ultra Rookies, 51 Rockies and Marlins, traded veteran players, and other major league veterans not included in the first series. The Rookie cards show a gold foil stamped Rookie "flag" as part of the card design. Randomly inserted in second series packs were a 20-card All-Stars subset, a ten-card All-Rookie Team subset, and a five-card Strikeout Kings subset. Rookie Cards in this set include Rene Arocha, Russ Davis, Greg McMichael, and J.T. Snow.

	MINT	EXC	G-VG
COMPLETE SET (650)	45.00	20.00	5.75
COMPLETE SERIES 1 (300)	20.00	9.00	2.50
COMPLETE SERIES 2 (350)	25.00	11.50	3.10
COMMON CARD (1-300)	.10	.05	.01
COMMON CARD (301-650)	.10	.05	.01

	MINT	EXC	G-VG
☐ 1 Steve Avery	.20	.09	.03
☐ 2 Rafael Belliard	.10	.05	.01
☐ 3 Damon Berryhill	.10	.05	.01
☐ 4 Sid Bream	.10	.05	.01
☐ 5 Ron Gant	.15	.07	.02
☐ 6 Tom Glavine	.20	.09	.03
☐ 7 Ryan Klesko	1.00	.45	.13
☐ 8 Mark Lemke	.10	.05	.01
☐ 9 Javy Lopez	.60	.25	.08
☐ 10 Greg Olson	.10	.05	.01
☐ 11 Terry Pendleton	.20	.09	.03
☐ 12 Deion Sanders	.50	.23	.06
☐ 13 Mike Stanton	.10	.05	.01
☐ 14 Paul Assenmacher	.10	.05	.01
☐ 15 Steve Buechele	.10	.05	.01
☐ 16 Frank Castillo	.10	.05	.01
☐ 17 Shawon Dunston	.10	.05	.01
☐ 18 Mark Grace	.20	.09	.03
☐ 19 Derrick May	.15	.07	.02
☐ 20 Chuck McElroy	.10	.05	.01
☐ 21 Mike Morgan	.10	.05	.01
☐ 22 Bob Scanlan	.10	.05	.01
☐ 23 Dwight Smith	.10	.05	.01
☐ 24 Sammy Sosa	.20	.09	.03
☐ 25 Rick Wilkins	.10	.05	.01
☐ 26 Tim Belcher	.10	.05	.01
☐ 27 Jeff Branson	.10	.05	.01
☐ 28 Bill Doran	.10	.05	.01
☐ 29 Chris Hammond	.10	.05	.01
☐ 30 Barry Larkin	.20	.09	.03
☐ 31 Hal Morris	.15	.07	.02
☐ 32 Joe Oliver	.10	.05	.01
☐ 33 Jose Rijo	.15	.07	.02
☐ 34 Bip Roberts	.10	.05	.01
☐ 35 Chris Sabo	.15	.07	.02
☐ 36 Reggie Sanders	.20	.09	.03
☐ 37 Craig Biggio	.15	.07	.02
☐ 38 Ken Caminiti	.15	.07	.02
☐ 39 Steve Finley	.10	.05	.01
☐ 40 Luis Gonzalez	.15	.07	.02
☐ 41 Juan Guerrero	.10	.05	.01
☐ 42 Pete Harnisch	.10	.05	.01
☐ 43 Xavier Hernandez	.10	.05	.01
☐ 44 Doug Jones	.10	.05	.01
☐ 45 Al Osuna	.10	.05	.01
☐ 46 Eddie Taubensee	.10	.05	.01
☐ 47 Scooter Tucker	.10	.05	.01
☐ 48 Brian Williams	.10	.05	.01
☐ 49 Pedro Astacio	.15	.07	.02
☐ 50 Rafael Bournigal	.15	.07	.02
☐ 51 Brett Butler	.15	.07	.02
☐ 52 Tom Candiotti	.10	.05	.01
☐ 53 Eric Davis	.10	.05	.01
☐ 54 Lenny Harris	.10	.05	.01
☐ 55 Orel Hershiser	.15	.07	.02
☐ 56 Eric Karros	.15	.07	.02
☐ 57 Pedro Martinez	.20	.09	.03
☐ 58 Roger McDowell	.10	.05	.01
☐ 59 Jose Offerman	.10	.05	.01
☐ 60 Mike Piazza	3.00	1.35	.40
☐ 61 Moises Alou	.20	.09	.03
☐ 62 Kent Bottenfield	.10	.05	.01
☐ 63 Archi Cianfrocco	.10	.05	.01
☐ 64 Greg Colbrunn	.10	.05	.01
☐ 65 Wil Cordero	.20	.09	.03
☐ 66 Delino DeShields	.15	.07	.02
☐ 67 Darrin Fletcher	.10	.05	.01
☐ 68 Ken Hill	.15	.07	.02
☐ 69 Chris Nabholz	.10	.05	.01
☐ 70 Mel Rojas	.10	.05	.01
☐ 71 Larry Walker	.20	.09	.03
☐ 72 Sid Fernandez	.10	.05	.01
☐ 73 John Franco	.10	.05	.01
☐ 74 Dave Gallagher	.10	.05	.01
☐ 75 Todd Hundley	.10	.05	.01
☐ 76 Howard Johnson	.10	.05	.01
☐ 77 Jeff Kent	.20	.09	.03
☐ 78 Eddie Murray	.20	.09	.03
☐ 79 Bret Saberhagen	.15	.07	.02
☐ 80 Chico Walker	.10	.05	.01
☐ 81 Anthony Young	.10	.05	.01
☐ 82 Kyle Abbott	.10	.05	.01
☐ 83 Ruben Amaro	.10	.05	.01
☐ 84 Juan Bell	.10	.05	.01
☐ 85 Wes Chamberlain	.10	.05	.01
☐ 86 Darren Daulton	.20	.09	.03
☐ 87 Mariano Duncan	.10	.05	.01
☐ 88 Dave Hollins	.20	.09	.03
☐ 89 Ricky Jordan	.10	.05	.01
☐ 90 John Kruk	.20	.09	.03
☐ 91 Mickey Morandini	.10	.05	.01
☐ 92 Terry Mulholland	.10	.05	.01
☐ 93 Ben Rivera	.10	.05	.01
☐ 94 Mike Williams	.10	.05	.01
☐ 95 Stan Belinda	.10	.05	.01
☐ 96 Jay Bell	.15	.07	.02
☐ 97 Jeff King	.10	.05	.01
☐ 98 Mike LaValliere	.10	.05	.01
☐ 99 Lloyd McClendon	.10	.05	.01
☐ 100 Orlando Merced	.15	.07	.02
☐ 101 Zane Smith	.10	.05	.01
☐ 102 Randy Tomlin	.10	.05	.01
☐ 103 Andy Van Slyke	.20	.09	.03
☐ 104 Tim Wakefield	.10	.05	.01
☐ 105 John Wehner	.10	.05	.01
☐ 106 Bernard Gilkey	.10	.05	.01
☐ 107 Brian Jordan	.15	.07	.02
☐ 108 Ray Lankford	.20	.09	.03
☐ 109 Donovan Osborne	.10	.05	.01
☐ 110 Tom Pagnozzi	.10	.05	.01
☐ 111 Mike Perez	.10	.05	.01
☐ 112 Lee Smith	.20	.09	.03
☐ 113 Ozzie Smith	.60	.25	.08
☐ 114 Bob Tewksbury	.10	.05	.01
☐ 115 Todd Zeile	.15	.07	.02
☐ 116 Andy Benes	.15	.07	.02
☐ 117 Greg W. Harris	.10	.05	.01
☐ 118 Darrin Jackson	.10	.05	.01
☐ 119 Fred McGriff	.40	.18	.05
☐ 120 Rich Rodriguez	.10	.05	.01
☐ 121 Frank Seminara	.10	.05	.01
☐ 122 Gary Sheffield	.20	.09	.03
☐ 123 Craig Shipley	.10	.05	.01
☐ 124 Kurt Stillwell	.10	.05	.01
☐ 125 Dan Walters	.10	.05	.01
☐ 126 Rod Beck	.20	.09	.03
☐ 127 Mike Benjamin	.10	.05	.01
☐ 128 Jeff Brantley	.10	.05	.01
☐ 129 John Burkett	.15	.07	.02
☐ 130 Will Clark	.40	.18	.05
☐ 131 Royce Clayton	.15	.07	.02
☐ 132 Steve Hosey	.10	.05	.01
☐ 133 Mike Jackson	.10	.05	.01
☐ 134 Darren Lewis	.10	.05	.01
☐ 135 Kirt Manwaring	.10	.05	.01
☐ 136 Bill Swift	.15	.07	.02
☐ 137 Robby Thompson	.10	.05	.01
☐ 138 Brady Anderson	.15	.07	.02
☐ 139 Glenn Davis	.10	.05	.01

☐ 140	Leo Gomez	.10	.05	.01
☐ 141	Chito Martinez	.10	.05	.01
☐ 142	Ben McDonald	.15	.07	.02
☐ 143	Alan Mills	.10	.05	.01
☐ 144	Mike Mussina	.60	.25	.08
☐ 145	Gregg Olson	.10	.05	.01
☐ 146	David Segui	.10	.05	.01
☐ 147	Jeff Tackett	.10	.05	.01
☐ 148	Jack Clark	.10	.05	.01
☐ 149	Scott Cooper	.15	.07	.02
☐ 150	Danny Darwin	.10	.05	.01
☐ 151	John Dopson	.10	.05	.01
☐ 152	Mike Greenwell	.15	.07	.02
☐ 153	Tim Naehring	.10	.05	.01
☐ 154	Tony Pena	.10	.05	.01
☐ 155	Paul Quantrill	.10	.05	.01
☐ 156	Mo Vaughn	.20	.09	.03
☐ 157	Frank Viola	.15	.07	.02
☐ 158	Bob Zupcic	.10	.05	.01
☐ 159	Chad Curtis	.15	.07	.02
☐ 160	Gary DiSarcina	.10	.05	.01
☐ 161	Damion Easley	.15	.07	.02
☐ 162	Chuck Finley	.10	.05	.01
☐ 163	Tim Fortugno	.10	.05	.01
☐ 164	Rene Gonzales	.10	.05	.01
☐ 165	Joe Grahe	.10	.05	.01
☐ 166	Mark Langston	.20	.09	.03
☐ 167	John Orton	.10	.05	.01
☐ 168	Luis Polonia	.10	.05	.01
☐ 169	Julio Valera	.10	.05	.01
☐ 170	Wilson Alvarez	.20	.09	.03
☐ 171	George Bell	.15	.07	.02
☐ 172	Joey Cora	.10	.05	.01
☐ 173	Alex Fernandez	.20	.09	.03
☐ 174	Lance Johnson	.10	.05	.01
☐ 175	Ron Karkovice	.10	.05	.01
☐ 176	Jack McDowell	.20	.09	.03
☐ 177	Scott Radinsky	.10	.05	.01
☐ 178	Tim Raines	.20	.09	.03
☐ 179	Steve Sax	.10	.05	.01
☐ 180	Bobby Thigpen	.10	.05	.01
☐ 181	Frank Thomas	3.00	1.35	.40
☐ 182	Sandy Alomar	.15	.07	.02
☐ 183	Carlos Baerga	.40	.18	.05
☐ 184	Felix Fermin	.10	.05	.01
☐ 185	Thomas Howard	.10	.05	.01
☐ 186	Mark Lewis	.10	.05	.01
☐ 187	Derek Lilliquist	.10	.05	.01
☐ 188	Carlos Martinez	.10	.05	.01
☐ 189	Charles Nagy	.10	.05	.01
☐ 190	Scott Scudder	.10	.05	.01
☐ 191	Paul Sorrento	.10	.05	.01
☐ 192	Jim Thome	.40	.18	.05
☐ 193	Mark Whiten	.15	.07	.02
☐ 194	Milt Cuyler UER (Reversed negative on card front)	.10	.05	.01
☐ 195	Rob Deer	.10	.05	.01
☐ 196	John Doherty	.10	.05	.01
☐ 197	Travis Fryman	.25	.11	.03
☐ 198	Dan Gladden	.10	.05	.01
☐ 199	Mike Henneman	.10	.05	.01
☐ 200	John Kiely	.10	.05	.01
☐ 201	Chad Kreuter	.10	.05	.01
☐ 202	Scott Livingstone	.10	.05	.01
☐ 203	Tony Phillips	.10	.05	.01
☐ 204	Alan Trammell	.20	.09	.03
☐ 205	Mike Boddicker	.10	.05	.01
☐ 206	George Brett	1.25	.55	.16
☐ 207	Tom Gordon	.10	.05	.01
☐ 208	Mark Gubicza	.10	.05	.01
☐ 209	Gregg Jefferies	.20	.09	.03
☐ 210	Wally Joyner	.15	.07	.02
☐ 211	Kevin Koslofski	.10	.05	.01
☐ 212	Brent Mayne	.10	.05	.01
☐ 213	Brian McRae	.20	.09	.03
☐ 214	Kevin McReynolds	.10	.05	.01
☐ 215	Rusty Meacham	.10	.05	.01
☐ 216	Steve Shifflett	.10	.05	.01
☐ 217	James Austin	.10	.05	.01
☐ 218	Cal Eldred	.15	.07	.02
☐ 219	Darryl Hamilton	.10	.05	.01
☐ 220	Doug Henry	.10	.05	.01
☐ 221	John Jaha	.15	.07	.02
☐ 222	Dave Nilsson	.15	.07	.02
☐ 223	Jesse Orosco	.10	.05	.01
☐ 224	B.J. Surhoff	.10	.05	.01
☐ 225	Greg Vaughn	.15	.07	.02
☐ 226	Bill Wegman	.10	.05	.01
☐ 227	Robin Yount UER (Born in Illinois, not in Virginia)	.40	.18	.05
☐ 228	Rick Aguilera	.15	.07	.02
☐ 229	J.T. Bruett	.10	.05	.01
☐ 230	Scott Erickson	.10	.05	.01
☐ 231	Kent Hrbek	.15	.07	.02
☐ 232	Terry Jorgensen	.10	.05	.01
☐ 233	Scott Leius	.10	.05	.01
☐ 234	Pat Mahomes	.10	.05	.01
☐ 235	Pedro Munoz	.10	.05	.01
☐ 236	Kirby Puckett	1.25	.55	.16
☐ 237	Kevin Tapani	.10	.05	.01
☐ 238	Lenny Webster	.10	.05	.01
☐ 239	Carl Willis	.10	.05	.01
☐ 240	Mike Gallego	.10	.05	.01
☐ 241	John Habyan	.10	.05	.01
☐ 242	Pat Kelly	.10	.05	.01
☐ 243	Kevin Maas	.10	.05	.01
☐ 244	Don Mattingly	1.25	.55	.16
☐ 245	Hensley Meulens	.10	.05	.01
☐ 246	Sam Militello	.10	.05	.01
☐ 247	Matt Nokes	.10	.05	.01
☐ 248	Melido Perez	.10	.05	.01
☐ 249	Andy Stankiewicz	.10	.05	.01
☐ 250	Randy Velarde	.10	.05	.01
☐ 251	Bob Wickman	.10	.05	.01
☐ 252	Bernie Williams	.15	.07	.02
☐ 253	Lance Blankenship	.10	.05	.01
☐ 254	Mike Bordick	.10	.05	.01
☐ 255	Jerry Browne	.10	.05	.01
☐ 256	Ron Darling	.10	.05	.01
☐ 257	Dennis Eckersley	.20	.09	.03
☐ 258	Rickey Henderson	.20	.09	.03
☐ 259	Vince Horsman	.10	.05	.01
☐ 260	Troy Neel	.15	.07	.02
☐ 261	Jeff Parrett	.10	.05	.01
☐ 262	Terry Steinbach	.15	.07	.02
☐ 263	Bob Welch	.10	.05	.01
☐ 264	Bobby Witt	.10	.05	.01
☐ 265	Rich Amaral	.10	.05	.01
☐ 266	Bret Boone	.20	.09	.03
☐ 267	Jay Buhner	.15	.07	.02
☐ 268	Dave Fleming	.15	.07	.02
☐ 269	Randy Johnson	.20	.09	.03
☐ 270	Edgar Martinez	.10	.05	.01
☐ 271	Mike Schooler	.10	.05	.01
☐ 272	Russ Swan	.10	.05	.01
☐ 273	Dave Valle	.10	.05	.01
☐ 274	Omar Vizquel	.10	.05	.01
☐ 275	Kerry Woodson	.10	.05	.01
☐ 276	Kevin Brown	.10	.05	.01
☐ 277	Julio Franco	.15	.07	.02
☐ 278	Jeff Frye	.10	.05	.01
☐ 279	Juan Gonzalez	1.00	.45	.13
☐ 280	Jeff Huson	.10	.05	.01
☐ 281	Rafael Palmeiro	.20	.09	.03

	No.	Player			
☐	282	Dean Palmer	.15	.07	.02
☐	283	Roger Pavlik	.15	.07	.02
☐	284	Ivan Rodriguez	.20	.09	.03
☐	285	Kenny Rogers	.10	.05	.01
☐	286	Derek Bell	.15	.07	.02
☐	287	Pat Borders	.10	.05	.01
☐	288	Joe Carter	.40	.18	.05
☐	289	Bob MacDonald	.10	.05	.01
☐	290	Jack Morris	.20	.09	.03
☐	291	John Olerud	.20	.09	.03
☐	292	Ed Sprague	.10	.05	.01
☐	293	Todd Stottlemyre	.10	.05	.01
☐	294	Mike Timlin	.10	.05	.01
☐	295	Duane Ward	.15	.07	.02
☐	296	David Wells	.10	.05	.01
☐	297	Devon White	.15	.07	.02
☐	298	Checklist 1-94 Ray Lankford	.10	.05	.01
☐	299	Checklist 95-193 Bobby Witt	.10	.05	.01
☐	300	Checklist 194-300 Mike Piazza	.20	.09	.03
☐	301	Steve Bedrosian	.10	.05	.01
☐	302	Jeff Blauser	.15	.07	.02
☐	303	Francisco Cabrera	.10	.05	.01
☐	304	Marvin Freeman	.10	.05	.01
☐	305	Brian Hunter	.10	.05	.01
☐	306	David Justice	.40	.18	.05
☐	307	Greg Maddux	.75	.35	.09
☐	308	Greg McMichael	.20	.09	.03
☐	309	Kent Mercker	.10	.05	.01
☐	310	Otis Nixon	.10	.05	.01
☐	311	Pete Smith	.10	.05	.01
☐	312	John Smoltz	.15	.07	.02
☐	313	Jose Guzman	.10	.05	.01
☐	314	Mike Harkey	.10	.05	.01
☐	315	Greg Hibbard	.10	.05	.01
☐	316	Candy Maldonado	.10	.05	.01
☐	317	Randy Myers	.15	.07	.02
☐	318	Dan Plesac	.10	.05	.01
☐	319	Rey Sanchez	.10	.05	.01
☐	320	Ryne Sandberg	1.00	.45	.13
☐	321	Tommy Shields	.15	.07	.02
☐	322	Jose Vizcaino	.10	.05	.01
☐	323	Matt Walbeck	.10	.05	.01
☐	324	Willie Wilson	.10	.05	.01
☐	325	Tom Browning	.10	.05	.01
☐	326	Tim Costo	.10	.05	.01
☐	327	Rob Dibble	.10	.05	.01
☐	328	Steve Foster	.10	.05	.01
☐	329	Roberto Kelly	.15	.07	.02
☐	330	Randy Milligan	.10	.05	.01
☐	331	Kevin Mitchell	.15	.07	.02
☐	332	Tim Pugh	.10	.05	.01
☐	333	Jeff Reardon	.15	.07	.02
☐	334	John Roper	.15	.07	.02
☐	335	Juan Samuel	.10	.05	.01
☐	336	John Smiley	.10	.05	.01
☐	337	Dan Wilson	.10	.05	.01
☐	338	Scott Aldred	.10	.05	.01
☐	339	Andy Ashby	.10	.05	.01
☐	340	Freddie Benavides	.10	.05	.01
☐	341	Dante Bichette	.20	.09	.03
☐	342	Willie Blair	.10	.05	.01
☐	343	Daryl Boston	.10	.05	.01
☐	344	Vinny Castilla	.10	.05	.01
☐	345	Jerald Clark	.10	.05	.01
☐	346	Alex Cole	.10	.05	.01
☐	347	Andres Galarraga	.20	.09	.03
☐	348	Joe Girardi	.10	.05	.01
☐	349	Ryan Hawblitzel	.10	.05	.01
☐	350	Charlie Hayes	.15	.07	.02
☐	351	Butch Henry	.10	.05	.01
☐	352	Darren Holmes	.10	.05	.01
☐	353	Dale Murphy	.20	.09	.03
☐	354	David Nied	.20	.09	.03
☐	355	Jeff Parrett	.10	.05	.01
☐	356	Steve Reed	.15	.07	.02
☐	357	Bruce Ruffin	.10	.05	.01
☐	358	Danny Sheaffer	.10	.05	.01
☐	359	Bryn Smith	.10	.05	.01
☐	360	Jim Tatum	.10	.05	.01
☐	361	Eric Young	.15	.07	.02
☐	362	Gerald Young	.10	.05	.01
☐	363	Luis Aquino	.10	.05	.01
☐	364	Alex Arias	.10	.05	.01
☐	365	Jack Armstrong	.10	.05	.01
☐	366	Bret Barberie	.10	.05	.01
☐	367	Ryan Bowen	.10	.05	.01
☐	368	Greg Briley	.10	.05	.01
☐	369	Cris Carpenter	.10	.05	.01
☐	370	Chuck Carr	.10	.05	.01
☐	371	Jeff Conine	.20	.09	.03
☐	372	Steve Decker	.10	.05	.01
☐	373	Orestes Destrade	.10	.05	.01
☐	374	Monty Fariss	.10	.05	.01
☐	375	Junior Felix	.10	.05	.01
☐	376	Chris Hammond	.10	.05	.01
☐	377	Bryan Harvey	.15	.07	.02
☐	378	Trevor Hoffman	.10	.05	.01
☐	379	Charlie Hough	.15	.07	.02
☐	380	Joe Klink	.10	.05	.01
☐	381	Richie Lewis	.10	.05	.01
☐	382	Dave Magadan	.10	.05	.01
☐	383	Bob McClure	.10	.05	.01
☐	384	Scott Pose	.10	.05	.01
☐	385	Rich Renteria	.10	.05	.01
☐	386	Benito Santiago	.10	.05	.01
☐	387	Walt Weiss	.10	.05	.01
☐	388	Nigel Wilson	.20	.09	.03
☐	389	Eric Anthony	.10	.05	.01
☐	390	Jeff Bagwell	1.50	.65	.19
☐	391	Andujar Cedeno	.15	.07	.02
☐	392	Doug Drabek	.20	.09	.03
☐	393	Darryl Kile	.15	.07	.02
☐	394	Mark Portugal	.10	.05	.01
☐	395	Karl Rhodes	.10	.05	.01
☐	396	Scott Servais	.10	.05	.01
☐	397	Greg Swindell	.10	.05	.01
☐	398	Tom Goodwin	.10	.05	.01
☐	399	Kevin Gross	.10	.05	.01
☐	400	Carlos Hernandez	.10	.05	.01
☐	401	Ramon Martinez	.15	.07	.02
☐	402	Raul Mondesi	2.00	.90	.25
☐	403	Jody Reed	.10	.05	.01
☐	404	Mike Sharperson	.10	.05	.01
☐	405	Cory Snyder	.10	.05	.01
☐	406	Darryl Strawberry	.15	.07	.02
☐	407	Rick Trlicek	.10	.05	.01
☐	408	Tim Wallach	.10	.05	.01
☐	409	Todd Worrell	.10	.05	.01
☐	410	Tavo Alvarez	.10	.05	.01
☐	411	Sean Berry	.10	.05	.01
☐	412	Frank Bolick	.10	.05	.01
☐	413	Cliff Floyd	1.00	.45	.13
☐	414	Mike Gardiner	.10	.05	.01
☐	415	Marquis Grissom	.20	.09	.03
☐	416	Tim Laker	.10	.05	.01
☐	417	Mike Lansing	.30	.14	[illegible]
☐	418	Dennis Martinez	.15	.07	[illegible]
☐	419	John Vander Wal	.10	.05	[illegible]
☐	420	John Wetteland	.10	.05	[illegible]
☐	421	Rondell White	.60	[illegible]	[illegible]
☐	422	Bobby Bonilla	.20	[illegible]	[illegible]
☐	423	Jeromy Burnitz	.15	[illegible]	[illegible]
☐	424	Vince Coleman	.10	[illegible]	[illegible]

No.	Player			
☐ 425	Mike Draper	.10	.05	.01
☐ 426	Tony Fernandez	.10	.05	.01
☐ 427	Dwight Gooden	.10	.05	.01
☐ 428	Jeff Innis	.10	.05	.01
☐ 429	Bobby Jones	.40	.18	.05
☐ 430	Mike Maddux	.10	.05	.01
☐ 431	Charlie O'Brien	.10	.05	.01
☐ 432	Joe Orsulak	.10	.05	.01
☐ 433	Pete Schourek	.10	.05	.01
☐ 434	Frank Tanana	.10	.05	.01
☐ 435	Ryan Thompson	.20	.09	.03
☐ 436	Kim Batiste	.10	.05	.01
☐ 437	Mark Davis	.10	.05	.01
☐ 438	Jose DeLeon	.10	.05	.01
☐ 439	Len Dykstra	.20	.09	.03
☐ 440	Jim Eisenreich	.10	.05	.01
☐ 441	Tommy Greene	.15	.07	.02
☐ 442	Pete Incaviglia	.10	.05	.01
☐ 443	Danny Jackson	.10	.05	.01
☐ 444	Todd Pratt	.10	.05	.01
☐ 445	Curt Schilling	.15	.07	.02
☐ 446	Milt Thompson	.10	.05	.01
☐ 447	David West	.10	.05	.01
☐ 448	Mitch Williams	.15	.07	.02
☐ 449	Steve Cooke	.10	.05	.01
☐ 450	Carlos Garcia	.15	.07	.02
☐ 451	Al Martin	.15	.07	.02
☐ 452	Blas Minor	.10	.05	.01
☐ 453	Dennis Moeller	.10	.05	.01
☐ 454	Denny Neagle	.10	.05	.01
☐ 455	Don Slaught	.10	.05	.01
☐ 456	Lonnie Smith	.10	.05	.01
☐ 457	Paul Wagner	.10	.05	.01
☐ 458	Bob Walk	.10	.05	.01
☐ 459	Kevin Young	.10	.05	.01
☐ 460	Rene Arocha	.20	.09	.03
☐ 461	Brian Barber	.15	.07	.02
☐ 462	Rheal Cormier	.10	.05	.01
☐ 463	Gregg Jefferies	.20	.09	.03
☐ 464	Joe Magrane	.10	.05	.01
☐ 465	Omar Olivares	.10	.05	.01
☐ 466	Geronimo Pena	.10	.05	.01
☐ 467	Allen Watson	.10	.05	.01
☐ 468	Mark Whiten	.15	.07	.02
☐ 469	Derek Bell	.15	.07	.02
☐ 470	Phil Clark	.10	.05	.01
☐ 471	Pat Gomez	.10	.05	.01
☐ 472	Tony Gwynn	.75	.35	.09
☐ 473	Jeremy Hernandez	.10	.05	.01
☐ 474	Bruce Hurst	.10	.05	.01
☐ 475	Phil Plantier	.20	.09	.03
☐ 476	Scott Sanders	.40	.18	.05
☐ 477	Tim Scott	.10	.05	.01
☐ 478	Darrell Sherman	.10	.05	.01
☐ 479	Guillermo Velasquez	.10	.05	.01
☐ 480	Tim Worrell	.10	.05	.01
☐ 481	Todd Benzinger	.10	.05	.01
☐ 482	Bud Black	.10	.05	.01
☐ 483	Barry Bonds	1.25	.55	.16
☐ 484	Dave Burba	.10	.05	.01
☐ 485	Bryan Hickerson	.10	.05	.01
☐ 486	Dave Martinez	.10	.05	.01
[illegible]	[illegible]	.15	.07	.02
[illegible]	[illegible]	.10	.05	.01
[illegible]	[illegible]	.10	.05	.01
[illegible]	[illegible]	.50	.23	.06
[illegible]	[illegible]	.10	.05	.01
[illegible]	[illegible]	.15	.07	.02
[illegible]	[illegible]	.15	.07	.02
[illegible]	[illegible]	.10	.05	.01
[illegible]	[illegible]	.15	.07	.02
[illegible]	[illegible]	.10	.05	.01
[illegible]	[illegible]	.20	.09	.03
☐ 498	Brad Pennington	.10	.05	.01
☐ 499	Harold Reynolds	.10	.05	.01
☐ 500	Arthur Rhodes	.10	.05	.01
☐ 501	Cal Ripken	2.25	1.00	.30
☐ 502	Rick Sutcliffe	.15	.07	.02
☐ 503	Fernando Valenzuela	.10	.05	.01
☐ 504	Mark Williamson	.10	.05	.01
☐ 505	Scott Bankhead	.10	.05	.01
☐ 506	Greg Blosser	.10	.05	.01
☐ 507	Ivan Calderon	.10	.05	.01
☐ 508	Roger Clemens	.75	.35	.09
☐ 509	Andre Dawson	.20	.09	.03
☐ 510	Scott Fletcher	.10	.05	.01
☐ 511	Greg A. Harris	.10	.05	.01
☐ 512	Billy Hatcher	.10	.05	.01
☐ 513	Bob Melvin	.10	.05	.01
☐ 514	Carlos Quintana	.10	.05	.01
☐ 515	Luis Rivera	.10	.05	.01
☐ 516	Jeff Russell	.10	.05	.01
☐ 517	Ken Ryan	.30	.14	.04
☐ 518	Chili Davis	.15	.07	.02
☐ 519	Jim Edmonds	.40	.18	.05
☐ 520	Gary Gaetti	.10	.05	.01
☐ 521	Torey Lovullo	.10	.05	.01
☐ 522	Troy Percival	.10	.05	.01
☐ 523	Tim Salmon	.50	.23	.06
☐ 524	Scott Sanderson	.10	.05	.01
☐ 525	J.T. Snow	.15	.07	.02
☐ 526	Jerome Walton	.10	.05	.01
☐ 527	Jason Bere	.75	.35	.09
☐ 528	Rod Bolton	.10	.05	.01
☐ 529	Ellis Burks	.15	.07	.02
☐ 530	Carlton Fisk	.20	.09	.03
☐ 531	Craig Grebeck	.10	.05	.01
☐ 532	Ozzie Guillen	.10	.05	.01
☐ 533	Roberto Hernandez	.10	.05	.01
☐ 534	Bo Jackson	.20	.09	.03
☐ 535	Kirk McCaskill	.10	.05	.01
☐ 536	Dave Stieb	.10	.05	.01
☐ 537	Robin Ventura	.20	.09	.03
☐ 538	Albert Belle	1.00	.45	.13
☐ 539	Mike Bielecki	.10	.05	.01
☐ 540	Glenallen Hill	.10	.05	.01
☐ 541	Reggie Jefferson	.10	.05	.01
☐ 542	Kenny Lofton	.75	.35	.09
☐ 543	Jeff Mutis	.10	.05	.01
☐ 544	Junior Ortiz	.10	.05	.01
☐ 545	Manny Ramirez	1.25	.55	.16
☐ 546	Jeff Treadway	.10	.05	.01
☐ 547	Kevin Wickander	.10	.05	.01
☐ 548	Cecil Fielder	.20	.09	.03
☐ 549	Kirk Gibson	.15	.07	.02
☐ 550	Greg Gohr	.10	.05	.01
☐ 551	David Haas	.10	.05	.01
☐ 552	Bill Krueger	.10	.05	.01
☐ 553	Mike Moore	.10	.05	.01
☐ 554	Mickey Tettleton	.15	.07	.02
☐ 555	Lou Whitaker	.20	.09	.03
☐ 556	Kevin Appier	.15	.07	.02
☐ 557	Billy Brewer	.15	.07	.02
☐ 558	David Cone	.20	.09	.03
☐ 559	Greg Gagne	.10	.05	.01
☐ 560	Mark Gardner	.10	.05	.01
☐ 561	Phil Hiatt	.10	.05	.01
☐ 562	Felix Jose	.10	.05	.01
☐ 563	Jose Lind	.10	.05	.01
☐ 564	Mike Macfarlane	.10	.05	.01
☐ 565	Keith Miller	.10	.05	.01
☐ 566	Jeff Montgomery	.15	.07	.02
☐ 567	Hipolito Pichardo	.10	.05	.01
☐ 568	Ricky Bones	.10	.05	.01
☐ 569	Tom Brunansky	.10	.05	.01
☐ 570	Joe Kmak	.10	.05	.01

	No.	Player	MINT	EXC	G-VG
☐	571	Pat Listach	.15	.07	.02
☐	572	Graeme Lloyd	.10	.05	.01
☐	573	Carlos Maldonado	.10	.05	.01
☐	574	Josias Manzanillo	.10	.05	.01
☐	575	Matt Mieske	.15	.07	.02
☐	576	Kevin Reimer	.10	.05	.01
☐	577	Bill Spiers	.10	.05	.01
☐	578	Dickie Thon	.10	.05	.01
☐	579	Willie Banks	.10	.05	.01
☐	580	Jim Deshaies	.10	.05	.01
☐	581	Mark Guthrie	.10	.05	.01
☐	582	Brian Harper	.10	.05	.01
☐	583	Chuck Knoblauch	.20	.09	.03
☐	584	Gene Larkin	.10	.05	.01
☐	585	Shane Mack	.15	.07	.02
☐	586	David McCarty	.15	.07	.02
☐	587	Mike Pagliarulo	.10	.05	.01
☐	588	Mike Trombley	.10	.05	.01
☐	589	Dave Winfield	.20	.09	.03
☐	590	Jim Abbott	.20	.09	.03
☐	591	Wade Boggs	.20	.09	.03
☐	592	Russ Davis	.40	.18	.05
☐	593	Steve Farr	.10	.05	.01
☐	594	Steve Howe	.10	.05	.01
☐	595	Mike Humphreys	.10	.05	.01
☐	596	Jimmy Key	.15	.07	.02
☐	597	Jim Leyritz	.10	.05	.01
☐	598	Bobby Munoz	.10	.05	.01
☐	599	Paul O'Neill	.15	.07	.02
☐	600	Spike Owen	.10	.05	.01
☐	601	Mike Stanley	.10	.05	.01
☐	602	Danny Tartabull	.15	.07	.02
☐	603	Scott Brosius	.10	.05	.01
☐	604	Storm Davis	.10	.05	.01
☐	605	Eric Fox	.10	.05	.01
☐	606	Rich Gossage	.20	.09	.03
☐	607	Scott Hemond	.10	.05	.01
☐	608	Dave Henderson	.10	.05	.01
☐	609	Mark McGwire	.20	.09	.03
☐	610	Mike Mohler	.10	.05	.01
☐	611	Edwin Nunez	.10	.05	.01
☐	612	Kevin Seitzer	.10	.05	.01
☐	613	Ruben Sierra	.20	.09	.03
☐	614	Chris Bosio	.10	.05	.01
☐	615	Norm Charlton	.10	.05	.01
☐	616	Jim Converse	.15	.07	.02
☐	617	John Cummings	.10	.05	.01
☐	618	Mike Felder	.10	.05	.01
☐	619	Ken Griffey Jr.	3.00	1.35	.40
☐	620	Mike Hampton	.10	.05	.01
☐	621	Erik Hanson	.10	.05	.01
☐	622	Bill Haselman	.10	.05	.01
☐	623	Tino Martinez	.15	.07	.02
☐	624	Lee Tinsley	.10	.05	.01
☐	625	Fernando Vina	.10	.05	.01
☐	626	David Wainhouse	.10	.05	.01
☐	627	Jose Canseco	.40	.18	.05
☐	628	Benji Gil	.15	.07	.02
☐	629	Tom Henke	.15	.07	.02
☐	630	David Hulse	.10	.05	.01
☐	631	Manny Lee	.10	.05	.01
☐	632	Craig Lefferts	.10	.05	.01
☐	633	Robb Nen	.10	.05	.01
☐	634	Gary Redus	.10	.05	.01
☐	635	Bill Ripken	.10	.05	.01
☐	636	Nolan Ryan	3.00	1.35	.40
☐	637	Dan Smith	.10	.05	.01
☐	638	Matt Whiteside	.10	.05	.01
☐	639	Roberto Alomar	.75	.35	.09
☐	640	Juan Guzman	.15	.07	.02
☐	641	Pat Hentgen	.15	.07	.02
☐	642	Darrin Jackson	.10	.05	.01
☐	643	Randy Knorr	.10	.05	.01
☐	644	Domingo Martinez	.10	.05	.01
☐	645	Paul Molitor	.40	.18	.05
☐	646	Dick Schofield	.10	.05	.01
☐	647	Dave Stewart	.15	.07	.02
☐	648	Checklist 301-421 Rey Sanchez	.10	.05	.01
☐	649	Checklist 422-537 Jeremy Hernandez	.10	.05	.01
☐	650	Checklist 538-650 Junior Ortiz	.10	.05	.01

1993 Ultra All-Rookies

Randomly inserted into series II packs, this ten-card standard-size (2 1/2" by 3 1/2") set features cutout color player action shots that are superposed upon a black background, which carries the player's uniform number, position, team name, and the set's title in multicolored lettering. The player's name appears in gold foil at the bottom. A posed color cutout player shot adorns the back, and is also projected upon a black background. The set's title appears at the top printed in gold foil and red lettering, and the player's name in gold foil precedes his career highlights, printed in white. The cards are numbered on the back in gold foil. The key cards in this set are Mike Piazza and Tim Salmon.

	MINT	EXC	G-VG
COMPLETE SET (10)	18.00	8.00	2.30
COMMON CARD (1-10)	.60	.25	.08

	No.	Player	MINT	EXC	G-VG
☐	1	Rene Arocha	.60	.25	.08
☐	2	Jeff Conine	1.25	.55	.16
☐	3	Phil Hiatt	.60	.25	.08
☐	4	Mike Lansing	.60	.25	.08
☐	5	Al Martin	.60	.25	.08
☐	6	David Nied	.60	.25	.08
☐	7	Mike Piazza	12.00	5.50	1.50
☐	8	Tim Salmon	3.50	1.55	.45
☐	9	J.T. Snow	.60	.25	.08
☐	10	Kevin Young	.60	.25	.08

1993 Ultra All-Stars

Randomly inserted into series II packs, this 20-card subset features National League (1-10) and American League (11-20) All-Stars. The gray-bordered fronts carry color

player action shots that are cutout and superposed upon their original, but faded and shifted, backgrounds. The player's name and the set's title are printed in gold foil upon simulated flames that issue from a baseball icon in the lower right. That same design of the player's name, the set's title, and flaming baseball icon appears again at the top of the gray-bordered back. The player's career highlights follow below. The cards are numbered on the back in gold foil.

	MINT	EXC	G-VG
COMPLETE SET (20)	50.00	23.00	6.25
COMMON CARD (1-20)	.60	.25	.08
□ 1 Darren Daulton	1.00	.45	.13
□ 2 Will Clark	2.25	1.00	.30
□ 3 Ryne Sandberg	5.00	2.30	.60
□ 4 Barry Larkin	1.00	.45	.13
□ 5 Gary Sheffield	1.00	.45	.13
□ 6 Barry Bonds	6.00	2.70	.75
□ 7 Ray Lankford	1.00	.45	.13
□ 8 Larry Walker	1.00	.45	.13
□ 9 Greg Maddux	4.00	1.80	.50
□ 10 Lee Smith	1.00	.45	.13
□ 11 Ivan Rodriguez	1.00	.45	.13
□ 12 Mark McGwire	.60	.25	.08
□ 13 Carlos Baerga	2.25	1.00	.30
□ 14 Cal Ripken	12.00	5.50	1.50
□ 15 Edgar Martinez	.60	.25	.08
□ 16 Juan Gonzalez	5.00	2.30	.60
□ 17 Ken Griffey Jr.	15.00	6.75	1.90
□ 18 Kirby Puckett	6.00	2.70	.75
□ 19 Frank Thomas	15.00	6.75	1.90
□ 20 Mike Mussina	3.00	1.35	.40

1993 Ultra Award Winners

Randomly inserted in first series packs, this first series of 1993 Ultra Award Winners presents the Top Glove for the National (1-9) and American (10-18) Leagues and other major league award winners (19-25). The 25 standard-size (2 1/2" by 3 1/2") cards comprising this set feature horizontal black-marbleized card designs and carry two color player photos: an action shot on the left and a posed photo on the right. The player's name appears in gold-foil cursive lettering near the bottom left. The category of award is shown in gold foil below. A gold-foil line highlights the card's lower edge. The horizontal and black-marbleized design continues on the back. A color player head shot appears on the left side. The player's name reappears in gold-foil cursive lettering near the top. Below is the player's award category in gold foil above a gold-foil underline. The player's career highlights are shown in white lettering below. The cards are numbered on the back.

	MINT	EXC	G-VG
COMPLETE SET (25)	40.00	18.00	5.00
COMMON CARD (1-25)	.60	.25	.08
□ 1 Greg Maddux	4.00	1.80	.50
□ 2 Tom Pagnozzi	.60	.25	.08
□ 3 Mark Grace	1.00	.45	.13
□ 4 Jose Lind	.60	.25	.08
□ 5 Terry Pendleton	.60	.25	.08
□ 6 Ozzie Smith	3.00	1.35	.40
□ 7 Barry Bonds	6.00	2.70	.75
□ 8 Andy Van Slyke	.60	.25	.08
□ 9 Larry Walker	1.00	.45	.13
□ 10 Mark Langston	.60	.25	.08
□ 11 Ivan Rodriguez	1.00	.45	.13
□ 12 Don Mattingly	6.00	2.70	.75
□ 13 Roberto Alomar	4.00	1.80	.50
□ 14 Robin Ventura	1.00	.45	.13
□ 15 Cal Ripken	12.00	5.50	1.50
□ 16 Ken Griffey Jr.	15.00	6.75	1.90
□ 17 Kirby Puckett	6.00	2.70	.75
□ 18 Devon White	1.00	.45	.13
□ 19 Pat Listach AL ROY	.60	.25	.08
□ 20 Eric Karros NL ROY	.60	.25	.08
□ 21 Pat Borders World Series MVP	.60	.25	.08
□ 22 Greg Maddux NL Cy Young	4.00	1.80	.50
□ 23 Dennis Eckersley AL MVP and Cy Young	1.00	.45	.13
□ 24 Barry Bonds NL MVP	6.00	2.70	.75
□ 25 Gary Sheffield Ultra POY	1.00	.45	.13

1993 Ultra Dennis Eckersley

Randomly inserted in first series foil packs, this 12-card (cards 11 and 12 were mail-aways) set salutes one of baseball's

greatest relief pitchers, Dennis Eckersley. The cards measure the standard size (2 1/2" by 3 1/2"). The color action player photos on the fronts are full-bleed except at the bottom where a black marbleized border carries the team and years in silver foil lettering. A silver foil "Dennis Eckersley Career Highlights" emblem rounds out the front. On the back, a full-bleed color photo provides the background for a transparent pastel purple panel presenting career highlights in silver foil lettering. The cards are numbered on the back. Two additional cards (11 and 12) were available through a mail-in offer for ten 1993 Fleer Ultra baseball wrappers plus 1.00 for postage and handling. Eckersley personally autographed more than 2,000 of these cards. The cards feature silver foil stamping on both sides.

	MINT	EXC	G-VG
COMPLETE SET (10)	6.00	2.70	.75
COMMON ECK (1-10)	.75	.35	.09
COMMON SEND-OFF (11-12)	2.00	.90	.25
☐ 1 Dennis Eckersley Perfection	.75	.35	.09
☐ 2 Dennis Eckersley The Kid	.75	.35	.09
☐ 3 Dennis Eckersley The Warrior	.75	.35	.09
☐ 4 Dennis Eckersley Beantown Blazer	.75	.35	.09
☐ 5 Dennis Eckersley Eckspeak	.75	.35	.09
☐ 6 Dennis Eckersley Down to Earth	.75	.35	.09
☐ 7 Dennis Eckersley Wrigley Bound	.75	.35	.09
☐ 8 Dennis Eckersley No Relief	.75	.35	.09
☐ 9 Dennis Eckersley In Control	.75	.35	.09
☐ 10 Dennis Eckersley Simply the Best	.75	.35	.09
☐ 11 Dennis Eckersley Reign of Perfection	2.00	.90	.25
☐ 12 Dennis Eckersley Leaving His Mark	2.00	.90	.25
☐ AU Dennis Eckersley AU (Certified autograph)	60.00	27.00	7.50

1993 Ultra Home Run Kings

Randomly inserted into all 1993 Ultra packs, this ten-card standard-size (2 1/2" by 3 1/2") set features the best long ball hitters in baseball. The borderless cards carry cutout color action player photos that are superposed upon an outer space scene, which includes a baseball "planet" and background stars. The player's name and team, along with the set's logo, are printed in gold foil and rest at the bottom. The horizontal black-and-stellar back carries a color player close-up on the left side, and the player's name, nickname, and career highlights in white lettering on the right side. The set's logo, printed in gold foil at the upper right, rounds out the card. The cards are numbered on the back in gold foil.

	MINT	EXC	G-VG
COMPLETE SET (10)	25.00	11.50	3.10
COMMON CARD (1-10)	1.00	.45	.13
☐ 1 Juan Gonzalez	5.00	2.30	.60
☐ 2 Mark McGwire	1.00	.45	.13
☐ 3 Cecil Fielder	1.50	.65	.19
☐ 4 Fred McGriff	2.25	1.00	.30
☐ 5 Albert Belle	4.00	1.80	.50
☐ 6 Barry Bonds	6.00	2.70	.75
☐ 7 Joe Carter	2.25	1.00	.30
☐ 8 Gary Sheffield	1.50	.65	.19
☐ 9 Darren Daulton	1.50	.65	.19
☐ 10 Dave Hollins	1.00	.45	.13

1993 Ultra Performers

This ten-card standard-size (2 1/2" by 3 1/2") set could only be ordered directly from Fleer by sending in 9.95, five Fleer/Fleer Ultra baseball wrappers, and an order blank found in hobby and sports periodicals. Each borderless front features a color player action shot superposed upon four other player photos, which are ghosted and color-screened. The player's name and the set name, both stamped in gold foil,

appear at the bottom. The Ultra Performers set logo, a gold-foil-rimmed baseball icon with a blue trail, lies just above. The gold-foil Fleer Ultra logo appears in an upper corner. The back features a borderless color player action photo that is ghosted and color-screened on one side, where the player's name and career highlights appear. The set logo and gold-foil-stamped name appear below. The set's production number (out of 150,000 produced) rests within a ghosted rectangle at the bottom. The cards are numbered on the back in gold foil.

	MINT	EXC	G-VG
COMPLETE SET (10)	20.00	9.00	2.50
COMMON CARD (1-10)	.50	.23	.06
☐ 1 Barry Bonds	3.00	1.35	.40
☐ 2 Juan Gonzalez	2.50	1.15	.30
☐ 3 Ken Griffey Jr.	8.00	3.60	1.00
☐ 4 Eric Karros	.50	.23	.06
☐ 5 Pat Listach	.50	.23	.06
☐ 6 Greg Maddux	2.00	.90	.25
☐ 7 David Nied	.50	.23	.06
☐ 8 Gary Sheffield	.50	.23	.06
☐ 9 J.T. Snow	.50	.23	.06
☐ 10 Frank Thomas	8.00	3.60	1.00

1993 Ultra Strikeout Kings

Randomly inserted into series II packs, this five-card set showcases outstanding pitchers from both leagues. The color cutout action player photo on the front of each card shows a pitcher on the mound superposed upon a background of stars and a metallic baseball. The player's name appears in gold foil at the bottom. The gold foil-stamped set logo also appears on the front. Upon a metallic-baseball-and-stellar background, the horizontal back carries a posed color player photo on the left side, and the player's career highlights in yellow lettering on the right side. The player's name and. team, as well as the set's logo, appear in gold foil at the top.

	MINT	EXC	G-VG
COMPLETE SET (5)	20.00	9.00	2.50
COMMON CARD (1-5)	1.00	.45	.13
☐ 1 Roger Clemens	4.00	1.80	.50
☐ 2 Juan Guzman	1.00	.45	.13
☐ 3 Randy Johnson	1.00	.45	.13
☐ 4 Nolan Ryan	15.00	6.75	1.90
☐ 5 John Smoltz	1.00	.45	.13

1994 Ultra

The 1994 Ultra baseball set consists of 600 standard-size cards that were issued in two series of 300. The front features a full-bleed color action player photo except at the bottom, where a gold foil strip edges the picture. The player's name, his position, team name, and company logo are gold foil stamped across the bottom of the front. The horizontal back has a montage of three different player cutouts on a action scene with a team color-coded border. Biography and statistics on a thin panel toward the bottom round out the back. The cards are numbered on the back, grouped alphabetically within teams, and checklisted below alphabetically according to teams for each league as follows: Baltimore Orioles (1-10/301-311), Boston Red Sox (11-19/312-319), California Angels (20-29/320-331), Chicago White Sox (30-39/332-341), Cleveland Indians (40-50/342-351), Detroit Tigers (51-60/352-358), Kansas City Royals (61-71/359-368), Milwaukee Brewers (72-82/369-381), Minnesota Twins (83-92/382-393), New York Yankees (93-103/394-401), Oakland Athletics (104-115/402-412), Seattle Mariners (116-125/413-424), Texas Rangers (126-134/425-433), Toronto Blue Jays (135-146/434-442), Atlanta Braves (147-158/443-453), Chicago Cubs (159-

169/454-466), Cincinnati Reds (170-179/467-476), Colorado Rockies (180-190/477-488), Florida Marlins (191-201/489-498), Houston Astros (202-211/499-512), Los Angeles Dodgers (212-221/513-522), Montreal Expos (222-233/523-528), New York Mets (234-241/529-540), Philadelphia Phillies (242-253/541-554), Pittsburgh Pirates (254-263/555-560), St. Louis Cardinals (264-274/561-570), San Diego Padres (275-284/571-585) and San Francisco Giants (285-296/586-595). Rookie Cards include Brian Anderson, Ray Durham, LaTroy Hawkins, Brooks Kieschnick, Chan Ho Park, Mac Suzuki and Terrell Wade.

	MINT	EXC	G-VG
COMPLETE SET (600)	50.00	23.00	6.25
COMPLETE SERIES 1 (300)	25.00	11.50	3.10
COMPLETE SERIES 2 (300)	25.00	11.50	3.10
COMMON CARD (1-300)	.10	.05	.01
COMMON CARD (301-600)	.10	.05	.01

	MINT	EXC	G-VG
☐ 1 Jeffrey Hammonds	.35	.16	.04
☐ 2 Chris Hoiles	.15	.07	.02
☐ 3 Ben McDonald	.15	.07	.02
☐ 4 Mark McLemore	.10	.05	.01
☐ 5 Alan Mills	.10	.05	.01
☐ 6 Jamie Moyer	.10	.05	.01
☐ 7 Brad Pennington	.10	.05	.01
☐ 8 Jim Poole	.10	.05	.01
☐ 9 Cal Ripken	2.25	1.00	.30
☐ 10 Jack Voigt	.10	.05	.01
☐ 11 Roger Clemens	.75	.35	.09
☐ 12 Danny Darwin	.10	.05	.01
☐ 13 Andre Dawson	.20	.09	.03
☐ 14 Scott Fletcher	.10	.05	.01
☐ 15 Greg A. Harris	.10	.05	.01
☐ 16 Billy Hatcher	.10	.05	.01
☐ 17 Jeff Russell	.10	.05	.01
☐ 18 Aaron Sele	.25	.11	.03
☐ 19 Mo Vaughn	.20	.09	.03
☐ 20 Mike Butcher	.10	.05	.01
☐ 21 Rod Correia	.10	.05	.01
☐ 22 Steve Frey	.10	.05	.01
☐ 23 Phil Leftwich	.10	.05	.01
☐ 24 Torey Lovullo	.10	.05	.01
☐ 25 Ken Patterson	.10	.05	.01
☐ 26 Eduardo Perez UER (listed as a Twin instead of Angel)	.15	.07	.02
☐ 27 Tim Salmon	.40	.18	.05
☐ 28 J.T. Snow	.15	.07	.02
☐ 29 Chris Turner	.10	.05	.01
☐ 30 Wilson Alvarez	.20	.09	.03
☐ 31 Jason Bere	.40	.18	.05
☐ 32 Joey Cora	.10	.05	.01
☐ 33 Alex Fernandez	.20	.09	.03
☐ 34 Roberto Hernandez	.10	.05	.01
☐ 35 Lance Johnson	.10	.05	.01
☐ 36 Ron Karkovice	.10	.05	.01
☐ 37 Kirk McCaskill	.10	.05	.01
☐ 38 Jeff Schwarz	.10	.05	.01
☐ 39 Frank Thomas	3.00	1.35	.40
☐ 40 Sandy Alomar Jr.	.15	.07	.02
☐ 41 Albert Belle	1.00	.45	.13
☐ 42 Felix Fermin	.10	.05	.01
☐ 43 Wayne Kirby	.15	.07	.02
☐ 44 Tom Kramer	.10	.05	.01
☐ 45 Kenny Lofton	.75	.35	.09
☐ 46 Jose Mesa	.10	.05	.01
☐ 47 Eric Plunk	.10	.05	.01
☐ 48 Paul Sorrento	.10	.05	.01
☐ 49 Jim Thome	.20	.09	.03
☐ 50 Bill Wertz	.10	.05	.01
☐ 51 John Doherty	.10	.05	.01
☐ 52 Cecil Fielder	.20	.09	.03
☐ 53 Travis Fryman	.25	.11	.03
☐ 54 Chris Gomez	.20	.09	.03
☐ 55 Mike Henneman	.10	.05	.01
☐ 56 Chad Kreuter	.10	.05	.01
☐ 57 Bob MacDonald	.10	.05	.01
☐ 58 Mike Moore	.10	.05	.01
☐ 59 Tony Phillips	.10	.05	.01
☐ 60 Lou Whitaker	.20	.09	.03
☐ 61 Kevin Appier	.15	.07	.02
☐ 62 Greg Gagne	.10	.05	.01
☐ 63 Chris Gwynn	.10	.05	.01
☐ 64 Bob Hamelin	.20	.09	.03
☐ 65 Chris Haney	.10	.05	.01
☐ 66 Phil Hiatt	.20	.09	.03
☐ 67 Felix Jose	.10	.05	.01
☐ 68 Jose Lind	.10	.05	.01
☐ 69 Mike Macfarlane	.10	.05	.01
☐ 70 Jeff Montgomery	.15	.07	.02
☐ 71 Hipolito Pichardo	.10	.05	.01
☐ 72 Juan Bell	.10	.05	.01
☐ 73 Cal Eldred	.15	.07	.02
☐ 74 Darryl Hamilton	.10	.05	.01
☐ 75 Doug Henry	.10	.05	.01
☐ 76 Mike Ignasiak	.10	.05	.01
☐ 77 John Jaha	.10	.05	.01
☐ 78 Graeme Lloyd	.15	.07	.02
☐ 79 Angel Miranda	.10	.05	.01
☐ 80 Dave Nilsson	.10	.05	.01
☐ 81 Troy O'Leary	.15	.07	.02
☐ 82 Kevin Reimer	.10	.05	.01
☐ 83 Willie Banks	.10	.05	.01
☐ 84 Larry Casian	.10	.05	.01
☐ 85 Scott Erickson	.10	.05	.01
☐ 86 Eddie Guardado	.10	.05	.01
☐ 87 Kent Hrbek	.15	.07	.02
☐ 88 Terry Jorgensen	.10	.05	.01
☐ 89 Chuck Knoblauch	.20	.09	.03
☐ 90 Pat Meares	.10	.05	.01
☐ 91 Mike Trombley	.10	.05	.01
☐ 92 Dave Winfield	.20	.09	.03
☐ 93 Wade Boggs	.20	.09	.03
☐ 94 Scott Kamieniecki	.10	.05	.01
☐ 95 Pat Kelly	.10	.05	.01
☐ 96 Jimmy Key	.15	.07	.02
☐ 97 Jim Leyritz	.10	.05	.01
☐ 98 Bobby Munoz	.10	.05	.01
☐ 99 Paul O'Neill	.10	.05	.01
☐ 100 Melido Perez	.10	.05	.01
☐ 101 Mike Stanley	.10	.05	.01
☐ 102 Danny Tartabull	.15	.07	.02
☐ 103 Bernie Williams	.15	.07	.02
☐ 104 Kurt Abbott	.30	.14	.04
☐ 105 Mike Bordick	.10	.05	.01
☐ 106 Ron Darling	.10	.05	.01
☐ 107 Brent Gates	.20	.09	.03
☐ 108 Miguel Jimenez	.15	.07	.02
☐ 109 Steve Karsay	.10	.05	.01
☐ 110 Scott Lydy	.10	.05	.01
☐ 111 Mark McGwire	.20	.09	.03
☐ 112 Troy Neel	.15	.07	.02
☐ 113 Craig Paquette	.10	.05	.01
☐ 114 Bob Welch	.10	.05	.01
☐ 115 Bobby Witt	.10	.05	.01
☐ 116 Rich Amaral	.10	.05	.01
☐ 117 Mike Blowers	.10	.05	.01
☐ 118 Jay Buhner	.15	.07	.02
☐ 119 Dave Fleming	.10	.05	.01
☐ 120 Ken Griffey Jr.	3.00	1.35	.40

☐ 121 Tino Martinez .10 .05 .01
☐ 122 Marc Newfield .20 .09 .03
☐ 123 Ted Power .10 .05 .01
☐ 124 Mackey Sasser .10 .05 .01
☐ 125 Omar Vizquel .10 .05 .01
☐ 126 Kevin Brown .10 .05 .01
☐ 127 Juan Gonzalez 1.00 .45 .13
☐ 128 Tom Henke .10 .05 .01
☐ 129 David Hulse .15 .07 .02
☐ 130 Dean Palmer .15 .07 .02
☐ 131 Roger Pavlik .15 .07 .02
☐ 132 Ivan Rodriguez .20 .09 .03
☐ 133 Kenny Rogers .10 .05 .01
☐ 134 Doug Strange .10 .05 .01
☐ 135 Pat Borders .10 .05 .01
☐ 136 Joe Carter .40 .18 .05
☐ 137 Darnell Coles .10 .05 .01
☐ 138 Pat Hentgen .15 .07 .02
☐ 139 Al Leiter .10 .05 .01
☐ 140 Paul Molitor .40 .18 .05
☐ 141 John Olerud .20 .09 .03
☐ 142 Ed Sprague .15 .07 .02
☐ 143 Dave Stewart .15 .07 .02
☐ 144 Mike Timlin .10 .05 .01
☐ 145 Duane Ward .15 .07 .02
☐ 146 Devon White .15 .07 .02
☐ 147 Steve Avery .20 .09 .03
☐ 148 Steve Bedrosian .10 .05 .01
☐ 149 Damon Berryhill .10 .05 .01
☐ 150 Jeff Blauser .15 .07 .02
☐ 151 Tom Glavine .20 .09 .03
☐ 152 Chipper Jones .40 .18 .05
☐ 153 Mark Lemke .10 .05 .01
☐ 154 Fred McGriff .40 .18 .05
☐ 155 Greg McMichael .15 .07 .02
☐ 156 Deion Sanders .50 .23 .06
☐ 157 John Smoltz .15 .07 .02
☐ 158 Mark Wohlers .10 .05 .01
☐ 159 Jose Bautista .10 .05 .01
☐ 160 Steve Buechele .10 .05 .01
☐ 161 Mike Harkey .10 .05 .01
☐ 162 Greg Hibbard .10 .05 .01
☐ 163 Chuck McElroy .10 .05 .01
☐ 164 Mike Morgan .10 .05 .01
☐ 165 Kevin Roberson .10 .05 .01
☐ 166 Ryne Sandberg 1.00 .45 .13
☐ 167 Jose Vizcaino .10 .05 .01
☐ 168 Rick Wilkins .10 .05 .01
☐ 169 Willie Wilson .10 .05 .01
☐ 170 Willie Greene .15 .07 .02
☐ 171 Roberto Kelly .15 .07 .02
☐ 172 Larry Luebbers .10 .05 .01
☐ 173 Kevin Mitchell .15 .07 .02
☐ 174 Joe Oliver .10 .05 .01
☐ 175 John Roper .20 .09 .03
☐ 176 Johnny Ruffin .10 .05 .01
☐ 177 Reggie Sanders .20 .09 .03
☐ 178 John Smiley .10 .05 .01
☐ 179 Jerry Spradlin .10 .05 .01
☐ 180 Freddie Benavides .10 .05 .01
☐ 181 Dante Bichette .20 .09 .03
☐ 182 Willie Blair .10 .05 .01
☐ 183 Kent Bottenfield .10 .05 .01
☐ 184 Jerald Clark .10 .05 .01
☐ 185 Joe Girardi .10 .05 .01
☐ 186 Roberto Mejia .15 .07 .02
☐ 187 Steve Reed .10 .05 .01
☐ 188 Armando Reynoso .10 .05 .01
☐ 189 Bruce Ruffin .10 .05 .01
☐ 190 Eric Young .15 .07 .02
☐ 191 Luis Aquino .10 .05 .01
☐ 192 Bret Barberie .10 .05 .01
☐ 193 Ryan Bowen .10 .05 .01
☐ 194 Chuck Carr .20 .09 .03
☐ 195 Orestes Destrade .15 .07 .02
☐ 196 Richie Lewis .15 .07 .02
☐ 197 Dave Magadan .10 .05 .01
☐ 198 Bob Natal .10 .05 .01
☐ 199 Gary Sheffield .20 .09 .03
☐ 200 Matt Turner .15 .07 .02
☐ 201 Darrell Whitmore .15 .07 .02
☐ 202 Eric Anthony .10 .05 .01
☐ 203 Jeff Bagwell 1.50 .65 .19
☐ 204 Andujar Cedeno .10 .05 .01
☐ 205 Luis Gonzalez .10 .05 .01
☐ 206 Xavier Hernandez .10 .05 .01
☐ 207 Doug Jones .10 .05 .01
☐ 208 Darryl Kile .15 .07 .02
☐ 209 Scott Servais .10 .05 .01
☐ 210 Greg Swindell .10 .05 .01
☐ 211 Brian Williams .15 .07 .02
☐ 212 Pedro Astacio .15 .07 .02
☐ 213 Brett Butler .15 .07 .02
☐ 214 Omar Daal .15 .07 .02
☐ 215 Jim Gott .10 .05 .01
☐ 216 Raul Mondesi 1.00 .45 .13
☐ 217 Jose Offerman .15 .07 .02
☐ 218 Mike Piazza 1.50 .65 .19
☐ 219 Cory Snyder .10 .05 .01
☐ 220 Tim Wallach .10 .05 .01
☐ 221 Todd Worrell .10 .05 .01
☐ 222 Moises Alou .20 .09 .03
☐ 223 Sean Berry .10 .05 .01
☐ 224 Wil Cordero .20 .09 .03
☐ 225 Jeff Fassero .10 .05 .01
☐ 226 Darrin Fletcher .10 .05 .01
☐ 227 Cliff Floyd .50 .23 .06
☐ 228 Marquis Grissom .20 .09 .03
☐ 229 Ken Hill .15 .07 .02
☐ 230 Mike Lansing .15 .07 .02
☐ 231 Kirk Rueter .10 .05 .01
☐ 232 John Wetteland .10 .05 .01
☐ 233 Rondell White .30 .14 .04
☐ 234 Tim Bogar .10 .05 .01
☐ 235 Jeromy Burnitz .15 .07 .02
☐ 236 Dwight Gooden .10 .05 .01
☐ 237 Todd Hundley .10 .05 .01
☐ 238 Jeff Kent .15 .07 .02
☐ 239 Josias Manzanillo .10 .05 .01
☐ 240 Joe Orsulak .10 .05 .01
☐ 241 Ryan Thompson .15 .07 .02
☐ 242 Kim Batiste .10 .05 .01
☐ 243 Darren Daulton .20 .09 .03
☐ 244 Tommy Greene .10 .05 .01
☐ 245 Dave Hollins .20 .09 .03
☐ 246 Pete Incaviglia .10 .05 .01
☐ 247 Danny Jackson .10 .05 .01
☐ 248 Ricky Jordan .10 .05 .01
☐ 249 John Kruk .20 .09 .03
☐ 250 Mickey Morandini .10 .05 .01
☐ 251 Terry Mulholland .15 .07 .02
☐ 252 Ben Rivera .10 .05 .01
☐ 253 Kevin Stocker .15 .07 .02
☐ 254 Jay Bell .15 .07 .02
☐ 255 Steve Cooke .10 .05 .01
☐ 256 Jeff King .10 .05 .01
☐ 257 Al Martin .10 .05 .01
☐ 258 Danny Miceli .15 .07 .02
☐ 259 Blas Minor .10 .05 .01
☐ 260 Don Slaught .10 .05 .01
☐ 261 Paul Wagner .10 .05 .01
☐ 262 Tim Wakefield .10 .05 .01
☐ 263 Kevin Young .10 .05 .01
☐ 264 Rene Arocha .15 .07 .02
☐ 265 Richard Batchelor .10 .05 .01
☐ 266 Gregg Jefferies .20 .09 .03

	No.	Player			
☐	267	Brian Jordan	.15	.07	.02
☐	268	Jose Oquendo	.10	.05	.01
☐	269	Donovan Osborne	.10	.05	.01
☐	270	Erik Pappas	.10	.05	.01
☐	271	Mike Perez	.10	.05	.01
☐	272	Bob Tewksbury	.10	.05	.01
☐	273	Mark Whiten	.15	.07	.02
☐	274	Todd Zeile	.15	.07	.02
☐	275	Andy Ashby	.10	.05	.01
☐	276	Brad Ausmus	.10	.05	.01
☐	277	Phil Clark	.10	.05	.01
☐	278	Jeff Gardner	.10	.05	.01
☐	279	Ricky Gutierrez	.10	.05	.01
☐	280	Tony Gwynn	.75	.35	.09
☐	281	Tim Mauser	.10	.05	.01
☐	282	Scott Sanders	.15	.07	.02
☐	283	Frank Seminara	.10	.05	.01
☐	284	Wally Whitehurst	.10	.05	.01
☐	285	Rod Beck	.15	.07	.02
☐	286	Barry Bonds	1.25	.55	.16
☐	287	Dave Burba	.10	.05	.01
☐	288	Mark Carreon	.10	.05	.01
☐	289	Royce Clayton	.15	.07	.02
☐	290	Mike Jackson	.10	.05	.01
☐	291	Darren Lewis	.10	.05	.01
☐	292	Kirt Manwaring	.10	.05	.01
☐	293	Dave Martinez	.10	.05	.01
☐	294	Billy Swift	.10	.05	.01
☐	295	Salomon Torres	.15	.07	.02
☐	296	Matt Williams	.60	.25	.08
☐	297	Checklist 1-75	.10	.05	.01
☐	298	Checklist 76-150	.10	.05	.01
☐	299	Checklist 151-225	.10	.05	.01
☐	300	Checklist 226-300	.10	.05	.01
☐	301	Brady Anderson	.15	.07	.02
☐	302	Harold Baines	.15	.07	.02
☐	303	Damon Buford	.10	.05	.01
☐	304	Mike Devereaux	.15	.07	.02
☐	305	Sid Fernandez	.10	.05	.01
☐	306	Rick Krivda	.30	.14	.04
☐	307	Mike Mussina	.40	.18	.05
☐	308	Rafael Palmeiro	.20	.09	.03
☐	309	Arthur Rhodes	.10	.05	.01
☐	310	Chris Sabo	.10	.05	.01
☐	311	Lee Smith	.20	.09	.03
☐	312	Gregg Zaun	.20	.09	.03
☐	313	Scott Cooper	.15	.07	.02
☐	314	Mike Greenwell	.15	.07	.02
☐	315	Tim Naehring	.10	.05	.01
☐	316	Otis Nixon	.10	.05	.01
☐	317	Paul Quantrill	.10	.05	.01
☐	318	John Valentin	.15	.07	.02
☐	319	Dave Valle	.10	.05	.01
☐	320	Frank Viola	.10	.05	.01
☐	321	Brian Anderson	.75	.35	.09
☐	322	Garret Anderson	.15	.07	.02
☐	323	Chad Curtis	.15	.07	.02
☐	324	Chili Davis	.15	.07	.02
☐	325	Gary DiSarcina	.10	.05	.01
☐	326	Damion Easley	.10	.05	.01
☐	327	Jim Edmonds	.10	.05	.01
☐	328	Chuck Finley	.10	.05	.01
☐	329	Joe Grahe	.10	.05	.01
☐	330	Bo Jackson	.20	.09	.03
☐	331	Mark Langston	.20	.09	.03
☐	332	Harold Reynolds	.10	.05	.01
☐	333	James Baldwin	.50	.23	.06
☐	334	Ray Durham	1.25	.55	.16
☐	335	Julio Franco	.15	.07	.02
☐	336	Craig Grebeck	.10	.05	.01
☐	337	Ozzie Guillen	.10	.05	.01
☐	338	Joe Hall	.10	.05	.01
☐	339	Darrin Jackson	.10	.05	.01
☐	340	Jack McDowell	.20	.09	.03
☐	341	Tim Raines	.20	.09	.03
☐	342	Robin Ventura	.15	.07	.02
☐	343	Carlos Baerga	.40	.18	.05
☐	344	Derek Lilliquist	.10	.05	.01
☐	345	Dennis Martinez	.15	.07	.02
☐	346	Jack Morris	.20	.09	.03
☐	347	Eddie Murray	.20	.09	.03
☐	348	Chris Nabholz	.10	.05	.01
☐	349	Charles Nagy	.10	.05	.01
☐	350	Chad Ogea	.15	.07	.02
☐	351	Manny Ramirez	.60	.25	.08
☐	352	Omar Vizquel	.10	.05	.01
☐	353	Tim Belcher	.10	.05	.01
☐	354	Eric Davis	.10	.05	.01
☐	355	Kirk Gibson	.15	.07	.02
☐	356	Rick Greene	.15	.07	.02
☐	357	Mickey Tettleton	.15	.07	.02
☐	358	Alan Trammell	.20	.09	.03
☐	359	David Wells	.10	.05	.01
☐	360	Stan Belinda	.10	.05	.01
☐	361	Vince Coleman	.10	.05	.01
☐	362	David Cone	.20	.09	.03
☐	363	Gary Gaetti	.10	.05	.01
☐	364	Tom Gordon	.10	.05	.01
☐	365	Dave Henderson	.10	.05	.01
☐	366	Wally Joyner	.15	.07	.02
☐	367	Brent Mayne	.10	.05	.01
☐	368	Brian McRae	.15	.07	.02
☐	369	Michael Tucker	.25	.11	.03
☐	370	Ricky Bones	.10	.05	.01
☐	371	Brian Harper	.10	.05	.01
☐	372	Tyrone Hill	.15	.07	.02
☐	373	Mark Kiefer	.10	.05	.01
☐	374	Pat Listach	.10	.05	.01
☐	375	Mike Matheny	.10	.05	.01
☐	376	Jose Mercedes	.15	.07	.02
☐	377	Jody Reed	.10	.05	.01
☐	378	Kevin Seitzer	.10	.05	.01
☐	379	B.J. Surhoff	.10	.05	.01
☐	380	Greg Vaughn	.15	.07	.02
☐	381	Turner Ward	.10	.05	.01
☐	382	Wes Weger	.10	.05	.01
☐	383	Bill Wegman	.10	.05	.01
☐	384	Rick Aguilera	.15	.07	.02
☐	385	Rich Becker	.15	.07	.02
☐	386	Alex Cole	.10	.05	.01
☐	387	Steve Dunn	.15	.07	.02
☐	388	Keith Garagozzo	.15	.07	.02
☐	389	LaTroy Hawkins	.75	.35	.09
☐	390	Shane Mack	.15	.07	.02
☐	391	David McCarty	.15	.07	.02
☐	392	Pedro Munoz	.10	.05	.01
☐	393	Derek Parks	.10	.05	.01
☐	394	Kirby Puckett	1.25	.55	.16
☐	395	Kevin Tapani	.10	.05	.01
☐	396	Matt Walbeck	.10	.05	.01
☐	397	Jim Abbott	.20	.09	.03
☐	398	Mike Gallego	.10	.05	.01
☐	399	Xavier Hernandez	.10	.05	.01
☐	400	Don Mattingly	1.25	.55	.16
☐	401	Terry Mulholland	.10	.05	.01
☐	402	Matt Nokes	.10	.05	.01
☐	403	Luis Polonia	.10	.05	.01
☐	404	Bob Wickman	.10	.05	.01
☐	405	Mark Acre	.20	.09	.03
☐	406	Fausto Cruz	.25	.11	.03
☐	407	Dennis Eckersley	.20	.09	.03
☐	408	Rickey Henderson	.20	.09	.03
☐	409	Stan Javier	.10	.05	.01
☐	410	Carlos Reyes	.10	.05	.01
☐	411	Ruben Sierra	.20	.09	.03
☐	412	Terry Steinbach	.15	.07	.02

	No.	Player	MINT	NRMT	EXC
☐	413	Bill Taylor	.10	.05	.01
☐	414	Todd Van Poppel	.15	.07	.02
☐	415	Eric Anthony	.10	.05	.01
☐	416	Bobby Ayala	.10	.05	.01
☐	417	Chris Bosio	.10	.05	.01
☐	418	Tim Davis	.10	.05	.01
☐	419	Randy Johnson	.20	.09	.03
☐	420	Kevin King	.10	.05	.01
☐	421	Anthony Manahan	.15	.07	.02
☐	422	Edgar Martinez	.10	.05	.01
☐	423	Keith Mitchell	.10	.05	.01
☐	424	Roger Salkeld	.10	.05	.01
☐	425	Mac Suzuki	.75	.35	.09
☐	426	Dan Wilson	.10	.05	.01
☐	427	Duff Brumley	.25	.11	.03
☐	428	Jose Canseco	.40	.18	.05
☐	429	Will Clark	.40	.18	.05
☐	430	Steve Dreyer	.25	.11	.03
☐	431	Rick Helling	.10	.05	.01
☐	432	Chris James	.10	.05	.01
☐	433	Matt Whiteside	.10	.05	.01
☐	434	Roberto Alomar	.75	.35	.09
☐	435	Scott Brow	.10	.05	.01
☐	436	Domingo Cedeno	.10	.05	.01
☐	437	Carlos Delgado	.50	.23	.06
☐	438	Juan Guzman	.15	.07	.02
☐	439	Paul Spoljaric	.10	.05	.01
☐	440	Todd Stottlemyre	.10	.05	.01
☐	441	Woody Williams	.10	.05	.01
☐	442	David Justice	.40	.18	.05
☐	443	Mike Kelly	.15	.07	.02
☐	444	Ryan Klesko	.50	.23	.06
☐	445	Javy Lopez	.30	.14	.04
☐	446	Greg Maddux	.60	.25	.08
☐	447	Kent Mercker	.10	.05	.01
☐	448	Charlie O'Brien	.10	.05	.01
☐	449	Terry Pendleton	.10	.05	.01
☐	450	Mike Stanton	.10	.05	.01
☐	451	Tony Tarasco	.20	.09	.03
☐	452	Terrell Wade	.75	.35	.09
☐	453	Willie Banks	.10	.05	.01
☐	454	Shawon Dunston	.10	.05	.01
☐	455	Mark Grace	.20	.09	.03
☐	456	Jose Guzman	.10	.05	.01
☐	457	Jose Hernandez	.10	.05	.01
☐	458	Glenallen Hill	.10	.05	.01
☐	459	Blaise Ilsley	.10	.05	.01
☐	460	Brooks Kieschnick	1.00	.45	.13
☐	461	Derrick May	.10	.05	.01
☐	462	Randy Myers	.10	.05	.01
☐	463	Karl Rhodes	.10	.05	.01
☐	464	Sammy Sosa	.20	.09	.03
☐	465	Steve Trachsel	.40	.18	.05
☐	466	Anthony Young	.10	.05	.01
☐	467	Eddie Zambrano	.10	.05	.01
☐	468	Bret Boone	.20	.09	.03
☐	469	Tom Browning	.10	.05	.01
☐	470	Hector Carrasco	.10	.05	.01
☐	471	Rob Dibble	.10	.05	.01
☐	472	Erik Hanson	.10	.05	.01
☐	473	Thomas Howard	.10	.05	.01
☐	474	Barry Larkin	.20	.09	.03
☐	475	Hal Morris	.15	.07	.02
☐	476	Jose Rijo	.15	.07	.02
☐	477	John Burke	.15	.07	.02
☐	478	Ellis Burks	.15	.07	.02
☐	479	Marvin Freeman	.10	.05	.01
☐	480	Andres Galarraga	.20	.09	.03
☐	481	Greg W. Harris	.10	.05	.01
☐	482	Charlie Hayes	.15	.07	.02
☐	483	Darren Holmes	.10	.05	.01
☐	484	Howard Johnson	.10	.05	.01
☐	485	Marcus Moore	.10	.05	.01
☐	486	David Nied	.20	.09	.03
☐	487	Mark Thompson	.15	.07	.02
☐	488	Walt Weiss	.10	.05	.01
☐	489	Kurt Abbott	.15	.07	.02
☐	490	Matias Carrillo	.15	.07	.02
☐	491	Jeff Conine	.20	.09	.03
☐	492	Chris Hammond	.10	.05	.01
☐	493	Bryan Harvey	.15	.07	.02
☐	494	Charlie Hough	.15	.07	.02
☐	495	Yorkis Perez	.10	.05	.01
☐	496	Pat Rapp	.10	.05	.01
☐	497	Benito Santiago	.10	.05	.01
☐	498	David Weathers	.10	.05	.01
☐	499	Craig Biggio	.15	.07	.02
☐	500	Ken Caminiti	.15	.07	.02
☐	501	Doug Drabek	.20	.09	.03
☐	502	Tony Eusebio	.10	.05	.01
☐	503	Steve Finley	.10	.05	.01
☐	504	Pete Harnisch	.10	.05	.01
☐	505	Brian L. Hunter	.50	.23	.06
☐	506	Domingo Jean	.10	.05	.01
☐	507	Todd Jones	.10	.05	.01
☐	508	Orlando Miller	.15	.07	.02
☐	509	James Mouton	.20	.09	.03
☐	510	Roberto Petagine	.15	.07	.02
☐	511	Shane Reynolds	.10	.05	.01
☐	512	Mitch Williams	.10	.05	.01
☐	513	Billy Ashley	.20	.09	.03
☐	514	Tom Candiotti	.10	.05	.01
☐	515	Delino DeShields	.15	.07	.02
☐	516	Kevin Gross	.10	.05	.01
☐	517	Orel Hershiser	.15	.07	.02
☐	518	Eric Karros	.15	.07	.02
☐	519	Ramon Martinez	.15	.07	.02
☐	520	Chan Ho Park	1.25	.55	.16
☐	521	Henry Rodriguez	.10	.05	.01
☐	522	Joey Eischen	.15	.07	.02
☐	523	Rod Henderson	.10	.05	.01
☐	524	Pedro J. Martinez	.20	.09	.03
☐	525	Mel Rojas	.10	.05	.01
☐	526	Larry Walker	.20	.09	.03
☐	527	Gabe White	.10	.05	.01
☐	528	Bobby Bonilla	.20	.09	.03
☐	529	Jonathan Hurst	.10	.05	.01
☐	530	Bobby Jones	.20	.09	.03
☐	531	Kevin McReynolds	.10	.05	.01
☐	532	Bill Pulsipher	.60	.25	.08
☐	533	Bret Saberhagen	.15	.07	.02
☐	534	David Segui	.10	.05	.01
☐	535	Pete Smith	.10	.05	.01
☐	536	Kelly Stinnett	.10	.05	.01
☐	537	Dave Telgheder	.10	.05	.01
☐	538	Quilvio Veras	.15	.07	.02
☐	539	Jose Vizcaino	.10	.05	.01
☐	540	Pete Walker	.10	.05	.01
☐	541	Ricky Bottalico	.30	.14	.04
☐	542	Wes Chamberlain	.10	.05	.01
☐	543	Mariano Duncan	.10	.05	.01
☐	544	Lenny Dykstra	.20	.09	.03
☐	545	Jim Eisenreich	.10	.05	.01
☐	546	Phil Geisler	.30	.14	.04
☐	547	Wayne Gomes	.25	.11	.03
☐	548	Doug Jones	.10	.05	.01
☐	549	Jeff Juden	.10	.05	.01
☐	550	Mike Lieberthal	.10	.05	.01
☐	551	Tony Longmire	.10	.05	.01
☐	552	Tom Marsh	.10	.05	.01
☐	553	Bobby Munoz	.10	.05	.01
☐	554	Curt Schilling	.10	.05	.01
☐	555	Carlos Garcia	.10	.05	.01
☐	556	Ravelo Manzanillo	.10	.05	.01
☐	557	Orlando Merced	.15	.07	.02
☐	558	Will Pennyfeather	.10	.05	.01

		MINT	EXC	G-VG
☐ 559	Zane Smith	.10	.05	.01
☐ 560	Andy Van Slyke	.20	.09	.03
☐ 561	Rick White	.10	.05	.01
☐ 562	Luis Alicea	.10	.05	.01
☐ 563	Brian Barber	.15	.07	.02
☐ 564	Clint Davis	.10	.05	.01
☐ 565	Bernard Gilkey	.10	.05	.01
☐ 566	Ray Lankford	.20	.09	.03
☐ 567	Tom Pagnozzi	.10	.05	.01
☐ 568	Ozzie Smith	.60	.25	.08
☐ 569	Rick Sutcliffe	.15	.07	.02
☐ 570	Allen Watson	.10	.05	.01
☐ 571	Dmitri Young	.10	.05	.01
☐ 572	Derek Bell	.15	.07	.02
☐ 573	Andy Benes	.15	.07	.02
☐ 574	Archi Cianfrocco	.10	.05	.01
☐ 575	Joey Hamilton	.60	.25	.08
☐ 576	Gene Harris	.10	.05	.01
☐ 577	Trevor Hoffman	.10	.05	.01
☐ 578	Tim Hyers	.20	.09	.03
☐ 579	Brian Johnson	.15	.07	.02
☐ 580	Keith Lockhart	.10	.05	.01
☐ 581	Pedro A. Martinez	.20	.09	.03
☐ 582	Ray McDavid	.10	.05	.01
☐ 583	Phil Plantier	.15	.07	.02
☐ 584	Bip Roberts	.10	.05	.01
☐ 585	Dave Staton	.10	.05	.01
☐ 586	Todd Benzinger	.10	.05	.01
☐ 587	John Burkett	.15	.07	.02
☐ 588	Bryan Hickerson	.10	.05	.01
☐ 589	Willie McGee	.10	.05	.01
☐ 590	John Patterson	.10	.05	.01
☐ 591	Mark Portugal	.10	.05	.01
☐ 592	Kevin Rogers	.10	.05	.01
☐ 593	Joe Rosselli	.10	.05	.01
☐ 594	Steve Soderstrom	.40	.18	.05
☐ 595	Robby Thompson	.10	.05	.01
☐ 596	125th Anniversary	.10	.05	.01
☐ 597	Checklist	.10	.05	.01
☐ 598	Checklist	.10	.05	.01
☐ 599	Checklist	.10	.05	.01
☐ 600	Checklist	.10	.05	.01

1994 Ultra All-Rookie Team

This 10-card set features top rookies of 1994. Randomly inserted in second series jumbo and foil packs at a rate of one in 10, these cards measure the standard size. Card fronts have a color player photo cut-out over a computer generated background that resembles volcanic activity. The player's name and All-Rookie Team logo appear in gold foil at the bottom. On the backs, the player cut-out appears toward the right with text on the left. The background is much the same as the front. Every second series Ultra hobby case included this set in jumbo (3 1/2" by 5") form. These jumbo versions are priced up to twice the values below.

	MINT	EXC	G-VG
COMPLETE SET (10)	20.00	9.00	2.50
COMMON CARD (1-10)	.50	.23	.06
*JUMBO ART's: 1X to 2X VALUES BELOW			

		MINT	EXC	G-VG
☐ 1	Kurt Abbott	.50	.23	.06
☐ 2	Carlos Delgado	3.00	1.35	.40
☐ 3	Cliff Floyd	3.00	1.35	.40
☐ 4	Jeffrey Hammonds	1.75	.80	.22
☐ 5	Ryan Klesko	3.00	1.35	.40
☐ 6	Javy Lopez	1.75	.80	.22
☐ 7	Raul Mondesi	6.00	2.70	.75
☐ 8	James Mouton	.50	.23	.06
☐ 9	Chan Ho Park	3.50	1.55	.45
☐ 10	Dave Staton	.50	.23	.06

1994 Ultra All-Stars

Randomly inserted in second series foil and jumbo packs at a rate of one in three, this 20-card set contains top major league stars. The fronts have a color player photo superimposed over a bright red (American League players) or dark blue (National League) background. The backs are much the same except they include highlights from 1993.

	MINT	EXC	G-VG
COMPLETE SET (20)	20.00	9.00	2.50
COMMON CARD (1-20)	.50	.23	.06

		MINT	EXC	G-VG
☐ 1	Chris Hoiles	.50	.23	.06
☐ 2	Frank Thomas	6.00	2.70	.75
☐ 3	Roberto Alomar	1.50	.65	.19
☐ 4	Cal Ripken	4.50	2.00	.55
☐ 5	Robin Ventura	.75	.35	.09
☐ 6	Albert Belle	2.00	.90	.25
☐ 7	Juan Gonzalez	2.00	.90	.25
☐ 8	Ken Griffey Jr.	6.00	2.70	.75
☐ 9	John Olerud	.75	.35	.09
☐ 10	Jack McDowell	.75	.35	.09
☐ 11	Mike Piazza	3.00	1.35	.40
☐ 12	Fred McGriff	.90	.40	.11

☐ 13 Ryne Sandberg	2.00	.90	.25
☐ 14 Jay Bell	.50	.23	.06
☐ 15 Matt Williams	1.25	.55	.16
☐ 16 Barry Bonds	2.50	1.15	.30
☐ 17 Lenny Dykstra	.75	.35	.09
☐ 18 David Justice	.90	.40	.11
☐ 19 Tom Glavine	.75	.35	.09
☐ 20 Greg Maddux	1.50	.65	.19
☐ 22 Jack McDowell AL POY	.75	.35	.09
☐ 23 Greg Maddux NL POY	1.50	.65	.19
☐ 24 Tim Salmon AL ROY	.90	.40	.11
☐ 25 Mike Piazza NL ROY	3.00	1.35	.40

1994 Ultra Award Winners

Randomly inserted in all first series packs at a rate of one in three, this 25-card standard-size set features three MVP's, two Rookies of the Year, and 18 Top Glove defensive standouts. The set is divided into American League Top Gloves (1-9), National League Top Gloves (10-18), and Award Winners (19-25). A horizontal design includes a color player cut-out over a gold background on front. Also on front, is a gold foil logo that indicates the honor. The backs have a small photo and text.

	MINT	EXC	G-VG
COMPLETE SET (25)	25.00	11.50	3.10
COMMON CARD (1-25)	.50	.23	.06
☐ 1 Ivan Rodriguez	.75	.35	.09
☐ 2 Don Mattingly	2.50	1.15	.30
☐ 3 Roberto Alomar	1.50	.65	.19
☐ 4 Robin Ventura	.75	.35	.09
☐ 5 Omar Vizquel	.50	.23	.06
☐ 6 Ken Griffey Jr.	6.00	2.70	.75
☐ 7 Kenny Lofton	1.50	.65	.19
☐ 8 Devon White	.75	.35	.09
☐ 9 Mark Langston	.50	.23	.06
☐ 10 Kirt Manwaring	.50	.23	.06
☐ 11 Mark Grace	.75	.35	.09
☐ 12 Robby Thompson	.50	.23	.06
☐ 13 Matt Williams	1.25	.55	.16
☐ 14 Jay Bell	.50	.23	.06
☐ 15 Barry Bonds	2.50	1.15	.30
☐ 16 Marquis Grissom	.75	.35	.09
☐ 17 Larry Walker	.75	.35	.09
☐ 18 Greg Maddux	1.50	.65	.19
☐ 19 Frank Thomas AL MVP	6.00	2.70	.75
☐ 20 Barry Bonds NL MVP	2.50	1.15	.30
☐ 21 Paul Molitor World Series MVP	.90	.40	.11

1994 Ultra Career Achievement

Randomly inserted in all first series packs at a rate of one in 21, this five card set highlights veteran stars and milestones they have reached during their brilliant careers. Horizontally designed cards have fronts that feature a color player photo superimposed over solid color background that contains another player photo. A photo of the player earlier in his career is on back along with text.

	MINT	EXC	G-VG
COMPLETE SET (5)	15.00	6.75	1.90
COMMON CARD (1-5)	1.25	.55	.16
☐ 1 Joe Carter	1.75	.80	.22
☐ 2 Paul Molitor	1.75	.80	.22
☐ 3 Cal Ripken	9.00	4.00	1.15
☐ 4 Ryne Sandberg	5.00	2.30	.60
☐ 5 Dave Winfield	1.25	.55	.16

1994 Ultra Firemen

Randomly inserted in all first series packs at a rate of one in 11, this ten-card standard-size set features ten of baseball's top relief pitchers. The fronts feature color player action cutouts superimposed upon borderless backgrounds consisting of pictures of fire-fighting equipment. The player's name appears in gold foil at the bottom. The horizontal back carries a color player head shot on one side, and career highlights inside a ghosted panel on the other, all on a borderless fire-fighting equipment background. The set is arranged according to American League (1-5) and National League (6-10) players.

	MINT	EXC	G-VG
COMPLETE SET (10)	8.00	3.60	1.00
COMMON CARD (1-10)	1.00	.45	.13
☐ 1 Jeff Montgomery	1.00	.45	.13
☐ 2 Duane Ward	1.00	.45	.13
☐ 3 Tom Henke	1.00	.45	.13
☐ 4 Roberto Hernandez	1.00	.45	.13
☐ 5 Dennis Eckersley	1.50	.65	.19
☐ 6 Randy Myers	1.00	.45	.13
☐ 7 Rod Beck	1.50	.65	.19
☐ 8 Bryan Harvey	1.00	.45	.13
☐ 9 John Wetteland	1.00	.45	.13
☐ 10 Mitch Williams	1.00	.45	.13

1994 Ultra Hitting Machines

Randomly inserted in all second series packs at a rate of one in five, this 10-card horizontally designed set features top hitters from 1993. The fronts have a color player cut-out over a "Hitting Machines" background. The back has a smaller player cut-out and text.

	MINT	EXC	G-VG
COMPLETE SET (10)	15.00	6.75	1.90
COMMON CARD (1-10)	.60	.25	.08
☐ 1 Roberto Alomar	1.50	.65	.19
☐ 2 Carlos Baerga	.90	.40	.11
☐ 3 Barry Bonds	2.50	1.15	.30
☐ 4 Andres Galarraga	.60	.25	.08
☐ 5 Juan Gonzalez	2.00	.90	.25
☐ 6 Tony Gwynn	1.50	.65	.19
☐ 7 Paul Molitor	.90	.40	.11
☐ 8 John Olerud	.60	.25	.08
☐ 9 Mike Piazza	3.00	1.35	.40
☐ 10 Frank Thomas	6.00	2.70	.75

1994 Ultra Home Run Kings

Randomly inserted exclusively in foil packs at a rate of one in 36, these 12 standard-size cards highlight home run hitters by an etched metalized look. Cards 1-6 feature American League Home Run Kings while cards 7-12 present National League Home Run Kings.

	MINT	EXC	G-VG
COMPLETE SET (12)	90.00	40.00	11.50
COMMON CARD (1-12)	2.00	.90	.25
☐ 1 Juan Gonzalez	8.00	3.60	1.00
☐ 2 Ken Griffey Jr.	25.00	11.50	3.10
☐ 3 Frank Thomas	25.00	11.50	3.10
☐ 4 Albert Belle	8.00	3.60	1.00
☐ 5 Rafael Palmeiro	2.00	.90	.25
☐ 6 Joe Carter	4.00	1.80	.50
☐ 7 Barry Bonds	10.00	4.50	1.25
☐ 8 David Justice	4.00	1.80	.50
☐ 9 Matt Williams	5.00	2.30	.60
☐ 10 Fred McGriff	4.00	1.80	.50
☐ 11 Ron Gant	2.00	.90	.25
☐ 12 Mike Piazza	12.00	5.50	1.50

1994 Ultra League Leaders

Randomly inserted in all packs at a rate of one in 11, this ten-card standard-size set features ten of 1993's most impressive hitters, runners, and pitchers. The fronts feature borderless color player action shots, with a color-screening that shades from being imperceptible at the top to washing out the photos' true colors at the bottom. The player's name in gold foil appears across the card face. The borderless back carries a color player head shot in a lower corner with his career highlights appearing

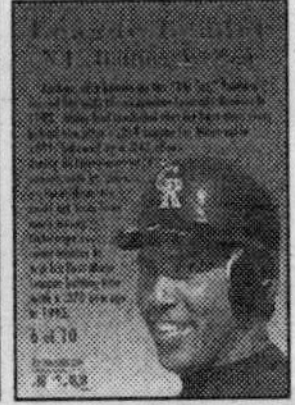

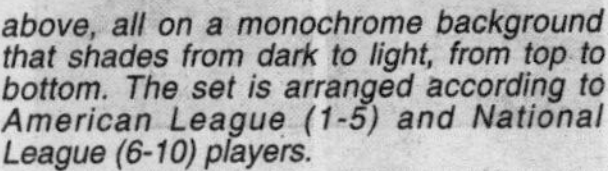

above, all on a monochrome background that shades from dark to light, from top to bottom. The set is arranged according to American League (1-5) and National League (6-10) players.

	MINT	EXC	G-VG
COMPLETE SET (10)	6.00	2.70	.75
COMMON CARD (1-10)	.50	.23	.06
☐ 1 John Olerud AL Batting Average Leader	1.00	.45	.13
☐ 2 Rafael Palmeiro AL Runs Scored Leader	1.00	.45	.13
☐ 3 Kenny Lofton AL Stolen Base Leader	2.00	.90	.25
☐ 4 Jack McDowell AL Winningest Pitcher	1.00	.45	.13
☐ 5 Randy Johnson AL Strikeout Leader	1.00	.45	.13
☐ 6 Andres Galarraga NL Batting Average Leader	1.00	.45	.13
☐ 7 Lenny Dykstra NL Runs Scored Leader	1.00	.45	.13
☐ 8 Chuck Carr NL Stolen Base Leader	.50	.23	.06
☐ 9 Tom Glavine NL Winningest Pitcher	1.00	.45	.13
☐ 10 Jose Rijo NL Strikeout Leader	.50	.23	.06

1994 Ultra On-Base Leaders

Randomly inserted in jumbo packs at a rate of one in 36, this 12-card set features those that were among the Major League leaders in on-base percentage. Card fronts have the player superimposed over a metallic background that simulates statistics from a sports page. The backs have a player cut-out and text over a statistical background that is not metallic.

	MINT	EXC	G-VG
COMPLETE SET (12)	225.00	100.00	28.00
COMMON CARD (1-12)	5.00	2.30	.60
☐ 1 Roberto Alomar	18.00	8.00	2.30
☐ 2 Barry Bonds	30.00	13.50	3.80
☐ 3 Lenny Dykstra	7.00	3.10	.85
☐ 4 Andres Galarraga	7.00	3.10	.85
☐ 5 Mark Grace	5.00	2.30	.60
☐ 6 Ken Griffey Jr.	75.00	34.00	9.50
☐ 7 Gregg Jefferies	7.00	3.10	.85
☐ 8 Orlando Merced	5.00	2.30	.60
☐ 9 Paul Molitor	12.00	5.50	1.50
☐ 10 John Olerud	7.00	3.10	.85
☐ 11 Tony Phillips	5.00	2.30	.60
☐ 12 Frank Thomas	75.00	34.00	9.50

1994 Ultra Phillies Finest

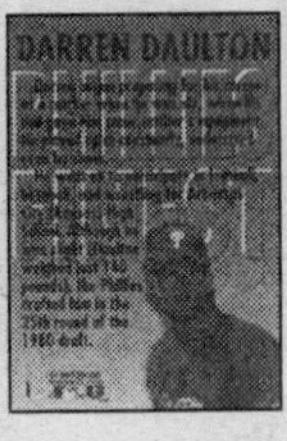

As the "Highlight Series" insert set, this 20-card standard-size set features Darren Daulton and John Kruk of the 1993 National League champion Philadelphia Phillies. The cards were inserted at a rate of one in six first series and one in 10 second series packs. Ten cards spotlight each player's career. Daulton and Kruk each signed more than 1,000 of their cards for random insertion. Moreover, the collector could receive four more cards (two of each player) through a mail-in offer by sending in ten 1994 series I wrappers plus 1.50 for postage and handling. The fronts feature borderless color player action shots. Behind the player, in "transparent" block lettering, the words "Phillies Finest" appear, followed by the player's name. His name also appears in gold foil in a lower corner. The

back carries a color player head shot in a lower corner, with career highlights appearing above, all on a borderless red background.

	MINT	EXC	G-VG
COMPLETE SET (20)	20.00	9.00	2.50
COMPLETE SERIES 1 (10)	10.00	4.50	1.25
COMPLETE SERIES 2 (10)	10.00	4.50	1.25
COMMON DAULTON (1-5/11-15)	1.00	.45	.13
COMMON KRUK (6-10/16-20)	1.00	.45	.13
COMMON MAIL-IN (M1-M4)	1.50	.65	.19
☐ 1 Darren Daulton (Standing behind home plate)	1.00	.45	.13
☐ 2 Darren Daulton (Swinging at a pitch)	1.00	.45	.13
☐ 3 Darren Daulton (Blocking home plate)	1.00	.45	.13
☐ 4 Darren Daulton (Just completed swing and is headed for fisrt)	1.00	.45	.13
☐ 5 Darren Daulton (Looking skyward after connecting with a pitch)	1.00	.45	.13
☐ 6 John Kruk (Swinging at a pitch)	1.00	.45	.13
☐ 7 John Kruk (Fielding)	1.00	.45	.13
☐ 8 John Kruk (Just completed a swing)	1.00	.45	.13
☐ 9 John Kruk (On deck)	1.00	.45	.13
☐ 10 John Kruk (Breaking out of batters box)	1.00	.45	.13
☐ 11 Darren Daulton (Looking skyward after swing)	1.00	.45	.13
☐ 12 Darren Daulton	1.00	.45	.13
☐ 13 Darren Daulton (Anticipating throw home)	1.00	.45	.13
☐ 14 Darren Daulton (Standing at home with ball in hand)	1.00	.45	.13
☐ 15 Darren Daulton (Running up first base line with in catching gear)	1.00	.45	.13
☐ 16 John Kruk (Follow through of swing)	1.00	.45	.13
☐ 17 John Kruk (Waiting on deck)	1.00	.45	.13
☐ 18 John Kruk (Follow through from first base dugout angle)	1.00	.45	.13
☐ 19 John Kruk (Swinging at pitch) chest high)	1.00	.45	.13
☐ 20 John Kruk (Looking out toward left field afer swinging)	1.00	.45	.13
☐ AU1 Darren Daulton	.00	.00	.00
☐ AU2 John Kruk	.00	.00	.00
☐ M1 Darren Daulton (About to throw down to second base)	1.50	.65	.19
☐ M2 John Kruk (Fielding position)	1.50	.65	.19
☐ M3 Darren Daulton (Awaiting pitch)	1.50	.65	.19
☐ M4 John Kruk (Running)	1.50	.65	.19

1994 Ultra Rising Stars

Randomly inserted in second series foil packs and jumbo packs at a rate of one in 36, this 12-card set spotlights top young major league stars. Metallic fronts have the player superimposed over icons resembling outer space. The backs feature the player in the same format along with text.

	MINT	EXC	G-VG
COMPLETE SET (12)	175.00	80.00	22.00
COMMON CARD (1-12)	5.00	2.30	.60
☐ 1 Carlos Baerga	12.00	5.50	1.50
☐ 2 Jeff Bagwell	35.00	16.00	4.40
☐ 3 Albert Belle	25.00	11.50	3.10
☐ 4 Cliff Floyd	12.00	5.50	1.50
☐ 5 Travis Fryman	5.00	2.30	.60
☐ 6 Marquis Grissom	6.00	2.70	.75
☐ 7 Kenny Lofton	20.00	9.00	2.50
☐ 8 John Olerud	5.00	2.30	.60
☐ 9 Mike Piazza	35.00	16.00	4.40
☐ 10 Kirk Rueter	5.00	2.30	.60
☐ 11 Tim Salmon	12.00	5.50	1.50
☐ 12 Aaron Sele	5.00	2.30	.60

1994 Ultra RBI Kings

Randomly inserted in first series jumbo packs at a rate of one in 36, this 12-card standard-size set features RBI leaders. These horizontal, metallized cards have a

color player photo on front that superimposes a player image.The backs have a write-up and a small color player photo. Cards 1-6 feature American League RBI Kings while cards 7-12 present National League RBI Kings.

	MINT	EXC	G-VG
COMPLETE SET (12)	230.00	105.00	29.00
COMMON CARD (1-12)	8.00	3.60	1.00
☐ 1 Albert Belle	25.00	11.50	3.10
☐ 2 Frank Thomas	75.00	34.00	9.50
☐ 3 Joe Carter	12.00	5.50	1.50
☐ 4 Juan Gonzalez	25.00	11.50	3.10
☐ 5 Cecil Fielder	8.00	3.60	1.00
☐ 6 Carlos Baerga	12.00	5.50	1.50
☐ 7 Barry Bonds	30.00	13.50	3.80
☐ 8 David Justice	12.00	5.50	1.50
☐ 9 Ron Gant	8.00	3.60	1.00
☐ 10 Mike Piazza	35.00	16.00	4.40
☐ 11 Matt Williams	14.00	6.25	1.75
☐ 12 Darren Daulton	8.00	3.60	1.00

1994 Ultra Second Year Standouts

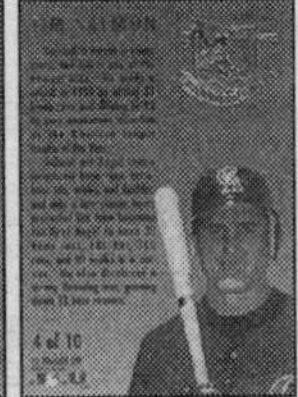

Randomly inserted in all first series packs at a rate of one in 11, this 10-card standard-size set includes 10 1993 outstanding rookies who are destined to become future stars. The fronts feature two color player action cutouts superimposed upon borderless team-colored backgrounds. The player's name appears in gold foil at the bottom. The back carries a color player head shot in a lower corner with his career highlights appearing alongside, all on a borderless team color-coded background. The set is arranged according to American League (1-5) and National League (6-10) players.

	MINT	EXC	G-VG
COMPLETE SET (10)	20.00	9.00	2.50
COMMON CARD (1-10)	.50	.23	.06
☐ 1 Jason Bere	2.50	1.15	.30
☐ 2 Brent Gates	.50	.23	.06
☐ 3 Jeffrey Hammonds	2.00	.90	.25
☐ 4 Tim Salmon	3.00	1.35	.40
☐ 5 Aaron Sele	1.50	.65	.19
☐ 6 Chuck Carr	.50	.23	.06
☐ 7 Jeff Conine	1.25	.55	.16
☐ 8 Greg McMichael	.50	.23	.06
☐ 9 Mike Piazza	10.00	4.50	1.25
☐ 10 Kevin Stocker	.50	.23	.06

1994 Ultra Strikeout Kings

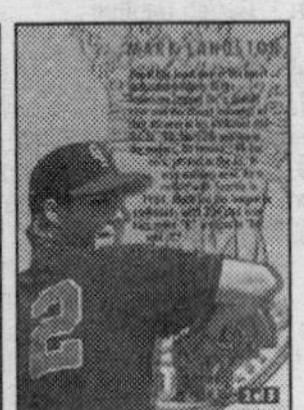

Randomly inserted in all second series packs at a rate of one in seven, this five-card standard-size set features top strikeout artists. Full-bleed fronts offer triple exposure photos and a gold foil Strikeout King logo. The backs contain a photo and write-up with the Strikeout King logo as background.

	MINT	EXC	G-VG
COMPLETE SET (5)	3.00	1.35	.40
COMMON CARD (1-5)	.50	.23	.06
☐ 1 Randy Johnson	.75	.35	.09
☐ 2 Mark Langston	.50	.23	.06
☐ 3 Greg Maddux	1.50	.65	.19
☐ 4 Jose Rijo	.50	.23	.06
☐ 5 John Smoltz	.50	.23	.06

1989 Upper Deck

This attractive 800-card set was introduced in 1989 as an additional fully licensed major card set. The cards feature full color on both the front and the back and are distinguished by the fact that each card has a

hologram on the reverse, thus making the cards essentially copy proof. The cards measure standard size, 2 1/2" by 3 1/2". Cards 668-693 feature a "Collector's Choice" (CC) colorful drawing of a player (by artist Vernon Wells) on the card front and a checklist of that team on the card back. Cards 1-26 are designated "Rookie Stars" by Upper Deck. On many cards "Rookie" and team logos can be found with either a "TM" or (R). Cards with missing or duplicate holograms appear to be relatively common and hence there is little, if any, premium value on these "variations". The more significant variations involving changed photos or changed type are listed below. According to the company, the Murphy and Sheridan cards were corrected very early, after only two percent of the cards had been produced. This means, for example, that out of 1,000,000 Dale Murphy '89 Upper Deck cards produced, there are only 20,000 Murphy error cards. Similarly, the Sheffield was corrected after 15 percent had been printed; Varsho, Gallego, and Schroeder were corrected after 20 percent; and Holton, Manrique, and Winningham were corrected 30 percent of the way through. Collectors should also note that many dealers consider that Upper Deck's "planned" production of 1,000,000 of each player was increased (perhaps even doubled) later in the year due to the explosion in popularity of the Upper Deck cards. Rookie Cards in the set include Jim Abbott, Sandy Alomar Jr., Dante Bichette, Norm Charlton, Junior Felix, Steve Finley, Ken Griffey Jr., Erik Hanson, Pete Harnisch, Charlie Hayes, Randy Johnson, Felix Jose, Ramon Martinez, Gregg Olson, Gary Sheffield, John Smoltz, Jerome Walton, and Todd Zeile. The high number cards (701-800) were made available three different ways: as part of the 800-card factory set, as a separate boxed set of 100 cards in a custom blue box, and in special high number foil packs.

	MINT	EXC	G-VG
COMPLETE SET (800)	110.00	50.00	14.00
COMPLETE FACT.SET (800)	120.00	55.00	15.00
COMPLETE LO SET (700)....	100.00	45.00	12.50
COMPLETE HI SET (100).......	10.00	4.50	1.25
COMPLETE HI FACT.SET (100)	10.00	4.50	1.25
COMMON CARD (1-700)...........	.10	.05	.01
COMMON CARD (701-800).......	.10	.05	.01

☐ 1 Ken Griffey Jr............... 75.00 19.00 3.80
☐ 2 Luis Medina..................... .10 .05 .01
☐ 3 Tony Chance................... .10 .05 .01
☐ 4 Dave Otto........................ .10 .05 .01
☐ 5 Sandy Alomar Jr. UER..... .50 .23 .06
(Born 6/16/66,
should be 6/18/66)
☐ 6 Rolando Roomes............ .10 .05 .01
☐ 7 Dave West....................... .15 .07 .02
☐ 8 Cris Carpenter.................. .10 .05 .01
☐ 9 Gregg Jefferies .... 1.50 .65 .19
☐ 10 Doug Dascenzo............. .10 .05 .01
☐ 11 Ron Jones...................... .10 .05 .01
☐ 12 Luis DeLosSantos.......... .10 .05 .01
☐ 13A Gary Sheffield ERR.... 5.00 2.30 .60
(SS upside down
on card front)
☐ 13B Gary Sheffield COR.... 5.00 2.30 .60
☐ 14 Mike Harkey................... .10 .05 .01
☐ 15 Lance Blankenship......... .10 .05 .01
☐ 16 William Brennan .... .10 .05 .01
☐ 17 John Smoltz................. 1.25 .55 .16
☐ 18 Ramon Martinez .... 1.25 .55 .16
☐ 19 Mark Lemke.................... .40 .18 .05
☐ 20 Juan Bell......................... .10 .05 .01
☐ 21 Rey Palacios .... .10 .05 .01
☐ 22 Felix Jose....................... .60 .25 .08
☐ 23 Van Snider .... .10 .05 .01
☐ 24 Dante Bichette............. 3.00 1.35 .40
☐ 25 Randy Johnson............ 3.00 1.35 .40
☐ 26 Carlos Quintana .... .10 .05 .01
☐ 27 Star Rookie CL............... .10 .05 .01
☐ 28 Mike Schooler................ .10 .05 .01
☐ 29 Randy St.Claire.............. .10 .05 .01
☐ 30 Jerald Clark.................... .10 .05 .01
☐ 31 Kevin Gross .... .10 .05 .01
☐ 32 Dan Firova...................... .10 .05 .01
☐ 33 Jeff Calhoun................... .10 .05 .01
☐ 34 Tommy Hinzo .... .10 .05 .01
☐ 35 Ricky Jordan.................. .25 .11 .03
☐ 36 Larry Parrish.................. .10 .05 .01
☐ 37 Bret Saberhagen UER .... .20 .09 .03
(Hit total 931,
should be 1031)
☐ 38 Mike Smithson............... .10 .05 .01
☐ 39 Dave Dravecky .... .15 .07 .02
☐ 40 Ed Romero..................... .10 .05 .01
☐ 41 Jeff Musselman .... .10 .05 .01
☐ 42 Ed Hearn .... .10 .05 .01
☐ 43 Rance Mulliniks .... .10 .05 .01
☐ 44 Jim Eisenreich .... .10 .05 .01
☐ 45 Sil Campusano............... .10 .05 .01
☐ 46 Mike Krukow................... .10 .05 .01
☐ 47 Paul Gibson .... .10 .05 .01
☐ 48 Mike LaCoss .... .10 .05 .01
☐ 49 Larry Herndon................ .10 .05 .01
☐ 50 Scott Garrelts................. .10 .05 .01
☐ 51 Dwayne Henry................ .10 .05 .01
☐ 52 Jim Acker........................ .10 .05 .01
☐ 53 Steve Sax........................ .10 .05 .01
☐ 54 Pete O'Brien................... .10 .05 .01
☐ 55 Paul Runge .... .10 .05 .01
☐ 56 Rick Rhoden .... .10 .05 .01
☐ 57 John Dopson .... .10 .05 .01
☐ 58 Casey Candaele UER...... .10 .05 .01
(No stats for Astros
for '88 season)
☐ 59 Dave Righetti .... .10 .05 .01
☐ 60 Joe Hesketh................... .10 .05 .01
☐ 61 Frank DiPino .... .10 .05 .01
☐ 62 Tim Laudner .... .10 .05 .01
☐ 63 Jamie Moyer................... .10 .05 .01
☐ 64 Fred Toliver.................... .10 .05 .01
☐ 65 Mitch Webster .... .10 .05 .01
☐ 66 John Tudor..................... .10 .05 .01
☐ 67 John Cangelosi .... .10 .05 .01
☐ 68 Mike Devereaux .... .15 .07 .02
☐ 69 Brian Fisher.................... .10 .05 .01
☐ 70 Mike Marshall .... .10 .05 .01
☐ 71 Zane Smith .... .10 .05 .01
☐ 72A Brian Holton ERR....... 1.25 .55 .16
(Photo actually
Shawn Hillegas)
☐ 72B Brian Holton COR .... .25 .11 .03
☐ 73 Jose Guzman .... .15 .07 .02
☐ 74 Rick Mahler.................... .10 .05 .01
☐ 75 John Shelby.................... .10 .05 .01
☐ 76 Jim Deshaies .... .10 .05 .01
☐ 77 Bobby Meacham .... .10 .05 .01

☐ 78 Bryn Smith .10 .05 .01
☐ 79 Joaquin Andujar .10 .05 .01
☐ 80 Richard Dotson .10 .05 .01
☐ 81 Charlie Lea .10 .05 .01
☐ 82 Calvin Schiraldi .10 .05 .01
☐ 83 Les Straker .10 .05 .01
☐ 84 Les Lancaster .10 .05 .01
☐ 85 Allan Anderson .10 .05 .01
☐ 86 Junior Ortiz .10 .05 .01
☐ 87 Jesse Orosco .10 .05 .01
☐ 88 Felix Fermin .10 .05 .01
☐ 89 Dave Anderson .10 .05 .01
☐ 90 Rafael Belliard UER .10 .05 .01
(Born '61, not '51)
☐ 91 Franklin Stubbs .10 .05 .01
☐ 92 Cecil Espy .10 .05 .01
☐ 93 Albert Hall .10 .05 .01
☐ 94 Tim Leary .10 .05 .01
☐ 95 Mitch Williams .15 .07 .02
☐ 96 Tracy Jones .10 .05 .01
☐ 97 Danny Darwin .10 .05 .01
☐ 98 Gary Ward .10 .05 .01
☐ 99 Neal Heaton .10 .05 .01
☐ 100 Jim Pankovits .10 .05 .01
☐ 101 Bill Doran .10 .05 .01
☐ 102 Tim Wallach .15 .07 .02
☐ 103 Joe Magrane .10 .05 .01
☐ 104 Ozzie Virgil .10 .05 .01
☐ 105 Alvin Davis .10 .05 .01
☐ 106 Tom Brookens .10 .05 .01
☐ 107 Shawon Dunston .15 .07 .02
☐ 108 Tracy Woodson .10 .05 .01
☐ 109 Nelson Liriano .10 .05 .01
☐ 110 Devon White UER .25 .11 .03
(Doubles total 46, should be 56)
☐ 111 Steve Balboni .10 .05 .01
☐ 112 Buddy Bell .15 .07 .02
☐ 113 German Jimenez .10 .05 .01
☐ 114 Ken Dayley .10 .05 .01
☐ 115 Andres Galarraga .75 .35 .09
☐ 116 Mike Scioscia .10 .05 .01
☐ 117 Gary Pettis .10 .05 .01
☐ 118 Ernie Whitt .10 .05 .01
☐ 119 Bob Boone .15 .07 .02
☐ 120 Ryne Sandberg 1.50 .65 .19
☐ 121 Bruce Benedict .10 .05 .01
☐ 122 Hubie Brooks .10 .05 .01
☐ 123 Mike Moore .10 .05 .01
☐ 124 Wallace Johnson .10 .05 .01
☐ 125 Bob Horner .10 .05 .01
☐ 126 Chili Davis .15 .07 .02
☐ 127 Manny Trillo .10 .05 .01
☐ 128 Chet Lemon .10 .05 .01
☐ 129 John Cerutti .10 .05 .01
☐ 130 Orel Hershiser .15 .07 .02
☐ 131 Terry Pendleton .10 .05 .01
☐ 132 Jeff Blauser .20 .09 .03
☐ 133 Mike Fitzgerald .10 .05 .01
☐ 134 Henry Cotto .10 .05 .01
☐ 135 Gerald Young .10 .05 .01
☐ 136 Luis Salazar .10 .05 .01
☐ 137 Alejandro Pena .10 .05 .01
☐ 138 Jack Howell .10 .05 .01
☐ 139 Tony Fernandez .15 .07 .02
☐ 140 Mark Grace .75 .35 .09
☐ 141 Ken Caminiti .20 .09 .03
☐ 142 Mike Jackson .10 .05 .01
☐ 143 Larry McWilliams .10 .05 .01
☐ 144 Andres Thomas .10 .05 .01
☐ 145 Nolan Ryan 3X 4.00 1.80 .50
☐ 146 Mike Davis .10 .05 .01
☐ 147 DeWayne Buice .10 .05 .01
☐ 148 Jody Davis .10 .05 .01
☐ 149 Jesse Barfield .10 .05 .01
☐ 150 Matt Nokes .10 .05 .01
☐ 151 Jerry Reuss .10 .05 .01
☐ 152 Rick Cerone .10 .05 .01
☐ 153 Storm Davis .10 .05 .01
☐ 154 Marvell Wynne .10 .05 .01
☐ 155 Will Clark 1.25 .55 .16
☐ 156 Luis Aguayo .10 .05 .01
☐ 157 Willie Upshaw .10 .05 .01
☐ 158 Randy Bush .10 .05 .01
☐ 159 Ron Darling .15 .07 .02
☐ 160 Kal Daniels .10 .05 .01
☐ 161 Spike Owen .10 .05 .01
☐ 162 Luis Polonia .15 .07 .02
☐ 163 Kevin Mitchell UER .20 .09 .03
('88/total HR's 18/52, should be 19/53)
☐ 164 Dave Gallagher .10 .05 .01
☐ 165 Benito Santiago .15 .07 .02
☐ 166 Greg Gagne .10 .05 .01
☐ 167 Ken Phelps .10 .05 .01
☐ 168 Sid Fernandez .15 .07 .02
☐ 169 Bo Diaz .10 .05 .01
☐ 170 Cory Snyder .10 .05 .01
☐ 171 Eric Show .10 .05 .01
☐ 172 Robby Thompson .15 .07 .02
☐ 173 Marty Barrett .10 .05 .01
☐ 174 Dave Henderson .10 .05 .01
☐ 175 Ozzie Guillen .15 .07 .02
☐ 176 Barry Lyons .10 .05 .01
☐ 177 Kelvin Torve .10 .05 .01
☐ 178 Don Slaught .10 .05 .01
☐ 179 Steve Lombardozzi .10 .05 .01
☐ 180 Chris Sabo .50 .23 .06
☐ 181 Jose Uribe .10 .05 .01
☐ 182 Shane Mack .15 .07 .02
☐ 183 Ron Karkovice .10 .05 .01
☐ 184 Todd Benzinger .10 .05 .01
☐ 185 Dave Stewart .15 .07 .02
☐ 186 Julio Franco .15 .07 .02
☐ 187 Ron Robinson .10 .05 .01
☐ 188 Wally Backman .10 .05 .01
☐ 189 Randy Velarde .10 .05 .01
☐ 190 Joe Carter 1.00 .45 .13
☐ 191 Bob Welch .15 .07 .02
☐ 192 Kelly Paris .10 .05 .01
☐ 193 Chris Brown .10 .05 .01
☐ 194 Rick Reuschel .10 .05 .01
☐ 195 Roger Clemens 1.25 .55 .16
☐ 196 Dave Concepcion .15 .07 .02
☐ 197 Al Newman .10 .05 .01
☐ 198 Brook Jacoby .10 .05 .01
☐ 199 Mookie Wilson .15 .07 .02
☐ 200 Don Mattingly 1.50 .65 .19
☐ 201 Dick Schofield .10 .05 .01
☐ 202 Mark Gubicza .10 .05 .01
☐ 203 Gary Gaetti .10 .05 .01
☐ 204 Dan Pasqua .10 .05 .01
☐ 205 Andre Dawson .50 .23 .06
☐ 206 Chris Speier .10 .05 .01
☐ 207 Kent Tekulve .10 .05 .01
☐ 208 Rod Scurry .10 .05 .01
☐ 209 Scott Bailes .10 .05 .01
☐ 210 Rickey Henderson UER .75 .35 .09
(Throws Right)
☐ 211 Harold Baines .15 .07 .02
☐ 212 Tony Armas .10 .05 .01
☐ 213 Kent Hrbek .15 .07 .02
☐ 214 Darrin Jackson .15 .07 .02
☐ 215 George Brett 1.50 .65 .19
☐ 216 Rafael Santana .10 .05 .01
☐ 217 Andy Allanson .10 .05 .01

☐ 218	Brett Butler	.15	.07	.02
☐ 219	Steve Jeltz	.10	.05	.01
☐ 220	Jay Buhner	.60	.25	.08
☐ 221	Bo Jackson	.75	.35	.09
☐ 222	Angel Salazar	.10	.05	.01
☐ 223	Kirk McCaskill	.10	.05	.01
☐ 224	Steve Lyons	.10	.05	.01
☐ 225	Bert Blyleven	.20	.09	.03
☐ 226	Scott Bradley	.10	.05	.01
☐ 227	Bob Melvin	.10	.05	.01
☐ 228	Ron Kittle	.10	.05	.01
☐ 229	Phil Bradley	.10	.05	.01
☐ 230	Tommy John	.20	.09	.03
☐ 231	Greg Walker	.10	.05	.01
☐ 232	Juan Berenguer	.10	.05	.01
☐ 233	Pat Tabler	.10	.05	.01
☐ 234	Terry Clark	.10	.05	.01
☐ 235	Rafael Palmeiro	1.00	.45	.13
☐ 236	Paul Zuvella	.10	.05	.01
☐ 237	Willie Randolph	.15	.07	.02
☐ 238	Bruce Fields	.10	.05	.01
☐ 239	Mike Aldrete	.10	.05	.01
☐ 240	Lance Parrish	.15	.07	.02
☐ 241	Greg Maddux	2.50	1.15	.30
☐ 242	John Moses	.10	.05	.01
☐ 243	Melido Perez	.10	.05	.01
☐ 244	Willie Wilson	.10	.05	.01
☐ 245	Mark McLemore	.10	.05	.01
☐ 246	Von Hayes	.10	.05	.01
☐ 247	Matt Williams	2.50	1.15	.30
☐ 248	John Candelaria UER (Listed as Yankee for part of '87, should be Mets)	.10	.05	.01
☐ 249	Harold Reynolds	.10	.05	.01
☐ 250	Greg Swindell	.15	.07	.02
☐ 251	Juan Agosto	.10	.05	.01
☐ 252	Mike Felder	.10	.05	.01
☐ 253	Vince Coleman	.15	.07	.02
☐ 254	Larry Sheets	.10	.05	.01
☐ 255	George Bell	.15	.07	.02
☐ 256	Terry Steinbach	.15	.07	.02
☐ 257	Jack Armstrong	.10	.05	.01
☐ 258	Dickie Thon	.10	.05	.01
☐ 259	Ray Knight	.15	.07	.02
☐ 260	Darryl Strawberry	.20	.09	.03
☐ 261	Doug Sisk	.10	.05	.01
☐ 262	Alex Trevino	.10	.05	.01
☐ 263	Jeffrey Leonard	.10	.05	.01
☐ 264	Tom Henke	.15	.07	.02
☐ 265	Ozzie Smith	.75	.35	.09
☐ 266	Dave Bergman	.10	.05	.01
☐ 267	Tony Phillips	.15	.07	.02
☐ 268	Mark Davis	.10	.05	.01
☐ 269	Kevin Elster	.10	.05	.01
☐ 270	Barry Larkin	.40	.18	.05
☐ 271	Manny Lee	.10	.05	.01
☐ 272	Tom Brunansky	.10	.05	.01
☐ 273	Craig Biggio	2.00	.90	.25
☐ 274	Jim Gantner	.10	.05	.01
☐ 275	Eddie Murray	.50	.23	.06
☐ 276	Jeff Reed	.10	.05	.01
☐ 277	Tim Teufel	.10	.05	.01
☐ 278	Rick Honeycutt	.10	.05	.01
☐ 279	Guillermo Hernandez	.10	.05	.01
☐ 280	John Kruk	.40	.18	.05
☐ 281	Luis Alicea	.10	.05	.01
☐ 282	Jim Clancy	.10	.05	.01
☐ 283	Billy Ripken	.10	.05	.01
☐ 284	Craig Reynolds	.10	.05	.01
☐ 285	Robin Yount	.75	.35	.09
☐ 286	Jimmy Jones	.10	.05	.01
☐ 287	Ron Oester	.10	.05	.01
☐ 288	Terry Leach	.10	.05	.01
☐ 289	Dennis Eckersley	.20	.09	.03
☐ 290	Alan Trammell	.20	.09	.03
☐ 291	Jimmy Key	.50	.23	.06
☐ 292	Chris Bosio	.10	.05	.01
☐ 293	Jose DeLeon	.10	.05	.01
☐ 294	Jim Traber	.10	.05	.01
☐ 295	Mike Scott	.10	.05	.01
☐ 296	Roger McDowell	.10	.05	.01
☐ 297	Garry Templeton	.10	.05	.01
☐ 298	Doyle Alexander	.10	.05	.01
☐ 299	Nick Esasky	.10	.05	.01
☐ 300	Mark McGwire UER (Doubles total 52, should be 51)	.75	.35	.09
☐ 301	Darryl Hamilton	.50	.23	.06
☐ 302	Dave Smith	.10	.05	.01
☐ 303	Rick Sutcliffe	.15	.07	.02
☐ 304	Dave Stapleton	.10	.05	.01
☐ 305	Alan Ashby	.10	.05	.01
☐ 306	Pedro Guerrero	.15	.07	.02
☐ 307	Ron Guidry	.15	.07	.02
☐ 308	Steve Farr	.10	.05	.01
☐ 309	Curt Ford	.10	.05	.01
☐ 310	Claudell Washington	.10	.05	.01
☐ 311	Tom Prince	.10	.05	.01
☐ 312	Chad Kreuter	.30	.14	.04
☐ 313	Ken Oberkfell	.10	.05	.01
☐ 314	Jerry Browne	.10	.05	.01
☐ 315	R.J. Reynolds	.10	.05	.01
☐ 316	Scott Bankhead	.10	.05	.01
☐ 317	Milt Thompson	.10	.05	.01
☐ 318	Mario Diaz	.10	.05	.01
☐ 319	Bruce Ruffin	.10	.05	.01
☐ 320	Dave Valle	.10	.05	.01
☐ 321A	Gary Varsho ERR (Back photo actually Mike Bielecki bunting)	2.00	.90	.25
☐ 321B	Gary Varsho COR (In road uniform)	.10	.05	.01
☐ 322	Paul Mirabella	.10	.05	.01
☐ 323	Chuck Jackson	.10	.05	.01
☐ 324	Drew Hall	.10	.05	.01
☐ 325	Don August	.10	.05	.01
☐ 326	Israel Sanchez	.10	.05	.01
☐ 327	Denny Walling	.10	.05	.01
☐ 328	Joel Skinner	.10	.05	.01
☐ 329	Danny Tartabull	.15	.07	.02
☐ 330	Tony Pena	.10	.05	.01
☐ 331	Jim Sundberg	.10	.05	.01
☐ 332	Jeff D. Robinson	.10	.05	.01
☐ 333	Oddibe McDowell	.10	.05	.01
☐ 334	Jose Lind	.10	.05	.01
☐ 335	Paul Kilgus	.10	.05	.01
☐ 336	Juan Samuel	.10	.05	.01
☐ 337	Mike Campbell	.10	.05	.01
☐ 338	Mike Maddux	.10	.05	.01
☐ 339	Darnell Coles	.10	.05	.01
☐ 340	Bob Dernier	.10	.05	.01
☐ 341	Rafael Ramirez	.10	.05	.01
☐ 342	Scott Sanderson	.10	.05	.01
☐ 343	B.J. Surhoff	.10	.05	.01
☐ 344	Billy Hatcher	.10	.05	.01
☐ 345	Pat Perry	.10	.05	.01
☐ 346	Jack Clark	.15	.07	.02
☐ 347	Gary Thurman	.10	.05	.01
☐ 348	Tim Jones	.10	.05	.01
☐ 349	Dave Winfield	.75	.35	.09
☐ 350	Frank White	.15	.07	.02
☐ 351	Dave Collins	.10	.05	.01
☐ 352	Jack Morris	.20	.09	.03
☐ 353	Eric Plunk	.10	.05	.01
☐ 354	Leon Durham	.10	.05	.01

No.	Player			
☐ 355	Ivan DeJesus	.10	.05	.01
☐ 356	Brian Holman	.10	.05	.01
☐ 357A	Dale Murphy ERR (Front has reverse negative)	35.00	16.00	4.40
☐ 357B	Dale Murphy COR	.25	.11	.03
☐ 358	Mark Portugal	.15	.07	.02
☐ 359	Andy McGaffigan	.10	.05	.01
☐ 360	Tom Glavine	1.25	.55	.16
☐ 361	Keith Moreland	.10	.05	.01
☐ 362	Todd Stottlemyre	.15	.07	.02
☐ 363	Dave Leiper	.10	.05	.01
☐ 364	Cecil Fielder	1.00	.45	.13
☐ 365	Carmelo Martinez	.10	.05	.01
☐ 366	Dwight Evans	.15	.07	.02
☐ 367	Kevin McReynolds	.15	.07	.02
☐ 368	Rich Gedman	.10	.05	.01
☐ 369	Len Dykstra	.50	.23	.06
☐ 370	Jody Reed	.10	.05	.01
☐ 371	Jose Canseco UER (Strikeout total 391, should be 491)	1.25	.55	.16
☐ 372	Rob Murphy	.10	.05	.01
☐ 373	Mike Henneman	.15	.07	.02
☐ 374	Walt Weiss	.10	.05	.01
☐ 375	Rob Dibble	.35	.16	.04
☐ 376	Kirby Puckett (Mark McGwire in background)	1.50	.65	.19
☐ 377	Dennis Martinez	.15	.07	.02
☐ 378	Ron Gant	1.00	.45	.13
☐ 379	Brian Harper	.15	.07	.02
☐ 380	Nelson Santovenia	.10	.05	.01
☐ 381	Lloyd Moseby	.10	.05	.01
☐ 382	Lance McCullers	.10	.05	.01
☐ 383	Dave Stieb	.15	.07	.02
☐ 384	Tony Gwynn	1.00	.45	.13
☐ 385	Mike Flanagan	.10	.05	.01
☐ 386	Bob Ojeda	.10	.05	.01
☐ 387	Bruce Hurst	.10	.05	.01
☐ 388	Dave Magadan	.10	.05	.01
☐ 389	Wade Boggs	.75	.35	.09
☐ 390	Gary Carter	.20	.09	.03
☐ 391	Frank Tanana	.10	.05	.01
☐ 392	Curt Young	.10	.05	.01
☐ 393	Jeff Treadway	.10	.05	.01
☐ 394	Darrell Evans	.15	.07	.02
☐ 395	Glenn Hubbard	.10	.05	.01
☐ 396	Chuck Cary	.10	.05	.01
☐ 397	Frank Viola	.15	.07	.02
☐ 398	Jeff Parrett	.10	.05	.01
☐ 399	Terry Blocker	.10	.05	.01
☐ 400	Dan Gladden	.10	.05	.01
☐ 401	Louie Meadows	.10	.05	.01
☐ 402	Tim Raines	.20	.09	.03
☐ 403	Joey Meyer	.10	.05	.01
☐ 404	Larry Andersen	.10	.05	.01
☐ 405	Rex Hudler	.10	.05	.01
☐ 406	Mike Schmidt	1.50	.65	.19
☐ 407	John Franco	.15	.07	.02
☐ 408	Brady Anderson	.75	.35	.09
☐ 409	Don Carman	.10	.05	.01
☐ 410	Eric Davis	.15	.07	.02
☐ 411	Bob Stanley	.10	.05	.01
☐ 412	Pete Smith	.10	.05	.01
☐ 413	Jim Rice	.20	.09	.03
☐ 414	Bruce Sutter	.15	.07	.02
☐ 415	Oil Can Boyd	.10	.05	.01
☐ 416	Ruben Sierra	.75	.35	.09
☐ 417	Mike LaValliere	.10	.05	.01
☐ 418	Steve Buechele	.10	.05	.01
☐ 419	Gary Redus	.10	.05	.01
☐ 420	Scott Fletcher	.10	.05	.01
☐ 421	Dale Sveum	.10	.05	.01
☐ 422	Bob Knepper	.10	.05	.01
☐ 423	Luis Rivera	.10	.05	.01
☐ 424	Ted Higuera	.10	.05	.01
☐ 425	Kevin Bass	.10	.05	.01
☐ 426	Ken Gerhart	.10	.05	.01
☐ 427	Shane Rawley	.10	.05	.01
☐ 428	Paul O'Neill	.40	.18	.05
☐ 429	Joe Orsulak	.10	.05	.01
☐ 430	Jackie Gutierrez	.10	.05	.01
☐ 431	Gerald Perry	.10	.05	.01
☐ 432	Mike Greenwell	.15	.07	.02
☐ 433	Jerry Royster	.10	.05	.01
☐ 434	Ellis Burks	.15	.07	.02
☐ 435	Ed Olwine	.10	.05	.01
☐ 436	Dave Rucker	.10	.05	.01
☐ 437	Charlie Hough	.15	.07	.02
☐ 438	Bob Walk	.10	.05	.01
☐ 439	Bob Brower	.10	.05	.01
☐ 440	Barry Bonds	2.00	.90	.25
☐ 441	Tom Foley	.10	.05	.01
☐ 442	Rob Deer	.10	.05	.01
☐ 443	Glenn Davis	.10	.05	.01
☐ 444	Dave Martinez	.10	.05	.01
☐ 445	Bill Wegman	.10	.05	.01
☐ 446	Lloyd McClendon	.10	.05	.01
☐ 447	Dave Schmidt	.10	.05	.01
☐ 448	Darren Daulton	.50	.23	.06
☐ 449	Frank Williams	.10	.05	.01
☐ 450	Don Aase	.10	.05	.01
☐ 451	Lou Whitaker	.20	.09	.03
☐ 452	Goose Gossage	.20	.09	.03
☐ 453	Ed Whitson	.10	.05	.01
☐ 454	Jim Walewander	.10	.05	.01
☐ 455	Damon Berryhill	.10	.05	.01
☐ 456	Tim Burke	.10	.05	.01
☐ 457	Barry Jones	.10	.05	.01
☐ 458	Joel Youngblood	.10	.05	.01
☐ 459	Floyd Youmans	.10	.05	.01
☐ 460	Mark Salas	.10	.05	.01
☐ 461	Jeff Russell	.10	.05	.01
☐ 462	Darrell Miller	.10	.05	.01
☐ 463	Jeff Kunkel	.10	.05	.01
☐ 464	Sherman Corbett	.10	.05	.01
☐ 465	Curtis Wilkerson	.10	.05	.01
☐ 466	Bud Black	.10	.05	.01
☐ 467	Cal Ripken	2.00	.90	.25
☐ 468	John Farrell	.10	.05	.01
☐ 469	Terry Kennedy	.10	.05	.01
☐ 470	Tom Candiotti	.10	.05	.01
☐ 471	Roberto Alomar	3.00	1.35	.40
☐ 472	Jeff M. Robinson	.10	.05	.01
☐ 473	Vance Law	.10	.05	.01
☐ 474	Randy Ready UER (Strikeout total 136, should be 115)	.10	.05	.01
☐ 475	Walt Terrell	.10	.05	.01
☐ 476	Kelly Downs	.10	.05	.01
☐ 477	Johnny Paredes	.10	.05	.01
☐ 478	Shawn Hillegas	.10	.05	.01
☐ 479	Bob Brenly	.10	.05	.01
☐ 480	Otis Nixon	.15	.07	.02
☐ 481	Johnny Ray	.10	.05	.01
☐ 482	Geno Petralli	.10	.05	.01
☐ 483	Stu Cliburn	.10	.05	.01
☐ 484	Pete Incaviglia	.15	.07	.02
☐ 485	Brian Downing	.10	.05	.01
☐ 486	Jeff Stone	.10	.05	.01
☐ 487	Carmen Castillo	.10	.05	.01
☐ 488	Tom Niedenfuer	.10	.05	.01
☐ 489	Jay Bell	.20	.09	.03
☐ 490	Rick Schu	.10	.05	.01
☐ 491	Jeff Pico	.10	.05	.01

	Card			
☐	492 Mark Parent	.10	.05	.01
☐	493 Eric King	.10	.05	.01
☐	494 Al Nipper	.10	.05	.01
☐	495 Andy Hawkins	.10	.05	.01
☐	496 Daryl Boston	.10	.05	.01
☐	497 Ernest Riles	.10	.05	.01
☐	498 Pascual Perez	.10	.05	.01
☐	499 Bill Long UER (Games started total 70, should be 44)	.10	.05	.01
☐	500 Kirt Manwaring	.10	.05	.01
☐	501 Chuck Crim	.10	.05	.01
☐	502 Candy Maldonado	.10	.05	.01
☐	503 Dennis Lamp	.10	.05	.01
☐	504 Glenn Braggs	.10	.05	.01
☐	505 Joe Price	.10	.05	.01
☐	506 Ken Williams	.10	.05	.01
☐	507 Bill Pecota	.10	.05	.01
☐	508 Rey Quinones	.10	.05	.01
☐	509 Jeff Bittiger	.10	.05	.01
☐	510 Kevin Seitzer	.10	.05	.01
☐	511 Steve Bedrosian	.10	.05	.01
☐	512 Todd Worrell	.10	.05	.01
☐	513 Chris James	.10	.05	.01
☐	514 Jose Oquendo	.10	.05	.01
☐	515 David Palmer	.10	.05	.01
☐	516 John Smiley	.10	.05	.01
☐	517 Dave Clark	.10	.05	.01
☐	518 Mike Dunne	.10	.05	.01
☐	519 Ron Washington	.10	.05	.01
☐	520 Bob Kipper	.10	.05	.01
☐	521 Lee Smith	.25	.11	.03
☐	522 Juan Castillo	.10	.05	.01
☐	523 Don Robinson	.10	.05	.01
☐	524 Kevin Romine	.10	.05	.01
☐	525 Paul Molitor	1.00	.45	.13
☐	526 Mark Langston	.20	.09	.03
☐	527 Donnie Hill	.10	.05	.01
☐	528 Larry Owen	.10	.05	.01
☐	529 Jerry Reed	.10	.05	.01
☐	530 Jack McDowell	1.00	.45	.13
☐	531 Greg Mathews	.10	.05	.01
☐	532 John Russell	.10	.05	.01
☐	533 Dan Quisenberry	.15	.07	.02
☐	534 Greg Gross	.10	.05	.01
☐	535 Danny Cox	.10	.05	.01
☐	536 Terry Francona	.10	.05	.01
☐	537 Andy Van Slyke	.20	.09	.03
☐	538 Mel Hall	.10	.05	.01
☐	539 Jim Gott	.10	.05	.01
☐	540 Doug Jones	.15	.07	.02
☐	541 Craig Lefferts	.10	.05	.01
☐	542 Mike Boddicker	.10	.05	.01
☐	543 Greg Brock	.10	.05	.01
☐	544 Atlee Hammaker	.10	.05	.01
☐	545 Tom Bolton	.10	.05	.01
☐	546 Mike Macfarlane	.50	.23	.06
☐	547 Rich Renteria	.10	.05	.01
☐	548 John Davis	.10	.05	.01
☐	549 Floyd Bannister	.10	.05	.01
☐	550 Mickey Brantley	.10	.05	.01
☐	551 Duane Ward	.15	.07	.02
☐	552 Dan Petry	.10	.05	.01
☐	553 Mickey Tettleton UER (Walks total 175, should be 136)	.15	.07	.02
☐	554 Rick Leach	.10	.05	.01
☐	555 Mike Witt	.10	.05	.01
☐	556 Sid Bream	.10	.05	.01
☐	557 Bobby Witt	.15	.07	.02
☐	558 Tommy Herr	.10	.05	.01
☐	559 Randy Milligan	.10	.05	.01
☐	560 Jose Cecena	.10	.05	.01
☐	561 Mackey Sasser	.10	.05	.01
☐	562 Carney Lansford	.15	.07	.02
☐	563 Rick Aguilera	.15	.07	.02
☐	564 Ron Hassey	.10	.05	.01
☐	565 Dwight Gooden	.15	.07	.02
☐	566 Paul Assenmacher	.10	.05	.01
☐	567 Neil Allen	.10	.05	.01
☐	568 Jim Morrison	.10	.05	.01
☐	569 Mike Pagliarulo	.10	.05	.01
☐	570 Ted Simmons	.15	.07	.02
☐	571 Mark Thurmond	.10	.05	.01
☐	572 Fred McGriff	1.25	.55	.16
☐	573 Wally Joyner	.15	.07	.02
☐	574 Jose Bautista	.10	.05	.01
☐	575 Kelly Gruber	.10	.05	.01
☐	576 Cecilio Guante	.10	.05	.01
☐	577 Mark Davidson	.10	.05	.01
☐	578 Bobby Bonilla UER (Total steals 2 in '87, should be 3)	.40	.18	.05
☐	579 Mike Stanley	.15	.07	.02
☐	580 Gene Larkin	.10	.05	.01
☐	581 Stan Javier	.10	.05	.01
☐	582 Howard Johnson	.15	.07	.02
☐	583A Mike Gallego ERR (Front reversed negative)	1.25	.55	.16
☐	583B Mike Gallego COR	.25	.11	.03
☐	584 David Cone	.60	.25	.08
☐	585 Doug Jennings	.10	.05	.01
☐	586 Charles Hudson	.10	.05	.01
☐	587 Dion James	.10	.05	.01
☐	588 Al Leiter	.10	.05	.01
☐	589 Charlie Puleo	.10	.05	.01
☐	590 Roberto Kelly	.50	.23	.06
☐	591 Thad Bosley	.10	.05	.01
☐	592 Pete Stanicek	.10	.05	.01
☐	593 Pat Borders	.50	.23	.06
☐	594 Bryan Harvey	.60	.25	.08
☐	595 Jeff Ballard	.10	.05	.01
☐	596 Jeff Reardon	.20	.09	.03
☐	597 Doug Drabek	.20	.09	.03
☐	598 Edwin Correa	.10	.05	.01
☐	599 Keith Atherton	.10	.05	.01
☐	600 Dave LaPoint	.10	.05	.01
☐	601 Don Baylor	.20	.09	.03
☐	602 Tom Pagnozzi	.10	.05	.01
☐	603 Tim Flannery	.10	.05	.01
☐	604 Gene Walter	.10	.05	.01
☐	605 Dave Parker	.20	.09	.03
☐	606 Mike Diaz	.10	.05	.01
☐	607 Chris Gwynn	.10	.05	.01
☐	608 Odell Jones	.10	.05	.01
☐	609 Carlton Fisk	.50	.23	.06
☐	610 Jay Howell	.10	.05	.01
☐	611 Tim Crews	.10	.05	.01
☐	612 Keith Hernandez	.15	.07	.02
☐	613 Willie Fraser	.10	.05	.01
☐	614 Jim Eppard	.10	.05	.01
☐	615 Jeff Hamilton	.10	.05	.01
☐	616 Kurt Stillwell	.10	.05	.01
☐	617 Tom Browning	.10	.05	.01
☐	618 Jeff Montgomery	.25	.11	.03
☐	619 Jose Rijo	.20	.09	.03
☐	620 Jamie Quirk	.10	.05	.01
☐	621 Willie McGee	.15	.07	.02
☐	622 Mark Grant UER (Glove on wrong hand)	.10	.05	.01
☐	623 Bill Swift	.15	.07	.02
☐	624 Orlando Mercado	.10	.05	.01
☐	625 John Costello	.10	.05	.01
☐	626 Jose Gonzalez	.10	.05	.01
☐	627A Bill Schroeder ERR	1.25	.55	.16

(Back photo actually
Ronn Reynolds buckling
shin guards)
☐ 627B Bill Schroeder COR .... .25 .11 .03
☐ 628A Fred Manrique ERR ... .35 .16 .04
(Back photo actually
Ozzie Guillen throwing)
☐ 628B Fred Manrique COR ... .10 .05 .01
(Swinging bat on back)
☐ 629 Ricky Horton .... .10 .05 .01
☐ 630 Dan Plesac .... .10 .05 .01
☐ 631 Alfredo Griffin .... .10 .05 .01
☐ 632 Chuck Finley .... .15 .07 .02
☐ 633 Kirk Gibson .... .15 .07 .02
☐ 634 Randy Myers.............. .15 .07 .02
☐ 635 Greg Minton............... .10 .05 .01
☐ 636A Herm Winningham .... .35 .16 .04
ERR (W1nningham
on back)
☐ 636B Herm Winningham COR .10 .05 .01
☐ 637 Charlie Leibrandt......... .10 .05 .01
☐ 638 Tim Birtsas .... .10 .05 .01
☐ 639 Bill Buckner................ .15 .07 .02
☐ 640 Danny Jackson .... .10 .05 .01
☐ 641 Greg Booker............... .10 .05 .01
☐ 642 Jim Presley .... .10 .05 .01
☐ 643 Gene Nelson .... .10 .05 .01
☐ 644 Rod Booker................. .10 .05 .01
☐ 645 Dennis Rasmussen...... .10 .05 .01
☐ 646 Juan Nieves .... .10 .05 .01
☐ 647 Bobby Thigpen............ .10 .05 .01
☐ 648 Tim Belcher................ .10 .05 .01
☐ 649 Mike Young................. .10 .05 .01
☐ 650 Ivan Calderon.............. .10 .05 .01
☐ 651 Oswaldo Peraza .... .10 .05 .01
☐ 652A Pat Sheridan ERR .. 12.00 5.50 1.50
(No position on front)
☐ 652B Pat Sheridan COR...... .10 .05 .01
☐ 653 Mike Morgan............... .10 .05 .01
☐ 654 Mike Heath.................. .10 .05 .01
☐ 655 Jay Tibbs .... .10 .05 .01
☐ 656 Fernando Valenzuela .... .10 .05 .01
☐ 657 Lee Mazzilli .... .10 .05 .01
☐ 658 Frank Viola AL CY .... .15 .07 .02
☐ 659A Jose Canseco AL MVP .60 .25 .08
(Eagle logo in black)
☐ 659B Jose Canseco AL MVP .60 .25 .08
(Eagle logo in blue)
☐ 660 Walt Weiss AL ROY ..... .15 .07 .02
☐ 661 Orel Hershiser NL CY.... .15 .07 .02
☐ 662 Kirk Gibson NL MVP .... .20 .09 .03
☐ 663 Chris Sabo NL ROY...... .15 .07 .02
☐ 664 D.Eckersley ALCS MVP .20 .09 .03
☐ 665 O.Hershiser NLCS MVP .15 .07 .02
☐ 666 Great WS Moment .... .20 .09 .03
(Kirk Gibson's homer)
☐ 667 Orel Hershiser WS MVP .15 .07 .02
☐ 668 Wally Joyner TC........... .15 .07 .02
California Angels
☐ 669 Nolan Ryan TC............ .75 .35 .09
Houston Astros
☐ 670 Jose Canseco TC .... .35 .16 .04
Oakland Athletics
☐ 671 Fred McGriff TC .... .35 .16 .04
Toronto Blue Jays
☐ 672 Dale Murphy TC........... .15 .07 .02
Atlanta Braves
☐ 673 Paul Molitor TC............ .25 .11 .03
Milwaukee Brewers
☐ 674 Ozzie Smith TC............ .15 .07 .02
St. Louis Cardinals
☐ 675 Ryne Sandberg TC....... .35 .16 .04
Chicago Cubs
☐ 676 Kirk Gibson TC............ .15 .07 .02
Los Angeles Dodgers
☐ 677 Andres Galarraga TC.... .20 .09 .03
Montreal Expos
☐ 678 Will Clark TC .... .40 .18 .05
San Francisco Giants
☐ 679 Cory Snyder TC........... .10 .05 .01
Cleveland Indians
☐ 680 Alvin Davis TC............. .10 .05 .01
Seattle Mariners
☐ 681 Darryl Strawberry TC .... .15 .07 .02
New York Mets
☐ 682 Cal Ripken TC .... .50 .23 .06
Baltimore Orioles
☐ 683 Tony Gwynn TC .... .25 .11 .03
San Diego Padres
☐ 684 Mike Schmidt TC .... .50 .23 .06
Philadelphia Phillies
☐ 685 Andy Van Slyke TC....... .15 .07 .02
Pittsburgh Pirates
UER (96 Junior Ortiz)
☐ 686 Ruben Sierra TC.......... .20 .09 .03
Texas Rangers
☐ 687 Wade Boggs TC .... .20 .09 .03
Boston Red Sox
☐ 688 Eric Davis TC .... .15 .07 .02
Cincinnati Reds
☐ 689 George Brett TC .... .30 .14 .04
Kansas City Royals
☐ 690 Alan Trammell TC .... .15 .07 .02
Detroit Tigers
☐ 691 Frank Viola TC............. .10 .05 .01
Minnesota Twins
☐ 692 Harold Baines TC .... .15 .07 .02
Chicago White Sox
☐ 693 Don Mattingly TC......... .30 .14 .04
New York Yankees
☐ 694 Checklist 1-100............ .10 .05 .01
☐ 695 Checklist 101-200........ .10 .05 .01
☐ 696 Checklist 201-300........ .10 .05 .01
☐ 697 Checklist 301-400........ .10 .05 .01
☐ 698 Checklist 401-500 UER .10 .05 .01
(467 Cal Ripkin Jr.)
☐ 699 Checklist 501-600 UER .10 .05 .01
(543 Greg Booker)
☐ 700 Checklist 601-700........ .10 .05 .01
☐ 701 Checklist 701-800........ .10 .05 .01
☐ 702 Jesse Barfield .... .10 .05 .01
☐ 703 Walt Terrell .... .10 .05 .01
☐ 704 Dickie Thon................. .10 .05 .01
☐ 705 Al Leiter .... .10 .05 .01
☐ 706 Dave LaPoint............... .10 .05 .01
☐ 707 Charlie Hayes .... 1.00 .45 .13
☐ 708 Andy Hawkins .... .10 .05 .01
☐ 709 Mickey Hatcher .... .10 .05 .01
☐ 710 Lance McCullers .... .10 .05 .01
☐ 711 Ron Kittle..................... .10 .05 .01
☐ 712 Bert Blyleven............... .20 .09 .03
☐ 713 Rick Dempsey............. .10 .05 .01
☐ 714 Ken Williams............... .10 .05 .01
☐ 715 Steve Rosenberg.......... .10 .05 .01
☐ 716 Joe Skalski.................. .10 .05 .01
☐ 717 Spike Owen................. .10 .05 .01
☐ 718 Todd Burns .... .10 .05 .01
☐ 719 Kevin Gross .... .10 .05 .01
☐ 720 Tommy Herr .... .10 .05 .01
☐ 721 Rob Ducey .... .10 .05 .01
☐ 722 Gary Green.................. .10 .05 .01
☐ 723 Gregg Olson................. .50 .23 .06
☐ 724 Greg W. Harris .... .10 .05 .01
☐ 725 Craig Worthington .... .10 .05 .01
☐ 726 Tom Howard................ .25 .11 .03
☐ 727 Dale Mohorcic............. .10 .05 .01

	No.	Player			
☐	728	Rich Yett	.10	.05	.01
☐	729	Mel Hall	.10	.05	.01
☐	730	Floyd Youmans	.10	.05	.01
☐	731	Lonnie Smith	.10	.05	.01
☐	732	Wally Backman	.10	.05	.01
☐	733	Trevor Wilson	.10	.05	.01
☐	734	Jose Alvarez	.10	.05	.01
☐	735	Bob Milacki	.10	.05	.01
☐	736	Tom Gordon	.50	.23	.06
☐	737	Wally Whitehurst	.12	.05	.02
☐	738	Mike Aldrete	.10	.05	.01
☐	739	Keith Miller	.10	.05	.01
☐	740	Randy Milligan	.10	.05	.01
☐	741	Jeff Parrett	.10	.05	.01
☐	742	Steve Finley	.40	.18	.05
☐	743	Junior Felix	.40	.18	.05
☐	744	Pete Harnisch	.50	.23	.06
☐	745	Bill Spiers	.10	.05	.01
☐	746	Hensley Meulens	.10	.05	.01
☐	747	Juan Bell	.10	.05	.01
☐	748	Steve Sax	.10	.05	.01
☐	749	Phil Bradley	.10	.05	.01
☐	750	Rey Quinones	.10	.05	.01
☐	751	Tommy Gregg	.10	.05	.01
☐	752	Kevin Brown	.15	.07	.02
☐	753	Derek Lilliquist	.10	.05	.01
☐	754	Todd Zeile	1.00	.45	.13
☐	755	Jim Abbott (Triple exposure)	2.00	.90	.25
☐	756	Ozzie Canseco	.10	.05	.01
☐	757	Nick Esasky	.10	.05	.01
☐	758	Mike Moore	.10	.05	.01
☐	759	Rob Murphy	.10	.05	.01
☐	760	Rick Mahler	.10	.05	.01
☐	761	Fred Lynn	.15	.07	.02
☐	762	Kevin Blankenship	.10	.05	.01
☐	763	Eddie Murray	.60	.25	.08
☐	764	Steve Searcy	.10	.05	.01
☐	765	Jerome Walton	.15	.07	.02
☐	766	Erik Hanson	.50	.23	.06
☐	767	Bob Boone	.15	.07	.02
☐	768	Edgar Martinez	.15	.07	.02
☐	769	Jose DeJesus	.10	.05	.01
☐	770	Greg Briley	.10	.05	.01
☐	771	Steve Peters	.10	.05	.01
☐	772	Rafael Palmeiro	1.00	.45	.13
☐	773	Jack Clark	.15	.07	.02
☐	774	Nolan Ryan (Throwing football)	4.00	1.80	.50
☐	775	Lance Parrish	.15	.07	.02
☐	776	Joe Girardi	.25	.11	.03
☐	777	Willie Randolph	.15	.07	.02
☐	778	Mitch Williams	.15	.07	.02
☐	779	Dennis Cook	.10	.05	.01
☐	780	Dwight Smith	.30	.14	.04
☐	781	Lenny Harris	.10	.05	.01
☐	782	Torey Lovullo	.10	.05	.01
☐	783	Norm Charlton	.25	.11	.03
☐	784	Chris Brown	.10	.05	.01
☐	785	Todd Benzinger	.10	.05	.01
☐	786	Shane Rawley	.10	.05	.01
☐	787	Omar Vizquel	.40	.18	.05
☐	788	LaVel Freeman	.10	.05	.01
☐	789	Jeffrey Leonard	.10	.05	.01
☐	790	Eddie Williams	.10	.05	.01
☐	791	Jamie Moyer	.10	.05	.01
☐	792	Bruce Hurst UER (Workd Series)	.10	.05	.01
☐	793	Julio Franco	.15	.07	.02
☐	794	Claudell Washington	.10	.05	.01
☐	795	Jody Davis	.10	.05	.01
☐	796	Oddibe McDowell	.10	.05	.01
☐	797	Paul Kilgus	.10	.05	.01
☐	798	Tracy Jones	.10	.05	.01
☐	799	Steve Wilson	.10	.05	.01
☐	800	Pete O'Brien	.10	.05	.01

1990 Upper Deck

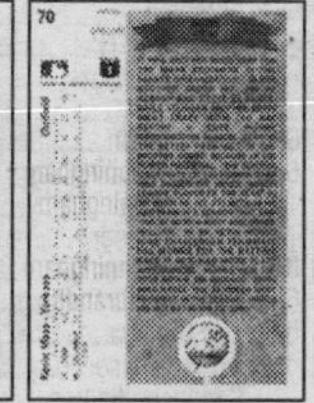

The 1990 Upper Deck set contains 800 standard-size (2 1/2" by 3 1/2") cards issued in two series, low numbers (1-700) and high numbers (701-800). The front and back borders are white, and both sides feature full-color photos. The horizontally oriented backs have recent stats and anti-counterfeiting holograms. Unlike the 1989 Upper Deck set, the team checklist cards are not grouped numerically at the end of the set, but are mixed in with the first 100 cards. Cards 101 through 199 have two minor varieties in that the cards either show or omit "Copyright 1990 Upper Deck Co. Printed in USA below the two licensing logos. Those without are considered minor errors; they were found in the High Number foil packs. The 1990 Upper Deck Extended Set (of high numbers) was issued in July 1990. The cards were in the same style as the first 700 cards of the 1990 Upper Deck set and were issued either as a separate set in its own collectors box, as part of the complete 1-800 factory set, as well as mixed in with the earlier numbered Upper Deck cards in late-season wax packs. The series also contains a Nolan Ryan variation; all cards produced before August 12th only discuss Ryan's sixth no-hitter while the later-issue cards include a stripe honoring Ryan's 300th victory. Rookie Cards in the set include Wilson Alvarez, Carlos Baerga, Alex Cole, Delino DeShields, Juan Gonzalez, Marquis Grissom, Bob Hamelin, Dave Hollins, David Justice, Ray Lankford, Derrick May, Ben McDonald, John Olerud, Dean Palmer, Sammy Sosa, and Larry Walker. Card 702 was originally scheduled to be Mike Witt. A few Witt cards with 702 on back and checklist cards showing 702 Witt escaped into early packs; they are characterized by a black rectangle covering much of the card's back.

	MINT	EXC	G-VG
COMPLETE SET (800)	25.00	11.50	3.10
COMPLETE FACT.SET (800)	25.00	11.50	3.10

COMPLETE LO SET (700)...... 20.00 9.00 2.50
COMPLETE HI SET (100)......... 5.00 2.30 .60
COMPLETE HI FACT.SET (100) 5.00 2.30 .60
COMMON CARD (1-700) .... .05 .02 .01
COMMON CARD (701-800) .... .05 .02 .01

☐ 1 Star Rookie Checklist....... .06 .03 .01
☐ 2 Randy Nosek.................... .05 .02 .01
☐ 3 Tom Drees UER................ .05 .02 .01
(11th line, hulred, should be hurled)
☐ 4 Curt Young .... .05 .02 .01
☐ 5 Devon White TC.............. .10 .05 .01
California Angels
☐ 6 Luis Salazar .... .05 .02 .01
☐ 7 Von Hayes TC..................... .05 .02 .01
Philadelphia Phillies
☐ 8 Jose Bautista .... .05 .02 .01
☐ 9 Marquis Grissom .... 1.00 .45 .13
☐ 10 Orel Hershiser TC........... .10 .05 .01
Los Angeles Dodgers
☐ 11 Rick Aguilera.................. .10 .05 .01
☐ 12 Benito Santiago TC .... .10 .05 .01
San Diego Padres
☐ 13 Deion Sanders .... 1.50 .65 .19
☐ 14 Marvell Wynne............... .05 .02 .01
☐ 15 Dave West...................... .05 .02 .01
☐ 16 Bobby Bonilla TC .... .10 .05 .01
Pittsburgh Pirates
☐ 17 Sammy Sosa............... 1.00 .45 .13
☐ 18 Steve Sax TC.................. .05 .02 .01
New York Yankees
☐ 19 Jack Howell.................... .05 .02 .01
☐ 20 Mike Schmidt Special .... .50 .23 .06
UER (Suprising, should be surprising)
☐ 21 Robin Ventura UER...... 1.25 .55 .16
(Samta Maria)
☐ 22 Brian Meyer .... .05 .02 .01
☐ 23 Blaine Beatty.................. .05 .02 .01
☐ 24 Ken Griffey Jr. TC........... .75 .35 .09
Seattle Mariners
☐ 25 Greg Vaughn UER.......... .50 .23 .06
(Association misspelled as assiocation)
☐ 26 Xavier Hernandez........... .05 .02 .01
☐ 27 Jason Grimsley............... .05 .02 .01
☐ 28 Eric Anthony UER .... .20 .09 .03
(Ashville, should be Asheville)
☐ 29 Tim Raines TC .... .10 .05 .01
Montreal Expos
UER (Wallach listed before Walker)
☐ 30 David Wells..................... .05 .02 .01
☐ 31 Hal Morris....................... .30 .14 .04
☐ 32 Bo Jackson TC .... .25 .11 .03
Kansas City Royals
☐ 33 Kelly Mann...................... .05 .02 .01
☐ 34 Nolan Ryan Special...... 1.00 .45 .13
☐ 35 Scott Service UER.......... .05 .02 .01
(Born Cincinatti on 7/27/67, should be Cincinnati 2/27)
☐ 36 Mark McGwire TC .... .10 .05 .01
Oakland A's
☐ 37 Tino Martinez................. .10 .05 .01
☐ 38 Chili Davis...................... .10 .05 .01
☐ 39 Scott Sanderson .... .05 .02 .01
☐ 40 Kevin Mitchell TC........... .10 .05 .01
San Francisco Giants
☐ 41 Lou Whitaker TC .... .10 .05 .01
Detroit Tigers
☐ 42 Scott Coolbaugh UER .... .05 .02 .01
(Definately)
☐ 43 Jose Cano UER.............. .05 .02 .01
(Born 9/7/62, should be 3/7/62)
☐ 44 Jose Vizcaino................. .05 .02 .01
☐ 45 Bob Hamelin .... 1.50 .65 .19
☐ 46 Jose Offerman UER .... .15 .07 .02
(Posesses)
☐ 47 Kevin Blankenship.......... .05 .02 .01
☐ 48 Kirby Puckett TC .... .25 .11 .03
Minnesota Twins
☐ 49 Tommy Greene UER ...... .25 .11 .03
(Livest, should be liveliest)
☐ 50 Will Clark Special........... .25 .11 .03
UER (Perenial, should be perennial)
☐ 51 Rob Nelson .... .05 .02 .01
☐ 52 Chris Hammond UER..... .15 .07 .02
(Chatanooga)
☐ 53 Joe Carter TC................. .15 .07 .02
Cleveland Indians
☐ 54A Ben McDonald ERR . 15.00 6.75 1.90
(No Rookie designation on card front)
☐ 54B Ben McDonald COR..... .75 .35 .09
☐ 55 Andy Benes UER............ .25 .11 .03
(Whichita)
☐ 56 John Olerud .... 1.00 .45 .13
☐ 57 Roger Clemens TC......... .25 .11 .03
Boston Red Sox
☐ 58 Tony Armas .... .05 .02 .01
☐ 59 George Canale................ .05 .02 .01
☐ 60A Mickey Tettleton TC... 2.50 1.15 .30
Baltimore Orioles
ERR (683 Jamie Weston)
☐ 60B Mickey Tettleton TC..... .10 .05 .01
Baltimore Orioles
COR (683 Mickey Weston)
☐ 61 Mike Stanton................... .05 .02 .01
☐ 62 Dwight Gooden TC......... .10 .05 .01
New York Mets
☐ 63 Kent Mercker UER .... .40 .18 .05
(Albuguerque)
☐ 64 Francisco Cabrera.......... .05 .02 .01
☐ 65 Steve Avery UER............ .75 .35 .09
(Born NJ, should be MI, Merker should be Mercker)
☐ 66 Jose Canseco................. .40 .18 .05
☐ 67 Matt Merullo .... .05 .02 .01
☐ 68 Vince Coleman TC.......... .05 .02 .01
St. Louis Cardinals
UER (Guererro)
☐ 69 Ron Karkovice................ .05 .02 .01
☐ 70 Kevin Maas .... .05 .02 .01
☐ 71 Dennis Cook UER........... .05 .02 .01
(Shown with righty glove on card back)
☐ 72 Juan Gonzalez UER...... 4.00 1.80 .50
(135 games for Tulsa in '89, should be 133)
☐ 73 Andre Dawson TC .... .10 .05 .01
Chicago Cubs
☐ 74 Dean Palmer UER .... .50 .23 .06
(Permanent misspelled as perminant)
☐ 75 Bo Jackson Special........ .30 .14 .04
UER (Monsterous, should be monstrous)
☐ 76 Rob Richie .... .05 .02 .01
☐ 77 Bobby Rose UER .... .10 .05 .01
(Pickin, should

be pick in)
☐ 78 Brian DuBois UER .... .05 .02 .01
(Commiting)
☐ 79 Ozzie Guillen TC .... .05 .02 .01
Chicago White Sox
☐ 80 Gene Nelson .... .05 .02 .01
☐ 81 Bob McClure.................. .05 .02 .01
☐ 82 Julio Franco TC .... .05 .02 .01
Texas Rangers
☐ 83 Greg Minton................... .05 .02 .01
☐ 84 John Smoltz TC UER...... .10 .05 .01
Atlanta Braves
(Oddibe not Odibbe)
☐ 85 Willie Fraser.................. .05 .02 .01
☐ 86 Neal Heaton .... .05 .02 .01
☐ 87 Kevin Tapani UER .... .35 .16 .04
(24th line has excpet,
should be except)
☐ 88 Mike Scott TC .... .05 .02 .01
Houston Astros
☐ 89A Jim Gott ERR............. 5.00 2.30 .60
(Photo actually
Rick Reed)
☐ 89B Jim Gott COR............... .10 .05 .01
☐ 90 Lance Johnson .... .10 .05 .01
☐ 91 Robin Yount TC UER...... .15 .07 .02
Milwaukee Brewers
(Checklist on back has
178 Rob Deer and
176 Mike Felder)
☐ 92 Jeff Parrett..................... .05 .02 .01
☐ 93 Julio Machado UER .... .05 .02 .01
(Valenzuelan, should
be Venezuelan)
☐ 94 Ron Jones...................... .05 .02 .01
☐ 95 George Bell TC .... .05 .02 .01
Toronto Blue Jays
☐ 96 Jerry Reuss.................... .05 .02 .01
☐ 97 Brian Fisher.................... .05 .02 .01
☐ 98 Kevin Ritz UER............... .05 .02 .01
(Amercian)
☐ 99 Barry Larkin TC .... .10 .05 .01
Cincinnati Reds
☐ 100 Checklist 1-100............ .06 .03 .01
☐ 101 Gerald Perry................. .05 .02 .01
☐ 102 Kevin Appier .... .75 .35 .09
☐ 103 Julio Franco .... .10 .05 .01
☐ 104 Craig Biggio .... .20 .09 .03
☐ 105 Bo Jackson UER .... .35 .16 .04
('89 BA wrong,
should be .256)
☐ 106 Junior Felix .... .05 .02 .01
☐ 107 Mike Harkey.................. .05 .02 .01
☐ 108 Fred McGriff.................. .40 .18 .05
☐ 109 Rick Sutcliffe................ .10 .05 .01
☐ 110 Pete O'Brien................. .05 .02 .01
☐ 111 Kelly Gruber.................. .05 .02 .01
☐ 112 Dwight Evans................ .10 .05 .01
☐ 113 Pat Borders................... .10 .05 .01
☐ 114 Dwight Gooden .... .10 .05 .01
☐ 115 Kevin Batiste .... .05 .02 .01
☐ 116 Eric Davis...................... .10 .05 .01
☐ 117 Kevin Mitchell UER ...... .10 .05 .01
(Career HR total 99,
should be 100)
☐ 118 Ron Oester.................... .05 .02 .01
☐ 119 Brett Butler .... .10 .05 .01
☐ 120 Danny Jackson .... .05 .02 .01
☐ 121 Tommy Gregg............... .05 .02 .01
☐ 122 Ken Caminiti .... .10 .05 .01
☐ 123 Kevin Brown .... .10 .05 .01
☐ 124 George Brett UER......... .50 .23 .06
(133 runs, should
be 1300)
☐ 125 Mike Scott..................... .05 .02 .01
☐ 126 Cory Snyder.................. .05 .02 .01
☐ 127 George Bell .... .10 .05 .01
☐ 128 Mark Grace .... .30 .14 .04
☐ 129 Devon White .... .10 .05 .01
☐ 130 Tony Fernandez............ .10 .05 .01
☐ 131 Don Aase .... .05 .02 .01
☐ 132 Rance Mulliniks .... .05 .02 .01
☐ 133 Marty Barrett................. .05 .02 .01
☐ 134 Nelson Liriano............... .05 .02 .01
☐ 135 Mark Carreon................ .05 .02 .01
☐ 136 Candy Maldonado .... .05 .02 .01
☐ 137 Tim Birtsas .... .05 .02 .01
☐ 138 Tom Brookens .... .05 .02 .01
☐ 139 John Franco.................. .10 .05 .01
☐ 140 Mike LaCoss .... .05 .02 .01
☐ 141 Jeff Treadway .... .05 .02 .01
☐ 142 Pat Tabler .... .05 .02 .01
☐ 143 Darrell Evans................ .10 .05 .01
☐ 144 Rafael Ramirez............. .05 .02 .01
☐ 145 Oddibe McDowell UER. .05 .02 .01
(Misspelled Odibbe)
☐ 146 Brian Downing .... .05 .02 .01
☐ 147 Curt Wilkerson .... .05 .02 .01
☐ 148 Ernie Whitt.................... .05 .02 .01
☐ 149 Bill Schroeder .... .05 .02 .01
☐ 150 Domingo Ramos UER.. .05 .02 .01
(Says throws right,
but shows him
throwing lefty)
☐ 151 Rick Honeycutt .... .05 .02 .01
☐ 152 Don Slaught.................. .05 .02 .01
☐ 153 Mitch Webster .... .05 .02 .01
☐ 154 Tony Phillips................. .10 .05 .01
☐ 155 Paul Kilgus.................... .05 .02 .01
☐ 156 Ken Griffey Jr. UER.... 6.00 2.70 .75
(Simultaniously)
☐ 157 Gary Sheffield .... .75 .35 .09
☐ 158 Wally Backman .... .05 .02 .01
☐ 159 B.J. Surhoff................... .05 .02 .01
☐ 160 Louie Meadows............ .05 .02 .01
☐ 161 Paul O'Neill................... .10 .05 .01
☐ 162 Jeff McKnight .... .05 .02 .01
☐ 163 Alvaro Espinoza .... .05 .02 .01
☐ 164 Scott Scudder............... .05 .02 .01
☐ 165 Jeff Reed....................... .05 .02 .01
☐ 166 Gregg Jefferies .... .40 .18 .05
☐ 167 Barry Larkin .... .20 .09 .03
☐ 168 Gary Carter .... .20 .09 .03
☐ 169 Robby Thompson .... .10 .05 .01
☐ 170 Rolando Roomes .... .05 .02 .01
☐ 171 Mark McGwire UER ..... .20 .09 .03
(Total games 427 and
hits 479, should be
467 and 427)
☐ 172 Steve Sax...................... .05 .02 .01
☐ 173 Mark Williamson........... .05 .02 .01
☐ 174 Mitch Williams.............. .10 .05 .01
☐ 175 Brian Holton.................. .05 .02 .01
☐ 176 Rob Deer....................... .05 .02 .01
☐ 177 Tim Raines.................... .20 .09 .03
☐ 178 Mike Felder................... .05 .02 .01
☐ 179 Harold Reynolds .... .05 .02 .01
☐ 180 Terry Francona............. .05 .02 .01
☐ 181 Chris Sabo .... .10 .05 .01
☐ 182 Darryl Strawberry .... .20 .09 .03
☐ 183 Willie Randolph............ .10 .05 .01
☐ 184 Bill Ripken..................... .05 .02 .01
☐ 185 Mackey Sasser............. .05 .02 .01
☐ 186 Todd Benzinger............ .05 .02 .01
☐ 187 Kevin Elster UER.......... .05 .02 .01
(16 homers in 1989,
should be 10)

☐ 188 Jose Uribe .05 .02 .01
☐ 189 Tom Browning .05 .02 .01
☐ 190 Keith Miller .05 .02 .01
☐ 191 Don Mattingly .60 .25 .08
☐ 192 Dave Parker .20 .09 .03
☐ 193 Roberto Kelly UER .10 .05 .01
(96 RBI, should be 62)
☐ 194 Phil Bradley .05 .02 .01
☐ 195 Ron Hassey .05 .02 .01
☐ 196 Gerald Young .05 .02 .01
☐ 197 Hubie Brooks .05 .02 .01
☐ 198 Bill Doran .05 .02 .01
☐ 199 Al Newman .05 .02 .01
☐ 200 Checklist 101-200 .06 .03 .01
☐ 201 Terry Puhl .05 .02 .01
☐ 202 Frank DiPino .05 .02 .01
☐ 203 Jim Clancy .05 .02 .01
☐ 204 Bob Ojeda .05 .02 .01
☐ 205 Alex Trevino .05 .02 .01
☐ 206 Dave Henderson .05 .02 .01
☐ 207 Henry Cotto .05 .02 .01
☐ 208 Rafael Belliard UER .05 .02 .01
(Born 1961, not 1951)
☐ 209 Stan Javier .05 .02 .01
☐ 210 Jerry Reed .05 .02 .01
☐ 211 Doug Dascenzo .05 .02 .01
☐ 212 Andres Thomas .05 .02 .01
☐ 213 Greg Maddux .60 .25 .08
☐ 214 Mike Schooler .05 .02 .01
☐ 215 Lonnie Smith .05 .02 .01
☐ 216 Jose Rijo .10 .05 .01
☐ 217 Greg Gagne .05 .02 .01
☐ 218 Jim Gantner .05 .02 .01
☐ 219 Allan Anderson .05 .02 .01
☐ 220 Rick Mahler .05 .02 .01
☐ 221 Jim Deshaies .05 .02 .01
☐ 222 Keith Hernandez .10 .05 .01
☐ 223 Vince Coleman .10 .05 .01
☐ 224 David Cone .25 .11 .03
☐ 225 Ozzie Smith .35 .16 .04
☐ 226 Matt Nokes .05 .02 .01
☐ 227 Barry Bonds 1.00 .45 .13
☐ 228 Felix Jose .10 .05 .01
☐ 229 Dennis Powell .05 .02 .01
☐ 230 Mike Gallego .05 .02 .01
☐ 231 Shawon Dunston UER .05 .02 .01
('89 stats are
Andre Dawson's)
☐ 232 Ron Gant .35 .16 .04
☐ 233 Omar Vizquel .05 .02 .01
☐ 234 Derek Lilliquist .05 .02 .01
☐ 235 Erik Hanson .05 .02 .01
☐ 236 Kirby Puckett UER .75 .35 .09
(824 games, should
be 924)
☐ 237 Bill Spiers .05 .02 .01
☐ 238 Dan Gladden .05 .02 .01
☐ 239 Bryan Clutterbuck .05 .02 .01
☐ 240 John Moses .05 .02 .01
☐ 241 Ron Darling .05 .02 .01
☐ 242 Joe Magrane .05 .02 .01
☐ 243 Dave Magadan .05 .02 .01
☐ 244 Pedro Guerrero UER .10 .05 .01
(Misspelled Guererro)
☐ 245 Glenn Davis .05 .02 .01
☐ 246 Terry Steinbach .10 .05 .01
☐ 247 Fred Lynn .10 .05 .01
☐ 248 Gary Redus .05 .02 .01
☐ 249 Ken Williams .05 .02 .01
☐ 250 Sid Bream .05 .02 .01
☐ 251 Bob Welch UER .05 .02 .01
(2587 career strike-
outs, should be 1587)
☐ 252 Bill Buckner .10 .05 .01
☐ 253 Carney Lansford .10 .05 .01
☐ 254 Paul Molitor .35 .16 .04
☐ 255 Jose DeJesus .05 .02 .01
☐ 256 Orel Hershiser .10 .05 .01
☐ 257 Tom Brunansky .05 .02 .01
☐ 258 Mike Davis .05 .02 .01
☐ 259 Jeff Ballard .05 .02 .01
☐ 260 Scott Terry .05 .02 .01
☐ 261 Sid Fernandez .10 .05 .01
☐ 262 Mike Marshall .05 .02 .01
☐ 263 Howard Johnson UER .10 .05 .01
(192 SO, should be 592)
☐ 264 Kirk Gibson UER .10 .05 .01
(659 runs, should
be 669)
☐ 265 Kevin McReynolds .05 .02 .01
☐ 266 Cal Ripken .75 .35 .09
☐ 267 Ozzie Guillen UER .05 .02 .01
(Career triples 27,
should be 29)
☐ 268 Jim Traber .05 .02 .01
☐ 269 Bobby Thigpen UER .05 .02 .01
(31 saves in 1989,
should be 34)
☐ 270 Joe Orsulak .05 .02 .01
☐ 271 Bob Boone .10 .05 .01
☐ 272 Dave Stewart UER .10 .05 .01
(Totals wrong due to
omission of '86 stats)
☐ 273 Tim Wallach .05 .02 .01
☐ 274 Luis Aquino UER .05 .02 .01
(Says throws lefty,
but shows him
throwing righty)
☐ 275 Mike Moore .05 .02 .01
☐ 276 Tony Pena .05 .02 .01
☐ 277 Eddie Murray UER .20 .09 .03
(Several typos in
career total stats)
☐ 278 Milt Thompson .05 .02 .01
☐ 279 Alejandro Pena .05 .02 .01
☐ 280 Ken Dayley .05 .02 .01
☐ 281 Carmen Castillo .05 .02 .01
☐ 282 Tom Henke .10 .05 .01
☐ 283 Mickey Hatcher .05 .02 .01
☐ 284 Roy Smith .05 .02 .01
☐ 285 Manny Lee .05 .02 .01
☐ 286 Dan Pasqua .05 .02 .01
☐ 287 Larry Sheets .05 .02 .01
☐ 288 Garry Templeton .05 .02 .01
☐ 289 Eddie Williams .05 .02 .01
☐ 290 Brady Anderson UER .10 .05 .01
(Home: Silver Springs,
not Siver Springs)
☐ 291 Spike Owen .05 .02 .01
☐ 292 Storm Davis .05 .02 .01
☐ 293 Chris Bosio .05 .02 .01
☐ 294 Jim Eisenreich .05 .02 .01
☐ 295 Don August .05 .02 .01
☐ 296 Jeff Hamilton .05 .02 .01
☐ 297 Mickey Tettleton .10 .05 .01
☐ 298 Mike Scioscia .05 .02 .01
☐ 299 Kevin Hickey .05 .02 .01
☐ 300 Checklist 201-300 .06 .03 .01
☐ 301 Shawn Abner .05 .02 .01
☐ 302 Kevin Bass .05 .02 .01
☐ 303 Bip Roberts .10 .05 .01
☐ 304 Joe Girardi .05 .02 .01
☐ 305 Danny Darwin .05 .02 .01
☐ 306 Mike Heath .05 .02 .01
☐ 307 Mike Macfarlane .05 .02 .01
☐ 308 Ed Whitson .05 .02 .01

☐ 309 Tracy Jones	.05	.02	.01
☐ 310 Scott Fletcher	.05	.02	.01
☐ 311 Darnell Coles	.05	.02	.01
☐ 312 Mike Brumley	.05	.02	.01
☐ 313 Bill Swift	.10	.05	.01
☐ 314 Charlie Hough	.10	.05	.01
☐ 315 Jim Presley	.05	.02	.01
☐ 316 Luis Polonia	.10	.05	.01
☐ 317 Mike Morgan	.05	.02	.01
☐ 318 Lee Guetterman	.05	.02	.01
☐ 319 Jose Oquendo	.05	.02	.01
☐ 320 Wayne Tolleson	.05	.02	.01
☐ 321 Jody Reed	.05	.02	.01
☐ 322 Damon Berryhill	.05	.02	.01
☐ 323 Roger Clemens	.50	.23	.06
☐ 324 Ryne Sandberg	.75	.35	.09
☐ 325 Benito Santiago UER (Misspelled Santago on card back)	.10	.05	.01
☐ 326 Bret Saberhagen UER (1140 hits, should be 1240; 56 CG, should be 52)	.10	.05	.01
☐ 327 Lou Whitaker	.20	.09	.03
☐ 328 Dave Gallagher	.05	.02	.01
☐ 329 Mike Pagliarulo	.05	.02	.01
☐ 330 Doyle Alexander	.05	.02	.01
☐ 331 Jeffrey Leonard	.05	.02	.01
☐ 332 Torey Lovullo	.05	.02	.01
☐ 333 Pete Incaviglia	.05	.02	.01
☐ 334 Rickey Henderson	.35	.16	.04
☐ 335 Rafael Palmeiro	.30	.14	.04
☐ 336 Ken Hill	.50	.23	.06
☐ 337 Dave Winfield UER (1418 RBI, should be 1438)	.35	.16	.04
☐ 338 Alfredo Griffin	.05	.02	.01
☐ 339 Andy Hawkins	.05	.02	.01
☐ 340 Ted Power	.05	.02	.01
☐ 341 Steve Wilson	.05	.02	.01
☐ 342 Jack Clark UER (916 BB, should be 1006; 1142 SO, should be 1130)	.10	.05	.01
☐ 343 Ellis Burks	.10	.05	.01
☐ 344 Tony Gwynn UER (Doubles stats on card back are wrong)	.50	.23	.06
☐ 345 Jerome Walton UER (Total At Bats 476, should be 475)	.05	.02	.01
☐ 346 Roberto Alomar UER (61 doubles, should be 51)	.75	.35	.09
☐ 347 Carlos Martinez UER (Born 8/11/64, should be 8/11/65)	.05	.02	.01
☐ 348 Chet Lemon	.05	.02	.01
☐ 349 Willie Wilson	.05	.02	.01
☐ 350 Greg Walker	.05	.02	.01
☐ 351 Tom Bolton	.05	.02	.01
☐ 352 German Gonzalez	.05	.02	.01
☐ 353 Harold Baines	.10	.05	.01
☐ 354 Mike Greenwell	.10	.05	.01
☐ 355 Ruben Sierra	.20	.09	.03
☐ 356 Andres Galarraga	.25	.11	.03
☐ 357 Andre Dawson	.20	.09	.03
☐ 358 Jeff Brantley	.05	.02	.01
☐ 359 Mike Bielecki	.05	.02	.01
☐ 360 Ken Oberkfell	.05	.02	.01
☐ 361 Kurt Stillwell	.05	.02	.01
☐ 362 Brian Holman	.05	.02	.01
☐ 363 Kevin Seitzer UER (Career triples total does not add up)	.05	.02	.01
☐ 364 Alvin Davis	.05	.02	.01
☐ 365 Tom Gordon	.10	.05	.01
☐ 366 Bobby Bonilla UER (Two steals in 1987, should be 3)	.20	.09	.03
☐ 367 Carlton Fisk	.20	.09	.03
☐ 368 Steve Carter UER (Charlotesville)	.05	.02	.01
☐ 369 Joel Skinner	.05	.02	.01
☐ 370 John Cangelosi	.05	.02	.01
☐ 371 Cecil Espy	.05	.02	.01
☐ 372 Gary Wayne	.05	.02	.01
☐ 373 Jim Rice	.20	.09	.03
☐ 374 Mike Dyer	.05	.02	.01
☐ 375 Joe Carter	.40	.18	.05
☐ 376 Dwight Smith	.05	.02	.01
☐ 377 John Wetteland	.10	.05	.01
☐ 378 Earnie Riles	.05	.02	.01
☐ 379 Otis Nixon	.10	.05	.01
☐ 380 Vance Law	.05	.02	.01
☐ 381 Dave Bergman	.05	.02	.01
☐ 382 Frank White	.10	.05	.01
☐ 383 Scott Bradley	.05	.02	.01
☐ 384 Israel Sanchez UER (Totals don't include '89 stats)	.05	.02	.01
☐ 385 Gary Pettis	.05	.02	.01
☐ 386 Donn Pall	.05	.02	.01
☐ 387 John Smiley	.05	.02	.01
☐ 388 Tom Candiotti	.05	.02	.01
☐ 389 Junior Ortiz	.05	.02	.01
☐ 390 Steve Lyons	.05	.02	.01
☐ 391 Brian Harper	.10	.05	.01
☐ 392 Fred Manrique	.05	.02	.01
☐ 393 Lee Smith	.20	.09	.03
☐ 394 Jeff Kunkel	.05	.02	.01
☐ 395 Claudell Washington	.05	.02	.01
☐ 396 John Tudor	.05	.02	.01
☐ 397 Terry Kennedy UER (Career totals all wrong)	.05	.02	.01
☐ 398 Lloyd McClendon	.05	.02	.01
☐ 399 Craig Lefferts	.05	.02	.01
☐ 400 Checklist 301-400	.06	.03	.01
☐ 401 Keith Moreland	.05	.02	.01
☐ 402 Rich Gedman	.05	.02	.01
☐ 403 Jeff D. Robinson	.05	.02	.01
☐ 404 Randy Ready	.05	.02	.01
☐ 405 Rick Cerone	.05	.02	.01
☐ 406 Jeff Blauser	.10	.05	.01
☐ 407 Larry Andersen	.05	.02	.01
☐ 408 Joe Boever	.05	.02	.01
☐ 409 Felix Fermin	.05	.02	.01
☐ 410 Glenn Wilson	.05	.02	.01
☐ 411 Rex Hudler	.05	.02	.01
☐ 412 Mark Grant	.05	.02	.01
☐ 413 Dennis Martinez	.10	.05	.01
☐ 414 Darrin Jackson	.05	.02	.01
☐ 415 Mike Aldrete	.05	.02	.01
☐ 416 Roger McDowell	.05	.02	.01
☐ 417 Jeff Reardon	.20	.09	.03
☐ 418 Darren Daulton	.20	.09	.03
☐ 419 Tim Laudner	.05	.02	.01
☐ 420 Don Carman	.05	.02	.01
☐ 421 Lloyd Moseby	.05	.02	.01
☐ 422 Doug Drabek	.20	.09	.03
☐ 423 Lenny Harris UER (Walks 2 in '89, should be 20)	.05	.02	.01
☐ 424 Jose Lind	.05	.02	.01
☐ 425 Dave Johnson (P)	.05	.02	.01

☐ 426 Jerry Browne .05 .02 .01
☐ 427 Eric Yelding .05 .02 .01
☐ 428 Brad Komminsk .05 .02 .01
☐ 429 Jody Davis .05 .02 .01
☐ 430 Mariano Duncan .05 .02 .01
☐ 431 Mark Davis .05 .02 .01
☐ 432 Nelson Santovenia .05 .02 .01
☐ 433 Bruce Hurst .05 .02 .01
☐ 434 Jeff Huson .05 .02 .01
☐ 435 Chris James .05 .02 .01
☐ 436 Mark Guthrie .05 .02 .01
☐ 437 Charlie Hayes .10 .05 .01
☐ 438 Shane Rawley .05 .02 .01
☐ 439 Dickie Thon .05 .02 .01
☐ 440 Juan Berenguer .05 .02 .01
☐ 441 Kevin Romine .05 .02 .01
☐ 442 Bill Landrum .05 .02 .01
☐ 443 Todd Frohwirth .05 .02 .01
☐ 444 Craig Worthington .05 .02 .01
☐ 445 Fernando Valenzuela .05 .02 .01
☐ 446 Joey Belle 3.00 1.35 .40
☐ 447 Ed Whited UER .05 .02 .01
(Ashville, should be Asheville)
☐ 448 Dave Smith .05 .02 .01
☐ 449 Dave Clark .05 .02 .01
☐ 450 Juan Agosto .05 .02 .01
☐ 451 Dave Valle .05 .02 .01
☐ 452 Kent Hrbek .10 .05 .01
☐ 453 Von Hayes .05 .02 .01
☐ 454 Gary Gaetti .05 .02 .01
☐ 455 Greg Briley .05 .02 .01
☐ 456 Glenn Braggs .05 .02 .01
☐ 457 Kirt Manwaring .05 .02 .01
☐ 458 Mel Hall .05 .02 .01
☐ 459 Brook Jacoby .05 .02 .01
☐ 460 Pat Sheridan .05 .02 .01
☐ 461 Rob Murphy .05 .02 .01
☐ 462 Jimmy Key .10 .05 .01
☐ 463 Nick Esasky .05 .02 .01
☐ 464 Rob Ducey .05 .02 .01
☐ 465 Carlos Quintana UER .05 .02 .01
(Internatinoal)
☐ 466 Larry Walker 1.00 .45 .13
☐ 467 Todd Worrell .05 .02 .01
☐ 468 Kevin Gross .05 .02 .01
☐ 469 Terry Pendleton .20 .09 .03
☐ 470 Dave Martinez .05 .02 .01
☐ 471 Gene Larkin .05 .02 .01
☐ 472 Len Dykstra UER .20 .09 .03
('89 and total runs understated by 10)
☐ 473 Barry Lyons .05 .02 .01
☐ 474 Terry Mulholland .10 .05 .01
☐ 475 Chip Hale .05 .02 .01
☐ 476 Jesse Barfield .05 .02 .01
☐ 477 Dan Plesac .05 .02 .01
☐ 478A Scott Garrelts ERR 3.00 1.35 .40
(Photo actually Bill Bathe)
☐ 478B Scott Garrelts COR .10 .05 .01
☐ 479 Dave Righetti .05 .02 .01
☐ 480 Gus Polidor UER .05 .02 .01
(Wearing 14 on front, but 10 on back)
☐ 481 Mookie Wilson .05 .02 .01
☐ 482 Luis Rivera .05 .02 .01
☐ 483 Mike Flanagan .05 .02 .01
☐ 484 Dennis Boyd .05 .02 .01
☐ 485 John Cerutti .05 .02 .01
☐ 486 John Costello .05 .02 .01
☐ 487 Pascual Perez .05 .02 .01
☐ 488 Tommy Herr .05 .02 .01
☐ 489 Tom Foley .05 .02 .01
☐ 490 Curt Ford .05 .02 .01
☐ 491 Steve Lake .05 .02 .01
☐ 492 Tim Teufel .05 .02 .01
☐ 493 Randy Bush .05 .02 .01
☐ 494 Mike Jackson .05 .02 .01
☐ 495 Steve Jeltz .05 .02 .01
☐ 496 Paul Gibson .05 .02 .01
☐ 497 Steve Balboni .05 .02 .01
☐ 498 Bud Black .05 .02 .01
☐ 499 Dale Sveum .05 .02 .01
☐ 500 Checklist 401-500 .06 .03 .01
☐ 501 Tim Jones .05 .02 .01
☐ 502 Mark Portugal .05 .02 .01
☐ 503 Ivan Calderon .05 .02 .01
☐ 504 Rick Rhoden .05 .02 .01
☐ 505 Willie McGee .10 .05 .01
☐ 506 Kirk McCaskill .05 .02 .01
☐ 507 Dave LaPoint .05 .02 .01
☐ 508 Jay Howell .05 .02 .01
☐ 509 Johnny Ray .05 .02 .01
☐ 510 Dave Anderson .05 .02 .01
☐ 511 Chuck Crim .05 .02 .01
☐ 512 Joe Hesketh .05 .02 .01
☐ 513 Dennis Eckersley .20 .09 .03
☐ 514 Greg Brock .05 .02 .01
☐ 515 Tim Burke .05 .02 .01
☐ 516 Frank Tanana .05 .02 .01
☐ 517 Jay Bell .10 .05 .01
☐ 518 Guillermo Hernandez .05 .02 .01
☐ 519 Randy Kramer UER .05 .02 .01
(Codiroli misspelled as Codoroli)
☐ 520 Charles Hudson .05 .02 .01
☐ 521 Jim Corsi .05 .02 .01
(Word "originally" is misspelled on back)
☐ 522 Steve Rosenberg .05 .02 .01
☐ 523 Cris Carpenter .05 .02 .01
☐ 524 Matt Winters .05 .02 .01
☐ 525 Melido Perez .05 .02 .01
☐ 526 Chris Gwynn UER .05 .02 .01
(Albeguergue)
☐ 527 Bert Blyleven UER .20 .09 .03
(Games career total is wrong, should be 644)
☐ 528 Chuck Cary .05 .02 .01
☐ 529 Daryl Boston .05 .02 .01
☐ 530 Dale Mohorcic .05 .02 .01
☐ 531 Geronimo Berroa .10 .05 .01
☐ 532 Edgar Martinez .10 .05 .01
☐ 533 Dale Murphy .20 .09 .03
☐ 534 Jay Buhner .20 .09 .03
☐ 535 John Smoltz UER .25 .11 .03
(HEA Stadium)
☐ 536 Andy Van Slyke .20 .09 .03
☐ 537 Mike Henneman .05 .02 .01
☐ 538 Miguel Garcia .05 .02 .01
☐ 539 Frank Williams .05 .02 .01
☐ 540 R.J. Reynolds .05 .02 .01
☐ 541 Shawn Hillegas .05 .02 .01
☐ 542 Walt Weiss .05 .02 .01
☐ 543 Greg Hibbard .05 .02 .01
☐ 544 Nolan Ryan 1.25 .55 .16
☐ 545 Todd Zeile .20 .09 .03
☐ 546 Hensley Meulens .05 .02 .01
☐ 547 Tim Belcher .05 .02 .01
☐ 548 Mike Witt .05 .02 .01
☐ 549 Greg Cadaret UER .05 .02 .01
(Aquiring, should be Acquiring)
☐ 550 Franklin Stubbs .05 .02 .01
☐ 551 Tony Castillo .05 .02 .01

	No.	Player			
☐	552	Jeff M. Robinson	.05	.02	.01
☐	553	Steve Olin	.10	.05	.01
☐	554	Alan Trammell	.20	.09	.03
☐	555	Wade Boggs 4X (Bo Jackson in background)	.30	.14	.04
☐	556	Will Clark	.50	.23	.06
☐	557	Jeff King	.10	.05	.01
☐	558	Mike Fitzgerald	.05	.02	.01
☐	559	Ken Howell	.05	.02	.01
☐	560	Bob Kipper	.05	.02	.01
☐	561	Scott Bankhead	.05	.02	.01
☐	562A	Jeff Innis ERR (Photo actually David West)	2.50	1.15	.30
☐	562B	Jeff Innis COR	.10	.05	.01
☐	563	Randy Johnson	.35	.16	.04
☐	564	Wally Whitehurst	.05	.02	.01
☐	565	Gene Harris	.05	.02	.01
☐	566	Norm Charlton	.10	.05	.01
☐	567	Robin Yount UER (7602 career hits, should be 2606)	.40	.18	.05
☐	568	Joe Oliver UER (Fl.orida)	.05	.02	.01
☐	569	Mark Parent	.05	.02	.01
☐	570	John Farrell UER (Loss total added wrong)	.05	.02	.01
☐	571	Tom Glavine	.40	.18	.05
☐	572	Rod Nichols	.05	.02	.01
☐	573	Jack Morris	.20	.09	.03
☐	574	Greg Swindell	.10	.05	.01
☐	575	Steve Searcy	.05	.02	.01
☐	576	Ricky Jordan	.05	.02	.01
☐	577	Matt Williams	.50	.23	.06
☐	578	Mike LaValliere	.05	.02	.01
☐	579	Bryn Smith	.05	.02	.01
☐	580	Bruce Ruffin	.05	.02	.01
☐	581	Randy Myers	.10	.05	.01
☐	582	Rick Wrona	.05	.02	.01
☐	583	Juan Samuel	.05	.02	.01
☐	584	Les Lancaster	.05	.02	.01
☐	585	Jeff Musselman	.05	.02	.01
☐	586	Rob Dibble	.10	.05	.01
☐	587	Eric Show	.05	.02	.01
☐	588	Jesse Orosco	.05	.02	.01
☐	589	Herm Winningham	.05	.02	.01
☐	590	Andy Allanson	.05	.02	.01
☐	591	Dion James	.05	.02	.01
☐	592	Carmelo Martinez	.05	.02	.01
☐	593	Luis Quinones	.05	.02	.01
☐	594	Dennis Rasmussen	.05	.02	.01
☐	595	Rich Yett	.05	.02	.01
☐	596	Bob Walk	.05	.02	.01
☐	597A	Andy McGaffigan ERR (Photo actually Rich Thompson)	.35	.16	.04
☐	597B	Andy McGaffigan COR	.10	.05	.01
☐	598	Billy Hatcher	.05	.02	.01
☐	599	Bob Knepper	.05	.02	.01
☐	600	Checklist 501-600 UER (599 Bob Kneppers)	.06	.03	.01
☐	601	Joey Cora	.05	.02	.01
☐	602	Steve Finley	.10	.05	.01
☐	603	Kal Daniels UER (12 hits in '87, should be 123; 335 runs, should be 235)	.05	.02	.01
☐	604	Gregg Olson	.10	.05	.01
☐	605	Dave Stieb	.10	.05	.01
☐	606	Kenny Rogers (Shown catching football)	.05	.02	.01
☐	607	Zane Smith	.05	.02	.01
☐	608	Bob Geren UER (Origionally)	.05	.02	.01
☐	609	Chad Kreuter	.05	.02	.01
☐	610	Mike Smithson	.05	.02	.01
☐	611	Jeff Wetherby	.05	.02	.01
☐	612	Gary Mielke	.05	.02	.01
☐	613	Pete Smith	.05	.02	.01
☐	614	Jack Daugherty UER (Born 7/30/60, should be 7/3/60; origionally)	.05	.02	.01
☐	615	Lance McCullers	.05	.02	.01
☐	616	Don Robinson	.05	.02	.01
☐	617	Jose Guzman	.05	.02	.01
☐	618	Steve Bedrosian	.05	.02	.01
☐	619	Jamie Moyer	.05	.02	.01
☐	620	Atlee Hammaker	.05	.02	.01
☐	621	Rick Luecken UER (Innings pitched wrong)	.05	.02	.01
☐	622	Greg W. Harris	.05	.02	.01
☐	623	Pete Harnisch	.10	.05	.01
☐	624	Jerald Clark	.05	.02	.01
☐	625	Jack McDowell UER (Career totals for Games and GS don't include 1987 season)	.35	.16	.04
☐	626	Frank Viola	.10	.05	.01
☐	627	Teddy Higuera	.05	.02	.01
☐	628	Marty Pevey	.05	.02	.01
☐	629	Bill Wegman	.05	.02	.01
☐	630	Eric Plunk	.05	.02	.01
☐	631	Drew Hall	.05	.02	.01
☐	632	Doug Jones	.05	.02	.01
☐	633	Geno Petralli UER (Sacremento)	.05	.02	.01
☐	634	Jose Alvarez	.05	.02	.01
☐	635	Bob Milacki	.05	.02	.01
☐	636	Bobby Witt	.05	.02	.01
☐	637	Trevor Wilson	.05	.02	.01
☐	638	Jeff Russell UER (Shutout stats wrong)	.05	.02	.01
☐	639	Mike Krukow	.05	.02	.01
☐	640	Rick Leach	.05	.02	.01
☐	641	Dave Schmidt	.05	.02	.01
☐	642	Terry Leach	.05	.02	.01
☐	643	Calvin Schiraldi	.05	.02	.01
☐	644	Bob Melvin	.05	.02	.01
☐	645	Jim Abbott	.20	.09	.03
☐	646	Jaime Navarro	.05	.02	.01
☐	647	Mark Langston UER (Several errors in stats totals)	.20	.09	.03
☐	648	Juan Nieves	.05	.02	.01
☐	649	Damaso Garcia	.05	.02	.01
☐	650	Charlie O'Brien	.05	.02	.01
☐	651	Eric King	.05	.02	.01
☐	652	Mike Boddicker	.05	.02	.01
☐	653	Duane Ward	.10	.05	.01
☐	654	Bob Stanley	.05	.02	.01
☐	655	Sandy Alomar Jr.	.10	.05	.01
☐	656	Danny Tartabull UER (395 BB, should be 295)	.10	.05	.01
☐	657	Randy McCament	.05	.02	.01
☐	658	Charlie Leibrandt	.05	.02	.01
☐	659	Dan Quisenberry	.10	.05	.01
☐	660	Paul Assenmacher	.05	.02	.01
☐	661	Walt Terrell	.05	.02	.01
☐	662	Tim Leary	.05	.02	.01
☐	663	Randy Milligan	.05	.02	.01
☐	664	Bo Diaz	.05	.02	.01
☐	665	Mark Lemke UER (Richmond misspelled as Richomond)	.10	.05	.01

☐ 666 Jose Gonzalez .05 .02 .01
☐ 667 Chuck Finley UER .10 .05 .01
(Born 11/16/62, should be 11/26/62)
☐ 668 John Kruk .20 .09 .03
☐ 669 Dick Schofield .05 .02 .01
☐ 670 Tim Crews .05 .02 .01
☐ 671 John Dopson .05 .02 .01
☐ 672 John Orton .05 .02 .01
☐ 673 Eric Hetzel .05 .02 .01
☐ 674 Lance Parrish .10 .05 .01
☐ 675 Ramon Martinez .20 .09 .03
☐ 676 Mark Gubicza .05 .02 .01
☐ 677 Greg Litton .05 .02 .01
☐ 678 Greg Mathews .05 .02 .01
☐ 679 Dave Dravecky .10 .05 .01
☐ 680 Steve Farr .05 .02 .01
☐ 681 Mike Devereaux .10 .05 .01
☐ 682 Ken Griffey .10 .05 .01
☐ 683A Mickey Weston ERR 2.50 1.15 .30
(Listed as Jamie on card)
☐ 683B Mickey Weston COR .10 .05 .01
(Technically still an error as birthdate is listed as 3/26/81)
☐ 684 Jack Armstrong .05 .02 .01
☐ 685 Steve Buechele .05 .02 .01
☐ 686 Bryan Harvey .10 .05 .01
☐ 687 Lance Blankenship .05 .02 .01
☐ 688 Dante Bichette .30 .14 .04
☐ 689 Todd Burns .05 .02 .01
☐ 690 Dan Petry .05 .02 .01
☐ 691 Kent Anderson .05 .02 .01
☐ 692 Todd Stottlemyre .10 .05 .01
☐ 693 Wally Joyner UER .10 .05 .01
(Several stats errors)
☐ 694 Mike Rochford .05 .02 .01
☐ 695 Floyd Bannister .05 .02 .01
☐ 696 Rick Reuschel .05 .02 .01
☐ 697 Jose DeLeon .05 .02 .01
☐ 698 Jeff Montgomery .10 .05 .01
☐ 699 Kelly Downs .05 .02 .01
☐ 700A Checklist 601-700 2.50 .20 .05
(683 Jamie Weston)
☐ 700B Checklist 601-700 .06 .03 .01
(683 Mickey Weston)
☐ 701 Jim Gott .05 .02 .01
☐ 702 Rookie Threats .75 .35 .09
Delino DeShields
Marquis Grissom
Larry Walker
☐ 703 Alejandro Pena .05 .02 .01
☐ 704 Willie Randolph .10 .05 .01
☐ 705 Tim Leary .05 .02 .01
☐ 706 Chuck McElroy .05 .02 .01
☐ 707 Gerald Perry .05 .02 .01
☐ 708 Tom Brunansky .05 .02 .01
☐ 709 John Franco .10 .05 .01
☐ 710 Mark Davis .05 .02 .01
☐ 711 David Justice 2.00 .90 .25
☐ 712 Storm Davis .05 .02 .01
☐ 713 Scott Ruskin .05 .02 .01
☐ 714 Glenn Braggs .05 .02 .01
☐ 715 Kevin Bearse .05 .02 .01
☐ 716 Jose Nunez .05 .02 .01
☐ 717 Tim Layana .05 .02 .01
☐ 718 Greg Myers .05 .02 .01
☐ 719 Pete O'Brien .05 .02 .01
☐ 720 John Candelaria .05 .02 .01
☐ 721 Craig Grebeck .05 .02 .01
☐ 722 Shawn Boskie .05 .02 .01
☐ 723 Jim Leyritz .25 .11 .03
☐ 724 Bill Sampen .05 .02 .01
☐ 725 Scott Radinsky .05 .02 .01
☐ 726 Todd Hundley .30 .14 .04
☐ 727 Scott Hemond .05 .02 .01
☐ 728 Lenny Webster .05 .02 .01
☐ 729 Jeff Reardon .20 .09 .03
☐ 730 Mitch Webster .05 .02 .01
☐ 731 Brian Bohanon .05 .02 .01
☐ 732 Rick Parker .05 .02 .01
☐ 733 Terry Shumpert .05 .02 .01
☐ 734A Ryan's 6th No-Hitter 6.00 2.70 .75
(No stripe on front)
☐ 734B Ryan's 6th No-Hitter 1.25 .55 .16
(stripe added on card front for 300th win)
☐ 735 John Burkett .50 .23 .06
☐ 736 Derrick May .35 .16 .04
☐ 737 Carlos Baerga 2.00 .90 .25
☐ 738 Greg Smith .05 .02 .01
☐ 739 Scott Sanderson .05 .02 .01
☐ 740 Joe Kraemer .05 .02 .01
☐ 741 Hector Villanueva .05 .02 .01
☐ 742 Mike Fetters .05 .02 .01
☐ 743 Mark Gardner .05 .02 .01
☐ 744 Matt Nokes .05 .02 .01
☐ 745 Dave Winfield .30 .14 .04
☐ 746 Delino DeShields .50 .23 .06
☐ 747 Dann Howitt .05 .02 .01
☐ 748 Tony Pena .05 .02 .01
☐ 749 Oil Can Boyd .05 .02 .01
☐ 750 Mike Benjamin .05 .02 .01
☐ 751 Alex Cole .10 .05 .01
☐ 752 Eric Gunderson .05 .02 .01
☐ 753 Howard Farmer .05 .02 .01
☐ 754 Joe Carter .40 .18 .05
☐ 755 Ray Lankford .75 .35 .09
☐ 756 Sandy Alomar Jr. .10 .05 .01
☐ 757 Alex Sanchez .05 .02 .01
☐ 758 Nick Esasky .05 .02 .01
☐ 759 Stan Belinda .05 .02 .01
☐ 760 Jim Presley .05 .02 .01
☐ 761 Gary DiSarcina .05 .02 .01
☐ 762 Wayne Edwards .05 .02 .01
☐ 763 Pat Combs .05 .02 .01
☐ 764 Mickey Pina .05 .02 .01
☐ 765 Wilson Alvarez 1.00 .45 .13
☐ 766 Dave Parker .20 .09 .03
☐ 767 Mike Blowers .05 .02 .01
☐ 768 Tony Phillips .10 .05 .01
☐ 769 Pascual Perez .05 .02 .01
☐ 770 Gary Pettis .05 .02 .01
☐ 771 Fred Lynn .10 .05 .01
☐ 772 Mel Rojas .10 .05 .01
☐ 773 David Segui .25 .11 .03
☐ 774 Gary Carter .20 .09 .03
☐ 775 Rafael Valdez .05 .02 .01
☐ 776 Glenallen Hill .05 .02 .01
☐ 777 Keith Hernandez .10 .05 .01
☐ 778 Billy Hatcher .05 .02 .01
☐ 779 Marty Clary .05 .02 .01
☐ 780 Candy Maldonado .05 .02 .01
☐ 781 Mike Marshall .05 .02 .01
☐ 782 Billy Joe Robidoux .05 .02 .01
☐ 783 Mark Langston .20 .09 .03
☐ 784 Paul Sorrento .25 .11 .03
☐ 785 Dave Hollins .50 .23 .06
☐ 786 Cecil Fielder .30 .14 .04
☐ 787 Matt Young .05 .02 .01
☐ 788 Jeff Huson .05 .02 .01
☐ 789 Lloyd Moseby .05 .02 .01
☐ 790 Ron Kittle .05 .02 .01
☐ 791 Hubie Brooks .05 .02 .01
☐ 792 Craig Lefferts .05 .02 .01

☐ 793	Kevin Bass	.05	.02	.01
☐ 794	Bryn Smith	.05	.02	.01
☐ 795	Juan Samuel	.05	.02	.01
☐ 796	Sam Horn	.05	.02	.01
☐ 797	Randy Myers	.10	.05	.01
☐ 798	Chris James	.05	.02	.01
☐ 799	Bill Gullickson	.05	.02	.01
☐ 800	Checklist 701-800	.05	.02	.01

1990 Upper Deck Reggie Jackson Heroes

This ten-card subset was issued as an insert in 1990 Upper Deck High Number packs as part of the Upper Deck promotional giveaway of 2,500 officially signed and personally numbered Reggie Jackson cards. These cards were the standard size (2 1/2" by 3 1/2") and cover Reggie's complete major league career. The complete set price refers only to the unautographed card set of ten. One-card packs of over-sized (3 1/2" by 5") versions of these cards were later inserted into retail blister repacks containing one foil pack each of 1993 Upper Deck Series I and II. These cards were later inserted into various forms of repackaging. The larger cards are also distinguishable by the Upper Deck Fifth Anniversary logo and "1993 Hall of Fame Inductee" logo on the front of the card. These over-sized cards were a limited (numbered) edition of 10,000 of each card and have no extra value than the basic cards.

	MINT	EXC	G-VG
COMPLETE SET (10)	20.00	9.00	2.50
COMMON REGGIE (1-9)	2.00	.90	.25

☐ 1	1969 Emerging Superstar	2.00	.90	.25
☐ 2	1973 An MVP Year	2.00	.90	.25
☐ 3	1977 Mr. October	2.00	.90	.25
☐ 4	1978 Jackson vs. Welch	2.00	.90	.25
☐ 5	1982 Under the Halo	2.00	.90	.25
☐ 6	1984 500 Homers	2.00	.90	.25
☐ 7	1986 Moving Up the List	2.00	.90	.25
☐ 8	1987 A Great Career Ends	2.00	.90	.25
☐ 9	Baseball Heroes Checklist	2.00	.90	.25
☐ NNO	Reggie Jackson Header Card	4.00	1.80	.50
☐ AU1	Reggie Jackson AU (Signed and Numbered out of 2500)	300.00	135.00	38.00

1991 Upper Deck

This set marked the third year Upper Deck has issued a 700-card set in January. The cards measure 2 1/2" by 3 1/2". The set features 26 star rookies to lead off the set as well as other special cards featuring multi-players. The set is made on the typical Upper Deck card stock and features full-color photos on both the front and the back. The team checklist (TC) cards in the set feature an attractive Vernon Wells drawing of a featured player for that particular team. A special Michael Jordan card (numbered SP1) was randomly included in packs on a somewhat limited basis; this Jordan card is not included in the set price below. The Hank Aaron hologram card was randomly inserted in the 1991 Upper Deck high number foil packs. The 100-card extended or high-number series was issued by Upper Deck several months after the release of their first series. The extended series features rookie players as well as players who switched teams between seasons. In the extended wax packs were low number cards, special cards featuring Hank Aaron as the next featured player in their baseball heroes series, and a special card honoring the May 1st exploits of Rickey Henderson and Nolan Ryan. For the first time in Upper Deck's three-year history, they did not issue a factory Extended set. Rookie Cards in this set include Jeff Bagwell, Wes Chamberlain, Jeff Conine, Wilfredo Cordero, Luis Gonzalez, Chipper Jones, Eric Karros, Brian McRae, Orlando Merced, Pedro Munoz, Mike Mussina, Phil Plantier, Reggie Sanders, and Todd Van Poppel.

	MINT	EXC	G-VG
COMPLETE SET (800)	20.00	9.00	2.50

COMPLETE FACT.SET (800)	20.00	9.00	2.50
COMPLETE LO SET (700)	16.00	7.25	2.00
COMPLETE HI SET (100)	4.00	1.80	.50
COMMON CARD (1-700)	.05	.02	.01
COMMON CARD (701-800)	.05	.02	.01

□ 1 Star Rookie Checklist	.05	.02	.01
□ 2 Phil Plantier	.40	.18	.05
□ 3 D.J. Dozier	.05	.02	.01
□ 4 Dave Hansen	.05	.02	.01
□ 5 Maurice Vaughn	.50	.23	.06
□ 6 Leo Gomez	.10	.05	.01
□ 7 Scott Aldred	.05	.02	.01
□ 8 Scott Chiamparino	.05	.02	.01
□ 9 Lance Dickson	.05	.02	.01
□ 10 Sean Berry	.15	.07	.02
□ 11 Bernie Williams	.10	.05	.01
□ 12 Brian Barnes UER (Photo either not him or in wrong jersey)	.05	.02	.01
□ 13 Narciso Elvira	.05	.02	.01
□ 14 Mike Gardiner	.05	.02	.01
□ 15 Greg Colbrunn	.10	.05	.01
□ 16 Bernard Gilkey	.10	.05	.01
□ 17 Mark Lewis	.10	.05	.01
□ 18 Mickey Morandini	.05	.02	.01
□ 19 Charles Nagy	.10	.05	.01
□ 20 Geronimo Pena	.05	.02	.01
□ 21 Henry Rodriguez	.20	.09	.03
□ 22 Scott Cooper	.10	.05	.01
□ 23 Andujar Cedeno UER (Shown batting left, back says right)	.10	.05	.01
□ 24 Eric Karros	.30	.14	.04
□ 25 Steve Decker UER (Lewis-Clark State College, not Lewis and Clark)	.05	.02	.01
□ 26 Kevin Belcher	.05	.02	.01
□ 27 Jeff Conine	.60	.25	.08
□ 28 Dave Stewart TC Oakland Athletics	.05	.02	.01
□ 29 Carlton Fisk TC Chicago White Sox	.10	.05	.01
□ 30 Rafael Palmeiro TC Texas Rangers	.10	.05	.01
□ 31 Chuck Finley TC California Angels	.05	.02	.01
□ 32 Harold Reynolds TC Seattle Mariners	.05	.02	.01
□ 33 Bret Saberhagen TC Kansas City Royals	.10	.05	.01
□ 34 Gary Gaetti TC Minnesota Twins	.05	.02	.01
□ 35 Scott Leius	.05	.02	.01
□ 36 Neal Heaton	.05	.02	.01
□ 37 Terry Lee	.05	.02	.01
□ 38 Gary Redus	.05	.02	.01
□ 39 Barry Jones	.05	.02	.01
□ 40 Chuck Knoblauch	.40	.18	.05
□ 41 Larry Andersen	.05	.02	.01
□ 42 Darryl Hamilton	.10	.05	.01
□ 43 Mike Greenwell TC Boston Red Sox	.05	.02	.01
□ 44 Kelly Gruber TC Toronto Blue Jays	.05	.02	.01
□ 45 Jack Morris TC Detroit Tigers	.10	.05	.01
□ 46 Sandy Alomar Jr. TC Cleveland Indians	.05	.02	.01
□ 47 Gregg Olson TC Baltimore Orioles	.05	.02	.01
□ 48 Dave Parker TC Milwaukee Brewers	.10	.05	.01
□ 49 Roberto Kelly TC New York Yankees	.05	.02	.01
□ 50 Top Prospect Checklist	.05	.02	.01
□ 51 Kyle Abbott	.05	.02	.01
□ 52 Jeff Juden	.10	.05	.01
□ 53 Todd Van Poppel UER (Born Arlington and attended John Martin HS, should say Hinsdale and James Martin HS)	.25	.11	.03
□ 54 Steve Karsay	.50	.23	.06
□ 55 Chipper Jones	1.50	.65	.19
□ 56 Chris Johnson UER (Called Tim on back)	.05	.02	.01
□ 57 John Ericks	.05	.02	.01
□ 58 Gary Scott	.05	.02	.01
□ 59 Kiki Jones	.05	.02	.01
□ 60 Wil Cordero	.60	.25	.08
□ 61 Royce Clayton	.35	.16	.04
□ 62 Tim Costo	.05	.02	.01
□ 63 Roger Salkeld	.05	.02	.01
□ 64 Brook Fordyce	.05	.02	.01
□ 65 Mike Mussina	1.50	.65	.19
□ 66 Dave Staton	.05	.02	.01
□ 67 Mike Lieberthal	.10	.05	.01
□ 68 Kurt Miller	.05	.02	.01
□ 69 Dan Peltier	.05	.02	.01
□ 70 Greg Blosser	.10	.05	.01
□ 71 Reggie Sanders	.50	.23	.06
□ 72 Brent Mayne	.05	.02	.01
□ 73 Rico Brogna	.30	.14	.04
□ 74 Willie Banks	.10	.05	.01
□ 75 Len Brutcher	.05	.02	.01
□ 76 Pat Kelly	.15	.07	.02
□ 77 Chris Sabo TC Cincinnati Reds	.05	.02	.01
□ 78 Ramon Martinez TC Los Angeles Dodgers	.05	.02	.01
□ 79 Matt Williams TC San Francisco Giants	.10	.05	.01
□ 80 Roberto Alomar TC San Diego Padres	.15	.07	.02
□ 81 Glenn Davis TC Houston Astros	.05	.02	.01
□ 82 Ron Gant TC Atlanta Braves	.10	.05	.01
□ 83 Fielder's Feat Cecil Fielder	.10	.05	.01
□ 84 Orlando Merced	.30	.14	.04
□ 85 Domingo Ramos	.05	.02	.01
□ 86 Tom Bolton	.05	.02	.01
□ 87 Andres Santana	.05	.02	.01
□ 88 John Dopson	.05	.02	.01
□ 89 Kenny Williams	.05	.02	.01
□ 90 Marty Barrett	.05	.02	.01
□ 91 Tom Pagnozzi	.05	.02	.01
□ 92 Carmelo Martinez	.05	.02	.01
□ 93 Bobby Thigpen (Save Master)	.05	.02	.01
□ 94 Barry Bonds TC Pittsburgh Pirates	.25	.11	.03
□ 95 Gregg Jefferies TC New York Mets	.10	.05	.01
□ 96 Tim Wallach TC Montreal Expos	.05	.02	.01
□ 97 Len Dykstra TC Philadelphia Phillies	.10	.05	.01
□ 98 Pedro Guerrero TC St.Louis Cardinals	.05	.02	.01
□ 99 Mark Grace TC Chicago Cubs	.10	.05	.01
□ 100 Checklist 1-100	.05	.02	.01
□ 101 Kevin Elster	.05	.02	.01

	No.	Player			
☐	102	Tom Brookens	.05	.02	.01
☐	103	Mackey Sasser	.05	.02	.01
☐	104	Felix Fermin	.05	.02	.01
☐	105	Kevin McReynolds	.05	.02	.01
☐	106	Dave Stieb	.10	.05	.01
☐	107	Jeffrey Leonard	.05	.02	.01
☐	108	Dave Henderson	.05	.02	.01
☐	109	Sid Bream	.05	.02	.01
☐	110	Henry Cotto	.05	.02	.01
☐	111	Shawon Dunston	.05	.02	.01
☐	112	Mariano Duncan	.05	.02	.01
☐	113	Joe Girardi	.05	.02	.01
☐	114	Billy Hatcher	.05	.02	.01
☐	115	Greg Maddux	.30	.14	.04
☐	116	Jerry Browne	.05	.02	.01
☐	117	Juan Samuel	.05	.02	.01
☐	118	Steve Olin	.05	.02	.01
☐	119	Alfredo Griffin	.05	.02	.01
☐	120	Mitch Webster	.05	.02	.01
☐	121	Joel Skinner	.05	.02	.01
☐	122	Frank Viola	.10	.05	.01
☐	123	Cory Snyder	.05	.02	.01
☐	124	Howard Johnson	.10	.05	.01
☐	125	Carlos Baerga	.40	.18	.05
☐	126	Tony Fernandez	.10	.05	.01
☐	127	Dave Stewart	.10	.05	.01
☐	128	Jay Buhner	.10	.05	.01
☐	129	Mike LaValliere	.05	.02	.01
☐	130	Scott Bradley	.05	.02	.01
☐	131	Tony Phillips	.05	.02	.01
☐	132	Ryne Sandberg	.35	.16	.04
☐	133	Paul O'Neill	.10	.05	.01
☐	134	Mark Grace	.15	.07	.02
☐	135	Chris Sabo	.10	.05	.01
☐	136	Ramon Martinez	.10	.05	.01
☐	137	Brook Jacoby	.05	.02	.01
☐	138	Candy Maldonado	.05	.02	.01
☐	139	Mike Scioscia	.05	.02	.01
☐	140	Chris James	.05	.02	.01
☐	141	Craig Worthington	.05	.02	.01
☐	142	Manny Lee	.05	.02	.01
☐	143	Tim Raines	.15	.07	.02
☐	144	Sandy Alomar Jr.	.10	.05	.01
☐	145	John Olerud	.20	.09	.03
☐	146	Ozzie Canseco (With Jose)	.05	.02	.01
☐	147	Pat Borders	.05	.02	.01
☐	148	Harold Reynolds	.05	.02	.01
☐	149	Tom Henke	.10	.05	.01
☐	150	R.J. Reynolds	.05	.02	.01
☐	151	Mike Gallego	.05	.02	.01
☐	152	Bobby Bonilla	.15	.07	.02
☐	153	Terry Steinbach	.10	.05	.01
☐	154	Barry Bonds	.50	.23	.06
☐	155	Jose Canseco	.30	.14	.04
☐	156	Gregg Jefferies	.15	.07	.02
☐	157	Matt Williams	.30	.14	.04
☐	158	Craig Biggio	.15	.07	.02
☐	159	Daryl Boston	.05	.02	.01
☐	160	Ricky Jordan	.05	.02	.01
☐	161	Stan Belinda	.05	.02	.01
☐	162	Ozzie Smith	.25	.11	.03
☐	163	Tom Brunansky	.05	.02	.01
☐	164	Todd Zeile	.10	.05	.01
☐	165	Mike Greenwell	.10	.05	.01
☐	166	Kal Daniels	.05	.02	.01
☐	167	Kent Hrbek	.10	.05	.01
☐	168	Franklin Stubbs	.05	.02	.01
☐	169	Dick Schofield	.05	.02	.01
☐	170	Junior Ortiz	.05	.02	.01
☐	171	Hector Villanueva	.05	.02	.01
☐	172	Dennis Eckersley	.15	.07	.02
☐	173	Mitch Williams	.10	.05	.01
☐	174	Mark McGwire	.15	.07	.02
☐	175	Fernando Valenzuela 3X	.05	.02	.01
☐	176	Gary Carter	.15	.07	.02
☐	177	Dave Magadan	.05	.02	.01
☐	178	Robby Thompson	.05	.02	.01
☐	179	Bob Ojeda	.05	.02	.01
☐	180	Ken Caminiti	.10	.05	.01
☐	181	Don Slaught	.05	.02	.01
☐	182	Luis Rivera	.05	.02	.01
☐	183	Jay Bell	.10	.05	.01
☐	184	Jody Reed	.05	.02	.01
☐	185	Wally Backman	.05	.02	.01
☐	186	Dave Martinez	.05	.02	.01
☐	187	Luis Polonia	.05	.02	.01
☐	188	Shane Mack	.10	.05	.01
☐	189	Spike Owen	.05	.02	.01
☐	190	Scott Bailes	.05	.02	.01
☐	191	John Russell	.05	.02	.01
☐	192	Walt Weiss	.05	.02	.01
☐	193	Jose Oquendo	.05	.02	.01
☐	194	Carney Lansford	.10	.05	.01
☐	195	Jeff Huson	.05	.02	.01
☐	196	Keith Miller	.05	.02	.01
☐	197	Eric Yelding	.05	.02	.01
☐	198	Ron Darling	.05	.02	.01
☐	199	John Kruk	.15	.07	.02
☐	200	Checklist 101-200	.05	.02	.01
☐	201	John Shelby	.05	.02	.01
☐	202	Bob Geren	.05	.02	.01
☐	203	Lance McCullers	.05	.02	.01
☐	204	Alvaro Espinoza	.05	.02	.01
☐	205	Mark Salas	.05	.02	.01
☐	206	Mike Pagliarulo	.05	.02	.01
☐	207	Jose Uribe	.05	.02	.01
☐	208	Jim Deshaies	.05	.02	.01
☐	209	Ron Karkovice	.05	.02	.01
☐	210	Rafael Ramirez	.05	.02	.01
☐	211	Donnie Hill	.05	.02	.01
☐	212	Brian Harper	.05	.02	.01
☐	213	Jack Howell	.05	.02	.01
☐	214	Wes Gardner	.05	.02	.01
☐	215	Tim Burke	.05	.02	.01
☐	216	Doug Jones	.05	.02	.01
☐	217	Hubie Brooks	.05	.02	.01
☐	218	Tom Candiotti	.05	.02	.01
☐	219	Gerald Perry	.05	.02	.01
☐	220	Jose DeLeon	.05	.02	.01
☐	221	Wally Whitehurst	.05	.02	.01
☐	222	Alan Mills	.05	.02	.01
☐	223	Alan Trammell	.15	.07	.02
☐	224	Dwight Gooden	.10	.05	.01
☐	225	Travis Fryman	.60	.25	.08
☐	226	Joe Carter	.25	.11	.03
☐	227	Julio Franco	.10	.05	.01
☐	228	Craig Lefferts	.05	.02	.01
☐	229	Gary Pettis	.05	.02	.01
☐	230	Dennis Rasmussen	.05	.02	.01
☐	231A	Brian Downing ERR (No position on front)	.25	.11	.03
☐	231B	Brian Downing COR (DH on front)	.40	.18	.05
☐	232	Carlos Quintana	.05	.02	.01
☐	233	Gary Gaetti	.05	.02	.01
☐	234	Mark Langston	.15	.07	.02
☐	235	Tim Wallach	.05	.02	.01
☐	236	Greg Swindell	.05	.02	.01
☐	237	Eddie Murray	.15	.07	.02
☐	238	Jeff Manto	.05	.02	.01
☐	239	Lenny Harris	.05	.02	.01
☐	240	Jesse Orosco	.05	.02	.01
☐	241	Scott Lusader	.05	.02	.01
☐	242	Sid Fernandez	.10	.05	.01
☐	243	Jim Leyritz	.05	.02	.01

- ☐ 244 Cecil Fielder .15 .07 .02
- ☐ 245 Darryl Strawberry .15 .07 .02
- ☐ 246 Frank Thomas UER 2.50 1.15 .30 (Comiskey Park misspelled Comisky)
- ☐ 247 Kevin Mitchell .10 .05 .01
- ☐ 248 Lance Johnson .05 .02 .01
- ☐ 249 Rick Reuschel .05 .02 .01
- ☐ 250 Mark Portugal .05 .02 .01
- ☐ 251 Derek Lilliquist .05 .02 .01
- ☐ 252 Brian Holman .05 .02 .01
- ☐ 253 Rafael Valdez UER .05 .02 .01 (Born 4/17/68, should be 12/17/67)
- ☐ 254 B.J. Surhoff .05 .02 .01
- ☐ 255 Tony Gwynn .25 .11 .03
- ☐ 256 Andy Van Slyke .15 .07 .02
- ☐ 257 Todd Stottlemyre .05 .02 .01
- ☐ 258 Jose Lind .05 .02 .01
- ☐ 259 Greg Myers .05 .02 .01
- ☐ 260 Jeff Ballard .05 .02 .01
- ☐ 261 Bobby Thigpen .05 .02 .01
- ☐ 262 Jimmy Kremers .05 .02 .01
- ☐ 263 Robin Ventura .35 .16 .04
- ☐ 264 John Smoltz .15 .07 .02
- ☐ 265 Sammy Sosa .15 .07 .02
- ☐ 266 Gary Sheffield .25 .11 .03
- ☐ 267 Len Dykstra .15 .07 .02
- ☐ 268 Bill Spiers .05 .02 .01
- ☐ 269 Charlie Hayes .10 .05 .01
- ☐ 270 Brett Butler .10 .05 .01
- ☐ 271 Bip Roberts .05 .02 .01
- ☐ 272 Rob Deer .05 .02 .01
- ☐ 273 Fred Lynn .10 .05 .01
- ☐ 274 Dave Parker .15 .07 .02
- ☐ 275 Andy Benes .15 .07 .02
- ☐ 276 Glenallen Hill .05 .02 .01
- ☐ 277 Steve Howard .05 .02 .01
- ☐ 278 Doug Drabek .15 .07 .02
- ☐ 279 Joe Oliver .05 .02 .01
- ☐ 280 Todd Benzinger .05 .02 .01
- ☐ 281 Eric King .05 .02 .01
- ☐ 282 Jim Presley .05 .02 .01
- ☐ 283 Ken Patterson .05 .02 .01
- ☐ 284 Jack Daugherty .05 .02 .01
- ☐ 285 Ivan Calderon .05 .02 .01
- ☐ 286 Edgar Diaz .05 .02 .01
- ☐ 287 Kevin Bass .05 .02 .01
- ☐ 288 Don Carman .05 .02 .01
- ☐ 289 Greg Brock .05 .02 .01
- ☐ 290 John Franco .10 .05 .01
- ☐ 291 Joey Cora .05 .02 .01
- ☐ 292 Bill Wegman .05 .02 .01
- ☐ 293 Eric Show .05 .02 .01
- ☐ 294 Scott Bankhead .05 .02 .01
- ☐ 295 Garry Templeton .05 .02 .01
- ☐ 296 Mickey Tettleton .10 .05 .01
- ☐ 297 Luis Sojo .05 .02 .01
- ☐ 298 Jose Rijo .10 .05 .01
- ☐ 299 Dave Johnson .05 .02 .01
- ☐ 300 Checklist 201-300 .05 .02 .01
- ☐ 301 Mark Grant .05 .02 .01
- ☐ 302 Pete Harnisch .10 .05 .01
- ☐ 303 Greg Olson .05 .02 .01
- ☐ 304 Anthony Telford .05 .02 .01
- ☐ 305 Lonnie Smith .05 .02 .01
- ☐ 306 Chris Hoiles .15 .07 .02
- ☐ 307 Bryn Smith .05 .02 .01
- ☐ 308 Mike Devereaux .10 .05 .01
- ☐ 309A Milt Thompson ERR .25 .11 .03 (Under yr information has print dot)
- ☐ 309B Milt Thompson COR .05 .02 .01 (Under yr information says 86)
- ☐ 310 Bob Melvin .05 .02 .01
- ☐ 311 Luis Salazar .05 .02 .01
- ☐ 312 Ed Whitson .05 .02 .01
- ☐ 313 Charlie Hough .10 .05 .01
- ☐ 314 Dave Clark .05 .02 .01
- ☐ 315 Eric Gunderson .05 .02 .01
- ☐ 316 Dan Petry .05 .02 .01
- ☐ 317 Dante Bichette UER .15 .07 .02 (Assists misspelled as assissts)
- ☐ 318 Mike Heath .05 .02 .01
- ☐ 319 Damon Berryhill .05 .02 .01
- ☐ 320 Walt Terrell .05 .02 .01
- ☐ 321 Scott Fletcher .05 .02 .01
- ☐ 322 Dan Plesac .05 .02 .01
- ☐ 323 Jack McDowell .15 .07 .02
- ☐ 324 Paul Molitor .20 .09 .03
- ☐ 325 Ozzie Guillen .05 .02 .01
- ☐ 326 Gregg Olson .10 .05 .01
- ☐ 327 Pedro Guerrero .10 .05 .01
- ☐ 328 Bob Milacki .05 .02 .01
- ☐ 329 John Tudor UER .05 .02 .01 ('90 Cardinals, should be '90 Dodgers)
- ☐ 330 Steve Finley UER .05 .02 .01 (Born 3/12/65, should be 5/12)
- ☐ 331 Jack Clark .10 .05 .01
- ☐ 332 Jerome Walton .05 .02 .01
- ☐ 333 Andy Hawkins .05 .02 .01
- ☐ 334 Derrick May .10 .05 .01
- ☐ 335 Roberto Alomar .40 .18 .05
- ☐ 336 Jack Morris .15 .07 .02
- ☐ 337 Dave Winfield .15 .07 .02
- ☐ 338 Steve Searcy .05 .02 .01
- ☐ 339 Chili Davis .10 .05 .01
- ☐ 340 Larry Sheets .05 .02 .01
- ☐ 341 Ted Higuera .05 .02 .01
- ☐ 342 David Segui .05 .02 .01
- ☐ 343 Greg Cadaret .05 .02 .01
- ☐ 344 Robin Yount .20 .09 .03
- ☐ 345 Nolan Ryan 1.00 .45 .13
- ☐ 346 Ray Lankford .15 .07 .02
- ☐ 347 Cal Ripken .50 .23 .06
- ☐ 348 Lee Smith .15 .07 .02
- ☐ 349 Brady Anderson .10 .05 .01
- ☐ 350 Frank DiPino .05 .02 .01
- ☐ 351 Hal Morris .10 .05 .01
- ☐ 352 Deion Sanders .35 .16 .04
- ☐ 353 Barry Larkin .15 .07 .02
- ☐ 354 Don Mattingly .35 .16 .04
- ☐ 355 Eric Davis .10 .05 .01
- ☐ 356 Jose Offerman .10 .05 .01
- ☐ 357 Mel Rojas .05 .02 .01
- ☐ 358 Rudy Seanez .05 .02 .01
- ☐ 359 Oil Can Boyd .05 .02 .01
- ☐ 360 Nelson Liriano .05 .02 .01
- ☐ 361 Ron Gant .10 .05 .01
- ☐ 362 Howard Farmer .05 .02 .01
- ☐ 363 David Justice .40 .18 .05
- ☐ 364 Delino DeShields .15 .07 .02
- ☐ 365 Steve Avery .25 .11 .03
- ☐ 366 David Cone .15 .07 .02
- ☐ 367 Lou Whitaker .15 .07 .02
- ☐ 368 Von Hayes .05 .02 .01
- ☐ 369 Frank Tanana .05 .02 .01
- ☐ 370 Tim Teufel .05 .02 .01
- ☐ 371 Randy Myers .10 .05 .01
- ☐ 372 Roberto Kelly .10 .05 .01
- ☐ 373 Jack Armstrong .05 .02 .01
- ☐ 374 Kelly Gruber .05 .02 .01

	#	Player			
☐	375	Kevin Maas	.05	.02	.01
☐	376	Randy Johnson	.15	.07	.02
☐	377	David West	.05	.02	.01
☐	378	Brent Knackert	.05	.02	.01
☐	379	Rick Honeycutt	.05	.02	.01
☐	380	Kevin Gross	.05	.02	.01
☐	381	Tom Foley	.05	.02	.01
☐	382	Jeff Blauser	.10	.05	.01
☐	383	Scott Ruskin	.05	.02	.01
☐	384	Andres Thomas	.05	.02	.01
☐	385	Dennis Martinez	.10	.05	.01
☐	386	Mike Henneman	.05	.02	.01
☐	387	Felix Jose	.10	.05	.01
☐	388	Alejandro Pena	.05	.02	.01
☐	389	Chet Lemon	.05	.02	.01
☐	390	Craig Wilson	.05	.02	.01
☐	391	Chuck Crim	.05	.02	.01
☐	392	Mel Hall	.05	.02	.01
☐	393	Mark Knudson	.05	.02	.01
☐	394	Norm Charlton	.05	.02	.01
☐	395	Mike Felder	.05	.02	.01
☐	396	Tim Layana	.05	.02	.01
☐	397	Steve Frey	.05	.02	.01
☐	398	Bill Doran	.05	.02	.01
☐	399	Dion James	.05	.02	.01
☐	400	Checklist 301-400	.05	.02	.01
☐	401	Ron Hassey	.05	.02	.01
☐	402	Don Robinson	.05	.02	.01
☐	403	Gene Nelson	.05	.02	.01
☐	404	Terry Kennedy	.05	.02	.01
☐	405	Todd Burns	.05	.02	.01
☐	406	Roger McDowell	.05	.02	.01
☐	407	Bob Kipper	.05	.02	.01
☐	408	Darren Daulton	.15	.07	.02
☐	409	Chuck Cary	.05	.02	.01
☐	410	Bruce Ruffin	.05	.02	.01
☐	411	Juan Berenguer	.05	.02	.01
☐	412	Gary Ward	.05	.02	.01
☐	413	Al Newman	.05	.02	.01
☐	414	Danny Jackson	.05	.02	.01
☐	415	Greg Gagne	.05	.02	.01
☐	416	Tom Herr	.05	.02	.01
☐	417	Jeff Parrett	.05	.02	.01
☐	418	Jeff Reardon	.10	.05	.01
☐	419	Mark Lemke	.05	.02	.01
☐	420	Charlie O'Brien	.05	.02	.01
☐	421	Willie Randolph	.10	.05	.01
☐	422	Steve Bedrosian	.05	.02	.01
☐	423	Mike Moore	.05	.02	.01
☐	424	Jeff Brantley	.05	.02	.01
☐	425	Bob Welch	.05	.02	.01
☐	426	Terry Mulholland	.05	.02	.01
☐	427	Willie Blair	.05	.02	.01
☐	428	Darrin Fletcher	.05	.02	.01
☐	429	Mike Witt	.05	.02	.01
☐	430	Joe Boever	.05	.02	.01
☐	431	Tom Gordon	.10	.05	.01
☐	432	Pedro Munoz	.15	.07	.02
☐	433	Kevin Seitzer	.05	.02	.01
☐	434	Kevin Tapani	.10	.05	.01
☐	435	Bret Saberhagen	.10	.05	.01
☐	436	Ellis Burks	.10	.05	.01
☐	437	Chuck Finley	.10	.05	.01
☐	438	Mike Boddicker	.05	.02	.01
☐	439	Francisco Cabrera	.05	.02	.01
☐	440	Todd Hundley	.10	.05	.01
☐	441	Kelly Downs	.05	.02	.01
☐	442	Dann Howitt	.05	.02	.01
☐	443	Scott Garrelts	.05	.02	.01
☐	444	Rickey Henderson 3X	.25	.11	.03
☐	445	Will Clark	.30	.14	.04
☐	446	Ben McDonald	.15	.07	.02
☐	447	Dale Murphy	.15	.07	.02
☐	448	Dave Righetti	.05	.02	.01
☐	449	Dickie Thon	.05	.02	.01
☐	450	Ted Power	.05	.02	.01
☐	451	Scott Coolbaugh	.05	.02	.01
☐	452	Dwight Smith	.05	.02	.01
☐	453	Pete Incaviglia	.05	.02	.01
☐	454	Andre Dawson	.15	.07	.02
☐	455	Ruben Sierra	.15	.07	.02
☐	456	Andres Galarraga	.15	.07	.02
☐	457	Alvin Davis	.05	.02	.01
☐	458	Tony Castillo	.05	.02	.01
☐	459	Pete O'Brien	.05	.02	.01
☐	460	Charlie Leibrandt	.05	.02	.01
☐	461	Vince Coleman	.05	.02	.01
☐	462	Steve Sax	.05	.02	.01
☐	463	Omar Olivares	.05	.02	.01
☐	464	Oscar Azocar	.05	.02	.01
☐	465	Joe Magrane	.05	.02	.01
☐	466	Karl Rhodes	.05	.02	.01
☐	467	Benito Santiago	.05	.02	.01
☐	468	Joe Klink	.05	.02	.01
☐	469	Sil Campusano	.05	.02	.01
☐	470	Mark Parent	.05	.02	.01
☐	471	Shawn Boskie UER (Depleted misspelled as depleated)	.05	.02	.01
☐	472	Kevin Brown	.10	.05	.01
☐	473	Rick Sutcliffe	.10	.05	.01
☐	474	Rafael Palmeiro	.25	.11	.03
☐	475	Mike Harkey	.05	.02	.01
☐	476	Jaime Navarro	.05	.02	.01
☐	477	Marquis Grissom UER (DeShields misspelled as DeSheilds)	.20	.09	.03
☐	478	Marty Clary	.05	.02	.01
☐	479	Greg Briley	.05	.02	.01
☐	480	Tom Glavine	.35	.16	.04
☐	481	Lee Guetterman	.05	.02	.01
☐	482	Rex Hudler	.05	.02	.01
☐	483	Dave LaPoint	.05	.02	.01
☐	484	Terry Pendleton	.15	.07	.02
☐	485	Jesse Barfield	.05	.02	.01
☐	486	Jose DeJesus	.05	.02	.01
☐	487	Paul Abbott	.05	.02	.01
☐	488	Ken Howell	.05	.02	.01
☐	489	Greg W. Harris	.05	.02	.01
☐	490	Roy Smith	.05	.02	.01
☐	491	Paul Assenmacher	.05	.02	.01
☐	492	Geno Petralli	.05	.02	.01
☐	493	Steve Wilson	.05	.02	.01
☐	494	Kevin Reimer	.05	.02	.01
☐	495	Bill Long	.05	.02	.01
☐	496	Mike Jackson	.05	.02	.01
☐	497	Oddibe McDowell	.05	.02	.01
☐	498	Bill Swift	.10	.05	.01
☐	499	Jeff Treadway	.05	.02	.01
☐	500	Checklist 401-500	.05	.02	.01
☐	501	Gene Larkin	.05	.02	.01
☐	502	Bob Boone	.10	.05	.01
☐	503	Allan Anderson	.05	.02	.01
☐	504	Luis Aquino	.05	.02	.01
☐	505	Mark Guthrie	.05	.02	.01
☐	506	Joe Orsulak	.05	.02	.01
☐	507	Dana Kiecker	.05	.02	.01
☐	508	Dave Gallagher	.05	.02	.01
☐	509	Greg A. Harris	.05	.02	.01
☐	510	Mark Williamson	.05	.02	.01
☐	511	Casey Candaele	.05	.02	.01
☐	512	Mookie Wilson	.05	.02	.01
☐	513	Dave Smith	.05	.02	.01
☐	514	Chuck Carr	.10	.05	.01
☐	515	Glenn Wilson	.05	.02	.01
☐	516	Mike Fitzgerald	.05	.02	.01

☐ 517 Devon White .10 .05 .01
☐ 518 Dave Hollins .15 .07 .02
☐ 519 Mark Eichhorn .05 .02 .01
☐ 520 Otis Nixon .10 .05 .01
☐ 521 Terry Shumpert .05 .02 .01
☐ 522 Scott Erickson .05 .02 .01
☐ 523 Danny Tartabull .10 .05 .01
☐ 524 Orel Hershiser .10 .05 .01
☐ 525 George Brett .35 .16 .04
☐ 526 Greg Vaughn .10 .05 .01
☐ 527 Tim Naehring .05 .02 .01
☐ 528 Curt Schilling .10 .05 .01
☐ 529 Chris Bosio .05 .02 .01
☐ 530 Sam Horn .05 .02 .01
☐ 531 Mike Scott .05 .02 .01
☐ 532 George Bell .10 .05 .01
☐ 533 Eric Anthony .10 .05 .01
☐ 534 Julio Valera .05 .02 .01
☐ 535 Glenn Davis .05 .02 .01
☐ 536 Larry Walker UER .20 .09 .03
(Should have comma after Expos in text)
☐ 537 Pat Combs .05 .02 .01
☐ 538 Chris Nabholz .05 .02 .01
☐ 539 Kirk McCaskill .05 .02 .01
☐ 540 Randy Ready .05 .02 .01
☐ 541 Mark Gubicza .05 .02 .01
☐ 542 Rick Aguilera .10 .05 .01
☐ 543 Brian McRae .40 .18 .05
☐ 544 Kirby Puckett .40 .18 .05
☐ 545 Bo Jackson .15 .07 .02
☐ 546 Wade Boggs .15 .07 .02
☐ 547 Tim McIntosh .05 .02 .01
☐ 548 Randy Milligan .05 .02 .01
☐ 549 Dwight Evans .10 .05 .01
☐ 550 Billy Ripken .05 .02 .01
☐ 551 Erik Hanson .05 .02 .01
☐ 552 Lance Parrish .10 .05 .01
☐ 553 Tino Martinez .10 .05 .01
☐ 554 Jim Abbott .15 .07 .02
☐ 555 Ken Griffey Jr. UER 2.50 1.15 .30
(Second most votes for 1991 All-Star Game)
☐ 556 Milt Cuyler .05 .02 .01
☐ 557 Mark Leonard .05 .02 .01
☐ 558 Jay Howell .05 .02 .01
☐ 559 Lloyd Moseby .05 .02 .01
☐ 560 Chris Gwynn .05 .02 .01
☐ 561 Mark Whiten .15 .07 .02
☐ 562 Harold Baines .10 .05 .01
☐ 563 Junior Felix .05 .02 .01
☐ 564 Darren Lewis .10 .05 .01
☐ 565 Fred McGriff .30 .14 .04
☐ 566 Kevin Appier .10 .05 .01
☐ 567 Luis Gonzalez .30 .14 .04
☐ 568 Frank White .10 .05 .01
☐ 569 Juan Agosto .05 .02 .01
☐ 570 Mike Macfarlane .05 .02 .01
☐ 571 Bert Blyleven .15 .07 .02
☐ 572 Ken Griffey Sr./Jr. .50 .23 .06
☐ 573 Lee Stevens .05 .02 .01
☐ 574 Edgar Martinez .10 .05 .01
☐ 575 Wally Joyner .10 .05 .01
☐ 576 Tim Belcher .05 .02 .01
☐ 577 John Burkett .10 .05 .01
☐ 578 Mike Morgan .05 .02 .01
☐ 579 Paul Gibson .05 .02 .01
☐ 580 Jose Vizcaino .05 .02 .01
☐ 581 Duane Ward .10 .05 .01
☐ 582 Scott Sanderson .05 .02 .01
☐ 583 David Wells .05 .02 .01
☐ 584 Willie McGee .10 .05 .01
☐ 585 John Cerutti .05 .02 .01
☐ 586 Danny Darwin .05 .02 .01
☐ 587 Kurt Stillwell .05 .02 .01
☐ 588 Rich Gedman .05 .02 .01
☐ 589 Mark Davis .05 .02 .01
☐ 590 Bill Gullickson .05 .02 .01
☐ 591 Matt Young .05 .02 .01
☐ 592 Bryan Harvey .10 .05 .01
☐ 593 Omar Vizquel .05 .02 .01
☐ 594 Scott Lewis .05 .02 .01
☐ 595 Dave Valle .05 .02 .01
☐ 596 Tim Crews .05 .02 .01
☐ 597 Mike Bielecki .05 .02 .01
☐ 598 Mike Sharperson .05 .02 .01
☐ 599 Dave Bergman .05 .02 .01
☐ 600 Checklist 501-600 .05 .02 .01
☐ 601 Steve Lyons .05 .02 .01
☐ 602 Bruce Hurst .05 .02 .01
☐ 603 Donn Pall .05 .02 .01
☐ 604 Jim Vatcher .05 .02 .01
☐ 605 Dan Pasqua .05 .02 .01
☐ 606 Kenny Rogers .05 .02 .01
☐ 607 Jeff Schulz .05 .02 .01
☐ 608 Brad Arnsberg .05 .02 .01
☐ 609 Willie Wilson .05 .02 .01
☐ 610 Jamie Moyer .05 .02 .01
☐ 611 Ron Oester .05 .02 .01
☐ 612 Dennis Cook .05 .02 .01
☐ 613 Rick Mahler .05 .02 .01
☐ 614 Bill Landrum .05 .02 .01
☐ 615 Scott Scudder .05 .02 .01
☐ 616 Tom Edens .05 .02 .01
☐ 617 1917 Revisited .05 .02 .01
(White Sox in vintage uniforms)
☐ 618 Jim Gantner .05 .02 .01
☐ 619 Darrel Akerfelds .05 .02 .01
☐ 620 Ron Robinson .05 .02 .01
☐ 621 Scott Radinsky .05 .02 .01
☐ 622 Pete Smith .05 .02 .01
☐ 623 Melido Perez .05 .02 .01
☐ 624 Jerald Clark .05 .02 .01
☐ 625 Carlos Martinez .05 .02 .01
☐ 626 Wes Chamberlain .05 .02 .01
☐ 627 Bobby Witt .05 .02 .01
☐ 628 Ken Dayley .05 .02 .01
☐ 629 John Barfield .05 .02 .01
☐ 630 Bob Tewksbury .10 .05 .01
☐ 631 Glenn Braggs .05 .02 .01
☐ 632 Jim Neidlinger .05 .02 .01
☐ 633 Tom Browning .05 .02 .01
☐ 634 Kirk Gibson .10 .05 .01
☐ 635 Rob Dibble .05 .02 .01
☐ 636A Stolen Base Leaders .25 .11 .03
(Rickey Henderson and Lou Brock in tuxedos and no date on card)
☐ 636B Stolen Base Leaders .50 .23 .06
(Dated May 1, 1991 on card front)
☐ 637 Jeff Montgomery .10 .05 .01
☐ 638 Mike Schooler .05 .02 .01
☐ 639 Storm Davis .05 .02 .01
☐ 640 Rich Rodriguez .05 .02 .01
☐ 641 Phil Bradley .05 .02 .01
☐ 642 Kent Mercker .10 .05 .01
☐ 643 Carlton Fisk .15 .07 .02
☐ 644 Mike Bell .05 .02 .01
☐ 645 Alex Fernandez .30 .14 .04
☐ 646 Juan Gonzalez 1.25 .55 .16
☐ 647 Ken Hill .15 .07 .02
☐ 648 Jeff Russell .05 .02 .01
☐ 649 Chuck Malone .05 .02 .01
☐ 650 Steve Buechele .05 .02 .01

☐	651 Mike Benjamin	.05	.02	.01
☐	652 Tony Pena	.05	.02	.01
☐	653 Trevor Wilson	.05	.02	.01
☐	654 Alex Cole	.05	.02	.01
☐	655 Roger Clemens	.30	.14	.04
☐	656 Mark McGwire (The Bashing Years)	.10	.05	.01
☐	657 Joe Grahe	.05	.02	.01
☐	658 Jim Eisenreich	.05	.02	.01
☐	659 Dan Gladden	.05	.02	.01
☐	660 Steve Farr	.05	.02	.01
☐	661 Bill Sampen	.05	.02	.01
☐	662 Dave Rohde	.05	.02	.01
☐	663 Mark Gardner	.05	.02	.01
☐	664 Mike Simms	.05	.02	.01
☐	665 Moises Alou	.35	.16	.04
☐	666 Mickey Hatcher	.05	.02	.01
☐	667 Jimmy Key	.10	.05	.01
☐	668 John Wetteland	.10	.05	.01
☐	669 John Smiley	.05	.02	.01
☐	670 Jim Acker	.05	.02	.01
☐	671 Pascual Perez	.05	.02	.01
☐	672 Reggie Harris UER (Opportunity misspelled as oppurtinty)	.05	.02	.01
☐	673 Matt Nokes	.05	.02	.01
☐	674 Rafael Novoa	.05	.02	.01
☐	675 Hensley Meulens	.05	.02	.01
☐	676 Jeff M. Robinson	.05	.02	.01
☐	677 Ground Breaking (New Comiskey Park; Carlton Fisk and Robin Ventura)	.20	.09	.03
☐	678 Johnny Ray	.05	.02	.01
☐	679 Greg Hibbard	.05	.02	.01
☐	680 Paul Sorrento	.10	.05	.01
☐	681 Mike Marshall	.05	.02	.01
☐	682 Jim Clancy	.05	.02	.01
☐	683 Rob Murphy	.05	.02	.01
☐	684 Dave Schmidt	.05	.02	.01
☐	685 Jeff Gray	.05	.02	.01
☐	686 Mike Hartley	.05	.02	.01
☐	687 Jeff King	.05	.02	.01
☐	688 Stan Javier	.05	.02	.01
☐	689 Bob Walk	.05	.02	.01
☐	690 Jim Gott	.05	.02	.01
☐	691 Mike LaCoss	.05	.02	.01
☐	692 John Farrell	.05	.02	.01
☐	693 Tim Leary	.05	.02	.01
☐	694 Mike Walker	.05	.02	.01
☐	695 Eric Plunk	.05	.02	.01
☐	696 Mike Fetters	.05	.02	.01
☐	697 Wayne Edwards	.05	.02	.01
☐	698 Tim Drummond	.05	.02	.01
☐	699 Willie Fraser	.05	.02	.01
☐	700 Checklist 601-700	.05	.02	.01
☐	701 Mike Heath	.05	.02	.01
☐	702 Rookie Threats Luis Gonzalez Karl Rhodes Jeff Bagwell	.75	.35	.09
☐	703 Jose Mesa	.05	.02	.01
☐	704 Dave Smith	.05	.02	.01
☐	705 Danny Darwin	.05	.02	.01
☐	706 Rafael Belliard	.05	.02	.01
☐	707 Rob Murphy	.05	.02	.01
☐	708 Terry Pendleton	.15	.07	.02
☐	709 Mike Pagliarulo	.05	.02	.01
☐	710 Sid Bream	.05	.02	.01
☐	711 Junior Felix	.05	.02	.01
☐	712 Dante Bichette	.15	.07	.02
☐	713 Kevin Gross	.05	.02	.01
☐	714 Luis Sojo	.05	.02	.01
☐	715 Bob Ojeda	.05	.02	.01
☐	716 Julio Machado	.05	.02	.01
☐	717 Steve Farr	.05	.02	.01
☐	718 Franklin Stubbs	.05	.02	.01
☐	719 Mike Boddicker	.05	.02	.01
☐	720 Willie Randolph	.10	.05	.01
☐	721 Willie McGee	.10	.05	.01
☐	722 Chili Davis	.10	.05	.01
☐	723 Danny Jackson	.05	.02	.01
☐	724 Cory Snyder	.05	.02	.01
☐	725 MVP Lineup Andre Dawson George Bell Ryne Sandberg	.15	.07	.02
☐	726 Rob Deer	.05	.02	.01
☐	727 Rich DeLucia	.05	.02	.01
☐	728 Mike Perez	.05	.02	.01
☐	729 Mickey Tettleton	.10	.05	.01
☐	730 Mike Blowers	.05	.02	.01
☐	731 Gary Gaetti	.05	.02	.01
☐	732 Brett Butler	.10	.05	.01
☐	733 Dave Parker	.15	.07	.02
☐	734 Eddie Zosky	.05	.02	.01
☐	735 Jack Clark	.10	.05	.01
☐	736 Jack Morris	.15	.07	.02
☐	737 Kirk Gibson	.10	.05	.01
☐	738 Steve Bedrosian	.05	.02	.01
☐	739 Candy Maldonado	.05	.02	.01
☐	740 Matt Young	.05	.02	.01
☐	741 Rich Garces	.05	.02	.01
☐	742 George Bell	.10	.05	.01
☐	743 Deion Sanders	.35	.16	.04
☐	744 Bo Jackson	.25	.11	.03
☐	745 Luis Mercedes	.05	.02	.01
☐	746 Reggie Jefferson UER (Throwing left on card; back has throws right)	.10	.05	.01
☐	747 Pete Incaviglia	.05	.02	.01
☐	748 Chris Hammond	.10	.05	.01
☐	749 Mike Stanton	.05	.02	.01
☐	750 Scott Sanderson	.05	.02	.01
☐	751 Paul Faries	.05	.02	.01
☐	752 Al Osuna	.05	.02	.01
☐	753 Steve Chitren	.05	.02	.01
☐	754 Tony Fernandez	.10	.05	.01
☐	755 Jeff Bagwell UER (Strikeout and walk totals reversed)	3.00	1.35	.40
☐	756 Kirk Dressendorfer	.05	.02	.01
☐	757 Glenn Davis	.05	.02	.01
☐	758 Gary Carter	.15	.07	.02
☐	759 Zane Smith	.05	.02	.01
☐	760 Vance Law	.05	.02	.01
☐	761 Denis Boucher	.05	.02	.01
☐	762 Turner Ward	.15	.07	.02
☐	763 Roberto Alomar	.40	.18	.05
☐	764 Albert Belle	.60	.25	.08
☐	765 Joe Carter	.25	.11	.03
☐	766 Pete Schourek	.05	.02	.01
☐	767 Heathcliff Slocumb	.05	.02	.01
☐	768 Vince Coleman	.05	.02	.01
☐	769 Mitch Williams	.10	.05	.01
☐	770 Brian Downing	.05	.02	.01
☐	771 Dana Allison	.05	.02	.01
☐	772 Pete Harnisch	.10	.05	.01
☐	773 Tim Raines	.15	.07	.02
☐	774 Darryl Kile	.15	.07	.02
☐	775 Fred McGriff	.30	.14	.04
☐	776 Dwight Evans	.10	.05	.01
☐	777 Joe Slusarski	.05	.02	.01
☐	778 Dave Righetti	.05	.02	.01
☐	779 Jeff Hamilton	.05	.02	.01
☐	780 Ernest Riles	.05	.02	.01

		MINT	EXC	G-VG
☐ 781	Ken Dayley	.05	.02	.01
☐ 782	Eric King	.05	.02	.01
☐ 783	Devon White	.10	.05	.01
☐ 784	Beau Allred	.05	.02	.01
☐ 785	Mike Timlin	.05	.02	.01
☐ 786	Ivan Calderon	.05	.02	.01
☐ 787	Hubie Brooks	.05	.02	.01
☐ 788	Juan Agosto	.05	.02	.01
☐ 789	Barry Jones	.05	.02	.01
☐ 790	Wally Backman	.05	.02	.01
☐ 791	Jim Presley	.05	.02	.01
☐ 792	Charlie Hough	.10	.05	.01
☐ 793	Larry Andersen	.05	.02	.01
☐ 794	Steve Finley	.05	.02	.01
☐ 795	Shawn Abner	.05	.02	.01
☐ 796	Jeff M. Robinson	.05	.02	.01
☐ 797	Joe Bitker	.05	.02	.01
☐ 798	Eric Show	.05	.02	.01
☐ 799	Bud Black	.05	.02	.01
☐ 800	Checklist 701-800	.05	.02	.01
☐ HH1	Hank Aaron Hologram	2.50	1.15	.30
☐ SP1	Michael Jordan SP (Shown batting in White Sox uniform)	16.00	7.25	2.00
☐ SP2	Henderson/Ryan (Rickey and Nolan) (Commemorating 5/1/91 record breaking)	4.00	1.80	.50

1991 Upper Deck Hank Aaron Heroes

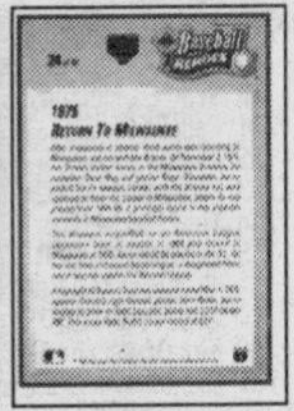

These standard-size (2 1/2" by 3 1/2") cards were issued in honor of Hall of Famer Hank Aaron and inserted in Upper Deck high number wax packs. The fronts have color player photos superimposed over a circular shot. Inside a red border stripe, a tan background fills in the rest of the card face. The Baseball Heroes logo adorns the card face. The backs have a similar design, except with an extended caption presented on a light gray background. Aaron autographed 2,500 of card number 27, which featured his portrait by noted sports artist Vernon Wells. The cards are numbered on the back in continuation of the Baseball Heroes set.

		MINT	EXC	G-VG
COMPLETE SET (10)		7.00	3.10	.85
COMMON AARON (19-27)		.50	.23	.06
☐ 19	1954: Rookie Year	.50	.23	.06
☐ 20	1957: MVP	.50	.23	.06
☐ 21	1966: Move to Atlanta	.50	.23	.06
☐ 22	1970: 3,000	.50	.23	.06
☐ 23	1974: 715	.50	.23	.06
☐ 24	1975: Return to Milwaukee	.50	.23	.06
☐ 25	1976: 755	.50	.23	.06
☐ 26	1982: Hall of Fame	.50	.23	.06
☐ 27	Checklist 19-27	.50	.23	.06
☐ NNO	Title/Header card SP	4.00	1.80	.50
☐ AU3	Hank Aaron AU (Signed and Numbered out of 2500)	300.00	135.00	38.00

1991 Upper Deck Heroes of Baseball

These standard-size (2 1/2" by 3 1/2") cards were (random) insert cards in Upper Deck Baseball Heroes wax packs. On a white card face, the fronts of the first three cards have sepia-toned player photos, with red, gold, and blue border stripes. The player's name appears in a gold border stripe beneath the picture, with the Upper Deck "Heroes of Baseball" logo in the lower right corner. The backs have a similar design to the fronts, except with a career summary and an advertisement for Upper Deck "Heroes of Baseball" games that will be played prior to regularly scheduled Major League games. The fourth card features a color portrait of the three players by noted sports artist Vernon Wells. The cards are numbered on the back.

		MINT	EXC	G-VG
COMPLETE SET (4)		45.00	20.00	5.75
COMMON CARD (H1-H4)		10.00	4.50	1.25
☐ H1	Harmon Killebrew	12.00	5.50	1.50
☐ H2	Gaylord Perry	10.00	4.50	1.25
☐ H3	Ferguson Jenkins	12.00	5.50	1.50
☐ H4	Header (Drawing of all three players)	15.00	6.75	1.90
☐ AU1	Harmon Killebrew AU (Signed and Numbered out of 3000)	100.00	45.00	12.50
☐ AU2	Gaylord Perry AU (Signed and Numbered out of 3000)	90.00	40.00	11.50

☐ AU3 Ferguson Jenkins AU (Signed and Numbered out of 3000)	100.00	45.00	12.50

1991 Upper Deck Nolan Ryan Heroes

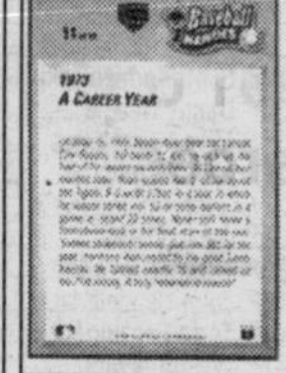

This nine-card standard size, 2 1/2" by 3 1/2", set was included in first series 1991 Upper Deck packs. The set which honors Nolan Ryan and is numbered as a continuation of the Baseball Heroes set which began with Reggie Jackson in 1990. This set honors Ryan's long career and his place in Baseball History. Card number 18 features the artwork of Vernon Wells while the other cards are photos. The complete set price below does not include the signed Ryan card of which only 2500 were made. These Ryan cards were apparently issued on 100-card sheets with the following configuration: ten each of the nine Ryan Baseball Heroes cards, five Michael Jordan cards and five Baseball Heroes header cards. The Baseball Heroes header card is a standard size card which explains the continuation of the Baseball Heroes series on the back while the front just says Baseball Heroes.

	MINT	EXC	G-VG
COMPLETE SET (10)	7.00	3.10	.85
COMMON RYAN (10-18)	.50	.23	.06
☐ 10 1968 Victory 1	.50	.23	.06
☐ 11 1973 A Career Year	.50	.23	.06
☐ 12 1975 Double Milestone	.50	.23	.06
☐ 13 1979 Back Home	.50	.23	.06
☐ 14 1981 All Time Leader	.50	.23	.06
☐ 15 1989 5,000 K's	.50	.23	.06
☐ 16 1990 6th No-Hitter	.50	.23	.06
☐ 17 1990 And Still Counting	.50	.23	.06
☐ 18 Checklist Card (Vernon Wells drawing with 5 poses of Ryan including each team he played for)	.50	.23	.06
☐ NNO Baseball Heroes SP (Header card)	4.00	1.80	.50
☐ AU2 Nolan Ryan AU (Signed and Numbered out of 2500)	600.00	275.00	75.00

1991 Upper Deck Silver Sluggers

The Upper Deck Silver Slugger set features nine players from each league, representing the nine batting positions on the team. The cards measure the standard size (2 1/2" by 3 1/2"). The fronts have glossy color action player photos, with white borders on three sides and a "Silver Slugger" bat serving as the border on the left side. The player's name appears in a tan stripe below the picture, with the team logo superimposed at the lower right corner. The card back is dominated by another color action photo with career highlights in a horizontally oriented rectangle to the left of the picture. The cards are numbered on the back with an SS prefix. The cards were issued one per 1991 Upper Deck jumbo pack.

	MINT	EXC	G-VG
COMPLETE SET (18)	20.00	9.00	2.50
COMMON CARD (SS1-SS18)	.50	.23	.06
☐ SS1 Julio Franco	.75	.35	.09
☐ SS2 Alan Trammell	.75	.35	.09
☐ SS3 Rickey Henderson	1.50	.65	.19
☐ SS4 Jose Canseco	2.50	1.15	.30
☐ SS5 Barry Bonds	4.00	1.80	.50
☐ SS6 Eddie Murray	1.00	.45	.13
☐ SS7 Kelly Gruber	.50	.23	.06
☐ SS8 Ryne Sandberg	3.00	1.35	.40
☐ SS9 Darryl Strawberry	.75	.35	.09
☐ SS10 Ellis Burks	.75	.35	.09
☐ SS11 Lance Parrish	.75	.35	.09
☐ SS12 Cecil Fielder	1.50	.65	.19
☐ SS13 Matt Williams	2.50	1.15	.30
☐ SS14 Dave Parker	.75	.35	.09
☐ SS15 Bobby Bonilla	.75	.35	.09
☐ SS16 Don Robinson	.50	.23	.06
☐ SS17 Benito Santiago	.75	.35	.09
☐ SS18 Barry Larkin	.75	.35	.09

1991 Upper Deck Final Edition

The 1991 Upper Deck Final Edition boxed set contains 100 cards and showcases players who made major contributions during their team's late-season pennant drive. In addition to the late season traded and impact rookie cards (22-78), the set includes two special subsets: Diamond Skills cards (1-21), depicting the best Minor League prospects, and All-Star cards (80-99). Six assorted hologram cards were issued with each set. The cards measure the standard size (2 1/2" by 3 1/2"). The fronts feature posed or action color player photos on a white card face, with the upper left corner of the picture cut out to provide space for the Upper Deck logo. The pictures are bordered in green on the left, with the player's name in a tan border below the picture. Two-thirds of the back are occupied by another color action photo, with biography, statistics, and career highlights in a horizontally oriented red rectangle to the left of the picture. The cards are numbered on the back with an F suffix. Among the outstanding Rookie Cards in this set are Ryan Klesko, Kenny Lofton, Pedro Martinez, Marc Newfield, Frankie Rodriguez, Ivan Rodriguez, Jim Thome, Rondell White, Rick Wilkins, and Dmitri Young.

	MINT	EXC	G-VG
COMPLETE FACT.SET (100)	6.00	2.70	.75
COMMON CARD (1F-100F)	.05	.02	.01

	MINT	EXC	G-VG
☐ 1F Diamond Skills Checklist Card (Ryan Klesko and Reggie Sanders)	.50	.23	.06
☐ 2F Pedro Martinez	.50	.23	.06
☐ 3F Lance Dickson	.05	.02	.01
☐ 4F Royce Clayton	.20	.09	.03
☐ 5F Scott Bryant	.05	.02	.01
☐ 6F Dan Wilson	.05	.02	.01
☐ 7F Dmitri Young	.40	.18	.05
☐ 8F Ryan Klesko	1.75	.80	.22
☐ 9F Tom Goodwin	.05	.02	.01
☐ 10F Rondell White	1.00	.45	.13
☐ 11F Reggie Sanders	.25	.11	.03
☐ 12F Todd Van Poppel	.15	.07	.02
☐ 13F Arthur Rhodes	.15	.07	.02
☐ 14F Eddie Zosky	.08	.04	.01
☐ 15F Gerald Williams	.05	.02	.01
☐ 16F Robert Eenhoorn	.05	.02	.01
☐ 17F Jim Thome	.75	.35	.09
☐ 18F Marc Newfield	.60	.25	.08
☐ 19F Kerwin Moore	.05	.02	.01
☐ 20F Jeff McNeely	.05	.02	.01
☐ 21F Frankie Rodriguez	.50	.23	.06
☐ 22F Andy Mota	.05	.02	.01
☐ 23F Chris Haney	.05	.02	.01
☐ 24F Kenny Lofton	2.00	.90	.25
☐ 25F Dave Nilsson	.40	.18	.05
☐ 26F Derek Bell	.08	.04	.01
☐ 27F Frank Castillo	.05	.02	.01
☐ 28F Candy Maldonado	.05	.02	.01
☐ 29F Chuck McElroy	.05	.02	.01
☐ 30F Chito Martinez	.05	.02	.01
☐ 31F Steve Howe	.05	.02	.01
☐ 32F Freddie Benavides	.05	.02	.01
☐ 33F Scott Kamieniecki	.05	.02	.01
☐ 34F Denny Neagle	.05	.02	.01
☐ 35F Mike Humphreys	.05	.02	.01
☐ 36F Mike Remlinger	.05	.02	.01
☐ 37F Scott Coolbaugh	.05	.02	.01
☐ 38F Darren Lewis	.08	.04	.01
☐ 39F Thomas Howard	.05	.02	.01
☐ 40F John Candelaria	.05	.02	.01
☐ 41F Todd Benzinger	.05	.02	.01
☐ 42F Wilson Alvarez	.30	.14	.04
☐ 43F Patrick Lennon	.05	.02	.01
☐ 44F Rusty Meacham	.05	.02	.01
☐ 45F Ryan Bowen	.05	.02	.01
☐ 46F Rick Wilkins	.15	.07	.02
☐ 47F Ed Sprague	.05	.02	.01
☐ 48F Bob Scanlan	.05	.02	.01
☐ 49F Tom Candiotti	.05	.02	.01
☐ 50F Dennis Martinez (Perfecto)	.08	.04	.01
☐ 51F Oil Can Boyd	.05	.02	.01
☐ 52F Glenallen Hill	.05	.02	.01
☐ 53F Scott Livingstone	.05	.02	.01
☐ 54F Brian R. Hunter	.15	.07	.02
☐ 55F Ivan Rodriguez	.60	.25	.08
☐ 56F Keith Mitchell	.15	.07	.02
☐ 57F Roger McDowell	.05	.02	.01
☐ 58F Otis Nixon	.08	.04	.01
☐ 59F Juan Bell	.05	.02	.01
☐ 60F Bill Krueger	.05	.02	.01
☐ 61F Chris Donnels	.05	.02	.01
☐ 62F Tommy Greene	.08	.04	.01
☐ 63F Doug Simons	.05	.02	.01
☐ 64F Andy Ashby	.05	.02	.01
☐ 65F Anthony Young	.05	.02	.01
☐ 66F Kevin Morton	.05	.02	.01
☐ 67F Bret Barberie	.15	.07	.02
☐ 68F Scott Servais	.05	.02	.01
☐ 69F Ron Darling	.05	.02	.01
☐ 70F Tim Burke	.05	.02	.01
☐ 71F Vicente Palacios	.05	.02	.01
☐ 72F Gerald Alexander	.05	.02	.01
☐ 73F Reggie Jefferson	.08	.04	.01
☐ 74F Dean Palmer	.08	.04	.01
☐ 75F Mark Whiten	.10	.05	.01
☐ 76F Randy Tomlin	.05	.02	.01
☐ 77F Mark Wohlers	.15	.07	.02
☐ 78F Brook Jacoby	.05	.02	.01
☐ 79F All-Star Checklist (Ken Griffey Jr. and Ryne Sandberg)	.40	.12	.04
☐ 80F Jack Morris AS	.10	.05	.01
☐ 81F Sandy Alomar Jr. AS	.05	.02	.01
☐ 82F Cecil Fielder AS	.10	.05	.01
☐ 83F Roberto Alomar AS	.25	.11	.03
☐ 84F Wade Boggs AS	.10	.05	.01
☐ 85F Cal Ripken AS	.50	.23	.06

☐ 86F Rickey Henderson AS...	.10	.05	.01
☐ 87F Ken Griffey Jr. AS.........	.75	.35	.09
☐ 88F Dave Henderson AS	.05	.02	.01
☐ 89F Danny Tartabull AS	.08	.04	.01
☐ 90F Tom Glavine AS	.10	.05	.01
☐ 91F Benito Santiago AS	.05	.02	.01
☐ 92F Will Clark AS	.20	.09	.03
☐ 93F Ryne Sandberg AS.......	.25	.11	.03
☐ 94F Chris Sabo AS..............	.05	.02	.01
☐ 95F Ozzie Smith AS.............	.08	.04	.01
☐ 96F Ivan Calderon AS	.05	.02	.01
☐ 97F Tony Gwynn AS	.15	.07	.02
☐ 98F Andre Dawson AS	.08	.04	.01
☐ 99F Bobby Bonilla AS	.08	.04	.01
☐ 100F Checklist 1-100..........	.05	.02	.01

1992 Upper Deck

The 1992 Upper Deck set contains 800 standard-size (2 1/2" by 3 1/2") cards. The set was produced in two series: a low-number series of 700 cards and a high-number series of 100 cards later in the season. Special subsets included in the set are Star Rookies (1-27; SR), Team Checklists (29-40, 86-99; TC), with player portraits by Vernon Wells; Top Prospects (52-77; TP); Bloodlines (79-85), and Diamond Skills (640-650; DS). Moreover, a nine-card Baseball Heroes subset (randomly inserted in packs) focuses on the career of Ted Williams. He autographed and numbered 2,500 cards, which were randomly inserted in low series foil packs. The cards are numbered on the back. By mailing in 15 1992 Upper Deck low number foil wrappers, a completed order form, and a handling fee, the collector could receive an 8 1/2" by 11" numbered, black and white lithograph picturing Ted Williams in his batting swing. A standard-size Ted Williams hologram card was randomly inserted in 1992 low number foil packs. The front design of the Williams hologram is horizontally oriented and features the artwork of Vernon Wells showing Williams in three different poses. The horizontally oriented back has a full-bleed sepia-tone photo of Williams and career highlights printed in black over the photo. Factory sets feature a unique gold-foil hologram on the card backs (in contrast to the silver hologram on foil pack cards). In addition to traded players and called-up rookies, the extended series features a National League Diamond Skills subset (711-721), a Diamond Debuts subset (771-780), two expansion-team player cards (701 Clemente Nunez and 710 Ryan Turner), and two commemorative cards highlighting Eddie Murray's 400th home run (728) and Rickey Henderson's 1,000th stolen base (782). Randomly inserted into high number foil packs were a 20-card Ted Williams' Best Hitters subset, a three-card hologram subset featuring College Player of the Year winners for 1989 through 1991, a ten-card Baseball Heroes subset highlighting the careers of Joe Morgan and Johnny Bench and featuring 2,500 dual autographed checklist cards. and a special card picturing Tom Selleck and Frank Thomas and commemorating the movie "Mr. Baseball." The fronts features shadow-bordered action color player photos on a white card face. The player's name appears above the photo, with the team name superimposed at the lower right corner. The backs include color action player photos and biography and statistics. The cards are numbered on the back. Rookie Cards in the set include Chad Curtis, Shawn Green, Tyler Green, Joey Hamilton, Mike Kelly, Pat Listach, David McCarty, Clemente Nunez, Eduardo Perez, Manny Ramirez, Mark Smith, Ryan Turner, Joe Vitiello, and Brian Williams.

	MINT	EXC	G-VG
COMPLETE SET (800)	20.00	9.00	2.50
COMPLETE FACT.SET (800)..	30.00	13.50	3.80
COMPLETE LO SET (700)......	16.00	7.25	2.00
COMPLETE HI SET (100).........	4.00	1.80	.50
COMMON CARD (1-700)	.05	.02	.01
COMMON CARD (701-800)	.05	.02	.01

☐ 1 Star Rookie Checklist....... Ryan Klesko Jim Thome	.30	.14	.04
☐ 2 Royce Clayton SR	.15	.07	.02
☐ 3 Brian Jordan SR...............	.15	.07	.02
☐ 4 Dave Fleming SR	.10	.05	.01
☐ 5 Jim Thome SR	.40	.18	.05
☐ 6 Jeff Juden SR	.10	.05	.01
☐ 7 Roberto Hernandez SR	.10	.05	.01
☐ 8 Kyle Abbott SR.................	.05	.02	.01
☐ 9 Chris George SR	.05	.02	.01
☐ 10 Rob Maurer SR..............	.10	.05	.01
☐ 11 Donald Harris SR	.05	.02	.01
☐ 12 Ted Wood SR.................	.05	.02	.01
☐ 13 Patrick Lennon SR	.05	.02	.01
☐ 14 Willie Banks SR	.05	.02	.01
☐ 15 Roger Salkeld SR UER... (Bill was his grand-father, not his father)	.10	.05	.01
☐ 16 Wil Cordero SR..............	.20	.09	.03
☐ 17 Arthur Rhodes SR...........	.10	.05	.01
☐ 18 Pedro Martinez SR.........	.25	.11	.03
☐ 19 Andy Ashby SR..............	.05	.02	.01
☐ 20 Tom Goodwin SR...........	.05	.02	.01
☐ 21 Braulio Castillo SR.........	.05	.02	.01
☐ 22 Todd Van Poppel SR......	.15	.07	.02
☐ 23 Brian Williams SR..........	.15	.07	.02
☐ 24 Ryan Klesko SR	1.00	.45	.13
☐ 25 Kenny Lofton SR..........	1.25	.55	.16
☐ 26 Derek Bell SR................	.10	.05	.01
☐ 27 Reggie Sanders SR........	.25	.11	.03
☐ 28 Dave Winfield's 400th....	.05	.02	.01
☐ 29 David Justice TC............	.10	.05	.01

Atlanta Braves
☐ 30 Rob Dibble TC .... .05 .02 .01
Cincinnati Reds
☐ 31 Craig Biggio TC .... .10 .05 .01
Houston Astros
☐ 32 Eddie Murray TC .... .10 .05 .01
Los Angeles Dodgers
☐ 33 Fred McGriff TC .... .10 .05 .01
San Diego Padres
☐ 34 Willie McGee TC .... .05 .02 .01
San Francisco Giants
☐ 35 Shawon Dunston TC .... .05 .02 .01
Chicago Cubs
☐ 36 Delino DeShields TC .... .10 .05 .01
Montreal Expos
☐ 37 Howard Johnson TC .... .05 .02 .01
New York Mets
☐ 38 John Kruk TC .... .10 .05 .01
Philadelphia Phillies
☐ 39 Doug Drabek TC .... .05 .02 .01
Pittsburgh Pirates
☐ 40 Todd Zeile TC .... .10 .05 .01
St. Louis Cardinals
☐ 41 Steve Avery .... .10 .05 .01
Playoff Perfection
☐ 42 Jeremy Hernandez .... .10 .05 .01
☐ 43 Doug Henry .... .05 .02 .01
☐ 44 Chris Donnels .... .05 .02 .01
☐ 45 Mo Sanford .... .05 .02 .01
☐ 46 Scott Kamieniecki .... .05 .02 .01
☐ 47 Mark Lemke .... .05 .02 .01
☐ 48 Steve Farr .... .05 .02 .01
☐ 49 Francisco Oliveras .... .05 .02 .01
☐ 50 Ced Landrum .... .05 .02 .01
☐ 51 Top Prospect Checklist .. .20 .06 .02
Rondell White
Craig Griffey
☐ 52 Eduardo Perez TP .... .20 .09 .03
☐ 53 Tom Nevers TP .... .10 .05 .01
☐ 54 David Zancanaro TP .... .10 .05 .01
☐ 55 Shawn Green TP .... .75 .35 .09
☐ 56 Mark Wohlers TP .... .10 .05 .01
☐ 57 Dave Nilsson TP .... .20 .09 .03
☐ 58 Dmitri Young TP .... .25 .11 .03
☐ 59 Ryan Hawblitzel TP .... .15 .07 .02
☐ 60 Raul Mondesi TP .... 2.00 .90 .25
☐ 61 Rondell White TP .... .60 .25 .08
☐ 62 Steve Hosey TP .... .10 .05 .01
☐ 63 Manny Ramirez TP .... 1.50 .65 .19
☐ 64 Marc Newfield TP .... .35 .16 .04
☐ 65 Jeromy Burnitz TP .... .05 .02 .01
☐ 66 Mark Smith TP .... .15 .07 .02
☐ 67 Joey Hamilton TP .... 1.00 .45 .13
☐ 68 Tyler Green TP .... .15 .07 .02
☐ 69 Jon Farrell TP .... .15 .07 .02
☐ 70 Kurt Miller TP .... .05 .02 .01
☐ 71 Jeff Plympton TP .... .10 .05 .01
☐ 72 Dan Wilson TP .... .05 .02 .01
☐ 73 Joe Vitiello TP .... .50 .23 .06
☐ 74 Rico Brogna TP .... .05 .02 .01
☐ 75 David McCarty TP .... .20 .09 .03
☐ 76 Bob Wickman TP .... .10 .05 .01
☐ 77 Carlos Rodriguez TP .... .05 .02 .01
☐ 78 Jim Abbott .... .10 .05 .01
Stay In School
☐ 79 Ramon Martinez .... .10 .05 .01
Pedro Martinez
☐ 80 Kevin Mitchell .... .05 .02 .01
Keith Mitchell
☐ 81 Sandy Alomar Jr. .... .10 .05 .01
Roberto Alomar
☐ 82 Cal Ripken .... .25 .11 .03
Billy Ripken
☐ 83 Tony Gwynn .... .10 .05 .01
Chris Gwynn
☐ 84 Dwight Gooden .... .10 .05 .01
Gary Sheffield
☐ 85 Ken Griffey Sr. .... .75 .35 .09
Ken Griffey Jr.
Craig Griffey
☐ 86 Jim Abbott TC .... .10 .05 .01
California Angels
☐ 87 Frank Thomas TC .... .75 .35 .09
Chicago White Sox
☐ 88 Danny Tartabull TC .... .10 .05 .01
Kansas City Royals
☐ 89 Scott Erickson TC .... .05 .02 .01
Minnesota Twins
☐ 90 Rickey Henderson TC .... .10 .05 .01
Oakland A's
☐ 91 Edgar Martinez TC .... .05 .02 .01
Seattle Mariners
☐ 92 Nolan Ryan TC .... .50 .23 .06
Texas Rangers
☐ 93 Ben McDonald TC .... .10 .05 .01
Baltimore Orioles
☐ 94 Ellis Burks TC .... .10 .05 .01
Boston Red Sox
☐ 95 Greg Swindell TC .... .05 .02 .01
Cleveland Indians
☐ 96 Cecil Fielder TC .... .10 .05 .01
Detroit Tigers
☐ 97 Greg Vaughn TC .... .10 .05 .01
Milwaukee Brewers
☐ 98 Kevin Maas TC .... .05 .02 .01
New York Yankees
☐ 99 Dave Stieb TC .... .05 .02 .01
Toronto Blue Jays
☐ 100 Checklist 1-100 .... .05 .02 .01
☐ 101 Joe Oliver .... .05 .02 .01
☐ 102 Hector Villanueva .... .05 .02 .01
☐ 103 Ed Whitson .... .05 .02 .01
☐ 104 Danny Jackson .... .05 .02 .01
☐ 105 Chris Hammond .... .05 .02 .01
☐ 106 Ricky Jordan .... .05 .02 .01
☐ 107 Kevin Bass .... .05 .02 .01
☐ 108 Darrin Fletcher .... .05 .02 .01
☐ 109 Junior Ortiz .... .05 .02 .01
☐ 110 Tom Bolton .... .05 .02 .01
☐ 111 Jeff King .... .05 .02 .01
☐ 112 Dave Magadan .... .05 .02 .01
☐ 113 Mike LaValliere .... .05 .02 .01
☐ 114 Hubie Brooks .... .05 .02 .01
☐ 115 Jay Bell .... .10 .05 .01
☐ 116 David Wells .... .05 .02 .01
☐ 117 Jim Leyritz .... .05 .02 .01
☐ 118 Manny Lee .... .05 .02 .01
☐ 119 Alvaro Espinoza .... .05 .02 .01
☐ 120 B.J. Surhoff .... .05 .02 .01
☐ 121 Hal Morris .... .10 .05 .01
☐ 122 Shawon Dawson .... .10 .05 .01
☐ 123 Chris Sabo .... .10 .05 .01
☐ 124 Andre Dawson .... .15 .07 .02
☐ 125 Eric Davis .... .05 .02 .01
☐ 126 Chili Davis .... .10 .05 .01
☐ 127 Dale Murphy .... .15 .07 .02
☐ 128 Kirk McCaskill .... .05 .02 .01
☐ 129 Terry Mulholland .... .05 .02 .01
☐ 130 Rick Aguilera .... .10 .05 .01
☐ 131 Vince Coleman .... .05 .02 .01
☐ 132 Andy Van Slyke .... .15 .07 .02
☐ 133 Gregg Jefferies .... .15 .07 .02
☐ 134 Barry Bonds .... .40 .18 .05
☐ 135 Dwight Gooden .... .10 .05 .01
☐ 136 Dave Stieb .... .10 .05 .01
☐ 137 Albert Belle .... .40 .18 .05

☐ 138 Teddy Higuera .05 .02 .01
☐ 139 Jesse Barfield .05 .02 .01
☐ 140 Pat Borders .05 .02 .01
☐ 141 Bip Roberts .05 .02 .01
☐ 142 Rob Dibble .05 .02 .01
☐ 143 Mark Grace .15 .07 .02
☐ 144 Barry Larkin .15 .07 .02
☐ 145 Ryne Sandberg .30 .14 .04
☐ 146 Scott Erickson .05 .02 .01
☐ 147 Luis Polonia .05 .02 .01
☐ 148 John Burkett .10 .05 .01
☐ 149 Luis Sojo .05 .02 .01
☐ 150 Dickie Thon .05 .02 .01
☐ 151 Walt Weiss .05 .02 .01
☐ 152 Mike Scioscia .05 .02 .01
☐ 153 Mark McGwire .15 .07 .02
☐ 154 Matt Williams .20 .09 .03
☐ 155 Rickey Henderson .15 .07 .02
☐ 156 Sandy Alomar Jr. .10 .05 .01
☐ 157 Brian McRae .15 .07 .02
☐ 158 Harold Baines .10 .05 .01
☐ 159 Kevin Appier .10 .05 .01
☐ 160 Felix Fermin .05 .02 .01
☐ 161 Leo Gomez .05 .02 .01
☐ 162 Craig Biggio .10 .05 .01
☐ 163 Ben McDonald .10 .05 .01
☐ 164 Randy Johnson .15 .07 .02
☐ 165 Cal Ripken .40 .18 .05
☐ 166 Frank Thomas 1.50 .65 .19
☐ 167 Delino DeShields .15 .07 .02
☐ 168 Greg Gagne .05 .02 .01
☐ 169 Ron Karkovice .05 .02 .01
☐ 170 Charlie Leibrandt .05 .02 .01
☐ 171 Dave Righetti .05 .02 .01
☐ 172 Dave Henderson .05 .02 .01
☐ 173 Steve Decker .05 .02 .01
☐ 174 Darryl Strawberry .10 .05 .01
☐ 175 Will Clark .20 .09 .03
☐ 176 Ruben Sierra .15 .07 .02
☐ 177 Ozzie Smith .20 .09 .03
☐ 178 Charles Nagy .05 .02 .01
☐ 179 Gary Pettis .05 .02 .01
☐ 180 Kirk Gibson .10 .05 .01
☐ 181 Randy Milligan .05 .02 .01
☐ 182 Dave Valle .05 .02 .01
☐ 183 Chris Hoiles .15 .07 .02
☐ 184 Tony Phillips .05 .02 .01
☐ 185 Brady Anderson .10 .05 .01
☐ 186 Scott Fletcher .05 .02 .01
☐ 187 Gene Larkin .05 .02 .01
☐ 188 Lance Johnson .05 .02 .01
☐ 189 Greg Olson .05 .02 .01
☐ 190 Melido Perez .05 .02 .01
☐ 191 Lenny Harris .05 .02 .01
☐ 192 Terry Kennedy .05 .02 .01
☐ 193 Mike Gallego .05 .02 .01
☐ 194 Willie McGee .10 .05 .01
☐ 195 Juan Samuel .05 .02 .01
☐ 196 Jeff Huson .05 .02 .01
(Shows Jose Canseco sliding into second)
☐ 197 Alex Cole .05 .02 .01
☐ 198 Ron Robinson .05 .02 .01
☐ 199 Joel Skinner .05 .02 .01
☐ 200 Checklist 101-200 .05 .02 .01
☐ 201 Kevin Reimer .05 .02 .01
☐ 202 Stan Belinda .05 .02 .01
☐ 203 Pat Tabler .05 .02 .01
☐ 204 Jose Guzman .05 .02 .01
☐ 205 Jose Lind .05 .02 .01
☐ 206 Spike Owen .05 .02 .01
☐ 207 Joe Orsulak .05 .02 .01
☐ 208 Charlie Hayes .10 .05 .01
☐ 209 Mike Devereaux .10 .05 .01
☐ 210 Mike Fitzgerald .05 .02 .01
☐ 211 Willie Randolph .10 .05 .01
☐ 212 Rod Nichols .05 .02 .01
☐ 213 Mike Boddicker .05 .02 .01
☐ 214 Bill Spiers .05 .02 .01
☐ 215 Steve Olin .05 .02 .01
☐ 216 David Howard .05 .02 .01
☐ 217 Gary Varsho .05 .02 .01
☐ 218 Mike Harkey .05 .02 .01
☐ 219 Luis Aquino .05 .02 .01
☐ 220 Chuck McElroy .05 .02 .01
☐ 221 Doug Drabek .15 .07 .02
☐ 222 Dave Winfield .15 .07 .02
☐ 223 Rafael Palmeiro .15 .07 .02
☐ 224 Joe Carter .20 .09 .03
☐ 225 Bobby Bonilla .15 .07 .02
☐ 226 Ivan Calderon .05 .02 .01
☐ 227 Gregg Olson .05 .02 .01
☐ 228 Tim Wallach .05 .02 .01
☐ 229 Terry Pendleton .15 .07 .02
☐ 230 Gilberto Reyes .05 .02 .01
☐ 231 Carlos Baerga .20 .09 .03
☐ 232 Greg Vaughn .10 .05 .01
☐ 233 Bret Saberhagen .10 .05 .01
☐ 234 Gary Sheffield .15 .07 .02
☐ 235 Mark Lewis .10 .05 .01
☐ 236 George Bell .10 .05 .01
☐ 237 Danny Tartabull .10 .05 .01
☐ 238 Willie Wilson .05 .02 .01
☐ 239 Doug Dascenzo .05 .02 .01
☐ 240 Bill Pecota .05 .02 .01
☐ 241 Julio Franco .10 .05 .01
☐ 242 Ed Sprague .10 .05 .01
☐ 243 Juan Gonzalez .60 .25 .08
☐ 244 Chuck Finley .05 .02 .01
☐ 245 Ivan Rodriguez .15 .07 .02
☐ 246 Len Dykstra .15 .07 .02
☐ 247 Deion Sanders .30 .14 .04
☐ 248 Dwight Evans .10 .05 .01
☐ 249 Larry Walker .15 .07 .02
☐ 250 Billy Ripken .05 .02 .01
☐ 251 Mickey Tettleton .10 .05 .01
☐ 252 Tony Pena .05 .02 .01
☐ 253 Benito Santiago .05 .02 .01
☐ 254 Kirby Puckett .35 .16 .04
☐ 255 Cecil Fielder .15 .07 .02
☐ 256 Howard Johnson .10 .05 .01
☐ 257 Andujar Cedeno .10 .05 .01
☐ 258 Jose Rijo .10 .05 .01
☐ 259 Al Osuna .05 .02 .01
☐ 260 Todd Hundley .05 .02 .01
☐ 261 Orel Hershiser .10 .05 .01
☐ 262 Ray Lankford .15 .07 .02
☐ 263 Robin Ventura .15 .07 .02
☐ 264 Felix Jose .10 .05 .01
☐ 265 Eddie Murray .15 .07 .02
☐ 266 Kevin Mitchell .10 .05 .01
☐ 267 Gary Carter .15 .07 .02
☐ 268 Mike Benjamin .05 .02 .01
☐ 269 Dick Schofield .05 .02 .01
☐ 270 Jose Uribe .05 .02 .01
☐ 271 Pete Incaviglia .05 .02 .01
☐ 272 Tony Fernandez .10 .05 .01
☐ 273 Alan Trammell .15 .07 .02
☐ 274 Tony Gwynn .25 .11 .03
☐ 275 Mike Greenwell .10 .05 .01
☐ 276 Jeff Bagwell .75 .35 .09
☐ 277 Frank Viola .10 .05 .01
☐ 278 Randy Myers .10 .05 .01
☐ 279 Ken Caminiti .10 .05 .01
☐ 280 Bill Doran .05 .02 .01
☐ 281 Dan Pasqua .05 .02 .01

☐ 282 Alfredo Griffin	.05	.02	.01
☐ 283 Jose Oquendo	.05	.02	.01
☐ 284 Kal Daniels	.05	.02	.01
☐ 285 Bobby Thigpen	.05	.02	.01
☐ 286 Robby Thompson	.05	.02	.01
☐ 287 Mark Eichhorn	.05	.02	.01
☐ 288 Mike Felder	.05	.02	.01
☐ 289 Dave Gallagher	.05	.02	.01
☐ 290 Dave Anderson	.05	.02	.01
☐ 291 Mel Hall	.05	.02	.01
☐ 292 Jerald Clark	.05	.02	.01
☐ 293 Al Newman	.05	.02	.01
☐ 294 Rob Deer	.05	.02	.01
☐ 295 Matt Nokes	.05	.02	.01
☐ 296 Jack Armstrong	.05	.02	.01
☐ 297 Jim Deshaies	.05	.02	.01
☐ 298 Jeff Innis	.05	.02	.01
☐ 299 Jeff Reed	.05	.02	.01
☐ 300 Checklist 201-300	.05	.02	.01
☐ 301 Lonnie Smith	.05	.02	.01
☐ 302 Jimmy Key	.10	.05	.01
☐ 303 Junior Felix	.05	.02	.01
☐ 304 Mike Heath	.05	.02	.01
☐ 305 Mark Langston	.15	.07	.02
☐ 306 Greg W. Harris	.05	.02	.01
☐ 307 Brett Butler	.10	.05	.01
☐ 308 Luis Rivera	.05	.02	.01
☐ 309 Bruce Ruffin	.05	.02	.01
☐ 310 Paul Faries	.05	.02	.01
☐ 311 Terry Leach	.05	.02	.01
☐ 312 Scott Brosius	.05	.02	.01
☐ 313 Scott Leius	.05	.02	.01
☐ 314 Harold Reynolds	.05	.02	.01
☐ 315 Jack Morris	.15	.07	.02
☐ 316 David Segui	.05	.02	.01
☐ 317 Bill Gullickson	.05	.02	.01
☐ 318 Todd Frohwirth	.05	.02	.01
☐ 319 Mark Leiter	.05	.02	.01
☐ 320 Jeff M. Robinson	.05	.02	.01
☐ 321 Gary Gaetti	.05	.02	.01
☐ 322 John Smoltz	.10	.05	.01
☐ 323 Andy Benes	.10	.05	.01
☐ 324 Kelly Gruber	.05	.02	.01
☐ 325 Jim Abbott	.15	.07	.02
☐ 326 John Kruk	.15	.07	.02
☐ 327 Kevin Seitzer	.05	.02	.01
☐ 328 Darrin Jackson	.05	.02	.01
☐ 329 Kurt Stillwell	.05	.02	.01
☐ 330 Mike Maddux	.05	.02	.01
☐ 331 Dennis Eckersley	.15	.07	.02
☐ 332 Dan Gladden	.05	.02	.01
☐ 333 Jose Canseco	.20	.09	.03
☐ 334 Kent Hrbek	.10	.05	.01
☐ 335 Ken Griffey	.10	.05	.01
☐ 336 Greg Swindell	.05	.02	.01
☐ 337 Trevor Wilson	.05	.02	.01
☐ 338 Sam Horn	.05	.02	.01
☐ 339 Mike Henneman	.05	.02	.01
☐ 340 Jerry Browne	.05	.02	.01
☐ 341 Glenn Braggs	.05	.02	.01
☐ 342 Tom Glavine	.15	.07	.02
☐ 343 Wally Joyner	.10	.05	.01
☐ 344 Fred McGriff	.20	.09	.03
☐ 345 Ron Gant	.10	.05	.01
☐ 346 Ramon Martinez	.10	.05	.01
☐ 347 Wes Chamberlain	.10	.05	.01
☐ 348 Terry Shumpert	.05	.02	.01
☐ 349 Tim Teufel	.05	.02	.01
☐ 350 Wally Backman	.05	.02	.01
☐ 351 Joe Girardi	.05	.02	.01
☐ 352 Devon White	.10	.05	.01
☐ 353 Greg Maddux	.20	.09	.03
☐ 354 Ryan Bowen	.05	.02	.01
☐ 355 Roberto Alomar	.25	.11	.03
☐ 356 Don Mattingly	.35	.16	.04
☐ 357 Pedro Guerrero	.10	.05	.01
☐ 358 Steve Sax	.05	.02	.01
☐ 359 Joey Cora	.05	.02	.01
☐ 360 Jim Gantner	.05	.02	.01
☐ 361 Brian Barnes	.05	.02	.01
☐ 362 Kevin McReynolds	.05	.02	.01
☐ 363 Bret Barberie	.05	.02	.01
☐ 364 David Cone	.15	.07	.02
☐ 365 Dennis Martinez	.10	.05	.01
☐ 366 Brian Hunter	.05	.02	.01
☐ 367 Edgar Martinez	.10	.05	.01
☐ 368 Steve Finley	.05	.02	.01
☐ 369 Greg Briley	.05	.02	.01
☐ 370 Jeff Blauser	.10	.05	.01
☐ 371 Todd Stottlemyre	.05	.02	.01
☐ 372 Luis Gonzalez	.10	.05	.01
☐ 373 Rick Wilkins	.10	.05	.01
☐ 374 Darryl Kile	.10	.05	.01
☐ 375 John Olerud	.15	.07	.02
☐ 376 Lee Smith	.15	.07	.02
☐ 377 Kevin Maas	.05	.02	.01
☐ 378 Dante Bichette	.15	.07	.02
☐ 379 Tom Pagnozzi	.05	.02	.01
☐ 380 Mike Flanagan	.05	.02	.01
☐ 381 Charlie O'Brien	.05	.02	.01
☐ 382 Dave Martinez	.05	.02	.01
☐ 383 Keith Miller	.05	.02	.01
☐ 384 Scott Ruskin	.05	.02	.01
☐ 385 Kevin Elster	.05	.02	.01
☐ 386 Alvin Davis	.05	.02	.01
☐ 387 Casey Candaele	.05	.02	.01
☐ 388 Pete O'Brien	.05	.02	.01
☐ 389 Jeff Treadway	.05	.02	.01
☐ 390 Scott Bradley	.05	.02	.01
☐ 391 Mookie Wilson	.05	.02	.01
☐ 392 Jimmy Jones	.05	.02	.01
☐ 393 Candy Maldonado	.05	.02	.01
☐ 394 Eric Yelding	.05	.02	.01
☐ 395 Tom Henke	.10	.05	.01
☐ 396 Franklin Stubbs	.05	.02	.01
☐ 397 Milt Thompson	.05	.02	.01
☐ 398 Mark Carreon	.05	.02	.01
☐ 399 Randy Velarde	.05	.02	.01
☐ 400 Checklist 301-400	.05	.02	.01
☐ 401 Omar Vizquel	.05	.02	.01
☐ 402 Joe Boever	.05	.02	.01
☐ 403 Bill Krueger	.05	.02	.01
☐ 404 Jody Reed	.05	.02	.01
☐ 405 Mike Schooler	.05	.02	.01
☐ 406 Jason Grimsley	.05	.02	.01
☐ 407 Greg Myers	.05	.02	.01
☐ 408 Randy Ready	.05	.02	.01
☐ 409 Mike Timlin	.05	.02	.01
☐ 410 Mitch Williams	.10	.05	.01
☐ 411 Garry Templeton	.05	.02	.01
☐ 412 Greg Cadaret	.05	.02	.01
☐ 413 Donnie Hill	.05	.02	.01
☐ 414 Wally Whitehurst	.05	.02	.01
☐ 415 Scott Sanderson	.05	.02	.01
☐ 416 Thomas Howard	.05	.02	.01
☐ 417 Neal Heaton	.05	.02	.01
☐ 418 Charlie Hough	.10	.05	.01
☐ 419 Jack Howell	.05	.02	.01
☐ 420 Greg Hibbard	.05	.02	.01
☐ 421 Carlos Quintana	.05	.02	.01
☐ 422 Kim Batiste	.05	.02	.01
☐ 423 Paul Molitor	.20	.09	.03
☐ 424 Ken Griffey Jr.	1.50	.65	.19
☐ 425 Phil Plantier	.15	.07	.02
☐ 426 Denny Neagle	.05	.02	.01
☐ 427 Von Hayes	.05	.02	.01

☐ 428 Shane Mack .10 .05 .01
☐ 429 Darren Daulton .15 .07 .02
☐ 430 Dwayne Henry .05 .02 .01
☐ 431 Lance Parrish .10 .05 .01
☐ 432 Mike Humphreys .10 .05 .01
☐ 433 Tim Burke .05 .02 .01
☐ 434 Bryan Harvey .10 .05 .01
☐ 435 Pat Kelly .10 .05 .01
☐ 436 Ozzie Guillen .05 .02 .01
☐ 437 Bruce Hurst .05 .02 .01
☐ 438 Sammy Sosa .15 .07 .02
☐ 439 Dennis Rasmussen .05 .02 .01
☐ 440 Ken Patterson .05 .02 .01
☐ 441 Jay Buhner .10 .05 .01
☐ 442 Pat Combs .05 .02 .01
☐ 443 Wade Boggs .15 .07 .02
☐ 444 George Brett .30 .14 .04
☐ 445 Mo Vaughn .20 .09 .03
☐ 446 Chuck Knoblauch .15 .07 .02
☐ 447 Tom Candiotti .05 .02 .01
☐ 448 Mark Portugal .05 .02 .01
☐ 449 Mickey Morandini .05 .02 .01
☐ 450 Duane Ward .10 .05 .01
☐ 451 Otis Nixon .10 .05 .01
☐ 452 Bob Welch .05 .02 .01
☐ 453 Rusty Meacham .05 .02 .01
☐ 454 Keith Mitchell .10 .05 .01
☐ 455 Marquis Grissom .15 .07 .02
☐ 456 Robin Yount .20 .09 .03
☐ 457 Harvey Pulliam .05 .02 .01
☐ 458 Jose DeLeon .05 .02 .01
☐ 459 Mark Gubicza .05 .02 .01
☐ 460 Darryl Hamilton .10 .05 .01
☐ 461 Tom Browning .05 .02 .01
☐ 462 Monty Fariss .05 .02 .01
☐ 463 Jerome Walton .05 .02 .01
☐ 464 Paul O'Neill .10 .05 .01
☐ 465 Dean Palmer .10 .05 .01
☐ 466 Travis Fryman .25 .11 .03
☐ 467 John Smiley .05 .02 .01
☐ 468 Lloyd Moseby .05 .02 .01
☐ 469 John Wehner .05 .02 .01
☐ 470 Skeeter Barnes .05 .02 .01
☐ 471 Steve Chitren .05 .02 .01
☐ 472 Kent Mercker .05 .02 .01
☐ 473 Terry Steinbach .10 .05 .01
☐ 474 Andres Galarraga .15 .07 .02
☐ 475 Steve Avery .15 .07 .02
☐ 476 Tom Gordon .05 .02 .01
☐ 477 Cal Eldred .05 .02 .01
☐ 478 Omar Olivares .05 .02 .01
☐ 479 Julio Machado .05 .02 .01
☐ 480 Bob Milacki .05 .02 .01
☐ 481 Les Lancaster .05 .02 .01
☐ 482 John Candelaria .05 .02 .01
☐ 483 Brian Downing .05 .02 .01
☐ 484 Roger McDowell .05 .02 .01
☐ 485 Scott Scudder .05 .02 .01
☐ 486 Zane Smith .05 .02 .01
☐ 487 John Cerutti .05 .02 .01
☐ 488 Steve Buechele .05 .02 .01
☐ 489 Paul Gibson .05 .02 .01
☐ 490 Curtis Wilkerson .05 .02 .01
☐ 491 Marvin Freeman .05 .02 .01
☐ 492 Tom Foley .05 .02 .01
☐ 493 Juan Berenguer .05 .02 .01
☐ 494 Ernest Riles .05 .02 .01
☐ 495 Sid Bream .05 .02 .01
☐ 496 Chuck Crim .05 .02 .01
☐ 497 Mike Macfarlane .05 .02 .01
☐ 498 Dale Sveum .05 .02 .01
☐ 499 Storm Davis .05 .02 .01
☐ 500 Checklist 401-500 .05 .02 .01
☐ 501 Jeff Reardon .10 .05 .01
☐ 502 Shawn Abner .05 .02 .01
☐ 503 Tony Fossas .05 .02 .01
☐ 504 Cory Snyder .05 .02 .01
☐ 505 Matt Young .05 .02 .01
☐ 506 Allan Anderson .05 .02 .01
☐ 507 Mark Lee .05 .02 .01
☐ 508 Gene Nelson .05 .02 .01
☐ 509 Mike Pagliarulo .05 .02 .01
☐ 510 Rafael Belliard .05 .02 .01
☐ 511 Jay Howell .05 .02 .01
☐ 512 Bob Tewksbury .05 .02 .01
☐ 513 Mike Morgan .05 .02 .01
☐ 514 John Franco .05 .02 .01
☐ 515 Kevin Gross .05 .02 .01
☐ 516 Lou Whitaker .15 .07 .02
☐ 517 Orlando Merced .10 .05 .01
☐ 518 Todd Benzinger .05 .02 .01
☐ 519 Gary Redus .05 .02 .01
☐ 520 Walt Terrell .05 .02 .01
☐ 521 Jack Clark .10 .05 .01
☐ 522 Dave Parker .15 .07 .02
☐ 523 Tim Naehring .05 .02 .01
☐ 524 Mark Whiten .10 .05 .01
☐ 525 Ellis Burks .10 .05 .01
☐ 526 Frank Castillo .05 .02 .01
☐ 527 Brian Harper .05 .02 .01
☐ 528 Brook Jacoby .05 .02 .01
☐ 529 Rick Sutcliffe .10 .05 .01
☐ 530 Joe Klink .05 .02 .01
☐ 531 Terry Bross .05 .02 .01
☐ 532 Jose Offerman .05 .02 .01
☐ 533 Todd Zeile .10 .05 .01
☐ 534 Eric Karros .15 .07 .02
☐ 535 Anthony Young .05 .02 .01
☐ 536 Milt Cuyler .05 .02 .01
☐ 537 Randy Tomlin .05 .02 .01
☐ 538 Scott Livingstone .05 .02 .01
☐ 539 Jim Eisenreich .05 .02 .01
☐ 540 Don Slaught .05 .02 .01
☐ 541 Scott Cooper .10 .05 .01
☐ 542 Joe Grahe .05 .02 .01
☐ 543 Tom Brunansky .05 .02 .01
☐ 544 Eddie Zosky .10 .05 .01
☐ 545 Roger Clemens .25 .11 .03
☐ 546 David Justice .20 .09 .03
☐ 547 Dave Stewart .10 .05 .01
☐ 548 David West .05 .02 .01
☐ 549 Dave Smith .05 .02 .01
☐ 550 Dan Plesac .05 .02 .01
☐ 551 Alex Fernandez .15 .07 .02
☐ 552 Bernard Gilkey .10 .05 .01
☐ 553 Jack McDowell .15 .07 .02
☐ 554 Tino Martinez .10 .05 .01
☐ 555 Bo Jackson .20 .09 .03
☐ 556 Bernie Williams .10 .05 .01
☐ 557 Mark Gardner .05 .02 .01
☐ 558 Glenallen Hill .05 .02 .01
☐ 559 Oil Can Boyd .05 .02 .01
☐ 560 Chris James .05 .02 .01
☐ 561 Scott Servais .05 .02 .01
☐ 562 Rey Sanchez .15 .07 .02
☐ 563 Paul McClellan .05 .02 .01
☐ 564 Andy Mota .05 .02 .01
☐ 565 Darren Lewis .10 .05 .01
☐ 566 Jose Melendez .05 .02 .01
☐ 567 Tommy Greene .10 .05 .01
☐ 568 Rich Rodriguez .05 .02 .01
☐ 569 Heathcliff Slocumb .05 .02 .01
☐ 570 Joe Hesketh .05 .02 .01
☐ 571 Carlton Fisk .15 .07 .02
☐ 572 Erik Hanson .05 .02 .01
☐ 573 Wilson Alvarez .15 .07 .02

☐	574 Rheal Cormier	.05	.02	.01
☐	575 Tim Raines	.15	.07	.02
☐	576 Bobby Witt	.05	.02	.01
☐	577 Roberto Kelly	.10	.05	.01
☐	578 Kevin Brown	.10	.05	.01
☐	579 Chris Nabholz	.05	.02	.01
☐	580 Jesse Orosco	.05	.02	.01
☐	581 Jeff Brantley	.05	.02	.01
☐	582 Rafael Ramirez	.05	.02	.01
☐	583 Kelly Downs	.05	.02	.01
☐	584 Mike Simms	.05	.02	.01
☐	585 Mike Remlinger	.05	.02	.01
☐	586 Dave Hollins	.15	.07	.02
☐	587 Larry Andersen	.05	.02	.01
☐	588 Mike Gardiner	.05	.02	.01
☐	589 Craig Lefferts	.05	.02	.01
☐	590 Paul Assenmacher	.05	.02	.01
☐	591 Bryn Smith	.05	.02	.01
☐	592 Donn Pall	.05	.02	.01
☐	593 Mike Jackson	.05	.02	.01
☐	594 Scott Radinsky	.05	.02	.01
☐	595 Brian Holman	.05	.02	.01
☐	596 Geronimo Pena	.05	.02	.01
☐	597 Mike Jeffcoat	.05	.02	.01
☐	598 Carlos Martinez	.05	.02	.01
☐	599 Geno Petralli	.05	.02	.01
☐	600 Checklist 501-600	.05	.02	.01
☐	601 Jerry Don Gleaton	.05	.02	.01
☐	602 Adam Peterson	.05	.02	.01
☐	603 Craig Grebeck	.05	.02	.01
☐	604 Mark Guthrie	.05	.02	.01
☐	605 Frank Tanana	.05	.02	.01
☐	606 Hensley Meulens	.05	.02	.01
☐	607 Mark Davis	.05	.02	.01
☐	608 Eric Plunk	.05	.02	.01
☐	609 Mark Williamson	.05	.02	.01
☐	610 Lee Guetterman	.05	.02	.01
☐	611 Bobby Rose	.05	.02	.01
☐	612 Bill Wegman	.05	.02	.01
☐	613 Mike Hartley	.05	.02	.01
☐	614 Chris Beasley	.05	.02	.01
☐	615 Chris Bosio	.05	.02	.01
☐	616 Henry Cotto	.05	.02	.01
☐	617 Chico Walker	.05	.02	.01
☐	618 Russ Swan	.05	.02	.01
☐	619 Bob Walk	.05	.02	.01
☐	620 Billy Swift	.10	.05	.01
☐	621 Warren Newson	.05	.02	.01
☐	622 Steve Bedrosian	.05	.02	.01
☐	623 Ricky Bones	.10	.05	.01
☐	624 Kevin Tapani	.05	.02	.01
☐	625 Juan Guzman	.10	.05	.01
☐	626 Jeff Johnson	.05	.02	.01
☐	627 Jeff Montgomery	.10	.05	.01
☐	628 Ken Hill	.10	.05	.01
☐	629 Gary Thurman	.05	.02	.01
☐	630 Steve Howe	.05	.02	.01
☐	631 Jose DeJesus	.05	.02	.01
☐	632 Kirk Dressendorfer	.05	.02	.01
☐	633 Jaime Navarro	.05	.02	.01
☐	634 Lee Stevens	.05	.02	.01
☐	635 Pete Harnisch	.10	.05	.01
☐	636 Bill Landrum	.05	.02	.01
☐	637 Rich DeLucia	.05	.02	.01
☐	638 Luis Salazar	.05	.02	.01
☐	639 Rob Murphy	.05	.02	.01
☐	640 Diamond Skills Checklist Jose Canseco Rickey Henderson	.10	.03	.01
☐	641 Roger Clemens DS	.15	.07	.02
☐	642 Jim Abbott DS	.10	.05	.01
☐	643 Travis Fryman DS	.15	.07	.02
☐	644 Jesse Barfield DS	.05	.02	.01
☐	645 Cal Ripken DS	.20	.09	.03
☐	646 Wade Boggs DS	.10	.05	.01
☐	647 Cecil Fielder DS	.10	.05	.01
☐	648 Rickey Henderson DS	.10	.05	.01
☐	649 Jose Canseco DS	.10	.05	.01
☐	650 Ken Griffey Jr. DS	.75	.35	.09
☐	651 Kenny Rogers	.05	.02	.01
☐	652 Luis Mercedes	.10	.05	.01
☐	653 Mike Stanton	.05	.02	.01
☐	654 Glenn Davis	.05	.02	.01
☐	655 Nolan Ryan	1.00	.45	.13
☐	656 Reggie Jefferson	.05	.02	.01
☐	657 Javier Ortiz	.05	.02	.01
☐	658 Greg A. Harris	.05	.02	.01
☐	659 Mariano Duncan	.05	.02	.01
☐	660 Jeff Shaw	.05	.02	.01
☐	661 Mike Moore	.05	.02	.01
☐	662 Chris Haney	.05	.02	.01
☐	663 Joe Slusarski	.05	.02	.01
☐	664 Wayne Housie	.10	.05	.01
☐	665 Carlos Garcia	.10	.05	.01
☐	666 Bob Ojeda	.05	.02	.01
☐	667 Bryan Hickerson	.05	.02	.01
☐	668 Tim Belcher	.05	.02	.01
☐	669 Ron Darling	.05	.02	.01
☐	670 Rex Hudler	.05	.02	.01
☐	671 Sid Fernandez	.10	.05	.01
☐	672 Chito Martinez	.05	.02	.01
☐	673 Pete Schourek	.05	.02	.01
☐	674 Armando Reynoso	.05	.02	.01
☐	675 Mike Mussina	.30	.14	.04
☐	676 Kevin Morton	.05	.02	.01
☐	677 Norm Charlton	.05	.02	.01
☐	678 Danny Darwin	.05	.02	.01
☐	679 Eric King	.05	.02	.01
☐	680 Ted Power	.05	.02	.01
☐	681 Barry Jones	.05	.02	.01
☐	682 Carney Lansford	.10	.05	.01
☐	683 Mel Rojas	.05	.02	.01
☐	684 Rick Honeycutt	.05	.02	.01
☐	685 Jeff Fassero	.05	.02	.01
☐	686 Cris Carpenter	.05	.02	.01
☐	687 Tim Crews	.05	.02	.01
☐	688 Scott Terry	.05	.02	.01
☐	689 Chris Gwynn	.05	.02	.01
☐	690 Gerald Perry	.05	.02	.01
☐	691 John Barfield	.05	.02	.01
☐	692 Bob Melvin	.05	.02	.01
☐	693 Juan Agosto	.05	.02	.01
☐	694 Alejandro Pena	.05	.02	.01
☐	695 Jeff Russell	.05	.02	.01
☐	696 Carmelo Martinez	.05	.02	.01
☐	697 Bud Black	.05	.02	.01
☐	698 Dave Otto	.05	.02	.01
☐	699 Billy Hatcher	.05	.02	.01
☐	700 Checklist 601-700	.05	.02	.01
☐	701 Clemente Nunez	.15	.07	.02
☐	702 Rookie Threats Mark Clark Donovan Osborne Brian Jordan	.05	.02	.01
☐	703 Mike Morgan	.05	.02	.01
☐	704 Keith Miller	.05	.02	.01
☐	705 Kurt Stillwell	.05	.02	.01
☐	706 Damon Berryhill	.05	.02	.01
☐	707 Von Hayes	.05	.02	.01
☐	708 Rick Sutcliffe	.10	.05	.01
☐	709 Hubie Brooks	.05	.02	.01
☐	710 Ryan Turner	.15	.07	.02
☐	711 Diamond Skills Checklist Barry Bonds	.15	.07	.02

Andy Van Slyke			
□ 712 Jose Rijo DS	.10	.05	.01
□ 713 Tom Glavine DS	.10	.05	.01
□ 714 Shawon Dunston DS	.05	.02	.01
□ 715 Andy Van Slyke DS	.10	.05	.01
□ 716 Ozzie Smith DS	.15	.07	.02
□ 717 Tony Gwynn DS	.20	.09	.03
□ 718 Will Clark DS	.10	.05	.01
□ 719 Marquis Grissom DS	.10	.05	.01
□ 720 Howard Johnson DS	.05	.02	.01
□ 721 Barry Bonds DS	.25	.11	.03
□ 722 Kirk McCaskill	.05	.02	.01
□ 723 Sammy Sosa	.15	.07	.02
□ 724 George Bell	.10	.05	.01
□ 725 Gregg Jefferies	.15	.07	.02
□ 726 Gary DiSarcina	.05	.02	.01
□ 727 Mike Bordick	.05	.02	.01
□ 728 Eddie Murray	.10	.05	.01
400 Home Run Club			
□ 729 Rene Gonzales	.05	.02	.01
□ 730 Mike Bielecki	.05	.02	.01
□ 731 Calvin Jones	.05	.02	.01
□ 732 Jack Morris	.15	.07	.02
□ 733 Frank Viola	.10	.05	.01
□ 734 Dave Winfield	.15	.07	.02
□ 735 Kevin Mitchell	.10	.05	.01
□ 736 Bill Swift	.10	.05	.01
□ 737 Dan Gladden	.05	.02	.01
□ 738 Mike Jackson	.05	.02	.01
□ 739 Mark Carreon	.05	.02	.01
□ 740 Kirt Manwaring	.05	.02	.01
□ 741 Randy Myers	.10	.05	.01
□ 742 Kevin McReynolds	.05	.02	.01
□ 743 Steve Sax	.05	.02	.01
□ 744 Wally Joyner	.10	.05	.01
□ 745 Gary Sheffield	.15	.07	.02
□ 746 Danny Tartabull	.10	.05	.01
□ 747 Julio Valera	.10	.05	.01
□ 748 Denny Neagle	.05	.02	.01
□ 749 Lance Blankenship	.05	.02	.01
□ 750 Mike Gallego	.05	.02	.01
□ 751 Bret Saberhagen	.10	.05	.01
□ 752 Ruben Amaro	.05	.02	.01
□ 753 Eddie Murray	.15	.07	.02
□ 754 Kyle Abbott	.05	.02	.01
□ 755 Bobby Bonilla	.15	.07	.02
□ 756 Eric Davis	.05	.02	.01
□ 757 Eddie Taubensee	.05	.02	.01
□ 758 Andres Galarraga	.15	.07	.02
□ 759 Pete Incaviglia	.05	.02	.01
□ 760 Tom Candiotti	.05	.02	.01
□ 761 Tim Belcher	.05	.02	.01
□ 762 Ricky Bones	.10	.05	.01
□ 763 Bip Roberts	.05	.02	.01
□ 764 Pedro Munoz	.10	.05	.01
□ 765 Greg Swindell	.05	.02	.01
□ 766 Kenny Lofton	1.25	.55	.16
□ 767 Gary Carter	.15	.07	.02
□ 768 Charlie Hayes	.10	.05	.01
□ 769 Dickie Thon	.05	.02	.01
□ 770 Donovan Osborne DD CL	.05	.02	.01
□ 771 Bret Boone DD	.25	.11	.03
□ 772 Archi Cianfrocco DD	.05	.02	.01
□ 773 Mark Clark DD	.20	.09	.03
□ 774 Chad Curtis DD	.15	.07	.02
□ 775 Pat Listach DD	.15	.07	.02
□ 776 Pat Mahomes DD	.15	.07	.02
□ 777 Donovan Osborne DD	.05	.02	.01
□ 778 John Patterson DD	.05	.02	.01
□ 779 Andy Stankiewicz DD	.05	.02	.01
□ 780 Turk Wendell DD	.15	.07	.02
□ 781 Bill Krueger	.05	.02	.01
□ 782 Rickey Henderson	.15	.07	.02
Grand Theft			
□ 783 Kevin Seitzer	.05	.02	.01
□ 784 Dave Martinez	.05	.02	.01
□ 785 John Smiley	.05	.02	.01
□ 786 Matt Stairs	.05	.02	.01
□ 787 Scott Scudder	.05	.02	.01
□ 788 John Wetteland	.05	.02	.01
□ 789 Jack Armstrong	.05	.02	.01
□ 790 Ken Hill	.10	.05	.01
□ 791 Dick Schofield	.05	.02	.01
□ 792 Mariano Duncan	.05	.02	.01
□ 793 Bill Pecota	.05	.02	.01
□ 794 Mike Kelly	.50	.23	.06
□ 795 Willie Randolph	.10	.05	.01
□ 796 Butch Henry	.10	.05	.01
□ 797 Carlos Hernandez	.05	.02	.01
□ 798 Doug Jones	.05	.02	.01
□ 799 Melido Perez	.05	.02	.01
□ 800 Checklist 701-800	.05	.02	.01
□ HH2 Ted Williams Hologram (Top left corner says, 91 Upper Deck 92)	2.00	.90	.25
□ SP3 Deion Sanders FB/BB	4.00	1.80	.50
□ SP4 Tom Selleck and Frank Thomas SP (Mr. Baseball)	6.00	2.70	.75

1992 Upper Deck Bench/Morgan Heroes

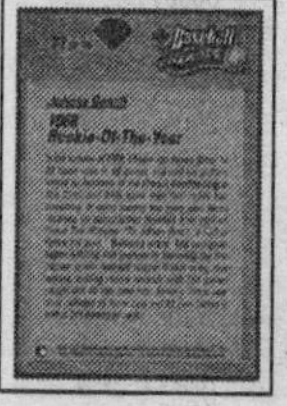

This standard size (2 1/2" by 3 1/2") 10-card set was randomly inserted in 1992 Upper Deck high number packs. Both Bench and Morgan autographed 2,500 of card number 45, which displays a portrait by sports artist Vernon Wells. The fronts feature color photos of Bench (37-39), Morgan (40-42), or both (43-44) at various stages of their baseball careers. These pictures are partially contained within a blue and white bordered circle. The photos rest on a parchment card face trimmed with a brick red and white border. The Upper Deck Baseball Heroes logo appears in the lower right corner. The back design displays career highlights on a gray plaque resting on the same parchment background as on the front. The cards are numbered on the back.

	MINT	EXC	G-VG
COMPLETE SET (10)	15.00	6.75	1.90
COMMON BENCH/MORG (37-45)	1.00	.45	.13
☐ 37 1968 Rookie-of-the-Year	1.00	.45	.13
☐ 38 1968-77 Ten Straight Gold Gloves	1.00	.45	.13
☐ 39 1970 and 1972 MVP	1.00	.45	.13
☐ 40 1965 Rookie Year	1.00	.45	.13
☐ 41 1975-76 Back-to-Back MVP	1.00	.45	.13
☐ 42 1980-83 The Golden Years	1.00	.45	.13
☐ 43 1972-79 Big Red Machine	1.00	.45	.13
☐ 44 1989 and 1990 Hall of Fame	1.00	.45	.13
☐ 45 Checklist-Heroes 37-45	1.00	.45	.13
☐ NNO Baseball Heroes SP (Header card)	6.00	2.70	.75
☐ AU5 Johnny Bench and Joe Morgan AU (Signed and Numbered of 2500)	275.00	125.00	34.00

1992 Upper Deck College POY Holograms

This three-card set was randomly inserted in 1992 Upper Deck foil packs. The subset features College Player of the Year winners for 1989 through 1991. The cards measure standard size (2 1/2" by 3 1/2). The full-bleed fronts display two action player holographic photos. The player's name is superimposed at the bottom edge over a team color-coded bar. The backs carry a second action player shot on the right side with the player's name and the year he made POY printed on a color-coded bar along the left side. In a vertical format, the player's career summary is printed on the left. The cards are numbered on the back with the prefix "CP".

	MINT	EXC	G-VG
COMPLETE SET (3)	2.00	.90	.25
COMMON CARD (CP1-CP3)	1.00	.45	.13
☐ CP1 David McCarty	1.00	.45	.13
☐ CP2 Mike Kelly	1.00	.45	.13
☐ CP3 Ben McDonald	1.00	.45	.13

1992 Upper Deck Heroes of Baseball

Continuing a popular subset introduced the previous year, Upper Deck produced four new commemorative cards, including three player cards and one portrait card by sports artist Vernon Wells. These cards were randomly inserted in 1992 Upper Deck baseball low number foil packs. Three thousand of each card were personally numbered and autographed by each player. On a white card face, the fronts carry sepia-tone player photos with red, gold, and blue border stripes. The player's name appears in a gold border stripe beneath the picture, with the Upper Deck "Heroes of Baseball" logo in the lower right corner. The backs have a similar design to the fronts except for a career summary and an advertisement for Upper Deck "Heroes of Baseball" games that will be played before regularly scheduled Major League games. The cards are arranged alphabetically and numbered on the back.

	MINT	EXC	G-VG
COMPLETE SET (4)	20.00	9.00	2.50
COMMON CARD (H5-H8)	5.00	2.30	.60
☐ H5 Vida Blue	5.00	2.30	.60
☐ H6 Lou Brock	8.00	3.60	1.00
☐ H7 Rollie Fingers	8.00	3.60	1.00
☐ H8 Header (Portrait of all three players)	8.00	3.60	1.00
☐ 5AU Vida Blue (Signed and Numbered out of 3000)	70.00	32.00	8.75
☐ 6AU Lou Brock (Signed and Numbered out of 3000)	90.00	40.00	11.50
☐ 7AU Rollie Fingers (Signed and Numbered out of 3000)	90.00	40.00	11.50

1992 Upper Deck Home Run Heroes

This 26-card subset measures the standard size (2 1/2" by 3 1/2") and was inserted one per pack into 1992 Upper Deck low series jumbo foil packs. The set spotlights the 1991 home run leaders from each of the 26 Major League teams. The fronts display color action player photos with a shadow strip around the picture for a three-dimensional effect. A gold bat icon runs vertically down the left side and contains the words "Homerun Heroes" printed in white. The backs have action photos in color and career highlights on a white background. AL players have their name printed in a red bar while NL players' names are printed in a green bar. The cards are numbered on the back with an "HR" prefix.

	MINT	EXC	G-VG
COMPLETE SET (26)	15.00	6.75	1.90
COMMON CARD (HR1-HR26)	.25	.11	.03
☐ HR1 Jose Canseco	1.00	.45	.13
☐ HR2 Cecil Fielder	.75	.35	.09
☐ HR3 Howard Johnson	.25	.11	.03
☐ HR4 Cal Ripken	2.50	1.15	.30
☐ HR5 Matt Williams	1.00	.45	.13
☐ HR6 Joe Carter	1.00	.45	.13
☐ HR7 Ron Gant	.25	.11	.03
☐ HR8 Frank Thomas	5.00	2.30	.60
☐ HR9 Andre Dawson	.50	.23	.06
☐ HR10 Fred McGriff	1.00	.45	.13
☐ HR11 Danny Tartabull	.50	.23	.06
☐ HR12 Chili Davis	.25	.11	.03
☐ HR13 Albert Belle	1.50	.65	.19
☐ HR14 Jack Clark	.25	.11	.03
☐ HR15 Paul O'Neill	.50	.23	.06
☐ HR16 Darryl Strawberry	.50	.23	.06
☐ HR17 Dave Winfield	.75	.35	.09
☐ HR18 Jay Buhner	.50	.23	.06
☐ HR19 Juan Gonzalez	2.00	.90	.25
☐ HR20 Greg Vaughn	.50	.23	.06
☐ HR21 Barry Bonds	1.50	.65	.19
☐ HR22 Matt Nokes	.25	.11	.03
☐ HR23 John Kruk	.50	.23	.06
☐ HR24 Ivan Calderon	.25	.11	.03
☐ HR25 Jeff Bagwell	2.50	1.15	.30
☐ HR26 Todd Zeile	.50	.23	.06

1992 Upper Deck Scouting Report

Randomly inserted one per high series jumbo pack, this 25-card set features outstanding prospects in baseball. The cards measure the standard size (2 1/2" by 3 1/2"). The fronts carry color action player photos that are full-bleed on the top and right, bordered below by a black stripe with the player's name, and by a black jagged left border that resembles torn paper. The words "Scouting Report" are printed vertically in silver lettering in the left border. The back design features a clipboard with three items held fast by the clamp: 1) a color player photo; 2) a 4" by 6" index card with major league rating in five categories (average, power, speed, fielding, and arm), and an 8 1/2" by 11" piece of paper typed with a player profile. The cards are numbered on the back with an SR prefix. The card numbering follows alphabetical order by player's name.

	MINT	EXC	G-VG
COMPLETE SET (25)	15.00	6.75	1.90
COMMON CARD (SR1-SR25)	.25	.11	.03
☐ SR1 Andy Ashby	.25	.11	.03
☐ SR2 Willie Banks	.25	.11	.03
☐ SR3 Kim Batiste	.25	.11	.03
☐ SR4 Derek Bell	.60	.25	.08
☐ SR5 Archi Cianfrocco	.25	.11	.03
☐ SR6 Royce Clayton	.40	.18	.05
☐ SR7 Gary DiSarcina	.25	.11	.03
☐ SR8 Dave Fleming	.35	.16	.04
☐ SR9 Butch Henry	.25	.11	.03
☐ SR10 Todd Hundley	.35	.16	.04
☐ SR11 Brian Jordan	.60	.25	.08
☐ SR12 Eric Karros	1.00	.45	.13
☐ SR13 Pat Listach	.50	.23	.06
☐ SR14 Scott Livingstone	.25	.11	.03
☐ SR15 Kenny Lofton	7.00	3.10	.85
☐ SR16 Pat Mahomes	.60	.25	.08
☐ SR17 Denny Neagle	.25	.11	.03
☐ SR18 Dave Nilsson	1.00	.45	.13
☐ SR19 Donovan Osborne	.25	.11	.03
☐ SR20 Reggie Sanders	1.50	.65	.19
☐ SR21 Andy Stankiewicz	.25	.11	.03
☐ SR22 Jim Thome	2.50	1.15	.30
☐ SR23 Julio Valera	.25	.11	.03
☐ SR24 Mark Wohlers	.25	.11	.03
☐ SR25 Anthony Young	.25	.11	.03

1992 Upper Deck Ted Williams Best

This 20-card set contains Ted Williams' choices of best current and future hitters in the game. The standard size cards (2 1/2" by 3 1/2") were randomly inserted in Upper Deck high number foil packs. The fronts feature full-bleed color action photos with the player's name in a black field separated from the picture by Ted Williams' gold-stamped signature. The back design displays a color close-up of the player in a purple and gold bordered oval on a gray cement-textured background. The upper right corner appears peeled back to reveal the Upper Deck hologram. A Ted Williams' quote about the player is included below the photo. Player's statistics in a purple and gold bordered box round out the card back. The cards are numbered on the back with a "T" prefix.

	MINT	EXC	G-VG
COMPLETE SET (20)	30.00	13.50	3.80
COMMON CARD (T1-T20)	.60	.25	.08
☐ T1 Wade Boggs	1.00	.45	.13
☐ T2 Barry Bonds	2.50	1.15	.30
☐ T3 Jose Canseco	1.50	.65	.19
☐ T4 Will Clark	1.50	.65	.19
☐ T5 Cecil Fielder	1.00	.45	.13
☐ T6 Tony Gwynn	1.50	.65	.19
☐ T7 Rickey Henderson	1.00	.45	.13
☐ T8 Fred McGriff	1.50	.65	.19
☐ T9 Kirby Puckett	2.50	1.15	.30
☐ T10 Ruben Sierra	.75	.35	.09
☐ T11 Roberto Alomar	1.75	.80	.22
☐ T12 Jeff Bagwell	4.00	1.80	.50
☐ T13 Albert Belle	2.50	1.15	.30
☐ T14 Juan Gonzalez	3.00	1.35	.40
☐ T15 Ken Griffey Jr.	8.00	3.60	1.00
☐ T16 Chris Hoiles	.60	.25	.08
☐ T17 David Justice	1.50	.65	.19
☐ T18 Phil Plantier	1.00	.45	.13
☐ T19 Frank Thomas	8.00	3.60	1.00
☐ T20 Robin Ventura	1.00	.45	.13

1992 Upper Deck Ted Williams Heroes

This standard size (2 1/2" by 3 1/2") ten-card set was randomly inserted in 1992 Upper Deck low number foil packs. Williams autographed 2,500 of card 36, which displays his portrait by sports artist Vernon Wells. The fronts features sepia-tone photos of Williams in various stages of his career that are partially contained within a blue and white bordered circle. The photos rest on a parchment card face trimmed with a brick red and white border. The Upper Deck Baseball Heroes logo appears in the lower right corner. The back design displays career highlights on a gray plaque resting on the same parchment background as on the front. The cards are numbered on the back.

	MINT	EXC	G-VG
COMPLETE SET (10)	7.00	3.10	.85
COMMON WILLIAMS (28-36)	.50	.23	.06
☐ 28 1939 Rookie Year	.50	.23	.06
☐ 29 1941 .406	.50	.23	.06
☐ 30 1942 Triple Crown Year	.50	.23	.06
☐ 31 1946 and 1949 MVP	.50	.23	.06
☐ 32 1947 2nd Triple Crown	.50	.23	.06
☐ 33 1950s Player of the Decade	.50	.23	.06
☐ 34 1960 500 Home Run Club	.50	.23	.06
☐ 35 1966 Hall of Fame	.50	.23	.06
☐ 36 Baseball Heroes CL	.50	.23	.06
☐ NNO Baseball Heroes SP (Header card)	4.00	1.80	.50
☐ AU4 Ted Williams (Signed and Numbered of 2500)	500.00	230.00	65.00

1993 Upper Deck

The 1993 Upper Deck set consists of two series of 420 cards each measuring the standard size, 2 1/2" by 3 1/2". The first series inserts included a ten-card hobby-only insert set featuring Triple Crown Contenders while a 26-card Walter Iooss

Collection was found in retail foil packs only. A ten-card Baseball Heroes insert set pays tribute to Willie Mays. Also a nine-card "Then And Now" hologram set was randomly inserted in foil packs and one card of a 28-card insert set was featured exclusively in each jumbo foil pack. A special card (SP5) was randomly inserted in first series packs to commemorate the 3,000th hit of Brett and Yount. Randomly inserted into second series foil packs were ten Future Heroes cards, a special card (SP6) commemorating Nolan Ryan's last season, a second nine-card Then and Now hologram subset, a 15-card Fifth Anniversary subset (hobby only), a 20-card Reggie Jackson's Clutch Performers subset (retail only), and a 25-card On Deck subset (jumbo packs only). The front designs features color action player photos bordered in white. The company name is printed along the photo surface of the card top. The player's name appears in script in a color stripe cutting across the bottom of the picture while the team name and his position appear in another color stripe immediately below. The backs have a color close-up photo on the upper portion and biography, statistics, and career higlights on the lower portion. Special subsets featured include Star Rookies (1-29), Community Heroes (30-40), and American League Teammates (41-55), Top Prospects (421-449), Inside the Numbers (450-470), Team Stars (471-485), Award Winners (486-499), and Diamond Debuts (500-510). The cards are numbered on the back. Rookie Cards in this set include Midre Cummings, Derek Jeter, Ray McDavid, Michael Moore, Chad Mottola, J.T. Snow, and Tony Tarasco.

	MINT	EXC	G-VG
COMPLETE SET (840)	40.00	18.00	5.00
COMPLETE FACT.SET (840)	45.00	20.00	5.75
COMPLETE SERIES 1 (420)	20.00	9.00	2.50
COMPLETE SERIES 2 (420)	20.00	9.00	2.50
COMMON CARD (1-420)	.05	.02	.01
COMMON CARD (421-840)	.05	.02	.01
COMMUNITY HEROES (30-40)	.05	.02	.01

*GOLD HOLOGRAM: 1.5X VALUES BELOW

	#	Card	MINT	EXC	G-VG
☐	1	Star Rookie CL Tim Salmon	.20	.06	.02
☐	2	Mike Piazza SR	2.00	.90	.25
☐	3	Rene Arocha SR	.15	.07	.02
☐	4	Willie Greene SR	.10	.05	.01
☐	5	Manny Alexander SR	.10	.05	.01
☐	6	Dan Wilson SR	.10	.05	.01
☐	7	Dan Smith SR	.10	.05	.01
☐	8	Kevin Rogers SR	.10	.05	.01
☐	9	Kurt Miller SR	.10	.05	.01
☐	10	Joe Vitko SR	.10	.05	.01
☐	11	Tim Costo SR	.10	.05	.01
☐	12	Alan Embree SR	.10	.05	.01
☐	13	Jim Tatum SR	.10	.05	.01
☐	14	Cris Colon SR	.10	.05	.01
☐	15	Steve Hosey SR	.10	.05	.01
☐	16	Sterling Hitchcock SR	.15	.07	.02
☐	17	Dave Mlicki SR	.10	.05	.01
☐	18	Jessie Hollins SR	.10	.05	.01
☐	19	Bobby Jones SR	.25	.11	.03
☐	20	Kurt Miller SR	.10	.05	.01
☐	21	Melvin Nieves SR	.15	.07	.02
☐	22	Billy Ashley SR	.35	.16	.04
☐	23	J.T. Snow SR	.15	.07	.02
☐	24	Chipper Jones SR	.50	.23	.06
☐	25	Tim Salmon SR	.40	.18	.05
☐	26	Tim Pugh SR	.10	.05	.01
☐	27	David Nied SR	.15	.07	.02
☐	28	Mike Trombley SR	.10	.05	.01
☐	29	Javy Lopez SR	.40	.18	.05
☐	30	Community Heroes CL Jim Abbott	.05	.02	.01
☐	31	Jim Abbott CH	.08	.04	.01
☐	32	Dale Murphy CH	.08	.04	.01
☐	33	Tony Pena CH	.05	.02	.01
☐	34	Kirby Puckett CH	.40	.18	.05
☐	35	Harold Reynolds CH	.05	.02	.01
☐	36	Cal Ripken CH	.75	.35	.09
☐	37	Nolan Ryan CH	1.00	.45	.13
☐	38	Ryne Sandberg CH	.35	.16	.04
☐	39	Dave Stewart CH	.08	.04	.01
☐	40	Dave Winfield CH	.08	.04	.01
☐	41	Teammates CL Joe Carter Mark McGwire	.05	.02	.01
☐	42	Blockbuster Trade Joe Carter Roberto Alomar	.15	.07	.02
☐	43	Brew Crew Paul Molitor Pat Listach Robin Yount	.15	.07	.02
☐	44	Iron and Steel Cal Ripken Brady Anderson	.20	.09	.03
☐	45	Youthful Tribe Albert Belle Sandy Alomar Jr. Jim Thome Carlos Baerga Kenny Lofton	.25	.11	.03
☐	46	Motown Mashers Cecil Fielder Mickey Tettleton	.05	.02	.01
☐	47	Yankee Pride Roberto Kelly Don Mattingly	.15	.07	.02
☐	48	Boston Cy Sox Frank Viola Roger Clemens	.15	.07	.02
☐	49	Bash Brothers Ruben Sierra Mark McGwire	.05	.02	.01
☐	50	Twin Titles Kent Hrbek Kirby Puckett	.15	.07	.02
☐	51	Southside Sluggers Robin Ventura Frank Thomas	.50	.23	.06
☐	52	Latin Stars	.20	.09	.03

	No.	Card			
		Juan Gonzalez			
		Jose Canseco			
		Ivan Rodriguez			
		Rafael Palmeiro			
☐	53	Lethal Lefties	.05	.02	.01
		Mark Langston			
		Jim Abbott			
		Chuck Finley			
☐	54	Royal Family	.15	.07	.02
		Wally Joyner			
		Gregg Jefferies			
		George Brett			
☐	55	Pacific Sock Exchange	.50	.23	.06
		Kevin Mitchell			
		Ken Griffey Jr.			
		Jay Buhner			
☐	56	George Brett	.75	.35	.09
☐	57	Scott Cooper	.08	.04	.01
☐	58	Mike Maddux	.05	.02	.01
☐	59	Rusty Meacham	.05	.02	.01
☐	60	Wil Cordero	.10	.05	.01
☐	61	Tim Teufel	.05	.02	.01
☐	62	Jeff Montgomery	.08	.04	.01
☐	63	Scott Livingstone	.08	.04	.01
☐	64	Doug Dascenzo	.05	.02	.01
☐	65	Bret Boone	.10	.05	.01
☐	66	Tim Wakefield	.05	.02	.01
☐	67	Curt Schilling	.08	.04	.01
☐	68	Frank Tanana	.05	.02	.01
☐	69	Len Dykstra	.10	.05	.01
☐	70	Derek Lilliquist	.05	.02	.01
☐	71	Anthony Young	.08	.04	.01
☐	72	Hipolito Pichardo	.05	.02	.01
☐	73	Rod Beck	.10	.05	.01
☐	74	Kent Hrbek	.08	.04	.01
☐	75	Tom Glavine	.10	.05	.01
☐	76	Kevin Brown	.05	.02	.01
☐	77	Chuck Finley	.05	.02	.01
☐	78	Bob Walk	.05	.02	.01
☐	79	Rheal Cormier UER (Born in New Brunswick, not British Columbia)	.05	.02	.01
☐	80	Rick Sutcliffe	.08	.04	.01
☐	81	Harold Baines	.08	.04	.01
☐	82	Lee Smith	.10	.05	.01
☐	83	Geno Petralli	.05	.02	.01
☐	84	Jose Oquendo	.05	.02	.01
☐	85	Mark Gubicza	.05	.02	.01
☐	86	Mickey Tettleton	.08	.04	.01
☐	87	Bobby Witt	.05	.02	.01
☐	88	Mark Lewis	.08	.04	.01
☐	89	Kevin Appier	.08	.04	.01
☐	90	Mike Stanton	.05	.02	.01
☐	91	Rafael Belliard	.05	.02	.01
☐	92	Kenny Rogers	.05	.02	.01
☐	93	Randy Velarde	.05	.02	.01
☐	94	Luis Sojo	.05	.02	.01
☐	95	Mark Leiter	.05	.02	.01
☐	96	Jody Reed	.05	.02	.01
☐	97	Pete Harnisch	.05	.02	.01
☐	98	Tom Candiotti	.05	.02	.01
☐	99	Mark Portugal	.05	.02	.01
☐	100	Dave Valle	.05	.02	.01
☐	101	Shawon Dunston	.05	.02	.01
☐	102	B.J. Surhoff	.05	.02	.01
☐	103	Jay Bell	.08	.04	.01
☐	104	Sid Bream	.05	.02	.01
☐	105	Checklist 1-105	.10	.05	.01
		Frank Thomas			
☐	106	Mike Morgan	.05	.02	.01
☐	107	Bill Doran	.05	.02	.01
☐	108	Lance Blankenship	.05	.02	.01
☐	109	Mark Lemke	.05	.02	.01

	No.	Card			
☐	110	Brian Harper	.05	.02	.01
☐	111	Brady Anderson	.08	.04	.01
☐	112	Bip Roberts	.05	.02	.01
☐	113	Mitch Williams	.08	.04	.01
☐	114	Craig Biggio	.08	.04	.01
☐	115	Eddie Murray	.10	.05	.01
☐	116	Matt Nokes	.05	.02	.01
☐	117	Lance Parrish	.08	.04	.01
☐	118	Bill Swift	.08	.04	.01
☐	119	Jeff Innis	.05	.02	.01
☐	120	Mike LaValliere	.05	.02	.01
☐	121	Hal Morris	.08	.04	.01
☐	122	Walt Weiss	.05	.02	.01
☐	123	Ivan Rodriguez	.10	.05	.01
☐	124	Andy Van Slyke	.10	.05	.01
☐	125	Roberto Alomar	.40	.18	.05
☐	126	Robby Thompson	.05	.02	.01
☐	127	Sammy Sosa	.10	.05	.01
☐	128	Mark Langston	.10	.05	.01
☐	129	Jerry Browne	.05	.02	.01
☐	130	Chuck McElroy	.05	.02	.01
☐	131	Frank Viola	.08	.04	.01
☐	132	Leo Gomez	.05	.02	.01
☐	133	Ramon Martinez	.08	.04	.01
☐	134	Don Mattingly	.75	.35	.09
☐	135	Roger Clemens	.50	.23	.06
☐	136	Rickey Henderson	.10	.05	.01
☐	137	Darren Daulton	.10	.05	.01
☐	138	Ken Hill	.08	.04	.01
☐	139	Ozzie Guillen	.05	.02	.01
☐	140	Jerald Clark	.05	.02	.01
☐	141	Dave Fleming	.08	.04	.01
☐	142	Delino DeShields	.08	.04	.01
☐	143	Matt Williams	.30	.14	.04
☐	144	Larry Walker	.10	.05	.01
☐	145	Ruben Sierra	.10	.05	.01
☐	146	Ozzie Smith	.40	.18	.05
☐	147	Chris Sabo	.08	.04	.01
☐	148	Carlos Hernandez	.08	.04	.01
☐	149	Pat Borders	.05	.02	.01
☐	150	Orlando Merced	.08	.04	.01
☐	151	Royce Clayton	.08	.04	.01
☐	152	Kurt Stillwell	.05	.02	.01
☐	153	Dave Hollins	.10	.05	.01
☐	154	Mike Greenwell	.08	.04	.01
☐	155	Nolan Ryan	2.00	.90	.25
☐	156	Felix Jose	.05	.02	.01
☐	157	Junior Felix	.05	.02	.01
☐	158	Derek Bell	.08	.04	.01
☐	159	Steve Buechele	.05	.02	.01
☐	160	John Burkett	.08	.04	.01
☐	161	Pat Howell	.05	.02	.01
☐	162	Milt Cuyler	.05	.02	.01
☐	163	Terry Pendleton	.10	.05	.01
☐	164	Jack Morris	.10	.05	.01
☐	165	Tony Gwynn	.50	.23	.06
☐	166	Deion Sanders	.40	.18	.05
☐	167	Mike Devereaux	.08	.04	.01
☐	168	Ron Darling	.05	.02	.01
☐	169	Orel Hershiser	.08	.04	.01
☐	170	Mike Jackson	.05	.02	.01
☐	171	Doug Jones	.05	.02	.01
☐	172	Dan Walters	.05	.02	.01
☐	173	Darren Lewis	.05	.02	.01
☐	174	Carlos Baerga	.30	.14	.04
☐	175	Ryne Sandberg	.60	.25	.08
☐	176	Gregg Jefferies	.10	.05	.01
☐	177	John Jaha	.08	.04	.01
☐	178	Luis Polonia	.05	.02	.01
☐	179	Kirt Manwaring	.05	.02	.01
☐	180	Mike Magnante	.05	.02	.01
☐	181	Billy Ripken	.05	.02	.01
☐	182	Mike Moore	.05	.02	.01

☐	183	Eric Anthony	.05	.02	.01
☐	184	Lenny Harris	.05	.02	.01
☐	185	Tony Pena	.05	.02	.01
☐	186	Mike Felder	.05	.02	.01
☐	187	Greg Olson	.05	.02	.01
☐	188	Rene Gonzales	.05	.02	.01
☐	189	Mike Bordick	.08	.04	.01
☐	190	Mel Rojas	.05	.02	.01
☐	191	Todd Frohwirth	.05	.02	.01
☐	192	Darryl Hamilton	.05	.02	.01
☐	193	Mike Fetters	.05	.02	.01
☐	194	Omar Olivares	.05	.02	.01
☐	195	Tony Phillips	.05	.02	.01
☐	196	Paul Sorrento	.05	.02	.01
☐	197	Trevor Wilson	.05	.02	.01
☐	198	Kevin Gross	.05	.02	.01
☐	199	Ron Karkovice	.05	.02	.01
☐	200	Brook Jacoby	.05	.02	.01
☐	201	Mariano Duncan	.05	.02	.01
☐	202	Dennis Cook	.05	.02	.01
☐	203	Daryl Boston	.05	.02	.01
☐	204	Mike Perez	.05	.02	.01
☐	205	Manny Lee	.05	.02	.01
☐	206	Steve Olin	.05	.02	.01
☐	207	Charlie Hough	.08	.04	.01
☐	208	Scott Scudder	.05	.02	.01
☐	209	Charlie O'Brien	.05	.02	.01
☐	210	Checklist 106-210 Barry Bonds	.05	.02	.01
☐	211	Jose Vizcaino	.05	.02	.01
☐	212	Scott Leius	.05	.02	.01
☐	213	Kevin Mitchell	.08	.04	.01
☐	214	Brian Barnes	.05	.02	.01
☐	215	Pat Kelly	.05	.02	.01
☐	216	Chris Hammond	.05	.02	.01
☐	217	Rob Deer	.05	.02	.01
☐	218	Cory Snyder	.05	.02	.01
☐	219	Gary Carter	.10	.05	.01
☐	220	Danny Darwin	.05	.02	.01
☐	221	Tom Gordon	.05	.02	.01
☐	222	Gary Sheffield	.10	.05	.01
☐	223	Joe Carter	.30	.14	.04
☐	224	Jay Buhner	.08	.04	.01
☐	225	Jose Offerman	.05	.02	.01
☐	226	Jose Rijo	.08	.04	.01
☐	227	Mark Whiten	.08	.04	.01
☐	228	Randy Milligan	.05	.02	.01
☐	229	Bud Black	.05	.02	.01
☐	230	Gary DiSarcina	.08	.04	.01
☐	231	Steve Finley	.05	.02	.01
☐	232	Dennis Martinez	.08	.04	.01
☐	233	Mike Mussina	.40	.18	.05
☐	234	Joe Oliver	.05	.02	.01
☐	235	Chad Curtis	.08	.04	.01
☐	236	Shane Mack	.08	.04	.01
☐	237	Jaime Navarro	.05	.02	.01
☐	238	Brian McRae	.10	.05	.01
☐	239	Chili Davis	.08	.04	.01
☐	240	Jeff King	.05	.02	.01
☐	241	Dean Palmer	.08	.04	.01
☐	242	Danny Tartabull	.08	.04	.01
☐	243	Charles Nagy	.05	.02	.01
☐	244	Ray Lankford	.10	.05	.01
☐	245	Barry Larkin	.10	.05	.01
☐	246	Steve Avery	.10	.05	.01
☐	247	John Kruk	.10	.05	.01
☐	248	Derrick May	.08	.04	.01
☐	249	Stan Javier	.05	.02	.01
☐	250	Roger McDowell	.05	.02	.01
☐	251	Dan Gladden	.05	.02	.01
☐	252	Wally Joyner	.08	.04	.01
☐	253	Pat Listach	.08	.04	.01
☐	254	Chuck Knoblauch	.10	.05	.01

☐	255	Sandy Alomar Jr.	.08	.04	.01
☐	256	Jeff Bagwell	1.00	.45	.13
☐	257	Andy Stankiewicz	.05	.02	.01
☐	258	Darrin Jackson	.05	.02	.01
☐	259	Brett Butler	.08	.04	.01
☐	260	Joe Orsulak	.05	.02	.01
☐	261	Andy Benes	.08	.04	.01
☐	262	Kenny Lofton	.50	.23	.06
☐	263	Robin Ventura	.10	.05	.01
☐	264	Ron Gant	.08	.04	.01
☐	265	Ellis Burks	.08	.04	.01
☐	266	Juan Guzman	.08	.04	.01
☐	267	Wes Chamberlain	.05	.02	.01
☐	268	John Smiley	.05	.02	.01
☐	269	Franklin Stubbs	.05	.02	.01
☐	270	Tom Browning	.05	.02	.01
☐	271	Dennis Eckersley	.10	.05	.01
☐	272	Carlton Fisk	.10	.05	.01
☐	273	Lou Whitaker	.10	.05	.01
☐	274	Phil Plantier	.10	.05	.01
☐	275	Bobby Bonilla	.10	.05	.01
☐	276	Ben McDonald	.08	.04	.01
☐	277	Bob Zupcic	.05	.02	.01
☐	278	Terry Steinbach	.08	.04	.01
☐	279	Terry Mulholland	.05	.02	.01
☐	280	Lance Johnson	.05	.02	.01
☐	281	Willie McGee	.08	.04	.01
☐	282	Bret Saberhagen	.08	.04	.01
☐	283	Randy Myers	.08	.04	.01
☐	284	Randy Tomlin	.05	.02	.01
☐	285	Mickey Morandini	.05	.02	.01
☐	286	Brian Williams	.05	.02	.01
☐	287	Tino Martinez	.08	.04	.01
☐	288	Jose Melendez	.05	.02	.01
☐	289	Jeff Huson	.05	.02	.01
☐	290	Joe Grahe	.05	.02	.01
☐	291	Mel Hall	.05	.02	.01
☐	292	Otis Nixon	.05	.02	.01
☐	293	Todd Hundley	.05	.02	.01
☐	294	Casey Candaele	.05	.02	.01
☐	295	Kevin Seitzer	.05	.02	.01
☐	296	Eddie Taubensee	.05	.02	.01
☐	297	Moises Alou	.10	.05	.01
☐	298	Scott Radinsky	.05	.02	.01
☐	299	Thomas Howard	.05	.02	.01
☐	300	Kyle Abbott	.05	.02	.01
☐	301	Omar Vizquel	.05	.02	.01
☐	302	Keith Miller	.05	.02	.01
☐	303	Rick Aguilera	.08	.04	.01
☐	304	Bruce Hurst	.05	.02	.01
☐	305	Ken Caminiti	.08	.04	.01
☐	306	Mike Pagliarulo	.05	.02	.01
☐	307	Frank Seminara	.05	.02	.01
☐	308	Andre Dawson	.10	.05	.01
☐	309	Jose Lind	.05	.02	.01
☐	310	Joe Boever	.05	.02	.01
☐	311	Jeff Parrett	.05	.02	.01
☐	312	Alan Mills	.05	.02	.01
☐	313	Kevin Tapani	.05	.02	.01
☐	314	Darryl Kile	.08	.04	.01
☐	315	Checklist 211-315 Will Clark	.05	.02	.01
☐	316	Mike Sharperson	.05	.02	.01
☐	317	John Orton	.05	.02	.01
☐	318	Bob Tewksbury	.05	.02	.01
☐	319	Xavier Hernandez	.05	.02	.01
☐	320	Paul Assenmacher	.05	.02	.01
☐	321	John Franco	.05	.02	.01
☐	322	Mike Timlin	.05	.02	.01
☐	323	Jose Guzman	.05	.02	.01
☐	324	Pedro Martinez	.10	.05	.01
☐	325	Bill Spiers	.05	.02	.01
☐	326	Melido Perez	.05	.02	.01

	No.	Player			
☐	327	Mike Macfarlane	.05	.02	.01
☐	328	Ricky Bones	.05	.02	.01
☐	329	Scott Bankhead	.05	.02	.01
☐	330	Rich Rodriguez	.05	.02	.01
☐	331	Geronimo Pena	.05	.02	.01
☐	332	Bernie Williams	.08	.04	.01
☐	333	Paul Molitor	.30	.14	.04
☐	334	Carlos Garcia	.08	.04	.01
☐	335	David Cone	.10	.05	.01
☐	336	Randy Johnson	.10	.05	.01
☐	337	Pat Mahomes	.05	.02	.01
☐	338	Erik Hanson	.05	.02	.01
☐	339	Duane Ward	.08	.04	.01
☐	340	Al Martin	.08	.04	.01
☐	341	Pedro Munoz	.05	.02	.01
☐	342	Greg Colbrunn	.05	.02	.01
☐	343	Julio Valera	.08	.04	.01
☐	344	John Olerud	.10	.05	.01
☐	345	George Bell	.08	.04	.01
☐	346	Devon White	.08	.04	.01
☐	347	Donovan Osborne	.05	.02	.01
☐	348	Mark Gardner	.05	.02	.01
☐	349	Zane Smith	.05	.02	.01
☐	350	Wilson Alvarez	.10	.05	.01
☐	351	Kevin Koslofski	.05	.02	.01
☐	352	Roberto Hernandez	.05	.02	.01
☐	353	Glenn Davis	.05	.02	.01
☐	354	Reggie Sanders	.10	.05	.01
☐	355	Ken Griffey Jr.	2.00	.90	.25
☐	356	Marquis Grissom	.10	.05	.01
☐	357	Jack McDowell	.10	.05	.01
☐	358	Jimmy Key	.08	.04	.01
☐	359	Stan Belinda	.05	.02	.01
☐	360	Gerald Williams	.05	.02	.01
☐	361	Sid Fernandez	.05	.02	.01
☐	362	Alex Fernandez	.10	.05	.01
☐	363	John Smoltz	.08	.04	.01
☐	364	Travis Fryman	.15	.07	.02
☐	365	Jose Canseco	.30	.14	.04
☐	366	David Justice	.30	.14	.04
☐	367	Pedro Astacio	.08	.04	.01
☐	368	Tim Belcher	.05	.02	.01
☐	369	Steve Sax	.05	.02	.01
☐	370	Gary Gaetti	.05	.02	.01
☐	371	Jeff Frye	.05	.02	.01
☐	372	Bob Wickman	.05	.02	.01
☐	373	Ryan Thompson	.10	.05	.01
☐	374	David Hulse	.05	.02	.01
☐	375	Cal Eldred	.08	.04	.01
☐	376	Ryan Klesko	.60	.25	.08
☐	377	Damion Easley	.08	.04	.01
☐	378	John Kiely	.05	.02	.01
☐	379	Jim Bullinger	.05	.02	.01
☐	380	Brian Bohanon	.05	.02	.01
☐	381	Rod Brewer	.05	.02	.01
☐	382	Fernando Ramsey	.08	.04	.01
☐	383	Sam Militello	.05	.02	.01
☐	384	Arthur Rhodes	.05	.02	.01
☐	385	Eric Karros	.08	.04	.01
☐	386	Rico Brogna	.05	.02	.01
☐	387	John Valentin	.08	.04	.01
☐	388	Kerry Woodson	.05	.02	.01
☐	389	Ben Rivera	.05	.02	.01
☐	390	Matt Whiteside	.05	.02	.01
☐	391	Henry Rodriguez	.05	.02	.01
☐	392	John Wetteland	.05	.02	.01
☐	393	Kent Mercker	.05	.02	.01
☐	394	Bernard Gilkey	.05	.02	.01
☐	395	Doug Henry	.05	.02	.01
☐	396	Mo Vaughn	.10	.05	.01
☐	397	Scott Erickson	.05	.02	.01
☐	398	Bill Gullickson	.05	.02	.01
☐	399	Mark Guthrie	.05	.02	.01
☐	400	Dave Martinez	.05	.02	.01
☐	401	Jeff Kent	.10	.05	.01
☐	402	Chris Hoiles	.08	.04	.01
☐	403	Mike Henneman	.05	.02	.01
☐	404	Chris Nabholz	.05	.02	.01
☐	405	Tom Pagnozzi	.05	.02	.01
☐	406	Kelly Gruber	.05	.02	.01
☐	407	Bob Welch	.05	.02	.01
☐	408	Frank Castillo	.05	.02	.01
☐	409	John Dopson	.05	.02	.01
☐	410	Steve Farr	.05	.02	.01
☐	411	Henry Cotto	.05	.02	.01
☐	412	Bob Patterson	.05	.02	.01
☐	413	Todd Stottlemyre	.05	.02	.01
☐	414	Greg A. Harris	.05	.02	.01
☐	415	Denny Neagle	.05	.02	.01
☐	416	Bill Wegman	.05	.02	.01
☐	417	Willie Wilson	.05	.02	.01
☐	418	Terry Leach	.05	.02	.01
☐	419	Willie Randolph	.08	.04	.01
☐	420	Checklist 316-420 Mark McGwire	.05	.02	.01
☐	421	Top Prospect CL Calvin Murray	.05	.02	.01
☐	422	Pete Janicki TP	.05	.02	.01
☐	423	Todd Jones TP	.05	.02	.01
☐	424	Mike Neill TP	.05	.02	.01
☐	425	Carlos Delgado TP	.60	.25	.08
☐	426	Jose Oliva TP	.25	.11	.03
☐	427	Tyrone Hill TP	.08	.04	.01
☐	428	Dmitri Young TP	.10	.05	.01
☐	429	Derek Wallace TP	.05	.02	.01
☐	430	Michael Moore TP	.20	.09	.03
☐	431	Cliff Floyd TP	.60	.25	.08
☐	432	Calvin Murray TP	.05	.02	.01
☐	433	Manny Ramirez TP	.75	.35	.09
☐	434	Marc Newfield TP	.25	.11	.03
☐	435	Charles Johnson TP	.35	.16	.04
☐	436	Butch Huskey TP	.05	.02	.01
☐	437	Brad Pennington TP	.05	.02	.01
☐	438	Ray McDavid TP	.30	.14	.04
☐	439	Chad McConnell TP	.05	.02	.01
☐	440	Midre Cummings TP	.60	.25	.08
☐	441	Benji Gil TP	.08	.04	.01
☐	442	Frankie Rodriguez TP	.10	.05	.01
☐	443	Chad Mottola TP	.20	.09	.03
☐	444	John Burke TP	.15	.07	.02
☐	445	Michael Tucker TP	.30	.14	.04
☐	446	Rick Greene TP	.08	.04	.01
☐	447	Rich Becker TP	.08	.04	.01
☐	448	Mike Robertson TP	.05	.02	.01
☐	449	Derek Jeter TP	2.00	.90	.25
☐	450	Inside the Numbers CL Ivan Rodriguez David McCarty	.05	.02	.01
☐	451	Jim Abbott IN	.08	.04	.01
☐	452	Jeff Bagwell IN	.50	.23	.06
☐	453	Jason Bere IN	.30	.14	.04
☐	454	Delino DeShields IN	.08	.04	.01
☐	455	Travis Fryman IN	.08	.04	.01
☐	456	Alex Gonzalez IN	.15	.07	.02
☐	457	Phil Hiatt IN	.05	.02	.01
☐	458	Dave Hollins IN	.08	.04	.01
☐	459	Chipper Jones IN	.25	.11	.03
☐	460	David Justice IN	.15	.07	.02
☐	461	Ray Lankford IN	.08	.04	.01
☐	462	David McCarty IN	.08	.04	.01
☐	463	Mike Mussina IN	.20	.09	.03
☐	464	Jose Offerman IN	.05	.02	.01
☐	465	Dean Palmer IN	.08	.04	.01
☐	466	Geronimo Pena IN	.05	.02	.01
☐	467	Eduardo Perez IN	.05	.02	.01
☐	468	Ivan Rodriguez IN	.08	.04	.01

□ 469 Reggie Sanders IN	.08	.04	.01
□ 470 Bernie Williams IN	.08	.04	.01
□ 471 Team Stars Checklist	.20	.09	.03
□ 472 Strike Force	.15	.07	.02
Greg Maddux			
Steve Avery			
John Smoltz			
Tom Glavine			
□ 473 Red October	.05	.02	.01
Jose Rijo			
Rob Dibble			
Roberto Kelly			
Reggie Sanders			
Barry Larkin			
□ 474 Four Corners	.15	.07	.02
Gary Sheffield			
Phil Plantier			
Tony Gwynn			
Fred McGriff			
□ 475 Shooting Stars	.05	.02	.01
Doug Drabek			
Craig Biggio			
Jeff Bagwell			
□ 476 Giant Sticks	.20	.09	.03
Will Clark			
Barry Bonds			
Matt Williams			
□ 477 Boyhood Friends	.08	.04	.01
Eric Davis			
Darryl Strawberry			
□ 478 Rock Solid Foundation	.15	.07	.02
Dante Bichette			
David Nied			
Andres Galarraga			
□ 479 Inaugural Catch	.05	.02	.01
Dave Magadan			
Orestes Destrade			
Bret Barberie			
Jeff Conine			
□ 480 Steel City Champions	.05	.02	.01
Tim Wakefield			
Andy Van Slyke			
Jay Bell			
□ 481 Les Grandes Etoiles	.05	.02	.01
Marquis Grissom			
Delino DeShields			
Dennis Martinez			
Larry Walker			
□ 482 Runnin' Redbirds	.08	.04	.01
Geronimo Pena			
Ray Lankford			
Ozzie Smith			
Bernard Gilkey			
□ 483 Ivy Leaguers	.15	.07	.02
Randy Myers			
Ryne Sandberg			
Mark Grace			
□ 484 Big Apple Power Switch	.05	.02	.01
Eddie Murray			
Howard Johnson			
Bobby Bonilla			
□ 485 Hammers and Nails	.10	.05	.01
John Kruk			
Dave Hollins			
Darren Daulton			
Len Dykstra			
□ 486 Barry Bonds AW	.40	.18	.05
□ 487 Dennis Eckersley AW	.08	.04	.01
□ 488 Greg Maddux AW	.20	.09	.03
□ 489 Dennis Eckersley AW	.08	.04	.01
□ 490 Eric Karros AW	.08	.04	.01
□ 491 Pat Listach AW	.05	.02	.01
□ 492 Gary Sheffield AW	.08	.04	.01
□ 493 Mark McGwire AW	.08	.04	.01
□ 494 Gary Sheffield AW	.08	.04	.01
□ 495 Edgar Martinez AW	.05	.02	.01
□ 496 Fred McGriff AW	.15	.07	.02
□ 497 Juan Gonzalez AW	.30	.14	.04
□ 498 Darren Daulton AW	.08	.04	.01
□ 499 Cecil Fielder AW	.08	.04	.01
□ 500 Diamond Debuts CL	.10	.05	.01
Brent Gates			
□ 501 Tavo Alvarez DD	.10	.05	.01
□ 502 Rod Bolton DD	.10	.05	.01
□ 503 John Cummings DD	.10	.05	.01
□ 504 Brent Gates DD	.15	.07	.02
□ 505 Tyler Green DD	.10	.05	.01
□ 506 Jose Martinez DD	.15	.07	.02
□ 507 Troy Percival DD	.10	.05	.01
□ 508 Kevin Stocker DD	.15	.07	.02
□ 509 Matt Walbeck DD	.10	.05	.01
□ 510 Rondell White DD	.40	.18	.05
□ 511 Billy Ripken	.05	.02	.01
□ 512 Mike Moore	.05	.02	.01
□ 513 Jose Lind	.05	.02	.01
□ 514 Chito Martinez	.05	.02	.01
□ 515 Jose Guzman	.05	.02	.01
□ 516 Kim Batiste	.05	.02	.01
□ 517 Jeff Tackett	.05	.02	.01
□ 518 Charlie Hough	.08	.04	.01
□ 519 Marvin Freeman	.05	.02	.01
□ 520 Carlos Martinez	.05	.02	.01
□ 521 Eric Young	.08	.04	.01
□ 522 Pete Incaviglia	.05	.02	.01
□ 523 Scott Fletcher	.05	.02	.01
□ 524 Orestes Destrade	.05	.02	.01
□ 525 Checklist 421-525	.10	.05	.01
Ken Griffey Jr.			
□ 526 Ellis Burks	.08	.04	.01
□ 527 Juan Samuel	.05	.02	.01
□ 528 Dave Magadan	.05	.02	.01
□ 529 Jeff Parrett	.05	.02	.01
□ 530 Bill Krueger	.05	.02	.01
□ 531 Frank Bolick	.05	.02	.01
□ 532 Alan Trammell	.10	.05	.01
□ 533 Walt Weiss	.05	.02	.01
□ 534 David Cone	.10	.05	.01
□ 535 Greg Maddux	.40	.18	.05
□ 536 Kevin Young	.05	.02	.01
□ 537 Dave Hansen	.05	.02	.01
□ 538 Alex Cole	.05	.02	.01
□ 539 Greg Hibbard	.05	.02	.01
□ 540 Gene Larkin	.05	.02	.01
□ 541 Jeff Reardon	.08	.04	.01
□ 542 Felix Jose	.05	.02	.01
□ 543 Jimmy Key	.08	.04	.01
□ 544 Reggie Jefferson	.05	.02	.01
□ 545 Gregg Jefferies	.10	.05	.01
□ 546 Dave Stewart	.08	.04	.01
□ 547 Tim Wallach	.05	.02	.01
□ 548 Spike Owen	.05	.02	.01
□ 549 Tommy Greene	.08	.04	.01
□ 550 Fernando Valenzuela	.05	.02	.01
□ 551 Rich Amaral	.05	.02	.01
□ 552 Bret Barberie	.05	.02	.01
□ 553 Edgar Martinez	.05	.02	.01
□ 554 Jim Abbott	.10	.05	.01
□ 555 Frank Thomas	2.00	.90	.25
□ 556 Wade Boggs	.10	.05	.01
□ 557 Tom Henke	.08	.04	.01
□ 558 Milt Thompson	.05	.02	.01
□ 559 Lloyd McClendon	.05	.02	.01
□ 560 Vinny Castilla	.05	.02	.01
□ 561 Ricky Jordan	.05	.02	.01
□ 562 Andujar Cedeno	.08	.04	.01
□ 563 Greg Vaughn	.08	.04	.01

☐ 564	Cecil Fielder	.10	.05	.01
☐ 565	Kirby Puckett	.75	.35	.09
☐ 566	Mark McGwire	.10	.05	.01
☐ 567	Barry Bonds	.75	.35	.09
☐ 568	Jody Reed	.05	.02	.01
☐ 569	Todd Zeile	.08	.04	.01
☐ 570	Mark Carreon	.05	.02	.01
☐ 571	Joe Girardi	.05	.02	.01
☐ 572	Luis Gonzalez	.08	.04	.01
☐ 573	Mark Grace	.10	.05	.01
☐ 574	Rafael Palmeiro	.10	.05	.01
☐ 575	Darryl Strawberry	.08	.04	.01
☐ 576	Will Clark	.30	.14	.04
☐ 577	Fred McGriff	.30	.14	.04
☐ 578	Kevin Reimer	.05	.02	.01
☐ 579	Dave Righetti	.05	.02	.01
☐ 580	Juan Bell	.05	.02	.01
☐ 581	Jeff Brantley	.05	.02	.01
☐ 582	Brian Hunter	.05	.02	.01
☐ 583	Tim Naehring	.05	.02	.01
☐ 584	Glenallen Hill	.05	.02	.01
☐ 585	Cal Ripken	1.50	.65	.19
☐ 586	Albert Belle	.60	.25	.08
☐ 587	Robin Yount	.30	.14	.04
☐ 588	Chris Bosio	.05	.02	.01
☐ 589	Pete Smith	.05	.02	.01
☐ 590	Chuck Carr	.05	.02	.01
☐ 591	Jeff Blauser	.08	.04	.01
☐ 592	Kevin McReynolds	.05	.02	.01
☐ 593	Andres Galarraga	.10	.05	.01
☐ 594	Kevin Maas	.05	.02	.01
☐ 595	Eric Davis	.05	.02	.01
☐ 596	Brian Jordan	.08	.04	.01
☐ 597	Tim Raines	.10	.05	.01
☐ 598	Rick Wilkins	.05	.02	.01
☐ 599	Steve Cooke	.05	.02	.01
☐ 600	Mike Gallego	.05	.02	.01
☐ 601	Mike Munoz	.05	.02	.01
☐ 602	Luis Rivera	.05	.02	.01
☐ 603	Junior Ortiz	.05	.02	.01
☐ 604	Brent Mayne	.05	.02	.01
☐ 605	Luis Alicea	.05	.02	.01
☐ 606	Damon Berryhill	.05	.02	.01
☐ 607	Dave Henderson	.05	.02	.01
☐ 608	Kirk McCaskill	.05	.02	.01
☐ 609	Jeff Fassero	.05	.02	.01
☐ 610	Mike Harkey	.05	.02	.01
☐ 611	Francisco Cabrera	.05	.02	.01
☐ 612	Rey Sanchez	.05	.02	.01
☐ 613	Scott Servais	.05	.02	.01
☐ 614	Darrin Fletcher	.05	.02	.01
☐ 615	Felix Fermin	.05	.02	.01
☐ 616	Kevin Seitzer	.05	.02	.01
☐ 617	Bob Scanlan	.05	.02	.01
☐ 618	Billy Hatcher	.05	.02	.01
☐ 619	John Vander Wal	.05	.02	.01
☐ 620	Joe Hesketh	.05	.02	.01
☐ 621	Hector Villanueva	.05	.02	.01
☐ 622	Randy Milligan	.05	.02	.01
☐ 623	Tony Tarasco	.25	.11	.03
☐ 624	Russ Swan	.05	.02	.01
☐ 625	Willie Wilson	.05	.02	.01
☐ 626	Frank Tanana	.05	.02	.01
☐ 627	Pete O'Brien	.05	.02	.01
☐ 628	Lenny Webster	.05	.02	.01
☐ 629	Mark Clark	.08	.04	.01
☐ 630	Checklist 526-630 Roger Clemens	.05	.02	.01
☐ 631	Alex Arias	.05	.02	.01
☐ 632	Chris Gwynn	.05	.02	.01
☐ 633	Tom Bolton	.05	.02	.01
☐ 634	Greg Briley	.05	.02	.01
☐ 635	Kent Bottenfield	.05	.02	.01
☐ 636	Kelly Downs	.05	.02	.01
☐ 637	Manny Lee	.05	.02	.01
☐ 638	Al Leiter	.05	.02	.01
☐ 639	Jeff Gardner	.05	.02	.01
☐ 640	Mike Gardiner	.05	.02	.01
☐ 641	Mark Gardner	.05	.02	.01
☐ 642	Jeff Branson	.05	.02	.01
☐ 643	Paul Wagner	.05	.02	.01
☐ 644	Sean Berry	.05	.02	.01
☐ 645	Phil Hiatt	.05	.02	.01
☐ 646	Kevin Mitchell	.08	.04	.01
☐ 647	Charlie Hayes	.08	.04	.01
☐ 648	Jim Deshaies	.05	.02	.01
☐ 649	Dan Pasqua	.05	.02	.01
☐ 650	Mike Maddux	.05	.02	.01
☐ 651	Domingo Martinez	.05	.02	.01
☐ 652	Greg McMichael	.15	.07	.02
☐ 653	Eric Wedge	.05	.02	.01
☐ 654	Mark Whiten	.08	.04	.01
☐ 655	Roberto Kelly	.08	.04	.01
☐ 656	Julio Franco	.08	.04	.01
☐ 657	Gene Harris	.05	.02	.01
☐ 658	Pete Schourek	.05	.02	.01
☐ 659	Mike Bielecki	.05	.02	.01
☐ 660	Ricky Gutierrez	.05	.02	.01
☐ 661	Chris Hammond	.05	.02	.01
☐ 662	Tim Scott	.05	.02	.01
☐ 663	Norm Charlton	.05	.02	.01
☐ 664	Doug Drabek	.10	.05	.01
☐ 665	Dwight Gooden	.05	.02	.01
☐ 666	Jim Gott	.05	.02	.01
☐ 667	Randy Myers	.08	.04	.01
☐ 668	Darren Holmes	.05	.02	.01
☐ 669	Tim Spehr	.05	.02	.01
☐ 670	Bruce Ruffin	.05	.02	.01
☐ 671	Bobby Thigpen	.05	.02	.01
☐ 672	Tony Fernandez	.05	.02	.01
☐ 673	Darrin Jackson	.05	.02	.01
☐ 674	Gregg Olson	.05	.02	.01
☐ 675	Rob Dibble	.05	.02	.01
☐ 676	Howard Johnson	.05	.02	.01
☐ 677	Mike Lansing	.20	.09	.03
☐ 678	Charlie Leibrandt	.05	.02	.01
☐ 679	Kevin Bass	.05	.02	.01
☐ 680	Hubie Brooks	.05	.02	.01
☐ 681	Scott Brosius	.05	.02	.01
☐ 682	Randy Knorr	.05	.02	.01
☐ 683	Dante Bichette	.10	.05	.01
☐ 684	Bryan Harvey	.08	.04	.01
☐ 685	Greg Gohr	.05	.02	.01
☐ 686	Willie Banks	.05	.02	.01
☐ 687	Robb Nen	.05	.02	.01
☐ 688	Mike Sciosia	.05	.02	.01
☐ 689	John Farrell	.05	.02	.01
☐ 690	John Candelaria	.05	.02	.01
☐ 691	Damon Buford	.05	.02	.01
☐ 692	Todd Worrell	.05	.02	.01
☐ 693	Pat Hentgen	.08	.04	.01
☐ 694	John Smiley	.05	.02	.01
☐ 695	Greg Swindell	.05	.02	.01
☐ 696	Derek Bell	.08	.04	.01
☐ 697	Terry Jorgensen	.05	.02	.01
☐ 698	Jimmy Jones	.05	.02	.01
☐ 699	David Wells	.05	.02	.01
☐ 700	Dave Martinez	.05	.02	.01
☐ 701	Steve Bedrosian	.05	.02	.01
☐ 702	Jeff Russell	.05	.02	.01
☐ 703	Joe Magrane	.05	.02	.01
☐ 704	Matt Mieske	.08	.04	.01
☐ 705	Paul Molitor	.30	.14	.04
☐ 706	Dale Murphy	.10	.05	.01
☐ 707	Steve Howe	.05	.02	.01
☐ 708	Greg Gagne	.05	.02	.01

☐ 709 Dave Eiland .05 .02 .01
☐ 710 David West .05 .02 .01
☐ 711 Luis Aquino .05 .02 .01
☐ 712 Joe Orsulak .05 .02 .01
☐ 713 Eric Plunk .05 .02 .01
☐ 714 Mike Felder .05 .02 .01
☐ 715 Joe Klink .05 .02 .01
☐ 716 Lonnie Smith .05 .02 .01
☐ 717 Monty Fariss .05 .02 .01
☐ 718 Craig Lefferts .05 .02 .01
☐ 719 John Habyan .05 .02 .01
☐ 720 Willie Blair .05 .02 .01
☐ 721 Darnell Coles .05 .02 .01
☐ 722 Mark Williamson .05 .02 .01
☐ 723 Bryn Smith .05 .02 .01
☐ 724 Greg W. Harris .05 .02 .01
☐ 725 Graeme Lloyd .05 .02 .01
☐ 726 Cris Carpenter .05 .02 .01
☐ 727 Chico Walker .05 .02 .01
☐ 728 Tracy Woodson .05 .02 .01
☐ 729 Jose Uribe .05 .02 .01
☐ 730 Stan Javier .05 .02 .01
☐ 731 Jay Howell .05 .02 .01
☐ 732 Freddie Benavides .05 .02 .01
☐ 733 Jeff Reboulet .05 .02 .01
☐ 734 Scott Sanderson .05 .02 .01
☐ 735 Checklist 631-735 .05 .02 .01
Ryne Sandberg
☐ 736 Archi Cianfrocco .05 .02 .01
☐ 737 Daryl Boston .05 .02 .01
☐ 738 Craig Grebeck .05 .02 .01
☐ 739 Doug Dascenzo .05 .02 .01
☐ 740 Gerald Young .05 .02 .01
☐ 741 Candy Maldonado .05 .02 .01
☐ 742 Joey Cora .05 .02 .01
☐ 743 Don Slaught .05 .02 .01
☐ 744 Steve Decker .05 .02 .01
☐ 745 Blas Minor .05 .02 .01
☐ 746 Storm Davis .05 .02 .01
☐ 747 Carlos Quintana .05 .02 .01
☐ 748 Vince Coleman .05 .02 .01
☐ 749 Todd Burns .05 .02 .01
☐ 750 Steve Frey .05 .02 .01
☐ 751 Ivan Calderon .05 .02 .01
☐ 752 Steve Reed .08 .04 .01
☐ 753 Danny Jackson .05 .02 .01
☐ 754 Jeff Conine .10 .05 .01
☐ 755 Juan Gonzalez .60 .25 .08
☐ 756 Mike Kelly .40 .18 .05
☐ 757 John Doherty .05 .02 .01
☐ 758 Jack Armstrong .05 .02 .01
☐ 759 John Wehner .05 .02 .01
☐ 760 Scott Bankhead .05 .02 .01
☐ 761 Jim Tatum .08 .04 .01
☐ 762 Scott Pose .05 .02 .01
☐ 763 Andy Ashby .05 .02 .01
☐ 764 Ed Sprague .05 .02 .01
☐ 765 Harold Baines .08 .04 .01
☐ 766 Kirk Gibson .08 .04 .01
☐ 767 Troy Neel .08 .04 .01
☐ 768 Dick Schofield .05 .02 .01
☐ 769 Dickie Thon .05 .02 .01
☐ 770 Butch Henry .05 .02 .01
☐ 771 Junior Felix .05 .02 .01
☐ 772 Ken Ryan .20 .09 .03
☐ 773 Trevor Hoffman .05 .02 .01
☐ 774 Phil Plantier .10 .05 .01
☐ 775 Bo Jackson .10 .05 .01
☐ 776 Benito Santiago .05 .02 .01
☐ 777 Andre Dawson .10 .05 .01
☐ 778 Bryan Hickerson .05 .02 .01
☐ 779 Dennis Moeller .05 .02 .01
☐ 780 Ryan Bowen .05 .02 .01
☐ 781 Eric Fox .05 .02 .01
☐ 782 Joe Kmak .05 .02 .01
☐ 783 Mike Hampton .05 .02 .01
☐ 784 Darrell Sherman .05 .02 .01
☐ 785 J.T. Snow .15 .07 .02
☐ 786 Dave Winfield .10 .05 .01
☐ 787 Jim Austin .05 .02 .01
☐ 788 Craig Shipley .05 .02 .01
☐ 789 Greg Myers .05 .02 .01
☐ 790 Todd Benzinger .05 .02 .01
☐ 791 Cory Snyder .05 .02 .01
☐ 792 David Segui .05 .02 .01
☐ 793 Armando Reynoso .05 .02 .01
☐ 794 Chili Davis .08 .04 .01
☐ 795 Dave Nilsson .08 .04 .01
☐ 796 Paul O'Neill .08 .04 .01
☐ 797 Jerald Clark .05 .02 .01
☐ 798 Jose Mesa .05 .02 .01
☐ 799 Brain Holman .05 .02 .01
☐ 800 Jim Eisenreich .05 .02 .01
☐ 801 Mark McLemore .05 .02 .01
☐ 802 Luis Sojo .05 .02 .01
☐ 803 Harold Reynolds .05 .02 .01
☐ 804 Dan Plesac .05 .02 .01
☐ 805 Dave Stieb .05 .02 .01
☐ 806 Tom Brunansky .05 .02 .01
☐ 807 Kelly Gruber .05 .02 .01
☐ 808 Bob Ojeda .05 .02 .01
☐ 809 Dave Burba .05 .02 .01
☐ 810 Joe Boever .05 .02 .01
☐ 811 Jeremy Hernandez .05 .02 .01
☐ 812 Tim Salmon TC .20 .09 .03
California Angels
☐ 813 Jeff Bagwell TC .50 .23 .06
Houston Astros
☐ 814 Dennis Eckersley TC .08 .04 .01
Oakland Athletics
☐ 815 Roberto Alomar TC .25 .11 .03
Toronto Blue Jays
☐ 816 Steve Avery TC .08 .04 .01
Atlanta Braves
☐ 817 Pat Listach TC .05 .02 .01
Milwaukee Brewers
☐ 818 Gregg Jefferies TC .08 .04 .01
St. Louis Cardinals
☐ 819 Sammy Sosa TC .08 .04 .01
Chicago Cubs
☐ 820 Darryl Strawberry TC .08 .04 .01
Los Angeles Dodgers
☐ 821 Dennis Martinez TC .05 .02 .01
Montreal Expos
☐ 822 Robby Thompson TC .05 .02 .01
San Francisco Giants
☐ 823 Albert Belle TC .30 .14 .04
Cleveland Indians
☐ 824 Randy Johnson TC .08 .04 .01
Seattle Mariners
☐ 825 Nigel Wilson TC .10 .05 .01
Florida Marlins
☐ 826 Bobby Bonilla TC .08 .04 .01
New York Mets
☐ 827 Glenn Davis TC .05 .02 .01
Baltimore Orioles
☐ 828 Gary Sheffield TC .08 .04 .01
San Diego Padres
☐ 829 Darren Daulton TC .08 .04 .01
Philadelphia Phillies
☐ 830 Jay Bell TC .05 .02 .01
Pittsburgh Pirates
☐ 831 Juan Gonzalez TC .30 .14 .04
Texas Rangers
☐ 832 Andre Dawson TC .08 .04 .01
Boston Red Sox

		MINT	EXC	G-VG
☐ 833	Hal Morris TC Cincinnati Reds	.05	.02	.01
☐ 834	David Nied TC Colorado Rockies	.08	.04	.01
☐ 835	Felix Jose TC Kansas City Royals	.05	.02	.01
☐ 836	Travis Fryman TC Detroit Tigers	.08	.04	.01
☐ 837	Shane Mack TC Minnesota Twins	.05	.02	.01
☐ 838	Robin Ventura TC Chicago White Sox	.08	.04	.01
☐ 839	Danny Tartabull TC New York Yankees	.08	.04	.01
☐ 840	Checklist 736-840 Roberto Alomar	.05	.02	.01
☐ SP5	George Brett and Robin Yount (Commemorating 3,000th Hit)	3.00	1.35	.40
☐ SP6	Nolan Ryan	6.00	2.70	.75

1993 Upper Deck Clutch Performers

These 20 standard-size (2 1/2" by 3 1/2") cards were randomly inserted into series II retail packs, and were also inserted one per series II retail jumbo packs. The fronts feature color player action shots that are borderless, except at the bottom, where a black stripe is set off by a gold-foil line and carries the set's title and Reggie Jackson's gold-foil signature. The player's name printed in white lettering rests at the bottom of the photo. The back carries a color player action shot below a black bar at the top that carries the player's name in gold-colored lettering. Below the picture appears a small black-and-white head shot of Reggie Jackson alongside his comments on the player. A player stat table appears below. The cards are numbered on the back with an "R" prefix and appear in alphabetical order. These 20 cards represent Reggie Jackson's selection of players who have come through under pressure.

		MINT	EXC	G-VG
COMPLETE SET (20)		20.00	9.00	2.50
COMMON CARD (R1-R20)		.35	.16	.04
☐ R1	Roberto Alomar	1.25	.55	.16
☐ R2	Wade Boggs	.35	.16	.04
☐ R3	Barry Bonds	2.00	.90	.25
☐ R4	Jose Canseco	.75	.35	.09
☐ R5	Joe Carter	.75	.35	.09
☐ R6	Will Clark	.75	.35	.09
☐ R7	Roger Clemens	1.25	.55	.16
☐ R8	Dennis Eckersley	.35	.16	.04
☐ R9	Cecil Fielder	.35	.16	.04
☐ R10	Juan Gonzalez	1.75	.80	.22
☐ R11	Ken Griffey Jr.	5.00	2.30	.60
☐ R12	Rickey Henderson	.35	.16	.04
☐ R13	Barry Larkin	.35	.16	.04
☐ R14	Don Mattingly	2.00	.90	.25
☐ R15	Fred McGriff	.75	.35	.09
☐ R16	Terry Pendleton	.35	.16	.04
☐ R17	Kirby Puckett	2.00	.90	.25
☐ R18	Ryne Sandberg	2.00	.90	.25
☐ R19	John Smoltz	.35	.16	.04
☐ R20	Frank Thomas	5.00	2.30	.60

1993 Upper Deck Fifth Anniversary

This 15-card set celebrates Upper Deck's five years in the sports card business. The cards are essentially reprinted versions of some of Upper Deck's most popular cards in the last five years. The standard-size (2 1/2" by 3 1/2") cards were randomly inserted in second series hobby packs. The black-bordered fronts feature player photos that previously appeared on an Upper Deck card. The Five-Year Anniversary logo is located in one of the corners and the player's name is printed in gold-foil along the lower black border. The black backs carry a picture of the original card on the left side with narrative historical information on Upper Deck and a brief career summary of the player. The gold-colored year of issue of the original card is prominently displayed in the middle of the text. The cards are numbered on the back with an A prefix. One over-sized (3 1/2" by 5") version of each of these cards was initially inserted into retail blister repacks, which contained one foil pack each of 1993 Upper Deck Series I and II. These cards are individually numbered out of 10,000 and were later inserted into various forms of repackaging. These over-sized cards are valued up to 2X the prices listed below.

		MINT	EXC	G-VG
COMPLETE SET (15)		20.00	9.00	2.50
COMMON CARD (A1-A15)		.35	.16	.04
☐ A1	Ken Griffey Jr.	8.00	3.60	1.00
☐ A2	Gary Sheffield	.35	.16	.04
☐ A3	Roberto Alomar	1.25	.55	.16
☐ A4	Jim Abbott	.35	.16	.04
☐ A5	Nolan Ryan	5.00	2.30	.60
☐ A6	Juan Gonzalez	1.75	.80	.22

☐ A7 David Justice	.75	.35	.09
☐ A8 Carlos Baerga	.75	.35	.09
☐ A9 Reggie Jackson	.75	.35	.09
☐ A10 Eric Karros	.35	.16	.04
☐ A11 Chipper Jones	1.00	.45	.13
☐ A12 Ivan Rodriguez	.35	.16	.04
☐ A13 Pat Listach	.35	.16	.04
☐ A14 Frank Thomas	5.00	2.30	.60
☐ A15 Tim Salmon	1.00	.45	.13

1993 Upper Deck Future Heroes

Randomly inserted in second series foil packs and continuing the Heroes insert set begun in the 1990 Upper Deck high-number set, this ten-card standard-size (2 1/2" by 3 1/2") set features eight different "Future Heroes" along with a checklist and header card. The fronts feature borderless color player action shots that bear the player's simulated autograph in gold foil in an upper corner. His name appears within a black stripe formed by the simulated tearing away of a piece of the photo. His team's name appears below. The back carries the player's name vertically within a black "tear-away" stripe along the right edge. Career highlights are displayed within a white, gray, and tan panel on the left. The cards are numbered on the back.

	MINT	EXC	G-VG
COMPLETE SET (10)	15.00	6.75	1.90
COMMON CARD (55-63)	.35	.16	.04
☐ 55 Roberto Alomar	1.25	.55	.16
☐ 56 Barry Bonds	2.00	.90	.25
☐ 57 Roger Clemens	1.25	.55	.16
☐ 58 Juan Gonzalez	1.75	.80	.22
☐ 59 Ken Griffey Jr.	5.00	2.30	.60
☐ 60 Mark McGwire	.35	.16	.04
☐ 61 Kirby Puckett	2.00	.90	.25
☐ 62 Frank Thomas	5.00	2.30	.60
☐ 63 Checklist	.35	.16	.04
☐ NNO Header Card SP	1.00	.45	.13

1993 Upper Deck Home Run Heroes

This 28-card set measures the standard size (2 1/2" by 3 1/2") and features the home run leader from each Major League team. Each 1993 first series 27-card jumbo pack contained one of these cards. The

cards feature action color player photos with a three-dimensional baseball bat design at the bottom. Featuring embossed printing, the bat looks and feels as if it stands off the card, and a shadow design below it adds to the effect. The words "Homerun Heroes" are printed vertically down the left. The backs show a team color-coded photo as the background for player information. The player's name appears in a white border on the right. The baseball bat design is repeated at the bottom. The cards are numbered on the back with an "HR" prefix and the set is arranged in descending order according to the number of home runs.

	MINT	EXC	G-VG
COMPLETE SET (28)	15.00	6.75	1.90
COMMON CARD (HR1-HR28)	.30	.14	.04
☐ HR1 Juan Gonzalez	1.75	.80	.22
☐ HR2 Mark McGwire	.30	.14	.04
☐ HR3 Cecil Fielder	.50	.23	.06
☐ HR4 Fred McGriff	.75	.35	.09
☐ HR5 Albert Belle	1.50	.65	.19
☐ HR6 Barry Bonds	2.00	.90	.25
☐ HR7 Joe Carter	.75	.35	.09
☐ HR8 Darren Daulton	.50	.23	.06
☐ HR9 Ken Griffey Jr.	5.00	2.30	.60
☐ HR10 Dave Hollins	.30	.14	.04
☐ HR11 Ryne Sandberg	1.75	.80	.22
☐ HR12 George Bell	.30	.14	.04
☐ HR13 Danny Tartabull	.30	.14	.04
☐ HR14 Mike Devereaux	.30	.14	.04
☐ HR15 Greg Vaughn	.30	.14	.04
☐ HR16 Larry Walker	.50	.23	.06
☐ HR17 David Justice	.75	.35	.09
☐ HR18 Terry Pendleton	.30	.14	.04
☐ HR19 Eric Karros	.30	.14	.04
☐ HR20 Ray Lankford	.50	.23	.06
☐ HR21 Matt Williams	1.00	.45	.13
☐ HR22 Eric Anthony	.30	.14	.04
☐ HR23 Bobby Bonilla	.30	.14	.04
☐ HR24 Kirby Puckett	2.00	.90	.25
☐ HR25 Mike Macfarlane	.30	.14	.04
☐ HR26 Tom Brunansky	.30	.14	.04
☐ HR27 Paul O'Neill	.30	.14	.04
☐ HR28 Gary Gaetti	.30	.14	.04

1993 Upper Deck Iooss Collection

This 27-card standard-size (2 1/2" by 3 1/2") set spotlights the work of famous sports photographer Walter Iooss Jr. by presenting 26 of the game's current greats

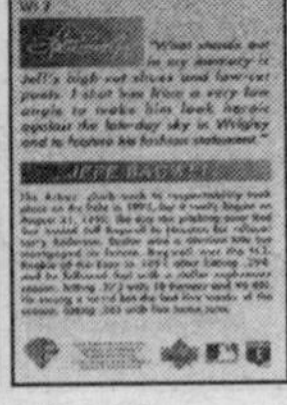

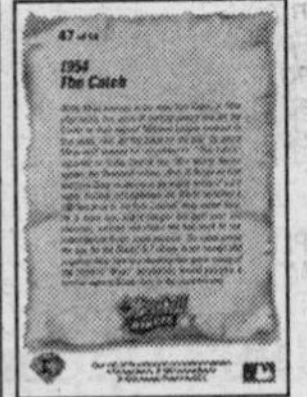

in a candid photo set. The cards were randomly inserted in series I foil packs purchased from major retail outlets only. The posed color player photos on the fronts are full-bleed and either horizontally or vertically oriented. The words "The Upper Deck Iooss Collection" are printed in gold foil. The back carries a quote from Iooss about the shoot and the player's career highlights. The text blocks on the card backs are separated by a gradated bars of varying colors. The cards are numbered on the back with a "WI" prefix. One over-sized version of each of these cards were initially inserted into retail blister repacks containing one foil pack each of 1993 Upper Deck Series I and II. These over-sized (3 1/2" by 5") cards are individually numbered out of 10,000 and were later inserted in various forms of repackaging. They are valued up to 2X the prices below.

	MINT	EXC	G-VG
COMPLETE SET (27)	25.00	11.50	3.10
COMMON CARD (WI1-WI26)	.35	.16	.04

	MINT	EXC	G-VG
☐ WI1 Tim Salmon	1.25	.55	.16
☐ WI2 Jeff Bagwell	3.00	1.35	.40
☐ WI3 Mark McGwire	.35	.16	.04
☐ WI4 Roberto Alomar	1.50	.65	.19
☐ WI5 Steve Avery	.60	.25	.08
☐ WI6 Paul Molitor	1.00	.45	.13
☐ WI7 Ozzie Smith	1.25	.55	.16
☐ WI8 Mark Grace	.35	.16	.04
☐ WI9 Eric Karros	.35	.16	.04
☐ WI10 Delino DeShields	.35	.16	.04
☐ WI11 Will Clark	1.00	.45	.13
☐ WI12 Albert Belle	1.75	.80	.22
☐ WI13 Ken Griffey Jr.	6.00	2.70	.75
☐ WI14 Howard Johnson	.35	.16	.04
☐ WI15 Cal Ripken	4.50	2.00	.55
☐ WI16 Fred McGriff	1.00	.45	.13
☐ WI17 Darren Daulton	.60	.25	.08
☐ WI18 Andy Van Slyke	.35	.16	.04
☐ WI19 Nolan Ryan	6.00	2.70	.75
☐ WI20 Wade Boggs	.60	.25	.08
☐ WI21 Barry Larkin	.60	.25	.08
☐ WI22 George Brett	2.50	1.15	.30
☐ WI23 Cecil Fielder	.60	.25	.08
☐ WI24 Kirby Puckett	2.50	1.15	.30
☐ WI25 Frank Thomas	6.00	2.70	.75
☐ WI26 Don Mattingly	2.50	1.15	.30
☐ NNO Title Card Iooss Header	.75	.35	.09

1993 Upper Deck Willie Mays Heroes

This standard size (2 1/2" by 3 1/2") ten-card set was randomly inserted in 1993 Upper Deck first series foil packs. The fronts feature color photos of Mays at various stages of his career that are partially contained within a black bordered circle. The photos rest on a rough-edged sports page from a newspaper. The Upper Deck Baseball Heroes logo appears in the lower right corner. The back design displays career highlights on a blank newspaper page. The cards are numbered on the back.

	MINT	EXC	G-VG
COMPLETE SET (10)	4.00	1.80	.50
COMMON MAYS (46-54)	.50	.23	.06

	MINT	EXC	G-VG
☐ 46 1951 Rookie-of-the-Year	.50	.23	.06
☐ 47 1954 The Catch	.50	.23	.06
☐ 48 1956-57 30-30 Club	.50	.23	.06
☐ 49 1961 Four-Homer Game	.50	.23	.06
☐ 50 1965 Most Valuable Player	.50	.23	.06
☐ 51 1969 600-Home Run Club	.50	.23	.06
☐ 52 1972 New York Homecoming	.50	.23	.06
☐ 53 1979 Hall of Fame	.50	.23	.06
☐ 54 Baseball Heroes CL (Portrait by Vernon Wells)	.50	.23	.06
☐ NNO Baseball Heroes SP (Header card)	1.00	.45	.13

1993 Upper Deck On Deck

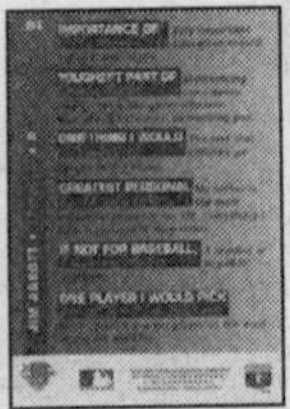

Inserted one per series II jumbo packs, these 25 standard-size (2 1/2" by 3 1/2") cards profile baseball's top players. The fronts feature borderless color player photos, some action, others posed, and carry the player's simulated gold-foil signature within a team color-coded stripe that appears as part of the set's logo. The gradated-tan-colored back carries the player's name, position, and team vertically within a team color-coded stripe near the left edge. The player's answers to personal questions rounds out the back. The cards are numbered on the back with a "D" prefix in alphabetical order by name.

	MINT	EXC	G-VG
COMPLETE SET (25)	20.00	9.00	2.50
COMMON CARD (D1-D25)	.35	.16	.04
☐ D1 Jim Abbott	.35	.16	.04
☐ D2 Roberto Alomar	1.25	.55	.16
☐ D3 Carlos Baerga	.75	.35	.09
☐ D4 Albert Belle	1.75	.80	.22
☐ D5 Wade Boggs	.55	.25	.07
☐ D6 George Brett	2.00	.90	.25
☐ D7 Jose Canseco	.75	.35	.09
☐ D8 Will Clark	.75	.35	.09
☐ D9 Roger Clemens	1.25	.55	.16
☐ D10 Dennis Eckersley	.55	.25	.07
☐ D11 Cecil Fielder	.55	.25	.07
☐ D12 Juan Gonzalez	1.75	.80	.22
☐ D13 Ken Griffey Jr.	5.00	2.30	.60
☐ D14 Tony Gwynn	1.25	.55	.16
☐ D15 Bo Jackson	.55	.25	.07
☐ D16 Chipper Jones	1.00	.45	.13
☐ D17 Eric Karros	.35	.16	.04
☐ D18 Mark McGwire	.35	.16	.04
☐ D19 Kirby Puckett	2.00	.90	.25
☐ D20 Nolan Ryan	5.00	2.30	.60
☐ D21 Tim Salmon	1.00	.45	.13
☐ D22 Ryne Sandberg	1.75	.80	.22
☐ D23 Darryl Strawberry	.35	.16	.04
☐ D24 Frank Thomas	5.00	2.30	.60
☐ D25 Andy Van Slyke	.35	.16	.04

1993 Upper Deck Season Highlights

This 20-card standard-size (2 1/2" by 3 1/2") insert set captures great moments of the 1992 Major League Baseball season. The set was randomly packed into specially marked cases that were available only at Upper Deck Heroes of Baseball Card Shows and through the purchase of a specified quantity of second series cases. The fronts display a full-bleed color action photo with a special "'92 Season Highlights" logo running across the bottom. The ribbon intersecting the logo is blue on the American League cards and red on the National League. The date of the player's outstanding achievement is gold-foil stamped at the lower right. On backs that fade from the league color to white, a description of the achievement is presented. The year 1992 is printed diagonally across the backs. The cards are numbered on the back with an "HI" prefix in alphabetical order by player's name.

	MINT	EXC	G-VG
COMPLETE SET (20)	150.00	70.00	19.00
COMMON CARD (HI1-HI20)	2.00	.90	.25
☐ HI1 Roberto Alomar 9th-inning homer off D. Eckersley in Game 4 of ALCS	12.00	5.50	1.50
☐ HI2 Steve Avery Extended NLCS shutout streak to LCS record 22 2/3 innings	2.00	.90	.25
☐ HI3 Harold Baines Game-winning home run in Game 1 of ALCS	2.00	.90	.25
☐ HI4 Damon Berryhill Three-run homer provided all Braves runs in WS Game 1 win	2.00	.90	.25
☐ HI5 Barry Bonds Two-time 30-30 player	20.00	9.00	2.50
☐ HI6 Bret Boone 1st third-generation player in Major Leagues	2.00	.90	.25
☐ HI7 George Brett 3,000th career hit	20.00	9.00	2.50
☐ HI8 Francisco Cabrera Game-winning, two-out, 9th-inning single in Game 7 of NLCS	2.00	.90	.25
☐ HI9 Ken Griffey Jr. All-Star Game MVP	50.00	23.00	6.25
☐ HI10 Rickey Henderson 1,000 career steals	2.00	.90	.25
☐ HI11 Kenny Lofton 1st rookie to lead AL in steals since 1956	12.00	5.50	1.50
☐ HI12 Mickey Morandini Unassisted triple play	2.00	.90	.25
☐ HI13 Eddie Murray 400th career home run	2.00	.90	.25
☐ HI14 David Nied 1st player taken in expansion draft	2.00	.90	.25
☐ HI15 Jeff Reardon Set record for career saves	2.00	.90	.25
☐ HI16 Bip Roberts Tied NL record with 10 consecutive hits	2.00	.90	.25
☐ HI17 Nolan Ryan Number retired by Angels	55.00	25.00	7.00
☐ HI18 Ed Sprague Game-winning, pitch-hit homer in Game 2 of WS	2.00	.90	.25
☐ HI19 Dave Winfield Game-winning, extra-inning double in Game 6 of WS	5.00	2.30	.60
☐ HI20 Robin Yount 3,000 career hit	8.00	3.60	1.00

1993 Upper Deck Then And Now

This 18-card, standard-size (2 1/2" by 3 1/2") hologram set highlights 18 veteran

stars in their rookie year and today, reflecting on how they and the game have changed. Cards 1-9 were randomly inserted in series I foil packs; cards 10-18 were randomly inserted in series II foil packs. The cards are numbered on the back with a "TN" prefix. The nine lithogram cards in the second series feature one card each of Hall of Famers Reggie Jackson, Mickey Mantle, and Willie Mays, as well as six active players. The second series cards are numbered on the back in continuation of the Then And Now Lithograms found in the 1993 Upper Deck first series baseball set. The horizontal fronts have a color close-up photo cutout and superimposed at the left corner of a full-bleed hologram portraying the player in an action scene. The skyline of the player's city serves as the background for the holograms. The player's name and the manufacturer's name form a right angle at the upper right corner. At the upper left corner, a "Then And Now" logo which includes the length of the player's career in years rounds out the front. On a sand-colored panel that resembles a postage stamp, the backs present career summary. The cards are numbered on the back with a "TN" prefix and arranged alphabetically within subgroup according to player's last name.

	MINT	EXC	G-VG
COMPLETE SET (18)	50.00	23.00	6.25
COMPLETE SERIES 1 (9)	25.00	11.50	3.10
COMPLETE SERIES 2 (9)	25.00	11.50	3.10
COMMON CARD (TN1-TN9)	.75	.35	.09
COMMON CARD (TN10-TN18)	.75	.35	.09
☐ TN1 Wade Boggs	1.25	.55	.16
☐ TN2 George Brett	4.00	1.80	.50
☐ TN3 Rickey Henderson	1.25	.55	.16
☐ TN4 Cal Ripken	7.50	3.40	.95
☐ TN5 Nolan Ryan	10.00	4.50	1.25
☐ TN6 Ryne Sandberg	3.50	1.55	.45
☐ TN7 Ozzie Smith	2.00	.90	.25
☐ TN8 Darryl Strawberry	.75	.35	.09
☐ TN9 Dave Winfield	1.25	.55	.16
☐ TN10 Dennis Eckersley	.75	.35	.09
☐ TN11 Tony Gwynn	2.50	1.15	.30
☐ TN12 Howard Johnson	.75	.35	.09
☐ TN13 Don Mattingly	4.00	1.80	.50
☐ TN14 Eddie Murray	1.25	.55	.16
☐ TN15 Robin Yount	1.50	.65	.19
☐ TN16 Reggie Jackson	4.00	1.80	.50
☐ TN17 Mickey Mantle	12.00	5.50	1.50
☐ TN18 Willie Mays	8.00	3.60	1.00

1993 Upper Deck Triple Crown

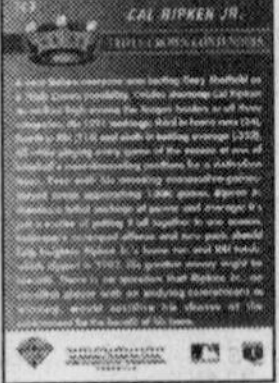

This ten-card, standard-size (2 1/2" by 3 1/2") subset highlights ten players who were selected by Upper Deck as having the best shot at winning Major League Baseball's Triple Crown. The cards were randomly inserted in series I foil packs sold by hobby dealers only. The fronts display glossy full-bleed color player photos. At the bottom, a purple ribbon edged in gold foil carries the words "Triple Crown Contenders," while the player's name appears in gold foil lettering immediately below on a gradated black background. A crown overlays the ribbon at the lower left corner and rounds out the front. On a gradated black background, the backs summarize the player's performance in home runs, RBIs, and batting average. The cards are numbered on the back with a "TC" prefix and arranged alphabetically by player's last name.

	MINT	EXC	G-VG
COMPLETE SET (10)	30.00	13.50	3.80
COMMON CARD (TC1-TC10)	1.00	.45	.13
☐ TC1 Barry Bonds	4.00	1.80	.50
☐ TC2 Jose Canseco	1.50	.65	.19
☐ TC3 Will Clark	1.50	.65	.19
☐ TC4 Ken Griffey Jr.	10.00	4.50	1.25
☐ TC5 Fred McGriff	1.50	.65	.19
☐ TC6 Kirby Puckett	4.00	1.80	.50
☐ TC7 Cal Ripken	7.50	3.40	.95
☐ TC8 Gary Sheffield	1.00	.45	.13
☐ TC9 Frank Thomas	10.00	4.50	1.25
☐ TC10 Larry Walker	1.00	.45	.13

1994 Upper Deck

The 1994 Upper Deck set was issued in two series of 280 and 270 cards for a total of

550. Card fronts feature a color photo of the player with a smaller version of the same photo along the left-hand border. The player's name appears in a black box in the upper left-hand corner. There are a number of subsets including Star Rookies (1-30), Fantasy Team (31-40), The Future is Now (41-55), Home Field Advantage (267-294), Upper Deck Classic Alumni (295-299), Diamond Debuts (511-522) and Top Prospects (523-550). Three autograph cards were randomly inserted in first series retail packs. They are Ken Griffey, Jr. (KG), Mickey Mantle (MM) and Griffey/Mantle (GM). An Alex Rodriguez (298A) autograph card was randomly inserted in second series retail packs. Rookie Cards include Brian Anderson, Alan Benes, John Hudek, Michael Jordan, Brooks Kieschnick, Chan Ho Park, Alex Rodriguez and Will VanLandingham.

	MINT	EXC	G-VG
COMPLETE SET (550)	50.00	23.00	6.25
COMPLETE SERIES 1 (280)	32.00	14.50	4.00
COMPLETE SERIES 2 (270)	18.00	8.00	2.30
COMMON CARD (1-280)	.10	.05	.01
COMMON CARD (281-550)	.10	.05	.01

	MINT	EXC	G-VG
☐ 1 Brian Anderson	.75	.35	.09
☐ 2 Shane Andrews	.15	.07	.02
☐ 3 James Baldwin	.50	.23	.06
☐ 4 Rich Becker	.15	.07	.02
☐ 5 Greg Blosser	.10	.05	.01
☐ 6 Ricky Bottalico	.30	.14	.04
☐ 7 Midre Cummings	.25	.11	.03
☐ 8 Carlos Delgado	.50	.23	.06
☐ 9 Steve Dreyer	.20	.09	.03
☐ 10 Joey Eischen	.15	.07	.02
☐ 11 Carl Everett	.15	.07	.02
☐ 12 Cliff Floyd UER	.50	.23	.06
(text indicates he throws left; should be right)			
☐ 13 Alex Gonzalez	.25	.11	.03
☐ 14 Jeff Granger	.15	.07	.02
☐ 15 Shawn Green	.50	.23	.06
☐ 16 Brian Hunter	.50	.23	.06
☐ 17 Butch Huskey	.10	.05	.01
☐ 18 Mark Hutton	.10	.05	.01
☐ 19 Michael Jordan	12.00	5.50	1.50
☐ 20 Steve Karsay	.10	.05	.01
☐ 21 Jeff McNeely	.10	.05	.01
☐ 22 Marc Newfield	.20	.09	.03
☐ 23 Manny Ramirez	.60	.25	.08
☐ 24 Alex Rodriguez	4.00	1.80	.50
☐ 25 Scott Ruffcorn UER	.20	.09	.03
(photo on back is Robert Ellis)			
☐ 26 Paul Spoljaric	.10	.05	.01
☐ 27 Salomon Torres	.15	.07	.02
☐ 28 Steve Trachsel	.40	.18	.05
☐ 29 Chris Turner	.10	.05	.01
☐ 30 Gabe White	.10	.05	.01
☐ 31 Randy Johnson FT	.15	.07	.02
☐ 32 John Wetteland FT	.10	.05	.01
☐ 33 Mike Piazza FT	.75	.35	.09
☐ 34 Rafael Palmeiro FT	.15	.07	.02
☐ 35 Roberto Alomar FT	.40	.18	.05
☐ 36 Matt Williams FT	.25	.11	.03
☐ 37 Travis Fryman FT	.15	.07	.02
☐ 38 Barry Bonds FT	.60	.25	.08
☐ 39 Marquis Grissom FT	.15	.07	.02
☐ 40 Albert Belle FT	.40	.18	.05
☐ 41 Steve Avery FUT	.20	.09	.03
☐ 42 Jason Bere FUT	.20	.09	.03
☐ 43 Alex Fernandez FUT	.15	.07	.02
☐ 44 Mike Mussina FUT	.25	.11	.03
☐ 45 Aaron Sele FUT	.20	.09	.03
☐ 46 Rod Beck FUT	.15	.07	.02
☐ 47 Mike Piazza FUT	.75	.35	.09
☐ 48 John Olerud FUT	.20	.09	.03
☐ 49 Carlos Baerga FUT	.20	.09	.03
☐ 50 Gary Sheffield FUT	.15	.07	.02
☐ 51 Travis Fryman FUT	.15	.07	.02
☐ 52 Juan Gonzalez FUT	.50	.23	.06
☐ 53 Ken Griffey Jr. FUT	1.50	.65	.19
☐ 54 Tim Salmon FUT	.25	.11	.03
☐ 55 Frank Thomas FUT	1.50	.65	.19
☐ 56 Tony Phillips	.10	.05	.01
☐ 57 Julio Franco	.15	.07	.02
☐ 58 Kevin Mitchell	.15	.07	.02
☐ 59 Raul Mondesi	1.00	.45	.13
☐ 60 Rickey Henderson	.20	.09	.03
☐ 61 Jay Buhner	.15	.07	.02
☐ 62 Bill Swift	.10	.05	.01
☐ 63 Brady Anderson	.15	.07	.02
☐ 64 Ryan Klesko	.50	.23	.06
☐ 65 Darren Daulton	.20	.09	.03
☐ 66 Damion Easley	.10	.05	.01
☐ 67 Mark McGwire	.20	.09	.03
☐ 68 John Roper	.15	.07	.02
☐ 69 Dave Telgheder	.10	.05	.01
☐ 70 Dave Nied	.20	.09	.03
☐ 71 Mo Vaughn	.20	.09	.03
☐ 72 Tyler Green	.10	.05	.01
☐ 73 Dave Magadan	.10	.05	.01
☐ 74 Chili Davis	.15	.07	.02
☐ 75 Archi Cianfrocco	.10	.05	.01
☐ 76 Joe Girardi	.10	.05	.01
☐ 77 Chris Hoiles	.15	.07	.02
☐ 78 Ryan Bowen	.10	.05	.01
☐ 79 Greg Gagne	.10	.05	.01
☐ 80 Aaron Sele	.25	.11	.03
☐ 81 Dave Winfield	.20	.09	.03
☐ 82 Chad Curtis	.15	.07	.02
☐ 83 Andy Van Slyke	.20	.09	.03
☐ 84 Kevin Stocker	.15	.07	.02
☐ 85 Deion Sanders	.50	.23	.06
☐ 86 Bernie Williams	.15	.07	.02
☐ 87 John Smoltz	.15	.07	.02
☐ 88 Ruben Santana	.10	.05	.01
☐ 89 Dave Stewart	.15	.07	.02
☐ 90 Don Mattingly	1.25	.55	.16
☐ 91 Joe Carter	.40	.18	.05
☐ 92 Ryne Sandberg	1.00	.45	.13
☐ 93 Chris Gomez	.20	.09	.03
☐ 94 Tino Martinez	.10	.05	.01
☐ 95 Terry Pendleton	.10	.05	.01
☐ 96 Andre Dawson	.20	.09	.03
☐ 97 Wil Cordero	.20	.09	.03
☐ 98 Kent Hrbek	.15	.07	.02
☐ 99 John Olerud	.20	.09	.03
☐ 100 Kirt Manwaring	.10	.05	.01
☐ 101 Tim Bogar	.10	.05	.01
☐ 102 Mike Mussina	.40	.18	.05
☐ 103 Nigel Wilson	.15	.07	.02
☐ 104 Ricky Gutierrez	.10	.05	.01
☐ 105 Roberto Mejia	.15	.07	.02
☐ 106 Tom Pagnozzi	.10	.05	.01
☐ 107 Mike Macfarlane	.10	.05	.01
☐ 108 Jose Bautista	.10	.05	.01
☐ 109 Luis Ortiz	.10	.05	.01
☐ 110 Brent Gates	.20	.09	.03
☐ 111 Tim Salmon	.40	.18	.05
☐ 112 Wade Boggs	.20	.09	.03
☐ 113 Tripp Cromer	.10	.05	.01
☐ 114 Denny Hocking	.10	.05	.01

No.	Player			
115	Carlos Baerga	.40	.18	.05
116	J.R. Phillips	.20	.09	.03
117	Bo Jackson	.20	.09	.03
118	Lance Johnson	.10	.05	.01
119	Bobby Jones	.20	.09	.03
120	Bobby Witt	.10	.05	.01
121	Ron Karkovice	.10	.05	.01
122	Jose Vizcaino	.10	.05	.01
123	Danny Darwin	.10	.05	.01
124	Eduardo Perez	.15	.07	.02
125	Brian Looney	.25	.11	.03
126	Pat Hentgen	.15	.07	.02
127	Frank Viola	.10	.05	.01
128	Darren Holmes	.10	.05	.01
129	Wally Whitehurst	.10	.05	.01
130	Matt Walbeck	.10	.05	.01
131	Albert Belle	1.00	.45	.13
132	Steve Cooke	.10	.05	.01
133	Kevin Appier	.15	.07	.02
134	Joe Oliver	.10	.05	.01
135	Benji Gil	.15	.07	.02
136	Steve Buechele	.10	.05	.01
137	Devon White	.10	.05	.01
138	Sterling Hitchcock UER (two losses for career; should be four)	.15	.07	.02
139	Phil Leftwich	.10	.05	.01
140	Jose Canseco	.40	.18	.05
141	Rick Aguilera	.15	.07	.02
142	Rod Beck	.15	.07	.02
143	Jose Rijo	.15	.07	.02
144	Tom Glavine	.20	.09	.03
145	Phil Plantier	.15	.07	.02
146	Jason Bere	.40	.18	.05
147	Jamie Moyer	.10	.05	.01
148	Wes Chamberlain	.10	.05	.01
149	Glenallen Hill	.10	.05	.01
150	Mark Whiten	.15	.07	.02
151	Bret Barberie	.10	.05	.01
152	Chuck Knoblauch	.20	.09	.03
153	Trevor Hoffman	.10	.05	.01
154	Rick Wilkins	.10	.05	.01
155	Juan Gonzalez	1.00	.45	.13
156	Ozzie Guillen	.10	.05	.01
157	Jim Eisenreich	.10	.05	.01
158	Pedro Astacio	.15	.07	.02
159	Joe Magrane	.10	.05	.01
160	Ryan Thompson	.15	.07	.02
161	Jose Lind	.10	.05	.01
162	Jeff Conine	.20	.09	.03
163	Todd Benzinger	.10	.05	.01
164	Roger Salkeld	.10	.05	.01
165	Gary DiSarcina	.10	.05	.01
166	Kevin Gross	.10	.05	.01
167	Charlie Hayes	.15	.07	.02
168	Tim Costo	.10	.05	.01
169	Wally Joyner	.15	.07	.02
170	Johnny Ruffin	.10	.05	.01
171	Kirk Rueter	.10	.05	.01
172	Lenny Dykstra	.20	.09	.03
173	Ken Hill	.15	.07	.02
174	Mike Bordick	.10	.05	.01
175	Billy Hall	.10	.05	.01
176	Rob Butler	.10	.05	.01
177	Jay Bell	.15	.07	.02
178	Jeff Kent	.15	.07	.02
179	David Wells	.10	.05	.01
180	Dean Palmer	.15	.07	.02
181	Mariano Duncan	.10	.05	.01
182	Orlando Merced	.15	.07	.02
183	Brett Butler	.15	.07	.02
184	Milt Thompson	.10	.05	.01
185	Chipper Jones	.40	.18	.05
186	Paul O'Neill	.15	.07	.02
187	Mike Greenwell	.15	.07	.02
188	Harold Baines	.15	.07	.02
189	Todd Stottlemyre	.10	.05	.01
190	Jeromy Burnitz	.15	.07	.02
191	Rene Arocha	.15	.07	.02
192	Jeff Fassero	.10	.05	.01
193	Robby Thompson	.10	.05	.01
194	Greg W. Harris	.10	.05	.01
195	Todd Van Poppel	.15	.07	.02
196	Jose Guzman	.10	.05	.01
197	Shane Mack	.15	.07	.02
198	Carlos Garcia	.10	.05	.01
199	Kevin Roberson	.10	.05	.01
200	David McCarty	.15	.07	.02
201	Alan Trammell	.20	.09	.03
202	Chuck Carr	.10	.05	.01
203	Tommy Greene	.10	.05	.01
204	Wilson Alvarez	.20	.09	.03
205	Dwight Gooden	.10	.05	.01
206	Tony Tarasco	.20	.09	.03
207	Darren Lewis	.10	.05	.01
208	Eric Karros	.15	.07	.02
209	Chris Hammond	.10	.05	.01
210	Jeffrey Hammonds	.30	.14	.04
211	Rich Amaral	.10	.05	.01
212	Danny Tartabull	.15	.07	.02
213	Jeff Russell	.10	.05	.01
214	Dave Staton	.10	.05	.01
215	Kenny Lofton	.75	.35	.09
216	Manny Lee	.10	.05	.01
217	Brian Koelling	.10	.05	.01
218	Scott Lydy	.10	.05	.01
219	Tony Gwynn	.75	.35	.09
220	Cecil Fielder	.20	.09	.03
221	Royce Clayton	.15	.07	.02
222	Reggie Sanders	.15	.07	.02
223	Brian Jordan	.15	.07	.02
224	Ken Griffey Jr.	3.00	1.35	.40
225	Fred McGriff	.40	.18	.05
226	Felix Jose	.10	.05	.01
227	Brad Pennington	.10	.05	.01
228	Chris Bosio	.10	.05	.01
229	Mike Stanley	.10	.05	.01
230	Willie Greene	.15	.07	.02
231	Alex Fernandez	.20	.09	.03
232	Brad Ausmus	.10	.05	.01
233	Darrell Whitmore	.15	.07	.02
234	Marcus Moore	.10	.05	.01
235	Allen Watson	.10	.05	.01
236	Jose Offerman	.10	.05	.01
237	Rondell White	.30	.14	.04
238	Jeff King	.10	.05	.01
239	Luis Alicea	.10	.05	.01
240	Dan Wilson	.10	.05	.01
241	Ed Sprague	.10	.05	.01
242	Todd Hundley	.10	.05	.01
243	Al Martin	.10	.05	.01
244	Mike Lansing	.15	.07	.02
245	Ivan Rodriguez	.20	.09	.03
246	Dave Fleming	.10	.05	.01
247	John Doherty	.10	.05	.01
248	Mark McLemore	.10	.05	.01
249	Bob Hamelin	.20	.09	.03
250	Curtis Pride	.30	.14	.04
251	Zane Smith	.10	.05	.01
252	Eric Young	.15	.07	.02
253	Brian McRae	.15	.07	.02
254	Tim Raines	.20	.09	.03
255	Javy Lopez	.30	.14	.04
256	Melvin Nieves	.20	.09	.03
257	Randy Myers	.10	.05	.01
258	Willie McGee	.10	.05	.01

☐ 259 Jimmy Key UER .15 .07 .02
(birthdate missing on back)
☐ 260 Tom Candiotti .10 .05 .01
☐ 261 Eric Davis .10 .05 .01
☐ 262 Craig Paquette .10 .05 .01
☐ 263 Robin Ventura .15 .07 .02
☐ 264 Pat Kelly .10 .05 .01
☐ 265 Gregg Jefferies .20 .09 .03
☐ 266 Cory Snyder .10 .05 .01
☐ 267 David Justice HFA .20 .09 .03
☐ 268 Sammy Sosa HFA .15 .07 .02
☐ 269 Barry Larkin HFA .15 .07 .02
☐ 270 Andres Galarraga HFA .15 .07 .02
☐ 271 Gary Sheffield HFA .15 .07 .02
☐ 272 Jeff Bagwell HFA .75 .35 .09
☐ 273 Mike Piazza HFA .75 .35 .09
☐ 274 Larry Walker HFA .15 .07 .02
☐ 275 Bobby Bonilla HFA .20 .09 .03
☐ 276 John Kruk HFA .15 .07 .02
☐ 277 Jay Bell HFA .10 .05 .01
☐ 278 Ozzie Smith HFA .30 .14 .04
☐ 279 Tony Gwynn HFA .40 .18 .05
☐ 280 Barry Bonds HFA .60 .25 .08
☐ 281 Cal Ripken HFA 1.00 .45 .13
☐ 282 Mo Vaughn HFA .10 .05 .01
☐ 283 Tim Salmon HFA .20 .09 .03
☐ 284 Frank Thomas HFA 1.50 .65 .19
☐ 285 Albert Belle HFA .50 .23 .06
☐ 286 Cecil Fielder HFA .15 .07 .02
☐ 287 Wally Joyner HFA .10 .05 .01
☐ 288 Greg Vaughn HFA .15 .07 .02
☐ 289 Kirby Puckett HFA .60 .25 .08
☐ 290 Don Mattingly HFA .60 .25 .08
☐ 291 Terry Steinbach HFA .10 .05 .01
☐ 292 Ken Griffey Jr. HFA 1.50 .65 .19
☐ 293 Juan Gonzalez HFA .50 .23 .06
☐ 294 Paul Molitor HFA .20 .09 .03
☐ 295 Tavo Alvarez UDCA .10 .05 .01
☐ 296 Matt Brunson UDCA .10 .05 .01
☐ 297 Shawn Green UDCA .30 .14 .04
☐ 298 Alex Rodriguez UDCA 2.00 .90 .25
☐ 299 Shannon Stewart UDCA .10 .05 .01
☐ 300 Frank Thomas 3.00 1.35 .40
☐ 301 Mickey Tettleton .15 .07 .02
☐ 302 Pedro Munoz .10 .05 .01
☐ 303 Jose Valentin .10 .05 .01
☐ 304 Orestes Destrade .10 .05 .01
☐ 305 Pat Listach .10 .05 .01
☐ 306 Scott Brosius .10 .05 .01
☐ 307 Kurt Miller .10 .05 .01
☐ 308 Rob Dibble .10 .05 .01
☐ 309 Mike Blowers .10 .05 .01
☐ 310 Jim Abbott .20 .09 .03
☐ 311 Mike Jackson .10 .05 .01
☐ 312 Craig Biggio .15 .07 .02
☐ 313 Kurt Abbott .30 .14 .04
☐ 314 Chuck Finley .10 .05 .01
☐ 315 Andres Galarraga .20 .09 .03
☐ 316 Mike Moore .10 .05 .01
☐ 317 Doug Strange .10 .05 .01
☐ 318 Pedro J. Martinez .20 .09 .03
☐ 319 Kevin McReynolds .10 .05 .01
☐ 320 Greg Maddux .60 .25 .08
☐ 321 Mike Henneman .10 .05 .01
☐ 322 Scott Leius .10 .05 .01
☐ 323 John Franco .10 .05 .01
☐ 324 Jeff Blauser .15 .07 .02
☐ 325 Kirby Puckett 1.25 .55 .16
☐ 326 Darryl Hamilton .10 .05 .01
☐ 327 John Smiley .10 .05 .01
☐ 328 Derrick May .10 .05 .01
☐ 329 Jose Vizcaino .10 .05 .01
☐ 330 Randy Johnson .20 .09 .03
☐ 331 Jack Morris .20 .09 .03
☐ 332 Graeme Lloyd .10 .05 .01
☐ 333 Dave Valle .10 .05 .01
☐ 334 Greg Myers .10 .05 .01
☐ 335 John Wetteland .10 .05 .01
☐ 336 Jim Gott .10 .05 .01
☐ 337 Tim Naehring .10 .05 .01
☐ 338 Mike Kelly .10 .05 .01
☐ 339 Jeff Montgomery .15 .07 .02
☐ 340 Rafael Palmeiro .20 .09 .03
☐ 341 Eddie Murray .20 .09 .03
☐ 342 Xavier Hernandez .10 .05 .01
☐ 343 Bobby Munoz .10 .05 .01
☐ 344 Bobby Bonilla .20 .09 .03
☐ 345 Travis Fryman .20 .09 .03
☐ 346 Steve Finley .10 .05 .01
☐ 347 Chris Sabo .10 .05 .01
☐ 348 Armando Reynoso .10 .05 .01
☐ 349 Ramon Martinez .15 .07 .02
☐ 350 Will Clark .40 .18 .05
☐ 351 Moises Alou .20 .09 .03
☐ 352 Jim Thome .20 .09 .03
☐ 353 Bob Tewksbury .10 .05 .01
☐ 354 Andujar Cedeno .10 .05 .01
☐ 355 Orel Hershiser .15 .07 .02
☐ 356 Mike Devereaux .15 .07 .02
☐ 357 Mike Perez .10 .05 .01
☐ 358 Dennis Martinez .15 .07 .02
☐ 359 Dave Nilsson .10 .05 .01
☐ 360 Ozzie Smith .60 .25 .08
☐ 361 Eric Anthony .10 .05 .01
☐ 362 Scott Sanders .10 .05 .01
☐ 363 Paul Sorrento .10 .05 .01
☐ 364 Tim Belcher .10 .05 .01
☐ 365 Dennis Eckersley .20 .09 .03
☐ 366 Mel Rojas .10 .05 .01
☐ 367 Tom Henke .10 .05 .01
☐ 368 Randy Tomlin .10 .05 .01
☐ 369 B.J. Surhoff .10 .05 .01
☐ 370 Larry Walker .20 .09 .03
☐ 371 Joey Cora .10 .05 .01
☐ 372 Mike Harkey .10 .05 .01
☐ 373 John Valentin .15 .07 .02
☐ 374 Doug Jones .10 .05 .01
☐ 375 David Justice .40 .18 .05
☐ 376 Vince Coleman .10 .05 .01
☐ 377 David Hulse .10 .05 .01
☐ 378 Kevin Seitzer .10 .05 .01
☐ 379 Pete Harnisch .10 .05 .01
☐ 380 Ruben Sierra .20 .09 .03
☐ 381 Mark Lewis .10 .05 .01
☐ 382 Bip Roberts .10 .05 .01
☐ 383 Paul Wagner .10 .05 .01
☐ 384 Stan Javier .10 .05 .01
☐ 385 Barry Larkin .20 .09 .03
☐ 386 Mark Portugal .10 .05 .01
☐ 387 Roberto Kelly .10 .05 .01
☐ 388 Andy Benes .15 .07 .02
☐ 389 Felix Fermin .10 .05 .01
☐ 390 Marquis Grissom .20 .09 .03
☐ 391 Troy Neel .15 .07 .02
☐ 392 Chad Kreuter .10 .05 .01
☐ 393 Gregg Olson .10 .05 .01
☐ 394 Charles Nagy .10 .05 .01
☐ 395 Jack McDowell .20 .09 .03
☐ 396 Luis Gonzalez .10 .05 .01
☐ 397 Benito Santiago .10 .05 .01
☐ 398 Chris James .10 .05 .01
☐ 399 Terry Mulholland .10 .05 .01
☐ 400 Barry Bonds 1.25 .55 .16
☐ 401 Joe Grahe .10 .05 .01
☐ 402 Duane Ward .10 .05 .01
☐ 403 John Burkett .15 .07 .02

☐ 404 Scott Servais .10 .05 .01
☐ 405 Bryan Harvey .15 .07 .02
☐ 406 Bernard Gilkey .10 .05 .01
☐ 407 Greg McMichael .15 .07 .02
☐ 408 Tim Wallach .10 .05 .01
☐ 409 Ken Caminiti .15 .07 .02
☐ 410 John Kruk .20 .09 .03
☐ 411 Darrin Jackson .10 .05 .01
☐ 412 Mike Gallego .10 .05 .01
☐ 413 David Cone .20 .09 .03
☐ 414 Lou Whitaker .20 .09 .03
☐ 415 Sandy Alomar Jr. .15 .07 .02
☐ 416 Bill Wegman .10 .05 .01
☐ 417 Pat Borders .10 .05 .01
☐ 418 Roger Pavlik .10 .05 .01
☐ 419 Pete Smith .10 .05 .01
☐ 420 Steve Avery .20 .09 .03
☐ 421 David Segui .10 .05 .01
☐ 422 Rheal Cormier .10 .05 .01
☐ 423 Harold Reynolds .10 .05 .01
☐ 424 Edgar Martinez .10 .05 .01
☐ 425 Cal Ripken 2.25 1.00 .30
☐ 426 Jaime Navarro .10 .05 .01
☐ 427 Sean Berry .10 .05 .01
☐ 428 Bret Saberhagen .15 .07 .02
☐ 429 Bob Welch .10 .05 .01
☐ 430 Juan Guzman .15 .07 .02
☐ 431 Cal Eldred .15 .07 .02
☐ 432 Dave Hollins .20 .09 .03
☐ 433 Sid Fernandez .10 .05 .01
☐ 434 Willie Banks .10 .05 .01
☐ 435 Darryl Kile .15 .07 .02
☐ 436 Henry Rodriguez .10 .05 .01
☐ 437 Tony Fernandez .10 .05 .01
☐ 438 Walt Weiss .10 .05 .01
☐ 439 Kevin Tapani .10 .05 .01
☐ 440 Mark Grace .20 .09 .03
☐ 441 Brian Harper .10 .05 .01
☐ 442 Kent Mercker .10 .05 .01
☐ 443 Anthony Young .10 .05 .01
☐ 444 Todd Zeile .15 .07 .02
☐ 445 Greg Vaughn .15 .07 .02
☐ 446 Ray Lankford .20 .09 .03
☐ 447 Dave Weathers .10 .05 .01
☐ 448 Bret Boone .20 .09 .03
☐ 449 Charlie Hough .15 .07 .02
☐ 450 Roger Clemens .75 .35 .09
☐ 451 Mike Morgan .10 .05 .01
☐ 452 Doug Drabek .20 .09 .03
☐ 453 Danny Jackson .10 .05 .01
☐ 454 Dante Bichette .20 .09 .03
☐ 455 Roberto Alomar .75 .35 .09
☐ 456 Ben McDonald .15 .07 .02
☐ 457 Kenny Rogers .10 .05 .01
☐ 458 Bill Gullickson .10 .05 .01
☐ 459 Darrin Fletcher .10 .05 .01
☐ 460 Curt Schilling .10 .05 .01
☐ 461 Billy Hatcher .10 .05 .01
☐ 462 Howard Johnson .10 .05 .01
☐ 463 Mickey Morandini .10 .05 .01
☐ 464 Frank Castillo .10 .05 .01
☐ 465 Delino DeShields .15 .07 .02
☐ 466 Gary Gaetti .10 .05 .01
☐ 467 Steve Farr .10 .05 .01
☐ 468 Roberto Hernandez .10 .05 .01
☐ 469 Jack Armstrong .10 .05 .01
☐ 470 Paul Molitor .40 .18 .05
☐ 471 Melido Perez .10 .05 .01
☐ 472 Greg Hibbard .10 .05 .01
☐ 473 Jody Reed .10 .05 .01
☐ 474 Tom Gordon .10 .05 .01
☐ 475 Gary Sheffield .20 .09 .03
☐ 476 John Jaha .10 .05 .01
☐ 477 Shawon Dunston .10 .05 .01
☐ 478 Reggie Jefferson .10 .05 .01
☐ 479 Don Slaught .10 .05 .01
☐ 480 Jeff Bagwell 1.50 .65 .19
☐ 481 Tim Pugh .10 .05 .01
☐ 482 Kevin Young .10 .05 .01
☐ 483 Ellis Burks .15 .07 .02
☐ 484 Greg Swindell .10 .05 .01
☐ 485 Mark Langston .20 .09 .03
☐ 486 Omar Vizquel .10 .05 .01
☐ 487 Kevin Brown .10 .05 .01
☐ 488 Terry Steinbach .15 .07 .02
☐ 489 Mark Lemke .10 .05 .01
☐ 490 Matt Williams .60 .25 .08
☐ 491 Pete Incaviglia .10 .05 .01
☐ 492 Karl Rhodes .10 .05 .01
☐ 493 Shawn Green .50 .23 .06
☐ 494 Hal Morris .15 .07 .02
☐ 495 Derek Bell .15 .07 .02
☐ 496 Luis Polonia .10 .05 .01
☐ 497 Otis Nixon .10 .05 .01
☐ 498 Ron Darling .10 .05 .01
☐ 499 Mitch Williams .10 .05 .01
☐ 500 Mike Piazza 1.50 .65 .19
☐ 501 Pat Meares .10 .05 .01
☐ 502 Scott Cooper .15 .07 .02
☐ 503 Scott Erickson .10 .05 .01
☐ 504 Jeff Juden .10 .05 .01
☐ 505 Lee Smith .20 .09 .03
☐ 506 Bobby Ayala .10 .05 .01
☐ 507 Dave Henderson .10 .05 .01
☐ 508 Erik Hanson .10 .05 .01
☐ 509 Bob Wickman .10 .05 .01
☐ 510 Sammy Sosa .20 .09 .03
☐ 511 Hector Carrasco DD .10 .05 .01
☐ 512 Tim Davis DD .10 .05 .01
☐ 513 Joey Hamilton DD .60 .25 .08
☐ 514 Robert Eenhoorn DD .10 .05 .01
☐ 515 Jorge Fabregas DD .10 .05 .01
☐ 516 Tim Hyers DD .10 .05 .01
☐ 517 John Hudek DD .75 .35 .09
☐ 518 James Mouton DD .20 .09 .03
☐ 519 Herbert Perry DD .25 .11 .03
☐ 520 Chan Ho Park DD 1.25 .55 .16
☐ 521 Bill Van Landingham DD 1.00 .45 .13
☐ 522 Paul Shuey DD .15 .07 .02
☐ 523 Ryan Hancock TP .30 .14 .04
☐ 524 Billy Wagner TP .60 .25 .08
☐ 525 Jason Giambi TP .10 .05 .01
☐ 526 Jose Silva TP .75 .35 .09
☐ 527 Terrell Wade TP .75 .35 .09
☐ 528 Todd Dunn TP .10 .05 .01
☐ 529 Alan Benes TP 1.00 .45 .13
☐ 530 Brooks Kieschnick TP 1.00 .45 .13
☐ 531 Todd Hollandsworth TP .60 .25 .08
☐ 532 Brad Fullmer TP .25 .11 .03
☐ 533 Steve Soderstrom TP .40 .18 .05
☐ 534 Daron Kirkreit TP .10 .05 .01
☐ 535 Arquimedez Pozo TP .75 .35 .09
☐ 536 Charles Johnson TP .30 .14 .04
☐ 537 Preston Wilson TP .10 .05 .01
☐ 538 Alex Ochoa TP .20 .09 .03
☐ 539 Derrek Lee TP .75 .35 .09
☐ 540 Wayne Gomes TP .25 .11 .03
☐ 541 Jermaine Allensworth TP .40 .18 .05
☐ 542 Mike Bell TP .40 .18 .05
☐ 543 Trot Nixon TP .75 .35 .09
☐ 544 Pokey Reese TP .10 .05 .01
☐ 545 Neifi Perez TP .25 .11 .03
☐ 546 Johnny Damon TP .40 .18 .05
☐ 547 Matt Brunson TP .30 .14 .04
☐ 548 LaTroy Hawkins TP .75 .35 .09
☐ 549 Eddie Pearson TP .50 .23 .06

☐ 550 Derek Jeter TP	.75	.35	.09
☐ AU298 Alex Rodriguez AU	100.00	45.00	12.50
☐ GM Griffey/Mantle AU/1000	600.00	275.00	75.00
☐ KG Griffey Jr. AU 1000	250.00	115.00	31.00
☐ MM Mantle AU/1000	300.00	135.00	38.00

1994 Upper Deck Electric Diamond

This 550-card set is a parellel issue to the basic 1994 Upper Deck cards. The cards were issued one per foil pack and two per mini jumbo. The only differences between these and the basic cards is the "Electric Diamond" in silver foil toward the bottom and the player's name is also in silver foil. Both differences appear on front.

	MINT	EXC	G-VG
COMPLETE SET (550)	125.00	57.50	15.50
COMPLETE SERIES 1 (280)	80.00	36.00	10.00
COMPLETE SERIES 2 (270)	50.00	23.00	6.25
COMMON CARD (1-280)	.10	.05	.01
COMMON CARD (281-550)	.10	.05	.01

*VETERAN STARS: 2X to 4X BASIC CARDS
*YOUNG STARS: 1.5X to 3X BASIC CARDS
*RCs: 1.25X to 2.5X BASIC CARDS

1994 Upper Deck Diamond Collection

This 30-card set was inserted regionally in first series hobby packs at a rate of one in 18. The three regions are Central (C1-C10), East (E1-E10) and West (W1-W10). While each card has the same horizontal format, the color scheme differs by region. The Central cards have a blue background, the East green and the West a deep shade of red. Color player photos are superimposed over the backgrounds. Each card has, "The Upper Deck Diamond Collection" as part of the background. The backs have a small photo and career highlights.

	MINT	EXC	G-VG
COMPLETE SET (30)	450.00	200.00	57.50
COMPLETE CENTRAL (10)	200.00	90.00	25.00
COMPLETE EAST (10)	90.00	40.00	11.50
COMPLETE WEST (10)	160.00	70.00	20.00
COMMON CENTRAL (C1-C10)	4.00	1.80	.50
COMMON EAST (E1-E10)	3.00	1.35	.40
COMMON WEST (W1-W10)	4.00	1.80	.50

☐ C1 Jeff Bagwell	30.00	13.50	3.80
☐ C2 Michael Jordan	60.00	27.00	7.50
☐ C3 Barry Larkin	4.00	1.80	.50
☐ C4 Kirby Puckett	25.00	11.50	3.10
☐ C5 Manny Ramirez	12.00	5.50	1.50
☐ C6 Ryne Sandberg	20.00	9.00	2.50
☐ C7 Ozzie Smith	12.00	5.50	1.50
☐ C8 Frank Thomas	60.00	27.00	7.50
☐ C9 Andy Van Slyke	4.00	1.80	.50
☐ C10 Robin Yount	9.00	4.00	1.15
☐ E1 Roberto Alomar	10.00	4.50	1.25
☐ E2 Roger Clemens	10.00	4.50	1.25
☐ E3 Lenny Dykstra	3.00	1.35	.40
☐ E4 Cecil Fielder	3.00	1.35	.40
☐ E5 Cliff Floyd	6.00	2.70	.75
☐ E6 Dwight Gooden	3.00	1.35	.40
☐ E7 David Justice	6.00	2.70	.75
☐ E8 Don Mattingly	16.00	7.25	2.00
☐ E9 Cal Ripken	30.00	13.50	3.80
☐ E10 Gary Sheffield	3.00	1.35	.40
☐ W1 Barry Bonds	25.00	11.50	3.10
☐ W2 Andres Galarraga	4.00	1.80	.50
☐ W3 Juan Gonzalez	20.00	9.00	2.50
☐ W4 Ken Griffey Jr.	60.00	27.00	7.50
☐ W5 Tony Gwynn	15.00	6.75	1.90
☐ W6 Rickey Henderson	4.00	1.80	.50
☐ W7 Bo Jackson	4.00	1.80	.50
☐ W8 Mark McGwire	4.00	1.80	.50
☐ W9 Mike Piazza	30.00	13.50	3.80
☐ W10 Tim Salmon	9.00	4.00	1.15

1994 Upper Deck Ken Griffey Jumbos

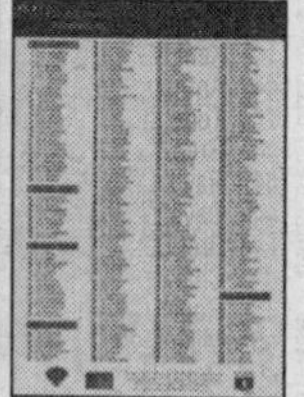

Measuring 4 7/8" by 6 13/16", these four Griffey cards serve as checklists for first series Upper Deck issues. They were issued one per first series hobby foil box. Card fronts have a full color photo with a small Griffey hologram. The first three cards provide a numerical, alphabetical and team organized checklist for the basic set. The fourth card is a checklist of inserts. Each card was printed in different quantities with CL1 the most plentiful and CL4 the more scarce. The backs are numbered with a CL prefix.

	MINT	EXC	G-VG
COMPLETE SET (4)	20.00	9.00	2.50
COMMON GRIFFEY (CL1-CL4)	4.00	1.80	.50

☐ CL1 Numerical CL TP	4.00	1.80	.50
☐ CL2 Alphabetical CL DP	5.00	2.30	.60
☐ CL3 Team CL	7.00	3.10	.85
☐ CL4 Insert CL SP	8.00	3.60	1.00

1994 Upper Deck Mantle Heroes

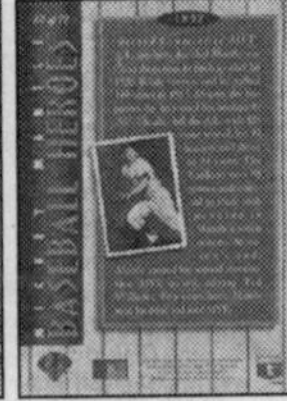

Randomly inserted in second series packs at a rate of one in 20, this 10-card set looks at various moments from The Mick's career. Metallic fronts feature a vintage photo with the card title at the bottom. The backs contain career highlights with a small scrapbook like photo. The numbering (64-72) is a continuation from previous Heroes sets.

	MINT	EXC	G-VG
COMPLETE SET (10)	75.00	34.00	9.50
COMMON MANTLE (64-72)	9.00	4.00	1.15
☐ 64 1951 The Early Years	9.00	4.00	1.15
☐ 65 1953 Tape-Measure Home Runs	9.00	4.00	1.15
☐ 66 1956 Triple Crown Season	9.00	4.00	1.15
☐ 67 1957 Second Consecutive MVP	9.00	4.00	1.15
☐ 68 1961 Chasing the Babe	9.00	4.00	1.15
☐ 69 1964 Series Home Run Record	9.00	4.00	1.15
☐ 70 1967 500th Home Run	9.00	4.00	1.15
☐ 71 1974 Hall of Fame	9.00	4.00	1.15
☐ 72 Checklist	9.00	4.00	1.15
☐ NNO Mantle Header Card	9.00	4.00	1.15

1994 Upper Deck Mantle's Long Shots

Randomly inserted in first series retail packs at a rate of one in 18, this 21-card silver foil set features top longball hitters as selected by Mickey Mantle. Two trade cards, were also random inserts and were redeemable (expiration: December 31, 1994) for either the basic silver foil set version (Silver Trade card) or the Electric Diamond version (blue Trade card). The Electric Diamond set and singles command up to 1.5X the values below. The only way to obtain the Electric Diamond version was through the trade card. These cards differ in that they have an Electric Diamond logo on front. Card fronts are horizontal with a color player photo standing out from a dulled holographic image. The backs have a vertical format with a player photo at the top, a small photo of Mickey Mantle, a quote from The Mick and career power numbers. The cards are numbered on the back with a "MM" prefix.

	MINT	EXC	G-VG
COMPLETE SET (21)	50.00	23.00	6.25
COMMON CARD (MM1-MM21)	.60	.25	.08
*ELECTRIC DIAMOND VERSIONS 1.25X VALUES BELOW			
☐ MM1 Jeff Bagwell	5.00	2.30	.60
☐ MM2 Albert Belle	3.50	1.55	.45
☐ MM3 Barry Bonds	4.00	1.80	.50
☐ MM4 Jose Canseco	1.50	.65	.19
☐ MM5 Joe Carter	1.50	.65	.19
☐ MM6 Carlos Delgado	1.50	.65	.19
☐ MM7 Cecil Fielder	1.10	.50	.14
☐ MM8 Cliff Floyd	1.50	.65	.19
☐ MM9 Juan Gonzalez	3.50	1.55	.45
☐ MM10 Ken Griffey Jr.	10.00	4.50	1.25
☐ MM11 David Justice	1.50	.65	.19
☐ MM12 Fred McGriff	1.50	.65	.19
☐ MM13 Mark McGwire	.60	.25	.08
☐ MM14 Dean Palmer	.60	.25	.08
☐ MM15 Mike Piazza	5.00	2.30	.60
☐ MM16 Manny Ramirez	2.00	.90	.25
☐ MM17 Tim Salmon	1.50	.65	.19
☐ MM18 Frank Thomas	10.00	4.50	1.25
☐ MM19 Mo Vaughn	1.10	.50	.14
☐ MM20 Matt Williams	2.00	.90	.25
☐ MM21 Mickey Mantle	12.00	5.50	1.50
☐ NNO Mantle ED LS Tr. Blue	7.50	3.40	.95
☐ NNO Mantle LS Tr. Silver	5.00	2.30	.60

1994 Upper Deck Next Generation

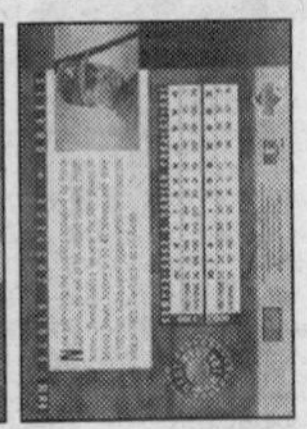

Randomly inserted in second series retail packs at a rate of one in 35, this 18-card set spotlights young established stars and promising prospects. Metallic fronts feature a color player photo on solid background. A small player hologram is halfway up the card on the right and comes between the player's first and last name. The Next Generation logo is at bottom left. Horizontal backs contain statistical comparisons,

where applicable, to Hall of Famers and brief write-up noting the comparisons. A Next Generation Electric Diamond Trade Card and a Next Generation Trade Card were randomly in second series hobby packs. Each card could be redeemed for that set. Expiration date for redemption was October 31, 1994. The Electric Diamond versions are priced at 1.25X the values below.

	MINT	EXC	G-VG
COMPLETE SET (18)	90.00	40.00	11.50
COMMON CARD (1-18)	1.50	.65	.19

*ELECTRIC DIAMOND VERSIONS 1.25X VALUES BELOW

	MINT	EXC	G-VG
☐ 1 Roberto Alomar	5.00	2.30	.60
☐ 2 Carlos Delgado	3.00	1.35	.40
☐ 3 Cliff Floyd	3.00	1.35	.40
☐ 4 Alex Gonzalez	1.50	.65	.19
☐ 5 Juan Gonzalez	7.00	3.10	.85
☐ 6 Ken Griffey Jr.	20.00	9.00	2.50
☐ 7 Jeffrey Hammonds	2.50	1.15	.30
☐ 8 Michael Jordan	20.00	9.00	2.50
☐ 9 David Justice	3.00	1.35	.40
☐ 10 Ryan Klesko	3.50	1.55	.45
☐ 11 Javy Lopez	2.00	.90	.25
☐ 12 Raul Mondesi	7.00	3.10	.85
☐ 13 Mike Piazza	10.00	4.50	1.25
☐ 14 Kirby Puckett	8.00	3.60	1.00
☐ 15 Manny Ramirez	4.00	1.80	.50
☐ 16 Alex Rodriguez	15.00	6.75	1.90
☐ 17 Tim Salmon	3.00	1.35	.40
☐ 18 Gary Sheffield	1.50	.65	.19
☐ NNO Expired ED Trade Card	6.00	2.70	.75
☐ NNO Expired NG Trade Card	5.00	2.30	.60

1993 Upper Deck SP

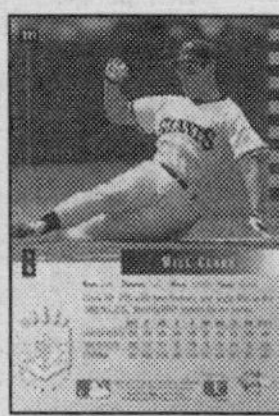

This 290-card standard-size (2 1/2" by 3 1/2") set features fronts with action color player photos. The player's name and position appear within a team-colored stripe at the bottom edge that shades from dark to light, left to right. A team color-checkered stripe is in the upper left and the team name in a gold-lettered arc appears at the top with a gold underline that extends down the right side. The copper foil-stamped SP logo appears at the bottom right. The back displays an action shot of the player in the top half with a team color-checkered stripe in the upper right. The bottom half carries the player's biography, statistics, and career highlights. Special subsets include All Star players (1-18) and Foil Prospects (271-290). Cards 19-270 are in alphabetical order by team nickname. The cards are numbered on the back. The six foil rookies are the key Rookie Cards in the set: Roger Cedeno, Johnny Damon, Russ Davis, Derek Jeter, Chad Mottola, and Todd Steverson. Other Rookie Cards in the set are Ray McDavid and Roberto Mejia.

	MINT	EXC	G-VG
COMPLETE SET (290)	100.00	45.00	12.50
COMMON CARD (1-290)	.25	.11	.03

	MINT	EXC	G-VG
☐ 1 Roberto Alomar AS	2.50	1.15	.30
☐ 2 Wade Boggs AS	.60	.25	.08
☐ 3 Joe Carter AS	1.50	.65	.19
☐ 4 Ken Griffey Jr. AS	12.00	5.50	1.50
☐ 5 Mark Langston AS	.50	.23	.06
☐ 6 John Olerud AS	.50	.23	.06
☐ 7 Kirby Puckett AS	4.00	1.80	.50
☐ 8 Cal Ripken AS	7.50	3.40	.95
☐ 9 Ivan Rodriguez AS	.50	.23	.06
☐ 10 Barry Bonds AS	3.50	1.55	.45
☐ 11 Darren Daulton AS	.50	.23	.06
☐ 12 Marquis Grissom AS	.50	.23	.06
☐ 13 David Justice AS	1.50	.65	.19
☐ 14 John Kruk AS	.50	.23	.06
☐ 15 Barry Larkin AS	.50	.23	.06
☐ 16 Terry Mulholland AS	.25	.11	.03
☐ 17 Ryne Sandberg AS	3.50	1.55	.45
☐ 18 Gary Sheffield AS	.50	.23	.06
☐ 19 Chad Curtis	.35	.16	.04
☐ 20 Chili Davis	.35	.16	.04
☐ 21 Gary DiSarcina	.25	.11	.03
☐ 22 Damion Easley	.35	.16	.04
☐ 23 Chuck Finley	.25	.11	.03
☐ 24 Luis Polonia	.25	.11	.03
☐ 25 Tim Salmon	2.00	.90	.25
☐ 26 J.T. Snow	.50	.23	.06
☐ 27 Russ Springer	.25	.11	.03
☐ 28 Jeff Bagwell	5.00	2.30	.60
☐ 29 Craig Biggio	.35	.16	.04
☐ 30 Ken Caminiti	.35	.16	.04
☐ 31 Andujar Cedeno	.35	.16	.04
☐ 32 Doug Drabek	.50	.23	.06
☐ 33 Steve Finley	.25	.11	.03
☐ 34 Luis Gonzalez	.35	.16	.04
☐ 35 Pete Harnisch	.25	.11	.03
☐ 36 Darryl Kile	.35	.16	.04
☐ 37 Mike Bordick	.25	.11	.03
☐ 38 Dennis Eckersley	.50	.23	.06
☐ 39 Brent Gates	.50	.23	.06
☐ 40 Rickey Henderson	.50	.23	.06
☐ 41 Mark McGwire	.50	.23	.06
☐ 42 Craig Paquette	.25	.11	.03
☐ 43 Ruben Sierra	.50	.23	.06
☐ 44 Terry Steinbach	.35	.16	.04
☐ 45 Todd Van Poppel	.35	.16	.04
☐ 46 Pat Borders	.25	.11	.03
☐ 47 Tony Fernandez	.25	.11	.03
☐ 48 Juan Guzman	.35	.16	.04
☐ 49 Pat Hentgen	.50	.23	.06
☐ 50 Paul Molitor	1.50	.65	.19
☐ 51 Jack Morris	.50	.23	.06
☐ 52 Ed Sprague	.25	.11	.03
☐ 53 Duane Ward	.35	.16	.04
☐ 54 Devon White	.35	.16	.04
☐ 55 Steve Avery	.50	.23	.06
☐ 56 Jeff Blauser	.35	.16	.04
☐ 57 Ron Gant	.35	.16	.04
☐ 58 Tom Glavine	.50	.23	.06
☐ 59 Greg Maddux	2.00	.90	.25
☐ 60 Fred McGriff	1.50	.65	.19
☐ 61 Terry Pendleton	.50	.23	.06
☐ 62 Deion Sanders	2.00	.90	.25
☐ 63 John Smoltz	.35	.16	.04

	Player			
☐ 64	Cal Eldred	.35	.16	.04
☐ 65	Darryl Hamilton	.25	.11	.03
☐ 66	John Jaha	.35	.16	.04
☐ 67	Pat Listach	.35	.16	.04
☐ 68	Jaime Navarro	.25	.11	.03
☐ 69	Kevin Reimer	.25	.11	.03
☐ 70	B.J. Surhoff	.25	.11	.03
☐ 71	Greg Vaughn	.35	.16	.04
☐ 72	Robin Yount	1.50	.65	.19
☐ 73	Rene Arocha	.60	.25	.08
☐ 74	Bernard Gilkey	.25	.11	.03
☐ 75	Gregg Jefferies	.50	.23	.06
☐ 76	Ray Lankford	.50	.23	.06
☐ 77	Tom Pagnozzi	.25	.11	.03
☐ 78	Lee Smith	.50	.23	.06
☐ 79	Ozzie Smith	2.00	.90	.25
☐ 80	Bob Tewksbury	.25	.11	.03
☐ 81	Mark Whiten	.35	.16	.04
☐ 82	Steve Buechele	.25	.11	.03
☐ 83	Mark Grace	.50	.23	.06
☐ 84	Jose Guzman	.25	.11	.03
☐ 85	Derrick May	.35	.16	.04
☐ 86	Mike Morgan	.25	.11	.03
☐ 87	Randy Myers	.35	.16	.04
☐ 88	Kevin Roberson	.25	.11	.03
☐ 89	Sammy Sosa	.50	.23	.06
☐ 90	Rick Wilkins	.25	.11	.03
☐ 91	Brett Butler	.35	.16	.04
☐ 92	Eric Davis	.25	.11	.03
☐ 93	Orel Hershiser	.35	.16	.04
☐ 94	Eric Karros	.35	.16	.04
☐ 95	Ramon Martinez	.35	.16	.04
☐ 96	Raul Mondesi	7.00	3.10	.85
☐ 97	Jose Offerman	.25	.11	.03
☐ 98	Mike Piazza	12.00	5.50	1.50
☐ 99	Darryl Strawberry	.35	.16	.04
☐ 100	Moises Alou	.50	.23	.06
☐ 101	Wil Cordero	.50	.23	.06
☐ 102	Delino DeShields	.35	.16	.04
☐ 103	Darrin Fletcher	.25	.11	.03
☐ 104	Ken Hill	.35	.16	.04
☐ 105	Mike Lansing	1.00	.45	.13
☐ 106	Dennis Martinez	.35	.16	.04
☐ 107	Larry Walker	.50	.23	.06
☐ 108	John Wetteland	.25	.11	.03
☐ 109	Rod Beck	.50	.23	.06
☐ 110	John Burkett	.35	.16	.04
☐ 111	Will Clark	1.50	.65	.19
☐ 112	Royce Clayton	.35	.16	.04
☐ 113	Darren Lewis	.25	.11	.03
☐ 114	Willie McGee	.35	.16	.04
☐ 115	Bill Swift	.35	.16	.04
☐ 116	Robby Thompson	.25	.11	.03
☐ 117	Matt Williams	2.00	.90	.25
☐ 118	Sandy Alomar Jr.	.35	.16	.04
☐ 119	Carlos Baerga	1.50	.65	.19
☐ 120	Albert Belle	3.50	1.55	.45
☐ 121	Reggie Jefferson	.25	.11	.03
☐ 122	Wayne Kirby	.25	.11	.03
☐ 123	Kenny Lofton	2.50	1.15	.30
☐ 124	Carlos Martinez	.25	.11	.03
☐ 125	Charles Nagy	.25	.11	.03
☐ 126	Paul Sorrento	.25	.11	.03
☐ 127	Rich Amaral	.25	.11	.03
☐ 128	Jay Buhner	.35	.16	.04
☐ 129	Norm Charlton	.25	.11	.03
☐ 130	Dave Fleming	.35	.16	.04
☐ 131	Erik Hanson	.25	.11	.03
☐ 132	Randy Johnson	.50	.23	.06
☐ 133	Edgar Martinez	.25	.11	.03
☐ 134	Tino Martinez	.35	.16	.04
☐ 135	Omar Vizquel	.25	.11	.03
☐ 136	Bret Barberie	.25	.11	.03
☐ 137	Chuck Carr	.25	.11	.03
☐ 138	Jeff Conine	.50	.23	.06
☐ 139	Orestes Destrade	.25	.11	.03
☐ 140	Chris Hammond	.25	.11	.03
☐ 141	Bryan Harvey	.35	.16	.04
☐ 142	Benito Santiago	.25	.11	.03
☐ 143	Walt Weiss	.25	.11	.03
☐ 144	Darrell Whitmore	.60	.25	.08
☐ 145	Tim Bogar	.25	.11	.03
☐ 146	Bobby Bonilla	.50	.23	.06
☐ 147	Jeromy Burnitz	.35	.16	.04
☐ 148	Vince Coleman	.25	.11	.03
☐ 149	Dwight Gooden	.25	.11	.03
☐ 150	Todd Hundley	.25	.11	.03
☐ 151	Howard Johnson	.25	.11	.03
☐ 152	Eddie Murray	.50	.23	.06
☐ 153	Bret Saberhagen	.35	.16	.04
☐ 154	Brady Anderson	.35	.16	.04
☐ 155	Mike Devereaux	.35	.16	.04
☐ 156	Jeffrey Hammonds	2.00	.90	.25
☐ 157	Chris Hoiles	.35	.16	.04
☐ 158	Ben McDonald	.35	.16	.04
☐ 159	Mark McLemore	.25	.11	.03
☐ 160	Mike Mussina	2.00	.90	.25
☐ 161	Gregg Olson	.25	.11	.03
☐ 162	David Segui	.25	.11	.03
☐ 163	Derek Bell	.35	.16	.04
☐ 164	Andy Benes	.35	.16	.04
☐ 165	Archi Cianfrocco	.25	.11	.03
☐ 166	Ricky Gutierrez	.25	.11	.03
☐ 167	Tony Gwynn	2.50	1.15	.30
☐ 168	Gene Harris	.25	.11	.03
☐ 169	Trevor Hoffman	.25	.11	.03
☐ 170	Ray McDavid	1.50	.65	.19
☐ 171	Phil Plantier	.50	.23	.06
☐ 172	Mariano Duncan	.25	.11	.03
☐ 173	Len Dykstra	.50	.23	.06
☐ 174	Tommy Greene	.35	.16	.04
☐ 175	Dave Hollins	.50	.23	.06
☐ 176	Pete Incaviglia	.25	.11	.03
☐ 177	Mickey Morandini	.25	.11	.03
☐ 178	Curt Schilling	.35	.16	.04
☐ 179	Kevin Stocker	.60	.25	.08
☐ 180	Mitch Williams	.35	.16	.04
☐ 181	Stan Belinda	.25	.11	.03
☐ 182	Jay Bell	.35	.16	.04
☐ 183	Steve Cooke	.25	.11	.03
☐ 184	Carlos Garcia	.35	.16	.04
☐ 185	Jeff King	.25	.11	.03
☐ 186	Orlando Merced	.35	.16	.04
☐ 187	Don Slaught	.25	.11	.03
☐ 188	Andy Van Slyke	.50	.23	.06
☐ 189	Kevin Young	.25	.11	.03
☐ 190	Kevin Brown	.25	.11	.03
☐ 191	Jose Canseco	1.50	.65	.19
☐ 192	Julio Franco	.35	.16	.04
☐ 193	Benji Gil	.50	.23	.06
☐ 194	Juan Gonzalez	3.50	1.55	.45
☐ 195	Tom Henke	.35	.16	.04
☐ 196	Rafael Palmeiro	.50	.23	.06
☐ 197	Dean Palmer	.35	.16	.04
☐ 198	Nolan Ryan	10.00	4.50	1.25
☐ 199	Roger Clemens	2.50	1.15	.30
☐ 200	Scott Cooper	.35	.16	.04
☐ 201	Andre Dawson	.50	.23	.06
☐ 202	Mike Greenwell	.35	.16	.04
☐ 203	Carlos Quintana	.25	.11	.03
☐ 204	Jeff Russell	.25	.11	.03
☐ 205	Aaron Sele	1.50	.65	.19
☐ 206	Mo Vaughn	.75	.35	.09
☐ 207	Frank Viola	.35	.16	.04
☐ 208	Rob Dibble	.25	.11	.03
☐ 209	Roberto Kelly	.35	.16	.04

	#	Player	MINT	EXC	G-VG
☐	210	Kevin Mitchell	.35	.16	.04
☐	211	Hal Morris	.35	.16	.04
☐	212	Joe Oliver	.25	.11	.03
☐	213	Jose Rijo	.35	.16	.04
☐	214	Bip Roberts	.25	.11	.03
☐	215	Chris Sabo	.35	.16	.04
☐	216	Reggie Sanders	.50	.23	.06
☐	217	Dante Bichette	.50	.23	.06
☐	218	Jerald Clark	.25	.11	.03
☐	219	Alex Cole	.25	.11	.03
☐	220	Andres Galarraga	.50	.23	.06
☐	221	Joe Girardi	.25	.11	.03
☐	222	Charlie Hayes	.35	.16	.04
☐	223	Roberto Mejia	.50	.23	.06
☐	224	Armando Reynoso	.25	.11	.03
☐	225	Eric Young	.35	.16	.04
☐	226	Kevin Appier	.35	.16	.04
☐	227	George Brett	4.00	1.80	.50
☐	228	David Cone	.50	.23	.06
☐	229	Phil Hiatt	.25	.11	.03
☐	230	Felix Jose	.25	.11	.03
☐	231	Wally Joyner	.35	.16	.04
☐	232	Mike Macfarlane	.25	.11	.03
☐	233	Brian McRae	.50	.23	.06
☐	234	Jeff Montgomery	.35	.16	.04
☐	235	Rob Deer	.25	.11	.03
☐	236	Cecil Fielder	.75	.35	.09
☐	237	Travis Fryman	.75	.35	.09
☐	238	Mike Henneman	.25	.11	.03
☐	239	Tony Phillips	.25	.11	.03
☐	240	Mickey Tettleton	.35	.16	.04
☐	241	Alan Trammell	.50	.23	.06
☐	242	David Wells	.25	.11	.03
☐	243	Lou Whitaker	.50	.23	.06
☐	244	Rick Aguilera	.35	.16	.04
☐	245	Scott Erickson	.25	.11	.03
☐	246	Brian Harper	.25	.11	.03
☐	247	Kent Hrbek	.35	.16	.04
☐	248	Chuck Knoblauch	.50	.23	.06
☐	249	Shane Mack	.35	.16	.04
☐	250	David McCarty	.35	.16	.04
☐	251	Pedro Munoz	.25	.11	.03
☐	252	Dave Winfield	.60	.25	.08
☐	253	Alex Fernandez	.50	.23	.06
☐	254	Ozzie Guillen	.25	.11	.03
☐	255	Bo Jackson	.50	.23	.06
☐	256	Lance Johnson	.25	.11	.03
☐	257	Ron Karkovice	.25	.11	.03
☐	258	Jack McDowell	.50	.23	.06
☐	259	Tim Raines	.50	.23	.06
☐	260	Frank Thomas	12.00	5.50	1.50
☐	261	Robin Ventura	.50	.23	.06
☐	262	Jim Abbott	.50	.23	.06
☐	263	Steve Farr	.25	.11	.03
☐	264	Jimmy Key	.35	.16	.04
☐	265	Don Mattingly	4.00	1.80	.50
☐	266	Paul O'Neill	.35	.16	.04
☐	267	Mike Stanley	.25	.11	.03
☐	268	Danny Tartabull	.35	.16	.04
☐	269	Bob Wickman	.25	.11	.03
☐	270	Bernie Williams	.35	.16	.04
☐	271	Jason Bere FOIL	4.00	1.80	.50
☐	272	Roger Cedeno FOIL	4.00	1.80	.50
☐	273	Johnny Damon FOIL	4.00	1.80	.50
☐	274	Russ Davis FOIL	1.50	.65	.19
☐	275	Carlos Delgado FOIL	5.00	2.30	.60
☐	276	Carl Everett FOIL	.75	.35	.09
☐	277	Cliff Floyd FOIL	5.00	2.30	.60
☐	278	Alex Gonzalez FOIL	2.00	.90	.25
☐	279	Derek Jeter FOIL	7.50	3.40	.95
☐	280	Chipper Jones FOIL	4.00	1.80	.50
☐	281	Javy Lopez FOIL	3.00	1.35	.40
☐	282	Chad Mottola FOIL	1.00	.45	.13
☐	283	Marc Newfield FOIL	1.50	.65	.19
☐	284	Eduardo Perez FOIL	.75	.35	.09
☐	285	Manny Ramirez FOIL	6.00	2.70	.75
☐	286	Todd Steverson FOIL	1.00	.45	.13
☐	287	Michael Tucker FOIL	2.00	.90	.25
☐	288	Allen Watson FOIL	.75	.35	.09
☐	289	Rondell White FOIL	3.00	1.35	.40
☐	290	Dmitri Young FOIL	1.25	.55	.16

1993 Upper Deck SP Platinum Power

Cards from this 20-card set were randomly inserted in packs. The standard-size (2 1/2" by 3 1/2") cards feature power hitters from the American and National Leagues. The color action cut-out shot is superimposed on a royal blue background that contains lettering for Upper Deck Platinum Power and about the player. The top edge of the front is cut out in an arc with a copper foil stripe containing the player's name. The copper foil-stamped Platinum Power logo appears in the lower right. The back displays a color action player photo over the same royal blue background as depicted on the front. On a white background below the player photo is a career summary. The cards are numbered on the back with a "PP" prefix alphabetically by player's name.

	MINT	EXC	G-VG
COMPLETE SET (20)	250.00	115.00	31.00
COMMON CARD (PP1-PP20)	6.00	2.70	.75

	#	Player	MINT	EXC	G-VG
☐	PP1	Albert Belle	20.00	9.00	2.50
☐	PP2	Barry Bonds	25.00	11.50	3.10
☐	PP3	Joe Carter	10.00	4.50	1.25
☐	PP4	Will Clark	10.00	4.50	1.25
☐	PP5	Darren Daulton	6.00	2.70	.75
☐	PP6	Cecil Fielder	6.00	2.70	.75
☐	PP7	Ron Gant	6.00	2.70	.75
☐	PP8	Juan Gonzalez	20.00	9.00	2.50
☐	PP9	Ken Griffey Jr.	65.00	29.00	8.25
☐	PP10	Dave Hollins	6.00	2.70	.75
☐	PP11	David Justice	10.00	4.50	1.25
☐	PP12	Fred McGriff	10.00	4.50	1.25
☐	PP13	Mark McGwire	6.00	2.70	.75
☐	PP14	Dean Palmer	6.00	2.70	.75
☐	PP15	Mike Piazza	40.00	18.00	5.00
☐	PP16	Tim Salmon	12.00	5.50	1.50
☐	PP17	Ryne Sandberg	25.00	11.50	3.10
☐	PP18	Gary Sheffield	6.00	2.70	.75
☐	PP19	Frank Thomas	65.00	29.00	8.25
☐	PP20	Matt Williams	12.00	5.50	1.50

1994 Upper Deck SP Previews

These 15 cards were distributed regionally as inserts in second series Upper Deck hobby packs. They were inserted at a rate of one in 35. The manner of distribution was five cards per Central, East and West region. The cards are nearly identical to the basic SP issue. Card fronts differ in that the region is at bottom right where the team name is located on the SP cards.

	MINT	EXC	G-VG
COMPLETE SET (15)	190.00	85.00	24.00
COMPLETE CENTRAL (5)	85.00	38.00	10.50
COMPLETE EAST (5)	40.00	18.00	5.00
COMPLETE WEST (5)	65.00	29.00	8.25
COMMON CENTRAL (CR1-CR5)	6.00	2.70	.75
COMMON EAST (ER1-ER5)	4.00	1.80	.50
COMMON WEST (WR1-WR5)	5.00	2.30	.60

		MINT	EXC	G-VG
☐ CR1	Jeff Bagwell	15.00	6.75	1.90
☐ CR2	Michael Jordan	30.00	13.50	3.80
☐ CR3	Kirby Puckett	12.00	5.50	1.50
☐ CR4	Manny Ramirez	6.00	2.70	.75
☐ CR5	Frank Thomas	30.00	13.50	3.80
☐ ER1	Roberto Alomar	8.00	3.60	1.00
☐ ER2	Cliff Floyd	5.00	2.30	.60
☐ ER3	Javy Lopez	4.00	1.80	.50
☐ ER4	Don Mattingly	12.00	5.50	1.50
☐ ER5	Cal Ripken	20.00	9.00	2.50
☐ WR1	Barry Bonds	12.00	5.50	1.50
☐ WR2	Juan Gonzalez	10.00	4.50	1.25
☐ WR3	Ken Griffey Jr.	30.00	13.50	3.80
☐ WR4	Mike Piazza	15.00	6.75	1.90
☐ WR5	Tim Salmon	5.00	2.30	.60

1994 Upper Deck SP

This 200-card set primarily contains the game's top players and prospects. The first 20 cards in the set are Foil Prospects which are brighter and more metallic than the rest of the set. In either case, card fronts have a metallic finish with color player photos and a gold right-hand border. The backs contain a color player photo, 1993, career and best season statistics. The left side has a black border. The Upper Deck hologram on back is gold. Rookie Cards include Brooks Kieschnick, Chan Ho Park, Alex Rodriguez and Glenn Williams.

	MINT	EXC	G-VG
COMPLETE SET (200)	50.00	23.00	6.25
COMMON CARD (1-200)	.15	.07	.02

		MINT	EXC	G-VG
☐ 1	Mike Bell FOIL	1.00	.45	.13
☐ 2	D.J. Boston FOIL	.50	.23	.06
☐ 3	Darren Dreifort FOIL	1.00	.45	.13
☐ 4	Brad Fullmer FOIL	.60	.25	.08
☐ 5	Joey Hamilton FOIL	1.50	.65	.19
☐ 6	Todd Hollandsworth FOIL	1.50	.65	.19
☐ 7	Brian Hunter FOIL	1.25	.55	.16
☐ 8	LaTroy Hawkins FOIL	2.00	.90	.25
☐ 9	Brooks Kieschnick FOIL	2.50	1.15	.30
☐ 10	Derrek Lee FOIL	2.00	.90	.25
☐ 11	Trot Nixon FOIL	2.00	.90	.25
☐ 12	Alex Ochoa FOIL	.40	.18	.05
☐ 13	Chan Ho Park FOIL	3.00	1.35	.40
☐ 14	Kirk Presley FOIL	2.00	.90	.25
☐ 15	Alex Rodriguez FOIL	10.00	4.50	1.25
☐ 16	Jose Silva FOIL	2.00	.90	.25
☐ 17	Terrell Wade FOIL	2.00	.90	.25
☐ 18	Billy Wagner FOIL	1.50	.65	.19
☐ 19	Glenn Williams FOIL	2.50	1.15	.30
☐ 20	Preston Wilson FOIL	.50	.23	.06
☐ 21	Brian Anderson	1.25	.55	.16
☐ 22	Chad Curtis	.15	.07	.02
☐ 23	Chili Davis	.20	.09	.03
☐ 24	Bo Jackson	.30	.14	.04
☐ 25	Mark Langston	.30	.14	.04
☐ 26	Tim Salmon	.75	.35	.09
☐ 27	Jeff Bagwell	2.50	1.15	.30
☐ 28	Craig Biggio	.20	.09	.03
☐ 29	Ken Caminiti	.20	.09	.03
☐ 30	Doug Drabek	.30	.14	.04
☐ 31	John Hudek	1.25	.55	.16
☐ 32	Greg Swindell	.15	.07	.02
☐ 33	Brent Gates	.30	.14	.04
☐ 34	Rickey Henderson	.30	.14	.04
☐ 35	Steve Karsay	.15	.07	.02
☐ 36	Mark McGwire	.30	.14	.04
☐ 37	Ruben Sierra	.30	.14	.04
☐ 38	Terry Steinbach	.20	.09	.03
☐ 39	Roberto Alomar	1.25	.55	.16
☐ 40	Joe Carter	.75	.35	.09
☐ 41	Carlos Delgado	.75	.35	.09
☐ 42	Alex Gonzalez	.50	.23	.06
☐ 43	Juan Guzman	.20	.09	.03
☐ 44	Paul Molitor	.75	.35	.09
☐ 45	John Olerud	.30	.14	.04
☐ 46	Devon White	.15	.07	.02
☐ 47	Steve Avery	.30	.14	.04
☐ 48	Jeff Blauser	.20	.09	.03
☐ 49	Tom Glavine	.30	.14	.04
☐ 50	David Justice	.75	.35	.09
☐ 51	Roberto Kelly	.15	.07	.02
☐ 52	Ryan Klesko	.75	.35	.09
☐ 53	Javy Lopez	.50	.23	.06
☐ 54	Greg Maddux	1.00	.45	.13
☐ 55	Fred McGriff	.75	.35	.09
☐ 56	Ricky Bones	.15	.07	.02
☐ 57	Cal Eldred	.20	.09	.03
☐ 58	Brian Harper	.15	.07	.02
☐ 59	Pat Listach	.15	.07	.02
☐ 60	B.J. Surhoff	.15	.07	.02
☐ 61	Greg Vaughn	.20	.09	.03
☐ 62	Bernard Gilkey	.15	.07	.02
☐ 63	Gregg Jefferies	.30	.14	.04
☐ 64	Ray Lankford	.30	.14	.04
☐ 65	Ozzie Smith	1.00	.45	.13
☐ 66	Bob Tewksbury	.15	.07	.02
☐ 67	Mark Whiten	.20	.09	.03
☐ 68	Todd Zeile	.20	.09	.03
☐ 69	Mark Grace	.30	.14	.04
☐ 70	Randy Myers	.15	.07	.02
☐ 71	Ryne Sandberg	1.75	.80	.22
☐ 72	Sammy Sosa	.30	.14	.04
☐ 73	Steve Trachsel	.60	.25	.08

☐ 74 Rick Wilkins .15 .07 .02
☐ 75 Brett Butler .20 .09 .03
☐ 76 Delino DeShields .20 .09 .03
☐ 77 Orel Hershiser .20 .09 .03
☐ 78 Eric Karros .20 .09 .03
☐ 79 Raul Mondesi 1.75 .80 .22
☐ 80 Mike Piazza 2.50 1.15 .30
☐ 81 Tim Wallach .15 .07 .02
☐ 82 Moises Alou .30 .14 .04
☐ 83 Cliff Floyd .75 .35 .09
☐ 84 Marquis Grissom .30 .14 .04
☐ 85 Pedro J. Martinez .30 .14 .04
☐ 86 Larry Walker .30 .14 .04
☐ 87 John Wetteland .15 .07 .02
☐ 88 Rondell White .50 .23 .06
☐ 89 Rod Beck .20 .09 .03
☐ 90 Barry Bonds 2.00 .90 .25
☐ 91 John Burkett .20 .09 .03
☐ 92 Royce Clayton .20 .09 .03
☐ 93 Billy Swift .15 .07 .02
☐ 94 Robby Thompson .15 .07 .02
☐ 95 Matt Williams .75 .35 .09
☐ 96 Carlos Baerga .75 .35 .09
☐ 97 Albert Belle 1.50 .65 .19
☐ 98 Kenny Lofton 1.25 .55 .16
☐ 99 Dennis Martinez .20 .09 .03
☐ 100 Eddie Murray .30 .14 .04
☐ 101 Manny Ramirez 1.00 .45 .13
☐ 102 Eric Anthony .15 .07 .02
☐ 103 Chris Bosio .15 .07 .02
☐ 104 Jay Buhner .20 .09 .03
☐ 105 Ken Griffey Jr. 5.00 2.30 .60
☐ 106 Randy Johnson .30 .14 .04
☐ 107 Edgar Martinez .15 .07 .02
☐ 108 Chuck Carr .15 .07 .02
☐ 109 Jeff Conine .30 .14 .04
☐ 110 Carl Everett .20 .09 .03
☐ 111 Chris Hammond .15 .07 .02
☐ 112 Bryan Harvey .20 .09 .03
☐ 113 Charles Johnson .50 .23 .06
☐ 114 Gary Sheffield .30 .14 .04
☐ 115 Bobby Bonilla .30 .14 .04
☐ 116 Dwight Gooden .15 .07 .02
☐ 117 Todd Hundley .15 .07 .02
☐ 118 Bobby Jones .35 .16 .04
☐ 119 Jeff Kent .20 .09 .03
☐ 120 Bret Saberhagen .20 .09 .03
☐ 121 Jeffrey Hammonds .50 .23 .06
☐ 122 Chris Hoiles .20 .09 .03
☐ 123 Ben McDonald .20 .09 .03
☐ 124 Mike Mussina .75 .35 .09
☐ 125 Rafael Palmeiro .30 .14 .04
☐ 126 Cal Ripken 4.00 1.80 .50
☐ 127 Lee Smith .30 .14 .04
☐ 128 Derek Bell .20 .09 .03
☐ 129 Andy Benes .20 .09 .03
☐ 130 Tony Gwynn 1.25 .55 .16
☐ 131 Trevor Hoffman .15 .07 .02
☐ 132 Phil Plantier .20 .09 .03
☐ 133 Bip Roberts .15 .07 .02
☐ 134 Darren Daulton .30 .14 .04
☐ 135 Lenny Dykstra .30 .14 .04
☐ 136 Dave Hollins .30 .14 .04
☐ 137 Danny Jackson .15 .07 .02
☐ 138 John Kruk .30 .14 .04
☐ 139 Kevin Stocker .20 .09 .03
☐ 140 Jay Bell .20 .09 .03
☐ 141 Carlos Garcia .15 .07 .02
☐ 142 Jeff King .15 .07 .02
☐ 143 Orlando Merced .20 .09 .03
☐ 144 Andy Van Slyke .30 .14 .04
☐ 145 Rick White .15 .07 .02
☐ 146 Jose Canseco .75 .35 .09
☐ 147 Will Clark .75 .35 .09
☐ 148 Juan Gonzalez 1.75 .80 .22
☐ 149 Rick Helling .15 .07 .02
☐ 150 Dean Palmer .20 .09 .03
☐ 151 Ivan Rodriguez .30 .14 .04
☐ 152 Roger Clemens 1.25 .55 .16
☐ 153 Scott Cooper .20 .09 .03
☐ 154 Andre Dawson .30 .14 .04
☐ 155 Mike Greenwell .20 .09 .03
☐ 156 Aaron Sele .40 .18 .05
☐ 157 Mo Vaughn .30 .14 .04
☐ 158 Bret Boone .30 .14 .04
☐ 159 Barry Larkin .30 .14 .04
☐ 160 Kevin Mitchell .20 .09 .03
☐ 161 Jose Rijo .20 .09 .03
☐ 162 Deion Sanders .75 .35 .09
☐ 163 Reggie Sanders .20 .09 .03
☐ 164 Dante Bichette .30 .14 .04
☐ 165 Ellis Burks .20 .09 .03
☐ 166 Andres Galarraga .30 .14 .04
☐ 167 Charlie Hayes .20 .09 .03
☐ 168 David Nied .30 .14 .04
☐ 169 Walt Weiss .15 .07 .02
☐ 170 Kevin Appier .20 .09 .03
☐ 171 David Cone .30 .14 .04
☐ 172 Jeff Granger .20 .09 .03
☐ 173 Felix Jose .15 .07 .02
☐ 174 Wally Joyner .20 .09 .03
☐ 175 Brian McRae .20 .09 .03
☐ 176 Cecil Fielder .30 .14 .04
☐ 177 Travis Fryman .35 .16 .04
☐ 178 Mike Henneman .15 .07 .02
☐ 179 Tony Phillips .15 .07 .02
☐ 180 Mickey Tettleton .20 .09 .03
☐ 181 Alan Trammell .30 .14 .04
☐ 182 Rick Aguilera .20 .09 .03
☐ 183 Rich Becker .20 .09 .03
☐ 184 Scott Erickson .15 .07 .02
☐ 185 Chuck Knoblauch .30 .14 .04
☐ 186 Kirby Puckett 2.00 .90 .25
☐ 187 Dave Winfield .30 .14 .04
☐ 188 Wilson Alvarez .30 .14 .04
☐ 189 Jason Bere .60 .25 .08
☐ 190 Alex Fernandez .30 .14 .04
☐ 191 Julio Franco .20 .09 .03
☐ 192 Jack McDowell .30 .14 .04
☐ 193 Frank Thomas 5.00 2.30 .60
☐ 194 Robin Ventura .20 .09 .03
☐ 195 Jim Abbott .30 .14 .04
☐ 196 Wade Boggs .30 .14 .04
☐ 197 Jimmy Key .20 .09 .03
☐ 198 Don Mattingly 2.00 .90 .25
☐ 199 Paul O'Neill .20 .09 .03
☐ 200 Danny Tartabull .20 .09 .03

1994 Upper Deck SP Die-Cut

This 200-card die-cut set is parallel to that of the basic SP issue. The cards were inserted one per SP pack. The difference, of course, is the unique die-cut shape. The backs have a silver Upper Deck hologram as opposed to gold on the basic issue.

	MINT	EXC	G-VG
COMPLETE SET (200)	175.00	80.00	22.00
COMMON CARD (1-200)	.25	.11	.03

*VETERAN STARS: 1.5X to 3X BASIC CARDS

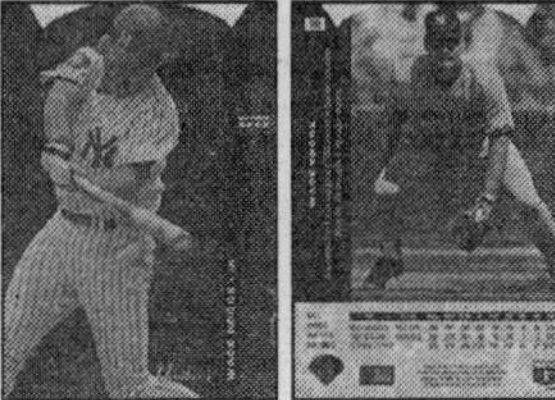

*YOUNG STARS: 1.25X to 2.5X BASIC CARDS
*RCs: 1X to 2X BASIC CARDS

1994 Upper Deck SP Holoview Blue

Randomly inserted in SP foil packs at a rate of one in five, this 38-card set contains top stars and prospects. Card fronts have a color player photo with a black and blue border to the right in which the player's name appears. A player hologram that runs the width of the card is at the bottom. The backs are primarily blue with a player photo and text.

	MINT	EXC	G-VG
COMPLETE SET (38)	175.00	80.00	22.00
COMMON CARD (1-38)	3.00	1.35	.40
☐ 1 Roberto Alomar	8.00	3.60	1.00
☐ 2 Kevin Appier	3.50	1.55	.45
☐ 3 Jeff Bagwell	15.00	6.75	1.90
☐ 4 Barry Bonds	5.00	2.30	.60
☐ 5 Roger Clemens	8.00	3.60	1.00
☐ 6 Carlos Delgado	5.00	2.30	.60
☐ 7 Cecil Fielder	4.00	1.80	.50
☐ 8 Cliff Floyd	5.00	2.30	.60
☐ 9 Travis Fryman	4.00	1.80	.50
☐ 10 Andres Galarraga	4.00	1.80	.50
☐ 11 Juan Gonzalez	10.00	4.50	1.25
☐ 12 Ken Griffey Jr.	30.00	13.50	3.80
☐ 13 Tony Gwynn	8.00	3.60	1.00
☐ 14 Jeffrey Hammonds	4.00	1.80	.50
☐ 15 Bo Jackson	3.50	1.55	.45
☐ 16 Michael Jordan	30.00	13.50	3.80
☐ 17 David Justice	4.50	2.00	.55
☐ 18 Steve Karsay	3.50	1.55	.45
☐ 19 Jeff Kent	3.00	1.35	.40
☐ 20 Brooks Kieschnick	5.00	2.30	.60
☐ 21 Ryan Klesko	5.00	2.30	.60
☐ 22 John Kruk	3.50	1.55	.45
☐ 23 Barry Larkin	4.00	1.80	.50
☐ 24 Pat Listach	3.00	1.35	.40
☐ 25 Don Mattingly	12.00	5.50	1.50
☐ 26 Mark McGwire	3.50	1.55	.45
☐ 27 Raul Mondesi	10.00	4.50	1.25
☐ 28 Trot Nixon	4.00	1.80	.50
☐ 29 Mike Piazza	15.00	6.75	1.90
☐ 30 Kirby Puckett	12.00	5.50	1.50
☐ 31 Manny Ramirez	6.00	2.70	.75
☐ 32 Cal Ripken	22.00	10.00	2.80
☐ 33 Alex Rodriguez	20.00	9.00	2.50
☐ 34 Tim Salmon	4.50	2.00	.55
☐ 35 Gary Sheffield	4.00	1.80	.50
☐ 36 Ozzie Smith	6.00	2.70	.75
☐ 37 Sammy Sosa	3.50	1.55	.45
☐ 38 Andy Van Slyke	3.50	1.55	.45

1994 Upper Deck SP Holoview Red

Parallel to the Holoview Blue set, this 38-card issue was also randomly inserted in SP packs. They are much more difficult to pull than the Blue version with an insertion rate of one in 75. Card fronts have a color player photo with a black and red border to the right in which the player's name appears. A player hologram that runs the width of the card is at the bottom. The backs are primarily red with a player photo and text.

	MINT	EXC	G-VG
COMPLETE SET (38)	2250.00	1000.00	275.00
COMMON CARD (1-38)	15.00	6.75	1.90
☐ 1 Roberto Alomar	55.00	25.00	7.00
☐ 2 Kevin Appier	18.00	8.00	2.30
☐ 3 Jeff Bagwell	125.00	57.50	15.50
☐ 4 Barry Bonds	40.00	18.00	5.00
☐ 5 Roger Clemens	55.00	25.00	7.00
☐ 6 Carlos Delgado	40.00	18.00	5.00
☐ 7 Cecil Fielder	25.00	11.50	3.10
☐ 8 Cliff Floyd	40.00	18.00	5.00
☐ 9 Travis Fryman	25.00	11.50	3.10
☐ 10 Andres Galarraga	20.00	9.00	2.50
☐ 11 Juan Gonzalez	75.00	34.00	9.50
☐ 12 Ken Griffey Jr.	240.00	110.00	30.00
☐ 13 Tony Gwynn	55.00	25.00	7.00
☐ 14 Jeffrey Hammonds	30.00	13.50	3.80
☐ 15 Bo Jackson	18.00	8.00	2.30
☐ 16 Michael Jordan	225.00	100.00	28.00
☐ 17 David Justice	35.00	16.00	4.40
☐ 18 Steve Karsay	18.00	8.00	2.30
☐ 19 Jeff Kent	15.00	6.75	1.90
☐ 20 Brooks Kieschnick	40.00	18.00	5.00
☐ 21 Ryan Klesko	40.00	18.00	5.00
☐ 22 John Kruk	18.00	8.00	2.30
☐ 23 Barry Larkin	20.00	9.00	2.50
☐ 24 Pat Listach	15.00	6.75	1.90
☐ 25 Don Mattingly	90.00	40.00	11.50
☐ 26 Mark McGwire	18.00	8.00	2.30
☐ 27 Raul Mondesi	75.00	34.00	9.50
☐ 28 Trot Nixon	35.00	16.00	4.40
☐ 29 Mike Piazza	110.00	50.00	14.00
☐ 30 Kirby Puckett	90.00	40.00	11.50
☐ 31 Manny Ramirez	55.00	25.00	7.00
☐ 32 Cal Ripken	175.00	80.00	22.00
☐ 33 Alex Rodriguez	150.00	70.00	19.00
☐ 34 Tim Salmon	30.00	13.50	3.80
☐ 35 Gary Sheffield	20.00	9.00	2.50
☐ 36 Ozzie Smith	45.00	20.00	5.75
☐ 37 Sammy Sosa	18.00	8.00	2.30
☐ 38 Andy Van Slyke	18.00	8.00	2.30